9/09

Sleuths, Sidekicks and Stooges

An annotated bibliography of detectives, their assistants
and their rivals in crime, mystery and adventure fiction,
1795-1995

Joseph Green and Jim Finch

Scolar Press

Published by:

Scolar Press
Gower House
Croft Road
Aldershot
Hants
GU11 3HR
England

Ashgate Publishing Company
Old Post Road
Brookfield
Vermont 05036-9704
USA

British Library Cataloguing in Publication Data

Sleuths, Sidekicks and Stooges: an annotated bibliography of detectives, their assistants and their rivals in crime, mystery and adventure fiction, 1795-1995
I. Green, Joseph II. Finch, Jim
016.82308720927

Library of Congress Cataloging-in-Publication Data

Green Joseph
Sleuths, sidekicks and stooges: an annotated bibliography of detectives, their assistants and their rivals in crime, mystery and adventure fiction, 1795-1995 / Joseph Green, Jim Finch.
Includes index.
ISBN 1-85928-192-3
1. Detective and mystery stories — Bibliography. 2. Detectives in literature — Bibliography. I. Finch, Jim II. Title.
Z5917.D5G74 1996
[PN3448.D4]
016.80883'872 — dc2095–49334
CIP

ISBN 1 85928 192 3

Typeset by The Authors
Printed in Great Britain at the University Press Cambridge

For Peter Ridgway Watt

Contents

Acknowledgements

We wish to thank all those who, in several ways, have contributed to the writing of this book: to Jill Grady, Liz Hernaman and Gaye Jones of the Elm Grove Library, Portsmouth, for their help in finding books and bibliographic sources and for whom no request was too much; to Maxim Jacubowski, who allowed us to roam freely among the cornucopian treasures of his unparalleled London bookshop, Murder One; to Peter Ridgway Watt, whose list of seventy-three detectives started it all and who read the manuscript and gave advice and expert help right to the end; to our wives who bore, with patience and fortitude, the five years' ordeal; and to Dilly, the French Briard puppy of one of us (JF), who lightened many of our dark hours and enjoyed eating one of our major sources as much as we enjoyed reading it. We express, finally, our gratitude to the many bibliographers, reviewers and critics, British and American, whose earlier researches in the field have enabled us to complete this work.

Preface

There have probably been what might broadly be termed 'detective stories' virtually since men have told tales and certainly since the beginnings of written fiction. If their elements can be regarded as being (a) a quest for an unknown or undiscovered object or person; (b) a conflict between two characters, a hero and a villain; (c) the existence of a 'crime' - that is, an offence against current morality; (d) a prize to be won; and (e) the triumph of some concept of justice - that is, the victory of the current right over the current wrong, then the rudiments of detective fiction are to be found throughout classical and medieval literature, from Virgil's *Aeniad* to Malory's *Morte D'Arthur*. However, if the underlying structure of such stories remains much the same, reflecting the excitement of enquiry and the joy of discovery as components of human inspiration, their content and style are variable and determined by the constraints of contemporary society. In these terms, the modern detective story is defined by the modern world, the type of society that developed in the West after the French and American Revolutions, the age of industry and conflict, but also, and fundamentally, one that produced the idea of political democracy. So critical is the latter that it would seem impossible for the modern detective story to have come into existence otherwise. It could not evolve in non-democratic societies and, indeed, it did not, for its essential elements are lacking in such societies. Furthermore, that it has been predominantly written in English (one hesitates to say it is dominantly Anglo-Saxon in form and content) cannot be disputed, although obvious and distinguished exceptions abound, and there are certainly social and political reasons why this is so. Not only is the modern detective story, or what may now be called the criminous genre of fiction, a special creation, uniquely a product of democratic Western societies, but it also says a great deal about those societies. Erik Routley, in his *The Puritan Pleasures of the Detective Story* (1972), makes the same point in stating that 'behind it all is an assumption that the reader accepts, admires and puts his faith in superiority of some kind - fundamentally, superiority of a law which keeps the peace and sees justice done, and in the foreground, superiority of intellect or of character'. He says, more succinctly, that the first condition in society for the detective story to flourish is, perhaps paradoxically but nevertheless appositely, 'a tradition of integrity in the police force'.

The detective story as we now know it cannot therefore be much more than about two hundred years old and, indeed, its history supports that view. The earliest works that can now, with hindsight, be regarded as primitive forms of the genre, date from the first decades of the nineteenth century, were written in England and France, and were, indeed, stories about policemen and police forces. By common consent, however, it is the American, Edgar Allan Poe, who is credited with the first completely formed detective story, featuring a true hero-detective whose methods and intellect place him above the lawful forces of correction in society and written as fiction for the reader's entertainment. He was swiftly followed in France by Emile Gaboriau and, in England, after a nod towards the genre from Charles Dickens in *Bleak House*, by Wilkie Collins, who in 1868 wrote the first novel that is a modern detective story, *The Moonstone*, described almost a century later by T S Eliot[1] as 'the first, the longest and the best detective story in the English language'. All three of that distinguished poet's statements are arguable, to say the least, if notice is to be taken of the perhaps over one hundred thousand detective works, novels and short stories that have been published since. If the publication rate has been remarkable, and it continues to be so, equally remarkable is the number of articles, essays, treatises, bibliographies and popular books that have been written *about* detective and mystery fiction.

Although it is impossible to define what is meant by a detective story or a mystery story or a crime story (the terms have often been used interchangeably) and their boundaries extend into the genres of spy fiction, fantasy, science fiction and even into the fringes of mainstream writing, several excellent classifications exist. Allen J Hubin's encyclopaedic bibliography, *Crime Fiction* (1994), which contains as complete a summary of the criminous genre as is at present available, lists about 80,000 titles. Walter Albert's *Mystery and Detective Fiction* (1984), a compendium of secondary sources (that is, books *about* detective fiction) has almost a thousand entries. Ronald Van der Waal's definitive bibliographic work, *The World Bibliography of Sherlock Holmes and Dr. Watson* - dealing with just one detective, albeit the greatest of them all - had, in 1976, about 6,000 entries. In recent years, valuable work has been done in collecting and annotating some of the earlier and more obscure parts of the genre; for example, Dorothy Glover and Graham Greene's *Victorian Detective Fiction* (1966); the rediscovery and the classification of at least a portion of the wealth of American pulp fiction published mostly between the years 1870 and 1910, as in Ron Goulart's *The Dime Detectives*; the pioneering research involved in such work as Gary Hoppenstand and Ray B Browne's *Defective Detectives in the Pulps* (1983); and several studies of the role of the female writer and the reasons for their dominance of certain aspects of the genre, exemplified by Victoria Nichols and Susan Thompson's *Silk Stalkings* (1988).

T J Binyon, in his rewarding study, *Murder will Out*: *The Detective in Fiction* (1990), has singled out the special characteristic of detective fiction as being constructed around the invention of the protagonist. He claims that 'uniquely, the genre grew out of the character, rather than vice versa... again uniquely, the character has so often overshadowed and become detached from the author. More people know of Sherlock Holmes and Hercule Poirot than of Conan Doyle and Agatha Christie.' Moreover, the special characteristic of protagonists in detective fiction is further exemplified by their ability to appear in series of stories, which may even be numbered in hundreds and appear over years or even decades. Although some may age a little, most seem not to be condemned by the passing years: the plots around them may change, but they themselves are often immutable. It is perhaps surprising that no major bibliographic index to fictional detectives exists. Certainly, many reference works, including Binyon's own, carry secondary indices of detective characters, but most - even including *A Catalogue of Crime* (1971), the classic study of over 3000 detective novels by Jacques Barzun and Wendel Hertig Taylor - mention detectives infrequently and inconsistently and discuss them only in passing. The more recent bibliographies and critical works continue to be author-orientated, although often citing detectives as part of their narrative structure. John Conquest, in his definitive work on private detectives, *Trouble is Their Business* (1990), indexes around a thousand detectives, in brief and delightfully informative narrative, but as structural subordinates to the main author index. The major publication, *Twentieth Century Crime & Mystery Writers, 3rd Edition* (Editor; Lesley Henderson) (1991), which is based on a detailed narrative discussion of almost a thousand authors, has no detective index. Steven Olderr's *Mystery Index*: *Subjects, Settings and Sleuths of 10,000 Titles'* (1987), although primarily author-indexed, provides a subsidiary index to several hundred detectives, but its value is hampered by taking its information only from 'books currently on the shelves of American libraries' and it contains many errors and omissions. Hubin's *Crime Fiction*, which is indexed by author, includes a subsidiary index of about 4000 detectives cited in its main text, but without further narrative information.

[1] Routley (loc. cit.) cites this statement.

The lack of a comprehensive and annotated index to the genre's key characters is to some extent understandable. Unlike the names of authors and the titles of books, which are already catalogued in several ways, fictional detectives must be found from the partial or secondary indices in other sources or by inspection of the books themselves. Even so, the task is formidable and, in some respects its resolution is not always satisfactory. Detective characters, unlike authors, are not always clearly definable, except in context. They may vary in the course of an author's work and they may disappear from it for a period, even of years, only to emerge again at some later date. They appear in every imaginable guise and even the most unimaginable situations. Authoritative sources may differ, and many indeed do, as to which of the several characters in a detective story is in fact the main detective.

The section entitled 'The Detectives' that is the substance of the present work is an attempt to fill the bibliographic gap. It cites nearly 8000 names of fictional characters that have either been directly identified from current books or catalogues or have been named, in context, by an authoritative source (Appendix 1) and it amplifies that data with narrative information on the detectives, their authors and their literary appearances. Further inspection has allowed the identification of several hundred characters designated as 'sidekicks'. Since no dedicated bibliography of detectives exists, it is not surprising that detectives' assistants, in spite of their acknowledged and often important role in detective fiction from its very inception, have not been bibliographically recognised. In a similar manner, an attempt has been made at the even more unrewarding task of identifying characters designated as 'stooges' - those protagonists that occur in many detective stories to oppose, hinder, negate or, contrariwise, even reluctantly to help the struggling but usually perspicacious sleuth. Clearly, both sidekicks and stooges are more difficult to discover than are detectives; and, in many cases, it is not easy to define them. Nevertheless, varying as they do over a vast range, from being 'poor mechanicals' to becoming linchpins of the plot, they appear to have been undeservedly neglected.

Certainly there must be many more sleuths, sidekicks and stooges to be discovered than appear in this book. The race against authors, of course, can never be won. If it were, more than one book would be needed to hold the information. However, perhaps writers, critics and researchers will enjoy reading about the extraordinary invention that authors, past and present, have used to create the ephemeral but eternally fascinating characters of detective fiction.

Introduction

The first works with identifiable characters that can be broadly regarded as detectives appeared towards the end of the eighteenth and beginning of the nineteenth century. The historical scope of the book is thus about two hundred years.

Detectives

Fictional detectives come in all shapes and sizes and sometimes they come in pairs, trebles or multiples. On the whole, it is usually clear from most crime and mystery fiction whether or not a protagonist may be considered to be a detective, even though the author may have other perspectives in view for his or her book. If a mystery is propounded or a crime committed and a character, hero or heroine, is invented to solve it, whether the author decides to call the protagonist a detective is, to a large extent, irrelevant. Detectives are defined, for inclusion in this book, as characters manifesting themselves as such by their action in the plot; or any character cited as a detective, in any context, by one of the sources from which the information is taken. Not all sources define detectives in the same way, of course, and there is often some difference of opinion as to which character is indeed the detective in any particular book. In addition to the main categories of detective, already wide in range, there are many species of characters - spies, secret agents, diplomats, bodyguards, hero-adventurers, detective-crooks and other minor types - who only enter the detective category transitorily or as a subsidiary part of their main activity. The principle for inclusion has more or less been that stated by John Conquest in his definitive book on private detectives, *Trouble is Their Business* : there he defends his decison on how to a define a private eye: 'It looks like a duck, it walks like a duck, it must be a duck'.

Some detectives are manifestly part of teams. The most popular team is a duo, in which two detectives do the sleuthing together and the author makes it clear that they do so, although their activities can be independent. Before the 1960s, police detectives operated mainly as strongly individual characters, although sometimes with a clear subordinate as a foil; but, since then, well-defined, equally balanced police duos, typified by Reginald Hill's British pair, Inspectors Dalziel and Pascoe, have appeared as inseparable detectives. Some of the most interesting modern police duos consist, however, of a higher ranking officer and a subordinate who each play an independent role in the sleuthing, in counterpoint, the second detective definitely playing a much greater part in the proceedings than would a sidekick, although sometimes the distinction is difficult to make. Private investigators also sometimes work as pairs. Even the American PI, whose habitat is typically a lonely one, occasionally operates in non-hierarchical collaboration, as do, for example, Frederick C Davis's pair, Luke Speare and Schyler Cole, who share their work fairly and entertainingly. British private investigators, much fewer in number, are traditionally lone birds and much prefer complaisant sidekicks. One cannot imagine Agatha Christie's Hercule Poirot working with anyone.

Introduction

Many duos, especially until the 1970s, comprise two amateurs. All permutations seem permissible: lawyers and clerks; professors and students; boys and their girlfriends; girls and their boyfriends; mothers and daughters; fathers and sons; hero-adventurers and their batmen, valets or what have you; rascals and do-gooders; geniuses and their narrators; reporters and photographers; and giants and dwarfs. A favourite of authors, especially from the 1930s to around the 1970s, but now less popular, is the husband-and-wife team, which became fashionable, particularly in the US, in the wake of the phenomenal success of Dashiell Hammett's famous pair, Nick and Nora Charles. The husband-and-wife team is predominantly amateur, but the married police duo is not unknown.

Sometimes amateurs work in harness with policemen, one or other of the pair perhaps being the leading character. This type of duo was not unusual in the 1930s and 1940s; but today it seems to be less common, since convincing amateurs are now less thick on the ground than they were and policemen are less inclined to be tolerant of them. The type of policeman and amateur duo that seems to have most credibility is when a policeman works with a professional scientist or doctor of some sort. This has been one of the more successful types of detective team, capable of vigorous and interesting potential in the hands of a skilled and knowledgeable author, and it has been extensively exploited. But is credibility of major importance in detective fiction?

On occasions it has been necessary to cite teams of three or more detectives. Sometimes this is because reference to the original publication fails to identify adequately the main detectives; and sometimes it is because the sources consulted disagree on who *is* the main detective. Wherever possible, a judgment has not been made and diverse views have been accommodated. Occasionally, three or more characters can truly be said to be detectives in parallel, a situation that appears most often in parodies. Indeed, one of the finest parodies in the literature, Marion Mainwairing's *Murder in Pastiche,* has nine detectives. They are all cited.

The rise of the so-called 'police procedural' poses special problems in the delineation of detectives. The form first emerged in the late 1950s in the police novels of Lawrence Treat and was developed in the 1960s by Ed McBain in his '87th Precinct' canon. It purports to give a realistic view of the collective nature of police work and was soon exploited by numerous American and British authors during the following two decades. Usually it was necessary for the authors of police procedurals to focus their plots around two or three key characters and, in such cases, they can be cited as conventional detectives. In cases where there is no such focus, as in the 87th Precinct novels, the collective itself is best cited as an entity, in full realisation that it is a variable one. The vogue for the police procedural seems, in the 1990s, to be in decline, and the gifted amateur, now often female rather than male, is venturing back in new and ingenious guises. However, under its influence, many American and not a few British police detectives are presently re-appearing in the old duo form, particularly as it is now becoming common to make one of them male and the other female. No wholly female police duos yet exist.

Fictional detectives fall into many categories but, for the classification purposes of 'The Detectives', they have been divided into eight main types. In real life, of course, and historically, detectives were certainly professional. In Tudor England, for example, Walsingham's spies and informers were, although *sub rosa,* part of the state's official system. In the eighteenth century, the London Bow Street Runners, the first professional police force, presumably did what detecting there was to be done. In fiction it is different. Fundamental to detective fiction is the detective's 'type', which is essentially determined by the author. Classically there were two types of person in detective stories who went around falling over bodies or stumbling across crimes and then went on to discover the why, when, how and who: the police and the gifted amateur. As the detective story developed, however, detectives diversified into several types. They were either official, professional and, in broader terms, agents of the law, or they had no official or legal standing and had some other interest in investigating a crime.

The first literary detectives were, in fact, only partially fictional. The Parisian sleuth, Vidocq, was a police spy and his literary exploits, although embroidered, were certainly based on his own experiences. The exploits of the early British sleuth, Richmond, are similarly based. However, when the detective story proper emerges, Poe's detective, Auguste Dupin, is not a professional but an interested and obsessed amateur, already equipped with the essential narrator or sidekick. Detective fiction developed only slowly after Poe's extraordinary leap and took place mainly in England, early policemen and amateurs (often lawyers of various kinds) still forming the bulk of mystery fiction's protagonists. Dorothy Glover and Graham Greene's collection was foremost in discovering the hidden features of Victorian mystery fiction and disclosing hitherto unrecognised police and amateur detectives.

In 1887, the second great revolution occurred when a young and obscure English doctor, with a penurious practice in Southsea, sent a short novel, *A Study in Scarlet,* to four publishers in turn, had it rejected and finally was paid £25 for it by Ward, Lock. Detective fiction has never been the same since. The role of the amateur detective was completely transformed by the appearance of Sherlock Holmes and, on both sides of the Atlantic, exploded in scope and size. The effects of this event are discussed later. For the moment, it is important as it necessitates the adoption of a better classification of detective types.

- ***Police***

All members of an official force are here designated as 'Police'. Nearly all have a rank or title, often with no relevance to their detective ability or job. Under this title, Scotland Yard Commanders and New York Police Commissioners may sleuth as much or as little as the humblest of constables. Included also are army cops and a few detectives who are virtually in police forces though they hold no rank. In the early days of Scotland Yard this was, indeed, sometimes the case and Victorian police detectives might use the plain title of 'Mr'.

- ***Professional Amateurs***

T J Binyon has divided amateurs into several groups. He considers all characters of the Sherlock Holmes type as 'professional amateurs', since they apparently do nothing apart from sleuthing. This concept is useful in separating a host of some of the most imposing figures in detective fiction from, say, the even larger group of amateur sleuths that would include demure lady librarians who find bodies instead of books on their shelves. However, Binyon does not define the category rigorously and includes, for example, not only doctors, lawyers and journalists, but also the large group of 'private eyes', who are clearly professionals taking fees. It is doubtful if Holmes or Poirot (both included by Binyon) normally received fees, although in the former's very first story, *A Study in Scarlet*, he said he did. They certainly never made their investigations dependent on their being paid. The failure to differentiate between the amateur who sets up his shingle and pronounces himself as an expert, ready to be consulted by lesser mortals, and the detective who can be hired to solve a case seems fundamental. The loose categorisation loses its usefulness if professionalism is merely a job description.

In the categorisation used here, the definition of the professional amateur is really that of Sherlock Holmes in *The Sign of Four*, in which he called himself an 'unofficial, consulting detective... The work itself, the pleasure of finding a field for my peculiar powers is my highest reward'. By the definition adopted, therefore, professional amateurs may seek out cases or receive cases without conditional payment: it makes no assumption about the cases, their creation, or the detective's own character or relationships. It includes many of the major detective figures in British and American fiction up to the 1970s, when, with the publication of Hercule Poirot's last case in 1975, the great era of the professional amateur more or less came to an end. The reasons for his demise are both explicit and implicit in post-war society; for amateurism has become linguistically identified with inferiority and even detectives who love their work expect to be paid for it, just as cricketers or baseball players do. A sad loss, but a clear case of *O Tempora! O Mores!*

- ***Private Detectives***

The separation of the professional amateur from the private investigator essentially follows Conquest's definitions for PIs. The category as defined here, however, is wider and includes, not only PIs, but all sleuths who act as consultants or investigators and thereby earn a living, which may be precarious, meagre or paid in kind in some way. The history of private detectives actually goes back to an era before Sherlock Holmes; and early examples, usually referred to as 'private investigators', certainly come to light in British Victorian novels, although fee-paying is hard to determine. After Holmes, several of his imitators were paid professionals. It seems clear that Arthur Morrison's Martin Hewitt, appearing in 1894, worked for fees, even though he was closely modelled on Sherlock Holmes, who usually did not. Almost all the early British lady detectives, such as Baroness Orczy's Lady Molly Mazaree, were strictly amateurs, for neither social status nor the times would have had it otherwise. Presumably this was true also for the best-known American girl sleuths of the 1920s, typified by Nancy Drew. But what about C L Pirkis's Loveday Brooke, who, in 1894, was said to be 'working for a Fleet Street Detective Agency' in London? And does the same apply to Reginald Wright Kauffman's Frances Baird, who, in 1906, was working for 'the Watkins Detective Agency' in New York?

Before 1930, virtually all British fictional detectives were either true amateurs or policemen, although some belonged to a general group (discussed below) that may be called 'professionals'. There was little social or financial promise, it seemed, in sleuthing for a living. However, the foundation in 1850 of Pinkerton's Agency in New York, was not only salutary for the detective profession but was eventually to set American detective fiction on a new course. Of the hundreds of detectives, most of them now lost or forgotten, who inhabited the pages of the American pulp magazines between the 1880s and the 1940s, it is quite unclear, in many cases, which of them or how many were amateur or professional. That changed with the appearance of Dashiell Hammett's pioneering professional, The Continental Op, in a short story in 1923, opening the floodgates for the detective type that was to dominate American fiction. The PI, the American shamus or gumshoe, sleuths for a fee. He may work alone from a shabby office or he may be head of an agency large enough to span continents. He may not *have* an office or even a roof over his head. He may hardly make a dollar a year; or, like Rex Stout's Nero Wolfe, he may receive ten thousand dollars for an hour's work between sessions in his orchid house. He may have assistants, sidekicks, secretaries or not a friend in the world. The police may entreat his services or threaten to run him out of town. He may have the highest degrees from Yale or simply be a muscular moron. He may be handsome, rich and desirable; or, and all too often, he may be nasty, unkempt, alcoholic, depressed, and unsound of limb. He may be black, white or something different; a lady-killer or celibate; a total roughneck or a namby-pamby. The American PI may be male, female, neither, or something in between; and, in the majority of cases, he (increasingly she) carries and is wont to use an offensive weapon, usually a gun. He may be anything at all providing only that he places an honest client above himself, his government and even his God - and that he is paid for it.

The American PI, by the end of the 1950s, had differentiated into two groups, which took detective fiction in different directions. The classic operative, descended from The Continental Op, with his Pinkertonian virtues, reached its zenith in Raymond Chandler's Philip Marlowe, who was the subject of Chandler's most often-quoted words in his essay, *The Simple Art of Murder* (1944): 'Down these mean streets a man must go who is not mean... He must be a complete man and a common man and yet an unusual man. He must be a man of honour, by instinct, by inevitability, without thought of it, and certainly without saying it. He must be the best man in the world and a good enough man for any world'. The great American detectives of later decades tended to fulfil and honour the ethos of this passage. However, the second school took a different path, becoming the 'hardboiled' detectives of the 1950s and after. These were men who were prepared to match violence with violence in a much more extreme way than had ever seemed morally justifiable either in life or in fiction, and were prepared to follow their private codes of justice, whether their criminal adversaries be private or public. Although the first detective of this type is customarily said to be Carroll John Daly's Race Williams, who surfaced in 1927, he was fairly moderate in his activities and was not widely imitated. The departure point for the new type came when Mickey Spillane introduced Mike Hammer in 1947, a detective who is as violent and sadistic as the criminals he brings to justice. Since then, the path of violence has been dominant in a considerable part of American and British detective fiction and is a characteristic that may appear in professionals and amateurs alike. Violence in detective fiction does not, in many cases, abrogate the co-existence of ingenious or even brilliant detection. Such is the case with Thomas Harris's Hannibal Lecter, the repulsive psychotic who is manifestly one of the most remarkable detectives in the literature.

In British fiction, the private investigator took a different turn from the 1930s onwards, existing largely in the novels of popular writers like John Creasey. Since Britain had nothing like Pinkerton's and, in fact, had little experience of real detective agencies, the British PI developed as an extension of that still important element in British fiction, itself the product of British middle-class values, the 'hero-crook-adventurer', exemplified by earlier creations like A J Raffles and Hugh 'Bulldog' Drummond. The British PI was racy, usually gentlemanly, soft-hearted to ladies and the poor, had a general dislike for foreigners of every description and usually spent much of his time in the shadier clubs of London's West End, which were, of course, a totally closed book to nearly everyone in Britain.

It is, in fact, no wonder that, in 1939, a quiet young Englishman sat down with some street maps of Los Angeles and San Francisco, a few American travel books, some old detective stories, and wrote a novel set in California and featuring a couple of larger-than-life American private eyes. *No Orchids for Miss Blandish*, rejected (as had been the first Sherlock Holmes story exactly fifty years earlier) by most British publishers, was finally accepted and became a publishing sensation. In the next two decades, James Hadley Chase (as the author decided to call himself), using much the same rustic methodology, turned out a series of best sellers in which American private eye clones and epigones flowed from his pen. The classic British PI trend having been well and truly bucked, many British writers, especially after 1945, turned to creating American PIs. None, however, has been as successful as Chase. Conquest considers that the poor quality of most British fiction of this sort is because of the cultural and linguistic gap between British and American concepts.

The revolutionary changes in information and entertainment technology in the 1970s initiated changes in British society that brought it closer to American society. Fictional trends began to follow each other closely, encouraged by the increasingly multi-national character of the publishing industry. These changes have seen the emergence of a true breed of British private investigator, far-removed from real life perhaps, but nevertheless immediately recognisable and ideologically acceptable to the new audience. The 1980s and 1990s have thus seen the arrival of many excellent British PIs, male and female, white and black, city and provincial, exemplified by Liza Cody's Anna Lee and Cynthia Harrod-Eagles' Bill Slider.

- ***Professional Investigators***

Two other groups can be reasonably differentiated. The first group, cited as 'Professional Investigator', comprises all those characters who work for official or legal institutions and whose job it is to carry out investigations of one kind or another, yet are not themselves members of a police force. It includes, for instance, scientists or doctors who work with the police; hero-adventurers on government missions; operatives in the armed services who track down political criminals, spies or terrorists; quasi-detectives on official business, such as tax inspectors, food inspectors, railway detectives, insurance investigators (who may edge into other types) and even meter readers. The large groups of lawyers and journalists have not been included here; for, although they may work closely with the police, they do not, as professionals, have a legal role in investigating, unless in court. These two important groups are best regarded as dedicated amateurs (see below).

- ***Secret Agents***

The second of the two groups is cited as 'Secret Agent'. Espionage is a human activity that has been recorded from the earliest times and there are many references to it even in Greek and Roman literature. European history is replete with spies and secret agents, especially in periods of instability and turmoil. It has been said that in Tudor England almost every personage of social standing was probably a spy for somebody else. Espionage and detection are, in one sense, twin activities, for each must encompass something of the other. It is not surprising then, that almost the first entry in European detective fiction, Vidocq, freely admits to being a police spy. Nevertheless, as has been seen, the development of detective fiction took other paths. It was not until after the end of the First World War that what were eventually secret agents became the central protagonists of tales that were really part adventure and part detective stories. Most of the early authors were British. Writers like William Le Queux (probably himself a secret agent), Sidney Horler (of Dr Fu Manchu fame), John Buchan, and even Somerset Maugham (almost certainly a secret agent) had a field day creating some of the best, and certainly some of the most credible, spies in fiction, even if they did sometimes veer towards the 'with one bound Jack was free' kind of activity. The United States, at the time, had turned politically towards isolation and major American authors were not at that time greatly concerned with secret agents.

During the Second World War and the succeeding decades of the Cold War, spies, although never out, became definitely and increasingly in - on both sides of the Atlantic. Exemplified by its best-known character, Ian Fleming's James Bond, the secret agent is part adventurer, part old-time hero and part assassin and, in many cases, a detective by any other name. He sleuths because he has to, sometimes just to stay alive. He usually works for a government, but not necessarily his own. He may even spy for a non-governmental organisation, for the vast corporations of the modern world are well able to afford their own agents; and, indeed, he may sell his services to the highest bidder. The ethics of the secret agent vary. Somerset Maugham's early example, Ashenden, was almost without commitment, whereas John Le Carré's George Smiley is totally involved with what he conceives as his country's just cause. Many citations in this group, particularly American ones, are essentially non-political agents, working to right wrongs for non-political reasons. Although most of the secret agents in the current literature cannot be classed as detectives, the citations included are for those who, in some way, behave as classic sleuths.

- ***Amateurs***

Probably the largest category of detectives is the 'Amateur'. Vast, amorphous and historically of great importance, the group as a whole is relatively definable, for the amateur will start detecting for any and every reason known to man or woman, except being paid for it. The amateur can be anybody, of any profession, race, creed or nationality. The temptation to subdivide the category has been resisted, for that would involve the designation of so many sub-types as to be confusing. Rather, the preferred method has been to give any relevant details or descriptions in the detective narrative.

Amateurs, as defined, include detectives whose activities impinge closely on those of the professional amateurs. Thus, Agatha Christie's Jane Marple does not behave so very differently from her Hercule Poirot. Ellery Queen's eponymous sleuth differs from S S

Van Dine's Philo Vance only in being even more brilliant. Before 1945, authors needed little excuse for their amateur detectives. In Britain, being of a superior class, at best an aristocrat, opened all doors, especially those closed to the peasantry of which the police were comprised in the books of most authors (although some did invent police detectives who appeared to come from some higher, if not the top, drawer). Dropping final g's, using jocular slang, fondness for phrases like 'Oh my Giddy Aunt', pipe-smoking, knowledge of good wines and a college education (if not an actual degree) were sufficient qualifications. The amateur detectives of the 1920s and 1930s found their own reasons for taking to detection. Many were clearly shown to be from a generation that had suffered terribly in the slaughter of the First World War. Disappointed by the state of society on their return, their class roots undermined, often personally hurt, they took to sleuthing, as Lord Peter Wimsey said, 'out of boredom' but also because it provided some of the undoubted excitement of the war itself. All the author had to do, in this context, was to invent reasons for the amateur to be on the scene and no more questions were asked. It was for similar reasons that another group of British amateurs took to at least part-time sleuthing. The 1920s saw the burgeoning of countless hero-adventurers, highly trained by the war and having enough in the way of worldly wealth to maintain them in a state of constant unemployment. Taking little notice of the law, they took it on themselves to hunt down criminals, spies, most foreigners and rotters of various kinds, rather as they did the Boche in 1914. The archetypal 'Bulldog' Drummond became, during his heyday, the most famous character in British fiction.

In America, where a college degree could actually be obtained by a member of the working classes, where childish slang was definitely not the thing, and neither campanology nor claret were well known, something more was definitely needed of the amateur detective of the 1920s and 1930s. The United States might have no nobility but, even so, the right college, the right religion, the right skin colour and a reasonable amount of money were regular requirements. The American amateur detective, like the PI, also differentiated into two main types. The first, the classic amateur, followed the British model, introducing genre giants like Philo Vance, geniuses like Ellery Queen and loveable characters like Nick and Nora Charles. They operated by skill and vast intellect and their cases were often the most ingenious intellectual puzzles, crimes of a personal and private nature.

A second group followed the trends being set by the professionals and came to depend on exotic, often abnormal and occasionally bizarre characteristics. A host of 'scientific detectives', typified by Arthur B Reeve's amazingly brainy Craig Kennedy, appeared and made use of baffling, up-to-the-minute but not necessarily real technology to defeat the poor, misguided criminal, who could not yet be expected to appreciate such arts. For detectives of this ilk, who usually had to teach the police what was what, even scientific methods often proved inadequate in their struggle against crime. Many of them turned out to be great athletes or magnificent boxers and they could usually shoot a hole in a dime at a hundred paces. Whereas, in Britain, scientific detectives, like John Rhodes' Dr Priestley, had their technical feet firmly on the ground even if they were as dull as ditchwater, their American cousins might suspend the second law of thermodynamics if the occasion demanded it, as long as the outcome provided excitement.

The American amateur tended, in many ways, to follow his antecedents from the pulps (see below), which, with their long history, continued to have a powerful effect. The American amateur might be one-armed, one-legged, haemophiliac, blind, deaf or crippled; but, in an extension of their detective skills, they could compensate in the most remarkable ways for life's little handicaps, proving more than a match for simple criminals who merely had the normal complement of limbs and senses. The trend continued and blossomed into a cluster of 'superman' detectives, to which American fiction has been more accommodating than has the British school. Some, like Bob Kane's Batman, are enjoyable in their own right as well as having reasonable detective credentials.

Introduction

Failing both a good family and great riches, on both sides of the Atlantic amateur detection was open country for lawyers. The law, as a profession, certainly provides the most excellent opportunity for entering the crime scene at any level and it has been taken advantage of by many authors. Although, in British fiction, lawyers (solicitors and barristers) have never, in recent times, comprised a major group of detectives, they appeared as amateur sleuths to a considerable extent in Victorian novels, whose plots were largely concerned with thefts of precious jewels, wills and inheritances. By the 1920s and 1930s, they were supplanted by non-professional amateurs, as already noted, although a few appear still.

In America, things were different, for there the legal profession is more closely allied with the police and, at all levels, is of great social importance, its members often being found in positions of political power. The American legal profession has probably provided more amateur detectives (although sometimes performing a professional inquisitional role) than any other. Some of the earliest American amateurs were lawyers, and country detectives were often judges or attorneys. The record number of appearances for any one detective, under one author, must surely be that of Erle Stanley Gardner's Perry Mason, the fighting, sleuthing legendary lawyer incarnate.

Outside the legal profession, it seems almost anybody can be an amateur detective. A major group, of course, is that of the meek, elderly ladies, typified by masterpieces like Jane Marple and Maud Silver, and of tough old ladies like Palmyra Pym and Mrs Bradley and continuing magnificently with creations like Dorothy Gilman's Mrs Pollifax and M C Beaton's Agatha Raisin. It is noticeable that all these are from British authors. On the whole, American authors do not care for elderly ladies as sleuths, meek or not, and have not created a major detective of this type. A few minor ones exist, however, such as Anita Blackmon's harridan, Adelaide Adams, and Richard Barth's bag-lady, Margaret Binton. There are, of course, American female amateurs in abundance, but few are little and hardly any are elderly. Quite the contrary.

Medical men of all kinds have proved useful, and perhaps the most credible, amateur sleuths. On the whole, British authors have gone for good solid physicians like Austin R Freeman's Dr Thorndyke and H C Bailey's Reggie Fortune, with the occasional brain surgeon or psychiatrist making only a fleeting appearance. American authors, on the other hand, have gone strongly for psychologists and psychiatrists, good snoopers all and certainly with sound credentials for investigating certain types of crime. As with lawyers, this too reflects the powerful role filled by psychiatric medicine in the United States, a phenomenon that has no real parallel in Britain. It is also true that many of the most highly regarded American authors have actually been practising psychologists and psychiatrists.

Academics of various sorts also provide a major source of amateur detectives. Professors, lecturers, and even students make excellent sleuths and have the built-in advantage of their cleverness being taken for granted. Murder on the campus is a field that has been mined exhaustively, for emotions run high in college and misdeeds abound in universities. British academics tend to be aloof, drink port and given to quoting from the classics, a sure way to increase the already existing bafflement of the police. American academics, on the other hand, are not unknown to take coffee with students, rarely know Greek and are prone to believe in social justice and racial tolerance. More difficult a group to use than it once was, it features some of the delights of detective fiction, introducing us to characters such as Edmund Crispin's Gervase Fen in Britain and Clyde B Classon's Theocritus Lucius Westborough in America.

Men of religion have always proved attractive as amateur sleuths, although their number is not large. In the main they have tended to be Catholic priests, whose work brings them into close contact with a community and provides them with excellent opportunities for asking questions. At the pinnacle, indisputably, stands G K Chesterton's Father Brown, but American authors have invented some excellent priest detectives, notably Ralph McInerny's

Father Dowling. In recent times, women have entered the field, with nuns like Kate Gallison's Mother Lavinia Grey and Carol Anne O'Marie's Sister Mary Helen emulating their brothers in the religious fold. In America too, although not yet in Britain, Jewish rabbis seem not forbidden to do a little sleuthing, as can be seen from Harry Kemelman's fine creation, David Small.

Murder, it would seem, is an occupational hazard of stage and film. Actors and actresses, but, interestingly, rarely directors, figure prominently among amateur detectives, for they exist in the kind of closed world that is so given to mayhem, where scenery is always falling on hated producers and stage daggers are frequently plunged into the splendid bosoms of leading ladies. Simon Brett's Charles Paris is a fine example of the modern trend in Britain, as is Jane Dentinger's Jocelyn O'Roarke in America. Pride of place may perhaps be accorded to Stuart M Kaminsky's unique inventions, featuring Hollywood in the 1930s and 1940s, in which the stars themselves assist in the sleuthing.

Among the professions, journalists, because of the nature of their work, are particularly useful as amateur sleuths. In America, where the investigative press has a more honoured place than it does in Britain, journalist sleuths have a long history, starting with the pulps. George Harmon Coxe's 'Flashgun' Casey, hero of several novels in the 1940s, started his career in the pulps. The use of reporters of various kinds is even more common now than in earlier days in both Britain and America, partly, one suspects, because the more traditional ways of allowing amateurs to investigate crimes have become less credible. Authors have an easy option with so-called 'investigative journalists', who seem to require little supportive evidence for their existence.

There has always been interest in historical detectives and this is a trend that has grown greatly since the 1970s. British authors, in particular, have been busy creating detectives, usually amateur, but sometimes connected to police forces or earlier official bodies. From the twelfth onwards, hardly a century has been left unravaged. Medieval detectives have proved highly attractive to writers with a good sense of history as well to distinguished professional historians with the ability to write. The mistress of the field is Edith Pargeter, a prolific writer of detective fiction, whose twelfth-century sleuth, Brother Caedfel has proved one of the most popular in current British fiction. Cardace M Robb is one of several authors to have captured the fourteenth century, with his ex-army detective, Owen Archer, and P C Doherty has created several sleuths bestriding the fifteenth, especially Matthew Jenkyn. Tudor detectives abound in the seventeenth century and are exemplified by P F Chisholm's Sir Robert Carey. Bruce Alexander's real-life figure, the blind magistrate, John Fielding, appears in the eighteenth, taking it over from other authors' Bow Street Runners. Not surprisingly, it is the nineteenth century that has been most exploited. Regency bucks like Kate Ross's Julian Kestrel appear in the early years, but it is the age of Victoria that is heaven-sent for the historical detective story, with its Keystone Cops police forces, the gaslight and hansom cabs, and, above all, formality, rules and boundaries, on which the genre has thrived from its very beginning. Fine Victorian detectives now occur in abundance and are exemplified by Anne Perry's husband-and-wife team of Thomas and Charlotte Pitt, solitary figures like Evelyn Hervey's Harriet Unwin and Emily Brightwell's recent addition, Mrs Jeffries.

American detective fiction has been hampered, of course, by the fact that American history is relatively short. American authors have, on the whole, tended to show less interest in creating historical detectives, although several recent PIs have been set back to the 1940s and 1950s, trading nostalgically on the aura surrounding the early gumshoe. However, there are signs that more American authors are now creating characters from their exciting past. A rich vein has been tapped by Elliott Roosevelt in his transformation of Eleanor Roosevelt, first lady in the 1930s, into a formidable sleuth in and around the White House, while her husband has other things on his mind. David Alexander has gone further back in his transmogrification of President Theodore Roosevelt, who had genuine police connections, into an amateur sleuth. Miriam Grace Monfredo has recently charted new areas with her invention of Glynis Tryon, who fights for women's rights and against slavery in the 1840s and 1850s but has to solve many a murder on the way. Further back into American history, the scientist, Benjamin Franklin, has been metamorphosed into a sleuth by at least three authors, especially Robert Lee Hall. The historically earliest detective found is S S Rafferty's Captain Cork, who does his sleuthing in the 1750s, when America was still a British colony.

Apart from the main groups of amateurs are all those hundreds of characters who appear in a vast range of books, often excellent but including others that must be regarded as in the nether end of fiction (for which Bill Pronzini's *Gun in Cheek* and *Son of Gun in Cheek* are compulsive as well as compulsory reading). They include the great eccentrics like Carter Dickson's Sir Henry Merrivale; oddballs like Michael Avallone's extraordinary Ed Noon; characters who appear just once but become known forever, like Iris Carr in Ethel Lina White's novel, *The Wheel Spins*, which was made into the classic film, *The Lady Vanishes*. They include the hundreds of young men who suspect that their uncle's death is not due, as the police think, to heart failure; the hundreds of young women who are to become the next victim of someone out there unless they do something about it; doctors who suspect their patients and patients who know the doctor did it; all butlers, of course; and nearly everyone who attended British country house parties in the 1930s. New and interesting ways of using amateurs to enter the crime scene continue to be invented and often give rise to vogues that last for some time before they too become discarded. A recent and really rather fascinating fashion is for amateur detectives who are in the food or catering business. Chefs, cooks, good plain cooks, haute cuisine cooks, hotel managers and innkeepers are surfacing like corks in a bath-tub. Not only is poison back on the criminous menu after its sad fictional decline, in recent years, in favour of (admittedly often inventive) thuggery, but some authors almost build their stories around meals. Indeed, the most enterprising provide menus and recipes in depth and as part of the narrative. Amy Myers' master chef, Auguste Didier, has three hats, being fascinatingly French, interestingly and historically Victorian, and brilliantly culinary. In America, where the trend is so pronounced that the stories are called 'Bed-and-Breakfast' mysteries, Claudia Bishop's engaging sisters, Sarah and Meg Quilliam, who run a hotel renowned through the state for its cuisine, meet mayhem continually.

- ***Pulp***

The final detective type categorised is called 'Pulp', a term intended to be historical and descriptive and in no sense derogatory. Although the term, in fact, covers a multitude of detectives of almost every category already discussed, separate treatment of this group seems warranted because of the special nature of the characters that can be gathered into it. Around the 1880s in the United States, in an age that saw rapid advances in printing processes, transport, communications and other facets of an expanding industrial society, several magazines appeared, usually 7 by 10 inches in size, with a glossy cover carrying a lurid picture, and about a hundred pages of cheap wood-pulp paper. The pulp magazines had arrived. They specialised in short stories, racy adventures, horror tales and mysteries at first, and later incorporated amazing new scientifically-based tales, designed for the new literate masses. Some of them were soon featuring home-grown detectives. Their numbers are virtually uncountable and many are certainly now lost. They were written rapidly by some of the most prolific writers of all time and they appeared in their hundreds. The New York Detective Library, for example, ran for 801 issues, between 1882 and 1888, and Gary Hoppenstand's collection, *The Dime Novel Detective,* cites several hundred names. The pulp detectives of the early era were essentially local, sometimes produced for just one or a very few stories. To maintain interest, the authors often endowed their detectives with some extraordinary power or attribute that could serve in good stead in their ceaseless fight against criminals. By the turn of the century, more enduring detectives were appearing, including several of the famous boy detectives and even girl detectives that were becoming popular among the young adult readership. There was no similar type of publication in Britain during this period, although many weekly and fortnightly magazines existed, usually filled with items of a domestic or religious nature, interspersed with romantic stories or simple mystery stories. The *Strand Magazine* of the late 1880s was read by middle-class gentlemen and sometimes their ladies; and, when it published the first Sherlock Holmes stories, it was being highly adventurous. However, in the first decade of the new century, British publishing magnates like Pearson and Harmsworth saw the potential in the new young adult readership and produced dozens of magazines aimed at that market. In many of them boy and girl detectives blossomed, although hardly ever in the same magazine and, of course, never together.

In America, the end of the First World War ushered in an era of moral relaxation and increasing lawlessness, which provided a vast new resource from which the old-time pulps profited immensely. During the 1920s and 1930s, literally hundreds of pulp magazines flourished, some for short periods, some lasting almost into the 1960s. Several were devoted entirely to crime fiction and, in their pages, appeared the classic pulp detectives, invented rapidly by fine professional authors and published even more quickly. They included amateurs, professionals, policemen, scientists and sportsmen; detectives on land, sea and in the air; boys and girls; detectives of many races and of many colours. This was the era that saw the birth of 'Two-gun' Race Williams, the legendary Nick Carter and the standard-bearing Nancy Drew. The pulps gave excitement to millions, even though they often stooped to a low level to do so, but they created a culture that has never disappeared from American detective fiction. The magazines had all but gone by the early 1960s, no longer having a place in a society that had grown up but had, in the process, lowered its standards. Although it would be impossible to include most of the pulp detectives, even if they could be found, a representative sample, with the slender information available, has been cited.

- ***Unidentified and Minor Types***

A few detectives clearly do not belong to the seven types listed above. For example, several detectives are policemen who have left the force for one reason or another and now practise independently, half amateur and half professional. They are cited as 'ex-Police'. There are a few sub-sets of detectives who operate in groups without individual identifications. Furthermore, although almost all the detectives in the Index belong to the species, *homo sapiens*, some authors have created animal detectives at least as plausible and often appearing to have considerably more of 'the little grey cells' than some of the human characters perforce included. Several cats and one dog qualify and they are cited, respectively as 'Cat' and 'Dog'. Other animal species do not occur but several non-terrestials do and are categorised as 'Alien'. If it has not been possible to arrive at a conclusion about a detective's type, the term 'Sleuth' has been used.

Sidekicks

The Detective record gives known associates (designated Sidekicks) of fictional detectives. Although the importance of sidekicks in detective fiction is well recognised, discovering them is more difficult than discovering detectives. As far as can be ascertained, only one major bibliographic source has provided an index and that is the *Encyclopaedia of Mystery and Detection*, edited by C Steinbrunner and O Penzler (1976), which contains a short section entitled 'Rogues and Helpers'. The key role of the sidekick in detective fiction was recognised in its misty beginnings by the founding fathers of the genre. Indeed, at first, it was a necessary invention. Poe, in his first story *The Murder in the Rue Morgue*, had Auguste Dupin relate the facts to a loyal but virtually uncomprehending assistant. Conan Doyle's sidekick *nonpareil*, Dr Watson, became so much the linchpin of Sherlock Holmes stories that it can be said that their remarkable success was, to a large extent, due to the author's stroke of genius in inventing him.

The earliest sidekicks were often unnamed, like Dupin's 'friend', and even when they narrated the stories they played a fairly passive role. Dr Watson changed all that; but, by the time of his creation, the stories themselves had changed. By the 1920s and 1930s, sidekicks became almost necessary and all the great detectives had one. They entered the stories properly, might narrate them, would provide a sounding-board for the detective's thoughts and would even carry out tasks that the great men might not wish to do or sometimes could not do. Their usefulness, of course varied. It would be impossible to imagine Nero Wolfe if it were not for the narrative, labours and deeply etched character of Archie Goodwin. But it became apparent to Agatha Christie, when her readers continued to yawn over Captain Hastings, that he was a complete bore and a drag on Hercule Poirot and she took the usual course of marrying him off. Albert Campion's brilliantly conceived, ex-burglar valet is of considerable use, for he can drive cars, pick locks, and mix with the underworld when he is not mixing the sleuth's drinks. Even the brilliant Ellery Queen could not have functioned without his father, Inspector Queen of the New York Police Department, available to feed him the facts and listen to his blatherings. The old-style amateurs, who could seemingly go anywhere and do anything, could take or leave sidekicks as they pleased, in one sense; for, in general, the baffled police were only too eager to seek their help. As detective fiction moved, in the 1940s and 1950s, just a little towards realism, the major problem for authors was increasingly how to get their amateur detectives into the crime scene. By now, the police were a little less stupid and a little more touchy about outsiders and entries of all sorts had to be invented. It even became acceptable for gifted amateurs to use friendly cops (to whom they might stand in various types of relationship) as legitimate sidekicks, for the purposes of moving the story along. If you were to appear in just one book in which you simply investigated a suspicious death because you were on the premises, you probably could do it on your own. If the author and the audience liked you so much that you had to be given the opportunity of solving cases *seriatim*, you could do worse than get yourself a sidekick.

Authors have exercised as little restraint in the invention of sidekicks as in the creation of the detectives themselves. They too can come in any size, sex, profession, anatomical and even zoological type. Dr Watson and even Archie Goodwin would not be out of place at a Church bazaar, but Peter Wimsey's Bunter could not mingle with the bourgeoisie and Albert Campion's ex-burglar sidekick, Magersfontein Lugg, would definitely be *de trop*. Series sidekicks over the decades have included characters as diverse as Inspector Schmidt's patiently toiling George Bagby; Perry Mason's unchangeable secretary, Della Street; the fictional Dr Sam Johnson's fictional narrator, James Boswell; Sexton Blake's (almost as famous and certainly as revered) Tinker; Carlotta Carlyle's feline Thomas C Carlyle; and Nick and Nora Charles' canine Asta. Many modern sidekicks have become, like many modern detectives, more grotesque or outrageous as authors attempt to keep them in the limelight. There are repulsive sidekicks like the saintly Bridget O'Toole's Harry Garnish; Jeremiah St John's delightfully shocking Michelle Farabaugh, who was sacked from an Ohio police force for posing for a magazine; Burke's collection of oddball sidekicks such as Max the Silent; and the unsavoury, streetwise Hawk, who has become attached to Robert B Parker's Spenser.

Male amateur sleuths have often been accompanied by female sidekicks. In most cases, especially in earlier days, the latter were strictly subordinate, helpful about the place, as it were, and often shown as adoring the boss; but sometimes they could be girlfriends, lovers or wives. Female detectives have occasionally had female assistants but have, in the main, tended to manage without them. It would be difficult to name a great female detective before 1980 (and there are many) who had a great female sidekick, although the numerous girl detectives, who mainly existed in years between the two world wars, almost always had impressionable and loyal chums. Things in this area are now changing too. As female detectives of all kinds continue to increase in number, their female sidekicks are becoming more prominent. That recent addition to the world of feminine sleuthing, the delightful Judith McMonigle Flynn, could hardly function without constant recourse to Cousin Renie. And with so many of the female additions being demonstrably and sometimes aggressively lesbian or even transvestite, female sidekicks are becoming more natural assistants. Indeed, the really tough sleuths on the distaff side are not above using male sidekicks.

Detectives created specifically for the teenage market, like Sexton Blake, mainly in the first half of the twentieth century, always had sidekicks in the shape of young adolescents, male or female depending on whether the stories were written for boys or girls, and they usually played vital roles in the stories. The numerous boy-detectives and girl-detectives, in Britain and America, often had loyal but subordinate sidekicks. A fascinating feature of the decades before 1939 was the extraordinary availability of clever dogs as sidekicks. A girl's best friend in the 1920s and 1930s was usually large, often Alsatian and nearly always male. It could open doors, jump through flames, deliver messages, bring help and rescue its mistress when necessary.

With the advent of the private eye in the 1930s and 1940s, sidekicks became less necessary to the detective. The very ethos of the early PI was that he was a man who stood on his own, a private man, without overt relationships. Such men as Philip Marlowe did not need sidekicks to do their dirty work, carry messages, interpret their thoughts or have police connections. The early PI's connections to officialdom were at best tenuous and often antagonistic. Paradoxically, as the PI developed and often became both more human and less human, he seemed in greater need of assistants. Many of them, like Mike Hammer, became kitted out with beautiful blonde secretaries, legmen, undercover operatives, henchmen, streetmen and even partners. Some of these sidekicks fulfilled, not just a major role in the detective work, but an essential structural part of the story-telling, as does Nero Wolfe's inimitable Archie Goodwin.

A major part of detective fiction has, of course, always used policemen as central characters. In the main, the early British and American police detectives tended to be sturdy individualists, rarely needing to shed the load or wishing to share the honours. Most of the great classic British policemen, from Inspector French to Inspector Appleby, had subordinates, sometimes named, but these were truly such and rarely functioned as important sidekicks. However, there are some notable exemptions. Ngaio Marsh's Inspector Alleyn was assisted by Inspector Fox, almost the best police sidekick ever invented - perhaps just as well, for he made up for the sad weaknesses in the detective abilities of his boss.

Early American cops followed much the same pattern but there was a greater tendency for them to work with partners, many of them taking only a subordinate role and qualifying as sidekicks. The development of the police procedural made it necessary for authors to pay much more attention to giving their lead policemen credible sidekicks. In the last two decades, hardly any self-respecting cop could exist without a rapidly manufactured sidekick, usually (in Britain at least) a rather dim-witted sergeant. In more recent times, police sidekicks have become more intelligent, have sometimes been to college, have domestic lives of their own and aspire to useful detective work. Commensurate with the growing numbers of female detectives of all kinds, it is becoming common for male cops to have female policewomen as sidekicks, a phenomenon almost unheard of until the late 1970s. At first it was obvious that authors invented them, in keeping with the times, solely for their mild sexual interest, but latterly they have played an increasingly important role. Not only have female sergeants or lieutenants become wives, lovers, and other kinds of sexual partners to erstwhile dominant male cops, but they are allowed to take a real part in detection. Many female police sidekicks, however, remain too obviously synthetic, pure devices to raise readers' temperatures. Senior women cops are still as rare in fiction as they are in life. The most senior by far is Jennie Melville's Charmian Daniels, who, like most women in other parts of detective fiction, seems not to need a sidekick.

Although fictional detectives, whether amateur, professional or official, have in the main operated singly, around ten per cent of all records in the Index refer to detective pairs. As has already been discussed, they may consist of two detectives of the same type (amateur or police for example) or be a duo composed of an official and amateur sleuth. Many types of combination are possible. Clearly it is not always possible to distinguish the detective-sidekick relationship from the detective duo or partnership and it has been necessary to make some arbitrary decisions. Reference to existing authoritative sources is unhelpful in this respect; for some do not admit detective pairs, while those that cite them do not distinguish sidekicks from partners. Authors generally find it difficult to balance detective roles between partners although their intentions may be to do so. With very few exceptions, most partnerships fail to maintain interest, the problem of dominance always manifesting itself. Where it is clearly the author's intention to create a partnership, it has nearly always been cited as such. Where the partnership tends to be a device or simply a bow to a trend, as with a number of modern police novels, the obviously subordinate member of the duo is cited as a sidekick. According to such criteria, sidekicks are distinguished, not by rank or other hierarchical order, but by being subordinate to the detective's motives and actions.

Stooges

The third type of character categorised is called 'Stooge'. From the very beginnings of detective fiction, authors have realised that additional dramatic tension can be created by facing their sleuths with adversaries other than the criminal. Wilkie Collins' Sergeant Cuff, the first police detective to occupy a central role in English fiction, already had a cross to bear in the shape of his superior, the stupidly arrogant Superintendent Seegrave. Sherlock Holmes had to suffer the ineptitude of Inspector Lestrade. The American PI, from his inception, was almost always being hounded, threatened and even arrested by unimpressed and antagonist cops. Rex Stout's Nero Wolfe saga would not be the classic it is were it not for the clashes between the detective and Inspector Cramer and their theatrical, climactic finishes.

The stooge is present in many types of detective fiction, although not always easy to identify. Where he is, he is worth citing. He (occasionally she) is considered to be a character who stands in apposition, although not always in opposition, to a story's hero-detective, both being in pursuit of the same ends. Virtually all amateur detectives have, perforce, to interact with the police. Although, from a textual point of view, this is totally unnecessary, such interaction provides the moral infrastructure without which, as Erik Routley says, civilised society would find detective fiction unacceptable. In the great days of amateur detectives, the interaction could be delayed or minimised by the author and, as already noted, early amateurs had little real trouble with the police. Certainly, early cops could be overbearing to gifted amateurs, but they could also be friendly, helpful and actively seek advice. In the modern era, when amateur entry in to the crime scene is constrained and has to be contrived by the author, police stooges must be better motivated. John Lutz's PI, Fred Carver, is faced with Insp McGregor, one of the best-drawn police stooges in the genre and one of the most evil characters to be found anywhere. Not all stooges are policeman behaving obnoxiously to amateurs. Police detectives themselves have sometimes to bear the brunt of stupid, browbeating, corrupt or malevolent superiors. Catherine Aird's Insp C D Sloan must suffer interminable discussions with his superior, the stupid and lazy Superintendent Leeyes, who somehow manages to help him solve his cases. But, like detectives, stooges can run the gamut of types. They need only to have one attribute; they must *never* be right about whodunnit.

Location

The Detective record, wherever possible, gives an idea of the specific or general location of a detective's operations. Although some locations can be stated concisely, some cannot and for various reasons. Sometimes authors do not state or clarify the locations of their books and do not wish to do so; sometimes detectives operate in several different locations; sometimes the locations are bizarre (including extra-terrestrial space) and cannot be identified. In general (an interesting sidelight this on cultural differences), American authors seem to like their country far more than British authors. Mostly they set, and have always tended to set, their crime stories in real places, usually named - New York, Chicago, San Francisco, Detroit and Boston. British authors shy away from such disclosures, although London has nearly always to be identified, since its milieu is unique and the majority of fictional as well as real crime occurs there. British authors become irritatingly vague when their books are set outside the great wen. Villages are invented with curious names; counties (and Britain has some superb ones) disappear and detectives operate in unbelievable places called Downshire and Upshire. Good solid British towns like Newcastle, Manchester and Birmingham, where crime is presumably not unknown, become monstrosities called Newcaster, Maningham and Riverford. This tradition must represent something deep in the national collective psyche, for it is already observable in the works of most of the great Victorian novelists. In the 1990s, however, things do seem to be changing and British provincial readers can sleep soundly at night, knowing that, at last, they are only a stone's throw away from a murder and that a detective is at hand to solve it.

Pastiches and Parodies

A feature of 'The Detectives' is its delineation of pastiches and parodies. A few detectives are of sufficient stature to have attracted authors other than their original creators. They fall into several categories:

1. When the death of an author has left the publishers an exceptional resource in the shape of his creation, that asset may be further exploitable if time, tide and the mood of the general public are right. When Margery Allingham died, her husband, Youngman Carter, wrote two more books featuring Albert Campion. After the death of Ian Fleming, several authors were induced to write further books featuring James Bond. Bruce Graeme's son, Roderic Jeffries, continued to write stories featuring his father's detective, Blackshirt, for many years. Barry Perowne took over E W Hornung's A J Raffles after the death of the creator. Several books featuring Rex Stout's Nero Wolfe have been written by Robert Goldsborough. Many such efforts at extension have a limited life, depending really on the classic potential of the detective, with all that is implied by that term. Clearly, characters like A J Raffles and James Bond are so much embedded in the constraints of their era that any potential readership must dwindle as the years pass. Only the truly great stay: Sherlock Holmes of course (see below); Philip Marlowe probably; and the jury must be considered to be still out on Nero Wolfe, depending on how future writers handle him. The works of secondary authors are cited as pastiches, which serves to identify them in the Detective record.
2. Some detectives and authors have, for diverse reasons, become industries in their own right. For over half a century, for example, there was, in Britain, a vast output of mostly ephemeral novels and short stories featuring popular detectives like Sexton Blake, Nelson Lee and Dixon Brett. The original begetters are now obscure and it is best to cite all such publications as original works rather than pastiches. For many years, Ellery Queen continued to be an author of novels featuring some of his earlier detectives - although not, it seems, Ellery Queen the detective - long after the original two cousins behind that illustrious name had died. Many detectives have become publishers' house names and continue in print under various hands. Where such as these appear, they are treated as independent detectives, not pastiches.

3. Some detectives appear under different authors' names, which are actually pseudonyms of the same author. These are not treated as pastiches.
4. Some detectives belonging to an author may be temporarily borrowed by another author, perhaps for one book and under joint authorship. Bill Pronzoni has enjoyed himself in this way, sharing detectives with Marcia Muller and John Lutz. Frances and Richard Lockridge published under three different by-lines, sharing the same detectives. None of these forgoing examples have been treated as pastiches.
5. Raymond Chandler's detective, Philip Marlowe, stands alone in American fiction. His classic qualities, archetypal, fathomless and infinitely exploitable, combine to make him a character of endless appeal to modern writers and he continues to be the subject of new novels and, especially, short stories. All those found have been individually cited and have been treated as pastiches.

Sherlock Holmes

The outstanding example of the detective who does not die is Sherlock Holmes. He stands unequivocally and absolutely at the top of any hierarchy it is possible to make and must be treated exceptionally. He has, almost from his inception and by some extraordinary magic, fascinated countless writers. Although Sir Arthur Conan Doyle wrote about him in only four novels and fifty-six short stories, such is his appeal that dozens of other authors have, for over a century, written stories with Holmes as the detective. They vary vastly in nature. There are short stories, in strict emulation of the master, incorporating rules that must be obeyed and obliquities that can be only be transgressed at the author's peril. There is a large group of such stories that base themselves on the allusions made in the original canon to unpublished cases, often offering tantalising scraps of information on which the pastiche writer can work. Doyle's son, Adrian Conan Doyle, collaborated with a modern master, John Dickson Carr, to write many such adventures; and June Thomson has, even within the last few years, produced three new volumes of such pastiches, in perfect style.

Some authors, spurning the short story form, have written full-length pastiche novels in which many of the characters from the canonical saga appear side by side with new ones. Nicholas Meyer's *The Seven Percent Solution* is a modern classic of the form. American authors have been among the foremost in the production of new Sherlock Holmes pastiches and have been at their most ingenious in devising new plots and situations. Holmes has been placed all over America and has been made to collaborate or vie with other detectives; he has been teamed up with a host of historical figures from Harry Houdini to the President of the United States; he has been induced to solve past crimes and future ones; he has sleuthed in Heaven and he has sleuthed in Hell, in the distant future and the dim past, in space and in the bowels of the earth.

Extending from the pastiches are the parodies. Clearly, even from the outset, there was something about Holmes that invited burlesque. Perhaps it was the fact that, not only was he always right, but that others were always wrong. Perhaps it was his extraordinary method. The parodies, as they are defined, feature detectives who deliberately and explicitly copy Holmes in mannerisms, situation or methodology. Often they are comic and come to grief, for the author is attempting to undermine the pedestal on which Holmes stands. By 1903, the American writer, John Kendrick Bangs, was already publishing stories featuring Shylock Homes; and parody writing has not ceased since, although perhaps the genre reached a peak with Robert Fish's series featuring Schlock Homes. There is, however, a group of more affectionate parodies, written in the style of the classic canon. Foremost amongst them are the stories written from the 1940s through the 1960s by August Derleth, which feature Solar Pons, a parody only by definition for he brilliantly emulates the master.

Extending beyond the more conventional parodies is a large group in which the detective is manifestly not Holmes or a parody of him but is in some way fictionally related to him. In this group are to be found some of the most delightful modern creations. There are

Holmes' sons, daughters, cousins and his brother Mycroft. Dr Watson himself has been used as a main detective by several authors and even Dr Watson's wife has appeared. Conan Doyle has teamed himself up with Holmes and even dear Mrs Hudson, the archetypal housekeeper at 221B Baker Street, has become a detective. As the eddies flow outwards, M J Trow has produced a marvellous series of Victorian parody-pastiches in which the detective hero is the fumbling Insp Lestrade, the persistent stooge in the Holmes canon. And of late, even Irene Adler, '*the* woman' as Holmes called her, who only ever appeared in *A Scandal in Bohemia*, is the detective-heroine of a new series.

In a bibliography of detectives it would be difficult to avoid either the importance of Sherlock Holmes as a phenomenon or the world-wide, never-ceasing interest he engenders. Accordingly, and in dedication, there is included in 'The Detectives', by title and reference, every original (canonical) story, pastiche and parody featuring Sherlock Holmes or related to the original canon that it has been possible to discover.

Guide to 'The Detectives'

This book is primarily about fictional detectives; but, although both the literary and bibliographic information relevant to full appreciation of them and their creators is rewarding, it is often complex. 'The Detectives'– the central part of this book attempts to provide that information in clear and logical form, so that the reader has access to it without necessarily having to consult subsidiary indexes. To achieve this, many of the Detective records are linked to others in such a way that the reader can obtain, at any point in the book, an accurate and comprehensive view of all the information concerning either a detective or an author that appears anywhere else in the book. This guide describes the structure of 'The Detectives' and how to use it.

A model detective record is shown on page 33. It consists of up to eighteen parts, some of which may be repeated, each giving a different kind of information relevant to the detective, author or publications. The guide discusses the components sequentially and, at appropriate points, parts from this record or other records are displayed in boxes to illustrate particular aspects of the subject matter.

Detective

Perry MASON

The citation gives, first, the full name (including a sobriquet, if known) of the detective and any title or rank he may have. In general, 'The Detectives' is arranged alphabetically by surname. However, some detectives have names or sobriquets that cannot sensibly be cited except as a whole: in such cases, the whole name is given, in alphabetical order. If a detective is known to appear, not only as the only detective, but in combination with one or more other detectives, every such combination is treated as a separate entity and is the subject of an individual citation, although the ancillary information is not repeated. Furthermore, the second detective of a pair or multiple is always cited (by name only) independently and in proper order and always points to the first detective, allowing for immediate access to information on the pair or multiple. Where a detective is cited, either solely or additionally, as appearing with at least two other detectives, the citation always points to the detective under whom the most information can be obtained. *The total sequential organisation of 'The Detectives' therefore facilitates immediate reference to every detective appearing anywhere in the book.*

It is remarkable how many different ranks or modes of address have been invented for sleuths. Over one hundred titles have been found, ranging from the humble 'Mr', through doctors, captains, generals, knights and earls, to the pinnacle of 'King of England' for the two British monarchs known to have been drafted into the genre.

In a sequence of detectives having the same surname the order is given by the forename without the rank, if cited, being relevant. Detective pairs and multiples follow the first name rule and, where their first detective is the same as a single detective, always follow that detective in order. The alphabetical order follows American rather than British classifications. Thus, names beginning with **Mc** are separated from those beginning with **Mac**. The abbreviation **St**, where it occurs at the beginning of a name, is regarded as a whole word and appears in its natural alphabetical order. Names containing apostrophes, such as M'Guire and O'Hara, are treated as if the apostrophe did not exist. Names preceded by a rank or title, or with any symbol or number, or with the indefinite or definite article, or with quotation marks, are treated as if that rank, title, symbol, number or quotation mark did not exist and they appear in normal surname order.

Detective's Narrative

is one of the great classic investigators of the genre, appearing in over eighty novels from 1933 to 1973 (that is, three years after the author's death)...

The detective's name is followed, in many cases, by a narrative that gives useful or important information about the character. It may include details of his appearance, qualities, mannerisms, mode of operating, the types of crime he may have investigated and, if important, reference to his progress through a series or canon of books. Where second or third detectives are cited, the same may be done for them.

The narratives attached to the various detectives vary considerably in length as well as scope, as some detectives are, for a number of reasons, more important than others. Their chronological emergence may be of significance in the history of detective fiction; they may have special attributes (even defective ones); they may use exceptional or novel methods; they may have appeared in exceptional books or at an exceptional time; or they may be innovatory in some particular respect. Some detectives are given longer narratives than others solely because of the eminence of the author, which may not necessarily be in the criminous field. The most detailed narratives are those given, on the whole, to detectives who have attracted most attention from critics and authoritative sources, often over long periods. Such figures are of exceptional importance in the study of the development of detective fiction, sometimes becoming legendary figures and frequently being reassessed historically, imitated, borrowed, and (the final accolade) parodied. The frequency of a detective's appearance is, in general, no guide to his or her importance and has not been taken to be so. Accordingly, a single appearance from one detective may warrant more attention than a dozen from another. *C'est la guerre!*

Many of the cited detectives have no narrative or only minimal information attached to them. In a perfect world, all should have something said about them, even though they may be lost forever and it would only be, as it were, *in memoriam*. That commentary is lacking from many is partly due to considerations of space and partly to the difficulty that presented itself in researching the books or stories in which they have appeared.

Detective's Statistics

American Male Amateur operating in New York

Following the detective's narrative text is a line consisting of four entries, each giving specific information about the detective as shown in the numbered sections below.

1. Nationality

The detective's nationality is real or apparent . 'Apparent' means, in fact, more than it seems to say; after all, it is not actually possible to know the nationality of a detective

An Example Record

Perry MASON
is one of the great classic investigators of the genre, appearing in over eighty novels from 1933 to 1973 (that is, three years after the author's death). He is a defence lawyer of great brilliance who takes on difficult cases, which he usually wins, often in spite of apparently damning evidence against his client. He nearly always has to set in motion considerable detective work so as to obtain the truth, which he uses, with devastating logic and panache in final courtroom dramas. He is aided, throughout the long canon, by a constant, devoted and apparently ageless team, almost as well known as he is. The cast of the books is also kept fairly constant, adding to their popularity, and there is a remarkable and foxy trio of stooges with whom he has many a struggle, in and out of the courtroom. The great detectives have a way of continuing after the death of their creators for both popular and commercial reasons. So it is with *Perry MASON*, who has been used in novels by at least one other author.

American Male Amateur operating in New York

Sidekick: Paul DRAKE
is a private detective who works, as far as we know, almost entirely on *Perry MASON's* cases. He is the detective's chief legman, acquiring much of the evidence that the great man usually needs. He is listed as a detective in his own right as well, but he must certainly be accounted as one of the most famous and overworked sidekicks in the whole genre.

American Male - Assistant

Sidekick: Della STREET
is perhaps the best-known secretary sidekick in the business and without her *MASON* would often be lost. As the canon goes on and on, there is sometimes more than a hint of a romantic attachment between the great attorney and this adoring, beautiful, completely efficient woman; but, the readers can rest assured, to her catching criminals is all good clean fun.

American Female - Secretary

Stooge: Lt FLAGG
is a consummate stooge, never quite believing *MASON*.

American Male

Stooge: Sgt HOLCOMB
is one of several police adversaries who confront *PERRY MASON* and live to regret it.

American Male

Stooge: Dist Att Hamilton BURGER
is often *MASON's* main adversary among the ranks of the police and the law. The two men are in frequent confrontation before and during the court cases that are the well-known climaxes of the books.

American Male

Thomas CHASTAIN 1900-1993 (American)
was born in Washington DC and was a newspaper editor.

Writer: Thomas CHASTAIN

Invented 4detectives - see J T 'Jake' SPANNER

Citation Record: 2 Books

The Case Of Too Many Murders - *Pastiche 1*
Morrow US (1989)

The Case Of The Burning Bequest - *Pastiche 2*
Morrow US (1990)

Erle Stanley GARDNER 1889-1970 (American)
was born in Malden, Massachusetts. He graduated from Palo Alto High School, California, 1909, and Valparaiso University, Indiana, 1909. Writer, reporter and lawyer, he wrote hundreds of stories for magazines and many novels during the 1920s, often using pseudonyms. He created many detectives, large and small, including the one for which he is renowned, the famed *Perry MASON*. He received the Mystery Writers of America Edgar Allan Poe award, 1952, their Grand Master award, 1961, and he has been honoured with degrees from several US universities.

Other Byline: A A FAIR

Other Detectives:

'Go Get 'Em' CARVER	Terry CLANE
Richard 'Speed' DASH	Sheriff Bill ELDON
Jax KEEN	Lester LEITH
Ed MIGRAINE	Paul PRY
Doug SELBY	Dane SKARLE
Peter WENNICK	'Gramps' WIGGINS
Sidney ZOOM	

Citation Record: 82 Books 1 Selected Short 2 Short Stories in 1 Collection

The Case Of The Velvet Claws - *First*
The very first of the long canon has blackmail, murder, suspicion falling on the detective, and a great ending.
Morrow US (1933); Harrap UK (1933)

The Case Of The Postponed Murder - *Last*
Morrow US (1973); Heinemann UK (1977)

The Case Of The Murderer's Bride
Davis US (1969)

The Case Of The Cautious Coquette - *Collection 1*
Morrow US (1949); Heinemann UK (1955)

unless the author states it implicitly. While it can be said absolutely that Lord Peter Wimsey is British because Dorothy Sayers, at considerable length, says so, one can only surmise (albeit with a large degree of probability) the nationality of Miss Marple. Race Williams is certainly American, but the true nationality of that great American detective, Nero Wolfe, might still be in doubt. To avoid excessive confusion, therefore, the detective's nationality is cited if it can be assumed with a reasonable degree of probability. Thus, the assumption has been made that British authors usually write about British detectives; and, if their books are located in the UK, their detectives can - in the absence of additional knowledge - be cited as British (where historical detectives operate in England before the Act of Union, they clearly must be called English). The same criteria, *mutatis mutandis,* apply to American authors and American detectives. However, vagaries occur and sometimes reasonable guesses must be made. During the 1950s and 1960s in particular, there was a vogue for British authors, eager to exploit the fastest growing trend in detective fiction, to create American private eyes, most of them execrable; American authors, such as Martha Grimes, have, on the contrary, created some very good British detectives; and sometimes it can never be clear, from internal evidence, whether a detective is British or American. Where more than one detective is the subject of the citation, both nationalities are cited, if they are known and differ. Many 'foreign' detectives are cited and, where known, their nationality is cited. If, for various reasons, it is not possible to make a reasonable statement about nationality, no statement is made.

2. Sex

In some citations, gender was not possible to ascertain from books not directly inspected and could not be attributed because of ambiguity in the detective's name. In a few other cases, the sex is not stated for other reasons, examples being sci-fi detectives and animal detectives.

3. Type

The detective is categorised as belonging to one of eight types, as cited by the author or, as judged most appropriate. For a discussion of these types reference should be made to the Introduction.

i Police
ii Professional Amateur
iii Private Detective
iv Professional Investigator
v Secret Agent
vi Amateur
vii Pulp (cited as Detective)
viii Sleuth

4. Location

Where possible, an idea of the specific or general location of the detective's operations is given. The data have been taken from the sources currently available or by direct inspection. Although some locations can be stated concisely, some cannot and for various reasons. Sometimes authors do not state or clarify the locations of their books and do not wish to do so; sometimes detectives operate in several different locations; sometimes the locations are so unusual (including extra-terrestrial space) that they cannot be identified. Where it is known, a town rather than a larger area, such as a county or a state, is given. When neither is known, the country may be stated. Where clearly the detective operates in several countries, they are given, if known, with the detective's home territory taking precedence. If they are not known, the citation says 'several places'. London means the whole area known as Greater London. New York includes the city and the state.

Sidekick

Sidekick: Paul DRAKE
is a private detective who works, as far as we know, almost entirely on *Perry MASON's* cases...
American Male - Assistant

The name and rank of the detective's sidekick, if one exists, follows and a narrative description may be included. Below that, a line gives the nationality and sex of the sidekick and his or her relationship to the detective. If other sidekicks are cited the same pattern is repeated.

Stooge

Stooge: Dist Att Hamilton BURGER
is often *MASON's* main adversary among the ranks of the police and the law. The two men are ...
American Male

The stooge record pattern is identical to that of the sidekick. If other stooges are cited the same pattern is repeated. For a detective who has several writers, it is assumed that all the writers refer to one set of sidekicks and stooges so these records are not repeated for subsequent writers.

Author

Erle Stanley GARDNER 1889-1970 (American)

The next line of the citation gives the author. This, by the definition used here, is the single or multiple name used by a writer (or writers), which identifies all the works published under the author's name. Such works may feature other detectives cited in other records. For further details on 'writer' see the following section.

Sometimes a detective has been written about by other authors in addition to the original inventor. Three possibilities arise. Sometimes the authors are simply different names used by the same writer; and this is often the case where writers publish under different names in the UK and US. Sometimes, mostly in the case of pastiches, a detective has been adopted by several authors. In a third case, a detective appears in books under a house name with the individual authors identified. In all these examples, the citations are made in alphabetical order but the original creator is always clearly indicated in the narrative.

The author's name is followed by statistics giving information on chronology and nationality. The author and writer may be linked in various ways. If there is a one-to-one relationship, as is generally the case, the information is given as for the author. Where more than one writer is cited, (see following section), and they have the same nationality, that is stated only once; if the writers have different nationalities, they are both stated. Where the possibility of ambiguity exists, as, for example, the author has one name and there are two writers, then the writer details are given as part of the writer data. Where the authorship is anonymous that is stated, but the designation 'Unknown' is used if the author is unidentifiable.

Author's Narrative

was born in Malden, Massachusetts. He graduated from Palo Alto High School, California, 1909, ...

Given here are the author's relevant biographical details, if available, and a summary of his or her literary output and awards.

Writer

Writer: Thomas CHASTAIN

The writer information, if shown, is the identity of the person or persons who use the names or names shown under author above. The concept of the writer, as distinct from the author, is central to the structure of 'The Detectives' for it connects all the entries relevant to the detectives and authors the writer has produced. The total output of a writer is made accessible by providing, in all records associated with that writer, pointers between the records. These pointers lead to a single detective record where the writer information can be found.

Two types of such record occur. If this is the only record for this writer it shows his or her name (or names) and the name of the author, which may be the same or different. Otherwise, the writer must have written under more than one byline and/or invented more than one detective. In these cases, 'Other Bylines' and/or 'Other Detectives' are part of the detective record as described below. Further explanations of the complex relationships which are possible between writers, authors and detectives are included in the next two sections.

Other Byline(s)

Other Byline: A A FAIR

Given here are all other names under which an author has published books that feature a detective cited elsewhere in the book. They thus include, not only all the pseudonyms of an author that are cited elsewhere in the book, but also his or her real name if that name appears also as an author.

If 'Other Bylines' appears in a record, it indicates that it is the destination for the pointers explained under 'Writer' above. The records that point to this record are governed by the following rules.

1. If the writer has invented more than one detective, each under a different byline, the Detective record containing those other bylines point to this record.

   Simon RATTRAY 1920- (British)
   For writer details see Richard VANESS

2. If the writer has invented more than one detective under the same byline then the reader is directed from all the other detective records to the 'main detective' record, which is this one.
3. If the writer has invented more than one detective under one byline and has invented more than one detective under another byline, he has created multiple 'main detectives'. One of those 'main detectives' is this one and the other 'main detectives' point to this record.
4. If the circumstances of the preceding rule apply and, in addition, the writer has invented other single detectives under individual bylines, this record has been chosen as the one with the writer information. All those single byline records and the other 'main detectives' records point to this record. In this case, there are two pointers:

   Edward RONNS 1916-1975 (American)
   For writer details see Sam DURELL
   Inventor of one other detective Reginald 'Beauty' BLACK

5. In certain other rare cases (always involving multiple pastiches, such as occur under Sexton Blake and Sherlock Holmes), where one detective has been written about by many authors, and one of these records has been chosen as the one to exhibit the writer details, then it is not sufficient to give a pointer to the detec-

tive only. In these circumstances, the author's name is appended to that of the Detective in the other records for this writer.

Other detectives

Other Detectives:
'Go Get 'Em' CARVER   Terry CLANE
Richard 'Speed' DASH   Sheriff Bill ELDON
Jax KEEN   Lester LEITH

The information here allows access to all the detectives created by the author. It may appear in one of five forms.

1. Listed here, in alphabetical order, are all the detectives created under the writer's byline that are cited elsewhere in the book. This form only appears where the record has been chosen as the 'main detective' from more than two detectives.

2. If this detective has been designated 'main detective' and the author has invented only two detectives, the pointer is:

   Elwyn JONES 1923- (British)
   Inventor of one other detective Dick BARTON

3. If this detective is not the 'main detective' and the author has invented only two detectives, the pointer is:

   Elwyn JONES 1923- (British)
   See main detective Supt Charles BARLOW

4. If the only other detective of an author is, in fact, a pastiche, the pointer is:

   Willoughby LANE (American)
   Adopter of one other detective Sherlock HOLMES

5. Where an author has invented more than two detectives, the pointer states the number invented and then gives the name of another of the author's detectives, referred to as the 'main detective' under which fuller information is given. It should be noted that the 'number invented' refers to the number of actual detective citations in 'The Detectives': that is, 'multiple detectives' or a 'detective pair' citation counts, for this purpose, as 'one detective'. Usually the name pointed to will, in fact, be the author's most important detective, if there clearly is one; but if the author has created several detectives, none of which is predominant, the choice is arbitrary. The pointer is:

   Invented 4 detectives - see J T 'Jake' SPANNER

Citation Record

Citation Record: 82 Books 1 Selected Short 2 Short Stories in 1 Collection

This section of the Detective record summarises the available information as to the frequency of a detective's appearances. No data from film, radio or TV are given. This book is not, by any means, intended to be a complete bibliography of either an author's work in the genre or the total bibliography of a detective's appearances in fiction. It is essentially detective-orientated and the purpose of the citation record is to give a useful and informative picture of the detective's chronological appearances and, where relevant, any significant information attached to those appearances. The citation record considers three types of publication. First, the number of 'books' featuring the detective is stated. It includes published plays as well as standard, full-length novels. This number must be taken, especially for earlier detectives, as a minimum figure. Secondly, a 'selected short story' number, which is rarely more than two, may be given. It is intended to be a representative number to indicate that the detective has appeared in (usually an unknown number of) short stories, from which those cited have been found or selected. Whereas the book number attempts to estimate the total number of books known to feature the detective, the selected short story number refers only to the number of stories actually listed by title (see below). Thirdly, a number may then be given for the total of 'short stories' (including novelettes) appearing in at least one 'collection'. The number of collections cited by title is stated and the title of every collection is then given in the following section (see Publications below). Where more than one collection is cited, the number of short stories is the total for all the collections. However, the number in an individual collection is always given under that collection's title. The number of short stories refers only to those in the collections that are known to feature the cited detective, but the total number of stories in an individual collection may also be stated in the text for that collection.

The short stories in which a detective appears are often of greater significance in assessing his genre importance and the scope of the author's work than the number of novels in which he is featured. In principle, therefore, and in contrast to the method used for citing the number of books, the citation includes all collections known to contain stories featuring the detective. Where a collection contains important short stories featuring more than one of the author's detectives, it is cited under both detectives with an appropriate narrative. Popular authors often have their stories published in several editions, sometimes with the contents rearranged. With rare exceptions, only the original publications have been cited. For the one detective where the number of collections has been judged too great, the first and last published collections only are cited, but the total number of stories featuring the detective is stated, the variation being clarified in a narrative.

Publications

The Case Of The Velvet Claws - *First*

Given here, by title, are the individual books, short stories, and collections referred to in the Detective record. If a publication has been entitled differently in Britain and America (sometimes also in other countries), both titles are given, with any further information concerning change of author byline. If the detective can only be found in one book and the author, as far as is known, may produce others, the book is designated as 'Single'. If the author has died and it is unlikely that the detective will appear in another book, it is designated 'Only'. Since it is clearly useful to have some concept of the chronological environment of a detective, it was decided that, if at least twenty years has elapsed since the detective's last known appearance in print, the book should also be coded as 'Only'. Apologies are due, in advance, to any author who, even now, is about to resuscitate one of his old detectives.

For the great majority of detectives, whatever the total number of books cited in the Detective record, only two titles are given in full. These are, by date, the first and last books featuring the detective known to have been published by the cited author, thus indicating the chronological extent of a series. The first is always coded 'First'; the second is coded 'Latest' if the author may produce others and 'Last' if the author has died or has not produced a book with the detective for at least twenty years. The 'author' refers, as always, only to the byline appearing in each individual record and does not necessarily mean that he or she may not have produced books with the same detective under another name. In the latter case, information about total publications will be linked by the pointers described above. Published plays are cited as 'Play', except when they are pastiches (see below) and are cited as such. A few collections of pastiches and parodies, written by more than one author, have special relevance and are cited as 'Anthology'. In a few cases, a book may be designated 'Special'.

The books shown are the first editions to appear under that title. Where the book has been republished under one or more new titles, they are all cited. For three authors of exceptional historical or literary significance (Sir Arthur Conan Doyle, Dashiell Hammett, and Raymond Chandler), the list of publications has been extended to include virtually every book and short story in which their several detectives are known to have appeared. The books and stories are then numbered sequentially.

Short stories are given by title next but, for reasons already stated, are not coded. Collections are coded in the same way as books and generally contain an additional statement as to the number of stories featuring the detective that they contain. Where not all the stories contain the detective or are not truly criminous or are unknown in number, that is stated in a narrative. Where the collections or short stories are entitled differently in Britain and America or appear under different bylines, both are given and they are cited appropriately for each country. Finally, collections of certain pastiches and parodies are followed by citations for all the individual stories (see below).

If any book, has been republished under one or mor titles differing from that cited as the original publication, the first title is coded 'First', 'Last', etc and the sequent titles are coded 'First*', 'Last*', etc. This rule applies not only when the title of an original publication differs, for example, in the Britain and the United States, but for all subsequent republications of the same item.

The order in which individual publications are cited is Books, Selected Short Stories, Short Stories, Collections, repeated under every author for any cited detective.

Publication Narrative

The very first of the long canon has blackmail, murder, suspicion falling on the detective, and a great ending.

Some publications need narratives of their own. This may be because there is something special to say about one book or story from a literary, historical, or publishing point of view. Sometimes a detective, especially if he is a recent one, may only have appeared in one book and is best amplified by giving certain details of that book. In all these instances, the information is given in a narrative section. The publication narrative is particularly useful in giving information on pastiches and parodies (see below).

Publication Data

Morrow US (1933); Harrap UK (1933)

The final section of the Detective record, which follows every publication item, gives the publishers of every book and collection cited, in both the UK and the US if both are relevant and known, and the publication dates, in chronological order. The country of first publication is cited first, provided the order does not conflict with the chronological order, which takes precedence. The following abbreviations have been used: AU=Australia; CA=Canada; EI=Eire; EN=England; FR=France; SA=South Africa. Short stories are treated likewise if they have appeared in an anthology or collection for which the publisher is known. The narrative texts may also include information on additional anthologies in which the story can be found. Many short stories first appear in magazines or newspapers and those sources are then given, with dates of their appearance, if available. Some of the pulp detectives cited have no publishers or sources appended.

Sherlock Holmes Pastiches and Parodies

The Detective records for Sherlock Holmes and the many pastiches and parodies are dealt with according to the following rules, which differ somewhat from those described for all other detectives:

1. For the original works by Conan Doyle, the four canonical books are cited first, in order of publication date. There follow the five canonical collections, again in order of publication. Under each collection are given all the original stories that were published in that collection, in alphabetical order for ease of reference, regardless of their original publication date but with the latter information always added.
2. For all pastiches and parodies, the normal order as for other detectives is followed. That is, books are cited first and in order of their publication date. Stories and then collections (designated as either pastiche or parody collections) follow and are dealt with similarly, in order of publication date. Under each collection, all the individual stories in that collection are then cited, in alphabetical order for ease of reference, regardless of their order in the original publication, the date only being relevant for the collection itself. Where the stories in a book are clearly sequential chapters, they are given in chapter order. All pastiche publications, regardless of type, are given individual pastiche numbers, which are sequential for each author.

Notes

1. In all narratives in 'The Detectives', the surname of any character, author or publication appearing in a citation elsewhere in the book is in italic capitals and so can be immediately identified.
2. As far as possible, abbreviations in the text have been avoided. The few that have been used are well known and need no explanation. However, detectives' and occasionally authors' ranks are sometimes cited as abbreviations, which are listed below.

Capt	Captain	Lt	Lieutenant
Cdr	Commander	Maj	Major
Ch	Chief	Mgr	Monsignor
Col	Colonel	Plce	Police
Commiss	Commissioner	Prof	Professor
Const	Constable	Pte	Private
Cpl	Corporal	Offr	Officer
Dep	Deputy	Rev	Reverend
Det	Detective	Sgt	Sergeant
Gen	General	Supt	Superintendent
Insp	Inspector		

3. The main sources used in the compilation of this book are given in Appendix 1.
4. Although the choice of data in 'The Detectives' is as accurate as possible, some discrepancies exist between the sources consulted. Sometimes manifest errors have been found: in the main they are minor; but sometimes, especially where they concern the names of detectives, they are more serious. Wherever possible, the original publications have been consulted. When that has not been possible, a judgment has been made as to the entry that is likely to be correct. In such cases the existence of a discrepancy or an important conflict of view is noted in the relevant Detective record and it is then listed in Appendix 2.
5. A complete list of the Sherlock Holmes parody detectives that appear in 'The Detectives' is given in Appendix 3.

6. Four indexes provide additional means of accessing 'The Detectives':

   The Authors

   The Books

   The Sidekicks

   The Stooges

   In each of these, all references are to the Detective records, from which all other information can be obtained, directly or indirectly.

7. In the Author index, all 'main detectives' are shown in a bold-italic typeface.

The Detectives

John ABBOT
British Male Amateur operating in England

Beryl WHITAKER 1916- (British)

Writer: Beryl Salisbury WHITAKER

Citation Record: 4 Books

The Chained Crocodile - *First*
Hale UK (1967)

The Man Who Wasn't There - *Last*
Hale UK (1968)

Supt ABBOTT
is called in to investigate a politically motivated kidnapping carried out by students at the fictional Quetley University.
British Policeman operating in England

Jeffrey ASHFORD 1926- (British)

Invented 9 detectives - see Det Insp Don KERRY

Citation Record: 1 Book

A Man Will Be Kidnapped - *Only*
Long UK (1972); Walker US (1972)

Ben ABBOTT
is a real estate agent who is trying to do a decent job but keeps falling over dead bodies.
American Male Amateur operating in USA

Justin SCOTT (American)

Citation Record: 2 Books

Hardscape - *First*
Penguin US (1994); HarperCollins UK (1994)

Stonedust - *Latest*
Penguin US (1995)

Jean ABBOTT
Second detective of Pat ABBOTT

Pat ABBOTT and Jean ABBOTT
are a husband-and-wife team. In the course of their long series of books, they progress from being typical, rather zany creations of the early 1940s into the era of the modern crime novel. In the early books the lady is still Jean Holly, living in an artists' colony in New Mexico. She meets tough private eye, *Pat ABBOTT*, and they marry. Travelling frequently to exotic and exciting places around the USA and Europe, where they sleuth happily together, he does the thinking and the lazing while she does the legwork and the worrying. In their later books, they have moved to New Orleans.
!See Appendix 2.
American Male Private Detective and American Female Private Detective operating in USA

Frances CRANE 1896-1981 (American)

was born in Lawrenceville, Illinois.

Writer: Francis Kirkwood CRANE

Citation Record: 25 Books

The Turquoise Shop - *First*
Lippincott US (1941); Hammond UK (1943)

The Amber Eyes - *Last*
Random House US (1962); Hammond UK (1962)

Samuel G ABBOTT
American Male Sleuth operating in Los Angeles

James R LANGHAM (American)

Citation Record: 2 Books

Sing A Song Of Homicide - *First*
Simon & Schuster US (1940)

Sing A Song Of Murder - *First**
Hale UK (1942)

A Pocket Full Of Clues - *Last*
Simon & Schuster US (1941)

A Pocketful Of Clues - *Last**
Hale UK (1943)

Luke ABEL
American Male Sleuth operating in Los Angeles

Nicholas CAIN (American)

Citation Record: 6 Books

Abel's War - *First*
Lynx US (1989)

White Death - *Latest*
Lynx US (1989)

An ABERDEEN DETECTIVE
Scottish Male Professional Investigator operating in Scotland

Robert WOODCROFT (British)

Citation Record: 23 Short Stories in 1 Collection

Memoirs Of An Aberdeen Detective - *Collection 1*
Rosemount UK (1903)

Uncle ABNER
is known only by his first name. He is the detective hero of a series of short stories, all set around 1850 in a mountain community in Virginia. His knowledge of the local people and the minutiae of the Bible enable him to solve all manner of local crimes. The stories are narrated in the first person by his nephew and he is sometimes assisted by a lawyer friend.
American Male Amateur operating in Virginia

Sidekick: Squire RANDOLPH
is a local justice, a remnant of an older English-style society in Virginia, who represents the legal side of *Uncle ABNER's* brilliant detective work.
American Male - Assistant

Melville Davisson POST 1871-1930 (American)

was born in Rominies Mills, West Virginia, and graduated at West Virginia University, Morgantown, in 1885. He practised criminal law and was an inveterate traveller until 1914, when he returned to his home state.

Other Detectives:
Col BRAXTON
Randolph MASON
Sir Henry MARQUIS
WALKER

Citation Record: 22 Short Stories in 2 Collections

Uncle Abner, Master Of Mysteries - *Collection 1*
Short stories - 18
Appleton US (1918); Stacey UK (1972)

The Methods Of Uncle Abner - *Collection 2*
Short stories - 4
Aspen US (1974)

Harvey ACE

American Male Sleuth operating in Los Angeles

Merle HORWITZ (American)

Citation Record: 2 Books

Bloody Silks - *First*
Knightsbridge US (1990)

Dead Heat - *Latest*
Knightsbridge US (1990)

Sgt ACKROYD

British Policeman operating in England

Jack S SCOTT 1922- (British)

Invented 3 detectives - see Det Insp Alf ROSHER

Citation Record: 1 Book

Corporal Smithers, Deceased - *Single*
Gollancz UK (1983); St Martin's US (1983)

Roger ACKROYD

is the fictional son of the fictional Roger Ackroyd, who was murdered in *Agatha CHRISTIE's* famous early novel, *THE MURDER OF ROGER ACKROYD.* He has become a PI and, while on a case, gets caught up in the life of his client.

British Male Private Detective operating in England

Jules FEIFFER 1929- (American)

Citation Record: 1 Book

Ackroyd - *Only*
Simon & Schuster US (1977); Hutchinson UK (1978)

Kit 'Marsden' ACTON

American Male Amateur operating in Cape Cod/Michigan

Marion BRAMHALL (American)

Citation Record: 5 Books

Button, Button - *First*
Doubleday US (1944)

Murder Is Contagious - *Last*
Doubleday US (1949)

The ACTRESS DETECTIVE

American Female Detective in Pulp Magazines operating in USA

ANON

Citation Record: 1 Book

The Actress Detective - *Only*
Aldine US

Eve ADAM

Czech Female Sleuth operating in Prague

Josef SKVORECKY 1924- (Czech)

See main detective Lt BORUVKA

Citation Record: 10 Short Stories in 1 Collection

Sins For Father Knox - *Collection 1*
is a translation from the Czech of *Hrichy Pro Patera Knoxe.*
Faber UK (1989); Norton US (1989)

ADAM 12

is in novelizations of episodes from a TV series.

American Male Sleuth operating in USA

Michael STRATFORD 1920- (American)

For writer details see Cash MADIGAN

Citation Record: 1 Book

The Sniper - *Only*
Award US (1974)

Chris STRATTON ?-1974? (American)

Writer: Richard HUBBARD
Other Byline: Nick CARTER

Citation Record: 1 Book

The Runaway - *Only*
Award US (1974)

Insp/Supt ADAMS

British Policeman operating in England

Leonard HOLLINGSWORTH (British)

Citation Record: 3 Books

The Body On The Bus - *First*
Murray UK (1930)

Dead Man's Alibi - *Last*
Murray UK (1933)

Abe ADAMS

American Male Amateur operating in USA

Tiffany THAYER 1902-1959 (American)

Writer: Tiffany Ellsworth THAYER

Citation Record: 1 Book

One Woman - *Only*
Morrow US (1933); Long UK (1939)

Adelaide ADAMS

is a tough old lady who resides at the Hotel Richelieu and solves cases of murder, 1937-style. !See Appendix 2.

American Female Amateur operating in USA

Anita BLACKMON 1893- (American)

Citation Record: 2 Books

Murder A La Richelieu - *First*
Doubleday US (1937)

The Hotel Richelieu Murders - *First**
Heinemann UK (1938)

There Is No Return - *Last*
Doubleday US (1938)

The Riddle Of The Dead Cats - *Last**
Butterworth UK (1939)

Anthony ADAMS

American Male Amateur operating in New York/Miami

Timothy BRACE 1901-1969 (American)

Writer: Theodore PRATT
Other Byline: Theodore PRATT

Citation Record: 4 Books

Murder Goes Fishing - *First*
Dutton US (1936)

Murder Goes To The World's Fair - *Last*
Dutton US (1939)

Theodore PRATT 1901-1969 (American)

For writer details see Anthony ADAMS

Murder Goes Fishing - *First*
Selwyn UK (1936)

Murder Goes To The World's Fair - *Last*
Diamond US (1945); Eldon UK (1951)

Bob ADAMS and Anne MINER

are students at an American university who solve a case of ingenious murder on the campus.

American Male Amateur and American Female Amateur operating in USA

William HARDY 1922- (American)

See main detective Karen GORDON

Citation Record: 1 Book

Lady Killer - *Only*
Dodd, Mead US (1957); Hamilton UK (1957)

Malice Domestic - *Only**
Detective Book Club US (1957)

Bradley ADAMS
American Male Amateur operating in Los Angeles

Maurice DEKOBRA 1885-1973 (French)
Writer: Ernest Maurice TESSIER
Citation Record: 2 Books
The Lady Is A Vamp - *First*
is a translation from the French of *Vamp ou Vestale* (Paris, 1957).
Allen UK (1958)
She Wore Pink Gloves - *Last*
is a translation from the French of *La Veuve aux Gants Roses* (Paris, 1956).
Allen UK (1958)

Brant ADAMS
American Male Detective in Pulp Magazines operating in USA

OLD SLEUTH (American)
was the pseudonym originally used by *Harlan Page HALSEY* for many of his detective stories in the pulps. His main detective was also given the name *OLD SLEUTH*. Both the author's and the detective's name were later used as house names for hundreds of stories, mainly written by other authors.

Other Detectives:
AMZI
The BICYCLE DETECTIVE
Henry BROCH
COOL TOM
CRESTON
DETECTIVE ARCHIE
DETECTIVE GAY
DETECTIVE KENNEDY
DETECTIVE PAYNE
GIPSY RENO
The IRISH DETECTIVE
JACK and GIL
KINGSLEY
The LADY DETECTIVE
MEAD
Billy MISCHIEF
OLD ELECTRICITY
OSCAR
RED CECIL
YANKEE RUE
Bruce ANGELO
Bertie BLAND
CLYDE
The COWBOY DETECTIVE
Desmond DARE
DETECTIVE DALE
DETECTIVE HANLEY
DETECTIVE MURDOCK
The GIANT DETECTIVE
GIPSY ROSE
IRON BURGESS
KEFTON
The KING'S DETECTIVE
MAGIC DICK
MEPHISTO
MURA
OLD SLEUTH
RAMSEY
TRUE BLUE

Citation Record: 1 Book
Brant Adams, The Emperor Of Detectives - *Only*
Aldine US

Dr Charlie ADAMS
is an oral surgeon with a lucrative practice in Cape Cod. His profound interest in the community and his quest for adventure lead him to investigate local crimes, in which pursuit he is considerably helped by his friends.
American Male Amateur operating in Massachusetts

Sidekick: Liatus ROANTIS
is a mercenary, a lethal veteran from Vietnam, who is useful to have around during he good doctor's adventures into detection.
American Male - Friend

Rick BOYER 1943- (American)
was born in Evanston, Illinois, and graduated with a BA at Denison University, Granville, Ohio, 1965. He has been a teacher of English and later a Professor of English at Western Carolina University. He received the Mystery Writers of America Edgar Allan Poe award, 1982.
Writer: Richard Lewis BOYER
Adopter of one other detective Sherlock HOLMES
Citation Record: 5 Books
Billingsgate Shoal - *First*
Houghton US (1982); Gollancz UK (1985)
Yellow Bird - *Latest*
Columbine US (1991)

Donald O'Keefe ADAMS
American Male Amateur operating in South America

Dana SAGE 1893?-1977 (American)
Writer: Glendon ALLVINE
Citation Record: 2 Books
The Moon Was Red - *First*
Simon & Schuster US (1944)
The 22 Brothers - *Last*
Simon & Schuster US (1950)

Gillian ADAMS
is a Canadian academic who, in two books separated by ten years, manages to meet murder in scientific circles. The police operate methodically and to no avail - but 'she asks questions that only a woman can'.
Canadian Female Amateur operating in England

Nora KELLY (American)
Citation Record: 2 Books
In The Shadow Of King's - *First*
St Martin's US (1985); Collins UK (1984)
Bad Chemistry - *Latest*
HarperCollins UK (1994)

Hilda ADAMS
is nicknamed 'Miss Pinkerton'; and, indeed, such is her proclivity for sleuthing that she is indexed under that name in some sources. She is, in fact, a nurse who seems to be invited rather frequently into the sick room of a family, only to find herself involved, not only in death, but in murder. Fortunately for the police, she is a friend of *Insp PATTON*, who encourages her to sleuth in circumstances in which he cannot.
American Female Amateur operating in USA

Stooge: Insp PATTON
is not unfriendly towards *Hilda ADAMS* but is baffled without her help.
American Male

Mary Roberts RINEHART 1876-1958 (American)
Invented 7 detectives - see Letitia CARBERRY
Citation Record: 2 Books
Miss Pinkerton - *First*
Farrar, Straus US (1932)
The Double Alibi - *First**
Cassell UK (1932)
Haunted Lady - *Last*
Farrar, Straus US (1942); Cassell UK (1942)

Insp Jeff ADAMS and Kate SHAW
When the Professor of Biochemistry and his wife are shot dead at the fictional Thorpe University in one of the eastern states, *Insp Jeff ADAMS* is called in. He is assisted in his investigation by *Kate SHAW*, a young and beautiful member of the History department, who is an expert on cryptograms, the deciphering of which play an important part in the plot.
American Policeman and American Female Amateur operating in USA

Scott KEECH 1936- (American)
Writer: John Scott KEECH
Citation Record: 1 Book
Ciphered - *Single*
Harper & Row US (1980)

Samantha ADAMS
American Female Sleuth operating in Atlanta

Sarah SHANKMAN (American)
Writer: Sarah SHANKMAN
Other Byline: Alice STOREY
Inventor of one other detective Annie TANNENBAUM
Citation Record: 5 Books
Now Let's Talk Of Graves - *First*
Pocket Books US (1990)

A

He Was Her Man - *Latest*
US (1993)

Alice STOREY (American)

For writer details see Samantha ADAMS

Citation Record: 2 Books

First Kill All The Lawyers - *First*
Pocket Books US (1988)

Then Hang All The Liars - *Latest*
Pocket Books US (1989)

Squire ADAMS

has, for various reasons, but one day to solve a murder case – which he does.

American Male Private Detective operating in New York

Horace BROWN 1908- (American)

Inventor of one other detective Napoleon B SMITH

Citation Record: 1 Book

The Penthouse Killings - *Only*
NewsStand US (1950)

The Four ADJUSTERS

Second detectives of Daphne WRAYNE

Harry ADKINS

sleuths in 1807-1808.

British Male Amateur operating in England

Raymond FOXALL 1916- (British)

Writer: Raymond Jehoiada Campbell FOXALL

Inventor of one other detective John CRISPIN

Citation Record: 4 Books

The Little Ferret - *First*
Hale UK (1968); St Martin's US (1974)

The Silver Goblet - *Last*
Hale UK (1974); St Martin's US (1974)

Irene ADLER

is the heroine of a recent series of near-Sherlockian parodies. '*The* Woman', as *Sherlock HOLMES* always called her, was almost the only person ever to have bested the great detective, which she did in the canonical story, *A SCANDAL IN BOHEMIA*. Not that *Irene ADLER* was exactly a criminal. She was simply a wronged lady and brilliant woman out to make things difficult for the King of Bohemia, which, in spite of *HOLMES'* intervention, she could well have done. She has emerged as the most revered female character in the whole Sherlockian canon. Now, with a delightful assistant, she is on the loose again, in a series of exciting adventures, ranging from the salons of Paris to the court of the Romanoffs.

German Female Amateur operating in Europe

Sidekick: Nell HUXLEIGH

accompanies her mistress everywhere and narrates her cases.

British Female - Companion

Carole Nelson DOUGLAS 1944- (American)

Other Detectives:

Kevin BLAKE MIDNIGHT LOUIE

Citation Record: 3 Books

Goodnight, Mr Holmes - *Pastiche 1*

is an ingenious pastiche novel, which features *Sherlock HOLMES* and *Dr WATSON* as incidental characters and retells the canonical story, *THE SCANDAL IN BOHEMIA,* from the viewpoint of *Irene ADLER.*

Tom Doherty Associates US (1992)

Irene At Large - *Pastiche 2*

is a second ingenious tale as retold by *Irene ADLER.*

Tom Doherty Associates US (1992)

Irene's Last Waltz - *Pastiche 3*
Tom Doherty Associates US (1994)

Johnny ADRANO

American Male Sleuth operating in USA

Michael BRADLEY 1938- (American)

Writer: Gary BLUMBERG

is, under his real name, the author of several genre books.

Citation Record: 4 Books

The Blood Bargain - *First*
Paperback Library US (1974)

The Swiss Shot - *Last*
Paperback Library US (1974)

Insp Christopher ADRIAN

British Policeman operating in England

Marguerite R SILVERMAN (British)

Writer: Marguerite Ruth SILVERMAN

Citation Record: 3 Books

The Vet It Was That Died - *First*
Nicholson & Watson UK (1945)

9 Had No Vet - *Last*
Nicholson & Watson UK (1951)

Robert AGNOLD

is unnamed in the first of the two books in which he appears. He is a young crime reporter on *The Evening Moon,* which enables him to solve two cases that are baffling the police.

British Male Amateur operating in London

B L FARJEON 1838-1903 (British)

was born in London of Jewish parents. After a quarrel with his family, he set off to prospect for gold in Australia. Later, he went to New Zealand, where he became the joint editor of the first daily paper to be produced in that country. He returned to London in 1868 and became well-known as a novelist and playwright. In his several criminous novels, which were to some extent based on his own experiences, his sleuth was often a reporter, as he had been.

Writer: Benjamin Leopold FARJEON

Other Detectives:

DEVLIN James DICKSON
Paul GODFREY George MILLINGTON
MOLESWORTH ROBSON and Edwin BOUSFIELD

Citation Record: 2 Books

Great Porter Square - *First*
UK (1885)

The Mystery Of M Felix - *Last*
White UK (1890); Lovell US (1890)

Charlie AGUTTER

British Male Sleuth operating in Scotland

Sam LLEWELLYN (British)

Writer: Samson LLEWELLYN

Citation Record: 4 Books

Dead Reckoning - *First*
Joseph UK (1987); Summit US (1988)

Deadeye - *Latest*
Joseph UK (1989); Summit US (1991)

Martin AINSWORTH

British Male Sleuth operating in England/Germany

Michael UNDERWOOD 1916-1992 (British)

Invented 6 detectives - see Rosa EPTON

Citation Record: 4 Books

The Unprofessional Spy - *First*
Macdonald UK (1964); Doubleday US (1964)

Reward For A Defector - *Last*
Macmillan UK (1973); St Martin's US (1973)

Martin AINSWORTH

Second detective of Rosa EPTON

ALBA

Second detective of Serge GORODISH

A

Jack ALBANY
is a bit-part actor who becomes involved in murders and usually bungles his way to solving them.
American Male Amateur operating in New York

John GODEY 1912- (American)
was born in Brooklyn, New York, graduated from New York University and served in the US Army, 1943-1946. He is the author of at least fourteen genre novels, not all with cited detectives.
Writer: Morton FREEDGOOD
Citation Record: 3 Books
The Reluctant Assassin - *First*
Simon & Schuster US (1967)
Never Put Off Till Tomorrow What You Can Kill Today - *Last*
Random House US (1970)

Sgt Karl ALBERG
Canadian Policeman operating in British Columbia

L R WRIGHT (Canadian)
received the Mystery Writers of America Edgar Allan Poe award, 1985.
Writer: Laurali Robson WRIGHT
Citation Record: 3 Books
The Suspect - *First*
Viking US (1985); Hale UK (1986)
Prized Possessions - *Latest*
US (1993)

Dr ALCAZAR
is a minor creation of this well-known author, appearing only in a few short stories (not individually cited) in the author's collection. He is a clairvoyant at a circus in California. Impressively handsome, with an Olympian brow, he is actually a charlatan; but, when his clients begin to die, he really has to solve the crimes.
American Male Amateur operating in California
Sidekick: Avie DU POIS
guesses people's weights at the circus and assists in the sleuthing.
American Male - Friend

Philip MACDONALD 1899-1981 (British)
Invented 5 detectives - see Col Anthony GETHRYN
Citation Record: 1 Collection
Something To Hide - *Collection 1*
Doubleday US (1952)
Fingers Of Fear - *Collection 1**
Collins UK (1953)

Peter ALCOTT and John ELLIS
American Male Amateurs operating in Havana

Joan SANGER (American)
Citation Record: 1 Book
The Case Of The Missing Corpse - *Only*
Green Circle US (1936)

Tom ALDER
specialises in tracing heirs.
American Male Private Detective operating in USA

Frank GRUBER 1904-1969 (American)
Invented 8 detectives - see Johnny FLETCHER and Sam CRAGG
Citation Record: 1 Book
Twenty Plus Two - *Only*
Dutton US (1961); Boardman UK (1961)

Rev Claire ALDINGTON
is an Episcopalian priest who investigates murders with an ecclesiastical background.
American Female Amateur operating in New York

Isabelle HOLLAND 1920- (American)
was born in Basel, Switzerland, and educated in England and the USA.
Inventor of one other detective pair Susan GRENELLE and Ch Mark CZERNICK
Citation Record: 3 Books
A Death At St Anselm's - *First*
Doubleday US (1984); Severn UK (1985)
A Lover Scorned - *Latest*
Doubleday US (1986); Severn UK (1987)

Finney ALETTER
American Male Sleuth operating in Denver

Yvonne MONTGOMERY (American)
Writer: Ewegan Yvonne MONTGOMERY
Citation Record: 2 Books
Scavengers - *First*
Avon US (1987)
Obstacle Course - *Latest*
Avon US (1990)

Pawang ALI
was called the Sherlock Holmes of Singapore. He appeared, 1928-1930, in several stories in *Clues*.
Malayan Male Detective in Pulp Magazines operating in Singapore

E Hoffman PRICE 1898-1988 (American)
Invented 4 detectives - see John CARMODY
No citations

Insp Pierre ALLAIN
Second detective of Supt William STEVENS

Rocky ALLAN
appears in one other book with the author's other detective, *Michael DUNDAS.*
American Male Amateur operating in California

Virginia RATH 1905- (American)
Writer: Virginia Anne RATH
Other Detectives:
Rocky ALLAN and Michael DUNDAS
Michael DUNDAS
Citation Record: 5 Books
Death At Dayton's Folly - *First*
Doubleday US (1935)
An Excellent Night For Murder - *Last*
Doubleday US (1937)

Rocky ALLAN and Michael DUNDAS
also appear individually in other books by this author.
American Male Amateurs operating in California

Virginia RATH 1905- (American)
Invented 3 detectives - see Rocky ALLAN
Citation Record: 1 Book
Murder With A Theme Song - *Only*
Doubleday US (1939)

Greg ALLARD
is an actor who once worked for the CIA. He solves an axe murder that took place in apparently 'impossible' circumstances.
American Male Professional Investigator

Cyril JOYCE ?-1992 (British)
Invented 3 detectives - see Insp Pat STOCKTON
Citation Record: 1 Book
Errant Sleuth - *Only*
Hale UK (1987)

Nick ALLARD
underwent a name change to *Jerry CORNELIUS* when the books were reissued under the author's other byline.
British Male Amateur operating in England

A

Bill BARCLAY 1939- (British)

For writer details see Jerry CORNELIUS

Citation Record: 2 Books

Printer's Devil - *First*
Compact UK (1966)

Somewhere In The Night - *Last*
Compact UK (1966)

Arthur ALLEN

is a barrister. He is one of the earliest examples of the investigative lawyer.

British Male Amateur operating in London

Edward Frederick KNIGHT 1852-1925 (British)

Citation Record: 1 Book

A Desperate Voyage - *Only*
Milne UK (1898)

Gracie ALLEN

Second detective of Philo VANCE

Peter ALLEN

British Male Amateur operating in England

Lindsay ANSON (British)

Citation Record: 2 Books

Such Natural Deaths - *First*
Collins UK (1930)

Even Doctors Die - *First**
Doubleday US (1939)

I Don't Like Cats - *Last*
Collins UK (1940); Doubleday US (1940)

Tom ALLEN

is a member of the English department at the fictional Kingsley University. When the librarian is found dead, he voices his suspicions and is asked by the president of the college to investigate.

American Male Amateur operating in Midwest USA

Marion BOYD ?-1974 (American)

is a mainstream novelist and poet who has taught at several universities.

Writer: Marion Boyd HAVIGHURST

Citation Record: 1 Book

Murder In The Stacks - *Only*
Lothrop US (1934)

Capt Jiggs ALLERMAN

is from the Chicago Detective Bureau and is in London to help Scotland Yard in their fight against two rival gangs of American criminals who are vying to set up protection rackets.

American Policeman operating in England

Edgar WALLACE 1875-1932 (British)

Invented 28 detectives - see J G REEDER

Citation Record: 1 Book

When The Gangs Came To London - *Only*
Long UK (1932); Doubleday US (1932)

Insp/Supt Roderick ALLEYN

is regarded as one of the big five of the British classic detectives of the Golden Age, appearing in books running from the 1930s to the 1980s. The books in which he features are variable in quality, often being pedestrian and cosy, with much peripheral and novelettish digression. He is, indeed, the last romantic hero in British detective fiction. Handsome, well-built, polite, educated at Oxford, and with a brief career in the diplomatic service behind him, he has vague aristocratic connections to boot. Steady as a rock, as is only to be expected with such a background, he never makes a mistake. A bachelor early in the series, he later meets the painter, Agatha Troy, and (this seems to be the fate of all Golden Age detectives created by British lady writers) marries her.

British Policeman operating in England/New Zealand

Sidekick: Insp FOX

is a large man, reliable, unambitious, efficient and courageous, altogether one of the best characterised police sidekicks in the business. He appears in nearly all the detective's cases.

British Male - Assistant

Sidekick: Nigel BATHGATE

was introduced in the early books as a young journalist, whose object was to try to help the detective. But the author seemed unable to accommodate him in her stories and she later disposed of him by the usual method, matrimony.

British Male - Assistant

Ngaio MARSH 1899-1982 (New Zealander)

Writer: Edith Ngaio MARSH

was born in Christchurch, New Zealand, and graduated from Canterbury University College School, Christchurch. She was to become distinguished for her work in creating and managing outlets for the drama in New Zealand and later in Great Britain. One of the great authors of the late Golden Age and beyond and recipient of the highest honours for her work in the theatrical world as well as the criminous genre, she received the Mystery Writers of America Grand Master award, 1977, and the British government gave her an OBE, 1948, and a DBE, 1966.

Citation Record: 32 Books 3 Short Stories in 1 Collection

A Man Lay Dead - *First*
Bles UK (1934); Sheridan US (1942)

Light Thickens - *Last*
Collins UK (1982); Little, Brown US (1982)

The Collected Short Fiction Of Ngaio Marsh - *Collection 1*
This collection of the seven of the author's short stories contains three with *ALLEYN.*
International Polygonics US (1989)

Insp ALLHOFF

is a police detective, still associated with the New York Police Department even if he does have no legs. He is one of the many 'defective detectives' that authors and presumably their readers found interesting, particularly in the inter-war years. He appeared in many short stories, 1938-1945, mainly in *Dime Detective.*

American Policeman operating in New York

D L CHAMPION 1903?-1968 (Australian)

Writer: D'Arcy Lyndon CHAMPION

Other Detectives:
Mariano MERCADO   Rex SACKLER
Richard Curtis (The Phantom) VAN LOAN

Citation Record: 2 Selected Short Stories

The Day Nobody Died
In 'Dime Detective' US (193?)

Lock The Death House Door
In 'Dime Detective' US (1938)

John ALLISON

British Male Sleuth operating in Austria/Africa

Richard MEADE 1926-1977 (British)

Writer: Benjamin Leopold HAAS

Citation Record: 2 Books

Beyond The Danube - *First*
Davies UK (1967)

The Danube Runs Red - *First**
Random House US (1968)

The Gun Runner - *First**
New English Library UK (1969)

A Score Of Arms - *Last*
Davies UK (1969)

The Lost Fräulein - *Last**
Random House US (1970)

A

Det Insp ALLPORT

appears in one other book with the author's other detective, *Insp George ANNERSLEY.*

British Policeman operating in England

Francis EVERTON 1883- (British)

Invented 4 detectives - see Insp George ANNESLEY

Citation Record: 3 Books

The Dalehouse Murder - *First*
Bobbs US (1927)

The Young Vanish - *Last*
Collins UK (1932); Morrow US (1932)

Det Insp ALLPORT and Insp George ANNESLEY

also appear individually in other books by this author.

British Policemen operating in England

Francis EVERTON 1883- (British)

Invented 4 detectives - see Insp George ANNESLEY

Citation Record: 1 Book

Murder May Pass Unpunished - *Only*
Collins UK (1936)

Dudley ALLWRIGHT

British Male Amateur

Philip MACDONALD 1899-1981 (British)

Invented 5 detectives - see Col Anthony GETHRYN

Citation Record: 1 Book

Escape - *Only*
Doubleday US (1932)

Mystery In Kensington Gore - *Only**
Collins UK (1932)

ALMACK

British Male Sleuth operating in England

E H CRAGG (British)

Citation Record: 1 Book

Almack, The Detective - *Only*
London Literary Society UK (1886)

Johnny ALOHA

Irish-Hawaiian Male Private Detective operating in California

Day KEENE ?-1969? (American)

wrote for the pulps in the 1930s and later for radio.

Inventor of one other detective Les FERRON

Citation Record: 2 Books

Dead In Bed - *First*
Pyramid US (1959)

Payola - *Last*
Pyramid US (1960)

Vino ALTOBELLI

Male Amateur operating in USA

Milton R BASS 1923- (American)

See main detective Benny FREEDMAN

Citation Record: 1 Book

The Broken-Hearted Detective - *Single*
Pocket Books US (1994)

Insp Enrique ALVAREZ

is head of the Spanish police force on the little island of Mallorca, which is known to harbour a sizeable British colony. Since its members are mainly respectable, quarrelsome, snooty, middle-class people, murders abound, many of them being just the sort of thing one might expect in an English village, being both dastardly and clever. *Enrique ALVAREZ* eats and drinks too much, but he brings official, and sometimes unofficial, justice to his little parish, in spite of being hounded, on the one hand, by cousin Dolores and, on the other, by 'the Superior Chief'.

Spanish Policeman operating in Spain

Stooge: Ch SALAS

is just a voice on the telephone. The 'Superior Chief' rings continually from 'some other place', attempting to interfere with *ALVAREZ's* theory and practice, which he usually regards as insubordinate and always calls idiotic.

Spanish Male

Roderic JEFFRIES 1926- (British)

was born in London, the son of the well-known genre writer, *Bruce GRAEME*. He was educated at Harrow View Preparatory School and the University of Southampton School of Navigation, served in the Merchant Navy, 1943-1949, studied Law and became a barrister in 1952. Starting in 1958, he began to write criminous novels in great numbers and he published them under several pseudonyms as well as his real name. He is the author, under the *Roderick GRAEME* byline, of at least twenty novels featuring his father's adventurer-detective, *BLACKSHIRT*, and has created several new series detectives. He has also written many books for children.

Writer: Roderic Graeme JEFFRIES

Other Bylines:
Peter ALDING — Jeffrey ASHFORD
Roderic GRAEME

Other Detectives:
Insp CLAYTON — Supt POPE
Bill STEMPLE

Citation Record: 18 Books

Mistakenly In Mallorca - *First*
Collins UK (1974)

An Arcadian Death - *Latest*
HarperCollins UK (1995)

Al AMATUCCI

American Male Amateur operating in USA

Carolyn BANKS 1941- (American)

Citation Record: 1 Book

The Darkroom - *Single*
Viking US (1980); Viking UK (1980)

Mynheer AMAYAT

Dutch Male Amateur operating in several locations

H De Vere STACPOOLE 1863-1951 (British)

Invented 3 detectives - see Capt SLOCUM

Citation Record: 14 Short Stories in 1 Collection

The Tales Of Mynheer Amayat - *Collection 1*
Newnes UK (1930)

Telzey AMBERDON and Trigger ARGEE

sleuth at some time in the future.

Male Sleuths

James H SCHMITZ 1911- (American)

Writer: James Henry SCHMITZ

Citation Record: 3 Books 4 Short Stories in 1 Collection

A Tale Of Two Clocks - *First*
Dodd, Mead US (1962)

Legacy - *First**
Ace US (1979)

The Lion Game - *Last*
Daw US (1973)

The Telzey Toy And Other Stories - *Collection 1*
Daw US (1973); Hamlyn UK (1983)

Frank AMBERLEY

is an accountant who, while travelling, finds a man dead in a car and a girl holding a gun. He helps the local police but solves the crime himself.

British Male Amateur operating in England

Georgette HEYER 1902-1974 (British)

Invented 3 detectives - see Supt HANNASYDE

A

Citation Record: 1 Book

Why Shoot A Butler? - *Only*
!See Appendix 2.
Longman UK (1933); Doubleday US (1936)

Marilyn AMBERS

American Female Amateur operating in USA

Elizabeth ST CLAIR 1938- (American)

Writer: Susan Handler COHEN

Citation Record: 3 Books

Murder In The Act - *First*
Zebra US (1978)

Trek Or Treat - *Latest*
Zebra US (1980)

Det Sgt AMBROSE

investigates the death of a don at a fictional English university.

British Policeman operating in England

Victor L WHITECHURCH 1868-1933 (British)

was born in Norham. He became the vicar of Blewbury, then a canon of Christ Church, Oxford, and later a rural dean. He wrote a number of criminous works.

Writer: Victor Lorenzo WHITECHURCH

Other Detectives:
Thorpe HAZELL
Capt Ivan KORAVITCH
Humphrey JUDD
Godfrey PAGE

Citation Record: 1 Book

Murder At The College - *Only*
Collins UK (1932)

Murder At Exbridge - *Only**
Dodd, Mead US (1932)

The AMERICAN DETECTIVE

American Male Detective in Pulp Magazines operating in England

A Frank PINKERTON (American)

Invented 5 detectives - see A Frank PINKERTON

Citation Record: 1 Book

The Whitechapel Murders; Or, An American Detective In London - *Only*
Laird & Lee US (1889)

Prof Leonidas AMES and Mr HOOPES

Leonidas AMES was formerly the Professor of Ornithology at an American university. Now retired, he is staying as one of several house-guests at the great mansion home of a Southern millionaire. When the latter is murdered, a private investigator from Washington, *Mr HOOPES*, is brought in to solve the case discreetly. However, he admits himself baffled and has to turn to *AMES* for help.

American Male Amateur and American Private Detective operating in USA

Cora JARRET 1877- (American)

was born in Norfolk, Virginia. Teacher and mainstream novelist, she used the KEENE byline for her detective fiction in the US, keeping her own name for publications in the UK.

Writer: Cora Hardy JARRET

Other Byline: Faraday KEENE

Citation Record: 1 Book

Pattern In Black And Red - *Only*
Barker UK (1934)

Faraday KEENE 1877- (American)

For writer details see Prof Leonidas AMES and Mr HOOPES

Citation Record: 1 Book

Pattern In Black And Red - *Only*
!See Appendix 2.
Houghton US (1934)

Martin AMES

American Male Amateur operating in New York

Alfred EICHLER 1908- (American)

Invented 3 detectives - see Insp KNICKMAN

Citation Record: 2 Books

Election By Murder - *First*
Lantern Press US (1946)

Pipeline To Death - *Last*
Hammond UK (1962)

Martin AMES

Second detective of Insp KNICKMAN

Russell AMES

American Male Private Detective operating in New York

Frank STEVENS 1909- (American)

Writer: Frank Edmund STEVENS

Citation Record: 1 Book

She Left A Silver Slipper - *Only*
Mill US (1954); Foulsham UK (1955)

Sid AMES

looks like an all-American boy and, when it comes to whisky and women, behaves like the all-American fictional private eye.

American Male Private Detective operating in New York

H W RODEN 1895-1963 (American)

Writer: Henry Wisdom RODEN

Citation Record: 4 Books

You Only Hang Once - *First*
Morrow US (1944); Hammond UK (1946)

Wake For A Lady - *Last*
Morrow US (1946); Hammond UK (1950)

Dr William AMES and Det LONEGAN

Dr AMES is a practising psychiatrist to whom *Det LONEGAN* of the New York Police Department brings cases that seem to require psychoanalytical investigation.

American Male Amateur and American Policeman operating in New York

Lucy FREEMAN 1916- (American)

Writer: Lucy Greenbaum FREEMAN

Citation Record: 3 Books

The Dream - *First*
Arbor US (1971)

The Case On Cloud Nine - *Last*
Arbor US (1975)

Reed AMHEARST

Second detective of Kate FANSLER

Robert AMISS

is an amateur undercover agent used by his policeman friend to solve difficult and bizarre cases of homicide.

British Male Amateur operating in England

Stooge: Det Sgt Ellis POOLEY
is *AMISS's* main antagonist at Scotland Yard.
British Male

Ruth Dudley EDWARDS 1944- (British)

Citation Record: 4 Books

Corridor Of Death - *First*
!See Appendix 2.
Quartet UK (1981); St Martin's US (1982)

Matricide At St Martha's - *Latest*
HarperCollins UK (1993)

Gregory AMOR

British Male Amateur operating in England

Milward KENNEDY 1894-1968 (British)

Invented 6 detectives - see Sir George BULL

Citation Record: 1 Book

Death To The Rescue - *Only*
Gollancz UK (1931)

Johnny AMSTERDAM

American Male Sleuth operating in USA

Michael LAWRENCE 1908-1981 (American)

For writer details see Mike WELLS

Citation Record: 2 Books

Naked And Alone - *First*
Popular Library UK (1953)

I Like It Cool - *Last*
Popular Library UK (1960)

AMZI

Male Detective in Pulp Magazines operating in USA

OLD SLEUTH (American)

Invented 40 detectives - see Brant ADAMS

Citation Record: 1 Book

Amzi, The Detective; Or, Morning, Noon And Night In New York - *Only*
Ogilvie US (1896)

Night And Morning; Or, A Detective's Shadow - *Only**
Ogilvie US (1900)

Insp/Supt ANDERS

British Policeman operating in England

Hamilton JOBSON 1914-1981 (British)

Citation Record: 13 Books

Therefore I Killed Him - *First*
Long UK (1968)

Exit To Violence - *Last*
Collins UK (1979)

Isobel ANDERS

returns home to clear up the death of her aunt and becomes a killer's target herself.

American Female Amateur operating in Florida

Mickey FRIEDMAN 1944- (American)

Writer: Michaele Thompson FRIEDMAN

Inventor of one other detective Georgia Lee MAXWELL

Citation Record: 1 Book

Riptide - *Single*
St Martin's US (1994)

Jonathan ANDERS

American Male Sleuth operating in USA

Christopher NICOLE 1930- (British)

For writer details see Jonas WILDE

Citation Record: 3 Books

Operation Destruct - *First*
Holt US (1969)

Operation Neptune - *Last*
Holt US (1972)

Tad ANDERS

British Male Secret Agent operating in Europe

Ted ALLBEURY 1917- (British)

was born in Stockport, Cheshire. Educated in Birmingham, he later worked as a draughtsman. During World War 2 he worked for British Intelligence.

Writer: Theodore Edward Le Bouthillier ALLBEURY

Other Byline: Richard BUTLER

Inventor of one other detective Max FARNE

Citation Record: 2 Books

Snowball - *First*
Davies UK (1974); Lippincott US (1974)

Palomino Blonde - *Last*
Davies UK (1975)

Omega-Minus - *Last**
was republished by *Perennial* (US 1983) under the UK title.
Viking US (1975)

Christine ANDERSEN

American Female Amateur operating in Washington DC

Merlda MACE (American)

Citation Record: 2 Books

Headlong For Murder - *First*
Messner US (1943)

Blondes Don't Cry - *Last*
Messner US (1945)

Ben ANDERSON

is a crime writer who can't resist sleuthing.

British Male Amateur operating in England

Guy COMPTON 1930- (British)

Writer: David Guy COMPTON

Citation Record: 2 Books

Medium For Murder - *First*
Long UK (1963)

Disguise For A Dead Gentleman - *Last*
Long UK (1964)

Dick ANDERSON

admits that his is not the brightest of intellects. However he keeps himself in good shape on a strict but boring diet.

American Male Private Detective operating in New York

Wolfe KAUFMAN (American)

Citation Record: 1 Book

I Hate Blondes - *Only*
Simon & Schuster US (1946)

Insp Everett ANDERSON

American Policeman operating in Maryland

K S DAIGER (American)

Writer: Katherine S DAIGER

Citation Record: 2 Books

Fourth Degree - *First*
Macrae, Smith US (1931); Harrap UK (1932)

Murder On Ghost Tree Island - *Last*
Macrae, Smith US (1934); Harrap UK (1934)

Lou 'Shifty' ANDERSON

is a race-track punter. A bit of a con-man, he nevertheless has the reputation of being something of a magician.

American Male Amateur operating in Los Angeles

William MURRAY 1926- (American)

Writer: William Buckley MURRAY

Citation Record: 8 Books

Tip On A Dead Crab - *First*
Viking US (1984); Penguin UK (1985)

Now You See Her, Now You Don't - *Latest*
Holt US (1994); Bantam UK (1994)

Malcolm ANDERSON

American Male Amateur operating in USA

John KATZENBACH 1950- (American)

Citation Record: 1 Book

In The Heat Of The Summer - *Single*
Atheneum US (1982)

The Mean Season - *Single**
Ballantine US (1985)

Sgt Pepper ANDERSON

appears in novelizations of the 'Policewoman' TV series.

American Policewoman operating in Los Angeles

Leslie TREVOR (American)

Citation Record: 3 Books

Code 1013: Assassin - *First*
Award US (1975)

The Rape - *Last*
Award US (1975); Tandem UK (1975)

Insp Tom ANDERSON

British Policeman operating in England

A

Louis SOUTHWORTH 1916- (British)
Writer: Thomas Louis GREALEY
Citation Record: 2 Books
Felon In Disguise - *First*
Hale UK (1966)
Corpse On London Bridge - *Last*
Hale UK (1969)

Tony ANDERSON
Second detective of Capt Jacques RADFORD

Hermann ANDERWELT
Male Amateur

Ellsworth DOUGLASS (British)
Citation Record: 9 Short Stories in 1 Collection
The Confessions Of A Coiner - *Collection 1*
Pearson UK (1899)

Fitzroy Maclean ANGEL
is a taxi-driver who, roaming around in an old black taxi he calls Armstrong, does some amateur sleuthing.
British Male Amateur operating in London

Mike RIPLEY 1952- (British)
Writer: Michael David RIPLEY
Citation Record: 5 Books
Just Another Angel - *First*
HarperCollins UK (1988)
Angel Confidential - *Latest*
HarperCollins UK (1995)

Harry ANGEL
specialises in finding missing persons. In his one case, though, he finds something he does not expect or can even conceive of.
American Male Private Detective operating in New York

William HJORTSBERG 1941- (American)
Inventor of one other detective pair Harry HOUDINI and Sir Arthur Conan DOYLE
Citation Record: 1 Book
Falling Angel - *Single*
Harcourt Brace US (1978); Hutchinson UK (1979)

Soeur ANGELE
French Female Amateur operating in France

Henri CATALAN 1885- (French)
Writer: Henri DUPUY-MAZUEL
Citation Record: 3 Books
Soeur Angele And The Embarrassed Ladies - *First*
is a translation from the French of *Le Cas de Soeur Angele* (Paris, 1953).
Sheed UK (1955)
The Embarrassed Ladies Affair - *First**
Sheed UK (1973)
Soeur Angele And The Bell Ringer's Niece - *Last*
Sheed UK (1957)

Bruce ANGELO
American Male Detective in Pulp Magazines operating in USA

Harlan Page HALSEY 1837-1898 (American)
Invented 6 detectives - see Kate GOELET
Citation Record: 1 Book
Bruce Angelo, The Old Time Detective - *Only*
Aldine US

OLD SLEUTH (American)
Invented 40 detectives - see Brant ADAMS
Citation Record: 1 Book
Bruce Angelo, The City Detective - *Only*
Street & Smith US (1887)

Pete ANGLICH
American Male Private Detective operating in USA

Raymond CHANDLER 1888-1959 (American)
Invented 9 detectives - see Philip MARLOWE
Citation Record: 1 Selected Short Story
Noon Street Nemesis
In 'Detective Fiction' US (1936)

Mici ANHALT
works for the Crime Victims' Compensation Board and, in the course of upholding the cause, needs to solve mystery and murder.
American Female Sleuth operating in New York

Lillian O'DONNELL 1926- (American)
Invented 3 detectives - see Policewoman Norah MULCAHANEY
Citation Record: 3 Books
Aftershock - *First*
Putnam US (1977); Hale UK (1979)
Wicked Designs - *Latest*
Putnam US (1980); Hale UK (1983)

Insp George ANNESLEY
appears also in one book with the author's other detective, *Det Insp ALLPORT.*
British Policeman operating in England

Francis EVERTON 1883- (British)
Writer: Francis William STOKES
Other Detectives:
Det Insp ALLPORT and Insp George ANNESLEY
Det Insp ALLPORT — Peter LINDSAY
Citation Record: 1 Book
Murder At Plenders - *Only*
Collins UK (1930)
Murder Through The Window - *Only**
Morrow US (1930)

Insp George ANNESLEY
Second detective of Det Insp ALLPORT

Margaret ANNISTER
appears once, sleuthing to some avail, in a farrago of a plot.
American Female Amateur operating in Nevada

Harry Stephen KEELER 1890-1967 (American)
Invented 14 detectives - see Angus MACWHORTER
Citation Record: 1 Book
The Case Of The Mysterious Moll - *Only*
Phoenix Press US (1945)
The Iron Ring - *Only**
Ward, Lock UK (1944)

Bill ANSTRUTHER
British Male Amateur operating in Singapore

Jerome NICHOLAS (British)
Citation Record: 4 Books
The Widow's Peak - *First*
Hodder & Stoughton UK (1946)
Deirdre - *Last*
Hodder & Stoughton UK (1952)

Colin ANSTRUTHER
British Male Amateur operating in England

Josephine PLAIN (British)
Citation Record: 3 Books
The Secret Of The Sandbanks - *First*
Butterworth UK (1934)
The Pazenger Problem - *Last*
Butterworth UK (1936)

Margot ANSTRUTHER and Gene VALERY
British Female Amateur and British Male Amateur operating in England

W Adolphe ROBERTS 1886-1962 (British)
Writer: Walter Adolphe ROBERTS

Citation Record: 1 Book

The Haunting Hand - *Only*
Hutchinson UK (1926); Macaulay US (1926)

Jim ANTHONY

was a trouble-shooter who appeared in short stories in *Super Detective* during the 1940s.

American Male Detective in Pulp Magazines operating in USA

John GRANGE (American)

Writers: Willis Todhunter BALLARD 1903-1980 and Robert Leslie BELLEM 1902-1968

No citations

Dr Wade ANTHONY

is a psychiatrist, an amateur criminologist, and a writer. He is, moreover, endowed with a number of the more batty theories about how to detect murderers. Fortunately he appears in books that are almost gothic in plot, in which anything can happen and usually does, as they say.

American Male Amateur operating in California

Sidekick: Penny LAKE
is the beautiful and not too unhelpful secretary who accompanies *Wade ANTHONY* on his cases.

American Female - Secretary

Eric HEATH (American)

Inventor of one other detective Cornelius CLIFT Jr

Citation Record: 2 Books

The Murder Pool - *First*
Arcadia US (1954)

Murder Of A Mystery Writer - *Last*
Arcadia US (1955)

ANTHROPOL

is a sci-fi detective who runs the Anthropol Detective Agency.

Male Private Detective operating in Space

Louis TRIMBLE 1917- (American)

Invented 3 detectives - see Martin ZANE

Citation Record: 2 Books

Anthropol - *First*
Ace US (1968)

The Noblest Experiment In The Galaxy - *Last*
Ace US (1970)

ANTOINE

French Male Sleuth operating in Paris

H Collinson OWEN 1882-1956 (British)

Writer: Harry Collinson OWEN

Citation Record: 7 Short Stories in 1 Collection

The Adventures Of Antoine - *Collection 1*
Hodder & Stoughton UK (1919)

Mark ANTONY

British Male Amateur operating in England

Colin CURZON 1917?- (British)

Citation Record: 2 Books

The Body In The Barrage Balloon ; Or, Who Killed The Corpse? - *First*
Hurst UK (1941); Macmillan US (1942)

The Case Of The Eighteenth Ostrich - *Last*
Hurst UK (1943); Macmillan US (1944)

Prof Jose APODACA

is a Professor of Archaeology who is a guest at a farm near New York when a best-selling novelist is murdered there. While drinking considerable amounts of whisky and knitting socks, his two beguiling occupations, this clever little man solves the crime well before the police.

Irish-Spanish Male Amateur operating in USA

Wirt VAN ARSDALE 1905-1952 (American)

was born in Denver, Colorado.

Writer: Martha Wirt DAVIS

Citation Record: 1 Book

The Professor Knits A Shroud - *Only*
Doubleday US (1951)

Insp/Commiss John APPLEBY

began life in 1936, a time when the breed of policemen who could also be English gentlemen was not only acceptable but fictionally fashionable. Although he was not considered to be of that peculiar class by birth, he certainly seems to be a gentleman by general consent, which is even more difficult. Good-mannered and rather reserved, he has a reasonable but not ostentatious degree of erudition and is moderately well educated. He rises through the ranks over a magnificent four decades; and, although perhaps his books get less interesting, he continues to appeal. His chief qualities are his patience, his equanimity and his sense of fairness and liberal values. During his long career, he acquires a wife and family and eventually a knighthood. His books vary widely and include tales of pure deduction, others that involve spies and fugitives, many that concern art thefts and some that are highly comic. Occasionally he appears with an old friend, another of the author's detectives, the brilliant university don, *Charles HONEYBATH.*

British Policeman operating in England

Michael INNES 1906-1994 (British)

was born in Edinburgh, Scotland. He was educated at Edinburgh Academy and Oriel College, Oxford, taking prizes and a BA in English, 1928. He was Professor of English at Adelaide, Australia, Fellow of Christ Church, Oxford, 1949-1973, Emeritus Reader in English Literature at Oxford, 1969-1973, and a visiting Professor at the University of Washington, Seattle. He used the pseudonym for his long series of highly regarded detective novels and criminous short stories, reserving his real name for all other works. Under the latter he wrote at least twenty non-genre novels, works of literary criticism and biographies of literary figures.

Writer: John Innes Mackintosh STEWART

Other Detectives:
Insp/Commiss John APPLEBY and Prof Charles HONEYBATH
Insp CADOGAN   Prof Charles HONEYBATH

Citation Record: 33 Books 56 Short Stories in 3 Collections

Death At The President's Lodging - *First*
Gollancz UK (1936)

Seven Suspects - *First**
Dodd, Mead US (1937)

Appleby And The Ospreys - *Last*
Gollancz UK (1987); Dodd, Mead US (1987)

Appleby Talking - *Collection 1*
Short stories - 23
Gollancz UK (1954); Dodd, Mead US (1954)

Dead Man's Shoes - *Collection 1**
Dodd, Mead US (1954)

Appleby Talks Again - *Collection 2*
Short stories - 18
Gollancz UK (1956); Dodd, Mead US (1957)

The Appleby File - *Collection 3*
Short stories - 15
Gollancz UK (1975); Dodd, Mead US (1976)

Insp/Commiss John APPLEBY and Prof Charles HONEYBATH

John APPLEBY is sometimes aided and sometimes hindered by his brilliant friend. The two detectives also appear individually in other books by this author.

British Policeman and British Male Amateur operating in England

Michael INNES 1906-1994 (British)

Invented 4 detectives - see Insp/Commiss John APPLEBY

Citation Record: 2 Books

Honeybath's Haven - *First*
Gollancz UK (1977); Dodd, Mead US (1978)

Appleby And Honeybath - *Last*
Gollancz UK (1983); Dodd, Mead US (1983)

Pecos APPLEBY

American Male Sleuth operating in New Mexico

A

Robert Portner KOEHLER 1905- (American)
Invented 4 detectives - see Les IVEY
Citation Record: 3 Books
Sing A Song Of Murder - *First*
Phoenix Press US (1941)
Here Come The Dead - *Last*
Phoenix Press US (1942)

Charles APPLEGATE
is a young man who, having written his first successful detective novel, becomes a teacher at a small private school, where he immediately runs into murder. Deciding to solve the problem on his own, he is drawn into a plot of almost global dimensions.
British Male Amateur operating in Kent

Julian SYMONS 1912-1994 (British)
Invented 11 detectives - see Insp CRAMBO
Citation Record: 1 Book
The Paper Chase - *Only*
Collins UK (1956)
Bogue's Fortune - *Only**
Harper & Row US (1957)

Luke APPLEGATE
sleuths in the Virginia of 1870.
American Male Amateur operating in USA

Paul Darcy BOLES (American)
Citation Record: 1 Book
The Limner - *Only*
Crowell US (1975)

Belle APPLEMAN
sleuths in the Boston of 1935.
American Female Amateur operating in Boston

Dorothy ROSEN 1916- and Sidney ROSEN 1916- (American)
Citation Record: 1 Book
Death And Blintzes - *Single*
Walker US (1985)

Arthur APPLEYARD
is a visiting British lecturer to the fictional Illinois State College, where he is to give lectures on swine husbandry. His work has certain military aspects and, because of that, murder ensues. He has to solve the problem himself, the local police being suitably baffled.
British Male Amateur operating in Illinois

Michael KENYON 1931- (British)
Invented 6 detectives - see Insp/Ch Insp Harry PECKOVER
Citation Record: 1 Book
The Whole Hog - *Only*
Collins UK (1967)
The Trouble With Series Three - *Only**
Morrow US (1967)

Danny APRIL
owns a small debt collection agency and, in the course of his work, needs to do a little light sleuthing.
American Male Private Detective operating in Chicago

William S BALLINGER 1912-1980 (American)
Invented 5 detectives - see Joaquin HAWKS
Citation Record: 1 Book
Portrait In Smoke - *Only*
Harper & Row US (1950); Reinhardt UK (1951)

Johnny APRIL
American Male Private Detective operating in Kansas

Mike ROSCOE (American)
Writers: John ROSCOE 1921-and Michael RUSO
Citation Record: 5 Books
Death Is A Round Black Ball - *First*
Crown US (1952); Foulsham UK (1954)
The Midnight Eye - *Last*
Ace US (1958)

Tomas ARAGON
is a Hispanic lawyer who is called on to investigate cases of disappearance and murder.
American Male Amateur operating in California

Margaret MILLAR 1915- (Canadian)
Invented 11 detectives - see Insp SANDS
Citation Record: 3 Books
Ask For Me Tomorrow - *First*
Random House US (1976); Gollancz UK (1977)
Mermaid - *Latest*
Gollancz UK (1982); Morrow US (1982)

Insp Carlo ARBATI
investigates death at the opera.
Italian Policeman operating in Florence

John Spencer HILL (Canadian)
is a Professor of English.
Citation Record: 1 Book
The Last Castrato - *Single*
Constable UK (1995)

Montrose ARBUTHNOT
British Male Amateur operating in England

N A TEMPLE-ELLIS 1894- (British)
Writer: Neville Aldridge HOLDAWAY
Other Detectives:
Montrose ARBUTHNOT and Edmund KING
Insp WREN
Citation Record: 1 Book
Dead In No Time - *Only*
Hodder & Stoughton UK (1935)
Murder In The Ruins - *Only**
Dial US (1936)

Montrose ARBUTHNOT and Edmund KING
British Male Amateurs operating in England

N A TEMPLE-ELLIS 1894- (British)
Invented 3 detectives - see Montrose ARBUTHNOT
Citation Record: 2 Books
The Inconsistent Villains - *First*
Methuen UK (1930); Dutton US (1929)
The Man Who Was There - *Latest*
Methuen UK (1930); Dutton US (1930)

Jonathan ARCANE and Vanessa ARCANE
American Male Amateur and American Female Amateur operating in USA

Ed FRIEND 1908-1977 (American)
For writer details see Lt Andy BASTIAN
Citation Record: 1 Book
The Corpse In The Castle - *Only*
Lancer US (1970)

Vanessa ARCANE
Second detective of Jonathan ARCANE

Alan ARCHBOLD
is an investigative journalist who clears up a seven-year-old case of murder.
British Male Amateur operating in England

Steve HAYWOOD (British)
Citation Record: 1 Book
Murderous Justice - *Single*
HarperCollins UK (1991)

Jill ARCHER
is one of the earliest of the hardboiled female private eyes. So much so that she thinks it expedient to conceal her gender

behind the name of the nominal head of her agency, which is called Secrets Inc.

American Female Private Detective operating in New York

Stephen RANSOME 1902-1977 (American)

Invented 4 detectives - see Lt Lee BARCELLO

Citation Record: 1 Book

A Shroud For Shylock - *Only*
Doubleday US (1939)

Lew ARCHER

is one of the key figures in modern detective fiction, although views on his credibility and performance vary. Formerly a cop and then in a branch of US Intelligence, once married and now divorced, he operates from an office on Sunset Boulevard. He is an excellent example of the American private eye with a social conscience.

American Male Private Detective operating in Los Angeles

John MACDONALD 1915- (American)

For writer details see Lew ARCHER

Citation Record: 2 Books

The Moving Target - *First*
was republished as *Harper* by *Pocket Books (US 1966)* under the *Ross MACDONALD* byline.
Knopf US (1949); Cassell UK (1951)

The Drowning Pool - *Last*
was also published as the first of the *Lew ARCHER* books under the *John Ross MACDONALD* byline.
Knopf US (1950); Cassell UK (1952)

John Ross MACDONALD 1915- (American)

was born in Los Gatos, California, and raised in Canada. Educated at the Kitchener-Waterloo Collegiate Institute, Ontario, where he graduated, 1932, he subsequently took degrees in English at universities in the Canada and the USA. After serving in the US Naval Reserve, 1944-1946, he continued his studies and taught English and History at the University of Michigan, Ann Arbor. He is universally recognised as one of the outstanding developers of American detective fiction; and his novels have, for over thirty-five years, received the highest acclaim, from readers and critics alike, for their superb plotting, social significance and literary quality. He received the Crime Writers Association Gold Dagger award, 1965, and the Mystery Writers of America Grand Master award, 1973. He married *Margaret MILLAR* (née Sturm), herself an admired author of detective novels, 1938. He has published his main works variously under the bylines of *John MACDONALD* and *John Ross MACDONALD*, occcasionally using the byline of *Ross MACDONALD* and sometimes his real name. Sometimes his works have appeared under the different bylines in the US and UK; and, moreover, republication has sometimes taken place under a changed byline.

Writer: Kenneth MILLAR

Other Bylines:
John MACDONALD   Ross MACDONALD

Other Detectives:
Howard CROSS   Herlock SHOLMES

Citation Record: 4 Books 7 Short Stories in 1 Collection

The Drowning Pool - *First*
was also published as the last of the *Lew ARCHER* books under the *John MACDONALD* byline.
Knopf US (1950); Cassell UK (1952)

Find A Victim - *Last*
Knopf US (1954); Cassell UK (1955)

The Name Is Archer - *Collection 1*
was republished, with two other stories, in a collection entitled *Lew Archer, Private Investigator* under the *Ross MACDONALD* byline.
Bantam UK (1955)

Ross MACDONALD 1915- (American)

Inventor of one other detective Bill GUNNERSON

Citation Record: 13 Books 9 Short Stories in 1 Collection

The Barbarous Coast - *First*
Knopf US (1956); Cassell UK (1957)

The Blue Hammer - *Last*
Knopf US (1976); Collins UK (1976)

Lew Archer, Private Investigator - *Collection 1*
is a republication of *THE NAME IS ARCHER*, with the addition of two more tales.
Mysterious Press US (1977)

Lew ARCHER

Appears with at least two other detectives - see Sherlock HOLMES.

Matt ARCHER

Male Amateur operating in Michigan

Clay HENRY (British)

Citation Record: 2 Books

Welcome Home, Lily Glow - *First*
Boardman UK (1960)

Nude On The Rocks - *Last*
Boardman UK (1965)

Maxwell ARCHER

British Male Amateur operating in England

Hugh CLEVELY 1898-1964 (British)

Writer: Hugh Desmond CLEVELY

Other Byline: Tod CLAYMORE

Other Detectives:
Sexton BLAKE   John MARTINSON
Insp WILLIAMS

Citation Record: 7 Books

Zero The 14th - *First*
Cassell UK (1937)

Blood And Thunder - *Last*
Cassell UK (1951)

Oceola ARCHER

American Male Amateur operating in Massachusetts/Georgia

Joseph Baker CARR (American)

Citation Record: 2 Books

Death Whispers - *First*
Viking US (1933); Cassell UK (1933)

The Man With Bated Breath - *Last*
Viking US (1934); Cassell UK (1935)

Owen ARCHER

is an ex-soldier in the fourteenth century, a former captain in the Archers. Finding corpses in York cathedral in his first book, he investigates. He continued his medieval sleuthing in a second book.

English Male Amateur operating in York

Candace M ROBB

Citation Record: 2 Books

The Apothecary Rose - *First*
Mandarin UK (1994)

The Lady Chapel - *Latest*
Mandarin UK (1994); St Martin's US (1994)

David ARDEN

British Male Amateur operating in England

Sheridan LE FANU 1814-1873 (Irish)

Writer: Joseph Sheridan LE FANU

Citation Record: 1 Book

Checkmate - *Only*
Chapman & Hall UK (1876)

Jan ARGAND

is a detective in the fictional country of Brabt, which seems rather like Spain or Turkey. He deals with crimes of politics and business.
!See Appendix 2.

Brabtian Male Professional Investigator operating in Brabt

Julian RATHBONE 1935- (British)

Invented 3 detectives - see Col Nur BEY

Citation Record: 3 Books

The Euro-Killers - *First*
Joseph UK (1979); Pantheon US (1990)

Watching The Detectives - *Latest*
Joseph UK (1983); Pantheon US (1984)

Trigger ARGEE

Second detective of Telzey AMBERDON

Albert ARGYLE

British Male Amateur operating in England

Jack Trevor STORY 1918-1991 (British)

Writer: Jack Trevor STORY

Other Bylines:
Bret HARDING   Richard WILLIAMS

Other Detectives:
Sexton BLAKE   Horace Spurgeon FENTON

Citation Record: 3 Books

Live Now, Pay Later - *First*
Secker & Warburg UK (1963)

The Urban District Lover - *Last*
Secker & Warburg UK (1964)

Jonathan ARGYLL

Appears with at least two other detectives - see Gen Taddeo BOTTANDO.

ARISTOTLE

is, indeed, the famous Greek philosopher and here he investigates a case in 332 BC.

Greek Male Amateur operating in Athens

Sidekick: STEPHANOS
Greek Male - Assistant

Margaret DOODY 1939- (British)

Citation Record: 1 Book

Aristotle, Detective - *Single*
Bodley Head UK (1978); Harper & Row US (1980)

Simon ARK

is a retired Coptic priest said to be 2000 years old. He appears only in short stories and is naturally better endowed with wisdom than most younger sleuths.

American Male Amateur operating in USA

Edward D HOCH 1930- (American)

Invented 20 detectives - see Capt LEOPOLD

Citation Record: 17 Short Stories in 3 Collections

The Judges Of Hades, And Other Simon Ark Stories - *Collection 1*
Short stories - 5
Leisure Books US (1971)

City Of Brass, And Other Simon Ark Stories - *Collection 2*
Short stories - 3
Leisure Books US (1971)

The Quests Of Simon Ark - *Collection 3*
Several of the stories are new.
Short stories - 9
Mysterious Press US (1984)

Oliver ARMISTON

is an oddity among detectives. A brilliant writer of detective stories himself, he is used (in the first of three books) by a master criminal, Godahl, to plan a great coup. In two subsequent books, he is actually employed by *Dep Commiss PARR* of the New York Police Department to solve difficult crimes, which he does by simply receiving information about the crimes and the suspects and then thinking around the problem until he arrives at the solution. The very model of an armchair detective, he takes no active steps himself, while *PARR* gets the credit.

American Male Professional Amateur operating in New York

Sidekick: Dep Commiss PARR
is a high-ranking officer in the New York Police Department and an oddity among sidekicks, as he actually employs the detective to solve crimes for him.
American Male - Employer

Frederick Irving ANDERSON 1877-1947 (American)

was born in Aurora, Illinois.

Citation Record: 23 Short Stories in 3 Collections

Adventures Of The Infallible Godahl - *Collection 1*
Short stories - 6
Crowell US (1914)

The Notorious Sophie Lang - *Collection 2*
Short stories - 7
Heinemann UK (1925)

The Book Of Murder - *Collection 3*
Short stories - 10
Dutton US (1930)

Bryan ARMITAGE

appears also in books with one of the author's other detectives, *Insp Cheviot BURMANN.*

British Male Amateur operating in England

Belton COBB 1892-1971 (British)

Invented 4 detectives - see Insp Cheviot BURMANN

Citation Record: 2 Books

Food For Felony - *First*
Allen UK (1969)

Scandal At Scotland Yard - *Last*
Allen UK (1969)

Bryan ARMITAGE

Second detective of Insp Cheviot BURMANN

Frances ARMITAGE

Female Amateur operating in England

Marion BABSON (American)

!See Appendix 2.

Invented 8 detectives - see Douglas PERKINS

Citation Record: 1 Book

Murder, Murder, Little Star - *Single*
Collins UK (1977); Walker US (1980)

Stephen ARMITAGE

British Male Sleuth operating in England

Hugh MCLEAVE 1923- (British)

Invented 3 detectives - see Paul BRODIE

Citation Record: 1 Book

Second Time Round - *Single*
Hale UK (1981); Walker US (1981)

Det Insp ARMSTRONG

British Policeman operating in England

Alan WHITE 1920- (British)

Inventor of one other detective Capt COLSON

Citation Record: 3 Books

Armstrong - *First*
Barrie & Jenkins UK (1973); Doubleday US (1977)

Death In Darkness - *Last*
Barrie & Jenkins UK (1975); Doubleday US (1977)

ARNHOLT

British Male Amateur operating in England

Gordon LATTA 1904- (British)

Citation Record: 3 Books

Arnholt Makes His Bow - *First*
Benn UK (1931)

The Toni Diamonds - *First**
Dial US (1931)

Exit Arnholt - *Last*
Bles UK (1935)

A

Insp Henry ARNOLD
Second detective of Desmond MERRION

James ARNOLD
British Male Amateur operating in England

Neil GORDON 1895-1941 (British)
Writer: Archibald Gordon MACDONELL
Other Detectives:
Insp DEWAR   Peter KERRIGAN
Citation Record: 1 Book
The Professor's Poison *- Only*
Longman UK (1928); Harcourt Brace US (1928)

Ch Insp Ralph ARNOTT
is called on to investigate the death of a barrister, but resigns from the force when Scotland Yard's Special Branch interferes. Spurred on by his sidekick, he continues to investigate the case privately.
British Policeman operating in England
Sidekick: Sgt Judy PULLEN
British Female - Subordinate

Vivien ARMSTRONG (British)
Inventor of one other detective Insp Lawrence ERSKINE
Citation Record: 1 Book
Sleight Of Hand *- Single*
HarperCollins UK (1991)

Frank ARROW
American Male Amateur operating in Hawaii/Mexico

Walter DEPTULA (American)
Writer: Walter J DEPTULA Jr
Citation Record: 2 Books
Naked Mistress *- First*
Curtis US (1974)
Wine, Women...And Death *- Last*
Curtis US (1974)

Sgt Steven ARROW
British Male Amateur operating in England

Laurie MANTELL 1917-
Writer: Mrs Lorraine MANTELL
Citation Record: 5 Books
Murder In Fancy Dress *- First*
!See Appendix 2.
Gollancz UK (1978); Walker US (1981)
Murder To Burn *- Last*
Gollancz UK (1983)

Sheriff Spencer ARROWWOOD
operates in rural Hamelin, where he runs into problems of ritualistic murders at the home of an old-style female folk-singer.
American Policeman operating in Tennessee

Sharyn MCCRUMB (American)
Invented 4 detectives - see Elizabeth MACPHERSON
Citation Record: 1 Book
If Ever I Return, Pretty Peggy-O *- Single*
Scribner's US (1990)

Dr ARTHUR
is a talkative but erudite sleuth of the old school.
American Male Private Detective operating in USA

Roger DELANCEY (American)
Citation Record: 1 Book
Murder Below Wall Street *- Only*
Appleton US (1934); Appleton UK (1934)

Simon ARTIFEX
British Male Amateur operating in several locations

Richard KEVERNE 1882-1950 (British)
Invented 4 detectives - see Insp MACE
Citation Record: 6 Short Stories in 2 Collections
Artifex Intervenes *- Collection 1*
contains three novelettes.
Short stories - 3
Constable UK (1934)
Crook Stuff *- Collection 2*
contains thirteen of the author's stories, three with *Simon ARTIFEX.*
Short stories - 3
Constable UK (1935)

The ARTIST DETECTIVE
American Male Detective in Pulp Magazines operating in USA

ANON
Citation Record: 1 Book
The Artist Detective *- Only*
Aldine US

Mrs ARTSIDE
British Female Amateur operating in England

Michael GILBERT 1912- (British)
Invented 11 detectives - see Insp HAZELRIGG
Citation Record: 1 Book
Sky High *- Only*
Hodder & Stoughton UK (1955)
The Country-House Burglar *- Only**
Harper & Row US (1955)

Jim ASBESTOS
American Male Amateur operating in Iowa

Leo F SCHMITT 1891- (American)
Writer: Leo Francis SCHMITT
Citation Record: 26 Short Stories in 1 Collection
The Shyster Lawyer *- Collection 1*
Schmitt US (1929)

Jacob ASCH
was a reporter but is now a PI who investigates crimes in several of the bizarre sub-cultures of southern California. Hardboiled he may be, yet he seems more compassionate and socially concerned than were the private eyes of the previous decade.
American Male Private Detective operating in California

Arthur LYONS 1946- (American)
was born in Los Angeles. He graduated from the University of California with a BA in Political Science.
Writer: Arthur LYONS Jr
Citation Record: 11 Books
The Dead Are Discreet *- First*
Robson UK (1977); Mason & Lipscomb US (1974)
False Pretences *- Latest*
Mysterious Press US (1994)

Lady ASENATH
British Female Amateur operating in England/Scotland

Basil THOMSON 1861-1939 (British)
Invented 5 detectives - see Insp RICHARDSON
Citation Record: 12 Short Stories in 1 Collection
The Indiscretions Of Lady Asenath *- Collection 1*
Not all the stories are criminous.
Innes UK (1898)

Supt Andrew ASH
appears also in six books with another of the author's detectives, *Ch Det Insp George MUIR.*
British Policeman operating in England

Francis GRIERSON 1888-1972 (British)
Invented 6 detectives - see Ch Det Insp George MUIR

Citation Record: 7 Books

Blackmail In Red - *First*
Hale UK (1954)

The Red Cobra - *Last*
Hale UK (1960)

Supt Andrew ASH and Ch Det Insp George MUIR

appear individually in other books by this author.

British Policemen operating in London/Paris

Francis GRIERSON 1888-1972 (British)

Invented 6 detectives - see Ch Det Insp George MUIR

Citation Record: 6 Books

No Wreaths For The Duchess - *First*
Hutchinson UK (1948)

Madame Shadow - *Last*
Hutchinson UK (1952)

Geoff ASHDEN

Male Amateur

Robert WESTALL 1929-

Writer: Robert Atkinson WESTALL

Citation Record: 7 Short Stories in 1 Collection

Antique Dust - *Collection 1*
Viking UK (1989); Viking US (1989)

Saxon ASHE

British Male Secret Agent operating in Europe

Saxon ASHE (British)

Citation Record: 2 Books

I Am Saxon Ashe - *First*
Hodder & Stoughton UK (1940); Alliance US (1941)

Saxon Ashe, Secret Agent - *Last*
Hodder & Stoughton UK (1941); Alliance US (1942)

Steve ASHE

American Male Sleuth operating in California/Colorado

James A HOWARD 1922- (American)

Writer: James Arch HOWARD

Inventor of one other detective Paul Kenneth KANE

Citation Record: 4 Books

I'll Get You Yet - *First*
Popular Library US (1954); Digit UK (1964)

Die On Easy Street - *Last*
Popular Library US (1957); Digit UK (1964)

ASHENDEN

appears only in short stories, written by one of the great masters of the form. He is a young writer who is drawn into espionage and then employed as an agent for British Intelligence during the First World War. His actual detective exploits are engineered for him, but he succeeds in the tasks he is given.

British Male Secret Agent operating in Europe

W S MAUGHAM 1874-1965 (British)

was born in Paris, France. Educated at King's School, Canterbury, he spent a year at Heidelberg University, Germany before graduating as a doctor at St Thomas' Hospital, London, 1897. He never practised medicine but served with British Intelligence during the First World War. He became a full-time writer in 1896 and travelled widely for many years. He lived in Cap Ferrat, France, from 1928 and in the USA during the Second World War. He wrote many novels and stage plays, but is now best known for his magnificent short stories. He wrote little in the criminous genre, apart from the famous *ASHENDEN* stories.

Writer: William Somerset MAUGHAM

Citation Record: 16 Short Stories in 1 Collection

Ashenden; Or The British Agent - *Collection 1*
Heinemann UK (1928); Doubleday US (1928)

Jacob ASHER

is an Israeli agent sent to London to train with the SIS. He manages to hunt down an escaped master spy, break up a spy ring and, *en passant*, he stops a nuclear holocaust.

Israeli Male Secret Agent operating in London

Barry WEIL (British)

Writer: Derek ROBERT

Citation Record: 1 Book

Dossier Ix - *Only*
Hamilton UK (1969); Bobbs Merrill US (1969)

Tim ASHER

American Male Amateur operating in Midwest USA

Helen Joan HULTMAN 1891- (American)

See main detective Insp Dave BRATTON

Citation Record: 2 Books

Find The Woman - *First*
Doubleday US (1929)

Death At Windward Hill - *Last*
Fiction League US (1931)

Grace ASHERTON

British Female Amateur operating in England

Dorothy EDEN 1912-1982 (British)

See main detective Kate TEMPEST

Citation Record: 1 Book

Waiting For Willa - *Only*
Hodder & Stoughton UK (1970); Coward McCann US (1970)

Col Robert Lee ASHLEY

American Male Amateur operating in USA

Chester K STEELE 1862-1930 (American)

See main detective Prof Irving SPENCER

Citation Record: 2 Books

The Diamond Cross Mystery - *First*
Sully US (1918); Jenkins UK (1920)

The Golf Course Mystery - *Last*
Sully US (1919)

Insp Carol ASHTON

Australian Policewoman operating in Sydney

Claire MCNAB (Australian)

Citation Record: 6 Books

Death Down Under - *First*
Allen AU (1990); Naiad UK (1990); Naiad US (1990)

Body Guard - *Latest*
Silver Moon UK (1994); Naiad US (1994)

Dany ASHTON

Second detective of Lash HOLDEN

Insp Simon ASHTON

Australian Policeman operating in Australia

Elizabeth ANTILL (Australian)

was born in Australia, but is now a British citizen

Writer: Elizabeth MIDDLETON

Citation Record: 2 Books

Murder In Mid-Atlantic - *First*
Hammond UK (1950)

Death On The Barrier Reef - *Last*
Hammond UK (1952)

ASHTON-KIRK

!See Appendix 2.

American Male Professional Investigator operating in USA

John MACINTYRE 1871-1951 (American)

Writer: John Thomas MACINTYRE

Other Byline: Kerry O'NEIL

Inventor of one other detective Duddington Pell CHALMERS

Citation Record: 4 Books

Ashton-Kirk: Investigator - *First*
Penn US (1910); Robinson UK (1921)

Ashton-Kirk: Criminologist - *Last*
Penn US (1918); Robinson UK (1921)

Dr John ASHWIN
is the Professor of Sanskrit at the University of California.
American Male Amateur operating in California

Anthony BOUCHER 1911-1968 (American)
Invented 7 detectives - see Fergus O'BREEN and Det Lt JACKSON
Citation Record: 1 Book
The Case Of The Seven Of Calvary - *Only*
Simon & Schuster (1937); Hamish Hamilton UK (1937)

Ch Insp Jim ASHWORTH
is head of the fictional Bridgetown CID.
British Policeman operating in England

Brian BATTISON (British)
was born in Northampton. He is an actor.
Citation Record: 2 Books
The Christmas Bow Murder - *First*
Constable UK (1994)
Fool's Ransom - *Latest*
Constable UK (1994)

Peter ASWELL
American Male Sleuth operating in New York

Wenzell BROWN (American)
Citation Record: 2 Books
Murder Seeks An Agent - *First*
Curzon UK (1947); Five Star US (1945)
The Rum And Coca-Cola Murders - *Last*
In 'Saint Mystery Library' US (1960)

The ASYLUM DETECTIVE
American Male Detective in Pulp Magazines operating in USA

Tom FOX (American)
Invented 4 detectives - see OLD DUDE
Citation Record: 1 Book
The Asylum Detective; Or, The Secret Of The Chest - *Only*
New York Detective Library US (1882-8)

Det Const ATHANA
British Policeman operating in England

Jeffrey ASHFORD 1926- (British)
Invented 9 detectives - see Det Insp Don KERRY
Citation Record: 1 Book
The Anger Of Fear - *Single*
Long UK (1979); Walker US (1979)

Brother ATHELSTAN
is a Dominican friar in London in 1378. A lowly figure, he is called on by his superiors to investigate mystery and murder.
English Male Amateur operating in London

Paul HARDING (British)
Citation Record: 5 Books
The Nightingale Gallery - *First*
Headline UK
By Murder's Bright Light - *Latest*
Headline UK (1994)

Maj Jack ATHERLEY
British Male Amateur operating in England

Charles ASHTON 1884- (British)
Other Detectives:
Insp MERTON   Richard SANGSTER
Citation Record: 2 Books
Murder In Make-Up - *First*
Nicholson & Watson UK (1934)
Death Greets A Guest - *Last*
Nicholson & Watson UK (1936)

The Earl of ATHERTON
leaves his house in Eaton Square every morning and drives his Bentley to Scotland Yard, where he has the rank of Detective Inspector.
British Policeman operating in England

Elizabeth GEORGE 1949- (American)
See main detective Insp Thomas LYNLEY
Citation Record: 1 Book
Missing Joseph - *Single*
Bantam UK (1993)

Nick ATWELL
British Male Amateur operating in England

Michael UNDERWOOD 1916-1992 (British)
Invented 6 detectives - see Rosa EPTON
Citation Record: 4 Books
The Juror - *First*
Macmillan UK (1975); St Martin's US (1975)
Crooked Wood - *Last*
Macmillan UK (1978); St Martin's US (1978)

Sharon ATWOOD
Second detective of Aileen DOUGLASS

Kenneth AUBREY
uncovers a conspiracy by Soviet Politburo members to undermine Russian bureaucracy.
British Male Secret Agent operating in Europe

Craig THOMAS 1942- (British)
Citation Record: 1 Book
Snow Falcon - *Single*
Joseph UK (1979); Holt US (1980)

Mme AUBRY
is an attractive widow who, being a lawyer and a handwriting expert, can solve mysteries that find the police out of their depth.
French Female Amateur operating in Paris

Hugh TRAVERS (British)
Writer: Hugh Travers MILLS
Citation Record: 2 Books
Madame Aubry And The Police - *First*
Elek UK (1966); Harper & Row US (1967)
Madame Aubry Dines With Death - *Last*
Elek UK (1967); Harper & Row US (1967)

Dr David AUDLEY
is a specialist in medieval history. A university don with the face of a prize-fighter, he is also an agent for British Intelligence.
British Male Secret Agent operating in several locations

Anthony PRICE 1928- (British)
was born in Hertfordshire. He was educated at King's School, Canterbury, and took a BA in History at Merton College, Oxford, 1952. Since then he has worked in publishing and on his series of genre novels, many of which have fascinating historical backgrounds and modern espionage plots. He received the Crime Writers Association Silver Dagger award, 1971, and their Gold Dagger award, 1975.
Writer: Alan Anthony PRICE
Other Detectives:
Frances FITZGIBBON   Dorothy Mayotte RIGBY
Citation Record: 19 Books
The Labyrinth Makers - *First*
Gollancz UK (1970); Doubleday US (1971)
The Memory Trap - *Latest*
Gollancz UK (1989); In 'Armchair Detective' US (1991)

Robert AUDLEY

A

is a young barrister who acts as the amateur sleuth – indeed, one of the earliest in the literature – in this classic Victorian novel.
British Male Amateur operating in England

M E BRADDON 1835-1915 (British)
was a former actress who, it is said, began to write fiction, which she could do at great speed, in order to save her lover, John Maxwell, from financial disaster. Her output of novels, historical romances and other types of fiction was large, but she is mainly remembered today for this one book.
Writer: Mary Elizabeth MAXWELL
Other Detectives:
Mr Henry CARTER
Lucius DAVOREN
Mr FAUNCE
George GERRARD
Valentine HAWKEHURST
Edward HEATHCOTE
Gilbert MONKTON
Coralie URQUHART
Citation Record: 1 Book
Lady Audley's Secret - *Only*
was said to have been inspired by those of *Wilkie COLLINS.* It was published first in the pages of *The Sixpenny Magazine* and it made the author's reputation for all time.
Tinsley UK (1862); Dick US (1863)

Marid AUDRAN
sleuths at some time in the future.
Sleuth

George Alec EFFINGER 1947- (American)
Adopter of one other detective Sherlock HOLMES
Citation Record: 3 Books
When Gravity Fails - *First*
Arbor US (1987); Bantam UK (1991)
The Exile Kiss - *Latest*
Doubleday US (1991)

Bill AUGUST
American Male Sleuth operating in USA

Joe BARRY 1909- (American)
Writer: Joe Barry LAKE
See main detective Rush HENRY
Citation Record: 1 Book
Three For The Money - *Only*
Handi-Books US (1950)

Maj Roderick AUSTEN
is an investigator for the Kentucky State Racing Commission, whose job it is to solve crimes on the course.
American Male Professional Investigator operating in Kentucky

Charles PARMER (American)
Writer: Charles B PARMER
Citation Record: 1 Book
Murder At The Kentucky Derby - *Only*
Doubleday US (1942)

Insp/Supt William AUSTEN
was a classic English cop in a period when the police were beginning to lose their earlier roughness and sense of social inferiority and could almost vie with the classic amateur sleuth. *William AUSTEN* was in the vanguard of the movements for change that were taking place. Oxford-educated, well-dressed, charming, he could be taken almost anywhere; and, indeed, as a Scotland Yard man, his cases took him all over England and abroad.
British Policeman operating in Europe/Africa
Sidekick: Insp CURTIS
British Male - Assistant
Sidekick: Sgt FLYTE
is one of the detective's two assistants.
British Male - Subordinate

Anne HOCKING 189?- (British)
Writer: Mona Naomi Anne Messel HOCKING
Citation Record: 28 Books
Old Mrs Fitzgerald - *First*
Bles UK (1939)
Deadly Is The Evil Tongue - *First**
Doubleday US (1940)
Murder Cries Out - *Last*
was the last of the author's books and was completed by Evelyn Healey.
Long UK (1968)

Bradley AUSTIN
American Male Sleuth operating in USA

Will MCMORROW (American)
Citation Record: 1 Selected Short Story
The House With The Red Door
appeared in the July number.
In 'Dime Detective' US (1938)

Steve AUSTIN
American Male Sleuth operating in USA

Martin CAIDIN (American)
Citation Record: 5 Books
The Mendelov Conspiracy - *First*
Meredith US (1969); Allen UK (1971)
Encounter Three - *First**
Pinnacle US (1978)
Cyborg IV - *Latest*
Arbor US (1975); Allen UK (1977)

Insp AUTUMN
is a stolid, working-class chap from Scotland Yard. He is, of course, a little out of his depth when it comes to investigating highly academic murder at the fictional, but delightfully typical, Warlock College at Oxford, not being armed with the numerous literary quotations often deemed necessary in such situations.
British Policeman operating in England

Robert ROBINSON 1929- (British)
was born in Liverpool and is known as an erudite newspaper columnist and broadcaster.
Writer: Robert Henry ROBINSON
Citation Record: 1 Book
Landscape With Dead Dons - *Only*
Gollancz UK (1956); Rinehart US (1956)

The AVENGERS
were dauntless righters of wrongs. They were headed by two rather strange characters, John Steed and Emma Peel, who appeared in a long-running British TV series.
British Male Sleuth and Female Sleuth operating in several locations

John GARFORTH (British)
Adopter of one other detective Sexton BLAKE
Citation Record: 4 Books
The Floating Game - *First*
Panther UK (1967); Berkley US (1967)
The Passing Of Gloria Munday - *Last*
Panther UK (1967); Berkley US (1967)

Insp/Supt Bill AVEYARD
has usually to investigate cases of rather nasty murder in normally tranquil English villages. The cases often have a strong background of horticultural activity and deal with aspects of rural or religious lore, which give them a special appeal.
British Policeman operating in England

James FRASER 1924- (British)
was born in Yorkshire. He is the author of many non-genre novels under his own name and the pseudonym.

Writer: Alan WHITE

Citation Record: 9 Books

The Evergreen Death - *First*
Jenkins UK (1968); Harcourt Brace US (1969)

Hearts Ease In Death - *Latest*
Barrie & Jenkins UK (1977); Doubleday US (1977)

Mick 'Brew' AXBREWDER

Second detective of Ginny FISTOULARI

Dave AXELROD

American Male Amateur operating in New York

E M BREZ (American)

Citation Record: 1 Book

Those Dark Eyes - *Single*
St Martin's US (1984)

Det AYLIFFE

British Policeman operating in London

Charles BENNETT 1899- (British)

Citation Record: 1 Book

Five Thousand Pounds Reward - *Only*
Warne UK (1899)

Jerome AYLWIN

British Male Amateur operating in England

Avon CURRY 1925- (British)

Writer: Jean BOWDEN

Citation Record: 2 Books

Derry Down Death - *First*
Allen UK (1960)

Dying High - *Last*
Allen UK (1961)

— B —

Offr Barbara BABALINO

Appears with at least two other detectives - see Det Joe LAWLESS.

Jyotish BABU

investigates an 'impossible' murder by poisoning in a locked room.

Bengali Male Amateur operating in India

Kennedy BRUCE (British)

Citation Record: 1 Book

The Poisoned Fang - *Only*
Jenkins UK (1930)

Ned BACHMAN

American Male Professional Investigator operating in New Orleans

Alan DALE 1861-1928 (American)

Writer: Alfred J COHEN

Citation Record: 1 Book

Ned Bachman, The New Orleans Detective - *Only*
Ogilvie US (1887)

Bud BACOLA

American Male Amateur operating in USA

Pamela CHAIS 1930- (American)

Writer: Pamela Herbert CHAIS

Citation Record: 1 Book

Final Cut - *Single*
Simon & Schuster US (1981)

Rex BADER

sleuths at some time in the future.

American Male Sleuth

Mack REYNOLDS 1917-1983 (American)

Writer: Dallas McCord REYNOLDS

Adopted one other detective Sherlock HOLMES

Citation Record: 4 Books

Satellite City - *First*
Ace US (1975)

Chaos In Lagrangia - *Latest*
Tor US (1984)

Insp BADGER

solves an extraordinary case of murder in which the victim is killed by being made to drink molten gold.

British Policeman operating in England

John REMENHAM 1877-1958 (British)

Writer: John Alexander VLASTO

Inventor of one other detective Insp BLISS

Citation Record: 1 Book

Sea Gold - *Only*
Skeffington UK (1930)

Insp BADGERY

is called in to investigate the murder of the wife of the guide of an educational tour in Yorkshire.

British Policeman operating in Yorkshire

R J WHITE 1905-1971 (British)

was born in Norwich, Norfolk. He was a Professor of History at Cambridge and an expert on eighteenth-century English history.

Writer: Reginald James WHITE

Inventor of one other detective Insp David BROCK

Citation Record: 1 Book

A Second-Hand Tomb - *Only*
Macmillan UK (1971); Harper & Row US (1971)

Ed BAER

is a partner in a venture capital business. He solves murders with a commercial background.

American Male Amateur operating in USA

Sidekick: Warren BAER
American Male

Herbert RESNICOW 1921- (American)

was born in New York City. He graduated with a BA in Engineering at the Polytechnic Institute of Brooklyn, New York, 1947, and later served as an engineer and architect with the US Army Corps at various locales in Asia. He has written several genre books, including some in collaboration with other, specialist co-authors.

Other Detectives:
Alexander Magnus GOLD   Giles SULLIVAN

Citation Record: 2 Books

The Dead Room - *First*
Dodd, Mead US (1987)

The Hot Place - *Latest*
St Martin's US (1990)

Frodo BAGGINS

is the hero of the great modern epic, *THE LORD OF THE RINGS.* In his quest for the Ring he must surely be accounted as one of the great 'questing' detectives, for he has clues to follow, puzzles to solve, and certainly he has to deal with many crimes. He has several main sidekicks, who accompany him at various stages.

Male Amateur operating in Middle Earth

Sidekick: Meriadoc BRANDYBUCK
Male - Companion

Sidekick: Sam GAMGEE
Male - Companion

Sidekick: Peregrine TOOK
Male - Guide

B

Sidekick: Wizard GANDALF
must be the most powerful sidekick in the business.
Male - Companion

J R TOLKIEN 1892-1973 (British)
was born at Blomfontein, South Africa. He was educated at King Edward VI School, Birmingham, Warwickshire, and graduated at Oxford University, where he became Professor of Anglo-Saxon, 1925-1945, and of English Language and Literature, 1945-1959.
Writer: John Ronald Reuel TOLKIEN
Citation Record: 1 Book
The Lord Of The Rings - *Only*
Allen & Unwin UK (1954)

Henry Napoleon BAGGS
British Male Amateur

Cecil H BULLIVANT 1882- (British)
Invented 5 detectives - see Garnett BELL
Citation Record: 2 Books
The Desert Lovers - *First*
Companion UK (1920)
The Enchanted Desert - *First**
was published under the byline of Mrs Frances Everhard and, rather remarkably, with the character of *Henry Napoleon BAGGS* omitted.
Wright UK (1930)
Whoso Diggeth A Pit - *Last*
Companion UK (1920)
The Fringe Of The Law - *Last**
Wright UK (1931)

Kate BAIER
is thirty-something and unmarried but with a live-in male lover. She progresses from being a freelance investigative journalist to setting up as a real private detective, although she behaves similarly in all her books. Ms *BAIER* is concerned with many social issues, such as feminism, anti-racism and socialism, which do not impede but rather enhance the books' qualities.
American Female Private Detective operating in London
Sidekick: CARMEN
is West Indian, beautiful and streetwise. She was taken on and, in a way, rescued by *Kate BAIER* during her third case. Although nominally her secretary, she proves a most useful assistant.
British Female - Secretary

Gillian SLOVO 1952- (South African)
was born in Johannesburg, the daughter of a famous couple, Joe Slovo and Ruth First. She attended Manchester University, England, where she took a degree in History. She now lives in London and writes detective novels of pace and ingenuity, in which the social issues of gender and race feature strongly.
Citation Record: 4 Books
Morbid Symptoms - *First*
Pluto UK (1984); Dembner US (1985)
Close Call - *Latest*
Joseph UK (1995)

Det Supt Geoffrey BAILEY
appears also in books with the author's other detective, *Helen WEST.*
British Policeman operating in England

Frances FYFIELD 1948- (British)
is a criminal lawyer.
Writer: Frances HEGARTY
Inventor of one other detective pair Helen WEST and Det Supt Geoffrey BAILEY
Citation Record: 1 Book
Shadows On The Mirror - *Single*
Heinemann UK (1989); Pocket Books US (1991)

Det Supt Geoffrey BAILEY
Second detective of Helen WEST

Hilary Dunsany BAILEY III and Hilea BAILEY
American Male Amateur and American Female Amateur operating in USA

Hilea BAILEY 1907- (American)
Writer: Ruth Lenore MARTING
Citation Record: 4 Books
What Night Will Bring - *First*
Doubleday US (1939)
Breathe No More, My Lady - *Last*
Doubleday US (1946)

Hilea BAILEY
Second detective of Hilary Dunsany BAILEY III

Jane BAILEY
is a bookstore owner. She sleuths, in a part-time capacity, for her private-eye boyfriend.
American Female Amateur operating in USA/West Indies

Margaret DOBSON (American)
Citation Record: 4 Books
Soothsayer - *First*
Dell US (1987)
Touchstone - *Latest*
Dell US (1987)

Red BAILEY
comes to a bad end.
American Male Private Detective operating in New York

Geoffrey HOMES 1902-1978 (American)
Invented 5 detectives - see Robin BISHOP
Citation Record: 1 Book
Build My Gallows High - *Only*
Morrow US (1946); Simon & Schuster UK (1988)

Stuart BAILEY
was formerly a government secret agent. Well-bred and intelligent as such men go, he now has to operate from a shabby little downtown office.
American Male Private Detective operating in Los Angeles

Roy HUGGINS 1914- (American)
Inventor of one other detective Danny FULLER
Citation Record: 1 Book 3 Short Stories in 1 Collection
The Double Take - *Only*
Morrow US (1946); Cassell UK (1947)
77 Sunset Strip - *Collection 1*
Three untitled novelettes.
Dell US (1959)

Insp BAILHACHE
appears in stories that form part of a book of puzzles and poems.
Policeman

Hubert PHILLIPS 1891- (British)
Citation Record: 5 Short Stories in 1 Collection
Heptameron - *Collection 1*
This collection of seven of the author's stories contains five with *Insp BAILHACHE.*
Eyre & Spottiswoode UK (1945)

Sheriff Joe BAIN
American Policeman operating in California

John Holbrook VANCE 1917- (American)
was born in San Francisco, California, and took a BA at the University of California, Berkeley, 1942. He is a distinguished writer of science fiction under the byline of *Jack VANCE,* being the author of at least thirty novels in that field. Using his real name and the same pseudonym, he is the author of

B

at least twenty genre novels, including three that he wrote under the *Ellery QUEEN (HOUSE NAME)* byline. He received the Mystery Writers of America Edgar Allen Poe award, 1960, and is the recipient of the highest honours for his science fiction.

Other Byline: Ellery QUEEN

Citation Record: 2 Books

The Fox Valley Murders - *First*
Bobbs US (1966); Hale UK (1967)

The Pleasant Grove Murders - *Last*
Bobbs US (1967); Hale UK (1968)

Joshua BAIN

American Male Sleuth operating in California

J Alexander MACKENZIE (American)

Citation Record: 3 Books

The Omega Document - *First*
Bethany UK (1979)

The Jordan Intercept - *Latest*
Bethany UK (1980)

Scattergood BAINES

American Male Amateur operating in USA

Clarence Budington KELLAND 1881-1964 (American)

Citation Record: 1 Book 32 Short Stories in 2 Collections

Scattergood Baines - *Single*
Harper & Row US (1921); Hodder & Stoughton UK (1942)

Scattergood Returns - *Collection 1*
Short stories - 16
Harper & Row US (1940)

Scattergood Baines Pulls The Strings - *Collection 2*
Short stories - 16
Harper & Row US (1941)

Frances BAIRD

is one of the genre's earliest female private detectives. Twenty-five years old, she is employed by the Watkins Private Detective Agency. She apprehends a man, falls in love with him, and then proves his innocence. In one other book by this author she renders assistance to *Sam BURTON*.

American Female Private Detective operating in New York

Reginald Wright KAUFFMAN 1877-1959 (American)

Writer: Reginald Wright KAUFFMAN

Inventor of one other detective pair Sam BURTON and Frances BAIRD

Citation Record: 1 Book

Miss Francis Baird, Detective: A Passage From Her Memoirs - *Only*
Page US (1906)

Frances BAIRD

Second detective of Sam BURTON

Insp/Supt BAKER

British Policeman operating in England

Osmington MILLS 1922- (British)

Writer: Vivian Collin BROOKS

Inventor of one other detective pair Patrick C SHIRLEY and Insp Rip IRVING

Citation Record: 8 Books

Unlucky Break - *First*
Bles UK (1955); Roy US (1957)

Traitor Betrayed - *Last*
Bles UK (1964); Roy US (1966)

Ch Charles BAKER

American Policeman operating in Washington DC

H C HUSTON (American)

Writer: Howard Chauncey HUSTON

Citation Record: 2 Books

With Murder For Some - *First*
Macmillan US (1953); Hodder & Stoughton US (1954)

The Blind Saw Murder - *Last*
Macmillan US (1954); Hodder & Stoughton US (1955)

Larry BAKER

is a Hollywood scriptwriter who is implicated in bizarre cases involving Hollywood cults.

American Male Amateur operating in Hollywood/New York

Sidekick: Boris SLIVKA
is nominally the detective's partner but is often too drunk to do much about it.
American Male - Partner

Carter BROWN 1923-1985 (Australian)

Invented 10 detectives - see Rick HOLMAN

Citation Record: 6 Books

Charlie Sent Me! - *First*
Horwitz AU (1963); Signet US (1963); Four Square UK (1965)

The Iron Maiden - *Last*
Horwitz AU (1975); Signet US (1975)

Paul BAKER

British Male Amateur operating in Spain

Barry NORMAN (British)

Citation Record: 2 Books

The Matter Of Mandrake - *First*
Allen UK (1967); Walker US (1968)

The Hounds Of Sparta - *Last*
Allen UK (1968)

Luis BALAM

is an ex-traffic cop from Mexico City who turns detective.

Mexican Male Sleuth operating in Yucatan

Gary ALEXANDER 1941- (American)

See main detective Supt Bamsan KIET

Citation Record: 2 Books

Blood Sacrifice - *First*
Doubleday US (1994)

Dead Dinosaurs - *Latest*
Doubleday US (1994)

T T BALDWIN

American Male Amateur operating in New York

Shannon OCORK (American)

!See Appendix 2.

Citation Record: 3 Books

Sports Freak - *First*
St Martin's US (1980)

Hell Bent For Heaven - *Latest*
St Martin's US (1983)

Elijah BALEY

was the most frequently used of this prolific author's detectives and he forms part of the author's scientific fantasy world. An Earth policeman of some future age, he solves crimes, which still seem to take place in classical fashion. However, he is unusually fortunate in being assisted by an extraordinary sidekick.

Policeman operating on Earth

Sidekick: R Danoel OLIVAW
is a robot from somewhere in outer space. Well, why not, considering who the detective is?
Unknown sex - Assistant

Isaac ASIMOV 1920-1992 (American)

was born in Petrovichi, Russia, and taken to the USA in 1923, becoming naturalised in 1928. He took a doctorate in chemistry at Columbia University, New York, and then held a number of teaching posts, which included a professorship. A true polymath, he was one of the most prolific of modern authors, his output ranging from some of the best science fiction and detective stories to straight scientific texts on a host of subjects.

B

Other Detectives:
The BLACK WIDOWERS
Darius JUST
The UNION CLUB
Lt Jack DOHERY and Lou BRADE
Wendell ORTH

Citation Record: 4 Books

The Caves Of Steel - *First*
Doubleday US (1954); Boardman UK (1954)

Robots And Empire - *Last*
Doubleday US (1965); Granada UK (1985)

Clinton BALL

American Male Amateur operating in USA

Albert ASHFORTH (American)

Citation Record: 1 Book

Murder After The Fact - *Single*
In 'The Gift' US (1984)

David BALLARD and Michelle Merrill BALLARD

American Male Amateur and American Female Amateur operating in California/Alaska

Carole Gift PAGE 1942- and Doris Elaine FELL (American)

Citation Record: 4 Books

Mist Over Morro Bay - *First*
Harvest House US (1985)

Beyond The Windswept Sea - *Latest*
Harvest House US (1987)

Michelle Merrill BALLARD

Second detective of David BALLARD

Gilead BALM

British Male Amateur operating in England

Bernard CAPES 1850?-1918 (British)

Writer: Bernard Edward Joseph CAPES

Citation Record: 11 Short Stories in 1 Collection

Gilead Balm, Knight Errant - *Collection 1*
Unwin UK (1911); Baker US (1911)

Gillian BALTIC

is a First World War veteran who returns to his home town to find corruption rife. He sets up as a PI and copes, mainly by behaving violently.

American Male Private Detective operating in USA

Dale CLARK (American)

Invented 4 detectives - see Mike O'HANNA

Citation Record: 1 Book

The Red Rods - *Only*
Messner US (1946)

The Blonde, The Gangster And The Private Eye - *Only**
Avon US (1959)

Ch of Plce Mario BALZIC

is the Chief of Police in the fictional small town of Rocksburg, Pennsylvania. He is overweight, drinks too much, is bad-tempered and beset with a host of personal problems. Yet, because of his sensitivity to the lives, problems and behaviour of his fellow-citizens, he is more than a match for the state cops who come into his territory to solve crimes.

American Policeman operating in Rocksburg

K C CONSTANTINE 1935- (American)

Writer: Karl KOSAK

Citation Record: 9 Books

The Rocksburg Railroad Murders - *First*
Saturday Review Press US (1972); Coronet UK (1989)

Sunshine Enemies - *Latest*
Hodder & Stoughton UK (1990)

Lisa BANCROFT

American Female Amateur operating in USA

Helen NIELSEN 1918- (American)

Invented 3 detectives - see Simon DRAKE

Citation Record: 1 Book

The Crime Is Murder - *Only*
Morrow US (1956); Gollancz UK (1957)

BANDBOX BOB

American Male Detective in Pulp Magazines operating in USA

S A D COX (American)

Citation Record: 1 Selected Short Story

Bandbox Bob, The Dandy Detective; Or, The Flying Dragon Of Devil's Gulch
Old Cap Collier Library US (18??)

Dan BANION

is an ex-journalist who, while drifting around California after the Second World War, solves cases of murder
!See Appendix 2.

American Male Amateur operating in San Francisco

Robert FINNEGAN 1906-1947 (American)

was born in San Francisco. He had little higher education and worked at many jobs, being active also in several social causes and a worker for movements on the political Left. He wrote only three detective novels, which have been highly regarded.

Writer: Paul William RYAN

Citation Record: 3 Books

The Bandaged Nude - *First*
Simon & Schuster US (1946); Boardman UK (1949)

Many A Monster - *Last*
Simon & Schuster US (1948); Boardman UK (1950)

Ch Insp Alan BANKS

British Policeman operating in England

Peter ROBINSON 1950- (British)

Citation Record: 6 Books

Gallows View - *First*
Penguin CA (1987); Viking UK (1987); Scribner's US (1990)

Past Reason Hated - *Latest*
Viking UK (1991)

Senator Brooks Urban BANNER

appeared in stories in several pulp magazines for over two decades. Tall, with white hair and a great red nose, he dresses like a tramp and speaks in gutter argot. In his time, it seems, he has been a soldier, hobo, salesman, circus barker, and even a county sheriff. Furthermore, he was once a graduate of Cornell University and Albany law-school. He solves many cases, including several ingenious and even seemingly 'impossible' murders.

American Male Professional Investigator operating in NYC

Joseph COMMINGS (American)

Invented 3 detectives - see Matt TUDOR

Citation Record: 2 Selected Short Stories

Murder Under Glass
In '10-Story Detective' US (1947)

The Grand Guignol Caper
In 'Mike Shayne Mystery Magazine' US (1984)

Rex BANNER

British Male Amateur operating in England

Robert CHAPMAN 1916- (British)

Writer: Robert Alec Mark CHAPMAN

Citation Record: 7 Books

One Jump Ahead - *First*
Laurie UK (1951)

The Downward Path - *Last*
Hale UK (1959)

Paul BANNERMAN

American Male Sleuth operating in Connecticut

John MAXIM 1937- (American)

Writer: John R MAXIM

B

Citation Record: 2 Books

The Bannerman Solution - *First*
Bantam US (1989)

The Bannerman Effect - *Latest*
Bantam US (1990)

Slim Jim BANNERMAN

is, in 1916, an operative for the Rocky Mountains office of the Gallows Detective Agency, San Francisco. He is certain death to wrongdoers, of whom he meets many.

American Male Private Detective operating in Denver

Jay FLYNN 1927-1985 (American)

For writer details see Burl STANNARD

Inventor of one other detective MCHUGH

Citation Record: 2 Books

Bannerman - *First*
Leisure Books US (1976)

Border Incident - *Last*
Leisure Books US (1976)

Bill BANNING

runs a detective agency when he is not writing crime stories; or vice versa, depending on the case situation.

British Male Private Detective operating in London

Nat EASTON (British)

Citation Record: 8 Books

Always The Wolf - *First*
Boardman UK (1957)

Forgive Me, Lively Lady - *Last*
Boardman UK (1961)

Burns BANNION

is an American ex-soldier now living in Japan. A karate expert, he becomes a PI by being mistaken for a well-known one. His cases are filled with quaint Japanese men and easy Japanese girls.

American Male Private Detective operating in Japan

Earl NORMAN (American)

Citation Record: 8 Books

Kill Me In Tokyo - *First*
Berkley US (1958)

Kill Me In Roppongi - *Last*
Berkley US (1967)

Dave BANNION

is up against the corruption of a big city when he tries to investigate the suicide of a colleague and the death of his own wife.

American Male Amateur operating in Philadelphia

William P MCGIVERN 1927-1982 (American)

was born in Chicago, Illinois. He was educated at the University of Birmingham and served with distinction in the US Army, 1943-1946. The author of at least twenty-five finely plotted genre novels, several of which have been used for films, he received the Mystery Writers of America Edgar Allan Poe award, 1952.

Writer: William Peter MCGIVERN

Other Byline: Bill PETERS

Other Detectives:
Insp HARRIGAN — Adam JAMES
Det Max PRIMA and Det Gypsy TONNELLI
Sam TERRELL

Citation Record: 1 Book

The Big Heat - *Only*
Dodd, Mead US (1952); Hamish Hamilton UK (1953)

Guy BANNISTER

British Male Amateur operating in England

Maude CROSSLEY 1879- (British)

Citation Record: 2 Books

The Forbidden Hour - *First*
Jenkins UK (1925)

Crookery Inn - *Last*
Jenkins UK (1931)

BANYON

is a TV detective, novelized in one book set in the 1930s.

American Male Private Detective operating in Los Angeles

William JOHNSTON 1924- (American)

Invented 7 detectives - see John WOODRUFF and Tony NOVELLO

Citation Record: 1 Book

Banyon - *Only*
Paperback Library US (1971)

Walter BARANOV

British Male Amateur operating on a ship.

Peter LOVESEY 1936- (British)

Invented 7 detectives - see Sgt CRIBB and Const THACKERAY

Citation Record: 1 Book

The False Inspector Dew - *Single*
Macmillan UK (1982); Pantheon US (1982)

Lt Lee BARCELLO

American Policeman operating in USA

Stephen RANSOME 1902-1977 (American)

For writer details see Luke SPEARE and Schyler COLE

Other Detectives:
Jill ARCHER — Stephen RANSOME
Luke SPEARE and Schyler COLE

Citation Record: 6 Books

The Night, The Woman - *First*
Dodd, Mead US (1963); Gollancz UK (1963)

Trap No 6 - *Last*
Doubleday US (1971); Gollancz UK (1972)

George BARCLAY

British Male Sleuth operating in England

Ernest PAUL 1896- (British)

Writer: Ernest FOCKE

Citation Record: 6 Books

Jewels In Jeopardy - *First*
Hale UK (1967)

The Reluctant Cloak And Dagger Man - *Last*
Hale UK (1971)

Kommissar Hans BARLACH

knows he is dying of stomach cancer and has only a year to live. In his two cases, he pits himself against amoral murderers, in ways that are unconventional and deserving of being described as Kafkaesque.

!See Appendix 2.

Swiss Policeman operating in Switzerland

Friedrich DUERRENMATT 1921- (Swiss)

was born in Konolfingen, Bern, Switzerland, the son of a pastor. A former painter, he became his country's most renowned playwright.

Citation Record: 2 Books

The Judge And His Hangman - *First*
is a translation from the German of *Der Richter und Sein Henker* (Einsiedeln, 1952).
Jenkins UK (1954); Harper & Row US (1955)

End Of The Game - *First**
Warner US (1976)

The Quarry - *Last*
is a translation from the German of *Der Verdacht* (Einsiedeln, 1959).
Cape UK (1962)

Supt Charles BARLOW

British Policeman operating in England

B

Elwyn JONES 1923- (British)

Inventor of one other detective Dick BARTON

Citation Record: 5 Books 6 Short Stories in 1 Collection

Barlow In Charge - *First*
Barker UK (1973)

Barlow Down Under - *Latest*
Weidenfeld & Nicolson UK (1977)

The Barlow Casebook - *Collection 1*
Barker UK (1973)

Margaret BARLOW

American Female Amateur operating in USA

David OSBORN (American)

Writer: David D OSBORN

Citation Record: 1 Book

Murder On The Chesapeake - *Single*
Zelnar UK (1993)

Nicholas BARLOW

is the president of an old family publishing house who meets murder, usually and irritatingly on the premises. Shuddering at the publicity that might ensue, he does the sleuthing himself.

American Male Amateur operating in USA

Robert A CARTER (American)

Citation Record: 2 Books

Casual Slaughter - *First*
Mysterious Press US (1992)

Final Edit - *Latest*
Mysterious Press US (1994)

Insp BARLOWE

British Policeman operating in England

C I D SMITH 1894- (British)

Citation Record: 2 Books

Thy Guilt Is Great - *First*
Jenkins UK (1939)

No Epitaph For Mr Zarke - *Last*
Jenkins UK (1941)

John BARMAN

British Male Private Detective operating in London

Arthur A BECKETT 1844-1909 (British)

Writer: Arthur William A BECKETT

Citation Record: 1 Book

Fallen Among Thieves: A Novel Of Interest - *Only*
Chapman & Hall UK (1870)

Brother BARNABAS

is a monk who does nice medieval sleuthing in England in 1379.

English Male Amateur operating in England

E M A ALLISON (American)

Writers: Eric W ALLISON 1947- and Mary Ann ALLISON 1949-

Citation Record: 1 Book

Through The Valley Of Death - *Single*
Doubleday US (1983); Hale UK (1985)

Dr George BARNABAS

is, in spite of her name, female. Which, of course, makes for endless surprise and talking points among the uninitiated. An American pathologist, she is now working at a hospital in East London, where the murders that occur seem every bit as ingenious as they are back home and the police are just as baffled.

American Female Amateur operating in London

Claire RAYNOR 1931-

is a popular novelist and newspaper columnist. She was once a nurse and knows a good deal about the medical matters she puts into her books.

Writer: Claire Berenice RAYNER

Citation Record: 2 Books

First Blood - *First*
Joseph UK (1993); Signet US (1994)

Second Opinion - *Latest*
Joseph UK (1994)

Capt BARNABY

American Policeman operating in USA

Leslie T WHITE 1903- (American)

Writer: Leslie Turner WHITE

Citation Record: 2 Books

Harness Bull - *First*
Harcourt Brace US (1937); Hamilton UK (1938)

Vice Squad - *First**
Bestseller US (1954)

Homicide - *Last*
Harcourt Brace US (1937); Hamilton UK (1938)

Insp BARNABY

is a tall, thin man. He investigates nice, old-fashioned cases of murder, usually at nice, old-fashioned British universities.

British Policeman operating in England

Howard SHAW 1934- (British)

Writer: Colin Howard SHAW

Citation Record: 2 Books

Killing No Murder - *First*
Hale UK (1972); Scribner's US (1981)

Death Of A Don - *Latest*
Scribner's US (1981)

Det Ch Insp Tom BARNABY

heads a detective squad dealing with cases of murder in English village settings, which are full of the usual crowd of irreproachable suspects.

British Policeman operating in England

Sidekick: Sgt TROY

is bumptious and irritating.

British Male - Subordinate

Caroline GRAHAM 1931- (British)

was born in Nuneaton, Warwickshire. She was educated at Nuneaton High School for Girls, Nuneaton, and received a BA from the Open University, 1982. She served in the WRNS, has run a marriage bureau and has also been a dancer, actress and stage manager. In addition to her criminous works, she has written mainstream novels and plays for radio and television.

Citation Record: 6 Books

The Killings At Badger's Drift - *First*
Century Hutchinson UK (1987); Adler & Adler US (1987)

Written In Blood - *Latest*
Headline UK (1994); Morrow US (1995)

Ch Insp BARNARD

British Policeman operating in England

T C H JACOBS 1899-1976 (British)

Writer: Jacques PENDOWER

Other Detectives:

Det Supt John BELLAMY, Temple FORTUNE
Jim MALONE, Dr Ian MCANDREW
Capt Jacques RADFORD and Tony ANDERSON
Reggie RUGGLES and Sgt TROTTER
Mike SETON

Citation Record: 13 Books

The Kestrel House Mystery - *First*
Paul UK (1932); Macaulay US (1933)

The Red Eyes Of Kali - *Last*
Paul UK (1950)

Col Richard BARNE

British Male Professional Investigator operating in England

B

E G COUSINS (British)

Writer: Edmund George COUSINS

Citation Record: 6 Books

Death By Marriage - *First*
Gifford UK (1959)

Death In A Quiet Place - *Last*
Gifford UK (1967)

Insp BARNES

is a member of the New York Police Department who sleuths during the closing years of the nineteenth century.

American Policeman operating in New York

James MATTHEWS 1852-1929 (American)

Writer: James Brander MATTHEWS

Citation Record: 1 Book

The Last Meeting - *Single*
Scribner's US (1885); Unwin UK (1885)

Al BARNES

was a cop with the Seattle police before he retired to become a PI. He now has to solve one last case.

American Male Amateur operating in Montana

Richard HUGO 1923-1982 (American)

Citation Record: 1 Book

Death And The Good Life - *Single*
St Martin's US (1981); Hale UK (1982)

Berkeley Hoy BARNES

was formerly a corporation lawyer and now works in the private sector. His activities are somewhat affected by the fact that he is a chronic hypochondriac. Meeting people, which the nature of his work renders rather essential, unfortunately does weird things to his insides.

American Male Private Detective operating in New York

Sidekick: Larry HOWE

was once a hippie but is now proving to be a valuable assistant – that is, when he is not chasing the fair sex. One of his jobs is to maintain a private pharmacopoeia on hand so as to deal with the everyday needs of his boss.

American Male - Assistant

Eugene FRANKLIN 1914-1987 (American)

Writer: Eugene Franklin BANDY Jr

Other Byline: Franklin BANDY

Citation Record: 3 Books

Murder Trapp - *First*
Stein US (1971)

The Bold House Murders - *Last*
Stein US (1973); Hale UK (1975)

Bromley BARNES

American Male Amateur operating in Washington DC

George BARTON 1866-1940 (American)

Citation Record: 2 Books 12 Short Stories in 1 Collection

The Mystery Of The Red Flame - *First*
Page US (1918)

The Pembroke Mason Affair - *Last*
Page US (1920)

The Strange Adventures Of Bromley Barnes - *Collection 1*
Page US (1918)

Ezell BARNES

is black, an ex-prizefighter and an ex-cop. He now operates in Newark, where he has a reputation for being tough, rough, honest and gallant.

American Male Private Detective operating in New Jersey

Richard HILARY (American)

Writers: Richard BODINO and Hilary CONNORS

Citation Record: 4 Books

Snake In The Grasses - *First*
Bantam US (1987)

Behind The Fact - *Latest*
Bantam US (1989)

Gerry BARNES

was in the government Secret Service

American Male Private Detective operating in New York

Robert Sidney BOWEN 1900-1977 (American)

Citation Record: 2 Books

Make Mine Murder - *First*
Crown US (1946)

Murder Gets Around - *Last*
Crown US (1947)

Humphrey BARNES

Second detective of Det Ch Supt Maurice KENDRICK

John BARNES

appears also in books with the author's other detective, *Robert Leroy MITCHELL.*

American Male Amateur operating in New York

Rodrigues OTTOLENGUI 1861-1937 (American)

See main detective pair Robert Leroy MITCHELL and John BARNES

Citation Record: 1 Book

A Modern Wizard - *Only*
Putnam US (1894)

John BARNES

Second detective of Robert Leroy MITCHELL

Michael BARNES

is an orange grower from Florida who, with just a few hours to while away in Manhattan, finds himself at the receiving end of practically everything in the way of skulduggery and mayhem that the city has to throw at innocent strangers. Stripped of his possessions, accused of robbery and murder, hunted by the police, he has just Christmas day to find out why it's all happening.

American Male Amateur operating in New York

Ed MCBAIN 1926- (American)

Invented 4 detectives - see The 87th PRECINCT

Citation Record: 1 Book

Downtown - *Single*
Morrow US (1989); Heinemann UK (1989)

Cory BARNETT

American Male Amateur operating in New York

Ben E MILLER (American)

Citation Record: 2 Books

Death Deal - *First*
Powell UK (1969)

The Set-Up - *Last*
Powell UK (1969)

Al BARNEY

American Male Private Detective operating in Florida

James Hadley CHASE 1906-1985 (British)

Invented 14 detectives - see Dave FENNER

Citation Record: 1 Book

An Ear To The Ground - *Only*
Hale UK (1968)

Al BARNEY

Second detective of Herman RADNITZ

Al BARNEY

Appears with at least two other detectives - see Steve HARMAS.

Dave BARNUM and Capt VAUGHN

Dave BARNUM is a lawyer who is supposed to watch over a millionaire in danger. When, in spite of his efforts, the latter is murdered, he naturally feels rather guilty and, aided by a local cop, decides to find out whodunnit.

American Male Amateur and American Policeman operating in Florida

B

George Harmon COXE 1901-1984 (American)

Invented 20 detectives - see Kent MURDOCK

Citation Record: 1 Book

Never Bet Your Life - *Only*
Knopf US (1952); Hammond UK (1955)

Bruce BARON

is a spy, also known as The Baron.

American Male Secret Agent operating in China

Norman DANIELS (American)

Invented 6 detectives - see Richard Curtis (Phantom) VAN LOAN

Citation Record: 2 Books

The Baron Of Hong Kong - *First*
Lancer US (1967)

Baron's Mission To Peking - *Last*
Lancer US (1968)

Hugo BARON

British Male Sleuth operating in England/Africa

John Michael BRETT 1923- (British)

For writer details see John SAMSON

Citation Record: 3 Books

A Plague Of Dragons - *First*
Barker UK (1965)

A Cargo Of Spent Evil - *Last*
Barker UK (1966)

Michael BRETT 1923- (British)

For writer details see John SAMSON

Citation Record: 1 Book

Diecast - *Only*
Barker UK (1964)

Lee BARON

American Male Private Detective operating in Florida

Gil BREWER 1922-1983 (American)

Invented 3 detectives - see Bill MADDERN

Citation Record: 1 Book

Wild - *Only*
Crest US (1958); Fawcett UK (1959)

Paul BARON

was a minor creation of this prolific writer for the pulps, but he was short-lived and seems only to have appeared in a few stories in *Black Mask Magazine.*

American Male Detective in Pulp Magazines operating in New York

George Harmon COXE 1901-1984 (American)

Invented 20 detectives - see Kent MURDOCK

No citations

Gideon BARR

appeared in a few stories in boys' magazines, particularly *Pluck,* during the late 1890s, when such inventions, after the emergence of *Sexton BLAKE,* were becoming popular. He was blonde, athletic and operated from his rooms in Bayard's Inn, off Holborn. This district, which is midway between the City of London and the West End, was well-known enough to mean something to a young audience and it was often used by the creators of detectives in this early era.

British Male Sleuth operating in London

UNKNOWN

No citations

Nile BARRABAS

American Male Professional Investigator operating in several locations

Jack HILD (American)

House name.

Citation Record: 1 Book

The Barrabas Blitz - *Only*
Gold Eagle US (1989)

Jack HILD (American)

Writer: William BAETZ

Citation Record: 2 Books

The Barrabas Fix - *First*
Gold Eagle US (1988)

The Barrabas Kill - *Latest*
Gold Eagle US (1989)

Jack HILD (American)

Writer: Jack GARSIDE

Other Byline: Nick CARTER

Citation Record: 2 Books

Alaska Deception - *First*
Gold Eagle US (1987)

Sakhalin Breakout - *Latest*
Gold Eagle US (1987)

Jack HILD (American)

Writer: Roland GREEN

Citation Record: 2 Books

The Barrabas Heist - *First*
Gold Eagle US (1989)

The Barrabas War - *Latest*
Gold Eagle US (1989)

Jack HILD (American)

Writer: Robin HARDY

Citation Record: 12 Books

Agile Retrieval - *First*
Gold Eagle US (1986)

No Safe Place - *Latest*
Gold Eagle US (1988)

Jack HILD (American)

Writer: Jim MADEVILLE

Citation Record: 1 Book

Tje Barrabas Fallout - *Only*
Gold Eagle US (1989)

Jack HILD (American)

Writer: Alan PHILIPSON

Citation Record: 2 Books

The Plains Of Fire - *First*
Gold Eagle US (1984)

The Barrabas Strike - *Latest*
Gold Eagle US (1988)

Jack HILD (American)

Writer: John PRESTON

Citation Record: 3 Books

The Barrabas Creed - *First*
Gold Eagle US (1988)

The Barrabas Raid- *Latest*
Gold Eagle US (1988)

Jack HILD (American)

See main detective Alex (The Protector) DARTANIAN

Citation Record: 3 Books

The Barrabas Fire - *First*
Gold Eagle US (1989)

The Barrabas Sweep - *Latest*
Gold Eagle US (1990)

Jack HILD (American)

Writer: Joe ROBERTS

Citation Record: 2 Books

The Barrabas Edge - *First*
Gold Eagle US (1988)

The Barrabas Hit - *Latest*
Gold Eagle US (1989)

Insp BARRACLOUGH

appears only in this short story, a fine example of vintage detection.

British Policeman operating in London

Frank FROEST and George DILNOT 1883-1951 (British)

Citation Record: 1 Selected Short Story

The Pink Edge
Little, Brown US (1941)

Lord BARRADINE

British Male Amateur operating in England

Edgar JEPSON 1863-1938 (British)

Writer: Edgar Alfred JEPSON

Other Detectives:
Lord Rupert GARTHOYLE TINKER

Citation Record: 10 Short Stories in 1 Collection

Barradine Detects - *Collection 1*
Jenkins UK (1937)

Dick BARRETT

was one of this author's numerous pulp detectives, his speciality being the recovery of stolen jewels. He appeared in stories in *Crime Busters Magazine.*

American Male Detective in Pulp Magazines operating in USA

Norwell PAGE (American)

Invented 3 detectives - see Ken CARTER

No citations

Prof Dennis BARRIE

American Male Amateur operating in USA

Adrian REYNOLDS 1904-1978 (American)

For writer details see Katherine 'Peter' PIPER

Citation Record: 3 Books

Formula For Murder - *First*
Phoenix Press US (1947)

The Round Table Murders - *Last*
Phoenix Press US (1952)

John BARRIN and Kate MARSH

British Male Amateur and British Female Amateur operating in England

Gret LANE (British)

Writer: Margaret LANE

Other Byline: Jennifer JONES

Invented 3 detectives - see Insp HOOK

Citation Record: 6 Books

The Curlew Coombe Mystery - *First*
Jenkins UK (1930)

The Guest With The Scythe - *Last*
Jenkins UK (1943)

Det Stone BARRINGTON

is a typical loner. Battling against authority and corruption among his colleagues in the New York Police Department, he jeopardises his own career to solve an important case.

American Policeman operating in New York

Stuart WOODS 1938- (American)

Citation Record: 1 Book

New York Dead - *Single*
HarperCollins UK (1992)

Janet BARRON

Second detective of Peter BARRON

Peter BARRON and Janet BARRON

American Male Amateurs operating in New York/Mexico

Ruth DARBY (American)

Citation Record: 5 Books

Death Boards The Lazy Lady - *First*
Doubleday US (1939)

Murder With Orange Blossoms - *Last*
Doubleday US (1943); Muller UK (1947)

Charles BARROW

is an investigator of insurance frauds.

American Male Professional Investigator operating in USA

Frank Jr PRICE 1890- (American)

Writer: Frank John PRICE Jr

Citation Record: 8 Short Stories in 1 Collection

Mind Wreckers, Limited, And Other Adventures Of Barrow - Ace Insurance Detective - *Collection 1*
Spectator US (1933)

Jake BARROW

American Male Private Detective operating in New York

Nick QUARRY 1924- (American)

For writer details see Pierre-Ange SAWYER

Citation Record: 6 Books

Trail Of A Tramp - *First*
GM US (1958); Muller UK (1960)

Some Die Hard - *Last*
GM US (1961); Muller UK (1963)

Winston BARROWS

British Male Amateur operating in England

M L EADES 1886-1935 (British)

Writer: Maud L EADES

Citation Record: 2 Books

The Crown Swindle - *First*
Jenkins UK (1925)

The Torrington Square Mystery - *Last*
Jenkins UK (1932)

Insp BARRY

American Policeman operating in New York

Anne ROWE (American)

See main detective Insp PETTENGILL

Citation Record: 3 Books

Cobra Venom - *First*
Gifford UK (1946)

Too Much Poison - *First**
Mill US (1944)

Deadly Intent - *Last*
Mill US (1946)

Dr Alun BARRY

British Male Amateur operating in England

Kenneth O'HARA 1928- (British)

is a movie scriptwriter.

Writer: Jean MORRIS

Inventor of one other detective Insp HOBDEN

Citation Record: 2 Books

A View To A Death - *First*
Cassell UK (1958)

Sleeping Dogs Lying - *Last*
Cassell UK (1960); Macmillan US (1962)

Herbert BARRY

solves a case of death by poisoning in a locked room.

American Male Amateur operating in USA

Edwin BAIRD 1886- (American)

Citation Record: 1 Selected Short Story

The Mystery Of The Locked Door
appeared in an anthology, *The World's Best One Hundred Detective Stories.*
Funk US (1929)

Percy BARSTONE

Second detective of Gilbert THRESHAM

Clifford BARTELLS

is an ex-cop. He resigned after exposing corruption in the force and now works for the Security Theft & Accident Insurance Company.

American Male Professional Investigator operating in Florida

John D MACDONALD 1916-1986 (American)

Invented 3 detectives - see Travis MCGEE

Citation Record: 1 Book

The Brass Cupcake - *Only*
GM US (1950); Muller UK (1955)

Kay BARTH
is a lawyer with an interest in crime fiction. She becomes involved in real murder cases, which she solves.
American Female Amateur operating in Colorado/Santa Fe

Norma SCHIER (American)

Citation Record: 4 Books

Death On The Slopes - *First*
Zebra US (1978)

Demon Of The Opera - *Latest*
Zebra US (1980)

Stephen BARTH
is hounded for the murder of his foster-father and has to solve his own case.
American Male Private Detective operating in USA

Philip KETCHUM 1902-1969 (American)

See main detective George CLAY

Citation Record: 1 Book

Death In The Library - *Only*
Crowell US (1937)

Peter BARTHOLOMEW
works in and around Nashtoba Island, near Cape Cod, and is called on to investigate murders that usually involve the local marine community.
American Male Amateur operating in Massachusetts

Sally GUNNING (American)

Citation Record: 6 Books

Hot Water - *First*
Pocket Books US (1990)

Rough Water - *Latest*
Pocket Books US (1994)

Bill BARTLETT
is a reporter who manages to solve some 'impossible' murder cases.
American Male Amateur operating in USA

Whitman CHAMBERS 1896- (American)

Invented 4 detectives - see Simon LAKE

Citation Record: 1 Book

The Campanile Murders - *Only*
Appleton US (1933)

Nell BARTLETT
American Female Amateur operating in New York

David ELIAS

Citation Record: 2 Books

The Cause Of The Screaming - *First*
Hammond UK (1954)

The Gory Details - *Last*
Hammond UK (1954)

John BARTLEY
American Male Amateur operating in New England

Charles Judson DUTTON 1888-1964 (American)

was born in Fall River, Massachusetts. He was a clergyman who wrote at least fifteen criminous novels.

Inventor of one other detective Prof Harley MANNERS

Citation Record: 8 Books

The Underwood Mystery - *First*
Dodd, Mead US (1921); Robinson UK (1922)

The Clutching Hand - *Last*
Dodd, Mead US (1928)

Ray BARTLEY
solves a case involving some nasty murders that take place in an old church.
American Male Amateur operating in USA

Madeleine BUCHANAN ?-1940 (American)

Writer: Madeleine Sharps BUCHANAN

Citation Record: 1 Book

Haunted Bells - *Only*
Chelsea US (1929); Skeffington UK (1931)

Susannah BARTOK
American Female Amateur operating in USA

Laird KOENIG (American)

Writer: Laird P KOENIG

Citation Record: 1 Book

Rockabye - *Single*
St Martin's US (1981); Piatkus UK (1982)

Alexander BARTON
British Male Amateur operating in Africa

Elspeth HUXLEY 1907- (British)

See main detective Supt VACHELL

Citation Record: 1 Book

The Merry Hippo - *Only*
Chatto UK (1963)

The Incident At The Merry Hippo - *Only**
Morrow US (1964)

Connie BARTON
Second detective of Steve BARTON

Dick BARTON
was one of the most popular of British radio detectives in the 1940s and 1950s. He was called a 'special agent' but it was never quite clear who or what he was an agent for. His adventures were often bizarre.
British Male Professional Investigator operating in England

Sidekick: Snowy WHITE
British Male - Assistant

Sidekick: Jock ANDERSON
Scottish Male - Assistant

Mike DORRELL (British)

Citation Record: 1 Book

Mystery Of The Missing Formula - *Only*
Star UK (1978)

Elwyn JONES 1923- (British)

See main detective Supt Charles BARLOW

Citation Record: 4 Short Stories in 1 Collection

Dick Barton, Special Agent - *Collection 1*
contains four novelettes.
Barker UK (1977)

Larry PRYCE (British)

Citation Record: 1 Book

The Gold Bullion Swindle - *Only*
Star UK (1979)

Alan RADNOR 1945- (British)

Writer: Richard LEWIS

Citation Record: 1 Book

The Case Of The Vanishing House - *Only*
Star UK (1978)

Geoffrey WEBB and Edward J MASON (British)

Citation Record: 9 Short Stories in 1 Collection

Dick Barton, Special Agent - *Collection 1*
The date of publication is uncertain.
Contact UK (?)

Steve BARTON and Connie BARTON
were fun-loving amateur detectives.
American Male Amateur and American Female Amateur operating in USA

Kelley ROOS (American)

Invented 3 detectives - see Jeff TROY and Haila TROY

Citation Record: 1 Book

The Blonde Died Dancing - *Only*
Dodd, Mead US (1956)

She Died Dancing - *Only**
Eyre & Spottiswoode UK (1947)

Victoria BARTON

Second detective of George JONES

Leora BARUCH

pursues an Arab terrorist who has murdered her colleague.

Israeli Female Secret Agent operating in Middle East

Allan TOPOL 1941-

Citation Record: 1 Book

A Woman Of Valor - *Single*
Morrow US (1980)

Jacob BARZENY

is an elderly immigrant who was formerly a policeman in Russia. He solves a case of murder, in which his chess-playing friend is a suspect.

Russian Male Ex-Policeman operating in USA

Richard BARTH 1943- (American)

was born in New Jersey. He graduated from Amherst College, Massachusetts, 1964, with an Honours BA. He is the sometime Assistant Professor in Jewellery Design in New York and also a sculptor.

Inventor of one other detective Margaret BINTON

Citation Record: 1 Book

Furnished For Murder - *Single*
St Martin's US (1990)

Ch David BAR-LEV

is the Chief of the Pattern Crimes Unit of the Jerusalem police force, specialising in crimes that appear to have a pattern attached to them, often threatening the security of Israel itself.

Israeli Policeman operating in Jerusalem

William BAYER 1939- (American)

Inventor of one other detective Frank JANEK

Citation Record: 1 Book

Pattern Crimes - *Single*
Villard US (1987); Joseph UK (1987)

Carver BASCOMBE

is a black PI operating in San Francisco. He is well educated and, in his early books, is trying to become a lawyer. Later, he studies and becomes a specialist in the field of paintings. His cases are thus concerned with the artistic world, in which his efforts for racial tolerance occupy a central place.

American Male Private Detective operating in San Francisco

Kenn DAVIS 1932- (American)

Citation Record: 8 Books

The Dark Side - *First*
Avon US (1976)

Blood Of Poets - *Latest*
Fawcett US (1990)

Insp BASIL

British Policeman operating in England

Polly HOBSON 1913- (British)

Writer: Julie Rendel EVANS

Citation Record: 3 Books

Murder Won't Out - *First*
Jenkins UK (1964)

The Three Graces - *Last*
Constable UK (1970); British Book Centre US (1971)

Andrew BASNETT

British Male Amateur operating in England

E X FERRARS 1907-1995 (British)

Invented 11 detectives - see Toby DYKE

Citation Record: 5 Books

Something Wicked - *First*
Doubleday US (1984)

Smoke Without Fire - *Last*
Doubleday US (1991)

Elizabeth FERRARS 1907-1995 (British)

Invented 10 detectives - see Toby DYKE

Citation Record: 5 Books

Something Wicked - *First*
Collins UK (1983)

Smoke Without Fire - *Last*
Collins UK (1990)

Insp BASS

British Policeman operating in England

George SELMARK 1892- (British)

For writer details see Insp BASS

Citation Record: 1 Book

Murder In Silence - *Only*
Cassell UK (1939); Doubleday US (1940)

Seldon TRUSS 1892- (British)

Invented 3 detectives - see Ch Insp GIDLEIGH

Citation Record: 2 Books

Rooksmiths - *First*
Hodder & Stoughton UK (1936)

Deadline For A Diplomat - *First**
In this republished edition, the detective's name was changed to that of the author's main detective, *Ch Insp GIDLEIGH.*
Merit UK (1954)

Foreign Bodies - *Last*
Hodder & Stoughton UK (1938)

Osgood BASS

American Male Amateur operating in New York

David SNELL 1942- (American)

Citation Record: 1 Book

Lights, Camera...Murder - *Single*
St Martin's US (1979)

Stanley BASS

is a part-time private eye and a full-time gambler. Based in San Francisco, he also operates in Las Vegas.

American Male Private Detective operating in USA

David ANTHONY 1929-1986 (American)

See main detective Morgan BUTLER

Citation Record: 2 Books

The Organization - *First*
Coward McCann US (1970); Collins UK (1971)

Stud Game - *Last*
Pocket Books US (1978); Collins UK (1977)

Ch Insp George BASSETT

British Policeman operating in England

Clive RYLAND 1892- (British)

Writer: Clive Ryland PRIESTLEY

Other Detectives:
Insp BECK — Supt SHANNON

Citation Record: 4 Books

Murder In Queer Street - *First*
Hutchinson UK (1941)

The Case Of The Back Seat Girl - *Last*
Hutchinson UK (1952)

Henry BASSETT

has retired from the force but still manages to get involved with cases of murder.

British Male Sleuth operating in England

B

Pat BURDEN (British)

Citation Record: 2 Books

Screaming Bones - *First*
HarperCollins UK (1989); Doubleday US (1990)

Wreath Of Honesty - *Latest*
HarperCollins UK (1990); Doubleday US (1991)

Justin BASSETT

Second detective of Scott GREGORY

Lt Andy BASTIAN

American Policeman operating in California

Richard WORMSER 1908-1977 (American)

was the author of fourteen genre novels, which were published under his real name and a pseudonym, as well eighteen non-genre novels, plays, screenplays and books for children. He received the Mystery Writers of America Edgar Allan Poe award, 1973.

Writer: Richard Edward WORMSER

Other Byline: Ed FRIEND

Inventor of one other detective Sgt Joe DIXON

Citation Record: 2 Books

Drive East On 66 - *First*
Fawcett US (1962)

A Nice Girl Like You - *Last*
Fawcett US (1963); Muller UK (1963)

Insp Roger BASTIDE

French Policeman operating in France

Howard R SIMPSON 1925- (American)

Writer: Howard Russell SIMPSON

Citation Record: 3 Books

The Jumpmaster - *First*
Doubleday US (1984)

A Gathering Of Gunmen - *Latest*
Doubleday US (1987)

Prof Luther BASTION

is an anthropologist with a penchant for criminology. Small, bald and middle-aged, he smokes a lot, loves the theatre, seems to do little work at his unnamed university and spends a lot of time sleuthing. A bachelor, he lives in an apartment near Charing Cross with his flatmate and sidekick.

British Male Amateur operating in England

Sidekick: Maj KETTERING-BEVIS

was badly wounded in the First World War. Even with only one eye, he is a great physical help to the weak but impetuous detective.

British Male - Assistant

Stooge: Insp BURCHELL

is reluctant to admit he needs help but ends up by taking his most baffling cases to BASTION.

British Male

Gavin HOLT 1891- (Australian)

has lived mainly in England and the USA.

Writer: Charles RODDA

Other Detectives:

Joel SABER — Sherrett YORK

Citation Record: 16 Books

Six Minutes Past Twelve - *First*
Hodder & Stoughton UK (1928)

Steel Shutters - *Last*
Hodder & Stoughton UK (1934)

Ch Insp William BASTION

British Policeman operating in England

Richard HARRISON 1901- (British)

Writer: Richard Motte HARRISON

Citation Record: 5 Books

Black Widow - *First*
Jarrolds UK (1946)

Rope Over Jezebel - *Last*
Jarrolds UK (1950)

Mary Lou 'Dunk' BATESON

is a gorgeous girl, her only 'fault' being self-consciousness about her height, which is six feet two (hence her basketball nickname). An expert rare-coin assessor, she becomes involved in the theft of a magnificent coin and the death that follows. To save herself she turns sleuth.

American Female Amateur operating in New York

Lawrence SANDERS 1920- (American)

Invented 6 detectives - see Ex-Plce Edward X DELANEY

Citation Record: 1 Book

The Eighth Commandment - *Single*
Putnam US (1986); New English Library UK (1986)

Anthony BATHURST

British Male Amateur operating in England

Brian FLYNN 1885- (British)

Citation Record: 53 Books

The Billiard-Room Mystery - *First*
Hamilton UK (1927); Macrae, Smith US (1929)

The Saints Are Sinister - *Last*
Long UK (1958)

Neil J BATHURST

American Male Private Detective operating in USA

Lawrence L LYNCH (American)

Writer: Emma M VAN DEVENTER

Other Detectives:

Rufus CARNES and Richard STANHOPE
Sheriff COOK — Francis FERRARS
Insp HAINES — Kenneth JASPER
Carl MASTERS — Ferriss MURTAGH
Madeline PAYNE — Policeman STANHOPE
Van VERNET

Citation Record: 2 Books

The Diamond Coterie - *First*
Loyd US (1882); Routledge UK (1887)

Out Of The Labyrinth - *Last*
Loyd US (1885); Ward, Lock UK (1887)

BATMAN

must be included in the genre, if only because of his popularity, which continues unabated. A fantasy figure, operating from the 1930s style Gotham City, he uses his bizarre powers to fight crime, in the course of which, it must be admitted, he does solve real mysteries.

American Male Professional Amateur operating in Gotham City

Sidekick: ROBIN

was originally called Dick Grayson but he soon became transmogrified into ROBIN and achieved lasting fame in the series of adventures undertaken by BATMAN.

American Male - Assistant

Bob KANE (American)

Citation Record: 2 Books 44 Short Stories in 3 Collections

Batman Vs The Joker - *First*
The first of two comic strip books.
Signet US (1966)

Batman Vs The Penguin - *Last*
The second of two comic strip books.
Signet US (1966)

Batman - *Collection 1*
Short stories - 6
Signet US (1966)

The Further Adventures Of Batman - *Collection 2*
Although published under this byline, the stories in this anthology were written by different authors, many of them the most distinguished in their fields.
Short stories - 13
Bantam US (1989)

The Greatest Batman Stories Ever Told - *Collection 3*
is a collection of comic strip stories.
Short stories - 25
Warner US (1989)

Winston LYON 1917- (American)
Writer: Winston WOOLFOLK
Citation Record: 2 Books
Batman Vs The Fearsome Foursome - *First*
Signet UK (1966)
Batman Vs The Three Villains Of Doom - *Last*
Four Square US (1966); Signet UK (1966)

BATTERY BOICE
American Male Detective in Pulp Magazines operating in USA

Ed STRAYER (American)
Invented 4 detectives - see Jack SHARPLEY
Citation Record: 1 Selected Short Story
Battery Boice, The Electric Detective; Or, Rounding Up The Race Track Swindlers
Old Cap Collier Library US (18??)

Supt BATTLE
was one of the author's favourite detectives in her early novels, but she lost interest in him in her later works. He appears in several books with some of her other detectives and, in later books, he appears as a stooge for the insufferably clever *Hercule POIROT.*
British Policeman operating in England

Agatha CHRISTIE 1890-1976 (British)
Invented 18 detectives - see Hercule POIROT
Citation Record: 4 Books
The Secret Of Chimneys - *First*
Lane UK (1925); Dodd, Mead US (1925)
Towards Zero - *Last*
Collins UK (1944); Dodd, Mead US (1944)

Supt BATTLE
Second detective of Lady Elaine 'Bundle' BRENT

Supt BATTLE
Appears with at least two other detectives - see Hercule POIROT.

Supt BATTLE and Luke FITZWILLIAMS
British Policeman and British Male Amateur operating in England

Agatha CHRISTIE 1890-1976 (British)
Invented 18 detectives - see Hercule POIROT
Citation Record: 1 Book
Easy To Kill - *Only*
Collins UK (1939); Dodd, Mead US (1939)

Singer BATTS
American Male Sleuth operating in Illinois

Thomas B DEWEY 1915- (American)
was born in Elkhart, Indiana. He graduated at the University of Iowa, Iowa City, 1938, and received a PhD at the University of California, Los Angeles, 1973. He was an editor and advertising manager who later was appointed Assistant Professor of English at Arizona State University, 1971-1977.
Writer: Thomas Blanchard DEWEY
Other Detectives:
MAC — Pete SCHOFIELD
Citation Record: 4 Books
Hue And Cry - *First*
Jefferson House US (1944)
Room For Murder - *First**
New American Library US (1950)
The Murder Of Marion Mason - *First**
Dakers UK (1951)
Handle With Fear - *Last*
Mill US (1951); Dakers UK (1955)

Bimbashi BAUK
Egyptian Male Sleuth operating in Egypt

Sax ROHMER 1883-1959 (British)
Invented 9 detectives - see Insp RYDER
Citation Record: 10 Short Stories in 1 Collection
Egyptian Nights - *Collection 1*
Hale UK (1944)
Bimbashi Baruk of Egypt - *Collection 1**
McBride US (1944)

Alfred BAUM
British Male Amateur operating in England/France

Derek KARTUN 1919- (British)
Citation Record: 4 Books
Beaver To Fox - *First*
Century UK (1983); St Martin's US (1986)
Safe House - *Latest*
Century UK (1989)

Prof Charles BAUMAN
is a college professor who, while in jail, solves a murder or two.
American Male Amateur operating in USA

Mitchell SMITH 1935- (American)
Citation Record: 1 Book
Stone City - *Single*
Simon & Schuster US (1990); Collins UK (1990)

Ch Insp BAXTER
British Policeman operating in England

Margaret MOORE (Irish)
was born in Ballymena, Ireland. She is an educational psychologist.
Citation Record: 4 Books
Forests Of The Night - *First*
Collins UK (1987)
Fringe Ending - *Latest*
HarperCollins UK (1991)

Roger BAXTER
appeared in juvenile books during the 1940s.
American Male Detective in Pulp Magazines operating in USA

Samuel EPSTEIN (American)
No citations

Tory BAXTER
American Sleuth operating in USA

Marcia BLAIR 1911- (American)
Writer: Marceil Genee Kolstad BAKER
Citation Record: 8 Books
The Final Pose - *First*
Zebra US (1978)
Finale - *Latest*
Zebra US (1980)

Charity BAY
once worked for a macho Californian PI, but she left and is now on her own in New York City. She is an updated, female, sexist *'Bulldog' DRUMMOND* in *Sam SPADE's* clothes.
American Female Private Detective operating in New York

Arthur KAPLAN 1925- (American)
Citation Record: 1 Book
A Killing For Charity - *Only*
Coward McCann US (1976)

Stephen BAYARD
British Male Amateur operating in England

Stacey BISHOP 1900-1959 (American)
Writer: George Johann Carl ANTHEIL

Citation Record: 1 Book

Death In The Dark - *Only*
Faber UK (1930)

B

China BAYLES
is a lawyer turned herbalist who investigates murders, which turn out to have strongly botanical elements.
American Female Amateur operating in USA

Susan Wittig ALBERT (American)
is a graduate of the University of California and a Professor of English.

Citation Record: 2 Books

Hangman's Root - *First*
Scribner's US (1994)

Witch's Bane - *Latest*
Scribner's US (1995)

Bert BAYLISS
is a wealthy New Yorker who decides to be a private detective just to amuse himself. He is always, he thinks, right; and to prove it he invents his own sidekick, who argues with him incessantly but always agrees with him in the end – as all good sidekicks, even imaginary ones, should.
American Male Amateur operating in New York

Sidekick: HARRIS
Male - Imaginary

Carolyn WELLS 1870-1942 (American)
Invented 7 detectives - see Fleming STONE

Citation Record: 1 Selected Short Story

Point Of Testimony
US (1911)

Pete BAYLISS
is a Korean War veteran trying to be a PI.
American Male Private Detective operating in Los Angeles

Blair TREYNOR (American)

Citation Record: 1 Book

Widow's Pique - *Only*
Mill US (1956); Ward, Lock UK (1958)

Warren BAYNE
has one case in which he is sent to guard a powerful client in Hollywood.
American Male Private Detective operating in Hollywood

C A BYERS 1879- (American)

Writer: Charles Alma BYERS

Citation Record: 1 Book

The Inverness Murder - *Only*
Dial US (1935)

Dr BAYNES
British Male Amateur operating in England

Vicars BELL 1904- (British)

Writer: Vicars Walker BELL

Citation Record: 6 Books

Death Under The Stars - *First*
Faber UK (1949)

Death Walks By The River - *Last*
Faber UK (1959)

Lt Oliver BAYNES and John Sherlock HOLMES
solve an 'impossible' murder case.
American Policeman and Male Sleuth operating in USA

Robert ARTHUR 1909-1969 (American)
Invented 6 detectives - see Max MILLION

Citation Record: 1 Selected Short Story

The Adventure Of The Single Footprint
In 'Ellery Queen's Mystery Magazine' US (1950)

BEACH
was a superintendent in the Bengal Police in the days of the British Raj.
British Male Ex-Policeman operating in India

Alan BROCK 1886- (British)

Writer: Alan St Hill BROCK

Citation Record: 1 Book

Miss Hamblett's Ghost - *Only*
Macdonald UK (1946)

Tony BEACH and Gregor MCGREGOR
British Male Amateurs operating in England

Dick FRANCIS 1920- (British)
Invented 18 detectives - see Sid HALLEY

Citation Record: 1 Book

Proof - *Single*
Putnam US (1985)

Amanda BEAGLE
Second detective of Lutie BEAGLE

Lutie BEAGLE and Amanda BEAGLE
are two sisters, both spinsters, who inherit their brother's business, the Beagle Detective Agency, and decide to continue it. They constitute what seems to be the first female partnership in private eye fiction.
American Female Private Detectives operating in New York

Torrey CHANSLOR 1899- (American)

Writer: Marjorie Torrey Hood CHANSLOR

Citation Record: 2 Books

Our First Murder - *First*
Stokes US (1940)

Our Second Murder - *Last*
Stokes US (1941)

Otis BEAGLE
runs the Beagle Detective Agency. A big man, he can be trusted about as much as his flashy finger rings can.
American Male Private Detective operating in Los Angeles

Sidekick: Joe PEEL
is the detective's long-suffering and overworked legman.
American Male - Assistant

Charles K BOSTON 1904-1969 (American)
For writer details see Johnny FLETCHER and Sam CRAGG

Citation Record: 1 Book

The Silver Jackass - *Only*
was republished under the author's real name.
Reynal US (1941)

Frank GRUBER 1904-1969 (American)
Invented 8 detectives - see Johnny FLETCHER and Sam CRAGG

Citation Record: 2 Books

The Silver Jackass - *First*
Cherry Tree US (1952)

Beagle Scented Murder - *Last*
Rinehart US (1956)

Insp Edward BEALE
British Policeman operating in England

Rupert PENNY (British)

Writer: Ernest Basil Charles THORNETT

Citation Record: 8 Books

The Talkative Policeman - *First*
Collins UK (1936)

Sealed-Room Murder - *Last*
Collins UK (1941)

Goldy BEAR
is a caterer supreme who has the knack of being in the wrong place at the wrong time, usually where and when a murder

B

has taken place. The books give real recipes for food as well as for crime.
American Amateur operating in Colorado

Diane Mott DAVIDSON (American)

Citation Record: 4 Books

Catering To Nobody - *First*
St Martin's US (1990)

The Last Suppers - *Latest*
Bantam US (1994)

Trajan BEARE

Appears with at least two other detectives - see Mallory KING.

Molly BEARPAW

is an investigator for the Cherokee tribe.
American Female Private Detective operating in USA

Jean HAGER 1932- (American)

Citation Record: 4 Books

Ravenmocker - *First*
Mysterious Press US (1992)

Seven Black Stones - *Latest*
Mysterious Press US (1994)

Clyde BEATTY

sleuths during the 1800s.
British Male Amateur operating in England

Basil COPPER 1924- (British)

Invented 3 detectives - see Solar PONS

Citation Record: 1 Book

Necropolis - *Single*
Sphere Books UK (1981); Arkham US (1980)

Insp Henry BEAUMONT

British Policeman operating in England

Meg Elizabeth ATKINS (British)

Citation Record: 4 Books

Palimpsest - *First*
Quartet UK (1981); St Martin's US (1982)

Tangle - *Latest*
Boyars UK (1988); Boyars US (1988)

Det J P BEAUMONT

has cases that occur in Rainy City and the deserts and Indian country for a long way around.
American Policeman operating in Seattle

J A JANCE 1944- (American)

Writer: Judith Ann JANCE

Inventor of one other detective Sheriff Joanna BRADY

Citation Record: 12 Books

Injustice For All - *First*
Avon US (1986); Severn UK (1993)

Lying In Wait - *Latest*
Morrow US (1994)

Jack BEAUMONT and Susan BRIGHT

sleuth in books set in various eras, from 1913 to 1953, not in that order.
American Male Amateur and American Female Amateur operating in USA

Michael MCDOWELL 1950- (American)

Citation Record: 3 Books

Jack And Susan In 1953 - *First*
Ballantine US (1985)

Jack And Susan In 1933 - *Latest*
Ballantine US (1987)

Ned BEAUMONT

is a political hanger-on and, in this classic novel, plays the part of a very amateur detective.
American Male Amateur operating in USA

Dashiell HAMMETT 1894-1961 (American)

Invented 7 detectives - see Sam SPADE

Citation Record: 1 Book

The Glass Key - *Only*
Knopf US (1931); Cassell UK (1931)

BEAUTIFUL JACK

was also called 'The Double-edged Detective'.
American Male Detective in Pulp Magazines operating in USA

ANON

Citation Record: 1 Book

Beautiful Jack, The Double-Edged Detective - *Only*
Aldine US

Insp BECK

British Policeman operating in England

Clive RYLAND 1892- (British)

Invented 3 detectives - see Ch Insp George BASSETT

Citation Record: 3 Books

The Blind Beggar Murder - *First*
Hutchinson UK (1935)

Murder On Bag Hill - *Last*
Hutchinson UK (1945)

Lucy BECK

British Female Amateur operating in England

Peter CONWAY 1929- (British)

Writer: Peter Claudius GAUTIER-SMITH

Citation Record: 3 Books

Motive For Revenge - *First*
Hale UK (1972)

Escape To Danger - *Last*
Hale UK (1974)

Insp Martin BECK

Dutch Policeman operating in Amsterdam

Maj SJOWALL 1935- (Dutch)

Citation Record: 10 Books

Roseanna - *First*
Pantheon US (1967); Gollancz UK (1968)

The Terrorists - *Latest*
Pantheon US (1976); Gollancz UK (1977)

Paul BECK

has, according to statements made by characters in his books, the reputation of being 'one of the cleverest detectives in London' and 'a worthy successor to the late Sherlock Holmes'. Unlike his mentor, however, he is stout, strongly built, bronzed, with red sidewhiskers and 'looks more like a retired milkman than a detective'. As to his methods, they too depart a little more than somewhat from his great predecessor: for, he says, 'I just go by rule of thumb and muddle and puzzle out my cases the best I can'. In the course of his work he meets the author's lady detective, *Dora MYRL*, whom he marries. Their son, *Paul BECK Jr*, is the detective in one book.
British Male Professional Amateur operating in London

Sidekick: Dora MYRL
is a lady detective, who appears in one collection of short stories on her own. In the course of time she marries *Paul BECK* and becomes his assistant.
British Female - Wife

M McDonnell BODKIN 1850-1933 (British)

was an Irish barrister who served as a judge in County Clare, Ireland, and as a Nationalist MP in the English parliament. He was the author of several mystery and detective novels.

Writer: Matthias McDonnell BODKIN

Other Detectives:
Paul BECK Jr — Dora MYRL

Citation Record: 2 Books 34 Short Stories in 3 Collections

B

The Capture Of Paul Beck - *First*
Unwin UK (1909); Little, Brown US (1911)

Pigeon Blood Rubies - *Last*
Nash UK (1915)

Paul Beck, The Rule Of Thumb Detective - *Collection 1*
Short stories - 12
Pearson UK (1898)

The Quests Of Paul Beck - *Collection 2*
Short stories - 12
Unwin UK (1908); Little, Brown US (1910)

Paul Beck, Detective - *Collection 3*
Short stories - 10
Talbot El (1929)

Paul BECK Jr

is the son of *Paul BECK* and *Dora MYRL*, the author's two main detectives. He becomes interested in detective work at college and appears in these short stories (his parents making brief appearances also), in which the author makes use of his own political experience and intimate knowledge of the House of Commons.

British Male Amateur operating in England

Sidekick: Lord KIRWOOD
is the son of a British peer and is thus able to help his detective friend in the ways that British peers were wont to at the time.
British Male - Friend

M McDonnell BODKIN 1850-1933 (British)

Invented 3 detectives - see Paul BECK

Citation Record: 12 Short Stories in 1 Collection

Young Beck, A Chip Off The Old Block - *Collection 1*
Unwin UK (1911); Little, Brown US (1912)

Lee BECKETT

American Male Sleuth operating in California

John CROWE 1924- (American)

For writer details see Kane JACKSON

Inventor of one other detective Ed GRAY

Citation Record: 6 Books

Another Way To Die - *First*
Random House US (1972)

Close To Death - *Latest*
Dodd, Mead US (1979); Hale UK (1983)

Sam BECKETT

appeared mainly in stories in *Dime Detective*.

American Male Detective in Pulp Magazines operating in USA

John LAURENCE 1885- (American)

Writer: John Laurence PRITCHARD
No citations

Raoul BECQ

French Male Amateur

William LEQUEUX 1864-1927 (British)

Invented 23 detectives - see Allan KENNEDY

Citation Record: 12 Short Stories in 1 Collection

Mysteries Of A Great City - *Collection 1*
was republished by *Mellifont* (UK 1934) in two volumes as *Mysteries of a Great City and More Mysteries of a Great City.*
Hodder & Stoughton UK (1920)

Sgt BEDDOES

Second detective of Insp EVANS

Lilia BEDDOES

American Female Amateur operating in New York

Thomas CHASTAIN (American)

Invented 4 detectives - see J T 'Jake' SPANNER

Citation Record: 1 Book

Nightscape - *Single*
Atheneum US (1982)

Father Simon BEDE

is an Anglican priest who is some kind of special aide to the Archbishop of Canterbury. His responsibilities take him to various parts of the world and he has a knack of meeting murder everywhere.

American Male Amateur operating in New York/Michigan

Sidekick: Helen BULLOCK
is a photographer who meets *Simon BEDE* on his first assignment and, being deeply religious herself, assists him in his investigations. In a later book by the author she acts as the main detective herself and her assistant is then *Fergus BEDE*.
American Female - Assistant

Barbara Ninde BYFIELD 1930- (American)

See main detective Helen BULLOCK

Citation Record: 3 Books

Solemn High Murder - *First*
Doubleday US (1975); Davies UK (1976)

A Harder Thing Than Triumph - *Latest*
Doubleday US (1977)

Tim BEDFORD

British Male Amateur operating in England

J B PRIESTLEY 1894-1984 (British)

Invented 3 detectives - see Lionel Humphrey SALT and Maggie CULTHORPE

Citation Record: 1 Book

Saturn Over The Water - *Only*
Heinemann UK (1961); Doubleday US (1961)

Insp BEDISON

British Policeman operating in England

Thomas COBB 1853-1932 (British)

See main detective Insp PARKER

Citation Record: 4 Books

The Crime Without A Clue - *First*
Benn UK (1929)

Who Closed The Casement? - *Last*
Benn UK (1932)

Sgt William BEEF

is that rare invention in the genre, a successfully portrayed comic detective. Plebeian and bucolic, the good sergeant appears first in a classic parody of a Golden Age locked-room mystery in which he has to pit his wits against parodies of *Peter WIMSEY, Hercule POIROT* and *Father BROWN*, all messing about interrogating house guests and servants, while *BEEF* knows whodunnit all along and is able to spend much of his time in the local pub drinking beer and playing darts. In his later books he has set up as a private detective and has his own sidekick to narrate his cases to the world.

British Policeman operating in England

Sidekick: Lionel TOWNSEND
is the Watsonian narrator of the good sergeant's cases, but, as he says, he would much prefer working for one of the more aristocratic sleuths with which British detective fiction abounded at the time.
British Male - Narrator

Stooge: Lord Simon PLIMSOLL
is a parody of *Dorothy SAYERS's* great detective, *Peter WIMSEY*, who, in concert with *Amer PICON* and *Mgr SMITH*, messes about in his usual irritating fashion trying to solve the case.
British Male Amateur

Stooge: Amer PICON
is a parody of *Agatha CHRISTIE's* great detective, *Hercule POIROT*. However, after spending much time fussing about the case in the fashion usually adopted by the latter, and in

concert with *Simon PLIMSOLL* and *Mgr SMITH*, he fails to solve it.
Belgian Male Professional Amateur

Stooge: Mgr SMITH
is a parody of *G K CHESTERTON's* great detective, *Father BROWN*, who, in concert with *Amer PICON* and *Simon PLIMSOLL*, perambulates religiously and fatuously, trying to solve the case.
British Male Amateur

Leo BRUCE 1903-1979 (British)
was born in Edenbridge, Kent, and educated in England and later at the University of Buenos Aires, 1923-1924. He served in the British Army, 1939-1946, and was awarded the British Empire Medal. A specialist in old books and a book critic for a London newspaper, the author wrote a great deal under his real name, including novels, plays, poetry, memoirs, books on history, games, cooking and the circus. He reserved the pseudonym for his criminous publications.
Writer: Rupert CROFT-COOKE
Inventor of one other detective Carolus DEENE
Citation Record: 8 Books
Case For Three Detectives - *First*
Bles UK (1936); Stokes US (1937)
Cold Blood - *Last*
Gollancz UK (1952); Academy US (1980)

Insp William (The Grouser) BEEKE
British Policeman operating in England

Edwy Searles BROOKS 1889-1965 (British)
Other Bylines:
Berkeley GRAY
Victor GUNN
Carlton ROSS
Other Detectives:
Sexton BLAKE
Nelson LEE
Ferrers LOCKE
ST FRANCIS SCHOOL
Citation Record: 2 Books
The Strange Case Of The Antlered Man - *First*
Harrap UK (1935)
The Grouser Investigates - *Last*
Harrap UK (1936)

Hymie BEERMAN
is a wise-cracking cab-driver in New York's Bronx district who plays at being an amateur detective. He appeared in several short stories published in *Detective Tales* during the 1940s.
American Male Detective in Pulp Magazines operating in New York

Parker BONNER 1903-1980 (American)
For writer details see Bill LENNOX
Citation Record: 2 Selected Short Stories
Hymie On The Spot
appeared in the January number.
In 'Detective Tales' US (1948)
Hymie And The Double-Dome
appeared in the May number.
In 'Detective Tales' US (1948)

Dr Villiers BEETHAM-SAUNDERS
British Male Amateur operating in England

William LEQUEUX 1864-1927 (British)
Invented 23 detectives - see Allan KENNEDY
Citation Record: 13 Short Stories in 1 Collection
"Cinders" Of Harley Street - *Collection 1*
Ward, Lock UK (1916)

Mr BEHRENS and Mr CALDER
are two British Counter-Intelligence agents and appear only in short stories, which have been praised as some of the very best in the whole genre of spy fiction.
British Male Professional Investigators operating in England

Michael GILBERT 1912- (British)
Invented 11 detectives - see Insp HAZELRIGG
Citation Record: 23 Short Stories in 2 Collections
Game Without Rules - *Collection 1*
Short stories - 11
Hodder & Stoughton UK (1968); Harper & Row US (1969)
Mr Calder And Mr Behrens - *Collection 2*
Short stories - 12
Hodder & Stoughton UK (1982); Harper & Row US (1982)

Robert BELCOURT
Male Sleuth operating in Tangier

Cameron ROUGVIE (British)
Citation Record: 4 Books
Medal From Pamplona - *First*
Barker UK (1964); Ballantine US (1964)
When Johnny Died - *Last*
Barker UK (1967)

Archibald BELDRUM and Nigel BLAIR
British Male Amateurs operating in England

L F HAY (British)
Writer: Lindsay Fitzgerald HAY
Citation Record: 3 Books
It Wasn't A Nightmare - *First*
Hutchinson UK (1937); Macmillan US (1937)
No Mean Tartar - *Last*
Hutchinson UK (1938)

Mr BELL and Mr WHITE
British Male Private Detectives operating in England

Mrs George CORBETT 1840- (British)
See main detective Annie CORY
Citation Record: 1 Book
Secrets Of A Private Enquiry Office - *Only*
Routledge UK (1891)

Charlie BELL
American Male Amateur operating in Chicago

David WAGONER 1926- (American)
Writer: David Russell WAGONER
Citation Record: 1 Book
The Man In The Middle - *Only*
Harcourt Brace US (1954); Gollancz UK (1955)

Garnett BELL
British Male Amateur operating in England

Cecil H BULLIVANT 1882- (British)
was a fairly well-known writer and editor of the pre-1914 era, when he was on the staff of several popular magazines, being an expert in English language and literature. He wrote several early detective works of a simple kind and re-established *HAWKSHAW* (the earliest detective to appear on the stage in the classic melodrama, *THE TICKET-OF-LEAVE MAN*).
Writer: Cecil Henry BULLIVANT
Other Byline: Alice MILLARD
Other Detectives:
Henry Napoleon BAGGS
May BERESFORD
Insp HAWKSHAW
Millie LYNNE
Citation Record: 1 Book 5 Short Stories in 1 Collection
Blood Money - *Only*
Long UK (1924)
Garnett Bell, Detective - *Collection 1*
Odhams UK (1920); Wright US (1935)

Jeremy BELL
British Male Amateur operating in England

Max PEMBERTON 1863-1950 (British)
Invented 4 detectives - see Bernard SUTTON

Citation Record: 6 Short Stories in 1 Collection

A Bagman In Jewels - *Collection 1*

This collection of sixteen of the author's stories contains six with *Jeremy BELL.*

Skeffington UK (1919)

John BELL

specialises in exposing crimes committed under the guise of 'occult' events.

British Male Professional Investigator operating in England

L T MEADE and Robert EUSTACE (British)

Invented 7 detectives - see Insp FROST and Dr GARLAND

Citation Record: 6 Short Stories in 1 Collection

A Master Of Mysteries - *Collection 1*

Ward, Lock UK (1898)

Samuel BELL

British Male Professional Investigator operating in several locations

Brian FREEMANTLE 1936- (British)

See main detective Charlie MUFFIN

Citation Record: 12 Short Stories in 1 Collection

The Factory - *Collection 1*

Century UK (1990)

The BELL BOY DETECTIIVE

American Male Detective in Pulp Magazines operating in USA

Harry ROCKWOOD 1859-1932 (American)

Invented 14 detectives - see Clarice DYKE

Citation Record: 1 Book

The Bell Boy Detective; Or, The Hotel Diamond Robbery

New York Detective Library US (1882-8)

Sir Harker BELLAMY

appears also in most of the books with one of the author's other detectives, *Timothy Overbury STANDISH.*

British Male Amateur operating in England

Sydney HORLER 1888-1954 (British)

was born in Leytonstone, Essex, and educated at Redcliffe and Colston schools, Bristol. He worked on newspapers in Bristol, 1905-1911, and by then had become a prolific writer of novels of detection, adventure and suspense, as well as of plays and other works. He was the natural successor to the supreme British thriller writers, *SAPPER* and *Edgar WALLACE;* but, while he inherited the reactionary ideas of the former and the speed in writing of the latter, he never reached the standard of either. He is credited with at least one hundred and twenty criminous novels, over twenty non-genre novels, six plays and several other works. The books contain many heroes, agents, sleuths, which are difficult to list or identify, as the author possessed narrative skill without the concomitant virtues of credibility, subtlety, organisation or plotting ability. His views, which he liked to express in his books, would now be regarded as bigoted, racist, and (according to some critics) showing evidence of mild madness. Although his work was popular at the time, it is hardly read today.

Other Detectives:

Brett CARSTAIRS
'Bunny' CHIPSTEAD
Insp H EMP
Sir Brian FORDINGHAME
Sir Brian FORDINGHAME and Baron VESSELOFFSKY
Gerald (Nighthawk) FROST
Ian HEATH
Martin HUISH
Sir William KIRBY
Sir Charles KNIGHTLEY
Gerald LISSENDALE
Justin (The Ace) MARCH
Ch Const George MEATYARD
Sebastian QUIN
Peter SCARLETT
Timothy Overbury 'Tiger' STANDISH
The Hon Timothy Overbury 'Tiger' STANDISH and Sir Harker BELLAMY
Baron VESSELOFFSKY
Robert WYNNTON

Citation Record: 1 Book

My Lady Dangerous - *Only*

Collins UK (1932); Harper & Row US (1933)

Sir Harker BELLAMY

Second detective of The Hon Timothy Overbury 'Tiger' STANDISH

James W BELLAMY

appears in the first story written by this highly regarded author and, as such, is well worth noting.

American Male Amateur operating in USA

Judson PHILIPS 1903-1989 (American)

Invented 4 detectives - see Peter STYLES

Citation Record: 1 Selected Short Story

Room Number Twenty-Three

is said to be the author's very first story.

US (1925)

Det Supt John BELLAMY

British Policeman operating in England

T C H JACOBS 1899-1976 (British)

Invented 8 detectives - see Ch Insp BARNARD

Citation Record: 5 Books

The Curse Of Khatra - *First*

Paul UK (1947)

Women Are Like That - *Last*

Hale UK (1960)

Mehatibel BELLAMY

is a reporter who solves an extraordinary case of death from the diving disease, 'the bends', that occurs in, of all places, a New York apartment.

American Female Amateur operating in New York

Dorothy WHEELOCK (American)

Citation Record: 1 Book

Dead Giveaway - *Only*

Phoenix Press US (1942)

Nick BELLAMY

British Male Private Detective operating in London

Peter CHEYNEY 1896-1951 (British)

Invented 11 detectives - see Lemmy CAUTION

Citation Record: 1 Book

Another Little Drink - *Only*

Collins UK (1940)

A Trap For Bellamy - *Only**

Dodd, Mead US (1941)

Premeditated Murder - *Only**

Avon US (1943)

Stephen BELLECROIX and Sheila ROATH

British Male Amateur and British Female Amateur operating in England

David CRAIG 1929- (British)

For writer details see Ch Supt Colin HARPUR

Citation Record: 2 Books

Young Men May Die - *First*

Cape UK (1970); Stein US (1970)

A Walk At Night - *Last*

Macmillan UK (1971); Stein US (1971)

Insp Frederic BELOT

French Policeman operating in France

Claude AVELINE 1901- (French)

Citation Record: 3 Books

The Fountain At Marlieu - *First*

is a translation from the French of *Le Jet d'Eau.*

Dobson UK (1954); Roy US (1954)

The Cat's Eye - *Last*

is a translation from the French of *L'Oeil-de-Chat* (Paris, 1970).

Dobson UK (1972); Doubleday US (1973)

Christopher BELSIZE

British Male Amateur operating in London

B

Vernon RENDALL 1869- (British)

Writer: Vernon Horace RENDALL

Citation Record: 14 Short Stories in 1 Collection

The London Nights Of Belsize - *Collection 1*
Lane UK (1917); Lane US (1917)

Becky BELSKI

is a lady who, when she is not deeply immersed in the Jewish life, is a computer hacker and an eager beaver of a detective.

American Female Amateur operating in New York

C A HADDAD (American)

See main detective David HAHAM

Citation Record: 2 Books

Caught In The Shadows - *First*
Severn US (1994); Severn UK (1994)

Root Canal - *Latest*
Severn US (1994); Severn UK (1994)

Valentine BELT

British Male Amateur operating in England

Fergus HUME 1859-1932 (British)

Invented 24 detectives - see Insp Samuel GORBY

Citation Record: 1 Book

Claude Duval Of Ninety-Five: A Romance Of The Road - *Only*
Digby, Long UK (1897); Dillingham US (1897)

BEN THE TRAMP

British Male Amateur operating in England

J Jefferson FARJEON 1883-1955 (British)

Invented 3 detectives - see Paul BISHOP

Citation Record: 7 Books

No 17 - *First*
Hodder & Stoughton UK (1926); Dial US (1926)

Ben On The Job - *Last*
Collins UK (1952)

Mike BENASQUE

Male Sleuth operating in South America

Alan CAILLOU 1914- (American)

Invented 4 detectives - see Matthew TOBIN

Citation Record: 4 Books

The Plotters - *First*
Harper & Row US (1960); Davies UK (1960)

Diamonds Wild - *Latest*
Avon UK (1979)

Angela BENBOW and Caledonia WINGATE

are two septuagenarians who live in a retirement community. Death there comes all too suddenly and frequently and, ever alert when the game's afoot, they become expert detectives.

American Female Amateurs operating in California

Corrine Holt SAWYER (American)

Citation Record: 4 Books

The J Alfred Prufrock Murders - *First*
Fine US (1988); Thorndike UK (1991)

Murder Has No Calories - *Latest*
Fine US (1994)

Juge d'Instruction Henri BENCOLIN

was the earliest of this important author's several detectives, although he was soon abandoned. A senior figure in the Paris police force and said to be 'one of the most dangerous policemen in Europe', he accepts fees for private detective work.

French Policeman operating in Paris

Sidekick: Jeff MARLE
narrates the cases and assists. He appears also as the main detective in one other book.

British Male - Narrator

John Dickson CARR 1906-1977 (American)

Invented 16 detectives - see Dr Gideon FELL

Citation Record: 5 Books 4 Short Stories in 1 Collection

It Walks By Night - *First*
Harper & Row US (1930); Hamish Hamilton UK (1976)

The Four False Weapons, Being The Return Of Bencolin - *Last*
Harper & Row US (1937); Hamish Hamilton UK (1938)

The Door To Doom And Other Detections - *Collection 1*
contains four *Henri BENCOLIN* stories, one *Gideon FELL* story and two *Sherlock HOLMES* stories (these are cited individually).
Harper & Row US (1980); Hamish Hamilton UK (1980)

Insp BENDER

is an early Scotland Yard detective.

British Policeman operating in London

Henry HERMAN 1832-1894 (British)

Inventor of one other detective George GREY

Citation Record: 1 Book

Lady Turpin - *Only*
Ward, Lock UK (1897)

Supt Edmund BENDILOW

British Policeman operating in England

Carlton WALLACE (British)

Citation Record: 5 Books

Mr Death Walks Abroad - *First*
Long UK (1933)

Mr Death - *First**
Doubleday US (1934)

Death In The Kettle - *Last*
Long UK (1938)

Det BENEDETTO

Second detective of Ch HAMMOND

Jerry BENEDICT

American Male Sleuth operating in USA

Edward RONNS 1916-1975 (American)

Writer details see Sam DURELL

Inventor of one other detective Reginald 'Beauty' BLACK

Citation Record: 2 Books

No Place To Live - *First*
was reprinted under the following byline.
McKay US (1947); Boardman UK (1950)

Lady, The Guy Is Dead - *First**
Avon US (1950)

Gift Of Death - *Last*
was reprinted under the following byline.
McKay US (1948)

Will B AARONS 1916-1975 (American)

See main detective Sam DURELL

Citation Record: 1 Book

No Place To Live - *First*
was previously published under the preceding byline.
MacFadden US (1964)

Gift Of Death - *Last*
was previously published under the preceding byline.
MacFadden US (1964)

Sam BENEDICT

appears in books written by three authors.

American Male Sleuth operating in San Francisco

Elsie LEE 1912- (American)

Citation Record: 1 Book

Sam Benedict: Cast The First Stone - *Only*
Lancer UK (1963)

Howard L OLECK 1911- (American)

Writer: Howard Leoner OLECK

Citation Record: 1 Book

B

A Singular Fury - *Pastiche 1*
World US (1968)

Brad WILLIAMS 1918- and W ERLICH 1900-1971 (American)

Citation Record: 2 Books

A Conflict Of Interests - *Pastiche 1*
Holt US (1971)

A Matter Of Confidence - *Pastiche 2*
Holt US (1973)

John BENHAM

British Male Amateur operating in England

Michael HOME 1885-1973 (British)

For writer details see Ludovic TRAVERS

Citation Record: 2 Books

The Strange Prisoner - *First*
Methuen UK (1947)

The Auber File - *Last*
Methuen UK (1953)

Paul BENJAMIN

appears in two novels. In the first he is a vigilante intent on discovering the killer of his wife. In the second he finds redemption.

American Male Amateur operating in New York/Chicago

Brian GARFIELD 1939- (American)

Invented 4 detectives - see Plce Sam WATCHMAN

Citation Record: 2 Books

Death Wish - *First*
McKay US (1972) ; Hodder & Stoughton UK (1973)

Death Sentence - *Last*
Evans US (1975); Macmillan UK (1976)

Al BENNET

American Male Amateur operating in USA

John M ASHENHURST (American)

Citation Record: 1 Book

The World's Fair Murders - *Only*
Houghton US (1933)

Scott BENNET

American Male Amateur operating in Chicago

Sidney MARSHALL (American)

Citation Record: 1 Book

Some Like It Hot - *Only*
Morrow US (1941)

Fred BENNETT

has been dismissed from the Los Angeles Police Department and is now an impoverished loner, working as an unlicensed detective. However, the city's cops still seek his aid in difficult or sensitive cases.

American Male Ex-Policeman operating in Los Angeles

Elliott LEWIS 1917-1990 (American)

Citation Record: 7 Books

Two Heads Are Better - *First*
Pinnacle US (1980)

Death And The Single Girl - *Last*
Pinnacle US (1983)

Hugh BENNETT

British Male Amateur operating in England

Julian SYMONS 1912-1994 (British)

Invented 11 detectives - see Insp CRAMBO

Citation Record: 1 Book

The Progress Of A Crime - *Only*
Collins UK (1960); Harper & Row US (1960)

Jim BENNETT

runs the Cleveland branch of an agency called American-International Inc. Unlike the norm in private eyes, he is well-heeled, middle-class and unusually concerned in his approach to his cases.

American Male Private Detective operating in Ohio

Robert MARTIN 1908-1976 (American)

For writer details see Lee FISKE

Citation Record: 13 Books

Dark Dream - *First*
Dodd, Mead US (1951); Muller UK (1954)

Bargain For Death - *Last*
Hale UK (1964); Curtis US (1972)

Maggie BENNETT

American Female Sleuth

Anne STUART (American)

Writer: Anne Kristine Stuart OHLRAGGE

Inventor of one other detective Ferris BYRD

Citation Record: 3 Books

At The Edge Of The Sun - *First*
Dell US (1987)

Escape Out Of Darkness - *Latest*
Dell US (1987)

Ch of Plce Reid BENNETT

is a tall, tough, divorced, dark, handsome Canadian who was in the Vietnam War as a volunteer. Formerly in the Toronto police force, he was dismissed for preferring private to official justice. However, time heals and he is now Chief of Police and, indeed, the only policeman in the fictional town of Murphy's Harbour, Ontario.

Canadian Policeman operating in Canada

Sidekick: SAM

is a German Shepherd dog who is the constant companion of the detective – which is as well, for murder is highly prevalent in Murphy's Harbour. He may be just a dog but he plays such an important part in the books that he is billed with the detective in the blurb.

Male - Pet Dog

Ted WOOD 1931- (Canadian)

was born in England and educated at Hartlebury Grammar School, Worcestershire, 1941-1946. After serving in the Royal Air Force, 1949-1953, he emigrated to Canada, where he spent three years in the Toronto police force. He then worked in advertising and became a full-time writer in 1974.

Writer: Edward John WOOD

Other Byline: Jack BARNAO

Citation Record: 8 Books

Dead In The Water - *First*
Scribner's US (1983); Collins UK (1984)

Snowjob - *Latest*
US (1990)

Maj Robert BENNION

is in his thirties. His cases usually arise through his involvement with a group of young people who interact with the plot in some way. There is often a cricket or golf background to the books, for the author was a keen sportsman. *Robert BENNION* cannot be regarded as one of the more intellectual detectives of the British Golden Age; indeed, his cases often tend to resolve themselves without his help. Besides which, he is often more chivalrous than ethical and sometimes less than honourable when it comes to strict adherence to the principles of law and justice. At some point in his long career he marries the chief suspect; and, in the later novels, written during the war years, he works for the British Intelligence Service.

British Male Amateur operating in England

Herbert ADAMS 1874-1958 (British)

Invented 3 detectives - see Jimmie HASWELL

Citation Record: 26 Books

Death Off The Fairway - *First*
Collins UK (1936)

B

Death Of A Viewer - *Last*
Macdonald UK (1958)

Const BENSKIN

British Policeman operating in England

E Phillips OPPENHEIM 1866-1946 (British)
Invented 27 detectives - see Nicholas GOADE
Citation Record: 12 Short Stories in 1 Collection
The Human Chase - *Collection 1*
Hodder & Stoughton UK (1929); Little, Brown US (1932)

Big Bull BENSON

is black, owns a Chicago hotel and does part-time detective work.

American Male Private Detective operating in Chicago

Percy Spurlark PARKER 1940- (American)
Citation Record: 1 Book
Good Girls Don't Get Murdered - *Only*
Scribner's US (1974)

Richard Henry (The Avenger) BENSON

was a late arrival in the seemingly unending sequence of American superman detectives. A small man, he makes up for his lack of stature by being, not only a billionaire, but extremely athletic into the bargain. Of supernormal intelligence, he is probably the most skilled man on the planet, there being nothing he does not know about medicine, science and engineering. Since his wife and daughter were killed by criminals, he quite understandably devotes his life to hunting down such nasty types. Armed with a gun he calls Mike and a knife he calls Ike, he patrols the underworld with the help of six loyal assistants.

American Male Amateur operating in USA/Europe

Kenneth ROBESON 1886- (American)
For writer details see Lt Jim RYAN
Citation Record: 24 Books
Stockholders In Death - *First*
Paperback Library US (1972)
Midnight Murder - *Last*
Paperback Library US (1974)

Kenneth ROBESON 1933- (American)
For writer details see Jake PACE and Hildy PACE
Citation Record: 12 Books
The Purple Zombie - *First*
Paperback Library US (1974)
Demon Island- *Last*
Paperback Library US (1975)

Dr John BENT

is a physician, although he practises hardly at all. Instead he drifts into detective work when, in his first book, he tries to find out who is poisoning a patient. He is low-key, drinks a lot of bourbon, and seems observant and able.

American Male Amateur operating in New York

H Clay BRANSON 1924- (American)
was born in Battle Creek, Michigan. He was educated at Princeton University, New Jersey, in the 1920s and took a BA at the University of Michigan, Ann Arbor, 1937.
Writer: Henry Clay BRANSON
Citation Record: 7 Books
I'll Eat You Last - *First*
Simon & Schuster US (1941); Lane UK (1943)
Beggar's Choice - *Last*
Simon & Schuster US (1953)

Dr BENTIRON

was one of the less successful attempts to produce an American *Sherlock HOLMES*. It transpired that having the detective wearing a green bathrobe and smoking endlessly in a mechanical easy chair was hardly good enough to last through more than one novel and a few short stories.

American Male Amateur operating in New York

Ernest M POATE (American)
Citation Record: 1 Book 3 Short Stories in 1 Collection
Behind Locked Doors - *Only*
Chelsea US (1923)
Doctor Bentiron: Detective - *Collection 1*
contains three novelettes.
Chelsea US (1930)

Steve BENTLEY

is a Washington accountant who does private investigating in the course of his work.

American Male Professional Investigator operating in Washington DC/Nassau

Robert DIETRICH 1918- (American)
For writer details see Jack NOVAK
Citation Record: 8 Books
Murder On The Rocks - *First*
Dell US (1957); Ward, Lock UK (1958)
My Body - *Last*
was republished under the following byline.
Lancer US (1962)

E Howard HUNT 1918- (American)
Invented 3 detectives - see Jack NOVAK
Citation Record: 1 Book
My Body - *Single*
was previously republished under the preceding byline.
Lancer US (1962)

Det George BENTON

works, as do others, in the terrible 'Precinct Siberia'. Known as 'The Bent One', he is a hypochondriac, but he is also a brilliant detective who has spent his life studying sex-killers.

American Policeman operating in New York

Tom PHILBIN (American)
Inventor of one other detective group Det Joe LAWLESS, Offr Barbara BABALINO and Det Leo GRADY
Citation Record: 1 Book
A Matter Of Degree - *Single*
GM US (1987); Sphere Books UK (1990)

May BERESFORD

British Female Amateur operating in London

Cecil H BULLIVANT 1882- (British)
Invented 5 detectives - see Garnett BELL
Citation Record: 16 Short Stories in 1 Collection
May Beresford, Typist - *Collection 1*
Lloyd UK (1917)

Michael BERESFORD

Australian Male Sleuth operating in Australia

Leon LE GRAND 1940- (Australian)
Citation Record: 3 Books
The Von Kessel Dossier - *First*
Fontana AU (1985); Critic US (1987)
The Whittington Pact - *Latest*
Collins AU (1988)

Tommy BERESFORD and Tuppence BERESFORD

are, in the slang of the time, rather 'dizzy'. A young husband and wife, they start their detective careers by placing an advert in a newspaper. Their books are more thrillers than effective detective stories, but the author liked these two characters enough to return to them on and off throughout her writing career.

British Male Amateur and British Female Amateur operating in England

Agatha CHRISTIE 1890-1976 (British)
Invented 18 detectives - see Hercule POIROT

B

Citation Record: 4 Books

The Secret Adversary - *First*
Lane UK (1922); Dodd, Mead US (1922)

Postern Of Fate - *Last*
Collins UK (1973); Dodd, Mead US (1973)

Tuppence BERESFORD

Second detective of Tommy BERESFORD

BERGERAC

appears in novelizations based on a long-running British TV series.

British Policeman operating in Jersey, Channel Islands

Michael HARDWICK 1924-1991 (British)

Invented 3 detectives - see Dr John H WATSON

Citation Record: 1 Book

Bergerac - *First*
BBC UK (1981); St Martin's US (1982)

Andrew SAVILLE (British)

Writer: UNKNOWN

Citation Record: 2 Books

Bergerac Is Back - *First*
Severn UK (1985)

Crimes Of The Season - *Latest*
Panther UK (1985)

George Stanhope BERKLEY

appears also in one book with another of the author's detectives, *Sir James ERSKINE.*

British Male Amateur operating in England

Laurence MEYNELL 1899-1989 (British)

Invented 5 detectives - see Hooky HEFFERMAN

Citation Record: 1 Book

Odds On Bluefeather - *Only*
Harrap UK (1934); Lippincott US (1935)

George Stanhope BERKLEY

Second detective of Sir James ERSKINE

Supt Luis BERNAL

is a policeman in Spain who meets crimes that usually have a political basis. He is middle-aged, paunchy, fond of good living, and has a loving mistress. However, his life is often made unbearable by his religious wife, Eugenia.

Spanish Policeman operating in Spain

David SERAFIN (British)

Writer: Ian MICHAEL

Citation Record: 6 Books

Saturday Of Glory - *First*
Collins UK (1979)

The Angel Of Torremolinos - *Latest*
Macmillan UK (1988)

Paul BERNARD

American Male Amateur operating in USA

Sinclair GLUCK 1887- (American)

Invented 3 detectives - see Jack CLAYTON

Citation Record: 2 Books

The Last Trap - *First*
Dodd, Mead US (1928); Mills UK (1928)

Shadow In The House - *Last*
Dodd, Mead US (1929)

Death Comes To Dinner - *Last**
Mills UK (1929)

Alan BERNHARDT

is an actor-producer who is moonlighting as a PI for Dancer Ltd, an agency run by the ruthless Hubert Dancer.

American Male Private Detective operating in San Francisco

Collin WILCOX 1924- (American)

Invented 4 detectives - see Lt Frank HASTINGS

Citation Record: 5 Books

Bernhardt's Edge - *First*
Tor US (1988)

Full Circle - *Latest*
Tom Doherty Associates US (1994)

Insp BERNSTEIN

American Policeman operating in USA

Elsa LEWIN (American)

Citation Record: 1 Book

I, Anna - *Single*
Otto Penzler US (1985)

Tommy BERREN

Male Amateur operating in India

Paul ROADARMEL 1942

Citation Record: 1 Book

The Kaligarh Fault - *Single*
Harper & Row US (1979)

BERYL

British Female Amateur operating in England

William LEQUEUX 1864-1927 (British)

Invented 23 detectives - see Allan KENNEDY

Citation Record: 6 Short Stories in 1 Collection

Beryl Of The Biplane - *Collection 1*
Pearson UK (1917)

Gen BESSERLEY

British Male Amateur operating in England

E Phillips OPPENHEIM 1866-1946 (British)

Invented 27 detectives - see Nicholas GOADE

Citation Record: 21 Short Stories in 2 Collections

General Besserley's Puzzle Box - *Collection 1*
Short stories - 9
Hodder & Stoughton UK (1935); Little, Brown US (1935)

General Besserley's Second Puzzle Box - *Collection 2*
Short stories - 12
Hodder & Stoughton UK (1939); Little, Brown US (1940)

Petunia BEST and Max FREUND

British Female Private Detective and British Male Private Detective operating in England

Bridget CHETWYND (British)

Citation Record: 2 Books

Death Has Ten Thousand Doors - *First*
Hutchinson UK (1951)

Rubies, Emeralds And Diamonds - *Last*
Hutchinson UK (1952)

Tom BETHANY

is a Vietnam War veteran who, although formerly a wrestler, is now a PI ready to take on only liberal or left-wing causes. A modern super-hero, he defends the environment, endangered species, oppressed women and minority groups against the machinations of FBI, the Mafiosi, Klansmen and Walt Disney.

American Male Private Detective operating in Boston

Jerome DOOLITTLE 1933- (American)

Writer: Jerome Hill DOOLITTLE

Citation Record: 5 Books
Hodder & Stoughton UK (1990); Pocket Books US (1991)

Half Nelson - *Latest*
Pocket Books US (1994)

Amadour BEVAN

is an antique dealer who turns sleuth.

British Male Amateur operating in England

Arthur HOUGHAM (British)

Citation Record: 1 Selected Short Story

The Night Of The Garter
appeared in an anthology, *Best Detective Stories.*
Faber UK (1929)

B

Jim BEVERLEY
British Male Amateur operating in England

Antony MARSDEN (British)

See main detective Insp BUCK

Citation Record: 2 Books

The Man In The Sandhills - *First*
Jarrolds UK (1927); Boni US (1927)

The Moonstone Mystery - *Last*
Jarrolds UK (1928)

Col Nur BEY
is a Turkish detective who investigates cases of smuggling, espionage and assassination involving British and other foreign visitors.
Turkish Policeman operating in Turkey

Julian RATHBONE 1935- (British)

was born in London. He was educated at Clayesmore School, Iwerne Minster, Dorset, and took a BA in English at Magdalene College, Cambridge, 1958. He was an English teacher in Turkey, 1959-1962.

Other Detectives:
Jan ARGAND John DANBY

Citation Record: 3 Books

Diamonds Bid - *First*
Joseph UK (1967); Walker US (1967)

Trip Trap - *Last*
Joseph UK (1972); St Martin's US (1972)

The BICYCLE DETECTIVE
was also known as Bicycle Jim.
American Male Detective in Pulp Magazines operating in USA

OLD SLEUTH (American)

Invented 40 detectives - see Brant ADAMS

Citation Record: 1 Book

Bicycle Jim - *Only*
Ogilvie US (1900)

Prof James Yates BIDDLE and Kay RITCHIE
When two men are found dead in the garden of *James BIDDLE*, Professor of Horticulture at Berkeley, he considers it his duty to find out whodunnit. In this socially admirable work he is assisted by *Kay RITCHIE*, a local reporter.
American Male Amateur and American Female Amateur operating in USA

Stooge: Insp Angus DRIFT
has a generally rather low opinion of professor-detectives and is far from pleased at their interference.
American Male

John MERSEREAU 1898- (American)

was born in Michigan. A successful writer for the movies, he wrote this one mystery novel.

Citation Record: 1 Book

Murder Loves Company - *Only*
Lippincott US (1940)

Insp BIDWELL
British Policeman operating in England

Sidekick: Sgt PRIMROSE
British Male - Subordinate

James ANDERSON 1936- (British)

Invented 5 detectives - see Insp WILKINS

Citation Record: 1 Book

Additional Evidence - *Single*
Doubleday US (1988)

Anthony BIGELOW
American Male Amateur operating in USA

Burton E STEVENSON 1872-1962 (American)

Writer: Burton Egbert STEVENSON

Inventor of one other detective Jim GODFREY

Citation Record: 1 Book

The Red Carnation - *Only*
Dodd, Mead US (1939); Cassell UK (1940)

BIGGERS
British Male Amateur operating in England

George STANLEY (British)

See main detective BLACK PILGRIM

Citation Record: 6 Short Stories in 1 Collection

Gangsters All - *Collection 1*
Mitre UK (1945)

Insp BIGGINS
investigates the murder of a village miser.
British Policeman operating in Wales

W BOORE 1904- (British)

Writer: Walter Hugh BOORE

Citation Record: 1 Book

The Valley And The Shadow - *Only*
Heinemann UK (1963)

'BIGGLES'
is one of the great creations of a special sub-genre – that combination of detective and adventure fiction for boys, which was so popular in Britain during the period between the two world wars and which, in fact, lasted well into the 1950s. James Bigglesworth, affectionately (and almost always) known as *'BIGGLES'*, holds a special place, as his adventures, rather than his detective skills were particularly appealing to the younger audience. He appeared first in short stories around 1934 and then in a novel published in 1935. He continued to appear in novels and countless other short stories until the publication of the seventy-ninth novel (there may be one or two more uncounted), in 1969, a year after the author's death.
Thirteen collections appeared during the author's lifetime, but there are several short stories that remain uncited. The particular appeal of *'BIGGLES'* was that, as a kind of non-cerebral *Sexton BLAKE*, he could apparently go anywhere, do anything, take part in any role in peace and, of course, in war. His adventures took him to all parts of the world; but he is particularly remembered for his activities as an early aviator, personifying the thrills of a generation for whom flying was the most magnificent of sports.
British Male Amateur operating in several locations

W E JOHNS 1893-1968 (British)

Writer: William Earl JOHNS

Other Detectives:
'Steeley' DELAROY Dr VANE

Citation Record: 79 Books 132 Short Stories in13 Collections

The Black Peril - *First*
Hamilton UK (1935)

Biggles And The Little Green God - *Last*
Brockhampton UK (1969)

"Biggles" Of The Camel Squadron - *Collection 1*
Short stories - 13
Brockhampton UK (1934)

Biggles Flies Again - *Collection 2*
Short stories - 13
Hamilton UK (1934)

Spitfire Parade - *Collection 3*
This collection, which includes some stories without *BIGGLES*, was published at the height of the air war over Britain during the Second World War and could not resist the appeal of the magnificent Spitfire aeroplane or placing *BIGGLES* in the thick of the fighting. The stories with *BIGGLES*, because of a degree of uncertainty, are not included in the total number cited.
Oxford UK (1941)

Biggles - Charter Pilot - *Collection 4*
Short stories - 16
Oxford UK (1943)

B

Biggles - Air Detective - *Collection 5*
Short stories - 7
Marks UK (1950)

Biggles Takes The Case - *Collection 6*
Short stories - 9
Hodder & Stoughton UK (1952)

Biggles Of The Special Air Police - *Collection 7*
Short stories - 14
Thames UK (1953)

Biggles And The Pirate Treasure, And Other Biggles Adventures - *Collection 8*
Short stories - 11
Brockhampton UK (1954)

Biggles' Chinese Puzzle - *Collection 9*
Short stories - 8
Brockhampton UK (1955)

Biggles Of The Interpol - *Collection 10*
Short stories - 11
Brockhampton UK (1957)

Biggles Presses On - *Collection 11*
Short stories - 11
Brockhampton UK (1958)

Biggles Flies To Work - *Collection 12*
Short stories - 11
Dean UK (1963)

Biggles Investigates - *Collection 13*
Short stories - 8
Brockhampton UK (1964)

Hamilton BIGGS

is a one-off spoof by the author, not under his usual pseudonym.

British Male Amateur operating in England

Shaun Lloyd MCCARTHY 1928- (British)

For writer details see Johnny FEDORA

Citation Record: 1 Book

Lucky Ham - *Only*
Macmillan UK (1977)

Commissaire Orestes BIGNON

French Policeman operating in Paris

Francis DIDELOT 1902- (French)

See main detective Insp LECAIN

Citation Record: 4 Books

The Tenth Leper - *First*
is a translation from the French of *Fer sur le Mage!* (Paris, 1956).
Macdonald UK (1962)

The Many Ways Of Death - *Last*
is a translation from the French of *Six Heures d'Anguisse* (Paris, 1955).
Belmont US (1966)

Gus BILINSKI

Second detective of Henrietta SNOOKS

Samuel T BILLINGHAM

British Male Amateur operating in France

E Phillips OPPENHEIM 1866-1946 (British)

Invented 27 detectives - see Nicholas GOADE

Citation Record: 10 Short Stories in 1 Collection

Mr Billingham, The Marquis And Madelon - *Collection 1*
Hodder & Stoughton UK (1927); Little, Brown US (1929)

Joshua BILLINGS

appears in a collection of adventure stories, some of which are criminous.

British Male Amateur operating in England

TAFFRAIL 1883-1968 (British)

Writer: Henry Taprell DORLING

Citation Record: 17 Short Stories in 1 Collection

"Oh, Joshua!" - *Collection 1*
Hodder & Stoughton UK (1920)

BILLY THE PAGE

is a young boy detective, clearly based on one of the street arabs used by *Sherlock HOLMES.* The character was given some importance in the famous American play (qv) by *William GILLETTE.*

British Male Amateur operating in London

Willoughby LANE (American)

Adopter of one other detective Sherlock HOLMES

Citation Record: 6 Short Stories in 1 Collection

The Exploits Of Billy The Page - *Collection 1*
Magico Press US (1986)

Joe BINNEY

is an ex-Navy diver, deafened by an explosion. He sets up as a PI, a profession in which his acquired acuteness at lip-reading is useful and is made much of.

American Male Private Detective operating in New York/Virginia

Jack LIVINGSTON (American)

Citation Record: 4 Books

A Piece Of The Silence - *First*
St Martin's US (1982); Hale UK (1983)

Hell-Bent For Election - *Latest*
St Martin's US (1988)

Hell-Bent For Homicide - *Latest**
Signet US (1991)

Margaret BINTON

is an elderly lady who, in her first book, is precipitated into solving a nasty case of professional murder. She finds sleuthing more interesting than sitting at home knitting and continues with it, receiving help in later books from her friends, The Rag Bag Clan.

American Female Amateur operating in New York

Richard BARTH 1943- (American)

See main detective Jacob BARZENY

Citation Record: 7 Books

The Rag Bag Clan - *First*
Dial US (1978); Gollancz UK (1979)

Deadly Climate - *Latest*
St Martin's US (1988); Thorndike UK (1989)

Jefferson BIRCH

is, although recently created, a detective in the Old West.

American Male Private Detective operating in USA (Old West)

W W LEE (American)

Writer: Wendi LEE

Citation Record: 2 Books

Rogue's Gold - *First*
Walker US (1989)

Rustler's Venom - *Latest*
Walker US (1990)

Miriam BIRDSEYE

is a rare invention; for, not only is she an interesting sleuth and a well-drawn and exciting character, but she appears in books that are successfully comic. A perfect period piece, typical of the numerous female bright (one used always to call them gay) young things who appeared in the 1940s and 1950s, she seems to be around forty and to have been a revue actress with an exciting, although unrevealed, past. She is the owner of an extraordinary detective agency called Birdseye et Cie, which she runs with the occasional help of her friend, *Natasha NEVKORINA.* Her only declared aim, she says, is 'to banish tedium and boredom', which she certainly does.

Miriam BIRDSEYE appears, not only in the four books cited, but also in two others with *Johnny DUVIVIEN*, who used to be

B

married to *NEVKORINA*, as a colleague in detection. The mad whirls of the books deliciously, if now somewhat boringly, echo the life and era of the author. Some have been reissued.

British Female Amateur operating in England

Sidekick: Natasha NEVKORINA

is a beautiful, lesbian ex-ballerina, who once worked for Diaghilev. Russian, of course, and with wonderfully comic diction, she is at once both dotty and appealing, an unlikely but valuable sidekick.

Russian Female - Assistant

Nancy SPAIN 1917-1964 (British)

was born in Newcastle, Tyneside. She was educated at Roedean School, Sussex, and served in the Women's Royal Navy Service, 1939-1945. She was a journalist, editor, early feminist ideologue and the author of some detective stories, books for children, and a cookbook. The 'modern woman incarnate' of the post-war world, she was killed – naturally, she would have said – in an aircraft crash, while travelling with a close woman friend to a race meeting.

Writer: Nancy Brooker SPAIN

Other Detectives:
Miriam BIRDSEYE and Johnny DUVIVIEN
Johnny DUVIVIEN

Citation Record: 4 Books

Cinderella Goes To The Morgue - *First*
Hutchinson UK (1950)

Minutes To Midnight - *First**
Duckworth UK (1978)

Out, Damned Tot! - *Last*
Duckworth UK (1952)

Miriam BIRDSEYE and Johnny DUVIVIEN

British Female Amateur and British Male Amateur operating in England

Nancy SPAIN 1917-1964 (British)

Invented 3 detectives - see Miriam BIRDSEYE

Citation Record: 2 Books

Death Goes On Skis - *First*
Hutchinson UK (1949)

Poison For Teacher - *Last*
Hutchinson UK (1949)

Verity 'Birdie' BIRDWOOD

Australian Female Amateur operating in Australia

Jennifer ROWE 1948- (Australian)

Citation Record: 2 Books 8 Short Stories in 1 Collection

Grim Pickings - *First*
Allen AU (1987); Century UK (1988); Bantam US (1991)

Murder By The Book - *Latest*
Allen AU (1989); Bantam US (1992)

Death In Store - *Collection 1*
Bantam US (1994)

Sam BIRGE

American Male Amateur operating in USA

William KRASNER 1917- (American)

Citation Record: 6 Books

Walk The Dark Streets - *First*
Harper & Row US (1949); Corgi UK (1952)

Death Of A Minor Poet - *Latest*
Scribner's US (1984); Chivers UK (1985)

Ch Insp Sam BIRKETT

is an amusing, self-parodying but highly logical copper, given to verbal pyrotechnics and satirical comment on a certain earlier detective who lived in Baker Street. He appears also in one book with another of the author's detectives, *Mark SAVAGE*.

British Policeman operating in London

Sidekick: Sgt SAUNDERS

British Male - Subordinate

Laurence PAYNE 1919- (British)

Invented 4 detectives - see Mark SAVAGE and Ch Insp Sam BIRKETT

Citation Record: 3 Books

The Nose On My Face - *First*
Hodder & Stoughton UK (1961); Macmillan US (1962)

The First Body - *First**
Avon US (1964)

Deep And Crisp And Even - *Last*
Hodder & Stoughton UK (1964)

Ch Insp Sam BIRKETT

Second detective of Mark SAVAGE

Arthur 'Turo' BIRONICO

is hired to investigate the smuggling of Mexican antiques *into* a museum.

American Male Private Detective operating in San Francisco

William L RIVERA (American)

Citation Record: 1 Book

Panic Walks Alone - *Only*
Major US (1976)

Mr BIRTLEY

British Male Amateur operating in England

Cyril A ALINGTON 1872-1955 (British)

See main detective pair John CRAGGS and James CASTLETON

Citation Record: 1 Book

Midnight Wireless - *Single*
Macdonald UK (1947)

Anton BIRUKOV

Male Amateur operating in USA

Mikhail CHERNYONOK

Citation Record: 1 Book

Losing Bet - *Single*
Doubleday US (1984)

Adrienne BISHOP

American Female Amateur operating in USA

Jan ELLERY (American)

Citation Record: 2 Books

The Last Set - *First*
Zebra US (1979)

High Strung - *Latest*
Zebra US (1980)

Prof Harry BISHOP

is the Professor of Political Science at the fictional John Jacob Astor College. He is a plain, dull, graying black sheep who investigates when academic murder occurs.

American Male Amateur operating in Oregon

Conrad HAYNES (American)

Citation Record: 2 Books

Bishop's Gambit - *First*
Bantam US (1987); Severn UK (1990)

Perpetual Check - *Latest*
Bantam US (1988)

Sacrifice Play - *Latest**
Severn UK (1990)

Hugo BISHOP

British Male Amateur operating in England

Simon RATTRAY 1920- (British)

For writer details see Richard VANESS

Citation Record: 6 Books

Knight Sinister - *First*
Boardman UK (1951); Pyramid US (1971)

Dead Sequence - *Last*
Boardman UK (1957)

Paul BISHOP

is an investigator called in to solve a difficult problem at a trial when the judge is incapacitated.

British Male Private Detective operating in England

B

J Jefferson FARJEON 1883-1955 (British)
was the son of the writer, *Benjamin Leopold FARJEON,* and the author of at least seventy criminous works, mostly thrillers, as well as short stories.
Writer: Joseph Jefferson FARJEON
Other Detectives:
BEN THE TRAMP   Insp KENDALL
Citation Record: 1 Book
The Judge Sums Up - *Only*
Collins UK (1942); Bobbs US (1942)

Robin BISHOP
is an alcoholic newspaperman who joins a shady agency and gets into cases in rural California. He appears in one other book with the author's other detective, *Humphrey CAMPBELL.*
American Male Private Detective operating in California

Geoffrey HOMES 1902-1978 (American)
was born in Dunlap, California. He was educated at Fresno State College, California, and then had a variety of jobs before becoming a journalist on a newspaper in San Francisco. He was later, in addition to being a writer of crime novels, a screenwriter and specialist in sound recording for Warner Brothers.
Writer: David MAINWARING
Other Detectives:
Red BAILEY   Humphrey CAMPBELL
Humphrey CAMPBELL and Robin BISHOP
Jose Manuel MADERO
Citation Record: 4 Books
The Doctor Died At Dusk - *First*
Morrow US (1936)
The Man Who Murdered Goliath - *Last*
Morrow US (1938); Eyre & Spottiswoode UK (1940)

Robin BISHOP
Second detective of Humphrey CAMPBELL

Shauna BISHOP
American Female Sleuth operating in USA

J J MONTAGUE (American)
Writer: James KEENAN
Citation Record: 4 Books
The Chinese Kiss - *First*
Canyon US (1974)
The Judas Kiss - *Last*
Canyon US (1975)

Max BITTERSOHN
is a specialist on art theft who not only marries another of the author's detectives, *Sarah KELLING,* but sleuths with her in other books. She makes brief appearances in the two books in which he is the main detective.
American Male Amateur operating in Boston

Charlotte MACLEOD 1922- (Canadian)
Invented 3 detectives - see Sarah KELLING and Max BITTERSOHN
Citation Record: 2 Books
The Withdrawing Room - *First*
Doubleday US (1980)
The Convivial Codfish - *Latest*
Doubleday US (1984)

Max BITTERSOHN
Second detective of Sarah KELLING

Calvin BIX
was formerly a policeman. Now a PI in Chicago, he seems to have none of the moral code of his fictional predecessors in that great city, working strictly for the loot.
American Male Private Detective operating in Chicago

Arthur MALING 1923- (American)
Invented 3 detectives - see Brockton POTTER
Citation Record: 1 Book
Lover And Thief - *Single*
Harper US (1988); Thorndike UK (1990)

BIZZY-QUIZZY
American Male Sleuth operating in USA

William Rushton BOWKER (American)
Citation Record: 8 Short Stories in 1 Collection
Bizzy-Quizzy The Great - *Collection 1*
Coronado US (1942)

BLACK
American Male Amateur operating in USA

Will MANSON
House name.
Citation Record: 4 Books
A Man Called Black - *First*
Caravelle US (1967)
A Very Black Deed - *Last*
Caravelle US (1968)

BLACK
American Male Sleuth operating in USA

Joseph NAZEL 1944- (American)
See main detective Henry Highland (Iceman) WEST
Citation Record: 2 Books
My Name Is Black! - *First*
Holloway US (1973)
Black Is Black - *Last*
Holloway US (1974)

Capt BLACK
British Male Sleuth operating in England

Max PEMBERTON 1863-1950 (British)
Invented 4 detectives - see Bernard SUTTON
Citation Record: 2 Books
The Iron Pirate: A Plain Tale Of Strange Happenings At Sea - *First*
Cassell UK (1893); Rand US (1897)
Captain Black - *Last*
Cassell UK (1911); Doran US (1911)

Col BLACK
Second detective of Peter COFFIN

Insp BLACK
British Policeman operating in London

UNKNOWN
Citation Record: 1 Collection
Scotland Yard Photo Crimes - *Collection 1*
UK (?)

Supt BLACK
appears in books with other detectives of this author.
British Policeman operating in England

John Newton CHANCE 1911-1983 (British)
Invented 8 detectives - see John Newton CHANCE
Citation Record: 1 Book
The Ghost Of Truth - *Only*
Gollancz UK (1939)

Supt BLACK
Second detective of Mr DeHAVILLAND

Alex BLACK
is a newspaper columnist on scientific matters who investigates the death of a swimmer, supposedly caused by a jellyfish sting. His computer provides the clues.
Male Amateur operating in Bermuda

Art SPIKOL 1936- (American)
Citation Record: 1 Book

The Physalia Incident - *Single*
Viking US (1988)

Johnny BLACK

runs the Black Eye Detective Agency in the seaside town of Torquay in Devon.

British Male Private Detective operating in Torquay

Neville STEED (British)

See main detective Peter MARKLIN

Citation Record: 2 Books

Black Eye - *First*
Weidenfeld & Nicolson UK (1989); St Martin's US (1990)

Black Mail - *Latest*
Weidenfeld & Nicolson UK (1990)

Ch Insp Jonathan BLACK

British Policeman operating in England

Roger GARNETT 1905-1986 (British)

For writer details see Mrs Palmyra Evangeline PYM

Other Detectives:
R I PERKINS
John YARDLEY
John YARDLEY and R I PERKINS

Citation Record: 4 Books

Death In Piccadilly - *First*
Wright & Brown UK (1937)

A Man Died Talking - *Last*
Wright & Brown UK (1943)

Maria BLACK

is often called 'Black Maria' by her pupils. An elderly schoolmistress in charge of a college for young ladies, she has a weakness for watching crime films and is led on to solve crimes, even including murder, committed around or by her charges. Often spurning modern forensic methods, she may even shame her suspect into a confession. In her first book she goes to the USA where she encounters the sidekick who, more or less, accompanies her in her later cases. In her second book, she has to deal with a really difficult police stooge.

British Female Amateur operating in several locations

Sidekick: 'Pulp' MARTIN
is a gentlemanly tough from the Bowery, encountered by the detective during her first case. A flamboyantly vulgar character, he stays on to protect her from the indignities she might otherwise suffer in her self-imposed tasks.

American Male - Bodyguard

Stooge: Insp 'Eyebrows' MORGAN
is so thick that he can only accentuate the detective's cleverness.

British Male

John SLATE 1908-1960

Writer: John Russell FEARN

Citation Record: 5 Books

Black Maria, MA - *First*
Rich & Cowan UK (1944)

Death In Silhouette - *Last*
Rich & Cowan UK (1950)

Reginald 'Beauty' BLACK

American Male Private Detective operating in New Jersey

Edward RONNS 1916-1975 (American)

See main detective Jerry BENEDICT

Citation Record: 1 Book

The Corpse Hangs High - *Only*
Phoenix Press US (1939)

Thomas BLACK

is an ex-cop who quit the police force after killing a young hoodlum. A bachelor of independent means, he is more interested in righting wrongs than in his fees. He abhors violence and, although he carries a gun, he will never use it. He rents an apartment to a lovely young woman, a novice attorney, with whom he has a close but celibate relationship, which he manages to continue through the series.

American Male Private Detective operating in Seattle

Sidekick: Kathy BIRCHFIELD
is a young attorney who, during her close relationship, with *BLACK* is instrumental in involving him in cases and sometimes helps to solve them. Although she romances others at times, he intends to keep her, even if it means proposing to her.

American Female - Friend

Earl W EMERSON 1948- (American)

was born in Tacoma, Washington. He graduated from the University of Washington, Seattle, 1968, and has been a lieutenant in the Seattle Fire Department from 1978.

Inventor of one other detective Sheriff (temp) Max FONTANA

Citation Record: 7 Books

The Rainy City - *First*
Avon US (1985)

The Portland Laugher - *Latest*
Morrow US (1994)

BLACK DOUGLASS

American Male Detective in Pulp Magazines operating in USA

Lieutenant CARLTON (American)

Invented 3 detectives - see Dan DECKER

Citation Record: 1 Selected Short Story

Black Douglass, The Jersey City Detective; Or, Tracing The Mystery Of A Great Crime
Old Cap Collier Library US (18??)

BLACK PILGRIM

British Male Amateur

George STANLEY (British)

Inventor of one other detective BIGGERS

Citation Record: 8 Short Stories in 2 Collections

The Adventures Of The Black Pilgrim - *Collection 1*
Short stories - 5
Modern Fiction UK (1945)

Further Adventures Of The Black Pilgrim - *Collection 2*
Short stories - 3
Modern Fiction UK (1945)

BLACK STAR

American Male Professional Investigator operating in USA

Johnston MCCULLEY 1883-1958 (American)

Invented 5 detectives - see John (The Thunderbolt) FLATCHLEY

Citation Record: 2 Books 4 Short Stories in 1 Collection

The Black Star - *First*
Chelsea US (1921); Hutchinson UK (1924)

Black Star's Return - *Last*
Chelsea US (1926); Hutchinson UK (1927)

Black Star's Revenge - *Collection 1*
contains four novelettes.
Chelsea US (19??)

Black Star Again - *Collection 1**
Hutchinson UK (1934)

The BLACK WIDOWERS

American Male Amateurs operating in USA

Isaac ASIMOV 1920-1992 (American)

Invented 6 detectives - see Elijah BALEY

Citation Record: 60 Short Stories in 5 Collections

Tales Of The Black Widowers - *Collection 1*
Short stories - 12
Doubleday US (1974); Gollancz UK (1975)

More Tales Of The Black Widowers - *Collection 2*
Short stories - 12
Doubleday US (1976); Gollancz UK (1976)

B

Casebook Of The Black Widowers - *Collection 3*
Short stories - 12
Doubleday US (1980); Gollancz UK (1980)

Banquets Of The Black Widowers - *Collection 4*
Short stories - 12
Doubleday US (1984); Granada UK (1985)

Puzzles Of The Black Widowers - *Collection 5*
Short stories - 12
Doubleday US (1990); Doubleday UK (1990)

Bobby BLACKBURN

solves a case of murder by stabbing in a locked room.
American Male Amateur operating in USA

Wadsworth CAMP 1879-1936 (American)
Writer: Charles Wadsworth CAMP
Other Detectives:
Insp GARTH   Arthur MCHUGH
Citation Record: 1 Book

The Abandoned Room - *Only*
Doubleday US (1917); Jarrolds UK (1919)

Jeffrey BLACKBURN

Second detective of Insp READ

Tim BLACKGROVE

British Male Sleuth operating in Antwerp

Ian MACKINTOSH 1940- (British)
Citation Record: 2 Books

A Slaying In September - *First*
Hale UK (1967)

A Drug Called Power - *Last*
Hale UK (1968)

Ian BLACKIE

investigates the death of a friend of his father, which he finds is linked to political skulduggery.
British Male Amateur operating in Scotland

Richard GRINDAL (British)
For writer details see John BRYANT
Citation Record: 1 Book

Over The Sea To Die - *First*
Macmillan UK (1989); St Martin's US (1990)

The Tartan Conspiracy - *Latest*
Macmillan UK (1992)

John BLACKMORE

British Male Amateur operating in several locations

Derwent STEELE 1896-1950 (British)
For writer details see Supt BUDD
Citation Record: 4 Books

The Avenger - *First*
Modern UK (1935)

The Poison Gang - *Last*
Modern UK (1937)

Paul BLACKSHEAR

investigates a case of attempted murder.
American Male Amateur operating in Los Angeles

Margaret MILLAR 1915- (Canadian)
Invented 11 detectives - see Insp SANDS
Citation Record: 1 Book

Beast In View - *Only*
Gollancz UK (1955); Random House US (1955)

BLACKSHIRT

is a delightful desperado in the long line of British gentleman-crook detectives, popular in the 1920s, 1930s and even into the 1940s. *BLACKSHIRT* is the sobriquet of one Richard Verrell, who was found on the streets as a boy and brought up by wealthy foster parents. He is a successful writer, but, for thrills, he dresses in black and takes to burglary, at which he is extremely efficient. Later, redeemed by the love of a woman, he robs the rich to help the deserving poor, detecting and handing out justice on the way. After being featured in dozens of short stories by *Bruce GRAEME*, he was re-worked by his son, *Roderic GRAEME* in later books, in which his morals were somewhat improved in accordance with changing tastes.
British Male Professional Amateur operating in England

Bruce GRAEME 1900-1982 (British)
was born in London and educated privately. A qualified lawyer, he was one of the founders of the Crime Writers Association, 1953. He wrote at least seventy-five genre books under this pseudonym but is perhaps best known for his many short stories featuring *BLACKSHIRT*. He adopted the *David GRAEME* byline for the publication of the series of books that feature the French counterpart of *BLACKSHIRT*.
Writer: Graham Montague JEFFRIES
Other Byline: David GRAEME
Other Detectives:
Lord Anthony BLACKSHIRT   Insp Auguste JANTRY
Det Sgt Robert MATHER
Supt William STEVENS and Insp Pierre ALLAIN
Theodore I TERHUNE
Citation Record: 16+ Short Stories in 10 Collections

Blackshirt - *Collection 1*
Short stories - 8
Unwin UK (1925); Dodd, Mead US (1925)

The Return Of Blackshirt - *Collection 2*
Short stories - 8
Unwin UK (1927); Dodd, Mead US (1927)

Blackshirt Again - *Collection 3*
Hutchinson UK (1929)

Adventures Of Blackshirt - *Collection 3**
Dodd, Mead US (1929)

Alias Blackshirt - *Collection 4*
Harrap UK (1932); Dodd, Mead US (1932)

Blackshirt The Audacious - *Collection 5*
Hutchinson UK (1935); Lippincott US (1936)

Blackshirt The Adventurer - *Collection 6*
Hutchinson UK (1936)

Blackshirt Takes A Hand - *Collection 7*
Hutchinson UK (1937)

Blackshirt, Counter-Spy - *Collection 8*
Hutchinson UK (1938)

Blackshirt Interferes - *Collection 9*
Hutchinson UK (1939)

Blackshirt Strikes Back - *Collection 10*
Hutchinson UK (1940)

Roderic GRAEME 1926- (British)
For writer details see Insp Enrique ALVAREZ
Citation Record: 20 Books

Concerning Blackshirt - *First*
Hutchinson UK (1952)

Blackshirt Stirs Thing Up - *Last*
Long UK (1969)

Monsieur BLACKSHIRT

is a supposed ancestor of the author's creation, *BLACKSHIRT*, operating in France during the seventeenth century. The stories, written under a slightly changed name, follow the pattern.
French Male Professional Amateur operating in France

David GRAEME 1900-1982 (British)
was the byline, with only a change of forename, chosen by the author for the publication of the series of books that feature the French counterpart of *BLACKSHIRT*.
For writer details see BLACKSHIRT
Citation Record: 4 Books

Monsieur Blackshirt - *First*
Harrap UK (1933); Lippincott US (1933)

The Inn Of Thirteen Swords - *Last*
Harrap UK (1938)

B

Lord Anthony BLACKSHIRT
is the son of *BLACKSHIRT*. He is elevated to the peerage, becomes *Lord BLACKSHIRT* and operates as a chip off the old block.
British Male Professional Amateur operating in England

Bruce GRAEME 1900-1982 (British)
Invented 6 detectives - see BLACKSHIRT
Citation Record: 3 Books
Son Of Blackshirt - *First*
Hutchinson UK (1941)
Calling Lord Blackshirt - *Last*
Hutchinson UK (1943)

Bow Street Runner Edmund BLACKSTONE
is one of this early force responsible for law and order during the early part of the nineteenth century. Although the settings are Victorian, he is very much an action-style cop, mixing it with every literary form of lowlife.
British Policeman operating in London

Richard FALKIRK 1929- (British)
was born in London. He was a journalist and foreign correspondent who wrote many genre novels, mainly thrillers, under his real name.
Writer: Derek William LAMBERT
Citation Record: 6 Books
Blackstone - *First*
Eyre & Spottiswoode UK (1972); Stein & Day US (1973)
Blackstone On Broadway - *Latest*
Eyre & Spottiswoode UK (1977)

Lincoln BLACKTHORNE
American Male Amateur operating in USA

Geoffrey MARSH (American)
Citation Record: 2 Books
The King Of Satan's Eyes - *First*
Doubleday US (1984)
The Fangs Of The Hooded Demon - *Latest*
Tor US (1988)

Riley BLACKWOOD
is a hotel detective.
American Male Amateur operating in USA

Vincent STARRETT 1886-1974 (American)
Invented 6 detectives - see Jimmie LAVENDER
Citation Record: 3 Books
The Great Hotel Murder - *First*
Doubleday US (1935); Nicholson & Watson UK (1935)
Murder In Peking - *Last*
Lantern Press US (1946); Edwards UK (1947)

Jud BLADE
American Male Sleuth operating in Oklahoma

Ken JACKSON (American)
Inventor of one other detective Nathan.NECESSARY
Citation Record: 2 Books
The Cutting Edge - *First*
Simon & Schuster US (1970)
The Sticking Point - *Last*
Simon & Schuster US (1971)

John BLAINE
is over six feet tall, weighs 220 lbs, and his body has the scars to show how he has lived. In his debut he is hired to find the drop-out son of a wealthy woman.
Irish Male Private Detective operating in Dublin

Vincent BANVILLE (Irish)
Citation Record: 1 Book
Death By Design - *Single*
Wolfhound EI (1993); No Exit Press US (1993)

Larry BLAINE
Second detective of Nora Hughes BLAINE

Nora Hughes BLAINE and Larry BLAINE
American Female Amateur and American Male Amateur operating in Connecticut

Lavinia R DAVIS 1909-1961 (American)
Writer: Lavinia Riker DAVIS
Citation Record: 2 Books
Evidence Unseen - *First*
Doubleday US (1945)
Taste Of Vengeance - *Last*
Doubleday US (1947)

Insp BLAIR
British Policeman operating in Scotland

M C BEATON 1936- (British)
Writer: Marion CHESNEY
Other Detectives:
Const Hamish MACBETH   Agatha RAISIN
Citation Record: 1 Book
Death Of A Gossip - *Single*
St Martin's US (1985)

Insp BLAIR
is a member of the CID in this Victorian novel.
British Policeman operating in London

Fergus HUME 1859-1932 (British)
Invented 24 detectives - see Insp Samuel GORBY
Citation Record: 1 Book
The Millionaire Mystery - *Only*
Chatto & Windus UK (1901); Buckles US (1901)

Elizabeth BLAIR and Max SHEPHERD
She is a widow from Virginia who runs a craft shop in the English town of Bath, in the West country. He is a private detective who lives upstairs. They investigate the death of a local lady in what could be the opening of a promising partnership.
American Female Amateur and British Male Amateur operating in Bath

Lisbie BROWN (British)
was born in Cornwall. A graduate of Sheffield University, she has written historical novels and short stories.
Citation Record: 1 Book
Turkey Tracks - *Single*
Constable UK (1995)

Gipsy BLAIR
was a typical character detective.
American Male Professional Investigator operating in USA

Judson R TAYLOR 1837-1898 (American)
Invented 4 detectives - see Phil SCOTT
Citation Record: 1 Book
Gipsy Blair, The Western Detective - *Only*
Ogilvie US (1882)

Margot BLAIR
is thirty-something and a partner in a public relations firm. She takes only female clients, who have the knack of involving her in cases of murder, blackmail and even espionage.
American Female Amateur operating in USA/Mexico

Kathleen Moore KNIGHT (American)
See main detective Elisha MACOMBER
Citation Record: 4 Books
Rendezvous With The Past - *First*
Doubleday US (1940); Withy Grove Press UK (1941)
Design In Diamonds - *Last*
Doubleday US (1944); Hammond UK (1945)

B

Mike BLAIR

appeared only in short stories, originally published during the 1930s in *Dime Detective* and now being collected.

American Male Private Detective operating in USA

Hank SEARLS 1922- (American)

Writer: Henry Hunt SEARLS

Citation Record: 7 Short Stories in 1 Collection

The Adventures Of Mike Blair - *Collection 1*
US (1988)

Nigel BLAIR

Second detective of Archibald BELDRUM

Maj Peter BLAIR

British Male Professional Investigator operating in several locations

J R L ANDERSON 1911-1981 (British)

See main detective Ch Const Piet DEVENTER

Citation Record: 8 Books

Death On The Rocks - *First*
Gollancz UK (1973); Stein US (1975)

Death In A High Latitude - *Latest*
Gollancz UK (1981)

Death In The High Latitude - *Latest**
Scribner's US (1984)

Robert BLAIR

is the lawyer who solves the mystery for his client, Marion Sharpe, in this well-known historical piece.

British Male Amateur operating in England

Josephine TEY 1897-1952 (British)

Invented 3 detectives - see Insp Alan GRANT

Citation Record: 1 Book

The Franchise Affair - *Only*
Davies UK (1948); Macmillan US (1949)

Ellis BLAISE

is a New York art dealer who goes to California to investigate art forgeries and is drawn into a case of murder, which he must solve.

American Male Amateur operating in California

Marco PAGE 1909-1968 (American)

Invented 3 detectives - see Joel GLASS

Citation Record: 1 Book

Reclining Figure - *Only*
Random House US (1952); Eyre & Spottiswoode UK (1952)

Modesty BLAISE

is a bizarre pop heroine who started life in a comic strip but graduated into books and short stories. Her later adventures have been published as graphic novels, which illuminate her physical rather than intellectual attributes. A far cry, one might safely say, from our own dear Loveday BROOKE.

British Female Professional Amateur operating in England

Peter O'DONNELL 1920- (British)

Citation Record: 20 Books 8 Short Stories in 2 Collections

Modesty Blaise - *First*
Souvenir UK (1965); Doubleday US (1965)

The Iron God - *Latest*
Titan UK (1989)

Pieces Of Modesty - *Collection 1*
Short stories - 6
Mysterious Press US (1972)

Uncle Happy - *Collection 2*
Short stories - 2
Mysterious Press US (1990)

Andy BLAKE

Second detective of Arab BLAKE

Arabella BLAKE and Andy BLAKE

American Female Amateur and American Male Amateur operating in Florida/Washington DC

Richard POWELL 1908- (American)

Writer: Richard Pitts POWELL

Citation Record: 5 Books

Don't Catch Me - *First*
Simon & Schuster US (1943); Hodder & Stoughton UK (1949)

The Case Of The Curious Chair - *First**
Handi-Books US (1944)

And Hope To Die - *Last*
Simon & Schuster US (1947); Hodder & Stoughton UK (1950)

Arthur 'Red' BLAKE and Dan WHEELER

American Male Private Detectives operating in Los Angeles

Edward LEE 1902- (American)

Writer: Edward Lee FOUTS

Citation Record: 2 Books

The Needle's Eye - *First*
Doubleday US (1941)

A Fish For Murder - *Last*
Doubleday US (1944); Hurst UK (1947)

Death Goes Fishing - *Last**
Abridged.
Thriller Novel Classics US (1944)

Lust To Kill - *Last**
Jonathan US (1955)

Glenda BLAKE

works for MI5 and investigates Nazi agents in wartime London.

British Female Secret Agent operating in several locations

Kathleen HEWITT 1893- (British)

Writer: Kathleen Douglas HEWITT

Citation Record: 1 Book

The Mice Are Not Amused - *Only*
Jarrolds UK (1942)

Hannah BLAKE

American Female Amateur operating in USA

Dorothy Salisbury DAVIS 1916- (American)

Invented 9 detectives - see Kate OSBORN

Citation Record: 1 Book

A Town Of Masks - *Only*
Scribner's US (1952)

Jacob C 'Jake' BLAKE

is shady and seedy and operates from a room in a hotel. In his one case, he has to protect the lovely but unstable wife of a prominent man about town, with dire consequences to himself.

American Male Private Detective operating in San Francisco

Charles WILLEFORD 1919-1988 (American)

See main detective Sgt Hoke MOSELEY

Citation Record: 1 Book

Wild Wives - *Only*
Beacon US (1956); Gollancz UK (1990)

Jana BLAKE

is not just a female PI but an ardent feminist to boot, so that she advertises her services 'for women only'. Not that she is against men. No mean looker herself, she is said to wear little under that trenchcoat.

American Female Private Detective operating in New York

Jim C CONAWAY (American)

Citation Record: 2 Books

Deadlier Than The Male - *First*
Belmont US (1977)

They Do It With Mirrors - *Latest*
Belmont US (1977)

Jim BLAKE

is, in the New Orleans of 1912, a reporter for *Harpers Weekly*. He investigates a case of murder and solves it.

American Male Amateur operating in New Orleans

B

John Dickson CARR 1906-1977 (American)

Invented 16 detectives - see Dr Gideon FELL

Citation Record: 1 Book

The Ghosts' High Noon - *Only*
Harper & Row US (1969); Hamilton UK (1970)

Jonathan BLAKE

is, in a long series, a pale shadow of the well-known *James BOND.*

British Male Secret Agent operating in several locations

John Newton CHANCE 1911-1983 (British)

Invented 8 detectives - see John Newton CHANCE

Citation Record: 33 Books

The Affair At Dead End - *First*
Hale UK (1966)

Hill Fog - *Last*
Hale UK (1975)

Kevin BLAKE

American Male Sleuth operating in Minnesota

Carole Nelson DOUGLAS 1944- (American)

Invented 3 detectives - see Irene ADLER

Citation Record: 2 Books

Probe - *First*
Tor US (1985)

Counterprobe - *Latest*
Tor US (1990)

Marty BLAKE

is down on his luck with no cases in hand. He is suddenly hired by a criminal lawyer to prove that a retarded man, who has pleaded guilty to murdering a woman, is innocent. He takes on an assistant to help in what becomes a dangerous game.

American Male Private Detective operating in USA

Sidekick: Sgt Bell KOSINSKI
is a misfit who, like *BLAKE*, is prepared to help in undoing a frame-up.

American Male - Assistant

Stephen SOLOMITA 1943- (American)

See main detective Stanley MOODROW

Citation Record: 1 Book

Last Chance For Glory - *Single*
Otto Penzler US (1994)

Richard BLAKE

investigates a suspicious death during a filming on set.

American Male Amateur operating in USA

Jonathan LATIMER 1906-1983 (American)

Invented 4 detectives - see Sam CLAY

Citation Record: 1 Book

Black Is The Fashion For Dying - *Only*
Random House US (1959)

The Mink-Lined Coffin - *Only**
Methuen UK (1960)

Sewell BLAKE

American Male Amateur operating in USA

Mignon G EBERHART 1899- (American)

Invented 9 detectives - see Sarah KEATE

Citation Record: 1 Book

Dead Men's Plays - *Only*
Random House US (1952); Collins UK (1953)

Sexton BLAKE

has been called the office-boy's *Sherlock HOLMES.* Aside from the latter detective, he has probably had more words written about him and appeared in more novels, more stories and, perhaps, even more translations, than any other detective in the whole criminous literature. He has been used as a detective by at least a hundred known authors (mostly British and many of them well-known authors outside the genre), as well as countless anonymous ones. He appeared first in a story in 1893 and was, at first, a blatant attempt to cash in on the *Sherlock HOLMES* phenomenon: certainly he was to prove the most successful. The story was *The Missing Millionaire* and it appeared in a magazine called *The Marvel*, published by Alfred Harmsworth, who was then establishing himself as the king of British popular publishing.

In the illustrations of the time, *BLAKE* was at first depicted as a typical Victorian gentleman, who operates from New Inn Chambers. He was, indeed, at that time shown as being in partnership with a French investigator, Jules Gervaise, the Gallic connection then being considered a distinction. The author of the first story was given as Hal Meredith, which was perhaps the pseudonym of Harry Blyth. In 1894, the rival publication, *Union Jack*, selling at a halfpenny, secured *BLAKE* and made him the most famous of all boys' detectives for many years thereafter, the first story in that magazine being *The Silver Arrow*. *BLAKE* was moved to Baker Street, following *HOLMES*, and given a housekeeper called Mrs Bardell to rival Mrs Hudson.

He had several assistants during his first years, including We-Wee, a Chinese boy, a waif called Griff and Wallace Lorrimer. However in 1904 he took on his famous assistant, *TINKER* (Edward Carter), a young man who admired and adored him for the next fifty years or so. The pair then settled down to fight every criminal, of every race known to literature, through two world wars and in every country of the globe.

In 1933, *Union Jack* became *Detective Weekly* and the stories continued until the magazine closed in 1940. But the detective had his own magazine, *The Sexton Blake Library*, which itself ran for nearly fifty years until it too closed in 1963. For a period *BLAKE* had a sort of female assistant called *Roxane HARFIELD*, who later operated on her own and is cited. He also sometimes worked with his lesser rival among the great British boys' detectives, *Nelson LEE*. One of his last adventures seems to have been *Company of Bandits*, written in 1972 by the English mainstream novelist, *Jack Trevor STOREY*.

British Male Professional Amateur operating in England

Sidekick: TINKER
was taken off the streets to become the most famous of all the boy assistants to the great *Sexton BLAKE*. They worked together in hundreds of short stories and novels.

British Male - Assistant

E W ALAIS 1864-1922 (British)

Writer: Ernest W ALAIS

Citation Record: 9 Books

A Case Of Blackmail - *First*
Amalgamated UK (1917)

In The Shadow Of Night - *Last*
Amalgamated UK (1922)

R C ARMOUR (Australian)

Writer: R Coutts ARMOUR

Other Byline: Coutts BRISBANE

Citation Record: 47 Books

Through Fire And Water - *First*
Amalgamated UK (1921)

The Masked Raiders - *Last*
Amalgamated UK (1930)

W Howard BAKER 1925-1991 (British)

See main detective Richard QUINTAIN

Citation Record: 20 Books

The Man Who Knew Too Much - *First*
Amalgamated UK (1955)

Treason Remembered - *Last*
Mayflower UK (1967)

B

W A BALLINGER 1925-1991 (British)
House name.
Citation Record: 2 Books
The Strange Face Of Murder - *First*
Mayflower UK (1965)
A Starlet For A Penny - *Last*
Mayflower UK (1966)

W A BALLINGER 1925-1991 (British)
See main detective Richard QUINTAIN
Citation Record: 17 Books
Epitaph To Treason - *First*
Amalgamated UK (1960)
The Green Grassy Slopes - *Last*
CorgiiUK (1969)

W A BALLINGER (British)
Writers: William Arthur Howard BAKER 1925-1991 and Wilfred MCNEILLY 1921-1983
Other bylines:
Desmond REID   Peter SAXON
Citation Record: 1 Book
A Corpse For Christmas - *Only*
Amalgamated UK (1962)

W A BALLINGER (British)
Writers: William Arthur Howard BAKER 1925-1991, George Mann and Wilfred MCNEILLY 1921-1983
Citation Record: 1 Book
The Last Tiger - *Only*
Amalgamated UK (1963)

W A BALLINGER 1921-1983 (British)
For writer details see Sexton BLAKE (Wilfred MCNEILLY)
Citation Record: 1 Book
Down Among The Ad Men - *Only*
Amalgamated UK (1968)

William J BAYFIELD 1871-1958 (British)
Writer: William John BAYFIELD
Other Bylines:
Allan BLAIR   Allan MAXWELL
Citation Record: 54 Books
When Conscience Sleeps - *First*
Amalgamated UK (1917)
The Masked Forgers - *Last*
Amalgamated UK (1929)

Lester BIDSTON 1884- (British)
Citation Record: 9 Books
The Phantom Of The Mill - *First*
Amalgamated UK (1927)
The Motor Coach Murder - *Last*
Amalgamated UK (1933)

Ladbroke BLACK 1877-1940 (British)
See main detective Mr PREED
Citation Record: 3 Books
The Case Of The Crook Banker - *First*
Amalgamated UK (1930)
The Mystery Militiaman - *Last*
Amalgamated UK (1940)

Allan BLAIR 1871-1958 (British)
Writer: William John BAYFIELD
Other Bylines:
William J BAYFIELD   Allan MAXWELL
Citation Record: 33 Books
The Lombard Street Mystery - *First*
Amalgamated UK (1930)
The Case Of The Dictator's Double - *Last*
Amalgamated UK (1940)

Stacey BLAKE 1878-1964 (British)
Citation Record: 3 Books
Prisoners Of The Desert - *First*
Amalgamated UK (1929)
On Ticket Of Leave - *Last*
Amalgamated UK (1944)

Stephen BLAKESLEY (British)
See main detective The CARDINAL
Citation Record: 3 Books
The Riddle Of The Blazing Bungalow - *First*
Amalgamated UK (1951)
The Man With A Number - *Last*
Amalgamated UK (1952)

John William BOBIN ?-1935 (British)
For writer details see Sylvia SILENCE
The Shadow Of His Crime - *First*
Amalgamated UK (1915)
The Secret Of The Surgery - *Last*
Amalgamated UK (1929)

Gerald BOWMAN ?-1967 (British)
See main detective Michael SHANNON
The Devil's Own - *First*
Amalgamated UK (1937)
The Hunchback Of Hatton Garden - *Last*
Amalgamated UK (1937)

John G BRANDON 1879-1941 (British)
Invented 5 detectives - see Sgt/Det Insp Patrick Aloysius MCCARTHY
The Taxi-Cab Murder - *First*
Amalgamated UK (1933)
Murder For A Million - *Last*
Wright UK (1942)

John BREARLEY (British)
Writer: John GARBUTT
The Flaming Frontier - *First*
Amalgamated UK (1939)
They Came To Spy - *Last*
Amalgamated UK (1939)

T C BRIDGES 1868-1944 (British)
Writer: Thomas Charles BRIDGES
The Crime On The Moor - *First*
Amalgamated UK (1935)

Coutts BRISBANE (Australian)
Writer: R Coutts ARMOUR
Other Byline: R C ARMOUR
The Gang's Deserter - *First*
Amalgamated UK (1930)
The Mystery Of The Red Tower - *Last*
Amalgamated UK (1940)

Edwy Searles BROOKS 1889-1965 (British)
Invented 5 detectives - see Insp William (The Grouser) BEEKE
Midst Balkan Perils - *First*
Amalgamated UK (1916)
The Midnight Lorry Crime - *Last*
Amalgamated UK (1937)

Leonard Harold BROOKS ?-1950 (British)
The Avenging Seven - *First*
Amalgamated UK (1920)
The Riddle Of The Lascar's Head - *Last*
Amalgamated UK (1926)

Lewis CARLTON 1886?- (British)
The Monomark Mystery - *First*
Amalgamated UK (1928)
The Case Of The Stranded Touring Company - *Last*
Amalgamated UK (1933)

Philip CHAMBERS 1936- (British)
Bullets To Baghdad - *First*
Amalgamated UK (1960)
Lotus Leaves And Larceny - *Last*
Amalgamated UK (1963)

Gilbert CHESTER 1888-1958 (British)
For writer details see Sexton BLAKE (H H Clifford GIBBONS)

Citation Record: 83 Books
The Green Room Crime - *First*
Amalgamated UK (1930)
The Secret Of The Snows - *Last*
Dean UK (1968)

Stephen CHRISTIE (British)
Writer: D S C KURUPPU
Citation Record: 2 Books
Crash And Carry - *First*
Mayflower UK (1967)
Slaughter In The Sun - *Last*
Baker US (1969)

Hugh CLEVELY 1898-1964 (British)
Invented 4 detectives - see Maxwell ARCHER
Citation Record: 12 Books
Calling Whitehall 1212 - *First*
Amalgamated UK (1952)
The Strange Affair Of The Widow's Diamonds - *Last*
Amalgamated UK (1955)

John CREASEY 1908-1973 (British)
Invented 6 detectives - see Insp Roger 'Handsome' WEST
Citation Record: 4 Books
The Case Of The Murdered Financier - *First*
Amalgamated UK (1937)
Private Carter's Crime - *Last*
Amalgamated UK (1943)

George DILNOT 1883-1951 (British)
Invented 5 detectives - see Val EMERY
Citation Record: 2 Books
The Black Ace - *First*
Amalgamated UK (1938)
The Case Of The Missing Bridegroom - *Last*
Amalgamated UK (1938)

Maurice B DIX 1889-1956 (British)
Invented 4 detectives - see Tommy MALINS
Citation Record: 5 Books
The Victim Of The Girl Spy - *First*
Amalgamated UK (1936)
The Affair Of The Smuggled Millions - *Last*
Amalgamated UK (1943)

Rex DOLPHIN 1915-1990 (British)
Writer: Rex Reginald Charles DOLPHIN
Other Byline: Richard WILLIAMS
Citation Record: 9 Books
Walk In The Shadows - *First*
Amalgamated UK (1959)
Driven To Kill - *Last*
Baker US (1969)

L C DOUTHWAITE 1878- (British)
Invented 3 detectives - see Const Jimmie WARDEN
Citation Record: 2 Books
Horror House - *First*
Amalgamated UK (1930)
The Army Defaulter's Secret - *Last*
Amalgamated UK (1943)

Sidney DREW 1878- (British)
Writer: Edgar Joyce MURRAY
Citation Record: 3 Books
The Gangster's Deputy - *First*
Amalgamated UK (1930)
The Fortnight Of Fear - *Last*
Amalgamated UK (1931)

J DRUMMOND 1911-1983 (British)
For writer details see John Newton CHANCE
Citation Record: 25 Books
The Manor House Menace - *First*
Amalgamated UK (1944)
The Teddy-Boy Mystery - *Last*
Amalgamated UK (1955)

Alfred EDGAR 1896- (British)
Citation Record: 6 Books
The Sign In The Sky - *First*
Amalgamated UK (1922)
The Cup Final Mystery - *Last*
Amalgamated UK (1927)

Walter EDWARDS ?-1940? (British)
Writer: Walter SHUTE
Citation Record: 13 Books
The Ambush - *First*
Amalgamated UK (1931)
The Great Stores Mystery - *Last*
Amalgamated UK (1940)

Gwyn EVANS 1899-1938 (British)
Invented 5 detectives - see Bill KELLAWAY
Citation Record: 21 Books
The Crook Of Fleet Street - *First*
Amalgamated UK (1926)
The Silent Jury - *Last*
Amalgamated UK (1930)

F Dubrez FAWCETT 1891-1968 (British)
Writer: Frank Dubrez FAWCETT
Citation Record: 1 Book
Journey To Genoa - *Only*
Amalgamated UK (1960)

Martin FRAZER 1895-1974 (British)
For writer details see Ferrers LOCKE (Percy A CLARKE)
Citation Record: 14 Books
Acquitted! - *First*
Wright UK (1937)
The Case Of The Dope Dealers - *Last*
Amalgamated UK (1952)

E J GANNON (British)
Citation Record: 4 Books
The Woolwich Arsenal Mystery - *First*
!See Appendix 2.
Amalgamated UK (1907)
The Sleepwalker - *Last*
Amalgamated UK (1908)

John GARFORTH (British)
See main detective The AVENGERS
Citation Record: 1 Book
Sexton Blake And The Demon God - *Only*
Mirror Books UK (1978)

Clifford GATES (British)
Citation Record: 1 Book
The Case Of The Murdered Caretaker - *Only*
Amalgamated UK (1940)

H H Clifford GIBBONS 1888-1958 (British)
Writer: Harry Hornaby Clifford GIBBONS
Other Byline: Gilbert CHESTER
Citation Record: 34 Books
Solved In Thirty-Six Hours! - *First*
Amalgamated UK (1923)
The Ballot Box Mystery - *Last*
Amalgamated UK (1929)

Norman GODDARD 1881-1917 (British)
Writer: Norman Molyneux GODDARD
Citation Record: 4 Books
Sexton Blake's Honour - *First*
Amalgamated UK (1907)
The Man With The Green Eyes - *Last*
Amalgamated UK (1917)

Richard GOYNE 1902-1957 (British)
Invented 4 detectives - see Supt 'Tubby' GREENE

B

Citation Record: 2 Books
The Cinema Crime - *First*
Amalgamated UK (1933)
The Kidnapper's Victim - *Last*
Amalgamated UK (1934)

Berkeley GRAY 1885-1965 (British)
See main detective Norman CONQUEST
Citation Record: 1 Book
Three Frightened Men - *Only*
Amalgamated UK (1938)

Robert Murray GRAYDON ?-1937 (British)
Citation Record: 4 Books
The Mysterious Mr Reece - *First*
Amalgamated UK (1917)
The Masked Marauder - *Last*
Amalgamated UK (1930)

W Murray GRAYDON 1864-1946 (British)
Writer: William Murray GRAYDON
Citation Record: 4 Books
The Case Of The Suppressed Will - *First*
Amalgamated UK (1916)
The Feud Of Fear - *Last*
Amalgamated UK (1930)

V J HANSON 1920- (British)
For writer details see 'Lefty' O'CONNOR
Citation Record: 1 Book
Death And Little Girl Blue - *Only*
Amalgamated UK (1962)

Rex HARDINGE 1904- (British)
See main detective pair MURPHY and MCTAVISH
Citation Record: 82 Books
The Midnight Mystery - *First*
Amalgamated UK (1929)
The Man With Five Enemies - *Last*
Amalgamated UK (1955)

A S HARDY 1873- (British)
Writer: Arthur Joseph STEFFENS
Citation Record: 12 Books
Traitor And Spy - *First*
Amalgamated UK (1917)
The Bookmaker's Crime - *Last*
Amalgamated UK (1935)

Edwin HARRISON (British)
Writer: Eric Alan BALLARD
Citation Record: 4 Books
Diamonds Can Be Trouble - *First*
Amalgamated UK (1958)
Killer's Playground - *Last*
Amalgamated UK (1959)

Harry Egbert HILL (British)
Citation Record: 13 Books
The Idol's Eye - *First*
Amalgamated UK (1921)
The Great Museum Mystery - *Last*
Amalgamated UK (1929)

C Malcolm HINCKS 1881-1954 (British)
See main detective PINCHER
Citation Record: 2 Books
The Riddle Of The Rovers - *First*
Amalgamated UK (1929)
The Throne Of Peril - *Last*
Amalgamated UK (1930)

Edward R HOME-GALL 1899- (British)
Writer: Edward Reginald HOME-GALL
Citation Record: 1 Book
State Secrets - *Only*
Amalgamated UK (1921)

Stephen HOOD (British)
Writer: Jack LEWIS
Other Bylines:
Lewis JACKSON   Jack LEWIS
Citation Record: 1 Book
The Crook From Chicago - *Only*
Amalgamated UK (1931)

Stanton HOPE 1889- 1961 (British)
See main detective Ferrers LOCKE
Citation Record: 13 Books
The Death Ship - *First*
Amalgamated UK (1931)
The Mystery Of The Engraved Skull - *Last*
Amalgamated UK (1954)

John HUNTER 1891-1961 (British)
See main detective Bill LANGLEY
Citation Record: 57 Books
Crook Cargo - *First*
Amalgamated UK (1936)
The Mystery Of The Vanished Trainer - *Last*
Amalgamated UK (1955)

Lewis JACKSON (British)
For writer details see Sexton BLAKE (Stephen HOOD)
Citation Record: 27 Books
The Case Of The Missing Stoker - *First*
Amalgamated UK (1942)
The Man From Persia - *Last*
Amalgamated UK (1951)

Warwick JARDINE (British)
For writer details see Ferrers LOCKE (Francis WARWICK)
Citation Record: 32 Books
The Great Dumping Mystery - *First*
Amalgamated UK (1932)
The Riddle Of The Green Cylinder - *Last*
Amalgamated UK (1955)

Gilbert JOHNS (British)
For writer details see Sexton BLAKE (James STAGG)
Citation Record: 2 Books
Thief Of Clubs - *First*
Amalgamated UK (1961)
Vote For Violence - *Last*
Amalgamated UK (1961)

J G JONES (British)
Citation Record: 1 Book
The Secret Of The Bucket Shop - *Only*
Amalgamated UK (1924)

Arthur KENT 1925- (British)
Writer: Arthur William Charles KENT
Citation Record: 5 Books
Inclining To Crime - *First*
Amalgamated UK (1956)
Corpse To Cuba - *Last*
Mayflower UK (1966); Macfadden UK (1967)

Hilary KING (British)
Writer: James Grierson DICKSON
Citation Record: 5 Books
Partners In Crime - *First*
Amalgamated UK (1951)
The Big Circus Mystery - *Last*
Amalgamated UK (1953)

Arthur KIRBY (British)
For writer details see Sexton BLAKE (Arthur MACLEAN)
Citation Record: 1 Book
Man On The Run! - *First*
Amalgamated UK (1960)
High Summer Homicide - *Last*
Amalgamated UK (1962)

B

Arthur KIRBY 1917-1989 (British)

For writer details see John GAIL

Citation Record: 1 Book

High Summer Homicide - *Only*
Amalgamated UK (1962)

Jack LEWIS (British)

For writer details see Sexton BLAKE (Stephen HOOD)

Citation Record: 15 Books

The Chink In The Armour - *First*
Amalgamated UK (1919)

The Case Of The Bendigo Heirlooms - *Last*
Amalgamated UK (1922)

Derek LONG (British)

Citation Record: 2 Books

The Case Of Lord Greyburn's Son - *First*
Amalgamated UK (1946)

The Mystery Of The Italian Ruins - *Last*
Amalgamated UK (1950)

Arthur MACLEAN 1927- (British)

Writer: George Paul MANN
Other Byline: Arthur KIRBY

Citation Record: 15 Books

Dark Frontier - *First*
Amalgamated UK (1956)

The Savage Squeeze - *Last*
Mayflower UK (1965)

Allan MAXWELL 1871-1958 (British)

Writer: William John BAYFIELD
Other Bylines:
William J BAYFIELD   Allan BLAIR

Citation Record: 1 Book

The Priest's Secret - *Only*
Amalgamated UK (1936)

Wilfred MCNEILLY 1921-1983 (British)

Writer: Wilfred Glassford MCNEILLY
Other Bylines:
W A BALLINGER   Desmond REID
Peter SAXON

Citation Record: 11 Books

Killer Pack - *First*
Amalgamated UK (1962)

The Case Of The Muckrakers - *Last*
Mayflower UK (1966); Macfadden UK (1967)

Peter MERITON 1891-1961 (British)

Invented 3 detectives - see Capt DACK

The Man From Madrid - *First*
Amalgamated UK (1943)

The Affair Of The Fraternizing Soldier - *Last*
Amalgamated UK (1946)

Oliver MERLAND (British)

Citation Record: 5 Books

The Branded Spy - *First*
Amalgamated UK (1919)

The Case Of Larachi The Lascar - *Last*
Amalgamated UK (1924)

Andrew MURRAY 1880-1929 (British)

For writer details see Ferrers LOCKE

Citation Record: 73 Books

Ill Gotten Gains - *First*
Amalgamated UK (1915)

The Secret Of The Green Lagoon - *Last*
Amalgamated UK (1928)

Edgar Joyce MURRAY 1878- (British)

Citation Record: 13 Books

The Case Of The Crimson Wizard - *First*
Amalgamated UK (1922)

The Riddle Of The Golden Fingers - *Last*
Amalgamated UK (1927)

Mark OSBORNE ?-1935 (British)

Writer: John William BOBIN
Other Bylines:
Adelie ASCOTT   Katherine GREENHALGH

Citation Record: 9 Books

The Boarding House Mystery - *First*
Amalgamated UK (1931)

The Dog Track Murder - *Last*
Amalgamated UK (1934)

Anthony PARSONS 1893-1963 (British)

Citation Record: 103 Books

The Secret Of The Ten Bales - *First*
Amalgamated UK (1937)

The Secret Of The Roman Temple - *Last*
Amalgamated UK (1955)

W J PASSINGHAM 1897- (British)

Writer: William John PASSINGHAM

Citation Record: 2 Books

The Case Of The Ace Accomplice - *First*
Amalgamated UK (1953)

The World Championship Mystery - *Last*
Amalgamated UK (1953)

John Nix PENTELOW 1872-1941 (British)

Citation Record: 2 Books

Missing In Mexico - *First*
Amalgamated UK (1925)

The Cleopatra Needle Mystery - *Last*
Amalgamated UK (1927)

George Norman PHILIPS 1888?- (British)

Citation Record: 14 Books

The Roumanian Envoy - *First*
Amalgamated UK (1921)

The Gangster's Revenge - *Last*
Amalgamated UK (1930)

Reginald Heber POOLE 1885- (British)

Citation Record: 8 Books

Unjustly Branded - *First*
Amalgamated UK (1919)

The Davenham Heritage - *Last*
Long UK (1928)

John PURLEY 1899-1956 (British)

For writer details see Vicky DARE

Citation Record: 1 Book

The Mansion On The Moor - *Only*
Amalgamated UK (1943)

Pierre QUIROULE 1892- (British)

For writer details see Barnaby GRAYLE

Citation Record: 17 Books

The Hour Of Recognition - *First*
Amalgamated UK (1932)

The Mystery Of The Missing Envoy - *Last*
Amalgamated UK (1939)

George REES (British)

Citation Record: 2 Books

The Secret Of The Jungle - *First*
Amalgamated UK (1953)

The Secret Of The Suez Canal - *Last*
Amalgamated UK (1954)

Desmond REID (British)

Writer: A CAHILL

Citation Record: 1 Book

Bullets Are Trumps - *Only*
Amalgamated UK (1961)

Desmond REID (British)

For writer details see Sexton BLAKE (Writer W A BALLINGER)

Citation Record: 1 Book

The Snowman Cometh - *Only*
Mayflower UK (1966

Desmond REID 1920- (British)
Writer: Sydney James BOUNDS
Other Byline: Peter SAXON
Citation Record: 1 Book
The Girl Who Saw Too Much - *Only*
Amalgamated UK (1963)

Desmond REID (British)
Writer: Noel BROWNE
Citation Record: 2 Books
Showdown In Sydney- *First*
Amalgamated UK (1959)
Contract For A Killer - *Last*
Amalgamated UK (1960)

Desmond REID 1922- (British)
For writer details see Dr Alexander CASPIAN
Citation Record: 1 Book
High Heels And Homicide - *Only*
Amalgamated UK (1958)

Desmond REID 1911-1983 (British)
For writer details see John Newton CHANCE
Citation Record: 1 Book
Anger At World's End - *Only*
Amalgamated UK (1963)

Desmond REID 1915-1990 (British)
For writer details see Sexton BLAKE (Rex DOLPHIN)
Citation Record: 1 Book
The World-Shakers - *Only*
Amalgamated UK (1960)

Desmond REID (British)
Writer: Anthony DOUSE
Citation Record: 1 Book
Dead On Cue - *Only*
Amalgamated UK (1962)

Desmond REID (British)
Writer: Robert Cowell ELLIOTT
Citation Record: 1 Book
Something To Kill About- *Only*
Mayflower UK (1961)

Desmond REID 1917-1989 (British)
For writer details see John GAIL
Citation Record: 1 Book
The Deadlier Of The Species - *Only*
Amalgamated UK (1966)

Desmond REID (British)
Writer: A GARSTIN
Citation Record: 1 Book
Hunt The Lady! - *Only*
Amalgamated UK (1961)

Desmond REID 1929- (British)
Writer: Anthony Arthur GLYNN
Citation Record: 1 Book
The Corpse Came Too - *Only*
Amalgamated UK (1961)

Desmond REID (British)
For writer details see 'Lefty' O'CONNOR
Citation Record: 2 Books
Death On A High Note - *First*
Amalgamated UK (1962)
Cult Of Darkness - *Last*
Amalgamated UK (1963)

Desmond REID (British)
Writer: Miss S HALL
Citation Record: 1 Book

Carribean Crisis - *Only*
Amalgamated UK (1962)

Desmond REID (British)
Writer: Frank LAMBE
Citation Record: 1 Book
Stand-In For Murder - *Only*
Amalgamated UK (1957)

Desmond REID 1945- (British)
Writer: Christopher LOWDER
Citation Record: 1 Book
The Abductors - *Only*
Mayflower UK (1968)

Desmond REID (British)
Writer: A L MARTIN
Citation Record: 1 Book
Roadhouse Girl - *Only*
Amalgamated UK (1957)

Desmond REID (British)
Writer: Brian MCARDLE
Citation Record: 1 Book
Flashpoint For Treason - *Only*
Amalgamated UK (1957)

Desmond REID 1921-1983 (British)
For writer details see Sexton BLAKE (Wilfred MCNEILLY)
Citation Record: 4 Books
Murder By Moonlight - *First*
Amalgamated UK (1961)
Frenzy In The Flesh - *Last*
Amalgamated UK (1966)

Desmond REID (British)
Writer: Eddie PLAYER
Citation Record: 1 Book
Murder Made Easy - *Only*
Amalgamated UK (1960)

Desmond REID (British)
Writer: Ross RICHARDS
Citation Record: 3 Books
Death On The Spike - *First*
Amalgamated UK (1966)
Dead Respectable - *Last*
Amalgamated UK (1967)

Desmond REID (British)
Writer: Lee ROBERTS
Citation Record: 1 Book
Victim Unknown - *Only*
Amalgamated UK (1957)

Desmond REID 1906-1980 (British)
For writer details see Mike REED
Citation Record: 1 Book
Deadly Persuasion - *Only*
Amalgamated UK (1961)

Desmond REID 1909(?)- (British)
Writer: Gordon SOWMAN
Citation Record: 3 Books
Homicide Blues - *First*
Amalgamated UK (1957)
Death In Dockland - *Last*
Amalgamated UK (1962)

Desmond REID (British)
For writer details see Sexton BLAKE (James STAGG)
Citation Record: 1 Book
Murder Comes Calling! - *Only*
Amalgamated UK (1960)

Desmond REID (British)
Writer: Rosamond Mary STORY
Citation Record: 1 Book

Witch-Hunt! - *Only*
Amalgamated UK (1960)

Desmond REID (British)
Writer: George Heber TEED
Citation Record: 1 Book
State Of Fear - *Only*
Amalgamated UK (1961)

Peter SAXON 1925-1991 (British)
For writer details see Richard QUINTAIN
Citation Record: 18 Books
The Voodoo Drum - *First*
Amalgamated UK (1948)
Woman Of Saigon - *Last*
Amalgamated UK (1968)

Peter SAXON (British)
For writer details see Sexton BLAKE (Writer W A BALLINGER)
Citation Record: 4 Books
The Darkest Night - *First*
Mayflower UK (1966); Paperback Library US (1967)
The Haunting Of Alan Mais - *Last*
Mayflower UK (1970); Berkley US (1969)

Peter SAXON (British)
For writer details see Sexton Blake (Writer Sydney James BOUNDS)
Citation Record: 1 Book
White Mercenary - *Only*
Amalgamated UK (1962))

Peter SAXON 1917-1989 (British)
For writer details see John GAIL
Citation Record: 1 Book
The Disorientated Man - *Only*
Mayflower UK (1966)
Scream And Scream Again - *Only**
Paperback Library US (1967)

Peter SAXON (British)
For writer details see Sexton Blake (Wilfred MCNEILLY)
Citation Record: 1 Book
Satan's Child - *Only*
Mayflower UK (1967); Lancer US (1968)

W W SAYER 1892- (British)
See main detective Barnaby GRAYLE
Citation Record: 25 Books
The Case Of The Strange Wireless Message - *First*
Amalgamated UK (1920)
The Ethiopian's Secret - *Last*
Amalgamated UK (1926)

Hedley SCOTT 1899-1955 (British)
See main detective Ferrers LOCKE
Citation Record: 2 Books
The Suspected Six - *First*
Amalgamated UK (1938)
The Mystery Of The Missing Refugee - *Last*
Amalgamated UK (1939)

Ernest SEMPHILL (British)
Citation Record: 2 Books
The Merrlyn Mystery - *First*
Amalgamated UK (1909)
The Ghost Of Robert Forbes - *Last*
Amalgamated UK (1913)

Stanley Gordon SHAW 1884-1938? (British)
Citation Record: 1 Book
The Secret Of The Monastery - *Only*
Amalgamated UK (1928)

Walter SHUTE ?-1940? (British)
Citation Record: 6 Books
The Affair Of The Rival Cinema Kings - *First*
Amalgamated UK (1928)
The "Talkie" Murder Mystery - *Last*
Amalgamated UK (1930)

Anthony SKENE 1888?- (British)
Writer: George Norman PHILIPS
Citation Record: 32 Books
The Crook's Accomplice - *First*
Amalgamated UK (1930)
The Ripper Returns - *Last*
Pemberton UK (1948)

James STAGG (British)
Writer: James STAGG
Other Byline: Gilbert JOHNS
Citation Record: 8 Books
Assignment In Beirut - *First*
Amalgamated UK (1956)
Desert Intrigue - *Last*
Amalgamated UK (1960)

Joseph STAMPER 1886- (British)
Citation Record: 1 Book
The Shipyard Menace - *Only*
Amalgamated UK (1943)

Donald William STEWARD 1896-1980 (British)
For writer details see Supt BUDD
Citation Record: 10 Books
The Clue Of The Second Tooth - *First*
Amalgamated UK (1927)
The Crime Of Four - *Last*
Amalgamated UK (1930)

Jack Trevor STORY 1918-1991 (British)
Invented 3 detectives - see Albert ARGYLE
Citation Record: 19 Books
Murder With Love - *First*
Amalgamated UK (1956)
Company Of Bandits - *Last*
Mayflower UK (1965)

Donald STUART 1896-1980 (British)
See main detective Lionel CRANE
Citation Record: 36 Books
The Hooded Terror - *First*
Amalgamated UK (1930)
The Secret Of The Hulk - *Last*
Amalgamated UK (1940)

F Addington SYMONDS 1893- (British)
See main detective Insp Maxwell QUAYNE
Citation Record: 13 Books
The Golden Casket - *First*
Amalgamated UK (1921)
Smile And Murder - *Last*
Boardman UK (1954)

G H TEED 1878-1939 (British)
Invented 6 detectives - see Roxane HARFIELD
Citation Record: 88 Books
The Yellow Tiger - *First*
Amalgamated UK (1915)
The Shadow Crook - *Last*
Smith US (1936)

Martin THOMAS 1913- (British)
Writer: Thomas Hector MARTIN
Citation Record: 24 Books
The Copy-Cat Killings - *First*
Amalgamated UK (1957)
The Mini-Skirt Murders - *Last*
Baker US (1969)

Walter TYRER 1900- (British)
Citation Record: 35 Books

B

The Curse Of The Carringtons - *First*
Amalgamated UK (1943)

The Case Of The Forbidden Island - *Last*
Amalgamated UK (1955)

Paul URQUHART 1877-1940 (British)

For writer details see Mr PREED

Citation Record: 23 Books

The Web - *First*
Ward, Lock UK (1907)

The Mystery Of The Lorry Driver - *Last*
Amalgamated UK (1939)

Trevor C WIGNALL 1884-1958 (British)

Citation Record: 2 Books

The Case Of The Japanese Detective - *First*
Amalgamated UK (1920)

The House With The Red Blinds - *Last*
Amalgamated UK (1920)

Richard WILLIAMS 1925-1991

For writer details see Richard QUINTAIN

Citation Record: 1 Book

Hurricane Warning - *Only*
Amalgamated UK (1960)

Richard WILLIAMS 1915-1990

For writer details see Sexton BLAKE (Rex DOLPHIN)

Citation Record: 1 Book

Speak Ill Of The Dead - *Only*
Amalgamated UK (1963)

Richard WILLIAMS 1917-1989

For writer details see John GAIL

Citation Record: 4 Books

Torment Was A Redhead - *First*
Amalgamated UK (1962)

The Man With The Iron Chest - *Last*
Mayflower UK (1965)

Richard WILLIAMS

Writers: Bob HOPKINS and Max MARQUIS

Citation Record: 1 Book

Murder By Proxy - *Only*
Amalgamated UK (1963)

Richard WILLIAMS 1917-

For writer details see Albert ARGYLE

Citation Record: 1 Book

Large Type Killer - *Only*
Amalgamated UK (1960)

Sexton BLAKE

Second detective of A J RAFFLES

Charles BLAKELOCK

Appears with at least two other detectives - see Insp MILD.

Insp BLANC

sleuths at some time in the early 1800s.

French Policeman operating in Paris/London

Bernard ST JAMES 1932- (American)

Writer: William TREISTER

Citation Record: 3 Books

April Thirteenth - *First*
Harper & Row US (1978)

The Seven Dreamers - *Latest*
Doubleday US (1982)

Insp BLAND

British Policeman operating in England

Julian SYMONS 1912-1994 (British)

Invented 11 detectives - see Insp CRAMBO

Citation Record: 3 Books

The Immaterial Murder Case - *First*
Gollancz UK (1945); Macmillan US (1957)

Bland Beginning - *Last*
Gollancz UK (1949); Harper & Row US (1949)

Bertie BLAND

American Male Detective in Pulp Magazines operating in USA

OLD SLEUTH (American)

Invented 40 detectives - see Brant ADAMS

Citation Record: 1 Book

Bertie Bland, The Detective - *Only*
Ogilvie US (1895)

Jim BLANEY

is a middle-aged insurance investigator.

American Male Professional Investigator operating in Los Angeles

Elliott WEST 1924- (American)

Citation Record: 1 Book

The Killing Kind - *Only*
Houghton US (1986); Futura UK (1986)

The Hon Everard BLATCHINGTON

appears also in books with another of the author's detectives, Supt Henry WILSON.

British Male Amateur operating in England

G D H COLE and Margaret COLE (British)

Invented 7 detectives - see Supt Henry WILSON

Citation Record: 1 Book

Scandal At School - *Only*
Collins UK (1935)

The Sleeping Death - *Only**
Doubleday US (1936)

The Hon Everard BLATCHINGTON

Second detective of Supt Henry WILSON

Edward BLAYNE

is a lawyer who has to turn detective to bring his case to a successful conclusion.

British Male Amateur operating in England

Victor MACCLURE 1887-1963 (British)

See main detective Ch Insp Archie BURFORD

Citation Record: 1 Book

The 'Crying Pig' Murder - *Only*
Harrap UK (1929); Morrow US (1930)

Kate BLAYNE

is one of the rare breed of early female newshounds. Working for the *New York Sun*, and often referred to as 'The Duchess', she regularly solved murders in *Detective Fiction Weekly.*

American Female Detective in Pulp Magazines operating in New York

Whitman CHAMBERS 1896- (American)

Invented 4 detectives - see Simon LAKE

No citations

Sebastian BLAYNE

American Male Amateur operating in New York/Connecticut

Sebastian BLAYNE (American)

Writer: Janet HUCKINS

Citation Record: 2 Books

Gay Ghastly Holiday - *First*
GM US (1951)

Terror In The Night - *Last*
GM US (1953); Muller UK (1953)

Joe BLAZE

American Male Sleuth operating in New York

Robert NOVAK (British)

Citation Record: 3 Books

The Big Payoff - *First*
Belmont US (1974)

The Concrete Cage - *Last*
Belmont US (1974)

B

The BLEEDER
is a haemophiliac and considered to be 'the world's most vulnerable dick'. He appeared in stories in *Dime Detective.*

American Male Detective in Pulp Magazines operating in USA

Edith JACOBSON and Ejler JACOBSON (American)

See main detective Nat PERRY

No citations

Det Dwight 'Bucky' BLEICHART
is the hero/antihero in the author's best known and most brilliant novel, corrupt only to serve the greater ends of human justice. Dedicated almost beyond reason, he puts his life out on a limb to solve the mystery of an unknown girl's murder and mutilation.

American Policeman operating in Los Angeles

James ELLROY 1948- (American)

Invented 4 detectives - see Fritz BROWN

Citation Record: 1 Book

The Black Dahlia - *Only*

Dealing as it does with one specific true-life crime, this novel is a masterpiece of style and plot, in which the detective can, perforce, only appear the once.

Mysterious Press US (1987); Century Hutchinson UK (1988)

BLEKE
British Male Amateur operating in England

William LEQUEUX 1864-1927 (British)

Invented 23 detectives - see Allan KENNEDY

Citation Record: 8 Short Stories in 1 Collection

Bleke, The Butler - *Collection 1*

Jarrolds UK (1924)

Insp BLESSINGAY
British Policeman operating in England

G J BARRETT 1928- (British)

Writer: Geoffrey John BARRETT

Citation Record: 4 Books

A Cup That Kills - *First*

Hale UK (1969)

His Own Funeral - *Last*

Hale UK (1972)

Charles BLESSINGTON
British Male Amateur operating in England

John SHERWOOD 1913- (British)

was born in Cheltenham, Gloucestershire. He was educated at Marlborough College, Wiltshire, and graduated at Oriel College, Oxford, 1935. After serving in the Intelligence Corps, 1940-1945, he worked for the British Broadcasting Corporation in a variety of capacities, 1946-1963.

Writer: John Herman Mulso SHERWOOD

Inventor of one other detective Celia GRANT

Citation Record: 5 Books

Disappearance Of Dr Bruderstein - *First*

Hodder & Stoughton UK (1949)

Dr Bruderstein Vanishes - *First**

Doubleday US (1949)

Vote Against Poison - *Last*

Hodder & Stoughton UK (1956)

Haskell BLEVINS
is 'the only hardboiled PI in Pigeon Fork, Kentucky. And it's hard to be a hardboiled PI in Pigeon Fork'.

American Male Private Detective operating in Kentucky

Taylor MCCAFFERTY (American)

Citation Record: 3 Books

Pet Peeves - *First*

Pocket Books US (1990)

Bed Bugs - *Latest*

Pocket Books US (1993)

Dulcie BLIGH
does her sleuthing in England around 1810.

British Female Amateur operating in England

Gail CLARK (American)

Citation Record: 2 Books

Dulcie Bligh - *First*

Putnam US (1978)

The Baroness Of Bow Street - *Latest*

Putnam US (1979)

Prof BLINKWELL
appears also in one book with another of the author's detectives, *Mr JELLIPOT.*

British Male Amateur operating in England

Sydney FOWLER 1874-1965 (British)

Invented 5 detectives - see Mr JELLIPOT

Citation Record: 2 Books

The Secret Of The Screen - *First*

Jarrolds UK (1933)

Who Murdered Reynard? - *Last*

Rich UK (1947)

Prof BLINKWELL and Mr JELLIPOT
also appear individually in other books by this author.

British Male Amateurs operating in England

Sydney FOWLER 1874-1965 (British)

Invented 5 detectives - see Mr JELLIPOT

Citation Record: 1 Book

The Bell Street Murders - *Only*

Harrap UK (1931); Macaulay US (1931)

Supt BLISS
is one of the author's lesser detectives but he is the main adversary of The Ringer, one of the author's finest creations, a shadowy, clever outlaw who specialises in bringing evildoers to justice - usually, however, by murdering them, to the considerable annoyance of the police. *Supt BLISS* is, in fact, a bit of a lay figure, secretive and working too much on his own. So, although always on the Ringer's track, he is always outwitted by him.

British Policeman operating in London

Edgar WALLACE 1875-1932 (British)

Invented 28 detectives - see J G REEDER

Citation Record: 1 Book

The Gaunt Stranger - *Only*

This justly famous book was, in all later publications, entitled *THE RINGER* in both the US and the UK.

Hodder & Stoughton UK (1925)

The Ringer - *Only**

Doubleday US (1926); Hodder & Stoughton UK (1929)

Insp BLISS
British Policeman operating in England

John REMENHAM 1877-1958 (British)

See main detective Insp BADGER

Citation Record: 3 Books

The Canal Mystery - *First*

Skeffington UK (1928)

The Dump - *Last*

Skeffington UK (1931)

Jim BLISS
American Male Amateur operating in Long Island

Christopher B BOOTH 1883-1924 (American)

Other Detectives:

Amos CLACKWORTHY

Bob FETHERSTON and Sgt QUINN

Citation Record: 2 Books

A Seaside Mystery - *First*

Chelsea US (1925)

Killing Jazz - *Last*
Chelsea US (1928)

Vicky BLISS

is an art historian who tracks down forgers, thieves and art smugglers. She is tall, beautiful, desirable, has a brilliant and quick-acting mind, and can outsmart most criminals. She has a transient sidekick, an art thief who says he is British.

American Female Amateur operating in Germany

Sidekick: Sir John SMYTHE
British Male - Assistant

Elizabeth PETERS 1927- (American)

was born in Canton, Illinois, and took three degrees at the Chicago Oriental Institute, 1947-1952. She has written, under her real name, several popular non-fictional works on Egyptology and Ancient Rome and is the author of detective novels and romantic suspense novels under pseudonyms.

Writer: Barbara Louise Gross MERTZ

Other Detectives:
Priest Amenhotep Sa HAPU   Jacqueline KIRBY
Amelia PEABODY

Citation Record: 5 Books

Borrower Of The Night - *First*
Dodd, Mead US (1973); Cassell UK (1974)

Night Train To Memphis - *Latest*
Warner US (1994)

Harvey BLISSBERG

is a baseball player who becomes an investigator of murder cases in sporting scenes.

American Male Amateur operating in New York/Boston

R D ROSEN 1949- (American)

was born in Chicago, Illinois. He was educated at Brown University, Providence, Rhode Island, and graduated with a BA at Harvard University, Cambridge, Massachusetts, 1972. He has been a chef, teacher and reporter.

Writer: Richard Dean ROSEN

Citation Record: 4 Books

Strike Three You're Dead - *First*
Walker US (1984)

A World Of Hurt - *Latest*
Walker US (1994)

Nils-Frederik BLIXEN

Male Amateur operating in Los Angeles

Charles LARSON 1922- (American)

Citation Record: 4 Books

Someone's Death - *First*
Lippincott US (1973)

The Portland Murders - *Latest*
Doubleday US (1983); Chivers UK (1985)

Insp BLOCK

British Policeman operating in England

Mary Christianna BRAND 1907-1988 (British)

Invented 6 detectives - see Insp COCKRILL and Insp CHARLESWORTH

Citation Record: 1 Selected Short Story

The Scapegoat
Joseph UK (1974); In 'Ellery Queen's Mystery Magazine' US (1970)

Mark BLOOD

American Male Sleuth operating in USA

Allan MORGAN

House name.

Citation Record: 2 Books

The Cat Cay Warrant - *First*
Award US (1974)

The Spandau Warrant - *Last*
Award US (1974); Tandem UK (1974)

Allan MORGAN

For writer details see Jeanne DONOVAN

Citation Record: 1 Book

Blood - *Only*
Award US (1974); Tandem UK (1974)

Leo G BLOODWORTH and Sarah 'Serendipity' DAHLQUIST

Leo BLOODWORTH is a middle-aged PI, thrice divorced, irritable as a bear with fleas, and all for the quiet life. He is asked to find a missing dog by *Sarah 'Serendipity' DAHLQUIST*, a fourteen-year-old girl, daughter of a movie actress, and an infant prodigy whose brilliance at reasoning runs rings round that of the putative sleuth. The two books in which they appear are sheer delights.

American Male Private Detective and American Female Amateur operating in Los Angeles

Dick LOCHTE 1937- (American)

was born in New Orleans, Louisiana. Reporter and critic for several journals, he received the Rex Stout Society's Nero Wolfe award, 1985.

Writer: Richard Samuel LOCHTE

Other Detectives:
Philip MARLOWE   Terry O'BANION

Citation Record: 2 Books

Sleeping Dog - *First*
Arbor US (1985); Macmillan UK (1986)

Laughing Dog - *Latest*
Arbor US (1988); Macmillan UK (1988)

Insp John Isidore BLOOM

British Policeman operating in England

Erik WARMAN 1904- (British)

Writer: William Erik WARMAN

Citation Record: 2 Books

Relative To Murder - *First*
Harrap UK (1940)

Pattern For Murder - *Last*
Harrap UK (1943)

Theo BLOOMER

is a retired florist who is drawn into mild crime mysteries, usually on foreign soil.

American Male Amateur operating in several locations

Joan HADLEY 1949- (American)

Writer: Joan HESS

Citation Record: 2 Books

The Night-Blooming Cereus - *First*
St Martin's US (1986)

The Deadly Ackee - *Latest*
St Martin's US (1988)

Kent BLOOMINGDALE

Second detective of Capt PACKER

Harry BLOUNT

British Male Professional Amateur operating in England

T J FLANAGAN (British)

Citation Record: 1 Book

Harry Blount, The Detective; Or, The Martin Mystery Solved - *Only*
Ogilvie US (1891)

Spike BLUDGEON

Appears with at least two other detectives - see Mallory KING.

Peter BLUE and Jean Henri ST AMAND

solve the disappearance of a man on board an aircraft. *Jean Henri St AMAND* also appears individually in one other book by this author.

Male Amateurs operating in Paris

B

Darwin L TEILHET 1904-1964 (American)

Other Detectives:
Herr KRESCH
Jean Henri ST AMAND

Citation Record: 1 Book

Murder In The Air - *Only*
Morrow US (1931)

Regina BLUE

solves a case of murder by stabbing in a locked room.

American Female Amateur operating in USA

Ted MARK (American)

Citation Record: 1 Book

Regina Blue - *Only*
Dell US (1972)

Sebastian BLUE

solves crimes of the 'impossible' kind.

American Male Professional Investigator operating in USA

Sidekick: Laura CHARME
American Female - Assistant

Edward D HOCH 1930- (American)

Invented 20 detectives - see Capt LEOPOLD

Citation Record: 1 Selected Short Story

Interpol: The Case Of The Modern Medusa
In 'Ellery Queen's Mystery Magazine' US (1973)

Sybil Sue BLUE

American Female Sleuth operating in Space

Rosel George BROWN 1926-1959 (American)

Citation Record: 2 Books

Sybil Sue Blue - *First*
Doubleday US (1966)

Galactic Sybil Sue Blue - *First**
Berkley US (1968)

The Waters Of Centaurus - *Last*
Doubleday US (1970)

BLUE PETE

Canadian Male Amateur operating in Canada

Luke ALLAN ?-1962 (British)

Writer: William Lacy AMY

Inventor of one other detective Gordon MULDREW

Citation Record: 18 Books

Blue Pete: Half-Breed - *First*
Jenkins UK (1921)

Blue Pete And The Kid - *Last*
Jenkins UK (1953)

Insp BLUNT

is called in to investigate some strange and murderous events at Oxford.

British Policeman operating in England

Rosalind ASHE (British)

Citation Record: 1 Book

Moths - *Single*
Hutchinson UK (1976); Holt US (1976)

Insp BLUNT

was a comic creation who appeared in one of the stories in the collection cited.

British Policeman operating in England

Mark TWAIN 1835-1910 (American)

Invented 5 detectives - see Tom SAWYER

Citation Record: 1 Book

The Stolen White Elephant, Etc - *Only*
Osgood US (1882); Chatto UK (1882)

Sandy BLUNT

American Sleuth operating in New York/Pennsylvania

Peter YATES 1922- (American)

Writer: William LONG

Citation Record: 2 Books

Death In The Hands Of Talent - *First*
Five Star US (1945)

The Dress Circle Murders - *Last*
Five Star US (1945)

Dorrit BLY

Second detective of Mr HUMBLE

Dr Martin BLYTHE

Second detective of Insp MELLISON

Max BLYTHE

Second detective of Carole TREVOR

Al BOCCA

is the eponymous invention of the pseudonymous author and purports to be a tough, slangy American PI. However, since the writer is British, he needs to be taken with a large pinch of salt.

American Male Private Detective operating in San Francisco

Al BOCCA 1918- (British)

is the author of many novels for the US market, most of which feature tough American private eyes.

Writer: Bevis Peter WINTER

Other Bylines:
Peter CAGNEY
Bevis WINTER

Citation Record: 32 Books

Blonde Dynamite - *First*
Scion UK (1950)

No Room At The Morgue - *Last*
Milestone UK (1954)

Asher BOCKHORN

works for an agency called MaxAmerica & Pacific in the year 2077. The cases still seem to be as tough as ever, with as many villains around as in the good old twentieth century.

American Male Private Detective operating in Space

Barney COHEN (American)

Citation Record: 2 Books

The Taking Of Satcon Station - *First*
Pinnacle US (1983)

Blood On The Moon - *Latest*
Pinnacle US (1984)

Maj BODDY

solves a case of murder by shooting in a locked room.

British Male Amateur operating in England

John BUDE 1901-1957 (British)

Invented 4 detectives - see Insp SHERWOOD

Citation Record: 1 Book

Death Knows No Calendar - *Only*
Cassell UK (1942)

Det BODKIN

is, in 1900, a detective at the newly formed Scotland Yard.

British Policeman operating in London

Henry BEAUCHAMP (British)

Citation Record: 1 Book

The Lost Emeralds Of Zarinthia - *Only*
Sands UK (1899); Knight US (1900)

Sam BOGGS

American Male Sleuth operating in USA

Mark WASHBURN 1948- (American)

Citation Record: 2 Books

The Armageddon Game - *First*
Putnam US (1977); Davies UK (1978)

The Omega Threat - *Latest*
Dell US (1980); Sphere UK (1982)

B

Simon BOGNOR

is a special investigator for the British Board of Trade, a position that, unexciting though it may sound, in fact brings him into situations of absurd but dastardly crime, especially murder. Mediocre in almost every respect, physically unprepossessing, although there are girls who fall for him, *Simon BOGNOR* is too stout, drinks and eats too much, and is a real flounderer. A truly comic anti-hero, hounded by his boss, Parkinson, and adored through thick and thin by his wife, Monica, he stumbles on the solutions to his cases almost accidentally.

British Male Professional Investigator operating in England

Tim HEALD 1944- (British)

was born in Dorchester, Dorset. He was educated at Sherborne School, Dorset, and took a BA in History at Balliol College, Oxford, 1965. He is a journalist and columnist.

Writer: Timothy Villiers HEALD

Inventor of one other detective Dorothy Mayotte RIGBY

Citation Record: 10 Books

Unbecoming Habits - *First*
Hutchinson UK (1973); Stein & Day US (1973)

Business Unusual - *Latest*
Macmillan UK (1989)

Mack (The Executioner) BOLAN

returns from the war in Vietnam disillusioned and vengeful, resolving to wipe out the American Mafia in a great number of books of extraordinary nonsense and full of cheap violence. In the course of his self-imposed career he does have to do some sleuthing.

American Male Sleuth operating in USA

Don PENDLETON 1927- (American)

Invented 3 detectives - see Joe COPP

Citation Record: 37 Books

War Against The Mafia - *First*
Pinnacle US (1969); Sphere UK (1973)

Satan's Sabbath - *Last*
Pinnacle US (1980); Corgi UK (1981)

Jim PETERSON 1929- (American)

For writer details see Colin STRYKER

Citation Record: 1 Book

Sicilian Slaughter - *Only*
Pinnacle US (1973); Corgi UK (1973)

Det Lou BOLDT and Daphne MATTHEWS

He is a police detective and she is a police psychologist and they work together to solve the now all too common maniacal crimes that seem to have ousted decent intellectual murder from our criminous pages.

American Policeman and American Female Professional Investigator in Seattle

Ridley PEARSON 1953- (American)

See main detective Det James DEWITT

Citation Record: 2 Books

Angel Maker - *First*
Hyperion US (1993)

No Witnesses - *Latest*
Hyperion US (1994); Pocket Books UK (1995)

Orson BOLES

Second detective of Kiel ST JAMES

John BOLSOVER

British Male Amateur operating in England

Una L SILBERRAD 1872-1955 (British)

Writer: Una Lucy SILBERRAD

Citation Record: 7 Short Stories in 1 Collection

The Affairs Of John Bolsover - *Collection 1*
Nelson UK (1911)

Dave (The Pro) BOLT

American Male Professional Investigator operating in USA

Richard CURTIS (American)

Citation Record: 4 Books

The $3 Million Turn-Over - *First*
Warner US (1974)

The Suicide Squad - *Last*
Warner US (1975)

John BOLT

American Male Sleuth operating in New York

Robert HAWKES (American)

For writer details see Hawthorne Albert HARKER

Citation Record: 9 Books

Narc - *First*
Lancer UK (1973)

Kill For It - *Last*
Signet UK (1975)

Bow Street Runner BOLTER

has, in fact, recently left the official force and is now a 'private enquiry agent'. He appears only in two collections of short stories (uncounted), published almost thirty years before the emergence of *Sherlock HOLMES*.

British Male Private Detective operating in London

Charles MARTEL 1810-1865 (British)

Writer: Thomas DELF

Citation Record: 2 Collections

The Detective's Note-Book - *Collection 1*
Ward, Lock UK (1860)

Diary Of An Ex-Detective - *Collection 2*
Ward, Lock UK (1860)

Judy BOLTON

was one of the most distinctive of the many American girl detectives to emerge in the inter-war years. A young lady from Pennsylvania, she was just fifteen when the stories began in 1932 and only twenty-two when they ceased in 1967.

American Female Amateur operating in USA

Margaret SUTTON (American)

Citation Record: 1 Selected Short Story

The Vanishing Shadow
was the first story in which *Judy BOLTON* appeared.
US (1932)

Raoul BOMFORTUNE

French Male Amateur operating in several locations

H C BAILEY 1878-1961 (British)

Invented 4 detectives - see Dr Reginald FORTUNE

Citation Record: 11 Short Stories in 1 Collection

Raoul: Gentleman Of Fortune - *Collection 1*
Hutchinson UK (1907)

Det Insp Napoleon BONAPARTE

is a unique creation. A tall, muscular, attractive man, half aboriginal and half white in descent, he joined the Queensland police force and has risen to a high rank because of his special qualities – his intimate knowledge of the bush and almost extra-sensory skills of the aborigine combined with the education usually reserved for the white population. In most of his cases, he tracks down criminals in difficult circumstances in the outbacks of Australia. The books, which were originally denigrated, are enriched with a fine feeling for Australian rural life and are now justly admired.

Australian Policeman operating in Queensland, Australia

Arthur W UPFIELD 1888-1964 (Australian)

was born in Gosport, Hampshire, England. His father shipped him to Australia in 1911 when he refused to work as a real estate surveyor and there he worked as a cowhand

and sheepherder. In 1914 he enlisted and fought with the Australian forces at Gallipoli and in France. On his return, he worked as a trapper, explorer and goldminer. He had already written four novels he knew would be unpublishable and he turned to writing for magazines, when a chance meeting gave him the model for his unique detective. His subsequent novels, although lacking in fine literary expertise, are of extraordinary quality in conveying the sense of the great Australian outbacks and the mysteries they hold.

Writer: Arthur William UPFIELD

Citation Record: 29 Books

The Barrakee Mystery - *First*
Hutchinson UK (1929)

The Lure Of The Bush - *First**
Doubleday US (1965)

The Lake Frome Monster - *Last*
was completed, after the author's death, by J L Price and Dorothy Strange.
Heinemann UK (1966)

Christopher BOND

American Male Sleuth operating in several locations

Wyndham MARTYN 1875- (British)

Invented 3 detectives - see Prof John SOUTHARD

Citation Record: 9 Books

The Spies Of Peace - *First*
Jenkins UK (1934)

The Chromium Cat - *Last*
Jenkins UK (1952)

Ed BOND

is a journalist who sleuths once.

British Male Amateur operating in England

Virgil MARKHAM 1899- (British)

Invented 5 detectives - see Insp Myles RUSBY

Citation Record: 1 Book

The Dead Are Prowling - *Only*
Collins UK (1934)

Israel 'Oy-Oy-7' BOND

is a Jewish super-spy, a *James BOND* spoof.

American Male Professional Investigator operating in several locations

Sol WEINSTEIN 1928- (American)

Citation Record: 4 Books

Loxfinger - *First*
Pocket Books US (1965)

You Only Live Until You Die - *Last*
Trident Press US (1968)

Cdr James BOND

is one of the seminal creations of the century. Known as Special Agent 007, he has imposed his presence, his name and his legendary ambience on circles far wider than the genre for which they were intended. Although the books were initially denigrated because of their novel introduction of themes of sex and violence into what was hitherto regarded (by experts and critics alike) as a rather gentlemanly game, they have now entered the realms of classic fiction and even folklore.

James BOND, indeed, is a continuation by other methods, as it were, of a long line of peculiarly British heroes, like *'Bulldog' DRUMMOND* and *Richard HANNAY*, as much at home in his era as they were in theirs. He is the hero-adventurer-detective brought into the post-1945 world, the world of the Cold War, of espionage gone mad, but not less thrilling for that. A gentleman, of course, a lover of good wines and bad women, always elegantly dressed and with every technical gadget in his suitcase, he fits cleverly into a society in which fast travel, exotic holidays and beautiful girls litter the pages of countless glossy magazines and the minds of the new generations whose dreams appear in them. As an agent on Her Majesty's Service, he had considerable classical detection to do in his earlier books, but the later ones rather turned to tricks and capers. Nevertheless, *BOND* now stands on a pedestal of the genre reserved for only a few. As a final accolade, the saga of his exploits was continued by other writers after the death of his creator.

British Male Secret Agent operating in several locations

Ian FLEMING 1908-1964 (British)

was born in London. He was educated at Durnford School, Isle of Purbeck, Eton College, and the Royal Military College, Sandhurst. He worked as a reporter for Reuters, 1929-1933, and later for firms of bankers and stockbrokers. At the outbreak of war he was made Lieutenant in the Royal Navy and became a personal assistant to the Director of Naval Intelligence, 1939-1945. After the war he worked in publishing until, in 1954, he published his first *James BOND* novel. In this he created one of the seminal characters of modern fiction.

Although the novels were received somewhat negatively when they first appeared, for reasons that now seem ludicrous and tendentious, it is clear that they predicted and reflected changes in the post-war world and the tensions they would cause.

FLEMING's style was novel too, with its throwaway advertising for drinks, cars, dress, food and perfume – in fact, exactly what the new, slightly-moneyed, lower-middle and working classes wanted to read about. It was a style that was to set new trends in criminous fiction and was emulated by many later authors. The success of his books was enormous and extraordinarily popular films were made from several of them. Abjured by critics, loved by publishers, it has been said that *Ian FLEMING* had the qualities of writers like *Charles DICKENS*, encompassing the practical and the universal elements of life in a mature literary style.

Writer: Ian Lancaster FLEMING

Citation Record: 12 Books 7 Short Stories in 2 Collections

Casino Royale - *First*
Cape UK (1954); Macmillan US (1954)

You Asked For It - *First**
Popular Library US (1955)

The Man With The Golden Gun - *Last*
Cape UK (1965); New American Library US (1965)

For Your Eyes Only - *Collection 1*
Short stories - 5
Cape UK (1960); Viking US (1960)

Octopussy And The Living Daylights - *Collection 2*
contains an uncounted number of the author's short stories.
Short stories - 2
Cape UK (1966)

Octopussy - *Collection 2**
Cape UK (1966)

John GARDNER 1926- (British)

Invented 5 detectives - see Boysie OAKES

Citation Record: 8 Books

Licence Renewed - *Pastiche 1*
The saga of *James BOND* was too much of a temptation to be given up by the publishers after the death of his creator. After much heart-searching, they put its continuation into the hands of an author who had already written the *Boysie OAKES* series and other spy thrillers. There may be many more *BOND* books to come.
Coward McCann US (1981)

Never Send Flowers - *Pastiche 2*
Hodder & Stoughton UK (1993)

Robert MARKHAM 1922- (British)

For writer details see Peter FURNEAUX

B

Citation Record: 1 Book

Colonel Sun - *Pastiche 1*
Cape UK (1968); Harper & Row US (1968)

Christopher WOOD 1935- (British)

Writer: Christopher Hovelle WOOD

Citation Record: 2 Books

James Bond, The Spy Who Loved Me - *Pastiche 1*
Cape UK (1977); Warner US (1977)

James Bond And Moonraker - *Pastiche 2*
Panther UK (1979); Jove US (1979)

Marty BOND

was once in the New York Police Department but was retired because of violent behaviour - not theirs but his. He now works as a house dick in a shady Manhattan hotel.

American Male Private Detective operating in New York

Ed LACY 1911-1968 (American)

Invented 8 detectives - see Toussaint 'Touie' MOORE

Citation Record: 1 Book

The Men From The Boys - *Only*
Harper & Row US (1956); Boardman UK (1960)

Insp Victor BONDURANT

is involved in murders that seem to occur in hospitals an inordinate number of times, even for Chicago. Usually he is the chief detective on the case, but in two books he is assisted in his sleuthing by *Paul RAVEL.*

American Policeman operating in Chicago

James G EDWARDS 1900-1954 (American)

Writer: James William MCQUEEN

Inventor of one other detective pair Insp Victor BONDURANT and Paul RAVEL

Citation Record: 6 Books

Murder In The Surgery - *First*
Doubleday US (1935)

But The Patient Died - *Last*
Doubleday US (1948); Cherry Tree UK (1949)

Insp Victor BONDURANT and Paul RAVEL

American Policeman and Sleuth operating in Chicago

James G EDWARDS 1900-1954 (American)

See main detective Insp Victor BONDURANT

Citation Record: 2 Books

The Private Pavilion - *First*
Doubleday US (1935)

F Corridor - *Last*
Doubleday US (1936)

BONE

awakes one day after falling asleep in Central Park to find he has no memory. It seems he might be a serial killer who is on the loose. However, since his innate intelligence is all that remains to him, he uses it to prove he is innocent and to solve the mystery of his own identity.

American Male Amateur operating in New York

George CHESBRO 1940- (American)

Invented 4 detectives - see Dr Robert 'Mongo' FREDERICKSON

Citation Record: 1 Book

Bone - *Single*
Mysterious Press US (1989)

Enoch BONE

efficiently and satisfactorily saves the USA from destruction by an arch-criminal, who will certainly not try it again.

American Male Private Detective operating in USA

Sidekick: John WESTON

American Male - Assistant

Gahan WILSON (American)

See main detective Eddy DECO

Citation Record: 1 Book

Everybody's Favorite Duck - *Single*
Mysterious Press US (1988)

Supt Robert BONE

is a straight-forward, no-nonsense British cop and a good detective.

British Policeman operating in England

Jill STAYNES and Margaret STOREY 1926- (British)

Citation Record: 5 Books

Goodbye, Nanny Gray - *First*
Bodley Head UK (1987); Summit US (1990)

The Late Lady - *Latest*
Century UK (1992)

Insp BONES

is a quintessential modern version of the British stage bobby, upgraded in rank in this, one of the great comic plays of the century. Brilliantly stupid, stupidly brilliant, he catches nobody and cannot be caught, for his logical processes are beyond comprehension.

British Policeman operating in England

Tom STOPPARD 1937- (British)

was born, as Thomas Straussler, in Zlin, Czechoslovakia, his father being a British officer who was later killed in the Second World War. Educated in Nottingham and Yorkshire, he was a journalist for a short time, but soon became a full-time writer and playwright. He is the author of several plays, some of which are considered to be among the finest to have been written this century.

Citation Record: 1 Book

Jumpers - *Play*
is a 2-act stage play.
Faber UK (1972)

Haricot BONES

is a *Sherlock HOLMES* parody.

Male Professional Amateur

Sidekick: Dr DAWSON
is his parody *WATSON*-like assistant.

Male - Assistant

John SUTHERLAND (American)

Citation Record: 1 Selected Short Story

The Struldbrugg Reaction - *Parody 1*
appeared in the July 1964 number.
In 'Magazine of Fantasy & Science Fiction' US (1964)

Norman BONES

is a boy detective who appeared in many British radio episodes as well as short stories during the 1950s. He was ably supported by his younger brother.

British Male Amateur operating in England

Sidekick: Henry BONES

British Male - Brother

Anthony C WILSON (British)

Citation Record: 1 Collection

Norman Bones, Detective - *Collection 1*
Methuen UK (1949)

Sherlock BONES

calls himself the world's only pet detective.

American Male Professional Investigator operating in USA

John KEANE (American)

Citation Record: 1 Book

Sherlock Bones, Tracer Of Missing Pets - *Parody 1*
Lippincott US (1079)

Thinlock BONES

is a *Sherlock HOLMES* parody.

Male Professional Amateur

B

Sidekick: WHATSONAME
is his parody *WATSON*-like assistant.
Male - Assistant

ZERO (British)
Writer: Allan RAMSAY
Citation Record: 1 Selected Short Story
The Adventure Of The Table Foot - *Parody 1*
appeared in the January number.
In 'The Bohemian' US (1894)

Warlock BONES
is a *Sherlock HOLMES* parody.
British Male Professional Amateur operating in England
Sidekick: GOSWELL
narrates this tale, rather in the manner of Dr Johnson's Boswell.
British Male - Narrator

G F FORREST
Citation Record: 1 Selected Short Story
The Adventure Of The Diamond Necklace - *Parody 1*
concerns the mystery of a jewel theft. It appeared in an anthology, *Misfits: A Book of Parodies.*
Frank Harvey UK (1905)

BONNER
American Male Sleuth operating in USA

Richard HARDING 1955?- (American)
For writer details see Det Insp Samuel 'Smudge' HUDDLESTON
Citation Record: 4 Books
The Outrider - *First*
Pinnacle US (1984)
Bay City Burnout - *Latest*
Pinnacle US (1985)

Theodora 'Dol' BONNER
was one of this famous author's earliest creations. Apparently she originally found it difficult to decide whether to be a landscape designer or a detective, but chose to be the latter. However, she tended to faint when confronted by a villain, a distinct disadvantage for an up-and-coming sleuth. The author soon discarded her in favour of better (and bigger!) things.
American Female Private Detective operating in New York

Rex STOUT 1886-1975 (American)
Invented 6 detectives - see Nero WOLFE
Citation Record: 1 Book
The Hand In The Glove - *Only*
Farrar & Rinehart US (1937)
Crime On Her Hands - *Only**
Collins UK (1939)

Const John BOODY
British Policeman operating in England

E Temple THURSTON 1879-1933 (British)
Writer: Ernest Temple THURSTON
Citation Record: 15 Short Stories in 1 Collection
John Boddy: Leaves From A Constable's Notebook - *Collection 1*
Ward, Lock UK (1931)

Sam BOOKER and Jimmy WEBB
are two unpleasant private eyes, hired by several men to find one woman.
American Male Private Detectives operating in USA

Jerome ODLUM 1905-1954 (American)
Invented 3 detectives - see John STEELE
Citation Record: 1 Book
The Morgue Is Always Open - *Only*
Scribner's US (1944)

Mallory BOOKOVER
American Male Amateur operating in USA

Mignon G EBERHART 1899- (American)
Invented 9 detectives - see Sarah KEATE
Citation Record: 1 Book
Casa Madrone - *Only*
Random House US (1980); Collins UK (1980)

Sgt John BOON
Second detective of Offr Tally WICKHAM

Jefferson (The Handyman) BOONE
American Male Professional Investigator operating in USA/Europe

Jon MESSMANN (American)
Writer: Jon J MESSMAN
Other Byline: Nick CARTER
Inventor of one other detective Ben (The Revenger) MARTIN
Citation Record: 7 Books
The Moneta Papers - *First*
Pyramid US (1973); New English Library UK (1977)
Ransom! - *Last*
Pyramid US (1975)

Insp BOOT
is an expert in gang warfare who is called in to solve what seems to be a case of murder at a residence for professional women.
American Policeman operating in USA

Q PATRICK 1901- (American)
Invented 5 detectives - see Lt Timothy TRANT
Citation Record: 1 Book
Murder At The Women's City Club - *Only*
Swain US (1932)
Death In The Dovecote - *Only**
Cassell UK (1934)

The BOOT BLACK DETECTIVE
American Male Detective in Pulp Magazines operating in USA

Allan ARNOLD (American)
Invented 6 detectives - see OLD SNAP
Citation Record: 1 Book
The Boot Black Detective; Or, The Youngest Man Hunter On The Force
New York Detective Library US (1882-8)

Silas BOOTH
is not averse to blackmailing his clients on the side. Definitely not a solid citizen!
American Male Private Detective operating in Los Angeles

J Lane LINKLATER (American)
Writer: Alex WATKINS
Citation Record: 7 Books
Black Opal - *First*
Mill US (1947); Boardman UK (1949)
A Tisket, A Casket - *Last*
Mystery House US (1959)

Insp BOOTLE
investigates in an English village in which dwell a remarkably large number of literary types, one of whom, not surprisingly, gets himself murdered.
British Policeman operating in England
Sidekick: SWIFT
British Male - Subordinate

Edwin DE CAIRE (British)
Writer: Edwin Alfred WILLIAMS
Citation Record: 1 Book
Death Among The Writers - *Only*
Hodder & Stoughton UK (1952)

El BORBAH
is one of a new generation of heroes and detectives based on comic strip characters. He looks like a Mexican wrestler, lives

B

on junk food, and meets crimes that are themselves comic strips, in which anything goes. Although a minor cult, such characters would not seem to be a major advance in the history of literature.

American Male Private Detective operating in New York

Charles BURNS (American)

Citation Record: 1 Book

Hard-Boiled Defective Stories - *Single*
Raw US (1988)

Johnny BORDELON

is Cajun French by extraction. A student at Tulane, he joined the police force when he ran into debt. Then he resigned, married, divorced, decided to be a painter and finally set up an agency on Rampart Street. When he isn't being a superb cook and a great man at karate, he does private detecting.

American Male Private Detective operating in New Orleans

George F OGAN 1912- (American)

Citation Record: 3 Books

To Kill A Judge - *First*
Raven US (1981)

Murder By Proxy - *Latest*
!See Appendix 2.
Raven US (1981)

Lizzie BORDEN

is, indeed, the young lady, accused thirty years before the novel begins of hacking her parents to death with an axe, and famed in lay and legend ever since. She now, in 1921, appears again on the scene of an axe murder and has to turn detective to clear herself from (all things considered, not unreasonable) suspicion.

American Female Amateur operating in New England

Walter SATTERTHWAIT (American)

Invented 3 detectives - see Rita MONDRAGON

Citation Record: 1 Book

Miss Lizzie - *Single*
St Martin's US (1989); Collins UK (1990)

Steve BORDEN

American Male Sleuth operating in New York

Bernard DOUGALL (American)

Citation Record: 2 Books

I Don't Scare Easy - *First*
Dodd, Mead US (1941)

The Singing Corpse - *Last*
Dodd, Mead US (1943); Boardman UK (1944)

The BORDER LINE DETECTIVE

American Male Detective in Pulp Magazines operating in USA

Police Captain HOWARD (American)

Invented 15 detectives - see LIGHTNING LUKE

Citation Record: 1 Book

The Border Line Detective; Or, Watching The Smugglers Of The Chinese
New York Detective Library US (1882-8)

Stephen BORG

British Male Sleuth operating in England

Carl A POSEY 1933- (British)

Writer: Carl Alfred POSEY

Citation Record: 2 Books

Kiev Footprint - *First*
Hale UK (1983); Dodd, Mead US (1983)

Prospero Drill - *Latest*
Hale UK (1984); St Martin's US (1985)

Insp Salvador BORGES

is a violet-eyed, softly-spoken policeman in the Brigade of Criminal Investigation.

Spanish Policeman operating in Spain

John BONETT 1906- (British)

wrote this one novel featuring *Insp BORGES* after writing several criminous works with his wife, including two others featuring *BORGES*.

Writer: John Hubert Arthur COULSON

Citation Record: 1 Book

Perish The Thought - *Only*
Hale UK (1984)

John BONETT and Emery BONETT (British)

are a husband-and-wife team. He was born in Benton, Northumberland, and she in Sheffield, Yorkshire. They both settled on the Costa Brava, Spain, in the early 1960s and did most of their writing there.

Writers: John Hubert Arthur COULSON 1906- and Felicity Winifred Carter COULSON 1907-

Inventor of one other detective Prof MANDRAKE

Citation Record: 5 Books

Better Dead - *First*
Joseph UK (1964)

Better Off Dead - *First**
Doubleday US (1964)

No Time To Kill - *Last*
Harrap UK (1972); Walker US (1972)

John BORHAM

British Male Amateur operating in England

Gordon BRODIE (British)

Citation Record: 3 Books

The Lady Had A Tiger - *First*
Hale UK (1968)

Who Called Diamonds? - *Last*
Hale UK (1970)

Billy BORKER

Australian Male Amateur operating in Australia

Frank HARDY (Australian)

Writer: Frank Joseph HARDY

Citation Record: 28 Short Stories in 1 Collection

The Yarns Of Billy Borker - *Collection 1*
Reed AU (1965)

Lt BORUVKA

Czech Policeman operating in Prague

Josef SKVORECKY 1924- (Czech)

Writer: Josef Vaclav SKVORECKY

Inventor of one other detective Eve ADAM

Citation Record: 1 Book 17 Short Stories in 2 Collections

The Return Of Lieutenant Boruvka - *Single*
is a translation from the Czech of *Navrat Porucika Boruvky.*
Faber UK (1990); Norton US (1991)

The Mournful Demeanour Of Lieutenant Boruvka - *Collection 1*
A translation from the Czech of *Smutek Porucika Boruvky.*
Short stories - 12
Gollancz UK (1973); Norton US (1987)

The End Of Lieutenant Boruvka - *Collection 2*
is a translation from the Czech of *Konec Porucika Boruvky.*
Short stories - 5
Faber UK (1990); Norton US (1990)

Det Harry BOSCH

of the Los Angeles Police Department is being demoted and investigated by a US committee on international affairs. Meanwhile he pursues his own cases. His name and the lunacies of the city he works in are a measured and deliberate parody of the times of his famous predecessor, the medieval painter, Hieronymus Bosch.

American Policeman operating in Los Angeles

B

Michael CONNELLY (American)

Citation Record: 3 Books

The Black Echo - *First*
Headline UK (1992)

The Concrete Blonde - *Latest*
Little, Brown US (1994)

Insp BOSCO OF THE YARD

British Policeman operating in London

Laura Kinn CHRISTOPHER

Citation Record: 3 Books

Inspector Bosco And The Cat Burglar. - *First*
UK (?)

Inspector Bosco And Lady Indiana - *Last*
UK (?)

Sgt/Supt Geoffrey BOSCOBELL

progresses from the rank of Sergeant to that of Superintendent at Scotland Yard in these books. In three later books he works with *Insp ELLERDINE*, who then replaces him in the series.

British Policeman operating in London

Cecil WILLS 1891- (British)

Writer: Maitland Cecil Melville WILLS

Other Detectives:
Supt Geoffrey BOSCOBELL and Insp Roger ELLERDINE
Insp Roger ELLERDINE PINKNEY

Citation Record: 9 Books

Author In Distress - *First*
Heritage UK (1934)

Number 18 - *First**
Lane UK (1934)

The Case Of The Calabar Bean - *Last*
Hodder & Stoughton UK (1939)

Supt Geoffrey BOSCOBELL and Insp Roger ELLERDINE

British Policemen operating in London

Cecil WILLS 1891- (British)

Invented 4 detectives - see Sgt/Supt Geoffrey BOSCOBELL

Citation Record: 3 Books

The Case Of The R E Pipe - *First*
Hodder & Stoughton UK (1940)

The Clue Of The Golden Ear-Ring - *Last*
Hodder & Stoughton UK (1950)

A BOSTON POLICE OFFICER

American Policeman operating in Boston

Edward H SAVAGE 1812-1893 (American)

Writer: Edward Hartwell SAVAGE

Citation Record: 50 Short Stories in 1 Collection

A Chronological History Of The Boston Watch And Police From 1681 To 1865 - *Collection 1*
Dale US (1873)

Gen Taddeo BOTTANDO, Flavia DI STEFANO and Jonathan ARGYLL

appear in cases involving forgery, theft and murder in the Italian art world, They operate as a real trio of detectives, each one playing an individual and essential part in the sleuthing. They are *Gen BOTTANDO*, Chief of the Rome Art Theft Squad, his assistant, *Flavia DI STEFANO*, and an English art historian, *Jonathan ARGYLL*, who is in Italy to buy pictures for a London gallery.

Italian Policeman, Italian Policewoman, and British Amateur operating in Rome

Ian PEARS 1955- (British)

Writer: Ian George PEARS

Citation Record: 2 Books

The Raphael Affair - *First*
Gollancz UK (1990); Harcourt Brace US (1992)

Giotto's Hand - *Latest*
Gollancz UK (1994)

Col BOTTESFORD

is a Crimean War veteran and the detective in this Victorian novel.

British Male Amateur operating in England

Albert D VANDAM 1843-1903 (British)

Writer: Albert Dresden VANDAM

Inventor of one other detective DAVENPORT

Citation Record: 1 Book

A Court Tragedy - *Only*
Chatto & Windus UK (1900)

Wencelaus BOTTWINK

is a Czech refugee who attends an English Christmas party at a castle that naturally becomes snowbound. Equally naturally, murders occur and he solves them elegantly.

Czech Male Amateur operating in England

Stooge: Sgt ROGERS
is quite out of his depth in this book, in which the academic *BOTTWINK* shows his brilliance.
British Male

Cyril HARE 1900-1958 (British)

Invented 4 detectives - see Insp MALLETT

Citation Record: 1 Book

An English Murder - *Only*
Faber UK (1951); Little, Brown US (1951)

The Christmas Murder - *Only**
Spivak US (1953)

Raymond BOUDRO

is a black criminal defence lawyer in San Antonio who elects to defend a white detective, a known racist, accused of murder.

American Male Amateur operating in Texas

Jay BRANDON (American)

Citation Record: 1 Book

Rules Of Evidence - *Single*
Joseph UK (1992)

Peter BOUNTY

American Male Sleuth operating in Texas/Mexico

Todd DOWNING 1902- (American)

See main detective Hugh RENNERT

Citation Record: 3 Books

Murder On The Tropic - *First*
Doubleday US (1935); Methuen UK (1936)

The Lazy Lawrence Murders - *Last*
Doubleday US (1941)

Insp BOURNE

British Policeman operating in England

R C FINNEY (British)

Writer: Robert Cecil FINNEY

Citation Record: 1 Book

Meet Inspector Bourne - *Only*
Newcoll UK (1945)

Ch Insp 'Daddy' BOURNE

British Policeman operating in Scotland

G V GALWEY 1912- (British)

Writer: Geoffrey Valentine GALWEY

Citation Record: 3 Books

Murder On Leave - *First*
Lane UK (1946)

Full Fathom Five - *Last*
Hodder & Stoughton UK (1951)

Edwin BOUSFIELD

Second detective of ROBSON

Insp BOW and Capt KEETCH

solve a case of shooting in a locked room.

British Policeman and British Sleuth operating in England

B

Paul HERRING (British)

Citation Record: 1 Book

The Murder Of Margot Midnight - *Only*
Low UK (1932)

The Midnight Murder - *Only**
Lippincott US (1932)

Geoffrey BOWEN

American Male Amateur operating in USA

Frances LOCKRIDGE and Richard LOCKRIDGE (American)

Invented 5 detectives - see Bernard SIMMONS

Citation Record: 1 Book

Catch As Catch Can - *Only*
Lippincott US (1958); Long UK (1960)

Sally BOWEN

investigates which of her seven aunts murdered her husband.

American Female Amateur operating in USA

Patricia MCGERR 1917-1985 (American)

See main detective Selena MEAD

Citation Record: 1 Book

The Seven Deadly Sisters - *Only*
Doubleday US (1947); Collins UK (1948)

BOWERY BILLY

was one of the several bootblack detectives popular in the 1930 pulps.

American Male Detective in Pulp Magazines operating in New York

UNKNOWN

No citations

Henry BOWFORT

solves a case of death by shooting in a snowbound hut.

American Male Amateur operating in USA

Edward D HOCH 1930- (American)

Invented 20 detectives - see Capt LEOPOLD

Citation Record: 1 Selected Short Story

The Impossible 'Impossible Crime'
In 'Ellery Queen's Mystery Magazine' US (1968)

Supt BOWMAN

British Policeman operating in England

Julie BURROWS (British)

Citation Record: 2 Books

No Need For Violence - *First*
Cassell UK (1970)

Like An Evening Gone - *Last*
Macmillan UK (1973)

Glenn BOWMAN

is a British creation and appeared in a great number of books in which he simulated a 'top American PI'.

American Male Private Detective operating in New York

Hartley HOWARD 1908-1979 (British)

For writer details see John PIPER

Inventor of one other detective Philip SCOTT

Citation Record: 38 Books

The Last Appointment - *First*
Collins UK (1951)

The Sealed Envelope - *Last*
Collins UK (1979)

Virginia BOX

British Female Sleuth

James MOFFATT 1922- (British)

Invented 3 detectives - see Johnny CANUCK

Citation Record: 2 Books

Virginia Box And The "Unsatisfied" - *First*
New English Library UK (1974)

Perfect Assignment - *Last*
New English Library UK (1975)

The BOY DETECTIVE

British Male Detective in Pulp Magazines operating in London

ANON

Citation Record: 1 Book

The Boy Detective; Or, The Crimes Of London - *Only*
Howe UK (ca 1865)

Sgt BOYCE

is a member of the newly formed CID at Scotland Yard.

British Policeman operating in London

Hawley SMART 1833-1893 (British)

Invented 8 detectives - see Insp POLLOCK

Citation Record: 1 Book

The Plunger: A Turf Tragedy Of Five-And-Twenty Years Ago - *Only*
White UK (1891); Lippincott US (1891)

Belle BOYD

American Female Detective in Pulp Magazines operating in Chicago

Allan ARNOLD (American)

Invented 6 detectives - see OLD SNAP

Citation Record: 1 Book

Belle Boyd, The Girl Detective; A Story Of Chicago And The West - *Only*
New York Detective Library US (1882-8)

Danny BOYD

is one of the author's several, unmemorable, Hollywood detectives.

American Male Private Detective operating in Hollywood/New York

Carter BROWN 1923-1985 (Australian)

Invented 10 detectives - see Rick HOLMAN

Citation Record: 29 Books

Suddenly By Violence - *First*
Horwitz AU (1959); Signet US (1959)

Death To A Downbeat - *Last*
Horwitz AU (1980); Tower US (1980)

Felix BOYD

American Male Private Detective operating in New York

Scott CAMPBELL 1858-1933 (American)

For writer details see Luke SPEARE and Schyler COLE

Citation Record: 58 Short Stories in 6 Collections

Below The Dead-Line - *Collection 1*
Short stories - 12
Street & Smith (Magnet #428) US (1906)

On The Trail Of 'Big Finger' - *Collection 2*
Short stories - 12
Street & Smith (Magnet #429) US (1906)

The Exploits Of A Private Detective - *Collection 3*
Short stories - 10
Street & Smith (New Magnet # US (1909)

The Adventures Of Felix Boyd - *Collection 4*
Short stories - 8
Street & Smith (Magnet #603) US (1909)

Felix Boyd's Revelations - *Collection 5*
Short stories - 8
Street & Smith (New Magnet # US (1909)

Felix Boyd's Final Problems - *Collection 6*
Short stories - 8
Street & Smith (New Magnet # US (1909)

Nile BOYD

American Male Amateur operating in New England/New York

Dana CHAMBERS 1895-1946 (American)

See main detective Jim STEELE

Citation Record: 1 Book

Blood On The Blonde - *Only*
was published earlier under the following byline as *WITCH'S MOON.*
Jonathan US (1952)

Giles JACKSON 1895-1946 (American)
For writer details see Jim STEELE
Citation Record: 2 Books
Witch's Moon - *First*
Dial US (1941); Museum Press UK (1943)
Court Of Shadows - *Last*
Dial US (1943); Museum Press UK (1945)

Helen BOYDEN

American Female Amateur operating in USA

Anna CLARKE 1919- (British)
Invented 4 detectives - see Paula GLENNING
Citation Record: 1 Book
Game, Set And Danger - *Single*
Doubleday US (1981); Hale UK (1983)

Tony BOYLE

is a large, tough, pistol-toting simpleton who, mercifully, has but one outing.
American Male Private Detective operating in USA

William WALL (American)
Citation Record: 1 Book
Wake Up Dead - *Only*
Papillon US (1974)
Quiet Terror - *Only**
Decade US (1980)

Neville BOYLES

is a *Sherlock HOLMES* parody.
British Male Professional Amateur operating in England
Sidekick: Dr WATCHPOT
is his parody *WATSON*-like assistant.
Male - Assistant

Acorn N DOYLE (American)
Writer: Jon WILMUNEN
Citation Record: 3 Selected Short Stories
The Adventure Of Sir Edward Pins - *Parody 1*
appeared in the September number.
In 'Baker Street Journal' US (1965)
The Adventure Of The Speckled Hand - *Parody 2*
appeared in the March number. The title parodies that of the canonical story, *THE ADVENTURE OF THE SPECKLED BAND.*
In 'Baker Street Journal' US (1966)
The Adventure Of The Tarred Captain - *Parody 3*
The title refers to the allusion made by *Dr WATSON* in the canonical story, *THE NAVAL TREATY,* to some notes he had of an unchronicled case.
In 'The Gamebag' US (1966)

Jerry BOYNE

American Male Amateur operating in San Francisco

Alice MACGOWAN 1858- and Perry NEWBERRY 1870-1938 (American)
Citation Record: 5 Books
The Million Dollar Suitcase - *First*
Stokes US (1922); Hutchinson UK (1922)
Who Is This Man? - *Last*
Stokes US (1927); Hutchinson UK (1927)

Emmy BRACE

does research on murder trials for a TV station and gets involved in a real live one.
American Female Amateur operating in New York

Mignon G EBERHART 1899- (American)
Invented 9 detectives - see Sarah KEATE
Citation Record: 1 Book
Alpine Condo Crossfire - *Only*
Random House US (1984); Collins UK (1985)

Nicholas BRACEWELL

sleuths in Tudor England around 1590.
English Male Amateur operating in England

Edward MARSTON (British)
Writer: Keith MILES
Other Byline: Keith MILES
Citation Record: 3 Books
The Queen's Head - *First*
Bantam UK (1988); St Martin's US (1989)
The Trip To Jerusalem - *Latest*
Corgi UK (1990); St Martin's US (1990)

Donald BRACKEN and James Rowland WOODWARD VII

American Male Amateurs operating in New York

J S BLAZER (American)
Writer: Justin Blazer SCOTT
Citation Record: 2 Books
Deal Me Out - *First*
Bobbs US (1973)
Lend A Hand - *Last*
Bobbs US (1975)

Walter BRACKETT

is British, bored, moderately boiled, and over fifty. He winds up in San Francisco and becomes a private eye for the firm of Brackett & Kemble.
British Male Private Detective operating in San Francisco

Derek MARLOWE 1938- (British)
was born in London. Educated at the Cardinal Vaughan School, London, he graduated at the University of London, 1960. His novels deal with the shady side of espionage and, latterly, more with detection.
Citation Record: 1 Book
Somebody's Sister - *Only*
Cape UK (1974); Viking US (1974)

Insp BRADBURY and Sgt RAYMOND

British Policemen operating in England

Norman LONGMATE 1925- (British)
Writer: Norman Richard LONGMATE
Citation Record: 5 Books
Death Won't Wash - *First*
Cassell UK (1957)
Death In Office - *Last*
Hale UK (1961)

Mark BRADDON

British Male Amateur operating in England

Herbert ADAMS 1874-1958 (British)
Invented 3 detectives - see Jimmie HASWELL
Citation Record: 1 Book
The Strange Murder Of Hatton, KC - *Only*
Lippincott US (1933)
The Knife - *Only**
Collins UK (1934)

Capt Courtney BRADE

American Male Professional Investigator operating in Minnesota

Katherine WOLFFE 1892- (American)
Writer: Marian Gallagher SCOTT
Citation Record: 2 Books
The Attic Room - *First*
Morrow US (1942)
Death's Long Shadow - *Last*
Five Star US (1946)

Lou BRADE
Second detective of Lt Jack DOHERY

Simon BRADE
sleuths in England, although created by an American author. He is eccentric, hates work, and plays with little Chinese ivory cubes, which somehow help him solve his cases.
British Male Professional Amateur operating in England

Harriette R CAMPBELL 1883- (American)
was born in New York. The daughter of the State Attorney-General, she married and settled in London, England, where she has set her books.
Writer: Harriette Russell CAMPBELL
Citation Record: 7 Books
The String Glove Mystery - *First*
Knopf US (1936); Heinemann UK (1936)
Crime In Crystal - *Last*
Harper & Row US (1946)

Stan BRADEN
has to find a missing girl, a case that leads him into the various and usual kinds of squalid situation.
American Male Private Detective operating in California

Jack USHER (American)
Citation Record: 1 Book
The Fix - *Only*
Mill US (1959)
The Girl In The White Mercedes - *Only**
Heinemann UK (1960)

Sgt/Insp Peter BRADFIELD
appears also in books with the author's other detective, *Insp CHARLTON.*
British Policeman operating in England

Clifford WITTING 1907- (British)
Invented 3 detectives - see Insp Harry CHARLTON
Citation Record: 3 Books
There Was A Crooked Man - *First*
Hodder & Stoughton UK (1960); British Book Centre US (1962)
Crime In Whispers - *Last*
Hodder & Stoughton UK (1964)

Insp Peter BRADFIELD
Second detective of Insp CHARLTON

Hank BRADFORD
was in the police force in Seattle; but, when his partner was killed, he took up PI work.
American Male Private Detective operating in Seattle

Mike WARDEN (American)
Citation Record: 6 Books
Death Beat - *First*
Carousel US (1980)
The Topless Corpse - *Latest*
Carousel US (1981)

Supt BRADLEY
British Policeman operating in England

Colin ROBERTSON 1906-1980 (British)
Invented 7 detectives - see Mike REED
Citation Record: 11 Books
Murder In The Morning - *First*
Long UK (1957)
The Green Diamonds - *Last*
Hale UK (1970)

Mrs Adela Beatrice Lestrange BRADLEY
is one of the famed creations of the genre, although not to everyone's taste, mainly because of the peculiarities of the novels, with their dabbling in the occult. *Mrs. BRADLEY* is an elderly lady and looks like a witch. She is, however, a psychologist who runs her own clinic and is, we are told, in some ill-defined way, a 'consultant to the Home Office'. That being so, she is involved in all manner of bizarre crimes in her many books, the police usually being baffled until she comes to their aid.
British Female Professional Investigator operating in England

Gladys MITCHELL 1901-1983 (British)
was born in Cowley, Oxfordshire. She was educated at Rothschild School, Brentford, Middlesex, and studied English and History at the University of London, 1919-1926. For most of her life she taught these subjects at various girls' schools in and near London. She was a prolific writer, whose work covered several genres, published under her own name and a number of pseudonyms. She is best known for her crime and detective fiction, which appeared over more than half a century.
Writer: Gladys Maude Winifred MITCHELL
Other Byline: Malcolm TORRIE
Citation Record: 68 Books
Speedy Death - *First*
Gollancz UK (1929); Dial US (1929)
The Crozier Pharaohs - *Last*
Joseph UK (1984); Joseph US (1985)

Bill BRADLEY and Noel MAYBERRY
American Male Amateurs operating in New York

Gregory TREE 1916-1981 (American)
See main detective pair Insp Stephen ELIOT and Arthur CRUMP
Citation Record: 2 Books
The Case Against Myself - *First*
Scribner's US (1950); Gollancz UK (1951)
The Case Against Butterfly - *Last*
Scribner's US (1951)

Bo BRADLEY
is a child abuse investigator, the only true manic depressive sleuth to have appeared in the genre so far.
American Female Professional Investigator operating in USA

Abigail PADGETT (American)
Citation Record: 3 Books
Strawgirl - *First*
Mysterious Press US (1994)
Turtle Baby - *Latest*
Mysterious Press US (1995)

Jason BRADLEY
American Male Amateur operating in California

Gaylord D LARSEN 1932- (American)
Invented 3 detectives - see Henry GARRETT
Citation Record: 2 Books
The 180 Degrees Murder - *First*
Ballantine US (1987)
Arascadero Island - *Latest*
Ballantine US (1989)

Jim BRADLEY
is in Mexico on the trail of the perpetrators of a large-scale robbery.
American Male Private Detective operating in Mexico

Frank O'ROURKE 1916-1989 (American)
is better known as a writer of westerns.
Citation Record: 1 Book
High Dive - *Only*
Random House US (1954)

Luke BRADLEY
American Male Amateur operating in USA

Hugh PENTECOST 1903-1989 (American)
Invented 12 detectives - see Pierre CHAMBRUN

B

Citation Record: 3 Books
Cancelled In Red - *First*
Dodd, Mead US (1939); Heinemann UK (1939)
The Brass Chills - *Last*
Dodd, Mead US (1943); Hale UK (1944)

Luke BRADLEY
British Male Amateur operating in England

Joyce Emerson Preston MUDDOCK 1843-1934 (British)
Citation Record: 1 Book
Whose Was The Hand? - *Only*
Digby, Long UK (1901)

Rupert BRADLEY
operates in London soon after the end of the Second World War.
British Male Private Detective operating in London

E B RONALD 1920-1976 (British)
Writer: Ronald Ernest BARKER
Other Byline: Ronald BARKER
Citation Record: 3 Books
The Cat And Fiddle Murders - *First*
Gollancz UK (1954); Rinehart US (1955)
A Sort Of Madness - *Last*
Boardman UK (1958); Abelard US (1959)

Vernon BRADLUSKY
Male Sleuth operating in Portugal

Steven BOSAK (American)
Citation Record: 1 Book
Gammon - *Single*
St Martin's US (1985)

Bow Street Runner BRADSHAW and Bow Street Runner FRASER
are members of what is generally regarded as the earliest fully professional police force in the world, taking its name from a police court established in 1749 in Bow Street, in the West End of London. Bow Street Runners, as they were called, could serve writs and act as detectives and were the forerunners of the Metropolitan police force in London, by which they were superseded in 1829. It is interesting that they appear, as fully fledged detectives, in this mid-Victorian novel, shortly after the creation of Insp BUCKET by Charles DICKENS.
British Policemen operating in London

Albany FONBLANQUE 1829-1924 (British)
Writer: Albany De Grenier FONBLANQUE
Citation Record: 1 Book
Tom Rocket - *Only*
Ward, Lock UK (1860)

BRADSHAW
American Male Detective in Pulp Magazines operating in USA

Anthony P MORRIS 1849-1921 (American)
Invented 5 detectives - see Mark MAGIC
Citation Record: 1 Selected Short Story
Bradshaw, The Wide Awake Detective; Or, Piping A Very Remarkable Case
Old Cap Collier Library US (18??)

Charlie BRADSHAW
was once in the police force, but is now a small-time PI in and around Saratoga, New York. A bit of a bumbler, he has to do a variety of other jobs to eke out a living, such as delivering milk or managing a hotel off-season. Somehow he gets involved in odd cases, which he solves with the help of equally odd friends, most of them layabouts or ex-convicts.
American Male Private Detective operating in Saratoga

Sidekick: Victor PLOTZ
may be a little over-enthusiastic when he has to deal with the opposite sex, but he is a good assistant for this dithering detective.
American Male - Friend

Stooge: Ch PETERSON
of the local police is a constant and typical official thorn in the side of amateur detectives.
American Male

Stephen DOBYNS 1941- (American)
was born in Orange, New Jersey. He took degrees at Wayne State University, Detroit, and the University of Iowa, Iowa City. He has been an instructor in English and a University lecturer and is also a distinguished poet who has received several prizes and awards for his work.
Inventor of one other detective Det LAZARD
Citation Record: 7 Books
Saratoga Longshot - *First*
Atheneum US (1976); Hale UK (1978)
Saratoga Haunting - *Latest*
Penguin US (1993)

Noah BRADSHAW
Male Amateur operating in Canada

Madeleine JOHNSTON
Citation Record: 2 Books
Death Casts A Lure - *First*
Doubleday US (1938)
Comets Have Long Tails - *Last*
Doubleday US (1938); Eyre & Spottiswoode UK (1939)

Steve BRADSHAW
runs a detective agency in the West End of London and, in his one appearance, solves the problem of the disappearance of two people, caused by a mysterious ray gun. Not at all the thing one likes to happen!
British Male Private Detective operating in England

Frank PEPPE (British)
Citation Record: 1 Book
The Riddle In Wax - *Only*
Paget UK (1950?)

Jane BRADSHAWE
goes in for 'psychic investigations', a branch of detective science once popular but now apparently only indulged in by police officers who are even more baffled than usual.
British Female Amateur operating in England

Mary Ann ALLEN 1951-
Writer: Rosemary PARDOE
Citation Record: 9 Short Stories in 1 Collection
The Angry Dead - *Collection 1*
Demsey UK (1986)

Hal BRADY
sleuths back in the 1920s.
American Male Amateur operating in North Dakota

Margaret SCHERF 1908-1979 (American)
Invented 5 detectives - see Rev Martin BUELL
Citation Record: 1 Book
Don't Wake Me Up While I'm Driving - *Only*
Doubleday US (1977); Hale UK (1978)

Sheriff Joanna BRADY
is the first lady sheriff in Cochise County, being appointed partly, it would seem, on the sentimental but reasonable grounds that her father once held the office and her husband was murdered while running for it. Formerly a suspect in a drugs case, she now enforces the law, meeting standard corpses and amazing twists of plot on the way. She triumphs; for, as the blurb says, 'Every woman in America is obviously not a sheriff but Joanna Brady is every woman'.
American Policewoman operating in USA

J A JANCE 1944- (American)

See main detective Det J P BEAUMONT

Citation Record: 2 Books

Desert Heat - *First*
Morrow US (1993)

Tombstone Courage - *Last*
Morrow US (1994)

Pete BRADY

American Male Sleuth operating in Louisiana

M S KARL (American)

For writer details see Micah DUNN

Citation Record: 2 Books

Killer's Ink - *First*
Dodd, Mead US (1988)

Death Notice - *Last*
St Martin's US (1990)

Const John BRAGG

British Policeman operating in England

Henry WADE 1887-1969 (British)

Invented 7 detectives - see Ch Insp POOLE

Citation Record: 1 Book 13 Short Stories in 1 Collection

Released For Death - *Only*
Constable UK (1938)

Here Comes The Copper - *Collection 1*
Constable UK (1938)

Sgt Joseph BRAGG

is a London policeman during the 1890s. Although only a sergeant, he is called on to do detective work, with which his superiors – usually being of a higher social class – do not wish to soil their hands. Coming from the lower middle class, *BRAGG* is subject to severe social restrictions and inhibitions as to what he may or may not do among the gentry, who, of course, usually commit the most interesting crimes. Fortunately, in an ingenious idea for role reversal, his sidekick, a lowly constable, is from an aristocratic family and so is able to help him out.

British Policeman operating in London

Sidekick: Const James MORTON

is the second son of an aristocratic English family. Since second sons had little to look forward to in Victorian times, he has joined the Metropolitan police force. He is of considerable help to *Sgt BRAGG*, who is not easily able to investigate the gentry, even its criminal members.

British Male - Subordinate

Ray HARRISON 1928- (British)

was born in Chorley, Lancashire. He was educated at Ormskirk Grammar School, Lancashire, and took a BA at Magdalene College, Cambridge, 1952, followed by an MA, 1954. He then took the post of Inspector of Taxes, 1952-1962, and later was a senior fraud investigator for the Inland Revenue. He was a sometime head of Lloyds, the London underwriting company.

Writer: Raymond HARRISON

Citation Record: 13 Books

French Ordinary Murder - *First*
Quartet UK (1983)

Why Kill Arthur Potter? - *First**
Scribner's US (1984)

Hallmark Of Murder - *Latest*
Constable UK (1995)

Peter BRAGG

is a Korean War veteran. Once a reporter in Seattle, he has set up as a PI in San Francisco – which doesn't seem too difficult to do there, if the numerous American detective novels set in California are any guide.

American Male Private Detective operating in San Francisco

Jack LYNCH (American)

Citation Record: 7 Books

Bragg's Hunch - *First*
GM US (1981)

Seattle - *Latest*
Warner US (1985)

Peter BRAID

is an ex-Marine and a Second World War veteran. Although he operates as a Manhattan PI, he really seems none too bright, having frequently to telephone *Mickey SPILLANE's* famous hardboiled detective, *Mike HAMMER*, to get advice about this, his only known case.

American Male Private Detective operating in New York

Sidekick: Mike HAMMER

is the well-known hardboiled detective created by *Mickey SPILLANE*. He is enlisted, in spirit if not in substance, to help out the rather inadequate sleuth.

American Male - Advisor

David J GARRITY 1923-1984 (American)

Writer: David James GARRITY

Citation Record: 1 Book

Dragon Hunt - *Only*
Signet US (1967)

Col BRAIN

appears also in books with the author's other detective, *Ambrose LOW*.

British Male Amateur operating in England

Henry CECIL 1902-1976 (British)

was born in London. He was educated at St Paul's School, London, and at King's College, Cambridge, where he studied Law, and was called to the English Bar, 1923. After serving in the Army, 1939-45, he continued at the Bar and became a judge. The successful author of at least twenty-five novels in the criminous genre, as well as several successful plays, he used series detectives only rarely.

Writer: Henry Cecil LEON

Other Detectives:
Col BRAIN and Ambrose LOW Rosamond CLINCH
Roger THURSBY

Citation Record: 1 Book

Natural Causes - *Only*
Chapman & Hall UK (1953)

Col BRAIN and Ambrose LOW

Colonel BRAIN works, perforce, in association with the ex-crook, *Ambrose LOW*, and together they unravel legal matters leading to the solution of murders. He appears alone in one other book.

British Male Amateurs operating in England

Henry CECIL 1902-1976 (British)

Invented 4 detectives - see Col BRAIN

Citation Record: 2 Books

No Bail For The Judge - *First*
Chapman & Hall UK (1952); Harper & Row US (1952)

According To The Evidence - *Last*
Chapman & Hall UK (1954); Harper & Row US (1954)

Roger BRAITHWAITE

solves a case of murder on a fictional East coast campus.

American Male Amateur operating in Connecticut

Henry SUTTON 1935- (American)

Writer: David Rytman SLAVITT

Citation Record: 1 Book

The Sacrifice - *Single*
Grosset US (1978); Sphere Books UK (1980)

Rev Theodora BRAITHWAITE

is a deacon in the fictional parish of St Sylvester's, which lies somewhere near Kensington in London. She is six feet tall,

B

attractive, and an inveterate amateur sleuth, particularly when it comes to solving crimes involving church matters.

British Female Amateur operating in England

D M GREENWOOD (British)

Citation Record: 5 Books

In Holy Terrors - *First*
Headline UK (1994)

Every Deadly Sin - *Latest*
Headline UK (1995)

Ed BRAKELY

is a US Government agent. An ex-Yale man, class of 1922, he is sent back, under cover, to investigate smuggling and murder involving the old *alma mater.*

American Male Professional Investigator operating in Connecticut

Francis W BRONSON 1901-1966 (American)

Writer: Francis Woolsey BRONSON

Citation Record: 1 Book

The Bulldog Has The Key - *Only*
Farrar, Straus US (1949)

Insp BRAMLEY

appears in this one book as the main detective and is the police stooge in two others by this author.

British Policeman operating in Cambridge

Adam BROOME 1888- (British)

See main detective Capt/Commiss Denzil GRIGSON

Citation Record: 2 Books

The Oxford Murders - *First*
Bles UK (1929)

The Cambridge Murders - *Last*
Bles UK (1936)

Sheriff BRAMLEY

investigates the murder of four men and has to go back in time to the era of the Klansmen to find the perpetrators.

American Policeman operating in Mississippi

John ARMISTEAD (American)

Citation Record: 1 Book

A Legacy Of Vengeance - *Single*
Carroll & Graf US (1994)

Supt BRANBURY

was used by the prolific author only once, in what seems to be one of his hastier efforts.

British Policeman operating in London

Edgar WALLACE 1875-1932 (British)

Invented 28 detectives - see J G REEDER

Citation Record: 1 Selected Short Story

Lord Exenham Created A Sensation
In 'Strand Magazine' UK (1918)

Delia BRAND

was an early invention of the author, before he embarked on his classic detective series with *Nero WOLFE*. He does not seem to have used her again.

American Female Amateur operating in Wyoming

Rex STOUT 1886-1975 (American)

Invented 6 detectives - see Nero WOLFE

Citation Record: 1 Book

Mountain Cat - *Only*
Farrar & Rinehart US (1939); Collins UK (1940)

The Mountain Cat Murders - *Only**
Dell US (1943)

Hilary BRAND

appears in eight books, of which six were written under the eponymous pseudonym by *James MOFFATT* and two, which appeared under the same byline, by *Stephen D FRANCES* .

British Amateur operating in England

Hilary BRAND 1922- (British)

Writer: James MOFFATT

Other Bylines:
Hank JANSON
James MOFFATT

Citation Record: 6 Books

Peak Of Frenzy - *First*
Compact UK (1964)

A Flair For Affairs - *Last*
Compact UK (1966)

Hilary BRAND 1917-1989 (British)

See main detective John GAIL

Citation Record: 2 Books

News Girl - *First*
Compact UK (1963)

Brand T - *Last*
Compact UK (1964)

Jake (The Liquidator) BRAND

British Male Amateur operating in Georgia/Florida

R L BRENT (American)

Writer: Larry POWELL

Other Byline: Nick CARTER

Citation Record: 5 Books

The Liquidator - *First*
Award US (1974); Tandem UK (1974)

The Exchange - *Latest*
Charter US (1978)

Mark BRAND

is a lawyer, often known simply as The Counsellor, who has to do detective work to win his cases.

British Male Professional Investigator operating in England

J J CONNINGTON 1880-1947 (British)

was educated at universities in Glasgow, London and Germany, receiving many degrees. He became a distinguished physical chemist, teaching at Glasgow University, and was later appointed Professor of Chemistry at Queen's University, Belfast. In addition to being the author of twenty-four detective novels, he wrote six excellent chemistry textbooks.

Writer: Alfred Walter STEWART

Other Detectives:
Ch Const Sir Clinton DRIFFIELD
Supt ROSS
Col SANDERSTEAD
Conway WESTENHANGER

Citation Record: 2 Books

The Counsellor - *First*
Hodder & Stoughton UK (1940); Little, Brown US (1940)

The Four Defences - *Last*
Hodder & Stoughton UK (1940)

The Four Defenses - *Last**
Little, Brown US (1940)

Kyle BRANDEIS

Male Sleuth operating in Europe/America

William ASH 1917- (British)

Writer: William Franklin ASH

Citation Record: 2 Books

Ride A Paper Tiger - *First*
Hutchinson UK (1968); Walker US (1969)

Take-Off - *Last*
Walker US (1969); Hutchinson UK (1970)

Anthony BRANDON

works for the SIS and is sent to foil the usual nefarious but flawed plots that Soviet and Chinese agents were prone to get up to.

British Male Secret Agent operating in Los Angeles/Hong Kong

Bryan PETERS 1924-1966 (British)

Writer: Peter Bryan GEORGE

Other Byline: Peter GEORGE

Citation Record: 2 Books

The Big H - *First*
Boardman UK (1961); Holt US (1963)
Hong Kong Kill - *Last*
Boardman UK (1958); Washburn US (1959)

Det Frank BRANDON and Dr Adrian LANCASTER

are given rotten pasts, perhaps to tap the reader's sympathies. They work together in the small town of Morganstown to solve a series of strange murders with roots in the good doctor's old life.

American Policeman and American Male Amateur operating in Michigan

Craig HOLDEN (American)
Citation Record: 1 Book
The River Sorrow - *Single*
Delacorte US (1994)

Lew BRANDON

was just one of the many American detectives created by this British writer, whose vivid imagination did not induce him to worry over much about their credibility. Described as a partner in a New York detective agency, *Lew BRANDON* sets out, in his one appearance, to avenge his partner's death in the usual corrupt Californian city that the author tended to invent.

American Male Private Detective operating in California

James Hadley CHASE 1906-1985 (British)
Invented 14 detectives - see Dave FENNER
Citation Record: 1 Book
The Guilty Are Afraid - *Only*
Hale UK (1957); New American Library US (1959)

Mark BRANDON

sleuths in Chicago, though he was created by a British author.

American Male Private Detective operating in Chicago

Vernon WARREN 1925- (British)
Invented 5 detectives - see Johnny MAQUIS
Citation Record: 6 Books
Brandon Takes Over - *First*
Gifford UK (1953)
Bullets For Brandon - *Last*
Gifford UK (1955)

Dave BRANDSTETTER

is between fifty and sixty years old, openly homosexual, and actually getting on in years for a Californian PI. Even so, he still gets a lot of work and, unlike most other private eyes, he does not have to bother too much about filthy lucre; for, not only is he unduly cultured, but he appears to be rather wealthy.

American Male Private Detective operating in Los Angeles

Joseph HANSEN 1923- (American)
was born in Aberdeen, South Dakota. He has been a teacher at the University of California and is the author of at least thirteen mainstream novels under his real name and pseudonyms.
Inventor of one other detective Alan TARR
Citation Record: 10 Books
Fadeout - *First*
Harper & Row US (1970); Harrap UK (1972)
Obedience - *Latest*
Mysterious Press US (1988)

Miss BRANDT

British Female Amateur operating in England

Margery LAWRENCE ?-1969 (British)
Writer: Margery H LAWRENCE
Inventor of one other detective Miles PENNOYER
Citation Record: 4 Short Stories in 1 Collection
Miss Brandt: Adventuress - *Collection 1*
contains four novelettes.
Hutchinson UK (1923)

Supt BRANNIGAN

British Policeman operating in England

Andrew MACKENZIE 1911- (British)
Writer: Andrew Carr MACKENZIE
Citation Record: 4 Books
Splash Of Red - *First*
Ward, Lock UK (1949)
The Man Who Wanted To Die - *Last*
Ward, Lock UK (1951)

Biff BRANNIGAN

Second detective of Gypsy Rose LEE

Kate BRANNIGAN

is a British female private detective, operating –refreshingly for the British genre – in the northern industrial and maritime town of Manchester. She is a welcome addition to a subspecies of the genre that has expanded considerably, and sometimes unbelievably, since the 1980s discovered that the sexes were equal and some were more equal than others.

British Female Private Detective operating in England

Val MCDERMID (British)
Citation Record: 3 Books
Dead Beat - *First*
Gollancz UK (1992)
Crack Down - *Latest*
HarperCollins UK (1994)

Geoffrey BRANSCOMBE

British Male Amateur operating in England

Hugh MATHESON 1897-1963 (British)
Writer: Hugh Lewis MACKAY
Citation Record: 2 Books
The Third Force - *First*
Wingate UK (1959); Washburn US (1960)
The Balance Of Fear - *Last*
Gibbs UK (1961)

Al BRANSON

American Male Amateur operating in California/Virginia

Robert Portner KOEHLER 1905- (American)
Invented 4 detectives - see Les IVEY
Citation Record: 3 Books
Steps To Murder - *First*
Phoenix Press US (1943); Boardman UK (1944)
Tread Gently, Death - *Last*
Phoenix Press US (1945)

John Lloyd BRANSON

American Male Amateur operating in Texas

D R MEREDITH (American)
was born in Oklahoma.
Writer: Doris R MEREDITH
Inventor of one other detective Sheriff Charles Timothy MATTHEWS
Citation Record: 2 Books
Murder By Impulse - *First*
Ballantine US (1988)
Murder By Deception - *Latest*
Ballantine US (1989)

Andrew BRANT

is the editor of a small newspaper who, finding that a local mill owner has been murdered, investigates the case himself.

American Male Amateur operating in Michigan

Donald Clough CAMERON 1909?- (American)
See main detective Abelard VOSS
Citation Record: 1 Book
White For A Shroud - *Only*
Mystery House US (1947); Boardman UK (1949)

B

Mason BRANT

American Male Amateur operating in Maine

Nevil Monroe HOPKINS 1873-1945 (American)

Citation Record: 1 Book 4 Short Stories in 1 Collection

The Raccoon Lake Mystery - *Only*
Lippincott US (1917)

The Strange Cases Of Mason Brant - *Collection 1*
Lippincott US (1916)

Pete BRASS

is Californian hardboiled.

American Male Private Detective operating in Los Angeles

Robert Donald LOCKE (American)

Citation Record: 1 Book

A Taste Of Brass - *Only*
Dell US (1957)

Insp Dave BRATTON

American Policeman operating in New York

Helen Joan HULTMAN 1891- (American)

Inventor of one other detective Tim ASHER

Citation Record: 1 Book

Murder In The French Room - *Only*
Mystery League US (1931)

Col BRAXTON

is a lawyer in old Virginia who solves crimes committed, he says, by the greedy.

American Male Amateur operating in USA

Sidekick: Dabney MASON
is a gentleman of the old South and the old school who assists in the sleuthing.
American Male - Friend

Melville Davisson POST 1871-1930 (American)

Invented 5 detectives - see Uncle ABNER

Citation Record: 13 Short Stories in 1 Collection

The Silent Witness - *Collection 1*
Farrar, Straus US (1930)

BRAY

Second detective of DELMASSO

Insp Bernard BRAY

appears also in books with the author's other detective, *Charles VENABLES.*

British Policeman operating in England

C St John SPRIGG 1907-1937 (British)

Invented 4 detectives - see Insp Charles MORGAN

Citation Record: 1 Book

Death Of An Airman - *Only*
Hutchinson UK (1934); Doubleday US (1935)

Insp Bernard BRAY and Charles VENABLES

are vintage British examples of the solid cop and clever amateur in combination.

British Policeman and British Male Amateur operating in England

C St John SPRIGG 1907-1937 (British)

Invented 4 detectives - see Insp Charles MORGAN

Citation Record: 2 Books

Crime In Kensington - *First*
Eldon UK (1933)

Pass The Body - *First**
Dial US (1933)

The Perfect Alibi - *Last*
Eldon UK (1934); Doubleday US (1934)

Nell BRAY

sleuths during the Edwardian era in rural England.

British Female Amateur operating in England

Gillian LINSCOTT (British)

See main detective Birdie LINNET

Citation Record: 4 Books

Stage Fright - *First*
Little, Brown UK (1993)

Widow's Peak - *Latest*
Little, Brown UK (1994)

Patrick BRAY

has retired to Long Island, after serving in the New York Police Department for many years. He has taken up chicken farming, but, bored with country life, he sets up as a private dick.

American Male Private Detective operating in New York

Irwin S COBB 1876-1944 (American)

See main detective Judge PRIEST

Citation Record: 1 Book

Murder Day By Day - *Only*
Bobbs US (1933); Cassell UK (1934)

Adam BRECK

is a CIA agent who foils plots hatched by the usual nasties.

American Male Secret Agent operating in USA

Kenneth ORVIS 1923- (Canadian)

was born in Montreal, Canada. He has been a professional hockey player and journalist.

Writer: Kenneth LEMIEUX

Citation Record: 2 Books

Night Without Darkness - *First*
Chatto UK (1965); Coward McCann US (1966)

The Doomsday List - *Last*
Hale UK (1974)

Father Joseph BREDDER

is a priest at the Convent of Holy Innocents. An ex-marine and ex-boxer, he is drawn into detective work by way of his religious duties. His cases often arise from neighbourhood events and people and, to solve them, he relies not merely on orthodox logic but on his spiritual understanding.

American Male Amateur operating in Los Angeles

Stooge: Lt MINARDI
is a friendly cop who generally opposes the good priest's meddling. He tries, but often fails, to solve the cases with which *Father BREDDER* is involved.
American Male

Leonard HOLTON 1915-1983 (American)

was born in Dublin, Ireland, and was educated at Ring College, Ireland, and El Camino College, Torrance, California. He has worked in Trinidad and the United States as a reporter and newspaper editor. He is the author, under his own name and various other pseudonyms, of many novels, plays and works for children, mainly in the realm of mainstream fiction and non-fiction. He has reserved the pseudonym of *HOLTON* for his criminous works.

Writer: Leonard WIBBERLY

Citation Record: 11 Books

The Saint Maker - *First*
Dodd, Mead US (1959); Hale UK (1960)

A Corner Of Paradise - *Last*
St Martin's US (1977)

Angela BREDON

Second detective of Miles BREDON

Miles BREDON

is a typical, but not particularly good, detective of the British Golden Age. Technically, he is an investigator for the ridiculously named Indescribable Life Assurance Company but that plays little or no part in his enquiries. In three books he sleuths alone, but in a further two he operates with *Angela BREDON,* his wife. He also appears in three (uncited) short stories.

British Male Professional Investigator operating in England/Scotland

B

Ronald A KNOX 1888-1957 (British)

was born in Knibworth, Leicestershire, the son of the Bishop of Manchester and brother of the well-known man of letters, E V Knox. He was educated at Summer Fields School, Oxford, 1896-1900, and Eton College, 1900-1906, and he then took a BA and many prizes at Balliol College, Oxford, 1910. He became an ordained priest in the Church of England, 1912, held several religious posts, worked in Military Intelligence, 1916-1918, and converted to Roman Catholicism, 1917. He was re-ordained priest, 1919, held teaching posts and finally became Catholic chaplain to Oxford University, 1926-1939. He later received several honours and awards.

KNOX was the author of numerous books and tracts on religion and was an illustrious editor and translator of biblical matters. His nine criminous novels are light-weight and do not compare in quality with the stories by his great contemporary and co-religionist, *G K CHESTERTON.* He is perhaps best remembered as being one of the earliest theorists of the detective story and of the *Sherlock HOLMES* canon in particular.

Writer: Ronald Arbuthnott KNOX

Other Detectives:
Miles BREDON and Angela BREDON
William CARMICHAEL Sherlock HOLMES

Citation Record: 3 Books

The Three Taps - *First*
Methuen UK (1927); Simon & Schuster US (1927)

The Body In The Silo - *Last*
Hodder & Stoughton UK (1933)

Settled Out Of Court - *Last**
Dutton US (1934)

Miles BREDON and Angela BREDON

After sleuthing alone in three books, with only occasional help from his wife, *Miles BREDON* appeared with her as part of a husband-and-wife team.

British Male Professional Investigator and British Female Amateur operating in England

Ronald A KNOX 1888-1957 (British)

Invented 4 detectives - see Miles BREDON

Citation Record: 2 Books

Still Dead - *First*
Hodder & Stoughton UK (1934); Dutton US (1934)

Double Cross Purposes - *Last*
Hodder & Stoughton UK (1937)

Barr BREED

was one of the author's first essays into the mystery and detective field. A laconic, intelligent operator, early post-*CHANDLER* in style, his two appearances were in cases bordering on the 'locked-room' variety.

American Male Private Detective operating in Chicago

William S BALLINGER 1912-1980 (American)

Invented 5 detectives - see Joaquin HAWKS

Citation Record: 2 Books

The Body In The Bed - *First*
Harper & Row US (1948); World Distributors UK (1960)

The Body Beautiful - *Last*
Harper & Row US (1949)
World Distributors UK (1960)

Jim BREEN

American Male Amateur operating in New York

Jack KARNEY 1911- (American)

Citation Record: 2 Books

The Knave Of Diamonds - *First*
Ace US (1959)

Layout For Murder - *Last*
Berkley US (1960)

Benedict BREEZE

investigates murder in hospital settings.

British Male Amateur operating in England

Isabella BAYNE (British)

Citation Record: 2 Books

Death And Benedict - *First*
Laurie UK (1952)

Cruel As The Grave - *Last*
Jarrolds UK (1956)

John BRELAND and Mike FREEMAN

British Male Amateurs operating in England

John PENN (British)

Invented 3 detectives - see Supt George THORNE

Citation Record: 1 Book

Deceitful Death - *Single*
Collins UK (1983)

Stag Dinner Death - *Single**
Scribner's US (1984)

Ernst BRENDEL

is a Viennese lawyer who visits the English university town of Oxford, where he brings his exceptional intellectual skill to bear on solving murders, one already committed, others still being contemplated.

Austrian Male Amateur operating in Oxford

J C MASTERMAN 1891-1877 (British)

was born in Kingston Hill, Surrey. He was educated at the Royal Naval College, Osborne, Isle of Wight, and took an MA at Worcester College, Oxford, 1913. He served in the Royal Navy during the First World War and in British Intelligence during the Second World War. A lecturer at Oxford for many years, he became Vice-Chancellor at Worcester College, 1957-1958. He was made an OBE, 1944, and a Knight Bachelor, 1959.

Writer: John Cecil MASTERMAN

Adopter of one other detective Sherlock HOLMES

Citation Record: 2 Books 2 Short Stories in 1 Collection

An Oxford Tragedy - *First*
Gollancz UK (1933); DeMer US (1981)

The Case Of The Four Friends - *Last*
Hodder & Stoughton UK (1957); British Book Centre US (1959)

Bits And Pieces - *Collection 1*
contains two stories with *BRENDEL* and one *Sherlock HOLMES* pastiche, which is cited separately.
Hodder & Stoughton UK (1961)

Michael BRENNAN

is divorced, depressed, disparaging, discourteous, dogged and drawing social benefit. That's the spirit, a private eye in the good old-fashioned mould and a man for the times!

American Male Private Detective operating in San Francisco

Fred ZACKEL (American)

Citation Record: 2 Books

Cocaine And Blue Eyes - *First*
Coward McCann US (1978)

Cinderella After Midnight - *Latest*
Coward McCann US (1980)

Jimmy BRENNON

solves a case of murder by shooting in a locked cabin aboard ship.

American Male Amateur operating on a ship

Kenneth GILBERT (American)

Citation Record: 1 Selected Short Story

Murder Is Aboard
In 'Pocket Detective US (1937)

Carey BRENT

American Male Amateur operating in Long Island

M W GLIDDEN (American)

Writer: Minna Maud Wesselhoft GLIDDEN

Citation Record: 2 Books

Death Strikes Home - *First*
Phoenix Press US (1937)

Come Dwell With Death - *First**
Abridged.
Black Knight US (1946)

The Long Island Murders - *Last*
Phoenix Press US (1937)

Dudley BRENT

Appears with at least two other detectives - see Insp SKANE.

Lady Elaine 'Bundle' BRENT and Supt BATTLE

make a rare example of a Golden Age British cop working in harmony with an amateur sleuth. In the Grand Dame's early books, the policeman was still the main sleuth and he probably had to accept help when it was forthcoming from a young lady who was, after all, the daughter of a lord of the realm. In this one excellent book they investigate a death after a village prank, which leads to involvement with a dangerous secret society and espionage.

British Female Amateur and British Policeman operating in England

Agatha CHRISTIE 1890-1976 (British)

Invented 18 detectives - see Hercule POIROT

Citation Record: 1 Book

The Seven Dials Mystery - *Only*
Collins UK (1929); Dodd, Mead US (1929)

Insp Jimmy BRENT

British Policeman operating in England

Harold KEMP 1896- (British)

Writer: Harold Curry KEMP

Citation Record: 4 Books

Murder Humane - *First*
Hammond UK (1947)

Mark Of A Witch - *Last*
Bles UK (1959)

Jimmy BRENT

British Male Amateur operating in England

Ed MARTIN (British)

Citation Record: 13 Short Stories in 1 Collection

To Hell With The Law - *Collection 1*
Columbine UK (1939)

Michael BRENT

Canadian Male Amateur operating in USA/Canada

Leslie MCFARLANE 1902-1977 (Canadian)

Citation Record: 2 Books

Streets Of Shadow - *First*
Dutton US (1930); Paul UK (1931)

The Murder Tree - *Last*
Dutton US (1931); Paul UK (1932)

Mike BRENT

American Male Amateur operating in Central America

George FENNELL (American)

Citation Record: 2 Books

Blood Patrol - *First*
Pinnacle US (1970)

Killer Patrol - *Last*
Pinnacle US (1970)

Det Ch Insp BRENTFORD

is a rather plodding cop who solves his cases more by probing into the psychology of suspects than by deductive reasoning.

British Policeman operating in England

S B HOUGH 1917- (British)

Writer: Stanley Bennett HOUGH

Citation Record: 4 Books

The Bronze Perseus - *First*
Secker & Warburg UK (1959); Walker US (1962)

The Tender Killer - *First**
Avon US (1963); Ian Henry UK (1975)

Fear Fortune, Father - *Last*
Gollancz UK (1974); Harper & Row US (1984)

Clifton BRENTWOOD

appears once to solve a 'locked-room' murder mystery.

American Male Amateur operating in USA

Kenneth WHIPPLE 1894- (American)

Citation Record: 1 Book

The Murders At Loon Lake - *Only*
King US (1933)

Alphonse Joseph BRESSIO

comes from an Italian family with links to the New York Mafia, which fact does not prevent him operating as a conscientious and very tough private eye.

American Male Private Detective operating in New York

Richard SAPIR 1936-1987 (American)

was the joint author, with *Warren B MURPHY,* of many of the thrillers featuring *Remo WIILIAMS,* a number of which appeared under his sole name. He was also the sole author of three genre books.

See main detective Remo (The Destroyer) WILLIAMS

Citation Record: 1 Book

Bressio - *Only*
Random House US (1975)

Alan BRETT

has a shady past and has had violent experience in the Korean War. These befit him admirably for the nasty work he has to do for the British and French governments.

Male Private Detective operating in Europe

Robert GARRETT

Citation Record: 2 Books

Run Down: The World Of Alan Brett - *First*
Joseph UK (1970); Atheneum US (1972)

Spiral: The World Of Alan Brett - *Last*
Joseph UK (1971); Atheneum US (1972)

Brian BRETT

was one of several insurance investigator-detectives that were created by the author, under this pseudonym and also under his own name.

American Male Professional Investigator operating in USA

Christopher MONIG 1910-1981 (American)

For writer details see Kim LOCKE

Citation Record: 4 Books

The Burned Man - *First*
Dutton US (1956); Boardman UK (1957)

Don't Count The Corpses - *First**
Dell US (1958)

The Lonely Graves - *Last*
Dutton US (1960); Boardman UK (1961)

Chester BRETT

British Male Amateur operating in England

Gwyn EVANS 1899-1938 (British)

Invented 5 detectives - see Bill KELLAWAY

Citation Record: 5 Books 3 Short Stories in 1 Collection

Castle Sinister - *First*
Wright UK (1936)

The Case Of The Climbing Corpse - *Last*
Wright UK (1939)

The Mysterious Miss Death - *Collection 1*
Wright UK (1937)

B

Chico BRETT

was born in Argentina of Irish-Spanish extraction. He operates from an office in Shepherd's Market, in the smart Mayfair district of London, but his cases mainly arise from skulduggery in the nearby and less salubrious district of Soho.

Argentine Male Private Detective operating in London

Kevin O'HARA 1892-1972 (British)

was the byline used by this prolific writer of detective stories for his London private eye novels.

Writer: Marten CUMBERLAND

Citation Record: 16 Books

The Customer's Always Wrong - *First*
Hurst UK (1951)

It's Your Funeral - *Last*
Long UK (1966)

David BRETT

Second detective of Ch Philip DECKER

Dixon BRETT

was, like *Sexton BLAKE* and *Nelson LEE*, one of several detectives, with a potentially vast audience of boy readers, to appear in British magazines during the late 1890s. Although not so well known as *BLAKE* or *LEE*, (he was never honoured by being given his own magazine) he was, in fact, already a seasoned performer when they were still feeling their way. Like them, he was locked in deadly combat with every shape and size of criminal for decades and had already dealt severe blows to the criminal anarchist fringe by the middle of the 1890s. He owned one of the first Mercedes racing cars, the 'Night Hawk', and was often to be found at its wheel, smoking a cigar and wearing immaculate evening dress under his fur-lined overcoat. In the 1920s he was concerned with the threat to private and public life in Britain by a number of oriental villains, typified by his great foe, the Chinese mandarin, Fan Chu Fang.

Dixon BRETT pursued his adventures mainly in short stories but he also appeared in at least two novels. He operated from rooms in the Lincoln's Inn district of London (much favoured by writers of the time) and, being rather brilliant at science, he had his own private laboratory. There he foiled many a fiendish plot by the use of chemistry and, of course, the new Röntgen rays. He had two young assistants, who ran the office when he was away, did the legwork, and could render help in tight corners.

British Male Professional Amateur operating in London

Sidekick: Pat MALONE
was the more important of *Dixon BRETT's* two assistants.
British Male - Assistant

Sidekick: Bill SLOOK
is one of the famous sleuth's several boy assistants.
British Male - Assistant

P W BATTEN (British)

Writer: Peter W BATTEN

Citation Record: 1 Book

The Stolen Girl - *Only*
Aldine UK (1926)

T Stanleyan KING (British)

Inventor of one other detective Scarsdale WARING

Citation Record: 3 Books

The Missing Mayor - *First*
Aldine UK (1926)

The Yellow Wolf - *Last*
UK (1926)

Talbot MAYNE (British)

Citation Record: 2 Books

The Passing Of Fan Chu Fang - *First*
Aldine UK (1922)

Hands Of Doom! - *Last*
Aldine UK (1923)

Richard WORTH (British)

Citation Record: 1 Book

The Murder In The Fog - *Only*
Lloyd UK (1921)

Jack WYLDE (British)

was the byline under which these two novels were published. It is known to have been a pseudonym and, on grounds of style, it has been suggested that it concealed the identity of *Richard Austin FREEMAN*. The vast majority of the *Dixon BRETT* stories were certainly penned by numerous other authors.

Citation Record: 2 Books

The Case Of The Mandarin's Mask - *First*
UK (1922)

The Whispering Death - *Last*
UK (1923)

Frances BRETT

becomes involved, in her first book, in a situation of child abuse and exploitation, leading to a crime.

British Female Amateur operating in England

Susan MOODY 1940- (British)

Invented 3 detectives - see Penny WANAWAKE

Citation Record: 1 Book

Playing With Fire - *Single*
Macdonald UK (1989)

John BRETT

American Male Private Detective operating in Los Angeles

John BRETT (British)

was born in England, the son of an earl, and now lives in America.

Citation Record: 1 Book

Who'd Hire Brett? - *Single*
St Martin's US (1981)

Mike BRETT

British Male Sleuth operating in England

Keith CAMPBELL (British)

Writer: Keith Campbell WEST-WATSON

Citation Record: 6 Books

That Was No Lady - *First*
Macdonald UK (1942)

Pardon My Gun - *Last*
Macdonald UK (1954)

Reginald BRETT

is an early member of the long line of lawyer detectives.

British Male Amateur operating in England

Louis TRACY 1863-1928 (British)

See main detective Insp Charles François FURNEAUX

Citation Record: 2 Books

The Albert Gate Affair - *First*
Ward, Lock UK (1904)

The Albert Gate Mystery - *First**
Fenno US (1904)

The Stowmarket Mystery - *Last*
Ward, Lock UK (1904); Fenno US (1904)

Charlie BREWER

is basically in the espionage game but he finds it necessary to act as a kind of private detective.

American Male Professional Investigator operating in USA

William H HALLAHAN (American)

was born in Brooklyn, New York, and graduated from Temple University, Philadelphia, with degrees in English and

B

Journalism. He received the Mystery Writers of America Edgar Allan Poe award, 1978.

Writer: William Henry HALLAHAN

Inventor of one other detective Arthur TANK

Citation Record: 2 Books

Foxcatcher - *First*
Morrow US (1986); Gollancz UK (1986)

Tripletrap - *Latest*
Morrow US (1989)

Insp William BREWER

British Policeman operating in England

Hugh MCELROY (British)

Writer: Hugh Francis MCELROY

Citation Record: 4 Books

The Silver Venus - *First*
Chapman & Hall UK (1942)

The House Of Malory - *Last*
Chapman & Hall UK (1948)

Insp BREWS

British Policeman operating in England

Vernon LODER 1881- (British)

Invented 3 detectives - see Insp CHACE

Citation Record: 2 Books

The Essex Murders - *First*
Collins UK (1930)

The Death Pool - *First**
Morrow US (1931)

Death Of An Editor - *Last*
Collins UK (1931); Morrow US (1931)

Amy BREWSTER

is not only a lawyer but a shrewd financier. A rather fat lady, she is also rather tough, smoking cigars incessantly and operating, it is said, like a Pershing tank. She helps friends in trouble by solving mysteries and murders for them.

American Female Amateur operating in New York

Sam Jr MERWIN 1910- (American)

Writer: Samuel Kimball Jr MERWIN

Citation Record: 3 Books

Message From A Corpse - *First*
Mystery House US (1945); Quality Press UK (1947)

A Matter Of Policy - *Last*
Mystery House US (1946); Quality Press UK (1952)

Nancy BREWSTER

Second detective of Timothy O'HARA

Andy BRICE

American Male Private Detective operating in USA

Lee ROBERTS 1908-1976 (American)

Invented 4 detectives - see Lee FISKE

Citation Record: 1 Book

Little Murder - *Only*
GM US (1952)

Jennie BRICE

American Female Amateur operating in Pittsburgh

Mary Roberts RINEHART 1876-1958 (American)

Invented 7 detectives - see Letitia CARBERRY

Citation Record: 1 Book

The Case Of Jennie Brice - *Only*
Bobbs US (1913); Hodder & Stoughton UK (1919)

Sgt Peter 'Obie' BRICHTER

American Policeman operating in USA

Mary Monica PULVER 1943- (American)

Writer: Kuhfield Mary Monica PULVER

Citation Record: 3 Books

Murder At The War - *First*
St Martin's US (1987)

Knight Fall - *First**
Diamond US (1991)

Ashes To Ashes - *Latest*
St Martin's US (1988)

BRICONI

Italian Male Sleuth operating in Italy/France

Beatrice BASKERVILLE (British)

Citation Record: 2 Books

By Whose Hand? - *First*
Hutchinson UK (1922)

The St Cloud Affair - *Last*
Hutchinson UK (1931)

Bob BRIDGER

British Male Detective in Pulp Magazines operating in USA

R M TAYLOR (American)

Citation Record: 1 Book

Detective Bob Bridger; Or, The Man From Scotland Yard - *Only*
Street & Smith US (1890)

Ronald BRIERCLIFFE

was cashiered out of the Army for drunkenness and is given a chance to redeem himself by working for British Intelligence.

British Male Professional Investigator operating in England/France

Francis BEEDING (British)

Invented 6 detectives - see Insp WILKINS

Citation Record: 2 Books

The Three Fishers - *First*
Hodder & Stoughton UK (1931); Little, Brown US (1931)

The Two Undertakers - *Last*
Hodder & Stoughton UK (1933); Little, Brown US (1933)

Prof Herman BRIERLY

is just 5 feet tall and a septuagenarian. Created in an era when amateur detectives were prone to be either intellectual giants or supermen and authors had a general awe of science, he is naturally a superb chemist, an expert physicist, a brilliant bacteriologist and many other things besides. It is no wonder that the police call on him when faced with the usual baffling cases.

American Male Amateur operating in USA

Sidekick: John MATTHEWS
is the adopted son of *Dr BRIERLY.* Like him he is a fine chemist; but he is also tall, tough and a fine boxer, which is even more useful when it comes to assisting Dad.

American Male - Son

Will LEVINREW 1881- (American)

Writer: William LEVINE

Citation Record: 4 Books

The Poison Plague - *First*
McBride US (1929); Cassell UK (1930)

Death Points A Finger - *Last*
Mystery League US (1933)

Frank BRIERS

British Male Amateur operating in England

C P SNOW 1905-1980 (British)

was born in Leicester, Leicestershire. He was educated in schools there and took degrees in Chemistry and Physics at Christ's College, Cambridge, where he was later a Fellow, 1930-1950. He soon gave up scientific research work, although he was a senior adviser to several governments during much of his life, for which work he was made a life Baron, 1964.

A powerful proponent for the popularisation of science, he invented the term 'two cultures' to describe the growing divorce between the arts and sciences in modern intellectual society: he worked through this theme in a long series of novels, which, however, were not judged to be of high

B

quality. He wrote two genre novels in the 1930s and this one detective story at the end of a distinguished life.

Writer: Charles Horace SNOW

Other Byline: Charles H SNOW

Citation Record: 1 Book

A Coat Of Varnish - *Only*
Macmillan UK (1979); Scribner's US (1979)

Robert (The Assassin) BRIGANTI

Male Sleuth operating in New York/New Orleans

Peter MCCURTIN (American)

Other Detectives:
Phillip (The Marksman) MAGELLAN
Jim (The Death Dealer) RAINEY
Pete SHAY

Citation Record: 2 Books

Manhattan Massacre - *First*
Dell US (1973); Mayflower UK (1975)

New Orleans Holocaust - *Last*
Dell US (1973); Mayflower UK (1975)

Insp BRIGG

of the CID is, in his one book, up against treachery and murder among the greyhound racing fraternity.

British Policeman operating in London

James CORBETT (British)

Invented 7 detectives - see Roy ENDICOTT

Citation Record: 1 Book

The Hound Of Death - *Only*
Jenkins UK (1944)

BRIGGS

Appears with at least two other detectives - see Carruthers SIMPSON.

Tommy BRIGGS

British Male Sleuth operating in England

Donald MACDONALD (British)

Citation Record: 6 Books

Briggs Investigates - *First*
Hale UK (1968)

Two Bullets For Briggs - *Last*
Hale UK (1971)

Rosie BRIGHT

British Female Amateur operating in England

Judge RUEGG 1854-1941 (British)

Writer: Judge Alfred Henry RUEGG

Citation Record: 2 Books

John Clutterbuck - *First*
Daniel UK (1923)

David Betterton - *Last*
Daniel UK (1941)

Nathan BRIGHTLIGHT

operates, not manifestly well, around Hollywood Boulevard.

American Male Private Detective operating in Hollywood

Trevor BERNARD (American)

Citation Record: 1 Book

Brightlight - *Single*
Manor US (1977)

Janna BRILL and Mahlon MAXWELL

appear in books set in America some time in the next century, when the criminal problems seem not to have changed noticeably.

American Sleuths operating in USA

Lee KILLOUGH 1942- (American)

Writer: Karen Lee KILLOUGH

Citation Record: 3 Books

The Doppelganger Gambit - *First*
Ballantine US (1979)

Dragon's Teeth - *Latest*
Questar US (1990)

Mark BRILL

American Male Amateur operating in Los Angeles

Nicholas MEYER 1945- (American)

was born in New York City. He was educated at Fieldston High School, Riverdale, New York, and took a BA at the University of Iowa, Iowa City.

Other Detectives:
Sherlock HOLMES and Sigmund FREUD
Sherlock HOLMES

Citation Record: 1 Book

Target Practice - *Only*
Harcourt Brace US (1974); Hodder & Stoughton UK (1975)

Sam BRIMMER

is a 'time detective', a blending of science fiction with detection.

American Male Private Detective operating in USA

Ron GOULART 1933- (American)

Invented 15 detectives - see Jake PACE and Hildy PACE

Citation Record: 1 Book

The Enormous Hour Glass - *Single*
Award US (1976)

BRINDLE

is a dog, a cross between a mastiff and a bull-terrier, and he is cited as the main detective in this Victorian novel. Although the genre has produced several well-known dogs as sidekicks, *BRINDLE* is rather special in being himself the detective, whilst his master (unnamed) is the sidekick.

American Male Canine operating in Boston

Sidekick: UNNAMED
is the owner and a sort of sidekick for the canine detective.
American Male - Owner

M M Lt MURRAY 1820-1895 (American)

Writer: Maturin M BALLOU

Citation Record: 1 Book

The Dog Detective And His Young Master - *Only*
Street & Smith US (1888)

Up The Ladder; Or, Morton Merrill's Pluck - *Only**
Street & Smith US (1899)

Max BRINDLE

American Male Amateur operating in California/Shanghai

A S FLEISCHMAN 1920- (American)

Writer: Albert Sidney FLEISCHMAN

Citation Record: 2 Books

The Straw Donkey Case - *First*
Phoenix Press US (1948)

Murder's No Accident - *Last*
Phoenix Press US (1949)

Sgt BRINKHAUS

appeared only in short stories, originally written for *Detective Action* and *Detective Fiction Weekly*. They do not seem to have been collected.

American Policeman operating in New York

Frederick NEBEL 1903-67 (American)

Invented 8 detectives - see Steve CARDIGAN

Citation Record: 2 Selected Short Stories

The Mystery At Pier 7
was the first of the eleven known stories featuring this detective.

Strangle Hold
In 'Detective Fiction' US (1933)

Sam BRISCOE

is an investigative journalist, pretty tough when it comes to getting a story and solving a case.

American Male Amateur operating in New York

Pete HAMILL 1935- (American)

Citation Record: 3 Books

Dirty Laundry - *First*
Bantam US (1978); Bantam UK (1979)

The Guns Of Heaven - *Latest*
Bantam US (1983)

Lt BRISSK

seems to have appeared in only this one book.

American Policeman operating in USA

Bruce ELLIOTT 1915?-1973 (American)

Writer: Bruce Walter Gardner Lively Stacy ELLIOTT

Citation Record: 1 Book

You'll Die Laughing - *Only*
Five Star US (1945)

Insp BRISTOL

is one of the detectives created by this extraordinary master of thriller-writing. In his one book he solves a case of murder by decapitation in a locked room.

British Policeman operating in England

Sax ROHMER 1883-1959 (British)

Invented 9 detectives - see Insp RYDER

Citation Record: 1 Book

The Quest Of The Sacred Slipper - *Only*
Pearson UK (1919); Doubleday US (1919)

Kate BRISTOL

appears only once and solves a case of murder in a spacecraft.

American Female Amateur operating in USA

Wilson TUCKER 1914- (American)

Invented 4 detectives - see Lt DANFORTH

Citation Record: 1 Book

To The Tombaugh Station - *Only*
Ace US (1960)

Jane BRITLAND

Second detective of Jack DEMARREST

Dr Daniel BRITLING

appears once and solves two cases of locked-room murder.

British Male Amateur operating in England

James RONALD 1905- (British)

Invented 3 detectives - see Supt WRENN

Citation Record: 1 Book

Six Were To Die - *Only*
Hodder & Stoughton UK (1932)

Kirk WALES 1905- (British)

Writer: James RONALD

Citation Record: 1 Book

Six Were To Die - *Only*
Mystery House US (1941)

William BRITTAIN

British Male Amateur operating in England/France

John COURAGE 1902-1957 (British)

For writer details see Supt 'Tubby' GREENE

Inventor of one other detective David CANE

Citation Record: 3 Books

Lakeland Tragedy - *First*
Paul UK (1947)

The Dread Cave - *Last*
Paul UK (1952)

Rickard 'Ricky' BRITTON

is more of a throwback to the days of the upper-class hero, a man-about-London type who comes complete with batman, than a modern detective.

British Male Private Detective operating in London

Deben HOLT (British)

Writer: UNKNOWN

Citation Record: 1 Book

Circle Of Shadows - *Only*
Gifford UK (1957)

Mike BRIXAN

British Male Professional Amateur operating in England

Edgar WALLACE 1875-1932 (British)

Invented 28 detectives - see J G REEDER

Citation Record: 1 Book

The Hairy Arm - *Only*
Small, Maynard US (1925)

The Avenger - *Only**
Long UK (1926)

BROADWAY BOB

Broadway Bob, The Bounder Detective - *Only*

American Male Detective in Pulp Magazines operating in USA

UNKNOWN

No citations

BROADWAY BILL

is one of the several bootblack detectives popular in the US pulps of the 1930s.

American Male Detective in Pulp Magazines operating in New York

UNKNOWN

No citations

Henry BROCH

American Male Detective in Pulp Magazines operating in USA

OLD SLEUTH (American)

Invented 40 detectives - see Brant ADAMS

Citation Record: 1 Book

Henry Broch, Old Sleuth's Assistant - *Only*
Royal US (ca 1908)

Insp David BROCK

investigates cases of murder set back into 1901-1902.

British Policeman operating in England

R J WHITE 1905-1971 (British)

See main detective Insp BADGERY

Citation Record: 2 Books

The Smartest Grave - *First*
Collins UK (1961); Harper & Row US (1961)

The Women Of Peasenhall - *Last*
Macmillan UK (1969); Harper & Row US (1970)

John BROCK

British Male Amateur operating in England

Desmond SKIRROW ?-1973 (British)

Citation Record: 3 Books

It Won't Get You Anywhere - *First*
Bodley Head UK (1966)

I'm Trying To Give It Up - *Last*
Bodley Head UK (1968); Doubleday US (1969)

Marge BROCK

is a free-lance researcher and single mother of three children. Whilst working on a crime book, she begins to suspect that a series of rapes and murders committed in England and the US have been committed by someone she knows.

American Female Amateur operating in Minneapolis

L A TAYLOR 1939- (American)

Invented 4 detectives - see Joseph 'JJ' JAMISON

Citation Record: 1 Book

Footnote To Murder - *Single*
Walker US (1983)

One For The Books - *Single**
Hale UK (1983)

B

Supt 'Badger' BROCK
heads the police force in the little fictional town of Melford and solves cases of espionage and murder.
British Policeman operating in England

John BINGHAM 1908-1988 (British)
was born in York, Yorkshire, and held the title of Lord Clanmorris. Educated at Cheltenham, he served in the Army during the Second World War and, for many years afterwards, he held senior posts at the Ministry of Defence, during which time he began writing thrillers, most of which dealt with the murky aspects of espionage. His work included several good detective stories, admired for their understanding of situations and characters.
Writer: John Michael Ward BINGHAM
Other Detectives:
Kenneth DUCANE   Det Ch Insp David MORGAN
Citation Record: 2 Books
Brock - *First*
Gollancz UK (1981)
Brock And The Defector - *Last*
Gollancz UK (1982); Doubleday US (1982)

William BROCKIE
Canadian Policeman operating in Canada

William BROCKIE
Citation Record: 17 Short Stories in 1 Collection
Tales Of The Mounted - *Collection 1*
Ryerson US (1949); Didier UK (1951)

Paul BRODER
American Male Private Detective operating in Tampa

James T DOYLE (American)
See main detective Dan CRONYN
Citation Record: 1 Book
Epitaph For A Loser - *Single*
Walker US (1988)

Paul BRODIE
is a government Intelligence officer who is sent to discover the reason why mysterious diseases and earthquakes are occurring together in Asia.
British Male Secret Agent operating in India

Hugh MCLEAVE 1923- (British)
Writer: Hugh George MCLEAVE
Other Byline: Richard COPELAND
Other Detectives:
Stephen ARMITAGE   Dr Gregor MACLEAN
Citation Record: 1 Book
A Borderline Case - *Single*
Gollancz UK (1979); Scribner's US (1979)

Peter BRODIE
Second detective of Michael DANEVITCH

Dan BRODSKY
is a mathematician at Berkeley who takes out a PI licence and uses his special skills at science in tracking down murderers.
American Male Private Detective operating in California

Erik ROSENTHAL (American)
Citation Record: 2 Books
The Calculus Of Murder - *First*
St Martin's US (1986); Gollancz UK (1987)
The Advanced Calculus Of Murder - *Latest*
St Martin's US (1988)

BRODY
is an American private eye, with a fashionable single name, invented by a British author. He did not reappear after this book.
American Male Private Detective operating in New York

Vern HANSEN 1920- (British)
For writer details see 'Lefty' O'CONNOR
Citation Record: 2 Book
Murder With Menaces - *First*
Digit UK (1962)
The Whisper Of Death - *Last*
Digit UK (1963)

Marc BRODY
is an antipodean reporter who, taking his name from the eponymous author, investigates a case of murder.
Australian Male Amateur operating in Australia

Marc BRODY 1906-
Writer: Richard WILKES-HUNTER
Citation Record: 1 Book
Murder Is A Maiden's Handicap - *Only*
Horwitz AU (1958)

Cole BROGAN
Male Sleuth operating in Ireland

Joe POYER 1939- (American)
Writer: Joseph John POYER Jr
Citation Record: 2 Books
The Shooting Of The Green - *First*
Doubleday US (1973); Barker UK (1974)
Hellshot - *First**
Sphere UK (1978)
The Contract - *Latest*
Atheneum US (1978); Gollancz UK (1978)

Jerry BROGAN
is a race-track announcer who is called on to solve cases connected with race-track crimes.
American Male Amateur operating in USA

Jon L BREEN 1943- (American)
Invented 6 detectives - see Rachel HENNINGS
Citation Record: 3 Books
Listen For The Click - *First*
Walker US (1983)
Vicar's Roses - *First**
Macmillan UK (1984)
Loose Lips - *Latest*
Simon & Schuster US (1990); Macmillan UK (1990)

Barry BROMLEY
British Male Amateur operating in England

Nat GOULD 1857-1919 (British)
See main detective Valentine MARTYN
Citation Record: 10 Short Stories in 1 Collection
The Racing Adventures Of Barry Bromley - *Collection 1*
Not all the stories, which were published posthumously, are criminous.
Long UK (1926)

BRONSON
is in a novelization of a TV pilot drama, later released as a film.
American Male Professional Investigator operating in USA

William JOHNSTON 1924- (American)
Invented 7 detectives - see John WOODRUFF and Tony NOVELLO
Citation Record: 1 Book
Then Came Bronson - *Only*
Pyramid US (1970)

Richard BRONSON
appears in novelizations of episodes from a TV series.
American Male Sleuth operating in USA

Philip RAWLS (American)
Citation Record: 3 Books

Blind Rage - *First*
Manor US (1975)

Switchblade - *Last*
Manor US (1975)

Supt BRONT

is on the trail of a homicidal maniac released from prison.

British Policeman operating in England

Sidekick: Det Const RICKS

British Male - Subordinate

Robert LAIT 1921- (British)

Citation Record: 1 Book

A Chance To Kill - *Only*
Macmillan UK (1968)

Roger BROOK

is a detective-adventurer who works for the British during the Napoleonic wars. He metes out justice to those dastardly Frenchies in confrontations that take place all over Europe.

British Male Amateur operating in France/Russia

Dennis WHEATLEY 1897-1977 (British)

Invented 4 detectives - see Julian DAY

Citation Record: 8 Books

The Man Who Killed The King - *First*
Hutchinson UK (1951); Putnam US (1965)

The Ravishing Of Lady Mary Ware - *Last*
Hutchinson UK (1971)

Clay BROOKE

American Male Amateur operating in New York/Los Angeles

Herbert CROOKER (American)

Citation Record: 2 Books

The Hollywood Murder Mystery - *First*
Macaulay US (1930); Long UK (1930)

The Crime In Washington Mews - *Last*
Macaulay US (1931)

Loveday BROOKE

was one of the very earliest female detectives and she appeared just a few years after the first Sherlock HOLMES stories were published. She was, it seems, employed by a Fleet Street agency and worked herself up the ladder over a period of six years. 'With poverty staring her in the face...she had forthwith defied conventions, and had chosen for herself a career that had cut her off sharply from her former associates and position in society'. Of medium build, neither dark nor fair, and neither handsome nor ugly, she usually dressed in black, Quaker-like, and her employer said that she was 'the most sensible and practical woman' he had ever met.

British Female Professional Amateur operating in England

C L PIRKIS ?-1910 (British)

was the granddaughter of the Reverend Richard Lyne and was married to a naval officer. She wrote fourteen rather indifferent novels, which are now little known, before embarking on her last work, the charming collection of stories cited here. In 1894, she gave up her writing and, with her husband, founded the National Canine Defence League, which thrives to this day.

Writer: Catherine Louisa PIRKIS

Citation Record: 7 Short Stories in 1 Collection

The Experiences Of Loveday Brooke, Lady Detective - *Collection 1*
Hutchinson UK (1894)

Loveday Brooke - *Collection 1**
Dover US (1896)

William BROOKE

British Male Amateur operating in Pakistan

Charlotte JAY 1919- (British)

was born in Adelaide, South Australia, and graduated from the University of Adelaide, 1941. She worked as a court stenographer in several countries in Asia before settling in England in 1958 to operate an antiques business, which she did until 1971, when she returned to Adelaide. Her genre novels are firmly based on her own experiences in foreign lands with often strange ethnic customs and practices. She received the Mystery Writers of America Edgar Allan Poe award for her second novel, 1953. She is the author, under her real name and the pseudonym, of eight genre books.

Writer: Geraldine Mary JAY
!See Appendix 2

Inventor of one other detective Emma WARWICK

Citation Record: 1 Book

The Yellow Turban - *Only*
Collins UK (1955); Harper & Row US (1955)

Xavier BROOKE

American Male Amateur operating in USA

A H Z CARR 1902-1971 (American)

Writer: Albert H Zolotkoff CARR

Citation Record: 1 Book

Finding Maubee - *Only*
Putnam US (1970)

The Calypso Murders - *Only**
Hale UK (1973)

B G BROOKS

works for the Association of American Memorial Parks. One day he finds a body where very definitely it ought not to be, in a park.

American Male Private Detective operating in USA

Wilson TUCKER 1914- (American)

Invented 4 detectives - see Lt DANFORTH

Citation Record: 1 Book

The Man In My Grave - *Only*
Rinehart US (1956); Macdonald UK (1958)

Bob BROOKS

American Male Detective in Pulp Magazines operating in USA

UNKNOWN

No citations

Courtney BROOKS

American Male Amateur

Zoe KAMITSES (American)

Citation Record: 1 Book

Moondreamer - *Single*
Little, Brown US (1983)

Mike BROOKS

British Male Sleuth operating in Europe/Africa

H T ROTHWELL 1921- (British)

Writer: Henry Talbot ROTHWELL

Citation Record: 5 Books

Dive Deep For Danger - *First*
Hale UK (1966); Roy US (1966)

No Honour Amongst Spies - *Last*
Hale UK (1969); Roy US (1969)

R J BROOKS

has put out his shingle in Manhattan, to say he is a 'Matrimonial Detective'. Alas, when he finds his famous showbiz mother dead on the floor he has to spread his wings a little.

American Male Private Detective operating in New York

Stephen BOGART (American)

Citation Record: 1 Book

Play It Again - *Single*
Macmillan UK (1994)

Andrew BROOM

is an investigative lawyer.

American Male Amateur operating in Indiana

B

Ralph MCINERNY 1929- (American)

See main detective Father Roger DOWLING

Citation Record: 4 Books

Cause And Effect - *First*
Atheneum US (1987); Landmark UK (1988)

Savings And Loam - *Latest*
Atheneum US (1990); Thorndike UK (1991)

Insp Herbert BROOM

British Policeman operating in England

Freda HURT 1911- (British)

Writer: Freda Mary Elizabeth HURT

Citation Record: 6 Books

Death By Bequest - *First*
Macdonald UK (1960)

A Cause For Malice - *Last*
Hale UK (1966)

Lt Kevin BROSKEY

American Policeman operating in Los Angeles

Ed NAHA 1950- (American)

Inventor of one other detective Harry PORTER

Citation Record: 2 Books

On The Edge - *First*
Pocket Books US (1989)

Razzle-Dazzle - *Latest*
Pocket Books US (1990)

Insp BROUSSE and Alan ESTERBROOKE

French Policeman and British Male Amateur operating in France

Cleveland MOFFETT 1863-1926 (British)

See main detective Paul COQUENIL

Citation Record: 1 Book

The Seine Mystery - *Only*
Melrose UK (1924); Dodd, Mead US (1925)

Father BROWN

must, for several reasons, be considered as one of the genre's very greatest detectives. He was, in fact, the first major amateur detective to have been created by a writer who was already a major mainstream author and established as a man of letters in other fields.

Father BROWN is a Catholic priest, physically a small man, but one who is possessed of great courage and the most profound religious belief. He is curious by nature and brilliantly deductive in his approach to life and its mysteries. Of his own life and background little is ever made clear. Even his first name is never used or even disclosed, although there is reason to believe (from a story in *THE INNOCENCE OF FATHER BROWN*) that its initial is J. In his youth, it seems, he was a prison chaplain in Chicago, but later he worked in Paris. He occupied several curacies in England, especially one in Essex, but, in his most active period, he is a priest at St Francis Xavier, Camberwell, in London. For all manner of reasons he encounters crimes, some of them terrible, which are often carried out by passionate or weak individuals. He solves them, not just by the extraordinary power of his reasoning, but by his deep insight into the human psyche. He rarely passes judgment on cases and never on fellow human beings, for he is more interested in saving souls than catching criminals.

Father BROWN only ever appeared in short stories, among which are certainly some of the very greatest in the genre. They extend the realm of the entertaining detective story into more profound regions of human enquiry.

British Male Amateur operating in London

G K CHESTERTON 1874-1936 (British)

was born in London and educated at St Paul's School, London. After an early career in publishing, he became one of the most distinguished literary figures of the English scene during the first part of the twentieth century. Author, critic, essayist, poet and illustrator, he received many literary and other honours for his work. Profoundly religious, in 1922 he converted to Roman Catholicism, which thenceforth influenced his life and his writing. After the First World War, he became one of the leaders of the political and economic movement of the far right known as Distributism, which collapsed in the late 1930s.

G K CHESTERTON is, ironically, perhaps best remembered today as the creator of the inimitable *Father BROWN*, the brilliant, deeply moralistic priest, who appeared many years before the author actually embraced the Catholic faith. There has recently been a suggestion that he might be put forward by the Roman Catholic Church as a candidate for beatification. Should that succeed, it will surely be an event unique in the annals of detective fiction.

Writer: Gilbert Keith CHESTERTON

Other Detectives:
Horne FISHER Gabriel GALE
Rupert GRANT and Basil GRANT
Dr HYDE Mr POND
SYME

Citation Record: 1 Selected Short Story 50 Short Stories in 5 Collections

The Donnington Affair
does not appear in any of the five canonical collections of *Father BROWN* stories. It was added to the second edition of a collection, *The Father Brown Omnibus* (US 1951) and may be found in a more recent collection of the author's short stories, *THIRTEEN DETECTIVES.*
Dodd, Mead US (1986); Xanadu UK (1988)

The Innocence Of Father Brown - *Collection 1*
Short stories - 12
Cassell UK (1911); Lane US (1911)

The Wisdom Of Father Brown - *Collection 2*
Short stories - 12
Cassell UK (1914); Lane US (1915)

The Incredulity Of Father Brown - *Collection 3*
Short stories - 8
Cassell UK (1926); Dodd, Mead US (1926)

The Secret Of Father Brown - *Collection 4*
Short stories - 10
Cassell UK (1927); Harper & Row US (1927)

The Scandal Of Father Brown - *Collection 5*
Short stories - 8
Cassell UK (1935); Dodd, Mead US (1935)

Thirteen Detectives - *Collection 6*
contains one *Father BROWN* story, two *Horne FISHER* stories, two *Gabriel GALE* stories, two *Rupert and Basil GRANT* stories and two *Mr POND* stories.
Short stories - 1
Dodd, Mead US (1986); Xanadu UK (1988)

Father BROWN

Appears with at least two other detectives - see Sherlock HOLMES.

Miss BROWN

seems only to have appeared in this novel.

British Female Amateur operating in London

E Phillips OPPENHEIM 1866-1946 (British)

Invented 27 detectives - see Nicholas GOADE

Citation Record: 1 Book

Miss Brown Of XYO - *Only*
Hodder & Stoughton UK (1927); Little, Brown US (1927)

Angel BROWN

British Male Sleuth operating in England

Graham MONTROSE 1924- (British)

Writer: Charles Roy MACKINNON

Citation Record: 13 Books

Angel Of Death - *First*
Hale UK (1968)

Angel And The Red Admiral - *Last*
Hale UK (1972)

Benvenuto BROWN

Male Sleuth operating in several locations

Elizabeth GILL (British)

Citation Record: 3 Books

Strange Holiday - *First*
Cassell UK (1931)

The Crime Coast - *First**
Doubleday US (1931)

Crime De Luxe - *Last*
Cassell UK (1933); Doubleday US (1933)

Chinese BROWN

British Policeman operating in London

Cecil BISHOP (British)

See main detective Ah FOO

Citation Record: 1 Book

Chinese Brown Of Scotland Yard - *Only*
Mellifont UK (1937)

Clio BROWN

is female, black, and the widow of a cop in St Louis. Inheriting a detective agency after the death of her father, who was 'the first black PI in the state of Missouri', she runs it herself, with the help of her mother and boyfriend.

American Female Private Detective operating in St Louis

Dolores KOMO (American)

Citation Record: 1 Book

Clio Brown: Private Investigator - *Single*
Crossing Press US (1988); Crossing Press UK (1989)

Dagobert BROWN and Jane BROWN

are one of the best-known and longest-lasting of the many husband-and-wife detective duos. *Dagobert BROWN* is said to be the black sheep of a titled family. He woos and marries *Jane* early in the series. Never, apparently, in need of full employment, they are always ready and able to push off to some odd corner of the globe because *Dagobert* gets a bright idea, usually one that absolves him from the threat of an imminent job. Good-humoured and easy-going, he is quite happy for *Jane* to start writing another book, a practice that enables her to keep them both. Wherever they are, however, his fine intellect and sense of impending or recent crime gets them both involved in murder and detection. She does the first-person narration.

British Male Amateur and British Female Amateur operating in Europe/USA

Delano AMES 1906- (American)

was born in Knox County, Ohio, and graduated from Yale University, New Haven, Connecticut. He is a specialist on French medieval history and translator of several works on the subject. He has set many of his books in Europe.

Writer: Delano L AMES

Inventor of one other detective Cpl Juan LLORCA

Citation Record: 12 Books

She Shall Have Murder - *First*
Hodder & Stoughton UK (1948); Rinehart US (1949)

Lucky Jane - *Last*
Hodder & Stoughton UK (1959); Rinehart US (1959)

Edmund BROWN

is a British secret agent, usually on assignments in Russia or France. Competent at neither espionage nor sex, he gets by in books that are basically thrillers.

British Male Secret Agent operating in England

Joyce PORTER 1924- (British)

Invented 3 detectives - see Insp Wilfred DOVER

Citation Record: 3 Books

Sour Cream With Everything - *First*
Cape UK (1966); Scribner's US (1966)

Neither A Candle Nor A Pitchfork - *Last*
Weidenfeld & Nicolson UK (1969); McCall US (1970)

Forsythia BROWN

Female Amateur

Rachel C PAYES 1922- (American)

Writer: Rachel Ruth Cosgrove PAYES

Citation Record: 2 Books

Forsythia Finds Murder - *First*
Avalon US (1960)

Memoirs Of Murder - *Last*
Avalon US (1964)

Fritz BROWN

is an ex-cop who runs a PI agency as a tax dodge, but makes his money by repossessing automobiles. Alcoholic and incurably romantic, in this, his first and last case, he is hired to watch the sister of a wealthy golf caddie, an exercise that leads inevitably to crime.

American Male Private Detective operating in USA

James ELLROY 1948- (American)

was born in Los Angeles.

Other Detectives:
Det Dwight 'Bucky' BLEICHART
Sgt Lloyd HOPKINS
Dudley SMITH and Det Fred UNDERHILL

Citation Record: 1 Book

Brown's Requiem - *Single*
Avon US (1981); Allison & Busby UK (1983)

Harry BROWN

infiltrates a group of IRA terrorists and becomes the target himself.

British Male Professional Investigator operating in Ireland

Gerald SEYMOUR (British)

Citation Record: 1 Book

Harry's Game - *Only*
Random House US (1975)

Dep Sheriff Jake BROWN

American Policeman operating in California

Owen CAMERON 1905- (American)

Writer: Courtney Owen CAMERON

Citation Record: 2 Books

Catch A Tiger - *First*
Simon & Schuster US (1952); Hammond UK (1954)

The Fire Trap - *Last*
Simon & Schuster US (1957); Hammond UK (1958)

The Devil Stirs - *Last**
Dell US (1958)

Jane BROWN

Second detective of Dagobert BROWN

Nic BROWN

American Male Detective in Pulp Magazines operating in Chicago

A Frank PINKERTON (American)

Invented 5 detectives - see A Frank PINKERTON

Citation Record: 1 Book

Saved At The Scaffold; Or, Nic Brown, The Chicago Detective - *Only*
Laird & Lee US (1888)

Nick BROWN

American Male Sleuth operating in Florida

Robert CORAM (American)

Citation Record: 3 Books

Narcs - *First*
Signet US (1988)

America's Heroes - *Latest*
Signet US (1990)

Rusty BROWN
British Male Sleuth operating in several locations

Cass REGAN (British)
Writer: Leslie T BARNARD
Citation Record: 4 Books
Assignment For Rusty Brown - *First*
Hamilton Stafford UK (1952)
Rusty Thumbs A Ride - *Last*
Hamilton Stafford UK (1952)

Sarah BROWN
is an early example of the American female detective. She is to be found only in one short book, published a dozen years or so after the appearance of *Sherlock HOLMES.*
American Female Amateur operating in USA

K F HILL 1884?-1925 (American)
Writer: Lucy A BAER
Citation Record: 1 Book
Sarah Brown, Detective; Or, The Mystery Of The Pavilion - *Only*
Ivers US (1901)

Vee BROWN
appeared in the pulp magazines of the 1930s before being featured in two novels. He is an early example of the hardboiled PI and is really not much more than just a tough, gun-toting cowboy loose in Manhattan. Unusual, though, for at night he is a writer of sentimental ballads and is wealthy to boot, living in a penthouse and riding around town in a chauffeur-driven limousine.
American Male Private Detective operating in New York

Carroll John DALY 1889-1958 (American)
Invented 6 detectives - see Race WILLIAMS
Citation Record: 2 Books
Murder Won't Wait - *First*
Washburn US (1933); Hutchinson UK (1934)
Emperor Of Evil - *Last*
Stokes US (1937); Hutchinson UK (1936)

'Encyclopedia' BROWN
is a boy detective with amazing insight and knowledge who appears only in a few short stories.
American Male Amateur operating in USA

Donald J SOBOL 1924- (American)
Citation Record: 1 Collection
Encyclopedia Brown And The Case Of The Secret Pitch - *Collection 1*
Nelson US (1965)

Det Ch Insp BROWNE
is a British cop in what may become a semi-procedural series.
British Policeman operating in England
Sidekick: Det Sgt Jerry HUNTER
is the assistant of *BROWNE* in one book but also appears as the main detective in another.
British Male - Subordinate

Pauline BELL 1928- (British)
Invented 3 detectives - see Det Sgt Jerry HUNTER
Citation Record: 1 Book
No Pleasure In Death - *Single*
Macmillan UK (1992)

Carl BROWNE
Second detective of Mark LEE

Freddie BROWNE and Jim FANSHAW
British Male Secret Agents operating in England

Michael POOLE 1885- (British)
Writer: Reginald Heber POOLE
Citation Record: 8 Books
Browne's First Case - *First*
Oxford UK (1935)
Browne Of The Secret Service - *Last*
Oxford UK (1940)

Galahad Urban BROWNE
is a strip cartoonist who, in one book, solves the problem of a shooting in a locked room.
British Male Amateur operating in England

Allan ALDOUS 1911- (British)
Writer: Allan Charles ALDOUS
Citation Record: 1 Book
It's Murder If You Say So - *Only*
Skeffington UK (1952)

Prof BROWNING
Appears with at least two other detectives - see Insp MILD.

Benjamin BROWNING
appears in this one book, a novelization of a children's film, in which he reincarnates as a dog to solve his own murder.
American Male Private Detective operating in USA

Joe CAMP (American)
Citation Record: 1 Book
Oh Heavenly Dog - *Single*
US (1980)

Richard BROWNING
is an Australian PI investigating crime in the underworld of Sydney.
Australian Male Private Detective operating in Sydney

Peter CORRIS 1942- (Australian)
was born in Stanwell, Victoria. A journalist and literary editor, author of over a dozen detective novels and several collections of short stories, he has also written several historical studies of Australian life.
Other Detectives:
Ray CRAWLEY Cliff HARDY
Citation Record: 3 Books
Box Office Browning - *First*
Viking US (1987); Penguin UK (1988)
Beverley Hills Browning - *Latest*
Penguin UK (1987)

Robert BROWNING
is, indeed, the renowned nineteenth-century English poet. He is living, in this book, in Florence, Italy – a location that was in fact dear to his heart. There he becomes involved in good old-fashioned mystery and murder, as well as spiritualism and Dante. His detective work is aided by the presence of his wife.
British Male Amateur operating in Florence
Sidekick: Mrs Elizabeth Barrett BROWNING
was a poetess, famed both in fact and subsequent fiction. She was renowned for her romantic attachment to her husband, with whom she eloped to Italy.
British Female - Wife

Michael DIBDIN 1947- (British)
Invented 3 detectives - see Commiss Aurelio ZEN
Citation Record: 1 Book
A Rich Full Death - *Single*
Cape UK (1986)

James BRUCE
British Male Amateur operating in several locations

Ronald JOHNSTON 1926- (British)
Citation Record: 2 Books
Disaster At Dungeness - *First*
Collins UK (1964)
Collision Ahead - *First**
Doubleday US (1965)

The Angry Ocean - *Last*
Collins UK (1968); Harcourt Brace US (1969)

Insp BRUMMEL

solves the rather strange disappearances of two men.
British Policeman operating in England

Robert VERRON (British)

Citation Record: 1 Book

The Curse Of Craig's End - *Only*
Wright UK (1953)

Jacques BRUNEL

French Male Amateur operating in France

Catherine GAVIN 1907- (British)

Writer: Catherine Irvine GAVIN

Citation Record: 2 Books

Traitor's Gate - *First*
Hodder & Stoughton UK (1976); St Martin's US (1977)

None Dare Call It Treason - *Last*
Hodder & Stoughton UK (1978); St Martin's US (1978)

Commiss Guido BRUNETTI

of the Venice Questura is one of those sound non-British, European policemen we have come to expect from the pens of British and American writers with a sound knowledge of their subject. Not for them the wild excesses of an earlier breed who may never have stepped on alien soil and garnered their information from city maps and their prose by reading foreign books. *Guido BRUNETTI*, careful, meticulous, with useless assistants, hounded by his elegant but incompetent chief, blessed with a clever wife from high-ranking Venetian society, moves seamlessly along the waterways and alleys in books that offer a fine feel for the old city and her ways.
Italian Policeman operating in Venice

Donna LEON (American)

was born in the United States but has lived most of her life abroad. At present she teaches English in Italy.

Citation Record: 4 Books

Death At La Fenice - *First*
Chapman & Hall UK (1992)

A Venetian Reckoning - *Latest*
Macmillan UK (1995)

Brother Felipe BRUNO

Male Amateur

Marjorie BOWEN 1886-1952 (British)

Writer: Gabrielle Margaret Vere Campbell LONG

Inventor of one other detective Capt HOARE

Citation Record: 14 Short Stories in 1 Collection

The Triumphant Beast - *Collection 1*
Bodley Head UK (1934)

Insp Thomas BRUNT

is as sound and solid as the hills on the Lancashire-Yorkshire borders among which, in the late part of the nineteenth century and the early part of the twentieth, he works. His murder cases are usually as strange and uncomfortable as the lives of the people in the isolated villages he knows so well.
British Policeman operating in Lancashire

John Buxton HILTON 1921-1986 (British)

was born in Buxton, Derbyshire. He was educated at The College, Buxton, and took a BA in languages at Pembroke College, Cambridge. He served with distinction in the Army and British Intelligence Corps, 1941-1946, and later became a school headmaster, language teacher and Inspector of Schools. He wrote twenty-nine genre works under his own name and a pseudonym.

Inventor of one other detective Supt/Ch Supt Simon KENWORTHY

Citation Record: 6 Books

Rescue From The Rose - *First*
Macmillan UK (1976); St Martin's US (1976)

Slickensides - *Last*
Collins UK (1987); St Martin's US (1987)

B

John BRYANT

British Male Amateur operating in England

Richard GRAYSON (British)

was born in Scotland, took a degree in history and, whilst writing his detective stories, finds time for his more vital work as an official with the Scottish Whisky Trade Association.

Writer: Richard GRINDAL

Other Byline: Richard GRINDAL

Inventor of one other detective Insp Jean-Paul GAUTIER

Citation Record: 4 Books

The Spiral Path - *First*
Hammond UK (1955)

Dead So Soon - *Last*
Hammond UK (1960)

Steve BRYANT

operates in Pacific City, California. His one case involves high-level city corruption.
American Male Private Detective operating in California

Peter GEORGE 1924-1966 (American)

For writer details see Anthony BRANDON

Citation Record: 1 Book

Come Blonde, Come Murder - *Only*
Harlequin US (1952); Boardman UK (1952)

Sydney BRYANT

is, in spite of her name, a very female PI, operating in and around San Diego, California.
American Female Private Detective operating in California

Patricia WALLACE (American)

Citation Record: 2 Books

Small Favors - *First*
Zebra US (1988)

Deadly Devotion - *Latest*
Zebra US (1994)

Emily BRYCE

Second detective of Henry BRYCE

Henry BRYCE and Emily BRYCE

are a husband-and-wife detective duo. They are unusual in being furnisher finishers for a firm of interior decorators in Manhattan, but they inevitably encounter murders needing their attention.
American Male Amateur and American Female Amateur operating in New York

Margaret SCHERF 1908-1979 (American)

Invented 5 detectives - see Rev Martin BUELL

Citation Record: 5 Books

Always Murder A Friend - *First*
Doubleday US (1948); Sampson, Low UK (1949)

The Diplomat And The Gold Piano - *Last*
Doubleday US (1963)

Death And The Diplomat - *Last**
!See Appendix 2.
Barker UK (1964)

Kevin BRYCE

American Male Sleuth operating in USA/Ireland

Deborah VALENTINE (American)

Citation Record: 3 Books

Unorthodox Methods - *First*
Gollancz UK (1989); Avon US (1991)

Fine Distinctions - *Latest*
Gollancz UK (1991)

B

Avis BRYDEN
British Female Amateur operating in England

Eden PHILLPOTTS 1862-1960 (British)

Invented 10 detectives - see Insp MIDWINTER

Citation Record: 4 Books

The Bred In The Bone - *First*
Hutchinson UK (1932); Macmillan US (1933)

The Book Of Avis - *Last*
Hutchinson UK (1936)

Ben BRYN
is a polio victim and stunted in growth; but he is exceptionally strong and muscular, a useful thing to be if you have to be up among the contenders in the pulps of the 1930s. His stories mainly appeared in *Dime Mystery.*

Male Detective in Pulp Magazines operating in USA

Russell GRAY 1908- (American)

was one of the pseudonyms used by this prolific author for stories in the pulps of the 1930s and 1940s.

Writer: Bruno FISCHER

Citation Record: 1 Selected Short Story

The Dead Hand Horrors
can be found in the anthology, *More Tales of the Defective Detective from the Pulps* (Editors; Gary Hoppenstand, Garyn G Roberts & Ray B Browne; US, 1985).
In 'Dime Mystery' US (1939)

Insp BRYSON
appears once, to solve a case of locked-room murder, typical of the period.

British Policeman operating in England

Van HARRISON (British)

Citation Record: 1 Selected Short Story

Alibi
is in the anthology, *Best Crime Stories* (*Faber*, UK 1934).
Faber UK (1934)

Bill BUCHANAN
American Male Amateur operating in Texas

Austin BAY (American)

Citation Record: 1 Book

The Coyote Cried Twice - *Single*
Arbor US (1985)

Johnny BUCHANAN
Australian Male Sleuth operating in Australia

John BRENNER (Australian)

Citation Record: 3 Books

Die My Lovely - *First*
Horwitz AU (1956)

Drag Me Down - *Last*
Horwitz AU (1956)

Johnny BUCHANAN
American Male Sleuth operating in New York/Miami

K T MCCALL (Australian)

Writers: Audrey ARMITAGE and Muriel WATKINS

Citation Record: 22 Books

A Redhead For Free - *First*
Horwitz AU (1957)

Dame On The Make - *Last*
Horwitz AU (1958)

Willie BUCHANAN
American Male Amateur operating in USA

Bryan TOBIN (American)

Citation Record: 1 Book

The Missing Person - *Single*
Otto Penzler US (1994)

Insp BUCK
British Policeman operating in England

Antony MARSDEN (British)

Writer: Graham SUTTON

Inventor of one other detective Jim BEVERLEY

Citation Record: 2 Books

Death On The Downs - *First*
Jarrolds UK (1929)

Death Strikes From The Rear - *Last*
Low UK (1934)

Zebulion BUCK
Second detective of Jim DUNN

Lionel BUCKBY
British Male Amateur operating in England

John GLOAG 1896-1981 (British)

Writer: John Edwards GLOAG

Citation Record: 4 Books

Ripe For Development - *First*
Cassell UK (1936)

Kind Uncle Buckby - *Last*
Cassell UK (1946)

Insp BUCKET
has the distinction of being the first professional detective in English literature, appearing just over a decade after the first fictional amateur detective of *Edgar Allan POE.* He is, indeed, called 'Inspector Bucket of the Detective' and the author apparently based him on a real policeman, Insp Charles Field, about whom he had written an article in 1850. *BUCKET* is described as a stodgy, middle-aged, honest, hardworking and thoughtful man. He is no intellectual, but he is a human bloodhound when it comes to following the trail. He invariably carries a stick on duty and he wears a mourning ring on his little finger, a not uncommon custom in mid-Victorian times. He is always active, obtaining his information – in these early formative years for his profession – simply by 'being there', by lurking and watching. He is, in fact, doubly distinguished, having perhaps the earliest sidekick in the literature; for his wife, *Mrs BUCKET,* clearly helps him in his elucidation of the mystery of Bleak House.

British Policeman operating in England

Sidekick: Mrs BUCKET
is perhaps the earliest real (and actually named) sidekick in the history of the genre. She is certainly of considerable, if unobtrusive, help to her husband in elucidating the mystery of Bleak House.

British Female - Wife

Charles DICKENS 1812-1870 (British)

was born at Landport, which was then a suburb of Portsmouth, Hampshire. The son of a poor Navy clerk, in 1814 he was taken to London and in 1916 to Chatham where he received a little schooling. In 1921, the family, being in financial trouble, removed to London, where the boy, at ten years old, entered the blacking factory of Day & Martin. His next years were hard and lonely, with little further schooling, and he got a job first as a clerk, then a junior reporter. He published his first magazine article in 1833 and the first number of *Pickwick Papers* in 1836. The rest, as they say, is history.

Charles DICKENS is regarded as by many as the greatest of all English novelists. He was, certainly, a true pioneer in all he did; and it is fitting, perhaps, that, among his many other distinctions, he must take the credit for having invented *Insp BUCKET,* the first professional detective to be described in English literature.

Writer: Charles John Huffam DICKENS

Citation Record: 1 Book

Bleak House - *Only*
This famous novel is the first in which a professional detective appears.
Bradbury & Evans UK (1853); Harper & Row US (1853)

Rev Ebenezer BUCKLE

British Male Amateur operating in England

Nicholas BRADY 1900-1945 (British)

For writer details see Mick CARDBY

Citation Record: 3 Books

The House Of Strange Guests - *First*
Bles UK (1932)

Ebenezer Investigates - *Last*
Bles UK (1934)

Supt BUDD

was one of many detective characters created by this author, who apparently had no conscience about borrowing them from other writers' books. Indeed, most of the books in which he appears seem to have been cobbled together from others.

British Policeman operating in London

Gerald VERNER 1896-1980 (British)

was a writer whose identity still remains unclear, although it is believed that he was born in London around 1896. He is known to have been a theatrical producer and he wrote over a hundred and thirty books (none of which seem to have been published in the US) under various names, taking other authors' and his own earlier plots and characters and stitching them together, sometimes more than once. A loveable rascal and, at his best, an enjoyable read, he created several detectives of his own and appropriated others from other authors.

Writer: Donald William STEWARD

Other Bylines:
Derwent STEELE
Donald STUART
Donald William STEWARD
Nigel VANE

Other Detectives:
Peter CHARD
Simon GALE
Trevor LOWE
Michael DENE
Felix HERON
Paul RIVINGTON

Citation Record: 19 Books

Green Mask - *First*
Wright & Brown UK (1934)

Mister Big - *Last*
Wright & Brown UK (1966)

Lanny BUDD

is the scion of a wealthy family and, taking it on himself to right the world's wrongs, becomes a prominent figure in the world of international politics and intrigue.

American Male Professional Investigator operating in USA

Upton SINCLAIR 1878-1968 (American)

was born in Baltimore, Maryland. A distinguished mainstream novelist and Pulitzer Prize winner, many of his works reflect his socialist outlook and were movers of public opinion during the early part of the twentieth century. Beginning in 1940, he wrote the *LANNY BUDD* novels, which, although in a popular genre, served as a final expression of his concern.

Writer: Upton Beall SINCLAIR

Citation Record: 7 Books

Presidential Agent - *First*
Viking US (1944)

The Return Of Lanny Budd - *Last*
Viking US (1953)

Rev Martin BUELL

is a portly, middle-aged, Episcopalian priest who lives in the rectory of Christ Church, Farrington, Montana. He has the most jaundiced views on life in general and his flock in particular. He seems to be right, for cases of murder crop up all around his parish. In spite of the disapproval of his housekeeper, he solves them.

American Male Amateur operating in Montana

Sidekick: Henry BEAVER
is *BUELL's* gardener and offers more advice than gardening.

American Male - Gardener

Margaret SCHERF 1908-1979 (American)

was born in Fairmont, West Virginia, and educated at public schools in New Jersey and Wyoming.

Writer: Margaret Louise SCHERF

Other Detectives:
Hal BRADY
Lt RYAN
Prof Grace SEVERANCE
Henry BRYCE and Emily BRYCE

Citation Record: 6 Books

Gilbert's Last Toothache - *First*
Doubleday US (1949)

For The Love Of Murder - *First**
Spivak US (1950)

The Corpse In The Flannel Nightgown - *Last*
Doubleday US (1965); Hale UK (1966)

Adele BUFFINGTON

is the head of the Hendricks Social Services Agency. She appeared as a minor character in earlier books and now returns as the main detective. After being assaulted in her office, forced to witness the burglary of her files and then involved in a murder, she decides – not unreasonably in the circumstances – to turn sleuth.

American Female Amateur operating in Indianapolis

Michael Z LEWIN 1942- (American)

Invented 3 detectives - see Albert SAMSON

Citation Record: 1 Book

And Baby Will Fall - *Single*
Morrow US (1988)

Child Proof - *Single**
Macmillan UK (1988)

Mr BUFFUM

British Male Amateur operating in England

Hugh DE SELINCOURT 1878-1951 (British)

Citation Record: 14 Short Stories in 1 Collection

Mr Buffum - *Collection 1*
Ward, Lock UK (1930)

Sir George BULL

is an oddity even by the flexible standards of the genre. A knight of the realm, he is a confidence trickster who assumes the role of a PI to gain entry to households and then has to carry on with the part, solving murder by necessity.

British Male Amateur operating in England

Milward KENNEDY 1894-1968 (British)

was educated at Winchester College and New College, Oxford. He had a distinguished career in the Civil Service, served in British Intelligence in the First World War, was decorated with the *Croix de Guerre*, and later played an important role in the world of the Press and in London literary circles. A member of the famous London Detection Club, he found time to write around twenty detective novels and many short stories.

Writer: Milward Rodon Kennedy BURGE

Other Byline: Robert Milward KENNEDY

Other Detectives:
Gregory AMOR
Insp CORNFORD
Mr TRUEFITT
Supt COLE
Supt GUEST

Citation Record: 2 Books

Bull's Eye - *First*
Gollancz UK (1933); Kinsey US (1933)

Corpse In Cold Storage - *Last*
Gollancz UK (1934); Kinsey US (1934)

B

Homer BULL
American Male Amateur operating in New York/Los Angeles

Lawrence LARIAR 1908-1981 (American)

Invented 3 detectives - see Mike WELLS

Citation Record: 4 Books

He Died Laughing - *First*
Phoenix Press US (1943); Boardman UK (1946)

The Girl With The Frightened Eyes - *Last*
Dodd, Mead US (1945); Cassell UK (1950)

Tom BULLEN
is a reluctant courier for some official but unnamed organisation. He becomes involved in a murder, with connections to stolen nuclear weaponry.
American Male Amateur operating in USA/Europe/Asia

Jack CURTIS (American)

Citation Record: 1 Book

Mirrors Kill - *Single*
Crown US (1995)

Insp BULLER
appears only once, to solve a most ingenious case of locked-room murder.
British Policeman operating in England

T H WHITE 1906-1964 (British)

Writer: Terence Hanbury WHITE

Citation Record: 1 Book

Darkness At Pemberley - *Only*
Gollancz UK (1932); Dover US (1978)

Supt Simon BULLION
British Policeman operating in England

Maurice B DIX 1889-1956 (British)

Invented 4 detectives - see Tommy MALINS

Citation Record: 2 Books

This Is My Murder - *First*
Ward, Lock UK (1938)

Murder Strikes Twice - *Last*
Ward, Lock UK (1939)

BULLOCK
of Scotland Yard is a Victorian detective of the pre-*HOLMES* era.
British Policeman operating in London

Hawley SMART 1833-1893 (British)

Invented 8 detectives - see Insp POLLOCK

Citation Record: 1 Book

False Cards - *Only*
Hurst & Blackett UK (1880)

Helen BULLOCK
is a photographer and appeared as the sidekick of *Simon BEDE* in earlier books by this author.
American Female Amateur operating in Marrakesh

Sidekick: Fergus BEDE
is the son of *Simon BEDE*, who was the detective in the author's earlier books.
British Male - Assistant

Barbara Ninde BYFIELD 1930- (American)

Inventor of one other detective Father Simon BEDE

Citation Record: 1 Book

A Parcel Of Their Fortunes - *Single*
Doubleday US (1979)

Turco BULLWORTHY
British Male Amateur operating in several locations

J S FLETCHER 1863-1935 (British)

Invented 9 detectives - see Paul CAMPENHAYE

Citation Record: 6 Short Stories in 1 Collection

The Adventures Of Turco Bullworthy - *Collection 1*
Washbourne UK (1912)

George BULMAN
appears in novelizations of episodes from a TV series.
British Male Professional Investigator operating in several locations

Robert P HOLDSTOCK 1948- (British)

Citation Record: 1 Book

One Of Our Pigeons Is Missing - *Single*
Futura UK (1984)

John RAYMOND 1947- (British)

Writer: John BROSNAN

Inventor of one other detective pair DEMPSEY and MAKEPEACE

Citation Record: 1 Book

Thin Ice - *Single*
Javelin UK (1987)

Jimmy BULSTRODE
British Male Amateur operating in England

Marie VAN VORST 1867-1936 (British)

Citation Record: 8 Short Stories in 1 Collection

The Sentimental Adventures Of Jimmy Bulstrode - *Collection 1*
Methuen UK (1908); Hurst US (1908)

Dr Nathaniel BUNCE
American Male Amateur operating in Naples

E M CURTISS (American)

Writer: Elizabeth Mangam CURTISS

Citation Record: 2 Books

Nine Doctors And A Madman - *First*
Simon & Schuster US (1937); Jenkins UK (1938)

Dead Dogs Bite - *Last*
Simon & Schuster US (1939)

Terry (Chopper Cop) BUNKER
American Male Sleuth operating in California

Paul ROSS

Writers: Bill AMIDON 1935- and Nathaniel FREEDLAND 1936-

Citation Record: 1 Book

Dynamite Monster Boogie Concert - *Only*
Popular Library US (1975)

Paul ROSS 1929-

For writer details see Colin STRYKER

Citation Record: 1 Book

The Assassin - *Only*
Manor US (1947)

Paul ROSS 1928-

For writer details see Michael HAWK

Citation Record: 2 Books

The Hitchhike Killer - *First*
Popular Library US (1972)

Valley Of Death - *Last*
Popular Library US (1972)

'Smiler' BUNN
British Male Amateur operating in England

Bertram ATKEY 1880-1952 (British)

Invented 4 detectives - see Prosper FAIR

Citation Record: 2 Books 75 Short Stories in 7 Collections

Arsenic And Gold - *First*
Jenkins UK (1939); Penn US (1939)

The Mystery Of The Glass Bullet - *Last*
Appleton US (1931)

The Amazing Mr Bunn - *Collection 1*
Short stories - 6
Newnes UK (1912)

The Smiler Bunn Brigade - *Collection 2*
Short stories - 12
Hodder & Stoughton UK (1916)

B

Smiler Bunn, Manhunter - *Collection 3*
Short stories - 7
Newnes UK (1920)

Smiler Bunn, Gentleman-Crook - *Collection 4*
Short stories - 9
Newnes UK (1923)

Smiler Bunn, Byewayman - *Collection 5*
contains an uncounted number of short stories.
Newnes UK (1925)

Smiler Bunn, Gentleman-Adventurer - *Collection 6*
Short stories - 11
Dial US (1927)

Smiler Bunn, Crook - *Collection 7*
includes all the stories in *SMILER BUNN, GENTLEMAN-CROOK* and thirty new stories.
Short stories - 39
Newnes UK (1929)

BURCHELL
Second detective of The Hon Augustus CHAMPNELL

Paul J BURDOCK and Joshua PRELL
American Male Amateurs operating in Washington DC

Walter J SHELDON 1917- (American)
Citation Record: 1 Book
The Rites Of Murder - *Single*
St Martin's US (1984)

Ch Insp Archie BURFORD
is a rather well-educated British cop for his period, the 1930s. When the game is afoot, his ears – we are informed – have the curious ability to tilt backwards. How this helps his sleuthing is difficult to see.
British Policeman operating in London

Victor MACCLURE 1887-1963 (British)
was born in Scotland. He became a sailor and, after an injury, turned to painting, architecture and journalism. Wounded at Gallipoli in the First World War, he began to write science fiction and crime stories.
Inventor of one other detective Edward BLAYNE
Citation Record: 6 Books
The Case Of The Dead Producer - *First*
Newnes UK (1930)
The Diva's Emeralds - *Last*
Harrap UK (1937)

Det BURGESS
is the laconic police detective in *WOOLRICH's* small masterpiece, the finest of the many novellas and short stories that the author wrote.
American Policeman operating in New York

William IRISH 1903-1968 (American)
was the pseudonym most often used by this author, one of the great early masters of the criminous short story.
For writer details see Hal JEFFRIES
Citation Record: 1 Book
Phantom Lady - *Only*
Lippincott US (1942); Hale UK (1945)

Barney BURGESS
is a PI in Chicago who models himself on the kind of detective often played in the movies by Humphrey Bogart.
American Male Private Detective operating in USA

Ellery QUEEN
was used as a house name from the 1960s and after the deaths of the two geniuses who wrote originally under this name. In some cases, the house name conceals the name of a well-known author, who has subsequently been identified.
Other Detectives:
Ellery QUEEN — Sherlock HOLMES
Citation Record: 1 Book
Kiss And Kill - *Single*
Dell US (1969)

Insp Jim BURGESS
British Policeman operating in England

Charles FRANKLIN 1909-1976 (British)
Writer: Frank Hugh USHER
Other Bylines:
Frank LESTER — Frank USHER
Other Detectives:
Maxine DANGERFIELD — Grant GARFIELD
Citation Record: 4 Books
Guilt For Innocence - *First*
Hale UK (1959)
Murder Before Dinner - *Last*
Hale UK (1963)

BURKE
is one of the toughest and most unusual of all American PIs, a mean man who hates delinquents and those who exploit the weak. He lives in New York, occupying an electronically equipped office, isolated from the outside world, with no phone and no paperwork, and guarded by *PANSY*, a mastiff, one of the fiercest in the large inventory of canine sidekicks that the genre has thrown up over the years. *BURKE* is himself an ex-convict and, with a fine mind and a photographic memory, he can negotiate with ease the mean streets, which he knows like the back of his hand, as he pursues his various villains. A self-appointed vigilante, he takes cases only if his conscience is pricked by them. He has several sidekicks, all of them fantastic or grotesque.
American Male Private Detective operating in New York

Sidekick: PANSY
is a 140-pound Neapolitan mastiff. Although female, she is certainly one of the fiercest and toughest canine sidekicks on record.
Female - Pet Dog

Sidekick: MAX THE SILENT
is a Mongolian giant, a man of great strength.
Mongolian Male - Assistant

Sidekick: MICHELLE
is a handsome, transvestite whore.
American Male - Assistant

Sidekick: The PROFESSOR
was once the prison companion and past mentor of *BURKE*, and has now become a street hustler. He speaks in rhyme as simple as his schemes are complex.
American Male - Assistant

Sidekick: The MOLE
is an expert Nazi hunter.
American Male - Assistant

Sidekick: Mama WONG
is an ageless, oriental restaurant owner.
American Female - Assistant

Andrew VACHSS 1942- (American)
was born in New York City. He took a BA at Case-Western Reserve University, Cleveland, Ohio, 1965, and a JD at the New England School of Law, Boston, Massachusetts. An attorney in New York, in a practice specialising in child delinquency, and holder of several government appointments in that field, he is the author of a number of criminous works.
Writer: Andrew Henry VACHSS
Citation Record: 7 Books
Flood - *First*
Fine US (1985); Collins UK (1985)
Down In The Zero - *Latest*
Knopf US (1994)

B

Det Caley BURKE
is a rookie cop.
American Policeman operating in USA

Bridget MCKENNA (American)
Citation Record: 1 Book
Dead Ahead - *Single*
Berkley US (1994)

Insp Curtis BURKE
British Policeman operating in England

Ralph TREVOR 1897- (British)
Writer: James Reginald WILMOT
Inventor of one other detective Insp LOCKET
Citation Record: 4 Books
Death Burns The Candle - *First*
Wright UK (1938)
Front Page Murder - *Last*
Wright UK (1942)

Eleanora BURKE
American Female Amateur operating in Los Angeles

Virginia PERDUE 1899-1905 (American)
Citation Record: 2 Books
The Case Of The Grieving Monkey - *First*
Doubleday US (1941)
The Case Of The Foster Father - *Last*
Doubleday US (1942); Jarrolds UK (1946)

Jerry BURKE
American Male Amateur operating in Texas

Asa BAKER 1904-1977 (American)
For writer details see Michael SHAYNE
Citation Record: 2 Books
Mum's The Word For Murder - *First*
Stokes US (1938); Gollancz UK (1939)
The Kissed Corpse - *Last*
Carlyle US (1939)

Shamus BURKE
British Male Amateur operating in England

H M WEBSTER (British)
Citation Record: 3 Books
The Ballycronin Mystery - *First*
Hurst UK (1947)
The Tontine Treasure - *Last*
Hurst UK (1951)

Dr BURKHALTER
solves a case of murder by stabbing in a locked room.
American Male Amateur operating in USA

Harry Stephen KEELER 1890-1967 (American)
Invented 14 detectives - see Angus MACWHORTER
Citation Record: 1 Selected Short Story
The Hand Of God
can be found in the anthology, *20 Great Tales of Murder.*
Random House US (1951); Hammond UK (1952)

James BURLANE
appears in action thrillers involving espionage and some detection.
American Male Secret Agent operating in USA

Richard HOYT 1941- (American)
Invented 3 detectives - see John DENSON
Citation Record: 4 Books
Trotsky's Run - *First*
Morrow US (1982); Severn UK (1987)
Siege - *Latest*
Tor US (1987); Grafton UK (1989)

Nestor BURMA
is the head (and, it seems, the only operative) of the Fiat Lux Detective Agency in Paris and is drawn into exciting cases that even the great *Jules MAIGRET* might not have heard of. They have, after forty years, only recently appeared in English.
French Male Private Detective operating in Paris

Leo MALET (French)
Citation Record: 2 Books
120 Rue De La Gare - *First*
Translated from the French.
Pan UK (?)
The Rats Of Montsouris - *Latest*
is a translation from the French of *Les Rats De Montsouris* (*Robert Laffont*, Paris, 1955).
Pan UK (1991)

BURMAN
solves a case of murder in which an actress is inexplicably shot on stage.
British Male Sleuth operating in England

John G BRANDON 1879-1941 (British)
Invented 5 detectives - see Sgt/Det Insp Patrick Aloysius MCCARTHY
Citation Record: 1 Book
The One-Minute Murder - *Only*
Methuen UK (1934); Dial US (1935)

Insp Cheviot BURMANN
appears also in other books with one of the author's other detectives, *Bryan ARMITAGE*.
British Policeman operating in England

Belton COBB 1892-1971 (British)
Writer: Geoffrey Belton COBB
Other Detectives:
Bryan ARMITAGE
Insp Cheviot BURMANN and Bryan ARMITAGE
Supt MANNING
Citation Record: 42 Books
No Alibi - *First*
Longman UK (1936)
Suspicion In Triplicate - *Last*
Allen UK (1971)

Insp Cheviot BURMANN and Bryan ARMITAGE
British Policeman and British Male Amateur operating in England

Belton COBB 1892-1971 (British)
Invented 4 detectives - see Insp Cheviot BURMANN
Citation Record: 2 Books
I Never Miss Twice - *First*
Allen UK (1965)
Secret Inquiry - *Last*
Allen UK (1968)

Insp John BURNELL
British Policeman operating in England

Francis VIVIAN 1906- (British)
Writer: Arthur Ernest ASHLEY
Other Detectives:
Sgt Ronnie DREW   Supt Gordon KNOLLIS
Citation Record: 2 Books
Death At The Salutation - *First*
Jenkins UK (1937)
Black Alibi - *Last*
Jenkins UK (1938)

Don BURNEY
was one of this author's numerous pulp detectives and appeared in short stories, mainly in *Dime Detective*.
American Male Detective in Pulp Magazines operating in USA

Ramon DECOLTA 1898-1945 (American)
Invented 5 detectives - see Dion DAVIES
No citations

B

Supt BURNIVAL
is described as 'lean and predatory', but is otherwise undistinguished and less interesting than his sidekick.
!See Appendix 2.
British Policeman operating in England

Sidekick: Dr Fabian HONEYCHURCH
is an eminent doctor who more than assists the detective work of *BURNIVAL.*
British Male - Assistant

Edward CANDY 1925- (British)
Writer: Barbara Alison Boodson NEVILLE
Citation Record: 2 Books
Which Doctor? - *First*
Gollancz UK (1953); Rinehart US (1954)
Bones Of Contention - *Last*
Gollancz UK (1954); Doubleday US (1983)

Insp BURNLEY, Insp LEFARGE and Insp Georges LA TOUCHE
appear in the first book by this important author, written before he embarked on his classic series with *Insp FRENCH.* The case starts in England, where it is investigated by *Insp BURNLEY;* but, still unsolved, it moves to Paris and is taken on successively by *Insp LA TOUCHE* and *Insp LEFARGE* before it can be resolved.
British Policeman and French Policemen operating in England/France

Freeman Wills CROFTS 1879-1957 (British)
Invented 4 detectives - see Insp Joseph FRENCH
Citation Record: 1 Book
The Cask - *Only*
Collins UK (1920); Seltzer US (1924)

Prof Carl BURNS
is the Professor of English at the fictional Hartley Gorman College in Pecan City, Texas, where he runs into murder most foul. He solves the cases, in spite of conflict with the overbearing local sheriff.
American Male Amateur operating in Texas

Stooge: Sheriff 'Boss' NAPIER
finds it hard to get along with the meddling professor.
American Male

Bill CRIDER 1941- (American)
was born in Mexia, Texas. He graduated with a BA from the University of Texas, Austin, 1963, and took a PhD, 1972. A sometime assistant Professor of English at Texan universities, he is the author of several mainstream novels as well as those in the crime and detective genre.
Writer: Allen Billy CRIDER
Inventor of one other detective Sheriff Dan RHODES
Citation Record: 2 Books
One Dead Dean - *First*
Walker US (1988)
Dying Voices - *Latest*
St Martin's US (1989)

Joe BURNS
has only one case but does not do well.
American Male Private Detective operating in New York

Michael JAFFE (American)
Citation Record: 1 Book
Death Goes To A Party - *Only*
Phoenix Press US (1942)

Harry BURNVILLE
American Male Amateur operating in USA

Victor LAURISTON 1881- (American)
Citation Record: 1 Book
The Twenty-First Burr - *Only*
Doran US (1922)

BURR
Second detective of DYKE

Jason BURR
American Male Amateur operating in USA

David KENT 1891-1958 (American)
Writer: Herman Hoffman BIRNEY
Citation Record: 2 Books
Jason Burr's First Case - *First*
Random House US (1941)
A Knife Is Silent - *Last*
Random House US (1947)

Marcus Aurelius BURR
was formerly a champion at gymnastics and is now a sports reporter. He is involved in murder cases with a sporting background.
American Male Amateur operating in USA

Herbert RESNICOW 1921- (American) and PELE (Argentinian)
Citation Record: 1 Book
The World Cup Murders - *Single*
Wynwood Press UK (1989)

Herbert RESNICOW 1921- (American) and Fran TARHENTON
Citation Record: 1 Book
Murder At The Superbowl - *Single*
Morrow US (1986)

Thad BURR
American Male Detective in Pulp Magazines operating in USA

ANON
Citation Record: 1 Book
Detective Burr's Seven Clues
Aldine US (?)

Mr Jacob BURRELL
is a private investigator of an early vintage, appearing only a decade or so after the appearance of *Sherlock HOLMES.*
British Male Private Detective operating in England

Guy BOOTHBY 1867-1905
Invented 3 detectives - see Dr NIKOLA
Citation Record: 2 Books
The Mystery Of The Clasped Hands - *First*
White UK (1901); Appleton US (1901)
A Millionaire's Love Story - *Last*
White UK (1901); Buckles US (1901)

Cheryl BURROUGHS
Second detective of Allan CONYERS

Julian 'Digger' BURROUGHS
is of mixed Irish-Jewish extraction. Once married, now divorced, he drinks a lot to forget the past and works freelance for a Life Insurance Company. He was mysteriously transformed by the author in 1983 into *Devlin TRACY,* who seems to be the same detective under a new name and appears in a further seven of the author's books.
American Male Private Detective operating in Las Vegas

Warren B MURPHY 1933- (American)
was born in Jersey City, New Jersey, and educated at St Peter's College, Jersey City. He is the author of at least thirty genre books, mainly novels of action, adventure and thrills, usually with supermen heroes. He also wrote, with *Richard SAPIR,* most of the novels of the *Remo WILLIAMS* series, many of which appeared under his name. He has received awards from various societies interested in the crime novel, in particular the Mystery Writers of America Edgar Allan Poe award twice, 1985 and 1986.

B

Other Detectives:
Justin GILEAD and Alexander ZHARKOV
Steve HOOKS Dr David Vincent LEONARDO
Ed RAZONI, William JACKSON and Devlin 'Trace' TRACY
Ed RAZONI and William JACKSON
Devlin 'Trace' TRACY Remo (The Destroyer) WILLIAMS

Citation Record: 4 Books

Smoked Out - *First*
Pocket Books US (1982)

Lucifer's Weekend - *Latest*
Pocket Books US (1982)

Caro BURSA

Second detective of Aaron GATES

Insp BURTON

appears also in one book with the author's other detective, *Mercedes QUERO*.

British Policeman operating in England

G E LOCKE 1887- (British)

Writer: Gladys Edson LOCKE

Other Detectives:
Insp BURTON and Mercedes QUERO
Mercedes QUERO

Citation Record: 3 Books

The Scarlet Macaw - *First*
Page US (1923)

The House On The Downs - *Last*
Page US (1925)

Dr BURTON

American Male Amateur operating in New York

Archibald Clavering GUNTER 1847-1907 (American)

Inventor of one other detective Thomas DUFF

Citation Record: 1 Book 9 Short Stories in 2 Collections

The Adventures Of Dr Burton - *Only*
Home US (1905)

Dr Burton - *Collection 1*
Short stories - 4
Ward, Lock UK (1907)

Dr Burton's Success - *Collection 2*
Short stories - 5
Ward, Lock UK (1908)

Insp BURTON and Mercedes QUERO

also appear individually in other books by this author.

British Policeman and Female Amateur operating in England

G E LOCKE 1887- (British)

Invented 3 detectives - see Insp BURTON

Citation Record: 1 Book

The Red Cavalier - *Only*
Page UK (1922)

Dr Clement BURTON

appears in this one Victorian novel.

British Male Amateur operating in England

Edmund YATES 1831-1894 (British)

Writer: Edmund Hodgson YATES

Citation Record: 1 Book

A Silent Witness - *Only*
Tinsley UK (1895); Gill US (1895)

Maj Dick BURTON

British Male Amateur operating in England

Mark BECKETT 1890- (British)

Writer: Marcus George TRUMAN

Citation Record: 6 Books

The Murder Of A Magnate - *First*
Eldon UK (1934)

The Bullet In The Cornice - *Last*
Eldon UK (1937)

Don BURTON

American Male Amateur operating in Connecticut

Philip OWEN 1903-1989 (American)

For writer details see Pierre CHAMBRUN

Citation Record: 1 Book

Mystery At A Country Inn - *Only*
Berkshire US (1979); Hale UK (1981)

Sam BURTON and Frances BAIRD

form a partnership in this one book. He is a reporter who becomes involved in a case of espionage. Fortunately he has *Frances BAIRD*, a lady detective with the Watkins Detective Agency, to help him. She appears on her own in another book by this author.

American Male Amateur and American Female Private Detective operating in New York

Reginald Wright KAUFFMAN 1877-1959 (American)

See main detective Frances BAIRD

Citation Record: 1 Book

My Heart And Stephanie: A Novel - *Only*
Page US (1910)

The BUTCHER

American Male Professional Investigator operating in USA/Europe

Stuart JASON

House name.

Citation Record: 24 Books

Kill Quick Or Die - *First*
Pinnacle US (1970)

Venetian Vendetta - *Last*
Pinnacle US (1977)

Stuart JASON (American)

For writer details see Ed NOON

Citation Record: 9 Books

The Judas Judge - *First*
Pinnacle US (1979)

The Man From White Hat - *Latest*
Pinnacle US (1982)

Stuart JASON (American)

Writer: Lee Floren

Citation Record: 2 Books

The Deadly Doctor - *First*
Pinnacle US (1974)

Valley Of Death - *Last*
Pinnacle US (1974)

BUTLER

American Male Sleuth operating in USA

Philip KIRK 1935- (American)

Writer: Leonard LEVINSON

Citation Record: 12 Books

The Hydra Conspiracy - *First*
Leisure Books US (1979)

The Midas Kill - *Latest*
Leisure Books US (1984)

Charles BUTLER

Second detective of MALLORY

Prof Brinsley BUTLER

is the young Professor of Drama at a fictional midwestern US University. He turns sleuth when an actress, with whom he is in love, becomes a murder suspect.

American Male Amateur operating in USA

Stooge: Attorney James DORGAN
is the State attorney and an important investigator on the same case. He is an excellent adversary but he will keep thinking that the wrong person dunnit until the professor puts him right as to whodunnit.
American Male

Henry Kitchell WEBSTER 1875-1932 (American)

was born in Evanston, Illinois. He was a prolific and very popular writer of novels and magazine stories.

B

Other Detectives:
Punch CORBIN
Arthur JEFFREY
Pete MURRAY

Citation Record: 1 Book

The Butterfly - *Only*
Appleton US (1914)

Morgan BUTLER

works for a San Francisco agency. He becomes a farmer and part-time PI outside Jordan, Ohio.

American Male Private Detective operating in San Francisco

David ANTHONY 1929-1986 (American)

was born in Holliday's Cove, West Virginia.

Writer: William Dale SMITH

Inventor of one other detective Stanley BASS

Citation Record: 3 Books

The Midnight Lady And The Mourning Man - *First*
Collins UK (1969); Bobbs US (1970)

The Long Hard Cure - *Last*
Collins UK (1979)

Patrick BUTLER

appears also in a book with one of the author's other detectives, *Gideon FELL.*

British Male Amateur operating in England

John Dickson CARR 1906-1977 (American)

Invented 16 detectives - see Dr Gideon FELL

Citation Record: 1 Book

Patrick Butler For The Defense - *Only*
Harper & Row US (1956); Hamilton UK (1956)

Patrick BUTLER

Second detective of Dr Gideon FELL

Harry BUTTEN

American Male Sleuth operating in USA

Jay BARBETTE (American)

is the pseudonym of a husband-and-wife team.

Writers: Bart SPICER and Betty Coe SPICER

Citation Record: 4 Books

Final Copy - *First*
Dodd, Mead US (1950); Barker UK (1952)

Look Behind You - *Last*
Dodd, Mead US (1960); Long UK (1961)

Jimmie BUTTERS

American Male Amateur operating in New Mexico

Glendon SWARTHOUT 1918-1992 (American)

Writer: Glendon Fred SWARTHOUT

Citation Record: 1 Book

Skeletons - *Only*
Doubleday US (1979); Secker & Warburg UK (1979)

Amelia BUTTERWORTH

Second detective of Det Ebenezer GRYCE

Insp George BYDE

British Policeman operating in England

H F WOOD (British)

Writer: Harry Freeman WOOD

Inventor of one other detective TOPPIN

Citation Record: 1 Book

The Passenger From Scotland Yard - *Only*
Chatto & Windus UK (1888); Munro US (1888)

The Night Mail; or, The Passenger From Scotland Yard - *Only**
Munro US (1888)

BYRD

Anna Katherine GREEN 1846-1935 (American)

Invented 9 detectives - see Det Ebenezer GRYCE

Citation Record: 1 Book

7 To 12: A Detective Story - *Only*
Putnam US (1887); Routledge UK (1887)

Ferris BYRD

American Male Amateur operating in San Francisco

Anne STUART (American)

See main detective Maggie BENNETT

Citation Record: 2 Books

Catspaw - *First*
Harlequin US (1985)

Catspaw II - *Latest*
Harlequin US (1988)

Det Supt James BYRD

disguises himself, in his one appearance to date, as one of the historic Yeoman Warders in order to infiltrate the guard at the Tower of London to see who is planning to steal the Crown Jewels. Rather odd behaviour for one of his rank, one might think; but it's just as well, since he meets murder and solves it.

British Policeman operating in London

Teresa COLLARD (British)

Citation Record: 1 Book

Murder At The Tower - *Single*
Severn UK (1991)

Insp BYRNE

British Policeman operating in England

E Charles VIVIAN 1882-1947 (British)

See main detective Insp HEAD

Citation Record: 3 Books

Girl In The Dark - *First*
Ward, Lock UK (1933)

Vain Escape - *Last*
Hale UK (1952)

Charlie BYRNE

American Male Amateur operating in New York

George ADAMS (American)

Citation Record: 1 Book

Insider's Price - *Single*
US (1993)

Edgar BYRNE

appears in this one short story, a departure in genre by one of the great British novelists of the twentieth century.

British Male Amateur operating in England

Joseph CONRAD 1857-1924 (British)

was born of Polish parents in Berdichev, then in Russia. After his family was exiled, he joined a British merchant ship and was a seaman for several years, obtaining the knowledge and interest that he later put into his novels. He became a British citizen in 1884. Although his novels are highly regarded, the short story was his true medium.

Citation Record: 1 Selected Short Story

The Inn Of Two Witches
is an unusual story, concerning a murder at an inn. It appeared in a collection of the author's stories, *Within the Tides.*
Dent UK (1915)

Insp BYRNES

American Policeman operating in New York

Julian HAWTHORNE 1846-1934 (American)

Invented 3 detectives - see Keppel DRAKE

Citation Record: 5 Books

An American Penman - *First*
Cassell US (1887); Cassell UK (1888)

Another's Crime - *Last*
Cassell US (1888); Cassell UK (1889)

Tom BYRNES

operates in the 15th Precinct and is interesting because of the book's title.

American Policeman operating in New York

Chandos FULTON 1839-1904 (American)

Citation Record: 1 Book

The Vidocq Of New York - *Only*
American News Company US (1891)

— C —

Brevet CABLE

British Male Sleuth operating in several locations

Brian CALLISON 1934- (British)

Writer: Brian Richard CALLISON

Citation Record: 2 Books

A Plague Of Sailors - *First*
Collins UK (1971); Putnam US (1971)

A Frenzy Of Merchantmen - *Latest*
Collins UK (1977)

An Act Of War - *Latest**
Dutton US (1977)

Sarah CABLE

British Female Amateur operating in Pakistan

Michael HARTLAND 1941- (British)

Inventor of one other detective David NAIRN

Citation Record: 2 Books

Seven Steps To Treason - *First*
Hodder & Stoughton UK (1984); Macmillan US (1984)

Frontier Of Fear - *Latest*
Hodder & Stoughton UK (1988); Macmillan US (1992)

Philip CABOT

seems to behave more like an old-fashioned British amateur detective than the American private eye he is; for, not only is he incessantly witty, but he gets on well with disgustingly rich members of society as well as with ordinary workaday cops.

American Male Private Detective operating in New York

Roman MCDOUGALD 1907?-1960 (American)

Citation Record: 3 Books

The Deaths Of Lora Karen - *First*
Simon & Schuster US (1944)

The Blushing Monkey - *Last*
Simon & Schuster US (1953); Boardman UK (1953)

Don CADEE

is a former US Marine, now Chief of Store Protection in a Fifth Avenue department store. He runs into a spectrum of crimes from shoplifting to murder and manages to solve them without too much help from the police.

American Male Professional Investigator operating in New York

Spencer DEAN 1895- (American)

For writer details see Fire Marshal Ben PEDLEY

Citation Record: 9 Books

The Frightened Fingers - *First*
Washburn US (1954); Boardman UK (1955)

Credit For A Murder - *Last*
Washburn US (1954); Boardman UK (1962)

Brother CADFAEL

is a Benedictine monk in the twelfth century, in the era of the battles between King Stephen and Empress Maud for the throne of England. Soldier, sailor, ex-Crusader and ex-lover, he has taken his vows late in life. His acute skills at observation and his vast experience enable him, on his travels from abbey to monastery, to detect and solve many a foul crime. The author, an expert in the medieval field and with an extensive history of criminous writing already behind her, has succeeded in creating one of the most presently popular characters in modern British fiction.

Welsh Male Amateur operating in England

Ellis PETERS 1913-1995 (British)

was born in Horsehay, Shropshire, and educated at local schools. She served in the Women's Royal Navy Service, 1940-1945, receiving the British Empire Medal, 1944. She has written crime novels from 1940 for over fifty years and, under her real name and other pseudonyms, is the author of at least thirty mainstream novels. She received the Mystery Writers of America Edgar Allen Poe award, 1963, and the Crime Writers Association Silver Dagger award, 1981.

Writer: Edith Mary PARGETER

Other Detectives:
George FELSE and Dominic FELSE
Francis KILLIAN
Det Insp MUSGRAVE

Citation Record: 20 Books

One Corpse Too Many - *First*
is *Brother CADFAEL's* stunning debut in which he solves the mystery of how there came to be one extra body among the many victims of a massacre, all of whom were known.
Macmillan UK (1979); Morrow US (1980)

Brother Cadfael's Penance - *Latest*
Headline UK (1992)

Insp CADMAN

British Policeman operating in England

Charles RUSHTON 1904- (British)

Writer: Charles Rushton SHORTT

Inventor of one other detective pair James O'HANNAY and Floyd EAST

Citation Record: 5 Books

Murder Out Of Tune - *First*
Jenkins UK (1939)

Devil's Power - *Last*
Jenkins UK (1952); Roy US (1956)

Insp CADOGAN

British Policeman operating in England

Michael INNES 1906-1994 (British)

Invented 4 detectives - see Insp/Commiss John APPLEBY

Citation Record: 1 Book

The Journeying Boy - *Only*
Gollancz UK (1949)

The Case Of The Journeying Boy - *Only**
Dodd, Mead US (1949)

Benjamin Franklin CAGE

is not a man who evokes admiration, for his morals seem as flexible as those of some of his clients.

American Male Private Detective operating in Los Angeles/Paris

Peter ISRAEL 1933- (American)

Writer: J Leon ISRAEL

Inventor of one other detective Charles CAMELOT

Citation Record: 3 Books

Hush Money - *First*
Crowell US (1974); Hodder & Stoughton UK (1975)

The Stiff Upper Lip - *Latest*
Crowell US (1978); Hodder & Stoughton UK (1979)

Huntingdon CAGE

manages to get by as a PI by using the fact that he has an identical twin who can usefully double for him in tricky situations. Altogether and definitely beyond the pale, even for the elastic ethics of the genre.

American Male Private Detective operating in New York

C

Alan RIEFE 1925- (American)
Inventor of one other detective Tygrus Gerald 'Tyger' DECKER
Citation Record: 5 Books
The Lady Killers - *First*
Popular Library US (1975); New English Library UK (1976)
The Silver Puma - *Latest*
Popular Library US (1976)

Colette CAHILL
investigates the death of a colleague, a courier, at Heathrow airport, which the police say was caused by a heart attack. Of course they would!
American Female Secret Agent operating in Washington DC

Margaret TRUMAN 1924- (American)
Invented 9 detectives - see Mr Ron FAIRCHILD
Citation Record: 1 Book
Murder In The CIA - *Single*
Random House US (1987); Severn UK (1988)

CAIN
American Male Sleuth operating in several locations

Sean A KEY 1924- (American)
For writer details see Rony RUSSO
Citation Record: 2 Books
The Mark Of Cain - *First*
Dell US (1980)
Cain's Chinese Puzzle - *Latest*
Dell US (1981)

Cabot CAIN
American Male Sleuth operating in Europe/Asia

Alan CAILLOU 1914- (American)
Invented 4 detectives - see Matthew TOBIN
Citation Record: 6 Books
Assault On Loveless - *First*
Avon UK (1969)
Assault On Aimata - *Last*
Avon UK (1975)

Jennifer CAIN
is the Director of the Port Frederick Civic Foundation in Newtown. She is involved in mystery and murder, which occur with great frequency and need solving, as the police seem inadequate.
American Female Amateur operating in Massachusetts

Nancy PICKARD 1945- (American)
was born in Kansas City, Missouri. She was a journalist and editor before turning to the writing of criminous works.
Citation Record: 9 Books
Generous Death - *First*
Avon US (1984)
Confession - *Latest*
Pocket Books US (1994); Macmillan UK (1994)

John CAIN
is a young book dealer who investigates the murder of a friend, who had declared a special interest in what seemed to be an ordinary old book.
British Male Amateur operating in England

John BLACKBURN 1923- (British)
Invented 4 detectives - see Gen Charles KIRK
Citation Record: 1 Book
Blue Octavo - *Only*
Cape US (1963)
Bound To Kill - *Only**
Mill US (1963)

Ned CAIN
solves a disappearance from a locked trunk.
American Male Sleuth operating in USA

Gene D ROBINSON (American)
Citation Record: 1 Selected Short Story
Hocus-Pocus Homicide
appeared in the April number.
In '10-Story Detective Magazine' US (1945)

Barney CAINE
searches for the formula for a secret fuel.
American Male Professional Investigator operating in several locations

Steve SHAGAN 1927- (American)
Citation Record: 1 Book
The Formula - *Single*
Morrow US (1979); Joseph UK (1980)

Nick CAINE
American Male Private Detective operating in Denver

Donald ZOCHERT 1938- (American)
Writer: Donald Paul ZOCHERT Jr
Inventor of one other detective Benjamin FRANKLIN
Citation Record: 2 Books
Another Weeping Woman - *First*
Holt US (1980); Hale UK (1983)
The Man Of Glass - *Latest*
Holt US (1982); Hale UK (1983)

Duncan CAINSFORTH
appears in books with the author's other detectives.
British Male Amateur operating in France

John MASKE (British)
Other Detectives:
Jeremy FLACK and Duncan CAINSFORTH
Clarence E HEMINGWAY and Jeremy FLACK
Citation Record: 1 Book
The Dinard Mystery - *Only*
Rich UK (1933)

Duncan CAINSFORTH
Second detective of Jeremy FLACK

Donald CAIRN
British Male Amateur operating in England

Vernon LODER 1881- (British)
Invented 3 detectives - see Insp CHACE
Citation Record: 2 Books
The Men With The Double Faces - *First*
Collins UK (1937)
A Wolf In The Fold - *Last*
Collins UK (1938)

Mr CALDER
Second detective of Mr BEHRENS

David CALDER
leaves his law practice and sets up as a private detective, working for an insurance company and searching for a lost Stradivarius violin.
American Male Private Detective operating in New York
Stooge: Lt FLUMMER
is the police end of the investigations.
American Male

Marco PAGE 1909-1968 (American)
Invented 3 detectives - see Joel GLASS
Citation Record: 1 Book
The Shadowy Third - *Only*
Dodd, Mead US (1946)
Suspects All - *Only**
Cherry Tree UK (1948)

Deborah CALDER
is the daughter of *Keith CALDER* and, as she grows up she starts to assist in his sleuthing. In this one book he is abroad and

she, as the steward of the local gun club, has to solve the usual crime that seems to bedevil this family.

British Female Amateur operating in Scotland

Gerald HAMMOND 1926- (British)

Invented 5 detectives - see Keith CALDER

Citation Record: 1 Book

A Brace Of Skeet - *Single*
Macmillan UK (1989)

C

Keith CALDER

is a countryman, a gun expert and skilled at solving crimes and mysteries depending on small clues, usually involving firearms. He is increasingly used by the local police in the fictional small town of Newton Lauder.

British Male Amateur operating in Scotland

Stooge: Ch Insp MUNRO
is the local law and is usually wrong about everything.
British Male

Gerald HAMMOND 1926- (British)

was born in Bournemouth, Hampshire. He was educated at St Edmund's School, Hindhead, and studied architecture at the Aberdeen School of Architecture, 1946-1952. He lives in Scotland, where most of his books are set, and is an expert on guns and shooting, subjects that provide the background for many of his detective stories.

Writer: Gerald Arthur Douglas HAMMOND
Other Byline: Arthur DOUGLAS
Other Detectives:
Deborah CALDER   John CUNNINGHAM
Simon PARBITTER and Keith CALDER
'Beau' PEPYS

Citation Record: 15 Books

Dead Game - *First*
Macmillan UK (1979)

Let Us Prey - *Latest*
Macmillan UK (1990)

Keith CALDER

Second detective of Simon PARBITTER

Harry CALDERWOOD

American Male Amateur operating in USA

Patrick A KELLEY 1951?- (American)

Writer: Patrick A KELLEY

Citation Record: 5 Books

Sleightly Murder - *First*
Avon US (1985)

Sleightly Guilty - *Latest*
Avon US (1988)

Prof CALDWELL

is the Professor of Psychology at the fictional North University. In his forties, a rather shabbily dressed bachelor, he takes to detective work 'because of his interest in the criminal mind'. He is a typical academic sleuth of the period, surrounded by books and pipe smoke whilst he indulges in deep thinking.

American Male Amateur operating in Chicago

Sidekick: Bendy BRINKS
is an admiring young assistant.
American Male - Assistant

Milton K OZAKI 1913- (American)

has been a reporter, artist, accountant and, at one time, the owner of a beauty salon. He has written under his own name and the pseudonym of *Richard SABER*, much of his output belonging to the sex and violence school.

Other Detectives:
Rusty FORBES   Carl GUARD

Citation Record: 3 Books

The Cuckoo Clock - *First*
Ziff-Davis US (1946)

Too Many Women - *First**
Handi-Books US (1950)

The Dummy Murder Case - *Last*
Graphic US (1951)

Martyn CALE

British Male Sleuth operating in England

Patrick LONG (British)

Citation Record: 2 Books

Heil Britannia - *First*
Everest UK (1973)

Eagle Six - *Last*
Everest UK (1975)

Dr Arthur CALGARY

is one of the author's minor sleuths.

British Male Amateur operating in England

Stooge: Supt HUISH
British Male

Agatha CHRISTIE 1890-1976 (British)

Invented 18 detectives - see Hercule POIROT

Citation Record: 1 Book

Ordeal By Innocence - *Only*
Collins UK (1958); Dodd, Mead US (1959)

Barney CALHOUN

was a policeman and is now a PI.

American Male Private Detective operating in Buffalo

Richard DEMING 1915-1983 (American)

Invented 4 detectives - see Manville MOON

Citation Record: 1 Book

Hit And Run - *Only*
Pocket Books US (1960)

Burt CALHOUN

works on a case involving studio blackmail.

American Male Private Detective operating in Hollywood

Weed DICKINSON (American)

Citation Record: 1 Book

Dead Man Talks Too Much - *Only*
Lippincott US (1947)

Cat CALIBAN

is middle-aged, has been married for nearly forty years and has raised three kids; but, for reasons difficult to fathom, since her contemporaries seem quite happy playing Bridge, she wants to be 'the best PI in Cincinnati'.

American Female Private Detective operating in Cincinnati

D B BORTON (American)

Citation Record: 5 Books

One For The Money - *First*
Diamond US (1993)

Three Is A Crowd - *Latest*
Berkley US (1994)

The CALIFORNIA DETECTIVE

American Male Detective in Pulp Magazines operating in USA

UNKNOWN

No citations

Rupert Patrick 'Slim' CALLAGHAN

is one of this prolific author's quasi-private eyes, who do not always fit comfortably into the British scene of the 1940s, but – trading perhaps on the appeal of their transatlantic counterparts – often offer exciting if unrealistic fare. *Patrick CALLAGHAN* is slim, down at heel and operates a sort of detective agency from a fourth-floor office somewhere off Chancery Lane in London. He can barely afford the rent or the salary of his redheaded secretary, Effie Perkins, who loves him dearly and unrequitedly. He smokes too much and, later, drinks too much.

C

but he has two useful attributes: his acquaintance with the ins and outs of journalism and journalists and his intimate knowledge of London's gaming clubs. He eventually does well under the tutelage of a not unhelpful police stooge and acquires a Canadian sidekick.

British Male Private Detective operating in London

Sidekick: Windermere NIKOLLS
is acquired as an assistant during the course of the series.
Canadian Male - Assistant

Stooge: Det Insp George Henry GRINGALL
is a not unfriendly cop from Scotland Yard who is helped by *CALLAGHAN* and in return helps him.
British Male

Peter CHEYNEY 1896-1951 (British)
Invented 11 detectives - see Lemmy CAUTION
Citation Record: 9 Books 12 Short Stories in 1 Collection
The Urgent Hangman - *First*
Collins UK (1938); Coward McCann US (1939)
Uneasy Terms - *Last*
Collins UK (1947); Dodd, Mead US (1946)
Calling Mr Callaghan - *Collection 1*
Three volumes of the author's short stories, some of which featured *Slim CALLAGHAN* were published. This is the last and most representative, but other stories are to be found scattered among the author's many and varied publications.
Todd UK (1943)

Col 'Steel' CALLAGHAN

British Male Secret Agent operating in England

Michael CHESNEY (British)
Citation Record: 3 Books
Callaghan Of Intelligence - *First*
Jenkins UK (1938)
Callaghan Meets His Fate - *Last*
Jenkins UK (1939)

Brock (The Rock) CALLAHAN

is an ex-football player, a giant of a man who has established an upmarket PI agency in Beverly Hills, taking good honest cases only.

American Male Private Detective operating in California

Sidekick: Corey RALEIGH
appears as the young assistant to *CALLAHAN* in later books of the series.
American Male - Assistant

William Campbell GAULT 1910- (American)
was born in Milwaukee, Wisconsin. He graduated from the University of Wisconsin, Madison, 1929, and served in the US Army, 1943-1945. In addition to being the author of at least twenty-nine genre books, he has been a prolific writer of short stories and the author of many books for children. He received the Mystery Writers of America Edgar Allan Poe award, 1953.

Other Detectives:
Mortimer JONES
Lee KAPRELIAN
Luke PILGRIM
Joe PUMA
Pete WORDEN

Citation Record: 11 Books
Ring Around Rosa - *First*
Dutton US (1955); Boardman UK (1955)
Murder In The Raw - *First**
Dell US (1956)
Cat And Mouse - *Latest*
St Martin's US (1988)

Nickie CALLAHAN

American Female Amateur operating in USA

Charlaine HARRIS 1951- (American)
Invented 3 detectives - see Catherine LINTON
Citation Record: 1 Book
A Secret Rage - *Single*
Houghton US (1984); Severn UK (1984)

David CALLAN

is a modern version of the British secret agent, updated from the *James BOND* model.

British Male Secret Agent operating in several locations

Sidekick: LONELY
is a musty, unwashed, smelly little man who acts as an unattractive and sometimes unwelcome legman.
American Male - Assistant

James MITCHELL 1926- (British)
Invented 3 detectives - see Joe CAVE
Citation Record: 4 Books
A Magnum For Schneider - *First*
Jenkins UK (1969)
A Red File For Callan - *First**
Simon & Schuster US (1971)
Callan - *First**
Corgi UK (1974)
Smear Job - *Last*
Hamish Hamilton UK (1975); Putnam US (1977)

Sarah CALLOWAY

is an investigative reporter who seems to act as if she was a private eye. Fond of wine, pasta dishes, and much human frailty, she sometimes needs to lean on a man friend or lover for support. However, she always succeeds in solving her cases, even though she is rather given to pursuing the kinds of vast criminal organisation that some of the greatest agents in the genre might have baulked at.

American Female Amateur operating in California/France

Jean WARMBOLD (American)
Citation Record: 3 Books
June Mail - *First*
Permanent US (1986)
Dead Man Running - *First**
!See Appendix 2.
Xanadu UK (1991)
The Third Way - *Latest*
Permanent US (1989)

Col CALPIN

British Male Sleuth operating in England

Roger PARKES 1933- (British)
Invented 3 detectives - see Insp Taff ROBERTS
Citation Record: 1 Book
The Guardians - *Only*
Constable UK (1973); St Martin's US (1974)

Insp CAM

British Policeman operating in England

Joan COCKIN 1919- (British)
Writer: Edith Joan BURBRIDGE
Citation Record: 3 Books
Curiosity Killed The Cat - *First*
Hodder & Stoughton UK (1947)
Deadly Ernest - *Last*
Hodder & Stoughton UK (1952)

Harry CAMBERT

was formerly a Detective Inspector in the police.

British Male Private Detective operating in London

Jill MCGOWN 1947- (British)
See main detective Ch Insp LLOYD
Citation Record: 1 Book
An Evil Hour - *Single*
Macmillan UK (1986); St Martin's US (1987)

Ronald CAMBERWELL

is a partner in the Chaney and Camberwell Detective Ager and has some undistinguished cases.

British Male Private Detective operating in England

J S FLETCHER 1863-1935 (British)

Invented 9 detectives - see Paul CAMPENHAYE

Citation Record: 11 Books

Murder At Wrides Park - *First*
Harrap UK (1931); Knopf US (1931)

Todmanhowe Grange - *Last*
Butterworth UK (1937)

The Mill House Murder - *Last**
Knopf US (1937)

Charlotte CAMBRY

British Female Amateur operating in England

E X FERRARS 1907-1995 (British)

Invented 11 detectives - see Toby DYKE

Citation Record: 1 Book

In At The Kill - *Only*
Doubleday US (1979)

Elizabeth FERRARS 1907-1995 (British)

Invented 10 detectives - see Toby DYKE

Citation Record: 1 Book

In At The Kill - *Only*
Collins UK (1978)

Richard (The Death Merchant) CAMELLION

American Male Sleuth operating in USA/Europe/Asia

Joseph ROSENBERGER (American)

See main detective Louis Luther (Murder Master) KING

Citation Record: 33 Books

The Death Merchant - *First*
Pinnacle US (1972); Corgi UK (1981)

The Burning Blue Death - *Latest*
Pinnacle US (1980)

Charles CAMELOT

is an unusually well-off and rather successful detective who operates from his excessively opulent Manhattan home.

American Male Private Detective operating in New York

Sidekick: Philip REVERE

acts as the legman for the home-loving and pampered sleuth.

American Male - Assistant

Peter ISRAEL 1933- (American)

See main detective Benjamin Franklin CAGE

Citation Record: 2 Books

I'll Cry When I Kill You - *First*
Mysterious Press US (1987)

If I Should Die Before I Die - *Latest*
Mysterious Press US (1989)

Cpl/Sgt Allan CAMERON

Canadian Policeman operating in Canada

Ralph CONNOR 1860-1937

Writer: Charles William GORDON

Citation Record: 2 Books

Corporal Cameron - *First*
Hodder & Stoughton UK (1912)

Corporal Cameron Of The North West Mounted Police - *First**
Doran US (1912)

The Patrol Of The Sun Dance - *Last*
Hodder & Stoughton UK (1914); Doran US (1914)

Janice CAMERON

Second detective of Lily WU

Commiss Kirker CAMERON

solves a case of death by poisoning in a locked room.

American Policeman operating in USA

William MORTON 1881-1967 (British)

See main detective 'Biff' CORRIGAN

Citation Record: 1 Book

The Mystery Of The Human Bookcase - *Only*
UK (1931)

Paul CAMERON

British Male Sleuth

Wade WRIGHT (British)

Writer: John WRIGHT

Inventor of one other detective Bart CONDOR

Citation Record: 3 Books

Shadows Don't Bleed - *First*
Hale UK (1967)

The Hades Hello - *Last*
Hale UK (1973)

Humphrey CAMPBELL

works for the Morgan Missing Persons Bureau. Part American Indian, he is a large, plump man who plays the accordion incessantly when on a case and, unlike most shamuses, drinks only milk. He appears also in one book with one of the author's other detectives, *Robin BISHOP.*

American Male Private Detective operating in California

Geoffrey HOMES 1902-1978 (American)

Invented 5 detectives - see Robin BISHOP

Citation Record: 4 Books

No Hands On The Clock - *First*
Morrow US (1939)

Six Silver Handles - *Last*
Morrow US (1944); Cherry Tree UK (1946)

The Case Of The Unhappy Angels - *Last**
Bantam US (1950)

Humphrey CAMPBELL and Robin BISHOP

American Male Private Detectives operating in California

Geoffrey HOMES 1902-1978 (American)

Invented 5 detectives - see Robin BISHOP

Citation Record: 1 Book

Then There Were Three - *Only*
Morrow US (1938); Cherry Tree UK (1945)

Pat CAMPBELL

is certainly one of the largest private eyes in the genre.

American Male Private Detective operating in California

Eli COLTER (American)

Writer: Elizabeth COLTER

Citation Record: 2 Books

The Gull Cove Murders - *First*
Mill US (1946); Pendulum UK (1946)

Cheer For The Dead - *Last*
Mill US (1947); Boardman UK (1949)

Paul CAMPENHAYE

British Male Professional Investigator operating in London

J S FLETCHER 1863-1935 (British)

was born in Halifax, Yorkshire. He was a journalist and a prolific writer of thrillers, detective stories and many other types of work. He is credited with at least ninety genre books, over thirty-five mainstream novels, about a dozen collections of poetry, as well as books on travel, history and biography. He was, in his time, a popular author, being specially admired (it is said, discovered) by that famous crime buff, President Woodrow Wilson. *FLETCHER* was, at the time, compared in stature with his great contemporary, *Edgar WALLACE*, at least in output, but his books, unlike the latter's, have not worn well.

Writer: Joseph Smith FLETCHER

Other Detectives:

Turco BULLWORTHY	Ronald CAMBERWELL
Sgt CHARLESWORTH	Archer DAWE
Richard GOULBURN	Mr POSKITT
Insp SKARRATT	Frank SPARGO

Citation Record: 1 Book 9 Short Stories in 1 Collection

The Secret Cargo - *Only*
Ward, Lock UK (1913)

C

Paul Campenhaye, Specialist In Criminology - *Collection 1*
The collection under this title, as published in the UK, did not include one story appearing in the US edition.
Ward, Lock UK (1918)

The Clue Of The Artificial Eye - *Collection 1**
The collection under this title, as published in the US, did not have one story included in the UK edition.
!See Appendix 2.
Hillman-Curl US (1939)

Albert CAMPION

is one of the great detective creations of the British Golden Age, although perhaps not in the class of *Peter WIIMSEY* or *Hercule POIROT.* Originally almost a caricature of the British amateur sleuth of the 1920s, he appears at first as a rich, indolent, brilliant man-about-town, who (it is only ever whispered) upstages certain contemporary British sleuths who are merely baronets and lords by being (possibly) related to the Royal Family. Naturally he has all the accoutrements of the 1930s detective: a bachelor flat in the best part of London; a faithful valet with a useful criminal past; and access to the highest in society. However, his importance to the developing genre is that he does truly reflect the changing features of English society around him and the changing views of an important English novelist about that society. By 1939 he has largely lost his comicality and vacuity, becoming a serious, dedicated, still brilliant, modern detective. The many novels and short stories in which he featured have been collected into several omnibuses.

British Male Amateur operating in London/Essex

Sidekick: Magersfontein LUGG
was named after the famous battle in the Boer War. A thoroughgoing Cockney and formerly a burglar, he is now the detective's valet and an invaluable assistant on investigational and sometimes illegal jaunts.
British Male - Valet

Stooge: Ch Stanislaus OATES
is one of the excellent but stolid police characters that appear in the many books of the series and who have difficulty in solving their cases.
British Male

Stooge: Insp Charlie LUKE
is a Scotland Yard man who, in several books, handles the police side of the cases with which *Albert CAMPION* becomes involved. In the novels of *Margery ALLINGHAM* the police are always depicted as very sound and doing a fine job on the most difficult crimes. *Charlie LUKE,* like all of them, is generally in error, but it is hardly the fault of the police of the Golden Age if they have neither the brilliant intellectual attributes nor the resources of an upper-class amateur detective. However, in later books, when the author saw how the Second World War had wrought irreversible changes on British society, she tended to elevate *LUKE* to a more dominant position with respect to *CAMPION,* especially in her finest novel, *The Tiger in the Smoke.*
British Male

Margery ALLINGHAM 1904-1966 (British)
was born in London. She was educated at Perse High School for Girls, Cambridge. The author of many criminous novels and short stories, her main detective is among the five greatest creations of British detective fiction between the two wars.

Writer: Margery Louise ALLINGHAM

Citation Record: 18 Books 27+ Short Stories in 6 Collections

Cargo Of Eagles - *Special*
This work remained unfinished at the author's death. It was completed by her husband, *P Youngman CARTER* and published posthumously.
Chatto UK (1968); Morrow US (1968)

The Black Dudley Murder - *First*
Doubleday US (1929)

The Crime At Black Dudley - *First**
Jarrolds UK (1929)

The Mind Readers - *Last*
was the last book to be completed by *Margery ALLINGHAM.*
Chatto & Windus UK (1965); Morrow US (1965)

Mr Campion: Criminologist - *Collection 1*
Short stories - 6
Doubleday US (1937)

Mr Campion And Others - *Collection 2*
Like several of the author's works, this collection appeared in differing forms, but the title cited contains nineteen stories, of which nine feature *CAMPION.*
Short stories - 9
Heinemann UK (1939); Jarrolds UK (1939)

The Case Book Of Mr Campion - *Collection 3*
Short stories - 7
Mercury US (1947)

The Allingham Case Book - *Collection 4*
contains some original stories featuring *CAMPION.*
Chatto UK (1969)

The Allingham Minibus - *Collection 5*
contains some original stories featuring *CAMPION.*
Chatto UK (1973); Morrow US (1973)

The Return Of Mr Campion - *Collection 6*
This collection of twelve of the author's short stories featuring *CAMPION* contains five previously uncollected.
Short stories - 5
Hodder & Stoughton UK (1989); St Martin's US (1990)

Youngman CARTER 1904-1969 (British)
was the husband of *Margery ALLINGHAM* and, after her death, he wrote two further books featuring her detective.

Writer: P Youngman CARTER

Citation Record: 2 Books

Mr Campion's Farthing - *First*
Heinemann UK (1969); Morrow US (1969)

Mr Campion's Falcon - *Last*
Heinemann UK (1970)

Mr Campion's Quarry - *Last**
Morrow US (1971)

Insp James CANDLISH

investigates a case involving impersonation and abduction.
British Policeman operating in England

R A V MORRIS (British)

Citation Record: 1 Book

The Lyttelton Case - *Only*
Collins UK (1922)

David CANE

British Male Amateur operating in England

John COURAGE 1902-1957 (British)
See main detective William BRITTAIN

Citation Record: 6 Books

Four Doors To Death - *First*
Paul UK (1936)

They All Came Back - *Last*
Paul UK (1945)

Tom CANE and CONDON

British Male Sleuths operating in Africa

David JORDAN (British)

Writer: J D F JONES

Citation Record: 2 Books

Nile Green - *First*
Joseph UK (1973); Day US (1974)

Black Account - *Last*
Joseph UK (1975)

C

Bill CANILLI

gets by through the use of superior but unpleasant violence against all and sundry.
!See Appendix 2.
American Male Private Detective operating in Philadelphia

Bill PETERS 1922-1982 (American)

For writer details see Dave BANNION

Citation Record: 1 Book

Blondes Die Young - *Only*
Dodd, Mead US (1952); Foulsham UK (1956)

Margaret CANNING

is an Oxford undergraduate who stumbles across a body whilst out hiking. She gets the local constable, only to find the body has disappeared. The police are unconvinced by her story, but she goes on sleuthing until she finds out whodunnit and why.
British Female Amateur operating in England

P M HUBBARD 1910-1980 (British)

Invented 3 detectives - see Peter GRANT

Citation Record: 1 Book

Flush As May - *Only*
Joseph UK (1963); London House US (1963)

CANNON

is a contender for the title of being the fattest of all private eyes. He appeared in novelizations of episodes from a TV series.
American Male Private Detective operating in USA

Paul DENVER (American)

Citation Record: 3 Books

The Golden Bullet - *First*
World Distributors UK (1973)

The Falling Blonde - *Last*
Star UK (1975)

Douglas ENEFER 1906- (American)

Citation Record: 2 Books

Farewell, Little Sister - *First*
Corgi UK (1978)

Shoot-Out - *Latest*
Corgi UK (1979)

Curt CANNON

is the one PI created by this famed author of detective stories, under the eponymous pseudonym. As a detective, he was once considered to be 'the best in New York' but he lost his licence after assaulting the man he found with his wife. However, unlicensed, he still functions.
American Male Private Detective operating in New York

Curt CANNON 1926- (American)

For writer details see The 87th PRECINCT

Citation Record: 1 Book 6 Short Stories in 1 Collection

I'm Cannon - For Hire - *Only*
Fawcett UK (1958)

I Like 'Em Tough - *Collection 1*
GM US (1958)

Dave CANNON

is an American antique dealer who is in England looking for rare pieces and he becomes involved in crimes related to the art and antique business. He appears in one other book with the author's other detective, Bob EDDISON, a Cherokee Indian who is also an antique dealer visiting England.
American Male Amateur operating in England

Michael DELVING 1914-1978

Invented 3 detectives - see Bob EDDISON

Citation Record: 4 Books

Smiling, The Boy Fell Dead - *First*
Scribner's US (1967); Macdonald UK (1967)

No Sign Of Life - *Last*
Strawberry Hill US (1979)

Dave CANNON and Bob EDDISON

also appear individually in other books by this author.
American Male Amateurs operating in England/Wales

Michael DELVING 1914-1978

Invented 3 detectives - see Bob EDDISON

Citation Record: 1 Book

The Devil Finds Work - *Only*
Scribner's US (1969); Collins UK (1970)

Roman CANTRELL

is a mercenary who now specialises in finding missing persons, for which purpose he has a head office in Miami and three others in Atlanta, Los Angeles and New York.
!See Appendix 2
American Male Private Detective operating in USA

Elaine Raco CHASE 1949- (American)

Citation Record: 2 Books

Dangerous Places - *First*
Bantam US (1987)

Dark Corners - *Latest*
Bantam US (1988)

Johnny CANUCK

is said to be one quarter Sioux. Presumably the rest is unnecessary to mention, being white immigrant British. A PI in the fictional city of Balmoral, he has to do more than the usual amount of physical fighting in the course of his investigations.
Canadian Male Private Detective operating in Canada

James MOFFATT 1922- (British)

For writer details see Hilary BRAND

Other Detectives:
Virginia BOX   Silas MANNERS

Citation Record: 8 Books

Time For Sleeping - *First*
Compact UK (1966); Leisure Books US (1970)

Terror-Go-Round - *Last*
Compact UK (1966)

Sgt/Ch Supt Merle CAPRICORN

comes from a family of stage magicians and is skilled in the art himself. However, he becomes a policeman, rising from the rank of Sergeant to that of Chief Superintendent at Scotland Yard during the series in which he appears. It goes without saying that his 'magical' skills are sometimes useful to him.
British Policeman operating in London

Pauline Glen WINSLOW (American)

was born in London and educated at schools in England. After going to the USA, she attended Columbia University, New York. She was a court reporter for the Federal Government, 1955-1963, for the United Nations, New York, 1963-1964, and a freelance court reporter, 1964-1973.

Citation Record: 6 Books

Death Of An Angel - *First*
St Martin's US (1975); Macmillan UK (1975)

The Rockefeller Gift - *Latest*
St Martin's US (1981); Collins UK (1982)

Rocky CAPUTO

is a crossword-puzzle compiler who solves this one case of 'impossible' crime.
American Male Amateur operating in New York

Robert B GILLESPIE 1917- (American)

Writer: Robert Byrne GILLESPIE

Inventor of one other detective Ralph SIMMONS

Citation Record: 1 Book

C

The Crossword Mystery - *Single*
Constable UK (1979); Raven US (1980)

The CARAVAN DETECTIVE
British Male Professional Investigator operating in England

S Clarke HOOK (British)
Writer: Samuel Clarke HOOK
Citation Record: 1 Book
The Caravan Detective - *Only*
Amalgamated UK (1912)

Jane CARBERRY
British Female Amateur operating in England/Belgium

Beryl SYMONS (British)
Writer: Beryl Mary Elizabeth Taubman SYMONS
Inventor of one other detective Insp Henry DOIGHT
Citation Record: 5 Books
Jane Carberry: Detective - *First*
Jenkins UK (1940)
Jane Carberry's Week-End - *Last*
Jenkins UK (1947)

Letitia CARBERRY
is a delightful character, zany and humorous, who appears in a number of short stories and novelettes, in which she sometimes plays at being an amateur detective and does it very well.
American Female Amateur operating in USA

Mary Roberts RINEHART 1876-1958 (American)
was born in Pittsburgh. She was a distinguished writer in several genres and a war correspondent in the First World War.
Other Detectives:
Hilda ADAMS | Jennie BRICE
Maj DANE | Insp HARRISON
Rachel INNES | Terrence O'BRIEN
Citation Record: 21 Short Stories in 5 Collections
The Amazing Adventures Of Letitia Carberry - *Collection 1*
contains three novelettes.
Short stories - 3
Bobbs US (1911); Hodder & Stoughton UK (1919)
Tish - *Collection 2*
Short stories - 5
Houghton US (1916); Hodder & Stoughton UK (1917)
More Tish - *Collection 3*
contains three novelettes.
Short stories - 3
Doran US (1921); Hodder & Stoughton UK (1921)
Tish Plays The Game - *Collection 4*
Short stories - 5
Doran US (1926); Hodder & Stoughton UK (1927)
Tish Marches On - *Collection 5*
Short stories - 5
Farrar, Straus US (1937)

CARBO
British Male Sleuth operating in England

James QUARTERMAIN 1920- (British)
For writer details see Richard WALKER
Citation Record: 4 Books
The Diamond Hook - *First*
Constable UK (1970); Doubleday US (1970)
The Diamond Hostage - *Last*
Constable UK (1975)

C CARD
operates in the San Francisco of 1942. In a gentle parody of the genre, he is so incompetent and so short of work that he has to operate from a phone booth.
American Male Private Detective operating in San Francisco

Richard BRAUTIGAN 1935-1984 (American)
Citation Record: 1 Book
Dreaming Of Babylon - *Only*
Delacorte US (1977); Cape UK (1978)

James CARD
was formerly in British Intelligence. In his one case, he acts as a bodyguard to a Lloyds insurance man on a trail of espionage and murder.
British Male Private Detective operating in England/France

Gavin LYALL 1932- (British)
Invented 4 detectives - see Bert KEMP
Citation Record: 1 Book
Blame The Dead - *Only*
Hodder & Stoughton UK (1972); Viking US (1973)

Mick CARDBY
sets up a London detective agency.
British Male Private Detective operating in London
Sidekick: CARDBY
is the detective's father. Formerly a Chief Inspector at Scotland Yard, he now joins his son, as an assistant, in the agency.
British Male - Father

David HUME 1900-1945 (British)
Writer: John Victor TURNER
Other Bylines:
Nicholas BRADY | J V TURNER
Other Detectives:
Tony CARTER | Det Insp SANDERSON
Citation Record: 27 Books
Bullets Bite Deep - *First*
Putnam UK (1932)
Heading For A Wreath - *Last*
Collins UK (1946)

Insp CARDIFF
British Policeman operating in England

Dulcie GRAY 1920- (British)
was born in Kuala Lumpur, Malaya, and was educated at schools in Malaya and England. She attended the Academy des Beaux Arts, London, became an actress and married Michael Denison, the well-known British actor, 1939. She has, since then, appeared continuously on the stage and in films, often with her husband. She was made a CBE, 1983, and is the recipient of several awards for her work on stage and other media. She has written eleven genre and six non-genre novels and at least one stage play.
Writer: Dulcie Winifred Catherine DENISON
Citation Record: 2 Books
Epitaph For A Dead Actor - *First*
Barker UK (1960)
Died In The Red - *Last*
Macdonald UK (1968)

Sally CARDIFF
is a bright young thing who is at the opera in Chicago when a wealthy woman is murdered in a neighbouring box. By clever observation of minute details, she discovers the murderer and astonishes the baffled police.
American Female Amateur operating in Chicago

Vincent STARRETT 1886-1974 (American)
Invented 6 detectives - see Jimmie LAVENDER
Citation Record: 1 Selected Short Story
The Bloody Crescendo
also appeared in 1943 in *Ellery Queen's Mystery Magazine* as *Murder at the Opera* and has appeared under that title in later collections.
In 'Real Detective Tales' US (1934)

Burgess 'Buzz' CARDIGAN
American Male Amateur operating in California

Don RICO 1913-1985 (American)
See main detective Casey GRANT

Citation Record: 2 Books

The Daisy Dilemma - *First*
Lancer US (1967)

The Man From Pansy - *Last*
Lancer US (1967)

Jack CARDIGAN

is an ex-cop, now a PI, who appeared in stories in *Dime Detective.*

American Male Detective in Pulp Magazines operating in USA

Frederick NEBEL 1903-67 (American)

Invented 8 detectives - see Steve CARDIGAN

No citations

Peter CARDIGAN

American Male Amateur operating in New York

Monte BARRETT 1897?-1949 (American)

Citation Record: 3 Books

The Pelham Murder Case - *First*
White House US (1930)

The Wedding March Murder - *Last*
Bobbs US (1933); Paul UK (1933)

Steve CARDIGAN

is one of the early examples of the truly hardboiled PI. He usually works for the Cosmos Detective Agency and appears in forty-four short stories, mainly written for *Dime Detective,* some of which are in the collection cited.

American Male Private Detective operating in New York

Frederick NEBEL 1903-67 (American)

was born in Staten Island, New York. He found casual and intermittent employment while writing a great number of short stories for the pulps and newspapers from the 1930s to the mid-1950s.

Writer: Louis Frederick NEBEL

Other Detectives:

Sgt BRINKHAUS	Jack CARDIGAN
Donny 'Tough Dick' DONAHUE	
Buck JASON	KENNEDY
Capt Steve MACBRIDE	Patricia SEAWARD

Citation Record: 6 Short Stories in 1 Collection

The Adventures Of Cardigan - *Collection 1*
Mysterious Press US (1988)

Insp James CARDINAL

British Policeman

Marion WALTON 1928- (British)

Citation Record: 2 Books

Cardinal Error - *First*
Hale UK (1973)

The Paduan Conspiracy - *Last*
Hale UK (1973)

The CARDINAL

British Male Amateur operating in England

Stephen BLAKESLEY (British)

Writer: F BOND

Adopter of one other detective Sexton BLAKE

Citation Record: 2 Books

A Case For The Cardinal - *First*
Fiction House UK (1946)

The Cardinal And The Corpse - *Last*
Fiction House UK (1947)

Hugh CARDING

British Male Amateur operating in England

Gilbert COLLINS 1900- (British)

Citation Record: 7 Books

Post-Mortem - *First*
Bles UK (1930)

Mystery In St James Square - *Last*
Ward, Lock UK (1937)

Frank CARDOLINI

American Male Amateur operating in New York

David J GERRITY 1923- (American)

Writer: David James GERRITY

Citation Record: 3 Books

The Never Contract - *First*
Signet US (1975)

The Numbers Man - *Last*
Signet US (1977)

Lt Vince CARDOZO

is a member of the New York Police Department and investigates some brutal murders, in spite of the opposition of his superiors.

American Policeman operating in New York

Edward STEWART 1938- (American)

Citation Record: 1 Book

Mortal Grace - *Single*
Headline UK (1993)

Ben CAREY

is one of this author's numerous pulp detectives and appeared in stories in *Dime Detective.*

American Male Detective in Pulp Magazines operating in USA

Ramon DECOLTA 1898-1945 (American)

Invented 5 detectives - see Dion DAVIES

No citations

Peter CAREY

American Male Amateur operating in New York

Richard North PATTERSON 1947- (American)

Invented 3 detectives - see Adam SHAW

Citation Record: 1 Book

Escape Into The Night - *Single*
Random House US (1983)

Rachel CAREY

American Female Amateur operating in USA

Doris Miles DISNEY 1907-1976 (American)

Invented 7 detectives - see Jefferson DIMARCO

Citation Record: 1 Book

Cry For Help - *Only*
Doubleday US (1975); Hale UK (1976)

Sir Robert CAREY

patrols the wilds of West March, the border lands between Wales and England, for queen and country. But murder was as foul in the sixteenth century as it is today.

English Male Amateur operating in England

P F CHISHOLM (British)

Writer: Pauline FINNEY

Citation Record: 2 Books

A Famine Of Horses - *First*
Coronet UK (1994); Walker US (1995)

A Season Of Knives - *Latest*
Hodder & Stoughton UK (1995)

Prof Richard CARFORD

is a young Professor of Bacteriology at a fictional medical school in London. When a research scientist is murdered, he is suspected, arrested, tried and subsequently acquitted. Not unreasonably, since he is innocent, he sets out to clear his name by discovering the real murderer, long after the police have given up.

British Male Amateur operating in England

Sidney FAIRWAY 1879- (British)

was a prominent doctor who wrote nine genre novels.

Writer: Sidney Herbert DAUKES

Citation Record: 1 Book

The Long Tunnel - *Only*
Paul UK (1935); Doubleday US (1936)

Alan CARLISLE
American Male Amateur operating in USA

George Harmon COXE 1901-1984 (American)
Invented 20 detectives - see Kent MURDOCK

Citation Record: 1 Book

Double Identity - *Only*
Knopf US (1970); Hale UK (1971)

Kenneth CARLISLE
was formerly a star of the silent movies. He gave it all up when the talkies came, not because his voice didn't suit but because he was fed up with the adulation. Now, thinking he has a flair for detective work, he has set up as a PI on Manhattan's East Side.

American Male Private Detective operating in New York

Carolyn WELLS 1870-1942 (American)
Invented 7 detectives - see Fleming STONE

Citation Record: 3 Books

Sleeping Dogs - *First*
Doubleday US (1929)

The Skeleton At The Feast - *Last*
Doubleday US (1931)

CARLITO
American Male Sleuth operating in New York

Edwin TORRES (American)

Citation Record: 2 Books

Carlito's Way - *First*
Saturday Review Press US (1975); Star UK (1977)

After Hours - *Latest*
Dial US (1979); Futura UK (1979)

Sal CARLUCCI
is a First World War veteran with a game leg. A part-time PI, he runs the Black Moon Saloon and organises the resolution of a case involving five assistant detectives in different parts of the country.

American Male Private Detective operating in USA

Robert J RANDISI 1951- (American)
was born in Brooklyn, New York, and educated at Canarsie High School, New York. After several jobs of a transient nature he became a full-time writer in 1982. He is the author of at least fourteen criminous novels (some with a collaborator) under his own name, and over thirty others under pseudonyms.

Writer: Robert Joseph RANDISI

Other Byline: Nick CARTER

Other Detectives:
Nick DELVECCHIO
Philip MARLOWE
Miles JACOBY
Henry PO

Citation Record: 1 Book

Black Moon - *Single*
Lynx US (1989)

Carlotta CARLYLE
is a detective in a town in which she has to compete, in fictional terms, with some of the very best private eyes in the business. A modern feminist invention, she is six feet tall, half Jewish but soundly Irish-American, red-haired, beautiful, and, being an ex-cop to boot, is a tough operator. Female shamuses are, of course, usually even more in need of a friend in the local police than are their male counterparts. Hers is a certain lieutenant who, for reasons best not questioned, seems quite unable or unwilling ever to solve a case without her. He is, indeed, typical of the modern American police stooge, who is now often more amiable than antagonistic. She has a friend too in her cat, whose name she lists as her own in the phone book. Clearly this important animal deserves to be cited as honorary sidekick.

American Female Private Detective operating in Boston

Sidekick: Thomas C CARLYLE
must be mentioned, for it is his name, not hers, that is listed in *Carlotta CARLYLE's* phone directory entry.
Male - Pet Cat

Stooge: Lt MOONEY
has to do so many things for *Carlotta CARLYLE* that he seems at times to render her almost unnecessary.
American Male

Linda J BARNES 1949- (American)
was born in Detroit, Michigan. She was experienced in many aspects of the theatre before beginning to write her highly successful criminous novels.

Writer: Linda Joyce BARNES

Inventor of one other detective Michael SPRAGGUE

Citation Record: 6 Books

A Trouble Of Fools - *First*
St Martin's US (1987); Hodder & Stoughton UK (1988)

Hardware - *Latest*
Delacorte US (1995)

Ted CARMADY
American Male Private Detective operating in USA

Raymond CHANDLER 1888-1959 (American)
Invented 9 detectives - see Philip MARLOWE

Citation Record: 4 Selected Short Stories

The Man Who Liked Dogs
The outline for this story was used by *CHANDLER* in his novel, *FAREWELL, MY LOVELY.*
In 'Black Mask Magazine' US (1936)

Goldfish
In 'Black Mask Magazine' US (1936)

The Curtain
This story was, in part, incorporated into the novel, *THE BIG SLEEP.*
In 'Black Mask Magazine' US (1936)

Try The Girl
was, in part, incorporated into the author's novel, *FAREWELL, MY LOVELY.*
In 'Black Mask Magazine' US (1937)

Nurse Agnes CARMICHAEL
perpetually finds herself in situations involving crime and murder. She is, of course a veritable hound-dog when it comes to finding out whodunnit; but, beyond that, she specialises in meting out her own private justice, even committing (or, at least, organising) homicide on the guilty party.

British Female Amateur operating in England

Anthea COHEN 1913- (British)
was born in Guildford, Surrey, and educated in a convent school in Northampton. A State Registered Nurse, she has worked in several hospitals.

Writer: Doris SIMPSON

Citation Record: 12 Books

Angel Without Mercy - *First*
Constable UK (1982); Doubleday US (1984)

Angel In Autumn - *Latest*
Constable UK (1995)

Casey CARMICHAEL
has grassed to the FBI on some communist friends, after which he has set up as a PI.

American Male Private Detective operating in Pittsburgh

John Nicholas DATESH 1950- (American)

Citation Record: 1 Book

The Janus Murder - *Single*
Leisure Books US (1979)

C

Justine CARMICHAEL
has retired from the police and is now bound to a wheelchair. He continues to solve cases.
Male Ex-Policeman operating in Mexico/California

Kip CHASE
Writer: Trevett Coburn CHASE
Citation Record: 3 Books
Where There's A Will - *First*
Hammond UK (1961)
Killer Be Killed - *Last*
Hammond UK (1963)

Michael CARMICHAEL
British Male Amateur

Paul DURST 1921- (British)
Citation Record: 2 Books
Backlash - *First*
Cassell UK (1967)
Badge Of Infamy - *Last*
Cassell UK (1968)

William CARMICHAEL
is a retired university don who, when four golfers find a body near their links, leads them in an attempt to solve the crime. He makes so many mistakes it is surprising they succeed.
British Male Sleuth operating in England

Ronald A KNOX 1888-1957 (British)
Invented 4 detectives - see Miles BREDON
Citation Record: 1 Book
The Viaduct Murder - *Only*
Methuen UK (1925); Simon & Schuster US (1925)

John CARMODY
appeared in stories in *Spicy Detective.*
American Male Detective in Pulp Magazines operating in San Francisco

E Hoffman PRICE 1898-1988 (American)
Writer: Edgar Hoffman PRICE
Other Detectives:
Pawang ALI
Cliff CRAGIN
Jeff DARGAN
No citations

Willie CARMODY
solves the disappearance of a thief inside a building.
American Male Amateur operating in USA

Robert C DENNIS 1920-1983 (American)
See main detective Paul REEDER
Citation Record: 1 Selected Short Story
Murder In The Mails
In 'Black Mask Magazine' US (1946)

Det Sgt CARNABY
British Policeman operating in England

Peter N WALKER 1936- (British)
See main detective Det Supt Mark PEMBERTON
Citation Record: 11 Books
Carnaby And The Hijackers - *First*
Hale UK (1967)
Carnaby And The Campaigners - *Latest*
Hale UK (1984)

CARNACKI
is an early example of the species, occult detective. In the far-off days of the genre he was easily able to solve mysteries by his magical powers, which the local police did not, to their eternal mortification, possess.
British Male Amateur operating in England

William Hope HODGSON 1875-1918 (British)
was born in Blackmore End, Essex. He was a seaman, founded a school of Physical Culture, 1899, and later entered the Army. He died in action at Ypres in the last months of the First World War.
Inventor of one other detective Capt GAULT
Citation Record: 9 Short Stories in 1 Collection
Carnacki, The Ghost Finder - *Collection 1*
The British edition contained six stories, but three more were added for the much later US edition.
Nash UK (1913); Mycroft & Moran US (1947)

Andrew CARNE
is a historian who becomes a post-war spy for British Intelligence and solves at least one murder.
British Male Amateur operating in Scotland

Allan MACKINNON (British)
Invented 4 detectives - see Don KENDRICK
Citation Record: 1 Book
Map Of Mistrust - *Only*
Collins UK (1948); Doubleday US (1948)

Simon CARNE
deserves, for historical reasons, a special mention. He seems to have been the very first of the long line of British and American gentleman-crook-detectives, antedating *Col CLAY* by two months and *A J RAFFLES* by two years. All members of the species had their own views on the balances to be struck between the law, their slightly criminal activities and their roles as detectives. *Simon CARNE* was certainly more crook than detective but, even so, he earns a place.
British Male Amateur operating in England

Guy BOOTHBY 1867-1905
Invented 3 detectives - see Dr NIKOLA
Citation Record: 6 Short Stories in 1 Collection
A Prince Of Swindlers - *Collection 1*
Ward, Lock UK (1897)
The Viceroy's Protegé - *Collection 1**
New Amsterdam US (1903)

Mary CARNER
works for a hotel detective. But, married to an obliging and house-trained husband, she is now well able to pursue her bent for amateur detection on her own.
American Female Amateur operating in New York

Zelda POPKIN 1898-1983 (American)
Citation Record: 5 Books
Death Wears A White Gardenia - *First*
Lippincott US (1938); Hutchinson UK (1939)
No Crime For A Lady - *Last*
Lippincott US (1942)

Rufus CARNES and Richard STANHOPE
American Male Sleuths operating in Chicago

Lawrence L LYNCH (American)
Invented 11 detectives - see Neil J BATHURST
Citation Record: 1 Book
A Slender Clue; Or, The Mystery Of Mardi-Gras - *Only*
Ward, Lock UK (1891)

Lucian CAROLUS
British Male Amateur operating in England

Eugene ASCHER 1900-1969 (British)
Writer: Harold Ernest KELLY
Citation Record: 2 Books 5 Short Stories in 1 Collection
The Grim Caretaker - *First*
In 'Everybody's' UK (1944)
There Were No Asper Ladies - *Last*
Mitre UK (1944)
To Kill A Corpse - *Last**
World Distributors UK (1959)
Uncanny Adventures - *Collection 1*
In 'Everybody's' UK (1944)

C

Ace CARPENTER
was once a professional guitarist and now sleuths.
American Male Private Detective operating in Los Angeles

Hamilton T CAINE (American)
was the sometime editor of *Mystery Magazine.*
Writer: Stephen SMOKE
Citation Record: 2 Books
Carpenter, Detective - *First*
Charter US (1980)
Hollywood Heroes - *Latest*
Berkley US (1986)

Hollis CARPENTER
is a sleuth whose lesbianism is made more of than her detective abilities.
American Female Sleuth operating in USA

Deborah POWELL (American)
Citation Record: 1 Book
Houston Town - *Single*
Naiad US (1992)

Charles CARR and Jack KELLY
are two aging, cynical, world-weary agents of the US Treasury Department. They sit in an office in Los Angeles and their job is to apprehend the most important counterfeiters in the country. This they do, but they have to solve a murder or two in the process.
American Male Professional Investigators operating in California

Gerald PETIEVICH 1944- (American)
was born in Los Angeles. He took a BA at California State University, Los Angeles, 1966, and served in the US Intelligence Corps, 1967-1970.
Citation Record: 2 Books 2 Short Stories in 1 Collection
To Die In Beverly Hills - *First*
Arbor US (1983)
The Quality Of The Informant - *Latest*
Arbor US (1985)
Money Men And One-Shot Deal - *Collection 1*
contains two novelettes.
Harcourt Brace US (1981); New English Library UK (1982)

Insp Dan CARR
American Policeman operating in New York

Willard K SMITH (American)
Citation Record: 2 Books
Bowery Murder - *First*
Doubleday US (1929); Collins UK (1930)
The Sultan's Skull - *Last*
Archer US (1933)

Iris CARR
is the amateur sleuth in this, one of the most famous of all 'disappearance' novels (the subject of an equally classic movie) in which she solves the mystery of a woman who disappears on a train.
British Female Amateur operating in a train

Ethel Lina WHITE 1887-1944 (British)
Inventor of one other detective Alan FOAM
Citation Record: 1 Book
The Wheel Spins - *Only*
Collins UK (1936); Harper & Row US (1936)
The Lady Vanishes - *Only**
Paperback Library US (1966)
It was under this now famous title that Alfred Hitchcock made his film.

Owen CARR
works on a case in which he does not know, and has to discover, the identity of a murder victim.
American Male Private Detective operating in Massachusetts

Walter WALKER 1949- (American)
See main detective Hector GRONIG
Citation Record: 1 Book
The Rules Of The Knife Fight - *Single*
Harper & Row US (1986)

Steve CARRADINE
British Male Sleuth

Manning K ROBERTSON (British)
Citation Record: 4 Books
Seek And Destroy - *First*
Badger UK (1965)
Night Passage - *Last*
Spencer UK (1967)

Max CARRADOS
is often regarded as one of the great detectives of the British Golden Age, although he only appears in one novel and less than thirty short stories. He was, in fact, a departure from the then current trend in sleuths and is one of the early 'defective' detectives. For *Max CARRADOS* is blind. His name, it was disclosed in an early story, was originally Max Wynn; but, when his blindness struck, he had the good fortune to inherit a fortune from an American benefactor on condition he adopted the latter's name. Although *CARRADOS* was not the very first blind detective to appear in the criminous literature, he was one of the earliest and is certainly the best and best-known. He is able to sleuth so amazingly well because the author has endowed him with extraordinarily enhanced other senses to make up for his blindness. He needs aid, of course, in certain ways, such as getting around to his cases, and so his sidekicks have more than usual to do, providing the thinking is left to him.
British Male Amateur operating in England
Sidekick: Louis CARLYLE
is a private inquiry agent but, it must be said, not a brilliant one. At the beginning of the canon he meets *CARRADOS*, whom he recognises as an old friend. Just as well; for, recognising the amazing abilities of the blind detective, he is then able to bring the latter many of his cases.
British Male - Friend
Sidekick: PARKINSON
is the blind detective's general factotum who takes him around on his cases and sometimes assists in them.
British Male - Butler

Ernest BRAMAH 1868-1942 (British)
was born in Lancashire. He was a farmer, then a newspaperman, then worked as secretary to Jerome K Jerome. Finally he became the editor of Jerome's magazine, *Today.* He wrote on a number of subjects and became particularly well-known for his series of short stories, told by an itinerant story-teller, Kai Lung, in a mock Chinese idiom and which are excellent mystery tales in their own right.
Citation Record: 1 Book 25 Short Stories in 3 Collections
The Bravo Of London - *Only*
Cassell UK (1934)
Max Carrados - *Collection 1*
Short stories - 8
Methuen UK (1914); Hyperion US (1975)
The Eyes Of Max Carrados - *Collection 2*
Short stories - 9
Grant Richards UK (1923); Doran US (1924)
Max Carrados Mysteries - *Collection 3*
Short stories - 8
Hodder & Stoughton UK (1927); Penguin US (1964)

Lt CARREAU
investigates the murder of an unliked theatrical manager.
American Policeman operating in New York

C

Daniel BROUN (American)

See main detective Harry EGYPT

Citation Record: 1 Book

Counterweight - *Only*
Holt US (1962)

Ch Offr Webb CARRICK

is captain of HMS Marlin and is engaged on the protection of the Scottish coast against poachers, smugglers, spies and gun-runners.

British Policeman operating in Scotland

Bill KNOX 1928- (British)

See main detective pair Det Ch Insp Colin THANE and Insp Phil MOSS

Citation Record: 14 Books

The Scavengers - *First*
Long UK (1964); Doubleday US (1964)

Dead Man's Mooring - *Latest*
Century Hutchinson UK (1987); Doubleday US (1988)

Derek CARRINGTON

Male Sleuth

Budleigh NETTON (British)

Citation Record: 3 Books

Guns In The Desert - *First*
Low UK (1937)

Desert Shadows - *Last*
Low UK (1939)

F T CARRINGTON

British Male Secret Agent operating in England

J Storer CLOUSTON 1870-1944 (British)

Writer: Joseph Storer CLOUSTON

Other Detectives:
Ursula DOLLING
Sherlock HOLMES
Francis MANDELL-ESSINGTON

Citation Record: 2 Books 11 Short Stories in 1 Collection

Simon - *First*
Blackwood UK (1919); Doran US (1919)

Beastmark The Spy - *Last*
Blackwood UK (1941)

Carrington's Cases - *Collection 1*
This collection of twelve of the author's stories contains eleven with *F T CARRINGTON.*
Blackwood UK (1948)

Laurence CARRINGTON

Second detective of Oliver POTTER

David CARROLL

American Male Amateur operating in USA

Octavus Roy COHEN 1891-1959 (American)

Invented 6 detectives - see Jim HANVEY

Citation Record: 4 Books

The Crimson Alibi - *First*
Dodd, Mead US (1919); Nash UK (1919)

Midnight - *Last*
Dodd, Mead US (1922); Nash UK (1922)

Jimmy CARROLL

British Male Sleuth operating in Europe

Hugh MCCUTCHEON 1909- (British)

Invented 6 detectives - see Insp MCKELLER

Citation Record: 5 Books

Treasure Of The Sun - *First*
Long UK (1964)

Something Wicked - *Last*
Long UK (1970)

Sam CARROLL

British Male Amateur operating in England

Robert LEIGH 1933- (British)

Citation Record: 1 Book

The Cheap Dream - *Single*
Macmillan UK (1982)

First And Last Murder - *Single**
St Martin's US (1983)

Dr CARRUTHERS

British Male Amateur operating in England

Hugo BLAYN 1908-1960

See main detective Insp GARTH

Citation Record: 2 Books

Flashpoint - *First*
Paul UK (1950)

What Happened To Hammond? - *Last*
Paul UK (1951)

CARRUTHERS

is, in this famous novel, a somewhat foppish British Foreign Office official who, against all the odds, uncovers a plan for the German invasion of England.

British Male Amateur operating in England

Erskine CHILDERS 1870-1922 (Irish)

was born in London. He was educated at Haileybury College and then at Trinity College, Cambridge, where he took a BA in 1893. He was a professional soldier, serving in the Boer War, and he then served as a high-ranking officer in the Royal Navy during the First World War, receiving the Distinguished Service Cross. He went to Dublin, 1919, became an Irish revolutionary and politician, and fought against the British in Ireland. He was subsequently court-martialled and executed for treason.

Writer: Robert Erskine CHILDERS

Citation Record: 1 Book

The Riddle Of The Sands - *Only*
Nelson UK (1900)

CARRUTHERS

Appears with at least two other detectives - see SIMPSON.

Det Lt Cathy CARRUTHERS

American Policewoman operating in USA

Mel D AMES (American)

Citation Record: 2 Selected Short Stories

A Matter Of Observation
appeared in the December number.
In 'Mike Shayne Mystery Magazine' US (1980)

The Christmas Eve Ghost
appeared in the December number.
In 'Mike Shayne Mystery Magazine' US (1983)

John CARRUTHERS

British Policeman operating in India

Sir Edmund C COX 1856- (British)

Writer: Sir Edmund Charles COX

Inventor of one other detective Kesho NAIK

Citation Record: 24 Short Stories in 2 Collections

John Carruthers: Indian Policeman - *Collection 1*
Short stories - 12
Cassell UK (1905)

The Achievements Of John Carruthers - *Collection 2*
Short stories - 12
Constable UK (1911)

Don CARSON

American Male Amateur operating in USA

Alan PRUITT (American)

Writer: Alvin Emanuel ROSE

Citation Record: 2 Books

The Restless Corpse - *First*
Ziff-Davis US (1947)

Typed For A Corpse - *Last*
Handi-Books US (1951)

C

Peter CARSON
American Male Sleuth operating in USA

Stephen GALLAGHER 1954- (American)

Citation Record: 1 Book

Chimera - *Single*
St Martin's US (1982); Sphere UK (1982)

Brett CARSTAIRS
British Male Amateur operating in England

Sydney HORLER 1888-1954 (British)

Invented 20 detectives - see Sir Harker BELLAMY

Citation Record: 2 Books

The Man Who Walked With Death - *First*
Hodder & Stoughton UK (1931); Knopf US (1931)

The Spy - *Last*
Hodder & Stoughton UK (1931)

Prof Charles CARSTAIRS
Second detective of Sylvia SNOW

John CARSTAIRS
American Male Professional Investigator operating in Space

Frank Belknap LONG 1903- (American)

Citation Record: 6 Short Stories in 1 Collection

John Carstairs, Space Detective - *Collection 1*
Fell US (1949); Cherry Tree UK (1951)

Dr Richard CARSTAIRS
British Male Amateur operating in England

A DE O (British)

Citation Record: 14 Short Stories in 1 Collection

The Indiscretions Of Dr Carstairs - *Collection 1*
Heinemann UK (1913)

'Apples' CARSTAIRS
British Male Sleuth

Simon MYLES 1949- (British)

For writer details see Piers ROPER

Citation Record: 2 Books

The Big Black - *First*
Everest UK (1974)

The Big Needle - *Last*
Everest UK (1974); Zebra US (1975)

Insp CARTER
is a Scotland Yard man and appears to have a brilliant gift for solving crimes, which are actually solved by his sergeant.

British Policeman operating in London

Sidekick: Sgt BELL
is really the detective, but his nasty superior takes the credit.
British Male - Subordinate

E R PUNSHON 1872-1956 (British)

See main detective Cdr Bobby OWEN

Citation Record: 5 Books

The Unexpected Legacy - *First*
Benn UK (1929)

Genius In Murder - *Last*
Benn UK (1932); Houghton Mifflin US (1933)

Mr Henry CARTER
is a Victorian private detective who may also be attached to Scotland Yard. He is called in by the novel's hero to solve a mystery.

British Male Private Detective operating in England

Sidekick: Clement AUSTIN
is responsible for calling in *CARTER* of the Yard and helps him with some amateur sleuthing.
British Male - Assistant

M E BRADDON 1835-1915 (British)

Invented 9 detectives - see Robert AUDLEY

Citation Record: 1 Book

Henry Dunbar: The Story Of An Outcast - *Only*
Maxwell UK (1864); Dick US (1867)

Jack CARTER
British Male Professional Investigator operating in England/USA

Ted LEWIS 1940- (British)

Writer: Ted Edward LEWIS

Citation Record: 3 Books

Jack's Return Home - *First*
Joseph UK (1970); Doubleday US (1970)

Jack Carter And The Mafia Pigeon - *Latest*
Joseph UK (1977)

Dr John CARTER
British Male Amateur operating in England

Kelvin I JONES (British)

Adopter of one other detective Sherlock HOLMES

Citation Record: 3 Short Stories in 1 Collection

The Obsidian And Other Stories - *Collection 1*
Hallmark UK (1990)

Ken CARTER
was one of this author's numerous pulp detectives. He was an ex-juggler whose skill was put to good use in stories in *Ten Detective Aces.*

American Male Detective in Pulp Magazines operating in USA

Norwell PAGE (American)

Other Detectives:
Dick BARRETT   Angus ST CLOUD
No citations

Det Insp Neil CARTER
of the Metropolitan Police has a loutish way of dealing with crimes that would surprise many an old-time British copper.

British Policeman operating in London

Eileen DEWHURST 1929- (British)

Invented 4 detectives - see Det Ch Supt Maurice KENDRICK and Humphrey BARNES

Citation Record: 5 Books

Curtain Fall - *First*
Macmillan UK (1977); Doubleday US (1982)

A Nice Little Business - *Latest*
Doubleday US (1987); Piatkus UK (1990)

Nick CARTER
can hardly be considered to occupy the exalted strata of detective fiction that are graced by such figures as *Sherlock HOLMES* and *Philip MARLOWE;* even so, he remains one of the seminal early figures of the genre. He was perhaps the first popular American detective to embody all the features that were to become the characteristics of the American superman hero and consolidate them into a figure and a name that would become legendary. His credentials were impeccable, for he actually appeared two years before *Sherlock HOLMES* and three years after his British counterpart, *Sexton BLAKE,* in a story written by *John Russell CORYELL* for the *New York Weekly.* It was published on September 18, 1886, in a serial that was aptly entitled *The Old Detective's Pupil,* since he was supposed to be the son of Sim (or Seth) Carter, a then well-known but now almost forgotten character of the even earlier pulps. It is said that the original idea for his creation came from Ormond G Smith, son of one of the founders of *Street & Smith.*

Young, handsome, and indomitable in his fight against crime, *Nick CARTER* was said to be 'of brilliant intelligence'. His mind was 'a storehouse of knowledge', he could disguise himself within minutes to be anything he chose, he could use any weapon, he could speak any known language and some unknown ones, and he could lip-read into the bargain. It is hardly surprising that villains stood little chance against him and his

C

two assistants. In addition to his mental superiority, his physical prowess was astounding. Indeed, 'giants were like children in his grasp. He could fell an ox with one blow of his small, compact fist'. *Sexton BLAKE*, of course, could do much the same, but he did it far less often and more politely. The two great contemporaneous detectives, one American and one British, are of considerable sociological interest, for they seem to have fulfilled some deep cultural need in the two societies that lasted for almost a century. Although they differed in their approach to crime and the methods they used to deal with it, they nevertheless had one thing in common. Their morals were of the highest where women were concerned.

In the later stories, from the 1960s, *Nick CARTER* lost much of his early individuality and took on many of the characteristics of the immoral, high-tech, international, sexually robust secret agent, then becoming overwhelmingly fashionable.

The *Nick CARTER* novels and short stories appeared in several magazines in America, some of which were named for him. The early adventures were published by *Street & Smith* in their *Magnet* series and, after 1907, in their *New Magnet* series, and many appeared after 1915 in the *Nick Carter Magazine*, also published by *Street & Smith.* They first appeared in Britain in 1912. The series were originally planned by *Frederick William DAVIES* (1858-1933), but most of the early stories were written by *Frederic Merrill Van Rensselaer DEY.* Numerous other stories were written by other authors and they mainly appeared under the house name of *Nicholas CARTER.* Where the writers have been identified they are cited individually below. After the Second World War, new *Nick CARTER* stories were published under the house name of *Nick CARTER*, the writers often being identified.

American Male Professional Amateur/Secret Agent operating in several locations

Sidekick: Chick CARTER

American Male - Assistant

Sidekick: Paddy GARVAN

American Male - Assistant

Nicholas CARTER

House name.

Citation Record: 45 Books 11 Short Stories in 1 Collection

Fighting Against Millions; Or, The Detective In The Jewel Caves Of Kurm - *First*

Street & Smith (Magnet #11) US (1897)

A Battle For The Rights; Or, A Clash Of Wits - *Last*

Street & Smith (New Magnet #1001) US (1919)

The Detective's Pretty Neighbour And Other Stories - *Collection 1*

Street & Smith (Magnet #89) US (1899)

Nicholas CARTER

Writer: ANDREWS

Citation Record: 1 Book

The Sandal Wood Slipper; Or, Nick Carter's Isle Of Safety - *Only*

Street & Smith (New Magnet #846) US (1914)

Nicholas CARTER

Writer: A L ARMAGNAC

Citation Record: 3 Books

The Key Ring Clew; Or, On The Edge Of Doom - *First*

Street & Smith (Magnet #415) US (1905)

When Honours Pall; Or, Not For Self Gain - *Last*

Street & Smith (New Magnet #905) US (1915)

Nicholas CARTER

Writer: BALL

Citation Record: 2 Books

A Triple Knavery; Or, Link By Link - *First*

Street & Smith (New Magnet #770) US (1912)

The Microbe Of Crime; Or, Nick Carter's Biggest Problem - *Last*

Street & Smith (New Magnet #861) US (1914)

Nicholas CARTER 1847-1923

Writer: William Perry BROWN

Citation Record: 1 Book

Nick Carter's Persistence; Or, At Danger's Call - *Only*

Street & Smith (New Magnet #671) US (1910)

Nicholas CARTER 1851-1930

Writer: George Waldo BROWNE

Citation Record: 1 Book

The Woman In Black; Or, Nick Carter's Clever Haul - *Only*

Street & Smith (New Magnet #769) US (1912)

Nicholas CARTER 1861-1909

Invented 4 detectives - see Patsy MURPHY

Citation Record: 16 Books

An Accidental Password - *First*

Street & Smith (Magnet #53) US (1898)

The Barrel Mystery; Or, A Murderer's Double - *Last*

Street & Smith (Magnet #314) US (1903)

Nicholas CARTER

Writer: O P CAYLOR

Citation Record: 1 Book

A Bonded Villain; Or, Nick Carter In Trouble - *Only*

Street & Smith (Magnet #286) US (1903)

Nicholas CARTER 1880-1935

Writer: Stephen CHALMERS

Citation Record: 1 Book

The Wages Of Rascality; Or, A Terrible Reward - *Only*

Street & Smith (New Magnet #880) US (1914)

Nicholas CARTER 1861-1922

Writer: Weldon J COBB

Citation Record: 16 Books 3 Short Stories in 1 Collection

Crossed Wires; Or, A Tangle Of Crime - *First*

Street & Smith (Magnet #138 US (1900)

Playing A Lone Hand; Or, Nick Carter On Top - *Last*

Street & Smith (Magnet #350) US (1904)

The Dumb Witness And Other Stories - *Collection 1*

Street & Smith (Magnet #220) US (1901)

Nicholas CARTER

Writer: William Wallace COOK

Citation Record: 2 Books

A Baffled Oath; Or, The Cost Of Deceit - *First*

Street & Smith (Magnet #396) US (1905)

Nick Carter's Egyptian Clew; Or, The Mystery Of The Mummy's Head - *Last*

Street & Smith (New Magnet #771) US (1912)

Nicholas CARTER 1851-1954

was the inventor of *Nick CARTER.*

Writer: John Russell CORYELL

Inventor of one other detective Wat DENTON

Citation Record: 1 Book 1 Selected Short Story

A Wall Street Haul; Or, A Bold Stroke For a Fortune - *Only*

Street & Smith (Magnet #6) US (1897)

The Old Detective's Pupil

is the first story in which *Nick CARTER* is known to have appeared.

New York Weekly US (1886)

Nicholas CARTER 1858-1933

See main detective Harrison KEITH (Writer Frederick William DAVIS)

Citation Record: 60 Books

A Framework Of Fate; Or, The One In Twenty - *First*

Street & Smith (Magnet #159) US (1900)

Blood Will Tell; Or, A Sacrifice For Nothing - *Last*

Street & Smith (New Magnet #973) US (1917)

Nicholas CARTER

Writer: E C DERBY and Vincent E SCOTT

Citation Record: 1 Book

The Prince Of Liars; Or, The Man Without A Soul - *Only*

Street & Smith (New Magnet #546) US (1908)

C

Nicholas CARTER 1861-1922
Writer: Frederic Merrill Van Rensselaer DEY
Other Detectives:
Harrison KEITH Doctor QUARTZ
Citation Record: 122 Books
Caught In The Toils; Or, Nick Carter And The Train Robbers *- First*
Street & Smith (Magnet #14) US (1897)
The Trail Of The Human Tiger; Or, Nick Carter's Mysterious Shadow *- Last*
Street & Smith (New Magnet #660) US (1916)

Nicholas CARTER
Writers: Frederic Merrill Van Rensselaer DEY1861-1922 and Charles Agnew MACLEAN1880-1928
Citation Record: 1 Book
The Chain Of Clues; Or, Nick Carter's Play To A Finish *- Only*
Street & Smith (New Magnet #486) US (1907)

Nicholas CARTER 1869-1929
Writer: Walter Bertram FOSTER
House writer for one other detective Harrison KEITH
Citation Record: 9 Books
The Last Move In The Game; Or, Crime's Horror *- First*
Street & Smith (New Magnet #634) US (1910)
The Vampire's Trail; Or, Nick Carter And The Policy King *- Last*
Street & Smith (New Magnet #739) US (1912)

Nicholas CARTER 1861-1929
Writer: Charles Witherle HOOKE
Citation Record: 1 Book 3 Short Stories in 1 Collection
The Bandits Of The Air; Or, Nick Carter's Aeroplane Trail *- Only*
Street & Smith (New Magnet #757) US (1912)
The Elevated Railway Mystery And Other Stories *- Collection 1*
Street & Smith (Magnet #105) US (1900)

Nicholas CARTER 1843-1915
Writer: Edward Cadwalader HUDSON
Citation Record: 10 Books
A Stroke Of Policy; Or, The Stolen Charter *- First*
Street & Smith (Magnet #266) US (1902)
A Checkmated Scoundrel; Or, After The Abductors *- Last*
Street & Smith (Magnet #276) US (1903)

Nicholas CARTER 1850-1929
Writer: George Charles JENKS
House writer for one other detective Harrison KEITH
Citation Record: 20 Books
The Bullion Mystery; Or, Nick Carter's Case From Overseas *- First*
Street & Smith (New Magnet #852) US (1914)
As A Crook Sows; Or, An Elusive Clew *- Last*
Street & Smith (New Magnet #895) US (1915)

Nicholas CARTER
See main detective Harrison KEITH (writer W L LARNED)
Citation Record: 6 Books
The Handcuff Wizard; Or, Nick Carter's Perplexity *- First*
Street & Smith (New Magnet #725) US (1911)
A Millionaire's Mania; Or, Nick Carter's Strange Client *- Last*
Street & Smith (New Magnet #801) US (1913)

Nicholas CARTER
Writer: MAKEE
Citation Record: 1 Book
The Pretty Stenographer Mystery; Or, On The Trail Of A Fiend *- Only*
Street & Smith (Magnet #407) US (1905)

Nicholas CARTER 1854-1938
Writer: St George Henry RATHBONE
Citation Record: 6 Books
The House Of Doom; Or, Nick Carter's Battle With The Crime Germ *- First*
Street & Smith (New Magnet #737) US (1911)
In The Face Of Evidence; Or, The House Of The Seven Gargoyles *- Last*
Street & Smith (New Magnet #740) US (1912)

Nicholas CARTER
Writer: RICH
Citation Record: 1 Book
Called To Account; Or, Nick Carter Takes a Hand *- Only*
Street & Smith (New Magnet #864) US (1914)

Nicholas CARTER
Writer: RUSSELL
Citation Record: 1 Book
In Suspicion's Shadow; Or, Nick Carter's Costly Error *- Only*
Street & Smith (New Magnet #838) US (1913)

Nicholas CARTER 1846-1924
For writer details see OLD QUARTZ
Citation Record: 6 Books 3 Short Stories in 1 Collection
The Man Of Mystery *- First*
Street & Smith (Magnet #189) US (1901)
In The Lap Of Danger; Or, The Man Who Would Not Hide *- Last*
Street & Smith (Magnet #458) US (1906)
The Steel Casket And Other Stories *- Collection 1*
Street & Smith (Magnet #201) US (1901)

Nicholas CARTER ?-1962
Writer: Samuel C SPALDING
Citation Record: 70 Books
The Connecting Link; Or, Nick Carter's Double Mystery *- First*
Street & Smith (New Magnet #773) US (1912)
The Secret Of The Marble Mantle *- Last*
Street & Smith (New Magnet #1021) US (1920)

Nicholas CARTER
Writer: SPLINT
Citation Record: 3 Books
King Of The Underworld; Or, With A Life At Stake *- First*
Street & Smith (New Magnet #704) US (1911)
A Gift Of The Gods; Or, The Path Of Sudden Death *- Last*
Street & Smith (New Magnet #712) US (1911)

Nicholas CARTER 1862-1930
For writer details see Nancy DREW
Citation Record: 1 Book
The Worst Case On Record; Or, A Murderer By Profession *- Only*
Street & Smith (New Magnet #526) US (1907)

Nicholas CARTER
Writer: Alfred B TOZER
Citation Record: 9 Books
The Crescent Brotherhood; Or, Nick Carter's Chicago Double *- First*
Street & Smith (Magnet #83) US (1899)
Broken On Crime's Wheel *- Last*
Street & Smith (New Magnet #702) US (1911)

Nicholas CARTER
Writer: TYSON
Citation Record: 1 Book
When Necessity Drives; Or, With The Speed Of Light *- Only*
Street & Smith (New Magnet #706) US (1911)

Nick CARTER
Writer: Frank ADDUCI Jr
Citation Record: 1 Book
Ten Times Dynamite *- Single*
Charter US (1980)

Nick CARTER
Writer: Bruce ALGOZIN
Citation Record: 2 Books
The Dominican Affair *- First*
Charter US (1980)
The Last Samaurai *- Latest*
Charter US (1982)

Nick CARTER

Writers: Michael Angelo AVALLONE 1924- and Valerie MOOLMAN

Citation Record: 2 Books

Safari For Spies - *First*
Award US (1964); Digit UK (1964)

Saigon - *Last*
Award US (1964); Digit UK (1965)

Nick CARTER 1903-1980

For writer details see Bill LENNOX

Citation Record: 1 Book

The Kremlin File - *Only*
Award US (1973); Tandem UK (1976)

Nick CARTER

For writer details see Peter WINSTON

Citation Record: 2 Books

Death Of The Falcon - *First*
Award US (1974)

A High Yield In Death - *Latest*
Award US (1976)

Nick CARTER

Writer: Nicholas BROWNE

Citation Record: 5 Books

Operation Starvation - *First*
Award US (1966); Tandem UK (1968)

The Bright Blue Death - *Last*
Award US (1967); Tandem UK (1968)

Nick CARTER

Writer: Jack CANON
Other Byline: Jack CANON

Citation Record: 33 Books

The Ebony Cross - *First*
Charter US (1978); Star UK (1979)

Ruby Red Death - *Latest*
Jove US (1990)

Nick CARTER 1920-

For writer details see Cash MADIGAN

Citation Record: 1 Book

The Spanish Connection - *Only*
Award US (1973); Tandem UK (1976)

Nick CARTER 1942-

For writer details see J T 'Jake' SPANNER

Citation Record: 1 Book

Assassination Brigade - *Only*
Award US (1973); Tandem UK (1974)

Nick CARTER

Writer: Robert COLBY

Citation Record: 1 Book

The Death's Head Conspiracy - *Only*
Award US (1973)

Nick CARTER

Writer: DeWitt S COPP

Citation Record: 2 Books

Six Bloody Summer Days - *First*
Award US (1975); Tandem UK (1978)

Under The Wall - *Latest*
Charter US (1978); Star UK (1982)

Nick CARTER

Writers: Allen Billy CRIDER (1941-) and Jack DAVIS

Citation Record: 1 Book

The Coyote Conection - *Single*
Charter US (1981)

Nick CARTER

Writer: Ron FELBER

Citation Record: 2 Books

Death Mission: Havana - *First*
Charter US (1980)

The Blue Ice Affair - *Latest*
Charter US (1985)

Nick CARTER

Writer: James FRITZHAND

Citation Record: 3 Books

Sign Of The Cobra - *First*
Award US (1974); Tandem UK (1977)

The List - *Latest*
Award US (1976); Tandem UK (1978)

Nick CARTER

For writer details see Nile BARRABAS(Writer Jack GARSIDE)

Citation Record: 11 Books

The Andropov File - *First*
Jove US (1988)

Arctic Abduction - *Latest*
Jove US (1990)

Nick CARTER 1929-

Writer: Joseph Lee GILMORE

Citation Record: 8 Books

War From The Clouds - *First*
Charter US (1980)

The Last Flight To Moscow - *Latest*
Charter US (1985)

Nick CARTER 1927-

For writer details see Jeanne DONOVAN

Citation Record: 1 Book

Assignment Intercept - *Single*
Award US (1976); Star UK (1978)

Nick CARTER 1942-

For writer details see Kirk MCGARVEY

Citation Record: 17 Books

The Sign Of The Prayer Shawl - *First*
Award US (1976)

The Vengeance Game - *Latest*
Charter US (1985)

Nick CARTER 1927-

For writer details see Mark STONER

Citation Record: 6 Books

Agent Counter Agent - *First*
Award US (1973); Tandem UK (1975)

Assassin - Code Name Vulture - *Last*
Award US (1974); Tandem UK (1975)

Nick CARTER

Writer: Al HINE

Citation Record: 2 Books

Our Agent In Rome Is Missing - *First*
Award US (1973); Tandem UK (1976)

Massacre In Milan - *Last*
Award US (1974); Tandem UK (1977)

Nick CARTER ?-1974(?)

For writer details see ADAM 12

Citation Record: 2 Books

The Liquidator - *First*
Award US (1973); Tandem UK (1974)

Target: Doomsday Island - *Last*
Award US (1973); Tandem UK (1974)

Nick CARTER 1944-

Writer: Frederick Vincent HUBER

Citation Record: 1 Book

Reich Four - *Single*
Charter US (1979); Star UK (1982)

Nick CARTER

Writer: H Edward HUNSBERGER

Citation Record: 1 Book

The Parisian Affair - *Single*
Charter US (1981)

Nick CARTER 1943-

For writer details see Jim ROCKFORD

Citation Record: 1 Book

Cauldron Of Hell - *Single*
Charter US (1981)

C

Nick CARTER
Writer: Bod LATONA
Citation Record: 1 Book
Plot For The Fourth Reich - *Single*
Award US (1977)

Nick CARTER
Writer: Leon LAZARUS
Citation Record: 2 Books
The Turncoat - *First*
Award US (1976); Tandem UK (1978)
The Jamaican Exchange - *Latest*
Charter US (1979)

Nick CARTER
For writer details see Don MILES
Citation Record: 1 Book
Operation Moon Rocket - *Only*
Award US (1968); Tandem UK (1968)

Nick CARTER 1924-
For writer details see Kane JACKSON
Citation Record: 12 Books
The N3 Conspiracy - *First*
Award US (1974); Tandem UK (1977)
Blood Of The Falcon - *Latest*
Charter US (1987)

Nick CARTER 1933(?)-1990
Writer: Douglas MARLAND
Citation Record: 1 Book
Counterfeit Agent - *Only*
Award US (1975)

Nick CARTER 1927(?)-1988
Writer: Arnold MARMOR
Citation Record: 1 Book
Peking - *Only*
Award US (1969)

Nick CARTER
For writer details see Jefferson (The Handyman) BOONE
Citation Record: 12 Books
The Amazon - *First*
Award US (1969); Tandem UK (1969)
The Death Strain - *Last*
Award US (1970); Tandem UK (1971)

Nick CARTER
Writer: Valerie MOOLMAN
Citation Record: 7 Books
Checkmate In Rio - *First*
Award US (1964); Digit UK (1965)
Hanoi - *Last*
Award US (1966); Mayflower UK (1968)

Nick CARTER 1915-1992
Writer: Homer MORRIS
Citation Record: 1 Book
The Z Document - *Only*
Award US (1975); Tandem UK (1978)

Nick CARTER
Writer: Craig NOVA
Citation Record: 2 Books
Dr Death - *First*
Award US (1975)
The Nichovev Plot - *Latest*
Award US (1976)

Nick CARTER
Writer: William ODELL
Citation Record: 3 Books
The Ultimate Code - *First*
Award US (1975)
The Nowhere Weapon - *Latest*
Charter US (1979); Star UK (1982)

Nick CARTER
Writer: Forrest V PERRIN
Citation Record: 1 Book
Beirut Incident - *Only*
Award US (1974)

Nick CARTER
For writer details see Jake (The Liquidator) BRAND
Citation Record: 1 Book
The Code - *Only*
Award US (1973); Tandem UK (1975)

Nick CARTER
Writer: Daniel C PRINCE
Citation Record: 1 Book
Hawaii - *Single*
Charter US (1976); Star UK (1982)

Nick CARTER 1951-
For writer details see Sal CARLUCCI
Citation Record: 6 Books
Pleasure Island - *First*
Charter US (1981)
Caribbean Coup - *Latest*
Charter US (1984)

Nick CARTER
Writer: Dan REARDON
Citation Record: 1 Book
The Tarantula Strike - *Single*
Charter US (1980)

Nick CARTER
For writer details see Mohawk DANIELS
Citation Record: 5 Books
Hood Of Death - *First*
Award US (1968); Tandem UK (1970)
The Human Time Bomb - *Last*
Award US (1969); Tandem UK (1970)

Nick CARTER
For writer details see Louis Luther (Murder Master) KING
Citation Record: 1 Book
Thunderstrike In Syria - *Single*
Charter US (1979); Star UK (1980)

Nick CARTER
Writer: Steve SIMMONS
Citation Record: 1 Book
Satellite City - *Single*
Charter US (1980)

Nick CARTER 1942-
For writer details see Roman GREY
Citation Record: 2 Books
Code Name: Werewolf - *First*
Award US (1973); Tandem UK (1973)
The Devil's Dozen - *Last*
Award US (1973); Tandem UK (1974)

Nick CARTER
Writer: George SNYDER
Citation Record: 6 Books
The Defector - *First*
Award US (1969); Tandem UK (1969)
Ice Bomb Zero - *Last*
Award US (1971); Tandem UK (1972)

Nick CARTER
Writer: Robert Derek STEELEY
Citation Record: 2 Books
Trouble In Paradise - *First*
Charter US (1978); Star UK (1980)
The Israeli Connection - *Latest*
Charter US (1982)

Nick CARTER
For writer details see John MARSHALL
Citation Record: 2 Books

Day Of The Dingo - *First*
Charter US (1980)

The Golden Bull - *Last*
Charter US (1981)

Nick CARTER

Writer: Linda STEWART

Citation Record: 2 Books

The Peking Dossier - *First*
Award US (1974)

The Jerusalem File - *Last*
Award US (1975); Star UK (1978)

Nick CARTER

For writer details see Barnaby JONES

Citation Record: 15 Books

The Eyes Of The Tiger - *First*
Award US (1965); Mayflower UK (1967)

The Black Death - *Last*
Award US (1970); Tandem UK (1972)

Nick CARTER 1921-

Writer: Bob STOKESBERRY

Citation Record: 1 Book

Tropical Deathpact - *Single*
Charter US (1979); Star UK (1982)

Nick CARTER 1915-1992

Writer: Dwight Vreeland SWAIN

Citation Record: 1 Book

The Pemex Chart - *Single*
Charter US (1979)

Nick CARTER

Writer: Lawrence VAN GELDER

Citation Record: 2 Books

The Man Who Sold Death - *First*
Award US (1974)

Deadly Doubles - *Latest*
Charter US (1978); Star UK (1980)

Nick CARTER

Writer: Robert E VARDEMAN

Citation Record: 8 Books

Eight Card Stud - *First*
Charter US (1980)

The Kali Death Cult - *Latest*
Charter US (1983)

Nick CARTER 1941-

Writer: Jeffrey Miner WALLMAN

Citation Record: 2 Books

Hour Of The Wolf - *First*
Award US (1973); Tandem UK (1975)

Ice Trap Terror - *Last*
Award US (1974); Tandem UK (1977)

Nick CARTER

Writer: George WARREN

Citation Record: 3 Books

The Vulcan Disaster - *First*
Award US (1976)

The Suicide Seat - *Latest*
Charter US (1980)

Nick CARTER 1921-

Writer: Saul WERNICK

Citation Record: 4 Books

The Aztec Avenger - *First*
Award US (1974); Tandem UK (1976)

Revenge Of The Generals - *Latest*
Charter US (1978); Star UK (1979)

Ralph CARTER

British Male Professional Investigator operating in England

Tom LILLEY 1924-1989 (British)

Writer: Thomas William LILLEY

Citation Record: 2 Books

The Projects Section - *First*
Macmillan UK (1970)

The Officer From Special Branch - *First**
Doubleday US (1971)

The K Section - *Last*
Macmillan UK (1972)

Steve CARTER

American Male Amateur operating in USA

Amelia Reynolds LONG 1904-1978 (American)

Invented 4 detectives - see Katherine 'Peter' PIPER

Citation Record: 7 Books

Murder To Type - *First*
Phoenix Press US (1943)

The House With Green Shutters - *Last*
Phoenix Press US (1950)

Tony CARTER

British Male Amateur operating in England

David HUME 1900-1945 (British)

Invented 3 detectives - see Mick CARDBY

Citation Record: 2 Books

You'll Catch Your Death - *First*
Collins UK (1940)

Requiem For Rogues - *Last*
Collins UK (1942)

Trim CARTER

American Male Detective in Pulp Magazines operating in USA

Nicholas CARTER 1861-1909

Invented 4 detectives - see Patsy MURPHY

Citation Record: 6 Books

The Clever Celestial; Or, The 'Salted' Mine Case- *First*
Street & Smith (Magnet #75) US (1899)

The Van Alstine Case- *Last*
Street & Smith (Magnet #77) US (1899)

Peter CARTHAGE

works for a private espionage firm and is sent to infiltrate a gang of assassins gathered in a monastery on Elba.

American Male Professional Investigator operating in Elba

Michael KURLAND 1938- (American)

Writer: Michael J KURLAND

Other Detectives:
Lord DARCY — Sherlock HOLMES

Citation Record: 1 Book

A Plague Of Spies - *Only*
Pyramid US (1969)

Yvonne CARTIER

originally appeared as one of the many assistants to *Sexton BLAKE*. In her early twenties, but already and properly widowed (this made her person sacrosanct), she was also the daughter of a woman who had been 'pitifully defrauded'. Swearing vengeance, therefore, on all wrongdoers, she became a detective in her own right and later appeared in several stories.

British Female Professional Investigator operating in England

G H TEED 1878-1939 (British)

Invented 6 detectives - see Roxane HARFIELD

Citation Record: 1 Selected Short Story

A Woman's Revenge
UK (?)

Bill CARTWRIGHT

American Male Sleuth operating in USA/Australia

Patrick MORGAN (American)

Writer: George SNYDE

Citation Record: 10 Books

Too Mini Murders - *First*
Macfadden UK (1969)

Freaked Out Stranger - *Last*
Manor US (1973)

Jinsie CARTWRIGHT

is a student at an unnamed American university and investigates the stabbing of her room-mate, which the police regard as suicide.

American Female Amateur operating in USA

Janet HART

Citation Record: 1 Book

File For Death - *Only*
Boardman UK (1965)

Philip Raines CARTWRIGHT

solves the mystery of the disappearance of a whole train.

British Male Amateur operating in England

Douglas TIMINS (British)

Citation Record: 1 Book

The Phantom Train - *Only*
Hutchinson UK (1926)

Enrico CARUSO

is, indeed, the most famous tenor ever to have sung a top C. Even so, it seems that he has found time to solve at least three cases of murder taking place in New York thespian circles, ca 1910. In the second of these he sleuths with the co-operation of the great American soprano, *Geraldine FERRAR.*

Italian Male Amateur operating in New York

Barbara PAUL (American)

Invented 8 detectives - see Lt TOOMEY

Citation Record: 2 Books

A Cadenza For Caruso - *First*
St Martin's US (1984)

A Chorus Of Detectives - *Latest*
St Martin's US (1987)

Enrico CARUSO and Geraldine FERRAR

make a formidable and unusual detective duo. The great tenor, who is the detective in two other books by this author, is here teamed with the most popular American operatic soprano of the era.

Italian Male Amateur and American Female Amateur operating in USA

Barbara PAUL (American)

Invented 8 detectives - see Lt TOOMEY

Citation Record: 1 Book

Prima Donna At Large - *Single*
St Martin's US (1985)

Michael CARUSO

American Male Private Detective operating in USA

K K BECK (American)

Invented 5 detectives - see Iris COOPER

Citation Record: 1 Book

Unwanted Attentions - *Single*
Walker US (1988)

Pepe CARVALHO

Spanish Male Private Detective operating in Barcelona

Manuel Vazquez MONTALBAN 1939- (Spanish)

was born in Barcelona. A sometime senior figure in the Spanish Communist Party, he has written several detective novels with political content.

Citation Record: 3 Books

Murder In The Central Committee - *First*
is a translation from the Spanish of *Asesinato En Al Comite Centrale* (1981).
Pluto UK (1984); Academy US (1985)

The Angst-Ridden Executive - *Latest*
is a translation from the Spanish of *Le Soledad Del Manager* (Barcelona, 1987).
Serpent's Tail UK (1989); Serpent's Tail US (1990)

Kelly CARVEL

is a professional spy-detective hero from the later work of one of the most prolific of American pulp story writers.

American Male Professional Investigator operating in California/Uruguay

Norman DANIELS (American)

Invented 6 detectives - see Richard Curtis (Phantom) VAN LOAN

Citation Record: 3 Books

The Rape Of A Town - *First*
Pyramid US (1970)

License To Kill - *Last*
Pyramid US (1972)

Insp CARVER

solves a case of death by shooting in a locked room.

British Policeman operating in London

Edgar WALLACE 1875-1932 (British)

Invented 28 detectives - see J G REEDER

Citation Record: 1 Book

The Clue Of The New Pin - *Only*
Hodder & Stoughton UK (1923); Small, Maynard US (1923)

Bruce CARVER

is an investigator for a British insurance company and is sent to New York on a job.

British Male ProfessionalInvestigator operating in New York

Dennis ALLAN 1900-1978 (British)

For writer details see Hiram POTTER

Citation Record: 1 Book

Brandon Is Missing - *Only*
Hamilton UK (1938); Mill US (1940)

Fred CARVER

was formerly a policeman. Now, invalided out of the force after being shot in the knee, he limps about with a heavy cane, which he can use when necessary as a lethal weapon, although he is more given to compassion than violence.

American Male Private Detective operating in Florida

Stooge: Lt MCGREGOR
must be the most evil police stooge in the whole literature. He never stops hounding and blackmailing *CARVER* for his own ends, with the perverse idea that he is the legitimate arm of official justice.
American Male

John LUTZ 1939- (American)

was born in Dallas, Texas. Educated at Meramec Community College, St Louis, he had many jobs before joining the St Louis Metropolitan Police. He has been a full-time writer since 1975.

Writer: John Thomas LUTZ

Other Detectives:
Sherlock HOLMES
Milo MORGAN
Philip MARLOWE
Alo NUDGER

Citation Record: 5 Books

Tropical Heat - *First*
Holt US (1986); Macmillan UK (1986)

Burn - *Latest*
Holt US (1995)

Humphrey CARVER

Second detective of Denys SARGENT

Rex CARVER

is the hero-agent-sleuth in books of thrilling action and fine story-telling, working for himself as well as British Intelligence.

British Male Private Detective operating in Europe

Victor CANNING 1911-1986 (British)

was born in Plymouth, Devon. He was educated at Plymouth Central School, Devon, and served in the Royal Artillery, 1940-1946. A highly regarded writer of non-genre novels, under his own name and pseudonyms, he was the author of at least thirty novels of suspense and crime, which were usually pervaded with an international flavour and had strong plots. He also wrote plays for radio and television and several of his books were used for films.

Other Detectives:
Joe CHRISTOPHER
Ch Alphonse GRAND
James HELDER
Edward MERCER
Robert ROLT

Citation Record: 4 Books

The Whip Hand - *First*
Heinemann UK (1965); Sloane US (1965)

The Melting Man - *Last*
Heinemann UK (1968); Morrow US (1969)

'Go Get 'Em' CARVER

is a little known pulp invention by a master of the art.

American Male Detective in Pulp Magazines operating in New York

Erle Stanley GARDNER 1889-1970 (American)

Invented 14 detectives - see Perry MASON

No citations

Bow Street Runner Victor CARYLL

British Policeman operating in London

Gerard FAIRLIE 1899-1983 (British)

Invented 4 detectives - see Johnny MACALL

Citation Record: 2 Books 6 Short Stories in 1 Collection

Scissors Cut Paper - *First*
Hodder & Stoughton UK (1927); Little, Brown US (1928)

Stone Blunts Scissors - *Last*
Hodder & Stoughton UK (1928); Little, Brown US (1929)

That Man Returns - *Collection 1*
This collection of twelve of the author's stories contains six with *Victor CARYLL.*
Hodder & Stoughton UK (1934); Little, Brown US (1934)

Charley CASE

operates in a world of cyberpunk, music and violence.

American Male Private Detective operating in Los Angeles

John SPENCER 1944- (British)

is a musician and songwriter.

Citation Record: 2 Books

A Case For Charley - *First*
Fontana UK (1984)

Charley Gets The Picture - *Latest*
Fontana US (1985)

Roy CASE

is an air pilot, involved in espionage and murder in the Middle East.

British Male Amateur operating in Middle East

Gavin LYALL 1932- (British)

Invented 4 detectives - see Bert KEMP

Citation Record: 1 Book

Judas Country - *Only*
Hodder & Stoughton UK (1975); Viking US (1975)

Ben CASEY

was one of this author's numerous pulp detectives, appearing in stories in *Black Mask Magazine.*

American Male Detective in Pulp Magazines operating in Los Angeles

Raoul WHITFIELD 1897-1945 (American)

Invented 3 detectives - see Ben JARDINN

Citation Record: 1 Selected Short Story

Cruise To Nowhere
In 'Black Mask Magazine' US (1933)

'Flashgun' CASEY

is a newspaper photographer, a large man, grumpy but a regular guy to his friends, and always after a story. His annals began in short stories in the pulps but he later appeared in novels.

American Male Amateur operating in Boston

George Harmon COXE 1901-1984 (American)

Invented 20 detectives - see Kent MURDOCK

Citation Record: 5 Books 4 Short Stories in 1 Collection

Silent Are The Dead - *First*
Knopf US (1952)

Deadly Image - *Last*
Knopf US (1964); Hammond UK (1964)

Flash Casey, Detective - *Collection 1*
contains four novelettes.
Avon US (1946)

Flash Casey - Hardboiled Detective - *Collection 1**
Avon US (1948)

Peter CASEY

American Male Amateur operating in Cape Cod

Russell MEAD (American)

Writer: Margaret Hudson KOEHLER

Citation Record: 3 Books

The Moses Bottle - *First*
Raven CA (1980)

The Nightingale Trivet - *Latest*
Raven CA (1981)

Phil CASEY

American Male Sleuth operating in USA

Hans LUGAR (British)

was a house name for a few authors gathered round the ephemeral publishers, *Scion,* who turned out a quantity of gangster novels during the 1950s, with various detectives.

Writer: Alistair John Blair PATERSON
Other Bylines: GRIFF, Ben SARTO

Citation Record: 4 Books

Appointment With Desire - *First*
Scion UK (1953)

Death By Appointment - *Last*
Scion UK (1954)

Sam CASH

New Zealander Male Amateur operating in New Zealand

Barry CRUMP (New Zealander)

Citation Record: 1 Book 39+ Short Stories in 3 Collections

Hang On A Minute, Mate - *Collection 1*
Short stories - 17
Reed AU (1961); Bodley Head UK (1963)

One Of Us - *Collection 2*
has an uncounted number of short stories.
Reed AU (1962)

There And Back - *Collection 3*
Short stories - 22
Reed AU (1963)

Steve CASH

comes up against city corruption at pretty high levels.

American Male Private Detective operating in Los Angeles

William FRANCIS (American)

See main detective Anthony MARTIN

Citation Record: 1 Book

Don't Dig Deeper - *Only*
Lion US (1953)

Carrie CASHIN

appeared in thirty-eight short stories in the pulps, 1937-1942. She used to let people think that her assistant, *Aleck BURTON,* a pretty dumb guy, was head of her outfit, the Cash & Carry Detective Agency, since, in those days, the paying public seemed to have little confidence in girl detectives.

American Female PrivateDetective in Pulp Magazines operating in New York

Sidekick: Aleck BURTON
is nominally the head of the agency owned and actually run by *Carrie CASHIN.*
American Male - Assistant

Theodore TINSLEY 1934- (American)
Other Detectives:
Maj John Tattersall LACY
Jerry TRACY and Insp FITZGERALD
Citation Record: 1 Selected Short Story
Riddle In Silk
appeared also in the anthology, *Hard-Boiled Dames; Stories featuring Women Detectives, Reporters, Adventurers and Criminals from the Pulp Fiction Magazines of the 1930s,* (US 1986) edited by Bernard Drew.
In 'Crime Busters Magazine' US (?)

Dr Alexander CASPIAN
solves cases set back into the late 1880s and early 1890s.
British Male Professional Amateur operating in England

John BURKE 1922- (British)
was born in Rye, Sussex and was educated at Holt High School, Liverpool. He served in the Royal Air Force and Royal Marines, 1942-1947. He is the author, under several bylines, of plays and novels, his detective stories forming only a small part of his large output.
Writer: John Frederick BURKE
Other Bylines:
Jonathan BURKE
Robert MIALL
Desmond REID
Citation Record: 3 Books
The Devil's Footsteps - *First*
Weidenfeld & Nicolson UK (1976); Coward McCann US (1976)
Ladygrove - *Latest*
Weidenfeld & Nicolson UK (1978); Coward McCann US (1978)

Jeff CASS
British Male Sleuth operating in Europe/Africa

Richard SEVERN (British)
Citation Record: 3 Books
Stalk A Long Shadow - *First*
Hale UK (1967)
The Killing Match - *Last*
Hale UK (1970)

Johnny CASS
was transmogrified in later stories into Johnny Can, both appearing, 1934-1941, mainly in *Dime Detective.*
American Male Detective in Pulp Magazines operating in USA

Roger TORREY (American)
Invented 7 detectives - see Pat MULLANCY
No citations

Steven CASSELL
British Male Amateur operating in England

Martin RUSSELL 1934- (British)
was born in Bromley, Kent, and educated at Bromley Grammar School. A reporter on provincial newspapers, he is the author of at least thirty-five criminous novels.
Writer: Martin James RUSSELL
Other Detectives:
Jim LARKIN
Mike WILLOUGHBY
Citation Record: 1 Book
Backlash - *Single*
Collins UK (1981); Walker US (1983)

Tony CASSELLA
is a man who has seen both sides of the law; for, not only was he a law student, but he was once a prison officer himself. He is thus singularly well equipped to investigate death and shady dealings amongst the members of the legal profession.
American Male Private Detective operating in New York

Larry BEINHART 1947- (American)
Citation Record: 2 Books
No One Rides For Free - *First*
Mysterious Press US (1986); Mysterious Press UK (1988)
You Get What You Pay For - *Latest*
Mysterious Press UK (1988)

Lew CASSIDAY
is a former football player. In his first case, in 1945, he joins a detective agency and gets into a plot involving escaping Nazis.
American Male Private Detective operating in USA

Thomas MAXWELL 1937- (American)
Writer: Thomas Eugene GIFFORD
Citation Record: 2 Books
Kiss Me Once - *First*
Mysterious Press US (1986); No Exit Press UK (1986)
Kiss Me Twice - *First*
Mysterious Press US (1988)

Horatio CASSIDY
American Male Sleuth operating in USA

John CROSBY 1912-1991 (American)
Writer: John Campbell CROSBY
Citation Record: 4 Books
Men In Arms - *First*
Constable UK (1984)
Wingwalker - *Last*
Stein US (1983); Constable UK (1989)

Insp Henri CASTANG
is a cop of medium seniority in an unnamed town somewhere in the north of France. Priding himself on being *bourgeois*, in the French sense, he works with patience and occasional flashes of brilliance, although much given to over-philosophising.
French Policeman operating in France

Nicholas FREELING 1927- (British)
Invented 4 detectives - see Insp Piet VAN DER VALK
Citation Record: 10 Books
A Dressing Of Diamond - *First*
Hamish Hamilton UK (1974); Harper & Row US (1974)
The Sea-coast Of Bohemia - *Latest*
Little, Brown UK (1994)

Darby CASTLE
American Male Sleuth operating in USA

Jan MICHAELS (American)
Writer: Jan MILELLA
Citation Record: 2 Books
Sing A Song Of Murder - *First*
Zebra US (1978)
Death On The Late Show - *Latest*
Zebra US (1979)

Julian CASTLE
Australian Male Sleuth operating in Australia

James CROWN (Australian)
Citation Record: 2 Books
Fragile Empires - *First*
Bantam AU (1988)
The December Conspiracy - *Latest*
Bantam AU (1989)

Peter CASTLE
appears also in books with the author's other detective, *'Twisted Face' STRAUSSMAN.*
British Male Amateur operating in England

G DAVISON 1892- (British)
Writer: Gilderoy DAVISON
Other Detectives:
Peter CASTLE and 'Twisted Face' STRAUSSMAN
'Twisted Face' STRAUSSMAN

Citation Record: 3 Books

Mystery Of The Red-Haired Valet - *First*
Jenkins UK (1934)

Exit Mr Brent - *Last*
Jenkins UK (1936)

C

Peter CASTLE and 'Twisted Face' STRAUSSMAN

also appear individually in other books by this author.

British Male Amateurs operating in England

G DAVISON 1892- (British)

Invented 3 detectives - see Peter CASTLE

Citation Record: 3 Books

The Man With The Twisted Face - *First*
Jenkins UK (1931)

A Dog Fight With Death - *Last*
Jenkins UK (1940)

Dr Marc CASTLEMAN

American Male Amateur operating in Long Island

Rosemary KUTAK 1908 - (American)

Citation Record: 2 Books

Darkness Of Slumber - *First*
Lippincott US (1944)

I Am The Cat - *Last*
Farrar, Straus US (1948)

James CASTLETON

Second detective of John CRAGGS

Det Supt Hilary CATCHPOLE

is a garrulous and clumsy cop. He was, alas, the last detective to be added to this author's select line of amateur and professional sleuths.

British Policeman operating in England

Sidekick: Sgt WILSON
British Male - Assistant

Julian SYMONS 1912-1994 (British)

Invented 11 detectives - see Insp CRAMBO

Citation Record: 1 Book

Playing Happy Families - *Only*
Macmillan UK (1994)

Molly CATES

is a crime reporter who, for eleven years, has been covering the story of a serial killer, now days away from execution. But when another similar crime is committed, can it all have gone wrong? Only *she* knows all the history of the crimes and has to act, not helped by the presence of an unwelcome and rather special cop.

American Female Amateur operating in Texas

Stooge: Lt Grady TRAYNOR
is *Molly CATES'* ex-husband and the investigating officer on the scene, making for a difficult relationship.
American Male

Mary Willis WALKER (American)

Citation Record: 1 Book

The Red Scream - *Single*
Doubleday US (1994)

Sam CATES

is an ex-Marine with a metal knee, who acts as some kind of loss adjuster for Home Protection Insurance, a job that seems to call for little brain and a good deal of brawn.

American Male Professional Investigator operating in New York

Paul ERNST 1886- (American)

Inventor of 6 detectives - see Lt Jim RYAN

Citation Record: 1 Book

The Bronze Mermaid - *Only*
Mill US (1952); Cassell UK (1954)

Sam CATES

American Male Amateur operating in USA

Ernest Jason FREDERICKS (American)

Citation Record: 1 Book

Shakedown Hotel - *Only*
Ace US (1958)

Lost Friday - *Only**
Hale UK (1959)

Capt CATLIN

American Male Sleuth operating in USA

Van Wyck MASON 1901-1978 (American)

was born in Boston, Massachusetts. He graduated with a BS at Harvard University, Cambridge, Massachusetts, 1924, and had a distinguished career in the US Army in both the First and Second World Wars, being the recipient of several military awards, including the French Legion of Honour. He was a full-time writer after 1928 and the author of at least fifty adventure and detective novels.

Writer: Francis Van Wyck MASON

Inventor of one other detective Capt/Maj/Col Hugh NORTH

Citation Record: 1 Book

Spider House - *Only*
Mystery League US (1932); Hale UK (1959)

Dr Paul CATO

Second detective of Dr Henry CHETWYND

Insp CAULDRON

British Policeman operating in England

Sydney FOWLER 1874-1965 (British)

Invented 5 detectives - see Mr JELLIPOT

Citation Record: 3 Books

A Bout With The Mildew Gang - *First*
Eyre & Spottiswoode UK (1941)

The End Of The Mildew Gang - *Last*
Eyre & Spottiswoode UK (1944)

Am CAULFIELD

was a hotel manager and is now a security chief at a vast hotel on the seashore at La Jolla Strand. The guests may be hilarious and the action bizarre, but murder can still rear its ugly head and, as in all the best (and worst) hotels, it has to be kept from the patrons and quietly solved.

American Male Amateur operating in California

Alan RUSSELL (American)

See main detective Stuart WINTER

Citation Record: 2 Books

The Hotel Detective - *First*
Mysterious Press US (1994)

The Fat Innkeeper - *Latest*
Mysterious Press US (1995)

Lemmy CAUTION

appeared in one of this prolific author's first novels. He was supposed to be a tough American 'G-man' (this school of British fiction was much influenced by the racy books and crime films that were, in the 1930s, flooding into Britain) who battled against (American) crime. He narrates his own cases in a hardboiled style that is so un-American that it can now be seen as hilarious. Even so, in the hands of such a skilled writer, the books were successful and paved the way for a long line of emulators.

American Male Sleuth operating in USA

Peter CHEYNEY 1896-1951 (British)

was born in London. Although he studied law, his career included diverse professions, such as journalism, songwriting and politics. He was the writer of many criminous works, often of the action-thriller variety. His

C

books were extremely popular at the time but their day has certainly passed.
Writer: Reginald Southouse CHEYNEY
Other Detectives:
Nick BELLAMY
Nicholas GALE
Alonzo MACTAVISH
Cary Wylde O'HARA
Everard Peter QUAYLE
Rupert Patrick 'Slim' CALLAGHAN
Michael KELLS
Terence O'DAY
Shaun O'MARA
Johnny VALLON
Citation Record: 10 Books 9 Short Stories in 1 Collection
This Man Is Dangerous - *First*
Collins UK (1936); Coward McCann US (1939)
I'll Say She Does! - *Last*
Collins UK (1945); Dodd, Mead US (1946)
Time For Caution - *Collection 1*
This collection of fourteen of the author's short stories contains nine with *Lemmy CAUTION*.
Foster UK (1946)

Mike CAVANAUGH

American Male Private Detective operating in Texas

Frank O'MALLEY 1916-1989 (American)
Writer: Frank O'ROURKE
Other Byline: Patrick O'MALLEY
Citation Record: 1 Book
The Best Go First - *Only*
Random House US (1950); Benn UK (1955)

Cpl John CAVANNAGH

is a Mountie in nineteenth-century Canada.
Canadian Policeman operating in Toronto

Ian ANDERSON (Australian)
has been a private detective in Australia and a Mountie in Canada.
Citation Record: 3 Books
Corporal Cavannagh - *First*
Seal CA (1983); Zebra US (1986)
The Flying Patrol - *Latest*
Zebra US (1988)

Joe CAVE

is a British agent, hunted by the KGB through Europe, Hong Kong, and even as far as Australia. Fortunately he has a useful sidekick.
British Male Secret Agent operating in Europe/Asia
Sidekick: Sandy KEITH
British Male - Assistant

James MITCHELL 1926- (British)
was born in South Shields, County Durham. He took a BA at St Edmund Hall, Oxford, 1948, and an MA, 1950. He has worked as an actor and lecturer.
Writer: James William MITCHELL
Other Byline: James MUNRO
Other Detectives:
David CALLAN
Ron HOGGETT
Citation Record: 1 Book
KGB Kill - *Single*
Hamish Hamilton UK (1984)

Kells CAVENAUGH

American Male Amateur operating in New York

Mary MCMULLEN 1920-1986 (American)
See main detective Eve FITZSIMMONS
Citation Record: 2 Books
Prudence Be Damned - *First*
Doubleday US (1978); Hale UK (1979)
Something Of The Night - *Last*
Doubleday US (1980); Collins UK (1982)

Alec CAVENDER

Male Sleuth operating in Africa/India

Elliot TOKSON (American)
Citation Record: 3 Books
Desert Captive - *First*
GM US (1977); Magnum UK (1980)
Appointment In Calcutta - *Latest*
GM US (1979); Magnum UK (1981)

Maude Teasdale CAVENDISH

is a young society reporter who, in 1916, unravels a ghastly plot by Germany to keep the US out of the First World War.
American Female Amateur operating in San Francisco

K K BECK (American)
Invented 5 detectives - see Iris COOPER
Citation Record: 1 Book
Young Mrs Cavendish And The Kaiser's Men - *Single*
Walker US (1987)

Supt CAWTHORNE

British Policeman operating in England

Roger SILVERWOOD 1932- (British)
Citation Record: 3 Books
Deadly Daffodils - *First*
Hale UK (1970)
The Illegitimate Spy - *Last*
Hale UK (1972)

Lois CAYLEY

was presented by the author as the prototype of the 'modern woman'. Girton graduate, sleuth and adventuress, she hunted tigers, rescued comrades, foiled thieves and found lost wills in her exciting tales.
British Female Amateur operating in several locations

Grant ALLEN 1848-1899 (British)
Invented 5 detectives - see Nurse Hilda WADE
Citation Record: 12 Short Stories in 1 Collection
Miss Cayley's Adventures - *Collection 1*
Richards UK (1899); Putnam US (1899)

The CELEBRATED DETECTIVE

American Male Detective in Pulp Magazines operating in USA

ANON
Citation Record: 1 Book
The Celebrated Detective - *Only*
Aldine US

Emmanuel CELLINI

believes he is descended from the Italian artist, Benvenuto Cellini. A psychiatrist turned detective, he formerly had a practice in New York but now works in London, solving crimes by means of his specialist knowledge – although that seems little enough – and then only after discussion with his plump, ex-ballerina wife.
Male Professional Investigator operating in London

Michael HALLIDAY 1908-1973 (British)
The *Dr CELLINI* books were published in the US under the following byline.
Inventor of one other detective pair Martin FANE and Richard FANE
For writer details see Insp Roger 'Handsome' WEST
Citation Record: 10 Books
Cunning As A Fox - *First*
Hodder & Stoughton UK (1965)
The Man Who Was Not Himself - *Last*
Hodder & Stoughton UK (1976)

Kyle HUNT 1908-1973 (British)
was the byline of the author for *Dr CELLINI* books in the USA.
For writer details see Insp Roger 'Handsome' WEST
Citation Record: 10 Books

C

Cunning As A Fox - *First*
Macmillan US (1965)
The Man Who Was Not Himself - *Last*
Stein & Day US (1976)

CENTERSHOT
American Male Detective in Pulp Magazines operating in USA

Allan ARNOLD (American)
Invented 6 detectives - see OLD SNAP
Citation Record: 1 Book
Centershot, The Scout Detective; Or, The Secret Of The Indian Graves
New York Detective Library US (1882-8)

Antonio 'Chico' CERVANTES
is involved with the US Drug Enforcement Agency and has cases of drug smuggling on his hands.
Mexican Male Private Detective operating in Los Angeles

Bruce COOK (American)
Citation Record: 2 Books
Mexican Standoff - *First*
Watts US (1988)
Rough Cut - *Latest*
St Martin's US (1990)

Insp CHACE
British Policeman operating in England

Vernon LODER 1881- (British)
For writer details see Penny MERCER and Vincent MERCER
Other Detectives:
Insp BREWS Donald CAIRN
Citation Record: 2 Books
Murder From Three Angles - *First*
Collins UK (1934)
Death At The Horse Show - *Last*
Collins UK (1935)

Denis CHAD
British Male Amateur

Mary ARCHER (Irish)
Writer: UNKNOWN
Citation Record: 2 Books
What - No Body? - *First*
Blackfriars UK (1947)
What - No Witnesses? - *Last*
Locker UK (1947)

Geoffrey CHADWICK
Canadian Male Amateur operating in Toronto/Montreal

Edward O PHILLIPS 1931- (Canadian)
Citation Record: 2 Books
Sunday's Child - *First*
McClelland & Stewart CA (1981); St Martin's US (1987)
Buried On Sunday - *Latest*
McClelland & Stewart CA (1986); St Martin's US (1988)

John CHADWICK
runs a small detective agency and comes upon his cases haphazardly.
British Male Private Detective operating in England

Guy COBDEN (British)
Citation Record: 7 Books
Murder Was My Neighbour - *First*
Rich UK (1955)
I Saw Murder - *Last*
Hale UK (1962)

Insp Chafik J CHAFIK
seems to have appeared only in short stories.
Iraqi Policeman operating in Baghdad

Charles B CHILD (British)
Citation Record: 1 Selected Short Story
Death Had A Voice
? (1948)

Henry CHALICE and Crying EDDIE
British Male Sleuths operating in England

Donald MACKENZIE 1908- (Canadian)
Invented 3 detectives - see John RAVEN
Citation Record: 3 Books
Death Is A Friend - *First*
Hodder & Stoughton UK (1966); Houghton US (1966)
Sleep Is For The Rich - *Last*
Macmillan UK (1971); Houghton US (1971)
The Chalice Caper - *Last**
Mayflower UK (1974)

Bart CHALLIS
has an office in the seediest part of town and his career as a detective has only just been on the right side of the law, a matter that brings him lots of trouble with the local police.
American Male Private Detective operating in Los Angeles
Stooge: Lt Lemmie KRAUSE
of the Los Angeles Police Department does not like private eyes.
American Male

William F NOLAN 1928- (American)
was born in Kansas City, Missouri. He was educated at San Diego State College and Los Angeles City College, California, 1947-1953. A prolific writer in many genres, he was also a reporter, editor, painter and cartoonist.
Writer: William Francis NOLAN
Other Detectives:
Nick CHALLIS Sam SPACE
Citation Record: 2 Books
Death Is For Losers - *First*
Sherbourne Press US (1968)
The White Cad Cross-Up - *Last*
Sherbourne Press US (1969)

Nick CHALLIS
is the younger half-brother of the author's *Bart CHALLIS* and appears only in a short story.
American Male Private Detective operating in USA

William F NOLAN 1928- (American)
Invented 3 detectives - see Bart CHALLIS
Citation Record: 1 Selected Short Story
The Pulpcon Kill
US (?)

Prof Ronald CHALLIS
is an American Professor of Archaeology who has retired to live in London, where he still lectures at some unnamed university. A bachelor, frail and weakened by chain-smoking, he writes learned monographs and indulges in his hobby of solving the murders that occur frequently in his circle of acquaintances. His *modus operandi* is simple enough: snooping around.
British Male Amateur operating in several locations

Shane MARTIN 1912-1970 (British)
Writer: George Henry JOHNSTON
Citation Record: 5 Books
Twelve Girls In The Garden - *First*
Collins UK (1957); Morrow US (1957)
A Wake For Mourning - *Last*
Collins UK (1962)
Mourner's Voyage - *Last**
Doubleday US (1963)

Insp CHALLON
solves a case of poisoning.
British Policeman operating in England

C

John S GLASBY 1928- (British)

Writer: A J MERAK

Citation Record: 1 Selected Short Story

Cyanide For Christmas
Michael O'Mara UK (1990)

Humphrey CHALLONER

British Male Amateur operating in England

R Austin FREEMAN 1862-1947 (British)

Invented 4 detectives - see Dr John Evelyn THORNDYKE

Citation Record: 7 Short Stories in 1 Collection

A Savant's Vendetta - *Collection 1*
Pearson UK (1920)

The Uttermost Farthing - *Collection 1**
Winston US (1914)

Duddington Pell CHALMERS

is a fat young man who loves eating. He solves a case of theft from a museum, involving peripheral blackmail and murder, simply by asking a lot of questions of a lot of people.

American Male Amateur operating in New York

John MACINTYRE 1871-1951 (American)

See main detective ASHTON-KIRK

Citation Record: 1 Book

The Museum Murder - *Only*
Doubleday US (1929); Bles UK (1930)

Det Sgt Harry CHAMBERLANE

British Policeman operating in London

Alan SEWART 1928- (British)

Citation Record: 1 Book

Smoker's Cough - *Single*
Hale UK (1982)

Insp CHAMBERS

British Policeman operating in England

Frank KING 1892-1958 (British)

Other Detectives:
Clive 'Dormouse' CONRAD
Insp GLOOM
Dr Frank KING
Clarence KNIGHT
O'ROURKE

Citation Record: 1 Book

Terror At Staups House - *Only*
Bles UK (1927); Watt US (1929)

Peter CHAMBERS

seems to get cases that are weird, sexy, rough and tough. They are narrated in a light and frivolously strange style, which does little to add to their appeal. He appears also in one book with the author's minor detective, *Marla TRENT.*

American Male Private Detective operating in New York

Henry KANE 1918- (American)

was born in New York City, practised as an attorney and later became a full-time writer.

Other Detectives:
Peter CHAMBERS and Marla TRENT
MCGREGOR
Marla TRENT

Citation Record: 29 Books 25+ Short Stories in 6 Collections

A Halo For Nobody - *First*
Simon & Schuster US (1947); Boardman UK (1950)

Martinis And Murder - *First**
Avon US (1956)

Kill For The Millions - *Last*
Lancer US (1972)

Report For A Corpse - *Collection 1*
Short stories - 6
Simon & Schuster US (1948); Boardman UK (1951)

Murder Of A Park Avenue Playgirl - *Collection 1**
Avon US (1957)

Trinity In Violence - *Collection 2*
The US collection with the same name contains different stories.
Short stories - 3
Boardman UK (1954); Avon US (1955)

The Case Of The Murdered Madame - *Collection 3*
Short stories - 3
Avon US (1955)

Triple Terror - *Collection 3**
Boardman UK (1958)

Trilogy In Jeopardy - *Collection 4*
Short stories - 3
Boardman UK (1955)

The Name Is Chambers - *Collection 5*
Short stories - 6
Pyramid US (1957)

Kiss! Kiss! Kill! Kill! - *Collection 6*
Short stories - 4
Lancer US (1970)

Peter CHAMBERS and Marla TRENT

also appear individually in other books by this author.

American Male Private Detective and American Female Private Detective operating in New York

Henry KANE 1918- (American)

Invented 4 detectives - see Peter CHAMBERS

Citation Record: 1 Book

Kisses Of Death - *Only*
Belmont US (1962)

Killer's Kiss - *Only**
Boardman UK (1962)

Pierre CHAMBRUN

was once a hero of the French resistance and is now in New York, managing the Hotel Beaumont. In the long series of books and short stories in which he appears, the hotel never runs short of crimes of theft, mayhem and murder, needing all his skill in detection and delicacy of approach to solve them.

French Male Amateur operating in New York

Hugh PENTECOST 1903-1989 (American)

was born in Northfield, Massachusetts, and graduated from Columbia University, New York, 1925. A prolific writer for the early pulps, creator of many fictional detectives, author of several dozen criminous books, mainly under this pseudonym and under his real name, he was a founding member of the Mystery Writers of America, receiving their Grand Master award, 1973, and the Nero Wolfe award, 1982.

Writer: Judson Pentecost PHILIPS

Other Bylines:
Philip OWEN
Judson PHILIPS

Other Detectives:
Luke BRADLEY
David COTTER
Uncle George CROWDER
Clyde HAVILAND
John JERICHO and Lt PASCAL
John JERICHO
Lt PASCAL
Julian QUIST
Grant SIMON and Lt PASCAL
Dr John SMITH
Mason TRASK

Citation Record: 20 Books 13 Short Stories in 1 Collection

The Cannibal Who Over Ate - *First*
Dodd, Mead US (1962); Boardman UK (1963)

Murder Goes Round And Round - *Last*
Dodd, Mead US (1988); Hale UK (1989)

Murder Round The Clock - *Collection 1*
Dodd, Mead US (1985)

Kyle CHAMPION

is a more or less conventional modern amateur sleuth, with a background in business and as an investigator in the TV world.

American Male Amateur operating in USA

Harold ADAMS 1923- (American)

See main detective Carl WILCOX

Citation Record: 1 Book

C

When Rich Men Die - *Single*
Doubleday US (1987); Landmark UK (1988)

The Hon Augustus CHAMPNELL

calls himself 'a confidential agent'. It is perhaps more comforting a job description than the later version, 'private eye'.
British Male Private Detective operating in England

Richard MARSH 1867-1915 (British)
Writer: Richard B HELDMANN
Other Detectives:
The Hon Augustus CHAMPNELL and BURCHELL
William CHARLECOT | Insp GARDNER
Matthew HOLMAN | Graham HUME
Insp IRELAND | Judith LEE
Augustus SHORT
George STONE, George DAVIS and FLETCHER
Citation Record: 1 Book 4 Short Stories in 1 Collection

The Beetle: A Mystery - *First*
Skeffington UK (1897); Mansfield US (1898)

An Aristocratic Detective - *Collection 1*
This collection of fourteen of the author's short stories contain four with *CHAMPNELL.*
Bell UK (1900)

The Hon Augustus CHAMPNELL and BURCHELL

Augustus CHAMPNELL also appears as the main detective in another book by this author. Here, however, he does his sleuthing in combination with a Scotland Yard man – not a policeman, however, but a clerk!
British Male Private Detective and British Male Amateur operating in London

Richard MARSH 1867-1915 (British)
Invented 10 detectives - see The Hon Augustus CHAMPNELL
Citation Record: 1 Book

The Seen And The Unseen - *Only*
Methuen UK (1900)

Sgt/Insp Charlie CHAN

is, thanks to countless radio and film scripts based on the original stories and many more invented ones, a member of that exclusive group, the detectives whom everyone knows. Indeed, he was a true original. Created in 1925, he appeared first as a Detective Sergeant and later an Inspector in the Honolulu Police Force and, it is said, was based on a real character. *Charlie CHAN* was a conscious attempt by the author to get away from the image of the wicked oriental that had populated so many thrillers until then and he soon became one of the seminal figures in detective fiction. He only appeared in six books solving cases only in Honolulu and the USA. Due to the numerous radio and film scripts that took him over in later years and which were written by numerous authors, he appeared in a vast number of cases having little relevance to the true canon. He eventually received the accolade of having a magazine devoted entirely to him and, after the death of *Earl Derr BIGGERS,* several other authors (one cited) continued the saga in print.
Chinese Policeman operating in Honolulu/California

Earl Derr BIGGERS 1884-1933 (American)
was born in Warren, Ohio. He was a reporter and writer, especially of plays, before inventing one of the classic American detectives.
Citation Record: 6 Books

The House Without A Key - *First*
Bobbs Merrill US (1925); Harrap UK (1926)

Keeper Of The Keys - *Last*
Bobbs Merrill US (1932); Cassell UK (1932)

Robert Hart DAVIS (American)
Inventor of one other detective pair Napoleon SOLO and Ilya KURYAKIN
Citation Record: 1 Book

The Pawns Of Death - *Only*
In 'Charlie Chan Mystery Magazine' US (1974)

Insp Charlie CHAN

Appears with at least two other detectives - see Sherlock HOLMES.

David CHAN

Male Sleuth operating in Japan

Charles LEADER 1938- (British)
Invented 4 detectives - see Paul MASON
Citation Record: 3 Books

A Wreath From Bangkok - *First*
Hale UK (1975)

A Wreath Of Cherry Blossom - *Latest*
Hale UK (1977)

Det Insp CHANCE

!See Appendix 2.
British Policeman operating in England

George R SIMS 1847-1922 (British)
Invented 5 detectives - see Dorcas DENE
Citation Record: 1 Book

Detective Inspector Chance - *Only*
Ferret Fantasy UK (1974)

John Newton CHANCE

British Male Sleuth operating in England

John Newton CHANCE 1911-1983 (British)
was born in London. He was the author, over a period of more than fifty years, of at least two hundred genre books, using many detectives and including about twenty *Sexton BLAKE* novels, the latter being an almost statuary task for prolific British crime writers in the 1930s, 1940s and 1950s.
Writer: John Newton CHANCE
Other Bylines:
J DRUMMOND | Desmond REID
Other Detectives:
Supt BLACK | Jonathan BLAKE
Mr DeHAVILLAND
Mr DeHAVILLAND and Supt BLACK
JASON | KEYES
John MARSH
Citation Record: 3 Books

The Screaming Fog - *First*
Macdonald UK (1946)

Death Stalks The Cobbled Square - *First**
McBride US (1946)

The Man In My Shoes - *Last*
Macdonald UK (1952)

Cliff CHANDLER

is hired to prevent crime on an ocean liner and, when there is a man overboard, he discovers that the passengers have both motives and weapons.
American Male Private Detective operating on a ship

Baynard KENDRICK 1894-1977 (American)
Invented 3 detectives - see Duncan MACLAIN
Citation Record: 1 Selected Short Story

Death At The Porthole
Duell US (1946); Hammond UK (1953)

Raymond CHANDLER

is, indeed, the famous author. He has been made over into a detective by at least two authors.
American Male Private Detective operating in USA

Richard DENBOW (American)
Citation Record: 1 Book

Chandler - *Single*
In which *CHANDLER,* depicted as an alcoholic, rescues a similarly soused *Dashiell HAMMETT* (yes, indeed, the equally famous author) from the clutches of gangsters. A case of double *lese-majesty,* it would seem!
Belmont US (1977)

Gaylord D LARSEN 1932- (American)

Invented 3 detectives - see Henry GARRETT

A Paramount Kill - *Single*

In which *CHANDLER* solves a case involving the Hollywood film director, Billy Wilder.

US (1987)

CHANDOS

appears sporadically in other books with the author's other detectives.

British Male Sleuth operating in England

Dornford YATES 1885-1960 (British)

Invented 4 detectives - see Supt FALCON

Citation Record: 1 Book

Blood Royal - *Only*

Hodder & Stoughton UK (1929); Minton US (1930)

Alexander (Check Force) CHANE and Vladimer KARLOV

American Male Professional Investigators operating in USA

Ralph HAYES 1927- (American)

Invented 4 detectives - see Mark STONER

Citation Record: 5 Books

Nightmare Island - *First*

Manor US (1975)

Seeds Of Doom - *Last*

Manor US (1976)

Ace CHANEY

is a member of a small town police department. After losing his job, he becomes an operator for Paragon International.

American Male Private Detective operating in USA

Christian GARRISON 1942- (American)

Writer: Christian Bascom GARRISON

Citation Record: 2 Books

Snake Doctor - *First*

Avon US (1980)

Paragon Man - *Latest*

Avon US (1981)

Mr CHANG

British Policeman operating in Canada

A E APPLE ?-1933 (Canadian)

Citation Record: 2 Books

Mr Chang Of Scotland Yard - *First*

Chelsea US (1926)

Mr Chang's Crime Ray - *Last*

Chelsea US (1928)

Gilbert CHANNAY

British Male Amateur operating in England

E Phillips OPPENHEIM 1866-1946 (British)

Invented 27 detectives - see Nicholas GOADE

Citation Record: 10 Short Stories in 1 Collection

The Channay Syndicate - *Collection 1*

Hodder & Stoughton UK (1927); Little, Brown US (1927)

Deborah CHANNING

American Female Amateur operating in New Mexico

Velda JOHNSTON (American)

is the author of at least thirty-three genre novels, many of them set in various parts of Europe in the nineteenth century.

Inventor of one other detective Catherine MAYHEW

Citation Record: 1 Book

Shadow Behind The Curtain - *Single*

Dodd, Mead US (1985); Severn UK (1986)

CHANTECOQ

French Male Sleuth operating in France

A BERNEDE 1871-1937 (French)

Writer: Arthur BERNEDE

Citation Record: 2 Books

The Mystery Of The Louvre - *First*

is a translation from the French of *Belphegor: Le Fantôme Noir* (Paris, 1927).

Reader's Library UK (1929); Worldwide US (1929)

The Haunted House - *Last*

is a translation from the French of *La Maison Hantée* (Paris, 1928).

Reader's Library UK (1930)

Jacob CHAOS

British Male Amateur operating in England

Shelley SMITH 1912- (British)

was born in Richmond, Surrey, and educated in France, graduating at the Sorbonne, Paris, 1931.

Writer: Nancy Hermione BODINGTON

Citation Record: 2 Books

Background For Murder - *First*

Swan UK (1942)

He Died Of Murder! - *Latest*

Collins UK (1947); Harper & Row US (1948)

CHARD

British Policeman operating in England

Cyril JOYCE ?-1992 (British)

Invented 3 detectives - see Insp Pat STOCKTON

Citation Record: 1 Book

A Calculated Risk - *Single*

Hale UK (1981)

Insp CHARD

British Policeman operating in London

Fergus HUME 1859-1932 (British)

Invented 24 detectives - see Insp Samuel GORBY

Citation Record: 1 Book

The Vanishing Of Tera - *Only*

White UK (1900)

Peter CHARD

British Male Amateur operating in England

Gerald VERNER 1886-1980 (British)

Invented 7 detectives - see Supt BUDD

Citation Record: 2 Books

Thirsty Evil - *First*

Westhouse UK (1946)

They Walk In Darkness - *Last*

Wright & Brown UK (1947)

Simon CHARD

British Male Amateur operating in England

Barbara MALIM (British)

Citation Record: 2 Books

Murder On Holiday - *First*

Murray UK (1937)

Seven Looked On - *Last*

Butterworth UK (1939)

William CHARLECOT

British Male Amateur operating in England

Richard MARSH 1867-1915 (British)

Invented 10 detectives - see The Hon Augustus CHAMPNELL

Citation Record: 1 Book

Mrs Musgrave And Her Husband - *Only*

Long UK (1901)

Mrs Edwina CHARLES

is a clairvoyante and amateur sleuth, living in the fictional village of Little Giddings and investigating the murders that occur around the place, time after time.

British Female Amateur operating in England/Wales

C

Mignon WARNER (Australian)

Citation Record: 8 Books

A Nice Way To Die - *First*
Hale UK (1976)

A Medium For Murder - *First**
McKay US (1977)

Exit Mr Punch - *Latest*
Doubleday US (1994)

Nick CHARLES and Nora CHARLES

hold a special place in detective literature, if only because of their countless followers and imitators. It seems impossible for them only to have existed in the one book. The author himself may have preferred to forget them and the cognoscenti may now find them an embarrassing creation of the great master, but they became an enormous success. A husband-and-wife detecting team seemed a remarkable invention at the time but it soon became remarkably attractive to other authors. *Nick CHARLES* is an Americanised Greek, originally with an unpronounceable second name, and he was once an ace operative for the Trans-American Detective Agency in San Francisco. Married to the wealthy *Nora*, he becomes involved in a murder case and decides to have a last go at it before retiring. It is of interest to note that, in the series of films that followed the book, *Nick CHARLES* came to be called The Thin Man, although in the book, of course, that name belonged to someone very different.

American Male Private Detective and American Female Amateur operating in San Francisco

Sidekick: ASTA

is a wire-haired, white Schnauzer and one of the most famous dogs in detective literature, accompanying the two detectives in their one authentic case.

Male - Pet Dog

Stooge: Det John GUILD

is the cop assigned to the case in the classic detective novel, *THE THIN MAN*. He gets into a terrible muddle before *Nick CHARLES* sees him through and, all in all, he must be the least remembered cop in any great detective novel.

American Male

Dashiell HAMMETT 1894-1961 (American)

Invented 7 detectives - see Sam SPADE

The Thin Man - *Only*

The author, one of the greatest names in the history of detective fiction, was later said to have been rather embarrassed by the success of this book, which proved to be lasting. It certainly started a powerful new trend by introducing the smart, modish, well-heeled, witty husband-and-wife detective team into the American ethos. It was made into a film (with William Powell and Myrna Loy as the loving pair) and was followed by scores of imitators. Even the dog became a household word and was copied too.

Knopf US (1934); Barker UK (1934)

Nora CHARLES

Second detective of Nick CHARLES

Sheriff Chick CHARLESTON

American Policeman operating in Montana/England

A B GUTHRIE Jr 1901-91 (American)

Writer: Alfred Bertram GUTHRIE Jr

Citation Record: 5 Books

Wild Pitch - *First*
Houghton UK (1973)

Murder In The Cotswolds - *Latest*
Houghton UK (1989)

Insp CHARLESWORTH

appears in books with one of the author's other detectives, *Insp COCKRILL*.

British Policeman operating in England

Mary Christianna BRAND 1907-1988 (British)

Invented 6 detectives - see Insp COCKRILL and Insp CHARLESWORTH

Citation Record: 2 Books

Death In High Heels - *First*
Lane UK (1941); Scribner's US (1954)

The Rose In Darkness - *Last*
Joseph UK (1979)

Insp CHARLESWORTH

Second detective of Insp COCKRILL

Sgt CHARLESWORTH

British Policeman operating in England

J S FLETCHER 1863-1935 (British)

Invented 9 detectives - see Paul CAMPENHAYE

Citation Record: 2 Books

The Borgia Cabinet - *First*
Jenkins UK (1932); Knopf US (1930)

The Burma Ruby - *Last*
Benn UK (1932); Dial US (1933)

James CHARLESWORTH

British Male Sleuth operating in England/Middle East

James SANDYS (British)

Invented 3 detectives - see Insp MILLWALL

Citation Record: 3 Books

A Stripe For A Stripe - *First*
Paul UK (1938)

Death Is Merciful - *Last*
Paul UK (1948)

Insp Harry CHARLTON

is a product of the old school of policemen, before post-war British police procedurals took root with their fast, violent action and often boring domesticity. He is a large man and seems always to be wearing an overcoat and bowler hat against the English weather. He is called 'The Doctor' by his colleagues in the fictional Downshire County police force, as his soft, avuncular, bedside manner often succeeds in gaining important clues, where others fail to do so. His sidekick, *Peter BRADFIELD*, appears first as a detective constable, then a sergeant. In later books, the two men are of equal rank and work together in a further six books.

British Policeman operating in England

Sidekick: Sgt Peter BRADFIELD

rises in the ranks during the series and eventually appears as the main detective in three books.

British Male - Subordinate

Clifford WITTING 1907- (British)

Other Detectives:
Insp Peter BRADFIELD
Insp Harry CHARLTON and Insp Peter BRADFIELD

Citation Record: 5 Books

Murder In Blue - *First*
Hodder & Stoughton UK (1937)

A Bullet For Rhino - *Last*
Hodder & Stoughton UK (1950)

Insp Harry CHARLTON and Insp Peter BRADFIELD

appear individually in other books by this author.

British Policemen operating in England

Clifford WITTING 1907- (British)

Invented 3 detectives - see Insp Harry CHARLTON

Citation Record: 6 Books

The Case Of The Michaelmas Goose - *First*
Hodder & Stoughton UK (1938)

Silence After Dinner - *Last*
Hodder & Stoughton UK (1952)

Supt CHARTER

investigates the murder of the Master of a local foxhunt.

British Policeman operating in England

Anne FLEMING (British)

Citation Record: 1 Book

There Goes Charlie - *Single*
Collins UK (1990)

Frank CHASE

is an ex-policeman who has retired to start a new life in a Boston suburb. There he is soon plunged into a mystery with roots in the past, which takes him back into the criminal underworld.

American Male Ex-Policeman operating in Boston

Andrew COBURN 1932- (American)

See main detective Rita Gardella O'DEA

Citation Record: 1 Book

Off Duty - *Single*
Norton US (1980); Secker & Warburg UK (1981)

Lt Jake CHASE

is a cop in the city of Grantham and is euphemistically described as 'not a legend in his own time – more of a cautionary tale – energetic, good-looking, kind-natured, very intelligent, and accident-prone: he had the X-rays to prove it'. He is involved in a most delightful detective caper story.

American Policeman operating in USA

Sidekick: Det Joe KAMINSKY
is surely one of the dumbest in the business.
American Male - Subordinate

Paula GOSLING 1939- (American)

Invented 7 detectives - see Lt Jack STRYKER

Citation Record: 1 Book

Hoodwink - *Single*
Doubleday US (1988); Macmillan UK (1988)

Erik CHATHAM

American Male Sleuth operating in Africa/China

Richard NEEBEL (American)

Citation Record: 2 Books

The Halo Solution - *First*
Charter US (1979)

The Yunnan Terminus - *Latest*
Charter US (1980)

Paul CHAVASSE

British Male Secret Agent operating in Europe/Asia

Martin FALLON 1929- (British)

For writer details see Liam DEVLIN

Citation Record: 6 Books

The Testament Of Caspar Schultz - *First*
was republished under the following byline.
Abelard Schuman UK (1962); Abelard Schuman US (1962)

A Fine Night For Dying - *Last*
Long UK (1969)

Jack HIGGINS 1929- (British)

Inventor of 3 detectives - see Liam DEVLIN

Citation Record: 1 Book

The Testament Of Caspar Schultz - *First*
was previously published under the preceding byline.
GM US (1978)

Ch Insp Charlie CHEADLE

is a middle-aged detective at Scotland Yard, whose style unites pensiveness with the ability to deduce much from small clues.

British Policeman operating in London

Sidekick: Sgt Derek ROBINSON
British Male - Assistant

Russell BRADDON 1921- (Australian)

was a prisoner of the Japanese during the Second World War. He came to England to recuperate, 1949, wrote his first book about his experiences and then turned to the criminous genre.

Writer: Russell Reading BRADDON

Citation Record: 1 Book

Funnelweb - *Single*
Constable UK (1990)

Sgt Jim CHEE

is a Navajo Indian police officer. He appears also in books with the author's other detective, *Joe LEAPHORN.*

American Policeman operating in Arizona

Tony HILLERMAN 1925- (American)

Invented 4 detectives - see Lt Joe LEAPHORN

Citation Record: 3 Books

People Of Darkness - *First*
Harper & Row US (1980); Gollancz UK (1982)

The Ghostway - *Latest*
Harper & Row US (1985); Gollancz UK (1985)

Sgt Jim CHEE

Second detective of Lt Joe LEAPHORN

Rodney CHELMARSH

Second detective of Doran FAIRWEATHER

CHERI-BIBI

French Male Amateur operating in France

Gaston LEROUX 1868-1927 (French)

See main detective Joseph ROULETABILLE

Citation Record: 4 Books

Cheri-Bibi and Cecily - *First*
is a translation from the French of *Cheri-Bibi et Cecily* (Paris, 1921).
Laurie UK (1923)

The Missing Men - *First**
Macaulay US (1923)

The New Idol - *Last*
is a translation from the French of *Le Coup d'Etat de Cheri-Bibi* (Paris, 1925).
Long UK (1928); Macaulay US (1929)

Prof Richard CHERRINGTON

is the Professor of Prehistory at the fictional Fisher's College in Cambridge and, an avid reader of detective fiction, fancies himself as a brilliant sleuth. In fact, he does solve two difficult cases for the police.

British Male Amateur operating in Wales

Glyn DANIEL 1914-1986 (British)

was born in Lampeter, Wales. After serving as an officer in British Intelligence in the Second World War, he returned to Cambridge where he was appointed first as a lecturer then as Professor of Archaeology.

Writer: Glyn Edmund DANIEL

Other Byline: Dilwyn REES

Citation Record: 1 Book

Welcome Death - *Only*
Gollancz UK (1954); Dodd, Mead US (1955)

Dilwyn REES 1914- (British)

For writer details see Prof Richard CHERRINGTON

Citation Record: 1 Book

The Cambridge Murders - *Only*
Gollancz UK (1945)

Insp CHERRY

British Policeman operating in England

Sidekick: Sgt DUFF
British Male - Subordinate

Peter VAN GREENAWAY 1929- (British)

was born on London. A practising lawyer, he is the author of sixteen genre novels, which have unusual plots and settings and are often based on real historical events.

Citation Record: 2 Books
Doppelganger - *First*
Gollancz UK (1975)
The Lazarus Lie - *Latest*
Gollancz UK (1982)

C

Henry CHESTERFIELD

sleuths in stories that have been set back into the early 1900s.
British Male Amateur operating in England

Clive BROOKS (British)
Writer: Clive Kenneth BROOKS
Adaapter of one other detective Sherlock HOLMES
Citation Record: 5 Short Stories in 1 Collection
Blood On The Tracks - *Collection 1*
contains five stories with *Henry CHESTERFIELD*, and also contains one *Sherlock HOLMES* pastiche, which is cited under that detective.
Kingfisher UK (1989)

G K CHESTERTON

is, indeed, the famous creator of *Father BROWN* and has been made the detective in this story in which he solves an 'impossible' mystery.
British Male Amateur

Edward D HOCH 1930- (American)
Invented 20 detectives - see Capt LEOPOLD
Citation Record: 1 Selected Short Story
The Bad Samaritan
This story, in which a whole circus apparently disappears, was first published in the December 9 number. It appears also in the anthology, *John Creasey's Crime Collection* (*Gollancz;* UK 1989).
In 'Alfred Hitchcock's Mystery Magazine' US (1981)

Dennis CHETWYND

British Male Amateur operating in England

Henry J FIDLER (British)
Citation Record: 10 Short Stories in 1 Collection
Chronicles Of Dennis Chetwynd - *Collection 1*
Hutchinson UK (1927)

Dr Henry CHETWYND and Dr Paul CATO

solve a series of murders that are apparently caused by supernatural means.
British Male Amateurs operating in England

L T MEADE and Robert EUSTACE (British)
Invented 7 detectives - see Insp FROST and Dr GARLAND
Citation Record: 12 Short Stories in 2 Collection
The Adventures Of A Man Of Science - *Collection 1*
This series of short stories appeared, 1896-1897, in Volumes XII-XIII.
Short stories - 6
In 'Strand Magazine' UK (1896)
The Sanctuary Club - *Collection 2*
Short stories - 6
Ward, Lock UK (1900)

Y CHEUNG

Chinese Male Professional Investigator operating in Indianapolis

Harry Stephen KEELER 1890-1967 (American)
Invented 14 detectives - see Angus MACWHORTER
Citation Record: 1 Book
Y Cheung, Business Detective - *Only*
Dutton US (1939)
Cheung, Detective - *Only**
Ward, Lock UK (1938)

Monsieur CHEVENARD

solves a case of death by strangulation in a locked room.
French Male Amateur operating in France

Jean JOSEPH-RENAUD (French)
!See Appendix 2
Inventor of one other detective pair Dr MEPHISTO and Monsieur HIGNETTE
Citation Record: 1 Book
The Phantom Violin - *Only*
is a translation from the French of *Le Violon Fantôme.*
Metropolitan UK (1948)

Insp John CHEVIOT

gets into a London taxi some time in the 1950s and, extraordinarily, emerges from a hackney carriage in 1859. He is able to use his modern skills to solve an old case of murder.
British Policeman operating in London

John Dickson CARR 1906-1977 (American)
Invented 16 detectives - see Dr Gideon FELL
Citation Record: 1 Book
Fire, Burn! - *Only*
Harper & Row US (1957); Hamish Hamilton UK (1957)

Col Allen CHEYNEY

British Male Professional Investigator operating in several locations

Patrick COSGRAVE 1941- (British)
Writer: Patrick John COSGRAVE
Citation Record: 3 Books
Cheyney's Law - *First*
Macmillan UK (1977)
Adventure Of State - *Latest*
Anderson UK (1984); St Martin's US (1986)

A CHICAGO DETECTIVE

American Male Detective in Pulp Magazines operating in Chicago

ANON
Citation Record: 1 Book
The Great Cronion Mystery; Or, The Irish Patriot's Fate - *Only*
Laird & Lee US (ca 1888)

Nelson CHIDDENHAM

is a crippled boy detective who solves local mysteries by means of his knowledge of the countryside and animal life, particularly of dogs.
British Male Amateur operating in England

Bertram ATKEY 1880-1952 (British)
Invented 4 detectives - see Prosper FAIR
No citations

Col CHIDDINGTON

Second detective of Supt WILKINS

Dr Russell V 'Chill' CHILDERS

American Male Amateur operating in several locations

Jory SHERMAN 1932- (American)
Writer: Jory Tecumseh SHERMAN
Citation Record: 6 Books
Chill - *First*
Pinnacle US (1978); New English Library UK (1979)
Shadows - *Latest*
Pinnacle US (1980)

Lydia CHIN

investigates protection rackets and shady art dealings in New York's Chinatown.
American Female Private Detective operating in New York

S J ROSEN (American)
Citation Record: 1 Book
China Trade - *Single*
St Martin's US (1994)

CHIN CHIN

is a Chinese detective who appeared in several stories in the pulps.
Chinese Male Amateur operating in USA

Albert W AIKEN 1846-1894 (American)

Invented 5 detectives - see Hilda SIRENE

Citation Record: 1 Book

Chin Chin, The Chinese Detective; Or, The Dark Work Of The Black Hands - *Only*
Westbrook US (1927)

CHIP

American Male Detective in Pulp Magazines operating in USA

Police Captain HOWARD (American)

Invented 15 detectives - see LIGHTNING LUKE

Citation Record: 1 Book

Chip, The Newsboy Detective; Or, The Plot To Steal A Million
New York Detective Library US (1882-8)

'Bunny' CHIPSTEAD

British Male Amateur operating in England

Sydney HORLER 1888-1954 (British)

Invented 20 detectives - see Sir Harker BELLAMY

Citation Record: 4 Books

In The Dark - *First*
Hodder & Stoughton UK (1927)

A Life For Sale - *First**
Doubleday US (1928)

The Enemy Within The Gates - *Last*
Hodder & Stoughton UK (1940)

CHISEL

is a gentleman's valet. Unusually for the period, it is he who solves the novel's mystery.

British Male Amateur operating in England

Hawley SMART 1833-1893 (British)

Invented 8 detectives - see Insp POLLOCK

Citation Record: 1 Book

Tie And Trick: A Melodramatic Story - *Only*
Chapman & Hall UK (1885)

Paul CHISHOLM

British Male Amateur operating in England

Alfred W EYLES 1896-1950 (British)

Citation Record: 3 Books

Murder In Hospital - *First*
World's Work UK (1944)

Murder At Out-Patients - *Last*
World's Work UK (1948)

Insp Lev CHISLENKO

investigates a case that seems to involve the appearance of ghosts, which, the author suggests, were strictly disallowed in the Soviet Union.

Russian Policeman operating in Russia

Reginald HILL 1936- (British)

Invented 4 detectives - see Supt Andrew DALZIEL and Sgt Peter PASCOE

Citation Record: 1 Selected Short Story

There Are No Ghosts In The Soviet Union
appeared in a collection of six of the author's stories, *There Are No Ghosts In The Soviet Union, And Other Stories.*
Collins UK (1987); Foul Play US (1988)

Ambrose CHITTERWICK

is a hen-pecked little man, not at all in the usual run of British amateur detectives of the 1920s, but he proves to be a brilliant solver of puzzles. He appears also in one book with the author's other detective, *Roger SHERINGHAM.*

British Male Amateur operating in England

Anthony BERKELEY 1893-1971 (British)

Invented 4 detectives - see Roger SHERINGHAM

Citation Record: 2 Books

The Piccadilly Murder - *First*
Collins UK (1929); Doubleday US (1930)

Trial And Error - *Last*
Hodder & Stoughton UK (1937); Doubleday US (1937)

Ambrose CHITTERWICK and Roger SHERINGHAM

also appear individually in other books by this author.

British Male Amateurs operating in England

Stooge: Insp MORESBY
is a classic British police stooge, eternally baffled by the cases that *SHERINGHAM* and *CHITTERWICK* solve (not together but in their respective books).
British Male

Anthony BERKELEY 1893-1971 (British)

Invented 4 detectives - see Roger SHERINGHAM

Citation Record: 1 Book

The Poisoned Chocolates Case - *Only*
Collins UK (1929)

Robin CHODOFF

investigates the kidnapping of her younger sister, at great risk to herself.

American Female Amateur operating in USA

Lucille FLETCHER 1912- (American)

was born in Brooklyn, New York. She took a BA at Vassar College, Poughkeepsie, New York, 1933, and then worked as a music librarian for the Columbia Broadcasting System, 1934-1939, after which she became a full-time writer. She received the Mystery Writers of America Edgar Allan Poe award, 1959.

Writer: Lucille Fletcher WALLOP

Citation Record: 1 Book

Mirror Image - *Only*
Morrow US (1988); Heywood UK (1989)

Bill CHORLEY

Male Amateur

F C TICKNER

Citation Record: 2 Books

Death At The Towers - *First*
Danceland ? (1946)

Murderers Three - *Last*
Danceland ? (1946)

Agatha CHRISTIE

is, indeed, the famous author and has been made the detective in this one novel. She is involved in a case of murder, supposedly occurring during her intriguing and still unresolved disappearance during 1926.

British Female Amateur operating in England

Kathleen TYNAN (British)

Citation Record: 1 Book

Agatha - *Only*
Weidenfeld & Nicolson UK (1978); Ballantine US (1978)

Det Sgt Bob CHRISTIE

Australian Policeman operating in Australia

James PRESTON 1913- (Australian)

Citation Record: 2 Books

Axes Of Hate - *First*
Long UK (1963)

Shattered Steel - *Last*
Long UK (1964)

Bob CHRISTOPHER

is a Vietnam war veteran who is now a field reporter for a TV channel. He has a weight problem, loves animals, and is generally a softie, even when he runs into murder – which he does most of the time.

American Male Amateur operating in Los Angeles

R R IRVINE 1936- (American)

was born in Salt Lake City, Utah. He was educated at the University of Utah, Salt Lake City, and at the University of

California, Berkeley, where he graduated, 1959, with a BA in Anthropology and Art History. He served in US Counter-Intelligence, 1959-1961, and later worked as a reporter and TV producer.

Writer: Robert Ralstone IRVINE

Other Byline: Robert IRVINE

Citation Record: 4 Books

Jump Cut - *First*
Popular Library US (1974)

Ratings Are Murder - *Latest*
Walker US (1985)

James (Operator 5) CHRISTOPHER

appeared in many pulp magazines during the 1930s.

American Male Professional Investigator operating in Los Angeles

Curtis STEELE 1902-1977 (American)

For writer details see Luke SPEARE and Schyler COLE

Citation Record: 11 Books

The Army Of The Dead - *First*
Corinth US (1966)

Cavern Of The Damned - *Last*
Pulp Press UK (1980)

Joe CHRISTOPHER

is enlisted by the British SIS, after one of its agents is murdered, to infiltrate a blackmail ring.

American Male Sleuth operating in France

Victor CANNING 1911-1986 (British)

Invented 6 detectives - see Rex CARVER

Citation Record: 1 Book

The Scorpio Letters - *Only*
Heinemann UK (1964); Sloane US (1964)

Paul CHRISTOPHER

is an American spy-detective, rather in the classic British style.

American Male Professional Investigator operating in several locations

Charles MCCARRY 1930- (American)

was born in Pittsburgh, Massachusetts. He has been a reporter and editor and served in the US Central Intelligence Agency, 1958-1967.

Citation Record: 3 Books

The Miernik Dossier - *First*
Saturday Review Press US (1973); Hutchinson UK (1974)

The Last Supper - *Latest*
Dutton US (1983); Hutchinson UK (1983)

Dr Gordon CHRISTY

is a newly graduated veterinarian from Fort Collins in Colorado. His cases involve much dog lore, especially that pertaining to Dobermans.

American Male Amateur operating in USA

Barbara MOORE 1934- (American)

Writer: Barbara Moore LEE

Citation Record: 2 Books

The Doberman Wore Black - *First*
St Martin's US (1983)

The Wolf Whispered Death - *Latest*
US (1985)

Insp CHUCKY

British Policeman operating in England/Wales

Mary Ann ASHE 1907-1988 (British)

For writer details see Insp COCKRILL and Insp CHARLESWORTH

Citation Record: 1 Books

A Ring Of Roses - *Only*
Star UK (1977)

Mary Christianna BRAND 1907-1988 (British)

Invented 6 detectives - see Insp COCKRILL and Insp CHARLESWORTH

Citation Record: 1 Books

Cat And Mouse - *Only*
was published, unusually, under the author's real name.
Joseph UK (1950); Knopf US (1950)

Harvey CHURCH

was, it seems, formerly a sheriff in Kentucky. His one case concerns murder at a stylish Long Island wedding.

American Male Private Detective operating in Long Island

Norman KLEIN 1897-1948 (American)

See main detective Kennedy JONES

Citation Record: 1 Book

Terror By Night - *Only*
Farrar, Straus US (1935)

Johnny CHURCH

American Male Amateur operating in Mexico/Las Vegas

Vechel HOWARD (American)

Writer: Howard Vechel RIGSBY

Other Byline: Howard RIGSBY

Citation Record: 2 Books

Murder On Her Mind - *First*
GM US (1959); Muller UK (1960)

Murder With Love - *Last*
GM US (1959); Muller UK (1960)

Prof Arthur CHURCHILL

Appears with at least two other detectives - see Lowell GAYLORD.

CHU-SHENG

Chinese Male Amateur operating in New York/Panama

Eugene THOMAS 1894- (American)

See main detective Mrs Caywood WESTON

Citation Record: 2 Books

Shadow Of Chu-Sheng - *First*
Sears US (1933)

Yellow Magic - *Last*
Sears US (1934)

Det Insp CICERO

British Policeman operating in England

Stooge: Supt TENCH
is the cop who plagues *CICERO.*
British Male

Patrick RUELL 1936- (British)

was born in Hartlepool, England. He has been a schoolmaster and writes, very successfully, under several bylines.

For writer details see Supt Andrew DALZIEL and Sgt/Det Ch Insp Peter PASCOE

Citation Record: 1 Book

The Only Game - *Single*
HarperCollins UK (1991)

Giuseppe CIGARINI

Italian Male Amateur operating in England

Gilbert FRANKAU 1884-1952 (British)

was a prolific author of light novels.

Other Detectives:
Marcus ORLANDO   Kyra SOKRATESCU

Citation Record: 6 Short Stories in 1 Collection

Wine, Women And Waiters - *Collection 1*
This collection of eighteen of the author's short stories contains six with *CIGARINI.*
Hutchinson UK (1932)

Joe CINQUEZ

is a Korean War veteran, now in his fifties and finding it difficult to use his training and skills professionally; for, although his skin is light, he counts as black in social circles where it seems to matter. Unlicensed, therefore, he does detective work for a lawyer friend.

American Male Professional Investigator operating in New York

Clifford MASON (American)

Citation Record: 2 Books

When Love Was Not Enough - *First*
Playboy US (1980)

Jamaica Run - *Latest*
UK (1987)

The CIRCUS DETECTIVE

The Circus Detective - *Only*

American Male Detective in Pulp Magazines operating in USA

ANON

Antoine CIRRET

French Male Amateur operating in Paris/Edinburgh

Elizabeth HELY 1913- (British)

Writer: Elizabeth Hely YOUNGER

Citation Record: 2 Books

Dominant Third - *First*
Heinemann UK (1959)

I'll Be Judge, I'll Be Jury - *First**
Scribner's US (1959)

A Mark Of Displeasure - *Last*
Scribner's US (1960); Heinemann UK (1961)

Morgan CITRON

!See Appendix 2.

American Male Amateur operating in Central America

Ross THOMAS 1926- (American)

was born in Oklahoma City, Oklahoma, He took a BA at the University of Oklahoma, Norman, 1949, after having served in the US Army, 1944-1946. He has been a reporter and US government consultant. Under his real name and a pseudonym, he is the author of at least twenty-two genre novels, mainly consisting of political and espionage thrillers. He received the Mystery Writers of America Edgar Allen Poe award twice, 1967 and 1985.

Writer: Ross Elmore THOMAS

Other Byline: Oliver BLEECK

Other Detectives:
Cyril MCCORKLE and Michael PADILLO
Jake POPE
Artie WU and Quincey DURANT

Citation Record: 1 Book

Missionary Stew - *Single*
Simon & Schuster US (1983); Hamish Hamilton UK (1984)

Amos CLACKWORTHY

American Male Amateur operating in Chicago

Christopher B BOOTH 1883-1924 (American)

Invented 3 detectives - see Jim BLISS

Citation Record: 2 Collections

Mr Clackworthy - *Collection 1*
contains an uncounted number of short stories.
Chelsea US (1926)

Mr Clackworthy, Con Man - *Collection 2*
contains an uncounted number of short stories.
Chelsea US (1927)

Frank CLAMART

Male Sleuth operating in Paris/New York

Henry C ROWLAND 1874-1933 (American)

Writer: Henry Cottrell ROWLAND

Citation Record: 2 Books

The Closing Net - *First*
Dodd, Mead US (1912); Hurst UK (1913)

The Return Of Frank Clamart - *Last*
Harper & Row US (1923)

Lt CLANCY

is an astute New York cop, based in the 52nd Precinct, whose detective ability enables him to solve difficult cases. His two sidekicks, however, do much of the legwork.

American Policeman operating in New York

Sidekick: KAPROSKI
American Male - Subordinate

Sidekick: STANTON
American Male - Subordinate

Robert L PIKE 1912-1981 (American)

See main detective Lt Jim REARDON

Citation Record: 3 Books

Mute Witness - *First*
Doubleday US (1963); Deutsch UK (1965)

Police Blotter - *Last*
Doubleday US (1965); Deutsch UK (1966)

Mike CLANCY

Second detective of Sidney 'Silky' PINCUS

Peter CLANCY

is a man-about-town and well set up in life. He practises as a private investigator in the days when every smart detective could have a valet – and he does, a very English one who doubles as a sidekick. His cases concern crimes that seem to occur frequently in well-to-do families and they take him to all parts of the USA and to Europe.

American Male Private Detective operating in New Jersey/California

Sidekick: WIGGAR
is always righteous and seems to be nearly always right.
British Male - Valet

Lee THAYER 1874-1973 (American)

was born in Troy, Pennsylvania. An artist, designer and book illustrator, she is also the author of a great many genre novels, all featuring one detective. She has the distinction of writing her last genre work at the age of ninety-two, which is probably a record.

Writer: Emma Bedington Lee THAYER

Citation Record: 60 Books

The Mystery Of The Thirteenth Floor - *First*
Century US (1919)

Dusty Death - *Last*
Dodd, Mead US (1966)

Death Walks In Shadow - *Last**
Long UK (1966)

Terry CLANE

American Male Amateur operating in San Francisco

Erle Stanley GARDNER 1889-1970 (American)

Invented 14 detectives - see Perry MASON

Citation Record: 2 Books

Murder Up My Sleeve - *First*
Morrow US (1937); Cassell UK (1938)

The Case Of The Backward Mule - *Last*
Morrow US (1946); Heinemann UK (1955)

Clarice CLAREMONT

American Female Amateur operating in USA

Claudia CRANSTON 1886-1947 (American)

Citation Record: 2 Books

The Murder On Fifth Avenue - *First*
Lippincott US (1934)

Murder Maritime - *Last*
Lippincott US (1935)

Sgt Bill CLARK and Det Randi STONER

investigate the murder of a woman, whose body is found naked in the trunk of a car in the police pound.

American Policemen operating in Dallas

Terry MARLOW (American)

Citation Record: 1 Book

Target Blue - *Single*
Putnam US (1991)

C

Max CLARK
was one of this author's numerous pulp detectives and appeared in several stories in *Dime Detective.*
American Male Detective in Pulp Magazines operating in USA

Norbert DAVIS 1909-1949 (American)
Invented 8 detectives - see Ben SHALEY
Citation Record: 1 Selected Short Story
The Gin Monkey
In 'Dime Detective' US (1935)

Insp CLARKE
British Policeman operating in England

John K LEYS 1846-1909 (British)
Writer: John Kirkwood LEYS
Citation Record: 1 Book
The Lawyer's Secret - *Only*
Warne UK (1897)

Henry CLARKE
was one of the detectives, purporting to be real, whose cases were published by this obscure author.
British Policeman operating in England/USA

WATERS (British)
Invented 6 detectives - see WATERS
Citation Record: 18 Short Stories in 1 Collection
Autobiography Of An English Detective - *Collection 1*
Maxwell UK (1863)
Autobiography Of A London Detective - *Collection 1**
Dick US (1864)

Horace CLARKE
American Male Sleuth operating in New York

Irwin LEWIS 1916- (American)
Citation Record: 2 Books
The Day They Invaded New York - *First*
Avon UK (1964)
The Day New York Trembled - *Last*
Avon UK (1967)

James CLARKSON-PARRY
British Male Amateur operating in England

B G QUIN (British)
Writer: Basil Godfrey QUIN
Citation Record: 4 Books
The Death Box - *First*
Hutchinson UK (1929); Greenberg US (1932)
The Phantom Murderer - *Last*
Hutchinson UK (1932)

Monsieur CLAUDE
French Policeman operating in France

M CLAUDE
Citation Record: 20 Short Stories in 1 Collection
Memoirs Of Monsieur Claude, Chief Of Police Under The Second Empire - *Collection 1*
Munro US (1892)

Theodore CLAW
was formerly a boxer, wrestler, baseball pitcher and soldier. He is now a lawyer, a PI, and a special agent.
American Male Private Detective operating in USA

Vincent PARADIS (American)
Citation Record: 2 Books
The Cocaine Caper - *First*
Manor US (1978)
The Castilian Caper - *Latest*
Manor US (1978)

Col CLAY
was a Victorian detective-adventurer.
British Male Amateur operating in several locations

Grant ALLEN 1848-1899 (British)
Invented 5 detectives - see Nurse Hilda WADE
Citation Record: 12 Short Stories in 1 Collection
An African Millionaire - *Collection 1*
Richards UK (1897); Arnold US (1897)

Cutty CLAY
American Male Amateur operating in New York/Paris

Harold MACGRATH 1871-1932 (American)
Citation Record: 2 Books
The Drums Of Jeopardy - *First*
Doubleday US (1920); Hodder & Stoughton UK (1923)
The Wolves Of Chaos - *Last*
Doubleday US (1929); Long UK (1929)

George CLAY
American Male Private Detective operating in USA

Philip KETCHUM 1902-1969 (American)
was born in Colorado.
Inventor of one other detective Stephen BARTH
Citation Record: 1 Book
Death In The Night - *Only*
Phoenix Press US (1939)
Good Night For Murder - *Only**
Dagger House US (1946)

Homer CLAY
American Male Amateur operating in Kentucky

Philip LAUBEN (American)
Citation Record: 2 Books
A Nice Sound Alibi - *First*
St Martin's US (1981); Hale UK (1981)
A Surfeit Of Alibis - *Latest*
Hale UK (1982); St Martin's US (1983)

Lucien CLAY
British Male Amateur operating in England

Robert GORE-BROWNE 1893- (British)
Citation Record: 2 Books
Murder Of An MP - *First*
Collins UK (1927)
In Search Of A Villain - *First**
Doubleday US (1928)
Death On Delivery - *Last*
Collins UK (1929)
By Way Of Confession - *Last**
Doubleday US (1930)

Sam CLAY
American Male Amateur operating in USA

Jonathan LATIMER 1906-1983 (American)
was born in Chicago, Illinois. He graduated from Knox College, Galesburg, Illinois, 1929, and served in the US Navy, 1942-1945, after which he worked mainly as a reporter in Chicago and as a screenwriter.
Writer: Jonathan Wyatt LATIMER
Other Byline: Peter COFFIN
Other Detectives:
Richard BLAKE
William CRANE
Steve CRAVEN
Citation Record: 1 Book
Sinners And Shrouds - *Only*
Simon & Schuster US (1955); Methuen UK (1956)

Stephen CLAY
American Male Amateur operating in New York/New England

Sidney E PORCELAIN (American)
Citation Record: 2 Books
The Purple Pony Murders - *First*
Phoenix Press US (1944); Partridge UK (1946)
The Crimson Cat Murders - *Last*
Phoenix Press US (1946)

C

Tod CLAYMORE

purports to be the pseudonymous author. A tennis professional who served with the Royal Air Force in the First World War, he has emigrated to America, where he is involved in exciting adventures that require a little light sleuthing.

British Male Amateur operating in New Orleans/Florida

Tod CLAYMORE 1898-1964 (British)

For writer details see Maxwell ARCHER

Citation Record: 6 Books

You Remember The Case - *First*
Nelson UK (1939)

This Is What Happened - *First**
Simon & Schuster US (1939)

Rendezvous On An Island - *Last*
Cassell UK (1957)

Insp CLAYTON

is the head of a small rural police force who is called in to a case of murder on a farm. He and his local knowledge are pushed to one side by one of the nastiest police stooges in the genre.

British Policeman operating in England

Stooge: Supt AKERS

is an offensive, bullying officer, sent from Scotland Yard, who almost fouls up the investigation of the gentle detective in charge of the case.

British Male

Roderic JEFFRIES 1926- (British)

Invented 4 detectives - see Insp Enrique ALVAREZ

Citation Record: 1 Book

Dead Man's Bluff - *Only*
Collins UK (1970)

Jack CLAYTON

Male Sleuth operating in New York/Far East

Sinclair GLUCK 1887- (American)

was born in Buffalo, New York, and educated in England and the United States.

Other Detectives:
Paul BERNARD   Ross MCCOY

Citation Record: 2 Books

The Golden Panther - *First*
Mills UK (1923)

The House Of The Missing - *First**
Dodd, Mead US (1924)

The Dragon In Harness - *Last*
Mills UK (1927); Dodd, Mead US (1932)

Jeff CLAYTON

American Male Amateur operating in USA

William WARD

House name.

Citation Record: 29 Books

Jeff Clayton's Triumph - *First*
Westbrook US (1910)

Jeff Clayton's Mexican Plot - *Last*
Westbrook US (1912)

Tom CLAYTON

solves a case of locked-room murder.

American Male Amateur operating in USA

Katherine VIRDEN (American)

Citation Record: 1 Book

The Crooked Eye - *Only*
Doubleday US (1930); Chapman & Hall UK (1930)

Jack CLEARY

American Male Sleuth operating in Los Angeles

appears in books that are novelizations of episodes from and American TV series.

David ELLIOTT (American)

Citation Record: 1 Book

Blue Movie - *Single*
Ivy US (1988)

T N ROBB (American)

Writer: Rob MACGREGOR

Citation Record: 2 Books

Private Eye - *First*
Ivy US (1988)

Flip Side - *Latest*
Ivy US (1988)

Clint CLEAVER

American Male Detective in Pulp Magazines operating in USA

F Lusk BROUGHTON (American)

Invented 10 detectives - see Harry WILLIAMS

Citation Record: 1 Selected Short Story

Clint Cleaver, The Grand Street Detective; Or, The Mystery Of The Headless Woman
Old Cap Collier Library US (18??)

Hamilton CLEEK

was a clever British cracksman, said to be the greatest ever, and the bane of Scotland Yard. He was known as 'The Man of Forty Faces', as he had the uncanny ability to change his features at will, reserving his true face for close friends, such as his sidekick, *DOLLOPS*, and his true love, Ailsa Lorne. He often warned the police of his forthcoming robberies and gave them a tithe of the proceeds to tease them. Eventually Ailsa prevailed on him to give up his life of crime and become a detective himself. He did and, as a result, he was of great help to the men of Scotland Yard in their tedious work. *Thomas HASHEW* wrote at least four of the early works, but the later books, although appearing under his name, were written by his wife and daughter. *CLEEK* appeared in a large number of stories of the 'locked-room' mystery type, in which he solves 'impossible' crimes. The short stories appeared in *Short Stories Magazine.*

British Male Amateur operating in England

Sidekick: DOLLOPS

is a Cockney urchin who assists *CLEEK* in his early robberies and later when he becomes a detective.

British Male - Assistant

Hazel Phillips HANSHEW (American)

was the daughter of *Thomas W HANSHEW* and *Mary E HANSHEW.* She was responsible for collecting many of their stories featuring *Hamilton CLEEK.*

Writer: Hazel Phillips HANSHEW

Other Byline: Mary E HANSHEW and Thomas W HANSHEW

Citation Record: 2 Books

The Riddle Of The Winged Death - *First*
Long UK (1931)

Murder In The Hotel - *Last*
Long UK (1932)

Mary E HANSHEW and Thomas W HANSHEW (American)

For first writer details see Hamilton CLEEK and Thomas W HANSHEW 1857-1914

Citation Record: 4 Books 16 Short Stories in 1 Collection

The Frozen Flame - *First*
Simpkin UK (1920)

The Riddle Of The Frozen Flame - *First**
Doubleday US (1920)

The House Of The Seven Keys - *Last*
Hutchinson UK (1925)

The Riddle Of The Mysterious Light - *Collection 1*

has a novel with the same title and sixteen short stories.

Doubleday US (1921)

C

Mary E HANSHEW and Hazel Phillips HANSHEW (American)

Writers: Mary E HANSHEW and *Hazel Phillips HANSHEW*

The Riddle Of The Purple Emperor - *Only*

Simpkin UK (1918); Doubleday US (1919)

Thomas W HANSHEW 1857-1914 (American)

was an actor and a novelist who wrote many of the early *Nick CARTER* stories for pulp magazines. He was later the author of several novels and over eighty short stories, often located in England or the East, about both of which locales he appeared to know little. His main and enduring detective, however, is successfully and endearingly British. After *Thomas HANSHEW's* death, his wife and daughter continued to write more novels and short stories, using the same detective. They were, at first, published under the original byline but later they appeared under the name of his daughter or as apparently joint works.

Citation Record: 1 Book 27 Short Stories in 3 Collections

The Riddle Of The Night - *Only*

Doubleday US (1915); Simpkin UK (1916)

The Man Of The Forty Faces - *Collection 1*

Short stories - 12

Cassell UK (1910)

Cleek, The Master Detective - *Collection 1**

Doubleday US (1918)

Cleek Of Scotland Yard - *Collection 2*

Short stories - 7

Cassell UK (1914); Doubleday US (1914)

Cleek's Greatest Riddles - *Collection 3*

Short stories - 8

Simpkin Marshall UK (1916)

Cleek's Government Cases - *Collection 3**

Doubleday US (1917)

Clifton CLEEVE

British Male Amateur operating in England

William LEQUEUX 1864-1927 (British)

Invented 23 detectives - see Allan KENNEDY

Citation Record: 1 Book

The Bond Of Black - *Only*

White UK (1899); Dillingham US (1899)

Prof CLEGHORN

is a Professor of Anthropology and a marine biologist. He is a droll, chubby man of about sixty who simply likes to solve murder cases when he comes across them.

British Male Amateur operating in Scotland

Thomas MUIR (British)

Inventor of one other detective Roger CRAMMOND

Citation Record: 1 Book

Death Under Virgo - *Only*

Hutchinson UK (1952)

Frank CLEMONS

is one of the considerably large sub-species of cops (mainly American but sometimes British) who are tortured by angst. With a daughter dead and an ex-wife, it is no wonder that he introspects so much while on his first two cases. In his third book, suffering even further because his partner has just been killed, he leaves the Atlanta force and becomes a PI in New York, finding life just hell if he can't catch a few criminals every now and then.

American Male Private Detective operating in New York

Thomas H COOK (American)

Inventor of one other detective Tom JACKSON

Citation Record: 3 Books

Sacrificial Ground - *First*

Collins UK (1989)

Night Secrets - *Latest*

HarperCollins UK (1991)

Mr CLERIHEW

British Male Amateur operating in England

Warner ALLEN 1881-1969 (British)

Invented 3 detectives - see George B EDGEHILL and Aristide GOVIN

Citation Record: 1 Book

Mr Clerihew: Wine Merchant - *Only*

Methuen UK (1933)

Insp CLEVELAND

British Policeman operating in England

Sydney FOWLER 1874-1965 (British)

Invented 5 detectives - see Mr JELLIPOT

Citation Record: 2 Books

The Hanging Of Constance Hillier - *First*

Jarrolds UK (1931); Macaulay US (1932)

Arresting Delia - *Last*

Jarrolds UK (1933); Macaulay US (1933)

David CLEVELAND

British Male Amateur operating in England

Dick FRANCIS 1920- (British)

Invented 18 detectives - see Sid HALLEY

Citation Record: 1 Book

Slayride - *Only*

Joseph UK (1970); Harper & Row US (1971)

Rosemary CLEVELAND

Second detective of Pete TANNER

Capt CLEW

American Male Detective in Pulp Magazines operating in USA

ANON

Citation Record: 1 Book

Captain Clew, The Flying Detective - *Only*

Aldine (?)

Caleb CLICKETT

American Male Professional Investigator operating in USA

Allen GRAVES (American)

Citation Record: 1 Book

Caleb Clickett, The Great Detective; Or, Tracked By A Finger-Nail - *Only*

Laird & Lee US (1890)

Bob CLIFFORD

American Male Amateur operating in New York

Leroy SCOTT 1875-1929. (American)

Citation Record: 2 Books 7 Short Stories in 1 Collection

Mary Regan - *First*

Houghton UK (1918)

Folly's Gold - *Last*

Houghton UK (1926)

Partners Of The Night - *Collection 1*

Century US (1916); Nash UK (1917)

Gillian CLIFFORD

is a distant member of a wealthy family whose members meet with unexplained fatalities. Bothered but not bewildered, she investigates and comes up with an awful truth.

American Female Amateur operating in Massachusetts

Barbara PAUL (American)

Invented 8 detectives - see Lt TOOMEY

Citation Record: 1 Book

In-Laws And Outlaws - *Single*

Scribner's US (1990)

Death Elsewhere - *Single**

Piatkus UK (1991)

Cornelius CLIFT Jr

American Male Private Detective operating in Los Angeles

C

Sidekick: Winnie PRESTON
is the narrator of the detective's cases. She eventually becomes his fiancée.
American Female - Fiancée

Eric HEATH (American)
See main detective Dr Wade ANTHONY
Citation Record: 2 Books
Death Takes A Dive - *First*
Hillman-Curl US (1938)
Murder In The Museum - *Last*
Hillman-Curl US (1939)

Jere CLINCH
American Male Detective in Pulp Magazines operating in USA

Gilbert JEROME (American)
Invented 5 detectives - see Jack DONAHUE
Citation Record: 1 Selected Short Story
Jere Clinch, The Eagle-Eyed Detective; Or, Guarding The Demdike Millions
Old Cap Collier Library US (18??)

Rosamond CLINCH
British Female Amateur operating in England

Henry CECIL 1902-1976 (British)
Invented 4 detectives - see Col BRAIN
Citation Record: 1 Book
The Long Arm - *Only*
Joseph UK (1957); Harper & Row US (1957)

Hortense CLINTON
Female Amateur operating in several locations

Miriam-Ann HAGEN 1903-1984 (American)
Citation Record: 3 Books
Plant Me Now - *First*
Doubleday US (1947)
Murder - But Natch - *Last*
Doubleday US (1951)

Donald CLIVE
is a criminologist who takes up PI work.
American Male Private Detective operating in USA

Marjorie STAFFORD (American)
Citation Record: 1 Book
Death Plays The Gramophone - *Only*
Macmillan US (1953)

Edmond CLIVE
has an office on Vine and Hollywood Boulevards and, in his one outing, sets out to discover the killer of his girlfriend.
American Male Private Detective operating in California

Leigh BRACKETT 1915-1978 (American)
was born in Los Angeles. She was the author of many novels and short stories but wrote only five crime novels. She is perhaps most renowned, however, for her part in the composition, with Nobel Laureate, *William FAULKNER*, of the screen play for Howard Hawk's film of *Raymond CHANDLER's* novel, *THE BIG SLEEP*. She was later responsible for other screenplays and TV scripts.
Writer: Leigh Douglas HAMILTON
!See Appendix 2.
Other Detectives:
Walter SHERRIS   Michael VICKERS
Citation Record: 1 Book
No Good From A Corpse - *Only*
Coward McCann US (1944); Simon & Schuster UK (1989)

Insp CLOUSEAU
appears in novelizations of two films written by Blake Edwards and featuring Peter Sellers.
French Policeman operating in France

Frank WALDMAN ?-1990
Citation Record: 2 Books
The Pink Panther Strikes Again - *First*
Futura UK (1976); Ballantine US (1976)
The Return Of The Pink Panther - *Latest*
Futura UK (1977); Ballantine US (1977)

Kitty CLOVER
is, by clever detection, able to prevent her sister marrying a scoundrel.
American Female Amateur operating in New York

Ella Wheeler WILCOX 1850-1919 (American)
was born at Johnstown Center, Wisconsin. She completed her first novel at the age of ten and later became a prolific writer of verse.
Citation Record: 1 Book
Detective Kitty - *Only*
US (1903)

Nancy CLUE
is a delightful modern parody of all those early American schoolgirl detectives, typified by the popular *Nancy DREW*. She appears in books, with her chum, of course, that echo many of those early adventures, when the world was more simple than it is today.
American Female Amateur operating in USA
Sidekick: Nurse Cherry AIMLESS
is a native of Idaho, the close chum of *Nancy CLUE*, always at her side in her adventures.
American Female - Friend

Mavis MANEY (American)
Citation Record: 2 Books
The Case Of The Not-So-Nice Nurse - *First*
Cleis Press US (1994)
The Case Of The Good-For-Nothing Girlfriend - *Latest*
Cleis Press US (1994)

Daniel J CLUER
is a copybook American PI from a British author. He is said to be the boss of the Manhattan Investigation Bureau and his cases seem to involve high politics.
American Male Private Detective operating in New York
Sidekick: BODINSKY
is an ex-convict and an inept assistant.
British Male - Assistant

W B M FERGUSON 1881-1967 (British)
See main detective 'Biff' CORRIGAN
Citation Record: 2 Books
Escape To Eternity - *First*
Long UK (1944)
The Shayne Case - *Last*
Long UK (1947)

Sgt Caleb CLUFF
is a slow but thoughtful policeman, known to all in the region around the fictional town of Gunnershaw. Although murders seem to happen frequently, the good sergeant always solves them.
British Policeman operating in Yorkshire

Gil NORTH 1916- (British)
was born in Skipton, Yorkshire. He was educated at Ermysted's Grammar School, Skipton, and took a BA at Christ's College, Cambridge, 1938, followed by an MA, 1942. He served in the Colonial Service in Nigeria and the Cameroons, 1938-1955.
Writer: Geoffrey HORNE
Inventor of one other detective Supt Kofi KATT
Citation Record: 11 Books
Sergeant Cluff Stands Firm - *First*
Chapman & Hall UK (1960)

C

Sergeant Cluff Rings True - *Last*
Eyre & Spottiswoode UK (1972)

Asaph CLUME

American Male Amateur operating in Los Angeles

Raymond Leslie GOLDMAN 1895- (American)

Citation Record: 6 Books

The Murder Of Harvey Blake - *First*
Skeffington UK (1931)

The Purple Shells - *Last*
Ziff-Davis US (1947); Boardman UK (1948)

Joshua CLUNK

is not cast in the common mould. Plump, small and owl-like in appearance, he is a rather rascally solicitor, working from an office in Covent Garden and running a Gospel Hall in his spare time. A psalm-singing hypocrite with a passion for sucking sweets, his legal speciality consists of defending rogues and getting them off. Nevertheless he stands for his own kind of rough justice and, often using not quite legal methods, succeeds in solving cases, to the chagrin of the police.

The author sometimes introduced *Joshua CLUNK* as a transient character into books featuring his main detective, *Reggie FORTUNE*, where, as usual, he is at cross purposes with the police.

British Male Amateur operating in London

Sidekick: JONES
is used by the devious *CLUNK* to ferret out useful information.
British Female - Employee

Sidekick: John SCOTT
works in the double-dealing *CLUNK's* office and is sometimes used by him as a legman.
British Male - Employee

Stooge: Supt BELL
is long-suffering, for his investigations invariably lead him across the path of *CLUNK*, one of the most cunning detective-rogues in fiction. The author sometimes introduced him into his series featuring his main detective, *Reggie FORTUNE*.
British Male

H C BAILEY 1878-1961 (British)

Invented 4 detectives - see Dr Reginald FORTUNE

Citation Record: 9 Books

Garstons - *First*
Methuen UK (1930)

The Garston Murder Case - *First**
Doubleday US (1930)

Shrouded Death - *Last*
Macdonald UK (1950); Doubleday US (1950)

CLUTHA

is a hardboiled private detective who is employed by a Glasgow shipyard to deal with the crime that abounds in the area.

British Male Private Detective operating in Glasgow

Hugh MUNRO (British)

Writer: Hugh MacFarlane MUNRO

Citation Record: 6 Books

Who Told Clutha? - *First*
Macdonald UK (1958); Washburn US (1958)

Get Clutha - *Last*
Hale UK (1974)

CLYDE

American Male Detective in Pulp Magazines operating in USA

OLD SLEUTH (American)

Invented 40 detectives - see Brant ADAMS

Citation Record: 1 Book

Clyde, The Resolute Detective; Or, His Own Mystery - *Only*
Parlor Car US (1897)

Viscount CLYMPING

Second detective of Insp Gregory PELLEW

Prof Ira COBB

is a Professor of English who has resigned his post after a bad fight with a fellow instructor, who, he discovers, was his wife's lover. Now he lives alone in a house by the sea in Nantucket, giving occasional lectures and writing detective stories under a pseudonym.

American Male Sleuth operating in Nantucket

Sidekick: Steve BARNES
is a young student who rises to become an Assistant Professor at Columbia. He is a most earnest assistant and narrates the cases.
American Male - Assistant

Stooge: Lt ROMANO
of the local police brings his difficult cases to *COBB* for solution.
American Male

Roy WINSOR 1912-1987 (American)

Citation Record: 3 Books

The Corpse That Walked - *First*
Fawcett US (1974)

Always Lock Your Bedroom Door - *Last*
Fawcett US (1976)

Matt COBB

was formerly in the military police, but is now a company detective for a TV network, in whose purlieus he encounters various kinds of nastiness. The narrator of his own cases, he sometimes seems arrogant, but his heart is in the right place and he merely aims to improve the state of the world in his own little way. On solving a case he assembles the suspects, in the good old-fashioned way, to tell them whodunnit. It is, of course, one of those foolish enough to be present.

American Male Professional Investigator operating in USA

Sidekick: SPOT
is an attack-trained Samoyed, one of the more useful kinds of sidekick in the business.
Male - Pet Dog

William L DEANDREA 1952- (American)

was born in Port Chester, New York, and graduated with a BS from Syracuse University, New York, 1974. He received the Mystery Writers of America Edgar Allan Poe award twice, 1978 and 1979.

Writer: William Louis DEANDREA

Other Byline: Philip DEGRAVE

Other Detectives:
Russ GARRETT　Ron GENTRY
Commiss Theodore ROOSEVELT

Citation Record: 5 Books

Killed In The Ratings - *First*
Harcourt Brace UK (1978)

Killed With A Passion - *First*
Doubleday US (1983)

Killed On The Rocks - *Latest*
Mysterious Press US (1990)

Constance COBBLE

is a writer who sleuths.

American Female Amateur operating in New England

Stanton FORBES 1923- (American)

was born in Kansas City, Missouri. She was educated at Wichita High School North, Kansas, Oklahoma State University and the University of Chicago. Under her real name and two main pseudonyms she has written at least forty genre books, whose situations usually involve local murders in small American towns.

Writer: Deloris Florine Stanton FORBES

Citation Record: 1 Book

The Last Will And Testament Of Constance Cobble - *Single*
Doubleday US (1980); Hale UK (1980)

Insp COCKRILL

is the best known of the author's several detectives. He is more the eccentric amateur than the normal policeman, being irascible, clever, shabbily dressed and, he admits, quite a coward. Smoking endless cigarettes, he is excellent at ferreting out the truth of a case from the usual mess of red herrings laid by this cunning author. He appears in other books with one of the author's other detectives, *Insp CHARLESWORTH.*

British Policeman operating in Kent

Mary Christianna BRAND 1907-1988 (British)

Invented 6 detectives - see Insp COCKRILL and Insp CHARLESWORTH

Citation Record: 5 Books 3 Short Stories in 1 Collection

Heads You Lose - *First*
is the story of a jealous spinster who is murdered and her behatted head is found in a ditch – after she has said she 'wouldn't be caught dead in a ditch wearing it'.
Lane UK (1941); Dodd, Mead US (1942)

The Three-Cornered Halo - *Last*
Joseph UK (1957); Scribner's US (1957)

What Dread Hand? - *Collection 1*
This collection of fifteen of the author's short stories contains three with *Insp COCKRILL.*
Joseph UK (1968)

Insp COCKRILL

Second detective of Insp CHARLESWORTH

Insp COCKRILL and Insp CHARLESWORTH

British Policemen operating in England

Mary Christianna BRAND 1907-1988 (British)
was born in Malaya. During her career she was a children's governess, dancer, model and secretary. As an author, she wrote novels and short stories as well as filmscripts, plays and children's' books. She is best known for her novel, *Green for Danger*, in which there was one of the most ingenious murders ever devised. She wrote many detective stories and was a sometime Chairwoman of the Crime Writers' Association.

Writer: Mary Christianna Milne LEWIS

Other Byline: Mary Ann ASHE

Other Detectives:

Insp BLOCK	Insp CHARLESWORTH
Insp CHUCKY	Insp COCKRILL
Mrs Dorinda JONES	

Citation Record: 2 Books

Death Of Jezebel - *First*
Dodd, Mead US (1948); Lane UK (1949)

London Particular - *Last*
Joseph UK (1952)

Fog Of Doubt - *Last**
Scribner's US (1953)

CODY

operates out of Fort Worth, Texas. Although he dresses like a cowboy, he is a PI who is also something of an intellectual.

American Male Private Detective operating in Texas

James M REASONER 1953?- (American)

Citation Record: 1 Book

Texas Wind - *Single*
Manor US (1980)

John CODY

American Male Sleuth operating in several locations

Jim CASE (American)

For writer details see Rock DUGAN

Citation Record: 7 Books

Assault Into Libya - *First*
Warner US (1986)

Sword Of The Prophet - *Latest*
Warner US (1988)

George COE

Second detective of David MALLIN

Dr Daniel Webster COFFEE and Lt Max RITTER

Dr COFFEE is a pathologist and the director of the Pasteur Hospital, Northbank, somewhere in the Midwest of the United States. He solves many cases, often with his microscope's evidence, for his friend in the local police force.

American Male Professional Investigator and American Policeman operating in USA

Sidekick: Motilal MOOKERJI
is as imperturbable and ingenious as would be expected of a Hindu assistant.

Indian Male - Assistant

Lawrence G BLOCHMAN 1900-1975 (American)
was born in San Diego, California, and graduated from the University of California, Berkeley, 1921. He had considerable expertise in forensic pathology and lived in Japan and India, working as an editor and feature writer for newspapers. He used his experiences in Asia as settings for many of his stories. He received the Mystery Writers of America Edgar Allan Poe award, 1950 and its Special award, 1958.

Writer: Lawrence Goldtree BLOCHMAN

Other Detectives:

Bill GABRIEL	Det KILKENNY
Roderick POPLAR	Insp Leonidas PRIKE

Citation Record: 1 Book 18 Short Stories in 2 Collections

Recipe For Homicide - *Only*
Lippincott US (1952); Hammond UK (1952)

Diagnosis: Homicide - *Collection 1*
Short stories - 8
Lippincott US (1950)

Clues For Dr Coffee - *Collection 2*
Short stories - 10
Lippincott US (1964)

Sgt/Insp John COFFIN

is a good example of the new type of police detective beginning to appear in English detective novels during the 1950s. He works a 'manor' in South London, somewhere near the river, rising in the ranks throughout the series, and acquiring on the way and then separating from an actress wife. His cases, although superficially modern, often involve the slightly bizarre, even gothic, circumstances so beloved of this author. He shared the detection in his first three books with *Insp WINTER,* but was on his own after that.

British Policeman operating in London

Sidekick: Sgt DOVE
is dull, practical and knowledgeable about his patch. A good legman, he makes a nice foil and useful contrast to his imaginative, thoughtful superior.

British Male - Subordinate

Gwendoline BUTLER 1922- (British)
was born in London. She was educated in London and took a BA in History at Oxford. Under her own name and pseudonyms, she is the author of about fifty crime and detective novels. She has received several awards for her work, including the Crime Writers Association Silver Dagger, 1973.

Writer: Gwendoline Williams BUTLER

Other Byline: Jennie MELVILLE

Inventor of one other detective pair Sgt/Insp John COFFIN and Insp/Supt William WINTER

Citation Record: 18 Books

Death Lives Next Door - *First*
Bles UK (1960)

Dine And Be Dead - *First**
Macmillan US (1960)

The Coffin Tree - *Latest*
HarperCollins UK (1994)

C

C

Sgt/Insp John COFFIN and Insp/Supt William WINTER

worked together on the first three cases in which *John COFFIN* appeared. From then on, the latter became the author's only detective.

British Policemen operating in England

Gwendoline BUTLER 1922- (British)

See main detective Sgt/Insp John COFFIN

Citation Record: 3 Books

Dead In A Row - *First*
Bles UK (1957)

The Murdering Kind - *Last*
Bles UK (1958); Roy US (1964)

Nicholas COFFIN

is an alchemist in Rome in the 1400s. That was the time of the Borgias, when murder, it is generally acknowledged, was not unusual. He is certainly better equipped than most of his fellow-citizens to do the sleuthing.

Male Amateur operating in Rome

C J STEVERMER 1955- (American)

Writer: Caroline J STEVERMER

Citation Record: 2 Books

Death Of A Borgia - *First*
Ace US (1980)

The Duke And The Veil - *Latest*
Ace US (1981)

Peter COFFIN and Col BLACK

American Male Amateurs operating in USA

Peter COFFIN 1906-1983 (American)

For writer details see Sam CLAY

Citation Record: 1 Book

The Search For My Great-Uncle's Head - *Only*
Doubleday US (1937)

Samson COGG

Male Amateur

Ronald CLARK 1903-

Writer: Ronald Harry CLARK

Citation Record: 16 Short Stories in 1 Collection

Some Adventures Of Samson Cogg - *Collection 1*
Not all the stories are criminous.
Goose ? (1975)

Insp Andrew COGGIN

solves two cases of murder, one monastical, the other operatical: they are both diabolical.

Canadian Policeman operating in Toronto

Sidekick: Sgt Fred SUMP

American Male - Subordinate

John REEVES 1926- (Canadian)

Citation Record: 2 Books

Murder Before Matins - *First*
Doubleday US (1984)

Murder With Muskets - *Latest*
Doubleday US (1985)

Insp COGHILL

British Policeman operating in England

Clive EGLETON 1927- (British)

was born in South Harrow, Middlesex. He graduated from the Army Staff College, Camberley, Surrey, 1957 and became a professional soldier, 1945-1975, rising to the rank of Lieutenant Colonel. He has worked all over the world and has had experience of Intelligence work, the flavour of which permeates his excellent novels.

Writer: Clive Frederick EGLETON

Other Detectives:
David GARNETT — Charles WINTER

Citation Record: 1 Book

A Conflict Of Interests - *Single*
Atheneum US (1983); Hodder & Stoughton UK (1984)

Insp COHEN

investigates the death of a hang-glider.

British Policeman operating in Glasgow

Francis LYALL (British)

Inventor of one other detective Supt MASON

Citation Record: 1 Book

Flying High - *Single*
HarperCollins UK (1991)

Larry COHEN

Second detective of John COMADAY

Mr Sherlock COHEN

was a *Sherlock HOLMES* parody who worked in the clothing business and with his partner, indulged in 'detectival misadventures' in a radio programme entitled 'Cohen the Detective', broadcast during 1943 from Station WJZ, New York. [This intriguing information is given in the introduction to *THE MISADVENTURES OF SHERLOCK HOLMES* (Editor; *Ellery QUEEN*).]

American Male Professional Amateur operating in New York

Sidekick: Mr WASSERMAN

acts as the *WATSON*-like parody assistant.

American Male - Partner

UNKNOWN

No citations

Al COLBY

American Male Private Detective operating in Mexico/South America

David DODGE 1910- (American)

was born in Berkeley, California. He is an accountant and a free-lance.

Writer: David Francis DODGE

Other Detectives:
John Abraham LINCOLN — John ROBIE
Whit WHITNEY

Citation Record: 3 Books

The Long Escape - *First*
Random House US (1948); Joseph UK (1950)

The Red Tassel - *Latest*
Random House US (1950); Joseph UK (1951)

Elsa COLBY

American Female Amateur operating in Chicago

Harry Stephen KEELER 1890-1967 (American)

Invented 14 detectives - see Angus MACWHORTER

Citation Record: 1 Book

The Case Of The Lavender Gripsack - *Only*
Phoenix Press US (1944)

The Lavender Gripsack - *Only**
Ward, Lock UK (1941)

Supt COLE

investigates the death of a rich spinster whose body is exhumed, as a result of village tattle, and is indeed found to be rather full of arsenic.

British Policeman operating in England

Milward KENNEDY 1894-1968 (British)

Invented 6 detectives - see Sir George BULL

Citation Record: 1 Book

Poison In The Parish - *Only*
Gollancz UK (1935)

Calvert COLE

American Male Detective in Pulp Magazines operating in USA

T W KING (American)

Citation Record: 1 Selected Short Story

Calvert Cole, Of California, The Pacific Slope Detective
Old Cap Collier Library US (18??)

C

Dr Carter COLE

is an early example of a 'casebook' detective. He appeared in stories in the pulps, especially *Dime Detective.*

American Male Amateur operating in USA

Frederick C DAVIS 1902-1977 (American)

Invented 4 detectives - see Luke SPEARE and Schyler COLE

Citation Record: 3 Selected Short Stories

Blood On The Block
In 'Dime Detective' US (1933)

The Case Of The Vanishing Venus
is a novelette published in the same volume as the following story
Sharman Ellis US (193?)

The Case Of The Concrete Corpse
is a novelette published in the same volume as the preceding story
Sharman Ellis US (193?)

Elvis COLE

is a Vietnam War veteran who loves his rather infantile past and seems to want to stay there. Even so, he is pretty literary for a shamus in West Hollywood, and not without humour and intellect.

American Male Private Detective operating in Hollywood

Sidekick: PIKE
is a 'survivalist' who makes a nice contrast and useful assistant to the detective.
American Male - Assistant

Robert CRAIS (American)

Adopter of one other detective Philip MARLOWE

Citation Record: 2 Books

The Monkey's Raincoat - *First*
Bantam US (1987); Piatkus UK (1989)

Stalking The Angel - *Latest*
Bantam US (1989); Piatkus UK (1990)

George COLE and Amanda DREW

British Male Amateur and British Female Amateur operating in England

Josephine BELL 1897-1987 (British)

Invented 10 detectives - see Dr David WINTRINGHAM

Citation Record: 1 Book

The Innocent - *Only*
Hodder & Stoughton UK (1983)

A Deadly Place To Stay - *Only**
Walker US (1984)

Harlan COLE

American Male Sleuth operating in Texas

Jack DONAHUE 1917- (American)

!See Appendix 2.

Real Name: Jack Clifford DONAHUE

Citation Record: 2 Books

Pray To The Hustlers' God - *First*
In 'Reader's Digest' UK (1977)

The Lady Loved Too Well - *Last*
McGraw UK (1978)

Lewis COLE

used to work for the Department of Defense until he was involved, by others, in something decidedly underhand. Now, at the age of thirty-five and a civilian magazine columnist, he is still getting involved with greed, murder and a reasonable number of dead bodies.

American Male Amateur operating in USA

Brendan DUBOIS (American)

Citation Record: 2 Books

Dead Sand - *First*
Otto Penzler US (1994)

Black Tide - *Latest*
Otto Penzler US (1995)

Marty COLE

American Male Private Detective operating in USA

Ben GRANT 1927- (American)

For writer details see Jeanne DONOVAN

Citation Record: 1 Book

Alice Dies Twice - *Only*
Major US (1975)

Schyler COLE

Second detective of Luke SPEARE

Capt/Insp COLIN

American Policeman operating in New York/Louisiana

Clement WOOD 1888-1950 (American)

Invented 3 detectives - see Skelton KYNE

Citation Record: 2 Books

The Shadow From The Bogue - *First*
Dutton US (1928)

The Tabloid Murders - *Last*
Macaulay US (1930)

Matthew COLL

!See Appendix 2.

British Male Amateur operating in England/Italy

Roy Harley LEWIS (British)

Citation Record: 5 Books

A Cracking Of Spines - *First*
Hale UK (1980); St Martin's US (1982)

Death In Verona - *Latest*
Hale UK (1989); St Martin's US (1989)

Insp Hugh COLLIER

British Policeman operating in England

Moray DALTON (British)

Inventor of one other detective Norman GLADE

Citation Record: 14 Books

One By One They Disappeared - *First*
Jarrolds UK (1929); Harper & Row US (1929)

Death Of A Spinster - *Last*
Low UK (1951)

Mr COLLIN

Male Amateur operating in England/Italy

Frank HELLER 1866-1947 (American)

Writer: Martin Gunnar SERNER

Citation Record: 2 Books 13 Short Stories in 2 Collections

The Grand Duke's Finances - *First*
Crowell US (1924); Jarrolds UK (1925)

Mr Collin Is Ruined - *Last*
Crowell US (1925)

The London Adventures Of Mr Collin - *Collection 1*
Short stories - 7
Crowell US (1924)

The Perilous Transactions Of Mr Collin - *Collection 1**
Lane UK (1924)

The Strange Adventures Of Mr Collin - *Collection 2*
Short stories - 6
Crowell US (1926)

Jem COLLINGHAM

British Male Amateur operating in England

Florence WARDEN 1857-1929 (British)

Invented 4 detectives - see Insp MAYNARD

Citation Record: 1 Book

A Sensational Case - *Only*
Ward, Lock UK (1898)

COLLINS and MCKECHNIE

American Male Sleuths operating in Los Angeles

Bert HITCHENS and Dolores HITCHENS (American)

were a husband-and-wife team. She wrote many criminous works on her own, but she also collaborated with her hus-

C

band, who had been a railway detective, on other stories dealing with crimes on the railway.

Writers: Hubert Allen HITCHENS and Julia Clara Catherine Dolores Birk Olsen HITCHENS 1907-1973

Other Detectives:
John FARREL
Michael KERNEHAN, Vic MOINE and Chuck REVES

Citation Record: 2 Books

FOB Murder - *First*
Doubleday US (1955); Boardman UK (1957)

The Man Who Followed Women - *Last*
Doubleday US (1959); Boardman UK (1960)

Emily COLLINS

Second detective of Dr Mary FINNEY

Henrietta O'Dwyer COLLINS

is known to her friends, and they are many, as Henrie O. She was a journalist and is now just a gal who sleuths. If ever you're in trouble, this is somebody to have at your side, although she would be the first to admit she's new to the work.

American Female Amateur operating in USA

Carolyn G HART 1936- (American)

See main detective Annie LAURANCE

Citation Record: 2 Books

Dead Man's Island - *First*
Bantam US (1993)

Scandal In Fair Haven - *Latest*
Bantam US (1994)

John COLLINS

is an US Army Intelligence detective whose cover is that of a boogie-woogie piano player. He appeared in several stories in *Black Mask Magazine* towards the end of its days.

American Male Detective in Pulp Magazines operating in USA

Norbert DAVIS 1909-1949 (American)

Invented 8 detectives - see Ben SHALEY

No citations

Insp Omar COLLINS

is a member of an unidentified police force somewhere in the middle of the USA.

American Policeman operating in USA

Ellery QUEEN 1917- (American)

Inventor of one other detective Insp TARR and Ann NELSON
For writer details see Sheriff Joe BAIN

Citation Record: 1 Book

The Mad Man Theory - *Single*
Pocket Books US (1966); Kinnell UK (1988)

Wilkie COLLINS

is, indeed, the famous British novelist whose classic novel started the vogue for crime. Here he has been transmuted into a detective by an almost equally famous author.

British Male Amateur operating in England

John Dickson CARR 1906-1977 (American)

Invented 16 detectives - see Dr Gideon FELL

Citation Record: 1 Book

The Hungry Goblin - *Only*
Harper & Row US (1972); Hamilton UK (1972)

Eve COLMAN

Second detective of Seth COLMAN

Seth COLMAN and Eve COLMAN

are a husband-and-wife team.

American Male Private Detective and American Female Amateur operating in New York

Lewis PADGETT 1914-1958 (American)

Writer: Henry KUTTNER
Other Byline: Henry KUTTNER
Citation Record: 1 Book

The Brass Ring - *Only*
Duell US (1946); Low UK (1947)

Murder In Brass - *Only**
Bantam US (1947)

Kat COLORADO

American Female Private Detective operating in Sacramento/Las Vegas

Karen KIJEWSKI (American)

Citation Record: 6 Books

Katwalk - *First*
St Martin's US (1989)

Alley Kat Blues - *Latest*
Pocket Books US (1995)

Aphra COLQUHOUN

works in a publishing house and one morning finds her boss dead. Since she herself is out on bail for another offence and a natural suspect, she has to clear herself by finding the real killer. She does, narrowly avoiding peril herself, and generally unearthing shady business in the financial world along the way.

British Female Amateur operating in London

Bronte ADAMS (British)

Citation Record: 1 Book

If Looks Could Kill - *Single*
Virago UK (1995)

Capt COLSON

operates in Europe during the Second World War.

British Male Professional Investigator operating in France/Holland

Alan WHITE 1920- (British)

See main detective Det Insp ARMSTRONG

Citation Record: 5 Books

The Long Night's Walk - *First*
Hodder & Stoughton UK (1968); Harcourt Brace US (1969)

The Long Silence - *Last*
Barrie & Jenkins UK (1976); Mason/Charter US (1977)

Commiss Thatcher COLT

comes from a wealthy family and rises to the top in the ranks of New York's finest. He has carried out several successful investigations for which, it seems, he has got little credit and his stories are now being told by his secretary and part-time sidekick. *Thatcher COLT* is a bachelor who lives in a five-story house on West 70th Street. He has his own gym, a library of 15,000 crime books, and a choice stock of wines. He also has the reputation of being the best-dressed man in New York. In an era when most of the good fictional detectives were amateurs, *COLT* is a consummate professional, solving his cases, not just by police procedure, but by using his own considerable powers of reasoning.

American Policeman operating in New York

Sidekick: Tony ABBOTT
is *COLT's* secretary. He narrates his cases and generally acts as a kind of assistant in the detective work.
American Male - Secretary

Stooge: Attorney Merle K DOUGHERTY
frequently clashes with the sleuth. He is a bachelor, a gourmand, a lover of noise and a routine would-be seducer of chorus girls. He is also overweight, homespun, eloquent, and usually wrong in his deductions.
American Male

Anthony ABBOT 1893-1952 (American)

Writer: Charles Fulton OURSLER

Citation Record: 8 Books

About The Murder Of Geraldine Foster - *First*
Covici US (1930)

The Murder Of Geraldine Foster - *First**
Collins UK (1931)

The Shudders - *Last*
Farrar, Straus US (1943)

Deadly Secret - *Last**
Collins UK (1943)

Stanford COLTON

Second detective of Prof Willis RAVENDEN

Thornley COLTON

is a blind detective who appeared on the American scene soon after the success of the British blind detective, *Max CARRAOS.*

American Male Professional Amateur operating in New York

Clinton H STAGG 1890-1916 (American)

Writer: Clinton Holland STAGG

Citation Record: 1 Book 8 Short Stories in 1 Collection

Silver Sandals - *Only*
Watt US (1916)

Thornton Colton, Blind Reader Of Hearts - *Only**
Simpkin UK (1915)

Thornley Colton, Blind Detective - *Collection 1*
Watt US (1923)

Stosh COLTRAY

American Male Sleuth operating in several locations

David ALEXANDER (American)

Citation Record: 4 Books

Hitler's Legacy - *First*
Leisure Books US (1989)

Pay The Devil - *Latest*
Leisure Books US (1990)

Lt COLUMBO

appears in novelizations, penned by several authors, of episodes from one of the most successful and endearing of all TV detective series. As the man in the old raincoat and with the old Peugot automobile, the small sleuth who never stops talking to his prime suspect is in danger of becoming legendary. Two books are cited, for illustrative purposes.

American Policeman operating in USA

Lee HAYS (American)

Citation Record: 1 Book

A Deadly State Of Mind - *Single*
Popular Library US (1976)

Bill MAGEE and Craig SCHENK (American)

Citation Record: 1 Book

Columbo And The Samurai Sword - *Single*
Black US (1980)

David COLWYN

British Male Amateur operating in England

Arthur J REES 1872-1942 (British)

Invented 3 detectives - see Insp LUCKRAFT

Citation Record: 2 Books

The Shrieking Pit - *First*
Lane UK (1919); Lane US (1919)

The Hand In The Dark - *Last*
Lane UK (1920); Lane US (1920)

John COMADAY and Larry COHEN

American Male Sleuths operating in New York

E V CUNNINGHAM 1914- (American)

Invented 4 detectives - see Det Sgt Masao MASUTO

Citation Record: 2 Books

Penelope - *First*
Doubleday US (1965); Deutsch UK (1966)

Margie - *Last*
Morrow US (1966); Deutsch UK (1968)

Oilock COMBS

is one of the earliest of the *Sherlock HOLMES* parodies.

Male Professional Amateur

Sidekick: Dr SPOTSON
is his parody *WATSON*-like assistant.

Male - Assistant

W B KAHN (American)

Citation Record: 1 Selected Short Story

More Adventures Of Oilock Combs: The Succored Beauty - *Parody 1*

An early American example of a *Sherlock HOLMES* parody. It appeared in the October issue of the magazine.
In 'The Smart Set' US (1905)

Shearlock COMBS

is a *Sherlock HOLMES* parody.

British Male Professional Amateur operating in London

Sidekick: Dr WITSEND
is his parody *WATSON*-like assistant.

British Male - Assistant

Stephen CLARKSON

Citation Record: 1 Selected Short Story

The Kimberley Diamond Mine Substitution Scandal - *Parody 1*
Privately printed (1970)

Insp COMFORT

British Policeman operating in England

Marten CUMBERLAND 1892-1972 (British)

See main detective Commissaire Saturnin DAX

Citation Record: 1 Selected Short Story

The Diary Of Death
was first published in an anthology, *The Best Detective Stories of the Year 1928* and later appeared in other anthologies and in *Ellery Queen's Mystery Magazine* for January 1943.
Faber UK (1929)

Steve CONACHER

operates from an office on 45th Street, Manhattan, and specialises in skip-tracing, most of which involves elementary detection. Tough he is, however, arriving at his solutions by brawn rather than excessive work in the upper story.

American Male Private Detective operating in New York/Paris

Adam KNIGHT 1908-1981 (American)

For writer details see Mike WELLS

Citation Record: 8 Books

Murder For Madame - *First*
Crown US (1951)

Triple Slay - *Last*
Signet US (1959)

CONDON

Second detective of Tom CANE

Bart CONDOR

is an American PI created by a British author in the era when that seemed possible.

American Male Private Detective operating in New York

Wade WRIGHT (British)

See main detective Paul CAMERON

Citation Record: 7 Books

Blood In The Ashes - *First*
Hale UK (1964)

Two Faces Of Death - *Last*
Hale UK (1970)

Timothy CONE

of the Haldering Detective Agency specialises in solving crimes in the world of high finance, which usually involves the deaths of high financiers.

American Male Private Detective operating in New York

C

Lawrence SANDERS 1920- (American)
Invented 6 detectives - see Ex-Plce Edward X DELANEY
Citation Record: 3 Books
The Timothy Files - *First*
Putnam US (1987); New English Library UK (1988)
Timothy's Game - *Latest*
Putnam US (1988); New English Library UK (1988)

Capt CONFETTI
British Male Amateur operating in London

F J DEE (British)
Citation Record: 6 Short Stories in 1 Collection
Captain Confetti - *Collection 1*
Simpkin UK (1928)

Peter CONGDON
American Male Private Detective operating in Philadelphia

Hillary WAUGH 1920- (American)
Invented 7 detectives - see Ch Fred FELLOWS
Citation Record: 1 Book
Run When I Say Go - *Only*
Doubleday US (1969); Gollancz UK (1969)

Jake CONGER
American Male Sleuth operating in USA

Ron GOULART 1933- (American)
Invented 15 detectives - see Jake PACE and Hildy PACE
Citation Record: 3 Books
A Talent For The Invisible - *First*
Daw US (1973)
Hello, Lemuria, Hello - *Latest*
Daw US (1979)

Rocco CONIGLIARO
visits his Italian family in Edinburgh and becomes drawn into investigating the murder of a theatre director, which seems to have political undercurrents.
American Male Private Detective operating in USA/Scotland

Gordon DE MARCO (American)
See main detective Riley KOVACHS
Citation Record: 1 Book
Murder At The Fringe - *Single*
Polygon US (1987)

Dan CONNELL
American Male Sleuth operating in California

Jack FOXX 1943- (American)
For writer details see NAMELESS DETECTIVE
Inventor of one other detective Fergus O'HARA
Citation Record: 2 Books
The Jade Figurine - *First*
Bobbs US (1972)
Dead Run - *Last*
Bobbs US (1975)

David CONNELL
British Male Amateur operating in England

John WEATHERHEAD (British)
Citation Record: 2 Books
A Force Of Innocence - *First*
Harrap UK (1966)
The Sacred Shaft - *Last*
Harrap UK (1967)

Shean CONNELL
plays the piano for fun but has to earn his living as a PI. He appeared also in short stories in *Detective Stories.*
American Male Private Detective operating in Reno
Sidekick: Lester HOYT
American Male - Assistant

Roger TORREY (American)
Invented 7 detectives - see Pat MULLANCY
Citation Record: 1 Book
42 Days For Murder - *Only*
Hillman-Curl US (1938)

'Doc' CONNOR
does his sleuthing on and around race-tracks, where crimes are legion.
American Male Amateur operating in New York/Cuba

Jack DOLPH 1894-1962 (American)
Citation Record: 5 Books
Odds-On Murder - *First*
Morrow US (1948); Boardman UK (1949)
Dead Angel - *Last*
Doubleday US (1953); Boardman UK (1954)

CONNORS
Male Sleuth

Samuel M GARDENHIRE 1885-1923
Writer: Samuel Major GARDENHIRE
Citation Record: 8 Short Stories in 1 Collection
The Long Arm - *Collection 1*
Harper & Row UK (1906)

Al CONNORS
American Male Amateur operating in USA

Raoul WHITFIELD 1897-1945 (American)
Invented 3 detectives - see Ben JARDINN
Citation Record: 1 Book
The Virgin Kills - *Only*
Knopf US (1932)

Liz CONNORS
Second detective of Det Jack LINGEMANN

Red CONNORS
is a stuntman in the movies who is hired to do some private investigating.
American Male Amateur operating in Mexico

John Carroll DALY 1889-1958 and C H WADDELL (American)
Citation Record: 1 Book
Two-Gun Gerta - *Single*
Chelsea US (1926)

Norman CONQUEST
was a pale copy of *Simon TEMPLAR* and appeared also in (uncited) short stories.
British Male Sleuth operating in England

Berkeley GRAY 1885-1965 (British)
Adopter of one other detective Sexton BLAKE
For writer details see Insp William (The Grouser) BEEKE
Citation Record: 51 Books
Vultures, Ltd - *First*
Collins UK (1938)
Conquest Calls The Tune - *Last*
Hale UK (1968)

Claire CONRAD
American Amateur operating in Los Angeles

Melody Johnson HOWE 1944?- (American)
Writer: Melody Johnson HOWE
Citation Record: 2 Books
The Mother Shadow - *First*
Viking US (1989); Deutsch UK (1990)
Beauty Dies - *Latest*
Viking US (1994)

Clive 'Dormouse' CONRAD
is one of that large species of British crook-detectives, working sometimes for and sometimes outside the law. Tougher

and rougher than *A J RAFFLES,* he is head of the Conrad Detective Agency in London, which acts as a cover for some of his more unlawful activities. Even so, he only steals from those who deserve to be stolen from. The police rather like him, although they would dearly like to catch him.
!See Appendix 2.

British Male Private Detective operating in London

Sidekick: Alice FAVENDEN
is the detective's beautiful partner. She becomes his wife and does useful work in covering up for him and generally bamboozling the police.

British Female - Wife

Frank KING 1892-1958 (British)

Invented 6 detectives - see Insp CHAMBERS

Citation Record: 20 Books

Enter The Dormouse - *First*
Hale UK (1936)

The Case Of The Frightened Brother - *Last*
Hale UK (1959)

Det CONROY and Det MCCARTHY

American Policemen operating in Chicago

Paul THORNE (American)

Citation Record: 1 Book

Murder In The Fog - *Only*
Penn US (1929)

Barney CONROY

tangles with crooked gamblers and their mobs.

American Male Private Detective operating in Las Vegas

Al FRAY (American)

Writer: Ralph SALAWAY

Citation Record: 1 Book

The Dame's The Game - *Only*
Popular Library US (1960)

Insp Thomas CONROY

American Policeman operating in New York

Herbert ASBURY 1891-1963 (American)

Citation Record: 2 Books

The Devil Of Pei-Ling - *First*
Macy-Masius US (1927)

The Crimson Rope - *First**
Jarrolds UK (1928)

The Tick Of The Clock - *Last*
Macy-Masius US (1928); Brentano's UK (1928)

Steve CONSIDINE

Second detective of Mike ZACHARIAS

Dr CONSTANTINE

British Male Amateur operating in England

Molly THYNNE (British)

Citation Record: 3 Books

The Crime At The "Noah's Ark" - *First*
Nelson UK (1931)

He Dies And Makes No Sign - *Last*
Hutchinson UK (1933)

Dora CONTI

is plump, pretty and married. She is really far too cuddly to be the very shrewd investigator of insurance frauds that she is. In her one appearance to date she has to deal with an enormous scam and three murders to boot, while keeping herself, with some difficulty, from breaking the seventh commandment with a too friendly cop. Altogether one of the author's most likeable creations!

American Female Professional Investigator operating in New York

Lawrence SANDERS 1920- (American)

Invented 6 detectives - see Ex-Plce Edward X DELANEY

Citation Record: 1 Book

The Seventh Commandment - *Single*
Putnam US (1991) ; New English Library UK (1991)

The CONTINENTAL OP

is one of detective fiction's greatest legends. Created by one of the genre's true innovators, he is, in fact, nameless in the three novels and few short stories in which he appears. He derives his name, posthumously as it were, from the fact that he is a private eye for the Continental Detective Agency in San Francisco, for whom the author took as a model a Pinkerton man, James Wright. Although there had been many fictional private detectives in preceding decades, it is fair to say that, on the whole, they were of a different sort. They were often wealthy amateurs or adventurers. Sometimes they were endowed with special or even amazing powers; or they were blind or lame. Occasionally they were doing it for their country; or they were doing it for remorse; or they just hated criminals and believed in justice. *The CONTINENTAL OP* is none of these. He is the progenitor, the very prototype of the modern American private eye, a professional detective who walks in the gutter even if at times he may lift his eyes to the stars. He does his detecting for the money and he is clinical in his approach. The criminals are patients, victims even, to be sought out, sympathised with perhaps, but brought to book according to the rules. *The OP* is described a being 'fat and forty', but he is also 'the toughest, hardest, strongest, fastest, sharpest, biggest, wisest, meanest man west of the Mississippi River' and he gave the next generation of private eyes any ethics and morals they might have. Comprehensive citation is difficult, as the short stories and even one novel appeared in pulp magazines between 1929 and 1934. The three novels and four main original collections of stories are however, all cited. They have appeared in many forms since.

American Male Private Detective operating in San Francisco

Dashiell HAMMETT 1894-1961 (American)

Invented 7 detectives - see Sam SPADE

Citation Record: 3 Books 14 Short Stories in 4 Collections

Red Harvest - *Book 1*
Knopf US (1929); Knopf UK (1929)

The Dain Curse - *Book 2*
Knopf US (1943); Knopf UK (1943)

$106,000 Blood Money - *Book 3*
Spivak US (1943)

Blood Money - *Book 3**
World US (1943)

The Big Knockover - *Book 3**
Spivak US (1948)

Hammett Homicides - *Collection 1*
This collection of six of the author's stories contains four with *The CONTINENTAL OP.*
Short stories - 4
Spivak US (1946)

Dead Yellow Women - *Collection 2*
This collection of six of the author's stories contains four with *The CONTINENTAL OP.*
Short stories - 4
Jonathan US (1947)

The Creeping Siamese - *Collection 3*
This collection of six of the author's stories contains three with *The CONTINENTAL OP.*
Short stories - 3
Jonathan US (1950)

Woman In The Dark - *Collection 4*
Short stories - 3
Headline UK (1988); Jonathan US (1951)

Sir Brian Dinsmore CONWAY

British Male Amateur operating in England

Simon STONE 1906- (British)

Writer: Howard BARRINGTON

Citation Record: 4 Books

Conway, KC - *First*
Hutchinson UK (1945)

Murder Gone Mad - *Last*
Hutchinson UK (1951)

David CONWAY

American Male Amateur operating in USA

L P DAVIES 1914- (British)

was born in Crewe, Cheshire. He was educated at the Manchester College of Science and Technology and qualified in optics. After serving in the Medical Corps in the First World War, he practised his profession in Wales and Tenerife. In addition to over a dozen criminous works, he has written numerous short stories and some science fiction.

Writer: Leslie Purnell DAVIES

Other Detectives:
Donald LOMAX and Peter CULLIMORE
John MORTON and Sgt DERWENT

Citation Record: 1 Book

The Reluctant Medium - *Only*
Doubleday US (1967)

George CONWAY

British Male Amateur operating in England

L T MEADE and Robert EUSTACE (British)

Invented 7 detectives - see Insp FROST and Dr GARLAND

Citation Record: 6 Short Stories in 1 Collection

The Gold Star Line - *Collection 1*
Ward, Lock UK (1899); New Amsterdam US (1899)

Insp James CONWAY

endures a host of dangers when solving a spate of political murders.

American Policeman operating in Boston

Charles Reed JONES (American)

See main detective Leighton SWIFT

Citation Record: 1 Book

The Rum Row Murders - *Only*
Macaulay US (1931)

Rupert CONWAY

British Male Amateur operating in Austria

Edwin LEATHER 1919- (British)

Writer: Edwin Hartley Cameron LEATHER

Citation Record: 3 Books

The Vienna Elephant - *First*
Dodd, Mead US (1977); Macmillan UK (1978)

The Duveen Letter - *Latest*
Macmillan UK (1980); Doubleday US (1980)

Det Steve CONWAY

is accused by his colleagues of being involved in the theft of a large ransom from a dead kidnapper. Deserted by his wife and his friends, he sets out to clear himself by discovering the true criminal.

American Policeman operating in New York

Earle BASINSKY 1921- (American)

Citation Record: 1 Book

The Big Steal - *Only*
Dutton US (1955); Boardman UK (1956)

Allan CONYERS and Cheryl BURROUGHS

American Male Amateur and British Female Amateur operating in Texas

Martha G WEBB 1943- (American)

See main detective Tommy INMAN

Citation Record: 1 Book

Darling Corey's Head - *Single*
Walker US (1984)

Sheriff COOK

American Policeman operating in USA

Lawrence L LYNCH (American)

Invented 11 detectives - see Neil J BATHURST

Citation Record: 1 Book

Under Fate's Wheel: A Story Of Mystery, Love And The Bicycle - *Only*
is surely one of the most delicious titles in the criminous genre!
Laird & Lee US (1900); Ward, Lock UK (1900)

Barney COOK

is one of the best boy detectives in the early literature, although only appearing in short stories.

American Male Amateur operating in New York

Harvey J O'HIGGINS 1876-1929 (Canadian)

See main detective Det John DUFF

Citation Record: 7 Short Stories in 1 Collection

The Adventures Of Detective Barney - *Collection 1*
Century US (1915)

Jeremy COOK

American Male Amateur operating in USA

David CARKEET 1946- (American)

Citation Record: 1 Book

Double Negative - *Single*
Dial US (1980)

Bertha COOL and Donald LAM

are an odd couple. She is a lady in her sixties, weighing in at over 200 lbs, who runs a detective agency called Cool & Lam, which she inherited from her late husband. She is rather given to the use of old-fashioned slang, showing her considerable temper, and is mean with money. Her partner is a small, skinny man, once an attorney but now disbarred. He does most of the legwork and is the narrator of their cases.

American Female Private Detective and American Male Private Detective operating in USA

A A FAIR 1889-1970 (American)

Writer: Erle Stanley GARDNER

Citation Record: 29 Books

The Bigger They Come - *First*
Morrow US (1939)

Lam To The Slaughter - *First**
Hamish Hamilton UK (1939)

All Grass Isn't Green - *Last*
Morrow US (1970); Heinemann UK (1970)

Jerry COOL

is rather an inadequate detective who, becoming involved in murder, has to work hard to clear himself.

American Male Private Detective operating in San Francisco

Gerry MADDREN (American)

Inventor of one other detective pair Ivy MIDDAUGH and Judith PERINO

Citation Record: 1 Book

The Case Of The Johannesberg Riesling - *Single*
Cliffhanger US (1988)

COOL CARTER

American Male Detective in Pulp Magazines operating in USA

Hawley SMART 1833-1893 (British)

Invented 8 detectives - see Insp POLLOCK

Citation Record: 1 Selected Short Story

Cool Carter, The Hocking Valley Detective; Or, Piping A Terrible Crime In The Iron Mines
Old Cap Collier Library US (18??)

COOL TOM

American Male Detective in Pulp Magazines operating in USA

OLD SLEUTH (American)

Invented 40 detectives - see Brant ADAMS

Citation Record: 1 Book

Cool Tom, The Sailor Boy Detective - *Only*
Ogilvie US (1897)

Dade COOLEY

American Male Amateur operating in Los Angeles/France

Gene THOMPSON 1924- (American)
Writer: Eugene Allen THOMPSON
Citation Record: 3 Books
Murder Mystery - *First*
Random House US (1980); Gollancz UK (1981)
A Cup Of Death - *Latest*
Random House US (1988)

Shilah COOMBES

is a *Sherlock HOLMES* parody.
British Male Professional Amateur operating in London
Sidekick: Dr THATSON
is his parody *WATSON*-like assistant.
British Male - Assistant

ANON
Citation Record: 1 Selected Short Story
The Adventure Of The Rubber Pipe - *Parody 1*
appeared in an anthology, *Twenty-five Detective Stories.*
Newnes UK (1910)

Sgt COOPER

investigates the murder of a wealthy old woman, which at first looks like suicide.
British Policeman operating in England

Minette WALTERS (British)
Invented 3 detectives - see Sgt Andy MCLOUGHLIN
Citation Record: 1 Book
The Scold's Bridle - *Single*
St Martin's US (1994)

Gary COOPER

Appears with at least two other detectives - see Toby PETERS.

Iris COOPER

is, in her first book, a nineteen-year-old girl travelling with her aunt on a voyage round the world during the 1920s. She meets a young reporter, with whose help she solves a case of murder on board. The two meet again later and solve mysteries in two more books.
American Female Amateur operating on a ship and in USA
Sidekick: Jack CLANCY
is a neophyte reporter who assists this intrepid, amateur sleuth.
American Male - Friend

K K BECK (American)
Writer: Kathrine MARRIS
Other Detectives:
Michael CARUSO
Maude Teasdale CAVENDISH
Jane DA SILVA
Sylvia SNOW and Prof Charles CARSTAIRS
Citation Record: 3 Books
Death In A Deckchair - *First*
Walker US (1984)
Peril Under The Palms - *Last*
Walker US (1989)

Lorna COOPER

British Female Amateur operating in England

Janice ROBINSON 1937- (British)
Citation Record: 1 Book
Deadly Inheritance - *Single*
Hale UK (1983)

Benny COOPERMAN

operates in the fictional Ontario town of Grantham, near Niagara. Cast in the classic mould of old-time private eyes, he is dogged rather than brilliant. He is Jewish, doesn't use a gun, drinks milk and gets sick when he sees a stiff. A bachelor so far, fond of his family and friendly with the cops, he has difficult cases that take some solving.
Canadian Male Private Detective operating in Ontario

Howard ENGEL 1931- (Canadian)
was born in Toronto, Canada. A former radio broadcaster and literary editor, he has been a full-time writer since 1985.
Citation Record: 7 Books
The Suicide Murders - *First*
Clarke Irwin CA (1980)
The Suicide Notice - *First**
St Martin's US (1980); Gollancz UK (1984)
Dead And Buried - *Latest*
Viking CA (1990)

COOPERSMITH

American Male Sleuth operating in USA

Robert J GRIFFIN (American)
Citation Record: 4 Books
Coopersmith - *First*
Pyramid US (1968)
Genghis Coopersmith - *Last*
Pyramid US (1972)

Insp David COPE

is a narcotics agent on vacation who is brought in to investigate poisonings and murder on a college campus near a rather English-style town.
American Policeman operating in South Africa

June DRUMMOND 1923- (South African)
See main detective James PORBEAGLE
Citation Record: 1 Book
Murder On A Bad Trip - *Only*
Holt US (1968)
The Gantry Episode - *Only**
Gollancz UK (1968)

Frank COPLESTONE

is blind and is the detective in this Victorian novel.
British Male Amateur operating in England

Henry Pottinger STEPHENS and Warham ST LEGER 1850- (British)
Citation Record: 1 Book
The Basilisk: A Story Of Today - *Only*
Swan, Sonnenschein UK (1889)

Joe COPP

is an ex-policeman, now a PI. Although macho to a pronounced degree, he seems to have not much on top.
American Male Private Detective operating in Los Angeles/Hawaii

Don PENDLETON 1927- (American)
was born in Little Rock, Arkansas. He served in the US Navy with distinction, receiving several battle honours. After 1945 he became an engineer and administrator at NASA. He was the author of a number of genre novels, mainly of the action thriller and hardboiled variety and his name was subsequently used as a house name by his main publishers, *Gold Eagle.*
Writer: Donald Eugene PENDLETON
Other Detectives:
Mack (The Executioner) BOLAN
Ashton FORD
Citation Record: 4 Books
Copp For Hire - *First*
Fine US (1987)
Copp In The Dark - *Latest*
Fine US (1990)

Maj COPPER

Appears with at least two other detectives - see Mark TREASURE.

C

COPPER DRIFT
American Male Detective in Pulp Magazines operating in USA

William S HALL (American)

Citation Record: 1 Book

Copper Drift, The Lake Detective
New York Detective Library US (1882-8)

Paul COQUENIL
French Male Amateur operating in Paris

Cleveland MOFFETT 1863-1926 (British)

Writer: Cleveland Langston MOFFETT

Inventor of one other detective pair Insp BROUSSE and Alan ESTERBROOKE

Citation Record: 2 Books

Through The Wall - *First*
Appleton US (1909); Melrose UK (1910)

The Master Mind - *Last*
Appleton UK (1927)

Capt (*Retired*) CORBETT
American Policeman operating in USA

Arthur PORGES (American)

Invented 13 detectives - see Arsène LUPIN

Citation Record: 1 Selected Short Story

The Unsolvable Crime
appeared in the March number.
In 'Ellery Queen's Mystery Magazine' US (1964)

Hugh CORBETT
is a 'Clerk to the King' during the late thirteenth and early fourteenth century. He is called in to solve several nasty cases of murder.

English Male Amateur operating in England

P C DOHERTY (British)

Writer: Paul C DOHERTY

Other Detectives:
Sir Godfrey EVESDEN   Matthew JENKYN

Citation Record: 6 Books

Satan In St Mary's - *First*
Hale UK (1986); St Martin's US (1987)

The Assassin In The Greenwood - *Latest*
Headline UK (1993)

Sgt Ben CORBIN
American Male Professional Investigator operating in Korea

Robert CRANE 1922- (American)

Writer: Connie Leslie SELLERS Jr

Citation Record: 2 Books

Sgt Corbin's War - *First*
Pyramid US (1964)

Time Running Out - *Last*
Papillon US (1974)

Punch CORBIN
American Male Amateur operating in USA

Henry Kitchell WEBSTER 1875-1932 (American)

Invented 4 detectives - see Prof Brinsley BUTLER

Citation Record: 1 Book

The Corbin Necklace - *Only*
Bobbs US (1926)

The Mystery Of The Corbin Necklace - *Only**
Hamilton UK (1929)

Insp CORBY
American Policeman operating in USA

Patricia HIGHSMITH 1921-1975 (American)

See main detective Tom RIPLEY

Citation Record: 1 Book

The Blunderer - *Only*
Coward McCann US (1954); Cresset UK (1956)

Lament For A Lover - *Only**
Popular Library US (1956)

Insp CORBY
British Policeman operating in England

Lettice COOPER 1897- (British)

Writer: Lettice Ulpha COOPER

Citation Record: 2 Books

Tea On Sunday - *First*
Gollancz UK (1973)

Unusual Behaviour - *Latest*
Gollancz UK (1986); Gollancz US (1987)

Talos CORD
Male Sleuth operating in Burma

Robert MACLEOD 1928- (British)

Invented 3 detectives - see Jonathan GAUNT

Citation Record: 6 Books

Cave Of Bats - *First*
Long UK (1964); Holt US (1966)

Nest Of Vultures - *Last*
Long UK (1973)

Geoffrey CORDELL
British Male Amateur operating in England

Leslie BRIDGMONT 1901- (British)

Writer: James Leslie BRIDGMONT

Citation Record: 1 Book

Unbriefed Mission - *Only*
Falcon US (1953)

Jason CORDRY
and his wife are movie extras who get involved with incredible villains and unbelievably bad murder cases. The latter he solves, with her help.

American Male Amateur operating in California/Arizona

Sidekick: Patricia CORDRY
American Female - Wife

James D O'HANLON (American)

Citation Record: 5 Books

Murder At Malibu - *First*
Phoenix Press US (1937)

Murder At Horsethief - *Last*
Phoenix Press US (1941); Boardman UK (1943)

Peter COREY
British Male Amateur operating in England

E X FERRARS 1907-1995 (British)

Invented 11 detectives - see Toby DYKE

Citation Record: 1 Book

Witness Before The Fact - *Only*
Doubleday US (1980)

Elizabeth FERRARS 1907-1995 (British)

Invented 10 detectives - see Toby DYKE

Citation Record: 1 Book

Witness Before The Fact - *Only*
Collins UK (1979)

Capt CORK
is (fictionally) perhaps the earliest American detective. He has a series of adventures around 1750 in colonial America.

American Male Amateur operating in Colonial America

S S RAFFERTY 1930- (American)

Writer: John Jerome HURLEY

Citation Record: 13 Short Stories in 1 Collection

Fatal Flourishes - *Collection 1*
Avon US (1979)

Cork Of The Colonies - *Collection 1**
International Polygonics US (1984)

Sgt CORK

is a Victorian policeman who originally appeared in a British TV series.

British Policeman operating in England

Arthur SWINSON 1915-1970 (British)

Citation Record: 6 Short Stories in 2 Collections

Sergeant Cork's Casebook - *Collection 1*
Short stories - 3
Arrow UK (1965)

Sergeant Cork's Second Casebook - *Collection 2*
Short stories - 3
Arrow UK (1966)

Montague CORK

is the manager of the Anchor Insurance Company. Although elderly, he is very smart at investigating false claims, which abound in his five cases.

British Male Professional Investigator operating in England

Macdonald HASTINGS 1909- (British)

Citation Record: 5 Books

Cork On The Water - *First*
Joseph UK (1951); Random House US (1951)

Fish And Kill - *First**
Mercury US (1952)

Cork On The Telly - *Last*
Joseph UK (1966)

Cork On Location - *Last**
Walker US (1967)

Jerry CORNELIUS

British Male Sleuth operating in several locations

Michael MOORCOCK 1939- (British)

Writer: Michael John MOORCOCK

Other Byline: Bill BARCLAY

Citation Record: 4 Books

The Chinese Agent - *First*
was a revision, with the protagonist's name changed, of *Somewhere in the Night*, originally published under the author's other byline.
Hutchinson UK (1970); Macmillan US (1970)

The Russian Intelligence - *Latest*
was a revision of *PRINTER'S DEVIL*, originally published under the author's other byline.
Savoy UK (1980)

Dr Alexander CORNELL

American Male Amateur operating in New York

M Scott MICHEL 1916- (American)

Writer: Milton Scott MICHEL

Other Byline: Milton SCOTT

Inventor of one other detective Wood JAXON

Citation Record: 1 Book

The Black Key - *Only*
Mystery House US (1946)

Milton SCOTT 1916- (American)

For writer details see Dr Alexander CORNELL

Citation Record: 1 Book

Dear, Dead Harry - *Only*
Phoenix Press US (1949)

Insp CORNFORD

British Policeman operating in England

Milward KENNEDY 1894-1968 (British)

Invented 6 detectives - see Sir George BULL

Citation Record: 2 Books

The Corpse On The Mat - *First*
was published in the US under the following byline.
Gollancz UK (1929)

Corpse Guard Parade - *Last*
Gollancz UK (1929); Doubleday US (1930)

Robert Milward KENNEDY 1894-1968 (British)

For writer details see Sir George BULL

The Man Who Rang The Bell - *Only*
was previously published as *THE CORPSE ON THE MAT* under the preceding byline.
Doubleday US (1929)

Kay CORNISH

Second detective of Adam DREW

Nicholas CORNISH

British Male Amateur operating in England

Virginia HANSON 1905-1968 (American)

Writer: Virginia L HANSON

Inventor of one other detective pair Adam DREW and Kay CORNISH

Citation Record: 5 Books

Three Hours To Hang - *First*
Boardman UK (1955)

A Man From The Past - *Last*
Boardman UK (1958)

Donald CORNWALL

investigates a death by electrocution in a locked room.

American Male Amateur operating in USA

Edwin BALMER and Philip WYLIE (American)

Writers: Edwin BALMER 1883-1959 and Philip Gordon WYLIE 1902-1971

Citation Record: 1 Book

Five Fatal Words - *Only*
Smith US (1932); Paul UK (1933)

'Biff' CORRIGAN

American Male Sleuth operating in New York

W B M FERGUSON 1881-1967 (British)

was one of several British authors who, in the 1940s (inspired perhaps by the remarkable success of *James Hadley CHASE*), thought it was easy to hijack the American PI and wrote detective novels to prove it. Of course, it wasn't and they didn't, demonstrating rather what a phenomenon *CHASE* was.

Writer: William Blair Morton FERGUSON

Other Byline: William MORTON

Inventor of one other detective Daniel J CLUER

Citation Record: 1 Book

The Pilditch Puzzle - *Only*
was published in the UK as *THE MURDERER* under the following byline.
Liveright US (1932)

William MORTON 1881-1967 (British)

For writer details see 'Biff' CORRIGAN

Inventor of one other detective Commiss Kirker CAMERON

Citation Record: 3 Books

Masquerade - *First*
Chelsea US (1927); Nelson UK (1928)

The Murderer - *Last*
was published in the US as *THE PILDITCH PUZZLE* under the preceding byline.
Hurst UK (1932)

Mark CORRIGAN

is a PI based in Philadelphia who was once in US Army Intelligence during the Second World War. Created by a British author, his various cases and adventures take him to many locales.

American Male Private Detective operating in USA

Mark CORRIGAN 1905-1962 (American)

For writer details see Insp Dick MASON

Citation Record: 30 Books

Bullets And Brown Eyes - *First*
Laurie UK (1948)

The Riddle Of The Spanish Circus - *Last*
Angus UK (1964)

Martin 'Brick-Top' CORRIGAN

is one of this British author's numerous American private eyes, constructed from reference books, and differing from his others only perhaps in being more unscrupulous. The books in which he appears under this pseudonym have usually been reprinted under the author's best-known byline, *James Hadley CHASE.*
!See Appendix 2.

American Male Private Detective operating in USA

Raymond MARSHALL 1906-1985 (British)
Invented 4 detectives - see Don MICKLEM
Citation Record: 2 Books
Mallory - *First*
Jarrolds UK (1950)
Why Pick On Me? - *Last*
Jarrolds UK (1951)

Tim CORRIGAN

American Male Sleuth operating in New York

Ellery QUEEN 1915-1983 (American)
Inventor of one other detective Micah 'Mike' MCCALL
For writer details see Manville MOON
Citation Record: 5 Books
Why So Dead? - *First*
Popular Library US (1966); Four Square UK (1967)
What Is The Dark? - *Last*
Popular Library US (1968)
When Fell The Night? - *Last**
Gollancz UK (1970)

Ellery QUEEN 1920 (American)
For writer details see Ed RIVERS
Citation Record: 2 Books
Where is Bianca? - *First*
Popular Library US (1966); Four Square UK (1966)
Who Spies, Who Kills? - *Last*
Popular Library US (1966); Four Square UK (1967)

Insp Franco CORTI

is a London copper, of large build, who comes from an Italian family. His manor is around the West End of London and he is in the 'Art and Antiques Squad' at Scotland Yard, whose work consists of impeding the numerous and varied art scams that abound in London and trying to solve the murder cases arising from them. He is himself something of an art connoisseur and his cases often take him to Venice or other delightful parts of Italy where the scams are even more numerous and varied. In an early book, he appeared under his anglicised name, *Frank SHORT.*

British Policeman operating in London/Venice

Peter INCHBALD 1919- (British)
is an artist and art connoisseur who has created a convincing series based on crime in the world of art and antiques.
Inventor of one other detective Insp Frank SHORT
Citation Record: 3 Books
Tondo For Short - *First*
Collins UK (1981); Doubleday US (1982)
Short Break In Venice - *Last*
Doubleday US (1983)

Manuel CORTINA

solves a case of murder by decapitation in a locked room.

American Male Amateur operating in USA

Joseph BOWEN 1871?- (American)
Citation Record: 1 Book
The Man Without A Head - *Only*
Covici US (1936); Butterworth UK (1937)

Annie CORY

is too lady-like to sleuth in her own and is helped by her father.

British Female Amateur operating in England

Mrs George CORBETT 1840- (British)
Writer: Burgoyne Elizabeth CORBETT
Inventor of one other detective pair Mr BELL and Mr WHITE
Citation Record: 1 Book
When The Sea Gives Up Its Dead: A Thrilling Detective Story - *Only*
Tower UK (1894)

Pete CORY

works for Boldman Investigations. He is hardboiled but not entirely without feelings.

American Male Private Detective operating in Seattle

Stuart BROCK 1917- (American)
Invented 3 detectives - see Steve ROURKE
Citation Record: 1 Book
Just Around The Corner - *Only*
Mill US (1948)

Ames CORYELL

investigates his wife's disappearance.

American Male Amateur operating in USA

Howard BROWNE 1908- (American)
See main detective Paul PINE
Citation Record: 1 Book
Thin Air - *Only*
Simon & Schuster US (1954); Gollancz UK (1955)

John Owen COSATELLI

is a musician who is suspected of murdering his girl-friend. He has to go on the run and solve the case himself.

American Male Amateur operating in USA

Paula GOSLING 1939- (American)
Invented 7 detectives - see Lt Jack STRYKER
Citation Record: 1 Book
Loser's Blues - *Single*
Macmillan UK (1980)
Solo Blues - *Single**
Coward McCann US (1981)

COSGROVE

Australian Male Sleuth operating in Australia

Murray M INNES
Citation Record: 4 Short Stories in 1 Collection
Cosgrove: Detective - *Collection 1*
Stockwell UK (1933)

Tony COSTAINE

Second detective of Bert MCCALL

COSTELLO

Male Professional Amateur operating in England

John NICHOLSON (British)
Writer: Norman Howe PARCELL
Citation Record: 8 Short Stories in 1 Collection
Costello - Psychic Investigator - *Collection 1*
Stockwell UK (1954)

Reginald COSWAY

is unusual in being a bit of a cad and actually getting killed in the course of the novel.

British Male Amateur operating in England

Carlton DAWE 1865-1935 (British)
See main detective Col Gantian LEATHERMOUTH
Citation Record: 1 Book
The Black Spider - *Only*
Nash UK (1911)

C

Neal COTTEN
American Male Private Detective operating in USA

Sam S TAYLOR (American)
Citation Record: 3 Books
Sleep No More - *First*
Dutton US (1949); Boardman UK (1951)
So Cold, My Bed - *Last*
Dutton US (1949); Foulsham UK (1955)

David COTTER
investigates the murder of an American politician.
American Male Amateur operating in New England

Hugh PENTECOST 1903-1989 (American)
Invented 12 detectives - see Pierre CHAMBRUN
Citation Record: 1 Book
Murder As Usual - *Only*
Dodd, Mead US (1977); Hale UK (1978)

Wellington COTTER
appears in novels set in Sydney in the 1880s.
Australian Male Amateur operating in Australia

Martin LONG (Australian)
is a journalist and music critic.
Citation Record: 3 Books
The Dark Gateway - *First*
Macmillan UK (1987)
The Music Room - *Latest*
Bantam AU (1990)

Martin COTTERELL
is an erudite archaeologist. Although he has lost one arm, this does not, it seems, prevent him from digging up as many murders as he does shards.
British Male Amateur operating in several locations

John TRENCH 1920- (British)
was born in Newick, Sussex. He was educated at Wellington College, Berkshire, and the Royal Military Academy, Woolwich, London. He served in the Army, 1939-1946, after which he had a career in publishing. His criminous novels often utilise his expert knowledge of local archaeology in Britain.
Writer: John Chevenix TRENCH
Citation Record: 3 Books
Docken Dead - *First*
Macdonald UK (1953); Macmillan US (1954)
What Rough Beast - *Last*
Macmillan US (1957)

Gunston COTTON
Male Secret Agent operating in Europe/USA

Rupert GRAYSON
Citation Record: 15 Books
Gun Cotton - Adventurer - *First*
Grayson UK (1933); Dutton US (1937)
Gun Cotton In Mexico - *Last*
Grayson UK (1937); Dutton US (1940)

John COTTON
is a reporter who finds the notebook of a murdered colleague, which offers clues to his death. In peril himself now, he must find the killer.
American Male Amateur operating in Oklahoma

Tony HILLERMAN 1925- (American)
Invented 4 detectives - see Lt Joe LEAPHORN
Citation Record: 1 Book
The Fly On The Wall - *Only*
Harper & Row US (1971)

Rex COULSON
British Male Amateur operating in England

Jack MANN 1882-1947 (British)
Writer: Evelyn Charles Henry VIVIAN
Other Byline: E Charles VIVIAN
Inventor of one other detective Gregory George Gordon GREEN
Citation Record: 6 Books
Reckless Coulson - *First*
Wright UK (1933)
Detective Coulson - *Last*
Wright UK (1936)

Det Insp COURTENAY
British Policeman operating in England

Norman BERROW 1902- (British)
Invented 4 detectives - see Michael REVEL
Citation Record: 2 Books
The Secret Dancer - *First*
Ward, Lock UK (1936)
One Thrilling Night - *Last*
Ward, Lock UK (1937)

Rose COURTENAY
who was the assistant of *Robert SPICER* in other books, acts alone in this Victorian novel.
British Female Private Detective operating in London

Milton DANVERS (British)
Inventor of one other detective Robert SPICER
Citation Record: 1 Book
The Fatal Finger Mark, Rose Courtenay's First Case - *Only*
Diprose & Bateman UK (1895)

Maggie COURTNEY
American Female Amateur operating in Mississippi

Ann PEARSON (American)
Citation Record: 3 Books
Murder By Degrees - *First*
Zebra US (1979)
Cat Got Your Tongue? - *Latest*
Zebra US (1980)

Lucifer COVE
American Male Sleuth operating in California

Virginia COFFMAN 1914- (American)
Writer: Virginia Edith COFFMAN
Inventor of one other detective MOURA
Citation Record: 6 Books
Priestess Of The Damned - *First*
Lancer UK (1970)
Chalet Diabolique - *Last*
Lancer UK (1971)

The COWBOY DETECTIVE
American Male Detective in Pulp Magazines operating in USA

OLD SLEUTH (American)
Invented 40 detectives - see Brant ADAMS
Citation Record: 1 Book
The Cowboy Detective - *Only*
Ogilvie US (1895)
A Little Cowboy In New York; Or, In Search Of His Dad - *Only**
Ogilvie US (1897)

The COWBOY 'TEC
American Male Detective in Pulp Magazines operating in USA

Jake DENVERS 1896- (British)
Writer: Alfred EDGAR
Citation Record: 1 Book
The Cowboy 'Tec - *Only*
Amalgamated UK (1924)

John COWPER
is an SIS agent sent to Italy to foil Italian plans to sink a British battleship.
British Policeman operating in Italy

C

Francis BEEDING (British)

Invented 6 detectives - see Insp WILKINS

Citation Record: 1 Book

The Black Arrows - *Only*
Hodder & Stoughton UK (1938); Harper & Row US (1938)

COYLE and DONOVAN

American Male Amateurs operating in USA

Judson PHILIPS 1903-1989 (American)

Invented 4 detectives - see Peter STYLES

Citation Record: 2 Books

Odds On The Hot Seat - *First*
Dodd, Mead US (1941); Hale UK (1946)

The Fourteenth Trump - *Last*
Dodd, Mead US (1942); Hale UK (1951)

Joseph COYLE

American Male Private Detective operating in Arizona

Louis TRIMBLE 1917- (American)

Invented 3 detectives - see Martin ZANE

Citation Record: 1 Book

Love Me And Die - *Only*
Ace US (1960)

Brady COYNE

is a Boston lawyer. He is highly skilled in court but he enjoys doing investigational work on his cases even more than he does in succeeding at subsequent trials. He is selective about his clients and always seems to choose rich ones so that his large fees can keep him in the style to which he is accustomed.

American Male Amateur operating in USA

William G TAPPLY 1940- (American)

was born in Waltham, Massachusetts. He took a BA in American Studies at Amherst College, Massachusetts, 1962, and later attended several other universities. He has been a teacher at schools and colleges.

Writer: William George TAPPLY

Citation Record: 12 Books

Death At Charity's Point - *First*
Scribner's US (1984); Collins UK (1985)

The Seventh Enemy - *Latest*
Otto Penzler US (1995)

The CRACKSHOT DETECTIVE

American Male Detective in Pulp Magazines operating in USA

ANON

Citation Record: 1 Book

The Crackshot Detective - *Only*
Aldine US

Carl CRADER and Earl JAZINE

do their detecting some time in the twenty-second century, when the problems do not seem to have changed much.

American Male Sleuths operating in USA

Edward D HOCH 1930- (American)

Invented 20 detectives - see Capt LEOPOLD

Citation Record: 3 Books

The Transvection Machine - *First*
Walker US (1971); Hale UK (1974)

The Frankenstein Factory - *Last*
Warner US (1975); Hale UK (1976)

Det CRAFFT

American Policeman operating in USA

Mignon G EBERHART 1899- (American)

Invented 9 detectives - see Sarah KEATE

Citation Record: 1 Book

The Dark Garden - *Only*
Doubleday US (1933)

Death In The Fog - *Only**
Lane UK (1934)

Sebald CRAFT

American Male Amateur operating in New York

Innis PATTERSON (American)

Writer: Isabella Innis PATTERSON

Citation Record: 2 Books

The Eppworth Case - *First*
Farrar, Straus US (1930)

The Standish Gaunt Case - *Last*
Farrar, Straus US (1931)

Sam CRAGG

Second detective of Johnny FLETCHER

CRAGGS

is a cleaning lady in the homes of top people. In the course of her homely duties she comes across crimes that baffle the police but which she is able to solve with common sense and humour.

British Female Amateur operating in London

Sidekick: MILHORNE

is the genteel, nervous friend of the forceful, investigating charlady.

British Female - Confidante

H R F KEATING 1926- (British)

Invented 6 detectives - see Insp Ganesh GHOTE

Citation Record: 14 Short Stories in 1 Collection

Mrs Craggs: Crimes Cleaned Up - *Collection 1*
Buchan & Enright UK (1985); St Martin's US (1986)

John CRAGGS and James CASTLETON

British Male Amateurs operating in England

Cyril A ALINGTON 1872-1955 (British)

was born in Lincolnshire. After a classical education he taught classics at Marlborough and Eton. He wrote extensively on theology and politics and eventually was appointed Dean of Durham and Chaplain to the King. He found time to write a dozen crime and mystery novels.

Writer: Reverend Cyril Argentine ALINGTON

Inventor of one other detective Mr BIRTLEY

Citation Record: 4 Books

Archdeacons Afloat - *First*
Faber UK (1946)

Gold And Gaiters - *Last*
Faber UK (1950)

Cliff CRAGIN

appeared mainly in stories in *Spicy Detective.*

American Male Detective in Pulp Magazines operating in USA

E Hoffman PRICE 1898-1988 (American)

Invented 4 detectives - see John CARMODY

Citation Record: 3 Short Stories in 1 Collection

Winds Of The World - *Collection 1*

contains three of the original stories.

In 'Spicy Detective Encores' US (1988)

Sgt CRAIG

Policeman

Ian JEFFERIES 1927- (British)

Writer: Peter HAYS

Citation Record: 3 Books

Thirteen Days - *First*
Cape UK (1959)

It Wasn't Me! - *Last*
Cape UK (1961)

Alan CRAIG

is a former detective from Scotland Yard who now is a private investigator.

British Male Private Detective operating in England

Malcolm GRAY 1927-1993 (British)

Writer: Ian STUART

Citation Record: 3 Books

Look Back On Murder - *First*
Ross Anderson UK (1985); Doubleday US (1986)

An Unwelcome Presence - *Latest*
Doubleday US (1989)

Prof Ian CRAIG

is Professor of Oriental Philosophy at the fictional Earl College. He is a rich, young, handsome bachelor and uses the methods, so he says, of oriental wisdom to solve baffling crimes.

American Male Amateur operating in USA

Babette Plechner HUGHES 1906- (American)

was born in Seattle, Washington. Although she only wrote two genre books, she was a considerable playwright and a successful businesswoman later in life.

Citation Record: 2 Books

Murder In The Zoo - *First*
Appleton US (1932); Benn UK (1932)

Murder In Church - *Last*
Appleton US (1934)

James CRAIG

is a British secret agent who lives in a rather more shabby world than did the classic *James BOND*. He endeavours to maintain some sort of ethic in his hazardous and often despicable work, in which he is manipulated by his loathsome boss. !See Appendix 2.

British Male Secret Agent operating in several locations

James MUNRO 1926- (British)

For writer details see Joe CAVE

Citation Record: 4 Books

The Man Who Sold Death - *First*
Hammond UK (1964); Knopf US (1965)

The Innocent Bystanders - *Last*
Jenkins UK (1969); Knopf US (1970)

Matthew CRAIG

is an attorney who investigates the murder of the dean at a university in Ohio.

American Male Professional Investigator operating in USA

Mary E CAMPBELL 1903-1984 (American)

was born in Cambridge, Ohio. Sometime lecturer in the English Department at Indiana University, she was the author of two genre books.

Writer: Mary Elizabeth CAMPBELL

Citation Record: 1 Book

Scandal Has Two Faces - *Only*
Doubleday US (1943)

Melissa CRAIG

is a detective story writer who has bought a cottage in a village in the Cotswolds, where she intends to work. Not a bit of it. She should know that English village life is literally seething with mayhem. In her very first book, her neighbour digs for vegetables in her garden and exhumes a corpse. Real life detection becomes not only the natural thing to do, but, once successful, becomes a habit, with no shortage of rural murder in the vicinity.

British Female Amateur operating in England

Betty ROWLANDS (British)

Citation Record: 5 Books

A Little Gentle Sleuthing - *First*
Hodder & Stoughton UK (1990)

Malice Poetic - *Latest*
Hodder & Stoughton UK (1995)

Nat CRAIG

British Male Private Detective operating in England

Ernest DUDLEY 1908- (British)

Invented 3 detectives - see Dr MORELLE

Citation Record: 30 Short Stories in 1 Collection

The Private Eye - *Collection 1*
Long UK (1950)

Peter CRAIG

British Male Secret Agent operating in Brazil/Middle East

Kenneth BENTON 1909- (British)

Writer: Kenneth Carter BENTON

Citation Record: 6 Books

24th Level - *First*
Collins UK (1969); Dodd, Mead US (1970)

Craig And The Midas Touch - *Last*
Macmillan UK (1975); Walker US (1976)

Robert CRAIG

runs a one-man agency that is going to be in dire straits unless he solves his big case. He does, even though it means getting himself temporarily committed as insane.

American Male Private Detective operating in New York

Carter CULLEN (American)

Writers: Mildred MACAULAY and Richard MACAULAY

Citation Record: 1 Book

The Deadly Chase - *Only*
GM US (1957); Fawcett UK (1958)

Steve CRAIG

is an American private eye, not a bad attempt by a British author.

American Male Private Detective operating in Santa Monica

Bevis WINTER 1918- (British)

For writer details see Al BOCCA

Citation Record: 9 Books

Redheads Cool Fast - *First*
Jenkins UK (1954)

The Dark And Deadly - *Last*
Jenkins UK (1961)

Tom CRAIG

British Male Amateur operating in New York

Virginia VAN URK (American)

Writer: Virginia Nellis VAN URK

Citation Record: 2 Books

Speaking Of Murder - *First*
Phoenix Press US (1951)

Grounds For Murder - *Last*
Arcadia US (1958)

Paul CRAINE

American Male Amateur operating in New York

Eugene P HEALY (American)

Citation Record: 2 Books

Craine's First Case - *First*
Holt US (1938); Hale UK (1939)

Mr Sandeman Loses His Life - *Last*
Holt US (1940)

Insp CRAMBO

British Policeman operating in England

Julian SYMONS 1912-1994 (British)

was born in London and educated at local schools. Editor, critic, poet and biographer, he also stands among the very highest in the field of crime and mystery fiction. His first writings were in the field of poetry and he was the founding editor, 1937-1939, of the important journal, *Twentieth Century Verse*. He wrote his first detective novel as a private joke in the 1930s but did not try to get it published until 1945. He was the author of at least twenty-six criminous novels, all admired for their meticulous plotting and eru-

C

dite form, but he rarely used series detectives as he considered they would stereotype his work. He wrote radio plays in the 1960s and 1970s and continued to write verse. He published a considerable number of works of literary criticism, biography and history and was the editor of many literary collections and omnibus editions, especially of crime fiction. Apart from his novels, he is renowned for his erudite, highly readable, critical account of the development of crime fiction, *Bloody Murder*, 1972, revised in 1985. He was a reviewer of books for the *Sunday Times* from 1958, a co-founder of the Crime Writers Association, 1953, and President of the Detection Club, 1976-1985. He received the Crime Writers Association Gold Dagger award, 1957; their Special Merit award, 1967; their Diamond Dagger award, 1990; the Mystery Writers of America Edgar Allan Poe award twice, 1961 and 1973; and their Grand Master award, 1982.

Writer: Julian Gustave SYMONS

Other Detectives:

Charles APPLEGATE	Hugh BENNETT
Insp BLAND	Det Supt Hilary CATCHPOLE
Sheridan HAYNES	Insp HAZELTON
Sherlock HOLMES	Dudley POTTER
Francis QUARLES	Paul VANDERVENT

Citation Record: 1 Book

The Gigantic Shadow - *Only*
Collins UK (1958)

The Pipe Dream - *Only**
Harper & Row US (1959)

Insp CRAMER

is the classic police stooge who appears, always baffled, in most of the *Nero WOLFE* books. The author, perhaps in commiseration, made him the successful detective in this one book.

American Policeman operating in New York

Rex STOUT 1886-1975 (American)

Invented 6 detectives - see Nero WOLFE

Citation Record: 1 Book

Red Threads - *Only*
Farrar, Straus US (1939); Collins UK (1941)

Roger CRAMMOND

British Male Amateur operating in Scotland

Thomas MUIR (British)

See main detective Prof CLEGHORN

Citation Record: 8 Books

Death In Reserve - *First*
Hutchinson UK (1948)

Death In Soundings - *Last*
Hutchinson UK (1955)

Ben CRANDEL

American Male Amateur operating in Los Angeles

Murray SINCLAIR 1950- (American)

Citation Record: 3 Books

Tough Luck, L A - *First*
Pinnacle US (1980); Black Lizard UK (1988)

Goodbye, L A - *Latest*
Black Lizard US (1988); Black Lizard UK (1988)

Insp CRANE

British Policeman operating in England

Jeffrey ASHFORD 1926- (British)

Invented 9 detectives - see Det Insp Don KERRY

Citation Record: 1 Book

Three Layers Of Guilt - *Single*
Long UK (1975); Walker US (1976)

Insp CRANE

Second detective of Insp Tom SWETMAN

Lionel CRANE

British Male Amateur operating in England

Donald STUART 1896-1980 (British)

was the byline also used by this author for his thirty-six *Sexton BLAKE* novels.

For writer details see Supt BUDD

Adopter of one other detective Sexton BLAKE

Citation Record: 2 Books

The White Friar - *First*
Wright & Brown UK (1934)

Midnight Murder - *Last*
Wright & Brown UK (1935)

Paul CRANE

American Male Sleuth operating in USA

Wade CURTIS 1933- (American)

For writer details see Paul CRANE

Citation Record: 2 Books

Red Heroin - *First*
was republished under the following byline.
Berkley US (1969)

Red Dragon - *Last*
was republished under the following byline.
Berkley US (1971)

Jerry POURNELLE 1933- (American)

Writer: Jerry POURNELLE

Other Byline: Wade CURTIS

Citation Record: 2 Books

Red Heroin - *First*
was previously published under the preceding byline.
Charter US (1985)

Red Dragon - *Last*
was previously published under the preceding byline.
Charter US (1985)

Simon CRANE

was accidentally shot by a colleague and was retired from the police force. To save his own life, he has to solve a case, fight both the Mafia and his old bosses, and see that justice is done.

American Male Sleuth operating in USA

Brian GARFIELD 1939- (American)

Invented 4 detectives - see Plce Sam WATCHMAN

Citation Record: 1 Book

The Hit - *Only*
Macmillan US (1970)

Steve CRANE

is a one-eyed Korean War veteran.

American Male Private Detective operating in New York

Morris HERSHMAN 1920- (American)

Citation Record: 1 Book

Guilty Witness - *Only*
Belmont US (1964)

William CRANE

is second in charge at Black's Detective Agency. He drinks to excess, tending to say, "I solve 'em, drunk or sober". It's as well that he has two sidekicks to help out.

American Male Private Detective operating in New York

Sidekick: 'Doc' WILLIAMS
provides muscle for the alcoholic sleuth.
American Male - Assistant

Sidekick: Tom O'MALLEY
does much the same.
American Male - Assistant

Jonathan LATIMER 1906-1983 (American)

Invented 4 detectives - see Sam CLAY

Citation Record: 5 Books

Murder In The Madhouse - *First*
Doubleday US (1935); Hurst UK (1935)

Red Gardenias - *Last*
Doubleday US (1939); Methuen UK (1939)

C

William Rutherford CRANE
Second detective of Bruce PERKINS

CRANG
Canadian Male Sleuth operating in Canada

Jack BATTEN 1932- (Canadian)

Citation Record: 3 Books

Crang Plays The Ace - *First*
Macmillan CA (1988)

Riviera Blues - *Latest*
Macmillan CA (1990)

Insp CRANKSHAW
British Policeman operating in England

E X FERRARS 1907-1995 (British)

Invented 11 detectives - see Toby DYKE

Citation Record: 1 Book

Depart This Life - *Only*
Doubleday US (1958)

Elizabeth FERRARS 1907-1995 (British)

Invented 10 detectives - see Toby DYKE

Citation Record: 1 Book

A Tale Of Two Murders - *Only*
Collins UK (1959)

Nick CRANLEY
American Male Sleuth operating in USA

Michael STORM (American)

Citation Record: 3 Books

Carmen Was A Virgin - *First*
Leisure Books US (1952)

This Woman Is Death - *Last*
Leisure Books US (1953)

Steve CRANMER
is head of Cranmer Investigations, in North May Avenue, Oklahoma City. Hardly the most admirable of private eyes, he is more interested in gambling than sleuthing. Even so, with the help of his appalling sidekick, he gets through two books with ease.

American Male Private Detective operating in Oklahoma

Sidekick: Butch MANERI
is a former pool hustler who smokes dope and is prey to stomach trouble. In spite of such interesting disabilities, he can go into action when needed to assist his equally offensive boss.

American Male - Assistant

Steve KNICKMEYER 1944- (American)

Citation Record: 2 Books

Straight - *First*
Random House US (1976); Harwood UK (1977)

Cranmer - *Latest*
Random House US (1978); Hamlyn UK (1980)

Lamont (The Shadow) CRANSTON
was one of those mysterious superman detectives who abounded in the early pulps. Originally an anonymous narrator of radio mysteries, he appeared in stories mostly written by *Walter B GIBSON*, several of which were later published under that name in book form. When Smith & Street began *The Shadow* magazine, the character was transformed into a mysterious, black-cloaked figure, a dreaded tracker of criminals, who could assume many identities, one of which was the millionaire explorer, *Lamont CRANSTON*. Many of the later stories were published or reprinted under the *Maxwell GRANT* house name and are so cited.

American Male Amateur operating in New York

Walter B GIBSON 1897-1985 (American)

was born in Philadelphia, Pennsylvania, and graduated from Colgate University, New York, 1919. Under several bylines he was the author of hundreds of genre novels, hundreds of short stories for the pulps in the 1930s and 1940s, novels for children and a large number of books on magic, witchcraft, tricks, puzzles, yoga, astronomy and the occult arts. He is renowned for the nearly three hundred short novels he wrote, under his real name and under the *Maxwell GRANT* byline, for the *Shadow Magazine*, featuring his new creation, *The SHADOW*. The pseudonym was eventually used as a house name for further stories.

Writer: Walter Brown GIBSON

Other Byline: Maxwell GRANT

Citation Record: 6 Books

Return Of The Shadow - *First*
Belmont US (1963)

The Shadow And The Golden Master - *Last*
Mysterious Press US (1984)

Maxwell GRANT 1897-1985 (American)

See main detective NORGIL

Citation Record: 34 Books

The Shadow Laughs! - *First*
Street US (1931)

The Silent Death - *Last*
Jove US (1978)

Maxwell GRANT 1924- (American)

For writer details see Kane JACKSON

Citation Record: 7 Books

The Shadow Strikes - *First*
Belmont US (1964)

Night Of The Shadow - *Last*
Belmont US (1966)

Steve CRAVEN
is in a strange book full of action. To call him hardboiled would be something of an understatement.

American Male Private Detective operating in St Louis

Jonathan LATIMER 1906-1983 (American)

Invented 4 detectives - see Sam CLAY

Citation Record: 1 Book

The Fifth Grave - *Only*
Popular Library US (1950)

Solomon's Vineyard - *Only**
Methuen UK (1941)

CRAWFORD
American Male Sleuth

Dan CUSHMAN 1909- (American)

Citation Record: 2 Books

Naked Ebony - *First*
GM US (1951); Fawcett UK (1953)

Savage Interlude - *Last*
GM US (1952); Fawcett UK (1953)

Liane CRAWFORD and Insp Hugh GORDON
British Female Amateur and British Policeman operating in Europe/Africa

Susan GILRUTH 1911- (British)

Citation Record: 7 Books

Sweet Revenge - *First*
Hale UK (1951)

The Snake Is Living Yet - *Last*
Hodder & Stoughton UK (1963)

Prof Theodora Wade CRAWFORD
is the Professor of Archaeology at the fictional University of Buriton, somewhere in Cornwall. She is married, but her husband is a prig, and she considers herself a modern woman and a free spirit. These qualities she confirms by sleeping around, getting tough and solving murders on the campus. She still has time for research.

British Female Amateur operating in England

C

Jessica MANN 1937- (British)

See main detective Tamara HOYLAND

Citation Record: 2 Books

The Only Security - *First*
Macmillan UK (1973)

Troublecross - *First**
McKay US (1973)

Captive Audience - *Last*
Macmillan UK (1975); McKay US (1975)

Ray CRAWLEY

Australian Male Private Detective operating in Sydney

Peter CORRIS 1942- (Australian)

Invented 3 detectives - see Richard BROWNING

Citation Record: 3 Books

Pokerface - *First*
Penguin AU (1985)

The Cargo Club - *Latest*
Penguin AU (1990)

Joseph P CRAY

British Male Amateur operating in England

E Phillips OPPENHEIM 1866-1946 (British)

Invented 27 detectives - see Nicholas GOADE

Citation Record: 9 Short Stories in 1 Collection

The Adventures Of Mr Joseph P Cray - *Collection 1*
Hodder & Stoughton UK (1925); Little, Brown US (1927)

Maj Jonathan CRAYTHORNE

British Male Sleuth operating in England

Arthur DOUGLAS 1926- (British)

Citation Record: 3 Books

Last Rights - *First*
Macmillan UK (1986); St Martin's US (1987)

A Worm Turns - *Latest*
Macmillan UK (1988); St Martin's US (1989)

Col Winston CREEVY

Male Sleuth operating in England/California

Jeremy LORD 1896-1961

Writer: Ben Ray REDMAN

Citation Record: 2 Books

The Bannerman Case - *First*
Hurst UK (1936); Doubleday US (1935)

Sixty-Nine Diamonds - *Last*
Hurst UK (1940); Doubleday US (1940)

Peter CREIGHTON

American Male Amateur operating in New York

Armstrong LIVINGSTON 1885- (American)

Inventor of one other detective Jimmy TREYNOR

Citation Record: 4 Books

On The Right Wrists - *First*
Chelsea US (1925); Jarrolds UK (1927)

Trackless Death - *Last*
Bobbs US (1930); Skeffington UK (1930)

CRESTON

American Male Detective in Pulp Magazines operating in USA

OLD SLEUTH (American)

Invented 40 detectives - see Brant ADAMS

Citation Record: 1 Book

Creston The Detective; Or, Following A Light Clew - *Only*
Parlor Car US (1897)

Barbara CREW

Second detective of Ch Rufus Albert JONES

CREWE

British Male Amateur operating in England

M ANDERSON (American)

See main detective Jason MARR

Citation Record: 2 Books

John R WATSON and Arthur J REES (British)

Writers: John Reay WATSON 1872- and Arthur John REES 1872-1942

Citation Record: 2 Books

The Hampstead Mystery - *First*
Lane UK (1916); Lane US (1916)

The Mystery Of The Downs - *Last*
Lane UK (1918); Lane US (1918)

CREWE (BIRGE MOREAU)

American Male Sleuth operating in New York

Varick VANARDY 1861-1922 (American)

See main detective Bingham HARVARD

Citation Record: 1 Book 3 Short Stories in 1 Collection

The Two-Faced Man - *Only*
Macaulay US (1918); Jarrolds UK (1920)

Something Doing - *Collection 1*
contains three novelettes.
Macaulay US (1919)

Sgt CRIBB and Const THACKERAY

sternly uphold the law and Victorian values in late nineteenth-century England, appearing in books that are superb pictures of various facets of life at the time. In the course of their duties they are often menaced by their overbearing boss.

British Policemen operating in London

Stooge: Insp JOWETT
is an unpleasant type, menacing and eager to reap the rewards of work done by these two detectives in particular.
British Male

Peter LOVESEY 1936- (British)

was born in Whitton, Middlesex. He was educated at Hampton Grammar School and took a BA in English at Reading University, Berkshire, 1958. After serving as an Education Officer in the Royal Air Force, he became a full-time writer and has since written some highly regarded detective novels, which he has often set in the Victorian and Edwardian eras in England. He received the Crime Writers Association Silver Dagger award, 1978, their Gold Dagger award, 1983, and the *Grand Prix de Littérature Policière*, 1985.

Writer: Peter Harmer LOVESEY

Other Detectives:
Walter BARANOV; Insp DEW
Supt Peter DIAMOND; Warwick EASTON
Dorothy Mayotte RIGBY
King of England Edward VII WINDSOR

Citation Record: 8 Books

Wobble To Death - *First*
Macmillan UK (1970); Dodd, Mead US (1970)

Waxwork - *Latest*
Macmillan UK (1978); Pantheon US (1978)

Tessa CRICHTON

is a modern *Miss MARPLE*, meeting murder in all sorts of situations, but mostly in the classic English cosy ones. Still, the pace is faster than in the old days and she is fortunate in being married to a policeman, who acts as a part-time, unofficial sidekick,

British Female Amateur operating in England

Sidekick: Det Robin PRICE
is married to *Tessa CRICHTON*, which is fortunate for her when action of the rough kind surfaces. Not only is he a perpetual sounding board for her ideas but, at times, has to rescue her from the hands of villains.
British Male - Husband

Anne MORICE 1918-1989 (British)

was born in Kent and educated privately in London, Paris and Munich. Her genre novels to date are all in the traditional mode. There is murder with a cast of suspects in a set situation, a number of clever but bewildering clues about the place, a nicely personal and personable female amateur detective, and a self-effacing sidekick of a husband in the police force. What could be more satisfying?

Writer: Felicity SHAW

Citation Record: 23 Books

Death In The Grand Manor - *First*
Macmillan UK (1970)

Planning For Murder - *Last*
Macmillan UK (1990); St Martin's US (1991)

Prof Adrian CRIDDLE

British Male Amateur operating in England

Ben STRONG (British)

Writers: Emmeric HULME-BEAMAN and William Senior ELLIS

Citation Record: 2 Books

The Track Of The Slayer - *First*
Hodder & Stoughton UK (1925)

The Secret Of Gnome Head - *Last*
Hodder & Stoughton UK (1928)

CRIMSON MASK

is one of the many shadowy, all-powerful crimebuster detectives of the era. He appeared, 1940-1944, in stories in *Detective Novels Magazine*, which were mainly written by the prolific pulp author, *Norman DANIELS*, under the cited byline. One story is cited for illustration purposes.

American Male Amateur operating in USA

Frank JOHNSON (American)

used this pseudonym mainly for his stories featuring *The CRIMSON MASK*.

Writer: Norman A DANIELS

Citation Record: 1 Selected Short Story

Enter The Crimson Mask
In 'Detective Novels Magazine' US (?)

Ch Const Colonel CRISP

solves a case of murder committed in a mine.

British Policeman operating in England

Roy VICKERS 1888-1965 (British)

Invented 9 detectives - see Insp J RASON

Citation Record: 1 Book

Murder Of A Snob - *Only*
Jenkins UK (1949); British Book Centre US (1958)

John CRISPIN

sleuths in the year 1750.

British Male Amateur operating in England

Raymond FOXALL 1916- (British)

See main detective Harry ADKINS

Citation Record: 3 Books

Society Of The Dispossessed - *First*
Hale UK (1978); Signet US (1976)

Noble Pirate - *Latest*
Signet US (1978); Hale UK (1980)

Det Fey CROAKER

investigates the death of a woman who seems to have had too many husbands, all of whom died leaving her their fortunes.

American Policewoman operating in Los Angeles

Paul BISHOP (American)

was born in England and served for several years in the Los Angeles police force.

Inventor of one other detective pair Calico Jack WALKER and Tina TAMIKO

Citation Record: 1 Book

Sins Of The Dead - *Single*
Pocket Books US (1994)

Fred CROCKETT

was once a cop and, it seems has graduated in 'Criminal Science'. Now, operating from an old office in a run-down part of town, and intimate with the street scene of the neighbourhood, he specialises in finding young runaways.

American Male Private Detective operating in Michigan

Brad LANG (American)

Citation Record: 3 Books

Crockett On The Loose - *First*
Leisure Books US (1975)

The Perdition Express - *Last*
Leisure Books US (1976)

Insp CROFT

British Policeman operating in England

Robert BARNARD 1936- (British)

Invented 13 detectives - see Insp Perry TRETHOWAN

Citation Record: 1 Book

Blood Brotherhood - *Single*
Penguin UK (1983)

Denham CROFT

was an early invention, soon discarded in favour of the better-known detectives created by this extraordinarily prolific writer. It is not clear where the stories appeared.

British Male Amateur operating in England

Charles HAMILTON 1876-1961 (British)

Invented 3 detectives - see Ferrers LOCKE

No citations

Freddie CROFT

is a jockey-trainer who investigates a racing stable crime.

British Male Amateur operating in England

Dick FRANCIS 1920- (British)

Invented 18 detectives - see Sid HALLEY

Citation Record: 1 Book

Driving Force - *Single*
Joseph UK (1992)

Danby CROKER

British Male Amateur operating in England

R Austin FREEMAN 1862-1947 (British)

Invented 4 detectives - see Dr John Evelyn THORNDYKE

Citation Record: 13 Short Stories in 1 Collection

The Exploits Of Danby Croker - *Collection 1*
Duckworth UK (1916)

Simon CROLE

is called on to investigate the shooting of another PI at a police banquet.

American Male Private Detective operating in Los Angeles

Robert FLEMING 1891- (American)

Citation Record: 1 Book

Night Freight Murders - *Only*
Smith & Durrell US (1942)

A Bullet In His Cap - *Only**
Handi-Books US (1942)

And Death Drove On - *Only**
Green Dragon US (194?)

Murder Comes To Dinner - *Only**
Long UK (1943)

Simon CROLE

is the head of a small detective agency. A PI of the same name and credentials is in a book by *Robert FLEMING* and the two authors may be the same person.

American Male Private Detective operating in Los Angeles

Robert H LEITFRED (American)

Citation Record: 3 Books

The Corpse That Spoke - *First*
Green Circle US (1936); Harrap UK (1937)

Death Cancels The Evidence - *Last*
Green Circle US (1938)

Murder Is My Racket - *Last**
Tech Mysteries US (194?)

Sam CROMBIE

operates from an office on 7th Avenue, Manhattan. He works on straightforward detective cases and, by the genre's current standards, is pretty soft-boiled.

American Male Private Detective operating in New York/Connecticut

George Harmon COXE 1901-1984 (American)

Invented 20 detectives - see Kent MURDOCK

Citation Record: 2 Books

The Frightened Fiancée - *First*
Knopf US (1950); Hammond UK (1953)

The Impetuous Mistress - *Last*
Knopf US (1958); Hammond UK (1959)

Derek CROME

is an instructor in psychology at a university somewhere in the eastern part of America and is writing a thesis on psychopathic murder. He is called in to help the police investigate a case of rape and brutal murder and is able to solve the crime and complete his thesis.

American Male Amateur operating in Massachusetts

Douglas Ross ANGUS 1909- (Canadian)

was born in Amherst, Nova Scotia, Canada.

Citation Record: 1 Book

Death On Jerusalem Road - *Only*
Random House US (1963)

Bill 'Ironsides' CROMWELL

British Policeman operating in England

Sidekick: Sgt LISTER

British Male - Subordinate

Victor GUNN 1889-1965 (British)

For writer details see Insp William (The Grouser) BEEKE

Citation Record: 43 Books

Footsteps Of Death - *First*
Collins UK (1939)

The Petticoat Lane Murders - *Last*
Collins UK (1966)

Dan CRONYN

is a small-time PI in a case involving political intrigues in Washington in the 1960s.

American Male Private Detective operating in Washington DC

James T DOYLE (American)

Inventor of one other detective Paul BRODER

Citation Record: 1 Book

Deadly Resurrection - *Single*
Walker US (1987)

Arthur G CROOK

is a rascally lawyer who has red hair, reddish suits and drives ridiculous sporty cars. Middle-aged, he lives in a disreputable part of town and spends a great deal of his time swilling beer with low acquaintances, to whom he distributes his business cards. It is thus no wonder that he is so often called on to rescue an innocent suspect or solve a crime that the police have already fouled up. In several of his many books he is by no means the main character, often being called in late on a case to untie the knots and tie up loose ends.

British Male Amateur operating in London

Anthony GILBERT 1899-1973 (British)

was born in London. Although the author reserved this pseudonym for her large output of criminous works, she wrote at least twenty mainstream novels and numerous radio plays under another pseudonym (uncited).

Writer: Lucy Beatrice MALLESON

Other Detectives:
Monsieur DUPUY   Scott EGERTON

Citation Record: 49 Books

Murder By Experts - *First*
Collins UK (1936); Dial US (1937)

A Nice Little Killing - *Last*
Collins UK (1974); Random House US (1974)

Paul CROOK

is working on a farm in the Australian outback when he is called on to take over a Sydney detective agency that has been left to his father, a stage comic, who is always on tour. Handsome, naive, a constant attraction to divers ladies, he really is not the greatest sleuth in the world – or, indeed, even in the antipodes. However, his inherited office staff help him get there in the end.

Australian Male Private Detective operating in Sydney

Charles WEST (British)

Citation Record: 3 Books

Stonefish - *First*
Collins UK (1990); Walker US (1991)

Little Ripper - *Latest*
HarperCollins UK (1991)

CROOKED COLE

American Male Detective in Pulp Magazines operating in USA

M H WILLIAMS (American)

Invented 4 detectives - see DAVENPORT BLAKE

Citation Record: 1 Selected Short Story

Crooked Cole, The Hunchback Detective; Or, Piping The Opium Dens
Old Cap Collier Library US (18??)

David CROSBIE

British Male Amateur operating in England

Alfred TACK 1906- (British)

Inventor of one other detective John HARLEY

Citation Record: 1 Book

Forecast - Murder - *Only*
Long UK (1967)

Prof CROSBY

American Male Amateur operating in USA

W S HASTINGS and Brian HOOKER (American)

Writer: (First author) Wells Southworth HASTINGS 1878-1923

Citation Record: 1 Book

The Professor's Mystery - *Only*
Bobbs US (1911)

David CROSBY

British Male Amateur operating in England

Harry Stephen KEELER 1890-1967 (American)

Invented 14 detectives - see Angus MACWHORTER

Citation Record: 1 Book

The Amazing Web - *Only*
Ward, Lock UK (1929); Dutton US (1930)

Herbert CROSBY

is said to be a DA's Assistant in the DA's office in St Louis. He fancies himself as a sleuth, having read books on the subject, but he is a pretty poor one.

American Male Professional Investigator operating in Wisconsin

Mary Semple SCOTT (American)

Citation Record: 1 Book

Crime Hound - *Single*
Scribner's US (1940)

Lee CROSLEY

American Male Secret Agent operating in USA

Robert TRALINS 1926- (American)

Writer: Stanley Robert TRALINS

Citation Record: 3 Books

The Chic Chic Spy - *First*
Belmont US (1966)
The Ring-A-Ding UFOs - *Last*
Belmont US (1967)

Det Alex CROSS
is black, has a PhD and carries a Glock semiautomatic to see him through the day in small towns in North Carolina.
American Policeman operating in North Carolina

James PATTERSON (American)
is the chairman of the J Walter Thompson advertising agency.
Citation Record: 2 Books
Along Came A Spider - *First*
Dell US (1994)
Kiss The Girls - *Latest*
Little, Brown US (1995)

Insp Frederick Jubilee 'Jumper' CROSS
British Policeman operating in England
Sidekick: Sgt John LAMB
British Male - Subordinate

John DONAVAN 1905-1986 (British)
Invented 3 detectives - see Sgt Johnny LAMB
Citation Record: 1 Book
The Case Of The Talking Dust - *Only*
Hale UK (1938); Mystery House US (1941)

Howard CROSS
American Male Sleuth operating in USA

John Ross MACDONALD 1915- (American)
Invented 3 detectives - see Lew ARCHER
Citation Record: 1 Book
Meet Me At The Morgue - *Only*
Knopf US (1953)
Experience With Evil - *Only**
Cassell UK (1954)

Peter CROSS
American Male Private Detective operating in New York

Jim THOMAS 1916- (American)
Writer: Thomas James Butler REAGAN
Citation Record: 1 Book
Cross Purposes - *Only*
McCall US (1971)

CROSSLEY
British Male Amateur operating in England

L T MEADE 1854-1914 (British)
Invented 4 detectives - see Rudolph GREY
Citation Record: 1 Book
A Son Of Ishmael - *Only*
White UK (1896); New Amsterdam US (1896)

Spencer CROSS-WADE
American Male Amateur operating in USA

William KATZ 1940- (American)
Citation Record: 2 Books
Death In December - *First*
McGraw US (1984)
Surprise Party - *Latest*
McGraw US (1984)

Insp CROUCH
is dogged and clever. He gets his man for murder – but probably not the right man.
British Policeman operating in London

Miles TRIPP 1923- (British)
See main detective John SAMSON
Citation Record: 1 Book
A Man Without Friends - *Only*
Macmillan UK (1970)

Insp CROW
is a stolid policeman in books that often have a strong legal setting, reflecting the author's own background.
British Policeman operating in Wales/England

Roy LEWIS 1933- (British)
Invented 3 detectives - see Arnold LANDON
Citation Record: 8 Books
A Lover Too Many - *First*
Collins UK (1969); World US (1971)
A Relative Distance - *Latest*
Collins UK (1981)

Ch Anderson CROW
is an oddity who appears in one novel and a collection of short stories published over a decade later. He is the entire police force of Tinkletown, New York, as well as occupying most of the town's other official posts. A rustic with absolute authority in his community, he sees to it that no crimes at all are ever committed.
American Policeman operating in New York

George Barr MCCUTCHEON 1866-1928 (American)
was born in Lafayette, Indiana. He worked as a reporter and is said to have made a large sum of money from one early book.
Citation Record: 1 Book 10 Short Stories in 1 Collection
The Daughter Of Anderson Crow - *Only*
Dodd, Mead US (1907); Hodder & Stoughton UK (1907)
Anderson Crow, Detective - *Collection 1*
Dodd, Mead US (1920)

Martin CROW
British Male Amateur operating in England

George NORSWORTHY (British)
Citation Record: 2 Books
A House-Party Mystery - *First*
Low UK (1935)
Crime At The Villa Gloria - *Last*
Low UK (1936); Greenberg US (1936)

Titus CROW
British Male Amateur

Brian LUMLEY 1937- (British)
Citation Record: 11 Short Stories in 1 Collection
The Compleat Crow - *Collection 1*
Ganley UK (1987)

Uncle George CROWDER
is one of the author's more minor detectives. An ex-lawyer who retired when he sent an innocent man to the electric chair, he spends time investigating local crimes around his rural community near Lakewood, assisted by his nephew.
American Male Amateur operating in Connecticut
Sidekick: Joey TRIMBLE
is twelve years old and is a clever assistant to his uncle.
American Male - Nephew

Hugh PENTECOST 1903-1989 (American)
Invented 12 detectives - see Pierre CHAMBRUN
Citation Record: 6 Books 9 Short Stories in 1 Collection
Choice Of Violence - *First*
Dodd, Mead US (1961); Boardman UK (1962)
Murder Sweet And Sour - *Last*
Dodd, Mead US (1985)
Around Dark Corners - *Collection 1*
Dodd, Mead US (1970)

Elisha CROWE
solves a case of death by shooting in a locked room.
British Male Amateur operating in England

C

Headon HILL 1857-1927 (British)

Invented 11 detectives - see Insp HERON

Citation Record: 1 Book

A Rogue In Ambush - *Only*
Ward, Lock UK (1911)

Insp CROWLEY

solves a case of death by poison gas in a locked room.

Policeman operating in Ireland

Gerald LEE (Irish)

Citation Record: 1 Book

Murder And Music - *Only*
Talbot EI (1943)

Ch Supt John CROWN

British Policeman operating in China/Macao

Terry HARKNETT 1936- (British)

Writer: Terry William HARKNETT

Other Bylines:

Joseph HEDGES Thomas H STONE

Inventor of one other detective Steve WAYNE

Citation Record: 3 Books

Crown: The Sweet And Sour Kill - *First*
Futura UK (1974); Pinnacle US (1974)

Crown: Bamboo Shoot-Out - *Last*
Futura UK (1975)

Nina CROWTHER

British Female Amateur operating in England

Margaret YORKE 1924- (British)

Invented 3 detectives - see Stephen DAWES

Citation Record: 1 Book

Find Me A Villain - *Single*
St Martin's US (1983)

CROYD

sleuths at some time in the future. He also appears in one book with the author's other detective, *Claudine ST CYR.*

Male Sleuth

Ian WALLACE 1912- (American)

Invented 3 detectives - see Claudine ST CYR

Citation Record: 3 Books

Croyd - *First*
Putnam UK (1967)

Door To Enigma - *Latest*
Daw US (1979)

CROYD

Second detective of Claudine ST CYR

Father Francis Xavier CRUMLISH

is the incumbent of St Brigid's, Lake City, near the Canadian border. He is elderly, arthritic, suffers from indigestion, and his bishop dogs him. His parishioners, however, seem more than somewhat addicted to robbery and murder, which he is called on by the local police to help solve.

American Male Amateur operating in USA

Alice Scanlon REACH (American)

Citation Record: 1 Selected Short Story

The Ordeal Of Father Crumlish
US (1963)

Arthur CRUMP

Second detective of Insp Stephen ELIOT

Jo CRUPPER

British Male Amateur operating in England

Thomas LE BRETON 1913- (British)

Writer: Auguste MONTFORT

Citation Record: 16 Short Stories in 1 Collection

Jo Crupper, Bus Conductor - *Collection 1*
Philpot UK (1925)

Edwina CRUSOE

American Female Amateur operating in USA

Mary KITTREDGE 1949- (American)

See main detective Charlotte KENT

Citation Record: 1 Book

Desperate Remedy - *Single*
St Martin's US (1993)

Det Carlos CRUZ

Appears with at least two other detectives - see Det Jay GOLDSTEIN.

Raymond CRUZ

American Male Amateur operating in USA

Elmore LEONARD 1935- (American)

Invented 6 detectives - see Frank RYAN

Citation Record: 1 Book

City Primaeval - *Single*
Delacorte US (1980)

Larry CRYSTAL

American Male Private Detective operating in Oklahoma

John MILES 1930- (American)

For writer details see Charity ROSS

Citation Record: 1 Book

Dally With A Deadly Doll - *Only*
Ace US (1961)

John Francis CUDDY

is an ex-soldier, recently widowed, who has resigned from an insurance company in Boston, where he was the head of the Claims Unit, to set up as a PI in an office near the Common.

American Male Private Detective operating in Boston

Jeremiah M HEALY 1948- (American)

was born in Teaneck, New Jersey. He took degrees at Rutgers University, New Brunswick, and Harvard University, Cambridge, Massachusetts. He is a practising lawyer.
!See Appendix 2.

Adopter of one other detective Philip MARLOWE

Citation Record: 10 Books

Blunt Darts - *First*
Walker US (1984); Macmillan UK (1986)

Rescue - *Latest*
Pocket Books US (1995)

Sgt CUFF

is one of the great classic detectives, as he appears in the first English novel to have the detective as a central character in the plot. *Insp BUCKET,* featured by *Charles DICKENS,* in *BLEAK HOUSE* is, although earlier, essentially a peripheral character. *Sgt CUFF,* who was based on a real policeman, Sergeant Whicher, is described as being elderly, thin, grizzled and having a passion for roses and throwaway lines. He is also said to be 'the finest detective in England'. He is called in to solve the mystery of the theft of the Moonstone at Frizinghall when the officer in charge, an ass if ever there was one, fails to make any sense of the case. *CUFF's* methods are simple and are based on solid, plodding work. Although he makes mistakes, he is human enough to admit them.

British Policeman operating in England

Stooge: Supt SEEGRAVE
must qualify as the very first police stooge in English literature. Tall, portly, brusque, imposing and with a military manner, he is a blundering fool of the first order and was to set the trend for countless followers.

British Male

Wilkie COLLINS 1824-1889 (British)

was a distinguished writer of the late Victorian period in Britain, author of many novels and recognised as the creator of one of the earliest and best characterised police detectives to appear in the genre. He was perhaps the first

C

writer to realise the new direction that a detective and his work could give to the novel. He is known to have toyed with the idea in a few later novels and short stories, but he did not take it any further.
Writer: William Wilkie COLLINS

Other Detectives:
Walter HARTWRIGHT | OLD SHARON
Griffith TROWBRIDGE | Valeria WOODVILLE

Citation Record: 1 Book

The Moonstone - *Only*
holds pride of place in detective fiction in being the first novel to have the detective as a major character and integral to the plot. The American poet and Nobel Laureate, T S Eliot, called it 'the first, the longest and the best detective story in the English language', a pontification with which, however, not all would agree.
Tinsley UK (1868); Harper & Row US (1868)

Kirk CULLEN
is a teacher of English at high school. He becomes a PI and is involved in a case with a touch of the occult about it.
American Male Private Detective operating in USA

James GUNN 1923- (American)
Writer: James Edwin GUNN
Inventor of one other detective Jerry PARKER
Citation Record: 1 Book
The Magicians - *Only*
Scribner's US (1976)

Peter CULLIMORE
Second detective of Donald LOMAX

Timothy CULLINAN
British Male Amateur operating in England

Oliver MARTIN 1873- (British)
Writer: Ernest DAVIES
Citation Record: 2 Books
The Iron Door - *First*
Hodder & Stoughton UK (1923)
The Mermaid - *Last*
Faber UK (1926)

Lucy CULPEPPER
does a little amateur sleuthing in this gothic mystery story by a famous author.
British Female Amateur operating in England

Joan Delano AIKEN 1924- (British)
was born in Rye, Sussex. She is the author of many admirable works of fiction, especially for children, and some mystery stories, usually romantic.
Citation Record: 1 Book
The Embroidered Sunset - *Only*
Gollancz UK (1970); Doubleday US (1970)

Maggie CULTHORPE
Second detective of Lionel Humphrey SALT

Dan CUMBERLAND
American Male Amateur operating in Minnesota

Vera KELSEY (American)
See main detective Lt DIEGO
Citation Record: 1 Book
Whisper Murder! - *Only*
Doubleday US (1946)

Ch Insp CUMMINGS
appears also in two books with the author's other detective, *Insp FILLINGER.*
British Policeman operating in England

Paul MCGUIRE 1903-1978 (Australian)
Invented 4 detectives - see Insp/Supt FILLINGER
Citation Record: 3 Books
Murder In Borstal - *First*
Skeffington UK (1931)
The Black Rose Murder - *First**
Brentano's US (1932)
7:30 Victoria - *Last*
Skeffington UK (1935)

Ch Insp CUMMINGS and Insp/Supt FILLINGER
also appear individually in other books.
British Policemen operating in England

Paul MCGUIRE 1903-1978 (Australian)
Invented 4 detectives - see Insp/Supt FILLINGER
Citation Record: 2 Books
Murder In Haste - *First*
Skeffington UK (1934)
Daylight Murder - *Last*
Skeffington UK (1934)
Murder At High Noon - *Last**
Doubleday US (1934)

Noel CUMMINGS
American Male Amateur operating in New York

Felice PICANO 1944- (American)
Citation Record: 1 Book
The Lure - *Single*
Delacorte US (1979); New English Library UK (1981)

Matt CUNEEN
American Male Amateur operating in USA

Charlotte ARMSTRONG 1905-1969 (American)
Invented 5 detectives - see Prof MacDougal DUFF
Citation Record: 1 Book
Dream Of A Fair Woman - *Only*
Coward McCann US (1966); Collins UK (1966)

Richard CUNLIFFE
British Male Professional Amateur operating in England

H FRANKISH (British)
Citation Record: 7 Short Stories in 1 Collection
Dr Cunliffe - Investigator - *Collection 1*
Heath UK (1913)

John CUNNINGHAM
is invalided out of the Army with a mysterious tropical disease and sets up as a breeder and trainer of gundogs. Simple enough, one might say, but – little known though it might be outside the world of the cognoscenti – there exist such things as gundog-associated robbery and murder. He is able to some solve baffling cases with the help of two female assistants.
British Male Amateur operating in England

Sidekick: Isobel KITTS
is a veterinarian who attends *John CUNNINGHAM's* dogs. In spite of a tendency to overindulge in drink and sex when celebrating, she is of great help in solving crimes.
British Female - Vet

Sidekick: Beth CANTRELL
is the sleuth's kennelmaid in his first book, but later becomes his wife. She is, moreover, a useful girl to have around when solving these doggy crimes.
British Female - Wife

Gerald HAMMOND 1926- (British)
Invented 5 detectives - see Keith CALDER
Citation Record: 3 Books
Dog In The Dark - *First*
Macmillan UK (1989)
Whose Dog Are You? - *Latest*
Macmillan UK (1990)

Maj 'Brains' CUNNINGHAM
British Male Sleuth operating in China/Haiti

C

E P THORNE (British)
Invented 3 detectives - see Quentin EADY
Citation Record: 13 Books
The Smile Of Cheng Su - *First*
Wright UK (1946)
The Caribbean Affair - *Last*
Wright UK (1966)

Max CURFEW
British Male Sleuth operating in Europe

John BRUNNER 1934-
Writer: John Kilian Houston BRUNNER
Citation Record: 3 Books
A Plague On Both Your Causes - *First*
Hodder & Stoughton UK (1969)
Backlash - *First**
Pyramid US (1969)
Honky In The Woodpile - *Last*
Constable UK (1971)

Nick CURRAN
American Male Private Detective operating in San Francisco

Richard OSBORNE (American)
Citation Record: 1 Book
Basic Instinct - *Single*
Signet UK (1992)

Vickie CURRAN
American Female Amateur operating in USA

Marie CASTOIRE and Richard POSNER 1944- (American)
Citation Record: 1 Book
Gold Shield - *Single*
Putnam US (1982); Sphere UK (1983)

Harry CURRY
Second detective of Insp GLOVER

Hugh CURTIS
British Male Amateur operating in England

Paul SOMERS 1908- (British)
For writer details see Max EASTERBROOK
Citation Record: 3 Books
Beginner's Luck - *First*
Collins UK (1958); Harper & Row US (1958)
The Shivering Mountain - *Last*
Collins UK (1959); Harper & Row US (1959)

Lyle CURTIS and Susan YATES
American Male Amateur and American Female Amateur operating in New York

Emma Lou FETTA (American)
was a journalist and foreign correspondent for American newspapers.
Citation Record: 3 Books
Murder In Style - *First*
Doubleday US (1939)
Dressed To Kill - *Last*
Doubleday US (1940)

Insp Peter CURWEN
appears also in books with another of the author's detectives, the amateur *Hugh STANTON.*
British Policeman operating in England

Roy VICKERS 1888-1965 (British)
Invented 9 detectives - see Insp J RASON
Citation Record: 1 Book 2 Short Stories in 1 Collection
Find The Innocent - *Only*
Jenkins UK (1959)
The Girl Who Wouldn't Talk - *Only**
In 'Detective Book Club' US (1959)
The Girl Who Wouldn't Talk - *Collection 1*
This collection of seven of the author's short stories contains two with *CURWEN.*
Faber UK (1959); In 'Detective Book Club' US (1959)

Insp Peter CURWEN and Hugh STANTON
British Policeman and British Male Amateur operating in England

Roy VICKERS 1888-1965 (British)
Invented 9 detectives - see Insp J RASON
Citation Record: 4 Books
Six Came To Dinner - *First*
Jenkins UK (1948)
Murder In Two Flats - *Last*
Jenkins UK (1951); Mill US (1952)

Amanda CURZON and Oscar SALLIS
British Female Amateur and British Male Amateur operating in England

Frank USHER 1909-1976 (British)
For writer details see Insp Jim BURGESS
Inventor of one other detective Daye SMITH
Citation Record: 3 Books
Fall Into My Grave - *First*
Hale UK (1962)
The Boston Crab - *Last*
Hale UK (1970)

Florence CUSACK
was one of the several lady detectives to appear shortly after the emergence of *Sherlock HOLMES.* She featured in a number of short stories, originally published during 1899 and 1900 in *The Harmsworth Magazine.*
British Female Amateur operating in London

L T MEADE and Robert EUSTACE (British)
Invented 7 detectives - see Insp FROST and Dr GARLAND
Citation Record: 2 Selected Short Stories
Mr Boyer's Unexpected Will
is the best-known story featuring *Florence CUSACK.* It is also to be found in an anthology, *Crime on her Mind* (*Pantheon*; US 1975; *Joseph;* UK 1976).
In 'The Harmsworth Magazine' UK (1899)
The Outside Ledge: A Cablegram Mystery
is the last of four stories in which *Florence CUSACK* is known to have appeared.
In 'The Harmsworth Magazine' UK (1900)

Det CUSH
American Male Professional Investigator operating in USA

Donald J MCKENZIE 1859-1932 (American)
For writer details see Clarice DYKE
Other Detectives:
The REPORTER DETECTIVE The WORKING MAN DETECTIVE
Citation Record: 1 Book
A Past Master Of Crime; Or, Detective Cush's Clever Work - *Only*
Street & Smith (Magnet) US (1899)

Bonny CUTLER
Second detective of Punch ROBERTS

Rusty CUTLER
American Male Amateur operating in Los Angeles

Marc RUBEL 1949- (American)
Writer: Marc Reid RUBEL
Citation Record: 1 Book
Flex - *Single*
St Martin's US (1983)

Dr Samuel CUTTING
American Male Amateur operating in Maine

Perrie D WESTBROOK 1916- (American)
Writer: Perrie Dickie WESTBROOK
Citation Record: 3 Books
Happy Deathday - *First*
Phoenix Press US (1947)
Infra Blood - *Last*
Phoenix Press US (1950)

C

Adam CYBER
Second detective of Jason STARR

Ch Mark CZERNICK
Second detective of Susan GRENELLE

Dr Jan CZISSAR
is a Czech policeman who, having fled his country in 1938, has come to England with a vague letter of introduction to the Home Office. He is a fussy little man and he hopes to set up as a detective in London, under the enforced tutelage of *Asst Commiss MERCER* of Scotland Yard.
Czech Policeman operating in London

Stooge: Asst Commiss MERCER
is responsible for bringing *CZISSAR* to England, but he is naturally irritated when the Czech meddles in his cases and, moreover, provides him with brilliant solutions.
British Male

Eric AMBLER 1909- (British)
was born in London. He took a degree at London University, 1928, and served in the Royal Artillery during the Second World War. He is the renowned author of numerous novels of crime, adventure, intrigue and espionage, as well as of many of the greatest film scripts. His works include some of the best examples of the various sub-genres for all media. He did not stick long with pure detective fiction, for his interests were in the political aspects of his absorbing plots. He received the Crime Writers Association's Gold Dagger four times, 1959, 1962, 1967, 1972, and their Diamond Dagger award, 1986. He received the Mystery Writers of America Edgar Allan Poe award, 1964, and their Grand Master award, 1975. In other years he has received awards of a similar nature from France and other countries. He was made an OBE, 1981.

Other Detectives:
Charles LATIMER
Arthur Abdul SIMPSON
VALESHOFF and TAMARA

Citation Record: 2 Selected Short Stories

Bird In The Trees
UK (1942)

The Case Of The Landlady's Brother
UK (1949)

— D —

Jane DA SILVA
is the one and only investigator for the Seattle Foundation for Righting Wrongs. A former cabaret singer and now in her thirties, she is said to walk as alluringly as Lauren Bacall in the movie, *The Big Sleep*, and to love good wine and good men.
American Female Professional Investigator operating in Seattle

K K BECK (American)
Invented 5 detectives - see Iris COOPER

Citation Record: 3 Books

A Hopeless Case - *First*
Mysterious Press US (1993)

Electric City - *Latest*
Mysterious Press US (1994)

Capt Jose DA SILVA
is a liaison officer between the Brazilian police and Interpol. Known to his friends as Ze, he is nearly forty, has a degree in criminology and always gets his man, whether in Brazilian jungles or on the streets of Manhattan, to which his cases sometimes take him.
Brazilian Policeman operating in Brazil/USA

Sidekick: Mr WILSON
is an official at the American Embassy in Rio. He has access to private information and acts as a kind of undercover aide to *DA SILVA*, usually meeting him in disguise.
American Male - Assistant

Robert L FISH 1912-1981 (American)
Invented 4 detectives - see Schlock HOMES

Citation Record: 10 Books

The Fugitive - *First*
Simon & Schuster US (1962); Boardman UK (1963)

Trouble In Paradise - *Last*
Doubleday US (1975)

Leonardo DA VINCI
is, indeed, the great Renaissance artist. He is the sleuth in one short story in the author's collection based on historical figures.
Italian Male Amateur operating in Italy

Theodore MATHIESON 1913- (American)

Other Detectives:
Benjamin FRANKLIN
Omar KHAYYAM

Citation Record: 1 Selected Short Story

Leonardo Da Vinci, Detective
appeared in the March number of the magazine and is also in the author's collection, *The Great "Detectives"* (*Simon*; US 1960).
In 'Ellery Queen's Mystery Magazine' US (1959)

Capt DACK
British Male Amateur operating in England

Peter MERITON 1891-1961 (British)
For writer details see Bill LANGLEY

Other Detectives:
Sexton BLAKE
Bill LANGLEY

Citation Record: 3 Books

Captain Dack - *First*
Hurst UK (1939)

Plunder - *Last*
Hurst UK (1948)

Mr DADDY
British Male Amateur operating in England

Collin BROOKS 1893- (British)
Invented 3 detectives - see Swete MCTAVISH

Citation Record: 1 Book

Mr Daddy - Detective - *Only*
Hutchinson UK (1933)

The DAGO DETECTIVE
American Male Detective in Pulp Magazines operating in USA

Lew WILLIAMS (American)
Inventor of one other detective The RELIANCE DETECTIVE

Citation Record: 1 Selected Short Story

The Dago Detective; Or, The Chum Of The Police Chief
Old Cap Collier Library US (18??)

Sarah 'Serendipity' DAHLQUIST
Second detective of Leo G BLOODWORTH

Stephen DAIN
American Male Sleuth operating in USA/Asia/Africa

Robert SHECKLEY 1928- (American)

Citation Record: 5 Books

Dead Run - *First*
Bantam UK (1961)

Time Limit - *Last*
Bantam US (1967); New English Library UK (1967)

D

Sam DAKKERS
American Male Amateur operating in New York

Mike BRETT (American)

Citation Record: 2 Books

The Guilty Bystander - *First*
Ace US (1959); Digit UK (1960)

Scream Street - *Last*
Ace US (1959); Digit UK (1960)

DAKOTA
is an American Indian.
American Male Private Detective operating in Nevada

Gilbert A RALSTON 1912- (American)

Writer: Gilbert Alexander RALSTON

Citation Record: 5 Books

Dakota Warpath - *First*
Pinnacle US (1973)

Chain Reaction - *Last*
Pinnacle US (1975)

Barlow DALE
British Male Amateur operating in England

Ruth SIVERNS (British)

Citat ion Record: 7 Short Stories in 1 Collection

Barlow Dale's Casebook - *Collection 1*
Macmillan UK (1981)

Edward DALE
British Male Amateur operating in England

Weatherby CHESNEY 1865-1944 (British)

For writer details see Capt Owen KETTLE

Inventor of one other detective Richard FELTON

Citation Record: 18 Short Stories in 1 Collection

The Adventures Of A Solicitor - *Collection 1*
Not all the stories are criminous.
Bowden UK (1898)

Insp James DALE
British Policeman operating in England

John C COOPER (British)

Writer: John CROYDON

Citation Record: 2 Books

The Body Was Of No Account - *First*
Boardman UK (1957)

Death In Aberration - *Last*
Boardman UK (1958)

Jimmie DALE
is a wealthy clubman who is a cracksman by night. A kind of Robin Hood character, he preys on criminals themselves, meting out his own justice in the tradition of *A J RAFFLES* and *Simon TEMPLAR*.
American Male Amateur operating in New York

Frank PACKARD 1877-1942 (Canadian)

was born in Montreal of American parents. He took a BSc at McGill University, Montreal, 1897, and later studied in Belgium. He was the author of many romantic thrillers, usually set in New York.

Writer: Frank Lucius PACKARD

Citation Record: 5 Books

The Adventures Of Jimmie Dale - *First*
Doran US (1917); Cassell UK (1918)

Jimmie Dale And The Missing Hour - *Last*
Doubleday US (1935); Hodder & Stoughton UK (1935)

Martin DALE
was one of the author's several detectives invented for juvenile magazines.
British Male Amateur operating in England

Maxwell SCOTT (British)

Invented 3 detectives - see Nelson LEE

Citation Record: 5 Books

The Secret Of The Ring - *First*
Amalgamated UK (1916)

The Silver Key - *Last*
Amalgamated UK (1917)

Roger DALE
American Male Amateur operating in USA

Steve ALLEN (American)

Writer: Stephen Valentine Patrick ALLEN

Citation Record: 1 Book

The Talk Show Murders - *Single*
Delacorte US (1982)

Insp/Cdr Adam DALGLIESH
is cast in the mould of the classic British policemen who go back to the Golden Age. Mainly created by women authors, they have usually been tall, dark, attractive, hard-worked, and vulnerable both physically and emotionally. They are also given to being highly literate, are armed with classical quotations, and have an exceptional knowledge of food and drink. *Adam DALGLEISH* is all of these and, moreover, he is a suffering widower too. A fine detective, he finds himself in books of quality and exquisite plotting that often, and regrettably, fizzle out in prolonged and violent endings (the British equivalent, it may be, of shoot-outs at the OK Corral).

DALGLEISH has paid the price, paid by others before him, of having a real life in which he ages as the books and authors age. It is the price of trying too hard to become a genre institution. Even the best fictional detectives, British or American, can rarely stand up to that and they almost always deteriorate. It is preferable, perhaps, that, in the words of the poet, 'They do not grow old as we that are left grow old'. He is now a Commander, the most senior serving rank in the British police force, and finally must leave most of the interesting detective work to others; especially, it seems, to his new lady assistant, taken on late in the series and, perhaps, merely bowing to present custom.
British Policeman operating in England

Sidekick: Det Insp Kate MISKIN
is the assistant to the great man in his later books. A high rank she may have and much work she may do; but, in such company, she can only be a sidekick.
British Female - Subordinate

P D JAMES 1920- (British)

was born in Oxford, Oxfordshire, and educated at Cambridge Girls' High School, 1931-1937. She later became an experienced administrator on various Hospital Boards, 1949-1962, in police departments and the Home Office. She received the Crime Writers Association Silver Dagger award three times, 1971, 1975, 1986, their Diamond Dagger award, 1987, and was made an OBE, 1983. Her criminous novels have been regarded, by several critics, as being some of the best since the days of the great English writers of the 1930s.

Writer: Phyllis Dorothy JAMES

Inventor of one other detective Cordelia GRAY

Citation Record: 12 Books

Cover Her Face - *First*
Faber UK (1962); Scribner's US (1966)

Original Sin - *Latest*
Faber UK (1994)

Dana DALLAS
American Male Sleuth operating in USA

Nat KARTA

House name.

Writer: Norman Austen LAZENBY

Citation Record: 2 Books

D

We The Condemned - *First*
Scion UK (1932)
A Guy Named Judas - *Last*
Muir-Watson UK (1952)

Johnny DALMAS

American Male Private Detective operating in USA

Raymond CHANDLER 1888-1959 (American)
Invented 9 detectives - see Philip MARLOWE
Citation Record: 4 Selected Short Stories
Mandarin's Jade
was used, in part, in the author's novel, *FAREWELL MY LOVELY.*
In 'Dime Detective' US (1937)
The Lady In The Lake
was used, in part, in the author's novel of the same title.
In 'Dime Detective' US (1939)

Prof DALY

taught English literature in Dublin for forty years before retiring to a nursing home in Galway. He is brought into difficult cases by an old friend in the police. Somehow the old buffer hits on the solutions.

British Male Amateur operating in Ireland
Stooge: Insp Mike KENNY
!See Appendix 2.
is the cop who introduces *DALY* to his cases.
Irish Male

Eilis DILLON 1920- (Irish)
See main detective Insp Mike KENNY
Citation Record: 2 Books
Death At Crane's Court - *First*
Faber UK (1953); Walker US (1963)
Death In The Quadrangle - *Last*
Faber UK (1956); Walker US (1968)

Maxwell DALY

British Male Private Detective operating in England

Roger BUSBY and Gerald HOLTHAM (British)
Writer: (First Author) Roger Charles BUSBY 1941-
Citation Record: 1 Book
Main Line Kill - *Only*
Cassell UK (1968); Walker US (1968)

Supt Andrew DALZIEL and Sgt/Det Ch Insp Peter PASCOE

appear together in semi-procedurals set in Yorkshire. *Andrew DALZIEL* is middle-aged, coarse, fat, indestructible, and a brilliant detective. *Peter PASCOE,* in his twenties, has a degree in social sciences and, to his senior's disgust, reads works on criminology. It is not surprising that, in the series, he rises to the rank of Detective Chief Inspector.

British Male Policemen operating in Yorkshire

Reginald HILL 1936- (British)
was born in Hartlepool, County Durham. He was educated in Carlisle and took a BA in English from St Catherine's College, Oxford, 1960. He has been a schoolmaster and lecturer, becoming a full-time writer in 1981.
Writer: Reginald Charles HILL
Other Byline: Patrick RUELL
Other Detectives:
Insp Lev CHISLENKO   Insp MCHARG
Joe SIXSMITH
Citation Record: 12 Books
A Clubbable Woman - *First*
Collins UK (1970); Foul Play US (1984)
Pictures Of Perfection - *Latest*
Delacorte US (1994)

Paul DAMIAN

American Male Private Detective operating in New York

Paul E WALSH (American)
Citation Record: 1 Book
The Murder Room - *Only*
Avon US (1957)

Insp DAMIOT

French Policeman operating in France

Vincent MCCONNOR 1907?- (American)
Other Detectives:
Zeke GAHAGAN   Eugène VIDOCQ
Citation Record: 3 Books
The Provence Puzzle - *First*
Macmillan US (1980)
The Riviera Puzzle - *Latest*
Macmillan US (1981)

Dan DAMON

American Male Amateur operating in New York

Gene GOLDSMITH (American)
Citation Record: 1 Book
Murder On His Mind - *Only*
Mill US (1947); Quality Press UK (1954)

Lingo DAN

American Male Amateur operating in USA

Percival POLLARD 1869-1911 (American)
Citation Record: 10 Short Stories in 1 Collection
Lingo Dan - *Collection 1*
Neale US (1903)

Jean DANA and Louise DANA

were sisters who were very much cast in the *Nancy DREW* style of early American schoolgirl detection.

American Female Amateurs operating in Pulp Magazines in USA
No citations

Louise DANA

Second detective of Jean DANA

Robin DANA

American Male Amateur operating in Arizona

Jake PAGE 1936- (American)
Writer: James Keena PAGE Jr
Citation Record: 1 Book
Shoot The Moon - *Single*
Bobbs US (1979); Hale UK (1980)

Don DANBY

American Male Sleuth operating in USA

GRIFF 1891-1968 (British)
See main detective Kinsey TARGET
Citation Record: 3 Books
Goodbye Tomorrow - *First*
Modern Fiction UK (1951)
Devil's Daughter - *Last*
Modern Fiction UK (1952)

John DANBY

meets murder in a complex thriller set in various parts of Europe.

British Male Professional Investigator operating in several locations

Julian RATHBONE 1935- (British)
Invented 3 detectives - see Col Nur BEY
Citation Record: 1 Book
The Pandora Option - *Single*
Heinemann UK (1990)

Charlie DANCE

sleuths in stories set back into the 1960s.

British Male Amateur operating in London

Tom BARLING (British)
Citation Record: 2 Books

The Smoke - *First*
Corgi UK (1986)
Dance With The Devil - *First**
Pocket Books US (1988)
God Is An Executioner - *Latest*
Corgi UK (1987)
Dance With Death - *Latest**
Pocket Books US (1988)

Elton DANCEY

is an unlicensed private detective who has to work in a city where the licensed detective competition is far from negligible.

American Male Professional Investigator operating in Los Angeles

R B PHILLIPS 1943- (American)
Writer: Roderick BRADLEY
Citation Record: 1 Book
Gun Play - *Single*
Foul Play US (1987)

Penni DANDRIDGE

investigates a death by poison on a moving train.

Female Amateur

William BANKIER 1925- (Canadian)
See main detective Harry LAWSON
Citation Record: 1 Selected Short Story
The Locked Roomette
appeared in the November number.
In 'Ellery Queen's Mystery Magazine' US (1990)

Maj DANE

American Male Amateur operating in Maine

Mary Roberts RINEHART 1876-1958 (American)
Invented 7 detectives - see Letitia CARBERRY
Citation Record: 1 Book
The Yellow Room - *Only*
Farrar, Straus US (1945); Cassell UK (1949)

Allen DANE

American Male Detective in Pulp Magazines operating in USA

Harry HAMMOND (American)
Inventor of one other detective OLD RUFE
Citation Record: 1 Book
Allen Dane, The Detective
New York Detective Library US (1882-8)

Bartholomew DANE

British Male Amateur operating in England

Rex DARK (British)
Citation Record: 8 Books
The Wardour Street Mystery - *First*
Wright UK (1936)
Spy 222 - *Last*
Wright UK (1940)

Christopher DANE

investigates, with the ambivalent help of a policeman.

British Male Amateur operating in England

Stooge: Det Supt Bill BARRY
is the police presence, doomed to fail.
British Male

Kingsley AMIS 1922-1995 (British)
See main detective Peter FURNEAUX
Citation Record: 1 Book
The Crime Of The Century - *Only*
was written, the author said, 'out of boredom'. It was published in the London newspaper, the *Sunday Times*, in six parts between August 13 and September 28, 1978.
Dent UK (1987)

Colwyn DANE

British Male Detective in Pulp Magazines operating in England

Mark GRIMSHAW 1896-1976 (British)
For writer details see Bill TRUSCOTT
Citation Record: 1 Book
Colwyn Dane - The Outlawed Detective - *Only*
Amalgamated UK (1937)

Timothy DANE

is a private eye in the classical tradition, but with a soft centre. Not really hardboiled, he is tender to women, non-violent, easy to foil, and generous and kind to those around him. He loves Broadway, movies and musicals and comes over as a decent, honest man who works hard at the job. His cases are related in a simple but vivid style, in which flashbacks explore his social roots.

American Male Private Detective operating in New York

William ARD 1922-1960 (American)
was born in Brooklyn, New York. He graduated from Dartmouth College, Hanover, New Hampshire, 1944, and served in the Marine Corps until 1945.
Writer: William Thomas ARD
Other Byline: Thomas WILLS
Other Detectives:
Mike FONTAINE
Danny FONTAINE
Barney GLINES
Lou LARGO
Citation Record: 9 Books
The Perfect Frame - *First*
Mill US (1951); Hammond UK (1953)
The Root Of His Evil - *Last*
Rinehart US (1957); Boardman UK (1958)
Deadly Beloved - *Last**
Dell US (1958)

Joe DANELLI

Second detective of Amanda ROBERTS

Michael DANEVITCH and Peter BRODIE

work together, the one a Czarist police official, the other an English detective.

Russian Policeman and British Male Sleuth operating in Russia

Dick DONOVAN 1842-1924 (British)
Invented 7 detectives - see Fabian FIELD
Citation Record: 10 Short Stories in 1 Collection
The Chronicles Of Michael Danevitch Of The Russian Secret Service - *Collection 1*
Chatto & Windus UK (1899)

Fred DANFORD

American Male Detective in Pulp Magazines operating in USA

Harry ROCKWOOD 1859-1932 (American)
Invented 14 detectives - see Clarice DYKE
Citation Record: 1 Book
Fred Danford, The Skillful Detective; Or, The Watertown Mystery - *Only*
Ogilvie US (1885)
The Watertown Mystery - *Only**
Street & Smith US (1901)

Lt DANFORTH

American Policeman operating in USA

Wilson TUCKER 1914- (American)
Writer: Arthur Wilson TUCKER
Other Detectives:
Kate BRISTOL
B G BROOKS
Charles HORNE
Citation Record: 1 Book
Time Bomb - *Only*
Rinehart US (1955)

Abigail Patience DANFORTH

is, during the last decade of the nineteenth century, a determined lady who, in her desire to emulate *Sherlock HOLMES,*

sets herself up as 'the world's first female consulting detective'. We are informed that '*Sir Arthur Conan DOYLE* himself advised against it, telling her to remember she was a lady'; but that '*Mark TWAIN* took the opposite view and encouraged her'.
British Female Professional Amateur operating in England

Marion J A JACKSON

Citation Record: 4 Books

The Arabian Pearl - *First*
Pinnacle US (1990)

The Sunken Treasure - *Latest*
Walker US (1994)

Maxine DANGERFIELD

British Female Sleuth operating in several locations

Charles FRANKLIN 1909-1976 (British)

Invented 3 detectives - see Insp Jim BURGESS

Citation Record: 4 Books

The Dangerous Ones - *First*
Hale UK (1964)

The Escape - *Last*
Hale UK (1968)

Vic DANIEL

Male Sleuth operating in Los Angeles

David M PIERCE (American)

Citation Record: 5 Books

Down In The Valley - *First*
Penguin US (1989); Penguin UK (1989)

Write Me A Letter - *Latest*
Scribner's UK (1992)

Supt DANIELS

British Policeman operating in England

Gregory BAXTER (British)

Writers: John Sellar Mathison RESSICH 1897- and Eric DE BANZIE 1894-

Citation Record: 4 Books

The Narrowing Lust - *First*
Selwyn UK (1928)

Death Strikes At Six Bells - *Last*
Benn UK (1930); Macaulay US (1934)

Det Insp Charmian DANIELS

is a graduate of Dundee University, Scotland. A dedicated and tough cop, she is, nevertheless, a woman with heart, someone who can be kind and benevolent to those who are in need. She has had to fight hard for her place in a man's police force; however, she is a fine detective and rises in the ranks during her long series of appearances.
British Policewoman operating in England

Jennie MELVILLE 1922- (British)

For writer details see Sgt/Insp John COFFIN

Citation Record: 16 Books

Come Home And Be Killed - *First*
Joseph UK (1962); British Book Centre US (1964)

The Morbid Kitchen - *Latest*
Macmillan UK (1995)

Mohawk DANIELS

is partly a cop and partly a private eye, being a detective employed by a railway company.
American Male Private Detective operating in New England

William L ROHDE (American)

Writer: William Laurence ROHDE

Other Byline: Nick CARTER

Citation Record: 1 Book

High Red For Dead - *Only*
GM US (1951); Fawcett UK (1953)

Murder On The Line - *Only**
GM US (1957)

Webster DANIELS

American Male Amateur operating in Chicago/New York

Terrence Lore SMITH 1942-1988 (American)

Citation Record: 2 Books

The Thief Who Came To Dinner - *First*
Doubleday US (1971)

The Devil And Webster Daniels - *Last*
Doubleday US (1975)

David DANNING

is a former colonel in the British OSS who has set up an agency specifically to carry out corporation trouble-shooting in the USA. His cases, however, often involve murder.
American Male Professional Investigator operating in USA/Hawaii

Don VON ELSNER 1909- (American)

Writer: Don Byron VON ELSNER

Inventor of one other detective Jake WINKMAN

Citation Record: 8 Books

Those Who Prey Together Slay Together - *First*
Signet US (1961); New English Library UK (1962)

A Bullet For Your Dreams - *Last*
Lancer US (1968)

Edik DANTE

solves a case of theatrical murder.
American Male Amateur operating in New York

Kay Nolte SMITH 1932- (American)

was born in Eveleth, Minnesota. She took a BA at the University of Minnesota, Minneapolis, 1952, and an MA at the University of Utah, Salt Lake City, 1955. A professional actress and a theatre and film critic, she wrote her first criminous novel in 1980, for which she received the Mystery Writers of America Edgar Allan Poe award, 1981.

Citation Record: 1 Book

Catching Fire - *Single*
Coward McCann US (1981)

Lt Joe DANTE

American Policeman operating in New York

Christopher NEWMAN (American)

Citation Record: 4 Books

The Sixth Precinct - *First*
GM US (1987); Corgi UK (1988)

Dead End Game - *Latest*
Putnam US (1994)

Ralph DANVERS

British Male Amateur operating in England

Mary CHOLMONDELEY 1859-1925 (British)

Citation Record: 1 Book

The Danvers Jewels - *Only*
Bentley UK (1887); Harper & Row US (1890)

Chris DANVILLE

American Male Amateur operating in Utah

Cleo JONES (American)

Citation Record: 1 Book

Prophet Motive - *Single*
St Martin's US (1984)

King DANWORTH and Martin LEROY

are part of an unusual triple parody. They are two detective story writers, their appearance as detectives in this book being a double parody on the famous cousins, *Fredric DANNAY* and *Manfred LEE*, who transformed themselves into the pseudonymous author, *Ellery QUEEN*. In the case of the two detectives cited, however, they have invented, in their own books, a detective called Leroy King (a fiction within a fiction) who is a parody of *Ellery QUEEN*, the detective. The two sleuths ap-

pear in a great number of short stories written for several of the main genre magazines from 1964 through 1984. Two good examples are listed for illustration purposes.
American Male Amateurs operating in New York

James HOLDING 1907- (American)
See main detective Hal JOHNSON
Citation Record: 2 Selected Short Stories
The Hongkong Jewel Mystery
In 'Ellery Queen's Mystery Magazine' US (1963)
The Tahitian Powder Box Mystery
was published in the October number.
In 'Ellery Queen's Mystery Magazine' US (1964)

D

Parrish DARBY
American Male Amateur operating in San Francisco/Hawaii

The ARESBYS (American)
Writers: Helen R BAMBERGER 1888- and Raymond S BAMBERGER
Citation Record: 2 Books
Who Killed Coralie? - *First*
Washburn US (1927); Skeffington UK (1929)
The Mark Of The Dead - *Last*
Washburn US (1929); Skeffington UK (1929)

Lord DARCY
Male Amateur operating in France/England

Randall GARRETT 1927-1987 (American)
Writer: Gordon Randall Phillips GARRETT
Invented 3 detectives - see Peter CARTHAGE
Citation Record: 1 Book 10 Short Stories in 3 Collections
Too Many Magicians - *Only*
Doubleday US (1967); Macdonald UK (1968)
Murder And Magic - *Collection 1*
Short stories - 4
Ace US (1979)
Lord Darcy Investigates - *Collection 2*
Short stories - 4
Ace US (1981)
The Best Of Randall Garrett - *Collection 3*
This collection of eight of the author's short stories contains two with *Lord DARCY.*
Short stories - 2
Timescape US (1982)

Michael KURLAND 1938- (American)
Invented 3 detectives - see Peter CARTHAGE
Citation Record: 2 Books
Ten Little Wizards - *Pastiche 1*
Ace US (1988)
A Study In Sorcery - *Pastiche 2*
Ace US (1989)

Desmond DARE
American Male Detective in Pulp Magazines operating in USA

OLD SLEUTH (American)
Invented 40 detectives - see Brant ADAMS
Citation Record: 1 Book
Desmond Dare; Or, Taking Desperate Chances - *Only*
Parlor Car US (1897)
A Desperate Chance; Or, Desmond Dare - *Only**
Ogilvie US (1900)

Eileen DARE
was an auxiliary of the early British boys' detective, *Nelson LEE.* Appearing first in 1916, she set out to avenge her father who was wrongly convicted of spying for Germany. But, excellent sleuth as she turned out to be, she stayed on a while as *LEE's* right-hand woman, appearing in several stories.
British Female Professional Investigator operating in England

E S BROOKE (British)
was the creator of *Nelson LEE,* who was second only to *Sexton BLAKE* in the hierarchy of detectives appealing to the young male audience of the time.
No citations

Lucille DARE
British Female Private Detective operating in England

Marie Conor LEIGHTON 1866-1941 (British)
Invented 3 detectives - see Michael DRED
Citation Record: 1 Book
Lucille Dare, Detective - *Only*
Ward, Lock UK (1919)

Susan DARE
was one of several female sleuths of the early decades of the twentieth century who shared the evocative surname of *DARE.*
American Female Amateur operating in USA
Sidekick: Jim BYRNE
is a smart reporter who assists the intrepid female sleuth, at a time when faithful young males were becoming more acceptable and were acknowledged to be more useful than Alsatian dogs.
American Male - Reporter

Mignon G EBERHART 1899- (American)
Invented 9 detectives - see Sarah KEATE
Citation Record: 6 Short Stories in 1 Collection
The Cases Of Susan Dare - *Collection 1*
Doubleday US (1934); Lane UK (1935)

Vicky DARE
was a schoolgirl detective who appeared, 1951-1953, in stories in *Girl's Crystal.* She never went anywhere without her canine sidekick.
British Female Amateur operating in England
Sidekick: REX
is an Alsatian dog.
Male - Pet Dog

Judy LEWIS 1899-1956 (British)
Writer: Reginald George THOMAS
Other Byline: John PURLEY
No citations

Jeff DARGAN
appeared mainly in stories in *Spicy Detective.*
American Male Detective in Pulp Magazines operating in USA

E Hoffman PRICE 1898-1988 (American)
Invented 4 detectives - see John CARMODY
No citations

Charlie DARK
is a CIA agent with moral scruples.
American Male Secret Agent operating in the world

Brian GARFIELD 1939- (American)
Invented 4 detectives - see Trooper Sam WATCHMAN
Citation Record: 12 Short Stories in 1 Collection
Checkpoint Charlie - *Collection 1*
Mysterious Press US (1981)

Dym DARKE
American Male Detective in Pulp Magazines operating in USA

F X HARNEY (American)
Citation Record: 1 Selected Short Story
Dym Darke, Detective; The History Of A Celebrated Case
Old Cap Collier Library US (18??)

Al DARLAN
is one of the author's many detectives, appearing in several short stories, sometimes with a sidekick.
American Male Private Detective operating in USA
Sidekick: Mike TRAPPER
appears only in some stories.
American Male - Assistant

D

Edward D HOCH 1930- (American)

Invented 20 detectives - see Capt LEOPOLD

Citation Record: 1 Selected Short Story

The Other Eye
is in an anthology, *The Mammoth Book of Private Eye Stories* (Editors: Bill Pronzini & Martin H Greenberg).
US (1988)

Hal DARLING

is an ex-boxer and judo expert who lives on a boat and specialises in solving crimes with a nautical touch about them. Built on the small side, he makes up for it by sheer brain power.

American Male Private Detective operating in USA

Ed LACY 1911-1968 (American)

Invented 8 detectives - see Toussaint 'Touie' MOORE

Citation Record: 1 Book

Strip For Violence - *Only*
Eton US (1953)

Janet DARLING

was one of the large crop of young female detectives, sometimes amateur, sometimes almost professional, to appear in British magazines during the first decade of the twentieth century. The nature of her cases can be judged from the fact that she was billed as 'The Girl Detective who will only help lovers'.

British Female Amateur operating in England

UNKNOWN

Citation Record: 1 Selected Short Story

Janet Darling, The Love Detective
In 'Forget-Me-Not' UK (1909)

Kiss DARLING

is a private eye with, surely, the most provocative name in the criminous genre. She has the utmost difficulty in preserving her oft-flaunted virginity, which is always in danger in the course of her investigations. Her name, of course, is not exactly calculated to rebuff predatory males – in particular the boss of the agency she works for.

American Female Private Detective operating in USA

James A YARDLEY (American)

Citation Record: 2 Books

Kiss The Boys And Make Them Die - *First*
Signet US (1970); Joseph UK (1970)

A Kiss A Day Keeps The Corpses Away - *Last*
Signet US (1971); Joseph UK (1971)

Dyke DARREL

American Male Professional Investigator operating in Chicago

A Frank PINKERTON (American)

Invented 5 detectives - see A Frank PINKERTON

Citation Record: 1 Book

Dyke Darrel, The Railroad Detective; Or, The Crime Of The Midnight Express - *Only*
Laird & Lee US (1886)

A Race For Life - *Only**
Laird & Lee US (1898)

The Crime Of The Midnight Express - *Only**
Routledge UK (1887)

Darke DARRELL

American Male Amateur operating in USA

Frank H STAUFFER 1832-1895 (American)

Writer: Frank Henry STAUFFER

Citation Record: 1 Book

Darke Darrell, The Boy Detective - *Only*
Street & Smith US (1888)

From Street To Mansion; Or, Darke Darrell's Success - *Only**
Street & Smith US (1903)

Frank DARRELL

British Male Amateur operating in England

Sidney STRAND (British)

Citation Record: 14 Short Stories in 1 Collection

The Phantom Crime - *Collection 1*
Pearson UK (1929)

Jeff DARRELL

American Male Amateur operating in Chicago

Harry Stephen KEELER 1890-1967 (American)

Invented 14 detectives - see Angus MACWHORTER

Citation Record: 1 Book

Find The Clock - *Only*
Hutchinson UK (1925); Dutton US (1927)

Capt Peter DARRELL

Second detective of Insp DUNCAN

Graham DARREN

British Male Sleuth operating in England

Anthony LENTON (British)

Citation Record: 2 Books

Murder Beat - *First*
Hale UK (1971)

Murder City - *Last*
Hale UK (1972)

Herbert DARRENT

British Male Private Detective operating in England

Norman HURST (British)

Citation Record: 1 Book

The Ivory Queen - *Only*
Milne UK (1899)

Mike DARROCH

British Male Sleuth operating in Middle East

Allan MACKINNON (British)

Invented 4 detectives - see Don KENDRICK

Citation Record: 2 Books

Red-Winged Angel - *First*
Collins UK (1958)

Summons From Baghdad - *First**
Doubleday US (1958)

Assignment In Iraq - *Last*
Collins UK (1960); Doubleday US (1960)

Percy DARROW

American Male Amateur operating in New York

Stewart Edward WHITE 1873-1946 (American)

See main detective Bobby ORDE

Citation Record: 1 Book

The Sign At Six - *Only*
Bobbs US (1912); Hodder & Stoughton UK (1912)

Steve DART

was once with the Drug Enforcement Administration, but, after being fired, he has set up as a PI, becoming involved in a case in which every kind of skulduggery is rampant.

American Male Private Detective operating in Dallas

Paul COGGINS (American)

Citation Record: 1 Book

The Lady Is The Tiger - *Single*
Avon US (1987)

Alex (The Protector) DARTANIAN

American Male Sleuth operating in USA

Rich RAINEY (American)

House writer for one other detective Nile BARRABAS

Citation Record: 6 Books

Venus Underground - *First*
Pinnacle US (1982)

The Dragon Slayings - *Latest*
Pinnacle US (1985)

Dick DARWENT

is, in 1815, about to be hanged for a murder he did not commit. Just in time, and by clever detective work, he discovers the identity of the true villain.

British Male Amateur operating in England

John Dickson CARR 1906-1977 (American)

Invented 16 detectives - see Dr Gideon FELL

Citation Record: 1 Book

The Bride Of Newgate - *Only*
Harper & Row US (1950); Hamish Hamilton UK (1950)

Jan DARZEK

is a sci-fi sleuth who heads a New York agency in what was then the future (1986) but is now the past. He spends much of his time elsewhere in the galaxy.

American Male Private Detective operating in New York

Lloyd BIGGLE 1923- (American)

Invented 5 detectives - see Bill RASTIN

Citation Record: 5 Books

All The Colors Of Darkness - *First*
Doubleday US (1963); Dobson UK (1964)

The Whirligig Of Time - *Latest*
Doubleday US (1979)

Richard 'Speed' DASH

was one of the master's many early pulp detectives, appearing first in 1925. Described as 'a human fly, as well as an amazing detective', he featured in twenty stories in *Top-Notch.*

American Male Detective in Pulp Magazines operating in USA

Erle Stanley GARDNER 1889-1970 (American)

Invented 14 detectives - see Perry MASON

Citation Record: 1 Selected Short Story

The Case Of The Misplaced Thumb
In 'Top-Notch Magazine' US (1925)

DAUNTLESS DAN

American Male Detective in Pulp Magazines operating in USA

Old Cap DARRELL (American)

Invented 5 detectives - see YOUNG SLEDGE

Citation Record: 1 Book

Dauntless Dan, The Boy Detective; Or, The Mysterious House In The Hollow
New York Detective Library US (1882-8)

P J DAVENANT

British Male Amateur/Secret Agent operating in England

Frederic Spencer HAMILTON 1856- (British)

Writer: Lord Frederic Spencer HAMILTON

Citation Record: 53 Short Stories in 6 Collections

The Holiday Adventures Of Mr P J Davenant - *Collection 1*
Short stories - 4
Nash UK (1915)

Some Further Adventures Of Mr P J Davenant - *Collection 2*
Short stories - 5
Nash UK (1915)

The Education Of Mr P J Davenant - *Collection 3*
Short stories - 24
Nash UK (1916)

The Beginnings Of Mr P J Davenant - *Collection 4*
Short stories - 6
Hodder & Stoughton UK (1917)

P J, The Secret Service Boy - *Collection 5*
Short stories - 8
Nelson UK (1922)

More About P J, The Secret Service Boy - *Collection 6*
Short stories - 6
Nelson UK (1923)

DAVENPORT

was described as a 'private detective' in this Victorian novel.

British Male Private Detective operating in England

Albert D VANDAM 1843-1903 (British)

See main detective Col BOTTESFORD

Citation Record: 1 Book

The Mystery Of The Patrician Club - *Only*
Chapman & Hall UK (1895)

DAVENPORT BLAKE

American Male Detective in Pulp Magazines operating in New York

M H WILLIAMS (American)

Other Detectives:
CROOKED COLE
DETECTIVE DAREDEATH
The THEATRE DETECTIVE

Citation Record: 1 Selected Short Story

Davenport Blake, The Metropolitan Detective; Or, Piping The Harlem Mystery
Old Cap Collier Library US (18??)

Lucas DAVENPORT

is a retired Homicide cop who still sleuths.

American Male Sleuth operating in Minneapolis

John SANDFORD (American)

Writer: John CAMP

Citation Record: 3 Books

Rules Of Prey - *First*
Putnam US (1989); Grafton UK (1990)

The Iceman - *Latest*
HarperCollins UK (1993)

Ben DAVIDGE

is a wealthy man who likes to work as a forester. He meets murder and investigates.

American Male Amateur operating in Tennessee

Leslie FORD 1898-1983 (American)

Invented 6 detectives - see Grace LATHAM

Citation Record: 1 Book

Burn Forever - *Only*
Farrar & Rinehart US (1935)

Mountain Madness - *Only**
Hutchinson UK (1935)

David DAVIDOWITZ

sets out to find a necklace stolen from his mother by the Nazis. He ends up foiling a neo-Nazi plot.

American Male Amateur operating in USA

Hershey H EISENBERG 1927- (American)

Citation Record: 1 Book

The Reinhard Action - *Single*
Morrow US (1980)

Dr R V DAVIE

is, although in his seventies, still teaching at St Nicholas College, Cambridge. An amateur detective in the classical tradition, he uses his long memory and experience to solve crimes that baffle the police. His methodology is simple in the extreme: eavesdropping on conversations.

British Male Amateur operating in Cambridge

V C CLINTON-BADDELEY 1900-1970 (British)

was born at Budleigh Salterton, Devon. He was educated at Sherborne School, Dorset, and took an MA at Jesus College, Cambridge. He was a professional historian and a well-known actor, touring extensively in America. He wrote many light plays for theatre and radio and five delightful crime novels.

Writer: Victor Vaughan Reynolds Geraint Clinton CLINTON-BADDELEY

Citation Record: 5 Books

Death's Bright Dart - *First*
Gollancz UK (1967); Morrow US (1970)

To Study A Long Silence - *Last*
Gollancz UK (1972)

Sheriff Bill DAVIES

American Policeman operating in Alabama

Sara Elizabeth MASON 1911- (American)

Citation Record: 2 Books

Murder Rents A Room - *First*
Doubleday US (1943)

The Crimson Feather - *Last*
Doubleday US (1945); Gordon Martin UK (1946)

Dangerous DAVIES

British Male Professional Investigator operating in England

Leslie THOMAS 1931- (British)

See main detective George ORMEROD

Citation Record: 2 Books

Dangerous Davies: The Last Detective - *First*
Eyre & Spottiswoode UK (1976); Dell US (1982)

Dangerous In Love - *Latest*
Methuen UK (1987)

Dion DAVIES

was one of this author's numerous pulp detectives and appeared in short stories in *Dime Detective.*

American Male Detective in Pulp Magazines operating in USA

Ramon DECOLTA 1898-1945 (American)

Writer: Raoul WHITFIELD

Other Detectives:

Don BURNEY	Ben CAREY
Jo GAR	Don TREE

No citations

Frank 'Lobo' DAVIES

goes to Greece in pursuit of fraudsters.
!See Appendix 2.

American Male Private Detective operating in Greece

James JONES 1921-1977 (American)

Citation Record: 1 Book

A Touch Of Danger - *Only*
Doubleday US (1973); Collins UK (1973)

John DAVIES

British Male Amateur operating in England

Margot BENNETT 1912-1980 (British)

was born in Lenzie, Scotland and educated at schools in Scotland and Australia. She worked in advertising in the 1930s, was a nurse in the Spanish Civil War, and published her first criminous work in 1946. Her output was small but of an exceptional quality.

Citation Record: 2 Books

Time To Change Hats - *First*
Nicholson & Watson UK (1945); Doubleday US (1946)

Away Went The Little Fish - *Last*
Nicholson & Watson UK (1946); Doubleday US (1946)

George DAVIS

Appears with at least two other detectives - see George STONE

John George DAVIS

British Male Amateur operating in England

Jack RIPLEY 1921- (British)

For writer details see Ch Insp/Supt LENNOX

Citation Record: 4 Books

Davis Doesn't Live Here Any More - *First*
Hamish Hamilton UK (1971); Doubleday US (1971)

My Word You Should Have Seen Us - *Last*
Hamish Hamilton UK (1972)

Lisa DAVIS

American Female Sleuth operating in Massachusetts

Lilla M WALTCH 1932- (American)

Citation Record: 2 Books

The Third Victim - *First*
Dodd, Mead US (1987)

Fearful Symmetry - *Latest*
Dodd, Mead US (1988)

Mavis DAVIS

American Female Private Detective operating in Texas

Susan BAKER (American)

Citation Record: 1 Book

My First Murder - *Single*
St Martin's US (1989)

Gilbert DAVISON

British Male Amateur operating in England

R J FLETCHER 1877- (British)

Writer: Robert James FLETCHER

Citation Record: 3 Books

Half Devil, Half Tiger - *First*
Murray UK (1929)

The Missing Doctor - *Last*
Murray UK (1930)

Owen DAVIS-WILLIAMS

is trying to write a novel about a real but so far unsolved murder. However, the murderer himself knows about the book and targets the writer as his next victim. The notional author must reach the solution before being killed himself.

American Male Amateur operating in Minnesota

L A TAYLOR 1939- (American)

Invented 4 detectives - see Joseph 'JJ' JAMISON

Citation Record: 1 Book

Poetic Justice - *Single*
Walker US (1988)

Lucius DAVOREN

is a surgeon who has to turn detective.

British Male Amateur operating in England

M E BRADDON 1835-1915 (British)

Invented 9 detectives - see Robert AUDLEY

Citation Record: 1 Book

Lucius Davoren; Or, Publicans And Sinners - *Only*
Maxwell UK (1873)

Publicans And Sinners; Or, Lucius Davoren - *Only**
Harper & Row US (1874)

Archer DAWE

British Male Professional Investigator operating in London

J S FLETCHER 1863-1935 (British)

Invented 9 detectives - see Paul CAMPENHAYE

Citation Record: 8 Short Stories in 1 Collection

The Adventures Of Archer Dawe, Sleuth-Hound - *Collection 1*
Digby, Long UK (1909)

The Contents Of The Coffin - *Collection 1**
Long UK (1928)

Ch Supt Peter DAWES

is in one classic short story that has often appeared in recent anthologies. It involves the almost impossible theft of a painting from a guarded gallery.

British Policeman operating in London

Edgar WALLACE 1875-1932 (British)

Invented 28 detectives - see J G REEDER

Citation Record: 1 Selected Short Story

The Missing Romney
appeared in the December 27 number. It is included in the

D

anthologies, *The Art of the Impossible* (*Xanadu*; UK 1990) and *Murder Impossible* (*Carroll*; US 1990).
In 'Weekly News' UK (1919)

Stephen DAWES

British Male Amateur operating in England

Margaret YORKE 1924- (British)

was born in Compton, Surrey. She was educated at Prior's Field, Godalming, Surrey, and served in the Women's Royal Naval Service, 1942-1945. A sometime librarian at Oxford, she is the author of at least eleven mainstream novels and twenty-one genre novels.

Writer: Margaret Beda NICHOLSON

Other Detectives:

Nina CROWTHER   Patrick GRANT

Citation Record: 1 Book

Intimate Kill - *Single*
Hutchinson UK (1985); St Martin's US (1985)

Supt DAWLE

solves a case of death by hanging in a locked study.
British Policeman operating in England

Henry WADE 1887-1969 (British)

Invented 7 detectives - see Ch Insp POOLE

Citation Record: 1 Book

The Hanging Captain - *Only*
Constable UK (1932); Harcourt Brace US (1933)

Patrick DAWLISH

is a huge man with a circle of tough friends, obsessed with their own ideas of justice, who set out to solve vicious crimes (then dealing with their perpetrators) when the police seem unable to do so. This unorthodox procedure is, naturally, frowned upon by officialdom, with which he is often in conflict. During the Second World War, however, *DAWLISH* turns his attention to the pursuit of Nazi agents and criminals, for which he is rewarded, when the war ends, with the post of Deputy Assistant Commissioner at Scotland Yard. In the last fifteen of his fifty books he becomes the boss of an organisation called The Crime Haters who seem to have regressed to the good old days. Now, however, they spend their twilight hours in fighting international crime.
British Male Amateur operating in England

Stooge: Insp TRIVETT
is from Scotland Yard and usually in conflict with *DAWLISH.*
British Male

Gordon ASHE 1908-1973 (British)

For writer details see Insp Roger 'Handsome' WEST

Citation Record: 51 Books

Death On Demand - *First*
Long UK (1939)

A Plague Of Demons - *Last*
Long UK (1976); Rinehart US (1977)

Paul DAWN

seems only to have appeared in short stories, many of them locked-room mysteries. A handsome young man, he has somehow persuaded the Commissioner of the New York Police Department to let him head something called The Department of Impossible Crimes, which is attached to the Homicide Squad. This is not at all pleasing to many of New York's finest.
American Male Amateur operating in New York

Stooge: Insp FLEDGE
is a middle-aged cop, a veritable human bloodhound who, while not unfriendly to *DAWN,* is not in the same class when it comes to solving cases.
American Male

James YAFFE 1927- (American)

Inventor of one other detective MOM

Citation Record: 2 Selected Short Stories

Department Of Impossible Crimes
appeared in the July number.
In 'Ellery Queen's Mystery Magazine' US (1943)

The Comic Opera Murders
is a translation of *Il Nome Della Rosa* (Milan, 1983).
In 'Ellery Queen's Mystery Magazine' US (1946)

Ch Insp DAWSON

British Policeman operating in England

Bennet COPPLESTONE 1867-1932 (British)

Writer: Frederick Harcourt KITCHIN

Citation Record: 8 Short Stories in 2 Collections

The Lost Naval Papers - *Collection 1*
Short stories - 4
Murray UK (1917); Dutton US (1917)

The Diversions Of Dawson - *Collection 2*
Short stories - 4
Murray UK (1923); Dutton US (1924)

Commissaire Saturnin DAX

is the Commissaire of the *Police Judiciaire* in Paris, a position, we are told, once held (fictionally) by the famous *Insp Jules MAIGRET.* A very big man, heavily moustached, with a sweet tooth and a love for Schubert's music, he appears in even more books that his great predecessor.
French Policeman operating in Paris

Marten CUMBERLAND 1892-1972 (British)

Inventor of one other detective Insp COMFORT

Citation Record: 34 Books

Someone Must Die - *First*
Hurst UK (1940)

No Sentiment In Murder - *Last*
Hutchinson UK (1966)

Julian DAY

British Male Amateur operating in Egypt/Hong Kong

Dennis WHEATLEY 1897-1977 (British)

was born in London. He was educated at Dulwich College, London, 1908, at HMS Worcester, 1909-1913, and privately in Germany. He served in the Army, 1914-1919, and held senior positions in the Royal Air Force, 1939-1946, being awarded the United States Army Bronze Star. Always fascinated by the macabre, the occult and historical romancing, he published his first novel in 1933 and continued to write novels, plays and short stories until his death. He wrote fifty-eight novels loosely in the criminous genre, his main themes being historical espionage, military adventure and the occult. His books were nearly all popular successes in their time, selling in their millions.

Writer: Dennis Yates WHEATLEY

Other Detectives:

Roger BROOK   Duke DE RICHLEAU
Gregory SALLUST

Citation Record: 3 Books

The Quest Of Julian Day - *First*
Hutchinson UK (1939)

Bill For The Use Of A Body - *Last*
Hutchinson UK (1964)

Marty DAY

was one of this author's numerous pulp detectives and appeared mainly in stories in *Black Mask Magazine.*
American Male Detective in Pulp Magazines operating in USA

Carroll John DALY 1889-1958 (American)

Invented 6 detectives - see Race WILLIAMS

No citations

Fred DAYMOND

owns a rundown detective agency and, happy not to have anything to do, is drawn into a case of blue film racketeering in which he shows he can slug it out with the best.

American Male Private Detective operating in Los Angeles

Russell GORDON (American)

Citation Record: 1 Book

Dead Level - *Only*
Morrow US (1948)

Guilhem DE COURDEVAL

Male Sleuth operating in San Francisco

Daniel RHODES (American)

Citation Record: 2 Books

Next, After Lucifer - *First*
St Martin's US (1988); New English Library UK (1988)

Adversary - *Latest*
St Martin's US (1989); New English Library UK (1989)

Sgt Rufus DE GIER

Second detective of Adjutent Henk GRIJPSTRA

Jules DE GRANDIN

Male Amateur operating in several locations

Seabury QUINN 1889-1969 (American)

Writer: Seabury Grandin QUINN

Citation Record: 1 Book 42 Short Stories in 6 Collections

The Devil's Bride - *Only*
Popular Library UK (1976)

The Phantom-Fighter - *Collection 1*
Short stories - 10
Mycroft & Moran US (1966)

The Casebook Of Jules De Grandin - *Collection 2*
Short stories - 7
Popular Library US (1974)

The Horror Chambers Of Jules De Grandin - *Collection 3*
Short stories - 6
Popular Library UK (1976)

The Adventures Of Jules De Grandin - *Collection 4*
Short stories - 7
Popular Library UK (1976)

The Skeleton Closet Of Jules De Grandin - *Collection 5*
Short stories - 6
Popular Library US (1976)

The Hellfire Files Of Jules De Grandin - *Collection 6*
Short stories - 6
Popular Library US (1976)

Baron DE HIRSCH

investigates the disappearance of a girl from a guarded house.

Male Amateur operating in USA

Robert ARTHUR 1909-1969 (American)

Invented 6 detectives - see Max MILLION

Citation Record: 1 Selected Short Story

The Glass Bridge
Scribner's US (1958)

Hubert Bonisseur DE LA BATH

French Male Amateur operating in France

Jean BRUCE 1921-1963 (French)

Writer: Jean Alexandre BROCHET

Citation Record: 15 Books

Deep Freeze - *First*
is a translation from the French of *Tactique Artique* (Paris, 1960)
Cassell UK (1963)

Strip Tease - *Last*
is a translation from the French of *Strip Tease pour OSS 117* (Paris, 1962).
Corgi UK (1968)

Marka DE LANCEY

American Male Amateur operating in New York

Barbara FROST (American)

was born in New York City. She was a sometime publicity manager for the US publishers, *Lippincott.*

Writer: Barbara Frost SHIVELY

Citation Record: 3 Books

The Corpse Said No - *First*
Coward McCann US (1949)

Innocent Bystander - *Last*
Coward McCann US (1955)

Lady Molly DE MAZEREEN

is always referred to as 'Lady Molly'. She married into exalted rank, we are told, but also, for some obscure reason, she has an ill-defined position as a detective at Scotland Yard. Her cases, related by her maid and semi-assistant, are interesting early examples of a new feminist approach to the detective story.

British Female Amateur operating in London

Sidekick: MARY
is a lady's maid who relates the cases of her distinguished mistress.
British Female - Maid

Stooge: Insp SAUNDERS
is a stolid British cop of the old school, quite antagonistic to the brilliance of *Lady Molly DE NAZAREEN.*
British Male

Baroness ORCZY 1865-1947 (British)

was British by marriage, but was born in Tarna-Ors, Hungary. She was educated in Brussels and Paris and developed into a considerable artist. However, she is now known mainly for her romantic novels and short stories, many of the latter being in the mildly criminous vein, although they are little read today. She is measured among the great, however, for her creation of the *SCARLET PIMPERNEL,* one of literature's lasting prototypes and, indeed, one that has become not just a legendary figure but a symbol for a whole code of selfless behaviour against the forces of evil.

Writer: Emma Magdalena Rosalia Maria Josifa Barbara ORCZY

Other Detectives:
FERNAND — Patrick MULLIGAN
The OLD MAN IN THE CORNER
Monsieur Hector RATICHON — The SCARLET PIMPERNEL

Citation Record: 12 Short Stories in 1 Collection

Lady Molly Of Scotland Yard - *Collection 1*
Cassell UK (1910); Arno US (1976)

Frank DE NARDO

operates from an office near Central Park, where, when not working, he can usually be found jogging. His Mafia connections are useful in a kidnapping case.

American Male Private Detective operating in New York

Philip CARLO (American)

Citation Record: 1 Book

Stolen Flower - *Single*
Dutton US (1988)

Reginald DE PUYSTER

was written into short stories for pulp magazines of the 1920s, before the author's better-known work. Wealthy, witty and devilishly clever, he is also a superb athlete who has punches in both fists for villains. He gets his cases through the O'Day Detective Agency on Broadway. One story is cited for illustration purposes.

American Male Amateur operating in New York

Rufus KING 1893-1966 (American)

Invented 5 detectives - see Cotton MOON

Citation Record: 1 Selected Short Story

The Man Who Didn't Exist
US (1925)

Carter DE RAVEN

appeared, 1939-1940, mainly in stories in *Double Detective.*

American Male Detective in Pulp Magazines operating in USA

D

D

Walter RIPPERGER (American)

No citations

Duke DE RICHLEAU

French Male Amateur operating in Moscow/Paris

Dennis WHEATLEY 1897-1977 (British)

Invented 4 detectives - see Julian DAY

Citation Record: 6 Books

The Forbidden Territory - *First*
Hutchinson UK (1933); Dutton US (1933)

The Prisoner In The Mask - *Last*
Hutchinson UK (1957)

Francis DE SALES

American Male Amateur operating in New York

Thomas BOYLE 1939- (American)

Citation Record: 2 Books

Only The Dead Know Brooklyn - *First*
Godine US (1985); Hodder & Stoughton UK (1986)

Post-Mortem Effects - *Latest*
Viking US (1987); Hodder & Stoughton UK (1988)

Mlle DE SCUDERI

solves a case of death by stabbing in locked apartments.

Female Amateur operating in USA

E T A HOFFMAN (American)

Citation Record: 1 Selected Short Story

Mademoiselle De Scuderi
is a novelette in an anthology, *Weird Tales.*
Scribner's US (1928)

William DEACON

is a free-lance journalist who becomes involved in murder cases.

American Male Amateur operating in New York

Herbert BREAN 1907-1963 (American)

Invented 3 detectives - see Reynold FRAME

Citation Record: 2 Books

The Traces Of Brillhart - *First*
Harper & Row US (1960); Heinemann UK (1961)

The Traces Of Merrilee - *Last*
Morrow US (1966); Harper & Row US (1966)

DEADWOOD DICK

American Male Detective in Pulp Magazines operating in USA

George CONDRICK (American)

No citations

DEADWOOD DICK

American Male Amateur operating in USA

Edward Lytton WHEELER 1854?-1885 (American)

Invented 6 detectives - see Nell NIBLO

Citation Record: 1 Book

Deadwood Dick's Last Shot - *Only*
Ogilvie US (1902)

Garry DEAN

American Male Amateur operating in USA

Paul WHELTON (American)

was born in Boston and has worked as a reporter.

Citation Record: 6 Books

Death And The Devil - *First*
Lippincott US (1944)

Flash - Hold For Murder - *First**
is an abridged version.
Graphic US (1949)

In Comes Death - *Last*
Lippincott US (1951); Gifford UK (1952)

Jeffrey DEAN

was a foreign correspondent and formerly a courier for the CIA. Now he deals in antique books and is a PI on the side.

American Male Private Detective operating in Los Angeles

Sidekick: Rachel SABIN
American Female - Assistant

Wayne WARGA (American)

Citation Record: 3 Books

Hardcover - *First*
Arbor US (1985)

Singapore Transfer - *Latest*
Viking US (1991)

Marc (The Mercenary) DEAN

American Male Professional Investigator operating in USA

Peter BUCK (American)

Citation Record: 9 Books

The Deadly Birdman - *First*
Signet US (1981)

The Megadeath Option - *Latest*
Signet US (1983)

Sgt Paul DEAN

appears also in one book with the author's other detective, *Insp GHENT.*

British Policeman operating in England

Basil FRANCIS 1906- (British)

Invented 3 detectives - see Insp GHENT

Citation Record: 4 Books

Slender Margin - *First*
Constable UK (1938)

Death For Safe Custody - *Last*
Quality Press UK (1944)

Sgt Paul DEAN

Second detective of Insp GHENT

Sally DEAN

is a member of the 'Ghost Squad' at Scotland Yard and works on undercover cases.

British Policewoman operating in London

Leonard GRIBBLE and Geraldine LAWS (British)

Writer: (First author) Leonard Reginald GRIBBLE 1908-1985

Citation Record: 1 Book

Sally Of Scotland Yard - *Only*
Allen UK (1954)

Samson DEAN

is one of London's young black generation. A hard-up reporter for a local paper, he investigates a case that takes him into the black community's underworld.

British Male Private Detective operating in London

Mike PHILLIPS (British)

was born in Guyana and has worked as a journalist, broadcaster and lecturer in London.

Citation Record: 2 Books

Blood Rights - *First*
Joseph UK (1989)

The Late Candidate - *Latest*
Joseph UK (1990); St Martin's US (1991)

Sarah DEANE and Dr Alex MCKENZIE

are young teachers, in the English and Medical departments respectively, at the fictional Bowmouth college in eastern America. They solve cases of murder in various locales.

American Male Amateur and American Female Amateur operating in USA

J S BORTHWICK (American)

Citation Record: 6 Books

The Case Of The Hook-Billed Kites - *First*
St Martin's US (1962)

The Bridled Groom - *Latest*
St Martin's US (1994)

DEATH SQUAD
American Sleuth operating in USA

Frank COLTER (American)

Citation Record: 2 Books

Gang War - *First*
Belmont US (1975)

Killers For Hire - *Last*
Belmont US (1975)

DEATH-FACE
American Male Sleuth operating in USA

ANON

Citation Record: 1 Book

Death-Face, The Detective - *Only*
Westbrook US (ca 1920)

Buzz DECKARD
sleuths in the Chicago of 1969.
American Male Amateur operating in Chicago

Ross H SPENCER 1921- (American)

Writer: Ross Harrison SPENCER

Other Detectives:
Rip DESTON, Birch KIRBY, Luke LASSITER, Lacy LOCKINGTON, Chance PURDUE, Tuthill WILLOW

Citation Record: 1 Book

The Missing Bishop - *Single*
Mysterious Press US (1985)

Rick DECKARD
is an ex-cop in the year 2019 pursuing outlawed androids in space.
American Male Private Detective operating in Space

Philip K DICK 1928-1982 (American)
is mainly a writer of science fiction.

Writer: Philip Kendred DICK

Citation Record: 1 Book

Do Androids Dream Of Electric Sheep? - *Only*
Doubleday US (1968); Rapp UK (1972)

Det Bill DECKER
Appears with at least two other detectives - see Jub FREEMAN.

Det Bill DECKER
Second detective of Det Jub FREEMAN

Dan DECKER
American Male Detective in Pulp Magazines operating in USA

Lieutenant CARLTON (American)

Other Detectives:
BLACK DOUGLASS, Gideon GAULT

Citation Record: 1 Selected Short Story

Dan Decker, The Strongest Detective In The Northwest; Or, The Quest Of The Stolen Five Million
Old Cap Collier Library US (18??)

Hugh DECKER
is an officer in the American Drug Enforcement Agency who investigates the murder of a colleague, a female agent, in the underworld of Hong Kong. He has a trio of sidekicks, bizarre in the extreme.
American Policeman operating in Hong Kong

Sidekick: 'Bumpy' LANDING
is a computer genius.
American Male - Assistant

Sidekick: Miriam The MOUTH
is the sexy one.
American Female - Assistant

Sidekick: Johnny RISOTTO
is more of a gourmet than a useful assistant.
American Male - Assistant

Tony KENRICK 1935- (Australian)
Invented 4 detectives - see Jimmy PELHAM

Citation Record: 1 Book

Neon Tough - *Single*
Joseph UK (1988); Putnam US (1988)

Paul DECKER
Male Sleuth

Andrew I ALBERT (American)

Citation Record: 2 Books

The Maori Murder Case - *First*
Vulcan US (1944)

Murder For A Hollow Shell - *Last*
Vulcan US (1945)

Gilbert HACKFORTH-JONES 1900- (British)

Writer: Frank Gilbert HACKFORTH-JONES

Other Detectives:
Joe GARTON, Earl (of) MILLINGTON

Citation Record: 6 Books

Chinese Poison - *First*
Hodder & Stoughton UK (1969)

Redoubtable Dexter - *Last*
Hodder & Stoughton UK (1975)

Det Peter DECKER
is a detective in a Los Angeles precinct who, in his first book, is called out to a case of rape and murder in a virtually closed Jewish religious community. He solves the case and becomes involved with a Jewish widow, Rina Lazarus. In later books their unusual relationship evolves and he deals with other horrific crimes. He has a female partner on the force with whom he also seems, at times, to be emotionally involved.
American Policeman operating in Los Angeles

Sidekick: Det Marge DUNN
American Female - Assistant

Faye KELLERMAN 1952- (American)
was born in St Louis, Missouri. She took an AB in Mathematics at the University of California, Los Angeles, 1974, and graduated in Dental Surgery, 1978. She married the well-known psychologist and crime writer, *Jonathan KELLERMAN*, 1972. A practising dentist, a skilled fencer, an expert guitar maker and the mother of three, she wrote her first crime novel in 1985 and received the Mystery Readers of America Macavity award, 1986.

Citation Record: 4 Books

The Ritual Bath - *First*
Arbor US (1985); Collins UK (1987)

Milk And Honey - *Latest*
Morrow US (1990); Headline UK (1990)

Ch Philip DECKER and David BRETT
work together in a small town, as policeman and chief suspect, to solve multiple murders, the origins of which go back to the Second World War.
American Policeman and American Male Amateur operating in USA

Sarah WOLF 1936- (American)

Writer: Sarah Elizabeth WOLF

Citation Record: 1 Book

Long Chain Of Death - *Single*
Walker US (1987); Collins UK (1988)

R J DECKER
is an ex-convict who has obtained a PI licence in Florida and investigates crime on the bass-fishing circuit.
American Male Private Detective operating in Florida

Carl HIAASEN 1933- (American)
was born in Fort Lauderdale, Florida. He was educated at Emory University, Atlanta, Georgia, and graduated with a BA in Journalism from the University of Florida, Gainesville, 1974.

Other Detectives:
Brian KEYES Mick STRANAHAN
Citation Record: 1 Book
Double Whammy - *Single*
Putnam US (1987); Century UK (1988)

Tygrus Gerald 'Tyger' DECKER
is based in Manhattan but also seems to practise abroad. He has a useful twin to bolster up his rather feeble efforts at being a detective, which must be regarded as being unfair to all those other hard-working sleuths in the genre.
American Male Private Detective operating in USA/Holland

Alan RIEFE 1925- (American)
See main detective Huntingdon CAGE
Citation Record: 2 Books
Tyger At Bay - *First*
Popular Library US (1976)
Tyger By The Tail - *Latest*
Popular Library US (1976)

Eddy DECO
is a parody of the hardboiled PI of the pre-1939 era.
American Male Private Detective operating in USA

Gahan WILSON (American)
Inventor of one other detective Enoch BONE
Citation Record: 1 Book
Eddy Deco's Last Caper - *Single*
Times Books US (1987)

The DECOY DETECTIVE
American Male Detective in Pulp Magazines operating in USA

ANON
Citation Record: 1 Book
The Decoy Detective - *Only*
Aldine US (?)

Mr DEE
British Male Amateur operating in England

Desmond CORY 1928- (British)
Invented 4 detectives - see Johnny FEDORA
Citation Record: 2 Books
Stranglehold - *First*
Muller UK (1961)
The Name Of The Game - *Last*
Muller UK (1964)

Judge Jen-djieh DEE
was based on Ti Jen-cheih, a Chinese statesman of the T'ang dynasty, who had a reputation as a solver of crimes. He lives in seventh-century China, where he achieves fame for his detective work, becoming eventually a minister at the imperial court. He appears in three novels and in fourteen collections, each consisting of three novelettes, some of which are apparently based on true records of crimes. For reasons of brevity and because of their standard format, the publications are all treated as single works, seventeen in all.
Chinese Male Professional Investigator operating in China

Sidekick: Liang HOONG
is the judge's trusted adviser on legal and other matters.
Chinese Male - Advisor

Robert VAN GULIK 1910-1967 (Dutch)
Writer: Robert Hans VAN GULIK
Citation Record: 17 Books
Dee Goong An - *First*
Van Gulik (1949); Arno US (1976)
was the first book to feature *Judge DEE* and was translated from the Chinese by the author and published privately by him. It consisted of a collection of three novelettes, the form that was used extensively for the many later publications.
Poets And Murder - *Last*
Heinemann UK (1968); Scribner's US (1972)

Ruth DEE
Second detective of Johnny STONE

Biff DEEGAN
Second detective of Hank MERCER

Carolus DEENE
is an ex-commando who is now the senior History master at the fictional Queen's School, Newminster. He solves crimes as a hobby, mainly using newspaper reports to get his clues. !See Appendix 2.
British Male Amateur operating in England

Sidekick: Rupert PRIGGLEY
is an unpleasant but clever pupil who encourages *DEENE* to play the detective and ends up by assisting him.
British Male - Pupil

Leo BRUCE 1903-1979 (British)
See main detective Sgt William BEEF
Citation Record: 23 Books
At Death's Door - *First*
Hamish Hamilton UK (1955)
Death Of A Bovver Boy - *Last*
Allen UK (1974)

Maj DEERING and George RYAN
British Male Amateurs operating in England

Cecil COURTENEY (British)
Citation Record: 1 Book
Link By Link - *Only*
Bevington UK (1886)

Insp/Supt DEERING
British Policeman operating in England

SIMON (British)
Writers: Roger d'Este BURFORD 1904- and Oswell 1907-BLAKESTON
Citation Record: 3 Books
Murder Among Friends - *First*
Wishart UK (1933)
The Cat With The Moustache - *Last*
Wishart UK (1935)
The Mystery Of The Hypnotic Room - *Last**
Curtis Warren UK (1950)

Chase DEFOE
American Male Sleuth operating in Pennsylvania

Deforest DAY 1941- (American)
Writer: Stephen Deforest DAY
Citation Record: 2 Books
August Ice - *First*
St Martin's US (1990)
A Cold Killing - *Latest*
Carroll & Graf US (1990)

Dr Gerritt DEGRAAF
American Male Professional Investigator operating in USA

Barbara D'AMATO 1938- (American)
See main detective Catherine 'Cat' MARSALA
Citation Record: 2 Books
The Hands Of Healing Murder - *First*
Charter US (1980)
The Eyes On Utopia Murders - *Latest*
Charter US (1981)

Mr DEHAVILLAND
British Male Amateur operating in England

John Newton CHANCE 1911-1983 (British)
Invented 8 detectives - see John Newton CHANCE
Citation Record: 6 Books
Maiden Possessed - *First*
Gollancz UK (1937)
Stormlight - *Last*
Hale UK (1965)

D

Mr DEHAVILLAND and Supt BLACK
British Male Amateur and British Policeman operating in England

John Newton CHANCE 1911-1983 (British)
Invented 8 detectives - see John Newton CHANCE

Citation Record: 2 Books

Wheels In The Forest - *First*
Gollancz UK (1935)

Death Of An Innocent - *Last*
Gollancz UK (1938)

Carl DEKKER
Male Sleuth operating in Europe/Asia

Carl DEKKER 1922-
Writer: John Alfred Charles LAFFIN

Citation Record: 10 Books

Blood On The Sand - *First*
Calvert AU (1954)

The War Model - *Last*
Calvert AU (1954)

Jake DEKKER
is an insurance claims investigator.
American Male Private Detective operating in New York

Stanley ELLIN 1916- (American)
was born in Brooklyn, New York, and graduated from Brooklyn College, New York, 1936. He has been a teacher, steelworker and farmer but has been a full-time writer since 1946. He is considered by many critics to be the finest exponent of the genre's short story division in the last fifty years, although his output has not been large. His genre novels use series detectives sparingly.
Writer: Stanley Bernard ELLIN

Other Detectives:
Mel GORDON — Murray KIRK
Johnny MILANO

Citation Record: 1 Book

The Bind - *Only*
Random House US (1970)

The Man From Nowhere - *Only**
Cape UK (1970)

Johnny DEKKER
is a former boxing champion. Created by the eponymous but obscure British author, he almost makes the grade as a foreign authored American PI.
American Male Private Detective operating in New York

Johnny DEKKER (British)
Citation Record: 6 Books

Dolls And Dollars - *First*
Martin ? (1948)

Streetcar To Hell - *Last*
Martin ? (1949)

Josh DEKKER
American Male Sleuth operating in France

Alex WEBB 1914- (American)
For writer details see Matthew TOBIN

Citation Record: 2 Books

Blood Run - *First*
Pinnacle US (1985)

Dekker's Demons - *Latest*
Pinnacle US (1985)

Det DELA
Policeman

Gerald Francis DI PEGO 1941- (American)
Citation Record: 1 Book

With A Vengeance - *Single*
McGraw US (1977); Macmillan UK (1977)

Dinah DELACROIX
acts as a true detective in this strange novel of suspense by a master of the form.
British Female Amateur operating in England

Elizabeth BOWEN 1899-1973 (British)
was the author of greatly esteemed mainstream novels and short stories.
Writer: Elizabeth Dorothea Cole BOWEN

Citation Record: 1 Book

The Little Girls - *Only*
UK (1964)

Det Kate DELAFIELD
is in the Los Angeles Police Department, novel only in being a lesbian who at first is closeted but in later books seems to like telling others about her sexual mores and problems. Otherwise she behaves like the traditional male cop, although her cases involve women, many of whom are lesbians too.
American Policewoman operating in Los Angeles

Sidekick: Det Ed TAYLOR
is nominally the partner of *Kate DELAFIELD*, but he acts really as a mere sidekick to the gal, given a role seemingly beyond his station in life.
American Male - Partner

Katherine V FORREST 1939- (Canadian)
was born in Windstorm, Ontario, Canada. A graduate of Wayne State University, Detroit, Michigan, and the University of California, Los Angeles, she has written several mainstream novels, all dealing with female sexuality and social problems in the USA.

Citation Record: 3 Books

Amateur City - *First*
Naiad US (1984); Women's Press UK (1987)

The Beverly Malibu - *Latest*
Naiad US (1989); Pandora UK (1989)

Mrs Mollie DELAMERE
is a widow who, to support herself, acts as a secret appraiser for a pearl broker. She detects and solves a crime, meanwhile bearing considerable physical hardship, in this Victorian novel.
British Female Amateur operating in England

Beatrice HERON-MAXWELL (British)
Citation Record: 1 Book

The Adventures Of A Lady Pearl-Broker - *Only*
New Century UK (1899)

Reginald DELAMERE
British Male Amateur operating in England

Jack KELSO (British)
Citation Record: 1 Book

The Murder Of Colonel Neville - *Only*
Popular Library UK (1935)

Al DELANEY
runs a detective agency in Chancellor City. He says he hates to see detectives resorting to violence, but he is no mean guy with a gun himself.
American Male Private Detective operating in USA

Sidekick: Dolly ADAMS
American Female - Assistant

Thomas B BLACK 1910- (American)
Citation Record: 4 Books

The 3-13 Murders - *First*
Reynal US (1946); Gannet UK (1954)

Four Dead Mice - *Last*
Rinehart US (1954)

Denis DELANEY
Australian Male Sleuth operating in Sydney

Bant SINGER 1900- (Australian)

Writer: Charles SHAW

Citation Record: 5 Books

You're Wrong, Delaney - *First*
Collins UK (1953); Crown US (1953)

Your Move, Delaney - *Last*
Collins UK (1956)

Eddie DELANEY

is a former policeman who, now nearly forty, lives alone in a hotel room, owes money and, for a British creation, is a convincingly realised American private eye.

American Male Private Detective operating in Los Angeles

Anthony GRAHAM (British)

Invented 3 detectives - see Eric MARSDEN

Citation Record: 1 Book

No Sale For Haloes - *Only*
Boardman UK (1954)

Ex-Plce Edward X DELANEY

is a retired chief of detectives who, in a fine first book, is drawn into the hunt for a serial killer and later investigates other murders in Manhattan. By his last appearance, however, his detective skills seem, regrettably, to be giving way to an excessive concentration on his blissful home life with his second wife, who makes lovey-dovey noises and nightly provides sex for the hard-working male.

American Male Amateur operating in New York

Lawrence SANDERS 1920- (American)

was born in Brooklyn, New York. He took a BA at Wabash College, Crawfordsville, Indiana, 1940, and served in the US Marine Corps, 1943-1946. He is the author of at least twenty-five highly regarded and successful genre novels and received the Mystery Writers of America Edgar Allan Poe award, 1970.

Other Detectives:
Mary Lou 'Dunk' BATESON
Timothy CONE
Dora CONTI
Archie McNally
Peter TANGENT

Citation Record: 4 Books

The First Deadly Sin - *First*
Putnam US (1973); Allen UK (1974)

The Fourth Deadly Sin - *Latest*
Putnam US (1985); New English Library UK (1985)

Jay DELANEY

British Male Amateur operating in France

Douglas RUTHERFORD 1915-1988 (British)

was born in Kilkenny, Ireland. He was educated at Sedbergh School, Yorkshire, and took an MA at Clare College, Cambridge, 1937. He served in the British Army Intelligence Corps, 1940-1946, after which he taught languages at Eton College, 1946-1973.

Writer: James Douglas Rutherford MCCONNELL

Inventor of one other detective Patrick MALONE

Citation Record: 1 Book

The Black Leather Murders - *Only*
Collins UK (1966); Walker US (1966)

Joe DELANEY

American Male Amateur operating in San Francisco

Frank ARCHER 1915-1975 (American)

For writer details see Lloyd NICOLSON

Citation Record: 3 Books

The Malabang Pearl - *First*
Doubleday US (1964); Hale UK (1966)

The Turquoise Spike - *Last*
GM US (1967); Jenkins UK (1968)

'Steeley' DELAROY

is, in some respects, similar to the author's classic hero, *BIGGLES*.

British Male Amateur operating in England

W E JOHNS 1893-1968 (British)

Invented 3 detectives - see BIGGLES

Citation Record: 4 Books

Steeley Flies Again - *First*
Newnes UK (1936)

Wings Of Romance - *Last*
Newnes UK (1939)

Dr Alex DELAWARE

is a clinical psychologist specialising in children's problems. He is in his early thirties, handsome, brilliant and now sufficiently well heeled to be able to select his own cases, many of which turn out to be modern-horrific in kind, involving young people in situations of crisis.
!See Appendix 2.

American Male Amateur operating in New York

Jonathan KELLERMAN 1949- (American)

was born in New York City. He took an AB in Psychology at the University of California, Los Angeles, 1971, an AM in Psychology, 1973, and a PhD, 1974. He married fellow writer *Faye KELLERMAN*, 1972, and has held many senior posts at hospitals in California. His genre novels all have a deeply authentic background in the author's own subjects, dealing especially with problems of aberrant child psychology. He received the Mystery Writers of America Edgar Allan Poe award, 1985, and the Boucher award, 1986.

Citation Record: 10 Books

When The Bough Breaks - *First*
Atheneum US (1985)

Shrunken Heads - *First**
Macdonald UK (1985)

Self-Defence - *Latest*
Little, Brown US (1994); Little, Brown UK (1994)

Tommy DELAYN

solves a mysterious theft from a locked room.

American Male Amateur operating in USA

SEAMARK ?-1929 (British)

Writer: Austin J SMALL

Inventor of one other detective Forrest ORD

Citation Record: 1 Book

The Master Mystery - *Only*
Hodder & Stoughton UK (1928); Doubleday US (1928)

Kit DELEEUW

has fulfilled one of the apparent dreams of the modern man with a wife and young family, being a 'househusband'. This does not stop him having a reputation as the 'Suburban Detective'. He does possess one useful attribute, not seen since the days of the pulps; for he is able to distinguish the innocent from the guilty by looking into their eyes – especially, it seems, when the peepers belong to one of the fair sex.

American Male Private Detective operating in USA

Jon KATZ (American)

Citation Record: 3 Books

The Family Stalker - *First*
Bantam US (1995)

The Last Housewife - *Latest*
Doubleday US (1995)

DELMASSO and BRAY

Male Sleuths operating in England

William LEQUEUX 1864-1927 (British)

Invented 23 detectives - see Allan KENNEDY

Citation Record: 12 Short Stories in 1 Collection

The Hotel X - *Collection 1*
Ward, Lock UK (1919)

Supt DELPHICK

Second detective of Emily SEETON

D

Stanley DELPHOND
American Male Amateur operating in New York/England

Fred HALLIDAY 1937- (American)

Citation Record: 3 Books

The Chocolate Mousse Murders - *First*
Pinnacle US (1974)

A Case Of Indelicate Champagne - *Latest*
Pinnacle US (1977)

Nick DELVECCHIO
American Male Private Detective operating in New York

Robert J RANDISI 1951- (American)

Invented 5 detectives - see Sal CARLUCCI

Citation Record: 1 Book

No Exit From Brooklyn - *Single*
St Martin's US (1987)

Sgt DELVES
British Policeman operating in England

Mrs Henry WOOD 1814-1887 (British)

was born Ellen Price but always wrote under her married name. She became a popular literary figure and the author of the most typical Victorian melodramas and romantic novels, including the famous melodrama, 'East Lynne'.

Writer: Ellen Price WOOD

Other Detectives:
Charlotte GUISE   TATTON

Citation Record: 1 Book

Mrs Halliburton's Troubles - *Only*
Ward, Lock UK (1900)

Katie DEMAIO
is a prosecutor in a small New Jersey town who witnesses a murder and has to seek out evidence to prosecute the killer.
American Female Amateur operating in New Jersey

Mary Higgins CLARK 1931- (American)

was born in New York City. A radio scriptwriter and producer, she has written a few crime and thriller novels with no real series detectives but generally with strong plots.

Other Detectives:
Elizabeth LANGE   Pat TRAYMORE

Citation Record: 1 Book

A Stranger Is Watching - *Only*
Simon & Schuster US (1978); Collins UK (1978)

Gregor DEMARKIAN
is of Armenian extraction. Once a detective for the FBI, he now solves friendly, local murders.
American Male Amateur operating in Philadelphia

Jane HADDAM 1951- (American)

Writer: Orania PAPAZOGLU

Citation Record: 13 Books

Not A Creature Was Stirring - *First*
Bantam US (1990)

Bleeding Hearts - *Latest*
Bantam US (1994)

Jack DEMARREST and Jane BRITLAND
American Male Sleuth and American Female Sleuth operating in USA

Ron L GERARD (American)

Citation Record: 2 Books

Deadly Aims - *First*
PaperJacks US (1986)

Deadly Sights - *Latest*
PaperJacks US (1987)

Richard DEMING
American Male Amateur operating in USA

R L F MCCOMBS 1897- (American)

Writer: Ralph L F MCCOMBS

Citation Record: 1 Book

Clue In Two Flats - *Only*
Mystery House US (1940); Eldon UK (1942)

The DEMON DETECTIVE
American Male Detective in Pulp Magazines operating in USA

No citations

DEMPSEY and MAKEPEACE
appear in novelizations of episodes from a TV series.
American Policeman and British Policewoman operating in England

John RAYMOND 1947- (British)

See main detective George BULMAN

Citation Record: 4 Books

Blind Eye - *First*
Futura UK (1985)

The Jericho Scam - *Latest*
Futura UK (1986)

Jack SAVAGE (British)

Citation Record: 1 Book

Love You To Death - *Single*
Futura UK (1986)

Sister Mary Teresa DEMPSEY
is a 5'2", 200-pound, elderly lady who lives in a Frank Lloyd house in Chicago, where she is writing a learned treatise on the history of ancient French monasteries. Unfortunately, this wholly admirable work is continually being interrupted by the murders that have a habit of occurring in and around her otherwise tranquil order. Simply so that she can get on with her writing, she decides to investigate. She solves the cases, of course, to the annoyance of the local police, who are usually quite baffled and irritated by her brilliance. Like her fat male counterpart, the great *Nero WOLFE*, she stirs herself little, preferring to sit and cogitate, leaving the legwork to two other admiring sisters.
American Female Amateur operating in Chicago

Sidekick: Sister KIM
American Female - Assistant

Sidekick: Sister JOYCE
American Female - Assistant

Monica QUILL 1929- (American)

For writer details see Father Roger DOWLING

Citation Record: 6 Books

Not A Blessed Thing! - *First*
Vanguard US (1981)

Veil Of Ignorance - *Latest*
Vanguard US (1988)

Dorcas DENE
is an interesting example of the several lady detectives who appeared within a few years of the emergence of *Sherlock HOLMES*. She was once an actress, a Miss Lester, who married a young artist. Unfortunately for her – but, it must be said, fortunately for us – he went blind and, to keep them both, she has taken up detective work.
British Female Private Detective operating in England

Sidekick: Mr SAXON
is a dramatist who befriends and assists *Dorcas DENE*. He also narrates her cases.
British Male - Narrator

George R SIMS 1847-1922 (British)

was born in London. He was the author of eleven genre novels and hundreds of short stories, which were generally published as collections.

Writer: George Robert SIMS

Other Detectives:
Det Insp CHANCE   Jabez DUCK
Det Insp HOGARTH   WESTON

Citation Record: 20 Short Stories in 2 Collections

Dorcas Dene, Detective - *Collection 1*
Short stories - 11
White UK (1897)

Dorcas Dene, Detective: Second Series - *Collection 2*
Short stories - 9
White UK (1898)

Michael DENE

British Male Amateur operating in England

Gerald VERNER 1886-1980 (British)

Invented 7 detectives - see Supt BUDD

Citation Record: 2 Books

The Seven Clues - *First*
Wright & Brown UK (1936)

The Heel Of Achilles - *Last*
Wright & Brown UK (1946)

Det Sgt Trevor DENE

is a young, bespectacled Scotland Yard man, who is said to be possessed of amazing powers of observation and deduction. Having appeared a few years earlier in one book with his superior, *Insp MANDERTON*, he is now involved in cases of suspicious death while on holiday in the Adirondacks and again while in Long Island.

British Policeman operating in England/USA

Valentine WILLIAMS 1883-1946 (British)

was born in London and educated in England and Germany. He entered the Irish Guards, 1915, was awarded the Military Cross, and had a distinguished career in the British Army, the War Office and British Intelligence in the Second World War. For much of his life he worked also as a journalist and foreign correspondent, operating in Europe and the USA. He wrote more than thirty genre novels, mainly works of suspense and espionage.

Writer: George Valentine WILLIAMS

Other Byline: Douglas VALENTINE

Other Detectives:
Robin GREVE, Mary TREVERT and Insp MANDERTON
Dr Adolph (Clubfoot) GRUNDT
Dr Adolph (Clubfoot) GRUNDT and Desmond OKEWOOD
Insp MANDERTON
Insp MANDERTON and Det Sgt Trevor DENE
Desmond OKEWOOD
Mr Horace B TREADGOLD

Citation Record: 3 Books

The Clock Ticks On - *First*
Hodder & Stoughton UK (1933); Houghton US (1933)

The Clue Of The Rising Moon - *Last*
Hodder & Stoughton UK (1935); Houghton US (1935)

Det Sgt Trevor DENE

Second detective of Insp MANDERTON

DENHAM

Second detective of Spencer TAIT

Curt DENMARK

leads an investigation into the murder of his own son.

American Male Amateur operating in USA

Marc BERENSON (American)

Citation Record: 1 Book

Kill All The Lawyers - *Single*
Zebra US (1994)

Ted DENNING

Second detective of Bob RAINIER

DENNISON

American Male Professional Investigator operating in USA

Adam LASSITER 1948- (American)

Writer: Stephen Mark KRAUZER

Citation Record: 6 Books

Dennison's War - *First*
Bantam US (1984); Bantam UK (1986)

Snowball In Hell - *Latest*
Bantam US (1986)

Hugh DENSMORE

is a black intern in Phoenix who is accused of murder and has to find the killer to clear himself.

American Male Amateur operating in Arizona

Dorothy B HUGHES 1904- (American)

Invented 4 detectives - see Insp TOBIN

Citation Record: 1 Book

The Expendable Man - *Only*
Random House US (1963); Deutsch UK (1964)

John DENSON

was a sometime journalist and Intelligence officer, but is now a private dick. Soft-boiled, low-profile, he carries no gun and often belittles himself. Although he seems just to get by in life, he more than gets by in solving tricky cases. He shares the sleuthing in his first book with *Pamela Yew.*

American Male Private Detective operating in Seattle

Richard HOYT 1941- (American)

was born in Hermiston, Oregon. He was educated at Umatilla High School, Oregon, and took degrees in Journalism at the University of Oregon, Eugene, 1963 and 1967. He later obtained further degrees while in Honolulu, where he worked as a reporter for several years. Latterly he has held professorial posts in Oregon, including that of Professor of Communications.

Writer: Richard Duane HOYT

Other Detectives:
James BURLANE
John DENSON and Pamela YEW

Citation Record: 2 Books

30 For A Harry - *First*
Evans US (1981); Hale UK (1982)

Fish Story - *Latest*
Viking US (1985); Hale UK (1986)

John DENSON and Pamela YEW

John DENSON, in his first outing, has to compete with the gorgeous *Pamela YEW*, a tough private eye from San Francisco. In later books, he sleuths on his own and she does not re-appear.

American Male Private Detective and American Female Private Detective operating in Seattle

Richard HOYT 1941- (American)

Invented 3 detectives - see John DENSON

Citation Record: 1 Book

Decoys - *Single*
Evans US (1980); Hale UK (1982)

Dan DENTON

American Male Detective in Pulp Magazines operating in USA

A F HILL (American)

Citation Record: 1 Book

Dan Denton, Detective; Or, The Crime Of The Conservatory
New York Detective Library US (1882-8)

Harry DENTON

is an easy-going sleuth with liberal political views, more likely to curl up with a good book than rush out on a car chase.

American Male Private Detective operating in Tennessee

Steven WOMACK (American)

is a newspaper reporter and mainstream novelist. His first book in this series received the Mystery Writers of America Edgar Allan Poe award.

Citation Record: 3 Books

Dead Folks' Blues - *First*
Ballantine US (1992)

Way Past Dead - *Latest*
Ballantine US (1995)

Mickey DENTON

appears also in one book with the author's other detective, *Johnny LIDDELL.*

American Male Sleuth operating in New York/Los Angeles

Frank KANE 1912-1968 (American)

Invented 3 detectives - see Johnny LIDDELL

Citation Record: 1 Book

Juke Box King - *First*
Dell US (1959)

Wat DENTON

American Male Detective in Pulp Magazines operating in USA

Nicholas CARTER 1851-1924

See main detective Nick CARTER (Writer John Russell Coryell)

Citation Record: 2 Books

A Titled Counterfeiter; Or, The American Detective In France - *First*
Street & Smith (Magnet #3) US (1897)

The Crime Of A Countess; Or, The American Detective And the Russian Nihilist - *Last*
Street & Smith (Magnet #5) US (1897)

Lucian DENZIL

is a barrister who sleuths, an early Victorian example of what was to become a favourite sub-genre.

British Male Amateur operating in London

Fergus HUME 1859-1932 (British)

Invented 24 detectives - see Insp Samuel GORBY

Citation Record: 1 Book

The Silent House - *Only*
Doscher US (1907)

The Silent House In Pimlico: A Detective Story - *Only**
Long UK (1899)

DEPARTMENT Z

British Male Policemen operating in London

John CREASEY 1908-1973 (British)

Invented 6 detectives - see Insp Roger 'Handsome' WEST

Citation Record: 29 Books

The Death Miser - *First*
Melrose UK (1932)

The Black Spiders - *Last*
Hodder & Stoughton UK (1957); Popular Library US (1975)

Det Insp Frank DERBEN

is in some ill-defined unit attached to the Flying Squad at Scotland Yard. According to him, the London underworld is mainly composed of foreigners and communists.

British Policeman operating in London

Sidekick: Sgt Tom KELLY

British Male - Subordinate

P A FOXALL (British)

Writer: Peter Augustus FOXALL

Citation Record: 3 Books

Inspector Derben's War - *First*
Hale UK (1976)

Taming The Furies - *Last*
Hale UK (1978)

Jonah DEREHAM

British Male Amateur operating in England

Dick FRANCIS 1920- (British)

Invented 18 detectives - see Sid HALLEY

Citation Record: 1 Book

Knock Down - *Only*
Harper & Row US (1975)

Lionel DERING

is an escaped prisoner who, wrongly accused of murder and disliking incarceration in a Victorian jail, not unreasonably turns detective to clear himself.

British Male Amateur operating in England

T W SPEIGHT 1830-1915 (British)

Invented 4 detectives - see Insp MALLESON

Citation Record: 1 Book

In The Dead Of Night - *Only*
Bentley UK (1874)

Richard DERRICK

British Male Amateur operating in England

H B Marriott WATSON 1863-1921 (British)

See main detective Dick RYDER

Citation Record: 4 Short Stories in 1 Collection

Ifs And Ans - *Collection 1*

This collection of fourteen of the author's stories contains four with *Richard DERRICK.*

Mills UK (1913)

Sgt DERWENT

Second detective of John MORTON

Frances DERWENT and Bobby JONES

do some extremely amateur detecting in one of the author's finest books.

British Female Amateur and British Male Amateur operating in England

Agatha CHRISTIE 1890-1976 (British)

Invented 18 detectives - see Hercule POIROT

Citation Record: 1 Book

Why Didn't They Ask Evans? - *Only*
Collins UK (1934)

The Boomerang Clue - *Only**
Dodd, Mead US (1935)

Brian DESMOND

American Male Private Detective operating in Boston

Kelly LAWRENCE (American)

Citation Record: 1 Book

The Gone Shots - *Single*
Watts US (1987)

Frank DESOUZA

Male Sleuth operating in Bombay

Freny OLBRICH (British)

Citation Record: 3 Books

Desouza Pays The Price - *First*
Heinemann UK (1978)

Sweet And Deadly - *Latest*
Heinemann UK (1979)

Frank DESPARD

British Male Amateur operating in England

Stanley GUISE (British)

Citation Record: 1 Book

The Falcon Mystery - *Only*
Long UK (1930)

Harcourt D'ESPINAL

appears also in one book with the author's other detective, *Paul HEDLEY.*

Male Amateur operating in Venice

Ben HEALEY 1908- (British)

Invented 3 detectives - see Paul HEDLEY

Citation Record: 3 Books

The Vespucci Papers - *First*
Hale UK (1972); Lippincott US (1972)

The Horstmann Inheritance - *Last*
Hale UK (1975)

Harcourt D'ESPINAL

Second detective of Paul HEDLEY

Rip DESTON

American Male Amateur operating in Illinois

Ross H SPENCER 1921- (American)

Invented 7 detectives - see Buzz DECKARD

Citation Record: 1 Book

Echoes Of Zero - *Single*
St Martin's US (1981)

DETECTIVE ARCHIE

American Male Detective in Pulp Magazines operating in USA

OLD SLEUTH (American)

Invented 40 detectives - see Brant ADAMS

Citation Record: 1 Book

Detective Archie - *Only*
Munro US (1895)

DETECTIVE DALE

American Male Detective in Pulp Magazines operating in USA

OLD SLEUTH (American)

Invented 40 detectives - see Brant ADAMS

Citation Record: 1 Book

Detective Dale; Or, Conflicting Testimonies - *Only*
Parlor Car US (1898)

DETECTIVE GAY

American Male Detective in Pulp Magazines operating in USA

OLD SLEUTH (American)

Invented 40 detectives - see Brant ADAMS

Citation Record: 1 Book

Detective Gay; Or, The King Of Disguises - *Only*
Ogilvie US (1896)

DETECTIVE HANLEY

American Male Detective in Pulp Magazines operating in USA

OLD SLEUTH (American)

Invented 40 detectives - see Brant ADAMS

Citation Record: 1 Book

Detective Hanley; Or, The Testimony Of A Face - *Only*
Ogilvie US (1896)

DETECTIVE KENNEDY

American Male Detective in Pulp Magazines operating in USA

OLD SLEUTH (American)

Invented 40 detectives - see Brant ADAMS

Citation Record: 1 Book

Detective Kennedy; Or, Always Ready - *Only*
Ogilvie US (11896)

DETECTIVE MURDOCK

American Male Detective in Pulp Magazines operating in USA

OLD SLEUTH (American)

Invented 40 detectives - see Brant ADAMS

Citation Record: 1 Book

Detective Murdock, The Silent; Or, A Captive For Ransom - *Only*
Royal US (ca 1908)

DETECTIVE PAYNE

American Male Detective in Pulp Magazines operating in USA

OLD SLEUTH (American)

Invented 40 detectives - see Brant ADAMS

Citation Record: 1 Book

Detective Payne; Or, A Shadow's Wonderful Adventures - *Only*
Ogilvie US (1899)

Detective Payne's Shadow; Or, A Remarkable Search - *Only**
Ogilvie US (1900)

DETECTIVE DAREDEATH

American Male Detective in Pulp Magazines operating in USA

M H WILLIAMS (American)

Invented 4 detectives - see DAVENPORT BLAKE

Citation Record: 1 Selected Short Story

Detective Daredeath, The Hero Of A Hundred Cases; Or The Five Points Tragedy
Old Cap Collier Library US (18??)

A DETECTIVE

American Male Professional Investigator operating in New York

Alfred Henry LEWIS 1857-1914 (American)

Citation Record: 5 Short Stories in 1 Collection

Confessions Of A Detective - *Collection 1*
Barnes US (1906)

A DETECTIVE

is in a collection published just three years after the appearance of the first *Sherlock HOLMES* story and already demonstrates its influence on the direction the criminous genre was to take.

British Male Professional Investigator operating in England

(Lt) A CARMICHAEL (British)

Writer: Archibald CARMICHAEL

Citation Record: 20 Short Stories in 1 Collection

Personal Adventures Of A Detective - *Collection 1*
Morison UK (1892)

A DETECTIVE

British Male Professional Investigator operating in England

E M Leader STURT (British)

Citation Record: 14 Short Stories in 1 Collection

A Detective's Memoirs And Other Stories - *Collection 1*
Drane UK (1921)

DETECTIVES

American Sleuths operating in Europe/USA

George S MCWATTERS

Citation Record: 31+ Short Stories in 3 Collections

Knots Untied; Or, Ways And Byways In The Hidden Life Of American Detectives - *Collection 1*
Short stories - 31
Burr US (1871)

Detectives In Europe And America; Or, Life In The Secret Service - *Collection 1**
Burr US (1877)

Forgers And Confidence Men; Or The Secrets Of The Detective Service Revealed - *Collection 2*
contains an uncounted number of short stories.
Laird & Lee US (1892)

The Gambler's Wax Finger And Other Startling Detective Experiences - *Collection 3*
contains an uncounted number of short stories.
Laird & Lee US (1892)

Richard DEUTSCH

Male Sleuth operating in Jerusalem/Middle East

John CHRISTIAN 1930- (British)

Writer: Roger DIXON

Citation Record: 2 Books

Five Gates To Armageddon - *First*
Harwood-Smart UK (1975); St Martin's US (1975)

The Persian Death-Trap - *Last*
Harwood UK (1976)

Ch Const Piet DEVENTER

is of Dutch extraction and once worked for the Metropolitan Police in London. Now he has been promoted to be the youngest Chief Constable in England, of the fictional North Wessex Constabulary. He excels in situations that require the author's knowledge of ships and the sea.

British Policeman operating in England

J R L ANDERSON 1911-1981 (British)

Writer: John Richard Lane ANDERSON

Inventor of one other detective Maj Peter BLAIR

Citation Record: 2 Books

A Sprig Of Sea Lavender - *First*
Gollancz UK (1978); St Martin's US (1979)

Festival - *Latest*
Gollancz UK (1979); St Martin's US (1980)

DEVEREAUX

is head of an American counter-intelligence section that investigates powerful plots against the state in Europe and the USA.

American Male Professional Investigator operating in several locations

Bill GRANGER 1941- (American)

was born in Chicago, Illinois. He graduated from De Paul University, Chicago, 1963, and then worked mainly as a reporter and columnist.

Inventor of one other detective pair Karen KOVAC and Jack DONOVAN

Citation Record: 10 Books

The November Man - *First*
Fawcett US (1979); New English Library UK (1981)

The Man Who Heard Too Much - *Latest*
Warner US (1989)

Johnny DEVEREAUX

American Male Sleuth operating in New York

John ROEBURT 1908?-1972 (American)

See main detective 'Jigger' MORAN

Citation Record: 2 Books

Tough Cop - *First*
Simon & Schuster US (1949)

The Hollow Man - *Last*
!See Appendix 2.
Simon & Schuster US (1954); Jarrolds UK (1955)

Rufus DEVILLE

British Policeman operating in England

John NOY 1892- (British)

Citation Record: 4 Books

Red Devil Of The Air Police - *First*
Hamilton UK (1937)

The Mystery Of The Crested Falcon - *Last*
Hamilton UK (1939)

DEVLIN

British Male Amateur operating in England

B L FARJEON 1838-1903 (British)

Invented 7 detectives - see Robert AGNOLD

Citation Record: 1 Book

Devlin The Barber - *Only*
Ward & Downey UK (1888)

Insp DEVLIN

British Policeman operating in England

Helen MCCLOY 1904-1993 (American)

Invented 5 detectives - see Dr Basil WILLING

Citation Record: 1 Book

The Further Side Of Fear - *Only*
Gollancz UK (1967)

Brock DEVLIN

American Male Sleuth operating in USA

Scott MITCHELL 1932- (British)

For writer details see Griff DEXTER

Citation Record: 12 Books

Deadly Persuasion - *First*
Hammond UK (1960)

You'll Never Get To Heaven - *Last*
Hale UK (1973)

Harry DEVLIN

is a lawyer who sleuths.

British Male Amateur operating in Liverpool

Martin EDWARDS (British)

Citation Record: 4 Books

All The Lonely People - *First*
Piatkus UK (1992)

Yesterday's Papers - *Latest*
Piatkus UK (1994)

D

Joe DEVLIN

has entered the detective business more or less accidentally and tries to be funny, succeeding less in that direction than in his hunt for a murderer.

American Male Private Detective operating in Chicago

Stephen ACRE 1904-1969 (American)

For writer details see Johnny FLETCHER and Sam CRAGG

Citation Record: 1 Book

The Yellow Overcoat - *Only*
Dodd, Mead US (1942); Boardman UK (1945)

Fall Guy For A Killer - *Only**
Jonathan US (1955)

Liam DEVLIN

British Male Professional Investigator operating in England

Jack HIGGINS 1929- (British)

was born in Newcastle-on-Tyne, Northumberland and, after taking a diploma course at Leeds Training College for Teachers, 1958, took a BSc in Sociology at the University of London, 1962. He is a history teacher and the author, under this byline, of at least eighteen highly regarded thrillers. Under his real name and various pseudonyms he has published at least thirty other novels of detection, adventure and suspense.

Writer: Harry PATTERSON

Other Bylines:
Martin FALLON — Harry PATTERSON

Other Detectives:
Paul CHAVASSE — Nick MILLER

Citation Record: 3 Books

The Eagle Has Landed - *First*
Collins UK (1975); Holt Rinehart US (1975)

Confessional - *Latest*
Collins UK (1985); Stein & Day US (1985)

Det Matt DEVLIN

is an Irish cop who, in the 1890s, is called in to investigate the murders of several young ladies in the opulent seaside resort of Newport.

American Policeman operating in Rhode Island

Mary KRUGER (American)

Citation Record: 1 Book

Death On The Cliff Walk - *Single*
Kensington US (1995)

Timothy DEVLIN

American Male Sleuth operating in USA/the Caribbean

Basil HEATTER 1918- (American)

Citation Record: 2 Books

Devlin's Triangle - *First*
Pinnacle US (1976)

The Golden Stag - *Last*
Pinnacle US (1976)

Dennis DEVORE

American Male Amateur operating in San Francisco

Dorothy BENNETT 1906- (American)

Citation Record: 2 Books

Murder Unleashed - *First*
Doubleday US (1935)

Come And Be Killed - *Last*
Select UK (1942)

Insp DEW

appears in this one book, a small masterpiece of detective fiction in which real and imaginary figures of the 1920s mingle. It won for the author the Crime Writers Association's Gold Dagger award.
British Policeman operating in England

Peter LOVESEY 1936- (British)
Invented 7 detectives - see Sgt CRIBB and Const THACKERAY
Citation Record: 1 Book
The False Inspector Dew: A Murder Mystery Aboard The SS Mauretania, 1921 - *Single*
Macmillan UK (1982); Pantheon US (1982)

Insp DEWAR

British Policeman operating in England

Neil GORDON 1895-1941 (British)
Invented 3 detectives - see James ARNOLD
Citation Record: 1 Book
The Silent Murders - *Only*
Longman UK (1929); Doubleday US (1930)

Det James DEWITT

is a forensic criminologist whose wife was murdered by a psychopath. Now, driven by a sense of guilt and his own personal demons, he has become a police detective who tracks down murders that seem like suicide.
American Policeman operating in California

Ridley PEARSON 1953- (American)
Inventor of one other detective pair Det Lou BOLDT and Daphne MATTHEWS
Citation Record: 1 Book
Probable Cause - *Single*
St Martin's US (1990); Macdonald UK (1991)

Manny DEWITT

is a company lawyer for a multinational firm, who is involved in industrial espionage and attendant crimes.
American Male Professional Investigator operating in USA

Peter RABE 1921-1990 (American)
Citation Record: 3 Books
Girl In A Big Brass Bed - *First*
GM US (1965); Fawcett UK (1965)
Code Name Gadget - *Last*
GM US (1967); Fawcett UK (1967)

D'Arcy DEWPOND

British Male Amateur operating in England

Will SLATER 1944- (British)
Citation Record: 7 Short Stories in 1 Collection
The Adventures Of D'Arcy Dewpond, Detective - *Collection 1*
Drane UK (1927)

Charles DEXTER

British Male Sleuth operating in England

John FREDMAN 1927- (British)
Writer: Henry John FREDMAN
Citation Record: 3 Books
The Fourth Agency - *First*
Hutchinson UK (1969); Bobbs US (1970)
Epitaph To A Bad Cop - *Last*
Hale UK (1973); McKay US (1973)

Edith DEXTER

was known as 'The Mill-Girl Detective', a young mill girl who solved all kinds of horrid crimes besetting her friends. She appeared in a series of short stories, written anonymously around the beginning of the twentieth century. They were published in *Golden Stories*, one of Lord Northcliffe's more ephemeral magazines, priced at one penny.
British Female Amateur operating in England

Sidekick: Nancy LEE
is the schoolgirl assistant and narrator of *Edith DEXTER's* cases.
British Female - Narrator
No citations

Griff DEXTER

is a typically ersatz American PI created by a British author. His one case concerns the murder of an aging movie sex-queen.
American Male Amateur operating in Los Angeles

Elliot KENNEDY 1922- (British)
Writer: Lionel Robert Holcombe GODFREY
Other Byline: Scott MITCHELL
Citation Record: 1 Book
The Dead Sleep Late - *Only*
Hale UK (1975)

Slippery Jim DI GRIZ

sleuths at some time in the thirtieth century.
Male Sleuth operating in Space

Harry HARRISON 1925- (British)
Writer: Harry Max HARRISON
Inventor of one other detective Tony HAWKIN
Citation Record: 6 Books
The Stainless Steel Rat - *First*
Pyramid UK (1961); Walker US (1973)
A Stainless Steel Rat Is Born - *Latest*
Titan UK (1985); Bantam US (1985)

Laura DI PALMA

is a young attorney who sleuths.
American Female Amateur operating in California

Lia MATERA (American)
See main detective Willa JANSSON
Citation Record: 2 Books
The Smart Money - *First*
Bantam US (1988)
The Good Fight - *Latest*
Some sources give the author's other detective, *Willa JANSSON*, as the main detective in this book.
Simon & Schuster US (1990)

Flavia DI STEFANO

Appears with at least two other detectives - see Gen Taddeo BOTTANDO.

Supt Peter DIAMOND

is an old-style copper, who prefers to ignore modern technology in favour of his instincts and old-fashioned procedures. His abrasive personality leads him to brilliant detective work but professional disaster. He has to quit the police and, in his second book, is a relentless but still skilled amateur.
British Policeman operating in England

Peter LOVESEY 1936- (British)
Invented 7 detectives - see Sgt CRIBB and Const THACKERAY
Citation Record: 3 Books
The Last Detective - *First*
Scribner's US (1991)
The Summons - *Latest*
Little Brown UK (1994)

Red DIAMOND

is a New York cab-driver called Simon Jaffe who, obsessed with pulp detectives, actually becomes one, *Red DIAMOND*, and then becomes involved in cases full of action and nostalgia about bygone sleuths.
American Male Private Detective operating in New York

Mark SCHORR 1953- (American)

was born in New York City. He graduated at the State University of New York, Binghampton, 1973.

Other Detectives:
Theodore ROOSEVELT and Jim WHITE
Robert STARK

Citation Record: 3 Books

Red Diamond: Private Eye - *First*
St Martin's US (1983)

Diamond Rock - *Latest*
St Martin's US (1985)

DIAMOND DAN

American Male Detective in Pulp Magazines operating in New York

Maro O ROLFE (American)

Citation Record: 1 Selected Short Story

Diamond Dan, The Brooklyn Divorce Detective; Or, The Strangest Tail Of Crime On Record
Old Cap Collier Library US (18??)

Don DIAVOLO

is a stage magician who perfects his tricks in a Greenwich Village basement. He is brought in by the police to solve their most difficult cases.

American Male Professional Amateur operating in New York

Stooge: Insp CHURCH
is thwarted, harassed and baffled in the course of his investigations and needs all the help he can get.
American Male

Stuart TOWNE 1906-1971 (American)

Writer: Clayton RAWSON

Citation Record: 4 Short Stories in 2 Collections

Death Out Of Thin Air - *Collection 1*
contains two novelettes.
Short stories - 2
Coward McCann US (1941); Cassell UK (1947)

Death From Nowhere - *Collection 2*
contains two novelettes.
Short stories - 2
Wiegers US (1949)

Willy DIAZ

is an ex-cop. Near-alcoholic and virtually down on his uppers, he operates in Spanish Harlem, with all that that connotes in terms of dangerous company.

American Male Private Detective operating in New York

Rider MCDOWELL (American)

Citation Record: 1 Book

The Mercy Man - *Single*
St Martin's US (1987)

Cdr Allan DICE

British Policeman operating in England

Peter HILL (British)

See main detective Insp Robert STAUNTON

Citation Record: 2 Books

The Fanatics - *First*
Davies UK (1977); Scribner's US (1978)

The Washermen - *Latest*
Davies UK (1979)

Lt Joseph DICKERSON

American Policeman operating in Boston

Eaton K GOLDTHWAITE 1907- (American)

Writer: Eaton Kenneth GOLDTHWAITE

Inventor of one other detective Frank MOERSON

Citation Record: 4 Books

You Did It - *First*
Duell US (1943); Jarrolds UK (1945)

Death Springs The Trap - *First**
Death House US (1944)

The Body Next Door - *First**
Handi-Books US (1946)

Root Of Evil - *Last*
Duell US (1948)

Insp DICKINS

British Policeman operating in England

E Phillips OPPENHEIM 1866-1946 (British)

Invented 27 detectives - see Nicholas GOADE

Citation Record: 10 Short Stories in 1 Collection

Inspector Dickens Retires - *Collection 1*
Hodder & Stoughton UK (1931)

Gangsters' Glory - *Collection 1**
Hodder & Stoughton UK (1931)

John DICKINSON

British Male Private Detective operating in England

Hawley SMART 1833-1893 (British)

Invented 8 detectives - see Insp POLLOCK

Citation Record: 1 Book

Without Love Or Licence: A Tale Of South Devon - *Only*
Chatto & Windus UK (1890)

James DICKSON

British Male Private Detective operating in England

B L FARJEON 1838-1903 (British)

Invented 7 detectives - see Robert AGNOLD

Citation Record: 1 Book

The Last Tenant - *Only*
Hutchinson UK (1893)

Auguste DIDIER

is a Frenchman and a master chef in London during the last days of Queen Victoria. He cooks for the greatest houses and has his own school of cuisine. Unfortunately, murders happen too often around him; and he has to use his brilliant deductive powers, which he often compares to culinary expertise, to solve them, usually in order to defend his own reputation. He has continually to deal with two friendly-unfriendly stooges in the police force.

French Male Amateur operating in England

Stooge: Insp Egbert ROSE
of Scotland Yard never solves a case, but he remains friendly, especially as he cannot resist *DIDIER's* cooking, which is as excellent as his sleuthing.
British Male

Stooge: Insp NASEBY
is always convinced that *DIDIER* is the one whodunnit, which generally means that he blunders into the wrong solution.
British Male

Amy MYERS (British)

Citation Record: 7 Books

Murder In A Pug's Parlour - *First*
Malvern UK (1987); Avon US (1992)

Murder In The Smokehouse - *Latest*
Headline UK (1994)

Lt DIEGO

American Policeman operating in USA/Brazil

Vera KELSEY (American)

Inventor of one other detective Dan CUMBERLAND

Citation Record: 2 Books

The Owl Sang Three Times - *First*
Doubleday US (1941)

Satan Has Six Fingers - *Last*
Doubleday US (1943)

Maureen DIETZ and Helen KATZ

American Female Amateurs operating in Los Angeles

D

Stuart M KAMINSKY 1934- (American)
Invented 18 detectives - see Toby PETERS and Errol FLYNN
Citation Record: 1 Book
Exercise In Terror - *Single*
St Martin's US (1985)

Howard DIGBURN
British Male Sleuth operating in England

Bruce SANDERS (British)
Citation Record: 4 Books
Secret Dragnet - *First*
Jenkins UK (1956); Roy US (1957)
Feminine For Spy - *Last*
Jenkins UK (1967)

Insp DIGBY
British Policeman operating in England

I WRAY (British)
Writer: Iris PALLISER
Citation Record: 2 Books
The Vye Murder - *First*
Methuen UK (1930)
Murder - And Ariadne - *Last*
Methuen UK (1931)

Athelstan DIGBY
British Male Amateur operating in England

William F HARVEY 1885-1937 (British)
Writer: William Fryer HARVEY
Citation Record: 1 Book 10 Short Stories in 1 Collection
The Mysterious Mr Badman - *Only*
Pawling UK (1934)
The Misadventures Of Athelstan Digby - *Collection 1*
Swarthmore UK (1920)

Matthew DILKE
!See Appendix 2.
Male Sleuth

Lindsay GUTTERIDGE 1923-
Writer: Thomas Gordon Lindsay GUTTERIDGE
Citation Record: 3 Books
Cold War In A Country Garden - *First*
Cape UK (1971); Putnam US (1971)
Fratricide Is A Gas - *Last*
Cape UK (1975)

Joseph 'Daffy' DILL and Insp HANLEY
Joseph DILL is a newspaper columnist who usually manages to solve murder cases with a little light help from the New York Police Department in the shape of *Insp HANLEY.* They appeared in short stories in *Black Mask Magazine.*
American Male Amateur and American Policeman operating in New York

Richard SALE 1911- (American)
Invented 5 detectives - see Calamity QUADE
No citations

Sheriff Steve DILLON
American Policeman operating in USA

Anna Katherine GREEN 1846-1935 (American)
Invented 9 detectives - see Det Ebenezer GRYCE
Citation Record: 1 Book
Miss Hurd: An Enigma - *Only*
Putnam US (1894)

Jefferson DIMARCO
is a claims adjuster for the Commonwealth Insurance Company. He hates fraud to the point of obsession and pursues its perpetrators relentlessly.
American Male Professional Investigator operating in Boston

Doris Miles DISNEY 1907-1976 (American)
was born in Glastonbury, Connecticut, and educated at schools there. She was the author of nearly fifty criminous novels, many of which exploit nicely the towns and villages and the past and present of New England, which she knew so well.
Other Detectives:
Rachel CAREY
Sarah LOWDEN
Jim O'NEILL
Griff HUGHES
David MADDEN
Aggie SCANLON
Citation Record: 7 Books
Dark Road - *First*
Doubleday US (1946); Nimmo UK (1947)
Dead Stop - *First**
Dell US (1956)
The Chandler Policy - *Last*
Putnam US (1971); Hale UK (1973)

Mike DIME
is, although created by a British author, a very creditable PI along classic lines, based in Philadelphia in 1948.
American Male Private Detective operating in Philadelphia

Barry FANTONI 1940- (British)
Citation Record: 2 Books
Mike Dime - *First*
Hodder & Stoughton UK (1980); Watts US (1981)
Stickman - *Latest*
Hodder & Stoughton UK (1982)

Alfred DIMMOCK
British Male Amateur operating in several locations

Fox RUSSELL (British)
Citation Record: 18 Short Stories in 1 Collection
The Escapades Of Mr Alfred Dimmock - *Collection 1*
Not all the stories are criminous.
Everett UK (1906)

James DINGLE and Glyn JONES
British Sleuths operating in Europe

Geoffrey OSBORNE 1930- (British)
Citation Record: 5 Books
Balance Of Fear - *First*
Hale UK (1968)
A Time For Vengeance - *Last*
Hale UK (1974)

Gil DISBRO
American Male Private Detective operating in Cleveland

James E MARTIN 1936- (American)
Citation Record: 2 Books
The Mercy Trap - *First*
Avon US (1989)
And Then You Die - *Latest*
Avon US (1992)

DISHER
may be British, but he seems a precursor of the great *Nero WOLFE.* He is certainly one of the fattest detectives in the literature. With long hair and a monocle, always tired, he never walks when he can ride and he never rides if he can get others to do it for him. He loves smoking big cigars and talking about himself and his detective prowess.
British Male Amateur operating in England

Will SCOTT 1894?-1964 (British)
was born in Leeds, Yorkshire. Cartoonist, feature writer, actor, playwright, producer, he is said to have written two thousand short stories as well as several plays that were produced on radio and later filmed.
Writer: William Matthew SCOTT
Inventor of one other detective GIGLAMPS
Citation Record: 3 Books
Disher - Detective - *First*
UK (1925)

The Black Stamp - *First**
US (1925)

The Mask - *Last*
UK (1928)

Tyler DIVINE

is overtly lesbian in her private life. Her well-meaning attempts at detection are involved with the activities of gays and lesbians, which tend to interfere with any interest in who or what dunnit.

American Female Private Detective operating in New Jersey

Dolores KLAICH 1936- (American)

Citation Record: 1 Book

Heavy Gilt - *Single*
Naiad US (1988)

Constantine DIX

British Male Amateur operating in England

Barry PAIN 1864-1928 (British)

See main detective Cdr DUMPHRY

Citation Record: 12 Short Stories in 1 Collection

The Memoirs Of Constantine Dix - *Collection 1*
Unwin UK (1905)

DIXON

British Male Sleuth operating in England

Edgar WALLACE 1875-1932 (British)

Invented 28 detectives - see J G REEDER

Citation Record: 8 Short Stories in 1 Collection

The Black - *Collection 1*
Reader's Library UK (1929)

Sgt George DIXON

is a memorable character in British detective fiction invented by *Ted WILLIS*. He appeared first in a minor film, cited here in the novelized version, and was later to appear in a long series of TV dramas, in which his homely wisdom at Dock Green police station more than made up for his lack of true detective skills.

British Policeman operating in London

George DIXON (British)

Writer: Charles HATTON

Citation Record: 16 Short Stories in 1 Collection

Dixon Of Dock Green - *Collection 1*
Kimber UK (1960)

Ted WILLIS 1918- (British)

was born in Tottenham, Middlesex, and educated at local schools. He has been one of the most prolific and one of the best writers of the post-war era, producing only a few novels but also numerous plays for TV, film and radio drama. His awards have been many and he was created a life peer, 1963.

Writer: Edward Henry WILLIS

Inventor of one other detective Cdr John KNOWLES

Citation Record: 4 Books

The Blue Lamp - *First*
Convoy UK (1950)

Seven Gates To Nowhere - *Last*
Parrish UK (1958)

Ted WILLIS (British) and Paul GRAHAM (British)

Writer: (First author) Edward Henry WILLIS

Citation Record: 1 Book

Dixon Of Dock Green - *Only*
Mayflower UK (1961)

Sgt Joe DIXON

American Policeman operating in New York

Richard WORMSER 1908-1977 (American)

See main detective Lt Andy BASTIAN

Citation Record: 2 Books

The Man With The Wax Face - *First*
Smith & Haas US (1934)

The Communist's Corpse - *Last*
Smith & Haas US (1935); Gollancz UK (1935)

DOAN

is a shamus in Bay City, California. An alcoholic (although always recovered by the next day), seemingly dim, but actually very bright, he is said to be 'one of the best in the West' by his bosses at the Severn International Detectives agency.

American Male Private Detective operating in California/Mexico

Sidekick: CARSTAIRS

is a Great Dane that was won by the detective in a poker game. He plays a considerable part in the latter's cases but generally takes a poor view of his master's abilities and way of life.

Male - Pet Dog

Norbert DAVIS 1909-1949 (American)

Invented 8 detectives - see Ben SHALEY

Citation Record: 3 Books

The Mouse In The Mountain - *First*
Morrow US (1943)

Poor Little Rich Girl - *First**
Handi-Books US (1945)

Rendezvous With Fear - *First**
Cherry Tree UK (1944)

Oh, Murderer Mine - *Last*
Handi-Books US (1946)

Dick DOBBS

is a juvenile detective who appeared in his own ephemeral magazine, *Dick Dobbs Detective Weekly.*

American Male Detective in Pulp Magazines operating in USA

ANON

No citations

John (The Ghost) DOBBS

British Male Amateur operating in England/France

R B SAXE (British)

Citation Record: 3 Books

The Ghost Knows His Greengages - *First*
Constable UK (1940)

The Ghost Pulls The Jackpot - *Last*
Long UK (1945)

Insp DOBSON

is a rather colourless figure from the early period of British police detective fiction, when policemen were expected to behave like servants and often did.

British Policeman operating in London

Henry WADE 1887-1969 (British)

Invented 7 detectives - see Ch Insp POOLE

Citation Record: 1 Book

The Verdict Of You All - *Only*
Constable UK (1926); Payson & Clarke US (1927)

Sgt/Insp DOCKER

British Policeman operating in England

Hal PINK (British)

Citation Record: 3 Books

The Green Triangle Mystery - *First*
Hutchinson UK (1938)

The Rodeo Murder Mystery - *Last*
Hutchinson UK (1941)

John DOCKRIDGE

is a young deputy District Attorney.

American Male Professional Investigator operating in USA

Arthur TRAIN 1875-1945 (American)

Invented 3 detectives - see Ephraim TUTT

Citation Record: 4 Short Stories 4 Short Stories in 1 Collection

McAllister And His Double - *Collection 1*
contains four stories with *DOCKRIDGE* and six with *MCALLISTER.*
Scribner's US (1905); Newnes UK (1905)

Insp DODD
British Policeman operating in England

Henry WADE 1887-1969 (British)
Invented 7 detectives - see Ch Insp POOLE
Citation Record: 1 Book
The Missing Partners - *Only*
Constable UK (1928); Payson & Clarke US (1928)

D

Cedric DODD
British Male Amateur operating in England

Kenneth LIVINGSTON 1894- (British)
Writer: Kenneth Livingston STEWART
Citation Record: 1 Book 6 Short Stories in 1 Collection
The Cloze Papers - *Only*
Rich UK (1936)
The Dodd Cases - *Collection 1*
Methuen UK (1933); Doubleday US (1934)

Elmer DODD
may now be a PI but previously has been a carpenter, seaman, military policeman and bible salesman.
American Male Private Detective operating in San Francisco

Margaret MILLAR 1915- (Canadian)
Invented 11 detectives - see Insp SANDS
Citation Record: 1 Book
The Listening Walls - *Only*
Gollancz UK (1959); Random House US (1959)

William 'Bail Bond' DODD
is a bail bondsman, in constant touch with the underworld of crime. He appeared in eight lengthy short stories in *Dime Detective.*
American Male Detective in Pulp Magazines operating in USA

Norbert DAVIS 1909-1949 (American)
Invented 8 detectives - see Ben SHALEY
No citations

Dr Septimus DODDS
British Male Amateur operating in England

Sutherland SCOTT (British)
Citation Record: 11 Books
Murder Without Mourners - *First*
Paul UK (1936)
Doctor Dodds' Experiment - *Last*
Paul UK (1956)

Insp DODSON
is a bumbling detective from Scotland Yard who appears in one incredibly rambling book about Egyptian mummies who, rather inexplicably, insist on moving about when brought into a decent English home.
British Policeman operating in England

Mary GAUNT 1872-1942 (British)
Citation Record: 1 Book
The Mummy Moves - *Only*
Laurie UK (1910); Clode US (1925)

Lt Jack DOHERY and Lou BRADE
solve a case of murder in a college chemistry laboratory.
American Policeman and American Male Sleuth operating in USA

Isaac ASIMOV 1920-1992 (American)
Invented 6 detectives - see Elijah BALEY
Citation Record: 1 Book
The Death Dealers - *Only*
Avon US (1958)
A Whiff Of Death - *Only**
Walker US (1968); Gollancz UK (1968)

Insp Henry DOIGHT
British Policeman operating in England

Beryl SYMONS (British)
See main detective Jane CARBERRY
Citation Record: 3 Books
The Devine Court Mystery - *First*
Jenkins UK (1928)
The Opal Murder Case - *Last*
Jenkins UK (1932)

Brad DOLAN
American Male Sleuth operating in Florida/Cuba

William O FULLER (American)
was a newspaperman, lecturer, eminent speaker and a friend of many of the great American literary figures of his time.
Adopter of one other detective Sherlock HOLMES
Citation Record: 6 Books
Back Country - *First*
Dell US (1954)
Tight Squeeze - *Last*
Dell US (1959); World Distributors UK (1960)

Trixie DOLAN and Evangeline SINCLAIR
are an engaging pair of ladies, involved in the film and entertainment business, who meet and unravel the murders with which that profession is always (fictionally) beset.
British Female Amateurs operating in England

Marion BABSON (American)
Invented 8 detectives - see Douglas PERKINS
Citation Record: 3 Books
Reel Murder - *First*
Collins UK (1986)
Shadows In Their Blood - *Latest*
Collins UK (1989)

Denver DOLL
American Female Private Detective operating in USA

Edward Lytton WHEELER 1854?-1885 (American)
Invented 6 detectives - see Nell NIBLO
Citation Record: 1 Book
Denver Doll, The Detective Queen - *Only*
US (?)

Cathy DOLLANGANGER
Second detective of Chris DOLLANGANGER

Chris DOLLANGANGER and Cathy DOLLANGANGER
American Male Amateur and American Female Amateur operating in USA

V C ANDREWS ?-1986 (American)
Writer: Virginia Cleo ANDREWS
Citation Record: 3 Books
Petals On The Wind - *First*
Pocket Books US (1980); Piatkus UK (1980)
Seeds Of Yesterday - *Last*
Pocket Books US (1984); Piatkus UK (1984)

Ursula DOLLING
British Female Amateur operating in England

J Storer CLOUSTON 1870-1944 (British)
Invented 4 detectives - see F T CARRINGTON
Citation Record: 2 Books
Colonel Dam - *First*
Blackwood UK (1930)
The Virtuous Vamp - *Last*
Blackwood UK (1931)

Charles DOMAY
sleuths at some time in the early 1800s.
Male Amateur operating in England

Annabel LAINE (British)
Citation Record: 1 Book

The Melancholy Virgin - *Single*
Macdonald UK (1981); St Martin's US (1982)

Donny 'Tough Dick' DONAHUE

appeared in fourteen short stories written for *Black Mask Magazine*, twelve of which are in the collection cited. Said to be 'iron-nerved', he works for the Inter-State Agency after being fired from the New York Police Department for 'raiding a joint in error'.

American Male Private Detective operating in New York

Frederick NEBEL 1903-67 (American)

Invented 8 detectives - see Steve CARDIGAN

Citation Record: 12 Short Stories in 1 Collection

Six Deadly Dames - *Collection 1*
Avon US (1950)

Jack DONAHUE

American Male Detective in Pulp Magazines operating in USA

Gilbert JEROME (American)

Other Detectives:

Jere CLINCH	The GREEK DETECTIVE
Isaac LAZARUS	Chris WREN

Citation Record: 1 Selected Short Story

Jack Donahue, The Mountain Detective; Or, Unraveling A Terrible Mystery
Old Cap Collier Library US (18??)

Lorna DONAHUE

American Female Amateur operating in Connecticut

Katharine HILL (American)

Citation Record: 2 Books

Dear Dead Mother-In-Law - *First*
Dutton US (1944)

Case For Equity - *Last*
Dutton US (1945)

The Case Of The Absent Corpse - *Last**
Mystery Novel Classics US (194?)

Edward DONALDSON

Appears with at least two other detectives - see Insp MILD.

Gil DONAN

American Female Amateur operating in USA

Margaret Page HOOD 1892- (American)

Citation Record: 4 Books

The Scarlet Thread - *First*
Coward McCann US (1956)

Drown The Wind - *Last*
Coward McCann US (1961)

Paul DONAVAN

Male Sleuth operating in England

Carter BROWN 1923-1985 (Australian)

Invented 10 detectives - see Rick HOLMAN

Citation Record: 4 Books

Donavan - *First*
Horwitz AU (1974); Signet US (1974)

Donavan's Delight - *Last*
Horwitz AU (1979); Belmont US (1979)

Dan 'DeeDee' DONER

American Male Amateur operating in New York/Cape Cod

Frank SHAY 1888-1954 (American)

Citation Record: 2 Books

The Charming Murder - *First*
Macaulay US (1930)

Murder On Cape Cod - *Last*
Macaulay US (1931)

The DONNA

American Female Amateur operating in New York/Washington DC

R T LARKIN 1935- (American)

Writer: Rochelle T LARKIN

Citation Record: 2 Books

The Godmother - *First*
Lancer UK (1971)

For Godmother And Country - *Last*
Lancer UK (1972)

Brihtvic DONNE

is a *Sherlock HOLMES* parody. When Queen Victoria tells him that enemies of the state have stolen the sacred Rules Britannia, he jumps into action to track down the former and recover the latter.

British Male Professional Amateur operating in London

Sidekick: Dr John H WESTON
is his parody *WATSON*-like assistant.
British Male - Assistant

Esther M FRIESNER 1951-

Citation Record: 1 Book

Druid's Blood - *Parody 1*
Penguin US (1988); Headline UK (1989)

Lt Peter DONNEGAN

American Policeman operating in Boston

Dorothy QUICK 1900-1962 (American)

was a journalist and poet.

Citation Record: 2 Books

The Fifth Dagger - *First*
Scribner's US (1947)

The Doctor Looks At Murder - *Last*
Arcadia US (1959)

Charles DONNELLY

is a lawyer who defends a client on a charge of murder, finding the real villain on the way.

American Male Amateur operating in California

Margaret MILLAR 1915- (Canadian)

Invented 11 detectives - see Insp SANDS

Citation Record: 1 Book

Spider Webs - *Single*
Gollancz UK (1987); Morrow US (1986)

Insp Fabian DONOGHUE

British Policeman operating in Scotland

Peter TURNBULL 1950- (British)

was born in Rotherham, Yorkshire. He attended Cambridge College of Arts and Technology, 1971-1974, and Cardiff University, Wales, 1976-1978, obtaining a diploma in social work. He has been a professional social worker since 1978 and is the author of several police procedurals, all set in Glasgow.

Citation Record: 4 Books

Deep And Crisp And Even - *First*
Collins UK (1981); St Martin's US (1982)

Condition Purple - *Latest*
Collins UK (1989); St Martin's US (1989)

DONOVAN

British Male Amateur operating in London

William LEQUEUX 1864-1927 (British)

Invented 23 detectives - see Allan KENNEDY

Citation Record: 9 Short Stories in 1 Collection

Donovan Of Whitehall - *Collection 1*
Pearson UK (1917)

DONOVAN

Second detective of COYLE

Insp DONOVAN

is a Scotland Yard detective in this Victorian novel.

British Policeman operating in London

Sir Gilbert CAMPBELL 1838-1899 (British)

Writer: Sir Gilbert Edward CAMPBELL

Inventor of one other detective Donald MACALPINE

Citation Record: 1 Book

The Mystery Of Mandeville Square - *Only*
Ward, Lock UK (1888)

Barry DONOVAN

Australian Male Sleuth operating in Australia

Steve WRIGHT (Australian)

Citation Record: 2 Books

A Drop In The Ocean - *First*
Pan AU (1990)

Love Avalon - *Latest*
Pan AU (1990)

Brigid DONOVAN

is hired by a women's inter-faith community to write the history of their foundation. She soon runs into a brutal case of murder, with deep family roots in the past.

American Female Amateur operating in Maine

Karen SAUM 1935- (American)

Citation Record: 1 Book

Murder Is Relative - *Single*
Naiad US (1990); Naiad UK (1990)

Det Dick DONOVAN

takes his name from the author himself. Appearing in well over a hundred short stories, he seems to be a hybrid of *Insp JAVERT,* the great French manhunter of *LES MISERABLES,* and a British, lower-class version of *Sherlock HOLMES,* with various other fictional policemen, already on the literary scene at the time, added.

British Policeman operating in England

Dick DONOVAN 1842-1924 (British)

Invented 7 detectives - see Fabian FIELD

Citation Record: 184 Short Stories 14 Collections

The Manhunter: Stories From The Notebook Of A Detective - *Collection 1*
Short stories - 13
Chatto & Windus UK (1888); Lovell US (1889)

Caught At Last! Leaves From The Notebook Of A Detective - *Collection 2*
Short stories - 15
Chatto UK (1889)

Who Poisoned Hetty Duncan? And Other Detective Stories - *Collection 3*
Short stories - 11
Chatto UK (1890)

Tracked And Taken: Detective Sketches - *Collection 4*
Short stories - 17
Chatto UK (1890)

Stories From The Note-Book Of A Detective - *Collection 4**
Street & Smith US (1900)

A Detective's Triumphs - *Collection 5*
Short stories - 11
Chatto UK (1891)

From Information Received - *Collection 6*
Short stories - 14
Chatto UK (1892)

In The Grip Of The Law - *Collection 7*
Short stories - 12
Chatto UK (1892)

Wanted! A Detective's Strange Adventures - *Collection 8*
Short stories - 22
Chatto UK (1892)

Link By Link - *Collection 9*
Short stories - 10
Chatto UK (1893)

Suspicion Aroused - *Collection 10*
Short stories - 13
Chatto UK (1893)

From Clue To Capture: A Series Of Thrilling Detective Stories - *Collection 11*
Short stories - 11
Hutchinson UK (1893)

Found And Fettered: A Series Of Thrilling Detective Stories - *Collection 12*
Short stories - 11
Hutchinson UK (1894)

Dark Deeds - *Collection 13*
Short stories - 16
Chatto UK (1895)

Riddles Read - *Collection 14*
Short stories - 8
Chatto UK (1896)

Ed DONOVAN

is an ex-cop who sets up his own agency in a fictional town called Lanford, where he is blacklisted by corrupt forces. Only a woman can save him from despair as he struggles with his one case.

American Male Private Detective operating in USA

John CREIGHTON (American)

See main detective Matt REBER

Citation Record: 1 Book

The Blonde Cried Murder - *Only*
Ace US (1961)

Eli DONOVAN

is an early example of the hardboiled female private eye. She did not endure.

American Female Private Detective operating in Los Angeles

James L RUBEL 1894- (American)

Writer: James Lyon RUBEL

Citation Record: 1 Book

No Business For A Lady - *Only*
GM US (1950); Fawcett UK (1952)

Jack DONOVAN

Second detective of Karen KOVAC

Jeanne DONOVAN

American Female Amateur operating in Los Angeles

M R HENDERSON 1927- (American)

Writer: Marilyn GRANBECK

Other Bylines:
Nick CARTER
Ben GRANT
Allan MORGAN

Citation Record: 2 Books

If I Should Die - *First*
Doubleday US (1985); Severn UK (1988)

By Reason Of - *Latest*
Doubleday US (1986); Severn UK (1987)

Johnny DOOLIN

was formerly a stuntman. He appears only in a few short stories.

American Male Private Detective operating in USA

Paul CAIN 1902-1966 (American)

was born in Des Moines, Iowa. He worked as an art director in early Hollywood films, but using pseudonyms, he spent much of the rest of his life writing stories for the pulps.

Writer: George Robert SIMS

Citation Record: 1 Collection

Seven Slayers - *Collection 1*
This collection of seven of the author's stories contains some with *Johnny DOOLIN.*
Saint Enterprises US (1946)

Christian DOOM

Australian Male Private Detective operating in Australia

Robert KENNY (Australian)

Citation Record: 1 Book

The Last Adventures Of Christian Doom, Private I - *Single*
Rigmarole AU (1982)

D

Sheridan DOOME

appears in one book under the author's real name as well as one under his pseudonym.

American Male Amateur operating in USA

Steve FISHER 1912-1980 (American)

Invented 4 detectives - see Joe SAXON

Citation Record: 1 Book

Murder Of The Pigboat Skipper - *Only*
Hillman-Curl US (1937)

Murder On The S-23 - *Only**
Mystery Book of the Month US (1938)

Stephen GOULD 1912-1980 (American)

For writer details see Joe SAXON

Citation Record: 1 Book

Murder Of The Admiral - *Only*
Macaulay US (1936)

John DOOWINKLE

American Male Amateur operating in USA

Harry M KLINGSBERG (American)

Citation Record: 9 Short Stories in 1 Collection

Doowinkle DA - *Collection 1*
Dial US (1940)

Urban DORMER

solves a case of murder by stabbing in a locked room.

British Male Amateur operating in England

Alex BARBER 1906- (British)

Citation Record: 1 Book

The Room With No Escape - *Only*
Hutchinson UK (1932)

DORRINGTON

is a rascally lawyer in Victorian London, senior partner in the firm of Dorrington & Hicks. He is villainous when it comes to making money from his clients, who are often involved in crimes of which they are innocent. Nevertheless, in order to extract exorbitant fees from them, he has to clear them. To do that, he has to do orthodox detective work.

British Male Amateurr operating in London

Sidekick: HICKS
is the cowed and subservient junior partner of *DORRINGTON* and is, often unwillingly, made to do some of the latter's devious sleuthing.
British Male - Partner

Arthur MORRISON 1863-1945 (British)

See main detective Martin HEWITT

Citation Record: 6 Short Stories in 1 Collection

The Dorrington Deed-Box - *Collection 1*
Ward, Lock UK (1897); New Amsterdam US (1900)

William DOUGAL

is a truly unusual character, a poor post-graduate student who is drawn into murder situations, which he tackles for thoroughly amoral reasons in an immoral world. Innovatory, if unlikeable!

British Male Amateur operating in England

Andrew TAYLOR 1951- (British)

See main detective Insp Richard THORNHILL

Citation Record: 6 Books

Caroline Minuscule - *First*
Gollancz UK (1982); Dodd, Mead US (1983)

Blood Relation - *Latest*
Gollancz UK (1990); Doubleday US (1991)

Andrew DOUGLAS

British Male Amateur operating in England

Dick FRANCIS 1920- (British)

Invented 18 detectives - see Sid HALLEY

Citation Record: 1 Book

The Danger - *Single*
Joseph UK (1983); Putnam US (1984)

Brian DOUGLAS

British Male Sleuth operating in Madrid/Algeria

John LEE 1931- (American)

Writer: John Darrell LEE

Citation Record: 2 Books

Caught In The Act - *First*
Morrow US (1968); Long UK (1969)

Assignment In Algeria - *Last*
Walker US (1971)

The Killing Wind - *Last**
Long UK (1972)

Catherine DOUGLAS

American Female Amateur operating in USA

Sidney SHELDON 1917- (American)

Citation Record: 2 Books

The Other Side Of Midnight - *First*
Morrow US (1974); Hodder & Stoughton UK (1974)

Memories Of Midnight - *Latest*
Morrow US (1990); Collins UK (1990)

Michael DOUGLAS

American Male Amateur operating in California

J D FORBES 1910- (American)

Writer: John Douglas FORBES

Citation Record: 2 Books

Murder...In Full View - *First*
Caravelle US (1968)

Death Warmed Over - *Last*
Pageant US (1971)

Micky DOUGLAS

is an author of children's books. She discovers the body of her illustrator dead in his bath and that sets her off on a sleuthing career. She seems to have a penchant for meeting murder in various antipodean locales.

Australian Female Amateur operating in Australia

Anne INFANTE (Australian)

Citation Record: 4 Books

Death On A Hot Summer Night - *First*
Collins UK (1989)

Death In Green - *Latest*
HarperCollins UK (1992)

Aileen DOUGLASS and Sharon ATWOOD

are two female private eyes, respectively tough and beautiful. They do what many female private eyes seem to be doing at present, emulating the worst features of their male counterparts by chasing villains in automobiles and finally indulging in unbelievable shoot-outs with them, adding, in the process, little to either the prestige or appeal of female sleuths.

American Female Private Detectives operating in San Francisco

Melisa C MICHAELS (American)

Citation Record: 1 Book

Through The Eyes Of The Dead - *Single*
Walker US (1989)

DOVE

is a detective at Scotland Yard in this Victorian novel.

British Policeman operating in England

Fergus HUME 1859-1932 (British)

Invented 24 detectives - see Insp Samuel GORBY

Citation Record: 1 Book

The Mystery Of Landy Court - *Only*
Jarrolds UK (1894)

D

Fidelity DOVE
appears sometimes on her own but is more usually accompanied by one of the author's other detectives, *Insp G RASON*. A female edition of *A J RAFFLES*, she is a type of detective-crook that endeared itself to many British authors of the 1920s. She was, perhaps, unusual in being the leader of a larceny gang that always managed to keep one step ahead of *RASON*, who called her 'the coolest crook in London and then some'.

British Female Amateur operating in England

David DURHAM 1888-1965 (British)

Invented 5 detectives - see Insp G RASON

Citation Record: 3 Short Stories in 1 Collection

The Exploits Of Fidelity Dove - *Collection 1*

contains nine stories in which *Fidelity DOVE* appears with *Insp G RASON* and three in which she is the only sleuth. It was republished under the *Roy VICKERS* byline.

Hodder & Stoughton UK (1924)

Roy VICKERS 1888-1965 (British)

Writer: Roy VICKERS

Other Bylines:

David DURHAM   Sefton KYLE

Invented 9 detectives - see Insp J RASON

Citation Record: 3 Short Stories in 1 Collection

The Exploits Of Fidelity Dove - *Collection 1*

was previously published under the *David DURHAM* byline.

Newnes UK (1935)

Fidelity DOVE
Second detective of Insp G RASON

Michael DOVE
is a down-at-heel thriller writer who is supposed to be irresistible to the ladies and is involved in a well-written but far-fetched spy and mayhem caper.

British Male Amateur operating in England

Michael STOREY 1941- (British)

Citation Record: 1 Book

Soft In The Middle - *Only*

Cape UK (1972); Knopf US (1972)

Insp Wilfred DOVER
is a splendid detective. But he is also gross, foul-mouthed, lazy, malicious, unhygienic, and has digestive problems, about which he does not hesitate to make the world around him aware. Outrageous and outrageously funny, he is assisted in his lumberings around the underworld by a sacrificial sidekick.

British Policeman operating in England

Sidekick: Sgt MCGREGOR

has the very great misfortune to be the assistant of *Insp DOVER*.

British Male - Subordinate

Joyce PORTER 1924- (British)

was born in Marple, Cheshire. Educated at the High School for Girls, Macclesfield, Cheshire, she took a BA at King's College, London, 1945, after which she served as a Flight Officer in the Women's Air Force, 1949-63. She is the creator of two of the most obnoxiously endearing detectives to grace the post-war era.

Other Detectives:

Edmund BROWN

The Hon Constance Ethel MORRISON-BURKE

Citation Record: 10 Books

Dover One - *First*

Cape UK (1964); Scribner's US (1964)

Dover Beats The Band - *Last*

Weidenfeld & Nicolson UK (1980); Foul Play US (1991)

Mr DOWKER
is a Victorian private enquiry agent.

British Male Private Detective operating in England

Fergus HUME 1859-1932 (British)

Invented 24 detectives - see Insp Samuel GORBY

Citation Record: 1 Book

The Piccadilly Puzzle: A Mysterious Puzzle - *Only*

White UK (1889); Lovell US (1889)

Father Roger DOWLING
is a middle-aged, Catholic priest at the fictional St Hilary's, in Fox River, supposedly near Chicago. It is a region where crimes abound and he, for one reason or another, is drawn into solving them. Once an alcoholic himself, he knows the down side of life and he is a man of great compassion who puts the religious needs of his clients above the requirements forced on him by his excellent detective work.

American Male Amateur operating in Chicago

Stooge: Capt Phil KEEGAN

may be a friendly cop but is still critical of the amateur sleuthing of the good priest, who happens to be always right.

American Male

Ralph MCINERNY 1929- (American)

was born in Minneapolis, Minnesota. He took a BA at the St Paul Seminary, Minnesota, 1951, an MA at the University of Minnesota, Minneapolis, 1952, and a PhD in Philosophy at Laval University, Quebec, 1954. He is a sometime Professor of Medieval Studies at the University of Notre Dame, Indiana.

Writer: Ralph Matthew MCINERNY

Other Bylines:

Edward MACKIN   Monica QUILL

Inventor of one other detective Andrew BROOM

Citation Record: 12 Books 4 Short Stories in 1 Collection

Her Death Of Cold - *First*

Vanguard US (1977); Hale UK (1979)

A Cardinal Offense - *Latest*

St Martin's US (1994)

Four On The Floor - *Collection 1*

contains four novelettes.

Worldwide US (1994)

Jerry DOWN
is hired as a bodyguard by an American living in England.

Irish Male Private Detective operating in England

Leo GREX 1908-1985 (British)

Invented 3 detectives - see Phil SANDERSON

Citation Record: 1 Book

The Man From Manhattan - *Only*

Hutchinson UK (1934); Doubleday US (1935)

Insp DOWNES and Sgt HOPKINS
Male Policemen operating in South Africa

Victor SAMPSON 1855-1940 (British)

Citation Record: 2 Books

The Murder Of Paul Rougier - *First*

Jenkins UK (1928)

The Komani Mystery - *Last*

Jenkins UK (1930)

Cpl DOWNEY
Canadian Policeman operating in Canada

James B HENDRYX 1880-1963 (Canadian)

Invented 3 detectives - see Connie MORGAN

Citation Record: 2 Books

Downey Of The Mounted - *First*

Hutchinson UK (1926); Putnam US (1926)

Badmen On Halfaday Creek - *Last*

Doubleday US (1950); Hammond UK (1956)

Sir Arthur Conan DOYLE
Second detective of Sherlock HOLMES

Sir Arthur Conan DOYLE
Second detective of Harry HOUDINI

Matt DOYLE and Carter WINFIELD
Matt DOYLE was a shamus in Chicago but had to flee the mob there when he began to interfere too much with their activities. He now runs an agency in San Diego, together with his partner, *Carter WINFIELD,* a former Secretary of State.
American Male Private Detectives operating in San Diego

Dale L GILBERT ?-1988 (American)
Citation Record: 2 Books
The Black Star Murders - *First*
St Martin's US (1988)
The Mother Murders - *Latest*
St Martin's US (1989)

Pat DOYLE
grew up in the slums of New York and dropped out of law school to become a PI. Still limping badly from an Army training accident, he goes to Dallas to investigate a vast oil theft.
American Male Private Detective operating in New York/Dallas

Mitchell CARLTON (American)
Citation Record: 1 Book
Hot Oil - *Single*
Belmont US (1980)

Det Patrick Michael DOYLE
American Policeman operating in New York

Audrey NEWELL (American)
Citation Record: 2 Books
Who Killed Cavelotti? - *First*
Century US (1930); Century UK (1930)
Murder Is Not Mute - *Last*
Macrae, Smith US (1940)

Dennis DOYNE
British Male Amateur operating in England

Cuthbert BAINES (British)
Writer: Cuthbert Edward BAINES
Citation Record: 2 Books
The Slip Coach - *First*
Arnold UK (1927)
A Drug In The Market - *Last*
Arnold UK (1928)

Pete DRACO
is a New Yorker who moves to Miami Beach and sets up an agency called Undercover Inc. He gets, as a result, an office, a white Cadillac, and lots of trouble from his cases and the Florida cops, who seem nastier than most.
American Male Private Detective operating in Miami

Richard FOSTER 1910-1981 (American)
Inventor of one other detective Chin Kwang KHAM
For writer details see Kim LOCKE
Citation Record: 2 Books
Bier For A Chaser - *First*
Fawcett US (1959); Muller UK (1960)
Too Late For Mourning - *Last*
Fawcett US (1960); Muller UK (1961)

Ransome DRAGOON and Vicky 'The Dish' GAINES
were two early examples of the many American agents spawned after the involvement of the US in the Second World War. They indulge in good, old-fashioned, adventurous detective work, before the (fictional) game became over-intellectualised.
American Male Secret Agent and American Female Secret Agent operating in New York

Frank DIAMOND (American)
Citation Record: 2 Books
Murder In Five Columns - *First*
Mystery House US (1944)
Murder Rides A Rocket - *Last*
Mystery House US (1946); Equerry UK (1947)

Frank DRAGOVICH
is Croatian by extraction and hardly blinks an eye when he meets a murder or three, which Chicago does not find it at all difficult to provide.
American Male Private Detective operating in Chicago

Barbara GREGORICH 1943- (American)
Citation Record: 1 Book
Dirty Proof - *Single*
Pageant US (1988)

Insp DRAKE
British Policeman operating in England

David TRISTAM
Citation Record: 1 Book
Inspector Drake's Last Case - *Play*
New Playwrights ? (1990)

Desmond DRAKE
British Male Amateur operating in England

SEA-LION 1909- (British)
Writer: Geoffrey Martin BENNETT
Inventor of one other detective John PRENTICE
Citation Record: 3 Books
Meet Desmond Drake - *First*
Hutchinson UK (1952)
Desmond Drake Goes West - *Last*
Hutchinson UK (1956)

Dexter DRAKE
American Male Amateur operating in Connecticut

Elsa BARKER 1869-1954 (American)
Citation Record: 2 Books 10 Short Stories in 1 Collection
The Cobra Candlestick - *First*
Sears US (1928); Hamilton UK (1930)
The Redman Cave Murder - *Last*
Sears US (1930)
The CID Of Dexter Drake - *Collection 1*
Sears US (1929); Hamilton UK (1931)

Earl DRAKE
is a thief who later becomes a Government secret agent.
American Male Secret Agent operating in Los Angeles/Florida

Dan J MARLOWE 1914- (American)
See main detective Johnny KILLAIN
Citation Record: 12 Books
The Name Of The Game Is Death - *First*
Fawcett US (1962); Muller UK (1963)
Operation Counterpunch - *Last*
Fawcett US (1976)

Det Jessica DRAKE
American Policewoman operating in New York

Rochelle Majer KRICH (American)
Citation Record: 2 Books
Fair Game - *First*
Mysterious Press US (1993)
Angel Of Death - *Latest*
Mysterious Press US (1994)

Keppel DRAKE
is a portrait painter who turns detective.
American Male Amateur operating in USA

D

Julian HAWTHORNE 1846-1934 (American)

Other Detectives:
Insp BYRNES Fred TYRREL

Citation Record: 1 Book

An American Monte Cristo - *Only*
Allen UK (1893)

Red DRAKE

is a racetrack detective who deals with crimes generated by gambling. He appeared only in short stories, published in *Black Mask Magazine, Crime Busters,* and *Mystery Magazine* during the 1930s and 1940s.

American Male Private Detective operating in USA

W T BALLARD 1903-1980 (American)

Invented 4 detectives - see Bill LENNOX

No citations

Simon DRAKE

is a lawyer who, being single and fond of the good life, is involved in several cases of murder.

American Male Amateur operating in USA

Michael MAGUIRE 1945- (British)

Citation Record: 3 Books

Shot Silk - *First*
Wingate UK (1975)

Scratchproof - *Last*
Allen UK (1976); St Martin's US (1977)

Helen NIELSEN 1918- (American)

was born in Roseville, Illinois. An engineer and artist, she was also the author of many crime and detective novels.

Writer: Helen Bernice NIELSEN

Other Detectives:
Lisa BANCROFT Ty LEANDER

Citation Record: 6 Books

Gold Coast Nocturne - *First*
Washburn US (1951)

Dead On The Level - *First**
Dell US (1954)

Murder By Proxy - *First**
Gollancz UK (1952)

The Brink Of Murder - *Last*
Gollancz UK (1976)

Stephen DRAKE

is a crime reporter who solves two cases of murder – mainly because of his improbable clairvoyant abilities.

American Male Amateur operating in San Francisco

Collin WILCOX 1924- (American)

Invented 4 detectives - see Lt Frank HASTINGS

Citation Record: 2 Books

The Black Door - *First*
Dodd, Mead US (1967); Cassell UK (1968)

The Third Figure - *Last*
Dodd, Mead US (1968); Hale UK (1969)

Steve DRAKE

is a Vietnam War veteran who has set up office on 44th Street, Manhattan.

American Male Private Detective operating in New York

Richard ELLINGTON 1914-1980 (American)

Citation Record: 5 Books

Shoot The Works - *First*
Morrow US (1948); Cassell UK (1956)

Just Killing Time - *Last*
Morrow US (1953); Boardman UK (1954)

Shakedown - *Last**
Bantam US (1955)

Dick DRANT

American Male Detective in Pulp Magazines operating in USA

F Lusk BROUGHTON (American)

Invented 10 detectives - see Harry WILLIAMS

Citation Record: 1 Selected Short Story

Dick Drant, The Reporter Detective; Or Running Down The Bank Wreckers
Old Cap Collier Library US (18??)

Paul DRAYER

investigates the disappearance of some important photographic negatives.

American Male Amateur operating in USA

Edward D HOCH 1930- (American)

Invented 20 detectives - see Capt LEOPOLD

Citation Record: 1 Selected Short Story

Murder Offstage
In 'Ellery Queen's Mystery Magazine' US (1969)

Michael DRED

British Male Private Detective operating in England

Marie Conor LEIGHTON 1866-1941 (British)

Writer: Marie Flora Barbara Conor LEIGHTON

Other Detectives:
Lucille DARE Joan MAR

Citation Record: 1 Book

Michael Dred, Detective - *Only*
Grant Richards UK (1899); Brentano's US (1899)

Adam DREW and Kay CORNISH

American Male Amateur and American Female Amateur operating in USA

Virginia HANSON 1905-1968 (American)

See main detective Nicholas CORNISH

Citation Record: 3 Books

Death Walks The Post - *First*
Doubleday US (1938)

Mystery For Mary - *Last*
Doubleday US (1942)

Amanda DREW

Second detective of George COLE

James DREW

British Male Sleuth operating in England/Scotland

William GARRETT 1890-1967 (British)

Writer: William A GARRETT

Citation Record: 2 Books

Friday To Monday - *First*
Hutchinson UK (1923); Appleton US (1923)

The Secret Of The Hills - *Last*
Jarrolds UK (1920)

Treasure Royal - *Last**
Appleton US (1926)

Nancy DREW

appeared first in 1929, the original American girl detective on which countless others, on both sides of the Atlantic, were based. She was a total contradiction, being sweet, feminine, moral, and good, but also tough and able to do anything, from flying a plane to stunning a bad guy with a single blow. She was created by Edward T Stratemeyer, writing as *Carolyn KEENE,* but he died after the first three stories (one cited). Others were then written by his daughter.

American Female Amateur operating in USA

Carolyn KEENE 1862-1930 (American)

Writer: Edward L STRATEMEYER

Other Bylines:
Chester K STEELE Nicholas CARTER

Citation Record: 1 Selected Short Story

The Secret Of The Old Clock - *Special*
was the first story in which *Nancy DREW* appeared.
US (1929)

D

Randall DREW
British Male Amateur operating in England

Dick FRANCIS 1920- (British)

Invented 18 detectives - see Sid HALLEY

Citation Record: 1 Book

Trial Run - *Single*
Harper & Row US (1979)

Sgt Ronnie DREW
British Policeman operating in England

Francis VIVIAN 1906- (British)

Invented 3 detectives - see Insp John BURNELL

Citation Record: 2 Books

The Arrow Of Death - *First*
Jenkins UK (1938)

Dark Moon - *Last*
Jenkins UK (1939)

Triggy DREW
solves a case of death by shooting in a locked room.
American Male Amateur operating in USA

Henry LEVERAGE 1885- (American)

Writer: Carl Henry LEVERAGE

Citation Record: 1 Book

Whispering Wires - *Only*
Moffat US (1918)

Valerie DREW
was one of the many schoolgirl detectives appearing in British girls' magazines of the inter-war years. She had violet eyes, red-gold hair (this was much favoured by writers in schoolgirl magazines) and, coming from a wealthy family, she lived in Park Lane. She was, of course, a skilled aviator and had a range of other abilities that could come in useful to a girl detective, as well as having the usual canine sidekick. She was created by *John William BOBIN* and all the stories from 1933 until his death in 1935 were written by him for *Schoolgirls' Weekly.* After that date they continued under the byline of *Isobel NORTON,* the last one appearing in 1939. The Second World War put an end to the whole ethos on which these and countless stories of other schoolgirl detectives was based.
British Female Amateur operating in England

Sidekick: FLASH
was a pretty brilliant detective for just a dog and was even allowed to appear in one or two stories on his own.
Male - Pet Dog

Isobel NORTON (British)

was probably the pseudonym of a male author who wrote the *Valerie DREW* stories after the death of their creator.

No citations

Timothy DREWER
British Male Amateur operating in England

Hilary LANDON 1902-1985 (British)

For writer details see George BELLAIRS

Citation Record: 2 Books

Murder At Morning Prayers - *First*
Gifford UK (1947)

Circle Round A Corpse - *Last*
Gifford UK (1948)

Ch Insp DREWRY
British Policeman operating in England

Nigel BURNABY 1882- (British)

See main detective Sir Timothy ROSSITER

Citation Record: 2 Books

The Clue Of The Green-Eyed Girl - *First*
Ward, Lock UK (1935)

Two Deaths For A Penny - *Last*
Ward, Lock UK (1935)

Quentin DREX
British Male Amateur operating in England

Gwyn EVANS 1899-1938 (British)

Invented 5 detectives - see Bill KELLAWAY

Citation Record: 1 Book 8 Short Stories in 2 Collections

His Majesty-The Crook - *Only*
Wright UK (1935)

The Man With The Scarlet Skull And Other Tales - *Collection 1*
Short stories - 5
Wright UK (1935)

Rogue Royal - *Collection 2*
contains three untitled novelettes.
Short stories - 3
Wright UK (1936)

Supt Michael DREXEL
British Policeman operating in England

Gray USHER 1903- (British)

Writer: John Gray USHER

Other Byline: Pete GARROWAY

Inventor of one other detective Pete GARROWAY

Citation Record: 4 Books

Death Sped The Plough - *First*
Long UK (1956)

Death In The Bag - *Last*
Long UK (1958)

Mortimer DREXEL
is a reporter who sleuths just the once.
American Male Amateur operating in USA

William R RANDALL (American)

Citation Record: 1 Book

The Syndicate Murders - *Only*
Greenberg US (1935)

Ch Const Sir Clinton DRIFFIELD
holds, although only in his thirties, high office, in that he is the Chief Constable of an English county. Created by an author who was a scientist of some standing, his cases, although having a period, upper-class flavour, often have detailed scientific content and are meticulously accurate when it comes to such things as footprints, ballistics and timetables, with which the books abound.
British Policeman operating in England

Sidekick: WENDOVER
is a local bigwig, often in conflict with *DRIFFIELD,* who usually addresses him as 'Squire'. However, he usually plays an important part in solving the latter's cases.
British Male - Friend

J J CONNINGTON 1880-1947 (British)

Invented 5 detectives - see Mark BRAND

Citation Record: 17 Books

Murder In The Maze - *First*
Benn UK (1927); Little, Brown US (1927)

Common Sense Is All You Need - *Last*
Hodder & Stoughton UK (1947)

William DRINK and Sam SLEEP
Australian Male Sleuths operating in Japan

Sam FINNEGAN (Australian)

Citation Record: 2 Books

It Blows Up In Your Face - *First*
Cleveland AU (?)

To Hell On Skates - *Latest*
Cleveland AU (?)

Prof Stuff DRISCOLL
is a young criminologist in a local sheriff's office, somewhere on the Florida coast.
American Male Professional Investigator operating in Florida

D

Rufus KING 1893-1966 (American)

Invented 5 detectives - see Cotton MOON

Citation Record: 22 Short Stories in 3 Collections

Malice In Wonderland - *Collection 1*

Short stories - 8
Doubleday US (1958)

The Steps To Murder - *Collection 2*

Short stories - 8
Doubleday US (1960)

The Faces Of Danger - *Collection 3*

Short stories - 6
Doubleday US (1964)

Theodore DROST

British Male Sleuth operating in England

William LEQUEUX 1864-1927 (British)

Invented 23 detectives - see Allan KENNEDY

Citation Record: 8 Short Stories in 1 Collection

The Bomb-Makers - *Collection 1*

Jarrolds UK (1917)

Dixon DRUCE

was one of the early rivals to the already famed *Sherlock HOLMES*, although he did not attempt to parody him.

British Male Professional Amateur operating in England

L T MEADE 1854-1914 (British)

Invented 4 detectives - see Rudolph GREY

Citation Record: 1 Selected Short Story

The Face Of The Abbot

appeared first in a collection of the author's stories, *The Sorceress of the Strand*, and was included in the anthology, *Rivals of Sherlock Holmes* (*Castle*; US 1978). This may be the American edition of Hugh Greene's 1970 collection (*Bodley Head*, UK, 1970; *Pantheon*, US, 1971).

Ward, Lock UK (1903)

Chester DRUM

is an ex-FBI man and runs the Drum Agency on F Street, Washington DC. He is involved in both detective and espionage work, often for government agencies, which takes him all over the world.

American Male Private Detective operating in USA/Yugoslavia

Stephen MARLOWE 1928- (American)

was born in New York City and educated at the College of William and Mary, Williamsburg, Virginia, graduating with a BA, 1949. After serving in the US army, 1954-1956, he became a full-time writer. The author of at least forty-six novels, he has, under several pseudonyms, published works in various genres, especially science fiction and books for children.

Writer: Milton LESSER

Citation Record: 20 Books

The Second Longest Night - *First*

GM US (1955); Fawcett UK (1958)

Drum Beat - Marianne - *Last*

GM US (1968)

Eve DRUM

is an agent of LUST (The League of Underground Spies and Terrorists) and solves a case of death by shooting in a locked library.

American Female Professional Investigator operating in USA

Rod GRAY (American)

Citation Record: 1 Book

Lay Me Odds - *Only*

Tower US (1967); K & G UK (1968)

Justus DRUM

is hired by seven men to find out which of them has murdered someone in a room to which only they have a key.

American Male Private Detective operating in USA

Carolynne LOGAN and Malcolm LOGAN (American)

Citation Record: 1 Book

One Of These Seven - *Only*

Mystery House US (1946); Quality Press UK (1948)

Supt DRUMLEY

British Policeman operating in England

T W SPEIGHT 1830-1915 (British)

Invented 4 detectives - see Insp MALLESON

Citation Record: 1 Book

The Crime In The Wood - *Only*

Long UK (1899)

Capt Hugh 'Bulldog' DRUMMOND

is the prototype of all those British heroes of the thriller and detective story who emerged during the inter-war years. Aristocratic, wealthy, military in experience and often in manner, speaking with a ghastly accent and in clichéd phrases, he appeared in books that had a tremendous appeal for a generation that had undergone the horrors of war and were seemingly denied the benefits of the peace. An undoubted xenophobe, he regarded it as his duty to seek out and punish criminals; and especially all those who would damage the security and welfare of Britain. His particular enemy was 'the filthy Boche' and his main personal antagonist was one Carl Peterson.

'Bulldog' DRUMMOND is probably the best known of the whole species of such hero-adventurers; and, indeed, he is one of the select few fictional types whose names have become generic, conjuring up a type, an era and an ethos. His exploits were used for many films and radio and stage dramas; and when the originals ran out, many more were written by unknown hands to make good the deficiency. He spawned countless imitators before the Second World War transformed the scene on which they depended.

British Male Amateur operating in England

Sidekick: Toby SINCLAIR

is available to *'Bulldog' DRUMMOND* whenever he sets out to defeat his country's enemies.

British Male - Friend

Sidekick: Ted JERNINGHAM

is a crack shot and master of disguise, a most useful combination of attributes.

British Male - Friend

Gerard FAIRLIE 1899-1983 (British)

continued the *'Bulldog' DRUMMOND* saga after the death of *H C MCNEILE*.

Invented 4 detectives - see Johnny MACALL

Citation Record: 7 Books

Bulldog Drummond On Dartmoor - *Pastiche 1*

Hodder & Stoughton UK (1938); Hillman-Curl US (1939)

The Return Of The Black Gang - *Pastiche 2*

(1954)

H C MCNEILE 1888-1937 (British)

For writer details see Capt Hugh 'Bulldog' DRUMMOND

Other Detectives:

Capt Hugh 'Bulldog' DRUMMOND and Ronald STANDISH
Jim MAITLAND

Citation Record: 7 Books

Bulldog Drummond: The Adventures Of A Demobilized Officer Who Found Peace Dull - *First*

Doran US (1920)

Bulldog Drummond Returns - *Last*

was published in the UK under the *SAPPER* byline and entitled *THE RETURN OF BULLDOG DRUMMOND*.

Doubleday US (1932)

SAPPER 1888-1937 (British)

was born in Bodmin, Cornwall. He was educated at Cheltenham College, Gloucestershire, attended Woolwich Military College and served in the Royal Engineers, 1907-19, reaching the rank of Lieutenant Colonel. He invented one of the most popular heroes in the history of the thriller and his stories were used for many films.

The UK books were published under this byline. The US books were published under the *MCNEILE* byline, which he also used in the UK for his short stories.

Writer: Herman Cyril MCNEILE

Other Byline: H C MCNEILE

Other Detectives:
Capt Hugh 'Bulldog' DRUMMOND and Ronald STANDISH
Jim MAITLAND
Ronald STANDISH

Citation Record: 7 Books

Bulldog Drummond: The Adventures Of A Demobilized Officer Who Found Peace Dull - *First*
Hodder & Stoughton UK (1920)

The Return Of Bulldog Drummond - *Last*
was published in the US under the *MCNEILE* byline and entitled *BULLDOG DRUMMOND RETURNS.*
Hodder & Stoughton UK (1937)

Capt Hugh 'Bulldog' DRUMMOND and Ronald STANDISH

Ronald STANDISH is a private detective who joins forces with *'Bulldog' DRUMMOND* in these books, although the latter's brawn is superior, it seems, to the former's brains. *STANDISH* appears on his own in some short stories and *DRUMMOND* appears separately in novels and short stories.

British Male Amateur and British Male Private Detective operating in England

H C MCNEILE 1888-1937 (British)

Invented 3 detectives - see Capt Hugh 'Bulldog' DRUMMOND

Citation Record: 3 Books

Tiny Carteret - *First*
Doubleday US (1930)

Challenge - *Last*
Doubleday US (1937)

SAPPER 1888-1937 (British)

Invented 4 detectives - see Capt Hugh 'Bulldog' DRUMMOND

Citation Record: 3 Books

Tiny Carteret - *First*
Hodder & Stoughton UK (1930)

Challenge - *Last*
Hodder & Stoughton UK (1937)

Insp Dennis DRURY

British Policeman operating in England

W Stanley SYKES 1894-1961 (British)

Writer: William Stanley SYKES

Citation Record: 2 Books

The Missing Money-Lender - *First*
Lane UK (1931)

The Man Who Was Dead - *First**
Dodd, Mead US (1931)

The Harness Of Death - *Last*
Lane UK (1932); Dodd, Mead US (1932)

'Dynamite' DRURY

South African Male Amateur operating in South Africa

L Patrick GREENE

Other Detectives:
Sgt LANCEY
Aubrey St John MAJOR
Aubrey St John MAJOR and Sgt LANCEY
Trooper USELESS

Citation Record: 19 Short Stories in 3 Collections

Dynamite Drury - *Collection 1*
Short stories - 7
Selwyn UK (1929)

Dynamite Drury Again - *Collection 2*
Short stories - 6
Jarrolds UK (1930)

Dynamite Drury Patrols - *Collection 3*
Short stories - 6
Devonshire UK (1946)

Supt Frank DRURY

British Policeman operating in England

Piers MARLOWE (British)

Inventor of one other detective pair Supt Frank DRURY and Insp Bill HAZARD

Citation Record: 1 Book

Promise To Kill - *Only*
Thriller Book Club UK (1965)

Supt Frank DRURY and Insp Bill HAZARD

British Male Policemen operating in England

Piers MARLOWE (British)

See main detective Supt Frank DRURY

Citation Record: 5 Books

The Dead Don't Scare - *First*
Gifford UK (1963)

Hire Me A Hearse - *Last*
Hale UK (1968)

Ben DRYDEN

South African Male Amateur operating in South Africa

Michael HARTMANN 1944- (British)

Citation Record: 2 Books

Shadow Of The Leopard - *First*
Heinemann UK (1978)

The Hunted - *First**
St Martin's US (1979)

Days Of Thunder - *Last*
Heinemann UK (1980); St Martin's US (1980)

John DRYDEN and Gwyneth JONES

solve a campus murder at an American university.

American Male Amateur and American Female Amateur operating in USA

Olivia DWIGHT 1928- (American)

Writer: Mary HAZZARD

Citation Record: 1 Book

Close His Eyes - *Only*
Harper & Row US (1961)

Det Insp DU CAS

British Policeman operating in England

Sir Henry IMBERT-TERRY 1854-1938 (British)

Writer: Sir Henry Machu IMBERT-TERRY

Citation Record: 3 Books

Acid - *First*
Skeffington UK (1928)

Weeds - *Last*
Skeffington UK (1933)

Stephen DUANE

American Male Secret Agent operating in Long Island/Boston

John L BENTON 1900-1976 (American)

Writer: Thomas Albert CURRY

Inventor of one other detective Jerry WADE

Citation Record: 2 Books

Duane Of The FBI - *First*
Dodge US (1937)

Duane And The G-Men - *First**
Cassell UK (1938)

The Art Treasure Murders - *Last*
Gateway US (1940)

Duane And The Art Murders - *Last**
Cassell UK (1939)

Kenneth DUCANE

is also called Vandoran.

British Male Secret Agent operating in England

John BINGHAM 1908-1988 (British)

Invented 3 detectives - see Supt 'Badger' BROCK

Citation Record: 3 Books

The Double Agent - *First*
Gollancz UK (1966); Dutton US (1967)

God's Defector - *Last*
Macmillan UK (1976)

Ministry Of Death - *Last**
Walker US (1977)

D

Jabez DUCK

calls himself a 'private enquiry agent' in this Victorian novel.

British Male Private Detective operating in London

George R SIMS 1847-1922 (British)

Invented 5 detectives - see Dorcas DENE

Citation Record: 1 Book

Rogues And Vagabonds - *Only*
Chatto & Windus UK (1885)

Sheriff Bugrus DUCKHOUSE

Second detective of Angus MACWHORTER

Phyllis DUDLEY

British Female Amateur operating in England

R Austin FREEMAN 1862-1947 (British)

Invented 4 detectives - see Dr John Evelyn THORNDYKE

Citation Record: 7 Short Stories in 1 Collection

Flighty Phyllis - *Collection 1*
Not all the stories are criminous.
Hodder & Stoughton UK (1928)

Derwent DUFF

solves a case of death by shooting in a locked room.

British Male Amateur operating in England

Cecil HAYTER 1871-1922 (British)

Writer: Cecil Goodenough HAYTER

Inventor of one other detective Mortimer KANE

Citation Record: 1 Selected Short Story

The Clue Of The Burnt Candle
appeared in the February number.
In 'Penny Pictorial Magazine' UK (1918)

Det John DUFF

was one of the first American detectives to propose a serious psychological approach to solving crimes. He appeared only in short stories and the collection cited, published after the author's death, was selected by *Queen's Quorum* as the most significant of the decade.

American Policeman operating in New York

Harvey J O'HIGGINS 1876-1929 (Canadian)

Writer: Harvey Jerrold O'HIGGINS

Inventor of one other detective Barney COOK

Citation Record: 8 Short Stories in 1 Collection

Detective Duff Unravels It - *Collection 1*
Liveright US (1929)

Prof MacDougal DUFF

is a Professor of American History and, as a hobby, solves mysteries solely from the accounts he reads in various newspapers.

American Male Amateur operating in New York/Michigan

Charlotte ARMSTRONG 1905-1969 (American)

was born in Vulcan, Michigan. She was educated at the University of Wisconsin, Madison, and graduated from Barnard College, New York.

Writer: Mrs Jack LEWI

Other Detectives:
Matt CUNEEN
Annabel O'SHEA
Charley IVES
Prof David WAKELY

Citation Record: 3 Books

Lay On, Macduff - *First*
Coward McCann US (1942); Gifford UK (1943)

The Innocent Flower - *Last*
Coward McCann US (1945)

Death Filled The Glass - *Last**
Cherry Tree UK (1945)

Thomas DUFF

investigates for the US Treasury Department.

American Male Professional Investigator operating in USA

Archibald Clavering GUNTER 1847-1907 (American)

See main detective Dr BURTON

Citation Record: 1 Book

Don Balasco Of Key West - *Only*
Home US (1896); Routledge UK (1897)

Father DUFFY and Sgt GOLDSMITH

American Male Amateur and American Policeman operating in USA

Dorothy Salisbury DAVIS 1916- (American)

Invented 9 detectives - see Kate OSBORN

Citation Record: 1 Book

A Gentle Murderer - *Only*
Scribner's US (1951)

Insp DUFFY

appears also in two books with the author's other detective, *Alan RUSSELL.*

Irish Policeman operating in Ireland

Nigel FITZGERALD 1906- (British)

Other Detectives:
Insp DUFFY and Alan RUSSELL
Alan RUSSELL

Citation Record: 7 Books

The House Is Falling - *First*
Collins UK (1955)

Affairs Of Death - *Last*
Collins UK (1967)

Insp DUFFY and Alan RUSSELL

also appear individually in other books by this author.

Irish Policeman and Male Sleuth operating in Ireland

Nigel FITZGERALD 1906- (British)

Invented 3 detectives - see Insp DUFFY

Citation Record: 2 Books

Midsummer Malice - *First*
Collins UK (1953); Macmillan US (1959)

The Rosy Pastor - *Last*
Collins UK (1954)

Cornelius DUFFY

is a penurious PI who, being without paying clients, does a good deed or two for the needy by solving cases for them.

American Male Private Detective operating in USA

William Gray BEYER (American)

Citation Record: 1 Book

Eenie, Meenie, Minie - Murder! - *Only*
Mystery House US (1945)

Murder By Arrangement - *Only**
Partridge UK (1946)

Nick DUFFY

is an ex-policeman who, having left the Metropolitan force in dubious circumstances, now practises as a downbeat PI in West London. His bisexuality is made much of and his detective skills are excellent.

British Male Private Detective operating in London

Dan KAVANAGH 1946- (British)

was born in Leicester, Leicestershire. He was educated at City of London School and took a BA in modern languages at Magdalen College, Oxford, 1968. He studied Law, became

a barrister and then worked as a reporter, editor, reviewer and critic for several illustrious London newspapers and journals. He has been a full-time writer since 1986 and his non-genre novels have won him many prizes and awards.
Writer: Julian BARNES
Citation Record: 4 Books
Duffy - *First*
Cape UK (1980); Pantheon US (1986)
Going To The Dogs - *Latest*
Viking UK (1985); Pantheon US (1985)

Lt Bud DUGAN
American Policeman operating in New York

Michael GELLER (American)
Inventor of one other detective Mickey 'Slots' RESNICK
Citation Record: 3 Books
Mayhem On The Coney Beat - *First*
Belmont US (1979)
A Corpse For A Candidate - *Latest*
Belmont US (1980)

Rock DUGAN
solves a case of death by stabbing in an aeroplane.
American Male Private Detective operating in USA

Stephen BRETT (American)
Writer: Stephen MERTZ
Other Byline: Jim CASE
Citation Record: 1 Book
Some Die Hard - *Single*
Manor US (1979)

Joe DUGGER
is a CIA agent who unearths a master plan to establish a Fourth Reich by nasties seeking a secret weapon buried in Africa.
American Male Secret Agent operating in USA/Africa

Jack BICKHAM 1930- (American)
See main detective Charity ROSS
Citation Record: 1 Book
The Regensburg Legacy - *Single*
Doubleday US (1980)

Theodore DUHAMEL
is a member of the French police and his cases, said to be adapted from French manuscripts, were written up by this obscure, pseudonymous, indefatigable, Victorian author.
French Policeman operating in France

WATERS (British)
Invented 6 detectives - see WATERS
Citation Record: 8 Short Stories in 1 Collection
The Experiences Of A French Police Officer - *Collection 1*
Clarke UK (1861)
The Experiences Of A French Detective Officer - *Collection 1**
Arno US (1876)

Casson DUKER
is a wine merchant who, in the course of his work, becomes involved in other people's crimes and does some effective sleuthing.
British Male Amateur operating in England

William MOLE 1917-1972 (British)
Writer: William Antony YOUNGER
Citation Record: 3 Books
The Hammersmith Maggot - *First*
Eyre & Spottiswoode UK (1955)
Small Venom - *First**
Dodd, Mead US (1956)
Shadow Of A Killer - *First**
Dell US (1959)
Skin Trap - *Last*
Eyre & Spottiswoode UK (1957)
You Pay For Pity - *Last**
Dodd, Mead US (1958)

Lois DULANE
Australian Female Sleuth operating in Sydney

Eddie SAINT (Australian)
Writer: Edward Carver SAINT
Citation Record: 3 Books
The Lady Is Lethal - *First*
In 'Action Comics' AU (?)
Naked Nemesis - *Last*
In 'Action Comics' AU (?)

Dove DULCET
American Amateur operating in USA

Christopher MORLEY 1890-1957 (American)
Writer: Christopher Darlington MORLEY
Citation Record: 1 Collection
The Ironing Board - *Collection 1*
Not all the stories feature *DULCET*.
Doubleday US (1949)

Supt DULLAC
French Policeman operating in France

JACQUEMARD-SENECAL (French)
have written many novels and plays together. *JACQUEMARD* was born in Algeria and is an authority on French literature. *SENECAL* was born in France and studied interior design.
Writers: Yves JACQUEMARD and Jean-Michel SENECAL
Citation Record: 1 Book
The Body Vanishes - *Single*
is a translation from the French of *Le Crime de la Maison Grun* (Paris, 1976).
Collins UK (1980); Dodd, Mead US (1980)

Peter DULUTH
was formerly a Broadway producer who, in his first book, is a patient in a sanatorium, drying out after two alcoholic years. There he meets murder, solves it and goes on to become a fine detective, meeting his wife, Iris, on the way. He appears also in one book with another of the author's detectives, *Lt Timothy TRANT*.
American Male Amateur operating in USA

Patrick QUENTIN (American)
was the pseudonym of a powerful writing partnership, two men who wrote together for almost three decades, under this byline and also as *Q PATRICK* and *Jonathan STAGGE*. Hugh Wheeler was born in Northwood, Middlesex, educated at Clayesmore School, Iwerne Minster, Dorset, and took a BA in English at London University, 1932. He emigrated to the USA, studied at Harvard and became a naturalised US citizen, 1942. Richard Webb was American. They were the joint authors, under the three bylines, of at least thirty-three genre novels and many short stories. Under his own name, Wheeler also wrote plays, librettos for musicals and screenplays. They received several awards in the theatrical field; the Tony award twice, 1973 and 1979; the New York Drama Critics Circle award three times, 1973, 1976, 1979; and the Mystery Writers of America Edgar Allan Poe award, 1962.
Writers: Hugh Callingham WHEELER 1912-1987 and Richard Wilson WEBB 1901-
Other Detectives:
Peter DULUTH and Lt Timothy TRANT
Andrew JORDAN
Nicky ROOD
Mark LIDDON
Lt Timothy TRANT
Citation Record: 8 Books
A Puzzle For Fools - *First*
Simon & Schuster US (1936); Gollancz UK (1936)
Black Widow - *Last*
Simon & Schuster US (1952)
Fatal Woman - *Last**
Gollancz UK (1953)

D

Peter DULUTH and Lt Timothy TRANT

American Male Amateur and American Policeman operating in New York

Patrick QUENTIN (American)

Invented 6 detectives - see Peter DULUTH

Citation Record: 1 Book

My Son, The Murderer - *Only*
Simon & Schuster US (1954)

The Wife Of Ronald Sheldon - *Only**
Gollancz UK (1954)

The DUMB DETECTIVE

British Male Detective in Pulp Magazines operating in England

ANON

Citation Record: 1 Book

The Dumb Detective - *Only*
In 'Boys of England' UK (1887)

Cdr DUMPHRY

British Male Amateur operating in England

Barry PAIN 1864-1928 (British)

Writer: Barry Eric Odell PAIN

Inventor of one other detective Constantine DIX

Citation Record: 16 Short Stories in 1 Collection

Dumphry - *Collection 1*
Not all the stories are criminous.
Ward, Lock UK (1927)

Judge DUNAWAY

solves a case of murder by shooting in a locked room.

American Male Amateur operating in USA

William N VAILE 1876-1927 (American)

Writer: William Newell VAILE

Citation Record: 1 Book

The Mystery Of The Golconda - *Only*
Doubleday US (1925); Cassell UK (1927)

Prof Clifford DUNBAR

is the Professor of English at Los Angeles University and is drawn into the investigation of the murder of a friend, which the police think is a mugging.

American Male Amateur operating in Los Angeles

Sidekick: Mona MOORE
American Female - Assistant

Will HARRISS 1922- (American)

Writer: Willard Irvin HARRISS

Citation Record: 2 Books

The Bay Psalm Book Murder - *First*
Walker US (1983); Hale UK (1983)

Timor Mortis - *Latest*
Walker US (1986)

Insp DUNCAN and Capt Peter DARRELL

solve a case of shooting in an 'impossible' situation.

British Policeman and British Male Amateur operating in England

Don BETTERIDGE 1897-1968 (British)

For writer details see Papa PONTIVY

Inventor of one other detective 'Tiger' LESTER

Citation Record: 1 Book

Cast Iron Alibi - *Only*
Jenkins UK (1939)

Hugh DUNCAN

has to take over a case from the author's *Insp POINTER.*

British Male Private Detective operating in Suffolk

A FIELDING 1884- (British)

See main detective Insp POINTER

Citation Record: 1 Book

Murder In Suffolk - *Only*
Collins UK (1938); Kinsey US (1938)

Jonas DUNCAN

American Male Private Detective operating in Seattle

Jackson GILLIS (American)

Writer: Jackson Clark GILLIS

Citation Record: 2 Books

The Killers Of Starfish - *First*
Lippincott US (1977); Hale UK (1979)

Chain Saw - *Latest*
US (1988)

Robbie DUNCAN

went to jail for defrauding a client. Out now, he manages to get to grips with murders galore and to make a profit.

British Male Private Detective operating in England

Dan BILLANY 1913-1945 (American)

Citation Record: 1 Book

It Takes A Thief - *Only*
Harper & Row US (1940)

The Opera House Murders - *Only**
Faber UK (1940)

Michael DUNDAS

appears also in one book with the author's other detective, *Rocky ALLAN.*

American Male Amateur operating in San Francisco

Virginia RATH 1905- (American)

Invented 3 detectives - see Rocky ALLAN

Citation Record: 7 Books

The Dark Cavalier - *First*
Doubleday US (1938)

A Shroud For Rowena - *Last*
Ziff-Davis US (1947)

Michael DUNDAS

Second detective of Rocky ALLAN

Insp James F 'Bonnie' DUNDEE

is a Yale man given to solving crimes in high society.

American Policeman operating in Midwest USA

Anne AUSTIN 1895- (American)

Citation Record: 5 Books

Murder Backstairs - *First*
Macmillan US (1930); Skeffington UK (1930)

Murdered But Not Dead - *Last*
Macmillan UK (1939)

Constance DUNLAP

appeared at a time when, even in the more liberated environment of America, ladies usually needed some deeply personal reason for taking up sleuthing, even of the amateur kind. And so it was with *Constance DUNLAP,* for she was once a criminal herself, having assisted her husband to commit forgery. He has committed suicide and she, stricken by remorse, turns to detective work so as to help others who may fall by the wayside. Her investigations, however, are dogged by the truly evil detective, *DRUMMOND,* who wishes to bring her to justice once more.

American Female Amateur operating in New York

Stooge: Det DRUMMOND
is one of most evil of early police adversaries. A detective himself, he deliberately dogs the investigations of the reformed *CONSTANCE DUNLAP* with the intent of harming them and her.
American Male

Arthur B REEVE 1880-1936 (American)

See main detective Prof Craig KENNEDY

Citation Record: 12 Selected Short Stories in1 Collection

Constance Dunlap, Woman Detective - *Collection 1*
Harper & Row US (1913); Hodder & Stoughton UK (1916)

D

Nan DUNLAP

American Female Amateur operating in New York

Miriam BORGENICHT 1915- (American)

Writer: Miriam Borgenicht KLEIN

Inventor of one other detective Ada WELLER

Citation Record: 1 Book

Fall From Grace - *Single*
St Martin's US (1984)

Michael DUNLOP

Second detective of Howard HYATT

Dan DUNN

was better known to his avid readers as Secret Operative 48. He was one of the many detectives in the pulps who waged battle with the wicked Wu Fang, one of the most dangerous oriental villains fictionally threatening the world.

American Male Professional Investigator operating in USA

Norman MARSH (American)

wrote largely for the pulps of the 1930s.

Citation Record: 1 Book

On The Trail Of Wu Fang
Whitman US (1938)

Dave DUNN

American Male Sleuth operating in USA

Michael AVALLONE 1924- (American)

Invented 5 detectives - see Ed NOON

Citation Record: 7 Short Stories in 1 Collection

Logbook Of The White Knight - *Collection 1*
Scholastic US (1977)

Jim DUNN and Zebulion BUCK

work for the Pine Detective Agency in Denver and solve crimes all over Colorado.

American Male Private Detectives operating in Denver

Hugh Lawrence NELSON 1907- (American)

See main detective Steve JOHNSON

Citation Record: 9 Books

Ring The Bell At Zero - *First*
Rinehart US (1949); Barker UK (1950)

Suspect - *Last*
Rinehart US (1954)

Micah DUNN

is hired to investigate the smuggling of Mexican antiques *into* a museum.

American Male Private Detective operating in New Orleans

M K SHUMAN (American)

Writer: Malcolm K SHUMAN

Other Byline: M S KARL

Citation Record: 2 Books

The Maya Stone Murders - *First*
St Martin's US (1989)

The Caesar Clue - *Latest*
St Martin's US (1990)

Otis DUNN

is a very small man, black, and an ex-FBI operator who still tracks criminals for the organisation.

American Male Private Detective operating in USA

Nat RICHARDS 1942- (American)

Writer: James Nathaniel RICHARDSON

Citation Record: 1 Book

Otis Dunn, Manhunter - *Only*
Ashley US (1974)

Sgt Sir Peter DUNN

British Policeman operating in England

Edgar WALLACE 1875-1932 (British)

Invented 28 detectives - see J G REEDER

Citation Record: 8 Short Stories in 1 Collection

Sergeant Sir Peter - *Collection 1*
Chapman & Hall UK (1932); Doubleday US (1933)

Sergeant Dunn, CID - *Collection 1**
Digit UK (1962)

Dudie DUNNE

was described as 'the detective of the age'.

American Female Private Detective operating in USA

Sidekick: Cad METTI
is Italian and calls herself a 'female detective strategist'. Whatever that is or was (the term must be unique in detective fiction) it seemed to demand a lot of cross-dressing, as was often necessary for women sleuths at the time.

Italian Female - Assistant

Harlan Page HALSEY 1837-1898 (American)

Invented 6 detectives - see Kate GOELET

Citation Record: 1 Book

Cad Metti, The Female Detective Strategist; Or, Dudie Dunne Again In The Field - *Only*
Ogilvie US (1895)

Joe DUNNE

is extra hardboiled, mercifully appearing only once.

American Male Private Detective operating in USA

Shepard RIFKIN 1918- (American)

See main detective Damian MCQUAID

Citation Record: 1 Book

The Murderer Vine - *Only*
Dodd, Mead US (1970); Hale UK (1973)

Lt Bret DUNNIGAN and Det Paige DUNNIGAN

are husband and wife, both young police officers in a small coastal town. A serial killer, of a type rapidly becoming an obsession with quick-draw authors, is on the loose. *Bret DUNNIGAN* is suspected and arrested. His wife disappears and he escapes, so as to clear himself and recover his wife. They finally find out whodunnit.

American Policeman and American Policewoman operating in Mississippi

Charles WILSON 1939- (American)

Citation Record: 1 Book

When First We Deceive - *Only*
Carroll & Graf US (1944)

Det Paige DUNNIGAN

Second detective of Lt Bret DUNNIGAN

Insp DUNNING

solves two murders that occur in 'impossible' situations.

British Policeman operating in England

Hugh DESMOND 1903- (British)

Although there appears to be some slight doubt as to the identity of this author as Kathleen Lindsay, it is cited as such here. If so, the putative author was an extraordinarily prolific writer of mystery and crime fiction under her own name and at least two pseudonyms, having around three hundred books listed.

Writer: Kathleen LINDSAY (?)

Inventor of one other detective Alan FRASER

Citation Record: 1 Book

The Jacaranda Murders - *Only*
Wright UK (1951)

Joe DUNSTAN and Eric FISHER

set up an international detective agency, called Dunstan Fisher. They have the ethics of hoodlums.

American Male Private Detectives operating in Europe

D

Evelyn ANTHONY 1928- (British)

See main detective Davina GRAHAM

Citation Record: 1 Book

The Poellenberg Inheritance - *Only*
Hutchinson UK (1972); Coward McCann US (1972)

Chevalier Auguste C DUPIN

has the distinction of being the very first real detective to appear in Anglo-American literature. The name of his inventor, *Edgar Allan POE*, is legendary.

DUPIN is a distinguished French aristocrat, a rich man who has great influence with the police, of whom he is rather contemptuous (the classic construction that was to become the model for detective fiction). He lives at 33 Rue Dunot, Fauberg St Germain, the smartest part of Paris, and solves crimes in his head; for not only is he an amateur and a member of high society, but he is an intellectual recluse, given to wearing green spectacles and strolling about the streets at night. The stories also introduce that other classic construction, the use of the 'narrator' or chronicler of the cases, to record the achievements of the great man. Here he is 'a friend', whose name we never know, but who often enjoys a meerschaum of tobacco with *DUPIN*, who is a heavy smoker.

More recently, this venerable detective has been resuscitated in a collection of short stories by *Michael HARRISON*.

French Male Amateur operating in Paris

Michael HARRISON 1907-1991 (British)

was born in Milton, Kent. He graduated at King's College, London, and studied at the School of Oriental and African Studies, London. He wrote only four genre novels but, in addition to his pastiches, a number of genre short stories. He was the author of at least eighteen mainstream novels and published many non-fiction books, including a great deal of literary and historical research and criticism. He wrote at least six books on *Sherlock HOLMES*.

Writer: Maurice Desmond ROHAN

Other Byline: Quentin DOWNES

Adopter of one other detective Sherlock HOLMES

Citation Record: 12 Short Stories in 1 Collection

The Exploits Of The Chevalier Dupin - *Collection 1*
The US publication contained only seven of the eventual twelve stories.
Mycroft & Moran US (1968)

Murder In The Rue Royale - *Collection 1**
Short stories - 12
Stacey UK (1972)

Edgar A POE 1809-1894 (American)

was born in Boston, Massachusetts, orphaned in his third year, and adopted by John Allan, a wealthy and childless merchant. The family spent time in England, 1815-1820, and the boy went to school in Stoke Newington, then a rural suburb of north London. Later, back in the USA, he attended the University of Virginia, 1826, but was removed because of 'dissipation and gambling debts'. He published his first poem in 1827, joined the army and rose to the rank of sergeant-major in 1829, when his patron bought him out. He then continued his literary career, writing poems and stories of extraordinary power and originality, which won him world-wide fame.

In 1837 he married his thirteen-year-old cousin, Virginia Clemm, who died of tuberculosis in 1847. His behaviour for this period of his life has been described as 'irregular, eccentric and querulous'. He attempted suicide in 1848, was hospitalised with acute alcoholism in June 1849, recovered, and went on a lecture tour. He then became engaged to a lady of means and set out north, in order to straighten out his affairs. However, he was found in a wretched condition in Baltimore and died in hospital there on September 3. His tormented genius created one of the most important legacies in all fiction.

Writer: Edgar Allan POE

Citation Record: 3 Selected Short Stories

The Murders In The Rue Morgue
In 'Graham's Magazine' US (1841); Wiley UK (1841)

The Purloined Letter
In 'The Gift' US (1845)

The Mystery Of Marie Roget
In 'Snowdon's Lady's Companion' US (1842)

Monsieur DUPUY

French Male Amateur operating in England

Anthony GILBERT 1899-1973 (British)

Invented 3 detectives - see Arthur G CROOK

Citation Record: 2 Books

The Man In The Button Boots - *First*
!See Appendix 2.
Collins UK (1934); Holt US (1935)

Courtier To Death - *Last*
Collins UK (1936)

The Dover Train Mystery - *Last**
Dial US (1936)

Dep Youngman DURAN and Hayden PAINE

Duran YOUNGMAN is a Hopi Indian who is a police deputy. With his colleague, *Hayden PAYNE*, a scientist, he investigates the death of an old medicine man on Indian territory.

American Policeman and American Male Amateur operating in USA

Martin Cruz SMITH 1942- (American)

Invented 3 detectives - see Roman GREY

Citation Record: 1 Book

Nightwing - *Single*
Norton US (1977); Deutsch UK (1977)

Quincey DURANT

Second detective of Artie WU

Insp Bertil DURELL

solves a case of death by carbon monoxide poisoning in a locked room.

Swedish Policeman operating in Sweden

Jan EKSTROM 1923- (Swedish)

Citation Record: 1 Book

The Ancestral Precipice - *Single*
is a translation from the Swedish of *Attestupan* (Stockholm, 1975).
Macmillan UK (1983)

Deadly Reunion - *Single**
Scribner's US (1983)

Sam DURELL

is hardly a detective in the classical sense, being more a violent operator of the modern school. He encounters, on his numerous assignments, enemies who are malevolent of brain or brawn or both and who often appear to be threatening the USA in some ghastly manner. The threat may be a force, an idea and even, in at least one case, a woman. He is, of course, involved with many women, most of whom succumb to his undoubted charms; and, at various times and in various books, they may become his aides. In his long career, *Sam DURELL* is ageless, except for a slight greying around the temples, which is introduced towards the end of the long series of books.

American Male Professional Investigator operating in USA/Europe/Asia

Edward Sydney AARONS 1916-1975 (American)

was born in Philadelphia, Pennsylvania. He graduated from Columbia University, New York, where he took degrees in History and English Literature, after which he had many jobs including that of a US coastguard, 1941-1945. He then

began to write a long succession of adventure-detective novels, many of which were first published under his main pseudonym, *Edward RONNS*.
Writer: Edward Sidney AARONS
Other Bylines:
Edward RONNS Will B AARONS
Citation Record: 41 Books
Assignment To Disaster - *First*
Fawcett US (1955); Fawcett UK (1956)
Assignment Afghan Dragon - *Last*
Fawcett US (1976); Coronet UK (1979)

Will B AARONS 1916-1975 (American)
Invented one other detective Jerry BENEDICT
Citation Record: 6 Books
Assignment Sheba - *First*
GM US (1976)
Assignment Tyrant's Bride - *Last*
GM US (1980)

Leo DURGAN
investigates frauds and the motivations of fraudsters.
American Male Private Detective operating in USA

Myrick LAND 1922- (American)
Writer: Myrick Ebben LAND
Citation Record: 1 Book
Search The Dark Woods - *Only*
Funk US (1955)
The Search - *Only**
Dell US (1959)

DURGON
American Male Detective in Pulp Magazines operating in USA

F Lusk BROUGHTON (American)
Invented 10 detectives - see Harry WILLIAMS
Citation Record: 1 Selected Short Story
Durgon, The Detective; Or, The Clerk's Crime
Old Cap Collier Library US (18??)

Dan DURKIN
American Male Amateur operating in New England/Texas

Arthur M CHASE 1875-1947 (American)
Writer: Arthur Mintum CHASE
Citation Record: 3 Books
The Party At The Penthouse - *First*
Dodd, Mead US (1932)
Twenty Minutes To Kill - *Last*
Dodd, Mead US (1936)

James DURKIN
American Male Amateur operating in New York

Arthur STRINGER 1874-1950 (American)
Writer: Arthur John Arbuthnott STRINGER
Other Detectives:
Witter KERFOOT Barbara 'Baddie' PRETLOW
Balmy RYMAL
Citation Record: 2 Books
The Wire Tappers - *First*
Little, Brown US (1906)
Phantom Wires - *Last*
Little, Brown US (1907); In 'Daily Mail' UK (1909)

Insp DURSLEY
solves two murders in 'impossible' situations.
British Policeman operating in England

Frank JOHNSTON 1900- (British)
Writer: Frank Norman Howard JOHNSTON
Citation Record: 1 Book
Li Kwang's Dagger - *Only*
Wright UK (1936)

James Gaylord DURSTINE
is a retired lawyer who sleuths out of interest.
American Male Amateur operating in Chicago

Sherwood KING 1904- (American)
was born in Yonkers, New York.
Writer: Raymond Sherwood KING
Citation Record: 1 Book
Between Murders - *Only*
Appleton US (1935)
Death Carries A Cane - *Only**
Cherry Tree UK (1941)

John DURSTON
British Male Amateur operating in England

William LEQUEUX 1864-1927 (British)
Invented 23 detectives - see Allan KENNEDY
Citation Record: 9 Short Stories in 1 Collection
The Rainbow Mystery - *Collection 1*
Hodder & Stoughton UK (1917)

Joe DUST
is, fictionally, a young gangster who worked with Dutch Schultz in the old days in the USA. Now reformed, he has come to London to set up the Medea Bureau of Missing Persons.
American Male Private Detective operating in London

Peter GRAAF 1922- (American)
Writer: Samuel Christopher YOUD
Citation Record: 3 Books
Give The Devil His Due - *First*
Mill US (1957)
Dust And The Curious Boy - *First**
Joseph UK (1957)
The Sapphire Conference - *Last*
Washburn US (1959); Joseph UK (1959)

Grace DUVALL
Second detective of Robert DUVALL

Richard DUVALL
American Male Amateur operating in New York

Arnold FREDERICKS 1873-1943 (American)
Writer: Frederick Arnold KUMMER
Other Byline: Frederick Arnold KUMMER
Citation Record: 5 Books
The Ivory Snuff Box - *First*
Watt US (1912); Simpkin UK (1916)
The Film Of Fear - *Last*
Watt US (1917); Hayes UK (1921)

Robert DUVALL and Grace DUVALL
were a husband-and-wife team who appeared in six pulp novels between 1912 and 1917, published in *The Cavalier*.
American Male Detective and American Female Detective in Pulp Magazines operating in USA
No citations

Johnny DUVIVIEN
is the owner of a night-club who has been married to *Natasha NEVKORINA*, who is cited as the sidekick of the author's other detective, *Miriam BIRDSEYE*. He appears, not only in the three books cited, in which he is more or less the sleuth, but also in two others in which he co-sleuths with *BIRDSEYE*. If it sounds like turmoil, so are the effusive but delightful books.
British Male Amateur operating in England

Nancy SPAIN 1917-1964 (British)
Invented 3 detectives - see Miriam BIRDSEYE
Citation Record: 3 Books
Death Before Wicket - *First*
Hutchinson UK (1946)
Murder, Bless It! - *Last*
Hutchinson UK (1948)

Johnny DUVIVIEN
Second detective of Miriam BIRDSEYE

D

Jack DWYER

was once a part-time actor and later a policeman. He is now a private eye in Cedar Rapids.

American Male Private Detective operating in Illinois

Ed GORMAN 1941- (American)

Invented 4 detectives - see Leo GUILD

Citation Record: 6 Books

New, Improved Murder - *First*
St Martin's US (1985)

The Night Remembers - *Latest*
St Martin's US (1991)

Harlan DYCE

was just three feet tall, but was the boss of the Dyce Detective Agency. He appeared mainly in short stories in *Clues.*

American Male Detective in Pulp Magazines operating in New York

Arthur J BURKS (American)

No citations

Henry DYER

is in his fifties and a real do-gooder, a modern, politically correct shamus in suitable conflict with society.

American Male Private Detective operating in Tucson

Raymond H RING 1949- (American)

Citation Record: 2 Books

Telluride Smile - *First*
Dodd, Mead US (1988)

Peregrine Dream - *Latest*
St Martin's US (1990)

DYKE and BURR

American Male Detectives in Pulp Magazines operating in USA

Harry ROCKWOOD 1859-1932 (American)

Invented 14 detectives - see Clarice DYKE

Citation Record: 1 Book

Dyke And Burr, The Rival Detectives - *Only*
Ogilvie US (1883)

The Rival Detectives - *Only**
Ogilvie US (1883)

Clarice DYKE

was one of the earliest American female professional detectives.

American Female Private Detective operating in USA

Harry ROCKWOOD 1859-1932 (American)

was a prolific writer of early detective stories, many of which featured the specialist and character detectives that were popular at the end of the nineteenth and beginning of the twentieth century.

Writer: Ernest Avon YOUNG

Other Byline: Donald J MCKENZIE

Other Detectives:

The BELL BOY DETECTIIVE, Fred DANFORD, Mrs Donald DYKE, DYKE and BURR, Donald DYKE, Abner FERRET, Nat FOSTER, Allan KEENE, Luke LEIGHTON, Neil NELSON, Harry PINKURTON, Harry SHARPE, Walt WHEELER

Citation Record: 1 Book

Clarice Dyke, The Female Detective - *Only*
Ogilvie US (1883)

Donald DYKE

American Male Detective in Pulp Magazines operating in USA

Harry ROCKWOOD 1859-1932 (American)

Invented 14 detectives - see Clarice DYKE

Citation Record: 1 Book

Donald Dyke, The Down-East Detective - *Only*
Ogilvie US (1882)

Donald Dyke, The Yankee Detective - *Only**
Street & Smith US (1900)

Mrs Donald DYKE

American Female Detective in Pulp Magazines operating in USA

Harry ROCKWOOD 1859-1932 (American)

Invented 14 detectives - see Clarice DYKE

Citation Record: 1 Book

Mrs Donald Dyke, Detective - *Only*
Street & Smith (Magnet #155) US (1901)

Toby DYKE

was the first detective to be created by this author. He is, in truth, a between-times sleuth, still carrying over some of the characteristics of the typical Golden Age amateur; but, by 1940, he has to appear to do some work and his whole bearing is harsher than was usual in that earlier time. Even so, he is still kitted out with bachelor's apartments in the West End of London and his sidekick is his valet. Whereas the Golden Age sleuth usually had the police kow-towing to his intellectual or class superiority, *Toby DYKE* has to work just that bit harder to keep in with the police.

British Male Amateur operating in England

Sidekick: GEORGE

is, like the detective, something of a between-times sidekick. He is an ex-convict and, although a valet to the master, has more to say for himself than would have been tolerated a decade earlier; and, in fact, he plays no inconsiderable part in solving the cases. Indeed, not only does he seem a better detective, but he is a comic Cockney to boot, making all sorts of witticisms before passing on his thoughts to his master. To make sure he is kept in his place, though, he has no need of a surname.

British Male - Valet

Stooge: Insp VANNER

is one of the best-drawn British police stooges of the period, being thoroughly vindictive towards *DYKE* because of past failures and generally being upstaged by him.

British Male

E X FERRARS 1907-1995 (British)

!See Appendix 2.

For writer details see Toby DYKE

Other Detectives:

Andrew BASNETT, Charlotte CAMBRY, Peter COREY, Insp CRANKSHAW, Virginia FREER and Felix FREER, Peter HARKNESS, Jonas P JONAS, Martin RHYMER, Emma RITCHIE, Matthew TIERNEY

Citation Record: 4Books

Rehersals For Murder - *First*
Doubleday US (1941)

Neck In A Noose - *Last*
was previously published under the *Elizabeth FERRARS* byline *as 'Your Neck In A Noose'.*
Doubleday US (1943)

Elizabeth FERRARS 1907-1995 (British)

was born in Rangoon, India, and has lived mainly in Britain. She was educated at Bedales School, Petersfield, Hampshire, and took a diploma in Journalism at University College, London, 1928. A founding member of the Crime Writers Association, 1953, she received their Silver Dagger award, 1981.

Writer: Moma Doris BROWN

Other Byline: E X FERRARS

Other Detectives:

Andrew BASNETT, Charlotte CAMBRY, Peter COREY, Insp CRANKSHAW, Virginia FREER and Felix FREER, Peter HARKNESS, Martin RHYMER, Emma RITCHIE, Matthew TIERNEY

Citation Record: 5 Books

Give A Corpse A Bad Name - *First*
Hodder & Stoughton UK (1940)

Your Neck In A Noose - *Last*
was republished under the *E X FERRARS* byline *as 'Neck In A Noose'.*
Hodder & Stoughton UK (1942)

Insp Lathom DYNES

British Policeman operating in England

Sidekick: Sgt BENWICK
British Male - Subordinate

Helen ROBERTSON 1913- (British)

Writer: Helen Jean Mary EDMISTON

Citation Record: 3 Books

Venice Of The Black Sea - *First*
Macdonald UK (1956)

The Chinese Goose - *Last*
Macdonald UK (1960)

Swan Song - *Last**
Doubleday US (1960)

DYSON and PHILIPPS

are two amateur detectives who spend much of their time daydreaming about solving macabre murders.

British Male Amateurs operating in England

Arthur MACHEN 1863-1947 (British)

was an actor, essayist and journalist who wrote many short stories with occult themes.

Writer: Arthur Llewellyn JONES

Citation Record: 13 Short Stories in 1 Collection

The Three Imposters - *Collection 1*
Lane UK (1895); Roberts US (1895)

D

— E —

Quentin EADY

British Male Amateur

E P THORNE (British)

Writer: Ernest Pollett THORNE

Other Detectives:
Maj 'Brains' CUNNINGHAM   Geoff FENNELL

Citation Record: 6 Books

Seven Red Herrings - *First*
Wright UK (1956)

Expect No Mercy - *Last*
Wright UK (1962)

John (The Expediter) EAGLE

is an Apache warrior who is also a US government agent. He is sent out on various hazardous investigations.

American Male Secret Agent operating in USA

Paul EDWARDS (American)

For writer details see Peter WINSTON

Citation Record: 4 Books

The Ice Goddess - *First*
Pyramid US (1974)

Last Poppies Of Death - *Last*
Pyramid US (1975)

Paul EDWARDS (American)

Writer: Robert LORY

Citation Record: 5 Books

The Laughing Death - *First*
Pyramid US (1973); New English Library UK (1976)

The Glyphs Of Gold - *Last*
Pyramid US (1974)

Paul EDWARDS (American)

For writer details see Barnaby JONES

Citation Record: 5 Books

The Brain Scavengers - *First*
Pyramid US (1973); New English Library UK (1976)

Silverskull - *Last*
Pyramid US (1975)

John EAKINS

American Male Amateur operating in USA

Dorothy Salisbury DAVIS 1916- (American)

Invented 9 detectives - see Kate OSBORN

Citation Record: 1 Book

Enemy And Brother - *Only*
Scribner's US (1966); Hodder & Stoughton UK (1967)

Linda EARLE

American Female Amateur operating in Pennsylvania

Phyllis A WHITNEY 1903- (American)

was born in Yokohama, Japan, and educated at schools in Japan, China and the USA, graduating finally from McKinley High School, Chicago, Illinois, 1924. She worked as a journalist and editor and in publishing and is the author of over thirty books that fall loosely in the criminous genre, although they are best described as novels of romantic suspense. She also wrote books on the art of writing and over thirty books for children. She received the Mystery Writers of America Edgar Allan Poe award for her books for children twice, 1961 and 1964 and their Grand Master award, 1988.

Writer: Phyllis Ayame WHITNEY

Inventor of one other detective Sylvester HERING

Citation Record: 1 Book

Snow Fire - *Only*
Doubleday US (1973); Heinemann UK (1973)

John EARLSTONE

is a reporter who sets up as a private detective, operating in the more seedy part of London's West End.

British Male Private Detective operating in London

Jack MONMOUTH (British)

See main detective Tom LANGLEY

Citation Record: 1 Book

Not Ready To Die - *Only*
Hale UK (1960)

Floyd EAST

Second detective of James O'HANNAY

Mark EAST

is one of an early breed of American private eyes, at a time when they were still gentlemanly, wealthy and educated. In his three fine appearances he receives sometimes unwanted, but often important, help from two little old lady amateur sleuths from New England, one scatty and the other rather clever.
!See Appendix 2.

American Male Private Detective operating in New York/New England

Sidekick: Beulah POND
is one of the two little old ladies.
American Female - Assistant

Sidekick: Bessy PETTY
is the other.
American Female - Assistant

Hilda LAWRENCE 1906?- (American)

was born in Baltimore, Maryland, and educated at Columbia School, Rochester, New York. She was a staff member of *Macmillan*, New York publishers.

Writer: Hildegarde LAWRENCE

Citation Record: 3 Books

Blood Upon The Snow - *First*
Simon & Schuster US (1944); Chapman & Hall UK (1946)

Death Of A Doll - *Last*
Simon & Schuster US (1947); Chapman & Hall UK (1948)

The EAST SIDE DETECTIVE

American Male Detective in Pulp Magazines operating in USA

ANON

Citation Record: 1 Book

The East Side Detective - *Only*
Aldine US

Mark EASTERBROOK and Ariadne OLIVER

The scholarly author, *Mark EASTERBROOK*, is the amateur sleuth in another of the author's novels and *Ariadne OLIVER* also appears in other books.

British Male Amateur and British Female Amateur operating in England

Stooge: Det Insp LE JEUNE
British Male

Agatha CHRISTIE 1890-1976 (British)

Invented 18 detectives - see Hercule POIROT

Citation Record: 1 Book

The Pale Horse - *Only*
Collins UK (1961); Dodd, Mead US (1962)

Max EASTERBROOK

British Male Amateur operating in England

Andrew GARVE 1908- (British)

was born in Leicester, Leicestershire and graduated with a BSc from the London School of Economics, 1928. Reporter and foreign correspondent, 1933-1946, and later a full-time writer, he has written at least thirty-five genre books under his two pseudonyms, as well as non-genre novels and political works under his real name and various pseudonyms.

Writer: Paul WINTERTON

Other Bylines:
Roger BAX
Paul SOMERS

Inventor of one other detective pair James RENISON and Carol RENISON

Citation Record: 1 Book

No Tears For Hilda - *Only*
Collins UK (1950); Harper & Row US (1950)

Lady Jane EASTINGS

solves a case of murder by gassing in a locked room.

British Female Amateur operating in England

SEAFORTH 1893- (British)

Writer: George Cecil FOSTER

Citation Record: 1 Book

Misprision Of Felony - *Only*
Jenkins UK (1941)

Warwick EASTON

is a British actor who, during the 1920s, finds himself in Hollywood and is given a job as one of the cops by Mack Sennett, who is making the famous Keystone Cops films. He is promptly dubbed 'Keystone', a pun on his name. When comedy on the set turns to murder, he does the sleuthing in this, one of the author's excellent historical pastiches.

British Male Amateur operating in Hollywood

Peter LOVESEY 1936- (British)

Invented 7 detectives - see Sgt CRIBB and Const THACKERAY

Citation Record: 1 Book

Keystone - *Single*
Macmillan UK (1983); Pantheon US (1983)

John EASY

operates on Sunset Strip, specialising in finding missing persons, who are usually beautiful female missing persons. As is not unusual in the work of this master of the genre, he seems to be the only sane man in an insane world, of which he has to make some sort of sense.

American Male Private Detective operating in Hollywood

Ron GOULART 1933- (American)

Invented 15 detectives - see Jake PACE and Hildy PACE

Citation Record: 4 Books

If Dying Was All - *First*
Ace US (1971)

One Grave Too Many - *Last*
Ace US (1974)

Jack EAVES

British Male Amateur operating in England

Allan PRIOR 1922- (British)

was born in Newcastle-on-Tyne, Northumberland. Educated at local schools, he served in the Royal Air Force, 1942-1946. His main work has been for radio, TV and films, for which media his output has been large.

Citation Record: 1 Book

The Interrogators - *Only*
Cassell UK (1965); Simon & Schuster US (1965)

Crying EDDIE

Second detective of Henry CHALICE

Bob EDDISON

American Male Amateur operating in England

Michael DELVING 1914-1978

Writer: Jay WILLIAMS

Other Detectives:
Dave CANNON and Bob EDDISON
Dave CANNON

Citation Record: 1 Book

A Shadow Of Himself - *Only*
Scribner's US (1972); Collins UK (1972)

Bob EDDISON

Second detective of Dave CANNON

John EDGARSON

works for Tobin-Global Investigations.

American Male Private Detective operating in USA

Donald E WESTLAKE 1933- (American)

See main detective Tim SMITH

Citation Record: 1 Book

Enough! - *Single*
Evans US (1977); Hodder & Stoughton UK (1980)

George B EDGEHILL and Aristide GOVIN

solve a number of locked-room mysteries in their one book.

British Male Amateurs operating in England

Warner ALLEN 1881-1969 (British)

Writer: Herbert Warner ALLEN

Other Detectives:
Mr CLERIHEW
Insp WAKE and Philip GAYMORE

Citation Record: 1 Book

The Devil That Slumbers - *Only*
Hamilton UK (1925)

Dr Catherine EDISON

teaches plant biology at the local university in Kingston and it seems she has everything going for her until her lover and then other members of her group of friends meet untimely and mysterious deaths. Trying to find out which one of her circle is actually doing it is difficult, especially when the local cop thinks she is responsible.

Canadian Female Amateur operating in Ontario

Stooge: Sgt John WARSHINSKY
represents the local police. He puts the first death down to misadventure; but, when others occur, he naturally suspects the amateur sleuth.
Canadian Male

Margaret HAFFNER (Canadian)

was born in Canada and educated there and in England. A professional scientist and expert in plant biotechnology, she is also a writer of books for children.

Citation Record: 1 Book

A Murder Of Crows - *Single*
HarperCollins UK (1992)

William EDMONDSON

is a young recruit to a New York detective agency in 1923. He is sent, with a veteran partner, to investigate a murder in a coal-mining town in West Virginia. When the older man is killed, he must solve the case on his own.

American Male Private Detective operating in New York/Virginia

John DOUGLAS (American)

Inventor of one other detective HARTER

Citation Record: 1 Book

Blind Spring Rambler - *Single*
St Martin's US (1988)

Dr Everett EDWARDS

British Male Amateur operating in England

Harry Stephen KEELER 1890-1967 and Hazel GOODWIN (American)

Invented 3 detectives - see Angus MACWHORTER

Citation Record: 1 Book

The Strange Will - *Only*
Ward, Lock UK (1949)

Jane Amanda EDWARDS

is unmarried, in her forties, and of independent means, all attributes that enable her to go about sleuthing in the American Midwest.

American Female Amateur operating in Illinois

Charlotte Murray RUSSELL (American)

Other Detectives:
Homer FITZGERALD   Wally KENT

Citation Record: 5 Books

Murder At The Old Stone House - *First*
Doubleday US (1935)

Hand Me A Crime - *Last*
Doubleday US (1949); Cherry Tree UK (1950)

Kate EDWARDS

appeared in the pulps surprisingly early for a lady detective.

American Female Detective in Pulp Magazines operating in USA

Harlan Page HALSEY 1837-1898 (American)

Invented 6 detectives - see Kate GOELET

Citation Record: 1 Book

Lady Kate, The Darling Detective - *Only*
US (1886)

Matt EDWARDS

is a hotel manager who solves the 'impossible' disappearance of a man from a locked apartment.

American Male Amateur operating in USA

MacKinlay KANTOR 1904-1977 (American)

was a prolific author of short stories, some criminous.

Other Detectives:
Max GRAME   Lt Cliff KENNEDY
Daniel ROSS

Citation Record: 1 Selected Short Story

The Light At Three O'clock
can also be found in a collection of the author's stories, *It's About Crime* (*Signet*; US 1960).
In 'Real Detective Tales' US (1930)

Scott EGERTON

British Male Sleuth operating in England

Anthony GILBERT 1899-1973 (British)

Invented 3 detectives - see Arthur G CROOK

Citation Record: 10 Books

The Tragedy At Freyne - *First*
Collins UK (1927); Dial US (1927)

The Man Who Was Too Clever - *Last*
Collins UK (1935)

Montague EGG

is a commercial traveller in wines and spirits who, in the course of his travels, meets and solves murder and other crimes.

British Male Amateur operating in England

Dorothy L SAYERS 1893-1957 (British)

See main detective Lord Peter WIMSEY

Citation Record: 11 Short Stories in 2 Collections

Hangman's Holiday - *Collection 1*
contains four *Peter WIMSEY* stories and six *Montague EGG* stories.
Short stories - 6
Gollancz UK (1933); Harcourt Brace US (1933)

In The Teeth Of The Evidence And Other Stories - *Collection 2*
contains seventeen of the author's short stories, not all of which were included in either the UK or the US edition. However, there are two *Peter WIMSEY* stories and five *Montague EGG* stories in the original publications. A later publication (*Gollancz*; UK 1972) added the last three known *Peter WIMSEY* stories and this is the one cited under the latter detective.
Short stories - 5
Gollancz UK (1939); Harcourt Brace US (1940)

Harry EGYPT

American Male Sleuth operating in New York

Daniel BROUN (American)

Inventor of one other detective Lt CARREAU

Citation Record: 2 Books

The Subject Of Harry Egypt - *First*
Holt US (1963); Gollancz UK (1963)

Egypt's Choice - *Last*
Holt US (1963); Gollancz UK (1964)

Jack EICHORD

American Male Sleuth operating in USA

Rex MILLER (American)

Citation Record: 5 Books

Slob - *First*
Signet US (1987); Pan UK (1988)

Slice - *Latest*
Onyx US (1990); Pan UK (1991)

Prof Christopher EKSHAW

solves the mystery of a death by poisoning.

British Male Amateur operating in England

L T MEADE and Robert EUSTACE (British)

Invented 7 detectives - see Insp FROST and Dr GARLAND

Citation Record: 1 Selected Short Story

The Invisible Enemy
In 'The Storyteller' UK (1906)

Sheriff Bill ELDON

American Policeman operating in California

Erle Stanley GARDNER 1889-1970 (American)

Invented 14 detectives - see Perry MASON

Citation Record: 1 Book

Two Clues
Morrow US (1947); Cassell UK (1951)

The ELECTRIC LIGHT DETECTIVE

American Male Detective in Pulp Magazines operating in USA

Alexander DOUGLAS (American)

Citation Record: 1 Selected Short Story

The Electric Light Detective; Or, Solving The Mysteries Of An Old Graveyard
New York Detective Library US (1882-8)

E

George Fort ELGIN
solves the 'impossible' disappearance of a jewel from a room under constant guard.
American Male Amateur operating in USA

Arthur PORGES (American)
Invented 13 detectives - see Arsène LUPIN
Citation Record: 1 Selected Short Story
Breath Of Suspicion
appeared in the January number.
In 'The Man From Uncle Magazine' US (1967)

Charlotte ELIOT
British Female Amateur

Macartney FILGATE (British)
Writer: C Macartney FILGATE
Citation Record: 2 Books
Bravo Charlie *- First*
Muller UK (1979)
Delta November *- Latest*
Muller UK (1979)

Insp Stephen ELIOT and Arthur CRUMP
solve a case of 'impossible' murder in an undisturbed room.
American Policeman and American Male Amateur operating in USA

Gregory TREE 1916-1981 (American)
was born in Cincinnati, Ohio.
Writer: John Franklin BARDIN
Other Byline: Douglas ASHE
Inventor of one other detective pair Bill BRADLEY and Noel MAYBERRY
Citation Record: 1 Book
A Shroud For Grandmama *- Only*
was published in the US under the following byline.
Gollancz UK (1951)

Douglas ASHE 1916-1981 (American)
For writer details see Insp Stephen ELIOT and Arthur CRUMP
Citation Record: 1 Book
A Shroud For Grandmama *- Only*
was published in the UK under the preceding byline.
Scribner's US (1951)
The Longstreet Legacy *- Only**
Paperback Library US (1970)

ELIZABETH
British Female Amateur operating in England

Florence KILPATRICK (British)
Citation Record: 1 Book 1 Collection
Elizabeth Finds The Body *- Only*
Jenkins UK (1949)
Elizabeth The Sleuth *- Collection 1*
contains stories spread across untitled chapters.
Jenkins UK (1946)

Lt Felix ELIZALDO
and his hapless assistant are involved in what must be some of the most extraordinary proceedings ever to have taken place in the whole history of the criminous genre.
American Policeman operating in the Philippines
Sidekick: Sgt Baptiste BANTOC
is of ancient head-hunting stock from the islands. It might seem that such a pedigree could be of value to a detective. Not a bit. He may be weird but he is essentially useless.
American Male - Subordinate

William MARSHALL 1944- (Australian)
See main detective pair Harry FEIFFER and YELLOWTHREAD STREET COPS
Citation Record: 2 Books
Manila Bay *- First*
Secker & Warburg UK (1986); Viking US (1986)
Whisper *- Latest*
Century UK (1988); Mysterious Press UK (1988)

Sgt/Insp ELK
is the most lugubrious and sardonic of the author's many detectives. A veritable bloodhound, he appears as a subordinate figure in several of the author's books but is the main detective in four novels and a play.
British Policeman operating in London

Edgar WALLACE 1875-1932 (British)
Invented 28 detectives - see J G REEDER
Citation Record: 5 Books
The Fellowship Of The Frog *- First*
Ward, Lock UK (1925); Small, Maynard US (1923)
The India-Rubber Men *- Last*
Doubleday US (1930); Hodder & Stoughton UK (1929)
The Terror *- Play*
Hodder & Stoughton UK (1929)

Sgt/Insp ELK and T B SMITH
British Policeman and British Male Amateur operating in London

Edgar WALLACE 1875-1932 (British)
Invented 28 detectives - see J G REEDER
Citation Record: 1 Book
The Nine Bears *- Only*
Ward, Lock UK (1910)
The Other Man *- Only**
Dodd, Mead US (1911)

Insp Roger ELLERDINE
is a brilliantly successful Scotland Yard detective. He appears in three earlier books with the author's other detective, *Supt BOSCOBELL.*
British Policeman operating in London
Sidekick: 'Cherry' BLOSSOM
British Male - Subordinate

Cecil WILLS 1891- (British)
Invented 4 detectives - see Sgt/Supt Geoffrey BOSCOBELL
Citation Record: 8 Books
Who Killed Brother Treasurer? *- First*
Hodder & Stoughton UK (1951)
Justice In Jeopardy *- Last*
Hale UK (1961)

Insp Roger ELLERDINE
Second detective of Supt Geoffrey BOSCOBELL

Maggie ELLIOTT
was not a PI in her first appearance but is now licensed and investigating the murder of a schoolmate at a Vassar reunion.
American Female Private Detective operating in San Francisco/New York

Elizabeth Atwood TAYLOR (American)
was born in San Antonio and has worked as a film editor, art therapist and social worker.
Citation Record: 2 Books
The Cable Car Murder *- First*
St Martin's US (1982); Hale UK (1983)
Murder At Vassar *- Latest*
Thorndike UK (1987)

Sgt ELLIS
solves a case of death by poisoning in a locked room.
British Policeman operating in England

Mileson HORTON and Thomas PEMBROKE (British)
Writer: Mileson Denis James HORTON 1899-
Citation Record: 1 Selected Short Story
Behind Locked Doors
is in an anthology, *Photocrimes.*
Barker UK (1936)

Bob ELLIS
is a lawyer who solves the case of an 'impossible' stabbing in a locked room.
American Male Sleuth operating in USA

Charles CHADWICK 1874-1950

See main detective Insp PRONTOUT

Citation Record: 1 Book

The Cactus - *Only*
Crowell US (1925)

John ELLIS

Second detective of Peter ALCOTT

Tony ELLIS

Second detective of Maj Avery GREGG

Capt Fox ELTON

Male Sleuth operating in Switzerland

Ared WHITE (American)

Citation Record: 2 Books

The Spy Net - *First*
Houghton US (1931); Eyre & Spottiswoode UK (1931)

Agent B-7 - *Last*
Houghton US (1930); Eyre & Spottiswoode UK (1935)

Horace Augustus ELVER

British Male Amateur operating in England

George DILNOT 1883-1951 (British)

Invented 5 detectives - see Val EMERY

Citation Record: 4 Books

Crook's Castle - *First*
Bles UK (1934); Houghton US (1934)

Murder At Scotland Yard - *Last*
Bles UK (1937)

EMERALD JIM

Irish Male Detective in Pulp Magazines operating in USA

Old Cap DARRELL (American)

Invented 5 detectives - see YOUNG SLEDGE

Citation Record: 1 Book

Emerald Jim, The Irish Boy Detective
New York Detective Library US (1882-8)

Val EMERY

British Male Amateur operating in England

George DILNOT 1883-1951 (British)

Other Detectives:
Sexton BLAKE
Horace Augustus ELVER
Jim STRANG
Insp STRICKLAND

Citation Record: 2 Books

Fighting Fool - *First*
Bles UK (1939)

Tiger Lily - *Last*
Bles UK (1939)

Caroline EMMET

American Male Amateur operating in USA

Ursula CURTISS 1923- (American)

Invented 5 detectives - see Lou FABIAN

Citation Record: 1 Book

The Deadly Climate - *Only*
Dodd, Mead US (1954); Eyre & Spottiswoode UK (1955)

Jason EMORY

is a tiny PI who works on cases centred on the art and fashion industries in New York city.

American Male Private Detective operating in New York

Samuel Melvin KOOTZ 1898-1982 (American)

is a lawyer and art expert.

Citation Record: 2 Books

Puzzle In Paint - *First*
Crown US (1943)

Puzzle In Petticoats - *Last*
Crown US (1944)

Insp H EMP

British Policeman operating in England

Sydney HORLER 1888-1954 (British)

Invented 19 detectives - see Sir Harker BELLAMY

Citation Record: 3 Books

Horror's Head - *First*
Hodder & Stoughton UK (1932)

Murderer At Large - *Last*
Hodder & Stoughton UK (1952)

Roy ENDICOTT

British Male Amateur operating in England

James CORBETT (British)

wrote around fifty thrillers and detective stories in the 1930s and 1940s, all published in the UK. Only one (uncited) seems ever to have attracted a US publisher.

Other Detectives:
Insp BRIGG
Det Insp Alan MELFORD
John PETERSON
Victor REDMAYNE
Victor SERGE
Insp Giles SEYMOUR

Citation Record: 1 Book

Red Farm Mystery - *Only*
Jenkins UK (1935)

Prof Paul ENGEL

solves a case of murder by shooting in a locked room.

American Male Sleuth operating in USA

Robert C SCHWEIK (American)

Citation Record: 1 Selected Short Story

Imagine A Murder
appeared in the June number.
In 'Ellery Queen's Mystery Magazine' US (1978)

Anthony ENGLAND

British Male Amateur operating in England

William J ELLIOTT 1886-1947? (British)

was the author of over thirty criminous books.

Writer: William James ELLLOTT

Other Detectives:
Royston FRERE
Ed GUNNING
Bren HARDY

Citation Record: 4 Books

'Silk' - *First*
Swan UK (1942)

Spun Silk - *Last*
Swan UK (1947)

Tricky ENRIGHT

was one of this author's numerous pulp detectives, appearing mainly in stories in *Dime Detective.*

American Male Detective in Pulp Magazines operating in California

John K BUTLER (American)

Invented 3 detectives - see Steve MIDNIGHT

No citations

Ebbie ENTWHISTLE

British Male Amateur operating in England

F A M WEBSTER 1886- (British)

Writer: Frederick Annesley Michael WEBSTER

Citation Record: 36 Short Stories in 3 Collections

Old Ebbie: Detective Up-To-Date - *Collection 1*
Short stories - 12
Chapman & Hall UK (1923)

Old Ebbie Returns - *Collection 2*
Short stories - 12
Chapman & Hall UK (1925)

The Crime Scientist - *Collection 3*
Short stories - 12
Warne UK (1930)

E

Rosa EPTON

started her fictional career as a minor clerk to a solicitor, but she studied and became a solicitor herself. Her work among the criminal fraternity enables her to solve some baffling cases. She appears also in one book with another of the author's detectives, *Martin AINSWORTH.*

British Female Amateur operating in England

Michael UNDERWOOD 1916-1992 (British)

was born in Worthing, Sussex. He was educated at Charterhouse School, Surrey, took an MA at Christ Church, Oxford, 1938, attended at Gray's Inn, London, and was called to the Bar, 1939. He served in the Army, 1939-1946, reaching the rank of Major, and held several senior government legal appointments, 1946-1976. He was the author of forty-five criminous novels, nearly all of which have honest or dishonest legal goings-on for their plots or backgrounds.

Writer: John Michael EVELYN

Other Detectives:
Martin AINSWORTH   Nick ATWELL
Rosa EPTON and Martin AINSWORTH
Insp/Supt Simon MANTON   Richard MONK

Citation Record: 13 Books

Crime Upon Crime - *First*
Macmillan UK (1980); St Martin's US (1981)

Rosa's Dilemma - *Latest*
Macmillan UK (1990); St Martin's US (1990)

Rosa EPTON and Martin AINSWORTH

also appear individually in other books by this author.

British Female Amateur and British Male Amateur operating in England

Michael UNDERWOOD 1916-1992 (British)

Invented 6 detectives - see Rosa EPTON

Citation Record: 1 Book

A Pinch Of Snuff - *Only*
Macmillan UK (1974); St Martin's US (1974)

Steven ERIKSON

American Male Private Detective operating in New York

Michael STARK 1908-1981 (American)

For writer details see Mike WELLS

Citation Record: 1 Book

Run For Your Life! - *Only*
Crown US (1946); Boardman UK (1948)

Kill-Box - *Only**
Ace US (1954)

ERNIE

solves a number of bucolic mysteries set in agricultural surroundings. Several of them are of the outdoor 'impossible' crime type.

American Male Amateur operating in USA

Fredric BROWN 1906-1972 (American)

Invented 8 detectives - see Ambrose HUNTER and Ed HUNTER

Citation Record: 1 Selected Short Story

The Case Of The Bewildering Barn

was later collected, with several others featuring *ERNIE*, in *The Water-Walker* (*Macmillan*; US 1990).

In 'Feedstuffs' US

Fiske ERRELL

was an early 'scientific detective' who appeared in stories in *Amazing Stories.*

American Male Detective in Pulp Magazines operating in USA

W F HAMMOND (American)

No citations

Matt ERRIDGE

is an engineer who, in many and varied locales, comes up against murders and has to solve them.

American Male Amateur operating in several locations

Aaron Marc STEIN 1906-1985 (American)

was born in New York City. He was educated at the Ethical Culture School, New York, and took an AB at Princeton University, New Jersey, 1927. Critic and newspaper columnist, he was the author of almost a hundred genre novels under his own name and pseudonyms. He received the Mystery Writers of America Grand Master award, 1979.

Inventor of one other detective pair Tim MULLIGAN and Elsie May HUNT

Citation Record: 23 Books

Sitting Up Dead - *First*
Doubleday US (1958); Macdonald UK (1959)

The Garbage Collector - *Last*
Doubleday US (1984)

Prof ERSKINE

Second detective of Insp HAWLING

Sir James ERSKINE

appears also in one book with another of the author's detectives, *George Stanhope BERKLEY.*

British Male Amateur operating in England

Laurence MEYNELL 1899-1989 (British)

Invented 5 detectives - see Hooky HEFFERMAN

Citation Record: 1 Book

Camouflage - *Only*
Harrap UK (1930)

The Mystery At Newton Ferry - *Only**
Lippincott US (1930)

Sir James ERSKINE and George Stanhope BERKLEY

British Male Amateurs operating in England

Laurence MEYNELL 1899-1989 (British)

Invented 5 detectives - see Hooky HEFFERMAN

Citation Record: 1 Book

Bluefeather - *Only*
Harrap UK (1928); Appleton US (1928)

Insp Lawrence ERSKINE

is a member of Scotland Yard's Special Branch. On his one outing, he investigates the drowning of a girl in the Thames and uncovers international complications.

British Policeman operating in London

Vivien ARMSTRONG (British)

See main detective Ch Insp Ralph ARNOTT

Citation Record: 1 Book

The Honey Trap - *Single*
HarperCollins UK (1992)

January ESPOSITO

Italian Male Sleuth operating in Italy

Gregory DOWLING (British)

was born and educated in Bristol, Gloucestershire. He graduated at Christ Church College, Oxford, and has lived and taught in Venice.

Citation Record: 2 Books

Double Take - *First*
Severn UK (1985); St Martin's US (1985)

Neapolitan Reel - *Latest*
Grafton UK (1988)

See Naples And Kill - *Latest**
St Martins US (1988)

Steve ESSEX

British Male Amateur operating in England

Simon WALDRON 1924- (British)

Writer: Albert KING

Other Byline: Paul MULLER

Citation Record: 2 Books

Leap Before You Look - *First*
Hale UK (1968)

Hot Ice - *Last*
Hale UK (1969)

Alan ESTERBROOKE
Second detective of Insp BROUSSE

Dr ESZTERHAZY
Male Amateur operating in several locations

Avram DAVIDSON (American)

Citation Record: 13 Short Stories in 2 Collections

The Enquiries Of Dr Eszterhazy - *Collection 1*
Short stories - 8
Warner US (1975)

The Adventures Of Doctor Eszterhazy - *Collection 2*
contains the eight stories published in the author's first collection (cited) and five new stories, cited thus.
Short stories - 5
Owlswick US (1990)

Frank ETHERIDGE
is an early example in the long line of lawyer detectives.
American Male Amateur operating in USA

Anna Katherine GREEN 1846-1935 (American)
Invented 9 detectives - see Det Ebenezer GRYCE

Citation Record: 1 Book

Cynthia Wakeham's Money - *Only*
Putnam US (1892); Putnam UK (1892)

Det Insp EVANS
British Policeman operating in England

William J MAKIN 1894- (British)

Writer: William James MAKIN

Other Detectives:
Det Insp GRAVES   Jonathan JOW

Citation Record: 2 Books

Murder At Covent Garden - *First*
Jarrolds UK (1930)

The Covent Garden Murder - *First**
Newnes UK (1938)

Red Mask - *Last*
Hamilton UK (1935)

Insp EVANS and Sgt BEDDOES
British Policemen operating in Wales

R W JONES 1941- (British)

Writer: Roger William JONES

Citation Record: 3 Books

Saving Grace - *First*
Joseph UK (1986); St Martin's US (1986)

The Green Reapers - *Latest*
Joseph UK (1988); St Martin's US (1989)

'Educated' EVANS
British Male Amateur operating in England

Edgar WALLACE 1875-1932 (British)
Invented 28 detectives - see J G REEDER

Citation Record: 42 Short Stories in 3 Collections

Educated Evans - *Collection 1*
Short stories - 13
Webster UK (1924)

Good Evans! - *Collection 2*
Short stories - 17
Webster UK (1926)

The Educated Man - *Collection 2**
Reader's Library UK (1929)

More Educated Evans - *Collection 3*
Short stories - 12
Webster UK (1926)

Homer EVANS
is one of the most outrageously comic, yet gifted detectives in the criminous genre. His cases begin in Paris shortly after the end of the First World War and then follow him to America, to which he returns with an entourage of bizarre characters, not least among which is a sidekick who is also his girlfriend.
American Male Amateur operating in USA/France

Sidekick: Miriam LEONARD
is an ex-cowgirl, a deadly sharpshooter, and the detective's girlfriend. All in all, an aide worth having.
American Female - Girlfriend

Elliot PAUL 1891-1958 (American)
was born in Malden, Massachusetts. He was a reporter in Paris until 1914 and served with the US Army in the First World War, returning later to live in Boston.

Writer: Elliot Harold PAUL

Citation Record: 9 Books

The Mysterious Mickey Finn; Or, Murder At The CaféDu Dôme - *First*
Modern Age US (1939); Penguin UK (1953)

The Black And The Red - *Last*
Random House US (1956)

John EVANS
Second detective of Tony RESECK

Louisa EVANS
is a reporter involved in murders.
American Female Amateur operating in New York

Jane JOHNSTON 1927- (American)

Citation Record: 2 Books

Pray For Ricky Foster - *First*
St Martin's US (1985)

Paint Her Face Dead - *Latest*
St Martin's US (1987)

Michael EVANS
British Male Sleuth operating in Middle East

Burton GRAHAM (American)

Citation Record: 2 Books

The Spy Trap - *First*
Dent UK (1971); Weybright US (1972)

Spy Or Die - *Last*
Dent UK (1972)

Tess EVELING
is a teenage detective in a novel written for the juvenile market.
British Female Amateur operating in England

John FOSTER (British)

Citation Record: 1 Book

Watch All Night - *Single*
Puffin UK (1980)

Don EVERHARD
British Male Amateur operating in England/USA

Paull STEWARD (British)

Citation Record: 3 Books

Dangerous Men - *First*
Harrap UK (1926)

Gaboreau The Terrible - *Last*
Harrap UK (1927)

Judith EVERSLEIGH
Second detective of Insp GREGG

Sir Godfrey EVESDEN
is a 'Special Commissioner' who does his sleuthing in the fourteenth century.
English Male Professional Investigator operating in London

Sidekick: Alexander MACBAIN
is a 'Clerk to the King'.
English Male - Assistant

P C DOHERTY (British)

Invented 3 detectives - see Hugh CORBETT

Citation Record: 1 Book

An Ancient Evil - *Single*
Headline UK (1994)

Sir Edgar EWART

British Male Amateur

A E WALTER and H C WALTER (British)

Writers: Alexia E WALTER and Hubert Conrad WALTER

Citation Record: 2 Books

The Patriot - *First*
Methuen UK (1928); Dutton US (1928)

Betrayed - *Last*
Methuen UK (1929); Dutton US (1930)

Ronald EWART

had featured in short stories before his appearance in one novel. In this, he sets out from London to Scotland, at the outbreak of the First World War, to unmask villains and spies who are using dastardly and very definitely unsporting ray guns.

!See Appendix 2.

British Male Amateur operating in Scotland

William LEQUEUX 1864-1927 (British)

Invented 23 detectives - see Allan KENNEDY

Citation Record: 1 Book 9 Short Stories in 1 Collection

The Mystery Of The Green Ray - *Only*
Hodder & Stoughton UK (1915)

The Green Ray - *Only**
Hodder & Stoughton UK (1916)

The Count's Chauffeur - *Collection 1*
Nash UK (1907)

The EYE

has been called by one critic 'the ultimate PI'. A unique creation in an unrepeatable book, he is a kind of modern symbolic Galahad, questing the highways and byways of America for his lost, dream-like daughter who always evades him.

American Male Private Detective operating in USA

Marc BEHM 1925- (American)

Citation Record: 1 Book

The Eye Of The Beholder - *Single*
Dial US (1980); Zomba UK (1980)

Susan Eyerly

Second detective Of Sheriff TOWNSEND

— F —

Armino FABBIO

is a tour guide who, conducting a group of English schoolteachers through a cathedral in Rome, stumbles across the body of a woman bearing a resemblance to his childhood nurse. He goes back to his birthplace and succeeds in unravelling the cause of the murder, which he finds is linked to other crimes.

Italian Male Amateur operating in Italy

Daphne DU MAURIER 1907-1989 (British)

was born in London, the daughter of the famous actor-manager, Sir Gerald Du Maurier. She was the author of a number of successful period romances and adventure stories, some of which have been made into successful films. Although many of her works deal in suspense, of which she was a mistress, few feature a real detective.

Citation Record: 1 Book

The Flight Of The Falcon - *Only*
Gollancz UK (1965); Doubleday US (1965)

Lou FABIAN

is a young woman who is menaced by an old crime and must turn sleuth to solve it.

American Female Amateur operating in USA

Ursula CURTISS 1923- (American)

was born in Yonkers, New York. She is the author of over twenty novels in the genre, usually dealing with individuals, especially women, in menacing situations or seeking vengeance. Her sleuths are nearly always ordinary people who have to turn to detective work to solve their special problems.

Writer: Ursula Reilly CURTISS

Other Detectives:
Caroline EMMET
Katy MEREDITH
Andrew SENTRY
Mrs TYRELL and Mrs LEEDS

Citation Record: 1 Book

The Face Of The Tiger - *Only*
Eyre & Spottiswoode UK (1960); Dodd, Mead US (1958)

Foster FADE

was one of this author's numerous pulp detectives and was called 'The Crime Spectacularist'.

American Male Detective in Pulp Magazines operating in USA

Lester DENT 1904-1959 (American)

Invented 9 detectives - see Chance MALLOY

No citations

Insp FAGERMO

Norwegian Policeman operating in Norway

Robert BARNARD 1936- (British)

Invented 13 detectives - see Insp Perry TRETHOWAN

Citation Record: 1 Book

Death In A Cold Climate - *Single*
Collins UK (1980); Scribner's US (1981)

Maj FAIDE

British Male Amateur operating in England

Henry WADE 1887-1969 (British)

Invented 7 detectives - see Ch Insp POOLE

Citation Record: 1 Book

The High Sheriff - *Only*
Constable UK (1937)

Prosper FAIR

is, we are told, the pseudonym of an English lord, the Duke of Devizes, a great eccentric who likes to solve mysteries.

British Male Amateur operating in England

Bertram ATKEY 1880-1952 (British)

was born in Wiltshire.

Other Detectives:
Smiler BUNN
Nelson CHIDDENHAM
Winnie O'WYNN

Citation Record: 2 Books

The Pyramid Of Lead - *First*
Hutchinson UK (1924); Appleton US (1925)

The Midnight Mystery - *Last*
Appleton UK (1928)

Hank FAIRBANKS

Second detective of Emma MARSH

Faith Sibley FAIRCHILD

is the wife of the local minister in a small town and is perpetually stumbling, even literally, over bodies. For divers reasons, she seems called on to investigate.

American Female Amateur operating in Maine

Katherine Hall PAGE 1947- (American)

Citation Record: 5 Books

The Body In The Belfry - *First*
St Martin's US (1990)

The Body In The Cast - *Latest*
St Martin's US (1994)

Mr Ron FAIRCHILD

is the President's own investigator and is called on to solve the murder of a Secretary of State.

American Male Amateur operating in Washington DC

Margaret TRUMAN 1924- (American)

Writer: Mary Margaret TRUMAN

Other Detectives:
Colette CAHILL
Mac HANRAHAN and Heather MCBEAN
Lydia JAMES
Ross LIZENBY and Chris SAKSIS
Sal MORIZIO Joe POTOMOS
Prof MacKenzie SMITH
Martin TELLER and Susanna PINSCHER

Citation Record: 1 Book

Murder In The White House - *Single*
Arbor US (1980); Severn UK (1981)

Phoebe FAIRFAX

investigates murder at an exclusive resort in the Canadian Rockies.

Canadian Female Amateur operating in Canada

Suzanne NORTH (Canadian)

Citation Record: 1 Book

Healthy, Wealthy And Dead - *Single*
NeWest US (1994)

Peggy FAIRFIELD

American Female Sleuth operating in USA

E S LIDDON 1897- (American)

Writer: Eloise S LIDDON

Citation Record: 2 Books

The Riddle Of The Russian Princess - *First*
Doubleday US (1934)

The Riddle Of The Florentine Folio - *Last*
Doubleday US (1935)

Insp FAIRFORD

is a young Scotland Yard man.

British Policeman operating in England

G D H COLE and Margaret COLE (British)

Invented 7 detectives - see Supt Henry WILSON

Citation Record: 2 Books

The Brothers Sackville - *First*
Collins UK (1936); Macmillan US (1937)

Off With Her Head - *Last*
Collins UK (1938); Macmillan US (1939)

Melville FAIRR

is a mediocre detective, a nondescript man in grey.

American Male Private Detective operating in New York

Michael VENNING 1908-1957 (American)

For writer details see John J MALONE

Citation Record: 3 Books

The Man Who Slept All Day - *First*
Coward McCann US (1943); Nicholson & Watson UK (1947)

Jethro Hammer - *Last*
Coward McCann US (1944); Nicholson & Watson UK (1947)

Doran FAIRWEATHER and Rodney CHELMARSH

Doran FAIRWEATHER is a feisty part-time antiques dealer. She and the vicar (later her husband), *Rodney CHELMARSH,* solve all manner of nasty crimes in rural Abbotsbourne.

British Female Amateur and British Male Amateur operating in England

Mollie HARDWICK (British)

Citation Record: 4 Books

Malice Domestic - *First*
Century UK (1986); St Martin's US (1986)

The Bandersnatch - *Latest*
Century Hutchinson UK (1989)

M Didius FALCO

is, in the year 70, a private eye cruising the exceedingly mean streets of Rome. Always in trouble and a republican to boot, he is, in his first book, hired to investigate a murder and a plot against the emperor. He goes on to investigate major crimes at home and abroad, even venturing as far as the bleak, cold island they called Britannia.

Roman Male Private Detective operating in Ancient Rome

Lindsey DAVIS (American)

Citation Record: 7 Books

Silver Pigs - *First*
Crown US (1989); Sidgwick & Jackson UK (1989)

A Time To Depart - *Latest*
Century UK (1995)

Ray FALCO

is a reporter who investigates the disappearance of a Haitian politician in exile.

American Male Amateur operating in USA/Haiti

David MADSEN (American)

Citation Record: 1 Book

Voudon - *Single*
Morrow US (1994)

Supt FALCON

appears sporadically in other books by this author with his other detectives.

British Policeman operating in England

Dornford YATES 1885-1960 (British)

was born in Upper Walmer, Kent. He attended Harrow School, 1899-1904, took a BA in Jurisprudence at University College, Oxford, 1907, attended at Inner Temple, London, and was called to the Bar, 1909. He was a practising solicitor for the rest of his life, interrupted only by his service with the army in both world wars. He lived in France after 1918 and in Rhodesia after 1945. He was the author of sixteen genre novels, all in the thriller category that had been so popularised by his contemporaries, *John BUCHAN* and *SAPPER.* Not so brilliant as the former but decidedly more palatable than the latter, his works are based firmly on his own experiences of crime and the law. Although they were still entrenched in outmoded ideas and are little read today, the stories themselves remain interesting.

Writer: Cecil William MERCER

Other Detectives:
CHANDOS Jonah MANSEL
Bertram PLEYDELL

Citation Record: 13 Short Stories in 1 Collection

Period Stuff - *Collection 1*
Ward, Lock UK (1942)

FALCON

British Male Professional Investigator operating in England

John CROZIER (British)

Citation Record: 2 Books

Murder In Public - *First*
Hutchinson UK (1934); Houghton US (1935)

Kidnapped Again - *Last*
Hutchinson UK (1935)

Gay Stanhope FALCON

is by way of being a phenomenon. He was invented by Michael Arlen, a naturalised British English novelist, for just one short story. He was taken up by film-makers of the post-war decade and much vulgarised and popularised in many stories and films, perhaps because he was a reworking of the old-style '*Bulldog' DRUMMOND* type, but more modern and so appearing at the right time for a new generation of movie makers.

FALCON, like others before him, is a gentleman- crook with the Robin Hood touch. He is a rogue, a burglar, a bit of a hero and, of course, good at anything he does. He is neither handsome nor charming, is indeed almost middle-aged, but women fall for him by the score. In the course of his crimes, many of which have an inverted justice about them, he often has to act the detective to clear himself of worse or to clear a woman accused of being a murderess or thief.

British Male Amateur operating in England

Michael ARLEN 1895-1956 (British)

was born in Bulgaria of Armenian parents. He came to England and became a naturalised citizen, 1922. He wrote a number of novels, the most famous of which was *The Green Hat*, which made his name and gave him a fortune. He then went to Hollywood, where he did nothing for two years as he hated writing. He created the legendary *FALCON* almost incidentally in one story. He never wrote another *FALCON* story, although many others did.

Writer: Dikran KUYUMJIAN

Citation Record: 1 Selected Short Story

Gay Falcon

was the progenitor of a host of plays and films that featured *The FALCON* as their romantic, tarnished hero.

UK (1940)

The FALCON

American Male Amateur operating in USA

Drexell DRAKE 1887?-1959 (American)

Writer: Charles H HUFF

Citation Record: 3 Books

The Falcon's Prey - *First*

Lippincott US (1936); Harrap UK (1937)

The Falcon Meets A Lady - *Last*

Lippincott US (1938)

Dan FALCONER

is hired as a bodyguard by a construction millionaire and becomes involved in nuclear power corruption.

American Male Private Detective operating in Phoenix

Edwin GAGE 1943- (American)

Citation Record: 1 Book

Phoenix No More - *Single*

Harper & Row US (1978)

Geoffrey FALCONER

British Male Amateur operating in England

William LEQUEUX 1864-1927 (British)

Invented 23 detectives - see Allan KENNEDY

Citation Record: 12 Short Stories in 1 Collection

Tracked By Wireless - *Collection 1*

Paul UK (1922); Moffat US (1922)

William FALCONER

is the Regent Master of Aristotle's Hall, Oxford, in the England of the thirteenth century. Experimenting with early aerodynamics, he is drawn away to investigate the murder of a townsman. The case involves medieval politics and the old rivalry between 'Town and Gown'.

English Male Amateur operating in Oxford

Ian MORSON (British)

Citation Record: 1 Book

Falconer's Crusade - *Single*

St Martin's US (1995)

Jesse FALKENSTEIN

Second detective of Det Vic VARALLO

Alexander FALLON

solves an 'impossible' crime.

American Male Amateur operating in USA

Neil HARRINGTON

Citation Record: 1 Selected Short Story

Too Much Evidence

appeared in the February number.

In 'Mike Shayne Mystery Magazine' US (1969)

Martin FANE and Richard FANE

British Male Amateurs operating in England

Michael HALLIDAY 1908-1973 (British)

See main detective Emmanuel CELLINI

Citation Record: 3 Books

Take A Body - *First*

was published in the US under the following byline.

Evans UK (1951)

Man On The Run - *Last*

was published in the US under the following byline.

Hodder & Stoughton UK (1972)

John CREASEY 1908-1973 (British)

Invented 6 detectives - see Insp Roger 'Handsome' WEST

Citation Record: 3 Books

Take A Body - *First*

was published in the UK under the preceding byline.

World US (1972)

Man On The Run - *Last*

was published in the UK under the preceding byline.

World US (1972)

Richard FANE

Second detective of Martin FANE

Fortune FANELLI

has come into money. He leaves the New York Police Department to set up as a PI in the SoHo district, whilst bringing up two kids left by their mother, the local butcher.

American Male Private Detective operating in New York

Jack EARLY 1936- (American)

Writer: Sandra SCOPPETONE

Inventor of one other detective Colin MAGUIRE

Citation Record: 1 Book

A Creative Kind Of Killer - *Single*

Watts US (1984)

Wu FANG

is one of those fictionally wily Chinese in the big cities of the Western world who are not quite inside, and not quite outside, the law and need to do a little private sleuthing to stay alive.

Chinese Male Amateur operating in London

Roland DANIEL 1880-1969 (British)

Invented 11 detectives - see Insp Neville LANGHAM

Citation Record: 4 Books

Wu Fang - *First*

Brentano's UK (1929)

The Return Of Wu Fang - *Last*

Wright UK (1937)

Octavius FANKS

is an idler who mixes with wealthy people prone to commit crimes, which he then solves.

British Male Amateur operating in England

Fergus HUME 1859-1932 (British)

Invented 24 detectives - see Insp Samuel GORBY

Citation Record: 2 Books

Monsieur Judas - *First*
Blackett UK (1891); Waverley US (1891)

The Carbuncle Clue - *Last*
Warne UK (1896)

Harry FANNIN

has been beaten up, shot at, and knifed more times than he can count, but on he goes with the good work.

American Male Private Detective operating in New York

David MARKSON 1927- (American)

Writer: David Merrill MARKSON

Citation Record: 3 Books

Epitaph For A Tramp - *First*
Dell US (1959)

Fannin - *First**
Belmont US (1971)

Miss Doll, Go Home - *Last*
Dell US (1965)

Capt Mark FANNING

solves a case of death by shooting in a locked room.

British Policeman operating in England

Vernon BARLOW (British)

Citation Record: 1 Book

The Green Murder - *Only*
Cranton UK (1931)

Jim FANSHAW

Second detective of Freddie BROWNE

Kate FANSLER

is the Professor of English in an American University where crimes on the campus seem almost part of the scenery. Fortunately for all concerned, with or without the help of the police, she is called on to solve them. Willowy, in her forties, and rather wealthy with it, *Kate FANSLER* is, however, a true academic, with a considerable knowledge of her main subject, Victorian literature. In two of her books she is associated with *Reed AMHEARST.*

American Female Amateur operating in New York

Amanda CROSS 1926- (American)

was born in East Orange, New Jersey. She graduated with a BA from Wellesley College, Massachusetts, 1947 and was awarded an MA at Columbia University, New York, 1951, and a PhD, 1959. She has been Professor of English at several US universities and has received many awards and fellowships. In addition to her criminous work, she has written specially on the role of women in literature.

Writer: Carolyn Gold HEILBRUN

Inventor of one other detective pair Kate FANSLER and Reed AMHEARST

Citation Record: 10 Books

In The Last Analysis - *First*
Macmillan US (1964); Gollancz UK (1964)

An Imperfect Spy - *Latest*
Ballantine US (1995)

Kate FANSLER and Reed AMHEARST

American Female Amateur and British Male Amateur operating in USA

Amanda CROSS 1926- (American)

See main detective Kate FANSLER

Citation Record: 2 Books

Poetic Justice - *First*
Knopf US (1970); Gollancz UK (1970)

The Theban Mysteries - *Last*
Knopf US (1971); Gollancz UK (1972)

FANTOMAS

French Male Amateur operating in France/England

Marcel ALLAIN 1885-1970 (French)

Citation Record: 5 Books

The Lord Of Terror - *First*
is a translation of *Fantomas Est Il Ressuscité?* (Paris, 1919).
Paul UK (1925); McKay US (1925)

Bulldog And Rats - *Last*
Paul UK (1928)

Pierre SOUVESTRE 1874-1910 and Marcel ALLAIN 1885-1970 (French)

Citation Record: 5 Books

Fantomas - *First*
Paul UK (1915); Brentano's US (1915)

Slippery As Sin - *Last*
Paul UK (1920); Moffat US (1923)

The FAR WEST DETECTIVE

American Male Detective in Pulp Magazines operating in USA

ANON

Citation Record: 1 Book

The Far West Detective - *Only*
Aldine US

Matt FARADAY

appears in books set in the Old West around the 1800s.

American Male Amateur operating in USA (Old West)

William GRANT (American)

Citation Record: 4 Books

The Iron Horse - *First*
Lynx US (1988)

The Trackwalker - *Latest*
Lynx US (1989)

Micah FARADAY

British Male Amateur operating in England

L T MEADE 1854-1914 (British)

Invented 4 detectives - see Rudolph GREY

Citation Record: 12 Short Stories in 1 Collection

Micah Faraday, Adventurer - *Collection 1*
Ward, Lock UK (1910)

Mike FARADAY

is one of the several imitation American private eyes invented by British authors. Appearing in a large number of books, he comes across as a fairly standard Californian PI, complete with beautiful secretary, with whom he never quite gets into bed, a fusty office and an old car. And, of course, he encounters murders and blondes without end under the hot sun.

American Male Private Detective operating in Los Angeles

Basil COPPER 1924- (British)

Invented 3 detectives - see Solar PONS

Citation Record: 52 Books

The Dark Mirror - *First*
Hale UK (1966)

Print-Out - *Latest*
Hale UK (1988)

Neil FARGO

American Male Private Detective operating in San Francisco

Joe GORES 1931- (American)

Invented 4 detectives - see Curt HALSTEAD

Citation Record: 1 Book

Interface - *Only*
Evans US (1974); Futura UK (1977)

William FARLAND

is a failed playwright, now a private eye.

American Male Private Detective operating in New York

Holly ROTH 1916-1964 (American)

Invented 4 detectives - see Insp MEDFORD

Citation Record: 1 Book

The Crimson In The Purple - *Only*
Simon & Schuster US (1956); Hamish Hamilton UK (1957)

F

Tom FARLEY

may look vacant and absent-minded but he is a first-class expert on cases of arson, which he investigates by the most up-to-date technical means.

American Male Private Detective operating in San Francisco

Jack SILER (American)

Citation Record: 1 Book

Triangle Of Fire - *Single*
Dell US (1984)

Max FARNE

British Male Sleuth operating in Italy

Richard BUTLER 1917- (British)

For writer details see Tad ANDERS

Citation Record: 2 Books

Where All The Girls Are Sweeter - *First*
was republished under the following byline.
Davies UK (1975)

Italian Assets - *Last*
was republished under the following byline.
Davies UK (1976)

Ted ALLBEURY 1917- (British)

See main detective Tad ANDERS

Citation Record: 2 Books

Where All The Girls Are Sweeter - *First*
was previously published under the preceding byline.
New English Library UK (1987)

Italian Assets - *Last*
was previously published under the preceding byline.
New English Library UK (1987)

Insp Jeremy FARO

is a Victorian cop who solves cases in and around Edinburgh. So skilled is he that even Queen Victoria is apt to call him in when she has a spot of bother at her castle over the border.

British Policeman operating in Edinburgh

Alanna KNIGHT (Scottish)

Citation Record: 4 Books

Enter Second Murderer - *First*
Macmillan UK (1988)

The Bull Slayers - *Latest*
UK (1995)

Insp Harry FARRANT

British Policeman operating in England

Lord GORELL 1884-1963 (British)

Invented 4 detectives - see Insp Gordon ROSS

Citation Record: 1 Book

The Devouring Fire - *Only*
Murray UK (1928)

Insp Michael FARRANT

British Policeman operating in England

P G LARBALESTIER (British)

Writer: Philip George LARBALESTIER

Citation Record: 3 Books

Darling, Don't Be Dumb - *First*
Gifford UK (1950)

Black Shrouds The Bride - *Last*
Gifford UK (1951)

Dr Francis FARRAR

solves a case of death by gassing in a locked room.

British Male Amateur operating in England

Kelman FROST (British)

Writer: Kelman Dalgety FROST

Inventor of one other detective Insp HYND

Citation Record: 1 Selected Short Story

The Late Edition
is in an anthology, *The Best Detective Stories of the Year 1928.*
Faber UK (1929)

John FARREL

is a railway detective.

American Male Private Detective operating in California

Bert HITCHENS and Dolores HITCHENS (American)

Invented 3 detectives - see COLLINS and MCKECHNIE

Citation Record: 2 Books

End Of The Line - *First*
Doubleday US (1957); Boardman UK (1958)

The Grudge - *Last*
Doubleday US (1963); Boardman UK (1964)

Mike FARREL

American Male Sleuth operating in Los Angeles

Carter BROWN 1923-1985 (Australian)

Invented 10 detectives - see Rick HOLMAN

Citation Record: 2 Books

The Million Dollar Babe - *First*
Signet US (1961); Horwitz AU (1962)

The Scarlet Flush - *Last*
Signet US (1963); Horwitz AU (1963)

Bruno FARRELL

sleuths in books set back into the 1920s.

American Male Amateur operating in Chicago

Ed MAZZARO (British)

Citation Record: 3 Books

One Death In The Red - *First*
New English Library UK (1976); Dale US (1979)

Chicago Deadline - *Latest*
New English Library UK (1978); Dale US (1978)

Johnny FARRELL

American Male Sleuth operating in USA

Johnny FARRELL (British)

Writer: George MAX

Other Byline: Hans LUGAR

Citation Record: 3 Books

Sugar, You're Swell - *First*
Scion UK (1952)

Curves And Angles - *Last*
Milestone UK (1953)

Hans LUGAR (British)

was a house name for a few authors gathered round the ephemeral publishers, *Scion,* who turned out a quantity of gangster novels during the 1950s, with various detectives.

For writer details see Johnny FARRELL

Citation Record: 1 Book

Midnight Sister - *Only*
Scion UK (1953)

Marcus Aurelius FARROW

is an ex-commando who is enlisted into industrial espionage and then into the British Intelligence Service. After appearing in one book on his own, he appears in later novels with his boss, *Charlie MCGOWAN.*

British Male Secret Agent operating in several locations

Angus ROSS 1927- (British)

was born in Dewsbury, Yorkshire.

Writer: Kenneth GIGGAL

Inventor of one other detective pair Marcus Aurelius FARROW and Charlie MCGOWAN

Citation Record: 1 Book

The Manchester Thing - *Only*
Long UK (1970)

The Manchester Connection - *Only**
Severn UK (1974)

Marcus Aurelius FARROW and Charlie MCGOWAN

British Male Secret Agents operating in several locations

Angus ROSS 1927- (British)

See main detective Marcus Aurelius FARROW

Citation Record: 18 Books

The Huddersfield Job - *First*
Long UK (1971)

Leipzig Manuscript - *Latest*
Firecrest UK (1990)

Insp FASKE

is a member of the CID.

British Policeman operating in England

Arthur GRIFFITHS 1838-1908 (British)

Writer: Arthur George Frederick GRIFFITHS

Other Detectives:
FLOCON
Insp LAMPETER
Mr LESLIE
Lionel MACNAUGHTEN-INNES
Insp PHILLIPSON
Plantagenet PLEWS
Col Theophilus ST CLAIR

Citation Record: 1 Book

Fast And Loose - *Only*
Chapman & Hall UK (1885); Munro US (1886)

Det Ch Supt Harry FATHERS

is the head of the Serious Crimes unit at Scotland Yard. His cases are complex rather than simple, protean rather than domestic, and the books are British semi-procedural in style.

British Policeman operating in London

D W SMITH 1951- (British)

Writer: Daniel Wubert SMITH

Citation Record: 3 Books

Father's Law - *First*
Macmillan UK (1986); Stuart US (1987)

The Fourth Crow - *Latest*
Macmillan UK (1989); St Martin's US (1990)

FATHOM

seems to be *Mr VERITY* (qv) under a different name and appears in this book published in the UK under the author's real names, which they rarely used. The change in the detective's name is inexplicable, but no more so than any of the other games played by these ingenious writers.

British Male Amateur operating in Sussex

Peter ANTONY (British)

See main detective pair Mr VERITY and Insp RAMBLER

Citation Record: 1 Book

Withered Murder - *First*
Macmillan US (1956)

Anthony SHAFFER and P SHAFFER (British)

Writers: Anthony Joshua SHAFFER 1926- and Peter Levin SHAFFER 1926-

Citation Record: 1 Book

Withered Murder - *First*
Gollancz UK (1955)

Reggie FAULKNER

British Male Amateur operating in England/Switzerland

Edmund SNELL 1889- (British)

Inventor of one other detective Peter PENNINGTON

Citation Record: 3 Books

The "Z" Ray - *First*
Skeffington UK (1932); Lippincott US (1932)

Murder In Switzerland - *Last*
Hale UK (1938); Hillman-Curl US (1938)

William FAULKNER

Appears with at least two other detectives - see Toby PETERS.

Mr FAUNCE

is with the Victorian CID at Bow Street.

British Policeman operating in London

M E BRADDON 1835-1915 (British)

Invented 9 detectives - see Robert AUDLEY

Citation Record: 2 Books

Rough Justice - *First*
Simpkin Marshall UK (1898)

His Darling Sin - *Last*
Simpkin Marshall UK (1899)

Insp FAVART

solves a case of death by stabbing in a locked room.

British Policeman operating in England

Robert BRENNAN 1881- (British)

Citation Record: 1 Book

The Toledo Dagger - *Only*
Hamilton UK (1927)

John FAY

American Male Detective in Pulp Magazines operating in USA

Old Cap LEE (American)

Citation Record: 1 Book

John Fay, Detective; Or, The Renegade's Plot
New York Detective Library US (1882-8)

Dave FEARLESS

American Male Detective in Pulp Magazines operating in USA

ANON

No citations

Johnny FEDORA

is an agent for British Intelligence who carries out many a desperate task, sometimes being pitted against brilliant Russian agents.

British Male Secret Agent operating in Europe

Desmond CORY 1928- (British)

was born in Lancing, Sussex. He took a BA in English at St Peter's College, Oxford, 1951, and a PhD at the University of Wales, Cardiff, 1976. He served in the Royal Marines, 1944-1948, and has since taught English at several universities in the Middle East.

Writer: Shaun Lloyd MCCARTHY

Other Byline: Shaun MCCARTHY

Other Detectives:
Mr DEE
Lindy GREY
Mr PILGRIM

Citation Record: 16 Books

Secret Ministry - *First*
Muller UK (1951)

The Nazi Assassins - *First**
Award US (1970)

Sunburst - *Last*
Hodder & Stoughton UK (1971); Walker US (1971)

Harry FEIFFER and YELLOWTHREAD STREET COPS

appear in police procedurals set in Hong Kong. *FEIFFER* and the cops of the zany *YELLOWTHREAD STREET PRECINCT* indulge in adventure, farce, searches and investigations.

Policemen operating in Hong Kong

William MARSHALL 1944- (Australian)

was born in Sydney, Australia, and graduated from the Australian National University, Canberra. Residing in England, he is the author of some of the most bizarre detective novels in the genre.

Writer: William Leonard MARSHALL

Inventor of one other detective Lt Felix ELIZALDO

Citation Record: 13 Books

Yellowthread Street - *First*
Hamilton UK (1975); Holt US (1976)

F

Out Of Nowhere - *Latest*
Mysterious Press US (1988); Chatto & Windus UK (1989)

Dr Gideon FELL

is one of the best known detectives in the criminous literature, the creation of one of the great masters of the genre. Bulging, bibulous and brilliant, he was modelled on the author's friend and fellow-writer in the genre, *G K CHESTERTON*. His cases, many of which were of the 'impossible crime' or locked-room kind, a sub-genre in which the author specialised and excelled, were usually solved to the astonishment of the police, who were often convinced that the crimes were so impossible that they were the work of occult forces. He appears also in one book with another of the author's detectives, *Patrick BUTLER*.

British Male Amateur operating in England/USA

Stooge: Insp Humphrey MASTERS
is, in fact, getting a little old for his job and is always confused by the cases that *FELL* finally solves.
British Male

John Dickson CARR 1906-1977 (American)

was born in Uniontown, Pennsylvania. He was educated at Haverford College, Pennsylvania, and then went abroad for further study, living in England, 1932-1948. He became one of the best and most prolific writers in the criminous field, the author of almost a hundred detective novels under his real name and his equally famous pseudonym, *Carter DICKSON*. He was a particular exponent of the locked-room or 'impossible' crime mystery and he was the inventor of some of the most ingenious murder methods ever to see the light of day. He was renowned for his enormous erudition, his meticulous attention to detail, and his historical knowledge and accuracy. He received the Mystery Writers of America Edgar Allan Poe award twice, 1949 and 1969, and their Grand Master award, 1962.

Writer: John Dickson CARR

Other Bylines:
Carr DICKSON
Carter DICKSON

Other Detectives:
Juge d'Instruction BENCOLIN
Jim BLAKE
Patrick BUTLER
Insp John CHEVIOT
Wilkie COLLINS
Dick DARWENT
Dr Gideon FELL and Patrick BUTLER
Prof Nicholas FENTON
Dr David GARTH and Det Insp TWIGG
Sherlock HOLMES
Jeff MARLE
Sir Henry MERRIVALE
Edward STEVENS
Clive STRICKLAND
Jeffrey WYNNE

Citation Record: 22 Books 10 Short Stories in 4 Collections

Hag's Nook - *First*
Hamish Hamilton UK (1933)

Dark Of The Moon - *Last*
Harper & Row US (1967); Hamish Hamilton UK (1968)

Dr Fell, Detective, And Other Stories - *Collection 1*
Short stories - 5
Mercury US (1947)

The Third Bullet And Other Stories - *Collection 2*
contains two *Gideon FELL* stories and one *Sir Henry MERRIVALE* story. In addition it contains the title novelette, originally published under the author's *Carter DICKSON* pseudonym.
Short stories - 2
Harper & Row US (1954); Hamish Hamilton UK (1954)

The Men Who Explained Miracles - *Collection 3*
Short stories - 2
Hamish Hamilton UK (1964); Harper & Row US (1963)

The Door To Doom And Other Detections - *Collection 4*
contains several stories with the author's other detectives.
Short stories - 1
Harper & Row US (1980); Hamish Hamilton UK (1981)

Dr Gideon FELL and Patrick BUTLER

British Male Amateurs operating in England

John Dickson CARR 1906-1977 (American)

Invented 16 detectives - see Dr Gideon FELL

Citation Record: 1 Book

Below Suspicion - *Only*
Harper & Row US (1949); Hamilton UK (1950)

Ch Fred FELLOWS

is the Chief of Police in the fictional little town of Stockford, Connecticut. He is a large man and growing larger, he fears, with age; but he is a fine policeman, firm with his staff but considerate of them, and his investigational methods are informal but patient, resembling those of the great French detective, *Jules MAIGRET*.

American Policeman operating in Connecticut

Sidekick: Lt Sid WILKS
American Male - Subordinate

Hillary WAUGH 1920- (American)

was born in Hew Haven, Connecticut. He was educated at Hillhouse High School, New Haven, took a BA at Yale University, New Haven, 1942 and served in the United States Navy Air Force, 1943-1945. Cartoonist, song writer, teacher of physics and mathematics, he is the author of at least forty-six genre novels. He received the Mystery Writers of America Grand Master award, 1981.

Writer: Hillary Baldwin WAUGH

Other Byline: H Baldwin TAYLOR

Other Detectives:
Peter CONGDON
Ch FORD
Simon KAYE
Philip MACADAM
Det Frank SESSIONS
Sheridan WESLEY

Citation Record: 11 Books

Sleep Long, My Love - *First*
Doubleday US (1959); Gollancz UK (1960)

The Con Game - *Last*
Doubleday US (1968); Gollancz UK (1968)

Morgan FELLOWS

British Male Amateur operating in England

J D BERESFORD 1873-1943 (British)

Writer: John Davys BERESFORD

Citation Record: 1 Book

The Instrument Of Destiny - *Only*
Collins UK (1928); Bobbs US (1928)

Dominic FELSE

Second detective of George FELSE

George FELSE and Dominic FELSE

are father and son. They and, at times, other members of their family, appear variously in at least thirteen books by this prolific author. The first was published under her real name, which she hardly ever used again for her large criminous output.

British Male Sleuths operating in several locations

Ellis PETERS 1913-1995 (British)

Invented 4 detectives - see Brother CADFAEL

Citation Record: 13 Books

Fallen Into The Pit - *First*
Heinemann UK (1951)

Rainbow's End - *Latest*
Macmillan UK (1978); Morrow US (1979)

Peter FELTHAM

British Male Sleuth operating in Cyprus

Berkley MATHER 1914- (British)

was a professional soldier for much of his life, serving in India, which is the background for many of his books and short stories.

Writer: John Evan Weston DAVIES

Other Detectives:
Idewal REES
James WAINWRIGHT

Citation Record: 2 Books

The Achilles Affair - *First*
Collins UK (1959); Scribner's US (1959)
With Extreme Prejudice - *Last*
Collins UK (1975); Scribner's US (1976)

Ray FELTON

British Male Amateur operating in England

John MARSH 1907- (British)

See main detective Simon LUCK
Citation Record: 4 Books
Murderer's Maze - *First*
Gifford UK (1957)
Small And Deadly - *Last*
Hale UK (1960)

Richard FELTON

is an engineer who solves the mystery of an inventor who disappears from his rooms. The story is to be found in the author's collection, *The Adventures of an Engineer.*

British Male Amateur operating in England

Weatherby CHESNEY 1865-1944 (British)

See main detective Edward DALE
Citation Record: 1 Selected Short Story
The Horror Of The Folding Bed
Bowden UK (1898)

Gervase FEN

is cast in the classic, although now somewhat outmoded, mould of the great British academic amateur detective. Modelled on one of the author's tutors at St John's College, Oxford, he is a large man, who customarily wears over-sized clothes and extraordinary hats. Given perhaps to excessive literary quotation, he is extremely clever, as befits a supposed Professor of English Language and Literature at Oxford University. Apart from the novels in which he appears, all of which have ingenious plots, he features in short stories on his own and with the author's other detective, *Insp HUMBLEBY.*

British Male Amateur operating in Oxford

Edmund CRISPIN 1921-1978 (British)

was born in Chesham Bois, Buckinghamshire. He was educated at Merchant Taylors' School, London, and at St John's College, Oxford. He was a schoolmaster, 1943-1945, after which he began work on his extraordinarily ingenious detective novels and short stories. He was also a composer of orchestral and choral music.

Writer: Robert Bruce MONTGOMERY
Other Detectives:
Gervase FEN and Insp HUMBLEBY
Insp HUMBLEBY
Citation Record: 11 Books 9 Short Stories in 1 Collection
The Case Of The Gilded Fly - *First*
Gollancz UK (1944)
Obsequies At Oxford - *First**
Lippincott US (1945)
The Glimpses Of The Moon - *Last*
Gollancz UK (1977); Walker US (1978)
Fen Country - *Collection 1*
contains nine stories with *Gervase FEN,* two with *Insp HUMBLEBY* and eight with both detectives.
Gollancz UK (1979); Walker US (1980)

Gervase FEN and Insp HUMBLEBY

British Male Amateurs operating in England

Edmund CRISPIN 1921-1978 (British)

Invented 3 detectives - see Gervase FEN
Citation Record: 8 Short Stories in 1 Collection
Fen Country - *Collection 1*
contains nine stories with *Gervase FEN,* two with *Insp HUMBLEBY* and eight with both detectives.
Gollancz UK (1979); Walker US (1980)

Insp FENBY

British Policeman operating in England

Richard HULL 1896-1973 (British)

was born in London, educated at Rugby School, Warwickshire, and served in the Army in both world wars. He was, by profession, a chartered accountant.

Writer: Richard Henry SAMPSON
Citation Record: 2 Books
The Murderers Of Monty - *First*
Faber UK (1937); Putnam US (1937)
Excellent Intentions - *Last*
Faber UK (1938)
Beyond Reasonable Doubt - *Last**
Messner US (1941)

F

George FENCHURCH

solves a case of murder by poison gas in order to clear himself of suspicion.

British Male Amateur operating in England/Spain

Edward WOODWARD (British)

See main detective Bill MARSHALL
Citation Record: 1 Book
The House Of Terror - *Only*
Selwyn UK (1929); Mystery League US (1930)

Ludovic FENDER

appears also in one book with the author's other detective, *Paul VENNEKER.*

Male Sleuth operating in Europe

Paul GEDDES 1922- (British)

Invented 3 detectives - see Paul VENNEKER
Citation Record: 4 Books
A November Wind - *First*
Joseph UK (1970); Coward McCann US (1971)
A Special Kind Of Nightmare - *Latest*
Bodley Head UK (1988); St Martin's US (1989)

Ludovic FENDER and Paul VENNEKER

also appear individually in other books by this author.

Male Sleuths operating in Europe

Paul GEDDES 1922- (British)

Invented 3 detectives - see Paul VENNEKER
Citation Record: 1 Book
The High Game - *Only*
Joseph UK (1968); Weybright US (1968)

Christopher FENN

American Male Amateur operating in New York/England

Manning Lee STOKES (American)

Invented 3 detectives - see Barnaby JONES
Citation Record: 2 Books
The Case Of The Presidents' Heads - *First*
Arcadia US (1956)
The Case Of The Judas Spoon - *Last*
Arcadia US (1957)

Geoff FENNELL

British Male Sleuth operating in Haiti/Middle East

E P THORNE (British)

Invented 3 detectives - see Quentin EADY
Citation Record: 2 Books
They Never Came Back - *First*
Wright UK (1961)
The Assignment Haiti - *Last*
Wright UK (1963)

Dave FENNER

is a crime reporter turned private eye. He was the very first of the author's many imitation American detectives.

American Male Private Detective operating in New York/Kansas

James Hadley CHASE 1906-1985 (British)

was, whether loved or loathed, admired or deprecated, a publishing phenomenon. Born in London, he was educated at King's School, Rochester, Kent, and later at Hastings University School, Sussex. He was, for a time, a bookseller and he served in the Royal Air Force as a Squadron Leader during the Second World War. He began to write his thrillers and detective novels in the late 1930s. Unusually, especially for the time, he set his books in America. However, it was an America that he had never visited and had learned about only from other writers' thrillers and his maps and street plans. His first book, *NO ORCHIDS FOR MISS BLANDISH,* was rejected as being impossibly corny by the English publishers, *Michael Joseph.* That must surely rank as one of the biggest mistakes in publishing history, for the book was eventually published and became one of the most famous and best-selling thrillers in the history of the genre.

James Hadley CHASE went on to write over eighty books, mainly under this pseudonym, but he also used others. Later editions have, however, tended to consolidate the endless reprints under the *CHASE* name. The books are often transparently false in their Californian and other American settings and the characters are sometimes pasteboard, yet the pace, ingenuity, and sheer power of the author's story-telling made them best-sellers in the USA as well as the UK. Initially denigrated by superior critics, but now recognised as a definite strand in the great fabric of the genre, they were loved by the audience. They continue to sell in paperbacks, in English and in translation, in their millions throughout the world.

Writer: Rene Brabazon RAYMOND

Other Byline: Raymond MARSHALL

Other Detectives:

Al BARNEY
Lew BRANDON
Mark GIRLAND
Mark GIRLAND and Herman RADNITZ
Mark GIRLAND, Lu SILK and Herman RADNITZ
Steve HARMAS
Steve HARMAS, Al BARNEY and Frank TERRELL
Floyd JACKSON
Vic MALLOY
Herman RADNITZ and Al BARNEY
Helga ROLFE
Frank TERRELL
Dirk WALLACE

Citation Record: 2 Books

No Orchids For Miss Blandish - *First*
Jarrolds UK (1939); Howell Soskin US (1942)

The Villain And The Virgin - *First**
Avon US (1948)

Twelve Chinks And A Woman - *Last*
Jarrolds UK (1940); Howell Soskin US (1940)

Twelve Chinamen And A Woman - *Last**
Novel Library US (1950)

The Doll's Bad News - *Last**
Panther US (1970)

Jack FENNER

appears also in books with another of the author's detectives, *Kent MURDOCK.*

American Male Private Detective operating in Boston

George Harmon COXE 1901-1984 (American)

Invented 20 detectives - see Kent MURDOCK

Citation Record: 1 Book

No Place For Murder - *Only*
Knopf US (1975); Hale UK (1976)

Joe FENNER

appeared in a number of stories, including the one cited, in which the crimes always had some new, and sometimes incredible, scientific or quasi-scientific methodology.

American Male Amateur operating in New York

Charles WOLFE (American)

Citation Record: 1 Selected Short Story

The Educated Harpoon

There were several stories with *Joe FENNER* in the April 1920 issue of this magazine and thereafter in its follower, *Science & Invention.*

In 'Electrical Experimenter' US (1920)

Maxwell FENNER

specialises in cases of fraud, which usually involve murder.

American Male Private Detective operating in New York

Louis F BOOTH (American)

Citation Record: 2 Books

The Bank Vault Mystery - *First*
Dodd, Mead US (1933); Hutchinson UK (1933)

Broker's End - *Last*
Dodd, Mead US (1935); Hutchinson UK (1935)

Hilary FENTON

Second detective of Insp HORROCKS

Horace Spurgeon FENTON

British Male Sleuth operating in several locations

Jack Trevor STORY 1918-1991 (British)

Invented 3 detectives - see Albert ARGYLE

Citation Record: 2 Books

One Last Mad Embrace - *First*
Allison & Busby UK (1970)

Hitler Needs You - *Last*
Allison & Busby UK (1971)

Lawrie FENTON

works in and out of diplomatic circles as a spy and counter-spy.

British Male Secret Agent operating in Europe

Michael ANNESLEY (British)

Citation Record: 14 Books

Room 14: A Secret Service Adventure - *First*
Harrap UK (1935)

Fenton Of The Foreign Service - *First**
Speller US (1937)

The Lights That Did Not Fail - *Last*
Paul UK (1949)

Prof Nicholas FENTON

strikes a bargain with the Devil, permitting him to go back to 1675 in order to solve a murder that took place in Cambridge.

British Male Amateur operating in England

John Dickson CARR 1906-1977 (American)

Invented 16 detectives - see Dr Gideon FELL

Citation Record: 1 Book

The Devil In Velvet - *Only*
Harper & Row US (1951); Hamilton UK (1951)

Sgt FENWICK

British Policeman operating in England

Reg BATCHELOR 1916- (British)

Writer: Lauran Bosworth PAINE

Other Byline: Mark CARREL

Citation Record: 2 Books

The Murder Game - *First*
Hale UK (1970)

Murderer's Row - *Last*
Hale UK (1970)

Charlie FENWICK

is a 'phonic criminologist' and solves an 'impossible' death by shooting in a locked room.

American Male Amateur operating in New York

George J BRENN 1888- (American)

Citation Record: 1 Book

Voices - *Only*
Century US (1923); Jenkins UK (1925)

Dr FERENC
Male Amateur operating in England

Richard SAVAGE 1913- (British)
Writer: Ivan ROE
Citation Record: 3 Books
Murder For Fun - *First*
Jarrolds UK (1947)
The Poison And The Root - *Last*
Jarrolds UK (1950)

Det FERGUSON
American Policeman operating in Washington DC

Natalie Sumner LINCOLN 1881-1935 (American)
See main detective Insp MITCHELL
Citation Record: 2 Books
The Red Seal - *First*
Appleton UK (1920)
The Unseen Ear - *Last*
Appleton UK (1921)

Connie FERGUSON and Gil FERGUSON
American Female Amateur and American Male Amateur operating in New Hampshire

Hy BRETT and Barbara BRETT (American)
Citation Record: 1 Book
Promises To Keep - *Only*
Harper & Row US (1981)

Gil FERGUSON
Second detective of Connie FERGUSON

Jim FERGUSON
is blacklisted after causing the death of a policeman and goes to work for a firm of management consultants.
American Male Amateur operating in USA

Winifred VAN ATTA 1910- (American)
Writer: Winifred Lowell VAN ATTA
Other Detectives:
Ken MITCHELL   Dale NELSON
Citation Record: 1 Book
A Good Place To Work And Die - *Only*
Doubleday US (1970); Hale UK (1971)

FERNAND
works as a spy for Napoleon in 1810.
French Male Secret Agent operating in France

Baroness ORCZY 1865-1947 (British)
Invented 6 detectives - see Lady Molly DE MAZEREEN
Citation Record: 9 Short Stories in 1 Collection
The Man In Grey - *Collection 1*
Cassell UK (1918); Doran US (1918)

FERNANDA
is a rough, would-be tough, beautiful but nasty private eye.
American Female Private Detective operating in New York

Victor B MILLER 1940- (American)
Writer: Victor Brooke MILLER
Inventor of one other detective Insp KOJAK
Citation Record: 1 Book
Fernanda - *Only*
Pocket Books US (1976)

Geraldine FERRAR
Second detective of Enrico CARUSO

Francis FERRARS
American Male Private Detective operating in Chicago

Lawrence L LYNCH (American)
Invented 11 detectives - see Neil J BATHURST
Citation Record: 2 Books
Shadowed By Three - *First*
Donnelly Gassette & Loyd US (1879)
The Last Stroke - *Last*
Laird & Lee US (1896); Ward, Lock UK (1897)

Hank FERRELL
American Male Private Detective operating in New Orleans

Genevieve HOLDEN 1919- (American)
Writer: Genevieve Long POU
Inventor of one other detective Lt Al WHITE
Citation Record: 1 Book
Deadlier Than The Male - *Only*
Doubleday US (1961)

Abner FERRET
American Male Detective in Pulp Magazines operating in USA

Harry ROCKWOOD 1859-1932 (American)
Invented 14 detectives - see Clarice DYKE
Citation Record: 1 Book
Abner Ferret, The Lawyer Detective - *Only*
Ogilvie US (1883)

The FERRET DETECTIVE
American Male Detective in Pulp Magazines operating in USA

ANON
No citations

Les FERRON
American Male Sleuth operating in Louisiana

Day KEENE ?-1969? (American)
See main detective Johnny ALOHA
Citation Record: 2 Books
Notorious - *First*
GM US (1955); Fawcett UK (1954)
Sleep With The Devil - *Last*
Lion US (1954)

Bernard FESTON
British Male Sleuth operating in Spain/Greece

Kevin FITZGERALD 1902- (British)
Citation Record: 3 Books
Quiet Under The Sun - *First*
Heinemann UK (1953); Little, Brown US (1954)
Dangerous To Lean Out - *Last*
Heinemann UK (1960); Macmillan US (1961)

Bob FETHERSTON and Sgt QUINN
American Male Amateur and American Policeman operating in USA

Christopher B BOOTH 1883-1924 (American)
Invented 3 detectives - see Jim BLISS
Citation Record: 1 Book
Deceiver's Door - *Only*
Chelsea US (1929)

Brig FFELLOWES
British Male Amateur operating in England

Sterling E LANIER 1927- (British)
Writer: Sterling Edmund LANIER
Citation Record: 7 Short Stories in 1 Collection
The Peculiar Exploits Of Brigadier Ffellowes - *Collection 1*
Sidgwick UK (1977)

FIDDLER
is rich but bored. He roams around California, drumming up tough cases, usually crowded with beautiful girls.
American Male Private Detective operating in California

A E MAXWELL 1944- (American)
Writers: Ann Elizabeth Lowell MAXWELL 1944- and Evan MAXWELL
Citation Record: 3 Books
Just Another Day In Paradise - *First*
Doubleday US (1985)

The Art Of Survival - *Latest*
Doubleday US (1989)

Sister FIDELMA

sleuths in medieval England.

English Female Amateur operating in England

Peter TREMAYNE (British)

Citation Record: 1 Book

Shroud For The Archbishop - *Single*
Headline UK (1995)

Fabian FIELD

British Male Professional Amateur operating in England

F

Dick DONOVAN 1842-1924 (British)

was born in Southampton, Hampshire. He was a journalist and the author of many books in various genres. Much of his work was in the form of short stories, the majority of them featuring his eponymous detective.

Writer: Joyce Emerson Preston MUDDOCK

Other Detectives:
Michael DANEVITCH and Peter BRODIE
Det Dick DONOVAN
Tyler TATLOCK
Det Vincent TRILL
Eugène VIDOCQ
Howel WALTER

Citation Record: 10 Short Stories in 1 Collection

The Triumphs Of Fabian Field, Criminologist - *Collection 1*
White UK (1912)

John FIELD

is 'a concert pianist, a world traveler, is handsome, witty and forever jinxed, for wherever he goes, murder is not far behind'. He goes to the fictional Fun City in Florida to give a concert, but someone orchestrates the perfect murder – reckoning, of course, without the sleuth of the shining ivories.

American Male Amateur operating in Florida

Joan HIGGINS (American)

has an MA in Music and has been a professional pianist.

Citation Record: 1 Book

A Little Death Music - *Single*
Dodd, Mead US (1987)

Latimer FIELD

British Male Amateur operating in England

Silas HOCKING 1850-1935 (British)

Writer: Silas Kitto HOCKING

Citation Record: 12 Short Stories in 1 Collection

Adventures Of Latimer Field - *Collection 1*
Warne UK (1903)

Insp Martin FIELD

American Policeman operating in San Francisco

Q PATRICK 1901- (American)

Invented 5 detectives - see Lt Timothy TRANT

Citation Record: 1 Selected Short Story

The 'Laughing Man' Murders
appeared in the August number.
In 'Ellery Queen's Mystery Magazine' US (1963)

Prof Henry Arthur FIELDING

is a Professor of Philology, formerly at Manchester University but now a free-lance intellectual in London. An amiable man, well sought after by cultured friends, he bumbles his way into his cases. He appears in two other books with an even greater bumbler, *Sheridan ORFORD.*

British Male Amateur operating in England

David SHARP (British)

Inventor of one other detective pair Sheridan ORFORD and Prof Henry Arthur FIELDING

Citation Record: 7 Books

When No Man Pursueth - *First*
Benn UK (1930)

The Frightened Sailor - *Last*
Jenkins UK (1939)

Prof Henry Arthur FIELDING

Second detective of Sheridan ORFORD

Sir John FIELDING

was, in fact, a magistrate for Westminster, London, in the latter half of the eighteenth century and he founded the Bow Street Runners, the first professional police force in the world. He has now been made a detective in this historical caper. Since he is blind, he needs must have a more than average assistant.

British Male Amateur operating in London

Sidekick: Jeremy PROCTER
is a precocious thirteen-year-old boy who leads the blind detective in his investigational jaunts and narrates the story.
British Male - Narrator

Bruce ALEXANDER (American)

Citation Record: 1 Book

Blind Justice - *Single*
Putnam US (1994)

Ch Jose Daniel FIERRO

is a thriller writer who is asked to take on the job of police chief in the town of Santa Ana. Little does he know that his two predecessors have both been killed – or that bullets and blood in real life are not the same as in print.

Mexican Policeman operating in Mexico

Paco Ignacio TAIBO II 1949-

Other Detectives:
Philip MARLOWE
Hector SHAYNE

Citation Record: 1 Book

Life Itself - *Single*
Mysterious Press US (1994)

Insp/Supt FILLINGER

British Policeman operating in England

Paul MCGUIRE 1903-1978 (Australian)

was born in South Australia. He attended the University of Adelaide and later served in the Royal Australian Naval Volunteer Reserve, 1939-1945. He was a lecturer in Australia and the USA for some years and then held several political posts for his government, being the Minister to Italy, 1954-1958, and Ambassador, 1958-1959. He was made a CBE, 1951, and received several foreign awards for his political work abroad. Although he did not settle in England, he set nearly all of his sixteen genre works there. In addition to those, he published two volumes of verse and several travel books.

Writer: Dominic Paul MCGUIRE

Other Detectives:
Ch Insp CUMMINGS
Ch Insp CUMMINGS and Insp/Supt FILLINGER
Insp WITTLER

Citation Record: 4 Books

Death Tolls The Bell - *First*
Coward McCann US (1933)

The Tower Mystery - *First**
Skeffington UK (1932)

Death Fugue - *Last*
Skeffington UK (1933)

Insp/Supt FILLINGER

Second detective of Ch Insp CUMMINGS

Charles FINCH and 'Stalky' HERON

solve a case of murder in which a shooting by an arrow takes place in a locked room.

British Male Amateurs operating in England

Ralph STEPHENSON 1910- (British)

See main detective Peter JACKSON

Citation Record: 1 Book

Darkest Death - *Only*
Gifford UK (1964)

Det Ch Insp Jack FINCH

is a good, old-fashioned English detective, with none of the more bizarre, yet increasingly standardised, attributes of the species that have emerged since the 1980s. He is a quiet man, a bachelor, who works patiently and painstakingly to solve his cases by pure detection. Although he has a number of personal problems in his own relationships, they do not obtrude into his cases. Indeed they often serve to enhance and illuminate them. For the US publications, he was renamed *RUDD* (qv) and is so cited.

British Policeman operating in England

Sidekick: Sgt Tom BOYCE

British Male - Subordinate

June THOMSON 1930- (British)

was born in Kent. She was educated at Chelmsford High School for Girls, Essex, and took a BA in English at Bedford College, London, 1952. A school teacher, 1953-1973, she then published her first detective novel in a series that continues. She is the author, also, of three exceptionally fine collections of *Sherlock HOLMES* pastiches, which capture the essence of the master as few others have done.

Writer: June Valerie THOMSON

Adopter of one other detective Sherlock HOLMES

Citation Record: 16 Books

Not One Of Us - *First*
Harper & Row US (1971); Constable UK (1972)

Past Reckoning - *Latest*
Constable UK (1990)

Martyn FINCH

British Male Amateur operating in Spain

Philip CLEIFE 1906- (British)

Writer: Kenneth Philip Hubert CLEIFE

Citation Record: 2 Books

The Pinchbeck Masterpiece - *First*
Macmillan UK (1970)

Tour De Force - *First**
Harper & Row US (1971)

The Slick And The Dead - *Last*
Macmillan UK (1972)

Insp Septimus FINCH

is a member of the London CID. A large, solemn and sensitive man, he is usually involved with strange happenings in peculiar surroundings or old houses with large casts of suspects.

British Policeman operating in England

Margaret ERSKINE ?-1984 (British)

Writer: Margaret Wetherby WILLIAMS

Citation Record: 22 Books

And Being Dead - *First*
Bles UK (1938)

The Limping Man - *First**
Doubleday US (1939)

The House In Hook Street - *Last*
Hale UK (1978); Doubleday US (1977)

Peter FINLEY

is a reporter for a New York City cable TV station who becomes involved in finding a former Miss America, now missing and presumed dead.

American Male Amateur operating in New York

Sidekick: Marty PEARL

provides the muscle and does the camera work.

American Male - Assistant

Mike LUPICA (American)

Citation Record: 1 Book

Dead Air - *Single*
Villard US (1986)

Rob FINN

British Male Amateur operating in England

Dick FRANCIS 1920- (British)

Invented 18 detectives - see Sid HALLEY

Citation Record: 1 Book

Nerve - *Only*
Joseph UK (1964); Harper & Row US (1964)

Cyrus FINNEGAN

British Male Amateur operating in England

Moncrieff WILLIAMSON 1915- (British)

Citation Record: 1 Book

Death In The Picture - *Single*
Beaufort US (1982)

Det Fin FINNEGAN

is, unusually for a fictional San Diego cop, one of nature's gentlemen. He would like to be an actor; but, instead, he is set difficult problems of murder and larceny, at first involving naval personnel and later some missing toxic waste.

American Policeman operating in San Diego

Joseph WAMBAUGH 1937- (American)

was born in East Pittsbugh, Pennsylvania. He was educated at Chaffey College, Alta Loma, California, and took a BA at California State College, Los Angeles, 1960. He served in the US Marine Corps, 1954-1957, and was a Detective Sergeant in the Los Angeles Police Department, 1960-1974. The author of at least eight greatly admired novels of chilling suspense, involving the best and worst aspects of American police work, creator of and consultant for TV police series, writer of plays for TV and films, he received the Mystery Writers of America Special award, 1973.

Citation Record: 1 Book

Finnegan's Week - *Single*
Bantam UK (1993)

John FINNEGAN

British Male Amateur operating in England

Norman FORREST 1905-1986 (British)

For writer details see Mrs Palmyra Evangeline PYM

Citation Record: 2 Books

Death Took A Publisher - *First*
Harrap UK (1936); Hillman US (1938)

Death Took A Greek God - *Latest*
Harrap UK (1937); Hillman US (1938)

Insp FINNEY and Graham LOUDON

Insp. FINNEY is called in to investigate the murder of a lecturer at the fictional Hardgate University and finds the usual lot of academic suspects. *Graham LOUDON,* dean of the Law faculty, is a prime suspect and turns sleuth to clear himself.

British Policeman and British Male Amateur operating in England

D M DEVINE 1920-1981 (British)

was the byline under which the author published his first six books.

Writer: Dominic DEVINE

Citation Record: 1 Book

The Devil At Your Elbow - *Only*
Collins UK (1966); Walker US (1967)

Dr Mary FINNEY and Emily COLLINS

are itinerant missionaries working around the town of Brazzaville, in the Congo. *Mary FINNEY,* red-haired and freckled, administers to problems of the flesh while *Emily COLLINS* looks after the soul end of the enterprise. They run into some pretty foul crimes, affecting both departments.

American Female Amateurs operating in Congo

Sidekick: Hooper TOLLIVER

assists in the investigations and narrates the stories.

American Male - Narrator

Matthew HEAD 1907-1985 (American)

was born in Fort Scott, Kansas. He graduated with a BA from the University of Texas, Austin, 1925, received an MA from Yale University, New Haven, Connecticut, 1932, and served in the US Marine Corps, 1943-1945. He is a historian and art critic and has held the post of visiting Professor at the University of Texas and received a doctorate from the University of Rochester, New York, 1973. He is the author, under his real name, of several works on art and art history.

Writer: John Edwin CANADAY

Citation Record: 4 Books

The Devil In The Bush - *First*
Simon & Schuster US (1945)

Murder At The Flea Club - *Last*
Simon & Schuster US (1955); Heinemann UK (1957)

Michael FINSBURY

is a lawyer who tracks down a body that is being moved from place to place in this comic crime novel, an unusual departure in style from one of the great masters of English literature.

British Male Amateur operating in England

Robert Louis STEVENSON (British) and Lloyd OSBOURNE (American)

Robert Louis STEVENSON was born in Edinburgh. He studied engineering for a time at the University of Edinburgh but, to follow the family calling, he transferred to study law, becoming an advocate in 1875. His health was poor and he suffered from consumption, which led him to go to Samoa, where he passed the last five years of his life. A brilliant essayist, poet and one of the masters of the nineteenth-century novel, he wrote several minor novels in conjunction with other authors. *Lloyd OSBOURNE* was, in fact, American, being born in San Francisco, the son of *STEVENSON's* second wife, Fanny Osbourne. He collaborated with his stepfather on several minor works.

Writer: Robert Louis Balfour STEVENSON 1850-1894 and Lloyd OSBOURNE 1869-1947

Citation Record: 1 Book

The Wrong Box - *Only*
Longman UK (1889)

Capt FIREBRACE

British Male Amateur operating in several locations

SEAFARER (British)

Writer: Clarence Hedley BARKER

Citation Record: 4 Books

Captain Firebrace - *First*
Ward, Lock UK (1958)

Smuggler's Pay For Firebrace - *Last*
Ward, Lock UK (1959)

Ian FIRTH and John SMITH

once worked with the British Colonial Police in Africa. Now they run a struggling detective agency in London and are involved in cases of crime and espionage in locales all over the world.

British Male Private Detectives operating in London

Sidekick: Godwin STAMBERGER

American Male - Assistant

Ludovic PETERS 1931-1984 (British)

Writer: Peter Ludwig BRENT

Citation Record: 6 Books

A Snatch Of Music - *First*
Abelard UK (1962); Abelard US (1962)

Riot '71 - *Last*
Hodder & Stoughton UK (1967); Walker US (1967)

Ch of Plce Ira FISCHER

investigates the murders of college girls in American academe.

American Policeman operating in USA

Ralph D CROSS 1931- (American)

Writer: Ralph Donald CROSS

Citation Record: 1 Book

Key To Murder - *Single*
Tower US (1980)

Ida FISCHMAN

Second detective of Nina FISCHMAN

Nina FISCHMAN and Ida FISCHMAN

are daughter and mother respectively. They investigate local murders involving, alas, their friends and neighbours. In later books *Nina FISCHMAN* sleuths mainly on her own.

American Female Amateurs operating in New York

Marissa PIESMAN (American)

See main detective Nina FISCHMAN

Citation Record: 1 Book

Unorthodox Practices - *Single*
Pocket Books US (1989)

Nina FISCHMAN

is a neurotic housing court attorney who appeared in an earlier book with her mother, *Ida FISCHMAN*. Despite her own romantic entanglements she is enmeshed in other peoples' problems, which usually become terminal.

American Female Amateur operating in New York

Marissa PIESMAN (American)

Inventor of one other detective pair Nina FISCHMAN and Ida FISCHMAN

Citation Record: 3 Books

Personal Effects - *First*
Pocket Books US (1991)

Close Quarters - *Latest*
Delacorte US (1994)

Syd FISH

Australian Male Sleuth operating in Australia

Susan GEASON 1946- (Australian)

was born in Tasmania and graduated in Toronto, Canada.

Citation Record: 10 Short Stories in 1 Collection

Shaved Fish - *Collection 1*
Allen AU (1990)

Cal FISHER

American Male Amateur operating in USA

Michael SELLERS 1941- (American)

Citation Record: 1 Book

Cache On The Rocks - *Single*
Doubleday US (1983)

Eric FISHER

Second detective of Joe DUNSTAN

Horne FISHER

is a minor invention of the great master and appears only in short stories, published in the two collections cited.

British Male Amateur operating in England

G K CHESTERTON 1874-1936 (British)

Invented 7 detectives - see Father BROWN

Citation Record: 10 Short Stories in 2 Collections

The Man Who Knew Too Much And Other Stories - *Collection 1*

contains eight *Horne FISHER* stories. The US edition contains three fewer stories than the UK edition.

Short stories - 8
Cassell UK (1922); Harper & Row US (1922)

Thirteen Detectives - *Collection 2*
contains one *Father BROWN* story, two *Horne FISHER* stories, two *Gabriel GALE* stories, two *Rupert and Basil GRANT* stories and two *Mr POND* stories.
Short stories - 2
Xanadu UK (1988); Dodd, Mead US (1986)

Natalie Dauntless FISHER

is lovely to look at, but that shouldn't fool anyone as to her toughness when, in her one appearance, she locks into a caper set up by a petty crook.
American Female Private Detective operating in San Francisco

Gerald LAURENCE 1948- (American)
Citation Record: 1 Book
One Bang-Up Job - *Single*
Berkley US (1989)

Phryne FISHER

Australian Female Sleuth operating in Australia

Kerry GREENWOOD (Australian)
Citation Record: 2 Books
Cocaine Blues - *First*
McPhee AU (1989)
Death By Misadventure - *First**
GM US (1991)
Flying Too High - *Latest*
McPhee AU (1990); GM US (1992)

Lee FISKE

American Male Private Detective operating in USA

Lee ROBERTS 1908-1976 (American)
Writer: Robert Lee MARTIN
Other Byline: Robert MARTIN
Other Detectives:
Andy BRICE
Chad PROCTOR
Dr Clinton SHANNON
Citation Record: 1 Book
The Case Of The Missing Lovers - *Only*
Dodd, Mead US (1957); Foulsham UK (1957)

Ginny FISTOULARI and Mick 'Brew' AXBREWDER

work together, a moral and physical cripple respectively. *Mick AXBREWDER* lost his PI licence after accidentally killing his policeman brother and he now works for *Ginny FISTOULARI*, who lost her hand in a bomb explosion. They dish out much violence to others to show how unhappy they feel about it all.
American Male Private Detective and American Female Private Detective operating in California

Reed STEPHENS 1927- (American)
Writer: Stephen R DONALDSON
Citation Record: 2 Books
The Man Who Killed His Brother - *First*
Ballantine US (1980); Fontana UK (1982)
The Man Who Risked His Partner - *Latest*
Ballantine US (1984); Fontana UK (1985)

Insp FITZGERALD

Second detective of Jerry TRACY

Ed FITZGERALD

is a reporter with a knack of solving murder cases.
American Male Amateur operating in USA

Don FLYNN 1928- (American)
Writer: Donald Robert FLYNN
Citation Record: 5 Books
Murder Isn't Enough - *First*
Walker US (1983); Hale UK (1986)
A Suitcase In Berlin - *Latest*
Walker US (1985)

F Scott 'Ritz' FITZGERALD

Second detective of Ernest 'Rhino' HEMINGWAY

Fiona FITZGERALD

American Female Amateur operating in Washington DC

Warren ADLER 1927- (American)
Citation Record: 3 Books
American Quartet - *First*
Arbor US (1982); Severn UK (1983)
The Ties That Bind - *Latest*
Fine US (1994)

Homer FITZGERALD

American Male Amateur operating in Midwest USA

Charlotte Murray RUSSELL (American)
Invented 3 detectives - see Jane Amanda EDWARDS
Citation Record: 3 Books
The Careless Mrs Christian - *First*
Doubleday US (1949)
June, Moon, And Murder - *Last*
Doubleday US (1952)

Kevin FITZGERALD

American Male Private Detective operating in New York

Tom TOPOR 1938- (American)
Citation Record: 2 Books
Bloodstar - *First*
Norton US (1978)
Coda - *Latest*
Scribner's US (1984)

Frances FITZGIBBON

British Female Amateur operating in England

Anthony PRICE 1928- (British)
Invented 3 detectives - see Dr David AUDLEY
Citation Record: 1 Book
Tomorrow's Ghost - *Single*
Gollancz UK (1979); Doubleday US (1979)

Det Ann FITZHUGH

American Policewoman operating in Washington DC

Carey ROBERTS 1935- (American)
Citation Record: 1 Book
Pray God To Die - *Single*
Avon US (1993)

Eve FITZSIMMONS

is a young copywriter newly employed in an advertising agency. In no time at all she has to discover who killed an unknown woman and inconsiderately left her naked body on the boardroom floor.
American Female Amateur operating in New York

Mary MCMULLEN 1920-1986 (American)
was born in Yonkers, New York. An artist and designer, she is also the author of several admired crime books, which usually do not have a main detective. She received the Mystery Writers of America Edgar Allan Poe award, 1952.
Writer: Mary Reilly WILSON
Inventor of one other detective Kells CAVENAUGH
Citation Record: 1 Book
Stranglehold - *Only*
Harper & Row US (1951)
Death Of Miss X - *Only**
Collins UK (1952)

Luke FITZWILLIAMS

Second detective of Supt BATTLE

Sir Hugh FITZ-HYFFEN

solves a case of 'impossible' murder in a locked room, the only key being in the victim's stomach.
British Male Amateur operating in England

R H W DILLARD 1937- (American)
Writer: Richard Henry Wilde DILLARD
Citation Record: 1 Book
The Book Of Changes - *Only*
Doubleday US (1974)

Det FIX
of New Scotland Yard is the sleuth in this famous Victorian novel.
British Policeman operating in England

Jules VERNE 1828-1905 (French)
was born in Nantes, France, studied law and wrote operatic *libretti*, 1848-1863, until he achieved sudden success with his new brand of fantasy science fiction.
Citation Record: 1 Book
Around The World In Eighty Days - *Only*
Sampson, Low UK (1875)

F

Jeremy FLACK
Second detective of Clarence E HEMINGWAY

Jeremy FLACK and Duncan CAINSFORTH
British Male Amateurs operating in France

John MASKE (British)
Invented 3 detectives - see Duncan CAINSFORTH
Citation Record: 1 Book
The Saint-Malo Mystery - *Only*
Rich UK (1933)

Insp FLAGG
British Policeman operating in England

John CASSELLS 1909-1975 (British)
For writer details see Supt MACNEILL
Inventor of one other detective Ludovic (The Picaroon) SAXON
Citation Record: 31 Books
Murder Comes To Rothesay - *First*
Melrose UK (1946)
Quest For Superintendent Flagg - *Last*
Long UK (1975)

W Murdoch DUNCAN 1909-1975 (British)
Invented 8 detectives - see Supt MACNEILL
Citation Record: 1 Book
Death Beckons Quietly - *Only*
Melrose UK (1946)

Conan FLAGG
is half Irish and half Nez Perce. He is rich, handsome, and was once in US Intelligence. Now he runs a bookstore in Holliday Beach, Oregon, concealing his activities as a private eye. He is ruled, and rightly so, by a feline.
American Male Private Detective operating in Oregon
Sidekick: MEG
is a beautiful blue-point Siamese cat and an honorary sidekick.
Female - Pet Cat

M K WREN 1938- (American)
Writer: Martha Kay RENFROE
Citation Record: 7 Books
Curiosity Didn't Kill The Cat - *First*
Doubleday US (1973); Hale UK (1975)
King Of The Mountain - *Latest*
Doubleday US (1995)

Curt FLAGG
American Male Detective in Pulp Magazines operating in New York

Lester DENT 1904-1959 (American)
Invented 9 detectives - see Chance MALLOY
No citations

Steven FLAGG
British Male Sleuth operating in Germany

Will B DAY (American)
Citation Record: 2 Books
Bravo 9 - *First*
Caravelle US (1967)
The Man From M O D - *Last*
Caravelle US (1968)

Webster FLAGG
is a Negro houseman to a wealthy man. An ex-butler, ex-cook, ex-actor and ex-singer, he is the amateur sleuth in two good novels involving cases affecting the family and household.
American Male Amateur operating in New York

Veronica Parker JOHNS 1907-1988 (American)
Inventor of one other detective Agatha WELCH
Citation Record: 2 Books
Murder By The Day - *First*
Doubleday US (1953)
Servant's Problem - *Last*
Doubleday US (1958)

Tim FLAHERTY
American Male Private Detective operating in New York

Gene HURLEY (American)
Citation Record: 1 Book
Have You Seen This Man? - *Only*
Bobbs US (1944)

Greg FLAMM
British Male Sleuth operating in Greece

Ivor WILSON 1924- (British)
Writer: Ivor Arthur WILSON
Citation Record: 4 Books
But Not For Love - *First*
Collins UK (1962)
Empty Tigers - *Last*
Collins UK (1965)

Jimmy FLANNERY
is a precinct captain in the 27th Ward of the crumbling Chicago Democratic Party machine. Though loyal and, indeed, hidebound by his loyalties, he is remarkably liberal in pursuing the perpetrators of crimes against minority groups and avenging their victims.
American Male Amateur operating in Chicago

Robert CAMPBELL 1927- (American)
Invented 5 detectives - see Jake HATCH
Citation Record: 7 Books
The Junkyard Dog - *First*
Signet US (1986); Arrow UK (1987)
Sauce For The Goose - *Latest*
New American Library US (1994); Coronet UK (1994)

John (The Thunderbolt) FLATCHLEY
American Male Sleuth operating in USA

Johnston MCCULLEY 1883-1958 (American)
Other Detectives:
BLACK STAR
Dalton (The Crimson Clown) PROUSE
Paul SELBON and Peter SELBON
John (The Spider) WARWICK
Citation Record: 2 Books
The Thunderbolt Collects - *First*
Lloyd UK (1921)
The Thunderbolt's Jest - *Last*
Chelsea US (1927)

Peter FLECK
is a hardboiled PI down under and sees a lot of hard action.
Australian Male Private Detective operating in Sydney

Richard CLAPPERTON 1934-

Citation Record: 2 Books

No News On Monday - *First*
Constable UK (1968)

You're A Long Time Dead - *First**
Putnam US (1968)

The Sentimental Kill - *Latest*
Constable UK (1976)

Insp James FLECKER

British Policeman operating in England

Josephine PULLEIN-THOMPSON (British)

Writer: Josephine Mary Wedderburn PULLEIN-THOMPSON

Citation Record: 3 Books

Gin And Murder - *First*
Hammond UK (1959)

Murder Strikes Pink - *Last*
Hammond UK (1963)

Detective FLEET

British Male Detective in Pulp Magazines operating in London

ANON

Citation Record: 1 Book

Detective Fleet Of London - *Only*
Aldine US (?)

Ian FLEMING

Appears with at least two other detectives - see Toby PETERS.

Prof Joanne FLEMING

is the Professor of Criminology at Florida State University and acts as a consultant to the local police. She is involved in the hunt for a psychopathic killer of girls on the campus.

American Female Sleuth operating in USA

Sidekick: Det Ken BLACKBURN
is a useful boyfriend to have around when the game is afoot. He's in the local police force.
American Male - Boyfriend

C Terry CLINE Jr 1935- (American)

was born in Birmingham, Alabama. He is the author of eight criminous books.

Citation Record: 1 Book

Missing Persons - *Single*
Arbor US (1982); Sphere UK (1983)

Laura FLEMING

American Female Amateur operating in USA

Toni L P KELNER (American)

Citation Record: 3 Books

Dead Ringer - *First*
Zebra US (1994)

Trouble Looking For A Place To Happen - *Latest*
Kensington US (1995)

Roger FLEMING

British Male Sleuth operating in several locations

Simon HARVESTER 1910-1875 (British)

Invented 4 detectives - see Dorian SILK

Citation Record: 7 Books

Let Them Prey - *First*
Rich & Cowan UK (1942)

The Vessel May Carry Explosives - *Last*
Jarrolds UK (1951)

FLETCHER

British Male Private Detective operating in England

Grant ALLEN 1848-1899 (British)

Invented 5 detectives - see Nurse Hilda WADE

Citation Record: 1 Book

A Splendid Sin - *Only*
White UK (1896); Buckles US (1899)

FLETCHER

Appears with at least two other detectives - see George STONE.

Irwin 'Fletch' FLETCHER

is a knave, yet an absolutely honest man. He is also, depending on one's views, a marginal sociopath who is thrust into playing the role of a detective in various bizarre situations. He appears also in one book with another of the author's detectives, *Francis Xavier FLYNN.*

American Male Amateur operating in several locations

Gregory MCDONALD 1937- (American)

was born in Shrewsbury, Massachusetts. He took a BA at Harvard University, Cambridge, Massachusetts, 1958, and later worked as a teacher and journalist. He received the Mystery Writers of America Edgar Allan Poe award twice, 1975 and 1977.

Writer: Gregory Christopher MCDONALD

Other Detectives:
Irwin 'Fletch' FLETCHER and Insp Francis Xavier FLYNN
Francis Xavier FLYNN

Citation Record: 9 Books

Fletch - *First*
Bobbs US (1974); Gollancz UK (1976)

Fletch Reflected - *Latest*
Putnam US (1994)

Irwin 'Fletch' FLETCHER and Insp Francis Xavier FLYNN

also appear individually in other books by this author.

American Male Amateurs operating in USA

Gregory MCDONALD 1937- (American)

Invented 3 detectives - see Irwin 'Fletch' FLETCHER

Citation Record: 1 Book

Confess, Fletch - *Single*
Avon US (1976); Gollancz UK (1977)

Jessica FLETCHER

is a delightful and homespun lady, very much a younger version of *Jane MARPLE* in her busybody, clever approach to domestic murder. She appears in novelizations of some of the stories from her long-running TV series, under at least two bylines.

American Female Amateur operating in Maine

James ANDERSON 1936- (British)

Invented 5 detectives - see Insp WILKINS

Citation Record: 2 Books

Hooray For Homicide - *First*
Avon US (1985); Star UK (1985)

The Murder Of Sherlock Holmes - *Latest*
Avon US (1985); Star UK (1985)

Jessica FLETCHER and Donald BAIN (American)

Citation Record: 1 Book

Gin And Daggers - *Single*
McGraw US (1989); Joseph UK (1990)

Johnny FLETCHER and Sam CRAGG

American Male Professional Investigators operating in New York

Frank GRUBER 1904-1969 (American)

was born in Elmer, Minnesota. He was one of the most prolific and admired of the early school of genre fiction in the USA, writing hundreds of short stories for the pulps as well as detective novels. He wrote, in addition, at least twenty-four novels not strictly in the criminous genre but which could loosely be termed thrillers. He was also the author of at least twenty-five screenplays, 1943-1965.

Other Detectives:
Tom ALDER
Otis BEAGLE
Simon LASH
Tom LOGAN
Oliver QUADE
Lt Cdr Frank SARGENT
Jim STRONG

Other Bylines:
Stephen ACRE
Charles K BOSTON
John K VEDDER

Citation Record: 14 Books

The French Key - *First*
Farrar, Straus US (1940); Hale UK (1941)

Swing Low, Swing Dead - *Last*
Belmont US (1964)

Phillip FLETCHER

is an actor who, in previous books by this author, was a murderer. In a novel that is now the first of a series he has risen in the acting profession and is rehearsing the part of Banquo in *Macbeth*. He is involved in the murder of a fellow actor and becomes the main suspect, having to track down the real culprit to clear himself. Apparently reformed, he continued to sleuth in later books.

British Male Amateur operating in England

Simon SHAW (British)

Citation Record: 3 Books

Bloody Instructions - *First*
Gollancz UK (1991)

The Villain Of The Earth - *Latest*
Gollancz UK (1994)

Stephen FLETCHER

British Male Secret Agent operating in Turkey

Geoffrey DAVISON 1927- (British)

Citation Record: 2 Books

The Spy Who Swopped Shoes - *First*
Hale UK (1967)

The Chessboard Spies - *Last*
Hale UK (1969); Roy US (1969)

Virgil FLETCHER

American Male Private Detective operating in New York

George P CRONIN 1933- (American)

Citation Record: 2 Books

Answer From A Dead Man - *First*
Condor US (1978)

Death Of A Delegate - *Latest*
Condor US (1978)

Robert W FLICK

is a Parole Officer who has to respond when his charges get into trouble. Apart from such admirable social work, he likes jazz and beautiful women.

American Male Professional Investigator operating in New York

Jack EHRLICH 1930- (American)

Writer: John Gunter EHRLICH

Citation Record: 3 Books

Parole - *First*
Dell US (1960)

The Girl Cage - *Latest*
Dell US (1967)

Insp Gil FLICKER

British Policeman operating in England

Edward J MILLWARD (British)

Citation Record: 2 Books

The Body Lies - *First*
Harrap UK (1936)

The Aero Clubs Mystery - *Last*
Harrap UK (1939)

Artemus FLINT

appears only in this collection of 'puzzle' short stories.

American Male Amateur operating in USA

Beryl GOLDSWEIG (American)

Citation Record: 35 Short Stories in 1 Collection

Artemus Flint: Detective - *Collection 1*
Scholastic US (1974)

James FLINT

is a lecturer in Economics at an unnamed London college who is led into sleuthing when he finds a photograph of an apparent murder in a book he has borrowed from Westminster Library. The case had been tried and the suspect found not guilty, but he is not satisfied and goes on to investigate the case further.

British Male Amateur operating in England

G D H COLE and Margaret COLE (British)

Invented 6 detectives - see Supt Henry WILSON

Citation Record: 1 Book

The Murder At Crome House - *Only*
Collins UK (1927); Macmillan US (1927)

Peter FLINT

is stated to be a 'detective extraordinary' and appeared in ten stories only in *Nugget Library* in 1913.

American Male Detective in Pulp Magazines operating in USA

Stephen H AGNEY (American)

No citations

Phineas FLINT

American Male Amateur operating in USA

Charles Edmonds WALK 1875- (American)

Citation Record: 2 Books

The Yellow Circle - *First*
McClurg US (1909)

The Time Lock - *Last*
McClurg US (1912)

Thorndyke FLINT

American Male Detective in Pulp Magazines operating in USA

Douglas GREY (American)

No citations

Anatole FLIQUE

Male Sleuth operating in California

Charles G BOOTH 1896-1949 (American)

Writer: Charles Gordon BOOTH

Other Detectives:
MCFEE
Kerry O'NEIL and Gail HOLLISTER

Citation Record: 2 Books

Murder At High Tide - *First*
Morrow US (1930); Hodder & Stoughton UK (1930)

The Cat And The Clock - *Last*
Doubleday US (1935); Cassell UK (1938)

FLOCON

French Male Sleuth operating in France

Arthur GRIFFITHS 1838-1908 (British)

Invented 8 detectives - see Insp FASKE

Citation Record: 1 Book

The Rome Express - *Only*
Milne UK (1896)

Det Const Caz FLOOD

is a feisty young policewoman in this English seaside town, well-known as one of the great watering holes for rogues. She does get a little help from a male colleague or two, but she solves two nasty cases of murder.

British Policewoman operating in Brighton

Alex KEEGAN (British)

Citation Record: 2 Books

Cuckoo - *First*
Headline UK (1994)

Vulture - *Latest*
Headline UK (1995)

Det Insp FLOWER
British Policeman operating in England

Moira FIELD (British)

Citation Record: 2 Books

Foreign Body - *First*
Bles UK (1950); Macmillan US (1951)

Gunpowder Treason And Plot - *Last*
Bles UK (1951)

Sheriff Gus FLOWERS
solves a case of murder in which the victim has been shot in a totally guarded room.

American Policeman operating in Colorado

Tyline PERRY (American)

See main detective Sheriff MACFARLAND

Citation Record: 1 Book

The Never Summer Mystery - *Only*
King US (1932)

Clifford FLUSH
British Male Amateur operating in England

Pamela BRANCH 1920-1967 (British)

Writer: Pamela Jean BRANCH

Citation Record: 2 Books

The Wooden Overcoat - *First*
Hale UK (1951)

Murder Every Monday - *Last*
Hale UK (1954)

Adam FLUTE
runs a detective agency from an apartment in the Bayswater Road, West London – not always strictly legally but in a steadfastly British way.

British Male Private Detective operating in London

Droo LAUNAY 1930- (British)

Writer: Andrew Joseph LAUNAY

Citation Record: 6 Books

She Modelled Her Coffin - *First*
Boardman UK (1961)

The Scream - *Last*
Boardman UK (1965)

Policeman FLYNN
American Policeman operating in USA

Elliott FLOWER 1863-1920 (American)

Citation Record: 25 Short Stories in 1 Collection

Policeman Flynn - *Collection 1*
Century US (1902)

Det FLYNN and Det TANNER
American Policemen operating in Los Angeles

Michael NEWTON 1951- (American)

See main detective Jon STEEL

Citation Record: 2 Books

Blood Sport - *First*
Dell US (1990)

Slay Ride - *Latest*
Dell US (1990)

Errol FLYNN
Second detective of Toby PETERS

Francis Xavier FLYNN
is an eccentric cop and international spy to boot. He appears also in books with another of the author's detectives, *Irwin FLETCHER.*

American Policeman operating in Boston

Gregory MCDONALD 1937- (American)

Invented 3 detectives - see Irwin 'Fletch' FLETCHER

Citation Record: 3 Books

Flynn - *First*
Avon US (1977); Gollancz UK (1978)

Flynn's In - *Latest*
Mysterious Press US (1984); Gollancz UK (1985)

Insp Francis Xavier FLYNN
Second detective of Irwin 'Fletch' FLETCHER

Judith McMonigle FLYNN
American Female Amateur operating in USA

Sidekick: COUSIN RENIE
is always so called and is the sleuth's constant companion and confidante.
American Female - Cousin

Mary DAHEIM (American)

See main detective Emma LORD

Citation Record: 7 Books

Just Desserts - *First*
Avon US (1991)

Major Vices - *Latest*
Avon US (1995)

Laura FLYNN
runs the Flynn Detective Agency in London.

British Female Private Detective operating in London

Lesley GRANT-ADAMSON 1942- (British)

See main detective Rain MORGAN

Citation Record: 1 Book

Flynn - *Single*
Faber UK (1991)

Peter FLYNN
has retired from the San Francisco Police Department because of extensive injuries to his face, received in a terrorist attack. Now, as a PI, he works on a case involving drugs, homosexuals, the Mafia and lots of girls.

American Male Private Detective operating in San Francisco

G P KENNEALY (American)

Writer: G P KENNEALY

Other Byline: Jerry KENNEALY

Citation Record: 1 Book

Nobody Wins - *Single*
Manor US (1977)

Terry FLYNN
Second detective of Karen KOVAC

Alan FOAM
solves the 'impossible' disappearance of a woman from a guarded house.

British Male Amateur

Ethel Lina WHITE 1887-1944 (British)

See main detective Iris CARR

Citation Record: 1 Book

She Faded Into Air - *Only*
Collins UK (1941); Harper & Row US (1941)

FOAMES
is a *Sherlock HOLMES* parody.

British Male Professional Amateur operating in England

Sidekick: SQUATSON
is his parody *WATSON*-like assistant.
British Male - Assistant

Ray RUSSELL 1924- (American)

See main detective Julian TRASK

Citation Record: 1 Selected Short Story

The Murder Of Conan Doyle - *Parody 1*
appeared in the May number.
Playboy US (1955)

Sgt FOGERTY and Philip WARING
When the murder of a Professor of Chemistry occurs at an

F

unnamed US university, *Sgt FOGERTY*, of the local Homicide Squad is called in, but he needs the help of *Philip WARING*, a junior colleague of the victim, to solve the case.
American Policeman and American Male Amateur operating in USA

John MILLER 1906-1980 (American)
was born in Trenton, New Jersey. A professional chemist, he became an associate Professor of Biochemistry in Chicago. A writer in several genres, he wrote only this one crime novel.
Writer: Joseph SAMACHSON
Citation Record: 1 Book
Murder Of A Professor - *Only*
Putnam US (1937); Hale UK (1937)

F

Prof FOLEY
Irish Male Amateur operating in Eire

Michael KENYON 1931- (British)
Invented 6 detectives - see Insp/Ch Insp Harry PECKOVER
Citation Record: 1 Book
May You Die In Ireland - *Only*
Collins UK (1965); Morrow US (1965)

Det FOLEY
is a persistent detective trying to get at the truth in this one haunting book.
American Policeman operating in Boston

George V HIGGINS 1939- (American)
was born in Brockton, Massachusetts. He was educated at Rockland High School, Massachusetts, and took degrees at Boston College, 1961, at Stanford University, California, 1962 and 1965, and at Boston Law School, Brighton, Massachusetts, 1967. Admitted to the US Bar, 1967, he has held many important legal posts, including that of US Attorney, has contributed articles and columns to newspapers and has taught at law schools and universities.
Writer: George Vincent HIGGINS
Inventor of one other detective Jerry KENNEDY
Citation Record: 1 Book
The Friends Of Eddie Coyle - *Only*
Knopf US (1972); Secker & Warburg UK (1972)

John FOLEY
is an ex-cop and is now a private eye. He is hired by a union boss to investigate the disappearance of his daughter, a junior at the local university.
American Male Private Detective operating in USA

Henry WOODFIN (American)
was born in Buffalo, New York.
Citation Record: 1 Book
Virginia's Thing - *Only*
Harper & Row US (1968)

Supt FOLLY
is a plain man's police detective in a series that this prolific author published under the *YORK* byline between 1941 and 1960. The cases are good solid crime stories without too much of the author's usual addiction to racy adventure to detract the attention.
British Policeman operating in England

Jeremy YORK 1908-1973 (British)
For writer details see Insp Roger 'Handsome' WEST
Inventor of one other detective Insp KENNEDY
Citation Record: 3 Books
Find The Body - *First*
Melrose UK (1945); Macmillan US (1967)
Close The Door On Murder - *Last*
was first published by *Melrose* (UK 1948), without *FOLLY.*
McKay US (1973)

Danny FONTAINE
was called *Mike FONTAINE* in the original hardcover edition of this book (qv), entitled *AS BAD AS I AM.*
American Male Private Detective operating in New York

William ARD 1922-1960 (American)
Invented 5 detectives - see Timothy DANE
Citation Record: 2 Books
When She Was Bad - *First*
Dell US (1960)
Wanted: Danny Fontaine - *Last*
was originally published by *Rinehart* (US 1959) entitled *AS BAD AS I AM*, with *Mike FONTAINE* as the detective.
Dell US (1960)

Mike FONTAINE
appeared in the book cited and was then reworked as *Danny FONTAINE.*
American Male Private Detective operating in New York
Sidekick: Barney GLINES
is both sidekick and partner to *FONTAINE.*
American Male - Partner

William ARD 1922-1960 (American)
Invented 5 detectives - see Timothy DANE
Citation Record: 1 Book
As Bad As I Am - *Only*
is a reworking of an earlier work called *Hell is a City*, which featured this author's main series detective, *Timothy DANE*, and was published by *Rinehart* (US 1955).
Rinehart US (1959); Boardman UK (1960)

Solange FONTAINE
assists her father in a police laboratory near Paris and is a herself half English, half French. Having the 'peculiar gift of feeling the presence of evil', she solves a number of cases, but is perhaps fortunate in usually receiving some supernatural help.
French-British Female Professional Investigator operating in Paris

F Tennyson JESSE 1888-1958 (British)
studied painting in Newlyn, Cornwall, then became a reporter and reviewer for several newspapers. He wrote only three genre novels but was the author of nine other novels and at least nine plays, most of which were produced on stage in London and elsewhere.
Writer: Fryniwyd Tennyson JESSE
Citation Record: 5 Short Stories in 1 Collection
The Solange Stories - *Collection 1*
Heinemann UK (1931); Macmillan US (1931)

Sheriff (temporary) Max FONTANA
is the head of the Fire Department and the temporary sheriff in a small town near Seattle.
American Policeman operating in Washington DC

Earl W EMERSON 1948- (American)
See main detective Thomas BLACK
Citation Record: 1 Book
Black Hearts And Slow Dancing - *Single*
Morrow US (1988)

Ah FOO
Chinese Male Amateur operating in England

Cecil BISHOP (British)
Inventor of one other detective Chinese BROWN
Citation Record: 1 Book
Adventures Of Ah Foo, The Chinese Sherlock Holmes - *Only*
Mitre UK (1943)

Mark FORAN
is a classic type of world-weary private eye, tough but innocent and honest, who faces the classic dilemma – easy money or his own conscience.
American Male Private Detective operating in Las Vegas

W T BALLARD 1903-1980 (American)
Invented 4 detectives - see Bill LENNOX
Citation Record: 1 Book
Murder Las Vegas Style - *Only*
Tower US (1973)

Horton FORBES

is on holiday when he stumbles across murder, which the local police dismiss as death by natural causes. He finds otherwise.
British Male Amateur operating in England

John HUNTINGDON 1884- (British)
!See Appendix 2.
Writer: Gerald William PHILLIPS
Citation Record: 1 Book
The Seven Black Chessmen - *Only*
Howe UK (1928); Holt US (1928)

Julian FORBES

American Male Amateur operating in Chicago

James Michael ULLMAN (American)
Other Detectives:
Max FULLER — Michael Dane JAMES
Citation Record: 1 Book
Lady On Fire - *Only*
Simon & Schuster US (1968); Cassell UK (1969)

Rusty FORBES

American Male Private Detective operating in Chicago

Milton K OZAKI 1913- (American)
Invented 3 detectives - see Prof CALDWELL
Citation Record: 1 Book
Dressed To Kill - *Only*
Graphic US (1954)

Ch FORD

American Policeman operating in USA

Hillary WAUGH 1920- (American)
Invented 7 detectives - see Ch Fred FELLOWS
Citation Record: 1 Book
Last Seen Wearing... - *Only*
Doubleday US (1952); Gollancz UK (1953)

Alan FORD

American Male Amateur operating in USA

Carolyn WELLS 1870-1942 (American)
Invented 7 detectives - see Fleming STONE
Citation Record: 4 Books
The Bride Of A Moment - *First*
Doran US (1916); Hodder & Stoughton UK (1920)
Murder Will In - *Last*
Lippincott US (1942)

Ashton FORD

is ex-Navy and has independent means. Now a PI, he is given to resolving his cases mainly by brute force. However, he is psychic to boot, a useful attribute, it must be admitted, and one that makes him a formidable opponent for your average villain, who is generally unacquainted with such potent forces.
American Male Private Detective operating in USA

Don PENDLETON 1927- (American)
Invented 3 detectives - see Joe COPP
Citation Record: 6 Books
Eye To Eye - *First*
Popular Library US (1986)
Heart To Heart - *Latest*
Popular Library US (1988)

Brad FORD

was once head of a Second World War Commando outfit and now runs a West End agency. He has the qualities of all the world's best detectives, but, alas, not the plots to go with them.
British Male Private Detective operating in London

Hank HOBSON 1908- (British)
Writer: Harry HOBSON
Other Byline: Hank JANSON
Citation Record: 5 Books
The Gallant Affair - *First*
Cassell UK (1957)
Beyond Tolerance - *Last*
Cassell UK (1960)

'Doc' FORD

American Male Amateur operating in Florida

Randy Wayn WHITE (American)
Citation Record: 1 Book
The Man Who Invented Florida
St Martin's US (1993)

Mr FORDHAM

appeared in a number of short stories, in one of which he solves the mystery of a robbery from a locked room.
British Male Amateur operating in England

Hubert GRAYLE (British)
Citation Record: 1 Selected Short Story
Three White Hairs
In 'Ludgate Magazine' UK (1893)

Det Ch Insp John FORDHAM

is a high-ranking cop who uses unofficial and even corrupt methods to pursue his own view of justice.
British Policeman operating in England

G F NEWMAN 1945- (British)
Invented 3 detectives - see Insp Terry SNEED
Citation Record: 1 Book
The Guvnor - *Only*
Hart Davis MacGibbon UK (1972)
Trade-Off - *Only**
Dell US (1979)

Sir Brian FORDINGHAME

is the head of a special department in British Intelligence and has to deal with all kinds of monstrous crimes against the nation inspired by a megalomaniac medical genius called Paul Vivanti.
British Male Professional Investigator operating in England

Sydney HORLER 1888-1954 (British)
Invented 20 detectives - see Sir Harker BELLAMY
Citation Record: 2 Books
The Murder Mask - *First*
Readers Library UK (1930)
The Prince Of Plunder - *Last*
Hodder & Stoughton UK (1934); Little, Brown US (1934)

Sir Brian FORDINGHAME and Baron VESSELOFFSKY

British Male Professional Investigator operating in England

Sydney HORLER 1888-1954 (British)
Invented 20 detectives - see Sir Harker BELLAMY
Citation Record: 1 Book
False-Face - *Only*
Hodder & Stoughton UK (1926); Doran US (1926)

Barney FORGE and Dr St George PEACHY

American Male Amateurs operating in Washington DC

Richard STARNES 1922- (American)
See main detective Maxwell SPEED
Citation Record: 3 Books

F

The Other Body In Grant's Tomb - *First*
Lippincott US (1951); Muller UK (1950)

Another Mug For The Bier - *Last*
Lippincott US (1951); Muller UK (1952)

Dan FORREST

American Male Sleuth operating in Washington DC

William BEECHCROFT 1924- (American)

Writer: William Finn HALLSTEAD

Citation Record: 2 Books

Chain Of Vengeance - *First*
Dodd, Mead US (1986)

Secret Kills - *Latest*
Dodd, Mead US (1988); Hale UK (1989)

F

Andrew FORRESTER Jr

does not seem to be identical with *Andrew FORRESTER*, created by the same author.

British Male Private Detective operating in England

Andrew FORRESTER Jr (British)

Invented 3 detectives - see Andrew FORRESTER

Citation Record: 13 Short Stories in 1 Collection

The Revelations Of A Private Detective - *Collection 1*
Ward, Lock UK (1863)

Andrew FORRESTER

does not seem to be identical with *Andrew FORRESTER Jr*, created by the same author.

British Male Professional Investigator operating in England

Andrew FORRESTER Jr (British)

Other Detectives:
Andrew FORRESTER Jr   Mrs GLADDEN

Citation Record: 1 Collection

Secret Service; Or, Recollections Of A City Detective - *Collection 1*
contains an uncounted number of short stories.
Ward, Lock UK (1864)

David FORRESTER

Second detective of Supt REDARREL

Dr Lily FORRESTER

is a District Attorney. Promoted to head a Sex Crimes Division, she is involved in an investigation of rape, which leads to an attack on herself and her daughter. She takes the law into her own hands.

American Female Amateur operating in USA

Nancy Taylor ROSENBERG (American)

was a photographer's model before she studied criminology and joined the police force in California as a probation officer.

Inventor of one other detective Judge Lara SANDERSTONE

Citation Record: 1 Book

Mitigating Circumstances - *Single*
Dutton US (1993); Orion UK (1993)

Michael FORRESTER and Theresa FORRESTER

American Male Professional Investigator and American Female Professional Investigator operating in USA

Frances Shelley WEES 1902- (American)

Citation Record: 2 Books

The Maestro Murders - *First*
Mystery League US (1931)

Detectives Ltd - *First**
Eyre & Spottiswoode UK (1933)

The Mystery Of The Creeping Man - *Last*
McCrae, Smith US (1931); Eyre & Spottiswoode UK (1934)

Robert FORRESTER

American Male Amateur operating in Chicago

Paul THORNE and Mabel THORNE (American)

Inventor of one other detective Dave MORGAN

Citation Record: 1 Book

The Secret Toll - *Only*
Dodd, Mead US (1922)

Theresa FORRESTER

Second detective of Michael FORRESTER

Andrew FORSTER

is a member of the famous Bow Street police and the detective in this Victorian magazine story.

British Policeman operating in London

ANON

Citation Record: 1 Book

Who Killed Peter Trueman? - *Only*
is a short novel that appeared in *The Halfpenny Surprise Illustrated*, Volume XL, Number 286.
Edwin J Brett UK (1900)

Robert FORSYTHE and Abigail 'Sandy' SANDERSON

Robert SANDERSON is a barrister who has a slightly shady past and, indeed, is never seen to practise. However, he and his secretary, *Abigail SANDERSON*, are so well thought of by the police because of their special skills that they are drawn by them into difficult cases. As the series continues, one or other of the two plays a dominant role in the proceedings.

British Male Amateur and British Female Amateur operating in England

E X GIROUX 1924- (Canadian)

was born in Elmira, New York, and educated at Napanee Collegiate Institute, Ontario, Canada, 1939-1942.

Writer: Doris SHANNON

Citation Record: 8 Books

A Death For Adonis - *First*
St Martin's US (1984); Hale UK (1986)

A Death For A Double - *Latest*
St Martin's US (1990)

John FORTESCUE

British Male Amateur operating in England

Charles BRANDON 1895- (British)

Writer: Charles Melville BRANDON

Citation Record: 3 Book

The Mystery Of King's Everard - *First*
Jenkins UK (1924)

The Phantom Musketeer - *Last*
Jenkins UK (1929)

Chester FORTUNE

British Male Sleuth

Thomas H STONE 1936- (British)

For writer details see Terry HARKNETT

Citation Record: 2 Books

Dead Set - *First*
New English Library UK (1972)

One Horse Race - *Last*
New English Library UK (1972)

Dan FORTUNE

is perhaps the finest creation of this prolific and highly regarded author. *Dan FORTUNE* is a New York private detective with an office on 28th Street in Manhattan. He is one-armed, having lost a limb as a juvenile delinquent, which gives him an extraordinary sense of anxiety when mixing with the violence that besets his many cases. He is portrayed as essentially a modern figure in the sense of being unusually concerned with the social implications of crime and his own work. His cases are complex studies of character and facets of American life as well as being hard-hitting and well plotted.

American Male Private Detective operating in New York/Los Angeles

Michael COLLINS 1924- (American)

was born in St Louis, Missouri. He was educated at several schools and colleges, graduating with a BA in Chemistry from Hofstra University, Hempstead, New York, 1949, and an MA in Journalism from Syracuse University, New York, 1951. He served in the US Army, 1943-1946, winning several major battle honours. He became the editor of various chemical industry journals and a full-time writer after 1960. He received the Mystery Writers of America Edgar Allan Poe award, 1968, and the Private Eye Writers of America Lifetime Achievement Award, 1988.

For writer details see Kane JACKSON

Citation Record: 16 Books

Act Of Fear - *First*
Dodd, Mead US (1967); Joseph UK (1968)

Cassandra In Red - *Latest*
Fine US (1992)

Hannibal FORTUNE

sleuths in the distant future, around 2500.

American Male Sleuth operating in Space

Larry MADDOCK 1931- (American)

Writer: Jack Owen JARDINE

Citation Record: 4 Books

The Flying Saucer Gambit - *First*
Ace US (1966)

The Time Trap Gambit - *Last*
Ace US (1969)

Dr Reginald FORTUNE

is a police surgeon, attached to the London CID, who uses his skills at observation and inference to help the police solve many a case. Plump and given to over-eating and over-drinking, he says of his methods, 'Just look at the facts, imagination is not needed'. Indeed ideology is conspicuously lacking in his books and *Reggie FORTUNE* is a prime example of the middle stratum of British Golden Age detection. His background is deliberately obscure and almost all we know about him is that he likes designing rose-gardens and loves children, although he does not seem to have any of his own. His greatest characteristic is his blistering anger at injustice, which he combines with a belief that the police force is totally unimaginative and inefficient. Though he was certainly no *Sherlock HOLMES*, he was considered to be the most popular of all English detectives in the inter-war years, perhaps because he fitted best the English conception of a decent, bluff chap – not an irritating know-all like *Peter WIMSEY* or an aristocratic buffoon like *Albert CAMPION* and certainly not a bumptious foreigner, however nice, like the insufferably egotistical *Hercule POIROT*. However, he too speaks in the conventional upper-class slang that British authors irritatingly gave their detectives at the time, dropping his 'g's and frequently betraying high emotion by saying things like 'My only aunt!'. The readers loved it and to prove it, *FORTUNE* had the distinction of appearing in more contemporary short story collections than any other British detective had done.

British Male Professional Investigator operating in England

Sidekick: Insp UNDERWOOD

represents the official side of the police, but he never seems to solve a case to which *FORTUNE* is called.

British Male - Assistant

H C BAILEY 1878-1961 (British)

was born in London and took a degree at Oxford. He was a sometime drama critic and later war correspondent for the London *Daily Telegraph* and wrote many novels outside the mystery and crime genre. He rarely used his forenames and his books were all published under the *H C BAILEY* byline.

Writer: Henry Christopher BAILEY

Other Detectives:
Raoul BOMFORTUNE
Joshua CLUNK
The Hon Victoria PUMPHREY

Citation Record: 8 Books 83 Short Stories in 12 Collections

Shadow On The Wall - *First*
Gollancz UK (1934); Doubleday US (1934)

Saving A Rope - *Last*
Macdonald UK (1948)

Save A Rope - *Last**
Doubleday US (1948)

Call Mr Fortune - *Collection 1*
Short stories - 6
Methuen UK (1920); Dutton US (1921)

Mr Fortune's Practice - *Collection 2*
Short stories - 7
Methuen UK (1923); Dutton US (1924)

Mr Fortune's Trials - *Collection 3*
Short stories - 6
Methuen UK (1925); Dutton US (1926)

Mr Fortune, Please - *Collection 4*
Short stories - 6
Methuen UK (1928); Dutton US (1928)

Mr Fortune Speaking - *Collection 5*
Short stories - 7
Ward, Lock UK (1929); Dutton US (1931)

Mr Fortune Explains - *Collection 6*
Short stories - 8
Ward, Lock UK (1930); Dutton US (1931)

Case For Mr Fortune - *Collection 7*
Short stories - 8
Ward, Lock UK (1932); Doubleday US (1932)

Mr Fortune Wonders - *Collection 8*
Short stories - 8
Ward, Lock UK (1933); Doubleday US (1933)

Mr Fortune Objects - *Collection 9*
Short stories - 6
Gollancz UK (1935); Doubleday US (1935)

A Clue For Mr Fortune - *Collection 10*
Short stories - 6
Gollancz UK (1936); Doubleday US (1936)

This Is Mr Fortune - *Collection 11*
Short stories - 6
Gollancz UK (1938); Doubleday US (1938)

Mr Fortune Here - *Collection 12*
Short stories - 9
Gollancz UK (1940); Doubleday US (1940)

Dr Reginald FORTUNE

Appears with at least two other detectives - see Sherlock HOLMES.

Temple FORTUNE

British Sleuth operating in England

T C H JACOBS 1899-1976 (British)

Invented 8 detectives - see Ch Insp BARNARD

Citation Record: 19 Books

Dangerous Fortune - *First*
Paul UK (1949)

House Of Horror - *Last*
Hale UK (1969)

Guy FOSSE

British Male Sleuth

Elliott CANNON (British)

Writer: Arthur ELLIOTT-CANNON

Other Byline: Nicholas FORDE

Citation Record: 2 Books

The Dumbo Dossier - *First*
Hale UK (1975)

The Big Chip - *Latest*
Hale UK (1976)

Gerald FOSTER

British Male Amateur operating in London

F

Fergus HUME 1859-1932 (British)

Invented 24 detectives - see Insp Samuel GORBY

Citation Record: 1 Book

The Girl From Malta - *Only*
Hansom Cab Publishing Co UK (1889)

Harry FOSTER

American Male Sleuth operating in USA/Haiti

Alan CULLIMORE (American)

Citation Record: 2 Books

A Good Place To Die - *First*
Tor US (1988)

A Bad Day In The Bahamas - *Latest*
Tor US (1989)

Nat FOSTER

American Male Detective in Pulp Magazines operating in USA

Harry ROCKWOOD 1859-1932 (American)

Invented 14 detectives - see Clarice DYKE

Citation Record: 1 Book

Nat Foster, The Boston Detective - *Only*
Ogilvie US (1883)

FOUR JUST MEN

are a group of four men intent on handing out private and harsh justice to criminals whom the police, for various reasons, are unable to touch. (Sometimes there were only three.)

British Male Amateurs operating in England

Edgar WALLACE 1875-1932 (British)

Invented 28 detectives - see J G REEDER

Citation Record: 3 Books 23 Short Stories in 2 Collections

The Four Just Men - *First*
Tallis UK (1905); Maynard US (1906)

The Three Just Men - *Last*
Hodder & Stoughton UK (1925); Doubleday US (1929)

The Law Of The Four Just Men - *Collection 1*
Short stories - 10
Hodder & Stoughton UK (1921)

Again The Three Just Men - *Collection 1**
Two different collections with this title were published.
Doubleday US (1933); Hodder & Stoughton UK (1928)

The Law Of The Three Just Men - *Collection 2*
Short stories - 13
Doubleday US (1931)

Sgt FOWELL

of the CID investigates murder in Gay Town Film Studios.

British Policeman operating in England

Samuel HOLMES (British)

Citation Record: 1 Book

Fade Into Murder - *Only*
Shakespeare Head UK (1947)

Dan FOWLER

is an FBI agent (created originally by George Fielding Eliot in 1936) who appears in twenty-six stories published in the early 1940s under several bylines used by various authors.

American Male Professional Investigator operating in Kansas/Rhode Island

Major George F ELIOT 1894- 1971 (American)

Writer: George Fielding ELIOT

Citation Record: 3 Books

Federal Bullets - *First*
Cassell US (1946); Caslon UK (1946)

The Navy Spy Murders - *Last*
Dodger UK (1947)

C K M SCANLON (American)

was a byline sometimes used by this prolific author for stories he wrote for the pulps. Particularly, he used it to relate the cases and adventures of *Dan FOWLER.*

For writer details see Richard Curtis (The Phantom) VAN LOAN

Inventor of one other detective The MASKED DETECTIVE

No citations

Grant FOWLER

American Male Sleuth operating in several locations

Paul RICHARDS

Writers: John J MESSMAN and George SNYDER

Citation Record: 1 Book

Our Spacecraft Is Missing! - *Only*
Award US (1970)

Paul RICHARDS

Writers: George SNYDER and Daniel Thomas STREIB 1928-

Citation Record: 1 Book

The President Has Been Kidnapped! - *Only*
Award US (1971)

Paul RICHARDS

Writers: Daniel Thomas STREIB 1928- and Chet CUNNINGHAM 1928-

Citation Record: 1 Book

Moscow At High Noon Is The Target - *Only*
Award US (1973)

John FOWLER

is a member of the English department of Dorset University, a fictional, high-ranking institution. He is suspected of the murder of a local businessman and has to hide out until he can discover the real killer and clear himself.

American Male Amateur operating in New England

Herbert DALMAS (American)

Citation Record: 1 Book

The Fowler Formula - *Only*
Doubleday US (1967); Gollancz UK (1968)

Timothy FOWLER

American Male Sleuth operating in New York

Colver HARRIS 1908- (American)

Writer: Anne COLVER

Citation Record: 4 Books

Hide And Go Seek - *First*
Minton Balch UK (1933)

Murder In Amber - *Last*
Hillman-Curl US (1938)

Tecumseh FOX

was this great author's early attempt at a PI. He looks rather intellectual for the job and operates from his own farm in Westchester County.

American Male Private Detective operating in New York

Rex STOUT 1886-1975 (American)

Invented 6 detectives - see Nero WOLFE

Citation Record: 3 Books

Double For Death - *First*
Farrar, Straus US (1939); Collins UK (1940)

The Broken Vase - *Last*
Farrar, Straus US (1941); Collins UK (1942)

Det Ch Supt Thomas FOX

is a shrewd, elegant, tough detective at the Yard, heading at least one part of Scotland Yard's select Flying Squad. The books are semi-procedurals, with *Thomas FOX* always satisfactorily in the lead. He appears also in one book with the author's other detective, *Supt John GAFFNEY.*

British Policeman operating in London

Sidekick: Det Insp Jack GILROY

is part of Scotland Yard's Criminal Intelligence Branch and is transferred to work with *FOX* in at least one book. He is tall, ascetic and looks not at all like a policeman.

British Male - Colleague

Graham ISON (British)

was, before retirement, a Chief Superintendent with the CID at Scotland Yard. His novels show a superb knowledge of his background.

Other Detectives:
Supt John GAFFNEY
Supt John GAFFNEY and Det Ch Supt Thomas FOX
Citation Record: 3 Books
Lead Me To The Slaughter - *First*
Macmillan UK (1990)
The Taming Of Tango Harris - *Latest*
Macmillan UK (1993)

Det Ch Supt Thomas FOX
Second detective of Supt John GAFFNEY

Charles FOX-BROWNE
solves a case of 'impossible' murder in which a man is drowned in a locked room.
British Male Amateur operating in England

Martin PORLOCK 1899-1981 (British)
Writer: Philip MACDONALD
Citation Record: 1 Book
Mystery At Friar's Pardon - *Only*
Collins UK (1931); Doubleday US (1932)

Supt Francis FOY
British Policeman operating in England

Lionel BLACK 1910-1980 (British)
Invented 3 detectives - see Kate THEOBALD
Citation Record: 3 Books
Breakaway - *First*
Collins UK (1970)
Flood - *First**
Stein & Day US (1971)
The Life And Death Of Peter Wade - *Last*
Collins UK (1973); Stein & Day US (1974)

Supt Heldon FOYLE
was not too distinguished a detective, but, as he rather wittily said in his own defence, he 'rarely wore a dressing gown and never played the violin'.
British Policeman operating in England

Frank FROEST (British)
was a sometime Superintendent in the CID.
Citation Record: 1 Book
The Grell Mystery - *Only*
Nash UK (1913); Clode US (1914)

Sgt Finnbar FRALEIGH
American Policeman operating in California

Joseph D MCNAMARA (American)
is a sometime Chief of Police in San Jose.
Citation Record: 3 Books
The First Detective - *First*
Crown US (1984); Collins UK (1985)
The Blue Mirage - *Latest*
Morrow US (1990)

Reynold FRAME
is a young newspaperman who is around when murders occur. The cases usually have a historical background.
American Male Amateur operating in New England

Herbert BREAN 1907-1963 (American)
was born in Detroit, Michigan, and graduated with a BA from the University of Michigan, Ann Arbor. He was a newspaperman and editor, working on Detroit papers.
Writer: Herbert J BREAN
Other Detectives:
William DEACON   Marty MALONE
Citation Record: 4 Books
Wilders Walk Away - *First*
Morrow US (1948); Heinemann UK (1949)
The Clock Strikes Thirteen - *Last*
Morrow US (1952); Heinemann UK (1954)

FRANCIS
is probably the best characterised animal detective (rather chillingly so) yet to have appeared in the criminous literature. He is a true detective, narrating his own remarkable sleuthing exploits in books that are totally non-anthropomorphic and completely feline in orientation.
Male Cat

Akif PIRINCCI (Turkish)
now lives in Germany and is an expert on cats.
Citation Record: 2 Books
Felidae - *First*
is a translation from the German.
Fourth Estate UK (1991)
Felidae On The Road - *Latest*
is a translation from the German.
Fourth Estate UK (1994)

Cesar Augustus FRANCK
American Male Amateur operating in Cincinnati

A M PYLE 1945- (American)
Writer: Albert M PYLE
Citation Record: 3 Books
Trouble Making Toys - *First*
Walker US (1985)
Pure Murder - *Latest*
St Martin's US (1990)

Benjamin FRANKLIN
is, indeed, the eighteenth-century American scientist. It is known, of course, that he possessed a high degree of curiosity about natural phenomena as well as taking part, later, in politics and so it is not surprising that at least three authors have used him as a sleuth, variously in Philadelphia and London.
American Male Amateur operating in Philadelphia

Robert Lee HALL 1941- (American)
Adopter of one other detective Sherlock HOLMES
Citation Record: 5 Books
Benjamin Franklin Takes The Case - *First*
St Martin's US (1988)
Benjamin Franklin And A Case Of Artful Murder - *Latest*
is set in England in the eighteenth century.
St Martin's US (1994)

Theodore MATHIESON 1913- (American)
Invented 3 detectives - see Leonardo DA VINCI
Citation Record: 1 Book
The Devil And Ben Franklin - *Only*
is set in Philadelphia in 1734.
Simon & Schuster US (1961)

Donald ZOCHERT 1938- (American)
See main detective Nick CAINE
Citation Record: 1 Collection
Murder In The Hellfire Club - *Collection 1*
Holt US (1978)

Ev FRANKLIN
appears also in a book with the author's other detective, *Hugh MORRISON.*
American Male Sleuth operating in New York

Frank ORENSTEIN 1919- (American)
Writer: Frank Everett ORENSTEIN
Other Detectives:
Ev FRANKLIN and Hugh MORRISON
Hugh MORRISON
Citation Record: 3 Books
Murder On Madison Avenue - *First*
St Martin's US (1983)
Paradise Of Death - *Latest*
St Martin's US (1988)

F

F

Ev FRANKLIN and Hugh MORRISON

also appear individually in other books by this author.

American Male Sleuths operating in New York

Frank ORENSTEIN 1919- (American)

Invented 3 detectives - see Ev FRANKLIN

Citation Record: 1 Book

The Man In The Grey Flannel Shroud - *Single*
St Martin's US (1984)

Margo FRANKLIN and Philip SPENCE

American Female Amateur and American Male Amateur operating in Chicago

Jerry JENKINS 1949- (American)

Invented 3 detectives - see Jennifer GREY

Citation Record: 11 Books

Margo - *First*
Moody US (1979)

The Woman At The Window - *First**
Nelson US (1991)

Lyssa - *Latest*
Moody US (1984)

Kit FRANKLYN

is a psychologist who works for the police on criminal cases.

American Female Professional Investigator operating in New Orleans

D J DONALDSON (American)

Citation Record: 2 Books

Blood On The Bayou - *First*
St Martin's US (1991)

No Mardi Gras For The Dead - *Latest*
Worldwide US (1995)

Arabella FRANT

British Female Amateur operating in England

Diana FEARON (British)

Citation Record: 2 Books

Death Before Breakfast - *First*
Hale UK (1959)

Murder-On-Thames - *Last*
Hale UK (1960)

Bow Street Runner FRASER

Second detective of Bow St Runner BRADSHAW

Alan FRASER

appeared in a large number of books, said by the author to have been based on real crimes.

British Male Private Detective operating in England/Czechoslovakia

Hugh DESMOND 1903- (British)

See main detective Insp DUNNING

Citation Record: 33 Books

The Hand Of Vengeance - *First*
Wright UK (1945)

We Walk With Death - *Last*
Wright UK (1968)

Bart FRASER

is a solicitor who becomes involved in an investigation in the wine trade, during which one crime leads to another, ending in murder.

British Male Amateur operating in England

Douglas STEWART (British)

Citation Record: 1 Book

Cellars' Market - *Single*
Collins UK (1983)

Donald FRASER

solves a case of murder by stabbing in a locked room.

Male Amateur operating in South Africa

Henry JUTA 1857-1939 (South African)

Writer: Sir Henry Hubert JUTA

Citation Record: 1 Book

Off The Track - *Only*

There would seem to be some mystery about this book. Although two sources give it as shown, there is a book with the same title that appeared in South Africa in 1895 by an author called Jacques Aanroy and published by *Juta*, which is the name of the author given in this citation.

Hutchinson UK (1925)

Insp Geoffrey FRASER

British Policeman operating in England

Elliott BAILEY 1887- (British)

Citation Record: 3 Books

Death In Quiet Places - *First*
Eldon UK (1933)

Revenge At Nightfall - *Last*
Eldon UK (1937)

James FRASER

British Male Sleuth

James WOOD 1918- (British)

Writer: James Alexander Fraser WOOD

Citation Record: 5 Books

The Sealer - *First*
Hutchinson UK (1959); Vanguard US (19601)

The Friday Run - *Last*
Hutchinson UK (1967); Vanguard US (1971)

Capt FRASS

British Male Amateur operating in England

John CHANCELLOR 1900-1971 (British)

See main detective pair Supt REDARREL and David FORRESTER

Citation Record: 2 Books

Frass - *First*
Hutchinson UK (1929)

The Return Of Frass - *Last*
Hutchinson UK (1930)

Ambrose FRAYNE and Dominique FRAYNE

are husband and wife and they run a detective agency together. He does most of the work, while she holds the fort, typing away as a good wife, it seems, should. Or might!

British Male Private Detective and American Female Private Detective operating in England

J T MCINTOSH 1925- (British)

Writer: James Murdoch MACGREGOR

Citation Record: 2 Books

Take A Pair Of Private Eyes - *First*

is a novelization of a TV play by *Peter O'DONNELL.*

Muller UK (1968); Doubleday US (1968)

A Coat Of Blackmail - *Last*
Muller UK (1970); Doubleday US (1971)

Dominique FRAYNE

Second detective of Ambrose FRAYNE

Tim FRAZER

British Male Amateur operating in England

Francis DURBRIDGE 1912- (British)

See main detective Paul TEMPLE

Citation Record: 3 Books

The World Of Tim Frazer - *First*
Hodder & Stoughton UK (1962); Dodd, Mead US (1962)

Tim Frazer Gets The Message - *Last*
Hodder & Stoughton UK (1978)

Dr Robert 'Mongo' FREDERICKSON

is an ex-circus acrobat who becomes the Professor of Criminology at some unnamed New York City university. In later books he sets up his own detective agency with his brother. *MONGO* himself is a dwarf, but he loves humanity to an extent that almost renders him an alien. He is involved in plots and adventures of the most bizarre kind, usually with strong occult and supernatural overtones. He appears in two books with the author's other detective, *Veil KENDRY.*

American Male Private Detective operating in New York

Sidekick: Garth FREDERICKSON

is almost a giant and a useful assistant to his tiny brother.

American Male - Brother

George CHESBRO 1940- (American)

was born in Washington DC and educated at Syracuse University, New York, where he graduated with a BS, 1962. He has held posts teaching English literature at several universities in the USA.

Writer: George Clark CHESBRO

Other Byline: David CROSS

Other Detectives:

BONE

Dr Robert 'Mongo' FREDERICKSON and Veil KENDRY

Veil KENDRY

Citation Record: 7 Books 10 Short Stories in 1 Collection

Shadow Of A Broken Man - *First*

Simon & Schuster US (1977); Severn UK (1981)

Dark Chant In A Crimson Key - *Latest*

Mysterious US (1992)

In The House Of Secret Enemies - *Collection 1*

Mysterious Press US (1990)

Dr Robert 'Mongo' FREDERICKSON and Veil KENDRY

American Male Private Detective and American Sleuth operating in New York

George CHESBRO 1940- (American)

Invented 4 detectives - see Dr Robert 'Mongo' FREDERICKSON

Citation Record: 2 Books

Two Songs This Archangel Sings - *First*

Atheneum US (1986)

The Cold Smell Of Sacred Stone - *Latest*

Atheneum US (1988)

Benny FREEDMAN

American Male Amateur operating in USA

Milton R BASS 1923- (American)

Writer: Milton Ralph BASS

Inventor of one other detective Vino ALTOBELLI

Citation Record: 2 Books

The Moving Finger - *First*

Signet US (1986); Hale UK (1986)

The Bandini Affair - *Latest*

Signet US (1987)

Maj FREEMAN

British Male Amateur operating in England

Sir William MAGNAY 1855-1917 (British)

Writer: Sir William MAGNAY

Inventor of one other detective Mr ROLF

Citation Record: 1 Book

The Hunt Ball Mystery - *Only*

Ward, Lock UK (1918); Brentano's UK (1918)

Det Insp John FREEMAN

British Policeman operating in England

John IRONSIDE (British)

Writer: Euphemia Margaret TAIT

Citation Record: 2 Books

The Red Symbol - *First*

Nash UK (1911); Little, Brown US (1910)

The Marten Mystery - *Last*

Arrowsmith UK (1933)

Det Jub FREEMAN

is a New York cop who appears in one book as the main detective and also in other books with the author's other detectives. The books are among the earliest examples of the American police procedural, in which various combinations of detectives enter and re-enter a series.

American Policeman operating in New York

Lawrence TREAT 1903- (American)

Invented 7 detectives - see Det Jub FREEMAN, Det Bill DECKER and Det Mitch TAYLOR

Citation Record: 1 Book

H As In Hunted - *Only*

Duell US (1946); Boardman UK (1950)

Det Jub FREEMAN and Det Bill DECKER

American Policemen operating in New York

Lawrence TREAT 1903- (American)

Invented 7 detectives - see Det Jub FREEMAN, Det Bill DECKER and Det Mitch TAYLOR

Citation Record: 2 Books

Over The Edge - *First*

Morrow US (1948); Boardman UK (1958)

F As In Flight - *Last*

Morrow US (1948); Boardman UK (1949)

Det Jub FREEMAN and Det Mitch TAYLOR

American Policemen operating in New York

Lawrence TREAT 1903- (American)

Invented 7 detectives - see Det Jub FREEMAN, Det Bill DECKER and Det Mitch TAYLOR

Citation Record: 4 Books

Q As In Quicksand - *First*

Duell US (1947)

Step Into Quicksand - *First**

Boardman UK (1959)

Lady, Drop Dead - *Last*

Abelard Schuman US (1960); Abelard Schuman UK (1960)

Det Jub FREEMAN and Det Carl WAYWARD

American Policemen operating in New York

Lawrence TREAT 1903- (American)

Invented 7 detectives - see Det Jub FREEMAN, Det Bill DECKER and Det Mitch TAYLOR

Citation Record: 1 Book

V As In Victim - *Only*

Duell US (1945); Rich UK (1950)

Det Jub FREEMAN, Det Bill DECKER and Det Mitch TAYLOR

All three detectives appear individually in other books by this author.

American Policemen operating in New York

Lawrence TREAT 1903- (American)

was born in New York City. He was educated at Dartmouth College, Hanover, New Hampshire, graduating with a BA, 1924, and then took an LLB at Columbia University School of Law, New York, 1927. He has taught mystery writing at several schools and universities, is the author of nine criminous novels and over a hundred genre short stories and is considered to have been the creator of the modern police procedural. He received the Mystery Writers of America Edgar Allan Poe award twice, 1965 and 1978.

Writer: Lawrence Arthur GOLDSTONE

Other Detectives:

Jub FREEMAN

Det Jub FREEMAN and Det Bill DECKER

Jub FREEMAN and Mitch TAYLOR

Det Jub FREEMAN and Det Carl WAYWARD

Hank GREENLEAF Carl WAYWARD

Citation Record: 1 Book

Big Shot - *Only*

Harper & Row US (1951); Boardman UK (1952)

Mike FREEMAN

Second detective of John BRELAND

Felix FREER
Second detective of Virginia FREER

Virginia FREER and Felix FREER
are a husband-and wife duo of an unusual kind. Separated, but not divorced, they find it impossible to live together. He is a bit of a ne'er-do-well but has a pretty good intellect. She becomes involved in mysteries and murders that she has to solve and she needs his help to do so. The highly skilled author finds no need to invent bizarre reasons for *Virginia FREER's* amateur sleuthing. When she finds a murder, clever lady and perpetual busybody that she is, she simply would just not dream of *not* interesting herself in discovering whodunnit.

British Female Amateur and British Male Amateur operating in England

E X FERRARS 1907-1995 (British)

Invented 11 detectives - see Toby DYKE

Citation Record: 1 Book

Last Will And Testament - *Only*
Doubleday US (1978)

Elizabeth FERRARS 1907-1995 (British)

Invented 10 detectives - see Toby DYKE

Citation Record: 4 Books

Last Will And Testament - *First*
Collins UK (1978)

Beware Of The Dog - *Last*
HarperCollins UK (1992)

Alan FRENCH
is a musician who, with his fellow players, is involved in murder and mystery at home, abroad, and even, it would seem, in transit.

American Male Amateur operating in USA/Europe

James GOLLIN (American)

Citation Record: 4 Books

The Philomel Foundation - *First*
St Martin's US (1980); Magnum UK (1982)

Broken Consort - *Latest*
St Martin's US (1989)

Lt Bill FRENCH
American Policeman operating in Michigan/Florida

Christopher HALE 1895-1948 (American)

Writer: Frances Moyer Ross STEVENS

Citation Record: 12 Books

Smoke Screen - *First*
Harcourt Brace US (1935); Boardman UK (1938)

He's Late This Morning - *Last*
Doubleday US (1949); Boardman UK (1951)

Charles 'Chickie' FRENCH
American Male Private Detective operating in USA

William KAYE (American)

Citation Record: 1 Book

Wrong Target - *Single*
Leisure Books US (1981)

Insp Joseph FRENCH
is, by any standards, one of the heroic figures of the British Golden Age and after. Before the advent of the police procedural, in which details of several policemen's' private lives seem to substitute for ideas as to how to go on with the detective work, fictional British policemen were really cast in the mould of the classic British amateur. The only change was that they were now given the backing and majesty of the law and more direct access to its machinery. So *Joseph FRENCH,* in a great series stretching from 1925 to 1957, plods his way through case after case, logical, pedantic, and sometimes a little mechanical as he solves ciphers, dissects minor clues and has no scruples about bringing criminals to justice. His private life remains a closed book. In his first appearance (qv) he had, in fact, shared the detective honours with two other detectives, but by 1924 he was on his own and remained so.

British Policeman operating in England

Freeman Wills CROFTS 1879-1957 (British)

was born in Dublin, Ireland. He was educated in Belfast and became a civil engineer. He suffered a severe illness in 1919 and then started writing his highly successful and ingenious detective novels, radio plays and short stories.

Other Detectives:
Insp BURNLEY, Insp LEFARGE and Insp Georges LA TOUCHE
Insp ROSS Insp TANNER

Citation Record: 29 Books 50 Short Stories in 3 Collections

Inspector French's Greatest Case - *First*
Collins UK (1924); Seltzer US (1925)

Anything To Declare? - *Latest*
Hodder & Stoughton UK (1957)

Murderers Make Mistakes - *Collection 1*
Short stories - 23
Hodder & Stoughton UK (1947)

Many A Slip - *Collection 2*
Short stories - 22
Hodder & Stoughton UK (1955)

The Mystery Of The Sleeping Car Express - *Collection 3*
contains ten of the author's stories, five of which feature *Insp FRENCH.*
Short stories - 5
Hodder & Stoughton UK (1956)

A FRENCH DETECTIVE OFFICER
is one of several ostensibly real-life detectives whose cases are related by this obscure but indefatigable author.

French Policeman operating in France

WATERS (British)

Invented 6 detectives - see WATERS

Citation Record: 8 Short Stories in 1 Collection

The Experiences Of A French Detective Officer - *Collection 1*
Clarke UK (1876)

Royston FRERE
American Male Sleuth operating in New York

William J ELLIOTT 1886-1947? (British)

Invented 4 detectives - see Anthony ENGLAND

Citation Record: 2 Books

Dope Devils - *First*
Swan UK (1942)

The Running Killer - *Last*
Swan UK (1946)

Brian FRESNEY
American Male Amateur operating in New York

Caroline CRANE 1930- (American)

See main detective Jessica HAYDEN

Citation Record: 1 Book

Trick Or Treat - *Single*
Dodd, Mead US (1983)

Sigmund FREUD
Second detective of Sherlock HOLMES

Max FREUND
Second detective of Petunia BEST

Kinky FRIEDMAN
is decidedly off-beat, sub-*MARLOWE* and sub-*HOLMES.* He appears in weird tales set mainly in Greenwich Village and is assisted by a sub-*WATSON.*

American Male Private Detective operating in New York

Sidekick: RATSO
was apparently based on a real character who worked for the *National Lampoon Magazine.*

American Male - Sidekick

Kinky FRIEDMAN (American)

was a singer in the 1970s. He has written several books starring an eponymous detective, based on his own life-style and views on American society.

Citation Record: 5 Books

When The Cat's Away - *First*
Beech Tree US (1980)

Elvis, Jesus And Coca-Cola - *Latest*
Bantam US (1994)

Abe FRIENDLY

American Male Amateur operating in New York

Richard NEELY (American)

is an advertising executive who has written more than a score of books in the criminous vein.

Citation Record: 1 Book

Death To My Beloved - *Only*
Signet US (1969)

FRISBEE

is a private eye given to studying law.

American Male Private Detective operating in USA

R D BROWN 1924- (American)

See main detective Cheney HAZZARD

Citation Record: 1 Selected Short Story

Frisbee In The Middle
In 'New Black Mask Quarterly' US (1985)

The FRISCO DETECTIVE

American Male Detective in Pulp Magazines operating in USA

ANON

Citation Record: 1 Book

The Frisco Detective - *Only*
Aldine US (?)

FRITZ

German Male Detective in Pulp Magazines operating in New York

Tony PASTOR 1837-1898 (American)

Invented 4 detectives - see O'Neil MCDARRAGH

Citation Record: 1 Book

Fritz, The German Detective - *Only*
Ogilvie US (1882)

FRITZ

American Male Detective in Pulp Magazines operating in USA

Edward Lytton WHEELER 1854?-1885 (American)

Invented 6 detectives - see Nell NIBLO

Citation Record: 2 Books

Fritz, The Bound Boy Detective - *First*
Westbrook US (ca 1920)

Fritz To The Front - *Last*
Westbrook US (ca 1920)

The FRONTIER DETECTIVE

American Male Detective in Pulp Magazines operating in USA

Edward Lytton WHEELER 1854?-1885 (American)

Invented 6 detectives - see Nell NIBLO

Citation Record: 1 Book

The Frontier Detective - *Only*
Westbrook US (ca 1920)

Insp FROST and Toni STAPLETON

British Policeman and British Female Amateur operating in England

Virgil MARKHAM 1899- (British)

Invented 5 detectives - see Insp Myles RUSBY

Citation Record: 1 Book

The Black Door - *Only*
Collins UK (1930)

Shock! - *Only**
Knopf UK (1930)

Insp FROST

British Policeman operating in England

H Maynard SMITH 1869-1949 (British)

Writer: Herbert Maynard SMITH

Citation Record: 7 Books

Inspector Frost's Jigsaw - *First*
Benn UK (1929); Doubleday US (1929)

Inspector Frost In The Background - *Last*
Faber UK (1941)

Insp FROST and Dr GARLAND

British Policeman and British Male Amateur operating in London

L T MEADE and Robert EUSTACE (British)

Writers: Elizabeth Thomasina Meade SMITH 1854-1914 and Eustace Robert BARTON 1854-1943

Other Detectives:
John BELL
Dr Henry CHETWYND and Dr Paul CATO
George CONWAY
Florence CUSACK
Prof Christopher EKSHAW
Norman HEAD

Citation Record: 1 Selected Short Story

The Man Who Disappeared
appeared in a collection, *Silenced*, in 1904 and, many years later was published in the May 1948 number of *Ellery Queen's Mystery Magazine*. It can also be found in an anthology, published by *IPL* (US 1987), entitled *Death Locked In*.
Ward, Lock UK (1904)

Gerald (Nighthawk) FROST

British Male Sleuth operating in England

Sydney HORLER 1888-1954 (British)

Invented 20 detectives - see Sir Harker BELLAMY

Citation Record: 7 Books

They Called Him Nighthawk - *First*
Hodder & Stoughton UK (1937)

Nighthawk Swears Vengeance - *Last*
Hodder & Stoughton UK (1954)

Hank (The Mercenary) FROST

American Male Professional Investigator operating in Central America

Axel KILGORE (American)

Citation Record: 3 Books

The Slaughter Run - *First*
Zebra US (1980)

The Killer Genesis - *Latest*
Zebra US (1980)

Dr Henry FROST

has retired, with his wife, to a quiet English village and any reader of detective fiction could have told him what that means.

British Male Professional Amateur operating in England

Josephine BELL 1897-1987 (British)

Invented 10 detectives - see Dr David WINTRINGHAM

Citation Record: 2 Books

The Upfold Witch - *First*
Hodder & Stoughton UK (1964); Macmillan US (1964)

Death On The Reserve - *Last*
Hodder & Stoughton UK (1966); Macmillan US (1967)

Det Insp Jack FROST

is a delightful newcomer to the British detective scene. Sloppy, scruffy, chaotic in his approach to desk work, rude, crude, insubordinate, the winner of the George Cross for gallantry, he is that rarely successful creation, a compulsively interesting and good detective of comic stature, the definitive answer to the modern, boring, British police procedural.

British Policeman operating in England

Sidekick: Det Sgt GILMORE
is one of the detective's two assistants.
British Male - Subordinate

F

Sidekick: Det Const Clive BARNARD
appears in the first of the *Insp Jack FROST* series. He is the nephew of the Chief Constable, a priggish young man, straight up from London and new to the force.
British Male - Subordinate

Stooge: Cdr MULLETT
is the superior of *FROST* but is officious, insufferable and in continuous battle with him over his cases.
British Male

R D WINGFIELD (British)
Writer: Rodney D WINGFIELD
Citation Record: 3 Books
Frost At Christmas - *First*
PaperJacks US (1984)
Night Frost - *Latest*
Constable UK (1992)

F

Reuben FROST

is a retired lawyer, a septuagenarian who investigates cases that sometimes start with business and fraud and usually end in murder.
American Male Professional Amateur operating in New York

Sidekick: Christine FROST
is the detective's wife and assists him.
American Female - Wife

Stooge: Lt Luis BAUTISTA
is ever present to handle the police end of *FROST's* detection work. *FROST* never fails to say how great a cop, whereas he seems to act pretty dumb.
American Male

Haughton MURPHY 1934- (American)
Writer: James Henry DUFFY
Citation Record: 6 Books
Murders And Acquisitions - *First*
Simon & Schuster US (1988); Collins UK (1988)
A Very Venetian Murder - *Latest*
Simon & Schuster US (1993)

Pete FRY

is an ex-journalist and is now a PI operating from an office off Covent Garden, in London's theatre-land.
British Male Private Detective operating in London

Pete FRY 1914- (British)
is the author of novels and plays and has written articles for various kinds of magazines, especially on the drama.
Writer: James Clifford KING
Citation Record: 15 Books
The Long Overcoat - *First*
Boardman UK (1957)
The Black Cotton Gloves - *Last*
Long UK (1970)

August FRYE

is a member of the English Department in Lyndon Johnson College and turns sleuth to solve the mystery of a colleague's untimely death.
American Male Amateur operating in USA

Edward MACKIN 1929- (American)
For writer details see Father Roger DOWLING
Citation Record: 1 Book
The Nominative Case - *Single*
Macmillan UK (1990); Walker US (1991)

Danny FULLER

appears but once, is corrupted and pays the price.
American Male Private Detective operating in Los Angeles

Roy HUGGINS 1914- (American)
See main detective Stuart BAILEY
Citation Record: 1 Book
Too Late For Tears - *Only*
Morrow US (1947); Cassell UK (1950)

Max FULLER

American Male Private Detective operating in Midwest USA

James Michael ULLMAN (American)
Invented 3 detectives - see Julian FORBES
Citation Record: 1 Book
The Neon Haystack - *Only*
Simon & Schuster US (1963); Cassell UK (1964)

Richard FURLING

British Male Amateur operating in England

Francis GRIERSON 1888-1972 (British)
Invented 6 detectives - see Ch Det Insp George MUIR
Citation Record: 3 Books
Murder In Mortimer Square - *First*
Collins UK (1932)
The Mystery Of The Golden Angel - *Last*
Collins UK (1933)

Insp Charles François FURNEAUX

British Policeman operating in England

Gordon HOLMES 1863-1928 (British)
For writer details see Insp Charles François FURNEAUX
Citation Record: 2 Books
By Force Of Circumstances - *First*
was republished under the following byline.
Mills UK (1910); Clode US (1909)
The Feldisham Mystery - *Last*
Amalgamated UK (1911)
The De Bercy Affair - *Last**
Clode US (1910)

Louis TRACY 1863-1928 (British)
was the author of much early science fiction, but also wrote a few detective stories.
Writer: Louis TRACY
Other Byline: Gordon HOLMES
Inventor of one other detective Reginald BRETT
Citation Record: 13 Books
Number Seventeen - *First*
Clode US (1915); Cassell UK (1916)
By Force Of Circumstances - *Last*
was previously published under the preceding byline.
Jarrolds UK (1932)

Peter FURNEAUX

is a boy of fourteen, just entering maturity, who is still bewildered and not a little bewitched by the opposite sex but is able to solve a murder carried out by a most cunning killer. The setting is that of the Golden Age whodunnit, an English country town, but textually the story is more advanced.
British Male Amateur operating in England

Kingsley AMIS 1922-1995 (British)
was born in London and took a degree at St John's College, Oxford. He was a considerable novelist, versifier, and writer in several genres, including the occasional detective story. Formerly an avant-garde figure, he later prided himself on being a conservative and *bon viveur*.
Writer: Sir Kingsley William AMIS
Other Byline: Robert MARKHAM
Inventor of one other detective Christopher DANE
Citation Record: 1 Book
The Riverside Villas Murder - *Only*
Harcourt Brace UK (1973); Cape US (1973)

Insp FURNIVAL

British Policeman operating in England

Annie HAYNES ?-1929 (British)
Inventor of one other detective Insp STODDART
Citation Record: 3 Books

The Abbey Court Murder - *First*
Bodley Head UK (1923)

The Crow's Inn Tragedy - *Last*
Bodley Head UK (1927); Dodd, Mead US (1927)

Insp Matthew FURNIVAL

British Policeman operating in England

Stella PHILLIPS 1927- (British)

Citation Record: 5 Books

Down To Death - *First*
Hale UK (1967)

The Hidden Wrath - *Last*
Hale UK (1968); Walker US (1982)

Dr FURNIVALL

Male Amateur

George BUTLER 1847-1921

Writer: George Frank BUTLER

Citation Record: 12 Short Stories in 1 Collection

The Exploits Of A Physician Detective - *Collection 1*
In 'Clinic' ? (1908)

Jackson FURY

American Male Private Detective operating in Dallas

Sidekick: Jillian FLETCHER
American Female - Assistant

Carol JERINA 1947- (American)

Citation Record: 2 Books

The Tall Dark Alibi - *First*
Charter US (1988)

Sweet Jeopardy - *Latest*
Charter US (1988)

Johnny FURY

American Male Private Detective operating in New York

Harrison WADE (American)

Citation Record: 1 Book

So Lovely To Kill - *Only*
Graphic US (1956)

Insp Robert FUSIL and Const KERR

work closely together. *Robert FUSIL* hates criminals to the point of obsession and, in cases where the evidence is not quite as it should be, is not beyond tampering with it a little in the interests of private justice. *KERR* is young, lusty and upright.

British Policemen operating in England

Peter ALDING 1926- (British)

For writer details see Insp Enrique ALVAREZ

Citation Record: 14 Books

The CID Room - *First*
Long UK (1967)

All Leads Negative - *First**
Harper & Row US (1967)

One Man's Justice - *Last*
Hale UK (1983)

Ch Insp David FYFE

British Policeman operating in Scotland

William PAUL (British)

Citation Record: 2 Books

Sleeping Dogs - *First*
Constable UK (1994)

Sleeping Pretty - *Latest*
Constable UK (1995)

Sgt/Insp Stanley FYLES

Canadian Policeman operating in Canada

Ridgwell CULLUM 1867-1943 (British)

Citation Record: 2 Books

The Law Breakers - *First*
Chapman & Hall UK (1914); Jacobs US (1914)

The Law Of The Gun - *Last*
Chapman & Hall UK (1918); Jacobs US (1918)

— G —

Bill GABRIEL

is a member of the Five Continents Detective Agency, so explaining what an American PI is doing in India.

American Male Private Detective operating in India

Lawrence G BLOCHMAN 1900-1975 (American)

Invented 5 detectives - see Dr Daniel Webster COFFEE and Lt Max RITTER

Citation Record: 1 Book

Wives To Burn - *Only*
Harcourt US (1940); Collins UK (1940)

Sheriff Matt GABRIEL

hears of an old crime in the dying words of a friend in Blackwater Bay. To solve it, he goes back through the treacherous past that engulfs the town in a web of murder and blackmail.

American Policeman operating in USA

Paula GOSLING 1939- (American)

Invented 7 detectives - see Lt Jack STRYKER

Citation Record: 1 Book

A Few Dying Words - *Only*
Mysterious Press US (1944)

Vic (Eagle Force) GABRIEL

American Male Sleuth operating in USA/Europe/Asia

Dan SCHMIDT (American)

Writer: Dan SCHMIDT

Other Byline: Dan KELLERMAN

Citation Record: 7 Books

Death Camp Columbia - *First*
Bantam US (1989)

Ring Of Fire - *Latest*
Bantam US (1990)

Oliver GAD

has psychic powers, which, perhaps not surprisingly, are put to use by British Intelligence.

Male Amateur

Stephen GELLER (British)

Citation Record: 1 Book

Gad - *Single*
Harper & Row US (1980)

Supt GADEN

British Policeman operating in England

P H POWELL (British)

Writer: Percival Henry POWELL

Citation Record: 2 Books

Why Kill A Butler? - *First*
Jenkins UK (1952); Roy US (1957)

Now Lying Dead - *Last*
Jenkins UK (1953)

Supt John GAFFNEY and Det Ch Supt Thomas FOX

also appear individually in other books by this author.

British Policemen operating in London

Graham ISON (British)

Invented 3 detectives - see Det Ch Supt Thomas FOX

Citation Record: 1 Book

The Home Secretary Will See You Now - *Single*
Macmillan UK (1989); St Martin's US (1990)

Supt John GAFFNEY

appears also in one book with the author's other detective, *Det Ch Supt Tommy FOX.*

British Policeman operating in London

Graham ISON (British)

Invented 3 detectives - see Det Ch Supt Thomas FOX

Citation Record: 3 Books

The Cold Light Of Dawn - *First*
Macmillan UK (1988)

A Damned Serious Business - *Latest*
Macmillan UK (1990)

Zeke GAHAGAN

is now eighty years old. An ex-Pinkerton man, he claims to have been trained by the famous author, *Dashiell HAMMETT*, as well as being the oldest PI in the business. He can still, it seems, handle a typical Hollywood murder case.

American Male Private Detective operating in Los Angeles

Vincent MCCONNOR 1907?- (American)

Invented 3 detectives - see Insp DAMIOT

Citation Record: 1 Book

The Man Who Knew Hammett - *Single*
Tor US (1988)

GAIL and MITCH

American Female Sleuth and American Male Sleuth operating in Los Angeles

The GORDONS (American)

Invented 3 detectives - see D C (Darn Cat) RANDALL

Citation Record: 2 Books

Night Before The Wedding - *First*
Doubleday US (1969); Macdonald UK (1969)

Night After The Wedding - *Last*
Doubleday US (1979); Macdonald UK (1980)

John GAIL

does a number of dirty jobs for the SIS.

British Male Secret Agent operating in England/Spain

Stephen D FRANCES 1917-1989 (British)

Writer: Stephen Daniel FRANCES
Other Bylines:
Hank JANSON
Arthur KIRBY
Desmond REID
Peter SAXON
Richard WILLIAMS

Inventor of one other detective Hilary BRAND

Citation Record: 7 Books

This Woman Is Death - *First*
Mayflower UK (1965); Award US (1969)

The Caress Of Conquest - *Last*
Mayflower UK (1968); Award US (1970)

Foster GAINES

Second detective of Frank LEONARD

Vicky 'The Dish' GAINES

Second detective of Ransome DRAGOON

George GALBRAITH

Australian Male Amateur operating in Australia

Osmar WHITE 1909-

Writer: Osmar Egmont Dorkin WHITE
!See Appendix 2.

Citation Record: 1 Book

A Silent Reach - *Single*
Macmillan UK (1978); Scribner's US (1980)

Carey GALBREATH

American Male Amateur operating in New York

Walbridge MCCULLY 1896-1980 (American)

Writer: Ethel Walbridge MCCULLY

Citation Record: 2 Books

Death Rides Tandem - *First*
Doubleday US (1942)

Doctors Beware! - *Last*
Doubleday US (1943)

Gabriel GALE

is a minor invention of the great master and appears only in short stories.

British Male Amateur operating in England

G K CHESTERTON 1874-1936 (British)

Invented 7 detectives - see Father BROWN

Citation Record: 10 Short Stories in 2 Collections

The Poet And The Lunatics: Episodes In The Life Of Gabriel Gale - *Collection 1*
Short stories - 8
Cassell UK (1929); Dodd, Mead US (1929)

Thirteen Detectives - *Collection 2*
contains one *Father BROWN* story, two *Horne FISHER* stories, two *Gabriel GALE* stories, two *Rupert and Basil GRANT* stories and two *Mr POND* stories.
Short stories - 2
Xanadu UK (1988); Dodd, Mead US (1986)

Nicholas GALE

British Male Private Detective operating in London

Peter CHEYNEY 1896-1951 (British)

Invented 11 detectives - see Lemmy CAUTION

Citation Record: 1 Book

Try Anything Twice - *Only*
Collins UK (1948); Dodd, Mead US (1948)

Undressed To Kill - *Only**
Avon US (1959)

Simon GALE

appeared in a radio series and is in these two novelizations by the author.

British Male Amateur operating in England

Gerald VERNER 1886-1980 (British)

Invented 7 detectives - see Supt BUDD

Citation Record: 2 Books

Noose For A Lady - *First*
Wright & Brown UK (1952)

Sorcerer's House - *Last*
Wright & Brown UK (1956)

Joe GALL

American Male Sleuth operating in USA/Europe/Asia

Philip ATLEE 1915-1991 (American)

Writer: James Atlee PHILLIPS
Other Byline: James Atlee PHILLIPS

Citation Record: 22 Books

The Green Wound - *First*
GM US (1963); Muller UK (1964)

The Green Wound Contract - *First**
GM US (1967)

The Last Domino Contract - *Last*
GM US (1976)

James Atlee PHILLIPS 1915-1991 (American)

Writer: James Atlee PHILLIPS
Other Byline: Philip ATLEE

Citation Record: 1 Book

Pagoda - *Only*
Macmillan US (1951); World's Work UK (1953)

Gale GALLAGHER

is a policeman's daughter and runs the Acme Investigating Bureau on Fifth Avenue, Manhattan. Young, pretty and tough, she is one of the earliest and most likeable of female private eyes. Her main line is that of skip-tracer, which seems simple enough; but, just in case, she carries a Colt .32 under her rather stunning clothes.

American Female Private Detective operating in New York

Gale GALLAGHER (American)

Writers: William Charles OURSLER 1913-1985 and Margaret SCOTT

Citation Record: 2 Books

I Found Him Dead - *First*
Coward McCann US (1947)

Chord In Crimson - *Last*
Coward McCann US (1949); Boardman UK (1950)

Gordon GALLAGHER

British Male Professional Investigator operating in several locations

Julian Jay SAVARIN (British)

See main detective David PROSS

Citation Record: 6 Books

Waterhole - *First*
Allison & Busby UK (1982); St Martin's US (1984)

Villiger - *Latest*
Allison & Busby UK (1989); St Martin's US (1991)

Gale GALLYON

British Female Amateur operating in England

Raymond BUXTON (British)

Writer: Raymond BUXTON

Other Bylines:
Spike GORDON   Don ROGAN

Inventor of one other detective LOU

Citation Record: 1 Book

No Gentle Lady - *Only*
Modern Fiction UK (1948)

Spike GORDON

House name.

For writer details see Gale GALLYON

Citation Record: 1 Book

Gale Gallyon Takes A Hand - *Only*
Modern Fiction UK (1951)

GALT

American Male Sleuth operating in New York

Joseph GOLLOMB 1881-1950 (American)

See main detective Insp Barton HAWLEY

Citation Record: 3 Books

The Portrait Invisible - *First*
Macmillan US (1928); Heinemann UK (1928)

The Curtain Of Storm - *Last*
Macmillan UK (1933)

Bradford GALT

is framed by his partner, goes to jail, comes out and sets about clearing things up.

American Male Private Detective operating in New York

Leo ROSTEN 1908- (American)

Writer: Leo Calvin ROSTEN

Other Byline: Leonord Q ROSS

See main detective pair Sidney 'Silky' PINCUS and Mike CLANCY

Citation Record: 1 Book

The Dark Corner - *Only*
was published in the UK under the following byline.
Century US (1945)

Leonard Q ROSS 1908- (American)

For writer details see Bradford GALT

Citation Record: 1 Book

The Dark Corner - *Only*
was published in the US under the preceding byline.
Edwards UK (1946)

Jason GALT

American Male Amateur operating in USA/England

Marc LOVELL 1930- (Australian)

For writer details see Norman PINK

Inventor of one other detective Appleton 'Apple' PORTER

Citation Record: 2 Books

The Blind Hypnotist - *First*
Doubleday US (1976)

The Second Vanetti Affair - *Latest*
Doubleday US (1977); Hale UK (1979)

Oliver GALT and Hugo TOWER

British Male Amateurs operating in England/France

Victor FRANCE (British)

Citation Record: 2 Books

The Carved Emerald - *First*
Selwyn UK (1926)

The Naked Five - *Last*
Selwyn UK (1927)

James GALVESTON

American Male Private Detective operating in USA

Sidekick: Emma TWIGGS
is in her seventies and not so useful as she would like to be.
American Female - Aunt

Helen CARPENTER and Lorri CARPENTER (American)

are a mother-and-daughter team

Citation Record: 1 Selected Short Story

The Disappearing Diamond
is in *The Woman Sleuth Anthology; Contemporary Mystery Stories by Women* (Editor; Irene Zahava).
US (1988)

Laurie GALVIN

Male Sleuth

Kenneth ROYCE 1920- (British)

Invented 3 detectives - see Willie 'Spider' SCOTT

Citation Record: 1 Book

The President Is Dead - *Single*
Hodder & Stoughton UK (1988)

Patriots - *Single**
Crown US (1988)

Clare GAMADGE

is the fictional widow of *Henry GAMADGE*, created by *Elizabeth DALY*. She now sleuths in her own right.

American Female Amateur operating in USA

Eleanor BOYLAN 1916- (American)

is the niece of *Elizabeth DALY*, who wrote the *Henry GAMADGE* books.

Citation Record: 2 Books

Working Murder - *First*
Holt US (1989)

Murder Observed - *Latest*
Holt US (1990)

Henry GAMADGE

is an author and bibliophile who lives in the select Murray Hill district of New York City. He consults on old books and his skills are of great use in the cases of theft, forgery and murder he encounters. He has a wife, a cat and an assistant he has raised from a child. He's a demon at Bridge, likes golf and music and, in general, makes *Lord Peter WIMSEY* seem an oaf. In a clever ploy, the author's niece, *Eleanor BOYLAN* (qv), has continued with a series featuring *Clare GAMADGE*, the fictional widow of *Henry GAMADGE*.

American Male Amateur operating in New York

Sidekick: Harold BANTZ
is a young man who, taken off the streets by *GAMADGE*, becomes his assistant.
American Male - Assistant

Elizabeth DALY 1878-1967 (American)

was born in New York City. She graduated with a BA from Bryn Mawr College, Pennsylvania, 1901, and with an MA from Columbia University, New York, 1902, then becoming Reader in English at Bryn Mawr College, 1904-1906. Her detective novels are simply those of the British Golden Age transferred to the New York of the 1940s.

Citation Record: 16 Books

Unexpected Night - *First*
Farrar & Rinehart US (1940); Gollancz UK (1940)

The Book Of The Crime - *Last*
Rinehart US (1951); Hammond UK (1954)

Charlie GAMBLE

American Male Amateur operating in Boston/New York

Don MATHESON (American)

Writer: Donald MATHESON

Citation Record: 2 Books

Stray Cat - *First*
Summit US (1987)

Ninth Life - *Latest*
Summit US (1989); Curley UK (1991)

Mike GANNON

American Male Amateur operating in Cleveland

Dean BALLENGER (American)

Citation Record: 3 Books

Blood For Breakfast - *First*
Manor US (1973)

Blood Beast - *Last*
Manor US (1974)

Peter GANNS

is a young American sleuth, taking snuff and holding forth, who is called in to investigate a remarkable case of sequential murder after a British detective has declared himself baffled.

American Male Amateur

Eden PHILLPOTTS 1862-1960 (British)

Invented 10 detectives - see Insp MIDWINTER

Citation Record: 1 Book

The Red Redmaynes - *Only*
Macmillan US (1922); Hutchinson UK (1923)

Steve GANT

is a skip-tracer. Suspected of murder, he has to discover the killer to clear himself.

American Male Private Detective operating in New York

Lawrence LARIAR 1908-1981 (American)

Invented 3 detectives - see Mike WELLS

Citation Record: 1 Book

Death Is Confidential - *Only*
Hillman US (1959)

Det Charlie GANTS

American Policeman operating in Texas

Richard K ABSHIRE and William R CLAIR (American)

are veteran police officers from Dallas.

Citation Record: 2 Books

Gants - *First*
Dell US (1987)

The Shaman Tree - *Latest*
St Martin's US (1989)

Barney GANTT

is a photographer and free-lance reporter who is usually to be found solving cases of murder, kidnapping or robbery.

American Male Amateur operating in USA

John Stephen STRANGE 1896- (American)

Invented 4 detectives - see Van Dusen ORMSBERRY

Citation Record: 8 Books

The Bell In The Fog - *First*
Doubleday US (1936); Collins UK (1937)

The House On 9th Street - *Last*
Doubleday US (1976)

Jennifer Norrington Aless GANZARELLO and Coleridge TUCKER

Female Sleuth and British Male Sleuth operating in Europe/Africa

Ivor DRUMMOND 1929- (British)

See main detective Colly TUCKER

Citation Record: 9 Books

The Man With The Tiny Head - *First*
Macmillan UK (1969); Harcourt Brace US (1970)

A Stench Of Poppies - *Latest*
Joseph UK (1978); St Martin's US (1978)

Jo GAR

was a hardboiled PI in Manila who appeared in eight short stories in the pulps. Some have recently appeared in anthologies and one is cited.

American Male Private Detective operating in Manila

Ramon DECOLTA 1898-1945 (American)

Invented 5 detectives - see Dion DAVIES

Citation Record: 1 Selected Short Story

Death In The Pasig
In 'Black Mask Magazine' US (1930)

Bill GARD

American Male Amateur operating in USA

William Atherton DUPUY 1876-1941 (American)

Citation Record: 12 Short Stories in 1 Collection

Uncle Sam, Detective - *Collection 1*
Stokes US (1916)

Vance (The Chameleon) GARDE

American Male Sleuth operating in USA

Jerry LA PLANTE (American)

Citation Record: 3 Books

In Garde We Trust - *First*
Zebra US (1978)

Garde Save The World - *Latest*
Zebra US (1979)

Ben GARDEN

American Male Amateur operating in Florida

Tom PACE 1929- (American)

Writer: Thomas C PACE Sr

Citation Record: 2 Books

The Treasure Hunt - *First*
Harper & Row US (1970)

Fisherman's Luck - *Last*
Harper & Row US (1971); White Lion UK (1973)

John GARDEN

British Male Amateur operating in England

Burford DELANNOY (British)

Invented 3 detectives - see Watson WARD

Citation Record: 1 Book

MRCS - *Only*
Ward, Lock UK (1903)

Insp GARDNER

is a Scotland Yard detective.

British Policeman operating in London

Richard MARSH 1867-1915 (British)

Invented 10 detectives - see The Hon Augustus CHAMPNELL

Citation Record: 1 Book

In Full Cry - *Only*
White UK (1891); Street & Smith US (1928)

Mr GARFIELD

British Policeman operating in England

F R BUCKLEY (British)

Writer: Frederick Robert BUCKLEY

Citation Record: 28 Short Stories in 2 Collections

The Blithe Sheriff - *Collection 1*
Short stories - 15
Bles UK (1926)
Re-Enter The Blithe Sheriff - *Collection 2*
Short stories - 13
Bles UK (1927)

Grant GARFIELD
British Male Sleuth operating in several locations

Charles FRANKLIN 1909-1976 (British)
Invented 3 detectives - see Insp Jim BURGESS
Citation Record: 19 Books
Rope Of Sand - *First*
Collins UK (1948)
Fear Runs Softly - *Last*
Hale UK (1961)

Lucas GARFIELD
foils a plot to take over the entire government of the United States.
American Male Secret Agent operating in USA

Frank ROSS (American)
Writers: Colin NORTHWAY and Michael EWINGS
Citation Record: 1 Book
The Sixty-Fifth Tape - *Single*
Atheneum US (1979); Macmillan UK (1979)

Mike GARFIN
is said to be of French-Irish lineage. His cases entail a daily round that takes him to nightclubs and other well-known dens of vice, and his activities involve him in a surfeit of violence and would-be eroticism that is almost hilarious in its attempts to be earnest.
Canadian Male Private Detective operating in Montreal

Martin BRETT 1922- (Canadian)
Writer: Ronald Douglas SANDERSON
Other Byline: Malcolm DOUGLAS
Citation Record: 3 Books
Hot Freeze - *First*
Dodd, Mead US (1954); Reinhardt UK (1954)
A Dum-Dum For The President - *Last*
Hammond UK (1961)

Dr GARLAND
Second detective of Insp FROST

Judy GARLAND
Second detective of Toby PETERS

Stan GARLAND
is what the young aspiring PI, only trying to do his best, is coming to in modern variations of the genre, when politics, a dash of mysticism, lashings of luck and martial arts take over.
British Male Private Detective operating in England

Paul MCDOWELL (British)
Citation Record: 1 Book
Dope Opera - *Single*
Pluto UK (1987); Allison US (1987)

George GARNER
British Male Amateur operating in England

Roy FULLER 1912- (British)
See main detective Harry SINTON
Citation Record: 1 Book
Second Curtain - *Only*
Verschoyle UK (1956); Macmillan US (1956)

GARNETT
British Policeman operating in England

R PHILMORE 1900- (British)
See main detective C J SWAN
Citation Record: 2 Books
Death In Arms - *First*
Collins UK (1939)
Procession Of Two - *Last*
Collins UK (1940)

David GARNETT
is a weary, war-worn resistance fighter. He now has to continue solving the problems of a deadly game.
British Male Professional Investigator operating in Europe

Clive EGLETON 1927- (British)
Invented 3 detectives - see Insp COGHILL
Citation Record: 3 Books
A Piece Of Resistance - *First*
Hodder & Stoughton UK (1970); Coward McCann US (1970)
The Judas Mandate - *Last*
Hodder & Stoughton UK (1972); Coward McCann US (1972)

Able GARRET
American Male Amateur operating in Los Angeles

Carol Houlihan FLYNN 1945- (American)
Citation Record: 1 Book
Washed In The Blood - *Single*
Seaview US (1983)

GARRETT
operates on another planet, where, it seems, they still haven't got round to giving private detectives first names. Nevertheless, things do seem a little different from what we have come expect on mother Earth. Inter-planetary war is common, crimes abound and magic rules. *GARRETT's* girlfriend is a witch, his partner has been dead for several hundred years, his hired help is an elf, and his client is a fairy. Never mind, the toughness of the cases and the hardboiled nature of the sleuth vividly recall our own dear times and climes!
Male Private Detective operating in Space

Glen COOK 1944- (American)
Writer: Glen Charles COOK
Citation Record: 5 Books
Sweet Silver Blues - *First*
Signet US (1987)
Dread Brass Shadows - *Latest*
ROC US (1990)

Charles GARRETT
British Male Sleuth

Frederick NOLAN 1931- (British)
Writer: Frederick W NOLAN
Other Byline: Donald SEVERN
Inventor of one other detective Joe PETROSINO
Citation Record: 2 Books
Sweet Sister Death - *First*
was published in the US, with a change of title, under the following byline.
Century UK (1989)
Designated Assassin - *Latest*
was published in the US under the following byline.
Century UK (1990)

Donald SEVERN 1931- (British)
For writer details see Charles GARRETT
Citation Record: 2 Books
A Time To Die - *First*
was published in the UK, with a change of title, under the preceding byline.
Lynx US (1989)
Designated Assassin - *Latest*
was published in the UK under the preceding byline.
Lynx US (1990)

Colin 'Big Brain' GARRETT
American Male Sleuth operating in USA

Gary BRANDNER 1933- (American)

Citation Record: 3 Books

The Aardvark Affair - *First*
Zebra US (1975); New English Library UK (1976)

Energy Zero - *Latest*
Zebra US (1976)

Henry GARRETT

American Male Sleuth operating in California

Gaylord D LARSEN 1932- (American)

Other Detectives:
Jason BRADLEY Raymond CHANDLER

Citation Record: 2 Books

The Kilbourne Connection - *First*
Bethany US (1980)

Trouble Crossing The Pyrenees - *Latest*
Regal US (1983)

An Educated Death - *Latest**
Ballantine US (1986)

G

Mike GARRETT

operates in Lancaster City in books set back to 1948. He was once, it seems, in the police force, but he was forced to retire. Naturally hurt by this, he takes to wearing old clothes and drinking too much.

American Male Private Detective operating in Pennsylvania

Richard BLAINE (American)

Citation Record: 2 Books

The Silver Setup - *First*
Pageant US (1988)

The Tainted Jade - *Latest*
Pageant US (1989)

Russ GARRETT

is a former minor league baseball player who, for various reasons, has to solve the murder of a Congressman.

American Male Amateur operating in USA

William L DEANDREA 1952- (American)

Invented 4 detectives - see Matt COBB

Citation Record: 1 Book

Five O'clock Lightning - *Single*
St Martin's US (1982)

Roger GARRISON

operates in the Hollywood of 1927. A well-known tough in his own right, he is just the operator to call in when the studios are plagued by murder.

American Male Private Detective operating in Hollywood

Jeff ROVIN 1951- (American)

Citation Record: 2 Books

Hollywood Detective: Garrison - *First*
Manor US (1975)

Hollywood Detective: The Wolf - *Last*
Manor US (1975)

Victor GARRISON

Male Sleuth operating in France

Dallas KIRBY (American)

Writer: David J GAMMON

Citation Record: 2 Books

Victor - *First*
Swan UK (1942)

Victor Versus Verhasst - *Last*
Swan UK (1943)

Callahan GARRITY

is said to be Atlanta's most inquisitive cleaning lady.

American Female Amateur operating in Atlanta

Kathy Hogan TROCHECK (American)

Citation Record: 4 Books

Homemade Sin - *First*
HarperCollins US (1994)

Happy Never After - *Latest*
Headline UK (1995)

Tony GARRITY

is half Irish and half Aztec. He once practised as an attorney but was disbarred after killing two men, in what he claimed was self-defence. Now he operates as a private eye, although unlicensed.

American Male Private Detective operating in Los Angeles

Allan NIXON 1918- (American)

Citation Record: 3 Books

Get Garrity - *First*
Avon US (1969)

Garrity - *First**
New English Library UK (1970)

Go For Garrity - *Last*
Avon US (1970)

Pete GARROWAY

American Male Sleuth operating in USA

Pete GARROWAY 1903- (American)

For writer details see Supt Michael DREXEL

Citation Record: 3 Books

A Dame Too Many - *First*
Milestone UK (1952)

Say Yes, Sugar - *Last*
Milestone UK (1953)

Gray USHER 1903- (British)

See main detective Supt Michael DREXEL

Citation Record: 2 Books

For Pete's Sake! - *First*
Scion UK (1951)

Don't Crowd Me! - *Last*
Scion UK (1952)

GARSON

American Male Sleuth operating in New York

Ellen RASKIN 1928-1984 (American)

Citation Record: 6 Short Stories in 1 Collection

The Tattooed Potato And Other Clues - *Collection 1*
Macmillan UK (1975)

GARSTANG

British Male Sleuth operating in England

R A J WALLING 1869-1949 (British)

Invented 3 detectives - see Philip TOLEFREE

Citation Record: 2 Books

The Stroke Of One - *First*
Methuen UK (1931); Morrow US (1931)

Behind The Yellow Blind - *Last*
Hodder & Stoughton UK (1932)

Murder At Midnight - *Last**
Morrow US (1932)

GARTH

Wadsworth CAMP 1879-1936 (American)

Invented 3 detectives - see Bobby BLACKBURN

Citation Record: 1 Book 3 Short Stories in 1 Collection

The Gray Mask - *Only*
Doubleday US (1920)

The Communicating Door - *Collection 1*
This collection of seven of the author's short stories contains three with *GARTH.*
Doubleday US (1923)

Insp GARTH

British Policeman operating in England/New York

Sidekick: Sgt WHITTAKER

British Male - Subordinate

Hugo BLAYN 1908-1960

For writer details see Maria BLACK

Inventor of one other detective Dr CARRUTHERS

Citation Record: 3 Books

Except For One Thing - *First*
Paul UK (1947)

The Silvered Cage - *Last*
Dragon UK (1955)

Dr David GARTH and Det Insp TWIGG

solve two 'impossible' murders by strangulation in a hut on an unmarked beach.

British Policemen operating in London

John Dickson CARR 1906-1977 (American)

Invented 16 detectives - see Dr Gideon FELL

Citation Record: 1 Book

The Witch Of The Low Tide; An Edwardian Melodrama - *Only*
Harper & Row US (1961); Hamish Hamilton UK (1961)

Lord Rupert GARTHOYLE

solves the mystery of a woman's disappearance from a locked room.

British Male Amateur operating in England

Edgar JEPSON 1863-1938 (British)

Invented 3 detectives - see Lord BARRADINE

Citation Record: 1 Selected Short Story

The House That Paid No Rent
appeared in a collection, *Garthoyle Gardens* published by *Hutchinson* (UK 1913) and as *Alice Devine* published by *Bobbs* (US 1916).
Hutchinson UK (1916)

Joe GARTON

British Male Amateur operating in England

Gilbert HACKFORTH-JONES 1900- (British)

Invented 3 detectives - see Paul DECKER

Citation Record: 2 Books

Danger Below - *First*
Hodder & Stoughton UK (1963)

I Am The Captain - *Last*
Hodder & Stoughton UK (1963)

Det Mick GARVEY

is in a West country police force and his life and work have, up to now, been dogged with disasters. However, he is given one more case and, as an old-fashioned cop approaching middle age, he does well in this one, in addition to training a new young assistant.

British Policeman operating in England

Sidekick: Det Frank COOPER

British Male - Subordinate

Roger BUSBY 1941- (British)

Invented 3 detectives - see Det Insp LERIC

Citation Record: 1 Book

Garvey's Code - *Single*
Collins UK (1978)

GATCH

Second detective of LYON

Aaron GATES and Caro BURSA

American Amateurs operating in USA

Thomas J GREEN 1946- (American)

Writer: Thomas John GREEN

Citation Record: 1 Book

The Flowered Box - *Single*
Beaufort US (1980)

Ben GATES

American Male Private Detective operating in New York

Robert KYLE 1914- (American)

For writer details see Michael SHAYNE

Citation Record: 5 Books

Blackmail, Inc - *First*
Dell US (1958)

Ben Gates Is Hot - *Last*
Dell US (1964); Mayflower UK (1966)

Carol GATES

American Female Amateur operating in New York/Vermont

Laura COLBURN (American)

Citation Record: 3 Books

Death In A Small World - *First*
Zebra US (1979)

Death Through The Mill - *Latest*
Zebra US (1979)

Capt GAULT

British Male Amateur operating in several locations

William Hope HODGSON 1875-1918 (British)

See main detective CARNACKI

Citation Record: 10 Short Stories in 1 Collection

Captain Gault - *Collection 1*
Nash UK (1917); McBride US (1918)

Gideon GAULT

American Male Detective in Pulp Magazines operating in USA

Lieutenant CARLTON (American)

Invented 3 detectives - see Dan DECKER

Citation Record: 1 Selected Short Story

Gideon Gault's Red Light Case; Or, Solving The Mystery Of The Bronx River
Old Cap Collier Library US (18??)

John GAUNT and Prof Michael TAIRLAINE

are an unusual team. *John GAUNT,* formerly a consultant in criminology to Scotland Yard, is now an alcoholic, whilst *Michael TAIRLAINE,* an ex-Harvard man, lectures on crime fiction. Together they solve what seems to be an impossible crime, a death by crossbow in an old English castle.

British Male Amateurs and American Male Amateur operating in England

Carr DICKSON 1906-1977 (American)

For writer details see Dr Gideon FELL

Citation Record: 1 Book

The Bowstring Murders - *Only*
Morrow US (1933); Heinemann UK (1934)

Jonathan GAUNT

is an agent for the Scottish Remembrancer's Office.

British Male Professional Investigator operating in Scotland/Germany

Robert MACLEOD 1928- (British)

was born in Glasgow and educated at local schools. He worked as a reporter and editor on newspapers in Scotland, 1944-1962, after which time he became a free-lance writer. He has written at least sixty criminous novels, using not only his real name, but several pseudonyms, which he varied between the UK and USA. He has also written radio plays and non-fiction works.

Writer: William KNOX

Other Bylines:
Michael KIRK; Bill KNOX; Noah WEBSTER

Other Detectives:
Talos CORD; Andrew LAIRD

Citation Record: 9 Books

A Property In Cyprus - *First*
was published in the US as *FLICKERING DEATH* under the following byline.
Long UK (1970)

G

The Money Mountain - *Latest*
was published in the US as *A FLIGHT FROM PARIS* under the following byline.
Century Hutchinson UK (1987)

Noah WEBSTER 1928- (British)
For writer details see Jonathan GAUNT
Inventor of one other detective Andrew LAIRD
Citation Record: 9 Books
Flickering Death - *First*
was published in the UK as *A PROPERTY IN CYPRUS* under the preceding byline.
Doubleday US (1971)
A Flight From Paris - *Latest*
was published in the UK as *THE MONEY MOUNTAIN* under the preceding byline.
Doubleday US (1987)

G

Michael GAUNT

British Male Amateur operating in Europe

George BRADDON 1903- (British)
Writer: George Alexis Milkomanovich MILKOMANE
Citation Record: 4 Books
Death In The Picture - *First*
Jenkins UK (1951)
Time Off For Death - *Last*
Jenkins UK (1952); Roy US (1958)

Insp Jean-Paul GAUTIER

stalks the streets of Paris in the early part of the twentieth century on behalf of the French *Sûreté*. Continually harassed by his Director-General, he solves many a crime and beds many a woman during his arduous work.
French Policeman operating in Paris

Richard GRAYSON (British)
See main detective John BRYANT
Citation Record: 8 Books
The Murders At Impasse Louvain - *First*
Gollancz UK (1978); St Martin's US (1979)
Death Off Stage - *Latest*
Macmillan UK (1991)

Rod (The Terminator) GAVIN

American Male Professional Investigator operating in USA

John QUINN (American)
Writer: Dennis RODRIGUEZ
Citation Record: 6 Books
Mercenary Kill - *First*
Pinnacle US (1982)
The Checkmate Kill - *Latest*
Pinnacle US (1985)

Supt GAYLORD

British Policeman operating in England

W Murdoch DUNCAN 1909-1975 (British)
Invented 8 detectives - see Supt MACNEILL
Citation Record: 2 Books
The Hooded Man - *First*
Long UK (1960)
The Nighthawk - *Last*
Long UK (1962)

Joe GAYLORD

American Male Private Detective operating in California

M S MARBLE 1913- (American)
See main detective Craig MCKENZIE
Citation Record: 1 Book
Die By Night - *Only*
Rinehart US (1947); Barker UK (1948)

Lowell GAYLORD, Prof Angus MCDERMOTT, Lens PENGA and Prof Arthur CHURCHILL

When mayhem and multiple murder descend on the fictional Chatham University, who is to be next? Four professors band together to solve the crimes. *Lowell GAYLORD*, their leader, is the portly head of the English Department.
American Male Amateurs operating in USA

Mortimer POST 1900- (American)
Writer: Walter BLAIR
Citation Record: 1 Book
Candidate For Murder - *Only*
Doubleday US (1936)

Philip GAYMORE

Second detective of Insp WAKE

June GAYNOR

was formerly the sidekick of *Noel RAYMOND* but began to appear in stories on her own in *Girl's Crystal* from 1940.
British Female Amateur operating in England

Ronald FLEMING (British)
See main detective Noel RAYMOND
No citations

Absolom GEBB

British Male Amateur operating in England

Fergus HUME 1859-1932 (British)
Invented 24 detectives - see Insp Samuel GORBY
Citation Record: 1 Book
The Lady From Nowhere - *Only*
Chatto & Windus UK (1900)

Dirk GENTLY

runs an agency at 33A Peckender Street, London, N1. Its catching, bravura motto is 'We solve the whole crime'. There are strong science fiction elements in the plotting, not surprising from this author.
British Male Private Detective operating in England

Douglas ADAMS 1952- (British)
Citation Record: 2 Books
Dirk Gently's Holistic Detective Agency - *First*
Heinemann UK (1987); Simon & Schuster US (1987)
The Long Dark Tea-Time Of The Soul - *Latest*
Heinemann UK (1988); Simon & Schuster US (1989)

Insp/Ch Supt George GENTLY

is in a long series. The stories are semi-procedural in style, but, on the whole, concentrate on the work of *George GENTLY* himself.
British Policeman operating in England

Alan HUNTER 1922- (British)
was born in Hoveton, Norfolk, and educated at Wroxham School, Norfolk, later serving in the Royal Air Force, 1940-1946. He has been a farmer, bookseller, journalist and columnist.
Writer: Alan James Herbert HUNTER
Citation Record: 37 Books
Gently Does It - *First*
Cassell UK (1955); Rinehart US (1955)
Bomber's Moon - *Latest*
Constable UK (1994)

Ron GENTRY

operates as a PI in Sparta, New York, only because, although tall and well-built, he failed the eyesight test of the New York Police Department.
American Male Private Detective operating in New York

William L DEANDREA 1952- (American)
Invented 4 detectives - see Matt COBB
Citation Record: 1 Book
The Hog Murders - *Single*
Avon US (1979)

G

GEORGE
Second detective of PAOLA

Edwin GEORGE
is an expert on coins and solves cases of murder that involve his special knowledge.
American Male Amateur operating in Washington DC

Charles A GOODRUM 1923- (American)
was born in Pittsburgh, Kansas. He was a sometime member of staff at the US Library of Congress.
Writer: Charles Alvin GOODRUM
Citation Record: 2 Books
Carnage Of The Realm - *First*
Crown US (1979)
Dead For A Penny - *First**
Gollancz UK (1980)
Dewey Decimated - *Latest*
Curley UK (1978); Crown US (1977)

The GEORGIA DETECTIVE
American Male Detective in Pulp Magazines operating in USA

ANON
No citations

Philip GERARD
Second detective of Jocelyn O'ROARKE

George GERRARD
is a surgeon turned amateur sleuth.
British Male Amateur operating in England

M E BRADDON 1835-1915 (British)
Invented 9 detectives - see Robert AUDLEY
Citation Record: 1 Book
The Cloven Foot - *Only*
Maxwell UK (1879)

Keith GERSEN
sleuths at some time in the future.
American Male Sleuth

Jack VANCE 1917- (American)
is mainly an author of science fiction, which often includes novels of crime and detection.
Writer: Jack VANCE
Other Detectives:
Miro HETZEL
Magnus RIDOLPH
Citation Record: 5 Books
The Star King - *First*
Berkley US (1964); Dobson UK (1966)
The Book Of Dreams - *Latest*
Daw US (1981)
The Palace Of Love - *Latest*
Coronet UK (1982)

Sawley GERSON
solves the disappearance of gold bullion from a locked bank vault.
Canadian Male Amateur operating in Canada

John Russell FEARN 1908-1960
See main detective Jenkinson Talbot MERRIDREW
Citation Record: 1 Book
Robbery Without Violence - *Only*
This novelette appeared in the December 14 number.
In 'Toronto Star Weekly' CA (1957)

Col Anthony GETHRYN
is a typical example of the British Golden Age detective. He is upper-class, handsome, moneyed and, of course, always able to solve mysteries baffling the police.
British Male Sleuth operating in England

Philip MACDONALD 1899-1981 (British)
was born in London. He served in a cavalry regiment in the First World War and later trained horses for the army. In 1931 he went to Hollywood, where he wrote scripts and bred dogs. He received the Mystery Writers of America Edgar Allan Poe award in 1953 and 1956.
Other Detectives:
Dr ALCAZAR
Dudley ALLWRIGHT
Supt Arnold PIKE
Supt SHANTER
Citation Record: 13 Books
The Rasp - *First*
Collins UK (1924); Dial US (1925)
The List Of Adrian Messenger - *Last*
Jenkins UK (1960); Doubleday US (1959)

Insp GHENT
appears in one book with the author's other detective, *Sgt Paul DEAN.*
British Policeman operating in England

Basil FRANCIS 1906- (British)
Writer: Basil Hoskins FRANCIS
Other Detectives:
Sgt Paul DEAN
Insp GHENT and Sgt Paul DEAN
Citation Record: 1 Book
Death In Act IV - *Only*
Jenkins UK (1954)

Insp GHENT and Sgt Paul DEAN
also appear individually in other books by this author.
British Policemen operating in England

Basil FRANCIS 1906- (British)
Invented 3 detectives - see Insp GHENT
Citation Record: 1 Book
Death On The Roof - *Only*
Quality Press UK (1946)

Chullunder GHOSE
appears also in books with the author's other detectives, *Athelstan KING* and *James Schuyler 'Jimgrim' GRIM.*
Indian Male Amateur operating in India

Talbot MUNDY 1879-1940 (British)
Writer: William Lancaster GRIBBON
Other Detectives:
James Schuyler 'Jimgrim' GRIM
James Schuyler 'Jimgrim' GRIM and Chullunder GHOSE
James Schuyler 'Jimgrim' GRIM Chullunder GHOSE and Athelstan KING
Cotswold OMMONY
Citation Record: 3 Books
CID - *First*
Hutchinson UK (1932); Century US (1932)
The Red Flame Of Erinpura - *Last*
Hutchinson UK (1934)

Chullunder GHOSE
Appears with at least two other detectives - see James Schuyler 'Jimgrim' GRIM.

Chullunder GHOSE
Second detective of James Schuyler 'Jimgrim' GRIM

Walter GHOST
is patterned rather on *Sherlock HOLMES,* although the author, a great expert on *HOLMES,* does not make him a real parody.
American Male Amateur operating in USA
Sidekick: MOLLOCK
is completely inept.
American Male - Assistant

Vincent STARRETT 1886-1974 (American)
Invented 6 detectives - see Jimmie LAVENDER
Citation Record: 3 Books
Murder On "B" Deck - *First*
Doubleday US (1929); World's Work UK (1936)
The End Of Mr Garment - *Last*
Doubleday US (1932)

G

Insp Ganesh GHOTE

is one of the more unusual inventions of the genre, although there have been earlier fictional detectives in the Indian police force, both British and Indian. However, *Insp GHOTE* of the Bombay CID is in a class of his own, not only for the excellence of his characterisation and the clever plotting of the books in which he appears, but for his staying power in the highest echelons of the current genre. Although the author has maintained that he only visited India for the first time several years after the creation of his detective, the novels seem vividly to exude the genuine character of Indian life – at least as understood by the British, who influenced much of it. They present, in delightful form, the unusual problems of a clever and wonderfully correct detective in a country that is searching for its future yet leans so much on its past under the British Raj.

Indian Policeman operating in Bombay

H R F KEATING 1926- (British)

was born in St Leonards-on Sea, Sussex. He was educated at Merchant Taylors' School, London, and took a BA at Trinity College, Dublin, 1952. He served in the Army, 1945-1948, and then worked as a reporter, 1953-1958, becoming a full-time writer when he had the first of his remarkable *Insp GHOTE* novels published. A sometime newspaper editor and reviewer of crime literature, he has received many awards for his outstanding contributions to the genre, including the Crime Writers Association Gold Dagger award, 1964, and the Mystery Writers of America Edgar Allan Poe award, 1965.

Writer: Henry Reymond Fitzwalter KEATING

Other Byline: Evelyn HERVEY

Other Detectives:

CRAGGS
Supt HOWARD
Insp SYLVESTER
Sherlock HOLMES
Dorothy Mayotte RIGBY

Citation Record: 20 Books 13 Short Stories in 1 Collection

The Perfect Murder - *First*
Collins UK (1964); Dutton US (1965)

Doing Wrong - *Latest*
Macmillan UK (1994)

Inspector Ghote, His Life And Crimes - *Collection 1*
Hutchinson UK (1989)

The GIANT DETECTIVE

American Male Detective in Pulp Magazines operating in USA

ANON

Citation Record: 1 Book

The Giant Detective In Ireland - *Only*
Aldine US (?)

OLD SLEUTH (American)

Invented 40 detectives - see Brant ADAMS

Citation Record: 3 Books

The Giant Detective; Or, Can't Be Downed - *First*
Munro US (1896)

A Little Giant; Or, Feats And Frolics Of An Athlete - *First**
Ogilvie US (1897)

The Giant Detective Among The Cowboys - *Last*
Westbrook US (1908)

Insp GIBBON

New Zealander Policeman operating in New Zealand

Barbara COOPER 1915- (British)

took a degree in economics and statistics at Nottingham University and emigrated to New Zealand in 1950.

Writer: Evelyn Barbara COOPER

Citation Record: 2 Books

Target For Malice - *First*
Hale UK (1964)

Drown Him Deep - *Last*
Hale UK (1966)

Bert GIBBONS

Second detective of Mike TOZZI

James Augustus GIBBS

demonstrates a lot of chess lore, while being deeply suspicious of the man who has hired him to solve this case.

American Male Private Detective operating in USA

Means DAVIS (American)

Inventor of one other detective Matthew HIGGINS

Citation Record: 1 Book

The Chess Murders - *Only*
Random House US (1937)

Insp GIBSON

British Policeman operating in England

V Vidal DIEHL

Citation Record: 1 Selected Short Story

The Room 31 Riddle
In '20-Story Magazine' UK (?)

Cassie GIBSON

manages to keep her father's detective agency going, but runs into nasty trouble in her one case.

American Male Private Detective operating in USA

Floyd MAHANNAH 1911- (American)

Inventor of one other detective Riley WADDELL

Citation Record: 1 Book

The Yellow Hearse - *Only*
Duell US (1950); Boardman UK (1951)

No Luck For A Lady - *Only**
Signet US (1951)

Christopher GIBSON

American Male Amateur operating in USA

Ione MONTGOMERY (American)

Citation Record: 2 Books

The Golden Dress - *First*
Doubleday US (1940); Boardman UK (1944)

Death Won A Prize - *Last*
Doubleday US (1941); Cherry Tree UK (1944)

Glen GIBSON

is an attorney who investigates an 'impossible' case of hanging in a locked room.

British Male Amateur operating in England

John BENTLEY (British)

Invented 3 detectives - see Sir Richard HERRIVELL

Citation Record: 4 Books

Bullets Make Holes - *First*
Hutchinson UK (1945)

It Was Murder, They Said - *Last*
Hutchinson UK (1948)

Henry GIBSON

British Male Amateur operating in England

Denis MACKAIL 1892- (British)

Writer: Denis George MACKAIL

Inventor of one other detective Hugo PEAK

Citation Record: 10 Short Stories in 1 Collection

According To Gibson - *Collection 1*
Not all the stories are criminous.
Heinemann UK (1923); Houghton US (1923)

Jeremiah X GIBSON and MAC

are Assistant District Attorneys in Manhattan. They investigate, solve and bring to trial cases in the New York area, with nice background material used in the narration.

American Male Professional Investigators operating in New York

Hampton STONE 1906-1985 (American)

For writer details see Insp SCHMIDT

Citation Record: 18 Books

The Corpse In The Corner Saloon - *First*
Simon & Schuster US (1948)
The Kid Who Came Home With A Corpse - *Last*
Simon & Schuster US (1972)

William GIBSON
is a Scotland Yard man in this Victorian novel.
British Policeman operating in London

Hume NISBET 1849-1921? (British)
Invented 3 detectives - see Nicodemus Dove TURTLE
Citation Record: 1 Book
Comrades Of The Black Cross: A Romance Of Love And Crime - *Only*
White UK (1899)

Cdr George GIDEON
In 1955, the incredibly prolific *John CREASEY*, master of almost every sub-genre in the criminous field, turned his hand to a series of police procedurals, a type that was then becoming fashionable and was to persist. He created, under the pseudonym of *J J MARRIC*, one of the best and most enduring of them – at least, as far as the British species is concerned. His detective, *Cdr George GIDEON* of Scotland Yard, heads a team that deals with case after case in book after book until 1976. After the death of *CREASEY*, the series was continued by *William Vivian BUTLER* until the latter's death in 1987.
British Policeman operating in England

William Vivian BUTLER 1927- (British)
Citation Record: 5 Books
Gideon's Force - *First*
Hodder & Stoughton UK (1978); Stein US (1985)
Gideon's Raid - *Last*
Hodder & Stoughton UK (1986); Stein US (1986)

J J MARRIC 1908-1973 (British)
Writer: John CREASEY
For writer details see Insp Roger 'Handsome' WEST
Citation Record: 22 Books
Gideon's Day - *First*
Hodder & Stoughton UK (1955); Harper & Row US (1955)
Gideon Of Scotland Yard - *First**
Berkley US (1958)
Gideon's Drive - *Last*
Hodder & Stoughton UK (1976); Harper & Row US (1976)
Gideon's Fear - *Play*
was an adaptation by the author of his second *GIDEON* novel, *Gideon's Week*. A novel with the same title, published by *Hodder & Stoughton* (UK 1990), appeared under the authorship of *William Vivian BUTLER*, who was responsible for continuing the *GIDEON* series after the death of *John CREASEY*.
Evans UK (1967)

Ch Insp GIDLEIGH
also appears in a book called *Deadline for a Diplomat*, which was a republication by *Merit* (UK 1954) of an earlier book by this author, entitled *ROOKSMITHS*, in which the protagonist was another of the author's detectives, *Insp BASS*.
British Policeman operating in England

Seldon TRUSS 1892- (British)
Writer: Leslie Seldon TRUSS
Other Byline: George SELMARK
Other Detectives:
Insp BASS   Det Insp SHANE
Citation Record: 23 Books
Draw The Blinds - *First*
Hodder & Stoughton UK (1936)
The Town That Went Sick - *Last*
Hale UK (1965)
The Crooks' Shepherd - *Last**
Lothrop US (1936)

Adam GIFFORD
is a crime reporter who works under cover for the British War Office and becomes involved in cases of espionage and murder.
British Male Professional Investigator operating in England

Anthony LEJEUNE 1928- (British)
was born in London. He was educated at Merchant Taylors' School, London, and graduated from Balliol College, Oxford, 1953. He has been a reporter, editor, critic, broadcaster and contributor to several British and American literary journals.
Writer: Edward Anthony THOMPSON
Inventor of one other detective Prof James GLOWREY
Citation Record: 3 Books
News Of Murder - *First*
Macdonald UK (1961)
The Dark Trade - *Last*
Macdonald UK (1965); Doubleday US (1966)
Death Of A Pornographer - *Last**
Lancer US (1967)

G

GIGLAMPS
is a tramp and a rogue who does detecting on his travels.
British Male Amateur operating in England

Will SCOTT 1894?-1964 (British)
See main detective DISHER
Citation Record: 13 Short Stories in 1 Collection
Giglamps - *Collection 1*
Cassell UK (1924)

GIL
Second detective of JACK

Deake GILBERT
solves a case of death by stabbing in a locked room.
American Male Amateur operating in USA

Frederick T HILL 1866-1930 (American)
Writer: Frederick Trevor HILL
Citation Record: 1 Book
The Accomplice - *Only*
Harper & Row US (1905)

Paul GILCHRIST
is a scientist who turns sleuth.
British Male Amateur operating in England

L T MEADE and Clifford HALIFAX (British)
Writers: Elizabeth Thomasina Meade SMITH 1854-1914 and Edgar BEAUMONT
Other Detectives:
Policeman William GREEN   Dr Clifford HALIFAX
Citation Record: 8 Short Stories in 1 Collection
A Race With The Sun - *Collection 1*
Ward, Lock UK (1901)

Justin GILEAD and Alexander ZHARKOV
American Male Sleuths operating in Russia

Warren B MURPHY 1933- (American)
Invented 8 detectives - see Julian 'Digger' BURROUGHS
Citation Record: 2 Books
Grandmaster - *First*
was written in collaboration with Molly Cochran.
Pinnacle US (1984); Futura UK (1985)
High Priest - *Latest*
New American Library US (1987); Futura UK (1988)

Eve GILL
British Female Amateur operating in England

Selwyn JEPSON 1899-1989 (British)
Invented 4 detectives - see Roger SPAIN
Citation Record: 6 Books
Man Running - *First*
Macdonald UK (1948)

Killer By Proxy - *First**
Macdonald UK (1950)

Outrun The Constable - *First**
Doubleday US (1948)

Fear In The Wind - *Last*
Allen UK (1954)

Insp GILLANDREW

solves the murder of a factor in a little Scottish community.

British Policeman operating in Scotland

Angus MACLEOD 1906- (British)

Inventor of one other detective Insp GILROY

Citation Record: 1 Book

The Tough And The Tender - *Only*
Robson UK (1960); Roy US (1960)

Patrick GILLARD

is an ex-soldier, wounded badly in the Falklands war and now a Major with a British undercover counter-espionage unit.

British Male Secret Agent operating in England

Margaret DUFFY (British)

Citation Record: 2 Books

A Murder Of Crows - *First*
Piatkus UK (1987)

Death Of A Raven - *Latest*
Piatkus UK (1989)

Geoffrey GILLESBY

British Male Private Detective operating in England

J Fitzgerald MOLLOY 1858-1908

Writer: Joseph Fitzgerald MOLLOY

Citation Record: 1 Book

An Excellent Knave - *Only*
Lovell US (1892); Hutchinson UK (1893)

Supt GILLIANT

British Policeman operating in England

John WAINWRIGHT 1921- (British)

Invented 9 detectives - see Ch Insp/Supt LENNOX

Citation Record: 3 Books

The Crystallised Carbon Pig - *First*
Collins UK (1966); Walker US (1967)

A Ripple Of Murders - *Latest*
Macmillan UK (1978); St Martin's US (1979)

Anthony GILLINGHAM

happens to be on the spot when the local police are faced with a most ingenious murder. He is upper-class, has a silly face and light manner, as befits his period, but he also has a brilliant mind. The case is, indeed, a most difficult and ingenious one and the police are suitably and conventionally baffled. The book is outstanding even by the standards of the best of the 1930s that were to follow.

British Male Amateur operating in England

Sidekick: Bill BEVERLEY

is a young man who is a friend of *GILLINGHAM* and is promoted to being his assistant in this one classic tale. He is a prototype for the kind of 'silly-ass' assistant, beloved of British authors of the 1920s and 1930s.

British Male - Narrator

A A MILNE 1882-1956 (British)

was born in London. He was educated at Westminster School, London, and took a BA in Mathematics at Trinity College, Cambridge, 1903. A journalist and playwright, he is renowned as the author of plays, stories and verse for children, the best known of which is the immortal *Winnie-the-Pooh.* He wrote only this one detective novel, shortly after his demobilisation in 1918. It has been reprinted many times and is still regarded by some as a masterpiece. Indeed, it pre-empted many of the conventions of the British Age of the late 1920s and 1930s. *MILNE's* only other entries into the criminous genre were a few short stories, a play and a *Sherlock HOLMES* parody.

Writer: Alan Alexander MILNE

Adopter of one other detective Sherlock HOLMES

Citation Record: 1 Book

The Red House Mystery - *Only*
Methuen UK (1922); Dutton US (1922)

Buckmaster GILLOON

solves the mystery of the disappearance of a body, dead or possibly still alive, from a gallows.

American Male Sleuth operating in USA

Bill PRONZINI 1943- (American)

Invented 5 detectives - see NAMELESS DETECTIVE

Citation Record: 1 Selected Short Story

The Arrowmont Prison Riddle
In 'Alfred Hitchcock's Mystery Magazine' US (1976)

Mr GILLY

British Male Amateur operating in England

W Murdoch DUNCAN 1909-1975 (British)

Invented 8 detectives - see Supt MACNEILL

Citation Record: 2 Books

The Crime Master - *First*
Long UK (1963)

Death And Mr Gilly - *Last*
Long UK (1974)

Supt Lawrence GILMARTIN

muddles his way through period pieces in England and sometimes France.

British Policeman operating in England/France

Charles BARRY 1877- (British)

Writer: Charles BRYSON

Citation Record: 15 Books

The Smaller Penny - *First*
Holden UK (1925); Dutton US (1928)

Nicholas Lattermole's Case - *Last*
Hurst UK (1939)

Insp GILMOUR

solves the mystery of several strange vanishings.

British Policeman operating in England

G McLeod WINSOR (British)

Writer: George McLeod WINSOR

Citation Record: 1 Book

The Mysterious Disappearances - *Only*
Faber UK (1926)

Vanishing Men - *Only**
Morrow US (1927)

Insp GILROY

solves the mystery of how two fishermen met their deaths at a Scottish fishing hotel.

British Policeman operating in Scotland

Angus MACLEOD 1906- (British)

See main detective Insp GILLANDREW

Citation Record: 1 Book

Blessed Among Women - *Only*
Dobson UK (1965); Roy US (1967)

Mr GIMBLET

British Male Amateur operating in England

Mrs Charles BRYCE (British)

Citation Record: 2 Books

Mrs Vanderstein's Jewels - *First*
Bodley Head UK (1914)

The Ashiel Mystery - *Last*
Bodley Head UK (1915)

GINGKO

is a so-called 'macrobiotic sage' who, accompanied by a bizarre group of characters, retraces the postulated journey of *Sherlock HOLMES* during the 'Great Hiatus', when the detective was presumed dead after his encounter with Professor Moriarty.

Chinese Policeman operating in Tibet

Sidekick: Jeff MILTON

is a journalist.

American Male - Friend

Alex JACK (American)

Citation Record: 1 Book

Inspector Gingko Tips His Hat To Sherlock Holmes - *Single*

One Peaceful World US (1994)

Eddie GINLEY

is a drop-out. An avid reader of detective stories, he gets into a real case after advertising himself as a PI. Exciting stuff, even so!

British Male Private Detective operating in Liverpool

Neville SMITH (British)

Citation Record: 1 Book

Gumshoe - *Only*

is a novelization of a film.

Collins UK (1971); Fontana US (1971)

GIPSY RENO

American Male Detective in Pulp Magazines operating in USA

OLD SLEUTH (American)

Invented 40 detectives - see Brant ADAMS

Citation Record: 1 Book

Gipsy Reno, The Detective - *Only*

Ogilvie US (1896)

GIPSY ROSE

American Female Detective in Pulp Magazines operating in USA

OLD SLEUTH (American)

Invented 40 detectives - see Brant ADAMS

Citation Record: 1 Book

Gipsy Rose, The Female Detective - *Only*

Ogilvie US (1898)

Abel GIRDLESTONE

is a detective at Scotland Yard in this Victorian novel.

British Policeman operating in London

Robert OVERTON (British)

Citation Record: 1 Book

A Chase Round The World: The Following-Up Of A Chain Of Mystery - *Only*

Warne UK (1899)

Mark GIRLAND

is an ex-CIA man who becomes a private investigator, sometimes operating in Paris and always involved in the usual racy, compelling but unbelievable world that this author has made his own. He appears also in other books with at least two of the author's other detectives, *Lu SILK* and *Herman RADNITZ*.

American Male Private Detective operating in California/Germany

Sidekick: Jack KERMAN

is a fast-talking, would-be comic legman for the detective and is borrowed from some of the author's other books.

American Male - Assistant

James Hadley CHASE 1906-1985 (British)

Invented 14 detectives - see Dave FENNER

Citation Record: 2 Books

You Have Yourself A Deal - *First*

Hale UK (1966); Walker US (1966)

Have This One On Me - *Last*

Hale UK (1967)

Mark GIRLAND and Herman RADNITZ

also appear individually in other books by this author.

American Male Private Detectives operating in several locations

James Hadley CHASE 1906-1985 (British)

Invented 14 detectives - see Dave FENNER

Citation Record: 1 Book

This Is For Real - *Only*

Hale UK (1965); Walker US (1967)

Mark GIRLAND, Lu SILK and Herman RADNITZ

are characters who have all appeared in other books by this author, who did tend to use whatever came to hand.

American Male Private Detectives operating in Florida

James Hadley CHASE 1906-1985 (British)

Invented 14 detectives - see Dave FENNER

Citation Record: 2 Books

Believed Violent - *First*

Hale UK (1968)

The Whiff Of Money - *Last*

Hale UK (1969); Pocket Books US (1972)

Steven GIROUX

American Male Amateur operating in USA

Bill PRONZINI 1943- (American)

Invented 5 detectives - see NAMELESS DETECTIVE

Citation Record: 1 Book

Masques - *Single*

Arbor US (1981)

Mrs GLADDEN

is arguably the very first fictional female detective, although most other sources claim *Mrs PASCHAL*. She is said to be a member of a London police force, which seems to engage also in some private detecting, using scientific methods, including chemical analysis.

British Policewoman operating in London

Andrew FORRESTER Jr (British)

Invented 3 detectives - see Andrew FORRESTER

Citation Record: 1 Book

The Female Detective - *Only*

Ward, Lock UK (1864)

Norman GLADE

British Male Amateur operating in England

Moray DALTON (British)

See main detective Insp Hugh COLLIER

Citation Record: 1 Book

The Body In The Road - *Only*

Low UK (1931); Harper & Row US (1930)

Dr Horatio GLASS

British Male Amateur operating in England

John Carter DICKSON (American) and John RHODE (British)

were, of course, two genre writers at the height of their powers when they wrote this one work jointly.

Writers: John Dickson CARR 1906-1977 and Cecil John Charles STREET 1884-1965

Citation Record: 1 Book

Drop To His Death - *Only*

Heinemann UK (1939)

Fatal Descent - *Only**

Dodd, Mead US (1939)

Joel GLASS

is a bookseller in search of some rare books, the disappearance of which leads to murder and his attempt to solve the crime.

American Male Amateur operating in New York

Marco PAGE 1909-1968 (American)

was born in Philadelphia.

Writer: Harry KURNITZ

Other Detectives:
Ellis BLAISE David CALDER
Citation Record: 1 Book
Fast Company - *Only*
Dodd, Mead US (1938); Heinemann UK (1938)

Alex GLAUBERMAN

calls himself a 'Semitic Sherlock Holmes'. In remission from lymphoma, he manages to solve a crime or two.

American Male Amateur operating in USA

Dick CLUSTER 1947- (American)

Citation Record: 2 Books
Return To Sender - *First*
Dutton US (1989)
Repulse Monkey - *Latest*
Dutton US (1989)

G

Elizabeth GLEN

British Female Amateur operating in England

Annie S SWAN (British)

Writer: Mrs Annie S Swan BURDETT-SMITH
Inventor of one other detective Anne HYDE
Citation Record: 12 Short Stories in 1 Collection
Elizabeth Glen, MB: The Experiences Of A Lady Doctor - *Collection 1*
Hutchinson UK (1895)

Mr GLENCANNON

American Male Amateur operating in several locations

Guy GILPATRIC 1896-1950

Citation Record: 57 Short Stories in 6 Collections
Scotch And Water - *Collection 1*
Not all the stories are criminous.
Short stories - 10
Lane UK (1931); Dodd, Mead US (1931)
Half-Seas Over - *Collection 2*
Not all the stories are criminous.
Short stories - 10
Lane UK (1932); Dodd, Mead US (1932)
Mr Glencannon - *Collection 3*
Short stories - 10
Dodd, Mead US (1934); Lane UK (1935)
Three Sheets In The Wind - *Collection 4*
Not all the stories are criminous.
Short stories - 9
Lane UK (1936); Dodd, Mead US (1936)
The Gentleman With The Walrus Moustache - *Collection 5*
Not all the stories are criminous.
Short stories - 10
Dodd, Mead US (1939)
Glencannon Afloat - *Collection 6*
Not all the stories are criminous.
Short stories - 8
Dodd, Mead US (1941)

Sir Toby GLENDOWER and Penelope SPRING

are archaeologists. As archaeologists are wont to do – in the criminous genre, that is – they unearth more than old bones. They find sleuthing just as fascinating as digging.

British Male Amateur and British Female Amateur operating in USA/Europe

Margot ARNOLD 1925-

Writer: Petronelle Marguerite Mary COOK
Citation Record: 7 Books
Exit Actors, Dying - *First*
Playboy US (1979); Chivers UK (1982)
Dirge For A Dorset Druid - *Latest*
Foul Play US (1993)

Al GLENNE

Male Sleuth operating in France/South America

M G BRAUN (French)

Writer: Maurice Gilles BRAUN
Citation Record: 4 Books
Operation Atlantis - *First*
Berkley US (1966)
That Girl From Istanbul - *Last*
Berkley US (1966)

Paula GLENNING

is something of a literary lioness, being the (fictional) Professor of Literature at the (real) Princess Elizabeth College, London. Her cases usually involves strong literary problems as well as murder and she is, in her later books, aided by *James GOFF*. In her first book, she is subsidiary, sleuth-wise, to *Richard GRIEVE*.

British Female Amateur operating in England

Sidekick: James GOFF
assists *Paula GLENNING* in her amateur sleuthing and becomes her lover.
British Male - Friend

Anna CLARKE 1919- (British)

was born in Cape Town, South Africa. She was educated at schools in Cape Town and in Montreal, and later took a BSc in Economics at the University of London, 1945. She has held senior positions in several English publishing houses and is the author of over twenty genre novels.

Other Detectives:
Helen BOYDEN
Richard GRIEVE, Paula GLENNING and James GOFF
Sally LIVINGSTONE
Citation Record: 7 Books
Cabin 3033 - *First*
Although she had previously appeared in *LAST JUDGMENT* (qv), this was the first book in which *Paula GLENNING* was the senior sleuth and was assisted by *James GOFF*.
Doubleday US (1986); Chivers UK (1988)
The Case Of The Paranoid Patient - *Latest*
Doubleday US (1994)

Paula GLENNING

Appears with at least two other detectives - see Richard GRIEVE.

Murray GLICK

American Male Private Detective operating in Chicago

Sidekick: Andy SUSSMAN
American Male - Assistant

Michael J KATZ 1951- (American)

Citation Record: 2 Books
Murder Off The Glass - *First*
Walker US (1987)
Last Dance At Redondo Beach - *Latest*
Putnam US (1989)

Barney GLINES

appears in other books by this author as the sidekick of *Mike FONTAINE*.

American Male Private Detective operating in USA

Thomas WILLS 1922-1960 (American)

For writer details see Timothy DANE
Citation Record: 1 Book
You'll Get Yours - *Only*
was republished under the following byline.
Lion US (1952)

William ARD 1922-1960 (American)

Invented 5 detectives - see Timothy DANE
Other Byline: Thomas WILLS
Citation Record: 1 Book
You'll Get Yours - *Only*
was previously published under the preceding byline.
Berkley US (1960)

Insp GLOOM

British Policeman operating in England

Frank KING 1892-1958 (British)

Invented 6 detectives - see Insp CHAMBERS

Citation Record: 3 Books

The Case Of The Painted Girl - *First*
Jarrolds UK (1931)

The Case Of The Vanishing Artist - *Last*
Hale UK (1956)

Insp GLOVER

Second detective of Supt QUILL

Insp GLOVER and Harry CURRY

are involved in murders at the fictional Penfield University in the Eastern USA, where *Harry CURRY* is the Professor of Sociology.

American Policeman and American Male Sleuth operating in USA

March EVERMAY 1893- (American)

was born in Washington DC. She wrote many romantic novels under her real name and two crime novels under the pseudonym.

Writer: Mathilder EIKER

Citation Record: 2 Books

They Talked Of Poison - *First*
Macmillan US (1938); Jarrolds UK (1939)

This Death Was Murder - *Last*
Macmillan US (1940); Jarrolds UK (1940)

Derek GLOVER

British Male Amateur operating in Africa

S C MASON (British)

Writer: Charles MASON

Citation Record: 2 Books

The Man On The Spot - *First*
Bles UK (1938)

Murder At Bador - *Last*
Bell US (1938)

Prof James GLOWREY

!See Appendix 2.

British Male Amateur operating in England

Anthony LEJEUNE 1928- (British)

See main detective Adam GIFFORD

Citation Record: 2 Books

Professor In Peril - *First*
Macmillan UK (1987); Doubleday US (1988)

Key Without A Door - *Latest*
Macmillan UK (1988); Doubleday US (1989)

Sheerluck GNOMES

is a *Sherlock HOLMES* parody.

British Male Professional Amateur operating in England

Sidekick: Dr POTSON

is his parody *WATSON*-like assistant.

British Male - Assistant

T P STAFFORD (British)

Citation Record: 1 Selected Short Story

The Bar Of Soap; Or, The Jew Au Jus - *Parody 1*

was one of the earliest *Sherlock HOLMES* parodies.

In 'The Modern Detective' UK (1898)

Nicholas GOADE

British Male Amateur operating in England

E Phillips OPPENHEIM 1866-1946 (British)

was born in London and educated at Wyggeston Grammar School, Leicester. Although he worked in his father's leather business until at least 1906, he published his first novel in 1887. He subsequently wrote at least a hundred novels, in divers genres, under his own name and under pseudonyms, as well as plays and many short stories, the latter often published as collections.

Writer: Edward Phillips OPPENHEIM

Other Detectives:

Const BENSKIN	Gen BESSERLEY
Samuel T BILLINGHAM	Miss BROWN
Gilbert CHANNAY	Joseph P CRAY
Insp DICKINS	Malcolm GOSSETT
Commodore JASEN	JENNERTON
The Hon Algernon KNOX	Ambrose LAVENDALE
John T LAXWORTHY	Benjamin LEVY
Baroness LINZ	Sir Joseph LONDE
Charles LYSON	MANNISTER
Lucie MOTT	Aaron RODD
Peter RUFF	Mr SABIN
Michael SAYERS	Sir Jasper SLANE
Grant SLATTERY	Insp SNELL

Citation Record: 10 Short Stories in 1 Collection

Nicholas Goade, Detective - *Collection 1*
Hodder & Stoughton UK (1927); Little, Brown US (1929)

Insp GODBOLD

British Policeman operating in England

Ben BOLT 1872- (British)

Invented 5 detectives - see Bob PONTING

Citation Record: 1 Book

The Green Lantern - *Only*
Ward, Lock UK (1935)

Insp GODBOLD and Bob PONTING

British Policeman and British Male Amateur operating in England

Ben BOLT 1872- (British)

Invented 5 detectives - see Bob PONTING

Citation Record: 1 Book

A Shot In The Dark - *Only*
Ward, Lock UK (1935)

Sgt GODBOLD

Second detective of Sgt TREVOR

Jim GODFREY

American Male Amateur operating in New York

Burton E STEVENSON 1872-1962 (American)

See main detective Anthony BIGELOW

Citation Record: 6 Books

The Holladay Case - *First*
Holt US (1903); Heinemann UK (1903)

The House Next Door - *Last*
Dodd, Mead US (1932); Hutchinson UK (1932)

Paul GODFREY

British Male Amateur operating in England

B L FARJEON 1838-1903 (British)

Invented 7 detectives - see Robert AGNOLD

Citation Record: 1 Book

The Betrayal Of John Fordham - *Only*
Hutchinson UK (1896)

Haggai GODIN

Male Sleuth operating in Europe/Africa

Owen JOHN 1918- (British)

Citation Record: 6 Books

Thirty Days Hath September - *First*
Joseph UK (1966); Dutton US (1967)

Sabotage - *Last*
Cassell UK (1973); Dutton US (1973)

Cynthia GODWIN

Second detective of Vincent STALLARD

Kate GOELET

was created by the daddy of pulp writers, the great *Harlan P HALSEY*, who was *OLD SLEUTH* himself. She appeared in a number of stories in pulp magazines around the 1880s and is probably the first fictional American female sleuth. Described as 'without parallel in New York', she was young and, later in the series, was married. A mistress of disguise, as was common at the time, she also possessed great courage and skill when it came to knives and other devices and weapons.

American Female Private Detective operating in New York

Harlan Page HALSEY 1837-1898 (American)

For writer details see Phil SCOTT

Other Detectives:

Bruce ANGELO | Dudie DUNNE
Kate EDWARDS | MANFRED
VAN

Citation Record: 1 Collection

The Lady Detective - *Collection 1*
US (1880)

James GOFF

Appears with at least two other detectives - see Richard GRIEVE.

Alexander Magnus GOLD

is an ex-engineer, now recovering from a heart attack and so not able to get around much. Even so, he runs his own detective agency. His cases often involve murder in locked rooms and other seemingly impossible crimes.

American Male Private Detective operating in New York

Sidekick: Norma GOLD
plays an important part in the work of her husband's agency, doing the legwork around New York while he thinks out the solutions to his rather unusual cases.

American Female - Wife

Herbert RESNICOW 1921- (American)

Invented 3 detectives - see Ed BAER

Citation Record: 5 Books

The Gold Solution - *First*
St Martin's US (1983); Hale UK (1984)

The Gold Gamble - *Latest*
St Martin's US (1988)

Benny GOLD

Appears with at least two other detectives - see Mark TREASURE.

Glad GOLD

solves cases of murder on the campus.

American Female Amateur operating in Massachusetts

Theodora WENDER (American)

Writer: Dorothea WENDER

Citation Record: 2 Books

Knight Must Fall - *First*
Avon US (1985)

Murder Gets A Degree - *Latest*
US (1986)

Marty GOLD

American Male Amateur operating in New York

Marvin KAYE 1938- (American)

Writer: Marvin Nathan KAYE

Other Detectives:

Sherlock HOLMES | Hilary QUAYLE

Citation Record: 2 Books

My Son, The Druggist - *First*
Doubleday US (1977)

My Brother, The Druggist - *Latest*
Doubleday US (1979)

Lt Max GOLD

American Policeman operating in New York

Octavus Roy COHEN 1891-1959 (American)

Invented 6 detectives - see Jim HANVEY

Citation Record: 3 Books

Danger In Paradise - *First*
Macmillan US (1945); Hale UK (1949)

Don't Ever Love Me - *Last*
Macmillan US (1947); Barker UK (1948)

Lt Paul GOLD and Tommy LARKIN

When an immigrant professor at the fictional Michigan State University is brutally murdered, *Lt GOLD* of the local police is called in. Assisted by the amateur sleuthing of *Tommy LARKIN*, the professor's research student, he solves a case that has its origins back in the Germany of the 1930s.

American Policeman and American Male Amateur operating in Michigan

Leonard GREENBAUM 1930- (American)

was born in Boston. He was the sometime Assistant Professor of English at the University of Michigan.

Citation Record: 1 Book

Out Of Shape - *Only*
Harper & Row US (1969); Gollancz UK (1970)

Rachel GOLD

American Female Sleuth operating in USA

Michael A KAHN 1952- (American)

Citation Record: 2 Books

Death Benefits - *First*
Dutton US (1992)

Firm Ambitions - *Latest*
Dutton US (1994)

Lt Ronnie GOLD

American Policeman operating in Chicago

Gary PAULSEN 1939- (American)

Citation Record: 2 Books

The Sweeper - *First*
Raven US (1980)

Clutterkill - *Latest*
Raven US (1981)

The GOLD STAR DETECTIVE

American Male Detective in Pulp Magazines operating in USA

ANON

No citations

GOLDBERG

American Male Sleuth operating in USA

Arnold GRISMAN (American)

Citation Record: 1 Book

The Winning Streak - *Single*
St Martin's US (1985)

Det Sgt Sammy GOLDEN and Father Joseph SHANLEY

seem, at first sight, an unlikely combination. *Sammy GOLDEN* is a lowly Jewish cop and *Father SHANLEY* is the local Roman Catholic priest. Together, however, they solve some rather good whodunnits, not without danger to *SHANLEY* and much rescue work by *GOLDEN*.

American Policeman and American Male Amateur operating in Los Angeles

Jack WEBB 1920- (American)

Citation Record: 9 Books

The Big Sin - *First*
Rinehart US (1952); Boardman UK (1953)

The Gilded Witch - *Last*
Regency US (1963); Boardman UK (1963)

Sgt GOLDSMITH

Second detective of Father DUFFY

Det Jay GOLDSTEIN, Det Carlos CRUZ and Carrie RAYBORN

In two books, the detectives are in the Oakland police force. In the first, they arrest *Carrie RAYBORN's* young daughter for a minor offence and then the three become closely involved in a case of murder. The trio, of two cops and one female amateur, is deliberate, novel and interesting. The format is continued into the second book, the female amateur now being *Jean TALBOT.*

Two American Policemen and one American Female Amateur operating in California

Marilyn WALLACE 1941- (American)

was born in Brooklyn, New York. She took a BA in English at the City University of New York in 1962 and attended the New School for Social Research, New York, 1963-1966. She has been an English teacher, was a qualified pastry chef, 1979, and became the vice-president of the Western Logic Corporation, California, 1981-1985.

Inventor of one other detective group Det Jay GOLDSTEIN, Det Carlos CRUZ and Jean TALBOT

Citation Record: 1 Book

A Case Of Loyalties - *Single*
St Martin's US (1986)

Det Jay GOLDSTEIN, Det Carlos CRUZ and Jean TALBOT

In the second of their two books, *Jay GOLDSTEIN* and *Carlos CRUZ* are involved in another detective trio with an amateur female sleuth.

Two American Policemen and one American Female Amateur operating in California

Marilyn WALLACE 1941- (American)

See main detective group Det Jay GOLDSTEIN, Det Carlos CRUZ and Carrie RAYBORN

Citation Record: 1 Book

Primary Target - *Single*
Bantam US (1988)

Comrade Sherslav GOLMSKY

In this delightful *Sherlock HOLMES* parody, *Comrade Sherslav GOLMSKY* and his sidekick, *Dr Ivan VATSOV*, solve the case of a missing football player, to the chagrin of the local cop, *Insp LESTRADSKY*.

Russian Male Professional Amateur operating in Russia

Sidekick: Dr Ivan VATSOV
is his parody *WATSON*-like assistant.
Russian Male - Narrator

Stooge: Insp LESTRADSKY
is a Russian cop who seems just as awkward a stooge as many a British or American one. His name gives a nod towards *Insp LESTRADE* of the *Sherlock HOLMES* canon.
Russian Male

John BOARDMAN (American)

Citation Record: 1 Selected Short Story

The Adventure Of The Sinister American - *Parody 1*
appeared in the November 1959 number.
In 'Double Action Detective & Mystery Stories' US (1959)

Pedro GONZALES

Spanish Male Amateur operating in Spain

Geoffrey HOUSEHOLD 1900-1988 (British)

See main detective Roger TAINE

Citation Record: 1 Book

Olura - *Only*
Joseph UK (1965); Little, Brown US (1965)

Carl GOOD

deals with cases in the gaudy, bawdy underworld of Chicago.

American Male Private Detective operating in Chicago

Robert O SABER 1913- (American)

Writer: Milton K OZAKI

Other Detectives:
Phil KEENE Max KEENE

Citation Record: 6 Books

The Dove - *First*
Handi-Books US (1951)

Sucker Bait - *Last*
Graphic US (1965)

Simon GOOD

British Male Amateur operating in England

George DAVIS (British)

Citation Record: 6 Books

Roag's Syndicate - *First*
Chapman & Hall UK (1960)

Death Of A Fire-Raiser - *Last*
Collins UK (1974)

Joe GOODEY

was fired from the San Francisco Police Department for accidentally killing the mayor's cousin. Well, anyone can make a mistake; but, surprisingly, he is given a PI licence to help the police solve a politically delicate case of murder.

American Male Private Detective operating in San Francisco

Charles ALVERSON 1935- (American)

Inventor of one other detective Alec HOERNER

Citation Record: 2 Books

Goodey's Last Stand - *First*
Houghton US (1975); Hamish Hamilton UK (1976)

Not Sleeping, Just Dead - *Latest*
Houghton US (1977); Hamish Hamilton UK (1978)

Insp George GOODMAN

appears in what is often said to be the first 'locked-room' or 'impossible' crime story, in which a man's throat is cut in a locked bedroom. He is a retired Inspector of the Metropolitan Police who is already, in 1892, showing the confidence and arrogance of *Sherlock HOLMES*, created only a few years earlier.

!See Appendix 2.

British Male Ex-Policeman operating in England

Israel ZANGWILL 1864-1926 (British)

was born in London. He had a simple upbringing but was able to graduate from London University. He became a journalist, subsequently became a confirmed Zionist, and wrote several novels with Jewish backgrounds, including a masterpiece, *Children of the Ghetto*.

Citation Record: 1 Book

The Big Bow Mystery - *Only*
is said to be the first locked-room detective story.
Henry UK (1892); Rand, McNally US (1895)

Rayford GOODMAN

is called 'The Private Eye to the Stars'.

American Male Private Detective operating in Hollywood

Sidekick: Mark BRADLEY
American Male - Aide

Stan CUTLER (American)

Citation Record: 1 Book

Rough Cut - *Single*
Ballantine US (1994)

Dr GOODRICH

was an early example of the new, so-called 'scientific detectives', but he did not last for more than a few issues. In the story cited he solves a locked-room murder case.

British Male Professional Investigator operating in England

Stoddard GOODHUE (British)

Citation Record: 1 Selected Short Story

The Locked Room
In 'Everybody's' UK (1922)

Robert GOODWIN

was one of the spate of 'scientific detectives' to appear in stories in the early issues of *Amazing Stories*, the first science fiction magazine.

American Male Detective in Pulp Magazines operating in USA

Merlin Moore TAYLOR (American)

No citations

Insp GOOLE
is the mysterious visitor who solves the problems of a family torn apart in this, the finest of the author's plays.
British Policeman operating in England

J B PRIESTLEY 1894-1984 (British)

Invented 3 detectives - see Lionel Humphrey SALT and Maggie CULTHORPE

Citation Record: 1 Book

An Inspector Calls - *Play*
Heinemann UK (1947)

Insp Samuel GORBY
was invented for what the author saw as a new market, the detective story in Australia. He holds an honoured place in the history of the genre, as *THE MYSTERY OF THE HANSOM CAB* is considered to be first detective *short* story by a British writer, pre-dating those of *Sir Arthur Conan DOYLE.*
Australian Policeman operating in Melbourne

G

Fergus HUME 1859-1932 (British)

was of New Zealand stock, but he himself was born in England. He returned to New Zealand to study Law at the University of Otago, being admitted to the Bar there in 1885. He returned to England to settle in 1888 and is known to be the author of more than a hundred and thirty novels, which are now little known.

Writer: Ferguson Wright HUME

Other Detectives:

Valentine BELT	Insp BLAIR
Insp CHARD	Lucian DENZIL
DOVE	Mr DOWKER
Octavius FANKS	Gerald FOSTER
Absolom GEBB	Maj Laurence JEN
Dr LUKE	Laurence MALLOW
Archie MAXWELL	Paul MEXTON
Det Sgt O'BYRNE	Insp PRINCE
Hagar STANLEY	Spencer TAIT and DENHAM
Gilbert THRESHAM and Percy BARSTONE	
Insp TINKLER	Mr TORRY
Insp TRUMPET	Insp WOKE

Citation Record: 1 Book

The Mystery Of A Hansom Cab - *Only*
was a key story in the history of the genre, although a very ordinary one by later standards. The first Australian edition is said to be the rarest book in crime literature and only two copies are known to exist. The author, who went on to become one of the most prolific writers of mystery fiction, wrote it swiftly when he learned that the detective stories of the famed *Emile GABORIAU* were enjoying a large sale in Australia. He then sold the rights of his book to a group of English investors for £50. It went on to sell, in paper covers, about half a million copies, a truly phenomenal success.
Kemp & Boyce AU (1886); Hume UK (1886); Munro US (1888)

Alison B GORDON
is an ex-CIA agent, beautiful naturally, sexy of course, and a great detective; for, not only does she save clients from danger, but sometimes she does the same for the US of A itself.
American Female Private Detective operating in USA

Walter WAGER 1924- (American)

Writer: Walter Herman WAGER

Citation Record: 3 Books

Blue Leader - *First*
Arbor US (1979)

Blue Murder - *Latest*
Arbor US (1981); Severn UK (1984)

Ben GORDON
solves cases of murder on the campus.
American Male Amateur operating in New York

Ivan T ROSS 1932- (American)

Writer: Robert ROSSNER

Citation Record: 4 Books

Murder Out Of School - *First*
Simon & Schuster US (1960); Heinemann UK (1960)

Teacher's Blood - *Last*
Doubleday US (1964); Hale UK (1966)

Chet GORDON
was created by the author under his real name and appeared several years before the author adopted the pseudonym of *Ross MACDONALD,* under which he created the series of novels featuring one of the classic American detectives, *Lew ARCHER.*
American Male Sleuth operating in Michigan

Kenneth MILLAR 1915-1983 (American)

Citation Record: 2 Books

The Dark Tunnel - *First*
Dodd, Mead US (1944)

I Die Slowly - *First**
Lion US (1955)

Trouble Follows Me - *Last*
Dodd, Mead US (1946)

Night Train - *Last**
Lion US (1955)

Ellie GORDON
is middle-aged, newly divorced, sharp, witty and nicely feminine. She signs on as the office manager of a firm of attorneys and becomes involved in cases of murder, which she solves.
American Female Amateur operating in California

Karin BERNE (American)

Writers: Sue BERNELL and Michaela KARNI

Citation Record: 3 Books

Bare Acquaintances - *First*
Popular Library US (1985)

False Impressions - *Latest*
Popular Library US (1986)

Insp Hugh GORDON
Second detective of Liane CRAWFORD

Karen GORDON
American Female Amateur operating in USA

William HARDY 1922- (American)

Writer: William Marion HARDY

Inventor of one other detective pair Bob ADAMS and Anne MINER

Citation Record: 1 Book

A Little Sin - *Only*
Dodd, Mead US (1958); Hamilton UK (1959)

Lee GORDON
solves the murder of a tycoon's mistress.
American Male Private Detective operating in USA

Douglas HEYES 1921- (American)

Invented 3 detectives - see Steve MALLORY

Citation Record: 1 Book

The 12th Of Never - *Only*
Random House US (1963); Boardman UK (1964)

Mel GORDON
is a screenwriter who solves the disappearance of a film producer from a guarded set.
American Male Amateur operating in USA

Stanley ELLIN 1916- (American)

Invented 4 detectives - see Jake DEKKER

Citation Record: 1 Selected Short Story

The Twelfth Statue
In 'Ellery Queen 's Mystery Magazine' US (1967)

Monte GORDON and Insp MEDFORD
American Male Sleuth and American Policeman operating in New York

Holly ROTH 1916-1964 (American)

Invented 4 detectives - see Insp MEDFORD

Citation Record: 1 Book

Shadow Of A Lady - *Only*
Simon & Schuster US (1957); Hamish Hamilton UK (1957)

Dr Yudel GORDON

is a South African prison psychiatrist. A white man, he is deeply concerned about the social and racial problems in his country. He becomes involved with cases involving injustice to black prisoners, on whom he has to pronounce medical judgment.

South African Male Professional Investigator operating in South Africa

Wessel Shalk EBERSOHN 1940- (South African)

Citation Record: 2 Books

A Lonely Place To Die - *First*
Gollancz UK (1979); Pantheon US (1979)

Divide The Night - *Latest*
Gollancz UK (1981); Pantheon US (1981)

Col GORE

is ex-Indian Army, an amateur in the first book, but later the founder of a detective agency. Lean, bronzed and standard British, he guesses rather than deduces. Even so, he is an interesting example of an early professional amateur.

British Male Professional Amateur operating in England

Lynn BROCK 1877-1943 (British)

Writer: Alister MACALISTER

Inventor of one other detective Sgt VENN

Citation Record: 7 Books

The Deductions Of Colonel Gore - *First*
Collins UK (1925); Harper & Row US (1925)

The Stoat - *Last*
Collins UK (1940)

Insp GORE

British Policeman operating in England

J M WALSH 1897-1952 (British)

Invented 7 detectives - see Insp QUAILE

Citation Record: 1 Book

The Hairpin Mystery - *Only*
Hamilton UK (1926)

Ed GORGON

is a baseball umpire who has to solve crimes committed on or around his turf.

American Male Amateur operating in USA

Jon L BREEN 1943- (American)

Invented 6 detectives - see Rachel HENNINGS

Citation Record: 1 Selected Short Story

The Number 12 Jinx
appeared in the May 1978 number of the magazine and is also to be found in an anthology, *All But Impossible* (*Ticknor* US 1981).
In 'Ellery Queen's Mystery Magazine' US (1978)

Eddie GORGON

American Male Amateur operating in New York

Russell HAUSFELD (Australian)

Citation Record: 2 Books

Eddie Gorgon Calls The Tune - *First*
Cleveland AU (?)

Eddie Gorgon Takes The Rap - *Last*
Cleveland AU (?)

Ch Insp GORHAM

British Policeman operating in England

Joan COWDROY (British)

Inventor of one other detective Li MOH

Citation Record: 2 Books

Framed Evidence - *First*
Hutchinson UK (1936)

Murder Out Of Court - *Last*
Hutchinson UK (1944)

Gilda GORHAM

is the cataloguer in a famous library on the campus of a prestigious university in the eastern US. When an assistant Professor of French is found rather dead of a broken neck, she sets out to prove that it was murder and discover whodunnit.

American Female Amateur operating in USA

W Bolingbroke JOHNSON 1893-1973 (American)

was born in Willard, New York. For many years Professor of Romance Languages at Cornell University, he was the author of textbooks, biographies, poetry and this one mystery novel.

Writer: Morris Gilbert BISHOP

Citation Record: 1 Book

The Widening Stain - *Only*
Knopf US (1942); Lane UK (1943)

Insp GORMAN and Const HALE

British Policemen operating in England

Desmond LOWDEN 1937-

Writer: Desmond Scott LOWDEN

Citation Record: 1 Book

Sunspot - *Single*
Macmillan UK (1981); Holt US (1982)

Insp GORMLEY

British Policeman operating in England

A E MARTIN 1885-1955 (Australian)

Writer: Archibald Edward MARTIN

Inventor of one other detective Pel PELHAM

Citation Record: 1 Book

Death In The Limelight - *Only*
Simon & Schuster US (1946); Reinhardt UK (1956)

Serge GORODISH and ALBA

Sleuths operating in USA/Europe

DELACORTA 1945- (French)

Writer: Daniel ODIER

Citation Record: 6 Books

Diva - *First*
Summit US (1983); Lane UK (1984)

Alba - *Latest*
Atlantic US (1989)

Nathaniel GOSS

British Male Amateur operating in England

Colin WILLOCK 1918- (British)

Writer: Colin Dennistoun WILLOCK

Citation Record: 3 Books

Death at Flight - *First*
Heinemann UK (1956)

Death In Covert - *Last*
Heinemann UK (1961)

Ch Insp Douglas GOSSAGE

solves a case of death by shooting in a locked room.

Canadian Policeman operating in Canada

Thornton AYRE (Canadian)

Writer: John Russell FEARNE

The Crimson Rambler - *Only*
This short book was printed complete in one edition of the *Toronto Star Weekly* on 31 May 1947.
In 'Toronto Star Weekly' CA (1947)

Malcolm GOSSETT

gave up a police career and set up as a private investigator to help innocent victims of crime.

British Male Private Detective operating in England

E Phillips OPPENHEIM 1866-1946 (British)

Invented 27 detectives - see Nicholas GOADE

Citation Record: 10 Short Stories in 1 Collection

The Ex-Detective - *Collection 1*
Hodder & Stoughton UK (1933); Little, Brown US (1933)

Richard GOULBURN

British Male Amateur operating in England

J S FLETCHER 1863-1935 (British)

Invented 9 detectives - see Paul CAMPENHAYE

Citation Record: 2 Books

The Mantle Of Ishmael - *First*
Nash UK (1909)

The Million-Dollar Diamond - *Last*
Jenkins UK (1923)

The Black House In Harley Street - *Last**
Doubleday US (1928)

G

Bart GOULD

is a special investigator for the President of the USA.

American Male Secret Agent operating in USA

Joseph MILTON (American)

Citation Record: 7 Books

Assignment - Assassination - *First*
Lancer US (1964)

The Man Who Bombed The World - *Last*
Lancer US (1966)

Harry GOULD

American Male Sleuth operating in Los Angeles

Raymond OBSTFELD 1952- (American)

Inventor of one other detective Cliff REMINGTON

Citation Record: 3 Books

The Goulden Fleece - *First*
Charter US (1979)

Dead Bolt - *Latest*
Charter US (1982)

Skipper GOULD

American Male Amateur operating in USA

Robert KALISH (American)

Citation Record: 3 Books

Bloodrun - *First*
Avon US (1984)

Bloodmoon - *Latest*
Avon US (1985)

Aristide GOVIN

Second detective of George B EDGEHILL

'Cuckoo' GOYLES

solves the mystery of a death in an escape tunnel during the Second World War.

British Male Amateur operating in Italy

Michael GILBERT 1912- (British)

Invented 11 detectives - see Insp HAZELRIGG

Citation Record: 1 Book

Death In Captivity - *Only*
Hodder & Stoughton UK (1952)

The Danger Within - *Only**
Harper & Row US (1952)

Henry GRACE

is an out-of-work but aspiring playwright who is suspected of murdering the wife of his best friend. He knows whodunnit and sets out to prove it.

American Male Amateur operating in New York

David E FISHER 1932- (American)

Writer: David Elimelech FISHER

Inventor of one other detective Katie MacGregor TOWNSEND

Citation Record: 1 Book

Variation On A Theme - *Single*
Doubleday US (1981); Quartet UK (1982)

Lt Bill GRADY

American Policeman operating in New York/California

Ione Sandberg SHRIBER 1911- (American)

Citation Record: 8 Books

The Dark Arbor - *First*
Farrar, Straus US (1940); Nicholson & Watson UK (1945)

The Last Straw - *Last*
Rinehart US (1946)

Det Leo GRADY

Appears with at least two other detectives - see Det Joe LAWLESS.

Jake GRAFTON

American Male Sleuth operating in several locations

Stephen COONTS 1946- (American)

Writer: Stephen Paul COONTS

Citation Record: 4 Books

Flight Of The Intruder - *First*
Sidgwick UK (1987); Naval Institute Press US (1986)

Under Siege - *Latest*
Pocket Books US (1990); Collins UK (1991)

Angel GRAHAM

belies his name, for he is very tough indeed. Born Angelo Grammone, he had a rough childhood, became a hobo for a time and then a private eye.

American Male Private Detective operating in New York

Richard RUSSELL (American)

Citation Record: 3 Books

Paperbag - *First*
Belmont US (1979)

Point Of Reference - *Latest*
Belmont US (1979)

Artemus GRAHAM

Second detective of Philip MACCRAY

Charlotte GRAHAM

is an actress who sleuths.

American Female Amateur operating in USA

Stefanie MATTESON (American)

Citation Record: 6 Books

Murder At The Spa - *First*
Diamond US (1990)

Murder On High - *Latest*
Berkley US (1994)

Davina GRAHAM

is a British Intelligence officer, in books of the Cold War period. She has to pit her skills against the KGB and various other forces said to be antagonistic to her country.

British Female Secret Agent operating in Europe

Evelyn ANTHONY 1928- (British)

was born in London and educated at the Convent of the Sacred Heart, Roehampton, Surrey, until 1944. She is the author of at least seventeen admired genre novels and at least thirteen other works, some of the latter being historical biographies.

Writer: Evelyn Bridget Patricia WARD-THOMAS

Inventor of one other detective pair Joe DUNSTAN and Eric FISHER

Citation Record: 4 Books

The Defector - *First*
Hutchinson UK (1980); Coward McCann US (1981)

The Company Of Saints - *Latest*
Hutchinson UK (1983); Putnam US (1984)

Kate GRAHAM

British Female Amateur operating in several locations

Joen ARLISS (British)
Writer: Ian MARTIN
Citation Record: 2 Books
The Shark Bait Affair - *First*
Zebra US (1979)
The Lady Killer Affair - *Latest*
Zebra US (1980)

Det Insp Liz GRAHAM
Second detective of Ch Insp Frank SHAPIRO

Peter GRAHAM
British Male Amateur operating in England

Basil THOMSON 1861-1939 (British)
Invented 5 detectives - see Insp RICHARDSON
Citation Record: 2 Books
The Metal Flask - *First*
Methuen UK (1929)
The Kidnapper - *Last*
Eldon UK (1933)

Richard GRAHAM
is a perfect English country gentleman who is, in fact, a secret agent and a friend of the author's other agent-detective, *Simon HERALD*. Retired he may be he still manages to become involved in plots of great suspense and has to do more than a little in the way of classical detection.
British Male Secret Agent operating in Europe

John WELCOME 1914- (Irish)
See main detective Simon HERALD
Citation Record: 5 Books
Run For Cover - *First*
Faber UK (1958); Knopf US (1959)
Go For Broke - *Last*
Faber UK (1972); Walker US (1972)

Rose GRAHAM
is a continuity girl in a film studio, who solves a case of murder by using her professional knowledge.
American Female Amateur operating in Hollywood

Karl DIETZER (American)
Citation Record: 1 Selected Short Story
Murder At The Movies
also appeared in the anthology published by *Little, Brown* (US 1943), *The Female of the Species: The Great Women Detectives and Criminals* (Editor: Ellery Queen).
In 'American Legion Monthly' US (1937)

Will GRAHAM
is an FBI agent who specialises in the pursuit and capture of psychotic criminals.
American Male Professional Investigator operating in USA

Thomas HARRIS 1940- (American)
See main detective pair Hannibal LECTER and Clarice STERLING
Citation Record: 1 Book
Red Dragon - *Single*
Putnam US (1981); Bodley Head UK (1986)
Manhunter - *Single**
Bantam US (1986)

Dawn GRAHAME
Second detective of Johnny MERAK

Insp Paul GRAINGER
is a widower, melancholy and rather given to quoting from the classics.
British Policeman operating in England

Fiona SINCLAIR (British)
Citation Record: 2 Books
Dead Of A Physician - *First*
Bles UK (1961)
But The Patient Died - *First**
Doubleday US (1962)
Most Unnatural Murder - *Last*
Bles UK (1965)

Max GRAME
solves the mystery of the 'impossible' disappearance of a grand piano from an upper floor.
American Male Amateur operating in USA

MacKinlay KANTOR 1904-1977 (American)
Invented 4 detectives - see Matt EDWARDS
Citation Record: 1 Selected Short Story
The Strange Case Of Steinkelwintz
appeared later in a collection of the author's short stories, *It's About Crime*, published by *Signet* (US 1960).
Chicago Daily News US (1929)

Insp GRAMPORT
British Policeman operating in England

Glyn BARNETT (British)
Citation Record: 4 Books
The Call-Box Murder - *First*
Low UK (1935)
Find The Lady - *Last*
Low UK (1946)

Col Alistair GRANBY
is a senior officer in the British Intelligence Service.
British Male Professional Investigator operating in several locations

Francis BEEDING (British)
Invented 6 detectives - see Insp WILKINS
Citation Record: 17 Books
The Six Proud Walkers - *First*
Little, Brown US (1928)
There Are Thirteen - *Last*
Hodder & Stoughton UK (1946); Harper & Row US (1946)

Ch Alphonse GRAND
is the head of the 'Department of Patterns', a rather special section of the French police, which is situated in the Quai D'Orsay. In his sixties and rather old-fashioned in his methods, his job is to seek out hitherto unobserved patterns in unsolved crimes and so solve them.
French Policeman operating in Paris

Victor CANNING 1911-1986 (British)
Invented 6 detectives - see Rex CARVER
Citation Record: 1 Selected Short Story
The Sunday Fishing Club
Random House US (1962); New English Library UK (1967)

Capt GRANDISON
British Male Sleuth operating in England

Ben BOLT 1872- (British)
Invented 5 detectives - see Bob PONTING
Citation Record: 2 Books
The Mystery Hand - *First*
Ward, Lock UK (1932)
The Green Arrow - *Last*
Ward, Lock UK (1933)

Insp Alan GRANT
was a latecomer to the last ranks of British gentlemen policemen. A bachelor, slightly built, handsome, well-dressed, wealthy and educated, he says he likes to work in the police force rather than do nothing. He has flair, which often misleads him, and he gets on with all sorts of people in spite of his background, although he sometimes seems to have difficulty concentrating on the case in hand. Luckily he has a good sergeant.
British Policeman operating in London

Sidekick: Sgt WILLIAMS
British Male - Subordinate

Gordon DAVIOT 1897-1952 (British)
was a early pseudonym used by the author and later abandoned.
For writer details see Insp Alan GRANT
Citation Record: 1 Book
The Man In The Queue - *Only*
was republished under the following byline.
Methuen UK (1929); Dutton US (1929)

Josephine TEY 1897-1952 (British)
was born in Inverness, Scotland, and educated at the Royal Academy, Inverness and the Anstey Physical Training College, Birmingham, Warwickshire. She taught physical education in the 1920s and later became the author of many admired historical novels and plays, her eight criminous novels being written between 1929 and 1952.
Writer: Elizabeth MACKINTOSH
Other Byline: Gordon DAVIOT
Other Detectives:
Robert BLAIR   Lucy PYM
Citation Record: 5 Books
A Shilling For Candles - *First*
Methuen UK (1936); Macmillan US (1954)
The Singing Sands - *Last*
Davies UK (1952); Macmillan US (1953)
Killer In The Crowd - *Special*
was a posthumous publication, in slightly abridged form, of the author's first book to feeature *Insp Alan GRANT*, which appeared originally under the preceding byline.
Spivak US (1954)

G

Basil GRANT
Second detective of Rupert GRANT

Casey GRANT
American Male Sleuth operating in USA

Don RICO 1913-1985 (American)
Inventor of one other detective Burgess 'Buzz' CARDIGAN
Citation Record: 3 Books
The Swinging Virgin - *First*
Paperback Library US (1969)
So Sweet, So Deadly - *Last*
Paperback Library US (1970)

Celia GRANT
is a widow and a devoted horticulturist, involved in cases of murder with a background of gardening, travel and botany, which occur, not only in her own village, but when she is abroad.
British Female Amateur operating in England
Sidekick: Bill WILKINS
is *GRANT's* gardener and handyman but he could be more to her than that. He certainly gives her more than advice on herbaceous borders; and, since he was formerly a male model, the neighbours are forever agog.
British Male - Assistant

John SHERWOOD 1913- (British)
See main detective Charles BLESSINGTON
Citation Record: 7 Books
Green Trigger Fingers - *First*
Gollancz UK (1984); Scribner's US (1984)
The Sunflower Plot - *Latest*
Macmillan UK (1990); Scribner's US (1990)

Clifford GRANT
American Male Private Detective operating in Seattle

Vernon WARREN 1925- (British)
Invented 5 detectives - see Johnny MAQUIS
Citation Record: 1 Book
Invitation To Kill - *Only*
Gifford UK (1963)

David GRANT
British Male Sleuth operating in Europe/Far East

George B MAIR 1914- (British)
Writer: George Brown MAIR
Citation Record: 10 Books
Death's Foot Forward - *First*
Jarrolds UK (1963); Random House US (1964)
Paradise Spells Danger - *Last*
Jarrolds UK (1973)

Dean GRANT
American Male Sleuth operating in Illinois/Florida

Robert W WALKER 1948- (American)
For writer details see Ryne LANARK
Citation Record: 4 Books
Dead Man's Float - *First*
Pinnacle US (1988)
Dying Breath - *Latest*
Pinnacle US (1989)

Ch Insp Douglas GRANT
British Policeman operating in England

Florence N MILLAR (British)
Citation Record: 2 Books
Fishing Is Dangerous - *First*
Gifford UK (1946)
Grant's Overture - *Last*
Gifford UK (1946)

Col Duncan GRANT
British Male Professional Investigator operating in France/Germany

Graham SETON 1890-1946 (British)
Writer: Graham Seton HUTCHISON
Citation Record: 7 Books
The W Plan - *First*
Butterworth UK (1929); Cosmopolitan US (1930)
The Red Colonel - *Last*
Hutchinson UK (1947)

Harry GRANT
British Male Sleuth operating in several locations

Brian FREEBORN 1939- (British)
Writer: Brian James FREEBORN
Citation Record: 2 Books
Good Luck, Mr Cain - *First*
Secker & Warburg UK (1976); St Martin's US (1977)
Ten Days, Mr Cain - *Latest*
Secker & Warburg UK (1977); St Martin's US (1978)

Jerry GRANT
solves the mystery of the defacing of a corpse in a morgue.
American Male Amateur operating in USA

Fredric BROWN 1906-1972 (American)
Invented 8 detectives - see Ambrose HUNTER and Ed HUNTER
Citation Record: 1 Selected Short Story
The Spherical Ghoul
can also be found in an anthology, *Death Locked In* (*IPL;* US 1987).
In 'The Saint Mystery Magazine' US (1961)

Laurie GRANT and Stewart NOBLE
British Male Sleuths operating in Spain/Italy

May MACKINTOSH (British)
Citation Record: 3 Books
Appointment In Andalusia - *First*
Collins UK (1972); Delacorte US (1972)
The Sicilian Affair - *Last*
Collins UK (1974); Delacorte US (1974)

Dark Paradise - *Last**
Dell US (1978)

Michael GRANT
runs an agency in the fictional town of Los Pagos.
American Male Private Detective operating in California

Roland DANIEL 1880-1969 (British)
Invented 11 detectives - see Insp Neville LANGHAM
Citation Record: 6 Books
Frightened Eyes - *First*
Wright UK (1956)
Murder In Ocean Drive - *Last*
Wright UK (1964)

Patrick GRANT
is an Oxford don, modelled on many fictional others before him, who does a bit of sleuthing. A bachelor and a Fellow of the fictional St Mark's College, he dresses well and is knowledgeable on art, music and suchlike matters. Having a nag of a sister, he spends much time abroad, where he invariably runs into murder most foul.
British Male Amateur operating in England
Stooge: Det Insp Colin SMITHERS
is really not unfriendly to *GRANT* but wishes he would play the detective game properly.
British Male

Margaret YORKE 1924- (British)
Invented 3 detectives - see Stephen DAWES
Citation Record: 5 Books
Dead In The Morning - *First*
Bles UK (1970)
Cast For Death - *Latest*
Hutchinson UK (1976); Walker US (1976)

Peter GRANT
British Male Amateur operating in England

P M HUBBARD 1910-1980 (British)
was born in Reading, Berkshire. He was educated at Elizabeth College, Guernsey, and graduated at Jesus College, Oxford, receiving the Newdigate Prize in 1933. He worked in the Indian Civil Service, 1934-1947, and is the author of at least sixteen genre novels.
Writer: Philip Maitland HUBBARD
Other Detectives:
Margaret CANNING Mark HAWKINS
Citation Record: 1 Book
The Causeway - *Only*
Macmillan UK (1976); Doubleday US (1978)

Rupert GRANT and Basil GRANT
appear only in short stories, which can be found in this recent collection of some of the author's lesser known works.
British Male Sleuths operating in England

G K CHESTERTON 1874-1936 (British)
Invented 7 detectives - see Father BROWN
Citation Record: 2 Short Stories in 1 Collection
Thirteen Detectives - *Collection 1*
contains one *Father BROWN* story, two *Horne FISHER* stories, two *Gabriel GALE* stories, two *Rupert and Basil GRANT* stories and two *Mr POND* stories.
Dodd, Mead US (1986); Xanadu UK (1988)

Victor GRANT
specialises in cases of fraud.
American Male Private Detective operating in New York

John B ETHAN (American)
Citation Record: 3 Books
The Black Gold Murders - *First*
In 'Detective Book Club' US (1959)
Murder On Wall Street - *Last*
Mill US (1960)

Clive GRANVILLE
British Male Secret Agent operating in Europe

Marthe MCKENNA 1892-1969 (British)
Citation Record: 2 Books
Lancer Spy - *First*
Jarrolds UK (1937)
The Spy In Khaki - *Last*
Jarrolds UK (1941)

Det Insp GRAVES
British Policeman operating in England

William J MAKIN 1894- (British)
Invented 3 detectives - see Det Insp EVANS
Citation Record: 2 Books
Gipsy In Evening Dress - *First*
Eldon UK (1935)
Murder At Full Moon - *Last*
Eldon UK (1937)

Insp GRAY
British Policeman operating in Edinburgh

Peter PIPER (British)
Writer: Theo LANG
Citation Record: 2 Books
Murder After The Blitz - *First*
Hurst UK (1943)
The Corpse That Came Back - *First**
Random House US (1954)
Death In The Canongate - *Last*
Hodder & Stoughton UK (1952)

Lt GRAY
American Policeman operating in Connecticut

Edwin LANHAM 1904-1979 (American)
Writer: Edwin Moutrie LANHAM
Other Detectives:
Frank LUTHER Lt MADIGAN
Citation Record: 2 Books
Death Of A Corinthian - *First*
Harcourt Brace US (1953); Boardman UK (1954)
The Case Of The Missing Corpse - *First**
Bestseller US (1955)
Death In The Wind - *Last*
Harcourt Brace US (1956); Boardman UK (1957)

Colin GRAY
is on secret missions for British Intelligence.
British Male Secret Agent operating in India/Tibet

Mark CHANNING (British)
Citation Record: 4 Books
King Cobra - *First*
Hutchinson UK (1933); Lippincott US (1934)
Nine Lives - *Last*
Harrap UK (1937); Lippincott US (1937)

Cordelia GRAY
is young and inexperienced when she becomes junior partner in Pryde's Detective Agency, in London's West End. When her partner commits suicide she inherits the business.
British Female Private Detective operating in London

P D JAMES 1920- (British)
See main detective Insp/Cdr Adam DALGLIESH
Citation Record: 2 Books
An Unsuitable Job For A Woman - *First*
Faber UK (1972); Scribner's US (1973)
The Skull Beneath The Skin - *Latest*
Faber UK (1982); Scribner's US (1982)

Eagle GRAY
American Male Detective in Pulp Magazines operating in USA

Morris REDWING 1847-1936 (American)
Writer: James Milford MERRILL
No citations

Ed GRAY
American Male Private Detective operating in California

John CROWE 1924- (American)
See main detective Lee BECKETT
Citation Record: 1 Book
Crooked Shadows - *Only*
Dodd, Mead US (1975)

Garamond GRAY
Second detective of Gwen GRAY

Gwen GRAY and Garamond GRAY
are cousins and operate as old-style private eyes in some far-distant future.
American Female Private Detective and American Male Private Detective operating in Space

Atanielle Annyn NOEL (American)
Citation Record: 1 Book
Murder On Usher's Planet - *Single*
Avon US (1987)

Dr Michael GRAY
is said to be a 'psychoanalyst-detective'.
American Male Amateur operating in San Francisco

Henry KUTTNER 1914-1958 (American)
was born in Los Angeles. He was a professional psychologist and wrote mainly science fiction.
Other Byline: Lewis PADGETT
Citation Record: 4 Books
The Murder Of Eleanor Pope - *First*
Permabooks US (1956)
Murder Of A Wife - *Last*
Permabooks US (1958); Banner UK (1958)

William S GRAY
is a lawyer who solves a case of death by shooting in a locked room.
American Male Amateur operating in USA

Leonard THOMPSON (American)
Citation Record: 1 Selected Short Story
Close Shave
appeared in the May number.
In 'Ellery Queen's Mystery Magazine' US (1946)

Will GRAY
solves a college murder.
American Male Amateur operating in South Dakota

Cathleen JORDAN (American)
Citation Record: 1 Book
A Carol In The Dark - *Single*
Walker US (1984)

The GRAY PHANTOM
was a man called Cuthbert Vanardy who became one of those early superman detectives. As was so boringly usual, he adopted a mysterious guise and went around righting wrongs. All the books with 'Gray' in the title became 'Grey' in the UK publications and are so cited.
American Male Amateur operating in New York/Maine

Herman LANDON 1882-1960 (American)
See main detective The PICAROON
Citation Record: 5 Books
The Gray Phantom - *First*
Watt US (1921)
The Grey Phantom - *First**
Long UK (1923)
Gray Magic - *Last*
Watt US (1925)
The Grey Phantom's Triumph - *Last**
Hutchinson UK (1927)

Steve GRAYCE
American Male Private Detective operating in USA

Raymond CHANDLER 1888-1959 (American)
Invented 9 detectives - see Philip MARLOWE
Citation Record: 1 Selected Short Story
The King In Yellow
In 'Dime Detective' US (1938)

Kendal GRAYDON
British Male Amateur operating in England

H E WHEELER (British)
See main detective Stephen RANT
Citation Record: 3 Books
Death Calls The Jester - *First*
Jenkins UK (1936)
Dead Men Turn Green - *Last*
Jenkins UK (1939)

Barnaby GRAYLE
British Male Amateur operating in England

W W SAYER 1892- (British)
Writer: Walter William SAYER
Other Byline: Pierre QUIROULE
Adopter of one other detective Sexton BLAKE
Citation Record: 3 Books
Sellers Of Death - *First*
Wright UK (1940)
Mine Sinister Host - *Last*
Wright UK (1948)

Peter GRAYLEIGH
British Male Sleuth operating in England

Colin ROBERTSON 1906-1980 (British)
Invented 7 detectives - see Mike REED
Citation Record: 15 Books
The Temple Of Dawn - *First*
Ward, Lock UK (1939)
A Lonely Place To Die - *Last*
Hale UK (1969)

Lester GRAYLING
is an investigative lawyer.
British Male Amateur operating in England

Leslie J LYNWOOD (British)
Citation Record: 9 Short Stories in 1 Collection
Lester Grayling, KC - *Collection 1*
Bale UK (1921)

Harvey GRAYMOOR and Laura GRAYMOOR
American Male Amateur and American Female Amateur operating in USA

George BAXT 1923- (American)
Invented 6 detectives - see Pharaoh LOVE
Citation Record: 1 Book
Process Of Elimination - *Single*
St Martin's US (1984)

Laura GRAYMOOR
Second detective of Harvey GRAYMOOR

GRAYSON
is a lawyer who decides to do a little detecting in these two Victorian stories.
British Male Amateur operating in London

C J Cutcliffe HYNE 1865-1944 (British)
Invented 4 detectives - see Capt Owen KETTLE
Citation Record: 2 Selected Short Stories

Tragedy Of A Third Class Smoker
appeared in the November number.
In 'The Harmsworth Magazine' UK (1898)

The Bank Note Forger
appeared in the September number.
In 'The Harmsworth Magazine' UK (1899)

Insp GRAZZONI

Italian Policeman operating in France

Sebastien JAPRISOT 1931- (French)

Writer: Jean Baptiste ROSSI

Citation Record: 1 Book

The 10:30 From Marseilles - *Only*
is a translation from the French of *Compartiment Tueurs* (Paris, 1962).
Doubleday US (1963); Souvenir UK (1964)

The Sleeping Car Murders - *Only**
Pocket Books US (1967)

The GREAT DETECTIVE

is a spoof on great fictional detectives by this admired writer of comic short stories. In this story the great man ends up by disguising himself as a dog, and he does it so well that he is caught and destroyed by dog-catchers.

Male Amateur operating in Canada

Stephen Butler LEACOCK 1869-1944 (Canadian)

was educated at the University of Toronto and became head of the Economics department at McGill University. He was a distinguished writer on politics, economics and the author of several biographical works. He is now mainly known for his humorous works.

Adopter of one other detective Sherlock HOLMES

Citation Record: 1 Selected Short Story

Maddened By Mystery; Or, The Defective Detective - *Pastiche 1*
is in a collection of stories by this author, *Nonsense Novels.*
Lane UK (1911)

Emma GREAVES

British Female Amateur operating in Italy/Africa

Lionel BLACK 1910-1980 (British)

Invented 3 detectives - see Kate THEOBALD

Citation Record: 3 Books

Chance To Die - *First*
Cassell UK (1965)

Two Ladies In Verona - *Last*
Cassell UK (1967)

The Lady Is A Spy - *Last**
Paperback Library US (1969)

The GREEK DETECTIVE

Greek Male Detective in Pulp Magazines operating in USA

Gilbert JEROME (American)

Invented 5 detectives - see Jack DONAHUE

Citation Record: 1 Selected Short Story

The Greek Detective; Or, On The Trail Of A Vitriol Thrower
Old Cap Collier Library US (18??)

Ch Insp Bill GREEN

Second detective of Insp/Ch Supt George MASTERS

Celery GREEN

solves the disappearance of a fabulous gem from a locked room.

American Female Amateur operating in USA

Arthur PORGES (American)

Invented 13 detectives - see Arsène LUPIN

Citation Record: 1 Selected Short Story

The Indian Diamond Mystery
In 'Ellery Queen's Mystery Magazine' US (1965)

Devillo GREEN

American Male Amateur operating in USA

Donald OLSON (American)

Citation Record: 1 Book

Sleep Before Evening - *Single*
St Martin's US (1979)

Edwin GREEN

is engaged in a hunt for treasure that involves murders galore in Paris and Monaco.

American Male Private Detective operating in New York

Hal Jason CALIN (American)

Citation Record: 1 Book

Rocks And Ruin - *Only*
Vanguard US (1954)

Payoff In Blood - *Only**
Jonathan US (1955)

Gregory George Gordon GREEN

is generally known as 'Gees'. He was once a cop; but, being rather wealthy, he is able to set up the Consult Gees Confidential Agency, which deals in everything, including the weird and supernatural.

British Male Private Detective operating in England

Jack MANN 1882-1947 (British)

See main detective Rex COULSON

Citation Record: 8 Books

Gees' First Case - *First*
Wright UK (1936); Bookfinger US (1970)

The Glass Too Many - *Last*
Wright UK (1940); Bookfinger US (1973)

Horatio GREEN

is short, fat, old and said to be 'a famous detective who has retired and now places his skills at the disposal of the police'. They would be baffled without him, particularly because his one remarkable attribute is his amazing sense of smell (not for nothing has he been called The Human Bloodhound), which of course enables him to solve impossible cases.

British Male Amateur operating in England

Beverley NICHOLS 1899-1983 (British)

was born in Bristol, Gloucestershire. He was educated at Marlborough College and graduated at Balliol College, Oxford. In his varied career he was a drama critic, essayist and journalist, but was best known in later life as an influential gossip columnist.

Writer: John Beverley NICHOLS

Citation Record: 5 Books

No Man's Street - *First*
Hutchinson UK (1954); Dutton US (1954)

Murder By Request - *Last*
Hutchinson UK (1960); Dutton US (1960)

Jeffrey GREEN

runs a one-man agency in New York, specialising in cases involving calligraphy and dubious documents.

American Male Private Detective operating in USA/Europe

Carlton KEITH 1914-1991 (American)

Writer: Keith Carlton ROBERTSON

Citation Record: 5 Books

The Diamond-Studded Typewriter - *First*
Macmillan US (1958); Heinemann UK (1960)

A Gem Of A Murder - *First**
Dell US (1959)

A Taste Of Sangria - *Last*
Doubleday US (1968)

The Missing Book-Keeper - *Last**
Hale UK (1969)

Margaret GREEN

Second detective of Raymond GREEN

Det Noah GREEN and Det Sam MCKIBBON

Noah GREEN is Jewish and a current American archetype – middle-aged, divorced, brooding, foul-mouthed, and hounded by a superior. He is a good cop, nevertheless, his own man, a guy who solves cases, deals toughly with criminals and naturally pulls in a sweet broad or two on the way. His partner, *Sam MCGIBBON*, is similarly archetypal. For he is young, tough and black.

American Policemen operating in New York

Nathan Irving HENTOFF 1925- (American)

is a sometime staff writer to New York newspapers and magazines. He is an authority on jazz, civil liberties, police work and education, about all of which he has written.

Citation Record: 2 Books

Blues For Charlie Darwin - *First*
Morrow US (1982); Constable UK (1983)

The Man From Internal Affairs - *Latest*
Mysterious Press US (1985)

G

Paul GREEN

solves some deaths at sea.

American Male Amateur operating in USA

W Shepard PLEASANTS (American)

Citation Record: 1 Book

The Stingaree Murders - *Only*
Mystery League US (1932)

Sgt Pembury GREEN

solves the mystery of how an immobilised man disappeared from a locked house.

British Policeman operating in England

John BUDE 1901-1957 (British)

Invented 4 detectives - see Insp SHERWOOD

Citation Record: 1 Book

Death On Paper - *Only*
Hale UK (1940)

Raymond GREEN and Margaret GREEN

together solve a murder in academia.

American Male Amateur and American Female Amateur operating in Virginia

William Harwood PEDEN 1913- (American)

Citation Record: 1 Book

Twilight At Monticello - *Only*
Houghton US (1973)

Policeman William GREEN

British Policeman operating in London

L T MEADE and Clifford HALIFAX (British)

Invented 3 detectives - see Paul GILCHRIST

Citation Record: 1 Book

This Troublesome World - *Only*
Chatto & Windus UK (1901)

Sophie GREENAWAY

is a 'food critic' who investigates political murders.

American Female Amateur operating in USA

Ellen HART (American)

See main detective Jane LAWLESS

Citation Record: 1 Book

This Little Piggy Went To Murder - *Single*
Ballantine US (1994)

Charlie GREENE

is a menopausal biology professor, whose speciality is the study of rodents and whose hobby is amateur sleuthing.

American Male Amateur operating in USA

Marlys MILLHISER 1938- (American)

Writer: Marlys Joy MILLHISER

Citation Record: 3 Books

Death Of The Office Witch - *First*
Otto Penzler US (1993)

Murder In A Hot Flash - *Latest*
Otto Penzler US (1995)

Marcus GREENE

American Male Private Detective operating in Chicago

Charles W RUNYON 1928- (American)

Citation Record: 1 Book

The Black Moth - *Only*
GM US (1967)

Supt 'Tubby' GREENE

British Policeman operating in Wales/England

Richard GOYNE 1902-1957 (British)

Other Byline: John GOURAGE

Other Detectives:
Sexton BLAKE
The PADRE
Paul TEMPLETON

Citation Record: 2 Books

Introducing The Super - *First*
Paul UK (1955)

The Missing Minx - *Last*
Paul UK (1957)

C B GREENFIELD

is the editor of the local newspaper; and since he is also an avid amateur sleuth, he has many chances to get first crack at a local theft or murder. A male chauvinist, he is always in conflict with his assistant.

American Male Amateur operating in Connecticut

Sidekick: Maggie ROME
is happily married and works as a part-time reporter for *GREENFIELD*. Often at loggerheads with him, especially over his macho attitude to women, she is more than a match for him. She fulfils, moreover, the role of legwoman when he starts sleuthing.

American Female - Assistant

Lucille KALLEN 1926- (American)

was born in Los Angeles, California. She has worked extensively in TV and has been a free-lance writer since 1954.

Citation Record: 5 Books

Introducing C B Greenfield - *First*
Crown US (1979); Collins UK (1979)

A Little Madness - *Latest*
Random House US (1986); Collins UK (1986)

Mr GREENLEAF

American Male Amateur operating in Washington DC

Herbert O YARDLEY 1889-1958

Writer: Herbert Osborn YARDLEY

Citation Record: 2 Books

The Blonde Countess - *First*
Longman US (1934); Faber UK (1934)

Red Sun Of Nippon - *Last*
Longman UK (1934)

Hank GREENLEAF

is perhaps the only PI created by the man who virtually invented the modern police procedural.

American Male Private Detective operating in New York

Lawrence TREAT 1903- (American)

Invented 7 detectives - see Det Jub FREEMAN, Det Bill DECKER and Det Mitch TAYLOR

Citation Record: 1 Book

Lady, Drop Dead - *Only*
Abelard US (1960); Abelard UK (1960)

GREENSLEEVES

British Male Sleuth operating in Scotland

W Murdoch DUNCAN 1909-1975 (British)

Invented 8 detectives - see Supt MACNEILL

Citation Record: 3 Books

Mystery On The Clyde - *First*
Melrose UK (1945)
Straight Ahead For Danger - *Last*
Melrose UK (1946)

Lt Claude GREENWAY

American Policeman operating in San Francisco

Lloyd S THOMPSON (American)
Citation Record: 2 Books
Death Stops The Show - *First*
Crown US (1946)
Hear Not My Steps - *Last*
Abelard UK (1953)

James GREER

solves a case of death by shooting in a sentry-box under constant observation.

British Male Amateur operating in England/USA

Newton GAYLE (British)
Writers: Maurice C GUINESS 1897- and Muna Lee De Munoz MARIN 1895-
Citation Record: 5 Books
Murder In The Haunted Sentry-Box - *First*
Gollancz UK (1935)
The Sentry-Box Murder - *First**
Scribner's US (1935)
Sinister Crag - *Last*
Gollancz UK (1938); Scribner's US (1939)

Insp GREGG and Judith EVERSLEIGH

Insp. GREGG and prime suspect *Judith EVERSLEIGH* have to sleuth together to solve a nasty case of murder in an antipodean advertising agency.

New Zealander Policeman and Female Amateur operating in New Zealand

Elizabeth MESSENGER 1908- (New Zealander)
wrote at least twelve genre novels, all set in New Zealand.
Writer: Elizabeth Margery Esson MESSENGER
Citation Record: 1 Book
Publicity For Murder - *Only*
Hale UK (1961)

Maj Avery GREGG and Tony ELLIS

work for a US Intelligence outfit, operate an enquiry agency in Los Angeles and are involved in cases throughout the Americas.

American Male Private Detectives operating in Central America/Mexico

Robert Portner KOEHLER 1905- (American)
Invented 4 detectives - see Les IVEY
Citation Record: 3 Books
The Road House Murders - *First*
Phoenix Press US (1946); Boardman UK (1948)
The Blue Parakeet Murders - *Last*
Phoenix Press US (1948)

Matt GREGG

is an ex-cop who moves to Pittsburgh, obtains a PI licence and works on a case involving pornography.

American Male Private Detective operating in Pittsburgh

David GUY 1948- (American)
Citation Record: 1 Book
The Man Who Loved Dirty Books - *Single*
New American Library US (1983)

Miss GREGORY

British Female Amateur operating in several locations

Perceval GIBBON 1879-1926 (British)
Inventor of one other detective The Vrouw GROBELAAR
Citation Record: 12 Short Stories in 1 Collection
The Adventures Of Miss Gregory - *Collection 1*
Dent UK (1912); Putnam US (1913)

Dan GREGORY

British Male Sleuth operating in the Caribbean

Leland JAMIESON 1904-1941 (British)
Writer: Leland Shattuck JAMIESON
Citation Record: 2 Books
Murder Island - *First*
Melrose UK (1935); Greenberg US (1936)
G-Men On Murder Island - *Last*
Swan UK (1947)

Scott GREGORY and Justin BASSETT

American Male Amateurs operating in Massachusetts

Roy STRATTON 1910-1985 (American)
Writer: Roy Olin STRATTON
Citation Record: 2 Books
The Decorated Corpse - *First*
Mill US (1962); Boardman UK (1963)
One Among None - *Last*
Mill US (1965); Boardman UK (1965)

Susan GRENELLE and Ch Mark CZERNICK

Susan GRENELLE returns to live near the campus of the fictional Grenelle College in Virginia, where, eleven years earlier, she was a student. When murder occurs, she investigates, aided by an old flame, now the local Chief of Police, *Mark CZERNICK*.

American Female Amateur and American Policeman operating in USA

Isabelle HOLLAND 1920- (American)
See main detective Rev Claire ALDINGTON
Citation Record: 1 Book
Grenelle - *Single*
Rawson Associates US (1976); Collins UK (1978)

Det GRENNON

British Policeman operating in England

Audrey Erskine LINDOP 1920-1986 (British)
Writer: Audrey Beatrice Noel LINDOP
Inventor of one other detective KEOGH
Citation Record: 1 Book
Journey Into Stone - *Only*
Doubleday US (1972); Macmillan UK (1973)

Digby GRESHAM

is said to be a 'noted criminal investigator' and appears in one amazing farrago in which mummies, islands, locked rooms, escaped convicts and stolen jewels all play a part. Notwithstanding, he also managed to appear in several stories published in the pulps during the 1920s and 1930s.

American Male Professional Amateur operating in USA

F M PETTEE 1888- (American)
Writer: Florence Mae PETTEE
Inventor of one other detective Beau QUICKSILVER
Citation Record: 1 Book
The Palgrave Mummy - *Only*
Payson & Clarke US (1929); Skeffington UK (1929)

Hubert GRESHAM

British Male Amateur operating in several locations

John Foster FRASER 1868-1936 (British)
Citation Record: 10 Short Stories in 1 Collection
The Red Passport - *Collection 1*
Chapman & Hall UK (1918)

Beverley GRETTON

British Male Amateur operating in England

Herbert CADETT (British)
Citation Record: 11 Short Stories in 1 Collection
The Adventures Of A Journalist - *Collection 1*
Sands UK (1900)

Ursula GRETTON
is an archaeologist who investigates the murder of her former lover's wife.
British Female Amateur

Ann GRANGER (British)

Inventor of one other detective pair Ch Insp Alan MARKBY and Meredith MITCHELL

Citation Record: 1 Book

Where Old Bones Lie - *Single*
St Martin's US (1994)

Det Ch Insp GREVE
investigates murder in a country house filled with shady suspects, all with motives for murdering their host.
British Policeman operating in England

Sidekick: Det Sgt Jim BRAILEY
British Female - Subordinate

G

Denis HADDOW (British)

Citation Record: 1 Book

Hanged By A Thread - *Only*
Hutchinson UK (1947)

Robin GREVE, Mary TREVERT and Insp MANDERTON
solve a case of death by shooting in a locked room.
!See Appendix 2.
British Male Amateur and British Female Amateur operating in England

Valentine WILLIAMS 1883-1946 (British)

Invented 8 detectives - see Det Sgt Trevor DENE

Citation Record: 1 Book

The Yellow Streak - *Only*
Jenkins UK (1922); Houghton US (1922)

Ana GREY
features, very credibly, in an everyday story of ordinary FBI folk.
American Female Sleuth operating in Los Angeles

April SMITH (American)

Citation Record: 1 Book

North Of Montana - *Single*
Hutchinson UK (1994)

Charles GREY
Second detective of Karl ZWEIG

Colwin GREY
British Male Amateur operating in England

Arthur J REES 1872-1942 (British)

Invented 3 detectives - see Insp LUCKRAFT

Citation Record: 3 Books 10 Short Stories in 1 Collection

The Threshold Of Fear - *First*
Hutchinson UK (1925); Dodd, Mead US (1926)

Greymarsh - *Last*
Jarrolds UK (1927); Dodd, Mead US (1927)

Investigations Of Colwin Grey - *Collection 1*
Jarrolds UK (1932)

Cyriack Skinner GREY
is in several short stories, most of them dealing with 'impossible' crimes. The one listed here is typical.
American Male Amateur operating in USA

Arthur PORGES (American)

Invented 13 detectives - see Arsène LUPIN

Citation Record: 1 Selected Short Story

The Impossible Gulf
appeared in the October number.
In 'Mike Shayne Mystery Magazine' US (1975)

George GREY
British Male Private Detective operating in England

Henry HERMAN 1832-1894 (British)

See main detective Insp BENDER

Citation Record: 1 Book

The Crime Of A Christmas Toy - *Only*
Ward, Lock UK (1894)

Jennifer GREY
American Female Amateur operating in Chicago

Jerry JENKINS 1949- (American)

Writer: Jerry Bruce JENKINS

Other Detectives:
Margo FRANKLIN and Philip SPENCE
Dallas O'NEIL

Citation Record: 5 Books

Heartbeat - *First*
Victor US (1983); Scripture Press UK (1990)

Veiled Threat - *Latest*
Victor US (1985)

Mother Lavinia GREY
is the vicar of the fictional St Bede's Episcopal Church. Given to compassionate causes, she is at loggerheads with her arrogant, business-like bishop. When he turns up dead, the police suspect her and she has to do the sleuthing herself.
American Female Amateur operating in USA

Kate GALLISON 1939- (American)

Inventor of one other detective Nick MAGARACZ

Citation Record: 1 Book

Bury The Bishop - *Single*
Dell US (1995)

Lindy GREY
!See Appendix 2.
British Female Sleuth operating in England

Desmond CORY 1928- (British)

Invented 4 detectives - see Johnny FEDORA

Citation Record: 4 Books

Begin, Murderer! - *First*
Muller UK (1951)

The Shaken Leaf - *Last*
Muller UK (1955)

Roman GREY
has gypsy origins and has inherited certain 'psychical qualities', which he uses successfully in his detective role.
American Male Amateur operating in USA

Martin Cruz SMITH 1942- (American)

was born in Reading, Pennsylvania. He took a BA at the University of Pennsylvania, Philadelphia, 1964. He is the author of several highly successful novels, which combine elements of the classic detective story with those of the action thriller, all set in unusual ethnic surroundings. He received the Crime Writers Association Gold Dagger award, 1982.

Writer: Martin Cruz SMITH

Other Bylines:
Nick CARTER Simon QUINN

Other Detectives:
Dep Youngman DURAN and Hayden PAINE
Investigator Arkady RENKO

Citation Record: 2 Books

Gypsy In Amber - *First*
Putnam US (1971); Barker UK (1975)

Canto For A Gypsy - *Last*
Putnam US (1972); Barker UK (1975)

Rudolph GREY
British Male Amateur operating in England

L T MEADE 1854-1914 (British)

was the author of a great number of semi-juvenile works and early detective stories. Indeed she is said to have written more books for young girls than any other author of her day. Many of them start with a mystery having an occult background, which is usually exposed as false by the detective she happens to be using. They are also full of supercriminals, secret societies and sensationally attractive and cunning women. Some were written with *Robert EUSTACE*, who himself collaborated with several other authors and whose real name was Robert Eustace Barton (1868-1943). *MEADE* too collaborated with several other authors.

Writer: Elizabeth Thomasina Meade SMITH

Other Detectives:
CROSSLEY
Dixon DRUCE
Micah FARADAY

Citation Record: 1 Book

The Red Ruth - *Only*
Laurie UK (1907)

Scout GREY

British Male Amateur operating in England

R L BELLAMY (British)

Writer: Robert Lowe BELLAMY

Citation Record: 2 Books

The Adventures Of Scout Grey - *First*
Low UK (1924)

Scout Grey - Detective - *Last*
Low UK (1927)

L F 'Scoop' GRIDDLE

American Male Amateur operating in USA

Thomas POLSKY 1908 (American)

Citation Record: 3 Books

Curtains For The Editor - *First*
Dutton US (1939)

Curtains For The Copper - *Last*
Dutton US (1941)

Insp GRIERSON

British Policeman operating in Scotland

H J WURR (British)

Citation Record: 2 Books

The Giant Hunchback - *First*
Rich UK (1939)

Who Dies Next? - *Last*
Rich UK (1939)

David GRIERSON

is a bank inspector who investigates crimes of some magnitude, usually with a financial background.

British Male Professional Investigator operating in England

Ian STUART 1927-1993 (British)

Invented 3 detectives - see Insp Neil LAMBERT

Citation Record: 5 Books

Death From Disclosure - *First*
Hale UK (1976)

A Growing Concern - *Latest*
Doubleday US (1985); Hale UK (1986)

Richard GRIEVE, Paula GLENNING and James GOFF

In the first book of the *Paula GLENNING* series (qv), the two main detectives are *Richard GRIEVE* and *James GOFF*, both Professors of English, in dispute over the literary remains of a great novelist. *GOFF*, in fact, becomes her aide and lover in later books.

Two British Male Amateurs and one British Female Amateur operating in England

Anna CLARKE 1919- (British)

Invented 4 detectives - see Paula GLENNING

Citation Record: 1 Book

Last Judgement - *Single*
Doubleday US (1985); Hale UK (1986)

Hamo GRIFFIN

British Male Amateur

Walter HAWES (British)

Citation Record: 6 Short Stories in 1 Collection

The Mystery Man - *Collection 1*
Ward, Lock UK (1905)

Jack GRIFFIN

investigates the disappearance of priceless porcelain from a closely guarded estate.

British Male Amateur operating in England

Charles CRUIKSHANK 1914- (British)

Writer: Charles Greig CRUIKSHANK

Citation Record: 1 Book

The Tang Murders - *Only*
Hale UK (1976)

Lew GRIFFIN

is black, intermittently alcoholic, naive and frequently violent. Pursued, in addition, by his own anxieties and inner devils, he is hardly the model of a detective.

American Male Private Detective operating in New Orleans

James SALLIS (American)

Citation Record: 3 Books

The Long-Legged Fly - *First*
Carroll & Graf US (1992)

Black Hornet - *Latest*
Carroll & Graf US (1994)

Wade GRIFFIN

was formerly in the Los Angeles Police Department and appears in this novelization of a TV drama.

American Male Private Detective operating in Los Angeles

Sidekick: S Michael MURDOCH
American Male - Assistant

Robert WEVERKA 1926- (American)

Citation Record: 1 Book

Griff - *Only*
Bantam US (1972)

Simona GRIFFO

returns to Rome and a tangled family life, meets murder at once and spends the remaining time solving it, while, at the same time, expounding on Italian cuisine. Recipes for delicious dishes seem to be becoming a new art form in the criminous genre.

Italian Female Amateur operating in Rome

Camilla T CRESPI

Citation Record: 1 Book

The Trouble With Going Home - *Single*
HarperCollins US (1995)

Neil GRIFFON

British Male Amateur operating in England

Dick FRANCIS 1920- (British)

Invented 18 detectives - see Sid HALLEY

Citation Record: 1 Book

Bonecrack - *Only*
Joseph UK (1971); Harper & Row US (1972)

Capt/Commiss Denzil GRIGSON

British Policeman operating in Africa

Adam BROOME 1888- (British)

Writer: Godfrey Warden JAMES

Inventor of one other detective Insp BRAMLEY

Citation Record: 8 Books

Crowner's Quest - *First*
Benn UK (1930)

Flame Of The Forest - *Last*
Bles UK (1943)

Adjutent Henk GRIJPSTRA and Sgt Rufus DE GIER
are police detectives in Amsterdam and their cases offer excellent plotting and fascinating background detail on the city itself. *GRIJPSTRA* is heavy and stolid and married. *DE GIER* is slim, attractive and romantically inclined. In spite of their differences they work well together, even to the point of playing drum and flute duets when off duty. Their books are partly police procedurals and introduce other detectives at times.
Dutch Policemen operating in Amsterdam

Janwillem VAN DE WETERING 1931- (Dutch)
was born in Rotterdam, Holland. He was educated at Delft University, Holland, 1948, Cambridge University, England, 1951, and the University of London, 1957-1958. He has worked in businesses in several parts of the world and has entered Buddhist monasteries and groups in Japan and the USA. A member of the Amsterdam Reserve Police from 1965, he now lives in the USA. The author of at least thirteen criminous novels, he received the *Grand Prix de Littérature Policière*, 1984.
Inventor of one other detective Insp SAITO
Citation Record: 12 Books 8 Short Stories in 1 Collection
Outsider In Amsterdam - *First*
Houghton US (1975); Heinemann UK (1976)
The Rattle-Rat - *Latest*
Pantheon US (1985); Gollancz UK (1986)
The Sergeant's Cat And Other Stories - *Collection 1*
This collection of fourteen of the author's stories contains eight with *GRIJPSTRA* and *DE GIER*.
Pantheon US (1987); Gollancz UK (1988)

James Schuyler 'JimGrim' GRIM
appears also in books with the author's other detectives, *Chullunder GHOSE* and *Athelstan KING*.
British Male Sleuth operating in India/Tibet

Talbot MUNDY 1879-1940 (British)
Invented 5 detectives - see Chullunder GHOSE
Citation Record: 8 Books
Ramsden - *First*
Hutchinson UK (1926)
The Devil's Guard - *First**
Bobbs US (1926)
Old Ugly Face - *Last*
Hutchinson UK (1939); Appleton US (1940)

James Schuyler 'Jimgrim' GRIM and Chullunder GHOSE
also appear individually in other books by this author.
British Male Sleuth and Indian Male Sleuth operating in India

Talbot MUNDY 1879-1940 (British)
Invented 5 detectives - see Chullunder GHOSE
Citation Record: 1 Book
Jimgrim - *Only*
Hutchinson UK (1931)
Jimgrim Sahib - *Only**
Universal UK (1953)

James Schuyler 'Jimgrim' GRIM, Chullunder GHOSE and Athelstan KING
British Male Sleuths and Indian Male Sleuth operating in India

Talbot MUNDY 1879-1940 (British)
Invented 5 detectives - see Chullunder GHOSE
Citation Record: 1 Book
The Nine Unknown - *Only*
Hutchinson UK (1924); Bobbs US (1924)

Detective GRIME
American Male Detective in Pulp Magazines operating in New York

Alexander ROBERTSON (American)
Inventor of one other detective OLD SPECIE
Citation Record: 1 Book
Detective Grime's Triumph - *Only*
Street & Smith US (1902)

'Doc' GRIP
American Male Detective in Pulp Magazines operating in USA

ANON
Citation Record: 1 Book
Doc Grip, The Sporting Detective; Or, The Vendetta - *Only*
Aldine US (?)

Simeon GRIST
was formerly a Professor of English in California. Now a PI, he has some weird cases to solve, and his work is not made easier by his mid-life crisis and a mother who puts him on the list of every wedding service specialist in town.
American Male Private Detective operating in Los Angeles

Timothy HALLINAN (American)
Citation Record: 4 Books
The Four Last Things - *First*
New American Library US (1989)
The Bone Polisher - *Latest*
Morrow US (1995)

The Vrouw GROBELAAR
South African Female Sleuth operating in South Africa

Perceval GIBBON 1879-1926 (British)
See main detective Miss GREGORY
Citation Record: 17 Short Stories in 1 Collection
The Vrouw Grobelaar's Leading Cases - *Collection 1*
Blackwood UK (1905)
Vrouw Grobelaar And Her Leading Cases - *Collection 1**
McClure US (1906)

Alan GROFIELD
is an actor, thief and agent for a secret government agency called 'Brand X'.
American Male Secret Agent operating in USA

Richard STARK 1933- (American)
For writer details see Tim SMITH
Inventor of one other detective PARKER
Citation Record: 8 Books
The Spy In The Ointment - *First*
Random House US (1966)
The Butcher's Moon - *Last*
Random House US (1974); Coronet UK (1977)

Insp GROGAN
is a straight, business-like cop from down under.
Australian Policeman operating in Sydney

Margot NEVILLE (Australian)
is the pseudonym of two writers, both born in Melbourne, Australia.
Writers: Margot GOYDER1903- and Anne Neville Goyder JOSKE 1893-
Citation Record: 19 Books
Murder In Rockwater - *First*
Bles UK (1944)
Lena Hates Men - *First**
Arcadia US (1943)
Head On The Sill - *Last*
Bles UK (1966)

Hector GRONIG
American Male Amateur operating in San Francisco

Walter WALKER 1949- (American)
Writer: Walter Herbert WALKER III
Inventor of one other detective Owen CARR
Citation Record: 1 Book
The Two-Dude Offense - *Single*
Harper & Row US (1985)

Mr GROODE

American Male Sleuth operating in USA/Europe/Middle East

George GRISWOLD 1904-1989 (American)

Writer: Robert George DEAN

Citation Record: 4 Books

A Gambit For Mr Groode - *First*
Dutton US (1952); Eyre & Spottiswoode UK (1953)

The Pinned Man - *Last*
Little, Brown US (1955); Eyre & Spottiswoode UK (1956)

Sam GROSS

was formerly a lawyer and insurance investigator but now operates as a PI.

American Male Private Detective operating in New York

James P WOHL 1937- (American)

Writer: James Paul WOHL

Citation Record: 2 Books

The Nirvana Contracts - *First*
Bobbs US (1977)

The Blind Trust Contracts - *Latest*
Bobbs US (1978); Hale UK (1980)

Dr Adolph (Clubfoot) GRUNDT

is a German spy of rather simian appearance and unpleasant manners.

German Male Secret Agent operating in Europe

Valentine WILLIAMS 1883-1946 (British)

Invented 8 detectives - see Det Sgt Trevor DENE

Citation Record: 4 Books

Clubfoot The Avenger - *First*
Jenkins UK (1924); Houghton US (1924)

Courier To Marrakesh - *Last*
Hodder & Stoughton UK (1944); Houghton US (1946)

Dr Adolph (Clubfoot) GRUNDT and Desmond OKEWOOD

also appear individually in other books by this author.

German Male Secret Agents and British Male Sleuth operating in Europe/Asia

Douglas VALENTINE 1893-1946 (British)

See main detective Desmond OKEWOOD

Citation Record: 1 Book

The Man With The Clubfoot - *Only*
was published in the US under the following byline.
Jenkins UK (1918)

Valentine WILLIAMS 1883-1946 (British)

Invented 8 detectives - see Det Sgt Trevor DENE

Citation Record: 2 Books

The Man With The Clubfoot - *First*
was published in the UK under the preceding byline.
McBride US (1918)

The Return Of Clubfoot - *Last*
Jenkins UK (1923)

Island Gold - *Last**
Houghton US (1923)

Simon GRUNDT

American Male Amateur operating in Chicago

Harry Stephen KEELER 1890-1967 (American)

Invented 14 detectives - see Angus MACWHORTER

Citation Record: 1 Book

The Green Jade Hand - *Only*
Dutton US (1930); Ward, Lock UK (1930)

Yevgeni Ivanovitch GRUSHKO

is one of the new breed of post-Cold War police detectives now falling within the sights of experienced Western authors, who use much inventiveness in imagining the Russian situation, usually to its detriment. *GRUSHKO* is stereotypically modelled on the Russian bears we have come to expect from the work of *John LE CARRE;* and the ruminations of him and all around him on the rotten state of post-Soviet Russia are endless. *Philip MARLOWE* did not, fortunately for posterity, gripe for so long about the mean streets.

Russian Policeman operating in St Petersburg

Philip KERR 1956- (British)

Invented 3 detectives - see Ch Insp 'Jake' JAKOWICZ

Citation Record: 1 Book

Dead Meat - *Single*
Chatto & Windus UK (1993)

Grushko - *Single**
Arrow UK (1994)

Det Ebenezer GRYCE

has the distinction of being the first major fictional detective to have been created by a woman author. A member of the New York Police Department, he is a portly, middle-aged man and highly competent at his job. However, he is a public servant and cannot be considered as a gentleman who can mix with the best of Manhattan society. This is unfortunate, as it is among them that he finds his cases, and so he must use two intermediary sidekicks in his delicate dealings with certain suspects. He appears also in books with other detectives of this author, *Caleb SWEETWATER* and *Amelia BUTTERWORTH.*

American Policeman operating in New York

Sidekick: Mr RAYMOND
is a gentlemanly lawyer who narrates *THE LEAVENWORTH CASE* and assists *GRYCE* in his deliberations.
American Male - Narrator

Sidekick: Mr Q
is employed by *GRYCE* to perform the more menial and less dignified jobs of his profession in an era when the social boundaries are rigid, even for policemen on duty.
American Male - Assistant

Anna Katherine GREEN 1846-1935 (American)

was born in Brooklyn, New York, and graduated with a BA from Ripley Female College, Poultney, Vermont, 1867. She wrote thirty-three genre books and is the acknowledged mother of the American detective story.

Other Detectives:
BYRD
Sheriff Steve DILLON
Frank ETHERIDGE
Det Ebenezer GRYCE and Amelia BUTTERWORTH
Det Ebenezer GRYCE and Caleb SWEETWATER
Violet STRANGE
Caleb SWEETWATER
Anthony TAMWORTH

Citation Record: 9 Books 1 Selected Short Story

The Leavenworth Case: A Lawyer's Story - *First*
Putnam US (1878); Routledge UK (1884)

One Of My Sons - *Last*
Putnam US (1901); Ward, Lock UK (1904)

The Golden Slipper
is in a collection of author's short stories, *THE GOLDEN SLIPPER AND OTHER PROBLEMS FOR VIOLET STRANGE.*
Putnam US (1915)

Det Ebenezer GRYCE and Caleb SWEETWATER

also appear individually in other books by this author.

American Policeman and American Male Amateur operating in USA

Anna Katherine GREEN 1846-1935 (American)

Invented 9 detectives - see Det Ebenezer GRYCE

Citation Record: 2 Books

Initials Only - *First*
Dodd, Mead US (1911); Nash UK (1912)

The Mystery Of The Hasty Arrow - *Last*
Dodd, Mead US (1917)

Det Ebenezer GRYCE and Amelia BUTTERWORTH

Ebenezer GRYCE finds it difficult to cross the portals of Manhattan society to pursue his cases and has to make use of friends who can. In this one book he works closely with the genteel but formidable *Amelia BUTTERWORTH.*

American Policeman and American Female Amateur operating in New York

Anna Katherine GREEN 1846-1935 (American)

Invented 9 detectives - see Det Ebenezer GRYCE

Citation Record: 1 Book

That Affair Next Door - *Only*
Putnam US (1897); Nash UK (1903)

Carl GUARD

American Male Private Detective operating in USA

Milton K OZAKI 1913- (American)

Invented 3 detectives - see Prof CALDWELL

Citation Record: 1 Book

Maid For Murder - *Only*
Ace US (1955)

G

Marshal Salva GUARNACCIA

is a likeable, taciturn, compassionate policeman based in Florence but working on cases all over his beloved Tuscany. Because of his methods, which are often intuitive rather than logical, and the background of family life against which his cases are related, he has often been said to be an Italian version of *Jules MAIGRET.*

Italian Policeman operating in Tuscany

Magdalen NABB 1947- (British)

was born in Lancashire. A professional potter for some years, she now writes full time and lives in Florence, Italy, which is the background for her novels.

Citation Record: 7 Books

Death Of An Englishman - *First*
Collins UK (1981); Scribner's US (1982)

The Marshal At The Villa Torini - *Latest*
HarperCollins UK (1993)

Philo GUBB

is a comic creation, for he is a paperhanger in a small town who has learned how to be a detective by a correspondence course from the Rising Sun Detective Agency. He is a fan of *Sherlock HOLMES* and, in an effort to emulate the master, wears a dressing-gown and smokes a calabash (the sage of Baker Street did not, in fact, smoke one). He uses a hundred disguises, which take in nobody, and he murders the English language as he progresses manfully through a series of failed cases.

American Male Amateur operating in USA

Ellis Parker BUTLER 1869-1937 (American)

was born in Muscatine, Iowa. Mainly a writer of humorous short stories, he also wrote some mystery stories.

Citation Record: 18 Short Stories in 1 Collection

Philo Gubb: Correspondence School Detective - *Collection 1*
Houghton Mifflin US (1919)

Mr GUELPA

Male Amateur operating in New York/Paris

Vance THOMPSON 1863-1925 (American)

Citation Record: 2 Books

The Pointed Tower - *First*
Bobbs US (1922); Hutchinson UK (1923)

Mr Guelpa - *Last*
Bobbs US (1925); Hutchinson UK (1926)

Kat GUERRERA

is the sobriquet of Maria Katerina Lorca Guerrera Alcazar, a feminist, bisexual, ex-revolutionary who is hired, in her one book, by a radical, feminist author for reasons that hardly seem credible.

American Female Private Detective operating in USA

M F BEAL (American)

Writer: Mary F BEAL

Citation Record: 1 Book

Angel Dance - *Single*
Daughters US (1977)

Supt GUEST

British Policeman operating in England

Milward KENNEDY 1894-1968 (British)

Invented 6 detectives - see Sir George BULL

Citation Record: 1 Book

Half-Mast Murder - *Only*
Gollancz UK (1930); Doubleday US (1930)

Leo GUILD

is a bounty hunter who does some excellent sleuthing in books set back into the 1890s.

American Male Professional Investigator operating in USA

Ed GORMAN 1941- (American)

was born in Cedar Rapids, Iowa, and educated at Coe College, Iowa.

Writer: Edward GORMAN

Other Detectives:
Jack DWYER
Philip MARLOWE
TOBIN

Citation Record: 3 Books

Guild - *First*
Evans US (1987)

Blood Game - *Latest*
Evans US (1989); Chivers UK (1991)

Ray GUINNESS

is a graduate of Ohio State University who goes to London to finish his studies but becomes involved as a paid assassin for a British secret department. In the course of his duties he does have to do some detecting.

American Male Amateur operating in USA/Europe

Nicholas GUILD 1944- (American)

Writer: Nicholas M GUILD

Inventor of one other detective William LUKES

Citation Record: 3 Books

The Summer Soldier - *First*
Seaview US (1978); Magnum UK (1979)

The Favor - *Latest*
St Martin's US (1981); Hale UK (1983)

Charlotte GUISE

French Female Amateur

Mrs Henry WOOD 1814-1887 (British)

Invented 3 detectives - see Sgt DELVES

Citation Record: 1 Book

The Master Of Greylands - *Only*
Bentley UK (1873)

Vladimir GULL

Male Sleuth operating in USA/Europe

Anthony STUART 1940- (American)

Writer: Julian Anthony Stuart HALE

Citation Record: 6 Books

Vicious Circles - *First*
Macdonald UK (1978); Arbor US (1979)

Russian Leave - *Latest*
Arbor US (1982)

Insp GULLIVER

British Policeman operating in England

George BURNETT 1918- (British)

Writer: George Stanley BURNETT

Citation Record: 2 Books

The Sheep And The Wolves - *First*
Hodder & Stoughton UK (1962)
Violent Security - *Last*
Hodder & Stoughton UK (1962)

Aaron GUNNER
is an Afro-American shamus who takes up cases involving the black militant minority, sometimes clearing white racists in the process.
American Male Private Detective operating in Los Angeles

Gar Anthony HAYWOOD (American)
Citation Record: 3 Books
Fear Of The Dark - *First*
St Martin's US (1988); Macmillan UK (1988)
You Can Die Trying - *Latest*
St Martin's US (1993)

Bill GUNNERSON
American Male Amateur operating in USA

Ross MACDONALD 1915- (American)
Writer: Kenneth MILLAR
See main detective Lew ARCHER
Citation Record: 1 Book
The Ferguson Affair - *Only*
Knopf US (1960); Collins UK (1961)

Ed GUNNING
Male Sleuth operating in England/USA

William J ELLIOTT 1886-1947? (British)
Invented 4 detectives - see Anthony ENGLAND
Citation Record: 4 Books
Freak Racket - *First*
Swan UK (1941)
Gunning In England - *Last*
Swan UK (1946)

Bernard GUNTHER
is a hardboiled PI in Berlin under the Nazi regime in the late 1930s. He investigates local murders, all the time having to tread warily and with the utmost professionalism, for he is conscious that, around him, vast crimes are being committed daily by the authorities and war is on the horizon.
German Male Private Detective operating in Berlin

Philip KERR 1956- (British)
Invented 3 detectives - see Ch Insp 'Jake' JAKOWICZ
Citation Record: 2 Books
March Violets - *First*
Viking UK (1989); Viking US (1989)
The Pale Criminal - *Latest*
Viking UK (1990); Viking US (1990)

Lt Joe GUNTHER
American Policeman operating in Vermont

Archer MAYOR 1950- (American)
Writer: Archer Huntingdon MAYOR
Citation Record: 5 Books
Open Season - *First*
Putnam US (1988); Piatkus UK (1989)
Fruits Of A Poisonous Tree - *Latest*
Piatkus UK (1994)

Percival GUNTRIP
is a Scotland Yard detective in this Victorian novel.
British Policeman operating in London

Eric A BAYLY (British)
Invented 3 detectives - see Oliver POTTER and Laurence CARRINGTON
Citation Record: 1 Book
The Man With The Parrots: A Story Of Events And The Shadows They Cast - *Only*
Sands UK (1901)

Ch Vince GUTIEREZ
Second detective of Meg HALLORAN

Max GUTTMAN
American Male Amateur operating in New York/California

Arthur D GOLDSTEIN 1937- (American)
See main detective Ben LOMAX
Citation Record: 3 Books
A Person Shouldn't Die Like That - *First*
Random House US (1972); Prior UK (1977)
Nobody's Sorry He Got Killed - *Latest*
Random House US (1976)

Brian GUY
American Male Amateur operating in USA/Italy

Jason RIDGWAY 1928- (American)
Writer: Stephen MARLOWE
Other Byline: Andrew FRAZER
Citation Record: 4 Books
Adam's Fall - *First*
Permabooks US (1960)
The Treasure Of The Cosa Nostra - *Last*
Pocket Books US (1966)

GWAYLOR
American Male Amateur operating in USA

George Clinton BESTOR (American)
Citation Record: 1 Book
The Postage Stamp Murder - *Only*
Dial US (1935); Low UK (1936)

The GYPSY DETECTIVE
American Male Detective in Pulp Magazines operating in USA

ANON
The Gypsy Detective
Aldine US (?)

G

— H —

Thackeray HACKETT
has had his licence withdrawn and goes to work for a publicity firm. There he comes upon a really nasty murder.
American Male Private Detective operating in New York

Murdo COOMBS 1902-1977 (American)
For writer details see Luke SPEARE and Schyler COLE
Citation Record: 1 Book
A Moment Of Need - *Only*
Dutton US (1947)

Dick HADDEN
solves a case of death by stabbing in a guarded office.
American Male Amateur operating in USA

Fred MACISAAC 1886-1940 (American)
was born in Massachusetts. A playwright and novelist, he wrote at least eighteen genre novels.
Writer: Frederick John MACISAAC
Other Detectives:
Frank LEONARD and Foster GAINES
Addison Frank MURPHY
Citation Record: 1 Book
The Winged Murderer - *Only*
Sovereign House US (1939)

Michael HADDEN
is hired by a woman to find the killer of her husband.
British Male Private Detective operating in England

Jan ROFFMAN ?-1979 (British)

Writer: Margaret SUMMERTON

Inventor of one other detective RATLIN

Citation Record: 1 Book

A Daze Of Fears - *Only*
Doubleday US (1968)

Leith HADLEY

American Male Amateur operating in Chicago

Michael GILLIAN (American)

Citation Record: 1 Book

Warrant For A Wanton - *Only*
Mill US (1952)

Jack HAGEE

American Male Private Detective operating in USA

C J HENDERSON (American)

Citation Record: 2 Books 11 Short Stories in 1 Collection

No Free Lunch - *First*
Diamond US (1992)

Something For Nothing - *Latest*
Jove US (1993)

What You Pay For - *Collection 1*
Gryphon US (1990)

H

Mort HAGEN

specialises in divorce cases.

American Male Private Detective operating in California

Whit MASTERSON (American)

See main detective John SHU

Citation Record: 1 Book

Dead She Was Beautiful - *Only*
Dodd, Mead US (1955); Allen UK (1955)

Forrest HAGGERTY

was formerly a Chief of Police. Now, retired, he leads three other geriatrics into amateur sleuthing and murder-solving.

American Male Sleuth operating in Connecticut

Susannah MCSHEA (American)

Writer: Susannah Hofmann MCSHEA

Citation Record: 2 Books

Hometown Heroes - *First*
St Martin's US (1990)

The Pumpkin-Shell Wife - *Latest*
St Martin's US (1992)

Leo HAGGERTY

specialises in finding missing persons.

American Male Private Detective operating in US and the Caribbean

Benjamin M SCHUTZ 1949- (American)

Adopter of one other detective Philip MARLOWE

Citation Record: 4 Books

Embrace The Wolf - *First*
Bluejay US (1985)

The Things We Do For Love - *Latest*
Scribner's US (1989)

David HAHAM

Israeli Male Sleuth operating in Israel

C A HADDAD (American)

Writer: Carolyn A HADDAD

Inventor of one other detective Becky BELSKI

Citation Record: 2 Books

Bloody September - *First*
Harper & Row US (1976)

Operation Apricot - *Latest*
Harper & Row US (1978)

Alec HAIG

American Male Sleuth operating in USA/Asia

Alec HAIG (American)

Writer: UNKNOWN

Citation Record: 3 Books

Sign On For Tokyo - *First*
Dodd, Mead US (1968); Heinemann UK (1968)

Flight From Montego Bay - *Last*
Dodd, Mead US (1972); Heinemann UK (1972)

Leo HAIG

is a fat, indolent, would-be detective, designed as a spoof on the famous *Nero WOLFE.* Whereas the latter is a genius with orchids, *HAIG* keeps fish. The novels are related by *Chip HARRISON,* who is likewise a parody of *WOLFE's* famous sidekick, *Archie GOODWIN.* Indeed, the US publications appeared under the byline of *Chip HARRISON,* although the UK editions were under the author's real name. The books are cited appropriately.

American Male Private Detective operating in New York

Sidekick: Chip HARRISON

was once a deputy sheriff in a brothel in North Carolina. He answers an ad in the New York Times placed by *Leo HAIG,* who *does* in fact want to set himself up as a *Nero WOLFE* parody and to employ a sidekick like the famous *Archie GOODWIN.*

American Male - Assistant

Lawrence BLOCK 1938- (American)

was born in Buffalo, New York, and educated at Antioch College, Yellow Springs, Ohio, from which he graduated, 1959. A highly regarded writer of criminous works, he is the creator of some of the best modern detectives in books that have received several awards, including the Mystery Writers of America Edgar Allan Poe award, 1985.

Other Bylines:
William ARD
Chip HARRISON

Other Detectives:
Ed LONDON
MARKHAM
Bernard Grimes RHODENBARR
Matt SCUDDER
Evan TANNER

Citation Record: 2 Books

Five Little Rich Girls - *First*
was previously published, with a change of title, under the following byline.
Allison US (1984)

The Topless Tulip Caper - *Latest*
was previously published under the following byline.
Allison US (1984)

Chip HARRISON 1938- (American)

For writer details see Leo HAIG

Citation Record: 2 Books

Make Out With Murder - *First*
was republished, with a change of title, under the preceding byline.
Fawcett US (1974)

The Topless Tulip Caper - *Latest*
was republished under the preceding byline.
Fawcett US (1975)

'Tubby' HAIG

British Male Amateur operating in England

ANON

Citation Record: 15 Books

The Cinema Crook - *First*
Newnes UK (?)

The Circle Of The Snake - *Last*
Newnes UK (?)

Insp 'Digger' HAIG

investigates cases with a classic Australian background, sometimes with aboriginal themes.

Australian Policeman operating in Australia

S H COURTIER 1904-1974 (Australian)
was born in Kangaroo Flat, Victoria, Australia. He is a school-teacher and writer of several non-genre novels.
Writer: Sidney Hobson COURTIER
Inventor of one other detective Insp Ambrose MAHON
Citation Record: 5 Books
Now Seek My Bones - *First*
Hammond UK (1957)
No Obelisk For Emily - *Latest*
Jenkins UK (1970)

Dr Eustace HAILEY
is a professional psychologist with rooms at 22 Harley Street in London. He is enormously fat, wears an eye-glass and takes snuff, both almost clichés of the time. He is usually called in by Scotland Yard to lend his expertise in strange cases.
British Male Amateur operating in London
Stooge: Insp BILES
seems to be utterly inept at his job and always has to be shown how to solve his cases by the fat doctor.
British Male

Anthony WYNNE 1882-1963 (British)
Writer: Robert McNair WILSON
Citation Record: 28 Books 12 Short Stories in 1 Collection
The Mystery Of The Ashes - *First*
Hutchinson UK (1927); Lippincott US (1927)
Death Of A Shadow - *Last*
Hutchinson UK (1950)
Sinners Go Secretly - *Collection 1*
Hutchinson UK (1927); Lippincott US (1927)

Insp HAINES
American Policeman operating in Chicago

Lawrence L LYNCH (American)
Invented 11 detectives - see Neil J BATHURST
Citation Record: 1 Book
The Unseen Hand - *Only*
Laird & Lee US (1898); Ward, Lock UK (1899)

Const HALE
Second detective of Insp GORMAN

Henry HALE
says he has learned a lot about detection by reading mystery novels. Asked by a friend to investigate the death of a local farmer, he solves the case, to the chagrin of the local cops.
American Male Amateur operating in USA
Stooge: Capt MACREADY
does not like amateur detectives who solve cases that baffle worthy and hard-working cops.
American Male

Peter STORME 1900- (American)
Writer: Philip Van Doren STERN
Citation Record: 1 Book
The Thing In The Brook - *Only*
Simon & Schuster US (1937); Hale UK (1937)

Max HALE
Male Sleuth operating in New Zealand

Kenneth SANDFORD 1915-
Writer: Kenneth Leslie SANDFORD
Citation Record: 2 Books
Dead Reckoning - *First*
Hutchinson UK (1955)
Dead Secret - *Last*
Long UK (1957)

Max Chauncy HALE
is one of several Boston private eyes created by this author. He is rather unusual in having had a good education and in having inherited some wealth, although he does his best to disguise both.
American Male Private Detective operating in Boston

George Harmon COXE 1901-1984 (American)
Invented 20 detectives - see Kent MURDOCK
Citation Record: 2 Books
Murder For The Asking - *First*
Knopf US (1939); Heinemann UK (1940)
The Lady Is Afraid - *Last*
Knopf US (1940); Heinemann UK (1940)

Ann HALES
British Female Amateur operating in England

Mary INGATE 1912-1991 (British)
Citation Record: 2 Books
The Sound Of The Weir - *First*
Macmillan UK (1974); Dodd, Mead US (1974)
Remembrance Of Miranda - *First**
Dell US (1977)
This Water Laps Gently - *Latest*
Macmillan UK (1977)

Jim HALEY
operates with the Private Enquiry Office in a California of the future that appears to be even more bizarre than it is at present.
American Male Private Detective operating in California

Ron GOULART 1933- (American)
Invented 15 detectives - see Jake PACE and Hildy PACE
Citation Record: 1 Book
After Things Fell Apart - *Only*
Ace US (1970); Arrow UK (1975)

Dr Clifford HALIFAX
has taken his name from one of the co-authors.
British Male Amateur operating in England

L T MEADE and Clifford HALIFAX (British)
Invented 3 detectives - see Paul GILCHRIST
Citation Record: 24 Short Stories in 2 Collections
Stories From The Diary Of A Doctor (1st Series) - *Collection 1*
Short stories - 12
Newnes UK (1894)
Stories From The Diary Of A Doctor (2nd Series) - *Collection 2*
Short stories - 12
Sands UK (1896)

Holderly HALL
American Male Amateur operating in Tennessee

Kate CAMERON 1924-1980 (American)
Writer: Elizabeth Lorinda DUBREUIL
Inventor of one other detective Whispering HILLS
Citation Record: 5 Books
Shadows Of The Past - *First*
Leisure Books US (1974)
Deadly Nightshade - *Last*
Leisure Books US (1975)

Satan HALL
American Male Private Detective operating in New York

Carroll John DALY 1889-1958 (American)
Invented 6 detectives - see Race WILLIAMS
Citation Record: 2 Books 4 Short Stories in 1 Collection
The Mystery Of The Smoking Gun - *First*
Stokes US (1936)
Death's Juggler - *First**
Hutchinson UK (1935)
Ready To Burn - *Last*
Museum Press UK (1951)
The Adventures Of Satan Hall - *Collection 1*
Mysterious Press US (1988)

Insp 'Tubby' HALL
British Policeman operating in England

Phyllis HAMBLEDON 1892- (British)
Writer: Phyllis MACVEAN
Citation Record: 2 Books
Keys For The Criminal - *First*
Hale UK (1958)
Murder And Miss Ming - *Last*
Hale UK (1959)

Anthony HALLAM

British Male Secret Agent operating in several locations

R J BUCKLEY (British)
Writer: Robert John BUCKLEY
Citation Record: 13 Short Stories in 1 Collection
The Master Spy - *Collection 1*
Ward, Lock UK (1902)

Lucas HALLAM

is an elderly ex-gunfighter of the Old West who, during the era of the silent movies, has gone to Hollywood to work as an extra. He also solves murders.

American Male Private Detective operating in California/Texas

L J WASHBURN (American)
Writer: Livia J WASHBURN
Citation Record: 3 Books
Wild Night - *First*
!See Appendix 2.
Tor US (1987); Curley UK (1990)
Dog Heavies - *Latest*
Tor US (1990)

Insp HALLAN and Sgt SPRATT

British Policemen operating in England

George DOUGLAS 1902-1981 (British)
Writer: Douglas George FISHER
Other Byline: Douglas FISHER
Inventor of one other detective Sgt/Insp Brian 'Bonny' LEE
Citation Record: 11 Books
Unwanted Witness - *First*
Hale UK (1966)
One To Jump - *Last*
Hale UK (1972)

Commiss Geoffrey HALLDEN

is a District Commissioner in British East Africa. When a man, who once worked for the government, is killed in a small town completely cut off by the rains, *HALLDEN* makes a good job of tracking down the murderer.

British Policeman operating in Tanganyika

Jean SCHOLEY (British)
Citation Record: 1 Book
The Dead Past - *Only*
Heinemann UK (1961); Macmillan US (1962)

Mike HALLER

is a Bostonian who now operates in California. He calls himself a specialist in finding missing persons.

American Male Private Detective operating in San Francisco

Max BYRD 1942- (American)
was born in Atlanta, Georgia. After studying at Harvard University, Cambridge, Massachusetts, and at King's College, Cambridge, England, he received degrees in English and History. He became Assistant Professor at Yale, 1975, and, later, Professor at the University of California, Berkeley.
Citation Record: 3 Books
California Thriller - *First*
Bantam US (1981); Allison & Busby UK (1984)
Finders Weepers - *Latest*
Bantam US (1983); Allison & Busby UK (1985)

Sid HALLEY

is an ex-jockey who lost a hand in a racing accident and now investigates cases of skulduggery around race-courses.

British Male Private Detective operating in England

Dick FRANCIS 1920- (British)
was born in Tenby, Pembrokeshire. He was educated at Maidenhead County Boys' School, Berkshire, and served with the Royal Air Force, 1940-1945. He was a first-rate amateur and then professional jockey and, on retirement, 1957, he became the Racing Correspondent of the London *Sunday Express* and a full-time writer. He is the author of over thirty novels, all of which deal with the varied aspects, often criminal, of horse-racing. He received the Crime Writers Association Silver Dagger award, 1965; their Gold Dagger award, 1980; their Diamond Dagger award, 1989; and the Mystery Writers of America Edgar Allan Poe award twice, 1969 and 1981.
Writer: Richard Stanley FRANCIS
Other Detectives:
Tony BEACH and Gregor MCGREGOR
David CLEVELAND
Freddie CROFT
Jonah DEREHAM
Andrew DOUGLAS
Randall DREW
Rob FINN
Neil GRIFFON
Gene HAWKINS and Dave TELLER
Kelly HUGHES
Thomas LYON
Philip NORE
Steven SCOTT
Matt SHORE
Charles TODD
James TYRONE
Alan YORK
Citation Record: 2 Books
Odds Against - *First*
Joseph UK (1965); Harper & Row US (1966)
Whip Hand - *Latest*
Joseph UK (1979); Harper & Row US (1980)

David HALLIDAY

American Male Amateur operating in Connecticut

H Baldwin TAYLOR 1920- (American)
See main detective Pete HOLLAND
Citation Record: 2 Books
The Duplicate - *First*
Doubleday US (1964); Heinemann UK (1965)
The Triumvirate - *Last*
Doubleday US (1966); Heinemann UK (1966)

Susan HALLIDAY

is an actress who has appeared for some years in a TV soap. When the story finds a parallel in real life, leading to murder, she turns detective.

British Female Amateur operating in England

Eileen DEWHURST 1929- (British)
Invented 4 detectives - see Det Ch Supt Maurice KENDRICK and Humphrey BARNES
Citation Record: 1 Book
The House That Jack Built - *Single*
Collins UK (1982); Doubleday US (1982)

Willie HALLIDAY

British Male Sleuth operating in England

Mike FREDMAN (British)
Citation Record: 2 Books
You Can Always Blame The Rain - *First*
Elek UK (1978); St Martin's US (1980)
Kisses Leave No Fingerprints - *Latest*
Elek UK (1979); St Martin's US (1980)

Meg HALLORAN and Ch Vince GUTIEREZ

Meg HALLORAN is a schoolteacher who, in her first book, receives anonymous letters, which are followed by the murder of the student she thinks wrote them. To save herself and her daughter from jeopardy, she investigates, with the help and understanding of the local Chief of Police. They form a relationship and continue to become involved in cases.

American Female Amateur and American Policeman operating in California/ Idaho

Janet LAPIERRE (American)
Citation Record: 3 Books

Children's Games - *First*
Scribner's US (1989); Virago UK (1990)

Old Enemies - *Latest*
US (199?)

Mick HALSEY

is a rich man's son, a drop-out from Stanford, a writer, an ex-cop and now a high-priced, under-worked PI.

American Male Private Detective operating in San Francisco

Charles MARTELL (American)

Citation Record: 2 Books

Halsey And The Dead Ringer - *First*
Pageant US (1988)

Halsey And The Fine Art Of Murder - *Latest*
Pageant US (1989)

Prof Richard HALSEY

is an American Professor of History, a widower in his forties, who is on a sabbatical in England, where he intends to do some research. Instead he finds a dead body, which then disappears to the not unreasonable chagrin of the police. He is in a difficult situation and has to do more sleuthing than researching. Fortune is kind; for not only does he solve the case, to the further annoyance of the police, but he finds a comely widow to take back to the States with him.

American Male Amateur operating in England

Robert BERNARD 1918- (American)

was born in La Harpe, Illinois. He taught in the English Department at Princeton University, 1951-1975 and is an authority on English Victorian literature.

Writer: Robert Bernard MARTIN

Other Detectives:
Millicent HETHEREGE
Lt MOYNAHAN , Millicent HETHEREGE and Bill STRATTON

Citation Record: 1 Book

Death Takes A Sabbatical - *Only*
Norton US (1967)

Death Takes The Last Train - *Only**
Constable UK (1967)

Arthur HALSTEAD

works for a New York agency dealing with crimes having an occult background.

American Male Private Detective operating in New York/Maryland

William Edward HAYES 1897- (American)

Citation Record: 3 Books

The Black Doll - *First*
Doubleday US (1936)

Black Chronicle - *Last*
Doubleday US (1938)

Curt HALSTEAD

is a Professor of Sociology. He tracks down the four men who raped his wife and were responsible for her suicide.

American Male Amateur operating in USA

Joe GORES 1931- (American)

was born in Rochester, Minnesota. He graduated with a BA from the University of Notre Dame, Indiana, 1953, and received an MA from Stanford University, California, 1961. He published his first short story in 1957 and has since written at least eight genre novels, over a hundred short stories, several stage plays and over twenty plays for television. He received two Edgar Allan Poe awards from the Mystery Writers of America, 1969, for a novel and a short story, and a third for a television play, 1975. He is the only writer to date to have been so honoured in all three categories.

Writer: Joseph N GORES

Other Detectives:
Neil FARGO
Dashiell HAMMETT
Dan KEARNEY ASSOCIATES

Citation Record: 1 Book

A Time Of Predators - *Only*
Random House US (1969); Allen UK (1970)

Kirk HALSTEAD

is a lawyer who re-investigates an unsolved case of murder that occurred seven years earlier.

British Male Amateur operating in England

Evelyn BERCKMAN 1900-1978 (British)

wrote over twenty excellent suspense novels, rarely using a main detective.

Writer: Evelyn Dominica BERCKMAN

Citation Record: 1 Book

No Known Grave - *Only*
Dodd, Mead US (1958); Eyre & Spottiswoode UK (1959)

Insp Rupert HAMBLEDON

British Policeman operating in England

Sidekick: Ronnie CUMMINGS

British Male - Assistant

John DELLBRIDGE 1887- (British)

Citation Record: 2 Books 11 Short Stories in 1 Collection

Unfit To Plead - *First*
Hurst & Blackett UK (1949)

The Lady In The Wood - *Last*
Hurst UK (1950)

Searchlight On Hambledon - *Collection 1*
UK (1947); Hurst UK (1947)

Tommy HAMBLEDON

is a British Secret Service agent who is involved in a long series of adventures on the international scene.

British Male Secret Agent operating in Europe

Manning COLES (British)

Cyril Henry COLES was born in London and served with British Intelligence in both world wars. He worked in Australia for several years from 1920, returning to England in 1928. *Adelaide MANNING* was born in London.

Writers: Adelaide Francis Oke MANNING 1891-1959 and Cyril Henry COLES 1899-1965

Other Byline: Francis GAITE

Inventor of one other detective pair Charles LATIMER and James LATIMER

Citation Record: 24 Books 12 Short Stories in 1 Collection

Drink To Yesterday - *First*
Hodder & Stoughton UK (1940); Knopf US (1941)

The House At Pluck's Gutter - *Last*
Hodder & Stoughton UK (1963); Pyramid US (1968)

Nothing To Declare - *Collection 1*
Doubleday US (1960)

Neil HAMEL

is a tough, witty, fast-talking, small-time lawyer in Albuquerque.

American Amateur operating in New Mexico

Judith VAN GIESON 1941- (American)

Citation Record: 4 Books

North Of The Border - *First*
Walker US (1988); Virago UK (1990)

The Lies That Bind - *Latest*
HarperCollins US (1994)

Barney HAMET

was once a PI and is now a (fictional) executive for the Mystery Writers of America, which is supposed to be holding its annual award-giving meeting. A distinguished guest is killed and he deduces whodunnit, no mean achievement in front of his peers.

American Male Amateur operating in New York

Edward D HOCH 1930- (American)

Invented 20 detectives - see Capt LEOPOLD

Citation Record: 1 Book

The Shattered Raven - *Only*
Lancer US (1969); Hale UK (1970)

Supt HAMILTON

solves a case of 'impossible' robbery.
British Policeman operating in England

Vincent CORNIER (British)
Invented 3 detectives - see Barnabas HILDRETH
Citation Record: 1 Selected Short Story
The Courtyard Of The Fly
appeared in the July number of the magazine. It has been collected by *Xanadu* (UK 1990) in an anthology, *The Art of the Impossible* and by *Carroll* (US 1990) in *Murder Impossible*.
Pearson UK (1937)

Anthony HAMILTON

foils Japanese schemes for war with the USA and several other threats of a lesser or greater nature.
American Male Secret Agent operating in several locations

H

Frederick FROST 1892-1944 (American)
For writer details see Terence RADWAY
Citation Record: 3 Books
Secret Agent Number One - *First*
Macrae US (1936); Harrap UK (1937)
Spy Meets Spy - *Last*
Macrae US (1937); Harrap UK (1937)

Gil HAMILTON

sleuths in the year 2124.
American Male Sleuth

Larry NIVEN 1938- (American)
Writer: Laurence Van Cott NIVEN
Citation Record: 1 Book 3 Short Stories in 1 Collection
The Patchwork Girl - *Single*
Ace US (1980)
The Long Arm Of Gil Hamilton - *Collection 1*
contains three novelettes.
Ballantine US (1976)

Steve HAMM

American Male Sleuth operating in several locations

Hank BOSTROM (American)
Writer: William H LOVEJOY
Citation Record: 2 Books
Gabriel's Flight - *First*
Lynx US (1988)
Pressure Point - *Latest*
Lynx US (1988)

Mike HAMMER

is perhaps the most denigrated of all American private eyes, his name having become identified with the most tasteless and viciously uncaring violence in the genre. Not all critics agree, however, and some have admired the novels and the detective. Without question, he has been outdone by the creations of more recent writers who have the skill to dress up their violence by making it appear significant and even literary.
American Male Private Detective operating in USA
Sidekick: VELDA
is not only his secretary but, since she holds a PI licence herself and can tote a handy gun, more than helps out.
American Female - Secretary

Mickey SPILLANE 1918- (American)
was born in Brooklyn, New York. He served with the United States Army Air Force in the Second World War. He started to write short stories in the 1930s while working in circuses and he became famous after the publication of his first book with *Mike HAMMER*, which appeared to set new and lower standards for the violence inherent to some extent in all hardboiled private eye fiction. Regarded, at first as beyond the pale, his works have become more acceptable as the genre has made progress backwards towards subjects that make his novels appear comic rather than sordid. The public, in any case, loved them and it is said that they achieved sales surpassing those of any other writer.
Writer: Frank Morrison SPILLANE
Other Detectives:
Dogeron KELLY   Tiger MANN
Citation Record: 12 Books
I, The Jury - *First*
Dutton US (1947); Barker UK (1952)
The Killing Man - *Latest*
Dutton US (1989)

Dashiell HAMMETT

is, indeed, the famous American author and the creator of *The CONTINENTAL OP.* He appears, as a fictional detective, in books by two authors.
American Male Private Detective operating in San Francisco

Joe GORES 1931- (American)
Invented 4 detectives - see Curt HALSTEAD
Citation Record: 1 Book
Hammett - *Only*
Putnam US (1975); Macdonald UK (1976)

Stephen WRIGHT (American)
Citation Record: 1 Book
The Adventures Of Sandy West, Private Eye - *Single*
In this book, *Dashiell HAMMETT,* the famous author, is a character in the late 1940s who now has writer's block and wishes to set up his own detective agency in New York. To this end he takes on *Sandy WEST* as an apprentice assistant.
Sidekick: Sandy WEST; Stephen Wright US (1986)

Ch HAMMOND and Det BENEDETTO

American Policemen operating in Chicago

Ronald E GETTEL 1931- (American)
Citation Record: 1 Book
Twice Burned - *Single*
Walker US (1983)

Andy HAMMOND

is an insurance investigator who appeared first in a film, *Lady Ice*.
American Male Private Detective operating in Florida

Malcolm BRALY 1925-1980 (American)
Citation Record: 1 Book
The Master - *Only*
Paperback Library US (1973)

August HAMMOND

American Male Private Detective operating in Phoenix

Mark COGGINS (American)
Citation Record: 1 Selected Short Story
There's No Such Things As Private Eyes
In 'New Black Mask Quarterly' US (1985)

John HAMMOND

is an ex-Marine who is sent by a Los Angeles law firm fronting for the CIA to investigate the 'accidental deaths' of political figures.
American Male Professional Investigator operating in USA

Hendrix JOHN (American)
Citation Record: 1 Book
The Carnellian Circle - *Only*
Atheneum US (1975)

Wade HAMMOND

American Male Private Detective operating in USA

Paul CHADWICK (American)

Citation Record: 1 Selected Short Story

Fangs Of The Cobra

can also be found in an anthology, *A Cent a Story! The Best from Ten Detective Aces* (Editor: Garyn G Roberts, US 1986).

In 'Ten Detective Aces' US (1933)

Insp HANAUD

is stout, provincial and bourgeois. He is thus typical material (fictionally and according, perhaps, to a British author of the period) to be an agent in the French *Sûreté*. He is patterned somewhat on the classic French detective, *LECOQ*, but he has more of a sense of humour and appreciation of his own fallibilities. During the course of his work in various parts of France, he is often concerned with crimes involving the English abroad.

French Policeman operating in France

Sidekick: Mr RICARDO

is an elderly, bibulous bachelor and is the close confidant of *Insp HANAUD*, who continually lays bare his thoughts to him.

French Male - Confidante

A E W MASON 1865-1948 (British)

was born in Camberwell, London. After reading Classics at Oxford and receiving his degrees there, he served in British Intelligence during the First World War. He later became an actor for a while but his interest in politics lead him to election as the Liberal MP for Coventry, 1906-10. His first novel was published in 1907 and he continued writing books, short stories and several kinds of plays for the London stage until his death. He is perhaps best remembered as the author of that classic novel of adventure and stiff upper lip ethics, *The Four Feathers*; but his few detective novels, written over a period of thirty years until late in his long life, are still highly readable.

Writer: Alfred Edward Woodley MASON

Citation Record: 5 Books 1 Selected Short Story

At The Villa Rose - *First*

A four-act play version was published by *Hodder & Stoughton* (UK 1928).

Hodder & Stoughton UK (1910); Scribner's US (1910)

The House In Lordship Lane - *Last*

Hodder & Stoughton UK (1946); Dodd, Mead US (1946)

The Affair At The Semiramis Hotel

is a long short story that was published at the same time in a collection, *The Four Corners of the World*.

Hodder & Stoughton UK (1917); Scribner's US (1917)

Christopher HAND

seems to solve mysteries in a mysterious way unrevealed to the reader.

American Male Private Detective operating in New York

Stanley Hart PAGE (American)

was born in New Jersey and was a journalist.

Citation Record: 5 Books

The Resurrection Murder Case - *First*

Knopf US (1932); Paul UK (1933)

The Tragic Curtain - *Last*

Dial US (1935)

HANDSOME HARRY

American Male Detective in Pulp Magazines operating in USA

ANON

No citations

Saul HANDY

is an ex-cop from Chicago who settles in New York to become a jewellery salesman on the 'Diamond Block' on Fifth Avenue. He uses his old skills to solve the murder of a bodyguard.

American Male Ex-Policeman operating in New York

Cornelius HIRSCHBERG 1901- (American)

Citation Record: 1 Book

Florentine Finish - *Only*

Harper & Row US (1963); Gollancz UK (1964)

Jack HANIGAN

was formerly with the New York Police Department. Now retired and living in Washington DC, he is a licensed PI who is hired by a victim's father to investigate serial murders committed by a killer who sets up blind dates by almost untraceable computer networks.

American Male Private Detective operating in Washington DC

Walter DILLON (American)

Citation Record: 1 Book

Deadly Intrusion - *Single*

Bantam US (1987)

Ch Arly HANKS

was formerly a policewoman in New York. She is now the Chief of Police in the tiny Arkansas town of Maggody, where she meets local backwoods crime.

American Policewoman operating in USA

Joan HESS 1949- (American)

See main detective Claire MALLOY

Citation Record: 7 Books

Malice In Maggody - *First*

St Martin's US (1987)

O Little Town Of Maggody - *Latest*

US (1994)

Insp HANLEY

Second detective of Joseph 'Daffy' DILL

George HANLON

sleuths at some time in the future.

British Male Sleuth

E Everett EVANS 1893-1958 (British)

Writer: Edward Everett EVANS

Citation Record: 2 Books

Man Of Many Minds - *First*

Fantasy Press UK (1953)

Alien Minds - *Last*

Fantasy Press UK (1955)

Red HANLON

American Male Amateur operating in New York/San Francisco

Mollie MERRICK (American)

was born in San Francisco. A well-known journalist, feature writer and music critic in Hollywood, she wrote only two genre novels.

Citation Record: 2 Books

Upper Case - *First*

Washburn US (1936)

The Mysterious Mr Frame - *Last*

Washburn US (1938)

Supt HANNASYDE

of Scotland Yard is a good, sound, old-fashioned policeman investigating English murders in English villages.

British Policeman operating in England

Sidekick: Insp HEMINGWAY

assists *HANNASYDE* and appears later in books as the main detective.

British Male - Assistant

Georgette HEYER 1902-1974 (British)

was born in Wimbledon, Surrey, and was educated at seminary schools and Westminster School, London. She is mainly known as the author of at least forty-four romantic and historical novels.

Other Detectives:

Frank AMBERLEY   Insp HEMINGWAY

Citation Record: 4 Books

Death In The Stocks - *First*
Longman UK (1935)

Merely Murder - *First**
Doubleday US (1935)

A Blunt Instrument - *Last*
Hodder & Stoughton UK (1938); Doubleday US (1938)

Richard HANNAY

was the finest creation of one of the great masters of British thriller and espionage fiction. In the superb first book in which he appears – he basis of at least two classic films since – he is a man caught up in a web of espionage, murder and treachery. Four subsequent novels featuring *Richard HANNAY* appeared during the next twenty years, although none attained the success of the first.

British Male Amateur operating in Europe

John BUCHAN 1875-1940 (British)

was born in Broughton Green, Peebles. He was educated in Glasgow and took a BA and many prizes at Brazenose College, Oxford, 1877-1899. His career was a distinguished one in the Army, in the world of the arts, in the universities, and in politics. Honours showered on him from universities and learned societies all over the world, and he was eventually made Baron Tweedsmuir. His output, on a variety of subjects, was large, but he is best remembered, perhaps, for his spy stories.

Other Detectives:
Sir Edward LEITHEN   Duncan MCCUNN

Citation Record: 5 Books

The Thirty-Nine Steps - *First*
One of the greatest of all stories of espionage, this book became a classic during the First World War and has remained so, being filmed several times. It concerns a mysterious organisation devoted to obtaining secret information and passing it to Germany by a most ingenious method.
Blackwood UK (1915); Doran US (1916)

The Island Of Sheep - *Last*
Hodder & Stoughton UK (1936)

The Man From The Norlands - *Last**
Houghton Mifflin US (1936)

Edge HANNEGAN

is an ex-gambler and ex-Army policeman.

American Male Private Detective operating in San Francisco

B E LOVELL 1920- (American)

Citation Record: 2 Books

...And Incidentally, Murder! - *First*
Bouregy US (1952)

A Rage To Kill - *Last*
Ace US (1957)

Joe HANNIBAL

is hardboiled and operates in the town of Rockford.

American Male Private Detective operating in Illinois

Wayne D DUNDEE (American)

Citation Record: 3 Books

The Burning Season - *First*
St Martin's US (1988)

The Brutal Ballet - *Latest*
St Martin's US (1992)

Chess HANRAHAN

has an independent income and can afford to be irreverent over many things he dislikes, mainly educational institutions and the press.

American Male Private Detective operating in New York

Edward CLINE (American)

Citation Record: 1 Book

First Prize - *Single*
Mysterious Press US (1988)

Mac HANRAHAN and Heather MCBEAN

American Male Amateur and American Female Amateur operating in Washington DC

Margaret TRUMAN 1924- (American)

Invented 9 detectives - see Mr Ron FAIRCHILD

Citation Record: 1 Book

Murder In The Smithsonian - *Single*
Arbor US (1983)

Insp HANSLET and Dr Lancelot PRIESTLEY

Insp HASLETT appears also in some of the early books of the *Lancelot PRIESTLEY* series as both accomplice and antagonist. He is cited as the main detective in some other books by this author.

British Policeman and British Male Amateur operating in England

John RHODE 1884-1965 (British)

Invented 3 detectives - see Dr Lancelot PRIESTLEY

Citation Record: 2 Books

The Davidson Case - *First*
Bles UK (1929)

Murder At Bratton Grange - *First**
Dodd, Mead US (1929)

Death Pays A Dividend - *Last*
Collins UK (1939); Dodd, Mead US (1939)

Sally HANSON

is a nurse who sleuths.

British Female Amateur operating in England

Grace RICHMOND (British)

Citation Record: 1 Book

Nurse Hanson's Strange Case - *Single*
Hale UK (1987)

Jim HANVEY

is a private detective of the old school in the American South, where he befriends criminals who have gone straight but is the terror of crooks who fail to see the error of their ways. A very fat man, he sits a lot, taking his shoes off and fondling a gold toothpick while he ratiocinates.

American Male Professional Amateur operating in USA

Octavus Roy COHEN 1891-1959 (American)

was born in Charleston, South Carolina. He graduated from Clemson Agricultural College, South Carolina, and became a qualified lawyer in 1913. He was a reporter for several Southern papers and later became a full-time writer. He wrote many stories about Negro life in the South as well as detective novels.

Other Detectives:
David CARROLL   Lt Max GOLD
Eric PETERS   Florian SLAPPEY
Lt Marty WALSH

Citation Record: 3 Books 7+ Short Stories in 2 Collections

The May Day Mystery - *First*
Appleton US (1929)

Star Of Earth - *Last*
Appleton US (1932)

Jim Hanvey, Detective - *Collection 1*
Short stories - 7
Dodd, Mead US (1923); Nash UK (1924)

Scrambled Yeggs - *Collection 2*
contains an uncounted number of *Jim HANVEY* stories.
Appleton US (1934)

Priest Amenhotep Sa HAPU

was created by an author skilled in the ways of detective archaeologists. He is a priest in ancient Egypt who solves the mystery of the theft of valuables from a locked tomb. Would he were alive today! He must be the earliest historical sleuth in the genre. To go back further would mean encountering the Stone Age.

Egyptian Male Professional Investigator operating in Ancient Egypt

Elizabeth PETERS 1927- (American)

Invented 4 detectives - see Vicky BLISS

Citation Record: 1 Selected Short Story

The Locked Tomb Mystery

is in an anthology, *Sisters in Crime.*

Berkley US (1989)

Johnny HARD

is a cop in the Los Angeles Police Department who sells his soul to the Devil so that he can go back in time and become a PI in order to solve his father's murder.

American Male Private Detective operating in Los Angeles

Robert DICHIARA (American)

Citation Record: 1 Book

The Dick And The Devil - *Single*

Tor US (1989)

Peter HARDCASTLE

is said to be 'a famous detective'. He is called in to solve mysterious 'locked-room' murders, only to fall victim himself.

British Male Professional Investigator operating in England

Eden PHILLPOTTS 1862-1960 (British)

Invented 10 detectives - see Insp MIDWINTER

Citation Record: 1 Book

The Grey Room - *Only*

Hurst UK (1921)

Will HARDESTY

investigates a strange case, the discovery of the remains of seven children buried in the desert.

American Male Private Detective operating in California

Richard BARRE (American)

Citation Record: 1 Book

The Innocents - *Single*

Walker US (1995)

Bart HARDIN

is a bachelor who lives above a Times Square Flea Circus. A Korean War hero, he is now a sporting columnist for the *Broadway Times.* Compassionate, humorous and flamboyant, he loves gambling and women – not necessarily in that order.

American Male Amateur operating in New York

Stooge: Lt ROMANO

of the New York Police Department is an ulcer-ridden, friendly rival working on the cases of *Bart HARDIN.* Sometimes he acts more like a sidekick than a stooge and, in one book, he is the main detective. *ROMANO* appears in all the books in which *HARDIN* is the main detective, except the first, considered to be the author's best, *TERROR ON BROADWAY.*

American Male

David ALEXANDER 1907-1973 (American)

was born in Shelbyville, Kentucky. Originally a sporting columnist for the *Broadway Times* and later the racing editor for the *New York Herald Tribune*, he served in the Second World War and then completed a course at the New York Institute of Criminology, graduating with the highest honours. Turning down several offers to enter detective agency work, he began to write fiction.

Other Detectives:

Marty LAND   Lt ROMANO

Tommy TWOTOES and Terry ROOKE

Citation Record: 8 Books

Terror On Broadway - *First*

Random House US (1954); Boardman UK (1957)

Dead Man, Dead - *Last*

Lippincott US (1960); Boardman UK (1961)

Mark (The Penetrator) HARDIN

American Male Sleuth operating in USA/Mexico/Japan

Lionel DERRICK (American)

was an alternating pseudonym for *Mark K ROBERTS* and Chet Cunningham, who wrote alternating titles in the series.

Citation Record: 53 Books

The Target Is H - *First*

Pinnacle US (1973)

Jungle Blitz - *Latest*

Pinnacle US (1984)

Prof Charles HARDING

is an American Professor of International Law but he seems to spend most of his time at English country houses, where, as is well known to all *aficionados*, murder is habitual. He is the silent cogitating type and helps the police with their enquiries, coming up with brilliant solutions before they do.

American Male Amateur operating in England

H H STANNERS 1894- (American)

Writer: Harold H STANNERS

Citation Record: 3 Books

Murder At Markendon Court - *First*

Eyre & Spottiswoode UK (1936)

The Crowning Murder - *Last*

Eyre & Spottiswoode UK (1938)

Jim HARDMAN

has left the Atlanta police force in disgrace and is now an unlicensed PI.

American Male Private Detective operating in Atlanta

Sidekick: Hump EVANS

is an ex-football player.

American Male - Assistant

Ralph DENNIS (American)

was born in South Carolina. He graduated from the University of North Carolina and was an instructor in radio and television.

Citation Record: 12 Books

Atlanta Deathwatch - *First*

Popular Library US (1974)

The Buy Back Blues - *Last*

Popular Library US (1977)

HARDSCRABBLE

American Male Detective in Pulp Magazines operating in USA

Bernard WAYDE (American)

Invented 3 detectives - see Larry MURTAGH

Citation Record: 1 Selected Short Story

Hardscrabble, The Detective; Or, Tracked By A Hair

Old Cap Collier Library US (18??)

Bill HARDTMANN

is sent to New York to investigate the death of a doctor who fell off a skyscraper after being involved in experiments with a secret drug.

American Male Secret Agent operating in New York

Thomas WISEMAN 1931- (American)

Citation Record: 1 Book

A Game Of Secrets - *Single*

Delacorte US (1979); Cape UK (1979)

Bren HARDY

American Female Sleuth operating in USA

William J ELLIOTT 1886-1947? (British)

Invented 4 detectives - see Anthony ENGLAND

Citation Record: 2 Books

Bren Hardy, Tough Dame - *First*

Swan UK (1942)

Bren Hardy Again - *Last*

Swan UK (1945)

Cliff HARDY

wears an old leather jacket and jeans in the office but, even so, seems able to act for a rich clientele in a series replete with mayhem and ingenious plotting, set against the vivid backdrop of a rundown Sydney landscape.

Australian Male Private Detective operating in Sydney

Peter CORRIS 1942- (Australian)

Invented 3 detectives - see Richard BROWNING

Citation Record: 10 Books 27 Short Stories in 3 Collections

The Dying Trade - *First*
McGraw US (1980); Pan AU (1982)

O'Fear - *Latest*
Bantam AU (1990); Doubleday US (1991)

Heroin Annie - *Collection 1*
Short stories - 10
Unwin AU (1984); GM US (1987)

The Big Drop And Other Cliff Hardy Stories - *Collection 2*
Short stories - 10
Unwin AU (1985); Unwin UK (1986); GM US (1991)

Man In The Shadows - *Collection 3*
Short stories - 7
Unwin AU (1989); Unwin UK (1989); Bantam US (1991)

H

Patrick HARDY

American Male Sleuth operating in New York

Martin MEYERS (American)

Citation Record: 5 Books

Kiss And Kill - *First*
Popular Library UK (1975)

Spy And Die - *Last*
Popular Library UK (1976)

The HARDY BOYS

were juvenile pulp detectives who first appeared in the 1920s and went on to the 1970s. Homespun, jolly, moral and clean, they were an industry in themselves.

American Male Detective in Pulp Magazines operating in USA

No citations

Roxane HARFIELD

came late into the canon of *Sexton BLAKE* stories. Although she, for a while, assisted the great man, she on occasion sleuthed on her own in some stories.

British Female Professional Investigator operating in England

G H TEED 1878-1939 (British)

Writer: George Hamilton TEED

Other Detectives:
Sexton BLAKE
Yvonne CARTIER
Lawrence MALONE
John RUMFORD
Grant RUSHTON

No citations

Derek HARING

British Male Amateur operating in England

Maurice WORTH (British)

Writers: Maurice H B MASH and Willan George BOSWORTH 1905-

Citation Record: 3 Books

The Golden Pheasant Mystery - *First*
Hutchinson UK (1927)

The Pagoda Mystery - *Last*
Hutchinson UK (1928)

HARKER

American Male Sleuth operating in USA

Nathan HOLLANDER (American)

Citation Record: 3 Books

The Harker File - *First*
Lynx US (1989)

Dead And Paid For - *Latest*
Lynx US (1989)

Harry HARKER

British Male Amateur operating in England

John WAINWRIGHT 1921- (British)

Invented 9 detectives - see Ch Insp/Supt LENNOX

Citation Record: 1 Book

Cul-De-Sac - *Single*
St Martin's US (1984)

Hawthorne Albert HARKER

American Male Amateur operating in Nevada

Marc OLDEN (American)

Writer: Mark OLDEN

Other Byline: Robert HAWKES

Inventor of one other detective Robert SAND

Citation Record: 4 Books

The Harker File - *First*
Signet UK (1976)

Kill The Reporter - *Latest*
Signet UK (1978)

Peter HARKNESS

finds himself at a country house in ominous circumstances and has to solve a murder.

British Male Amateur operating in England

E X FERRARS 1907-1995 (British)

Invented 11 detectives - see Toby DYKE

Citation Record: 1 Book

The Cup And The Lip - *Only*
Doubleday US (1975)

Elizabeth FERRARS 1907-1995 (British)

Invented 10 detectives - see Toby DYKE

Citation Record: 1 Book

The Cup And The Lip - *Only*
Collins UK (1975)

William HARKNESS

British Male Amateur operating in Scotland

Milligan WARRICK (British)

Citation Record: 2 Books

The Yawning Lion - *First*
Grant UK (1932)

The Bandit Trust - *Last*
Moray UK (1934)

John HARLAND

American Male Amateur operating in New York

Rae FOLEY 1900-1978 (American)

See main detective Hiram POTTER

Citation Record: 3 Books

The Girl From Nowhere - *First*
Dodd, Mead US (1949)

An Ape In Velvet - *Last*
Dodd, Mead US (1951); Boardman UK (1952)

Robert HARLAND

Male Amateur operating in Germany

B Fletcher ROBINSON and J Malcolm FRASER (British)

Writer: (First author) Bertram Fletcher ROBINSON

Citation Record: 6 Short Stories in 1 Collection

The Trail Of The Dead - *Collection 1*
Ward, Lock UK (1904)

George HARLEQUIN

British Male Sleuth operating in Italy

Morris L WEST 1916- (British)

Writer: Morris Langlo WEST

Citation Record: 2 Books

The Big Story - *First*
Heinemann UK (1957)

The Crooked Road - *First**
Morrow US (1957)

Harlequin - *Last*
Collins UK (1974); Morrow US (1974)

John HARLEY

British Male Private Detective operating in London

Alfred TACK 1906- (British)

See main detective David CROSBIE

Citation Record: 4 Books

Selling's Murder - *First*
Jenkins UK (1946)

Death Takes A Dive - *Last*
Jenkins UK (1950); Roy US (1957)

Paul HARLEY

British Male Amateur operating in several locations

Sax ROHMER 1883-1959 (British)

Invented 9 detectives - see Insp RYDER

Citation Record: 2 Books

Bat-Wing - *First*
Cassell UK (1921); Doubleday US (1921)

Fire-Tongue - *Last*
Cassell UK (1921); Doubleday US (1922)

Wilson HARLEY

is a member of the English department at the fictional Spotswood University. When a pupil who has threatened him is found murdered with *HARLEY's* scissors in his back, it is no great wonder that the latter is suspected by the cops and has to solve the case to clear himself. He does so, by 'the pure Baconian method', as he calls it, consisting, it would seem, of putting facts on index cards and shuffling them.

American Male Amateur operating in Virginia

William MANER (American)

Inventor of one other detective Parker ROWE

Citation Record: 1 Book

Die Of A Rose - *Only*
Doubleday US (1970)

Mike HARMAN

British Male Sleuth operating in England

J M WALSH 1897-1952 (British)

Invented 7 detectives - see Insp QUAILE

Citation Record: 3 Books

Express Delivery - *First*
Collins UK (1946)

Time To Kill - *Last*
Collins UK (1949)

Steve HARMAS

works for an insurance company, National Fidelity. He is specially involved in large-scale insurance frauds, usually with murder attached, and is assisted by his beautiful wife. He appears also in books with this author's other detectives, *Al BARNEY* and *Frank TERRELL*.

American Male Private Detective operating in California/Florida

Sidekick: Helen HARMAS
American Female - Wife

James Hadley CHASE 1906-1985 (British)

Invented 14 detectives - see Dave FENNER

Citation Record: 4 Books

The Double Shuffle - *First*
Hale UK (1952); Dutton US (1953)

Tell It To The Birds - *Last*
Hale UK (1963); Pocket Books US (1974)

Steve HARMAS, Al BARNEY and Frank TERRELL

have all appeared in other books by this author, who did tend to use whichever of his many detectives came to hand.

American Male Private Detectives operating in USA

James Hadley CHASE 1906-1985 (British)

Invented 14 detectives - see Dave FENNER

Citation Record: 1 Book

An Ear To The Ground - *Only*
Hale UK (1968)

Fritz HARMON

German Male Private Detective operating in USA

Tony PASTOR 1837-1898 (American)

Writer: Harlan Page HALSEY

Other Byline: Judson R TAYLOR

Invented 4 detectives - see O'Neil MCDARRAGH

Citation Record: 1 Book

Fritz, The German Detective - *Only*
Ogilvie US (1885); Cameron UK (1886)

Dr Robert HARMON

Male Amateur operating in Jamaica/Nicaragua

Richard ELMAN 1934- (American)

Writer: Richard M ELMAN

Citation Record: 2 Books

The Breadfruit Lotteries - *First*
Methuen US (1980)

The Menu Cypher - *Latest*
Macmillan US (1982)

Det Sigrid HAROLD

has a professional life that is impeccable and devoted to the New York Police Department. Her private life is a disaster, though a funny one.

American Policewoman operating in New York

Margaret MARON (American)

Inventor of one other detective Judge Deborah KNOTT

Citation Record: 6 Books

One Coffee With - *First*
Raven US (1981); Headline UK (1988)

Corpus Christmas - *Latest*
Doubleday US (1989); Severn UK (1990)

Porteus Alexander HARP

is a Professor of Geology who solves the mystery of the appearance of a corpse in a holiday cabin.

American Male Amateur operating in USA

Leslie FORD 1898-1983 (American)

Invented 6 detectives - see Grace LATHAM

Citation Record: 1 Selected Short Story

Death Stops At A Tourist Camp
is a novelette that appeared in the October number.
In 'The Saint Mystery Magazine' US (1955)

Angela HARPE

belongs to the worst period of writing in the whole genre, the liberated 1970s, when authors thought that by writing about anything previously regarded as forbidden they could make up for lack of anything else. *Angela HARPE* is indeed a product of the times, a modern fantasy of the genre, being a beautiful model, a high-priced prostitute, an ex-policewoman who knows all about karate, electronics, athletics, swimming and, of course, shooting – in fact, a veritable update of the worst of superheroes.

American Female Private Detective operating in Detroit

James D LAWRENCE (American)

Citation Record: 4 Books

The Dream Girl Caper - *First*
Pyramid US (1975)

The Godmother Caper - *Last*
Pyramid US (1975)

HARPER

British Male Sleuth operating in several locations

Marcus AYLWARD 1929- (British)

Writer: Mark ALEXANDER

Citation Record: 2 Books

H

Harper's Folly - *First*
Barker UK (1984)
Harper's Luck - *Latest*
Weidenfeld & Nicolson UK (1985)

Nancy HARPER

British Female Amateur operating in England

Marion BABSON (American)
Invented 8 detectives - see Douglas PERKINS
Citation Record: 1 Book
Death Swap - *Single*
Collins UK (1984); Walker US (1985)

Det Insp Stephen HARPER

American Policeman operating in USA

Walter C BROWN (American)
Citation Record: 3 Books
The Second Chance - *First*
Lippincott US (1929)
Murder At Mocking House - *Last*
Lippincott US (1933)

H

Ch Supt Colin HARPUR

is a good example of the modern tough British cop mixing it with British nasties.
British Policeman operating in London

Bill JAMES 1929- (British)
Writer: Allan James TUCKER
Other Byline: David CRAIG
Citation Record: 6 Books
You'd Better Believe It - *First*
Constable UK (1985); St Martin's US (1986)
Roses, Roses - *Latest*
Macmillan UK (1993)

Steve HARRAGAN

Male Sleuth operating in England/USA

Steve HARRAGAN (British)
Citation Record: 9 Books
The Bigamy Kiss - *First*
Universal UK (1952)
Carney's Burlesque - *Last*
Universal UK (1953)

Insp HARRIGAN

American Policeman operating in Chicago

William P MCGIVERN 1927-1982 (American)
Invented 5 detectives - see Dave BANNION
Citation Record: 1 Book
Heaven Ran Last - *Only*
Dodd, Mead US (1949); Digit UK (1958)

HARRIGAN and HOEFFLER

American Male Sleuths operating in California/New Mexico

Patrick O'MALLEY 1916-1989 (American)
For writer details see Mike CAVANAUGH
Citation Record: 7 Books
The Affair Of The Red Mosaic - *First*
Mill US (1961)
The Affair Of The Blue Pig - *Last*
Mill US (1965)

Tex HARRIGAN

American Male Sleuth operating in USA

August DERLETH 1909-1971 (American)
Invented 4 detectives - see Solar PONS
Citation Record: 17 Short Stories in 1 Collection
Harrigan's File - *Collection 1*
Not all the stories are criminous.
Arkham US (1975)

HARRINGTON

is a US Army veteran who graduates at Law from New York University and eventually becomes an attorney in Manhattan. He is in constant trouble, as he has lost his last ten cases, cannot pay his rent for his apartment in Greenwich Village and is spurned incessantly by his girl-friend. At the end of his tether, he takes this case of a young man who has apparently killed someone whilst on drugs. He solves the case, without fee.
American Male Professional Amateur operating in New York

Mel ARRIGHI 1933- (American)
Inventor of one other detective pair Hank MERCER and Biff DEEGAN
Citation Record: 1 Book
Freak-Out - *Only*
Putnam US (1968)

John HARRINGTON

British Male Amateur operating in India

Brian COOPER 1919- (American)
Invented 3 detectives - see Rod MCKINNON
Citation Record: 1 Book
A Mission For Betty Smith - *Only*
Heinemann UK (1967)
Monsoon Murder - *Only**
Vanguard US (1968)

Insp HARRIS

investigates a death by bludgeoning in a locked room
British Policeman operating in England

Ronald BARKER 1920-1976 (British)
Writer: Ronald Ernest BARKER
Other Byline: E B RONALD
Citation Record: 1 Book
Clue For Murder - *Only*
Abelard UK (1962); Abelard US (1962)

Insp HARRIS

British Policeman operating in England
Sidekick: Sgt LEEDS
British Male - Subordinate

John ROSENBERG and Elizabeth ROSENBERG (British)
Writers: John ROSENBERG 1931-1991 and Elizabeth ROSENBERG
Citation Record: 1 Book
Out Brief Candle - *Only*
Hogarth UK (1959)

Albie HARRIS

is a middle-aged widower who lives with his sister at Ogg Lake, where only the occasional murder alleviates the boredom.
American Male Amateur operating in New York

Amber DEAN 1902- (American)
Citation Record: 5 Books
Dead Man's Float - *First*
Doubleday US (1944)
Snipe Hunt - *Last*
Doubleday US (1949)

Barney HARRIS

is an ex-auto mechanic who specialises in dealing with car crimes.
American Male Private Detective operating in New York

Ed LACY 1911-1968 (American)
Invented 8 detectives - see Toussaint 'Touie' MOORE
Citation Record: 1 Book
The Best That Ever Did It - *Only*
Harper & Row US (1955); Hutchinson UK (1957)
Visa To Death - *Only**
Permabooks US (1956)

David S HARRIS

was a 'scientific detective' who appeared in short stories in the pulps, mainly in *Amazing Stories.*

American Male Detective in Pulp Magazines operating in USA

Charles CLOUKEY (American)

No citations

Jim HARRIS and Kate HARRIS

American Male Amateur and American Female Amateur operating in New York

Travis MACRAE 1926- (American)

Writer: Anita Macrae FEAGLES

Citation Record: 2 Books

Death In View - *First*
Holt US (1960); Hammond UK (1961)

Twenty Per Cent - *Last*
Holt US (1961)

Multiple Murder - *Last**
Hammond UK (1962)

Joseph HARRIS

is the father of a student at Dartmouth. When three other students are murdered, it is only natural that the University should ask him to find out whodunnit.

American Male Amateur operating in USA

Clifford ORR 1899-1951 (American)

See main detective 'Spider' MEECH

Citation Record: 1 Book

The Dartmouth Murders - *Only*
Farrar, Straus US (1929); Hamilton UK (1931)

Kate HARRIS

Second detective of Jim HARRIS

Leonard HARRIS

Second detective of Franklin PARRY

Mike HARRIS and Trixie MEEHAN

Mike HARRIS is the head of the Blaine Detective Agency and his partner is *Trixie MEEHAN*, who is, we are told, beautiful, tough and very brainy.

American Male Private Detective and American Female Private Detective operating in USA

T T FLYNN 1902- (American)

Writer: Thomas Theodore FLYNN

Inventor of one other detective Mr MADDOX

Citation Record: 1 Selected Short Story

The Deadly Orchid
was first published in the pulps and appears also in the anthology, *Hard-Boiled Dames; Stories featuring Women Detectives, Reporters, Adventurers and Criminals from the Pulp Fiction Magazines of the 1930s*, (US 1986) edited by Bernard Drew.
In 'Detective Fiction Weekly' US (1933)

Paul HARRIS

is a Scot who, in his first book, is in China as an engineering advisor and salesman. In this and subsequent books he sleuths in the East and later in Scotland.

British Male Amateur operating in Far East

Gavin BLACK 1913- (British)

is a Scot who was born in Tokyo. He was educated in Japan and later in the USA and Scotland. He served in the British Army, 1940-1945, and has since been a full-time writer.

Writer: Oswald Morris WYND

Citation Record: 13 Books

Suddenly, At Singapore - *First*
Collins UK (1961)

Night Run From Java - *Latest*
Collins UK (1979)

Sam HARRIS

British Male Amateur operating in England

Michael CRONIN 1907- (British)

Writer: Brendan Leo CRONIN

Other Detectives:
James HELLIER; Richard (The Pilgrim) MAIDMENT

Citation Record: 4 Books

A Black Leather Case - *First*
Hale UK (1971)

The Big Tickle - *Last*
Hale UK (1974)

Insp HARRISON

American Policeman operating in USA

Mary Roberts RINEHART 1876-1958 (American)

Invented 7 detectives - see Letitia CARBERRY

Citation Record: 1 Book

The Door - *Only*
Farrar, Straus US (1930); Hodder & Stoughton UK (1930)

H

Clay HARRISON

British Male Private Detective operating in England

Clifton ROBBINS 1890- (British)

Inventor of one other detective STAVELEY

Citation Record: 5 Books

Dusty Death - *First*
Benn UK (1931); Appleton US (1932)

Methylated Murder - *Last*
Butterworth UK (1935)

Richard HARRISON

is a diocesan official sent to investigate nasty goings-on at Canterbury cathedral.

British Male Amateur operating in England

Michael David ANTHONY (British)

Citation Record: 1 Book

The Becket Factor - *Single*
Collins UK (1990); St Martin's US (1991)

Insp HARROW

British Policeman operating in England

Shipley ADAMS (British)

Citation Record: 4 Books

Murder Unsolved - *First*
Boardman UK (1947)

Murder Well Done - *Last*
Boardman UK (1950)

Jennifer HART

Second detective of Jonathan HART

Jonathan HART and Jennifer HART

American Male Amateur and American Female Amateur operating in USA

Roger BOWDLER 1934- (British)

Citation Record: 6 Short Stories in 1 Collection

Hart To Hart - *Collection 1*
contains novelizations of episodes from an American TV series.
Granada UK (1981)

Kirby HART

of Probe Associates, is an ex-Marine. In his one book he is the victim of a frame-up and has to clear himself.

American Male Private Detective operating in USA

Dexter ST CLAIR 1895- (American)

For writer details see Fire Marshal Ben PEDLEY

Citation Record: 1 Book

The Lady's Not For Living - *Only*
GM US (1963); Muller UK (1964)

Nicol HART
solves a murder and so saves an accused friend.
British Male Private Detective operating in England

Harrington HEXT 1862-1960 (British)
See main detective Insp MIDWINTER
Citation Record: 1 Book
Who Killed Diana - *Only*
Butterworth UK (1924)
Who Killed Cock Robin? - *Only**
Macmillan US (1924)

HARTER
American Male Sleuth operating in Virginia

John DOUGLAS (American)
See main detective William EDMONDSON
Citation Record: 2 Books
Shawnee Alley Fire - *First*
St Martin's US (1987)
Haunts - *Latest*
St Martin's US (1990)

H

'Hashknife' HARTLEY
American Male Sleuth operating in USA

W C TUTTLE 1883- (American)
mostly wrote Westerns, some of which have criminous plots and detective elements. Many of his books were only published in the UK.
Writer: Wilbur Coleman TUTTLE
Citation Record: 20 Books
The Medicine-Man - *First*
Houghton US (1939); Collins UK (1925)
Medicine Maker - *Last*
Collins UK (1967)

Roger HARTLEY
British Male Amateur operating in England

Geoffrey ELLNGER (British)
Citation Record: 2 Books
The Trap In The Tunnel - *First*
Jenkins UK (1941)
The Return Of Cardannesley - *Last*
Heritage UK (1944)

Walter HARTWRIGHT
is a drawing teacher who vaguely sleuths in this classic novel.
British Male Amateur operating in London

Wilkie COLLINS 1824-1889 (British)
Invented 5 detectives - see Sgt CUFF
Citation Record: 1 Book
The Woman In White - *Only*
Sampson, Low UK (1860); Harper & Row US (1860)

Sgt Cass HARTY
!See Appendix 2.
American Policeman operating in New York

Joel Y DANE 1905- (American)
Writer: Joseph Francis DELANEY
Citation Record: 4 Books
Murder Cum Laude - *First*
Smith & Haas US (1935)
Murder In College - *First**
Bell UK (1935)
The Christmas Tree Murders - *Last*
Doubleday US (1938)

Bingham HARVARD
American Male Amateur operating in USA

Varick VANARDY 1861-1922 (American)
Writer: Frederic Merril Van Reuss DAY
Inventor of one other detective CREWE (BIRGE MOREAU)
Citation Record: 4 Books
Alias The Night Wind - *First*
Dillingham US (1913)
The Lady Of The Night Wind - *Last*
Macaulay US (1919); Skeffington UK (1926)

Paul HARVARD
British Male Sleuth

C H GIBBS-SMITH 1909-1981
Writer: Charles Harvard GIBBS-SMITH
Citation Record: 2 Books
Operation Caroline - *First*
Heinemann UK (1953)
The Caroline Affair - *First**
Viking US (1954)
Escape And Be Secret - *Last*
Hutchinson UK (1957)

Steve HARVESTER
succeeds in saving the free world from various diabolical schemes hatched by its enemies.
American Male Secret Agent operating in USA/Europe

James M FOX (American)
was born in The Hague, Netherlands and educated at the Universities of Leiden and Utrecht. He emigrated to the USA, 1946, and became a naturalised citizen, 1949. He was a lawyer and advisor to the Dutch government in exile during the Second World War.
Writer: Johannes Matthijs Willem KNIPSCHEER
Other Byline: Grant HOLMES
Other Detectives:
Sgt Jerry LONG
John MARSHALL and Suzy MARSHALL
Citation Record: 2 Books
Dark Crusade - *First*
was published in the UK under the following byline.
Little, Brown US (1954)
Operation Dancing Dog - *Last*
Walker US (1974)

Grant HOLMES (American)
For writer details see Steve HARVESTER
Citation Record: 1 Book
Dark Crusade - *Only*
was published in the US under the preceding byline.
Cassell UK (1955)

HARVEY
British Male Sleuth operating in England

Douglas HURD 1930- (British)
Writer: Douglas Richard HURD
Citation Record: 2 Books
Send Him Victorious - *First*
was written with Andrew Osmond.
Collins UK (1968); Macmillan US (1969)
The Smile On The Face Of The Tiger - *Last*
was written with Andrew Osmond.
Collins UK (1969); Macmillan US (1970)

'Bump' HARWELL
is involved in a nonsensical foreign adventure.
American Male Sleuth operating in York

Burt HIRSCHFIELD 1923- (American)
Citation Record: 1 Book
The Verdugo Affair - *Single*
Dell US (1984)

Insp HASKELL
British Policeman operating in England

William SUTHERLAND 1908- (British)
Writer: John Murray COOPE
Citation Record: 2 Books

Behind The Head-Lines - *First*
Arrowsmith UK (1933)
The Proverbial Murder Case - *Last*
Arrowsmith UK (1935)

Ellie Simons HASKELL

!See Appendix 2.

British Female Amateur operating in England

Dorothy CANNELL (British)
now lives in the United States.

Inventor of one other detective pair Hyacinth TRAMWELL and Primrose TRAMWELL

Citation Record: 3 Books
The Thin Woman - *First*
St Martin's US (1984); Bantam UK (1990)
Mum's The Word - *Latest*
Bantam US (1990); Bantam UK (1992)

Vejay HASKELL

is a meter reader for a large Californian electrical power company in the fictional resort of Russian River. Her ability to enter other people's homes, combined with her curiosity and cleverness, get her involved in detection. The local crimes are many and varied.

American Female Amateur operating in California

Susan DUNLAP 1943- (American)
was born in New York City. She graduated with a BA from Bucknell University, Lewisburg, Pennsylvania, 1943.
Writer: Susan D DUNLAP
Other Detectives:
Kiernan O'SHAUNESSY Jill SMITH
Citation Record: 3 Books
An Equal Opportunity Death - *First*
St Martin's US (1984); Hale UK (1986)
The Last Annual Slugfest - *Latest*
St Martin's US (1986)

Lt HASS

solves the fascinating mystery of how a severed hand got into a locked safe.

American Policeman operating in USA

Seth BAILEY (American)
Citation Record: 1 Selected Short Story
The Hand In The Cobbler's Safe
Apparently a true story, this appeared in a collection with the same title.
Bartholomew US (1944)

Ben HASSETT

Second detective of Charles Hendesley MANNING

Bill HASTINGS and Coco HASTINGS

are one of the many husband-and-wife detective teams of the period. He is a businessman involved, we are told, in electrical engineering. That seems hardly the most exciting of professions for an amateur sleuth!

American Male Amateur and American Female Amateur operating in California/Idaho

Lenore Glen OFFORD 1905- (American)
See main detective Todd MCKINNON
Citation Record: 2 Books
Murder On Russian Hill - *First*
Macrae, Smith US (1938)
Murder Before Breakfast - *First**
Jarrolds UK (1938)
Clues To Burn - *Latest*
Duell US (1942); Grayson UK (1943)

Coco HASTINGS

Second detective of Bill HASTINGS

Lt Frank HASTINGS

was formerly a football professional. Now he is with the San Francisco Homicide Squad and appears in books that are virtually police procedurals.

American Policeman operating in San Francisco

Sidekick: Lt Pete FRIEDMAN
is an obese ex-actor who works on most of his cases.
American Male - Partner

Collin WILCOX 1924- (American)
was born in Detroit, Michigan. He graduated with a BA from Antioch College, Yellow Springs, Ohio, 1948, has been a teacher and business-man, and became a full-time writer in 1970. Most of his genre novels fall loosely into the police procedural category.
Other Detectives:
Alan BERNHARDT Stephen DRAKE
Marshall MCCLOUD
Citation Record: 14 Books
The Lonely Hunter - *First*
Random House US (1969); Hale UK (1971)
A Death Before Dying - *Latest*
Holt US (1990)

Lt Frank HASTINGS

Second detective of NAMELESS DETECTIVE

Jefferson HASTINGS

American Male Amateur operating in Washington DC

James HAY Jr 1881-1936 (American)
Citation Record: 3 Books
The Melwood Mystery - *First*
Dodd, Mead US (1920)
The Bellamy Case - *Last*
Dodd, Mead US (1925)

Jimmy HASTINGS

American Male Amateur operating in USA

Charles G GIVENS 1899-1964 (American)
Writer: Charles Garland GIVENS
Citation Record: 2 Books
The Rose Petal Murders - *First*
Bobbs US (1935)
The Jig-Time Murders - *Last*
Bobbs US (1936)

Stanley HASTINGS

is impoverished and usually does legwork for a lawyer. He becomes a PI only because the call board of his New York office says so, and he is quite surprised that anyone should actually want his services.

American Male Private Detective operating in New York

Parnell HALL (American)
Writer: Parnell HALL
Other Byline: J P HAILEY
Citation Record: 6 Books
Detective - *First*
Fine US (1987)
Juror - *Latest*
Fine US (1990)

Jimmie HASWELL

is a barrister and well versed in the legal background that was so dear to the author's heart. His cases are typical of the period, well plotted and descriptive of English middle-class life in the era before 1939.

British Male Professional Amateur operating in England

Herbert ADAMS 1874-1958 (British)
was born in London. He was a surveyor by profession.
Other Detectives:
Maj Robert BENNION Mark BRADDON

Citation Record: 8 Books

The Secret Of Bogey House - *First*
Methuen UK (1924); Lippincott US (1925)

The Woman In Black - *Last*
Lippincott US (1932); Methuen UK (1933)

Prof Cyrus HATCH

is the son of New York's Police Commissioner and is the Professor of Criminology at the fictional Knickerbocker College. Tall, handsome and something of a media personality, he becomes involved in several cases of murder.

American Male Professional Investigator operating in New York

Sidekick: Danny DELEVAN
is both bodyguard and assistant.
American Male - Bodyguard

Frederick C DAVIS 1902-1977 (American)

Invented 4 detectives - see Luke SPEARE and Schyler COLE

Citation Record: 8 Books

Coffins For Three - *First*
Doubleday US (1938)

One Murder Too Many - *First**
Heinemann UK (1938)

Gone Tomorrow - *Last*
Doubleday US (1948)

H

Jake HATCH

is a railway cop for Burlington Northern, operating out of Omaha.

American Male Professional Investigator operating in Omaha

Robert CAMPBELL 1927- (American)

was born in Newark, New Jersey. He is an illustrator, playwright, and screenwriter and the author of some criminous works.

Writer: Robert Wright CAMPBELL

Other Detectives:
Jimmy FLANNERY
Philip MARLOWE
Panama HEATH
WHISTLER

Citation Record: 2 Books

Plugged Nickel - *First*
Pocket Books US (1988)

Red Cent - *Latest*
Pocket Books US (1989)

Amos HATCHER

is an art historian who is also an investigator for an association of art dealers. He meets the usual chicanery to be found in the fictional art world.

American Male Amateur operating in Boston/Rome

Oliver BANKS 1941- (American)

Writer: Oliver T BANKS

Citation Record: 2 Books

The Rembrandt Panel - *First*
Little, Brown US (1980)

The Rembrandt File - *First**
Gollancz UK (1984)

The Caravaggio Obsession - *Latest*
Little, Brown US (1984); Gollancz UK (1985)

Frank HATCHER

American Male Sleuth operating in USA/Asia

Don MERRITT 1945- (American)

Citation Record: 3 Books

Hatch's Island - *First*
Bantam US (1986)

Hatch's Mission - *Latest*
Bantam US (1987)

Madge HATCHETT

is affectionately known as Madge The Badge. She is also called The Black Widow and she did not get her reputation for nothing. Once a female cop in Chicago, she has done very well, lives luxuriously, beats suspects up in the line of duty and is, they say, lovely to look at.

American Female Private Detective operating in Chicago

Lee MCGRAW (American)

Citation Record: 1 Book

Hatchett - *Single*
Ballantine US (1976)

Jim HATFIELD

is a Western detective in the pulps.

American Male Detective in Pulp Magazines operating in USA

Jackson COLE (American)

Writer: A Leslie SCOTT

No citations

Prof Paul HATFIELD

is the Professor of Chemistry at the fictional Woodside University in the US Midwest. He is fond of bird-watching and bicycling and is the consultant to the local police, managing to solve three cases of academic murder for them.

American Male Amateur operating in Midwest USA

Samuel ROGERS 1904- (American)

was born in Newport, Rhode Island. He is the author of several mainstream novels and is a sometime Professor of French at the University of Wisconsin.

Writer: Samuel Greene Arnold ROGERS

Citation Record: 3 Books

Don't Look Behind You! - *First*
Harper & Row US (1944)

You Leave Me Cold! - *Last*
Harper & Row US (1946)

James HATTON

is, in Victorian times, on a bicycling holiday in Brittany, where he is able to assist the baffled French police with their enquiries.

British Male Amateur operating in France

Basil THOMSON 1861-1939 (British)

Invented 5 detectives - see Insp RICHARDSON

Citation Record: 1 Book

A Court Intrigue - *Only*
Heinemann UK (1896)

Jonathan HATWOOD

British Male Private Detective operating in London

E T COLLIS (British)

Citation Record: 1 Book

Murder By Warrant - *Only*
Kelvin Glen UK (1898)

Camilla HAVEN

Second detective of Simon LESTER

Clyde HAVILAND

solves the mystery of a how a bus, carrying children, has come to disappear.

American Male Amateur operating in USA

Hugh PENTECOST 1903-1989 (American)

Invented 12 detectives - see Pierre CHAMBRUN

Citation Record: 1 Book

The Day The Children Vanished - *Only*
was published originally as a short story but due to its subsequent popularity, it was converted to a novel.
Pocket Books US (1976); Hale UK (1977)

Anthony HAVILLAND

British Male Amateur operating in England

Val GIELGUD 1900-1981 (British)

Invented 3 detectives - see Det Insp Simon SPEARS

Citation Record: 4 Books

Gravelhanger - *First*
Cassell UK (1934)

The Ruse Of The Vanished Women - *First**
!See Appendix 2.
Doubleday US (1934)

Special Delivery - *Last*
Collins UK (1950)

Johnny HAVOC

is small, handsome, bright, but unlicensed. Even so, he finds sleuthing and laying the dames easy enough.

American Male Private Detective operating in USA

John JAKES 1932- (American)

is a prolific writer of crime stories himself and was commissioned, after *Lawrence BLOCK*, to continue writing books featuring *William ARD's* detective.

Writer: John William JAKES

Other Byline: William ARD

Citation Record: 4 Books

Johnny Havoc - *First*
Belmont US (1960)

Making It Big - *Last*
Belmont US (1968)

Michael HAWK

American Male Sleuth operating in USA/Australia

Dan STREIB 1928- (American)

Writer: Daniel Thomas STREIB

Other Bylines:
Mark CRUZ Paul ROSS

Citation Record: 4 Books

The Mind Twisters - *First*
Jove US (1980); Sphere UK (1982)

The Predators - *Latest*
Jove US (1980); Sphere UK (1982)

Nathan HAWK

comes from New York but now runs a little agency in Sun City, Florida. In the course of his work he gets a lot of opposition from the local police.

American Male Private Detective operating in Florida

Stooge: Lt Tobias DUANE
is not altogether unfriendly but he is a formidable adversary.
American Male

Bob MACKNIGHT 1906- (American)

Citation Record: 12 Books

Downwind - *First*
Ace US (1957)

Homicide Handicap - *Last*
Ace US (1963)

Dixon HAWKE

was a relative latecomer to those ranks of British detectives whose adventures, during the early part of the twentieth century, were aimed solely at the juvenile market. He appeared shortly after the end of the First World War in Thomson publications, especially the *Dixon Hawke Library*, which was created for him and which ran for 576 numbers until 1941. Several hundred stories have been published in twenty collections, only the first and last of which are cited.

British Male Amateur operating in England

UNKNOWN

Citation Record: 60 Short Stories in 2 Collections

Dixon Hawke's Case Book. No 1 - *Collection 1*
Short stories - 40
Thomson UK (1939)

Dixon Hawke's Case Book. No 20 - *Collection 2*
Short stories - 20
Thomson UK (1948?)

Kitty HAWKE

was a schoolgirl detective who, though still in her young teens, was a skilled aviatrix. She appeared, during the early 1950s, in the magazine, *Girl.*

British Female Amateur operating in England

ANON

No citations

Valentine HAWKEHURST

British Male Amateur

M E BRADDON 1835-1915 (British)

Invented 9 detectives - see Robert AUDLEY

Citation Record: 2 Books

Birds Of Prey - *First*
Ward, Lock UK (1867); Harper & Row US (1867)

Charlotte's Inheritance - *Last*
Ward, Lock UK (1868); Harper & Row US (1868)

Don HAWKER

is a sports journalist who becomes involved in murders with a sporting background and undertakes the investigations himself.

British Male Amateur operating in England

Martin INIGO (British)

Citation Record: 2 Books

Stone Dead - *First*
Sphere Books UK (1991)

Touch Play - *Latest*
Sphere Books UK (1991)

James HAWKER

American Male Sleuth operating in USA

Carl RAMM (American)

Citation Record: 11 Books

Deadly In New York - *First*
Dell US (1984)

Denver Strike - *Latest*
Dell US (1986)

A B C HAWKES

is a *Sherlock HOLMES* parody.

British Male Professional Amateur operating in London

EPHESIAN 1894-1949 (British)

Writer: Carl Eric Bechhofer ROBERTS

Citation Record: 1 Book 23 Short Stories in 2 Collections

ABC's Test Case - *Parody 1*
Jarrolds UK (1933)

ABC Investigates - *Parody Collection 1*
Short stories - 18
Jarrolds UK (1937)

ABC Solves Five - *Parody Collection 2*
Short stories - 5
Jarrolds UK (1937)

Sidekick: JOHNSTONE
is his parody *WATSON*-like assistant.
British Male - Assistant

Carl Eric Bechhofer ROBERTS (British)

Citation Record: 1 Selected Short Story

The Persistent House-Hunters - *Parody 1*
appeared in the July number, published posthumously under the author's real name. He had, almost twenty years earlier, published a number of stories featuring *HAWKES,* under his unusual pseudonym.
In 'Ellery Queen's Mystery Magazine' US (1954)

Tony HAWKIN

Male Sleuth operating in several locations

Harry HARRISON 1925- (British)

See main detective Slippery Jim DI GRIZ

Citation Record: 2 Books

Montezuma's Revenge - *First*
Doubleday US (1972)
Queen Victoria's Revenge - *Last*
Doubleday US (1974); Severn UK (1977)

Dr HAWKINS

solves a case of death by stabbing in a locked room.

British Male Amateur operating in England

Sidney GAINSLEY (British)

Citation Record: 1 Book
Love And Dr Hawkins - *Only*
Brown UK (1945)

Gene HAWKINS and Dave TELLER

British Male Amateurs operating in England

Dick FRANCIS 1920- (British)

Invented 18 detectives - see Sid HALLEY
Citation Record: 1 Book
Blood Sport - *Only*
Joseph UK (1967); Harper & Row US (1967)

H

J D HAWKINS

is an ex-cop. Now, confined to a wheelchair, he writes crime novels when he isn't sleuthing.

American Male Private Detective operating in Boston

W R PHILBRICK (American)

Invented 4 detectives - see Connie KALE
Citation Record: 3 Books
Shadow Kills - *First*
Beaufort US (1985)
Slow Grave - *First**
Hale UK (1986)
Paint It Black - *Latest*
St Martin's US (1989)

Mark HAWKINS

British Male Amateur operating in England

P M HUBBARD 1910-1980 (British)

Invented 3 detectives - see Peter GRANT
Citation Record: 1 Book
The Dancing Man - *Only*
Macmillan UK (1971); Atheneum US (1971)

Sam HAWKINS

is a part-time gigolo, hired by an invalid woman to find her uncle.

American Male Private Detective operating in Palm Beach

Preston PAIRO III (American)

Citation Record: 1 Book
Razor Moon - *Single*
GM US (1988)

Joaquin HAWKS

is half Spanish, half Indian and a skilled CIA agent.

American Male Secret Agent operating in Far East/China

William S BALLINGER 1912-1980 (American)

was born in Oskaloosa, Iowa and graduated from the University of Wisconsin, Madison, 1934. He worked in radio and television as a writer and received the Mystery Writers of America Edgar Allan Poe award, 1960. A prolific writer of mystery and detective stories, he was the recipient of many other awards for his fiction.

Writer: William Sanborn BALLINGER
Other Detectives:
Danny APRIL — Barr BREED
Van MARS — Bryce PATCH
Citation Record: 5 Books
The Chinese Mask - *First*
Signet US (1965)
The Spy In The Java Sea - *Last*
Signet US (1966)

Star HAWKS

American Male Sleuth operating in USA

Ron GOULART 1933- (American)

Invented 15 detectives - see Jake PACE and Hildy PACE
Citation Record: 2 Books
Empire 99 - *First*
Playboy US (1980)
The Cyborg King - *Latest*
Playboy US (1981)

Insp HAWKSHAW

appears in what is apparently a re-working of *Tom TAYLOR's* play (qv) into a detective novel.

British Policeman operating in England

Cecil H BULLIVANT 1882- (British)

Invented 5 detectives - see Garnett BELL
Citation Record: 1 Book
The Ticket-Of-Leave Man - *Only*
Mellifont UK (1935)

Tim J KELLY 1937- (American)

was a prolific playwright who specialised in converting famous criminous novels into stage plays.

Adopter of one other detective Sherlock HOLMES
Citation Record: 1 Book
Hawkshaw The Detective - *Play*
Pioneer US (1976)

Tom TAYLOR 1817-1870 (British)

was born in Sunderland and studied at Glasgow and Cambridge. A well-known writer of Scottish drama and also Professor of English in London, he was called to the Bar in 1845 and then worked in various government departments. He was the editor of *Punch*, art critic for *The Times*, and is said to have written or adapted over a hundred pieces for the theatre. The play cited is probably his best known work and was staged in London and New York.

Citation Record: 1 Book
The Ticket-Of-Leave Man - *Play*
has the distinction of being the first stage play to contain a detective as the main character. The plot concerns a young man duped by forgers. Over seventy years later, it was reworked into a detective novel, with the same title, by *Cecil H BULLIVANT.*
Lacy's UK (1863)

Sgt HAWKSLEY

Second detective of Rosalind LEIGH

Insp HAWKSMOOR

is a mysterious twentieth-century detective who becomes involved in solving the mystery of a strange death that occurred in the late eighteenth century in the Spitalfields district of London.

British Policeman operating in London

Peter ACKROYD 1949- (British)

is a biographer and author of several novels with a historical background.

Citation Record: 1 Book
Hawksmoor - *Single*
Hamish Hamilton UK (1985); Harper & Row US (1986)

Insp Barton HAWLEY

solves a case of murder in which an 'impossible' fingerprint renders the case exceptionally difficult.

British Policeman operating in England

Joseph GOLLOMB 1881-1950 (American)

Inventor of one other detective GALT
Citation Record: 1 Book

The Girl In The Fog - *Only*
Boni US (1923); Long UK (1924)

Bill HAWLEY

is the town undertaker. He doubles as a shamus, as he believes the two professions go well together – probably with some justification.

American Male Private Detective operating in USA

Leo AXLER (American)

Citation Record: 3 Books

Double Plot - *First*
Berkley US (1994)

Grave Matters - *Latest*
Berkley US (1995)

Insp HAWLING and Prof ERSKINE

solves a case of death by cyanide poisoning of a lecturer in front of his class.

British Policemen and British Male Amateur operating in England

Michael BURNING and Althea GREY (British)

Citation Record: 1 Book

Dusty Death - *Only*
Jenkins UK (1949)

Vincent HAWTHORN

is said to be a 'psychiatric detective'.

American Male Private Detective operating in USA

Ron GOULART 1933- (American)

Invented 15 detectives - see Jake PACE and Hildy PACE

Citation Record: 1 Selected Short Story

Monte Cristo Complex
is in a collection of the author's short stories, *What's Become of Screwloose?*
Sidgwick & Jackson UK (1971); Scribner's US (1971)

Dr Sam HAWTHORNE

appears in at least forty short stories, mostly of the 'impossible crime' variety. Only one is cited.

American Male Professional Investigator operating in USA

Edward D HOCH 1930- (American)

Invented 20 detectives - see Capt LEOPOLD

Citation Record: 1 Selected Short Story

The Problem Of Cell 16
appeared in the March issue.
In 'Ellery Queen's Mystery Magazine' US (1977)

Jessica HAYDEN

American Female Amateur operating in France

Caroline CRANE 1930- (American)

is the author of over a dozen genre books.

Inventor of one other detective Brian FRESNEY

Citation Record: 1 Book

Coasts Of Fear - *Single*
!See Appendix 2.
Dodd, Mead US (1980); Hale UK (1981)

Det Stuart HAYDON

is a Homicide detective who believes in saving lost souls as much as bringing criminals to justice. He does both, in various parts of the two Americas.

American Policeman operating in Texas

David L LINDSEY (American)

Citation Record: 6 Books

A Cold Mind - *First*
Harper & Row US (1983); Arlington UK (1984)

Body Of Truth - *Latest*
Doubleday US (1992); Bantam UK (1993)

George HAYDUKE

American Male Amateur operating in USA

Edward ABBEY 1927-1989 (American)

Citation Record: 2 Books

The Monkey Wrench Gang - *First*
Lippincott US (1975); Canongate UK (1978)

Hayduke Lives! - *Last*
Little, Brown US (1990)

Father HAYES

Male Amateur

Peter LESLIE 1922-

trained as a geologist and practised as a journalist in England before going to the USA. He is the author of at least twenty genre novels and has specialised in novelizations of TV series.

Citation Record: 2 Books

Father Hayes - *First*
Zebra US (1976)

The Holy Spirit - *Latest*
Zebra US (1977)

Judith HAYES

Canadian Female Amateur operating in Canada

Anna PORTER (Canadian)

Citation Record: 2 Books

Hidden Agenda - *First*
Irwin CA (1985); Dutton US (1986); Allison & Busby UK (1988)

Mortal Sins - *Latest*
New American Library US (1988); Allen UK (1989)

Julia HAYES

has set up a fortune-telling shop in a seedy part of New York and becomes involved in local murders, which – with a little help from the police – she solves.

American Female Amateur operating in New York

Dorothy Salisbury DAVIS 1916- (American)

Invented 9 detectives - see Kate OSBORN

Citation Record: 4 Books

A Death In The Life - *First*
Scribner's US (1976); Gollancz UK (1977)

The Habit Of Fear - *Latest*
Scribner's US (1987); Chivers UK (1989)

Lee HAYES

American Policeman operating in New York

Ed LACY 1911-1968 (American)

Invented 8 detectives - see Toussaint 'Touie' MOORE

Citation Record: 2 Books

Harlem Underground - *First*
Pyramid US (1965)

In Black And Whitey - *Latest*
Lancer US (1967)

Sheridan HAYNES

is an actor who is playing the part of *Sherlock HOLMES* in a TV series. The character of the great detective obsesses him and, while the series is collapsing because of his strange behaviour, he sets about solving three murders, which seem to be connected. He crosses the paths of the police; but, following his obsession, he solves the case in an extraordinary fashion that would have done credit to the master himself.

British Male Amateur operating in England

Stooge: Supt Roger DEVENISH
heads the police enquiries in this one book, in which he crosses swords with *Sheridan HAYNES,* whom he regards as slightly crazy. Even so, he is wrong and it is the amateur who comes up with the most unlikely of murderers.
British Male

Julian SYMONS 1912-1994 (British)

Invented 11 detectives - see Insp CRAMBO

H

Citation Record: 1 Book

A Three-Pipe Problem - *Only*

The title of this most ingenious detective story is taken from the famous remark made by *Sherlock HOLMES* when faced with a difficult case, to the effect that it was 'a three-pipe problem'.

Collins UK (1975); Harper & Row US (1975)

Dr Frank HAYVIER, Dr Love Rees PONS, Dr Malcolm PLECKS and Prof Knott Coe MITTLE

are four psychologists, all of different orientations, who, when a passenger is murdered on an ocean liner, attempt to use their ideologies and skills to solve the case.

American Male Amateurs operating on a ship

C Daly KING 1895-1963 (American)

Invented 3 detectives - see Lt Michael LORD

Citation Record: 1 Book

Obelists At Sea - *Only*

Heritage UK (1932); Knopf US (1933)

H

Insp Bill HAZARD

Second detective of Supt Frank DRURY

Eric HAZARD

American Male Private Detective operating in Connecticut

Lee CROSBY 1905-1967 (American)

was a reporter, feature writer and foreign correspondent.

Writer: Ware TORREY

Citation Record: 2 Books

Terror By Night - *First*

Dutton US (1938)

Too Many Doors - *Last*

Dutton US (1941)

Doors To Death - *Last**

Thriller Novel Classic US (194?)

Norman O HAZARD

American Male Private Detective operating in California

F L WALLACE (American)

Writer: Floyd L WALLACE

Citation Record: 1 Book

Three Times A Victim - *Only*

Ace US (1957)

James HAZELL

is one of the best British private eyes. An ex-policeman and a cured alcoholic, he is a true East Londoner and can speak Cockney rhyming slang along with the crooks. He may have an office in smart Shepherd's Market, Mayfair, but he is more at home among the villains of East and South London. His detective work is helped at times by the fact that he may be only just on the right side of the law.

British Male Private Detective operating in London

P B YUILL (British)

Gordon WILLIAMS was born in Paisley, Renfrewshire, and is a reporter and author of at least fifteen novels. *Terry VENABLES* was born in Dagenham, Essex, was a well-known football player and has since had a career in the top echelons of British football management.

Writers: Gordon MacLean WILLIAMS 1934- and Terry VENABLES 1943-

Citation Record: 3 Books

Hazell Plays Solomon - *First*

Macmillan UK (1974); Walker US (1975)

Hazell And The Menacing Jester - *Last*

Macmillan UK (1976)

Thorpe HAZELL

is a gentleman of independent means, a health fanatic, vegetarian and bibliophile. He is consulted by railway companies with mysteries to solve, which often involve the complexities of timetables, rolling stock and signalling. These are all subjects on which *HAZELL* has vast knowledge.

British Male Professional Amateur operating in England

Victor L WHITECHURCH 1868-1933 (British)

Invented 5 detectives - see Det Sgt AMBROSE

Citation Record: 9 Short Stories in 1 Collection

Thrilling Stories Of The Railway - *Collection 1*

This collection of fifteen of the author's short stories contains nine with *Thorpe HAZELL*.

Pearson UK (1912)

Stories Of The Railway - *Collection 1**

Routledge UK (1977)

Insp HAZELRIGG

is stolid and sturdily British.

British Policeman operating in England

Sidekick: Sgt POLLOCK

British Male - Subordinate

Michael GILBERT 1912- (British)

was born in Billinghay, Lincolnshire. He was educated at St Peter's School, Seaford, Sussex, and at Blundell's School, Tiverton, graduating at London University, where he took an LLB, 1937. He served in the Army with distinction, 1939-1945, and afterwards became a lawyer of some repute. Even so, he found time, from 1947 onwards, to write at least twenty-five genre novels, many of which have a superb legal background, and of which one, at least, is a masterpiece of detective fiction. In addition, he wrote short stories, plays for stage, radio and television and some critical works with a legal or criminous background. He was a founding member of the Crime Writers Association, 1953, and he received the Mystery Writers of America Grand Master award, 1988. He was made a CBE, 1980.

Writer: Michael Francis GILBERT

Other Detectives:

Mrs ARTSIDE	Mr BEHRENS and Mr CALDER
'Cuckoo' GOYLES	Sherlock HOLMES
Ch Supt KNOTT	Peter MANCIPLE
Insp MERCER	Const/Ch Insp Patrick PETRELLA
Dorothy Mayotte RIGBY	James SCOTLAND

Citation Record: 6 Books 2 Short Stories in 1 Collection

Close Quarters - *First*

Hodder & Stoughton UK (1947); Walker US (1963)

Fear To Tread - *Last*

Hodder & Stoughton UK (1953); Harper & Row US (1953)

Stay Of Execution - *Collection 1*

This collection of thirteen of the author's short stories contains two with *Insp HAZELRIGG*.

Hodder & Stoughton UK (1971)

Insp HAZELTON

British Policeman operating in England

Julian SYMONS 1912-1994 (British)

Invented 11 detectives - see Insp CRAMBO

Citation Record: 1 Book

The Players And The Game - *Only*

Collins UK (1972); Harper & Row US (1972)

Cheney HAZZARD

is a security specialist in Brownsville. Using his intelligence rather than muscle power, he solves two difficult cases of narcotic smuggling and associated murder.

American Male Private Detective operating in Texas

R D BROWN 1924- (American)

Writer: Robert D BROWN

Inventor of one other detective FRISBEE

Citation Record: 2 Books

Hazzard - *First*

Bantam US (1986)

The Villa Head - *Latest*

Bantam US (1987)

Sir Christopher HAZZARD

is actually Sir Christopher Hazzard of St James, an eighteenth-century aristocrat. He is rightly concerned about Napoleon, whose army is threatening an attack on England. However, he does have time to solve the occasional mystery, 'for the excitement of the chase', he says.

British Male Amateur operating in England

Sidekick: Jem VAUGHAN

British Male - Valet

Richard KEVERNE 1882-1950 (British)

Invented 4 detectives - see Insp MACE

Citation Record: 1 Short Story in 1 Collection

More Crook Stuff - *Collection 1*

This collection of sixteen of the author's short stories contains one with *Sir CHRISTOPHER HAZZARD.*

Constable UK (1938)

Insp HEAD

British Policeman operating in England

E Charles VIVIAN 1882-1947 (British)

For writer details see Rex COULSON

Inventor of one other detective Insp BYRNE

Citation Record: 11 Books 1 Selected Short Story

Accessory After - *First*

Ward, Lock UK (1934)

Problem By Rail - *Last*

Ward, Lock UK (1939)

Locked In

is in an anthology, *My Best Mystery Stories.*

Faber UK (1939)

Norman HEAD

is a philosopher and a recluse.

British Male Amateur operating in England

L T MEADE and Robert EUSTACE (British)

Invented 7 detectives - see Insp FROST and Dr GARLAND

Citation Record: 10 Short Stories in 1 Collection

The Brotherhood Of The Seven Kings - *Collection 1*

Ward, Lock UK (1899)

Insp HEADCORN

appears also in one book with the author's other detective, *Tommy ROSTETTER.*

British Policeman operating in England

Alice CAMPBELL 1887- (American)

Invented 3 detectives - see Tommy ROSTETTER

Citation Record: 4 Books

Death Framed In Silver - *First*

Collins UK (1937)

The Cockroach Sings - *Last*

Collins UK (1946)

With Bated Breath - *Last**

Random House US (1946)

Insp HEADCORN and Tommy ROSTETTER

also appear individually in other books by this author.

British Policeman and British Male Amateur operating in England

Alice CAMPBELL 1887- (American)

Invented 3 detectives - see Tommy ROSTETTER

Citation Record: 1 Book

The Bloodstained Toy - *Only*

Collins UK (1948)

Insp HEADLEY

British Policeman operating in England

T B MORRIS 1900- (British)

Writer: Thomas Baden MORRIS

Citation Record: 4 Books

The Papyrus Murder - *First*

Hale UK (1958)

Orchids With Murder - *Last*

Hale UK (1966)

Max HEALD

was a squadron-leader in the Royal Air Force in the Second World War. Posted to an unnamed SIS outfit, he uses his talents to crack some difficult cases.

British Male Secret Agent operating in several locations

Harry HOSSENT 1916- (British)

Citation Record: 8 Books

Spies Die At Dawn - *First*

Long UK (1958)

Gangster Movies - *Last*

Long UK (1976)

'Bunjy' HEARNE

British Amateur operating in England

Thurlow CRAIG 1901- (British)

Writer: Charles William Thurlow CRAIG

Citation Record: 3 Books

White Girls Eastward - *First*

Hutchinson UK (1938)

Plague Over London - *Last*

Hutchinson UK (1939)

Warren HEARST and Harry HERBOLD

solve a case involving a double indemnity insurance claim.

American Male Private Detectives operating in Los Angeles

Robert CARSON 1909-1983 (American)

Citation Record: 1 Book

The Quality Of Mercy - *Only*

Holt US (1954); Hale UK (1955)

The HEART OF OAK DETECTIVE

American Male Detective in Pulp Magazines operating in USA

E A ST MOX 1840-1916 (American)

Writer: Edward Sylvester ELLIS

Citation Record: 1 Book

The Heart Of Oak Detective; Or, Zig-Zag's Full Hand - *Only*

Ivers US (1902)

Edward Lytton WHEELER 1854?-1885 (American)

Invented 6 detectives - see Nell NIBLO

Citation Record: 1 Book

The Heart Of Oak Detective - *Only*

Westbrook US (ca 1920)

Ian HEATH

toils away to unmask devilish goings-on in a typical farrago by this author, involving supernatural events on Dartmoor.

British Male Secret Agent operating in England

Sydney HORLER 1888-1954 (British)

Invented 20 detectives - see Sir Harker BELLAMY

Citation Record: 1 Book

The Curse Of Doone - *Only*

Hodder & Stoughton UK (1928); Mystery League US (1930)

Jennifer HEATH

American Female Amateur operating in France/Italy

Alison TYLER (American)

Writer: Elsie TITLE

Citation Record: 3 Books

Chase The Storm - *First*

Dell US (1987)

Chase The Wind - *Latest*

Dell US (1987)

Panama HEATH

is a tough detective in a Vice Squad.

American Policeman operating in USA

Robert CAMPBELL 1927- (American)
Invented 5 detectives - see Jake HATCH
Citation Record: 1 Book
Juice - *Single*
Poseidon Press US (1989)

Edward HEATHCOTE
British Male Amateur operating in England

M E BRADDON 1835-1915 (British)
Invented 9 detectives - see Robert AUDLEY
Citation Record: 1 Book
Wyllard's Weird - *Only*
Maxwell UK (1885); Harper & Row US (1885)

Arthur HEATHER
British Male Amateur operating in England

William LEQUEUX 1864-1927 (British)
Invented 23 detectives - see Allan KENNEDY
Citation Record: 12 Short Stories in 1 Collection
The Secret Telephone - *Collection 1*
Jarrolds UK (1921)

H

Marshall HEDLEY
British Male Amateur operating in England

F A FAWKES (British)
Writer: Frank Attfield FAWKES
Citation Record: 15 Short Stories in 1 Collection
Adventures Of A Chemist - *Collection 1*
Simpkin UK (1930)

Paul HEDLEY
appears also in one book with the author's other detective, *Harcourt D'ESPINAL.*
British Male Amateur operating in England/France

Ben HEALEY 1908- (British)
was born in Birmingham, Warwickshire. He attended Birmingham University, 1923-1926, after which he worked as a scenic artist, stage designer and theatre director, 1926-1967, except when he served in the Royal Air Force, 1940-1945. He has written at least twenty genre novels under his real name and a pseudonym and several other novels.
Writer: Benjamin James HEALEY
Other Bylines:
J G JEFFREYS   Jeremy STURROCK
Other Detectives:
Harcourt D'ESPINAL
Paul HEDLEY and Harcourt D'ESPINAL
Citation Record: 7 Books
Waiting For A Tiger - *First*
Hale UK (1965); Harper & Row US (1965)
The Snapdragon Murders - *Latest*
Hale UK (1978)

Paul HEDLEY and Harcourt D'ESPINAL
British Male Amateurs operating in England

Ben HEALEY 1908- (British)
Invented 3 detectives - see Paul HEDLEY
Citation Record: 1 Book
Last Ferry From The Lido - *Single*
Hale UK (1981)
Midnight Ferry To Venice - *Single**
Walker US (1982)

Insp John HEENAN
solves a case of death by poisoning in a locked office.
British Policeman operating in England

Herbert METCALFE (British)
Citation Record: 1 Book
The Packet Of Death - *Only*
Church UK (1967)

Hooky HEFFERMAN
operates from a seedy office in Gerrard Mews in London's Soho district. His terrifying aunt, Mrs Theresa Page-Foley, is often instrumental in starting him on his cases, which he solves not so much by intelligence, as by knocking around the pubs and haunts of London and listening to his friends.
British Male Private Detective operating in London

Laurence MEYNELL 1899-1989 (British)
was born in Wolverhampton, Staffordshire. He was educated at St Edmund's College, Ware, Hertfordshire, and served in the Army during the First World War and with distinction in the Royal Air Force, 1939-1945. He wrote, under his own name and several pseudonyms, over a hundred novels of various kinds, many of them vaguely criminous, as well as short stories and works for children. It was in the latter part of his long life that he wrote the large series of detective novels cited.
Writer: Laurence Walter MEYNELL
Other Detectives:
George Stanhope BERKLEY   Sir James ERSKINE
Sir James ERSKINE and George Stanhope BERKLEY
Insp Kingsley HYLTON
Citation Record: 22 Books
The Frightened Man - *First*
Collins UK (1952)
Hooky Hooked - *Last*
Macmillan UK (1988)

Capt/Insp Merton HEIMRICH
American Policeman operating in New York

Richard LOCKRIDGE 1898-1982 (American)
Writer: Richard Orson LOCKRIDGE
Other Detectives:
Det Nathan SHAPIRO   Bernard SIMMONS
Citation Record: 7 Books
Murder Roundabout - *First*
Lippincott US (1966); Long UK (1967)
The Tenth Life - *Last*
Lippincott US (1977); Long UK (1979)

Richard LOCKRIDGE and Frances LOCKRIDGE (American)
Writers: Richard Orson LOCKRIDGE 1898-1982 and Frances Louise Davis LOCKRIDGE 1896-1963
Citation Record: 16 Books
Think Of Death - *First*
Lippincott US (1947)
The Distant Clue - *Last*
Lippincott US (1963); Long UK (1964)

HEINE
Male Sleuth operating in England

Edgar WALLACE 1875-1932 (British)
Invented 28 detectives - see J G REEDER
Citation Record: 4 Short Stories in 1 Collection
The Adventures Of Heine - *Collection 1*
contains four novelettes.
Ward, Lock UK (1919)

Johnny HELDAR
Second detective of Sally HELDAR

Sally HELDAR and Johnny HELDAR
British Female Amateur and British Male Amateur operating in England/Scotland

Henrietta HAMILTON 1920- (British)
was born in Scotland and took a degree in Modern Languages at Oxford.
Citation Record: 4 Books
The Two Hundred Ghost - *First*
Hodder & Stoughton UK (1956)

At Night To Die - *Last*
Hodder & Stoughton UK (1959)

James HELDER

British Male Private Detective operating in England

Victor CANNING 1911-1986 (British)
Invented 6 detectives - see Rex CARVER
Citation Record: 1 Book
A Fall From Grace - *Single*
Heinemann UK (1980); Morrow US (1981)

Carl HELLER

dropped out from law school, preferring to raise cattle in Colorado Springs, where local crime springs eternal. Without police support, he solves cases to his neighbours' satisfaction, which they express more than generously.

American Male Private Detective operating in USA

Frank RODERUS 1942- (American)
Citation Record: 6 Books
The Oil Rig - *First*
Bantam US (1984)
The Dead Heat - *Latest*
Bantam US (1985)

Jesse HELLER

American Male Sleuth operating in Texas

Dan KELLERMAN (American)
For writer details see Vic (Eagle Force) GABRIEL
Citation Record: 2 Books
Blood Run - *First*
Pinnacle US (1985)
Hellrider - *Latest*
Pinnacle US (1985)

Nate HELLER

quits the corrupt police force in the Chicago of the 1930s and sets up as a PI, working on cases whose period backgrounds are particularly well researched.

American Male Private Detective operating in Chicago

Max Allan COLLINS 1948- (American)
was born in Muscatine, Iowa. He was educated at Muscatine Community College and graduated with a BA from the University of Iowa, Iowa City, 1970. He was a musician and reporter and wrote the Dick Tracy comic strips from 1977.
Writer: Max Allan COLLINS Jr
Other Detectives:
MALLORY — Philip MARLOWE
NOLAN — QUARRY
Citation Record: 4 Books
True Detective - *First*
St Martin's US (1983); Sphere Books UK (1984)
Neon Mirage - *Latest*
St Martin's US (1988); Gollancz UK (1989)

James HELLIER

British Male Amateur operating in England

Michael CRONIN 1907- (British)
Invented 3 detectives - see Sam HARRIS
Citation Record: 6 Books
Man Alive - *First*
Hale UK (1968)
The Big C - *Last*
Hale UK (1973)

Ben HELM

was once in the police and is now a likeable PI. He lectures on criminology and uses brains rather than brawn to solve his cases.

American Male Private Detective operating in New York

Bruno FISCHER 1908- (American)
was born in Berlin, Germany and was taken to the USA, 1913. He was educated at Richmond High School, Long Island, New York, and at the Rand School of Social Sciences, New York. He became a prolific writer of short stories for the pulps, especially during the 1940s, and he wrote at least twenty-five genre novels.
Inventor of one other detective Rick TRAIN
Citation Record: 6 Books
The Dead Men Grin - *First*
McKay US (1945); Quality Press UK (1947)
The Paper Circle - *Last*
Dodd, Mead US (1951); Boardman UK (1952)
Stripped For Murder - *Last**
Signet US (1953)

Matt HELM

is an American secret agent, licensed to kill. Modelled on the classic British agent, *James BOND,* he manages to do more serious sleuthing than the latter did.

American Male Secret Agent operating in USA/Canada

Donald HAMILTON 1916- (American)
was born in Uppsala, Sweden. He emigrated to the USA, 1924, became a naturalised citizen, 1926, and graduated with a BS from the University of Chicago, Illinois, 1938. He is the author of several non-genre novels.
Writer: Donald Bengtsson HAMILTON
Citation Record: 25 Books
Death Of A Citizen - *First*
Fawcett US (1960); Muller UK (1960)
The Frighteners - *Latest*
Fawcett US (1989)

Insp HEMINGWAY

British Policeman operating in England

Georgette HEYER 1902-1974 (British)
Invented 3 detectives - see Supt HANNASYDE
Citation Record: 4 Books
No Wind Of Blame - *First*
Hodder & Stoughton UK (1939); Doubleday US (1939)
Detection Unlimited - *Last*
Heinemann UK (1953); Dutton US (1969)

Clarence E HEMINGWAY and Jeremy FLACK

British Male Amateurs operating in France

John MASKE (British)
Invented 3 detectives - see Duncan CAINSFORTH
Citation Record: 2 Books
The Cherbourg Mystery - *First*
Rich UK (1934)
Ghost Of A Cardinal - *Last*
Rich UK (1935)

Ernest 'Rhino' HEMINGWAY and F Scott 'Ritz' FITZGERALD

Yes, indeed, these are two of the most famous American novelists of the 1920s and 1930s, here setting up a detective agency together at 314 Union Street.

American Male Amateurs operating in San Francisco

Keith ABBOTT 1944- (American)
Writer: Keith George ABBOTT
Citation Record: 1 Book
Rhino Ritz - *Single*
is an improbable pastiche concerning the disappearance of prominent literary figures such as *Gertrude STEIN.*
Blue Wind US (1979)

Ernest HEMINGWAY

Appears with at least two other detectives - see Toby PETERS.

Prof Jonathan HEMLOCK

is a Professor of Art History, a mountain climber and – to earn a decent stipend – an assassin (on the right side of justice) for a US government agency.

American Male Professional Investigator operating in several locations

TREVANIAN 1931- (American)

was born in Granville, New York, and graduated with several degrees from American universities, including a PhD in Communications.

Writer: Rodney WHITAKER

Inventor of one other detective Lt Claude LAPOINTE

Citation Record: 2 Books

The Eiger Sanction - *First*
Crown US (1972); Heinemann UK (1973)

The Loo Sanction - *Last*
Crown US (1973); Heinemann UK (1974)

HEMMINGS

British Policeman operating in England

Dominic DEVINE 1920-1981 (British)

Invented 4 detectives - see Det Insp Maurice NICOLSON

Citation Record: 1 Book

Illegal Tender - *Only*
Collins UK (1970); Walker US (1970)

H

Billy HEMPLE

American Male Amateur operating in Chicago

Harry Stephen KEELER 1890-1967 (American)

Invented 14 detectives - see Angus MACWHORTER

Citation Record: 1 Book

The Mystery Of The Fiddling Cracksman - *Only*
Dutton US (1934)

The Fiddling Cracksman - *Only**
Ward, Lock UK (1934)

Maj Maurice HEMYOCK

British Male Amateur operating in England

Douglas G BROWNE 1884-1963 (British)

Invented 4 detectives - see LEGARDE

Citation Record: 3 Books

The Dead Don't Bite - *First*
Methuen UK (1933)

The May-Week Murders - *Last*
Longman UK (1937)

Insp HENDERSON

British Policeman operating in England

Charles BARLING 1904- (British)

See main detective Insp George MARSHALL

Citation Record: 1 Book

Death Of A Shrew - *Only*
Hale UK (1968)

Pamela BARRINGTON 1904- (British)

Invented 3 detectives - see Insp George MARSHALL

Citation Record: 1 Book

Accessory To Murder - *Only*
Hale UK (1968)

Mervyn HENDERSON

solves a case of death by poisoning.

British Male Amateur operating in England

Dorothea CONYERS 1873-1949 (British)

Writer: Dorothea Smyth CONYERS

Other Detectives:
Mr JONES   SANDY

Citation Record: 1 Selected Short Story

The Poisoning Of Hector Alhuson
appeared in a collection, *Hunting and Hunted.*
Hutchinson UK (1930)

Vincent CORNIER (British)

Invented 3 detectives - see Barnabas HILDRETH

Citation Record: 1 Selected Short Story

The Brother Of Heaven
appeared in the October number.
Pearson UK (1933)

Ralph HENDERSON

is perhaps the first detective to have appeared in a serialised format, which he did ten years after the appearance of *Insp BUCKET,* created by *Charles DICKENS.* He can thus be said to represent a true landmark in the development of detective fiction. Featured, during 1862, in eight instalments of a novel in an obscure magazine, he has a private enquiry office in Clement's Inn, Holborn, and the novel tells of his one case, a complex plot of inheritance and murder of a type so beloved by the Victorian era. The serial then appeared in book form in 1865, published by *Saunders, Otley & Co* and reappeared in a collection of Victorian novels, *Novels of Mystery from the Victorian Age,* published by *Pilot Press* (UK 1945). More recently it has been republished by *Arno* (? 1976).

British Male Professional Amateur operating in London

Charles FELIX (British)

Writer: John RETCLIFF

Citation Record: 1 Book

The Notting Hill Mystery - *Only*
In 'Once A Week Magazine' UK (1862)

Ch Const William HENDERSON

was the Chief Constable of Edinburgh and is both the detective in, and the author of, this book.

British Policeman operating in Edinburgh

William HENDERSON (British)

Citation Record: 9 Short Stories in 1 Collection

Clues; Or, Leaves From A Chief Constable's Note Book - *Collection 1*
Oliphant, Anderson UK (1889); White & Allen US (1890)

Ch Const HENDON

British Policeman operating in England

Walter S MASTERMAN 1876- (British)

Invented 3 detectives - see Dick SELDON

Citation Record: 1 Book

The Green Toad - *Only*
Gollancz UK (1928); Dutton US (1929)

Jack HENLEY

solves a case of death by shooting in a locked room.

American Male Amateur operating in USA

Henry Smith WILLIAMS 1863-1943 (American)

Citation Record: 1 Book

The Witness Of The Sun - *First*
Doubleday US (1920)

Jack HENLEY

British Male Amateur operating in England

Stuart KAY (British)

Citation Record: 2 Books

Bad Debt - *First*
Severn UK (1987)

Something Rotten - *Latest*
Severn UK (1988); Severn US (1988)

Rachel HENNINGS

is the owner of a bookshop who solves cases of murder connected with the shop and the book trade.

American Female Amateur operating in USA

Sidekick: Stu WELLMAN

American Male - Lover

Jon L BREEN 1943- (American)

was born in Montgomery, Alabama. He took a BA at Pepperdine College, Los Angeles, 1965, and later studied Library Sciences. A well-known sports writer and broadcaster, as well as a critic and reviewer of crime fiction, he has written several novels and many short stories. He is particularly well-known for his parodies and pastiches of classic detective story writers. He received the Mystery Writers of America Edgar Allan Poe award for non-fiction twice, 1981 and 1984.

Writer: Jon Linn BREEN

Other Detectives:

Jerry BROGAN
Ed GORGON
Sherlock HOLMES
Sir Gideon MERRIMAC
Dr Sid SHOEHORN

Citation Record: 2 Books

The Gathering Place - *First*
Macmillan UK (1984); Walker US (1984)

Touch Of The Past - *Latest*
Macmillan UK (1988); Walker US (1988)

HENRICKSEN

Norwegian Male Amateur operating in Oslo

Thomas HENEGE (American)

is a prominent figure in the world of banking and author of several criminous works.

Writer: Albert F GILLOTTI

Citation Record: 1 Book

Death Of A Shipowner - *Single*
Dodd, Mead US (1981)

A Cargo Of Tin - *Single**
Deutsch UK (1982)

Ben HENRY

is an ex-journalist. He drives a cab to make ends meet but is also a part-time detective.

American Male Private Detective operating in San Francisco

Mike WEISS (American)

Citation Record: 2 Books

No Go On Jackson Street - *First*
Scribner's US (1987); Thorndike UK (1988)

All Points Bulletin - *Latest*
Avon US (1989)

George Herbert HENRY

writes unwanted songs for a living, which he thus has to eke out by working as a private eye.

American Male Private Detective operating in New York

Jack SHARKEY 1931- (American)

Writer: John Michael SHARKEY

Citation Record: 2 Books

Murder, Maestro, Please - *First*
Abelard US (1960); Abelard UK (1960)

Death For Auld Lang Syne - *Last*
Holt US (1962); Joseph UK (1963)

Gilmore HENRY

is a lawyer in Calhoun County, Kentucky, who has to do a lot of investigating to clear his clients, which he does in dazzling courtroom finishes.

American Male Amateur operating in Kentucky

C W GRAFTON 1909-1982 (American)

was born in China of missionary parents. He later practised journalism and law in Kentucky.

Writer: Cornelius Warren GRAFTON

Citation Record: 2 Books

The Rat Began To Gnaw The Rope - *First*
Farrar & Rinehart US (1943); Gollancz UK (1944)

The Rope Began To Hang The Butcher - *Last*
Farrar & Rinehart US (1944); Gollancz UK (1945)

Henri HENRY

French Male Sleuth operating in Paris

Leon GROC 1882- (French)

Citation Record: 1 Book

The Bus That Vanished - *Only*
is a translation from the French of *L'Autobus Evanoui* (Paris, 1914).
Macaulay US (1928)

Kate HENRY

is a sports reporter, based in Toronto, who investigates murders at ball games.

Canadian Female Amateur operating in Canada

Alison GORDON 1943- (Canadian)

Writer: Alison Kate GORDON

Citation Record: 2 Books

The Dead Pull Hitter - *First*
St Martin's US (1988)

Safe At Home - *Latest*
St Martin's US (1991)

Rush HENRY

is vintage hardboiled and there is much gore and guts on the floor – usually other people's – when he uses what few brains he has to solve a case.

American Male Private Detective operating in Chicago

Joe BARRY 1909- (American)

Writer: Joe Barry LAKE

Inventor of one other detective Bill AUGUST

Citation Record: 5 Books

The Third Degree - *First*
Mystery House US (1943)

The Pay-Off - *Last*
Mystery House US (1953)

Susan HENSHAW

American Female Amateur operating in Connecticut

Valerie WOLZIEN (American)

Citation Record: 2 Books

Murder At The PTA Luncheon - *First*
St Martin's US (1988)

The Fortieth Birthday Party - *Latest*
St Martin's US (1989)

H

Max HENSIG

appears in a story based on a historic murder case, written by a master of suspense and the chill occult.

American Male Amateur operating in New York

Algernon BLACKWOOD 1869-1951 (British)

See main detective John SILENCE

Citation Record: 1 Selected Short Story

Max Hensig - Bacteriologist And Murderer
is in a collection of nine of the author's stories, *The Listener and Other Stories.*
Nash UK (1907); Vaughan US (1907)

Insp Maurice HEPBURN

appears also in books with another of the author's detectives, *Evelyn TEMPLE.*

British Policeman operating in England

Lord GORELL 1884-1963 (British)

Invented 4 detectives - see Insp Gordon ROSS

Citation Record: 2 Books

Devil's Drum - *First*
Murray UK (1929)

Murder At Mavering - *Last*
Murray UK (1943)

Insp Maurice HEPBURN and Evelyn TEMPLE

Insp HEPBURN appears as the sole detective in two other books by this author.

British Policeman and British Female Amateur operating in England

Lord GORELL 1884-1963 (British)

Invented 4 detectives - see Insp Gordon ROSS

Citation Record: 2 Books

D E Q - *First*
Murray UK (1922)

Red Lilac - *Last*
Murray UK (1935)

Franz HEPPEL
Male Amateur operating in Italy

Hugh Travers MILLS (American)

Citation Record: 1 Book

In Pursuit Of Evil - *Only*
Lippincott US (1967); Triton UK (1967)

Simon HERALD
is a former spy, a friend of the author's other agent-detective, *Richard GRAHAM.* Once a racing driver, now with marital problems, he faces overwhelming odds in novels of great suspense, which include considerable detection.
!See Appendix 2.
British Male Sleuth operating in Europe

H

John WELCOME 1914- (Irish)
was born in Wexford, Ireland. He was educated at Sedburgh School, Yorkshire, and took a BA in Law at Exeter College, Oxford, 1936. He served in the British Army, 1940-1942, and then practised as a solicitor.

Writer: John Needham Huggard BRENNAN

Inventor of one other detective Richard GRAHAM

Citation Record: 2 Books

Stop At Nothing - *First*
Faber UK (1959); Knopf US (1960)

Wanted For Killing - *Last*
Faber UK (1965); Holt US (1967)

Harry HERBOLD
Second detective of Warren HEARST

Sylvester HERING
American Male Amateur operating in Chicago

Phyllis A WHITNEY 1903- (American)

See main detective Linda EARLE

Citation Record: 1 Book

Red Is For Murder - *Only*
Ziff-Davis US (1943)

The Red Carnelian - *Only**
Coronet UK (1976)

Rowland HERN
British Male Amateur operating in England

Nicholas OLDE (British)

Citation Record: 11 Short Stories in 1 Collection

The Incredible Adventures Of Rowland Hern - *Collection 1*
Heinemann UK (1928)

Alexander HERO
British Male Amateur operating in USA/England

Paul GALLICO 1897-1976 (American)

Writer: Paul William GALLICO

Other Detectives:
Hiram HOLLIDAY
Sally Holmes LANE

Citation Record: 2 Books

Too Many Ghosts - *First*
Doubleday US (1959); Joseph UK (1961)

The Hand Of Mary Constable - *Last*
Doubleday US (1964); Heinemann UK (1964)

Pepperoni HERO
American Male Amateur operating in USA/Mexico

Bill KELLY (American)

Citation Record: 2 Books

Peanut Butter & Jelly Is Not For Kids - *First*
Zebra US (1975)

Sandwiches Are Not My Business - *Last*
Zebra US (1975)

Insp HERON
is a detective at Scotland Yard in this one Victorian novel.
British Policeman operating in London

Headon HILL 1857-1927 (British)

Writer: Francis Edward GRAINGER

Other Detectives:
Elisha CROWE
Franklin KENNARD
Pte Amos MEARS
Laura METCALF
Kala PERSAD
Radford SHONE
Mark TAVERNER
Sgt TREVOR and Sgt GODBOLD
Montague WARDROP
Sebastian ZAMBRA

Citation Record: 1 Book

Guilty Gold: A Romance Of Financial Fraud And City Crime - *Only*
Pearson UK (1896)

Felix HERON
British Male Amateur operating in England

Gerald VERNER 1886-1980 (British)

Invented 7 detectives - see Supt BUDD

Citation Record: 2 Books

The Tudor Garden Mystery - *First*
Wright & Brown UK (1966)

Dead Secret - *Last*
Wright & Brown UK (1967)

Patrick HERON
British Male Sleuth operating in England

Colm BROGAN 1902- (British)

Citation Record: 2 Books

The Ghost Walks - *First*
Skeffington UK (1932)

The Plunge - *Last*
Skeffington UK (1933)

'Stalky' HERON
Second detective of Charles FINCH

HERRIG
is a Scotland Yard officer who investigates the disappearance of a heavy gun.
British Policeman operating in London

L E WIENER

Citation Record: 1 Selected Short Story

The Disappearing Monster
In 'Detective Magazine' UK (1923)

James 'Kipper' HERRING
investigates death by strangulation in a locked room.
British Male Amateur operating in England

Hugo MORRISON (British)

Citation Record: 1 Book

The Low Road - *Only*
Methuen UK (1930)

Timothy HERRING
British Male Amateur operating in England

Malcolm TORRIE 1901-1983 (British)

Writer: Gladys Maude Winifred MITCHELL

Other Byline: Gladys MITCHELL

Citation Record: 6 Books

Heavy As Lead - *First*
Joseph UK (1966)

Bismarck Herrings - *Last*
Joseph UK (1971)

Sir Richard HERRIVELL
British Male Amateur operating in England

John BENTLEY (British)

Other Detectives:
Glen GIBSON — Dick MARLOW

Citation Record: 9 Books

The Berg Case - *First*
Eldon UK (1934)

The Eyes Of Death - *First**
Doubleday US (1934)

The Hartland Case - *Last*
Chapman & Hall UK (1939)

Steve HERSHEY

is a pretty small guy for a PI, but he makes up for it by his work at the gym when not in his office on 23rd Street, Manhattan.

American Male Private Detective operating in New York

Vernon HINKLE 1935- (American)

Inventor of one other detective Martin WEBB

Citation Record: 1 Book

Murder After A Fashion - *Single*
Leisure Books US (1986); Chivers UK (1987)

Millicent HETHEREGE

appeared in a previous book with other detectives of this author and now solves another murder.

British Female Amateur operating in New England

Robert BERNARD 1918- (American)

Invented 3 detectives - see Prof Richard HALSEY

Citation Record: 1 Book

Illegal Entry - *Only*
Norton US (1972); Faber UK (1973)

Millicent HETHEREGE

Appears with at least two other detectives - see Lt MOYNAHAN.

Miro HETZEL

sleuths at some time in the future.

Male Sleuth

Jack VANCE 1917- (American)

Invented 3 detectives - see Keith GERSEN

Citation Record: 3 Short Stories in 1 Collection

Galactic Effectuator - *Collection 1*
contains three novelettes.
Underwood US (1980)

Barrington (The Peacemaker) HEWES-BRADFORD

American Male Sleuth operating in Africa/Asia

Adam HAMILTON (American)

Writers: Marilyn GRANBECK1927- and Arthur MOORE

Citation Record: 4 Books

The Xander Pursuit - *First*
Berkley US (1974)

The Wyss Pursuit - *Last*
Berkley US (1975)

Jefferson HEWITT

operates in Cheyenne, Wyoming, during the 1880s. An ex-Pinkerton man, he travels for a bonding company in which he is a partner.

American Male Private Detective operating in Wyoming/Kansas

John REESE (American)

Writer: John Henry REESE

Citation Record: 3 Books

Weapon Heavy - *First*
Doubleday US (1973); Milton House UK (1975)

Wes Hardin's Gun - *Last*
Doubleday US (1975); Hale UK (1978)

Martin HEWITT

was one of the earliest rivals to appear on the criminous scene after it had undergone its major upheaval by the arrival of *Sherlock HOLMES*. Unlike many others that have come and gone, however, he remains an important creation in the genre's history. In contrast to *HOLMES*, he is of ordinary appearance, rather stout in fact, and considerably more amiable. He was a lawyer's clerk before deciding to set up as a private investigator and, in some respects, he is more attuned to the modern world than was *HOLMES*, in that he actually has an office in an old building near the Strand in London, with a glass door engraved with his name and unlike *HOLMES*, he actively invites clients. His cases are related by a journalist friend, less of a true sidekick than *Dr WATSON*, but clearly an attempt to copy him. There is no doubt that *Martin HEWITT* must be classed as a PI, however, as he clearly seeks payment for his work.

British Male Private Detective operating in London

Sidekick: Mr BRETT
is a journalist friend who acts as the detective's assistant and narrates the stories.

Stooge: Insp PLUMMER
was probably modelled on *HOLMES'* main police adversary, *Insp LESTRADE*, and is depicted, similarly, as a typical blundering Scotland Yard policeman of the period.

British Male

Arthur MORRISON 1863-1945 (British)

was born in London. He became a practising journalist and, while still a novice, wrote two classic works on the East End of Victorian London, in which he laid bare much of the poverty and crime that lay below its surface. Later he seems to have abandoned his literary career and was to become well known as a collector of Chinese art: later in his life, he was made Inspector of Constabulary in Essex. He wrote these detective stories during the 1890s.

Inventor of one other detective DORRINGTON

Citation Record: 26 Short Stories in 4 Collections

Martin Hewitt, Investigator - *Collection 1*
Short stories - 7
Ward, Lock UK (1894); Harper & Row US (1894)

Chronicles Of Martin Hewitt - *Collection 2*
Short stories - 7
Ward, Lock UK (1895); Appleton US (1896)

Adventures Of Martin Hewitt - *Collection 3*
Short stories - 6
Ward, Lock UK (1896)

The Red Triangle - *Collection 4*
Short stories - 6
Nash UK (1903); Page US (1903)

Pete HEYSEN

Australian Male Sleuth operating in Australia

Ian HAMILTON 1935- (Australian)

was born in Melbourne and has been a copywriter and TV scriptwriter.

Citation Record: 4 Books

The Persecutor - *First*
Constable UK (1965); Lippincott US (1965)

The Thrill Machine - *Last*
Collins UK (1972)

'Alphabet' HICKS

is thus called because he is so fond of word games. A disbarred lawyer, he is now a private eye.

American Male Private Detective operating in USA

Rex STOUT 1886-1975 (American)

Invented 6 detectives - see Nero WOLFE

Citation Record: 1 Book

Alphabet Hicks - *Only*
Farrar & Rinehart US (1941); Collins UK (1942)

The Sound Of Murder - *Only**
Pyramid US (1965)

Algernon HIGGINS
is described as a 'government servant' in this Victorian novel.
British Male Amateur operating in England

ANON
Citation Record: 1 Book
A Strange Case: With Full Particulars First Made Public
Tinsley UK (1870)

Insp Cuthbert HIGGINS
British Policeman operating in England

Cecil Freeman GREGG 1898- (British)
See main detective Henry PRINCE
Citation Record: 35 Books
The Murdered Manservant - *First*
Hutchinson UK (1928)
The Body In The Safe - *First**
Dial US (1930)
Professional Jealousy - *Last*
Methuen UK (1960)

H

Matthew HIGGINS
American Male Amateur operating in USA

Means DAVIS (American)
See main detective James Augustus GIBBS
Citation Record: 2 Books
The Hospital Murders - *First*
Smith US (1934); Bell UK (1934)
Murder Without Weapons - *Last*
Smith US (1934); Bell UK (1935)

HIGHWAY
American Male Sleuth operating in Los Angeles

Garnett WESTON (American)
Writer: Garnett James WESTON
Citation Record: 3 Books
Murder In Haste - *First*
Stokes US (1935)
Death Never Forgets - *First**
Hutchinson UK (1935)
The Undertaker Dies - *Last*
Hutchinson UK (1940)

Monsieur HIGNETTE
Second detective of Dr MEPHISTO

Barnabas HILDRETH
appeared in several short stories. He was clearly modelled on the famed Dr THORNDYKE and, like him, used modern scientific methods in his investigations. He was sometimes known as 'The Black Monk'.
British Male Amateur operating in England

Vincent CORNIER (British)
Other Detectives:
Supt HAMILTON   Mervyn HENDERSON
Citation Record: 1 Selected Short Story
The Brother Of Heaven
appeared in the December number.
In 'Ellery Queen's Mystery Magazine' US (1948)

Lady Jane HILDRETH
British Female Amateur operating in England

Michael SPICER 1943- (British)
Citation Record: 2 Books
Cotswold Manners - *First*
Severn UK (1988); St Martin's US (1989)
Cotswold Murders - *Latest*
St Martin's US (1990); Constable UK (1991)

Asmun HILL
British Male Amateur operating in England

Hector HAWTON 1901- (British)
See main detective pair Peter MAXWELL and Susan MAXWELL
Citation Record: 6 Books
Murder At HQ - *First*
Ward, Lock UK (1945)
Rope For The Judge - *Last*
Ward, Lock UK (1954)

Dave HILL
American Male Amateur operating in Mexico

Bill ADKINS (American)
Citation Record: 3 Books
The Entry From San Sebastian - *First*
Popular Library UK (1976)
Prison At Obregon - *Last*
Popular Library UK (1976)

Lt Charles HILLARY
American Policeman operating in Ohio

Fenn MCGREW (American)
Writers: Julia MCGREW and Caroline K FENN
Citation Record: 2 Books
Taste Of Death - *First*
Rinehart US (1953)
Made For Murder - *Last*
Rinehart US (1954)

Gregory HILLER
American Male Secret Agent operating in New York/Russia

Jack LAFLIN (American)
See main detective Peter WINSTON
Citation Record: 3 Books
The Spy Who Loved America - *First*
Belmont US (1964)
The Reluctant Spy - *Last*
Belmont US (1966)

Jay HILLER
is an ex-CIA man who, with only a photograph and one code word to go on, must locate and rescue the President of the United States, who has been kidnapped.
American Male Amateur operating in USA

Mal KARMAN 1944- (American)
Citation Record: 1 Book
The Foxbat Spiral - *Single*
Dell US (1980)

Whispering HILLS
American Male Amateur operating in Indiana

Kate CAMERON 1924-1980 (American)
See main detective Holderly HALL
Citation Record: 6 Books
Evil At Whispering Hills - *First*
Leisure Books US (1973)
The Awakening Dream - *Last*
Leisure Books US (1974)

Alec HILLSDEN
British Male Amateur operating in England

Bryan FORBES 1926- (British)
Citation Record: 2 Books
The Endless Game - *First*
Collins UK (1986); Random House US (1986)
A Song At Twilight - *Latest*
Collins UK (1989)
A Spy At Twilight - *Latest**
Random House US (1990)

Insp Rodney HILTON
solves a case of death by strangulation in a guarded room.
British Policeman operating in England

Mary DURHAM (British)

See main detective Insp YORK

Citation Record: 1 Book

Murder Hath Charms - *Only*
Skeffington UK (1948)

Insp HINKLEY

solves a case of death by poisoning.

British Policeman operating in England

Gavin MONRO 1905- (British)

Writer: Gertrude MONRO-HIGGS

Citation Record: 1 Book

Marked With A Cross - *Only*
Hale UK (1968)

Sgt/Insp HISCOCK

British Policeman operating in England

Jeremy POTTER 1922- (British)

Citation Record: 2 Books

Death In Office - *First*
Constable UK (1965)

The Dance Of Death - *Last*
Constable UK (1968); Walker US (1969)

Quinny HITE

was busted from the New York Police Department for political reasons. He now operates privately from a room in the Hotel du Nord, near Times Square. His main aim in life is to wed his girlfriend, Joan – which he is continually prevented from doing by becoming involved in murder cases.

American Male Private Detective operating in New York

Richard BURKE 1884-1963 (American)

was born in Los Angeles. He worked as a newspaperman and wrote several criminous novels during the 1940s.

Citation Record: 5 Books

The Dead Take No Bows - *First*
Houghton UK (1941)

Sinister Street - *Last*
Ziff-Davis US (1948); World Distributors UK (1950)

Stewart HOAG

American Male Sleuth operating in New York/London

David HANDLER (American)

is a journalist and scriptwriter.

Citation Record: 4 Books

The Man Who Died Laughing - *First*
Bantam US (1988)

The Man Who Cancelled Himself - *Latest*
Bantam US (1994)

Sherwood HOAKES

is a *Sherlock HOLMES* parody.

British Male Professional Amateur operating in England

C C ROTHWELL (British)

Citation Record: 1 Selected Short Story

Adventures Of Sherwood Hoakes. Adventure 1 - An Interrupted Honeymoon - *Parody 1*

In which the sleuth solves the remarkable disappearance of a man before the eyes of his wife. The story appeared in the issue of the magazine for April 9, under the punning pseudonym of *A. Cone and Oil.* It is to be found in a collection, *My Evening with Sherlock Holmes* published by *Ferret* (UK 1981).
In 'Ludgate Magazine' UK (1892)

Capt HOARE

solves the mystery of a stabbing in a locked room.

British Policeman operating in London

Marjorie BOWEN 1886-1952 (British)

See main detective Brother Felipe BRUNO

Citation Record: 1 Selected Short Story

The Orford Mystery: Covent Garden 1734
is a locked-room mystery. It is also to be found in an anthology, *Old Patch's Medley.*
Selwyn UK (1930)

Insp Felix HOBBINGDON

is a bright, quiet and observant Scotland Yard man in a confused and old-fashioned tale.

British Policeman operating in England

Olwen REES (British)

Citation Record: 1 Book

Death Of Virginia - *Only*
Gifford UK (1945)

Const HOBBS

solves a case of death by stabbing, in a story that was one of the earliest examples of the locked-room mystery.

British Policeman operating in England

Henry FLETCHER (British)

Citation Record: 1 Book

The North Shore Mystery - *Only*
Swan, Sonnenschein UK (1899)

Sgt HOBBS

Michael LEWIS 1890-1970 (British)

Writer: Michael Arthur LEWIS

Citation Record: 2 Books

The Brand Of The Beast - *First*
Allen UK (1925); Dial US (1925)

The Island Of Disaster - *Last*
Allen UK (1926)

Insp HOBDEN

British Policeman operating in England

Sidekick: Sgt CHEAL

American Male - Subordinate

Kenneth O'HARA 1928- (British)

See main detective Dr Alun BARRY

Citation Record: 1 Book

Nightmare's Nest - *Single*
Gollancz UK (1982); Doubleday US (1983)

Det Neil 'Hock' HOCKADAY

American Policeman operating in New York

Thomas Larry ADCOCK (American)

Writer: Thomas Larry ADCOCK

Other Byline: Buck SANDERS

Citation Record: 3 Books

Sea Of Green - *First*
Mysterious Press US (1989)

Drown All The Dogs - *Latest*
Simon & Schuster US (1994)

Greg HOCKING

teaches history at the fictional Oswaldson College of Further Education, somewhere in northern England. Murder, nicely involved with literary mystery, is committed and he decides to investigate. The book is an elegant spoof on all those academic mayhem novels.

British Male Amateur operating in England

Robert BARNARD 1936- (British)

Invented 13 detectives - see Insp Perry TRETHOWAN

Citation Record: 1 Book

Posthumous Papers - *Single*
Collins UK (1979)

Death Of A Literary Widow - *Single**
Scribner's US (1980)

Robert HOCKNEY

American Male Amateur operating in Miami

Arnaud DE BORCHGRAVE 1926- and Robert MOSS 1946-

Citation Record: 2 Books

The Spike - *First*
Weidenfeld & Nicolson UK (1980); Crown US (1980)

Monimbo - *Latest*
Simon & Schuster US (1983)

Mr HODSON

British Male Amateur operating in England

Margaret BIDWELL (British)

Citation Record: 2 Books

Death On The Agenda - *First*
Hurst UK (1939)

Death And His Brother - *Last*
Hurst UK (1940)

HOEFFLER

Second detective of HARRIGAN

H

Alec HOERNER

was one of the more vicious private eyes in the genre and, unregrettably, appeared only once.

American Male Private Detective operating in New York

Charles ALVERSON 1935- (American)

See main detective Joe GOODEY

Citation Record: 1 Book

Fighting Back - *Only*
Bobbs US (1973); Hamish Hamilton UK (1978)

Dr Joel HOFFMAN

appears in several short stories in which he solves 'impossible' crimes. One only is cited.

American Male Amateur operating in USA

Arthur PORGES (American)

Invented 13 detectives - see Arsène LUPIN

Citation Record: 1 Selected Short Story

Birds Of One Feather
appeared in the January 1963 number.
In 'Alfred Hitchcock's Mystery Magazine' US (1963)

Det Insp HOGARTH

solves a case of a stabbing in a locked room.

British Policeman operating in England

Celia DALE 1912- (British)

Writer: Celia Marjorie DALE

Citation Record: 1 Book

Helping With Inquiries - *Single*
Macmillan UK (1979)

The Deception - *Single**
Harper & Row US (1980)

George R SIMS 1847-1922 (British)

Invented 5 detectives - see Dorcas DENE

Citation Record: 1 Selected Short Story

The Mystery Of The Studio Suite
is in a collection of seventeen of the author's short stories, *A Cabinet Minister's Wife and Other Tales.*
Paul UK (1910)

Flora HOGG

is a schoolmistress and, being the daughter of a senior British cop, very naturally decides to set up as a private detective. She is in her middle years and looks it, wears pince-nez, goes to church, and is fussy about the types of cases and clients she takes on.

British Female Private Detective operating in London

Austin LEE 1904-1965 (British)

Citation Record: 9 Books

Sheep's Clothing - *First*
Cape UK (1955)

Miss Hogg's Last Case - *Last*
Cape UK (1963)

Gentle HOGGERTY

!See Appendix 2

American Male Sleuth operating in USA

GRIFF (British)

House name.

For writer details see Phil CASEY

Citation Record: 3 Books

The Poisonous Angel - *First*
Modern Fiction UK (1953)

Main Street Morgue - *Last*
Modern Fiction UK (1953)

Ben SARTO (British)

For writer details see Phil CASEY

Dread - *First*
Modern Fiction UK (1955)

Fear- *Last*
Modern Fiction UK (1955)

Ron HOGGETT

seems to be running a detective agency, although that is sometimes difficult to realise. His speciality is finding 'lost' items, especially valuable ones that other people want.

British Male Private Detective operating in London

Sidekick: Dave BAXTER
provides a rather essential muscular backup for his partner.
British Male - Assistant

James MITCHELL 1926- (British)

Invented 3 detectives - see Joe CAVE

Citation Record: 3 Books

Sometimes You Could Die - *First*
Hamish Hamilton UK (1985)

Dying Day - *Latest*
Hamish Hamilton UK (1988); Holt US (1989)

Mr HOLBROOK

is a *Sherlock HOLMES* parody.

British Male Professional Amateur operating in England

Sidekick: Mr WILSON
is his parody *WATSON*-like assistant.
British Male - Assistant

Charles PETERSON

Citation Record: 1 Selected Short Story

The Adventure Of The Mocking Devil - *Parody 1*
appeared in the January number.
In 'Mike Shayne Mystery Magazine' US (1982)

Noel HOLCROFT

seeks an old document drawn up by his father and other Nazi leaders, in order to make recompense.

American Male Professional Investigator operating in several locations

Robert LUDLUM 1927- (American)

Invented 3 detectives - see John TANNER

Citation Record: 1 Book

The Holcroft Covenant - *Single*
Marek US (1978); Hart Davis UK (1978)

Hugo HOLD

is a Scottish barrister who investigates a case of murder on behalf of his client.

British Male Amateur operating in Scotland

Helen MATHERS 1853-1920 (British)

was born in Somerset. She wrote several novels, mainly in the romantic genre.

Writer: Helen Buckingham MATHERS

Citation Record: 1 Book

Murder Or Manslaughter - *Only*
Routledge UK (1885)

Dan HOLDEN

loses his hearing in a shoot-out but learns to lip-read. This enables him to fool everyone, especially villains.
American Male Private Detective operating in New York

Leon BRYNE (American)

Citation Record: 1 Selected Short Story

The Society Of The Singing Death
can also be found in the anthology, *More Tales of the Defective Detective from the Pulps* (Editors: Gary Hoppenstand, Garyn G Roberts & Ray B Browne, US 1985).
In 'Dime Mystery' US (1939)

Lash HOLDEN and Dany ASHTON

British Male Amateur and Female Amateur operating in Africa

M M KAYE 1909- (British)

Writer: Mary Margaret KAYE

Inventor of one other detective Copper RANDAL

Citation Record: 1 Book

The House Of Shade - *Only*
Longman UK (1959); Coward McCann US (1959)

Death In Zanzibar - *Only**
Revised.
St Martin's US (1983)

Sydney HOLDEN

American Male Amateur operating in USA

Jerome CHARYN 1937- (American)

See main detective Dep Commiss Isaac SIDEL

Citation Record: 1 Book

Paradise Man - *Single*
Fine US (1987); Joseph UK (1988)

Picklock HOLES

is a *Sherlock HOLMES* parody who first appeared in eight stories that were published in *Punch* between August 12 and November 4, 1893. They appeared originally under the author's punning pseudonym and are so cited. The eight stories were later published in a collection under the author's own name and it is also so cited. Almost a century later, in 1980, a further eight stories were published in a collection under the author's real name. The collection and the new stories are all cited.
British Male Professional Amateur operating in London

Sidekick: Dr POTSON
is his parody *WATSON*-like assistant.
British Male - Assistant

R C LEHMANN 1856-1929 (British)

was a lawyer, journalist, sometime newspaper editor, and on the staff of *Punch*. Later he became a Member of Parliament and wrote several books on politics and law.

Writer: Rudolph Chambers LEHMAN
Other Byline: Cunnin TOIL

Citation Record: 16 Short Stories in 2 Collections

The Adventures Of Picklock Holes, Together With A Perversion And A Burlesque - *Parody Collection 1*
The stories in this collection are those originally published under the pseudonym and are so cited.
Short stories - 8
Aspen US (1975)

The Return Of Picklock Holes - *Parody Collection 2*
is the collection of newly discovered stories, which are cited immediately below.
Short stories - 8
Magico US (1980)

The Adventure Of The Swiss Banker - *Parody 1*
The King Of Paflagonia - *Parody 2*
The Notch In The Tulwar - *Parody 3*
Picky Pack, Being Passages From The Re-Incarnation Of Picklock Holes - *Parody 4*
Scotland Yard - *Parody 5*
The Story Of The Lost Picklock - *Parody 6*
The Story Of The Lamplighter - *Parody 7*
The Story Of The Princess - *Parody 8*

Cunnin TOIL 1856-1929 (British)

For writer details see Picklock HOLES

Citation Record: 8 Short Stories in 1 Collection

The Adventures Of Picklock Holes, Together With A Perversion And A Burlesque - *Parody Collection 1*
These are the stories originally published in *Punch*. They are cited immediately below. They were republished by *Aspen* (US 1975) under the author's real name.
Short stories - 8
Bradbury & Agnew UK (1901)

The Bishop's Crime - *Parody 1*
The Duke's Feather - *Parody 2*
The Escape Of The Bulldog - *Parody 3*
The Hungarian Diamond - *Parody 4*
Lady Hilda's Mystery - *Parody 5*
Picklock's Disappearance - *Parody 6*
The Stolen March - *Parody 7*
The Umbrosa Burglary - *Parody 8*

Peter HOLGATE

behaves like an old-fashioned amateur in an American version of the old-fashioned British whodunnit.
American Male Private Detective operating in New York

Edith HOWIE (American)

Inventor of one other detective Ross LANGDON

Citation Record: 1 Book

Murder For Christmas - *Only*
Farrar, Straus US (1941); Boardman UK (1942)

Bernard HOLLAND

was formerly with British Intelligence and now runs the Rapid Results Agency in Belfast.
British Male Private Detective operating in Belfast

Mike SHELLEY (British)

See main detective Barney HUGGINS

Citation Record: 1 Book

The Last Private Eye In Belfast - *Single*
Domino UK (1984)

Henry HOLLAND

British Male Amateur operating in England

Henry ANDOVER (British)

Writer: Henry HOPE

Citation Record: 2 Books

Death On The Pack Road - *First*
Eyre & Spottiswoode UK (1931)

The Dennisdale Tragedy - *Last*
Eyre & Spottiswoode UK (1936)

Jenny HOLLAND

American Female Amateur operating in USA

Joyce HARRINGTON (American)

was born in Jersey City, New Jersey. She is the author of several dozen short stories, nearly all in the criminous genre, and her very first won for her a Mystery Writers of America Edgar Allan Poe award, 1973.

Other Detectives:
Philip MARLOWE
John Conan WATSON

Citation Record: 1 Book

Family Reunion - *Single*
St Martin's US (1982); Severn UK (1983)

H

Mark HOLLAND
British Male Sleuth operating in Europe

Paul MYERS 1932- (British)

Citation Record: 6 Books

Deadly Variations - *First*
Constable UK (1985); Vanguard US (1986)

Deadly Crescendo - *Latest*
Constable UK (1989); Doubleday US (1990)

Pete HOLLAND
was once with US Intelligence but now works for Abaco Private Investigation Services, which operates on 48th Street in Manhattan.
American Male Private Detective operating in New York

H Baldwin TAYLOR 1920- (American)
For writer details see Ch Fred FELLOWS
Inventor of one other detective David HALLIDAY

Citation Record: 1 Book

The Trouble With Tycoons - *Only*
Doubleday US (1967)

The Missing Tycoon - *Only**
Hale UK (1967)

Matthew HOLLEY
is the security chief at the fictional Stanton College, a distinguished male preserve. When a professor is murdered, he, though more used to giving out parking tickets than sleuthing, solves the crime.
American Male Amateur operating in USA

Elizabeth FENWICK 1920- (American)

Writer: Elizabeth Fenwick WAY

Citation Record: 1 Book

A Long Way Down - *Only*
Harper & Row US (1959); Gollancz UK (1959)

Felix HOLLIDAY
British Male Amateur operating in England

Arthur E JONES (British)

Citation Record: 3 Books

You Know The Way It Is - *First*
Hutchinson UK (1956)

It Makes You Think - *Last*
Long UK (1958)

Hiram HOLLIDAY
British Male Amateur operating in England

Paul GALLICO 1897-1976 (American)
Invented 3 detectives - see Alexander HERO

Citation Record: 1 Book 6 Short Stories in 1 Collection

The Secret Front - *Only*
Knopf US (1944)

The Adventures Of Hiram Holliday - *Collection 1*
Knopf US (1939); Joseph UK (1939)

Gail HOLLISTER
Second detective of Kerry O'NEIL

Insp HOLLY
British Policeman operating in England

Raymond POSTGATE 1896-1971 (British)
was born in Cambridge, educated at Perse School, Cambridge, and graduated at St John's College, Oxford. Journalist and editor of repute, he was the author of many learned books on politics and history.

Writer: Raymond William POSTGATE

Citation Record: 2 Books

Somebody At The Door - *First*
Knopf US (1943)

The Ledger Is Kept - *Last*
Joseph UK (1953)

Matthew HOLMAN
is a Scotland Yard detective in this one Victorian novel.
British Policeman operating in London

Richard MARSH 1867-1915 (British)
Invented 10 detectives - see The Hon Augustus CHAMPNELL

Citation Record: 1 Book

The Crime And The Criminal - *Only*
Ward, Lock UK (1897)

Rick HOLMAN
is a Hollywood detective, solving cases in and around the studios among the great and the not so good. His work involves inspecting many corpses and quite a few blondes.
American Male Private Detective operating in Hollywood/Florida

Carter BROWN 1923-1985 (Australian)
was the pseudonym of a writer who was something of a publishing phenomenon. Born in London, he went to Australia and took up citizenship in 1948. He served in the Royal Navy and, after several different kinds of work, became a full-time writer from 1953 until his death in 1985. He wrote a great number of crime and detective novels and short stories, mostly published in Australia. They were in the old pulp magazine style always and not of the highest quality, but they sold in their millions. So many were there, especially after 1958 in the United States, that they made him one of the largest selling genre authors of all time.

BROWN created a number of mainly forgettable detectives, usually patterned on those of other authors, and he set his books in the USA and in Hollywood particularly, although his knowledge of these venues and of the American idiom has been adjudged as shaky in the extreme.

Writer: Alan Geoffrey YATES

Other Detectives:
Larry BAKER
Paul DONAVAN
Andy KANE
Max ROYAL
Lt Al WHEELER
Danny BOYD
Mike FARREL
Randy ROBERTS
Mavis SEIDLITZ

Citation Record: 35 Books

Zelda - *First*
Horwitz AU (1961); New American Library US (1961); New English Library UK (1962)

The Swingers - *Latest*
Horwitz AU (1980); Tower US (1980)

Bill HOLMES
British Male Amateur operating in England

G F HUGHES (British)

Writer: George Fieldon HUGHES

Citation Record: 5 Short Stories in 1 Collection

The Adventures Of Bill Holmes - *Collection 1*
Oxford UK (1950)

Charlotte HOLMES
purports to be the sister of *Sherlock HOLMES*. In a collection of stories, and with the assistance another canonical character, she undertakes a little light sleuthing on her own, the master himself intervening only marginally.
British Female Amateur operating in England

Sidekick: Mrs Mary WATSON
purports to be the wife of the canonical *Dr John H WATSON*.
British Female - Assistant

Stooge: Insp Jules LESTRADE
is a parody of the canonical *Insp LESTRADE*. The author states that his forename has been changed to make him seem 'more English'. But did the original actually *have* a forename?
British Male

Hilary BAILEY (British)

Citation Record: 7 Short Stories in 1 Collection

The Strange Adventures Of Charlotte Holmes - *Parody Collection 1*
The individual stories, in chapters, are cited immediately below.
Constable UK (1994)
Introducing Miss Holmes And Her Friend - *Parody 1*
The Kravonian Adventure - *Parody 2*
The Adventure In Whitechapel - *Parody 3*
Who Killed The Little Cockney Nightingale - *Parody 4*
A Missing Boy And A Royal Connection - *Parody 5*
The New Monster - *Parody 6*
Mary Watson Takes A Hand - *Parody 7*

Creighton HOLMES

purports to be the grandson of *Sherlock HOLMES* and is alive and detecting in England during the 1930s.
British Male Amateur operating in England

Ned HUBBELL (American)
Writer: Lois W HUBBELL
Citation Record: 7 Short Stories in 1 Collection
The Adventures Of Creighton Holmes - *Parody Collection 1*
Popular Library US (1979)

Doorlock HOLMES

is a *Sherlock HOLMES* parody.
British Male Professional Amateur operating in London
Sidekick: Dr WHATSON
is his parody *WATSON*-like assistant.
British Male - Assistant

Paul NIZZA
Citation Record: 1 Selected Short Story
The Adventure Of The Five Puce Map Tacks - *Parody 1*
Fibonacci Corporation US (1976)

Fellock HOLMES

is a *Sherlock HOLMES* parody.
British Male Professional Amateur operating in London
Sidekick: Dr WATSO
is his parody *WATSON*-like assistant.
British Male - Assistant

Bill CONKLIN (American)
Citation Record: 1 Selected Short Story
Caught In The Act - *Parody 1*
appeared in the August 26 number.
In 'Saturday Evening Post' US (1967)

Hairlock HOLMES

is a *Sherlock HOLMES* parody.
Male Professional Amateur

Floyd R HOROWITZ (American)
Adopter of one other detective Sherlock HOLMES
Citation Record: 1 Selected Short Story
Hairlock Holmes, Detective, Solves An Anachronistic Mystery - *Parody 1*
was originally broadcast in Iowa in a radio series for children. It was published later in the December number of the magazine.
In 'Baker Street Journal' US (1964)

Hemlock HOLMES

is a *Sherlock HOLMES* parody.
Male Professional Amateur
Sidekick: Dr WATTS
is his parody *WATSON*-like assistant.
Male - Assistant

John MCGOLDRICK (American)
Citation Record: 1 Selected Short Story
The Adventure Of The Artissium Murder - *Parody 1*
In 'Sidelights on Holmes' US (1967)

Hemlock HOLMES

is a *Sherlock HOLMES* parody.
Male Professional Amateur
Sidekick: Dr WATSON
is not presumably the same person as the eminent *Dr John H WATSON.*
Male - Narrator
Stooge: Insp LETSTRAYED
is a parody of *Insp LESTRADE,* the classic police antagonist of *Sherlock HOLMES.*
Male

James Francis THIERRY (American)
Citation Record: 1 Book
The Adventure Of The Eleven Cuff-Buttons - *Parody 1*
is a novelette in which the great detective triumphs over *Insp LETSTRAYED.*
Neale US (1918)

H

John Sherlock HOLMES

Second detective of Lt Oliver BAYNES

Mycroft HOLMES and Sherlock HOLMES

Mycroft HOLMES is the brother of *Sherlock HOLMES* and appeared in some of the canonical stories. He worked in some mysterious capacity for the government and was said, by his famous brother, in a rare display of coyness, to have an even finer intellect than himself. Several later authors have used him in parodies and pastiches, usually as the main detective, but sometimes, as here, with *Sherlock HOLMES* as well.
British Male Amateur and British Professional Amateur operating in London

Charlton ANDREWS 1874-1939 (American)
Invented 4 detectives - see Derek WHITBY
Citation Record: 3 Short Stories in 1 Collection
The Resources Of Mycroft Holmes - *Pastiche Collection 1*
The individual stories are cited immediately below.
Aspen US (1973)
He Repudiates Sherlock - *Pastiche 1*
He Solves The Mystery Of The Man In The Iron Mask - *Pastiche 2*
He Solves The Mystery Of The Shakespearean Authorship - *Pastiche 3*

Michael P HODEL and Sean M WRIGHT (American)
The two authors, one a radio writer and the other an expert on Sherlockiana, collaborated on one novel.
Citation Record: 1 Book
Enter The Lion - *Pastiche 1*
Hawthorn US (1979); Dent UK (1980)

Mycroft HOLMES

appears also with *Sherlock HOLMES* in books by at least one other author. *Sherlock* appears as a subsidiary character in these books.
British Male Amateur operating in England

Glen PETRIE 1931- (British)
was born in Glasgow, brought up in the Lake District and then served in Malaya, 1949-1951. He returned to Balliol College, Oxford, to read History and taught and pursued his studies in historical research in London and Exeter. He became a full-time writer in 1977 and has published biographies and historical novels.
Citation Record: 3 Books
The Dorking Gap Affair - *Pastiche 1*
Bantam UK (1989)
The Monstrous Regiment - *Pastiche 2*
Bantam UK (1990)
The Hampstead Poisonings - *Pastiche 3*
UK (1995)

Raffles HOLMES

was an early and ingenious combination of the moral, intellectual *Sherlock HOLMES* and *E W Hornung's* immoral, adventurous, gentleman-detective-crook, *A J RAFFLES.*

British Male Professional Amateur operating in England

Sidekick: Dr JENKINS

narrates the stories and is himself a combination of *Dr WATSON* and *Bunny MANDERS*, the original sidekicks of the two parodied detectives.

British Male - Narrator

John Kendrick BANGS 1862-1922 (American)

devoted much of his writing career to short stories, parodies and pastiches, many of which he published in collections.

Other Detectives:

Sherlock HOLMES　　Shylock HOMES
Mrs A J VAN RAFFLES

Citation Record: 10 Selected Short Stories in 1 Collection

R Holmes & Co; Being The Remarkable Adventures Of Raffles Holmes, Esq, Detective And Amateur Cracksman By Birth - *Parody Collection 1*

contains ten parodies, which originally appeared in *Harper's Weekly*, from July 22 through August 26, 1905. The individual stories are cited immediately below.

Short stories - 10
Harper US (1906)

The Adventure Of Mrs Burlingame's Diamond Stomacher - *Parody 1*

The Adventure Of Room 407 - *Parody 2*

The Adventure Of The Brass Check - *Parody 3*

The Adventure Of The Dorrington Ruby Seal - *Parody 4*

The Adventure Of The Hired Burglar - *Parody 5*

The Adventure Of The Missing Pendants - *Parody 6*

Introducing Mr Raffles Holmes - *Parody 7*

The Major-General's Pepper-Pots - *Parody 8*

The Nostalgia Of Nervy Jim The Snatcher - *Parody 9*

The Redemption Of Young Billington Rand - *Parody 10*

Sharlock HOLMES

is a *Sherlock HOLMES* parody.

British Male Professional Amateur operating in London

Sidekick: Nigel WATSON

is his parody *WATSON*-like assistant.

British Male - Assistant

Tom MENGERT (American)

Citation Record: 1 Selected Short Story

A Study In Stagnation - *Parody 1*

appeared in the March number.

In 'The Victorian Journal' US (1971)

Sherlock HOLMES

is, without any doubt, the best-known character in detective fiction and is, indeed, one of the greatest creations to have ever appeared in English literature. Invented by a penurious doctor with an ailing practice in the seaside town of Southsea, he is said to have been based on Dr Joseph Bell, a surgeon at Edinburgh University, where *Sir Arthur Conan DOYLE* attended lectures as a medical student. Bell apparently possessed amazingly acute powers of observation and deduction, which he used in diagnosis. *DOYLE*, indeed, dedicated his first collection of short stories, *THE ADVENTURES OF SHERLOCK HOLMES*, to him.

What is it about *Sherlock HOLMES* that, almost from the time of his inception and continuing to this day, hundreds of writers have written about him, critics have become obsessed with him and literary historians have spent years, sometimes their lives, sifting every minute scrap of information from the canon (a mere four short novels and fifty-six short stories), in order to reconstruct this fictional figure's life? Dozens of authors have, for over a century, created imitations of *HOLMES* and penned pastiches, parodies and burlesques in an extraordinary fashion, so declaring that there is something about him that has become significant at a deep artistic level. Dozens of societies exist, and not only in English-speaking countries, to discuss the stories, to discuss the detective, to play games around his invented life, habits and character, to publish journals containing essays, apocrypha and new pastiches. They take their names from passages in the canon itself; the Baker Street Journal, the Shades of Sherlock, the Amateur Mendicant Society, the Persian Slipper Club, and Dr Watson's Neglected Patients are just a few of literally hundreds. None of this was the author's intention, so how was it done?

In fact, *DOYLE* declared on many occasions that he was thoroughly fed up with his detective and, as we know, he tried to kill him off quite early in the canon. The unique stature of *HOLMES* is evidenced by the fact that he has become something that he shares with only a few other fictional creations, that is, a permanent part of British culture. In this respect he can be likened to Lewis Carroll's Alice, W S Gilbert's Mikado, Emily Brontë's Heathcliff, Bernard Shaw's Eliza Doolittle and Oscar Wilde's Lady Bracknell. Civilised, cultivated people are expected to be able to quote appropriately from *THE HOUND OF THE BASKERVILLES* as they do from *Alice in Wonderland*, *The Mikado* or *The Importance Of Being Earnest.* It is in that sense that *HOLMES* stands apart from all other detectives. Georges Simenon's *Jules MAIGRET*, for example, is as brilliant and is perhaps the only detective in European fiction who can be said to be on a par with *HOLMES*. He too appears in a canon of novels that are among the greatest in detective fiction; he too makes a city his own; and he too spans an era of at least forty years. Even so, only sketches of his character emerge and it would be impossible to imagine that thousands of pieces, articles, essays, historical and mock-historical studies, quasi-biographies and pseudo-chronologies could be written about him. At the end of a *MAIGRET* story, it is possible to know everything about the people of Montmartre, the café-owners, the prostitutes and the concierges, while learning almost nothing about the detective himself. In the *HOLMES* stories, on the other hand, the characters often remain symbols, cut-out pieces only necessary to get the plot going, and we learn more and more about the detective himself. Everything that can be known about *HOLMES* is, of course, in the stories. The rest, and it is vast, is all embroidery and invention. But it is delightful embroidery and brilliant invention and now so interwoven with the facts that emerge in the stories themselves that it has become legendary. It is known, throughout the world, as Sherlockiana.

In this world of sub-textual analysis, it is generally agreed that *HOLMES* must have been born around 1854, that he attended the university at either Oxford or Cambridge (the debate continues) and was perhaps taught mathematics by the brilliant Professor Moriarty, later to become his arch-enemy. He showed his analytical skills early and, allied to his extraordinary knowledge of many fields, they placed him in the forefront of criminal detection. He seems to have come to London in 1877 or 1878 and there he took rooms in Montague Street, near the British Museum, where he continued to study. He is presumed to have met *Dr WATSON* in 1881, after the latter had encountered a mutual acquaintance at the Criterion Bar and was looking for an apartment. The two then took rooms together at 221B Baker Street, in London's West End, which was to become the most famous address in fiction.

The first case to be published was *A STUDY IN SCARLET*, in which *WATSON* says, 'Your merits should be publicly recognised. You should publish an account of the case. If you won't,

I will for you'. So began what was, chronologically, one of the longest series in detective fiction and the best known. Although the first story did not appear until November 1887, internal evidence suggests that the episode occurred in 1881, and several other cases in the canon are presumed to have taken place in the intervening years. By 1889, *HOLMES* was able to say he had worked on 'some five hundred cases'.

In 1893 *THE FINAL PROBLEM* appeared. In this story *WATSON* relates the case, regarded as having occurred in 1891, in which the detective had his last struggle with Moriarty at the Reichenbach Falls in Switzerland, both being presumed killed in the process. This attempt by the author to kill off his detective appalled his public, many of whom paraded outside his house wearing black arm-bands and wrote constant, often abusive, letters to him. Although the novel, *THE HOUND OF THE BASKERVILLES,* was published in 1902, this was canonically a 'posthumous' work and it was not until 1903 that, under some financial pressure, the author brought *HOLMES* back to life in *THE ADVENTURE OF THE EMPTY HOUSE,* presumed to have taken place in 1894. The years 1891 to 1894 are referred to as 'The Great Hiatus', when it seems that the detective travelled abroad, mainly to Tibet and France. The details given by *WATSON* are vague and manifestly full of errors, but they have proved a fertile field for several inventive writers of pastiches.

Readers of the *Strand Magazine* in December, 1904 were traumatised yet again in learning, in *THE SECOND STAIN,* that *HOLMES* had 'definitely retired from London and betaken himself to study and bee-farming on the Sussex Downs'. The penultimate part of the canon, the collection, *HIS LAST BOW,* was published in 1914 and the story of the same name is of a case presumed to have taken place in 1914. The last collection of short stories, *THE CASE-BOOK OF SHERLOCK HOLMES,* purported to narrate cases from a rather earlier period.

DOYLE died in 1930, but not his creation. In fact, the legend grew apace and the era of analysis and reconstruction began. The famous society, The Baker Street Irregulars, was founded in New York in 1934 by Christopher Morley and the Sherlock Holmes Society met for the first time in London in 1935. Several authors, including *Anthony BOUCHER,* have suggested that *HOLMES* must have continued his work for the British government during the First World War and have written pastiches to prove it. *Strand Magazine* finally published an obituary of *HOLMES,* written by *E V KNOX,* in 1948 and the magazine itself published its last number in 1950, an event that truly signified the end of an era. The expert W S Baring-Gould, however, after much research, gave the date of the detective's death as January 6, 1957, at the age of 103.

The indispensable *The World Bibliography of Sherlock Holmes and Dr Watson* (Editor: Ronald Burt De Waal), 1974, lists 6221 items of Sherlockiana extant at that time. The total might well have reached the five figure mark by now. They discuss endlessly and fascinatingly every conceivable facet of the detective's fictional life; subjects as important as the colour of the Persian slipper in which the detective kept his tobacco; the kind of knife that transfixed his correspondence to the wall; whether or not he actually took cocaine; how many dressing-gowns he actually had; was he colour-blind?; how much he really knew about chemistry, anatomy and other sciences; why he distrusted women; and a thousand other matters. Certainly nothing else like the *Sherlock HOLMES* phenomenon exists. He sums himself up and, indeed, the whole ethos of the detective story, in *THE SIGN OF FOUR:* 'I am the last and highest court of appeal in detection. When Gregson, or Lestrade, or Athelney Jones are out of their depths – which, by the way, is their normal state – the matter is laid before me. I examine the data, as an expert, and pronounce a specialist's opinion. I claim no credit in such cases. My name figures in no newspaper. The work itself, the pleasure of finding a field for my peculiar powers, is my highest reward'.

In recognition of *HOLMES',* exceptional status, every story, pastiche and parody connected to the genre's greatest detective that it has been possible to find, with any appropriate information on them, is cited. Plays, but none of the numerous works in any other medium, are admitted.

[The indexing and citation methods used are necessarily more difficult here than in other parts of the book. The appropriate section of the Introduction should be consulted.]

British Male Amateur operating in London

Sidekick: Dr John H WATSON

is the assistant of *Sherlock HOLMES* and the narrator of almost all his cases. He must be accounted the greatest and best known of all detective fiction's sidekicks and a legend in his own right, giving the word 'Watsonian' to the language. The good doctor's biography has been studied and annotated by experts almost as assiduously as that of his mentor and what does not appear in the canon of stories has been invented.

WATSON's greatness is almost as difficult to understand as that of *HOLMES* himself, but so it is with all outstanding literary creations. He is introduced to us in a phrase that was to resound through the next century. 'You have been in Afghanistan, I perceive', says *HOLMES* when he meets the young doctor, who is introduced to him by the latter's former dresser at St Batholomew's Hospital after a meeting at the Criterion Bar in London's West End. It was a meeting that was certainly the most momentous in criminous fiction.

WATSON was in his thirties when he first met the detective, hard up and, he says, 'as free as air'. He had served in the British wars on the Indian borders, he was wounded (whether in the arm or the leg or both is never quite clear and has been hotly debated since) and he has a practice near (but not too near as to be considered posh) the West End. When the stories get going, he sometimes lives with *HOLMES,* but during his (second) married state, he lives, of course, with his wife. Whenever and wherever, though, he is always able to stop work and join his friend when the game is afoot. He is a bumbler, he never understands what *HOLMES* is up to and has to be told. He carries a gun for the chase on occasions, but it is an old piece left over from his army days. He does use it on the odd villain and he sometimes tends the wounded in action. So what is it about him that has made scholars on both sides of the Atlantic write papers on the question as to whether he was wounded in the arm or the leg; or what name his middle H stood for? Perhaps he is just loveable. Certainly the author, in creating him, set a pattern for a man and a relationship that was to pervade the detective genre for ever. He has appeared in hundreds of *HOLMES* pastiches and has been parodied as much as *HOLMES* himself. He has even been made over into a detective in pastiches by some authors.

British Male - Narrator

Stooge: Insp LESTRADE

is perhaps the best-known police stooge in the whole detective literature. Described as 'lean and ferret-like', he appears frequently in the *Sherlock HOLMES* canon and is a brilliant creation in his own right, the plodding Scotland Yard man who is nominally in charge of many of the cases but is sometimes inept and always baffled by them. He sometimes works in opposition to *HOLMES* but occasionally, in desperation or conscious of his own lowly social standing in an era in which the police detective was still looked down on, he brings a case to him. He is sometimes helpful but, of course, he is never right.

British Male

Stooge: Insp Tobias GREGSON
is the second of the main police adversaries who occur in the *Sherlock HOLMES* canon. He is less well known than *LESTRADE* and appears only in *A STUDY IN SCARLET* and one or two short stories. Unlike *LESTRADE*, he is tall, lean and flaxen-haired. *HOLMES* opines, with only slight condescension, that he is 'the cleverest of all Scotland Yard detectives'.
British Male

Stooge: Athelney JONES
is a Scotland Yard officer. Described as 'red-faced, burly and plethoric', he was in charge of the police in *THE SIGN OF FOUR* and made the usual fool of himself.

Poul ANDERSON 1926- (American)

Invented 4 detectives - see Trygve YAMAMURA

Citation Record: 1 Selected Short Story

The Adventure Of The Misplaced Hound - *Pastiche 1*
is in a collection of six of the author's short stories, *Earthman's Burden*. It is included in the anthology, *SHERLOCK HOLMES THROUGH TIME AND SPACE* (Editors; *Isaac ASIMOV, Martin Harry Greenberg and Charles G WAUGH).*
Gnome US (1957)

H

Charlton ANDREWS 1874-1939 (American)

Invented 4 detectives - see Derek WHITBY

Citation Record: 1 Selected Short Story

The Bound Of The Astorbilts: A Modern Detective Story - *Pastiche 1*
The publication of this pastiche in 1902 illustrates how early was the effect of the *Sherlock HOLMES* stories on other authors.
In 'The Bookman' US (1902)

Val ANDREWS (American)

Citation Record: 9 Books

The Beekeeper - *Pastiche 1*
Magico Press US (1983)

The Fair - *Pastiche 2*
Magico Press US (1983)

The Fowlhaven Werewolf - *Pastiche 3*
Magico Press US (1983)

The Last Reunion - *Pastiche 4*
Magico Press US (1983)

The Carriage Clock - *Pastiche 5*
Magico Press US (1983)

Sherlock Holmes And The Brighton Pavilion Mystery - *Pastiche 6*
Ian Henry UK (1989)

Sherlock Holmes And The Eminent Thespian - *Pastiche 7*
Ian Henry UK (1992)

Sherlock Holmes And The Greyfriars School Mystery - *Pastiche 8*
? (1993)

Sherlock Holmes And The Egyptian Hall Adventure - *Pastiche 9*
? (1993); Ian Henry UK (1989)

Val ANDREWS and H PENN (American)

Citation Record: 4 Books

Sherlock Holmes And The Arthritic Clergyman - *Pastiche 1*
Magico Press US (1980)

The Case Of The Chief Rabbi's Problem - *Pastiche 2*
Magico Press US (1980)

The Mystery Of The Sealed Room - *Pastiche 3*
Magico Press US (1980)

Sherlock Holmes And A Theatrical Mystery - *Pastiche 4*
Magico Press US (1980)

ANON

Citation Record: 1 Selected Short Story

The Adventure Of The Clawed Horrors Of Limehouse - *Pastiche 1*
There have been several ribald *Sherlock HOLMES* pastiches over the years and this is one of the most scandalous. The brief text is accompanied by ninety-three photographs purporting to be of 'The Naked Street Irregulars'. It is, in a way, rather a tribute to the extraordinary ability of *HOLMES* to impose his presence on most literary forms.
In 'Naked' US (1968)

Allan ARNOLD

Invented 6 detectives - see OLD SNAP

Citation Record: 1 Book

Young Sherlock Holmes - *Pastiche 1*
is a novelization of a film made by Paramount in 1985.
Pocket Books US (1985); Dragon UK (1986)

Mark ARONSON (American)

Citation Record: 1 Selected Short Story

The Adventure Of The Second Scarf - *Pastiche 1*
has the great detective solving a case of murder for a visitor from another planet. The story, the title of which refers to the canonical story, *THE ADVENTURE OF THE SECOND STAIN*, is in the anthology, *SHERLOCK HOLMES IN ORBIT* (Editors; *Mike RESNICK and Martin H GREENBERG*).
Daw US (1995)

Ralph A ASHTON

Citation Record: 1 Selected Short Story

The Adventure Of The Pius Missal - *Pastiche 1*
purports to have been discovered 'in the barrel of an express rifle' (unlike the pastiches of several other authors that are usually said to have been found in *Dr WATSON's* old tin dispatch box). It tells the story of 'the politician, the lighthouse and the trained cormorant', which was alluded to as a hitherto unrecorded case by *WATSON*, in the canonical story, *THE ADVENTURE OF THE VEILED LODGER*. For further information see *THE POLITICIAN, LIGHTHOUSE AND TRAINED CORMORANT*, written by *Clive BROOKS*. Several other authors have used the allusion as the basis for a pastiche.
In 'Baker Street Journal' US (1957)

Isaac ASIMOV 1920-1992, Martin Harry GREENBERG and Charles G WAUGH (American)

are the editors of the cited anthology.

Citation Record: 4 Short Stories in 1 Collection

Sherlock Holmes Through Time And Space - *Parody and Pastiche Anthology 1*
The theme of the anthology is an extension of some of the characteristics of the original canon into modern and futuristic settings, often with a strong helping of sci-fi. Several authors submitted stories, some of which are cited under the appropriate byline. Only four of the thirteen stories are considered relevant.
St Martin's US (1984); Severn UK (1985)

Forrest ATHEY (American)

Citation Record: 1 Selected Short Story

The Adventure Of The Soporific Cipher - *Pastiche 1*
In 'Baker Street Journal' US (1969)

Edmund AUBREY (American)

Writer: Edmond S IONS

Citation Record: 1 Book

Sherlock Holmes In Dallas - *Pastiche 1*
Dodd, Mead US (1980)

Bliss AUSTIN

Citation Record: 1 Selected Short Story

The Final Problem - *Pastiche 1*
In 'The Queen's Awards' US (1946)

John BALL 1911-1988 (American)

Inventor of 3 detectives - see Virgil TIBBS

Citation Record: 1 Selected Short Story

The Ripe Moment - *Pastiche 1*
appeared in the September number. It refers to the allusion made by *Dr WATSON* in the canonical story, *THE PROBLEM OF THOR BRIDGE*, and purports to elucidate an unchronicled

case, the disappearance of Mr James Phillimore, 'who, stepping back into his house to get an umbrella, was never more seen in this world'. Other authors have used the allusion as the basis for a pastiche or parody.
In 'Baker Street Journal' US (1968)

Francis BAMFORD (British)

Citation Record: 1 Selected Short Story

The Case Of The Crippled Bridegroom - *Pastiche 1*
In which an eighteenth-century case of murder is solved, mainly by *Dr WATSON.*
Return to Cottington UK (1946)

John Kendrick BANGS 1862-1922 (American)

Invented 4 detectives - see Raffles HOLMES

Citation Record: 1 Selected Short Story 2 Collections

The Mystery Of Pinkham's Diamond Stud - *Pastiche 1*
In 'Harper's Bazaar' US (1899)

The Pursuit Of The House Boat - *Pastiche Collection 1*
contains connected chapters in which the shades of some great figures, including *Sherlock HOLMES,* take part in bizarre shenanigans.
Harper & Row US (1897)

The Enchanted Type-Writer - *Pastiche Collection 2*
contains connected stories or chapters in which several famous figures, including *Sherlock HOLMES,* have descended to Hades.
Harper & Row US (1899)

Maurice BARING 1874-1945 (British)

was a well-known novelist and dramatist, but he wrote little in the criminous genre apart from the one pastiche cited.

Citation Record: 1 Selected Short Story

From The Diary Of Sherlock Holmes - *Pastiche 1*
purports to be the record of a case taken from the diary of *Sherlock HOLMES* himself. It first appeared in an English magazine and later in an anthology, *Lost Diaries* (*Duckworth*; UK 1913). It can also be found in the more recent anthology, *THE MISADVENTURES OF SHERLOCK HOLMES* (Editor: *Sebastian WOLFE).*
In 'The Eye-Witness' UK (1911)

Stephen BARR (American)

See main detective Dr Sylvan MOORE

Citation Record: 1 Selected Short Story

The Procurator Of Justice - *Pastiche 1*
appeared in the February number. It refers to the allusion made by *Dr WATSON* in the canonical story, *THE PROBLEM OF THOR BRIDGE,* to an unchronicled case concerning the disappearance of Mr James Phillimore, 'who, stepping back into his house to get an umbrella, was never more seen in this world'. The pastiche purports to solve the mystery. Other authors have used the allusion as the basis for a pastiche or parody.
In 'Ellery Queen's Mystery Magazine' US (1950)

James M BARRIE 1860-1937 (British)

Writer: Sir James Matthew BARRIE

Citation Record: 1 Selected Short Story

The Adventure Of The Two Collaborators - *Pastiche 1*
was admired by *Sir Arthur Conan DOYLE* and he included it in a miscellany he published in 1924, *Memoirs and Adventures.* It appears also in *THE MISADVENTURES OF SHERLOCK HOLMES* (Editor: *Ellery QUEEN).*
Hodder & Stoughton UK (1924)

Hill BARTON (American)

Writer: J W SOVINE

Citation Record: 2 Selected Short Stories

The Adventure Of The Command Performance - *Pastiche 1*
appeared in the January number.
In 'Baker Street Journal' US (1958)

The Adventure Of The Brimstone Chalice - *Pastiche 2*
appeared in the Christmas Annual.
In 'Baker Street Journal' US (1959)

William BARTON and Michael CAPOBIANCO

Citation Record: 1 Selected Short Story

The Adventure Of The Russian Grave - *Pastiche 1*
In which the great detective, in 1908 and after he has retired, is nearly led to his death by a diabolical scheme hatched by Professor Moriarty, which takes him to Russia. The story is in the anthology, *SHERLOCK HOLMES IN ORBIT* (Editors: *Mike RESNICK and Martin H GREENBERG*).
Daw US (1995)

H BEDFORD-JONES 1887-1949 (British)

Writer: Henry James O'Brien BEDFORD-JONES

Citation Record: 1 Selected Short Story

The Affair Of The Aluminium Crutch - *Pastiche 1*
was reprinted in the January 1946 number of the *Baker Street Journal.* It refers to the allusion made by *Sherlock HOLMES* in the canonical story, *THE MUSGRAVE RITUAL,* to one of his early, unpublished cases, 'the singular affair of the aluminium crutch', which had apparently occurred before he met *Dr WATSON.* Other authors have used the allusion as the basis for a pastiche or parody.
In 'Palm Springs News' US (1936)

Nathan L BENGIS

Citation Record: 2 Selected Short Stories

A Course Of Miss Violet De Merville - *Pastiche 1*
is a one-act play, purporting to be a dramatisation of the critical meeting between *Sherlock HOLMES* and Violet De Merville (beautiful, but with the ethereal other-worldly beauty of some fanatic whose thoughts are set on high), which occurred in the canonical story, *THE ADVENTURE OF THE ILLUSTRIOUS CLIENT.*
In 'Sherlock Holmes Journal' UK (1958)

Sorry, Mr Sherlock Is Engaged Just Now - *Pastiche 2*
In 'Sherlock Holmes Journal' UK (1963)

D R BENSEN 1927- (American)

Writer: Donald R BENSEN

Citation Record: 2 Books

Sherlock Holmes In New York - *Pastiche 1*
is a novelization of a TV movie.
Ballantine US (1977)

Irene, Good Night - *Pastiche 2*
The lady whose name appears in the title is, of course, none other than *Irene ADLER*, '*the* woman' of the canonical story, *A SCANDAL IN BOHEMIA.*
Targ US (1982)

R H BIBOLET 1937- (British)

Writer: Tim J KELLY

Citation Record: 1 Book

Sherlock Holmes' First Case - *Pastiche 1*
is a two-act stage play.
Performance ? (1976)

Lloyd BIGGLE 1923- (American)

Invented 5 detectives - see Bill RASTIN

Citation Record: 1 Book

The Quallsford Inheritance - *Pastiche 1*
St Martin's US (1986)

Rolfe BOSWELL (American)

Citation Record: 1 Selected Short Story

Colonel Warburton's Madness - *Pastiche 1*
refers to the allusion made by *Dr WATSON* in the canonical story, *THE ADVENTURE OF THE ENGINEER'S THUMB,* to an unrecorded case. Other authors have used the allusion as the basis for a pastiche or parody.
In 'Baker Street Journal' US (1962)

Anthony BOUCHER 1911-1968 (American)

Invented 7 detectives - see Fergus O'BREEN and Det Lt JACKSON

Citation Record: 4 Selected Short Stories

The Adventure Of The Illustrious Imposter - *Pastiche 1*

In this story, set in 1941, *Sherlock HOLMES* (although not actually mentioned by name) is now a very old man, retired to his farm in Sussex. He convinces a very old *Dr WATSON* that the German, Rudolf Hess, who flew to Britain that year 'to make peace' was, in fact, an impostor. The story (the title of which is itself a parody of the canonical *HOLMES* story, *THE ADVENTURE OF THE ILLUSTRIOUS CLIENT)* appeared first in the anthology, *THE MISADVENTURES OF SHERLOCK HOLMES* (Editor: *Ellery QUEEN).*

Little, Brown US (1944)

The Adventure Of The Bogle-Wolf - *Pastiche 2*

In which *Sherlock HOLMES* proves that Red Ridinghood's grandmother was a werewolf. It appears in 'The Illustrious Clients' Second Casebook' (Editor: *J N WILLIAMSON*).

In 'The Illustrious Clients' US (1949)

H

The Anomaly Of The Empty Man - *Pastiche 3*

is to be found in several collections, including *Cream of the Crime* (*Holt*; US 1962; *Harrap*; UK 1964) and latterly in *THE MISADVENTURES OF SHERLOCK HOLMES* (Editor; *Sebastian WOLFE).*

In 'Magazine of Fantasy & Science Fiction' US (1952)

The Greatest Tertian - *Pastiche 4*

In which a Martian reports to an unbelieving alien audience on the Earth genius known as Sherk Ohms. The story appeared in a collection, *Invaders of Earth* (Editor; Groff Conklin.)

Vanguard US (1952)

Mark BOURNE

Citation Record: 1 Selected Short Story

The Case Of The Detective's Smile - *Pastiche 1*

In which the great detective has a strange encounter with Alice Pleasance Hargreaves (née Liddell), the original model for *Alice in Wonderland*, who informs him preternaturally, of the death of Lewis Carroll. The story is in the anthology, *SHERLOCK HOLMES IN ORBIT* (Editors; *Mike RESNICK and Martin H GREENBERG*).

(1995)

Craig BOWLSBY (Canadian)

Citation Record: 1 Book

The Hound Of London - *Pastiche 1*

is the titular two-act play in a collection of the same name, the other entries not featuring *Sherlock HOLMES.*

Intrepid CA (1988)

Rick BOYER 1943- (American)

See main detective Dr Charlie ADAMS

Citation Record: 1 Book

The Giant Rat Of Sumatra - *Pastiche 1*

is one of the finest and most sincere of modern pastiches, a classic in its own right. It refers to the allusion made by *Dr WATSON* in the canonical story, *THE ADVENTURE OF THE SUSSEX VAMPIRE*, to an unchronicled case concerning 'the giant rat of Sumatra, a story for which the world is not yet prepared'. The allusion has been used by other authors as the basis for a pastiche or parody.

Warner US (1976); Allen UK (1977)

Worthen BRADLEY (American)

Citation Record: 1 Selected Short Story

Bad Day On Baker Street - *Pastiche 1*

appeared in the July number.

In 'Baker Street Journal' US (1959)

Jon L BREEN 1943- (American)

Invented 6 detectives - see Rachel HENNINGS

Citation Record: 1 Selected short Story

The Adventure Of The Unique Holmes - *Pastiche 1*

is in *THE NEW ADVENTURES OF SHERLOCK HOLMES* (Editors; *Martin H GREENBERG and Carol-Lynn Rossel WAUGH).*

Carroll & Graf US (1987)

Gregory BREITMAN

Citation Record: 1 Selected Short Story

The Marriage Of Sherlock Holmes - *Pastiche 1*

is a translation by Benjamin Block of a Russian pastiche.

In 'Beau: The Man's Magazine' US (1926)

Charles BROOKFIELD and Edward Seymour HICKS 1871-1949 (British)

were eminent British actors during the late Victorian and early Edwardian eras. *Edward Seymour HICKS* was born in Jersey, Channel Islands. He first appeared on the stage in Islington in 1887 and made his reputation originally as a light comedian. He later wrote several popular plays, in which he usually appeared himself. He became a famous actor-manager and was knighted, 1935.

Citation Record: 1 Book

Under The Clock - *Pastiche 1*

This extravanganza in one act has the distinction of being the first vehicle for the stage in which *Sherlock HOLMES* and *Dr WATSON* were portrayed, an already visible sign of their extraordinary impact on current media and a portent of things to come. The play was put on at the Court Theatre, London, on November 25, 1893 and ran for ninety-two performances through March 3, 1894. The authors themselves played (respectively) the two main characters. A review appeared in *The Times* on November 27, 1893.

Clive BROOKS (British)

See main detective Henry CHESTERFIELD

Citation Record: 17 Short Stories in 4 Collections

Blood On The Tracks - *Collection 1*

contains six of the author's short stories, five of which feature *Henry CHESTERFIELD* and one cited immediately below with *Sherlock HOLMES.*

Kingfisher UK (1989)

The Mid-Hants Affair - *Pastiche 1*

The Memoirs Of Professor Moriarty - *Pastiche Collection 1*

The individual stories are cited immediately below.

Short stories - 4
Spy Glass UK (1990)

The Ascot Gamble - *Pastiche 2*

Spy Glass UK (1990)

An Explosive Encounter - *Pastiche 3*

Spy Glass UK (1990)

Ordeal By Fire - *Pastiche 4*

Spy Glass UK (1990)

The Ultimate Confrontation - *Pastiche 5*

Spy Glass UK (1990)

Sherlock Holmes Revisited - *Pastiche Collection 2*

The individual stories are cited immediately below.

Short stories - 7
Hallmark UK (1990)

The Abergavenny Adventure - *Pastiche 6*

refers to the allusion made by *Dr WATSON* in the canonical story, *THE ADVENTURE OF THE PRIORY SCHOOL,* to a case 'coming up for trial'.

The Adventure Of The Alicia Cutter - *Pastiche 7*

refers to the allusion made by *Dr WATSON* in the canonical story, *THE PROBLEM OF THOR BRIDGE,* to an unchronicled case concerning 'the Alicia Cutter, which sailed one spring morning into a small patch of mist from where she never again emerged, nor was anything further ever heard of herself or her crew'.

The Adventure Of The Aluminium Crutch - *Pastiche 8*

refers to the allusion made by *Sherlock HOLMES* in the canonical story, *THE MUSGRAVE RITUAL,* to an unchronicled case concerning 'the singular affair of the aluminium crutch'. The allusion has been used by other authors as the basis for a pastiche or parody.

The Case Of The Red Leech - *Pastiche 9*

The Conk-Singleton Affair - *Pastiche 10*
refers to the allusion made by *Sherlock HOLMES* at the end of the canonical story, *THE ADVENTURE OF THE SIX NAPOLEONS,* where he asks *Dr WATSON* 'to get out the papers of the Conk-Singleton forgery case', which was never chronicled. Other authors have used the allusion as the basis for a pastiche or parody.

The Disappearance Of James Phillimore - *Pastiche 11*
refers to the allusion made by *Dr WATSON* in the canonical story, *THE PROBLEM OF THOR BRIDGE,* to an unchronicled case concerning 'Mr James Phillimore, who, stepping back into his house to get an umbrella, was never more seen in this world'. Other authors have used the allusion as the basis for a pastiche or parody and, indeed, it remains one of the most frequently adopted, perhaps because of the peculiar attraction of the mysterious and unresolved event.

The Problem Of The Peculiar Pipes - *Pastiche 12*

Sherlock Holmes Revisited: Volume 2 - *Pastiche Collection 3*
The individual stories are cited immediately below.
Short stories - 5
Spy Glass UK (1990)

The Abernathy Affair - *Pastiche 13*
may, although the spelling is different, refer to the allusion made by *Sherlock HOLMES* himself in the canonical story, *THE ADVENTURE OF THE SIX NAPOLEONS,* to how 'the dreadful business of the Abernetty family was first brought to my notice by the depth to which the parsley had sunk into the butter on a hot day'.

The Adventure Of The Amateur Mendicants - *Pastiche 14*
refers to the allusion made by *Dr WATSON* in the canonical story, *THE FIVE ORANGE PIPS,* to an unchronicled case of 1987, in which *Sherlock HOLMES* had investigated the 'Amateur Mendicant Society, who held a luxurious club in the lower vault of a furniture warehouse'. Other authors have used the allusion as the basis for a pastiche or parody.

The Case Of The Canary Trainer - *Pastiche 15*
refers to the allusion made by *Dr WATSON* in the canonical story, *THE ADVENTURE OF BLACK PETER,* to an unrecorded case in which *Sherlock HOLMES* had arrested 'Wilson, the notorious canary-trainer, which removed a plague-spot from the East End of London'.

The Friesland Case - *Pastiche 16*
refers to the allusion made by *Dr WATSON* in the canonical story, *THE ADVENTURE OF THE NORWOOD BUILDER,* to an unchronicled case, 'the shocking affair of the Dutch steamship "Friesland", which so nearly cost us both our lives'.

The Politician, Lighthouse And Trained Cormorant - *Pastiche 17*
refers to the allusion made by *Dr WATSON* in the canonical story, *THE ADVENTURE OF THE VEILED LODGER,* that, 'in the event of certain outrages being repeated', he had 'Mr Holmes's authority for saying that the whole story concerning the politician, the lighthouse and the trained cormorant will be given to the public'. Other authors have used the allusion as the basis for a pastiche or parody. Indeed, it has been a favourite source of later stories.

Russell A BROWN

Citation Record: 1 Book

Sherlock Holmes And The Mysterious Friend Of Oscar Wilde - *Pastiche 1*
St Martin's US (1988)

C D S BRYAN

Citation Record: 1 Selected Short Story

The Jefferson Nickel: An Astonishing Sherlock Holmes Adventure - *Pastiche 1*
In which the American CIA, a little out of its era, appeals for help to *Sherlock HOLMES.*
Monocle US (1963)

Anthony BURGESS 1917-1993 (British)

was acknowledged as one of the outstanding writers of mainstream fiction of the century. Like so many other great writers he could not resist writing one *HOLMES* pastiche.

Writer: John Anthony Burgess WILSON

Citation Record: 1 Selected Short Story

Murder To Music - *Pastiche 1*
appears in a collection of nine of the author's short stories, *The Devil's Mode.*
Hutchinson UK (1989)

Sidekick: Dr DOVER
British Male - Assistant

John Dickson CARR 1906-1977 (American)

Invented 16 detectives - see Dr Gideon FELL

Citation Record: 2 Short Stories in 1 Collection

The Door To Doom And Other Detections - *Pastiche Collection 1*
Harper & Row US (1980); Hamish Hamilton UK (1981)

The Adventure Of The Paradol Chamber - *Pastiche 1*
is a short play that was first performed at the annual meeting of the Mystery Writers of America in 1949. It is also be found in the anthology, *THE MISADVENTURES OF SHERLOCK HOLMES* (Editor; *Sebastian WOLFE).* The story refers to the allusion made by *Dr WATSON* in the canonical story, *THE FIVE ORANGE PIPS,* to an unchronicled case. Other authors have used the allusion as the basis for a pastiche or parody.
Citadel US (1991)

The Adventure Of The Conk-Singleton Papers - *Pastiche 2*
is a short playlet that was first performed at the annual meeting of the Mystery Writers of America in 1948. It is also in the anthology, *THE MISADVENTURES OF SHERLOCK HOLMES* (Editor; *Sebastian WOLFE*). The pastiche refers to the allusion made by *Dr WATSON* in the canonical story, *THE ADVENTURE OF THE SIX NAPOLEONS,* to a case that the detective was working on at the time, 'the Conk-Singleton forgery'.
Citadel US (1991)

Susan CASPER

Citation Record: 1 Selected Short Story

Holmes Ex Machina - *Pastiche 1*
has the detective, in the 1990s, getting the best of computer technology. The story is in the anthology, *SHERLOCK HOLMES IN ORBIT* (Editors; *Mike RESNICK and Martin H GREENBERG*).
Daw US (1995)

Jules CASTIER (American)

Citation Record: 1 Selected Short Story

The Footprints On The Ceiling - *Pastiche 1*
was originally published in an anthology, *Rather Like...* (Jenkins; UK 1920) and is to be found in the anthology, *THE MISADVENTURES OF SHERLOCK HOLMES* (Editor; *Ellery QUEEN).*
Lippincott US (1920); Jenkins UK (1920)

Dick CHARLTON (British)

Citation Record: 3 Short Stories in 1 Collection

Sherlock Holmes Comedy Trilogy - *Pastiche Collection 1*
contains three short plays, individually cited immediately below.
Hanbury UK (1988)

The Affair Of Lady Carfax - *Pastiche 1*
The title refers to the canonical story, *THE DISAPPEARANCE OF LADY CARFAX.*

The Golden Limping Stick - *Pastiche 2*

The Venus Figurine - *Pastiche 3*

Frank CHIN (American)

Citation Record: 1 Selected Short Story

Sherlock Holmes - *Pastiche 1*

This story, although featuring *Sherlock HOLMES,* is perhaps more parody than pastiche. It concerns a case solved by 'the Detective of Bacon Street' and purports to have been written by 'Sir Arthur Conning Tower'.
In 'The California Pelican' US (1959)

Agatha CHRISTIE 1890-1976 (British)

Invented 18 detectives - see Hercule POIROT

Citation Record: 1 Selected Short Story

The Case Of The Missing Lady - *Pastiche 1*

In which the author's own two detectives, *Tommy* and *Tuppence BERESFORD,* try to pass themselves off as *Sherlock HOLMES* and *Dr WATSON.* The story is in a collection of the author's short stories, *Partners in Crime,* and also in the anthology, *THE MISADVENTURES OF SHERLOCK HOLMES* (Editor: *Ellery QUEEN).*
Collins UK (1929); Dodd, Mead US (1929)

H

Anatole CHUJOY

Citation Record: 1 Selected Short Story

The Adventure Of The Tainted Worm - *Pastiche 1*

appeared in the July number. It refers to the allusion made by *Dr WATSON* in the canonical story, *THE PROBLEM OF THOR BRIDGE,* to an unchronicled case concerning 'Isodora Persano, the well-known journalist and duellist, who was found stark staring mad with a matchbox in front of him which contained a remarkable worm, said to be unknown to science'. Other authors have used the allusion as the basis for a pastiche or parody.
In 'Baker Street Journal' US (1955)

François Paulus P CILLIE

was the author of a *Sherlock HOLMES* pastiche short story, which won joint First Prize (see also under the author, *Miles MASTERS*) in the 1967 competition organised by the *Sunday Times of South Africa.*

Citation Record: 1 Selected Short Story

The Adventure Of The Second Stain - *Pastiche 1*

The title is identical with that of the canonical story and it is to be found in the anthology, *THE FURTHER ADVENTURES OF SHERLOCK HOLMES* (Editor: *Richard Lancelyn GREEN*), where it is retitled *The Adventure of the Green Empress.* Other authors have used the canonical story as the basis for a pastiche or parody.
In 'Sunday Times News Magazine' SA (1967)

Benjamin S CLARK (American)

Citation Record: 1 Selected Short Story

Sunshine, Sunshine - *Pastiche 1*

was published in the Christmas Annual Edition of 1960 and refers to the allusion made by *Dr WATSON* in the canonical story, *THE PROBLEM OF THOR BRIDGE,* to an unchronicled case involving the mysterious disappearance of 'Mr James Phillimore, who, stepping back into his own house to get his umbrella, was never more seen in this world'. Other authors have used the allusion as the basis for a pastiche or parody.
In 'Baker Street Journal' US (1960)

Logan CLENDENING (American)

Citation Record: 1 Selected Short Story

The Case Of The Missing Patriarchs - *Pastiche 1*

was published in a limited edition of thirty copies in 1934 and is to be found in the anthology, *THE MISADVENTURES OF SHERLOCK HOLMES* (Editor: *Ellery QUEEN).* In what must be one of shortest pastiches on record, the great detective, recently dead, is still carrying on his work in Heaven, where he solves a case that is puzzling the Almighty. In this short piece, there is not even room for *Dr WATSON.*
Edwin B Hill US (1934)

J Storer CLOUSTON 1870-1944 (British)

Invented 4 detectives - see F T CARRINGTON

Citation Record: 1 Selected Short Story

The Truthful Lady - *Pastiche 1*

appears in the author's collection, *CARRINGTON'S CASES.* It is unusual in that the great detective remains invisible throughout.
Blackwood UK (1920)

Allen COHEN

Citation Record: 1 Selected Short Story

The Adventure Of Vigor, The Hammersmith Wonder - *Pastiche 1*

refers to the allusion made by *Dr WATSON* in the canonical story, *THE ADVENTURE OF THE SUSSEX VAMPIRE,* to an unchronicled case concerning 'Vigor, the Hammersmith wonder'.
In 'Baker Street Pages' US (1966)

Howard COLLINS (American)

Citation Record: 1 Selected Short Story

The Affair Of The Politician, The Lighthouse, And The Trained Cormorant - *Pastiche 1*

refers to the allusion made by *Dr WATSON* in the canonical story, *THE ADVENTURE OF THE VEILED LODGER.* For further information see *THE POLITICIAN, LIGHTHOUSE AND TRAINED CORMORANT,* written by *Clive BROOKS.* Other authors have used the allusion as the basis for a pastiche or parody.
In 'Baker Street Journal (Old Series)' US (1947)

Randall COLLINS 1941- (American)

graduated from the University of California, Berkeley and is a prominent sociologist.

Citation Record: 1 Book

The Case Of The Philosopher's Ring - *Pastiche 1*

In which *Sherlock HOLMES* and *Dr WATSON* travel to Cambridge to investigate the strange behaviour of the philosopher, Ludwig Wittgenstein.
Crown US (1978); Harvester UK (1980)

A CON and O YLE (American)

used the punning byline for their pastiche.

Writers: Robert W HAHN and John H NIEMINSKI

Citation Record: 1 Selected Short Story

The Adventure Of The Copper's Breeches - *Pastiche 1*

makes punning reference to the canonical story, *THE ADVENTURE OF THE COPPER BEECHES.*
In 'Devon County Chronicles' US (1967)

Alistair COOKE (British)

first broadcast this story in his 'Letters from America' Series.

Citation Record: 1 Selected Short Story

The Case of the November Sun-Tan - *Pastiche 1*

Hart Davis UK

J W COURTNEY (American)

Citation Record: 1 Selected Short Story

Dr Watson And Mr Holmes; Or, The Worm That Turned - *Pastiche 1*

In 'Boston Medical & Surgical Journal' US (1904)

A B COX 1893-1970 (British)

For writer details see Roger SHERINGHAM

Citation Record: 1 Selected Short Story

Holmes And The Dasher - *Pastiche 1*

appeared first in a collection of the author's stories, *Jugged Journalism,* and is also to be found in the anthology, *THE MISADVENTURES OF SHERLOCK HOLMES* (Editor: *Ellery*

QUEEN). The author decided to write it in what was the then current style of *P G WODEHOUSE* and, although the story is true pastiche rather than parody, *HOLMES'* sidekick is called Bertie!
Jenkins UK (1925)

Sidekick: Bertie WATSON
is the parody *WATSON*-like assistant of *HOLMES* in this curious little pastiche.

Milt CREIGHTON (American)

Citation Record: 2 Books

The Dynamiters - *Pastiche 1*
A book of games.
Berkley US (1988)

The Royal Flush - *Pastiche 2*
A book of games.
Berkley US (1988)

Robert A CUTTER (American)

Citation Record: 1 Selected Short Story

A Tall Adventure Of Sherlock Holmes - *Pastiche 1*
appeared in the author's collection, *Sherlockian Studies.*
In 'Baker Street Press' US (1947)

Susan Elizabeth DAHLINGER (American)

Citation Record: 2 Selected Short Stories

The Adventure Of The Aluminium Crutch - *Pastiche 1*
refers to the allusion made by *Sherlock HOLMES* in the canonical story, *THE MUSGRAVE RITUAL,* to a case he had undertaken before his meeting with *Dr WATSON,* 'the singular affair of the aluminium crutch'.
In 'Baker Street Journal' US (1969)

The Cask Of Amontillado - *Pastiche 2*
appeared in an anthology, *A Curious Collection* (Editor; William J Walsh). It relates how *Sherlock HOLMES* offers his own solution to the famous tale of this name by *Edgar Allan POE.*
The Musgrave Ritualists' US (1971)

DARVAS Robert, Norman V HART and Paul STERN (American)

Citation Record: 1 Selected Short Story

Elementary, My Dear Watson (The Tale Of 4 Clubs) - *Pastiche 1*
appeared in a collection, *Right through the Pack* and is a puzzle based on a hand at Bridge and solved by *HOLMES.*
Stuyvesant House US (1948)

David Stuart DAVIES

Citation Record: 2 Books

The Tangled Skein - *Pastiche 1*
Ian Henry UK (19??)

Sherlock Holmes And The Hentzau Affair - *Pastiche 2*
Ian Henry UK (1991)

Lillian DE LA TORRE 1902- (American)

See main detective Dr Sam JOHNSON

Citation Record: 1 Selected Short Story

The Adventure Of The Persistent Marksman - *Pastiche 1*
concerns a case in which an attempt is made to make a dupe of the great detective, but he solves it by his knowledge of forensic science and ballistics. The story is in *THE NEW ADVENTURES OF SHERLOCK HOLMES* (Editors; *Martin H GREENBERG and Carol-Lynn Rossel WAUGH).*
Carroll & Graf US (1987)

John DECHANCIE

Citation Record: 1 Selected Short Story

The Richmond Enigma - *Pastiche 1*
In which the great detective is called on to investigate a house in Richmond, Surrey, where events connected with a Time Machine have been deemed to occur and they seem associated with a young man rather like *H G WELLS.* The story is in the anthology, *SHERLOCK HOLMES IN ORBIT* (Editors; *Mike RESNICK and Martin H GREENBERG)*
Daw US (1995)

August DERLETH 1909-1971 (American)

Invented 4 detectives - see Solar PONS

Citation Record: 1 Selected Short Story

The Adventure Of The Circular Room - *Pastiche 1*
first appeared in the July 1946 number of the Baker Street Journal, where the names of the detective and sidekick were changed from *Solar PONS* and *Dr PARKER* to *Sherlock HOLMES* and *Dr WATSON.* The story is accordingly cited under both sets of names. Its first appearance with the names of *Solar PONS* and *Dr PARKER* was in *THE MEMOIRS OF SOLAR PONS.*
In 'Baker Street Journal' US (1946)

Michael DIBDIN 1947- (British)

Invented 3 detectives - see Commiss Aurelio ZEN

Citation Record: 1 Book

The Last Sherlock Holmes Story - *Pastiche 1*
In which *Sherlock HOLMES* and an increasingly perplexed *Dr WATSON* are involved in a final clash with Professor Moriarty. Other authors have invented 'final clashes', none of which seems to live up to the name, any more than did the famous one in the canonical story, *THE FINAL PROBLEM.*
Cape UK (1978); Pantheon US (1978)

Donald McNutt DOUGLASS 1899-1975 (American)

See main detective Det Bolivar MANCHENIL

Citation Record: 1 Selected Short Story

The Case Of The Sunburned Peer - *Pastiche 1*
Privately printed (1965)

Adrian Conan DOYLE and John Dickson CARR (British)

Writers: Adrian Malcolm Conan DOYLE 1910-1970 and John Dickson CARR 1906-1977

Citation Record: 12 Short Stories in 1 Collection

The Exploits Of Sherlock Holmes - *Pastiche Collection 1*
contains stories that were all first published in either *Collier's* or *Life* during 1952 and 1953. They were mostly based on the several allusions made by *Dr WATSON* to unchronicled cases. Unlike many other pastiche writers, however, *Adrian Conan DOYLE* and *John Dickson CARR* did not use the allusions for their titles. The stories are individually cited immediately below.
Murray UK (1954); Random House US (1954)

The Adventure Of The Abbas Ruby - *Pastiche 1*

The Adventure Of The Black Baronet - *Pastiche 2*

The Adventure Of The Dark Angels - *Pastiche 3*
The title of this story when it was first published was 'The Adventure of the Demon Angeles'. It was included in the author's collection under the title cited, by which name it is now generally known.

The Adventure Of The Deptford Horror - *Pastiche 4*

The Adventure Of Foulkes Rath - *Pastiche 5*

The Adventure Of The Gold Hunter - *Pastiche 6*
purports to be an account of the 'Camberwell poisoning', an unchronicled case alluded to by *Dr WATSON* in the canonical story, *THE FIVE ORANGE PIPS.*

The Adventure Of The Highgate Miracle - *Pastiche 7*
purports to offer a solution to the unchronicled case alluded to by *Dr WATSON* in the canonical story, *THE PROBLEM OF THOR BRIDGE,* concerning 'Mr James Phillimore, who, stepping back into his own house to get his umbrella, was never more seen in this world'. The allusion has been used by other authors as the basis for a pastiche or parody.

The Adventure Of The Red Widow - *Pastiche 8*
appears also in *THE FURTHER ADVENTURES OF SHERLOCK HOLMES* (Editor; *Richard Lancelyn GREEN*), where it is entitled *The Adventure of Arnsworth Castle.*

The Adventure Of The Sealed Room - *Pastiche 9*
purports to be an account of an unchronicled case, alluded to by *Dr WATSON* in the canonical story, *THE ADVENTURE OF THE ENGINEER'S THUMB*, concerning 'the affair of Colonel Warburton's madness'. The allusion has been used by other authors as the basis for a pastiche or parody.

The Adventure Of The Seven Clocks - *Pastiche 10*

The Adventure Of The Two Women - *Pastiche 11*

The Adventure Of The Wax Gamblers - *Pastiche 12*

Sir Arthur Conan DOYLE 1859-1930 (British)
was born in Edinburgh, Scotland. He was educated at the Hodder School, Lancashire, 1868-1970, Stonyhurst College, Lancashire, 1870-1875, and at the Jesuit School, Feldkirch, Austria. He studied medicine at the University of Edinburgh, 1876-1881, receiving his MB, 1881 and an MD, 1886. He set up practice as a physician in Southsea, Hampshire, 1882-1890, and served in a field hospital in South Africa during the Boer War, 1899-1902, after which he received a knighthood. He began his writing while at Southsea, completing his first *Sherlock HOLMES* short story there. He lived in London after 1902 but, because of his rapidly increasing fame as a writer, he gave up medicine. He wrote many novels, some of which are still full of interest, but he has never been considered to be in the first rank of mainstream novelists. He became interested, in the latter part of his life, in spiritualism and devoted much of his time, money and writings to it.

He is, of course, known the world over for his creation of the greatest of all fictional detectives, *Sherlock HOLMES*, who is, without doubt, the *nonpareil*, the key turning point in the history of detective fiction. Created originally in a short story, he was an instant success. Deservedly so; for, in retrospect, it is immediately clear how superior the first few stories were to anything in detective fiction that had appeared before. Soon, they acquired an immense public, who could not get enough of them and clamoured for more. Such was their appeal that they were almost immediately pirated, pastiched and parodied, in the United States as well as in Britain.

DOYLE continued to produce the stories, although not in great numbers and bowing reluctantly to public pressure, for almost forty years. They made him a great fortune but he himself remained sceptical and even appalled at the public's apparently insatiable demand for more. He regarded the stories as interfering with his work as a historical novelist and serious writer. In fact, he tried to kill off *HOLMES* in *THE FINAL PROBLEM* but was made to revivify him when it became clear that the public would not stand for his demise. When the famous American actor-playwright, *William GILLETTE*, the author of the most famous play dramatising the sage of Baker Street, cabled *DOYLE* to ask, 'May I marry Holmes?', his creator replied, 'You may marry or murder him or do what you like with him.'

DOYLE was the author of sixteen non-genre novels, some of high quality, a dozen or so plays, four volumes of verse, over fifty volumes of works on subjects as diverse as travel, war, politics, history and, especially, photography and spiritualism (the latter two subjects became major interests in the latter part of his life). However, the irony of history has dictated that he is mainly remembered and acclaimed as the begetter of the greatest detective in fiction.

Writer: Sir Arthur Conan DOYLE

Inventor of one other detective Pharaoh JONES

Citation Record: 4 books 1 Play 56 Short Stories 5 Collections

A Study In Scarlet - *Book 1*
In 'Beeton's Christmas Annual' UK (1887); Ward, Lock UK (1887); Lippincott US (1890)

The Sign Of Four - *Book 2*
Blackett UK (1890); Lippincott US (1890)

The Hound Of The Baskervilles - *Book 3*
Newnes UK (1902); McClure US (1902)

The Valley Of Fear - *Book 4*
Smith, Elder UK (1915); Doran US (1915)

The Speckled Band - *Play*
The already rich and famous creator of *Sherlock HOLMES* had little success with his historical novels and his attempts as a playwright failed miserably in the theatre. Determined to outdo the success of *William GILLETTE's* play, in 1910 he rapidly wrote this play, in three acts, based on his own story, *THE ADVENTURE OF THE SPECKLED BAND*. It was put on at the Adelphi theatre in London on June 4 and proved an enormous and highly profitable success, particularly as it had as its star the venerated H H Saintbury, who had already played the role of the detective in *GILLETTE's* play over a thousand times.
UK (1910)

The Adventures Of Sherlock Holmes - *Collection 1*
The stories cited immediately below are given in the order in which they appeared in the canonical collection, together with details of their original publication.
Short stories - 12
Newnes UK (1892); Harper & Row US (1892)

A Scandal In Bohemia
In 'Strand Magazine' UK (1891)

The Red-Headed League
In 'Strand Magazine' UK (1891)

A Case Of Identity
In 'Strand Magazine' UK (1891)

The Boscombe Valley Mystery
In 'Strand Magazine' UK (1891)

The Five Orange Pips
In 'Strand Magazine' UK (1891)

The Man with The Twisted Lip
In 'Strand Magazine' UK (1891)

The Adventure Of The Blue Carbuncle
In 'Strand Magazine' UK (1892)

The Adventure Of The Speckled Band
In 'Strand Magazine' UK (1892)

The Adventure Of The Engineer's Thumb
In 'Strand Magazine' UK (1892)

The Adventure Of The Noble Bachelor
In 'Strand Magazine' UK (1892)

The Adventure Of The Beryl Coronet
In 'Strand Magazine' UK (1892)

The Adventure Of The Copper Beeches
In 'Strand Magazine' UK (1892)

The Memoirs Of Sherlock Holmes - *Collection 2*
The stories cited immediately below are given in the order in which they appeared in the canonical collection, together with details of their original publication.
Short stories - 12
Newnes UK (1894); Harper & Row US (1894)

Silver Blaze
In 'Strand Magazine' UK (1892)

The Cardboard Box
appeared only in some editions of this collection and was also collected later in *HIS LAST BOW*.
In 'Strand Magazine' UK (1893)

The Yellow Face
In 'Strand Magazine' UK (1893)

The Stockbroker's Clerk
In 'Strand Magazine' UK (1893)

The 'Gloria Scott'
In 'Strand Magazine' UK (1893)

The Musgrave Ritual
In 'Strand Magazine' UK (1893)

The Reigate Squires
was also called *The Reigate Puzzle* in the US.
In 'Strand Magazine' UK (1893).

The Crooked Man
In 'Strand Magazine' UK (1893)

The Resident Patient
In 'Strand Magazine' UK (1893)

The Greek Interpreter
In 'Strand Magazine' UK (1893)

The Naval Treaty
In 'Strand Magazine' UK (1893)

The Final Problem
In 'Strand Magazine' UK (1893)

The Return Of Sherlock Holmes - *Collection 3*
The stories cited immediately below are given in the order in which they appeared in the canonical collection, together with details of their original publication.
Short stories - 13
Newnes UK (1905); McClure US (1905)

The Adventure Of The Empty House
In 'Collier's Magazine' US (1903)

The Adventure Of The Norwood Builder
In 'Collier's Magazine' US (1903)

The Adventure Of The Dancing Men
In 'Strand Magazine' UK (1903)

The Adventure Of The Solitary Cyclist
In 'Collier's Magazine' US (1903)

The Adventure Of The Priory School
In 'Collier's Magazine' US (1904)

The Adventure Of Black Peter
In 'Collier's Magazine' US (1904)

The Adventure Of Charles Augustus Milverton
In 'Strand Magazine' UK (1904)

The Adventure Of The Six Napoleons
In 'Collier's Magazine' US (1904)

The Adventure Of The Three Students
In 'Strand Magazine' UK (1904)

The Adventure Of The Golden Pince-Nez
In 'Strand Magazine' UK (1904)

The Adventure Of The Missing Three-Quarter
In 'Strand Magazine' UK (1904)

The Adventure Of The Abbey Grange
In 'Strand Magazine' UK (1904)

The Adventure Of The Second Stain
In 'Strand Magazine' UK (1904)

His Last Bow - *Collection 4*
The stories cited immediately below are given in the order in which they appeared in the canonical collection, together with details of their original publication.
Short stories - 7
Murray UK (1917); Doran US (1917)

Wisteria Lodge
In 'Strand Magazine' UK (1908)

The Adventure Of The Bruce-Partington Plans
In 'Strand Magazine' UK (1908)

The Adventure Of The Devil's Foot
In 'Strand Magazine' UK (1910)

The Adventure Of The Red Circle
In 'Strand Magazine' UK (1911)

The Disappearance Of Lady Francis Carfax
appeared in *Ellery Queen's Challenge to the Reader: An Anthology* (*Stokes*; US 1938) and the names of *Sherlock HOLMES* and *Dr WATSON* were changed to *Pharaoh JONES* and *Dr DOVER* respectively.
In 'Strand Magazine' UK (1911)

The Adventure Of The Dying Detective
In 'Collier's Magazine' US (1913)

His Last Bow: The War Service Of Sherlock Holmes
In 'Strand Magazine' UK (1917)

The Case-Book Of Sherlock Holmes - *Collection 5*
The stories cited immediately below are given in the order in which they appeared in the canonical collection, together with details of their original publication.
Short stories - 12
Murray UK (1927); Doran US (1927)

The Adventure Of The Mazarin Stone
In 'Strand Magazine' UK (1921)

The Problem Of Thor Bridge
In 'Strand Magazine' UK (1922)

The Adventure Of The Creeping Man
In 'Strand Magazine' UK (1923)

The Adventure Of The Sussex Vampire
In 'Strand Magazine' UK (1924)

The Adventure Of The Three Garridebs
In 'Collier's Magazine' US (1924)

The Adventure Of The Illustrious Client
In 'Collier's Magazine' US (1924)

The Adventure Of The Three Gables
Liberty US (1926)

The Adventure Of The Blanched Soldier
In 'Strand Magazine' UK (1926)

The Adventure Of The Lion's Mane
Liberty US (1926)

The Adventure Of The Retired Colourman
In 'Collier's Magazine' US (1926)

The Adventure Of The Veiled Lodger
Liberty US (1927)

The Adventure Of Shoscombe Old Place
Newnes UK (1905); Liberty US (1927)

B Conan DOYLIE (American)

is presumably a punning pseudonym.

Citation Record: 1 Selected Short Story

The Adventure Of The Missing Bit - *Pastiche 1*
In which the great detective discovers, really quite early on in the 1960s, that a computer is the murderer.
Datamation US (1964)

William E DUDLEY

Citation Record: 1 Collection

The Untold Sherlock Holmes - *Pastiche Collection 1*
contains an uncounted number of stories.
Magico Press US (1983)

David DVORKIN 1943- (American)

Citation Record: 1 Book

Time For Sherlock Holmes - *Pastiche 1*
Dodd, Mead US (1983)

Marcel D'AGNEAU

Citation Record: 1 Book

The Curse Of The Nibelung: Being The Last Case Of Lord Holmes Of Baker Street And Sir John Watson - *Pastiche 1*
It seems that the great detective, in old age, has been elevated to the peerage by a grateful monarch and the most famous sidekick in the criminous literature has received a much deserved knighthood.
Arlington UK (1981)

Herbert EATON (American)

Citation Record: 1 Selected Short Story

The Adventure Of The Addleton Tragedy - *Pastiche 1*
refers to the allusion made by *Dr WATSON* in the canonical story, *THE ADVENTURE OF THE GOLDEN PINCE-NEZ*, to an unchronicled case concerning 'the Addleton tragedy'.
Pontine US (1975)

George Alec EFFINGER 1947- (American)

See main detective Marid AUDRAN

Citation Record: 1 Selected Short Story

The Musgrave Version - *Pastiche 1*
The great detective possibly attended Cambridge University in his youth and, in this story, he is introduced by his friend, Mr Reginald Musgrave (see the canonical story, *THE MUSGRAVE RITUAL*), to a mysterious and brilliant young Chinaman by the name of Fu Manchu! The story is in the anthology, *SHERLOCK HOLMES IN ORBIT* (Editors; *Mike RESNICK and Martin H GREENBERG*).
Daw US (1995)

Loren D ESTLEMAN 1952- (American)

Invented 7 detectives - see Amos WALKER

Citation Record: 2 Books

Sherlock Holmes Vs Dracula: Or, The Adventures Of The Sanguinary Count - *Pastiche 1*

Doubleday US (1978); New English Library UK (1978)

Dr Jekyll And Mr Holmes - *Pastiche 2*

Doubleday US (1979); Penguin UK (1980)

Frank J EUSTACE (American)

Citation Record: 2 Selected Short Stories

The Adventure Of The Highest Beast - *Pastiche 1*

appeared in the March number. It purports to take place during the time of 'The Great Hiatus', when Sherlock HOLMES was, for three years, presumed dead but, he said, was travelling in Tibet. On a climbing expedition to Everest, he has, it seems, solved the mystery of the Abominable Snowman.

In 'Baker Street Journal' US (1961)

A Commission To The Sultan Of Turkey - *Pastiche 2*

appeared in the March number.

In 'Baker Street Journal' US (1965)

H

EVOE 1881-1971 (British)

was an esteemed comic writer and parodist, associated for many years with *Punch*, the long-lived but now defunct British humorous journal.

Writer: Edmund George Valpy KNOX

Citation Record: 1 Selected Short Story

Conan Doyle In Space - *Pastiche 1*

It seems that the great detective has become the first man in space.

In 'Punch' UK (1960)

Mary FANTINA

Citation Record: 1 Book

The Adventure Of The Smiling Judge - *Pastiche 1*

May Press ? (1986)

Philip Jose FARMER (American)

is the author of a number of literary parodies and pastiches.

Citation Record: 1 Book 2 Selected Short stories

The Adventure Of The Peerless Peer - *Pastiche 1*

has *Sherlock HOLMES* and *Dr WATSON* on a secret mission to Cairo in 1916, in pursuit of Van Bork, the German master spy who appeared in the canonical story, *HIS LAST BOW.* They encounter Lord Greystoke, later known as Tarzan of the Apes.

UK (1974)

The Adventure Of The Three Madmen - *Pastiche 2*

is in the anthology, *THE MISADVENTURES OF SHERLOCK HOLMES* (Editor; *Sebastian WOLFE).*

Berkley US (1984)

The Problem Of The Sore Bridge - Among Others - *Pastiche 3*

is in the anthology, *SHERLOCK HOLMES THROUGH TIME AND SPACE* (Editors; *Isaac ASIMOV, Martin Harry GREENBERG and Charles G WAUGH).*

S FEANADY

Citation Record: 1 Book

Sherlock Holmes In Gibraltar - *Pastiche 1*

UK (199?)

Rachel FERGUSON 1893-1957 (British)

Citation Record: 1 Selected Short Story

His Last Scrape: Or, Holmes, Sweet Holmes - *Pastiche 1*

appeared in a collection of the author's parodies, *Nymphs and Satires*, and is also to be found in *THE MISADVENTURES OF SHERLOCK HOLMES* (Editor: *Ellery QUEEN).* The story is cited in the authoritative bibliography, *The World Bibliography of Sherlock Holmes and Dr Watson* (Editor; Ronald Burt de Waal) under the title, *Home! Sweet Holmes!.*

Benn UK (1932)

Lewis FEUER 1912-

Writer: Lewis Samuel FEUER

Citation Record: 1 Book

The Case Of The Revolutionist's Daughter: Sherlock Holmes Meets Karl Marx - *Pastiche 1*

In 1881, the detective is consulted by Frederick Engels, the friend and main colleague of Karl Marx, about certain personal troubles besetting the latter.

Prometheus ? (1983)

Cindy FISCHER (American)

Citation Record: 1 Book

The Adventure Of The Copper Beeches - *Pastiche 1*

bears the same title as the canonical story by *Sir Arthur Conan DOYLE.*

Last Bow US (1978)

Charles FISHER (American)

Citation Record: 7 Short Stories in 1 Collection

Some Unaccountable Exploits Of Sherlock Holmes - *Pastiche Collection 1*

The stories, which are cited immediately below, had all appeared previously in the now defunct *Philadelphia Record* in 1939 and 1940.

Privately printed (1956)

The Case Of The Beleaguered Detective - *Pastiche 1*

The Problem Of The Empty Magnums - *Pastiche 2*

The Adventure Of The Foiled Revenge - *Pastiche 3*

The Case Of The Haunted Ball Park - *Pastiche 4*

The Problem Of The Importunate Landlady - *Pastiche 5*

The Problem Of The Mysterious Client - *Pastiche 6*

The Puzzle Of The Strange Visage - *Pastiche 7*

Corey FORD 1902-1969 (American)

Citation Record: 1 Selected Short Story

The Rollo Boys With Sherlock In Mayfair - *Pastiche 1*

is in an anthology, *Three Rousing Cheers for the Rollo Boys.*

Doran US (1925)

Morris D FORKOSCH (American)

Citation Record: 1 Selected Short Story

The Case Of The Curious Kerchief - *Pastiche 1*

appeared in the December number.

In 'Baker Street Journal' US (1970)

John FORSTER, Greer WOODWARD and Rick CUMMINS

Citation Record: 1 Book

Sherlock Holmes And The Red-Headed League - *Pastiche 1*

A stage play.

French UK (1989)

Berkley FORSYTHE (American)

Citation Record: 1 Book

Expo '98: Sherlock Holmes In Omaha - *Pastiche 1*

takes place in 1898.

Simmons-Boardman US (1987)

Mark FROST (American)

Citation Record: 1 Book

The List Of Seven - *Pastiche 1*

Morrow US (1993)

William O FULLER (American)

See main detective Brad DOLAN

Citation Record: 2 Selected Short Stories

A Night With Sherlock Holmes - *Pastiche 1*

Privately printed (1929)

The Mary Queen Of Scots Jewel - *Pastiche 2*

was first published as a private edition, limited to two hundred copies, printed by *The Riverside Press* (Cambridge, Massachusetts, 1929) under the title, *A NIGHT WITH SHERLOCK HOLMES.* It is to found, somewhat amended,

under its new title, in *THE MISADVENTURES OF SHERLOCK HOLMES* (Editor: *Ellery QUEEN*).
Little, Brown US (1944)

Craig Shaw GARDNER

Citation Record: 1 Selected Short Story

The Sherlock Solution - *Pastiche 1*
has the great detective, in the 1990s, dealing with a computer virus called Moriarty. The story is in the anthology, *SHERLOCK HOLMES IN ORBIT* (Editors; *Mike RESNICK and Martin H GREENBERG*).
Daw US (1995)

John GARDNER 1926- (British)

Invented 5 detectives - see Boysie OAKES

Citation Record: 2 Books

The Return Of Moriarty - *Pastiche 1*
In which the evil professor takes advantage of the disappearance and suspected death of *Sherlock HOLMES* by expanding his vast criminal empire. Alas for him!
Weidenfeld & Nicolson UK (1974); Pan US (1976)

The Revenge Of Moriarty - *Pastiche 2*
In the second of the author's pastiche novels, Moriarty and the sage of Baker Street continue to slug it out.
Weidenfeld & Nicolson UK (1975); Putnam US (1976)

Martin GARDNER 1914-

Citation Record: 1 Selected Short Story

The Missing Walnuts - *Pastiche 1*
appeared in the February number.
In 'Ellery Queen's Mystery Magazine' US (1956)

Lawrence GARLAND (American)

Writers: Lawrence TOPPMAN and Steven GARLAND

Citation Record: 1 Book

The Affair Of The Unprincipled Publisher - *Pastiche 1*
Oak Knoll US (1983)

Charles GEORGE 1893-1960 (American)

Citation Record: 1 Book

Sherlock Holmes - *Pastiche 1*
is a three-act play, based on the canonical novel, *A STUDY IN SCARLET*.
Baker US (1936)

Isaac S GEORGE (American)

Citation Record: 1 Selected Short Story

The Sudden Death Of Cardinal Tosca - *Pastiche 1*
appeared in the January number. It refers to the allusion made by *Dr WATSON* in the canonical story, *THE ADVENTURE OF BLACK PETER*, to an unchronicled case of 1895 in which *Sherlock HOLMES* had been called in 'at the express desire of his Holiness the Pope' to investigate 'the sudden death of Cardinal Tosca'.
In 'Baker Street Journal' US (1948)

David GERROLD

Citation Record: 1 Selected Short Story

The Fan Who Molded Himself - *Pastiche 1*
In which the great detective, according to a manuscript purporting to have been discovered in the 1990s, was not all he was supposed to have been and, in fact, spent much time in his Time Machine, perhaps still being with us! The story is in the anthology, *SHERLOCK HOLMES IN ORBIT* (Editors; *Mike RESNICK and Martin H GREENBERG*).
Daw US (1995)

Theodore W GIBSON

Citation Record: 2 Selected Short Stories

Watson's No 8 In B Minor - *Pastiche 1*
appeared in the Christmas Annual.
In 'Baker Street Journal' US (1960)

The Adventure Of The Thinking(?) Machine - *Pastiche 2*
appeared in the December number.
In 'Baker Street Journal' US (1964)

Michael GILBERT 1912- (British)

Invented 11 detectives - see Insp HAZELRIGG

Citation Record: 1 Selected Short Story

The Two Footmen - *Pastiche 1*
is seemingly the only pastiche by this master of the detective novel. It appears in the anthology, *THE NEW ADVENTURES OF SHERLOCK HOLMES* (Editors; *Martin H GREENBERG and Carol-Lynn Rossel WAUGH*).
Carroll & Graf US (1987)

William GILLETTE 1855-1937 (American)

was an actor-manager who is now best known for his long-running play, which was loosely based on two or three of the early *Sherlock HOLMES* stories that he knitted together. He himself acted in the play when it was first performed; and Charlie Chaplin, when he was a young man, appeared in it as the great detective's chief 'street Arab', Billy. Although *GILLETTE* had never read any of the *HOLMES* stories previously, he became an expert on the saga and a great friend of *Sir Arthur Conan DOYLE*, whom he always billed as a joint author of the play. He gave, during his lifetime, over 1300 performances; and, even in real life, he often walked around in cloak and deerstalker hat, puffing a pipe made to the specification described in the canon. He retired in 1910 but continued to perform the play on occasions.

Writer: William Hooker GILLETTE

Citation Record: 2 Books

Sherlock Holmes - *Pastiche 1*
is the published version of the most famous of all the plays in which *Sherlock HOLMES* is portrayed. *William GILLETTE* wrote the play (after, it is said, apocryphally, that *Sir Arthur Conan DOYLE* had suggested that he would be a great actor to personify his detective), basing it on two canonical stories, *A SCANDAL IN BOHEMIA* and *THE FINAL PROBLEM*. He premiered it at Buffalo on October 23, 1899, under joint authorship with *DOYLE*, and then in New York on November 6. He subsequently played the lead until 1910, making many and constant alterations, and adjusting plot and character as the mood took him. The play did as much to immortalise the eternal conception of *HOLMES* as did the stories themselves. It consolidated the image of the detective, in cloak and deerstalker hat, puffing at a pipe, that has survived almost a hundred years, in spite of the fact that the original illustrations to the stories depicted *HOLMES* as debonair and conventionally dressed. And the play gave the world what was to become one of its most remembered lines, 'oh, this is elementary, my dear Watson', a phrase that occurs nowhere in the canonical stories.
French UK (1922)

The Painful Predicament Of Sherlock Holmes - *Pastiche 2*
This play was *GILLETTE's* revenge on the critics who had, over, the years attacked his acting style (it had, in fact, degenerated with time and countless performances) in his famous first play, *SHERLOCK HOLMES*. It was a spoof, a comedy in one act, and was first performed on March 24, 1905, with the author playing the lead opposite Ethel Barrymore. All the lines were given to her and the great detective said not a word. The critics loved it and it had many later performances.
Abramson US (1955)

George GOODEN and Frank THOMAS 1926-

Citation Record: 1 Selected Short Story

Sherlock Holmes, Bridge Detective - *Pastiche 1*
is a Bridge instruction book, in which the great man solves two mysteries – by a finesse, as it were.
Thomas ? (1973)

Glenn GRAVATT (American)

Citation Record: 1 Book

The Adventure Of The Mysterious Lodger - *Pastiche 1*
Magico Press US (1979)

Richard Lancelyn GREEN (British)

is one of the world's experts on *Sir Arthur Conan DOYLE.* He is the editor of the cited anthology.

Citation Record: 11 Short Stories in 1 Collection

The Further Adventures Of Sherlock Holmes - *Pastiche Anthology 1*
contains eleven stories, written by different authors, with detailed documentation as to their history. The stories are all cited individually under the appropriate author's name.
Penguin UK (1985)

Martin H GREENBERG and Carol-Lynn Rossel WAUGH (American)

are the editors of the cited anthology.

Citation Record: 15 Short Stories in 1 Collection

The New Adventures Of Sherlock Holmes - *Parody and Pastiche Anthology 1*
This anthology contains thirteen pastiches and two parodies written, by different authors, specially for this publication. The stories are cited individually under the appropriate author's name.
Carroll & Graf US (1987)

Ken GREENWALD 1936- (American)

Citation Record: 13 Short Stories in 1 Collection

The Lost Adventures Of Sherlock Holmes - *Pastiche Collection 1*
The individual stories are cited immediately below.
Mallard US (1989)

The Adventure Of The Headless Monk - *Pastiche 1*

The Adventure Of The Iron Box - *Pastiche 2*

The Adventure Of The Notorious Canary Trainer - *Pastiche 3*
refers to the allusion made by *Dr WATSON* in the canonical story, *THE ADVENTURE OF BLACK PETER,* to an unrecorded case in which *Sherlock HOLMES* had arrested 'Wilson, the notorious canary-trainer, which removed a plague-spot from the East End of London'. The allusion has been used by other authors as the basis for a pastiche or parody.

The Adventure Of The Out-Of-Date Murder - *Pastiche 4*

The Adventure Of The Second Generation - *Pastiche 5*

The April Fool's Adventure - *Pastiche 6*

The Case Of The Amateur Mendicants - *Pastiche 7*
refers to the allusion made by *Dr WATSON* in the canonical story, *THE FIVE ORANGE PIPS,* to an unchronicled case of 1897 concerning 'the Amateur Mendicant Society, who held a luxurious club in the lower vault of a furniture warehouse'. The allusion has been used by other authors as the basis for a pastiche or parody.

The Case Of The Baconian Cipher - *Pastiche 8*

The Case Of The Camberwell Poisoners - *Pastiche 9*
refers to the allusion made by *Dr WATSON* in the canonical story, *THE FIVE ORANGE PIPS,* to an unchronicled case concerning the 'Camberwell poisoning'. The allusion has been used by other authors as the basis for a pastiche or parody.

The Case Of The Demon Barber - *Pastiche 10*

The Case Of The Girl With The Gazelle - *Pastiche 11*

The Case Of The Uneasy Easy Chair - *Pastiche 12*
!See Appendix 2.

Murder Beyond The Mountains - *Pastiche 13*

L B GREENWOOD 1932- (American)

Writer: Lillian Bethel GREENWOOD

Citation Record: 3 Books

Sherlock Holmes And The Raleigh Legacy - *Pastiche 1*
Atheneum US (1986); Chivers UK (1988)

Sherlock Holmes And The Case Of Sabina Hall - *Pastiche 2*
Simon & Schuster US (1988)

Sherlock Holmes And The Thistle Of Scotland - *Pastiche 3*
Simon & Schuster US (1989)

Vernon HALL (American)

Citation Record: 1 Selected Short Story

Sherlock Holmes And The Wife Of Bath - *Pastiche 1*
appeared in the January number. It has the great detective, now retired to Sussex, telling *Dr WATSON* about a discovery he has made concerning Chaucer's famous story.
In 'Baker Street Journal (Old Series)' US (1948)

Leslie HALLIWELL 1929- (British)

Citation Record: 1 Selected Short Story

The Ghost Of Sherlock Holmes - *Pastiche 1*
is in a collection of the author's short stories with the same title.
Granada UK (1984); Academy US (1984)

David L HAMMER (American)

Citation Record: 1 Book

The Twentysecond Man; Or, Re Sherlock Holmes, German Agent - *Pastiche 1*
Gasogene Press US (1989)

Thomas HAMMOND (American)

Citation Record: 1 Selected Short Story

The Singular Affair Of The Tintype Woman - *Pastiche 1*
In 'Shades of Sherlock' US (1969)

Michael HARDWICK 1924-1991 (British)

Invented 3 detectives - see Dr John H WATSON

Citation Record: 4 Books 1 Collection

Prisoner Of The Devil: Sherlock Holmes And The Dreyfus Case - *Pastiche 1*
Proteus UK (1979); Proteus US (1980)

The Private Life Of Dr Watson - *Pastiche 2*
Dutton US (1983); Weidenfeld & Nicolson UK (1985)

Sherlock Holmes: My Life And Crimes - *Pastiche 3*
Doubleday US (1984)

Four Sherlock Holmes Plays - *Pastiche Collection 1*
contains plays based on the original *Sherlock HOLMES* stories.
Murray UK (1964)

Michael HARDWICK and Mollie HARDWICK 1924-1991 (British)

Citation Record: 1 Book 2 Collections

The Private Life Of Sherlock Holmes - *Pastiche 1*
Mayflower UK (1970); Bantam US (1971)

The Game's Afoot - *Pastiche Collection 1*
contains plays based on the original *Sherlock HOLMES* stories.
Murray UK (1969)

Four More Sherlock Holmes Plays - *Pastiche Collection 2*
contains plays based on the original *Sherlock HOLMES* stories.
Murray UK (1973)

Edward B HARMA

Citation Record: 1 Book

The Whitechapel Horrors - *Pastiche 1*
Carroll & Graf US (1992)

Michael HARRISON 1907-1991 (British)

See main detective Chevalier Auguste C DUPIN

Citation Record: 1 Book 1 Selected Short Story

I, Sherlock Holmes - *Pastiche 1*
Dutton US (1977)

Sherlock Holmes And 'The Woman' - *Pastiche 2*
is in the anthology *THE NEW ADVENTURES OF SHERLOCK HOLMES* (Editors: *Martin H GREENBERG and Carol-Lynn Rossel WAUGH).*
Carroll & Graf US (1987)

Peter HARTLEY 1956-

Citation Record: 1 Book

The Sherlock Holmes Solution - *Pastiche 1*
is a play.
New Playwrights ? (1988)

W HEIDENFELD (American)

See main detective Dr John H WATSON

Citation Record: 1 Selected Short Story

The True Adventure Of The Second Stain - *Pastiche 1*

refers to the title of the canonical story, *THE ADVENTURE OF THE SECOND STAIN*. Other authors have used this story as the basis for a pastiche or parody.

In 'Ellery Queen's Mystery Magazine' US (1959)

Evelyn HERZOG (American)

Citation Record: 1 Selected Short Story

The Second Case Of The Speckled Band - *Pastiche 1*

appeared in the Spring number of what seems to have been a college magazine. Sherlock HOLMES is almost hoaxed by students but triumphs in the end. The title parodies that of the canonical story, *THE ADVENTURE OF THE SPECKLED BAND*.

Albertinium US (1966)

James Alfred HITT

Citation Record: 1 Book

Sherlock Holmes And The Curious Adventure Of The Clockwork Prince - *Pastiche 1*

is a three-act stage play.

French UK (1980)

Edward D HOCH 1930- (American)

Invented 20 detectives - see Capt LEOPOLD

Citation Record: 1 Selected Short Story

The Return Of The Speckled Band - *Pastiche 1*

appears in the anthology, *THE NEW ADVENTURES OF SHERLOCK HOLMES* (Editors; Martin H GREENBERG and Carol-Lynn WAUGH). It purports to be a sequel to the canonical story, *THE ADVENTURE OF THE SPECKLED BAND*.

Carroll & Graf US (1987)

Ebbe Curtis HOFF and Phebe M HOFF (American)

Citation Record: 2 Selected Short Stories

The Problem Of Biffley Vicarage - *Pastiche 1*

appeared in the September number.

In 'Baker Street Journal' US (1964)

The Adventure Of The Hadderly Formula - *Pastiche 2*

appeared in the March number.

In 'Baker Street Journal' US (1966)

Banesh HOFFMAN

Citation Record: 1 Selected Short Story

Shakespeare The Physicist - *Pastiche 1*

first appeared in the April 1951 issue of *Scientific American*, but was later enlarged and appeared in the February 1966 issue of *Ellery Queen's Mystery Magazine*, where it was retitled, *Sherlock, Shakespeare and the Bomb*. In it, Sherlock HOLMES proves that SHAKESPEARE anticipated radar, relativity and the atom bomb.

In 'Scientific American' US (1951)

John C HOGAN

Citation Record: 4 Short Stories 4 Short Stories in 1 Collection

Sherlock Holmes In Hongkong - *Pastiche Collection 1*

contains four stories, which appeared between March 30 and April 20. The stories are cited immediately below.

In 'Hongkong Standard' HK (1969)

The Adventure Of The Calabash Pipe - *Pastiche 1*

Although Sherlock HOLMES was greatly given to smoking and used many kinds of pipe, often described in the canonical stories, there is a commonly held belief that he smoked a calabash pipe. There seems little evidence for it.

The Giant Rat Of *Sumatra* - *Pastiche 2*

refers to the allusion made by Dr WATSON in the canonical story, *THE ADVENTURE OF THE SUSSEX VAMPIRE*, to an unchronicled case concerning 'the giant rat of Sumatra, a story for which the world is not yet prepared'. Other authors have used the allusion as the basis for a pastiche or parody.

The Hound Of The Basket-Maker - *Pastiche 3*

The title parodies that of the canonical story, *THE HOUND OF THE BASKERVILES*.

The Persian Slipper - *Pastiche 4*

The title pays homage to the most famous slipper in literary history, the one in which the great detective kept his tobacco and the very epitome of his apartment in Baker Street.

Floyd R HOROWITZ (American)

See main detective Hairlock HOLMES

Citation Record: 1 Selected Short Story

The Case Of The Schweinitz Portrait - *Pastiche 1*

appeared in the December number.

In 'Baker Street Journal' US (1965)

H

Wayne HOWELL (Canadian)

Citation Record: 1 Selected Short Story

The Bacchus Club Mystery - *Pastiche 1*

is a novelette. It is not only a pastiche but an excellent wine primer, for over sixty fine wines are discussed by the great detective.

UK (1991)

Dorothy B HUGHES 1904- (American)

Invented 4 detectives - see Insp TOBIN

Citation Record: 1 Selected Short Story

Sherlock Holmes And The Muffin - *Pastiche 1*

is in *THE NEW ADVENTURES OF SHERLOCK HOLMES*. (Editors; Martin H GREENBERG and Carol-Lynn WAUGH) .

Carroll & Graf US (1987)

James C IRALDI 1907-1990

Citation Record: 1 Book

The Problem Of The Purple Maculas: A Sherlock Holmes Adventure - *Pastiche 1*

is a novelette that was first published in an edition limited to five hundred copies. Its plot would seem to refer to an episode in the canonical story, *THE ADVENTURE OF THE MISSING THREE-QUARTER*, concerning a handwriting impression, a *macula* so-called, although the word does not seem to occur in the story.

Luther Norris US (1968)

Colin JACK (British)

Citation Record: 1 Selected Short Story

Sherlock Holmes Investigates The EPR Paradox - *Pastiche 1*

In which the detective (almost) solves the most baffling problem in modern physics.

In 'Physics World' UK (1995)

Donald W JACKSON (American)

Citation Record: 1 Selected Short Story

Denouement - *Pastiche 1*

appeared in the December number.

In 'Baker Street Journal' US (1966)

John JACOBSON (American)

See main detective Tide POOLES

Citation Record: 1 Selected Short Story

The Phantom Anarchist - *Pastiche 1*

appeared in the February number.

In 'Baker Street Pages' US (1967)

Mary JAFFEE and Irvine JAFFEE

Citation Record: 5 Short Stories in 1 Collection

Beyond Baker Street - *Pastiche Collection 1*

The individual stories are cited immediately below.

Pontine US (1973)

The Case Of The Doomed Dissertation - *Pastiche 1*
The Case Of The Missing Scotch - *Pastiche 2*
The Case Of The Purloined Mummy - *Pastiche 3*
The Case Of The Sinister Squeeze - *Pastiche 4*
The Case Of The Unhappy Medium - *Pastiche 5*

J Jeremy JOHNSTON (American)

Citation Record: 1 Selected Short Story

The Giant Rat Of Sumatra: A Story For Which The World Is Now, At Last, Prepared - *Pastiche 1*
appeared in the November 14 number The title refers to the allusion made by *Dr WATSON,* in the canonical story, *THE ADVENTURE OF THE SUSSEX VAMPIRE,* to an unchronicled case concerning 'the giant rat of Sumatra, a story for which the world is not yet prepared'. Other authors have used the allusion as the basis for a pastiche or parody.
In 'The Harvard Lampoon' US (1962)

Barry JONES (British)

Citation Record: 1 Selected Short Story

The Shadows On The Lawn - *Pastiche 1*
is in *THE NEW ADVENTURES OF SHERLOCK HOLMES* (Editors; *Martin H GREENBERG and Carol-Lynn Rossel WAUGH).*
Carroll & Graf US (1987)

H

Kelvin I JONES (British)

See main detective Dr John CARTER

Citation Record: 1 Book

Sherlock Holmes, Consulting Detective - *Pastiche 1*
Sir Hugo UK (1990)

Stuart M KAMINSKY 1934- (American)

Invented 18 detectives - see Toby PETERS and Errol FLYNN

Citation Record: 1 Selected Short Story

The Final Toast - *Pastiche 1*
is in *THE NEW ADVENTURES OF SHERLOCK HOLMES* (Editors; *Martin H GREENBERG and Carol-Lynn Rossel WAUGH).*
Carroll & Graf US (1987)

Marvin KAYE 1938- (American)

Invented 3 detectives - see Marty GOLD

Citation Record: 1 Book

The Incredible Umbrella - *Pastiche 1*
refers to the allusion made by *Dr WATSON* in the canonical story, *THE PROBLEM OF THOR BRIDGE,* to an unchronicled case concerning 'Mr James Phillimore, who, stepping back into his own house to get his umbrella, was never more seen in this world'. Other authors have used the allusion as the basis for a pastiche or parody.
US (19??)

H R F KEATING 1926- (British)

Invented 6 detectives - see Insp Ganesh GHOTE

Citation Record: 1 Selected Short Story

A Trifling Affair - *Pastiche 1*
first appeared in an anthology, *John Creasey's Crime Collection.* It can also be found in *THE MISADVENTURES OF SHERLOCK HOLMES* (Editor; *Sebastian WOLFE.*
Gollancz UK (1980)

Tim J KELLY 1937- (American)

See main detective Insp HAWKSHAW

Citation Record: 6 Books

If Sherlock Holmes Were A Woman - *Pastiche 1*
is a one-act play.
Baker US (1970)

The Last Of Sherlock Holmes - *Pastiche 2*
is a one-act play.
Baker US (1970)

Sherlock Holmes Meets The Phantom - *Pastiche 3*
is a one-act play.
Pioneer US (1975); Hanbury UK (1985)

The Hound Of The Baskervilles - *Pastiche 4*
is a play based on the canonical story of the same title.
French UK (1976)

Sherlock Holmes - *Pastiche 5*
is an adaptation of the famous play by *William GILLETTE,* itself based on two canonical stories.
Pioneer US (1977)

The Adventure Of The Speckled Band - *Pastiche 6*
is a play based on the canonical story of the same title.
Clark US (1981)

Tim J KELLY 1937- and Jack SHARKEY 1931-1992 (American)

Citation Record: 1 Book

Sherlock Holmes And The Giant Rat Of Sumatra - *Pastiche 1*
is a two-act play based on the allusion made by *Dr WATSON,* in the canonical story, *THE ADVENTURE OF THE SUSSEX VAMPIRE,* to an unchronicled case concerning 'the giant rat of Sumatra, a story for which the world is not yet prepared'. Other authors have used the allusion as the basis for a pastiche or parody.
Baker US (1987)

Bruce KENNEDY

Citation Record: 5 Selected Short Stories

The Adventure Of The Amesbury Disappearance - *Pastiche 1*
appeared in the Christmas Annual.
In 'Baker Street Pages' US (1966)

The Adventure Of The Carved Knife - *Pastiche 2*
appeared in the December number.
In 'Baker Street Pages' US (1965)

The Adventure Of The Dover Ghost - *Pastiche 3*
appeared in the society's Annual in January.
In 'Shades of Sherlock' US (1967)

The Adventure Of The Headless Torso - *Pastiche 4*
appeared in the March-April number.
In 'Baker Street Pages' US (1966)

The Adventure Of The Prophetic Poet - *Pastiche 5*
appeared in the society's Annual in January.
In 'Shades of Sherlock' US (1968)

Laurie R KING (American)

See main detective pair Det Kate MARTINELLI and Al HAWKINS

Citation Record: 1 Book

The Beekeeper's Apprentice; Or, The Segregation Of The Queen - *Pastiche 1*
tells of an aging *Sherlock HOLMES,* engaged, as we know, in keeping bees during his retirement in Sussex. A young girl comes to see him in 1914: he decides to make her an apprentice and teach her his old arts and skills. They solve a few local cases and then encounter a vast criminal plot.
St Martin's US (1994)

Sidekick: Mary RUSSELL
is the great man's noviciate.
British Female - Assistant

Stephen KING 1947- (American)

Citation Record: 1 Book

The Doctor's Case - *Pastiche 1*
Carroll & Graf US (1987); Arlington UK (1988)

Ronald A KNOX 1888-1957 (British)

Invented 4 detectives - see Miles BREDON

Citation Record: 1 Selected Short Story

The Adventure Of The First-Class Carriage - *Pastiche 1*
appeared first in the February number and is included in the anthology, *THE FURTHER ADVENTURES OF SHERLOCK HOLMES* (Editor; *Richard Lancelyn GREEN*).
In 'Strand Magazine' UK (1947)

Michael KURLAND 1938- (American)

Invented 3 detectives - see Peter CARTHAGE

Citation Record: 2 Books

The Infernal Device - *Pastiche 1*
Signet US (1979); New English Library UK (1979)

Death By Gaslight - *Pastiche 2*
Signet US (1982)

Michael LAMBE

Citation Record: 1 Book

The Private Lives Of Sherlock Holmes - *Pastiche 1*
is a play.
New Playwrights ? (1988)

Willoughby LANE (American)

See main detective BILLY THE PAGE

Citation Record: 2 Books

Sherlock Holmes And The Wood Green Empire Mystery - *Pastiche 1*
Magico Press US (1985)

Sherlock Holmes And The London Zoo Mystery - *Pastiche 2*
Magico Press US (1987)

Henry LEDGARD and Andrew SINGER (American)

Citation Record: 1 Book

Elementary Pascal - *Pastiche 1*
is a serious introduction to computer language in which *Dr WATSON* asks the questions and *Sherlock HOLMES* provides the answers.
Vintage Books US (1982)

F Andrew LESLIE 1927- (American)

Writer: Frank Andrew LESLIE

Citation Record: 1 Book

The Hound Of The Baskervilles - *Pastiche 1*
is a two-act play based on the canonical story of the same title.
Dramatists US (1977)

Anthony LEWIS

Citation Record: 1 Selected Short Story

The Adventure Of The Illegal Alien - *Pastiche 1*
is set in the future, when the great detective is still having to circumvent dastardly attempts on his life by Professor Moriarty. The story is in the anthology, *SHERLOCK HOLMES IN ORBIT* (Editors; *Mike RESNICK and Martin H GREENBERG*).
Daw US (1995)

Fritz LIEBER

Citation Record: 1 Selected Short Story

The Moriarty Gambit - *Pastiche 1*
In which *Sherlock HOLMES* tells *Dr WATSON* how he defeated Moriarty in the London International Chess Tournament of 1883.
Chess Review ? (1962)

Gerald LIENTZ (American)

Citation Record: 5 Books

Death At Appledore Towers - *Pastiche 1*
A book of games.
Berkley US (1987)

Murder At The Diogenes Club - *Pastiche 2*
A book of games.
Berkley US (1987)

The Crown Vs Dr Watson - *Pastiche 3*
A book of games.
Berkley US (1988)

The Honor Of The Yorkshire Light Artillery - *Pastiche 4*
A book of games.
Berkley US (1988)

The Lost Heir - *Pastiche 5*
A book of games.
Berkley US (1988)

Herman Anthony LITZINGER (American)

Citation Record: 10 Short Stories in 1 Collection

Traveling With Sherlock Holmes And Dr Watson - *Pastiche Collection 1*
The individual stories are cited immediately below.

The Chapel Bell At Derby Drabbs - *Pastiche 1*

A Hidden Masterpiece In Westminster - *Pastiche 2*

The Midnight Sonata At Colliers End - *Pastiche 3*

The Night At The Lighthouse Inn On The Beach At Blackpool - *Pastiche 4*

The Night In The Asylum At Torrence - *Pastiche 5*

The Night In The Burial Vault Under The Sanitarium At Soames Meadow - *Pastiche 6*

The Night In The Elizabethan Concert Hall In The Very Heart Of London - *Pastiche 7*

The Night In The Wax Museum At Llangollen - *Pastiche 8*

A Treasure From Treasure Island - *Pastiche 9*

The Wolfman At Milburn - *Pastiche 10*

A LLOYD-TAYLOR

Citation Record: 1 Selected Short Story

The Wine Merchant: A Hitherto Unpublished Case Of Sherlock Holmes As Recorded By Dr Watson -*Pastiche 1*
In 'Sherlock Holmes Journal' UK (1959)

J LOVISI

Citation Record: 1 Book

The Grey Nun Legacy - *Pastiche 1*
Gryphon UK (1992)

John LUTZ 1939- (American)

Invented 5 detectives - see Fred CARVER

Citation Record: 1 Selected Short Story

The Infernal Machine - *Pastiche 1*
In which the great detective encounters the invention of the Gatling gun and broods on the future of mankind. It appears in *THE NEW ADVENTURES OF SHERLOCK HOLMES* (Editors; *Martin H GREENBERG and Carol-Lynn Rossel WAUGH).*
Carroll & Graf US (1987)

Bohun LYNCH and Reginald BERKELEY (British)

Writers: John Gilbert Bohun LYNCH 1884- and Reginald Cheyne BERKELEY 1890-

Citation Record: 1 Selected Short Story

The Adventure Of The Chuckle-Headed Doctor: A Positively Final Story Of Sherlock Holmes - *Pastiche 1*
appeared in an anthology, *Decorations and Absurdities.* Many pastiche and parody writers have threatened to kill off *Sherlock HOLMES*, something that even *Sir Arthur Conan DOYLE* failed to do.
Collins UK (1923)

W R Duncan MACMILLAN (British)

Citation Record: 1 Selected Short Story

Holmes In Scotland - *Pastiche 1*
appeared first in the magazine's September number. The story is based on the allusion made by *Dr WATSON* in the canonical story, *THE ADVENTURE OF THE VEILED LODGER*, to an unchronicled case concerning 'the politician, the lighthouse and the trained cormorant'. The story is included in the anthology, *THE FURTHER ADVENTURES OF SHERLOCK HOLMES* (Editor; *Richard Lancelyn GREEN*), where it is, indeed, retitled *The Adventure of the Trained Cormorant.* For further information on the origin of the title, see *THE POLITICIAN, LIGHTHOUSE AND TRAINED CORMORANT,* written by *Clive BROOKS.*
In 'Blackwood's Magazine' UK (1953)

Brinsley MACNAMARA (Irish)

Writer: A E WELDON

Citation Record: 1 Selected Short Story

The Man Who Knew Sherlock Holmes - *Pastiche 1*
is in the author's collection of short stories, *Some Curious People.*
Talbot EI (1945)

Bill MAJESKI 1927-

Writer: William MAJESKI

Citation Record: 1 Book

The Very Great Grandson Of Sherlock Holmes - *Pastiche 1*
is a three-act play.
Dramatic ? (1976)

Richard MALLETT 1910- (British)

Citation Record: 5 Selected Short Stories

The Case Of The Pearls - *Pastiche 1*

appeared in the November 21 number.

In 'Punch' UK (1934)

The Case Of The Pursuit - *Pastiche 2*

appeared in the January 23 number.

In 'Punch' UK (1934)

The Case Of The Traveller - *Pastiche 3*

appeared in the December 26 number.

In 'Punch' UK (1934)

The Case Of The Diabolical Plot - *Pastiche 4*

appeared first in the magazine's June 12 number. It is also in the anthology, *THE MISADVENTURES OF SHERLOCK HOLMES* (Editor; *Ellery QUEEN*).

In 'Punch' UK (1935)

The Case Of The Impersonation - *Pastiche 5*

appeared in the May 8 number.

In 'Punch' UK (1935)

H

Charles MAROWITZ

Citation Record: 1 Collection

Sherlock's Last Case - *Pastiche 1*

is a two-act play.

Dramatists US (1984)

J C MASTERMAN 1891-1877 (British)

See main detective Ernst BRENDEL

Citation Record: 1 Selected Short Story

The Case Of The Gifted Amateur - *Pastiche 1*

In 'MacKills Mystery Magazine' US (1952)

Miles MASTERS

is the author of a *Sherlock HOLMES* pastiche that won joint First Prize (see also under the author, *François Paulus CILLIE*) in a *Sunday Times of South Africa* competition, which asked entrants to submit a pastiche based on the canonical story, *THE ADVENTURE OF THE SECOND STAIN*, which *Dr WATSON* said he had been hesitant about publishing and which Sherlockians consider must refer to three different cases.

Citation Record: 1 Selected Short Story

The Adventure Of The Second Stain - *Pastiche 1*

bears the same title as the canonical story by *Sir Arthur Conan DOYLE* .

In 'Sunday Times News Magazine' SA (1967)

Lee A MATTHIAS (American)

Citation Record: 1 Book

The Pandora Plague - *Pastiche 1*

Leisure Books US (1981)

Robert MAURO

Citation Record: 2 Books

Elementary, My Dear Holmes - *Pastiche 1*

is a play.

Hanbury UK (1986)

Sherlock Holmes And A Near Case Of Murder - *Pastiche 2*

is a play.

Bakers ? (1983)

Stanley MCCOMAS (American)

Citation Record: 1 Selected Short Story

The Case Of The Crazy Americans - *Pastiche 1*

appeared in an anthology, *Illustrious Client's Second Casebook* (Editor; *J N WILLIAMSON*).

In 'The Illustrious Clients' US (1948)

Vonda N MCINTYRE

Citation Record: 1 Selected Short Story

The Adventure Of The Field Theorems - *Pastiche 1*

In which the great detective takes on *Sir Arthur Conan DOYLE* as a client, the latter wanting him to investigate mysterious happenings, apparently in outer space. The story is in the anthology, *SHERLOCK HOLMES IN ORBIT* (Editors; *Mike RESNICK and Martin H GREENBERG*).

Daw US (1995)

Russell MCLAUCHLIN (American)

Citation Record: 1 Selected Short Story

The Adventure Of The Paradol Chamber - *Pastiche 1*

refers to the allusion made by *Dr WATSON* in the canonical story, *THE FIVE ORANGE PIPS*, to an unchronicled case of 1887, of which he gives no details. Other authors have used the allusion as the basis for a pastiche or parody.

In 'Baker Street Journal' US (1965)

Nicholas MEYER 1945- (American)

Invented 3 detectives - see Mark BRILL

Citation Record: 2 Books

The West End Horror - *Pastiche 1*

HOLMES almost certainly was well acquainted with the London theatre and, as a young man, may have been an actor. In this pastiche novel he has to deal with ferocious murders in theatreland.

Dutton US (1976); Hodder & Stoughton UK (1976)

The Canary Trainer - *Pastiche 2*

purports to tell of an unchronicled case in the canon that took place during the years of 'The Great Hiatus', 1891-1894, when *Sherlock HOLMES* was presumed dead. In the canonical story, *THE ADVENTURE OF THE EMPTY HOUSE*, in which all manner of reasons are given for the great detective's disappearance, it is said that for part of the time he was in France, although many Sherlockians have disputed the evidence for that. However, *Nicholas MEYER's* story suggests that the detective was, in fact, tracking down the Phantom of the Opera in Paris, getting mixed up, yet again, with '*the* woman', *Irene ADLER*. The title of the pastiche pays distant homage to the allusion made by *Dr WATSON* in the canonical story, *THE ADVENTURE OF BLACK PETER*, to 'the arrest of Wilson, the notorious canary-trainer, which removed a plague-spot from the East End of London'. Other authors have used the allusion as the basis for a pastiche or parody.

Norton US (1993)

W F MIKSCH (American)

Citation Record: 1 Selected Short Story

The Singular Case Of The Plural Twosome - *Pastiche 1*

is one of several pastiches by writers who like to imagine *Dr WATSON* out-deducing *Sherlock HOLMES*.

In 'Collier's Magazine' US (1951)

Roy S MILLER (British)

Citation Record: 2 Selected Short Stories

The Truth At Last: An Authentic Case Of Some Baker Street Irregularities - *Pastiche 1*

In which *Dr WATSON* complains about *Sherlock HOLMES* and confesses that, in fact, he hardly knew the fellow.

Courier UK (1963)

Inspector Lestrade Lets The Cat Out Of The Bag - *Pastiche 2*

The venerable stooge himself is the hero of the piece.

In 'London Mystery Selection' UK (1967)

Thomas Kent MILLER

Citation Record: 1 Book

Sherlock Holmes On The Roof Of The World; Or, The Adventure Of The Wayfaring God - *Pastiche 1*

Rosemill ? (1989)

A A MILNE 1882-1956 (British)

See main detective Anthony GILLINGHAM

Citation Record: 1 Selected Short Story

The Rape Of The Sherlock - *Pastiche 1*

An early piece by a great English writer, but one for which there is little information.

In 'Vanity Fair' UK (?)

Angela MILNE (British)

Citation Record: 1 Selected Short Story

The Postmaster-General: A Further Adventure Of Sherlock Holmes - *Pastiche 1*

appeared in the November 1 number.

In 'Punch' UK (1967)

Austin MITCHELSON and Nicholas UTECHIN (American)

Citation Record: 2 Books

The Earthquake Machine - *Pastiche 1*
Belmont US (1976)

Sherlock Holmes And The Hellbirds - *Pastiche 2*
Belmont US (1976)

Roberts MORGAN (American)

Citation Record: 1 Book

Spotlight On A Simple Case; Or, Wiggins, Who Was That Horse I Saw You With Last Night? - *Pastiche 1*
The 'Wiggins' of this oddly-titled story may allude to the apparent head of *HOLMES'* Baker Street Irregulars, who appears in *A STUDY IN SCARLET.*
Cedar Tree US (1959)

R L MUNKITTRICK

Citation Record: 1 Selected Short Story

The Sign Of The '400': Being A Continuation Of The Adventures Of Sherlock Holmes - *Pastiche 1*
It is one the most remarkable features of literary history that, such was the impact of *Sherlock HOLMES,* several writers were already producing pastiches and parodies in the early 1890s and already setting the trend for using or parodying the canonical titles. This early example, which parodies the canonical novel of 1890, *THE SIGN OF FOUR,* is also to be found in *THE MISADVENTURES OF SHERLOCK HOLMES* (Editor: *Ellery QUEEN).*
In 'Puck' ? (1894)

Terence MUSTOO

Citation Record: 1 Book

The Deerstalker - *Pastiche 1*
is a two-act musical play.
Henry UK (1985)

Carl MUUSMANN 1863-1936 (Danish)

Writer: Carl Quistgaard MUUSMANN

Citation Record: 1 Selected Short Story

Sherlock Holmes At Elsinore - *Pastiche 1*
Baker Street Irregulars US (1956)

Sena Jeter NASLUND (American)

is a sometime teacher at the University of Louisville.

Citation Record: 1 Book

Sherlock In Love - *Pastiche 1*
has all the canonical characters appearing in a story that purports to chronicle the details of the sage's one true love. It has a real mystery story thrown in.
Godine US (1993)

John NASSIVERA 1950-

Citation Record: 1 Book

The Penultimate Problem Of Sherlock Holmes - *Pastiche 1*
is a play.
French UK (1980)

Jack NIMERSSHEIM (American)

Citation Record: 1 Selected Short Story

Moriarty By Modem - *Pastiche 1*
is set in the future, when the struggle between *Sherlock HOLMES* and Professor Moriarty is continued by computer technology. The story is in the anthology, *SHERLOCK HOLMES IN ORBIT* (Editors: *Mike RESNICK and Martin H GREENBERG*).
Daw US (1995)

Margaret NORRIS

Citation Record: 1 Selected Short Story

A Case Of Identities - *Pastiche 1*
appeared in the April number.
In 'Ellery Queen's Mystery Magazine' US (1966)

John NORTH (British)

Citation Record: 2 Books

Sherlock Holmes And The Arabian Princess - *Pastiche 1*
is a novel based on the musical play, *THE DEERSTALKER.*
Ian Henry UK (1990)

Sherlock Holmes And The German Nanny - *Pastiche 2*
Ian Henry UK (1990); Ian Henry US (1991)

Graham NOWN (American)

Citation Record: 1 Book

Elementary, My Dear Watson - *Pastiche 1*
Salem US (1986)

A E P

Citation Record: 1 Selected Short Story

The End Of Sherlock Holmes - *Pastiche 1*
In which the great detective falls foul of a three-year-old prodigy, who happens to be his own son. The story first appeared in the newspaper, the *Manchester Guardian,* July 7, and is also in the anthology, *THE MISADVENTURES OF SHERLOCK HOLMES* (Editor: *Ellery QUEEN).*
Manchester Guardian UK (1927)

Stuart PALMER 1905-1968 (American)

Invented 3 detectives - see Hildegarde WITHERS

Citation Record: 2 Selected Short Stories

The Adventure Of The Remarkable Worm - *Pastiche 1*
refers to the allusion made by *Dr WATSON* in the canonical story, *THE PROBLEM OF THOR BRIDGE,* to the case of 'Isadora Persano, the well-known journalist and duellist, who was found stark staring mad with a matchbox in front of him which contained a remarkable worm, said to be unknown to science'. It appeared first in the anthology, *THE MISADVENTURES OF SHERLOCK HOLMES* (Editor: *Ellery QUEEN).* Other authors have used the allusion as the basis for a pastiche or parody.
Little, Brown US (1944)

The Adventure Of The Marked Man - *Pastiche 2*
appeared in the July number and can also be found in *THE FURTHER ADVENTURES OF SHERLOCK HOLMES* (Editor: *Richard Lancelyn GREEN*). More recently it has appeared in the author's book, published by *Aspen* (US 1973), *THE ADVENTURE OF THE MARKED MAN AND ONE OTHER.*
In 'Ellery Queen's Mystery Magazine' US (1944)

Jeremy PAUL (British)

Citation Record: 1 Book

The Secret Of Sherlock Holmes - *Pastiche 1*
Ian Henry UK (1989)

Gilbert PEARLMAN (American)

Citation Record: 1 Book

The Adventure Of Sherlock Holmes' Smarter Brother - *Pastiche 1*
Ballantine US (1975); Futura UK (1977)

Ronald PEARSALL 1927- (British)

Citation Record: 1 Book

Sherlock Holmes Investigates The Murder In Euston Square - *Pastiche 1*
David & Charles UK (1989)

Edmund PEARSON 1880-1937 (American)

Writer: Edmund Lester PEARSON

Citation Record: 1 Book 2 Short Stories in 1 Collection

Sherlock Holmes And The Drood Mystery - *Pastiche 1*
Aspen US (1973)

The Adventure Of The Lost Manuscripts, And One Other - *Pastiche Collection 1*
The individual stories are cited immediately below.
Short stories - 2
Aspen US (1974)

The Adventure Of The Lost Manuscripts - *Pastiche 1*

Help! Help! Sherlock! - *Pastiche 2*

S J PERELMAN 1904-1979 (American)

See main detective Mike NOONAN

Citation Record: 1 Selected Short Story

The Affair Of The Razor's Edge - *Pastiche 1*
appeared in the January number.
In 'Diplomat Magazine' US (1966)

Rohase PIERCY (American)

Citation Record: 1 Selected Short Story

My Dearest Holmes - *Pastiche 1*
GMP UK (1988)

H Beam PIPER 1904-1964 and John J M MCGUIRE (American)

Citation Record: 1 Selected Short Story

The Return - *Pastiche 1*
appeared in the January number. It relates how, after an atomic war in the twenty-second century, the shades of *Sherlock HOLMES* and *Dr WATSON* return to pervade a new religion that is sweeping through what remains of humanity and to whose disciples they have become reverential images.
In 'Astounding Science Fiction' US (1954)

Arthur PORGES (American)

Invented 13 detectives - see Arsène LUPIN

Citation Record: 1 Selected Short Story

The Singular Affair Of The Aluminium Crutch - *Pastiche 1*
is in the author's collection, *THREE PORGES PARODIES AND A PASTICHE*. The title refers to the allusion made by *Sherlock HOLMES* in the canonical story, *THE MUSGRAVE RITUAL*, to a case he had undertaken before his meeting with *Dr WATSON*, 'the singular affair of the aluminium crutch. Other authors have used the allusion as the basis for a pastiche or parody.
Magico Press US (1988)

H

Bill PRONZINI 1943- (American)

Invented 5 detectives - see NAMELESS DETECTIVE

Citation Record: 1 Selected Short Story

Who's Afraid Of Sherlock Holmes? - *Pastiche 1*
appeared in the April number.
In 'Mike Shayne Mystery Magazine' US (1968)

Ellery QUEEN (American)

House writer for 3 detectives - see Barney BURGESS

Citation Record: 1 Book 1 Selected Short Story 33 Short Stories in 1 Collection

A Study In Terror - *Pastiche 1*
is a novelization of a screenplay, which pits *Sherlock HOLMES* against the famous British serial killer of 1888, Jack The Ripper, with surprising results. Other authors have been intrigued by the proximity of the murders and the date of the great detective's first appearance and have used it as the basis for a pastiche or parody.
Lancer US (1966)

Sherlock Holmes Versus Jack The Ripper - *Pastiche 1**
Gollancz UK (1967)

The Disappearance Of Mr James Phillimore - *Pastiche 2*
refers to the allusion made by *Dr WATSON* in the canonical story, *THE PROBLEM OF THOR BRIDGE*, to an unchronicled case concerning 'Mr James Phillimore, who, stepping back into his own house to get his umbrella, was never more seen in this world'. The pastiche, in the form of a short play, first appeared in the author's classic anthology, *THE MISADVENTURES OF SHERLOCK HOLMES* (Editor: *Ellery QUEEN*). It is updated to New York in the 1940s and it is the grandson of the original Mr Phillimore who disappears. Furthermore, although it is the author's own brilliant detective, *Ellery QUEEN*, who solves the mystery, it is made clear that *Sherlock HOLMES* is present 'in spirit'. Other authors have used the allusion as the basis for a pastiche or parody.
Little, Brown US (1944)

The Misadventures Of Sherlock Holmes - *Pastiche Anthology 1*
remains a classic. The product of indefatigable research, this was one of the earliest attempts to collect the best examples of the then extant *Sherlock HOLMES* pastiches. Justly famous and of the highest quality, the anthology is an indispensable source for researchers into Sherlockiana. The individual stories are cited under the appropriate authors.
Little, Brown US (1944)

Chris REDMOND

Citation Record: 1 Selected Short Story

The Tale Of Copperella - *Pastiche 1*
was published by the author.
Redmond ? (1985)

Laura RESNICK (American)

Citation Record: 1 Selected Short Story

The Adventure Of The Missing Coffin - *Pastiche 1*
In which a late-night visitor to Baker Street tells of a missing coffin and seems to bear a close resemblance to Count Dracula. The story is in the anthology, *SHERLOCK HOLMES IN ORBIT* (Editors: *Mike RESNICK and Martin H GREENBERG*).
Daw US (1995)

Mike RESNICK and Martin H GREENBERG (American)

are the editors of the cited anthology

Writers: Michael Diamond RESNICK 1942- and Martin Harry Greenberg

Citation Record: 26 Short Stories in 1 Collection

Sherlock Holmes In Orbit - *Pastiche Anthology 1*
contains twenty-six specially written pastiches, set in various times, from the 1880s to the far distant future. They present the great detective as he was, will be and even after death, while remaining true to the spirit of the canonical stories, to which frequent allusion is made. The individual stories are cited under the appropriate authors.
Daw US (1995)

Mack REYNOLDS (American)

See main detective Rex BADER

Citation Record: 1 Selected Short Story

The Adventure Of The Extraterrestrial - *Pastiche 1*

Maurice RICHARDSON

Citation Record: 1 Selected Short Story

The Last Detective Story In The World - *Pastiche 1*
appeared in the February number. It describes yet another 'final battle' between *Sherlock HOLMES* and Professor Moriarty.
In 'Ellery Queen's Mystery Magazine' US (1947)

Robert RICHARDSON 1940- (British)

See main detective Augustus MALTRAVERS

Citation Record: 1 Book

The Attwater Firewitch - *Pastiche 1*
The author not only ingeniously involves the great detective in the discovery of an unknown story by *Sir Arthur Conan DOYLE* (his own creator), but gives that story, complete, in the novel. It is, in its own right, a most entertaining addition to the pastiche bibliography and deserves to be noted as such.
Gollancz UK (1989)

Barrie ROBERTS (British)

Citation Record: 1 Book

Sherlock Holmes And The Railway Maniac - *Pastiche 1*
A fiend is responsible for a series of railway disasters and the police are at their wits' ends. At the request of his brother, *Sherlock HOLMES* emerges from his retirement in Sussex to deal with the matter. The game's afoot, once more!
Constable UK (1994)

Ralph ROBERTS

Citation Record: 1 Selected Short Story

The Greatest Detective Of All Time - *Pastiche 1*
is set at some time in the future, when the great detective circumvents a highly technical trap set for him by Professor Moriarty. The story is in the anthology, *SHERLOCK HOLMES IN ORBIT* (Editors: *Mike RESNICK and Martin H GREENBERG*).
Daw US (1995)

S C ROBERTS 1887- (British)

Writer: Sidney Castle ROBERTS

Citation Record: 4 Selected Short Stories

Christmas Eve: An Unrecorded Adventure Of Sherlock Holmes - *Pastiche 1*
is a short playlet that first appeared in an edition limited to one hundred copies and privately printed by Cambridge University Press in 1936. The story tells how, on Christmas Eve, the great detective not only solves a crime but actually pardons a sinner. It is to be found in *THE MISADVENTURES OF SHERLOCK HOLMES* (Editor; *Ellery QUEEN).*
Privately printed (1936)

The Strange Case Of The Megatherium Thefts - *Pastiche 2*
was privately printed in 1945 in an edition limited to 125 copies and appeared in the author's book, *Holmes and Watson: A Miscellany* (*Oxford University Press*; UK 1953). It is included in the anthology, *THE FURTHER ADVENTURES OF SHERLOCK HOLMES* (Editor; *Richard Lancelyn GREEN*), where the title has been changed to *The Adventure of the Megatherium Thefts*, bringing it into concordance with the titles of most of the canonical stories.
In 'Sherlock Holmes Journal' UK (1945)

The Death Of Cardinal Tosca - *Pastiche 3*
appeared first in the June number of the *Sherlock Holmes Journal* and was included in the author's book, *Holmes and Watson: A Miscellany* (*Oxford University Press*; UK 1953). The title refers to the allusion made by *Dr WATSON* in the canonical tale, *THE ADVENTURE OF BLACK PETER,* to an unchronicled case concerning 'the sudden death of Cardinal Tosca', which *Sherlock HOLMES* had investigated in 1895 'at the express desire of his Holiness the Pope'. Other authors have used the allusion as the basis for a pastiche or parody.
In 'Sherlock Holmes Journal' UK (1953)

The Missing Quarto - *Pastiche 4*
appeared in the Spring number. It relates how the great detective is called on to recover a rare copy of a Shakespearean play.
In 'Sherlock Holmes Journal' UK (1963)

Frank M ROBINSON

Citation Record: 1 Selected Short Story

The Phantom Of The Barbary Coast - *Pastiche 1*
In which the detective is asked by his brother, *Mycroft HOLMES*, to go to San Francisco to investigate the disappearance of a talented singer, who turns out to be the sister of *Irene ADLER*, the only woman who had ever bested him (see the canonical story, *A SCANDAL IN BOHEMIA).* The story is in the anthology, *SHERLOCK HOLMES IN ORBIT* (Editors; *Mike RESNICK and Martin H GREENBERG*).
Daw US (1995)

Dennis ROSA

Citation Record: 1 Book

Sherlock Holmes And The Curse Of The Sign Of Four; Or, 'The Mark Of Timber Toe' - *Pastiche 1*
is a play based on *THE SIGN OF FOUR* by *Sir Arthur Conan DOYLE.*
Dramatists US (1975)

Pat ROSENKJAR (American)

Citation Record: 2 Selected Short Stories

The Adventure Of The Persecuted Millionaire - *Pastiche 1*
appeared in the December number. It refers to the allusion made by *Dr WATSON* in the canonical story, *THE ADVENTURE OF THE SOLITARY CYCLIST,* to a case in 1895, 'a very abstruse and complicated problem concerning the peculiar persecution to which John Vincent Harden, the well-known tobacco millionaire, had been subjected'.
In 'Studies in Scarlet' US (1965)

The Little Affair Of The Vatican Cameos - *Pastiche 2*
appeared in the August number.
In 'Baker Street Pages' US (1969)

Anne Oakins ROSSO

Citation Record: 1 Selected Short Story

The Adventure Of The Tired Housewife - *Pastiche 1*
La Crosse US (1952)

Peter ROWLAND (British)

Citation Record: 1 Book

The Disappearance Of Edwin Drood - *Pastiche 1*
In which the great man attempts to solve one of literature's great mysteries.
Constable UK (1991)

Kristine Kathryn RUSCH (American)

Citation Record: 1 Selected Short Story

Second Fiddle - *Pastiche 1*
Holmes in the 1990s, seems to be operating as a PI in the United States. The story is in the anthology, *SHERLOCK HOLMES IN ORBIT* (Editors; *Mike RESNICK and Martin H GREENBERG*).
Daw US (1995)

Gary Alan RUSE 1946- (American)

Citation Record: 2 Selected Short Stories

The Phantom Chamber - *Pastiche 1*
In which the great detective investigates some strange happenings at an English country house. It is included in *THE NEW ADVENTURES OF SHERLOCK HOLMES* (Editors; *Martin H GREENBERG and Carol-Lynn Rossel WAUGH).*
Carroll & Graf US (1987)

The Holmes Team Advantage - *Pastiche 2*
In which the great detective runs into a bizarre case of people cloning. The story is in the anthology, *SHERLOCK HOLMES IN ORBIT* (Editors; *Mike RESNICK and Martin H GREENBERG*).
(1995)

Howard M SABERHAGEN 1928- (American)

Writer: Howard Morley SABERHAGEN

Citation Record: 1 Book

The Holmes-Dracula File - *Pastiche 1*
Ace US (1978)

Paula SALO (American)

Citation Record: 2 Selected Short Stories

The Adventure Of The Giant Rat Of Sumatra - *Pastiche 1*
appeared in a privately printed collection, *West By One And By One*. The title of the pastiche refers to the allusion made by *Dr WATSON* in the canonical story, *THE ADVENTURE OF THE SUSSEX VAMPIRE,* to an unchronicled case concerning 'the giant rat of Sumatra, a story for which the world is not yet prepared'. Other authors have used the allusion as the basis for a pastiche or parody.
Privately printed (1965)

The Caper Of The Politician, The Lighthouse, And Trained Cormorant - *Pastiche 2*
first appeared in a private collection, *West By One And By One*. The title oth this pastiche refers to the allusion made by *Dr WATSON* in the canonical story, *THE ADVENTURE OF THE VEILED LODGER,* to an unchronicled case. For further information on the derivation of the title, see *THE POLITICIAN, LIGHTHOUSE AMD TRAINED CORMORANT,* written by *Clive BROOKS*. Other authors have used the allusion as the basis for a pastiche or parody.
Privately printed (1965)

Robert J SAWYER (American)

Citation Record: 1 Selected Short Story

You See But You Do Not Observe - *Pastiche 1*
In which the detective travels two centuries into the future, so that he can resolve some of the great mysteries of physics, including the paradox of Schrodinger's cat! The title refers to the famous remark made by *HOLMES* to *Dr WATSON* in the canonical story, *A SCANDAL IN BOHEMIA.* The story is in the anthology, *SHERLOCK HOLMES IN ORBIT* (Editors; *Mike RESNICK and Martin H GREENBERG*).
Daw US (1995)

Lawrence SCHIMEL

Citation Record: 1 Selected Short Story

Alimentary, My Dear Watson - *Pastiche 1*
In which the great detective becomes rather too mixed up with characters from *Alice in Wonderland.* The story is in the anthology, *SHERLOCK HOLMES IN ORBIT* (Editors; *Mike RESNICK and Martin H GREENBERG*).
Daw US (1995)

Crighton SELLERS (American)
Citation Record: 1 Selected Short Story
The Dilemma Of The Distressed Savoyard - *Pastiche 1*
appeared in the October number. Surprisingly perhaps, there is no mention in the canon of the Gilbert and Sullivan comic operas running at the Savoy Theatre in London contemporaneously.
In 'Baker Street Journal (Old Series)' US (1946)

Jay SHAKLEY (Canadian)
Citation Record: 3 Short Stories in 1 Collection
The Villars-Manningham Papers And Other Stories Of Sherlock Holmes - *Pastiche Collection 1*
The individual stories are cited immediately below.
Catalyst CA (1978)
The Shred Of Lace - *Pastiche 1*
The Strange Death Of The Heir Apparent - *Pastiche 2*
The Villars-Manningham Papers - *Pastiche 3*

Stephen A SHALET (American)
Citation Record: 1 Selected Short Story
The Adventure Of The Three Golden Chessmen - *Pastiche 1*
appeared in the September number.
In 'Baker Street Journal' US (1961)

Allen SHARP (British)
See main detective Spencer HOLMES
Citation Record: 11 Books
The Unsolved Case Of Sherlock Holmes - *Pastiche 1*
Storytrails UK (1984)
The Meyringen Papers - *Pastiche 2*
Storytrails UK (1986)
The Case Of The Dancing Bees - *Pastiche 3*
Storytrails UK (1987)
The Case Of The Baffled Policemen - *Pastiche 4*
Cambridge University UK (1989)
The Case Of The Devil's Hoofmarks - *Pastiche 5*
Cambridge University UK (1989)
The Case Of The Frightened Heiress - *Pastiche 6*
Cambridge University UK (1989)
The Case Of The Gentle Conspirators - *Pastiche 7*
Cambridge University UK (1989)
The Case Of The Buchanan Curse - *Pastiche 8*
Cambridge University UK (1990)
The Case Of The Howling Dog - *Pastiche 9*
Cambridge University UK (1990)
The Case Of The Man Who Followed Himself - *Pastiche 10*
Cambridge University UK (1990)
The Case Of The Silent Canary - *Pastiche 11*
Cambridge University UK (1990)

Luke SHARP 1850-1912 (British)
See main detective Sherlaw KOMBS
Citation Record: 1 Selected Short Story
The Adventure Of The Second Swag - *Pastiche 1*
is a recent publication, under a punning pseudonym, of an early, previously unpublished pastiche by the author of several early *Sherlock HOLMES* parodies. Its title parodies that of the canonical story, *THE ADVENTURE OF THE SECOND STAIN.*
Ferret Fantasy UK (1990)

Stanley SHAW (British)
Citation Record: 2 Books
Sherlock Holmes Meets Annie Oakley - *Pastiche 1*
It is 1897 and the legendary American sharpshooter is on a visit to London. She has a problem for the great man.
Allen UK (1986); Magico Press US (1986)
Sherlock Holmes At The 1902 Fifth Test - *Pastiche 2*
The English cricket team is in serious trouble in this match against the visiting Australians.
Allen UK (1985); Magico Press US (1986)

Josepha SHERMAN
Citation Record: 1 Selected Short Story
The Case Of The Purloined L'isitek - *Pastiche 1*
is set in the far future, somewhere in space. The story is in the anthology, *SHERLOCK HOLMES IN ORBIT* (Editors; *Mike RESNICK and Martin H GREENBERG*).
Daw US (1995)

Floyd SHERROD
Citation Record: 1 Book
The Secret Adventure Of The Thoroughbred Ghost - *Pastiche 1*
Privately printed (1972)

Sam SICILANO
Citation Record: 1 Book
The Angel Of The Opera - *Pastiche 1*
Simon & Schuster Us (1994)

John SIKORSKI (American)
Citation Record: 1 Selected Short Story
The Adventure Of The Five Green Gasogenes - *Pastiche 1*
In 'Sidelights on Holmes' US (1968)

D O SMITH 1948- (British)
Writer: Dennis O SMITH
Citation Record: 4 Books 1 Selected Short Story
The Adventure Of The Purple Hand - *Pastiche 1*
was originally privately printed. It is included in the anthology, *THE FURTHER ADVENTURES OF SHERLOCK HOLMES* (Editor; *Richard Lancelyn GREEN*).
Privately printed (1982)
The Adventure Of The Christmas Visitor - *Pastiche 2*
Diogenes UK (1985)
The Adventure Of The Unseen Traveler - *Pastiche 3*
Diogenes UK (1983)
The Adventure Of The Zodiac Plate - *Pastiche 4*
Diogenes UK (1984)
The Secret Of Shoreswood Hall - *Pastiche 5*
Diogenes UK (1985)

Dean Wesley SMITH (American)
Citation Record: 1 Selected Short Story
Two Roads, No Choices - *Pastiche 1*
In which the great detective is involved with a time switch in which the sinking of the Titanic might or might not have occurred. The story is in the anthology, *SHERLOCK HOLMES IN ORBIT* (Editors; *Mike RESNICK and Martin H GREENBERG*).
Daw US (1995)

George Hudson SMITH (American)
Citation Record: 1 Selected Short Story
The Adventure Of The Wrong Time - *Pastiche 1*
In 'Famous Detective Stories' US (1955)

George H SMITH 1922- (American)
Writer: George Henry SMITH
Citation Record: 1 Book
The Second War Of Worlds - *Pastiche 1*
The action takes place at some time in the future.
Daw US (1978)

P SMITH
Citation Record: 1 Book
The Loss Of The British Bark, Sophy Anderson - *Pastiche 1*
refers to the allusion made by *Dr WATSON* in the canonical story, *THE FIVE ORANGE PIPS*, to an unchronicled case of 1887.
Gryphon UK (1992)

Raymond SMULLYAN 1919- (American)
Writer: Raymond Merrill SMULLYAN
Citation Record: 1 Book
The Chess Mysteries Of Sherlock Holmes - *Pastiche 1*
chess problems with a linking *Sherlock HOLMES* narrative.
Knopf US (1979); Hutchinson UK (1979)

Vincent STARRETT 1886-1974 (American)

Invented 6 detectives - see Jimmie LAVENDER

Citation Record: 2 Selected Short Stories

The Adventure Of The Unique Hamlet - *Pastiche 1*

is one of the truly great *Sherlock HOLMES* pastiches. Privately printed for the author in 1920, it has since appeared in several anthologies, including *THE MISADVENTURES OF SHERLOCK HOLMES* (Editor; *Ellery QUEEN*) and *THE FURTHER ADVENTURES OF SHERLOCK HOLMES* (Editor; *Richard Lancelyn GREEN*).

Privately printed (1920)

Monologue In Baker Street - *Pastiche 2*

In 'Baker Street Journal' US (1956)

Frederic Dorr STEELE (American)

was the most eminent of the American illustrators of the *Sherlock HOLMES* stories.

Citation Record: 3 Selected Short Stories

The Adventure Of The Missing Hatrack: A Story Of Mr Sherlock Holmes - *Pastiche 1*

appeared in the October number. It was republished in the December 1963 number of the *Baker Street Journal.*

In 'The Players Bulletin' US (1926)

The Attempted Murder Of Malcolm Duncan: A Reminiscence Of Mr Sherlock Holmes - *Pastiche 2*

appeared in the June number.

In 'The Players Bulletin' US (1932)

The Adventure Of The Murdered Art Editor: A Reminiscence Of Mr Sherlock Holmes - *Pastiche 3*

appeared first in an anthology, *Spoofs*, edited by Richard Butler Glaenzer. It is also in the anthology, *THE MISADVENTURES OF SHERLOCK HOLMES* (Editor; *Ellery QUEEN*).

McBride US (1933)

Shane STEVENS 1941- (American)

Citation Record: 1 Selected Short Story

The Final Adventure - *Pastiche 1*

appeared in the February number.

In 'Ellery Queen's Mystery Magazine' US (1969)

Ian STEWART (American)

Citation Record: 1 Selected Short Story

The Great Drain Robbery - *Pastiche 1*

is one of the monthly 'mathematical recreations' for which the magazine is justly famous. Trenchant deductions by the great detective find the shortest way round a circle.

In 'Scientific American' US (1995)

Arthur M STOKES (American)

Citation Record: 1 Book

Checkmate! - *Pastiche 1*

Goldscheider US (1980)

Richard STONE (British)

Citation Record: 1 Collection

Mysteries Suspended - *Pastiche Collection 1*

contains an uncounted number of stories.

UK (1993)

Julian SYMONS 1912-1994 (British)

Invented 11 detectives - see Insp CRAMBO

Citation Record: 1 Selected Short Story

How A Hermit Was Disturbed In His Retirement - *Pastiche 1*

purports to take place when *Sherlock HOLMES*, now an old man, is in his country retirement. *Dr WATSON*, perhaps dead by then, does not appear. The story first appeared in the author's collection, *The Great Detectives: Seven Original Investigations*, 1981, and is included in the anthology, *THE FURTHER ADVENTURES OF SHERLOCK HOLMES* (Editor; *Richard Lancelyn GREEN*), where it is entitled, *The Adventure of Hillerman Hall*, bringing it into concordance with most of the canonical stories.

Orbis UK (1981); Abrams US (1981)

Bert L TAYLOR 1866-1921 (American)

Writer: Bert Leston TAYLOR

Citation Record: 1 Selected Short Story

The Adventure Of The Double Santa Claus - *Pastiche 1*

Written in 1904, this story appeared in *The Illustrious Client's Second Case-Book* (Editor; *J N WILLIAMSON*).

In 'The Illustrious Clients' US (1949)

Byron TETRICK

Citation Record: 1 Selected Short Story

The Future Engine - *Pastiche 1*

In which the great detective is consulted by Charles Babbage about a novel analytical engine he has invented but whose parts have been stolen (by Professor Moriarty, it would seem). The story is in the anthology, *SHERLOCK HOLMES IN ORBIT* (Editors; *Mike RESNICK and Martin H GREENBERG*).

Daw US (1995)

Frank THOMAS 1926- (American)

Citation Record: 4 Books

Sherlock Holmes And The Golden Bird - *Pastiche 1*

Pinnacle US (1979); LSP Books UK (1980)

Sherlock Holmes And The Sacred Sword - *Pastiche 2*

LSP Books UK (1980)

Sherlock Holmes And The Treasure Train - *Pastiche 3*

Pinnacle US (1985)

Sherlock Holmes And The Masquerade Murders - *Pastiche 4*

Medallion US (1986)

Brian M THOMSEN

Citation Record: 1 Selected Short Story

Mouse And The Master - *Pastiche 1*

In which the great detective finds it necessary to collaborate with the 'second greatest consulting detective in all of London', one Malcolm Chandler, alias Mouse. The story is in the anthology, *SHERLOCK HOLMES IN ORBIT* (Editors; *Mike RESNICK and Martin H GREENBERG*).

Daw US (1995)

June THOMSON 1930- (British)

See main detective Det Ch Insp Jack FINCH

Citation Record: 21 Short Stories in 3 Collections

Constable UK (1990)

The Secret Files Of Sherlock Holmes - *Pastiche Collection 1*

The individual stories are cited immediately below.

Short stories - 7

Constable UK (1990)

The Case Of The Abandoned Lighthouse - *Pastiche 1*

refers to the allusion made by *Dr WATSON* in the canonical story, *THE ADVENTURE OF THE VEILED LODGER*, to an unchronicled case concerning 'the politician, the lighthouse and the trained cormorant'. Other authors have used the allusion as the basis for a pastiche or parody.

Constable UK (1990)

The Case Of The Amateur Mendicants - *Pastiche 2*

refers to the allusion by *Dr WATSON* in the canonical story, *THE FIVE ORANGE PIPS*, to an unchronicled case of 1887 concerning 'the Amateur Mendicant Society, who held a luxurious club in the lower vault of a furniture warehouse'. Other authors have used the allusion as the basis for a pastiche or parody.

The Case Of The Exalted Client - *Pastiche 3*

The title pays homage to the canonical story, *THE ADVENTURE OF THE ILLUSTRIOUS CLIENT.*

The Case Of The Itinerant Yeggman - *Pastiche 4*

The Case Of The Notorious Canary-Trainer - *Pastiche 5*

refers to the allusion made by *Dr WATSON* in the canonical story, *THE ADVENTURE OF BLACK PETER*, to a case that *Sherlock HOLMES* had undertaken in 1895, during which he had arrested 'Wilson, the notorious canary-trainer, which removed a plague-spot from the East End of London'. Other authors have used the allusion as the basis for a pastiche or parody.

The Case Of The Remarkable Worm - *Pastiche 6*
refers to the allusion made by *Dr WATSON* in the canonical story, *THE PROBLEM OF THE THOR BRIDGE,* to an unchronicled case concerning 'Isodora Persano, the well-known journalist and duellist, who was found stark staring mad with a matchbox in front of him which contained a remarkable worm, said to be unknown to science'. Other authors have used the allusion as the basis for a pastiche or parody.

The Case Of The Vanishing Head-Waiter - *Pastiche 7*

The Secret Chronicles Of Sherlock Holmes - *Pastiche Collection 2*
The individual stories are cited immediately below.
Short stories - 7
Constable UK (1992)

The Case Of The Camberwell Poisoning - *Pastiche 8*
purports to be an account of the 'Camberwell poisoning', an unchronicled case alluded to by *Dr WATSON* in the canonical story, *THE FIVE ORANGE PIPS.*

H

The Case Of The Hammersmith Wonder - *Pastiche 9*
refers to the allusion made by *Dr WATSON* in the canonical story, *THE ADVENTURE OF THE SUSSEX VAMPIRE,* to an unchronicled case concerning 'Vigor, the Hammersmith wonder'. Other authors have used the allusion as the basis for a pastiche or parody.

The Case Of The Harley Street Specialist - *Pastiche 10*

The Case Of The Maplestead Magpie - *Pastiche 11*

The Case Of The Old Russian Woman - *Pastiche 12*
refers to the allusion made by *Sherlock HOLMES* in the canonical story, *THE MUSGRAVE RITUAL,* to an unchronicled case he had undertaken before his meeting with *Dr WATSON,* concerning 'the adventure of the old Russian woman'.

The Case Of The Paradol Chamber - *Pastiche 13*
refers to the allusion made by *Dr WATSON* in the canonical story, *THE CASE OF THE FIVE ORANGE PIPS,* to an unchronicled case. Other authors have used the allusion as the basis for a pastiche or parody.

The Case Of The Sumatran Rat - *Pastiche 14*
refers to the allusion made by *Dr WATSON* in the canonical story, *THE ADVENTURE OF THE SUSSEX VAMPIRE,* to an unchronicled case about 'the giant rat of Sumatra, a story for which the world is not yet prepared'. Other authors have used the allusion as the basis for a pastiche or parody.

The Secret Journals Of Sherlock Holmes - *Pastiche Collection 3*
The individual stories are cited immediately below.
Short stories - 7
Constable UK (1993)

The Case Of The Addleton Tragedy - *Pastiche 15*
refers to the allusion made by *Dr WATSON* in the canonical story, *THE ADVENTURE OF THE GOLDEN PINCE-NEZ,* to an unchronicled case concerning 'the Addleton tragedy'.

The Case Of The Colonel's Madness - *Pastiche 16*
refers to the allusion made by *Dr WATSON* in the canonical story, *THE ADVENTURE OF THE ENGINEER'S THUMB,* to an unchronicled case (one of the only two that he had himself introduced to *Sherlock HOLMES),* 'that of Colonel Warburton's madness'. Other authors have used the allusion as the basis for a pastiche or parody.

The Case Of The Friesland Outrage - *Pastiche 17*
refers to the allusion made by *Dr WATSON* in the canonical story, *THE ADVENTURE OF THE NORWOOD BUILDER,* to an unchronicled case, 'the shocking affair of the Dutch steamship, "Friesland", which so nearly cost us both our lives'.

The Case Of The Maupertuis Scandal - *Pastiche 18*
refers to the allusion made by *Dr WATSON* in the canonical story, *THE REIGATE SQUIRES,* to an unchronicled case, saying 'The whole question of the Netherland-Sumatra Company and of the colossal schemes of Baron Maupertuis are too recent in the minds of the public, and are too intimately concerned with politics and finance, to be a fitting subject for this series of sketches'.

The Case Of The Millionaire's Persecution - *Pastiche 19*
refers to the allusion made by *Dr WATSON* in the canonical story, *THE ADVENTURE OF THE SOLITARY CYCLIST,* to an unchronicled case concerning 'the abstruse and complicated problem concerning the peculiar persecution to which John Vincent Harden, the well-known tobacco millionaire, had been subjected'.

The Case Of The Shopkeeper's Terror - *Pastiche 20*
refers to the allusion made by *Dr WATSON* in the canonical story, *THE DISAPPEARANCE OF LADY CARFAX,* to a case on which *Sherlock HOLMES* was working, saying that he could not 'possibly leave London while old Abrahams is in such mortal terror of his life'.

The Case Of The Smith-Mortimer Succession - *Pastiche 21*
refers to the allusion made by *Dr WATSON* in the canonical story, *THE ADVENTURE OF THE GOLDEN PINCE-NEZ,* to an unchronicled case concerning 'the famous Smith-Mortimer succession'.

Larry TOWNSHEND (American)

Citation Record: 3 Short Stories in 1 Collection

The Sexual Adventures Of Sherlock Holmes - *Pastiche Collection 1*
The individual stories are cited immediately below.
Olympia Press US (1971)

A Study In Lavender Lace - *Pastiche 1*

The Queer Affair Of The Greek Interpreter - *Pastiche 2*

The Final Solution - *Pastiche 3*

Mark TWAIN 1835-1910 (American)

Invented 5 detectives - see Tom SAWYER

Citation Record: 1 Book

A Double-Barrelled Detective Story - *Pastiche 1*
In which the great detective operates in an American western setting.

Sidekick: Fetlock JONES
is supposed to be the nephew of *Sherlock HOLMES* and acts as his assistant in these pastiches.
American Male - Nephew
Harper & Row US (1902); Chatto UK (1902)

Nicholas UTECHIN (American)

See main detective Porlock MOANS

Citation Record: 1 Book

Sherlock Holmes At Oxford - *Pastiche 1*
Dugdale US (1977)

Cay VAN ASH 1918- (American)

Citation Record: 1 Book

Ten Years Beyond Baker Street - *Pastiche 1*
In which the great detective clashes with the greatest of all yellow perils, that famous creation of *Sax ROHMER,* the dastardly Dr Fu Manchu.
Harper & Row US (1984)

Ralph VAUGHAN

Citation Record: 2 Books

Sherlock Holmes: The Adventure Of The Ancient Gods - *Pastiche 1*
The action takes place in the USA.
Gryphon UK (1990)

The Dreaming Detective - *Pastiche 2*
Gryphon UK (199?)

Daniel D VICTOR (American)

Citation Record: 1 Book

The Seventh Bullet And Others - *Pastiche 1*
the great detective operates in New York and Washington.
St Martin's US (1992)

Ian WALKER (British)

Citation Record: 1 Book

The Singular Case Of The Duplicate Holmes - *Pastiche 1*

Ian Henry UK (1994)

William J WALSH (American)

Citation Record: 1 Selected Short Story

The Adventure Of The Harassed Prussian - *Pastiche 1*

appeared in the July number.

In 'Shades of Sherlock' US (1969)

Edward WELLEN 1919-

Writer: Edward Paul WELLEN

Citation Record: 2 Selected Short Stories

The House That Jack Built - *Pastiche 1*

is in *THE NEW ADVENTURES OF SHERLOCK HOLMES* (Editors; *Martin H GREENBERG and Carol-Lynn Rossel WAUGH).*

Carroll & Graf US (1987)

Voiceover - *Pastiche 2*

is in the anthology, *SHERLOCK HOLMES THROUGH TIME AND SPACE* (Editors; *Isaac ASIMOV, Martin Harry GREENBERG and Charles G WAUGH).*

Manly Wade WELLMAN 1905- (American)

Invented 5 detectives - see David RETURN

Citation Record: 2 Selected Short Stories

But Our Hero Was Not Dead - *Pastiche 1*

appeared in the August number. The great detective is now, in 1941, very old and living in his cottage in Sussex, being looked after by his old landlady, *Mrs HUDSON.* He is able to trap a German paratrooper by using his old methods of analysis. The story was reworked as *THE MAN WHO WAS NOT DEAD.*

In 'Argosy' US (1941)

The Man Who Was Not Dead - *Pastiche 2*

A reworking of the earlier story, *BUT OUR HERO WAS NOT DEAD,* included in *THE MISADVENTURES OF SHERLOCK HOLMES* (Editor; *Ellery QUEEN).*

Little, Brown US (1944)

Manly Wade WELLMAN 1905- and Wade WELLMAN 1939- (American)

Citation Record: 1 Book

Sherlock Holmes's War Of The Worlds - *Pastiche 1*

Warner US (1975)

Carolyn WELLS 1870-1942 (American)

Invented 7 detectives - see Fleming STONE

Citation Record: 1 Selected Short Story

The Adventure Of The Clothes-Line - *Pastiche 1*

first appeared in May 1915 in *The Century* and is included in *THE MISADVENTURES OF SHERLOCK HOLMES* (Editor; *Ellery QUEEN). HOLMES* is the president of the Society of Infallible Detectives and solves a case in which a lady is observed hanging by her hands on a high line, which baffles almost a dozen of the finest fictional detectives (all named).

Little, Brown US (1944)

J W WELLS

Citation Record: 1 Selected Short Story

His First Bow - *Pastiche 1*

appeared in the December number.

In 'Ellery Queen's Mystery Magazine' US (1951)

Ronald C WEYMAN (Canadian)

served in the Canadian Navy during the Second World War. He produces of plays and other works for TV and the stage.

Citation Record: 2 Books 5 Short Stories in 1 Collection

Sherlock Holmes And The Mark Of The Beast - *Pastiche 1*

The great detective, in 1891 (the year in which he disappeared, presumed dead), seems to be operating in Canada.

Simon & Pierre CA (1990)

Sherlock Holmes And The Ultimate Disguise - *Pastiche 2*

UK (1992)

Travels In The Canadian West - *Pastiche Collection 1*

The individual stories are cited immediately below.

Simon & Pierre CA (1994)

The Case Of The Smiling Buddha - *Pastiche 1*

The Lady Of The Camellias - *Pastiche 2*

The Mystery Of Headless Valley - *Pastiche 3*

Sherlock Holmes And The King Of Siam - *Pastiche 4*

Sherlock Holmes And The Wendigo - *Pastiche 5*

Arthur WHITAKER 1882-1949 (British)

See main detective Harold QUEST

Citation Record: 1 Selected Short Story

The Case Of The Man Who Was Wanted

was written in 1911 but was first published by *Cosmopolitan* in 1948. Its chequered history is given in some detail in the introduction to the anthology, *THE FURTHER ADVENTURES OF SHERLOCK HOLMES* (Editor; *Richard Lancelyn GREEN*), in which it is included, its title being changed to *The Adventure of the Sheffield Banker*, bringing it into concordance with the titles of most of the canonical stories.

Cosmopolitan US (1948)

Frank Marshall WHITE (American)

Citation Record: 1 Selected Short Story

The Recrudescence Of Sherlock Holmes - *Pastiche 1*

This remarkably early pastiche places the detective in New York.

In 'Life' US (1894)

H

Jerry Neal WILLIAMSON (American)

Invented 3 detectives - see Sheerback TONES

Citation Record: 2 Selected Short Stories

The Adventure Of The Politician, The Lighthouse, And The Trained Cormorant - *Pastiche 1*

is in the author's collection, *The Illustrious Client's Second Case-Book*. The title refers to the allusion made by *Dr WATSON* in the canonical story, *THE ADVENTURE OF THE VEILED LODGER,* and further information is given in *THE POLITICIAN, LIGHTHOUSE AND TRAINED CORMORANT,* written by *Clive BROOKS.* Other authors have used the allusion as the basis for a pastiche or parody.

In 'The Illustrious Clients' US (1949)

The Terrible Death Of Crosby, The Banker - *Pastiche 2*

appeared in the author's collection, *The Illustrious Client's Case-book* (Editors; *J N WILLIAMSON* & H B Williams).

In 'The Illustrious Clients' US (1948)

Alan WILSON (American)

Citation Record: 2 Selected Short Stories

The Adventure Of The Tired Captain - *Pastiche 1*

refers to an allusion made by *Dr WATSON* in the canonical story, *THE NAVAL TREATY,* to an unchronicled case.

In 'Sherlock Holmes Journal' UK (1958)

The Adventure Of The Paradol Chamber - *Pastiche 2*

refers to the allusion made by *Dr WATSON* in the canonical story, *THE FIVE ORANGE PIPS,* to an unchronicled case concerning 'the adventure of the Paradol Chamber'. Other authors have used the allusion as the basis for a pastiche or parody.

In 'Sherlock Holmes Journal' UK (1961)

John A WILSON

Citation Record: 1 Selected Short Story

The Case Of The Two Coptic Patriarchs - *Pastiche 1*

appeared in the January number.

In 'Baker Street Journal' US (1949)

Richard WINCOR (American)

Citation Record: 1 Book

Sherlock Holmes In Tibet - *Pastiche 1*

purports to provide some information on the whereabouts of *Sherlock HOLMES* during 'The Great Hiatus', 1891-1894, when the great detective was presumed dead. He was said to have been travelling widely, especially in Tibet and Persia. The pastiche purports to give his experiences in Tibet, where he was supposed to be disguised as the Norwegian explorer, Ole Sigerson (actually a favourite alias of *HOLMES*

and mentioned in the canonical story, *THE ADVENTURE OF THE EMPTY HOUSE)*, cavorting with a number of strange characters at 'Llassa University' (one of *Dr WATSON's* several errors in that story).
Weybright US (1968)

Sebastian WOLFE (American)

is the editor of a recent anthology of *Sherlock HOLMES* pastiches, parodies and burlesques. He regrettably chose the same title for his anthology as was used in 1944 for the classic anthology edited by *Ellery QUEEN.*

Citation Record: 14 Short Stories in 1 Collection

The Misadventures Of Sherlock Holmes - *Parody and Pastiche Anthology 1*

pastiches, parodies and burlesques of *Sherlock HOLMES*, each cited individually under the appropriate authors.
Citadel US (1991)

Leah A ZELDES

Citation Record: 1 Selected Short Story

A Study In Sussex - *Pastiche 1*

In which the great detective, in late retirement, is experimenting with bee venom. The story is in the anthology, *SHERLOCK HOLMES IN ORBIT* (Editors; *Mike RESNICK and Martin H GREENBERG*).
Daw US (1995)

H

Sherlock HOLMES

Second detective of Mycroft HOLMES

Sherlock HOLMES

Second detective of Mrs HUDSON

Sherlock HOLMES

Second detective of Edward Porter JONES

Sherlock HOLMES

Second detective of Insp/Supt Sholto LESTRADE

Sherlock HOLMES

is, here, not the sage of Baker Street himself, but an actor who – having played the part of the great detective on the stage – sets up in business as a private investigator under the same name. He even finds himself a suitable sidekick.

British Male Professional Amateur operating in London

Sidekick: Dr WATSON

is not the great sidekick of the *Sir Arthur Conan DOYLE* stories but an actor who is taken on by the facsimile *Sherlock HOLMES.*

British Male - Assistant

Robert ZIMLER and Michael ZIMLER (American)

Citation Record: 1 Selected Short Story

Home Office: 221b Baker Street; Or, A Study In Cement - *Pastiche 1*

appeared in the February number.
In 'Ellery Queen's Mystery Magazine' US (1963)

Sherlock HOLMES and Sir Arthur Conan DOYLE

British Male Professional Amateur and British Male Amateur operating in London

Ray WALSH 1949- (British)

Citation Record: 1 Book

The Mycroft Memoranda - *Pastiche 1*

In which *Sherlock HOLMES* and his creator, *Sir Arthur Conan DOYLE*, are, rather ingeniously, made to sleuth together.
St Martin's US (1985)

Sherlock HOLMES and Sigmund FREUD

In which *Sherlock HOLMES* visits Vienna in 1890 and solves a mystery in collaboration with *Sigmund FREUD*, the founder of psychiatric medicine, who was also practising at that time. The same pair have been more recently used as detectives in a mainstream novel by *Keith OATLEY.*

British Male Professional Amateur and Austrian Amateur operating in London

Nicholas MEYER 1945- (American)

Invented 3 detectives - see Mark BRILL

Citation Record: 1 Book

The Seven Per-Cent Solution - *Pastiche 1*

Dutton US (1974); Hodder & Stoughton UK (1975)

Keith OATLEY (British)

Citation Record: 1 Book

The Case Of Emily V - *Pastiche 1*

? (1993)

Sherlock HOLMES and Harry HOUDINI

In which *Sherlock HOLMES* collaborates with the greatest magician and escapologist of all time, *Harry HOUDINI.*

British Male Professional Amateur and American Amateur operating in London

Daniel STASHOWER 1960- (American)

Writer: Daniel Meyer STASHOWER

Citation Record: 1 Selected Short Story

The Adventures Of The Ectoplasmic Man - *Pastiche 1*

Morrow US (1985)

Sherlock HOLMES and Arsène LUPIN

Arsène LUPIN, the great French detective and *Sherlock HOLMES*, the sage of Baker Street, are at loggerheads in this remarkable parody-pastiche.

British Male Professional Amateur and French Male Professional Amateur operating in France

Jacob BRUSSELL

Citation Record: 1 Book

Sherlock Holmes Versus Arsène Lupin: The Case Of The Golden Blonde - *Pastiche 1*

was not a translation but a new adaptation of *ARSENE LUPIN CONTRE HERLOCK SHOLMES.*
Atomic Books US (1946)

Sherlock HOLMES and Fergus O'BREEN

In which *Fergus O'BREEN*, who appears in other novels by this author, is outflanked by the great *Sherlock HOLMES* himself.

British Male Professional Amateur and American Private Detective operating in USA

Anthony BOUCHER 1911-1968 (American)

Invented 7 detectives - see Fergus O'BREEN and Det Lt JACKSON

Citation Record: 1 Book

The Case Of The Baker Street Irregulars - *Pastiche 1*

Simon & Schuster US (1940)

Sherlock HOLMES and A J RAFFLES

are respectively the detectives of *Sir Arthur Conan DOYLE* and *E W HORNUNG.*

British Male Professional Amateur and British Male Amateur operating in London

Hugh KINGSMILL 1889-1949 (British)

Writer: Hugh Kingsmill LUNN

Citation Record: 1 Selected Short Story

The Ruby Of Khitmandu - *Pastiche 1*

When an Indian Maharajah is staying at Claridges in London he is robbed of a famous ruby. *Sherlock HOLMES* traces the theft to *A J RAFFLES*, who agrees to hand it over if proceedings are not taken against him.
In 'The Bookman' US (1932)

Sherlock HOLMES and Theodore ROOSEVELT

HOLMES collaborates with the some-time President of the United States, and they discover a conspiracy that threatens the US. Their investigation, it is suggested, occurred in 1880, before *HOLMES* met *Dr WATSON*, or *ROOSEVELT* entered politics.

British Male Professional Amateur and American Male Amateur operating in USA

H Paul JEFFERS 1934- (American)

Invented 3 detectives - see David MORGAN

Citation Record: 1 Book

The Adventure Of The Stalwart Companions - *Pastiche 1*
!See Appendix 2.
Cassell UK (1979); Harper & Row US (1978)

Sherlock HOLMES, Lew ARCHER, Nero WOLFE, Father BROWN and Hercule POIROT

are the detectives of five different authors. They have come together to solve a most difficult problem.
Two American, two British, and one Belgian Male Private Detectives operating in Rome

Charles DICKENS (British), Carlo FRUTTERO and Francio LUCENTINI

Writer: (First author) Charles John Huffam DICKENS (1812-1870)

Citation Record: 1 Book

The D Case; Or, The Truth About The Mystery Of Edwin Drood - *Pastiche 1*
At an international conference in Rome, five of the world's greatest detectives try to solve the greatest mystery in literature: in *Charles DICKENS'* novel, who killed Edwin Drood?
Harcourt Brace UK (1992)

Sherlock HOLMES, Insp Charlie CHAN and Hercule POIROT

are the detectives of three different authors.
One American, one British, and one Belgian Male Private Detectives operating in London

P H JONES

Invented 3 detectives - see Sherlock HOLMES, Insp Charlie CHAN and Hercule POIROT

Citation Record: 1 Selected Short Story

Master Minds At Play - *Pastiche 1*
The detectives play a hand at Bridge and *HOLMES* performs an amazing feat in making an almost impossible contract of four spades.
In 'Bridge Quarterly' ? (1958)

Sherlock HOLMES, Dr Reginald FORTUNE and Dr John Evelyn THORNDYKE

In this triple pastiche novel, the detectives (qqv) are the creations of three different authors.
British Male Detectives, of different types, operating in England

Alfred C WARD (American)

Citation Record: 1 Book

Sherlock Holmes Versus John Thorndyke And Reginald Fortune - *Pastiche 1*
Goldscheider US (1982)

Shirlick HOLMES

appears in a story for children. She is a young girl in a small American town who solves the mystery of thefts of furniture, using the great detective's methods.
American Female Amateur operating in USA

Jane YOLEN (American)

Citation Record: 1 Book

Shirlick Holmes And The Case Of The Wandering Wardrobe - *Parody 1*
Coward, McCann & Geoghegan US (1981)

Shirley HOLMES

is a *Sherlock HOLMES* parody, purporting to be the great man's daughter.
British Female Amateur operating in England

Sidekick: Joan WATSON
is understood to be the daughter of *Dr WATSON*.
British Female - Sidekick

Frederic Arnold KUMMER 1873-1943 and Basil MITCHELL (American)

Citation Record: 2 Selected Short Stories

The Adventure Of The Queen Bee - *Parody 1*
appeared as a four-part serial in the numbers from July through October.
In 'Mystery Magazine' US (1933)

The Canterbury Cathedral Murder - *Parody 2*
appeared first in the December number. It is also in the anthology, *THE MISADVENTURES OF SHERLOCK HOLMES* (Editor: *Ellery QUEEN*).
In 'Mystery Magazine' US (1933)

Shirley HOLMES

is a *Sherlock HOLMES* parody, not identical with the detective cited immediately above.
Female Sleuth

Sidekick: Jean WATSON
is her parody *WATSON*-like assistant.
Female - Sidekick

Viola Brothers SHORE 1895- (American)

See main detective pair Colin KEATS and Gwynn LEITH

Citation Record: 1 Selected Short Story

A Case Of Facsimile - *Parody 1*
appeared in the October number.
In 'Ellery Queen's Mystery Magazine' US (1948)

Shrock HOLMES

is a *Sherlock HOLMES* parody.
British Male Professional Amateur operating in London

Sidekick: Dr HARCOURT
is his parody *WATSON*-like assistant.
British Male - Assistant

Bradley KJELL (American)

See main detctive Tide POOLES

Citation Record: 1 Selected Short Story

The Adventure Of The Psychodelic Sleuth - *Parody 6*
had *Shrock HOLMES* as the detective when it first appeared. It was republished in the June & August issues of *Shades of Sherlock*, when the detective was the parody, *TIDE POOLES*.
In 'The Loft' US (1968)

Spencer HOLMES

purports to be the grandson of *Sherlock HOLMES*.
American Male Amateur operating in San Francisco

Denny Martin FLINN (American)

Citation Record: 1 Book

San Francisco Kills - *Parody 1*
Bantam US (1991)

William HOLMES

British Male Amateur operating in England

Conrad Voss BARK (British)

Citation Record: 7 Books

Mr Holmes At Sea - *First*
Macdonald UK (1962); Macmillan US (1962)

The Second Red Dragon - *Last*
Gollancz UK (1968); Walker US (1968)

Zinsheimer HOLMES

is a *Sherlock HOLMES* parody.
Male Professional Amateur operating in USA

Harold KELLOCK

Citation Record: 2 Selected Short Stories

The Adventure Of The East Side Ball - *Parody 1*
appears in the author's collection of short stories, *Mr Hobby*.
Century US (1913)

The Adventure Of The Pudgy Leg - *Parody 2*
appears in the author's collection of short stories, *Mr Hobby*.
Century US (1913)

Shirley HOLMQUIST

is a *Sherlock HOLMES* parody.
Female Professional Amateur

Sidekick: AUNT WILMA
is her parody *WATSON*-like assistant.
Female - Aunt

Janet Letnes MARTIN (American)
was born in North Dakota.
Citation Record: 14 Short Stories in 1 Collection
Shirley Holmquist And Aunt Wilma: Whodunnit? - *Parody Collection 1*
The individual stories are cited immediately below.
Martin ? (1989)
The Case Of The Anonymous Doorstep Donors - *Parody 1*
The Case Of The Burgled Bulb - *Parody 2*
The Case Of The Character Lines In Chenille - *Parody 3*
The Case Of The Communist Plot To Conquer Heartsberg - *Parody 4*
The Case Of The Cool-Headed Claim Jumper - *Parody 5*
The Case Of The Edberg Boy Who Never Married - *Parody 6*
The Case Of The Fire At The Flickertail Lounge And Grill - *Parody 7*
The Case Of The Forbidden Fruit - *Parody 8*
The Case Of The Laundry That Came Up Short - *Parody 9*
The Case Of The Lutefisk Heist - *Parody 10*
The Case Of The Missing Merger Pamphlets - *Parody 11*
The Case Of The Misplaced Lutheran Hymnal - *Parody 12*
The Case Of The Ribbon Snatchers - *Parody 13*
The Case Of The Telltale Slop Pail - *Parody 14*

Clay HOLT
was one of this author's numerous pulp detectives and mainly in stories in *Dime Detective.*
American Male Detective in Pulp Magazines operating in USA

Carroll John DALY 1889-1958 (American)
Invented 6 detectives - see Race WILLIAMS
No citations

Essington HOLT
Male Amateur operating in Melbourne

Robert WALLACE (Australian)
Writer: Robin WALLACE-CRABBE
Citation Record: 3 Books
To Catch A Forger - *First*
Gollancz UK (1988); St Martin's US (1989)
Paint Out - *Latest*
Gollancz UK (1990)

Harrison HOLT
solves a case of murder by shooting in a locked room.
American Male Amateur operating in USA
Sidekick: Bobby WEATHERBY
American Male - Narrator

Roy EASTMAN O 1883- (American)
Citation Record: 1 Book
The Mysteries Of Blair House - *Only*
Conjure US (1948)

Herbert HOLT
British Male Amateur operating in England

Ernest DE WIL (British)
Citation Record: 1 Book
The Brookham Mystery - *Only*
International Publishing UK (1893)

Ken HOLT
American Male Detective in Pulp Magazines operating in USA

Bruce CAMPBELL (American)
No citations

Ch Mitchell HOLT and Megan O'MALLEY
investigate the disappearance of young boy in the quiet little town of Deer Lake.
American Policeman and American Policewoman operating in Minnesota

Tami HOAG (American)
is a writer of mainstream novels.
Citation Record: 1 Book
Night Sins - *Single*
Bantam US (1995)

Samantha HOLT
is a veterinary sleuth.
American Female Amateur operating in Florida

Karen Ann WILSON (American)
Citation Record: 1 Book
Eight Dogs Flying - *Single*
Berkley US (1994)

Samuel HOLT
American Male Sleuth operating in USA

Samuel HOLT 1933- (American)
For writer details see Tim SMITH
Citation Record: 1 Book
What I Tell You Three Times Is False - *Single*
Tor US (1987)

Dr Paul HOLTON
British Male Amateur operating in England

Charlotte HUNT 1915- (American)
Writer: Doris Marjorie HODGES
Citation Record: 6 Books
Chambered Tomb - *First*
Ace US (1975)
The Gilded Sarcophagus - *Last*
Ace US (1967)

Chubb-Lock HOMES
was an early *Sherlock HOLMES* parody who appeared in a comic paper.
British Male Professional Amateur operating in London

ANON
Citation Record: 33 Short Stories in 1 Collection
The Adventures Of Chubb-Lock Homes - *Parody Collection 1*
The stories (uncited) appeared in issues from November 1893 through September 1894.
In 'Comic Cuts' UK (1893/4)

Padlock HOMES
was a *Sherlock HOLMES* parody who appeared during 1944 in a comic magazine called *Speed Comics.* [This information is in the introduction to *THE MISADVENTURES OF SHERLOCK HOLMES* (Editor; *Ellery QUEEN*)]
Male Professional Amateur
Sidekick: Dr WATSIS
was his parody *WATSON*-like assistant.
Male - Assistant
No citations

Rex HOMES
is a *Sherlock HOLMES* parody.
Male Professional Amateur
Sidekick: Dr HOTBUN
is his parody *WATSON*-like assistant.
Male - Assistant

Albert J BROMLEY (American)
Citation Record: 1 Selected Short Story
The Grate Fur Koat Mistery - *Parody 1*
appears in a collection of miscellaneous stories by this author, entitled *Snowshoe Al's Bed Time Storries (and uther times)* (sic!). It also appeared in *Illustrious Client's Third Case-Book* (Editors: *J N WILLIAMSON* & H B Williams: US 1953).
Minton US (1926)

Schlock HOMES
British Male Professional Amateur operating in England
is one of the best-known of all the numerous *Sherlock HOLMES*

parodies, although, at times, he seems nearer to burlesque. His adventures appear in a number of short stories that have appeared in the author's collections and their titles are often the most delightful parodies of those of the canonical stories. The stories themselves include a panoply of exotic but easily identified figures, who parody those in the canonical stories. They include, for example, a sidekick who is the narrator, a buffoon from Scotland Yard, an arch-criminal, Professor Marty (a parody of the canonical Moriarty), Colonel Moron (a parody of the canonical Colonel Moran, 'the second most dangerous man in London'), and a long-suffering housekeeper, Mrs Essex, who presides over the comforts at the great detective's rooms at 221B Bagel Street.
Schlock HOMES appeared in stories in magazines over many years. The stories have been collected into three volumes and are cited under them.
British Male Professional Amateur operating in England

Sidekick: Dr J WATNEY
is his parody *WATSON*-like assistant.
British Male - Assistant

Stooge: Insp BALUSTRADE
is the usual type of baffled police detective and parodies the canonical *Insp LESTRADE.*
British Male

Robert L FISH 1912-1981 (American)
was born in Cleveland, Ohio, and graduated with a BS at the Case School of Applied Science, Cleveland, Ohio, 1933. A distinguished engineer in the plastics industry, he began writing detective stories in 1962 under his own name and his punning pseudonym.
Writer: Robert Lloyd FISH
Other Byline: Robert L PIKE
Other Detectives:
Capt Jose DA SILVA
Kek HUUYGENS
SIMPSON, CARRUTHERS and BRIGGS
Citation Record: 32 Short Stories in 3 Collections

The Incredible Schlock Homes - *Parody Collection 1*
The individual stories are cited immediately below, with the original publication also cited, if known.
Short stories - 12
Simon & Schuster US (1966)

The Adventure Of The Adam Bomb - *Parody 1*
In 'Ellery Queen's Mystery Magazine' US (1960)

The Adventure Of The Artist's Mottle - *Parody 2*
In 'Ellery Queen's Mystery Magazine' US (1961)

The Adventure Of The Ascot Tie - *Parody 3*
In 'Ellery Queen's Mystery Magazine' US (1960)

The Adventure Of The Counterfeit Sovereign - *Parody 4*
In 'Ellery Queen's Mystery Magazine' US (1963)

The Adventure Of The Double-Bogey Man - *Parody 5*
In 'Ellery Queen's Mystery Magazine' US (1962)

The Adventure Of The Lost Prince - *Parody 6*
was entitled *The Adventure of the Missing Prince* when it first appeared.
In 'Ellery Queen's Mystery Magazine' US (1962)

The Adventure Of The Missing Cheyne-Stroke - *Parody 7*
In 'Ellery Queen's Mystery Magazine' US (1961)

The Adventure Of The Printer's Inc - *Parody 8*
In 'Ellery Queen's Mystery Magazine' US (1960)

The Adventure Of The Snared Drummer - *Parody 9*
In 'Ellery Queen's Mystery Magazine' US (1963)

The Adventure Of The Spectacled Band - *Parody 10*
In 'Ellery Queen's Mystery Magazine' US (1960)

The Adventure Of The Stockbroker's Clark - *Parody 11*
In 'Ellery Queen's Mystery Magazine' US (1961)

The Adventure Of The Final Problem - *Parody 12*
In 'Ellery Queen's Mystery Magazine' US (1964)

The Memoirs Of Schlock Homes - *Parody Collection 2*
Bobbs Merrill US (1974)
The individual stories are cited immediately below, with the original publication also cited, if known.
Short stories - 11
Bobbs US (1974)

The Adventure Of Black, Peter - *Parody 13*

The Adventure Of The Big Plunger - *Parody 14*
In 'Ellery Queen's Mystery Magazine' US (1965)

The Adventure Of The Briary School - *Parody 15*

The Adventure Of The Disappearance Of Whistler's Mother - *Parody 16*
In 'Ellery Queen's Mystery Magazine' US (1968)

The Adventure Of The Dog In The Knight - *Parody 17*
can also be found in the anthology, *THE MISADVENTURES OF SHERLOCK HOLMES* (Editor; *Sebastian WOLFE).*
In 'Ellery Queen's Mystery Magazine' US (1970)

The Adventure Of The Great Train Robbery - *Parody 18*

The Adventure Of The Hansom Ransom - *Parody 19*

The Adventure Of The Missing Three-Quarters - *Parody 20*
In 'Ellery Queen's Mystery Magazine' US (1967)

The Adventure Of The Perforated Ulster - *Parody 21*
In 'Ellery Queen's Mystery Magazine' US (1967)

The Adventure Of The Widow's Weeds - *Parody 22*
In 'Ellery Queen's Mystery Magazine' US (1966)

The Return Of Schlock Homes - *Parody 23*
In 'Ellery Queen's Mystery Magazine' US (1964)

Schlock Homes: The Complete Bagel Street Saga - *Parody Collection 3*
contains the twenty-three stories of the two earlier collections and nine previously uncollected stories, which are cited individually below.
Short stories - 32
Gaslight US (1990)

The Adventure Of The Animal Fare - *Parody 24*

The Adventure Of The Belles Letters - *Parody 25*

The Adventure Of The Common Code - *Parody 26*

The Adventure Of The Elite Type - *Parody 27*

The Adventure Of The Odd Lotteries - *Parody 28*

The Adventure Of The Patient Resident - *Parody 29*

The Adventure Of The Pie-Eyed Piper - *Parody 30*

The Adventure Of The Short Fuse - *Parody 31*

The Adventure Of The Ukrainian Foundling Orphans - *Parody 32*

Shylar HOMES

is a *Sherlock HOLMES* parody who operates out of 221B Barlow Street, Houston, Texas.
American Male Professional Amateur operating in Texas

Sidekick: Dr WHATLEY
is his parody *WATSON*-like assistant.
American Male - Assistant

Stephen Daniel WILLIAMS (American)
Citation Record: 3 Short Stories in 1 Collection

The Adventures Of Shylar Homes - *Parody Collection 1*
The individual stories are cited immediately below.
Carlton US (1966)

The Adventure Of The Bradley Tragedy - *Parody 1*

The Adventure Of The Missing Bullet - *Parody 2*

The Adventure Of The Pendleton Jewels - *Parody 3*

Shylock HOMES

is a *Sherlock HOLMES* parody who appeared in ten stories in *The New York Herald, Literary Section,* 1903, which were collected later into an anthology.
Male Professional Amateur

John Kendrick BANGS 1862-1922 (American)
Invented 4 detectives - see Raffles HOLMES
Citation Record: 10 Short Stories in 1 Collection

Shylock Homes: His Posthumous Memoirs - *Parody Collection 1*

The individual stories, which were all published between February 1 and April 5, 1903, are cited immediately below. The collection was republished by *Dispatch Box Press* (US 1973).
In 'New York Herald' US (1903)

Mr Homes Acts As Attorney For Solomon - *Parody 1*

Mr Homes Foils A Conspiracy And Gains A Fortune - *Parody 2*

Mr Homes Makes An Important Confession - *Parody 3*

Mr Homes Radiates A Wireless Message - *Parody 4*

Mr Homes Reaches An Unhistorical Conclusion - *Parody 5*

Mr Homes Shatters An Alibi - *Parody 6*

Mr Homes Shatters A Tradition - *Parody 7*

Mr Homes Solves A Question Of Authorship - *Parody 8*

Mr Homes Tackles A "Hard Case" - *Parody 9*

Shylock Homes: His Posthumous Memoirs - *Parody 10*
bears the same title as the collection.

H

Stately HOMES

is a *Sherlock HOLMES* parody.
British Male Professional Amateur operating in England

Sidekick: Sun WAT
is his parody *WATSON*-like assistant.
Chinese Male - Assistant

Arthur PORGES (American)

is the author of many short stories, often of a bizarre character or having, as a theme, a seemingly impossible crime. In this pastiche, *LUPIN* solves the mystery of how a priceless ruby is stolen from a room under constant guard.

Other Detectives:

Capt (Retired) CORBETT	George Fort ELGIN
Celery GREEN	Cyriack Skinner GREY
Dr Joel HOFFMAN	Sherlock HOLMES
Stately HOMES	Ben JOYCE
Alfred LEWIS	Ulysses Price MIDDLEBIE
Lt SELBY	Julian Morse TROWBRIDGE

Citation Record: 1 Selected Short Story 3 Short Stories in 1 Collection

Her Last Bow; Or, An Adventure Of Stately Homes - *Parody 1*
In 'Ellery Queen's Mystery Magazine' US (1957)

Three Porges Parodies And A Pastiche - *Parody Collection 1*
contains a *Sherlock HOLMES* pastiche short story (cited under that detective) and three parodies, cited immediately below, with their original publications, if known.
Magico Press US (1988)

An Adventure Of Stately Homes - *Parody 1*

Another Adventure Of Stately Homes - *Parody 2*
In 'The Saint Mystery Magazine' US (1964)

Stately Homes...And The Box: A Mystery - *Parody 3*
In 'Diner's Club Magazine' US (1965)

Surly HOMES

is a *Sherlock HOLMES* parody.
Male Professional Amateur

Sidekick: Dr WATCHSON
is his parody *WATSON*-like assistant.
Male - Assistant

Edward LUDWIG (American)

Citation Record: 1 Selected Short Story

The Martian Who Hated People - *Parody 1*
In which *HOMES* detects a visitor from another planet. The story appeared in the January 1955 number of *Inside and Science Fiction Advertiser* and later in an anthology, *The SHsf Fanthology* (Editor: Ruth Berman), published by *The Professor Challenger Society* (US 1971).
In 'Inside & Science Fiction Advertiser' US (1955)

Sure-They-Lock HOMEZ

is a *Sherlock HOLMES* parody.
Male Professional Amateur

Sidekick: 'Doc' WHOOSON
is his parody *WATSON*-like assistant.
Male - Assistant

Jerry Neal WILLIAMSON (American)

Invented 3 detectives - see Sheerback TONES

Citation Record: 1 Selected Short Story

The Gig Of The Man (With The Twist) - *Parody 1*
appeared in the March number.
In 'Baker Street Journal' US (1966)

HOMONYMOUS

is a *Sherlock HOLMES* parody.
British Male Professional Amateur operating in England

Sidekick: Dr Ernest WHOPPER
is his parody *WATSON*-like assistant.
British Male - Assistant

Helan HALBACH (American)

Citation Record: 2 Selected Short Stories

Caedmon, Caedmonk - *Parody 1*
appeared in the December number. The detective pretends to be senile but is actually about to enter a contract with Caedmon Records for an exclusive on his cases.
In 'Baker Street Journal' US (1965)

A Whale Of A Tale - *Parody 2*
Vermissa Herald (New Series) ? (1969)

Purlock HONE

is a *Sherlock HOLMES* parody.
British Male Professional Amateur operating in England

Sidekick: Dr JOBSON
is his parody *WATSON*-like assistant.
British Male - Assistant

Oswald CRAWFURD 1834-1909 (British)

See main detective Det Insp MORGAN

Citation Record: 1 Selected Short Story

Our Mr Smith - *Parody 1*
appeared in the introduction to the US edition of the author's collection of detective stories *THE REVELATIONS OF INSPECTOR MORGAN*. The author made it known that he, like everybody else, was satiated with *Sherlock HOLMES* and the dozens of imitations that had already appeared. So, in a piece that took a swipe at the whole species, he has the great man shown up as an ass. It was meant to be a potent antidote to the fashion for making amateur detectives so superior to the police force. The story is included in *THE MISADVENTURES OF SHERLOCK HOLMES* (Editor: *Ellery QUEEN*).
Dodd, Mead US (1907)

Lt/Capt George HONEGGER

American Policeman operating in USA

John Stephen STRANGE 1896- (American)

Invented 4 detectives - see Van Dusen ORMSBERRY

Citation Record: 3 Books

Murder Gives A Lovely Light - *First*
Doubleday US (1941); Collins UK (1942)

Eye Witness - *Last*
Doubleday US (1961); Collins UK (1962)

Prof Charles HONEYBATH

is a brilliant professor who is a friend of *Insp John APPLEBY* and appears in at least two other books with him. Here he mainly does the sleuthing alone.
British Male Amateur operating in England

Michael INNES 1906-1994 (British)

Invented 4 detectives - see Insp/Commiss John APPLEBY

Citation Record: 2 Books

The Mysterious Commission - *First*
Gollancz UK (1974); Dodd, Mead US (1975)

Lord Mullion's Secret - *Last*
Gollancz UK (1981); Dodd, Mead US (1981)

Prof Charles HONEYBATH

Second detective of Insp/Commiss John APPLEBY

Nora HONEYCUTT

finds herself in a small town in Colorado to clear up the effects of her sister who died, it was said, accidentally. Not true, it seems, for there are dark secrets in this town and they need unearthing if the truth is to be known and a murderer found.

American Female Amateur operating in Colorado

Sidekick: Thomas WHITNEY
assists the detective and falls in love with her.
American Male - Friend

Stooge: Ch FELLOWES
American Male

Michael ALLEGRETTO 1944- (American)
See main detective Jacob LOMAX
Citation Record: 1 Book
Shadow House - *Single*
Carroll & Graf US (1994)

Adam HOOD

British Male Secret Agent operating in England

Nicholas RICH (British)
Citation Record: 2 Books
The Blayne Document - *First*
Hale UK (1972)
Spy Now, Pay Later - *Last*
Hale UK (1972)

Charles HOOD

is cast in the *JAMES BOND* mould, but is in stories even more bizarre and violent. He is an art dealer, elegant, wealthy, and a lover of beautiful girls. Underneath this amazing, if well-worn, facade, however, he works for British Intelligence and outwits most of the Queen's enemies.

British Male Secret Agent operating in Europe/Asia

James MAYO 1913- (British)
served in the Royal Navy and British Intelligence. A journalist and the author of several novels under his real name, he wrote at least ten genre novels.
Writer: Stephen COULTER
Citation Record: 6 Books
Hammerhead - *First*
Deutsch UK (1952); Morrow US (1952)
Asking For It - *Last*
Heinemann UK (1971)

Mark HOOD

Male Secret Agent operating in several locations

James DARK 1917- (Australian)
Writer: James Edmond MACDONNELL
Citation Record: 12 Books
Spy From The Grave - *First*
Horwitz AU (1964)
Sea Scrape - *Last*
Signet UK (1971)

Mortimer HOOD

is a scientist involved in some weird goings-on in a temple, during which a naked priestess disappears. That seems a not unreasonable price to pay for meddling with the unknown.

British Male Amateur operating in England

Huxley HERNE 1888-1955 (British)
Writer: Bertram BROOKER
Citation Record: 1 Book
The Tangled Miracle - *Only*
Nelson UK (1936)

HOODOOED HOWARD

American Male Detective in Pulp Magazines operating in USA

F Lusk BROUGHTON (American)
Invented 10 detectives - see Harry WILLIAMS
Citation Record: 1 Selected Short Story
Hoodooed Howard, The Detective; Or, The River Pirates - *Only*
Old Cap Collier Library US (18??)

Insp HOOK

British Policeman operating in England

Gret LANE (British)
Writer: Margaret LANE
Other Byline: Jennifer JONES
Other Detectives:
John BARRIN and Kate MARSH
Kate MARSH
Citation Record: 2 Books
Three Dead That Night - *First*
Jenkins UK (1937)
The Red Mirror Mystery - *Last*
Jenkins UK (1938)

Sam HOOK

American Male Secret Agent operating in France/China

Hildegarde Tolman TEILHET 1906- (American)
Citation Record: 2 Books
The Double Agent - *First*
Doubleday US (1945); Gollancz UK (1946)
The Assassins - *Last*
Doubleday US (1946); Gollancz UK (1947)

Hildegarde TOLMAN 1906- (American)
Writer: Hildegarde Tolman TEILHET
Citation Record: 1 Book
Hero By Proxy - *Only*
Little, Brown US (1942); Gollancz UK (1943)

Steve HOOKS

was formerly in the Secret Service. Now, with a badly injured leg, he sleuths privately.

American Male Private Detective operating in USA

Warren B MURPHY 1933- (American)
Invented 8 detectives - see Julian 'Digger' BURROUGHS
Citation Record: 1 Book
The Ceiling Of Hell - *Single*
GM US (1984)

Mr HOOPES

Second detective of Leonidas AMES

Insp HOPE

solves a case of death by gassing in a locked room.

British Policeman operating in England

Joan FLEMING 1908-1980 (British)
Invented 3 detectives - see Nuri ISKIRLAK
Citation Record: 1 Book
Polly Put The Kettle On - *Only*
Hutchinson UK (1952)

Matthew HOPE

is an attorney in a small town in Florida and is drawn into cases (usually of murder) because of a client's involvement. The book titles all allude to the names of nursery rhymes or tales.

American Male Amateur operating in Florida

Ed MCBAIN 1926- (American)
Invented 4 detectives - see The 87th PRECINCT
Citation Record: 10 Books
Goldilocks - *First*
Arbor US (1977); Hamish Hamilton UK (1978)

There Was A Little Girl - *Latest*
Warner US (1994); Hodder & Stoughton UK (1994)

Insp HOPKINS

solves a case of murder and mutilation of an American actress visiting this otherwise old and idyllic island, where such things do not usually happen.

British Policeman operating in Bermuda

David BURNHAM 1907-

Citation Record: 1 Book

Last Act In Bermuda - *Only*
Scribner's US (1940)

Sgt HOPKINS

Second detective of Insp DOWNES

John HOPKINS

British Male Amateur operating in England

Roland DANIEL 1880-1969 (British)

appears in other books as the sidekick of *Insp Neville LANGHAM*

Invented 11 detectives - see Insp Neville LANGHAM

Citation Record: 1 Book

The Shooting Of Sergius Leroy - *Only*
Wright UK (1932)

Sgt Lloyd HOPKINS

is in the Homicide Division of the Los Angeles Police Department. Brilliant, aggressive, morally ambivalent, he is another of the author's somewhat deranged cops, almost psychotic and suicidal in the face of the cases he meets.

American Policeman operating in Los Angeles

James ELLROY 1948- (American)

Invented 4 detectives - see Fritz BROWN

Citation Record: 3 Books

Blood On The Moon - *First*
Mysterious Press US (1984); Allison & Busby UK (1985)

Suicide Kill - *Latest*
Mysterious Press US (1986)

Insp HOPTON

British Policeman operating in England

John C WOODIWISS (British)

Writer: John Cecil WOODIWISS

Citation Record: 2 Books

Death's Visiting Card - *First*
Melrose UK (1936)

The Ebony Torso - *Last*
Gifford UK (1939)

Max HORN

sleuths in the twenty-first century.

American Male Sleuth operating in New York

Ben SLOAN (American)

Writer: Stephen R COX

Citation Record: 2 Books

Blown Dead - *First*
Gold Eagle US (1990)

Hot Zone - *Latest*
Gold Eagle US (1990)

Larry HORNBLOWER

is an ex-cabdriver who gets plenty of divorce work after putting an ad in *Yellow Pages.*

American Male Private Detective operating in New York

John BROWNER (American)

Citation Record: 1 Book

Death Of A Punk - *Single*
Pocket Books US (1980)

Charles HORNE

operates in the small town of Boone for an agency called Confidential Services.

American Male Private Detective operating in Illinois

Wilson TUCKER 1914- (American)

Invented 4 detectives - see Lt DANFORTH

Citation Record: 5 Books

The Chinese Doll - *First*
Rinehart US (1946); Cassell UK (1948)

Red Herring - *Last*
Rinehart US (1951)

Harry HORNE

American Male Amateur operating in USA

John GONZALES 1914- (American)

For writer details see Michael SHAYNE

Citation Record: 3 Books

End Of A JD - *First*
GM US (1960)

Follow That Hearse! - *Last*
GM US (1963)

Lewis HORNE

British Male Sleuth

Michael MOLLOY 1940- (British)

Writer: Michael John MOLLOY

Citation Record: 2 Books

The Black Dwarf - *First*
Hodder & Stoughton UK (1985); Hodder & Stoughton US (1987)

The Kid From Riga - *Latest*
Hodder & Stoughton UK (1987)

Insp Michael HORNSLEY

Australian Policeman operating in Australia/New Zealand

Elizabeth SALTER 1925-1980 (Australian)

Writer: Elizabeth Fulton SALTER

Citation Record: 5 Books

Death In A Mist - *First*
Bles UK (1957); Ace US (1968)

Once Upon A Tombstone - *Last*
Hutchinson UK (1965); Ace US (1967)

Helen HOROWITZ

Second detective of Lt Jacob HOROWITZ

Lt Jacob HOROWITZ and Helen HOROWITZ

Jacob HOROWITZ is a cop in the fictional small town of Tri-Town. A brilliant detective himself, he is, latterly, aided by his wife, *Helen HOROWITZ,* who has set up business as a PI.

American Policeman and American Female Private Investigator operating in USA

David DELMAN 1924- (American)

Citation Record: 10 Books

Sudden Death - *First*
Doubleday US (1972); Collins UK (1973 .)

The Liar's League - *Latest*
Collins UK (1989)

Insp HORROCKS and Hilary FENTON

British Policeman and American Amateur operating in Cambridge

When there is murder at the fictional All Saints College, the investigating cop is aided by an American student.

Q PATRICK 1901- (American)

Invented 5 detectives - see Lt Timothy TRANT

Citation Record: 1 Book

Murder At The Varsity - *Only*
Longman UK (1933)

Murder At Cambridge - *Only**
Farrar, Straus US (1933)

Mr HORROCKS
is a purser on board ship, which post gives him many opportunities for discovering misdeeds.
British Male Amateur operating on a ship

C J Cutcliffe HYNE 1865-1944 (British)
Invented 4 detectives - see Capt Owen KETTLE
Citation Record: 6 Short Stories in 1 Collection

Mr Horrocks, Purser - *Collection 1*
This collection of seventeen of the author's short stories contains six with *Mr HORROCKS.*
Methuen UK (1902)

HORTON and JORDAN
British Male Amateurs operating in England

Leslie BUTLER (British)
Citation Record: 3 Books

Night And The Judgement - *First*
Hale UK (1964)

The Man Who Crawled Away - *Last*
Hale UK (1966)

Sam HOSKINS
British Male Sleuth operating in England

Richard DACRE (British)
Citation Record: 3 Books

The Blood Runs Hot - *First*
Macmillan UK (1988)

Money With Menaces - *Latest*
Macmillan UK (1989)

Harry HOUDINI and Sir Arthur Conan DOYLE
were, in fact, close friends. *Sir Arthur Conan DOYLE,* the writer, became passionately convinced of the truth of spiritualism, a cult that was fast becoming fashionable in the 1920s, and he believed that *Harry HOUDINI,* the American magician and escapologist, had paranormal powers. The latter, a profound sceptic, scorned the very idea and offered to repeat any 'psychic' phenomenon by his own trickery. In this ingenious novel, a maniacal serial killer is committing murders in the style of *Edgar Allan POE* and, it seems, has *HOUDINI* on his list. The two men, both skilled in their own brands of mystery, track him down.
American Male Amateur and British Male Amateur operating in USA

William HJORTSBERG 1941- (American)
See main detective Harry ANGEL
Citation Record: 1 Book

Nevermore - *Single*
Grove US (1994)

Harry HOUDINI
Second detective of Sherlock HOLMES

Ch Insp Bill HOUGHTON
British Policeman operating in England

Maurice CULPAN 1918- (British)
Citation Record: 5 Books

A Nice Place To Die - *First*
Collins UK (1965)

Bloody Success - *Last*
Collins UK (1969)

Duffy HOUSE
investigates arson and murder, mixed up with baseball fever, in a hot town.
American Male Amateur operating in Detroit

Crabbe EVERS (American)
Citation Record: 1 Book

Tigers Burning - *Single*
Avon US (1995)

Sam HOUSTON
is an investigator for a Hospital Society, in spite of which he runs into rough cases of murder, which he just manages to solve.
American Male Professional Investigator operating in California

E Spence DE PUY 1872- (American)
!See Appendix 2.
Writer: Edward Spence DE PUY [DE PUE]
Citation Record: 2 Books

The Long Knife - *First*
Doubleday US (1936)

The Hospital Homicides - *Last*
Phoenix Press US (1937)

Supt HOWARD
British Policeman operating in India

H R F KEATING 1926- (British)
Invented 6 detectives - see Insp Ganesh GHOTE
Citation Record: 1 Book

The Murder Of The Maharajah - *Single*
Collins UK (1980); Doubleday US (1980)

Anthony HOWARD
is a sort of private eye who, being British, is an ex-Naval officer and the son of a knight to boot. He appears also in books with another of this author's detectives, *Insp MCKELLER.*
!See Appendix 2.
British Male Private Detective operating in England

Hugh MCCUTCHEON 1909- (British)
Invented 6 detectives - see Insp MCKELLER
Citation Record: 1 Book

The Long Night Through - *Only*
Rich UK (1956)

Anthony HOWARD
Second detective of Insp MCKELLER

Charlie HOWARD
is sacked from an electronics firm as a security risk but decides to investigate the investigators.
British Male Amateur operating in England

Leonard BRAIN 1906- (British)
Writer: Leonard PECK
Citation Record: 1 Book

It's A Free Country - *Only*
Longman UK (1965); Coward McCann US (1966)

Jeri HOWARD
American Female Private Detective operating in California

Janet DAWSON (American)
Citation Record: 4 Books

Kindred Crimes - *First*
St Martin's US (1990); Macmillan UK (1990)

Don't Turn Your Back On The Ocean - *Latest*
Fawcett US (1994); Headline UK (1994)

Roz HOWARD
American Female Amateur operating in Maine

Susan KENNEY 1941- (American)
Writer: Susan McIlvaine KENNEY
Citation Record: 2 Books

Garden Of Malice - *First*
Scribner's US (1983); Hale UK (1985)

Graves In Academe - *Latest*
Viking US (1985)

Russell HOWARD
Male Amateur

A E JOBSON (Australian)

Citation Record: 12 Short Stories in 1 Collection

The Adventures Of Russell Howard - *Collection 1*
Bookstall AU (1909)

Tom HOWARD
Australian Male Amateur operating in Australia

Tom HOWARD 1937- (Australian)

Writer: John T H REID

Citation Record: 4 Books 15 Short Stories in 1 Collection

The Beach-Front Murders - *First*
Rastar AU (1985)

A Way Of Life - *Latest*
Rastar AU (1989)

The Last Generation - *Collection 1*
Rastar AU (1986)

H

John HOWDEN
British Male Sleuth operating in England/Holland

Woosnam MILLS (British)

See main detective John MELROSE

Citation Record: 4 Books

Shadow Crusade - *First*
Hodder & Stoughton UK (1941)

Dusty Coinage - *Last*
Hodder & Stoughton UK (1953)

Bob HOWE
Male Amateur

Jeffrey ASHFORD 1926- (British)

Invented 9 detectives - see Det Insp Don KERRY

Citation Record: 1 Book

Guilt With Honor - *Single*
Walker US (1982)

Holly HOWE
Canadian Female Amateur operating in Canada

Alisa CRAIG 1922- (Canadian)

For writer details see Sarah KELLING and Max BITTERSOHN

Other Detectives:
Dittany MONK and Osbert MONK
Policeman Madoc RHYS

Citation Record: 1 Book

The Terrible Tide - *Single*
Doubleday US (1983); Hale UK (1985)

Mr HOYLAND
British Male Amateur operating in England

P C WILLIAMS (British)

Writer: Philip Claxton WILLIAMS

Citation Record: 1 Book 9 Short Stories in 3 Collections

Murder Will Out - *Only*
In 'Pictorial Art' UK (1946)

Mr Hoyland Looks Round - *Collection 1*
Short stories - 4
Hale UK (1941)

Hoyland Intervenes - *Collection 2*
Short stories - 2
Atlas UK (1944)

Hoyland Steps Out - *Collection 3*
Short stories - 3
In 'Pictorial Art' UK (1946)

Tamara HOYLAND
is an archaeologist who is also employed by a mysterious Department E in the British Secret Service.
British Female Amateur/Secret Agent operating in several locations

Jessica MANN 1937- (British)

was born in London. She was educated at St Paul's Girls' School, London, and took a BA in Archaeology and Anglo-Saxon at Newnham College, Cambridge. She later took an LLB at the University of Leicester.

Inventor of one other detective Prof Theodora Wade CRAWFORD

Citation Record: 4 Books

Funeral Rites - *First*
Macmillan UK (1981); Doubleday US (1982)

Death Beyond The Nile - *Latest*
Macmillan UK (1988); St Martin's US (1988)

Sarah HOYT
American Female Amateur operating in California

Barbara ABERCROMBIE 1939- (American)

Writer: Barbara Mattas ABERCROMBIE

Citation Record: 1 Book

Run For Your Life - *Single*
Morrow US (1984); Macdonald UK (1984)

Mike HUBBARD
British Male Sleuth operating in several locations

Muir SEUFFERT (British)

Citation Record: 3 Books

Hand Of A Killer - *First*
Hale UK (1967)

Devil At The Door - *Last*
Hale UK (1972)

Harriet HUBBLEY
is said to be a 'down-to earth dyke from Montreal and self-appointed sleuth'. In her one outing to date she takes refuge in a deserted motel and, as all those who have seen Alfred Hitchcock's film, *Psycho*, will at once appreciate, that is not at all the thing to do.
American Female Sleuth operating in Montreal

Jackie MANTHORNE (American)

Citation Record: 1 Book

The Ghost Motel - *Single*
Gynergy ? (1994)

Det Insp Samuel 'Smudge' HUDDLESTON
is an aging Scotland Yard officer, almost on the scrap-heap, who – in this comic novel set in a fictional England of the future – is given the task of solving a series of murders patterned on those of Jack the Ripper, not being helped much by the silly sergeant assigned to him.
!See Appendix 2.
British Policeman operating in London

Sidekick: Det Sgt Tony PIDGEON
is a brash young man who is assigned to HUDDLESTON on the latter's last case.
British Male - Subordinate

Robert TINE 1955?- (American)

Writer: Robert TINE

Other Byline: Richard HARDING

Citation Record: 1 Book

Uneasy Lies The Head - *Single*
Viking US (1982); Collins UK (1983)

Dr HUDSON
solves a case of death by poisoning in a locked room.
British Male Amateur operating in London

T A FRASER (British)

Citation Record: 1 Selected Short Story

The Pink Carnation
is in a collection, *The Eye of Jinas*.
Fraser UK (1923)

Mrs HUDSON and Sherlock HOLMES

In this short pastiche, *Sherlock HOLMES* is sick, his nephew is in hiding from arrest and *Mrs HUDSON*, the revered landlady of 221B Baker Street, becomes a detective and foils a dastardly plot.

British Female Amateur and Male Professional Amateur operating in London

Ardath MAYHAR 1930-

Citation Record: 1 Selected Short Story

The Affair Of The Midnight Midget - *Pastiche 1*

appears in the anthology, *THE MISADVENTURES OF SHERLOCK HOLMES* (Editor: *Sebastian WOLFE*).

Citadel US (1991)

Robin HUDSON

is a television reporter who becomes the chief suspect in a case of murder. She reluctantly turns to sleuthing to save herself.

American Female Amateur operating in USA

Sparkle HAYTER (American)

Citation Record: 1 Book

What's A Girl Gotta Do? - *Single*

Penguin US (1994)

Percy Aloysius HUFF

British Male Amateur operating in several locations

Charman EDWARDS 1896- (British)

Writer: Frederick Anthony EDWARDS

Citation Record: 6 Books

The Blue Macaw - *First*

Ward, Lock UK (1935)

Confetti For A Killing - *Last*

Ward, Lock UK (1937)

Barney HUGGINS

is a veteran of the Korean War, returned to England and now attempting to make a living as a PI in London's seedy Soho district.

British Male Private Detective operating in London

Mike SHELLEY (British)

Inventor of one other detective Bernard HOLLAND

Citation Record: 2 Books

The Terror Of Her Ways - *First*

Domino UK (1984)

Madame Ellie's Chamber Of Horrors - *Latest*

Domino UK (1984)

Byron HUGHES

American Male Amateur operating in USA

Eugene JONES (American)

Citation Record: 1 Book

Who Killed Gregory? - *Only*

Stokes US (1928)

The Last Clue - *Only**

Selwyn UK (1931)

Det Insp Elwyn HUGHES

British Policeman operating in England/Wales

D W F HARDIE 1906- (British)

Writer: David William Ferguson HARDIE

Citation Record: 4 Books

The Iron Egg - *First*

Nicholson & Watson UK (1947)

A Grave For Miss Carling - *Last*

Nicholson & Watson UK (1952)

Griff HUGHES

of the Hughes Agency, Worcester, solves a case of murder that occurred over forty years earlier.

American Male Private Detective operating in Connecticut

Doris Miles DISNEY 1907-1976 (American)

Invented 7 detectives - see Jefferson DIMARCO

Citation Record: 1 Book

Here Lies - *Only*

Doubleday US (1963); Hale UK (1964)

Howard HUGHES

Appears with at least two other detectives - see Toby PETERS.

Jack HUGHES

operates, at the end of the twentieth century, in a kind of deteriorating sci-fi world in which things are not at all what they used to be.

American Male Private Detective operating in New York

David BEAR 1949- (American)

Citation Record: 1 Book

Keeping Time - *Single*

St Martin's US (1979)

Jo HUGHES

is an astrologer who is a part-time PI.

British Private Detective operating in England

Linda MATHER (British)

Citation Record: 1 Book

Beware Taurus - *Single*

Macmillan UK (1994)

Kelly HUGHES

is one of the author's many racing sleuths.

British Male Amateur operating in England

Dick FRANCIS 1920- (British)

Invented 18 detectives - see Sid HALLEY

Citation Record: 1 Book

Enquiry - *Only*

Joseph UK (1969); Harper & Row US (1969)

Matt HUGHES

American Male Sleuth operating in Los Angeles

Aylwin Lee MARTIN (American)

Citation Record: 4 Books

Death On A Ferris Wheel - *First*

GM US (1952)

The Crimson Frame - *Last*

GM US (1952)

John HUGO

is a real estate manager who was once in the police.

American Male Sleuth operating in Florida

Alan GREEN 1906-1975 (American)

Writer: Alan Baer GREEN

Citation Record: 2 Books

What A Body! - *First*

Simon & Schuster US (1949); Redman UK (1950)

They Died Laughing - *Last*

Simon & Schuster US (1952); Panther UK (1957)

Martin HUISH

British Male Secret Agent operating in England

Sydney HORLER 1888-1954 (British)

Invented 20 detectives - see Sir Harker BELLAMY

Citation Record: 2 Books

The Secret Service Man - *First*

Hodder & Stoughton UK (1929); Knopf US (1930)

The Evil Messenger - *Last*

Hodder & Stoughton UK (1938)

Mark HULL

was one of this author's numerous pulp detectives, appearing mainly in stories in *Black Mask Magazine.*

American Male Detective in Pulp Magazines operating in USA

Norbert DAVIS 1909-1949 (American)

Invented 8 detectives - see Ben SHALEY

Citation Record: 1 Selected Short Story

Kansas City Flash
In 'Black Mask Magazine' US (1933)

Sarah HULL

appears in a collection of mini-mysteries.

American Female Sleuth operating in USA

Julia Remine PIGGIN (American)

Citation Record: 25 Short Stories in 1 Collection

Mini-Mysteries - *Collection 1*
Scholastic US (1973)

Horatio HUMBERTON

was a part-time undertaker and part-time detective who appeared in stories in *Dime Detective* in the 1930s.

American Male Detective in Pulp Magazines operating in USA

H

J Paul SUTER (American)

No citations

Mr HUMBLE and Dorrit BLY

Male Amateur and Female Amateur

Frank BUNCE 1907

Writer: Frank David BUNCE

Citation Record: 2 Books

So Young A Body - *First*
Simon & Schuster US (1950)

Rehearsal For Murder - *Last*
Abelard UK (1956); Abelard US (1956)

Insp HUMBLEBY

appears only in two short stories as the main detective, but also in eight with the author's other detective, *Gervase FEN.*

British Policeman operating in England

Edmund CRISPIN 1921-1978 (British)

Invented 3 detectives - see Gervase FEN

Citation Record: 2 Selected Short Stories

A Case In Camera
Gollancz UK (1979); Walker US (1980)

Blood Sport
is in the author's collection of miscellaneous stories, *FEN COUNTRY.*
Gollancz UK (1979); Walker US (1980)

Insp HUMBLEBY

Second detective of Gervase FEN

Graham HUME

is a brain specialist who sleuths in this one Victorian novel.

British Male Amateur operating in England

Richard MARSH 1867-1915 (British)

Invented 10 detectives - see The Hon Augustus CHAMPNELL

Citation Record: 1 Book

The Goddess, A Demon - *Only*
White UK (1900)

Hampton HUME

American Male Amateur operating in New York

Brandon BIRD 1906- (American)

were a husband-and wife writing team.

Writers: George Bird EVANS1906- and Kay Harris EVANS 1906-

Citation Record: 3 Books

Never Wake A Dead Man - *First*
Dodd, Mead US (1950); Constable UK (1952)

Downbeat For A Dirge - *Last*
Dodd, Mead US (1952)

Dead And Gone - *Last**
Dell US (1955)

Insp Laurie HUME

British Policeman operating in England

W Murdoch DUNCAN 1909-1975 (British)

Invented 8 detectives - see Supt MACNEILL

Citation Record: 3 Books

Murder Calls The Tune - *First*
Rich UK (1957)

The Murder Man - *Last*
Long UK (1959)

HUMPTY DUMPTY DICK

American Male Detective in Pulp Magazines operating in USA

C LITTLE (American)

See main detective Laura KEEN

Citation Record: 1 Selected Short Story

Humpty Dumpty Dick; Or, The Harlequin Detective
New York Detective Library US (1882-8)

Bow St Runner HUNT

British Policeman operating in London

Robert Louis STEVENSON and William Ernest HENLEY (British)

Robert Louis STEVENSON, the illustrious author, wrote several tales of horror and adventure, a vogue greatly popular at the time. *William HENLEY* was born in Gloucester and was a poet, editor and minor playwright. He too was a consumptive and, in fact, met *STEVENSON* after his stay in Edinburgh Infirmary, 1873-1875. The two men collaborated on three plays, none of which has ever been professionally performed. The one cited has a detective as a main character.

Writer: Robert Louis Balfour STEVENSON 1850-1894 and William Ernest HENLEY 1849-1903

Citation Record: 1 Book

Deacon Brodie; Or, The Double Life - *Play*
was described as 'a Melodrama in 5 acts and 8 Tableaux' and was privately printed.
Edinburgh University Press UK (1888)

Elsie May HUNT

Second detective of Tim MULLIGAN

Frederick HUNT

American Male Amateur operating in New York

Lillian DAY 1893- (American)

Citation Record: 2 Books

Murder In Time - *First*
Furman US (1936); Cassell UK (1935)

Death Comes On Friday - *Last*
Dutton US (1937); Cassell UK (1937)

Lucius HUNT

American Male Amateur operating in New York/Georgia

James WELLARD 1909- (American)

Writer: James Howard WELLARD

Citation Record: 2 Books

The Snake In The Grass - *First*
Dodd, Mead US (1942); United Authors UK (1946)

A Moment In Time - *Last*
Dodd, Mead US (1947)

Spotlight On Murder - *Last**
Foulsham UK (1949)

Norman HUNT

American Male Private Detective operating in Florida

Geoffrey NORMAN (American)

is a past editor of *Playboy* and *Esquire* magazines.

Citation Record: 2 Books

Sweetwater Ranch - *First*
Atlantic US (1990)

Blue Chipper - *Latest*
US (1992)

Adam HUNTER
American Male Secret Agent operating in USA

Norman CONWAY (American)

Citation Record: 2 Books

The Omega Operation - *First*
Canyon US (1974)

Operation: Alpha Death - *Last*
Canyon US (1975)

Ambrose HUNTER and Ed HUNTER
Am HUNTER, a retired circus performer, is the uncle of the young, brash *Ed HUNTER* and comes to Chicago to investigate the murder of his brother. As a result of their success, they set up the Hunter and Hunter Detective Agency and continue to solve crimes.

American Male Private Detectives operating in Chicago

Fredric BROWN 1906-1972 (American)

was born in Cincinnati, Ohio, and received only minimal education at Hanover College, Indiana. He wrote only seven books with his best-known detective pair, a dozen or so other good crime books, a considerable number of short stories about crime, some science fiction and several books for children. He received the Mystery Writers of America Edgar Allan Poe award, 1948.

Writer: Fredric William BROWN

Other Detectives:
ERNIE
Jerry GRANT
Det Frank RAMOS
Mr Henry SMITH
'Doc' STOEGER
SWEENEY
Roger L YOUNG

Citation Record: 7 Books

The Fabulous Clipjoint - *First*
Dutton US (1947); Boardman UK (1949)

Mrs Murphy's Underpants - *Last*
Dutton US (1963); Boardman UK (1965)

Anthony HUNTER
works for the Imperator Schmidt Agency on 49th Street, Manhattan. He gets the cases others won't touch.

American Male Private Detective operating in New York

Sidekick: Bill GRIFFITH
American Male - Assistant

Robert George DEAN (American)

Inventor of one other detective Pat THOMPSON

Citation Record: 10 Books

Murder Makes A Merry Widow - *First*
Doubleday US (1938)

Affair At Lover's Leap - *Last*
Doubleday US (1953)

Death At Lover's Leap - *Last**
Boardman UK (1954)

Ed HUNTER
Second detective of Ambrose HUNTER

Jazz HUNTER and Wynn HUNTER
are the wife and sister respectively of a man killed by a scorpion while looking after animals and running a safari business. When they discover that the scorpion was a venomous species not native to Africa, they naturally suspect foul play and seek out the murderer.

American Female Amateurs operating in Kenya

Karin MCQUILLAN 1950- (American)

Citation Record: 1 Book

The Cheetah Chase - *Single*
Ballantine US (1994)

Det Sgt Jerry HUNTER
British Policeman operating in England

Pauline BELL 1928- (British)

was born in Yorkshire and was a teacher before turning to criminous writing.

Other Detectives:
Det Ch Insp BROWNE
Sgt Benedict MITCHELL

Citation Record: 1 Book

Feast Into Mourning - *Single*
Macmillan UK (1991)

Leah HUNTER
begins her very first page in the way that is becoming almost obligatory, but none-the-less agreeable. She is, indeed, the kind of feisty young female sleuth who, in the subconscious of the criminous dream world, has replaced the male amateur know-all. She says of herself, a trifle ungrammatically, 'I'm twenty-five, brown hair, brown eyes, and single from choice; but don't run away with the idea that I hate men, because I don't, men are all right – in their place. I was born and live in Yorkshire, where puddings and cricket have about equal status.'

Leah HUNTER epitomises the new wave. A working girl, she is a tax inspector in the fictional small town of Bramfield, which seems to have more going for it in the way of crime and vice than Miami. Zany she may be, but she is delightful and dedicated, and her job gives her a useful way of turning amateur detective when she stumbles across unexplained corpses whose problems now have little to do with tax evasion.

British Female Professional Investigator operating in England

Sarah LACEY

Citation Record: 4 Books

File Under: Deceased - *First*
Hodder & Stoughton UK (1992)

File Under: Jeopardy - *Latest*
Hodder & Stoughton UK (1995)

Lt Max HUNTER
is in the Las Vegas police force and, relating his own cases, seems a hardened, world-weary cop.

American Policeman operating in Las Vegas

W T BALLARD 1903-1980 (American)

Invented 4 detectives - see Bill LENNOX

Citation Record: 3 Books

Pretty Miss Murder - *First*
Permabooks US (1961)

Three For The Money - *Last*
Permabooks US (1963)

Ch Insp Max HUNTER and Prof Stephen PILGRIM
Insp. HUNTER, investigating a double murder in Dorset and nicely baffled, sends for his old friend, *Stephen PILGRIM,* an affluent young man who is a 'Professor of Criminology' to help out.

British Policeman and British Male Amateur operating in Dorset

Dexter MUIR 1908- (British)

For writer details see Supt Anthony SLADE

Citation Record: 1 Book

The Pilgrims Meet Murder - *Only*
Jenkins UK (1948)

Pete HUNTER
operates in an unnamed city, which is not noted for its standards of morality or justice.

American Male Private Detective operating in USA

A A MARCUS (American)

Writer: Arthur A MARCUS

Citation Record: 3 Books

The Widow Gay - *First*
McKay US (1948)

Post-Mark Homicide - *First**
Graphic US (1953)

Make Way For Murder - *Last*
Graphic US (1955)

Det Supt Philip HUNTER
operates in the fictional small town of Yoreborough in the north of England. He is a British cop of the new procedural era, tough, abrasive and solving his cases by mixing with criminals rather than by fine, classic detective work.
British Policeman operating in England

Maurice PROCTER 1906-1973 (British)
Invented 3 detectives - see Det Insp Harry MARTINEAU
Citation Record: 2 Books
The Chief Inspector's Statement - *First*
Hutchinson UK (1951)
The Pennycross Murders - *First**
Harper & Row US (1953)
I Will Speak Daggers - *Last*
Hutchinson UK (1956)
The Ripper - *Last**
Harper & Row US (1956)

H

Robert Lee HUNTER
is in his thirties. Unusually wealthy for a detective, he lives in a nineteenth-century pile on a Delaware River island and is usually to be found hunting vicious criminals.
American Male Private Detective operating in New York

Eric SAUTER 1948- (American)
was born in Bay City, Michigan. He graduated with a BA at Michigan State University, East Lansing, 1971, and has worked as a reporter and editor.
Other Detectives:
Det PAIGE   Det YATES
Citation Record: 3 Books
Hunter - *First*
Avon US (1983)
Hunter And The Raven - *Latest*
Avon US (1984)

Sam HUNTER
has cases that involve a very great deal of violence.
American Male Private Detective operating in Los Angeles

L A MORSE 1945- (American)
See main detective Jake SPANNER
Citation Record: 2 Books
The Big Enchilada - *First*
Avon US (1982); Avon UK (1983)
Slease - *Latest*
Avon US (1985)

Wynn HUNTER
Second detective of Jazz HUNTER

Capt Colin HUNTINGTON
American Male Professional Investigator operating in USA

Richard CONDON 1915- (American)
was born in New York City. His main work has been with several film studios in Hollywood, but he has written several highly acclaimed genre and non-genre novels, the former usually dealing with crime or espionage.
Writer: Richard Thomas CONDON
Citation Record: 2 Books
Arigato - *First*
Weidenfeld & Nicolson UK (1972); Dial US (1972)
Bandicoot - *Latest*
Dial US (1978); Hutchinson UK (1978)

Joe HUSSEY
has a front suggesting he is a garage attendant in North London. But actually he is a PI and an undercover espionage agent with vague government connections.
!See Appendix 2.
British Male Private Detective operating in London

Colin DUNNE (British)
Citation Record: 2 Books
Ratcatcher - *First*
Secker & Warburg UK (1985); Secker & Warburg US (1986)
Hooligan - *Latest*
Secker & Warburg UK (1987); Norton US (1988)

HUTCH
Second detective of STARSKY

Robert HUTCH
British Male Amateur operating in England

H M RICHARDSON 1876- (British)
Writer: Harry Marriott RICHARDSON
Citation Record: 1 Book
The Rock Of Justice - *Only*
Hutchinson UK (1928)

Judy HUTCHINGS
British Female Amateur

Dominic DEVINE 1920-1981 (British)
Invented 4 detectives - see Det Insp Maurice NICOLSON
Citation Record: 1 Book
Sunk Without A Trace - *Only*
Collins UK (1978); St Martin's US (1979)

Kail HUTTON
American Male Detective in Pulp Magazines operating in Cincinnati

Will WINCH (American)
Invented 5 detectives - see The LAWYER DETECTIVE
Citation Record: 1 Selected Short Story
Kail Hutton, The Cincinnati Detective; Or, The Mystery Of The Phantom Hand
Old Cap Collier Library US (18??)

Kek HUUYGENS
Male Sleuth operating in Lisbon

Robert L FISH 1912-1981 (American)
Invented 4 detectives - see Schlock HOMES
Citation Record: 3 Books 7 Short Stories in 1 Collection
The Hochmann Miniatures - *First*
New American Library US (1967)
The Wager - *Last*
Putnam US (1974); Hale UK (1976)
Kek Huuygens, Smuggler - *Collection 1*
Mysterious Press US (1976)

Rex HUXFORD
is said to be a 'criminologist' and appears in two novels, the extraordinary and complex ineptitude of which can only be admired. The plots are too complicated to reveal, as are *HUXFORD's* detective methods.
American Male Amateur operating in USA
Sidekick: Spike SALIENO
American Male - Assistant
Sidekick: 'Plugger' MARTIN
American Male - Assistant

Cromwell GIBBONS 1893- (American)
Citation Record: 2 Books
Murder In Hollywood - *First*
Kemp US (1936)
The Bat Woman - *Last*
World US (1938)

HUY
must be one of the most ancient of all detectives in the history of the genre. He is a problem-solver and former scribe in the reign of Tutankhamun in Egypt. No mean detective, he is a loner who frequents the mean streets of town, more of a *MARLOWE* than a *HOLMES*, but with a bit of the gloomy *MORSE* and a touch of the patient *MAIGRET* about him.
Egyptian Male Private Detective operating in Ancient Egypt

Anton GILL (British)

Citation Record: 1 Book

City Of Dreams - *Single*
Bloomsbury UK (1993)

HYACINTH
Second detective of Sister JOHN

Howard HYATT and Michael DUNLOP
American Male Amateurs operating in California

Margaret MILLAR 1915- (Canadian)

Invented 11 detectives - see Insp SANDS

Citation Record: 1 Book

Banshee - *Single*
Morrow US (1983)

Insp HYDE
is a tall gourmet. He manages, but only just, to solve the murder of a lewd comedian who is shot on stage at a summer theatre.

British Policeman operating in England

Anthony HECKSTALL-SMITH 1904- (British)

Citation Record: 1 Book

Murder On The Brain - *Only*
Wingate UK (1958); Roy US (1958)

Dr HYDE
British Male Amateur operating in England

G K CHESTERTON 1874-1936 (British)

Invented 7 detectives - see Father BROWN

Citation Record: 1 Selected Short Story

The White Pillar Murders
is in the anthology, *To The Queen's Taste* (Editor; *Ellery QUEEN)* and also in the author's own collection, *THIRTEEN DETECTIVES*. An alternative title for this story may be *Dr Hyde, Detective*.
!See Appendix 2.
Little, Brown US (1946)

Anne HYDE
British Female Amateur operating in England

Annie S SWAN (British)

See main detective Elizabeth GLEN

Citation Record: 12 Short Stories in 1 Collection

Anne Hyde, Travelling Companion - *Collection 1*
Hodder & Stoughton UK (1908)

Barney HYDE
was once a Scotland Yard detective-sergeant, but is now the London manager for Global Investigations Inc of New York. In his cases, usually semi-boiled mid-Atlantic in style, he is accompanied by a useful canine sidekick.

British Male Private Detective operating in London

Sidekick: KURT
Male - Pet Dog

Nigel BRENT 1905- (British)

Writer: Cecil Gordon Eugene WIMHURST

Citation Record: 11 Books

The Scarlet Lily - *First*
Muller UK (1953)

Spider In The Web - *Last*
Muller UK (1960)

John Byron HYDE
is a Vietnam War hero who works with an agency in California and makes good use of his skills in karate.

American Male Private Detective operating in California/England

Benjamin WOLFF (American)

Citation Record: 2 Books

Hyde And Seek - *First*
Avon US (1984)

Hyde In Deep Cover - *Latest*
Avon US (1985)

John George Norman HYDE
British Male Amateur operating in England

John BOLAND 1913-1976 (British)

Writer: Bertram John BOLAND

Other Byline: James TREVOR

Inventor of one other detective Kim SMITH

Citation Record: 3 Books

The League Of Gentlemen - *First*
Boardman UK (1958); Beacon US (1961)

The Gentlemen At Large - *Last*
Boardman UK (1962); Award US (1968)

Hank HYER
was raised in Chicago but, still in his twenties, moves to New York and sets up as a PI on Bank Street in Greenwich Village, pricing his services very high indeed.

American Male Private Detective operating in New York

Sidekick: Orson QUICK
is taken on as an assistant in the sixth book of the series.
American Male - Assistant

Kurt STEEL 1904-1946 (American)

was born in Tuscola, Illinois. He is a sometime Professor of Philosophy at New York University.

Writer: Rudolph Harnaday KAGEY

Citation Record: 9 Books

Murder Of A Dead Man - *First*
Bobbs US (1935)

The Traveling Corpses - *First**
Abridged.
Crime Novel Selection US (1942)

Ambush House - *Last*
Harcourt Brace US (1943)

Insp Kingsley HYLTON
investigates the murder of a lecherous miser in a little village, where sexual activity seems to be as rife as murder.

British Policeman operating in England

Laurence MEYNELL 1899-1989 (British)

Invented 5 detectives - see Hooky HEFFERMAN

Citation Record: 1 Book

"On The Night Of The 18th..." - *Only*
Nicholson & Watson UK (1936); Harper & Row US (1936)

Insp HYND
solves a case of death by bludgeoning in a locked room.

British Policeman operating in England

Kelman FROST (British)

See main detective Dr Francis FARRAR

Citation Record: 1 Book

Death Registers At The Eagle Arms - *Only*
Oberon UK (1948)

The HYPNOTIST DETECTIVE
American Male Detective in Pulp Magazines operating in USA

ANON

No citations

Mr H-LM-S
is a *Sherlock HOLMES* parody.

British Male Professional Amateur operating in London

Allen UPWARD 1863-1926 (British)

Invented 6 detectives - see Charles PRESCOTT

Citation Record: 1 Selected Short Story

The Adventure Of The Stolen Doormat - *Parody 1*
appears in *THE WONDERFUL CAREER OF EBENEZER LOBB.*
Hurst & Blackett UK (1900)

Simon IFF
British Male Amateur operating in England

Alistair CROWLEY 1875-1947 (British)

was a writer who became interested in the occult while an undergraduate at Cambridge at the time of the 'magic revival' during the last years of the nineteenth century. He joined one of the 'magic orders' that were then the rage but was expelled for what were called 'extreme practices'. He started his own order and for the rest of his life travelled with 'disciples'. His name was connected with malpractices of various kinds and, for a while, he became notorious as 'the wickedest man in the world', a title he revelled in and which the newspapers loved. He found little time for writing and it is perhaps surprising that this little collection has surfaced.

Writer: Edward Alexander CROWLEY

Citation Record: 6 Short Stories in 1 Collection

The Scrutinies Of Simon Iff - *Collection 1*
Teitan ? (1987)

IMPEY
British Male Amateur operating in London

Horace Annesley VACHELL 1861-1955 (British)

See main detective Joe QUINNEY

Citation Record: 15 Short Stories in 1 Collection

Experiences Of A Bond Street Jeweller - *Collection 1*
Cassell UK (1932)

Insp John INCH
British Policeman operating in England

Jesse TEMPLETON 1888-1969 (British)

Writer: George GOODCHILD

Other Byline: George GOODCHILD

Invented 5 detectives - see Insp MCLEAN

Citation Record: 21 Short Stories in 1 Collection

Inch Of The CID- *Collection 1*
contains twenty-one untitled chapters, each a short story. It was republished under the following byline.
Ward, Lock UK (1932)

George GOODCHILD 1888-1969 (British)

For writer details see Insp John INCH

Citation Record: 21 Short Stories in 1 Collection

Inch Of The CID- *Collection 1*
was previously published under the preceding byline.
Ward, Lock UK (1936)

Det Johnny INCH
is a young man, at first attached to Scotland Yard's Criminal Investigation Department but later becoming a private investigator.

British Male Ex-Policeman operating in London

J F STRAKER 1904- (British)

was born in Farnborough, Hampshire. He was educated at Framlingham College, Suffolk, and served in the Army, 1940-1945. He taught mathematics at several schools, 1927-1976, and is the author of at least twenty-five genre novels.

Writer: John Foster STRAKER

Other Detectives:
Insp PITT David WRIGHT

Citation Record: 4 Books

Sin And Johnny Inch - *First*
Harrap UK (1968)

The Goat - *Last*
Harrap UK (1972)

The INDEPENDENT DETECTIVE
American Male Detective in Pulp Magazines operating in USA

ANON

Citation Record: 1 Book

The Independent Detective - *Only*
Aldine US

Bonnie INDERMILL
is a part-time investigator who solves cases that all have a legal angle.

American Female Professional Investigator operating in New York

Carole BERRY (American)

Citation Record: 4 Books

The Letter Of The Law - *First*
St Martin's US (1988)

The Death Of A Difficult Woman - *Latest*
St Martin's US (1994)

Insp Archibald INGE
is, for obvious reasons, known as 'The Archdeacon'.

British Policeman operating in England

Q PATRICK 1901- (American)

Invented 5 detectives - see Lt Timothy TRANT

Citation Record: 1 Book

Cottage Sinister - *Single*
Swain US (1931); Longman UK (1932)

John INGLES and Madeline SMITH
sleuth together in Glasgow in 1857.

Male Amateur and Female Amateur operating in Scotland

Pamela WEST (American)

Writers: Pamela West KATKIN and Samuel Leonard RUBENSTEIN 1922-

Citation Record: 1 Book

Madeline - *Single*
St Martin's US (1983)

Gerald INGRAM
is a member of the British Embassy staff in Paris.

British Male Amateur operating in Paris

William LEQUEUX 1864-1927 (British)

Invented 23 detectives - see Allan KENNEDY

Citation Record: 1 Book

Her Majesty's Minister - *Only*
Hodder & Stoughton UK (1901)

John INGRAM
American Male Amateur operating in several locations

Charles WILLIAMS 1909-1975 (American)

was born in San Angelo, Texas, and educated at Brownsville High School, Texas. He worked in the field of radio electronics, much of the time for the United States Merchant Marine and Navy and was the author of twenty-three genre novels and several screenplays.

Citation Record: 2 Books

Aground - *First*
Viking US (1960); Cassell UK (1961)

Dead Calm - *Last*
Viking US (1963); Cassell UK (1964)

Supt INKBARROW
has to solve a case of murder, which he does magnificently only using the telephone and without cheating. He is quite a character and it is a pity he has not been used more often.

British Policeman operating in England

John ROSSITER 1916- (British)

was born in Staverton, Devon. He was himself a Detective Chief Superintendent in the Wiltshire Constabulary, which gives his main line of detective stories a special edge.

Inventor of one other detective Roger TALLIS

Citation Record: 1 Selected Short Story

Yes, Sir: No, Sir
is in an anthology, *John Creasey's Crime Collection.*
Gollancz UK (1978)

Tommy INMAN
American Male Amateur operating in Texas

Martha G WEBB 1943- (American)

Writer: Martha Anne Guice Wingate WEBB

Inventor of one other detective pair Allan CONYERS and Cheryl BURROUGHS

Citation Record: 2 Books

A White Male Running - *First*
Walker US (1985)

Even Cops' Daughters - *Latest*
Walker US (1986)

Kate INNES

The scene is set in an eastern American girls' school, at which the Professor of English is killed. Although a number of people try to solve the mystery, it is *Kate INNES*, 'the staff psychiatrist', who solves it. Did American girls' schools really have staff psychiatrists in 1946? The mind boggles.

American Male Amateur operating in USA

Helen White EUSTIS 1916- (American)

was born in Cincinnati, Ohio, and is mainly known for this one acclaimed novel, her first, for which she received the Mystery Writers of America Edgar Allan Poe award, 1947. She wrote only one other novel afterwards.

Citation Record: 1 Book

The Horizontal Man - *Only*
Harper & Row US (1946); Hamish Hamilton UK (1947)

Rachel INNES

is a middle-aged spinster who investigates the deaths of a bank president and his son.

American Female Amateur operating in California

Mary Roberts RINEHART 1876-1958 (American)

Invented 7 detectives - see Letitia CARBERRY

Citation Record: 1 Book

The Circular Staircase - *Only*
Bobbs US (1908); Cassell UK (1909)

INSPECTOR F

British Policeman operating in England

WATERS (British)

Invented 6 detectives - see WATERS

Citation Record: 1 Collection

Experiences Of A Real Detective - *Collection 1*
Ward, Lock UK (1862)

Wayman INSTONE

solves a case of death by bludgeoning in an observatory.

American Male Amateur operating in USA

Arlton EADIE ?-1935 (American)

Citation Record: 1 Selected Short Story

The Clue From Mars
appeared in the February number.
In 'Detective Story Magazine' US (1924)

The INSURANCE DETECTIVE

American Male Detective in Pulp Magazines operating in USA

Tom FOX (American)

Invented 4 detectives - see OLD DUDE

Citation Record: 1 Book

The Insurance Detective; Or, Unearthing A Great Fraud - *Only*
New York Detective Library US (1882-8)

Insp IRELAND

British Policeman operating in London

Richard MARSH 1867-1915 (British)

Invented 10 detectives - see The Hon Augustus CHAMPNELL

Citation Record: 1 Book

The Datchet Diamonds - *Only*
Ward, Lock UK (1898)

Sam IRELAND

American Male Private Detective operating in Vermont

William BRANDON 1914- (American)

Writer: William E BRANDON

Citation Record: 1 Book

The Dangerous Dead - *Only*
Dodd, Mead US (1943)

Jeremiah IRISH

American Male Amateur operating in Los Angeles

Nellise CHILD (American)

Citation Record: 2 Books

Murder Comes Home - *First*
Knopf US (1933); Collins UK (1933)

The Diamond Ransom Murders - *Last*
Knopf US (1935); Collins UK (1939)

The IRISH DETECTIVE

Irish Male Detective in Pulp Magazines operating in USA

OLD SLEUTH (American)

Invented 40 detectives - see Brant ADAMS

Citation Record: 1 Book

The Irish Detective; Or, Fergus Connor's Greatest Case - *Only*
Munro US (1892)

The IRISH POLICE OFFICER

Irish Policeman operating in Ireland

Robert CURTIS (British)

Citation Record: 6 Short Stories in 1 Collection

The Irish Police Officer - *Collection 1*
Ward, Lock UK (1861)

IRON BURGESS

American Male Detective in Pulp Magazines operating in USA

OLD SLEUTH (American)

Invented 40 detectives - see Brant ADAMS

Citation Record: 1 Book

Iron Burgess, The Government Detective - *Only*
Royal US (ca 1908)

Paul IRVING

British Male Amateur operating in England

Leo GREX 1908-1985 (British)

Invented 3 detectives - see Phil SANDERSON

Citation Record: 6 Books

The Tragedy At Draythorpe - *First*
Hutchinson UK (1931)

Ace Of Danger - *Last*
Hutchinson UK (1952)

Insp Rip IRVING

Second detective of Patrick C SHIRLEY

Jack IRWIN and Robert MARTINEAU

JACK IRWIN is a young London barrister and *Robert MARTINEAU* a medical student at Guy's Hospital. They sleuth jointly in a story published in this rare Victorian magazine.

British Male Amateurs operating in London

ANON

Citation Record: 1 Book

Struck Dead - *Only*
In 'Boys of England' UK (1888)

Nuri ISKIRLAK

is a Turkish philosopher. His first case involves opium smuggling in Turkey and his second, on a visit to England, the death of a friend's son in Oxford.

Turkish Male Amateur operating in England/Turkey

Joan FLEMING 1908-1980 (British)

was born in Horwich, Lancashire. She was educated at Brighthelmston School, Southport, Lancashire, and at

Lausanne University, Switzerland. She was the author of at least thirty-two genre books, whose overall style has been compared in technique and quality with that of *Patricia HIGHSMITH*. Her books are thus not standard detective stories – indeed, she rarely used a series detective – but psychological investigations of her characters, innocent and guilty alike. She received the Crime Writers Association Golden Dagger award twice, 1962 and 1970.

Writer: Joan Margaret FLEMING

Other Detectives:
Insp HOPE   Nat SAPPERTON

Citation Record: 2 Books

When I Grow Rich - *First*
Collins UK (1962); Washburn US (1962)

Nothing Is The Number When You Die - *Last*
Collins UK (1965); Washburn US (1965)

Charley IVES

solves the mystery of why and how a woman's double appears in so many places.

American Male Amateur operating in New York

Sidekick: Olivia HUDSON
Female - Assistant

I

Charlotte ARMSTRONG 1905-1969 (American)

Invented 5 detectives - see Prof MacDougal DUFF

Citation Record: 1 Book

The Dream Walker - *Only*
Coward McCann US (1955); Davies UK (1955)

Alibi For Murder - *Only**
Pocket Books US (1956)

Les IVEY

American Male Private Detective operating in USA

Robert Portner KOEHLER 1905- (American)

Other Detectives:
Pecos APPLEBY   Al BRANSON
Maj Avery GREGG and Tony ELLIS

Citation Record: 1 Book

Corpse In The Wind - *Only*
Phoenix Press US (1944)

Eric IVORSEN

American Male Sleuth operating in USA

Rick SPENCER (American)

Citation Record: 5 Books

All That Glitters - *First*
Signet US (1983)

The Devil's Mirror - *Latest*
Signet US (1984)

Kate IVORY

is a novelist who takes to sleuthing.

British Female Amateur operating in England

Veronica STALLWOOD (British)

Citation Record: 3 Books

Deathspell - *First*
Macmillan UK (1992)

Oxford Exit - *Latest*
Macmillan UK (1994)

Baron IXELL

Male Amateur operating in New York

Oscar SCHISGALL 1901-1984 (American)

Citation Record: 4 Short Stories in 1 Collection

Baron Ixell, Crime Breaker - *Collection 1*
contains four novelettes.
Longman US (1929); Longman UK (1929)

— J —

JACARA

Male Sleuth

Victor NORWOOD 1920-1983 (British)

Writer: Victor George Charles NORWOOD

Other Byline: Hank JANSON

Citation Record: 6 Books

The Caves Of Death - *First*
Scion UK (1951)

Cry Of The Beast - *Last*
Scion UK (1953)

JACK and GIL

American Male Detective and American Female Detective in Pulp Magazines operating in USA

OLD SLEUTH (American)

Invented 40 detectives - see Brant ADAMS

Citation Record: 1 Book

Two Wonderful Detectives; Or, Jack And Gil's Marvellous Skill - *Only*
Ogilvie US (1898)

Insp Wilton JACKS

American Policeman operating in New York

J H WALLIS 1885-1958 (American)

Writer: James Harold WALLIS

Citation Record: 6 Books

Murder By Formula - *First*
Dutton US (1931); Jarrolds UK (1932)

Murder Mansion - *Last*
Dutton US (1934)

House Of Murder - *Last**
Jarrolds UK (1934)

Det Lt JACKSON

Second detective of Fergus O'BREEN

Ed JACKSON

American Male Sleuth operating in Washington DC

Nora ROBERTS 1950- (American)

Citation Record: 2 Books

Sacred Sins - *First*
Bantam US (1987); Thorndike UK (1988)

Brazen Virtue - *Latest*
Bantam US (1988)

Floyd JACKSON

American Male Private Detective operating in California

James Hadley CHASE 1906-1985 (British)

Invented 14 detectives - see Dave FENNER

Citation Record: 1 Book

You Never Know With Women - *Only*
Jarrolds UK (1949); Pocket Books US (1972)

Insp John Jay 'Jailbird' JACKSON

British Policeman operating in England

David T LINDSAY (British)

Citation Record: 3 Books

Inspector Jackson Investigates - *First*
Hamilton UK (1936)

Inspector Jackson Goes North - *Last*
Hamilton UK (1939)

Juliet JACKSON

American Female Amateur operating in New York/New Jersey

Margaret TURNBULL ?-1942 (American)

Citation Record: 4 Books

Madame Judas - *First*
Lippincott US (1926); Jenkins UK (1926)

The Coast Road Murder - *Last*
Lippincott US (1934)

Kane JACKSON

is an industrial spy, employed by a large US pharmaceutical company. In the course of his work he has to solve several murders and track down a rather large number of villains.

American Male Professional Investigator operating in New York/New Jersey

William ARDEN 1924- (American)

was born in St Louis, Missouri.

Writer: Dennis LYNDS

Other Bylines:

Michael COLLINS John CROWE
Maxwell GRANT Dennis LYNDS
Mark SADLER

Inventor of one other detective Sgt Joseph MARX

Citation Record: 5 Books

A Dark Power - *First*
Dodd, Mead US (1968); Hale UK (1970)

Deadly Legacy - *Last*
Dodd, Mead US (1973); Hale UK (1974)

Peter JACKSON

is a broadcaster who solves a case of murder by strangulation in a locked room.

British Male Amateur operating in England

Ralph STEPHENSON 1910- (British)

Writer: William Ralph Ewing STEPHENSON

Inventor of one other detective pair Charles FINCH and 'Stalky' HERON

Citation Record: 1 Book

Body In My Arms - *Only*
Gifford UK (1963)

'Slow and Sure' JACKSON

British Male Sleuth operating in England

W A MACKENZIE 1870- (British)

Writer: William Andrew MACKENZIE

Inventor of one other detective Sir Nigel LACAITA

Citation Record: 1 Book

The Flower O' The Peach - *Only*
Ward, Lock UK (1916)

Tom JACKSON

American Male Amateur operating in Salt Lake City

Thomas H COOK (American)

See main detective Frank CLEMONS

Citation Record: 1 Book

Tabernacle - *Single*
Houghton US (1983)

Walter JACKSON

American Male Amateur operating in USA

Arthur MALING 1923- (American)

Invented 3 detectives - see Brockton POTTER

Citation Record: 1 Book

Bent Man - *Only*
Harper & Row US (1975); Prior UK (1976)

William JACKSON

Second detective of Ed RAZONI

William JACKSON

Appears with at least two other detectives - see Ed RAZONI

Det Insp 'Jacko' JACKSON

is one of the best of the modern breed of British cops. Well characterised, well balanced, sound in wind and limb, with no hangups, a satisfactory love life, and dedication without overbearing intellectual wisdom, he is a creation that manages to encompass the special quality of the old-style amateur within the strict and very realistic world of police procedure. His cases, nicely original in being set around the provincial and real town of Nottingham, steer well away from the yawn-provoking police procedurals of many a British crime novel; and, thankfully, he manages to do without that other invention, the boring British sergeant sidekick with sexual problems. Altogether, a welcome departure!

British Policeman operating in England

Frank PALMER (British)

Citation Record: 5 Books

Testimony - *First*
Constable UK (1992)

China Hand - *Latest*
Constable UK (1994)

Callista JACOBS

American Female Amateur operating in Boston

Kathryn Lasky KNIGHT (American)

Citation Record: 3 Books

Trace Elements - *First*
Norton US (1986); Thorndike UK (1988)

Dark Swan - *Latest*
St Martin's US (1994)

Miles JACOBY

is an ex-boxer who, when his former boss is killed, takes over a small-time New York agency, which seems to operate out of a bar called Bogies.

American Male Private Detective operating in New York

Sidekick: Caroline MCWILLIAMS

is taken on as a novice detective.

American Female - Assistant

Robert J RANDISI 1951- (American)

Invented 5 detectives - see Sal CARLUCCI

Citation Record: 7 Books

Eye In The Ring - *First*
Avon US (1982)

Stand-Up - *Latest*
Walker US (1994)

Quentin JACOBY

is retired from the force and, widowed and bored, practises as a PI, although he has no licence.

American Male Amateur operating in New York

J C S SMITH 1947- (American)

Writer: Jane C S SMITH

Citation Record: 2 Books

Jacoby's First Case - *First*
Atheneum US (1980); Hale UK (1981)

Nightcap - *Latest*
Atheneum US (1984); Quartet UK (1985)

Milan JACOVICH

is middle-aged and perpetually worried about his Slav roots. Formerly a US Army policeman and later a civilian cop, he is now a PI. Sadder and wiser than he once was, he comes over as a sound detective with compassion.

American Male Private Detective operating in Cleveland

Les ROBERTS 1937- (American)

was born in Chicago, Illinois. He has been a professional singer, jazz pianist, TV writer and theatrical producer.

Inventor of one other detective SAXON

Citation Record: 5 Books

Pepper Pike - *First*
St Martin's US (1988); Coronet UK (1990)

The Lake Effect - *Latest*
St Martin's US (1994)

Monsieur JACQUOT and Monsieur LEVERT

solve a case of death by bludgeoning in a locked room.

French Male Amateurs operating in France

Jean TOUSSAINT-SAMAT 1865- (French)

See main detective Monsieur LEVERT

Citation Record: 2 Books

Shoes That Had Walked Twice - *Only*
is a translation from the French of *L'Horrible Mort de Miss Gildchrist.*
Lippincott US (1933)

Curt 'Nazi Hunter' JAEGER
American Male Professional Investigator operating in several locations

Mark MANDELL (American)

Citation Record: 5 Books

Nazi Hunter - *First*
Pinnacle US (1981)

Hell Nest - *Latest*
Pinnacle US (1983)

Karl JAEGER
is a large, tough, ex-Army Intelligence policeman who, at some time in the future, is apparently the last PI. Notwithstanding, he still has to deal with the usual bunch of nasty aliens from another planet.
American Male Private Detective

Gardner DOZOIS and George EFFINGER (American)

Citation Record: 1 Book

Nightmare Blue - *First*
Berkley US (1975)

J

Mick JAGGER
British Male Sleuth

William GARNER 1920- (American)

Citation Record: 4 Books

Overkill - *First*
New American Library US (1966); Collins UK (1966)

A Big Enough Wreath - *Last*
Collins UK (1974); Putnam US (1975)

JAGGERS
British Male Professional Investigator operating in England

John TEMPLER (British)

Citation Record: 1 Book 20 Short Stories in 2 Collections

Jaggers At Bay - *Only*
Oxford UK (1938)

Jaggers, Air Detective - *Collection 1*
Short stories - 10
Oxford UK (1936)

Jaggers Swoops Again - *Collection 2*
Short stories - 10
Oxford UK (1937)

Ch Insp 'Jake' JAKOWICZ
is a heroine who sleuths in the London of the future, in 2013, where communal crime is rife and police methods, though advanced, are certainly odd.
British Policewoman operating in England

Philip KERR 1956- (British)
was born in Edinburgh.

Other Detectives:
Yevgeni Ivanovitch GRUSHKO Bernard GUNTHER

Citation Record: 1 Book

A Philosophical Investigation - *Single*
is an involved intellectual study and an example of new avenues being explored by the advance guard of the genre.
Chatto & Windus UK (1992)

Insp JAMES
is a rarity among the author's inventions, an ordinary English country policeman. In a tale of sinister violence, his simple sleuthing succeeds in trapping an evil murderer.
British Policeman operating in England

Sidekick: Const George ROGERS
British Male - Subordinate

Raymond MARSHALL 1906-1985 (British)
Invented 4 detectives - see Don MICKLEM

Citation Record: 1 Book

Trusted Like The Fox - *Only*
is one of the few novels by the author set in England and one for which he chose a new pseudonym. Although not a specially good novel, the story, like all those by this author, is sinister and exciting. Later reprints have tended to use the *James Hadley CHASE* byline, for obvious commercial reasons.
Jarrolds UK (1948)

Insp JAMES
British Policeman operating in England

Roger BAX 1908- (British)
For writer details see Max EASTERBROOK

Citation Record: 2 Books

Blueprint For Murder - *First*
Hutchinson UK (1948)

The Trouble With Murder - *First**
Harper & Row US (1948)

A Grave Case Of Murder - *Last*
Hutchinson UK (1951); Harper & Row US (1951)

Abby JAMES
solves a theatrical murder case.
American Female Amateur operating in New York

Barbara PAUL (American)
Invented 8 detectives - see Lt TOOMEY

Citation Record: 1 Book

The Fourth Wall - *Single*
Doubleday US (1979); Women's Press UK (1988)

Adam JAMES
is a foreign correspondent on the Orient Express. Murder is committed, as seems to be common on this train, but he unmasks the killer.
Male Amateur operating in Middle East

William P MCGIVERN 1927-1982 (American)
Invented 5 detectives - see Dave BANNION

Citation Record: 1 Selected Short Story

The Last Word
appeared in the February number.
In 'Ellery Queen's Mystery Magazine' US (1963)

Dewey JAMES
is a librarian in a small town and naturally she takes to amateur sleuthing, as all good fictional librarians must.
American Female Amateur operating in Kentucky

Kate MORGAN (American)

Citation Record: 5 Books

A Slay At The Races - *First*
Berkley US (1990)

Wanted: Dude Or Alive - *Latest*
Berkley US (1995)

Frank JAMES
American Male Amateur operating in USA

Elizabeth FACKLER 1947- (American)

Citation Record: 1 Book

Arson - *Single*
Dodd, Mead US (1984)

Insp Harry JAMES
British Policeman operating in England

Sidekick: Sgt HONEYBODY
British Male - Subordinate

Kenneth GILES 1922-1972 (British)

Citation Record: 9 Books

Some Beasts No More - *First*
Gollancz UK (1965); Walker US (1968)

A File On Death - *Last*
Gollancz UK (1973); Walker US (1973)

Jessica JAMES

American Female Amateur operating in New York/Rochester

Meg O'BRIEN (American)

Citation Record: 3 Books

Salmon In The Soup - *First*
Bantam US (1990); Women's Press UK (1993)

Eagles Die Too - *Latest*
Doubleday US (1992)

Lydia JAMES

is a Congress Committee counsel who investigates the murder of a US senator.

American Female Amateur operating in Washington DC

Margaret TRUMAN 1924- (American)

Invented 9 detectives - see Mr Ron FAIRCHILD

Citation Record: 1 Book

Murder On Capitol Hill - *Single*
Arbor US (1981)

Michael Dane JAMES

is head of an investigation agency specialising in industrial espionage prevention. Once a professional football player, he is now middle-aged, wears horn-rimmed glasses and sports a crew cut.

American Male Professional Investigator operating in New York

James Michael ULLMAN (American)

Invented 3 detectives - see Julian FORBES

Citation Record: 1 Selected Short Story

The Stock Market Detective
US (1962)

Mike JAMES

is a young man from Chicago who is learning the private eye business as he goes.
!See Appendix 2.

American Male Private Detective operating in Chicago/Long Island

Denis SCOTT (American)

Writers: Mary MEANS and Theodore SAUNDERS

Citation Record: 2 Books

Murder Makes A Villain - *First*
!See Appendix 2.
Bobbs US (1944); Hammond UK (1955)

The Beckoning Shadow - *Last*
!See Appendix 2.
Bobbs US (1946); Hammond UK (1956)

Walter JAMES

leaves an agency in Atlanta in order to investigate a colleague's death that has occurred in San Diego.

American Male Private Detective operating in San Diego

Wade MILLER (American)

See main detective Max THURSDAY

Citation Record: 1 Book

Deadly Weapon - *Only*
Farrar, Straus US (1946); Low UK (1947)

Cass JAMESON

is a Brooklyn attorney who gets drawn into her first investigation when the police seem to be bungling the case of her murdered lover.

American Female Amateur operating in New York

Carolyn WHEAT (American)

is a New York attorney.

Citation Record: 2 Books

Dead Man's Thoughts - *First*
St Martin's US (1983)

Where Nobody Dies - *Latest*
St Martin's US (1986)

JAMIESON

is described as 'a businessman' and is the detective in this one Victorian novel.

British Male Amateur operating in England

Percy ANDREAE 1858- (British)

Citation Record: 1 Book

Stanhope Of Chester - *Only*
Smith, Elder UK (1894)

Joseph 'JJ' JAMISON

is a consultant engineer whose work leads him to detection.

American Male Amateur operating in Minneapolis

L A TAYLOR 1939- (American)

Writer: Laurie Aylma TAYLOR

Other Detectives:
Marge BROCK
Owen DAVIS-WILLIAMS
Ethel PECK

Citation Record: 3 Books

Only Half A Hoax - *First*
Walker US (1983); Hale UK (1984)

Shed Light On Death - *Latest*
Walker US (1985)

Frank JANEK

American Male Amateur operating in New York

William BAYER 1939- (American)

See main detective Ch David BAR-LEV

Citation Record: 2 Books

Switch - *First*
Simon & Schuster US (1984); Joseph UK (1985)

Twice Removed - *Latest*
Simon & Schuster US (1984)

Cliff JANEWAY

is a former cop who now runs a bookstore. He becomes involved in fascinating mysteries concerned with the oddities of the rare book trade, which usually lead to murder.

American Male Amateur operating in Denver

John DUNNING (American)

Citation Record: 2 Books

Booked To Die - *First*
Scribner's US (1992)

The Bookman's Wake - *Latest*
Scribner's US (1995)

JANSON

is a Scotland Yard officer.

British Policeman operating in London

Burford DELANNOY (British)

Invented 3 detectives - see Watson WARD

Citation Record: 1 Book

Between The Lines: A Detective Story - *Only*
Ward, Lock UK (1901)

Hank JANSON

American Male Sleuth operating in several locations

Hank JANSON

House name.

Citation Record: 43 Books

Hell's Angel - *First*
Moring US (1956)

Dead Certainty - *Last*
Compact US (1966)

Hank JANSON 1917-1989 (British)

For writer details see John GAIL

Citation Record: 60 Books
When Dames Get Tough - *First*
Ward & Hitchon US (1946)
Nymph In The Night - *Last*
Roberts UK (1962)

Hank JANSON 1908- (British)
For writer details see Brad FORD
Citation Record: 57 Books
Beauty And The Beat - *First*
Roberts UK (1962)
Caribbean Caper - *Last*
Gold UK (1971)

Hank JANSON 1922-
For writer details see Hilary BRAND
Citation Record: 13 Books
Depravity - *First*
Compact UK (1964)
Abomination - *Last*
Compact UK (1965)

Hank JANSON
Writer: Colin SIMPSON
Citation Record: 11 Books
Bid For Beauty - *First*
Compact US (1966)
Grass Widow - *Last*
Gold UK (1971)

Hank JANSON 1920-1983 (British)
For writer details see JACARA
Citation Record: 6 Books
Blood Bath - *First*
Roberts UK (1962)
Top Ten - *Last*
Compact UK (1964)

Willa JANSSON

is a lawyer who solves legal problems and is drawn into investigating the murders that seem to be attached to them.

American Female Amateur operating in New York/San Francisco

Lia MATERA (American)
Inventor of one other detective Laura DI PALMA
Citation Record: 3 Books
Where Lawyers Fear To Tread - *First*
Bantam US (1987)
A Radical Departure - *Latest*
Bantam US (1988)

John Kenneth Galbraith JANTARRO

is of Basque descent. He has only one arm.

Canadian Male Private Detective operating in Toronto

Simon RITCHIE 1944- (Canadian)
Writer: Simon R FODDEN
Citation Record: 2 Books
The Hollow Woman - *First*
Scribner's US (1986)
Work For A Dead Man - *Latest*
Scribner's US (1989)

Insp Auguste JANTRY

sleuths during the 1800s.

French Policeman operating in Paris

Bruce GRAEME 1900-1982 (British)
Invented 6 detectives - see BLACKSHIRT
Citation Record: 2 Books
Cherchez La Femme - *First*
Hutchinson UK (1951)
Lady In Black - *Last*
Hutchinson UK (1952)

Ben JARDINN

was the very first of the real Hollywood private eyes, appearing soon after *Dashiell HAMMETT's* first books.

American Male Private Detective operating in Hollywood

Sidekick: Max COHN
American Male - Assistant

Raoul WHITFIELD 1897-1945 (American)
was born in New York City, raised in the Philippines and served in the US Army in the First World War. He is the author of five genre novels but is mainly remembered for the many stories he wrote for *Black Mask Magazine* in the 1920s and 1930s.
Other Detectives:
Ben CASEY   Al CONNORS
Citation Record: 1 Book
Death In A Bowl - *Only*
Knopf US (1931)

James JARNEGAN

American Male Private Detective operating in New York

Will F JENKINS 1896-1975 (American)
Writer: William Fitzgerald JENKINS
Citation Record: 1 Book
The Man Who Feared - *Only*
Gateway US (1942)

Rev Jabel JARRETT

New Zealander Male Amateur operating in New Zealand

Freda BREAM
Citation Record: 2 Books
The Vicar Done It - *First*
Hale UK (1983)
The Vicar Investigates - *Latest*
Hale UK (1983)

Det Elena JARVIS

is the first female detective to be enrolled in the police force of the fictional city of Los Santos. She is designated 'Crimes against the Person Detective', a specification that seems to have particular relevance in this totally mixed-up part of Texas.

American Policewoman operating in Texas

Nancy HERNDON (American)
Citation Record: 1 Book
Acid Bath - *Single*
Berkley US (1995)

Milton JARVIS

was a 'scientific detective' who appeared in short stories in *Amazing Stories.*

American Male Detective in Pulp Magazines operating in USA

Edward S SEARS (American)
No citations

Commodore JASEN

British Male Amateur operating in several locations

E Phillips OPPENHEIM 1866-1946 (British)
Invented 27 detectives - see Nicholas GOADE
Citation Record: 10 Short Stories in 1 Collection
Crooks In The Sunshine - *Collection 1*
Hodder & Stoughton UK (1932); Little, Brown US (1933)

JASON

British Male Sleuth operating in England

John Newton CHANCE 1911-1983 (British)
Invented 8 detectives - see John Newton CHANCE
Citation Record: 2 Books
The Jason Affair - *First*
Macdonald UK (1953)
Up To Her Neck - *First**
The US edition had a text somewhat different from that of the UK edition.
Popular Library US (1955)
Jason Goes West - *Last*
Macdonald UK (1955)

J

JASON
Male Sleuth operating in several locations

JASON (Australian)

Citation Record: 7 Books

Death Is A Circus - *First*
Webster AU (1958)

Honolulu Slay Ride - *Last*
Webster AU (1959)

Alex (The Enforcer) JASON
American Male Sleuth operating in New York

Andrew SUGAR (American)

Citation Record: 4 Books

Kill City - *First*
Lancer UK (1973)

Bio Blitz - *Last*
Manor US (1975)

Buck JASON
American Male Sleuth operating in New York

Frederick NEBEL 1903-1967 (American)

Invented 8 detectives - see Steve CARDIGAN

Citation Record: 2 Selected Short Stories

China Silk
appeared in the March number.
In 'Black Mask Magazine' US (1927)

Emeralds Of Shade
appeared in the August number.
In 'Black Mask Magazine' US (1927)

Kenneth JASPER
is a young criminal lawyer who becomes a private investigator, a precedent for the long line of US lawyers who do much the same.
American Male Private Detective operating in USA

Lawrence L LYNCH (American)

Invented 11 detectives - see Neil J BATHURST

Citation Record: 1 Book

No Proof - *Only*
Rand, McNally US (1895)

Emma Murdoch VAN DEVENTER (American)

Citation Record: 1 Book

No Proof - *Only*
Ward, Lock UK (1895)

Smilla JASPERSON
investigates the apparently accidental death of a boy in Copenhagen and pursues her quarry into the snow of the Arctic Circle.
Greenlander Female Amateur operating in Denmark

Peter HOEG

Citation Record: 1 Book

Miss Smilla's Feeling For Snow - *Single*
Flamingo UK (1994)

Insp JAVETT
is one of the very great creations of nineteenth-century literature and one of its most finely drawn detectives, though strangely omitted from most bibliographic works on detective fiction. Indeed, more is known about the physiology and psychology of *Insp JAVETT* than of almost any other fictional detective. Described in great depth in a classic novel, he is the great French policeman, a bulldog and a bloodhound combined, as he undertakes his relentless quest for an abstract justice and the soul and body of Jean Valjean. A stoutish man, fifty-two years old, with a snub nose and bushy whiskers, *JAVETT* is awesome and fearsome, bearing allegiance only to established authority and believing that all crimes are a rebellion against it. His card, indeed, carries this message on it: Surveillance and Vigilance. He is no solver of puzzles, but a tracker of men. At the end of this great book, he cannot face the decision he has to make and walks into the Seine.
French Policeman operating in France

Victor Marie HUGO 1802-1885 (French)
was born at Besancon, France and educated in Paris.

Citation Record: 1 Book

Les Miserables - *Only*
is a great novel and a classic of detective literature, although not referred to, surprisingly, by many sources.
UK (1853)

Wood JAXON
gives little evidence of the intellectual prowess he claims, but the line impresses his lady clients.
!See Appendix 2.
American Male Private Detective operating in New York

M Scott MICHEL 1916- (American)

See main detective Dr Alexander CORNELL

Citation Record: 2 Books

The X-Ray Murders - *First*
Coward McCann US (1942); Hammond UK (1945)

Sweet Murder - *Last*
Coward McCann US (1943); Hammond UK (1945)

Dr JAZ
Male Amateur operating in England

Margaret VIVIAN (British)

Citation Record: 12 Short Stories in 1 Collection

Doctor Jaz - *Collection 1*
Stockwell UK (1933)

Earl JAZINE
Second detective of Carl CRADER

Jerry JEETER
American Male Amateur operating in Los Angeles

Stephen ROBINETT 1941- (American)

Writer: Stephen Allen ROBINETT

Citation Record: 2 Books

Final Option - *First*
Avon US (1990)

Unfinished Business - *Latest*
Avon US (1990)

Jack JEFFCOAT
is an ex-thief turned detective.
British Male Professional Investigator operating in London

Charles H ROSS 1842-1897 (British)

Writer: Charles Henry ROSS

Citation Record: 1 Book

A Private Enquiry - *Only*
Tinsley UK (1870)

Arthur JEFFREY
American Male Amateur operating in New York

Henry Kitchell WEBSTER 1875-1932 (American)

Invented 4 detectives - see Prof Brinsley BUTLER

Citation Record: 2 Books

The Whispering Man - *First*
Appleton US (1908); Nash UK (1908)

The Ghost Girl - *Last*
Appleton UK (1913)

Sheriff JEFFRIES and Mr PIGEON
American Policeman and American Male Amateur operating in Illinois

Jean POTTS 1910- (American)
was born in St Paul, Nebraska, and educated at Nebraska Wesleyan University, Lincoln. Author of at least fourteen genre novels, she received the Mystery Writers of America Edgar Allan Poe award, 1954.

Citation Record: 1 Book

Go, Lovely Rose - *Only*
Scribner's US (1954); Gollancz UK (1955)

Mrs JEFFRIES and Insp WITHERSPOON

Mrs JEFFRIES is the landlady of *Insp WITHERSPOON*, who is a copper in Victorian England. And just as well, for he is pretty inept, and she, with the assistance of maid, cook, footman and coachman, solves his cases and raises his stock at the Yard most considerably.
British Female Amateur and British Policeman operating in London

Emily BRIGHTWELL

Citation Record: 2 Books

Mrs Jeffries On The Ball - *First*
Berkley US (1994)

Mrs Jeffries On The Trail - *Latest*
Berkley US (1995)

Mrs JEFFRIES

Second detective of Insp WITHERSPOON

Hal JEFFRIES

American Male Amateur operating in USA

Stooge: Lt BYRNE
will not believe that *Hal JEFFRIES* can be right all the time and pays the price accordingly.
American Male

J

Cornell WOOLRICH 1903-1968 (American)

was born in New York City. He was raised partly in South America but attended Columbia University, New York. Under his real name and under his pseudonym, *William IRISH*, he elevated the pulp fiction of the 1940s to previously unknown heights and his best tales are of extraordinary power and quality. He wrote, under the two bylines, at least twelve genre novels, six non-genre novels and many short stories. He received the Mystery Writers of America Edgar Allan Poe award for a short story, 1948.

Writer: Cornell George Hopley WOOLRICH
Other Byline: William IRISH
Other Detectives:
'Angel Face' REARDON   Prudence ROBERTS
Citation Record: 1 Selected Short Story

It Had To Be Murder
In 'Dime Detective' US (1942)

Jane JEFFRY

is a widow with three children. Agreeing to let a movie be made in her backyard, she is drawn into a case of blackmail and murder, which she has to solve so that her forthcoming weekend with a lusty local cop is not to be forgone. There may, somewhere in the genre, be less important motives for amateurs wanting to turn detective.
American Female Amateur operating in USA

Jill CHURCHILL (American)

Writer: Janice Young BROOKS
Citation Record: 1 Book

A Knife To Remember - *Single*
Avon US (1994)

Mr JELLIPOT

appears also in one book with another of the author's detectives, *Prof BLINKWELL*.
British Male Amateur operating in England

Sydney FOWLER 1874-1965 (British)

Writer: Sydney Fowler WRIGHT
Other Detectives:
Prof BLINKWELL and Mr JELLIPOT
Prof BLINKWELL   Insp CAULDRON
Insp CLEVELAND
Citation Record: 8 Books

The Attic Murder - *First*
Butterworth UK (1936)

With Cause Enough? - *Last*
Harvill UK (1954)

Mr JELLIPOT

Second detective of Prof BLINKWELL

Maj Laurence JEN

British Male Amateur

Fergus HUME 1859-1932 (British)

Invented 24 detectives - see Insp Samuel GORBY

Citation Record: 1 Book

The Devil-Stick - *Only*
Downey UK (1898)

Joe JENKINS

Male Amateur operating in Denmark

Paul ROSENHAYN 1877-1929

Citation Record: 24 Short Stories in 2 Collections

Joe Jenkins: Detective - *Collection 1*
Short stories - 13
Heinemann UK (1929); Doubleday US (1930)

Joe Jenkins' Casebook - *Collection 2*
Short stories - 11
Heinemann UK (1930)

Matthew JENKYN

sleuths in the early part of the fifteenth century.
English Male Amateur operating in England

P C DOHERTY (British)

Invented 3 detectives - see Hugh CORBETT

Citation Record: 2 Books

The Whyte Hart - *First*
Hale UK (1988); St Martin's US (1988)

The Serpent Among The Lilies - *Latest*
Hale UK (1990); St Martin's US (1990)

Jim JENNER

is an ex-policeman who, having lost a foot in a terrorist outrage, sets up as a private eye in Canning Town, a dockland area in East London.
British Male Private Detective operating in London

John MILNE 1952- (British)

was born in London. He took a BA in Fine Art at the Ravensbourne School of Art, London, 1980. He has worked at several jobs and served in the Police.

Citation Record: 4 Books

Dead Birds - *First*
Hamish Hamilton UK (1986); Viking US (1987)

Daddy's Girl - *Latest*
UK (1988)

JENNERTON

British Male Amateur operating in England

E Phillips OPPENHEIM 1866-1946 (British)

Invented 27 detectives - see Nicholas GOADE

Citation Record: 10 Short Stories in 1 Collection

Jennerton & Co - *Collection 1*
Hodder & Stoughton UK (1929); Little, Brown US (1931)

Det Christopher JENSEN and Prof Natalie KEITH

Christopher JENSEN is a young police detective who gets involved with campus murders and forms a close relationship with *Natalie KEITH*, an attractive, middle-aged Professor of Archaeology and Anthropology, whose personal history is overbearingly sentimental. Even so, she provides him with crucial information about the crimes he is investigating and shares her theories about them with him. So much so that she is actually given an official police badge!
American Policeman and American Female Amateur operating in USA

Lee LANGLEY 1927- (American)
has practised as a journalist and later as an occupational therapist.
Writer: Sarah LANGLEY
Citation Record: 2 Books
Osiris Died In Autumn - *First*
Doubleday US (1964)
Twilight Of Death - *First**
Hale UK (1965)
Dead Center - *Last*
Doubleday US (1968)
Dead Centre - *Last**
Hale UK (1969)

Ch Insp Peter JENSEN
Swedish Policeman operating in Stockholm

Per WAHLOO 1926-1975 (Swedish)
Writer: Per Peter WAHLOO
Citation Record: 2 Books
Murder On The Thirty-First Floor - *First*
Joseph UK (1966)
The Thirty-First Floor - *First**
Knopf US (1966)
The Steel Spring - *Last*
Joseph UK (1970); Delacorte US (1970)

Mr JEREMY
British Male Amateur operating in England

J Bradley WHITTON (British)
Citation Record: 1 Book
Mr Jeremy, Detective - *Only*
Digby UK (1891)

John JERICHO
is tall, red-bearded and looks like a Viking. A good painter and an even better champion of lost causes, he does a lot of detection in the pleasant surroundings of New England. He appears in books with another of the author's detectives, *Lt PASCAL.*
American Male Amateur operating in Connecticut
Sidekick: Arthur HALLAM
not only narrates but assists.
American Male - Narrator

Hugh PENTECOST 1903-1989 (American)
Invented 12 detectives - see Pierre CHAMBRUN
Citation Record: 4 Books
Sniper - *First*
Dodd, Mead US (1965); Boardman UK (1966)
A Plague Of Violence - *Last*
Dodd, Mead US (1970); Hale UK (1972)

John JERICHO and Lt PASCAL
also appear individually in other books by this author.
American Male Amateur and American Policeman operating in Connecticut

Hugh PENTECOST 1903-1989 (American)
Invented 12 detectives - see Pierre CHAMBRUN
Citation Record: 2 Books
The Creeping Hours - *First*
Dodd, Mead US (1966); Boardman UK (1967)
Dead Woman Of The Year - *Last*
Dodd, Mead US (1967); Macdonald UK (1968)

Peter JERNINGHAM
American Male Amateur operating in Pennsylvania

Isabel Briggs MYERS (American)
Citation Record: 2 Books
Murder Yet To Come - *First*
Stokes US (1930)
Give Me Death - *Last*
Stokes US (1934); Gollancz UK (1935)

JERRY
Second detective of TOM

The JEW DETECTIVE
American Male Detective in Pulp Magazines operating in USA

ANON
No citations

JIMSIE
appears in one short story in the collection, *THE INVISIBLE PICKPOCKET,* which mainly features *M'GOVAN.*
British Male Amateur operating in Edinburgh

James M'GOVAN (British)
Invented 3 detectives - see James M'GOVAN
Citation Record: 1 Selected Short Story
Jimsie, The Horse Detective
Menzies UK (1922)

Sister JOAN and Det Sgt Alan MILL
Sister JOAN is a nun of the 'Order of the Daughters of Compassion', who, with the official but rather bewildered *Det Sgt Alan MILL* at her spiritual side to render some assistance, finds a surprising number of murders that seem to fall within her province.
British Female Amateur and British Policeman operating in England

Veronica BLACK (American)
Citation Record: 5 Books
A Vow Of Silence - *First*
St Martin's US (1990); Hale UK (1990)
A Vow Of Devotion - *Latest*
St Martin's US (1994)

JOCKEY JOE
American Male Detective in Pulp Magazines operating in USA

Warne MILLER (American)
Invented 4 detectives - see Silas QUIRK
Citation Record: 1 Selected Short Story
Jockey Joe, The Race Track Detective
Old Cap Collier Library US (18??)

Sister JOHN and HYACINTH
American Female Amateurs operating in New York

Dorothy GILMAN 1923- (American)
Invented 3 detectives - see Mrs Emily POLLIFAX
Citation Record: 1 Book
A Nun In The Closet - *Only*
Doubleday US (1975)
A Nun In The Cupboard - *Only**
Hale UK (1976)

Insp JOHNSON
British Policeman operating in England

Denzil BATCHELOR 1906-1969 (British)
Writer: Denzil Stanley BATCHELOR
Citation Record: 3 Books
The Man Who Loved Chocolates - *First*
Heinemann UK (1961)
The Sedulous Ape - *Last*
Macdonald UK (1965)

Anthony JOHNSON
British Male Amateur operating in England

Ruth RENDELL 1930- (British)
See main detective Ch Insp Reginald WEXFORD
Citation Record: 1 Book
A Demon In My View - *Single*
Hutchinson UK (1976); Doubleday US (1977)

Chet JOHNSON
was formerly a fireman.
American Male Private Detective operating in Minneapolis

Joel HELGERSON (American)
Slow Burn - *Only*
US (1987)

Det 'Coffin' Ed JOHNSON
Second detective of Det 'Grave Digger' JONES

Hal JOHNSON

was once a Homicide cop. Now, retired, he has the strange job of recovering stolen and long overdue books from the public library. Called thus 'The Library Fuzz', he runs into serious crimes including murder. He appears in a number of short stories, of which one is cited for illustration purposes.

American Male Professional Investigator operating in New York

James HOLDING 1907- (American)

was born in Pittsburgh, Pennsylvania, and educated at Yale University, New Haven, Connecticut. A distinguished poet and professional copywriter, he is the author of hundreds of short stories, the majority of them being in the criminous mode.

Inventor of one other detective pair King DANWORTH and Martin LEROY

Citation Record: 1 Selected Short Story

The Search For Tamerlane

appeared in the May 1981 number.

In 'Ellery Queen's Mystery Magazine' US (1981)

Johnson JOHNSON

American Male Amateur operating in USA/Scotland

Dorothy DUNNETT 1923- (British)

was born in Dunfermline, Fife, Scotland. She has held several appointments in Scottish governmental departments, is a professional portrait painter and has written several non-genre novels. Her detective novels were originally published under her maiden name, *Dorothy HALLIDAY*, in the UK.

Citation Record: 6 Books

The Photogenic Soprano - *First*

Houghton US (1968)

Dolly And The Bird Of Paradise - *Latest*

Knopf US (1984)

Dorothy HALLIDAY (British)

Citation Record: 6 Books

Dolly And The Singing Bird - *First*

Cassell UK (1968); Vanguard US (1982)

Dolly And The Bird Of Paradise - *Latest*

Cassell UK (1984)

Dr Sam JOHNSON

is, indeed, the eminent English man of letters. In this series of short stories, the author has made him an amateur sleuth who uses his fine brain to solve mystery and murder in and around eighteenth-century London. There are no prizes for guessing who his sidekick is.

British Male Amateur operating in London

Sidekick: James BOSWELL

must be the sidekick of *Dr JOHNSON* and, naturally, he narrates his cases.

British Male - Narrator

Lillian DE LA TORRE 1902- (American)

was born in New York City and educated at the College of New Rochelle, New York. She later studied at Columbia University, New York, the University of Munich, Harvard University, Cambridge, Massachusetts, and the University of Colorado, Boulder, Colorado. Formerly a technical advisor to Twentieth Century Fox, she is now a full-time writer.

Writer: Lillian De La Torre Bueno MCCUE

Adopter of one other detective Sherlock HOLMES

Citation Record: 31 Short Stories in 4 Collections

Dr Sam: Johnson, Detector - *Collection 1*

Knopf US (1946); Joseph UK (1948)

Short stories - 9

The Detections Of Dr Sam: Johnson - *Collection 2*

Short stories - 8

Knopf US (1960); Xanadu UK (1989)

The Return Of Dr Sam: Johnson, Detector - *Collection 3*

Short stories - 7

International Polygonics US (1984)

The Exploits Of Dr Sam: Johnson, Detector - *Collection 4*

Short stories - 7

International Polygonics US (1987); Xanadu UK (1990)

Steve JOHNSON

American Male Amateur operating in San Francisco

Hugh Lawrence NELSON 1907- (American)

Inventor of one other detective pair Jim DUNN and Zebulion BUCK

Citation Record: 3 Books

The Title Is Murder - *First*

Rinehart US (1947); Barker UK (1947)

Dead Giveaway - *Last*

Rinehart US (1950); Barker UK (1951)

Wellaby JOHNSON

British Male Amateur operating in England

Oliver BOOTH (British)

Citation Record: 14 Short Stories in 1 Collection

The Adventures Of Mr Wellaby Johnson - *Collection 1*

Arrowsmith UK (1914)

Insp JOLIVET

French Policeman operating in Paris

Joan SHEPHERD (American)

worked in Hollywood studios, mainly as a writer.

Writer: Betty Joan BUCHANAN

Citation Record: 2 Books

The Girl On The Left Bank - *First*

Washburn US (1953)

Tender Is The Knife - *Last*

Washburn US (1956)

Sgt JOLLEY

British Policeman operating in England

David FLETCHER 1940-1988 (British)

Invented 3 detectives - see Det Insp RUBY

Citation Record: 1 Book

Dismal Ravens Crying - *Only*

Macmillan UK (1989)

Shamrock JOLNES

is a *Sherlock HOLMES* parody.

American Male Professional Amateur operating in USA

Sidekick: Dr WATSUP

is his parody *WATSON*-like assistant.

American Male - Assistant

Sidekick: JUGGINS

For some reason the author decided to change *JOLNES'* sidekick and have him play a superior role.

American Male - Assistant

Sidekick: Avery KNIGHT

For some reason the author decided to change *JOLNES'* sidekick yet again.

American Male - Assistant

O HENRY 1862-1910 (American)

was born in Greensboro, North Carolina. He had a poor upbringing, took money from a bank to help his consumptive wife, served three years in jail for embezzlement and later roamed the streets of New York to find material for his tales. He became one of the most illustrious of American short story writers. Although he rarely mentioned detectives among his host of characters, he did write the two *Sherlock HOLMES* parodies and the two *VIDOCQ* parodies cited, which were published posthumously in collections.

Writer: William Sydney PORTER

Inventor of one other detective TICTOCQ

Citation Record: 3 Selected Short Stories

The Adventures Of Shamrock Jolnes - *Parody 1*

appeared in a collection of the author's stories, *Sixes and Sevens*.

Doubleday US (1911); Hodder & Stoughton UK (1916)

The Sleuths - *Parody 2*
appeared in a collection of the author's stories, *Sixes and Sevens.*
Doubleday US (1911); Hodder & Stoughton UK (1916)
The Detective Detector - *Parody 3*
appeared in a collection of the author's stories, *Waifs and Strays.*
Doubleday US (1917); Hodder & Stoughton UK (1920)

Ben JOLSON

is one of this author's several space detectives of the future. This one operates in the 'Barnum System'. He is employed by the Briggs Interplanetary Detective Service and is called a 'shapechanger'.
American Male Private Detective operating in Space

Ron GOULART 1933- (American)
Invented 15 detectives - see Jake PACE and Hildy PACE
Citation Record: 1 Book 6 Short Stories in 1 Collection
Daredevils, Ltd - *Single*
St Martin's US (1987)
The Chameleon Corps - *Collection 1*
This collection of ten of the author's short stories contains six with *Ben JOLSON.*
Macmillan US (1972)

Jonas P JONAS

is a garrulous old man who claims to have been a private detective. His niece is persuaded to relate some of his memoirs. In this story he has to ask only two questions to solve a case of murder.
British Male Amateur operating in England

E X FERRARS 1907-1995 (British)
Invented 11 detectives - see Toby DYKE
Citation Record: 1 Selected Short Story
The Case Of The Two Questions
appeared originally in the *Evening Standard* (London), December 8, 1958, and then in the August number of the cited magazine.
In 'Ellery Queen's Mystery Magazine' US (1959)

JONES

is a Scotland Yard officer in this one Victorian novel.
British Policeman operating in London

Walter H MAYSON 1835-1904 (British)
Writer: Walter Henry MAYSON
Citation Record: 1 Book
The Stolen Fiddle - *Only*
Warne UK (1897)

Mr JONES

British Male Amateur operating in England

Dorothea CONYERS 1873-1949 (British)
Invented 3 detectives - see Mervyn HENDERSON
Citation Record: 5 Short Stories in 2 Collections
A Mixed Pack - *Collection 1*
This collection of eighteen of the author's stories contains two with *Mr JONES.*
Short stories - 2
Methuen UK (1915)
Irish Stew - *Collection 2*
This collection of twelve of the author's stories contains three with *Mr JONES.*
Short stories - 3
Skeffington UK (1920)

A V R E 'Average' JONES

is a good-looking young man whose unusual sobriquet conceals his real forenames of Adrian Reypen Egerton. Always impeccably dressed, he describes himself as an advertising advisor and he seems to reside at something called the Cosmic Club, situated in Baltimore. He is blessed with more erudite knowledge and has more useful forces at his disposal than are wholly believable, but these do enable him to solve, rather creditably, several cases of crime in his home town.
American Male Amateur operating in USA

Samuel Hopkins ADAMS 1871-1958 (American)
Inventor of one other detective pair Prof Willis RAVENDEN and Stanford COLTON
Citation Record: 10 Short Stories in 1 Collection
Average Jones - *Collection 1*
Bobbs US (1911); Palmer UK (1911)

Amelia JONES

American Female Amateur operating in USA

Dorothy GILMAN 1923- (American)
Invented 3 detectives - see Mrs Emily POLLIFAX
Citation Record: 1 Book
The Tightrope Walker - *Single*
Doubleday US (1979); Hale UK (1980)

Barnaby JONES

!See Appendix 2.
American Male Private Detective operating in Illinois

Manning Lee STOKES (American)
Other Bylines:
Nick CARTER   Paul EDWARDS
Ken STANTON
Other Detectives:
Christopher FENN   Steve PAGET
Citation Record: 2 Books
The Wolf Howls "Murder" - *First*
Phoenix Press US (1945)
Green For A Grave - *Last*
Phoenix Press US (1946)

Bobby JONES

Second detective of Frances DERWENT

Candid JONES and Insp Harry RENTANO

Candid JONES is a photographer for the *New York Chronicle.* He packs a Luger as well as a camera and solves some unusual murder cases, with the co-operation of *Insp Harry RENTANO.*
American Male Amateur and American Policeman in Pulp Magazines

Richard SALE 1911- (American)
Invented 5 detectives - see Calamity QUADE
No citations

Cleopatra JONES

appears in books that are novelizations of films.
American Female Amateur operating in USA

Ron GOULART 1933- (American)
Invented 15 detectives - see Jake PACE and Hildy PACE
Citation Record: 2 Books
Cleopatra Jones - *First*
Paperback Library US (1973)
Cleopatra Jones And The Casino Of Gold - *Last*
Paperback Library US (1975)

Mrs Dorinda JONES

solves the disappearance of a man who is believed to have committed murder in a Rolls-Royce limousine.
British Female Amateur operating in England

Mary Christianna BRAND 1907-1988 (British)
Invented 6 detectives - see Insp COCKRILL and Insp CHARLESWORTH
Citation Record: 1 Selected Short Story
Upon Reflection
In 'Ellery Queen's Mystery Magazine' US (1977)

Edmund 'Jupiter' JONES

is a brilliant student at Harvard who, during the series,

progresses to become an assistant professor in the little fictional town of Saxon. Tall, thin, eventually married, he sleuths simply, he says, because he likes to.

American Male Amateur operating in USA

Sidekick: SYLVESTER

is black and the detective's supportive and earnest valet, as well as being a useful assistant.

American Male - Valet

Timothy FULLER 1914-1971 (American)

was born in Newell, Massachusetts.

Citation Record: 5 Books

Harvard Has A Homicide - *First*
Little, Brown US (1936)

J For Jupiter - *First**
Collins UK (1937)

Keep Cool, Mr Jones - *Last*
Little, Brown US (1950); Heinemann UK (1951)

Edward Porter JONES and Sherlock HOLMES

Edward JONES was, when a small boy in London, one of the 'Baker Street Irregulars', that gang of street arabs used by *Sherlock HOLMES* for extra-mural sleuthing. He now resides in Wales and *HOLMES* and *Dr WATSON* come to him for help in what seems to be a very Welsh case.

Welsh Male Amateur and British Male Professional Amateur operating in Wales

Sidekick: Dr John H WATSON

British Male - Narrator

Lloyd BIGGLE 1923- (American)

Invented 5 detectives - see Bill RASTIN

Citation Record: 1 Book

The Glendower Conspiracy - *Pastiche 1*
Council Oaks Books US (1990)

George Helmfleet JONES

a sci-fi sleuth who solves the problem of an unusual theft from a space rocket.

American Male Professional Investigator operating in USA

Fletcher PRATT 1897-1956 (American)

Writer: Murray Fletcher PRATT

Inventor of one other detective Ellis PARKER

Citation Record: 1 Book

Double Jeopardy - *Only*
Doubleday US (1952)

George JONES and Victoria BARTON

solves the mystery of a disappearing hotel room in this well-known story.

British Male Amateur and British Female Amateur operating in Paris

Anthony THORNE 1904-

Writer: Eric Anthony THORNE

Citation Record: 1 Book

So Long At The Fair - *Only*
Heinemann UK (1947); Random House US (1947)

Glyn JONES

Second detective of James DINGLE

Guinevere JONES

Second detective of Zachariah JUSTIS

Gwyneth JONES

Second detective of John DRYDEN

Hemlock JONES

is a *Sherlock HOLMES* parody and not a very nice one.

British Male Professional Amateur operating in London

Bret HARTE 1836-1902 (American)

was born in Albany, New York and went to San Francisco in 1854 to become a compositor. He later became a journalist and a famed writer of short stories, especially ballads of the Californian mining camps, for which he is best known. He was a US Consul in Glasgow, Scotland, 1880-1885, and then lived in London until his death.

Writer: Francis Brett HARTE

Adopter of one other detective Sherlock HOLMES

Citation Record: 1 Selected Short Story

The Stolen Cigar Case - *Parody 1*

is in the author's second series of *Condensed Novels*, his last work. It is a humorous but savage attack on all the brouhaha surrounding the great detective. It was included in *THE MISADVENTURES OF SHERLOCK HOLMES* (Editor: *Ellery QUEEN*).
Houghton Mifflin US (1902)

Jason JONES and 'Necessary' SMITH

are two of this author's several sleuths who are insurance investigators.

American Male Professional Investigators operating in New York

Ken CROSSEN 1910-1981 (American)

See main detective Kim LOCKE

Citation Record: 2 Books

The Case Of The Curious Heel - *First*
Vulcan US (1944)

The Case Of The Phantom Fingerprints - *Last*
Vulcan US (1945)

Kennedy JONES

American Male Private Detective operating in New York

Norman KLEIN 1897-1948 (American)

Inventor of one other detective Harvey CHURCH

Citation Record: 1 Book

The Destroying Angel - *Only*
Farrar, Straus US (1933)

Morocco JONES

is a tough fighting man, formerly in counter-espionage, and now working for an agency specialising in the recovery of valuables that have, for one reason or another, gone astray. The perpetrators of such acts have extreme cause to regret their misdeeds by the time he has finished with them.

American Male Private Detective operating in Chicago

Jack BAYNES (American)

Writer: Bertram B FOWLER

Citation Record: 5 Books

Meet Morocco Jones - *First*
Crest US (1956); Crest UK (1957)

Morocco Jones In The Case Of The Golden Angel - *Last*
Crest US (1959)

Mortimer JONES

appeared mainly in stories in *Dime Detective*.

American Male Detective in Pulp Magazines operating in USA

William Campbell GAULT 1910- (American)

Invented 6 detectives - see Brock (The Rock) CALLAHAN

No citations

Pharaoh JONES

When *Sir Arthur Conan DOYLE's* story, *THE DISAPPEARANCE OF LADY FRANCIS CARFAX* appeared in *Ellery Queen's Challenge to the Reader: an Anthology* in 1938, the names of *Sherlock HOLMES* and *Dr WATSON* were changed to *Pharaoh JONES* and *Dr DOVER* in order not to give obvious clues to the reader.

British Male Professional Amateur operating in London

Sidekick: Dr DOVER

British Male - Narrator

Sir Arthur Conan DOYLE 1859-1930 (British)

See main detective Sherlock HOLMES

Citation Record: 1 Book

The Disappearance Of Lady Francis Carfax
Stokes US (1938)

Pine-Top JONES

American Male Private Detective operating in USA (Old West)

Bret HARDING 1918-1991 (British)

For writer details see Albert ARGYLE

Citation Record: 10 Books

Pine-Top Jones: Renegade - *First*
Milestone UK (1953)

Corpse To Colorado - *Last*
Hamilton UK (1955)

Ch Rufus Albert JONES and Barbara CREW

When the Professor of Chemistry at the fictional Roseview College, a women's college in the eastern USA, is murdered, the list of suspects is large. Chief of Police *JONES*, unaccountably helped by a temporary assistant, a pretty student called *Barbara CREW*, discovers whodunnit.

American Policeman and American Female Amateur operating in USA

K Alison LA ROCHE (American)

Citation Record: 1 Book

Dear Dead Professor - *Only*
Phoenix Press US (1944)

Russell JONES

is a photo-journalist who, in his first book, is involved in murder in Burma. His second book takes him to Spain, where he investigates the murder of his brother.

British Male Amateur operating in Spain/Burma

Max MUNDY 1918- (British)

Writer: Sylvia Anne Matheson SCHOFIELD

Citation Record: 2 Books

Pagan Pagoda - *First*
Long UK (1965)

Death Cries Olé - *Last*
Long UK (1966)

Samuel JONES

American Male Amateur operating in USA

Volney MATHISON (American)

Citation Record: 12 Short Stories in 1 Collection

The Radiobuster - *Collection 1*
Stokes US (1924)

Sheerluck JONES

is a *Sherlock HOLMES* parody who appears in a burlesque play.

British Male Professional Amateur operating in London

Sidekick: Dr J ROTSON
is his parody *WATSON*-like assistant.
British Male - Assistant

Malcolm WATSON and Edward LA SERRE (American)

Citation Record: 1 Book

Sheerluck Jones - *Parody 1*
is a parody of a pastiche, being a burlesque on the play, *SHERLOCK HOLMES*, by *William GILLETTE*.
Peter Schoffer US (1982)

Sherlock JONES

is a *Sherlock HOLMES* parody.

British Male Professional Amateur operating in London

Lester HEATH (American)

Citation Record: 1 Selected Short Story

The Case Of The Aluminium Crutch - *Parody 1*
was written for children. The title refers to the allusion made by *Sherlock HOLMES* in the canonical story, *THE MUSGRAVE RITUAL*, to one of his early, unpublished cases, 'the singular affair of the aluminium crutch', which had apparently occurred before he met *Dr WATSON*. Other authors have used the allusion as the basis for a pastiche or parody.
Dell US (1963)

Tom JONES

British Male Ex-Policeman operating in England

Andrew PUCKET (British)

is a professional microbiologist.

Citation Record: 3 Books

Bloodstains - *First*
Collins UK (1987); Doubleday US (1987)

Terminus - *Latest*
Collins UK (1990); Doubleday US (1991)

Victoria JONES

is fired from her job in London, goes to Baghdad and solves an espionage plot, designed to endanger world peace.

British Female Amateur operating in Baghdad

Agatha CHRISTIE 1890-1976 (British)

Invented 18 detectives - see Hercule POIROT

Citation Record: 1 Book

They Came To Baghdad - *Only*
Collins UK (1951); Dodd, Mead US (1951)

X JONES

British Policeman operating in London

Harry Stephen KEELER 1890-1967 (American)

Invented 14 detectives - see Angus MACWHORTER

Citation Record: 1 Book

X Jones Of Scotland Yard - *Only*
Dutton US (1936)

X Jones - *Only**
Ward, Lock UK (1936)

Zachary JONES

American Male Amateur operating in USA

Hy STEIRMAN 1921- (American)

Citation Record: 2 Books

Strike Terror - *First*
Paperback Library US (1968)

Cry Of The Hawk - *Last*
Paperback Library US (1970)

Det 'Grave Digger' JONES and Det 'Coffin' Ed JOHNSON

are two tough, often violent, black cops based on the Harlem district of the New York Police Department. Their cases are often built around the lives and special struggles of the New York black community.

American Policemen operating in New York

Chester HIMES 1909-1984 (American)

was born in Jefferson City, Missouri. He was educated at Glenville High School, Cleveland, and graduated at Ohio State University, 1928. He was imprisoned for armed robbery, 1928, and served eight years in Ohio State Penitentiary. After his release he worked on newspapers in the USA, but in 1953 he emigrated to live in France and Spain. He received the *Grand Prix de Littérature Policière*, 1958.

Writer: Chester Bomar HIMES

Citation Record: 8 Books

For Love Of Imabelle - *First*
GM US (1957)

A Rage In Heaven - *First**
Avon US (1965)

Blind Man With A Pistol - *Last*
Morrow US (1969); Hodder & Stoughton UK (1969)

Hot Day Hot Night - *Last**
Dell US (1970)

Ben JONSON

is an Oxford archaeologist who is enlisted into a Secret Service unit, which puts his special skills to good use in unusual ways.

British Male Amateur operating in Europe

Peter LEVI 1931- (British)
Writer: Chad TIGAR
Citation Record: 2 Books
Grave Witness - *First*
Quartet UK (1985); St Martin's US (1985)
Knit One, Drop Two - *Latest*
Quartet UK (1986); Walker US (1987)

JORDAN
Second detective of HORTON

Andrew JORDAN
investigates the murder of his wife who may or may not have been cheating on him.
American Male Amateur operating in New York

Patrick QUENTIN (American)
Invented 6 detectives - see Peter DULUTH
Citation Record: 1 Book
The Green-Eyed Monster - *Only*
Random House US (1960); Gollancz UK (1960)

Barry JORDAN
works for a lowly agency, falls for a suspect, ought to know better and is framed for murder.
American Male Private Detective operating in Hollywood

J

Donald MACKENZIE 1908- (Canadian)
Invented 3 detectives - see John RAVEN
Citation Record: 1 Book
The Kyle Contract - *First*
Houghton US (1970); Hodder & Stoughton UK (1971)

Dan JORDAN
is extremely hardboiled and excessively alcoholic.
American Male Private Detective operating in Seattle

Harlan REED (American)
Citation Record: 2 Books
The Case Of The Crawling Cockroach - *First*
Dutton US (1937)
The Swing Music Murder - *Last*
Dutton US (1938)

Jack JORDAN
Male Sleuth operating in Connecticut/Bahamas

William DU BOIS 1903- (American)
Citation Record: 3 Books
The Case Of The Frightened Fish - *First*
Little, Brown US (1940); Swan UK (1947)
The Case Of The Haunted Brides - *Last*
Little, Brown US (1941); Swan UK (1947)

Marc JORDAN
American Male Amateur operating in USA

R M LAURENSON (American)
Writer: Robert Mark LAURENSON
Citation Record: 2 Books
The Case Of The Six Bullets - *First*
Phoenix Press US (1949); Foulsham UK (1950)
The Railroad Murder Case - *Last*
Phoenix Press US (1948); Foulsham UK (1950)

Scott JORDAN
is a lawyer whose cases are usually concerned with fine points of law. During his investigations he meets a fair share of murders and more than his fair share of beautiful dames. He is a classical music addict, but his main contact with the Orphean art is by way of the blunt instruments that frequently connect with his skull.
American Male Amateur operating in New York

Stooge: Det John NOLA
of New York's Homicide division is friendly as police stooges go, but is usually at odds with *JORDAN* over his handling of the cases.
American Male

Harold Q MASUR 1909- (American)
was educated at Bordentown Military Institute, 1926-1928, and took a BA at New York University, 1932. He later took a Law degree and served in the US Air Force.
Inventor of one other detective Mike RYAN
Citation Record: 11 Books 10 Short Stories in 1 Collection
Bury Me Deep - *First*
Simon & Schuster US (1947); Boardman UK (1948)
The Mourning After - *Latest*
Gollancz UK (1983)
The Name Is Jordan - *Collection 1*
Random House US (1962)

Tony JORDAN
American Male Amateur operating in Washington DC

Lawrence MEYER 1941-
Writer: Lawrence Robert MEYER
Citation Record: 1 Book
A Capitol Crime - *Single*
Collins UK (1977); Viking US (1977)

Joseph JORKENS
appeared in over a hundred short stories by this master of the form. Although not all of them are criminous, he does a reasonable amount of sleuthing.
British Male Amateur operating in England

Lord DUNSANY 1878-1957 (British)
Invented 3 detectives - see Mr LINLEY
Citation Record: 128 Short Stories in 5 Collections
The Travel Tales Of Mr Joseph Jorkens - *Collection 1*
Short stories - 13
Putnam UK (1931); Putnam US (1931)
Mr Jorkens Remembers Africa - *Collection 2*
Short stories - 21
Heinemann UK (1934)
Jorkens Has A Large Whisky - *Collection 3*
Short stories - 26
Putnam UK (1940)
The Fourth Book Of Jorkens - *Collection 4*
Short stories - 34
Jarrolds UK (1948); Arkham US (1948)
Jorkens Borrows Another Whisky - *Collection 5*
Short stories - 34
Joseph UK (1954)

John Howard JOURNEY
American Male Amateur operating in Chicago

Jay Robert NASH 1937- (American)
Citation Record: 2 Books
A Crime Story - *First*
Delacorte US (1981)
The Mafia Diaries - *Latest*
Delacorte US (1984)

Jonathan JOW
British Male Amateur operating in England

William J MAKIN 1894- (British)
Invented 3 detectives - see Det Insp EVANS
Citation Record: 6 Short Stories in 1 Collection
The Exploits Of Jonathan Jow - *Collection 1*
Pearson UK (1936)

Ben JOYCE
is an insurance claims investigator.
American Male Professional Investigator operating in USA

Arthur PORGES (American)
Invented 13 detectives - see Arsène LUPIN
Citation Record: 1 Selected Short Story
The Bet
appeared in the March number.
In 'Alfred Hitchcock's Mystery Magazine' US (1967)

Michael JOYCE
American Male Amateur operating in New York/Oklahoma

Louis CORNELL (American)
Citation Record: 2 Books
Poison Case Number 10 - *First*
Brentano's UK (1931)
Murder Case Number 33 - *Last*
Brentano's UK (1932)

Anthea JUBB
solves a case of death by shooting.
British Female Amateur operating in England

Ralph RODD 1869- (British)
Writer: William NORTH
Citation Record: 1 Book
Sleuth Of The World - *Only*
Collins UK (1933)

Insp George JUDD
is a stolid policeman in a Central London division and solves his cases by patient plodding rather than intellectual bravura.
British Policeman operating in England

Eric BRUTON 1915- (British)
was born in London. He served in the Royal Air Force, 1940-1946. He is an engineer and IS known as an expert in horology and jewellery, on which subjects he has lectured extensively.
Writer: Eric Moore BRUTON
Inventor of one other detective Stephen KELLY
Citation Record: 5 Books
The Laughing Policeman - *First*
Boardman UK (1963)
The Fire Bug - *Last*
Boardman UK (1967)

Humphrey JUDD
appeared in short stories published by *Pearsons* around 1899. Some have been collected.
British Male Amateur operating in England

Victor L WHITECHURCH 1868-1933 (British)
Invented 5 detectives - see Det Sgt AMBROSE
Citation Record: 6 Short Stories in 1 Collection
The Chronicles Of Humprey Judd - *Collection 1*
Ferret Fantasy UK (1990)

Toby JUDD
solves a case of 'impossible' murder involving a supposedly dead dwarf.
British Male Amateur operating in England

Eric HARDING (British)
Citation Record: 1 Book
Pray For The Dawn - *Only*
Low UK (1946)

Anastasia JUGEDINSKI
is a complete emotional mess, being the bastard of a police chief and having been raped at an early age.
!See Appendix 2.
American Female Private Detective operating in USA

Phyllis SWAN (American)
Citation Record: 4 Books
Trigger Lady - *First*
Leisure Books US (1979)
The Death Inheritance - *Latest*
Leisure Books US (1980)

Jack JUGG
British Male Amateur operating in England

Donald SUDDABY (British)
Writer: William Donald SUDDABY
Citation Record: 8 Short Stories in 1 Collection
Merry Jack Jugg - Highwayman - *Collection 1*
Blackie UK (1954)

Insp Ben JURNET
of the Norfolk CID is dark and good-looking. He usually meets his murders under bizarre circumstances and they often seem to have some hidden religious background or pagan significance. *JURNET* is not without problems of his own, for he wants to marry Miriam, who is orthodox Jewish and wants him to convert to Judaism.
British Policeman operating in Norfolk
Sidekick: Det Sgt Jack ELLERS
British Male - Subordinate

S T HAYMON 1918- (British)
was born in Norwich, Norfolk. She has worked in journalism, public relations and farming. She received the Crime Writers Association Silver Dagger award, 1983.
Writer: Sylvia T HAYMON
Citation Record: 6 Books
Death And The Pregnant Virgin - *First*
Constable UK (1980); St Martin's US (1980)
A Beautiful Death - *Latest*
Constable UK (1993); St Martin's US (1993)

J

Insp Richard JURY
of Scotland Yard carries on the classic tradition of British policemen. He operates in and around fictional villages deep in the heart of England, which involve him in the (only to be expected but nicely updated) mystery and mayhem that is known to occur in such outwardly tranquil places. He is especially concerned with Long Piddleton and its rich bunch of characters.
British Policeman operating in England
Sidekick: Melrose PLANT
seems to weave in and out of the cases by accident. He is, as a matter of fact, aristocratic, handsome, cultured and rather clever, with more than a touch of the old *WIMSEY* about him. These are all virtues that can, of course, be of solid use to a stolid policeman at his wit's end among the English yeomanry.
British Male - Assistant
Sidekick: Sgt WIGGINS
is *JURY's* official assistant, a hypochondriac with comic importance in the novels.
British Male - Subordinate
Stooge: Ch Supt RACER
is *JURY's* boss and tries to browbeat him at every opportunity, fortunately always being in the wrong – as all good stooges should be.
British Male

Martha GRIMES (American)
was born in Pittsburgh, Pennsylvania. She took a BA and MA at the University of Maryland and has been sometime Professor of English at Montgomery College, Maryland. She has set her books in rural England, with lots of literary allusions and use of English pubs, often using the names of the latter for her book titles.
Citation Record: 12 Books
The Man With A Load Of Mischief - *First*
Little, Brown US (1981)
Rainbow's End - *Latest*
Little, Brown US (1995)

Darius JUST
American Male Amateur operating in USA

Isaac ASIMOV 1920-1992 (American)
Invented 6 detectives - see Elijah BALEY

Citation Record: 1 Book

Murder At The ABA - *Only*
Doubleday US (1976)

Authorized Murder - *Only**
Gollancz UK (1976)

Capt John Valcourt JUSTICE

indulges in adventures, with some detection, in 1804, a time of great tension between the two countries.

British Male Professional Investigator operating in England/France

Anthony FORREST (British)

Writers: Antony BROWN and Norman Ian MACKENZIE 1921-

Citation Record: 3 Books

Captain Justice - *First*
Lane UK (1981); Hill US (1981)

A Balance Of Dangers - *Latest*
Lane UK (1984); Hill US (1984)

Peter JUSTICE

British Male Amateur operating in England

Francis DUNCAN (British)

See main detective Mordecai Euripides TREMAINE

Citation Record: 5 Books

The League Of Justice - *First*
Jenkins UK (1937)

The Hand Of Justice - *Last*
Jenkins UK (1945)

J

William JUSTICE

American Male Sleuth operating in several locations

Jack ARNETT (American)

Writer: Mike MACQUAY

Other Byline: Mike MACQUAY

Citation Record: 4 Books

Genocide Express - *First*
Bantam US (1989)

Death Force - *Latest*
Bantam US (1990)

Zachariah JUSTIS and Guinevere JONES

Zachariah JONES is tall, dark and handsome and appears in romantic variations on the PI novel, falling for *Guinevere JONES*, a beautiful PI who works for Camelot Investigations of Seattle. !See Appendix 2.

American Male Private Detective and American Female Private Detective operating in Seattle/Washington DC

Jayne CASTLE (American)

Writer: Jayne Ann KRENTZ

Citation Record: 4 Books

The Desperate Game - *First*
!See Appendix 2.
Dell US (1986)

The Chilling Deception - *Latest*
!See Appendix 2.
Dell US (1988)

Helene JUSTUS

Appears with at least two other detectives - see Jake JUSTUS

Jake JUSTUS, Helene JUSTUS and John J MALONE

Two American Male Amateurs and one American Female Amateur operating in Chicago

Craig RICE 1908-1957 (American)

Invented 3 detectives - see John J MALONE

Citation Record: 10 Books

Eight Faces At Three - *First*
Simon & Schuster US (1939); Eyre & Spottiswoode UK (1939)

Murder Stops The Clock - *First**
Mystery Novel of the Month US (1941)

Death At Three - *First**
Cherry Tree UK (1941)

But The Doctor Died - *Last*
appears to have been published ten years after the author's death.
Lancer US (1967)

Lavie JUTT

British Amateur operating in England

Marguerite BARCLAY and Armiger BARCLAY (British)

Citation Record: 11 Short Stories in 1 Collection

The Activities Of Lavie Jutt - *Collection 1*
Paul UK (1911)

— K —

Connie KALE

tried to be a top golf pro, failed, and returned to her home town in New England, where she has set up as a private detective.

American Female Private Detective operating in New England

W R PHILBRICK (American)

Writer: W Rodman PHILBRICK

Other Detectives:
J D HAWKINS — Philip MARLOWE
T D STASH

Citation Record: 1 Book

Slow Dancer - *Single*
St Martin's US (1984)

Stephen KALE

American Male Amateur operating in England

Montague JON (British)

Citation Record: 2 Books

The Wallington Case - *First*
Macmillan UK (1981); St Martin's US (1982)

A Question Of Law - *Latest*
Macmillan UK (1981); St Martin's US (1982)

Li KAO

lives in the Peking of a thousand years ago. A former thief, having just become a centenarian and needing to be carried around, he decides to become a professional detective. Surely he must be the oldest practitioner in the business!

Chinese Male Professional Investigator operating in Peking

Sidekick: Lu YU
is the immensely strong assistant of *Li KAO* and helps him in every way, even to the point of carrying him on his travels.

Chinese Male - Assistant

Barry HUGHART (American)

Citation Record: 2 Books

Bridge Of Birds - *First*
US (1986)

The Story Of The Stone - *Latest*
US (1988)

Sir Bruton KAMES

Second detective of Harvey TUKE

KAMUS OF KADIZAR

Male Sleuth

J Michael REAVES (American)

Citation Record: 4 Short Stories in 1 Collection

Darkworld Detective - *Collection 1*
Bantam US (1982)

Insp KANE

American Policeman operating in Boston

Roger SCARLETT (American)
Writers: Dorothy BLAIR 1903- and Evelyn PAGE 1902-
Citation Record: 4 Books
The Back Bay Murders - *First*
Doubleday US (1930); Selwyn UK (1931)
Murder Among The Angells - *Last*
Doubleday US (1932)

Adam KANE
British Male Amateur operating in England

W R BENNETT 1921- (British)
Writer: William Robert BENNETT
Citation Record: 2 Books
The Man From Checkmate - *First*
Hale UK (1971)
Dossier On A Mantis - *Last*
Hale UK (1972)

Andy KANE
American Male Sleuth operating in USA/Hong Kong

Carter BROWN 1923-1985 (Australian)
Invented 10 detectives - see Rick HOLMAN
Citation Record: 2 Books
The Hong Kong Caper - *First*
was first published (perhaps 1957) in Australia by *Horwitz* as *Blonde, Bad, and Beautiful.*
Horwitz AU (1962); Four Square UK (1963); Signet US (1962)
Bird In A Guilt-Edged Cage - *Last*
Horwitz AU (1963)
The Guilt-Edged Cage - *Last**
Four Square UK (1963); Signet US (1962)

Ben KANE
American Male Sleuth operating in the Caribbean

Nick STONE (American)
Citation Record: 7 Books
The Assassin - *First*
Ivy US (1987)
Killer Cruise - *Latest*
Ivy US (1988)

Elias KANE
sleuths at some time in the future.
American Male Professional Investigator

Steven G SPRUILL 1946- (American)
Writer: Stephen Gregory SPRUILL
Citation Record: 3 Books
The Psychopath Plague - *First*
Doubleday US (1978); Hale UK (1978)
Paradox Planet - *Latest*
Doubleday US (1988)

Martin KANE
Male Sleuth operating in USA

KANE (Australian)
Writer: C J MCKENZIE
Citation Record: 14 Books
Hands Off The Lovely - *First*
Webster AU (1958)
Margin For Murder - *Last*
Webster AU (1959)

Mortimer KANE
solves a case of death by bludgeoning in locked and bolted offices.
British Male Amateur operating in England

Cecil HAYTER 1871-1922 (British)
See main detective Derwent DUFF
Citation Record: 1 Selected Short Story
The Maddox House Murder
In 'The Red Magazine' UK

Paul Kenneth KANE
American Male Amateur operating in Illinois

James A HOWARD 1922- (American)
See main detective Steve ASHE
Citation Record: 1 Book
The Bullet-Proof Martyr - *Only*
Dutton US (1961)

Peter KANE
appeared mainly in stories in *Dime Detective.*
American Male Detective in Pulp Magazines operating in USA

Hugh B CAVE (American)
No citations

Det Ch Insp Phelim KANE
solves a case of death by bludgeoning in a locked library.
Irish Policeman operating in Ireland

David BRALY
Citation Record: 1 Selected Short Story
The Gallowglass
appeared in the August number.
In 'Alfred Hitchcock's Mystery Magazine' US (1986)

Solomon KANE
was an 'occult' detective.
American Male Detective in Pulp Magazines operating in USA

Robert E HOWARD 1906-1936 (American)
Writer: Robert Erwin HOWARD
Inventor of one other detective King KULL
No citations

'Sugar' KANE
is a former military policeman and middleweight boxing champion. He runs a London detective agency and ploughs his way through many cases in many books.
British Male Private Detective operating in London

Lovat MARSHALL 1909-1975 (British)
For writer details see Supt MACNEILL
Citation Record: 28 Books
Sugar For The Lady - *First*
Hurst UK (1955)
Murder To Order - *Last*
Hale UK (1975)

Nash KANZLER
was once a reporter, became a small-time PI, and then retired. A reporter on a local paper brings him back to investigate the murders of black leaders.
American Male Private Detective operating in Newark

Nathan GOTTLIEB (American)
Citation Record: 1 Book
Stinger - *Single*
Jove US (1978)

Morris KAPLAN
is about forty years old and a self-styled PI who sets up a crummy detective agency.
American Male Private Detective operating in San Francisco

Bob BIDERMAN 1960- (American)
See main detective Joseph RADKIN
Citation Record: 1 Book
Death Order Of A Left-Wing Student - *Single*

Lee KAPRELIAN
is of Armenian extraction and works in his father's carpet business. Infatuated with a beautiful woman, he is drawn into a case of murder and has to do a little sleuthing.
American Male Amateur operating in Milwaukee

William Campbell GAULT 1910- (American)
Invented 6 detectives - see Brock (The Rock) CALLAHAN
Citation Record: 1 Book
The Bloody Bokhara - *Only*
Dutton US (1952)
The Bloodstained Bokhara - *Only**
Boardman UK (1953)

Vladimer KAR
Second detective of Alexander (Check Force) CHANE

Joe KARNS
Male Sleuth operating in several locations

Gene DEWEESE and Robert Stratton COULSON 1918-(American)
Writer: (First author) Thomas Eugene DEWEESE 1934-
Citation Record: 2 Books
Now You See It-Him-Them - *First*
Doubleday US (1975); Hale UK (1976)
Charles Fort Never Mentioned Wombats - *Latest*
Doubleday US (1977); Hale UK (1978)

Roger 'Butch' KARP
American Male Sleuth operating in New York

Robert K TANENBAUM (American)
Citation Record: 2 Books
No Lesser Plea - *First*
Watts US (1987); Sidgwick UK (1988)
Depraved Indifference - *Latest*
New American Library US (1989)

Ginny KARR
is reluctantly forced to investigate the death of an old college friend.
American Female Amateur operating in New York

James ELWARD (American)
Citation Record: 1 Book
Monday's Child Is Dead - *Single*
Carroll & Graf US (1995)

Supt Kofi KATT
is the son of a wealthy English trader and a black African mother. He is a policeman in some unnamed African state.
African Policeman operating in Africa

Gil NORTH 1916- (British)
See main detective Sgt Caleb CLUFF
Citation Record: 1 Book
A Corpse For Kofi Katt - *Only*
Hale UK (1978)

Helen KATZ
Second detective of Maureen DIETZ

Dep Ch Insp Max KAUFFMAN and J T 'Jake' SPANNER
MAX KAUFFMAN is not only a top cop but is a wealthy man in his own right. He appears in a number of police procedurals, nearly always involving ingenious capers and amazing heists. In some books he works closely with *J T SPANNER*, a PI who is assisted off and on by his ex-wives.
American Policeman and American Male Private Detective operating in New York

Thomas CHASTAIN (American)
Invented 4 detectives - see J T 'Jake' SPANNER
Citation Record: 6 Books
Pandora's Box - *First*
Mason/Charter US (1974); Cassell US (1975)
The Diamond Exchange - *Latest*
Doubleday US (1981); Hale UK (1981)

Philip KAUFMAN
Canadian Male Private Detective operating in Montreal

Joel NEWMAN 1951- (Canadian)
Citation Record: 1 Book
Dead Man's Tears - *Single*
Beaufort US (1981)

Knock-Out KAVANAGH
British Male Amateur operating in several locations

Brian STUART (British)
Writer: Brian Arthur WORTHINGTON-STUART
Citation Record: 2 Books
Knock-Out Kavanagh - *First*
Ward, Lock UK (1948)
The Silver Phantom Murder - *Last*
Ward, Lock UK (1950)

Bromley KAY
British Male Amateur operating in England

J M WALSH 1897-1952 (British)
Invented 7 detectives - see Insp QUAILE
Citation Record: 3 Books
The League Of Missing Men - *First*
Hamilton UK (1932)
The White Mask - *Last*
Hamilton UK (1925); Doran US (1927)

Simon KAYE
is a classic-style gumshoe who is good at solving the kind of problems that dames get themselves into.
American Male Private Detective operating in USA

Hillary WAUGH 1920- (American)
Invented 7 detectives - see Ch Fred FELLOWS
Citation Record: 6 Books
The Glenna Powers Case - *First*
Raven US (1980); Gollancz UK (1981)
The Priscilla Copperwaite Case - *Latest*
Gollancz UK (1986); Curley US (1988)

Peter KAYIRA
American Male Amateur operating in USA

S Joshua L ZAKE (Ugandan)
was a former Ugandan Minister of Education, later Ambassador to the United States.
Citation Record: 1 Book
Truckful Of Gold - *Single*
Regnery US (1980)

Dan KEARNEY ASSOCIATES
is a team of auto repossessors, debt collectors and skip tracers operating out of Golden Gate Avenue. It includes Dan Kearney himself and his chief assistant, Larry Ballard, but also others.
American Male Private Detectives operating in San Francisco

Joe GORES 1931- (American)
Invented 4 detectives - see Curt HALSTEAD
Citation Record: 4 Books
Dead Skip - *First*
Random House US (1973); Gollancz UK (1974)
32 Cadillacs - *Latest*
Mysterious Press US (1992)

Max KEARNY
is an 'occult' detective.
American Male Private Detective operating in USA

Ron GOULART 1933- (American)
Invented 15 detectives - see Jake PACE and Hildy PACE
Citation Record: 1 Selected Short Story
Kearny's Last Case
is in a collection of the author's short stories, *Ghost Breaker*.
Ace US (1971)

Sarah KEATE
had appeared, many years earlier, in several books with another of the author's detectives, *Lance O'LEARY.* Literarily resuscitated, she is now the sole detective.
American Female Amateur operating in USA

Mignon G EBERHART 1899- (American)
was born in University Place, Nebraska, and graduated from Nebraska Wesleyan University, Lincoln, 1920. Acknowledged as one of the mistresses of the genre, with over fifty novels to her credit, she has used her two main series detectives sparingly, usually inventing new ones for the exotic locales she often uses in her work.
Writer: Mignon Good EBERHART
Other Detectives:
Sewell BLAKE
Mallory BOOKOVER
Emmy BRACE
Det CRAFFT
Susan DARE
Sarah KEATE and Det Lance O'LEARY
Mady SMITH
Mr WICKWIRE
Citation Record: 2 Books
Wolf In Man's Clothing - *First*
Random House US (1942); Collins UK (1943)
Man Missing - *Last*
Random House US (1954); Collins UK (1954)

Sarah KEATE and Det Lance O'LEARY
Sarah KEATE, who appeared on her own in two books, ten and twenty years after these, her first appearances, is a middle-aged spinster in a midwestern American town and works in hospital as a nurse. She stumbles, time and time again, on ingenious medical crimes and solves them with the help of a friendly, young police detective, *Lance O'LEARY.* The books were made into successful films in the 1930s.
American Female Amateur and American Policeman operating in USA

Mignon G EBERHART 1899- (American)
Invented 9 detectives - see Sarah KEATE
Citation Record: 5 Books
The Patient In Room 18 - *First*
Doubleday US (1929); Heinemann UK (1929)
Murder By An Aristocrat - *Last*
Doubleday US (1932)

Sarah KEATE
Second detective of Det Lance O'LEARY

Kyra KEATON
is, around the turn of the twentieth century, a rich, beautiful, progressive woman who runs a detective agency from her Broad Street mansion in Philadelphia. Believing she can sleuth as well as any man, she does so in a first book set in 1899. She does so again in a second book, set in 1907 and in Virginia.
American Female Private Detective operating in Philadelphia/Virginia

Teona TONE 1944- (American)
Citation Record: 2 Books
Lady On The Line - *First*
GM US (1983)
Full Cry - *Latest*
GM US (1985)

Colin KEATS
Second detective of Gwynn LEITH

John H W KEATS
is a newsman who solves a case of death by shooting in a locked room.
American Male Amateur operating in USA

Theodore ROSCOE (American)
was an expert on naval affairs, on which he advised the US government.
Citation Record: 1 Book
I'll Grind Their Bones - *Only*
Dodge US (1936); Harrap UK (1937)

Magnus KEEBLE
British Male Amateur operating in England

Andrew WOOD 1890- (British)
Writer: Samuel Andrew WOOD
Inventor of one other detective KOREGORVSKY
Citation Record: 4 Books
The Prom Concert Murders - *First*
Hurst UK (1948)
Murder By The Minute - *Last*
Dragon UK (1955)

Michael KEEFE
American Male Sleuth operating in Vietnam/Panama

Michael WOLFE 1917- (American)
Writer: Gilbert MacLean WILLIAMS
Citation Record: 4 Books
Man On A String - *First*
Harper & Row US (1973)
The Panama Paradox - *Last*
Harper & Row US (1977)

KEEGAN
British Male Sleuth operating in England

Brian BALL 1932- (British)
Writer: Brian Neville BALL
Citation Record: 2 Books 2 Short Stories in 1 Collection
Keegan: The No-Option Contract - *First*
Barker UK (1975)
Keegan: The One-Way Deal - *Last*
Barker UK (1976)
The Baker Street Boys - *Collection 1*
contains two novelizations from a TV series.
BBC UK (1983)

Daniel KEEL
American Male Sleuth operating in USA

T A SCHOCK (American)
Citation Record: 3 Books
Deadpan - *First*
Leisure Books US (1981); Star UK (1982)
Pratfall - *Latest*
Leisure Books US (1981)

Insp KEEN
British Policeman operating in England

Philip LORAINE (British)
Writer: Robert ESTRIDGE
Inventor of one other detective Catherine WALDEN
Citation Record: 1 Book
White Lie The Dead - *Only*
Hodder & Stoughton UK (1950)
And To My Beloved Husband - *Only**
Mill US (1950)

Franklyn KEEN
British Male Amateur operating in England/France

Harman LONG (British)
Citation Record: 2 Books
Seven To Die - *First*
Rich UK (1946)
The Golden Cat - *Last*
Rich UK (1947)

Gregory KEEN
British Male Amateur operating in England/Macao

Lindsay HARDY (Australian)
is a writer for TV, now living in the USA.
Citation Record: 2 Books

Requiem For A Redhead - *First*
Appleton UK (1953)
The Nightshade Ring - *Last*
Appleton US (1954); Hale UK (1955)

Hal KEEN
Male Detective in Pulp Magazines

Hugh LLOYD
Writer: Percy Keese FITZHUGH
No citations

Jax KEEN
appeared in two novelettes, both set in a movie studio, written by a master of the art in his early days and published, 1939, in *Double Detective.*
American Male Detective in Pulp Magazines operating in Hollywood

Erle Stanley GARDNER 1889-1970 (American)
Invented 14 detectives - see Perry MASON
No citations

Laura KEEN
was a kind of avant-garde girl sleuth who appeared in short stories in the pulps. Her main claim to fame was that, in a still rather gentle era, she travelled around with a brace of pistols, a bowie knife, and accompanied by a 'darky bootblack and an Indian'.
American Female Detective in Pulp Magazines operating in USA

C LITTLE (American)
Inventor of one other detective HUMPTY DUMPTY DICK
Citation Record: 1 Selected Short Story
Laura Keen, The Queen Of Detectives
New York Detective Library US (1892)

Riley KEENAN
was Irish-American and appeared mainly in stories in *Private Detective* in the 1940s.
American Male Detective in Pulp Magazines operating in USA

Roger TORREY (American)
Invented 7 detectives - see Pat MULLANCY
No citations

KEENE
is a lawyer.
British Male Amateur operating in England

Frank BARRETT 1848-1926 (British)
Invented 5 detectives - see Capt Thomas VERNAN
Citation Record: 3 Books
A Recoiling Vengeance - *First*
Watt & Downey UK (1888); Appleton US (1888)
Under A Strange Mask - *Last*
Cassell UK (1889); Lovell US (1889)

Allan KEENE
American Male Detective in Pulp Magazines operating in USA

Harry ROCKWOOD 1859-1932 (American)
Invented 14 detectives - see Clarice DYKE
Citation Record: 1 Book
Allan Keene, The War Detective - *Only*
Ogilvie US (1884)

Arnold KEENE and Bernard YOUNG
British Male Amateurs operating in England

Eric WOOD 1887-1940 (British)
Writer: Frank Knowles CAMPLING
Citation Record: 3 Books
Death In The Mews - *First*
Hamilton UK (1937)
Death Of An Oddfellow - *Last*
Hamilton UK (1938)

Max KEENE
American Male Private Detective operating in Chicago
Sidekick: Carl GOOD
is the assistant to *Max KEENE* and is somehow transmuted into *Carl GUARD* in another book, in which he appears on his own.
American Male - Assistant

Robert O SABER 1913- (American)
Invented 3 detectives - see Carl GOOD
Citation Record: 2 Books
A Dame Called Murder - *First*
Graphic US (1955)
A Time For Murder - *Last*
Graphic US (1956)

Oliver KEENE
British Male Secret Agent operating in several locations

J M WALSH 1897-1952 (British)
Invented 7 detectives - see Insp QUAILE
Citation Record: 11 Books
Island Of Spies - *First*
Collins UK (1937)
Whispers In The Dark - *Last*
Collins UK (1945)

Phil KEENE
solves murders committed in absolute darkness.
American Male Amateur operating in USA

Robert O SABER 1913- (American)
Invented 3 detectives - see Carl GOOD
Citation Record: 1 Book
The Black Dark Murders - *Only*
Handi-Books US (1949); Jewel UK (1949)

Capt KEETCH
Second detective of Insp BOW

KEFTON
American Male Detective in Pulp Magazines operating in USA

OLD SLEUTH (American)
Invented 40 detectives - see Brant ADAMS
Citation Record: 1 Book
Kefton, The Detective; Or, The Wonder Of The Age - *Only*
Ogilvie US (1895)

Harrison KEITH
features, as did many other detectives appearing under house names, in a large, uncounted number of stories published around the end of the nineteenth and beginning of the twentieth century and published in book form, mainly by *Street & Smith* in their *Magnet* and *New Magnet* libraries.
American Male Detective in Pulp Magazines operating in USA

Nicholas CARTER
House name.
Citation Record: 1 Book 12 Short Stories in 1 Collection
Harrison Keith's Poison Problem; Or, The Quest Of The Blue Cobra - *Only*
Street & Smith (New Magnet #635) US (1910)
The Adventures Of Harrison Keith, Detective - *Collection 1*
Street & Smith (Magnet #93) US (1899)

Nicholas CARTER
Writer: S A D COX
Citation Record: 1 Book
Harrison Keith's Perilous Contract; Or, Crime's Bitterest Foe - *Only*
Street & Smith (New Magnet #638) US (1910)

Nicholas CARTER 1858-1933
Writer: Frederick William DAVIS
House writer for one other detective Nick CARTER

Citation Record: 6 Books

Harrison Keith's Death Compact - *First*
Street & Smith (New Magnet #590) US (1909)

Harrison Keith's Triple Tragedy - *Last*
Street & Smith (New Magnet #629) US (1909)

Nicholas CARTER 1861-1922

Invented 3 detectives - see Nick CARTER (Writer Frederic Merrill Van Rensselaer DEY)

Citation Record: 1 Book

Harrison Keith, Sleuth; Or, The Army Puzzle - *Only*
Street & Smith (New Magnet #489) US (1907)

Nicholas CARTER 1869-1929

See main detective Nick CARTER (Writer Walter Bertram FOSTER)

Citation Record: 3 Books

Harrison Keith's Greatest Task; Or, An Unbearable Burden - *First*
Street & Smith (New Magnet #521) US (1907)

Harrison Keith's Drag Net - *Last*
Street & Smith (New Magnet #541) US (1908)

Nicholas CARTER 1850-1929

See main detective Nick CARTER (George Charles JENKS)

Citation Record: 3 Books

Harrison Keith's Queer Clue; Or, Among The 'Reds' - *First*
Street & Smith (New Magnet #561) US (1908)

Harrison Keith's Lucky Strike; Or, The Plot That Failed - *Last*
Street & Smith (New Magnet #581) US (1909)

Nicholas CARTER

Writer: W L LARNED

House writer for one other detective Nick Carter

Citation Record: 12 Books

Harrison Keith's Abduction Tangle; Or, Lifting A Veil Of Mystery - *First*
Street & Smith (New Magnet #620) US (1909)

Harrison Keith's Cyclone Clue; Or, Through The Air - *Last*
Street & Smith (New Magnet #621) US (1910)

Nicholas CARTER 1880-1928

Writer: Charles Agnew MACLEAN

Citation Record: 12 Books

Harrison Keith's Danger; Or, Out Of The Jaws Of Death - *First*
Street & Smith (New Magnet #497) US (1907)

Harrison Keith's Diamond Case; Or, The Most Exciting Case On Record - *Last*
Street & Smith (New Magnet #549) US (1908)

John KEITH

is one of this prolific author's later creations, a counter-espionage detective of the more vulgar kind, also known as 'The Man from APE'.

American Male Professional Investigator operating in USA/Germany

Norman DANIELS (American)

Invented 6 detectives - see Richard Curtis (Phantom) VAN LOAN

Citation Record: 8 Books

The Hunt Club - *First*
Pyramid US (1964)

Operation S-L - *Last*
Pyramid US (1971)

Prof Natalie KEITH

Second detective of Christopher JENSEN

Bill KELLAWAY

British Male Amateur operating in England

Gwyn EVANS 1899-1938 (British)

Writer: Gwynfil Arthur EVANS

Other Detectives:

Sexton BLAKE — Chester BRETT
Quentin DREX — Double O'DAY

Citation Record: 2 Books 3 Short Stories in 1 Collection

Hercules Esq - *First*
Shaylor UK (1930)

Mr Hercules - *First**
Dial US (1931)

Satan Ltd - *Last*
Wright UK (1935); Godwin US (1935)

The Return Of Hercules, Esq - *Collection 1*
contains three novelettes.
Wright UK (1937)

Det Sgt Joe KELLER and Det Sgt Joe RYKER

operate together in the Homicide division of the New York Police Department. *Joe RYKER* also appears on his own in other books by this author.

American Policemen operating in New York

Nelson DE MILLE 1943- (American)

was born in New York City. He graduated with a BA in Political Science and History from Hofstra University, New York, 1970, and later saw distinguished service in the US Army, 1966-1969, receiving decorations for gallantry. Later he became an art dealer and editorial assistant.

Writer: Nelson Richard DE MILLE

Other Byline: Jack CANNON

Inventor of one other detective Det Sgt Joe RYKER

Citation Record: 3 Books

The Smack Man - *First*
was republished under the following byline.
Manor US (1975)

Night Of The Phoenix - *Last*
was republished under the following byline.
Manor US (1975)

Jack CANNON 1943- (American)

For writer details see Det Sgt Joe KELLER and Det Sgt Joe RYKER

Citation Record: 2 Books

The Smack Man - *First*
was previously published under the preceding byline.
Pocket Books US (1989); Grafton UK (1991)

Night Of The Phoenix - *Last*
was previously published under the preceding byline.
Pocket Books US (1989)

Supt Konstantin KELLER

German Policeman operating in Munich

Hans Hellmut KIRST 1914-1989 (German)

was the author of at least seventeen genre novels, which have appeared in English translation.

Citation Record: 3 Books

A Time For Scandal - *First*
is a translation from the German of *Verdammt zum Erfolg* (Munich, 1971).
Collins UK (1973)

Damned To Success - *First**
Coward McCann US (1973)

A Time For Payment - *Last*
is a translation from the German of *Alles Hat Seinen Preis* (Hamburg, 1974).
Collins UK (1976)

Everything Has Its Price - *Last**
Coward McCann US (1976)

Insp KELLERWAY

British Policeman operating in England

W H L CRAUFORD 1886- (British)

Writer: William Harold Lane CRAUFORD

Citation Record: 2 Books

The Missing Ace - *First*
Ward, Lock UK (1931)

Murder To Music - *Last*
Ward, Lock UK (1936)

Sarah KELLING and Max BITTERSOHN

SARAH KELLING is a member of a wealthy family clan on Boston's Beacon Hill. Their number is augmented by *Max*

BITTERSOHN, who, as it happens, is a specialist in solving art thefts. He appears on his own in other books by this author.

American Female Amateur and American Male Amateur operating in Boston

Charlotte MACLEOD 1922- (Canadian)

was born in Bath, New Brunswick, Canada. Educated at schools in Weymouth, Massachusetts, she has been an artist and sometime vice-president of an advertising business.

Writer: Charlotte Matilda Hughes MACLEOD

Other Byline: Alisa CRAIG

Other Detectives:

Max BITTERSOHN Prof Peter SHANDY

Citation Record: 9 Books

The Family Vault - *First*
Collins UK (1980); Doubleday US (1980)

The Odd Job - *Latest*
HarperCollins UK (1995)

Casey KELLOG and Al KRUG

!See Appendix 2.

American Female Amateur and American Male Amateur operating in Los Angeles

Carolyn WESTON 1921- (American)

Citation Record: 3 Books

Poor, Poor Ophelia - *First*
Random House US (1972)

Rouse The Demon - *Latest*
Random House US (1976); Gollancz UK (1977)

K

Benson KELLOGG

is an investigative lawyer whose cases end in powerful courtroom dramas.

American Male Amateur operating in USA

Bart SPICER 1918- (American)

Invented 3 detectives - see Carney WILDE

Citation Record: 2 Books

Act Of Anger - *First*
Atheneum US (1962); Barker UK (1963)

Kellogg Junction - *Last*
Atheneum US (1969); Hodder & Stoughton UK (1970)

Michael KELLS

British Male Amateur operating in England

Peter CHEYNEY 1896-1951 (British)

Invented 11 detectives - see Lemmy CAUTION

Citation Record: 2 Books

Sinister Errand - *First*
Collins UK (1945); Dodd, Mead US (1945)

Sinister Murders - *First**
Avon US (1957)

Ladies Won't Wait - *Last*
Collins UK (1951); Dodd, Mead US (1951)

Cocktails And The Killer - *Last**
Avon US (1957)

Lt KELLY

American Policeman operating in New York

Holly ROTH 1916-1964 (American)

Invented 4 detectives - see Insp MEDFORD

Citation Record: 2 Books

The Content Assignment - *First*
Simon & Schuster US (1954); Hamish Hamilton UK (1954)

The Shocking Secret - *First**
Dell US (1955)

Button, Button - *Last*
Harcourt Brace US (1966); Hamish Hamilton UK (1967)

Aloysius KELLY

British Male Amateur operating in England

Barbara WORSLEY-GOUGH 1903- (British)

Writer: Barbara Kathleen WORSLEY-GOUGH

Citation Record: 2 Books

Alibi Innings - *First*
Joseph UK (1954)

Lantern Hill - *Last*
Joseph UK (1957)

Dogeron KELLY

American Male Amateur operating in USA

Mickey SPILLANE 1918- (American)

Invented 3 detectives - see Mike HAMMER

Citation Record: 1 Book

The Erection Set - *Only*
Dutton US (1972); Allen UK (1972)

Emmett KELLY

Second detective of Toby PETERS

Homer KELLY

is an attorney, scholar and sometime detective whose cases occur in the literary belt and combine the best of American genre erudition with some mayhem and good puzzles.

American Male Amateur operating in Massachusetts

Jane LANGTON 1922- (American)

was born in Boston. She was educated at Wellesley College, Michigan, and graduated with a BS from the University of Michigan, Ann Arbor, 1944, and an MA, 1945. She studied at the Boston Museum School of Art, 1958-1959, and has since been an artist, teacher and writer of crime fiction and books for children.

Writer: Jane Gillson LANGTON

Citation Record: 8 Books

The Transcendental Murder - *First*
Harper & Row US (1964)

The Minuteman Murder - *First**
Dell US (1976)

The Dante Game - *Latest*
Gollancz UK (1991)

Irene KELLY

is a newshound who does a little cosy amateur sleuthing in situations fraught with danger.

American Female Amateur operating in USA

Jan BURKE (American)

Citation Record: 2 Books

Sweet Dreams, Irene - *First*
Simon & Schuster US (1994)

Dear Irene - *Latest*
Simon & Schuster US (1995)

Jack KELLY

Second detective of Charles CARR

Joe KELLY

American Male Amateur operating in Connecticut

Robert AVERY 1911-1983 (American)

Writer: Robert J AVERY Jr

Citation Record: 2 Books

A Murder A Day! - *First*
Mystery House US (1940)

A Fat Man With A Dollar - *Last*
Arcadia US (1947)

Lt Joseph KELLY

American Policeman operating in Maryland

Leslie FORD 1898-1983 (American)

Invented 6 detectives - see Grace LATHAM

Citation Record: 2 Books

Murder In Maryland - *First*
Farrar & Rinehart US (1932); Hutchinson UK (1933)

The Clue Of The Judas Tree - *Last*
Farrar & Rinehart US (1933)

Neil KELLY
is a middle-aged Professor of English at the fictional Old Hampton College in a small town in Massachusetts. A sad widower, he is addicted to his research and to teaching but is reluctantly drawn into investigating the terrible murder of a beloved student. Thus initiated, he continues his sleuthing in further books.

American Male Amateur operating in USA

S F X DEAN (American)

probably invented his strange pseudonym in dedication to the classic fictional detective, *Prof S F X VAN DUSEN*, the Thinking Machine.

Writer: Francis SMITH

Citation Record: 6 Books

By Frequent Anguish - *First*
Walker US (1982); Collins UK (1982)

Nantucket Soap Opera - *Latest*
Atheneum US (1987)

Samuel Moses KELLY
is an Afro-American ex-cop, now a part-time private eye and house detective in the Hotel Castelreagh, Manhattan. He has a cat named Baudelaire and consorts with an amiable blonde who runs the local brothel. With so much going for him, is it surprising that he meets several murders in the line of duty?

American Male Private Detective operating in New York

J F BURKE 1915-1992 (American)

Writer: Jackson Frederick BURKE

Inventor of one other detective Joe STREETER

Citation Record: 3 Books

Location Shots - *First*
Harper & Row US (1974); Constable UK (1974)

Kelly Among The Nightingales - *Last*
Dutton US (1979)

'Slot-machine' KELLY
appeared only in short stories. A tough operator in the Chelsea district of New York, he has only one arm and takes his nickname from being considered a one-armed bandit, like the famous slot-machine. He is the perhaps the prototype for the author's better-known one-armed detective, *Dan FORTUNE.*

American Male Private Detective operating in New York

Dennis LYNDS 1924- (American)

For writer details see Kane JACKSON

No citations

Stephen KELLY
is an artist working in the offices of a Fleet Street magazine. When murder occurs he sets about discovering whodunnit. !See Appendix 2.

British Male Amateur operating in London

Stooge: Insp REYNOLDS
British Male

Eric BRUTON 1915- (British)

See main detective Insp George JUDD

Citation Record: 1 Book

Death In Ten Point Bold - *Only*
Jenkins UK (1957)

Virginia KELLY
is an Afro-American girl who goes home to a small town in the Midwest for Christmas. In addition to having to explain to her parents that she is lesbian and still grieving for her dead lover, she has to investigate a murder.

American Female Sleuth operating in USA

Nikki BAKER (American)

Citation Record: 1 Book

The Long Goodbyes - *Single*
Naiad US (1993)

Insp KELSEY
British Policeman operating in England

Sidekick: Sgt LAMBERT
British Male - Subordinate

Emma PAGE (British)

Writer: Honoria TIRBUTT

Citation Record: 12 Books

Missing Woman - *First*
Hale UK (1980)

Mortal Remains - *Latest*
HarperCollins UK (1991)

Sgt George KELSO
American Policeman operating in Indianapolis

Malcolm MCCLINTICK (American)

Citation Record: 4 Books

Mary's Grave - *First*
Doubleday US (1987)

Joe Nix Is Dead - *Latest*
Doubleday US (1990)

Ruth KELSTERN
appeared in one famous short story, which has found its way into several anthologies, because of interest in its ingenious method of murder, which took place in an unusual 'locked-room' situation, a Turkish Bath. Her father is the victim and her lover is the suspect. To clear him she must solve a most puzzling crime.

British Female Amateur operating in England

Edgar JEPSON and Robert EUSTACE (British)

Writers: Edgar Alfred JEPSON 1863-1938 and Eustace Robert BARTON 1854-1943

Citation Record: 1 Selected Short Story

The Tea Leaf

appeared first in the October 1925 number of *Strand Magazine.* It is to be found in several anthologies: *Great Short Stories of Detection, Mystery and Horror* (*Gollancz*; UK 1928); *101 Years' Entertainment* (*Little, Brown*; US 1941); and *Detective Stories* (*Octopus*; US 1980).
In 'Strand Magazine' UK (1925)

Matthew KELTON
American Male Amateur operating on a ship

Richard CONNELL 1893-1949

Writer: Richard Edward CONNELL

Inventor of one other detective Mr POTTLE

Citation Record: 1 Book

Murder At Sea - *Only*
Jarrolds UK (1929); Minton US (1929)

Bert KEMP
is an art specialist and gun dealer, and solves a crime in the art world.

British Male Amateur operating in England

Gavin LYALL 1932- (British)

was born in Birmingham, Warwickshire. He was educated at King Edward VI School, Birmingham, and took a BA in English at Pembroke College, Cambridge, 1956. Journalist, film director and writer of thrillers, he has latterly written detective novels. He received the Crime Writers Association Silver Dagger award twice, 1964 and 1965.

Writer: Gavin Tudor LYALL

Other Detectives:
James CARD | Roy CASE
Maj Harry MAXIM

Citation Record: 1 Book

Venus With Pistol - *Only*
Hodder & Stoughton UK (1969); Scribner's US (1969)

Lennox KEMP
is a disbarred lawyer who, in the first book in which he appears, is having to work for Mcready's Detective Agency in

East London. By the second book he is reinstated and subsequently appears as an investigating lawyer.
British Male Professional Investigator operating in London

M R D MEEK 1918- (British)
was born in Greenock, Renfrewshire. She was educated at Birkenhead Girls' School, Cheshire, and took an LLB at the University of London, 1966.
Writer: Margaret Reid Duncan MEEK
Citation Record: 7 Books
Hang The Consequences - *First*
Collins UK (1984); Scribner's US (1985)
A Loose Connection - *Latest*
Collins UK (1989); Scribner's US (1989)

Supt KEMPSON
investigates the disappearance of two elderly people, newly married, in Italy.
British Policeman operating in Italy

E C R LORAC 1894-1958 (British)
See main detective Insp/Supt MACDONALD
Citation Record: 1 Book
Death In Triplicate - *Only*
Collins UK (1958)
People Will Talk - *Only**
Doubleday US (1958)

Insp KENDALL
British Policeman operating in England

J Jefferson FARJEON 1883-1955 (British)
Invented 3 detectives - see Paul BISHOP
Citation Record: 2 Books
Thirteen Guests - *First*
Collins UK (1936); Bobbs US (1938)
Seven Dead - *Last*
Collins UK (1939); Bobbs US (1939)

Don KENDRICK
British Male Amateur operating in Scotland

Allan MACKINNON (British)
Other Detectives:
Andrew CARNE
Mike DARROCH
Det Insp Duncan MACCALLUM
Citation Record: 2 Books
Dead On Departure - *First*
Long UK (1964)
Report From Argyll - *First**
Doubleday US (1964)
No Wreath From Manuela - *Last*
Long UK (1965)
Man Overboard - *Last**
Doubleday US (1965)

Det Ch Supt Maurice KENDRICK and Humphrey BARNES
pursue parallel but independent investigations in the hunt for a serial killer in a seaside town.
British Policeman and British Male Amateur operating in England

Eileen DEWHURST 1929- (British)
was born in Liverpool, Lancashire. She took a BA in English at St Anne's College, Oxford, 1951, and an MA, 1956. She has been a journalist and has held several administrative posts in the Universities of London and Liverpool.
Writer: Eileen Mary DEWHURST
Other Detectives:
Det Insp Neil CARTER
Susan HALLIDAY
Helen MARKHAM
Citation Record: 1 Book
A Private Prosecution - *Single*
Collins UK (1986); Doubleday US (1987)

Veil KENDRY
appears also in books with the author's other detective, *Dr Robert FREDERICKSON.*
American Sleuth operating in USA

George CHESBRO 1940- (American)
Invented 4 detectives - see Dr Robert 'Mongo' FREDERICKSON
Citation Record: 2 Books
Veil - *First*
Mysterious Press US (1986)
Jungle Of Steel And Stone - *Latest*
Mysterious Press US (1988)

Veil KENDRY
Second detective of Dr Robert 'Mongo' FREDERICKSON

Franklin KENNARD
British Male Private Detective operating in England

Headon HILL 1857-1927 (British)
Invented 11 detectives - see Insp HERON
Citation Record: 1 Book
The Queen Of Night - *Only*
Ward, Lock UK (1896)

Insp KENNEDY
British Policeman operating in England

Jeremy YORK 1908-1973 (British)
See main detective Supt FOLLY
Citation Record: 1 Book
Missing - *Only*
Scribner's US (1959)

KENNEDY
was a reporter for the *Richmond City Free Press* and appeared in about three dozen short stories in *Black Mask Magazine.*
American Male Detective in Pulp Magazines operating in USA

Frederick NEBEL 1903-1967 (American)
Invented 8 detectives - see Steve CARDIGAN
No citations

Allan KENNEDY
British Male Amateur operating in England

William LEQUEUX 1864-1927 (British)
was born in London and educated in London and Pegli, Italy. After studying art in Paris, he became a distinguished reporter and editor for British papers. Later he served abroad as a British consul and may have been, in fact, an undercover agent. He wrote books in many genres and a great many short stories. He was certainly one of the founders of the art of the modern spy story, often appearing to use his own intimate knowledge of espionage.
Writer: William Tufnell LEQUEUX
Other Detectives:
Raoul BECQ
Dr Villiers BEETHAM-SAUNDERS
BERYL
BLEKE
Clifton CLEEVE
DELMASSO and BRAY
DONOVAN
Theodore DROST
John DURSTON
Ronald EWART
Geoffrey FALCONER
Arthur HEATHER
Gerald INGRAM
Kershaw KIRK
William LEQUEUX
Helen MARKLOVE
MARTIN
Harry NETTLEFIELD
SANT
George STRATFIELD
Frank URWIN
Rex YELVERTON
Citation Record: 1 Book
The Closed Book - *Only*
Methuen UK (1904); In 'The Smart Set' US (1904)

Bill KENNEDY
British Male Amateur operating in England

Leslie CHARTERIS 1907- (American)
Invented 3 detectives - see Simon (The Saint) TEMPLAR

Citation Record: 2 Books

X Esquire - *First*
Ward, Lock UK (1927)

The White Rider - *Last*
Doubleday US (1930); Ward, Lock UK (1928)

Lt Cliff KENNEDY

American Policeman operating in USA

MacKinlay KANTOR 1904-1977 (American)

Invented 4 detectives - see Matt EDWARDS

Citation Record: 1 Selected Short Story

Wolf! Wolf!
appears also in the collection of the author's short stories, *It's About Crime* (*Signet*, US 1960).
In 'Real Detective Tales' US (1932)

Prof Craig KENNEDY

was often referred to as 'the American Sherlock Holmes' because of the brilliance of his deductive powers. However, his range was wider and more developed than that of his great British predecessor, for he worked sometimes as a private investigator and later for the New York Police Department and the Federal government. He was highly knowledgeable about the latest scientific advances and many of the stories are, in fact, concerned with such matters.

American Male Professional Amateur operating in USA

Sidekick: Walter JAMESON
is a reporter and friend who rooms with *KENNEDY* and follows him on a kind of roving brief, reporting his cases for his newspaper.
American Male - Friend

Arthur B REEVE 1880-1936 (American)

was born in Patchogue, Long Island, New York. He took an AB at Princeton University, New York, 1903, and attended New York Law School, later becoming a magazine editor and the author of several genre novels, short stories and plays. He is mainly remembered for his creation of *Craig KENNEDY*, one of the most significant and popular of early American detectives. His knowledge of science allowed him to incorporate the most modern methods, such as the use of dictaphones, X-rays, blood sampling and handwriting analysis, into his stories. During the First World War, he advised on the creation of a most advanced scientific laboratory for the US government for the detection of spies and saboteurs. Many of his stories were made into films, for which he wrote the screenplays.

Writer: Arthur Benjamin REEVE

Inventor of one other detective Constance DUNLAP

Citation Record: 4 Books 181 Short Stories in 15 Collections

The Soul Scar - *First*
Harper & Row US (1919)

The Stars Scream Murder - *Last*
Appleton US (1936)

The Poisoned Pen - *Collection 1*
Short stories - 12
Harper & Row US (1911); Hodder & Stoughton UK (1916)

The Silent Bullet: Adventures Of Craig Kennedy, Scientific Detective - *Collection 2*
Short stories - 11
Dodd, Mead US (1912)

The Black Hand - *Collection 2**
Nash UK (1912)

The Dream Doctor - *Collection 3*
Short stories - 12
Hearst's US (1914); Hodder & Stoughton UK (1916)

The War Terror - *Collection 4*
Short stories - 12
Hearst's US (1915)

Gold Of The Gods - *Collection 5*
Short stories - 25
Hearst's US (1915); Hodder & Stoughton UK (1916)

The Exploits Of Elaine - *Collection 6*
Short stories - 14
Hearst's US (1915); Hodder & Stoughton UK (1915)

The Romance Of Elaine - *Collection 7*
Short stories - 23
Hearst's US (1916); Hodder & Stoughton UK (1916)

The Triumph Of Elaine - *Collection 8*
Short stories - 12
Hodder & Stoughton UK (1916)

The Social Gangster - *Collection 9*
Short stories - 12
Hearst's US (1916)

The Diamond Queen - *Collection 9**
Hodder & Stoughton UK (1917)

The Treasure Train - *Collection 10*
Short stories - 12
Harper & Row US (1917); Collins UK (1920)

The Panama Plot - *Collection 11*
Short stories - 10
Harper & Row US (1918); Collins UK (1920)

Craig Kennedy Listens In - *Collection 12*
Short stories - 6
Harper & Row US (1923); Hodder & Stoughton UK (1924)

The Boy Scout's Craig Kennedy - *Collection 13*
Short stories - 6
Harper & Row US (1925)

Craig Kennedy On The Farm - *Collection 14*
Short stories - 10
Harper & Row US (1925)

Enter Craig Kennedy - *Collection 15*
Almost the last work by this gifted author, the collection contains four novelettes.
Short stories - 4
Macaulay US (1935)

George KENNEDY

American Male Amateur operating in USA/Mexico

George KENNEDY (American)

is an actor in films and on TV and the creator of the eponymous *GEORGE KENNEDY*, in books said to be ghosted by Walter J Sheldon.

Citation Record: 2 Books

Murder On Location - *First*
Avon US (1983); Hale UK (1983)

Murder On High - *Latest*
Avon US (1984)

Jerry KENNEDY

American Male Professional Investigator operating in Boston

George V HIGGINS 1939- (American)

See main detective Det FOLEY

Citation Record: 2 Books

Kennedy For The Defense - *First*
Knopf US (1980); Secker & Warburg UK (1980)

Penance For Jerry Kennedy - *Latest*
Holt US (1985); Deutsch UK (1985)

Nick KENNEDY

appeared, with his River Police, in a British boys' magazine, *Bullseye*, which appeared weekly for some years in the 1920s and 1930s. He was in eternal conflict with the Red Shadow Tong, a nasty gang of Chinese in London's Limehouse.

British Male Detective in Pulp Magazines operating in London

No citations

Ch of Plce KENNY

American Policeman operating in USA

Donald Bayne HOBART (American)

Citation Record: 1 Book

The Cell Murder Mystery - *Only*
Fiction League US (1931)

Dr KENT

American Male Amateur operating in Chicago

Rufus HEED (American)

Citation Record: 1 Book

Ghosts Never Die - *Only*
Vantage US (1954)

Addison KENT

American Male Amateur operating in New York

Hopkins MOORHOUSE 1882- (American)

Writer: Herbert Joseph MOORHOUSE

Citation Record: 2 Books

The Gauntlet Of Alceste - *First*
Musson CA (1921); Hodder & Stoughton US (1922)

The Golden Scarab - *Last*
Hodder & Stoughton UK (1926)

Brice KENT

American Male Private Detective operating in New York/Connecticut

Guy Elwyn GILES 1904- (American)

Citation Record: 2 Books

Three Died Variously - *First*
Reynal US (1941)

Target For Murder - *Last*
Morrow US (1943)

K

Charlotte KENT

is a freelance writer, later a magazine editor, who solves murder cases.

American Female Amateur operating in USA

Mary KITTREDGE 1949- (American)

Inventor of one other detective Edwina CRUSOE

Citation Record: 5 Books

Murder In Mendocino - *First*
Walker US (1987)

Cadaver - *Latest*
St Martin's US (1993)

David KENT

was once in the Hong Kong police and now works for MI5 investigating deaths whose roots go back to the war in Malaya in 1953.

British Male Professional Investigator operating in London

George BROWN (British)

was born in London. He has been a journalist and photographer and has had extensive experience with the police in Malaya.

Citation Record: 1 Book

The Double Tenth - *Single*
Century UK (1992)

Harry KENT

British Male Private Detective operating in London

Christopher LANDON 1911- (British)

Writer: Christopher Guy LANDON

Inventor of one other detective Bob ROSS

Citation Record: 1 Book

The Shadow Of Time - *Only*
Heinemann UK (1957)

Unseen Enemy - *Only**
Doubleday US (1957)

Lawrence Patrick 'Larry' KENT

is an American shamus who has offices in San Francisco and Sydney, Australia. He has appeared in a large but uncounted number of books, of which over four hundred have so far been identified. They were published originally in Australia in paperback form, always undated, but beginning around 1953 and continuing into the 1980s. Although many appeared under the byline of the author cited, others appeared anonymously, although possibly written by the same author.

American Male Private Detective operating in USA/England/Australia

Don HARING (American)

is believed to have been an American who settled in Australia after the end of the Second World War and died some time in the 1980s. If he was the single author of the books appearing under his name, he must hold the all-time record for the genre.

Citation Record: 400 Books

The Yellow Dragon - *First*
appeared around 1953 and is cited for illustration purposes.
Cleveland AU

Level With Me - *Latest*
appeared around 1983 and is cited for illustration purposes.
Cleveland AU

Susan KENT

American Female Amateur operating in France

Ruth Sawtell WALLIS 1895-1978 (American)

See main detective Eric LUND

Citation Record: 1 Book

Blood From A Stone - *Only*
Dodd, Mead US (1945); Hammond UK (1955)

Wally KENT

American Male Amateur operating in Chicago

Charlotte Murray RUSSELL (American)

Invented 3 detectives - see Jane Amanda EDWARDS

Citation Record: 1 Book

The Case Of The Topaz Flower - *Only*
Doubleday US (1939)

Jimmie KENTLAND

American Male Amateur operating in Chicago

Harry Stephen KEELER 1890-1967 (American)

Invented 14 detectives - see Angus MACWHORTER

Citation Record: 1 Book

The Face Of The Man From Saturn - *Only*
Dutton US (1933)

The Crilly Court Mystery - *Only**
Ward, Lock UK (1933)

Malcolm KENTON

is an engineer who, in exotic locations in Asia, meets trouble and murder.

British Male Amateur operating in Far East

Simon HARVESTER 1910-1975 (British)

Invented 4 detectives - see Dorian SILK

Citation Record: 5 Books

The Bamboo Screen - *First*
Jarrolds UK (1955); Walker US (1963)

The Golden Fear - *Last*
Jarrolds UK (1957)

The KENTUCKY DETECTIVE

American Male Detective in Pulp Magazines operating in USA

ANON

Citation Record: 1 Book

The Kentucky Detective - *Only*
Aldine US

Supt/Ch Supt Simon KENWORTHY

is, in a series of early police procedurals, a Scotland Yard man who rises to Chief Superintendent. On retirement he becomes a private investigator.

British Policeman operating in England

John Buxton HILTON 1921-1986 (British)

See main detective Insp Thomas BRUNT

Citation Record: 17 Books

Death Of An Alderman - *First*
Cassell UK (1968); Walker US (1968)

Displaced Persons - *Last*
Collins UK (1987); St Martin's US (1988)

KENYATTA

Male Sleuth operating in Detroit/Las Vegas

Al C CLARK 1937-1974 (American)

Writer: Donald GOINES

Citation Record: 2 Books

Crime Partners - *First*
Holloway US (1974)

Kenyatta's Last Hit - *Last*
Holloway US (1975)

Sidney KENYON

British Male Amateur operating in England

N J CRISP 1923- (British)

Writer: Norman James CRISP

Citation Record: 2 Books

The Gotland Deal - *First*
Weidenfeld & Nicolson UK (1976); Viking US (1976)

The London Deal - *Latest*
Macdonald UK (1978); St Martin's US (1979)

KEOGH

Male Amateur operating in Mexico

Audrey Erskine LINDOP 1920-1986 (British)

See main detective Det GRENNON

Citation Record: 2 Books

The Singer Not The Song - *First*
Heinemann UK (1953); Appleton US (1953)

The Judas Figures - *Last*
Heinemann UK (1956); Appleton US (1956)

Helen KEREMOS

is a Navy veteran operating from a dingy upper-storey office in Vancouver's Chinatown. Tough, streetwise, supposedly lesbian, hardly believable, she says things to a new client like 'Helen Keremos. I detect'.

Canadian Female Private Detective operating in Canada

Eve ZAREMBA 1930- (Canadian)

Citation Record: 3 Books

A Reason To Kill - *First*
PaperJacks US (1978)

Beyond Hope - *Latest*
Virago UK (1989)

Witter KERFOOT

American Male Amateur operating in New York

Arthur STRINGER 1874-1950 (American)

Invented 4 detectives - see James DURKIN

Citation Record: 3 Short Stories in 1 Collection

The Man Who Couldn't Sleep - *Collection 1*
This collection of ten stories contains three with *KERFOOT.*
Bobbs US (1919)

Michael KERNEHAN, Chuck REVES and Vic MOINE

are three of the author's several 'railway detectives'.

American Male Professional Investigators operating in USA

Bert HITCHENS and Dolores HITCHENS (American)

Invented 3 detectives - see COLLINS and MCKECHNIE

Citation Record: 1 Book

One-Way Ticket - *Only*
Doubleday US (1956); Boardman UK (1958)

Annette KERNER

ran the Mayfair Detective Agency in London for twenty years and wrote a book about her own experiences.

British Female Private Detective operating in London

Annette KERNER (British)

Citation Record: 1 Book

Woman Detective - *Only*
features the author herself as the detective.
Laurie UK (1954?)

Sam KERNOCHAN

is a rather alcoholic reporter who is hired by a woman friend to find the murderer of her husband.

American Male Amateur operating in New York

Arthur Somers ROCHE 1883-1935 (American)

Citation Record: 1 Book

The Case Against Mr Ames - *Only*
Dodd, Mead US (1934); Archer US (1935)

Const KERR

Second detective of Insp Robert FUSIL

Duncan KERR

fights against a sinister organisation, set to take over the world, but foiled in an English country setting. Organisations that aim to take over the world should certainly avoid English villages.

British Male Amateur operating in England

David DALHEATH (British)

Citation Record: 1 Book

The Shadow Of The Cobra - *Only*
Hale UK (1975)

Lt Francis X KERRIGAN

is an Irish-American Catholic cop, in his thirties and a bachelor. Honest, conscientious and courteous, he is, however, not exactly the intellectual type; but he is tireless in his questioning of suspects, a procedure that gets him there in the end.

American Policeman operating in New York

Sidekick: Det Jane BOARDMAN

American Female - Colleague

Joseph HARRINGTON 1903- (American)

Writer: Joseph James HARRINGTON

Citation Record: 3 Books

The Last Known Address - *First*
Lippincott US (1965); Hale UK (1966)

The Last Doorbell - *Last*
Lippincott US (1969); Hale UK (1970)

Peter KERRIGAN

British Male Amateur operating in England

Neil GORDON 1895-1941 (British)

Invented 3 detectives - see James ARNOLD

Citation Record: 2 Books

Murder In Earl's Court - *First*
Lane UK (1931)

The Shakespeare Murders - *Last*
Barker UK (1933); Holt US (1933)

Marion KERRISON

is a clever female lawyer who uses all her legal and detective skills in a case of murder.

British Female Amateur operating in England

Edward GRIERSON 1914-1975 (British)

was born in Bedford, Bedfordshire. He was educated at St Paul's School, London, and at Exeter College, Oxford, where he took a BA in Jurisprudence. He became a barrister in 1937 and served in the Army, 1939-1946, reaching the rank of Lieutenant-Colonel. He has written several non-genre novels and plays.

Writer: Edward Dobbyn GRIERSON

Citation Record: 1 Book

The Second Man - *Only*
Chatto UK (1956); Knopf US (1956)

K

Ch Insp Daniel 'Red' KERRY

is one of the author's rare police detectives, but he too does battle with the author's usual run of nasty oriental criminals.

British Policeman operating in England

Sax ROHMER 1883-1959 (British)

Invented 9 detectives - see Insp RYDER

Citation Record: 2 Books

Dope - *First*
Cassell UK (1919); McBride US (1919)

Yellow Shadows - *Last*
Cassell UK (1925); Doubleday US (1926)

Det Insp Don KERRY

has been called the epitome of the British hardworking policeman.

British Policeman operating in England

Jeffrey ASHFORD 1926- (British)

For writer details see Insp Enrique ALVAREZ

Other Detectives:
Supt ABBOTT
Det Const ATHANA
Insp CRANE
Bob HOWE
Det Sgt Peter NOYES
Bill STENEM
Miba STERLING
Gary WESTON

Citation Record: 2 Books

Investigations Are Proceeding - *First*
Long UK (1961)

The DI - *First**
Harper & Row US (1962)

Enquiries Are Continuing - *Last*
Long UK (1964)

The Superintendent's Room - *Last**
Harper & Row US (1965)

Maj Charles Douglas KERWOOD

!See Appendix 2.

British Male Amateur

Allan DUNCAN (British)

Citation Record: 2 Books

An Official Secret - *First*
Hutchinson UK (1937)

A Cabinet Minister Resigns - *Last*
Hutchinson UK (1939)

Julian KESTREL

is a nineteenth-century detective in Regency London, a kind of ante-dated *Peter WIMSEY* in costume, stalking the streets and clubs, where murders tend to be nasty and bodies lie thick on the ground – or the double bed.

British Male Amateur operating in London

Kate ROSS (American)

Citation Record: 3 Books

Cut To The Quick - *First*
Hodder & Stoughton UK (1994); Viking US (1994)

Whom The Gods Love - *Latest*
Hodder & Stoughton UK (1995); Viking US (1995)

Det Jack KETHERIDGE

When a key player dies during an important football game at the fictional State College, *Det KETHERIDGE* reconstructs the entire game to solve the mystery of the murder.
!See Appendix 2.

American Policeman operating in USA

Courtland FITZSIMMONS 1883-1949 (American)

Other Detectives:
Arthur MARTINSON
Prof Percy PEACOCK
Ethel THOMAS

Citation Record: 1 Book

70,000 Witnesses - *Only*
McBride US (1931)

Capt Owen KETTLE

is a loveable rogue of a sea captain who, over the years between about 1898 and 1930, featured in adventures far and wide and in various transmutations. Not all the stories, certainly, can be truly regarded as crime or detective stories; but, by and large, *Capt KETTLE* has to do a considerable amount of ingenious detective work during his long career.

British Male Amateur operating in several locations

C J Cutcliffe HYNE 1865-1944 (British)

Writer: Charles John Cutcliffe Wright HYNE

Other Byline: Weatherby CHESNEY

Other Detectives:
GRAYSON
Mr HORROCKS
Cdr MCTURK

Citation Record: 2 Books 81 Short Stories in 7 Collections

Mr Kettle, Third Mate - *First*
Ward, Lock UK (1931)

The Marriage Of Kettle - *First**
Heinemann UK (1912)

The Marriage Of Captain Kettle - *Last*
Bobbs US (1912)

The Adventures Of Captain Kettle - *Collection 1*
Short stories - 11
Pearson UK (1898); Doubleday US (1898)

Further Adventures Of Captain Kettle - *Collection 2*
Short stories - 12
Pearson UK (1900)

A Master Of Fortune - *Collection 2**
Dillingham US (1901)

Captain Kettle, KCB - *Collection 3*
Short stories - 12
Pearson UK (1903)

More Adventures Of Captain Kettle, KCB - *Collection 3**
Federal US (1903)

Captain Kettle On The War-Path - *Collection 4*
Short stories - 10
Methuen UK (1916)

Captain Kettle's Bit - *Collection 5*
Short stories - 8
Hodder & Stoughton UK (1918)

The Rev Captain Kettle - *Collection 6*
Short stories - 16
Harrap UK (1925)

President Kettle - *Collection 7*
Short stories - 12
Nash UK (1929)

Sebastian KETTLE

British Male Sleuth operating in Europe

James Dillon WHITE 1913- (British)

Writer: Stanley WHITE

Citation Record: 2 Books

The Salzberg Affair - *First*
Hutchinson UK (1977)

The Brandenburg Affair - *Latest*
Hutchinson UK (1979)

Capt KEYES

solves a case of 'impossible' murder of a woman in front of witnesses.

American Policeman operating in New York

Adam BLISS (American)

See main detective Alice PENNY

Citation Record: 1 Book

The Campden Ruby Murder - *Only*
Barse US (1931); Rich UK (1934)

KEYES

is some sort of private detective, ill-defined and not up to the standards set by this prolific author.

British Male Private Detective operating in London

John Newton CHANCE 1911-1983 (British)

Invented 8 detectives - see John Newton CHANCE

Citation Record: 1 Book

Looking For Samson - *Only*
Hale UK (1984)

Brian KEYES

was a reporter. Now a PI, he investigates the strange death of a powerful business figure in Miami.

American Male Private Detective operating in Miami

Carl HIAASEN 1933- (American)

Invented 3 detectives - see R J DECKER

Citation Record: 1 Book

Tourist Season - *Single*
Putnam US (1986); Futura UK (1987)

Chin Kwang KHAM

Tibetan Male Amateur operating in Los Angeles/Cleveland

Richard FOSTER 1910-1981 (American)

See main detective Pete DRACO

Citation Record: 2 Books

The Laughing Buddha Murders - *First*
Vulcan US (1944)

The Invisible Man Murders - *Last*
Green US (1945)

Asaf KHAN

Indian Male Amateur operating in India

AFGHAN (British)

Citation Record: 1 Book 12 Short Stories in 1 Collection

The Wanderings Of Asaf - *Only*
Jenkins UK (1923)

Exploits Of Asaf Khan - *Collection 1*
Jenkins UK (1922)

KHARDUNI

Male Sleuth operating in England

Andrew SOUTAR 1879-1941 (British)

See main detective Phineas SPINNET

Citation Record: 3 Books

Kharduni - *First*
Hutchinson UK (1933); Macaulay US (1934)

Justice Is Done - *Last*
Hutchinson UK (1936)

Omar KHAYYAM

is, indeed, the famous poet and teller of tales.

Persian Male Amateur

Theodore MATHIESON 1913- (American)

Invented 3 detectives - see Leonardo DA VINCI

Citation Record: 1 Selected Short Story

Omar Khayyam, Detective
appeared first in the February number of the magazine and is also to be found in the author's book, *The Great "Detectives"* (*Simon*; US 1960).
In 'Ellery Queen's Mystery Magazine' US (1960)

Randy KIDD

American Male Sleuth operating in USA

DAGMAR (American)

Citation Record: 2 Books

The Spy Who Came In From The Copa - *First*
was ghost-written by Lou Cameron, the author of several genre novels.
Lancer UK (1967)

The Spy With The Blue Kazoo - *Last*
was also ghost-written by Lou Cameron.
Lancer UK (1967)

Gyp KIDNADZE

Female Amateur operating in England

Lady Kitty VINCENT 1887- (British)

Writer: Lady Kitty Edith Blanche VINCENT

Citation Record: 3 Books

No 3 - *First*
Jenkins UK (1924)

An Untold Tale - *Last*
Jenkins UK (1934)

Supt Bamsan KIET

is a hardworking cop in an imaginary country in the Far East.

Policeman

Gary ALEXANDER 1941- (American)

Inventor of one other detective Luis BALAM

Citation Record: 4 Books

Pigeon Blood - *First*
Walker US (1988)

Kiet And The Opium War - *Latest*
St Martin's US (1990)

Insp KILBY

British Policeman operating in England

J C LENEHAN (British)

Writer: John Christopher LENEHAN

Inventor of one other detective Charlie RYAN

Citation Record: 3 Books

The Tunnel Mystery - *First*
Jenkins UK (1929); Mystery League US (1931)

The Mansfield Mystery - *Last*
Jenkins UK (1932)

K

Mark KILBY

is an arrogant British PI in the USA and not a very good one. He was created by an author who would try his hand at anything under one of his armoury of pseudonyms.

British Male Amateur operating in New York

Robert Caine FRAZER 1908-1973 (British)

For writer details see Insp Roger 'Handsome' WEST

Citation Record: 6 Books

Mark Kilby Solves A Murder - *First*
Pocket Books US (1959)

RISC - *First**
Collins UK (1962)

The Timid Tycoon - *First**
Fontana US (1965)

Mark Kilby Takes A Risk - *Latest*
Pocket Books US (1962)

Dr KILDARE

is the doctor who became one of America's best-known and best-loved amateur detectives, appearing in countless short stories, books, radio programmes and movies.

American Male Amateur operating in New York

Max BRAND 1892-1944 (American)

See main detective Terence RADWAY

No citations

Xavier KILGARVAN

American Male Amateur operating in USA

Joyce Carol OATES 1938- (American)

is a mainstream novel writer.

Citation Record: 1 Book

Mysteries Of Winterthurn - *Single*
Dutton US (1984); Cape UK (1984)

Paul KILGERRIN

is in his forties and is said to be gaunt of countenance, with remarkable eyes. Seriously wounded in the First World War but still as strong and hardboiled as they come, he now works for US Army Intelligence and other government departments, dealing firmly with his country's many enemies. He is aided in this weary work by a most useful lady friend.

American Male Secret Agent operating in Europe/USA

Sidekick: Gerry CORDENT
is an attractive widow, seemingly always at hand when the US is in peril.
American Female - Friend

Charles L LEONARD 1906- (American)
For writer details see Desmond SHANNON
Citation Record: 11 Books
The Stolen Squadron - *First*
Doubleday US (1942)
Treachery In Trieste - *Last*
Doubleday US (1951)

George KILGORE
American Male Amateur operating in California

David Rains WALLACE 1945- (American)
Citation Record: 1 Book
The Turquoise Dragon - *Single*
Sierra Club US (1985); Bodley Head UK (1986)

Det KILKENNY
solves a case involving fast women, gigolos, crooks of all descriptions, and an early use of scientific tissue analysis.
American Policeman operating in USA

Lawrence G BLOCHMAN 1900-1975 (American)
Invented 5 detectives - see Dr Daniel Webster COFFEE and Lt Max RITTER
Citation Record: 1 Book
See You At The Morgue - *Only*
Duell US (1941); Cassell UK (1946)

Johnny KILLAIN
operates from the Hotel Duarte, and is pretty hardboiled.
American Male Amateur operating in New York

Dan J MARLOWE 1914- (American)
was born in Lowell, Massachusetts. He has worked on newspapers in Michigan and is the author of at least twenty-five genre novels and many short stories.
Writer: Dan James MARLOWE
Inventor of one other detective Earl DRAKE
Citation Record: 5 Books
Doorway To Death - *First*
Avon US (1959); Digit UK (1959)
Shake A Crooked Town - *Last*
Avon US (1961)

Coley KILLEBREW
was once a jockey. His career ruined by scandal, he takes to sleuthing on behalf of friends.
American Male Amateur operating in USA

Bill SHOEMAKER (American)
Citation Record: 2 Books
Stalking Horse - *First*
Fawcett US (1994)
Fire Horse - *Latest*
Fawcett US (1995)

Francis KILLIAN
is hired by a lady singer to clear up the suspicious death of a gentleman friend.
British Male Private Detective operating in England

Ellis PETERS 1913-1995 (British)
Invented 4 detectives - see Brother CADFAEL
Citation Record: 1 Book
The House Of Green Turf - *Only*
Collins UK (1969); Morrow US (1969)

Jedediah KILLINGER III
American Male Amateur operating in California

P K PALMER (American)
Citation Record: 2 Books
The Rainbow/Seagreen Case - *First*
Pinnacle US (1974)
The Turquoise/Yellow Case - *Last*
Pinnacle US (1974)

Francis X (The Inquisitor) KILLY
American Male Sleuth operating in USA

Simon QUINN 1942- (American)
For writer details see Roman GREY
Citation Record: 6 Books
His Eminence, Death - *First*
Dell US (1974)
Last Rites For The Vulture - *Last*
Dell US (1975)

Col KILMAIN
British Male Amateur

W Clark RUSSELL 1844-1911 (British)
was the author of many sea stories, which were highly popular at the time.
For writer details see WATERS
Inventor of one other detective Jock THIRLSTANE
Citation Record: 1 Book
Is He The Man? - *Only*
Tinsley UK (1876)
The Copsford Mystery; Or, Is He The Man? - *Only**
US (1896)

Osmo KILPI
Finnish Male Sleuth operating in Finland

Mauri SARIOLA (Finnish)
was born in Helsinki.
Citation Record: 1 Book
The Helsinki Affair - *Only*
is a translation from the Finnish of *Lavaen tien Laki* (Finland, 1970).
Cassell UK (1970); Walker US (1971)

Ben KINCAID
is a lawyer who wins his cases by careful sleuthing before they come to court.
American Male Amateur operating in Oklahoma

William BERNHARDT (American)
Citation Record: 3 Books
Blind Justice - *First*
Ballantine US (1992)
Perfect Justice - *Latest*
Ballantine US (1993)

Duncan KINCAID
is an overworked Scotland Yard man, in his late thirties, taking a week's holiday at a country house hotel in Yorkshire. There he meets murder, fumbling by the local police, and a whole cast of suspects among the guests. He has to discover whodunnit, which he seems quite unable to do without summoning his female sergeant from her week's leave.
British Policeman operating in England

Sidekick: Sgt Gemma JAMES
is the now obligatory female sergeant without whom no modern British cop can be expected to function, let alone solve a case. She is in her twenties, red-haired, clever, safely divorced, and so well placed for a growing relationship in future books.
British Female - Subordinate

Deborah CROMBIE (American)
has lived in England and Scotland and, although living in the USA, likes typically English mysteries.
Citation Record: 2 Books
A Share In Death - *First*
Scribner's US (1993); Macmillan UK (1993)
Leave The Grave Green - *Latest*
Scribner's US (1995)

Roger KINCAID

solves a number of 'impossible' crimes.

American Male Amateur operating in USA

Sidekick: Svetozar VOK

Male - Assistant

Hake TALBOT 1900-1986 (American)

Writer: Nenning HELMS

Citation Record: 2 Books 1 Selected Short Story

The Hangman's Handyman - *First*
Simon & Schuster US (1942)

Rim Of The Pit - *Last*
Simon & Schuster US (1944); Stacey UK (1972)

The Other Side
is to be found in the anthologies, *The Art of the Impossible* (*Xanadu*; UK 1990) and *Murder Impossible* (*Carroll*; US 1990).

Tom KINCAID

appeared in early pulp stories written by this prolific writer and later in three novels. He is a professional gambler who practises detection and trouble-shooting among his numerous and nefarious acquaintances.

American Male Private Detective operating in Nevada

William R COX 1901-1989 (American)

was born in Peapack, New Jersey, and graduated from Rutgers University, New Brunswick, and Princeton University, New Jersey. He was a journalist and the prolific writer of hundreds of stories for the pulp magazines of the 1930s and 1940s.

Writer: William Robert COX

Other Byline: Joel REEVE

Other Detectives:
Malachi MANATEE   Dan TROUT
John WADE

Citation Record: 3 Books

Hell To Pay - *First*
Signet UK (1958); New American Library US (1960)

Death On Location - *Last*
New American Library US (1962); Signet UK (1962)

Bill KINDERMAN

American Male Amateur operating in USA

William Peter BLATTY 1928- (American)

Citation Record: 2 Books

The Exorcist - *First*
Harper & Row US (1971); Blond UK (1971)

Legion - *Latest*
Simon & Schuster US (1983); Collins UK (1983)

Athelstan KING

appears in books with other detectives of this author, *Chullunder GHOSE* and *James Schuyler (Jimgrim) GRIM.*

British Male Amateur operating in India

Talbot MUNDY 1879-1940 (British)

Invented 6 detectives - see Chullunder GHOSE

Citation Record: 2 Books

King Of The Khyber Rifles - *First*
Bobbs US (1916); Constable UK (1917)

Caves Of Terror - *Last*
Hutchinson UK (1932)

Athelstan KING

Appears with at least two other detectives - see James Schuyler (Jimgrim) GRIM

Bill KING

is a reporter who solves a bizarre case of murder carried out by cutting the victim's leg artery.

American Male Amateur operating in San Francisco

B J MAYLON (American)

Citation Record: 1 Book

The Corpse With The Knee-Action - *Only*
Phoenix Press US (1940)

Clifford KING

is a barrister who sleuths in this one Victorian novel.

British Male Amateur operating in England

Florence WARDEN 1857-1929 (British)

Invented 4 detectives - see Insp MAYNARD

Citation Record: 1 Book

The Mystery Of The Inn By The Shore - *Only*
Bonner US (1875)

The Inn By The Shore - *Only**
Jarrolds UK (1897)

Edmund KING

Second detective of Montrose ARBUTHNOT

Dr Frank KING

British Male Amateur operating in England

Frank KING 1892-1958 (British)

Invented 6 detectives - see Insp CHAMBERS

Citation Record: 4 Books

Death Of A Halo - *First*
Hale UK (1950)

Death Has A Double - *Last*
Hale UK (1955)

Jason KING

appears in novelizations of episodes from a TV series.

British Male Sleuth operating in England

Robert MIALL 1922- (British)

For writer details see John BURKE

Citation Record: 4 Books

Jason King - *First*
Pan AU (1972)

Kill Jason King - *Last*
Pan AU (1972)

Louis Luther (Murder Master) KING

American Male Sleuth operating in Illinois/the Caribbean

Joseph ROSENBERGER (American)

Writer: Joseph ROSENBERGER

Other Byline: Nick CARTER

Inventor of one other detective Richard (The Death Merchant) CAMELLION

Citation Record: 2 Books

Death Trap - *First*
Manor US (1973)

The Caribbean Caper - *Last*
Manor US (1974)

Mallory KING, Insp Jon NAPPLEBY, Jerry PASON, Atlas POIREAU, Simon QUINSEY, Fan SLIVER, Insp Broderick TOURNEUR, Spike BLUDGEON and Trajan BEARE

The nine detectives are all parodies of other author's detectives, as follows: *Mallory KING* of *Ellery QUEEN; Jon NAPPLEBY* of *John APPLEBY; Jerry PASON* of *Perry MASON; Atlas POIROT* of *Hercule POIROT; Simon QUINSEY* of *Peter WIMSEY; Fan SLIVER* of *Maud SILVER; Broderick TOURNEUR* of *Roderick ALLEYN; Spike BLUDGEON* of *Mike HAMMER;* and *Trajan BEARE* of *Nero WOLFE*. The parodied detectives are all cited elsewhere in the citation index.

American, British (and one Belgian) Detectives operating on a ship

Marion MAINWARING (American)

See main detective Toby SAMPSON

Citation Record: 1 Book

Murder In Pastiche - *Parody 1*
was subtitled *Nine Detectives all at Sea* and features nine immediately recognisable parodies of famous fictional detectives of the day, all on board an ocean liner. When a mur-

der occurs, they go about trying to solve the case, each in his own identifiable way and excellently described. All prove to be in error and the solution is arrived at by somebody else. More parody than true pastiche, this ingenious novel is a veritable *tour de force*.
Macmillan US (1954); Gollancz UK (1955)

Mike KING
British Male Amateur operating in England

Graham FISHER 1920- (British)
For writer details see Rogue RANSOM
Citation Record: 3 Books
Face Of Danger - *First*
Macdonald UK (1970)
Villain Of The Piece - *Latest*
Macdonald UK (1977)

Peter KING
American Male Amateur operating in USA

Anthony BURTON (American)
Citation Record: 1 Book
Embrace Of The Butcher - *Single*
Dodd, Mead US (1982)

Reefe KING
American Male Amateur operating in New York

Albert BARKER 1900- (American)
Writer: Albert W BARKER
Inventor of one other detective Hawk MACRAE
Citation Record: 2 Books
Gift From Berlin - *First*
Award US (1969)
The Apollo Legacy - *Last*
Award US (1970)

Sam KING
runs a detective agency specialising in the recovery of stolen goods, but he takes on a murder case or two when business is slack.
American Male Private Detective operating in Los Angeles

Raymond E BANKS 1918?- (American)
Citation Record: 2 Books
Meet Me In Darkness - *First*
Popular Press US (1961)
The Computer Kill - *Last*
Popular Press US (1961)

Willow KING
is an internal investigator for the Inland Revenue authorities and meets all manner of crimes, of which tax evasion is the least serious.
British Female Professional Investigator operating in England

Natasha COOPER (British)
Writer: Daphne WRIGHT
Citation Record: 5 Books
Festering Lilies - *First*
Simon & Schuster UK (1990)
A Common Death - *First**
Crown US (1991)
Rotten Apples - *Latest*
Simon & Schuster UK (1995)

Wylie KING and Nels LUNDBERG
American Male Sleuths operating in New York

Lawrence SAUNDERS (American)
Writers: Clare Ogden DAVIS 1893- and Burton DAVIS 1892-
Citation Record: 2 Books
The Columnist Murder - *First*
Farrar, Straus US (1931)
The Devil's Den - *Last*
Covici US (1933)

KING DAN
American Male Professional Investigator operating in Massachusetts

George W GOODE (American)
Inventor of one other detective The POST-OFFICE DETECTIVE
Citation Record: 1 Book
King Dan, The Factory Detective - *Only*
Katahdin US (1896)

KINGSLEY
American Male Detective in Pulp Magazines operating in USA

OLD SLEUTH (American)
Invented 40 detectives - see Brant ADAMS
Citation Record: 1 Book
Kingsley The Detective; Or, A Single Clew - *Only*
Ogilvie US (1897)
A Single Clew - *Only**
Ogilvie US (1900)

Belle KINGSTON
American Female Detective in Pulp Magazines operating in USA

F Lusk BROUGHTON (American)
Invented 10 detectives - see Harry WILLIAMS
Citation Record: 1 Selected Short Story
Belle Kingston, The Detective Queen; Or, The Stolen Bonds
Old Cap Collier Library US (18??)

Keedy KINGSTON
British Male Amateur operating in England

Keedy KINGSTON (British)
Citation Record: 1 Book
The Great Pimlico Mystery: A Well-Kept Secret Disclosed - *Only*
Diprose & Bateman UK (1896)

The KING'S DETECTIVE
American Male Detective in Pulp Magazines operating in USA

OLD SLEUTH (American)
Invented 40 detectives - see Brant ADAMS
Citation Record: 1 Book
The King's Detective; Or, A New York Detective's Great Quest - *Only*
Parlor Car US (1898)

Kate KINSELLA
is a state general nurse who does part-time work at hospitals and clinics in the fictional country town of Longborough. What better way of describing her than in her own remark to a prospective client who has overdosed, been a rape victim and is in fear of her life: 'My name's Kate Kinsella and I run a detective agency from an office in the High Street – above Humberstone's, the funeral directors. Come and see me when you feel better and perhaps together we can sort this out?' A novice she may be, unattractive and overweight she is, but learn she will. A real charmer, with the nose of a bloodhound and the Devil's own luck in getting out of threatening situations.!
British Female Private Detective operating in England

Sidekick: Hubert HUMBERSTONE
is the landlord of *KINSELLA's* dingy, unfurnished office. Downstairs he operates an undertaker's business, determined to run the Co-op out of town. A middle-aged, friendly, foot-fetishist, he gives much advice to the inept lady sleuth and is there to protect her when she needs it.
Male - Landlord

Christine GREEN 1944- (British)
was born in Luton and trained as a nurse in London. She is married, now lives in Northampton and does occasional nursing.
Citation Record: 3 Books

Deadly Errand - *First*
Macmillan UK

Deadly Practice - *Latest*
Macmillan UK (1994)

Birch KIRBY

is an aging ex-CIA man, now inept at his job and played for a fall guy in his last case.

American Male Private Detective operating in Chicago

Ross H SPENCER 1921- (American)

Invented 7 detectives - see Buzz DECKARD

Citation Record: 1 Book

Kirby's Last Circus - *Single*
Fine US (1987)

Grant KIRBY

American Male Sleuth operating in New York/New Orleans

Clay RICHARDS 1910-1981 (American)

See main detective Kim LOCKE

Citation Record: 2 Books

The Marble Jungle - *First*
Oboleniky UK (1961); Cassell US (1963)

Death Of An Angel - *Last*
Bobbs US (1963)

Jacqueline KIRBY

is a middle-aged American college librarian with a vast knowledge of arcane subjects and later a writer of steamy romances. Such qualities enable her to solve erudite murder mysteries, which baffle the police.

American Female Amateur operating in USA

Elizabeth PETERS 1927- (American)

Invented 4 detectives - see Vicky BLISS

Citation Record: 4 Books

The Seventh Sinner - *First*
Dodd, Mead US (1972); Coronet UK (1975)

Naked Once More - *Latest*
Warner US (1989); Piatkus UK (1990)

Sir William KIRBY

British Male Amateur operating in England

Sydney HORLER 1888-1954 (British)

Invented 20 detectives - see Sir Harker BELLAMY

Citation Record: 1 Book

The Lessing Murder Case - *Only*
Collins UK (1935)

Gen Charles KIRK

is in British Intelligence and has to do a lot of smart detecting and hunting to solve a variety of problems, usually of devastating importance.

British Male Secret Agent operating in Europe/Mexico

John BLACKBURN 1923- (British)

was born in Corbridge-on-Tyne, Northumberland. He took a BA at Durham University, 1949, served in the Merchant Navy during the Second World War and later worked as a schoolmaster in London and Berlin.

Writer: John Fenwick BLACKBURN

Other Detectives:
John CAIN | Marcus LEVIN
J Molden MOTT

Citation Record: 6 Books

A Scent Of New-Mown Hay - *First*
Secker & Warburg UK (1958); Mill US (1958)

The Reluctant Spy - *First**
Lancer US (1966)

A Ring Of Roses - *Last*
Cape US (1965)

A Wreath Of Roses - *Last**
Mill US (1965)

Devlin KIRK

is a drop-out from Stanford Law School and an ex-government agent. Now a partner in a security firm, he is involved in cases of industrial espionage.

American Male Private Detective operating in Colorado

Rex BURNS 1935- (American)

See main detective Det Gabriel WAGER

Citation Record: 3 Books

Suicide Season - *First*
Viking US (1987); Penguin UK (1988)

Body Guard - *Latest*
Viking US (1991)

Kershaw KIRK

British Male Amateur operating in England

William LEQUEUX 1864-1927 (British)

Invented 23 detectives - see Allan KENNEDY

Citation Record: 1 Book

The Red Room - *Only*
Cassell UK (1909); Little, Brown US (1911)

Murray KIRK

is head of an agency called Conmy & Kirk and is tough, but has a sentimental streak.

American Male Private Detective operating in New York

Stanley ELLIN 1916- (American)

Invented 4 detectives - see Jake DEKKER

Citation Record: 1 Book

The Eighth Circle - *Only*
Random House US (1958); Boardman UK (1959)

Peter KIRK

American Male Private Detective operating in Mississippi

William E VANCE 1911-1986 (American)

Citation Record: 1 Book

Homicide Lost - *Only*
Graphic US (1956)

Steven KIRK

is a lapsed CIA agent in political thrillers.

American Male Professional Investigator operating in USA

Stooge: SMITH
of the Operations Directorate of the CIA is the mysterious manipulator of geopolitical events who bugs *Steven KIRK*.
American Male

Doug HORNIG 1943- (American)

See main detective Loren SWIFT

Citation Record: 2 Books

Waterman - *First*
Mysterious Press US (1987)

Stinger - *Latest*
New American Library US (1990)

Bruce KIRKWOOD

was formerly a mercenary soldier. On his return to England he sets up as a PI.

British Male Private Detective operating in England

Bill TURNER 1927- (British)

Writer: William Price TURNER

Inventor of one other detective Sgt Louis SOLDEN

Citation Record: 1 Book

Another Little Death - *Only*
Constable UK (1970); Walker US (1971)

Claude 'Snake' KIRLIN and F T ZEVICH

American Male Sleuths operating in Tennessee

Art BOURGEAU (American)

Citation Record: 4 Books

A Lonely Way To Die - *First*
Charter US (1980)

The Elvis Murders - *Latest*
Charter US (1985)

Helen KITTEREGE

British Female Amateur

Robert BARNARD 1936- (British)

Invented 13 detectives - see Insp Perry TRETHOWAN

Citation Record: 1 Book

The Disposal Of The Living - *Single*
Collins UK (1985)

Fete Fatale - *Single**
Scribner's US (1985)

Morris KLAW

usually solved his cases, some of which are excellent locked-room mysteries, by 'psychic' methods.

British Male Professional Investigator operating in England

Sax ROHMER 1883-1959 (British)

Invented 9 detectives - see Insp RYDER

Citation Record: 10 Short Stories in 1 Collection

The Dream-Detective - *Collection 1*
Only nine of the ten stories appeared in the UK publication.
Jarrolds UK (1920); Doubleday US (1925)

K

KLEIN

investigates the kidnapping of the wife of a TV personality.

American Policeman operating in USA

Don BLOCK (American)

Citation Record: 1 Book

Double Take - *Single*
US (?)

Dylan KLEIN and Johnny MCCLOUGH

investigate murders with roots in the Cold War.

American Male Amateur and American Male Ex-Policeman operating in New York

Reed Farrell COLEMAN (American)

was born in Brooklyn and had a variety of unskilled jobs before becoming a writer.

Citation Record: 1 Book

Life Goes Sleeping - *Single*
Permanent US (1991)

Max KLEIN

was once a college baseball player and is now a down-at-heel shamus on Broadway. He takes a case involving a former baseball star and his sexy wife.

American Male Private Detective operating in New York

Paul BENJAMIN 1947- (American)

was born in New Jersey. He abandoned the straight detective story after this one book and, under his real name, published three unusual and highly praised novels with surrealistic crime content.

Writer: Paul AUSTER

Citation Record: 1 Book

Squeeze Play - *Single*
Alpha-Omega UK (1982); Avon US (1984)

Lt Rocco KLEIN

is a Homicide detective in a disastrous, rundown, urban landscape, somewhere in an unnamed American city. Overweight, overworked and middle-aged he certainly is, but he remains a good cop in a book that extends the detective story into the sphere of the American social novel.

American Policeman operating in USA

Sidekick: Det MAZELLI

Male - Assistant

Richard PRICE 1949- (American)

Citation Record: 1 Book

Clockers - *Single*
Bloomsbury UK (1992)

Chris KLICK

is a 6' 4" skip-tracer who has to sleuth to survive.

American Male Private Detective operating in Idaho

Wendell MCCALL 1953- (American)

Writer: Ridley PEARSON

Citation Record: 2 Books

Dead Aim - *First*
St Martin's US (1988)

Aim For The Heart - *Latest*
St Martin's US (1990)

John KLINE

appears in novelizations of episodes from the TV series.

American Male Sleuth

Philip MARTIN (American)

Citation Record: 2 Books

Gangsters - *First*
Sphere UK (1977)

Gangsters #2 - *Latest*
Sphere UK (1977)

Dr KLOTZ

appears in a complicated farrago of a plot, mainly about seances and disappearances.

American Male Amateur operating in Wisconsin

Horatio WINSLOW and Leslie QUIRK (British)

Writers: Horatio Gates WINSLOW 1882- and Leslie W QUIRK 1882-

Citation Record: 1 Book

Into Thin Air - *Only*
Gollancz UK (1928); Doubleday US (1929)

KLUTE

appears in a novelization of a film.

American Male Sleuth operating in USA

William JOHNSTON 1924- (American)

Invented 7 detectives - see John WOODRUFF and Tony NOVELLO

Citation Record: 1 Book

Klute - *Only*
Paperback Library US (1971); Sphere UK (1971)

Olga KNARESBROOK

is bored with her small-town existence and sets up as a private detective.

British Female Private Detective operating in England

Sidekick: Molly KINGSLEY
is a reporter who is taken on to assist the rather strange *Olga KNARESBROOK*. She discovers that the detective-presumptive is a drug addict who needs psychological help, so she commits a variety of crimes so that the boss can solve them and boost her morale.

British Female - Assistant

Hazel CAMPBELL (British)

Citation Record: 1 Book

Olga Knaresbrook: Detective - *Only*
Long UK (1933)

Insp KNICKMAN

appears also in books with the author's other detective, *Martin AMES*.

American Policeman operating in New York/Los Angeles

Alfred EICHLER 1908- (American)

Other Detectives:
Martin AMES | Insp KNICKMAN and Martin AMES

Citation Record: 2 Books

Moment For Murder - *First*
Arcadia US (1956); Hammond UK (1957)
Bury In Haste - *Last*
Arcadia US (1957)

Insp KNICKMAN and Martin AMES

also appear individually in other books by this author.
American Policeman and American Male Amateur operating in New York

Alfred EICHLER 1908- (American)
Invented 3 detectives - see Insp KNICKMAN
Citation Record: 4 Books
Murder In The Radio Department - *First*
Gold Label US (1943); Hammond UK (1953)
Death Of An Artist - *Last*
Arcadia US (1955); Hammond UK (1955)

Anna KNIGHT

is an investigative reporter who witnesses the murder of a member of Parliament and sets out to discover whodunnit and why.
British Female Amateur operating in England

Barbara CROSSLEY 1952- (British)
was born in Saddleworth, on the borders of Lancashire and Yorkshire.
Citation Record: 1 Book
Candy Floss Coast - *Single*
Virago UK (1991)

Bill KNIGHT

British Male Amateur operating in England

Maurice PROCTER 1906-1973 (British)
Invented 3 detectives - see Det Insp Harry MARTINEAU
Citation Record: 1 Book
The Pub Crawler - *Only*
Hutchinson UK (1956); Harper & Row US (1957)

Clarence KNIGHT

British Male Amateur operating in England

Frank KING 1892-1958 (British)
Invented 6 detectives - see Insp CHAMBERS
Citation Record: 3 Books
The Ghoul - *First*
Bles UK (1928); Watt US (1929)
The Owl - *Last*
Jarrolds UK (1930); Watt US (1930)

Micky KNIGHT

Female Sleuth

J M REDMAN
Citation Record: 1 Book
Deaths Of Jacosta
(1992)

Peter KNIGHT

solves a case in which a derelict yacht is found abandoned at sea.
Male Amateur operating on a ship

William ALLISON (American)
Citation Record: 1 Book
The Secret Of The Sea - *Only*
Doubleday US (1920)

Sam KNIGHT

American Male Amateur operating in New York

David Keith COHLER 1940- (American)
Citation Record: 2 Books
Gamemaker - *First*
Doubleday US (1980); Allen UK (1980)
Freemartin - *Latest*
Little, Brown US (1981)

Sir Charles KNIGHTLEY

British Male Amateur operating in England

Sydney HORLER 1888-1954 (British)
Invented 20 detectives - see Sir Harker BELLAMY
Citation Record: 1 Book 1 Short Story in 1 Collection
Death At Court Lady - *Last*
Collins UK (1936)
The Man Who Shook The Earth - *Collection 1*
contains three novelettes, one of which features *Sir Charles KNIGHTLEY.*
Hutchinson UK (1933)

KNIGHTSBRIDGE

is a Vietnam War veteran who works for an agency called Joe Venice Investigations, based aboard a boat on the Charles River in Boston. He drives around the streets in an old cab and has a sidekick in the shape of one of the most menacing dogs in the whole criminous genre. In this one book he searches for a missing urn in Wyoming.
American Male Private Detective operating in Wyoming
Sidekick: GAYLORD
is probably the roughest, toughest canine sidekick in the business.
Unknown sex - Pet Dog

Conall RYAN (American)
Citation Record: 1 Book
Black Gravity - *Single*
Ballantine US (1985)

Supt Gordon KNOLLIS

British Policeman operating in England

Francis VIVIAN 1906- (British)
Invented 3 detectives - see Insp John BURNELL
Citation Record: 7 Books
The Three Short Men - *First*
Jenkins UK (1939)
Darkling Death - *Last*
Jenkins UK (1956); Roy US (1957)

Ch Supt KNOTT

is a bumptious, overbearing, ambitious detective from Scotland Yard, sent to solve a case of murder in the territory of a small rural force.
British Policeman operating in England

Michael GILBERT 1912- (British)
Invented 11 detectives - see Insp HAZELRIGG
Citation Record: 1 Book
Death Of A Favourite Girl - *Single*
Hodder & Stoughton UK (1980)
The Killing Of Katie Steelstock - *Single**
Harper & Row US (1980)

Judge Deborah KNOTT

is a liberal-minded attorney in a fine community in a state that is struggling to free itself from its old racial and political divisions. She fights to become a judge, solving murders old and new on the way.
American Female Amateur operating in North Carolina

Margaret MARON (American)
See main detective Det Sigrid HAROLD
Citation Record: 3 Books
Bootlegger's Daughter - *First*
is the only book in the genre to have been given the Edgar Allan Poe award, the Agatha award, the Anthony award and the Macavity award.
Mysterious Press US (1992); Headline UK (1994)
Shooting At Loons - *Latest*
Mysterious Press US (1994)

Det KNOWLES
Policeman

Marion BABSON (American)
Invented 8 detectives - see Douglas PERKINS
Citation Record: 1 Book
The Twelve Deaths Of Christmas - *Single*
Collins UK (1979); Walker US (1980)

Colin KNOWLES
British Male Amateur operating in England

Roger EAST 1904- (British)
See main detective Ex-Supt 'Simmy' SIMMONDS
Citation Record: 2 Books
Murder Rehearsal - *First*
Collins UK (1933); Knopf US (1934)
Detectives In Gum Boots - *Last*
Collins UK (1936)

Cdr John KNOWLES
British Male Sleuth operating in England

Ted WILLIS 1918- (British)
See main detective Sgt George DIXON
Citation Record: 1 Book
Death May Surprise Us - *Only*
Macmillan UK (1974)
Westminster One - *Only**
Putnam US (1975)

K

Libby KNOWLES
is a female bodyguard who solves a case of murder by throat-cutting in a locked room.
American Female Private Detective operating in New York

Edward D HOCH 1930- (American)
Invented 20 detectives - see Capt LEOPOLD
Citation Record: 1 Selected Short Story
The Invisible Intruder
In 'Ellery Queen's Mystery Magazine' US (1984)

The Hon Algernon KNOX
British Male Amateur operating in England

E Phillips OPPENHEIM 1866-1946 (British)
Invented 27 detectives - see Nicholas GOADE
Citation Record: 12 Short Stories in 1 Collection
The Honourable Algernon Knox, Detective - *Collection 1*
Hodder & Stoughton UK (1920)

Jonathan KNOX
American Male Amateur operating in Louisville

Emmett MCDOWELL 1914-1975 (American)
Writer: Robert Emmett MCDOWELL
Inventor of one other detective Jamie MACRAE
Citation Record: 4 Books
Stamped For Death - *First*
Ace US (1958)
In At The Kill - *Last*
Ace US (1960)

Mr KNUCKLESTONE
British Male Amateur operating in England

Fred J PROCTOR (British)
Citation Record: 1 Book
Timothy Twill's Secret - *Only*
Tarstow, Denver UK (1891)

Komako KOA
Male Amateur operating in Hawaii

Max LONG 1890- (American)
Writer: Max Freedom LONG
Citation Record: 3 Books
Murder Between Dark And Dark - *First*
Lippincott US (1939); Hutchinson UK (1940)
Death Goes Native - *Last*
Lippincott US (1941)

Charles KOENIG
Second detective of Cobb TAKAMURA

Father Robert KOESLER
is a Catholic priest who solves difficult crimes that have religious backgrounds and often religious plots. He is often asked by the local police for his help.
American Male Amateur operating in Detroit

William X KIENZLE 1928- (American)
was born in Detroit, Michigan. He was educated at Sacred Heart Seminary College, Detroit, 1946-1950, and at St John's Seminary, Plymouth, Michigan, 1950-1954, becoming an ordained priest in the Roman Catholic Church, 1954.
Writer: William Xavier KIENZLE
Citation Record: 13 Books
The Rosary Murders - *First*
Andrews US (1979); Hodder & Stoughton UK (1979)
Body Count - *Latest*
Andrews & McMeel US (1992)

Larry KOHARIK
American Policeman operating in USA

John M ESHLEMAN 1914(?)- (American)
Writer: John Morton ESHLEMAN
Citation Record: 2 Books
The Long Window - *First*
Washburn US (1953)
Death Of A Cheat - *First**
Mercury US (1955)
The Long Chase - *Last*
Washburn US (1954)
The Deadly Chase - *Last**
Mercury US (1955)

André KOHL
Male Sleuth operating in USA

Pierre SALINGER 1925- (American)
Writer: Pierre Emile George SALINGER
Citation Record: 2 Books
On The Instruction Of My Government - *First*
Doubleday US (1971)
For The Eyes Of The President Only - *First**
Collins UK (1971)
The Dossier - *Latest*
Doubleday US (1984); Deutsch UK (1984)

Hermann KOHLER
Second detective of Insp ST CYR

Insp KOJAK
appears in novelizations of episodes from a TV series.
American Policeman operating in New York

Victor B MILLER 1940- (American)
See main detective FERNANDA
Citation Record: 9 Books
Requiem For A Cop - *First*
Pocket Books US (1974); Wingate UK (1976)
Death Is Not A Passing Grade - *Last*
Pocket Books US (1975)
Marked For Murder - *Last**
Star UK (1976)

Viera KOLAROVA
Female Amateur operating in New York

Elizabeth POWERS 1944- (American)
Citation Record: 2 Books

The All That Glitters: The Case Of The Ice-Cold Diamond - *First*
!See Appendix 2.
Doubleday US (1981)
On Account Of Murder - *Latest*
Avon US (1984)

Carl KOLCHAK

appears in novelizations of TV movies.
American Male Sleuth operating in Las Vegas/Seattle

Jeff RICE 1944- (American)
was born in Rhode Island. He is a journalist and screenwriter.
Citation Record: 2 Books
The Night Stalker - *First*
Pocket Books US (1973)
The Night Strangler - *Last*
Pocket Books US (1974)

Ch Insp Lars KOLLIN

Swedish Policeman operating in Stockholm

Olle HOGSTRAND 1933- (Swedish)
Writer: Olle Edvard HOGSTRAND
Citation Record: 3 Books
On The Prime Minister's Account - *First*
is a translation from the Swedish of *Maskerat Brott* (Stockholm, 1971).
Gollancz UK (1972); Pantheon US (1972)
The Gambler - *Last*
Pantheon US (1974); Hale UK (1976)

Sherlaw KOMBS

is a *Sherlock HOLMES* parody. He was probably the very earliest of the species, appearing in a story, complete with parody sidekick, in 1892 and published under the author's punning pseudonym of *Luke SHARP.* He appeared later in another story under the author's real name.
British Male Professional Amateur operating in London
Sidekick: Dr WHATSON
is his parody *WATSON*-like assistant.
British Male - Narrator
Stooge: Insp GREGORY
is a parody of *Insp GREGSON,* a minor police adversary of *Sherlock HOLMES.*
British Male

Robert BARR 1850-1912 (British)
Invented 4 detectives - see Nick NICHOLSON
Citation Record: 1 Selected Short Story
The Great Pegram Mystery - *Parody 1*
appeared first in the author's own collection, *The Face and the Mask.* It was included in the anthology, *THE MISADVENTURES OF SHERLOCK HOLMES* (Editor: *Ellery QUEEN*).
Hutchinson UK (1894); Stokes US (1895)

Luke SHARP 1850-1912 (British)
Writer: Robert BARR
Other Byline: Robert BARR
Adopter of one other detective Sherlock HOLMES
Citation Record: 1 Selected Short Story
Detective Stories Gone Wrong: The Adventures Of Sherlaw Kombs - *Parody 1*
was published in this British magazine just a few years after the first appearance of *Sherlock HOLMES.* It is, according to Ronald Burt De Waal, 'the first and one of the funniest Sherlockian parodies ever written'. The detective, faced with a death in a railway carriage, makes a series of most ingenious deductions, all of them completely wrong as it turns out, the case being solved by the plodders at Scotland Yard. Two years after its first publication, the story appeared in *The Face and the Mask,* a collection of short stories by the author under his real name, and it was then entitled, *THE GREAT PEGRAM MYSTERY.*
In 'The Idler' UK (1892)
The Adventures Of Sherlaw Kombs - *Parody 1**
Aspen US (1979)

Paul KONIG

American Male Amateur operating in New York

Herbert LIEBERMAN 1933- (American)
See main detective Det Sgt Francis MOONEY
Citation Record: 1 Book
City Of The Dead - *Only*
Simon & Schuster US (1976); Hutchinson UK (1976)

Olga von KOPF

Russian Female Secret Agent operating in Russia

Henry DE HALSALLE 1872- (British)
Citation Record: 1 Book 8 Short Stories in 1 Collection
A Secret Service Woman - *Only*
Laurie UK (1917)
A Woman Spy - *Collection 1*
Skeffington UK (1918)

Capt Ivan KORAVITCH

Russian Male Amateur operating in Europe

Victor L WHITECHURCH 1868-1933 (British)
Invented 5 detectives - see Det Sgt AMBROSE
Citation Record: 12 Short Stories in 1 Collection
The Adventures Of Captain Ivan Koravitch - *Collection 1*
Blackwood UK (1925)

K

KOREGORVSKY

Male Sleuth operating in England

Andrew WOOD 1890- (British)
See main detective Magnus KEEBLE
Citation Record: 2 Books
Bright Angel - *First*
Ward, Lock UK (1933); Dutton US (1933)
Red Square - *Last*
Ward, Lock UK (1934); Dutton US (1934)

Karen KOVAC and Jack DONOVAN

Karen KOVAC appears also with the one of the author's other detectives, *Terry FLYNN,* in two books written by the author under his real name.
American Female Amateur and American Male Amateur operating in USA

Bill GRANGER 1941- (American)
Writer: Bill GRANGER
See main detective DEVEREAUX
Citation Record: 1 Book
Public Murders - *Single*
Jove US (1980); New English Library UK (1981)

Karen KOVAC and Terry FLYNN

Karen KOVAC appears also in one book (under the author's real name) with another detective, *Jack DONOVAN.*
American Female Amateur and American Male Amateur operating in USA

Joe GASH (American)
Writer: Bill GRANGER
Citation Record: 2 Books
Priestly Murders - *First*
Holt US (1984)
Newspaper Murders - *Latest*
Holt US (1985)

Riley KOVACHS

sleuths in San Francisco back in the 1950s and is involved in cases with political undertones.
!See Appendix 2.
American Male Private Detective operating in San Francisco

Gordon DE MARCO (American)
Inventor of one other detective Rocco CONIGLIARO
Citation Record: 3 Books

October Heat - *First*
Germinal US (1979); Pluto UK (1984)
Frisco Blues - *Latest*
Pluto US (1985); Pluto UK (1985)

Shaun KOVACK
American Male Sleuth operating in USA

Spike MORELLI 1923- (American)
Writer: William Simpson NEWTON
Other Bylines:
Gilroy MITCHAM Gene ROSS
Citation Record: 2 Books
Give It To Me Straight - *First*
Harborough US (1953)
No Place For Me - *Last*
Harborough US (1953)

Sheriff Milton KOVAK
American Policeman operating in Oklahoma

Susan Rogers COOPER 1947- (American)
Inventor of one other detective Kimmy KRUSE
Citation Record: 4 Books
The Man In The Green Chevy - *First*
St Martin's US (1989)
Chasing Away The Devil - *Latest*
St Martin's US (1991)

Stash KOVAL
American Male Amateur operating in New York

Ron PETERS (American)
Citation Record: 2 Books
The Big Stash - *First*
Curtis US (1972)
Stash Spots A Murder - *Last*
Curtis US (1973)

Spaceman KOWALSKI and Blue MAGUIRE
American Male Sleuths operating in Los Angeles

Teri WHITE 1946- (American)
was born in Topeka, Kansas, and educated at several schools in the USA. She received the Mystery Writers of America Edgar Allan Poe award, 1983.
Citation Record: 3 Books
Triangle - *First*
Mysterious Press US (1981)
Tightrope - *Latest*
Mysterious Press US (1986); Mysterious Press UK (1988)

KOYALA
Male Sleuth operating in Borneo

John Charles BEECHAM (British)
Citation Record: 2 Books
The Argus Pheasant - *First*
Watt US (1918); Methuen UK (1920)
The Yellow Spider - *Last*
Watt US (1920); Methuen UK (1921)

Det Insp Abraham KOZMINSKI
British Policeman operating in England

Quentin DOWNES 1907-1991 (British)
For writer details see Chevalier Auguste C DUPIN
Citation Record: 3 Books
No Smoke, No Fire - *First*
Wingate UK (1952); Roy US (1956)
They Hadn't A Clue - *Last*
Arco UK (1954)

Asbjorn (Osborne Crag) KRAG
Norwegian Male Sleuth operating in Norway/Denmark

Sven ELVESTAD 1894-1934 (Norwegian)
Writer: Sven Christopher Svendson ELVESTAD
Citation Record: 3 Books
The Man Who Plundered The City - *First*
is a translation from the Norwegian of *Manden Som Vilde Plyndre Kristiania* (Oslo 1915), under the byline of Stein Riverton.
McBride US (1924)
The Case Of Robert Robertson - *Last*
is a translation from the Norwegian of *Faenomenet Robert Robertson* (Oslo, 1923), as by Stein Riverton.
Lane UK (1930); Knopf US (1930)

Lt Ben KRAHMER
American Policeman operating in Philadelphia

Samuel A KRASNEY 1922- (American)
Inventor of one other detective Lt Abe LARSON
Citation Record: 2 Books
Morals Squad - *First*
Ace US (1959); WDL UK (1960)
A Mania For Blondes - *Last*
Ace US (1961)

Josh KRALES
American Male Amateur operating in New York

Heywood GOULD (American)
Citation Record: 2 Books
One Dead Debutante - *First*
St Martin's US (1975)
Glitterburn - *Latest*
St Martin's US (1977)

Phil KRAMER
is a lawyer who takes clients suspected of murder and goes on to find the real culprits.
American Male Amateur operating in USA

Paul KRUGER 1917- (American)
See main detective Vince LATIMER
Citation Record: 5 Books
Weep For Willow Green - *First*
Simon & Schuster US (1967); Hale UK (1971)
The Cold Ones - *Last*
Simon & Schuster US (1972)

Lt Tromp KRAMER
is a white policeman in racially divided South Africa, based in the fictional town of Trekkersburg. His cases are excellent studies in classic detection, while giving a vivid picture of the social realities lying behind them.
South African Policeman operating in South Africa
Sidekick: Sgt ZONDI
is a young Kaffir policeman, clever, fairly well educated and highly skilled in the arts of observation and tracking. He has a close and nicely balanced friendship with his boss in the hard world of the South African police, in which racial division is deep and endemic. His outstanding virtues are his loyalty and his ability to investigate among his black and coloured countrymen.
South African Male - Subordinate

James MCCLURE 1939- (South African)
was born in Johannesburg, South Africa. He graduated at Maritzburg College, Natal, 1958, and worked as a photographer, artist, and reporter in South Africa and England during the 1960s and 1970s. He has been successful in creating detective stories of quality and, at the same time, portraying believable characters and relationships against a most difficult background. He received the Crime Writers Association Gold Dagger award, 1971, and their Silver Dagger award, 1976.
Writer: James Howe MCCLURE
Citation Record: 8 Books

The Steam Pig - *First*
Gollancz UK (1971); Harper & Row US (1972)
Imago: A Modern Comedy Of Manners - *Latest*
Mysterious Press US (1988)

Stan KRAYCHIK

is a gay hairdresser who, in the course of his work, hears much gossip and runs into many cases of murder, which he is prevailed upon to do something about.
American Male Amateur operating in Boston

Grant MICHAELS (American)
Citation Record: 3 Books
A Body To Dye For - *First*
St Martin's US (1992)
Dead On Your Feet - *Latest*
St Martin's US (1993)

Herr KRESCH

German Policeman operating in Germany

Darwin L TEILHET 1904-1964 (American)
Invented 3 detectives - see Peter BLUE and Jean Henri ST AMAND
Citation Record: 1 Book
The Talking Sparrow Murder - *Only*
!See Appendix 2.
Morrow US (1934); Gollancz UK (1934)

Henry KRETZNER

runs a radio show in the tiny town of Hamelin and becomes involved in a struggle to prove the innocence of a man, imprisoned for murder, who has escaped.
American Male Amateur operating in Tennessee

Sharyn MCCRUMB (American)
Invented 4 detectives - see Elizabeth MACPHERSON
Citation Record: 1 Book
She Walks These Hills - *Single*
Scribner's US (1994)

Maj KRIM

appears also in one book with other detectives of this author.
American Male Amateur operating in New York/California

Dwight MARFIELD 1868-1955 (American)
Writer: Dwight Steele MARFIELD
Other Detectives:
Insp SKANE
Insp SKANE, Dudley BRENT and Maj KRIM
Insp SKANE, Gail MCGURK and Dudley BRENT
Citation Record: 1 Book
The Ghost On The Balcony - *Only*
Dutton US (1939)

Maj KRIM

Appears with at least two other detectives - see Insp SKANE

Harvey KRIM

is an insurance investigator who sleuths. Although undoubtedly clever, he is a pretty mean and undesirable character.
American Male Professional Investigator operating in New York

E V CUNNINGHAM 1914- (American)
Invented 4 detectives - see Det Sgt Masao MASUTO
Citation Record: 2 Books
Lydia - *First*
Doubleday US (1964); Deutsch UK (1965)
Cynthia - *Latest*
Morrow US (1968); Deutsch UK (1969)

Al KRUG

Second detective of Casey KELLOG

Dan KRUGER

is an ex-rock musician and ex-cop; a sleuth who hates violence, does not carry a gun, can't fight, drinks too much, and would rather play in a group in a cellar than walk the mean streets above.
American Male Private Detective operating in Chicago

Michael CORMANY (American)
Citation Record: 4 Books
Lost Daughter - *First*
Stuart US (1988)
Polaroid Man - *Latest*
Carol US (1991)

Herbie KRUGER

is a brilliant but flawed senior member of British Intelligence who becomes involved in the most tortuous of proceedings, laced with despair and deceit. He emerges with some honour.
British Male Secret Agent operating in several locations

John GARDNER 1926- (British)
Invented 5 detectives - see Boysie OAKES
Citation Record: 4 Books
The Nostradamus Traitor - *First*
Hodder & Stoughton UK (1979); Doubleday US (1979)
The Secret Families - *Latest*
Bantam UK (1989); Putnam US (1989)

Kimmy KRUSE

is a comedian on tour. When she is called back home, murder strikes and she investigates.
American Female Amateur operating in Louisiana

Susan Rogers COOPER 1947- (American)
See main detective Sheriff Milton KOVAK
Citation Record: 1 Book
Funny As A Dead Relative - *Single*
St Martin's US (1994)

King KULL

was an 'occult' detective.
American Male Detective in Pulp Magazines operating in USA

Robert E HOWARD 1906-1936 (American)
See main detective Solomon KANE
No citations

Lt KUPFERMAN

solves a case of death by shooting in a locked room.
American Policeman operating in Los Angeles

Joseph NATHENSON (American)
Citation Record: 1 Book
A Puzzle For Experts - *Single*
Shades of Sherlock US (1985)

Burt KURRIE

American Male Amateur operating in USA

Ron GOULART 1933- (American)
Invented 15 detectives - see Jake PACE and Hildy PACE
Citation Record: 1 Book
A Graveyard Of My Own - *Single*
Walker US (1985)

Ilya KURYAKIN

Second detective of Napoleon SOLO

'Handsome' KUSAK

Second detective of 'Bingo' RIGGS

Det Ivan KUVAKIN

Russian Male Sleuth operating in Russia

Anthony OLCOTT 1950- (American)
Citation Record: 2 Books
Murder At The Red October - *First*
Academy US (1981); Hodder & Stoughton UK (1983)
Mayday In Magadan - *Latest*
Bantam US (1983); Macmillan UK (1984)

Thomas KYD

is a Vietnam war veteran who has recently become a widower. Not surprisingly, he comes over as tough and cynical.

American Male Private Detective operating in Los Angeles

Timothy HARRIS 1946- (American)

was born in Los Angeles, California. He took a BA at Peterhouse College, Cambridge, 1969, and received an MA, 1974.

Writer: Timothy Hyde HARRIS

Citation Record: 2 Books

Kyd For Hire - *First*
Gollancz UK (1977); Dell US (1978)

Good Night And Goodbye - *Latest*
Delacorte US (1979); Pandora UK (1981); Pan AU (1981)

Insp KYLE

British Policeman operating in England

Roy VICKERS 1888-1965 (British)

Invented 9 detectives - see Insp J RASON

Citation Record: 1 Book

Murdering Mr Velfrage - *Only*
Faber UK (1950)

Maid To Murder - *Only**
Mill US (1950)

Harry KYLE and Angela ROLLASON

British Male Amateur and British Female Amateur operating in Wales

Roger ORMEROD 1920- (British)

Invented 4 detectives - see Philipa LOWE

Citation Record: 1 Book

Seeing Red - *Single*
Constable UK (1985); Scribner's US (1984)

Jack KYLE

American Male Private Detective operating in Dallas

Richard ABSHIRE (American)

Citation Record: 3 Books

Dallas Drop - *First*
Coronet UK (1990)

The Dallas Deception - *Latest*
Morrow US (1991)

John KYMMERLY

American Male Amateur operating in Chicago

Eleanor A BLAKE 1899- (American)

Writer: Eleanor Blake Atkinson Cox PRATT

Citation Record: 1 Book

The Jade Green Cats - *Only*
McBride US (1931)

Skelton KYNE

American Male Amateur operating in USA

Clement WOOD 1888-1950 (American)

was born in Alabama. He was a lawyer, a novelist and a poet.

Other Detectives:
Capt/Insp COLIN   Lal REED

Citation Record: 2 Books

The Corpse In The Guest Room - *First*
Arcadia US (1945)

Double Jeopardy - *Last*
Arcadia US (1947)

Sir John KYNNERSLEY

British Male Amateur operating in England

A C FOX-DAVIES 1871-1928 (British)

Writer: Arthur Charles FOX-DAVIES

Other Detectives:
Col MARWOOD   Ashley TEMPEST

Citation Record: 13 Short Stories in 1 Collection

The Finances Of Sir John Kinnersley - *Collection 1*
Lane UK (1908); Lane US (1908)

K

— L —

Papa LA BAS

is a kind of Ju-Ju man in New York's Harlem who works as a private eye.

American Male Private Detective operating in USA

Ishmael REED 1938- (American)

Citation Record: 2 Books

Mumbo-Jumbo - *First*
Doubleday US (1972)

The Last Days Of Louisiana Red - *Latest*
Random House US (1974)

Joe LA BRAVA

American Male Amateur operating in Miami

Elmore LEONARD 1935- (American)

Invented 6 detectives - see Frank RYAN

Citation Record: 1 Book

La Brava - *Single*
Arbor US (1983); Viking UK (1983)

LA MARMOSET

is always in disguise and has been called 'the most expert agent...in all France'.

French Female Private Detective operating in France

Albert W AIKEN 1846-1894 (American)

Invented 5 detectives - see Hilda SIRENE

Citation Record: 1 Book

La Marmoset, The Detective Queen; Or, The Lost Heir Of Morel - *Only*
Beadle & Adams US (1882)

Offr Michael LA RUE

solves a case of murder by shooting, which takes place in a locked upper-story apartment.

American Policeman operating in New York

Will OURSLER 1913-1985 (American)

See main detective pair Philip STRONG and James MATTHEWS

Citation Record: 1 Book

Murder Memo: The Carl Houston Case - *Only*
Simon & Schuster US (1950)

Insp Georges LA TOUCHE

Appears with at least two other detectives - see Insp BURNLEY

Sir Nigel LACAITA

British Male Amateur operating in England

W A MACKENZIE 1870- (British)

See main detective 'Slow and Sure' JACKSON

Citation Record: 4 Books

The Drexel Dream - *First*
Chatto UK (1904)

The Bite Of The Leech - *Last*
Holden UK (1914)

Meg LACEY

takes on a case involving child abuse and pornography.

American Female Private Detective operating in Vancouver

Elizabeth BOWERS (Canadian)

Citation Record: 1 Book

Ladies' Night - *Single*
Seal US (1988); Seal UK (1989)

A Lincoln LACY
American Male Amateur operating in New York/Chicago

Marion STROBEL 1895- (American)

Citation Record: 2 Books

Ice Before Killing - *First*
Scribner's US (1943)

Kiss And Kill - *Last*
Scribner's US (1946)

Maj John Tattersall LACY
was in a machine-gun brigade during the First World War and became a kind of vigilante operator, appearing in stories in *Black Aces.*
American Male Detective in Pulp Magazines operating in USA

Theodore TINSLEY 1934- (American)

Invented 3 detectives - see Carrie CASHIN

No citations

Tim LACY
was formerly a secret agent and is now head of a security firm specially concerned with the world of art and antiques, a *milieu* that generates much mayhem and murder.
British Male Private Detective operating in England

Derek WILSON (British)

is an historian, biographer and author of novels and travel books.

Citation Record: 3 Books

The Triarchs - *First*
Headline UK (1994)

The Hellfire Papers - *Latest*
Headline UK (1995)

The LADY DETECTIVE
American Female Detective in Pulp Magazines operating in USA

OLD SLEUTH (American)

Invented 40 detectives - see Brant ADAMS

Citation Record: 1 Book

The Lady Detective - *Only*
Munro US (1892)

LADY KATE
American Female Detective in Pulp Magazines operating in USA

No citations

Jack LAIDLAW
is a tough policeman but a compassionate man in a hard city.
British Policeman operating in Glasgow

Sidekick: Sgt HARKNESS
Scottish Male - Subordinate

William MCILVANNEY 1936- (British)

was born in Kilmarnock, Ayrshire, Scotland. He took an MA at Glasgow University, 1959, and then worked as a teacher in Scotland and in France. He received the Crime Writers Association Silver Dagger award, 1984.

Citation Record: 3 Books

Laidlaw - *First*
Hodder & Stoughton UK (1977); Pantheon US (1977)

Strange Loyalties - *Latest*
Hodder & Stoughton UK (1991)

Insp Martin LAIDMAN
British Policeman operating in England

Stuart SEATON (British)

Citation Record: 2 Books

Don't Take It To Heart - *First*
Boardman UK (1955)

Dust In Your Eyes - *Last*
Boardman UK (1957)

Patrick LAING
American Male Amateur operating in USA

Patrick LAING 1904-1978 (American)

Writer: Amelia Reynolds LONG

Other Bylines:
Amelia Reynolds LONG   Adrian REYNOLDS

Citation Record: 6 Books

If I Should Murder - *First*
Phoenix Press US (1945)

The Shadow Of Murder - *Last*
Phoenix Press US (1957)

Andrew LAIRD
is a Marine Insurance investigator. The books were published in the US under the pseudonym of *Michael KIRK.*
British Male Professional Investigator operating in Scotland/France

Michael KIRK 1928- (British)

For writer details see Jonathan GAUNT

Citation Record: 1 Book

All Other Perils - *First*
Doubleday US (1975)

Robert MACLEOD 1928- (British)

Invented 3 detectives - see Jonathan GAUNT

Citation Record: 6 Books

All Other Perils - *First*
Long UK (1974)

Witchline - *Last*
Century Hutchinson UK (1988)

Noah WEBSTER 1928- (British)

See main detective Jonathan GAUNT

Citation Record: 1 Book

Witchline - *Single*
Doubleday US (1988)

Louis LAIT
investigates a robbery and finds a public figure very dead. He naturally has to find out whodunnit.
American Male Private Detective operating in New York

Kermit JAEDIKER (American)

was born in New York City and worked there as a crime reporter.

Citation Record: 1 Book

Tall, Dark And Dead - *Only*
Mystery House US (1947)

Harry LAKE
is a Vietnam War veteran who was taken prisoner. He then joined the police, resigned, and is now a pretty sad PI.
American Male Private Detective operating in California

Peter Heath FINE 1938- (American)

Citation Record: 1 Book

Troubled Waters - *Single*
Pinnacle US (1981)

Simon LAKE
American Male Private Detective operating in New York

Whitman CHAMBERS 1896- (American)

Writer: Elwyn Whitman CHAMBERS

Other Detectives:
Bill BARTLETT   Kate BLAYNE
Pierre O'BRIEN

Citation Record: 1 Book

Dead Men Leave No Fingerprints - *Only*
Doubleday US (1935); Cassell UK (1935)

LAKIN
solves the mystery of various shootings that take place in 'inaccessible' rooms.
British Policeman operating in England

Justin ATHOLL (British)

Citation Record: 1 Book

L

The Trackless Thing - *Only*
In 'Everybody's' UK (1945)

Donald LAM
Second detective of Bertha COOL

Jack LAMARRE and Alison PRENDERGAST
British Male Amateur and British Female Amateur operating in USA

Peter FOX 1946- (British)
is a research scientist specialising in mathematical physics.
Writer: Peter F FOX
Citation Record: 1 Book
Kensington Gore - *Single*
Macmillan UK (1983)
The Trail Of The Reaper - *Single**
!See Appendix 2.
St Martin's US (1983)

Insp Ernest LAMB
appears in many of the author's books featuring her main detective, *Maud SILVER.* He is really not a very good detective, but he succeeds in solving his cases without the help of the formidable lady sleuth in at least three books.
British Policeman operating in England

Patricia WENTWORTH 1878-1961 (British)
See main detective Maud Hephzibah SILVER
Citation Record: 3 Books
The Blind Side - *First*
Hodder & Stoughton UK (1939); Lippincott US (1939)
Pursuit Of A Parcel - *Last*
Hodder & Stoughton UK (1942); Lippincott US (1942)

Sgt Johnny LAMB
British Policeman operating in London

John DONAVAN 1905-1986 (British)
For writer details see Mrs Palmyra Evangeline PYM
Other Detectives:
Insp Frederick Jubilee 'Jumper' CROSS
Sir Benjamin SCARLE
Citation Record: 5 Books
The Case Of The Rusted Room - *First*
Hale UK (1937); Hillman-Curl US (1937)
The Case Of The Plastic Man - *Last*
Hodder & Stoughton UK (1940)
The Case Of The Plastic Mask - *Last**
Arcadia US (1941)

Johnny LAMB
was once a reporter. Fired for being drunk, he is now a PI who resolves to do better.
American Male Private Detective operating in Los Angeles

Robert DUNDEE 1922-1980 (American)
Writer: Robert R KIRSCH
Citation Record: 1 Book
Pandora's Box - *Only*
Signet US (1962)

Allan LAMBERT
British Male Amateur operating in Spain

Frances Parkinson KEYES 1885-1970 (American)
Citation Record: 1 Book
Station Wagon In Spain - *Only*
Farrar, Straus US (1955)
The Letter From Spain - *Only**
Eyre & Spottiswoode UK (1959)

Supt John LAMBERT
is a member of some undisclosed, fictional, English county police force and is a good standard English detective of the traditional school.
British Policeman operating in England

Sidekick: Sgt Bert HOOK
British Male - Subordinate

J M GREGSON (British)
Citation Record: 3 Books
For Sale - With Corpse - *First*
Collins UK (1990); Collins US (1991)
Bring Forth Your Dead - *Latest*
Collins UK (1991)

Insp Neil LAMBERT
investigates the murder of a nasty TV comedian.
British Policeman operating in London

Ian STUART 1927-1993 (British)
was born in Royston, Hertfordshire. He worked as a staff member of Barclay's Bank, 1943-1984, and then become a full-time writer.
Other Detectives:
David GRIERSON
Graham LORIMER
Citation Record: 1 Book
Stab In The Back - *Single*
Doubleday US (1986)

Valerie LAMBERT
American Female Amateur operating in several locations

Joan ALLAN (American)
Writer: Martin GROVE
Citation Record: 3 Books
Who Killed Me? - *First*
Zebra US (1979)
Who's Next? - *Last*
Zebra US (1979)

Duca LAMBERTI
Italian Male Sleuth operating in Milan

Giorgio SCERBANECO 1911-1969 (Italian)
Citation Record: 1 Book
Duca And The Milan Murders - *Only*
is a translation from the Italian of *Traditori di Tutti* (Milan, 1966).
Cassell UK (1970); Walker US (1970)

Insp LAMPETER
of Scotland Yard is in one Victorian novel.
British Policeman operating in England

Arthur GRIFFITHS 1838-1908 (British)
Invented 8 detectives - see Insp FASKE
Citation Record: 1 Book
The Brand Of The Broad Arrow - *Only*
Pearson UK (1900)

Jack LANAGAN
American Male Amateur operating in San Francisco

Edward H HURLBUT (American)
Citation Record: 10 Short Stories in 1 Collection
Lanagan, Amateur Detective - *Collection 1*
Sturgis US (1913)

Ryne LANARK
American Male Amateur operating in Chicago

Stephen ROBERTSON 1948- (American)
Writer: Robert Wayne WALKER
Other Byline: Robert W WALKER
Citation Record: 3 Books
Blood Tells - *First*
Pinnacle US (1989)
Blood Ties - *Latest*
Pinnacle US (1989)

Dr Adrian LANCASTER
Second detective of Det Frank BRANDON

Sgt LANCEY
appears also in a collection of stories with one of the author's other detectives, *Aubrey St John MAJOR.*
Policeman operating in South Africa

L Patrick GREENE
Invented 5 detectives - see 'Dynamite' DRURY
Citation Record: 19 Short Stories in 3 Collections
Sergeant Lancey Reports *- Collection 1*
Short stories - 6
Hamilton UK (1931)
Sergeant Lancey Carries On *- Collection 2*
Short stories - 4
Hamilton UK (1933)
Sergeant Lancey Tells The Tale *- Collection 3*
Short stories - 9
Devonshire UK (1947)

Sgt LANCEY
Second detective of Aubrey St John MAJOR

Hannah LAND
is tall, lanky, red-haired, attractive, and an Assistant Professor in Political Science at Duke University, Durham, North Carolina. In her mid-thirties, once married, now comfortably divorced, she becomes involved in detection when death strikes, as it often seems to, on the American campus. Although the official cop is reasonably friendly and can go places and do things she can't be expected to, he is baffled. So she shows him how to do it.
American Female Amateur operating in North Carolina

Stooge: Det Lt Robert E JENKINS
is called in to solve murder. He fails in that but falls for *Hannah LAND.* And why not, indeed, as she is not only pretty but solves his cases for him?
American Male

Amanda MACKAY (American)
Writer: Amanda MacKay SMITH
Citation Record: 2 Books
Death Is Academic *- First*
McKay US (1976); Hale UK (1980)
Death On The Eno *- Latest*
Little, Brown US (1981)
Death On The River *- Latest**
Gollancz UK (1983)

Marty LAND
is a lawyer, working mainly around Broadway, and he crops up in some of the books featuring the author's detective, *Bart HARDIN.* In the two books cited here he is the main detective.
American Male Amateur operating in New York

David ALEXANDER 1907-1973 (American)
Invented 4 detectives - see Bart HARDIN
Citation Record: 2 Books
The Death Of Daddy-O *- First*
Lippincott US (1960); Boardman UK (1960)
Bloodstain *- Last*
Lippincott US (1961); Boardman UK (1962)

LANDER
American Male Sleuth operating in USA

P B MAXON 1944- (American)
Writer: Ann Elizabeth Lowell MAXWELL
Other Byline: A E MAXWELL
Citation Record: 1 Book
The Waltz Of Death *- Only*
Mystery House US (1941)

Mayor Thomas LANDIN
American Male Professional Investigator operating in USA

Joseph COMMINGS (American)
Invented 3 detectives - see Matt TUDOR
Citation Record: 1 Selected Short Story
The Black Friar Murders
In 'Ten Detective Aces' US (1948)

Arnold LANDON
is a planning officer who works on government buildings and frequently meets murder on site.
British Male Amateur operating in England

Roy LEWIS 1933- (British)
was born in Rhondda, Glamorganshire. He was educated at Pentre Grammar School and graduated with an LLB from Bristol University, 1954. He was called to the Bar, 1965, and practised as a lawyer, later holding many senior posts in education. He has written over thirty genre novels and many learned works on law.
Writer: John Royston LEWIS
Other Detectives:
Insp CROW — Eric WARD
Citation Record: 3 Books
A Gathering Of Ghosts *- First*
Collins UK (1982); St Martin's US (1983)
A Short-Lived Ghost *- Latest*
HarperCollins UK (1995)

Geoffrey LANDON
British Male Sleuth operating in Germany

Gerald SINSTADT (British)
Citation Record: 2 Books
The Fidelio Score *- First*
Long UK (1965); Lancer US (1967)
Whisper In A Lonely Place *- Last*
Long UK (1966)
Ship Of Spies *- Last**
Lancer US (1967)

Harvey LANDON
British Male Amateur operating in England

James PATTINSON 1915- (British)
Citation Record: 2 Books
The Liberators *- First*
Harrap UK (1961)
The Last Stronghold *- Last*
Hale UK (1968)

Richard LANDON
searches for stolen plutonium.
American Male Secret Agent operating in Greece

Leo KATCHER 1911-1991 (American)
Citation Record: 1 Book
The Blind Cave *- Only*
Viking US (1966)

Bob LANDRELL
solves a case of theft of a necklace from a locked room.
American Male Amateur operating in USA

Harry Stephen KEELER 1890-1967 (American)
Invented 14 detectives - see Angus MACWHORTER
Citation Record: 1 Book
The Case Of The Two Strange Ladies *- Only*
Phoenix Press US (1943)
Two Strange Ladies *- Only**
Ward, Lock UK (1945)

Jeff LANDRUM
Second detective of Howard MATTHEWS

LANDSDOWNE
appears in what seem to be the autobiographical memoirs of a Scotland Yard detective.
British Policeman operating in London

Andrew LANDSDOWNE (British)

Inventor of one other detective A SCOTLAND YARD DETECTIVE

Citation Record: 21 Short Stories in 1 Collection

A Life's Reminiscences At Scotland Yard - *Collection 1*
Leadenhall UK (1890); Scribner's US (1890)

Drury LANE

was created by the two great masters in their salad days, under a pseudonym they did not use again for other works. *Drury LANE* is an elderly Shakespearean actor who, it seems, was forced to retire when he went deaf, whereupon he fashioned his own Elizabethan community in a castle overlooking the Hudson river. His brilliant mind has enabled him to become an extraordinary solver of problems and he is called on by the police to investigate some truly terrible crimes.

American Male Amateur operating in New York

Stooge: Insp THUMM
is a stooge by definition, being always and suitably baffled by his cases, which he takes to *LANE.*
American Male

Barnaby ROSS (American)

is the pseudonym under which the most famous writing team in American fiction published four ingenious mysteries.

For writer details see Ellery QUEEN

Citation Record: 4 Books

The Tragedy Of X - *First*
Viking US (1932); Cassell UK (1932)

Drury Lane's Last Case - *Last*
Viking US (1933); Cassell UK (1933)

L

Lorimer LANE

American Male Amateur operating in USA

Carolyn WELLS 1870-1942 (American)

Invented 7 detectives - see Fleming STONE

Citation Record: 2 Books

More Lives Than One - *First*
Boni US (1923); Hutchinson UK (1924)

The Fourteenth Key - *Last*
Putnam US (1924)

Paul LANE

American Male Amateur operating in New York

Frances LOCKRIDGE and Richard LOCKRIDGE (American)

Invented 5 detectives - see, Bernard SIMMONS

Citation Record: 2 Books

Night Of Shadows - *First*
Lippincott US (1962); Long UK (1964)

Quest For The Bogeyman - *Last*
Lippincott US (1964); Hutchinson UK (1965)

Sally 'Sherlock Holmes' LANE

is an ace reporter who stumbles on a baby-killing racket.

American Female Amateur operating in USA

Paul GALLICO 1897-1976 (American)

Invented 3 detectives - see Alexander HERO

Citation Record: 1 Selected Short Story

Solo Job
is in the anthology, *The Female of the Species* (Editor; *Ellery QUEEN*, US 1943).
Cosmopolitan US (1937)

Foy LANEER

American Male Private Detective operating in USA

David A BOWMAN (American)

Citation Record: 1 Selected Short Story

Pincushion
In 'New Black Mask Quarterly' US (1985)

Henry LANEHAM

is a nerve specialist who solves a case of death by electrocution in a locked room.

American Male Amateur operating in USA

Arthur E MACFARLANE 1896- (American)

Writer: Arthur Emerson MACFARLANE

Citation Record: 1 Book

Behind The Bolted Door? - *Only*
Dodd, Mead US (1916); Nash UK (1916)

Sherwood LANG

British Male Amateur operating in England

C Delves WARREN (British)

Citation Record: 4 Short Stories in 1 Collection

Some Cases Of Sherwood Lang, Detective - *Collection 1*
Drane UK (1923)

Ross LANGDON

American Male Private Detective operating in Midwest USA

Edith HOWIE (American)

See main detective Peter HOLGATE

Citation Record: 1 Book

Cry Murder - *Only*
Mill US (1944); Boardman UK (1950)

Offr Skip LANGDON

is a Southern girl of good family who was too tall and too big to qualify as a belle. Instead she has become a rookie cop in the Homicide division of New Orleans, a city she knows well.

American Policewoman operating in New Orleans

Julie SMITH 1944- (American)

Invented 4 detectives - see Paul MACDONALD

Citation Record: 2 Books

New Orleans Mourning - *First*
St Martin's US (1990)

The Axeman's Jazz - *Latest*
Ballantine US (1991)

Elizabeth LANGE

investigates the mysterious death of her sister and proves it was murder.

American Female Amateur operating in California

Mary Higgins CLARK 1931- (American)

Invented 3 detectives - see Katie DEMAIO

Citation Record: 1 Book

Weep No More, My Lady - *Single*
Simon & Schuster US (1987); Collins UK (1987)

John LANGE

solves a case of death by bludgeoning in a locked room.

American Male Sleuth operating in USA

Thomas CHASTAIN and Bill ADLER (American)

Inventors of one other detective Capt Gregory WALTHAM

Citation Record: 1 Book

The Picture-Perfect Murders - *Single*
Morrow US (1987)

Insp Neville LANGHAM

British Policeman operating in England

Sidekick: Sgt HOPKINS
British Male - Subordinate

Roland DANIEL 1880-1969 (British)

was British but was raised in Florida. He was the author of many crime novels, which featured all kinds of British and American detectives, most of whom seemed to have problems with mysterious and usualy malevolent orientals.

Writer: William Roland DANIEL

Other Detectives:

Wu FANG	Michael GRANT
John HOPKINS	Buddy MUSTARD
Brian O'MALLEY	Insp Jack PEARSON
The REMOVER	Bill SAVILLE
Insp John WALK	Michael WALLACE

Citation Record: 2 Books

The Brown Murder Case - *First*
Shaylor UK (1930)

The Rosario Murder Case - *First*
Brentano's UK (1930)

Bill LANGLEY

appears in one book under the author's real name and in one under his pseudonym.

American Male Private Detective operating in London

John HUNTER 1891-1961 (British)

Writer: Alfred John HUNTER
Other Byline: Peter MERITON

Adopter of one other detective Sexton BLAKE

Citation Record: 1 Book

Three Die At Midnight - *Only*
Hurst UK (1937); Dutton US (1937)

Peter MERITON 1891-1961 (British)

Invented 3 detectives - see Capt DACK

Citation Record: 1 Book

After Darvray Died - *Only*
Hurst UK (1938)

Tom LANGLEY

is an investigative reporter.

British Male Private Detective operating in London

Jack MONMOUTH (British)

Writer: William Leonard PEMBER

Inventor of one other detective John EARLSTONE

Citation Record: 4 Books

The Donovan Case - *First*
Jarrolds UK (1955)

Lightning Over Mayfair - *Last*
Hale UK (1958)

Jimmy LANGRY

British Male Amateur operating in England

Francis LESLIE (British)

Citation Record: 2 Books

Study Of Death - *First*
Hurst UK (1943)

Who Keeps The Keys? - *Last*
Hurst UK (1948)

Maj Clifford LANSING

solves an 'impossible' case of death by bludgeoning.

Male Professional Investigator

W L FIELDHOUSE (American)

Citation Record: 1 Selected Short Story

Murder Under The Christmas Tree
In 'Mike Shayne Mystery Magazine' US (1980)

Harry LANSING

American Male Amateur operating in USA

Martina D'ALTON (American)

Citation Record: 1 Book

Fatal Finish - *Single*
Walker US (1982)

Mike LANSON

American Male Amateur operating in USA

J Harvey BOND 1904-1971 (American)

Writer: Russell Robert WINTERBOTHAM

Citation Record: 4 Books

Murder Isn't Funny - *First*
Ace US (1958); Digit UK (1958)

If Wishes Were Hearses - *Last*
Ace US (1961)

Tony LANTZ

does the brain work while his sidekick does the rest.

American Male Private Detective operating in New York

Sidekick: Eddie WRIGHT
is the brawn to the detective's undoubted brain but has to take the kicks and do the legwork as well as having to narrate the books.

American Male - Narrator

Clarence MULLEN 1907- (American)

Citation Record: 2 Books

Thereby Hangs A Corpse - *First*
Mystery House US (1946)

A Good Place For Murder - *Last*
Phoenix Press US (1948)

Michael LANYARD

was also known as The Lone Wolf, an early member of the species of outlaw-detective, and it was said that the author based him on *Arsène LUPIN.* He typifies the 'bent hero', the noble outcast who has been made a criminal by society because of his struggle in a just but long-forgotten cause. Now, having given up his old ways for the love of a good woman, he uses his skills to hunt down other criminals. His exploits provided material for a series of films in the 1930s, with William Warren often playing the hero.

American Male Amateur operating in USA

Louis Joseph VANCE 1879-1933 (American)

was born in Washington DC and educated at Brooklyn Polytechnic Institute, New York. He was the author of hundreds of short stories for magazines before attaining success as an author. He wrote, 1906-1933, at least twenty-nine genre novels.

Inventor of one other detective Terence O'ROURKE

Citation Record: 8 Books

The Lone Wolf - *First*
Little, Brown US (1914); Nash UK (1915)

The Lone Wolf's Last Prowl - *Last*
Lippincott US (1934); Jarrolds UK (1935)

Lt Claude LAPOINTE

is a lonely, burnt-out cop in Montreal who investigates, on his own and by old-fashioned methods, a case of murder.

Canadian Policeman operating in Montreal

TREVANIAN 1931- (American)

See main detective Prof Jonathan HEMLOCK

Citation Record: 1 Book

The Main - *Single*
Harcourt Brace US (1976); Hart Davis UK (1977)

Sgt Marian LARCH

American Policewoman operating in New York

Barbara PAUL (American)

Invented 8 detectives - see Lt TOOMEY

Citation Record: 3 Books

The Renewable Virgin - *First*
Collins UK (1984); Scribner's US (1985)

He Huffed And He Puffed - *Latest*
Scribner's US (1989); Macmillan UK (1989)

Marius LARCHE

is in his forties and a senior Interpol officer, based in Lyons, France. He seems to have so many emotional problems and spends so much time, when involved in his cases, lusting after anything that moves, female or male, that it is a wonder he has attained his official position. Certainly intellectual brilliance and detective skills do not seem to account for it.

French Policeman operating in Europe

Sidekick: Det Supt Alison ROWE
is seconded from Scotland Yard, in *LARCHE's* second book. Although this is supposed to be because of her 'special knowledge', one suspects it is to provide a sexual lift for a

wearisome detective. Not speaking Spanish seems no hindrance.
British Male - Assistant

Anthony MASTERS 1940- (British)
is a distinguished mainstream novelist, biographer and short story writer, winner of the John Llewellyn Rhys Memorial Prize. He has written a number of thrillers under a pseudonym.
Citation Record: 3 Books
Murder Is A Long Time Coming - *First*
Constable UK (1991)
Confessional - *Latest*
Constable UK (1993)

Lou LARGO

was based in a office on Times Square. One of this author's hardboiled private eyes, he appeared in only two books actually written by *ARD* before his untimely death. In the next two years, four new *Lou LARGO* books, ghost-written, appeared under his name.
American Male Private Detective operating in New York/Florida

William ARD 1922-1960 (American)
Invented 5 detectives - see Timothy DANE
Citation Record: 2 Books
All I Can Get - *First*
Derby US (1959)
Like Ice She Was - *Last*
Monarch US (1960)

William ARD 1938- (American)
For writer details see Leo HAIG
Citation Record: 1 Book
Babe In The Woods - *Only*
Monarch US (1960)

William ARD 1932- (American)
For writer details see Johnny HAVOC
Citation Record: 3 Books
Make Mine Mavis - *First*
Monarch US (1961)
And So To Bed - *Last*
Monarch US (1962)

Rick LARKAN

American Male Private Detective operating in Miami

Marston LA FRANCE 1917?- (American)
Citation Record: 1 Book
Miami Merry-Go-Round - *Only*
World US (1951)

Jim LARKIN

is a reporter on a provincial newspaper who has a nose for murder.
British Male Amateur operating in England

Martin RUSSELL 1934- (British)
Invented 3 detectives - see Steven CASSELL
Citation Record: 5 Books
Deadline - *First*
Collins UK (1971)
Murder By The Mile - *Last*
Collins UK (1975)

Tommy LARKIN

Second detective of Lt Paul GOLD

Gilbert LAROSE

Male Amateur operating in Australia

Arthur GASK 1872- (British)
Writer: Arthur Cecil GASK
Citation Record: 26 Books
Cloud The Smiter - *First*
Jenkins UK (1926)
Crime Upon Crime - *Last*
Jenkins UK (1952); Roy US (1957)

Simon LARREN

British Male Amateur operating in England

Robert CHARLES 1938- (British)
For writer details see Paul MASON
Inventor of one other detective Supt Mark NICOLSON
Citation Record: 10 Books
Nothing To Lose - *First*
Hale UK (1963)
Strikefast - *Last*
Hale UK (1969)

Tracy LARRIMORE and Mike THOMPSON

American Female Amateur and American Male Amateur operating in USA

Jessica PAULL (American)
Writers: Julia PERCEVAL and Rosaylmer BURGER
Citation Record: 3 Books
Destination: Terror - *First*
Award US (1968)
Rendezvous With Death - *Last*
Award US (1969)

Max Van LARSEN

Second detective of Sylvia PLOTKIN

Lt Abe LARSON

American Policeman operating in New York

Samuel A KRASNEY 1922- (American)
See main detective Lt Ben KRAHMER
Citation Record: 4 Books
Death Cries In The Street - *First*
Rinehart US (1955); Muller UK (1956)
Homicide Call - *Last*
Morrow US (1962); Allen UK (1963)

Lt LASALA

American Policeman operating in USA

Seymour SHUBIN 1921- (American)
Citation Record: 1 Book
The Captain - *Single*
Stein US (1982)

Lynn LASH

was one of the best-known 'scientific detectives' of the 1930s. He spent most of his time outwitting wily orientals whose main aim in life was, apparently, to destroy the USA. He did so, seemingly exclusively, in stories in *Ten Detective Aces.*
American Male Detective in Pulp Magazines operating in USA

Lester DENT 1904-1959 (American)
Invented 9 detectives - see Chance MALLOY
Citation Record: 3 Novelets in 1 collection
The Sinister Ray - *Only*
Gryphon US (1987)

Simon LASH

is a hardboiled, cynical ex-lawyer who now works as a private detective from his home on Harper Avenue, Hollywood. His main interest in life is his collection of books, and they play an important part in his cases.
American Male Private Detective operating in Hollywood
Sidekick: Eddie SLOCUM
American Male - Assistant

Frank GRUBER 1904-1969 (American)
Invented 8 detectives - see Johnny FLETCHER and Sam CRAGG
Citation Record: 3 Books
Simon Lash, Private Detective - *First*
Farrar & Rinehart US (1941)

Simon Lash, Detective - *First**
Nicholson & Watson UK (1943)

Murder 97 - *Last*
Rinehart US (1948); Barker UK (1956)

Dan LASSITER

is a medical student faced with the dissection of his first cadaver. He comes to believe that the dead young man was the victim of foul play and sets out to discover the truth.

American Male Amateur operating in Boston

Marshall GOLDBERG (American)

is a surgeon, a director of medical education and a TV scriptwriter.

Citation Record: 1 Book

The Anatomy Lesson - *Only*
Putnam US (1974)

Jake LASSITER

is a high-priced lawyer who investigates complex cases of theft and murder.

American Male Amateur operating in Florida

Paul LEVINE 1948- (American)

Citation Record: 5 Books

To Speak For The Dead - *First*
Bantam US (1990); Hamish Hamilton UK (1990)

Slashback - *Latest*
Morrow US (1995)

Luke LASSITER

American Male Private Detective operating in Chicago

Ross H SPENCER 1921- (American)

Invented 7 detectives - see Buzz DECKARD

Citation Record: 1 Book

Monastery Nightmares - *Single*
Mysterious Press US (1986)

Grace LATHAM

is a beautiful widow, in her thirties, from Georgetown. In a subsequent series she meets *Col PRIMROSE* and together they make a formidable sleuthing duo. However, in this book she manages to do the necessary without him.

American Female Private Detective operating in USA

Leslie FORD 1898-1983 (American)

was born in Smith River, California. She graduated from the University of Washington, Seattle, 1921, and later held several teaching posts at US universities before becoming a full-time writer in 1927. She lived in England with her husband in the 1930s and her early books were set in England and writtten under the byline of *David FROME.*

She became a war correspondent in the Second World War and then returned to the USA.

Writer: Mrs Zenith Jones BROWN

Other Detectives:

Ben DAVIDGE	Porteus Alexander HARP
Lt Joseph KELLY	Col John PRIMROSE
Col John PRIMROSE and Grace LATHAM	

Citation Record: 1 Book

Three Bright Pebbles - *Only*
Farrar & Rinehart US (1938); Collins UK (1938)

Grace LATHAM

Second detective of Col John PRIMROSE

Charles LATIMER

is a novelist living in Greece and neighbouring parts in the period just before the outbreak of the Second World War. He is the protagonist in this thrilling story of espionage.

British Male Amateur operating in Middle East

Eric AMBLER 1909- (British)

Invented 4 detectives - see Dr Jan CZISSAR

Citation Record: 1 Book

The Mask Of Demetrios - *Only*
Hodder & Stoughton UK (1939)

A Coffin For Demetrios - *Only**
Knopf US (1939)

Charles LATIMER and James LATIMER

are two cousins who were killed in 1870, during the Franco-Prussian war. They return as spirits in order to help out their descendants and others, solving mysteries as they do so.

British Male Amateurs operating in France

Manning COLES (British)

See main detective Tommy HAMBLEDON

Citation Record: 3 Books

Brief Candles - *First*
Doubleday US (1954)

Come And Go - *Last*
Doubleday US (1958)

Francis GAITE 1891-1959 (British)

For writer details see Tommy HAMBLEDON

Citation Record: 3 Books

Brief Candles - *First*
Hodder & Stoughton UK (1954)

Come And Go - *Last*
Hodder & Stoughton UK (1958)

James LATIMER

Second detective of Charles LATIMER

Vince LATIMER

American Male Private Detective operating in Western USA

Paul KRUGER 1917- (American)

Writer: Roberta Elizabeth SEBENTHAL

Inventor of one other detective Phil KRAMER

Citation Record: 1 Book

A Bullet For A Blonde - *Only*
Dell US (1958)

Max LATIN

was one of this author's numerous pulp detectives. He appeared in many short stories, some of which are in the collection cited. Well-dressed always, he ran a restaurant, and his reputation for being a crook stood him in good stead when it came to solving his cases.

American Male Private Detective operating in USA

Sidekick: GUITERREZ

was the chef in *LATIN's* restaurant and fronted for him when necessary.

American Male - Chef

Norbert DAVIS 1909-1949 (American)

Invented 8 detectives - see Ben SHALEY

Citation Record: 5 Short Stories in 1 Collection

The Adventures Of Max Latin - *Collection 1*
Mysterious Press US (1988)

Annie LAURANCE

is a bookseller and owns a shop called Death on Demand on Broward's Rock Island, South Carolina. This coastal resort is plagued by murders, most of which seem to revolve around the bookshop. Fortunately she is an excellent amateur sleuth, especially so when assisted by her boyfriend.

American Female Amateur operating in USA

Sidekick: Max DARLING

American Male - Boyfriend

Carolyn G HART 1936- (American)

was born in Oklahoma City and graduated from the University of Oklahoma with a BA in Journalism, 1958. She has been a reporter and subsequently was appointed Professor of Journalism at the University of Oklahoma.

Writer: Carolyn Gimpel HART

Inventor of one other detective Henrietta O'Dwyer COLLINS

Citation Record: 8 Books
Death On Demand - *First*
Bantam US (1987)
Southern Ghost - *Latest*
Bantam US (1992)

Lauren LAURANO

is single, of Italian descent and in her middle forties. She lives in Greenwich Village and is a liberal in politics and lesbian by nature. She endured an early rape, studied law, joined the New York Police Department, and was retired after accidentally shooting her partner in a stake-out (a distressingly common feat, it seems, among American cops, male and female, whose creators wish to give them experience and then get them out into the private sector). She now runs a one-woman private detective agency, carries three guns and solves crimes brilliantly. In books that are highly entertaining, wonderfully plotted, beautifully literate and totally unbelievable, she is a good example of the modern fantasy that the American PI has become – particularly the female of the species. She has a police stooge, of course, to give her some legitimacy: he must be one of the dumbest and most useless in the history of the genre.

American Female Private Detective operating in New York

Stooge: Lt Peter CECCHI
is a friendly cop who can't credit a female detective's abilities. Yet he himself seems so useless when it comes to crimebusting that it is difficult to see how he ever got into the New York police force.
American Male

L

Sandra SCOPPETONE 1936- (American)
For writer details see Fortune FANELLI
Citation Record: 2 Books
Everything You Have Is Mine - *First*
Little, Brown US (1991); Virago UK (1992)
My Sweet Untraceable You - *Latest*
Little, Brown US (1994)

Det Insp Arvo LAURILA

is a Finnish police detective in investigatory mood.

Finnish Policeman operating in Finland/Italy

Ona LOW
Citation Record: 2 Books
To His Just Deserts - *First*
Collins UK (1986)
Murky Shallows - *Latest*
Collins UK (1987)

Ambrose LAVENDALE

British Male Amateur operating in several locations

E Phillips OPPENHEIM 1866-1946 (British)
Invented 27 detectives - see Nicholas GOADE
Citation Record: 8 Short Stories in 1 Collection
Ambrose Lavendale, Diplomat - *Collection 1*
Hodder & Stoughton UK (1920)

Jimmie LAVENDER

was named by the author after a famous Chicago Cubs baseball pitcher. He appears in a number of mainly puzzle-type stories.

American Male Private Detective operating in USA

Vincent STARRETT 1886-1974 (American)
was born in Toronto, Canada, and educated at public schools in Chicago. A journalist, war correspondent and editor, he wrote several genre novels and was the author of literary studies and biographies. He is best known as one of the founding fathers of the researches undertaken into what is now called Sherlockiana and was the co-founder, with Christopher Morley, of the Baker Street Irregulars. He himself wrote one of the finest of all *Sherlock HOLMES* pastiches. He received the Mystery Writers of America Grand Master award, 1957.
Writer: Charles Vincent Emerson STARRETT
Other Detectives:
Riley BLACKWOOD, Sally CARDIFF, Walter GHOST, Sherlock HOLMES, George Washington TROXELL
Citation Record: 12 Short Stories in 1 Collection
The Case Book Of Jimmie Lavender - *Collection 1*
Gold Label US (1944)

Lt/Cdr Frank H LAWLESS

British Male Amateur operating in several locations

Rolf BENNETT (British)
See main detective James TURNER
Citation Record: 16 Short Stories in 2 Collections
The Adventures Of Lieutenant Lawless - *Collection 1*
Short stories - 8
Hodder & Stoughton UK (1915)
Commander Lawless, VC - *Collection 2*
Short stories - 8
Hodder & Stoughton UK (1916)

Jane LAWLESS

is a restaurateur, overt lesbian and part-time sleuth – a combination not altogether easy to handle.

American Female Amateur operating in Minneapolis

Sidekick: Cordelia THORN
is a theatrical friend who assists.
Female - Friend

Ellen HART (American)
Inventor of one other detective Sophie GREENAWAY
Citation Record: 5 Books
Hallowed Murder - *First*
Seal US (1989); Seal UK (1989)
A Small Sacrifice - *Latest*
Seal US (1994)

Det Joe LAWLESS, Offr Barbara BABALINO and Det Leo GRADY

Joe LAWLESS is a tough, street-smart, ruthless cop and his battles with the brass have landed him in Siberia (the squad's name for the 53rd Precinct, where particularly hard types hang out). Also in Siberia is *Barbara BABALINO,* who has been sent there by her venomous boss as a punishment for resisting his advances. And there too is *Leo GRADY,* nearing retirement, who thinks that, with a flask of vodka in his pocket, he can take it easy. But nothing's easy in Siberia.

Two American Policemen and one American Policewoman operating in New York

Tom PHILBIN (American)
See main detective George BENTON
Citation Record: 7 Books
Precinct: Siberia - *First*
GM US (1985); Sphere Books UK (1989)
Death Sentence - *Latest*
GM US (1990)

Algy LAWRENCE

solves a case of death by strangulation in a locked room.

British Male Amateur operating in England

Derek SMITH (British)
Citation Record: 1 Book
Whistle Up The Devil - *Only*
Gifford UK (1953)

Merrick LAWRENCE

British Sleuth

N Wesley FIRTH 1920-1949 (British)
See main detective Al MCFEE

Citation Record: 3 Books

Deceit - *First*
Hamilton Stafford UK (1946)

Good Time Lady - *Last*
Hughes UK (ca 1947)

Mignon LAWRENCE

works as a spy for the New York Police Department, setting up a barber shop in the fictional mining town of Bearopolis in New Mexico.

American Female Private Detective operating in New Mexico

Stooge: Joe PHOENIX
American Male

Albert W AIKEN 1846-1894 (American)

Invented 5 detectives - see Hilda SIRENE

Citation Record: 1 Book

The Female Barber Detective; Or, Joe Phoenix In Silver City - *Only*
Beadle & Adams US (1895)

Harry LAWSON

is a former stage magician. One of the author's few series detectives, he appears in several short stories.

Canadian Male Amateur operating in Montreal

William BANKIER 1925- (Canadian)

was born in Belleville, Ontario, Canada. An advertising copywriter and radio announcer, he was also a most prolific writer of short stories in both the criminous and romantic genres. He is probably unique in having had several dozen detective stories published in *Ellery Queen's Mystery Magazine* and several dozen romantic stories (under various feminine bylines) in *Woman's Weekly*. He seems to have had neither the time nor the inclination to write a novel.

Inventor of one other detective Penni DANDRIDGE

Citation Record: 1 Selected Short Story

Wednesday Night At The Forum
appeared in the August number.
In 'Alfred Hitchcock's Mystery Magazine' US (1977)

Loretta LAWSON

is a young social worker, in the usual trouble with husband and boyfriend. She manages to become involved with various kinds of murder, which she investigates.

British Female Amateur operating in England

Joan SMITH 1953- (British)

was born in London.

Citation Record: 5 Books

A Masculine Ending - *First*
Faber UK (1987); Scribner's US (1988)

Full Stop - *Latest*
Chatto & Windus UK (1995)

The LAWYER DETECTIVE

American Male Detective in Pulp Magazines operating in USA

Will WINCH (American)

Other Detectives:

Kail HUTTON	LITTLE BRAVO
The MARINE DETECTIVE	WOLVERINE WAIF

Citation Record: 1 Selected Short Story

The Lawyer Detective; Or, The Mystery At Three Oaks Ranch
Old Cap Collier Library US (18??)

Prof LAXTON

solves a case in which a man is murdered in the presence of several witnesses, one of whom must be guilty.

British Male Amateur operating in England

R A J WALLING 1869-1949 (British)

Invented 3 detectives - see Philip TOLEFREE

Citation Record: 1 Book

Murder At The Keyhole - *Only*
Methuen UK (1929); Morrow US (1929)

John T LAXWORTHY

British Male Amateur operating in France

E Phillips OPPENHEIM 1866-1946 (British)

Invented 27 detectives - see Nicholas GOADE

Citation Record: 12 Short Stories in 1 Collection

Mr Laxworthy's Adventures - *Collection 1*
Cassell UK (1913)

Austin LAYMAN

is a famous biographer of Emerson and belongs to an exclusive literary society. When a member is murdered, he is invited to investigate so that the scandal of a police investigation can be circumvented.

American Male Amateur operating in Boston

John MCALEER 1923- (American)

Writer: John Joseph MCALEER

Citation Record: 1 Book

Coign Of Vantage; Or, The Boston Athenaeum Murders - *Single*
Foul Play US (1988)

Anne LAYTON and David LAYTON

British Female Amateur and British Male Amateur operating in Burma

Marion ROBERTS (British)

Citation Record: 2 Books

Red Greed - *First*
Eldon UK (1934)

A Mask For Crime - *Last*
Eldon UK (1935)

David LAYTON

Second detective of Anne LAYTON

Peter LAYTON

has to find a National Intelligence Agency colleague who has defected. He then has to try to kill him.

American Male Professional Investigator operating in USA

Richard P FRENCH (American)

Citation Record: 1 Book

A Spy Is Forever - *Only*
Tuttle US (1970)

Det LAZARD

American Policeman operating in USA

Stephen DOBYNS 1941- (American)

See main detective Charlie BRADSHAW

Citation Record: 1 Book

Dancer With One Leg - *Single*
Dutton US (1983)

Isaac LAZARUS

Egyptian Male Detective in Pulp Magazines operating in USA

Gilbert JEROME (American)

Invented 5 detectives - see Jack DONAHUE

Citation Record: 1 Selected Short Story

Isaac Lazarus, The Egyptian Detective
Old Cap Collier Library US (18??)

Miles LE BRETON

American Male Amateur operating in New England

John ESTEVEN 1888-1954 (American)

See main detective Insp Rae NORSE

Citation Record: 2 Books

By Night At Dinsmore - *First*
Doubleday US (1935); Harrap UK (1935)

While Murder Waits - *Last*
Doubleday US (1937); Harrap UK (1936)

Richard LE GRANDE

American Male Sleuth operating in USA/Vietnam

Irwin R BLACKER 1919- (British)

Writer: Irwin Robert BLACKER

Citation Record: 2 Books

The Kilroy Gambit - *First*
World US (1960)

Search And Destroy - *Last*
Random House US (1966)

The Valley Of Hanoi - *Last**
Cassell UK (1966)

Frank LE ROUX

appears in this spoof detective story as a young, black and most beautiful woman, with the reputation of being the finest investigator in the world. She is specially summoned to Cambridge to solve a case of world-shattering importance.

American Female Professional Amateur operating in Cambridge

Hosanna BROWN

Citation Record: 1 Book

I Spy, You Die - *Single*
Gollancz UK (1984)

Rolf LE ROUX

is benign of countenance and an inveterate pipe smoker. Behind his bushy whiskers, however, is a razor-sharp intellect, which he uses to solve the cases of his nephew, Inspector Joubert of the Capetown police. He appeared, mainly in US magazines of the early 1950s, in several short stories, many of them being of the locked-room mystery kind.

South African Male Amateur operating in Capetown

L

Peter GODFREY 1917-1992 (South African)

Citation Record: 2 Selected Short Stories

The Flung-Back Lid
involves a stabbing in a cable car in which the victim was alone. It also appears in *John Creasey's Crime Collection 1979*.
In 'John Creasey's Crime Magazine' UK (1979)

Kill And Tell
In 'Ellery Queen's Mystery Magazine' US (1950)

Ty LEANDER

American Male Amateur operating in USA

Helen NIELSEN 1918- (American)

Invented 3 detectives - see Simon DRAKE

Citation Record: 1 Book

Sin Me A Murder - *Only*
Morrow US (1960); Gollancz UK (1961)

Lt Joe LEAPHORN

is a police officer who is also a member of the Navajo tribe. A lieutenant in the Navajo Tribal Police, his cases are heavily involved with Indian custom and law. He appears also in other books with the author's other detective, *Sgt Jim CHEE.*

American Policeman operating in Arizona

Tony HILLERMAN 1925- (American)

was born in Sacred Heart, Oklahoma. He was raised among US Indian tribes and later attended Oklahoma State University, Stillwater, and the University of Oklahoma to study Journalism. He received an MA in English from the University of New Mexico, Albuquerque, 1965. He served with distinction in the US Army in the Second World War, being awarded the Bronze Star and Purple Heart. A distinguished reporter and the sometime Professor of Journalism at the University of New Mexico, he received the Mystery Writers of America Edgar Allan Poe award, 1974.

Writer: Anthony Grove HILLERMAN

Other Detectives:
Sgt Jim CHEE   John COTTON
Lt Joe LEAPHORN and Sgt Jim CHEE

Citation Record: 3 Books

The Blessing Way - *First*
Harper & Row US (1970); Macmillan UK (1970)

Listening Woman - *Latest*
Harper & Row US (1978); Macmillan UK (1979)

Lt Joe LEAPHORN and Sgt Jim CHEE

also appear individually in other books by this author.

American Policemen operating in Arizona

Tony HILLERMAN 1925- (American)

Invented 4 detectives - see Lt Joe LEAPHORN

Citation Record: 6 Books

Skinwalkers - *First*
Harper & Row US (1987); Joseph UK (1988)

Sacred Clowns - *Latest*
Joseph UK (1993)

Danny LEATHER

British Male Amateur operating in England

David LAWRENCE 1920- (British)

Writer: David Henry St Lawrence MORRIS

Citation Record: 2 Books

Dead Orchid - *First*
Ward, Lock UK (1958)

Death Has Two Hands - *Last*
Ward, Lock UK (1958)

Col Gantian LEATHERMOUTH

British Male Professional Investigator operating in several locations

Carlton DAWE 1865-1935 (British)

Writer: William Carlton Lanyon DAWE

Inventor of one other detective Reginald COSWAY

Citation Record: 10 Books

Leathermouth - *First*
Ward, Lock UK (1931)

Tough Company - *Last*
Ward, Lock UK (1936)

Commissaire LEBEL

is a latter-day *Insp JAVETT* and his hunt to find the assassin known as the Jackal is surely one of the most thrilling in contemporary fiction.

French Policeman operating in France

Sidekick: Insp CARON
is the assistant of *LEBEL* and does important work in tracking down the Jackal in this one outstanding novel.
French Male - Assistant

Frederick FORSYTH 1938- (British)

was born in Ashford, Kent, and educated at Tonbridge School, Kent. He worked as a journalist for newspapers and Reuters, and as a diplomatic correspondent for British radio and TV. His first book was an outstanding success and has been followed by less than half a dozen more. He received the Mystery Writers of America award, 1971.

Citation Record: 1 Book

The Day Of The Jackal - *Only*
Hutchinson UK (1971); Viking US (1971)

Paula LEBETWOOD

Second detective of Supt SALT

Insp LECAIN

French Policeman operating in Paris

Francis DIDELOT 1902- (French)

Writer: Roger Francis DIDELOT

Inventor of one other detective Commissaire Orestes BIGNON

Citation Record: 2 Books

Murder In The Bath - *First*
is a translation from the French.
Lippincott US (1933)

Death Of The Deputy - *Last*
is a translation from the French of *L'Assassin du Député.*
Lippincott US (1935)

Monsieur LECOQ

French Male Amateur operating in France

Sidekick: Father ABSINTHE
is usually drunk but aids the detective in his first case.
French Male - Assistant

Emile GABORIAU 1833-1873 (French)

is second in importance only to *Edgar Allan POE* in the history of detective fiction, for he was the first to write a full-length detective novel, for which he followed and elaborated the rules already laid down by *POE.* The British detective story was to follow his pattern rather than the one set by *Wilkie COLLINS,* which had placed the detective into the framework of the conventional English novel.

Citation Record: 3 Books

The Mystery Of Orcival - *First*
Holt US (1871); Routledge UK (1887)

Crime At Orcival - *First**
Abridged.
Harvill UK (1952)

The Slaves Of Paris - *Last*
Estes US (1882); Routledge UK (1897)

Hannibal LECTER and Clarice STERLING

Hannibal LECTER is a psychotic killer, a psychiatrist so mentally brilliant, so demonic physically, that he must be kept in isolation. For complex reasons, he uses his detective powers to help a young FBI trainee, *Clarice STERLING,* in her search for another serial killer.
American Male Amateur and American Policewoman operating in USA

Thomas HARRIS 1940- (American)

was born in Mississippi, Missouri.
Inventor of one other detective Will GRAHAM

Citation Record: 1 Book

The Silence Of The Lambs - *Single*
St Martin's US (1988); Heinemann UK (1988)

Romulus LEDBETTER

is Afro-American, a past musician of some genius, a paranoid personality who has dropped out of Manhattan life, and he lives in some sort of cave in the Park. When a frozen corpse is discovered nearby, the entire brains of New York's finest are baffled. They despair not, however, for the disturbed, troglodytic ex-troubadour does things his way.
American Male Amateur operating in New York

George Dawes GREEN (American)

was born in Idaho and practises as a journalist.

Citation Record: 1 Book

Caveman - *Single*
Little, Brown US (1994)

Const LEE

British Policeman operating in London

Edgar WALLACE 1875-1932 (British)

Invented 28 detectives - see J G REEDER

Citation Record: 9 Short Stories in 1 Collection

The Undisclosed Client - *Collection 1*
contains stories that had appeared in various magazines earlier.
Digit UK (1963)

Capt Andrew LEE

Second detective of Bill MANDELL

Anna LEE

works for the London detective agency, Brierly Security.
British Female Private Detective operating in London

Sidekick: Bernie SCHILLER
is the detective's main assistant.
Male - Assistant

Liza CODY 1944- (British)

was born in London. Although her real name has not been disclosed, she is said to be a painter and graphic artist as well as the author of a highly successful series of books with a lively female detective.

Citation Record: 5 Books

Dupe - *First*
Collins UK (1980); Scribner's US (1983)

Under Contract - *Latest*
Collins UK (1986); Scribner's US (1987)

Sgt/Insp Brian 'Bonny' LEE

British Policeman operating in England

George DOUGLAS 1902-1981 (British)

See main detective pair Insp HALLAN and Sgt SPRATT

Citation Record: 3 Books

Death On The Doorstep - *First*
Hale UK (1973)

Crime Without Reason - *Last*
Hale UK (1975)

David LEE

appears in this gothic tale of horror and mystery.
American Male Amateur operating in New Jersey

Charles Lee SWEM (American)

was a secretary to the US president, Woodrow Wilson.

Citation Record: 1 Book

Werewolf - *Only*
Hutchinson UK (1928); Doubleday US (1929)

L

Gaff LEE

Australian Male Amateur operating in Australia

W T STEWART (Australian)

Writer: William Thomas STEWART

Citation Record: 4 Books

Gaff Lee, Detective - *First*
New Century AU (1940)

Red Agents - *Last*
Condor AU (1944)

Gerry LEE

is a London-based newspaperman who visits the University of Texas to give some lectures. When the Professor of English dies in suspicious circumstances, he turns sleuth.
British Male Amateur operating in England/Texas

Kenneth HOPKINS 1914-1988 (British)

See main detective pair Prof Gideon MANCIPLE and Dr William BLOW

Citation Record: 4 Books

The Girl Who Died - *First*
Macdonald UK (1955)

Campus Corpse - *Last*
Macdonald UK (1963)

Gypsy Rose LEE and Biff BRANNIGAN

Gypsy Rose LEE is, indeed, the famous strip-tease artiste who made her art fashionable. *Biff BRANNIGAN* is a comic who works in burlesque with her. They sleuth together in at least the first book, solve two cases of murder and are eventually married.
American Female Amateur and American Male Amateur operating in New York/Texas

Gypsy Rose LEE 1914-1970 (American)

was a famous burlesque actress. She became renowned as the strip-tease artiste who lifted her act into the *milieu* of respectability. Her two books, ostensibly dealing with murder behind the scenes, were published under her stage name although they were, in fact, written by *Craig RICE.*

Writer: Rose Louise HOVICK

Citation Record: 2 Books

The G-String Murders - *First*
Simon & Schuster US (1941)
Lady Of Burlesque - *First**
Tower US (1942)
The Strip-Tease Murders - *First**
Lane UK (1943)
Mother Finds A Body - *Last*
Simon & Schuster US (1944); Lane UK (1944)

Judith LEE

is a teacher of deaf and dumb children and an expert at lip-reading, an attribute that enables her to stumble across crimes that others are not aware of.

British Female Amateur operating in several locations

Richard MARSH 1867-1915 (British)

Invented 10 detectives - see The Hon Augustus CHAMPNELL

Citation Record: 12 Short Stories in 1 Collection

Judith Lee, Some Pages From Her Life - *Collection 1*
Methuen UK (1912)

The Adventures Of Judith Lee - *Collection 1**
Methuen UK (1916)

Largely LEE

British Male Amateur operating in England

Evelyn HARRIS (British)

Citation Record: 2 Books

Largely Luck - *First*
Hale UK (1985)

Largely Trouble - *Latest*
Hale UK (1986)

L

Mark LEE and Carl BROWNE

American Male Sleuths operating in USA

Bob HAM (American)

Citation Record: 8 Books

Atlanta Burn - *First*
Bantam US (1989)

Nebraska Nightmare - *Latest*
Bantam US (1990)

Nelson LEE

was, after *Sexton BLAKE*, the best-known of the detectives that flooded British boys' magazines after the advent of *Sherlock HOLMES*. He appeared first in 1894, in the Harmsworth magazine, *Pluck*, his creator being *Maxwell SCOTT*.

Nelson LEE had his headquarters in Gray's Inn Road, in Holborn. He was very *HOLMES*-like at first, hawk-faced and much given to wearing a dressing-gown and knitting his brows in thought. In early stories he worked with a French detective, Jean Moreau, the French connection then being fashionable. However, the latter was soon discarded and *LEE* worked his way through adventures in many magazines of the period until, in 1915, he was given his own magazine, *The Nelson Lee Library*, to which many authors contributed stories, which ran into hundreds. He shared many of his early adventures with *Eileen DARE*, a girl detective who was an invaluable and, it goes without saying, inviolate assistant.

LEE eventually went to St Frank's, a fictional British public school, similar to the more famous Greyfriars of *Frank HAMILTON*, to help solve a crime there. He stayed on and became a detective-schoolmaster, only occasionally going back to Gray's Inn Road to deal with special cases, often at the government's request.

The Nelson Lee Library closed in 1933, merging with the new magazine for boys, *The Gem*, where his detective exploits continued for some years. An illustrative selection of stories by several authors is cited.

British Male Amateur operating in England

Sidekick: NIPPER
was a street urchin who was taken in by *LEE* and became his most important assistant in countless stories. He appeared in the very first story and continued to appear in stories until the end. When *Nelson LEE* went to St Frank's, *NIPPER* was found a place as a pupil.
British Male - Assistant

John ANDREWS 1880-1929 (British)

See main detective Ferrers LOCKE

Citation Record: 1 Book

The Beggars Of Kashapore - *Only*
was an adaptation of a *Sexton BLAKE* story, *The Rajah's Revenge*.
Amalgamated UK (1938)

Edwy Searles BROOKS 1889-1965 (British)

Invented 5 detectives - see Insp William (The Grouser) BEEKE

Citation Record: 2 Books

The Return Of Zingrave - *First*
Amalgamated UK (1923)

The Wonder Craft - *Last*
Amalgamated UK (1923)

Maxwell SCOTT (American)

Writer: John STANIWORTH

Other Detectives:
Martin DALE   Vernon READ

Citation Record: 12 Books

A Dead Man's Secret - *Special*
is the story in which *Nelson LEE* and *NIPPER* first appeared. It was published later in book form by *Amalgamated* (UK 1907) as *The Great Unknown*.
Pluck UK (1894)

Birds Of Prey - *First*
Amalgamated UK (1906)

Detective Warder Nelson Lee - *Last*
Amalgamated UK (1920)

Norma 'Nicky' LEE

was also known as 'The Beautiful Gunner'.

American Female Sleuth operating in New York

Norma LEE (American)

Citation Record: 4 Books

The Beautiful Gunner - *First*
Laurie UK (1953)

The Broadway Jungle - *Last*
Laurie UK (1954)

Quong LEE

is one of the wonderful London characters of the 1920s and 1930s that this author was so brilliant at depicting. The settings for the *Quong LEE* stories is Limehouse, London's Chinatown at that time, which had an unsavoury if undeserved reputation.

Chinese Male Amateur operating in London

Thomas BURKE 1886-1945 (British)

was born in London. Brought up in an orphanage, he had little formal education, and he did several kinds of job until, in 1913, he had his first work published. He wrote his detective stories only as a side-line, for his life was devoted to writing about the London he knew and loved. His books have a most enduring and endearing quality and deserve a place of honour to themselves.

Citation Record: 29 Short Stories 2 Collections

Limehouse Nights - *Collection 1*
Short stories - 13
Richards UK (1916); McBride US (1917)

The Pleasantries Of Old Quong - *Collection 2*
Short stories - 16
Constable UK (1931)

A Tea-Shop In Limehouse - *Collection 2**
Little, Brown US (1931)

Steve LEE
American Male Private Detective operating in Memphis

Charlie WELLS (American)
Writer: Charles Harding WELLS
Citation Record: 1 Book
The Last Kill - *Only*
Signet US (1955)

Tommy LEE
is half Chinese and half Russian. After working for US Military Intelligence in Vietnam he now heads East-West Investigations, an agency that has offices in the USA and Asia.
Eurasian Male Private Detective operating in San Francisco

Owen PARK (American)
House name.
Citation Record: 1 Book
The Chinatown Connection - *First*
Pinnacle US (1977)

Mrs LEEDS
Second detective of Mrs TYRELL

Insp LEFARGE
Appears with at least two other detectives - see Insp BURNLEY

Lucius LEFFING
is a private detective and psychic investigator who lives in an old house at 7 Autumn Street, New Haven. An old-fashioned man who wishes he were a Victorian, he consumes vast amounts of that old-fashioned drink, sarsaparilla, when doing his detecting, in which activity he is assisted by the author himself.
American Male Professional Amateur operating in Connecticut
Sidekick: Joseph Payne BRENNAN
is the author of the stories and also appears in them as their fictional narrator.
American Male - Narrator

Joseph Payne BRENNAN 1918-1990 (American)
was the sometime librarian at Yale University. He was a writer almost exclusively of poetry and short stories, most of which deal with the weird and supernatural.
Citation Record: 38 Short Stories in 3 Collections
The Casebook Of Lucius Leffing - *Collection 1*
Short stories - 17
Macabre House UK (1973)
The Chronicles Of Lucius Leffing - *Collection 2*
Short stories - 8
Grant UK (1977)
The Adventures Of Lucius Leffing - *Collection 3*
Short stories - 13
Grant US (1990)

Insp Richard LEFT
British Policeman operating in England/Turkey

Charles FORSYTE (British)
is the joint pseudonym of a husband-and-wife team.
Writers: UNKNOWN and UNKNOWN
Inventor of one other detective Christopher MILNER-BROWN
Citation Record: 3 Books
Diplomatic Death - *First*
Cassell UK (1961); Morrow US (1961)
Double Death - *Last*
Cassell UK (1965)

LEGARDE
solves the mystery of how and why a boat-train has been made to disappear.
French Male Sleuth operating in England

Douglas G BROWNE 1884-1963 (British)
Writer: Douglas Gordon BROWNE
Other Detectives:
Maj Maurice HEMYOCK   Insp H H THEW
Harvey TUKE and Sir Bruton KAMES
Citation Record: 1 Book
The Stolen Boat-Train - *Only*
Methuen UK (1935)

Constance LEIDL
Second detective of Charles MEIKLEJOHN

David LEIGH
solves the disappearance of a body from a locked room.
British Male Amateur operating in England

Frank BARRETT 1848-1926 (British)
Invented 5 detectives - see Capt Thomas VERNAN
Citation Record: 1 Book
The Justification Of Andrew Lebrun - *Only*
Heinemann UK (1894); Appleton US (1894)

David LEIGH
solves the mystery of how and why a bullion coach disappeared from a moving train.
British Male Amateur operating in England

E G BARTLETT 1920- (British)
Writer: Eric George BARTLETT
Citation Record: 1 Book
The Case Of The Thirteenth Coach - *Only*
Staples UK (1958)

Rosalind LEIGH and Sgt HAWKSLEY
Rosalind LEIGH is a writer who is given a chance to write up the story of a woman serving a long sentence for matricide. Working with *Sgt HAWKSLEY*, who was the arresting officer, she becomes convinced that the real killer is still at large and sets out to learn the truth, which puts both sleuths at risk.
British Female Amateur and British Male Ex-Policeman operating in England

Minette WALTERS (British)
Invented 3 detectives - see Sgt Andy MCLOUGHLIN
Citation Record: 1 Book
The Sculptress - *Single*
Macmillan UK (1993); St Martin's US (1993)

Simon LEIGH
British Male Secret Agent operating in several locations

Richard TEMPLE (British)
Citation Record: 2 Books
Spy Is A Dirty Word - *First*
Hale UK (1970)
The Schulsinger Affair - *Last*
Hale UK (1971)

Alex LEIGHTON
was once a 'cult de-programmer' and is now a detective on a case in India, in search of a woman who has disappeared.
British Male Private Detective operating in India

Joyce SPARLING
Citation Record: 1 Book
North Of Delhi, East Of Heaven - *Single*
Walker US (1988)

Luke LEIGHTON
American Male Detective in Pulp Magazines operating in USA

Harry ROCKWOOD 1859-1932 (American)
Invented 14 detectives - see Clarice DYKE
Citation Record: 1 Book
Luke Leighton, The Government Detective - *Only*
Ogilvie US (1884)

Shirley LEIGHTON and Bill HARPER
American Female Detective and American Male Amateurs operating in Miami

Paul ERNST 1886- (American)

Inventor of 5detectives - see Lt Jim RYAN, Shirley LEIGHTON and Bill HARPER

Citation Record: 1 Book

Lady, Get Your Gun - *Only*
Mill US (1955)

A Rose From The Dead - *Only**
Cassell UK (1956)

Shirley LEIGHTON and Bill HARPER

Second detective pair of Lt Jim RYAN

Gwynn LEITH and Colin KEATS

are husband and wife. She is a famous writer who is very good at both discovering and solving cases of murder. He assists.

American Male Amateur and American Female Amateur operating in USA

Viola Brothers SHORE 1895- (American)

Inventor of one other detective Shirley HOLMES

Citation Record: 2 Books

The Beauty-Mask Murder - *First*
Smith US (1930)

The Beauty-Mask Mystery - *First*
Hamilton UK (1932)

Murder On The Glass Floor - *Last*
Smith US (1932); Harrap UK (1933)

Lester LEITH

was formerly a confidence trickster. Now an amateur sleuth, he is a Robin Hood character who takes from crooks to give to others, including himself. He appeared, 1929-1941, in stories (uncited) in *Detective Fiction Weekly.*

American Male Amateur operating in USA

L

Erle Stanley GARDNER 1889-1970 (American)

Invented 14 detectives - see Perry MASON

Citation Record: 1 Selected Short Story

The Exact Opposite
appeared in the December number.
In 'Ellery Queen's Mystery Magazine' US (1951)

Sir Edward LEITHEN

is a lawyer, a rather quiet man, who becomes involved in treachery and espionage. He was the second of the author's spy-detectives, although his books did not have the staying power of those with *Richard HANNAY.*

British Male Professional Amateur operating in England

John BUCHAN 1875-1940 (British)

Invented 3 detectives - see Richard HANNAY

Citation Record: 3 Books

The Power-House - *First*
Blackwood UK (1916); Doran US (1916)

Sick Heart River - *Last*
Hodder & Stoughton UK (1941)

Mountain Meadow - *Last**
Houghton Mifflin US (1941)

Joe LELAND

was in the Army Air Force and was once a cop. He has set up an agency called Leland Associates in Malibu.

American Male Private Detective operating in Malibu Beach

Roderick THORP 1936- (American)

Writer: Roderick Mayne THORP Jr

Citation Record: 2 Books

The Detective - *First*
Dial US (1966); Barker UK (1967)

Nothing Lasts Forever - *Latest*
Norton US (1979); Corgi UK (1981)

Die Hard - *Latest**
Ivy US (1988)

Quinn LELAND

American Male Sleuth operating in Far East

Franklin DAVIS 1918-1981 (American)

Writer: Franklin Milton DAVIS

Citation Record: 2 Books

Kiss The Tiger - *First*
Pyramid US (1961)

Secret Hong Kong - *Last*
Pyramid US (1962)

Miriam LEMAIRE

British Female Amateur operating in England

Coralie STANTON (British)

Writers: Alice Cecil Seymour HOSKEN 1877- and Ernest Charles Heath HOSKEN

Citation Record: 12 Short Stories in 1 Collection

Miriam Lemaire, Moneylender - *Collection 1*
Cassell UK (1906)

The Adventuress - *Collection 1**
McBride US (1907)

Ch Insp/Supt LENNOX

British Policeman operating in England

John WAINWRIGHT 1921- (British)

was born in Leeds, Yorkshire. Educated at local schools, he took an external LLB from the University of London, 1956. He saw active service with the Royal Air Force, 1940-1945, and served as a police officer in Yorkshire, 1947-1969. He is the author of at least seventy-seven genre novels, in which he has created several police detectives, nearly always as individuals rather than as team members of police procedurals.

Writer: John William WAINWRIGHT

Other Byline: Jack RIPLEY

Other Detectives:

Supt GILLIANT	Harry HARKER
Supt LEWIS	Insp David LYLE
Tom PILTER	RIPLEY
Asst Ch Const SULLIVAN	Harry THOMPSON

Citation Record: 3 Books

The Evidence I Shall Give - *First*
Macmillan UK (1974)

Dominoes - *Latest*
!See Appendix 2.
Macmillan UK (1980); St Martin's US (1980)

Bill LENNOX

appeared in the author's first short story for *Black Mask Magazine* in 1933 and then in twenty-six other stories by 1942. He then featured in four novels, of which one appeared under the *SHEPHERD* byline. *LENNOX* is not a true PI but a troubleshooter for General Consolidated Studios in Hollywood. In the later novels he has moved into the world of Las Vegas, which is well described. Early hardboiled, he was more than the stereotyped pulp detective and he was copied, in essence, by many later fictional Hollywood and Californian detectives.

American Male Professional Amateur operating in Hollywood/Las Vegas

W T BALLARD 1903-1980 (American)

was born in Cleveland, Ohio. He was a prolific writer and used nearly twenty pseudonyms. He began by writing countless short stories for the pulp magazines of the 1930s and 1940s. Later he turned to writing Western crime stories and he created (with *R J BELLEM)* the legendary *Dan TURNER,* Hollywood Detective. In the late 1950s he returned to detective fiction and created several new detectives.

Writer: Willis Todhunter BALLARD

Other Bylines:

Parker BONNER	Walt BRUCE
Nick CARTER	Neil MACNEIL
John SHEPHERD	

Other Detectives:

Red DRAKE	Mark FORAN
Lt Max HUNTER	

Citation Record: 2 Books 5 Short Stories in 1 Collection

Say Yes To Murder - *First*
was republished, with a change of title, under the following byline.
Putnam US (1942)

Murder Can't Stop - *Last*
McKay US (1946); Banner UK (ca 1950)

Hollywood Troubleshooter - *Collection 1*
Popular Library US (1984)

John SHEPHERD 1903-1980 (American)
For writer details see Bill LENNOX

Citation Record: 2 Books

Lights, Camera, Murder - *First*
Belmont US (1960)

Demise Of A Louse - *Last*
was previoulsy published, with a change of title, under the preceding byline.
Belmont US (1962)

Ursula LENORME
British Female Amateur operating in England

T W SPEIGHT 1830-1915 (British)
Invented 4 detectives - see Insp MALLESON

Citation Record: 1 Collection

Ursula Lenorme: Lady Companion - *Collection 1*
The stories in this book are spread across the chapters.
Digby UK (1909)

Insp LEONARD
British Policeman operating in England

Christopher LEE (British)

Citation Record: 1 Book

The Bath Detective - *Single*
Mandarin UK (1995)

Frank LEONARD and Foster GAINES
Frank LEONARD is a Harvard professor and inventor who is involved with *Foster GAINES*, a private investigator, in a semi-sci-fi mystery.
American Male Amateur and American Male Private Detective operating in New York

Fred MACISAAC 1886-1940 (American)
Invented 3 detectives - see Dick HADDEN

Citation Record: 1 Book

The Vanishing Professor - *Only*
Henry Waterson US (1927); Methuen UK (1939)

Dr David Vincent LEONARDO
solves a case of death by bludgeoning in a locked room.
American Male Amateur operating in USA

Warren B MURPHY 1933- (American)
Invented 8 detectives - see Julian 'Digger' BURROUGHS

Citation Record: 1 Book

Leonardo's Law - *Single*
Carlyle US (1978)

Capt LEOPOLD
is somewhat of an expert in solving 'impossible' crimes. He has appeared in many short stories, of which two are cited. Some have been collected.
American Policeman operating in USA

Edward D HOCH 1930- (American)
was born in Rochester, New York and educated at the University of Rochester, 1947-1949. One of the great names in modern mystery and detective fiction, he has written several novels. However, he is specially renowned for his work as a prolific writer of short stories, which number around seven hundred. He received the Mystery Writers of America Edgar Allan Poe short story award, 1968.

Writer: Edward Dentinger HOCH
Other Byline: Ellery QUEEN
Other Detectives:

Simon ARK	Sebastian BLUE
Henry BOWFORT	G K CHESTERTON
Carl CRADER and Earl JAZINE	Al DARLAN
Paul DRAYER	Barney HAMET
Dr Sam HAWTHORNE	Sherlock HOLMES
Libby KNOWLES	Philip MARLOWE
MCLOVE	Sir Gideon PARROT
Harry PONDER	Tommy PRESTON
RAND	Sgt ROMANO
Nick VELVET	

Citation Record: 2 Selected Short Stories 19 Short Stories in 1 Collection

Captain Leopold And The Vanishing Men - *Latest*
appeared in the July number.
In 'Alfred Hitchcock's Mystery Magazine' US (1979)

The Vanishing Of Velma
appeared in the August number.
In 'Alfred Hitchcock's Mystery Magazine' US (1969)

Leopold's Way - *Collection 1*
contains stories that had appeared previously in various magazines.
Southern Illinois University US (1985)

Arsène LEPINE
Second detective of Herlock SOAMES

Louis LEPINE
has to solve a dastardly crime in the Paris of 1911.
French Male Amateur operating in France

Martin PAGE 1938- (American)

Citation Record: 1 Book

The Man Who Stole The Mona Lisa - *Single*
Pantheon US (1984)

Set A Thief - *Single**
Bodley Head UK (1984)

William LEQUEUX
British Male Amateur operating in England

William LEQUEUX 1864-1927 (British)
Invented 23 detectives - see Allan KENNEDY

Citation Record: 12 Short Stories in 1 Collection

In Secret - *Collection 1*
Odhams UK (1921)

Det Insp LERIC
is a member of a Midlands police force. He appears in police procedurals, having a great knowledge of police work because he was once a crime reporter.
British Policeman operating in England

Roger BUSBY 1941- (British)
was born in Leicester, Leicestershire. He has been a journalist and police information officer in the West Country.

Writer: Roger Charles BUSBY
Other Detectives:
Det Mick GARVEY   Det Sgt Tony ROWLEY

Citation Record: 5 Books

Robbery Blue - *First*
Collins UK (1969)

Pattern Of Violence - *Last*
Collins UK (1973)

Martin LEROY
Second detective of King DANWORTH

R J 'Rick' LEROY
appears also in two books with the author's main detective, *A J RAFFLES*.
British Male Amateur operating in several locations

Barry PEROWNE 1908-1985 (British)
was born in Redlynch, Wiltshire. He was educated at Central School, Oxford, and served in the Army, 1940-1943, and

in the Intelligence Corps, 1943-1945. An editor and publisher by profession, he wrote several novels and short stories, as well as a number of stories that continued the adventures of that great British crook-detective, *A J RAFFLES*, who was the creation of *E W HORNUNG*. In these later stories the hero, in accordance with the times, is rather more of a moral character than he once was. At any rate, he seems to do less in the way of burglary and more in the way of helping out the baffled police by his clever detective work.

Writer: Philip ATKEY

Other Detectives:
A J RAFFLES
A J RAFFLES and R J 'Rick' LEROY
A J RAFFLES and Sexton BLAKE

Citation Record: 1 Book 6 Short Stories in 2 Collections

I'm No Murderer - *Only*
Cassell UK (1938); Hillman-Curl US (1939)

Arrest These Men! - *Collection 1*
contains three novelettes.
Short stories - 3
Cassell UK (1932)

Ask No Mercy - *Collection 2*
contains three novelettes.
Short stories - 3
Cassell UK (1937)

R J 'Rick' LEROY
Second detective of A J RAFFLES

Mr LESLIE
is a lawyer who turns detective in this one Victorian novel.
British Male Amateur operating in London

Arthur GRIFFITHS 1838-1908 (British)
Invented 8 detectives - see Insp FASKE
Citation Record: 1 Book
Number 99 - *Only*
Chapman & Hall UK (1885); Munro US (1885)

Supt LESLIE
British Policeman operating in England

W Murdoch DUNCAN 1909-1975 (British)
Invented 8 detectives - see Supt MACNEILL
Citation Record: 2 Books
The Council Of Comforters - *First*
Long UK (1967)
The Green Triangle - *Last*
Long UK (1969)

LESSINGER
appears also in books with the author's other detective, *Insp SLADE*.
British Male Amateur operating in London

Richard ESSEX 1878- (British)
Writer: Richard Henry STARR
Inventor of one other detective pair Insp John SLADE and LESSINGER
Citation Record: 4 Books
Lessinger's Lapse - *First*
Amalgamated UK (1936)
Assisted By Lessinger - *Last*
Jenkins UK (1939)

LESSINGER
Second detective of Insp John SLADE

Dr Edward LESTER
American Male Amateur operating in Jacksonville

Eric LEVISON (American)
Citation Record: 3 Books
Hidden Eyes - *First*
Bobbs US (1920)
Ashes Of Evidence - *Last*
Bobbs US (1921)

Simon LESTER and Camilla HAVEN
British Male Amateur and British Female Amateur operating in Greece

Mary STEWART 1916- (British)
Invented 3 detectives - see Charity SELBOURNE
Citation Record: 1 Book
My Brother Michael - *Only*
Hodder & Stoughton UK (1960); Mill US (1960)

'Tiger' LESTER
British Male Secret Agent operating in several locations

Don BETTERIDGE 1897-1968 (British)
See main detective pair Insp DUNCAN and Capt Peter DARRELL
Citation Record: 12 Books
Balkan Spy - *First*
Jenkins UK (1942)
The Package Holiday Spy Case - *Last*
Hale UK (1962)

Insp/Supt Sholto LESTRADE
is, indeed, the famous plodding police stooge who appears, always in need of help, in several of the canonical *Sherlock HOLMES* stories. *M J TROW* has made him a detective in his own right, in a series of novels, all set in late-Victorian or Edwardian England. He is now his own butt. Comic, brilliant at puns, prone to accidents, usually outsmarted by an amateur, often wrong about the situation or plot, he nevertheless obeys the rules and he usually gets his man – not always by means of his own intellect. The canonical stories do not, it may be noted, appear to reveal a first name for *Insp LESTRADE*.
British Policeman operating in London

Sidekick: Sgt DICKENS
is one of four knockabout assistants who appear at times in the stories. All four of the buffoon detective's sidekicks are named after famed (and still extant) stores opened in Edwardian London, in this case, Dickens & Jones.
British Male - Assistant

Sidekick: Sgt JONES
is another assistant of *LESTRADE*, being named after famous stores opened in Edwardian London, in this case, Dickens & Jones.
British Male - Assistant

Sidekick: Sgt MARSHALL
is another assistant of *LESTRADE*, being named after a famous store opened in Edwardian London, in this case, Marshall & Snelgrove.
British Male - Assistant

Sidekick: Sgt SNELGROVE
is another assistant of *LESTRADE*, being named after a famous store opened in Edwardian London, in this case Marshall & Snelgrove.
British Male - Assistant

Sidekick: Emma LESTRADE
is *LESTRADE's* daughter. She joins in his hunt for the murderer of her lost lover.
British Female - Daughter

Stooge: Ch Supt ABBERLINE
appears in several of the author's novels featuring *LESTRADE*. A senior officer in the Metropolitan Police he was, in fact, an historical figure, who played no small part, it is now believed, in fouling up the investigations into the Jack the Ripper murders that occurred in London during 1888. Here, the author makes *LESTRADE* responsible to *ABBERLINE*, who is portrayed as a doddering and blundering ass.
British Male

Stooge: Sherlock HOLMES
appears, in one book of the series, as a kind of stooge in reverse. He is shown as being sadly in error in his deductions when his old, traditionally inept, police adversary, *LESTRADE*, shows him how it is done.
British Male

M J TROW 1949- (British)

Writer: Meirion James TROW

Citation Record: 10 Books

The Adventures Of Inspector Lestrade - *First*
Constable UK (1985)

The Supreme Adventure Of Inspector Lestrade - *First**
Stein & Day US (1985)

Lestrade And The Sign Of Nine - *Latest*
Constable UK (1992)

Insp/Supt Sholto LESTRADE and Sherlock HOLMES

British Policeman and British Male Professional Amateur operating in England

Sidekick: Dr John H WATSON

British Male - Narrator

UNKNOWN

Citation Record: 1 Book

Lestrade And The Mirror Of Murder - *Single*
Constable UK (1993)

Monsieur LEVERT

also appears, with *JACQUOT*, in another book by this author.

French Male Amateur operating in France

Jean TOUSSAINT-SAMAT 1865- (French)

Inventor of one other detective pair Monsieur JACQUOT and Monsieur LEVERT

Citation Record: 1 Book

The Dead Man At The Window - *Only*
is a translation from the French of *Le Mort à la Fenêtre*.
Lippincott US (1934)

Monsieur LEVERT

Second detective of Monsieur JACQUOT

Marcus LEVIN

Male Amateur operating in Mexico

Sidekick: Tania LEVIN

Russian Female - Assistant

John BLACKBURN 1923- (British)

Invented 4 detectives - see Gen Charles KIRK

Citation Record: 1 Book

The Young Man From Lima - *Only*
Cape US (1968)

Roger LEVIN

is an unlicensed private eye. Formerly the owner of a Chinese restaurant, he now operates around town on a kind of cash and carry basis.

American Male Private Detective operating in New York

Alan FURST 1941- (American)

Citation Record: 3 Books

Your Day In The Barrel - *First*
Atheneum US (1976)

The Caribbean Account - *Latest*
Delacorte US (1981); Quartet UK (1983)

Jack LEVINE

works on cases set back into the 1940s. Middle-aged, overweight, and Jewish with hang-ups, he operates from an office near Broadway.

American Male Private Detective operating in New York/Hollywood

Andrew BERGMAN 1946- (American)

Citation Record: 2 Books

The Big Kiss-Off Of 1944 - *First*
Holt US (1974); Hale UK (1974)

Hollywood And Levine - *Last*
Holt US (1975); Hutchinson UK (1976)

Lt LEVY

upholds the social order while working on crimes that seem chaotic and destructive.

American Policeman operating in New York

Elizabeth Sanxay HOLDING 1889-1955 (American)

was born in Brooklyn, New York.

Citation Record: 3 Books

The Blank Wall - *First*
Simon & Schuster US (1947)

Widow's Mite - *Last*
Simon & Schuster US (1953); Muller UK (1954)

Benjamin LEVY

British Male Amateur operating in London

E Phillips OPPENHEIM 1866-1946 (British)

Invented 27 detectives - see Nicholas GOADE

Citation Record: 1 Book

The Mystery Of Mr Bernard Brown - *Only*
Bentley UK (1901); Little, Brown US (1910)

The New Tenant - *Only**
Collier UK (1912)

His Father's Crime - *Only**
Street & Smith US (1929)

Joe LEVY

American Male Amateur operating in Wyoming

George SZANTO 1940- (American)

Writer: George H SZANTO

Citation Record: 1 Book

Not Working - *Single*
St Martin's US (1982)

Supt LEWIS

British Policeman operating in England

John WAINWRIGHT 1921- (British)

Invented 9 detectives - see Ch Insp/Supt LENNOX

Citation Record: 1 Book

Death In A Sleeping City - *Only*
Collins UK (1965)

Alfred LEWIS

is a pathologist who solves a case of 'impossible' murder by shooting.

American Male Professional Investigator operating in USA

Arthur PORGES (American)

Invented 13 detectives - see Arsène LUPIN

Citation Record: 1 Selected Short Story

First Degree Murder
appeared in the March number.
In 'Mike Shayne Mystery Magazine' US (1962)

Maj Gregory LEWIS

British Male Sleuth operating in England

David FROME 1898-1983 (American)

Invented 3 detectives - see Evan PINKERTON

Citation Record: 2 Books

The Murder Of An Old Man - *First*
Methuen UK (1929)

The Strange Death Of Martin Green - *Last*
Doubleday US (1931)

The Murder On The Sixth Hole - *Last**
Methuen UK (1931)

Hunter LEWIS

Second detective of Jenny Gilette LEWIS

Jenny Gilette LEWIS and Hunter LEWIS

American Female Amateur and American Male Amateur operating in New York

Elizabeth GRESHAM 1904- (American)

Writer: Elizabeth Fenner GRESHAM

Other Byline: Robin GREY

Citation Record: 4 Books

Puzzle In Paisley - *First*
Curtis US (1972)

Puzzle In Parquet - *Last*
Curtis US (1973)

Robin GREY 1904-1986 (American)

For writer details see Jenny Gilette LEWIS and Hunter LEWIS

Citation Record: 4 Books

Puzzle In Porcelain - *First*
Duell US (1945)

Puzzle In Pewter - *Last*
Duell US (1947)

Lord Louis LEWIS

British Male Amateur operating in England

Roland PERTWEE 1885-1963 (British)

Citation Record: 9 Short Stories in 1 Collection

The Transactions Of Lord Louis Lewis - *Collection 1*
Murray UK (1917); Dodd, Mead US (1918)

Sir Abercrombie LEWKER

is an eminent actor-manager, bald, heavy of jowl, and hot on Shakespearean quotations. A skilled mountaineer, once a Commando in the Second World War, he is continually running up against murder in the hills.

British Male Amateur operating in several locations

Glyn CARR 1908- (British)

For writer details see Sir Abercrombie LEWKER

Citation Record: 15 Books

Death On Milestone Buttress - *First*
Bles UK (1951)

Fat Man's Agony - *Last*
Bles UK (1969)

Showell STYLES 1908- (British)

was born in Four Oaks, Warwickshire. He was a commander in the Royal Navy in the Second World War and was a journalist, explorer, traveller, and author of adventure books for children. He published his first three books featuring *LEWKER* under his own name, which he later only used for books without this detective. The later books with *LEWKER* were all published under the pseudonym of *Glyn CARR.*

Writer: Frank Showell STYLES

Other Byline: Glyn CARR

Citation Record: 3 Books

Traitor's Mountain - *First*
Selwyn UK (1945); Macmillan US (1946)

Hammer Island - *Last*
Selwyn UK (1947)

Alexander L'HIBOUX

is of mixed origin, having African, Indian and Irish antecedents. Always on the streets on a case, hardly needing sleep and never having much in the way of possessions or a lifestyle, he is a fine invention for the bleak 1980s.

American Male Private Detective operating in Los Angeles

Robert L FORWARD 1932- (American)

Writer: Robert Lull FORWARD

Citation Record: 1 Book

The Owl - *Single*
Pinnacle US (1984)

The LIBERATOR

is one of the author's several adventurer-detectives who mete out rough justice to international crooks.

British Male Professional Investigator

Norman DEANE 1908-1973 (British)

See main detective Bruce MURDOCH

Citation Record: 3 Books

Return To Adventure - *First*
Hurst & Blackett UK (1943)

Come Home To Crime - *Last*
Hurst & Blackett UK (1945)

Johnny LIDDELL

is in books that are fast and full of action rather than high-quality detection. In his early books he is an operative for the Acme Detective Agency; but, later, he sets up on his own on West 42nd Street. He appears also in one book with the author's other detective, *Mickey DENTON.*

American Male Private Detective operating in New York/Los Angeles

Frank KANE 1912-1968 (American)

was born in New York City. He was educated at City College, New York, and studied Law at night-school at St John's University, Jamaica, New York, 1939-1941. A businessman, TV and radio producer and editor, he was the author of many crime novels, as well as radio and TV plays.

Other Detectives:
Mickey DENTON
Johnny LIDDELL and Mickey DENTON

Citation Record: 26 Books 16 Short Stories in 2 Collections

About Face - *First*
Curl US (1947)

Death About Face - *First**
Quin US (1948)

The Fatal Foursome - *First**
Dell US (1958)

Margin For Terror - *Latest*
Dell US (1967)

Johnny Liddel's Morgue - *Collection 1*
Short stories - 8
Mayflower UK (1956)

Stacked Deck - *Collection 2*
Short stories - 8
Washburn US (1961)

Johnny LIDDELL and Mickey DENTON

also appear individually in other books by this author.

American Male Sleuths operating in Los Angeles

Frank KANE 1912-1968 (American)

Invented 3 detectives - see Johnny LIDDELL

Citation Record: 1 Book

Dead Rite - *Last*
Dell US (1962); Mayflower UK (1968)

Mark LIDDON

returns home to find his wife missing and a corpse on the floor. He follows a trail to Mexico, having to solve the mystery and regain his wife before the cops foul up the case.

American Male Amateur operating in Mexico

Patrick QUENTIN (American)

Invented 6 detectives - see Peter DULUTH

Citation Record: 1 Book

The Follower - *Only*
Simon & Schuster US (1950); Gollancz UK (1950)

Jake LIEBERMAN

operates an agency called Confidential Investigations Unlimited from a rundown little office on Vermont Avenue. His vaunted homosexuality is neither a help nor a hindrance, merely an act of authorial supererogation.

American Male Private Detective operating in Los Angeles

Stephen LEWIS 1948?- (American)

Writer: Teri WHITE

Citation Record: 1 Book

Cowboy Blues - *Single*
Alyson US (1985); Alyson UK (1986)

Yakov LIEBERMAN

is an elderly Nazi hunter who foils a mad plot by a former SS doctor to clone doubles of Hitler.

American Male Amateur operating in USA

Ira LEVIN 1929- (American)

was born in New York City and took a degree in English at New York University, 1950. He is specially noted for his few mainstream novels, most of which have been used for some highly regarded films. He received the Mystery Writers of America Edgar Allan Poe award, 1954, and their Special award, 1980.

Citation Record: 1 Book

The Boys From Brazil - *Only*
Random House US (1976); Joseph UK (1976)

Lt LIEBERMANN

solves the problem of a throat being cut in a weaponless bathroom.

American Policeman operating in USA

Anthony BOUCHER 1911-1968 (American)

Invented 7 detectives - see Fergus O'BREEN and Det Lt JACKSON

Citation Record: 1 Selected Short Story

The Smoke Filled Room
Random House US (1968)

Robin LIGHT

is the gutsy widow of a late and unlamented cocaine king and she inherits little more than a pet shop in Syracuse. When, however, her assistant is mysteriously killed by what appears to be a snakebite, she becomes a dab hand at the amateur shamus business.

American Female Amateur operating in Syracuse

Barbara BLOCK (American)

Citation Record: 1 Book

Chutes And Adders - *Single*
Kensington US (1994)

Insp LIGHTFOOT

British Policeman operating in England

Arthur T RICH (British)

Citation Record: 1 Book

The Curate Finds The Corpse - *Only*
Bear UK (1945)

LIGHTNING LUKE

American Male Detective in Pulp Magazines operating in USA

Police Captain HOWARD (American)

Other Detectives:

The BORDER LINE DETECTIVE
CHIP
LITTLE FERRET
MONTE
MOUNTED POLICEMAN MARK
Nick NEVERSEEN
OLD DOUBLE FACE
OLD SAFETY
OLD WOLF
SILENT
SLENDER SAUL
Wade WESTON
YOUNG FEARLESS
YOUNG WEASEL

Citation Record: 1 Book

Lightning Luke, The Photographer Detective; Or, Caught By The Instantaneous Camera
New York Detective Library US (1882-8)

LIGHTNING GRIP

American Male Detective in Pulp Magazines operating in USA

ANON

Citation Record: 1 Selected Short Story

Lightning Grip, The Cautious Detective; Or Piping The Nathan Murder Mystery
Old Cap Collier Library US (18??)

Little LIGHTNING

American Male Detective in Pulp Magazines operating in USA

Police Captain JAMES (American)

Inventor of one other detective The REVENUE DETECTIVE

Citation Record: 1 Book

Little Lightning, The Shadow Detective; Or, The Twenty-Third Street Mystery - *Only*
Street & Smith US (1888)

Abraham LINCOLN

American Male Amateur operating in USA

Walter H CARNAHAN 1891- (American)

Writer: Walter Hervey CARNAHAN

Citation Record: 1 Book

Hoffman's Row - *Only*
Bobbs US (1963)

Edward EGGLESTON 1837-1902 (American)

Citation Record: 1 Book

The Graysons - *Only*
Century US (1887)

John Abraham LINCOLN

American Male Sleuth operating in USA/Asia

David DODGE 1910- (American)

Invented 4 detectives - see Al COLBY

Citation Record: 2 Books

Hooligan - *First*
Macmillan US (1969)

Hatchet-Man - *First**
!See Appendix 2.
Joseph UK (1970)

Troubleshooter - *Last*
Macmillan US (1971); Joseph UK (1972)

Matt LINCOLN

is in novelizations of episodes from a TV series.

American Male Amateur operating in USA

Ed GARTH 1924- (American)

For writer details see John WOODRUFF and Tony NOVELLO

Citation Record: 2 Books

The Revolutionist - *First*
Lancer US (1970)

The Hostage - *Last*
Lancer US (1971)

Wylie LINCOLN

is black, a Harvard graduate, and an ex-cop. He now runs the Cerberus School for Dogs, on the corner of 25th Street and Second Avenue in Manhattan. He does some smart detection in a case where lots of canine (and sexual) information seems to be necessary.

American Male Private Detective operating in New York

Sidekick: Russ TURNER
is an ex-convict whose jail experience is useful.

American Male - Partner

Eric CORDER (American)

Writer: Jerrold MUNDIS

Citation Record: 1 Book

The Bite - *Only*
Dell US (1976); Allen UK (1976)

Richard LIND

investigates death on an ocean liner.

American Male Amateur operating on a ship

Hugh BAKER (American)

Citation Record: 1 Book

Cartwright Is Dead, Sir! - *Only*
Houghton US (1936)

Peter LINDSAY

British Male Amateur operating in England

Francis EVERTON 1883- (British)

Invented 4 detectives - see Insp George ANNESLEY

Citation Record: 1 Book

Insoluble - *Only*
Collins UK (1934)

Hobart LINDSEY and Det Marvia PLUM

make an unusual and useful combination, he being an insurance investigator and she being a cop in the Los Angeles Police Department. The themes of the books are interestingly interwoven with classic movies, classic cars, old comic books and other historical phenomena.

American Male Professional Investigator and American Policewoman operating in Los Angeles

Richard A LUPOFF 1935- (American)

Writer: Richard Allen LUPOFF

Citation Record: 4 Books

The Comic Book Killer - *First*
Offspring US (1988)

The Sepia Siren Killer - *Latest*
St Martin's US (1994)

Trooper Ralph LINDSEY

is a young State Trooper, dedicated to his job but rebellious against authority, tending to become involved more than he should with his cases.

American Policeman operating in Massachusetts

Benjamin BENSON 1915-1959 (American)

See main detective Capt Wade PARIS

Citation Record: 7 Books

The Venus Death - *First*
Mill US (1953)

Seven Steps East - *Last*
Mill US (1959)

Karen LINDSTROM

is a would-be writer of mystery novels, who investigates the death of a friend whose work has been plagiarised.

American Female Amateur operating in New York

Marie R RENO (American)

Writer: Marie Roth RENO

Citation Record: 1 Book

Final Proof - *Single*
Harper & Row US (1976)

Malko LINGE

French Male Sleuth operating in Italy/Japan

Gerard DE VILLIERS 1929- (French)

Citation Record: 16 Books

West Of Jerusalem - *First*
is a translation from the French of *A L'Ouest de Jerusalem* (Paris, 1967).
New English Library UK (1969); Pinnacle US (1973)

Hostage In Tokyo - *Last*
is a translation from the French of *Les Ostages de Tokyo* (Paris, 1975).
Pinnacle US (1976)

Det Jack LINGEMANN and Liz CONNORS

Homicide detective, *Jack LINGEMANN*, is the boyfriend of *Liz CONNORS*, who is an Assistant Professor of English and teaches at the Cambridge Police Academy, Massachusetts. A fortunate partnership, for they are able to be together while solving cases of murder in a surprising number of Bostonian establishments!

American Policeman and American Female Amateur operating in Boston

Susan KELLY (American)

Inventor of one other detective Ch Insp Nick TREVELLYAN

Citation Record: 6 Books

The Gemini Man - *First*
Walker US (1985)

Out Of The Darkness - *Latest*
Walker US (1992)

Sam LINKUM

American Male Sleuth operating in USA

Herbert MITGANG (American)

Citation Record: 2 Books

The Montauk Fault - *First*
Arbor US (1981)

Kings In The Counting House - *Latest*
Arbor US (1983)

Mr LINLEY

appears, alas, in only a few of the many short stories written by this master teller of tales. A strange contemplative man, he solves the most baffling cases by pure ratiocination.

British Male Amateur operating in England

Lord DUNSANY 1878-1957 (British)

was an 18th Baron of Irish descent. A distinguished novelist and playwright, he served in the Army during the Boer War and in the First World War. Later he was appointed Byron Professor of Literature in Athens. He wrote a large number of short stories, some with ingenious criminous content.

Writer: Edward John Moreton Drax PLUNKETT

Other Detectives:
Joseph JORKENS RIPLEY

Citation Record: 8 Short Stories in 1 Collection

The Little Tales Of Smethers, And Other Stories - *Collection 1*
This collection contains five stories featuring *RIPLEY* and eight featuring *LINLEY.*
Jarrolds UK (1952)

Nicholas LINNEAR

American Male Sleuth operating in New York/Tokyo

Eric VAN LUSTBADER 1946-

Invented 3 detectives - see Jake MAROC

Citation Record: 2 Books

The Ninja - *First*
Granada UK (1980); Evans US (1980)

The Miko - *Latest*
Granada UK (1984); Villard US (1984)

'Birdie' LINNET

has left the police force because of some undisclosed conflict with his superiors about 'justice and the law'. Middle-aged, divorced and with a youngish mistress, he is drawn into cases that either do not interest or simply baffle the cops.

British Male Amateur operating in England

Sidekick: Nimue HAWTHORNE
is the mistress of and assistant to the detective.
British Female - Mistress

Gillian LINSCOTT (British)

is a civil servant, market gardener, journalist and playwright.

Inventor of one other detective Nell BRAY

Citation Record: 4 Books

A Healthy Body - *First*
Macmillan UK (1984)

A Whiff Of Sulphur - *Latest*
Macmillan UK (1987); St Martin's US (1987)

Insp LINSCOTT

solves a case of death by stabbing in a locked room.

British Policeman operating in England

John HAWK 1893- (British)

See main detective Mortimer SARK

Citation Record: 1 Book

The Locked Door - *Only*
Skeffington UK (1929)

It Was Locked - *Only**
Farrar, Straus US (1930)

Lord Arthur LINTON

solves a case of poisoning in the British House of Commons.

British Male Amateur operating in London

Anthony BERKELEY 1893-1971 (British)

Invented 4 detectives - see Roger SHERINGHAM

Citation Record: 1 Selected Short Story

Death In The House
Hodder & Stoughton UK (1939); Doubleday US (1939)

Catherine LINTON

American Female Amateur operating in Louisiana

Charlaine HARRIS 1951- (American)

Other Detectives:
Nickie CALLAHAN　　Aurora 'Rose' TEAGARDEN

Citation Record: 1 Book

Sweet And Deadly - *Single*
Houghton US (1981)

Dead Dog - *Single**
Hale UK (1982)

Insp John Joseph LINTOTT

is a Scotland Yard policeman in Victorian London.

British Policeman operating in London

Jean STUBBS 1926- (British)

was born in Denton, Lancashire. She was educated at the Manchester High School for Girls and attended the Manchester School of Art, 1944-1947.

Citation Record: 3 Books

Dear Laura - *First*
Macmillan UK (1973); Stein & Day US (1973)

The Golden Crucible - *Latest*
Macmillan UK (1976); Stein & Day US (1976)

Baroness Clara LINZ

operates Advice Limited, in Adam Street in London's West End.

Hungarian Female Private Detective operating in London

E Phillips OPPENHEIM 1866-1946 (British)

Invented 27 detectives - see Nicholas GOADE

Citation Record: 11 Short Stories in 1 Collection

Advice Limited - *Collection 1*
When some of the stories appeared in *Woman's Home Companion* (1933-34), the lady detective was mysteriously transformed into a young Englishwoman, Elizabeth Martin.
Hodder & Stoughton UK (1935); Little, Brown US (1936)

Insp LIPINSKI

appears in short stories about the detection of illicit diamond smuggling.

British Policeman operating in England

George GRIFFITH 1859-1906 (British)

Citation Record: 9 Short Stories in 1 Collection

Knaves Of Diamonds, Being Tales Of Mine And Veld - *Collection 1*
Pearson UK (1899)

The Memoirs Of An Inspector - *Collection 1**
UK (1904)

Darina LISLE

is, like her creator, a culinary expert and caterer. Regrettably for her clients, however, whether she's laying on plain fare for the hoipolloi or banquets for the elite, she inevitably runs into murder. To protect her good name or simply because of her zest for sleuthing, she investigates. In this she is rather fortunate, being affianced to a senior copper in the local force, who provides her with useful information and sometimes physical back-up.

British Policewoman operating in England

Sidekick: Det Insp William PIGRAM
is, although a senior policeman, merely a useful but necessary appendage to the sleuthing chefette as she plunges into her gastronomic homicide cases. Certainly a reversal of the normal order of things!
British Male - Boyfriend

Janet LAURENCE (British)

lives in Somerset and is a culinary guru. She writes on cooking and gastronomy for several newspapers and magazines and uses her expert knowledge as a basis for her detective novels.

Citation Record: 6 Books

A Deepe Coffyn - *First*
!See Appendix 2.
Macmillan UK (1989); Doubleday US (1990)

Death A La Provençale - *Latest*
Macmillan UK (1995)

Lila LISLE

was often called 'the Girl Problem Investigator' and appeared in short stories in *Schoolgirls' Own* from 1930. She had red-gold hair and was stylish, active and modern, as befitted the new type of girl-detective image.

British Female Amateur operating in England

Adelie ASCOTT ?-1935 (British)

For writer details see Sylvia SILENCE

Citation Record: 1 Selected Short Story

The Haunted Grange
is one of many that featured *Lila LISLE.*
In 'Schoolgirls' Own' UK (1930)

Gerald LISSENDALE

British Male Amateur operating in England

Sydney HORLER 1888-1954 (British)

Invented 20 detectives - see Sir Harker BELLAMY

Citation Record: 2 Books

The Closed Door - *First*
Pilot UK (1948)

The Blade Is Bright - *Last*
Eyre & Spottiswoode UK (1952)

Jim LITTLE

American Male Amateur operating in USA

Maude PARKER 189?-1959 (American)

Citation Record: 3 Books

Which Mrs Torr? - *First*
Rinehart US (1951); Hodder & Stoughton UK (1952)

Murder In Jackson Hole - *Last*
Rinehart US (1955)

LITTLE BRAVO

American Male Detective in Pulp Magazines operating in USA

Will WINCH (American)

Invented 5 detectives - see The LAWYER DETECTIVE

Citation Record: 1 Selected Short Story

Little Mink, The Bravo Detective; Or, Traps And Trails Of The Southwest Border
Old Cap Collier Library US (18??)

LITTLE FERRET

American Male Detective in Pulp Magazines operating in USA

Police Captain HOWARD (American)

Invented 15 detectives - see LIGHTNING LUKE

Citation Record: 1 Book

Little Ferret, The Boy Detective
New York Detective Library US (1882-8)

Ch Insp John George LITTLECHILD

British Policeman operating in London

John George LITTLECHILD (British)

Citation Record: 22 Short Stories in 1 Collection

The Reminiscences Of Chief-Inspector Littlechild - *Collection 1*
Leadenhall UK (1894)

Det Insp/Supt Thomas LITTLEJOHN

featured in a series that stretched over nearly thirty years. A good standard British policeman, he worked on cases in England, the Isle of Man, and especially in France, where he had connections. As the series of books evolved, he advanced in rank and was assisted by a succession of uninspiring sidekicks.

British Policeman operating in Europe

Sidekick: Insp HOPKINSON

British Male - Subordinate

Sidekick: Supt CROMWELL

British Male - Subordinate

George BELLAIRS 1902-1985 (British)

was born in Heywood, Lancashire. He took a BSc at the London School of Economics, 1928. A banker by profession, he began writing the *LITTLEJOHN* books in 1941 and continued to write them for the next thirty-nine years.

Writer: Harold BLUNDELL

Other Byline: Hilary LANDON

Citation Record: 57 Books

Littlejohn On Leave - *First*
Gifford UK (1941)

Old Man Dies - *Last*
Gifford UK (1980)

John LITTLETON

solves a case of death by stabbing in a locked room.

American Male Sleuth operating in USA

William MARCH 1894-1954 (American)

Writer: William Edward March CAMPBELL

Citation Record: 1 Selected Short Story

The Bird House

appeared in the February number of the magazine and is also in the anthology, *Ellery Queen's Best Bets* (*Pyramid*; US 1972).

In 'Ellery Queen's Mystery Magazine' US (1954)

L

Sally LIVINGSTONE

sleuths in a book set back into 1939.

British Female Amateur operating in England

Anna CLARKE 1919- (British)

Invented 4 detectives - see Paula GLENNING

Citation Record: 1 Book

The Last Voyage - *Only*
Collins UK (1976); St Martin's US (1982)

Ross LIZENBY and Chris SAKSIS

American Male Amateurs operating in Washington DC

Margaret TRUMAN 1924- (American)

Invented 9 detectives - see Mr Ron FAIRCHILD

Citation Record: 1 Book

Murder At The FBI - *Single*
Arbor US (1985)

LI-SIN

Chinese Male Amateur operating in England

Nigel VANE 1896-1980 (British)

See main detective Philip QUEST

Citation Record: 2 Books

The Menace Of Li-Sin - *First*
Modern UK (193?)

The Vengeance Of Li-Sin - *Last*
Modern UK (1935)

Charles LLEWELLYN

American Male Amateur operating in USA

Paula GOSLING 1939- (American)

Invented 7 detectives - see Lt Jack STRYKER

Citation Record: 1 Book

The Woman In Red - *Single*
Doubleday US (1984)

Cpl Juan LLORCA

commands a force of only six men, who constitute the Civil Guard of Madrigal del Mar, an island off the coast of Spain. The plots deal with the lives and activities of British expatriates, who are often living in the way they could not afford to in Britain. As a result, their problems continually engender crime.

Spanish Policeman operating in Spain

Delano AMES 1906- (American)

Writer: Delano L AMES

See main detective pair Dagobert BROWN and Jane BROWN

Citation Record: 4 Books

The Man In The Tricorn Hat - *First*
Methuen UK (1960); Regnery US (1966)

The Man With Three Passports - *Last*
Methuen UK (1967)

Ch Insp LLOYD

British Policeman operating in England

Sidekick: Judy HILL

is the detective's assistant and lover.

British Female - Assistant

Jill MCGOWN 1947- (British)

was born in Campbeltown, Argyll, Scotland, and educated at Kettering Technical College, Northampton.

Inventor of one other detective Harry CAMBERT

Citation Record: 4 Books

A Perfect Match - *First*
Macmillan UK (1983); St Martin's US (1983)

The Other Woman - *Latest*
Macmillan UK (1992)

Sheriff Bill LLOYD

American Policeman operating in New York

Wallace REED (American)

Citation Record: 4 Books

Time To Kill - *First*
Phoenix Press US (1940)

Motive For Murder - *Last*
Arcadia US (1957)

Turlock LOAMS

is a *Sherlock HOLMES* parody, operating out of 221b Quaker Street, San Francisco. The titles of the books are themselves amusing parodies on the titles of the canonical short stories written by *Sir Arthur Conan DOYLE.*

American Male Professional Amateur operating in San Francisco

Sidekick: Dr FATSO

is his parody *WATSON*-like assistant.

American Male -

John RUYLE (American)

The author of the twenty-two parodies cited, all featuring *Turlock LOAMS*, published the parodies himself, mainly under the imprint of the so-called *Pequod Press*, but sometimes under the aegis of other fictitious and eccentrically named publishers.

Citation Record: 22 Books

The Adventure Of The Dancing Hen - *Parody 1*
Pequod US (1978)

The Adventure Of The Freckled Hand - *Parody 2*
Pequod US (1975)

The Adventure Of The Giant Bat Of Sonoma - *Parody 3*
Pequod US (1976)

The Adventure Of The Jogging Man - *Parody 4*
Pequod US (1979)

The Adventure Of The Logophagous Client - *Parody 5*
Pequod US (1976)

The Adventure Of The Missing Third Quarter - *Parody 6*
Pequod US (1977)

The Adventure Of The Retired Weatherman - *Parody 7*

was revised by the author and republished under the punning imprint of a new and fictitious publishing house, *Quaker Street Irregulars* (US 1978).

Pequod US (1976)

His Last Vow - *Parody 8*
Pequod US (1977)
The Adventure Of Blue Peter - *Parody 9*
Pequod US (1987)
The Adventure Of The Cardboard Lox - *Parody 10*
Dowson & Miles US (1989)
The Adventure Of The Cheesemonger's Bark - *Parody 11*
Ross & Mangles US (1988)
The Adventure Of The Fairfax Umpire - *Parody 12*
Pequod US (1988)
The Adventure Of The Frail Codger - *Parody 13*
Biddle, Haywood & Moffat US (1988)
The Adventure Of The Soledad Cyclist - *Parody 14*
was revised by the author and republished as by the fictitious publishers, *Nimble & Quick* (US 1986).
Pequod US (1974)
The Muscatel Ritual - *Parody 15*
Beaune-Again US (1989)
The Napa Valley Mystery - *Parody 16*
Pycroft & Doran US (1989)
The Prenatal Entreaty - *Parody 17*
Tonga & Small US (1989)
A Scandal In Bulimia - *Parody 18*
Pequod US (1986)
Silver Haze - *Parody 29*
Pequod US (1978)
The Adventure Of The Five Buffalo Chips - *Parody 20*
Pequod US (1975)
The Adventure Of The Frying Detective - *Parody 21*
Trout & Milk US (1990)
The Geek Interpreter - *Parody 22*
Trout-in-the-Milk US (1990)

Ebenezer LOBB

British Male Amateur operating in England

Allen UPWARD 1863-1926 (British)
Invented 6 detectives - see Charles PRESCOTT
Citation Record: 23 Short Stories in 1 Collection
The Wonderful Career Of Ebenezer Lobb - *Collection 1*
Hurst UK (1900)

Ferrers LOCKE

first appeared in 1907 and was one of the many 'boys' detectives' of the inter-war years, being continually summoned to either Greyfriars or St Jim's (fictional public schools) to solve crimes. He was used by many authors, often writing under a house name, to replace the original detective, such as *Sexton BLAKE*, in earlier stories.
British Male Amateur operating in England

John ANDREWS 1880-1929 (British)
was a house name used by several British authors during the 1930s for writing or ghosting the innumerable stories for boys' magazines then so popular. Often the stories were reworkings of others.
Writer: Andrew Nicholas MURRAY
Other Bylines:
Nicholas ISLAY
Andrew MURRAY
Inventor of one other detective Nelson LEE
Citation Record: 5 Books
The Peril Pit - *First*
was an adaptation of a *Sexton BLAKE* story, *The Man From Kura-Kura*.
Amalgamated UK (1931)
The Secret Of The Reef - *Last*
was an adaptation of a *Sexton BLAKE* story, *The Barrier Reef Mystery*.
Amalgamated UK (1933)

Edwy Searles BROOKS 1889-1965 (British)
Invented 5 detectives - see Insp William (The Grouser) BEEKE
Citation Record: 1 Book
The Terror Of Tibet - *Only*
Amalgamated UK (1930)

Percy A CLARKE 1895- 1974 (British)
Writer: Percy Arthur CLARKE
Other Bylines:
Martin FRAZER
Steve ROGERS
St John WATSON
Citation Record: 1 Book
The Secret Of The Tower - *Only*
Amalgamated UK (1931)

Charles HAMILTON 1876-1961 (British)
is the real name of the most famous of all authors of schoolboys' stories. He wrote countless such stories over a period of nearly sixty years and is said to have been the second most prolific writer ever to have lived, his output being reckoned at about 100,000,000 words (the most prolific writer in history is said to have been Lope Felix de Vega Carpio, 1562-1635, of Spain). *HAMILTON* published most of his stories as long, almost never-ending series in the many popular magazines that flourished in the first half of the twentieth century. He used many pseudonyms, which have yet to be catalogued adequately.
Writer: Charles Harold St John HAMILTON
Other Byline: Peter TODD
Other Detectives:
Denham CROFT
Sedley SHARPE
No citations

Stanton HOPE 1889- 1961 (British)
was born in London and travelled widely in later life, writing on various subjects as well as being the author of many novels.
Writer: William Edward Stanton HOPE
Adopter of one other detective Sexton BLAKE
Citation Record: 1 Book
The Yellow Spider - *Only*
Amalgamated UK (1924)

Steve ROGERS 1895- 1974 (British)
For writer details see Ferrers LOCKE (Writer Percy A CLARKE)
Citation Record: 1 Book
The Wolf Of Texas - *Only*
Amalgamated UK (1939)

Hedley SCOTT 1899-1955 (British)
Writer: Hedley Percival Angelo O'MANT
Adopter of one other detective Sexton BLAKE
Citation Record: 14 Books
A Marked Man - *First*
Amalgamated UK (1925)
The Football Crooks - *Last*
Amalgamated UK (1938)

John SYLVESTER 1901- (British)
For writer details see Peter MAXWELL and Susan MAXWELL
Citation Record: 1 Book
The Masked Death - *Only*
Amalgamated UK (1931)

Francis WARWICK (British)
Writer: Francis Alister WARWICK
Other Byline: Warwick JARDINE
Citation Record: 1 Book
The Mystery Of Lone Manor - *Only*
Amalgamated UK (1928)

St John WATSON 1895- 1974 (British)
For writer details see Ferrers LOCKE (Writer Percy A CLARKE)
Citation Record: 1 Book
The Mystery Of The War - *Only*
Amalgamated UK (1934)

Jeremy LOCKE

British Male Amateur operating in England

Mary CHALLIS 1922-1985 (British)
For writer details see Antony MAITLAND

Citation Record: 2 Books

Burden Of Proof - *First*
Raven CA (1980)

Crimes Past - *Latest*
Raven CA (1980)

John LOCKE

is a Toronto bodyguard. A graduate of both Cambridge, England, and Harvard, USA, and once in the British SAS, he runs an agency that offers its clients 'physical assurance' but his work for them is as much intellectual as physical.

British Male Private Detective operating in Toronto

Jack BARNAO 1931- (Canadian)

Writer: Edward John WOOD

Other Byline: Ted WOOD

Citation Record: 2 Books

Hammer Locke - *First*
Scribner's US (1986)

Lockestep - *Latest*
Scribner's US (1987)

John LOCKE

American Male Sleuth operating in Bali/Far East

Sterling SILLIPHANT 1918- (American)

Writer: Sterling Dale SILLIPHANT

Citation Record: 3 Books

Steel Tiger - *First*
Ballantine US (1983); Severn UK (1986)

Silver Star - *Latest*
Ballantine US (1986)

L

Kim LOCKE

works for the CIA in undercover operations.

American Male Secret Agent operating in USA/ Asia

Ken CROSSEN 1910-1981 (American)

was born in Albany, Ohio, and educated at the Rio Grande College, Ohio. He worked as an insurance investigator and has cast his several detectives in that mould.

Other Byline: Clay RICHARDS

Inventor of one other detective pair Jason JONES and 'Necessary' SMITH

Citation Record: 2 Books

The Tortured Path - *First*
Dutton US (1957); Eyre & Spottiswoode UK (1958)

The Big Dive - *Last*
Dutton US (1959); Eyre & Spottiswoode UK (1959)

Clay RICHARDS 1910-1981 (American)

continued with the *Kim LOCKE* character in one book that appeared under this byline.

For writer details see Kim LOCKE

Inventor of one other detective Grant KIRBY

Citation Record: 1 Book

The Gentle Assassin - *Only*
Bobbs US (1964); Boardman UK (1965)

Mike LOCKEN

American Male Sleuth

Robert ROSTAND (American)

Writer: Robert S HOPKINS

Other Byline: R Thurston HOPKINS

Citation Record: 3 Books

The Killer Elite - *First*
Delacorte US (1973); Hodder & Stoughton UK (1974)

A Killing In Rome - *Latest*
Delacorte US (1977); Hutchinson UK (1977)

Insp LOCKET

solves a case of murder by induced heart attack.

British Policeman operating in England

Ralph TREVOR 1897- (British)

See main detective Insp Curtis BURKE

Citation Record: 1 Book

Behind The Green Mask - *Only*
Wright UK (1940)

Lacy LOCKINGTON

was suspended from the Chicago police force because of his regrettable tendency to kill more criminals than was the acceptable average. He now works for a private agency.

American Male Private Detective operating in Chicago

Ross H SPENCER 1921- (American)

Invented 7 detectives - see Buzz DECKARD

Citation Record: 2 Books

The Fifth Script - *First*
Fine US (1989)

The Devereaux File - *Latest*
Fine US (1990); Curley UK (1991)

Bill (The Hook) LOCKWOOD

is a First World War veteran. An ex-boxer and subsequently a law graduate, he is a tough operator for Transatlantic Underwriters in novels set back into the 1930s.

American Male Private Detective operating in New York

Brad LATHAM (American)

Citation Record: 5 Books

The Gilded Canary - *First*
Warner US (1981)

Corpses In The Cellar - *Latest*
Warner US (1982)

LOGAN

American Male Sleuth

Alan JOSEPH (American)

Citation Record: 2 Books

Logan - *First*
Belmont US (1970)

Killers At Sea - *Last*
Belmont US (1970)

Ben LOGAN

American Male Detective in Pulp Magazines operating in USA

Charles C MORGAN (American)

Citation Record: 1 Selected Short Story

Ben Logan, The Castle Garden Detective; Or, Trading The Best Of Diamonds
Old Cap Collier Library US (18??)

Mike LOGAN

appears also in two books with the author's main detective, *Insp Jim SILVER.*

British Male Amateur operating in England

Henry HOLT (British)

Invented 3 detectives - see Insp Jim SILVER

Citation Record: 1 Book

No Lilies - *Only*
Hale UK (1947)

Mike LOGAN

Second detective of Insp Jim SILVER

Richard LOGAN

appears also in one book with another of the author's detectives, *Insp MCKELLER.*

British Male Sleuth operating in Vienna

Hugh MCCUTCHEON 1909- (British)

Invented 6 detectives - see Insp MCKELLER

Citation Record: 1 Book

Suddenly, In Vienna - *Only*
Long UK (1963)

Richard LOGAN

Second detective of Insp MCKELLER

Tom LOGAN

is a disbarred lawyer who works for the Boss agency in Beverly Hills.

American Male Private Detective operating in California

Frank GRUBER 1904-1969 (American)

Invented 8 detectives - see Johnny FLETCHER and Sam CRAGG

Citation Record: 1 Book

The Etruscan Bull - *Only*
Dutton US (1969); Hale UK (1970)

Insp Ernst LOHMANN

appears in novels set back into the 1930s, just before the outbreak of war.

German Policeman operating in England/Germany

Jack GERSON (British)

was born in Glasgow and is a TV scriptwriter.

Citation Record: 3 Books

Death's Head Berlin - *First*
Allen UK (1987); St Martin's US (1989)

Deathwatch - *Latest*
Allen UK (1990); St Martin's US (1991)

Ben LOMAX

was retired from the New York Police Department after being crippled by a gunshot. However, with the aid of a walking cane, he is now able to operate privately.

American Male Private Detective operating in New York

Arthur D GOLDSTEIN 1937- (American)

Writer: Arthur David GOLDSTEIN

Inventor of one other detective Max GUTTMAN

Citation Record: 1 Book

If I Knew What I Was Doing... - *Only*
Random House US (1974)

Donald LOMAX and Peter CULLIMORE

investigate a strange case involving the disappearance of a car on the road.

Male Amateurs

L P DAVIES 1914- (British)

Invented 3 detectives - see David CONWAY

Citation Record: 1 Book

Adventure Holidays, Ltd - *Only*
Doubleday US (1970)

Jacob LOMAX

retired from the police after the unsolved rape and murder of his wife. He has set up as a PI and, morose and introverted, he is a real loner, eating and sleeping casually. He narrates his own tales.

American Male Private Detective operating in Denver

Michael ALLEGRETTO 1944- (American)

was born in Florida. He graduated from the University of Denver, Colorado, 1965, and Santa Monica City College, California, 1970. He has been a bookseller and a printer.

Inventor of one other detective Nora HONEYCUTT

Citation Record: 4 Books

Death On The Rocks - *First*
Scribner's US (1987); Macmillan UK (1988)

Blood Relative - *Latest*
Scribner's US (1992)

Sir Joseph LONDE

British Male Amateur operating in England

E Phillips OPPENHEIM 1866-1946 (British)

invented 27 detectives - see Nicholas GOADE

Citation Record: 10 Short Stories in 1 Collection

The Terrible Hobby Of Sir Joseph Londe, Baronet - *Collection 1*
Hodder & Stoughton UK (1924); Little, Brown US (1927)

Ed LONDON

American Male Private Detective operating in New York

Lawrence BLOCK 1938- (American)

Invented 6 detectives - see Leo HAIG

Citation Record: 1 Book

Death Pulls A Double Cross - *Only*
Fawcett US (1961)

Coward's Kiss - *Only**
Foul Play US (1987)

Lavinia LONDON

is a retired actress who recognises a murder scene when she sees it, as she usually does. She uses her theatrical skills to solve some interesting cases.

American Female Amateur operating in New York

James R MCCAHERY (American)

Citation Record: 2 Books

Grave Undertaking - *First*
Knightsbridge US (1990)

What Evil Lurks - *Latest*
Kensington US (1995)

Max LONDON

is half English, half Swedish. A former boxer, he is now a PI at Vista Beach.

British-Swedish Male Private Detective operating in California

Robert ARTHUR 1909-1969 (American)

Invented 6 detectives - see Max MILLION

Citation Record: 1 Book

Somebody's Walking Over My Grave - *Only*
Ace US (1961)

L

Teddy LONDON

is a shamus who 'has an eerie knack of solving eerie crimes'. That seems hardly surprising, since, as well as having a gun he calls Betty and a knife he calls Veronica, he has contacts both in this world and the one beyond.

American Male Private Detective operating in USA

Robert A MORGAN (American)

Citation Record: 6 Books

All Things Under The Moon - *First*
Berkley US (1994)

Some Things Come Back - *Latest*
Berkley US (1995)

The LONDON DETECTIVE

British Male Detective in Pulp Magazines operating in England

ANON

No citations

Det LONEGAN

Second detective of Dr William AMES

Mitchell LONEMAN

works for a food co-operative. When murder occurs he has to find whodunnit, so as to protect his suspected wife and the firm.

American Male Amateur operating in USA

Lester DENT 1904-1959 (American)

Invented 9 detectives - see Chance MALLOY

Citation Record: 1 Book

Lady In Peril - *Only*
Ace US (1959)

Rex LONERGAN

was a hardboiled cop who appeared in stories in *Dime Detective.*

American Male Detective in Pulp Magazines operating in San Francisco

John K BUTLER (American)

Invented 3 detectives - see Steve MIDNIGHT

No citations

Insp Arnold 'Betcher' LONG
solves a case of death by shooting in a locked room.
British Policeman operating in London

Edgar WALLACE 1875-1932 (British)
Invented 28 detectives - see J G REEDER
Citation Record: 1 Book
The Terrible People - *Only*
Doubleday US (1926); Hodder & Stoughton UK (1927)

Chester LONG
American Male Amateur operating in New York

Carleton CARPENTER 1926- (American)
is an actor in radio, TV and films.
Citation Record: 2 Books
Only Her Hairdresser Knew - *First*
Curtis US (1973)
Deadhead - *Last*
Curtis US (1974)

Sgt Jerry LONG
is given assignments that involve him and his sidekick in more mayhem than detective work.
American Policeman operating in USA
Sidekick: Sgt Chuck CONLEY
American Male - Partner

James M FOX (American)
Invented 3 detectives - see Steve HARVESTER
Citation Record: 3 Books
Code Three - *First*
Little, Brown US (1953); Hammond UK (1956)
Dead Pigeon - *Last*
Hammond UK (1967)
The Dead Canary - *Last**
Major US (1979)

L

Lydford LONG
British Male Amateur operating in England

Henry CARSTAIRS (British)
Citation Record: 13 Books
Harpinger's Hunch - *First*
Ward, Lock UK (1943)
The Winton Street Mystery - *Last*
Ward, Lock UK (1955)

Michael LONG
is in novelizations of episodes from a TV series.
American Male Professional Investigator operating in USA

Glen A LARSON 1937?- and Roger HILL (American)
Citation Record: 5 Books
Knight Rider - *First*
Pinnacle US (1983); Star UK (1985)
Mirror Image - *Latest*
Target US (1985)

Pusher LONG
British Male Amateur operating in England

Derwent MIALL (British)
Citation Record: 12 Short Stories in 1 Collection
Disclosures Of A Press Agent - *Collection 1*
Greening UK (1912)

Dr Sebastian LONG
solves a case of death by wrist-slashing in a locked bathroom.
British Male Amateur operating in England

Gordon FURNIVALL (American)
Citation Record: 1 Book
The Tracker Tracked - *Only*
Jenkins UK (1928)

Timothy LONG
British Male Amateur operating in England

Josephine BELL 1897-1987 (British)
Invented 10 detectives - see Dr David WINTRINGHAM
Citation Record: 1 Book
No Escape - *Only*
Hodder & Stoughton UK (1965); Macmillan US (1966)

LONG BRANCH DETECTIVE
American Male Detective in Pulp Magazines operating in USA

ANON
Citation Record: 1 Book
The Long Branch Detective - *Only*
Aldine US

Det LONNIE THE FED
American Policeman operating in USA

Hans LUGAR (British)
See main detective Hans LUGAR
Citation Record: 6 Books
Come Out With Your Hands Up! - *First*
Scion UK (1951)
Handle With Care - *Last*
Scion UK (1952)

Tony LONTO
American Policeman operating in USA

E Richard JOHNSON 1937- (American)
was born in Printice, Wisconsin. He served in US Army Intelligence, 1956-1961, has worked as a logger and ranch-hand and, since 1964, has been an inmate of Stillwater State Prison, Minnesota. He is the author of at least eleven genre books, which deal in great depth with the underworld of American society, in which the deeds are dark and the characters even darker. He received the Mystery Writers of America Edgar Allan Poe award for his first book, 1968.
Writer: Emil Richard JOHNSON
Citation Record: 2 Books
Silver Street - *First*
Harper & Row US (1968)
The Silver Street Killer - *First**
Hale UK (1969)
The Inside Man - *Last*
Harper & Row US (1969); Macmillan UK (1970)

Clay LOOMIS
American Male Sleuth operating in USA

Leonard SANDERS 1929- (American)
Citation Record: 2 Books
The Hamlet Warning - *First*
Scribner's US (1976); Allen UK (1977)
The Hamlet Ultimatum - *Latest*
Scribner's US (1979)

Ch Insp LORD
British Policeman operating in England

David FROME 1898-1983 (American)
Invented 3 detectives - see Evan PINKERTON
Citation Record: 1 Book
That's Your Man, Inspector! - *Single*
Longman UK (1934)

Emma LORD
is a newspaperwoman who works in the Pacific Northwest.
American Female Amateur operating in USA

Mary DAHEIM (American)
Inventor of one other detective Judith McMonigle FLYNN
Citation Record: 5 Books
The Alpine Advocate - *First*
Ballantine US (1992)

The Alpine Escape - *Latest*
Ballantine US (1995)

Lt Michael LORD

of the New York Police Department is a highly educated young man, given to ratiocination as a means of solving crimes.

American Policeman operating in New York

Sidekick: Dr Love Rees PONS
is a plump, intelligent but rather bumbling psychologist who works with *Michael LORD* in most of his cases and is one of a group of detectives appearing in one other book by this author.

American Male - Assistant

C Daly KING 1895-1963 (American)

was born in New York City. He served in the US Army and graduated in Psychology, afterwards writing several treatises on the subject.

Writer: Charles Daly KING

Other Detectives:
Dr Frank HAYVIER, Dr Love Rees PONS, Dr Malcolm PLECKS and Prof Knott Coe MITTLE
Mr Trevis TARRANT

Citation Record: 4 Books

Obelists En Route - *First*
Collins UK (1934)

Bermuda Burial - *Last*
Collins UK (1940); Funk US (1941)

Nelson LORD

British Male Secret Agent operating in several locations

George WINDSOR (British)

Citation Record: 1 Book

Nelson Lord - One Of Our Agents - *Only*
Stockwell UK (1974)

Graham LORIMER

is a dedicated official of the British Home Office who is sent to investigate financial crimes on an international scale.

British Male Professional Investigator operating in several locations

Ian STUART 1927-1993 (British)

Invented 3 detectives - see Insp Neil LAMBERT

Citation Record: 3 Books

Sandscreen - *First*
Doubleday US (1987)

Master Plan - *Latest*
Doubleday US (1990)

Richard LORYAT

British Male Amateur operating in England

J B HARRIS-BURLAND 1870- (British)

See main detective Insp STRODE

Citation Record: 1 Book

The Shadow Of Malreward - *Only*
Chapman & Hall UK (1911); Knopf US (1919)

LOTTA

American Male Detective in Pulp Magazines operating in USA

Fred HAZEL (American)

Citation Record: 1 Book

Lotta, The Young Lady Detective - *Only*
Old Cap Collier Library US (18??)

LOU

American Female Amateur operating in USA

Raymond BUXTON (British)

See main detective Gale GALLYON

Citation Record: 1 Book

A Rope For A Gal Called Lou - *Only*
Modern Fiction UK (1950)

Don ROGAN (British)

For writer details see Gale GALLYON

Citation Record: 1 Book

Dames Take To Crime - *Only*
Modern Fiction UK (1950)

Graham LOUDON

Second detective of Insp FINNEY

Ben LOUIS

American Male Amateur operating in Massachusetts

E S RUSSELL (American)

Writer: Enid S RUSSELL

Citation Record: 2 Books

She Should Have Cried On Monday - *First*
Doubleday US (1968); Hale UK (1969)

Nice Enough To Murder - *Last*
Doubleday US (1971)

Joe LOUIS

Second detective of Toby PETERS

Dr Jason LOVE

is an English country doctor whose Second World War record persuades British Intelligence to use him in a series of adventures in exotic locales. Although an outsider in an environment he finds baffling, he succeeds where others fail.

British Male Professional Amateur operating in several locations

James LEASOR 1923- (British)

was born in Erith, Kent. He was educated at the City of London School and took a BA in English at Oriel College, Oxford, 1948, followed by an MA, 1952, and served in the Army, 1942-1946. He has been a reporter, newspaper columnist and foreign correspondent. In addition to his genre novels he is the author of at least seven non-genre novels, short stories and plays.

Writer: Thomas James LEASOR

Inventor of one other detective Dorothy Mayotte RIGBY

Citation Record: 7 Books

Passport To Oblivion - *First*
Heinemann UK (1964); Lippincott US (1965)

Where The Spies Are - *First**
Pan UK (1965); Signet US (1965)

Love Down Under - *Latest*
UK (1992)

Det Pharaoh LOVE

is black, homosexual, and a cop. His work involves all three of these aspects of his existence. He appears in one book with another of this author's detectives, *Satan STAGG.*

American Policeman operating in New York

George BAXT 1923- (American)

Other Detectives:
Harvey GRAYMOOR and Laura GRAYMOOR
Pharaoh LOVE and Det Satan STAGG
Valentine NORTON
Dorothy PARKER and Alexander WOOLLCOTT
Sylvia PLOTKIN and Max Van LARSEN

Citation Record: 2 Books

A Queer Kind Of Death - *First*
Simon & Schuster US (1966); Cape UK (1967)

Swing Low, Sweet Harriet - *Last*
Simon & Schuster US (1967)

Det Pharaoh LOVE and Det Satan STAGG

Although *Pharaoh LOVE* features in the author's last novel, centre stage is taken by another policeman, also black, *Satan STAGG.*

American Policemen operating in New York

George BAXT 1923- (American)

was born in New York City. He is the author of plays, short

L

stories and several genre novels, often set back into the 1920s and using famous actors and film directors as characters.

Invented 6 detectives - see Pharoh LOVE

Citation Record: 1 Book

Topsy And Evil - *Only*
Simon & Schuster US (1968)

LOVEJOY

is one of the most successful British creations of the 1980s, partly because of the intrinsic interest of his background, the slightly shady world of antiques. *LOVEJOY* is himself a dealer in antiques, seemingly scruffy and always short of money. But he is a loveable rogue, never quite on the wrong side of the law, and women fall for him all the time. Ever on the lookout for a rare or underpriced piece, often trying to help out a friend, he becomes involved in squalid crimes in and around the world of antiques. They somehow have a way of being solved to his credit and profit.

British Male Amateur operating in England

Sidekick: TINKER

is a vague, almost tramp-like figure, superb at finding valuable antiques, who assists *LOVEJOY* in his numerous exploits.

British Male - Assistant

Jonathan GASH 1933- (British)

was born in Bolton, Lancashire. He was educated at the University of London and the Royal College of Surgeons and Physicians, London, where he received his medical degrees, 1958. A doctor, pathologist, and microbiologist of some renown, who is still in private practice, he has created a popular and fascinating amateur sleuth who has appeared in TV series over several years.

Writer: John GRANT

Citation Record: 17 Books

The Judas Pair - *First*
Collins UK (1977); Harper & Row US (1977)

The Grace In Older Women - *Latest*
Random Century UK (1994)

Jack LOVEL

British Male Amateur operating in England

O J CURRINGTON 1924- (British)

Writer: Owen Josiah CURRINGTON

Citation Record: 2 Books

A Bad Night's Work - *First*
Deutsch UK (1974)

Break-Out - *Latest*
Deutsch UK (1978)

Clarisse LOVELACE

Second detective of Daniel VALENTINE

Insp LOVICK

British Policeman operating in Norfolk

Gertrude M Bryan WILSON 1899-1986 (British)

Writer: Gertrude Mary Bryan WILSON

Citation Record: 15 Books

Bury That Poker - *First*
Hale UK (1957)

Death On A Broomstick - *Last*
Hale UK (1977)

Ambrose LOW

Second detective of Col BRAIN

Sarah LOWDEN

investigates old diaries to discover why she has been left out of a will. Her curiosity leads to her solving a murder.

American Female Amateur operating in Connecticut

Doris Miles DISNEY 1907-1976 (American)

Invented 7 detectives - see Jefferson DIMARCO

Citation Record: 1 Book

Who Rides A Tiger - *Only*
Doubleday US (1946)

Sow The Wind - *Only*
Nimmo UK (1948)

Philipa LOWE

is the daughter of a police detective, and a career woman who, curious beyond belief, gets involved in murder.

British Female Amateur operating in England

Roger ORMEROD 1920- (British)

was born in Wolverhampton, Staffordshire.

Other Detectives:
Harry KYLE and Angela ROLLASON
David MALLIN and George COE
Richard PATTON and Amelia PATTON

Citation Record: 2 Books

Hung In The Balance - *First*
Constable UK (1990)

Bury Him Darkly - *Latest*
Constable UK (1991)

Selby LOWE

solves a case of death by stabbing in a locked room.

British Male Amateur operating in England

Edgar WALLACE 1875-1932 (British)

Invented 28 detectives - see J G REEDER

Citation Record: 1 Book

A King By Night - *Only*
Long UK (1925); Doubleday US (1926)

Trevor LOWE

British Male Amateur operating in England

Gerald VERNER 1886-1980 (British)

Invented 7 detectives - see Supt BUDD

Citation Record: 13 Books

Phantom Hollow - *First*
Wright & Brown UK (1933)

Death Set In Diamonds - *Last*
Wright & Brown UK (1965)

LOWELL

American Male Amateur operating in New York

A MERRITT 1884-1943 (American)

Writer: Abraham MERRITT

Citation Record: 2 Books

Burn, Witch, Burn! - *First*
Liveright US (1933); Methuen UK (1934)

Creep, Shadow! - *Last*
Doubleday US (1934)

Creep, Shadow, Creep! - *Last**
Methuen UK (1935)

Sgt Shelly LOWENKOPF

American Policeman operating in New York/Los Angeles

Richard FLIEGEL (American)

Citation Record: 4 Books

The Next To Die - *First*
Bantam US (1986)

Time To Kill - *Latest*
Pocket Books US (1990)

Ch Insp LUBBOCK and Det Insp TENCH

operate in police procedurals.

British Policemen operating in England

Brian COOPER 1919- (American)

Invented 3 detectives - see Rod MCKINNON

Citation Record: 3 Books

The Cross Of San Vincente - *First*
Constable UK (1991)

Covenant For Death - *Latest*
Constable UK (1994)

Det Insp Rory LUCCAN

British Policeman operating in London

Nigel MORLAND 1905-1986 (British)

Invented 4 detectives - see Mrs Palmyra Evangeline PYM

Citation Record: 2 Books

Death When She Wakes - *First*
Evans UK (1951)

A Girl Died Singing - *Last*
Evans UK (1952)

Ben LUCIUS

American Male Amateur operating in Detroit

Royce HOWES 1901-1973 (American)

Writer: Royce Bucknam HOWES

Citation Record: 4 Books

Night Of The Garter Murder - *First*
Doubleday US (1937)

The Case Of The Copy-Book Killing - *Last*
!See Appendix 2.
Dutton US (1945)

Simon LUCK

British Male Amateur operating in England

John MARSH 1907- (British)

Inventor of one other detective Ray FELTON

Citation Record: 2 Books

The Reluctant Executioner - *First*
Hale UK (1959)

Girl In A Net - *Last*
Hale UK (1962)

Insp LUCKRAFT

British Policeman operating in England

Arthur J REES 1872-1942 (British)

Writer: Arthur John REES

Other Detectives:
David COLWYN   Colwin GREY

Citation Record: 5 Books

The Pavilion By The Lake - *First*
Lane UK (1930); Dodd, Mead US (1930)

The Corpse That Traveled - *Last*
Dodd, Mead US (1938)

Adam LUDLOW

is a lecturer in English at the fictional North London College. Middle-aged, thin, introspective, a bachelor, and antagonistic to most aspects of modern American culture, he likes to look at art and meditate. He is first drawn into detection by a death in the college and, in later books, he solves cases with the grudging help of the police - and to their annoyance.

British Male Amateur operating in London

Stooge: Insp Herbert MONTERO
of the Yard considers *LUDLOW* a meddling amateur but agrees that he does seem to solve his cases for him.
British Male

Simon NASH 1924- (British)

was born in Cardiff, Wales. He is a sometime lecturer in English at the London School of Economics.

Writer: Raymond CHAPMAN

Citation Record: 5 Books

Dead Of A Counterplot - *First*
Bles UK (1962); Perennial US (1985)

Unhallowed Murder - *Last*
Bles UK (1966); Roy US (1966)

Chris LUDLOW

is an upper-crust golf caddie who solves murders on the golf course.

British Male Amateur operating in England

Malcolm HAMER (British)

is a sportsman and an expert golfer himself. He has been the sports columnist for several newspapers and is also the author of some guide books.

Citation Record: 4 Books

A Deadly Lie - *First*
Headline UK (1992)

Shadows On The Green - *Latest*
Headline UK (1993)

Hans LUGAR

American Male Sleuth operating in USA

Hans LUGAR (British)

was a house name for a few authors gathered round the ephemeral publishers, *Scion*, who turned out a quantity of gangster novels during the 1950s, with various detectives.

Writer: QUINN

Inventor of one other detective Det LONNIE THE FED

Citation Record: 2 Books

Six Foot Deep - *First*
Scion UK (1950)

The Lady Can Lose - *Last*
Scion UK (1951)

Bela LUGOSI

Appears with at least two other detectives - see Toby PETERS

Jimmy LUJACK

was formerly in the Los Angeles Police Department's Vice Squad. Now he operates as a part-time bookie and a PI who investigates crime in the professional football fraternity.

American Male Private Detective operating in Los Angeles

David THOREAU (American)

Citation Record: 2 Books

The Good Book - *First*
Pocket Books US (1988)

The Book Of Numbers - *Last*
Pocket Books US (1990)

Dr LUKE

British Male Amateur operating in England

Fergus HUME 1859-1932 (British)

Invented 24 detectives - see Insp Samuel GORBY

Citation Record: 1 Book

A Marriage Mystery - *Only*
Digby, Long UK (1896)

William LUKES

American Male Amateur operating in Switzerland

Nicholas GUILD 1944- (American)

See main detective Ray GUINNESS

Citation Record: 1 Book

The Lost And Found Man - *Only*
Harper's Magazine Press US (1975); Hale UK (1977)

Tommy LUMB and Peter MARSHAM

British Male Amateurs operating in England

Laurence CROSS (British)

Citation Record: 2 Books

The Dope Dealers - *First*
Jarrolds UK (1928)

The White Chalet - *Last*
Jarrolds UK (1929)

Archie LUMSDEN

British Male Amateur operating in Europe/Turkey

Max SALTMARSH (British)

Citation Record: 3 Books

Highly Inflammable - *First*
Joseph UK (1936); Little, Brown US (1936)

Indigo Death - *Last*
Joseph UK (1938)

Eric LUND

is an ex-FBI agent who takes up amateur sleuthing.

American Male Amateur operating in Massachusetts/Minnesota

Ruth Sawtell WALLIS 1895-1978 (American)

Writer: Ruth Otis Sawtell WALLIS

Inventor of one other detective Susan KENT

Citation Record: 3 Books

No Bones About It - *First*
Dodd, Mead US (1944); Hammond UK (1950)

Forget My Fate - *Last*
Dodd, Mead US (1950)

Nels LUNDBERG

Second detective of Wylie KING

Auguste LUPA

is said to be the son of *Sherlock HOLMES*, and solves vital state problems in France and Russia in the years preceding the First World War.

French Male Amateur operating in Russia

Sidekick: Jules GIRAUD

French Male - Assistant

L

John T LESCROART 1948- (American)

Citation Record: 2 Books

Son Of Holmes - *First*
Fine US (1986)

Rasputin's Revenge - *Latest*
Fine US (1987)

Arsène LUPIN

was a popular French version of the crook-detective, creation that leaned heavily on earlier characters like *LECOCQ*, *A J RAFFLES*, and even *Sherlock HOLMES*. His adventures were amusing and his sardonic view of authority appealed to readers. He became higly regarded, especially since he usually outwitted the police and rarely committed crimes for personal gain. In his later adventures, however, he reformed somewhat and tended to work with the police.

LUPIN appeared in a number of short stories and in novels, the latter being less successful than the former. The best stories have appeared in English under several titles and in several collections.

French Male Professional Amateur operating in France

Edgar JEPSON (British) and Maurice LEBLANC (French)

Writers: Edgar Alfred JEPSON 1863-1938 and Maurice Marie Emile LEBLANC 1864-1941

Citation Record: 1 Book

Arsène Lupin - *Only*
is a novelization in English of the play by *LEBLANC*.
Mills UK (1909); Doubleday US (1909)

Maurice LEBLANC 1864-1941 (French)

was a crime reporter, a playwright, and a hack writer. He is now mainly remembered for his creation of *Arsène LUPIN*.

Writer: Maurice Marie Emile LEBLANC

Other Detectives:
Arsène LUPIN and Herlock SHOLMES
Holmlock SHEARS and Arsène LUPIN

Citation Record: 7 Books 19 Short Stories in 2 Collections

The Crystal Stopper - *First*
Is a translation from the French of *Le Bouchon de Cristal* (Paris, 1912).
Hurst UK (1913); Doubleday US (1913)

The Return Of Arsène Lupin - *Last*
Is a translation from the French of *Victor, de la Brigade Mondaine* (Paris, 1933).
Short Stories - 9
Skeffington UK (1933); Macaulay US (1933)

The Exploits Of Arsène Lupin - *Collection 1*
Is a translation from the French of *Arsène Lupin, Gentleman-Cambrioleur* (Paris, 1907).
Harper US (1909); Cassell UK (1909)

The Seven Of Hearts - *Collection 1**
Cassell UK (1908)

The Confessions of Arsène Lupin - *Collection 2*
Is a translation from the French of *Les Confidences d'Arsène Lupin* (Paris, 1913).
Short Stories - 10
Mills UK (1912); Doubleday US (1913)

Arthur PORGES (American)

Invented 13 detectives - see Stately HOMES

Citation Record: 1 Selected Short Story

In Compartment 813 - *Pastiche 1*
appeared in the June number.
In 'Ellery Queen's Mystery Magazine' US (1966)

Arsène LUPIN

Second detective of Sherlock HOLMES

Arsène LUPIN

Second detective of Holmlock SHEARS

Arsène LUPIN and Herlock SHOLMES

Arsène LUPIN and *Herlock SHOLMES* appeared as co-detectives in this early parody, in which the latter, a *Sherlock HOLMES* parody, is portrayed as just a dunderheaded plodder when compared with the brilliant French detective, *Arsène LUPIN*, who is a parody of *Edgar Allan POE's* detective, *Auguste DUPIN*. The original French novel had a somewhat strange English language publishing history in which *SHOLMES* appeared successively as *HOLMLOCK SHEARS* and finally as *SHERLOCK HOLMES* (the latter in an adaptation by *JACOB BRUSSELL*.

French Male Professional Amateur and British Male Professional Amateur operating in France

Maurice LEBLANC 1864-1941 (French)

Invented 3 detectives - see Arsène LUPIN

Citation Record: 8 Short Stories 1 Collection

Arsène Lupin Versus Holmlock Shears - *Collection 1*
Richards UK (1909)
Is a translation from the French of *Arsène Lupin contre Herlock Sholmes* (Paris, 1908).

The Blonde Lady - *Collection 1**
Doubleday US (1910)
appeared in France in 1908 and it had subsequently a rather chequered English publishing history. The English detective was originally called *Herlock SHEARS*. The book then appeared in English as *THE FAIR-HAIRED LADY* and also as *ARSENE LUPIN VERSUS HERLOCK SHOLMES*, but was then republished as *ARSENE LUPIN VERSUS HOLMLOCK SHEARS*. In 1946, it reappeared as *SHERLOCK HOLMES VERSUS ARSENE LUPIN*.
Pierre Lafitte FR (1908)

The Fair-Haired Lady - *Collection 1**
was the first English version of the *Sherlock HOLMES* parody, *ARSENE LUPIN CONTRE HERLOCK SHEARS*, which was translated by Alexander Teixeira de Mattos. It later appeared as *ARSENE LUPIN VERSUS HOLMLOCK SHEARS* and still later as *SHERLOCK HOLMES VERSUS ARSENE LUPIN*.
Grant Richards UK (1909)

Frank LUTHER

American Male Amateur operating in New York

Edwin LANHAM 1904-1979 (American)

Invented 3 detectives - see Lt GRAY

Citation Record: 2 Books

Murder On My Street - *First*
Harcourt Brace US (1958); Gollancz UK (1958)

No Hiding Place - *Last*
Harcourt Brace US (1962); Gollancz UK (1962)

George LYDNEY

British Male Amateur operating in England

Sebastian FOX 1893-1958 (British)

Writer: Gerald William BULLETT

Citation Record: 2 Books

One Man's Poison - *First*
Chatto UK (1956)

Odd Woman Out - *Last*
Dent UK (1958)

Insp LYLE

is a detective at Scotland Yard in this one Victorian novel.

British Policeman operating in London

Richard Harding DAVIS 1864-1901 (British)

Inventor of one other detective VAN BIBBER

Citation Record: 1 Book

In The Fog - *Only*
Ward, Lock UK (1901); Russell US (1901)

Prof Austin LYLE

is a Professor of Chemistry, who solves an ingenious case of murder by poisoning.

Male Amateur

Lynwood SAWYER

Citation Record: 1 Selected Short Story

The Shredded Rose
In 'Ellery Queen's Mystery Magazine' US (1978)

Insp David LYLE

British Policeman operating in England

John WAINWRIGHT 1921- (British)

Invented 9 detectives - see Ch Insp/Supt LENNOX

Citation Record: 2 Books

Duty Elsewhere - *First*
Macmillan UK (1979); St Martin's US (1979)

Brainwash - *Latest*
Macmillan UK (1979); St Martin's US (1979)

Samuel LYLE

American Male Professional Amateur operating in New England

Arthur CRABB (American)

Writer: UNKNOWN

Citation Record: 1 Book 11 Short Stories in 1 Collection

Ghosts - *Single*
Century US (1921)

Mrs Brown's Pearls - *Single**
Page UK (1921)

Samuel Lyle, Criminologist - *Collection 1*
Century US (1920)

Bertram LYNCH

is an investigator attached to the League of Nations and is sent to a number of exotic tropical locales to deal with crimes of various kinds.

American Male Professional Investigator operating in Fiji/Haiti

Sidekick: Prof Robert DEANE

is a Professor of Medieval History who is sent to accompany *LYNCH* and narrates the cases.

American Male - Narrator

John W VANDERCOOK 1902-1963 (American)

was born in London. He was a reporter for US papers and spent several years as an explorer in the tropical locations that he used in his books.

Writer: John Womack VANDERCOOK

Citation Record: 4 Books

Murder In Trinidad - *First*
Doubleday US (1933); Heinemann UK (1934)

Murder In New Guinea - *Last*
Macmillan US (1959); Allen UK (1960)

Colin LYNCH

British Male Secret Agent operating in several locations

Paul MANN

Citation Record: 2 Books

The Libyan Contract - *First*
Macmillan AU (1988); Macmillan UK (1988)

The Beirut Contract - *Latest*
Pan AU (1989); Pan UK (1991)

Paul LYNDE

is said to have been the first detective to have been created by an American author after the pioneering stories of *Edgar Allan POE.*

American Male Amateur operating in New Hampshire

Thomas Bailey ALDRICH 1836-1907 (American)

was born in Portsmouth, New Hampshire. A poet, novelist and playwright, he covered the Civil War as a journalist for the prestigious *Atlantic Monthly*. He was, in addition, one of the pioneers of the detective story.

Inventor of one other detective TAGGETT

Citation Record: 1 Book

Out Of His Head - *Only*

constitutes a landmark in the history of detective fiction, for it was the first to contain a complete detective story (in chapters 11 to 14) written by an American since the tales of *Edgar Allan POE*. Furthermore, it was one of the very earliest stories of the 'locked-room' type. And it has the final distinction of being the first in which the detective is the murderer.

Carlton US (1862)

Insp Thomas LYNLEY

is, in fact, 'the 8th Earl of Asherton' and has an appointment at Scotland Yard. As befits such a man, however, he is usually called on to solve cases deep in rural England, which quite naturally exhibit historic overtones, sexual undercurrents, and a deal of gore, resulting in the total bafflement of the local cops. While doing the necessary sleuthing, he is building a complex relationship with his delectable female sergeant, his constant assistant: it is a development – not to be wholly welcomed, on literary rather than moral grounds – that seems to be reaching epidemic proportions in the fictional British police force.

British Policeman operating in England

Sidekick: Sgt Barbara HAVERS

lacks self-confidence in her relationship with her guv. She fights to make good in her job, although she senses that the relationship is becoming more than just official.

British Female - Subordinate

Elizabeth GEORGE 1949- (American)

was born in Warren, Ohio. She graduated from the University of California with a BA in English and has since been an English teacher at several American universities. Her detective stories, all of which have British settings, have been awarded the *Grand Prix de Littérature Policière*, 1990.

Inventor of one other detective The Earl of ATHERTON

Citation Record: 7 Books

A Great Deliverance - *First*
Bantam US (1988); Bantam UK (1989)

Playing For The Ashes - *Latest*
Bantam US (1994); Bantam UK (1994)

Millie LYNNE

!See Appendix 2.

British Female Professional Investigator operating in England

L

Cecil H BULLIVANT 1882- (British)

Invented 5 detectives - see Garnett BELL

Citation Record: 13 Short Stories in 1 Collection

Millie Lynne - Shop Investigator - *Collection 1*
Odhams UK (1920)

Jason LYNX

is an interior decorator and antique dealer in Denver, Colorado, who runs into murders. He is an excellent amateur sleuth, but is more than fortunate in having a close girl-friend who is a detective in the local police.

American Male Amateur operating in Colorado

Sidekick: Det Grace WILLIS
may be in the local police but she acts just like a good old-fashioned sidekick to a good old-fashioned amateur sleuth.
American Female - Girl-friend

A J ORDE 1929- (American)

Citation Record: 3 Books

Death And The Dogwalker - *First*
Doubleday US (1990); Collins UK (1990)

Death For Old Time's Sake - *Latest*
Collins UK (1992)

LYNX-EYE

American Male Detective in Pulp Magazines operating in USA

No citations

LYON and GATCH

American Male Private Detectives operating in USA

ANON

Citation Record: 1 Book

The Wolves Of Washington - *Only*
Aldine US (1895)

Insp LYON

Australian Policeman operating in Australia

Patrick WINN 1906- (British)

Inventor of one other detective Lee SEDDON

Citation Record: 3 Books

Postscript To Murder - *First*
Hale UK (1964)

Dead Innocent - *Last*
Hale UK (1966)

Thomas LYON

has horse-racing in his blood, although he is a successful maker of films. While shooting a film near Newmarket, he is able to use both his skills to solve an old case of murder.

British Male Amateur operating in England

Dick FRANCIS 1920- (British)

Invented 18 detectives - see Sid HALLEY

Citation Record: 1 Book

Wild Horses - *Single*
Joseph UK (1994); Putnam US (1994)

Pauline LYONS

American Female Amateur operating in Atlanta

Elizabeth ANTHONY (American)

Writers: Anthony TRAYNOR and Page TRAYNOR

Citation Record: 2 Books

Ballet Of Death - *First*
Zebra US (1979)

Ballet Of Fear - *Latest*
Zebra US (1979)

Charles LYSON

British Male Amateur operating in England

E Phillips OPPENHEIM 1866-1946 (British)

Invented 27 detectives - see Nicholas GOADE

Citation Record: 20 Short Stories in 2 Collections

A Pulpit In The Grill Room - *Collection 1*
Short stories - 10
Hodder & Stoughton UK (1938); Little, Brown US (1939)

The Milan Grill Room - *Collection 2*
Short stories - 10
Hodder & Stoughton UK (1940); Little, Brown US (1941)

—M—

Nicholas MAASTEN

Male Secret Agent operating in several locations

Owen SELA (British)

Citation Record: 3 Books

The Bearer Plot - *First*
Hodder & Stoughton UK (1972); Pantheon US (1973)

The Portuguese Fragment - *Last*
Pantheon US (1973); Hodder & Stoughton UK (1974)

MAC

appeared in over a dozen books before it was disclosed that he had a surname, which turned out, most disappointingly, to be Robinson. He is, however, the archetypal American private eye who perhaps needs no other name. He lives alone with no revealed private life and, although he is usually chaste, women throw themselves at him. He operates at first in Chicago and later in New York City. Ageless through the series, he narrates his own cases, which are real puzzles, well clued and without overt violence.

American Male Private Detective operating in New York/Chicago

Sidekick: Det DONOVAN
is a veteran police officer who sometimes brings cases to *MAC* and occasionally assists him in solving them.
American Male - Aide

Thomas B DEWEY 1915- (American)

Invented 3 detectives - see Singer BATTS

Citation Record: 16 Books

Draw The Curtain Close - *First*
Jefferson House US (1947); Dakers UK (1951)

The Taurus Trip - *Last*
Simon & Schuster US (1970)

MAC

Second detective of Jeremiah X GIBSON

Philip MACADAM

American Male Private Detective operating in USA

Hillary WAUGH 1920- (American)

Invented 7 detectives - see Ch Fred FELLOWS

Citation Record: 1 Book

The Girl Who Cried Wolf - *Only*
Doubleday US (1958); Foulsham UK (1960)

Johnny MACALL

is a former London police superintendent who operates privately in some very nasty cases.

British Male Private Detective operating in London

Gerard FAIRLIE 1899-1983 (British)

was born in London. Educated in Brussels and the Royal Military Academy, Sandhurst, he served in the Army, 1918-1924, and again in 1939-1945, receiving the *Croix de Guerre.* He was a fine boxer and skier, and was the sports correspondent for newspapers in the 1930s as well as a screen writer. He continued the *'Bulldog' DRUMMOND* stories after the death of the latter's creator, and his several new novels brought the character up-to-date. He also wrote about twenty other criminous books.

Other Detectives:
Bow St Runner Victor CARYLL Capt Hugh 'Bulldog' DRUMMOND Mr MALCOLM
Citation Record: 6 Books
Winner Take All - *First*
Hodder & Stoughton UK (1953); Dodd, Mead US (1953)
Please Kill My Cousin - *Last*
Hodder & Stoughton UK (1961)

Frank MACALLISTER
British Male Private Detective operating in several locations

Ritchie PERRY 1942- (British)
See main detective Arthur PHILIS
Citation Record: 2 Books
MacAllister - *First*
Doubleday US (1984); Hale UK (1986)
Presumed Dead - *Latest*
Doubleday US (1987)

Ross MACALLISTER
British Male Amateur operating in England

Christopher CORAM 1936- (British)
For writer details see Det Supt Mark PEMBERTON
Citation Record: 2 Books
Murder By The Lake - *First*
Hale UK (1975)
Death In Ptarmigan Forest - *Last*
Hale UK (1970)

Donald MACALPINE
British Male Amateur operating in Tibet

Sir Gilbert CAMPBELL 1838-1899 (British)
See main detective Insp DONOVAN
Citation Record: 1 Book
The Vanishing Diamonds: Or, The Treasure-Seekers Of Tibet - *Only*
Ward, Lock UK (1890)

Prof Adam MACAMERON
Second detective of Dr Henry RIDDLE

Ian MACARTHUR
British Male Amateur operating in England

Selwyn JEPSON 1899-1989 (British)
Invented 4 detectives - see Roger SPAIN
Citation Record: 1 Book
The Qualified Adventurer - *Only*
Hutchinson UK (1922); Harcourt US (1922)
Manchu Jade - *Only**
Mellifont UK (1935)

Mr MACAULEY
British Male Amateur operating in England

Russell THORNDYKE 1885-1972 (British)
See main detective Dr SYN
Citation Record: 2 Books
The Slype - *First*
Holden UK (1927); Dial US (1928)
Herod's Peal - *Last*
Butterworth UK (1931)
The Devil In The Belfry - *Last**
Dial US (1932)

Const Hamish MACBETH
polices the sleepy Highland village of Lochdubh, where the peace is continually being shattered, it seems, by unimaginable crimes.
British Policeman operating in Scotland

M C BEATON 1936- (British)
Invented 3 detectives - see Insp BLAIR
Citation Record: 7 Books
Death Of A Gossip - *First*
Bravos UK (1985); St Martin's US (1985)
Death Of A Charming Man - *Latest*
Mysterious Press US (1994)

Frank MACBRIDE and Pete RYAN
MACBRIDE is an old retired cop and *RYAN* is an ex-crook. They appear in novelizations of episodes from a TV series.
American Male Private Detective and American Male Amateur operating in USA

Michael JAHN 1943- (American)
See main detective Jim ROCKFORD
Citation Record: 2 Books
Switch - *First*
Berkley US (1976); Star UK (1976)
Switch 2 - *Latest*
Berkley US (1976)

Capt Steve MACBRIDE
is a Homicide cop in the New York Police Department, as tough as nails as he stalks through his cases in stories virtually all written originally for *Black Mask Magazine.*
American Policeman operating in New York

Sidekick: KENNEDY
is a reporter for *Free Press* who invariably accompanies *MACBRIDE* in his cases and acts as a light foil to the latter's heaviness.
American Male - Assistant

Frederick NEBEL 1903-1967 (American)
Invented 8 detectives - see Steve CARDIGAN
Citation Record: 2 Selected Short Stories
The Crimes Of Richmond City
is the first of thirty-four known stories.
In 'Black Mask Magazine' US (1928)
Deep Red
is the last of thirty-four known stories.
In 'Black Mask Magazine' US (1936)

Det Insp Duncan MACCALLUM
British Policeman operating in several locations

Allan MACKINNON (British)
Invented 4 detectives - see Don KENDRICK
Citation Record: 2 Books
Nine Day's Murder - *First*
Collins UK (1945)
Money On The Black - *First**
Doubleday US (1946)
House Of Darkness - *Last*
Collins UK (1947); Doubleday US (1947)

Cam MACCARDLE
lives at Fort Lauderdale in a house, rather than in a boat like his hero, the fictional *Travis MCGEE*. Invalided from the Marines and an ex-football player, he carries out investigations for a law firm.
American Male Private Detective operating in Florida

Tucker HALLERAN (American)
Inventor of one other detective King Edward VII WINDSOR
Citation Record: 2 Books
A Cool Clear Death - *First*
St Martin's US (1985)
Sudden Death Finish - *Latest*
St Martin's US (1985)

Philip MACCRAY
appears also with one of the author's other detectives, *Artemus GRAHAM.*
American Male Amateur operating in Chicago/Los Angeles

Owen Fox JEROME 1897-1963 (American)
Invented 3 detectives - see George ROBIN
Citation Record: 5 Books

M

The Hand Of Horror - *First*
Clode US (1927); Skeffington UK (1929)

Leave Everything To Me - *Last*
Mystery House US (1959)

Philip MACCRAY and Artemus GRAHAM

Although usually on his own, *Philip MACCRAY* shares the honours in this one book.

American Male Amateurs operating in Chicago

Owen Fox JEROME 1897-1963 (American)

Writer: Oscar Jerome FRIEND

Invented 3 detectives - see George ROBIN

Citation Record: 1 Book

The Red Kite Clue - *Only*
Clode US (1928); Skeffington UK (1929)

Insp/Supt MACDONALD

is a London Scot, the son of a newspaperman, who joined the Metropolitan Police after service in the First World War. A bachelor, he lives alone, looked after by his old batman. Tall, lean and active, he is also a rather clever detective – as he must be to have lasted in an exceptionally long series spanning nearly three decades.

British Policeman operating in London

Sidekick: Sgt REEVES
British Male - Subordinate

E C R LORAC 1894-1958 (British)

was born in London. She was the author of over seventy genre books, mostly conventional police thrillers.

Writer: Edith Caroline RIVETT

Other Byline: Carol CARNAC

Inventor of one other detective Supt KEMPSON

Citation Record: 46 Books

The Murder On The Burrows - *First*
Sampson, Low UK (1931); Macaulay US (1932)

Dishonour Among Thieves - *Last*
Collins UK (1959)

The Last Escape - *Last**
Doubleday US (1959)

Lynn MACDONALD

runs a female-staffed detective agency based in Oregon but sometimes takes on cases elsewhere.

American Female Private Detective operating in Oregon

Kay Cleaver STRAHAN 1888-1941 (American)

Citation Record: 7 Books

The Desert Moon Mystery - *First*
Doubleday US (1928); Gollancz UK (1928)

The Desert Lake Mystery - *Last*
Bobbs US (1936); Methuen UK (1937)

Paul MACDONALD

is a journalist who has worked himself out and a writer of books that do not sell. He prepares reports for a PI who is murdered and, suspected, has to turn sleuth to save himself. He seems to be going on with the detective work.
!See Appendix 2.

American Male Private Detective operating in San Francisco

Julie SMITH 1944- (American)

was born in Annapolis, Maryland. She has been a reporter in San Francisco.

Other Detectives:
Offr Skip LANGDON
Philip MARLOWE
Rebecca SCHWARTZ

Citation Record: 2 Books

True-Life Adventure - *First*
Mysterious Press US (1985)

Huckleberry Fiend - *Latest*
Mysterious Press US (1987)

Insp MACE and Prof Heinrich UNTERMENSCH

When murder occurs in connection with a great London museum, *Insp MACE* is on the case, but he needs expert assistance from the famous *Prof UNTERMENSCH* to solve it.

British Policeman and Male Amateur operating in London

Penelope FITZGERALD 1916- (British)

was born in Lincoln, Lincolnshire, daughter of the distinguished writer, *E V KNOX*.

Citation Record: 1 Book

The Golden Child - *Only*
Duckworth UK (1977); Scribner's US (1979)

Insp MACE

British Policeman operating in England

Richard KEVERNE 1882-1950 (British)

Writer: Clifford James Wheeler HOSKEN

Other Detectives:
Simon ARTIFEX
Sir Christopher HAZZARD
Franklin PARRY and Leonard HARRIS

Citation Record: 2 Books

White Gas - *First*
Constable UK (1937)

Open Verdict - *Last*
Constable UK (1940)

MACE

Male Sleuth operating in several locations

James GRANT 1933-

Writer: Bruce Ian CROWTHER

Citation Record: 2 Books

Mace! - *First*
Piatkus UK (1984); Critic US (1984)

Mace's Luck - *Latest*
Piatkus UK (1985)

Leonard MACE

solves what appears an 'impossible' murder by shooting.

American Male Amateur operating in USA

Curtis T GARDNER (American)

See main detective Valentine VICKERS

Citation Record: 1 Selected Short Story

Death's Bright Angel
Street & Smith US (1948)

Sheriff MACFARLAND

solves a case of murder in a mine.

American Policeman operating in USA

Tyline PERRY (American)

Inventor of one other detective Sheriff Gus FLOWERS

Citation Record: 1 Book

The Owner Lies Dead - *Only*
Covici US (1930); Gollancz UK (1930)

'Mac' MACFARLAND

is a reporter who is out of a job and has just had his wife leave him. His life begins to pick up, however, when he gets to solving murders.

American Male Amateur operating in Chicago

Douglas KIKER 1930-1991 (American)

Citation Record: 3 Books

Murder On Clam Pond - *First*
Random House US (19868)

Last Death Below Deck - *Latest*
Random House US (1991)

Rev P J MACFARLANE

British Male Amateur operating in Scotland

Angus MACVICAR 1908- (British)

See main detective Bruce MCLINTOCK

M

Citation Record: 2 Books

The Temple Falls - *First*
Paul UK (1935)

The Crouching Spy - *Last*
Paul UK (1941)

Maggie MACGOWEN

is an investigative film-maker who is trying to help a young prostitute. When the latter is murdered, she finds out why and whodunnit.

American Female Amateur operating in USA

Wendy HORNSBY (American)

is a sometime Professor of History at the University of California.

Inventor of one other detective Roger TEJEDA

Citation Record: 1 Book

Midnight Baby - *Single*
Dutton US (1993)

Capt James Donald MACGREGOR

British Male Professional Investigator operating in Middle East

Robert MASON (British)

Citation Record: 13 Short Stories in 2 Collections

Cairo Communiqué - *Collection 1*
Short stories - 4
Hurst UK (1942)

More News From Middle East - *Collection 2*
Short stories - 9
Hurst UK (1943)

Niccolò MACHIAVELLI

is, indeed, the great early sixteenth-century Florentine politician and here he solves a case in which jewels have been removed from a guarded room.

Italian Male Amateur operating in Italy

Thomas FLANAGAN 1923- (American)

was born in Greenwich, Connecticut.

Inventor of one other detective Maj TENNENTE

Citation Record: 1 Selected Short Story

The Fine Italian Hand

appeared in the May number and has since been included in several anthologies, the latest being *8 Doors to Death* (*Dell*; US 1970).
In 'Ellery Queen's Mystery Magazine' US (1949)

Kevin MACINNES

is a 'Psychological Stress Detector Expert', which is a useful thing to be if you are a PI in Manhattan and are fond of the good life.

American Male Private Detective operating in New York/Ohio

Franklin BANDY 1914-1987 (American)

For writer details see Berkeley Hoy BARNES

Citation Record: 3 Books

Deceit And Deadly Lies - *First*
Charter US (1978); Magnum UK (1979)

The Blackstock Affair - *Latest*
Charter US (1980)

Urbino MACINTYRE

is an American expatriate who is drawn into mysteries and murders among the old Venetian aristocracy, usually involving skulduggery in the art world.

American Male Amateur operating in Venice

Edward SKLEPOWICH (American)

is an American Fulbright scholar who lives in Venice.

Citation Record: 3 Books

Death In A Serene City - *First*
Morrow US (1990)

Liquid Desires - *Latest*
Avon US (1993)

Dr Johnny MACK

American Male Amateur operating in New York

Theodore S DRACHMAN 1904-1988 (American)

Writer: Theodore Solomon DRACHMAN

Citation Record: 3 Books

Cry Plague! - *First*
Ace US (1953)

The Deadly Dream - *Last*
Erikson US (1982)

Madelyn MACK

is twenty-five years old, golden-haired, and beautiful. Described as 'a college girl confronted suddenly with the necessity of earning her own living', she first appeared in a collection of short stories in 1914 and is important in the history of the genre as she is clearly an updated female version of *Sherlock HOLMES*, using his methods, and even given to taking coca berries as a stimulant. She solved some difficult cases, including two of the locked-room variety.

American Female Professional Amateur operating in New York

Sidekick: Nora NORAKER

is a gushing and adoring young reporter who narrates the stories. She is blessed, we are told, 'with a card-index' brain, which is, of course, of inestimable value to the hard-pressed female sleuth.

American Female - Assistant and Narrator

Hugh C WEIR 1884-1934 (American)

Writer: Hugh Cosgro WEIR

Citation Record: 5 Short Stories in 1 Collection

Miss Madelyn Mack, Detective - *Collection 1*
Page US (1914)

Terry MACK

has been called the very first hardboiled PI in detective fiction. He actually calls himself a 'Private Investigator' and habitually carries three guns to prove he is in at the beginning of a new era that would have suited *Philo VANCE* not at all. His first appearance was in a short story called *Three Gun Terry*.

American Male Private Detective operating in New England

Carroll John DALY 1889-1958 (American)

Invented 6 detectives - see Race WILLIAMS

Citation Record: 1 Book

The Man In The Shadows - *Only*
Clode US (1928); Hutchinson UK (1924)

Insp MACKAY

Canadian Policeman operating in Canada

E Louise CUSHING (Canadian)

Citation Record: 3 Books

Murder Without Regret - *First*
Arcadia US (1954)

The Unexpected Corpse - *Last*
Arcadia US (1957)

Kathryn MACKAY

is a District Attorney who, in her first book, gets cryptic notes from a serial killer and realises that the next chosen victim is herself. What can a girl do but go out and get him before he gets her?

American Female Amateur operating in USA

Christine MCGUIRE (American)

Citation Record: 1 Book

Until Proven Guilty - *Single*
Pocket Books US (1994)

Edmond MACKELL

solves a case of thefts from a locked room.

Irish Male Private Detective operating in Eire

James Vincent NOLAN

Citation Record: 1 Book

Murder Walks Alone - *Only*
Grafton El (1945)

Shane MACKENZIE

British Male Amateur operating in several locations

Ronald MAGOWAN (British)

Citation Record: 4 Books

Monopoly To Murder - *First*
Hale UK (1968)

Fox In The Sea - *Last*
Hale UK (1975)

Clay MACKINNON

works in Castile, and the people he meets say he can be very tough indeed.

American Male Private Detective operating in Florida

Steve BRACKEEN (American)

Citation Record: 1 Book

Delfina - *Only*
GM US (1962); Muller UK (1963)

Alan MACKLIN

is a minor operator hired by a billionaire to investigate his bride.

American Male Private Detective operating in USA

E V CUNNINGHAM 1914- (American)

Invented 4 detectives - see Det Sgt Masao MASUTO

Citation Record: 1 Book

Sylvia - *Only*
Doubleday US (1962); Deutsch UK (1962)

M

Peter MACKLIN

American Male Sleuth operating in USA

Loren D ESTLEMAN 1952- (American)

Invented 7 detectives - see Amos WALKER

Citation Record: 3 Books

Kill Zone - *First*
Mysterious Press US (1984); Mysterious Press UK (1984)

Any Man's Death - *Latest*
Mysterious Press US (1986); Mysterious Press UK (1986)

Duncan MACLAIN

was formerly a US Intelligence officer. Blinded in the First World War, he is now a PI, operating from his elegant penthouse in Manhattan. In books of adventure and detection, he is aided not only by his partner but by his two German Shepherd dogs. Like all blind detectives, *MACLAIN* is pretty good at things like shooting at the merest sound.

American Male Private Detective operating in New York

Sidekick: Spud SAVAGE
is technically the partner of *MACLAIN* but acts as a sidekick.
American Male - Assistant

Sidekick: SCHNUCKE
is the more docile of the detective's two dogs and is, in fact, his seeing eye.
Female - Pet Dog

Sidekick: DREIST
has been trained to attack in an instant at the detective's command, a most useful attribute in a canine sidekick.
Male - Pet Dog

Stooge: Insp Larry DAVIS
of the New York Police Department seems a pretty stupid fellow when *MACLAIN* is around.
American Male

Baynard KENDRICK 1894-1977 (American)

was born in Philadelphia, Pennsylvania. He was educated at Tome School, Port Deposit, Maryland, and the Episcopal Academy, Philadelphia. He served with the Canadian Army, 1914-1918, and as an instructor for blind veterans in the Second World War, later working as a writer and editor on several newspapers and as a free-lance writer, 1932. He was a founder and the first President of the Mystery Writers of America, 1945, and received their Grand Master award, 1967.

Writer: Baynard Hardwick KENDRICK

Other Detectives:
Cliff CHANDLER   Miles Standish RICE

Citation Record: 13 Books

The Last Express - *First*
Doubleday US (1937); Methuen UK (1938)

Frankincense And Murder - *Last*
Dodd, Mead US (1961); Hale UK (1962)

Supt Steve MACLAREN

British Policeman operating in Malaysia

Bruce SCOTT (British)

Citation Record: 2 Books

The Prayer Mat - *First*
Hale US (1971)

The Secret Of the Elephant - *Last*
Hale US (1967)

Dr Gregor MACLEAN

sleuths in rural England in novels set back to the Edwardian era.

British Male Amateur operating in England

Richard COPELAND 1923- (British)

For writer details see Paul BRODIE

Citation Record: 1 Book

No Face In The Mirror - *Only*
Macmillan UK (1980)

Hugh MCLEAVE 1923- (British)

Invented 3 detectives - see Paul BRODIE

Citation Record: 3 Books

A Question Of Negligence - *First*
Collins UK (1973); Harcourt Brace US (1970)

Death Masque - *Latest*
Hale UK (1985); Walker US (1986)

Mike MACLEAN

is a journalist who investigates the disposal of toxic waste and stumbles across murder.

British Male Amateur operating in England

Paul ADAM (British)

Citation Record: 1 Book

Toxin - *Single*
HarperCollins UK (1995)

Roy MACLEAN

British Male Amateur operating in Scotland

Bill GASTON 1927- (British)

Writer: William James GASTON

Citation Record: 2 Books

Deep Green Death - *First*
Hammond UK (1963)

Drifting Death - *Last*
Hammond UK (1964)

Cooper MACLEISH

finds it difficult to make ends meet by working as a cab-driver and is involved in various scams. However, his activities do lead him to solve some nasty cases of murder, though not as a fine art.

American Male Amateur operating in Chicago

Sam REAVES (American)

Citation Record: 3 Books

A Long Cold Fall - *First*
Putnam US (1991)

Bury It Deep - *Latest*
St Martin's US (1994)

Insp Neil MACLEOD

British Policeman operating in England

Allan Campbell MCLEAN 1922- (British)

Citation Record: 3 Books

The Carpet-Slipper Murder - *First*
Ward, Lock UK (1956); Washburn US (1957)

Death On All Hallows - *Last*
Washburn US (1958)

Murder By Invitation - *Last**
Ward, Lock UK (1959)

Insp Marcus MACLURG

is a traditional British policeman solving traditional whodunnits.

British Policeman operating in England

Rhona PETRIE 1922- (British)

Writer: Eileen-Marie Duell BUCHANAN

Inventor of one other detective Dr Nassim PRIDE

Citation Record: 5 Books

Death In Deakins Wood - *First*
Gollancz UK (1963); Dodd, Mead US (1964)

MacLurg Goes West - *Last*
Gollancz UK (1968)

Insp MACMASTERS

solves a case of death by poison in the middle of a tennis match at Wimbledon.

British Policeman operating in London

Helen WILLS and Robert W MURPHY (British)

Writers: Helen Newington WILLS 1906- and Robert William MURPHY 1902-1971

Citation Record: 1 Book

Death Serves An Ace - *Only*
Hutchinson UK (1939); Scribner's US (1939)

Francis MACNAB

British Male Amateur operating in England

John FERGUSON 1873- (British)

Writer: John Alexander FERGUSON

Citation Record: 5 Books

The Man In The Dark - *First*
Lane UK (1928); Dodd, Mead US (1928)

The Death Of Mr Dodsley - *Last*
Collins UK (1937)

Angus MACNAIR

of Scotland Yard solves a case of drowning in a locked bathroom.

British Policeman operating in England

R E SWARTWOUT (British)

Writer: Robert Egerton SWARTWOUT

Citation Record: 1 Book

The Boat Race Murder - *Only*
Grayson UK (1933)

Lionel MACNAUGHTEN-INNES

British Male Amateur operating in several locations

Arthur GRIFFITHS 1838-1908 (British)

Invented 8 detectives - see Insp FASKE

Citation Record: 16 Short Stories in 1 Collection

In Tight Places: Some Experiences Of An Amateur Detective - *Collection 1*
Jarrolds UK (1900)

Harry MACNEIL

is an ex-cop who lives in an apartment over a jazz club in 52nd Street, Manhattan. He prefers playing the clarinet to sleuthing.

American Male Private Detective operating in New York

H Paul JEFFERS 1934- (American)

Invented 3 detectives - see David MORGAN

Citation Record: 3 Books

Rubout At The Onyx - *First*
Ticknor & Fields US (1981)

The Rag Doll Murder - *Latest*
St Martin's US (1987)

Supt MACNEILL

British Policeman operating in England

W Murdoch DUNCAN 1909-1975 (British)

was born in Glasgow. A historian, he is the author of at least thirty-three genre novels.

Writer: William Murdoch DUNCAN

Other Bylines:
John CASSELLS — Neill GRAHAM
Peter MALLOCH — Lovat MARSHALL

Other Detectives:
Insp FLAGG — Supt GAYLORD
Mr GILLY — GREENSLEEVES
Insp Laurie HUME — Supt LESLIE
Supt Donald (The Dreamer) REAMER

Citation Record: 3 Books

Death Stands Round The Corner - *First*
Rich UK (1955)

Pennies For His Eyes - *Last*
Long UK (1956)

Elisha MACOMBER

is an important figure in Martha's Vineyard and is able to solve many cases of local murder before the police can.

American Male Amateur operating in Cape Cod

Kathleen Moore KNIGHT (American)

Inventor of one other detective Margot BLAIR

Citation Record: 16 Books

Death Blew Out The Match - *First*
Doubleday US (1935); Heinemann UK (1935)

Beauty Is A Beast - *Last*
Doubleday US (1959); Hammond UK (1960)

Elizabeth MACPHERSON

is, when she first appears, just a young lady with a passion for sleuthing. She eventually marries a marine biologist whose work takes him to various places in the USA and Europe, where she naturally encounters murder and can continue practising her hobby.

American Female Amateur operating in USA/Europe

Sharyn MCCRUMB (American)

Other Detectives:
Sheriff Spencer ARROWWOOD
Henry KRETZNER — Jay OMEGA

Citation Record: 6 Books

Sick Of Shadows - *First*
Avon US (1984); Severn UK (1992)

Missing Susan - *Latest*
Ballantine US (1991)

Det Supt George MACRAE and Det Sgt Leopold SILVER

are a British duo, operating from London's Cannon Row police station, illustrating most of what's wrong with the modern British police.

British Policemen operating in London

Alan SCHOLEFIELD 1931- (British)

Citation Record: 4 Books

Dirty Weekend - *First*
Macmillan UK (1990)

Threats And Menaces - *Latest*
Macmillan UK (1993)

Hawk MACRAE

American Male Sleuth operating in Europe/China

Albert BARKER 1900- (American)

See main detective Reefe KING

Citation Record: 5 Books

The Dragon In Spring - *First*
Curtis US (1973)

The Diamond Fix - *Last*
Curtis US (1974)

Jamie MACRAE

finds out that the life of a PI is not quite like it is in the books he reads.

American Male Private Detective operating in Kentucky

Emmett MCDOWELL 1914-1975 (American)

See main detective Jonathan KNOX

Citation Record: 1 Book

Switcheroo - *Only*
Ace US (1954)

Sheriff MACREADY

American Policeman operating in South Carolina

Hugh HOLMAN 1914-1981 (American)

Writer: Clarence Hugh HOLMAN

Inventor of one other detective Norman TRAVIS

Citation Record: 4 Books

Trout In The Milk - *First*
Mill US (1945); Boardman UK (1951)

Another Man's Poison - *Last*
Mill US (1947); Foulsham UK (1950)

Insp MACSPORRAN

British Policeman operating in Scotland

Lawrence HILL (British)

Citation Record: 2 Books

Dagger Drawn - *First*
Collins UK (1939)

Corpse Without Boots - *Last*
Collins UK (1940)

M

Alonzo MACTAVISH

British Male Amateur operating in several locations

Peter CHEYNEY 1896-1951 (British)

Invented 11 detectives - see Lemmy CAUTION

Citation Record: 1 Book 23 Short Stories in 2 Collections

Alonzo MacTavish Again - *Only*
Polybooks UK (1943)

The Adventures Of Alonzo MacTavish - *Collection 1*
Short stories - 4
Polybooks UK (1943)

He Walked In Her Sleep - *Collection 2*
Short stories - 19
Todd UK (1954)

MacTavish - *Collection 2**
Belmont US (1973)

Capt Andy MACVEIGH

is an investigator for the New York, Chicago & Western Railroad.

American Male Professional Investigator operating in USA

Sidekick: Susie MACVEIGH
assists her husband and narrates his cases.
American Female - Wife

Sue MACVEIGH 1898?- (American)

Writer: Elizabeth Custer NEARING

Citation Record: 4 Books

Murder Under Construction - *First*
Houghton US (1939)

The Corpse And The Three Ex-Husbands - *Last*
Houghton US (1941)

Angus MACWHORTER

is incompetent and lazy, yet he manages to solve the most terrifying of cases by the power of coincidences.

American Male Amateur operating in Chicago

Harry Stephen KEELER 1890-1967 (American)

was born in Chicago, Illinois, and educated at the Armour Institute, graduating with a degree in Electrical Engineering. He was the author of over seventy mildly criminous works, often of a bizarre, farcical, and almost incomprehensible nature. His novels became larger and more convoluted with time, packed with grotesque characters and exotic knowledge, the strange outpourings of an eccentric genius.

Other Detectives:
Margaret ANNISTER
Dr BURKHALTER
Y CHEUNG
Elsa COLBY
David CROSBY
Jeff DARRELL
Simon GRUNDT
Billy HEMPLE
X JONES
Jimmie KENTLAND
Bob LANDRELL
Angus MACWHORTER and Sheriff Bugrus DUCKHOUSE
Terry O'ROURKE

Citation Record: 2 Books

The Case Of The Jeweled Ragpicker - *Last*
Phoenix Press US (1948)

The Ace Of Spades Murder - *Last**
Ward, Lock UK (1949)

Harry Stephen KEELER 1890-1967 and Hazel GOODWIN (American)

Other Detectives:
Dr Everett EDWARDS
Tuddleton TROTTER

Citation Record: 1 Book

Stand By - London Calling - *Only*
Ward, Lock UK (1953)

Angus MACWHORTER and Sheriff Bugrus DUCKHOUSE

Angus MACWHORTER also appears on his own in other books by this author.

American Male Amateur and American Policeman operating in USA

Harry Stephen KEELER 1890-1967 (American)

Invented 14 detectives - see Angus MACWHORTER

Citation Record: 2 Books

The Vanishing Gold Truck - *First*
Dutton US (1941); Ward, Lock UK (1942)

Eve MACWILLIAMS

American Female Amateur operating in Maine

Marie BLIZARD (American)

Citation Record: 2 Books

The Late, Lamented Lady - *First*
Mystery House US (1946)

The Men In Her Death - *Last*
Mystery House US (1947)

Con MADDEN

investigates, on behalf of a murder suspect, a murder trail that has long gone cold.

British Male Private Detective operating in England

Maurice WALSH 1879-1964 (British)

Citation Record: 1 Book

The Man In Brown - *Only*
Chambers UK (1945)

Nine Strings To Your Bow - *Only**
Lippincott US (1945)

David MADDEN

is a lonely, hardworking Postal Inspector for the US Mail, and his cases are concerned with theft.

American Male Professional Investigator operating in Connecticut

Doris Miles DISNEY 1907-1976 (American)

Invented 7 detectives - see Jefferson DIMARCO

Citation Record: 3 Books

Unappointed Rounds - *First*
Doubleday US (1956)

The Post Office Case - *First**
Foulsham UK (1957)

Mrs Meeker's Money - *Last*
Doubleday US (1961); Hale UK (1963)

Joseph (The Vigilante) MADDEN

American Male Sleuth operating in Los Angeles/Washington

V J SANTIAGO

House name.

Citation Record: 6 Books

Detour To A Funeral - *First*
Pinnacle US (1975)

This Gun For Justice - *Latest*
Pinnacle US (1978)

Bill MADDERN

American Male Private Detective operating in Florida

Gil BREWER 1922-1983 (American)

Other Byline: Ellery QUEEN

Other Detectives:
Lee BARON   Al MUNDY

Citation Record: 1 Book

So Rich, So Dead - *Only*
GM US (1951); New Fiction UK (1952)

Mr MADDOX

is a bookie who gets involved in murders at racetracks all over the USA. He appeared in thirty-five short stories, 1938-1950, in *Dime Detective*.

American Male Detective in Pulp Magazines operating in USA

T T FLYNN 1902- (American)

See main detective pair Mike HARRIS and Trixie MEEHAN

Citation Record: 1 Selected Short Story

The Devil's Derby
In 'Dime Detective' US (1933)

Sgt Ivor MADDOX

works for the Hollywood Police Department in California and is assisted on and off during a long series by divers detectives and sidekicks. His books were published under the *LININGTON* byline in the US and under the *BLAISDELL* byline in the UK.

American Policeman operating in Hollywood

Sidekick: Det D'ARCY
American Male - Assistant

Sidekick: Policewoman Sue CARSTAIRS
American Female - Assistant

Anne BLAISDELL 1921-1988 (American)

For writer details see Sgt Ivor MADDOX

Citation Record: 13 Books

Greenmask! - *First*
Gollancz UK (1965)

Strange Felony - *Last*
!See Appendix 2
Gollancz UK (1987)

Elizabeth LININGTON 1921-1988 (American)

was born in Aurora, Illinois. She attended local schools and graduated from Herbert Hoover High School. She was the author of about eighty genre novels under her own name and her two main pseudonyms, which she used for different types of detective story.

Writer: Barbara Elizabeth LININGTON

Other Bylines:
Elizabeth LININGTON   Dell SHANNON
Anne BLAISDELL

Citation Record: 13 Books

Greenmask! - *First*
Harper & Row US (1964)

Strange Felony - *Last*
Doubleday US (1987)

Det Ch Insp Kate MADDOX

British Policewoman operating in several locations

Erica QUEST (American)

is the pseudonym of a husband-and-wife team.

Writers: John SAWYER 1919- and Nancy Buckingham SAWYER 1924-

Inventor of one other detective Tess PENNICOTT

Citation Record: 3 Books

Death Walk - *First*
Doubleday US (1988); Piatkus UK (1990)

Model Murder - *Latest*
Piatkus UK (1991)

MADEMOISELLE LUCIE

French Female Private Detective operating in France

UNKNOWN

Citation Record: 1 Book

Mademoiselle Lucie, The French Lady Detective
US (?)

Jose Manuel MADERO

Mexican Male Amateur operating in USA/Mexico

Geoffrey HOMES 1902-1978 (American)

Invented 5 detectives - see Robin BISHOP

Citation Record: 2 Books

The Street Of The Crying Woman - *First*
Morrow US (1942)

The Case Of The Mexican Knife - *First**
Bantam US (1948)

Seven Died - *First**
Cherry Tree UK (1943)

The Hill Of The Terrified Monk - *Last*
Morrow US (1943)

Dead As A Dummy - *Last**
Bantam US (1949)

Lt MADIGAN

American Policeman operating in New York

Edwin LANHAM 1904-1979 (American)

Invented 3 detectives - see Lt GRAY

Citation Record: 3 Books

Slug It Slay - *First*
Harcourt Brace US (1946); Boardman UK (1948)

Headlined For Murder - *First**
Bantam US (1948)

Headline For Murder - *First**
Boardman UK (1950)

One Murder Too Many - *Last*
Harcourt Brace US (1952); Boardman UK (1953)

Cash MADIGAN

specialises in crimes of bond violation. He is tough and a fatal attraction to women.

American Male Private Detective operating in New York

Bruce CASSIDAY 1920- (American)

Writer: Bruce Bingham CASSIDAY

Other Bylines:
Nick CARTER   Michael STRATFORD

Inventor of one other detective Johnny MIDAS

Citation Record: 2 Books

The Buried Motive - *First*
Ace US (1957)

While Murder Waits - *Last*
Graphic US (1957)

Jane MADISON

American Female Amateur operating in USA

Willo Davis ROBERTS 1928- (American)

was born in Grand Rapids, Michigan.

Citation Record: 1 Book

The Sniper - *Single*
Doubleday US (1984)

Ken MADISON

is in a novelization of an episode from a TV series.

American Male Private Detective operating in Miami Beach

J M FLYNN 1927-1985 (American)

See main detective Burl STANNARD

Citation Record: 1 Book

Surfside 6 - *Only*
Dell US (1962)

Lacey MADISON

finds her sister missing, her brother-in-law dead, and their four-months-old baby feeling pretty hungry. Being an ace reporter, it seems only proper that she should scoop the child up, press on with the milk feeds, and discover what is at the root of all this.

American Female Amateur operating in Los Angeles

Barbara PRONIN (American)

Citation Record: 1 Book

Thicker Than Water - *Single*
Dell US (1995)

George MADO

British Male Sleuth operating in Greece/Egypt

Warren TUTE 1914-1989 (British)

Writer: Warren Stanley TUTE

Citation Record: 6 Books

A Matter Of Diplomacy - *First*
Dent UK (1969); Coward McCann US (1970)

The Cairo Sleeper - *Last*
Constable UK (1977)

M

Paul MADRIANI

is a lawyer who is first met defending an innocent person by discovering the true villain. On his second appearance, the murders and plots follow a twisting path, as do the usual ramifications of his domestic and sexual life. Helped by a willing neighbour, hounded by a rotten cop, he still manages to take a swipe at the US system of justice.

American Male Amateur in USA

Sidekick: Harry HINDS
is an office-suite neighbour of *MADRIANI*. World-weary and iconoclastic in the extreme, he begins to act as an unofficial partner.

American Male - Neighbour

Stooge: Jimmy LAMA
is a cop who not only hates *MADRIANI* enough to oppose his efforts but is prepared to perjure himself, fabricate evidence, and hush up facts to do so.

American Male

Steve MARTINI (American)

Citation Record: 2 Books

Prime Witness - *First*
Headline UK (1993)

Undue Influence - *Latest*
Putnam US (1994)

Nick MAGARACZ

American Male Private Detective operating in New Jersey

Kate GALLISON 1939- (American)

See main detective Mother Lavinia GREY

Citation Record: 2 Books

Unbalanced Accounts - *First*
Little, Brown US (1986)

The Death Tape - *Latest*
Little, Brown US (1987)

Phillip (The Marksman) MAGELLAN

American Male Sleuth operating in New York/California

Aaron FLETCHER (American)

Writer: UNKNOWN

Citation Record: 2 Books

The Card Game - *First*
Tower US (1980)

The Reckoning - *Latest*
Leisure Books US (1981)

Peter MCCURTIN (American)

Invented 4 detectives - see Robert (The Assassin) BRIGANTI

Citation Record: 2 Books

Death Hunt - *First*
Belmont US (1973)

Vendetta - *Last*
Belmont US (1973)

Frank SCARPETTA

For writer details see Johnny ROCK

Citation Record: 20 Books

Death To The Mafia - *First*
Belmont US (1973)

The Times Square Connection - *Last*
Belmont US (1976)

Mark MAGIC

American Male Amateur operating in Baltimore

Anthony P MORRIS 1849-1921 (American)

Writer: Anthony Paschel MORRIS

Other Detectives:
BRADSHAW, Jack PARKER, Jack SIMONS, Tom TURNER

Citation Record: 2 Books

Mark Magic, The Detective; Or, A Story Of A Beautiful Woman's Strange Career - *First*
Westbrook US (1901)

The Cipher Detective; Or, Fighting For Fortune - *Last*
Ivers US (1902)

The Cipher Detective; Or, Mark Magic On A New Trail - *Last**
Westbrook US (1920)

MAGIC DICK

American Male Detective in Pulp Magazines operating in USA

OLD SLEUTH (American)

Invented 40 detectives - see Brant ADAMS

Citation Record: 1 Book

Magic Dick, A Boy Detective; Or, Out Of The Streets Of New York - *Only*
Ogilvie US (1898)

Dick, The Boy Detective; Or, Out Of The Streets Of New York - *Only**
Ogilvie US (1900)

Sheriff Moss MAGILL

American Policeman operating in New York/Colorado

Dorothy GARDINER 1894-1979

Inventor of one other detective Mr WATSON

Citation Record: 3 Books

What Crime Is It? - *First*
Doubleday US (1956)

The Case Of The Hula Clock - *First**
Hammond UK (1957)

Lion In Wait - *Last*
Doubleday US (1963)

Lion? Or Murder? - *Last**
Hammond UK (1964)

Cuddy MAGNUM and Justine SAVILE

American Amateurs operating in North Carolina

Michael MALONE 1942- (American)

Writer: Michael Christopher MALONE

Citation Record: 2 Books

Uncivil Seasons - *First*
!See Appendix 2.
Delacorte US (1983)
Time's Witnesses - *Latest*
Little, Brown US (1989); Chatto UK (1989)

Arnold MAGNUSON

appears in one remarkable book about an ex-cop who heads an army of investigators in a thrilling and tension-filled hunt for a serial killer in Chicago.
!See Appendix 2.
American Male Private Detective operating in Chicago

Mark SMITH 1935- (American)
Writer: Mark Richard SMITH
Citation Record: 1 Book
The Death Of The Detective - *First*
Knopf US (1974); Secker & Warburg UK (1975)

Insp John B MAGRUDER

has had some forty years experience in the New York Police Department. He wears an old brown suit and is a manhunter rather than an intellectual, as it were.
American Policeman operating in New York

Jerome PRINCE and Harold PRINCE (American)
Citation Record: 1 Selected Short Story
Can You Solve This Crime?
was one of the first short stories to use a plot involving television.
US (1950)

Blue MAGUIRE

Second detective of Spaceman KOWALSKI

Colin MAGUIRE

American Male Amateur operating in USA

Jack EARLY (American)
See main detective Fortune FANELLI
Citation Record: 1 Book
Razzamatazz - *Single*
Watts US (1985)

Joe (The Illusionist) MAGUIRE

American Male Sleuth operating in USA

John P RADFORD (American)
Writer: William BENTLEY
Citation Record: 4 Books
All Of Our Aircraft Are Missing! - *First*
Canyon US (1974)
The Game Show Girls - *Last*
Canyon US (1975)

John Patrick Aloysius MAGUIRE

is a lawyer who also practises as a private eye. Raised on the streets of Chicago, he can mix it with the worst of hoodlums.
American Male Private Detective operating in USA

Richard HIMMEL (American)
was born in Chicago, Illinois. A painter and designer, he is the author of at least fourteen genre books.
Citation Record: 7 Books
I'll Find You - *First*
GM US (1950); Fawcett UK (1958)
It's Murder, Maguire - *First**
Jenkins UK (1962)
The Name's Maguire - *Last*
Jenkins UK (1963)

Insp Ambrose MAHON

Australian Policeman operating in Australia

S H COURTIER 1904-1974 (Australian)
See main detective Insp 'Digger' HAIG
Citation Record: 8 Books
The Glass Spear - *First*
Wyn US (1950); Dakers UK (1952)
Mimic A Murderer - *Last*
Hammond UK (1964)

John MAHONEY

Second detective of Wallace MAHONEY

Wallace MAHONEY and John MAHONEY

American Male Sleuths operating in several locations

Sean FLANNERY 1942- (American)
For writer details see Kirk MCGARVEY
Citation Record: 7 Books
The Kremlin Conspiracy - *First*
Charter US (1979)
Counterstrike - *Latest*
Morrow US (1990); Piatkus UK (1991)

Nicky MAHOUN

British Male Amateur operating in Scotland

Clark SMITH 1919- (British)
was born in Glasgow and has practised as a chartered accountant.
Writer: Alexander Clark SMITH
Citation Record: 3 Books
The Speaking Eye - *First*
Hammond UK (1955)
The Case Of Torches - *Last*
Hammond UK (1957)

Richard (The Pilgrim) MAIDMENT

British Male Sleuth

Michael CRONIN 1907- (British)
Invented 3 detectives - see Sam HARRIS
Citation Record: 5 Books
I Can Cope - *First*
Museum Press UK (1955)
Curtain Call - *Last*
Hale UK (1961)

Insp Jules MAIGRET

is one of the genre's greatest and most endearing creations, without question the best-known of all French detectives. Although the complete canon has probably not yet been put together and, for various reasons, the UK and US publication data are difficult to decipher, *Insp Jules MAIGRET* has certainly appeared in many dozens of novels (unusually and deliberately short by modern standards) and several short stories. The action of the series mainly takes place in Paris, although sometimes the detective is called to a case in the countryside or meets one when he is on vacation. He even solves one case while visiting America to study police work there.

MAIGRET stands apart from both his British and American contemporaries of the 1930s and 1940s. Just a senior cop in the *Police Judiciaire*, stolidly bourgeois, living happily with his childless wife in an upper-story apartment on the Boulevard Richard-Lenoir in Paris, slow-moving, slightly grumpy, and compassionate, he exudes the very feel of France, the odour of *Gauloises*, the image of zinc-topped bars, the taste of Calvados, and the sights and sounds of Pigalle and Montmartre. No detective has more knowledge of the criminal classes or the motivation behind their crimes. His methods are unique; for he stands alone in his ability to solve the most obscure crimes by empathy with his surroundings, by soaking up the atmosphere of a place, an action, a gesture, a word.

MAIGRET is a patient man, deeply cognisant of human behaviour. Not for him the magnifying glass, the crossed bicycle treads, the dust on a shoulder or the knowledge that the cigar ash on the carpet came from one plantation in Cuba! He is a camera. He sits in a café near the scene of the crime and thinks about why, not how, it was done; and, although his stories

reveal much about the characters involved in a case, they say little about the detective himself. Most of what is known is learned from his wife during the infrequent occasions when we find him at home, enjoying the *tête de veau* she has made for him and drinking a favourite glass of plum brandy.
French Policeman operating in Paris

Sidekick: Insp JANVIER
appears in many novels and is one of the detective's most trusted assistants.
French Male - Subordinate

Sidekick: Insp LAPOINTE
is the youngest, least experienced and most emotional of the inspectors who regularly assist *Insp MAIGRET*. He is also, throughout the canon, clearly the great man's favourite.
French Male - Subordinate

Sidekick: Insp LUCAS
is the closest associate of *Insp MAIGRET* and his most senior assistant. He appears in most of the novels.
French Male - Subordinate

Georges SIMENON 1903-1989 (French)
was born in Liege, Belgium, and began work, at the age of sixteen, as a journalist. He subsequently went to France, where he lived for much of his life, and later to Lausanne, Switzerland, which he made his permanent home. The author of over two hundred novels, his work has had a great influence on the French cinema in particular and more than forty of his novels have been filmed. He is renowned, however, for his creation of *Insp MAIGRET*, certainly one of the very best detectives ever to have graced the genre. In a series of short novels, each one written, according to the author, in an intense eleven days, they convey, as do few other detective stories, the sense of location (in this case, Paris and rural France) and the hidden tensions that lurk beneath the surface of bourgeois family life, exploding at times into violence and crime. They can deservedly be placed in the highest echelons of crime fiction.

Citation Record: 77 Books 26 Short Stories in 3 Collections

The Strange Case Of Peter The Lett - *First*
is a translation from the French of *Pietr-le Letton* (Paris, 1931).
Hurst UK (1933); Covici US (1933)

Maigret And The Enigmatic Lett - *First**
Penguin UK (1966)

The Patience Of Maigret - *Last*
is a translation from the French of *La Patience de Maigret* (Paris, 1965).
Hamish Hamilton UK (1966)

Maigret Bides His Time - *Last**
Harcourt Brace US (1985)

The Short Cases Of Inspector Maigret - *Collection 1*
Short stories - 5
Doubleday US (1959)

Maigret's Christmas - *Collection 2*
contains one story from the preceding collection.
Short stories - 9
Hamish Hamilton UK (1976); Harcourt US (1977)

Maigret's Pipe - *Collection 3*
contains four stories from the preceding collection.
Short stories - 17
Hamish Hamilton UK (1977); Harcourt US (1977)

Insp Edward MAINE

solves an ingenious case in which a body appears to come to life inside a sealed coffin.
British Policeman operating in England

Eden PHILLPOTTS 1862-1960 (British)
Invented 10 detectives - see Insp MIDWINTER

Citation Record: 1 Selected Short Story

The Witching Hour
Hutchinson UK (1936)

Robert MAINE

solves some seemingly occult problems.
British Male Amateur operating in England

Jacques PENDOWER 1899-1976 (British)
See main detective Slade MCGINTY

Citation Record: 1 Book

Walking On Air - *Only*
Hale UK (1966)

Antony MAITLAND

is a lawyer who investigates crime and brings villains to justice, often in courtroom dramas not unlike those of his great American counterpart, *Perry MASON*. In a long and unfolding series in which characters abound, he is ably and morally supported by his wife, Jenny, and especially by his uncle, Sir Nicholas Harding.
British Male Professional Investigator operating in London

Sara WOODS 1922-1985 (British)
was born in Bradford, Yorkshire, and educated privately and at the Convent of the Sacred Heart, Filey, Yorkshire, 1932-1937. She is the author of at least forty-five classical detective novels, with a firmly characterised series detective, and often set against fascinating legal backgrounds.

Writer: Sara Hutton BOWEN-JUDD

Other Bylines:
Anne BURTON
Mary CHALLIS
Margaret LEEK

Citation Record: 47 Books

Bloody Instructions - *First*
Macmillan UK (1962); Holt US (1962)

Naked Villain - *Latest*
St Martin's US (1987)

George MAITLAND

American Male Amateur operating in Boston

Martin SEVERY 1873- (American)

Writer: Martin Linwood SEVERY

Citation Record: 3 Books

Jim MAITLAND

is one of the author's several ruffians passing for the era's hero-detectives and simply carries on where *'Bulldog' DRUMMOND* left off.
British Male Amateur operating in England

H C MCNEILE 1888-1937 (British)
Invented 3 detectives - see Capt Hugh 'Bulldog' DRUMMOND

Citation Record: 1 Book 12 Short Stories in 1 Collection

Guardians Of The Treasure - *Only*
Doubleday US (1931)

Jim Maitland - *Collection 1*
Doran US (1924)

SAPPER 1888-1937 (British)

Writer: Herman Cyril MCNEILE

Other Byline: H C MCNEILE

Invented 4 detectives - see Capt Hugh 'Bulldog' DRUMMOND

Citation Record: 1 Book 12 Short Stories in 1 Collection

The Island Of Terror - *Only*
Hodder & Stoughton UK (1931)

Jim Maitland - *Collection 1*
Hodder & Stoughton UK (1923)

Aubrey St John MAJOR

appears in a collection of short stories with one of the author's other detectives, *Sgt LANCEY*.
Male Sleuth operating in South Africa

L Patrick GREENE
Invented 5 detectives - see 'Dynamite' DRURY

Citation Record: 9 Books 67 Short Stories in 9 Collections

The Devil's Kloof - *First*
Hamilton UK (1928)
Escape From Liberty - *Last*
Hamilton UK (1939)
The Major - Diamond Buyer - *Collection 1*
Short stories - 10
Hamilton UK (1926); Doubleday US (1924)
Major Adventures - *Collection 2*
Short stories - 6
Heinemann UK (1928)
The Major - Knight Errant - *Collection 3*
Short stories - 6
Heinemann UK (1929)
White Man's Stride - *Collection 4*
Short stories - 6
Selwyn UK (1929)
Major Exploits - *Collection 5*
Short stories - 6
Selwyn UK (1930)
Major Occasions - *Collection 6*
Short stories - 6
Hamilton UK (1931)
Major Developments - *Collection 7*
Short stories - 6
Hamilton UK (1931)
Major Hazards - *Collection 8*
Short stories - 6
Hamilton UK (1932)
Face Value - *Collection 9*
Short stories - 15
Hamilton UK (1939)

Aubrey St John MAJOR and Sgt LANCEY

also appear individually in other books by this author.
Male Sleuth and Policeman operating in South Africa

L Patrick GREENE
Invented 5 detectives - see 'Dynamite' DRURY
Citation Record: 6 Short Stories in 1 Collection
The Point Of A Thousand Spears - *Collection 1*
Hamilton UK (1934)

MAKEPEACE

Second detective of DEMPSEY

Mike MALCHECK

is a police officer who was once a crack Army sniper. He is now employed on duties to track down criminal snipers.
American Policeman operating in USA

Paula GOSLING 1939- (American)
Invented 7 detectives - see Lt Jack STRYKER
Citation Record: 1 Book
A Running Duck - *Single*
Coward McCann US (1978); Macmillan UK (1978)

Mr MALCOLM

British Male Amateur operating in England

Gerard FAIRLIE 1899-1983 (British)
Invented 4 detectives - see Johnny MACALL
Citation Record: 4 Books
Unfair Lady - *First*
Hodder & Stoughton UK (1931)
Men For Counters - *Last*
Hodder & Stoughton UK (1933)

James 'Solo' MALCOLM

British Male Private Detective operating in England

Neill GRAHAM 1909-1975 (British)
For writer details see Supt MACNEILL
Inventor of one other detective Mr SANDYMAN
Citation Record: 37 Books
Play It Solo - *First*
Jarrolds UK (1955)
Motive For Murder - *Last*
Long UK (1977)

Tommy MALINS

British Male Amateur operating in England

Maurice B DIX 1889-1956 (British)
wrote about twenty crime novels in the 1930s, including the obligatory several with *Sexton BLAKE.*
Writer: Maurice Buxton DIX
Other Detectives:
Sexton BLAKE
Supt Simon BULLION
Ch Insp James MILLER
Citation Record: 2 Books
Twisted Evidence - *First*
Ward, Lock UK (1933)
Beacons Of Death - *Last*
Ward, Lock UK (1937)

James MALLABY

British Male Amateur operating in England

Bruce NORMAN (British)
Inventor of one other detective Jocelyn PINNER
Citation Record: 2 Books
The Thousand Hands - *First*
Arrowsmith UK (1926); Dial US (1927)
The Black Pawn - *Last*
Arrowsmith UK (1927); Dial US (1927)

Det Insp 'Duck' MALLARD

British Policeman operating in England

Andrew SPILLER (British)
Citation Record: 17 Books
What's In A Name? - *First*
Archer US (1947)
Murder On A Shoestring - *Last*
Long UK (1958)

M

Insp MALLESON

of Scotland Yard is in this one Victorian novel.
British Policeman operating in London

T W SPEIGHT 1830-1915 (British)
Writer: Thomas Wilkinson SPEIGHT
Other Detectives:
Lionel DERING
Supt DRUMLEY
Ursula LENORME
Citation Record: 1 Book
The Sandycroft Mystery - *Only*
Chatto & Windus UK (1890)

Insp/Supt MALLETT

is a straightforward, stolid, Scottish policeman, red-haired, moustached, and green-eyed, who barely solves his cases.
British Policeman operating in Scotland
Sidekick: Dr FITZBROWN
British Male - Assistant

Mary FITT 1897-1959 (British)
graduated from the University College of South Wales and Monmouthshire, Cardiff, 1918, and stayed on as a lecturer in Greek, 1919-1946. She was the author of many criminous novels, for which she always used the pseudonym, whilst, under her real name, she wrote novels and works of history and philosophy. She was also the translator of philosophical works from the Greek and the author of books for children.
Writer: Kathleen FREEMAN
Citation Record: 16 Books 12 Short Stories in 1 Collection
Expected Death - *First*
Nicholson & Watson UK (1938)
Mizmaze - *Last*
Joseph UK (1958); British Book Centre US (1959)
The Man Who Shot Birds And Other Tales - *Collection 1*
Macdonald UK (1954)

Insp MALLETT
is a sound Scotland Yard policeman in solid mystery cases, usually with excellent legal and courtroom backgrounds. In a further three books he matches wits with *Francis PETTIGREW*, a brilliant but unsuccessful lawyer, who appears later on his own.
British Policeman operating in London
Sidekick: Sgt FRANT
British Male - Subordinate

Cyril HARE 1900-1958 (British)
was born in Mickleham, Surrey. He was educated at Rugby School, Warwickshire, took a BA in History at New College, Oxford, and became a barrister in 1924.
Writer: Alfred Alexander Gordon CLARK
Other Detectives:
Wencelaus BOTTWINK
Francis PETTIGREW
MALLETT and PETTIGREW
Citation Record: 3 Books
Tenant For Death - *First*
Faber UK (1937); Dodd, Mead US (1937)
Suicide Excepted - *Last*
Faber UK (1939); Macmillan US (1939)

Insp MALLETT and Francis PETTIGREW
also appear individually in other books by this author.
British Policeman and Male Amateur operating in London
Sidekick: Sgt FRANT
British Male - Subordinate

Cyril HARE 1900-1958 (British)
Invented 4 detectives - see Insp MALLETT
Citation Record: 3 Books
Tragedy At Law - *First*
is considered by many critics to be one of the masterpieces of the British detective genre.
Faber UK (1942); Harcourt Brace US (1943)
He Should Have Died Hereafter - *Last*
was republished by *Hogarth* (UK 1987) under the US title.
Faber UK (1958)
Untimely Death - *Last**
Macmillan US (1958)

Dan MALLETT
British Male Amateur operating in England

Frank PARRISH 1929- (British)
For writer details see Coleridge TUCKER
Citation Record: 8 Books
Fire In The Barley - *First*
Constable UK (1977); Dodd, Mead US (1979)
Voices From The Dark - *Latest*
Constable UK (1993)

William MALLETT
British Male Sleuth operating in Italy/the Caribbean

Douglas ORGILL 1922- (British)
Writer: Douglas William ORGILL
Citation Record: 2 Books
The Death Bringers - *First*
Davies UK (1962)
Journey Into Violence - *First**
Morrow US (1963)
Ride A Tiger - *Last*
Davies UK (1963)
The Cautious Assassin - *Last**
Morrow US (1964)

David MALLIN and George COE
British Male Private Detectives operating in England

Roger ORMEROD 1920- (British)
Invented 4 detectives - see Philipa LOWE
Citation Record: 14 Books
Time To Kill - *First*
Hale UK (1974)
One Deathless Hour - *Latest*
Hale UK (1981)

William Arthur MALLINGHAM
is the curator of the fictional University of Mansterbridge Anthropological Museum, and solves the murder of a young girl.
British Male Amateur operating in England

C E VULLIAMY 1886-1971 (British)
Writer: Colwyn Edward VULLIAMY
Citation Record: 1 Book
Tea At The Abbey - *Only*
Joseph UK (1961)

Ch Reuben MALLOCK
investigates murder at an American liberal arts college.
American Policeman operating in USA

David MACDUFF 1905- (American)
Citation Record: 1 Book
Murder Strikes Three - *Only*
In 'Modern Age' US (1937)

MALLORY
was the third and last of the author's one-name heroes and the first to be unequivocally on the right side of the law. He is a young mystery writer who works at delivering hot meals to the elderly citizens of a small town in Iowa; but he becomes involved in real-life murders, which he solves.
American Male Amateur operating in Iowa
Stooge: Sheriff BRENNAN
is the local law who is continually telling *MALLORY* to keep out of his cases.
American Male

Max Allan COLLINS 1948- (American)
Invented 5 detectives - see Nate HELLER
Citation Record: 4 Books
The Baby Blue Rip-Off - *First*
Walker US (1983); Hale UK (1984)
A Shroud For Aquarius - *Latest*
Walker US (1985)

MALLORY
American Male Private Detective operating in USA

Raymond CHANDLER 1888-1959 (American)
Invented 9 detectives - see Philip MARLOWE
Citation Record: 2 Selected Short Stories
Blackmailers Don't Shoot
is in a collection of five stories by the author, *Five Murderers*.
In 'Black Mask Magazine' US (1933)
Smart-Aleck Kill
is in a collection of twelve stories by the author, *The Simple Art Of Murder*.
In 'Black Mask Magazine' US (1934)

Capt MALLORY
British Male Professional Investigator operating in Turkey/Yugoslavia

Alistair MACLEAN 1922- (British)
was born in Daviot, Inverness, Scotland. He took a BA in English at Glasgow University and later served in the Royal Navy, 1941-1945. He was a teacher during the 1950s and ran hotels in the 1960s. His acclaimed novels, twenty-eight in number, are mainly action-packed adventure stories that contain elements of mystery and detection. His heroes, cast usually in the classic mould, play for large stakes. The stories are all immensely readable.
Writer: Alistair Stuart MACLEAN
Citation Record: 2 Books

The Guns Of Navarone - *First*
Collins UK (1957); Doubleday US (1957)
Force 10 From Navarone - *Last*
Collins UK (1968); Doubleday US (1968)

T J R SENNOCKE (British)

Citation Record: 3 Books
Inquest On A Lady - *First*
Rudkin UK (1941)
Inquest On A Mistress - *Last*
Rudkin UK (1943)

Bert MALLORY

American Male Private Detective operating in USA

Tom REAMY 1935-1977 (American)

Citation Record: 1 Selected Short Story
The Detweiler Boy
is in an anthology, *San Diego Lightfoot & Other Stories.*
Ace US (1979)

David MALLORY

solves a case of death by stabbing in a guarded hotel room.
American Male Amateur operating in USA

Frederick F VAN DE WATER 1890-1968 (American)

See main detective John TARLETON
Citation Record: 1 Book
Hidden Ways - *Only*
Bobbs US (1935); Jenkins UK (1937)

James Maxwell MALLORY

has quit law school at Harvard and set up as a PI in the belief that he can thus achieve justice better than he could in law practice.
American Male Private Detective operating in Boston

Richard N SMITH 1937- (American)

Citation Record: 2 Books
A Secret Singing - *First*
New American Library US (1988)
Wild Justice - *Latest*
St Martin's US (1990)

John Justin MALLORY

takes to the bottle when his partner runs off with his wife. He is saved when an elf appears and offers him $10,000 to find a lost unicorn.
American Male Private Detective operating in New York

Mike RESNICK 1942- (American)

Writer: Michael Diamond RESNICK
Citation Record: 1 Book
Stalking The Unicorn: A Fable For Tonight - *Single*
Tor US (1987); Arrow UK (1987)

Mrs Sheila MALLORY

is widowed, literary, and becomes an amateur sleuth when drawn into murder in the traditional English country fashion, in England and Pennsylvania.
British Female Amateur operating in England/USA

Hazel HOLT 1928- (British)

Citation Record: 6 Books
Gone Away - *First*
Macmillan UK (1989)
Mrs Mallory Investigates - *First**
St Martin's US (1990)
Superfluous Death - *Latest*
Macmillan UK (1995)

Steve MALLORY

American Male Private Detective operating in Los Angeles

Douglas HEYES 1921- (American)

Other Detectives:
Lee GORDON   Ray RIPLEY
Citation Record: 1 Book
The Kiss-Off - *Only*
Simon & Schuster US (1951)
Goodbye Stranger - *Only**
Redman UK (1952)

MALLORY and Charles BUTLER

are an unusually matched duo. *MALLORY* was once a thief, taken off the streets, when a child, by a loving Jewish cop and his wife. She is now a cool detective in a Special Crimes unit and a crack shot to boot. When the cop is killed while working on gruesome murders in Gramercy Park, she turns to his friend *Charles BUTLER* Together they hunt the serial killer, she working wizardry on her computer and he absorbing the results into his remarkable brain until he enables her to come up with the answer.
American Policewoman and American Male Amateur operating in New York

Carol O'CONNELL (American)

Citation Record: 1 Book
Mallory's Oracle - *Only*
St Martin's US (1992)

Laurence MALLOW

is a journalist who sleuths in this one Victorian novel.
British Male Amateur operating in London

Fergus HUME 1859-1932 (British)

Invented 24 detectives - see Insp Samuel GORBY
Citation Record: 1 Book
The Indian Bangle - *Only*
Sampson, Low UK (1899)

Chance MALLOY

is one of the prolific author's minor detectives. He works for an airline company and is involved in his two cases because of it.
American Male Amateur operating in USA

Lester DENT 1904-1959 (American)

was born in La Plata, Missouri. Telegrapher, house writer for *Dell*, aerial photographer and freelance journalist, he became a prolific writer for the pulps during the 1930s. Later he wrote detective novels, for which he invented innumerable minor and ephemeral detectives. He is best known for the two hundred or so detective-adventure novels he wrote, under his main pseudonym, featuring *'Doc' SAVAGE,* in which the plots involve intrigue and character rather than violence.
Other Byline: Kenneth ROBESON
Other Detectives:
Foster FADE   Curt FLAGG
Lynn LASH   Mitchell LONEMAN
Chance MALLOY   John MARKS
Lee NACE   Oscar SAIL
Citation Record: 2 Books
Dead At The Take-Off - *First*
Doubleday US (1946); Cassell UK (1948)
High Stakes - *First**
Ace US (1953)
Lady To Kill - *Last*
Doubleday US (1946); Cassell UK (1949)

Claire MALLOY

is the widow of a Professor of English and lives in the fictional town of Fabersville, where she runs a bookstore called The Book Depot in a refurbished old train station. There she runs into much murder, which she deals with cleverly; sometimes with the help of, often to the chagrin of, an amiable local cop
American Female Amateur operating in Arkansas

Stooge: Lt Peter ROSEN
is friendly but sort of can't understand why he can't solve the cases.
American Male

Joan HESS 1949- (American)

graduated from the University of Arkansas, Fayetteville, with a BA in Art, 1972.

Inventor of one other detective Ch Arly HANKS

Citation Record: 5 Books

Strangled Prose - *First*
St Martin's US (1986)

Death By The Light Of The Moon - *Latest*
St Martin's US (1992)

Jim MALLOY

Canadian Male Sleuth operating in Canada

Charles STODDARD 1906-1962

Writer: Charles Stanley STRONG

Citation Record: 9 Books

The Killer At Port Norman - *First*
Arcadia US (1944)

The Caribou Patrol - *Last*
Foulsham UK (1957)

Vic MALLOY

is one of this author's many, and largely indistinguishable, American detectives. He runs Universal Services, an up-market agency in the mythical Orchid City, somewhere on the Californian seaboard. He takes on cases for its rich and often corrupt inhabitants and runs into beautiful women, some good, many bad, with whom he does not get sexually involved. He rarely carries a gun and solves his cases through pretty ordinary, but always exciting, legwork. He has various assistants, some of whom get killed.

American Male Private Detective operating in California

Sidekick: Jack KERMAN

is a fast-talking, would-be comic legman for the detective.

American Male - Assistant

Stooge: Lt Tim MIFFLIN

is not a dumb stooge and he does carry out some of the necessary police work in the *MALLOY* books. However, he never comes to any sensible conclusions.

American Male

James Hadley CHASE 1906-1985 (British)

Invented 14 detectives - see Dave FENNER

Citation Record: 4 Books

You're Lonely When You're Dead - *First*
Hale UK (1949); Duell US (1950)

Lay Her Among The Lilies - *Last*
Hale UK (1950)

Too Dangerous To Be Free - *Last**
Duell US (1951)

MALONE

is an ex-FBI man, a widower and a Catholic ex-seminarian.

American Male Private Detective operating in Jersey City

J W RIDER (American)

Writer: Shane MARTIN

Citation Record: 2 Books

Jersey Tomatoes - *First*
US (1986)

Hot Tickets - *Latest*
US (1988)

Insp MALONE

British Policeman operating in England

D J MURPHY 1905- (British)

Writer: David John MURPHY

Citation Record: 1 Book

Inspector Malone Sails In - *Only*
Selwyn UK (1947)

David MALONE

American Male Sleuth operating in New York

William J CAUNITZ 1935- (American)

Citation Record: 1 Book

One Police Plaza - *Single*
Crown US (1984)

Jim MALONE

British Male Amateur operating in France

T C H JACOBS 1899-1976 (British)

Writer: Jacques PENDOWER

Invented 8 detectives - see Ch Insp BARNARD

Citation Record: 2 Books

Let Him Stay Dead - *First*
Hale UK (1961)

The Red Net - *Last*
Hale UK (1962)

John J MALONE

was created by *Craig RICE*. He is a lawyer who investigates crimes in order to win his cases in the manner made famous forever by the great *Perry MASON*. Indeed, he is something of a parody, a cross between the archetypal great American investigative lawyer and the tough private eye. Thus we hear a lot about his prowess in court, although no courtroom drama is ever actually depicted; and, like all good shamuses should, he smokes endless cigars and keeps the hooch in a drawer in his filing cabinet labelled 'Confidential'. Much of his time, however, is actually spent in Joe the Angel's bar, where he tends to solve his cases by contemplation over a rye whisky. He is continually involved with a madcap couple, *Jake JUSTUS* and *Helene JUSTUS*, who believe that, according to well-established American tradition, husband-and-wife duos with money to spare and not much else to do, are pretty good at being detectives. Alas, this is not true and their charming ineptness interferes with *MALONE's* sleuthing on more than one occasion.

John J MALONE appeared in ten books with *John and Helen JUSTUS*. He was also the main detective in a number of short stories, which appeared in a collection published shortly after *Craig RICE's* death.

American Male Amateur operating in Chicago

Larry M HARRIS 1933- (American)

adopted the detective for one book shortly after the death of *Craig RICE*.

Writer: Larry Mark HARRIS

Citation Record: 1 Book

The Pickled Poodles - *Pastiche 1*
Random House US (1960); Boardman UK (1961)

Craig RICE 1908-1957 (American)

was born in Chicago, Illinois, and educated privately.

Writer: Georgiana Ann Randolph CRAIG

Other Byline: Michael VENNING

Other Detectives:
Jake JUSTUS, Helene JUSTUS and John J MALONE
'Bingo' RIGGS and 'Handsome' KUSAK

Citation Record: 10 Short Stories in 1 Collection

The Name Is Malone - *Collection 1*
Pyramid US (1958); Hammond UK (1960)

John J MALONE

Appears with at least two other detectives - see Jake JUSTUS

John J MALONE

Second detective of Hildegarde WITHERS

Johnny MALONE

American Male Sleuth operating in New York

Ferguson FINDLEY 1910- (American)

Writer: Charles Weiser FREY

Citation Record: 2 Books

My Old Man's Badge - *First*
Duell US (1950); Reinhardt UK (1950)

M

Killer Cop - *First**
Monarch US (1959)
Waterfront - *Last*
Duell US (1951)
Remember That Face! - *Last**
Reinhardt UK (1950)

Kenneth MALONE

did his sleuthing in what was then the future (1973).

American Male Amateur operating in New York

Mark PHILLIPS (American)
Writers: Larry Mark HARRIS 1933- and Randall Phillips GARRETT 1927-1987
Citation Record: 3 Books
Brain Twister - *First*
Pyramid US (1962)
Supermind - *Last*
Pyramid US (1963)

Lawrence MALONE

British Male Amateur operating in England

G H TEED 1878-1939 (British)
Invented 6 detectives - see Roxane HARFIELD
Citation Record: 3 Books
Night On The Broads - *First*
Mellifont UK (1935)
Missing At Lloyds - *Last*
Mellifont UK (1935)

Marty MALONE

is a bus driver who solves a case of murder on his bus.

American Male Amateur operating in USA

Herbert BREAN 1907-1963 (American)
Invented 3 detectives - see Reynold FRAME
Citation Record: 1 Selected Short Story
Murder Buys A Ticket
was also published in the December 1957 number of *Ellery Queen's Mystery Magazine.*
In 'Exciting Detective' US (1941)

Pat MALONE

was an Irish-American detective appearing in stories in *Private Detective* in the 1940s.

American Male Detective in Pulp Magazines operating in USA

Roger TORREY (American)
Invented 7 detectives - see Pat MULLANCY
No citations

Patrick MALONE

British Male Amateur

Douglas RUTHERFORD 1915-1988 (British)
See main detective Jay DELANEY
Citation Record: 1 Book
Turbo - *Single*
Macmillan UK (1980); St Martin's US (1980)

Scobie MALONE

is a tough, professional operator who works on large-scale crimes, usually with international or political significance. The identity of the criminals is often known to the police; but, for various reasons, they are unable to act and so they use *MALONE* to see that justice is done.

Australian Male Professional Investigator operating in Australia

Jon CLEARY 1917- (Australian)
was born in Sydney, Australia. He served in the Australian Imperial Forces, 1940-1945. Broadcaster, artist and journalist, he has written many thrillers and detective novels as well as other novels and plays outside the genre. He received the Mystery Writers of America Edgar Allan Poe award, 1974.
Writer: Jon Stephen CLEARY
Inventor of one other detective Jim MCKECHNIE
Citation Record: 9 Books
The High Commissioner - *First*
Collins UK (1966); Morrow US (1966)y
Autumn Maze - *Latest*
HarperCollins UK (1994)

Steven MALONE

British Male Amateur operating in England

Nigel MORLAND 1905-1986 (British)
Invented 4 detectives - see Mrs Palmyra Evangeline PYM
Citation Record: 2 Books
Strangely She Died - *First*
Jenkins UK (1946)
Death Takes An Editor - *Last*
Aldor UK (1949)

Augustus MALTRAVERS

is a journalist and a writer who turns to sleuthing. Definitely a modern sixty-years-on *Peter WIMSEY*-ish type, he resembles his predecessor in style, culture, intelligence, and cerebral method. Unlike him, however, he has the misfortune to be rather poor and to have few friends in high positions and absolutely none among the police. The official force is perhaps more tolerant of his private sleuthing than is strictly believable, but they are as baffled as ever when faced with difficult murder cases and are only too glad of his help.

British Male Amateur operating in England

Robert RICHARDSON 1940- (British)
Adopter of one other detective Sherlock HOLMES
Citation Record: 3 Books
The Latimer Mercy - *First*
Gollancz UK (1985); St Martin's US (1986)
The Book Of The Dead - *Latest*
Gollancz UK (1989)

Ted MALVERN

American Male Private Detective operating in USA

Raymond CHANDLER 1888-1959 (American)
Invented 9 detectives - see Philip MARLOWE
Citation Record: 1 Selected Short Story
Guns At Cyrano's
In 'Black Mask Magazine' US (1936)

George MAN

is a member of an early eighteenth-century police force in London, the Parish Watch. He runs into cases of robbery and murder that require considerable period detective work.

British Policeman operating in London

Keith HELLER 1949- (British)
Citation Record: 3 Books
Man's Illegal Life - *First*
Collins UK (1984); Scribner's US (1985)
Man's Loving Family - *Latest*
Collins UK (1986)

Malachi MANATEE

appeared in short stories in *Dime Detective,* where he was mainly engaged in eliminating political villains.

American Male Detective in Pulp Magazines operating in USA

William R COX 1901-1989 (American)
Invented 4 detectives - see Tom KINCAID
No citations

Det Bolivar MANCHENIL

is a black cop who narrates his own tales, ratiocinating more than actually detecting.

American Policeman operating in the Caribbean

Donald McNutt DOUGLASS 1899-1975 (American)
Adopter of one other detective Sherlock HOLMES
Citation Record: 3 Books

Rebecca's Pride - *First*
Harper & Row US (1956); Eyre & Spottiswoode UK (1956)

Saba's Treasure - *Last*
Harper & Row US (1961); Eyre & Spottiswoode UK (1963)

Prof Gideon MANCIPLE and Dr William BLOW

Gideon MANCIPLE is over eighty and a retired Professor of Numismatics. A bachelor, he lives in a London boarding house and studies coins at the British Museum. His friend, *Dr William BLOW,* is also over eighty and together they think they have a talent for criminal investigation, for which they use many disguises. The authorities regard them as nuisances; yet, even though they get the clues muddled, they somehow succeed in solving cases that baffle the police.

British Male Amateurs operating in England

Kenneth HOPKINS 1914-1988 (British)

was born in Bournemouth, Hampshire. He has written many kinds of fiction, as well as poetry and travel books.

Writer: Hector Kenneth HOPKINS

Inventor of one other detective Gerry LEE

Citation Record: 3 Books

She Died Because... - *First*
Macdonald UK (1957); Holt US (1964)

Body Blow - *Last*
Macdonald UK (1962); Holt US (1962)

Peter MANCIPLE

British Male Amateur operating in England

Michael GILBERT 1912- (British)

Invented 11 detectives - see Insp HAZELRIGG

Citation Record: 1 Book

The Empty House - *Single*
Hodder & Stoughton UK (1978); Harper & Row US (1979)

M

Bill MANDELL and Capt Andrew LEE

are, in a single book containing about a dozen separate plots, engaged in a desperate struggle against Japanese no-gooders bent on the most felonious and underhand crimes against the USA. *MANDELL* is fat, jolly and has spent his whole life in the Secret Service. *LEE* is young, handsome and an Army captain who is, it seems, on loan to him.

American Male Secret Agent and American Male Professional Investigator operating in San Francisco

Tom ROAN (American)

Citation Record: 1 Book

The Dragon Strikes Back - *Only*
Messner US (1936); Melrose UK (1936)

Francis MANDELL-ESSINGTON

British Male Amateur operating in England

J Storer CLOUSTON 1870-1944 (British)

Invented 4 detectives - see F T CARRINGTON

Citation Record: 6 Books

The Lunatic At Large - *First*
Blackwood UK (1899); Appleton US (1900)

The Best Story Ever - *Last*
Blackwood UK (1932)

Insp MANDERTON

appears also with another of this author's detectives, *Sgt Trevor DENE.*

British Policeman operating in England

Valentine WILLIAMS 1883-1946 (British)

Invented 8 detectives - see Det Sgt Trevor DENE

Citation Record: 2 Books

The Yellow Streak - *First*
Jenkins UK (1922); Houghton US (1922)

The Orange Divan - *Last*
Jenkins UK (1923); Houghton US (1923)

Insp MANDERTON

Appears with at least two other detectives - see Robin GREVE

Insp MANDERTON and Det Sgt Trevor DENE

also appear individually in other books by this author.

British Policemen operating in England

Valentine WILLIAMS 1883-1946 (British)

Invented 8 detectives - see Det Sgt Trevor DENE

Citation Record: 2 Books

The Eye In Attendance - *First*
Hodder & Stoughton UK (1927); Houghton US (1927)

Death Answers The Bell- *Last*
Hodder & Stoughton UK (1931); Houghton US (1932)

Prof MANDRAKE

is old, fat, and ugly. An anthropologist, author, and media personality, he stumbles into murder mysteries and delights in meddling until he solves them.

British Male Amateur operating in England

John BONETT and Emery BONETT (British)

See main detective Insp Salvador BORGES

Citation Record: 3 Books

Dead Lion - *First*
Joseph UK (1949); Doubleday US (1949)

No Grave For A Lady - *Latest*
Joseph UK (1960); Doubleday US (1959)

Oliver MANDRAKE

British Male Sleuth operating in several locations

John HAYTHORNE (British)

has been a senior member of the British diplomatic service.

Writer: Sir Richard PERSONS

Citation Record: 4 Books

None Of Us Cared For Kate - *First*
Cassell UK (1968); Dutton US (1968)

Mandrake In The Monastery - *Latest*
Anderson UK (1985)

Augustus MANDRELL

American Male Amateur operating in USA

Frank MCAULIFFE 1926- (American)

Writer: Frank MALACHY

Citation Record: 12 Short Stories in 3 Collections

Of All The Bloody Cheek - *Collection 1*
contains four novelettes.
Short stories - 4
Ballantine US (1965); New English Library UK (1971)

Rather A Vicious Gentleman - *Collection 2*
contains four novelettes.
Short stories - 4
Ballantine US (1968)

For Murder I Charge More - *Collection 3*
Short stories - 4
Ballantine US (1971)

MANFRED

is a ventriloquist detective.

American Male Amateur operating in USA

Harlan Page HALSEY 1837-1898 (American)

Invented 6 detectives - see Kate GOELET

Citation Record: 1 Book

The West Shore Mystery - *Only*
Munro US (1886)

Judge MANFRED

American Male Amateur operating in USA

A R HILLIARD 1908- (American)

Writer: Alec Rowley HILLIARD

Citation Record: 2 Books

Justice Be Damned - *First*
Farrar, Straus US (1941); Cassell UK (1944)

Outlaw Island - *Last*
Farrar, Straus US (1942); Cassell UK (1947)

'Tiger' MANN
American Male Secret Agent operating in USA

Mickey SPILLANE 1918- (American)
Invented 3 detectives - see Mike HAMMER
Citation Record: 4 Books
Day Of The Guns - *First*
Dutton US (1964); Barker UK (1965)
The By-Pass Control - *Last*
Dutton US (1966); Barker UK (1967)

John MANNERING
was one of his author's several gentleman adventurers and he had a very long run. Usually known as The Baron, he was a reformed jewel thief who used his talents to aid the law, often to the chagrin of the official police.
British Male Amateur operating in England
Stooge: Supt BRISTOW
frequently clashed with *John MANNERING,* being suspicious that he might return to his old criminal ways rather than pursue the lines of justice.
British Male

Anthony MORTON 1908-1973 (British)
For writer details see Insp Roger 'Handsome' WEST
Inventor of one other detective Mr QUENTIN
Citation Record: 47 Books
Meet The Baron - *First*
Harrap UK (1937)
The Man In The Blue Mask - *First**
Lippincott US (1937)
Love For The Baron - *Last*
Hodder & Stoughton UK (1979)

Randolph MANNERING
British Male Amateur operating in England

George Sidney PATERNOSTER 1866- (British)
Citation Record: 2 Books
The Motor Pirate - *First*
Chatto UK (1903); Page US (1904)
The Cruise Of The Motor-Boat Conqueror - *Last*
Page US (1906)

Insp MANNERS
British Policeman operating in England

Jean MARSH 1897- (British)
Writer: Evelyn MARSHALL
Citation Record: 1 Book
The Shore House Mystery - *Only*
Hamilton UK (1928)

MANNERS
British Male Amateur operating in England

James Patrick MCGINITY (British)
Citation Record: 2 Short Stories in 1 Collection
Whirlpools - *Collection 1*
This collection of seven of the author's short stories contains two with *Dr MANNERS.*
Stockwell UK (1925)

Prof Harley MANNERS
is a Professor of Abnormal Psychology at an unnamed university in the eastern USA. Tall, young, a bachelor and a chain-smoker, he is a man of great inherited wealth who takes up sleuthing as an extension of his work on human motivation, which seems a not unreasonable thing to do
American Male Amateur operating in New England

Charles Judson DUTTON 1888-1964 (American)
See main detective John BARTLEY
Citation Record: 6 Books
Streaked With Crimson - *First*
Dodd, Mead US (1929)
Black Fog - *Latest*
Dodd, Mead US (1933); Hurst UK (1933)

Silas MANNERS
British Male Sleuth

James MOFFATT 1922- (British)
Invented 3 detectives - see Johnny CANUCK
Citation Record: 2 Books
The Sleeping Bomb - *First*
New English Library UK (1970)
The Cambri Plot - *First**
Tower US (1973)
Justice For A Dead Spy - *Last*
New English Library UK (1971)

Supt MANNING
British Policeman operating in England

Belton COBB 1892-1971 (British)
Invented 4 detectives - see Insp Cheviot BURMANN
Citation Record: 6 Books
Early Morning Poison - *First*
Longman UK (1947)
No Charge For The Poison - *Last*
Methuen UK (1950)

Charles Hendesley MANNING and Ben HASSETT
Charles MANNING is an agent for Wabon & Co, said to be 'the largest private enquiry agents in Britain'. He is sent on a case to Australia, where he works on other cases with *Ben HASSETT.*
British Male Private Detectives operating in Australia

Herbert DE HAMEL (Australian)
Citation Record: 11 Short Stories in 1 Collection
Many Thanks - Ben Hassett - *Collection 1*
Simpkin Marshall UK (1915); Congreve AU (1948)

Johnny MANNING
American Male Sleuth operating in USA

Michael DINES 1916- (British)
Citation Record: 3 Books
Operation-Deadline - *First*
Ward, Lock UK (1967)
Operation - Kill Or Be Killed - *Last*
Hale UK (1969)

Det Steve MANNING
appeared in some short stories as a variant on the author's main detective, *Pete SELBY.*
American Policeman operating in New York
Sidekick: Det Walt LOGAN
American Male - Partner

Jonathan CRAIG 1919- (American)
was a senior advisory analyst to the Pentagon and Joint Chiefs of Staff in the Second World War.
Writer: Frank E SMITH
Inventor of one other detective Det Pete SELBY
No citations

MANNISTER
British Male Amateur operating in England

E Phillips OPPENHEIM 1866-1946 (British)
Invented 27 detectives - see Nicholas GOADE
Citation Record: 10 Short Stories in 1 Collection
The Long Arm Of Mannister - *Collection 1*
Little, Brown US (1908)
The Long Arm - *Collection 1**
Ward, Lock UK (1909)

Harrison MANNIX
investigates a case of death by decapitation in a locked room and comes up with an extraordinary solution.
American Male Amateur operating in USA

Robert ARTHUR 1909-1969 (American)
Invented 6 detectives - see Max MILLION

Citation Record: 1 Selected Short Story
The 51st Sealed Room; Or, The MWA Murder
appeared in the October number and is also in the anthology, *Tantalizing Locked Room Mysteries* (*Walker*; US 1962).
In 'Ellery Queen's Mystery Magazine' US (1951)

Joe MANNIX

is a TV private eye whose activities have been novelized by at least two authors.
American Male Private Detective operating in New York

Michael AVALLONE 1924- (American)
Invented 5 detectives - see Ed NOON
Citation Record: 1 Book
Mannix - *Only*
Popular Library US (1968)

J T MACCARGO (American)
Citation Record: 4 Books
The Faces Of Murder - *First*
Belmont US (1975)
A Walk On The Blond Side - *Last*
Belmont US (1975)

Jonah MANSEL

appears sporadically in other books by this author and with his other detectives.
British Male Amateur operating in England

Dornford YATES 1885-1960 (British)
Invented 4 detectives - see Supt FALCON
Citation Record: 1 Book
Shoal Water - *Only*
Ward, Lock UK (1940); Putnam US (1941)

Dr MANSON

British Male Amateur operating in England

E RADFORD and M A MANGAN (British)
Writers: Edwin RADFORD 1891- and Mona Augusta MANGAN
Inventor of one other detective Prof Marcus STUBBS
Citation Record: 35 Books
Murder Jigsaw - *First*
Melrose UK (1944)
Death Has Two Faces - *Last*
Hale UK (1972)

Insp MANTIS

appears in stories, with strong insect connections, that are *Sherlock HOLMES* parodies.
Policeman operating in Bugland

William KOTZWINKLE 1938- (American)
See main detective Paul PICARD
Citation Record: 5 Short Stories in 1 Collection
Trouble In Bugland: A Collection Of Inspector Mantis Mysteries - *Parody Collection 1*
is a collection of *Sherlock HOLMES* parodies, in which insects play the parts. The individual stories are cited below.
Godine US (1983)
The Case Of The Caterpillar's Hand - *Parody 1*
The Case Of The Emperor's Crown - *Parody 2*
The Case Of The Frightened Scholar - *Parody 3*
The Case Of The Headlmess Monster - *Parody 4*
The Case Of The Missing Butterfly - *Parody 5*

Insp/Supt Simon MANTON

British Policeman operating in England

Michael UNDERWOOD 1916-1992 (British)
Invented 6 detectives - see Rosa EPTON
Citation Record: 13 Books
Murder On Trial - *First*
Hammond UK (1954); Washburn US (1958)
The Anxious Conspirator - *Last*
Macdonald UK (1965); Doubleday US (1965)

Philip MANWEARING

British Male Amateur operating in England

Douglas NEWTON 1884-1951 (British)
Writer: Wilfred Douglas NEWTON
Inventor of one other detective pair Raphael PHARE and Martin SONDES
Citation Record: 1 Book 10 Short Stories in 1 Collection
Philip In Particular - *Single*
Simpkin UK (1916)
Philip And The Flappers - *Collection 1*
Pearson UK (1918)

Amos Lee MAPPIN

is a wealthy author and criminologist, described as looking like Mr Pickwick. He can afford to have his sleuthing done by friends while he thinks up the solutions.
American Male Professional Amateur operating in New York

Hulbert FOOTNER 1879-1944 (Canadian)
See main detective Mme Rosika STOREY
Citation Record: 10 Books
The Mystery Of The Folded Paper - *First*
Harper & Row US (1930)
The Folded Paper Mystery - *First**
Collins UK (1930)
Orchids To Murder - *Latest*
Collins UK (1945); Harper & Row US (1945)

Johnny MAQUIS

American Male Private Detective operating in USA

Vernon WARREN 1925- (British)
specialised in ersatz American private eyes, of whom this is one.
Writer: George Warren Vernon CHAPMAN
Other Detectives:

Mark BRANDON	Clifford GRANT
Glen RANSOM	Brad STERLING

Citation Record: 1 Book
Backlash - *Only*
Gifford UK (1960)

Joan MAR

British Female Private Detective operating in England

Marie Conor LEIGHTON 1866-1941 (British)
Invented 3 detectives - see Michael DRED
Citation Record: 1 Book
Joan Mar, Detective - *Only*
Ward, Lock UK (1910)

Col MARCH

is assigned by Scotland Yard to head a curious body, the Department of Queer Complaints, mainly because nothing has ever been known to surprise him. Pipe-smoking, amiable, with a bushy moustache, he is the caricature of a dull British colonel, but he is a storehouse of apparently useless knowledge that proves invaluable for the solution of his truly astonishing cases. Although he appears almost wholly in the short stories published in the collection under the *Carter DICKSON* byline, he does appear in one story in a collection published under the *John Dickson CARR* name.
British Policeman operating in England

Sidekick: Insp ROBERTS
served under *MARCH* in the Army and is now his assistant.
British Male - Assistant

Carter DICKSON 1906-1977 (American)
See main detective Sir Henry MERRIVALE
Citation Record: 8 Short Stories in 2 Collections
The Department Of Queer Complaints - *Collection 1*
This collection of eleven of the author's short stories contains seven with *Col MARCH*.
Short stories - 7
Morrow US (1940)
Scotland Yard: Department of Queer Complaints - *Collection 1**
Dell US (1944)

The Men Who Explained Miracles - *Collection 2*
contains two *Gideon FELL* stories, one *Col MARCH* story and one *Sir Henry MERRIVALE* story.
Short stories - 1
Harper & Row US (1963); Hamish Hamilton UK (1964)

Erik MARCH

operates on Sunset Boulevard and charges the high rate of $1000 a day for investigating crime in large corporations. He is even tough enough to accompany *Honey WEST* in one book.
American Male Private Detective operating in Los Angeles

G G FICKLING (American)
Invented 3 detectives - see Honey WEST
Citation Record: 3 Books
Naughty But Dead - *First*
Belmont US (1962)
The Crazy Mixed-Up Nude - *Last*
Belmont US (1964)

Erik MARCH

Second detective of Honey WEST

Justin (The Ace) MARCH

British Male Sleuth operating in England

Sydney HORLER 1888-1954 (British)
Invented 20 detectives - see Sir Harker BELLAMY
Citation Record: 2 Books
Enter The Ace - *First*
Hodder & Stoughton UK (1941)
The Dark Night - *Last*
Hodder & Stoughton UK (1953)

Milo MARCH

is an insurance claims investigator who is also a sometime CIA agent. He works for the Intercontinental Insurance Company and, whatever his role at the moment, he is always in pursuit of something or someone lost or stolen, sometimes in exotic locations.
American Male Professional Investigator operating in California/Nevada

M E CHABER 1910-1981 (American)
For writer details see Kim LOCKE
Citation Record: 22 Books
Hangman's Harvest - *First*
Holt US (1952)
Don't Get Caught - *First**
Popular Library US (1953)
Born To Be Hanged - *Last*
Holt US (1973)

Septimus MARCH

British Male Amateur operating in England

Lilian BAMBURG (British)
Citation Record: 2 Books
Beads Of Silence - *First*
Selwyn UK (1926); Dutton US (1927)
Rays Of Darkness - *Last*
Selwyn UK (1927)

Urgan MARCH

is called to a case on Zombi Island, South Carolina, to discover which of seven guests killed their hostess.
American Male Private Detective operating in South Carolina

Benson WHEELER 1905- and Claire Lee PURDY 1906- (American)
Citation Record: 1 Book
The Riddle Of The Eighth Guest - *Only*
Speller US (1936)

David MARCHANT

solves a case of death by shooting in a locked room.
British Male Amateur operating in England

Max DALMAN (British)
See main detective pair Supt WILKINS and Col CHIDDINGTON
Citation Record: 1 Book
The Hidden Light - *Only*
Ward, Lock UK (1937)

Det Billy MARCUS

works in the Vice squad in Atlanta. When his partner is killed he sets out to avenge him, smashing a drugs ring in the process.
American Policeman operating in Atlanta

Tony KENRICK 1935- (Australian)
Invented 4 detectives - see Jimmy PELHAM
Citation Record: 1 Book
China White - *Single*
!See Appendix 2.
Coronet UK (1986)

Lt Joseph MARCUS

solves a case of a man killed while mowing a lawn.
American Policeman operating in USA

Fletcher FLORA 1914-1968 (American)
was born in Parsons, Kansas, and graduated at Kansas State College, Manhattan, and the University of Kansas, Lawrence, 1938-1940, later serving in the US Army, 1943-1945. He wrote short stories for the late pulps in the 1950s and is the author of at least sixteen genre novels.
Citation Record: 1 Selected Short Story
A Word For Murder
appeared in the October number.
In 'Mike Shayne Mystery Magazine' US (1964)

Jean MAREUIL

French Male Sleuth operating in France

Maurice RENARD 1875-1939 (French)
Citation Record: 1 Book
The Snake Of Luvercy - *Only*
is a translation from the French of *Lui* (Paris, 1927).
Dutton US (1930)

Sgt/Insp/Supt MARGETSON

British Policeman operating in England

E M KEATE (British)
Writer: Edith Murray KEATE
Citation Record: 4 Books
A Wild-Cat Scheme - *First*
Rivers UK (1930)
Demon Again - *Last*
Eldon UK (1937)

Eddie MARGOLIS

is a reformed alcoholic who joins Murphy's Detective Agency and works on his first case during Murphy's absence.
American Male Private Detective operating in New York

Stephen Paul COHEN (American)
Citation Record: 2 Books
Heartless - *First*
Morrow US (1986)
Island Of Steel - *Latest*
Morrow US (1988)

The MARINE DETECTIVE

American Male Detective in Pulp Magazines operating in USA

Will WINCH (American)
Invented 5 detectives - see The LAWYER DETECTIVE
Citation Record: 1 Selected Short Story
The Marine Detective; Or, Tracking The Ship Insurance
Old Cap Collier Library US (18??)

Ch Insp Alan MARKBY and Meredith MITCHELL

are ill-matched, he being the head of a rural CID and she a high ranking member of the British consular staff abroad. Nevertheless, when they do come together (they have more than just their common interest in sleuthing to talk about on long winter evenings) they act independently yet co-operatively.
British Policeman and British Female Amateur operating in England

M

Ann GRANGER (British)

See main detective Ursula GRETTON

Citation Record: 4 Books

Say It With Poison - *First*
Headline UK

Murder Among Us - *Latest*
Headline UK (1993)

Frank MARKER

is in a novelization of a TV drama, operating as a small-time PI in Birmingham, in the English Midlands.

British Male Private Detective operating in Birmingham

Anthony MARRIOTT (British)

Citation Record: 1 Book

Marker Calls The Tune - *Only*
Fontana UK (1968)

Audley SOUTHCOTT (British)

Citation Record: 1 Book

Cross That Palm When I Come To It - *Only*
Sphere UK (1974)

MARKHAM

was intended for a TV drama starring Ray Milland, but the author decided to make a novel of it instead.

American Male Private Detective operating in USA

Lawrence BLOCK 1938- (American)

Invented 6 detectives - see Leo HAIG

Citation Record: 1 Book

The Case Of The Pornographic Photos - *Only*
is a novelization of an episode from a TV series.
Belmont US (1961); Consul UK (1965)

You Could Call It Murder - *Only**
Chivers UK (1989)

M

Helen MARKHAM

is an actress who marries an officer in British Intelligence (becoming Helen Johnson, under which name she is sometimes indexed). Because of his work she becomes involved in murder cases, which she solves.

British Female Amateur operating in England

Eileen DEWHURST 1929- (British)

Invented 4 detectives - see Det Ch Supt Maurice KENDRICK and Humphrey BARNES

Citation Record: 2 Books

Whoever I Am - *First*
Collins UK (1982); Doubleday US (1984)

Playing Safe - *Latest*
Collins UK (1984); Doubleday US (1987)

Peter MARKLIN

is a dealer and expert in antique toys who becomes involved in cases of murder, mostly in connection with his profession. He solves the crimes, to the annoyance of the police.

British Male Amateur operating in Dorset

Sidekick: Augustus TRIBBLE
is large, dirty, friendly, simple of mind, and over-eager to help.
British Male - Friend

Sidekick: Arabella TRENCH
is more than a pretty face. Close to *MARKLIN*, she plays an important part in the detection.
British Female - Girlfriend

Stooge: Insp Digby WHETSTONE
is a real terror when he hears that *MARKLIN* is meddling in yet another of his cases, and continually warns him about the perils of obstructing the police.
British Male

Neville STEED (British)

Inventor of one other detective Johnny BLACK

Citation Record: 5 Books

Tinplate - *First*
Weidenfeld & Nicolson UK (1986)

Wind-Up - *Latest*
Weidenfeld & Nicolson UK (1990)

Helen MARKLOVE

British Female Amateur operating in England

William LEQUEUX 1864-1927 (British)

Invented 23 detectives - see Allan KENNEDY

Citation Record: 6 Short Stories in 1 Collection

The Peril Of Helen Marklove And Other Stories - *Collection 1*
This collection of ten of the author's short stories contain six with *Helen MARKLOVE*.
Jarrolds UK (1928)

John MARKS

searches for his uncle's killer.

American Male Amateur operating in USA

Lester DENT 1904-1959 (American)

Invented 9 detectives - see Chance MALLOY

Citation Record: 1 Book

Cry At Dusk - *Only*
Fawcett US (1952); Fawcett UK (1959)

Jonathan MARKS

American Male Private Detective operating in USA

Glenn M BARNS (American)

was born in Washington DC and is a practising attorney.

Writer: Glenn Miller BARNS

Citation Record: 3 Books

Murder Is A Gamble - *First*
Phoenix Press US (1952); Foulsham UK (1954)

Murder Is Insane - *Last*
Lippincott US (1956); Foulsham UK (1958)

Sara MARKS

American Female Amateur operating in USA

Laura MUNDER (American)

is a clinical psychologist as well as the author of criminous works.

Citation Record: 1 Book

Therapy For Murder - *Single*
St Martin's US (1984)

Jeff MARLE

is the valued assistant of *Henri BENCOLIN* in the latter's books, but here he acts on his own.

Male Amateur operating in Pennsylvania

John Dickson CARR 1906-1977 (American)

Invented 16 detectives - see Dr Gideon FELL

Citation Record: 1 Book

Poison In Jest - *Only*
Harper & Row US (1932); Hamish Hamilton UK (1932)

James MARLEY

is a Vietnam War veteran who becomes a Quaker as well as a private eye. He sleuths among the local Quaker community.

American Male Private Detective operating in Boston

Philip ROSS 1932- (American)

is a Professor of Creative Writing.

Writer: UNKNOWN

Inventor of one other detective Tom TALLEY

Citation Record: 2 Books

Blue Heron - *First*
Tor US (1985)

White Flower - *Latest*
US (1989)

Lawrence MARLEY

British Male Sleuth

Jerry WALKER (British)

Citation Record: 2 Books

Mission Accomplished - *First*
Mitre UK (1948)

A Date With Destiny - *Last*
Cosmos US (1947); Cosmos US (1949)

Daisy MARLOW

is widowed, rude, and generally unpleasant. She makes up for any deficiencies in the plots by being a bit of a character – that is, by behaving like many obnoxious male shamuses, being especially given to drinking and swearing.

American Female Private Detective operating in USA

D Miller MORGAN (American)

Citation Record: 2 Books

Money Leads To Murder - *First*
UK (1987)

A Lovely Night To Kill - *Latest*
UK (1988)

Dick MARLOW

British Male Private Detective operating in England

John BENTLEY (British)

Invented 3 detectives - see Sir Richard HERRIVELL

Citation Record: 6 Books

Mr Marlow Takes To Rye - *First*
Houghton US (1942)

Dangerous Waters - *First**
Hutchinson UK (1939)

The Dead Do Talk - *Last*
Hutchinson UK (1944)

Peter MARLOW

is an agent and a spy, one of many spawned by the era of the Cold War.

British Male Secret Agent operating in Europe/Africa

Joseph HONE 1937- (Irish)

was born in London and educated at the University of London. He has worked in radio and films, and as a teacher in Ireland and Egypt.

Citation Record: 4 Books

The Private Sector - *First*
Hamish Hamilton UK (1971); Dutton US (1972)

The Valley Of The Fox - *Latest*
Secker & Warburg UK (1982); St Martin's US (1984)

Sam MARLOW

has had plastic surgery to make him look like Humphrey Bogart and takes his (slightly curtailed) name in an act of homage to *Raymond CHANDLER*. To complete the image he sets up on Larchmont and Beverley, drives a 1939 Plymouth and hires a blonde secretary, generally having lots of fun.

American Male Private Detective operating in Los Angeles

Andrew J FENADY 1928- (American)

is a film producer.

Citation Record: 2 Books

The Man With Bogart's Face - *First*
Regnery US (1977)

The Secret Of Sam Marlow - *Latest*
Contemporary Books US (1980)

Supt 'Cissie' MARLOW

British Policeman operating in England

Grierson DICKSON (British)

Citation Record: 4 Books

The Devil's Torch - *First*
Hutchinson UK (1936)

Knight's Gambit - *Last*
Hutchinson UK (1950)

MARLOWE

is a twenty-first-century person who is allowed to appear as a copy of the 1940s detective, *Philip MARLOWE*. He gets involved in a case involving the missing sister of a beautiful female client. A reminiscence, perhaps, of *THE LITTLE SISTER?*

American Male Private Detective operating in USA

Mick FARREN (American)

Citation Record: 1 Book

The Long Orbit - *Single*
Del Ray US (1988)

MARLOWE

appears in an illustrated novel.

American Male Private Detective operating in USA

STERANKO (American)

was the inventor of many innovative forms of Op Art, which he used to illustrate novels.

Citation Record: 1 Book

Red Tide - *Only*
US (1976)

Greg MARLOWE

Male Secret Agent operating in Canada

Greg MARLOWE

Writer: Leslie T Barnard

Citation Record: 2 Books

Behind The Enemy - *First*
Hamilton Stafford UK (1952)

Death-Mask Of War - *Last*
Hamilton Stafford UK (1952)

Greg MARLOWE

Writer: James MCCORMICK

Citation Record: 2 Books

Burma Battle - *First*
Hamilton Stafford UK (1953)

Espionage! - *Last*
Hamilton Stafford UK (1953)

Philip MARLOWE

was one of the turning points in the development of modern detective fiction: the most admired, most copied, most eulogised, most anthologised private eye in American detective fiction. Relatively hardboiled he is, but he has also been called a product of the author's 'romantic aestheticism'. It is he, above all others, who gave American private eye fiction both the style and the ethos that were to follow. From the moment he crossed the threshold of General Sternwood's house in *THE BIG SLEEP* to the final tragedy of *PLAYBACK*, it was clear that he was something new, a true knight errant in the modern, sleazy world of Southern California. Certainly it was the combination of *Raymond CHANDLER's* British roots combined with his American experience that created this singular and great detective. As a man, physically, we know almost nothing about him; but, as a symbol of honesty and morality, we wish the rest of the world was like him.

Philip MARLOWE has also been adopted and parodied by several other authors, there being no greater accolade for the truly greats. In homage, all the canonical works and the pastiches are cited below. Except where stated, all the pastiches by authors other than *Raymond CHANDLER* appeared in the celebration centenary anthology, *RAYMOND CHANDLER'S MARLOWE* (US 1988).

American Male Private Detective operating in California

Simon BRETT 1945- (British)

Invented 3 detectives - see Charles PARIS

Citation Record: 1 Selected Short Story

Stardust Kills - *Pastiche 1*

M

Robert CAMPBELL 1927- (American)

Invented 5 detectives - see Jake HATCH

Citation Record: 1 Selected Short Story

Mice - *Pastiche 1*

Raymond CHANDLER 1888-1959 (American)

was born in Chicago, Illinois. He was educated in England at Dulwich College, London, and later studied in France and Germany. He worked on newspapers in England, 1908-1912, and returned to the United States, 1912. He then worked at various jobs, as a rancher, a salesman, and an accountant. He served in the Canadian Army in the First World War and for a year in the British Royal Air Force, 1918-1919. He worked for the Dabney Oil Syndicate, Los Angeles, 1922-1932 and then became a full-time writer. He is, by general consensus, regarded as one of the three finest American writers of detective fiction, being renowned, not only for his superb creation, *Philip MARLOWE,* the prototype of the modern private eye, but for the high literary standards and moral quality of all his writing. He was President of the Mystery Writers of America, 1959.

Writer: Raymond Thornton CHANDLER

Other Detectives:

Pete ANGLICH
Ted CARMADY
Johnny DALMAS
Steve GRAYCE
MALLORY
Ted MALVERN
Tony RESECK and John EVANS
Lt WALDMAN

Citation Record: 8 Books

The Big Sleep - *Book 1*
Knopf US (1939); Hamish Hamilton UK (1939)

Farewell, My Lovely - *Book 2*
Knopf US (1940); Hamish Hamilton UK (1940)

The High Window - *Book 3*
Knopf US (1942); Hamish Hamilton UK (1943)

The Lady In The Lake - *Book 4*
Knopf US (1943); Hamish Hamilton UK (1944)

The Little Sister - *Book 5*
Houghton Mifflin US (1949); Hamish Hamilton UK (1949)

The Long Goodbye - *Book 6*
Hamish Hamilton UK (1953); Houghton Mifflin US (1954)

Playback - *Book 7*
Hamish Hamilton UK (1940); Houghton Mifflin US (1958)

Poodle Springs - *Book 8*
Putnam US (1989); Macdonald UK (1990)

Max Allan COLLINS 1948- (American)

Invented 5 detectives - see Nate HELLER

Citation Record: 1 Selected Short Story

The Perfect Crime - *Pastiche 1*

Hiber CONTERIS (Uruguayan)

wrote, with the permission of the *CHANDLER* estate, an adulatory pastiche of a *Philip MARLOWE* novel.

Citation Record: 1 Book

Ten Percent Of Life - *Pastiche 1*

In which *Philip MARLOWE* supposedly investigates the alleged 1956 suicide of his literary agent.
Fireside US (1987)

Robert CRAIS (American)

See main detective Elvis COLE

Citation Record: 1 Selected Short Story

The Man Who Knew Dick Bong - *Pastiche 1*

Loren D ESTLEMAN 1952- (American)

Invented 7 detectives - see Amos WALKER

Citation Record: 1 Selected Short Story

Gun Music - *Pastiche 1*

Ed GORMAN 1941- (American)

Invented 4 detectives - see Leo GUILD

Citation Record: 1 Selected Short Story

The Alibi - *Pastiche 1*

M

James GRADY 1949- (American)

See main detective John RANKIN

Citation Record: 1 Selected Short Story

The Devil's Playground - *Pastiche 1*

Joyce HARRINGTON (American)

Invented 3 detectives - see Jenny HOLLAND

Citation Record: 1 Selected Short Story

Saving Grace - *Pastiche 1*

Jeremiah M HEALY 1948- (American)

See main detective John Francis CUDDY

Citation Record: 1 Selected Short Story

In The Line Of Duty - *Pastiche 5*

Edward D HOCH 1930- (American)

Invented 20 detectives - see Capt LEOPOLD

Citation Record: 1 Selected Short Story

Essence D'Orient - *Pastiche 1*

Stuart M KAMINSKY 1934- (American)

Invented 18 detectives - see Toby PETERS and Errol FLYNN

Citation Record: 1 Selected Short Story

Bitter Lemons - *Pastiche 1*

Dick LOCHTE 1937- (American)

Invented 3 detectives - see Leo G BLOODWORTH and Sarah 'Serendipity' DAHLQUIST

Sad-Eyed Blonde - *Pastiche 1*

Eric Van LUSTBADER 1946- (American)

Invented 3 detectives - see Jake Maroc

Citation Record: 1 Selected Short Story

Asia - *Pastiche 1*

John LUTZ 1939- (American)

Invented 5 detectives - see Fred CARVER

Citation Record: 1 Selected Short Story

Star Bright - *Pastiche 1*

Francis M NEVINS Jr 1943- (American)

Invented 3 detectives - see Loren MENSING

Citation Record: 1 Selected Short Story

Consultation In The Dark - *Pastiche 1*

Sara PARETSKY 1947- (American)

See main detective Victoria Iphigenia 'VI' WARSHAWSKI

Citation Record: 1 Selected Short Story

Dealer's Choice - *Pastiche 1*

Robert B PARKER 1932- (American)

See main detective SPENSER

Citation Record: 1 Book

Perchance To Dream - *Pastiche 1*

purports to be a sequel to the famed *THE BIG SLEEP*.
Macdonald UK (1991)

W R PHILBRICK (American)

Invented 4 detectives - see Connie KALE

Citation Record: 1 Selected Short Story

The Empty Sleeve - *Pastiche 1*

Byron PREISS (American)

Citation Record: 1 Book

Raymond Chandler's Marlowe - *Anthology*

was published in celebration of the centenary of the birth of *Raymond CHANDLER* and contained twenty-four pastiche short stories featuring *Philip MARLOWE,* contributed by many of the most distinguished writers in the genre. In homage, they are all cited and appear under the names of the appropriate authors.
Putnam US (1988)

Robert J RANDISI 1951- (American)

Invented 5 detectives - see Sal CARLUCCI

Citation Record: 1 Selected Short Story

Locker 246 - *Pastiche 1*

Benjamin M SCHUTZ 1949- (American)

See main detective Leo HAGGERTY

Citation Record: 1 Selected Short Story

The Black-Eyed Blonde - *Pastiche 1*

Roger L SIMON 1943- (American)

See main detective Moses VINE

Citation Record: 1 Selected Short Story

In The Jungle Of Cities - *Pastiche 1*

Julie SMITH 1944- (American)

Invented 4 detectives - see Paul MACDONALD

Citation Record: 1 Selected Short Story

Red Rock - *Pastiche 1*

Paco Ignacio TAIBO II 1949-

Invented 3 detectives - see Ch Jose Daniel FIERRO

Citation Record: 1 Selected Short Story

The Deepest South - *Pastiche 1*

Jonathan VALIN 1948- (American)

See main detective Harry STONER

Citation Record: 1 Selected Short Story

Malibu Tag Team - *Pastiche 1*

John MARNE

British Male Amateur operating in England

William KEENAN (British)

Citation Record: 3 Books

Lonely Mosaic - *First*
Hale UK (1967)

Murder In Melancholy - *Last*
Hale UK (1971)

Jake MAROC

Male Sleuth operating in Far East

Eric VAN LUSTBADER 1946-

Other Detectives:
Nicholas LINNEAR   Philip MARLOWE

Citation Record: 2 Books

Jian - *First*
Granada UK (1985); Villard US (1985)

Shan - *Latest*
Grafton UK (1987); Random House US (1987)

Jane MARPLE

is one of the author's finest and most lasting creations. An elderly spinster in a small English village, St. Mary Mead, she is drawn into the most ingenious of problems, which she solves by her acuity of observation and by picking up nuances of behaviour and clues that go unobserved by the police. Unperturbed by the most frightening crimes, she knits away as she asks seemingly unimportant questions of neighbours and, of course, of the baffled police. Although she sometimes has to set a trap for a murderer, this means only that she has already caught him in her head.

British Female Amateur operating in England

Agatha CHRISTIE 1890-1976 (British)

Invented 18 detectives - see Hercule POIROT

Citation Record: 13 Books 20 Short Stories in 1 Collection

The Murder At The Vicarage - *First*
Collins UK (1930); Dodd, Mead US (1930)

Sleeping Murder - *Last*
Collins UK (1976); Dodd, Mead US (1976)

Miss Marple: Complete Short Stories - *Collection 1*

Short stories featuring *Jane MARPLE* appeared at various times and in several collections. This is the first publication to contain all the stories.

Dodd, Mead US (1985)

Sir Henry MARQUIS

British Male Amateur operating in England

Melville Davisson POST 1871-1930 (American)

Invented 5 detectives - see Uncle ABNER

Citation Record: 21 Short Stories in 2 Collections

The Sleuth Of St James's Square - *Collection 1*
Short stories - 16
Appleton US (1920)

The Bradmoor Murder - *Collection 2*

This collection of seven of the author's short stories contains five with *Sir Henry MARQUIS.*

Short stories - 5
Sears US (1929)

The Garden Of Asia - *Collection 2**
Brentano's UK (1929)

Lt Marty MARQUIS

is said to be the ruthless, amoral head of the Broadway Squad, keeping law and order during the Depression years.

American Policeman operating in New York

John LAWRENCE 1922- (American)

Citation Record: 1 Book

Love Is The Victim - *Single*
New Horizon US (1982)

Jason MARR

is a tough and violent man with a scarred face, the colour of which varies with the intensity of his brutal emotions. Fortunately for the well-being of the genre he seems to have restricted his sleuthing to one book.

American Male Private Detective operating in New York

M ANDERSON (American)

Inventor of one other detective CREWE

Citation Record: 1 Book

Her Mother's Husband - *Only*
NewsStand US (1960)

Peter MARRELL

American Male Amateur operating in Long Island

Stanley HOPKINS Jr (American)

Writer: Blythe MORLEY

Citation Record: 2 Books

Murder By Inches - *First*
Harcourt Brace UK (1943)

The Parchment Key - *Last*
Harcourt Brace UK (1944)

Richard MARRETT

American Male Amateur operating in New York

Thomas HAUSER 1946- (American)

Citation Record: 1 Book

The Beethoven Conspiracy - *Single*
Macmillan US (1984)

Judo MARRIOTT

American Male Amateur operating in USA

Martin J FREEMAN 1899- (American)

Writer: Martin Joseph FREEMAN

See main detective Jerry TODD

Citation Record: 1 Book

The Murder Of A Midget - *Only*
Dutton US (1931); Eldon UK (1933)

Stephen MARRYAT

British Male Amateur operating in England

Margaret LEEK 1922-1985 (British)

For writer details see Antony MAITLAND

Citation Record: 3 Books

The Healthy Grave - *First*
Raven CA (1980)

Voice Of The Past - *Last*
Raven CA (1981)

Van MARS

is a sleuth from this important author's experimental phase and has been called 'a cerebral sleuth in a classic detective story.' He deals with an apparent suicide leap over Brooklyn Bridge, which is, in fact, a murder.

American Male Amateur operating in New York

William S BALLINGER 1912-1980 (American)

Invented 5 detectives - see Joaquin HAWKS

Citation Record: 1 Book

Formula For Murder - *Only*
New American Library US (1958)

Catherine 'Cat' MARSALA

is an investigative reporter and no mean one at that.

American Female Amateur operating in several locations

Barbara D'AMATO 1938- (American)

Inventor of one other detective Dr Gerritt DEGRAAF

Citation Record: 4 Books

Hardball - *First*
Scribner's US (1990)

Hard Case - *Latest*
Scribner's US (1994)

Insp Christopher MARSDEN

Australian Policeman operating in Australia

BACKHOUSE (British)

Writer: Enid Elizabeth BACKHOUSE

Inventor of one other detective Insp PRENTIS

Citation Record: 2 Books

Death Came Uninvited - *First*
Hale UK (1957)

The Night Has Eyes - *Last*
Hale UK (1961)

M

Eric MARSDEN

Male Sleuth

Anthony GRAHAM (British)

Other Detectives:
Eddie DELANEY   Frank RICHMOND

Citation Record: 1 Book

The Veetols - *Only*
Boardman UK (1965)

Clio MARSH and Det Supt Harry MARSH

are a husband-and wife team. She was a doctor and now writes crime fiction. Since he is a cop, she is at hand when murder occurs. Although he bears the official police burden, she not only does the real sleuthing but narrates breezily.

British Female Amateur and British Policeman operating in England/Scotland

Jo BANNISTER 1951- (British)

was born in Rochdale, Lancashire. She has received several awards for her writing, including the Young Journalist of the Year Award.

Inventor of one other detective pair Ch Insp Frank SHAPIRO and Det Insp Liz GRAHAM

Citation Record: 2 Books

Gilgamesh - *First*
Piatkus UK (1989); Doubleday US (1989)

The Going Down Of The Sun - *Latest*
Doubleday US (1989); Piatkus UK (1990)

Emma MARSH and Hank FAIRBANKS

Emma MARSH runs an antique shop in Boston and has a fondness for night life. The two activities, although by no means incompatible, bring her close to murders, which she solves with the aid of her friend, *Hank FAIRBANKS.*

American Female Amateur and American Male Amateur operating in Boston/Colorado

Elizabeth DEAN (American)

Citation Record: 3 Books

Murder Is A Collector's Item - *First*
Doubleday US (1939); Cassell UK (1939)

Murder A Mile High - *Last*
Doubleday US (1944); Boardman UK (1948)

Det Supt Harry MARSH

Second detective of Clio MARSH

John MARSH

British Male Sleuth operating in England

John Newton CHANCE 1911-1983 (British)

Invented 8 detectives - see John Newton CHANCE

Citation Record: 3 Books

The Case Of The Death Computer - *First*
Hale UK (1947); Hale UK (1967)

The Thug Executive - *Last*
Hale UK (1967)

Justin MARSH

British Male Amateur operating in France

Leslie BERESFORD 1899- (British)

was the author of at least eight genre books.

Writer: Leslie George BERESFORD

Citation Record: 1 Book

What's At The End? - *Only*
Jenkins UK (1937)

Kate MARSH

appears also in books with another of the author's detectives, *John BARRIN.*

British Female Amateur operating in England

Gret LANE (British)

Writer: Margaret LANE

Other Byline: Jennifer JONES (with Enid JOHNSON)

Invented 3 detectives - see Insp HOOK

Citation Record: 1 Book

The Lantern House Affair - *Only*
Jenkins UK (1931)

Kate MARSH

Second detective of John BARRIN

Lt MARSHALL and Judy MEADOWS

When a nasty type is murdered at the fictional Greene University, *Lt MARSHALL* of the local police takes charge; but, to solve the case, he needs the assistance of *Judy MEADOWS,* a new member of the Humanities department.

American Policeman and American Female Amateur operating in USA

R I WAKEFIELD 1915- (American)

was born in Pawtucket, Rhode Island and was a teacher and sometime Professor of English at Oakland University, Michigan.

Writer: Gertrude Mason WHITE

Citation Record: 1 Book

You Will Die Today! - *Only*
Dodd, Mead US (1953)

Sgt/Insp MARSHALL

is in the 'Special Branch' at Scotland Yard and roves around Europe dealing with plots and murder, while lecturing to select audiences on police methods.

British Policeman operating in England/Italy

Bernard NEWMAN 1897-1968 (British)

Invented 3 detectives - see Papa PONTIVY

Citation Record: 3 Books

Secret Servant - *First*
Gollancz UK (1935); Hillman-Curl US (1936)

The Mussolini Murder Plot - *Last*
Hutchinson UK (1936); Hillman-Curl US (1939)

Bill MARSHALL

is called a 'Turf Sleuth' and appears only in short stories.

British Male Professional Investigator operating in England

Edward WOODWARD (British)

wrote a large number of genre novels between 1924 and 1950, but he did not use series detectives, except in short stories.

Writer: Edward Emberlin WOODWARD

Inventor of one other detective George FENCHURCH

Citation Record: 10 Short Stories in 1 Collection

Bill Marshall, Turf Sleuth - *Collection 1*
Mellifont UK (1942)

Clive MARSHALL

American Male Sleuth

James WILLARD 1909-

Citation Record: 1 Book

The Affair In Arcady - *Only*
Reynal US (1959)

Insp George MARSHALL

British Policeman operating in England

Charles BARLING 1904- (British)

For writer details see Insp George MARSHALL

Inventor of one other detective Insp HENDERSON

Citation Record: 5 Books

Motive For Murder - *First*
Hale UK (1963)

Confession Of Murder - *Last*
Hale UK (1967)

Pamela BARRINGTON 1904- (British)

Writer: Muriel Vere Mant BARLING

Other Byline: Charles BARLING

Other Detectives:
Insp HENDERSON   Insp George TRAVERS

Citation Record: 7 Books

The Rest Is Silence - *First*
Evans UK (1951)

Slow Poison - *Last*
Hale UK (1967)

John MARSHALL

American Male Sleuth operating in Europe/USA

Mark DENNING (American)

Writer: John STEVENSON

Other Bylines:
Nick CARTER   Bruno ROSSI

Citation Record: 4 Books

Die Fast, Die Happy - *First*
Pyramid US (1976)

The Golden Lure - *Latest*
Tower US (1981)

John MARSHALL and Suzy MARSHALL

are a husband-and-wife team, he being a major in the US Army Intelligence Corps before his honourable discharge. In their first book they solve a murder as amateurs, but then he goes on to obtain a PI licence and thereafter they work as professionals. They have, following on the success of other such duos, got themselves a canine sidekick.

American Male Private Detective and American Female Private Detective operating in Los Angeles

Sidekick: KHAN
is a Great Dane.

Male - Pet Dog

James M FOX (American)

Invented 3 detectives - see Steve HARVESTER

Citation Record: 12 Books

Journey Into Danger - *First*
Withy Grove Press UK (1943)

Rites For A Killer - *First**
Jonathan US (1957)

Bright Serpent - *Last*
Little, Brown US (1953); Hammond UK (1956)

Megan MARSHALL

has been called by one authoritative critic 'the silliest sleuth of the season'. She is really an art-gallery director who gets involved in cases concerning paintings.

American Female Amateur operating in New York

Michelle COLLINS (American)

Citation Record: 2 Books

Murder At Willow Run - *First*
Zebra US (1979)

Premiere At Willow Run - *Latest*
Zebra US (1980)

Nick MARSHALL

operates in London but still manages to suffer from the 'murdered partner' syndrome, for which the great Dashiell HAMMETT must take full responsibility. Alas, where he led, others do not find it possible to follow.

British Male Private Detective operating in London

Gilroy MITCHAM 1923- (British)

For writer details see Shaun KOVACK

Citation Record: 3 Books

The Full Stop - *First*
Dobson UK (1957); Roy US (1957)

The Dead Reckoning - *Last*
Dobson UK (1960); Roy US (1960)

Suzy MARSHALL

Second detective of John MARSHALL

Peter MARSHAM

Second detective of Tommy LUMB

Meldrum MARSHFIELD

British Male Amateur operating in England

Egerton CASTLE 1858-1920 (British)

Citation Record: 6 Short Stories in 1 Collection

Marshfield The Observer - *Collection 1*
Six of the seven stories in this collection feature *MARSHFIELD*.
Macmillan UK (1900); Stone US (1900)

Paul MARSTON

runs an agency specialising in corporate crime in Southern California.

American Male Private Detective operating in California

Sidekick: Angel CANTINI
is a self-appointed assistant and turns out to be of considerable use, she being not just clever and beautiful, but a female boxing champion.

American Female - Assistant

Robert EVERSZ 1954- (American)

Citation Record: 2 Books

The Bottom Line Is Murder - *First*
Viking US (1988)

False Profit - *Latest*
Viking US (1990)

Bill MARTELL

American Male Amateur operating in USA

Alan Dennis BURKE 1949- (American)

Citation Record: 1 Book

Getting Away With Murder - *Single*
Little, Brown US (1981)

MARTEN

of Scotland Yard is in this one Victorian novel.

British Policeman operating in London

Coulson KERNAHAN 1858-1943 (British)

See main detective RISSLER

Citation Record: 1 Book

Scoundrels & Co - *Only*
Stone US (1899); Ward, Lock UK (1900)

Balthazar MARTEN

Male Sleuth operating in San Juan

M J ADAMSON 1935- (American)

Writer: Mary Jo ADAMSON

Citation Record: 5 Books

Not Till A Hot January - *First*
Bantam US (1987)

May's New Fangled Mirth - *Latest*
Bantam US (1989)

Insp MARTIN

is the head of the local police force in the fictional town of Camley and solves local murders, involving blackmail, espionage, and much else.

British Policeman operating in England

Richard AMBERLEY 1916- (British)

Writer: Paul Henry James BOURQUIN

Citation Record: 2 Books

Dead On The Stone - *First*
Hale UK (1969)

Incitement To Murder - *Last*
Hale UK (1968)

MARTIN

British Male Amateur operating in Monte Carlo

William LEQUEUX 1864-1927 (British)

Invented 23 detectives - see Allan KENNEDY

Citation Record: 23 Short Stories in 2 Collection

The Secrets Of Monte Carlo - *Collection 1*
Short stories - 11
White UK (1899); Dillingham US (1900)

The Secret Telephone - *Collection 1*
Short stories - 12
McCann US (1920)

M

Anthony MARTIN

is hardboiled and handsome.

American Male Private Detective operating in Los Angeles

William FRANCIS (American)

Writer: William Francis URELL

Inventor of one other detective Steve CASH

Citation Record: 2 Books

Rough On Rats - *First*
Morrow US (1942)

IOU - Murder - *First**
Signet US (1951)

Bury Me Not - *Latest*
Morrow US (1943); Boardman UK (1950)

Ben (The Revenger) MARTIN

American Male Sleuth operating in New York

Jon MESSMANN (American)

See main detective Jefferson (The Handyman) BOONE

Citation Record: 6 Books

The Revenger - *First*
Signet UK (1973)

A Promise Of Death - *Last*
Signet UK (1975)

Chris MARTIN

British Male Amateur operating in England

Annette ROOME 1946- (British)

Citation Record: 2 Books

A Real Shot In The Arm - *First*
Hodder & Stoughton UK (1989); Crown US (1991)

A Second Shot In The Dark - *Latest*
Hodder & Stoughton UK (1990); Crown US (1992)

Insp Clancy MARTIN

British Policeman operating in England

Wallace JACKSON 1898- (British)

Writer: William John BUDD

Inventor of one other detective Archibald PENNY

Citation Record: 3 Books

Two Knocks For Death - *First*
Low UK (1934); Hopkins US (1935)

The Diamonds Of Death - *Last*
Low UK (1936); Hopkins US (1937)

Supt Donald MARTIN

British Policeman operating in England

Michael BARDSLEY (British)

Citation Record: 3 Books

Murder For Sale - *First*
Hale UK (1970); Roy US (1971)

Murder On Ice - *Last*
Hale UK (1972)

Emil MARTIN

American Male Amateur operating in Nevada

Mary Ann TAYLOR 1912- (American)

Citation Record: 2 Books

Red Is For Shrouds - *First*
Raven US (1980)

Return To Murder - *Latest*
Raven US (1980)

Insp George MARTIN

is a fine, upstanding man, the son of a doctor, and a political Conservative. He is in conflict, in many ways, therefore, with his assistant.

British Policeman operating in England

Sidekick: Insp CROSBY
has attained his rank by hard work. He is contrasted to the upper-class *MARTIN*, in the class-conscious society of Britain, by being from the working class and rather left-wing in his politics.
British Male - Colleague

Francis BEEDING (British)

Invented 6 detectives - see Insp WILKINS

Citation Record: 3 Books

The Norwich Victims - *First*
Hodder & Stoughton UK (1935); Harper & Row US (1935)

He Could Not Have Slipped - *Last*
Hodder & Stoughton UK (1939); Harper & Row US (1939)

Jake MARTIN

American Male Amateur operating in California

Elizabeth C WARD 1936- (American)

Writer: Elizabeth Campbell WARD

Citation Record: 1 Book

Coast Highway - *Single*
Walker US (1983)

Jim MARTIN

British Male Amateur operating in England

Frederick SLEATH (British)

Citation Record: 10 Short Stories in 1 Collection

The Breaker Of Ships - *Collection 1*
Not all the stories are criminous.
Hutchinson UK (1922)

Ray (The Bodyguard) MARTIN

American Male Sleuth operating in USA

Richard REINSMITH 1930- (American)

Writer: Richard Rein SMITH

Citation Record: 5 Books

The Blonde Target - *First*
Tower UK (1980)
The Five And Dime Murders - *Latest*
Tower UK (1980)

Tavey MARTIN

British Male Sleuth operating in several locations

Diana WINSOR 1946- (British)
was born in Belfast and has been a journalist and a painter.
Citation Record: 2 Books
Red On Wight - *First*
Macmillan UK (1972); Stein US (1978)
The Death Convention - *Last*
Macmillan UK (1974); Stein US (1978)

William (Tiger Shark) MARTIN

American Male Sleuth operating in USA

Ken STANTON (American)
For writer details see Barnaby JONES
Citation Record: 11 Books
Cold Blue Death - *First*
Macfadden UK (1970)
Operation Mermaid - *Last*
Manor US (1974)

Det Insp Harry MARTINEAU

operates in the fictional industrial town of Grantchester in the north of England. He is almost the last in the long line of British gentleman police detectives and stands at the beginning of the era of police procedurals. He loves to play the piano, is kind to witnesses and highly supportive of his juniors. His cases are good, solid stuff, depending less on modern techniques than on old-fashioned detective work.
British Policeman operating in England

Maurice PROCTER 1906-1973 (British)
was born in Nelson, Lancashire. He served in the Yorkshire police force, 1927-1946.
Other Detectives:
Det Supt Philip HUNTER   Bill KNIGHT
Citation Record: 14 Books
Hell Is A City - *First*
Hutchinson UK (1954)
Somewhere In This City - *First**
Harper & Row US (1954)
Hideaway - *Last*
Hutchinson UK (1968); Harper & Row US (1968)

Robert MARTINEAU

Second detective of Jack IRWIN

Det Kate MARTINELLI and Det Al HAWKINS

Kate MARTINELLI is an overt lesbian, which propensity makes her fairly safe when in the company of her partner, *Al HAWKINS.*
American Policewoman and American Policeman operating in San Francisco

Laurie R KING (American)
Adopter of one other detective Sherlock HOLMES
Citation Record: 2 Books
A Grave Talent - *First*
St Martin's US (1993)
To Play The Fool - *Latest*
St Martin's US (1995)

David MARTINI

British Male Sleuth

Richard RAINE 1923- (British)
For writer details see TWEED
Citation Record: 3 Books
A Wreath For America - *First*
Heinemann UK (1967)
The Corder Index - *First**
Harcourt Brace US (1967)
Bombshell - *Last*
Dent UK (1970); Harcourt Brace US (1970)

Arthur MARTINSON

American Male Amateur operating in New York

Courtland FITZSIMMONS 1883-1949 (American)
Invented 4 detectives - see Det Jack KETHERIDGE
Citation Record: 2 Books
The Bainbridge Murder - *First*
McBride US (1930); Eyre & Spottiswoode UK (1930)
The Manville Murders - *Last*
McBride US (1930)

John MARTINSON

British Male Amateur operating in England

Hugh CLEVELY 1898-1964 (British)
Invented 4 detectives - see Maxwell ARCHER
Citation Record: 2 Books
The Gang Smasher - *First*
Hutchinson UK (1928); Clode US (1930)
The Gang Smasher Again - *Last*
Cassell UK (1938)

Paul MARTINY

British Male Secret Agent operating in England/Cyprus

William HAGGARD 1907- (British)
yInvented 4 detectives - see Col Charles RUSSELL
Citation Record: 2 Books
The Protectors - *First*
Cassell UK (1972); Walker US (1972)
The Kinsmen - *Last*
Cassell UK (1974); Walker US (1974)

Valentine MARTYN

spends his professional time uncovering the misdeeds, legion in number, that take place at race meetings.
British Male Professional Investigator operating in England

Nat GOULD 1857-1919 (British)
Writer: Nathaniel GOULD
Inventor of one other detective Barry BROMLEY
Citation Record: 6 Short Stories in 1 Collection
The Exploits Of A Race-Course Detective - *Collection 1*
This collection of fifteen of the author's short stories contains six with *Valentine MARTYN.*
Long UK (1927)

Dr Joan MARVIN

British Female Amateur operating in England

Leonora EYLES 1889-1960 (British)
Writer: Margaret Leonora Pitcairn EYLES
Citation Record: 2 Books
Death Of A Dog - *First*
Hutchinson UK (1936)
They Wanted Him Dead! - *Last*
Hutchinson UK (1936)

Pete MARVIN

American Male Amateur operating in Colorado

Brent EDMUNDS (American)
Citation Record: 4 Books
A Gun In My Back - *First*
Laurie UK (1955)
Spiders In The Night - *Last*
Laurie UK (1956)

Col MARWOOD

British Male Amateur operating in England

A C FOX-DAVIES 1871-1928 (British)
Invented 3 detectives - see Sir John KYNNERSLEY
Citation Record: 15 Short Stories in 1 Collection
The Troubles Of Colonel Marwood - *Collection 1*
White UK (1909)

Sgt Joseph MARX
solves a case of death by bludgeoning in a locked room.
American Policeman operating in USA

William ARDEN 1924- (American)
See main detective Kane JACKSON
Citation Record: 1 Selected Short Story
The Bizarre Case Expert
appeared in the June number. It is also in the anthology, *Ellery Queen Masters of Mystery* (*Galahad*; US 1987).
In 'Ellery Queen's Mystery Magazine' US (1970)

MARX BROTHERS
appear with at least two other detectives - see Toby PETERS

Insp MARX and Dr RHINEWALD
American Policeman and American Male Amateur operating in USA

Samuel SPEWACK 1899-1971 (American)
Citation Record: 1 Book
The Skyscraper Murder - *Only*
Macaulay US (1928)

Sister MARY HELEN
is an elderly nun who, now retired, has been sent to Mount St Francis College for Women in San Francisco. A cross between *Father BROWN* and *Miss MARPLE*, she is continually coming across (and solving) murders.
American Female Amateur operating in San Francisco
Stooge: Det Kate MURPHY
of the San Francisco Police Department is friendly enough but finds herself continually outwitted and upstaged by the detective ability of the elderly nun.
American Female

M

Sister Carol Anne O'MARIE 1933- (American)
Citation Record: 4 Books
A Novena For Murder - *First*
Scribner's US (1984)
Murder Makes A Pilgrimage - *Latest*
Delacorte US (1994)

The MASKED DETECTIVE
was one of this prolific writer's several pulp magazine crimebusters. He appeared, under a new pseudonym, in several stories, 1940-1942, in *Masked Detective Magazine.*
American Male Amateur operating in USA

C K M SCANLON (American)
See main detective Dan FOWLER
Citation Record: 1 Selected Short Story
Alias The Masked Detective
In 'Masked Detective Magazine' US

MASON
solves a case of death by stabbing in a locked room. He is to be noted as an early and minor creation by the most famous author not to have been awarded the Nobel Prize for Literature!
British Policeman operating in England

Graham GREENE 1904-1991 (British)
was born in Berkhampstead, Hertfordshire, and was educated at Berkhampstead School and Balliol College, Oxford. He was a reporter on *The Times*, 1926-1930, was their film critic, 1937-1940, and then served in the Foreign Office, London, 1941-1944. Regarded as one of the most important writers of the century, he wrote novels, short stories, plays, film scripts, verse, books for children, and critical studies. Many of his books can loosely be termed thrillers but they all deal with deep psychological or religious and moral problems. He rarely used detectives as main characters, however. He received literary and other awards from all over the world and in 1986 was given the Order of Merit, the highest of all British non-military distinctions.
Citation Record: 1 Selected Short Story
Murder For The Wrong Reason
appears also in an anthology, *The Last Word* (*Reinhardt*; UK 1990)
In 'The Graphic' UK (1929)

Insp MASON
solves a case of death by stabbing while the victim is under continual watch.
British Policeman operating in England
Sidekick: Sgt ELK
assists in this one investigation at a time when he still occupied the rank of sergeant, although chronologically the book appeared later than those in which he held a higher rank.
British Male - Subordinate

Edgar WALLACE 1875-1932 (British)
Invented 28 detectives - see J G REEDER
Citation Record: 1 Book
White Face - *Only*
Hodder & Stoughton UK (1930); Doubleday US (1931)

Supt MASON
investigates the death of a guest at a spa in the Scottish Highlands.
British Policeman operating in Scotland

Francis LYALL (British)
See main detective Insp COHEN
Citation Record: 1 Book
The Croaking Of The Raven - *Single*
HarperCollins UK (1990); St Martin's US (1992)

Insp Dick MASON
British Policeman operating in England

Raymond ARMSTRONG 1905-1962 (British)
was a British author who invented would-be American detectives in might-be American situations.
Writer: Norman LEE
Other Bylines:
Mark CORRIGAN   Robertson HOBART
Other Detectives:
Insp Dick MASON and Laura SCUDAMORE
J Rockingham STONE
J Rockingham STONE, Laura SCUDAMORE and Insp Dick MASON
Citation Record: 2 Books
Dangerous Limelight - *First*
Long UK (1947)
Sinister Playhouse - *Last*
Long UK (1949)

Insp Dick MASON
Appears with at least two other detectives - see J Rockingham STONE, Laura SCUDAMORE and Insp Dick MASON

Insp Dick MASON and Laura SCUDAMORE
British Policeman and British Female Amateur operating in England

Raymond ARMSTRONG 1905-1962 (British)
Invented 4 detectives - see Insp Dick MASON
Citation Record: 5 Books
The Sinister Widow - *First*
Long UK (1951)
The Sinister Widow At Sea - *Last*
Long UK (1959)

Paul MASON
British Male Amateur operating in England

Charles LEADER 1938- (British)
Writer: Robert Charles SMITH
Other Byline: Robert CHARLES
Other Detectives:
David CHAN   Ric MCADDEN
Mike MCCALL

Citation Record: 2 Books

Frontiers Of Violence - *First*
Hale UK (1966)

Strangler's Moon - *Last*
Hale UK (1968)

Perry MASON

is one of the great classic investigators of the genre, appearing in over eighty novels from 1933 to 1973 (that is, three years after the author's death). He is a defence lawyer of great brilliance who takes on difficult cases, which he usually wins, often in spite of apparently damning evidence against his client. He nearly always has to set in motion considerable detective work so as to obtain the truth, which he uses, with devastating logic and panache in final courtroom dramas. He is aided, throughout the long canon, by a constant, devoted and apparently ageless team, almost as well-known as he is. The cast of the books is also kept fairly constant, adding to their popularity, and there is a remarkable and foxy trio of stooges with whom he has many a struggle, in and out of the courtroom. The great detectives have a way of continuing after the death of their creators for both popular and commercial reasons. So it is with *Perry MASON,* who has been used in novels by at least one other author.

American Male Amateur operating in New York

Sidekick: Paul DRAKE
is a private detective who works, as far as we know, almost entirely on *Perry MASON's* cases. He is the detective's chief legman, acquiring much of the evidence that the great man usually needs. He is listed as a detective in his own right as well, but he must certainly be accounted as one of the most famous and overworked sidekicks in the whole genre.
American Male - Assistant

Sidekick: Della STREET
is perhaps the best-known secretary sidekick in the business and without her *MASON* would often be lost. As the canon goes on and on, there is sometimes more than a hint of a romantic attachment between the great attorney and this adoring, beautiful, completely efficient girl; but, the readers can rest assured, to her catching criminals is all good clean fun.
American Female - Secretary

Stooge: Lt FLAGG
is a consummate stooge, never quite believing *MASON.*
American Male

Stooge: Sgt HOLCOMB
is one of several police adversaries who confront *PERRY MASON* and live to regret it.
American Male

Stooge: Dist Att Hamilton BURGER
is often *MASON's* main adversary among the ranks of the police and the law. The two men are in frequent confrontation before and during the court cases that are the well-known climaxes of the books.
American Male

Thomas CHASTAIN (American)
was born in Washington DC and was a newspaper editor.
Invented 4 detectives - see J T 'Jake' SPANNER

Citation Record: 2 Books

The Case Of Too Many Murders - *Pastiche 1*
Morrow US (1989)

The Case Of The Burning Bequest - *Pastiche 2*
Morrow US (1990)

Erle Stanley GARDNER 1889-1970 (American)
was born in Malden, Massachusetts. He graduated from Palo Alto High School, California, 1909, and Valparaiso University, Indiana, 1909. Writer, reporter and lawyer, he wrote hundreds of stories for magazines and many novels during the 1920s, often using pseudonyms. He created many detectives, large and small, including the one for which he is renowned, the famed *Perry MASON.* He received the Mystery Writers of America Edgar Allan Poe award, 1952, their Grand Master award, 1961, and he has been honoured with degrees from several US universities.

Other Byline: A A FAIR

Other Detectives:

'Go Get 'Em' CARVER	Terry CLANE
Richard 'Speed' DASH	Sheriff Bill ELDON
Jax KEEN	Lester LEITH
Ed MIGRAINE	Paul PRY
Doug SELBY	Dane SKARLE
Peter WENNICK	'Gramps' WIGGINS
Sidney ZOOM	

Citation Record: 82 Books 1 Selected Short Story 2 Short Stories in 1 Collection

The Case Of The Velvet Claws - *First*
The very first of the long canon has blackmail, murder, suspicion falling on the detective, and a great ending.
Morrow US (1933); Harrap UK (1933)

The Case Of The Postponed Murder - *Last*
Morrow US (1973); Heinemann UK (1977)

The Case Of The Murderer's Bride
is in the author's collection of the same name, in which another of his detectives, *Lester LEITH,* appears.
Davis US (1969)

The Case Of The Cautious Coquette - *Collection 1*
Morrow US (1949); Heinemann UK (1955)

Randolph MASON

American Male Amateur operating in USA

Melville Davisson POST 1871-1930 (American)
Invented 5 detectives - see Uncle ABNER

Citation Record: 25 Short Stories in 3 Collections

The Strange Schemes Of Randolph Mason - *Collection 1*
Short stories - 7
Putnam US (1896)

Randolph Mason: The Strange Schemes - *Collection 1**
Putnam US (1922)

The Man Of Last Resort; Or, The Clients Of Randolph Mason - *Collection 2*
Short stories - 5
Putnam US (1897)

Randolph Mason: The Clients - *Collection 2**
Putnam US (1923)

The Corrector Of Destinies - *Collection 3*
Short stories - 13
Clode US (1908)

Rick MASON

American Male Private Detective operating in China

Paul W FAIRMAN 1916-1977 (American)
Inventor of one other detective Wally WATTS

Citation Record: 1 Book

The Glass Ladder - *Only*
Handi-Books US (1950)

Tom MASON

American Male Amateur operating in Chicago

Mark Richard ZUBRO (American)

Citation Record: 2 Books

A Simple Suburban Murder - *First*
St Martin's US (1989)

Why Isn't Becky Twitchell Dead? - *Latest*
St Martin's US (1990)

Richard MASSEY

American Male Amateur operating in New York/Virginia

Van SILLER (American)

Writer: Hilda Van SILLER

Other Detectives:

Pete RECTOR	Alan STEWART

Citation Record: 2 Books
Echo Of A Bomb - *First*
Doubleday US (1943); Jarrolds UK (1944)
The Curtain Between - *Latest*
Doubleday US (1947); Jarrolds UK (1949)
Fatal Bride - *Latest**
Mercury US (1948)

Lisa MASSINGHAM

solves the mystery of an airliner's disappearance.
British Female Amateur operating in England

Karen CAMPBELL 1922- (British)
Writer: Betty BEATY
Citation Record: 1 Book
Suddenly, In The Air - *Only*
Collins UK (1969)
The Broken Spectre - *Only**
Fontana US (1972)

Carl MASTERS

American Policeman operating in Chicago

Lawrence L LYNCH (American)
Invented 11 detectives - see Neil J BATHURST
Citation Record: 3 Books
Against Odds - *First*
Rand US (1894); Ward, Lock UK (1894)
Man And Master - *Last*
Laird & Lee US (1908); Ward, Lock UK (1909)

Insp/Ch Supt George MASTERS and Ch Insp Bill GREEN

feature in a long series of police procedurals, often concerned with cases involving a medical or scientific problem and often with unusual poisons and ingenious criminal methods. *George MASTERS* is suave and educated, with a good knowledge of toxicology and forensics, and contrasts in his approach and behaviour with *Bill GREEN,* his partner, who really doesn't like him.
British Policemen operating in England
Sidekick: Sgt REED
British Male - Subordinate
Sidekick: Sgt BERGER
British Male - Subordinate

Douglas CLARK 1919- (British)
was born in Lincolnshire. He was educated at the University of London and was a professional soldier, 1939-1956.
Writer: Douglas Malcolm Jackson CLARK
Citation Record: 26 Books
Nobody's Perfect - *First*
Cassell UK (1969); Stein & Day US (1969)
Plain Sailing - *Latest*
Gollancz UK (1987); Harper & Row US (1988)

J C K 'Jigger' MASTERS

is an early example of the American super-detective who can out-shoot, out-fight, and generally outwit any of the ordinary super-criminals that might come his way.
American Male Private Detective operating in Long Island

Anthony M RUD 1893-1942 (American)
Writer: Anthony Melville RUD
Citation Record: 3 Books
The Rose Bath Riddle - *First*
Macaulay US (1934)
The Stuffed Men - *Last*
Macaulay US (1935); Newnes UK (1936)

Det Sgt Masao MASUTO

is a Zen Buddhist, a happy family man, a karate expert, and keen gardener. He solves several cases that arise among the corrupt rich around Los Angeles.
Japanese Policeman operating in California

E V CUNNINGHAM 1914- (American)
was born in New York City. A distinguished American man of letters, he has been a war correspondent and is the author of over forty books under his real name, as well as plays, poetry, children's books, political and critical works. A leading figure of radical movements and of the political left, imprisoned during the McCarthy years, and recipient of many literary and other awards, he has found time to write around two dozen books in the criminous genre, creating several interesting detectives.
Writer: Howard Melvin FAST
Other Detectives:
John COMADAY and Larry COHEN
Harvey KRIM — Alan MACKLIN
Citation Record: 7 Books
Samantha - *First*
Morrow US (1967); Deutsch UK (1968)
The Case Of The Angry Actress - *First**
Dell US (1984)
The Case Of The Murdered MacKenzie - *Latest*
Delacorte US (1984); Gollancz UK (1985)

Hoani MATA

Male Sleuth

V Merle GRAYLAND (British)
Writer: Valerie Merle Spanner GRAYLAND
Citation Record: 4 Books
The Dead Men Of Eden - *First*
Hale UK (1962)
Jest Of Darkness - *Last*
Hale UK (1965)

Sgt MATCH

is the police presence in one of the author's best comic plays. He is brilliantly inept, easily traduced, and a wonderful addition to the great and lasting tradition of British stage cops.
British Policeman operating in England

Joe ORTON 1933-1967 (British)
See main detective Insp TRUSCOTT
Citation Record: 1 Book
What The Butler Saw - *Play*
Methuen UK (1969)

The MATCHLESS DETECTIVE

American Male Detective in Pulp Magazines operating in USA

ANON
No citations

Det Sgt Robert MATHER

British Policeman operating in England

Bruce GRAEME 1900-1982 (British)
Invented 6 detectives - see BLACKSHIRT
Citation Record: 8 Books
The Quiet Ones - *First*
Hutchinson UK (1970)
Mather Investigates - *Latest*
Hale UK (1980)

James MATLOCK

is a Connecticut professor who is employed by the US Justice Department to penetrate a narcotic operation.
American Male Amateur operating in USA

Robert LUDLUM 1927- (American)
Invented 3 detectives - see John TANNER
Citation Record: 1 Book
The Matlock Paper - *Only*
Dial US (1973); Hart Davis MacGibbon UK (1973)

James MATRIC

is a criminal cop who investigates the murders of semi-retired prostitutes and tries to frame an innocent man.
American Policeman operating in USA

Mark MCSHANE 1930- (Australian)

Invented 3 detectives - see Norman PINK

Citation Record: 1 Book

Untimely Ripped - *Only*
Cassell UK (1962); Doubleday US (1963)

Sgt Gunnar MATSON

American Policeman operating in San Francisco

Breni JAMES (American)

was born in Denver.

Writer: Breni James PEVERHOUSE

Citation Record: 2 Books

Night Of The Kill - *First*
Simon & Schuster US (1961); Hammond UK (1963)

The Shake-Up - *Last*
Simon & Schuster US (1964)

Patrick MATSON

British Male Sleuth operating in England

Michael BALDWIN 1930- (British)

Citation Record: 3 Books

The Gamecock - *First*
Faber UK (1980)

Holfernes - *Latest*
Macdonald UK (1989)

MATTHEWS

British Policeman operating in England

Norman BERROW 1902- (British)

Invented 4 detectives - see Michael REVEL

Citation Record: 1 Book

Ghost House - *Only*
Ward, Lock UK (1940); St Martin's US (1979)

Sheriff Charles Timothy MATTHEWS

American Policeman operating in USA

D R MEREDITH (American)

See main detective John Lloyd BRANSON

Citation Record: 3 Books

The Sheriff And The Panhandle Murders - *First*
Walker US (1984)

The Sheriff And The Folsom Man Murders - *Latest*
Walker US (1987)

Daphne MATTHEWS

Second detective of Det Lou BOLDT

Freye MATTHEWS

Second detective of Guy PLANTE

Howard MATTHEWS and Jeff LANDRUM

solve a case involving a man who mysteriously disappears.

American Male Amateurs operating in USA

Robert ARTHUR 1909-1969 (American)

Invented 6 detectives - see Max MILLION

Citation Record: 1 Book

The Mystery Of The Man Who Evaporated - *Only*
Random House US (1963)

James MATTHEWS

Second detective of Philip STRONG

Lt Barney MATTINGLEY

Second detective of Prof Clifford WELLS

Mark MATURIN

British Male Amateur operating in England

F Cowley WHITEHOUSE (British)

Writer: Frank Cowley WHITEHOUSE

Citation Record: 16 Short Stories in 1 Collection

Mark Maturin, Parson - *Collection 1*
Ward, Lock UK (1906)

Leslie MAUGHAN

is the daughter of a high-ranking Scotland Yard man. Although she has no need to earn her own living, 'detection is in her blood' and she has worked her way up to a senior position in the CID.

British Policewoman operating in London

Edgar WALLACE 1875-1932 (British)

Invented 28 detectives - see J G REEDER

Citation Record: 1 Book

The Square Emerald - *Only*
Hodder & Stoughton UK (1926)

The Girl From Scotland Yard - *Only**
Doubleday US (1927)

Victor MAURY

French Male Professional Investigator operating in Paris

George REYNOLDS (American)

Citation Record: 1 Book

Victor Maury, The French Detective - *Only*
Ogilvie US (1882)

Bucketeer MAV

is a three-shouldered alien detective in this sci-fi novel. He solves a nasty case of murder by explosion in a locked room.

Sleuth operating in Space

L Neil SMITH (American)

Citation Record: 1 Book

Their Majesties' Bucketeers - *Single*
Ballantine US (1981)

Lawrence MAVER

British Male Amateur operating in Italy

Alan NIXON 1937- (British)

Citation Record: 2 Books

Item 7 - *First*
Bodley Head UK (1970); Simon & Schuster US (1971)

The Attack On Vienna - *Last*
Bodley Head UK (1971); St Martin's US (1972)

Gaston MAX

is one of the author's hero-detectives, doing battle with some of the author's usual gangs of arch-criminals who threaten world order.

Male Amateur operating in several locations

Sax ROHMER 1883-1959 (British)

Invented 9 detectives - see Insp RYDER

Citation Record: 4 Books

The Yellow Claw - *First*
Methuen UK (1915); McBride US (1915)

Seven Sins - *Last*
McBride US (1943); Cassell UK (1944)

Maj Harry MAXIM

is an agent in some special service unit, countering spies and encountering the usual mayhem.

British Male Secret Agent operating in Europe

Gavin LYALL 1932- (British)

Invented 4 detectives - see Bert KEMP

Citation Record: 4 Books

The Secret Servant - *First*
Hodder & Stoughton UK (1980); Viking US (1980)

Uncle Target - *Latest*
Hodder & Stoughton UK (1988); Viking US (1988)

Alan MAXWELL

is fleeing from his wife, only to be caught up in murder. A suspect himself, he has to find out whodunnit to save himself.

American Male Amateur operating in the Caribbean

George Harmon COXE 1901-1984 (American)

Invented 20 detectives - see Kent MURDOCK

Citation Record: 1 Book

Woman With A Gun - *Only*
Knopf US (1972); Hale UK (1974)

Archie MAXWELL

is an engineer who turns sleuth in this one Victorian novel.

British Male Amateur

Fergus HUME 1859-1932 (British)

Invented 24 detectives - see Insp Samuel GORBY

Citation Record: 1 Book

The Fever Of Life - *Only*
Sampson, Low UK (1893)

Georgia Lee MAXWELL

is a society editor for the *Bay City Sun* who investigates a case of murder.

American Female Amateur operating in Florida

Mickey FRIEDMAN 1944- (American)

See main detective Isobel ANDERS

Citation Record: 2 Books

Magic Mirror - *First*
Viking US (1988)

Deadly Reflections - *First**
Gollancz UK (1989)

A Temporary Ghost - *Latest*
Gollancz UK (1990); Viking US (1991)

Lauren MAXWELL

is based in Anchorage, Alaska, and works as an investigator for the Wild America Society to protect the wild life and environment in the snowy wastes. Naturally, there are those who do not wish to protect either, and it is as well that the lady packs her trusty .38 calibre revolver.

American Female Professional Investigator operating in Alaska

Elizabeth QUINN (American)

Citation Record: 1 Book

Murder Most Grizzly - *Single*
Pocket Books US (1993)

Mahlon MAXWELL

Second detective of Janna BRILL

Peter MAXWELL and Susan MAXWELL

solve a case of murder in which the victim was apparently killed by a poisoned dart while in a locked bathroom.

British Male Amateur and British Female Amateur operating in England

Hector HAWTON 1901- (British)

Writer: Hector HAWTON

Other Byline: John SYLVESTER

Inventor of one other detective Asmun HILL

Citation Record: 1 Book

Death Of A Witch - *Only*
Ward, Lock UK (1952)

Susan MAXWELL

Second detective of Peter MAXWELL

Tina MAY

British Female Amateur operating in England

Sarah KEMP 1924- (British)

is the pseudonym of an author of several excellent crime novels without a series detective.

Writer: Michael BUTTERWORTH

Citation Record: 2 Books

The Lure Of Sweet Death - *First*
Century UK (1986); Doubleday US (1986)

What Dread Hand? - *Latest*
Century UK (1987); Doubleday US (1987)

Noel MAYBERRY

Second detective of Bill BRADLEY

Det Ch Insp Tom MAYBRIDGE

British Policeman operating in England

B M GILL 1921- (British)

was born in Holyhead, Anglesey, Wales. She was educated at Le Bon Sauveur Convent, Holyhead, and Redland College, Bristol. A professional chiropodist, she became a full-time writer of detective novels and, under a pseudonym, at least eight mainstream novels. She received the Crime Writers Association Gold Dagger award, 1984.

Writer: Barbara Margaret TRIMBLE

Citation Record: 3 Books

Victims - *First*
Hodder & Stoughton UK (1980)

Suspect - *First**
Scribner's US (1981)

The Fifth Rapunzel - *Latest*
Hodder & Stoughton UK (1991)

Catherine MAYHEW

American Female Amateur operating in Maine

Velda JOHNSTON (American)

See main detective Deborah CHANNING

Citation Record: 1 Book

The Other Karen - *Single*
Dodd, Mead US (1983)

Lt Stephen MAYHEW

is the main detective in these two books and appears in other books with other detectives of this author.

American Policeman operating in San Francisco

D B OLSEN 1907-1973 (American)

was born in Texas.

Writer: Julia Clara Catherine Dolores Berk Olsen HITCHENS

Other Byline: Dolores HITCHENS

Other Detectives:
Rachel MURDOCK, Jennifer MURDOCK and Lt Stephen MAYHEW
Rachel MURDOCK and Jennifer MURDOCK
Prof A PENNYFEATHER Mr PUCKETT

Citation Record: 2 Books

The Clue In The Clay - *First*
Phoenix Press US (1938)

The Ticking Heart - *Last*
Doubleday US (1940)

Lt Stephen MAYHEW

Appears with at least two other detectives - see Rachel MURDOCK

Insp MAYNARD

of Scotland Yard is in this one Victorian novel.

British Policeman operating in London

Florence WARDEN 1857-1929 (British)

Writer: Florence Alice Price JAMES

Other Detectives:
Jem COLLINGHAM Clifford KING
Gerald STAUNTON

Citation Record: 1 Book

The House On The Marsh - *Only*
Munro US (1883); Stevens UK (1884)

Garrett MAYNARD

lives in a lighthouse off the shore of Maryland, from which he does his sleuthing.

American Male Private Detective operating in Maryland

Howard SWIGGETT 1891-1957 (American)

Citation Record: 2 Books

The Corpse In The Derby Hat - *First*
Little, Brown US (1937)

The Stairs Lead Nowhere - *First**
Heinemann UK (1937)

Most Secret...Most Immediate - *Last*
Houghton US (1944)

Nigel MAYNE

solves some 'impossible' deaths in locked-room situations.

American Male Amateur operating in USA

Gerald BENEDICT (American)

Citation Record: 1 Book

The Case Of The Deadly Drops - *Only*
Phoenix Press US (1941)

Asey MAYO

of Wellfleet, Cape Cod, is a plain Yankee, tall, thin, and much given to chewing tobacco. An ex-sailor and motor mechanic, he is called by his friends the Codfish Sherlock, for he has the knack of being able to solve all manner of crimes and mysteries around the area.

American Male Amateur operating in Massachusetts

Sidekick: 'Doc' CUMMINGS
American Male - Friend

Phoebe Atwood TAYLOR 1909-1976 (American)

was born in Boston, Massachusetts, and graduated with a BA from Barnard College, New York, 1930. She was the author of two series of detective novels, all set against the New England background she loved so much.

Citation Record: 24 Books

The Cape Cod Mystery - *First*
Bobbs US (1931)

Diplomatic Corpse - *Last*
Little, Brown US (1951); Collins UK (1951)

Insp Gil MAYO

is head of a CID force in rural England and does good standard investigation.

British Policeman operating in England

Sidekick: Sgt KITE
British Male - Subordinate

Marjorie ECCLES (American)

Citation Record: 4 Books

Cast A Cold Eye - *First*
Doubleday US (1988)

More Deaths Than One - *Latest*
Collins UK (1991)

Ric MCADDEN

British Male Sleuth operating in Saigon

Charles LEADER 1938- (British)

Invented 4 detectives - see Paul MASON

Citation Record: 2 Books

The Golden Lure - *First*
Hale UK (1967)

Cargo To Saigon - *Last*
Hale UK (1969)

MCALLISTER

is a wealthy clubman whose minor detective successes are aided by the fact that his valet, a convicted felon, looks just like him.

American Male Amateur operating in New York

Arthur TRAIN 1875-1945 (American)

Invented 3 detectives - see Ephraim TUTT

Citation Record: 6 Short Stories in 1 Collection

McAllister And His Double - *Collection 1*

This collection contains four stories with *DOCKRIDGE* and six with *MCALLISTER.*
Scribner's US (1905); Newnes UK (1905)

William MCALPIN

American Male Amateur operating in New York

Richard H R SMITHIES 1936- (American)

Writer: Richard Hugo Ripman SMITHIES

Citation Record: 2 Books

An Academic Question - *First*
Horizon US (1965)

Death Gets An A - *First**
Signet US (1968)

Disposing Mind - *Last*
Horizon US (1966)

Death Takes A Gamble - *Last**
Signet US (1968)

Philip MCALPINE

British Male Amateur operating in England

Adam DIMENT 1945?- (British)

Citation Record: 4 Books

The Dolly Dolly Spy - *First*
Joseph UK (1967); Dutton US (1967)

Think Inc - *Last*
Joseph UK (1971)

Dr Ian MCANDREW

solves a case of death by decapitation in a locked room.

British Male Amateur operating in England

T C H JACOBS 1899-1976 (British)

Invented 8 detectives - see Ch Insp BARNARD

Citation Record: 1 Book

Black Trinity - *Only*
Long UK (1959)

Victor MCBAIN

is a 'Specialist Investigator', one of the old politely British names for the private eye. He takes cases passed to him from other types of agency.

British Male Private Detective operating in London

Colin ROBERTSON 1906-1980 (British)

Invented 7 detectives - see Mike REED

Citation Record: 8 Books

The Tiger's Claws - *First*
Ward, Lock UK (1951)

Murder Sits Pretty - *Last*
Hale UK (1961)

Heather MCBEAN

Second detective of Mac HANRAHAN

Capt MCBLAID

British Male Professional Investigator operating in England

Rowland WALKER 1876- (British)

Inventor of one other detective Devil MCKEENE

Citation Record: 1 Book

Captain McBlaid Of The Air Police - *Only*
Partridge UK (1932)

Jane MCBRIDE

takes a job in Sitka, Alaska, is warned off, and finds herself in the role of sleuth.

American Female Amateur operating in Alaska

Susan FROETSCHEL (American)

Citation Record: 1 Book

Alaska Gray - *Single*
St Martin's US (1994)

Rex MCBRIDE

is nominally an insurance investigator. Actually, he is a womaniser, a drinker, and a liar. He is a prototype and a portent of a new species, hardboiled, vicious, violent, and without redeeming features.

American Male Private Detective operating in Los Angeles

Cleve F ADAMS 1895-1949 (American)

was born in Chicago, Illinois. He worked as a miner, in films, and as a detective before becoming a full-time writer in the 1930s.

Writer: Cleve Franklin ADAMS

M

Other Byline: John SPAIN

Other Detectives:

Stephen MCCLOUD
John J SHANNON
Violet MCDADE
Insp THOMAS

Citation Record: 6 Books

And Sudden Death - *First*
Dutton US (1940)

Shady Lady - *Last*
Completed by *Robert Leslie BELLEM* and *W T BALLARD* and published after the death of *Cleve F ADAMS.*
Dutton US (1955); Ace US (1955)

Det Insp Carl MCCADDEN

is 'unshaven, unorthodox and unliked by his superiors'. He investigates the shabby underside of the cut-glass world of Waterford.

Irish Policeman operating in Eire

Jim LUMSBY (Irish)

Citation Record: 1 Book

Making The Cut - *Single*
Gollancz UK (1994)

Insp MCCAIG

British Policeman operating in Scotland

Hugh C RAE 1935- (British)

was born in Glasgow.

Writer: Hugh Crawford RAE

Other Byline: Robert CRAWFORD

Citation Record: 2 Books

A Few Small Bones - *First*
Bland UK (1968)

The House At Balnesmoor - *First**
Coward McCann US (1969)

The Shooting Gallery - *Last*
Constable UK (1972); Coward McCann US (1972)

M

Marmaduke 'Duke' MCCALE

had to leave Chicago, as the police there seemed of the unanimous opinion that he should. He now works in Boston on cases of politically motivated murder among the upper crust.

American Male Private Detective operating in Boston

Gerald BROWN (American)

Citation Record: 2 Books

Murder On Beacon Hill - *First*
Phoenix Press US (1941)

Murder In Plain Sight - *Last*
Phoenix Press US (1945)

Andrew MCCALL

British Male Amateur operating in several locations

Mark CARREL 1916- (British)

For writer details see Sgt FENWICK

Citation Record: 4 Books

The Blood Pit - *First*
Hale UK (1967)

Tears Of Blood - *Last*
Hale UK (1967)

Bert MCCALL and Tony COSTAINE

are said to be the most expensive private eyes in New York. Tough, smart, and handsome, and with Secret Service backgrounds, who would want to argue?

American Male Private Detectives operating in New York

Neil MACNEIL 1903-1980 (American)

For writer details see Bill LENNOX

Citation Record: 7 Books

Death Takes An Option - *First*
GM US (1958); Fawcett UK (1960)

The Spy Catchers - *Last*
Fawcett UK (1966)

Matt MCCALL

American Male Sleuth operating in San Antonio

C C RISENHOOVER 1936- (American)

was born in Oklahoma. He has been a reporter and Professor of Journalism.

Citation Record: 3 Books

Dead Even - *First*
McLennan US (1986)

Child Stalker - *Latest*
McLennan US (1987)

Micah 'Mike' MCCALL

is a kind of professional trouble-shooter, a forgettable and unadmirable type.

American Male Professional Investigator operating in USA

Ellery QUEEN 1922-1983 (American)

For writer details see Bill MADDERN

Citation Record: 1 Book

The Campus Murders - *Only*
Lancer US (1970)

Ellery QUEEN 1915-1983 (American)

See main detective Tim CORRIGAN

Citation Record: 1 Book

The Black Hearts Murder - *Only*
Lancer US (1970)

Ellery QUEEN 1930- (American)

For writer details see Capt LEOPOLD

Citation Record: 1 Book

The Blue Movies Murder - *Only*
Lancer US (1972); Gollancz UK (1973)

Mike MCCALL

British Male Amateur operating in England

Charles LEADER 1938- (British)

Invented 4 detectives - see Paul MASON

Citation Record: 3 Books

The Double M Man - *First*
Hale UK (1969)

Salesman Of Death - *Last*
Hale UK (1971)

Dick MCCAREY

solves a case of death by shooting in a locked room.

American Male Amateur operating in USA

Ben HECHT 1894-1964 (American)

was born in New York. One of the great names of the cinema, he wrote some of the finest motion picture scripts, which were used by many Hollywood producers. He also wrote a number of novels and short stories, some with a criminous content.

Citation Record: 1 Selected Short Story

The Mystery Of The Fabulous Laundryman
was first published by *Faber* (UK 1933) in an anthology, *Best Mysteries of the Year.* It was later published by *Covici* (US 1936) in an anthology, *Actor's Blood* and by *Pyramid* (US 1972) in *Ellery Queen's Best Bets.*
Faber UK (1933)

Det MCCARTHY

Second detective of Det CONROY

Sgt/Det Insp Patrick Aloysius MCCARTHY

appears also in books with the author's other detective, *Arthur Stukeley PENNINGTON.*

British Policeman operating in England

John G BRANDON 1879-1941 (British)

is the author of several criminous works and the inventor of several detectives. His main output, however, consisted of a large number of novels featuring *Sexton BLAKE.*

Writer: John Gordon BRANDON

Other Detectives:
Sexton BLAKE
BURMAN
Arthur Stukeley PENNINGTON and Det Insp Patrick Aloysius MCCARTHY
Arthur Stukeley PENNINGTON

Citation Record: 22 Books

Red Altars - *First*
Cassell UK (1928)

The Secret Brotherhood - *First**
Dial US (1928)

M For Murder - *Last*
Wright UK (1949)

Det Insp Patrick Aloysius MCCARTHY

Second detective of Arthur Stukeley PENNINGTON

Timothy MCCARTY

American Male Sleuth operating in New York

Isabel OSTRANDER 1883-1924 (American)

For writer details see Barry O'DELL

Citation Record: 5 Books

The Clue In The Air - *First*
Watt US (1917); Skeffington UK (1920)

Annihilation - *Last*
Hurst UK (1923); McBride US (1924)

Manx MCCATTY

is, in this charming fantasy, a feline PI who goes down the mean streets of San Francisco in his relentless pursuit of the wicked *Gatto Nostro.*

American Male Cat operating in San Francisco

Christopher REED (American)

Citation Record: 1 Book

The Big Scratch - *Single*
Ballantine US (1988)

Quint MCCAULEY

is the Chief of Security for a Chicago store and is pretty hardboiled.

American Male Private Detective operating in Chicago

D C BROD (American)

Citation Record: 4 Books

Murder In Store - *First*
Walker US (1989); Piatkus UK (1990)

Framed In Blue - *Latest*
Diamond US (1993)

Sam MCCHESNEY

American Male Amateur operating in Vermont

Richard HUGHES 1927- (American)

Writer: Richard Edmund HUGHES

Citation Record: 1 Book

Unholy Communion - *Single*
Doubleday US (1982); Hale UK (1983)

Mike MCCLEARY

Second detective of Quin ST JAMES

MCCLOUD

is in novelizations of episodes from a TV series. A former marshal in a small rural community, he has come to the big city to continue his fight against the criminal fraternity.

American Male Sleuth operating in New York/Mexico

Collin WILCOX 1924- (American)

Invented 4 detectives - see Lt Frank HASTINGS

Citation Record: 2 Books

McCloud - *First*
Award US (1973)

The New Mexican Connection - *Last*
Award US (1974); Tandem UK (1974)

David WILSON (American)

Citation Record: 4 Books

The Corpse Maker - *First*
Award US (1974); Tandem UK (1974)

Park Avenue Executioner - *Last*
Award US (1975); Tandem UK (1975)

Stephen MCCLOUD

works for an insurance company and meets plenty of trouble from dames as well as murderers in the one book in which he appears.

American Male Private Detective operating in USA

Cleve F ADAMS 1895-1949 (American)

Invented 5 detectives - see Rex MCBRIDE

Citation Record: 1 Book

What Price Murder - *Only*
Dutton US (1942)

Johnny MCCLOUGH

Second detective of Dylan KLEIN

Ferris MCCLUE

American Male Amateur operating in Paris/South Pacific

Harvey WICKHAM 1872-1930 (American)

Citation Record: 3 Books

The Scarlet X - *First*
Clode US (1922); Brentano's UK (1923)

The Trail Of The Squid - *Last*
Clode US (1924)

Anna MCCOLL

is a psychologist who finds her patients involved in murder. Her attempts at investigation puts her in peril herself.

British Female Amateur operating in England

Penny KLINE (British)

Citation Record: 3 Books

Dying To Help - *First*
Macmillan UK (1993)

A Crushing Blow - *Latest*
Macmillan UK (1995)

Lynn MCCOLL

Second detective of Jason PROPHET

Miles MCCONAUGHY

Irish Male Amateur

Arthur D Howden SMITH 1887-1945

Writer: Arthur Douglas Howden SMITH

Citation Record: 7 Short Stories in 1 Collection

The Audacious Adventures Of Miles McConaughy - *Collection 1*
Skeffington UK (1919); Doran US (1918)

Sharon MCCONE

was one of the first of the modern generation of true female private eyes. Of mixed Scottish-Irish-Shosone Indian ancestry, she is portrayed as a fine example of American womanhood, progressive in her ideas, and only packing a .38 when necessary. She is retained by a legal services co-operative and, in her many appearances, wrangles with authority and tangles with the police. In one other book, written by this author with *Bill PRONZINI*, she shares the honours with the latter's detective, *NAMELESS.*

American Female Private Detective operating in San Francisco

Marcia MULLER 1944- (American)

was born in Detroit, Michigan. She took a BA in English, 1966, and an MA in Journalism, 1971, at the University of Michigan, Ann Arbor.

Other Detectives:
Elena OLIVEREZ
Joanna STARK

Citation Record: 15 Books

Edwin Of The Iron Shoes - *First*
McKay US (1977)

Till The Butchers Cut Him Down - *Latest*
Mysterious Press US (1994); Women's Press UK (1995)

Sharon MCCONE

Second detective of NAMELESS DETECTIVE

Cyril MCCORKLE and Michael PADILLO

are mysterious figures, apparently with past involvements in government espionage work in Europe, who now run a restaurant in Washington that appears to be a centre for various exciting happenings.

American Male Amateurs operating in Germany/Washington DC

Ross THOMAS 1926- (American)

Invented 4 detectives - see Morgan CITRON

Citation Record: 4 Books

The Cold War Swap - *First*
Morrow US (1966)

The Spy In The Vodka - *First**
Hodder & Stoughton UK (1967)

Twilight At Mac's Place - *Latest*
Mysterious Press US (1990); Scribner's US (1991)

MCCOY

American Male Sleuth operating in Dallas

Gary CLIFTON 1939- (American)

is an ex-federal agent.

Citation Record: 2 Books

Burn Sugar Burn - *First*
McLennan US (1987)

When The Dragon Flies - *Latest*
McLennan US (1987)

Doyle Dean MCCOY and Jerry ZALMAN

MCCOY is an ex-convict, a layabout who now runs an outfit that hires out guard dogs as well as operating as a detective agency among the more wealthy citizens of California. He works closely with lawyer, *JERRY ZALMAN.*

American Male Private Detective and American Male Amateur operating in California

Gabrielle KRAFT (American)

Citation Record: 4 Books

Bullshot - *First*
Pocket Books US (1987)

Bloody Mary - *Latest*
Pocket Books US (1990)

Johnny MCCOY

American Male Sleuth operating in Texas

John WOLFE (American)

Citation Record: 2 Books

The Wrong Target - *First*
Major US (1978)

Drilling For Death - *Latest*
Raven US (1980)

Pete MCCOY

is a PI in modern Los Angeles, but most of the action is recalled from the 1930s.

American Male Private Detective operating in Los Angeles

Terence KINGSLEY-SMITH 1940- (American)

Citation Record: 1 Book

The Murder Of An Old-Time Movie Star - *Single*
Pinnacle US (1983)

Ross MCCOY

American Male Amateur operating in New York

Sinclair GLUCK 1887- (American)

Invented 3 detectives - see Jack CLAYTON

Citation Record: 2 Books

The Man Who Never Blundered - *First*
Mills UK (1928); Dodd, Mead US (1929)

The Blind Fury - *Last*
Dodd, Mead US (1930); Mills UK (1930)

Shamus MCCOY

appears in a novelization of a film, in which he is a PI who hustles pool on the seamier side of New York.

American Male Private Detective operating in New York

Raymond GILES 1926- (American)

Writer: John Robert HOLT

Citation Record: 1 Book

Shamus - *Only*
Lancer US (1973)

Blaine MCCRACKEN

operates at some time in the future.

American Sleuth

Jon LAND (American)

Citation Record: 3 Books

The Omega Command - *First*
GM US (1986)

The Alpha Deception - *Latest*
GM US (1988); Grafton UK (1990)

Duncan MCCUNN

British Male Amateur operating in Scotland

John BUCHAN 1875-1940 (British)

Invented 3 detectives - see Richard HANNAY

Citation Record: 3 Books

Huntingtower - *First*
Hodder & Stoughton UK (1922); Doran US (1922)

The House Of The Four Winds - *Last*
Hodder & Stoughton UK (1935); Houghton US (1935)

Violet MCDADE

is in one of this author's many short stories that appeared in *Clues.* Once a circus fat lady, she can fell any guy to the floor with a single blow; not an entirely useless attribute for a gal who now runs her own detective agency.

American Female Detective in Pulp Magazines operating in USA

Sidekick: Nevada ALVARADO
Hispanic Male - Partner

Cleve F ADAMS 1895-1949 (American)

Invented 5 detectives - see Rex MCBRIDE

Citation Record: 1 Selected Short Story

Flowers For Violet
can also be found in an anthology, *Hard-Boiled Dames* (Editor; Bernard Drew).
In 'Clues' US (1936)

O'Neil MCDARRAGH

American Male Professional Investigator operating in USA

Tony PASTOR 1837-1898 (American)

For writer details see Phil SCOTT

Other Detectives:
FRITZ — Fritz HARMON
TOM and JERRY

Citation Record: 1 Book

O'Neil McDarragh, The Detective - *Only*
American News Company US (1877)

Prof Angus MCDERMOTT

Appears with at least two other detectives - see Lowell GAYLORD

Insp Walter MCDUMONT

Canadian Policeman operating in Canada

Hugh GARNER 1913-1979 (Canadian)

Citation Record: 3 Books

The Sin Sniper - *First*
Pocket Books CA (1970)

Stone Cold Dead - *First**
PaperJacks US (1978)

Murder Has Your Number - *Last*
McGraw CA (1978); PaperJacks US (1984)

Nina MCFALL and Lt Dino ROSSI

American Female Amateur and American Policeman operating in New York

Eileen FULTON (American)

Citation Record: 6 Books

Death Of A Golden Girl - *First*
Ivy US (1988)

Fatal Flashback - *Latest*
Ivy US (1989)

MCFEE

American Male Sleuth

Charles G BOOTH 1896-1949 (American)

Invented 3 detectives - see Anatole FLIQUE

Citation Record: 3 Short Stories in 1 Collection

Murder Strikes Thrice - *Collection 1*
contains three novelettes.
Bond US (1946)

Al MCFEE

Male Sleuth

N Wesley FIRTH 1920-1949 (British)

Writer: Norman FIRTH

Inventor of one other detective Merrick LAWRENCE

Citation Record: 2 Books

The Striptease Murders - *First*
Mitre UK (ca 1946)

Gangster Pay-Off - *Last*
Hughes UK (ca 1948)

Bernard MCFOY

British Male Amateur operating in England

J M SHROG (British)

Citation Record: 2 Books

Hag Wood - *First*
Stockwell UK (1936)

White Circle - *Last*
Stockwell UK (1936)

Mack MCGANN

American Male Private Detective operating in USA

Fred DICKENSON (American)

Citation Record: 1 Book

Kill 'Em With Kindness - *Only*
Bell US (1950)

Insp Peter MCGARR

of the *Garda Siochana* in Dublin was formerly, one hears, with the 'French police and Interpol' Now back on home ground, he has to deal with various killings, some with connections to the paramilitary struggle in Ulster, but the more interesting ones being comfortably domestic. A Dubliner himself, short, balding, and middle-aged, he is a tough tenacious cop (a retired one, it seems, in his latest appearance) and married to a woman twenty years his junior.

Irish Policeman operating in Eire

Sidekick: Noreen MCGARR
is in her late twenties, the wife of the detective, and an art historian. Her specialist knowledge is often able to assist him in his enquiries and, on occasions, she has even put herself directly in the line of fire.

Irish Female - Wife

Bartholomew GILL 1943- (American)

was born in Holyoke, Massachusetts. He graduated with a BA from Brown University, Providence, Rhode Island, 1966, and received a D Litt from Trinity College, Dublin, 1971. He has been a reporter, insurance investigator and, since 1971, a full-time writer.

Writer: Mark MCGARRITY

Citation Record: 11 Books

McGarr And The Politician's Wife - *First*
Scribner's US (1977); Hale UK (1978)

Death Of An Ardent Bibliophile - *Latest*
Morrow US (1995)

Det Dan MCGARRY

American Policeman operating in New York

Matt TAYLOR (American)

Citation Record: 2 Short Stories in 1 Collection

The Famous McGarry Stories - *Collection 1*
In 'Detective Book Club' US (1958)

Kirk MCGARVEY

American Male Sleuth operating in USA

David HAGBERG 1942- (American)

Writer: David James HAGBERG

Other Bylines:
Nick CARTER
Sean FLANNERY

Citation Record: 2 Books

Without Honor - *First*
Tor US (1989)

Countdown - *Latest*
St Martin's US (1990)

Luther MCGAVOCK

appeared in eleven novelettes in *Black Mask Magazine.*

American Male Detective in Pulp Magazines operating in Memphis

Merle CONSTINER (American)

Writer: Francis Merle CONSTINER

Inventor of one other detective Dean Wardlow ROCK

Citation Record: 1 Selected Short Story

The Turkey Buzzard Blues
In 'Black Mask Magazine' US (1943)

Travis MCGEE

is one of the best and most individual creations in the genre. Although he does not, in fact, claim to be a detective, referring to himself as a 'salvage consultant'. as near as makes no difference, he operates as a classic private eye. Indeed, he is one of the best. A large, strong man, once a football player, and a Korean War veteran, he is involved with cases that nominally involve the recovery of goods, money, or people; and always murder. Furthermore, he often has to salvage emotionally or physically hurt women, who end up by staying a while, until he parts from them with love and no regret. He lives on a luxurious boat, *The Busted Flush*, which he won in a poker game, moored in Slip F-18, Bahia Mar, Fort Lauderdale, Florida. He is assisted in his difficult and often dangerous cases by *MEYER,* one of the most useful and most endearing of all sidekicks. In his later books *MCGEE* is given to much moralising on the state of humanity and the world in general, both of which he deplores.
!See Appendix 2.

American Male Professional Investigator operating in Florida

Sidekick: MEYER
is a hairy (but balding), chess-playing, retired, Jewish economist and a profound philosopher. He, like *McGEE,* lives on a boat, the *John Maynard Keynes*, in the Florida Keys. (It was actually - and for the exigencies of the plot - exploded in a late book and replaced by another called the *Thorstein Veblen*). *MEYER* is a key figure in this highly regarded canon of novels. He plays a great part in discussing the latter's cases, especially the morality of them. He is also of considerable importance in the actual physical development of the various stories. All in all, he is certainly one of the best characterised sidekicks in the literature, exemplifying what such a role in detective fiction can contribute to its significance. A far cry from *Dr WATSON* and an even farther cry from dear old *Magersfontein LUGG.*

American Male - Friend

John D MACDONALD 1916-1986 (American)
was born in Sharon, Pennsylvania. He was educated at the University of Pennsylvania, Philadelphia, and subsequently graduated with a BS from Syracuse University, New York, 1938, after which he served, as Lieutenant-Colonel, with the US Strategic Services, 1940-1946. He was the author of at least sixty-nine novels in various genres, and all his work carries with it his deep commitment to human values and morality. His knowledge of maritime matters, economics and philosophy is always impressive. He received the *Grand Prix de Littérature Policière*, 1964, and the Mystery Writers of America Grand Master award, 1972.
Writer: John Dann MACDONALD
Other Detectives:
Clifford BARTELLS Paul STANIAL
Citation Record: 21 Books
The Deep Blue Goodbye - *First*
!See Appendix 2.
Lippincott US (1964); Hale UK (1965)
The Lonely Silver Rain - *Last*
Knopf US (1985); Macdonald UK (1985)

Mgr Thomas O MCGILLICUDDY
solves a case of death by throat-cutting in a locked cabin.
American Male Amateur operating in USA

William Lodevick DOTY 1919- (American)
Citation Record: 1 Book
Button, Button... - *Only*
In 'Our Sunday Visitor' UK (1979)

Slade MCGINTY
works, mainly abroad, for the Karton Agency. Tall, handsome and tough, he is a secret agent as well as a PI.
British Male Private Detective operating in several locations

Jacques PENDOWER 1899-1976 (British)
Inventor of one other detective Robert MAINE
Citation Record: 5 Books
The Perfect Wife - *First*
Hale UK (1962)
Traitor's Island - *Last*
Hale UK (1967)

Charlie MCGOWAN
Second detective of Marcus Aurelius FARROW

Pete MCGRATH
has an office on 34th Street, Manhattan, that he rarely visits, since he hates working for a living. He has an obsession about world pollution and talks much to himself about it, since no-one else is listening. Even so, he seems to get work and certainly is involved in some strange and action-filled cases.
American Male Private Detective operating in New York

Michael BRETT 1928- (American)
Citation Record: 10 Books
Kill Him Quickly, Its Raining - *First*
Pocket Books US (1966)
Slit My Throat Gently - *Last*
Pocket Books US (1968)

MCGREGOR
was once in the New York Police Department; but he has grown wealthy by making sound investments and, now in his fifties, charges a lot for his services as a PI.
American Male Private Detective operating in New York

Henry KANE 1918- (American)
Invented 4 detectives - see Peter CHAMBERS
Citation Record: 3 Books
The Midnight Man - *First*
Macmillan US (1965)
Other Sins Only Speak - *First**
Boardman UK (1960)
Laughter In The Alehouse - *Last*
Macmillan US (1968); Penguin UK (1978)

Gregor MCGREGOR
Second detective of Tony BEACH

Maggie MCGUANE
Second detective of Fritz THIERINGER

Amos MCGUFFIN
became a PI as a result of reading too many detective pulps in his youth. He lives on an old ferryboat and drinks too much, but manages to solve his cases.
!See Appendix 2.
American Male Private Detective operating in San Francisco/New York

Robert UPTON (American)
Citation Record: 5 Books
Who'd Want To Kill Old George? - *First*
Putnam US (1977)
A Killing In Real Estate - *Latest*
Dutton US (1990)

Jack MCGUIRE
was a 'government investigator' who appeared, 1930-1932, in three stories in *Black Mask Magazine.*
American Male Detective in Pulp Magazines operating in Los Angeles

J J DES ORMEAUX (American)
Writer: Forrest ROSAIRE
Citation Record: 2 Selected Short Stories
Murder's Night
In 'Black Mask Magazine' US (1930)
The Devil's Suit
In 'Black Mask Magazine' US (1932)

Lt Joe MCGUIRE
American Policeman operating in Boston

John Lawrence REYNOLDS (American)
Citation Record: 2 Books
The Man Who Murdered God - *First*
Viking US (1989)
And Leave Her Lay Dying - *Latest*
Viking US (1990)

Gail MCGURK
Appears with at least two other detectives - see Insp SKANE

Ch Insp MCHALE
is a rather stupid policeman who, in his one case, pins the murder on the wrong suspect.
British Policeman operating in England

Robert BARNARD 1936- (British)
Invented 13 detectives - see Insp Perry TRETHOWAN
Citation Record: 1 Book
Mother's Boys - *Single*
Collins UK (1981)
Death Of A Perfect Mother - *Single**
Scribner's US (1981)

Insp MCHARG
British Policeman operating in England

Reginald HILL 1936- (British)
Invented 4 detectives - see Supt Andrew DALZIEL and Sgt Peter PASCOE
Citation Record: 1 Book
Who Guards The Prince? - *Single*
Pantheon US (1982)

MCHUGH
American Male Sleuth operating in San Francisco/Switzerland

Jay FLYNN 1927-1985 (American)
See main detective Slim Jim BANNERMAN

Citation Record: 5 Books

McHugh - *First*
Avon US (1959); Consul UK(1961)

The Five Faces Of Murder - *Last*
Avon US (1962); Consul US (1965)

Arthur MCHUGH

American Male Amateur operating in USA

Wadsworth CAMP 1879-1936 (American)

Invented 3 detectives - see Bobby BLACKBURN

Citation Record: 1 Book

The House Of Fear - *Only*
Doubleday US (1916); Hodder & Stoughton UK (1917)

The Last Warning - *Only**
Reader's Library UK (1929)

Mac MCINTYRE

American Male Amateur operating in Chicago

M E CORNE (American)

Writer: Molly E CORNE

Citation Record: 3 Books

Death At A Masquerade - *First*
Mill US (1938)

Death Is No Lady - *First**
Black Knight US (1946)

A Magnet For Murder - *Last*
Mill US (1939)

Jealousy Pulls The Trigger - *Last**
Double Action Detective US (1943)

Tony MCINTYRE

investigates nefarious goings-on in the mountains of Ararat.

American Male Secret Agent operating in Turkey

Robert KATZ 1933- (American)

Inventor of one other detective Zack ROBERTS

Citation Record: 1 Book

The Spoils Of Ararat - *Single*
Houghton Mifflin US (1978); Sphere UK (1979)

Houston MCIVER

American Male Private Detective operating in El Paso

William WOODY (American)

Writer: Woodbury William FAGETTE

Citation Record: 1 Book

Mistress Of Horror House - *Only*
Ace US (1959)

Insp Ellis MCKAY

British Policeman operating in England

L A G STRONG 1896-1958 (British)

is the author of many mainstream novels.

Writer: Leonard Alfred George STRONG

Citation Record: 4 Books

All Fall Down - *First*
Collins UK (1944); Doubleday US (1944)

Treason In The Egg - *Last*
Collins UK (1950)

Jenny MCKAY

American Female Sleuth operating in USA

Dick BELSKY (American)

See main detective Lucy SHANNON

Citation Record: 1 Book

The Mourning Show - *Single*
Berkley US (1994)

Robin MCKAY

British Male Amateur operating in Jamaica

John MORRIS (British)

Writers: John Edgar Caulwell HEARNE 1926- and Morris CARGILL 1914-

Citation Record: 3 Books

Fever Grass - *First*
Collins UK (1969); Putnam US (1969)

The Checkerboard Caper - *Last*
Citadel US (1975)

MCKECHNIE

Second detective of COLLINS

Jim MCKECHNIE

American Male Amateur operating in USA

Jon CLEARY 1917- (Australian)

See main detective Scobie MALONE

Citation Record: 1 Book

Vortex - *Single*
Collins UK (1977); Morrow US (1978)

Insp Christopher MCKEE

is head of the Manhattan Homicide Squad. Of Scottish origin, he claims to solve his cases by using his instinct for the truth rather than by following conventional clues.

American Policeman operating in New York

Helen REILLY 1891-1962 (American)

Citation Record: 32 Books

The Diamond Feather - *First*
Doubleday US (1930)

The Day She Died - *Last*
Random House US (1962); Hale UK (1963)

Deville MCKEENE

British Male Amateur operating in England

Rowland WALKER 1876- (British)

See main detective Capt MCBLAID

Citation Record: 2 Books

Deville McKeene, The British Ace - *First*
Partridge UK (1919)

The Exploits Of Capt McKeene - *Last*
Aldine US (1926)

Ross MCKELLAR

American Male Private Detective operating in New York

Niles N PEEBLES (American)

Citation Record: 2 Books

See The Red Blood Run - *First*
Pyramid US (1968)

Blood Brother, Blood Brother - *Last*
Pyramid US (1969)

Insp MCKELLER

appears also in books with the author's other detectives, Anthony HOWARD and Richard LOGAN.

British Policeman operating in England

Hugh MCCUTCHEON 1909- (British)

Writer: Hugh Davie-Martin MCCUTCHEON

Other Detectives:
Jimmy CARROLL
Anthony HOWARD
Richard LOGAN
Insp MCKELLER and Richard LOGAN
Insp MCKELLER and Anthony HOWARD

Citation Record: 1 Book

None Shall Sleep Tonight - *Only*
Rich UK (1953); Dutton US (1953)

Insp MCKELLER and Anthony HOWARD

also appear individually in other books by this author.

British Policeman and British Male Amateur operating in England

Hugh MCCUTCHEON 1909- (British)

Invented 6 detectives - see Insp MCKELLER

Citation Record: 2 Books

The Angel Of Light - *First*
Rich UK (1951)

Murder At "The Angel" - *First**
Dutton US (1952)

Cover Her Face - *Last*
Rich UK (1954)

Insp MCKELLER and Richard LOGAN

also appear individually in other books by this author.

British Policeman and British Male Amateur operating in England

Hugh MCCUTCHEON 1909- (British)

Invented 6 detectives - see Insp MCKELLER

Citation Record: 1 Book

To Dusty Death - *Only*
Long UK (1960)

Graydon MCKELVIE

American Male Amateur operating in New York

Marion HARVEY 1900- (American)

Citation Record: 4 Books

The Mystery Of The Hidden Room - *First*
Clode US (1922); Brentano's UK (1923)

The Dragon Of Lung Wang - *Last*
Clode US (1928); Wright UK (1934)

'Bugs' MCKENNA

has done a stretch in jail but is now the house detective in a hotel in an oil town.

American Male Private Detective operating in Texas

Jim THOMPSON 1906-1977 (American)

was born in Oklahoma and graduated with a BA from the University of Nebraska. He had a variety of jobs, was a reporter, and wrote at least thirty genre novels.

Writer: James Myers THOMPSON

Citation Record: 1 Book

Wild Town - *Only*
Signet US (1957)

M

Patience MCKENNA

is very tall, very slim, and a writer of romantic novels. She also has the unfortunate habit of stumbling over dead bodies when her mind is on higher things. She knows murder when she sees it, however, and sets out on paths of detection, to the enormous chagrin of the New York Police Department's Homicide squad.

American Female Amateur operating in New York

Stooge: Lt Luis MARTINEZ
works for the New York Police Department and is irritated by the success of *Patience MCKENNA.*

American Male

Ornia PAPAZOGLU 1951- (American)

Citation Record: 5 Books

Sweet, Savage Death - *First*
Doubleday US (1984)

Once And Always Murder - *Latest*
Doubleday US (1990)

Dr Alex MCKENZIE

Second detective of Sarah DEANE

Craig MCKENZIE

American Male Private Detective operating in California

M S MARBLE 1913- (American)

Writer: Margaret Sharp MARBLE

Inventor of one other detective Joe GAYLORD

Citation Record: 1 Book

Everybody Makes Mistakes - *Only*
Rinehart US (1946); Barker UK (1947)

Victoria MCKENZIE

is an Oxford historian who, in a tale of revenge and guilt, does most of the detective work, being given both moral and intellectual support by her mentor, *Ambrose USHER,* who is the author's main detective in all his previous books.

British Female Amateur operating in England

Sidekick: Ambrose USHER
is the detective in the first six of the seven books in which he appears; but, in his last book, he is prepared to play second fiddle to *MCKENZIE,* giving her the benefit of his special knowledge and experience.

British Male - Aide

Jocelyn DAVEY 1908-1994 (British)

See main detective Ambrose USHER

Citation Record: 1 Book

A Dangerous Liaison - *Only*
Walker US (1988)

Walter MCKENZIE

is an industrial consultant who also practises as a private investigator.

American Male Private Detective operating in Illinois

Al GUTHRIE ?-1992 (American)

Citation Record: 2 Books

Private Murder - *First*
Bantam US (1989)

Grave Murder - *Latest*
Zebra US (1990)

Det Sam MCKIBBON

Second detective of Det Noah GREEN

Rod MCKINNON

British Male Amateur operating in England

Brian COOPER 1919- (American)

was born in Stockport, Cheshire, and served, during the Second World War, in the Army and Intelligence Corps. He took an MA at Jesus College, Cambridge, 1945, and has been a teacher at various schools.

Writer: Brian Newman COOPER

Other Detectives:
John HARRINGTON
Ch Insp LUBBOCK and Det Insp TENCH

Citation Record: 1 Book

Giselle - *Only*
Vanguard US (1958)

A Path To The Bridge - *Only**
Heinemann UK (1958)

Todd MCKINNON

is a writer of mystery stories for a pulp magazine. He lives with wife and daughter in Berkeley, where he gets involved in murders at the daughter's local dramatic company. He solves the cases; but how is anyone's guess!

American Male Amateur operating in California/Oregon

Lenore Glen OFFORD 1905- (American)

was born in Spokane, Washington. Music critic of the San Francisco Chronicle, 1950-1982, reviewer of detective fiction elsewhere, writer of light verse, she has written several criminous works.

Inventor of one other detective pair Bill HASTINGS and Coco HASTINGS

Citation Record: 4 Books

Skeleton Key - *First*
Duell US (1943); Eldon UK (1944)

Walking Shadow - *Last*
Simon & Schuster US (1959); Ward, Lock UK (1961)

John T MCLAREN

is a deputy sheriff, a part-time PI, and not a nice guy at all.

American Male Private Detective operating in New Mexico

Will COOPER 1929- (American)

Citation Record: 1 Book

Death Has A Thousand Doors - *Single*
Bobbs US (1976); Hale UK (1979)

Insp MCLEAN

appears in at least sixteen novels and thirty-seven collections of short stories, published over four decades and certainly numbering several hundreds. The collections in which he appears often contain eighteen untitled stories, but some carry stories with individual titles. The first and last novels and first and last collections only are cited; but, in view of the importance of giving a faithful record of the author's immense output, and in a departure from the normal citation practice, the publishing record cites the total number of collections and stories they carry.

British Policeman operating in England

Sidekick: Sgt BROOK
British Male - Subordinate

George GOODCHILD 1888-1969 (British)

was a prolific author of criminous works under his own name and various pseudonyms. He is specially noted for his vast number of short stories featuring *Insp MCLEAN.*

Other Detectives:
Insp John INCH
Insp Laurence OGILVIE
Nigel REX
John Q TRELAWNY

Citation Record: 16 Books 792 Short Stories in 37 Collections

The Triumph Of McLean - *First*
Hodder & Stoughton UK (1933); Houghton US (1933)

Savage Encounter - *Last*
Jarrolds UK (1962)

McLean Of Scotland Yard - *Collection 1*
Short stories - 16
Hodder & Stoughton UK (1929)

McLean Takes Over - *Collection 2*
Short stories - 16
Long UK (1966)

Anne 'Davvie' Davenport MCLEAN

American Female Amateur operating in Cuba/Hawaii/Midway Island

Margaret Tayler YATES 1887- (American)

Writer: Margaret Evelyn Tayler YATES

Citation Record: 4 Books

The Hush-Hush Murders - *First*
Macmillan US (1937); Dickson UK (1938)

Murder By The Yard - *Last*
Macmillan US (1942)

Bruce MCLINTOCK

British Male Amateur operating in Scotland

Angus MACVICAR 1908- (British)

Inventor of one other detective Rev P J MACFARLANE

Citation Record: 2 Books

The Golden Venus Affair - *First*
Long UK (1972)

The Painted Doll Affair - *Last*
Long UK (1973)

Sgt Andy MCLOUGHLIN

is a man of brooding intensity, given to quoting from English literature in a manner above his apparent station - or so the suspects believe. A bit mixed up sexually and with only average sleuthing ability, he appears in a fine, if flawed, first novel.

British Policeman operating in Hampshire

Minette WALTERS (British)

has been a magazine editor and a writer of romantic novels. Her recent turn to crime has already resulted in her first book receiving the John Creasey award.

Other Detectives:
Sgt COOPER
Rosalind LEIGH and Sgt HAWKSLEY

Citation Record: 1 Book

The Ice House - *Single*
Macmillan UK (1992)

MCLOVE

solved the mystery of how a man who jumped off a building reappeared.

American Male Sleuth operating in USA

Edward D HOCH 1930- (American)

Invented 20 detectives - see Capt LEOPOLD

Citation Record: 1 Selected Short Story

The Long Way Down

appeared first in the February number and has since appeared in several anthologies, including *Best American Detective Stories of the Year 16th Series* (Dutton; US 1966).

In 'Alfred Hitchcock's Mystery Magazine' US (1965)

Father MCMAHON

is a priest in a seedy parish of New York who is drawn into a murder case, which he solves.

American Male Amateur operating in USA

Dorothy Salisbury DAVIS 1916- (American)

Invented 9 detectives - see Kate OSBORN

Citation Record: 1 Book

Where The Dark Streets Go - *Only*
Scribner's US (1969); Hodder & Stoughton UK (1970)

Insp MCMASTER

British Policeman operating in England

George LIMNELIUS 1886- (British)

Writer: Lewis George ROBINSON
Other Byline: Lewis ROBINSON

Inventor of one other detective Maj Weston PRYME

Citation Record: 1 Book

The Medbury Fort Murder - *Only*
Benn UK (1929); Doubleday US (1929)

Jack MCMORROW

is the editor of a small-town paper. He comes up against resistance when he investigates the murder of one of his photographers.

American Male Amateur operating in New England

Gerry BOYLE (American)

Citation Record: 1 Book

Deadline - *Single*
Berkley US (1995)

Ch Insp Andy MCMURDO

British Policeman operating in England

Nigel MORLAND 1905-1986 (British)

Invented 4 detectives - see Mrs Palmyra Evangeline PYM

Citation Record: 8 Books

She Didn't Like Dying - *First*
Sampson, Low UK (1948)

Death To The Ladies - *Last*
Hale UK (1959)

Archie MCNALLY

is said to be a cross between *Lord Peter WIMSEY* and Bertie WOOSTER.

American Male Private Detective operating in Florida

Lawrence SANDERS (American)

Invented 6 detectives - see Ex-Plce Edward X DELANEY

Citation Record: 3 Books

McNally's Secret - *First*
Putnam US (1992)

McNally's Risk - *Latest*
Putnam US (1993)

Dr Jeffrey MCNEILL

is a physician.

American Male Amateur operating in New England

Sidekick: Anne MCNEILL
is a nurse. She assists her husband and narrates his cases.
American Female - Wife

Theodora DU BOIS 1890- (American)

was born in Brooklyn, New York, He has written several books for children.

Writer: Theodora McCormick DU BOIS

Citation Record: 19 Books

Armed With A New Terror - *First*
Houghton US (1936); Heinemann UK (1937)

Seeing Red - *Last*
Doubleday US (1954); Collins UK (1955)

Const MCNINCH

Irish Policeman operating in Ulster

T M ALBERT (Irish)

Writer: T M Albert SIMPSON

Citation Record: 16 Short Stories in 1 Collection

Tales Of An Ulster Detective - *Collection 1*
Albert UK (1989)

MCPHERSON

is an alcoholic. He becomes involved in a case of very odd happenings.

American Male Private Detective operating in USA

R Howard LINDSAY 1910- (Canadian)

was born in Ontario, Canada.

Writer: Robert Howard LINDSAY

Citation Record: 1 Book

Fowl Murder - *Only*
Little, Brown US (1941)

Det Mark MCPHERSON

is the hero detective in one outstanding book, which was dramatised and screened.

American Policeman operating in New York

Vera CASPARY 1904-1987 (American)

was born in Chicago. She wrote several novels of suspense and other fiction also; but she was especially renowned for the masterly screenplays she wrote, 1935-1961, for some of the finest directors in Hollywood.

Citation Record: 1 Book

Laura - *Only*
Houghton US (1943); Eyre & Spottiswoode UK (1944)

MCQUADE

is a young PI brought in to investigate burglaries at the University of California.

American Male Private Detective operating in Berkeley

Nancy GREENWALD (American)

Citation Record: 1 Book

Ladycat - *Single*
Crown US (1980)

Damian MCQUAID

American Male Sleuth operating in New York/Los Angeles

Shepard RIFKIN 1918- (American)

Inventor of one other detective Joe DUNNE

Citation Record: 3 Books

McQuaid - *First*
Putnam US (1974); Hale UK (1975)

McQuaid In August - *Latest*
Doubleday US (1979); Hale UK (1980)

MCTAVISH

Second detective of MURPHY

Stoner MCTAVISH

American Female Amateur operating in USA

Sidekick: Gwen
American Female - Friend

Sarah DREHER (British)

Citation Record: 4 Books

Stoner McTavish - *First*
New Victoria US (1985); Pandora UK (1987)

Captive In Time - *Latest*
Pandora UK (1990); New Victoria US (1990)

Swete MCTAVISH

British Male Amateur operating in England

Collin BROOKS 1893- (British)

Writer: William Collin BROOKS

Other Detectives:
Mr DADDY — Raeburn STEEL

Citation Record: 3 Books

O Sweet McTavish - *First*
Hutchinson UK (1930)

Three Yards Of Cord - *Last*
Hutchinson UK (1931)

Cdr MCTURK

British Male Amateur operating in several locations

C J Cutcliffe HYNE 1865-1944 (British)

Invented 4 detectives - see Capt Owen KETTLE

Citation Record: 12 Short Stories in 1 Collection

The Trials Of Commander McTurk - *Collection 1*
Not all the stories are criminous.
Murray UK (1906); Dutton US (1906)

Mike (American Avenger) MCVEIGH

American Male Professional Investigator operating in Europe/Africa

Robert EMMETT (American)

Citation Record: 5 Books

Beat A Distant Drum - *First*
Signet US (1981)

The Devil's Finger - *Latest*
Signet US (1982)

Trish MCWHINNEY

American Female Sleuth operating in Vermont

B COMFORT (American)

Writer: Barbara COMFORT

Citation Record: 1 Book

Grave Consequences - *Single*
Landgrove US (1989)

MEAD

American Male Detective in Pulp Magazines operating in USA

OLD SLEUTH (American)

Invented 40 detectives - see Brant ADAMS

Citation Record: 1 Book

A Close Call; Or, Detective Mead's Dilemma - *Only*
Parlor Car US (1897)

Selena MEAD

is a Washington DC socialite, who is also a counter-espionage agent and has to investigate murder.

American Male Secret Agent operating in Washington DC

Patricia MCGERR 1917-1985 (American)

was born in Falls City, Nebraska. She was educated at Trinity College, Washington DC, took a BA at the University of Nebraska, Lincoln, and an MS in Journalism at Columbia University, New York. She received the *Grand Prix de Littérature Policière*, 1952.

Inventor of one other detective Sally BOWEN

Citation Record: 2 Books

Is There A Traitor In The House? - *First*
Doubleday US (1964); Collins UK (1965)

Legacy Of Danger - *Last*
Luce US (1970)

Desdemona 'Squeakie' MEADOW

may look as if butter wouldn't melt in her mouth but, in several short stories, she continually startles her husband by solving crimes.

Female Amateur

Margaret MANNERS

Citation Record: 2 Selected Short Stories

Squeakie's First Case
In 'Ellery Queen's Mystery Magazine' US

Matter For A May Morning
In 'Ellery Queen's Mystery Magazine' US

Supt MEADOWS

British Policeman operating in England

Arden WINCH (British)

Citation Record: 1 Book

Blood Money - *Single*
BBC UK (1981)

Blood Royal - *Single**
Viking US (1982)

Judy MEADOWS

Second detective of Lt MARSHALL

Pte Amos MEARS

British Male Amateur

Headon HILL 1857-1927 (British)

Invented 11 detectives - see Insp HERON

Citation Record: 1 Book

The Zone Of Fire - *Only*
Pearson UK (1897)

Ch Const George MEATYARD

British Policeman operating in England

Sydney HORLER 1888-1954 (British)

Invented 20 detectives - see Sir Harker BELLAMY

Citation Record: 2 Books

Here Is An SOS - *First*
Hodder & Stoughton UK (1939)

The Man Who Loved Spiders - *Last*
Barker UK (1948)

Insp MEDFORD

appears also in one book with the author's other detective, *Monte GORDON.*

Policeman operating on a ship

Holly ROTH 1916-1964 (American)

was born in Chicago, Illinois.

Other Detectives:
William FARLAND
Monte GORDON and Insp MEDFORD
Lt KELLY

Citation Record: 1 Book

Too Many Doctors - *Only*
Random House US (1962)

Operation Doctors - *Only**
Hamilton UK (1962)

Insp MEDFORD

Second detective of Monte GORDON

Joe MEDFORD

is a tough, witty reporter in and around the Hollywood of the period, whose cases are as much about fun as detection.

American Male Amateur operating in Los Angeles

Jimmy STARR 1904-1990 (American)

was born in Texas and worked as a publicity agent in Hollywood.

Writer: James A STARR

Citation Record: 3 Books

Three Short Biers - *First*
Murray US (1945)

The Corpse Came C O D - *Last*
Murray US (1944); Coker UK (1951)

David MEDINA

British Male Sleuth operating in Middle East

A M KABAL

Writer: H S BHABRA

Citation Record: 2 Books

The Adversary - *First*
Allison & Busby UK (1985); Walker US (1987)

Bad Money - *Latest*
Allison & Busby UK (1986); Dutton US (1988)

Julian MEDOZA

British Male Amateur operating in England

James RONALD 1905- (British)

Invented 3 detectives - see Supt WRENN

Citation Record: 2 Books

Cross Marks The Spot - *First*
Hodder & Stoughton UK (1933)

Death Croons The Blues - *Last*
Hodder & Stoughton UK (1934); Phoenix Press US (1940)

'Spider' MEECH

solves a case of death by stabbing in a locked cupola.

American Male Sleuth operating in USA

Clifford ORR 1899-1951 (American)

was born in Portland, Maine. For many years he was an editor on *The New Yorker.*

Inventor of one other detective Joseph HARRIS

Citation Record: 1 Book

The Wailing Rock Murders - *First*
Farrar, Straus US (1932); Cassell UK (1933)

Eric MEECHAM

is a defence lawyer who investigates his client's case and does a stunning job in court.

American Male Amateur operating in USA

Margaret MILLAR 1915- (Canadian)

Invented 11 detectives - see Insp SANDS

Citation Record: 1 Book

Vanish In An Instant - *Only*
Random House US (1952); Museum Press UK (1953)

Trixie MEEHAN

Second detective of Mike HARRIS

Supt Ceal MEGARRY

is highly moral and filled with angst and integrity, which is not surprising as he has to solve murders in the seedy, violent whiskey-laden atmosphere of South Antrim.

Irish Policeman operating in Belfast

Eugene MCELDOWNEY (Irish)

Citation Record: 2 Books

A Kind Of Homecoming - *First*
Heinemann UK (1994)

A Stone Of The Heart - *Last*
Heinemann UK (1995)

Charles MEIKLEJOHN and Constance LEIDL

Charlie MEIKLEJOHN was in the New York Police Department and is married to *Constance LEIDL,* his former psychology professor. They form a modern variation on the old American husband-wife detective partnership, being not the bright young things of the 1930s and 1940s but serious, high-tech people.

American Male Private Detective and American Female Amateur operating in New York/Oregon

Kate WILHELM 1928- (American)

Writer: Kate Wilhelm KNIGHT

Citation Record: 4 Books 5 Short Stories in 1 Collection

The Hamlet Trap - *First*
St Martin's US (1987); Gollancz UK (1988)

Sweet, Sweet Poison - *Latest*
St Martin's US (1990); Hale UK (1991)

Children Of The Wind - *Collection 1*
St Martin's US (1989)

Lynn MELCHAN
has a supersensitive auditory ability, which causes him considerable pain but is also jolly useful; for, while engaged in sleuthing, he can hear the slightest sound or whisper that anyone makes.
American Male Private Detective operating in USA

Warren LUCAS (American)
Citation Record: 1 Selected Short Story
The Devil Beats Death's Drums
In 'Dime Mystery' US (1938)

'Tiny' MELDRUM
Second detective of Insp 'Dusty' MULLER

Det Insp Alan MELFORD
British Policeman operating in London

James CORBETT (British)
Invented 7 detectives - see Roy ENDICOTT
Citation Record: 1 Book
Who Was The Killer? - *Only*
Jenkins UK (1939)

Prof Hugh MELLING
is some sort of professional trouble-shooter used by the highest echelons in the governments of the USA and the UK, who need him to save the world from terrible evils.
British Male Secret Agent operating in several locations

Leon PHILLIPS (British)
Citation Record: 3 Books
Fire In His Hand - *First*
Hale UK (1979)
Ritual Fire Dance - *Latest*
Hale UK (1981)

M

Molly MELLINGER
is an editor of mystery novels who solves the murder of one of her authors.
American Female Amateur operating in New York

Kin PLATT 1911- (American)
See main detective Max ROPER
Citation Record: 1 Book
Dead As They Come - *Only*
Random House US (1972); Hale UK (1974)

Insp MELLISON and Dr Martin BLYTHE
solve a case of death by cyanide in a laboratory.
British Policeman and British Male Amateur operating in England

T L DAVIDSON 1901-1964 (British)
was born in Aberdeen, Scotland. For many years he was the Professor of Biochemistry at McGill University in Montreal.
Writer: David Landsborough THOMPSON
Citation Record: 1 Book
The Murder In The Laboratory - *Only*
Methuen UK (1929); Dutton US (1929)

Claude MELNOTTE
American Male Private Detective operating in New York

Allan PINKERTON 1819-1884 (American)
See main detective Allan PINKERTON
Citation Record: 3 Short Stories in 1 Collection
Claude Melnotte As A Detective, And Other Stories - *Collection 1*
Keen, Cooke US (1875)

John MELROSE
British Male Amateur operating in England

Woosnam MILLS (British)
Writer: Harry Roland Woosnam MILLS
Inventor of one other detective John HOWDEN
Citation Record: 4 Books
Grim Chancery - *First*
Nelson UK (1937)
Biting Fortune - *Last*
Nelson UK (1939)

Austin MELVILLE
British Male Professional Investigator operating in England

Harold GRAHAM (British)
Citation Record: 1 Book
Austin Melville, Turf Investigator - *Only*
Aldine US (1926)

Susan MELVILLE
American Female Amateur operating in New York

Evelyn E SMITH 1927- (American)
Citation Record: 3 Books
Miss Melville Regrets - *First*
Fine US (1986); Collins UK (1987)
Miss Melville's Revenge - *Latest*
Fine US (1989)

Lt Luis MENDOZA
is of Mexican heritage and latterly in the Los Angeles Police Department. Scholarly, gentlemanly, and rather wealthy – having inherited his money from a disreputable grandfather – he loves cars and adores cats. He manages to solve his cases by the classic use of logic and reason.
American Policeman operating in USA
Sidekick: Det Arthur HACKETT
is big, tough and has a degree in psychology.
American Male - Assistant
Sidekick: Det George HIGGINS
American Male - Assistant

Dell SHANNON 1921-1988 (American)
For writer details see Sgt Ivor MADDOX
Citation Record: 38 Books
Case Pending - *First*
Harper & Row US (1960); Gollancz UK (1960)
The Dispossessed - *Latest*
Morrow US (1988)

Insp Miguel MENENDEZ
is massively built and is an Inspector in the Police Department at San Luis, Mexico. He is an erudite, intelligent man, who despises his dull sergeant and his own ultra-religious family.
Mexican Policeman operating in Mexico

Suzanne BLANC (American)
Citation Record: 3 Books
The Green Stone - *First*
Harper & Row US (1961); Cassell UK (1962)
The Rose Window - *Last*
Doubleday US (1967); Cassell UK (1968)

Loren MENSING
is Professor of Law at the fictional City University in the American midwest. With inherited wealth, in his late thirties, a bachelor, a writer, and a researcher, he has a high standing in academia and is strong on social justice. He is called in to solve crimes by the local authorities, who usually admit themselves baffled. He seems to do most of his detecting by sitting in the local law library, an unremarkable activity that somehow has lovely ladies falling over themselves to get at him.
American Male Amateur In Illinois

Francis M NEVINS Jr 1943- (American)
was born in Bayonne, New Jersey. He was educated at St Peter's College, Jersey City, graduating with an AB, 1964. After studying at New York University of Law he was admitted to

the New Jersey Bar, 1967. An expert on law and an esteemed crime literature critic, he has written only a few genre novels but many short stories.
Writer: Francis Michael NEVINS
Other Detectives:
Philip MARLOWE   Milo TURNER
Citation Record: 2 Books
Publish And Perish - *First*
Putnam US (1975); Hale UK (1977)
Corrupt And Ensnare - *Latest*
Putnam US (1978); Hale UK (1979)

Dr MEPHISTO and Monsieur HIGNETTE

solve cases of 'impossible' murder in locked-room situations.
French Male Sleuths

Jean JOSEPH-RENAUD (French)
See main detective Monsieur CHEVENARD
Citation Record: 1 Book
Dr Mephisto - *Only*
Hutchinson UK (1929)

MEPHISTO

American Male Detective in Pulp Magazines operating in USA

OLD SLEUTH (American)
Invented 40 detectives - see Brant ADAMS
Citation Record: 1 Book
The Man Of Mystery; Or, Mephisto The Detective - *Only*
Ogilvie US (1900)

Johnny MERAK and Dawn GRAHAME

investigate a case of death by cyanide.
British Male Amateur and British Female Amateur operating in England

A J MERAK 1928- (British)
Writer: John Stephen GLASBY
Other Byline: John S GLASBY
Citation Record: 1 Book
This Time Forever - *Only*
Spencer UK (1957)

Mariano MERCADO

is a hypochondriac sleuth who appeared in eight novelettes, 1944-1948, in *Dime Detective.*
American Male Detective in Pulp Magazines operating in USA

D L CHAMPION 1903?-1968 (Australian)
Invented 4 detectives - see Insp ALLHOFF
No citations

Insp MERCER

British Policeman operating in England

Michael GILBERT 1912- (British)
Invented 11 detectives - see Insp HAZELRIGG
Citation Record: 1 Book
The Body Of A Girl - *Only*
Hodder & Stoughton UK (1972); Harper & Row US (1972)

Edward MERCER

tries to find a missing man in Italy.
British Male Private Detective operating in Venice

Victor CANNING 1911-1986 (British)
Invented 6 detectives - see Rex CARVER
Citation Record: 1 Book
Venetian Bird - *Only*
Hodder & Stoughton UK (1951)
Bird Of Prey - *Only**
Mill US (1951)

Hank MERCER and Biff DEEGAN

Hank MERCER is a writer of mystery stories who would like to dispense with his fictional detective, *Biff DEEGAN*, but finds him more and more indispensable in solving a real-life case.
American Male Private Detectives operating in New York

Mel ARRIGHI 1933- (American)
See main detective HARRINGTON
Citation Record: 1 Book
Alter Ego - *Single*
St Martin's US (1983); Quartet UK (1984)

Penny MERCER

Appears with at least two other detectives - see William POWER

Penny MERCER and Vincent MERCER

appear also in books with the author's other detective, *William POWER.*
British Female Amateur and British Male Amateur operating in England

Henrietta CLANDON 1881- (British)
Writer: John George Haslette VAHEY
Other Bylines:
Vernon LODER   Walter PROUDFOOT
Other Detectives:
William POWER, Penny MERCER and Vincent MERCER
William POWER
Citation Record: 1 Book
Fog Off Weymouth - *Only*
Bles UK (1938)

Vincent MERCER

Second detective of Penny MERCER

Vincent MERCER

Appears with at least two other detectives - see William POWER

Insp MEREDITH

British Policeman operating in England

John BUDE 1901-1957 (British)
Invented 4 detectives - see Insp SHERWOOD
Citation Record: 26 Books
The Lake District Murder - *First*
Skeffington UK (1935)
Another Man's Shadow - *Last*
Macdonald UK (1957)

Lt MEREDITH

American Policeman operating in New York

Diana RAMSAY
Writer: Rhoda BRANDES
Citation Record: 3 Books
A Little Murder Music - *First*
Collins UK (1972)
No Cause To Kill - *Last*
Collins UK (1974)

Idwal MEREDITH

investigates the death by poisoning of a writer of detective fiction, who seems to be hated by all and sundry.
British Policeman operating in England

Robert BARNARD 1936- (British)
Invented 13 detectives - see Insp Perry TRETHOWAN
Citation Record: 1 Book
Unruly Son - *Single*
Collins UK (1978)
Death Of A Mystery Writer - *Single**
Scribner's US (1979)

Sir John MEREDITH

British Male Amateur operating in England

Francis GERARD 1906-1962? (South African)
was the son of a Frenchman and spent his boyhood in France. He came to Britain and served as a major in the Essex Regiment during the First World War. He lived in London until 1946, when he emigrated to South Africa, taking up citizenship there. An admirer of *Edgar WALLACE*, he wrote three *SANDERS* novels after the latter's death.
Adopter of one other detective Commiss SANDERS

Citation Record: 17 Books

The Black Emperor - *First*
Rich UK (1936)

Bare Bodkin - *Last*
Macdonald UK (1951)

Katy MEREDITH

is menaced by the existence of an old crime, and has to turn sleuth to solve it.

American Female Amateur operating in USA

Ursula CURTISS 1923- (American)

Invented 5 detectives - see Lou FABIAN

Citation Record: 1 Book

Voice Out Of Darkness - *Only*
Dodd, Mead US (1948); Evans UK (1949)

Commiss T X MEREDITH

solves a case of death by shooting in a locked room.

British Policeman operating in London

Edgar WALLACE 1875-1932 (British)

Invented 28 detectives - see J G REEDER

Citation Record: 1 Book

The Clue Of The Twisted Candle - *Only*
Small, Maynard US (1916); Newnes UK (1918)

MEREN

is a Theban master spy in Egypt around 2000 BC. When a high priest is murdered and the young Tutankhamun is in danger, not only must he walk any mean streets there may have been among the pyramids, but he has to deal with the mystical beliefs of rival parties as well, making his sleuthing not all that easy.

Theban Male Secret Agent operating in Thebes

Lynda S ROBINSON (American)

Citation Record: 1 Book

Family Album - *Single*
Scribner's US (1995)

Brooke MERIT

Second detective of Jason PRICE

The Great MERLINI

is a stage magician who has written has written several books about magic. He meets murder on and around the stage, real mysteries, often of the 'impossible' kind, which turn into real mysteries that he is called on to solve.

American Male Amateur operating in New York

Clayton RAWSON 1906-1971 (American)

was born in Elyria, Ohio. He took a BA at Ohio State University, Columbus, 1929, and studied further at the Chicago Art Institute. He was, at various times, the editor of a number of prestigious detective and mystery magazines, 1942-1970.

Citation Record: 4 Books 12 Short Stories in 1 Collection

Death From A Top Hat - *First*
Putnam US (1938); Collins UK (1938)

No Coffin For The Corpse - *Last*
Little, Brown US (1942); Stacey UK (1972)

The Great Merlini: The Complete Stories Of The Great Magician - *Collection 1*
Gregg US (1979)

Nick MERLOTTI

American Male Sleuth operating in New York/Miami

Jim DEANE (American)

Citation Record: 2 Books

The Great Pretender - *First*
Signet UK (1974)

Moon Over Miami - *Last*
Signet UK (1975)

MERRICK

American Male Private Detective operating in New York

A Maynard BARBOUR 1862-1941 (American)

Writer: Anna Mary BARBOUR

Citation Record: 1 Book

That Mainwaring Affair - *Only*
Lippincott US (1900); Ward, Lock UK (1901)

Jenkinson Talbot MERRIDREW

is a 300-lb English butler in the US midwest who solves a case of murder by poison gas in the middle of a desert.

British Male Amateur operating in USA

John Russell FEARN 1908-1960

For writer details see Maria BLACK

Inventor of one other detective Sawley GERSON

Citation Record: 1 Book

Merridrew Marches On - *Only*
World's Work UK (1951)

Sir Gideon MERRIMAC

is a parody, a combination of *Gideon FELL* and *Sir Henry MERRIVALE*, the two classic detectives of *John Dickson CARR* and his alter ego, *Carter DICKSON*. In this one delightful short story he solves a case of 'impossible' murder that would have appealed to the genius of his literary mentor.

British Male Amateur operating in England

Jon L BREEN 1943- (American)

Invented 6 detectives - see Rachel HENNINGS

Citation Record: 1 Selected Short Story

The House Of The Shrill Whispers
involves a shooting in a guarded house surrounded by artificial snow. It appeared in the August number of the magazine and is also in a collection, *Hair of the Sleuthhound* (*Scarecrow*; US 1982)
In 'Ellery Queen's Mystery Magazine' US (1972)

Mike MERRIMAN

British Male Amateur operating in England

Jonathan BURKE 1922- (British)

For writer details see John BURKE

Citation Record: 2 Books

Fear By Instalments - *First*
Long UK (1960)

Deadly Downbeat - *Last*
Long UK (1962)

Desmond MERRION and Insp Henry ARNOLD

Desmond MERRION is an unofficial consultant on crime to Scotland Yard, brilliant, imaginative, and even whimsical rather than pedantically logical. He likes driving cars and smoking cigarettes and, in one of the largest series of British detective novels, he works closely with *Insp Henry ARNOLD*, a sound but unimaginative standard British cop. The cases are interesting and the books excellent.

British Male Amateur and British Policeman operating in England

Miles BURTON 1884-1964 (British)

For writer details see Dr Lancelot PRIESTLEY

Citation Record: 61 Books

The Secret Of High Eldersham - *First*
Collins UK (1930); Mystery League US (1931)

The Mystery Of High Eldersham - *First**
Collins UK (1933)

Death Paints A Picture - *Last*
Collins UK (1960)

Vic MERRITT

American Male Sleuth operating in New Jersey

Jake CAFFERTY (American)

Citation Record: 1 Book

The Death On The Boardwalk - *Single*
Critic US (1986)

James CALLAHAN (American)

Citation Record: 1 Book

The Carnation Killer - *Single*
Critic US (1987)

Sir Henry MERRIVALE KC

is usually known simply as HM and is perhaps the most famous of this remarkable author's detectives. Loosely copied from *Gideon FELL*, the author's other great detective (created under the *John Dickson CARR* byline) he too is a large man, erratic, ebullient, and talkative. A barrister, a King's Counsel, and earnest sleuth, he is said to be the holder of one of the oldest baronetcies in England. Described as being bald-headed, pigeon-toed, and given to temper and childishness, he can often appear comic; but he is brilliant at solving the most complex and diabolical crimes, often of an 'impossible' nature. He features in a series of novels over two decades and in at least two short stories, included in collections published under the *CARR* byline.

British Male Amateur operating in England

John Dickson CARR 1906-1977 (American)

Invented 16 detectives - see Dr Gideon FELL

Citation Record: 2 Short Stories in 2 Collections

The Third Bullet And Other Stories - *Collection 1*

contains two *Gideon FELL* stories and one *Sir Henry MERRIVALE* story. In addition it contains the title novelette, originally published under the author's *Carter DICKSON* pseudonym.

Short stories - 1
Harper & Row US (1954); Hamish Hamilton UK (1954)

The Men Who Explained Miracles - *Collection 2*

contains two *Gideon FELL* stories, one *Col MARCH* story, and one *Sir Henry MERRIVALE* story.

Short stories - 1
Harper & Row US (1963); Hamish Hamilton UK (1964)

Carter DICKSON 1906-1977 (American)

For writer details see Dr Gideon FELL

Inventor of one other detective Col MARCH

Citation Record: 22 Books

The Plague Court Murders - *First*
Morrow US (1934); Heinemann UK (1935)

The Cavalier's Cup - *Latest*
Morrow US (1953); Heinemann UK (1954)

John MERRY

American Male Detective in Pulp Magazines operating in USA

Jack HOWARD (American)

Inventor of one other detective OLD BRIGHTON

Citation Record: 1 Selected Short Story

John Merry, The Alert Detective
Old Cap Collier Library US (18??)

Supt MERSEY

British Policeman operating in England

Frank A CLEMENT (British)

Citation Record: 3 Books

Picture Him Dead - *First*
Longman UK (1935)

Scandal At The Home Office - *Last*
Longman UK (1937)

Insp MERTON

solves a case of death by stabbing in a locked library.

British Policeman operating in England

Charles ASHTON 1884- (British)

Invented 3 detectives - see Maj Jack ATHERLEY

Citation Record: 1 Book

Dance For A Dead Uncle - *Only*
Methuen UK (1948)

Mr MERTON

of Scotland Yard is in this one Victorian novel.

British Policeman operating in London

Eric A BAYLY (British)

Invented 3 detectives - see Oliver POTTER and Laurence CARRINGTON

Citation Record: 1 Book

The Secret Of Scotland Yard: A Mystery - *Only*
Sands UK (1900)

Laura METCALF

British Female Amateur operating in England

Headon HILL 1857-1927 (British)

Invented 11 detectives - see Insp HERON

Citation Record: 1 Book

By A Hair's-Breadth - *Only*
Cassell UK (1897); Dodd, Mead US (1897)

Paul MEXTON

is a reporter who sleuths in this one Victorian novel.

British Male Amateur operating in England

Fergus HUME 1859-1932 (British)

Invented 24 detectives - see Insp Samuel GORBY

Citation Record: 1 Book

The Rainbow Feather - *Only*
Digby, Long UK (1898)

David MEYNELL

British Male Amateur operating in England

Ivon BAKER 1928- (British)

Citation Record: 4 Books

Grave Doubt - *First*
Hale UK (1972); Washburn US (1972)

Death And Variations - *Latest*
Hale UK (1977); St Martin's US (1977)

James M'GOVAN

is on the Edinburgh police force and appears in a large number of short stories, published in collections over almost half a century, as if written by himself.

British Policeman operating in Edinburgh

James M'GOVAN (British)

Writer: William Crawford HONEYMAN

Other Detectives:

JIMSIE WEE PUNCH

Citation Record: 169 Short Stories in 7 Collections

Brought To Bay; Or, Experiences Of A City Detective - *Collection 1*

was republished in 1884 by *Menzies*, also in Edinburgh.

Short stories - 23
Edinburgh Publishing Co UK (1878)

Hunted Down; Or, Recollections Of A City Detective - *Collection 2*

Short stories - 17
Menzies UK (1878)

Strange Clues; Or, Chronicles Of A City Detective - *Collection 3*

was republished in 1885 by *Menzies*, also of Edinburgh.

Short stories - 30
Simpkin Marshall UK (1881)

Traced And Tracked; Or, Memoirs Of A City Detective - *Collection 4*

Short stories - 24
Menzies UK (1884)

Solved Mysteries; Or, Revelations Of A City Detective - *Collection 5*

Short stories - 31
Menzies UK (1888)

Criminals Caught; Or, Records Of A City Detective - *Collection 6*
Short stories - 24
Jenkins UK (1921)

The Invisible Pickpocket; Or, Records Of A City Detective - *Collection 7*
contains the short story featuring *JIMSIE.*
Short stories - 20
Menzies UK (1922)

Insp M'GUIRE
British Policeman operating in England

Gilbert COVERACK 1886- (British)
For writer details see Insp M'GUIRE
Citation Record: 2 Books
Time For A Murder - *First*
was published in the US under the following byline.
Hurst UK (1941)
The Magpie Murder - *Last*
was published in the US under the following byline.
Earl UK (1947)

J Russell WARREN 1886- (British)
was a journalist and writer of several criminous novels.
Writer: John Russell WARREN
Other Byline: Gilbert COVERACK
Citation Record: 3 Books
Time For A Murder - *First*
was published in the UK under the preceding byline.
Sheridan US (1942)
The Magpie Murder - *Last*
was published in the UK under the preceding byline.
Sheridan US (1952)

M

Lt MICHAELS
is quite naturally concerned with deaths that are occurring much too frequently among a group of people.
American Policeman operating in USA

E L WITHERS 1930- (American)
Writer: George William POTTER Jr
Citation Record: 1 Book
Diminishing Returns - *Only*
Rinehart US (1960); Harrap UK (1961)

Danny MICHAELS
American Male Sleuth operating in Chicago

North BAKER and William BOLTON (American)
Writer: (First author) Howell North BAKER 1912-
Citation Record: 1 Book
Dead To The World - *Only*
Doubleday US (1944)

Richard MICHAELSON
solves a murder recorded on tape.
American Male Amateur operating in USA

Michael BOWEN (American)
Citation Record: 1 Book
Washington Deceased - *Single*
St Martin's US (1990)

Father MICKLE
solves a case of death by poisoning in a locked library.
American Male Amateur operating in USA
Sidekick: Hilary MEREDITH
is a reporter
American Male - Assistant

Henry C BECK 1902- (American)
Writer: Henry Charlton BECK
Citation Record: 1 Book
Death By Clue - *Only*
Dutton US (1933)

Don MICKLEM
is a millionaire playboy who likes sleuthing.
British Male Amateur operating in Venice

Raymond MARSHALL 1906-1985 (British)
For writer details see Dave FENNER
Other Detectives:
Martin 'Brick-Top' CORRIGAN
Insp JAMES
Marc SPENCER
Citation Record: 2 Books
Mission To Venice - *First*
Hale UK (1954)
Mission To Siena - *Last*
Hale UK (1955)

Johnny MIDAS
is a skiptracer.
American Male Private Detective operating in New York

Bruce CASSIDAY 1920- (American)
See main detective Cash MADIGAN
Citation Record: 1 Book
The Brass Shroud - *Only*
Ace US (1956)

Ivy MIDDAUGH and Judith PERINO
are a mother-and-daughter team, hitherto a rare kind of combination in the criminous genre.
American Female Private Detectives operating in USA

Gerry MADDREN (American)
See main detective Jerry COOL
Citation Record: 1 Selected Short Story
Fit For Felony
is in an anthology, *The Woman Sleuth Anthology: Contemporary Mystery Stories by Women* (Editor; Irene Zahava; US 1988).
US (1988)

Ulysses Price MIDDLEBIE
appears in several short stories.
American Male Amateur operating in USA

Arthur PORGES (American)
Invented 13 detectives - see Arsène LUPIN
Citation Record: 1 Selected Short Story
Blood Will Tell
appeared in the February number.
In 'Alfred Hitchcock's Mystery Magazine' US (1964)

Mr MIDDLETON
American Male Amateur operating in several locations

Wardon Allan CURTIS (American)
Citation Record: 15 Short Stories in 1 Collection
The Strange Adventures Of Mr Middleton - *Collection 1*
Stone US (1903)

David MIDDLETON-BROWNE
is a lawyer who is continually being drawn into cases of murder in and around churches and clergymen, it seeming that ecclesiastical crimes are rampant in Britain, the police being powerless to either stop or solve them. He is aided by his admirable sidekick.
British Male Amateur operating in England
Sidekick: Lucy KINGSLEY
is the lover of *David MIDDLETON-BROWNE* and he wishes she was his wife, his intentions being reasonably honourable, especially as she is of enormous help in solving the churchy crimes she often lays on his figurative doorstep.
British Female - Lover

Kate CHARLES (British)
Citation Record: 4 Books

Appointment To Die - *First*
Headline UK (1992)
A Dead Man Out Of Mind - *Latest*
Headline UK (1994)

Steve MIDNIGHT

was a former playboy. He now drives a cab and, somewhat surprisingly, is a detective who appeared in eight stories in *Dime Detective.*

American Male Private Detective operating in Los Angeles

John K BUTLER (American)

Other Detectives:
Tricky ENRIGHT   Rex LONERGAN
Citation Record: 1 Selected Short Story
The Saint In Silver
In 'Dime Detective' US (1941)

MIDNIGHT LOUIE and Temple BARR

MIDNIGHT LOUIE is an adorable feline and is called variously by his companions, 'tough cat extraordinaire' and 'a combination of Nathan Detroit and Sam Spade'. On his prowls he often stumbles across a dead (human) body or two, which he needs to investigate the causes of. This he does with the help of *Temple BARR,* a petite, red-headed, lady publicist who is at his every beck and call. They tell the story in alternate chapters, he in racy Runyonese, she more conventionally. Delightful, and compulsive reading for all cat-lovers!

American Male Cat and American Female Amateur operating in Las Vegas

Carole Nelson DOUGLAS 1944- (American)

Invented 3 detectives - see Irene ADLER
Citation Record: 4 Books
Crystal Days - *First*
Bantam US (1990)
Cat In A Crimson Haze - *Latest*
Bantam US (1995)

Insp MIDWINTER

British Policeman operating in England

Harrington HEXT 1862-1960 (British)

For writer details see Insp MIDWINTER
Inventor of one other detective Nicol HART
Citation Record: 1 Book
The Thing At Their Heels - *Only*
Butterworth UK (1923); Macmillan US (1923)

Eden PHILLPOTTS 1862-1960 (British)

was born in Mount Aboo, India, and educated in England. During his long life he was the author of over a hundred novels, thirty stage plays, many plays for radio, a large number of short stories and a vast amount of poetry, much of his work featuring the aspects of English country life he loved. Among his work there are at least forty novels loosely in the criminous genre, including a number of good detective stories.

Writer: Eden PHILLPOTTS
Other Byline: Harrington HEXT
Other Detectives:
Avis BRYDEN   Peter GANNS
Peter HARDCASTLE   Insp Edward MAINE
PETERS   John RINGROSE
Richard SILVER and Insp Tarrant TINKLER
Dr THORNE   Insp Thomas WARNER
Citation Record: 1 Book
The Captain's Curio - *Only*
Hutchinson UK (1933); Macmillan US (1933)

Montague MIGGLEWADE

British Male Amateur operating in England

Edgar HALE (British)

See main detective Insp Michael REGAN
Citation Record: 2 Books
Blue Murder - *First*
Ward, Lock UK (1948)
Coffee For One - *Last*
Ward, Lock UK (1949)

Ed MIGRAINE

was one of the master's early pulp detectives, appearing in stories in *Double Detective.*

American Male Detective in Pulp Magazines operating in USA

Erle Stanley GARDNER 1889-1970 (American)

Invented 14 detectives - see Perry MASON
No citations

Johnny MILANO

American Male Private Detective operating in New York

Stanley ELLIN 1916- (American)

Invented 4 detectives - see Jake DEKKER
Citation Record: 2 Books
Star Light, Star Bright - *First*
Random House US (1979); Cape UK (1979)
The Dark Fantastic - *Latest*
Mysterious Press US (1983)

Insp MILD, Charles BLAKELOCK, Edward DONALDSON, Andrew MUIR, John QUINCE and Prof BROWNING

In a spoof of all those delightful Oxbridge detective stories, a most unpleasant don is killed with an eighteenth-century pistol in his rooms at the fictional St Saviour's College at Oxford. *Insp MILD* knows that all such academic murders have their roots in literary quotations and spends much of his time studying the works of lesser British writers in the hope of coming across the odd clue. He has to contend, however, not only with four self-appointed amateur sleuths who are undergraduates, but with a visiting professor from Harvard who insists on getting into the detective act. A real muddle and a glittering prize.

British Male Amateurs and American Amateur operating in Oxford

Timothy ROBINSON 1934- (British)

was born in Croydon, Surrey.
Writer: Timothy Michael ROBINSON
Citation Record: 1 Book
When Scholars Fall - *Only*
Hutchinson UK (1961)

Geoffrey MILDMAY

American Male Sleuth operating in Washington DC/France

Burke WILKINSON 1914- (American)

Writer: John Burke WILKINSON
Citation Record: 3 Books
Proceed At Will - *First*
Little, Brown US (1948); Hodder & Stoughton UK (1949)
Last Clear Chance - *Last*
Little, Brown US (1954); Hodder & Stoughton UK (1954)

Don MILES

does his sleuthing at the automobile races at Le Mans, Monte Carlo, and Indianapolis.

American Male Amateur operating in USA/France

Larry KENYON (American)

Writer: Lew LOUDERBACK
Other Byline: Nick CARTER
Citation Record: 4 Books
Challenge At Le Mans - *First*
Avon UK (1967)
Revenge At Indy - *Last*
Avon UK (1967)

Jeff MILES

is an ex-convict who is employed by a detective agency on an unusual case.

American Male Private Detective operating in California

Dana LYON 1897-1982 (American)

See main detective Hilda TRENTON

Citation Record: 1 Book

It's My Own Funeral - *Only*
Farrar, Straus US (1944); Hammond UK (1948)

Robert MILES

was once a professional baseball player. He now works for the Mid-Continental Op agency in Springfield, investigating political crime.

American Male Private Detective operating in Illinois

David EVERSON 1941- (American)

Citation Record: 5 Books

Recount - *First*
Ivy US (1987)

A Capital Killing - *Latest*
Ivy US (1990)

Det Sgt Alan MILL

Second detective of Sister JOAN

Alan MILLER

American Male Amateur operating in New York

Peter HUNT (American)

Writers: George Worthing YATES and Charles Hunt MARSHALL

Citation Record: 3 Books

Murders At Scandal House - *First*
Appleton UK (1933)

Murder For Breakfast - *Last*
Vanguard US (1934)

'Doc' MILLER

American Male Amateur operating in USA

M

Herman PETERSEN 1893- (American)

Citation Record: 3 Books

Murder In The Making - *First*
McBride US (1940)

Old Bones - *Last*
Duell US (1943); Swan UK (1950)

Ch Insp James MILLER

British Policeman operating in England

Sidekick: Insp Gordon FREWIN

British Male - Subordinate

Maurice B DIX 1889-1956 (British)

Invented 4 detectives - see Tommy MALINS

Citation Record: 2 Books

Murder At Grassmere Abbey
Ward, Lock UK (1933)

The Fleetwood Mansions Mystery - *Last*
Ward, Lock UK (1934)

Nick MILLER

British Male Professional Investigator operating in England

Harry PATTERSON 1929- (British)

For writer details see Liam DEVLIN

Citation Record: 3 Books

The Graveyard Shift - *First*
Long UK (1965)

Hell Is Always Today - *Last*
was republished in the UK and US under the following byline.
Long UK (1968)

Jack HIGGINS 1929- (British)

Inventor of 3 detectives - see Liam DEVLIN

Citation Record: 1 Book

Hell Is Always Today - *Only*
was previously published in the UK under the preceding byline.
Coronet UK (1968); GM US (1974)

Penny MILLER

is a researcher for a glossy travel magazine who solves the mystery of a murder that took place long ago in the family she is researching.
!See Appendix 2.

American Female Amateur operating in Rhode Island

Margaret LAMB 1936- (American)

was born in North Dakota. She was educated at the University of New York and is an authority on the works of Shakespeare.

Citation Record: 1 Book

Chains Of Gold - *Single*
St Martin's US (1985)

Robin MILLER

appears also in a collection of stories with one of the author's other detectives, *Aubrey St John MAJOR.*

American Female Amateur operating in California

Jaye MAIMAN (American)

Citation Record: 3 Books

I Left My Heart - *First*
Naiad US (1991); Silver Moon UK (1992)

Under My Skin - *Latest*
Naiad US (1993)

Kinsey MILLHONE

is at the top end of the great American Female Detective boom, a tough, bright, somewhat dishonest, likeable, and feminine PI, operating beautifully, according to the best rules of the genre, in the fictional town of Santa Teresa. Her books have titles that are in alphabetical order and it seems a pity that the English alphabet has only twenty-six letters to play with.
!See Appendix 2.

American Female Private Detective operating in California

Sue GRAFTON 1940- (American)

was born in Louisville, Kentucky, the daughter of the genre writer, *Cornelius Warren GRAFTON.* She graduated with a BA in English from the University of Louisville, Kentucky, 1961, published her first genre novel in 1967, and has since embarked on the most interesting and clever series of detective novels, with a superb female private eye, of the post-war period. She received the Private Eye Writers of America Shamus award, 1986, and has since received other awards for her short stories and television plays.

Citation Record: 11 Books

A Is For Alibi - *First*
Holt US (1982); Macmillan UK (1986)

K Is For Killer - *Latest*
Holt US (1994); Macmillan UK (1994)

Earl (of) MILLINGTON

British Male Amateur operating in England

Gilbert HACKFORTH-JONES 1900- (British)

Invented 3 detectives - see Paul DECKER

Citation Record: 4 Books 17 Short Stories in 1 Collection

Submarine Flotilla - *First*
Hodder & Stoughton UK (1940)

The Questing Hound - *Last*
Hodder & Stoughton UK (1947)

Sixteen Bells - *Collection 1*
Not all the stories are criminous.
Hodder & Stoughton UK (1946)

George MILLINGTON

British Male Private Detective operating in England

B L FARJEON 1838-1903 (British)

Invented 7 detectives - see Robert AGNOLD

Citation Record: 1 Book

The March Of Fate - *Only*
White UK (1893)

Max MILLION

American Male Amateur operating in USA

Robert ARTHUR 1909-1969 (American)

Writer: Robert FEDER

Other Detectives:
Lt Oliver BAYNES and John Sherlock HOLMES
Baron DE HIRSCH Max LONDON
Harrison MANNIX
Howard MATTHEWS and Jeff LANDRUM

Citation Record: 1 Book

The Case Of The Murderous Mice
Tower US (1933)

Mark MILLNER

American Male Private Detective operating in USA

Julian SHORE (American)

Citation Record: 1 Book

Rattle His Bones - *Only*
Morrow US (1941)

MILLS

British Male Sleuth operating in several locations

Manning O'BRINE 1915- (British)

See main detective Michael the O'KELLY

Citation Record: 2 Books

Mills - *First*
Jenkins UK (1969); Lippincott US (1969)

No Earth For Foxes - *Last*
Barrie & Jenkins UK (1974); Delacorte US (1975)

Francesca MILLS

American Female Amateur operating in Texas

Robert MCCOLLUM (American)

Citation Record: 1 Book

And Then They Die - *Single*
St Martin's US (1985)

Insp MILLWALL

British Policeman operating in England

James SANDYS (British)

Other Detectives:
James CHARLESWORTH Mr SPRINGFIELD

Citation Record: 2 Books

The Vengeance Due - *First*
Paul UK (1938)

Green Eye Of Death - *Last*
Paul UK (1943)

Larry MILNER

British Male Amateur operating in England

Stooge: Sgt EVANS
British Male

Michael CROMBIE (British)

Citation Record: 1 Book

The Sealed Room Murder - *Only*
Arthur Gray UK (1934)

Terence MILNER

is a member of the British Admiralty Secret Service.

British Male Professional Investigator operating in England

Laurence CLARKE (British)

Writer: Laurence Aycough CLARKE

Citation Record: 1 Selected Short Story

Flashlight
In 'Strand Magazine' UK (1918)

Christopher MILNER-BROWN

British Male Amateur

Charles FORSYTE (British)

Writers: UNKNOWN and UNKNOWN

See main detective Insp Richard LEFT

Citation Record: 1 Book

Murder With Minarets - *Only*
Cassell UK (1968)

Milton Chester MILODRAGOVITCH

operates out of Meriwether, Montana, and is an idealised PI of the post-Vietnam War generation, so beloved by their creators in the 1970s. A bad lot, a cocaine addict, an alcoholic, and a compulsive chaser of women, he lives in a sleazy world of underdogs and cast-offs, rich misfits, and psychopaths, among whom crime abounds.

American Male Private Detective operating in Montana

James CRUMLEY 1939- (American)

See main detective Chauncy Wayne SUGHRUE

Citation Record: 2 Books

The Wrong Case - *First*
Random House US (1975); Hart Davis MacGibbon UK (1976)

Dancing Bear - *Latest*
Random House US (1983); Penguin UK (1987)

Det Sgt Arthur MILTON

British Policeman operating in England

Laurence HENDERSON 1928- (British)

Citation Record: 4 Books

With Intent - *First*
Harrap UK (1968); St Martin's US (1971)

Major Enquiry - *Latest*
Harrap UK (1976); St Martin's US (1976)

Anne MINER

Second detective of Bob ADAMS

Mike MINER

solves a case of campus murder.

American Male Amateur operating in USA

Jacquelyn NOWAK (American)

is an art historian and playwright.

Citation Record: 1 Book

Death At The Crossings - *Single*
Dodd, Mead US (1985)

Sgt Matt MINOGUE

of the Dublin Murder Squad investigates the murder of an elderly Englishman, a case that could have security implications.

Irish Policeman operating in Dublin

John BRADLEY 1955- (Irish)

Writer: John Mary BRADLEY

Citation Record: 4 Books

Unholy Ground - *First*
Constable UK (1989)

All Souls - *Last*
Constable UK (1993)

Connie MINOR

is a veteran newspaperman, now working in obscurity for an advertising agency. He is given a chance to make it big again by promoting a secret new car, but soon finds that he is immersed in chicanery and murder, which he must deal with.

American Male Amateur operating in Detroit

Loren D ESTLEMAN 1952- (American)

Invented 7 detectives - see Amos WALKER

Citation Record: 1 Book

Edsel - *Single*
Mysterious Press US (1995)

Supt MINTER

is otherwise known as The Sooper, one of the author's most likeable police detectives. He appeared only in one novelette and a few short stories. Some of the latter are in the collection cited.

British Policeman operating in London

Edgar WALLACE 1875-1932 (British)

Invented 28 detectives - see J G REEDER

Citation Record: 1 Book 4 Short Stories in 1 Collection

Big Foot - *Only*
Long UK (1927)

The Lone House Mystery - *Collection 1*
contains the title novelette and three short stories.
Collins UK (1929)

MINTO

investigates, while at his sister's wedding, the death of a tiger-tamer in a travelling circus.

Male Amateur operating in England

Alan MELVILLE 1910-1983 (British)

was a well-known literary figure who wrote several light plays, performed in London. He also wrote at least six crime novels, of which only this one is a detective story.

Writer: William Melville CAVERHILL

Citation Record: 1 Book

Death Of Anton - *Only*
Skeffington UK (1936)

Tori MIRACLE

is a New York journalist who investigates a murder at the Rose Rent Festival in Amish country.

American Female Amateur operating in USA

Valerie S MALMONT (American)

Citation Record: 1 Book

Death Pays The Rose Rent - *Single*
Simon & Schuster US (1994)

MIRO

investigates political murders.

American Male Secret Agent operating in several locations

Shaun HERRON 1912- (American)

Citation Record: 5 Books

Miro - *First*
Random House US (1969)

The Miro Papers - *First**
Hale UK (1971)

The Bird In Last Year's Nest - *Last*
Cape US (1974); Evans UK (1974)

Billy MISCHIEF

American Male Detective in Pulp Magazines operating in USA

OLD SLEUTH (American)

Invented 40 detectives - see Brant ADAMS

Citation Record: 1 Book

Billy Mischief, A Regular Trained Detective - *Only*
Royal US (ca 1908)

MITCH

Second detective of GAIL

Victor MITCHEL

appears in this science fiction work, in which a murder is committed by some invisible agency.

American Male Sleuth operating in USA

Curme GRAY (American)

Citation Record: 1 Book

Murder In Millenium Vi - *Only*
Shasta US (1951)

Insp MITCHELL

American Policeman operating in Washington DC

Natalie Sumner LINCOLN 1881-1935 (American)

Inventor of one other detective Det FERGUSON

Citation Record: 8 Books

I Spy - *First*
Appleton UK (1916)

PPC - *Last*
Appleton UK (1927)

Sgt Benedict MITCHELL

is young, and this is his first case. Although it is under the direction of other officers, it is he who really solves it.

British Policeman operating in England

Pauline BELL 1928- (British)

Invented 3 detectives - see Det Sgt Jerry HUNTER

Citation Record: 1 Book

The Dead Do Not Praise - *Single*
Macmillan UK (1990)

Sgt/Lt Charley MITCHELL

American Policeman operating in New York

William Almon WOLFF 1885-1933 (American)

Citation Record: 2 Books

Manhattan Night - *First*
Minton US (1930)

Murder At Endor - *Last*
Minton US (1933); Putnam UK (1933)

Harry MITCHELL

American Male Amateur operating in Detroit

Elmore LEONARD 1935- (American)

Invented 6 detectives - see Frank RYAN

Citation Record: 1 Book

Fifty-Two Pickup - *Only*
Delacorte US (1974); Secker & Warburg UK (1974)

Ken MITCHELL

American Male Amateur operating in Illinois

Winifred VAN ATTA 1910- (American)

Invented 3 detectives - see Jim FERGUSON

Citation Record: 1 Book

Hatchet Man - *Only*
Doubleday US (1962); Boardman UK (1964)

Meredith MITCHELL

Second detective of Ch Insp Alan MARKBY

Peter MITCHELL

British Male Amateur operating in England

G Walter COOKE 1924- (British)

Writer: Geoffrey Walter COOKE

Citation Record: 3 Books

Death Can Wait - *First*
Bles UK (1957)

Death Is The End - *Last*
Bles UK (1965)

Robert Leroy MITCHELL and John BARNES

John BARNES appears also in one other book by this author.

American Male Amateurs operating in New York

Rodrigues OTTOLENGUI 1861-1937 (American)

Inventor of one other detective John BARNES

Citation Record: 3 Books 12 Short Stories in 1 Collection

An Artist In Crime - *First*
Putnam US (1892)

The Crime Of The Century - *Last*
Putnam US (1896)

Final Proof Or, The Value Of Evidence - *Collection 1*
Putnam US (1898)

Scott MITCHELL

British Male Private Detective operating in England

John HARVEY 1938- (British)

See main detective Insp Charlie RESNICK

Citation Record: 4 Books

The Geranium Kiss - *First*
Sphere UK (1976)

Junkyard Angel - *Latest*
Sphere UK (1977)

Insp Steven MITCHELL

of Scotland Yard nearly always shares, in other books, the detective work with the author's favourite amateur detectives, *Dr David WINTRINGHAM* and *Claude WARRINGTON-REEVE*, and it is he, in fact, who often makes the real deductions from the clues the amateur sleuths find. In this one book he is, in the main, on his own.

British Policeman operating in England

Josephine BELL 1897-1987 (British)

Invented 10 detectives - see Dr David WINTRINGHAM

Citation Record: 1 Book

The Port Of London Murders - *Only*
Longman UK (1938); Macmillan US (1958)

Insp Steven MITCHELL

Second detective of Claude WARRINGTON-REEVE

Insp Steven MITCHELL

Second detective of Dr David WINTRINGHAM

William MITCHELL

British Male Amateur operating in England

Harold A WRENN 1909- (British)

Writer: Harold Albert WRENN

Citation Record: 5 Books

Tangle - *First*
Hammond UK (1953)

Unguarded Moment - *Last*
Hale UK (1959)

Prof Knott Coe MITTLE

Appears with at least two other detectives - see Dr Frank HAYVIER

Porlock MOANS

of Bacon Street is a *SHERLOCK HOLMES* parody.

Male Professional Amateur

Sidekick: Dr POTSDAM
is his parody *WATSON*-like assistant.
Male - Assistant

Nicholas UTECHIN (American)

Adopter of one other detective Sherlock HOLMES

Citation Record: 1 Selected Short Story

The Adventures Of Porlock Moans - *Parody 1*
appeared in the July number.
In 'Shades of Sherlock' US (1970)

Sheercrocked MOANS

is a *SHERLOCK HOLMES* parody.

Male Professional Amateur

Sidekick: Dr WATSDOTTER
is his parody *WATSON*-like assistant.
Male - Assistant

Gayle Lange PUHL (American)

Citation Record: 2 Selected Short Stories

The Adventure Of Basil Rathbone - *Parody 1*
appeared in the January 6 number.
In 'Shades of Sherlock US' (1962)

The Adventure Of Stocksen Bonds - *Parody 2*
appeared in the June number. *Sheercrocked MOANS* helps a famous international agent, Bonds, to smash an organisation called 'Spasm', headed by the terrible Professor Artymore.
In 'Baker Street Journal' US (1968)

The MOD SQUAD

were a group of detectives in novelizations of episodes from a TV series.

American Policemen operating in USA

Richard DEMING 1915-1983 (American)

Invented 4 detectives - see Manville MOON

Citation Record: 5 Books

The Greek God Affair - *First*
Pyramid US (1968)

The Hit - *Last*
Pyramid US (1970)

Frank MOERSON

American Male Amateur operating in USA

Eaton K GOLDTHWAITE 1907- (American)

See main detective Lt Joseph DICKERSON

Citation Record: 1 Book

First You Have To Find Him - *Single*
Doubleday US (1981); Hale UK (1982)

Li MOH

Chinese Male Amateur operating in England

Joan COWDROY (British)

See main detective Ch Insp GORHAM

Citation Record: 6 Books

Watch Mr Moh - *First*
Hutchinson UK (1931.)

The Flying Dagger Murder - *First**
McBride US (1932)

Merry-Go-Round - *Last*
Hutchinson UK (1940)

Insp Raj MOHAMED

Indian Policeman operating in India

Innocent SOUSA (British)

Citation Record: 5 Short Stories in 1 Collection

Twixt Night And Morn - *Collection 1*
Drane UK (1925)

Peter MOHUNE

British Male Amateur operating in several locations

Pelham GROOM (British)

Writer: Arthur John Pelham GROOM

Citation Record: 5 Books

Sabotage Unlimited - *First*
Hamilton UK (1938)

The Purple Twilight - *Last*
Laurie UK (1948)

Vic MOINE

Appears with at least two other detectives - see Michael KERNEHAN

MOLESWORTH

British Male Amateur operating in England

B L FARJEON 1838-1903 (British)

Invented 7 detectives - see Robert AGNOLD

Citation Record: 1 Book

For The Defence - *Only*
Trischler UK (1891); Lovell US (1891)

Herr MOLLNAR

is an elderly agent who, during the occupation of Austria after the Second World War, solves the murder of a British journalist in the Russian zone of Vienna.

Austrian Male Secret Agent operating in Vienna

Sarah GAINHAM 1922- (British)

was the Central Europe corespondent for *The Spectator*, London, 1956-1966.

Writer: Sarah Rachel Stainer AMES

Citation Record: 1 Book

Time Right Deadly - *Only*
Barker UK (1956); Walker US (1961)

Jacob MOLNAR

American Male Amateur operating in USA

Peter CLOTHIER 1936- (American)

Writer: Peter Dean CLOTHIER

Citation Record: 1 Book
Chiaroscuro - *Single*
St Martin's US (1985)

MOM

appeared in the 1950s and 1960s in short stories, which have not been collected. A Jewish lady, she often had her policeman son, David, and his wife round for Friday night supper. He usually brought his superior, *Insp MILNER,* and together they would discuss the latter's perplexing cases, which generally had plots with strong musical connections, which she solved. Over two decades later she has emerged in at least two novels.

American Female Amateur operating in New York/Colorado

Stooge: Insp MILNER
American Male

James YAFFE 1927- (American)
See main detective Paul DAWN
Citation Record: 2 Books 2 Selected Short Stories
A Nice Murder For Mom - *First*
St Martin's US (1988)
Mom Meets Her Maker - *Latest*
St Martin's US (1990)
Mom In The Spring
US (1954)
Mom Sings An Aria
US (1966)

Rosie MONAGHAN

British Female Amateur

Alan MCDONALD 1949- (British)
Writer: Alan Patrick MCDONALD
Citation Record: 2 Books
Rosie Among Thorns - *First*
Futura UK (1989)
Unofficial Rosie - *Latest*
Futura UK (1989)

MONDO

Male Sleuth operating in USA

Anthony DE STEPHANO (American)
Citation Record: 3 Books
Mondo - *First*
Manor US (1975)
Cocaine Kill - *Latest*
Manor US (1977)

Rita MONDRAGON

runs her own detective agency from a wheelchair, down in New Mexico.

Mexican Female Private Detective operating in New Mexico

Sidekick: Joshua CROFT
is the sidekick, legman and lover of the crippled *Rita MONDRAGON.*
American Male - Assistant

Walter SATTERTHWAIT (American)
Writer: Walter Aiden SATTERTHWAIT
Other Detectives:
Lizzie BORDEN   Oscar WILDE
Citation Record: 3 Books
Wall Of Glass - *First*
HarperCollins UK (1988)
The Death Card - *Latest*
St Martin's US (1993); HarperCollins UK (1993)

Rachael MONETTE

When her husband, a member of staff at the fictional Williams College, is murdered and her son kidnapped for racial motives, *Rachael MONETTE* takes a trail that leads her to Europe and Israel in order to solve the crimes.
!See Appendix 2.

American Female Amateur operating in USA

Peter ABRAHAMS 1947- (American)
Citation Record: 1 Book
The Fury Of Rachael Monette - *Single*
Macmillan US (1980); Muller UK (1981)

Cummings King MONK

Male Amateur operating in Scotland

M P SHIEL 1865-1947 (British)
See main detective Prince ZALESKI
Citation Record: 3 Short Stories in 1 Collection
Prince Zaleski And Cummings King Monk - *Collection 1*
contains three *Cummings King MONK* stories and four *Prince ZALESKI* stories.
Arkham US (1977)

Dittany MONK and Osbert MONK

sleuth together in zany murder cases that seem to occur rather frequently in Lobelia Falls, deep in the heart of rural Canada.

Canadian Female Amateur and Canadian Male Amateur operating in Canada

Alisa CRAIG 1922- (Canadian)
Invented 3 detectives - see Holly HOWE
Citation Record: 4 Books
The Grub-And-Stakers Move A Mountain - *First*
Doubleday US (1981)
The Grub-And-Stakers Spin A Yarn - *Latest*
Avon US (1990)

Osbert MONK

Second detective of Dittany MONK

Richard MONK

British Male Amateur operating in England

Michael UNDERWOOD 1916-1992 (British)
Invented 6 detectives - see Rosa EPTON
Citation Record: 2 Books
The Man Who Died On Friday - *First*
Macdonald UK (1967)
The Man Who Killed Too Soon - *Last*
Macdonald UK (1968)

Sherlock MONK

was a *Sherlock HOLMES* animal parody, a monkey detective wearing a deerstalker hat and smoking a calabash pipe, who appeared during 1944 in a comic magazine called *Funny Animals.* [This information is in the introduction to *THE MISADVENTURES OF SHERLOCK HOLMES* (Editor: *Ellery QUEEN).*]

Male Sleuth operating in New York

Sidekick: CHUCK
is a duck who wears a flat, wide-brimmed, straw hat and does most of the detecting.
Unknown sex - Assistant
No citations

Insp William MONK

is an 'agent of inquiry' in the 1850s, sleuthing in England and Scotland.

British Policeman operating in London

Anne PERRY 1938- (British)
See main detective pair Insp Thomas PITT and Charlotte PITT
Citation Record: 6 Books
A Sudden, Fearful Death - *First*
Headline UK (1993); Ballantine US (1994)
Defend And Betray - *Latest*
Headline UK (1994)

Gilbert MONKTON

British Male Amateur operating in England

M E BRADDON 1835-1915 (British)
Invented 9 detectives - see Robert AUDLEY
Citation Record: 1 Book

Eleanor's Victory - *Only*
Tinsley UK (1863); Harper & Row US (1863)

MONTE
French Male Detective in Pulp Magazines operating in USA

Police Captain HOWARD (American)
Invented 15 detectives - see LIGHTNING LUKE
Citation Record: 1 Book
Monte, The French Detective; Or, The Man Of Many Disguises
New York Detective Library US (1882-8)

Frank MONTGOMERY
American Male Amateur operating in USA

Michael A SMITH 1942- (American)
Writer: Michael Anthony SMITH
Citation Record: 1 Book
Secrets - *Single*
St Martin's US (1981)

Dr Kirke MONTGOMERY
American Male Amateur operating in New York

Arthur MALLORY (American)
Citation Record: 2 Books
The Black Valley Murders - *First*
Chelsea US (1930)
Mysteries Of Black Valley - *Last*
Chelsea US (1930)

Percival MONTGOMERY
British Male Amateur operating in England

Muirhead ROBERTSON (British)
Writer: Henry JOHNSON
Citation Record: 1 Book
A Lombard Street Mystery - *Only*
Bartholomew US (1888)

Insp Richard MONTGOMERY
British Policeman operating in England
Sidekick: Sgt William BIRD
British Male - Subordinate

Stella SHEPHERD (British)
Citation Record: 3 Books
Black Justice - *First*
Constable UK (1988); Doubleday US (1989)
Thinner Than Blood - *Latest*
Constable UK (1991)

Jane MONTIGNY
is a journalist who seeks to learn the true fate of her mother, an American secret agent during the Second World War.
American Female Amateur operating in Europe

David GURR 1936-
Citation Record: 1 Book
A Woman Called Scylla - *Single*
Viking US (1981)

Pierre MONTIGNY
Canadian Male Amateur operating in New York/Montreal

Edwin Dial TORGERSON
Citation Record: 2 Books
The Murderer Returns - *First*
Smith US (1930); Lane UK (1931)
The Cold Finger Curse - *Last*
Falcon US (1933)

Dr Jean MONTROSE
is a middle-aged doctor, complete with busy surgery, husband, and daughters. Because of her medical knowledge and 'profound understanding of the psychology of murder', she is able to help the otherwise baffled local police to solve their cases.
British Female Amateur operating in Scotland

Stooge: Insp Douglas NIVEN
has to call in *Jean MONTROSE* in cases that involve specialised medical knowledge.
British Male

C F ROE (British)
Citation Record: 6 Books
The Lumsden Baby - *First*
Headline UK (1990)
A Nasty Bit Of Murder - *First**
Signet US (1992)
A Death In The Family - *Latest*
Headline UK (1993)

Stanley MOODROW
American Male Sleuth operating in New York

Stephen SOLOMITA 1943- (American)
Inventor of one other detective Marty BLAKE
Citation Record: 3 Books
A Twist Of The Knife - *First*
Putnam US (1988); Futura UK (1990)
Forced Entry - *Latest*
Putnam US (1990)

Hank MOODY
American Male Sleuth operating in New York

Robert CHAMBERS 1933- (American)
Citation Record: 3 Books
Moth In A Rag Shop - *First*
Bobbs US (1968); Hale UK (1969)
Village East - *First**
Dell US (1970)
The Neon Preacher - *Latest*
Mason UK (1977)

Nathaniel MOODY
British Male Amateur operating in England

E C LESTER (British)
Writer: Edward Castellain LESTER
Citation Record: 2 Books
The Guy Fawkes Murder - *First*
Long UK (1936)
The Murder Of Martin Fotherill - *Last*
Long UK (1937)

Charles 'Spotted' MOON
is a lawyer and a partner in Ogilvie, Tallant & Moon of San Francisco. He is part American Indian, which makes him feel an outsider in the society in which he moves.
American Male Amateur operating in USA

Chelsea Quinn YARBRO 1942- (American)
Citation Record: 2 Books
Ogilvie, Tallant & Moon - *First*
Putnam US (1976)
Music When Sweet Voices Die - *Latest*
Putnam US (1979)

Cotton MOON
is an oddball. He has a mania for edible nuts, and charges $30,000 a case to support his yacht, *Coquilla*, on which he roams the oceans in search of nuts.
American Male Private Detective operating on a ship
Sidekick: Bert STANLEY
American Male - Secretary

Rufus KING 1893-1966 (American)
was born in New York City. He attended Yale University, New Haven, Connecticut, and later served in the US Cavalry and Merchant Marine and then in Field Artillery in France during the First World War. He began writing magazine stories in the 1920s and is the author of at least twenty-two genre novels.
Writer: Rufus Frederick KING

M

Other Detectives:
Reginald DE PUYSTER | Prof Stuff DRISCOLL
Dr Colin STARR | Lt VALCOUR

Citation Record: 1 Book

Holiday Homicide - *Only*
Doubleday US (1940); Methuen UK (1941)

Manville MOON

does not have an office, preferring to operate from the premises of the El Patio Café. Although somewhat handicapped by having an artificial leg, he is tough enough, as well as being honest and even pleasingly comic.

American Male Private Detective operating in California

Sidekick: Fausta MORENI
is not just a lovely girlfriend. She comes in useful when the game's afoot.

American Female - Girlfriend

Richard DEMING 1915-1983 (American)
was born in Des Moines, Iowa. He graduated from Washington University, St Louis, 1937, and took an MA at the University of Iowa, Iowa City, 1939, after which he served in the US Army, 1941-1945. A prolific writer for the late pulps and then for magazines and paperbacks, he created two main series detectives and several 'group detectives'. The latter kind were usually invented for TV and later novelized.

Other Byline: Ellery QUEEN

Other Detectives:
Barney CALHOUN | The MOD SQUAD
Matt RUDD

Citation Record: 4 Books

The Gallows In My Garden - *First*
Rinehart US (1952); Boardman UK (1953)

Juvenile Delinquent - *Last*
Boardman UK (1958)

M

Martin MOON

Male Sleuth

Lester MALLOY (British)

Writer: Leonard F MEARES

Citation Record: 3 Books

The Happiest Ghost In Town - *First*
Hale UK (1981)

The Bullet-Proof Toga - *Latest*
Hale UK (1984)

Reggie MOON

has to go back to the 1840s to solve an old murder case.

American Male Private Detective operating in USA

William Dorsey BLAKE (American)

Citation Record: 1 Book

My Time Or Yours - *Single*
Manor US (1979)

Supt MOONEY

British Policeman operating in England

David MAGARSHACK 1899-1977 (British)

Citation Record: 3 Books

Big Ben Strikes Eleven - *First*
Constable UK (1934)

Three Dead - *Last*
Constable UK (1937)

Al MOONEY

is an ex-Marine who, as a PI, operates more or less on the skids, his main aim in life apparently being to prevent his aged Chrysler from being repossessed.

American Male Private Detective operating in Los Angeles

John J MCCALL (American)

Citation Record: 1 Book

Is Money Everything? - *Only*
Consul UK(1964)

Det Sgt Francis MOONEY

is overweight, argumentative, passed over, and nearing retirement from the ranks of New York's finest. In his first book there is a serial killer about who drops concrete blocks from tall buildings; an unsocial practice it is true, but one that hardly worries the police, for the deaths look accidental if coincidental. Only *MOONEY* believes that there is a pattern to the murders and, although it takes some years, tracks down the killer patiently and with great ingenuity.

American Policeman operating in New York

Herbert LIEBERMAN 1933- (American)

Writer: Herbert Henry LIEBERMAN

Inventor of one other detective Paul KONIG

Citation Record: 2 Books

Nightbloom - *First*
Putnam US (1984); Hutchinson UK (1984)

Shadow Dancers - *Latest*
Little, Brown US (1989); Hutchinson UK (1989)

Jerry MOONEY

is an ex-cop. He knows his city and its underworld so well that he has no difficulty in solving cases before the police do.

American Male Private Detective operating in Philadelphia

Kerry O'NEIL 1871-1951 (American)

For writer details see ASHTON-KIRK

Citation Record: 4 Books

Mooney Moves Around - *First*
Reynal US (1939)

Death Strikes At Heron House - *Last*
Farrar, Straus US (1944)

MOONSHINER JACK

American Male Detective in Pulp Magazines operating in USA

Mark MERRICK (American)

Invented 3 detectives - see OLD GOLD-EYE

Citation Record: 1 Selected Short Story

Moonshiner Jack, The Mountain Detective
Old Cap Collier Library US (18??)

John MOORE

American Male Amateur operating in Atlanta

John LOGUE 1933- (American)

Citation Record: 3 Books

Follow The Leader - *First*
Crown US (1949)

Flawless Execution - *Latest*
Ballantine US (1986); Futura UK (1986)

Macon MOORE

American Male Professional Investigator operating in USA

Judson R TAYLOR 1837-1898 (American)

Invented 4 detectives - see Phil SCOTT

Citation Record: 1 Book

Macon Moore, The Southern Detective - *Only*
Ogilvie US (1882)

Dr Sylvan MOORE

investigates a death by shooting in a locked room and the disappearance of the body.

American Male Professional Amateur operating in USA

Stephen BARR (American)

Adopter of one other detective Sherlock HOLMES

Citation Record: 1 Selected Short Story

The Locked House
appeared in the August number.
In 'Ellery Queen's Mystery Magazine' US (1965)

Toussaint 'Touie' MOORE

is black and a veteran of the Second World War and the Ko-

rean War. He worked as a postman before setting up in Harlem as a PI for the Ted Bailey Agency.
American Male Private Detective operating in New York/Ohio/Mexico

Ed LACY 1911-1968 (American)
was born in New York City. He wrote at least twenty-eight genre novels and a great many criminous short stories, 1956-1969, which were published in many of the main crime magazines. He received the Mystery Writers of America Edgar Allan Poe award, 1958.
Writer: Len ZINBERG
Other Detectives:
Marty BOND
Hal DARLING
Barney HARRIS
Lee HAYES
Matt RANZINO
William WALLACE
Dave WINTINO
Citation Record: 2 Books
Room To Swing - *First*
Harper & Row US (1957); Boardman UK (1958)
Moment Of Untruth - *Last*
Lancer US (1964); Boardman UK (1965)

Policeman William MOORE
solves a case of death by strangulation in a locked hospital ward.
American Policeman operating in USA

Fredric NEUMAN 1934- (American)
See main detective Abe REDDEN
Citation Record: 1 Book
The Seclusion Room - *Single*
Viking US (1978); Gollancz UK (1979)

Vincent MORA
American Male Amateur operating in New Jersey

Elmore LEONARD 1935- (American)
Invented 6 detectives - see Frank RYAN
Citation Record: 1 Book
Glitz - *Only*
Arbor US (1975); Viking UK (1975)

'Jigger' MORAN
is a disbarred attorney and a gambling man who likes to live well. He earns a crust as a cab-driver and practises as an unlicensed PI, operating from a front, a News Service on Broadway. His reputation goes before him and his clients are legion.
American Male Private Detective operating in New York

John ROEBURT 1908?-1972 (American)
Inventor of one other detective Johnny DEVEREAUX
Citation Record: 3 Books
Jigger Moran - *First*
Greenberg US (1944); Wells Gardner UK (1948)
Corpse On The Town - *Last*
Graphic US (1950)
The Case Of The Hypnotized Virgin - *Last**
Avon US (1956)

Peter MORAN
is a handyman by day, but at night he is a student of the Acme International Detective Correspondence School. He appears in a number of humorous short stories and has a perfect record in that he is never right about a case.
American Male Private Detective operating in New England

Percival WILDE 1887-1953 (American)
See main detective Bill PARMELEE
Citation Record: 7 Short Stories in 1 Collection
P Moran, Operative - *Collection 1*
Random House US (1947); Gollancz UK (1947)

Bob MORANE
French Male Amateur operating in France

Henri VERNES (French)
Writer: Charles DEWISME
Citation Record: 5 Books
The Dinosaur - *First*
Corgi UK (1966)
Operation Parrot - *Last*
Corgi UK (1968)

Insp Jonas MORCK
Danish Policeman operating in Denmark

Poul ORUM 1919- (Danish)
Citation Record: 2 Books
The Whipping Boy - *First*
is a translation from the Danish of *Syndebuk* (Copenhagen, 1972).
Gollancz UK (1975)
Scapegoat - *First**
Pantheon US (1975)
Nothing But The Truth - *Last*
Gollancz UK (1976); Pantheon US (1976)

Andrew MORDENT
solves a case of death by shooting in a locked library.
British Male Amateur operating in England

Arthur APPLIN 1883-1948? (British)
Citation Record: 1 Book
The Actress - *Only*
Hurst UK (1927); Duffield US (1930)

Dr MORELLE
Male Professional Amateur operating in England

Ernest DUDLEY 1908- (British)
Writer: Vivian Ernest COLTMAN-ALLEN
Other Detectives:
Nat CRAIG
Jimmy STRANGE
Citation Record: 11 Books 37 Short Stories in 3 Collections
Dr Morelle And The Drummer Girl - *First*
Hodder & Stoughton UK (1950)
Nightmare For Dr Morelle - *Last*
Hale UK (1960)
Meet Dr Morelle - *Collection 1*
Short stories - 15
Long UK (1943)
Meet Dr Morelle Again - *Collection 2*
Short stories - 15
Long UK (1944)
Dr Morelle Meets Murder And Other Adventures - *Collection 3*
Short stories - 7
Findon UK (1948)

M

Pedro MORENO
Mexican Male Sleuth operating in Mexico City

Pablo MORALES
Citation Record: 2 Books
Victim For Hire - *First*
Leisure Books US (1979)
Big Deal In Veragua - *Latest*
Leisure Books US (1979)

Cdr MORETON
British Male Amateur operating in several locations

Denis BOYLE (British)
Citation Record: 2 Books
Strange Corpse On Murder Mile - *First*
Hale UK (1960)
Death At Devil-Fish Point - *Last*
Hale UK (1961)

Paddy MORETTI
is a sports reporter who investigates murders in various parts of America, set back into the last two decades of the nineteenth century.
American Male Amateur operating in USA

James SHERBURNE 1925- (American)

Writer: James Robert SHERBURNE

Citation Record: 4 Books

Death's Pale Horse - *First*
Houghton US (1980)

Death's Bright Arrow - *Latest*
Houghton US (1989)

Det Insp MORGAN

British Policeman operating in England

Oswald CRAWFURD 1834-1909 (British)

Writer: Oswald John Frederick CRAWFURD

Inventor of one other detective Purlock HONE

Citation Record: 8 Short Stories in 2 Collections

The Revelations Of Inspector Morgan - *Collection 1*
contains four novelettes.
Short stories - 4
Chapman & Hall UK (1906); Dodd, Mead US (1907)

The League Of The White Hand - *Collection 2*
contains four novelettes.
Short stories - 4
Chapman & Hall UK (1909)

Insp Charles MORGAN

British Policeman operating in England

C St John SPRIGG 1907-1937 (British)

Writer: Christopher St John SPRIGG

Other Detectives:
Insp Bernard BRAY
Insp Bernard BRAY and Charles VENABLES
Charles VENABLES

Citation Record: 1 Book

The Six Queer Things - *Only*
Jenkins UK (1937); Doubleday US (1937)

M

Connie MORGAN

Canadian Female Amateur operating in Alaska/Canada

James B HENDRYX 1880-1963 (Canadian)

Writer: James Beardsley HENDRYX

Other Detectives:
Cpl DOWNEY Policeman Black John SMITH

Citation Record: 9 Books

Connie Morgan In Alaska - *First*
Jarrolds UK (1919); Putnam US (1916)

Connie Morgan In The Arctic - *Last*
Jarrolds UK (1936); Putnam US (1936)

Dave MORGAN

American Male Amateur operating in Chicago

Paul THORNE and Mabel THORNE (American)

See main detective Robert FORRESTER

Citation Record: 1 Book

The Sheridan Road Mystery - *Only*
Dodd, Mead US (1921)

Det Ch Insp David MORGAN

British Policeman operating in England

John BINGHAM 1908-1988 (British)

Invented 3 detectives - see Supt 'Badger' BROCK

Citation Record: 1 Book

The Paton Street Case - *Only*
Gollancz UK (1955)

Inspector Morgan's Dilemma - *Only**
Dodd, Mead US (1956)

David MORGAN

is a member of the Baker Street Irregulars, who are holding their annual dinner. Murder is planned against them and *MORGAN* finds himself in England investigating the crime by the methods of the great Sherlock HOLMES.

American Male Amateur operating in England

H Paul JEFFERS 1934- (American)

Writer: Harry Paul JEFFERS

Other Detectives:
Sherlock HOLMES and Theodore ROOSEVELT
Harry MACNEIL

Citation Record: 1 Book

Murder Most Irregular - *Single*
St Martin's US (1983); Hale UK (1984)

Insp Elwyn MORGAN

British Policeman operating in England

Stewart FARRAR (British)

Citation Record: 3 Books

The Snake On 99 - *First*
Collins UK (1958); Washburn US (1959)

Zero In The Gate - *Last*
Collins UK (1960); Walker US (1961)

Glyn MORGAN

British Male Amateur operating in France

Rosa LAMBERT and Dudley LAMBERT (British)

Citation Record: 4 Books

The Mediterranean Murder - *First*
Wishart UK (1930)

Crime In Quarantine - *Last*
Nelson UK (1938)

Joe MORGAN

is a low-key SIS agent who cracks an international drug network.

British Male Secret Agent operating in Italy

John HOWLETT 1940- (British)

Writer: John Reginald HOWLETT

Citation Record: 1 Book

The Christmas Spy - *Only*
Hutchinson UK (1975); Harcourt Brace US (1975)

Milo MORGAN

American Male Sleuth operating in USA

John LUTZ 1939- (American)

Invented 5 detectives - see Fred CARVER

Citation Record: 1 Selected Short Story

The Case Of The Canine Accomplice
appeared in the March number of the magazine and is to be found in the anthologies, *The Art of the Impossible* (*Xanadu*; UK 1990) and *Murder Impossible* (*Carroll*; US 1990).
In 'Alfred Hitchcock's Mystery Magazine' US (1982)

Mordecai 'Maudie' MORGAN

British Male Amateur operating in England

Peter LACEY (British)

Citation Record: 2 Books

The Limit - *First*
Hodder & Stoughton UK (1988); Doubleday US (1989)

The Bagman - *Latest*
Hodder & Stoughton UK (1989); Doubleday US (1990)

Owen MORGAN

British Male Amateur operating in England

Frederic Arnold KUMMER 1873-1943 (American)

Other Detectives:
Judge Henry TYSON Elinor VANCE

Citation Record: 1 Book

The Green God - *Only*
Watt US (1911)

Rain MORGAN

is a gossip columnist whose enquiries lead her into various cases of murder, which she investigates with much old-fashioned peril to herself.

British Female Amateur operating in England

Lesley GRANT-ADAMSON 1942- (British)

was born in London. She has had an extensive career as a reporter and screenwriter.

Inventor of one other detective Laura FLYNN

Citation Record: 5 Books

Patterns In The Dust - *First*
Faber UK (1985)

Death On Widows Walk - *First**
Scribner's US (1985)

Curse The Darkness - *Latest*
Faber UK (1990); St Martin's US (1990)

Ruff MORGAN

is hardboiled but one of the most stupid private eyes in the genre. He has to stop a bunch of hoodlums stealing a priceless formula for a new narcotic. This he does, mainly by shooting them, not being easily able to think of anything else.

American Male Private Detective operating in New York

Jimmy SHANNON (American)

Citation Record: 1 Book

The Devil's Passkey - *Only*
Appleton US (1952)

'Gutsy' MORGAN

American Male Sleuth operating in USA

Duff JOHNSON 1920- (British)

For writer details see Rogue RANSOM

Citation Record: 2 Books

The Chiseller - *First*
Hamilton Stafford UK (1951)

Rocky Mountain - *Last*
Hamilton Stafford UK (1951)

Molly MORGANTHAU

American Female Amateur operating in New York/New Jersey

Geraldine BONNER 1870-1930 (American)

Citation Record: 2 Books

The Girl At Central - *First*
Appleton UK (1915)

The Black Eagle Mystery - *Last*
Appleton UK (1916)

Johnny MORINI

American Male Sleuth operating in New Orleans

Al CONROY 1924- (American)

For writer details see Pierre-Ange SAWYER

Citation Record: 5 Books

Blood Run - *First*
Lancer UK (1973)

Murder Mission - *Last*
Lancer UK (1973)

Max MORITZ

is a newspaperman who investigates a series of murders and much fornication in Paris.

Male Amateur operating in Paris

Irving MARDER (British)

Citation Record: 1 Book

The Paris Bit - *Only*
Collins UK (1967); Dodd, Mead US (1968)

Sal MORIZIO

American Female Amateur operating in Washington DC

Margaret TRUMAN 1924- (American)

Invented 9 detectives - see Mr Ron FAIRCHILD

Citation Record: 1 Book

Murder On Embassy Row - *Single*
Arbor US (1984)

Leon MORLEY

was used by this prolific author only once. This is hardly surprising, for *MORLEY* is not at all a nice guy and is in the business strictly for the dough.

American Male Private Detective operating in USA

George Harmon COXE 1901-1984 (American)

Invented 20 detectives - see Kent MURDOCK

Citation Record: 1 Book

Alias The Dead - *Only*
Knopf US (1943); Hammond UK (1945)

Pat MORLEY

American Male Sleuth operating in several locations

James BURKE 1921- (American)

Citation Record: 2 Books

A Present For Santa - *First*
St Martin's US (1986); Dent UK (1988)

Spy Story - *Latest*
St Martin's US (1989)

Hugh MORRIS

is an expert on all kinds of rare objects in addition to being an enthusiastic amateur sleuth. Just as well; for, in his one outing, he encounters maniacally obsessed bibliophiles, rare books, and murder.

American Male Amateur operating in Chicago

William TARG 1907- and Louis HERMAN 1905- (American)

Citation Record: 1 Book

The Case Of Mr Cassidy - *Only*
Phoenix Press US (1939)

Wesley MORRIS

British Male Amateur operating in England

Peter DICKINSON 1927- (British)

Invented 3 detectives - see Supt James PIBBLE

Citation Record: 1 Book

The Poison Oracle - *Only*
Hodder & Stoughton UK (1974); Pantheon US (1974)

Ben MORRISON

solves a case of a stabbing in a locked room.

American Male Amateur operating in USA

Sidney WILLIAMS 1878-1949 (American)

was born in Maine and worked as a reporter, editor and drama critic on newspapers in Maine and neighbouring states.

Writer: Sidney Clark WILLIAMS

Inventor of one other detective Jabez TWOMBLEY

Citation Record: 1 Book

The Body In The Blue Room - *Only*
Penn US (1922); Hurst UK (1924)

Dan MORRISON

American Male Sleuth operating in Philadelphia

Joseph SHALLITT (American)

Citation Record: 4 Books

Kiss The Killer - *First*
Lippincott US (1942); Hammond UK (1954)

Juvenile Hoods - *First**
Avon US (1957)

Lady, Don't Die On My Doorstep - *Last*
Lippincott US (1951); Hammond UK (1952)

Edward Gascoyne MORRISON

was the detective in this famous play, later filmed, in which a train disappears at night.

British Policeman operating in England

Arnold RIDLEY 1896- (British)

Citation Record: 1 Book

M

The Ghost Train - *Play*
French UK (1930); French US (1931)

Hugh MORRISON

appears in one book with the author's other detective, *Ev FRANKLIN.*

American Male Sleuth operating in New York

Frank ORENSTEIN 1919- (American)

Invented 3 detectives - see Ev FRANKLIN

Citation Record: 1 Book

A Killing In Real Estate - *Single*
St Martin's US (1989)

Hugh MORRISON

Second detective of Ev FRANKLIN

Nigel MORRISON

British Male Sleuth operating in Paris

Norman FISHER 1910-1972 (British)

Citation Record: 3 Books

Walk At A Steady Pace - *First*
Triton UK (1970); Walker US (1971)

The Last Assignment - *Last*
Triton UK (1972); Walker US (1973)

The Hon Constance Ethel MORRISON-BURKE

is usually known as The Hon Con. She has taken to detecting, she says, as callisthenics fail to satisfy her inner drive and energy. A gentlewomen of independent means and a spinster, she is almost a grotesque in her own mild way. She manages to solve cases more by ineptitude than intellect.

British Female Amateur operating in England

Sidekick: JONES
is the long-suffering companion and assistant of the ineffable *MORRISON-BURKE.*

British Female - Companion

M

Joyce PORTER 1924- (British)

Invented 3 detectives - see Insp Wilfred DOVER

Citation Record: 5 Books

Rather A Common Sort Of Crime - *First*
Weidenfeld & Nicolson UK (1970); McCall US (1970)

The Cart Before The Crime - *Latest*
Weidenfeld & Nicolson UK (1979)

Det Ch Insp John MORRISSEY

British Policeman operating in England

Kay MITCHELL

Citation Record: 4 Books

A Strange Desire - *First*
Constable UK (1993)

A Portion For Foxes - *Latest*
Hodder & Stoughton UK (1995)

Nick MORRO

American Male Sleuth operating in New York

Prosper BURANELLI 1890-1960 (American)

was the editor of Movietone News.

Citation Record: 3 Books

Big Nick - *First*
Doubleday US (1931)

News Reel Murder - *Last*
Funk US (1940)

Bill MORROW and Jacqueline PINKER

British Male Amateur and British Female Amateur operating in England

Carlton ROSS 1889-1965 (British)

For writer details see Insp William (The Grouser) BEEKE

Citation Record: 1 Book

The Black Skull Murders - *Only*
Swan UK (1942)

Insp MORSE

is based in Oxford. His cases are delightful intellectual puzzles as well as being superb exercises in detection. We never know his first name, as is often the case for brilliant cops. He loves music, especially Wagner and Mozart, drinks too much beer, is a bachelor by choice, is often irascible, and suffers fools badly.

British Policeman operating in Oxford

Sidekick: Sgt LEWIS
is an amiable family man, a well characterised sidekick, contrasting admirably with his illustrious superior.

British Male - Subordinate

Colin DEXTER 1930- (British)

was born in Stamford, Lincolnshire. He was educated at Stamford School, 1940-1949, and took a BA in Classics at Christ's College, Cambridge, 1953, followed by an MA, 1958. A Classics teacher at various schools, he published his first detective novel in 1975. Since then he has written less than a dozen detective novels, but they have all been highly acclaimed and justly honoured. He received the Crime Writers Association Silver Dagger award twice, 1979 and 1981, and the Gold Dagger award, 1989.

Writer: Norman Colin DEXTER

Citation Record: 9 Books

Last Bus To Woodstock - *First*
Macmillan UK (1975); St Martin's US (1975)

The Daughters Of Cain - *Latest*
Macmillan UK (1994)

William DIEHL 1924- (British)

Writer: William Francis DIEHL Jr

Citation Record: 1 Book

Inspector Morse's Greatest Mystery - *Only*
UK (1995)

Charlie MORTDECAI

British Male Sleuth operating in England/Channel Islands

Kyril BONFIGLIOLI 1929?-1983?

Citation Record: 3 Books

Don't Point That Thing At Me - *First*
Weidenfeld & Nicolson UK (1972)

Mortdecai's Endgame - *First**
Simon & Schuster US (1973)

After You With The Pistol - *Last*
Secker & Warburg UK (1979); Doubleday US (1980)

Sir Julian MORTHOE

sleuths in 1893, 1909 and 1912.

British Male Amateur operating in England

P W WILSON 1875-1956

Writer: Philip Whitwell WILSON

Citation Record: 3 Books

Bride's Castle - *First*
Boardman UK (1946); Farrar, Straus US (1944)

The Old Mill - *Last*
Boardman UK (1948); Rinehart US (1946)

John MORTON and Sgt DERWENT

British Male Amateur and British Policeman operating in England

L P DAVIES 1914- (British)

Invented 3 detectives - see David CONWAY

Citation Record: 1 Book

A Grave Matter - *Only*
Doubleday US (1967)

Harry MOSEBY

is an introspective, chess-obsessed apology for a shamus who fails to come up with the answers.

American Male Private Detective operating in USA

Alan SHARP 1934- (American)

Citation Record: 1 Book

Night Moves - *Only*
Paperback Library US (1975); Corgi UK (1975)

Sgt Hoke MOSELEY

is in the Homicide division of the Miami Police Force and is usually involved in trying to solve strange cases left over by other detectives on the force. He is middle-aged, lean, and very tough. But he is also intelligent, sensitive, and tolerant in an area not specially noted for those virtues.
!See Appendix 2.

American Policeman operating in Florida

Charles WILLEFORD 1919-1988 (American)

was both a soldier and a Professor of English. His literary work, although not extensive, gives an exquisite picture of the lower end of life in South Florida, within the narrow compass of the hardboiled detective story.

Writer: Charles Ray WILLEFORD III

Inventor of one other detective Jacob C 'Jake' BLAKE

Citation Record: 4 Books

Miami Blues - *First*
St Martin's US (1984); Futura UK (1985)

The Way We Die Now - *Latest*
Macmillan US (1988); Random House US (1989)

Insp MOSER

appears in stories based on real experiences and told by himself.

British Policeman operating in London

Maurice Moser and Charles F RIDEAL (British)

Citation Record: 32 Short Stories in 2 Collection

Stories From Scotland Yard - *Collection 1*
Short stories - 21
Routledge UK (1890)

True Detective Stories - *Collection 2*
Short stories - 11
Trischler UK (1889); Lovell US (1890)

Insp MOSLEY

is a lonely man, in his middle fifties, usually shabbily dressed but always wearing a black Homberg on his head as he polices the bleak Lancashire-Yorkshire border country that is his life. Difficult to work with, not trusted by his superiors, he is a kind of one-man police force, solving crimes by slow patient work and by knowing everything about his territory and the ways of the people in it. Sometimes he metes out his own private form of justice, but always within the law.

British Policeman operating in Lancashire/Yorkshire

Stooge: Det Supt GRIMSHAW
is *MOSLEY's* superior and hounds him incessantly, never understanding how he works, or even where he is, and constantly wondering if he can get on without him.
British Male

John GREENWOOD 1921-1986 (British)

Writer: John Buxton HILTON

Citation Record: 6 Books

Murder, Mr Mosley - *First*
Quartet UK (1983); Walker US (1983)

What Me, Mr Mosley? - *Last*
Quartet UK (1988); Walker US (1988)

Max MOSS

American Male Sleuth operating in USA/Australia

Steven L THOMPSON 1948- (American)

Writer: Steven Lynn THOMPSON

Citation Record: 4 Books

Recovery - *First*
Warner US (1980); New English Library UK (1981)

Top End - *Latest*
Worldwide US (1989)

Insp Phil MOSS

Second detective of Det Ch Insp Colin THANE

Maj MOSSON

British Male Amateur operating in England

Leslie CARGILL (British)

Inventor of one other detective Morrison SHARPE

Citation Record: 4 Books

It Might Have Meant Murder - *First*
Jenkins UK (1940)

Next Door To Murder - *Last*
Jenkins UK (1948)

Col MOSTYN

continues the long line of British adventurer-heroes, doing a little detecting in the course of his undercover jobs for the government.

British Male Secret Agent operating in England/Germany

Mark HEBDEN 1916- (British)

See main detective Insp Clovis Desire PEL

Citation Record: 3 Books

Mask Of Violence - *First*
Harcourt Brace US (1970); Joseph UK (1971)

A Pride Of Dolphins - *Last*
Joseph UK (1974); Harcourt Brace UK (1975)

Mr MOTO

is a Japanese, well-educated aristocrat, speaking many languages, including flawless English. In exotic locales, he is involved with Americans in trouble and he uses his unusually acute qualities to solve some difficult problems. He appeared in a number of films, so popular was he in the 1940s.

Japanese Male Amateur operating in Far East

John P MARQUAND 1893-1960 (American)

was born in Wilmington, Delaware. Educated at Newbury High School, Massachusetts, he took a an AB at Harvard University, Cambridge, Massachusetts, 1915. He had a distinguished career in the US Army in the First World War and was a war correspondent in the Second World War. Author of novels, plays, and stories in several fields, he received the Pulitzer Prize, 1938, and many other literary awards and honours from American universities.

Writer: John Phillips MARQUAND

Citation Record: 6 Books

No Hero - *First*
Little, Brown US (1935)

Mr Moto Takes A Hand - *First**
Hale UK (1940)

Your Turn, Mr Moto - *First**
Berkley US (1963)

Stopover: Tokyo - *Last*
Little, Brown US (1957); Collins UK (1957)

The Last Of Mr Moto - *Last**
Berkley US (1963)

Right You Are, Mr Moto - *Last**
Popular Library US (1977)

Daisy Jane MOTT

American Female Amateur operating in New York

Jennifer JONES (American)

Writers: Margaret LANE and Enid JOHNSON

Citation Record: 3 Books

Murder-On-Hudson - *First*
Crowell US (1937)

Murder Al Fresco - *Last*
Doubleday US (1939)

J Molden MOTT

is an explorer and big-game hunter who turns amateur detective.

British Male Amateur operating in Russia

Sidekick: Tania LEVIN
Russian Female - Assistant

John BLACKBURN 1923- (British)
Invented 4 detectives - see Gen Charles KIRK
Citation Record: 1 Book
Dead Man Running - *Only*
Secker & Warburg UK (1960); Mill US (1961)

Lucie MOTT
runs Mott's Enquiry Agency and is a rather unsuccessful detective, failing in most of the cases that comprise the stories in this collection.
British Female Private Detective operating in London

E Phillips OPPENHEIM 1866-1946 (British)
Invented 27 detectives - see Nicholas GOADE
Citation Record: 10 Short Stories in 1 Collection
Ask Miss Mott - *Collection 1*
Hodder & Stoughton UK (1936); Little, Brown US (1937)

Winslow MOULT
British Male Amateur operating in several locations

B L JACOT 1898-1977
Writer: Bernard Louis Jacot DE BOINOD
Citation Record: 10 Short Stories in 1 Collection
Winslow Moult - *Collection 1*
Not all the stories are criminous.
Rich UK (1934)

Capt MOUNSELL
British Male Amateur operating in Spain

W Willmott DIXON 1843- (British)
Writer: Willmott Willmott DIXON
Citation Record: 14 Short Stories in 1 Collection
The Adventures Of Captain Mounsell - *Collection 1*
Everett UK (1902)

MOUNTED POLICEMAN MARK
American Male Detective in Pulp Magazines operating in New York

Police Captain HOWARD (American)
Invented 15 detectives - see LIGHTNING LUKE
Citation Record: 1 Selected Short Story
Mounted Policeman Mark; Or, The Central Park Detective's Great Cremation Case
New York Detective Library US (1882-8)

MOURA
sleuths during the Napoleonic Wars, 1793-1815.
Sleuth operating in France/Italy

Virginia COFFMAN 1914- (American)
See main detective Lucifer COVE
Citation Record: 4 Books
Moura - *First*
Crown US (1959)
The Dark Gondola - *Last*
Ace US (1968)
The Dark Beyond Moura - *Last**
Ace US (1977)

Lt MOYNAHAN, Millicent HETHEREGE and Bill STRATTON
American Male Policeman, American Female Amateur, and American Male Amateur operating in USA

Robert BERNARD 1918- (American)
Invented 3 detectives - see Prof Richard HALSEY
Citation Record: 1 Book
Deadly Meeting - *Only*
Norton US (1970)

Dr MUCH
American Male Amateur operating in New Zealand

Simon JAY 1920- (New Zealander)
Writer: Colin James ALEXANDER
Citation Record: 1 Book
Death Of A Skin Diver - *Only*
Collins UK (1964); Doubleday US (1964)

Charlie MUFFIN
is a loner and a loser, working for British Intelligence in a series of sordid adventures, in which both sides are rotten. Deceived by his spymasters time and time again, he is always blackmailed into going back to work for them.
British Male Professional Investigator operating in several locations

Brian FREEMANTLE 1936- (British)
was born in Southampton, Hampshire. He worked as a foreign correspondent and editor on several London newspapers before turning to full-time writing. He is the author of at least thirty genre novels under his real name and a pseudonym.
Writer: Brian Harry FREEMANTLE
Inventor of one other detective Samuel BELL
Citation Record: 9 Books
Charlie Muffin - *First*
Cape UK (1977)
Charlie M - *First**
Doubleday US (1977)
Comrade Charlie - *Latest*
Century UK (1989)

Andrew MUIR
Appears with at least two other detectives - see Insp MILD

Ch Det Insp George MUIR
appears also in books with another of the author's detectives, *Supt Andrew ASH.*
British Policeman operating in England

Francis GRIERSON 1888-1972 (British)
was a journalist and editor and the author of over fifty genre novels.
Writer: Francis Durham GRIERSON
Other Detectives:
Supt Andrew ASH
Supt Andrew ASH and Ch Det Insp George MUIR
Richard FURLING
Commissaire PATRAS
Prof WELLS
Citation Record: 9 Books
The Cabaret Crime - *First*
Butterworth UK (1938)
Boomerang Murder - *Last*
Hutchinson UK (1951)

Ch Det Insp George MUIR
Second detective of Supt Andrew ASH

Steve MUIRHEAD
American Male Amateur operating in New York

Lyon MEARSON 1888-1966 (American)
Citation Record: 1 Book
Phantom Fingers - *Only*
Macaulay US (1927); Hutchinson UK (1929)

Policewoman Norah MULCAHANEY
is a policewoman who plays a leading role in what are virtually minimal police procedurals. The series of books follows developments in her work, her marriage, and her eventual widowing.
American Policewoman operating in New York

Lillian O'DONNELL 1926- (American)
was born in Trieste, which was then in Italy. An actress on stage and later in TV, she has found the time to write many detective novels.
Writer: Lillian Udvardy O'DONNELL

Other Detectives:

Mici ANHALT	Gwen RAMADGE

Citation Record: 11 Books

The Phone Calls - *First*
Putnam US (1972); Hodder & Stoughton UK (1972)

The Other Side Of The Door - *Latest*
Putnam US (1987)

Eugene MULCAHY

British Male Amateur operating in England

James STREET (British)

See main detective Supt ROMER

Citation Record: 2 Books

Death In An Armchair - *First*
Jenkins UK (1936)

A Wastrel Goes West - *Last*
Low UK (1937)

Kate MULCAY

American Female Private Detective operating in Atlanta

Celestine SIBLEY (American)

Citation Record: 1 Book

A Plague Of Kinfolks - *Single*
HarperCollins US (1995)

Kip MULDANE

appeared in stories in *Black Mask Magazine* in the 1930s.

Hawaiian Male Private Detective operating in Hawaii

Steve FISHER 1912-1980 (American)

Invented 4 detectives - see Joe SAXON

No citations

Hart MULDOON

Male Sleuth operating in Cairo/the Caribbean

John FLAGG (American)

Writer: John GEARON

Citation Record: 5 Books

Woman Of Cairo - *First*
GM US (1953); Muller UK (1954)

The Paradise Gun - *Last*
GM US (1961); Muller UK (1962)

Gordon MULDREW

British Male Amateur operating in England/USA

Luke ALLAN ?-1962 (British)

See main detective BLUE PETE

Citation Record: 7 Books

The Jungle Crime - *First*
Arrowsmith UK (1931)

Murder At The Club - *Last*
Arrowsmith UK (1933)

Sgt MULHEISEN

American Policeman operating in Detroit

Jon A JACKSON 1938- (American)

Writer: Jon Anthony JACKSON

Citation Record: 3 Books

The Diehard - *First*
Random House US (1977); Hale UK (1978)

Groota - *Latest*
Foul Play US (1992)

Pat MULLANCY

was an Irish-American detective appearing in stories in *Private Detective* in the 1940s.

American Male Detective in Pulp Magazines operating in USA

Roger TORREY (American)

Other Detectives:

Johnny CASS	Shean CONNELL
Riley KEENAN	Pat MALONE
Pat O'LEARY	John RYAN

No citations

A B C MULLER

appears in a strange story of a case within a case, in which a minor character, *MULLER*, takes over the analysis from the orthodox detective, Smith, proving everybody else wrong, although in the end we do not know whether *MULLER* is actually right.

American Male Amateur operating in Hollywood

Cameron MCCABE 1915- (American)

Writer: Ernest W J BORNEMAN

Citation Record: 1 Book

The Face On The Cutting Room Floor - *Only*
Gregg US (1981); Gollancz UK (1937)

Joe MULLER

!See Appendix 2.

Austrian Male Amateur operating in Austria/Middle East

Grace Isabel COLBRON 1869-1948 (American) and Augusta GRONER 1850- (Austrian)

Citation Record: 5 Short Stories in 1 Collection

Joe Muller, Detective - *Collection 1*
Duffield US (1910)

Augusta GRONER 1850- (Austrian)

Citation Record: 2 Books

The Man With The Black Cord - *First*
Chatto UK (1911); Duffield US (1911)

Mene Tekel: A Tale Of Strange Happenings - *Last*
Duffield US (1912)

Augusta GRONER 1850- (Austrian) and Grace Isobel COLBRON 1869-1948 (American)

Citation Record: 1 Book

The Lady In Blue - *Only*
Duffield US (1922)

Paul MULLER

is an American PI created by a British author, with the usual consequences. He operates in the fictional town of Anfield, somewhere in the western part of the USA.

American Male Private Detective operating in USA

Paul MULLER 1924- (British)

Writer: Albert KING

Other Byline: Simon WALDRON

Citation Record: 15 Books

Make Mine Mayhem - *First*
Hale UK (1967)

A Viper In Her Bosom - *Last*
Hale UK (1975)

Insp 'Dusty' MULLER and 'Tiny' MELDRUM

British Policeman and British Male Sleuth operating in England

Alec GLANVILLE 1902- (British)

Writer: Alexander Haig Glanville GRIEVE

Citation Record: 2 Books

Death Goes Ashore - *First*
Harrap UK (1936)

The Body In The Trawl - *Last*
Harrap UK (1938)

Patrick MULLIGAN

is an Irish lawyer practising in England who, as he becomes involved in the usual types of society case of the era, finds he must do detective as well as legal work. His morals are in doubt, it seems, as he is occasionally seen with a French novel in his coat pocket.

Irish Male Amateur operating in England

Baroness ORCZY 1865-1947 (British)

Invented 6 detectives - see Lady Molly DE MAZEREEN

Citation Record: 12 Short Stories in 1 Collection

Skin O' My Tooth - *Collection 1*
Hodder & Stoughton UK (1928); Doubleday US (1928)

Tim MULLIGAN and Elsie May HUNT

are archaeologists who seem to meet murder in every exotic location at which they dig.

American Male Amateur and American Female Amateur operating in several locations

Aaron Marc STEIN 1906-1985 (American)

See main detective Matt ERRIDGE

Citation Record: 18 Books

The Sun Is A Witness - *First*
Doubleday US (1940)

Moonmilk And Murder - *Last*
Doubleday US (1955); Macdonald UK (1956)

Adrian MULLINER

is perhaps a relative of the author's classic creation, Mr Mulliner, for here he is in a London Club telling a story in which he analyses certain aspects of the *Sherlock HOLMES* canon and concludes that *HOLMES* was in fact *Professor MORIARTY*, the arch-criminal. Interestingly enough, it is an idea that has been exploited by others.

British Male Private Detective operating in London

P G WODEHOUSE 1881-1975 (British)

was born in England, where he lived and wrote during the early part of his life, but he went to the USA in the 1920s and stayed to write many more books and to collaborate on the librettos of musicals. The author of many novels, much verse, plays, and pastiches, he is without doubt the greatest British comic writer of the twentieth century. He is the author of at least this one criminous story, which, although not quite a *Sherlock HOLMES* pastiche, almost deserves to be treated as one.

Writer: Pelham Grenville WODEHOUSE

Citation Record: 1 Selected Short Story

From A Detective's Notebook - *Parody 1*
appeared in the May number and is also in the anthology, *THE MISADVENTURES OF SHERLOCK HOLMES* (Editor; *Sebastian WOLFE*).
In 'Punch' UK (1959)

M

Insp MULLINS

British Policeman operating in England

Scobie MACKENZIE 1906- (American)

Citation Record: 1 Book

Three Dead, One Hurt - *Only*
Eyre & Spottiswoode UK (1934)

Jane D MULROY

operates from an office in Woodward Avenue, Birmingham, near Detroit. As Irish as they come, she gives the appearance of being just a sweet little thing. But do not be fooled. She totes a .32 and has the assistance of a formidable sidekick should she get into trouble during her sleuthing.

American Female Private Detective operating in Michigan/Florida

Sidekick: Ahmad DAKAR
is an ex-professional baseball player (with the Miami Dolphins) and a karate black belt. How useful for the little female sleuth in whose mouth butter would not even soften!

American Male - Assistant

Richard R WERRY 1916- (American)

Citation Record: 2 Books

Casket For A Living Lady - *First*
Dodd, Mead US (1985)

A Delicately Personal Matter - *Latest*
Dodd, Mead US (1986)

Al MUNDY

is in novelizations of episodes from a TV series.

Male Sleuth operating in Switzerland/Brazil

Gil BREWER 1922-1983 (American)

Invented 3 detectives - see Bill MADDERN

Citation Record: 3 Books

Appointment In Hell - *First*
Monarch US (1961)

The Devil In Davos - *Last*
Ace US (1969)

MUNPA

Male Sleuth

Alexandra DAVID-NEEL and Lama YONGDEN (American)

Citation Record: 1 Book

The Power Of Nothingness - *Single*
Houghton US (1982)

Peter MUNRO

foils KGB plots.

British Male Secret Agent operating in Greece/Lebanon

Ian Stuart BLACK 1915- (British)

Citation Record: 2 Books

The Man On The Bridge - *First*
Constable UK (1975); St Martin's US (1977)

Journey To A Safe Place - *Last*
Constable UK (1979); St Martin's US (1979)

Stephen MUNRO

is a temporary footman who solves the mystery of the disappearance of a woman during a seance.

British Male Amateur operating in England

A Monmouth PLATTS 1893-1971 (British)

was a pseudonym that the famous author only used once for a genre novel.

For writer details see Roger SHERINGHAM

Citation Record: 1 Book

Cicely Disappears - *Only*
Long UK (1927)

MURA

American Female Detective in Pulp Magazines operating in USA

OLD SLEUTH (American)

Invented 40 detectives - see Brant ADAMS

Citation Record: 1 Book

Mura, The Western Lady Detective - *Only*
Munro US

Sam MURCHISON

American Male Private Detective operating in New York

Antoine DE CAUNES (French)

Citation Record: 1 Book

Good - But Hot - *Single*
Fourth Estate UK (1991)

Const MURDOCH

solves a case of 'impossible' murder, in which a man is shot in open country.

British Policeman operating in England

Lynton BLOW (British)

Citation Record: 1 Book

The Bournewick Murders - *Only*
Butterworth UK (1935)

Bruce MURDOCH

is one of this author's racy adventurers fighting crime and appearing under a special byline.

British Male Professional Investigator operating in Europe

Norman DEANE 1908-1973 (British)

For writer details see Insp Roger 'Handsome' WEST

Inventor of one other detective The LIBERATOR

Citation Record: 6 Books

Secret Errand - *First*
Hurst & Blackett UK (1939); McKay US (1974)

Where Is The Withered Man? - *Last*
Hurst & Blackett UK (1941); McKay US (1972)

Jennifer MURDOCK

Appears with at least two other detectives - see Rachel MURDOCK

Jennifer MURDOCK

Second detective of Rachel MURDOCK

Joyce MURDOCK

Second detective of Kent MURDOCK

Kent MURDOCK

is a newspaper photographer who is frequently brought into contact with crimes and sets out to solve them. He is more socially sophisticated than the author's other photographer sleuth, *Flashgun CASEY*. He appears also in books with another of the author's detectives, *Jack FENNER*.

American Male Amateur operating in Boston

George Harmon COXE 1901-1984 (American)

was born in Olean, New York. He graduated from Purdue University, West Lafayette, Indiana, and Cornell University, Ithaca, New York, 1921. He was a journalist and prolific writer of short stories for the pulps of the 1930s, 1940s and 1950s. He was also the author of many detective novels, creating several detectives and private eyes, usually locating them in Boston. He received the Mystery Writers of America Grand Master award, 1964.

Other Detectives:
Dave BARNUM and Capt VAUGHN
Paul BARON
Alan CARLISLE
'Flashgun' CASEY
Sam CROMBIE
Jack FENNER
Max Chauncy HALE
Alan MAXWELL
Leon MORLEY
Kent MURDOCK and Jack FENNER
Kent MURDOCK and Joyce MURDOCK
Jerry NASON
Larry PALMER
Bill RAEBURN
Knox RANDALL
Spence RANKIN
Capt Alan SCOTT
Dr Paul STANDISH
Andrew TALBOT

Citation Record: 15 Books

The Barotique Mystery - *First*
Knopf US (1936); Heinemann UK (1937)

Murdock's Acid Test - *First**
Dell US (1947)

An Easy Way To Go - *Last*
Knopf US (1969); Hale UK (1969)

Kent MURDOCK and Joyce MURDOCK

Kent MURDOCK, the author's long-running sleuth, is married to *Joyce MURDOCK* and they worked together in one book. However, she proved so strong a character that she stole the limelight from her husband and the author subsequently dropped her.

American Male Amateur and American Female Amateur operating in USA

George Harmon COXE 1901-1984 (American)

Invented 20 detectives - see Kent MURDOCK

Citation Record: 1 Book

Mrs Murdock Takes A Case - *Only*
Knopf US (1941); Swan UK (1949)

Kent MURDOCK and Jack FENNER

also appear individually in other books by this author.

American Male Amateur and American Male Private Detective operating in Boston/New York

George Harmon COXE 1901-1984 (American)

Invented 20 detectives - see Kent MURDOCK

Citation Record: 6 Books

Murder With Pictures - *First*
Knopf US (1935); Heinemann UK (1937)

The Silent Witness - *Last*
Knopf US (1973); Hale UK (1974)

Matt MURDOCK

American Male Private Detective operating in California

Robert RAY 1935- (American)

Writer: Robert Joseph RAY

Inventor of one other detective Clayton 'Yankee' TAGGART

Citation Record: 3 Books

Murdock For Hire - *First*
US (1987)

Dial 'M' For Murdock - *Latest*
US (1988)

Page MURDOCK

American Male Amateur operating in USA

Loren D ESTLEMAN 1952- (American)

Invented 7 detectives - see Amos WALKER

Citation Record: 1 Book

The Stranglers - *Single*
Doubleday US (1984)

Rachel MURDOCK and Jennifer MURDOCK

are elderly spinsters. *Jennifer MURDOCK* is two years older than her sister, notices everything and is a veritable battle-axe of an old lady. *Rachel MURDOCK* is slim, tiny, zany, out for any good time she can get, and is always accompanied by her black cat, Samantha, who figures largely in the books. Their contrasting characters make them a formidable pair of sleuths when Californian-style murder arrives, as it often does. In some books they are joined in friendly rivalry by the author's other detective, *Lt Stephen MAYHEW*.

American Female Amateurs operating in California

D B OLSEN 1907-1973 (American)

Invented 5 detectives - see Lt Stephen MAYHEW

Citation Record: 8 Books

The Alarm Of The Black Cat - *First*
Doubleday US (1942)

Death Walks On Cat's Feet - *Last*
Doubleday US (1956)

Rachel MURDOCK, Jennifer MURDOCK and Lt Stephen MAYHEW

Two American Female Amateurs and one American Policeman operating in USA

D B OLSEN 1907-1973 (American)

Invented 5 detectives - see Lt Stephen MAYHEW

Citation Record: 5 Books

The Cat Saw Murder - *First*
Doubleday US (1939); Heinemann UK (1940)

Cats Don't Need Coffins - *Last*
Doubleday US (1946)

William MURGATROYD

American Male Amateur operating in New York

William Hamilton OSBORNE 1873-1942 (American)

Citation Record: 2 Books

The Red Mouse - *First*
Dodd, Mead US (1909); Hodder & Stoughton UK (1916)

The Running Fight - *Last*
Dodd, Mead US (1910)

Heron MURMER

British Male Professional Investigator operating in Far East

Simon HARVESTER 1910-1875 (British)

Invented 4 detectives - see Dorian SILK

Citation Record: 2 Books

The Chinese Hammer - *First*
Jarrolds UK (1960); Walker US (1961)

Troika - *Last*
Jarrolds UK (1962)

The Flying Horse - *Last*
Walker US (1974)

Patrolman MURPHY
was called The Neighbourhood Cop. He appeared in stories, 1944-1952, in *Blue Book.*

American Policeman operating in USA

Joel REEVE 1901-1985 (American)

For writer details see Tom KINCAID

Citation Record: 2 Selected Short Stories

A Lady Swings Her Right
In 'Blue Book' US (1944)

Set A Thief
In 'Blue Book' US (1962)

MURPHY and MCTAVISH
solve a case of death by shooting in a locked room containing secret codes.

British Male Sleuths operating in England

Rex HARDINGE 1904- (British)

was born in India and educated in England, where he mainly lived. He wrote many novels and short stories set in India or Africa, usually under the other byline.

Writer: Charles Wrexe HARDINGE

Other Byline: "CAPSTAN"

Adopter of one other detective Sexton BLAKE

Citation Record: 1 Book

The Problem In Ciphers - *Only*
Wright UK (1952)

Mrs MURPHY
is a cat who is said to be 'the greatest detective on four legs'. Assisted by a mentally inferior Welsh Corgi, she sleuths delightfully.

Female Cat operating in Virginia

Rita Mae BROWN 1944- (American)

Citation Record: 3 Books

Wish You Were Here - *First*
Bantam US (1990); Curley UK (1992)

Murder At Monticello - *Latest*
Bantam US (1994)

Addison Frank MURPHY
was a peripatetic newspaperman, known as 'The Rambler', who roved the United States working for various newspapers in the Depression years of the 1930s.

American Male Amateur operating in USA

Fred MACISAAC 1886-1940 (American)

Invented 3 detectives - see Dick HADDEN

No citations

Frank MURPHY
American Male Sleuth operating in Philadelphia

Daniel LYNCH (American)

Citation Record: 4 Books

Deadly Ernest - *First*
Zebra US (1986)

Bad Fortune - *Latest*
Pinnacle US (1989)

Sgt Jake MURPHY
formerly trained for the priesthood; but he abandoned his studies, married, and had three children. He now works as a cop in the Homicide division. He appears in a gothic tale of unbelievable dimensions, in which he seems to do very little except exude his powers of inner spirituality. His case concerns drugs, homosexuality, pornography, blackmail, robbery, kidnapping, murder, to name but a few. He solves it, of course. He commits, in the process, the once inadmissible, but now apparently tolerated, sin of bedding the heroine-suspect half way through the book.

American Policeman operating in Boston

Alex JUNIPER

Writer: UNKNOWN

Citation Record: 1 Book

A Very Proper Death - *Single*
Virago UK (1992)

Patsy MURPHY
American Detective in Pulp Magazines operating in USA

Nicholas CARTER 1861-1909 (American)

Writer: Frederick Russell BURTON

Other Detectives:
Nick CARTER, Trim CARTER, Harvey STOKES

Citation Record: 10 Books

At Odds With Scotland Yard - *First*
Street & Smith (Magnet #49) US (1898)

The King's Prisoner; Or, Patsy Plays a Lone Hand - *Last*
Street & Smith (New Magnet #677) US (1908)

Insp Bill MURRAY
!See Appendix 2.

British Policeman operating in England

Aubrey COLIN (British)

Citation Record: 2 Books

Hands Of Death - *First*
Hammond UK (1963)

Death Comes To Dinner - *Last*
Hammond UK (1965)

Pete MURRAY
American Male Amateur operating in Illinois

Henry Kitchell WEBSTER 1875-1932 (American)

Invented 4 detectives - see Prof Brinsley BUTLER

Citation Record: 1 Book

Who Is The Next? - *Only*
Bobbs US (1931); Garland UK (1976)

Ferriss MURTAGH
American Male Private Detective operating in Chicago

Lawrence L LYNCH (American)

Invented 11 detectives - see Neil J BATHURST

Citation Record: 1 Book

A Dead Man's Step: A Detective Story - *Only*
Rand, McNally US (1893); Ward, Lock UK (1893)

Larry MURTAGH
American Male Detective in Pulp Magazines operating in USA

Bernard WAYDE (American)

Other Detectives:
HARDSCRABBLE, Rody ROGAN

Citation Record: 1 Selected Short Story

Larry Murtagh's Missing Ear Case; Or, A Clew To The Murder Of Langley, The Broker
Old Cap Collier Library US (18??)

Lt Janus MURTAUGH
is a cop in the New York Police Department, hunting a remarkable serial killer who murders for a fee.

American Policeman operating in New York

Sidekick: Sgt EBERHART
American Male - Subordinate

Barbara PAUL (American)

Invented 8 detectives - see Lt TOOMEY

Citation Record: 1 Book

Kill Fee - *Single*
Scribner's US (1985); Collins UK (1985)

Det Insp MUSGRAVE
investigates the murder of the baritone of an opera company, an episode that threatens the production of Mozart's masterpiece.

British Policeman operating in England

Ellis PETERS 1913-1995 (British)

Invented 4 detectives - see Brother CADFAEL

Citation Record: 1 Book

The Funeral Of Figaro - *Only*
Collins UK (1962); Morrow US (1964)

MUSH and POKE

American Male Sleuths operating in USA

Arthur Le Roy KASER 1890-1956 (American)

Citation Record: 1 Book

Mush And Poke, Detectives - *Play*
Denison US (1930)

Buddy MUSTARD

is British but seems like a mixed-up American PI. He runs Mustard Investigations in Piccadilly.

British Male Private Detective operating in London

Roland DANIEL 1880-1969 (British)

Invented 11 detectives - see Insp Neville LANGHAM

Citation Record: 13 Books

The Crawshay Jewel Mystery - *First*
Wright UK (1941)

The Gangster's Daughter - *Last*
Wright UK (1964)

Mr MYCROFT

is a detective who, we are told 'keeps bees in the English countryside'. He is, in fact, a delightful and mild parody of *Sherlock HOLMES*, who, of course, also retired to keep bees in Sussex. His name is an allusion to the latter's brilliant brother and, for all Sherlockians, the other allusions in the books are there to enjoy.

British Male Amateur operating in England/California

Sidekick: SILCHESTER

British Male - Narrator

H F HEARD 1889-1971 (British)

was born in London. He took a BA in History at Gonville and Caius College, Cambridge, 1911. A journalist, he emigrated to the USA, 1937, where he lectured on science and religion.

Writer: Henry Fitzgerald HEARD

Citation Record: 3 Books

A Taste For Honey - *First*
Cassell UK (1942); Vanguard US (1941)

A Taste For Murder - *First**
Avon US (1955)

The Notched Hairpin - *Last*
Cassell UK (1951); Vanguard US (1949)

Rosie MYERS

American Female Sleuth operating in USA

Susan ISAACS 1943- (American)

Inventor of one other detective pair Nelson SHARPE and Judith SINGER

Citation Record: 1 Book

After All These Years - *Single*
HarperCollins UK (1993)

Dora MYRL

is one of the earliest lady detectives in British fiction, appearing also as a sidekick in books featuring the author's other detective, *Paul BECK*.

British Female Professional Amateur operating in London

M McDonnell BODKIN 1850-1933 (British)

Invented 3 detectives - see Paul BECK

Citation Record: 12 Short Stories in 1 Collection

Dora Myrl, The Lady Detective - *Collection 1*
Chatto UK (1900)

— N —

Lee NACE

was a 'scientific' detective in the pulps who was known as The Blond Adder because of a snake-like scar on his forehead, acquired when a wicked Chinaman threw a knife at him.
!See Appendix 2.

American Male Detective in Pulp Magazines operating in USA

Lester DENT 1904-1959 (American)

Invented 9 detectives - see Chance MALLOY

Citation Record: 1 Selected Short Story

The Tank Of Terror
is also in an anthology, *A Cent A Story! The Best from Ten Detective Aces* (Editor; Garyn G. Roberts; 1986).
In 'Ten Detective Aces' US (1933)

Kesho NAIK

Indian Male Amateur operating in India

Sir Edmund C COX 1856- (British)

See main detective John CARRUTHERS

Citation Record: 12 Short Stories in 1 Collection

The Exploits Of Kesho Naik, Dacoit - *Collection 1*
Constable UK (1912)

David NAIRN

British Male Sleuth operating in Asia

Michael HARTLAND 1941- (British)

See main detective Sarah CABLE

Citation Record: 2 Books

Down Among The Dead Men - *First*
Hodder & Stoughton UK (1983); Macmillan US (1983)

The Third Betrayal - *Latest*
Hodder & Stoughton UK (1986); Macmillan US (1987)

NAMELESS DETECTIVE

is a large man, middle-aged, an ex-policeman of Italian extraction who now operates from an office on Drumm Street. His real name is never disclosed but his character is open for all to see. An avid reader of pulp magazines (he owns over 6000 titles), he is a PI who, while not made out to be brilliant, is absolutely right in his job. He is in the line of all the classic Californian private eyes descended from *The CONTINENTAL OP*, upholding the public law rather than a private code and he has no need of a gun to enforce it. His only worries are his health, whether or not he has cancer, his increasing girth, and the sorry state of his bank balance. He appears also in some books with other authors' detectives, notably *Sharon MCCONE* and *Lt Frank HASTINGS*.

American Male Private Detective operating in San Francisco

Bill PRONZINI 1943- (American)

was born in Petaluma, California. One of the modern masters of detective fiction, he is a prolific writer of novels, short stories, critical works and biography. Although he has created several excellent detectives, he likes working with other genre authors, taking over their detectives and even combining his with theirs.

Writer: William John PRONZINI

Other Byline: Jack FOXX

Other Detectives:

Buckmaster GILLOON	Steven GIROUX
Sherlock HOLMES	John QUINCANNON

Citation Record: 17 Books 10 Short Stories in 1 Collection

The Snatch - *First*
Random House US (1971); Hale UK (1974)

Demons - *Latest*
Delacorte US (1993)

Casefile: The Best Of The 'Nameless Detective' Stories - *Collection 1*
St Martin's US (1983)

NAMELESS DETECTIVE and Lt Frank HASTINGS

The NAMELESS DETECTIVE, the creation of *Bill PRONZINI,* appears in books on his own and in books with another author's detective, the latter written under joint authorship. Here he appears with *Frank HASTINGS,* the police detective created by *Collin WILCOX.*

American Male Private Detective and American Policeman operating in San Francisco

Bill PRONZINI and Collin WILCOX (American)

have each published many works in the criminous field and have created other detectives. *Bill PRONZINI* has collaborated with other authors to produce works in which their respective detectives work jointly.

Writers: William John PRONZINI 1943- and Collin WILCOX 1924-

Citation Record: 1 Book

Twospot - *Single*
Putnam US (1978)

NAMELESS DETECTIVE and Sharon MCCONE

The NAMELESS DETECTIVE, created by *Bill PRONZINI,* appears here with *Sharon MCCONE,* the creation of *Marcia MULLER.*

American Male Private Detective and American Female Private Detective operating in San Francisco

Bill PRONZINI and Marcia MULLER (American)

Writer: William John PRONZINI 1943- and Marcia MULLER 1944-

Inventor of one other detective pair Elena OLIVEREZ and John QUINCANNON

Citation Record: 1 Book

Double - *Single*
St Martin's US (1984)

N

Georgie NAPPER

appears in an American play of the late Victorian era, a farce in which she sets out to capture a crook called Burglar Bill.

American Female Amateur operating in USA

Sarah Folsom ENNEBUSKE (American)

Citation Record: 1 Book

A Detective In Petticoats: A Comedy In Three Acts For Female Characters Only - *Play*
US (1900)

Insp Jon NAPPLEBY

is a parody of *Michael INNES'* detective, *John APPLEBY.*

Appears with at least two other detectives. For more information, if available see under Mallory KING

Capt Prem NARAYAN

Indian Policeman operating in India

Melvin A CASBERG 1909- (American)

Citation Record: 3 Books

Death Stalks The Punjab - *First*
Strawberry Hill US (1980)

Dowry Of Death - *Latest*
Strawberry Hill US (1984)

Insp NARROCOTT

British Policeman operating in England

Agatha CHRISTIE 1890-1976 (British)

Invented 18 detectives - see Hercule POIROT

Citation Record: 1 Book

The Sittaford Mystery - *Only*
Collins UK (1931)

Murder At Hazelmoor - *Only**
Dodd, Mead US (1931)

Aubrey NASH

American Male Private Detective operating in New York/Connecticut

Tech DAVIS (American)

Citation Record: 3 Books

Terror On Compass Lake - *First*
Doubleday US (1935)

Murder On Alternate Tuesdays - *Last*
Doubleday US (1938)

Capt George NASH

British Male Amateur operating in England

Ragan BUTLER 1930- (British)

Writer: Raymond Ragan BUTLER

Citation Record: 2 Books

Captain Nash And The Honour Of England - *First*
Harwood UK (1975); St Martin's US (1977)

Captain Nash And The Wroth Inheritance - *Latest*
St Martin's US (1976)

Montgomery NASH

is a tongue-in-cheek send-up of a tough Cold War spy, who is involved in outrageously absurd situations during his work for the 'Department of Counter-Intelligence'.

American Male Professional Investigator operating in USA

Richard TELFAIR 1925-1982 (American)

Writer: Richard JESSUP

Citation Record: 5 Books

The Bloody Medallion - *First*
Fawcett US (1959); Muller UK (1960)

The Slavers - *Last*
Fawcett US (1961); Muller UK (1962)

Jerry NASON

is a fashion photographer who uses his special skills to solve a case of theft and murder.

American Male Amateur operating in New York

George Harmon COXE 1901-1984 (American)

Invented 20 detectives - see Kent MURDOCK

Citation Record: 1 Book

Fashioned For Murder - *Only*
Knopf US (1947); Hammond UK (1950)

The NAVAL DETECTIVE

American Male Amateur operating in USA

Edward Zane Carroll JUDSON 1821-1866

Citation Record: 1 Book

The Naval Detective's Chase - *Only*
Aldine US

Rudy NAVARRO

is an operative with The Ajax Novelty Company.

American Male Private Detective operating in Florida

Ron GOULART 1933- (American)

Invented 15 detectives - see Jake PACE and Hildy PACE

Citation Record: 1 Book

The Wisemann Originals - *Single*
Walker US (1989)

NEBRASKA

was once a PI, but now he is a struggling writer who accepts assignments while writing some great work, which, one knows, will never be completed. Married once, but now divorced, he is an interesting character who is both hardboiled and compassionate. The name he has taken may seem strange; but, as he says, that's where I am, so why not?

American Male Amateur operating in Omaha

William J REYNOLDS 1956- (American)

was born in Omaha, Nebraska. He graduated with a BA in Political Science at Creighton University, Omaha, 1979, and has since worked as a magazine editor and in advertising.

Citation Record: 5 Books

The Nebraska Quotient - *First*
St Martin's US (1984); Macmillan UK (1986)

The Naked Eye - *Latest*
Putnam US (1990)

Nathan NECESSARY

American Male Sleuth operating in Oklahoma

Ken JACKSON (American)

See main detective Jud BLADE

Citation Record: 2 Books

Necessary - *First*
St Martin's US (1986)

Control - *Latest*
St Martin's US (1987)

NEEDLE MIKE

is an artist who is also a millionaire playboy and loves adventures in the underworld of St Louis. He appeared mainly in short stories in *Dime Detective.*

American Male Detective in Pulp Magazines operating in St Louis

William E BARRETT 1900- (American)

Writer: William Edmund BARRETT

No citations

NELLIE

American Female Detective in Pulp Magazines operating in USA

Detective EDENHOPE (American)

Citation Record: 1 Selected Short Story

Nellie, The Girl Detective; Or, The Mystery Of The Mason Mansion
Old Cap Collier Library US (18??)

Ann NELSON

Second detective of Insp TARR

Dale NELSON

American Male Amateur operating in Illinois

Winifred VAN ATTA 1910- (American)

Invented 3 detectives - see Jim FERGUSON

Citation Record: 1 Book

Shock Treatment - *Only*
Doubleday US (1961); Boardman UK (1964)

Ed NELSON

British Male Amateur operating in England

Frank NORMAN 1930-1980 (British)

Citation Record: 2 Books

The Dead Butler Caper - *First*
Macdonald UK (1978); St Martin's US (1979)

Too Many Crooks Spoil The Caper - *Last*
Macdonald UK (1979); St Martin's US (1980)

Capt Gridley NELSON

American Policeman operating in New York

Ruth FENISONG ?-1978 (American)

Inventor of one other detective Victoria TARRANT

Citation Record: 13 Books

Murder Needs A Name - *First*
Doubleday US (1942); Swan UK (1950)

Dead Weight - *Last*
Doubleday US (1962); Hale UK (1964)

Jerry NELSON

American Male Private Detective operating in New York

Howard SCHOENFELD (American)

Citation Record: 1 Book

Let Them Eat Bullets - *Only*
GM US (1954); Fawcett UK (1955)

Neil NELSON

American Male Detective in Pulp Magazines operating in New York

Harry ROCKWOOD 1859-1932 (American)

Invented 14 detectives - see Clarice DYKE

Citation Record: 1 Book

Neil Nelson, The Veteran Detective; Or, Tracking Mail Robbers - *Only*
Ogilvie US (1885)

NEMO

American Male Detective in Pulp Magazines operating in USA

F Lusk BROUGHTON (American)

Invented 10 detectives - see Harry WILLIAMS

Citation Record: 1 Book

Nemo, The Shadow Detective - *Only*
Ogilvie US (1885)

NETTERLY

British Policeman operating in England

Henry WADE 1887-1969 (British)

Invented 7 detectives - see Ch Insp POOLE

Citation Record: 1 Book

A Dying Fall - *Only*
Constable UK (1955); Macmillan US (1955)

Harry NETTLEFIELD

British Male Secret Agent operating in England

William LEQUEUX 1864-1927 (British)

Invented 23 detectives - see Allan KENNEDY

Citation Record: 9 Short Stories in 1 Collection

The Spy Hunter - *Collection 1*
Pearson UK (1916)

Lt NEUMAN

American Policeman operating in New York

Sidekick: Sgt REDFIELD
American Male - Subordinate

Jerry OSTER 1943- (American)

See main detective Eve ZABRISKIE

Citation Record: 3 Books

Sweet Justice - *First*
Harper & Row US (1985)

Rough Justice - *First**
Collins UK (1985)

Club Dead - *Latest*
Harper & Row US (1988)

Billy NEVERS

American Male Private Detective operating in New York

Joseph Mark GLAZNER 1945- (American)

Citation Record: 5 Books

Smart Money Doesn't Sing Or Dance - *First*
Warner US (1979); Hamlyn UK (1980)

Hot Money Can Cook Your Goose - *Latest*
Warner US (1981)

Nick NEVERSEEN

American Male Detective in Pulp Magazines operating in USA

Police Captain HOWARD (American)

Invented 15 detectives - see LIGHTNING LUKE

Citation Record: 1 Book

Nick Neverseen, The Invisible Detective; Or, A Startling Story Of Two Great Cities
New York Detective Library US (1882-8)

The NEVER-FAIL DETECTIVE

American Male Detective in Pulp Magazines operating in USA

Capt Howard HOLMES 1849-1924 (American)

Writer: Thomas Chalmers HARBAUGH

No citations

Rocky NEVINS

American Male Private Detective operating in Los Angeles

N

Verne CHUTE 1917- (American)

!See Appendix 2.

Citation Record: 1 Book

Wayward Angel - *Only*
Knopf US (1948)

Blackmail - *Only**
Museum Press UK (1951)

Yuri NEVSKY

Russian Male Private Detective operating in Pittsburgh

Dimitri GAT 1936-

Writer: Dimitri Vsevolod GAT

Citation Record: 2 Books

Nevsky's Return - *First*
Avon US (1982)

Nevsky's Demon - *Latest*
Avon US (1983)

A NEW YORK DETECTIVE

is so described in a collection of short stories that appeared just a few years after the tales of Edgar Allan POE.

American Male Professional Investigator operating in New York

ANON

Citation Record: 11 Short Stories in 1 Collection

The Thrilling Adventures Of A New York Detective - *Collection 1*
Lupton US (1893)

A NEW YORK DETECTIVE

American Policeman operating in New York

John Babington WILLIAMS (American)

was the author of one of the earliest US collections of detective stories.

Citation Record: 29 Short Stories in 1 Collection

Leaves From The Notebook Of A New York Detective - *Collection 1*
is perhaps the earliest collection of stories with one detective throughout.
Dick US (1864)

N

The New York Detective Police Officer - *Collection 1**
Maxwell UK (1865)

Millicent NEWBERRY

appears quite early on in the history of female private eyes, for she runs a New York detective agency in 1909. To solve her cases she makes use of this new-fangled thing called psychiatry and, in fact, calls herself a 'mind-nurse'. The precursor of many later shamuses, she does tend, however, to mete out private justice when the law, in her opinion, fails to do so. She has one other claim to fame. She must be the very first lady detective to indulge in knitting while solving a case.

American Female Private Detective operating in New York

Jennette LEE 1860-1951 (American)

Writer: Jennette Barbour Perry LEE

Citation Record: 4 Books

The Green Jacket - *First*
Scribner's US (1909)

Dead Right - *Last*
Scribner's US (1925)

Sgt Roger NEWMAN

Second detective of Supt Robert TOWNLEY

Insp NEWSOM

British Policeman operating in Fiji

Flora STEWART (British)

Citation Record: 2 Books

Deadly Nightcap - *First*
Jenkins UK (1966)

Blood Relations - *Last*
Jenkins UK (1967)

Anthony NEWTON

British Male Amateur operating in England

Edgar WALLACE 1875-1932 (British)

Invented 28 detectives - see J G REEDER

Citation Record: 12 Short Stories in 1 Collection

The Brigand - *Collection 1*
Hodder & Stoughton UK (1927)

Nell NIBLO

was reared on the streets of old New York. She is a rough diamond who works for the 'New York Detective Force' but also seems to be a PI.

American Female Private Detective operating in New York

Edward Lytton WHEELER 1854?-1885 (American)

Writer: Edward Lytton WHEELER

Other Detectives:
DEADWOOD DICK; Denver DOLL
FRITZ; The FRONTIER DETECTIVE
The HEART OF OAK DETECTIVE

Citation Record: 1 Book

New York Nell, The Boy-Girl Detective - *Only*
Beadle & Adams US (1886)

Capt NICE

is in a novelization of an episode for a TV series.

Male Sleuth

William JOHNSTON 1924- (American)

Invented 7 detectives - see John WOODRUFF and Tony NOVELLO

Citation Record: 1 Book

Captain Nice - *Only*
Tempo UK (1967)

Insp Trevor NICHOLLS

British Policeman operating in Australia/Antarctic

Geoffrey PETERS 1910- (British)

Writer: Madelyn PALMER

Citation Record: 7 Books

The Claw Of A Cat - *First*
Ward, Lock UK (1964)

The Chill Of A Corpse - *Last*
Ward, Lock UK (1968)

NICHOLSON

British Male Sleuth operating in England

Mary KELLY 1927- (British)

See main detective Insp Brett NIGHTINGALE

Citation Record: 2 Books

The Spoilt Kill - *First*
Joseph UK (1961); British Book Centre US (1961)

Due To A Death - *Last*
Joseph UK (1962)

The Dead Of Summer - *Last**
Mill US (1963)

Nick NICHOLSON

British Male Amateur operating in The Hebrides

Robert BARR 1850-1912 (British)

was born in Glasgow. He was educated in Canada, worked in the USA, and returned to England in 1881 to edit several publications. In 1892 he and Jerome K Jerome established the periodical, *The Idler*.

Writer: Robert BARR

Other Byline: Luke SHARP

Other Detectives:
Sherlaw KOMBS; Lord STRANLEIGH
Eugène VALMONT

Citation Record: 2 Books

The Dark Island - *First*
Allen UK (1972); Bobbs US (1973)

The Edge Of The Forest - *Last*
Allen UK (1973)

Det Brub NICOLAI

investigates serial killings that come very close to home.

American Policeman operating in Los Angeles

Dorothy B HUGHES 1904- (American)

Invented 4 detectives - see Insp TOBIN

Citation Record: 1 Book

In A Lonely Place - *Only*
Duell US (1947); Nicholson & Watson UK (1950)

Nick NICOLETTI

American Male Sleuth operating in USA

Kara GEORGE (American)

Citation Record: 1 Book

Murder At Tomorrow - *Single*
Walker US (1982)

Lloyd NICOLSON

American Male Professional Investigator operating in USA/Canada

Patrick WAYLAND 1915-1975 (American)

Writer: Richard O'CONNOR

Other Byline: Frank ARCHER

Citation Record: 3 Books

Counterstroke - *First*
Doubleday US (1964); Hale UK (1965)

The Waiting Game - *Last*
Doubleday US (1965); Hale UK (1967)

Supt Mark NICOLSON

British Policeman operating in England/France

Robert CHARLES 1938- (British)

See main detective Simon LARREN

Citation Record: 3 Books

The Hour Of The Wolf - *First*
Hale UK (1974); Pinnacle US (1975)

The Flight Of The Raven - *Last*
Hale UK (1975); Pinnacle US (1975)

Det Insp Maurice NICOLSON

unravels a tortuous crime involving a boy's disappearance.

British Policeman operating in Scotland

Dominic DEVINE 1920-1981 (British)

was born in Greenock, Renfrewshire, Scotland. He took a degree in Law at London University and then became Registrar at St Andrews in Scotland. He wrote his first six books under the byline of *D M DEVINE.*

Other Detectives:
HEMMINGS — Judy HUTCHINGS
John PRESCOTT

Citation Record: 1 Book

His Own Appointed Day - *Only*
Collins UK (1965); Walker US (1966)

Antonia NIELSEN

is a classical scholar doing research in Crete, where she runs into a mystery involving a theft and girl's murder, with abstruse classical clues that only she can solve. The local cop in charge is bewildered, for he never had the opportunity, it seems, of reading Homer.

American Female Amateur operating in Crete

Stooge: Lt CARACCI
is continually stumped by the significance of the classical clues to the mystery in this book, which only *NIELSEN* has enough understanding to solve.
Greek Male

Carol CLEMEAU 1935- (American)

is a Professor of Classics at an American university

Writer: Carol Clemeau ESLER

Citation Record: 1 Book

The Ariadne Clue - *Single*
Collins UK (1983)

Amanda NIGHTINGALE

British Female Amateur operating in France/Germany

George REVELLI (British)

Citation Record: 5 Books

Commander Amanda Nightingale - *First*
Grove US (1968); New English Library UK (1969)

Amanda In Berlin - *Latest*
Mayflower UK (1978)

Insp Brett NIGHTINGALE

British Policeman operating in England

Mary KELLY 1927- (British)

was born in London and took an MA at the University of Edinburgh, 1951. She wrote ten genre novels, 1956-1974, receiving the Crime Writers Association Gold Dagger award, 1961.

Writer: Mary Theresa KELLY

Inventor of one other detective NICHOLSON

Citation Record: 3 Books

A Cold Coming - *First*
Secker & Warburg UK (1956); Walker US (1968)

The Christmas Egg - *Last*
Secker & Warburg UK (1958); Holt US (1966)

Dr NIKOLA

Italian Male Amateur operating in Italy

Guy BOOTHBY 1867-1905

was born in Adelaide, South Australia, but was educated in England, where he lived for most of his life. He was the author of many non-genre novels, plays and some genre novels.

Writer: Guy Newell BOOTHBY

Other Detectives:
Simon CARNE — Mr Jacob BURRELL

Citation Record: 4 Books

A Bid For Fortune; Or Dr Nikola's Vendetta - *First*
Ward, Lock UK (1895); Appleton US (1895)

Enter Dr Nikola - *First**
Newcastle (1975)

Farewell Nikola - *Last*
Ward, Lock UK (1901); Lippincott US (1901)

Pam NILSEN

is modern, female, left-wing, socially embroiled and feminist. She runs a printing press for good causes and becomes involved in murders, all of which have vast substructures of social awareness.

American Female Amateur operating in Seattle

Barbara WILSON 1950- (American)

was born in Long Beach, California.

Writer: Barbara Ellen WILSON

Inventor of one other detective Cassandra REILLY

Citation Record: 3 Books

Murder In The Collective - *First*
Seal US (1984); Women's Press UK (1984)

The Dog Collar Murders - *Latest*
Seal US (1989); Virago UK (1989)

Sgt Rudolf NILSEN

Norwegian Policeman operating in Norway

Ella GRIFFITHS

Citation Record: 2 Books

Murder On Page Three - *First*
is a translation from the Norwegian of *Mord Pa Side 3.*
Quartet UK (1984)

The Water Widow - *Latest*
is a translation from the Norwegian.
Quartet UK (1986)

NIMBLE IKE

American Male Detective in Pulp Magazines operating in USA

NIMBLE IKE (American)

Inventor of one other detective NORVAL

Citation Record: 3 Books

Nimble Ike, The Trick Ventriloquist - *First*
Ogilvie US (1894)

Nimble Ike, The Detective; Or, Solving A Mystery - *Last*
Ogilvie US (1900)

Branders NOBLE

British Male Amateur operating in England

A Richard MARTIN (British)

Citation Record: 2 Books

The Cassiodore Case - *First*
Methuen UK (1927); McBride US (1928)

The Death Of The Claimant - *Last*
Methuen UK (1929); McBride US (1929)

Nick NOBLE

is an ex-cop. He is also an alcoholic and an armchair detective who solves some very strange cases.

American Male Amateur operating in USA

Anthony BOUCHER 1911-1968 (American)

Invented 7 detectives - see Fergus O'BREEN and Det Lt JACKSON

Citation Record: 8 Short Stories in 1 Collection

Exeunt Murderers - *Collection 1*
contains eight *Nick NOBLE* stories and two *Sister URSULA* stories.
South Illinois University Press US (1983)

Stewart NOBLE

Second detective of Laurie GRANT

NOLAN

is an aging thief. Nevertheless, as the author maintains, he frequently behaves as a private eye in the way he serves the ends of a greater justice by dealing with organised and often violent crime.

American Male Professional Investigator operating in USA

Sidekick: Jon X
American Male - Assistant

Max Allan COLLINS 1948- (American)

Invented 5 detectives - see Nate HELLER

Citation Record: 6 Books

Bait Money - *First*
Curtis US (1973); New English Library UK (1976)

Scratch Fever - *Latest*
Pinnacle US (1982)

John NOLAN

American Male Amateur operating in New York/San Francisco

Charles NICOLAI (American)

Citation Record: 3 Books

A Killer Is Loose - *First*
Hammond UK (1954)

Murder In The Fine Arts - *Last*
Hammond UK (1964)

Ed NOON

is a most remarkable creation and he seems to live in a private world of his own. He has an office on Central Park and was once, it seems, an investigator for a disgraced ex-President. He hates eggheads, Communists, hippies, feminists, militant blacks, pacifists – all of them 'traitors to the John Wayne ethos'. By dwelling on *NOON's* obsession for old movies, baseball, and other deeply ingrained aspects of American culture, the author creates a strange world of inane plots, misplaced English, mangled prose and strange characters, in which detection plays an important, if hardly essential, part.

American Male Private Detective operating in New York

Michael AVALLONE 1924- (American)

was born in Manhattan, New York. He graduated from the Theodore Roosevelt High School, Bronx, and later served in the US Army, 1943-1946. A prolific author in the criminous genre under many pseudonyms, he became known as 'the fastest typewriter in the East'. In all he wrote nearly two hundred novels, mostly published as paperbacks. He wrote in almost every popular genre – thrillers, gothic romances, juvenile stories, soft pornography and espionage action thrillers. A mine of knowledge on a variety of subjects, his plots are as unusual as the man himself.

Writer: Michael Angelo AVALLONE Jr

Other Byline: Stuart JASON

Other Detectives:
Dave DUNN
Joe MANNIX
Satan SLEUTH

Napoleon SOLO and Ilya KURYAKIN

Citation Record: 32 Books

The Tall Dolores - *First*
Holt Rinehart US (1953); Barker UK (1956)

High Noon At Midnight - *Latest*
PaperJacks US (1988)

Insp NOONAN

solves a case of double poisoning in a locked room.

American Policeman operating in USA

Willard RICH (American)

Writer: UNKNOWN

Citation Record: 1 Book

Brain-Waves And Death - *Only*
Scribner's US (1940)

Giovanni Alberto NOONAN

is an Irish-American ex-cop and ex-Pinkerton man. Tough, impoverished and constantly in debt, he manages to run the phone-directory-friendly AAAA Private Investigations Agency from an office on West 17th Street, Manhattan.

American Male Private Detective operating in New York

Daniel HEARN (American)

was born in Washington DC. Educated at the University of Maryland, he has been an actor, courier and salesman.

Citation Record: 1 Book

Bad August - *Single*
St Martin's US (1987)

Mike NOONAN

is a parody detective, created by one of America's greatest satirists.

American Male Private Detective operating in USA

S J PERELMAN 1904-1979 (American)

was one of the great comic writers of all time. He wrote stories, articles, film scripts and plays, all endowed with his remarkable gift for humour in all its forms. He did, however, honour the genre by creating one minor detective and, it goes without saying, he wrote one *Sherlock HOLMES* pastiche.

Writer: Sydney Joseph PERELMAN

Adopter of one other detective Sherlock HOLMES

Citation Record: 1 Selected Short Story

Farewell, My Lovely Appetizer
appears in a collection of the author's stories, *Keep It Crisp.*
Random House US (1946); Heinemann UK (1947)

Rita NOONAN

is a recent addition to the female PI catalogue and better than most. A fairly normal, though tough American girl, she is just doing an honest job working for a seedy agency, run by an aging PI. Although at times she has to act as a male substitute, she is also agreeably feminine and, trying to work her way into a partnership, succeeds in doing so.

American Female Private Detective operating in New York

Michael HENDRICKS (American)

Citation Record: 1 Book

Money To Burn - *Single*
Dutton US (1989); Macmillan UK (1990)

Bert NORDEN

American Male Private Detective operating in Washington DC

Stuart BROCK 1917- (American)

Invented 3 detectives - see Steve ROURKE

Citation Record: 1 Book

Killer's Choice - *Only*
Graphic US (1956)

Philip NORE

British Male Amateur operating in England

Dick FRANCIS 1920- (British)

Invented 18 detectives - see Sid HALLEY

Citation Record: 1 Book

Reflex - *Single*
Joseph UK (1980); Putnam US (1981)

NORGIL

is one of the many magician detectives appearing in pulp stories before the Second World War. His were chiefly in *Crime Busters Magazine* during 1938 and 1939. Two collections have recently appeared.

American Male Detective in Pulp Magazines operating in USA

Maxwell GRANT 1897-1985 (American)

House writer for one other detective Lamont (The Shadow) CRANSTON
For writer details see Lamont (The Shadow) CRANSTON (Walter B GIBSON)

Citation Record: 16 Short Stories in 2 Collections

Norgil The Magician - *Collection 1*
Short stories - 8
Mysterious Press US (1977)

Norgil: More Tales Of Prestidigitection - *Collection 2*
Short stories - 8
Mysterious Press US (1979)

Mrs Annie NORRIS

appears also in books with one of the author's other detectives, *Jasper TULLY.*

American Female Amateur operating in Washington DC

Dorothy Salisbury DAVIS 1916- (American)

Invented 9 detectives - see Kate OSBORN

Citation Record: 1 Book 1 Selected Short Story

Old Sinners Never Die - *Only*
Scribner's US (1959); Secker & Warburg UK (1960)

Mrs Norris Observes
appears in the author's collection, *Tales For A Stormy Night.*
Foul Play US (1984)

Mrs Annie NORRIS

Second detective of Jasper TULLY

Jacqueline NORRIS

Second detective of Anthony READ

Philip NORRIS

is an investigative lawyer in this one Victorian novel.

British Male Professional Amateur operating in England

Hugh CONWAY 1840-1885 (British)

Writer: Frederick John FARGUS

Citation Record: 1 Book

Living Or Dead - *Only*
Macmillan UK (1886)

Yorke NORROY

American Male Professional Investigator operating in several locations

George BRONSON-HOWARD 1833- 1922 (American)

Writer: George FitzAlan BRONSON-HOWARD

Citation Record: 11 Short Stories in 2 Collections

Norroy, Diplomatic Agent - *Collection 1*
Short stories - 6
Saalfield UK (1907)

Slaves Of The Lamp - *Collection 2*
Short stories - 5
Watt US (1917)

Insp Rae NORSE

American Male Amateur operating in New England

John ESTEVEN 1888-1954 (American)

Writer: Samuel SHELLABARGER

Inventor of one other detective Miles LE BRETON

Citation Record: 2 Books

The Door Of Death - *First*
Century US (1928); Methuen UK (1929)

Voodoo - *Last*
Doubleday US (1930); Hutchinson UK (1930)

Dr NORTH

solves the mystery of how two patients came to be electrocuted while embracing in hospital gardens.

American Male Amateur operating in USA

James D PERRY 1895- (American)

Writer: James Dewolfe PERRY

Citation Record: 1 Book

Murder Walks The Corridors - *Only*
Macmillan US (1937)

Corridor Of Fear - *Only**
Constable UK (1937)

Edward NORTH

British Male Amateur operating in England

Colin ROBERTSON 1906-1980 (British)

Invented 7 detectives - see Mike REED

Citation Record: 4 Books

Dusky Limelight - *First*
Ward, Lock UK (1950)

No Trial - No Error - *Last*
Allen UK (1953)

Gerry NORTH

Male Amateur operating in USA

Gerry NORTH

Writer: UNKNOWN

Citation Record: 2 Books

Meet Gerry North - *First*
Horwitz AU (1959)

Gerry North Collects - *Last*
Horwitz AU (1959)

Capt/Maj/Col Hugh NORTH

is usually concerned with crimes involving the English abroad.

American Male Secret Agent operating in several locations

Sidekick: Dr Walter ALLAN
narrates the first two books featuring *NORTH* but then disappears from the transactions.
American Male - Narrator

Van Wyck MASON 1901-1978 (American)

See main detective Capt CATLIN

Citation Record: 25 Books 4 Short Stories in 1 Collection

Seeds Of Murder - *First*
Doubleday US (1930); Eldon UK (1937)

The Deadly Orbit Mission - *Last*
Doubleday US (1968); Hale UK (1968)

The Seven Seas Murders - *Collection 1*
contains four novelettes.
Doubleday US (1936); Eldon UK (1937)

Jerry NORTH

Second detective of Pam NORTH

N

Norah NORTH

British Female Amateur operating in England

Madelaine DUKE 1925- (British)

Writer: Madelaine Elizabeth DUKE

Citation Record: 3 Books

Death Of A Holy Murderer - *First*
Joseph UK (1975)

Death Of A Dandie Dinmont - *Latest*
Joseph UK (1978)

Pam NORTH and Jerry NORTH

are a husband-and-wife team, one of the most successful of the duos created by American writers in the 1930s, 1940s and 1950s. Like most others of their kind, they tend to dash about New York and the surrounding countryside, solving murders galore. Their cases usually end with an exciting chase, often with the distaff side being in imminent and terminal danger. She survives, of course; for, otherwise, who would look after their adored cats?

American Female Amateur and American Male Amateur operating in New York

Frances LOCKRIDGE and Richard LOCKRIDGE (American)

Invented 5 detectives - see Bernard SIMMONS

Citation Record: 26 Books

The Norths Meet Murder - *First*
Stokes US (1940); Joseph UK (1940)

Murder By The Book - *Last*
Lippincott US (1963); Hutchinson UK (1964)

Philip NORTH

is a Member of Parliament who goes in for sleuthing when political murders occur.

British Male Amateur operating in London

Nigel WEST (British)

Citation Record: 1 Book

Murder In The Lords - *Single*
Macmillan UK (1994)

N

Sam NORTH

British Male Amateur operating in London

Sam NORTH (British)

Citation Record: 1 Book

209 Thriller Road - *Single*
New English Library UK (1979); St Martin's US (1980)

Insp Guy NORTHEAST

is young but plodding, the son of a farmer and not gentlemanly at all.

British Policeman operating in England

Joanna CANNAN 1898-1961 (British)

was born in Oxford, Oxfordshire. A mainstream author of repute, she has written twelve genre books.

Writer: Joanna Maxwell Cannan PULLEIN-THOMPSON

Inventor of one other detective Insp Ronald PRICE

Citation Record: 2 Books

They Rang Up The Police - *First*
Gollancz UK (1939)

Death At The Dog - *Last*
Gollancz UK (1940); Reynal US (1941)

Dr NORTON

is a coroner who solves a case of death by bludgeoning in a locked study.

American Male Professional Investigator operating in USA

Wilder ANTHONY (American)

Citation Record: 1 Book

Deep Valley - *Only*
Dorrance US (1940)

Alec NORTON

is a reporter who solves the murder of a second-rate actress.

Male Amateur

Helen MCCLOY 1904-1993 (American)

Invented 5 detectives - see Dr Basil WILLING

Citation Record: 1 Selected Short Story

The Black Disk

appeared in the April issue. It was a reworking of an earlier story, *The Nameless Clue*, published in 1941.
In 'Ellery Queen's Mystery Magazine' US (1961)

Dave NORTON

British Male Amateur operating in England

Peter MALLOCH 1909-1976 (British)

For writer details see Supt MACNEILL

Inventor of one other detective pair Insp Tom SWETMAN and Insp CRANE

Citation Record: 2 Books

Blood On Pale Fingers - *First*
Long UK (1969)

The Slugger - *Last*
Long UK (1971)

Les NORTON

Australian Male Amateur operating in Australia

Robert G BARRETT (Australian)

Citation Record: 2 Books 2 Selected Short Stories

The Boys From Binjiwunyawunya - *First*
Pan AU (1987)

The Godson - *Latest*
Pan AU (1989)

Prof Myrl Adler NORTON

is the Professor of Logic at Smith College. Interestingly enough, she is just two steps away from the great Sherlock HOLMES himself, being the daughter of Irene ADLER, his most female famous antagonist. She seems to have inherited many of the latter's abilities as she starts her amateur career in criminal investigation. [Ms ADLER has recently appeared in several books by another author as a sleuth in her own right. It may also be noted that one of Prof NORTON's forenames alludes to an early British lady detective, Dora MYRL.]

American Female Amateur operating in USA

Abbey Penn BAKER (American)

Citation Record: 1 Book

In The Dead Of Winter - *Single*
St Martin's US (1994)

Valentine NORTON

American Male Amateur operating in USA

George BAXT 1923- (American)

Invented 6 detectives - see Pharaoh LOVE

Citation Record: 1 Book

The Neon Graveyard - *Single*
St Martin's US (1979)

NORVAL

American Male Detective in Pulp Magazines operating in USA

NIMBLE IKE (American)

See main detective NIMBLE IKE

Citation Record: 1 Book

Norval The Detective; Or, A Detective's Shadow - *Only*
Ogilvie US (1895)

Jack NOVAK

appears in Cold War action thrillers.

American Male Secret Agent operating in several locations

E Howard HUNT 1918- (American)

was born in Hamburg, New York. He graduated from Brown University, Providence, Rhode Island, 1940, served with the US Army Air Force, 1943-1946, and was also a distinguished war correspondent. Latterly he held posts, in the USA and abroad, for the US government. Consultant to President

Nixon, 1971-1972, he was implicated in the Watergate scandal and served two terms in a federal prison. He is the author of at least forty-two genre novels under his real name and pseudonyms, many of them dealing with secret agents and having exciting plots, reflecting his own life and experiences.

Writer: Everette Howard HUNT

Other Bylines:
Gordon DAVIS — Robert DIETRICH
David ST JOHN

Other Detectives:
Steve BENTLEY — Pete NOVAK

Citation Record: 3 Books

Cozumel - *First*
Stein & Day US (1985)

Mazatlan - *Latest*
Stein & Day US (1987)

Pete NOVAK

is a house dick in a Washington hotel who finds a corpse, hides it while he solves the crime, and doesn't find it at all necessary to notify the police.

American Male Private Detective operating in Washington DC

Gordon DAVIS 1918- (American)

was a CIA man who played a prominent part in the Watergate scandal.

For writer details see Jack NOVAK

Citation Record: 1 Book

House Dick - *Only*
was republished, with a change of title, under the following byline.
GM US (1961); Muller UK (1962)

E Howard HUNT 1918- (American)

Invented 3 detectives - see Jack NOVAK

Washington Payoff - *Only*
was previously published, with a change of title, under the preceding byline.
Pinnacle US (1975)

Tony NOVELLO

Second detective of John WOODRUFF

NOVEMBER JOE

uses his native skills for detective purposes in the frozen wilds.

Canadian Male Amateur operating in Canada

Hesketh PRICHARD 1876-1922 (British)

was born in India and taken as a small child to England, where he was educated. A great traveller and hunter, he put many of his own experiences into his stories.

Writer: Vernon Hesketh PRICHARD

Citation Record: 16 Short Stories in 1 Collection

November Joe, The Detective Of The Woods - *Collection 1*
Hodder & Stoughton UK (1913); Houghton US (1913)

Det Sgt Peter NOYES

solves a case of murder committed forty years earlier.

British Policeman operating in England

Jeffrey ASHFORD 1926- (British)

Invented 9 detectives - see Det Insp Don KERRY

Citation Record: 1 Book

A Crime Remembered - *Single*
Collins UK (1987); St Martin's US (1988)

Alo NUDGER

is less than medium-boiled, far from brave, often down on his uppers, and always pursued by his ex-wife for alimony payments. His personal integrity and compassion see him through in some excellent books.

American Male Private Detective operating in St Louis

John LUTZ 1939- (American)

Invented 5 detectives - see Fred CARVER

Citation Record: 7 Books

Buyer Beware - *First*
Putnam US (1976); Hale UK (1977)

Thicker Than Blood - *Latest*
St Martin's US (1992)

— O —

Blackford OAKES

is a CIA agent, recruited from Yale. He features in novels of adventure, espionage, and murder, vignettes of the Cold War era, in which he saves the USA from certain destruction on more than one occasion. He is a hero, however, who has more than the usual quota of moral underpinnings, although these are not always to be admired or countenanced.

American Male Secret Agent operating in several locations

William F BUCKLEY 1925- (American)

was born in New York. Ex-Yale, ex-Army, ex-CIA, he is one of America's best known literary figures, renowned especially for having founded the *National Review*, the prestigious conservative journal. He has written widely on a variety of subjects as well as being the author of eight detective novels, all with curious yet appealing titles. His work has received awards and honours from the worlds of literature and television, and he himself has received honours from universities and learned societies all over the United States.

Writer: William Frank BUCKLEY

Citation Record: 8 Books

Saving The Queen - *First*
Doubleday US (1976); Allen UK (1976)

Mongoose, Rip - *Latest*
Random House US (1988); Muller UK (1988)

Boysie OAKES

appeared, at first, to be a mere pastiche of or even an antidote to the already famous *James BOND*. However, he eventually became a character in his own right, although he has not lasted well. He too was in British Intelligence; but, unlike his prototype, he was initially portrayed as a blundering oaf, although he does improve in manners if not in interest.

British Male Secret Agent operating in several locations

John GARDNER 1926- (British)

was born in Seaton Delavel, Northumberland. He took a BA in Theology at St John's College, Cambridge, 1950, and an MA, 1951. He served in the Commandos and the Marines, 1943-7, later becoming a Chaplain in the Royal Air Force. He now lives in the USA and is the creator of several detectives in his at least thirty-two genre novels. He has been honoured by being allowed to continue the *James BOND* saga.

Writer: John Edmund GARDNER

Other Detectives:
Lt James BOND — Sherlock HOLMES
Herbie KRUGER — Derek TORRY

Citation Record: 7 Books 2 Short Stories in 1 Collection

The Liquidator - *First*
Muller UK (1964); Viking US (1964)

A Killer For A Song - *Last*
Hodder & Stoughton UK (1975)

Hideaway - *Collection 1*
contains two stories with *Boysie OAKES*.
Corgi UK (1968)

Quintus OAKES

American Male Amateur operating in New York

Charles Ross JACKSON 1867-1915 (American)

Citation Record: 2 Books

The Third Degree - *First*
Dillingham US (1903); Unwin UK (1903)

Quintus Oakes - *Last*
Dillingham US (1904); Unwin UK (1904)

Hamish OATH

British Male Amateur operating in England

Digby DURRANT 1926- (British)

Citation Record: 2 Books

With My Little Eye - *First*
Gollancz UK (1975); St Martin's US (1978)

Trunch - *Latest*
Bachman UK (1978)

Terry O'BANION

is an alcoholic who always gets his man.

American Male Private Detective operating in New Orleans

Sidekick: Nadia WELLS

was once a madam in a brothel. Now, more or less legitimised, she works as a kind of PI with and for *Terry O'BANION.*

American Female - Assistant

Dick LOCHTE 1937- (American)

Invented 3 detectives - see Leo G BLOODWORTH and Sarah 'Serendipity' DAHLQUIST

Citation Record: 2 Books

Blue Bayou - *First*
Ballantine US (1992)

The Neon Smile - *Latest*
Ballantine US (1995)

Fergus O'BREEN

Second detective of Sherlock HOLMES

Fergus O'BREEN and Det Lt JACKSON

Fergus O'BREEN is deliberately stage Irish. He wears loud checks, speaks with a brogue, and drives a bright yellow automobile, but he has winning ways and is bright enough to run his own agency. He usually works on cases being investigated by a member of the Los Angeles Police Department, *Det Lt JACKSON.*

American Male Private Detective and American Policeman operating in Los Angeles

Anthony BOUCHER 1911-1968 (American)

was born in Oakland, California, and educated at the University of California, Berkeley, after which he entered a distinguished career as a writer, critic, publisher, and editor in several branches of literature and music. He holds an esteemed place in the history of modern crime fiction, not only through his own contributions to the genre, but also because of his learned and critical approach to the subject. He was, for twenty-six years from 1951, the writer of the famous 'Criminals at Large' column in the *New York Times Book Review*, which made him the most popular and influential critic of crime and mystery fiction. He was President of the Mystery Writers of America, 1951, and received the Edgar Allan Poe award for non-fiction three times, 1946, 1950, and 1953. After his death an annual convention of mystery writers, the Bouchercon, was named for him.

Writer: William Anthony Parker WHITE

Other Byline: H H HOLMES

Other Detectives:
Dr John ASHWIN; Sherlock HOLMES; Sherlock HOLMES and Fergus O'BREEN; Lt LIEBERMANN; Nick NOBLE; Sister URSULA

Citation Record: 3 Books

The Case Of The Crumpled Knave - *First*
Simon & Schuster US (1939); Harrap UK (1939)

The Case Of The Seven Sneezes - *Last*
Simon & Schuster US (1942); United Authors UK (1946)

Kenneth O'BRIEN

British Male Amateur operating in England

Edward GELLIBRAND (British)

Citation Record: 2 Books

The End Of A Cigarette - *First*
Long UK (1924)

The Windblow Mystery - *Last*
Hamilton UK (1926)

Patrick O'BRIEN

American Male Amateur operating in Boston/Cape Cod

Inez Haynes IRWIN 1873-1970 (American)

Citation Record: 5 Books

Murder In Fancy Dress - *First*
Heinemann UK (1935)

Murder Masquerade - *First**
Smith & Haas US (1935)

The Women Swore Revenge - *Last*
Random House US (1946); Boardman UK (1948)

Pierre O'BRIEN

American Male Private Detective operating in New York

Whitman CHAMBERS 1896- (American)

Invented 4 detectives - see Simon LAKE

Citation Record: 1 Book

Dog Eat Dog - *Only*
Doubleday US (1938)

Murder In The Mist - *Only**
Cassell UK (1938)

Sarah O'BRIEN

American Female Amateur operating in USA

Melba MARLETT 1909- (American)

Writer: Melba Balmat MARLETT

Citation Record: 2 Books

Death Has A Thousand Doors - *First*
Doubleday US (1941)

Another Day Toward Dying - *Last*
Doubleday US (1943)

Witness In Peril - *Last**
Cherry Tree UK (1948)

Terrence O'BRIEN

American Male Amateur operating in New York

Mary Roberts RINEHART 1876-1958 (American)

Invented 7 detectives - see Letitia CARBERRY

Citation Record: 1 Book

The Swimming Pool - *Only*
Rinehart US (1952)

The Pool - *Only**
Cassell UK (1952)

Det Sgt O'BRIEN and Det Sgt O'NEILL

Irish Policemen operating in Eire

Michael HENRY (British)

Citation Record: 1 Book

Murder In The Old Jail - *Only*
Hamilton UK (1938)

Det Sgt O'BYRNE

Irish Policeman

Fergus HUME 1859-1932 (British)

Invented 24 detectives - see Insp Samuel GORBY

Citation Record: 1 Book

The Last Straw - *Only*

was published posthumously, the last work by an author who has an assured place in the hall of fame for his first detective story, *THE MYSTERY OF A HANSOM CAB,* written almost half a century earlier.

Hutchinson UK (1932)

Cat O'CONNELL

is forty-five, a mother, a lawyer, is 'stroppy, congenitally unable to put a sock in it and, however hard she tries, she can't quite hide her heart of gold'. For reasons difficult to appreciate, she can't think of anything better in life than to be a PI in Glasgow. Perhaps not surprisingly, she has difficulty finding work.

American Female Private Detective operating in Glasgow

Pat SWEET (British)

was born in Dundee and has worked for the Inland Revenue.

Citation Record: 1 Book

Troubled Waters - *Single*
Virago UK (1994)

Father O'CONNOR

Irish Male Amateur

D G ROWLANDS

Citation Record: 6 Short Stories in 1 Collection

Eye Hath Not Seen... - *Collection 1*
Pardoe (1990)

'Lefty' O'CONNOR

American Male Sleuth operating in USA

Brad SHANNON 1920- (American)

Writer: Victor Joseph HANSON

Other Bylines:
Vern HANSEN
V J Hanson
Desmond REID

Citation Record: 7 Books

Lefty O'Connor Moves In - *First*
Scion US (1950)

Lefty Takes Over - *Last*
Scion US (1952)

Chauncey O'DAY

is fat and comic.

American Male Private Detective operating in Washington DC/Virginia

Sidekick: Cassie STORM

is not only the detective's fiancée but is a nurse who administers to his various ailments, assists his sleuthing and narrates his cases.

American Female - Narrator

Audrey GAINES (American)

Writer: Audrey Gaines SCHULTZ

Inventor of one other detective Jeff STRANGE

Citation Record: 3 Books

The Old Must Die - *First*
Crowell US (1939)

The Voodoo Goat - *Last*
Crowell US (1942)

Double O'DAY

British Male Amateur operating in England

Gwyn EVANS 1899-1938 (British)

Invented 5 detectives - see Bill KELLAWAY

Citation Record: 4 Books

Bluebeard's Keys - *First*
Wright UK (1937)

The Sleepless Man - *Last*
Wright UK (1940)

Terence O'DAY

British Male Private Detective operating in London

Peter CHEYNEY 1896-1951 (British)

Invented 11 detectives - see Lemmy CAUTION

Citation Record: 1 Book

One Of Those Things - *Only*
Collins UK (1949); Dodd, Mead US (1950)

Mistress Murder - *Only**
Avon US (1951)

Supt Mike ODDIE

investigates a death among writers, which was a favourite theme of the author.

British Policeman operating in England

Robert BARNARD 1936- (British)

Invented 13 detectives - see Insp Perry TRETHOWAN

Citation Record: 1 Book

A Hovering Of Vultures - *Single*
Bantam UK (1993)

Rita Gardella O'DEA

American Female Amateur operating in USA

Andrew COBURN 1932- (American)

was born in Exeter, New Hampshire, and graduated at Suffolk University, Boston. He is a journalist, editor, and political columnist.

Inventor of one other detective Frank CHASE

Citation Record: 3 Books

Sweetheart - *First*
Macmillan US (1985); Secker & Warburg UK (1985)

Goldilocks - *Latest*
Scribner's US (1989); Secker & Warburg UK (1989)

Barry O'DELL

American Male Amateur operating in New York

Robert Orr CHIPPERFIELD 1883-1929 (American)

Writer: Isabel Egenton OSTRANDER

Other Bylines:
David FOX
Isabel OSTRANDER

Other Detectives:
Geoffrey PETERS
The SHADOWERS INC

Citation Record: 2 Books

Unseen Hands - *First*
McBride US (1920); Hurst UK (1920)

The Man In The Jury Box - *Last*
McBride US (1921); Hurst UK (1921)

Philip ODELL

British Male Sleuth operating in Europe

Lester POWELL 1912- (British)

Writer: Lester Edwin POWELL

Citation Record: 5 Books

A Count Of Six - *First*
Collins UK (1948)

The Black Casket - *Last*
Collins UK (1953)

Ch Insp ODHIAMBO

African Policeman operating in Kenya/England

Dennis CASLEY (British)

was born at Mullion, Cornwall. A graduate of University College, London, he has worked for the Colonial Office and the World Health Organisation in several African countries.

Citation Record: 2 Books

Death Underfoot - *First*
Constable UK (1993)

Death Undertow - *Latest*
Constable UK (1994)

Sheriff Hiram ODOM

American Policeman operating in Texas/New Mexico

Marjorie BONIFACE (American)

Citation Record: 3 Books

Murder As An Ornament - *First*
Doubleday US (1940)

Wings Of Death - *Last*
McBride US (1946)

Insp O'DONOVAN

British Policeman operating in England

Brian CLEEVE 1921- (British)

was born in Thorpe Bay, Essex. He was educated at St Edward's School, Oxford, 1935-1938, took a BA from the University of South Africa, Johannesburg, 1953, and received a PhD from the National University of Ireland, Dublin, 1956. He served in the British Merchant Navy, 1939-1945, was a journalist and broadcaster in Ireland and South Africa, and is the author of many genre books as well as others, including several political and literary studies.

Writer: Brian Brendan Talbot CLEEVE

Inventor of one other detective Sean RYAN

Citation Record: 1 Book

Death Of A Wicked Servant - *Only*
Hammond UK (1963); Random House US (1964)

Lee OFSTED

is a pro golfer who finds the body of a tour star on the course. She investigates, at some considerable peril to herself from the unknown killer.

American Female Amateur operating in California

Charlotte ELKINS and Aaron ELKINS (American)

Citation Record: 1 Book

A Wicked Slice - *Single*
St Martin's US (1989)

Insp Laurence OGILVIE

investigates a case of locked-room murder, with a suspicion of the occult at work.

British Policeman operating in England

George GOODCHILD 1888-1969 (British)

Invented 5 detectives - see Insp MCLEAN

Citation Record: 1 Book

Cauldron, Bubble - *Only*
Macdonald UK (1946)

O

Capt O'HAGAN

British Male Amateur operating in several locations

Sax ROHMER 1883-1959 (British)

Invented 9 detectives - see Insp RYDER

Citation Record: 6 Short Stories in 1 Collection

The Exploits Of Captain O'Hagan - *Collection 1*
Jarrolds UK (1916); Bookfinger US (1968)

Mike O'HANNA

is a house dick in a small Californian hotel, appearing mainly in stories in *Dime Detective.*

American Male Detective in Pulp Magazines operating in California

Dale CLARK (American)

was the author of hundreds of short stories and a teacher of writing.

Writer: Ronal KAYSER

Other Detectives:

Gillian BALTIC
Highland PRICE
'Plates' O'RION

No citations

James O'HANNAY and Floyd EAST

British Male Amateurs operating in England/Germany

Charles RUSHTON 1904- (British)

See main detective Insp CADMAN

Citation Record: 3 Books

The Trail Of Blood - *First*
Jenkins UK (1929)

No Second Stroke - *Last*
Jenkins UK (1938)

Cary Wylde O'HARA

British Male Private Detective operating in London

Peter CHEYNEY 1896-1951 (British)

Invented 11 detectives - see Lemmy CAUTION

Citation Record: 1 Book

Dance Without Music - *Only*
Collins UK (1947); Dodd, Mead US (1948)

Deirdre O'HARA

is a Montreal lawyer, seemingly a top insurance case expert, whose clients pay her large fees, which she earns by continually solving murder cases.

Canadian Female Amateur operating in Montreal

Maurice GAGNON 1912- (Canadian)

Citation Record: 3 Books

The Inner Ring - *First*
Collins UK (1985)

Doubtful Motives - *Latest*
Collins UK (1987)

Fergus O'HARA

is a Pinkerton agent who, in 1863, is engaged on a case in San Francisco and later on a river steamer.

American Male Private Detective operating in San Francisco

Sidekick: Hattie O'HARA

assists her husband in his one case, being useful in enquiring about things that a man cannot.

American Female - Wife

Jack FOXX 1943- (American)

See main detective Dan CONNELL

Citation Record: 1 Book

Freebooty - *Only*
Bobbs US (1976)

Isamu OHARA

American Male Amateur operating in Los Angeles

Nan HAMILTON (American)

Writer: Nanoni Patricia Maude Hamilton BALL

Citation Record: 2 Books

Killer's Rights - *First*
Walker US (1984); Hale UK (1986)

The Shape Of Fear - *Latest*
Dodd, Mead US (1986)

Pixie O'HARA

British Female Amateur

Dudley STURROCK (British)

Citation Record: 12 Short Stories in 1 Collection

Pixie At The Wheel - *Collection 1*
Hodder & Stoughton UK (1923)

Terence O'HARA

British Male Sleuth

Paul COSTELLO (British)

Citation Record: 4 Books

The Long Silence - *First*
Hale UK (1957)

Blue Diamond - *Last*
Cassell UK (1962)

Timothy O'HARA and Nancy BREWSTER

Timothy O'HARA is an aging, broken-down operative who is sent by his agency to investigate what is considered as a hopelessly insoluble case of murder. He solves it, however, with the help of *Nancy BREWSTER.*

American Male Private Detective and American Female Amateur operating in New York

Kelley ROOS (American)

Invented 3 detectives - see Jeff TROY and Haila TROY

Citation Record: 1 Book

Murder On Martha's Vineyard - *Single*
Walker US (1981); Hale UK (1982)

Insp O'HARE

investigates the death of Professor Larkin, famous Egyptologist, which does seem rather suspicious as he is not only dead but also mummified.

American Policeman operating in USA

Frederick G EBERHARD 1889- (American)

was born in South Whitley, Indiana. A practising physician, he wrote a few detective novels, usually replete with scientific mumbo-jumbo.

Writer: Frederick George EBERHARD

Inventor of one other detective Ch of Plce SUTHERLAND

Citation Record: 1 Book

The Microbe Murders - *Only*

!See Appendix 2.

Macaulay US (1935)

Sheerluck OHMS

is a *Sherlock HOLMES* parody.

British Male Professional Amateur operating in London

Sidekick: Dr Watts ION

is his parody *WATSON*-like assistant.

British Male - Narrator

Dr Watts ION (American)

Writer: UNKNOWN

Citation Record: 15 Short Stories in 2 Collections

The Adventures Of Sheerluck Ohms - *Parody Collection 1*

The stories in this collection – the titles of some of which parody some of the titles of the canonical *Sherlock HOLMES* stories – appeared, June 1947 through March 1951, in what was clearly a local journal, *The Anaconda Wire*, and the names of the detective and author are manifestly references to matters electrical. The twelve stories are cited individually. The collection has more recently been republished by *Magico* with two alterations of the names of the individual stories and with the addition of three further stories, which are also individually cited below.

Short stories i - 12

In 'The Anaconda Wire' US (1947-51)

The Case Of The Account That Got Away - *Parody 1*

The Case Of The Alphabetical Vandal - *Parody 2*

The Case Of The Chain Reaction - *Parody 3*

The Case Of The Counterfeit Cent - *Parody 4*

The Case Of The Cummuppance Cup - *Parody 5*

In the edition published by *Magico* the title appears as *The Case Of The Comeuppance Cup.*

The Case Of "Eye-Strained" Door - *Parody 6*

The title appears thus in *The World Bibliography of Sherlock Holmes and Dr Watson* by Robert Burt De Waal. In the edition published by *Magico*, the title is given as *The Case of the Eye-Stained Door*, thus missing the joke as well as changing the sense.

In 'The Anaconda Wire' US (1947-51)

The Case Of The Fish That Wouldn't Keep - *Parody 7*

The Case Of The Gushwell Ghost - *Parody 8*

The Case Of The Limping Man - *Parody 9*

parodies the title of the canonical story, *THE ADVENTURE OF THE CREEPING MAN.*

The Case Of The Persian Parsnip - *Parody 10*

The Case Of The Second Santa - *Parody 11*

parodies the title of the canonical story, *THE ADVENTURE OF THE SECOND STAIN.*

The Case Of The Tootsbury Typist - *Parody 12*

The Adventures Of Sheerluck Ohms - *Parody Collection 2*

contains the twelve stories of the first collection, with the titles of two somewhat altered, and three additional stories, cited individually immediately under.

Short stories - 3

Magico Press US (1980)

The Case Of The Clockport Catnapper - *Parody 13*

Magico Press US (1980)

The Case Of The Confounded Counterfeiter - *Parody 14*

Magico Press US (1980)

The Case Of The Purloined Pickle - *Parody 15*

Magico Press US (1980)

Sherlock OHMS

is a *Sherlock HOLMES* parody.

Male Professional Amateur

Sidekick: Dr WATTS

is his parody *WATSON*-like assistant.

Male - Assistant

Steven TOMASHEFSKY (American)

Citation Record: 1 Selected Short Story

The Adventure Of Isadora Persano - *Parody 1*

appeared in the December number. It refers to the allusion made by *Dr WATSON* in the canonical story, *THE PROBLEM OF THOR BRIDGE,* to an unchronicled case concerning 'Isadora Persano, a well-known journalist and duellist, who was found stark staring mad with a matchbox in front of him which contained a remarkable worm said to be unknown to science'. The allusion has been used by other authors as the basis for a pastiche or parody.

In 'Baker Street Journal' US (1966)

Michael the O'KELLY

Irish Male Amateur operating in Rome

Manning O'BRINE 1915- (British)

Writer: Padraic Manning O'BRINE

Inventor of one other detective MILLS

Citation Record: 7 Books

Killers Must Eat - *First*

Hammond UK (1951)

Dagger Before Me - *Last*

Hammond UK (1957)

Desmond OKEWOOD

appears also in books with one of the author's other detectives, *Dr Adolph GRUNDT.*

British Male Secret Agent operating in Europe

Douglas VALENTINE 1893-1946 (British)

For writer details see Det Sgt Trevor DENE

Inventor of one other detective pair Dr Adolph GRUNDT and Desmond OKEWOOD

Citation Record: 1 Book

The Secret Hand - *Only*

was published in the US with a change in title and under the following byline.

Jenkins UK (1919)

Valentine WILLIAMS 1883-1946 (British)

Invented 8 detectives - see Det Sgt Trevor DENE

Citation Record: 1 Book

Okewood Of The Secret Service - *Only*

was published in the UK with a change in title and under the preceding byline.

McBride US (1919)

Desmond OKEWOOD

Second detective of Dr Adolph GRUNDT

OLD BRIGHTON

American Male Detective in Pulp Magazines operating in New York

Jack HOWARD (American)

See main detective John MERRY

Citation Record: 1 Selected Short Story

Old Brighton, The Coney Island Detective; Or, Solving The Great Coffin Mystery

Old Cap Collier Library US (18??)

OLD DECEIVER

American Male Detective in Pulp Magazines operating in USA

F Lusk BROUGHTON (American)

Invented 10 detectives - see Harry WILLIAMS

Citation Record: 1 Selected Short Story

Old Deceiver, The Private Detective; Or, Trailing His Own Cast
Old Cap Collier Library US (18??)

OLD DOUBLE FACE

American Male Detective in Pulp Magazines operating in USA

Police Captain HOWARD (American)

Invented 15 detectives - see LIGHTNING LUKE

Citation Record: 1 Book

Old Double Face, The Veteran Detective
New York Detective Library US (1882-8)

OLD DUDE

American Male Detective in Pulp Magazines operating in USA

Tom FOX (American)

Other Detectives:
The ASYLUM DETECTIVE The INSURANCE DETECTIVE
The PAN HANDLE DETECIVE

Citation Record: 1 Book

Old Dude, The Detective; Or, Working For A Life
New York Detective Library US (1882-8)

OLD ELECTRICITY

American Male Detective in Pulp Magazines operating in USA

OLD SLEUTH (American)

Invented 40 detectives - see Brant ADAMS

Citation Record: 1 Book

Old Electricity, The Lightning Detective - *Only*
Munro US (1892)

OLD GOLD-EYE

American Male Detective in Pulp Magazines operating in USA

Mark MERRICK (American)

Other Detectives:
MOONSHINER JACK OLD GRIMES

Citation Record: 1 Selected Short Story

Old Gold-Eye, The Miner Detective; Or, Piping The Mystery Of Sandy Gulch
Old Cap Collier Library US (18??)

OLD GRIMES

American Male Detective in Pulp Magazines operating in USA

Mark MERRICK (American)

Invented 3 detectives - see OLD GOLD-EYE

Citation Record: 1 Selected Short Story

Old Grimes, The 'Get-There' Detective; Or, Tracking The Mystery Of The Vault
Old Cap Collier Library US (18??)

OLD HUMPY

American Male Detective in Pulp Magazines operating in USA

David DRUID (American)

Invented 4 detectives - see Sam SMART

Citation Record: 1 Selected Short Story

Old Humpy, The Dwarf Detective; Or, Thwarting A Career Of Crime
Old Cap Collier Library US (18??)

The OLD MAN IN THE CORNER

was one of the earliest of the many armchair detectives that have graced the genre, appearing originally in stories carried in *The Royal Magazine* between 1901 and 1904. They were published over the next twenty-five years or so in the author's various collections and a new series, regarded as inferior to the earlier ones, appeared in 1925. Although this untypical detective is invariably called by the author *THE OLD MAN IN THE CORNER*, it was eventually disclosed by the author that his real name was, in fact, Bill Owen, a fact that must be regarded as of minimal importance to the history of detective fiction. That being so, his methods of detection are certainly unusual and still have an appeal; he simply sits in the corner of a London tea-shop, playing with a length of string, and solves cases, all of which are baffling the police, by the power of ratiocination only. The cases are usually brought to him by a young lady reporter with whom he has become acquainted. At other times he merely picks up a case from a newspaper.

British Male Amateur operating in London

Sidekick: Polly BURTON
has the most diverse of connections in London society, which is seemingly brimming with crimes of theft and murder. She often brings such cases to *THE OLD MAN IN THE CORNER*, although, sometimes, she just listens as he unravels crimes he has read about in the papers.
British Female - Friend

Baroness ORCZY 1865-1947 (British)

Writer: Emma Magdalena Rosalia Maria Josifa Barbara ORCZY

Invented 6 detectives - see Lady Molly DE MAZEREEN

Citation Record: 47 Short Stories 3 Collections

The Case Of Miss Elliott - *Collection 1*
was comprised of the third series of stories that had appeared in *The Royal Magazine.*
Short stories - 12
Unwin UK (1905)

The Old Man In The Corner - *Collection 2*
was comprised of the first and second series of stories that had appeared in *The Royal Magazine.* Not all of them appeared in the US publication.
Short stories - 22
Greening UK (1909)

The Man In The Corner - *Collection 2**
was comprised of the first and second series of stories that had appeared in *The Royal Magazine.* Not all them appeared in the UK publication.
Dodd, Mead US (1909)

Unravelled Knots - *Collection 3*
appeared many years after the first stories had been published.
Short stories - 13
Hutchinson UK (1925); Doran US (1926)

OLD MYSTAGOGNE

American Male Detective in Pulp Magazines operating in USA

F Lusk BROUGHTON (American)

Invented 10 detectives - see Harry WILLIAMS

Citation Record: 1 Selected Short Story

Old Mistagogne, The Protean Detective; Or, Tracking The Prince Of Rogues
Old Cap Collier Library US (18??)

OLD NEVERSLEEP

American Male Detective in Pulp Magazines operating in USA

Walter FENTON (American)

Citation Record: 1 Book

Old Neversleep, The Government Detective
New York Detective Library US (1882-8)

OLD PITCHER

American Male Detective in Pulp Magazines operating in USA

David DRUID (American)

Invented 4 detectives - see Sam SMART

Citation Record: 1 Selected Short Story

Old Pitcher, The Baseball Detective; Or, Sharp Work On The Diamond
Old Cap Collier Library US (18??)

OLD PURITAN

American Male Detective in Pulp Magazines operating in USA

ANON

No citations

OLD QUARTZ

American Male Detective in Pulp Magazines operating in Nevada

Eugene T SAWYER 1846-1924 (American)

Real Name: Eugene T SAWYER

Other Byline: Nicholas CARTER

Citation Record: 1 Book

Old Quartz, The Nevada Detective - *Only*
Street & Smith (Magnet #118) US (1900)

OLD RUFE

American Male Detective in Pulp Magazines operating in USA

Harry HAMMOND (American)

See main detective Allen DANE

Citation Record: 1 Book

Old Rufe, The Secret Service Detective
New York Detective Library US (1882-8)

OLD SADDLE-BAGS

American Male Detective in Pulp Magazines operating in USA

D W STEVENS (American)

See main detective Sam SIX KILLER

Citation Record: 1 Book

Old Saddle-Bags, The Preacher Detective; Or, The James Boys In A Fix
New York Detective Library US (1882-8)

OLD SAFETY

American Male Detective in Pulp Magazines operating in USA

Police Captain HOWARD (American)

Invented 15 detectives - see LIGHTNING LUKE

Citation Record: 1 Book

Old Safety, The Denver Detective; Or, Piping The Mail Robbers
New York Detective Library US (1882-8)

OLD SHARON

is an eccentric private detective.

British Male Professional Amateur operating in England

Wilkie COLLINS 1824-1889 (British)

Invented 5 detectives - see Sgt CUFF

Citation Record: 1 Book

My Lady's Money - *Only*
UK (1878)

OLD SLEUTH

appeared, over several decades, in a large number of pulp stories under this byline and also anonymously. Many were written by *Harlan Page HALSEY*. An early and a late book are cited for illustrative purposes.

American Male Detective in Pulp Magazines operating in USA

OLD SLEUTH (American)

Invented 40 detectives - see Brant ADAMS

Citation Record: 2 Books

Old Sleuth, The Detective; Or, The Bay Ridge Mystery - *First*
Munro US (1891)

Old Sleuth's Greatest Case - *Last*
Westbrook US (ca 1920)

OLD SNAP

American Male Detective in Pulp Magazines operating in USA

Allan ARNOLD (American)

Other Detectives:

The BOOT BLACK DETECTIVE
Belle BOYD
CENTERSHOT
Sherlock HOLMES
YANKEE JED

Citation Record: 1 Book

Old Snap, The Postal Service Detective
New York Detective Library US (1882-8)

OLD SPECIE

American Male Detective in Pulp Magazines operating in New York

Alexander ROBERTSON (American)

See main detective Detective GRIME

Citation Record: 1 Book

Old Specie, The Treasury Detective; Or, The Harbor Lights Of New York - *Only*
Street & Smith US (1890)

OLD STONEWALL

American Male Professional Investigator operating in Colorado

Judson R TAYLOR 1837-1898 (American)

Invented 4 detectives - see Phil SCOTT

Citation Record: 1 Book

Old Stonewall, The Colorado Detective - *Only*
Street & Smith US (1888)

OLD TERRIBLE

American Male Detective in Pulp Magazines operating in USA

ANON

Citation Record: 1 Book

The Iron Arm Detective - *Only*
Aldine US

OLD TRAMP

American Male Detective in Pulp Magazines operating in USA

Old Cap COLLIER (American)

Citation Record: 1 Selected Short Story

Old Tramp, The Hermit Detective; Or, Tracking The Opium Smugglers Of San Francisco
Old Cap Collier Library US (18??)

OLD WOLF

American Male Detective in Pulp Magazines operating in USA

Police Captain HOWARD (American)

Invented 15 detectives - see LIGHTNING LUKE

Citation Record: 1 Book

Old Wolf, The Secret Service Detective
New York Detective Library US (1882-8)

Det Lance O'LEARY

Second detective of Sarah KEATE

Pat O'LEARY

is a female PI who sets out to solve one last case before she gets married.

American Female Private Detective operating in USA

Lois EBY and John C FLEMING (American)

See main detective Zachary STONE

Citation Record: 1 Book

Hell Hath No Fury - *Only*
Dutton US (1947)

Pat O'LEARY

was an Irish-American detective appearing in stories in *Private Detective* in the 1940s.

American Male Detective in Pulp Magazines operating in USA

Roger TORREY (American)

Invented 7 detectives - see Pat MULLANCY

No citations

Mrs Ariadne OLIVER

Second detective of Mark EASTERBROOK

Mrs Ariadne OLIVER

Second detective of Hercule POIROT

Mrs Ariadne OLIVER

Appears with at least two other detectives - see Hercule POIROT

Gideon OLIVER

is a physical anthropologist and an expert in forensic anthropology who meets murder, past and present, in various exotic and well-researched locales. Tall, good-looking and attractive to women, he marries, in his third book, *Julie TENDLER*, who becomes an important assistant in his sleuthing activities.

American Male Professional Amateur operating in several locations

Sidekick: Julie TENDLER
is a National Park ranger who becomes the assistant to *Gideon OLIVER* and, in the third book of the series, marries him.

American Female - Wife

Aaron J ELKINS 1935- (American)

was born in Brooklyn, New York. He has received several degrees from universities in New York and in California, and has had a career as a management consultant and as a professor at Californian colleges. He received the Mystery Writers of America Edgar Allan Poe award, 1988.

Citation Record: 6 Books

Fellowship Of Fear - *First*
Walker US (1982)

Dead Men's Hearts - *Latest*
Mysterious Press US (1995)

Elena OLIVEREZ

is a Chicana Indian. She works in a highly specialised field, being concerned with combating crimes connected with museums and the world of art. She also appears in one book with *QUINCANNON*, the creation of *Bill PRONZINI*.

American Female Professional Investigator operating in California

Marcia MULLER 1944- (American)

Invented 3 detectives - see Sharon MCCONE

Citation Record: 2 Books

The Tree Of Death - *First*
Walker US (1983); Hale UK (1986)

The Legend Of The Slain Soldiers - *Latest*
Walker US (1985); Hale UK (1986)

O

Elena OLIVEREZ and John QUINCANNON

Elena OLIVEREZ, the creation of *Marcia MULLER*, is a modern sleuth who, in this one unusual book, is able to use her special knowledge to solve a case, involving stolen religious artefacts, which *QUINCANNON*, the nineteenth-century sleuth of *Bill PRONZINI* had failed to solve.

American Female Professional Investigator and American Male Amateur operating in California

Bill PRONZINI and Marcia MULLER 1944- (American)

See main detective pair NAMELESS DETECTIVE and Sharon MCCONE

Citation Record: 1 Book

Beyond The Grave - *Single*
Walker US (1986)

Mrs Emily OLLERBY

was one of the first of a crop of British lady detectives appearing after the end of the First World War. Elderly, fat and very strong, she is said to be 'one of the cleverest woman detectives of Scotland Yard'.

British Policewoman operating in London

Edgar WALLACE 1875-1932 (British)

Invented 28 detectives - see J G REEDER

Citation Record: 1 Book

The Traitor's Gate - *Only*
Hodder & Stoughton UK (1927); Doubleday US (1927)

Cerlocio OLMEZ

is a *Sherlock HOLMES* parody.

Spanish Male Professional Amateur

Sidekick: ATSONEZ
is his parody *WATSON*-like assistant.

Male - Assistant

Katherine E KARLSON (American)

Citation Record: 1 Selected Short Story

A Case Of Identity II: Or, Art In The Soup Can Take The Strangest Forms - *Pastiche 1*
appeared in the September number.
In 'Baker Street Journal' US (1970)

Sheriff John Charles OLSON

American Policeman operating in USA

M G CHUTE 1907- (American)

Writer: Mary Grace CHUTE

Citation Record: 9 Short Stories in 1 Collection

Sheriff Olson - *Collection 1*
Appleton US (1942)

O'MALLEY

appears in short stories, being presented as a 'dumb cop' who turns out to be smart. He starts each story by saying the case cannot be solved and then proving himself wrong by solving it.

American Policeman operating in USA

William MACHARG 1872-1951 (American)

was born in Dover Plains, New York. A journalist and author of several novels and detective fiction works, he collaborated with *Edwin BALMER* in some works.

Writer: William Briggs MACHARG

Citation Record: 33 Short Stories in 1 Collection

The Affairs Of O'Malley - *Collection 1*
Dial US (1940)

Supt O'MALLEY

appears also in one book with the author's other detective, *Harry PECKOVER*.

Irish Policeman operating in Ireland

Michael KENYON 1931- (British)

Invented 6 detectives - see Insp/Ch Insp Harry PECKOVER

Citation Record: 4 Books

The 100,000 Welcomes - *First*
Collins UK (1970); Coward McCann US (1970)

The Rapist - *Latest*
Collins UK (1977); Coward McCann US (1977)

Supt O'MALLEY

Second detective of Insp/Ch Insp Harry PECKOVER

Benjamin O'MALLEY

American Male Amateur operating in USA

Brian LYSAGHT (American)

Citation Record: 2 Books

Special Circumstances - *First*
St Martin's US (1983); Severn UK (1983)

Sweet Deals - *Latest*
St Martin's US (1985)

Brian O'MALLEY

British Male Amateur operating in England

Roland DANIEL 1880-1969 (British)

Invented 11 detectives - see Insp Neville LANGHAM

Citation Record: 4 Books

Arrested For Murder - *First*
Wright UK (1950)

The Devil Woman - *Last*
Wright UK (1964)

Megan O'MALLEY

Second detective of Ch Mitchell HOLT

Shaun O'MALLEY

American Male Sleuth operating in California

Gene ROSS 1923- (American)

For writer details see Shaun KOVACK

Citation Record: 3 Books

Two Smart Dames - *First*
Archer US (1949)

Step Up, Sucker - *Last*
Harborough US (1950)

Prince Abdull OMAR

was an 'occult' detective, also known as Semi-Dual, who appeared in many stories in the pulps, 1912-1935.
Male Detective in Pulp Magazines operating in USA

J U GIESY and Junius B SMITH (American)

Writer: (First author) John Ulrich GIESY 1877-1947
No citations

Shaun O'MARA

Irish Male Amateur operating in France

Peter CHEYNEY 1896-1951 (British)

Invented 11 detectives - see Lemmy CAUTION

Citation Record: 1 Book

Dark Interlude - *Only*
Collins UK (1947); Dodd, Mead US (1947)

The Terrible Night - *Only**
Avon US (1955)

Jay OMEGA

is a writer of science fiction who turns amateur sleuth.
American Male Amateur operating in USA

Sharyn MCCRUMB (American)

Invented 4 detectives - see Elizabeth MACPHERSON

Citation Record: 2 Books

Bimbos Of The Death Sun - *First*
TSR US (1987); Penguin UK (1989)

Zombies Of The Gene Pool - *Latest*
Simon & Schuster US (1992)

Cotswold OMMONY

British Male Amateur operating in India

Talbot MUNDY 1879-1940 (British)

Invented 5 detectives - see Chullunder GHOSE

Citation Record: 2 Books

Om: The Secret Of Ahbor Valley - *First*
Hutchinson UK (1924); Bobbs US (1924)

Jungle Jest - *Last*
Hutchinson UK (1931); Century US (1932)

Andrew ONE

is a statistician who solves a case of murder on a transatlantic plane.
American Male Amateur operating on a plane

Thomas KYD 1901-1976 (American)

Invented 3 detectives - see Det Sam PHELAN

Citation Record: 1 Selected Short Story

High Court
appeared in the October issue.
In 'Ellery Queen's Mystery Magazine' US (1953)

Caitlin O'NEAL

was, after ten years, discharged from the Los Angeles Police Department when she broke her captain's jaw during an investigation. Now she commands the night shift in the Sheriff's department in a small Oregon town. Things do not stay quite as restful as she expected and she has to use her old skills.
American Female Ex-Policewoman operating in Oregon

John ANGUS (American)

Citation Record: 1 Book

The Monster Squad - *Single*
St Martin's US (1994)

Father Fernando O'NEAL

became a priest to avoid the Vietnam war. Married, and with a drink problem, he is working in the border town of El Sol when he runs into murder. Threatened himself, he turns detective.
American Male Amateur operating in USA/Mexico

Paul SPIKE 1947- (American)

Citation Record: 1 Book

Last Rites - *Single*
US (1981); Granada UK (1982)

Dallas O'NEIL

American Male Sleuth operating in USA

Jerry JENKINS 1949- (American)

Invented 3 detectives - see Jennifer GREY

Citation Record: 8 Books

Mystery Of The Kidnapped Kid - *First*
Moody US (1988)

Mystery Of The Golden Palomino - *Latest*
Moody US (1989)

Jason T O'NEIL

investigates salacious crime on the campus at Boston.
American Male Private Detective operating in Boston

Lawrence KINSLEY (American)

Citation Record: 1 Book

The Red-Light Victim - *Single*
Tower US (1981)

Kerry O'NEIL and Gail HOLLISTER

solve the mystery of a death by strangulation in a locked house.
American Male Amateur and American Female Amateur operating in USA

Charles G BOOTH 1896-1949 (American)

Invented 3 detectives - see Anatole FLIQUE

Citation Record: 1 Book

Sinister House - *Only*
Morrow US (1926); Hodder & Stoughton UK (1927)

O

Tip O'NEIL

is a poor sleuth but quick with the repartee. An authority has called him 'the first of the smart-ass detectives of the 1930s and poor stuff indeed in a bad book'.
American Male Private Detective operating in USA

Sidekick: LILLY
has a name that could mislead the innocent. Criminals know that, in fact, he can be very, very tough when it comes to it.
American Male - Assistant

James Edward GRANT 1905-1966 (American)

is the son of the Chief Investigator for the Illinois State Attorney. He was a former prize-fighter and later a journalist for a Chicago newspaper.

Citation Record: 1 Book

The Green Shadow - *Only*
Hartney US (1935)

Det Sgt O'NEILL

Second detective of Det Sgt O'BRIEN

Jim O'NEILL

is a cop in a small town, who is concerned with problems of crime in the US Mail.
American Policeman operating in Connecticut

Doris Miles DISNEY 1907-1976 (American)

Invented 7 detectives - see Jefferson DIMARCO

Citation Record: 5 Books

A Compound For Death - *First*
Doubleday US (1943)

The Last Straw - *Last*
Doubleday US (1954)

Driven To Kill - *Last**
Foulsham UK (1957)

Jimmy O'NEILL

American Male Sleuth operating in Chicago

Andrew M GREELEY 1928- (American)

was born in Oak Park, Illinois. He was educated at St Mary of the Lake Seminary and took an MA at the University of Chicago, Illinois, 1961, and a PhD, 1962. He became an ordained priest in the Roman Catholic Church, 1954, and has since held several religious posts in Chicago and elsewhere. He is the author of works on religious subjects as well as being author of over a dozen criminous works.

Writer: Andrew Moran GREELEY

Inventor of one other detective Mnsgnr John Blackwood 'Blackie' RYAN

Citation Record: 1 Book

Death In April - *Single*
McGraw US (1980); Futura UK (1987)

Peggy O'NEILL

is a 'university cop',

American Female Sleuth operating in Minneapolis

M D LAKE (American)

is the sometime Professor of Scandinavian Studies at the University of Minnesota.

Writer: James Allen SIMPSON

Citation Record: 5 Books

Amends For Murder - *First*
Avon US (1989); Chivers UK (1991)

Murder By Mail - *Latest*
Avon US (1993)

Policewoman Christie OPARA

is the widow of a cop killed on duty and mother of a young son. The only woman in the Manhattan District Attorney's office, she is a First Grade detective.

American Policewoman operating in New York

O

Stooge: Casey REARDON
is, in fact, her departmental superior but he is just an overbearing source of pain to *Christie OPARA*, for he is always trying to manipulate her and direct her work.

American Male

Dorothy UHNAK 1933- (American)

was born in New York City. She was educated at City College, New York, and graduated around 1970 from the John Jay College of Criminal Justice. She served in the New York police force until 1967.

Other Detectives:
Joe PETERS   Miranda TORRES

Citation Record: 3 Books

The Bait - *First*
Simon & Schuster US (1958); Hodder & Stoughton UK (1958)

The Ledger - *Last*
Simon & Schuster US (1970); Hodder & Stoughton UK (1971)

Insp ORD

British Policeman operating in England

Austen ALLEN 1887- (British)

Citation Record: 4 Books

Menace To Mrs Kershaw - *First*
Bles UK (1929); Harper & Row US (1930)

The Loose Rib - *Last*
Bles UK (1932); Kinsey US (1933)

Forrest ORD

British Male Amateur operating in England

SEAMARK ?-1929 (British)

See main detective Tommy DELAYN

Citation Record: 1 Book

The Web Of Destiny - *Only*
was published in the US with a change in title and under the author's real name.
Hodder & Stoughton UK (1929)

Austin J SMALL ?-1929 (British)

Citation Record: 1 Book

The Web Of Murder - *Only*
Doubleday US (1929)

Bobby ORDE

American Male Amateur operating in USA

Stewart Edward WHITE 1873-1946 (American)

Inventor of one other detective Percy DARROW

Citation Record: 25 Short Stories in 1 Collection

The Adventures Of Bobby Orde - *Collection 1*
Not all the stories are criminous.
Doubleday US (1910); Unwin UK (1912)

Dr Robert ORDWAY

was created for a radio series in 1940. One of the first psychiatrist-detectives, he usually dealt with mentally aberrant people.

American Male Professional Investigator operating in USA

Max MARCIN 1879-1948 (American)

was born in Posan, Germany (now in Poland) and was taken to the USA as a child. He wrote several plays, which were used as the basis for silent films, 1918-1919.

No citations

Sheridan ORFORD and Prof Henry Arthur FIELDING

Sheridan OFFORD is a dilettante amateur who, just the twice, helps the author's main detective, *Prof FIELDING* out of trouble.

British Male Amateurs operating in England

David SHARP (British)

See main detective Prof Henry Arthur FIELDING

Citation Record: 2 Books

None Of My Business - *First*
Benn UK (1931)

The Code-Letter-Mystery - *First**
Houghton US (1932)

I, The Criminal - *Last*
Benn UK (1932); Houghton US (1933)

Dr Owen ORIENT

Male Amateur

Frank LAURIA 1935- (American)

Writer: Frank Jonathan LAURIA

Citation Record: 5 Books

Dr Orient - *First*
Bantam UK (1970)

The Seth Papers - *Latest*
Ballantine US (1979)

'Plates' O'RION

appeared in several stories in *Dime Detective*.

American Male Detective in Pulp Magazines operating in USA

Dale CLARK (American)

Invented 4 detectives - see Mike O'HANNA

No citations

Doug ORLANDO

sleuths among the gay community.

American Male Amateur operating in New York

Steve JOHNSON (American)

Citation Record: 1 Book

False Confessions - *Single*
Dutton US (1993)

Marcus ORLANDO
Male Amateur operating in England

Gilbert FRANKAU 1884-1952 (British)
Invented 3 detectives - see Giuseppe CIGARINI
Citation Record: 6 Short Stories in 1 Collection
Secret Services - *Collection 1*
This collection of sixteen of the author's stories contains six with *ORLANDO.*
Hutchinson UK (1934)

Commissaire ORLOFF
French Policeman operating in France

Isobel LAMBOT 1926- (British)
Writer: Isobel Mary LAMBOT
Citation Record: 1 Book
Still Waters Run Deadly - *Single*
Macmillan UK (1987)

George ORMEROD
British Male Professional Investigator operating in France

Leslie THOMAS 1931- (British)
Writer: Leslie John THOMAS
Inventor of one other detective Dangerous DAVIES
Citation Record: 1 Book
Ormerod's Landing - *Single*
Eyre & Spottiswoode UK (1978); St Martin's US (1979)

Col ORMISTON
British Male Professional Investigator operating in Egypt/Spain

J M WALSH 1897-1952 (British)
Invented 7 detectives - see Insp QUAILE
Citation Record: 8 Books
King's Messenger - *First*
Collins UK (1933)
Spies In Spain - *Last*
Collins UK (1937)

Van Dusen ORMSBERRY
is a consultant to the New York Police Commissioner, but he has to solve certain crimes himself.
American Professional Investigator operating in New York

John Stephen STRANGE 1896- (American)
Writer: Dorothy Stockbridge TILLETT
Other Detectives:
Barney GANTT — Lt/Capt George HONEGGER
Sgt POTTER
Citation Record: 3 Books
The Man Who Killed Fortescue - *First*
Doubleday US (1928); Collins UK (1929)
Murder On The Ten-Yard Line - *Last*
Doubleday US (1931)
Murder Game - *Last**
Collins UK (1931)

Jocelyn O'ROARKE and Philip GERARD
Jocelyn O'ROARKE, is an Irish-American actress. With the aid of a friend, *Philip GERARD,* she solves many cases of sudden death, to which theatrical people are fictionally rather prone.
American Female Amateur and American Male Amateur operating in New York

Jane DENTINGER (American)
is a director of, and actress in, drama off Broadway and in regional houses.
Citation Record: 5 Books
Murder On Cue - *First*
Doubleday US (1983); Gollancz UK (1985)
The Queen Is Dead - *Latest*
Viking US (1994)

O'ROURKE
British Male Amateur

Frank KING 1892-1958 (British)
Invented 6 detectives - see Insp CHAMBERS
Citation Record: 1 Collection
Molly On The Spot - *Collection 1*
This collection of seventeen of the author's stories contains several with *O'ROURKE.*
Hale UK (1940)

Terence O'ROURKE
American Male Amateur operating in USA

Louis Joseph VANCE 1879-1933 (American)
See main detective Michael LANYARD
Citation Record: 2 Books
Terence O'Rourke, Gentleman Adventurer - *First*
Wessels US (1905); Richards UK (1906)
The Pool Of Flame - *Last*
Dodd, Mead US (1909); Richards UK (1910)

Terry O'ROURKE
British Male Amateur

Harry Stephen KEELER 1890-1967 (American)
Invented 14 detectives - see Angus MACWHORTER
Citation Record: 1 Book
Behind That Mask - *Only*
Ward, Lock UK (1933); Dutton US (1938)

Sarah ORPINGTON
British Female Amateur operating in England

Marion BABSON (American)
Invented 8 detectives - see Douglas PERKINS
Citation Record: 1 Book
Bejewelled Death - *Single*
Collins UK (1981); Walker US (1982)

Wendell ORTH
American Male Amateur operating in USA

Isaac ASIMOV 1920-1992 (American)
Invented 6 detectives - see Elijah BALEY
Citation Record: 1 Collection
Asimov's Mysteries - *Collection 1*
This collection of twelve of the author's short stories contains several with *Wendell ORTH.*
Doubleday US (1968); Rapp UK (1968)

Johnny ORTIZ
American Male Sleuth operating in New Mexico

Richard Martin STERN 1915- (American)
was born in Fresno, California. He graduated from Harvard University, Cambridge, Massachusetts, and worked as an engineer for Lockheed Aircraft, 1940-1945. Author of many short stories and novellas for several magazines, he has written at least nineteen genre novels and at least eight mainstream novels. He received the Mystery Writers of America of America Edgar Allan Poe award, 1958.
Other Detectives:
Dorothy Mayotte RIGBY — Walter SPENSE
Citation Record: 7 Books
Murder In The Walls - *First*
Scribner's US (1971); Hale UK (1973)
Interloper - *Latest*
Pocket Books US (1990)

Kate OSBORN
is an investigative reporter who goes to the fictional State University of Venice, Illinois, to get a story, but has to investigate the murder of one of the professors.
!See Appendix 2.
American Female Amateur operating in USA

Dorothy Salisbury DAVIS 1916- (American)
was born in Chicago, Illinois and graduated at Barat College, Lake Forest, Illinois. Distinguished in the literary and arts

O

world, she has received major awards for her criminous work, including the Mystery Writers of America Grand Master award and the Bouchercon Lifetime Achievement award.

Other Detectives:
Hannah BLAKE
Father DUFFY and Sgt GOLDSMITH
John EAKINS
Julia HAYES
Father MCMAHON
Mrs Annie NORRIS
Jasper TULLY and Mrs Annie NORRIS
Sheriff WILLETS

Citation Record: 1 Book

Shock Wave - *Only*
Scribner's US (1972); Barker UK (1974)

OSCAR
American Male Detective in Pulp Magazines operating in USA

OLD SLEUTH (American)
Invented 40 detectives - see Brant ADAMS
Citation Record: 1 Book

Oscar, The Detective - *Only*
Parlor Car US (1897)

Kiernan O'SHAUNESSY
is a forensic pathologist who gives up her work to become a PI.
American Female Private Detective operating in USA

Sidekick: Brad TCHERNACK
is an ex-footballer, a huge man who is the cook-cum-housekeeper of *O'SHAUNESSY* and is only too eager to act as her sidekick.
American Male - Cook

Susan DUNLAP 1943- (American)
Invented 3 detectives - see Vejay HASKELL
Citation Record: 1 Book

High Fall - *Single*
Delacorte US (1994)

Annabel O'SHEA
American Female Amateur operating in USA

Charlotte ARMSTRONG 1905-1969 (American)
Invented 5 detectives - see Prof MacDougal DUFF
Citation Record: 1 Book

The Witch's House - *Only*
Coward McCann US (1963); Collins UK (1964)

O'SULLIVAN
is a reporter who, while investigating for his paper, solves a case of murder by shooting in a locked room.
American Male Amateur operating in USA

Jerome ODLUM 1905-1954 (American)
Invented 3 detectives - see John STEELE
Citation Record: 1 Book

Nine Lives Are Not Enough - *Only*
Sheridan US (1940); Boardman UK (1944)

Insp OSWALD
solves a case of death by shooting in a locked study.
British Policeman operating in England

Christopher WILSON (British)
Citation Record: 1 Book

For A Woman's Honour - *Only*
Paul UK (1911)

Supt Tetsuo OTANI
is head of Japan's third largest police force.
Japanese Policeman operating in Tokyo

Sidekick: Insp Jiro KIMURA
is one of *OTANI's* two assistants, being responsible for the security of foreign residents. He has a liking for appearing in disguises. He also has a liking for Western girls.
Japanese Male - Assistant

Sidekick: Insp 'Ninja' NOGUCHI
is the second of *OTANI's* two assistants. He looks like a crook and perhaps that is why he is in charge of drug control in Tokyo.
Japanese Male - Assistant

James MELVILLE 1931- (British)
was born in London. He was educated at Highbury Grammar School, London, and took a BA and an MA at Birkbeck College, London, 1953 and 1956. After working as a schoolteacher, he became a Local Government officer and then held several posts abroad for the British Council. He has been, since 1979, a cultural counsellor at the British Embassy, Tokyo.
Writer: Roy Peter Martin MELVILLE
Citation Record: 13 Books

The Wages Of Zen - *First*
Secker & Warburg UK (1979); Methuen US (1981)

The Body Wore Brocade - *Latest*
Scribner's US (1993)

Miss OTIS
Female Sleuth

Ben SARTO 1891-1968 (British)
House name.
For writer details see Kinsey TARGET
Citation Record: 18 Books

Miss Otis Throws A Come-Back - *First*
Modern Fiction UK (1947)

Miss Otis Relents - *Last*
Milestone US (1954)

Gerald OTLEY
British Male Amateur operating in England

Martin WADDELL 1941- (British)
Citation Record: 4 Books

Otley - *First*
Hodder & Stoughton UK (1966); Stein US (1966)

Otley Victorious - *Last*
Hodder & Stoughton UK (1969); Stein US (1969)

Bridget O'TOOLE
is an elderly nun who takes over her sick father's agency in Chicago and runs it with the help of a fallible and repulsive sidekick.
American Female Private Detective operating in Chicago

Sidekick: Harry GARNISH
is a lying, alcoholic, coarse man. Even so, he is an assistant for the elderly ex-nun when she decides to play detective.
American Male - Assistant

Frank D MCCONNELL 1942- (American)
Writer: Frank Demay MCCONNELL
Citation Record: 3 Books

Murder Among Friends - *First*
Walker US (1983)

The Frog King - *Latest*
Walker US (1987)

Kerry OTT
is a deaf writer who solves a case of double murder in a locked apartment.
American Male Amateur operating in USA

Joel Townsley ROGERS 1896-1984 (American)
was born in Sedalia, Missouri. He wrote four novels and a few short stories and is renowned for the genre masterpiece, *THE RED RIGHT HAND.*
Inventor of one other detective pair Dr Henry RIDDLE and Prof Adam MACAMERON
Citation Record: 1 Selected Short Story

The Hanging Rope
is also in the anthologies, *The Art of the Impossible* (*Xanadu*; UK 1990) and *Murder Impossible* (*Carroll*; US 1990).
In 'New Detective Magazine' US (1946)

Rostron OUTFIT
American Male Sleuths operating in USA/Mexico

Dean MORGAN 1920- (American)
See main detective Rogue RANSOM
Citation Record: 7 Books
Four Of A Kind - *First*
Hamilton Stafford UK (1951)
Rostron Outfit In Mexico - *Last*
Hamilton Stafford UK (1952)

Marise OVERTON
solves a case of death by stabbing in a locked room.
Female Amateur

Earle DANESFORD
Citation Record: 1 Selected Short Story
Beyond The Second Door
In 'Violet Magazine' (1926)

Capt OWEN
is head of the Political Secret Police in Egypt under British rule, before the Second World War. He is called upon to investigate various crimes, which usually have implications for the British government.
British Policeman operating in Egypt

Michael PEARCE 1933- (British)
Citation Record: 5 Books
The Mamur Zapt And The Return Of The Carpet - *First*
Collins UK (1988); Doubleday US (1990)
The Mamur Zapt And The Spoils Of Egypt - *Latest*
HarperCollins UK (1992)

Cdr Bobby OWEN
is set firmly in the mainstream of English detective fiction in the era between the two world wars. He is definitely in the tradition of the gentleman policeman, yet the books are often different from the usual run, being intense and sometimes melodramatic. He starts off his long series as a young man in a rural police force, but later he goes to London's Scotland Yard, eventually attaining the most senior rank.
British Policeman operating in England

E R PUNSHON 1872-1956 (British)
was born in London. He was the author of at least sixty criminous novels.
Writer: Ernest Robertson PUNSHON
Inventor of one other detective Insp CARTER
Citation Record: 35 Books
Information Received - *First*
Benn UK (1933); Houghton Mifflin US (1934)
Six Were Present - *Last*
Gollancz UK (1956)

Dr Hillis OWEN
is a psychiatrist with a practice on Park Avenue. He is drawn into cases of murder involving his patients.
American Male Amateur operating in New York
Sidekick: Grace POMEROY
is a nurse who works for *OWEN* and assists him in his cases. In one other book, which comes between the two cited, 'when he is away on war service', she sleuths on her own.
American Female - Assistant

Anna Mary WELLS 1906- (American)
See main detective Grace POMEROY
Citation Record: 2 Books
A Talent For Murder - *First*
Knopf US (1942); Hammond UK (1948)
Sin Of Angels - *Last*
Simon & Schuster US (1948); Hammond UK (1951)

Richard OWEN
American Male Sleuth operating in Mexico

Marilyn SHARP (American)
Citation Record: 2 Books
Sunflower - *First*
Marek US (1979); Macmillan UK (1979)
Falseface - *Latest*
St Martin's US (1984)

Jerry OWENS
American Male Detective in Pulp Magazines operating in New York

Robert MAYNARD (American)
Citation Record: 1 Book
Jerry Owens, The Young Western Detective
New York Detective Library US (1882-8)

Molly OWENS
is a Western detective.
American Female Amateur operating in USA

Stephen OVERHOLSER 1944- (American)
Citation Record: 6 Books
Molly And The Confidence Man - *First*
Doubleday US (1975)
Molly And The Gambler - *Latest*
Bantam US (1984)

Winnie O'WYNN
British Female Amateur operating in England

Bertram ATKEY 1880-1952 (British)
Invented 4 detectives - see Prosper FAIR
Citation Record: 19 Short Stories in 2 Collections
Winnie O'Wynn And The Wolves - *Collection 1*
Short stories - 6
Hutchinson UK (1921)
Winnie O'Wynn And The Dark Horses - *Collection 2*
Short stories - 13
Hutchinson UK (1925)

E L OXMAN and Art TOBIN
American Male Sleuths operating in USA

Bill PRONZINI and John LUTZ (American)
Writers: William John PRONZINI 1943- and John Thomas LUTZ 1949-
Citation Record: 1 Book
The Eye - *Single*
Mysterious Press US (1984)

The OZARK DETECTIVE
American Male Detective in Pulp Magazines operating in USA

Old Cap DARRELL (American)
Invented 5 detectives - see YOUNG SLEDGE
Citation Record: 1 Selected Short Story
The Ozark Detective; Or, Wild Life Among The Bald Knobbers
New York Detective Library US (1882-8)

OZMAR
Male Sleuth

Emeric HULME-BEAMAN (British)
Citation Record: 2 Books
Ozmar The Mystic - *First*
Sands UK (1896)
The Prince's Diamond - *Last*
Hutchinson UK (1898)

Hildy PACE
Second detective of Jake PACE

Jake PACE and Hildy PACE
are a husband-and-wife team in the twenty-first century. They work for Odd Jobs Inc, one of the most prestigious investigation agencies in the galaxy, which takes on all the bizarre jobs that no sane operatives in outer space will touch.
American Male Private Detective and American Female Private Detective operating in Connecticut

Ron GOULART 1933- (American)
was born in Berkeley, California and graduated with a BA from the University of California, Berkeley, 1955. He is a prolific author of novels and short stories in the genres of science fiction, mystery, detection, and sometimes strange mixtures of all three (often under one of his numerous male or female pseudonyms). He is also a respected writer on, and critic of, all aspects of detective and crime fiction and is an authority on the early American pulps. Although his stories are rich in characters, among which are several private eyes, he has created relatively few series detectives. He received the Mystery Writers of America Edgar Allan Poe award, 1971.
Writer: Ronald Joseph GOULART
Other Bylines:
Josephine KAINS — Kenneth ROBESON
Other Detectives:
Sam BRIMMER — Jake CONGER
John EASY — Jim HALEY
Star HAWKS — Vincent HAWTHORN
Ben JOLSON — Cleopatra JONES
Max KEARNY — Burt KURRIE
Rudy NAVARRO — Jared SMITH
'Skyrocket' STEELE — Jack SUMMER
Citation Record: 4 Books 7 Short Stories in 1 Collection
Calling Dr Patchwork - *First*
Daw US (1978)
Brainz, Inc - *Latest*
Daw US (1985)
Odd Job #101 & Other Future Crimes And Intrigues - *Collection 1*
Scribner's US (1975); Hale UK (1976)

P

Quentin PACE
American Male Amateur operating in USA

Roger DENBIE (American)
Writers: Alan Baer GREEN 1906-1975 and Julian Paul BRODIE 1908-
Citation Record: 2 Books
Death On The Limited - *First*
Morrow US (1933)
The Timetable Murder - *First**
Nicholson & Watson UK (1934)
Death Cruises South - *Last*
Morrow US (1934); Nicholson & Watson UK (1934)

James PACKARD
is a fairly typical professional agent of the period, who does do some detecting in the course of his duties.
British Male Secret Agent operating in several locations

Robert Conington GALWAY 1920- (British)
For writer details see Cdr Esmonde SHAW
Citation Record: 11 Books
Assignment New York - *First*
Hale UK (1963)
The Negative Man - *Last*
Hale UK (1971)

Capt PACKER and Kent BLOOMINGDALE
solve a case of murder on the campus.
American Policeman and American Male Amateur operating in USA

Addison SIMMONS 1902- (American)
Citation Record: 1 Book
Death On The Campus - *Only*
Crowell US (1935)

Penny PACKER and Det Jim SCOTT
Penny PACKER was a newshound for the *New York Clarion* who solved murders with the aid of Homicide Detective, *Jim SCOTT*. They appeared mainly in the pages of *Popular Detective.*
American Female Amateur and American Policeman operating in New York

Richard SALE 1911- (American)
Invented 5 detectives - see Calamity QUADE
No citations

Michael PADILLO
Second detective of Cyril MCCORKLE

The PADRE
British Male Amateur operating in England

Richard GOYNE 1902-1957 (British)
Invented 4 detectives - see Supt 'Tubby' GREENE
Citation Record: 5 Books
The Crime Philosopher - *First*
Paul UK (1945)
Traitor's Tide - *Last*
Paul UK (1948)

Godfrey PAGE
British Male Amateur operating in England

Victor L WHITECHURCH 1868-1933 (British)
Invented 5 detectives - see Det Sgt AMBROSE
Citation Record: 6 Short Stories in 1 Collection
The Investigations Of Godfrey Page, Railwayac - *Collection 1*
Sic!
Ferret Fantasy UK (1990)

Lorraine PAGE
is a former police lieutenant, now a wife and mother and a reformed alcoholic. She helps her old buddies still in the force to track down a serial killer.
American Female Ex-Policewoman operating in California

Lynda LA PLANTE (British)
has written some excellent crime dramas for TV and is now writing detective novels.
Citation Record: 1 Book
Cold Shoulder - *Single*
Macmillan UK (1994)

Christopher PAGET
American Male Amateur operating in USA

Richard North PATTERSON 1947- (American)
Invented 3 detectives - see Adam SHAW
Citation Record: 1 Book
The Lasko Tangent - *Single*
Norton US (1979); Hale UK (1980)

Steve PAGET
is hardboiled, always broke and operates in Steel City.
American Male Private Detective operating in USA

Manning Lee STOKES (American)
Invented 3 detectives - see Barnaby JONES
Citation Record: 1 Book
The Crooked Circle - *Only*
Graphic US (1951)
Too Many Murderers - *Only**
Graphic US (1955)

Pte PAGETT
British Male Amateur operating in England

W P DRURY 1861-1949 (British)

Writer: William Price DRURY

Citation Record: 11 Short Stories in 2 Collections

Men At Arms - *Collection 1*

Only three of the stories in this early collection of twelve of the author's short stories feature *Pte PAGETT,* who appears in a collection devoted to him twenty-four years later.

Short stories - 3
Chapman & Hall UK (1906)

Pagett Calling - *Collection 2*

Short stories - 8
Chapman & Hall UK (1930)

Det PAIGE

American Policeman operating in Philadelphia

Eric SAUTER 1948- (American)

Invented 3 detectives - see Robert Lee HUNTER

Citation Record: 1 Book

Skeletons - *Single*
Dutton US (1990)

Henry PAIGE

is an ex-cop and ex-Pinkerton man.

American Male Private Detective operating in Ohio

Dick STODGHILL (American)

Citation Record: 1 Selected Short Story

Wrongful Death
is included in *Mean Streets: The Second Private Eye Writers of America Anthology* (Editor: Robert J Randisi).
US (1986)

Tom PAIGE

British Male Amateur operating in England

Marion BABSON (American)

Invented 8 detectives - see Douglas PERKINS

Citation Record: 1 Book

Dangerous To Know - *Single*
Collins UK (1980); Walker US (1981)

Hayden PAINE

Second detective of Dep Youngman DURAN

Jack PAINE

is a reformed alcoholic who tries to solve the mystery of his client's death.

American Male Private Detective operating in USA

Al SARRANTONIO (American)

Citation Record: 1 Book

Cold Night - *Single*
Tor US (1989)

Dr PALFREY

was in charge of one of the several Intelligence agencies created by this author, all dealing with spies and enemies of the realm. This was fine during the Second World War and for a few years afterwards, but later the stories developed into science fiction.

British Male Professional Investigator operating in Europe

John CREASEY 1908-1973 (British)

Invented 6 detectives - see Insp Roger 'Handsome' WEST

Citation Record: 30 Books

Traitors' Doom - *First*
Long UK (1942); Hodder & Stoughton UK (1970)

The Whirlwind - *Last*
Walker US (1979)

Nick PALLADINO

looks like a 1940s gangster and dresses like a 1980s one.

American Male Private Detective operating in New York

Sidekick: Jane MYERS
American Female - Assistant

Abby ROBINSON 1947- (American)

Citation Record: 1 Book

The Dick And The Jane - *Single*
Delacorte US (1985)

Insp PALMER

tracks an unusual blackmailer.

British Policeman operating in England

James ANDERSON 1936- (British)

Invented 5 detectives - see Insp WILKINS

Citation Record: 1 Book

The Alpha List - *Only*
Constable UK (1972); Walker US (1972)

Harry PALMER

was, in fact, nameless in the original book, but was given the cited name in a famous film made from it.

British Male Secret Agent operating in several locations

Len DEIGHTON 1929- (British)

See main detective Bernard SAMSON

Citation Record: 6 Books

The Ipcress File - *First*
Hodder & Stoughton UK (1962); Simon & Schuster US (1963)

An Expensive Place To Die - *Last*
Cape UK (1967); Putnam US (1967)

Larry PALMER

is the ace reporter for the *Bulletin* and saves his newspaper from collapse by solving the murder of a minor film star.

American Male Amateur operating in USA

George Harmon COXE 1901-1984 (American)

Invented 20 detectives - see Kent MURDOCK

Citation Record: 1 Book

Top Assignment - *Only*
Knopf US (1955); Hammond UK (1955)

George PALMER-JONES

is a retired Home Office official, used to authority, which he now misses, and a devoted ornithologist. It is the latter occupation that gets him involved in detection; for, as soon as goes on a bird-watching trip, he runs into murder. The books are full of interesting bird lore, on which the author is an expert.

British Male Amateur operating in England/Scotland

Ann CLEEVES 1954- (British)

See main detective Insp Stephen RAMSAY

Citation Record: 6 Books

A Bird In The Hand - *First*
Century UK (1986); Fawcett US (1986)

Sea Fever - *Latest*
Fawcett US (1991); Macmillan UK (1993)

Monsieur Aristide PAMPLEMOUSSE

French Male Amateur operating in France

Michael BOND 1943- (American)

Writer: Michael Thomas BOND

Citation Record: 9 Books

Monsieur Pamplemousse - *First*
Beaufort US (1985)

Monsieur Pamplemousse Takes The Train - *Last*
Fawcett US (1992)

The PAN HANDLE DETECEIVE

American Male Detective in Pulp Magazines operating in USA

Tom FOX (American)

Invented 4 detectives - see OLD DUDE

Citation Record: 1 Book

The Pan Handle Detective; Or, Working Up The Great Railroad Robbery
New York Detective Library US (1882-8)

Marques Don PANCHO

is supposed to be 'the most famous detective in South America'. Created by British authors, he did not survive the 1950s.

Mexican Policeman operating in Mexico

Bruce BUCKINGHAM (British)

Writers: Peter LILLEY 1919- and Anthony STANSFIELD 1924-

Citation Record: 2 Books

Three Bad Nights - *First*
Joseph UK (1956)

Broiled Alive - *Latest*
Joseph UK (1957)

Colin PANTON

works in TV, has a penchant for smelling out things that just don't seem right and, not surprisingly, gets into one case of murder after another.
!See Appendix 2.

British Male Amateur operating in England

Philip PURSER 1925- (British)

was born in Letchworth, Hertfordshire. He was educated at Birkenhead School, Cheshire, attended King's College, Cambridge, and took an MA in English and History at St Andrew's University, Scotland. He served in the Army, 1943-1947, and then worked as a historian, journalist, and TV critic for several newspapers.

Writer: Philip John PURSER

Citation Record: 3 Books

Peregrination 22 - *First*
Cape UK (1962)

The Holy Father's Navy - *Last*
Hodder & Stoughton UK (1971)

Magistrate PAO

is a fictional character who is supposed to have lived in China around 1100. The author has 'translated' the records of his cases.

Chinese Male Professional Investigator operating in China

Leon COMBER (British)

is an expert on Oriental Studies and has worked in Hong Kong.

Citation Record: 6 Short Stories in 1 Collection

The Strange Cases Of Magistrate Pao - *Collection 1*
Tuttle US (1964)

PAOLA and GEORGE

British Female Amateur and British Male Amateur

George SAMPSON 1916- (British)

Writer: George Richard SAMPSON

Citation Record: 2 Books

A Drug On The Market - *First*
Hale UK (1967)

Playing With Fire - *Last*
Hale UK (1968)

Mike PARADISE

American Male Sleuth operating in USA

Jack CANON (American)

For writer details see Nick CARTER (Writer Jack CANON)

Citation Record: 3 Books

An Angel For Paradise - *First*
Charter US (1979)

A Hangman For Paradise - *Latest*
Charter US (1980)

Simon PARBITTER and Keith CALDER

Simon PARBITTER is a town-bred detective story writer who comes to Newton Lauder to claim his inheritance and has to solve the murder of his uncle. He is assisted in his enquiries by *KEITH CALDER*, who is the main detective in other books by this author.

British Male Amateurs operating in Scotland

Stooge: Ch Insp MUNRO
is the local law and is usually wrong as far as *CALDER* is concerned.

British Male

Gerald HAMMOND 1926- (British)

Invented 5 detectives - see Keith CALDER

Citation Record: 2 Books

Adverse Report - *First*
Macmillan UK (1987)

Stray Shot - *Latest*
Macmillan UK (1988)

Tom PARCHER

American Male Amateur operating in USA

James POWERS (American)

Citation Record: 1 Book

Estate Of Grace - *Only*
Harper & Row US (1979)

Ch Insp Dan PARDOE

is tall, in his forties, intelligent and cultured, clearly still possessing most of the attributes given to old-style British amateur detectives of the 1930s. His cases usually involve nasty poisons and much in the way of literary allusions.

British Policeman operating in England

Sidekick: Sgt SALT

British Male - Subordinate

Dorothy BOWERS 1904- (British)

Writer: Dorothy Violet BOWERS

Inventor of one other detective Insp RAIKES

Citation Record: 4 Books

Shadows Before - *First*
Hodder & Stoughton UK (1939); Doubleday US (1940)

Fear For Miss Betony - *Last*
Hodder & Stoughton UK (1941)

Fear And Miss Betony - *Last**
Doubleday US (1942)

Thibault PAREW

is an authority on most of the things that the well-turned-out amateur sleuth of the 1930s was expected to be. Not surprisingly, his behaviour and speech reflect his manifest and manifold abilities.

American Male Amateur operating in California

Gilbert ELDREDGE (American)

Citation Record: 2 Books

Death For The Surgeon - *First*
Phoenix Press US (1939)

Murder In The Stratosphere - *Last*
Phoenix Press US (1940)

Melita PARGETER

is a widow who, in her first book, becomes involved in a mystery and has to turn amateur detective. Since her late husband was a crook himself, she has considerable knowledge of the seamier side of life; this enables her to leave the police standing when it comes to discovering and solving crimes, which she later goes on doing for curiosity's sake.

British Female Amateur operating in England

Simon BRETT 1945- (British)

Invented 3 detectives - see Charles PARIS

Citation Record: 3 Books

A Nice Class Of Corpse - *First*
Macmillan UK (1986); Scribner's US (1986)

Mrs, Presumed Dead - *Latest*
Gollancz UK (1989); Scribner's US (1989)

Charles PARIS

is a second-class actor who, during the course of his theatrical work, becomes involved in murders galore. He solves them under the noses of the police, even when they do not recognise that a crime has been committed. He drinks too much (always Bell's whisky), has an agreeable ex-wife, beds available females, and lives in an aura of theatre and TV, which the author describes most convincingly.

British Male Amateur operating in London

Simon BRETT 1945- (British)

was born in Worcester Park, Surrey. He was educated at Dulwich College, London, 1956-1964, and took a BA in English at Wadham College, Oxford, 1967.

Writer: Simon Anthony Lee BRETT

Other Detectives:

Philip MARLOWE　　Melita PARGETER

Citation Record: 15 Books

Cast, In Order Of Disappearance - *First*
Gollancz UK (1975); Scribner's US (1975)

A Reconstructed Corpse - *Latest*
Gollancz UK (1993)

Evan PARIS

was once a drop-out. But he discovered the science of criminology and, working at it, became a millionaire several times over. Then his wife was murdered – a seemingly occupational hazard of modern American private eyes, which is getting distressingly more frequent. This event, not surprisingly, made him cynical and disillusioned and he has withdrawn from business into a mountain retreat. Fortunately, he is persuaded to take up arms again.

American Male Private Detective operating in Santa Monica

Joseph LOUIS (American)

Citation Record: 2 Books

Madelaine - *First*
Bantam US (1987); Mysterious Press UK (1987)

The Trouble With Stephanie - *Latest*
Bantam US (1988)

Capt Wade PARIS

operates in 'Eastern City', modelled on Boston, which the author knew well. The settings are rural rather than urban and, unlike police procedurals, the novels mainly deal with single, workmanlike detective cases. Called 'Old Icewater' by his colleagues, *PARIS* is mature, tough, invulnerable and devoid of most human weaknesses.

American Policeman operating in Massachusetts

Benjamin BENSON 1915-1959 (American)

was born in Boston, Massachusetts, and graduated from the Suffolk University Law School, Boston. He served in the US army and received the Purple Heart and other battle decorations during the Second World War, during which he was seriously wounded. He began writing around 1950 and published some twenty criminous works, mostly set in and around Boston, before his untimely death.

Inventor of one other detective Trooper Ralph LINDSEY

Citation Record: 10 Books

Beware The Pale Horse - *First*
Mill US (1951); Muller UK (1952)

The Huntress Is Dead - *Last*
Mill US (1960)

PARKER

American Male Sleuth operating in New York

Richard STARK 1933- (American)

See main detective Alan GROFIELD

Citation Record: 15 Books

The Score - *First*
Pocket Books US (1960)

Killtown - *First**
Coronet UK (1971)

Deadly Edge - *Last*
Random House US (1971); Coronet UK (1972)

Insp PARKER

of Scotland Yard is in this Victorian short story, which appeared in an obscure publication.

British Policeman operating in London

Thomas COBB 1853-1932 (British)

Inventor of one other detective Insp BEDISON

Citation Record: 1 Book

Wedderburn's Will - *Only*
Lifebuoy Library UK (1892)

Insp PARKER

British Policeman operating in England

John AUSTWICK 1904-1965 (British)

Writer: Austin LEE

Citation Record: 2 Books

Highland Homicide - *First*
Hale UK (1957)

Murder In The Borough Library - *Last*
Hale UK (1959)

Det Claire PARKER

Second detective of Det Jack WILLOWS

Dorothy PARKER and Alexander WOOLLCOTT

American Female Amateur and American Male Amateur operating in New York

George BAXT 1923- (American)

Invented 6 detectives - see Pharaoh LOVE

Citation Record: 1 Book

The Dorothy Parker Murder Case - *Only*
is an excellent whodunnit set among the *literati* of New York, 1926.
St Martin's US (1984); Collins UK (1985)

Ellis PARKER

American Male Professional Investigator operating in New Jersey

Fletcher PRATT 1897-1956 (American)

See main detective George Helmfleet JONES

Citation Record: 12 Short Stories in 1 Collection

The Cunning Mulatto And Other Cases Of Ellis Parker, American Detective - *Collection 1*
Smith & Haas US (1935)

Detective No 1 - *Collection 1**
Methuen UK (1936)

Dr Eric PARKER

American Male Amateur operating in Los Angeles

Thomas T NOGUCHI and Arthur LYONS Jr (American)

Citation Record: 2 Books

Unnatural Causes - *First*
Putnam US (1988); Pan UK (1991)

Physical Evidence - *Latest*
Putnam US (1990)

Horatio PARKER

is a millionaire reporter.

Male Amateur

Lew MATTHEWS

Citation Record: 1 Book

A Conviction Of Guilt - *Single*
HarperCollins UK (1993)

Jack PARKER

American Male Detective in Pulp Magazines operating in USA

Anthony P MORRIS 1849-1921 (American)

Invented 5 detectives - see Mark MAGIC

Citation Record: 1 Selected Short Story

Jack Parker, The 'All-Round' Detective; Or, The Trail Of The Letter 'A'
Old Cap Collier Library US (18??)

Jerry PARKER

British Male Amateur operating in England

James GUNN

See main detective Kirk CULLEN

Citation Record: 6 Short Stories in 1 Collection

The Adventures Of Jerry Parker, Mobile Investigator - *Collection 1*
Nuffield UK (?)

Quinn PARKER

American Male Sleuth operating in USA

Bruce ZIMMERMAN 1952- (American)

Citation Record: 1 Book

Thicker Than Water - *Single*
HarperCollins US (1993)

Christopher PARKINS

British Male Amateur operating in several locations

R L DEARDEN 1883- (British)

Writer: Richard Lionel DEARDEN

Citation Record: 15 Short Stories in 1 Collection

Christopher Parkins, RN - *Collection 1*
Unwin UK (1925)

Eddie PARKS

appeared only in a few short stories.

American Male Amateur operating in USA

George ADE 1866-1944 (American)

Citation Record: 7 Short Stories in 1 Collection

Bang! Bang! - *Collection 1*
This collection of eleven of the author's short stories contains seven with *Eddie PARKS.*
Sears US (1928)

P

Bill PARMELEE

is a professional cardsharp and, in short stories involving cardplay, has to solve mysteries connected with his games.

American Male Private Detective operating in USA

Percival WILDE 1887-1953 (American)

Inventor of one other detective Peter MORAN

Citation Record: 8 Short Stories in 1 Collection

Rogues In Clover - *Collection 1*
Appleton US (1929)

Sophie PARNELL

sets out to investigate the death of her cousin and ends up in a mess of corrupt wealth, drugs and the occult before she succeeds.

Australian Female Private Detective operating in Sydney

Tom BEAUFORT 1944- (Australian)

was born in New Zealand, educated at Cambridge in the UK, and is now an Australian citizen.

Writer: John SLIGO

Citation Record: 1 Book

Whatever Happened To Rosie Dunn? - *Single*
Penguin UK (1989)

Tim PARNELL

was once with the CIA but has gone to Holland, where he operates near Amsterdam Airport.

American Male Private Detective operating in Amsterdam

Don SMITH 1909- (American)

See main detective Phil SHERMAN

Citation Record: 4 Books

The Man Who Played Thief - *First*
GM US (1969); Hale UK (1971)

Corsican Takeover - *Last*
GM US (1974); Coronet UK (1974)

Insp PARR

solves a case of murder by poison gas in a locked-room situation.

British Policeman operating in London

Edgar WALLACE 1875-1932 (British)

Invented 28 detectives - see J G REEDER

Citation Record: 1 Book

The Crimson Circle - *Only*
Hodder & Stoughton UK (1922); Doubleday US (1929)

Insp PARRISH

investigates a murder that occurs while a radio programme is being broadcast from an English village to its twin town in the USA.

British Policeman operating in England

Robert BARNARD 1936- (British)

Invented 13 detectives - see Insp Perry TRETHOWAN

Citation Record: 1 Book

A Little Local Murder - *Single*
Collins UK (1976); Scribner's US (1983)

Sir Gideon PARROT

solves the mystery of a woman's 'impossible' disappearance from a locked room.

British Male Amateur operating in England

Edward D HOCH 1930- (American)

Invented 20 detectives - see Capt LEOPOLD

Citation Record: 1 Selected Short Story

Lady Of The Impossible
In 'Ellery Queen's Mystery Magazine' US (1981)

Liz PARROTT

American Female Amateur operating in New York

Manning LONG 1906- (American)

Citation Record: 6 Books

Vicious Circle - *First*
Duell US (1942); Hammond UK (1946)

Savage Breast - *Last*
Duell US (1948); Hammond UK (1951)

Franklin PARRY and Leonard HARRIS

British Male Amateurs operating in England

Richard KEVERNE 1882-1950 (British)

Invented 4 detectives - see Insp MACE

Citation Record: 2 Books

William Cook - Antique Dealer - *First*
Constable UK (1928)

The Strange Case Of William Cook - *First**
Harper & Row US (1928)

Menace - *Last*
Constable UK (1933)

Insp Lane PARRY

British Policeman operating in England

Maureen SARSFIELD (British)

Citation Record: 2 Books

Green December Fills The Graveyard - *First*
Pilot Press UK (1945); Coward McCann US (1946)

Dinner For None - *Last*
Nicholson & Watson UK (1948)

A Party For Lawty - *Last**
Coward McCann US (1948)

Ch Insp Peter PARSON

investigates a girl's death in a fall from a lover's leap.

British Policeman operating in England

Sidekick: Sgt 'Wammo' WIMBUSH
British Male - Subordinate

Jack S SCOTT 1922- (British)
Invented 3 detectives - see Det Insp Alf ROSHER
Citation Record: 1 Book
A Little Darling, Dead - *Single*
Collins UK (1985); St Martin's US (1986)

Lt PASCAL
is even-tempered, soft-spoken, and a most dedicated cop. He appears also with two of the author's other detectives: in two books with *Grant SIMON,* and in two books with *John JERICHO.*
American Policeman operating in New York

Hugh PENTECOST 1903-1989 (American)
Invented 12 detectives - see Pierre CHAMBRUN
Citation Record: 1 Book 3 Short Stories in 1 Collection
Only The Rich Die Young - *Only*
Dodd, Mead US (1964); Boardman UK (1964)
Lieutenant Pascal's Tastes In Homicides - *Collection 1*
contains three novelettes.
Dodd, Mead US (1954); Boardman UK (1955)

Lt PASCAL
Second detective of John JERICHO

Lt PASCAL
Second detective of Grant SIMON

Mrs PASCHAL
is considered by many sources to be the first female detective in the literature (but see under *Mrs GLADDEN* for rival claims). She is a member of the London police force and is employed by Colonel Warren, 'Chief of London Police Detectives'. She is around the age of forty, well-educated, well-born, was a widow when her police work began, and was, rather delightfully, called 'one of the much-dreaded, but little-known people called Female Detectives'. Ah, Marple! Ah, Millhone!
British Policewoman operating in London

Hayward W STEPHENS (British)
Citation Record: 10 Short Stories in 1 Collection
The Experiences Of A Lady Detective - *Collection 1*
narrates three cases in which *Mrs PASCHAL* works with the police, and seven in which she undertakes a private investigation.
Clarke UK (1864)

Sgt Peter PASCOE
Second detective of Supt Andrew DALZIEL

Jerry PASON
is a parody of *Erle Stanley GARDNER's* detective, *Perry MASON.*
Appears with at least two other detectives - see Mallory KING

Bryce PATCH
was formerly in the Military Police. Now he runs the Amsterdam Investigation Bureau, East 12th Street, Manhattan.
American Male Private Detective operating in New York

William S BALLINGER 1912-1980 (American)
Invented 5 detectives - see Joaquin HAWKS
Citation Record: 1 Book
Heist Me Higher - *Only*
Signet US (1969); Hale UK (1971)

Col PATERNOSTER
British Male Sleuth operating in England

Ralph INCHBALD 1902- (British)
Writer: Ralph Mordaunt Elliot INCHBALD
Citation Record: 3 Books
Colonel Paternoster - *First*
Hodder & Stoughton UK (1951)
September Story - *Last*
Hodder & Stoughton UK (1955)

Kate PATERSON
visits the grave of her lover, a mountain climber, and is told that his death was the result of a clash between the CIA and the KGB. She resolves to bring those responsible to justice.
British Female Secret Agent operating in Austria

Hester ROWAN 1928- (British)
Writer: Sheila Mary ROBINSON
Other Byline: Sheila RADLEY
Citation Record: 1 Book
Snowfall - *Single*
Collins UK (1978)
Alpine Encounter - *Single**
Scribner's US (1979)

Det Insp Ross PATERSON
British Policeman operating in England

Katherine FIELD (British)
Citation Record: 3 Books
Disappearance Of A Niece - *First*
Murray UK (1941)
Murder To Follow - *Last*
Jenkins UK (1944)

Commissaire PATRAS
French Policeman operating in Paris

Francis GRIERSON 1888-1972 (British)
Invented 6 detectives - see Ch Det Insp George MUIR
Citation Record: 3 Books
Heart In The Box - *First*
Butterworth UK (1936)
The Man From Madagascar - *Last*
Butterworth UK (1937)

Roger PATTEN
British Male Secret Agent operating in several locations

Anthony A RANDALL 1923- (British)
Writer: Anthony Asheton RANDALL
Citation Record: 2 Books
Ride A Tiger - *First*
Hale UK (1965)
Flashpoint - *Last*
Hale UK (1966)

Amelia PATTON
Second detective of Richard PATTON

Richard PATTON and Amelia PATTON
are husband and wife. He is now retired from his position as Detective-Inspector in a local police force but still manages to becomes involved in solving case after case, with unending help from her. It seems fortunate that they each have an upmarket car, for both are frequently mentioned and appear to be essential for the resolution of some ingenious plots.
British Male Ex-Policeman and British Female Amateur operating in England

Roger ORMEROD 1920- (British)
Invented 4 detectives - see Philipa LOWE
Citation Record: 8 Books
Face Value - *First*
Constable UK (1983)
The Hanging Doll Murder - *First**
Scribner's US (1984)
Mask Of Innocence - *Latest*
Constable UK (1994)

Mother PAUL
is a nun who solves her one case by 'seeing things in peoples' eyes'. That would seem a most useful adjunct to conventional police work!
Female Amateur

June WRIGHT (Australian)

Citation Record: 1 Book

Make-Up For Murder - *Only*
Long UK (1966)

Don PAULSON

runs across murder in triplicate. The police naturally suspect him and he has to discover whodunnit (or them) to clear himself.

American Male Amateur operating in USA

J F HUTTON (American)

Writer: Joy Ferris HUTTON

Citation Record: 1 Book

Too Good To Be True - *Only*
Simon & Schuster US (1948)

Dead Man Friday - *Only**
Ace US (1953)

The Dolphin Mystery - *Only**
Foulsham UK (1949)

Gregory 'Grischa' PAVLOV

American Male Amateur operating in USA

Jessica RYAN 1914?-1972 (American)

Writer: Jessica Cadwalader RYAN

Citation Record: 2 Books

The Man Who Asked Why - *First*
Doubleday US (1945)

Exit The Harlequin - *Last*
Doubleday US (1947)

The Clue Of The Frightening Coin - *Last**
Novel Selections US (194?)

Madeline PAYNE

American Female Professional Investigator operating in USA

Lawrence L LYNCH (American)

Invented 11 detectives - see Neil J BATHURST

Citation Record: 2 Books

Madeline Payne, The Detective's Daughter - *First*
Loyd US (1884)

The Detective's Daughter; Or, Madeline Payne - *First**
Ward, Lock UK (1887)

Moina; Or, Against The Mighty - *Last*
Laird & Lee US (1891)

Moina - *Last**
Ward, Lock UK (1891)

P

Ritchie PAYNE

Second detective of Walter PAYNE

Sham PAYNE

American Sleuth operating in USA

Kelliher SECRIST (American)

was a pseudonym for two reporters in Kansas City.

Writers: Dan T KELLIHER and W G SECRIST

Citation Record: 2 Books

Murder Melody - *First*
Phoenix Press US (1939)

She Screamed Blue Murder - *First**
Green Dragon US (1946)

Murder Makes By-Lines - *Last*
Mystery House US (1941)

Walter PAYNE and Ritchie PAYNE

Walter PAYNE, an octogenarian, is a retired Professor of English, now living in Iowa. With the help of his grand-nephew, he investigates a strange case of murder and burial that takes place when an aeroplane lands near his farm.

American Male Amateurs operating in Iowa

Laurence Davis LAFORE 1917- (American)

Citation Record: 1 Book

Nine Seven Juliet - *Only*
Doubleday US (1969)

Commissaire PAYRAN

Policeman operating in Geneva

Elizabeth NISOT 1893- (American)

Writer: Mavis Elizabeth Hocking NISOT

Citation Record: 4 Books

Twelve To Dine - *First*
Paul UK (1935)

Unnatural Deeds - *Last*
Paul UK (1939)

Amelia PEABODY

is a Victorian archaeologist who attracts mystery and mayhem whenever and wherever she is digging. She is married to another archaeologist who acts as a support at such grievous times.

British Female Amateur operating in England/Egypt

Sidekick: Radcliff EMERSON

is, like his wife, an archaeologist. Definitely a second fiddle, he assists her on her excavations and in the mysteries she encounters.

British Male - Husband

Elizabeth PETERS 1927- (American)

Invented 4 detectives - see Vicky BLISS

Citation Record: 6 Books

Crocodile On The Sandbank - *First*
Dodd, Mead US (1975); Cassell UK (1976)

The Last Camel Died At Noon - *Latest*
Warner US (1992); Piatkus UK (1991)

Addington PEACE

British Male Amateur operating in England

B Fletcher ROBINSON (British)

Writer: Bertram Fletcher ROBINSON

Citation Record: 8 Short Stories in 1 Collection

The Chronicles Of Addington Peace - *Collection 1*
Harper & Row UK (1905)

Charlie PEACE

appears also in two books with the author's other detective, *Insp Perry TRETHOWAN.*

British Male Amateur operating in England

Robert BARNARD 1936- (British)

Invented 13 detectives - see Insp Perry TRETHOWAN

Citation Record: 1 Book

Death And The Chaste Apprentice - *Single*
Collins UK (1989); Scribner's US (1989)

Charlie PEACE

Second detective of Insp Perry TRETHOWAN

Cdr Geoffrey PEACE

British Male Professional Investigator operating in Africa

Geoffrey JENKINS 1920- (British)

Citation Record: 2 Books

A Twist Of Sand - *First*
Collins UK (1959); Viking US (1960)

Hunter-Killer - *Last*
Collins UK (1966); Putnam US (1967)

Dr St George PEACHY

Second detective of Barney FORGE

Prof Percy PEACOCK

is a Professor of Psychology in California, a bachelor, an amateur actor and an amateur detective.

American Male Amateur operating in Cape Cod/California

Courtland FITZSIMMONS 1883-1949 (American)

Invented 4 detectives - see Det Jack KETHERIDGE

Citation Record: 2 Books

Death Rings A Bell - *First*
Lippincott US (1942); Boardman UK (1943)
Tied For Murder - *Last*
Lippincott US (1943); Boardman UK (1945)

Hugo PEAK
British Male Amateur operating in England

Denis MACKAIL 1892- (British)
See main detective Henry GIBSON
Citation Record: 10 Short Stories in 1 Collection
According To Gibson - *Collection 1*
Not all the stories are criminous.
Heinemann UK (1926); Houghton US (1926)

Supt Andrew PEARSON
British Policeman operating in England

Eric SHEPHERD 1892- (British)
Citation Record: 2 Books
Murder In A Nunnery - *First*
Sheed UK (1940)
More Murder In A Nunnery - *Last*
Sheed UK (1954)

Insp Jack PEARSON
British Policeman operating in England

Roland DANIEL 1880-1969 (British)
Invented 11 detectives - see Insp Neville LANGHAM
Citation Record: 4 Books
The Crackswoman - *First*
Wright UK (1932)
Murder At Little Malling - *Last*
Wright UK (1946)

Dave PECK
American Male Amateur operating in USA

Thomas Patrick MCMAHON (American)
Citation Record: 1 Book
The Issue Of The Bishop's Blood - *Only*
Doubleday US (1972); Collins UK (1973)

Judge Ephraim Peabody PECK
lives in Sac Prairie, Wisconsin, and is a shrewd local detective in the classical style, solving classical murder mysteries.
American Male Professional Investigator operating in Wisconsin

August DERLETH 1909-1971 (American)
Invented 4 detectives - see Solar PONS
Citation Record: 10 Books
Murder Stalks The Wakely Family - *First*
Loring & Mussey US (1934)
Death Stalks The Wakely Family - *First**
Newnes UK (1937)
Fell Purpose - *Last*
Arcadia US (1953)

Ethel PECK
American Female Amateur operating in Minneapolis

L A TAYLOR 1939- (American)
Invented 4 detectives - see Joseph 'JJ' JAMISON
Citation Record: 1 Book
Love Of Money - *Single*
Walker US (1976)

Lou PECKINPAUGH
is in a novelization of a film.
American Male Private Detective operating in San Francisco

Robert GROSSBACH 1941- (American)
Citation Record: 1 Book
The Cheap Detective - *Single*
is a novelization of a film, set in San Francisco in 1940, and is a satire on the classic story, *THE MALTESE FALCON.*
Warner US (1978)

Insp/Ch Insp Harry PECKOVER
fits none too well into Scotland Yard. A London cockney, a bit of a bruiser, a lowly poet, a lover of beer and brown hats, and a stickler for law and order, he becomes involved in some of the oddest crimes and situations. He appears also in one book with the author's other detective, *Supt O'MALLEY.*
British Policeman operating in England

Sidekick: Det Const Jason TWITTY
is tall, black, intellectual, and was a pupil at Harrow. All of which makes him a stunningly effective assistant for a short, white, cockney detective!
British Male - Subordinate

Michael KENYON 1931- (British)
was born in Huddersfield, Yorkshire. He was educated at Leighton Park School, Reading, Berkshire, and took an MA in History at Wadham College, Oxford, 1954. He studied, 1954-1955, at Duke University, Durham, North Carolina, and later practised and taught journalism in England and the USA. He is the author of at least twenty genre books.
Other Detectives:
Arthur APPLEYARD
Prof FOLEY
Supt O'MALLEY
Insp/Ch Insp Harry PECKOVER and Supt O'MALLEY
Det Const Jason TWITTY
Citation Record: 5 Books
The Elgar Variations - *First*
Putnam US (1981)
Peckover And The Bog Man - *Latest*
Macmillan UK (1994)

Insp/Ch Insp Harry PECKOVER and Supt O'MALLEY
also appear individually in other books by this author.
British Policemen operating in Ireland

Michael KENYON 1931- (British)
Invented 6 detectives - see Insp/Ch Insp Harry PECKOVER
Citation Record: 1 Book
Zigzag - *Single*
Collins UK (1981)

Det Carl PEDERSON
American Policeman operating in California

Jeanne HART 1919-1990 (American)
Writer: Jeanne Hart SHRAGER
Citation Record: 3 Books
Fetish - *First*
St Martin's US (1987)
A Personal Possession - *First**
Collins UK (1989)
A Decent Killer - *Latest*
HarperCollins UK (1991); Hall US (1995)

Fire Marshal Ben PEDLEY
hates fire-raisers but, in the course of his job as a Fire Marshal, runs into them an extraordinary number of times. Hunting for clues to arson and sabotage, he certainly gets into thrilling situations.
American Male Professional Investigator operating in USA

Stewart STERLING 1895- (American)
was born in Illinois. He was a journalist, editor and radio programme producer.
Writer: Prentice WINCHELL
Other Bylines:
Spencer DEAN
Dexter ST CLAIR
Inventor of one other detective Gil VINE
Citation Record: 9 Books
Fire Alarm Funeral - *First*
Putnam US (1942)
Too Hot To Handle - *Last*
Random House US (1961); Boardman UK (1962)

Emma PEEL
Second detective of John STEELE

Robert PEGRAM
is a lawyer in this one Victorian novel.
British Male Amateur operating in England

Hawley SMART 1833-1893 (British)
Invented 8 detectives - see Insp POLLOCK
Citation Record: 1 Book
The Great Tontine - *Only*
Chapman & Hall UK (1881)

Insp Clovis Desire PEL
appears in a long series of books, stylistically police procedurals but unusual in being set in Burgundy, France. *Clovis PEL* is a senior member of the *Brigade Criminelle* and appears to be a good cop. He is also a hypochondriac and seems to dislike most things, but especially anything not Burgundian. As in all police procedurals, wherever they are located, he has a bewildering number of sidekicks, intelligent, stupid, and comic. They may be of interest to the author but they are of doubtful interest to the reader. Only two are cited.
French Policeman operating in Burgundy
Sidekick: Insp Daniel DARCY
is something of a ladies' man. However, he is a brilliant investigator and *PEL's* main assistant in the field.
French Male - Assistant
Sidekick: Sgt Jean-Luc NOSJEAN
is another of *PEL's* assistants. This one seems to spend much of his time unsuccessfully courting girls.
French Male - Subordinate

Mark HEBDEN 1916- (British)
was born in Rotherham, Yorkshire, and was educated at Rotherham Grammar School, 1924-1932. He served in the Royal Air Force, 1939-1945, and later worked as a history teacher, journalist and cartoonist, becoming a full-time writer in the 1950s. Apart from his criminous work, he is the author, under his real name, of at least thirty-four non-genre novels and many other books of various kinds.
Writer: John HARRIS
Inventor of one other detective Col MOSTYN
Citation Record: 17 Books
Death Set To Music - *First*
Hamish Hamilton UK (1979); Walker US (1983)
Pel And The Sepulchre Job - *Latest*
Constable UK (1992)

Lexey Jane PELAZONI
American Female Amateur operating in USA

Lee HEAD 1931- (American)
Writer: Joanne Lee HEAD
Citation Record: 2 Books
The Terrarium - *First*
Putnam US (1976)
The Crystal Clear Case - *Latest*
Putnam US (1977)

Ida PELHAM
American Female Amateur operating in Philadelphia

Kage BOOTON 1919- (American)
wrote nearly a dozen criminous novels.
Writer: Catherine Kage BOOTON
Citation Record: 1 Book
Who Knows Julie Gordon? - *Single*
Doubleday US (1980); Hale UK (1981)

Jimmy PELHAM
is an insurance agent who accidentally stumbles on a plot by post-war Nazis to detonate an atom bomb in London. By clever sleuthing, however, he foils them.
British Male Professional Investigator operating in London
Sidekick: ROSSI
is a dizzy, beautiful lady who is of invaluable support.
Swiss Female - Aide

Tony KENRICK 1935- (Australian)
was born in Sydney, New South Wales, Australia. He was educated at Sydney High School and served in the Royal Australian Navy, 1953. He is the author of some delicious caper novels, many of which have exotic backgrounds.
Other Detectives:
Hugh DECKER
Det Billy MARCUS
Bill VERECKER
Citation Record: 1 Book
The 81st Site - *Single*
Granada UK (1980); New American Library US (1980)

Pel PELHAM
Australian Male Sleuth operating in Australia

A E MARTIN 1885-1955 (Australian)
See main detective Insp GORMLEY
Citation Record: 2 Books
The Common People - *First*
Consolidated AU (1944)
The Outsiders - *First**
Simon & Schuster US (1945); Nimmo UK (1948)
The Bridal Bed Murders - *Last*
Simon & Schuster US (1954)
The Chinese Bed Mystery - *Last**
Reinhardt UK (1955)

Insp Gregory PELLEW and Viscount CLYMPING
comprise one of the more unusual duos of British crime fiction, for here a local policeman calls for aid on a bohemian English lord who happens to be in the vicinity. In the later books of the series they actually set up a detective agency together.
British Policeman and British Male Amateur operating in England

Val GIELGUD 1900-1981 (British)
Invented 3 detectives - see Det Insp Simon SPEARS
Citation Record: 10 Books
Gallows' Foot - *First*
Collins UK (1958)
A Fearful Thing - *Last*
Macmillan UK (1975)

Det Supt Mark PEMBERTON
British Policeman operating in England
Sidekick: Policewoman Amanda WALLBRIDGE
British Female - Subordinate

Peter N WALKER 1936- (British)
Writer: Peter Norman WALKER
Other Bylines:
Christopher CORAM
Nicholas RHEA
Inventor of one other detective Det Sgt CARNABY
Citation Record: 1 Book
False Alibi - *Single*
Constable UK (1991)

Dick PEMBERTY and Peter WEBB
solve the mystery of an aerodrome that disappears.
British Male Amateurs operating in England

Philip CONDE (British)
Invented 3 detectives - see Dick PEMBERTY
Citation Record: 1 Book
Mystery Of The Vanishing Aerodrome - *Only*
Wright UK (1939)

Dick PEMBERTY
British Male Amateur operating in England

Philip CONDE (British)

Other Detectives:
Dick PEMBERTY and Peter WEBB
Irving TODD

Citation Record: 7 Books

Death From The Air - *First*
Wright UK (1936)

Death Laughs Aloft - *Last*
Wright UK (1940)

Mr PENDLEBURY

British Male Amateur operating in England

Anthony WEBB 1901- (British)

Writer: Norman Scarlyn WILSON

Citation Record: 9 Books

Mr Pendlebury's Hat Trick - *First*
Harrap UK (1938)

A Queer Bag Of Bodies - *Last*
Harrap UK (1947)

John Hawkdale PENDRAGON

operates in England during the middle years of the nineteenth century.

British Male Amateur operating in England

Robert TREVELYAN 1929- (British)

Writer: Robert FORREST-WEBB

Citation Record: 5 Books

Pendragon, Late Of Prince Albert's Own - *First*
Hodder & Stoughton UK (1975); Saturday Review Press US (1975)

Pendragon, The Illusionist - *Latest*
Hodder & Stoughton UK (1980)

Lens PENGA

Appears with at least two other detectives - see Lowell GAYLORD

Insp PENK

British Policeman operating in England

Jan GORDON 1882-1944 (British)

Writer: Jan GORDON

Other Byline: William GORE

Citation Record: 1 Book

Death In The Wheelbarrow - *Only*
was previously published under the following byline.
Mystery House US (1940)

William GORE 1882-1944 (British)

For writer details see Insp PENK

Citation Record: 2 Books

Death In The Wheelbarrow - *First*
was republished under the preceding byline.
Harrap UK (1935)

Murder Most Artistic - *Last*
Harrap UK (1937)

The Mystery Of The Painted Nude - *Last**
Doubleday US (1938)

David PENN

is a writer in London during the Second World War who believes that a friend of his has been murdered. He searches for the killers and, not only does he find them, but he also succeeds in foiling a plot by Nazi agents.

British Male Amateur operating in England

Storm JAMESON 1897-1986 (British)

was the author of several admired mainstream novels.

Writer: Margaret Storm JAMESON

Citation Record: 1 Book

Before The Crossing - *Only*
Macmillan UK (1947)

Tess PENNICOTT

Female Amateur operating in England

Erica QUEST 1919- (American)

See main detective Det Ch Insp Kate MADDOX

Citation Record: 1 Book

The October Cabaret - *Single*
Doubleday US (1979); Hale UK (1986)

Arthur Stukeley PENNINGTON

appears also with *Insp Patrick Aloysius MCCARTHY* in other books by this author and by *Gordon BRANDON.*

British Male Amateur operating in England

John G BRANDON 1879-1941 (British)

Writer: John Gordon BRANDON

Invented 5 detectives - see Sgt/Det Insp Patrick Aloysius MCCARTHY

Citation Record: 3 Books

Murder In Mayfair - *First*
Methuen UK (1934)

The Case Of The Would-Be Widow - *Last*
Wright UK (1950)

Arthur Stukeley PENNINGTON and Det Insp Patrick Aloysius MCCARTHY

appeared originally in a long series of books by *John G GORDON.* After his death in 1941, they were also featured in two further books written by *Gordon BRANDON,* who was probably related to their originator. Both detectives also appear individually in other books written by the latter author.

British Male Amateur and British Policeman operating in England

Gordon BRANDON (British)

See main detective pair Michael TERRENCE and "Terry" TERRENCE

Other Byline: John G BRANDON

Citation Record: 2 Books

Murder Comes Smiling - *Pastiche 1*
Wright UK (1959)

Death Of A Mermaid - *Pastiche 2*
Wright UK (1960)

John G BRANDON 1879-1941 (British)

Invented 5 detectives - see Sgt/Det Insp Patrick Aloysius MCCARTHY

Citation Record: 25 Books

West End - *First*
Methuen UK (1933)

Death Stalks In Soho - *Last*
Wright UK (1959)

Peter PENNINGTON

British Male Amateur operating in England/Far East

Edmund SNELL 1889- (British)

See main detective Reggie FAULKNER

Citation Record: 2 Books

The Yellow Seven - *First*
Unwin UK (1923); Century US (1923)

Yellow Jacket - *Last*
Skeffington UK (1936)

Miles PENNOYER

British Male Amateur operating in England

Margery LAWRENCE ?-1969 (British)

See main detective Miss BRANDT

Citation Record: 9 Short Stories in 2 Collections

Number Seven Queer Street - *Collection 1*

Short stories - 5
Hale UK (1945); Mycroft & Moran US (1969)

Master Of Shadows - *Collection 2*

Short stories - 4
Hale UK (1959)

Mr PENNY

British Male Amateur operating in England

Maurice MOISEIWITSCH (British)

Inventor of one other detective Woolf SARASON

Citation Record: 2 Books 10 Short Stories in 1 Collection

Mr Penny - *First*
Muller UK (1938)
Mr Penny At War - *Last*
Angus UK (1942)
Mr Penny Comes Down Heads - *Collection 1*
Angus UK (1945)

Alice PENNY

American Female Amateur operating in USA

Adam BLISS (American)
Writers: Robert Ferdinand BURKHARDT 1892-1947 and Eva BURKHARDT 1899-
Inventor of one other detective Capt KEYES
Citation Record: 2 Books
Murder Upstairs - *First*
Macrae UK (1934); Hamilton UK (1935)
Four Times A Widower - *Last*
Macrae UK (1936); Hamilton UK (1938)

Archibald PENNY

British Male Amateur operating in England

Wallace JACKSON 1898- (British)
See main detective Insp Clancy MARTIN
Citation Record: 2 Books
The Zadda Street Affair - *First*
Low UK (1934)
The Extraordinary Case Of Mr Bell - *Last*
Low UK (1935); Hopkins US (1936)

Prof A PENNYFEATHER

is the Professor of English at the fictional Clarendon College in Southern California. Although elderly, he does some very fancy sleuthing when asked by friends or relatives to solve mysteries that are, as usual, baffling the cops.
American Male Amateur operating in USA

D B OLSEN 1907-1973 (American)
Invented 5 detectives - see Lt Stephen MAYHEW
Citation Record: 6 Books
Bring The Bride A Shroud - *First*
Doubleday US (1945); Aldor UK (1945)
Enrollment Cancelled - *Last*
Doubleday US (1952)
Dead Babes In The Wood - *Last**
Dell US (1954)

Mr PEPPER

is an American enthusiast who poses as a great private eye and does solve some mysteries.
American Male Amateur operating in England

Basil THOMSON 1861-1939 (British)
Invented 5 detectives - see Insp RICHARDSON
Citation Record: 15 Short Stories in 1 Collection
Mr Pepper, Investigator - *Collection 1*
Castle UK (1925)

Supt PEPPER

Canadian Policeman operating in Canada

Frank A SMITH 1927- (Canadian)
Writer: Frank Allen SMITH
Citation Record: 2 Books
Corpse In Handcuffs - *First*
Macmillan CA (1969); Hale UK (1969)
Defectors Are Dead Men - *Last*
Macmillan CA (1971); Hale UK (1971)

Amanda PEPPER

is a teacher in a local school and investigates local murder.
American Female Amateur operating in Philadelphia

Gillian ROBERTS (American)
Writer: Judith GREBER
Citation Record: 3 Books
Caught Dead In Philadelphia - *First*
Scribner's US (1987)
I'd Rather Be In Philadelphia - *Latest*
Ballantine US (1992)

'Beau' PEPYS

is an expert in automobile racing. He investigates cases with a motor-racing background.
British Male Amateur operating in England

Gerald HAMMOND 1926- (British)
Invented 5 detectives - see Keith CALDER
Citation Record: 2 Books
Fred In Situ - *First*
Hodder & Stoughton UK (1965)
The Loose Screw - *Last*
Hodder & Stoughton UK (1966)

Johnny PERFECT

American Male Sleuth operating in USA

Jeffrey NOEL (American)
Citation Record: 2 Books
The Trouble With Crime - *First*
Sphere UK (1976)
The Trouble With Guns - *Last*
Sphere UK (1976)

Judith PERINO

Second detective of Ivy MIDDAUGH

Andrea PERKINS

American Female Amateur operating in England/Italy

Carolyn COKER (American)
Citation Record: 4 Books
The Other David - *First*
Dodd, Mead US (1984); Hale UK (1986)
The Hand Of The Lion - *Latest*
Dodd, Mead US (1987)

Ben PERKINS

was formerly employed in the automobile industry as an intermediary in union negotiations; this seems a good start for someone now practising as an unlicensed PI in Motown.
American Male Private Detective operating in Detroit

Rob KANTNER (American)
Citation Record: 5 Books
The Back Door Man - *First*
Bantam US (1986)
Made In Detroit - *Latest*
Bantam US (1990)

Bruce PERKINS

solved a campus mystery once before, with *William CRANE.* He now appears on his own.
American Male Amateur operating in New York

Jean LILLY (American)
Inventor of one other detective pair Bruce PERKINS and William Rutherford CRANE
Citation Record: 2 Books
Death In B-Minor - *First*
Dutton US (1934); Cassell UK (1935)
Death Thumbs A Ride - *Last*
Dutton US (1940)

Bruce PERKINS and William Rutherford CRANE

When a student is murdered at the fictional Jefferson University, his girl-friend's father, *William CRANE,* and the victim's brother, *Bruce PERKINS,* in spite of the police presence, do the sleuthing. The latter appears later in other books on his own.
American Male Amateurs operating in USA

P

Stooge: Insp MANNIE

American Male

Jean LILLY (American)

See main detective Bruce PERKINS

Citation Record: 1 Book

False Face - *Only*

Dutton US (1929)

Douglas PERKINS

is a partner in a publicity firm that is attempting to publicise a troupe of hillbillies. Murder ensues and he, a conventional amateur detective but a good one, comes up with the solutions. In later books he has acquired a sidekick.

American Male Amateur operating in England

Sidekick: Gerry TATE

Male - Assistant

Marion BABSON (American)

was born in Salem, Massachusetts, but has mainly lived in London since 1960. Her books have usually been set in England, though she often uses American characters.

Writer: Ruth STENSTROM

Other Detectives:

Frances ARMITAGE

Trixie DOLAN and Evangeline SINCLAIR

Nancy HARPER | Det KNOWLES

Sarah ORPINGTON | Tom PAIGE

Douglas PERKINS and Gerry TATE

Citation Record: 2 Books

Cover-Up Story - *First*

Collins UK (1971); St Martin's US (1988)

Murder On Show - *Latest*

Collins UK (1971)

Murder At The Cat Show - *Latest**

St Martins US (1989)

Douglas PERKINS and Gerry TATE

Douglas PERKINS was in two early books by this author and now works with *TATE,* who was his sidekick in earlier books.

American Male Amateurs operating in England

Marion BABSON (American)

Invented 8 detectives - see Douglas PERKINS

Citation Record: 2 Books

Tourists Are For Trapping - *First*

St Martin's US (1989)

In The Teeth Of Adversity - *Latest*

St Martin's US (1990)

R I PERKINS

appears also in one book with the author's other detective, *John YARDLEY.*

British Male Amateur operating in England

Roger GARNETT 1905-1986 (British)

Invented 4 detectives - see Ch Insp Jonathan BLACK

Citation Record: 1 Book

The Killing Of Paris Norton - *Only*

Wright & Brown UK (1938)

R I PERKINS

Second detective of John YARDLEY

Willis PERKINS

is a mild, ex-bank clerk who styles himself a detective and solves a crime involving a bank raid.

American Male Amateur operating in New York

Philip WYLIE 1902-1971 (American)

Citation Record: 1 Selected Short Story

Perkins Finds $3,400,000

US (1931)

Matilda PERKS

is a plump little woman, with a hooked nose, a pronounced moustache, and a gruff voice. A former school-teacher and not exactly prepossessing, she has a bark that is definitely not worse than her bite: both are formidable.

British Female Amateur operating in England

R C WOODTHORPE 1886- (British)

Writer: Ralph Carter WOODTHORPE

Inventor of one other detective Nicholas SLADE

Citation Record: 2 Books

Death In A Little Town - *First*

Nicholson & Watson UK (1935); Doubleday US (1935)

The Shadow On The Downs - *Last*

Nicholson & Watson UK (1935); Doubleday US (1935)

Insp Achille PERONI

is a Neapolitan cop operating in Italian locales, expertly realised.

Italian Policeman operating in London/Venice

Timothy HOLME 1928-1987 (British)

Citation Record: 5 Books

The Neapolitan Streak - *First*

Macmillan UK (1980); Coward McCann US (1980)

At The Lake Of Sudden Death - *Latest*

Macmillan UK (1987); Coward McCann US (1987)

Christopher PERRIN

is enlisted, in time-honoured period style, by Scotland Yard when its force is totally baffled.

British Male Private Detective operating in London

Cecil WAYE (British)

Citation Record: 4 Books

The Figure Of Eight - *First*

Hodder & Stoughton UK (1931); Kinsey US (1933)

The Prime Minister's Pencil - *Last*

Hodder & Stoughton UK (1933); Kinsey US (1933)

John PERRIN

British Male Amateur operating in Tunisia

Selwyn JEPSON 1899-1989 (British)

Invented 4 detectives - see Roger SPAIN

Citation Record: 1 Book

The Death Gong - *Only*

Harrap UK (1927); Watt US (1927)

Det Sgt Jane PERRY

was in the London force but has taken a new post in the police force of a cathedral city, where she imagines the work might be less stressful. In the face of considerable male chauvinism, she investigates a girl's disappearance and hunts a murderer successfully.

British Policewoman operating in Kent

Frances FERGUSON (British)

Citation Record: 1 Book

Missing Person - *Single*

Headline UK (1993)

Justin (The Assassin) PERRY

American Male Professional Investigator operating in USA

John D REVERE (American)

Citation Record: 5 Books

The Assassin - *First*

Pinnacle US (1983)

Death's Running Mate - *Latest*

Pinnacle US (1985)

Nat PERRY

is a haemophiliac and, for him, a mere scratch can mean danger or even death. Still, so tough is he that it is those who come up against him who don't live to tell the tale. He appeared in stories in *Dime Mystery,* some of which have recently appeared in collections.

American Male Private Detective operating in USA

P

Edith JACOBSON and Ejler JACOBSON (American)

Writers: Edith JACOBSON and Ejler JACOBSON

Inventor of one other detective The BLEEDER

Citation Record: 1 Selected Short Story

Dead Man Killer

is also in the anthology, *The Defective Detective in the Pulps* (Editors: Gary Hoppenstand & Ray B Browne, US 1983).

In 'Dime Mystery' US (1939)

Kala PERSAD

Male Sleuth operating in several locations

Headon HILL 1857-1927 (British)

Invented 11 detectives - see Insp HERON

Citation Record: 11 Short Stories in 1 Collection

The Divinations Of Kala Persad And Other Stories - *Collection 1*

contains eleven stories with *PERSAD* and one with the author's other detective, *Sebastian ZAMBRA*.

Ward, Lock UK (1895)

PETERS

is an English schoolboy who tries to emulate *Sherlock HOLMES*.

British Male Amateur operating in England

Eden PHILLPOTTS 1862-1960 (British)

Invented 10 detectives - see Insp MIDWINTER

Citation Record: 1 Selected Short Story

Peters, Detective - *Parody 1*

appeared in the April number.

In 'Ellery Queen's Mystery Magazine' US (1954)

Anna PETERS

is a girl who has worked her way up a variety of ladders in industry and commerce, using honest and dishonest methods as it suited her, until she sets up as a PI in Florida. Her cases take her to Paris and Scotland also.

American Female Private Detective operating in USA/Europe

Janice LAW 1941- (American)

was born in Sharon, Connecticut.

Writer: Janice Law TRECKER

Citation Record: 5 Books

The Big Payoff - *First*

Hale UK (1976); Houghton US (1978)

Death Under Par - *Latest*

Houghton US (1981); Houghton UK (1982)

Casey PETERS

American Male Amateur operating in North Carolina

H F S MOORE (American)

Writer: Harry F S MOORE

Citation Record: 2 Books

Murder Goes Rolling Along - *First*

Doubleday US (1942)

Shed A Bitter Tear - *Last*

Doubleday US (1944)

Eric PETERS

American Male Amateur operating in USA

Octavus Roy COHEN 1891-1959 (American)

Invented 6 detectives - see Jim HANVEY

Citation Record: 8 Short Stories in 1 Collection

Eric Peters, Pullman Porter - *Collection 1*

Appleton US (1930)

Geoffrey PETERS

British Male Amateur operating in England

Robert Orr CHIPPERFIELD 1883-1929 (American)

Invented 3 detectives - see Barry O'DELL

Citation Record: 1 Book

Above Suspicion - *Only*

McBride US (1923); Hurst UK (1923)

George PETERS

is an ex-prison warder.

British Male Amateur operating in England

Virgil MARKHAM 1899- (British)

Invented 5 detectives - see Insp Myles RUSBY

Citation Record: 1 Book

The Devil Drives - *Only*

Collins UK (1932); Knopf US (1932)

Joe PETERS

American Male Amateur operating in New York

Dorothy UHNAK 1933- (American)

Invented 3 detectives - see Policewoman Christie OPARA

Citation Record: 1 Book

The Investigation - *Single*

Simon & Schuster US (1977); Hodder & Stoughton UK (1977)

Toby PETERS, Gary COOPER and Ernest HEMINGWAY

Toby PETERS takes on a case involving the great film star of the 1930s, *Gary COOPER*, and the eminent author, *Ernest HEMINGWAY*, who was around writing scripts for the movies at the time.

One American Private Detective and two American Male Amateurs operating in Los Angeles

Stuart M KAMINSKY 1934- (American)

Invented 18 detectives - see Toby PETERS and Errol FLYNN

Citation Record: 1 Book

High Midnight - *Single*

St Martin's US (1981)

Toby PETERS and Bette DAVIS

Toby PETERS has a hard job in this one as he has to work with one of the silver screen's most redoubtable actresses, *Bette DAVIS*.

American Male Private Detective and American Female Amateur operating in Los Angeles

Stuart M KAMINSKY 1934- (American)

Invented 18 detectives - see Toby PETERS and Errol FLYNN

Citation Record: 1 Book

The Devil Met A Lady - *Single*

Mysterious Press US (1993)

Toby PETERS, William FAULKNER and Bela LUGOSI

Toby PETERS here shares the sleuthing honours with the virtuoso of horror movies, 'Count Dracula' himself, the great *Bela LUGOSI*, and the winner of the Nobel Prize for Literature, *William FAULKNER*, who was employed for a time by the studios writing film scripts.

One American Private Detective and two American Male Amateurs operating in Los Angeles

Stuart M KAMINSKY 1934- (American)

Invented 18 detectives - see Toby PETERS and Errol FLYNN

Citation Record: 1 Book

Never Cross A Vampire - *Single*

St Martin's US (1980)

Toby PETERS, Ian FLEMING and MARX BROTHERS

Toby PETERS collaborates with the British author, *Ian FLEMING*, and the famous comedy quartet, *The MARX BROTHERS*.

One American Private Detective and several Male Amateurs operating in Los Angeles

Stuart M KAMINSKY 1934- (American)

Invented 18 detectives - see Toby PETERS and Errol FLYNN

Citation Record: 1 Book

You Bet Your Life - *Single*

St Martin's US (1979)

Toby PETERS and Errol FLYNN

Toby PETERS is a private eye who spends most of his time hanging around the studios in Hollywood during the 1930s and 1940s. He is divorced but still sees a lot of his ex-wife, with whom his relationship is never quite severed. So impoverished is he for most of the time that he has to share his rooms with a local dentist, who pays the rent.

PETERS has police contacts through the good offices of his brother, who is on the local force, and his cases usually arise when distinguished figures in the film world find they need non-official help to extricate them from difficult situations, which may involve threats or blackmail. These characters share some of the sleuthing with him, appearing in stories that are replete with nostalgia and full of excellent background material on the great days of Hollywood. The titles the author has given his books are a delight in themselves, often referring to old films or other episodes in the lives of the movie stars, producers, musicians, and writers who join in the detection.

In the first book of the series it is *Errol FLYNN,* the dashing hero of some of the greatest adventure movies, who shares the honours with him.

American Male Private Detective and American Male Amateur operating in Los Angeles

Stuart M KAMINSKY 1934- (American)

was born in Chicago, Illinois. He graduated from the University of Illinois, Urbana, with a BS in Journalism, 1957 and an MA in English, 1959, followed by a PhD in Speech from Northwestern University, Evanston, Illinois, 1972. He served in the Army, 1957-1959, and has since held many distinguished professorships and directorships at universities and other establishments, especially those connected with entertainment and the mass media. He has declared himself a passionate addict of historical nostalgia, especially of that surrounding the giant figures of the early movie industry. His novels, many of which are set in the Hollywood of the 1930s and 1940s, are unusual in their involvement of real and famous characters with his slightly seedy detective. *KAMINSKY* received the Mystery Writers of America Edgar Allan Poe award, 1989 and the *Prix du Roman d'Aventures,* 1990.

Writer: Stuart Melvin KAMINSKY

Other Detectives:
Maureen DIETZ and Helen KATZ
Sherlock HOLMES
Philip MARLOWE
Toby PETERS, Gary COOPER and Ernest HEMINGWAY
Toby PETERS and Bette DAVIS
Toby PETERS, William FAULKNER and Bela LUGOSI
Toby PETERS, Ian FLEMING and MARX BROTHERS
Toby PETERS and Clark GABLE
Toby PETERS and Judy GARLAND
Toby PETERS and Dashiell HAMMETT
Toby PETERS, Howard HUGHES and Basil RATHBONE
Toby PETERS and Emmett KELLY
Toby PETERS and Eleanor ROOSEVELT
Toby PETERS and Joe LOUIS
Toby PETERS and Leopold STOKOWSKI
Toby PETERS and Mae WEST
Insp Porfiry Petrovich ROSTNIKOV

Citation Record: 1 Book

Bullet For A Star - *Only*
St Martin's US (1977); Curley UK (1978)

Toby PETERS and Clark GABLE

Toby PETERS sleuths here with the greatest leading man in Hollywood during the 1940s, *Clark GABLE,* who has received a death threat.

American Male Private Detective and American Male Amateur operating in Los Angeles

Stuart M KAMINSKY 1934- (American)

Invented 18 detectives - see Toby PETERS and Errol FLYNN

Citation Record: 1 Book

Tomorrow Is Another Day - *Single*
Mysterious Press US (1995)

Toby PETERS and Judy GARLAND

Toby PETERS works on a case with the famous movie star, *Judy GARLAND.*

American Male Private Detective and American Female Amateur operating in Los Angeles

Stuart M KAMINSKY 1934- (American)

Invented 18 detectives - see Toby PETERS and Errol FLYNN

Citation Record: 1 Book

Murder On The Yellow Brick Road - *Single*
St Martin's US (1978); Curley UK (1979)

Toby PETERS and Dashiell HAMMETT

The peripatetic private eye and the famous author work together in a desperate search for the lost papers of General Douglas MacArthur.

American Male Private Detective and American Male Amateur operating in Los Angeles

Stuart M KAMINSKY 1934- (American)

Invented 18 detectives - see Toby PETERS and Errol FLYNN

Citation Record: 1 Book

Buried Caesars - *Single*
Mysterious Press US (1989); Severn UK (1990)

Toby PETERS, Howard HUGHES and Basil RATHBONE

Toby PETERS finds himself on a case in which he shares some of the sleuthing with *Basil RATHBONE,* movie actor and the screen's greatest interpreter of *Sherlock HOLMES,* and the eccentric Hollywood producer, *Howard HUGHES.*

One American Private Detective and two American Male Amateurs operating in Los Angeles

Stuart M KAMINSKY 1934- (American)

Invented 18 detectives - see Toby PETERS and Errol FLYNN

Citation Record: 1 Book

The Howard Hughes Affair - *Single*
St Martin's US (1979); Severn UK (1980)

Toby PETERS and Emmett KELLY

American Male Private Detective and American Male Amateur operating in Los Angeles

Stuart M KAMINSKY 1934- (American)

Invented 18 detectives - see Toby PETERS and Errol FLYNN

Citation Record: 1 Book

Catch A Falling Clown - *Single*
St Martin's US (1982)

Toby PETERS and Joe LOUIS

Toby PETERS works on a case with *Joe LOUIS,* the famous heavyweight world boxing champion.

American Male Private Detective and American Male Amateur operating in Los Angeles

Stuart M KAMINSKY 1934- (American)

Invented 18 detectives - see Toby PETERS and Errol FLYNN

Citation Record: 1 Book

Down For The Count - *Single*
St Martin's US (1985)

Toby PETERS and Eleanor ROOSEVELT

Toby PETERS works on a case with *Eleanor ROOSEVELT,* America's first lady.

American Male Private Detective and American Female Amateur operating in Los Angeles

Stuart M KAMINSKY 1934- (American)

Invented 18 detectives - see Toby PETERS and Errol FLYNN

Citation Record: 1 Book

The Fala Factor - *Single*
St Martin's US (1984)

Toby PETERS and Leopold STOKOWSKI

In this one, *Toby PETERS* has to pull all the stops out when he is called in to solve the problems of the eminent conductor, *Leopold STOKOWSKI.*

American Male Private Detective and American Male Amateur operating in Hollywood

Stuart M KAMINSKY 1934- (American)

Invented 18 detectives - see Toby PETERS and Errol FLYNN

Citation Record: 1 Book

Poor Butterfly - *Single*
Mysterious Press US (1990)

Toby PETERS and Mae WEST

Toby PETERS works on a case involving the sparkling sex idol of the 1930s, *Mae WEST.*

American Male Private Detective and American Female Amateur operating in Los Angeles

Stuart M KAMINSKY 1934- (American)

Invented 18 detectives - see Toby PETERS and Errol FLYNN

Citation Record: 1 Book

He Done Her Wrong - *Single*
St Martin's US (1983)

'Chink' PETERS

American Male Amateur operating in New York

Vance BOURJAILY 1922- (American)

Writer: Vance Nye BOURJAILY

Citation Record: 1 Book

A Game Men Play - *Single*
Dial US (1980)

Brian PETERSEN

American Male Sleuth operating in Washington DC

James P CODY 1926- (American)

Writer: Peter Thomas ROHRBACH

Citation Record: 4 Books

Search And Destroy - *First*
Berkley US (1974)

Your Daughter Will Die! - *Last*
Berkley US (1975)

P

John PETERSON

British Male Professional Amateur operating in England

James CORBETT (British)

Invented 7 detectives - see Roy ENDICOTT

Citation Record: 1 Book

Murder At Red Grange - *Only*
Jenkins UK (1931)

Phil PETERSON

American Male Detective in Pulp Magazines operating in USA

Police Captain GRACE (American)

Citation Record: 1 Selected Short Story

Phil Peterson, The Detective; Or, Trailing Down A Murderer
Old Cap Collier Library US (18??)

Const/Ch Insp Patrick PETRELLA

is half Spanish, half English. A lowly member of the Metropolitan Police when he first appeared around 1970, he has many skills, of which lockpicking is not the least, and he is fluent at languages. Such qualities aid his rise from being a cop on the beat to the rank of Chief Inspector. *PETRELLA* has been appearing in short stories for over twenty years and they have been published in the three main collections cited. A few also appear in other collections of the author's stories (not cited) and he has recently featured in his first novel.

British Policeman operating in England

Michael GILBERT 1912- (British)

Invented 11 detectives - see Insp HAZELRIGG

Citation Record: 1 Book 36 Short Stories in 3 Collections

Blood And Judgment - *Only*
Hodder & Stoughton UK (1959); Harper & Row US (1959)

Petrella At Q - *Collection 1*
Short stories - 15
Hodder & Stoughton UK (1977); Harper & Row US (1977)

Young Petrella - *Collection 2*
Short stories - 12
Hodder & Stoughton UK (1988); Harper & Row US (1988)

Anything For A Quiet Life - *Collection 3*
Short stories - 9
Hodder & Stoughton UK (1990); Carroll & Graf US (1990)

Amos PETRIE

solves a case of murder in the boxing ring.

British Male Amateur operating in England

J V TURNER 1900-1945 (British)

For writer details see Mick CARDBY

Citation Record: 7 Books

First Round Murder - *First*
Holt US (1932)

Death Must Have Laughed - *First**
Putnam UK (1932)

Below The Clock - *Last*
Collins UK (1936); Appleton US (1936)

Mikael Josef PETROS

Male Sleuth

James ANDERSON 1936- (British)

Invented 5 detectives - see Insp WILKINS

Citation Record: 2 Books

Assassin - *First*
Constable UK (1969); Simon & Schuster US (1971)

The Abolition Of Death - *Last*
Constable UK (1974); Walker US (1975)

Joe PETROSINO

American Male Sleuth operating in New York

Frederick NOLAN 1931- (British)

Other Byline: Donald SEVERN

See main detective Charles GARRETT

Citation Record: 1 Book

Kill Petrosino! - *Only*
Barker UK (1975)

Insp PETROVICH

is one of the great seminal detectives in what is certainly one of the finest novels ever written. He pursues the wretched Raskolnikov until the latter breaks down and confesses.

Russian Policeman operating in Moscow

Fyodor Mikhailovich DOSTOIEVSKI 1821-1881 (Russian)

was born in Moscow. Although his output was not large, he is acknowledged as one of the world's greatest novelists. His best-known work, cited, is seminal in its understanding of the psychology of crime.

Citation Record: 1 Book

Crime And Punishment - *Only*
Vizetelly UK (1886); Crowell US (1886)

Insp PETTENGILL

American Policeman operating in Maine

Anne ROWE (American)

Writer: Anne Von Meibom ROWE

Inventor of one other detective Insp BARRY

Citation Record: 2 Books

The Little Dog Barked - *First*
Morrow US (1942); Gifford UK (1944)

The Painted Monster - *Last*
Gifford UK (1945)

PETTIGREW

Second detective of MALLETT

Francis PETTIGREW

is an elderly and not very successful lawyer who matches wits with the author's other detective, *Insp MALLETT*, in some books, and goes on to be the protagonist in the books cited, in which he solves difficult cases by the power of sheer logic.

British Male Amateur Investigator operating in London

Cyril HARE 1900-1958 (British)

Invented 4 detectives - see Insp MALLETT

Citation Record: 2 Books

When The Wind Blows - *First*
Faber UK (1949)

The Wind Blows Death - *First**
Little, Brown US (1950)

That Yew Tree's Shade - *Last*
Faber UK (1954)

Death Walks The Woods - *Last**
Little, Brown US (1954)

The PHANTOM

Male Sleuth operating in Middle East

Lee FALK 1915- (British)

Writer: Lee Harrison FALK

Citation Record: 15 Books

The Slave Market Of Mucar - *First*
Avon UK (1972)

The Assassins - *Last*
Avon UK (1975)

Raphael PHARE and Martin SONDES

appeared in a series of stories in *Detective Fiction Weekly* in which they waged continuous battle with the villainous Odoric Dyn, whose simple enough aim was to conquer the entire world.

Male Amateurs operating in several locations

Douglas NEWTON 1884-1951 (British)

See main detective Philip MANWEARING

No citations

John P PHELAN

is a Hollywood PI, tough in action but weak when it comes to gambling.

American Male Private Detective operating in Hollywood

James P DUFF (American)

Citation Record: 2 Books

Some Die Young - *First*
Graphic US (1956)

Who Dies There? - *Last*
Graphic US (1956)

Det Sam PHELAN

is an ex-boxer, a little literary, dogged rather than brilliant, who is thrown into cases by his chief, Cleveland Jones.

American Policeman operating in Philadelphia

Thomas KYD 1901-1976 (American)

was born in Philadelphia, Pennsylvania, and took several degrees at the University of Pennsylvania, Philadelphia. He became a Professor of English at the University of Pennsylvania, 1942-1947, at Columbia University, New York, 1947-1952, and at Harvard University, Cambridge, Massachusetts. He was a renowned Shakespearean scholar and received many awards for his work.

Writer: Alfred Bennett HARBAGE

Other Detectives:
Andrew ONE   Gilbert E WHELDON

Citation Record: 3 Books

Blood Is A Beggar - *First*
Lippincott US (1946); Hammond UK (1949)

Blood On The Bosom Divine - *Last*
Lippincott US (1948)

Chet PHELPS

American Male Amateur operating in USA

George CHILDERNESS (American)

Citation Record: 2 Books

Murder In False Face - *First*
Phoenix Press US (1943)

Too Many Murderers - *Last*
Phoenix Press US (1944); Pemberton UK (1946)

Dr PHIBES

appears in novelizations of films.

Male Sleuth

William GOLDSTEIN 1932- (American)

Writer: William Isaac GOLDSTEIN

Citation Record: 2 Books

Dr Phibes - *First*
Award US (1971)

Dr Phibes Rises Again - *Last*
Award US (1972)

PHILIPPS

Second detective of DYSON

Arthur PHILIS

is a small-time smuggler in Brazil who is recruited into a branch of British Intelligence by his boss, Pawson, but is used more as a pawn for overt operations. However, he does a fair deal of detective work in his battles with international criminals and spies.

British Male Secret Agent operating in several locations

Ritchie PERRY 1942- (British)

was born in King's Lynn, Norfolk. He was educated at King Edward's School, King's Lynn, Norfolk, and took a BA in History at St John's College, Oxford, 1964.

Writer: Ritchie John Allen PERRY

Inventor of one other detective Frank MACALLISTER

Citation Record: 14 Books

The Fall Guy - *First*
Collins UK (1972); Houghton US (1972)

The Creepy Tale - *Latest*
Hutchinson UK (1989)

Bono PHILLIPS

is a white-haired, albino, crime lawyer entangled in a case of murder, corruption and vice. He is hardboiled and scatological, with hardly a redeeming feature.

American Male Amateur operating in Texas

A W GRAY 1940- (American)

is said to be serving a term in the penitentiary for fraud.

Citation Record: 1 Book

Bino - *Single*
Joseph UK (1988)

Dr Hal PHILLIPS

British Male Professional Amateur operating in England

Nieves MATHEWS 1917- (British)

Writer: Nieves M MATHEWS

Citation Record: 1 Book

She Died Without Light - *Only*
Hodder & Stoughton UK (1954)

Det Jake PHILLIPS

American Policeman operating in Chicago

Nick GAITANO (American)

Citation Record: 2 Books

Special Victims - *First*
Simon & Schuster US (1994)
Mr X - *Latest*
Simon & Schuster US (1995)

Madeleine PHILLIPS

American Female Sleuth operating in USA

R D ZIMMERMAN 1952- (American)
Writer: Robert Dingwall ZIMMERMAN
Citation Record: 1 Book
Death Trance - *Single*
US (1992)

Nathan PHILLIPS

is a poor, aesthetic, angry young man, whose partner has just been killed in a car crash. Can he take over the agency? He can and he does, having the good fortune to be assisted by his cat.

American Male Private Detective operating in Minneapolis

Sidekick: MARLOWE
is an honorary sidekick, with an honoured name, and is greatly loved by the detective.
Male - Pet Cat

Nick O'DONOHOE (American)
Citation Record: 3 Books
April Snow - *First*
Raven US (1981)
Open Season - *Latest*
PaperJacks US (1986)

Insp PHILLIPSON

is a member of the London CID in this one Victorian novel.

British Policeman operating in London

Arthur GRIFFITHS 1838-1908 (British)
Invented 8 detectives - see Insp FASKE
Citation Record: 1 Book
A Set Of Flats - *Only*
Milne UK (1901)

Freddy PHILPOTTS

American Male Amateur operating in New York/Pennsylvania

Alfred Betts CALDWELL (American)
Citation Record: 3 Books
Turquoise Hazard - *First*
Doubleday US (1936)
Death Rattle - *Last*
Doubleday US (1940)

Thackeray PHIN

British Male Amateur operating in England

John SLADEK 1937- (British)
Writer: John Thomas SLADEK
Citation Record: 2 Books
Black Aura - *First*
Cape UK (1974); Walker US (1979)
Invisible Green - *Latest*
Gollancz UK (1977); Walker US (1979)

Marian PHIPPS

is an elderly spinster who appears only in a few short stories. She solves her little cases by homespun wisdom and the use of her rather bright intellect. She first appeared, according to one source, in 1937 (no details) and then again in 1954, in a short story that won a prize in an annual *Ellery Queen's Mystery Magazine* competition. However, she really doesn't come up to the standards set by this well-known author in her mainstream novels.

British Female Amateur operating in England

Phyllis BENTLEY 1894-1977 (British)
was born in Halifax, Yorkshire. A well-known English novelist, she occasionally turned her hand to mystery stories, mainly featuring *Marian PHIPPS*.
Writer: Phyllis Eleanor BENTLEY
Citation Record: 1 Selected Short Story
Chain Of Witnesses
In 'Ellery Queen's Mystery Magazine' US (1954)

Joe PHOENIX

American Male Private Detective operating in New York

Albert W AIKEN 1846-1894 (American)
Invented 5 detectives - see Hilda SIRENE
Citation Record: 2 Books
Joe Phoenix, The Police Spy - *First*
Ivers US (1901)
Joe Phoenix, Private Detective; Or, The League Of Skeleton Keys - *Last*
Ivers US (1901)

Supt James PIBBLE

of Scotland Yard is a quiet man, solving his cases in the classical manner by shrewdly suspecting the right people and following up the clues. The plots of his books, however, are sometimes rather bizarre.

British Policeman operating in England

Peter DICKINSON 1927- (British)
was born in Livingstone, Zambia. He was educated at Eton College and took a BA in English at King's College, Cambridge, 1951. A sometime assistant editor of *Punch*, he has written many crime novels, children's books and other works of fiction. He has received many awards for his work, including the Crime Writers Association Gold Dagger twice, 1968 and 1969.
Writer: Malcolm DE BRISSAC
Other Detectives:
Wesley MORRIS — Paul ROGERS
Citation Record: 6 Books
Skin Deep - *First*
Hodder & Stoughton UK (1968)
The Glass-Sided Ants' Nest - *First**
Harper & Row US (1968)
One Foot In The Grave - *Latest*
Hodder & Stoughton UK (1979); Pantheon US (1980)

Paul PICARD

American Male Amateur operating in USA

William KOTZWINKLE 1938- (American)
Inventor of one other detective Insp MANTIS
Citation Record: 1 Book
Fata Morgana - *Single*
Knopf US (1977); Hutchinson UK (1977)

The PICAROON

appeared mainly in books that each contained three short novels (not individually cited).

American Male Sleuth operating in New York

Herman LANDON 1882-1960 (American)
Inventor of one other detective The GRAY PHANTOM
Citation Record: 8 Books
The Green Shadow - *First*
Cassell UK (1927); Dial US (1928)
The Picaroon And The Burglar Tools - *Last*
Thacker (Bombay) (1944)

Nora PICKHAM

is a senior student who investigates when three fellow students are murdered at the fictional Carodac College.

American Female Amateur operating in USA

M R HODGKIN 1917- (American)
Writer: Marion Rous HODGKIN
Citation Record: 1 Book
Student Body - *Only*
Scribner's US (1949); Gollancz UK (1950)

Athena PIERCE

American Female Amateur operating in San Diego

Richard PURTILL 1931- (American)
Writer: Richard L PURTILL
Citation Record: 1 Book
Murdercon - *Single*
!See Appendix 2.
Doubleday US (1982)

Jim PIERCE
is rough, tough, bloody and, unregrettably, appears just the once.
American Male Private Detective operating in Baltimore

Adam RING (American)
Writer: Blair REED
Citation Record: 1 Book
Killers Play Rough - *Only*
Crown US (1946)

Perry PIERCE
is a boy detective who appeared in four stories only.
American Male Detective in Pulp Magazines operating in USA

Clinton W LOCKE (American)
No citations

Mr PIGEON
Second detective of Sheriff JEFFRIES

Anna PIGEON
has fled the Big Apple to become a national park ranger. She soon finds a colleague dead, seemingly killed by a mountain lion, but it looks suspiciously like murder to her..
American Female Amateur operating in Nevada

Nevada BARR (American)
is a national park ranger.
Citation Record: 3 Books
Track Of The Cat - *First*
Avon US (1994)
Ill Wind - *Latest*
Putnam US (1995)

Supt Arnold PIKE
British Policeman operating in England

Philip MACDONALD 1899-1981 (British)
Invented 5 detectives - see Col Anthony GETHRYN
Citation Record: 1 Book
Murder Gone Mad - *Only*
Collins UK (1931); Doubleday US (1931)

Daniel PIKE
is a tough Scot, operating in Glasgow as a PI and part-time debt-collector. He was originally in a TV series and this is a novelization from it.
British Male Private Detective operating in Glasgow

Bill KNOX and Edward BOYD (British)
Writer: (First author) William KNOX 1928-
Citation Record: 5 Short Stories in 1 Collection
The View From Daniel Pike - *Only*
Arrow UK (1974); St Martin's US (1974)

Stella PIKE
American Female Amateur operating in San Francisco/Peru

Victoria WEBB (American)
Writer: UNKNOWN
Citation Record: 1 Book
A Little Lady Killing - *Single*
Dial US (1982)

Mr PILGRIM
British Male Sleuth operating in Germany

Desmond CORY 1928- (British)
Invented 4 detectives - see Johnny FEDORA
Citation Record: 2 Books
Pilgrim At The Gate - *First*
Muller UK (1957); Washburn US (1958)
Pilgrim On The Island - *Last*
Muller UK (1959); Walker US (1961)

Luke PILGRIM
is a professional boxer, once a middleweight champion. Concussed after a fight, he does not know how he spent a night out with a lady who is found murdered. Defending his life and career, he turns sleuth.
American Male Amateur operating in California

William Campbell GAULT 1910- (American)
Invented 6 detectives - see Brock (The Rock) CALLAHAN
Citation Record: 1 Book
The Canvas Coffin - *Only*
Dutton US (1953); Boardman UK (1953)

Prof Stephen PILGRIM
Second detective of Ch Insp Max HUNTER

PILKINGTON
British Male Amateur operating in England

William CAINE 1873-1975 (British)
Citation Record: 11 Short Stories in 1 Collection
Pilkington - *Collection 1*
Ward, Lock UK (1906)

Tom PILTER
British Male Amateur operating in England

John WAINWRIGHT 1921- (British)
Invented 9 detectives - see Ch Insp/Supt LENNOX
Citation Record: 1 Book
The Eye Of The Beholder - *Single*
Macmillan UK (1980); St Martin's US (1980)

Steve PINATA
is a Mexican orphan who has worked his way up in San Felice to become a bail bondsman and finally a fully operative PI.
American Male Private Detective operating in California

Margaret MILLAR 1915- (Canadian)
Invented 11 detectives - see Insp SANDS
Citation Record: 1 Book
A Stranger In My Grave - *Only*
Gollancz UK (1960); Random House US (1960)

P

Insp PINAUD
is the creation of a British writer who set his detective stories, written over a period of at least forty years, in France, which he knew well. The author's France is a strange one, English-mythical in concept and a geographical nightmare to decipher. No matter, for *PINAUD* of the *Sûreté* is above such things. Paid a pittance and subject to constant appraisal by *Monsieur le Chef*, he is a man who is both honourable and comic, a decidedly Gallic *bon viveur*. In the course of his cases he often stumbles over nude women who are dead and various other women who are alive and decidedly more attractive. The latter he resists for love of his wife, Germaine.
French Policeman operating in France

Pierre AUDEMARS 1909-1989 (British)
was born in London. After serving in the army during the Second World War he seems to have spent the rest of his working life first as a salesman, and then a manager for various European firms involved in the jewellery and watch trades, finding time, however, to write over thirty detective novels.
Inventor of one other detective Insp Hercule RENARD
Citation Record: 26 Books
The Two Imposters - *First*
Long UK (1958)
A Small Slain Body - *Last*
Hale UK (1985)

Dearborn V PINCH

American Male Amateur operating in USA/Havana

Edith Pinero GREEN 1929- (American)

Citation Record: 3 Books

Rotten Apples - *First*
Dutton US (1977); Curley UK (1980)

Sneaks - *Latest*
Dutton US (1979); Curley UK (1981)

PINCHER

British Male Amateur operating in several locations

C Malcolm HINCKS 1881-1954 (British)

Writer: Cyril Malcolm HINCKS

Adopter of one other detective Sexton BLAKE

Citation Record: 18 Short Stories in 1 Collection

Pincher In Peace And War - *Collection 1*
Not all the stories are criminous.
Pearson UK (1916)

Sidney 'Silky' PINCUS and Mike CLANCY

Sidney PINCUS is a partner in a detective agency called Watson & Holmes Inc, on Sixtieth and First in Manhattan, and is Jewish. The other partner is *Mike CLANCY*, who is Irish and speaks Yiddish with a brogue. Both are comical caricatures of the type to be expected from this author.

American Male Private Detectives operating in USA

Sidekick: Isadore GOLDBERG
is a Schnauzer who has been raised by a rabbi. He only accepts commands in Yiddish and will only eat kosher food.
Male - Pet Dog

Leo ROSTEN 1908- (American)

Inventor of one other detective Bradford GALT

Citation Record: 2 Books

Silky! - *First*
Harper & Row US (1979)

King Silky! - *Latest*
Harper & Row US (1980)

Paul PINE

P

is a typical hardboiled private eye of the post-*CHANDLER* era. Formerly on the staff at the State Attorney General's Office, he now operates on his own from an office in Clawson Building, East Jackson. The first and last books in which he appeared were published under the author's pseudonym.

American Male Private Detective operating in Chicago

Howard BROWNE 1908- (American)

Inventor of one other detective Ames CORYELL

Citation Record: 2 Books

The Taste Of Ashes - *First*
Simon & Schuster US (1957); Gollancz UK (1958)

The Paper Gun - *Latest*
Still incomplete, the last novel was published almost forty years after the first.
Macmillan US (1985)

John EVANS 1908- (American)

Writer: Howard BROWNE

Citation Record: 3 Books

Halo In Blood - *First*
Bobbs Merrill US (1946); No Exit Press UK (1988)

Halo In Brass - *Last*
Bobbs US (1949); Foulsham UK (1951)

Melinda PINK

is a novelist, a mountaineer, and a British magistrate to boot. She travels, writes, and climbs in Britain and the United States, meeting murder everywhere, especially well above sea level. She proves to be an excellent detective, which is as well, for the police of both nations are equally baffled.

British Female Amateur operating in several locations

Gwen MOFFAT 1924- (British)

was born in Brighton, Sussex. She was educated at Hove County Grammar School, Sussex, and served in the Auxiliary Territorial Service, 1943-1947. She is an expert on mountaineering, a subject that forms the background for her detective novels.

Inventor of one other detective Ruth STANTON

Citation Record: 12 Books

Lady With A Cool Eye - *First*
Gollancz UK (1973)

The Raptor Zone - *Latest*
Macmillan UK (1990)

Norman PINK

has retired from the Birmingham, England, police force, in which he was a detective sergeant, to set up Peerless Private Enquiry Agents Limited.

British Male Private Detective operating in Birmingham

Mark MCSHANE 1930- (Australian)

was born in Sydney, Australia, and educated in Blackpool, Lancashire. He is the author, under his own name and the *LOVELL* byline, of at least fifty genre novels of various types, including detective stories, espionage and adventure stories and mystery novels.

Writer: Mark MCSHANE

Other Byline: Marc LOVELL

Other Detectives:
James MATRIC — Myra SAVAGE

Citation Record: 3 Books

The Girl Nobody Knows - *First*
Doubleday US (1965); Hale UK (1966)

The Way To Nowhere - *Last*
Hale UK (1967)

Jacqueline PINKER

Second detective of Bill MORROW

Private PINKERTON

British Male Amateur operating in England

Harold ASHTON (British)

Citation Record: 23 Short Stories in 1 Collection

Private Pinkerton, Millionaire - *Collection 1*
Simpkin UK (1916)

A Frank PINKERTON

American Male Private Detective operating in USA

A Frank PINKERTON (American)

was the son of *Allan PINKERTON*. Like his father, he wrote a number of books and stories with various detectives, including one with himself.

Other Detectives:
The AMERICAN DETECTIVE — Nic BROWN
Dyke DARREL — Det Patrick RYAN

Citation Record: 1 Book

Jim Cummings; Or, The Great Adams Express Robbery - *Only*
Laird & Lee US (1887)

The Great Adams Express Robbery - *Only**
Routledge UK (1889)

Allan PINKERTON

tells his own tales. He is, indeed, the founder of Pinkertons, the first professional detective agency in the USA.

American Male Private Detective operating in USA

Allan PINKERTON 1819-1884 (American)

was born in Glasgow, Scotland, the son of a policeman who moved to Chicago, Illinois, in 1842. There he became a detective and soon founded the Pinkerton National Detective Agency. Its symbol, the open eye, and the slogan, 'We Never Sleep' became famous the world over and his name became almost synonymous with 'professional detective' or 'private eye'. He wrote a number of detective stories, which were published in various collections.

Inventor of one other detective Claude MELNOTTE

Citation Record: 2 Books 22 Short Stories in 1 Collection

The Expressman And The Detective - *First*

The first edition revealed, for the first time, the open eye logo and the famous slogan.

Keen, Cooke US (1874)

Criminal Reminiscences And Detective Sketches - *Collection 1*

Carlton US (1884)

Evan PINKERTON

is a timid little Welshman whose domineering and miserly wife has died and left him a large sum of money. He can now do all the things he wants to, mainly going to the movies and solving mysteries with the help of *Sgt (later Insp) BULL.*

Welsh Male Amateur operating in England

Sidekick: Insp Humphrey BULL

was formerly a police constable who used to occupy a room in Mrs Pinkerton's Boarding house. He welcomes the help of his friend, *Mr PINKERTON,* who has the knack of solving his cases.

British Male - Friend

David FROME 1898-1983 (American)

For writer details see Grace LATHAM

Other Detectives:

Maj Gregory LEWIS   Ch Insp LORD

Citation Record: 11 Books

The Hammersmith Murders - *First*

Methuen UK (1930); Doubleday US (1930)

Murder On The Square - *Last*

Hale UK (1951)

Homicide House: Mr Pinkerton Returns - *Last**

Rinehart US (1950)

Nat PINKERTON

American Male Detective in Pulp Magazines operating in USA

UNKNOWN

No citations

PINKNEY

British Male Sleuth operating in England

Cecil WILLS 1891- (British)

Invented 4 detectives - see Sgt/Supt Geoffrey BOSCOBELL

Citation Record: 2 Books

Death Of A Best Seller - *First*

Hale UK (1959)

The Colonel's Foxhound - *Last*

Hale UK (1960)

Harry PINKURTON

American Male Detective in Pulp Magazines operating in USA

Harry ROCKWOOD 1859-1932 (American)

Invented 14 detectives - see Clarice DYKE

Citation Record: 1 Book

Harry Pinkurton, The King Of Detectives - *Only*

Ogilvie US (1882)

Harry Pinkurton, The Boy Detective - *Only**

Untied States Book US (1891)

Jocelyn PINNER

British Male Amateur operating in England

Bruce NORMAN (British)

See main detective James MALLABY

Citation Record: 10 Short Stories in 1 Collection

The Luck Of Jocelyn Pinner, RN - *Collection 1*

Not all the stories are criminous.

Arrowsmith UK (1931)

Centenier PINOT

French Male Amateur operating in England

Wilfred J L BOWEN (British)

Citation Record: 1 Selected Short Story

The Bungalow Mystery

Mitre UK (1929)

Susanna PINSCHER

Second detective of Martin TELLER

John PIPER

appears also in books with the author's other detective, *QUINN.*

British Male Professional Investigator operating in England

Harry CARMICHAEL 1908-1979 (British)

was born in Montreal, Canada, and, as a boy, was educated at Rutherglen Academy, Lanarkshire. He worked as a journalist, became a writer and published about eighty genre novels, consistently using the same protagonists and detectives.

Writer: Leopold Horace OGNALL

Other Byline: Hartley HOWARD

Other Detectives:

John PIPER and QUINN   QUINN

Citation Record: 4 Books

The Vanishing Track - *First*

Collins UK (1952)

Emergency Exit - *Last*

Collins UK (1957)

John PIPER and QUINN

appear mainly together, although occasionally in books on their own. *John PIPER* is an insurance assessor who investigates deaths that occur under shady circumstances, he not being satisfied with the official police view of things. He does it quietly, probing and prodding suspects until the killer gives way. *QUINN* is a crime reporter for the *Morning Post* who works with him. Brash, given to drink, untidy, and often unpleasant, he is the perfect foil. No mean sleuth, though, he tends to do most of the work in the last ten books of the cycle.

British Male Professional Investigator and British Male Amateur operating in England

Harry CARMICHAEL 1908-1979 (British)

Invented 3 detectives - see John PIPER

Citation Record: 33 Books

Death Leaves A Diary - *First*

Collins UK (1952)

Life Cycle - *Last*

Collins UK (1978)

Katherine 'Peter' PIPER

is a writer of mystery novels who manages to become involved with, and eventually to solve, murders taking place in the American South and in academia. She appears also in one book with another of the author's detectives, *Edward TRELAWNEY.* !See Appendix 2.

American Female Amateur operating in Louisiana

Amelia Reynolds LONG 1904-1978 (American)

Writer: Amelia Reynolds LONG

Other Bylines:

Patrick LAING   Adrian REYNOLDS

Other Detectives:

Steve CARTER

Katherine 'Peter' PIPER and Edward TRELAWNEY

Edward TRELAWNY

Citation Record: 6 Books

Four Feet In The Grave - *First*

Phoenix Press US (1941)

It's Death, My Darling! - *Last*

Mystery House US (1948)

Katherine 'Peter' PIPER and Edward TRELAWNEY

appear individually in other books by this author.

American Female Amateur and American Male Amateur operating in Philadelphia

Amelia Reynolds LONG 1904-1978 (American)

Invented 4 detectives - see Katherine 'Peter' PIPER

Citation Record: 1 Book

Death Looks Down - *Only*
Ziff-Davis US (1944)

Peter PIPER

American Male Amateur operating in San Francisco

Nancy Barr MAVITY 1890- (American)

Citation Record: 5 Books

The Body On The Floor - *First*
Doubleday US (1929); Collins UK (1929)

The Man Who Didn't Mind Hanging - *Last*
Doubleday US (1932)

He Didn't Mind Hanging - *Last**
Collins UK (1932)

Eliza PIREX

runs her own little agency in Oakland, with the help of the man who trained her so she could get her licence. Being lesbian, she can, of course, have no feelings for him other than strictly business-like ones.

American Female Private Detective operating in California

Sidekick: Dennis ECKENBERG

American Male - Teacher

Diana MCRAE (American)

Citation Record: 1 Book

All The Muscle You Need - *Single*
Spinsters US (1988); Spinsters UK (1988)

PIRON

is a red-headed American who works for a large, unnamed, American detective agency, which gets its cases from the US Embassy and the British government.

American Male Private Detective operating in England

Sidekick: HOGG

British Male - Assistant

Edmund MCGIRR 1922-1972 (British)

Writer: Kenneth GILES

Other Byline: Charles DRUMMOND

Citation Record: 9 Books

The Funeral Was In Spain - *First*
Gollancz UK (1966)

A Murderous Journey - *Last*
Gollancz UK (1974); Walker US (1975)

Mr PITKIN

British Male Amateur operating in England

Basil BOOTHROYD 1910-1988 (British)

Writer: John Basil BOOTHROYD

Citation Record: 14 Short Stories in 1 Collection

The Adventures Of Mr Pitkin - *Collection 1*
Causton (1937)

Insp PITT

is a quiet, elderly, old-fashioned British policeman who asks nothing more of his readers than to be allowed to get on with solving good old-fashioned British murder cases.

British Policeman operating in England

J F STRAKER 1904- (British)

Invented 3 detectives - see Det Johnny INCH

Citation Record: 7 Books

Postman's Knock - *First*
Harrap UK (1954)

Murder For Miss Emily - *Last*
Harrap UK (1961)

Charlotte PITT

Second detective of Insp Thomas PITT

Det Dave PITT

is on what seems to be his last case, an apparent hit-and-run death that turns out to be murder.

American Policeman operating in USA

Laurence FISHER 1923- (American)

Citation Record: 1 Book

Die A Little Every Day - *Only*
Random House US (1963)

Dirk PITT

is the Special Projects Director of the US National Underwater and Marine Agency. It is a job that gets him into plenty of trouble and provides opportunities for some detection and thrilling adventures, mainly consisting of rescuing women and killing nasty adversaries. He is nothing more than *'Bulldog' DRUMMOND,* writ large for the modern age.

American Male Professional Investigator operating in USA

Clive CUSSLER 1921- (American)

was born in Aurora, Illinois, and graduated at California State University, Los Angeles.

Writer: Clive Eric CUSSLER

Citation Record: 10 Books

Iceberg - *First*
Dodd, Mead US (1975); Sphere Books UK (1976)

Dragon - *Latest*
Simon & Schuster US (1990); Hamish Hamilton UK (1990)

Insp Thomas PITT and Charlotte PITT

are a husband-and-wife team in late Victorian London. He is a policeman in the Metropolitan force and, although he holds a relatively senior rank, he comes from the lower classes and so finds certain aspects of his detective work made difficult for him. His wife is a gentlewoman who is considered by one and all to have married beneath her. However, her background gives her access to the drawing rooms of society that her poor husband could not very well enter, and so she is of great help to him in his work.

British Policeman and British Female Amateur operating in London

Sidekick: EMILY

is *Charlotte PITTS's* sister and has a place in the upper echelons of London society. She is thus often able, in a genteel way, to render assistance to the two detectives.

British Female - Sister

Anne PERRY 1938- (British)

was born in London and privately educated.

Inventor of one other detective Insp William MONK

Citation Record: 15 Books

The Cater Street Hangman - *First*
Hale UK (1979); St Martin's US (1979)

Traitor's Gate - *Latest*
Fawcett US (1995)

Duke PIZZATELLO

is in one awful book in which he puffs continuously at cigarettes (usually in other guys' eyes), is armed to the teeth, is known as The Wop, is partial to dames, and likes knocking off unfriendly gunsels.

American Male Private Detective operating in USA

Robert Leslie BELLEM 1902-1968 (American)

Other Byline: John A SAXON

See main detective Dan TURNER

Citation Record: 1 Book

Blue Murder - *Only*
Phoenix Press US (1938)

Thackeray PLACE

American Male Amateur operating in USA

Kirby WILLIAMS (American)

Writer: UNKNOWN

Citation Record: 2 Books

The CVC Murders - *First*
Doubleday US (1929); Hutchinson UK (1929)

The Opera Murders - *Last*
Scribner's US (1933)

PLACER DAN

American Male Detective in Pulp Magazines operating in USA

Ed STRAYER (American)

Invented 4 detectives - see Jack SHARPLEY

Citation Record: 1 Selected Short Story

Placer Dan, The Yukon Detective; Or, The Missing Nuggets Of Gold
Old Cap Collier Library US (18??)

Guy PLANTE and Freye MATTHEWS

British Male Amateur and British Female Amateur operating in several locations

John PALMER 1904- (British)

Writer: Edgar John Palmer WATTS

Citation Record: 2 Books

Above And Below - *First*
Hodder & Stoughton UK (1967)

So Much For Gennaro - *Last*
Hodder & Stoughton UK (1968)

Dr Malcolm PLECKS

Appears with at least two other detectives - see Dr Frank HAYVIER

Jay PLETCHER

American Male Private Detective operating in Ohio

Sidekick: Raina LAMBERT
American Female - Assistant

Lloyd BIGGLE 1923- (American)

Invented 5 detectives - see Bill RASTIN

Citation Record: 3 Book

Interface For Murder - *First*
Doubleday US (1987)

Where Dead Soldiers Walk - *Latest*
St Martin's US (1994)

Plantagenet PLEWS

is an early 'private enquiry agent' in this one Victorian novel.

British Male Private Detective operating in England

Arthur GRIFFITHS 1838-1908 (British)

Invented 8 detectives - see Insp FASKE

Citation Record: 1 Book

Ford's Folly Ltd - *Only*
MacQueen UK (1900)

Bertram PLEYDELL

appears sporadically in other books by this author with his other detectives.

British Male Amateur operating in Europe

Dornford YATES 1885-1960 (British)

Invented 4 detectives - see Supt FALCON

Citation Record: 1 Book 34 Short Stories in 4 Collections

Adele & Co - *Only*
Minton US (1931); Hodder & Stoughton UK (1932)

The Courts Of Idleness - *Collection 1*
This collection of twelve stories contains six with *PLEYDELL*, not all criminous.
Short stories - 6
Ward, Lock UK (1920)

Jonah And Co - *Collection 2*
Not all the stories are criminous.
Short stories - 12
Ward, Lock UK (1922); Minton US (1927)

And Berry Came Too - *Collection 3*
Short stories - 8
Putnam US (1935); Ward, Lock UK (1936)

The Berry Scene - *Collection 4*
Short stories - 8
Ward, Lock UK (1947); Putnam US (1947)

Sylvia PLOTKIN and Max Van LARSEN

American Female Amateur and American Male Amateur operating in New York

George BAXT 1923- (American)

Invented 6 detectives - see Pharaoh LOVE

Citation Record: 3 Books

A Parade Of Cockeyed Creatures; Or, Did Someone Murder Our Wandering Boy? - *First*
Random House US (1967); Cape UK (1968)

Satan Is A Woman - *Latest*
International Polygonics US (1987)

Det Marvia PLUM

Second detective of Hobart LINDSEY

Stephanie PLUM

is a New Jersey bounty hunter whose first assignment is to bring in an ex-cop who has skipped on a murder charge.

American Female Professional Investigator operating in USA

Janet EVANOVICH (American)

Citation Record: 1 Book

One For The Money - *Single*
Scribner's US (1994)

Emma PLUME

British Female Amateur operating in England

Peter CURTIS 1904-1983 (British)

Writer: Norah Ethel Robinson LOFTS

Other Byline: Norah LOFTS

Citation Record: 1 Book

Dead March In Three Keys - *Only*
was republished under the following byline.
Davies UK (1940)

No Question Of Murder - *Only**
Doubleday US (1959)

The Bride Of Moat House - *Only**
Dell US (1969)

Norah LOFTS 1904-1983 (British)

For writer details see Emma PLUME

Citation Record: 1 Book

Dead March In Three Keys - *Only*
was previously published under the preceding byline.
Hodder & Stoughton UK (1970)

George PLUMMER

was the so-called 'Renegade Detective Sergeant of Scotland Yard'.

British Male Detective in Pulp Magazines operating in USA

UNKNOWN

No citations

Jeff PLUMMER

British Male Sleuth operating in England

Dan LEES 1927- (British)

Citation Record: 3 Books

The Rainbow Conspiracy - *First*
Constable UK (1971); Walker US (1972)

Rape Of A Quiet Town - *Last*
Constable UK (1973); Walker US (1973)

Lincoln PLUMMER

American Male Sleuth operating in USA

Clayton MATTHEWS 1917- (British)

Writer: Clayton Hartley MATTHEWS

Citation Record: 1 Selected Short Story

Into Thin Air
In 'Alfred Hitchcock's Mystery Magazine' US (1978)

Det Supt Horace PLUMMMET

of Scotland Yard is brought in to solve a case of murder in a little English village.

British Policeman operating in London

Evelyn HEALEY (British)

Citation Record: 1 Book

The Blaydin Mystery - *Only*
Long UK (1963)

Paul PLUSH

is a Professor of Latin at a girls' school who stumbles around, solving murder (and almost getting murdered) as he goes.

American Male Amateur operating in New York/Germany

Oliver KEYSTONE (American)

Writer: James M MANTINBAND

Citation Record: 3 Books

Major Crime - *First*
Phoenix Press US (1948)

Arsenic For The Teacher - *Last*
Phoenix Press US (1950)

Henry PO

works almost always for the New York Racing Club.

American Male Private Detective operating in New York

Robert J RANDISI 1951- (American)

Invented 5 detectives - see Sal CARLUCCI

Citation Record: 1 Book

The Disappearance Of Penny - *Single*
Ace US (1980)

Christopher POE

American Male Amateur operating in USA

Robert Carlton BROWN 1886-1959 (American)

Citation Record: 12 Short Stories in 1 Collection

The Remarkable Adventures Of Christopher Poe - *Collection 1*
Browne US (1913)

P

Edgar Allan POE

is, indeed, the famous founder of the detective story himself and it is a bold author who has the temerity to make him a detective. Even so, here he is!

American Male Amateur operating in USA

Barbara STEWARD and Dwight STEWARD (American)

were both born in Chicago and are sometime Professors of English at Delaware State College.

Citation Record: 2 Books

Evermore - *First*
The action occurs in Paris, France.
Morrow US (1978)

The Lincoln Diddle - *Latest*
The action occurs in the USA.
Morrow US (1979)

Dwight STEWARD (American)

Citation Record: 1 Selected Short Story

Genesis
is in an anthology, *Crime Wave.*
Collins UK (1981)

Prof Henry POGGIOLI

is the Professor of Psychology at Ohio State University and spends much of his time around places in the Caribbean and in Latin America. In short stories only, he is involved in cases that scare him as they involve bizarre happenings and strange drugs. His approach to mystery is rational and shows sympathy for the poor people of other races.

American Male Amateur operating in USA/the Caribbean

T S STRIBLING 1881-1965 (American)

was born in Clifton, Tennessee. He graduated from Southern Normal College, Florence, Alabama, 1903 and then studied at the University of Alabama, Tuscaloo, where he received an LLB, 1905. He practised as a lawyer for only a year before becoming a full-time writer. A well-known mainstream novelist, he received the Pulitzer Prize, 1932.

Writer: Thomas Sigismund STRIBLING

Citation Record: 20 Short Stories in 2 Collections

Clues Of The Caribbees, Being Certain Criminal Investigations Of Henry Poggioli, Ph D - *Collection 1*
Short stories - 5
Doubleday US (1929); Heinemann UK (1930)

Best Dr Poggioli Detective Stories - *Collection 2*
Short stories - 15
Dover US (1975); Dover UK (1976)

Insp POINTER

is young, handsome, and has made it into the senior ranks, it seems, rather easily. He lives in an apartment in Bayswater, a then fashionable and salubrious part of inner London, where he is looked after by a landlady-cum-cook. His cases are many and mostly unmemorable.

British Policeman operating in England

A FIELDING 1884- (British)

Writer: Dorothy FIELDING

Inventor of one other detective Hugh DUNCAN

Citation Record: 23 Books

The Eames-Erskine Case - *First*
Collins UK (1924); Knopf US (1925)

Pointer To A Crime - *Last*
Collins UK (1944); Arcadia US (1945)

Atlas POIREAU

is a parody of *Agatha CHRISTIE's* detective, *Hercule POIROT.*

Appears with at least two other detectives - see Mallory KING

Hercule POIROT

is the greatest and best-known of this remarkable author's detectives and the books in which he features continue to sell in their tens of millions all over the world. This dapper little man, vain, irritatingly arrogant at times, kind to others, always impeccably dressed (often in morning coat and spats), with his funny moustache, brilliantined hair and foreign accent, could be said virtually to have created the essentials of the British Golden Age. Observant he certainly is, but material clues are not of prime importance to him. Rather he takes in, subliminally, the merest nuances of a crime, the merest traces of disorder where there should be order. By the use of the famous 'little grey cells' he solves some of the most fiendishly plotted puzzles in the history of the genre, the ingenuity of which has never been bettered. Between 1927 and 1975 he appeared in at least twenty-eight novels and many short stories, usually as the sole detective but also in books with one or other of the author's other detectives, including *Jane MARPLE, Ariadne OLIVER* and *Col RACE.* In the early books he seemed to need the assistance of a sidekick and the author duly created one, but he was so ineffectual that he only appeared sporadically later. In the course of the long canon, *Hercule POIROT* has, of course, many encounters with police stooges, friendly and unfriendly. Some dislike him; but all, in the end, bow to him. The books in which he appeared have provided the basis for seemingly unending radio and TV programmes as well as films, both British and American.

Belgian Male Professional Amateur operating in England

Sidekick: Capt HASTINGS
has been invalided out of the Army and, after the First World War, meets the great *POIROT* at the very onset of the latter's detective career in Britain. Although he was clearly a

rather silly and ineffectual man (usually the case with early British sidekicks in even the best novels of the British Golden Age) the little, stuck-up Belgian genius took to him and asked him to accompany him on several of his early cases, saying he needed someone to help him understand British ways but, more probably, because he liked having someone around with a vastly inferior brain to his own. Which is more than the author did, for she dropped *HASTINGS* from most of her later books!

British Male - Assistant

Sidekick: Dr James SHEPPARD

narrates *THE MURDER OF ROGER ACKROYD*, a classic case of *POIROT's*, and endeavours to assist him. However, he is a most unusual sidekick, as reference to the story will disclose.

British Male - Assistant

Stooge: Insp Jimmy JAPP

is the police end of many investigations that *POIROT* is called on to solve. He is not at all an antagonistic adversary, much less so indeed than is *LESTRADE* to *HOLMES*. Nevertheless, an excellent character, he plods through the cases, sometimes believing he is right, but in the end appealing to *POIROT* for help.

British Male

Stooge: Supt BATTLE

appears in several novels as the main police detective, but in some of the author's books he acts as a typical police foil for *POIROT*.

British Male

Stooge: Insp RAGLAN

is a classic example of the British Golden Age police stooge, wrong in almost everything he says and does.

British Male

Agatha CHRISTIE 1890-1976 (British)

was born in Torquay, Devon and educated privately. She married the archaeologist, Max Mallowan, in 1930 and served as a nurse during the First World War and in a hospital in London during the Second World War. She accompanied her husband on several of his expeditions in the Middle East, which she used as a background for several of her novels. Acknowledged as being, after *Sir Arthur Conan DOYLE*, perhaps the greatest of all writers of English detective fiction, she created many strongly characterised detectives, among them at least two that must be regarded as among the best in the history of the detective story. She wrote over fifty novels and many short stories and her books continue to sell in hundreds of millions in almost every language in the world. Many of them have been used for films, radio and TV scripts and plays. Her own play, *The Mousetrap*, is the longest running play in the history of the theatre. During her lifetime she received many awards for her writing as well as civil awards, including the Mystery Writers of America Grand Master award, 1954, and, from the British government, a CBE, 1956, and a DBE, 1971.

Writer: Agatha Mary Clarissa CHRISTIE

Other Detectives:

Supt BATTLE
Supt BATTLE and Luke FITZWILLIAMS
Tommy BERESFORD and Tuppence BERESFORD
Lady Elaine 'Bundle' BRENT and Supt BATTLE
Dr Arthur CALGARY
Frances DERWENT and Bobby JONES
Mark EASTERBROOK and Ariadne OLIVER
Sherlock HOLMES
Victoria JONES
Jane MARPLE
Insp NARROCOTT
Hercule POIROT and Mrs Ariadne OLIVER
Hercule POIROT, Supt BATTLE, Col RACE and Mrs Ariadne OLIVER
Parker PYNE
Harley QUIN
Col RACE
Insp TAVERNER

Citation Record: 28 Books 50 Short Stories in 1 Collection

The Mysterious Affair At Styles - *Book 1*
Lane UK (1920); Grosset US (1920)

The Murder Of Roger Ackroyd - *Book 2*
is justly considered to be one of the author's finest novels. It is cited because, in it, *Hercule POIROT* has a very special kind of sidekick, who is also the story's narrator. As a bonus, it also features what must be one of the classic Golden Age stooges, a policeman who has absolutely no idea who did what and says so.
Collins UK (1926); Dodd, Mead US (1926)

Curtain: Hercule Poirot's Last Case - *Book 3*
Collins UK (1975); Dodd, Mead US (1975)

Hercule Poirot's Casebook: Fifty Stories - *Collection 1*
Dodd, Mead US (1984); Fontana UK (1989)

Hercule POIROT

Appears with at least two other detectives - see Sherlock HOLMES

Hercule POIROT, Supt BATTLE, Col RACE and Mrs Ariadne OLIVER

all appear, sometimes individually and sometimes with another detective, in other books by this author.

Belgian Professional Amateur, British Policeman, and two British Amateurs operating in England

Agatha CHRISTIE 1890-1976 (British)

Invented 18 detectives - see Hercule POIROT

Citation Record: 1 Book

Cards On The Table - *Only*
Collins UK (1936); Dodd, Mead US (1937)

Hercule POIROT and Mrs Ariadne OLIVER

Mrs OLIVER seems to have been a deliberate self-caricature by the author. A middle-aged writer of detective stories, she has a most difficult time in producing books featuring an inept Finnish sleuth. The two detectives cited also appear either alone or with other detectives in other books by this author.

Belgian Male Amateur and British Female Amateur operating in England

Agatha CHRISTIE 1890-1976 (British)

Invented 18 detectives - see Hercule POIROT

Citation Record: 5 Books

Mrs McGinty's Dead - *First*
Collins UK (1952); Dodd, Mead US (1952)

Elephants Can Remember - *Last*
Collins UK (1972); Dodd, Mead US (1972)

POKE

Second detective of MUSH

POLACK ANNIE

American Female Amateur operating in New York/Chicago

Jack LAIT 1882-1954 (American)

Writer: Jack Jaquin L LAIT

Citation Record: 2 Books

Gangster Girl - *First*
Grosset US (1930)

Put On The Spot - *Last*
Grosset US (1930)

Det Supt Tom POLLARD

of Scotland Yard deals with mysteries constructed in the classical fashion, although lately veering towards the police procedural, as the series details the development of the detective through the ranks – which is understandable, and of his family life, which is in danger of becoming tedious.

British Policeman operating in England

Sidekick: Det Insp Gregory TOYE

British Male - Subordinate

Elizabeth LEMARCHAND 1906- (British)

was born in Barnstaple, Devon. She was educated at the Ursuline Convent, Bideford, Devon, and at Exeter University, later taking a BA and an MA from London University.

She had a career as a teacher and headmistress at several schools until becoming a full-time writer.

Writer: Elizabeth Wharton LEMARCHAND

Inventor of one other detective Insp Tom WHARTON

Citation Record: 17 Books

Death Of An Older Girl - *First*
Hart Davis UK (1967); Award US (1970)

The Glade Manor Murder - *Latest*
Piatkus UK (1988); Walker US (1989)

Mrs Emily POLLIFAX

is a sweet, elderly widow who, almost unbelievably, applies for and gets a position with the CIA. Because her appearance is so remarkably impossible for an agent, she is soon doing adventurous jobs all over the place.

American Female Secret Agent operating in USA/Asia/Africa

Dorothy GILMAN 1923- (American)

was born in New Brunswick, New Jersey, and is an artist and art teacher. In addition to her criminous works, she has written at least fifteen books for children.

Writer: Dorothy Gilman BUTTERS

Other Detectives:
Sister JOHN and HYACINTH   Amelia JONES

Citation Record: 12 Books

The Unexpected Mrs Pollifax - *First*
Doubleday US (1966); Hale UK (1967)

Mrs Pollifax, Spy - *First**
Tandem UK (1971)

Mrs Pollifax Pursued - *Latest*
Fawcett US (1995)

Insp POLLOCK

of the Plymouth Police is in this one Victorian novel.

British Policeman operating in Devonshire

Hawley SMART 1833-1893 (British)

Other Detectives:
Sgt BOYCE   BULLOCK
CHISEL   COOL CARTER
John DICKINSON   Robert PEGRAM
Sgt Silas USHER

Citation Record: 1 Book

Struck Down: A Tale Of Devon - *Only*
Warne UK (1885)

William POLLOK

British Male Amateur operating in several locations

Gerald GROGAN 1894-1918

Citation Record: 16 Short Stories in 1 Collection

William Pollok And Other Tales - *Collection 1*
Lane UK (1919); Lane US (1919)

Kira POLLY

is professional, hard-hearted, and one of the last of the old breed of Edwardian lady detectives.

British Female Private Detective operating in London

James OPPENHEIM (British)

Citation Record: 1 Selected Short Story

Mrs Judas
In 'The Storyteller' UK (1916)

Nick POLO

is smart-mouthed, low-key, and makes very little out of his rather dangerous cases.

American Male Private Detective operating in San Francisco

Jerry KENNEALY (American)

For writer details see Peter FLYNN

Citation Record: 9 Books

Polo Solo - *First*
St Martin's US (1987)

Beggar's Choice - *Latest*
St Martin's US (1994)

Grace POMEROY

is a nurse who has specialised in treating psychiatric cases and has now joined the Keen Detective Agency.

American Female Private Detective operating in New York

Anna Mary WELLS 1906- (American)

Inventor of one other detective Dr Hillis OWEN

Citation Record: 1 Book

Murderer's Choice - *Only*
Knopf US (1943); Hammond UK (1950)

Maria PONCE

Second detective of Pablo WAITZ

Mr POND

British Male Amateur operating in England

G K CHESTERTON 1874-1936 (British)

Invented 7 detectives - see Father BROWN

Citation Record: 10 Short Stories in 2 Collections

The Paradoxes Of Mr Pond - *Collection 1*
Short stories - 8
Cassell UK (1936); Dodd, Mead US (1937)

Thirteen Detectives - *Collection 2*
contains one *Father BROWN* story, two *Horne FISHER* stories, two *Gabriel GALE* stories, two *Rupert and Basil GRANT* stories and two *Mr POND* stories.
Short stories - 2
Dodd, Mead US (1986); Xanadu UK (1988)

Harry PONDER

American Male Sleuth operating in USA

Edward D HOCH 1930- (American)

Invented 20 detectives - see Capt LEOPOLD

Citation Record: 1 Selected Short Story

The Magic Bullet
appeared first in the January number of the magazine and is also in the anthology, *Best Detective Stories of the Year 24th Annual Collection* (Dutton, US 1970).
In 'Argosy' US (1969)

Mr PONDERY

is a village postmaster and the detective in this one Victorian novel.

British Male Amateur operating in England

Arnold GOLSWORTHY 1865- (British)

Citation Record: 1 Book

A Cry In The Night - *Only*
Greening UK (1899)

Dr Love Rees PONS

Appears with at least two other detectives - see Dr Frank HAYVIER

Solar PONS

is not so much a parody of *Sherlock HOLMES* as a dedicated copy, created by the American writer, *August DERLETH*, who so admired the work of *Sir Arthur Conan DOYLE* that he resolved to emulate his hero by devoting much of his literary output to his new detective's adventures. *Solar PONS* lives at 7B Praed Street, which is not too near and not too far from Baker Street, although it is (or was) less salubrious, and he has a parody sidekick in *Dr Lyndon PARKER*. *PONS* is certainly the most faithful of all the *HOLMES* parodies and the stories are of a high standard. In time they attracted their own dedicated following and led to the formation of various clubs and a journal, *The Pontine Dossier*. The first story was published in *Dragnet Magazine* in February 1929, and other stories appeared in the years following. By the time of his death, *DERLETH* had published virtually the whole canon of his remarkable parodies in six collections. A seventh, with some remaining stories, was published posthumously. The complete canon was published in 1982. The collections and the indi-

vidual stories are all individually cited. After the death of *DERLETH*, many new stories were written by the British writer, *Basil COPPER*, and these too have been published in four collections, which are all cited with their individual stories.
British Male Professional Amateur operating in London

Sidekick: Dr Lyndon PARKER
was modelled on the inimitable *Dr WATSON*. He is a solid Englishman who once spent some years in the US and now lives with *PONS* and narrates his cases.
British Male - Assistant

Stooge: Insp Tobias ATHELNEY
appears in one story. He arrives from the planet Terra with a problem for *Solar PONS*.
Terraist Male

Basil COPPER 1924- (British)
is a journalist who has written many books outside the genre with a strong leaning towards the occult and macabre.
Other Detectives:
Clyde BEATTY   Mike FARADAY
Citation Record: 16 Short Stories in 4 Collections
The Dossier Of Solar Pons - *Parody Collection 1*
contains six stories, which are cited immediately below.
Short stories - 6
Pinnacle US (1979); LSP Books UK (1980)
The Adventure Of Buffington Old Grange - *Parody 1*
The Adventure Of The Hammer Of Hate - *Parody 2*
The Adventure Of The Ipi Idol - *Parody 3*
The Adventure Of The Perplexed Photographer - *Parody 4*
The Adventure Of The Six Gold Doubloons - *Parody 5*
The Sealed Spire Mystery - *Parody 6*
The Further Adventures Of Solar Pons - *Parody Collection 2*
contains four stories, which are cited immediately below.
Short stories - 4
Pinnacle US (1979); LSP Books UK (1980)
The Adventure Of The Defeated Doctor - *Parody 7*
The Adventure Of The Frightened Governess - *Parody 8*
The Adventure Of The Shaft Of Death - *Parody 9*
Murder At The Zoo - *Parody 10*
The Secret Files Of Solar Pons - *Parody Collection 3*
contains four stories, which are cited immediately below.
Short stories - 4
Pinnacle US (1979)
The Adventure Of The Anguished Actor - *Parody 11*
The Adventure Of The Anguished Actress - *Parody 12*
The Adventure Of The Crawling Horror - *Parody 13*
The Adventure Of The Ignored Idols - *Parody 14*
The Uncollected Cases Of Solar Pons - *Parody Collection 4*
contains four stories, two of which appear in earlier collections. The two new stories are cited immediately below.
Short stories - 2
Pinnacle US (1980)
The Adventure Of The Haunted Rectory - *Parody 15*
The Adventure Of The Singular Sandwich - *Parody 16*

August DERLETH 1909-1971 (American)
was born in Sauk City, Wisconsin. He graduated with a BA from the University of Wisconsin, Madison, 1930. Publisher, editor, poet, writer of crime and many other types of novel as well as many non-fiction works, he was the creator of the best of all *Sherlock HOLMES* parodies, *Solar PONS*, whose adventures were (almost) as lovingly and meticulously recounted as were those of his great predecessor.
Writer: August William DERLETH
Other Detectives:
Tex HARRIGAN   Sherlock HOLMES
Judge Ephraim Peabody PECK
Citation Record: 1 Book 70 Short Stories in 8 Collections
Mr Fairlie's Final Journey - *Only*
Mycroft & Moran US (1968)
In Re Sherlock Holmes: The Adventures Of Solar Pons - *Parody Collection 1*
The individual stories are cited immediately below. The title of this first collection of *Solar PONS* stories was chosen by the author in homage to the *Sherlock HOLMES* canon, which the author said had had such a large influence on his writing career. Being rather unwieldy, however, the title was changed for the first UK publication and the collection was also retitled when republished by *Pinnacle* (US 1974) as *Regarding Sherlock Holmes*. Some of the stories first appeared in magazines and, for those, the date and place of the original publication are given.
Short stories - 12
Mycroft & Moran US (1945)
The Adventures Of Solar Pons - *Parody Collection 1**
Robson UK (1975)
The Adventure Of The Black Narcissus - *Parody 1*
appeared first in the February 1929 number of 'Dragnet Magazine'.
The Adventure Of The Frightened Baronet - *Parody 2*
The Adventure Of The Late Mr Faversham - *Parody 3*
appeared first in the December 1929 number of 'Dragnet Magazine'.
The Adventure Of The Limping Man - *Parody 4*
appeared first in the December 1929 number of *Detective Trails*. The title parodies that of the canonical *Sherlock HOLMES* story, *THE ADVENTURE OF THE CREEPING MAN*.
The Adventure Of The Lost Holiday - *Parody 5*
The Adventure Of The Man With The Broken Face - *Parody 6*
The Adventure Of The Norcross Riddle - *Parody 7*
appeared first, it would seem, in the classic anthology, *THE MISADVENTURES OF SHERLOCK HOLMES* (Editor; *Ellery QUEEN*). In his introduction to the tale, the editor suggested that it may have been written as early as 1928. The following year it was included in the author's first published collection of *Solar PONS* stories, *IN RE SHERLOCK HOLMES. THE ADVENTURES OF SOLAR PONS*.
The Adventure Of The Purloined Periapt - *Parody 8*
The Adventure Of The Retired Novelist - *Parody 9*
parodies the title of the canonical *Sherlock HOLMES* story, *THE ADVENTURE OF THE RETIRED COLOURMAN*.
The Adventure Of The Seven Passengers - *Parody 10*
The Adventure Of The Sotheby Salesman - *Parody 11*
The Adventure Of The Three Red Dwarfs - *Parody 12*
The Memoirs Of Solar Pons - *Parody Collection 2*
The individual stories are cited immediately below. Some appeared first in magazines and, for those, the date and place of the original publication are given.
Short stories - 11
Mycroft & Moran US (1951)
The Adventure Of Ricoletti Of The Club Foot - *Parody 13*
refers to an allusion made by *Sherlock HOLMES* in the canonical story, *THE MUSGRAVE RITUAL*, to an unchronicled case of his, before he had met *Dr WATSON*, concerning 'Ricoletti of the club foot and his abominable wife'.
The Adventure Of The Broken Chessman - *Parody 14*
appeared first in the September 1929 number of 'Dragnet Magazine'.
The Adventure Of The Circular Room - *Parody 15*
appeared first in the July 1946 number of the Baker Street Journal, where the names of the detective and sidekick were changed from *Solar PONS* and *Dr PARKER* to *Sherlock HOLMES* and *Dr WATSON*. The story is accordingly cited under both sets of names.
The Adventure Of The Dog In The Manger - *Parody 16*
The Adventure Of The Five Royal Coachmen - *Parody 17*
The Adventure Of The Lost Locomotive - *Parody 18*

The Adventure Of The Paralytic Mendicant - *Parody 19*
refers to the allusion made by *Dr WATSON* in the canonical story, *THE FIVE ORANGE PIPS*, to the 'Amateur Mendicant Society, who held a luxurious club in the lower vault of a furniture warehouse'. The allusion has been used by other authors as the basis for a pastiche or parody.

The Adventure Of The Perfect Husband - *Parody 20*

The Adventure Of The Proper Comma - *Parody 21*

The Adventure Of The Six Silver Spiders - *Parody 22*
appeared first in the October 1950 number of *Ellery Queen's Mystery Magazine* as *The Six Silver Spiders.*

The Adventure Of The Tottenham Werewolf - *Parody 23*

The Return Of Solar Pons - *Parody Collection 3*
The individual stories are cited immediately below. Some appeared first in magazines and, for those, the date and place of the original publication are given.
Short stories - 13
Mycroft & Moran US (1958)

The Adventure Of The Camberwell Beauty - *Parody 24*
appeared first in a minor collection, which contained only three stories and was limited to 996 copies, *Three Problems for Solar Pons.* The title refers to the allusion by *Dr WATSON* in the canonical story, *THE FIVE ORANGE PIPS*, to the unchronicled case of 'the Camberwell Poisoning'.

The Adventure Of The Devil's Footprints - *Parody 25*
appeared first in *Double Action Detective Stories* in 1956.

The Adventure Of The Dorrington Inheritance - *Parody 26*
appeared first in the March 1958 number of *The Saint Mystery Magazine* as *The Dorrington Inheritance.*

The Adventure Of The Grice-Paterson Curse - *Parody 27*
appeared first in the November 1956 number of *Pursuit Detective Story Magazine* as *The Curse of Grice-Paterson.* The title refers to an allusion made by *Dr WATSON* in the canonical story, *THE FIVE ORANGE PIPS*, to an unchronicled case involving 'the singular adventures of Grice Patersons in the island of Uffa'.

The Adventure Of The Little Hangman - *Parody 28*
appeared first in the January 1959 number of *The Saint Mystery Magazine.*

P

The Adventure Of The Lost Dutchman - *Parody 29*
appeared first in the November 1955 number of *Pursuit Detective Story Magazine* as *The Case of the Lost Dutchman.*

The Adventure Of The Penny Magenta - *Parody 30*
appeared first in the November 1954 issue of *The Saint Mystery Magazine.*

The Adventure Of The Remarkable Worm - *Parody 31*
appeared first in *Three Problems for Solar Pons.* The title refers to the allusion made by *Dr WATSON* in the canonical story, *THE PROBLEM OF THOR BRIDGE*, to an unchronicled case concerning 'Isadora Persano, a well-known journalist and duellist, who was found stark staring mad with a match box in front of him which contained a remarkable worm, said to be unknown to science'. The allusion has been used by other authors as the basis for a pastiche or parody.

The Adventure Of The Rydberg Numbers - *Parody 32*
appeared first in *Three Problems for Solar Pons.*

The Adventure Of The Stone Of Scone - *Parody 33*

The Adventure Of The Swedenborg Signatures - *Parody 34*
appeared first in the May 1954 number of Nero Wolfe Mystery Magazine.

The Adventure Of The Trained Cormorant - *Parody 35*
appeared first in the October 1956 number of *The Saint Mystery Magazine.* The title refers to the allusion made by *Dr WATSON* in the canonical story, *THE ADVENTURE OF THE VEILED LODGER*, to an unchronicled case. For further information see the *Sherlock HOLMES* pastiche, *THE POLITICIAN, LIGHTHOUSE AND TRAINED CORMORANT* written by *Clive BROOKS.*
(1956)

The Adventure Of The 'Triple Kent' - *Parody 36*
appeared first in the April 1957 number of *The Saint Mystery Magazine.*

The Reminiscences Of Solar Pons - *Parody Collection 4*
The individual stories are cited immediately below. Some appeared first in magazines and, for those, the date and place of the original publication are given.
Short stories - 8
Mycroft & Moran US (1961)

The Adventure Of The Black Cardinal - *Parody 37*
appeared first in the March 1930 number of *Gangster Stories.*

The Adventure Of The Blind Clairaudient - *Parody 38*
appeared first in the September 1961 number of *The Saint Mystery Magazine.*

The Adventure Of The Cloverdale Kennels - *Parody 39*
appeared first in the June 1960 number of *The Saint Mystery Magazine.*

The Adventure Of The Mazarine Blue - *Parody 40*
appeared first in the June 1956 number of *The Hunted* as *The Thirteenth Coffin.* The title refers to the canonical *Sherlock HOLMES* story, *THE ADVENTURE OF THE MAZARIN STONE.*

The Adventure Of The Mosaic Cylinders - *Parody 41*
appeared first in the August 1959 number of *The Saint Mystery Magazine.*

The Adventure Of The Praed Street Irregulars - *Parody 42*

The Adventure Of The Hats Of M Dulac - *Parody 43*
appeared first in the January 1959 number of *The Saint Mystery Magazine* as *The Adventure of the Stolen Hats.*

The Adventure Of The Troubled Magistrate - *Parody 44*
appeared first in the February 1961 number of *Alfred Hitchcock's Mystery Magazine* as *Others Deal in Death.*

The Casebook Of Solar Pons - *Parody Collection 5*
The individual stories are cited immediately below. Some appeared first in magazines and, for those, the date and place of the original publication are given.
Short stories - 12
Mycroft & Moran US (1965)

The Adventure Of The Amateur Philologist - *Parody 45*
appeared first in the September 1964 number of *Alfred Hitchcock's Mystery Magazine.*

The Adventure Of The Ascot Scandal - *Parody 46*

The Adventure Of The China Cottage - *Parody 47*
appeared first in the March 1965 issue of *Alfred Hitchcock's Mystery Magazine.*

The Adventure Of The Crouching Dog - *Parody 48*
appeared first in the July 1964 number of *The Saint Mystery Magazine.*

The Adventure Of The Fatal Glance - *Parody 49*
appeared first in the March 1963 number of *The Saint Mystery Magazine.*
!See Appendix 2.

The Adventure Of The Haunted Library - *Parody 50*
appeared first in the November 1963 number of *Alfred Hitchcock's Mystery Magazine.*

The Adventure Of The Innkeeper's Clerk - *Parody 51*
appeared first in the January 1966 number of *The Saint Mystery Magazine.*

The Adventure Of The Intarsia Box - *Parody 52*
appeared first in the March 1964 number of *Alfred Hitchcock's Mystery Magazine.* The title refers, obliquely and ingeniously, to the canonical *Sherlock HOLMES* story, *THE CARDBOARD BOX*, 'intarsia' being a form of Italian inlaid woodwork.

The Adventure Of The Missing Huntsman - *Parody 53*

The Adventure Of The Spurious Tamerlane - *Parody 54*
appeared first in the December 1964 number of *The Saint Mystery Magazine.*

The Adventure Of The Sussex Archers - *Parody 55*
appeared first in the October 1962 number of *Alfred Hitchcock's Mystery Magazine* as *Adventures of the Sussex Archers.* The title refers obliquely to that of the canonical story, *THE ADVENTURE OF THE SUSSEX VAMPIRE.*

The Adventure Of The Whispering Knights - *Parody 56*
appeared first in the September 1963 number of *The Saint Mystery Magazine.*

A Praed Street Dossier - *Parody Collection 6*
The individual stories are cited immediately below. Some appeared first in magazines and, for those, the date and place of the original publication are given.
!See Appendix 2.
Short stories - 3
Mycroft & Moran US (1968)

The Adventure Of The Ball Of Nostradamus - *Parody 57*
appeared first in the June 1955 number of *Alfred Hitchcock's Mystery Magazine.*

The Adventure Of The Bookseller's Clerk - *Parody 58*

From The Notebooks Of Dr Lyndon Parker - *Parody 59*

The Chronicles Of Solar Pons - *Parody Collection 7*
The individual stories are cited immediately below. Some appeared first in magazines and, for those, the date and place of the original publication are given.
Short stories - 10
Mycroft & Moran US (1973); Robson UK (1975)

The Adventure Of The Aluminium Crutch - *Parody 60*
refers to a remark made by *Sherlock HOLMES* in the canonical story, *THE MUSGRAVE RITUAL,* to an unchronicled case concerning 'the singular affair of the aluminium crutch'. The allusion has been used by other authors as the basis for a pastiche or parody.

The Adventure Of The Benin Bronze - *Parody 61*

The Adventure Of The Bishop's Companion - *Parody 62*

The Adventure Of The Golden Bracelet - *Parody 63*
makes oblique reference to the title of the canonical *Sherlock HOLMES* story, *THE ADVENTURE OF THE GOLDEN PINCE-NEZ.*

The Adventure Of The Missing Tenants - *Parody 64*
appeared first in the June 1929 number of *Dragnet Magazine.*

The Adventure Of The Obrisset Snuff Box - *Parody 65*
!See Appendix 2.

The Adventure Of The Orient Express - *Parody 66*
was first published by *Candlelight Press* (US 1965).

The Adventure Of The Red Leech - *Parody 67*
appeared first in the October 1966 number of *Alfred Hitchcock's Mystery Magazine.* The title refers to the allusion made by *Dr WATSON* in the canonical story, *THE ADVENTURE OF THE GOLDEN PINCE-NEZ,* to an unchronicled case, 'the repulsive story of the red leech'.
(1966)

The Adventure Of The Seven Sisters - *Parody 68*

The Adventure Of The Shaplow Millions - *Parody 69*

The Adventure Of The Unique Dickensians - *Parody 70*

The Solar Pons Omnibus - *Parody Collection 8*
This, the most recent collection, contains all the short stories featuring *Solar PONS* previously published.
Short stories - 70
Arkham US (1982)

August DERLETH and Mack REYNOLDS (American)
were the joint authors of the only *Solar PONS* story that *DERLETH* did not write on his own.
Writers: August William DERLETH 1909-1971 and Dallas McCord REYNOLDS 1917-
Citation Record: 1 Selected Short Story

The Adventure Of The Snitch In Time - *Parody 1*
concerns a visit from a police stooge from another planet, Terra, with a problem for the detective. The story appeared first in the July 1953 number of *The Magazine of Fantasy and Science Fiction* and is also in the anthology, *THE MISADVENTURES OF SHERLOCK HOLMES* (Editor; *Sebastian WOLFE).*

Peter PONSONBY

American Male Amateur operating in California

Jean LESLIE (American)
was born in Omaha and was a lecturer in Psychology. She is the author of at least nine genre books.
Citation Record: 3 Books

One Cried Murder - *First*
Doubleday US (1945); Edwards UK (1946)

Three-Cornered Murder - *Last*
Doubleday US (1947); Hodder & Stoughton UK (1948)

Bob PONTING

British Male Amateur operating in England

Ben BOLT 1872- (British)
Writer: Ottwell BINNS
Other Detectives:
Insp GODBOLD
Insp GODBOLD and Bob PONTING
Capt GRANDISON John SCARLETT
Citation Record: 2 Books

A Shot In The Night - *First*
Ward, Lock UK (1934)

The Five Red Stars - *Last*
Ward, Lock UK (1936)

Papa PONTIVY

is a typical spy-detective of the era and operates all over Europe.

Male Secret Agent operating in several locations

Bernard NEWMAN 1897-1968 (British)
was born in Ibstock, Leicestershire. He served in the Army in the First World War and in the Ministry of Information during the Second World War. He was the author of thirty-four genre novels under his own name and fourteen under his main pseudonym, *Don BETTERIDGE.* They are, for the most part, spy thrillers based on world events at the time and with strong links to detection. He also wrote a few mainstream novels, a dozen or more plays, and over fifty books on travel, current events and espionage.
Writer: Bernard Charles NEWMAN
Other Byline: Don BETTERIDGE
Other Detectives:
Sgt/Insp MARSHALL Insp Nicholas PRINCE
Citation Record: 15 Books 4 Short Stories in 1 Collection

Death To The Spy - *First*
Gollancz UK (1939)

The Spy At Number 10 - *Last*
Hale UK (1965)

Spy Catchers - *Collection 1*
Only four of the stories in this collection of thirty of the author's stories feature *PONTIVY.*
Gollancz UK (1945)

Ch Insp POOLE

was a student at Oxford, where he read Law. A tall man, handsome and a fine athlete, he decided to become a copper and did so well that, although called to the Bar, he rose to become a senior member of the CID at Scotland Yard. He is, in fact, clearly designed as an antidote to the brilliant amateurs of the British Golden Age.

British Policeman operating in England

Sidekick: Sgt BRAGG
British Male - Subordinate

Henry WADE 1887-1969 (British)
was born in Leigh, Surrey, a 6th Baronet. He was educated at Eton College and attended New College, Oxford. He served in the Grenadier Guards, 1908-1920, was mentioned in dispatches, and was awarded the Distinguished Service Order and the *Croix de Guerre*. In the Second World War, he served in the Guards again, 1940-1945. He succeeded to the baronetcy, 1937, and received several honours in later life. A master of the police novel, he was a major writer during the years of the British Golden Age and then resumed writing after 1945. The author of twenty-one fine criminous novels, his books are widely read in the UK although few were published in the USA.
Writer: Sir Henry Lancelot AUBREY-FLETCHER
Other Detectives:
Const John BRAGG
Insp Inspector DOBSON
Maj FAIDE
Supt DAWLE
Insp DODD
NETTERLY
Citation Record: 9 Books 6 Short Stories in 1 Collection
The Duke Of York's Steps - *First*
Constable UK (1929); Payson & Clarke US (1929)
Gold Was Our Grave - *Last*
Constable UK (1954); Macmillan US (1954)
Policeman's Lot - *Collection 1*
This collection of thirteen of the author's stories contains six with *Insp POOLE*.
Constable UK (1933)

Insp POOLE
investigates when, at an unnamed university, the mistress of the Professor of Archaeology is found with her head stove in. He solves not only the murder but a lot of archaeological mysteries too.
British Policeman operating in England

Kathleen FREEMAN 1897-1959 (British)
was born in Birmingham, Warwickshire. She was a lecturer in Greek at Cardiff University, Wales. A prolific writer of mystery fiction under her main pseudonym, *Mary FITT*, she published this one novel under her real name.
Citation Record: 1 Book
Gown And Shroud - *Only*
Macdonald UK (1947)

P

Bill POOLE
American Male Detective in Pulp Magazines operating in USA

Paul WARREN (American)
Inventor of one other detective SKILLFUL CHARLIE
Citation Record: 1 Selected Short Story
Bill Poole, The Louisville Detective; Or, In The Lair Of The 'Red Ribbon'.
Old Cap Collier Library US (18??)

Jaspar POOLE
solves the mystery of a girl's disappearance inside a locked house.
British Male Amateur operating in England

Joseph HOCKING 1860-1937 (British)
Citation Record: 1 Book
The Case Of Miss Dunstable - *Only*
Hodder & Stoughton UK (1923); Wright US (1936)

Tide POOLES
is a *Sherlock HOLMES* parody.
British Male Professional Amateur operating in England
Sidekick: Dr HARCOURT
is his parody *WATSON*-like assistant.
British Male - Assistant

John JACOBSON (American)
Adopter of one other detective Sherlock HOLMES
Citation Record: 6 Selected Short Stories
The Adventure Of The Misleading Murder - *Parody 1*
appeared in the June number.
In 'Baker Street Journal' US (1967)
The Opera Murder - *Parody 2*
appeared in the June, August and October numbers.
In 'Shades of Sherlock' US (1967)
The Return Of The Redheaded League - *Parody 3*
appeared in the Annual in January 1967.
In 'Shades of Sherlock' US (1967)
The Adventure Of The Spot Of Tea - *Parody 4*
appeared in the March number.
In 'Baker Street Journal' US (1967)
Inspector Kirchner's Own Case - *Parody 5*
appeared in the June number.
In 'Baker Street Pages' US (1969)
The Adventure Of The Stone Of Henge - *Parody 6*
appeared in the September number.
In 'Astounding Deductions' US (1970)

Bradley KJELL (American)
Inventor of one other detective Shrock HOLMES
Citation Record: 7 Selected Short Stories
The Adventure Of The Missing Scuttle - *Parody 1*
appeared in the November number.
In 'Shades of Sherlock' US (1966)
The Adventure Of The Sick Sleuth - *Parody 2*
appeared in the Christmas Annual.
In 'Baker Street Pages' US (1966)
The Adventure Of The Bored Professor - *Parody 3*
In 'Baker Street Journal' US (1967)
The Adventure Of The Unstrung Fiddler - *Parody 4*
appeared in the May number.
In 'Baker Street Journal' US (1967)
The Adventure Of The Mowed Lawn - *Parody 5*
appeared in February.
In 'Shades of Sherlock' US (1967)
The Adventure Of The Synthetic Soup - *Parody 6*
appeared in the Annual for 1968.
In 'Shades of Sherlock' US (1968)
The Adventure Of The Perilous Protoplasm - *Parody 7*
appeared in the September number.
In 'Astounding Deductions' US (1970)

Supt POPE
investigates a complex case, in which two people falsely confess to murder and are found not guilty at their trial.
British Policeman operating in England

Roderic JEFFRIES 1926- (British)
Invented 4 detectives - see Insp Enrique ALVAREZ
Citation Record: 1 Book
Evidence Of The Accused - *Only*
Collins UK (1961); London House US (1963)

Jake POPE
is a Virginian who joins an agency in Los Angeles, where he makes good, particularly after he inherits a fortune on the death of his wife.
American Male Private Detective operating in Los Angeles

Ross THOMAS 1926- (American)
Invented 4 detectives - see Morgan CITRON
Citation Record: 1 Book
The Money Harvest - *Only*
Morrow US (1975); Hamish Hamilton UK (1975)

Paul POPE and Roy POPE
are a father and son who track down a member of what is perhaps becoming an over-popular species, the villain of the 1990s, the serial killer. This one, it seems, has been hacking

up people for years and 'the detectives are at a loss'. The two sleuths, however, have so much gone awry in their own lives (rape, abduction, assault and murder, to name but a few) that they are spurred on to solve the mystery of who is doing what; and, presumably, why.
American Male Amateurs operating in Arizona

Philip GERARD (American)

Citation Record: 1 Book

Desert Kill - *Single*
Morrow US (1994)

Roy POPE

Second detective of Paul POPE

Roderick POPLAR

works for the Abraxus Detective Agency.
American Male Professional Investigator operating in USA

Lawrence G BLOCHMAN 1900-1975 (American)

Invented 5 detectives - see Dr Daniel Webster COFFEE and Lt Max RITTER

Citation Record: 1 Selected Short Story

Reprieve
In 'Private Detective Stories' US (1943)

Max POPPER

is a failed literary agent who investigates the death of his neighbour, a private detective who was trying to find a lost film.
American Male Amateur operating in New York

Michael WOLK (American)

Citation Record: 1 Book

The Big Picture - *Single*
Signet US (1985); Severn UK (1987)

James PORBEAGLE

is a thirty-year-old bachelor, a lecturer in English at Cape Town University, who investigates the death of the grandmother of a young female student.
South African Male Amateur operating in Cape Town

June DRUMMOND 1923- (South African)

was born in Durban, Natal, and took a BA at the University of Cape Town, 1944. A journalist and social worker in many causes, she is the author of nearly twenty mystery and crime novels, many of which are set in South Africa.

Inventor of one other detective Insp David COPE

Citation Record: 1 Book

Welcome, Proud Lady - *Only*
Gollancz UK (1964); Holt US (1968)

Appleton 'Apple' PORTER

is a quirky, lanky spy who is involved in grotesque but often comic assignments.
British Male Secret Agent operating in several locations

Marc LOVELL 1930- (Australian)

See main detective Jason GALT

Citation Record: 14 Books

The Spy Game - *First*
Doubleday US (1980); Hale UK (1981)

Comfort Me With Spies - *Latest*
Doubleday US (1990)

Ben PORTER and Carrie PORTER

American Male Amateur and American Female Amateur operating in USA/ France

Elizabeth TRAVIS 1920- (American)

Writer: Elizabeth Frances Chandler TRAVIS

Citation Record: 2 Books

Under The Influence - *First*
St Martin's US (1989)

Finders, Keepers - *Latest*
St Martin's US (1990)

Carrie PORTER

Second detective of Ben PORTER

Harry PORTER

sleuths at some time in the future.
American Male Sleuth

Ed NAHA 1950- (American)

See main detective Lt Kevin BROSKEY

Citation Record: 2 Books

The Paradise Plot - *First*
Bantam US (1980)

The Suicide Plague - *Latest*
Bantam US (1982)

Jessamyn POSEY

American Female Amateur operating in California

Dorothy BRYANT 1930- (American)

Citation Record: 1 Book

Killing Wonder - *Single*
A & A Books US (1981)

Mr POSKITT

British Male Amateur operating in England

J S FLETCHER 1863-1935 (British)

Invented 9 detectives - see Paul CAMPENHAYE

Citation Record: 25 Short Stories in 2 Collections

Mr Poskitt - *Collection 1*
Not all these stories are criminous.
Short stories - 11
Nash UK (1907)

Mr Poskitt's Nightcaps - *Collection 2*
Not all these stories are criminous.
Short stories - 14
Nash UK (1910)

Joe POSNER

American Male Amateur operating in New Jersey

Jeremy PIKSER (American)

Citation Record: 1 Book

Junk On The Hill - *Single*
Pluto UK (1984); Carroll & Graf US (1985)

Insp 'Steady as a Rock' POSSE

British Policeman operating in England

Adrian ALINGTON 1895-1958 (British)

Writer: Adrian Richard ALINGTON

Citation Record: 2 Books

The Vanishing Celebrities - *First*
Chatto UK (1938)

The Amazing Test Match Crime - *Last*
Chatto UK (1939)

Anthony POST

American Male Amateur operating in USA

Alexander IRVING 1922-1980 (American)

Writers: Ruth FOX and Anne FARHENKOPF

Citation Record: 2 Books

Bitter Ending - *First*
Dodd, Mead US (1946)

Symphony In Two Time - *Last*
Dodd, Mead US (1948)

The POST-OFFICE DETECTIVE

American Male Professional Investigator operating in USA

George W GOODE (American)

See main detective KING DAN

Citation Record: 1 Book

The Post-Office Detective; Or, A Mystery In The Mails - *Only*
Street & Smith US (1888)

Jordan POTEET
is the librarian in a small town. He investigates, quite naturally, when he finds a corpse in his store room.
American Male Amateur operating in Texas

Jeff ABBOTT (American)
Citation Record: 1 Book
Do Unto Others - *Single*
Ballantine US (1994)

Ralph POTEET
is downbeat, strapped for cash and fairly typical of the modern species.
American Male Private Detective operating in Detroit

Loren D ESTLEMAN 1952- (American)
Invented 7 detectives - see Amos WALKER
Citation Record: 1 Selected Short Story
State Of Grace
is in an anthology, *An Eye For Justice* (Editor: Robert J Randisi).
Mysterious Press US (1988)

Joe POTOMOS
is a crime reporter who investigates the death of a senator's daughter, in spite of political pressure to prevent him.
American Male Amateur operating in Washington DC

Margaret TRUMAN 1924- (American)
Invented 9 detectives - see Mr Ron FAIRCHILD
Citation Record: 1 Book
Murder In Georgetown - *Single*
Arbor US (1986); Chivers UK (1986)

Sgt POTTER
is, rather fancifully, said to be a member of 'The New London Police'. Even so, he solves a family mystery and a murder that goes with it.
American Policeman operating in Connecticut

John Stephen STRANGE 1896- (American)
Invented 4 detectives - see Van Dusen ORMSBERRY
Citation Record: 1 Book
Black Hawthorn - *Only*
Doubleday US (1933)
The Chinese Jar Mystery - *Only**
Collins UK (1934)

Brockton POTTER
is a researcher with a New York brokerage firm who runs up against business crimes, which he has to solve.
American Male Amateur operating in New York/Phoenix

Arthur MALING 1923- (American)
was born in Chicago, Illinois. He was educated at the Francis W Parker School, Chicago, and later took degrees and honours at Harvard University, Cambridge, Massachusetts. Reporter and crime editor, he has been an executive in the Maling Brothers shoe chain in Chicago, 1946-1972. He received the Mystery Writers of America Edgar Allan Poe award, 1980.
Writer: Arthur Gordon MALING
Other Detectives:
Calvin BIX — Walter JACKSON
Citation Record: 5 Books
Ripoff - *First*
Harper & Row US (1976); Hale UK (1977)
A Taste Of Treason - *Latest*
Harper & Row US (1983); Gollancz UK (1983)

Dudley POTTER
British Male Amateur operating in England

Julian SYMONS 1912-1994 (British)
Invented 11 detectives - see Insp CRAMBO
Citation Record: 1 Book
The Name Of Annabel Lee - *Single*
Viking US (1983)

Eugenia POTTER
is a wealthy widow, in her sixties, who has a ranch in Arizona but solves murders in Harrington, Iowa.
American Female Amateur operating in USA

Virginia RICH 1914-1985 (American)
Citation Record: 3 Books
The Cooking School Murders - *First*
Dutton US (1982)
The Nantucket Diet Murders - *Latest*
Delacorte US (1985)

Hiram POTTER
lives in Gramercy Park and is rich and idle; but, when interested in a case, he turns into a quick-witted amateur sleuth with a sense of moral outrage.
American Male Amateur operating in New York

Rae FOLEY 1900-1978 (American)
was the author of many novels in both the criminous and romantic genres, for which she used different bylines.
Writer: Elinore DENNISTON
Other Byline: Dennis ALLAN
Inventor of one other detective John HARLAND
Citation Record: 11 Books
Death And Mr Potter - *First*
Dodd, Mead US (1955); Boardman UK (1955)
The Peacock Is A Bird Of Prey - *First**
Dell US (1976)
A Calculated Risk - *Last*
Dodd, Mead US (1970); Hale UK (1972)

Dr Neal POTTER
is a doctor in South Africa. He suspects that a black patient has been murdered and investigates, to his own peril.
South African Male Amateur operating in South Africa

Lawrie REZNEK (South African)
was born in South Africa. He was a doctor and psychiatrist in Cape Town, later practising in England.
Citation Record: 1 Book
The Medicine Men - *Single*
Collins UK (1990)

Oliver POTTER and Laurence CARRINGTON
British Male Professional Investigator and Amateur operating in England

Eric A BAYLY (British)
Other Detectives:
Percival GUNTRIP — Mr MERTON
Citation Record: 1 Book
The House Of Strange Secrets - *Only*
Sands UK (1899); Dutton US (1899)

Det Insp Simon POTTER
has sandy hair and pale eyes and is said to look 'like a weary solicitor at the end of a long day'.
British Policeman operating in London

Terence BLACKER (British)
is a journalist.
Writer: Harvey PORLOCK
Citation Record: 1 Book
The Fame Hotel - *Single*
Bloomsbury UK (1992)

Mr POTTLE
Male Amateur

Richard CONNELL 1893-1949
See main detective Matthew KELTON

Citation Record: 11 Short Stories in 1 Collection

Mr Braddy's Bottle And Other Humorous Tales - *Collection 1*
Chapman & Hall UK (1922)

Gen Stepan POVIN

Male Professional Investigator

John TRENHAILE 1949- (British)

Writer: John Stevens TRENHAILE

Inventor of one other detective Simon YOUNG

Citation Record: 2 Books

Kyril - *First*
Severn UK (1981)

A Man Called Kyril - *First**
Congdon US (1983)

Nocturne For The General - *Latest*
Bodley Head UK (1985); Congdon US (1985)

Lt Leroy POWDER

American Policeman operating in Indianapolis

Michael Z LEWIN 1942- (American)

Invented 3 detectives - see Albert SAMSON

Citation Record: 3 Books

Night Cover - *First*
Knopf US (1976); Hamilton UK (1976)

Late Payments - *Latest*
Morrow US (1986); Macmillan UK (1986)

Kit POWELL

is a 'sportscaster'. In splendid parody of the modern female PI, she says, 'My name is Kit Powell and I carry a notebook'. She deserves a medal. Assigned to cover events and sporting stars, instead she finds murder, kidnapping and racism in various forms.

American Female Amateur operating in USA

Julie ROBITAILLE (American)

Citation Record: 2 Books

Jinx - *First*
County Oak US (1994)

Iced - *Latest*
St Martin's US (1994)

Richard POWELL

British Male Amateur operating in England

Anthony FOWLES (British)

Citation Record: 2 Books

Dupe Negative - *First*
Allen UK (1970); Simon & Schuster US (1972)

Double Feature - *Last*
Allen UK (1972); Simon & Schuster US (1973)

William POWER

appears also in books with the author's other detectives, *Penny MERCER and Vincent MERCER.*

British Male Amateur operating in England

Henrietta CLANDON 1881- (British)

Invented 3 detectives - see Penny MERCER and Vincent MERCER

Citation Record: 1 Book

Good By Stealth - *Only*
Bles UK (1936)

William POWER, Penny MERCER and Vincent MERCER

all appear individually in other books by this author.

Two British Male Amateurs and one British Female Amateur operating in England

Henrietta CLANDON 1881- (British)

Invented 3 detectives - see Penny MERCER and Vincent MERCER

Citation Record: 3 Books

Rope By Arrangement - *First*
Bles UK (1935)

Power On The Scent - *Last*
Bles UK (1937)

Georgina POWERS

is a tough, lively journalist who is involved in some nasty goings-on during her doubtless honest duties.

American Female Amateur operating in New York

Denise DANKS (American)

Citation Record: 4 Books

The Pizza House Crash - *First*
Constable UK (1989)

Wink A Hopeful Eye - *Latest*
Macmillan UK (1993)

Johnny POWERS

American Male Private Detective operating in San Francisco

Joe RAYTER (American)

Writer: Mary F MCCHESNEY

Citation Record: 2 Books

The Victim Was Important - *First*
Scribner's US (1954); Reinhardt UK (1954)

Asking For Trouble - *Last*
Mill US (1955); Ward, Lock UK (1957)

Lt POWLEDGE

American Policeman operating in Chicago

M P REA (American)

Writer: Margaret Lucille Paine REA

Citation Record: 3 Books

A Curtain For Crime - *First*
Doubleday US (1941)

Death Of An Angel - *Last*
Doubleday US (1943)

Roger POYNINGS

British Male Amateur operating in England

Michael BURT 1900- (British)

Citation Record: 3 Books

The Case Of The Fast Young Lady - *First*
Ward, Lock UK (1942)

The Case Of The Laughing Jesuit - *Last*
Ward, Lock UK (1948)

The PRAIRIE DETECTIVE

American Male Detective in Pulp Magazines operating in USA

ANON

No citations

PREACHER

American Male Sleuth operating in USA

Ted THACKREY Jr 1918- (American)

Citation Record: 3 Books

Preacher - *First*
Jove US (1988)

King Of Diamonds - *Latest*
Jove US (1989)

The 87th PRECINCT

appears in a series of books that has become almost legendary. Although the author did not actually invent the new form of detective story that was to become known as the police procedural, he was one of the very first to use it extensively. In this sub-genre there is no single detective doing the sleuthing, but rather there are several officers, of different grades, who are investigating different aspects of one case or several cases at once, which may or may not overlap each other. There is, it is true, almost always a protagonist, the novel's hero, who is highlighted. He may be in charge, or he may be a more lowly figure, and he may vary from book to book in a series. The police procedural is often successful, mainly because of modern interest in the details of police work rather than in the intellectual puzzles of the classic detective story. But it contains many pitfalls and can be simply boring. It is an amazing feat of *MCBAIN's* to have maintained a high quality over so many years and all the books in the long series are outstanding for the skill in their plotting and characterisation. The three main characters in the series have been, Steve Carella, Meyer Meyer and Bert Kling.

American Policemen operating in New York

Ed MCBAIN 1926- (American)

was born in New York City and named Salvatore A Lombino. He was educated at Cooper Union, New York, and graduated with a BA at Hunter College, New York, 1950. He later chose the name of Evan Hunter and became a high school teacher. In the 1950s he turned to writing and has been the author of numerous novels, short stories and plays under his own name and several pseudonyms. Most of his criminous novels have been published under the pseudonym cited and take place against the background of an imaginary city, clearly New York by another name. He received the Mystery Writers of America Edgar Allan Poe award, 1957, and their Grand Master award, 1987.

Writer: Evan HUNTER

Other Byline: Curt CANNON

Other Detectives:

Michael BARNES — Matthew HOPE

Benjamin SMOKE

Citation Record: 33 Books

Cop Hater - *First*

Simon & Schuster US (1956); Boardman UK (1958)

Lullaby - *Latest*

Morrow US (1989); Hamilton UK (1989)

Mr PREED

British Male Amateur operating in England

Ladbroke BLACK 1877-1940 (British)

Writer: Ladbroke Lionel Day BLACK

Other Byline: Paul URQUHART

Adopter of one other detective Sexton BLAKE

Citation Record: 3 Books

The Killer At Large - *First*

Paul UK (1937)

Mr Preed's Gangster - *Last*

Nelson UK (1939)

P

Joshua PRELL

Second detective of Paul J BURDOCK

Alison PRENDERGAST

Second detective of Jack LAMARRE

John PRENTICE

British Male Amateur operating in England

SEA-LION 1909- (British)

See main detective Desmond DRAKE

Citation Record: 5 Books

Phantom Fleet - *First*

Collins UK (1946)

When Danger Threatens - *Last*

Collins UK (1949)

Insp PRENTIS

Australian Policeman operating in Australia

BACKHOUSE (British)

See main detective Insp Christopher MARSDEN

Citation Record: 2 Books

The Web Of Shadows - *First*

Hale UK (1960)

Death Climbs A Hill - *Last*

Hale UK (1963)

Julian PRESCOT

British Male Amateur operating in England

Julian PRESCOT (British)

Writer: John BUDD

Citation Record: 9 Books

Both Sides Of The Case - *First*

Barker UK (1958)

The Krakatoa Cult - *Last*

Barker UK (1966)

Amy PRESCOTT

is a forensic investigator.

American Female Professional Investigator operating in Idaho

Louise HENDRICKSON (American)

Citation Record: 1 Book

Grave Secrets - *Single*

Zebra US (1994)

Charles PRESCOTT

is a Queen's Counsel who plays the detective in this one Victorian novel.

British Male Amateur operating in England

Allen UPWARD 1863-1926 (British)

Other Detectives:

Mr H-LM-S — Ebenezer LOBB

Dr Frank TARLETON — Monsieur V

VERRITER

Citation Record: 1 Book

The Queen Against Owen - *Only*

Chatto & Windus UK (1894)

Jane PRESCOTT

Female Amateur operating in Japan

Shizuko NATSUKI 1938- (Japanese)

is the author of about a hundred novels and short stories in and out of the criminous genre.

Citation Record: 1 Book

Murder At Mt Fuji - *Single*

St Martin's US (1984)

John PRESCOTT

British Male Amateur

Dominic DEVINE 1920-1981 (British)

Invented 4 detectives - see Det Insp Maurice NICOLSON

Citation Record: 1 Book

The Sleeping Tiger - *Only*

Collins UK (1968); Walker US (1968)

Johnny PRESTON

American Male Private Detective operating in California

Peter CHESTER 1924- (British)

See main detective Johnny VINCENT

Citation Record: 1 Book

Killing Comes Easy - *Only*

Jenkins UK (1958); Roy US (1959)

Mark PRESTON

is an imitation American PI created by a prolific British author. Tough, moral and honest, he operates in a fast, sleazy, imaginary city in California.

British Male Private Detective operating in California

Peter CHAMBERS 1924- (British)

was born in London. He was educated at Westminster City School, London, 1935-1940, and served in the Royal Air Force, 1942-1947. He has been a professional jazz musician and has written over a dozen non-genre novels under his real name as well as many detective novels, under the pseudonym by which he is best known.

Writer: Dennis John Andrew PHILLIPS

Other Byline: Peter CHESTER

Citation Record: 38 Books

Murder Is For Keeps - *First*
Hale UK (1961); Abelard Schuman US (1962)

The Day The Thames Caught Fire - *Latest*
Chivers UK (1989); St Martin's US (1990)

Matt PRESTON

is an oil man caught in a case of murder and espionage that he must solve to survive.

British Male Amateur operating in Middle East

Kenneth ROYCE 1920- (British)

Invented 3 detectives - see Willie 'Spider' SCOTT

Citation Record: 1 Book

Bones In The Sand - *Only*
Cassell UK (1967)

Thomas PRESTON

is a travelling salesman in Europe, becomes involved in skulduggery manipulated by Professor Kreutzemark, who is the villain, but is cited as a 'detective' by some authorities. !See Appendix 2.

British Male Amateur operating in Europe

Francis BEEDING (British)

Invented 6 detectives - see Insp WILKINS

Citation Record: 2 Books

The Seven Sleepers - *First*
Hutchinson UK (1925); Little, Brown US (1925)

The Hidden Kingdom - *Last*
Hodder & Stoughton UK (1927); Little, Brown US (1927)

Tommy PRESTON

American Male Amateur operating in USA

Edward D HOCH 1930- (American)

Invented 20 detectives - see Capt LEOPOLD

Citation Record: 1 Selected Short Story

The Stolen Sapphire
Grosset US (1978)

Barbara 'Baddie' PRETLOW

is a true early female PI, relating her own tale.

American Female Private Detective operating in USA

Arthur STRINGER 1874-1950 (American)

Invented 4 detectives - see James DURKIN

Citation Record: 1 Book

The House Of Intrigue - *Only*
Burt US (1918)

Lady Margaret PRIAM

is an aristocratic English lady, who lives in Manhattan and has the reputation of being the neighbourhood busybody. She specialises in solving local crimes; but only, she never ceases to emphasise, when they occur among upper-class people.

British Female Amateur operating in New York

Joyce CHRISTMAS (American)

Inventor of one other detective Betty TRENKA

Citation Record: 4 Books

Suddenly In Her Sorbet - *First*
GM US (1988)

It's Her Funeral - *Latest*
GM US (1992)

Highland PRICE

appeared mainly in stories in *Dime Detective.*

American Male Detective in Pulp Magazines operating in USA

Dale CLARK (American)

Invented 4 detectives - see Mike O'HANNA

No citations

Jason PRICE and Brooke MERIT

American Male Amateur and American Female Amateur operating in Los Angeles

Alan COCHRAN (American)

Citation Record: 1 Book

Two Plus Two - *Single*
Doubleday US (1980)

Jimmy 'Wiggly' PRICE

American Male Amateur operating in New York

John Jay CHICHESTER (American)

Inventor of one other detective Maxwell SANDERSON

Citation Record: 5 Books

The Porcelain Mask - *First*
Jenkins UK (1925); Chelsea US (1929)

Sanderson's Diamond Loot - *Last*
Chelsea US (1935); Hutchinson UK (1935)

Sgt Morgan PRICE

investigates a case in which corpses, fresh and putrefied, abound.

American Policeman operating in USA

Lou CAMERON 1924- (American)

Inventor of one other detective Steve WARREN

Citation Record: 1 Book

Behind The Scarlet Door - *Only*
Fawcett US (1971); World Distributors UK (1972)

Lt Price PRICE

is such a bad detective he lets down the force. He does conjuring tricks to fool his suspects and confides his blow-by-blow progress, such as it is, to the reader.

American Policeman operating in San Francisco

Sidekick: Nikky PRICE
is both beautiful and clever. She needs to be.

American Female - Wife

Knight RHOADES (American)

Citation Record: 1 Book

She Died On The Stairway - *Only*
Arcadia US (1947)

Insp Ronald PRICE

is efficient and a man of high integrity. However, he must be one of the most unprepossessing and unlikeable policemen to have appeared from a British author. The definitive answer to the fine, upstanding cops that went before him, men like *Roderick ALLEYN* and *Sir John APPLEBY,* he is an unlovely product, bullying and even malignant. Not only that, he has a shrewish wife and unpleasant kids to distract him.

British Policeman operating in England

Joanna CANNAN 1898-1961 (British)

See main detective Insp Guy NORTHEAST

Citation Record: 5 Books

Murder Included - *First*
Gollancz UK (1950)

Poisonous Relations - *First**
Morrow US (1951)

All Is Discovered - *Last*
Gollancz UK (1962)

Insp Joseph PRICKETT

is a Scotland Yard police inspector who would seem to be the protagonist in the book by *David Christie MURRAY* as well as the book by *Inspector MURRAY,* who may well be the same person.

British Policeman operating in London

David Christie MURRAY 1847-1901 (British)

was born in West Bromwich, Staffordshire. Journalist, novelist and lecturer, he worked for many years as a police reporter and used much of his experience in the courts for his criminous novels and short stories (only one collection of which featured a main detective). Around the turn of the century he worked incessantly on behalf of the campaign in Britain and France for the release of Alfred Dreyfus.

Inventor of one other detective John PYM

Citation Record: 1 Book

A Race For Millions - *Only*
Chatto & Windus UK (1898)

Inspector MURRAY (British)

Writer: Alexander Duke BAILIE

Citation Record: 1 Book

Joseph Prickett, The Scotland Yard Detective - *Only*
Laird & Lee US (1889)

Duncan PRIDE

was once a football player. Crippled by the mob for disobeying game-fixing instructions, he is now a PI, specialising in cases involving the game.

American Male Private Detective operating in New York

Andrew FRAZER 1928- (American)

Writer: Stephen MARLOWE

Other Bylines:
Stephen MARLOWE Jason RIDGWAY

Citation Record: 2 Books

Find Eileen Hardin – Alive! - *First*
Avon US (1959)

The Fall Of Marty Moon - *Last*
Avon US (1960); Avon UK (1960)

Jeff PRIDE

appears in one book under the author's real name and four others under his pseudonym.

Male Sleuth operating in Europe/Israel

Jim HENAGHAN 1919- (American)

Writer: Jim HENAGHAN

Other Byline: Archie O'NEILL

Citation Record: 1 Book

Azor! - *Only*
St Martin's US (1977)

Archie O'NEILL 1919- (American)

For writer details see Jeff PRIDE

Citation Record: 4 Books

The Da Vinci Rose - *First*
Bantam UK (1973)

High Bid For Murder - *Last*
Bantam UK (1974)

Dr Nassim PRIDE

is an Anglo-Sudanese forensic scientist who applies his relentless logic to the solution of murders in the best traditional manner.

Sudanese Male Professional Investigator operating in England

Rhona PETRIE 1922- (British)

See main detective Insp Marcus MACLURG

Citation Record: 2 Books

Foreign Bodies - *First*
Gollancz UK (1967)

Despatch Of A Dove - *Last*
Gollancz UK (1969)

Judge PRIEST

American Male Professional Investigator operating in USA

Irwin S COBB 1876-1944 (American)

Writer: Irwin Shrewsbury COBB

Inventor of one other detective Patrick BRAY

Citation Record: 1 Book 63 Short Stories in 6 Collections

Judge Priest Turns Detective - *Only*
Bobbs US (1937)

Back Home - *Collection 1*
Short stories - 9
Doran US (1912)

The Escape Of Mr Trimm - *Collection 2*
Short stories - 9
Doran US (1913)

Old Judge Priest - *Collection 3*
Short stories - 9
Doran US (1916)

Snake Doctor - *Collection 4*
Short stories - 9
Doran US (1923)

Down Yonder With Judge Priest - *Collection 5*
Short stories - 12
Long & Smith US (1932)

Faith, Hope And Charity - *Collection 6*
Short stories - 15
Bobbs US (1934)

Det Insp Charles PRIEST

British Policeman operating in Yorkshire

Stuart PAWSON (British)

Citation Record: 1 Book

The Mushroom Man - *Single*
Headline UK (1995)

Eddie PRIEST

is an ex-lawyer and star athlete.

American Male Amateur operating in Florida

Sterling WATSON (American)

has practised as a lawyer.

Citation Record: 1 Book

Deadly Sweet - *Single*
Headline UK (1994)

Dr Lancelot PRIESTLEY

was something of a breakaway from the range of wealthy young amateurs who were the mainstay of the British detective story in the 1920s. Here was a man, an amateur it is true, but one who was up-to-date in scientific expertise and who dedicated it to the solving of crimes with or without the aid of the police. He was once a Professor of Mathematics, it seems, but he fell out with the authorities and resigned. Since then he has written erudite works on the subject and applied the principle of strict logic to the cases that are brought to him by his friends at Scotland Yard, especially *Supt HANSLET* and his junior, *Insp WAGHORN*. In the early books of this long series *HANSLET* was given to denigrating *PRIESTLEY's* efforts. However he is also cited by some authorities as a main detective. *WAGHORN* works closely with *PRIESTLEY* and, in the later books, when the latter hardly ever leaves the house, does the legwork.

British Male Professional Amateur operating in London

Sidekick: Insp James WAGHORN

British Male - Friend

Stooge: Supt HANSLET

is a standard British police officer of the period and, in at least the early books of the important series featuring *PRIESTLEY*, denigrates the latter's amateur sleuthing, only to be shown the error of his ways. In later books of the long series, however, he is of considerable help to the amateur detective.

British Male

John RHODE 1884-1965 (British)

was a serving Army officer. He was the recipient of the Military Cross and was made an OBE. He was the author, under his real name and his main pseudonym, *Miles BURTON*, of over a hundred detective novels.

Writer: Cecil John Charles STREET

Other Byline: Miles BURTON

Other Detectives:
Insp HANSLET and Dr Lancelot PRIESTLEY
Jimmy WAGHORN

Citation Record: 67 Books

The Paddington Mystery - *First*
Bles UK (1925)

The Vanishing Diary - *Last*
Bles UK (1961); Dodd, Mead US (1961)

Lancelot PRIESTLEY

Second detective of Insp HANSLET

Insp Leonidas PRIKE

is a member of the British CID in India during the colonial period. He is described as a dynamic little man, with a head as bald as an ostrich egg, who patiently ferrets out information to solve his cases.

Eurasian Policeman operating in India

Lawrence G BLOCHMAN 1900-1975 (American)

Invented 5 detectives - see Dr Daniel Webster COFFEE and Lt Max RITTER

Citation Record: 3 Books

Bombay Mail - *First*
is a famed novel, concerning the murder on a train of the Governor of Bengal, whose body is found in a second-class lavatory.
Little, Brown US (1934); Collins UK (1934)

Red Snow At Darjeeling - *Last*
Collins UK (1938); In 'Saint Mystery Library' US (1960)

Det Max PRIMA and Det Gypsy TONNELLI

stalk a psychopathic killer in the South Bronx.

American Policemen operating in New York

William P MCGIVERN 1927-1982 (American)

Invented 5 detectives - see Dave BANNION

Citation Record: 1 Book

Night Of The Juggler - *Only*
Putnam US (1975); Collins UK (1975)

Col John PRIMROSE

is an ex-Army Intelligence officer who chooses to continue his work as an investigator, always in cases involving wealthy or positioned people. Short and rather plump, he lives in a bachelor flat in Georgetown, Washington DC, and is ably assisted by his old aide, *Sgt Phineas BUCK.* In his second book he meets the beautiful widow, *Grace LATHAM,* and, in all the following books of the series, sleuths with her. Although doing her best, she nearly always has to be saved from death, or worse than death, by *PRIMROSE,* who invariably manages to be in the right place at the right time.

American Male Private Detective operating in Los Angeles

Sidekick: Sgt Phineas BUCK
was in the Army as the aide of *PRIMROSE* and now assists him on his sleuthing ventures.

American Male - Assistant

Leslie FORD 1898-1983 (American)

Invented 6 detectives - see Grace LATHAM

Citation Record: 1 Book

The Strangled Witness - *Only*
Farrar & Rinehart US (1934)

Col John PRIMROSE and Grace LATHAM

meet each other in his second book and, as loving but platonic friends, sleuth together. They each appear in other books on their own.

American Male Private Detective and American Female Private Detective operating in USA

Leslie FORD 1898-1983 (American)

Invented 6 detectives - see Grace LATHAM

Citation Record: 14 Books

Ill Met By Moonlight - *First*
Farrar & Rinehart US (1937); Collins UK (1937)

Washington Whispers Murder - *Last*
Scribner's US (1953)

The Lying Jade - *Last**
Collins UK (1953)

Insp PRINCE

British Policeman operating in England

Fergus HUME 1859-1932 (British)

Invented 24 detectives - see Insp Samuel GORBY

Citation Record: 1 Book

A Woman's Burden - *Only*
Jarrolds UK (1901)

David PRINCE

British Male Amateur operating in England

Geoffrey WEBB (British)

Citation Record: 5 Short Stories in 1 Collection

Prince Has Five Aces - *Collection 1*
Mandeville UK (1953)

Hank PRINCE

American Male Private Detective operating in Atlanta

Philip Lee WILLIAMS (American)

Citation Record: 1 Book

Slow Dance In Autumn - *Single*
Peachtree US (1988)

Henry PRINCE

British Male Amateur operating in England

Cecil Freeman GREGG 1898- (British)

Inventor of one other detective Insp Cuthbert HIGGINS

Citation Record: 3 Books

The Ten Black Pearls - *First*
Methuen UK (1935)

The Murder Of Estelle Cantor - *First**
Dial US (1936)

The Return Of Henry Prince - *Last*
Methuen UK (1943)

Napoleon PRINCE

British Male Amateur operating in several locations

May EDGINTON 1883-1957 (British)

Writer: May Helen Marion Edginton BAILEY

Citation Record: 12 Short Stories in 1 Collection

The Adventures Of Napoleon Prince - *Collection 1*
Cassell UK (1912); Cassell US (1912)

Insp Nicholas PRINCE

hunts for a murderer at a football match.

British Policeman operating in England

Bernard NEWMAN 1897-1968 (British)

Invented 3 detectives - see Papa PONTIVY

Citation Record: 1 Book

The Cup Final Murder - *Only*
Gollancz UK (1950)

The PRINCELY DETECTIVE

American Male Detective in Pulp Magazines operating in USA

ANON

Citation Record: 1 Book

The Princely Detective - *Only*
Butler US (?)

Laura PRINCIPAL

British Female Private Detective operating in Norfolk

Michelle SPRING (Canadian)

Citation Record: 2 Books

Every Breath You Take - *First*
Pocket Books US (1994)

Running For Shelter - *Latest*
Orion UK (1995)

G D H PRINGLE

is a retired Tax Inspector and so has a good eye for fraud. He meets more than that in his books. We never hear his first name and he may look weak, but he is strongly supported by the florid ex-barmaid who is his 'lady-friend'.

British Male Amateur operating in England

Sidekick: Mavis BIGNELL
seems to help in more ways than one.
British Female - Friend

Nancy LIVINGSTON 1935- (British)

was born in Stockton-on-Tees, County Durham. She has been an actress, musician, TV worker and secretary.

Citation Record: 6 Books

The Trouble At Aquitaine - *First*
Gollancz UK (1985); St Martin's US (1986)

Mayhem At Parva - *Latest*
Gollancz UK (1990); St Martin's US (1991)

Romney PRINGLE

belongs to that wonderful group of amateur detectives, sometimes a little crooked, sometimes adventurers, sometimes rogues, who festooned the pages of English short story writing during the decades between the advent of *Sherlock HOLMES* and the start of the First World War, after which they were, as a species, converted to more dynamic figures. Like many of them, *PRINGLE* has an office in Holborn, and his sign at 33 Furnival Inn says 'Literary Agent', which is the last thing he is. Chronically hard up, inquisitive by nature, he apparently detects for the sheer fun of it, while not above taking a few ill-gotten gains. He was created by an author who, without his collaborator, was to become one of the masters of the British detective story.

British Male Amateur operating in London

Clifford ASHDOWN 1862-1943 (British)

After co-authoring these stories about yet another early *Sherlock HOLMES* imitator, now largely forgotten, *Richard Austin FREEMAN* went on to write the classic series of detective stories featuring *Dr THORNDYKE*.

Writers: Richard Austin FREEMAN 1862-1943 and John James PITCAIRN 1860-1936

Citation Record: 12 Short Stories in 2 Collections

The Adventures Of Romney Pringle - *Collection 1*
Short stories - 6
Ward, Lock UK (1902); Oswald Train US (1968)

The Further Adventures Of Romney Pringle - *Collection 2*
Short stories - 6
Oswald Train US (1970)

Matthew PRIOR

is a British playwright who goes to a Canadian University to direct one of his plays. Unfortunately, someone keeps murdering members of his cast. The police are baffled and proving difficult, so he has to solve the crimes himself.

British Male Amateur operating in Ontario

Stooge: Sgt KOZETSKY
is the suitably mystified cop.
Canadian Male

Anthony QUOGAN (British)

was educated at Cambridge, England, and Toronto, Canada. He is the sometime Professor of Theatre at York University, Ontario, Canada.

Citation Record: 1 Book

The Fine Art Of Murder - *Single*
Macmillan UK (1988); St Martin's US (1988)

Insp PROBYN

appears in a collection of puzzle stories.

British Policeman operating in England

Morley ADAMS (British)

Citation Record: 6 Short Stories in 1 Collection

Puzzle Parade - *Collection 1*
Faber UK (1948)

Julia PROBYN

is young, beautiful, wealthy and unfettered. A freelance journalist whose job takes her to many parts of the world, she is involved in murders galore.

British Female Amateur operating in several locations

Ann BRIDGE 1889-1974 (British)

Writer: Lady Mary Dolling Saunders O'MALLEY

Citation Record: 10 Books

The Lighthearted Quest - *First*
Chatto UK (1956); Macmillan US (1956)

Julia In Ireland - *Last*
US (1973)

Chad PROCTOR

American Male Private Detective operating in USA

Lee ROBERTS 1908-1976 (American)

Invented 4 detectives - see Lee FISKE

Citation Record: 1 Book

The Pale Door - *Only*
Dodd, Mead US (1955); Foulsham UK (1956)

Insp PRONTOUT

solves the mystery of how two men disappeared from a guarded windmill.

Policeman operating in France

Charles CHADWICK 1874-1950

Inventor of one other detective Bob ELLIS

Citation Record: 1 Book

The Moving House Of Foscaldo - *Only*
Cassell UK (1926)

Jason PROPHET and Lynn MCCOLL

American Male Private Detective and American Female Private Detective operating in San Francisco

J T MORROW (American)

Citation Record: 1 Book

Prophet - *Single*
PaperJacks US (1988)

David PROSS

British Male Sleuth operating in Tibet and other locations

Julian Jay SAVARIN (British)

was born in Dominica, which he left at an early age to become a resident in England. He is a professional rock musician and, in addition to his criminous works, has written several science fiction novels.

Inventor of one other detective Gordon GALLAGHER

Citation Record: 3 Books

Gunship - *First*
St Martin's US (1985); Secker & Warburg UK (1988)

Warhawk - *Latest*
Secker & Warburg UK (1988)

Dalton (The Crimson Clown) PROUSE

American Male Professional Investigator operating in USA

Johnston MCCULLEY 1883-1958 (American)

Invented 5 detectives - see John (The Thunderbolt) FLATCHLEY

Citation Record: 8 Short Stories in 2 Collections

The Crimson Clown - *Collection 1*
Short stories - 4
Cassell UK (1927); Chelsea US (1928)

The Crimson Clown Again - *Collection 2*
Short stories - 4
Chelsea US (192?); Cassell UK (1928)

Paul PRY

was one of this author's many pulp detectives, appearing in twenty stories in *Gang World* and a further five in *Dime Detective,* all 1930-1939.

American Male Detective in Pulp Magazines operating in USA

Erle Stanley GARDNER 1889-1970 (American)

Invented 14 detectives - see Perry MASON

No citations

Dr Paul PRYE

is a psychiatrist, rather given to poetic quotation, who turns to detection. He appears in two books on his own and in another with one of the author's other detectives, *Insp SANDS.*

Male Amateur operating in Detroit

Margaret MILLAR 1915- (Canadian)

Invented 11 detectives - see Insp SANDS

Citation Record: 2 Books

The Invisible Worm - *First*
Doubleday US (1941); Long UK (1943)

The Weak-Eyed Bat - *Last*
Doubleday US (1942)

Dr Paul PRYE

Second detective of Insp SANDS

Maj Weston PRYME

British Male Amateur operating in England

George LIMNELIUS 1886- (British)

See main detective Insp MCMASTER

Citation Record: 1 Book

The Manuscript Murder - *Only*
Doubleday US (1934)

Lewis ROBINSON 1886- (British)

For writer details see Insp MCMASTER

Citation Record: 1 Book

The Manuscript Murder - *Only*
Barker UK (1933)

Mr PUCKETT

American Male Amateur operating in USA

D B OLSEN 1907-1973 (American)

Invented 5 detectives - see Lt Stephen MAYHEW

Citation Record: 1 Book

Widows Ought To Weep - *Only*
Ziff-Davis US (1947)

Aristide PUJOL

French Male Amateur operating in Europe

W J LOCKE 1863-1930 (British)

Writer: William John LOCKE

Citation Record: 9 Short Stories in 1 Collection

The Joyous Adventures Of Aristide Pujol - *Collection 1*
Lane UK (1912); Lane US (1912)

Joe PUMA

is a Beverly Hills gumshoe, altogether tougher, rougher and serving a lower kind of clientele than some of the author's other detectives. Indeed, in the last book, he comes to a deservedly sticky end.

American Male Private Detective operating in California

William Campbell GAULT 1910- (American)

Invented 6 detectives - see Brock (The Rock) CALLAHAN

Citation Record: 6 Books

End Of A Call Girl - *First*
Crest US (1958)

Don't Call Tonight - *First**
Boardman UK (1960)

The Hundred-Dollar Girl - *Last*
Dutton US (1961); Boardman UK (1963)

Roney SCOTT 1910- (American)

Writer: William Campbell GAULT

Citation Record: 1 Book

Shakedown - *Only*
Ace US (1953)

Insp Mike PUMFREY

is in the CID of a fictional English county. With little to distinguish him except his sleek black hair and little black moustache, he investigates pranks at a boys' school, which lead to murder.

British Policeman operating in England

Robert BARNARD 1936- (British)

Invented 13 detectives - see Insp Perry TRETHOWAN

Citation Record: 1 Book

Little Victims - *Single*
Scribner's US (1983)

School For Murder - *Single**
Scribner's US (1984)

The Hon Victoria PUMPHREY

is a young, aristocratic Amazon of a girl who sets up a kind of amiable amateur private detective agency, solving mysteries for friends.

British Female Amateur operating in England

H C BAILEY 1878-1961 (British)

Invented 4 detectives - see Dr Reginald FORTUNE

Citation Record: 1 Book

A Matter Of Speculation
In 'Ellery Queen's Mystery Magazine' US (1961)

Insp PURBRIGHT

operates in the fictional English town of Flaxborough, where the goings-on are as far removed from those at *Miss MARPLE's* home patch, St Mary Mead, as it is possible to imagine. The books are comic in the richest sense, abounding with eccentrics, minor crooks, randy aldermen, corrupt doctors, fraudulent ladies, drunken journalists, male sex fetishists, nymphomaniacs, brothels and witches' covens. It is no wonder that he has both his hands full.

British Policeman operating in England

Sidekick: Sgt LOVE
British Male - Subordinate

Colin WATSON 1920-1982 (British)

was born in Croydon, Surrey and educated at Whitgift School, Croydon, 1930-1936. He worked as a journalist, in publishing, and in radio.

Citation Record: 11 Books

Coffin Scarcely Used - *First*
Eyre & Spottiswoode UK (1958); Putnam US (1967)

Whatever's Been Going On At Mumblesby? - *Latest*
Methuen UK (1982); Doubleday US (1983)

Chance PURDUE

is so tough he only has time to speak in clipped sentences. Paragraphs seem completely beyond him.
!See Appendix 2.

American Male Private Detective operating in Chicago

Ross H SPENCER 1921- (American)

Invented 7 detectives - see Buzz DECKARD

Citation Record: 5 Books

The Dada Caper - *First*
Avon US (1978)

The Radish River Caper - *Latest*
Avon US (1981)

Judge Keith Hilary PURSUIVANT

uses 'psychic powers' to aid his detection.

American Male Amateur operating in USA

P

Manly Wade WELLMAN 1905- (American)

Invented 5 detectives - see David RETURN

Citation Record: 4 Short Stories in 1 Collection

Lonely Vigils - *Collection 1*

This collection of twenty stories contains four with *PURSUIVANT* and fifteen with *THUNSTONE*.

Carcosa US (1981)

Sheriff Buford PUSSER

is in a novelization of a film.

American Policeman operating in Tennessee

Webster CAREY (American)

Citation Record: 1 Book

Walking Tall: Part 2 - *Only*

Bantam UK (1975)

W R MORRIS (American)

Citation Record: 1 Book

The Twelfth Of August - *Only*

Bantam UK (1974)

Sgt David PUTNAM

American Policeman operating in New York/Massachusetts

Leslie STEPHAN 1933- (American)

Writer: Leslie Bates STEPHAN

Citation Record: 3 Books

Murder R F D - *First*

Scribner's US (1978)

Murder In The Family - *First**

Hale UK (1979)

Reprise - *Latest*

St Martin's US (1988)

Henry Lancaster PYM

is a zoologist who, with a private income, lives in Cornwall and solves cases using his excellent deductive powers.

British Male Amateur operating in Cornwall

W J BURLEY 1914- (British)

was born in Falmouth, Devon and graduated with a BA at Balliol College, Oxford, 1953. He is a professional engineer and a biologist but became a full-time writer in 1974.

Writer: William John BURLEY

Inventor of one other detective Supt Charles WYCLIFFE

Citation Record: 2 Books

A Taste Of Power - *First*

Gollancz UK (1966)

Death In Willow Pattern - *Last*

Gollancz UK (1969); Walker US (1970)

P

John PYM

British Male Amateur operating in England

David Christie MURRAY 1847-1901 (British)

See main detective Insp Joseph PRICKETT

Citation Record: 7 Short Stories in 1 Collection

The Investigations Of John Pym - *Collection 1*

UK (1895)

Lucy PYM

is middle-aged, pert and plump. Fancying herself as a psychologist, she comes to lecture at a training college run by an old friend and is called on to investigate the murder of an unpleasant girl student.

British Female Amateur operating in England

Josephine TEY 1897-1952 (British)

Invented 3 detectives - see Insp Alan GRANT

Citation Record: 1 Book

Miss Pym Disposes - *Only*

Davies UK (1946); Macmillan US (1948)

Nicholas PYM

British Male Amateur operating in France

John SANDERS 1930- (British)

Writer: John Edward SANDERS

Citation Record: 5 Books

A Firework For Oliver - *First*

Heinemann UK (1964); Walker US (1965)

Roundhead Retreat - *Last*

Hale UK (1971)

Mrs Palmyra Evangeline PYM

is an employee of the British War Department seconded to Scotland Yard for 'special work'. Whatever that is never becomes clear; but, a hard-bitten lady, she is a terror to villains, as tough as nails and totally oblivious to police regulations.

British Policewoman operating in London

Nigel MORLAND 1905-1986 (British)

was born in London and educated privately. From an early age he worked on newspapers in England and the Far East, being the editor of newspapers and journals in many cities. He was, for a time, the secretary of the famous British crime writer, *Edgar WALLACE*, from whom he learned much. He had a lifelong absorbing interest in crime, criminology, and forensic science and, after the master's death, he began to write his many thrillers and detective stories, for which he used his own name and several pseudonyms. He was one of the founders of the Crime Writers Association, 1953.

Writer: Nigel MORLAND

Other Bylines:

John DONAVAN; Norman FORREST; Roger GARNETT; Neal SHEPHERD

Other Detectives:

Det Insp Rory LUCCAN; Steven MALONE; Ch Insp Andy MCMURDO

Citation Record: 23 Books 57 Short Stories in 4 Collections

The Clue Of The Bricklayer's Aunt - *First*

Cassell UK (1936); Farrar & Rinehart US (1937)

The Dear, Dead Girls - *Last*

Cassell UK (1961)

Mrs Pym Of Scotland Yard - *Collection 1*

Short stories - 9

Vallancey UK (1946)

The Case Of The Innocent Wife - *Collection 2*

Short stories - 5

Martin (ca 1947)

26 Three-Minute Thrillers - *Collection 3*

Short stories - 26

Martin (1947)

Mrs Pym And Other Stories - *Collection 4*

Short stories - 17

Ellis UK (1976)

Whit PYNCHON and Annie TYSON-TYREE

American Male Sleuth and American Female Sleuth operating in Virginia

Dave PEDNEAU 1947-1990 (American)

Writer: David Elliott PEDNEAU

Citation Record: 4 Books

APB - *First*

Ballantine US (1987)

AKA - *Last*

Ballantine US (1990)

Parker PYNE

appears in the short stories cited as the main detective, and he also appears in collections with other detectives of this author, especially *Jane MARPLE*, *Ariadne OLIVER* and *Hercule POIROT*.

British Male Professional Investigator operating in England

Agatha CHRISTIE 1890-1976 (British)

Invented 18 detectives - see Hercule POIROT

Citation Record: 12 Short Stories in 1 Collection

Parker Pyne Investigates - *Collection 1*

Collins UK (1934)

Mr Parker Pyne, Detective - *Collection 1**

Dodd, Mead US (1934)

Don Q

Spanish Male Amateur operating in Spain

K PRICHARD and Hesketh PRICHARD (British)

Writers: Katherine O'Brien PRICHARD and Vernon Hesketh PRICHARD 1876-1922

Citation Record: 1 Book 24 Short Stories in 2 Collections

Don Q's Love Story - *Only*
Greening UK (1909); Grosset US (1925)

The Chronicles Of Don Q - *Collection 1*
Short stories - 12
Chapman & Hall UK (1904); Lippincott US (1904)

The New Chronicles Of Don Q - *Collection 2*
Short stories - 12
Unwin UK (1906)

Don Q In The Sierras - *Collection 2**
Lippincott US (1906)

Calamity QUADE

appeared mainly in short stories in *Double Detective.*

American Male Detective in Pulp Magazines operating in USA

Richard SALE 1911- (American)

was born in New York City and educated at Lee University, Lexington, Virginia. He has been a writer and director in all media.

Writer: Richard Bernard SALE

Other Detectives:
Joseph 'Daffy' DILL and Insp HANLEY
Candid JONES and Insp Harry RENTANO
Penny PACKER and Det Jim SCOTT
Det Daniel WEBSTER

No citations

Oliver QUADE

calls himself 'The Human Encyclopedia', and he certainly makes a living by hawking books around. Even so, he manages to get himself involved in murders wherever he goes.

American Male Amateur operating in USA

Sidekick: Charlie BOSTON
is the straight man for the itinerant salesman-sleuth.
American Male - Assistant

Frank GRUBER 1904-1969 (American)

Invented 8 detectives - see Johnny FLETCHER and Sam CRAGG

Citation Record: 9 Short Stories in 1 Collection

Brass Knuckles - *Collection 1*
Sherbourne Press US (1966)

Insp QUAILE

British Policeman operating in England

J M WALSH 1897-1952 (British)

Writer: James Morgan WALSH

Other Byline: Stephen MADDOCK

Other Detectives:
Insp GORE
Bromley KAY
Col ORMISTON
Mike HARMAN
Oliver KEENE
Insp STORM

Citation Record: 3 Books

The Hand Of Doom - *First*
Hamilton UK (1927)

Lady Incognito - *Last*
Collins UK (1932)

Supt Samuel QUAN

British Policeman operating in England

Garston BEGBIE (British)

Citation Record: 2 Books

Sudden Death At Scotland Yard - *First*
Jenkins UK (1933)

Murder Mask - *Last*
Jenkins UK (1934)

Det Ch Insp Douglas QUANTRILL

is the head of the fictional Breckham Market CID in Suffolk. A slow but methodical cop, he is middle-aged, married and has a son – none of which preclude him from a hankering after one or two ladies, including, on and off, the clever young female sergeant who becomes his assistant in later books.

British Policeman operating in Suffolk

Sidekick: Sgt Martin TATE
is the assistant of *QUANTRILL* in his early books.
British Male - Subordinate

Sidekick: Sgt Hilary LLOYD
is a very good detective who may go far. Although the boss has cast more than an official eye on her, she has tactfully resisted, which seems to be good for all concerned.
British Female - Subordinate

Sheila RADLEY 1928- (British)

was born in Cogenhoe, Northamptonshire. She took a BA in History at Bedford College, London, 1951. She lives in Norfolk and, under the pseudonym of Hester Rowan, is the author of several non-genre novels.

Writer: Sheila Mary ROBINSON

Other Byline: Hester ROWAN

Citation Record: 9 Books

Death And The Maiden - *First*
Hamilton UK (1978)

Death In The Morning - *First**
Scribner's US (1979)

Fair Game - *Latest*
Constable UK (1994)

Christopher QUARLES

is a college professor who detects only in numerous short stories.

British Male Amateur operating in England

Percy BREBNER 1864-1922 (American)

Writer: Percy James BREBNER

Citation Record: 31 Short Stories in 2 Collections

Christopher Quarles, College Professor And Master Detective - *Collection 1*
Short stories - 16
Dutton US (1914); Holden UK (1921)

The Master Detective - *Collection 2*
Short stories - 15
Dutton US (1916); Holden UK (1922)

Francis QUARLES

is a vain and rather lazy private eye. The eminent author used him only in short stories.

British Male Private Detective operating in England

Julian SYMONS 1912-1994 (British)

Invented 11 detectives - see Insp CRAMBO

Citation Record: 36 Short Stories in 2 Collections

Murder! Murder! - *Collection 1*
Short stories - 21
Fontana UK (1961)

Francis Quarles Investigates - *Collection 2*
Short stories - 15
Panther UK (1965)

QUARRY

is an embittered Vietnam War veteran who now hires himself out as a professional killer. Even so, he has to do considerable detection.

American Male Professional Investigator operating in Wisconsin

Max Allan COLLINS 1948- (American)

Invented 5 detectives - see Nate HELLER

Citation Record: 5 Books

The Broker - *First*
Berkley US (1976)

Primary Target - *Latest*
Countryman Press US (1987)

Simon QUARRY

British Male Amateur operating in Europe

Robin HUNTER 1935- (British)

Writer: Robin NEILLANDS

Citation Record: 3 Books

The Fourth Angel - *First*
Macmillan UK (1985); Arbor US (1986)

The London Connection - *Latest*
Morrow US (1990)

Dr QUARSHIE

Male Amateur operating in Africa

John WYLLIE 1914- (American)

!See Appendix 2.

Writer: John Vectis Carew WYLLIE

Citation Record: 8 Books

Skull Still Bone - *First*
Doubleday US (1975); Barrie & Jenkins UK (1975)

The Long, Dark Night Of Baron Samedi - *Latest*
Doubleday US (1981)

Doctor QUARTZ

American Male Detective in Pulp Magazines operating in USA

Nicholas CARTER 1861-1922

Invented 3 detectives - see Nick CARTER (Writer Frederic Merrill Van Rensselaer DEY)

Citation Record: 4 Books

Doctor Quartz, Magician; Or, The Most Dangerous Criminal Alive - *First*
Street & Smith (Magnet #444) US (1906)

Doctor Quartz's Quick Move; Or, Cleverness Personified - *Last*
Street & Smith (Magnet #450) US (1906)

Everard Peter QUAYLE

heads a secret British counter-espionage unit operating in Britain and continental Europe during the Second World War.

British Male Secret Agent operating in Europe

Peter CHEYNEY 1896-1951 (British)

Invented 11 detectives - see Lemmy CAUTION

Citation Record: 4 Books

The Stars Are Dark - *First*
Collins UK (1943); Dodd, Mead US (1943)

Dark Wanton - *Last*
Collins UK (1948); Dodd, Mead US (1949)

Q

Hilary QUAYLE

is a public relations lady in show business who, confident of her ability as a detective, sets up as a PI. For various reasons, she has difficulty in getting her licence; but she is able to persuade GENE, once a PI himself, to get his own licence again and act as her assistant.

American Female Private Detective operating in New York

Sidekick: GENE

is an effective legman for the frustrated PI.

American Male - Assistant

Marvin KAYE 1938- (American)

Invented 3 detectives - see Marty GOLD

Citation Record: 5 Books

A Lively Game Of Death - *First*
Dutton US (1972); Barker UK (1974)

The Soap Opera Slaughter - *Latest*
Doubleday US (1982)

Ian QUAYLE

American Male Sleuth operating in Middle East

Alan CAILLOU 1914- (American)

Invented 4 detectives - see Matthew TOBIN

Citation Record: 2 Books

A League Of Hawks - *First*
Critic US (1986)

The Sword Of God - *Latest*
Critic US (1987)

Kit QUAYLE

British Male Amateur operating in England

James ALDRIDGE 1918- (British)

See main detective Rupert ROYCE

Citation Record: 2 Books

A Sporting Proposition - *First*
Joseph UK (1973); Little, Brown US (1973)

The Untouchable Juli - *Last*
Joseph UK (1975); Little, Brown US (1976)

Peter QUAYLE

British Policeman operating in England

Paul TRENT (American)

Writer: Edward PLATT

Citation Record: 2 Books

Quayle Of The Yard - *First*
Ward, Lock UK (1935)

The London Spy Murders - *First**
Avon US (1944)

Quayle's First Case - *Last*
Ward, Lock UK (1936)

The Case Of The Dark Wanton - *Last**
Avon US (1958)

Crispin QUAYNE

British Male Amateur operating in England

Edwin KILVINGTON (British)

Citation Record: 2 Books

Mystery In Glass - *First*
Houghton UK (1931)

Window In The Dark - *Last*
Houghton UK (1932)

Insp Maxwell QUAYNE

British Policeman operating in England

F Addington SYMONDS 1893- (British)

Writer: Francis Addington SYMONDS

Adaptor of one other detective Sexton BLAKE

Citation Record: 3 Books

Stone Dead - *First*
Ward, Lock UK (1961)

Spotlight On Murder - *Last*
Ward, Lock UK (1962)

Quentin QUAYNE

is an obscure detective by an obscure author. He occurs in short stories and is said to have 'a psychological approach' to the solution of his cases.

British Male Amateur operating in England

Sidekick: CREIGHTON

British Male - Narrator

F Britten AUSTIN 1885-1941 (British)

Writer: Frederick Britten AUSTIN

Citation Record: 1 Selected Short Story

The Fourth Degree

is in the anthology, *Fifty Famous Detectives of Fiction*.
Odhams UK (1948)

Ellery QUEEN

was, from his first appearance in 1929, destined to become one of the greatest of all fictional detectives. This is not simply because of the books, some of which are masterpieces in their own right, but because of the influence he and his creators had on the subsequent development of the genre. Ellery QUEEN, when first met, is young, tall, athletic, wears pince-nez when he has a mind to, and has an encyclopaedic knowledge and the most brilliant of intellects. In his first cycle of novels, based on patterned titles of countries, he took the American whodunnit out of the static hands of Philo VANCE into new realms of imaginative detection and deduction. In later books he mellows somewhat, becoming less of a machine and more compassionate. His father, *Insp Richard QUEEN,* is the instrument by which he is introduced to his cases and is his constant support and sounding board. Indeed, he has a vital part to play in the books by providing the police evidence and the necessary investigatory apparatus; for, above all, these authors play absolutely fair. *Ellery QUEEN* appeared in over fifty original publications, including novels and short story collections, until the death of one of the two authors.

American Male Amateur operating in New York

Sidekick: Insp Richard QUEEN
is in the New York Police Department. The father of one of the genre's most prestigious detectives, he is an important figure in the canon, for it is he who is the main purveyor of clues and police discoveries to *Ellery QUEEN.* He must be, structurally, one of the most powerful and important sidekicks in the genre.

American Male - Father

Stooge: Sgt VELIE
appears throughout the canon. Large, stolid, staunch, and apparently without an inquisitory thought in his head, he does the hack work necessary to set up the scene for the one of the most cerebral detectives ever to grace the criminous page.

American Male

Ellery QUEEN (American)

is the pseudonym of two cousins who formed the most famous writing team in the history of the criminous genre. Using one of the best-known bylines in American mystery fiction, they were perhaps the most scholarly investigators into the art, craft and history of the detective story since its beginnings. Their influence on the development of the detective story has, indeed, been immense; for they wrote, collected, catalogued, philosophised and created in every nook and cranny of detective fiction.

Their major original invention was the eponymous *Ellery QUEEN,* named identically and deliberately with their own joint pseudonym, which, after their deaths, was used generically for other novels and the continuation of their magazine. *Frederic DANNAY* was born Daniel Nathan in Brooklyn, New York, and was educated at Boys' High School, Brooklyn. He was the art director for an advertising agency before 1931. *Manfred Bennington LEE* was born Manfred Lepofsky in Brooklyn, New York, and attended New York University. He was a publicity writer before 1931. They wrote their first detective novel in 1929 and it was a sensation. The next five years saw the publication of their most brilliant work, which set new standards in the realm of classical, intellectual puzzles. The novels continued to appear until the death of *LEE* in 1971 but, although still of great ingenuity, showed a decline in spirit and force.

The cousins turned out short stories and great numbers of editorial works and collections, all of high quality. They founded *Ellery Queen's Mystery Magazine,* 1941, and edited it; they wrote many *Ellery Queen Adventure Stories* for radio, 1939-1948; and they were co-founders and co-presidents of the Mystery Writers of America, receiving the Edgar Allan Poe award three times, 1945, 1947 and 1949, Special awards twice, 1951 and 1958, and the Grand Master award, 1960.

Writers: Frederic DANNAY 1905-1982 and Manfred Bennington LEE 1905-1971
Other Byline: Barnaby ROSS

Adopter of one other detective Sherlock HOLMES

Citation Record: 47 Books 59 Short Stories in 5 Collections

The Roman Hat Mystery - *First*
Stokes US (1929); Gollancz UK (1929)

A Fine And Private Place - *Last*
was the last work featuring *Ellery QUEEN* to have been written by the original authors.
World US (1971); Gollancz UK (1971)

The Adventures Of Ellery Queen - *Collection 1*
Short stories - 11
Stokes US (1934); Gollancz UK (1935)

The New Adventures Of Ellery Queen - *Collection 2*
Short stories - 9
Stokes US (1940); Gollancz UK (1940)

QBI: Queen's Bureau Of Investigation - *Collection 3*
Short stories - 18
Little, Brown US (1954); Gollancz UK (1955)

Queens Full - *Collection 4*
Short stories - 5
Random House US (1965); Gollancz UK (1966)

QED: Queen's Experiments In Detection - *Collection 5*
Short stories - 16
New American Library US (1968); Gollancz UK (1969)

Ellery QUEEN (American)

House writer for 3 detectives - see Barney BURGESS

Citation Record: 4 Books

The Penthouse Mystery - *First*
is a novelization of a film.
Grossett US (1942)

The Murdered Millionaire - *Last*
is a novelization of a radio play.
Whitman US (1942)

Mr QUENTIN

British Male Amateur operating in England

Anthony MORTON 1908-1973 (British)

See main detective John MANNERING

Citation Record: 1 Book

Mr Quentin Investigates - *Only*
Low UK (1943)

Andrew QUENTIN and Jane WINFIELD

Male Amateur and Female Amateur operating in England/France

Audrey PETERSON

Citation Record: 5 Books

The Nocturne Murder - *First*
Arbor US (1987)

Elegy In A Country Graveyard - *Latest*
Pocket Books US (1990)

Peter QUENTIN

British Male Amateur operating in England

Rodney QUEST 1897- (British)

Citation Record: 3 Books

The Cerebus Murders - *First*
Harrap UK (1969); McCall US (1970)

Death Of A Sinner - *Last*
Harrap UK (1971)

Mercedes QUERO

appears also in one book with the author's other detective, *Insp BURTON.*

Spanish Female Amateur operating in England

G E LOCKE 1887- (British)

Invented 3 detectives - see Insp BURTON

Citation Record: 1 Book

That Affair At Portstead Manor - *Only*
Sherman UK (1914)

Mercedes QUERO

Second detective of Insp BURTON

Harold QUEST

British Male Amateur operating in England

Arthur WHITAKER 1882-1949 (British)

Adopter of one other detective Sherlock HOLMES

Citation Record: 1 Selected Short Story

The Missing Bales
In 'Novel Magazine' UK (1913)

Peter QUEST

is going blind from glaucoma, which does not stop him from tackling dangerous cases. He appeared mainly in short stories published in *Dime Mystery.*

American Male Detective in Pulp Magazines operating in New York

John KOBLER (American)

Citation Record: 1 Selected Short Story

The Brain Murders

can also be found in the anthology, *The Defective Detectives In The Pulps* (Editors; Gary Hoppenstand & Ray B Browne; US 1983).

In 'Dime Mystery' US (1939)

Philip QUEST

British Male Amateur operating in England/Spain

Peter TOWNEND 1935- (British)

Writer: Peter Robert Gascoigne TOWNEND

Citation Record: 2 Books

Out Of Focus - *First*
Heinemann UK (1971); St Martin's US (1972)

Triple Exposure - *Latest*
Pinnacle US (1977)

Nigel VANE 1896-1980 (British)

For writer details see Supt BUDD

Inventor of one other detective LI-SIN

Citation Record: 2 Books

The Vanishing Death - *First*
Modern UK (193?)

The Veils Of Death - *Last*
Modern UK (1935)

Beau QUICKSILVER

seems to have been modelled on several other amateur detectives of the 1920s, coming complete with silver-topped cane, would-be brilliant wit, much repartee and rather amazing powers of reasoning. He appeared in seven short stories in a pulp magazine and then vanished.

American Male Detective in Pulp Magazines operating in USA

F M PETTEE 1888- (American)

See main detective Digby GRESHAM

Citation Record: 7 Short Stories in 1 Collection

Exploits Of Beau Quicksilver - *Collection 1*
In 'Argosy' US (1923)

Q

Jim QUIGLEY

investigates the mysterious death of a man shot by an arrow while inside a locked room.

American Male Sleuth operating in USA

David DUNCAN 1913- (American)

Citation Record: 1 Book

The Shade Of Time - *Only*
Random House US (1946); Grey Walls Press UK (1948)

Supt QUILL and Insp GLOVER

British Policemen operating in England

Lynton LAMB 1907-1977 (British)

Writer: Lynton Harold LAMB

Citation Record: 4 Books

Death Of A Dissenter - *First*
Gollancz UK (1969)

Man In A Mist - *Last*
Gollancz UK (1974)

Insp Adam QUILL

appeared in several farcical novels in the 1930s and 1940s, mostly concerned with an improbable Russian Ballet in England, the Troupe Stroganoff. Murders sometimes occur and, although the novels are hardly detective stories, there strides through them *Insp Adam QUILL*, who uses his Detective's Handbook extensively but seldom solves a case.

British Policeman operating in England

Caryl BRAHMS and S J SIMON (British)

were the pseudonymous authors of several very funny and highly admired books with an ingenious narrative style and mostly about the deeds and misdeeds of the members of a ballet company, full of zany Russians, eccentrics and neurotics.

Writers: Doris Caroline ABRAHAMS 1901-1982 and Simon Jasha SKIDELSKY

Citation Record: 3 Books

A Bullet In The Ballet - *First*
Joseph UK (1937); Doubleday US (1938)

Envoy On Excursion - *Last*
Joseph UK (1940)

QUILLER

is a cold, emotionless, ruthless, British agent in the era of the Cold War, pitting his wits against the machinations of the Soviets and other forces considered hostile to the security of the West. There have been many like him in the genre books of the era, but he is one of the best and most long-lasting.

British Male Secret Agent operating in Moscow

Adam HALL 1920- (British)

was born in Bromley, Kent. He was educated at Sevenoaks School, Kent, and served in the Royal Air Force, 1939-1945. He lived for many years in France and, after 1973, in the USA. The author of over seventy genre novels, for which he has used several pseudonyms, he has also written many books for children and at least four stage plays, all of which have been produced on stage. He received the Mystery Writers of America Edgar Allan Poe award, 1965, and the *Grand Prix Littérature Policière*, 1965.

Writer: Trevor Dudley SMITH

Citation Record: 17 Books

The Berlin Memorandum - *First*
Collins UK (1965)

The Quiller Memorandum - *First**
Simon & Schuster US (1965)

Quiller Solitaire - *Latest*
Headline UK (1993)

Meg QUILLIAM

Second detective of Sarah QUILLIAM

Sarah QUILLIAM and Meg QUILLIAM

are two sisters who run a gastronomic hideaway, the Hemlock Falls Inn, in upstate New York. The cooking is marvellous, but murder occurs rather often and the charming pair must, for the sake of their good names, do the sleuthing.

American Female Amateurs operating in New York

Claudia BISHOP (American)

Citation Record: 2 Books

A Taste For Murder - *First*
Berkley US (1994)

A Dash Of Death - *Latest*
Berkley US (1995)

Harley QUIN

is a strange, probably supernatural, gentleman who turns up mysteriously to solve puzzles, crimes and sometimes see that justice is done. He appears, by himself, in a collection of short stories and in collections with other *Agatha CHRISTIE* detectives.

British Male Amateur operating in England

Agatha CHRISTIE 1890-1976 (British)

Invented 18 detectives - see Hercule POIROT

Citation Record: 12 Short Stories in 1 Collection

The Mysterious Mr Quin - *Collection 1*
Collins UK (1930); Dodd, Mead US (1930)

Sebastian QUIN

British Male Amateur operating in England

Sydney HORLER 1888-1954 (British)

Invented 20 detectives - see Sir Harker BELLAMY

Citation Record: 1 Book

Fear Walked Behind - *Only*
Hale UK (1942)

John QUINCANNON

sleuths in California during the 1890s. He appears also in one book with *Elena OLIVEREZ*, the creation of *Marcia MULLER*, written under joint authorship.

American Male Amateur operating in San Francisco

Bill PRONZINI 1943- (American)

Invented 5 detectives - see NAMELESS DETECTIVE

Citation Record: 1 Book

Quincannon - *Single*
Walker US (1985)

John QUINCANNON

Second detective of Elena OLIVEREZ

Dion QUINCE

is a famous writer who is also an undercover PI for 'Univest, the largest detective agency in the world'.

American Male Private Detective operating in California

Patrick CAKE 1935- (American)

Writer: Timothy L WELCH

Citation Record: 1 Book

The Pro-Am Murders - *Single*
Proteus US (1979); Proteus UK (1979)

Timothy L WELCH 1935- (American)

Citation Record: 1 Book

The Tennis Murders - *Single*
Popular Library US (1976)

John QUINCE

Appears with at least two other detectives - see Insp MILD

Charlie QUINLAN

is an ex-actor.

American Male Private Detective operating in Los Angeles

Brad SOLOMON 1945- (American)

Writer: Neal Bradley SOLOMON

Inventor of one other detective pair Fritz THIERINGER and Maggie MCGUANE

Citation Record: 1 Book

The Gone Man - *Single*
Random House US (1977); New English Library UK (1978)

QUINN

appears, unusually, without the author's main detective, *John PIPER*, in this one book.

British Male Amateur operating in England

Harry CARMICHAEL 1908-1979 (British)

Invented 3 detectives - see John PIPER

Citation Record: 1 Book

A Slightly Bitter Taste - *Only*
Collins UK (1968)

Noel SCANLON

Citation Record: 1 Book

Quinn - *First*
Murray UK (1973)

Quinn And The Desert Oil - *Last*
Murray UK (1975)

Sgt QUINN

Second detective of Bob FETHERSTON

QUINN

Second detective of John PIPER

Joe QUINN

has to leave his office in Reno, where he works as a casino security officer, in rather a hurry, having mixed a little too much pleasure with business. He heads for California, there becoming involved with a religious community having problems.

American Male Private Detective operating in Nevada

Margaret MILLAR 1915- (Canadian)

Invented 11 detectives - see Insp SANDS

Citation Record: 1 Book

How Like An Angel - *Only*
Gollancz UK (1962); Random House US (1962)

Rupert QUINN

British Male Sleuth operating in Algeria

Alan WILLIAMS 1935- (British)

Writer: Alan Emlyn WILLIAMS

Citation Record: 2 Books

Long Run South - *First*
Blond UK (1962); Little, Brown US (1962)

Barbourze - *Last*
Blond UK (1964)

Tony (Black Bat) QUINN

is a district attorney who dons the usual cloak and mask (they were deemed necessary at the time if one was to deal properly with criminals), in order to become a detective and crime fighter. Generally known by those who feared him as 'The Black Bat', he was created, under a special pseudonym, by this most prolific of authors and appeared in over sixty short novels in *Black Book Detective* between 1939 and 1952.

American Male Professional Investigator operating in USA

G Wayman JONES (American)

used this byline, which later became a house name, specifically for his books featuring *The BLACK BAT*.

For writer details see Richard Curtis (The Phantom) VAN LOAN

Citation Record: 1 Selected Short Story

Brand Of The Black Bat
In 'Black Book Detective' US

Lon QUINNCANNON

is an Irish-American lawyer in New York around the middle of the nineteenth century, who is drawn into cases of murder and solves them.

American Male Professional Investigator operating in New York

Raymond PAUL 1940- (American)

Inventor of one other detective Christopher RANDOLPH

Citation Record: 2 Books

The Thomas Street Horror - *First*
Viking US (1982)

The Bond Street Burlesque - *Latest*
Norton US (1987)

Murder By Gaslight - *Latest**
Allison & Busby UK (1990)

Joe QUINNEY

British Male Amateur operating in England

Horace Annesley VACHELL 1861-1955 (British)

was born in Sydenham, Kent. He was the author of many plays and over a hundred books.

Inventor of one other detective IMPEY

Citation Record: 1 Book 37 Short Stories in 3 Collections

Quinney's - *Only*
!See Appendix 2.
Murray UK (1914); Doran US (1914)

Quinney's Adventures - *Collection 1*
Short stories - 12
Murray UK (1924); Doran US (1924)

Joe Quinney's Jodie - *Collection 2*
Short stories - 13
Ward, Lock UK (1936)

Quinney's For Quality - *Collection 3*
Short stories - 12
Ward, Lock UK (1938)

Simon QUINSEY

is a parody of *Dorothy SAYERS'* detective, *Peter WIMSEY.*

Appears with at least two other detectives - see Mallory KING

Hugh QUINT

American Male Private Detective operating in New Hampshire

Steve SHERMAN 1938- (American)

Writer: Steve Barry SHERMAN

Citation Record: 2 Books

The Maple Sugar Murders - *First*
Walker US (1987)

The White Mountain Murders - *Latest*
Walker US (1989)

Peter QUINT

American Male Amateur operating in USA

Hugh AUSTIN (American)

Writer: Hugh Austin EVANS

Inventor of one other detective William (Sultans' Harem) SULTAN

Citation Record: 5 Books

It Couldn't Be Murder - *First*
Doubleday US (1935); Heinemann UK (1935)

The Upside Down Murders - *Last*
Doubleday US (1937); Heinemann UK (1938)

Richard QUINTAIN

Male Sleuth operating in Vietnam/Haiti

W Howard BAKER 1925-1991 (British)

Writer: William Arthur Howard BAKER

Adaptor of one other detective Sexton BLAKE

Other Bylines:
W A BALLINGER
Peter SAXON
Richard WILLIAMS

Citation Record: 9 Books

Destination Dieppe - *First*
Mayflower UK (1965)

The Judas Diary - *Last*
Lancer UK (1969); Baker US (1969)

W A BALLINGER (British)

For writer details see Richard QUINTAIN

House writer for one other detective Sexton BLAKE

Citation Record: 2 Books

Unfriendly Persuasion - *First*
Consul US (1964)

Drums Of The Dark Gods - *Last*
Mayflower UK (1966); Paperback Library US (1967)

Gimiendo Hernande QUINTO

Spanish Male Sleuth operating in China

James NORMAN 1912- (American)

Writer: James Norman SCHMIDT

Citation Record: 3 Books

Murder, Chop Chop - *First*
Morrow US (1942); Joseph UK (1943)

The Nightwalkers - *Last*
Ziff-Davis US (1947); Joseph UK (1948)

Silas QUIRK

American Male Detective in Pulp Magazines operating in USA

Warne MILLER (American)

Other Detectives:
JOCKY JOE
John RUGBY
Zeb TAYLOR

Citation Record: 1 Selected Short Story

Silas Quirk, The Diamond Detective; Or, The Mystery Of The False Jewels
Old Cap Collier Library US (18??)

Adam QUIRKE

is a scientist of the then future (the 1990s) who, in his first book, solves a locked-room murder involving spider bites.

British Male Amateur operating in England

Volsted GRIDBAN 1908-1960

For writer details see Maria BLACK

Citation Record: 2 Books

The Master Must Die - *First*
Scion UK (1953)

The Lonely Astronomer - *Last*
Scion UK (1954)

Gregory QUIST

is a special investigator for the Texas & Arizona Southern Railroad, operating out of El Paso.

American Male Private Detective operating in Texas

William Colt MACDONALD 1891- (American)

was born in Michigan and lived most of his life in the West. He wrote many straight westerns as well as detective novels.

Writer: Allen William Colt MACDONALD

Inventor of one other detective pair Brady RUSKIN and Whit TRAXLER

Citation Record: 9 Books

Law And Order, Unlimited - *First*
Doubleday US (1953); Hodder & Stoughton UK (1955)

The Osage Bow - *Last*
Hodder & Stoughton UK (1964)

Julian QUIST

is blond, handsome and head of a New York public relations firm. He finds it very necessary to do his own detective work.

American Male Amateur operating in New York

Sidekick: Bobby HILLIARD

American Male - Partner

Hugh PENTECOST 1903-1989 (American)

Invented 12 detectives - see Pierre CHAMBRUN

Citation Record: 11 Books

Don't Drop Dead Tomorrow - *First*
Dodd, Mead US (1971); Hale UK (1973)

Past, Present, And Murder - *Last*
Dodd, Mead US (1982); Hale UK (1983)

Imogen QUY

is a young college nurse at the mythical St Agatha's College, Cambridge. She calmly and reticently solves typically British murders, with bodies in the library and encouragingly literary mysteries involving rare books.

British Female Amateur operating in Cambridge

Jill Paton WALSH (British)

is the author of several novels for children.

Citation Record: 2 Books

The Wyndham Case - *First*
Hodder & Stoughton UK (1993)

A Piece Of Justice - *Latest*
Hodder & Stoughton UK (1995)

Jim QWILLERAN

is a writer, a reformed alcoholic who takes a job as an art critic on a paper; but, in fact, he becomes involved in mysteries and murders, which he sets about solving, in various parts of the country. He is aided and abetted by two of the strangest and most loveable sidekicks in the genre, Siamese cats, who, by their feline ways, contribute to the solutions as much as did

any village constable in the old days.
American Male Amateur operating in Midwest USA
Sidekick: KOKO
Siamese Male - Pet Cat
Sidekick: YUM YUM
Siamese Female - Pet Cat

Lillian Jackson BRAUN (American)
Citation Record: 15 Books
The Cat Who Could Read Backwards - *First*
Dutton US (1966)
The Cat Who Blew The Whistle - *Latest*
Putnam US (1995); Headline UK (1995)

— R —

Col RACE
is an ex-Army man who appears also in novels with the author's other detectives, *Hercule POIROT* and *Insp BATTLE.*
British Male Amateur operating in England

Agatha CHRISTIE 1890-1976 (British)
Invented 18 detectives - see Hercule POIROT
Citation Record: 2 Books
The Man In The Brown Suit - *First*
Lane UK (1924); Dodd, Mead US (1924)
Sparkling Cyanide - *Last*
Collins UK (1945)
Remembered Death - *Last**
Dodd, Mead US (1945)

Col RACE
Appears with at least two other detectives - see Hercule POIROT

Christopher RACE
British Male Amateur operating in England

C N WILLIAMSON and A M WILLIAMSON (British)
Writers: Charles Norris WILLIAMSON 1859-1920 and Alice Muriel Livingston WILLIAMSON
Citation Record: 12 Short Stories in 1 Collection
The Scarlet Runner - *Collection 1*
Methuen UK (1908)

'Blue Jean' Billy RACE
American Male Amateur operating in New England

Charles W TYLER 1841-1920 (American)
Writer: Charles Waller TYLER
Citation Record: 2 Books
Blue Jean Billy - *First*
Lloyd UK (1921); Chelsea US (1926)
Quality Bill's Girl - *Last*
Chelsea US (1925); Hutchinson UK (1925)

RADCLIFF
American Male Sleuth operating in New York

Roosevelt MALLORY (American)
Citation Record: 3 Books
Harlem Hit - *First*
Holloway US (1973)
New Jersey Showdown - *Latest*
Holloway US (1976)

Capt Jacques RADFORD and Tony ANDERSON
investigate an ingenious robbery from a totally guarded room.
British Male Amateurs operating in England

T C H JACOBS 1899-1976 (British)
Invented 8 detectives - see Ch Insp BARNARD
Citation Record: 1 Book
The Terror Of Torlands - *Only*
Paul UK (1930)

Joseph RADKIN
American Male Private Detective operating in USA/England

Bob BIDERMAN 1960- (American)
was born in Ohio.
Inventor of one other detective Morris KAPLAN
Citation Record: 4 Books
Strange Inheritance - *First*
Pluto UK (1985)
Paper Cuts - *Latest*
Gollancz UK (1990)

John RADMELL
is a journalist who investigates the death of a man under 'impossible' circumstances.
British Male Amateur operating in England

Mark ASHTON (British)
Citation Record: 1 Book
A Silence Of Birds - *Single*
Hale UK (1979)

Herman RADNITZ
Second detective of Mark GIRLAND

Herman RADNITZ
Appears with at least two other detectives - see Mark GIRLAND

Herman RADNITZ and Al BARNEY
also appear individually and in books with some of the author's other detectives.
American Male Private Detectives operating in California

James Hadley CHASE 1906-1985 (British)
Invented 14 detectives - see Dave FENNER
Citation Record: 1 Book
You're Dead Without Money - *Only*
Hale UK (1972)

Jacques RADOUB
French Male Amateur operating in several locations

H De Vere STACPOOLE 1863-1951 (British)
Invented 3 detectives - see Capt SLOCUM
Citation Record: 7 Short Stories in 1 Collection
Corporal Jacques Of The Foreign Legion - *Collection 1*
Hutchinson UK (1916)

Terence RADWAY
American Male Amateur operating in USA

Max BRAND 1892-1944 (American)
Writer: Frederick Schiller FAUST
Other Byline: Frederick FROST
Inventor of one other detective Dr KILDARE
Citation Record: 1 Book
Big Game - *Only*
Paperback Library US (1973)

Barry RAEBURN
British Male Private Detective operating in England

Alastair MacTavish DUNNETT 1908- (British)
Citation Record: 1 Book
No Thanks To The Duke - *Single*
Cape UK (1978); Doubleday US (1981)

Bill RAEBURN
American Male Amateur operating in USA

George Harmon COXE 1901-1984 (American)
Invented 20 detectives - see Kent MURDOCK
Citation Record: 1 Book
Venturous Lady - *Only*
Knopf US (1948); Hammond UK (1951)

Mark RAEBURN

was formerly in a famous Scottish regiment serving in the Korean War and was also a member of the Metropolitan Police. He sets up a private enquiry agency in London, where he is familiar with most of the crooks.

British Male Private Detective operating in England/Switzerland

Malcolm GAIR (British)

Writer: John Dick SCOTT

Citation Record: 6 Books

Sapphires On Wednesday - *First*
Collins UK (1957); Doubleday US (1957)

Snow Job - *Last*
Collins UK (1962); Doubleday US (1962)

RAFFERTY

is an ex-cop, fired for insubordination, who practises as a PI according to his own rules, which seem to allow him an excessive use of violence.

American Male Private Detective operating in Dallas

Sidekick: COWBOY
is one half of an independent husband-and-wife team of very tough helpers for *RAFFERTY,* whose brain power is unfortunately not strong enough to enable him to solve cases by brilliant feats of intellect.

American Male - Aide

Sidekick: MIMI
is the other half.

American Female - Aide

W Glenn DUNCAN (American)

Citation Record: 3 Books

Rafferty's Rules - *First*
GM US (1987)

Rafferty: Poor Dead Cricket - *Latest*
GM US (1988)

Insp Joseph Aloysius RAFFERTY

is red-haired and appears to be Irish.

British Policeman operating in England

Sidekick: Sgt Dafydd LLEWELLYN
is Welsh and quotes much from literature, being superior in class to his boss.

British Male - Subordinate

Geraldine EVANS (British)

was born in London.

Citation Record: 1 Book

Dead Before Morning - *Single*
Macmillan UK (1993)

Neal RAFFERTY

has to quit the police force, being hounded by a powerful politician he has offended. He now operates as a private eye from the Jesuit Fathers Building.

American Male Private Detective operating in New Orleans

Chris WILTZ (American)

Writer: Christine WILTZ

Citation Record: 2 Books

The Killing Circle - *First*
Macmillan US (1981); Hale UK (1982)

A Diamond Before You Die - *Latest*
Mysterious Press US (1987); Mysterious Press UK (1988)

Pat RAFFIGAN

American Male Private Detective operating in USA

Harry WHITTINGTON 1915- (American)

was born in Ocala, Florida, and educated at public schools. He edited several magazines, 1938-1975, was a prolific writer of thrillers and westerns, and certainly wrote over a hundred novels under his many pseudonyms.

Writer: Harry Benjamin WHITTINGTON

Citation Record: 1 Book

The Lady Was A Tramp - *Only*
Handi-Books US (1951)

A J RAFFLES

is one of the earliest, and certainly one of the best, of a long line of British and American gentleman crook-detectives. Indeed, he remains one of the great creations of the genre, fairly deplorable though his criminal habits might be, and he is one of the few characters from fiction to have attained legendary status: his name itself epitomises a species. He appeared in only one novel but in a great number of short stories, which were published by the author in various collections. After the death of *E W HORNUNG,* further stories were written by at least two authors, especially by *Barry PEROWNE,* who also teamed him in two books with his other detective, *J R LEROY* and even, in one book, with the protean *Sexton BLAKE.*

A J RAFFLES is an English gentleman, young, bold and attractive. A man-about-town, mingling with the best that society has to offer, he naturally plays for England at cricket, being a first-class batsman. However, beneath it all, he loves excitement; and, since he rarely has enough funds to maintain his way of life, he takes to crime. Of course, it is as well that, among his other attributes, he is the finest cracksman in the country and is never caught. He uses his skill to commit the most difficult and audacious burglaries, often under the eyes of the police; but he always obeys the English gentleman's code of honour and, although he revels in the excitement, he often robs the rich or crooked to help a deserving cause or person. His work is dangerous and involves considerable sleuthing, not only when he is planning his adventures, but also when he has to clear his name of crimes he has not committed. He is blessed with one of the most loyal and endearing sidekicks in the business.

British Male Amateur operating in England

Sidekick: Bunny MANDERS
is the close and completely loyal friend of *RAFFLES,* who once, we are told, saved him from 'utter disgrace'. He accompanies him on many of his adventures but he disapproves of his activities and often tries to make him reform.

British Male - Friend

David FLETCHER 1940-1988 (British)

Invented 3 detectives - see Det Insp RUBY

Citation Record: 7 Short Stories in 1 Collection

Raffles - *Collection 1*
Macmillan UK (1977); Putnam US (1977)

E W HORNUNG 1866-1921 (British)

was born in Middlesborough, Yorkshire. The brother-in-law of *Sir Arthur Conan DOYLE,* he began writing under the latter's influence. Although he wrote a considerable number of novels he is remembered mainly for his creation of *A J RAFFLES.*

Writer: Ernest William HORNUNG

Citation Record: 1 Book 26 Short Stories in 3 Collections

Mr Justice Raffles - *Only*
Smith, Elder UK (1909); Scribner's US (1909)

The Amateur Cracksman - *Collection 1*
Short stories - 8
Methuen UK (1899); Scribner's US (1899)

Raffles, The Amateur Cracksman - *Collection 1**
Nash UK (1906)

Raffles: Further Adventures Of The Amateur Cracksman - *Collection 2*
Short stories - 8
Scribner's US (1901)

The Black Mask - *Collection 2**
Richards UK (1901)

A Thief In The Night - *Collection 3*
Short stories - 10
Chatto & Windus UK (1905); Scribner's US (1905)

Barry PEROWNE 1908-1985 (British)

Invented 4 detectives - see J R 'Rick' LEROY

Citation Record: 1 Book 46 Short Stories in 6 Collections

She Married Raffles - *Pastiche 1*
Cassell UK (1936)

Raffles After Dark - *Collection 1*
contains three novelettes.
Short stories - 3
Cassell UK (1933)

The Return Of Raffles - *Collection 1**
Day US (1933)

Raffles In Pursuit - *Collection 2*
contains three novelettes.
Short stories - 3
Cassell UK (1934)

Raffles Under Sentence - *Collection 3*
contains four novelettes.
Short stories - 4
Cassell UK (1936)

Raffles Revisited - *Collection 4*
Short stories - 14
Hamish Hamilton UK (1975); Harper & Row US (1974)

Raffles Of The Albany - *Collection 5*
Short stories - 11
Hamish Hamilton UK (1976); St Martin's US (1977)

Raffles Of The MCC - *Collection 6*
Short stories - 11
Macmillan UK (1979)

A J RAFFLES

Second detective of Sherlock HOLMES

A J RAFFLES and Sexton BLAKE

are a formidable duo in this one book, a pastiche in which the author borrows not one, but two of the best known detectives in the whole genre.

British Male Amateur and British Male Professional Amateur operating in England

Barry PEROWNE 1908-1985 (British)

Invented 4 detectives - see J R 'Rick' LEROY

Citation Record: 1 Book

Raffles Vs Sexton Blake - *Pastiche 1*
Amalgamated UK (1937)

A J RAFFLES and R J 'Rick' LEROY

also appear individually in other books by this author.

British Male Amateurs operating in Europe

Barry PEROWNE 1908-1985 (British)

Invented 4 detectives - see J R 'Rick' LEROY

Citation Record: 2 Books

Raffles' Crime In Gibraltar - *First*
The UK edition included a brief episode with Sexton BLAKE, who happened to be passing through Gibraltar on another case at the time. It was omitted from the US edition.
Amalgamated UK (1937)

They Hang Them In Gibraltar - *First**
Hillman-Curl US (1939)

Raffles And The Key Man - *Last*
Lippincott US (1940)

Tom RAGNON

American Male Sleuth operating in Arizona/Mexico

Richard HARPER (American)

Citation Record: 2 Books

Death To The Dancing Masters - *First*
GM US (1980); Hale UK (1985)

Kinderkill - *Latest*
Lynx US (1989)

Noel RAID

was a secret agent during the Second World War and he returns, after twenty years, to the Middle East.

British Male Professional Investigator operating in several locations

Alec WAUGH 1898-1981 (American)

Writer: Alexander Rabin WAUGH

Citation Record: 1 Book

The Mule On The Minaret - *Only*
Farrar, Straus US (1966); Allen UK (1966)

Insp RAIKES

is from Scotland Yard and appears once, descending on a quiet little village to solve a problem involving blackmail, forced suicide, murder and other typical goings-on in rural England in the 1940s.

British Policeman operating in England

Dorothy BOWERS 1904- (British)

See main detective Ch Insp Dan PARDOE

Citation Record: 1 Book

The Bells At Old Bailey - *Only*
Hodder & Stoughton UK (1947)

The Bells Of Old Bailey - *Only**
Doubleday US (1947)

The RAILWAY DETECTIVE

American Male Detective in Pulp Magazines operating in USA

ANON

Citation Record: 1 Book

The Railway Detective
Butler US

Doll RAINBOW

is a pickpocket who is the detective in this one Victorian novel.

British Female Amateur operating in London

Thomas WRIGHT 1859-1936 (British)

Citation Record: 1 Book

The Mystery Of St Dunstans - *Only*
Sampson, Low UK (1892)

Jim (The Death Dealer) RAINEY

Male Sleuth operating in Lebanon/Haiti

Peter MCCURTIN (American)

Invented 4 detectives - see Robert (The Assassin) BRIGANTI

Citation Record: 9 Books

Spoils Of War - *First*
Belmont US (1976); New English Library UK (1978)

Battle Pay - *Latest*
Belmont US (1978)

Bob RAINIER and Ted DENNING

are, respectively, a white PI and a black PI. They appear in one book, which uses the comic strip form.

American Male Private Detectives operating in USA

Don MCGREGOR and Gene COLAN (American)

Citation Record: 1 Book

Detectives Inc - *Single*
US (1986)

Agatha RAISIN

lives in a small English country town and is said to be 'a cross between Miss Marple, Aunt Mame and Lucille Ball'.

British Female Amateur operating in England

M C BEATON 1936- (British)

Invented 3 detectives - see Insp BLAIR

Citation Record: 3 Books

Agatha Raisin And The Quiche Of Death - *First*
Bantam US (1992)

Agatha Raisin And The Walkers Of Dembley - *Latest*
Bantam US (1995)

RAKER

American Male Professional Investigator operating in USA

Don SCOTT (American)

Citation Record: 2 Books

Raker - *First*
Pinnacle US (1982)
Tijuana Traffic - *Latest*
Pinnacle US (1982)

Det Deb RALSTON

is on the police force at Fort Worth. On the tough side, she has been with the Homicide squad for around fifteen years.

American Policewoman operating in Fort Worth

Lee MARTIN 1943- (American)
Writer: Martha Anne Guice WINGATE
Other Byline: Anne WINGATE
Citation Record: 10 Books
Too Sane A Murder - *First*
St Martin's US (1984); Quartet UK (1986)
Hacker - *Latest*
St Martin's US (1992)

Gwen RAMADGE

American Female Amateur operating in USA

Lillian O'DONNELL 1926- (American)
Invented 3 detectives - see Policewoman Norah MULCAHANEY
Citation Record: 2 Books
A Wreath For The Bride - *First*
Putnam US (1990); Piatkus UK (1991)
Used To Kill - *Latest*
Putnam US (1993)

Insp RAMBLER

Second detective of Mr VERITY

Carmen RAMIREZ

is a newspaper copy-editor who investigates new and sometimes old crimes.

American Female Amateur operating in Oklahoma

Lisa HADDOCK (American)
Citation Record: 1 Book
Edited Out - *Single*
Naiad US (1994)

Det Frank RAMOS

is up against prejudice, both in race and class, as he tries to solve a crime in Tucson.

Mexican Policeman operating in Tucson

Fredric BROWN 1906-1972 (American)
Invented 8 detectives - see Ambrose HUNTER and Ed HUNTER
Citation Record: 1 Book
The Lenient Beast - *Only*
Dutton US (1956); Boardman UK (1957)

Andrea Reid RAMSAY and David RAMSAY

American Female Amateur and American Male Amateur operating in Louisiana/Georgia

Cecile Hulse MATSCHAT 1895?-1976 (American)
Citation Record: 2 Books
Murder At The Black Crook - *First*
Farrar, Straus US (1943); Cassell UK (1945)
Murder In Okefenokee - *Last*
Farrar, Straus US (1941)

Charles RAMSAY

is an expert on fine art and antiques who becomes involved in the usual nasty goings-on to which the fictional art world is prone.

British Male Amateur operating in England

William ARDIN (British)
was educated in Worcester and graduated at Oxford. He has worked in the research department of ICI, the large British chemical firm.
Citation Record: 2 Books
Some Dark Antiquities - *First*
Headline UK (1994)
Light At Midnight - *Latest*
Headline UK (1995)

David RAMSAY

Second detective of Andrea Reid RAMSAY

Insp Stephen RAMSAY

operates in Northumberland and Scotland. Impulsive, he is given to error during his cases and is heartily disliked by his colleagues.

British Policeman operating in England

Ann CLEEVES 1954- (British)
was born in Hereford, Herefordshire. She has been a social worker and is an experienced bird observer in England and Scotland.
Inventor of one other detective George PALMER-JONES
Citation Record: 3 Books
A Lesson In Dying - *First*
Century UK (1990)
A Day In The Death Of Dorothea Cassidy - *Latest*
Macmillan UK (1992)

Steve RAMSAY

American Male Sleuth operating in Belgian Congo

C H WALLACE (American)
Writer: Rosaylmer BURGER
Citation Record: 4 Books
Crashlanding In The Congo - *First*
Belmont US (1965)
E T A For Death - *Last*
Belmont US (1967)

Lucy RAMSDALE and Insp James MACDOUGAL

Lucy RAMSDALE is an artist who, in her sixties and lately widowed, lives in the small town of Wingate. Together with *Insp James MACDOUGAL*, who has been forced to resign from the local police 'because of circumstances surrounding his divorce', she solves several cases of local murder.

American Female Amateur and American Policeman operating in Connecticut

Hildegarde DOLSON 1908-1981 (American)
Citation Record: 4 Books
To Spite Her Face - *First*
Lippincott US (1971); Curley UK (1979)
Beauty Sleep - *Last*
Lippincott US (1977); Hale UK (1979)

RAMSEY

American Male Detective in Pulp Magazines operating in USA

OLD SLEUTH (American)
Invented 40 detectives - see Brant ADAMS
Citation Record: 1 Book
Ramsey, The Detective - *Only*
Parlor Car US (1898)

Deuce RAMSEY

was forced to retire from the police force in Yellow, Texas, as he was too honest for his superiors. Big, tough and ugly, he finds missing persons.

American Male Private Detective operating in Texas

Jamie MANDELKAU (American)
Citation Record: 1 Book
The Leo Wyoming Caper - *Single*
Putnam US (1977)

RAND

is a cipher expert who works for the Department of Concealed Communications, a mythical branch of British Intelligence.

British Male Secret Agent operating in several locations

Edward D HOCH 1930- (American)
Invented 20 detectives - see Capt LEOPOLD
Citation Record: 12 Short Stories in 2 Collections
The Spy And The Thief - *Collection 1*
This collection has seven stories with *RAND* and seven with *Nick VELVET.*
Short stories - 7
Walker US (1971)
The Spy Who Read Latin And Other Stories - *Collection 2*
Short stories - 5
Walker US (1990)

Col Jefferson Davis RAND

is an expert on antique guns and uses his knowledge of the peculiar psychology of collectors to crack a difficult case.
American Male Private Detective operating in USA

H Beam PIPER 1904-1964 (American)
Writer: Henry Beam PIPER
Citation Record: 1 Book
Murder In The Gunroom - *Only*
Knopf US (1953)

Miller RAND

was one of the more unusual inventions among the spate of 'scientific detectives' of the 1920s and 1930s. He was called the Electrical Man, since his clothes were electrified by 'radio waves' so as to stun any man who touched him – a useful attribute that many of our sleuths might profit from today. He appeared mainly in stories in *Amazing Detective Tales.*
American Male Detective in Pulp Magazines operating in USA

Neil R JONES (American)
No citations

Copper RANDAL

is a young girl who resides in British government circles in India under the Raj. She turns amateur sleuth when murder is done in Government House on Ross Island.
British Female Amateur operating in India

M M KAYE 1909- (British)
See main detective pair Lash HOLDEN and Dany ASHTON
Citation Record: 1 Book
Death In The Andamans - *Only*
seems to have appeared originally as *Night on the Island* in 1960.
Viking UK (1985); St Martin's US (1986)

D C (Darn Cat) RANDALL

is a twenty-five-pound black cat who is the (not very proud) owner of a Californian family called the Randalls. A sweet bruiser and a soft tiger by turns, he is the hero-detective in cases that have the local police stumped. He is not usually grateful for any aid they give him.
American Male Cat operating in Los Angeles

The GORDONS (American)
were a husband-and wife team. *Mildred GORDON* graduated with a BA from the University of Arizona, Tucson, 1930, and married *Gordon GORDON*, 1932. He was a journalist and publicist for Twentieth Century Fox, Hollywood, and later was a counter-espionage agent for the FBI. Their first detective-espionage novel appeared in 1946 and their comic series featuring the cat, *D C RANDALL*, in 1963. They received the Writers Guild of America award, 1965 and the American Humor Society award, 1965.
Writers: Mildred GORDON 1905-1979 and Gordon GORDON 1906-
Other Detectives:
GAIL and MITCH
John RIPLEY
Citation Record: 3 Books
Undercover Cat - *First*
Doubleday US (1963); Macdonald UK (1964)
That Darn Cat - *First**
Bantam US (1966); Corgi UK (1966)
Catnapped: The Further Adventures Of Undercover Cat - *Last*
Doubleday US (1974); Macdonald UK (1975)

Knox RANDALL

is hired to pilot a boat to sea from Florida, but has to solve two murders on the way.
American Male Amateur operating in Florida

George Harmon COXE 1901-1984 (American)
Invented 20 detectives - see Kent MURDOCK
Citation Record: 1 Book
Inland Passage - *Single*
Knopf US (1949); Hammond UK (1952)

Mark RANDALL

British Male Sleuth operating in Europe/Africa

Charles ELAND 1906- (British)
Writer: Charles Adolph VON RIMANOCZY
Citation Record: 3 Books
Dossier Closed - *First*
Hale UK (1970)
The Gold Hijack - *Last*
Hale UK (1973)

Peter Carstan RANDALL

becomes accidentally involved in a complex crime committed in the African bush and, by clever detective work, solves it.
South African Male Amateur operating in Africa

R H LEES (British)
Citation Record: 1 Book
A Question Of Murder - *Single*
Hale UK (1981)

Rev Cesare RANDOLLPH

American Male Amateur operating in USA

Charles Merrill SMITH (American)
Citation Record: 6 Books
Reverend Randollph And The Wages Of Sin - *First*
Putnam US (1974); Barker UK (1975)
Reverend Randollph And The Splendid Samaritian - *Last*
Barker UK (1986)

Christopher RANDOLPH

sleuths in the year 1832.
American Male Amateur operating in New England

Raymond PAUL 1940- (American)
See main detective Lon QUINNCANNON
Citation Record: 1 Book
The Tragedy At Tiverton - *Single*
Viking US (1984)

Steve RANDOM

solves a case of 'impossible' murder of a man in a hotel room.
American Male Sleuth operating in USA

Davis DRESSER 1904-1977 (American)
usually wrote under a pseudonym but published this story under his own name.
!See Appendix 2.
Citation Record: 1 Selected Short Story
Murder Takes A Ride
In 'Mystery Book Magazine' US (1946)

Arthur RANELEIGH

American Male Amateur operating in Los Angeles

Mark Lee LUTHER 1872- (American)
Citation Record: 2 Books

Card 13 - *First*
Bobbs US (1930)
The Saranoff Murder - *Last*
Bobbs US (1930)

John RANKIN
has an office on Capitol Hill and flashes a dirty silver Porsche just to show he's up there with the best of them.
American Male Private Detective operating in Washington DC

James GRADY 1949- (American)
Writer: James Thomas GRADY
Adopter of one other detective Philip MARLOWE
Citation Record: 2 Books
Runner On The Streets - *First*
!See Appendix 2.
Macmillan US (1984)
Hard Bargains - *Latest*
Macmillan US (1985)

Spence RANKIN
American Male Amateur operating in USA

George Harmon COXE 1901-1984 (American)
Invented 20 detectives - see Kent MURDOCK
Citation Record: 1 Book
Dangerous Legacy - *Only*
Knopf US (1946); Hammond UK (1949)

Det Tommy RANKIN
is a young detective in the Homicide Division of the Philadelphia Police Force.
American Policeman operating in USA

Milton PROPPER 1906-1962 (American)
was born in Philadelphia, Pennsylvania. He graduated with a BA from the University of Pennsylvania, Philadelphia, 1926, followed by an LLB, 1929. Called to the Bar, 1929, he has also worked as a literary and drama critic.
Writer: Milton Morris PROPPER
Citation Record: 14 Books
The Strange Disappearance Of Mary Young - *First*
Harper & Row US (1929); Harrap UK (1932)
The Blood Transfusion Murders - *Last*
Harper & Row US (1943)
Murders In Sequence - *Last**
Jenkins UK (1947)

R

Glen RANSOM
American Male Private Detective operating in New York

Vernon WARREN 1925- (British)
Invented 5 detectives - see Johnny MAQUIS
Citation Record: 1 Book
Appointment In Hell - *Only*
Gifford UK (1956)

Rogue RANSOM
American Male Amateur operating in USA/Mexico

Dean MORGAN 1920- (American)
Writer: Graham FISHER
Other Bylines:
Graham FISHER   Duff JOHNSON
Inventor of one other detective Rostron OUTFIT
Citation Record: 3 Books
Rogue Ransom - Racket Buster - *First*
Hamilton Stafford UK (1952)
Rogue Ransom - Triggerman - *Last*
Hamilton Stafford UK (1952)

Stephen RANSOME
American Male Amateur operating in New York

Stephen RANSOME 1902-1977 (American)
Invented 4 detectives - see Lt Lee BARCELLO
Citation Record: 2 Books
Hear No Evil - *First*
Doubleday US (1953); Gollancz UK (1954)
The Shroud Off Her Back - *Last*
Doubleday US (1953); Gollancz UK (1953)

Lamaar RANSOM
appears in a Chandleresque parody set back into 1942. She has a smart office and a black male secretary who likes to change his sex appearance from time to time, which concerns her not a jot as she herself is proudly lesbian.
American Female Private Detective operating in Los Angeles
Sidekick: Lavender TREVELYAN
is male, black, transvestite, and the detective's secretary and assistant.
American Male - Secretary

David GALLOWAY 1937- (American)
Writer: David Darryl GALLOWAY
Citation Record: 1 Book
Lamaar Ransom - Private Eye - *Single*
Riverrun US (1979)

Stephen RANT
British Male Amateur operating in England

H E WHEELER (British)
Inventor of one other detective Kendal GRAYDON
Citation Record: 2 Books
Death Takes A Ride - *First*
Jenkins UK (1942)
The Third Attempt - *Last*
Jenkins UK (1946)

Matt RANZINO
is a Korean War veteran. He has tuberculosis but can still mix it with the best of them.
American Male Private Detective operating in USA

Ed LACY 1911-1968 (American)
Invented 8 detectives - see Toussaint 'Touie' MOORE
Citation Record: 1 Book
Sin In Their Blood - *Only*
Eton US (1952)
Death In Passing - *Only**
Boardman UK (1959)

Dr Louis RAPHAEL
is a pathologist who uses his specialised knowledge to solve mysteries, some of the locked-room murder variety.
British Male Professional Amateur operating in England
Sidekick: MEREDITH
is the detective's secretary and assistant.
British Male - Secretary

Augustus MUIR 1892-1989 (British)
Writer: Charles Augustus Carlow MUIR
Citation Record: 12 Short Stories in 1 Collection
Raphael, MD - *Collection 1*
Methuen UK (1935)

Insp G RASON
seems to be the same man as *Insp J RASON* created by the author under other bylines. Apart from the one novel, he appears also in short stories with the one of the author's other detectives, *Fidelity DOVE.*
British Policeman operating in England

David DURHAM 1888-1965 (British)
For writer details see Insp J RASON
Other Detectives:
Fidelity DOVE   Insp J RASON
Insp G RASON and Fidelity DOVE
James SEGROVE
Citation Record: 1 Book
Hounded Down - *Only*
was republished under the following byline.
Hodder & Stoughton UK (1923)

Roy VICKERS 1888-1965 (British)

Invented 9 detectives - see Insp J RASON

Hounded Down - *Only*
was originally published under the preceding byline.
Newnes UK (1935)

Insp G RASON and Fidelity DOVE

also appear individually in other books by this author.
British Policeman and British Female Amateur operating in England

David DURHAM 1888-1965 (British)

Invented 5 detectives - see Insp G RASON

Citation Record: 9 Short Stories in 1 Collection

The Exploits Of Fidelity Dove - *Collection 1*
contains nine stories in which *Fidelity DOVE* appears with *Insp G RASON* and three in which she is the only sleuth. It was republished under the following byline.
Hodder & Stoughton UK (1924)

Roy VICKERS 1888-1965 (British)

Invented 9 detectives - see Insp J RASON

Citation Record: 3 Short Stories in 1 Collection

The Exploits Of Fidelity Dove - *Collection 1*
was previously published under the preceding byline.
Newnes UK (1935)

Insp J RASON

is a sound British copper who appears in books and short stories under the *Roy VICKERS* byline, others under the *Sefton KYLE* byline and occasionally in other books under pseudonymous titles. He was particularly associated with the Department of Dead Ends, a fictitious section at Scotland Yard, where detectives sit around to pick up the ends of old, unsolved cases.
British Policeman operating in England

David DURHAM 1888-1965 (British)

Invented 5 detectives - see Insp G RASON

Citation Record: 1 Book

The Pearl-Headed Pin - *Only*
Hodder & Stoughton UK (1925)

Sefton KYLE 1888-1965 (British)

For writer details see Insp J RASON

Citation Record: 8 Books

The Man In The Shadow - *First*
Jenkins UK (1924)

The Girl Known As D 13 - *Last*
Jenkins UK (1940)

Roy VICKERS 1888-1965 (British)

was educated at Charterhouse School, Surrey. A journalist and editor, he was the author of sixty-three criminous novels under his real name and two pseudonyms, as well as many short stories, which he published in collections.

Writer: Roy VICKERS

Other Bylines:
David DURHAM | Sefton KYLE

Other Detectives:
Ch Const Colonel CRISP | Insp Peter CURWEN
Insp Peter CURWEN and Hugh STANTON
Fidelity DOVE | Insp KYLE
Insp G RASON | Insp G RASON and Fidelity DOVE
James SEGROVE

Citation Record: 8 Books 19 Short Stories 3 Collections

The Mystery Of The Scented Death - *First*
Jenkins UK (1922)

She Walked In Fear - *Last*
Jenkins UK (1940)

The Department Of Dead Ends - *Collection 1*
Short stories - 7
Spivak US (1947); Faber UK (1949)

Murder Will Out - *Collection 2*
Short stories - 8
Faber UK (1950); In 'Detective Book Club' US (1950)

Eight Murders In The Suburbs - *Collection 3*
This collection of eight of the author's stories contains four with *RASON.*
Short stories - 4
Jenkins UK (1954)

Six Murders In The Suburbs - *Collection 3**
The US edition had only six stories, retaining the four with *RASON.*
In 'Detective Book Club' US (1958)

Alex RASSMUSSEN

is hired to investigate the murder of a Cambodian immigrant.
American Male Private Detective operating in USA

David DANIEL (American)

Citation Record: 1 Book

The Heaven Stone - *Single*
St Martin's US (1994)

Bill RASTIN

appears in several short stories and is usually known as 'Grandfather' in the little town of Borgville, Michigan, where he lives. One of the geriatric wonders of detective fiction, he is said to be also 'even more conceited than *Hercule POIROT*'. He has a good, sharp mind, however, which he uses to solve the crimes to which this community seems prone. He is sensitive about his baldness, often being called 'the antique Yul Brynner', and he says he lost his hair driving an open car in the cold winter of 1928.
American Male Amateur operating in Michigan

Stooge: Sheriff PILKINS
is not endeared to *Bill RASTIN,* who has the knack of being proved right about the cases he himself ought to be solving.
American Male

Lloyd BIGGLE 1923- (American)

Writer: Lloyd BIGGLE Jr

Other Detectives:
Jan DARZEK | Sherlock HOLMES
Edward Porter JONES and Sherlock HOLMES
Jay PLETCHER

Citation Record: 1 Selected Short Story

The Great Horseshoe Mystery
US (1962)

Oliver RATER

British Male Amateur operating in England

Edgar WALLACE 1875-1932 (British)

Invented 28 detectives - see J G REEDER

Citation Record: 12 Short Stories in 1 Collection

The Orator - *Collection 1*
Hutchinson UK (1928)

Basil RATHBONE

Appears with at least two other detectives - see Toby PETERS

Monsieur Hector RATICHON

is an unscrupulous 'volunteer police agent' in Paris during 1813. His detective work is often for his own ends.
French Policeman operating in Paris

Baroness ORCZY 1865-1947 (British)

Invented 6 detectives - see Lady Molly DE MAZEREEN

Citation Record: 7 Short Stories in 1 Collection

Castles In The Air - *Collection 1*
Cassell UK (1921); Doran US (1922)

RATLIN

British Policeman operating in England

Jan ROFFMAN ?-1979 (British)

See main detective Michael HADDEN

Citation Record: 2 Books

A Penny For The Guy - *First*
Bles UK (1965); Doubleday US (1965)

Mask Of Words - *First**
Ace US (1973)

The Hanging Woman - *Last*
Bles UK (1965)

RATS

is a north-country, working-class girl, an ardent feminist, who discovers a body in a Rolls Royce. Instead of telling the police, she does the fictionally sensible thing and, rather messily, investigates the mystery. She virtually solves it but fails to bring her investigation to a conclusion, apparently because of her own emotional problems.

British Female Amateur operating in London

Rebecca O'ROURKE (British)

Citation Record: 1 Book

Jumping The Cracks - *Single*
Virago UK (1987)

Claude RAVEL

French Male Amateur operating in England/France

Bradshaw JONES 1904-

Writer: Malcolm Henry Bradshaw JONES

Citation Record: 9 Books

The Hamlet Problem - *First*
Long UK (1962)

A Den Of Savage Men - *Last*
Long UK (1967)

Paul RAVEL

Second detective of Insp Victor BONDURANT

John RAVEN

was once a Detective Inspector in the London police. He was a loner who consistently broke the rules in his singular and passionate war on criminals. Now, no longer in the police, he lives in a houseboat on the Thames and continues to pursue criminals with obsessive zeal, enormous skill and great patience. In his private search for justice he is often in serious conflict with the police.

British Male Professional Amateur operating in England

Stooge: Cdr DRAKE

is one of the few truly evil police adversaries in the literature. A senior policeman, he is malevolent and corrupt as he attempts to outwit and betray his ex-colleague.

British Male

R

Donald MACKENZIE 1908- (Canadian)

was born in Toronto, Canada and educated in England, Canada and Switzerland. He has described himself as being a professional thief from 1930 to 1948 and, consequentially, served time in jail. He has been a full-time author since 1948.

Other Detectives:
Henry CHALICE and Crying EDDIE
Barry JORDAN

Citation Record: 10 Books

Zaleski's Percentage - *First*
Macmillan UK (1974); Houghton Mifflin US (1974)

Raven's Shadow - *Latest*
Macmillan UK (1984); Doubleday US (1985)

Max RAVEN

has to understand the life of the woman he is investigating before he can come to the right conclusion in a blackmail case.

American Male Private Detective operating in Chicago

O G BENSON (American)

Citation Record: 1 Book

Cain's Woman - *Single*
Dell US (1985)

Richard RAVEN

British Male Sleuth

John GRIFFIN 1934- (British)

Writer: Michael John CLAY

Citation Record: 10 Books

The Midas Operation - *First*
Hale UK (1976)

The Camelot Conundrum - *Latest*
Hale UK (1979)

Schlomo RAVEN

appears in an illustrated novel. Although only three feet tall, he wears the conventional and fictional rig of the hardboiled PI, especially the military-style raincoat and fedora.

American Male Private Detective operating in USA

Tom SUTTON (American)

Writer: Byron PREISS

Citation Record: 1 Book

Raven - *Only*
US (1975)

Prof Willis RAVENDEN and Stanford COLTON

solve a case of 'impossible murder' of a man on a stretch of sand where there are no footprints.

American Male Amateurs operating in USA

Samuel Hopkins ADAMS 1871-1958 (American)

See main detective A V R E 'Average' JONES

Citation Record: 1 Book

The Flying Death - *Only*
McClure US (1908)

Anthony RAVENHILL

British Male Amateur operating in England

R Francis FOSTER 1896-1975 (British)

Writer: Reginald Francis FOSTER

Citation Record: 4 Books 12 Short Stories in 1 Collection

The Lift Murder - *First*
Jarrolds UK (1924)

The Body In The Shaft - *First**
Siebel US (1925)

Something Wrong At Chillery - *Last*
Nash UK (1931)

The Mystery At Chillery - *Last**
Fiction League US (1931)

The Chillery Court Mystery - *Last**
Mellifont UK (1936)

Anthony Ravenhill, Crime Merchant - *Collection 1*
Jarrolds UK (1926)

'Little John' RAWLINGS

American Male Sleuth operating in New York

John MINAHAN 1933- (American)

Citation Record: 5 Books

The Great Hotel Robbery - *First*
Norton US (1982)

The Great Grave Robbery - *Latest*
Norton US (1989); Curley UK (1990)

'Easy' RAWLINS

is a black PI and operates in situations set back into the 1950s and 1960s. He has more than the usual problems in getting by, let alone doing his job.

American Male Private Detective operating in Los Angeles

Walter MOSLEY (American)

Citation Record: 4 Books

Devil In A Blue Dress - *First*
Norton US (1990); Serpent's Tail UK (1991)

Black Betty - *Latest*
Norton US (1994)

Insp RAWLINSON

British Policeman operating in England

Josephine BELL 1897-1987 (British)

Invented 10 detectives - see Dr David WINTRINGHAM

Citation Record: 1 Book

Death Of A Con Man - *Only*
Hodder & Stoughton UK (1968); Lippincott US (1968)

Carrie RAYBORN

Appears with at least two other detectives - see Det Jay GOLDSTEIN

Sgt RAYMOND

Second detective of Insp BRADBURY

Nimrod RAYMOND

works for the United States Treasury Department.

American Male Professional Investigator operating in Washington DC

Clayton W COBB (American)

Writer: J A PATTEN

Citation Record: 1 Book

The Mountaineer Detective - *Only*
Street & Smith US (1889)

Noel RAYMOND

was the first male detective to appear in the pages of British girls' magazines in the inter-war years. This startling innovation began in 1935 and, in fact, continued until 1951 in stories in *Girl's Crystal. Noel RAYMOND* was pleasant, clean, well-dressed and debonair. Although without a touch of sex to distract young readers' minds, he was strong and masculine, and his appearance signified bad news to all those canine sidekicks that had formerly frequented the pages of schoolgirl magazines. Instead, from 1937, he had an assistant called *June GAYNOR*, a considerable advance, who, after 1940, appeared as the detective in her own stories.

British Male Professional Amateur operating in England

Sidekick: June GAYNOR

was the assistant to *Noel RAYMOND* in stories from 1937 to 1940, after which she appeared as the main detective.

British Female - Assistant

Ronald FLEMING (British)

Inventor of one other detective June GAYNOR

No citations

Proteus RAYMOND

was one of the several 'scientific detectives' to appear after the success of *Craig KENNEDY* in 1910, appearing in stories in *Top-Notch Magazine* during 1911.

American Male Amateur operating in USA

No citations

Rick RAZIO

American Male Sleuth operating in Chicago

Rick RAZIO (American)

Citation Record: 2 Books

Blondie Beg Your Bullet - *First*
MC Publications US (1950?)

Blondie Kiss Your Doom - *Last*
MC Publications US (1950?)

Ed RAZONI and William JACKSON

re-appeared a decade later in one book with another of the author's detectives, *Devlin TRACY.*

American Male Sleuths operating in New York

Warren B MURPHY 1933- (American)

Invented 8 detectives - see Julian 'Digger' BURROUGHS

Citation Record: 6 Books

Dead End Street - *First*
Pinnacle US (1973)

On The Dead Run - *Last*
Pinnacle US (1975)

Ed RAZONI, William JACKSON and Devlin TRACY

American Male Sleuths operating in New York

Warren B MURPHY 1933- (American)

Invented 8 detectives - see Julian 'Digger' BURROUGHS

Citation Record: 1 Book

Too Old A Cat - *Single*
Signet US (1986)

Insp READ and Jeffrey BLACKBURN

British Policeman and British Male Amateur operating in England

Max AFFORD 1906-1954 (British)

Citation Record: 4 Books

Blood On His Hands! - *First*
Long UK (1936)

Fly By Night - *Last*
Long UK (1942)

The Owl Of Darkness - *Last**
Angus UK (1942)

Anthony READ and Jacqueline NORRIS

are cipher solvers who solve a case of locked-room murder.

British Male Professional Investigator and British Female Professional Investigator operating in England

Stanley P TOYE (British)

Writer: Stanley Percival TOYE

Citation Record: 4 Books

Cyanide! - *First*
Nelson UK (1940)

The Laughing Cat - *Last*
Melrose UK (1950)

Vernon READ

British Male Amateur operating in England

Maxwell SCOTT (American)

Invented 3 detectives - see Nelson LEE

Citation Record: 3 Books

The Iron Skull - *First*
Amalgamated UK (1921)

Lorimer's Legacy - *Last*
Amalgamated UK (1924)

Supt Donald (The Dreamer) REAMER

British Policeman operating in England

W Murdoch DUNCAN 1909-1975 (British)

Invented 8 detectives - see Supt MACNEILL

Citation Record: 12 Books

Meet The Dreamer - *First*
Long UK (1963)

The Dreamer At Large - *Last*
Long UK (1972)

Lt Jim REARDON

is no slouch when it comes to detective work or dalliance with the ladies, to both of which activities he is greatly attracted.

American Policeman operating in San Francisco

Robert L PIKE 1912-1981 (American)

For writer details see Schlock HOMES

Inventor of one other detective Lt CLANCY

Citation Record: 4 Books

Reardon - *First*
Doubleday US (1970)

Deadline: 2 AM - *Last*
Doubleday US (1976); Hale UK (1977)

'Angel Face' REARDON

American Male Sleuth operating in USA

Cornell WOOLRICH 1903-1968 (American)

Invented 3 detectives - see Hal JEFFRIES

Citation Record: 1 Book

Murder In Wax - *Only*
US (19??)

Matt REBER
American Male Private Detective operating in Los Angeles

John CREIGHTON (American)
Writer: Joseph L CHADWICK
Inventor of one other detective Ed DONOVAN
Citation Record: 1 Book
A Half Interest In Murder - *Only*
Ace US (1960)

Insp REBUS
British Policeman operating in Edinburgh

Ian RANKIN 1960- (British)
Writer: Ian James RANKIN
Citation Record: 6 Books
Knots And Crosses - *First*
Bodley Head UK (1987); Doubleday US (1987)
Mortal Causes - *Latest*
Orion UK (1994)

Pete RECTOR
American Male Amateur operating in Washington DC/Montana

Van SILLER (American)
Invented 3 detectives - see Richard MASSEY
Citation Record: 2 Books
Good Night, Ladies - *First*
Doubleday US (1943); Jarrolds UK (1945)
Under A Cloud - *Last*
Doubleday US (1944); Jarrolds UK (1946)

RED CECIL
American Male Detective in Pulp Magazines operating in USA

OLD SLEUTH (American)
Invented 40 detectives - see Brant ADAMS
Citation Record: 1 Book
Red Cecil, The Detective; Or, A Steady Pursuit - *Only*
Ogilvie US (1898)

Supt REDARREL and David FORRESTER
solve a case of murder by stabbing in a locked room.
British Policeman and British Male Amateur operating in England

John CHANCELLOR 1900-1971 (British)
Writer: Charles De Balzac RIDEAUX
Inventor of one other detective Capt FRASS
Citation Record: 1 Book
The Mystery Of Norman's Court - *Only*
Hutchinson UK (1923); Small, Maynard US (1924)

R

Abe REDDEN
American Male Sleuth operating in USA

Fredric NEUMAN 1934- (American)
Writer: Fredric Jay NEUMAN
Inventor of one other detective Policeman William MOORE
Citation Record: 1 Book
Maneuvers - *Single*
Dial US (1982)

Joe REDDMAN
was raised by a Cheyenne foster mother and, although not himself Indian, he has much of the Indian lore and culture in him. Cool, patient, brilliant at observation in the wilderness, he is a pretty good detective, or so the Denver police think.
American Male Private Detective operating in Colorado

Warwick DOWNING 1931- (American)
Citation Record: 2 Books
The Player - *First*
Dutton US (1974)
The Gambler, The Minstrel And The Dance Hall Queen - *Latest*
Dutton US (1976)

Victor REDMAYNE
witnesses a shooting attack on a man in the heart of London and sets out to discover whodunnit and why.
British Male Amateur operating in London

James CORBETT (British)
Invented 7 detectives - see Roy ENDICOTT
Citation Record: 1 Book
The Man With Nine Lives - *Only*
Jenkins UK (1938)

Anne REDMOND
is the wife of a young instructor at the fictional Hoyt College in the American Berkshire Mountains, an institution whose English department seems no freer from murder than most other such establishments in the genre. Certainly she must investigate.
American Female Amateur operating in New York

Edith TAYLOR 1913- (American)
was born in New York City. She is a teacher of English and creative writing.
Citation Record: 1 Book
The Serpent Under It - *Only*
Norton US (1973); Barker UK (1974)

RED-LIGHT WILL
American Male Detective in Pulp Magazines operating in USA

ANON
No citations

Caitlin REECE
Canadian Female Private Detective operating in British Columbia

Lauren Wright DOUGLAS
Citation Record: 6 Books
The Always Anonymous Beast - *First*
Naiad US (1987); Pandora UK (1989)
A Rage Of Maidens - *Latest*
Naiad US (1994)

Sgt REED
of Scotland Yard is a fine detective but inclined to be bibulous, awkward and prone to rule-bending; qualities that get him into no end of trouble with his superiors.
British Policeman operating in England

Charles DRUMMOND 1922-1972 (British)
For writer details see PIRON
Citation Record: 5 Books
Death At The Furlong Post - *First*
Gollancz UK (1967); Walker US (1968)
A Death At The Bar - *Latest*
Gollancz UK (1972); Walker US (1973)

James REED
was once with Scotland Yard in England but now sleuths privately in Malibu Beach.
British Male Private Detective operating in USA/England

Jimmy SANGSTER 1927- (British)
Other Detectives:
John SMITH   Katy TOUCHFEATHER
Citation Record: 3 Books
Snowball - *First*
Holt US (1986); Hale UK (1989)
Hardball - *Latest*
Holt US (1988); Hale UK (1990)

Lal REED
American Male Amateur operating in Argentine/Turkey

Clement WOOD 1888-1950 (American)
Invented 3 detectives - see Skelton KYNE

Citation Record: 2 Books

Death In Ankara - *First*
Mystery House US (1944)

Death On The Pampas - *Last*
Mystery House US (1944)

Mike REED

is a newspaperman who solves a case of murder by gas in a locked room.

British Male Amateur operating in England

Colin ROBERTSON 1906-1980 (British)

Other Byline: Desmond REID

Other Detectives:

Supt BRADLEY, Peter GRAYLEIGH, Victor MCBAIN, Edward NORTH, Alan STEEL, Insp Robert STRONG

Citation Record: 1 Book

Ghost Fingers - *Only*
Ward, Lock UK (1941)

J G REEDER

is one of this extraordinary author's finest detectives. A meek little man, middle-aged, with mutton-chop whiskers, he wears pince-nez and is dressed soberly. To add to the milksop image, he carries a furled umbrella, which, however, has a knife blade concealed in its handle. He has, it seems, 'something to do with the Public Prosecutor's Office' and his superb memory and brilliant mind enable him to hunt down criminals like a veritable tiger.

British Male Professional Investigator operating in London

Edgar WALLACE 1875-1932 (British)

was born in Greenwich, London and educated in Camberwell. He served in the army, 1893-1899, and his subsequent jobs were as varied as they were numerous. He worked in factories, as a labourer, as a merchant seaman, and finally as a journalist, a career that he pursued for the rest of his life. He worked on many London newspapers and was the racing correspondent for many of them. His written output subsequently covered the whole field of popular journalism and literature and its scale was immense. He wrote innumerable stories and novels, mostly thrillers and detective stories, but also stage plays, screenplays, verse and critical works, usually at great speed. His work was not always of a high standard but his narrative power was virtually unmatched. He created many memorable detectives and other characters, a few of which have endured, and he remains one of the great pinnacles in the history of the English detective and mystery story.

Writer: Richard Horatio Edgar WALLACE

Other Detectives:

Capt Jiggs ALLERMAN, Supt BLISS, Supt BRANBURY, Mike BRIXAN, Insp CARVER, Ch Supt Peter DAWES, DIXON, Sgt Sir Peter DUNN, 'Educated' EVANS, Sgt/Insp ELK, Sgt/Insp ELK and T B SMITH, FOUR JUST MEN, HEINE, Const LEE, Insp Arnold 'Betcher' LONG, Selby LOWE, Insp MASON, Leslie MAUGHAN, Commiss T X MEREDITH, Supt MINTER, Anthony NEWTON, Mrs Emily OLLERBY, Insp PARR, Oliver RATER, Commiss SANDERS, T B SMITH, York SYMON

Citation Record: 2 Books 16 Short Stories in 3 Collections

Room 13 - *First*
Long UK (1924)

Terror Keep - *Last*
Hodder & Stoughton UK (1927); Doubleday US (1927)

The Mind Of Mr J G Reeder - *Collection 1*

Short stories - 8
Hodder & Stoughton UK (1925)

The Murder Book Of Mr J G Reeder - *Collection 1**
Doubleday US (1929)

The Guv'nor And Other Stories - *Collection 2*

Short stories - 5
Collins UK (1932)

Mr J G Reeder Returns - *Collection 2**
Doubleday US (1932)

Red Aces - *Collection 3*

contains three novelettes.

Short stories - 3
Hodder & Stoughton UK (1929); Doubleday US (1930)

Paul REEDER

American Male Amateur operating in California

Robert C DENNIS 1920-1983 (American)

Inventor of one other detective Willie CARMODY

Citation Record: 2 Books

The Sweat Of Fear - *First*
Bobbs US (1973); Gollancz UK (1973)

Conversations With A Corpse - *Last*
Bobbs US (1974)

Insp David REEFE

solves a case of death by poisoning in a locked house.

British Policeman operating in England

Richard Marr BURMAH (British)

Citation Record: 1 Book

The Smith Slayer - *Only*
Gardner UK (1939)

Idewal REES

British Male Secret Agent operating in India

Berkley MATHER 1914- (British)

Invented 3 detectives - see Peter FELTHAM

Citation Record: 3 Books

The Pass Beyond Kashmir - *First*
Collins UK (1961); Scribner's US (1961)

Snowline - *Last*
Collins UK (1973); Scribner's US (1973)

Det Insp Jack REGAN

is in novelizations of episodes from a TV series.

British Policeman operating in England/USA

Joe BALHAM (British)

Citation Record: 7 Books

Regan And The Snout Who Cried Wolf - *First*
Futura UK (1977)

Regan And The Venetian Virgin - *Latest*
Futura UK (1978)

Ian Kennedy MARTIN 1936- (British)

Citation Record: 3 Books

Regan - *First*
Barker UK (1975); Holt US (1975)

Regan And The Deal Of The Century - *Latest*
Barker UK (1977)

Insp Michael REGAN

British Policeman operating in England

Edgar HALE (British)

Inventor of one other detective Montague MIGGLEWADE

Citation Record: 5 Books

Devil's Tears - *First*
Ward, Lock UK (1946)

So The Lady Died - *Last*
Ward, Lock UK (1949)

Mark REGISTER

British Male Amateur operating in England

Arthur DOUGLAS 1928- (British)

Writer: Douglas Arthur MORETON

Citation Record: 3 Books

The Noah's Ark Murders - *First*
Milton House UK (1974)

The Decoy Murders - *Last*
Milton House UK (1975)

James REHM

only appeared twice but upset the Chicago cops each time.
American Male Private Detective operating in Chicago

William HERBER 1920- (American)

Writer: William Edward HERBER

Citation Record: 2 Books

King-Sized Murder - *First*
Lippincott US (1954); Foulsham UK (1955)

Some Die Slow - *First**
Bantam US (1956)

Live Bait For Murder - *Last*
Lippincott US (1955); Foulsham UK (1956)

Cassandra REILLY

is an Irish-American translator in Barcelona who becomes involved in comic and serious crime.
American Female Amateur operating in Barcelona

Barbara WILSON 1950- (American)

See main detective Pam NILSEN

Citation Record: 1 Book

Gaudi Afternoon - *Single*
Seal US (1990); Virago UK (1991)

Harry REILLY

American Male Sleuth operating in USA

Gary CORBIN (American)

Citation Record: 2 Books

The Last Time I Saw Mary - *First*
Jade US (1963)

Cosa Nostra Circus - *Last*
Nite Time US (1964)

Regan REILLY

American Female Private Detective operating in USA

Carol Higgins CLARK

Citation Record: 2 Books

Decked - *First*
Warner US (1992)

Slagged - *Latest*
Warner US (1993)

R

The RELIANCE DETECTIVE

American Male Detective in Pulp Magazines operating in USA

Lew WILLIAMS (American)

See main detective The DAGO DETECTIVE

Citation Record: 1 Selected Short Story

The Reliance Detective; Or, Tracking The Great Grain Steal
Old Cap Collier Library US (18??)

Cliff REMINGTON

American Male Sleuth operating in USA

Raymond OBSTFELD 1952- (American)

See main detective Harry GOULD

Citation Record: 2 Books

The Remington Factor - *First*
Charter US (1985)

The Remington Contract - *Latest*
Worldwide US (1988)

J A 'Rem' REMINGTON

British Male Amateur operating in England

Robert LADLINE (British)

Citation Record: 6 Books

The Man Who Made A King - *First*
Jenkins UK (1936)

Stop That Man! - *Last*
Jenkins UK (1940)

The REMOVER

British Male Sleuth operating in England

Roland DANIEL 1880-1969 (British)

Invented 11 detectives - see Insp Neville LANGHAM

Citation Record: 4 Books

The Remover - *First*
Wright UK (1933)

Again The Remover - *Last*
Wright UK (1939)

REMSEN

American Male Sleuth operating in USA

David MONTROSS 1914-1986 (American)

Writer: Jean Louise BACKUS

Citation Record: 3 Books

Traitor's Wife - *First*
Doubleday US (1962); Gollancz UK (1962)

Fellow-Traveler - *Last*
Doubleday US (1965); Hale UK (1966)

Insp Hercule RENARD

French Policeman operating in France

Pierre AUDEMARS 1909-1989 (British)

See main detective Insp PINAUD

Citation Record: 3 Books

The Temptation Of Hercule - *First*
Pilot Press UK (1945)

The Confession Of Hercule - *Last*
Low UK (1947)

The RENEGADE DETECTIVE

American Male Detective in Pulp Magazines operating in USA

Hal HAWK (American)

See main detective Oscar SLICK

Citation Record: 1 Book

The Renegade Detective; Or, Playing A Double Role
New York Detective Library US (1882-8)

Douglas RENFREW

Canadian Policeman operating in Canada

Laurie York ERSKINE 1894-1976 (Canadian)

Citation Record: 9 Books

Renfrew Of The Royal Mounted - *First*
Appleton US (1922)

Renfrew Flies Again - *Last*
Appleton US (1941)

Carol RENISON

Second detective of James RENISON

James RENISON and Carol RENISON

hunt down the murderer of her twin sister.
British Male Amateur and British Female Amateur operating in England

Andrew GARVE 1908- (British)

See main detective Max EASTERBROOK

Citation Record: 1 Book

The Far Sands - *Only*
Harper & Row US (1960); Collins UK (1961)

Investigator Arkady RENKO

is, in his first classic book, a dedicated policeman who pursues the murderer of three people amid a labyrinth of bureaucracy and criminality. He appears later in other books, which are in no way comparable.
Russian Policeman operating in Moscow

Martin Cruz SMITH 1942- (American)
Invented 3 detectives - see Roman GREY
Citation Record: 3 Books
Gorky Park - *First*
Random House US (1981); Collins UK (1981)
Red Square - *Latest*
Random House US (1989); HarperCollins UK (1993)

Hugh RENNERT
American Male Amateur operating in Texas/Mexico

Todd DOWNING 1902- (American)
Writer: George Todd DOWNING
Inventor of one other detective Peter BOUNTY
Citation Record: 6 Books
Murder On Tour - *First*
Putnam US (1933)
Night Over Mexico - *Last*
Doubleday US (1937); Methuen UK (1938)

Pete RENO
was fired from the New York Police Department for killing two dangerous drug dealers and, not unreasonably piqued at this, he now runs his own agency, Total Protection Services Inc. Through a pal who happens to be a priest, he is hired – perhaps a little surprisingly, one might think – by certain forces in the Vatican to investigate some peculiar pecuniary peccadilloes of an out-of-town Italian priest. They prove to have alarming consequences.
American Male Private Detective operating in New York/Italy

Robert ROSENBLUM 1938- (American)
Writer: Robert J ROSENBLUM
Citation Record: 1 Book
The Good Thief - *Only*
Doubleday US (1974); Hart Davis UK (1975)

Insp Harry RENTANO
Second detective of Candid JONES

Florence RENWICK
is happily married and a millionairess, but she wishes to undertake a little sleuthing – in disguise, naturally.
American Female Amateur operating in New York

Richard Henry SAVAGE 1846-1903 (American)
Citation Record: 1 Book
Checked Through. Missing Trunk No 17850: A Story Of New York City Life - *Only*
Rand, McNally US (1876); Routledge UK (1876)

Gifford RENWICK
solves a case of an 'impossible' theft of a vial of radium.
British Male Amateur operating in England

Albert DORRINGTON
Citation Record: 1 Book
The Radium Terrors - *Only*
Nash UK (1912); Doubleday US (1912)

Mark RENZLER
was once a professional baseball player but retired when he lost the sight of an eye in a game. After two years in the New York Police Department he has set up as a PI on West 72nd Street, Manhattan. His cases, all set back into the early 1960s, are concerned with baseball.
American Male Private Detective operating in New York

Paul ENGLEMAN (American)
Citation Record: 3 Books
Dead In Center Field - *First*
Ballantine US (1983)
Murder-In-Law - *Latest*
US (1987)

The REPORTER DETECTIVE
American Male Detective in Pulp Magazines operating in USA

Donald J MCKENZIE 1859-1932 (American)
Invented 3 detectives - see Det CUSH
Citation Record: 1 Book
The Reporter Detective - *Only*
Street & Smith (Magnet) US (1900)

Frank REPPA
American Male Sleuth operating in New York

David NEMEC 1938- (American)
Citation Record: 1 Book
Mad Blood - *Single*
Dial US (1983)

Tony RESECK and John EVANS
appear in a short story, later used in the author's novel, *LADY IN THE LAKE.*
American Male Private Detectives operating in USA

Raymond CHANDLER 1888-1959 (American)
Invented 9 detectives - see Philip MARLOWE
Citation Record: 1 Selected Short Story
I'll Be Waiting
In 'Saturday Evening Post' US (1939)

Insp Charlie RESNICK
is perhaps half Polish or half Jewish and is a cop in a gritty Midlands town where life has never been easy. His cases are modern British police procedural, with all its advantages and boredoms, but he himself is an interesting character, with his love of food and jazz, his flawed yet stubborn nature, and his self-doubts.
British Policeman operating in England

John HARVEY 1938- (British)
Inventor of one other detective Scott MITCHELL
Citation Record: 6 Books
Lonely Hearts - *First*
Viking UK (1989); Holt US (1989)
Living Proof - *Latest*
UK (1995)

Mickey 'Slots' RESNICK
was formerly a baseball player. Injured and forced to retire, he entered the New York Police Department, a career that was cut short when he had a brush with his superior. Now a PI, he drives a red Porsche and has an office on 33rd Street, Manhattan.
American Male Private Detective operating in New York

Michael GELLER (American)
See main detective Lt Bud DUGAN
Citation Record: 2 Books
Heroes Also Die - *First*
US (1988)
Major League Murder - *Latest*
US (1988)

David RETURN
is an American Indian and an Indian Agency policeman on a reservation. He uses modern methods of detection, as well as his tribal knowledge, to solve crimes.
American Policeman operating in USA

Manly Wade WELLMAN 1905- (American)
Other Detectives:
Sherlock HOLMES
Judge Keith Hilary PURSUIVANT
John THUNSTONE
Stonewall Jackson YATES and J D THATCHER
Citation Record: 2 Selected Short Stories
Star For A Warrior
US (1946)
Knife Between Brothers
US (1947)

Michael REVEL
British Male Amateur operating in England

Norman BERROW 1902- (British)
was born in England but lived mainly in Australia and New Zealand.
Writer: Cyril Norman BERROW
Other Detectives:
Det Insp COURTENAY MATTHEWS
Det Insp Lancelot Carolus SMITH
Citation Record: 4 Books

Fingers For Ransom - *First*
Ward, Lock UK (1939)

The Singing Room - *Last*
Ward, Lock UK (1948)

Colin REVELL
has come down from Oxford and is living in London, where he is trying to write a lengthy poetic drama (much quoted in the book). He is an old boy of Oakington School and, when a murder occurs there, the headmaster asks him to investigate. Unwillingly he agrees – with dire results.
British Male Amateur operating in England

Glen TREVOR 1900-1954 (British)
For writer details see Colin REVELL
Citation Record: 1 Book

Murder At School - *Only*
Benn UK (1931)

Was It Murder? - *Only**
was republished under the following byline.
Harper & Row US (1933)

James HILTON 1900-1954 (British)
Writer: James HILTON
Other Byline: Glen TREVOR
Citation Record: 1 Book

Was It Murder? - *Only*
was previously published under the preceding byline.
Dover UK (1989)

The REVENUE DETECTIVE
American Male Detective in Pulp Magazines operating in USA

Police Captain JAMES (American)
See main detective Little LIGHTNING
Citation Record: 1 Book

The Revenue Detective - *Only*
Street & Smith US (1889)

Chuck REVES
Appears with at least two other detectives - see Michael KERNEHAN

Nigel REX
British Male Amateur operating in England

George GOODCHILD 1888-1969 (British)
Invented 5 detectives - see Insp MCLEAN
Citation Record: 2 Books

The Quest Of Nigel Rex - *First*
Ward, Lock UK (1934)

Knock And Come In - *Last*
Ward, Lock UK (1935)

Insp REYNOLDS
British Policeman operating in England/France

Elaine HAMILTON (British)
Citation Record: 8 Books

Some Unknown Hand - *First*
Paul UK (1930)

The Westminster Mystery - *First**
Century US (1931)

Murder Before Tuesday - *Last*
Ward, Lock UK (1937)

R

Maxine REYNOLDS
is red-haired, green-eyed, rather lovely, and dashes about California and New York, mixing with movie stars and murder.
American Female Amateur operating in England/USA

Marjorie GROVE (American)
Citation Record: 7 Books

You'll Die When You Hear This - *First*
Zebra US (1978)

You'll Die Tonight - *Latest*
Zebra US (1979)

Jimmie REZAIRE
British Male Amateur operating in England

Anthony ARMSTRONG 1897-1976 (British)
was a soldier in the British army and later joined the Royal Air Force. He was a well-known essayist and wrote a number of crime plays as well as novels.
Writer: George Anthony Armstrong WILLIS
Citation Record: 5 Books

Jimmie Rezaire - *First*
Paul UK (1927)

The Trail Of Fear - *First**
Macrae, Smith US (1927)

The Poison Trail - *Last*
Benn UK (1932)

Const Nick RHEA
British Policeman operating in England

Nicholas RHEA 1936- (British)
For writer details see Det Supt Mark PEMBERTON
Citation Record: 14 Books

Constable On The Hill - *First*
Hale UK (1979)

Constable In The Shrubbery - *Latest*
Hale UK (1995)

Michael RHINEHEART
operates in Louisville. A widower, he lives in a furnished apartment, drives an old car, drinks too much and sleeps around. His cases revolve around bloodstock and the Kentucky races. !See Appendix 2.
American Male Private Detective operating in Kentucky

John BIRKETT (American)
Citation Record: 2 Books

The Last Private Eye - *First*
Avon US (1988)

The Queen's Mare - *Latest*
Avon US (1990)

Dr RHINEWALD
Second detective of Insp MARX

Steve RHODEN
American Male Amateur operating in Colorado/Kentucky

Ira WALKER 1921- (American)
Writer: Irma Ruth Roden WALKER
Other Byline: Irma WALKER
Citation Record: 2 Books

Someone's Stolen Nellie Gray - *First*
Abelard US (1963); Abelard UK (1963)

The Man In The Driver's Seat - *Last*
Abelard US (1964); Abelard UK (1964)

Irma WALKER 1921- (American)
For writer details see Steve RHODEN
Citation Record: 1 Book

Murder In 25 Words Or Less - *Single*
Raven US (1980)

Bernard Grimes RHODENBARR
is a burglar who is usually engaged in some highly specialised, skilled, but strictly non-violent robbery when, to his chagrin,

he becomes involved in murder, often whilst actually on the scene of the crime. He then has to solve the case in order to clear himself.

American Male Amateur operating in New York

Lawrence BLOCK 1938- (American)

Invented 6 detectives - see Leo HAIG

Citation Record: 6 Books

Burglars Can't Be Choosers - *First*
Random House US (1977); Hale UK (1978)

The Burglar Who Thought He Was Bogart - *Latest*
Dutton US (1995)

Sheriff Dan RHODES

is the Sheriff of Blacklin County, Texas, recently widowed and with a grown-up daughter. In a rural atmosphere, he has to deal with the usual crop of robberies and murders.

American Policeman operating in Texas

Bill CRIDER 1941- (American)

See main detective Prof Carl BURNS

Citation Record: 7 Books

Too Late To Die - *First*
Walker US (1986)

Murder Most Fowl - *Latest*
St Martin's US (1994)

James RHODES

American Male Amateur operating in USA

Don GOBER 1944- (American)

For writer details see Henry Highland (Iceman) WEST

Citation Record: 4 Books

Black Cop - *First*
Holloway US (1974)

Killing Ground! - *Latest*
Holloway US (1976)

Prof Arnold RHYMER

British Male Amateur operating in England

Sam KEY 1874- (British)

Writer: Samuel Whittell KEY

Citation Record: 1 Book 5 Short Stories in 1 Collection

Yellow Death - *Only*
Books Limited UK (1921)

The Broken Fang And Other Experiences Of A Specialist In Spooks - *Collection 1*
Hodder & Stoughton UK (1920)

Martin RHYMER

British Male Amateur operating in England

E X FERRARS 1907-1995 (British)

Invented 11 detectives - see Toby DYKE

Citation Record: 1 Book

The Pretty Pink Shroud - *Only*
Doubleday US (1977)

Elizabeth FERRARS 1907-1995 (British)

Invented 10 detectives - see Toby DYKE

Citation Record: 1 Book

The Pretty Pink Shroud - *Only*
Collins UK (1977)

Hartley RHYS

is 'an investigator and trouble-shooter for the Sword Shipping Line of Singapore'.

Male Professional Amateur operating in Australia

Charlotte YARBOROUGH

Citation Record: 1 Book

Murder On The Long Straight - *Single*
Leisure Books US (1979)

Policeman Madoc RHYS

is in the Royal Canadian Mounted Police and, more or less, always gets his man.

Canadian Policeman operating in Canada

Alisa CRAIG 1922- (Canadian)

Invented 3 detectives - see Holly HOWE

Citation Record: 5 Books

A Pint Of Murder - *First*
Doubleday US (1980)

The Wrong Rite - *Latest*
Morrow US (1992)

George RIAM

American Male Sleuth operating in New England

David O WOODBURY 1896-1981 (American)

Writer: David Oakes WOODBURY

Citation Record: 2 Books

Five Days To Oblivion - *First*
Devin-Adair US (1963)

Mr Faraday's Formula - *Last*
Devin-Adair US (1965)

Bill RICE

British Male Amateur operating in England

Marguerite STAND (British)

See main detective Const ROBINS

Citation Record: 7 Books

Escape From Murder - *First*
Hale UK (1964)

Death Came In The Studio - *Last*
Hale UK (1969)

Miles Standish RICE

is a Miami PI who was once a deputy Sheriff. His main interest seems to be eating, but he does detect a little.

American Male Private Detective operating in Miami

Baynard KENDRICK 1894-1977 (American)

Invented 3 detectives - see Duncan MACLAIN

Citation Record: 3 Books

The Iron Spiders - *First*
Greenberg US (1936); Methuen UK (1938)

Death Beyond The Go-Thru - *Last*
Doubleday US (1938)

Mickey RICHARDS

American Male Amateur operating in Chicago

Franklin JAMES 1908- (American)

Writer: Robert GODLEY

Citation Record: 1 Book

Killer In The Kitchen - *Only*
Lantern Press US (1947)

Paul RICHARDS

British Male Professional Amateur operating in England

Duncan DALLAS (British)

Citation Record: 1 Book 7 Short Stories in 1 Collection

I L F - *Only*
Ouseley UK (1909)

Paul Richards - Detective - *Collection 1*
Ouseley UK (1908)

Insp RICHARDSON

solves a case of death by shooting in a locked room.

British Policeman operating in England

Ronald S L HARDING (British)

Citation Record: 1 Book

The Library Of Death - *Only*
Modern UK (1938)

Insp RICHARDSON

British Policeman operating in England

Basil THOMSON 1861-1939 (British)

was the son of the then Archbishop of York. He was educated at Eton College, graduated from New College, Oxford,

and, after attendance at Inner Temple, London, he was called to the Bar. He worked in the Foreign Service and was appointed Prime Minister of Tonga, a British colony, at the age of twenty-nine. Later he was appointed Head of Dartmoor Prison, Devon, 1907, and subsequently held positions in the CID and British Intelligence, receiving several medals and other public honours for his work. He was the author of several criminous novels and other works.
Writer: Sir Basil Home THOMSON
Other Detectives:
Lady ASENATH
James HATTON
Peter GRAHAM
Mr PEPPER
Citation Record: 8 Books
PC Richardson's First Case - *First*
Eldon UK (1933); Doubleday US (1933)
A Murder Arranged - *Last*
Eldon UK (1937)
When Thieves Fall Out - *Last**
Doubleday US (1937)

Paul RICHARDSON
American Male Amateur operating in USA

Harold L KLAWANS 1937- (American)
Writer: Harold Leo KLAWANS
Citation Record: 1 Book
Sins Of Commission - *Single*
Contemporary Books US (1982)

Frank RICHMOND
Male Amateur operating in Los Angeles

Anthony GRAHAM (British)
Invented 3 detectives - see Eric MARSDEN
Citation Record: 2 Books
The Deadly Lovers - *First*
Boardman UK (1966)
The Death Business - *Last*
Boardman UK (1967)

Bow Street Runner Thomas RICHMOND
is a young criminal who, tiring of his way of life, joins the Bow Street Runners. He appears, in five stories, in what would seem to be the earliest collection of detective stories published. The cases seem to be real ones and, although they are technically poor, they actually antedate *THE MURDERS IN THE RUE MORGUE* by two decades. Soon forgotten apparently, they did not influence the future of the detective story as *POE's* story did.
British Policeman operating in London

ANON
Citation Record: 7 Short Stories in 1 Collection
Richmond; Or Scenes In The Life Of A Bow Street Runner - *Collection 1*
has the distinction of being the first collection of detective or police short stories to be published.
UK (1827)

Maj Morven RICKMAN
is a soldier of fortune engaged in defeating various organisations and forces of evil in strange and gothic circumstances.
British Male Professional Investigator operating in several locations

Jon Manchip WHITE 1924- (British)
was born in Cardiff, Glamorganshire. He took an MA in English at St Catherine's College, Cambridge, 1950, and also studied archaeology and oriental languages. He served in the Royal Navy and the Army, 1942-1946, worked in radio and films, 1950-1957, was Professor of English at the University of Texas, El Paso, 1967-1977, and since then has been a Professor of English at the University of Tennessee, Knoxville. His seven criminous novels are all tales of strange, often gothic, adventure; but he has also written mainstream novels, plays for all media, and works on archaeology, anthropology and ancient history.
Writer: Jon Ewbank Manchip WHITE
Citation Record: 3 Books
Nightclimber - *First*
Chatto UK (1968); Morrow US (1968)
The Garden Game - *Last*
Chatto UK (1973); Bobbs US (1974)

Dr Henry RIDDLE and Prof Adam MACAMERON
investigate a series of seemingly maniacal murders of extraordinary ingenuity.
American Male Amateurs operating in USA

Joel Townsley ROGERS 1896-1984 (American)
See main detective Kerry OTT
Citation Record: 1 Book
The Red Right Hand - *Only*
Simon & Schuster US (1945); Panther UK (1956)

Martin RIDGWAY
British Male Sleuth operating in Europe

Peter HELM 1916- (British)
Writer: Peter James HELM
Citation Record: 2 Books
Dead Man's Fingers - *First*
Long UK (1960)
A Walk Into Murder - *First**
Scribner's US (1960)
The Man With No Bones - *Last*
Long UK (1966)

Nat RIDLEY
American Male Amateur operating in USA

Nat RIDLEY Jr
House name.
Citation Record: 2 Books
The Crime On The Limited; Or, Nat Ridley In The Follies - *First*
Garden City UK (1926)
The Western Express Robbery; Or, Nat Ridley And The Mail Thieves - *Last*
Garden City UK (1927)

Magnus RIDOLPH
is an interstellar con-man in the distant future who investigates murder, and rights wrongs for a fee.
Male Professional Investigator operating in Space

Jack VANCE 1917- (American)
Invented 3 detectives - see Keith GERSEN
Citation Record: 10 Short Stories in 2 Collections
The Many Worlds Of Magnus Ridolph - *Collection 1*
contains stories that appeared first in magazines of the 1940s.
Short stories - 6
Ace US (1966)
The Complete Magnus Ridolph - *Collection 2*
added four stories to the first collection.
Short stories - 10
Dobson UK (1977); Underwood US (1984)

Dorothy Mayotte RIGBY
appears in an anthology, *The Rigby File*, (Hodder & Stoughton; UK 1989) comprising thirteen short stories, each one of which was written by a different author.
British Female Amateur operating in England

Angela CHEYNE
Citation Record: 1 Selected Short Story

R

Run Rabbit Run Run Run

John EHRLICHMAN 1925- (American)

Citation Record: 1 Selected Short Story

An Affair Of The Couch

Michael GILBERT 1912- (British)

Invented 11 detectives - see Insp HAZELRIGG

Citation Record: 1 Selected Short Story

The Rules Of The Game

Paula GOSLING 1939- (American)

Invented 7 detectives - see Lt Jack STRYKER

Citation Record: 1 Selected Short Story

A Little Learning

William HAGGARD 1907- (British)

Invented 4 detectives - see Col Charles RUSSELL

Citation Record: 1 Selected Short Story

The Great Divide

Tim HEALD 1944- (British)

See main detective Simon BOGNOR

Citation Record: 1 Selected Short Story

We Are Not Amused

H R F KEATING 1926- (British)

Invented 6 detectives - see Insp Ganesh GHOTE

Citation Record: 1 Selected Short Story

In Disgrace

Duncan KYLE 1930- (British)

Writer: John Franklin BROXHOLME

Citation Record: 1 Selected Short Story

The Breathless Hush

James LEASOR 1923- (British)

Writer: Thomas James LEASOR

See main detective Dr Jason LOVE

Citation Record: 1 Selected Short Story

At Rest At Last

Peter LOVESEY 1936- (British)

Invented 7 detectives - see Sgt CRIBB and Const THACKERAY

Citation Record: 1 Selected Short Story

The Munich Posture

Minette MARRIN (American)

was born in California and raised in England, where she resides.

Citation Record: 1 Selected Short Story

A Man Of God

Anthony PRICE 1928- (British)

Invented 3 detectives - see Dr David AUDLEY

Citation Record: 1 Selected Short Story

The Road To Suez

Richard Martin STERN 1915- (American)

Invented 3 detectives - see Johnny ORTIZ

Citation Record: 1 Selected Short Story

The Bomb

'Bingo' RIGGS and 'Handsome' KUSAK

are two street photographers – an old American way of getting amateurs into crime cases.

American Male Amateurs operating in USA

Craig RICE 1908-1957 (American)

Invented 3 detectives - see John J MALONE

Citation Record: 2 Books

The Sunday Pigeon Murders - *First*
Simon & Schuster US (1942); Nicholson & Watson UK (1948)

The Thursday Turkey Murders - *Last*
Simon & Schuster US (1943); Nicholson & Watson UK (1946)

Craig RICE and Ed MCBAIN (American)

Ed MCBAIN completed this book after the death of *Craig RICE*.

Writers: Georgiana Ann Randolph CRAIG 1908-1957 and Evan HUNTER 1926-

Citation Record: 1 Book

The April Robin Murders - *Only*
Random House US (1958); Hammond UK (1959)

Insp RILEY

British Policeman operating in London

Leonard GRIBBLE 1908-1985

See main detective Supt Anthony SLADE

Citation Record: 1 Book

Riley Of The Special Branch - *Only*
Harrap UK (1936)

Ed RILEY

is a house detective in the Hotel Demerest and meets trouble all the way.

American Male Professional Investigator operating in USA

Huntley PALMER (American)

Citation Record: 1 Selected Short Story

A Shamus And A Sheba

can also be found in an anthology, *Spicy Detective Stories* (Editor: Tom Mason; US 1989).
In 'Spicy Detective Stories' US (1937)

Pete RILEY

British Male Private Detective operating in England

Patrick QUINN (British)

Citation Record: 5 Books

Once Upon A Private Eye - *First*
Hale UK (1968)

The Bid Game - *Last*
Hale UK (1970)

Anthony RILLINGTON

British Male Amateur operating in England

Nigel ORDE-POWLETT 1900- (British)

Writer: Nigel Amyas ORDE-POWLETT

Citation Record: 2 Books

The Cast Of Death - *First*
Benn UK (1932); Houghton US (1932)

Driven Death - *Last*
Benn UK (1933)

John RINGROSE

is an ex-Scotland Yard man, now elderly but still a good detective.

British Male Amateur operating in England

Eden PHILLPOTTS 1862-1960 (British)

Invented 10 detectives - see Insp MIDWINTER

Citation Record: 2 Books

A Voice From The Dark - *First*
Hutchinson UK (1925); Macmillan US (1925)

The Marylebone Miser - *Last*
Hutchinson UK (1926)

Jigsaw - *Last**
Macmillan US (1926)

Stephen RINGWAY

British Male Amateur operating in England

S Makepeace LOTT (British)

Writer: Stanley Makepeace LOTT

Citation Record: 2 Books

Twopence For A Rat's Tail - *First*
Rich UK (1947)

The Judge Will Call It Murder - *Last*
Rich UK (1951)

Insp Richard RINGWOOD

is a policeman of the 1950s but one who still has the characteristics of the old pre-1939 amateurs, being an Oxford man, handsome, a classical scholar, and literary too. He has a beautiful young assistant in his earlier books and, sharing the fate of so many British amateurs created by lady writers, he later marries her.

British Policeman operating in England/France

Sidekick: Sgt PLUMMER

British Male - Subordinate

Sidekick: Clare LIDDICOTE

is the detective's pre-nuptial assistant.

British Female - Wife

Katherine FARRER 1911- (British)

was born in Chippenham, Wiltshire, and graduated at St Anne's College, Oxford.

Writer: Katherine Dorothy FARRER

Citation Record: 3 Books

The Missing Link - *First*
Collins UK (1952)

Gownsman's Gallows - *Last*
Hodder & Stoughton UK (1957)

Linus RINTOUL

is a government veterinarian who becomes involved in nasty crimes connected with the doggy world.

British Male Amateur operating in England

Janet EDMONDS (British)

Citation Record: 3 Books

Dog's Body - *First*
Collins UK (1988)

Judge And Be Damned - *Latest*
Collins UK (1990)

Delia RIORDAN

American Female Amateur operating in USA

Lesley EGAN 1921-88 (American)

See main detective pair Det Vic VARALLO and Jesse FALKENSTEIN

Citation Record: 1 Book

A Choice Of Crimes - *Only*
Doubleday US (1980); Gollancz UK (1981)

Matthew RIORDAN

American Male Sleuth operating in Seattle

Frederick D HUEBNER 1955- (American)

Citation Record: 4 Books

The Joshua Sequence - *First*
GM US (1986)

Picture Postcard - *Latest*
Columbine UK (1990)

R

Pat RIORDAN

seems to have enough troubles of his own, leaving him little time to spare for the sleuthing he manages to get done.

American Male Private Detective operating in California

Roy GILLIGAN (American)

Citation Record: 2 Books

Chinese Restaurants Never Serve Breakfast - *First*
Perseverance US (1986)

Live Oaks Also Die - *Latest*
Brendan US (1990)

Preston John RIORDAN

American Male Amateur operating in Alaska

Sean HANLON 1952?- (American)

Citation Record: 3 Books

The Big Dark - *First*
Pocket Books US (1989)

The Frozen Franklin - *Latest*
Pocket Books US (1990)

Tom RIORDAN

investigates the disappearance of a young girl.

American Male Private Detective operating in New Jersey

Dick RILEY 1946- (American)

Citation Record: 1 Book

Rite Of Expiation - *Single*
Putnam US (1976)

Henry RIOS

American Policeman operating in USA

Michael NAVA (American)

Citation Record: 1 Book

The Hidden Law - *Single*
HarperCollins US (1992)

RIPLEY

British Policeman operating in England

John WAINWRIGHT 1921- (British)

Invented 9 detectives - see Ch Insp/Supt LENNOX

Citation Record: 6 Books

Evil Intent - *First*
Collins UK (1966)

Death Of A Big Man - *Latest*
Macmillan UK (1975); St Martin's US (1975)

RIPLEY

British Male Amateur operating in England

Lord DUNSANY 1878-1957 (British)

Invented 3 detectives - see Mr LINLEY

Citation Record: 5 Short Stories in 1 Collection

The Little Tales Of Smethers, And Other Stories - *Collection 1*

contains five stories featuring *RIPLEY* and eight featuring *LINLEY.*

Jarrolds UK (1952)

John RIPLEY

American Male Secret Agent operating in Chicago

The GORDONS (American)

Invented 3 detectives - see D C (Darn Cat) RANDALL

Citation Record: 5 Books

FBI Story - *First*
Doubleday US (1950); Corgi UK (1957)

The Informant - *Last*
Doubleday US (1973); Macdonald UK (1973)

Ray RIPLEY

is an ex-cop, now a PI, who sleuths in a book set back into 1938.

American Male Private Detective operating in Los Angeles

Douglas HEYES 1921- (American)

Invented 3 detectives - see Steve MALLORY

Citation Record: 1 Book

The Kill - *Single*
Ballantine US (1985)

Tom RIPLEY

is a modern member of that great line of rogues who also, for one reason or another, function as detectives. However, as would be expected from an author of this calibre, he is a much deeper character than most that have gone before, more serious and, in many ways, more deadly. He is a man who likes the good life and succeeds in attaining it, although, to his regret, he has to do away with several unfortunates who get in his way. His detective skills are considerable, as they have to be if he is to avoid the continual threats to his equilibrium and keep the police at bay, which he manages to do over many years. *Tom RIPLEY* is certainly one of the most outstanding of all hero-villains.

American Male Amateur operating in Europe

Patricia HIGHSMITH 1921-1995 (American)

was born Mary Patricia Plaugman in Fort Worth, Texas, but took her stepfather's name. She was educated at Julia Richmond High School, New York, and graduated with a BA from Barnard College, New York, 1942. She lived in Europe from 1963 and set many of her later works in European locations. She was the author of some of the most admired works in the modern criminous genre, in a style altogether her own and rarely approached, although often imitated, by others. She received the *Grand Prix de Littérature Policière*, 1957, and the Mystery Writers of America Silver Dagger award, 1964.

Writer: Mary Patricia Plaugman HIGHSMITH

Inventor of one other detective Insp CORBY

Citation Record: 4 Books

The Talented Mr Ripley - *First*
Coward McCann US (1955); Cresset UK (1957)

Ripley Under Water - *Last*
Bloomsbury UK (1991)

RISSLER

is an author who is the detective in this one Victorian novel.

British Male Amateur operating in England

Coulson KERNAHAN 1858-1943 (British)

Writer: John Coulson KERNAHAN

Inventor of one other detective MARTEN

Citation Record: 1 Book

Captain Shannon - *Only*
Ward, Lock UK (1897)

Emma RITCHIE

British Female Amateur operating in England

E X FERRARS 1907-1995 (British)

Invented 11 detectives - see Toby DYKE

Citation Record: 1 Book

Experiment With Death - *Only*
Doubleday US (1981)

Elizabeth FERRARS 1907-1995 (British)

Invented 10 detectives - see Toby DYKE

Citation Record: 1 Book

Experiment With Death - *Only*
Collins UK (1981)

Kay RITCHIE

Second detective of Prof James Yates BIDDLE

Lt Max RITTER

Second detective of Dr Daniel Webster COFFEE

Carlito RIVERA

is a Puerto-Rican lawyer who is as sharp as a needle. He investigates the frame-up of a Rican youth and, in a brilliant court performance, gets him off and finds the murderer.

American Male Amateur operating in New York

Carson WOLFE (American)

Writer: UNKNOWN

Citation Record: 1 Book

Murder At La Marimba - *Single*
St Martin's US (1984); Hale UK (1985)

Ed RIVERS

is a middle-aged ex-cop from New Jersey who is a PI in Tampa, Florida, where he is in charge of a branch of the Nationwide Detective Agency. He carries a sheathknife round his neck in case his gun is not sufficient for dealing with the various violent characters he is apt to meet around the place.

American Male Private Detective operating in Florida

Talmage POWELL 1920- (American)

was born in Hendersonville, North Carolina, He is best known as the author of many criminous short stories, published at first in the pulps of the 1940s and later in most of the main crime magazines.

Other Byline: Ellery QUEEN

Citation Record: 5 Books

The Killer Is Mine - *First*
Pocket Books US (1959)

Corpus Delectable - *Last*
Pocket Books US (1964)

Ch Insp Julian RIVERS

is a cut above the ordinary British cop, being an art connoisseur and a romantic, neither of which qualities prevent him solving some tricky cases.

British Policeman operating in England

Carol CARNAC 1894-1958 (British)

See main detective Insp RYVET

Citation Record: 15 Books

A Double For Detection - *First*
Macdonald UK (1945)

Clue Sinister - *Last*
Macdonald UK (1967)

Mabelle RIVERS

British Female Amateur operating in England

Alice MILLARD 1882- (British)

For writer details see Garnett BELL

Citation Record: 1 Book

Mabelle Rivers, Girl Detective - *Only*
In 'Girl's Friend' UK (ca 1915)

Paul RIVINGTON

British Male Amateur operating in England

Gerald VERNER 1886-1980 (British)

Invented 7 detectives - see Supt BUDD

Citation Record: 2 Books

The Con Man - *First*
Wright & Brown UK (1934)

White Wig - *Last*
Wright & Brown UK (1935)

Capt RIZZI

Policeman operating in Venice

Thomas STERLING 1921- (American)

Writer: Thomas L STERLING

Citation Record: 2 Books

The Evil Of The Day - *First*
Simon & Schuster US (1955); Gollancz UK (1955)

Murder In Venice - *First**
Dell US (1959)

The Silent Siren - *Last*
Simon & Schuster US (1958); Gollancz UK (1958)

Supt ROACH

solves a case of death by shooting in a locked room.

British Policeman operating in England

A C TREVOR 1902- (British)

Writer: Norman George PULSFORD

Citation Record: 1 Book

Death Haunts The Lounge - *Only*
Harrap UK (1936)

Sampson ROACH

tracks a missing heiress through the low life of New York.

American Male Private Detective operating in New York

Will SQUERENT (American)

Writer: Will Wilbur BRADBURY

Citation Record: 1 Book

Your Golden Jugular - *Only*
Macmillan US (1970); Hale UK (1971)

Sheila ROATH

Second detective of Stephen BELLECROIX

Donald ROBAK

is a crusading criminal lawyer in the fictional riverside town of Bington. He takes on cases solely to help the outcasts of society, whom the law cannot or will not help.

American Male Amateur operating in Indiana

Joe L HENSLEY 1926- (American)

was born in Bloomington, Indiana. He graduated at Indiana University, Bloomington, with a BA, 1950, and an LLB, 1955. He has since had a distinguished career at the US Bar, being appointed a judge, 1977.

Writer: Joseph Louis HENSLEY

Citation Record: 8 Books 1 Collection

Deliver Us To Evil - *First*
Doubleday US (1971)

Robak's Run - *Latest*
Doubleday US (1990)

Robak's Firm - *Collection 1*
Doubleday US (1987)

Dave ROBBINS and Max THERINGER

ROBBINS is a man in advertising and *THERINGER* is a crime reporter.

American Male Amateurs operating in New York

Henry SLESAR 1927- (American)

See main detective Steve TYNER

Citation Record: 1 Book

The Gray Flannel Shroud - *Only*
Random House US (1959); Deutsch UK (1960)

Amanda ROBERTS and Joe DANELLI

American Female Amateur and American Male Amateur operating in Georgia

Sherryl WOODS 1944- (American)

Citation Record: 3 Books

Body And Soul - *First*
Popular Library US (1989); Severn UK (1990)

Stolen Moments - *Latest*
Popular Library US (1990); Severn UK (1991)

George ROBERTS

British Male Amateur operating in England

Maurice SYMONS 1904- (British)

Writer: Maurice Albert SYMONS

Citation Record: 3 Books

The Girl In Ocean View - *First*
Boardman UK (1961)

Lot 41 - Dead Auctioneer - *Last*
Boardman UK (1964)

Mitch ROBERTS

appears in cases set back into the 1950s.

American Male Private Detective operating in Wichita

Gaylord DOLD (American)

is an attorney in Kansas.

Citation Record: 4 Books

Hot Summer, Cold Murder - *First*
Avon US (1987)

Bonepile - *Latest*
US (1988)

Prudence ROBERTS

American Female Amateur operating in USA

Cornell WOOLRICH 1903-1968 (American)

Invented 3 detectives - see Hal JEFFRIES

Citation Record: 1 Book

The Book That Squealed
US (19??)

Punch ROBERTS and Bonny CUTLER

American Male Amateur and American Female Amateur operating in Los Angeles

Joe HYAMS 1923- (American)

Citation Record: 1 Book

Murder At The Academy Awards - *Single*
St Martin's US (1983)

Randy ROBERTS

is a lawyer who chases women as much as he chases cases.

American Male Amateur operating in San Francisco

Carter BROWN 1923-1985 (Australian)

Invented 10 detectives - see Rick HOLMAN

Citation Record: 4 Books

Murder In The Family Way - *First*
Signet US (1971); Horwitz AU (1972)

Sex Trap - *Last*
Signet US (1975); Horwitz AU (1975)

Insp Taff ROBERTS

British Policeman operating in England

Roger PARKES 1933- (British)

Writer: Roger Graham PARKES

Other Detectives:
Col CALPIN — Supt WALSH

Citation Record: 2 Books

An Abuse Of Justice - *First*
Collins UK (1988)

Camelord - *Latest*
Collins UK (1990)

Zack ROBERTS

is assisted by a friendly CIA agent as he works to halt a terrorist plot to detonate an atomic bomb at the North Pole.

American Male Sleuth operating in the Arctic

Robert KATZ 1933- (American)

See main detective Tony MCINTYRE

Citation Record: 1 Book

Ziggurat - *Single*
Houghton Mifflin US (1977); Eyre & Spottiswoode UK (1978)

Det Dave ROBICHAUX

is in the New Orleans Police Department. A Cajun, a war veteran and an ex-alcoholic, he works the town with his roughneck partner, always tangling with authority and the sleazy side of politics in the Big Easy. He resigns from the force in disgust and thereafter works, usually for personal reasons, on some bad cases. *ROBICHAUX* is not a run of the mill detective. He is a flawed knight, deeply conscious of the imperfections of the world around him and the need to do something about them.

American Policeman operating in Louisiana

Sidekick: Cletus PURCEL
is rough and tough. He was the detective's partner in the force and returned to work with him after he resigned.
American Male - Assistant

James Lee BURKE 1936- (American)

was born in Houston, Texas, and graduated with a BA in English from the University of Missouri, Columbia, 1959. He has worked in various professions in the Southern states, especially as a Lecturer in English. He has written several non-genre and criminous novels and received the Mystery Writers of America Edgar Allan Poe award, 1989.

Citation Record: 6 Books

The Neon Rain - *First*
Holt US (1987); Mysterious Press UK (1989)

Dixie City Jam - *Latest*
Hyperion US (1994)

John ROBIE
American Male Amateur

David DODGE 1910- (American)

Invented 4 detectives - see Al COLBY

Citation Record: 1 Book

To Catch A Thief - *Only*
Random House US (1952); Joseph UK (1953)

George ROBIN
is mystified by bodies that come and go.
American Male Private Detective operating in New York

Owen Fox JEROME 1897-1963 (American)

Writer: Oscar Jerome FRIEND

Other Detectives:
Philip MACCRAY
Philip MACCRAY and Artemus GRAHAM

Citation Record: 1 Book

The Corpse Awaits - *Only*
Mystery House US (1946); Wells Gardner UK (1948)

Wilmurt ROBIN
solves a case of theft from a guarded room.
American Male Amateur operating in USA

Russell HUGHES

Citation Record: 1 Selected Short Story

Seeing Is Believing
In 'Ellery Queen's Mystery Magazine' US (1944)

Insp ROBINET
British Policeman operating in England

Kem BENNETT 1919- (British)

Writer: Kemys Deverell BENNETT

Citation Record: 1 Book

The Wink - *Only*
Hart UK (1951)

The Fabulous Wink - *Only**
Pellegrini US (1951)

Const ROBINS
British Policeman operating in England

Marguerite STAND (British)

Inventor of one other detective Bill RICE

Citation Record: 2 Books

Murder In The Camp - *First*
Hale UK (1964)

Diana Is Dead - *Last*
Hale UK (1967)

Nan ROBINSON
is an attorney for the California State Bar and a relentless investigator.
American Female Amateur operating in California

Taffy CANNON (American)

Citation Record: 2 Books

A Pocketful Of Khama - *First*
Carroll & Graf US (1993)

Tangled Roots - *Latest*
Carroll & Graf US (1995)

ROBSON and Edwin BOUSFIELD
provide an early example of a Scotland Yard detective and private investigator working together to solve a case of murder.
British Policeman and British Male Private Detective operating in London

B L FARJEON 1838-1903 (British)

Invented 7 detectives - see Robert AGNOLD

Citation Record: 1 Book

Samuel Boyd Of Catchpole Square: A Mystery - *Only*
Hutchinson UK (1899)

Dean Wardlow ROCK
appeared in eighteen stories in *Dime Detective,* his cases being narrated by his sidekick.
American Male Detective in Pulp Magazines operating in USA

Sidekick: Ben MATTHEWS
American Male - Narrator

Merle CONSTINER (American)

See main detective Luther MCGAVOCK

Citation Record: 1 Selected Short Story

Strangler's Kill
In 'Dime Detective' US (1940)

Johnny ROCK
American Male Sleuth operating in USA

Bruno ROSSI (American)

House Name.

Citation Record: 9 Books

The Killing Machine - *First*
Leisure Books US (1973)

A Dirty Way To Die - *Last*
Leisure Books US (1975)

Bruno ROSSI (American)

Writer: Paul HOFRICHTER

Citation Record: 2 Books

Savage Slaughter - *First*
Leisure Books US (1975)

Scar Faced Killer - *Last*
Leisure Books US (1975)

Bruno ROSSI 1935- (American)

Writer: Leonard LEVINSON

Citation Record: 3 Books

Head Crusher - *First*
Leisure Books US (1974)

The Worst Way TO Die - *Last*
Leisure Books US (1974)

Bruno ROSSI (American)

sometimes wrote *Phillip (The Marksman) MAGELLAN* stories (uncited) as *Frank SCARPETTA.*

Writer: Russell SMITH

Citation Record: 1 Book

Trigger Man - *Only*
Leisure Books US (1975)

Bruno ROSSI (American)

For writer details see John MARSHALL

Citation Record: 2 Books

Hit Man - *First*
Leisure Books US (1974)

Las Vegas Vengeance - *Last*
Leisure Books US (1975)

Jim ROCKFORD
appears in novelizations of episodes from a TV series.
American Male Private Detective operating in USA

Michael JAHN 1943- (American)

Writer: Joseph Michael JAHN
Other Byline: Nick CARTER

Inventor of one other detective pair Frank MACBRIDE and Pete RYAN

Citation Record: 2 Books

The Unfortunate Replacement - *First*
Popular Library US (1975)

The Deadliest Game - *Latest*
Popular Library US (1976)

Chris ROCKWELL and Sarah SABER
are intimate lovers but work independently in solving overlapping cases for an agency calling itself Inquiries Inc. which specialises in corporate crime.
American Male Private Detective and American Female Private Detective operating in Connecticut

R

David LINZEE 1952- (American)

Writer: David Augustine Anthony LINZEE

Citation Record: 2 Books

Discretion - *First*
Seaview US (1977); Hale UK (1981)

Belgravia - *Latest*
Seaview US (1979); Hale UK (1982)

Nick ROCKWELL

British Male Amateur operating in England

A M BURRAGE 1889-1956 (British)

Writer: Alfred McLelland BURRAGE

Citation Record: 1 Book

Don't Break The Seal - *Only*
Swan UK (1946)

Rocky ROCKWELL

American Male Amateur operating in USA/Europe

Jack IAMS 1910-1990 (American)

Writer: Samuel Harvey IAMS Jr

Citation Record: 3 Books

Do Not Murder Before Christmas - *First*
Morrow US (1949)

What Rhymes With Murder? - *Last*
Morrow US (1950); Gollancz UK (1951)

Aaron RODD

British Male Amateur operating in England

E Phillips OPPENHEIM 1866-1946 (British)

Invented 27 detectives - see Nicholas GOADE

Citation Record: 10 Short Stories in 1 Collection

Aaron Rodd, Diviner - *Collection 1*
Hodder & Stoughton UK (1920); Little, Brown US (1927)

Sheriff Jess RODEN

is a bachelor and a backwoodsman who is the sheriff of Deer Lick, Kentucky. He uses his keen powers of observation and the skill of his five hunting dogs to solve local crimes.

American Policeman operating in Kentucky

A B CUNNINGHAM 1888-1962 (American)

Writer: Albert Benjamin CUNNINGHAM

Citation Record: 20 Books

Murder At Deer Lick - *First*
Dutton US (1939)

Strange Return - *Last*
Dutton US (1952)

R

Insp RODERICKS

Canadian Policeman operating in Canada

Dougal MCLEISH (Canadian)

!See Appendix 2.

Writer: D J GOODSPEED

Citation Record: 1 Book

The Valentine Victim - *Only*
Houghton US (1969)

Insp RODWAY

British Policeman operating in England

John Knox RYLAND (British)

Citation Record: 3 Books

The Tragedy Near Tring - *First*
Paul UK (1934)

Death Meets The Coroner - *Last*
Paul UK (1936)

Jerry 'Renegade' ROE and Stuart WORTH

Jerry ROE is half Cherokee Indian and half Irish, and looks like it. Libidinous to the extreme, he runs a detective agency with his puritanical partner, *Stuart WORTH.*

American Male Private Detectives operating in New Orleans

L V ROPER (American)

Writer: Lester V ROPER

Inventor of one other detective Michael SAXON

Citation Record: 2 Books

The Red Horse Caper - *First*
Popular Library US (1975)

The Emerald Chicks Caper - *Last*
Popular Library US (1976)

Sgt Edmund ROERSCH

American Policeman operating in New York

Herbert D KASTLE 1924- (American)

Writer: Herbert David KASTLE

Citation Record: 2 Books

The Gang - *First*
Dell US (1976); Allen UK (1977)

Death Squad - *Last*
Delacorte US (1977); Allen UK (1978)

Hit Squad - *Last**
Mayflower UK (1978)

Rody ROGAN

Irish Male Detective in Pulp Magazines operating in USA

Bernard WAYDE (American)

Invented 3 detectives - see Larry MURTAGH

Citation Record: 1 Selected Short Story

Rody Rogan, The Detective From Ireland; Or, In Search Of The Thug With The Yellow Club
Old Cap Collier Library US (18??)

ROGER THE CHAPMAN

is a pedlar from Bristol who travels to London in the year 1741 and is asked to investigate the disappearance of a merchant's son. He continues to be called in to deal with crimes and murders.

British Male Amateur operating in London

Kate SEDLEY (British)

Citation Record: 4 Books

Death And The Chapman - *First*
HarperCollins UK

The Holy Innocents - *Latest*
HarperCollins UK (1994)

'Bull' ROGERS

Male Sleuth

Arnold BREDE (American)

Citation Record: 2 Books

The Climbing Corpse - *First*
Cooper UK (1952)

An Outside Job - *Last*
Cooper UK (1952)

Det Supt George ROGERS

is a senior cop in the fictional town of Thurnholme, somewhere towards England's bleak north. Just reaching middle-age, *George ROGERS* is divorced and taking full advantage of his newly acquired bachelor state; for he is irascible, intelligent and lustful, enjoying the chase as much as eventual victory. In his work he is a sleuth in the classic mode, appearing in a series of elegantly designed detective stories. To prove it, he speaks in an amazing style of convoluted but beautifully composed prose, which even *Lord Peter WIMSEY* or his transatlantic cousin, *Ellery QUEEN,* might envy – if they could get the gist.

British Policeman operating in England

Sidekick: Ch Insp LINGARD
is surprisingly elegant and well-mannered for this rough game. With his tailored clothes, his snuff-taking and his habit of saying 'Egad' at times, he is an excellent second-in-command and foil for his clever but rather scruffy boss.
British Male - Subordinate

Jonathan ROSS 1916- (British)
was born in Staverton, Devon, and educated at military schools in England. He served in the Royal Air Force, 1943-1945, and as a detective in the Wiltshire police force, 1939-69.
Writer: John ROSSITER
Citation Record: 17 Books
The Blood Running Cold - *First*
Cassell UK (1968)
Dead Eye - *Latest*
Constable UK (1992)

Prof Huntoon ROGERS

is a Professor of English at a university in Los Angeles. He is in his thirties, grim-faced but pleasant, and seems to do very little in the way of professorial work. Instead he has to devote his time to solving murder cases, which crop up not only near home but in various exotic locales to which he is inexplicably called.

American Male Amateur operating in California

Clifford KNIGHT 1886- (American)
was born in Fulton, Kansas. He was educated at the University of Michigan, Ann Arbor, and became a newspaper editor and crime writer.
Writer: Clifford Reynolds KNIGHT
Citation Record: 18 Books
The Affair Of The Scarlet Crab - *First*
Dodd, Mead US (1937); Gollancz UK (1937)
The Affair Of The Sixth Button - *Last*
McKay US (1947)

Jay ROGERS

becomes involved in a case involving a girl who escapes after her arrest for murder.

American Male Private Detective operating in San Francisco

Leslie EDGELY 1912- (American)
is the author of at least ten genre books.
Citation Record: 1 Book
Fear No More - *Only*
Simon & Schuster US (1946); Barker UK (1948)

Paul ROGERS

British Male Amateur operating in England

Peter DICKINSON 1927- (British)
Invented 3 detectives - see Supt James PIBBLE
Citation Record: 1 Book
Hindsight - *Single*
Bodley Head UK (1983); Pantheon US (1983)

Pogy ROGERS

Second detective of Beau SMITH

Leo ROI

is both a lawyer and private eye. Unlike the usual run of shamuses, however, he is the son of a French baron who imported fine liquor for Al Capone. Enormously wealthy, he lives on the shore of Lake Michigan and simply loves doing detective work.

French Male Private Detective operating in France

Phillips LORE 1942-1988 (American)
Writer: Terrence Lore SMITH
Citation Record: 3 Books
Who Killed The Pie Man? - *First*
Saturday Review Press US (1975)
Murder Behind Closed Doors - *Latest*
Playboy US (1980)

Guy ROLAND

has taken over a detective agency owned by a benefactor who reared him and gave him his name. His one case is to discover his own identity.

French Male Private Detective operating in Paris

Patrick MODIANO 1945- (French)
Writer: Patrick Jean MODIANO
Citation Record: 1 Book
Missing Person - *Single*
is a translation from the French of *Rue Des Boutiques Obscures* (Paris, 1978).
Cape US (1980)

Det Insp James ROLAND

is the enigmatic head of the CID in the fictional small town of Felstone in Suffolk.

British Policeman operating in England

Sidekick: Sgt Patrick MANSFIELD
British Male - Subordinate

Ann QUINTON (British)
is a librarian, artis, and professional musician.
Citation Record: 3 Books
Death Of A Dear Friend - *First*
Piatkus UK (1990)
Fatal End - *Latest*
Piatkus UK (1992)

Mr ROLF

British Policeman operating in England

Sir William MAGNAY 1855-1917 (British)
See main detective Maj FREEMAN
Citation Record: 1 Book
The Cloak Of Darkness - *Only*
Ward, Lock UK (1918)

Sergei ROLF

Male Secret Agent

Terence KELLY (American)
Writer: Terence KELLY
Other Byline: Charles RUSSELL
Citation Record: 2 Books
Long Live The Spy - *First*
was published in the US under the following byline.
Hale UK (1990)
The Spy Is Dead - *Latest*
was published in the US under the following byline.
Hale UK (1990)

Charles RUSSELL (American)
Writer: Terence KELLY
Other Byline: Terence KELLY
Citation Record: 2 Books
Long Live The Spy - *First*
was published in the UK under the preceding byline.
Doubleday US (1987)
The Spy Is Dead - *Latest*
was published in the UK under the preceding byline.
Doubleday US (1988)

Zachariah Tobias ROLF

works for the casinos, his main task being to catch the many kinds of frauds and cheats who frequent them. This he seems to do, not by high-powered intellectual activity, but by driving around ostentatiously in his Porsche.

American Male Private Detective operating in Las Vegas

J J LAMB (American)
Citation Record: 3 Books
Nickel Jackpot - *First*
Ballantine US (1976)
Losers Take All - *Latest*
Carlyle US (1979)

Helga ROLFE

is a powerful and wealthy lady who, ill-used, gets her own back – and does it twice.

American Female Sleuth operating in USA

James Hadley CHASE 1906-1985 (British)

Invented 14 detectives - see Dave FENNER

Citation Record: 2 Books

An Ace Up My Sleeve - *First*
Hale UK (1971)

The Joker In The Deck - *Last*
Hale UK (1975)

Simon ROLFE

is a so-called 'crime analyst' and says he solves his cases by 'psychological logic'. He tries to emulate his hero, *Sherlock HOLMES*, and even has his tales told by an aptly named sidekick.

American Male Professional Amateur operating in Long Island

Sidekick: Henry F WATSON

American Male - Narrator

Joseph L BONNEY (American)

Citation Record: 2 Books

Death By Dynamite - *First*
Carrick & Evans US (1940)

Murder Without Clues - *Last*
Carrick & Evans US (1940)

No Man's Hand - *Last**
Heinemann UK (1940)

Angela ROLLASON

Second detective of Harry KYLE

Bob ROLLINS

American Male Amateur operating in Chicago

Maurice C JOHNSON (American)

Citation Record: 1 Book

Damning Trifles - *Only*
Knopf US (1932)

Richard (The Toff) ROLLISON

was one of this remarkable author's earlier creations, although he continued to appear in a series that lasted over four decades. A gentleman-adventurer like *The SAINT* of *Leslie CHARTERIS*, he was cast in a mould that was more morally acceptable; for he was no crook – unlike so many of his contemporary gentleman-detectives. He worked *with* Scotland Yard on many occasions, although his activities were not restricted by their official approach. Indeed, he often befriended minor criminals in his relentless pursuit of major ones; and, in the course of his many adventures, he unmasked many a master criminal and rescued many a damsel in distress by his own methods, which were sometimes not quite legal.

R

ROLLISON's background was impeccably English: Charterhouse and Cambridge, a cricketing blue, a First in classics, and great wealth, which allowed him to have a flat at 25G Gresham Terrace in Mayfair, London, and a cottage in the New Forest. He was known as 'The Toff', because of his immaculate dress, courtesy and his ornate visiting cards; and, naturally he had a 'gentleman's gentleman' of a valet, perhaps hardly a real sidekick but so well known that he must be cited.

British Male Professional Amateur operating in England

Sidekick: JOLLY

British Male - Valet

John CREASEY 1908-1973 (British)

Invented 6 detectives - see Insp Roger 'Handsome' WEST

Citation Record: 58 Books

Introducing The Toff - *First*
Long UK (1938)

The Toff And The Dead Man's Finger - *Latest*
Hodder & Stoughton UK (1978)

Robert ROLT

British Male Amateur operating in Europe

Victor CANNING 1911-1986 (British)

Invented 6 detectives - see Rex CARVER

Citation Record: 1 Book

The Finger Of Saturn - *Only*
Heinemann UK (1973); Morrow US (1974)

Dan ROMAN

is a Vietnam War veteran who joined the Dallas police force but quit to set up as a PI. He operates in a plain, business-like, but concerned manner.

American Male Private Detective operating in Texas

Edward MATHIS 1927-1988 (American)

Citation Record: 6 Books

From A High Place - *First*
Scribner's US (1985)

Another Path, Another Dragon - *Latest*
Scribner's US (1988)

Lt ROMANO

has been cited as a stooge for *Bart HARDIN*. He also operates as a detective on his own and appears thus in one book, actually antedating the appearance of *HARDIN*.

American Policeman operating in New York

David ALEXANDER 1907-1973 (American)

Invented 4 detectives - see Bart HARDIN

Citation Record: 1 Book

Murder Points A Finger - *Only*
Random House US (1953); Boardman UK (1955)

Sgt ROMANO

solves the mystery of the disappearance of an apartment and its occupant.

American Policeman operating in USA

Edward D HOCH 1930- (American)

Invented 20 detectives - see Capt LEOPOLD

Citation Record: 1 Selected Short Story

Behind Closed Doors
In 'Woman's World' US (1982)

Tony ROME

is an ex-cop from Miami. A compulsive gambler, he quit the force after his father's suicide and now lives on a boat, *The Straight Pass*, which he won in a card game. He works as a PI solely to earn enough money to get to Las Vegas, intending to break the bank there.

American Male Private Detective operating in Miami

Anthony ROME 1924- (American)

For writer details see Pierre-Ange SAWYER

Citation Record: 3 Books

Miami Mayhem - *First*
was republished under the following byline.
Pocket Books US (1960); Hale UK (1961)

My Kind Of Game - *Last*
Dell US (1962)

Marvin H ALBERT 1924- (American)

See main detective Pierre-Ange SAWYER

Citation Record: 1 Book

Miami Mayhem - *Only*
was previously published under the preceding byline.
Dell US (1967)

Supt ROMER

solves a case of poisoning by carbon monoxide.

British Policeman operating in England

James STREET (British)

Inventor of one other detective Eugene MULCAHY

Citation Record: 1 Book

Carbon Monoxide - *Only*
Low UK (1937)

Sebastian ROMM
Male Sleuth

Philip FREUND 1909-

Citation Record: 7 Short Stories in 1 Collection

The Beholder: Seven Tales For Sebastian Romm - *Collection 1*
Allen UK (1961); British Book Centre US (1963)

Nick RONGETTI
is white-haired and has a purple birthmark on his swarthy face, ideal qualifications for a cop on Broadway in the era of the pulps. He appeared only in short stories, mainly in *Black Aces.*
American Male Detective in Pulp Magazines operating in New York

George BRUCE 1898- (American)

No citations

Nicky ROOD
is a teenager who, to prove his actress mother innocent of the murder of a rival, discovers whodunnit.
American Male Amateur operating in Los Angeles

Patrick QUENTIN 1912-1987 (American)

Invented 6 detectives - see Peter DULUTH

Citation Record: 1 Book

Suspicious Circumstances - *Only*
Simon & Schuster US (1957); Gollancz UK (1957)

Howie ROOK
is a middle-aged, overweight newspaperman who becomes a Hollywood private eye.
American Male Private Detective operating in Hollywood

Stuart PALMER 1905-1968 (American)

Invented 3 detectives - see Hildegarde WITHERS

Citation Record: 2 Books

Death In Grease Paint - *First*
Collins UK (1956)

Unhappy Hooligan - *First**
Harper & Row US (1956)

Rook Takes Knight - *Last*
Random House US (1968)

Terry ROOKE
Second detective of Tommy TWOTOES

The ROOKERY DETECTIVE
American Male Detective in Pulp Magazines operating in USA

ANON

Citation Record: 1 Book

The Rookery Detective - *Only*
Aldine US

Eleanor ROOSEVELT
is indeed the niece, 1882-1962, of *Theodore Roosevelt*, a former President of the United States (also transformed into a fictional detective), and the wife of Franklin D Roosevelt, the President of the United States, 1932-1945. She played an important, even dominant part, in several aspects of American political life and has been made over into a clever amateur detective who solves crimes in the highest political echelons.
American Female Amateur operating in USA

Elliott ROOSEVELT 1910-1990 (American)

is the byline, but it is known that at least some of his books were ghost-written by William Harrington.

Citation Record: 12 Books

Murder And The First Lady - *First*
St Martin's US (1984)

Murder In The Red Room - *Last*
Avon US (1994)

Eleanor ROOSEVELT
Second detective of Toby PETERS

Commiss Theodore ROOSEVELT
is, indeed, the man who went on to become President of the United States in 1891. However, during 1895 to 1897 he was the Commissioner of Police in New York, and three authors to date have utilised him as a fictional detective.
American Policeman operating in New York

Lawrence ALEXANDER 1939- (American)

Citation Record: 3 Books

The Big Stick - *First*
Doubleday US (1986)

The Strenuous Life - *Latest*
US (199?)

William L DEANDREA 1952- (American)

Invented 4 detectives - see Matt COBB

Citation Record: 1 Book

The Lunatic Fringe - *Single*
Evans US (1980)

Theodore ROOSEVELT and Jim WHITE
Theodore ROOSEVELT is, indeed, the one-time President of the United States. It seems here that he has become a target for blackmail, so he sends for an old and trusted friend, *Jim WHITE*, and together they root out the criminal.
American Male Amateurs operating in Washington DC

Mark SCHORR 1953- (American)

Invented 3 detectives - see Red DIAMOND

Citation Record: 1 Book

Bully! - *Single*
St Martin's US (1985)

Theodore ROOSEVELT
Second detective of Sherlock HOLMES

Charlie ROPE
American Male Amateur operating in USA

John ELLER 1935- (American)

Citation Record: 2 Books

Charlie And The Ice Man - *First*
St Martin's US (1981)

Rage Of Heaven - *Latest*
St Martin's US (1982)

Supt ROPER
is a sound British cop in a fictional force somewhere in England. He meets murder cases in which, quite properly, bodies are found in the first chapter and murderers leave substantial clues, such as good old-fashioned cigarette stubs on the scene of the crime. But, regrettably, somebody called the SOCO, a much loved creation of the British crime writer of the last decade, nowadays does much of the work that decent detectives like *ROPER* used to do. For the blissfully uninformed, still blinkered by the British Golden Age, the acronym stands for 'Scene of Crime Officer', and he comes armed with lots of plastic bags in case the real detective should touch anything.
British Policeman operating in England

Sidekick: Insp PRICE
is a regular dummy, a now conventional appendage, whose main function is to say at intervals, 'I hadn't thought of that, Super' or variations on it.
British Male - Subordinate

Roy HART 1930- (British)

Citation Record: 8 Books

A Position Of Trust - *First*
Hale UK (1985); St Martin's US (1985)

Breach Of Promise - *Latest*
Macmillan UK (1990)

Det Ch Insp Ian ROPER

is head of the fictional Rickenham Green police force. He investigates murders in quiet English villages, the kind of locale known to be given to that sort of thing in the British criminous canon.

British Policeman operating in England

Janie BOLITHO (British)

was born in Falmouth, Cornwall. She has been a clerk, a debt collector and a nurse.

Citation Record: 3 Books

Kindness Can Kill - *First*
Constable UK (1993)

Motive For Murder - *Latest*
Constable UK (1994)

Max ROPER

works for some unspecified organisation in Santa Monica and specialises in cases involving crime in the world of sport.

American Male Private Detective operating in California

Kin PLATT 1911- (American)

Inventor of one other detective Molly MELLINGER

Citation Record: 7 Books

The Pushbutton Butterfly - *First*
Random House US (1970); Hale UK (1971)

The Screwball King Murder - *Last*
Random House US (1978)

Piers ROPER

British Male Sleuth operating in several locations

Ken FOLLETT 1949- (British)

was born in Cardiff, Glamorganshire. He took a BA in Philosophy at University College, London, 1949, and has been a reporter, editor, and professional musician and, from 1977, a full-time writer. His books are mainly action thrillers, which usually depend on turning historical events and situations to literary advantage. He received the Mystery Writers of America Edgar Allan Poe award, 1979.

Writer: Kenneth Martin FOLLETT

Other Byline: Simon MYLES

Citation Record: 2 Books

The Shakeout - *First*
Harwood UK (1975)

The Bear Raid - *Last*
Harwood UK (1976)

Konrad ROQUE

Male Amateur operating in England

Guy MORTON 1896-1968 (British)

Writer: Guy Mainwaring MORTON

Citation Record: 3 Books

The Perrin Murder Case - *First*
Skeffington UK (1930); Greenberg US (1934)

The Ragged Robin Murders - *Last*
Skeffington UK (1935); Greenberg US (1937)

Det Insp Alf ROSHER

is a delightful creation, a provincial cop who seems to be everything the British police force can do without. Fat, crude, in dated clothes, lusting, coarse, he is nevertheless – to the absolute incredulity of his superiors – a fine detective who succeeds where others fail.

British Policeman operating in England

Jack S SCOTT 1922- (British)

was born in London. He was an actor, singer and comedian in all media and even had a short career as a singing cowboy.

Writer: Jonathan ESCOTT

Other Detectives:

Sgt ACKROYD — Ch Insp Peter PARSON

Citation Record: 10 Books

The Poor Old Lady's Dead - *First*
Hale UK (1976); Harper & Row US (1976)

A Knife Between The Ribs - *Latest*
Collins UK (1986); St Martin's US (1987)

Supt ROSS

British Policeman operating in England

J J CONNINGTON 1880-1947 (British)

Invented 5 detectives - see Mark BRAND

Citation Record: 2 Books

The Eye In The Museum - *First*
Gollancz UK (1929); Little, Brown US (1930)

The Two Tickets Puzzle - *Last*
Gollancz UK (1930)

The Two Ticket Puzzle - *Last**
Little, Brown US (1930)

Insp ROSS

British Policeman operating in England

Freeman Wills CROFTS 1879-1957 (British)

Invented 4 detectives - see Insp Joseph FRENCH

Citation Record: 1 Book

The Groote Park Murder - *Only*
Collins UK (1924); Seltzer US (1925)

Insp ROSS

American Policeman operating in USA

Lucretia GRINDLE (American)

Citation Record: 1 Book

So Little To Die For - *Single*
Pocket Books US (1994)

Bob ROSS

was in the Military Police before he set up privately. He handles a case of murder on the Stock Exchange.

British Male Private Detective operating in London

Christopher LANDON 1911- (British)

See main detective Harry KENT

Citation Record: 1 Book

Stone Cold Dead In The Market - *Only*
Heinemann UK (1955)

Charity ROSS

American Female Amateur operating in USA

Jack BICKHAM 1930- (American)

Writer: John Miles BICKHAM

Other Byline: John MILES

Inventor of one other detective Joe DUGGER

Citation Record: 2 Books

The War Against Charity Ross - *First*
Doubleday US (1967)

Target: Charity Ross - *Last*
Doubleday US (1968)

Daniel ROSS

American Male Amateur operating in USA

MacKinlay KANTOR 1904-1977 (American)

Invented 4 detectives - see Matt EDWARDS

Citation Record: 1 Selected Short Story

Nobody Saw Him Fall

can also be found in the author's collection, *It's about Crime* (*Signet*, US 1960).

In 'Detective Fiction Weekly' US (1933)

Insp Gordon ROSS

British Policeman operating in England

Lord GORELL 1884-1963 (British)

Writer: Ronald Gorell BARNES

Other Detectives:

Insp Harry FARRANT — Maurice HEPBURN

Maurice HEPBURN and Evelyn TEMPLE

Citation Record: 2 Books

Let Not Thy Left Hand - *First*
Ward, Lock UK (1949)

Murder At Manor House - *Last*
Ward, Lock UK (1954)

Jack ROSS

American Male Private Detective operating in Nevada

Bernard SCHOPEN (American)

was born in South Dakota. He is a sometime Professor of English at Saint Anselm College.

Citation Record: 2 Books

The Big Silence - *First*
Mysterious Press US (1989)

The Desert Look - *Latest*
Mysterious Press US (1990)

Jimmy ROSS

solves the mystery of the disappearance of a house.

American Male Amateur operating in USA

Norman DANIELS (American)

Invented 6 detectives - see Richard Curtis (Phantom) VAN LOAN

Citation Record: 1 Selected Short Story

Enigma Of The Talking Wraith
In '10-Story Detective Magazine' US (1942)

John Thomas ROSS

is an operator for the Mackelroy Agency in Albany, New York.

American Male Private Detective operating in New York

Thomas BUNN 1944- (American)

Citation Record: 1 Book

Closet Bones - *Single*
Putnam US (1977)

Martin ROSS

British Male Private Detective operating in England

Alan ALLYSON (British)

Citation Record: 3 Books

Don't Mess With Murder - *First*
Hale UK (1972)

The Lady Said No - *Last*
Hale UK (1972); Drake US (1977)

Mike ROSS

may be an ordinary PI by day but, at night, he turns into a Superman clone, called The Hitman, who deals peremptorily with villains.

American Male Private Detective operating in Los Angeles

Kirby CARR 1911- (American)

Writer: Kin PLATT

Citation Record: 7 Books

The Girls Who Came To Murder - *First*
Canyon US (1974)

You're Hired; You're Dead - *Last*
Major US (1975)

Lt Dino ROSSI

Second detective of Nina MCFALL

Sir Timothy ROSSITER

British Male Amateur operating in England

Nigel BURNABY 1882- (British)

Writer: Harold Pincton ELLETT

Inventor of one other detective Ch Insp DREWRY

Citation Record: 1 Book

The Clue Of The Green-Eyed Girl - *Only*
Ward, Lock UK (1935)

Tommy ROSTETTER

appears also in one book with the author's other detective, *Insp HEADCORN.*

Male Sleuth operating in Paris

Alice CAMPBELL 1887- (American)

was born in Georgia but emigrated to England, where she wrote over twenty criminous novels.

Writer: Alice Ormond CAMPBELL

Other Detectives:
Insp HEADCORN
Insp HEADCORN and Tommy ROSTETTER

Citation Record: 3 Books

The Click Of The Gate - *First*
Farrar, Straus US (1931); Collins UK (1932)

Flying Blind - *Last*
Collins UK (1938)

Tommy ROSTETTER

Second detective of Insp HEADCORN

Insp Porfiry Petrovich ROSTNIKOV

is a policeman in Soviet Russia. A wounded war veteran, he is an outsider who must manipulate the system to achieve the ends of justice. Unless he can raise a warrant to get the use of a police car, he travels to his cases by public transport. He is an avid reader of the Russian classics and also of 'forbidden' American crime fiction, being an admirer of *Ed MCBAIN.* Called 'Washtub' by his colleagues, he spends his spare time in weight-lifting and repairing bad plumbing. The latter skill often allows him to enter premises to obtain information from unwilling witnesses.

Russian Policeman operating in Moscow

Sidekick: SASHA

is a young man whose sense of humour helps alleviate the dreariness of some of his superior's cases.

Russian Male - Assistant

Sidekick: KARPO

is a Tartar and an obsessive cop who never gives up. Like his boss, he too endures pain from a bad war wound.

Russian Male - Assistant

Stuart M KAMINSKY 1934- (American)

Invented 18 detectives - see Toby PETERS and Errol FLYNN

Citation Record: 6 Books

Black Knight In Red Square - *First*
Berkley US (1984); Macdonald UK (1988)

Death Of A Russian Priest - *Latest*
Scribner's US (1992)

Max ROTH

British Male Sleuth operating in several locations

Harry ARVAY 1925- (British)

was the author of several criminous books, most of them apparently ghosted by *Gil BREWER.*

Citation Record: 9 Books

The Meirovitz Plan - *First*
Corgi UK (1975)

The Swiss Deal - *Last*
Corgi UK (1976)

Rosalind ROTH

American Female Amateur operating in Pennsylvania

Betsy ASWAD 1939- (American)

Citation Record: 1 Book

Winds Of The Old Day - *Single*
Dial US (1980)

Joseph ROULETABILLE

appeared in two historic tales that set new dimensions in the development of the early detective story. An eighteen-year-old reporter who gets his name from the fact that his head resembles a billiard-ball, he is rather given to making mysterious remarks that baffle his assistant and most other people. However, he does solve two locked-room mysteries that seem insoluble.

French Male Amateur operating in France

Sidekick: SAINCLAIR
is a lawyer. He narrates the cases of the detective and is, in some respects, a true antecedent of the great *Dr WATSON*, being absolutely loyal and always perplexed.
French Male - Narrator

Gaston LEROUX 1868-1927 (French)
Inventor of one other detective CHERI-BIBI
Citation Record: 4 Books
The Mystery Of The Yellow Room - *First*
is a translation from the French of *Le Mystère de la Chambre Jaune* (Paris, 1908).
In 'Daily Mail' UK (1908); Brentano's US (1908)
Murder In The Bedroom - *First**
Brussel (1945)
The Sleuth Hound - *Last*
Long UK (1926)
The Octopus Of Paris - *Last**
Macaulay US (1927)

Stonewall ROUNTREE
solves a case of death by shooting in a locked room.
American Male Sleuth operating in USA

Jesse CARMACK (American)
Citation Record: 1 Book
The Tell-Tale Clock Mystery - *Only*
Stokes US (1937)

Peter ROURKE
Male Sleuth operating in Hong Kong/India

David C COOKE 1917-
Writer: David Coxe COOKE
Citation Record: 3 Books
The 14th Agent - *First*
Dodd, Mead US (1967); Hale UK (1968)
C/o American Embassy - *Last*
Dodd, Mead US (1967); Hale UK (1968)

Steve ROURKE
works on a case for a timber millionaire.
American Male Professional Investigator operating in Washington DC

Stuart BROCK 1917- (American)
For writer details see Martin ZANE
Other Detectives:
Pete CORY   Bert NORDEN
Citation Record: 1 Book
Death Is My Lover - *Only*
Mill US (1948)

R

Timothy ROURKE
Male Sleuth operating in California

Jack WOLF 1922- (British)
Writer: Jack Clifford WOLF
Citation Record: 2 Books
Two Shadows For Death - *First*
Hammond UK (1961)
Payoff On Fever Street - *Last*
Hammond UK (1962)

George ROWE
American Male Amateur operating in USA

Edmund G LOVE 1912- (American)
Writer: Edmund George LOVE
Citation Record: 1 Book
Set-Up - *Single*
Doubleday US (1980)
Set A Trap - *Single**
Hale UK (1981)

Parker ROWE
American Male Private Detective operating in North Carolina

William MANER (American)
See main detective Wilson HARLEY
Citation Record: 1 Book
The Image Killer - *Only*
Doubleday US (1968); Hale UK (1970)

Zachary T ROWLAND
is a lawyer and part-time government secret agent who cracks a Nazi spy plot in Bermuda.
American Male Professional Investigator operating in Bermuda

David GARTH 1908- (American)
Citation Record: 1 Book
Bermuda Calling - *Only*
Putnam US (1944)

Det Supt Bill ROWLANDS
is a big wheel in the Scotland Yard Murder Squad.
British Policeman operating in England

Norman LUCAS (British)
Citation Record: 4 Books
Corner In Crime - *First*
Jenkins UK (1952); Roy US (1957)
Situations Vacant - *Last*
Jenkins UK (1956)

Det Sgt Tony ROWLEY
is a Scotland Yard cop who goes to New York on a manhunt and comes up against power politics from both the British and American authorities.
British Policeman operating in London

Roger BUSBY 1941- (British)
Invented 3 detectives - see Det Insp LERIC
Citation Record: 2 Books
The Hunter - *First*
Collins UK (1985); Doubleday US (1989)
Crackshot - *Latest*
Collins UK (1990)

Max ROYAL
works for the Cranmer Detective Agency.
American Male Private Detective operating in USA

Carter BROWN 1923-1985 (Australian)
Invented 10 detectives - see Rick HOLMAN
Citation Record: 1 Book
A Siren Sounds Off - *Only*
Horwitz AU (1958)
The Myopic Mermaid - *Only**
New American Library US (1961)

ROYCE
Canadian Policeman operating in Canada

Amos MOORE 1884-1958 (Canadian)
Writer: George Barron HUBBARD
Citation Record: 1 Book
Royce Of The Royal Mounted - *Only*
Harlequin US (1950)

Rupert ROYCE
British Male Sleuth

James ALDRIDGE 1918- (British)
Writer: Harold Edward James ALDRIDGE
Inventor of one other detective Kit QUAYLE
Citation Record: 2 Books
A Captive In The Land - *First*
Hamilton UK (1962); Doubleday US (1963)
The Statesman's Game - *Last*
Hamish Hamilton UK (1966); Doubleday US (1966)

Insp ROYLE

is slow-witted, corrupt, unpleasant and unlikeable. However, he solves the murder of a visiting professor from Oxford in the fictional University of Drummondville in a remote part of Australia.

Australian Policeman operating in Australia

Robert BARNARD 1936- (British)

Invented 13 detectives - see Insp Perry TRETHOWAN

Citation Record: 1 Book

Death Of An Old Goat - *Only*
Collins UK (1974); Walker US (1977)

Joan Daisy ROYLE

American Female Amateur operating in USA

Edwin BALMER 1883-1959 (American)

was born in Chicago. He graduated with an AB from Northwestern University, Evanston, Illinois, 1902, and took an AM at Harvard University, Cambridge, Massachusetts, 1903. Reporter and publisher, he wrote several early detective novels under his own name as well as with collaborators.

Citation Record: 1 Book

That Royle Girl - *Only*
Dodd, Mead US (1925)

Det Insp RUBY

British Policeman operating in Edinburgh

David FLETCHER 1940-1988 (British)

was born in Reading, Berkshire. He graduated, 1959, from Leeds University, Yorkshire, and later worked mainly in publishing. He wrote twelve genre books under this pseudonym and mainstream novels under other names, as well as critical literary works.

Writer: Dulan Friar Whilberton BARBER

Other Detectives:
Sgt JOLLEY   A J RAFFLES

Citation Record: 1 Book

A Lovable Man - *Only*
Macmillan UK (1974)

Hugh RUDD

British Male Amateur operating in England

Howard Charles DAVIS 1909- (British)

Inventor of one other detective Edward TOPE

Citation Record: 2 Books

The Waxworks Spies - *First*
Ward, Lock UK (1962)

Murder Starts From Fishguard - *Last*
Long UK (1966)

Matt RUDD

is a Vice cop in the fictional town of St Cecilia, where corruption and vice abound. His real name was Mateus Ruddiski.

American Policeman operating in California

Richard DEMING 1915-1983 (American)

Invented 4 detectives - see Manville MOON

Citation Record: 3 Books

Vice Cop - *First*
Belmont US (1961)

Death Of A Pusher - *Last*
Pocket Books US (1964)

Insp RUDGE

appeared in a remarkable book written by *The DETECTION CLUB*, a closed society of British detective writers during the 1930s. In 1931, twelve of the most revered crime writers in the land got together and wrote one chapter each, without prior consultation, of a novel, *THE FLOATING ADMIRAL*. The twelfth, *Anthony BERKELEY* no less, provided what he regarded as the solution, although some of the others also wrote short solutions of their own. The authors were, in order of writing, *Victor L WHITECHURCH, G D H & Margaret COLE, Henry WADE, Agatha CHRISTIE, John RHODE, Milward KENNEDY, Dorothy L SAYERS, Ronald A KNOX, Freeman Wills CROFTS, Edgar JEPSON, Clemence DANE* and *Anthony BERKELEY*. A prologue was written by *G K CHESTERTON*.

British Policeman operating in England

The DETECTION CLUB (British)

was a coterie of some of the best British authors of the 1930s who had the bright idea of writing a book or two together, often with each author doing one chapter.

Citation Record: 1 Book

The Floating Admiral - *Only*
concerns the murder of a retired Admiral of the British Navy, whose body is found afloat on a small boat in an English river. Clever and still very worth reading.
Macmillan UK (1931)

Dan RUDNICKI

is from a Ukrainian family, now in Canada.

Canadian Male Private Detective operating in Canada

Paul GRESCOE 1931- (Canadian)

was born in Winnipeg and is a reporter and columnist for Canadian newspapers.

Citation Record: 2 Books

Flesh Wound - *First*
McClelland & Stewart CA (1992)

Blood Vessel - *Latest*
McClelland & Stewart CA (1993)

Bob RUFF

brilliantly solves a case of tax racketeering.

American Male Private Detective operating in Chicago

Carl G HODGES 1902-1964 (American)

Citation Record: 1 Book

Murder By The Pack - *Only*
Ace US (1953)

Peter RUFF

British Male Amateur operating in England

E Phillips OPPENHEIM 1866-1946 (British)

Invented 27 detectives - see Nicholas GOADE

Citation Record: 12 Short Stories in 1 Collection

Peter Ruff - *Collection 1*
Hodder & Stoughton UK (1912)

Peter Ruff And The Double Four - *Collection 1**
Little, Brown US (1912)

R

Peter RUFF

British Male Amateur operating in England

Reginald E SALWAY (British)

Writer: Reginald Ernest SALWAY

Citation Record: 10 Short Stories in 1 Collection

My Masters; Or, The Strange Experiences Of Peter Ruff In Domestic Service - *Collection 1*
Not all the stories are criminous.
Heath UK (1920)

Ch Matt RUFFINS

is called in to solve a murder or two at the fictional Jonas B Steele College for Women in New England, where the usual odd academic types provide suspects thick on the campus.

American Policeman operating in New England

Chad PILGRIM (American)

Citation Record: 1 Book

The Silent Slain - *Only*
Abelard Schuman US (1958); Abelard Schuman UK (1958)

John RUGBY

American Male Detective in Pulp Magazines operating in USA

Warne MILLER (American)
Invented 4 detectives - see Silas QUIRK
Citation Record: 1 Selected Short Story
John Rugby, The Ferryboat Detective; Or, The North River Mystery
Old Cap Collier Library US (18??)

Reggie RUGGLES and Sgt TROTTER
get to grips with all kinds of nonsensical goings-on during seances.
British Male Amateur and British Policeman operating in England

T C H JACOBS 1899-1976 (British)
Invented 8 detectives - see Ch Insp BARNARD
Citation Record: 1 Book
Appointment With The Hangman - *Only*
Paul UK (1936); Macaulay US (1936)

John RUMFORD
British Male Amateur operating in England

G H TEED 1878-1939 (British)
Invented 6 detectives - see Roxane HARFIELD
Citation Record: 2 Books
The Digger 'Tec - *First*
Amalgamated UK (1927)
The Three Gold Feathers - *Last*
Amalgamated UK (1927)

Horace RUMPOLE
is a brilliant but rascally lawyer who solves many a case and wins many a court encounter.
British Male Amateur operating in London

John MORTIMER 1923- (British)
was born in London. He was educated at Harrow School, Middlesex, took a BA at Brasenose College, Oxford, 1942, and was called to the Bar, 1948. He became a Queen's Counsel, 1966, and Master of the Bench, Inner Temple, 1975. He has been the drama critic for several journals and has written plays, filmscripts, and works for all media, in addition to works of biography. He has received several awards for his literary work and was made a CBE, 1986.
Writer: John Clifford MORTIMER
Citation Record: 1 Book 44 Short Stories in 7 Collections
Rumpole's Return - *Single*
Penguin UK (1980); Penguin US (1982)
Rumpole Of The Bailey - *Collection 1*
Short stories - 6
Penguin UK (1978); Penguin US (1978)
The Trials Of Rumpole - *Collection 2*
Short stories - 6
Penguin UK (1979); Penguin US (1981)
Regina V Rumpole - *Collection 3*
Short stories - 7
Lane UK (1981)
Rumpole And The Golden Thread - *Collection 4*
Short stories - 6
Penguin UK (1983); Penguin US (1984)
Rumpole's Last Case - *Collection 5*
Short stories - 6
Penguin UK (1987); Penguin US (1988)
Rumpole And The Age Of Miracles - *Collection 6*
Short stories - 7
Penguin UK (1988); Penguin US (1989)
Rumpole A La Carte - *Collection 7*
Short stories - 6
Viking UK (1990); Viking US (1990)

RUNE
American Male Sleuth operating in New York

Jeffrey Wilds DEAVER (American)
Citation Record: 2 Books
Manhattan Is My Beat - *First*
Bantam US (1989)
Death Of A Blue Movie Star - *Latest*
Bantam US (1990)

Insp Myles RUSBY
British Policeman operating in England

Virgil MARKHAM 1899- (British)
Other Detectives:
Ed BOND
Insp FROST and Toni STAPLETON
George PETERS
Supt SALT and Paula LEBETWOOD
Citation Record: 2 Books
Inspector Rusby's Finale - *First*
Collins UK (1933); Farrar, Straus US (1933)
The Deadly Jest - *Last*
Collins UK (1935)

Alexander RUSH
is a disgraced ex-cop who is now a PI. He appears only in some short stories by the distinguished author.
American Male Private Detective operating in USA

Dashiell HAMMETT 1894-1961 (American)
Invented 7 detectives - see Sam SPADE
Citation Record: 1 Selected Short Story
The Assistant Murderer
In 'Black Mask Magazine' US (1926)

Click RUSH
was one of this author's numerous pulp detectives. Tall, wiry, fond of brown suits and brown everything else, he was known as 'The Gadget Man' as he was always inventing gizmos to catch crooks.
American Male Detective in Pulp Magazines operating in USA

Lester DENT 1904-1959 (American)
Invented 9 detectives - see Chance MALLOY
No citations

Grant RUSHTON
British Male Amateur operating in Egypt/Haiti

G H TEED 1878-1939 (British)
Invented 6 detectives - see Roxane HARFIELD
Citation Record: 3 Books
Bottom Of Suez - *First*
Columbine UK (1939)
Voodoo Island - *Last*
Columbine UK (1939)

Brady RUSKIN and Whit TRAXLER
American Male Sleuths operating in California

William Colt MACDONALD 1891- (American)
See main detective Gregory QUIST
Citation Record: 1 Book
The Gloved Saskia - *Only*
Avalon US (1964); Hodder & Stoughton UK (1965)

Alan RUSSELL
appears also in two books with the author's other detective, *Insp DUFFY.*
British Male Amateur operating in Ireland

Nigel FITZGERALD 1906- (British)
Invented 3 detectives - see Insp DUFFY
Citation Record: 2 Books
The Candles Are All Out - *First*
Collins UK (1960); Macmillan US (1961)
Ghost In The Making - *Last*
Collins UK (1960)

Alan RUSSELL
Second detective of Insp DUFFY

Col Charles RUSSELL

is the head of some sort of secret service unit run by the British government. Although basically a man of action, he does the usual amount of sleuthing necessary when dealing with the usual foreign rotters.

British Male Secret Agent operating in several locations

William HAGGARD 1907- (British)

was born in Croydon, Surrey. He was educated at Lancing College, Sussex, and took a BA at Christ Church College, Oxford. He served in the Indian Civil Service, 1931-1939, and in the Indian Army, 1939-1946, reaching the rank of Lieutenant Colonel.

Writer: Richard Henry Michael CLAYTON

Other Detectives:
Paul MARTINY
Dorothy Mayotte RIGBY
William Wilberforce SMITH

Citation Record: 22 Books

Slow Burner - *First*
Cassell UK (1958); Little, Brown US (1958)

The Vendettists - *Latest*
Hodder & Stoughton UK (1990)

Franklin RUSSELL

American Male Amateur operating in USA

Richard M BAKER 1896- (American)

Writer: Richard Merriam BAKER

Citation Record: 1 Book

Death Stops The Manuscript - *First*
Scribner's US (1936)

Death Stops The Bells - *Last*
Scribner's US (1938)

Rony RUSSO

American Male Amateur operating in USA

William J COUGHLIN 1924- (American)

Writer: William Jeremiah COUGHLIN

Other Byline: Sean A KEY

Citation Record: 1 Book

The Stalking Man - *Single*
Delacorte US (1979); Magnum UK (1981)

Barney RUSSOM

investigates the death of his twin brother, whom the Air Force decided to bury in a sealed coffin.

American Male Secret Agent operating in USA

Richard M GARVIN and Edmond G ADDEO (American)

Writer: (First author) Richard McClellan GARVIN 1934-

Citation Record: 1 Book

The Fortec Conspiracy - *Only*
Sherbourne Press US (1968)

Anthea RUTHERFORD and Justin RUTHERFORD

sleuth together in Regency England.

British Female Amateur and British Male Amateur operating in England

Alice Chetwynd LEY 1915- (British)

Citation Record: 3 Books

A Reputation Dies - *First*
Methuen UK (1984); St Martin's US (1985)

Masquerade Of Vengeance - *Latest*
Severn UK (1989); Severn US (1989)

Justin RUTHERFORD

Second detective of Anthea RUTHERFORD

'Jumbo' RUTHERFORD

British Male Amateur operating in England

Norman LESLIE (British)

Citation Record: 2 Books

Raid Over England - *First*
Ward, Lock UK (1938)

The Kiwi Club - *Last*
Ward, Lock UK (1939)

Lt RYAN

American Policeman operating in USA

Margaret SCHERF 1908-1979 (American)

Invented 5 detectives - see Rev Martin BUELL

Citation Record: 2 Books

The Owl In The Cellar - *First*
Doubleday US (1945); Nimmo UK (1947)

Murder Makes Me Nervous - *Last*
Doubleday US (1948); Sampson, Low UK (1952)

Bill RYAN

is a stuntman in the movies. In his several stories, he is involved in improbable plots and adventures and uses his special acrobatic skills to help out his inept detective ability.

American Male Amateur operating in Los Angeles

Michael MORGAN (American)

was the byline of two important publicity men in Hollywood during the 1940s.

Writers: C E 'Teet' CARLE and Dean M DORN

Citation Record: 2 Books

Nine More Lives - *First*
Random House US (1947)

The Blonde Body - *First**
Lion US (1949)

Decoy - *Last*
Ace US (1953)

Charlie RYAN

British Male Amateur operating in England

J C LENEHAN (British)

See main detective Insp KILBY

Citation Record: 5 Books

Death Dances Thrice - *First*
Jenkins UK (1933)

Driven To Death - *Last*
Jenkins UK (1944)

Frank RYAN

was a thief in his first book, but later became a first-rate process server and obtained his PI licence.

American Male Private Detective operating in Detroit

Elmore LEONARD 1935- (American)

was born in New Orleans, Louisiana. He took a PhD in English at the University of Detroit, 1950, and later worked in journalism, advertising and films. He is the author of at least twenty criminous novels, several non-genre novels and some screenplays. He received the Mystery Writers of America Edgar Allan Poe award, 1984.

Other Detectives:
Raymond CRUZ
Joe LA BRAVA
Harry MITCHELL
Vincent MORA
Nolen TYNER

Citation Record: 2 Books

Swag - *First*
Delacorte US (1976); Penguin UK (1976)

Ryan's Rules - *First**
Dell US (1978)

Unknown Man #89 - *Latest*
Delacorte US (1977); Secker & Warburg UK (1977)

George RYAN

Second detective of Maj DEERING

Jack RYAN

is a CIA analyst who becomes involved in the most massive and ingenious adventures of the Cold War, in which American and Russian strategists try to outwit each other. The vic-

R

tory of the CIA, standing in for American democracy, is not in doubt for long.

American Male Secret Agent operating in USA

Tom CLANCY 1947- (American)

Citation Record: 5 Books

The Hunt For Red October - *First*
Naval Institute Press US (1984); Collins UK (1985)

Debt Of Honour - *Latest*
Putnam US (1994); Collins UK (1994)

Lt Jim RYAN, Shirley LEIGHTON and Bill HARPER

These detectives were used in several combinations resulting in very few books and short stories.

American Policeman, American Female Detective and American Male Detective operating in New York

Paul ERNST 1886- (American)

Other Byline: Kenneth ROBESON

Other Detectives:
Sam CATES and Lt Jim RYAN
Shirley LEIGHTON and Bill HARPER
Dr SATAN
SEEKAY

Citation Record: 1 Book

Hangman's Hat - *Only*
Mill US (1951); Muller UK (1952)

Mgr John Blackwood 'Blackie' RYAN

is a priest in a parish near Chicago. He comes upon terrible crimes, all with a religious or spiritual aspect, and solves them.

American Male Amateur operating in USA

Andrew M GREELEY 1928- (American)

See main detective Jimmy O'NEILL

Citation Record: 9 Books

Happy Are The Meek - *First*
Warner US (1985); Macdonald UK (1986)

Blessed Are The Poor In Spirit - *Latest*
Jove US (1994)

John RYAN

was an Irish-American detective appearing in stories in *Private Detective* in the 1940s.

American Male Detective in Pulp Magazines operating in USA

Roger TORREY (American)

Invented 7 detectives - see Pat MULLANCY

No citations

R

Johnny RYAN

seems to be a failure, sharing a telephone and a room with other tenants. However, his one case changes his life.

American Male Private Detective operating in New York

Steve FISHER 1912-1980 (American)

Invented 4 detectives - see Joe SAXON

Citation Record: 1 Book

Winter Kill - *Only*
Dodd, Mead US (1946)

Maggie RYAN

is a brilliant undergraduate who, in the course of the series, becomes a superb amateur sleuth.

American Female Amateur operating in New York

P M CARLSON 1940- (American)

Writer: Patricia McEvoy CARLSON

Citation Record: 8 Books

Audition For Murder - *First*
Avon US (1985)

Murder In The Dog Days - *Latest*
Bantam US (1991); Doubleday US (1991)

Mike RYAN

American Male Amateur operating in USA

Harold Q MASUR 1909- (American)

See main detective Scott JORDAN

Citation Record: 1 Book

The Broker - *Single*
St Martin's US (1981)

Det Patrick RYAN

American Policeman operating in USA

A Frank PINKERTON (American)

Invented 5 detectives - see A Frank PINKERTON

Citation Record: 1 Book

A Daring Horse Thief - *Only*
Laird & Lee US (1890)

Pete RYAN

Second detective of Frank MACBRIDE

Sean RYAN

is a disillusioned Irish ex-revolutionary recruited by British Intelligence to infiltrate groups, all over the world, that threaten Britain's security. Such groups are usually terrorist or fascist and *RYAN* is able to justify his often horrendous violence by destroying them, although in the process he is left as cynical as ever.

Irish Male Professional Investigator operating in Ireland/Italy

Brian CLEEVE 1921- (British)

See main detective Insp O'DONOVAN

Citation Record: 4 Books

Vote X For Treason - *First*
Collins UK (1964); Random House US (1965)

Counterspy - *First**
Lancer US (1966)

Violent Death Of A Bitter Englishman - *Last*
Random House US (1967); Corgi UK (1969)

Insp RYDER

solves a case in which two women are murdered in locked rooms.

British Policeman operating in England

Sax ROHMER 1883-1959 (British)

was born in Birmingham, Warwickshire, and invariably used his well-known pseudonym for all his writing; later he used it even in his private life. After a difficult childhood in a poor family, he obtained work as a reporter and started writing short stories in 1910, at first without success. He became interested in the occult and, on a newspaper assignment, visited Limehouse, the then Chinese district of London, still virtually unknown to outsiders. The visit changed his life and, in a sense, the history of mystery and thriller fiction until at least the beginning of the Second World War.

Sax ROHMER is now almost wholly remembered for his creation of the Chinese master criminal, Dr Fu Manchu, whose endless and ingenious villainies and countless tussles with Caucasian heroes continued in stories and films for a generation. Although he did not invent the concept of the wicked oriental criminal, on which the Yellow Peril school of journalism and fiction was based, he was the prime figure in its popularisation. The author of over fifty novels and many short stories, he created several quasi-detective heroes as well as true detectives to do battle with the various kinds of criminal, often oriental, master-minds he invented. His books certainly succeeded because they appealed to the concept of white supremacy that reigned in the West between the two great wars; but his work, though now of-

ten derided, featured carefully researched backgrounds and good plots.
Writer: Arthur Henry Sarsfield WARD
Other Detectives:

Bimbashi BAUK	Insp BRISTOL
Paul HARLEY	Ch Insp Daniel 'Red' KERRY
Morris KLAW	Gaston MAX
Capt O'HAGAN	Insp SHEFFIELD

Citation Record: 1 Book
The Moon Is Red - *Only*
Cassell UK (1954); Bookfinger US (1976)

Dick RYDER
British Male Amateur operating in England

H B Marriott WATSON 1863-1921 (British)
Writer: Henry Brereton Marriott WATSON
Inventor of one other detective Richard DERRICK
Citation Record: 36 Short Stories in 4 Collections
Galloping Dick - *Collection 1*
Short stories - 6
Lane UK (1896)
The High Toby - *Collection 2*
Short stories - 11
Methuen UK (1906)
The King's Highway - *Collection 3*
Short stories - 12
Mills UK (1910)
As It Chanced - *Collection 4*
This collection of thirteen stories contains seven with *Dick RYDER.*
Short stories - 7
Methuen UK (1916)

Harry RYDER
American Male Sleuth operating in Far East

Robert FOOTMAN 1916- (American)
Writer: Robert Henry FOOTMAN
Citation Record: 3 Books
Once A Spy - *First*
Dodd, Mead US (1980)
China Spy - *Latest*
Dodd, Mead US (1988)

William 'Tiny' RYDER
American Male Professional Investigator operating in USA

William BOYLES and Hank NUYER (American)
Citation Record: 4 Books
A Killing Trade - *First*
Playboy US (1981)
Blood Mountain - *Latest*
Playboy US (1982)

William RYE
is a trouble-shooter for an oil magnate and in both his books has to solve a murder to get his boss off a hook.
American Male Professional Investigator operating in California

John SPAIN 1895-1949 (American)
For writer details see Rex MCBRIDE
Citation Record: 2 Books
Dig Me A Grave - *First*
Dutton US (1942)
Death Is Like That - *Last*
Dutton US (1943)

RYKER
American Male Sleuth operating in New York

Edson HAMILL (American)
Citation Record: 4 Books
The Sadist - *First*
Leisure Books US (1975)
The Slasher - *Latest*
Leisure Books US (1976)

Det Sgt Joe RYKER
is a tough cop in the Homicide division of the New York Police Department. He appears also in books with the author's other detective, *Sgt JOE KELLER.*
American Policeman operating in New York

Nelson DE MILLE 1943- (American)
See main detective pair Det Sgt Joe KELLER and Det Sgt Joe RYKER
Citation Record: 4 Books
The Sniper - *First*
was republished in the US and UK under the following byline.
Leisure Books US (1974)
The Agent Of Death - *Last*
was republished in the US, with a change of title, under the following byline.
Leisure Books US (1974)

Jack CANNON 1943- (American)
For writer details see Det Sgt Joe KELLER and Det Sgt Joe RYKER
Citation Record: 4 Books
The Sniper - *First*
was previously published in the US under the preceding byline.
Pocket Books US (1989); Grafton UK (1991)
The Death Squad - *Last*
was previously published in the US, with a change of title, under the preceding byline.
Pocket Books US (1990)

Det Sgt Joe RYKER
Second detective of Det Sgt Joe KELLER

Garth RYLAND
American Male Amateur operating in Wisconsin

John R RIGGS 1945- (American)
Writer: John Raymond RIGGS
Citation Record: 5 Books
The Last Laugh - *First*
Dembner US (1984)
Cold Hearts And Gentle People - *Latest*
Dembner US (1994)

Balmy RYMAL
works as an investigator for the Jewellers' Protective Alliance. In her relentless pursuit of criminals, 'she is forced to hide her sentimental nature behind a tough exterior'. Splendid! !See Appendix 2.
American Female Professional Investigator operating in New York

Arthur STRINGER 1874-1950 (American)
Invented 4 detectives - see James DURKIN
Citation Record: 8 Short Stories in 1 Collection
The Diamond Thieves - *Collection 1*
Bobbs Merrill US (1923)

Insp RYVET
preceded the better known *Insp RIVERS* in the author's series.
British Policeman operating in England

Carol CARNAC 1894-1958 (British)
For writer details see Insp/Supt MACDONALD
Inventor of one other detective Ch Insp Julian RIVERS
Citation Record: 6 Books
Triple Death - *First*
Butterworth UK (1936)
Death In The Diving-Pool - *Last*
Davies UK (1950)

Joel SABER
is an ex-Scotland Yard Inspector who is now a PI.
British Male Private Detective operating in England

Sidekick: Winton 'Ritzy' TRIPP-TYLER
knows everything about everything. A useful man to have around!
British Male - Assistant

Gavin HOLT 1891- (Australian)
Invented 3 detectives - see Prof Luther BASTION
Citation Record: 6 Books
The Theme Is Murder - *First*
Gollancz UK (1938); Simon & Schuster US (1939)
Ladies In Ermine - *Last*
Hodder & Stoughton UK (1947)

Sarah SABER
Second detective of Chris ROCKWELL

Mr SABIN
Male Amateur operating in England

E Phillips OPPENHEIM 1866-1946 (British)
Invented 27 detectives - see Nicholas GOADE
Citation Record: 2 Books
Mysterious Mr Sabin - *First*
Ward, Lock UK (1898); Little, Brown US (1905)
The Yellow Crayon - *Last*
Ward, Lock UK (1903); Dodd, Mead US (1903)

Rex SACKLER
is a penny-pinching detective who appeared in stories in *Dime Detective* and later, 1930-1950, in *Black Mask Magazine.*
American Male Detective in Pulp Magazines operating in USA

Sidekick: Joey GRAHAM
is the detective's junior partner.
American Male - Partner

D L CHAMPION 1903?-1968 (Australian)
Invented 4 detectives - see Insp ALLHOFF
No citations

Jim SADER
is a partner in the agency of Sader & Scarborough, and as hardboiled as they come.
American Male Private Detective operating in Long Beach

Dolores HITCHENS 1907-1973 (American)
For writer details see Lt Stephen MAYHEW
Citation Record: 2 Books
Sleep With Strangers - *First*
Doubleday US (1955); Macdonald UK (1956)
Sleep With Slander - *Last*
Doubleday US (1960); Boardman UK (1961)

Benton SAFFORD
is a congressman from Ohio who is forced to investigate mayhem and murder in high places.
American Male Amateur operating in Washington DC

R B DOMINIC (American)
Writers: Mary J LATIS1927- and Martha HENNISSART 1929(?)-
Citation Record: 7 Books
Murder Sunny Side Up - *First*
Abelard Schuman US (1968); Abelard Schuman UK (1968)
A Flaw In The System - *Latest*
Macmillan UK (1983)
Unexpected Developments - *Latest**
St Martin's US (1984)

Malcolm SAGE
was a rather unsuccessful attempt to produce a copy of the great *Sherlock HOLMES.*
British Male Professional Amateur operating in England

Herbert JENKINS 1876-1923 (British)
Writer: Herbert George JENKINS
Inventor of one other detective Mr STIFFSON
Citation Record: 17 Short Stories in 1 Collection
Malcolm Sage, Detective - *Collection 1*
Jenkins UK (1921); Doran US (1921)

Oscar SAIL
lives on a boat in the Miami City Yacht Basin.
American Male Private Detective operating in Miami

Lester DENT 1904-1959 (American)
Invented 9 detectives - see Chance MALLOY
Citation Record: 2 Selected Short Stories
Sail
can also be found in the anthology, *The Hard-Boiled Omnibus; Early Stories From Black Mask* (Editor; Joseph Shaw; 1946)
In 'Black Mask Magazine' US (1936)
Angelfish
can also be found in the anthology, *The Hard-Boiled Detective; Stories From Black Mask Magazine 1920-1951* (Editor; Herbert Ruhm; 1977).
In 'Black Mask Magazine' US (1936)

Insp SAITO
Japanese Policeman operating in Japan

Janwillem VAN DE WETERING 1931- (Dutch)
See main detective pair Adjutent Henk GRIJPSTRA and Sgt Rufus DE GIER
Citation Record: 11 Short Stories in 1 Collection
Inspector Saito's Small Satori - *Collection 1*
Putnam US (1985)

Chris SAKSIS
Second detective of Ross LIZENBY

Jo SALIS
British Male Secret Agent operating in Europe/Asia

William Oliver GREENER 1862- (British)
Citation Record: 1 Book 16 Short Stories in 1 Collection
A Secret Agent In Port Arthur - *Only*
Constable UK (1905)
The Exploits Of Jo Salis, A British Spy - *Collection 1*
This collection of twenty-one short stories by the author contains sixteen with *Jo SALIS.*
Hurst UK (1905)

Arthur SALISBURY and Frank SHEARER
British Male Amateurs operating in England

Robert CRAWFORD 1935- (British)
For writer details see Insp MCCAIG
Citation Record: 2 Books
Cockleburr - *First*
Constable UK (1969); Putnam US (1970)
Pay As You Die - *First**
Berkley US (1971)
Kiss The Boss Goodbye - *Last*
Constable UK (1970); Putnam US (1971)

Oscar SALLIS
Second detective of Amanda CURZON

Gregory SALLUST
British Male Amateur operating in several locations

Dennis WHEATLEY 1897-1977 (British)
Invented 4 detectives - see Julian DAY
Citation Record: 9 Books
Black August - *First*
Hutchinson UK (1934); Dutton US (1934)
The White Witch Of The South Seas - *Last*
Hutchinson UK (1968)

Andrew SALMOND
British Male Amateur operating in South America

Lawrence DUNDAS (British)

Writer: Lawrence George Donicio DUNDAS

Citation Record: 3 Books

A Spider At The Elvira - *First*
Hammond UK (1949)

The Strange Smell Of Murder - *Last*
Hammond UK (1965)

Supt SALT and Paula LEBETWOOD
British Policeman and British Female Amateur operating in Wales

Virgil MARKHAM 1899- (British)

Invented 5 detectives - see Insp Myles RUSBY

Citation Record: 1 Book

Death In The Dusk - *Only*
Knopf UK (1928); Knopf US (1928)

Lionel Humphrey SALT and Maggie CULTHORPE
British Male Amateur and British Female Amateur operating in England

J B PRIESTLEY 1894- 1984(British)

was born in Bradford, Yorkshire. He was educated at local schools and took an MA at Trinity Hall, Cambridge, after which he served in the Army, 1914-1919. He was one of the most distinguished writers and literary figures of the twentieth century and his output was large, consisting of novels, plays, essays, and critical works on a great variety of subjects. His incursion into the detective and mystery genre was, however, merely an exercise.

Writer: John Boynton PRIESTLEY

Other Detectives
Tim BEDFORD   Insp GOOLE

Citation Record: 1 Book

Salt Is Leaving - *Only*
Pandora UK (1966); Harper & Row US (1975)

Insp Charlie SALTER
appears in books that are almost police procedurals.
Canadian Policeman operating in Toronto

Sidekick: Sgt Frank GATENBY
is an occasional sidekick.
Canadian Male - Subordinate

Eric WRIGHT 1929- (Canadian)

was born in London and educated at Mitcham Grammar School. He went to Canada and took a BA at the University of Manitoba, Winnipeg, 1957. He received the Crime Writers Association John Creasey award, 1983, and the Crime Writers of Canada award, 1983.

Citation Record: 8 Books

The Night The Gods Smiled - *First*
Collins UK (1983); Scribner's US (1983)

Final Cut - *Latest*
HarperCollins UK (1991)

Toby SAMPSON
is a district attorney who unravels a case of murder at the fictional Collins College.
American Male Professional Investigator operating in New England

Marion MAINWARING (American)

was born in Boston. She was a teacher of English, a European newspaper correspondent, and a worker for UNESCO. In addition to the criminous novel cited here, she was the author of a parody to outdo all parodies, *MURDER IN PASTICHE.*

Inventor of one other detective group Mallory KING, Insp Jon NAPPLEBY, Jerry PASON, Atlas POIREAU, Simon QUINSEY, Fan SLIVER, Insp Broderick TOURNEUR, Spike BLUDGEON and Trajan BEARE

Citation Record: 1 Book

Murder At Midyears - *Only*
Macmillan US (1953); Gollancz UK (1954)

Charlotte SAMS
is a free-lance reporter who, when a philandering elephant keeper is pushed to his death one night at the Columbus Zoo by a hand that seems to be more human than pachydermous, is determined to get a scoop by solving his murder.
American Male Amateur operating in USA

Alson GLEN (American)

Citation Record: 1 Book

Trunk Show - *Single*
Simon & Schuster US (1995)

Capt SAMSON
British Male Amateur

Gavin DOUGLAS (British)

Citation Record: 3 Books

The Obstinate Captain Samson - *First*
Collins UK (1936); Putnam US (1937)

Captain Samson, A B - *Last*
Collins UK (1937); Putnam US (1937)

Albert SAMSON
dropped out of college and, with very little going for him, has set up as a private eye. Medium-boiled, always broke, and shabbily dressed, he changes offices a lot because he has to. He drives an old car, is hardly a hero, and will not carry a gun. His cases, which are set, rather unusually, in the mean streets of Indianapolis, are often nasty and sometimes slightly comic, but they deal with important aspects of the social life of the people he investigates. He gives a discount on his fees to any client naive enough to employ him.
American Male Private Detective operating in Indianapolis

Michael Z LEWIN 1942- (American)

was born in Springfield, Massachusetts. He took an AB at Harvard University, Cambridge, Massachusetts, 1964, and later studied at Cambridge, England. He has taught science and been a reporter.

Writer: Michael Zinn LEWIN

Other Detectives:
Adele BUFFINGTON   Lt Leroy POWDER

Citation Record: 7 Books

Ask The Right Question - *First*
Putnam US (1971); Hamilton UK (1972)

Called By A Panther - *Latest*
Macmillan UK (1991)

Bernard SAMSON
is one of the finest creations in the sub-genre of British spy fiction, from the pen of a master. He appears in two trilogies to date and (as of 1995) two parts of a third trilogy, all of them historically fascinating and complex in structure. Because of their inter-related nature, the books are all cited.
British Male Secret Agent operating in several locations

Len DEIGHTON 1929- (British)

was born in London and educated at Marylebone Grammar School, London. After studying at the Royal College of Art, London, he served for a while in the Royal Air Force. He has worked on the railways, as a cook, a waiter, an illustrator, and as a photographer. His first novel, combining the espionage and detective genres, was highly successful. Since then he has gone from strength to strength in a succession of books, partially in the detective genre but largely biased towards the highly complex novel of espionage. He is now regarded as one of the supreme masters of this type of fiction.

Writer: Leonard Cyril DEIGHTON

Inventor of one other detective Harry PALMER

Citation Record: 8 Books

Berlin Game - *Book 1*
The first part of the first trilogy.
Hutchinson UK (1983); Knopf US (1983)

Mexico Set - *Book 2*
The second part of the first trilogy.
Hutchinson UK (1984); Knopf US (1985)

London Match - *Book 3*
The third part of the first trilogy.
Hutchinson UK (1985); Knopf US (1986)

Spy Hook - *Book 4*
The first part of the second trilogy.
Hutchinson UK (1988); Knopf US (1988)

Spy Line - *Book 5*
The second part of the second trilogy.
Hutchinson UK (1989); Knopf US (1989)

Spy Sinker - *Book 6*
The third part of the second trilogy.
Hutchinson UK (1990); Harper & Row US (1990)

Faith - *Book 7*
The first part of the third trilogy.
HarperCollins UK (1994); HarperCollins US (1994)

Hope - *Book 8*
The second part of the third trilogy.
HarperCollins UK (1995)

Jake SAMSON

was in the Chicago police force, but moved to Oakland, California, became a hippie, then began to practise as an unlicensed PI.

American Male Private Detective operating in California

Sidekick: Rosie VICENTE
is female but only just. She is a carpenter who is, in fact, *SAMSON's* tenant and is useful in assisting him in his unlicensed PI activities.
American Female - Assistant

Rochelle SINGER 1939- (American)
Other Byline: Shelley SINGER
Citation Record: 1 Book
Samson's Deal - *Single*
St Martin's US (1983)

Shelley SINGER 1939- (American)
Writer: Rochelle SINGER
Other Byline: Rochelle SINGER
Citation Record: 4 Books
Free Draw - *First*
St Martin's US (1985)
Suicide King - *Latest*
St Martin's US (1988)

S

John SAMSON

is, if not quite as fat as *Nero WOLFE*, certainly overweight. He inherited a debt-collecting agency in South London and got into the business of private investigation as a result.

British Male Private Detective operating in London

Miles TRIPP 1923- (British)
was born in Ganwick Corner, Hertfordshire. He was educated at Queen Elizabeth's Grammar School, Barnet, Hertfordshire, and served in the Royal Air Force, 1942-1946. A practising solicitor since 1950, he is the author of at least twenty-seven genre novels under his real name and a pseudonym. His books have unusual, often legal, themes and the early ones did not have a series detective.
Writer: Miles Barton TRIPP
Other Bylines:
John Michael BRETT Michael BRETT
Inventor of one other detective Insp CROUCH
Citation Record: 10 Books
Obsession - *First*
Macmillan UK (1973)
The Cords Of Vanity - *Latest*
Macmillan UK (1989); St Martin's US (1990)

SAN ANTONIO

French Male Amateur operating in France

SAN ANTONIO 1921- (French)
is a journalist who has written many novels featuring this detective, some uncounted.
Writer: Frederic DARD
Citation Record: 65 Books
Tough Justice - *First*
is a translation from the French of *Messieurs les Hommes* (Paris, 1955).
Duckworth UK (1967); Norton US (1969)
Alien Archipelago - *Last*
is a translation from the French of *L'Archipel des Malotrus* (Paris, 1969).
Joseph UK (1971)

Robert SAND

American Male Sleuth operating in several locations

Marc OLDEN (American)
See main detective Hawthorne Albert HARKER
Citation Record: 3 Books
Black Samurai - *First*
Signet UK (1974)
The Deadly Pearl - *Last*
Signet UK (1974)

Commiss SANDERS

was both a policeman and the administrator of justice in British West Africa, exercising the rule of the white minority but showing more than usual sympathy for the native people for whom he was, under colonial rule, responsible. He remains one of *Edgar WALLACE's* most interesting creations and, after the latter's death, was the hero of a number of stories by *Francis GERARD.*

British Policeman operating in Africa

Francis GERARD 1906-1962? (South African)
See main detective Sir John MEREDITH
Citation Record: 34 Short Stories in 3 Collections
The Return Of Sanders Of The River - *Collection 1*
Short stories - 12
Rich UK (1938); Dutton US (1939)
The Law Of The River - *Collection 2*
Short stories - 10
Rich UK (1939); Dutton US (1940)
The Justice Of Sanders - *Collection 3*
Short stories - 12
Rich UK (1951)

Edgar WALLACE 1875-1932 (British)
Invented 28 detectives - see J G REEDER
Citation Record: 141 Short Stories in 11 Collections
Sanders Of The River - *Collection 1*
Short stories - 14
Ward, Lock UK (1911); Doubleday US (1930)
The People Of The River - *Collection 2*
Short stories - 17
Ward, Lock UK (1912)
Bosambo Of The River - *Collection 3*
Short stories - 13
Ward, Lock UK (1914)
Bones - *Collection 4*
Short stories - 13
Ward, Lock UK (1915)
The Keepers Of The King's Peace - *Collection 5*
Short stories - 12
Ward, Lock UK (1917)
Lieutenant Bones - *Collection 6*
Short stories - 14
Ward, Lock UK (1918)
Bones In London - *Collection 7*
Short stories - 12
Ward, Lock UK (1921)

Sandi, The King Maker - *Collection 8*
Short stories - 12
Ward, Lock UK (1922)

Bones Of The River - *Collection 9*
Short stories - 12
Newnes UK (1923)

Sanders - *Collection 10*
Short stories - 10
Hodder & Stoughton UK (1926)

Mr Commissioner Sanders - *Collection 10**
Doubleday US (1930)

Again Sanders - *Collection 11*
Short stories - 12
Hodder & Stoughton UK (1928); Doubleday US (1929)

Insp John SANDERS

Canadian Policeman operating in Toronto/Ottawa

Medora SALE (Canadian)

is an authority on medieval studies and a teacher of English in Toronto.

Citation Record: 4 Books

Murder On The Run - *First*
PaperJacks US (1986)

Short Cut To Santa Fe - *Latest*
Scribner's US (1994)

Det Insp SANDERSON

British Policeman operating in England

David HUME 1900-1945 (British)

Invented 3 detectives - see Mick CARDBY

Citation Record: 6 Short Stories in 2 Collections

Call In The Yard - *Collection 1*
Short stories - 3
Collins UK (1935)

The Crime Combine - *Collection 2*
Short stories - 3
Collins UK (1936)

Abigail 'Sandy' SANDERSON

Second detective of Robert FORSYTHE

Maxwell SANDERSON

American Male Amateur operating in New York

John Jay CHICHESTER (American)

See main detective Jimmy 'Wiggly' PRICE

Citation Record: 2 Books

The Bigamist - *First*
Chelsea US (1925); Hutchinson UK (1927)

The House Of The Moving Room - *Last*
Chelsea US (1926); Hutchinson UK (1926)

Ned SANDERSON

British Male Private Detective operating in London

Arthur WISE 1923-1982? (British)

Other Byline: Brian SWIFT

Citation Record: 1 Book

The Death's-Head - *Only*
Cassell UK (1962)

Phil SANDERSON

British Male Amateur operating in England

Leo GREX 1908-1985 (British)

For writer details see Supt Anthony SLADE

Other Detectives:

Jerry DOWN	Paul IRVING

Citation Record: 2 Books

Violent Keepsake - *First*
Long UK (1967)

The Hard Kill - *Last*
Long UK (1969)

Col SANDERSTEAD

is a country squire who bumbles his way into solving a country crime.

British Male Amateur operating in England

J J CONNINGTON 1880-1947 (British)

Invented 5 detectives - see Mark BRAND

Citation Record: 1 Book

Death At Swaythling Court - *Only*
Benn UK (1926); Little, Brown US (1926)

Judge Lara SANDERSTONE

is a young and dedicated court judge whose sister is brutally murdered. She investigates and realises that she herself may have been responsible for releasing a killer. Her own life is now on the line unless she can prove it.

American Female Amateur operating in California

Nancy Taylor ROSENBERG (American)

See main detective Dr Lily FORRESTER

Citation Record: 1 Book

Interest Of Justice - *Single*
Orion UK (1993)

George SANDFORD

has telepathic powers. Which is just as well for a PI trying to do a moderately honest job in the New York of the future (1999), a city with two billion people.

American Male Private Detective operating in New York

Katherine MACLEAN 1925- (American)

Citation Record: 1 Book

Missing Man - *Only*
Berkley US (1975)

Insp SANDS

appears also in one book with the author's other detective, *Paul PRYE.*

Canadian Policeman operating in Toronto

Margaret MILLAR 1915- (Canadian)

was born in Kitchener, Ontario, Canada, and educated at the Kitchener-Waterloo Collegiate Institute and the University of Toronto. She married the distinguished genre novelist, *Kenneth MILLAR*, 1938, and published the first of at least twenty-six criminous novels, 1941. She received the Mystery Writers of America Edgar Allan Poe award, 1956, and their Grand Master award, 1982.

Writer: Margaret Ellis Sturm MILLAR

Other Detectives:

Tomas ARAGON	Paul BLACKSHEAR
Elmer DODD	Charles DONNELLY
Howard HYATT and Michael DUNLOP	
Eric MEECHAM	Steve PINATA
Dr Paul PRYE	Joe QUINN
Insp SANDS and Dr Paul PRYE	

Citation Record: 2 Books

Wall Of Eyes - *First*
Lancer UK (1966); Random House US (1943)

The Iron Gates - *Last*
Random House US (1945)

Taste Of Fears - *Last**
Hale UK (1950)

Insp SANDS and Dr Paul PRYE

also appear individually in other books by this author.

Canadian Policeman and Canadian Male Amateur operating in Toronto

Margaret MILLAR 1915- (Canadian)

Invented 11 detectives - see Insp SANDS

Citation Record: 1 Book

The Devil Loves Me - *Only*
Doubleday US (1942)

Jake SANDS

seeks the killer of a girl described as a 'sexy beach bunny'.

American Male Sleuth operating in USA

Ron ELY (American)

Citation Record: 1 Book

East Beach - *Single*

Simon & Schuster US (1995)

Jim SANDS

American Male Amateur operating in USA

Robert J CASEY 1890-1962 (British)

Citation Record: 5 Books

The Secret Of Thirty-Seven Hardy Street - *First*

Bobbs US (1929); Mathews UK (1930)

The Third Owl - *Last*

Nicholson & Watson UK (1934); Bobbs US (1934)

John SANDS

British Male Amateur operating in England

Hammond INNES 1913- (British)

was born in Horsham, Sussex. He was educated at Cranbrook School, Kent, worked on the staff of the *Financial Times*, 1934-1940, and served in the Army, 1940-1946. He is the author of at least thirty genre novels in a realm he has made his own. They deal with the struggle, not only of man against man, but of man against the great forces of nature in all its aspects. He is also the author of at least a dozen fine books on travel and historical exploration. He was made a CBE, 1978, and awarded a D Litt from Bristol University, 1985.

Writer: Ralph Hammond INNES

Citation Record: 1 Book

The Mary Deare - *Only*

Collins UK (1956)

The Wreck Of The Mary Deare - *Only**

Knopf US (1956)

Nick SANDS

is hired by a woman to find God.

American Male Private Detective operating in San Francisco

Stephen SMOKE (American)

Citation Record: 1 Book

Trick Of The Light - *Single*

In 'Beyond Worlds' US (1988)

SANDY

is in Bonn to find out who killed his partner.

American Male Private Detective operating in Germany

Samuel FULLER 1911- (American)

Writer: Samuel William FULLER

Citation Record: 1 Book

Dead Pigeon On Beethoven Street - *Only*

Pyramid US (1974)

SANDY

British Male Amateur operating in England

Dorothea CONYERS 1873-1949 (British)

Invented 3 detectives - see Mervyn HENDERSON

Citation Record: 12 Short Stories in 1 Collection

Sandy And Others - *Collection 1*

Not all the stories are criminous.

Mills UK (1925)

Mr SANDYMAN

British Male Amateur operating in England

Neill GRAHAM 1909-1975 (British)

See main detective James 'Solo' MALCOLM

Citation Record: 7 Books

The Symbol Of The Cat - *First*

Melrose UK (1948)

Salute Mr Sandyman - *Last*

Jarrolds UK (1953)

Joe SANFORD

American Male Sleuth operating in Far East

Franklin M PROUD 1920- (Canadian)

Citation Record: 2 Books

The Golden Triangle - *First*

Sphere UK (1976); St Martin's US (1978)

The Walking Wind - *Latest*

St Martin's US (1979)

Richard SANGSTER

solves a case of locked-room murder.

British Male Amateur operating in England

Charles ASHTON 1884- (British)

Invented 3 detectives - see Maj Jack ATHERLEY

Citation Record: 1 Book

Here's Murder Done - *Only*

Hale UK (1943)

SANT

British Male Secret Agent operating in several locations

William LEQUEUX 1864-1927 (British)

Invented 23 detectives - see Allan KENNEDY

Citation Record: 1 Collection

Sant Of The Secret Service - *Collection 1*

has several chapters devoted to the exploits of this detective.

Odhams UK (1918)

Minnie SANTANGELO

American Female Amateur operating in New York

Anthony MANCINI 1939- (American)

Citation Record: 2 Books

Minnie Santangelo's Mortal Sin - *First*

Coward McCann US (1975)

Minnie Santangelo And The Evil Eye - *Last*

Coward McCann US (1977)

Basil SANTOINE

is a lawyer and is blind. The author may have been influenced by the appearance in 1914 of the most famous of all blind detectives, *Max CARRADOS*.

American Male Professional Amateur operating in USA

Edwin BALMER and William MACHARG 1872-1951 (American)

See main detective Luther TRANT

Citation Record: 1 Book

The Blind Man's Eyes - *Only*

Little, Brown US (1916); Nash UK (1916)

Domingo SANTOS

Male Professional Investigator operating in Texas

W B BANNERMAN

Citation Record: 3 Books

Bad End Valley - *First*

Low UK (1937)

Santos, Border Detective - *Last*

Quality Press UK (1940)

Nat SAPPERTON

was once a member of a secret British agency abroad and is now drawn into a case of home-grown and ingenious murder.

British Male Amateur operating in England

Joan FLEMING 1908-1980 (British)

Invented 3 detectives - see Nuri ISKIRLAK

Citation Record: 1 Book

Every Inch A Lady - *Only*

Collins UK (1977); Putnam US (1978)

Woolf SARASON

British Male Secret Agent operating in England

Maurice MOISEIWITSCH (British)

See main detective Mr PENNY

Citation Record: 1 Book

Woolf Sarason, Special Agent - *Only*
Muller UK (1941)

Richard SAREL

British Male Amateur operating in Italy

John BRYAN 1916- (British)

Writer: Josephine DELVES-BROUGHTON

Citation Record: 3 Books

The Contessa Came Too - *First*
Faber UK (1957)

The Man Who Came Back - *Last*
Faber UK (1958); London House US (1959)

Denys SARGENT and Humphrey CARVER

When the body of a Professor of Egyptology, or possibly a mummy, is found incinerated after a fire at the fictional Beaufort College, Oxford, the university dons naturally want to cover up any scandal, but these two students decide to investigate further.

British Male Amateurs operating in Oxford

Dermot MORRAH 1896-1974 (British)

was a fellow of All Souls College, Oxford, and later a distinguished editor, historian, and man of letters. He seems to have written only one genre novel.

Writer: Dermot Michael MacGregor MORRAH

Citation Record: 1 Book

The Mummy Case - *Only*
Faber UK (1933)

The Mummy Case Mystery - *Only**
Harper & Row US (1933)

Lt Cdr Frank SARGENT

ia a Vietnam War hero who escaped from a prison camp.

American Male Amateur operating in Chicago

Frank GRUBER 1904-1969 (American)

Invented 8 detectives - see Johnny FLETCHER and Sam CRAGG

Citation Record: 2 Books

Kiss The Boss Goodbye - *First*
was previously published, with a change of title, under the following byline.
Mercury US (1954)

The Gold Gap - *Last*
Dutton US (1968); Hale UK (1968)

John K VEDDER 1904-1969 (American)

For writer details see Johnny FLETCHER and Sam CRAGG

Citation Record: 1 Book

The Last Doorbell - *Only*
was republished, with a change of title, under the preceding byline.
Mercury US (1954)

Mortimer SARK

British Male Amateur operating in England

John HAWK 1893- (British)

Inventor of one other detective Insp LINSCOTT

Citation Record: 5 Books

The Lone Lodge Mystery - *First*
Hodder & Stoughton UK (1926); Doran US (1926)

Murder At Arondale Farm - *Last*
Skeffington UK (1931); Farrar, Straus US (1932)

Dr SATAN

Male Sleuth

Paul ERNST 1886- (American)

Inventor of 5detectives - see Lt Jim RYAN, Shirley LEIGHTON and Bill HARPER

Citation Record: 5 Short stories in 1 Collection

Dr Satan - *Collection 1*
Weinberg US (1974)

Johnny SATURDAY

works for Coastal Mutual Insurance, and deals with some violent situations and characters.

American Male Private Detective operating in California

Lawrence GOLDMAN (American)

Writer: Lawrence Louis GOLDMAN

Citation Record: 2 Books

Fall Guy For Murder - *First*
Dutton US (1943); Gifford UK (1945)

Tiger By The Tail - *Last*
McKay US (1946)

Gordon SAULT

American Male Amateur operating in Washington DC

Henry ALLEN (American)

was the sometime editor of the *Washington Post.*

Citation Record: 1 Book

Fool's Mercy - *Single*
Houghton US (1982)

Sir John SAUMAREZ

was born plain Jim Simmonds, but he has risen to become one of England's premier actor-managers. With a penchant for detection, he solves several theatrical murders, which, as is well known in the criminous genre, occur with unusual frequency among thespians.

British Male Amateur operating in England

Clemence DANE and Helen SIMPSON (British)

Writers: Winifred ASHTON 1888-1965 and Helen De Guerry SIMPSON 1897-1940

Citation Record: 3 Books

Enter Sir John - *First*
Hodder & Stoughton UK (1928); Cosmopolitan US (1928)

Re-Enter Sir John - *Last*
Hodder & Stoughton UK (1932); Farrar, Straus US (1932)

Dick SAUNDERS

British Male Amateur operating in several locations

SCOBER (British)

Citation Record: 2 Short Stories in 1 Collection

The Spirit House And Other Stories - *Collection 1*
This collection of seven of the author's short stories contains two with *Dick SAUNDERS.*
Stockwell UK (1926)

Jeff SAUNDERS

Male Sleuth operating in Israel

Michael BAR-ZOHAR 1938- (Israeli)

Other Byline: Michael HASTINGS

Citation Record: 2 Books

The Third Truth - *First*
is a translation from the French of *La Troisieme Verité* (Paris, 1972). It was republished under the following byline.
Houghton US (1973); Hodder & Stoughton UK (1973)

The Spy Who Died Twice - *Last*
is a translation from the Hebrew of *Ha-ish She-Met Pa'amayim.*
Houghton US (1975); Weidenfeld & Nicolson UK (1976)

Michael HASTINGS 1938- (Israeli)

Other Byline: Michael BAR-ZOHAR

Citation Record: 1 Book

The Third Truth - *Single*
was previously published under the preceding byline.
Collier US (1988)

'Doc' SAVAGE

is a detective-adventurer who appears in the pulps. About two hundred stories written by several prolific authors were republished as books and thirteen collections from 1967 to 1985. All these authors used the house name cited.

American Male Amateur operating in USA

Kenneth ROBESON 1907-1977 (American)

Writer: William BOGART

Adopter of one other detective Johnny SAXON

Citation Record: 8 Books

The Flying Goblin - *First*
Bantam US (1977); Bantam UK 1977

Bequest Of Evil - *Last*
Bantam US (1990)

Kenneth ROBESON 1902-1955 (American)

Writer: Harold A DAVIS

Citation Record: 6 Books

Merchants Of Disaster - *First*
Bantam US (1969)

Devils Of The Deep - *Last*
Bantam US (1984)

Kenneth ROBESON 1905-1969 (American)

For writer details see Chance MALLOY

Citation Record: 131 Books

Quest Of The Spider - *First*
Street & Smith US (1935)

The Goblins - *Last*
Bantam US (1985)

Kenneth ROBESON (American)

Writer: Lester DENT 1905-1969 and William BOGART 1907-1977

Citation Record: 6 Books

The Spotted Men - *First*
Bantam US (1977)

Fire And Ice - *Last*
Bantam US (1988)

Kenneth ROBESON (American)

Writer: Lester DENT 1905-1969 and Harold A DAVIS 1902-1955

Citation Record: 9 Books

The Seven Agate Devils - *First*
Bantam US (1973)

The Exploding Lake - *Last*
Bantam US (1980)

Kenneth ROBESON (American)

Writer: Lester DENT 1905-1969 and Walter Ryerson JOHNSON 1902-

Citation Record: 9 Books

Land Of Always-Night - *First*
Bantam US (1966)

The Motion Menace - *Last*
Bantam US (1971)

Kenneth ROBESON (American)

Writer: Laurence DONOVAN

Citation Record: 8 Books

Murder Melody - *First*
Bantam US (1967)

The Black Spot - *Last*
Bantam US (1974)

Kenneth ROBESON (American)

Writer: Alan HATHWAY

Citation Record: 9 Books

The Flaming Falcons - *First*
Bantam US (1968); Bantam UK (1969)

The Rustling Death - *Last*
Bantam US (1987)

John SAVAGE

Male Amateur operating in South America

James TREVOR 1913-1976 (British)

For writer details see John Byron HYDE

Citation Record: 2 Books

The Savage Game - *First*
Gibbs UK (1967); Award US (1967)

The Savage Height - *Last*
Award US (1969); Tandem UK (1970)

Mark SAVAGE

British Male Sleuth operating in England

Matthew EDEN (Canadian)

Citation Record: 4 Books

Countdown To Crisis - *First*
Hale UK (1968)

Conquest Before Autumn - *Last*
Abelard UK (1973)

Mark SAVAGE

was formerly, under another name, a film stuntman and a movie star, but, following an accident, his actress wife left him and he retired. He became an alcoholic, then recovered, and was reborn as a PI, putting out his shingle near St Paul's in the City of London. He appears also in one book with another of the author's detectives, *Sam BIRKETT.*

British Male Private Detective operating in London

Laurence PAYNE 1919- (British)

Invented 4 detectives - see Mark SAVAGE and Ch Insp Sam BIRKETT

Citation Record: 4 Books

Take The Money And Run - *First*
Hodder & Stoughton UK (1982); Doubleday US (1984)

Late Knight - *Latest*
Hodder & Stoughton UK (1987)

Knight Fall - *Latest**
Doubleday US (1987)

Mark SAVAGE and Ch Insp Sam BIRKETT

operate together in this book, solving a mystery unusually located in Wales, in which *BIRKETT* now makes only a 'ghostly' appearance. They also appear individually in other books by this author.

British Male Private Detective and British Policeman operating in Wales

Sidekick: Sgt SAUNDERS
British Male - Subordinate

Laurence PAYNE 1919- (British)

was born in London. He is a professional actor, appearing on film, TV, and stage, and is a drama teacher at the Royal College of Music, London.

Other Detectives:
Ch Insp Sam BIRKETT   Mark SAVAGE
John TIBBETT

Citation Record: 1 Book

Dead For A Ducat - *Single*
Hodder & Stoughton UK (1985); Doubleday US (1986)

Matt SAVAGE

Male Sleuth operating in USA

Craig COOPER (British)

Citation Record: 5 Books

Blackmail Is Murder - *First*
Hale UK (1968)

Catch And Squeeze - *Last*
Hale UK (1968); Roy US (1969)

Myra SAVAGE

is a medium who cannot decide whether she is genuine or simply a self-deluded fake. In her first book, she tries to determine the matter by getting her weak husband to kidnap a child so that she can play the detective and discover it. Her second book does little to enhance her reputation.

American Female Amateur operating in USA

Mark MCSHANE 1930- (Australian)

Invented 3 detectives - see Norman PINK

Citation Record: 2 Books

Seance On A Wet Afternoon - *First*
Cassell UK (1961)
Seance - *First**
Doubleday US (1962)
Seance For Two - *Last*
Doubleday US (1972); Hale UK (1974)

Rampion SAVAGE

British Male Amateur operating in England

James TURNER 1909- (British)
Writer: James Ernest TURNER
Citation Record: 12 Books
Murder At Landred Hall - *First*
Cassell UK (1954)
The Stone Dormitory - *Last*
Cassell UK (1971)

Spencer Monroe SAVAGE

American Male Amateur operating in London

Paul THEROUX 1941- (British)
Citation Record: 38 Short Stories in 2 Collections
The Consul's File - *Collection 1*
Short stories - 20
Hamish Hamilton UK (1977); Houghton US (1977)
The London Embassy - *Collection 2*
Short stories - 18
Hamish Hamilton UK (1982); Houghton US (1983)

Steve SAVAGE

American Male Sleuth operating in Norway

David LEWIS (American)
Writer: David Lewis PATTON
Citation Record: 2 Books
The Andromeda Assignment - *First*
Pinnacle US (1976)
The Omega Assignment - *Last*
Pinnacle US (1976)

Justine SAVILE

Second detective of Cuddy MAGNUM

Bill SAVILLE

British Male Amateur operating in England

Roland DANIEL 1880-1969 (British)
Invented 11 detectives - see Insp Neville LANGHAM
Citation Record: 1 Book
The Society Of The Spiders - *Only*
Brentano's UK (1928)

Paul SAVOY

American Male Amateur operating in California

Jackson GREGORY 1882-1943 (American)
Citation Record: 3 Books
The House Of The Opal - *First*
Scribner's US (1932)
The First Case Of Mr Paul Savoy - *First**
Hodder & Stoughton UK (1933)
The Emerald Murder Trap - *Last*
Scribner's US (1934)
The Third Case Of Mr Paul Savoy - *Last**
Hodder & Stoughton UK (1934)

Pierre-Ange SAWYER

is half American and half French and was raised in Chicago. After he upset several powerful figures during his work as a private investigator in Washington DC, he went to France, where he is now able to work as a PI, although he has to be rather careful of the authorities for fear of losing his work permit. His office is in Paris but he works, often on missing person cases, on the Riviera.

American Male Private Detective operating in France

Sidekick: Fritz DONHOFF
is an expert in many things, guns especially. Although German, he now has French citizenship because of his work with the French Resistance during the Second World War 2.
German Male - Assistant

Marvin H ALBERT 1924- (American)
was born in Philadelphia, Pennsylvania. He has been a magazine editor and literary researcher for various US papers but he now lives mainly in France.
Writer: Marvin Hubert ALBERT
Other Bylines:
Al CONROY
Nick QUARRY
Anthony ROME
Inventor of one other detective Tony ROME
Citation Record: 7 Books
Stone Angel - *First*
Fawcett US (1946); Macmillan UK (1947)
Bimbo Heaven - *Latest*
Fawcett US (1990); Macmillan UK (1990)

Quincy Adams SAWYER

is a rural character who does a little sleuthing.

American Male Amateur operating in Massachusetts

Charles Felton PIDGIN 1844-1923 (American)
was born in Roxbury, Massachusetts. He was nearly blind when he wrote his stories and the second book (a collection, cited below) was written with a co-author.
Citation Record: 1 Book
The Further Adventures Of Quincy Adams Sawyer - *Only*
Page US (1909)

Charles Felton PIDGIN 1844-1923 and John M TAYLOR 1988- (American)
Citation Record: 7 Short Stories in 1 Collection
The Chronicles Of Quincy Adams Sawyer, Detective - *Collection 1*
Page US (1912)

Tom SAWYER

is one of the great characters of American fiction. He is of such an enquiring nature that he can certainly be called a sleuth; and, judging by the title of the collection, the author thought so too. In the story giving the book its title, he solves a case for a $2000 reward – not without help from his almost equally famous young friend.

American Male Amateur operating in Mississippi

Sidekick: Huckleberry FINN
American Male - Friend

Mark TWAIN 1835-1910 (American)
was born in Florida, Missouri. He worked as a printer, riverboat pilot, gold miner, and newspaperman, finally becoming a writer, taking his pen-name from the call (by the mark, twain) made by riverboat men when sounding. Apart from the humorous works for which he is famous, he wrote several short stories and one or two novels with a detective background, including one *Sherlock HOLMES* pastiche.
Writer: Samuel Langhorne CLEMENS
Other Detectives:
Insp BLUNT
Sherlock HOLMES
Simon WHEELER
David 'Pudd'nhead' WILSON
Citation Record: 5 Short Stories in 1 Collection
Tom Sawyer Abroad, Tom Sawyer, Detective & Other Stories - *Collection 1*
Harper & Row US (1896)
Tom Sawyer, Detective, As Told By Huck Finn - *Collection 1**
Chatto UK (1897)

Christopher SAXE

American Male Amateur operating in New York

Susannah SHANE 1896-1946 (American)
Writer: Harriette Cora ASHBROOK
Other Byline: H ASHBROOK

Citation Record: 4 Books

Lady In Danger - *First*
Dodd, Mead US (1942); Nicholson & Watson UK (1948)

Diamonds In The Dumplings - *Last*
Doubleday US (1946)

SAXON

is an Easterner now living in Los Angeles. Not only is he a part-time actor and part-time chef, but he manages to run the Saxon agency. He is honest, muscular, not especially violent, courteous to ladies, and good to lowly types.

American Male Private Detective operating in Los Angeles

Les ROBERTS 1937- (American)

See main detective Milan JACOVICH

Citation Record: 6 Books

An Infinite Number Of Monkeys - *First*
St Martin's US (1987); Macmillan UK (1987)

The Lemon Chicken Jones - *Latest*
St Martin's US (1994)

Alan SAXON

British Male Amateur operating in Scotland/USA

Keith MILES (British)

For writer details see Nicholas BRACEWELL

Citation Record: 3 Books

Bullet Hole - *First*
Deutsch UK (1986); Harper & Row US (1987)

Green Murder - *Latest*
Macdonald UK (1990)

Joe SAXON

is a stage magician whose female assistant really does disappear. He has to use his skills to solve the mystery.

American Male Amateur operating in USA

Steve FISHER 1912-1980 (American)

was a prolific writer of short stories for the pulps of the 1930s and 1940s. Many of his stories also appeared in magazines and collections of the 1940s and 1950s. He wrote at least nineteen criminous books and a great number of screenplays between 1940 and 1975.

Writer: Stephen Gould FISHER

Other Byline: Stephen GOULD

Other Detectives:
Sheridan DOOME
Kip MULDANE
Johnny RYAN

Citation Record: 1 Book

Saxon's Ghost - *Only*
Sherbourne Press US (1969)

S

Johnny SAXON

is a writer of pulp detective stories who operates as a private eye.

American Male Private Detective operating in New York

William BOGART 1903-1977 (American)

See main detective 'Doc' SAVAGE

Citation Record: 4 Books

Hell On Friday - *First*
Swift US (1941)

The Queen City Murder Case - *Last*
Mystery House US (1946)

Ludovic (The Picaroon) SAXON

British Male Sleuth operating in England

John CASSELLS 1909-1975 (British)

See main detective Insp FLAGG

Citation Record: 20 Books

Meet The Picaroon - *First*
Long UK (1957)

Action Of The Picaroon - *Last*
Long UK (1975)

Michael SAXON

charges very high rates for his rather mediocre services.

American Male Private Detective operating in California

William D BLANKENSHIP 1924- (American)

Writer: William Douglas BLANKENSHIP

Citation Record: 1 Book

The Programmed Man - *Only*
Walker US (1973); Barker UK (1973)

Michael SAXON

American Male Private Detective operating in Kansas City

L V ROPER (American)

See main detective pair Jerry 'Renegade' ROE and Stuart WORTH

Citation Record: 1 Book

Hookers Don't Go To Heaven - *Single*
Popular Library US (1976)

Simeon SAXON

was one of this author's numerous detectives, appearing mainly in stories in *Detective Fiction Weekly.*

American Male Detective in Pulp Magazines operating in California

Norbert DAVIS 1909-1949 (American)

Invented 8 detectives - see Ben SHALEY

No citations

Michael SAYERS

British Male Amateur operating in England

E Phillips OPPENHEIM 1866-1946 (British)

Invented 27 detectives - see Nicholas GOADE

Citation Record: 11 Short Stories in 1 Collection

Michael's Evil Deeds - *Collection 1*
Little, Brown US (1923); Hodder & Stoughton UK (1924)

Catherine SAYLOR

is a cop's daughter and specialises in solving the rather superior kinds of crime associated with the technocracy around San Francisco.

American Female Private Detective operating in San Francisco

Sidekick: Pete HARMAN
is, in fact, a PI himself.
American Male - Friend

Linda GRANT (American)

Writer: Linda V WILLIAMS

Citation Record: 2 Books

Random Access Murder - *First*
Avon US (1988)

Blind Trust - *Latest*
Scribner's US (1990)

Aggie SCANLON

American Female Amateur operating in USA

Doris Miles DISNEY 1907-1976 (American)

Invented 7 detectives - see Jefferson DIMARCO

Citation Record: 1 Book

Room For Murder - *Only*
Doubleday US (1955); Foulsham UK (1957)

Jerry SCANT

British Male Amateur operating in England

Leonard KNIGHT 1895- (British)

See main detective Colby STACK

Citation Record: 5 Books

Deadman's Bay - *First*
Low UK (1930)

The Solander Box Mystery - *Last*
Low UK (1940)

Paul SCARF

British Male Amateur operating in England

Raymond BOYD (British)

Citation Record: 2 Books

Fetch Me A Rope - *First*
Hammond UK (1947)

Murder Is A Furtive Thing - *Last*
Hammond UK (1950)

Det/Sgt/Supt SCARFE

British Policeman operating in England

John GOODWIN 1878- (British)

Writer: Sidney Floyd GOWING

Citation Record: 2 Books

The Shadow Man - *First*
Putnam UK (1932); Sears US (1932)

In Full Cry - *Last*
Jenkins UK (1941)

Sir Benjamin SCARLE

solves a case of death by poisoning in a locked study.

British Male Amateur operating in England

John DONAVAN 1905-1986 (British)

Invented 3 detectives - see Sgt Johnny LAMB

Citation Record: 1 Book

The Dead Have No Friends - *Only*
Home US (1952)

The SCARLET PIMPERNEL

was the brilliant invention of the author when she was still young and a struggling newcomer to England. He was, of course, the English aristocrat, Sir Percy Blakeney, who, while giving the appearance of foppish decadence, became the daring adventurer and hero responsible, in the years of the Terror after the French Revolution, for rescuing French 'aristos' from the guillotine. He was to become not only a legend for his own, fictional time, but for all time. Although the author went on writing about his adventures for the next thirty-five years, the novels and short stories gradually lost their earlier fine quality and appeal.

The SCARLET PIMPERNEL has featured as a character in several films, serious and comic.

British Male Amateur operating in England/France

Baroness ORCZY 1865-1947 (British)

Invented 6 detectives - see Lady Molly DE MAZEREEN

Citation Record: 10 Books 19 Short Stories in 2 Collections

The Scarlet Pimpernel - *First*
Greening UK (1905); Putnam US (1905)

Mam'zelle Guillotine - *Last*
Hodder & Stoughton UK (1940)

The League Of The Scarlet Pimpernel - *Collection 1*
Short stories in this collection - 11
Castle UK (1919); Doran US (1919)

Adventures Of The Scarlet Pimpernel - *Collection 2*
Short stories in this collection - 8
Hutchinson UK (1929); Doran US (1929)

Dr SCARLETT

American Male Amateur operating in Far East

Alexander LAING 1903-1976 (American)

Writer: Alexander Kinnan LAING

Citation Record: 2 Books

Dr Scarlett - *First*
Farrar, Straus US (1936); Rich UK (1937)

The Methods Of Dr Scarlett - *Last*
Farrar, Straus US (1937); Cassell UK (1938)

John SCARLETT

British Male Amateur operating in England

Ben BOLT 1872- (British)

Invented 5 detectives - see Bob PONTING

Citation Record: 1 Book

The Girl In The Train - *Only*
Ward, Lock UK (1939)

Peter SCARLETT

British Policeman operating in England

Sydney HORLER 1888-1954 (British)

Invented 20 detectives - see Sir Harker BELLAMY

Citation Record: 2 Books

Scarlett - Special Branch - *First*
Foulsham UK (1950)

Scarlett Gets The Kidnapper - *Last*
Foulsham UK (1951)

Dr Kay SCARPETTA

is a Chief Medical Examiner, usually up to her elbows in gore, who uses her exceptional forensic skills to trap murderers.

American Female Professional Investigator operating in USA

Patricia D CORNWELL 1956- (American)

was a computer analyst in the Chief Medical Examiner's Office at Richmond, Virginia, before turning to writing. Her first detective novel won several prestigious awards.

Citation Record: 6 Books

Postmortem - *First*
Little, Brown US

Body Farm - *Latest*
Scribner's US (1994); Little, Brown UK (1994)

William SCHAEFER

is tall and very large. He worked for the Worldwide Detective Agency in Manhattan before setting up on his own. He may seem a little soft: but beware!

American Male Private Detective operating in New York

Sidekick: Ann LANG
American Female - Partner

Daniel ESTOW (American)

Citation Record: 2 Books

The Moment Of Fiction - *First*
Carlyle US (1979)

The Moment Of Silence - *Latest*
Carlyle US (1980)

Insp SCHMIDT

of Manhattan's Homicide Squad appears in a long series of straight whodunnits. The greatly admired books give a wonderful picture of New York, the background and backdrop for nearly all *SCHMIDT's* cases, and we sympathise continually with the detective, whose feet are always aching and who has to put on slippers before he can do his thinking.

American Policeman operating in New York

Sidekick: George BAGBY
was ostensibly sent by a publisher to help *SCHMIDT* with his memoirs. To do so, however, he becomes his constant sidekick, accompanying him on many of his cases and sometimes getting into trouble from which he has to be rescued. He also narrates the stories.
American Male - Narrator

George BAGBY 1906-1985 (American)

Writer: Aaron Marc STEIN

Other Byline: Hampton STONE

Citation Record: 51 Books

Murder At The Piano - *First*
Covici US (1935); Sampson, Low UK (1936)

The Most Wanted - *Last*
Doubleday US (1983); Hale UK (1984)

Pete SCHOFIELD

is a little unusual for a PI in being a happily married man, which, indeed, has raised objections from some critics, who maintain that what the British actress, Mrs Patrick Campbell, called the 'deep, deep peace of the double bed after the hurly-burly of the *chaise-longue'* is not, as it were, compatible with the work of an honest gumshoe.

American Male Private Detective operating in Los Angeles/Nevada

Thomas B DEWEY 1915- (American)

Invented 3 detectives - see Singer BATTS

Citation Record: 9 Books

And Where She Stops - *First*
Popular Library US (1957)

IOU Murder - *First**
Boardman UK (1958)

Nude In Nevada - *Last*
Dell US (1965); Boardman UK (1966)

Lenny SCHWARTZ

American Male Amateur operating in New York

Irving WEINMAN 1937- (American)

Citation Record: 3 Books

Tailor's Dummy - *First*
Atheneum US (1986); Arlington UK (1988)

Virgil's Ghost - *Latest*
Columbine UK (1990)

Rebecca SCHWARTZ

is a lawyer, feminine and feminist, who deals with lively cases of murder in full Californian colour.

American Female Amateur operating in San Francisco

Julie SMITH 1944- (American)

Invented 4 detectives - see Paul MACDONALD

Citation Record: 4 Books

Death Turns A Trick - *First*
Walker US (1982)

Dead In The Water - *Latest*
Berkley US (1993)

Danny SCIPIO

appears in novelizations of episodes from a TV series.

Male Sleuth operating in several locations

Tudor GATES

Citation Record: 3 Books

I Was Walking Down Below - *First*
Corgi UK (1967)

Ancora Scipio - *Last*
Muller UK (1970)

Sherbert SCONES

is a *Sherlock HOLMES* parody.

Male Professional Amateur

Hugh LOFTING 1886-1947 (American)

Citation Record: 1 Selected Short Story

The Food Mystery Story - *Parody 1*
is to be found in *Gub Gub's Book.*
Stokes US (1932)

James SCOTLAND

British Male Amateur operating in England

Michael GILBERT 1912- (British)

Invented 11 detectives - see Insp HAZELRIGG

Citation Record: 1 Book

The Black Seraphim - *Single*
Harper & Row US (1984)

A SCOTLAND YARD DETECTIVE

British Policeman operating in England

G H GREENHAM (British)

Writer: George Hepburn GREENHAM

Citation Record: 38 Short Stories in 1 Collection

Scotland Yard Experiences - *Collection 1*
Routledge UK (1904)

A SCOTLAND YARD DETECTIVE

British Policeman operating in London

Andrew LANDSDOWNE (British)

See main detective LANDSDOWNE

Citation Record: 21 Short Stories in 1 Collection

A Life's Reminiscences Of Scotland Yard - *Collection 1*
Leadenhall UK (1890); Scribner's US (1890)

Capt Alan SCOTT

is the captain of a cruise ship who, when a passenger is murdered, turns detective and solves the crime before the police can.

American Male Amateur operating in Barbados

George Harmon COXE 1901-1984 (American)

Invented 20 detectives - see Kent MURDOCK

Citation Record: 1 Book

Uninvited Guest - *Only*
Knopf US (1953); Hammond UK (1956)

Aline SCOTT

American Female Sleuth operating in Florida

Alison DRAKE 1947- (American)

Writer: Trish JANESCHUTZ

Citation Record: 3 Books

Tango Key - *First*
Ballantine US (1988)

Black Moon - *Latest*
Ballantine US (1989)

Griffin SCOTT

is a psychologist who solves a case of death by shooting in a locked room.

American Male Professional Investigator operating in USA

Rufus GILLMORE 1879-1935 (American)

Writer: Rufus Hamilton GILLMORE

Citation Record: 1 Book

The Ebony Bed Murder - *Only*
Mystery League US (1932)

Det Jim SCOTT

Second detective of Penny PACKER

Sir Patrick SCOTT

is a prominent Queen's Counsel and a Fellow of a fictional Cambridge college. His decisive detective work is duly acknowledged by the local police, who seem to know their place in the scheme of things.

British Male Amateur operating in Cambridge

Anthony APPIAH 1954- (British)

was born in London. He took a double first in Philosophy at Clare College, Cambridge, followed by a PhD, and is now Professor of Philosophy at Duke University, North Carolina.

Citation Record: 2 Books

Avenging Angel - *First*
Constable UK (1991)

Nobody Likes Letitia - *Latest*
Constable UK (1994)

Phil SCOTT

American Male Professional Investigator operating in USA

Judson R TAYLOR 1837-1898 (American)

was the author of many stories featuring character detectives, a feature of the genre that was popular around the beginning of the twentieth century. Most were published in magazines.

Writer: Harlan Page HALSEY

Other Byline: Tony PASTOR

Other Detectives:
Gipsy BLAIR — Macon MOORE
OLD STONEWALL

Citation Record: 1 Book

Phil Scott, The Indian Detective - *Only*
Ogilvie US (1888)

Philip SCOTT

British Male Professional Investigator operating in England

Hartley HOWARD 1908-1979 (British)

See main detective Glenn BOWMAN

Citation Record: 2 Books

Department K - *First*
Collins UK (1964)

Assignment K - *First**
Pyramid US (1968)

The Eye Of The Hurricane - *Last*
Collins UK (1968)

Robert SCOTT

of Scotland Yard is in this one Victorian novel.

British Policeman operating in London

Hume NISBET 1849-1921? (British)

Invented 3 detectives - see Nicodemus Dove TURTLE

Citation Record: 1 Book

A Singular Crime - *Only*
White UK (1894)

Sarah SCOTT

American Female Amateur operating in California

Karl ALEXANDER (American)

Inventor of one other detective H G WELLS

Citation Record: 1 Book

A Private Investigation - *Single*
Delacorte US (1980); Severn UK (1981)

Shell SCOTT

has been, for over twenty-five years, a legend and a loved phenomenon in the field of American detection. An ex-Marine, well over six feet tall, with a snow-white crew cut an inch high and a rather battered face, he owns and largely operates the Sheldon Scott Agency on Broadway, Los Angeles. He has handled, he often says, 'half the crimes in the California Penal Code'. No avenger, no man with a mission, he simply has a refreshingly good time being a detective, driving around town in his distinctive blue Cadillac, finding cases, catching crooks, bedding the ladies, and generally getting into the most enjoyable and unusual situations. He appears in one book under the author's pseudonym.

American Male Private Detective operating in Los Angeles

Stooge: Capt Phil SAMPSON
of the Los Angeles Police Department's Homicide division often tangles with *Shell SCOTT,* but he is not, on the whole, unfriendly, seeing that he is inevitably beaten to the solution of his cases.
American Male

David KNIGHT 1921- (American)

For writer details see Shell SCOTT

Citation Record: 1 Book

Pattern For Murder - *Only*
was republished, with a change of title, under the *Richard S PRATHER* byline.
Graphic US (1952)

Richard PRATHER 1921- (American)

was born in Santa Ana, California, and educated at Riverside Junior College, California. Marine, fireman and engineer, he has been a full-time writer since 1949.

Writer: Richard Scott PRATHER

Other Bylines:
David KNIGHT — Richard S PRATHER

Citation Record: 34 Books 18 Short Stories in 3 Collections

Case Of The Vanishing Beauty - *First*
Fawcett US (1950); Fawcett UK (1957)

Shellshock - *Latest*
Tor US (1987)

Have Gat - Will Travel - *Collection 1*
Short stories - 6
GM US (1957); Fawcett UK (1958)

Shell Scott's Seven Slaughters - *Collection 2*
Short stories - 7
GM US (1961); Muller UK (1962)

The Shell Scott Sampler - *Collection 3*
Short stories - 5
Pocket Books US (1969)

Richard S PRATHER 1921- (American)

For writer details see Shell SCOTT

Citation Record: 1 Book

The Scrambled Yeggs - *Only*
was previously published, with a change of title, under the *David KNIGHT* byline.
GM US (1958); Muller UK (1961)

Steven SCOTT

British Male Amateur operating in England

Dick FRANCIS 1920- (British)

Invented 18 detectives - see Sid HALLEY

Citation Record: 1 Book

High Stakes - *Single*
Harper & Row US (1976)

Willie 'Spider' SCOTT

is an ex-burglar who has been recruited, for special duties in connection with his profession, by British Intelligence.

British Male Professional Investigator operating in England

Kenneth ROYCE 1920- (British)

was born in Croydon, Surrey. He served in the Army, 1939-46, then became a businessman and writer of thrillers.

Writer: Kenneth Royce GANDLEY

Other Detectives:
Laurie GALVIN — Matt PRESTON

Citation Record: 7 Books

The XYY Man - *First*
Hodder & Stoughton UK (1970); McKay US (1970)

No Way Back - *Latest*
Hodder & Stoughton UK (1986)

Hashimi's Revenge - *Latest**
Stein US (1987)

Mr John Cornelius SCOTTER

is too brusque and ill-mannered to be loveable, but he does a creditable job.

British Male Private Detective operating in England

Thurman WARRINER (British)

Citation Record: 7 Books

Method In His Murder - *First*
Hodder & Stoughton UK (1950); Macmillan US (1950)

Heavenly Bodies - *Last*
Hodder & Stoughton UK (1960)

Publius Manlius SCRIBO

sleuths in a historical whodunnit, set in Rome around 50 BC.

Roman Male Amateur operating in Rome

Wallace IRWIN 1876-1959 (American)

was born in New York City and worked there for many years as a newspaper editor.

Writer: Wallace Admah IRWIN

Citation Record: 1 Book

The Julius Caesar Murder Case - *Only*
Appleton US (1935)

Laura SCUDAMORE

Second detective of Insp Dick MASON

Laura SCUDAMORE

Appears with at least two other detectives - see J Rockingham STONE

Matt SCUDDER

is first introduced as an ex-cop from the New York Police Department, retired after having accidentally killed a young girl.

Filled with remorse and guilt, he leaves his family, becomes an alcoholic, and goes to live in a hotel on West 57th Street. He is unlicensed but resumes his life as a private detective when he begins to solve cases connected with his friends, many of them involving murder. He gives a tenth of his fees to any nearby church and sends most of the rest to his family.

American Male Private Detective operating in New York

Sidekick: TJ
is black, streetwise and has appeared in the last three books with *SCUDDER*.
American Male - Assistant

Lawrence BLOCK 1938- (American)
Invented 6 detectives - see Leo HAIG
Citation Record: 12 Books
The Sins Of The Fathers *- First*
Dell US (1976); Hale UK (1979)
The Devil Knows You're Dead *- Latest*
Morrow US (1995)

Maj Hutton SEARY

British Male Amateur operating in England

John ROSS 1912-1987 (Irish)
Writer: Rudolph Clifford JONES
Citation Record: 3 Books
The Moccasin Men *- First*
Hodder & Stoughton UK (1936)
The Major Steps Out *- Last*
Hodder & Stoughton UK (1939)

Patricia SEAWARD

American Female Private Detective operating in New York

Frederick NEBEL 1903-1967 (American)
Invented 8 detectives - see Steve CARDIGAN
Citation Record: 1 Selected Short Story
Murder By Mail
In 'Dime Detective' US (1933)

SEBASTIAN

American Male Secret Agent operating in Israel/The Arctic

James L JOHNSON 1927- (American)
Writer: James Leonard JOHNSON
Citation Record: 4 Books
Code Name Sebastian *- First*
Lippincott US (1967)
A Piece Of The Moon Is Missing *- Last*
Holman UK (1974)

S

SECRET AGENT X-9

American Male Secret Agent operating in USA

Dashiell HAMMETT 1894-1961 (American)
Invented 7 detectives - see Sam SPADE
Citation Record: 1 Book 3 Short Stories in 1 Collection
Secret Agent X-9: Book Two *- Only*
McKay US (1934)
Secret Agent X-9 *- Collection 1*
McKay US (1934)

Harry SEDDAL

British Male Sleuth

J K MAYO (British)
Citation Record: 5 Books
The Hunting Season *- First*
Collins UK (1985); Holt US (1986)
The Masterless Men *- Latest*
UK (1995); Harvill UK (1995)

Lee SEDDON

British Male Amateur operating in England

Patrick WINN 1906- (British)
See main detective Insp LYON

Citation Record: 1 Book
Invisible Evidence *- Only*
Hale UK (1963)

SEEKAY

is a specialist in solving difficult cases. He has a face so mutilated that, when he interviews clients, he covers it with a plain plastic shield. He prefers to wear an artificial face when he goes out.

American Male Private Detective operating in Chicago

Paul ERNST 1886- (American)
Inventor of 5detectives - see Lt Jim RYAN, Shirley LEIGHTON and Bill HARPER
Citation Record: 1 Selected Short Story
Madam Murder - And The Corpse Brigade
can also be found in the anthology, *'The Defective Detective In The Pulps* (Editors; Gary Hoppenstand & Ray B Browne; 1983).
In 'Strange Detective Mysteries' US (1937)

Emily SEETON and Supt DELPHICK

Miss EMILY SEETON is a frail, elderly art teacher, in love with the opera and ballet in London. She has recently inherited a house in the country and becomes involved, for a variety of reasons, in crimes, which she solves – with the assistance of her friend, *Supt DELPHICK* (called The Oracle, for obvious reasons) and his assistant. After the death of their creator, *Heron CARVIC*, the detectives reappeared under the authorship of *Hampton CHARLES.*

British Female Amateur and British Policeman operating in London

Sidekick: Det Sgt RANGER
British Male - Subordinate

Heron CARVIC ?-1980
Citation Record: 5 Books
Picture Miss Seeton *- First*
Bles UK (1968); Harper & Row US (1968)
Odds On Miss Seeton *- Last*
Davies UK (1976); Harper & Row US (1976)

Hampton CHARLES 1931- (American)
Writer: Roy Peter MARTIN
Citation Record: 3 Books
Advantage Miss Seeton *- First*
Berkley US (1990)
Miss Seeton, By Appointment *- Latest*
Berkley US (1990)

James SEGROVE

British Male Amateur operating in England

David DURHAM 1888-1965 (British)
Invented 5 detectives - see Insp G RASON
Citation Record: 1 Book
The Woman Accused *- Only*
was republished by *Newnes* (UK 1936) under the author's real name.
Hodder & Stoughton UK (1923)

Roy VICKERS 1888-1965 (British)
Invented 9 detectives - see Insp J RASON
Citation Record: 3 Books
The Vengeance Of Henry Jarroman *- First*
Jenkins UK (1923)
Four Past Four *- Last*
Jenkins UK (1925); Jefferson House US (1945)

Martin SEGUNDO

British Male Sleuth operating in Scotland/Argentine

Bob LANGLEY 1936- (British)
Writer: Robert LANGLEY
Citation Record: 2 Books

Conquistadores - *First*
Joseph UK (1985)
Falklands Gambit - *First**
Walker US (1985)
Avenge The Belgrano - *Latest*
Joseph UK (1988); Walker US (1988)
Conqueror Down - *Latest**
Bantam US (1991)

Mavis SEIDLITZ

is just one of this extraordinary writer's detective creations, all of them in books coming pretty far down the scale as far as the standards of most critics are concerned, although they are good racy reads that have sold in their millions. *Mavis SEIDLITZ*, blonde, zany, lovely and loveable, has, indeed, been called by one critic 'a cross between Gracie Allen and Candy Christian, whose looks outweigh by far her mental ability'; and, by another, 'the most improbable PI of all time'. Regardless of such snide comments, she manages to function as a private detective in several books, in which she has a vague, fluctuating association with *Johnny RIO*.

American Female Private Detective operating in California

Sidekick: Johnny RIO
is not quite a partner and not quite a sidekick.
American Male - Partner

Carter BROWN 1923-1985 (Australian)
Invented 10 detectives - see Rick HOLMAN
Citation Record: 12 Books
A Bullet For My Baby - *First*
Horwitz-Transport AU (1955)
And The Undead Sing - *Last*
Signet US (1974)

Paul SELBON and Peter SELBON

American Male Amateurs operating in USA

Johnston MCCULLEY 1883-1958 (American)
Invented 5 detectives - see John (The Thunderbolt) FLATCHLEY
Citation Record: 2 Books
The Avenging Twins - *First*
Chelsea US (1927); Hutchinson UK (1927)
The Avenging Twins Collect - *Last*
Chelsea US (1927)

Peter SELBON

Second detective of Paul SELBON

Charity SELBOURNE

British Male Amateur operating in France

Mary STEWART 1916- (British)
was born in Sunderland, County Durham. She was educated at Eden Hall, Penrith, Cumberland, and took a BA at St Hild's Hall, University of Durham, 1938. She has taught English at Durham University, 1941-1956, and is the author of at least twelve genre novels, five mainstream novels, plays for radio and books for children. She received the Crime Writers Association Silver Dagger award, 1961.
Writer: Mary Florence Elinor STEWART
Other Detectives:
Simon LESTER and Camilla HAVEN
Jennifer SILVER
Citation Record: 1 Book
Madam, Will You Talk? - *Only*
Hodder & Stoughton UK (1955); Morrow US (1956)

Lt SELBY

investigates a murder in a locked prison cell.

American Policeman operating in USA

Arthur PORGES (American)
Invented 13 detectives - see Arsène LUPIN
Citation Record: 1 Selected Short Story
Murder Of A Priest
In 'Ellery Queen's Mystery Magazine' US (1967)

Doug SELBY

is a small-town attorney who is a prosecuting counsel, having usually to prove his cases in spite of shady work by the defence.

American Male Amateur operating in California

Sidekick: Sylvia MARTIN
is a beautiful reporter on the *Clarion* who assists *SELBY* and falls in love with him too.
American Female - Aide

Erle Stanley GARDNER 1889-1970 (American)
Invented 14 detectives - see Perry MASON
Citation Record: 6 Books
The DA Calls It Murder - *First*
Morrow US (1937); Cassell UK (1937)
The DA Breaks An Egg - *Last*
Morrow US (1949); Heinemann UK (1957)

Det Pete SELBY

is a detective in Manhattan's 6th Precinct and appears in books that are early police procedurals.

American Policeman operating in New York

Sidekick: Det Stan RAYDER
American Male - Partner

Jonathan CRAIG 1919- (American)
See main detective Det Steve MANNING
Citation Record: 10 Books
The Dead Darling - *First*
Fawcett US (1955); Miller UK (1958)
Case Of The Brazen Beauty - *Last*
GM US (1966)

Dick SELDON

British Male Amateur operating in England

Walter S MASTERMAN 1876- (British)
Writer: Walter Sidney MASTERMAN
Other Detectives:
Ch Const HENDON Sir Arthur SINCLAIR
Citation Record: 2 Books
The Bloodhounds Bay - *First*
Jarrolds UK (1936); Dutton US (1936)
The Border Line - *Last*
Jarrolds UK (1936); Dutton US (1937)

Andrew SENTRY

American Male Amateur

Ursula CURTISS 1923- (American)
Invented 5 detectives - see Lou FABIAN
Citation Record: 1 Book
The Noonday Devil - *Only*
Dodd, Mead US (1951); Eyre & Spottiswoode UK (1953)

Victor SERGE

is, it would seem, a famous amateur detective who is often called in by those dunces at Scotland Yard, so highly do they think of his skills. Based in a magnificent apartment in Jermyn Street, wealthy, an expert in arts and sciences, he is, however, a throwback to an earlier detective era. In his one book, he is called to a country mansion to solve a series of murders that are puzzling the police. Using remarkable but totally unbelievable methods, including his 'occult pointer', the exact principle of which remains unexplained, he solves the case.

British Male Professional Amateur operating in London

Sidekick: Ralph MORETON
is a novelist and the detective's close friend. He accompanies him on his cases and tries to help, but most things have to be explained to him – sometimes twice.
British Male - Friend

Stooge: Insp BANCROFT
is a Scotland Yard man, suitably baffled, which is not surprising as he must be one of the most inept cops ever invented.
British Male

James CORBETT (British)
Invented 7 detectives - see Roy ENDICOTT
Citation Record: 1 Book
The Merrivale Mystery - *Only*
Mystery League US (1931)

Jock SERGEANT

American Male Sleuth operating in California/New York

Daniel DA CRUZ 1921- (American)
Writer: Daniel DA CRUZ Jr
Inventor of one other detective Ape SWAIN
Citation Record: 4 Books
Double Kill - *First*
GM US (1973); Coronet UK (1973)
Fire Kill - *Last*
GM US (1976); Coronet UK (1976)

Peter Cutler SERGEANT

is a public relations expert, ladies man and amateur sleuth. His books are high class on style and language, but he is a pretty mediocre sleuth.

American Male Amateur operating in New York

Edgar BOX 1925- (American)
was born at West Point, New York, and educated in New Mexico and New Hampshire. The author of many novels, histories, biographies, screenplays and critical studies, he wrote three pot-boiler detective novels in the 1950s and has written none since.
Writer: Gore VIDAL
Citation Record: 3 Books
Death In The Fifth Position - *First*
Dutton US (1952); Heinemann UK (1954)
Death Likes It Hot - *Last*
Dutton US (1954); Heinemann UK (1955)

Det Frank SESSIONS

is in the Homicide division of Manhattan North in the New York Police Department and is a gentlemanly cop compared to many that could be named.

American Policeman operating in New York

Hillary WAUGH 1920- (American)
Invented 7 detectives - see Ch Fred FELLOWS
Citation Record: 3 Books
30 Manhattan East - *First*
Doubleday US (1968); Gollancz UK (1969)
Finish Me Off - *Last*
Doubleday US (1970); Gollancz UK (1971)

S

Cleavers SETON

lives at 2 Wigmore Street, just a stone's throw away from a certain address in Baker Street.

British Male Professional Amateur operating in London

Stooge: Insp MARTIN
British Male

W A H BROOKER (British)
Citation Record: 1 Book
The Mystery Of Castle Royal - *Only*
Heath Cranton UK (1931)

Mike SETON

British Male Sleuth operating in Paris/Tunisia

T C H JACOBS 1899-1976 (British)
Invented 8 detectives - see Ch Insp BARNARD
Citation Record: 2 Books
Target For Terror - *First*
Hale UK (1961)
The Elusive Mr Drago - *Last*
Hale UK (1965)

Prof Grace SEVERANCE

is a retired Professor of Pathology, unmarried and now living in a small town in Arizona. Forthright and not very sociable, she gets drawn into solving murder cases that baffle the police, something that she is able to do because of her expert forensic knowledge.

American Female Amateur operating in Arizona

Margaret SCHERF 1908-1979 (American)
Invented 5 detectives - see Rev Martin BUELL
Citation Record: 4 Books
The Banker's Bones - *First*
Doubleday US (1968); Hale UK (1969)
The Beaded Banana - *Latest*
Doubleday US (1978); Hale UK (1979)

Insp SEVERN

is in the Devonshire police force.

British Policeman operating in England

Gordon BROMLEY 1910- (British)
Citation Record: 3 Books
In The Absence Of The Body - *First*
Collins UK (1972)
A Midsummer Night's Crime - *Last*
Hale UK (1977)

Det Knute SEVERSON

American Policeman operating in Boston

Tobias WELLS 1923- (American)
Writer: Deloris Florine STANTON
Citation Record: 15 Books
A Matter Of Love And Death - *First*
Doubleday US (1966); Gollancz UK (1966)
A Creature Was Stirring - *Latest*
Doubleday US (1977); Hale UK (1978)

Insp SEVREL

American Policeman operating in California/New York

Cedric WORTH 1900- (American)
Citation Record: 2 Books
The Trail Of The Serpent - *First*
Dutton US (1940)
The Corpse That Knew Everybody - *Last*
Dutton US (1941)

Insp Giles SEYMOUR

British Policeman operating in England

James CORBETT (British)
Invented 7 detectives - see Roy ENDICOTT
Citation Record: 1 Book
The Body In The Bungalow - *Only*
Jenkins UK (1938)

Ned SHACKLETON

American Male Amateur operating in Africa

Raymond CRAWLEY
Citation Record: 2 Books
The Valley Of Creeping Men - *First*
Harper & Row US (1930)
Chattering Gods - *Last*
Harper & Row US (1931)

Det Rene SHADE

is a detective in the fictional town of St Bruno, in the deep bayou country, and investigates killings among the dregs of society there.

American Policeman operating in Louisiana

Daniel WOODRELL 1953- (American)
Citation Record: 1 Book
Under The Bright Lights - *Single*
Mysterious Press UK (1986)

Grey SHADOW

British Male Sleuth operating in England

Geo E ROCHESTER 1898- (British)

Writer: George Ernest ROCHESTER

Citation Record: 2 Books

Grey Shadow - *First*
Hamilton UK (1936)

The Return Of Grey Shadow - *Last*
Eldon UK (1949)

The SHADOWERS INC

American Male Sleuths operating in New York

David FOX 1883-1924 (American)

For writer details see Barry O'DELL

Citation Record: 4 Books

The Man Who Convicted Himself - *First*
was published in the UK under the following byline.
McBride US (1920)

The Handwriting On The Wall - *Last*
was published in the UK under the following byline.
McBride US (1924)

Robert Orr CHIPPERFIELD 1883-1924 (American)

Invented 3 detectives - see Barry O'DELL

Citation Record: 4 Books

The Man Who Convicted Himself - *First*
was published in the US under the preceding byline.
Hurst UK (1923)

The Handwriting On The Wall - *Last*
was published in the US under the preceding byline.
Hurst UK (1925)

John SHAFT

is a big, tough, black, Vietnam War hero, an ex-marine who has set up as a PI on 46th Street, Manhattan. He is more intelligent than many of his ilk.

American Male Private Detective operating in New York

Ernest TIDYMAN 1928-1984 (American)

was born in Cleveland, Ohio, and educated at public schools. He worked for many years as a reporter, wrote stories for magazines and was a film producer. He is renowned, however, for his creation of *SHAFT*, a black detective for the 1970s, who was not only cast in the prevailing mould of hardboiled violence but appeared as a new sexual model and super-hero. Not surprisingly, he was featured in several films and TV dramas, and *TIDYMAN* wrote or collaborated on the scripts. When the first of the short series of novels was published, the author received the Mystery Writers of America Edgar Allan Poe award, 1972, and the Academy Award for his screenplay derived from it in the same year.

Citation Record: 7 Books

Shaft - *First*
Macmillan US (1970); Joseph UK (1971)

The Last Shaft - *Last*
Weidenfeld & Nicolson UK (1975)

Will SHAKESPEAR

British Male Amateur operating in England

Mark HAYMAN (British)

Citation Record: 1 Book

The Nice Lady - *Single*
Hale UK (1979)

William SHAKESPEARE

is, indeed, the famed playwright.

English Male Amateur operating in England

J F PEIRCE (American)

See main detective Capt ZACHARY

Citation Record: 1 Selected Short Story

Cassandra's Castle; Or, The Devious Disappearances
In 'Ellery Queen's Mystery Magazine' US (1975)

Sylvia SHALE

is a young lady, said to be 'very refined and with nothing mannish about her appearance', and is employed by a New York detective agency. She foregoes marriage, stating, rather unaccountably, that her one aim in life is to outwit and unmask Notorious Nick, the international master criminal.

American Female Private Detective operating in New York

Mrs Sidney GROOM (British)

Writer: GROOM

Citation Record: 1 Book

Detective Sylvia Shale - *Only*
Hurst & Blackett UK (1923)

Ben SHALEY

is one of this author's numerous pulp detectives, appearing in stories in *Black Mask Magazine*.

American Male Private Detective operating in USA

Norbert DAVIS 1909-1949 (American)

is regarded as one of the best of all the pulp writers of the 1930s.

Other Detectives:
Max CLARK
John COLLINS
DOAN
William 'Bail Bond' DODD
Mark HULL
Max LATIN
Simeon SAXON

Citation Record: 1 Selected Short Story

Red Goose
In 'Black Mask Magazine' US (1934)

Roger SHALLOT

sleuths in England during the sixteenth century.

English Male Amateur operating in England

Michael CLYNES (British)

Citation Record: 4 Books

The Grail Murders - *First*
Otto Penzler US (1993)

A Brood Of Vipers - *Latest*
Headline UK (1994)

The SHAM DETECTIVE

American Male Detective in Pulp Magazines operating in USA

ANON

Citation Record: 1 Book

The Sham Detective - *Only*
Aldine US

Prof Peter SHANDY

works at the Balaclava Agricultural College on the East Coast and becomes involved in sometimes bizarre cases of murder in and around the place. Short, overweight and bespectacled, he is neither imposing nor gracious, and his sleuthing often borders on the frenetic.

American Male Amateur operating in Massachusetts

Charlotte MACLEOD 1922- (Canadian)

Invented 3 detectives - see Sarah KELLING and Max BITTERSOHN

Citation Record: 7 Books

Rest You Merry - *First*
Doubleday US (1978); Collins UK (1979)

Vane Pursuit - *Latest*
Collins UK (1989); Mysterious Press US (1989)

Det Insp SHANE

British Policeman operating in England

Seldon TRUSS 1892- (British)

Invented 3 detectives - see Ch Insp GIDLEIGH

Citation Record: 4 Books

Gallows Bait - *First*
Butterworth UK (1928)

The Living Alibi - *First**
Coward McCann US (1929)

Murder Paves The Way - *Last*
Hodder & Stoughton UK (1936)

Maj Peter Utley SHANE

teaches sociology and criminology at the University of Chicago. Described by others as 'the man in grey', he has grey hair, grey eyes, and wears grey clothes. He remains calm in the face of all disasters and is terribly brilliant at his deductive work. His cases, during the Second World War, take place in Washington DC, where he holds the rank of Major in Military Intelligence.

American Male Professional Investigator operating in Washington DC/Chicago

Sidekick: Francis BONNAMY
was formerly *SHANE's* assistant, when he taught criminology, and now narrates his cases.
American Male - Narrator

Francis BONNAMY 1906-1983 (American)

Writer: Audrey WALZ

Citation Record: 8 Books

Death By Appointment - *First*
Doubleday US (1931)

The Man In The Mist - *Last*
Duell US (1951); Murray UK (1952)

Hana SHANER

American Female Sleuth operating in Pennsylvania

Rona GRETH (American)

Citation Record: 2 Books

Now You Don't - *First*
Pageant US (1988); Chivers UK (1992)

Plain Murder - *Latest*
Pageant US (1989)

Father Joseph SHANLEY

Second detective of Det Sgt Sammy GOLDEN

Supt SHANNON

British Policeman operating in England

Clive RYLAND 1892- (British)

Invented 3 detectives - see Ch Insp George BASSETT

Citation Record: 3 Books

The Notting Hill Murder - *First*
Grayson UK (1932)

Murder On The Common - *Last*
Hutchinson UK (1939)

Dr Clinton SHANNON

American Male Amateur operating in Ohio/New York

S

Lee ROBERTS 1908-1976 (American)

Invented 4 detectives - see Lee FISKE

Citation Record: 4 Books

Once A Widow - *First*
Dodd, Mead US (1957); Hale UK (1961)

Suspicion - *Last*
Hale UK (1964); Curtis US (1971)

Desmond SHANNON

of the Boothe & Shannon Agency is tough and said to be the highest paid PI in New York.

American Male Private Detective operating in New York

M V HEBERDEN 1906- (American)

was born in England but has travelled widely in her business of timber importing. Most of the books that she published under her real name are set in New York and its environs, whilst she reserved her pseudonym, *Charles LEONARD,* mainly for books set in various European countries.

Writer: Mary Violet HEBERDEN

Other Byline: Charles L LEONARD

Inventor of one other detective Rick VANNER

Citation Record: 17 Books

Death On The Doormat - *First*
Doubleday US (1939)

Subscription To Murder - *First*
Doubleday US (1940)

Murder Unlimited - *Last*
Doubleday US (1953); Hale UK (1954)

John J SHANNON

is an ex-cop from the Los Angeles Police department and, tending to drink to excess, is not a loveable character.

American Male Private Detective operating in Los Angeles/Arizona

Cleve F ADAMS 1895-1949 (American)

Invented 5 detectives - see Rex MCBRIDE

Citation Record: 2 Books

The Private Eye - *First*
Reynal US (1942)

No Wings On A Cop - *Last*
Quin US (1950); Handi-Books US (1950)

Lucy SHANNON

American Female Amateur operating in USA

Dick BELSKY (American)

was the sometime City editor of the *New York Post.*

Inventor of one other detective Jenny MCKAY

Citation Record: 1 Book

One For The Money - *Single*
Academy US (1985)

Michael SHANNON

British Male Amateur operating in England

Gerald BOWMAN ?-1967 (British)

Adopter of one other detective Sexton BLAKE

Citation Record: 3 Books

Pattern In Poison-Ivy - *First*
Laurie UK (1948)

The Quick And The Wed - *Last*
Laurie UK (1950)

Patrick SHANNON

American Male Amateur operating in New York

Jake QUINN (American)

Writer: Jim C CONAWAY

Citation Record: 3 Books

Shallow Grave - *First*
Leisure Books US (1974)

The Mindbenders - *Last*
Leisure Books US (1975)

Supt SHANTER

British Policeman operating in England

Philip MACDONALD 1899-1981 (British)

Invented 5 detectives - see Col Anthony GETHRYN

Citation Record: 1 Book

Rynox - *Only*
Collins UK (1930)

The Rynox Mystery - *Only**
Collins UK (1933)

The Rynox Murder Mystery - *Only**
Doubleday US (1931)

The Rynox Murder - *Only**
Avon US (1968)

Ch Insp Frank SHAPIRO and Det Insp Liz GRAHAM

work together in the fictional town of Castlemere.

British Policeman and British Policewoman operating in England

Jo BANNISTER 1951- (British)

See main detective pair Clio MARSH and Det Supt Harry MARSH

Citation Record: 2 Books

A Bleeding Of Innocents - *First*
Macmillan UK (1993)

Sins Of The Heart - *Latest*
Macmillan UK (1994)

Det Nathan SHAPIRO

is a Jewish cop in the New York Homicide Squad. He appears with other detectives in the sprawling, interconnected, police novels of the two authors.

American Policeman operating in New York

Frances LOCKRIDGE and Richard LOCKRIDGE (American)

Invented 5 detectives - see Bernard SIMMONS

Citation Record: 4 Books

The Faceless Adversary - *First*
Lippincott US (1956)

The Drill Is Death - *Last*
Lippincott US (1961); Long UK (1963)

Richard LOCKRIDGE 1898-1982 (American)

Invented 3 detectives - see Capt/Insp Merton HEIMRICH

Citation Record: 8 Books

Murder Can't Wait - *First*
Lippincott US (1964); Long UK (1965)

The Case Of The Murdered Redhead - *First**
Avon US (1957)

Murder For Art's Sake - *Last*
Lippincott US (1968); Long UK (1967)

Harvey SHAPMAN

British Male Professional Investigator operating in England

Roland PUCCETTI 1924-

Writer: Roland Peter PUCCETTI

Citation Record: 1 Book

The Trial Of John And Henry Norton - *Only*
Hutchinson UK (1973)

Det Ch Supt Simon SHARD

of Scotland Yard is seconded to the Foreign Office for special duties.

British Policeman operating in several locations

Philip MCCUTCHAN 1920- (British)

See main detective Cdr Esmonde SHAW

Citation Record: 6 Books

Call For Simon Shard - *First*
Harrap UK (1974)

The Executioners - *Latest*
Hodder & Stoughton UK (1986)

Nick SHARMAN

is a private detective in South London, as sleazy and nasty as his surroundings. He seems to get a little work, but mostly he becomes involved in crime by accident.

British Male Private Detective operating in London

Mark TIMLIN (British)

Citation Record: 9 Books

A Good Year For Little Roses - *First*
Corgi UK (1988)

Ashes By Now - *Latest*
Gollancz UK (1993)

SHARP

is the Police Superintendent of the Grand National Trunk Line and is the detective in this one Victorian novel.

British Policeman operating in England

R M BALLANTYNE 1825-1894 (British)

Writer: Robert Michael BALLANTYNE

Citation Record: 1 Book

The Iron Horse Or Life On The Line - *Only*
Nisbet UK (1891)

Silas SHARP

American Male Detective in Pulp Magazines operating in USA

UNKNOWN

No citations

Terence Everard Christopher SHARP

British Male Professional Investigator operating in England

John M HOWARD (British)

Citation Record: 1 Collection

T E C Sharp, The Football Sleuth - *Collection 1*
has several chapters in which the detective investigates various footballing misdeeds.
Amalgamated UK (1931)

Harry SHARPE

American Male Detective in Pulp Magazines operating in USA

Harry ROCKWOOD 1859-1932 (American)

Invented 14 detectives - see Clarice DYKE

Citation Record: 1 Book

Harry Sharpe, The New York Detective - *Only*
Ogilvie US (1893)

Morrison SHARPE

is a chess and puzzle expert, whose skills enable him to solve crimes before the police do.

British Male Amateur operating in England

Leslie CARGILL (British)

See main detective Maj MOSSON

Citation Record: 2 Books

Death Goes By Bus - *First*
Jenkins UK (1936)

Heads You Lose - *Last*
Jenkins UK (1938)

Nelson SHARPE and Judith SINGER

American Male Amateur and American Female Amateur operating in Long Island

Susan ISAACS 1943- (American)

See main detective Rosie MYERS

Citation Record: 1 Book

Compromising Positions - *Single*
Times Books US (1978); Lane UK (1978)

Sedley SHARPE

British Male Amateur operating in England

Charles HAMILTON 1876-1961 (British)

Invented 3 detectives - see Ferrers LOCKE

No citations

William SHARPE

British Policeman operating in England

WATERS (British)

Invented 6 detectives - see WATERS

Citation Record: 1 Book

Recollections Of A Sheriff's Officer - *Only*
Thompson UK (1860)

Jack SHARPLEY

American Male Detective in Pulp Magazines operating in USA

Ed STRAYER (American)

Other Detectives:
BATTERY BOICE PLACER DAN
VASCO

Citation Record: 1 Selected Short Story

Jack Sharpley, The Always-Ready Detective; Or, Hunting Down The Red Hand Gang
Old Cap Collier Library US (18??)

B K SHARRETTS

British Male Professional Amateur operating in England

P H WOODWARD (British)

Citation Record: 7 Short Stories in 1 Collection

Sharretts The Detective - *Collection 1*
Warne UK (1894)

Adam SHAW

American Male Amateur operating in USA

Richard North PATTERSON 1947- (American)

Other Detectives:
Peter CAREY Christopher PAGET

Citation Record: 1 Book

The Outside Man - *Single*
Little, Brown US (1981)

Donald SHAW

Second detective of Robert WEST

Emma SHAW

is a continuity girl, working for a film company that is making a movie in Italy. When death begins to cut down on the members, she seems to be the one to solve the problems.

British Female Amateur operating in Rome

Hazel Wynn JONES ?-1990 (British)

was a director of documentary films.

Citation Record: 1 Book

Death And The Trumpets Of Tuscany - *Single*
Collins UK (1988)

Cdr Esmonde SHAW

is a standard example of the post-war British detective-agent in the thrills and adventures of the Cold War. Initially in Naval Intelligence, he moves in later books to 6D2, a secret outfit.

British Male Secret Agent operating in several locations

Philip MCCUTCHAN 1920- (British)

was born in Cambridge, England. He was educated at St Helens' College, Southsea, Hampshire, and at the Royal Military College, Sandhurst. After serving in the Royal Navy Volunteer Reserve, 1939-1945, he had several different jobs before becoming a full-time writer in 1960. He is the author of at least forty-six criminous and detective novels under his real name, eleven under the *GALWAY* pseudonym, at least thirty-five action thrillers of the sea, also under his own name, and at least seventeen adventure novels with a military background under other bylines.

Writer: Philip Donald MCCUTCHAN

Other Byline: Robert Conington GALWAY

Inventor of one other detective Det Ch Supt Simon SHARD

Citation Record: 20 Books

Gibraltar Road - *First*
Harrap UK (1960); Berkley US (1965)

Burn-Out - *Latest*
Hodder & Stoughton UK (1995)

S

James SHAW

was formerly in US Army Intelligence and has taken over an impoverished detective agency belonging to a relative.

American Male Private Detective operating in New York

Isidore HAIBLUM 1935- (American)

Citation Record: 2 Books

Murder In Yiddish - *First*
St Martin's US (1988)

Bad Neighbours - *Latest*
St Martin's US (1990)

Joe SHAW

American Male Private Detective operating in USA

Keith LAUMER 1925- (American)

Writer: John Keith LAUMER

Citation Record: 1 Book

Deadfall - *Only*
Doubleday US (1971); Hale UK (1974)

Fat Chance - *Only**
Pocket Books US (1975)

Kate SHAW

Second detective of Insp Jeff ADAMS

Paul SHAW

works for an agency in New York and Los Angeles. He is well-heeled, drives a Ferrari about town, and is specially hard on liberals or those he considers to be such.

American Male Private Detective operating in USA

Mark SADLER 1924- (American)

For writer details see Kane JACKSON

Citation Record: 6 Books

The Falling Man - *First*
Random House US (1973)

The Deadly Innocent - *Latest*
US (1988)

Pete SHAY

American Male Private Detective operating in New York

Peter MCCURTIN (American)

Invented 4 detectives - see Robert (The Assassin) BRIGANTI

Citation Record: 1 Book

Minnesota Strip - *Single*
Belmont US (1979)

Hector SHAYNE

Mexican Male Private Detective

Paco Ignacio TAIBO II 1949-

Invented 3 detectives - see Ch Jose Daniel FIERRO

Citation Record: 1 Book

No Happy Ending
Mysterious Press US (1993)

Michael SHAYNE

is an example of the archetypal, first-generation, American private eye. Extremely popular at many levels, he appeared in novels, short stories, radio shows and films, and later achieved the supreme accolade of getting his own magazine. *Michael SHAYNE* is Irish-American, has red hair, drinks hard liquor, and fights a lot, although at the time he was around guns were not often used by private eyes. He operates out of an office on Flagler Street and solves his cases with what seems today to be lightning speed. After his creator's death, the books and the character were taken over by others, especially *Robert TERRAIL*.

American Male Private Detective operating in Miami

Brett HALLIDAY 1904-1977 (American)

was born in Chicago, Illinois, and raised in Texas. He joined the US Cavalry at the age of fourteen and later went to Tri-State College, Angola, Indiana, graduating in Civil Engineering. He worked at a number of jobs in the old-time West and, from 1927, began to write, rapidly turning out countless novels and stories under several names, many them being standard Westerns and adventure yarns for the pulps. After 1958 his name was used as a byline for similar stories by other ghost-writers. His main detective creation was the famed *Mike SHAYNE* and he was the founding editor of the *Mike Shayne Mystery Magazine,* which not only continues but still carries stories under the *Brett HALLIDAY* byline.

Writer: Davis DRESSER

Other Bylines:
Asa BAKER Matthew BLOOD

Citation Record: 71 Books

Dividend On Death - *First*
Holt US (1939); Jarrolds UK (1941)

Win Some, Lose Some - *Last*
Dell US (1976)

Ryerson JOHNSON 1901- (American)

Writer: Walter Ryerson JOHNSON

Citation Record: 2 Books

Dolls Are Deadly - *First*
US (1960)

Killers From The Keys - *Last*
US (1961)

James REACH 1909(?)-1970 (American)

See main detective WING

Citation Record: 2 Plays

Mrder Is My Business
Samuel French US (1958)

Murder Over Miami
Samuel French US (19??)

Robert TERRALL 1914- (American)

Writer: Robert TERRALL
Other Bylines:
John GONZALES Robert KYLE

Citation Record: 22 Books

Fit To Kill - *First*
US (1959)

Million Dollar Handle - *Latest*
US (1976)

Tim SHEA

British Male Amateur operating in England

Joseph DELMONT 1873-1975 (British)

Citation Record: 6 Short Stories in 1 Collection

Beasts And Escapades - *Collection 1*
This collection of twenty-nine of the author's stories contains six with *Tim SHEA.*
Hutchinson UK (1934)

Frank SHEARER

Second detective of Arthur SALISBURY

Holmlock SHEARS and Arsène LUPIN

feature in this early *SHERLOCK HOLMES* parody. It would appear that the author first used the name *Herlock SHOLMES* in the original French version of the book, *ARSENE LUPIN CONTRE HERLOCK SHOLMES.* The much later American author, *Ross MACDONALD,* seems to have been the only other author to have used the name *Herlock SHOLMES* for a *Sherlock HOLMES* parody, which he did in one early short story, seemingly antedating his well-known novels.

British Male Professional Amateur and French Professional Amateur operating in France

Maurice LEBLANC 1864-1941 (French)

Invented 3 detectives - see Arsène LUPIN

Citation Record: 1 Book 1 Selected Short Story

The Blonde Lady: Being A Record Of The Duel Of Wits Between Arsène Lupin And The English Detective - *Parody 1*
was published in the UK as *ARSENE LUPIN VERSUS HOLMLOCK SHEARS,* being translated, unlike the UK edition, by Alexander Teixeira de Mattos. Both books were translated from the French original, *ARSENE LUPIN CONTRE HERLOCK SHOLMES,* in which the parody detective's name is given as *Herlock SHOLMES.* The latter book was first published in the UK as *THE FAIR-HAIRED LADY.*
Doubleday US (1910)

Arsène Lupin Versus Holmlock Shears - *Parody 1**
Richards UK (1909)

Holmlock Shears Arrives Too Late - *Parody 2*
appeared originally as part of the collection, *THE EXPLOITS OF ARSENE LUPIN,* featuring the French detective, *Arsène LUPIN.* It is to be found, in an English translation, in the anthology, *THE MISADVENTURES OF SHERLOCK HOLMES,* (Editor; *Ellery QUEEN).*
Little, Brown US (1944)

Insp SHEFFIELD

British Policeman operating in England

Sax ROHMER 1883-1959 (British)

Invented 9 detectives - see Insp RYDER

Citation Record: 1 Selected Short Story

A White Orchid
Cassell UK (1914); Bookfinger US (1967)

Richard SHEILAN

American Male Sleuth operating in USA

William KROHN (American)

Citation Record: 1 Selected Short Story

The Impossible Murder Of Dr Satanus
appeared in the April number.
In 'Ellery Queen's Mystery Magazine' US (1967)

Insp SHELLEY

British Policeman operating in England

John ROWLAND 1907- (British)

Writer: John Herbert Shelley ROWLAND

Citation Record: 17 Books

Bloodshed In Bayswater - *First*
Jenkins UK (1935)

Calamity In Kent - *Last*
Jenkins UK (1950)

Max SHEPHERD

Second detective of Elizabeth BLAIR

Tom SHEPHERD

is the sole member of the Laguna Beach Homicide Division and has to investigate killings with a motive that is forty years old.

American Policeman operating in Los Angeles

T Jefferson PARKER (American)

is a journalist in California.

Citation Record: 1 Book

Laguna Heat - *Single*
St Martin's US (1985); Bodley Head UK (1986)

Dan SHERIDAN

is a District Attorney who has a reputation for defending 'every faker, fraud, embezzler, scalawag, drunk driver, narcotics dealer, bookie and hooker who has congested the streets of Boston'. No wonder a prominent surgeon, suspected of murder, turns to him for help!

American Male Amateur operating in Boston

Barry REED (American)

Citation Record: 1 Book

The Indictment - *Single*
Crown US (1994)

David SHERIDAN

British Male Sleuth operating in several locations

Colin DAVY 1896- (British)

Writer: Colin Kayser DAVY

Citation Record: 2 Books

Mariella - Spy! - *First*
Harrap UK (1935)

Agents Of The League - *Last*
Harrap UK (1936)

Jim SHERIDAN

sleuths in books set back into the 1920s.

American Male Amateur operating in Chicago

Vincente TORRIO

Citation Record: 4 Books

Bootlegger - *First*
New English Library UK (1975)

Dealer - *Latest*
New English Library UK (1976)

Timothy Seamus Wolfe SHERIDAN

is a writer of crime fiction who investigates the nasty murders of friends and relations.

American Male Amateur operating in New York

Stephen F WILCOX (American)

Citation Record: 2 Books

The Dry White Tear - *First*
St Martin's US (1989)

The Twenty-Acre Plot - *Latest*
St Martin's US (1991)

Michael (The Shield) SHERIFF

American Male Professional Investigator operating in USA

Preston MACADAM 1945- (American)

Writers: John PRESTON 1945- and UNKNOWN

Citation Record: 3 Books

African Assignment - *First*
Avon US (1985)

Island Intrigue - *Latest*
Avon US (1985)

Roger SHERINGHAM

holds an honoured place in the genre's history as being a departure from the type of amateur detective that was common before 1925. He was an author, given to pipe-smoking, and a master of the witty conversation that was mandatory at the time. Even so, he was naturalistic, no intellectual giant but simply a methodical sleuth. Indeed, he was often fallible and was certainly this author's favourite detective.

British Male Amateur operating in England

Stooge: Insp MORESBY
is a classic British police stooge, eternally baffled by the cases that *SHERINGHAM* and *CHITTERWICK* solve in their respective books.
British Male

Anthony BERKELEY 1893-1971 (British)

was born in Watford, Hertfordshire, and educated at Sherborne School, Dorset, and University College, London. He was a book reviewer and critic for several newspapers between 1930 and 1970. A seminal figure in the history of the detective story, he used this pseudonym for most of his crime fiction. Although his trail-blazing work was mainly published under the *Francis ILES* name, the books with *SHERINGHAM* took the English detective story of the 1920s into new realms of plot, ingenuity, and delightfully contrived comedy and satire, on which the major writers of the 1930s were to build.

S

Writer: Anthony Berkeley COX

Other Bylines:
A B COX
A Monmouth PLATTS

Other Detectives:
Ambrose CHITTERWICK and Roger SHERINGHAM
Ambrose CHITTERWICK
Lord Arthur LINTON

Citation Record: 10 Books

The Layton Court Mystery - *First*
was originally published as by '?'.
Jenkins UK (1925); Doubleday US (1929)

Panic Party - *Last*
Hodder & Stoughton UK (1934)

Mr Pidgeon's Island - *Last**
Doubleday US (1934)

Roger SHERINGHAM

Second detective of Ambrose CHITTERWICK

Boyd SHERMAN

is a reformed drunk, ex-sports writer and would-be shamus who investigates murder among the racing fraternity.

American Male Private Detective operating in Wyoming

Geoff PETERSON (American)

Citation Record: 1 Book

Medicine Dog - *Single*
St Martin's US (1989)

Phil SHERMAN

American Male Secret Agent operating in several locations

Don SMITH 1909- (American)

Writer: Donald Taylor SMITH

Inventor of one other detective Tim PARNELL

Citation Record: 20 Books

Secret Mission: Prague - *First*
Award US (1968); Tandem UK (1971)

The Strausser Transfer - *Latest*
Charter US (1978)

Winston Marlowe SHERMAN

American Male Sleuth operating in New York

M K LORENZ 1945- (American)

Writer: Margaret KEILSTRUP

Citation Record: 3 Books

Deception Island - *First*
Bantam US (1990)

Sweet Narcissus - *Latest*
Bantam US (1990)

SHERRARD

of Scotland Yard is in this one Victorian novel.

British Policeman operating in London

Grant ALLEN 1848-1899 (British)

Invented 5 detectives - see Nurse Hilda WADE

Citation Record: 1 Book

The Scallywag - *Only*
Chatto & Windus UK (1893); Cassell US (1893)

Walter SHERRIS

is the victim of a brutal mugging. He sets out to identify the perpetrators and bring them to justice.

American Male Amateur operating in USA

Leigh BRACKETT 1915-1978 (American)

Invented 3 detectives - see Edmond CLIVE

Citation Record: 1 Book

The Tiger Among Us
Doubleday US (1957); Boardman UK (1958)

Insp SHERWOOD

British Policeman operating in England

John BUDE 1901-1957 (British)

Writer: Ernest Carpenter ELMORE

Other Detectives:
Maj BODDY
Sgt Pembury GREEN
Insp MEREDITH

Citation Record: 2 Books

The Night The Fog Came Down - *First*
Macdonald UK (1958); Washburn US (1958)

A Twist Of The Rope - *Last*
Macdonald UK (1958)

Ned SHERWOOD

operates from an office on 36th Street, Manhattan, but his only known case is in Havana.

American Male Private Detective operating in New York/Havana

Robert SYLVESTER 1907-1975 (American)

Writer: Robert McPhierson SYLVESTER

Citation Record: 1 Book

The Big Boodle - *Only*
Random House US (1954); Hammond UK (1957)

A Night In Havana - *Only**
Corgi UK (1958)

Jefferson SHIELDS

British Male Amateur operating in England

Patricia CARLON (British)

Writer: Patricia Bernadette CARLON

Citation Record: 2 Books

Death By Demonstration - *First*
Hodder & Stoughton UK (1970)

The Souvenir - *Last*
Hodder & Stoughton UK (1970)

John SHIELDS

solves a double murder in Fordham.

American Male Private Detective operating in Texas

Ada E LINGO (American)

Citation Record: 1 Book

Murder In Texas - *Only*
Houghton US (1935)

Mark SHIGATA

American Male Sleuth operating in Texas

Anne WINGATE 1943- (American)

For writer details see Det Deb RALSTON

Citation Record: 2 Books

Death By Deception - *First*
Walker US (1988)

The Eye Of Anna - *Latest*
Walker US (1990)

Harold SHILLING

is a San Diego ex-cop, a bit the worse for wear.

American Male Private Detective operating in San Diego

Eric BERCOVICI (American)

Citation Record: 1 Book

So Little Cause For Caroline - *Single*
Atheneum US (1981)

Insp Tami SHIMONI

is in a secret force (GAG) set up to combat terrorism.

Israeli Policeman operating in Israel

Olga HESKY ?-1974 (American)

Citation Record: 2 Books

The Serpent's Smile - *First*
Long UK (1966); Dodd, Mead US (1967)

The Different Night - *Last*
Long UK (1970); Random House US (1971)

Charley SHIPTON

American Male Professional Investigator operating in USA

Charles H SIMPSON (American)

Citation Record: 1 Book

Life In The Far West; Or, A Detective's Adventures Among The Indians And Outlaws Of Montana - *Only*
Rhodes, McClure US (1897)

Patrick C SHIRLEY and Insp Rip IRVING

British Male Amateur and British Policeman operating in England

Osmington MILLS 1922- (British)

See main detective Insp/Supt BAKER

Citation Record: 4 Books

Enemies Of The Bride - *First*
Bles UK (1966); Roy US (1967)

Many A Slip - *Last*
Bles UK (1967)

Benjamin SHOCK and Charity TUCKER

Benjamin SHOCK is an ex-cop who runs an unlicensed detective agency with ex-reporter, *Charity TUCKER*. She, blond, beautiful, and now sexually frigid, was a rape victim. To the displeasure of the official force, he killed the man who raped her.

American Male Private Detective and Female Private Detective operating in USA/England

Patrick BUCHANAN 1931-1981 (American)

Writers: Edwin Raymond CORLEY 1931-1981 and Jack MURPHY

Citation Record: 4 Books

A Murder Of Crows - *First*
Stein US (1970); Hale UK (1973)

A Sounder Of Swine - *Last*
Dodd, Mead US (1974)

Dr Sid SHOEHORN

is an affectionate parody of *Sam HAWTHORNE*, created by *Ed HOCH*. In his one appearance he investigates how a whole town seems to have vanished.

American Male Amateur operating in USA

Jon L BREEN 1943- (American)

Invented 6 detectives - see Rachel HENNINGS

Citation Record: 1 Selected Short Story

The Problem Of The Vanishing Town
appeared in the November number.
In 'Ellery Queen's Mystery Magazine' US (1979)

Eddie SHOESTRING

appears in novelizations of episodes from a British TV series.

British Male Private Detective operating in Bristol

Paul ABLEMAN 1927- (British)

!See Appendix 2.

Citation Record: 2 Books

Shoestring - *First*
BBC UK (1979); Parkhurst US (1984)

Shoestring's Finest Hour - *Latest*
BBC UK (1980); Parkhurst US (1985)

Herlock SHOLMES

is a *Sherlock HOLMES* parody who appears in a little-known story (undated) written by this illustrious author of crime fiction when still a young novice. It is quite fortuitous, it seems, that he chose the same name for his parody as had been used many years earlier by *Maurice LEBLANC* and then by the immortal *Charles HAMILTON*, writing as *Peter TODD.*

British Male Professional Amateur operating in London

Sidekick: Dr John H WATSON

British Male - Narrator

John Ross MACDONALD 1915- (American)

See main detective Lew ARCHER

Citation Record: 1 Selected Short Story

The South Sea Soup Company - *Parody 1*

Herlock SHOLMES

The name *Herlock SHOLMES* for a *Sherlock HOLMES* parody was certainly invented by *Maurice LEBLANC* in a story in which he appears with *Arsène LUPIN*, and was re-invented by *Ross MACDONALD* in a much later story. However, its main adoption was by *Peter TODD*, who was, in fact, the extraordinary British writer of humorous tales and schoolboy stories, perhaps the second most prolific writer who has ever lived. During his long life *TODD* wrote almost a hundred short stories featuring *SHOLMES*. The stories, some being obvious parodies of the *HOLMES* stories, began in 1915 in the *Greyfriars Herald* and continued through 1925, some being published in the two main boys' magazines of the era, *Magnet* and *The Gem*. They ended in 1952, after an interval of twenty-five years, with two stories in *Tom Merry's Own Annual*. *SHOLMES* has a narrator-assistant in *Dr JOTSON* and his landlady is a Mrs Spudson, a parody on *Mrs HUDSON*, the landlady at 221B Baker Street and herself transformed, by another author, into a fictional parody detective. All these remarkable characters reside at an apartment in the fictional Shaker Street, somewhere in the West End of London.

The stories have recently been collected into one volume, *The Complete Casebook of Herlock Sholmes* (*Hawk Books*;

UK 1989) and the individual stories are all cited below in the order in which they originally appeared.

British Male Professional Amateur operating in London

Sidekick: Dr JOTSON
is his parody *WATSON*-like assistant.
British Male - Narrator

Peter TODD 1876-1961 (British)

For writer details see Ferrers LOCKE (Writer Charles HAMILTON)

Citation Record: 95 Selected Short Stories

The Adventure Of The Diamond Pins
In 'Greyfriars Herald' UK (1915)

The Case Of The Biscuit Tin
In 'Greyfriars Herald' UK (1915)

The Bound Of The Haskervilles
In 'Greyfriars Herald' UK (1915)

The Freckled Hand
In 'Greyfriars Herald' UK (1915)

The Sign Of Fourty Four
In 'Greyfriars Herald' UK (1915)

The Death Of Sholmes
In 'Greyfriars Herald' UK (1915)

The Return Of Herlock Sholmes
In 'Greyfriars Herald' UK (1916)

The Missing Mother-In-Law
In 'Greyfriars Herald' UK (1916)

The Adventure Of The Brixton Builder
In 'Greyfriars Herald' UK (1916)

The Case Of The American Millionaire
In 'Greyfriars Herald' UK (1916)

The Foreign Spy
In 'Greyfriars Herald' UK (1916)

The Case Of The Pipe-Clay Department
In 'Greyfriars Herald' UK (1916)

The Case Of The Pawned Pickle Jar
In 'Greyfriars Herald' UK (1916)

The Munition Mystery
In 'Greyfriars Herald' UK (1916)

The Captured Submarines
In 'Greyfriars Herald' UK (1916)

The Sham Huns
In 'Greyfriars Herald' UK (1916)

The Kaiser's Code
In 'Greyfriars Herald' UK (1916)

The Yellow Phiz
In 'Greyfriars Herald' UK (1916)

The Case Of His Lordship's Engagement
In 'The Magnet' UK (1917)

The Missing Minister
In 'The Magnet' UK (1917)

The Clue Of The Chanting Cheese
In 'The Magnet' UK (1917)

The Missing Moke
In 'The Magnet' UK (1917)

The Vanished Aliens
In 'The Magnet' UK (1917)

The Red Tape Mystery
In 'The Gem' UK (1917)

The Case Of The Escaped Hun
In 'The Gem' UK (1917)

The Case Of The Currant Bun
In 'The Gem' UK (1917)

The Case Of The Russian Revolution
In 'The Gem' UK (1917)

The Last Of The Potatoes
In 'The Gem' UK (1917)

On The Scent
In 'The Gem' UK (1917)

The Case Of The Teuton's Trousers
In 'The Gem' UK (1917)

The Missing Margarine
In 'The Gem' UK (1917)

The Mystery Of The Dustbin
In 'The Magnet' UK (1917)

The Case Of The American Clock
In 'The Magnet' UK (1917)

The Case Of The Hidden Hun
In 'The Magnet' UK (1917)

The Secretary's Double
In 'The Magnet' UK (1917)

The Lottery Ticket
In 'The Magnet' UK (1917)

Herlock Sholmes At Monte Carlo
In 'The Magnet' UK (1918)

The Case Of The Financier
In 'The Magnet' UK (1918)

A Murder Mystery
In 'The Magnet' UK (1918)

The Case Of The Missing Wife
In 'The Magnet' UK (1918)

The Case Of The Missing Manuscript
In 'The Magnet' UK (1918)

The Case Of The Airman's Medal
In 'The Gem' UK (1919)

The Missing Cricketer
In 'Greyfriars Herald' UK (1920)

The Bacon Mystery
In 'Greyfriars Herald' UK (1920)

The Chopstein Venus
In 'Greyfriars Herald' UK (1920)

The Case Of The Missing Heir
In 'Greyfriars Herald' UK (1920)

The Mystery Of The Studio
In 'Greyfriars Herald' UK (1920)

The Case Of The Musician
In 'Greyfriars Herald' UK (1920)

The Mystery Of The Taxi-Cab
In 'Greyfriars Herald' UK (1920)

The Case Of The Stolen Car
In 'Greyfriars Herald' UK (1920)

The Case Of The Ball Dress
In 'Greyfriars Herald' UK (1920)

The Disappearance Of Lord Adolphus
In 'Greyfriars Herald' UK (1920)

The Mystery Of The Garden Suburb
In 'Greyfriars Herald' UK (1920)

The Case Of The Sinn Feiners
In 'Greyfriars Herald' UK (1920)

The Case Of The Mysterious Soprano
In 'Greyfriars Herald' UK (1920)

The Mysterious Bottle
In 'Greyfriars Herald' UK (1920)

The Case Of The Missing Patient
In 'Greyfriars Herald' UK (1920)

The Purloined Pork
In 'Greyfriars Herald' UK (1920)

The Case Of The Bolshevik!
In 'Greyfriars Herald' UK (1920)

The Case Of The Orator
In 'Greyfriars Herald' UK (1920)

The Trunk Mystery
In 'Greyfriars Herald' UK (1920)

The Disappearance Of Dr Jotson
In 'Greyfriars Herald' UK (1920)

The Case Of The Boat Club
In 'Greyfriars Herald' UK (1920)

The Case Of The Gunpowder Plot
In 'Greyfriars Herald' UK (1920)

The Case Of The Lost Chord
In 'Greyfriars Herald' UK (1920)

The Case Of The Charlady
In 'Greyfriars Herald' UK (1920)

The Case Of The Corn-Plaster
In 'Greyfriars Herald' UK (1920)

The Case Of Podgers MP
In 'Greyfriars Herald' UK (1920)

The Case Of The Cubist
In 'Greyfriars Herald' UK (1920)

The Case Of The Dentist
In 'Greyfriars Herald' UK (1920)

The Mystery Of The Mince-Pie
In 'Greyfriars Herald' UK (1920)
Pinkeye's New Year Resolution
In 'Greyfriars Herald' UK (1921)
The Case Of The Pink Rat
In 'Greyfriars Herald' UK (1921)
The Case Of The Lame Snail
In 'Greyfriars Herald' UK (1921)
The Case Of The Potato Jacket
In 'Penny Popular' UK (1921)
The Sarah Jane Mystery
In 'The Magnet' UK (1921)
The Mystery Of The Vacant House
In 'Penny Popular' UK (1921)
The Case Of The Lost Sapphire
In 'The Magnet' UK (1921)
The Case Of The Haunted Coal Shed
In 'The Magnet' UK (1921)
The Case Of The Creeping Krooboy!
In 'The Magnet' UK (1921)
The Case Of The Lost Nugget
In 'The Magnet' UK (1921)
The Ghostly Xmas Knight
In 'The Magnet' UK (1922)
The Lost Persian
In 'The Magnet' UK (1922)
The Schwotten Ray
In 'Penny Popular' UK (1924)
The Golden Cow
In 'Penny Popular' UK (1924)
The White Rabbit
In 'Penny Popular' UK (1924)
The Unguarded Goal
In 'Penny Popular' UK (1924)
The Mystery Of Moldy Manor
In 'Penny Popular' UK (1924)
The Silver Wishbone
In 'Penny Popular' UK (1924)
The Secret In The Pudding Bag
In 'Penny Popular' UK (1924)
The Great Waxworks Mystery
In 'Penny Popular' UK (1925)
The Nabob's Elephant
In 'Penny Popular' UK (1925)
The Missing Millionaire
In 'Tom Merry's Own Annual' UK (1950)
The Case Of The Perplexed Painter
In 'Tom Merry's Own Annual' UK (1950)

Herlock SHOLMES

Second detective of Arsène LUPIN

Sam SHOLTO

British Male Sleuth operating in Europe/Asia

Duff HART-DAVIS 1946- (British)

Citation Record: 2 Books
The Gold Of St Matthew - *First*
Constable UK (1970)
The Gold-Trackers - *First**
Doubleday US (1970)
Spider In The Morning - *Last*
Constable UK (1972); Doubleday US (1972)

Lt Shomri SHOMAR

is an Israeli detective on loan to the New York Police Department.

Israeli Policeman operating in New York/Israel

Henry KLINGER ?-1980 (American)

Citation Record: 4 Books
Wanton For Murder - *First*
Permabooks US (1961)
Lust For Murder - *Last*
Trident Press US (1966)

Mrs Julia Herlock SHOMES

is a female *Sherlock HOLMES* parody. The recently widowed wife of Mr Shomes, a reputedly great detective, she becomes a PI, assisted by a *Mrs Lucilla WIGGINS*, a quiet little lady who knits while *Julia SHOMES* sits, smokes, thinks and takes decisions that are usually wrong.

British Female Private Detective operating in England

Sidekick: Mrs Lucilla WIGGINS
is her parody *WATSON*-like assistant.
British Female - Assistant

KA (British)

Citation Record: 2 Selected Short Stories
The Adventure Of The Tomato On The Wall - *Parody 1*
appeared first in *The Student: a Journal for University Extension students* in 1894.
Ferret Fantasy UK (1975)
The Identity Of Miss Angela Vespers - *Parody 2*
appeared first in *The Student: a Journal for University Extension Students* in 1894.
Ferret Fantasy UK (1975)

Kerlock SHOMES

is a *Sherlock HOLMES* parody. He appeared originally, in stories with a philatelic emphasis, in a magazine devoted to the study of stamps. Nine stories have been published in a collection.

Male Professional Amateur

Sidekick: Dr WARSAW
is his parody *WATSON*-like assistant.
Male - Assistant

E Tudor GROSS (American)

Citation Record: 9 Short Stories in 1 Collection
The Adventures Of Kerlock Shomes And Dr Warsaw - *Parody Collection 1*
The individual stories are cited immediately below. Some of the stories first appeared elsewhere and, for those, the date and place of original publication are given.
Magico Press US (1980)
I Am Not A Candidate...But - *Parody 1*
The Kidnapping Of Mr Chasebrook - *Parody 2*
appeared first in the December 1943 number of *Stamps.*
Hail To The Chief - *Parody 3*
The Mystery Of The Carrier Of The One Cent - *Parody 4*
The Mystery Of The Goya Nude - *Parody 5*
The Mystery Of The 1c August Cover - *Parody 6*
The Mystery Of The 10-20-Thirt - *Parody 7*
The Theft Of The World's Rarest Stamp - *Parody 8*
appeared first in the September 1943 number of *Stamps.*
The Worm Will Turn - *Parody 9*

Amos SHOMRON

Male Amateur operating in USA

Emanuel LITVINOFF 1915- (American)

Citation Record: 1 Book
Falls The Shadow - *Single*
Stein & Day US (1983)

Radford SHONE

British Male Amateur operating in London

Headon HILL 1857-1927 (British)

Invented 11 detectives - see Insp HERON
Citation Record: 12 Short Stories in 1 Collection
Radford Shone - *Collection 1*
Ward, Lock UK (1908)

Jemima SHORE

is really an update of the old British Golden Age amateur sleuth, except that she is now female. Middle-class, well-heeled, well-educated, Protestant by religion, but with a convent upbringing (like that of the distinguished lady of letters, her author), privileged, able to move in social circles (in which, of course the police flounder), she is more like *Peter WIMSEY* than *Miss MARPLE*. She usually becomes involved in cases because of her presence as an insider, but her undoubted intellect and catholicism of outlook are enlisted in her solutions. Her books continue to appear and, in addition to the collection of short stories cited, there has been a TV series, from which the individual stories have been novelized by divers authors and published in a collection, *Jemima Shore Investigates* (*Methuen;* UK 1983).

British Female Amateur operating in England/Scotland

Antonia FRASER 1932- (British)

was born in London, 1932, daughter of the writer, Lord Longford. She was educated at the Dragon School, Oxford, the Godolphin School, Salisbury, and at St Mary's Convent, Ascot, Berkshire, then taking a BA in History at St Margaret's Hall, Oxford, 1953. She was an already distinguished lady of letters and historian, the recipient of awards in both fields, when she entered the criminous genre in 1977, presumably for relaxation. Her criminous works, like her excellent historical biographies, have been generally admired.

Writer: Lady Antonia Pakenham FRASER

Citation Record: 8 Books 5 Short Stories in 1 Collection

Quiet As A Nun - *First*
Weidenfeld & Nicolson UK (1977); Viking US (1977)

Political Death - *Latest*
Heinemann UK (1994)

Jemima Shore's First Case - *Collection 1*
This collection of twelve of the author's short stories contains five with *Jemima SHORE*.
Weidenfeld & Nicolson UK (1986); Norton US (1987)

Matt SHORE

British Male Amateur operating in England

Dick FRANCIS 1920- (British)

Invented 18 detectives - see Sid HALLEY

Citation Record: 1 Book

Rat Race - *Only*
Joseph UK (1970); Harper & Row US (1971)

Augustus SHORT

British Male Amateur operating in England

Richard MARSH 1867-1915 (British)

Invented 10 detectives - see The Hon Augustus CHAMPNELL

Citation Record: 9 Short Stories in 1 Collection

The Adventures Of Augustus Short - *Collection 1*
Not all the stories are criminous.
Treherne UK (1902)

S

Insp Frank SHORT

is the same man as *Franco CORTI*, who, in later books and for family reasons, prefers to show his Italian ancestry by taking up the Italian version of his name.

British Policeman operating in London

Peter INCHBALD 1919- (British)

See main detective Insp Franco CORTI

Citation Record: 1 Book

The Sweet Short Grass - *Only*
Doubleday US (1982)

James SHORT

is a lawyer who sleuths in this one Victorian novel.

British Male Professional Investigator operating in England

Rider HAGGARD 1856-1925 (British)

was born at Bradenham Hall, Norfolk, and educated at Ipswich Grammar School, Norfolk. He went to Natal as secretary to Sir Henry Bulwer, 1875, and then to the Transvaal. He returned to England, 1879, married, and settled down to a literary life. He is the author of several well-known adventure stories, which included the classic *King Solomon's Mines*. He was knighted, 1912.

Writer: Henry Rider HAGGARD

Citation Record: 1 Book

Mr Meeson's Will - *Only*
Spencer Blackett UK (1888)

Sgt Jasper SHRIG

is a would-be comic creation. Based at the famous Bow Street police station, he investigates in a book containing murder, romance and low comedy.

British Policeman operating in London

Jeffrey FARNOL 1878-1952 (British)

Writer: John Jeffrey FARNOL

Citation Record: 8 Books

The Amateur Gentleman - *First*
Low UK (1913); Little, Brown US (1913)

Waif Of The River - *Last*
Low UK (1952)

John SHU

American Male Amateur operating in USA

Whit MASTERSON 1920- (American)

For writer details see Max THURSDAY

Inventor of one other detective Mort HAGEN

Citation Record: 1 Book

The Slow Gallows - *Only*
Dodd, Mead US (1979); Hale UK (1979)

Kate SHUGAK

American Female Sleuth operating in Alaska

Dana STABENOW (American)

Citation Record: 4 Books

Dead In The Water - *First*
US (199?)

Play With Fire - *Latest*
Berkley US (1995)

Dep Commiss Isaac SIDEL

is in the New York Police Department. A highly idiosyncratic figure with a gnawing conscience, 'a Sherlock Holmes with a tapeworm instead of a fiddle', he appears in books with eccentric plots that require high quality detective work.

American Policeman operating in New York

Jerome CHARYN 1937- (American)

was born in New York City. He studied at Columbia University and later became Professor of English at a number of universities in the USA. He is the author of several non-genre novels as well as critical studies on literature and films.

Inventor of one other detective Sydney HOLDEN

Citation Record: 8 Books

Blue Eyes - *First*
Simon & Schuster US (1975)

Montezuma's Man - *Latest*
Mysterious Press US (1995)

Phoebe SIEGEL

was formerly in the police but has turned PI, specialising 'in investigations with an attitude', we are told, and working among the Crow Indians.

American Female Private Detective operating in Montana

Sandra West PROWELL (American)

Citation Record: 2 Books

By Evil Means - *First*
Bantam US (1994)

The Killing Of Monday Brown - *Latest*
Walker US (1994)

Randall Gatsby SIERRA

investigates the senseless murder of a rising young baseball star.

American Male Private Detective operating in USA

Richard HILL (American)

Citation Record: 1 Book

Kill The Hundredth Monkey - *Single*
St Martin's US (1995)

SIGISMONDO

is a professional soldier in the turmoil of Renaissance Italy. He is hired by a minor prince to find out who is trying to murder him.

Italian Male Amateur operating in Italy

Sidekick: BENNO
Italian Male - Servant

Elizabeth EYRE (British)

Writers: Jill STAYNES and Margaret STOREY

Citation Record: 1 Book

Poison For The Prince - *Single*
Harcourt Brace UK (1994)

SILBER

Male Sleuth

Gunnar JOHNSTON

Citation Record: 2 Books

The Claws Of The Scorpion - *First*
Rider UK (1935)

The Two Kings - *Last*
Rider UK (1936)

John SILENCE

is an 'occult detective' who specialises in treating patients with mysterious problems of supernatural dimensions.

British Male Professional Amateur operating in England

Algernon BLACKWOOD 1869-1951 (British)

was born in Kent. Educated in Germany and Scotland, he went to Canada, where he worked first as a farmer and then as a journalist for several Canadian and American papers, returning to England, 1899. He was one of the best-known Edwardian writers and was the author of novels, plays and especially short stories, many of which had plots dealing with the occult, a subject in which he was interested all his life. He was an early writer for television and was made a CBE, 1949.

Writer: Algernon Henry BLACKWOOD

Inventor of one other detective Max HENSIG

Citation Record: 5 Short Stories in 1 Collection

John Silence, Physician Extraordinary - *Collection 1*
Nash UK (1908); Luce US (1909)

Sylvia SILENCE

was one of the many British girl sleuths appearing in magazines of the 1920s. She came into the business, it was disclosed, because her father, a famous detective, 'wanted her to follow in his footsteps'. With such touching parental concern to guide her and with her monkey, Jacko, and her dog, *WOLF*, at her side, she appeared in stories in *Schoolgirls' Weekly* from October 1922.

British Female Amateur operating in England

Sidekick: WOLF
is an Alsatian dog, the inseparable companion of and assistant to the young girl sleuth.
Male - Pet Dog

Katherine GREENHALGH ?-1935 (British)

was one of the evocative female names that *BOBIN* used for his stories in the English schoolgirl magazines of the inter-war years.

Writer: John William BOBIN

Other Bylines:
Adelie ASCOTT
John William BOBIN
Mark OSBORNE

Citation Record: 1 Selected Short Story

The Case Of The Missing Pendant
In 'Schoolgirls' Weekly' UK (1922)

SILENT

American Male Detective in Pulp Magazines operating in USA

Police Captain HOWARD (American)

Invented 15 detectives - see LIGHTNING LUKE

Citation Record: 1 Book

Silent, The Harbor Detective; Or, Tracking A Gang Of Thieves
New York Detective Library US (1882-8)

Dorian SILK

is an updated version of the British hero-adventurer, dealing with the Queen's enemies in a thoroughly old-fashioned British way. This is something he is able to do readily, being a master of disguise, languages and foreign customs.

British Male Secret Agent operating in Iran/Russia

Sidekick: Giles PRIEST
British Male - Co-worker

Simon HARVESTER 1910-1975 (British)

was educated at Marlborough College, Wiltshire, and studied painting at several schools in Europe. He was a journalist, farmer, and the author of many thrillers under his main pseudonym. In addition he published at least nineteen non-genre novels and several travel books under his real name.

Writer: Henry St John Clair RUMBOLD-GIBBS

Other Detectives:
Roger FLEMING
Malcolm KENTON
Heron MURMER

Citation Record: 13 Books

Dragon Road - *First*
Jarrolds UK (1956); Walker US (1969)

Siberian Road - *Last*
Hutchinson UK (1976); Walker US (1976)

Lu SILK

Appears with at least two other detectives - see Mark GIRLAND

Steve SILK

is an ex-boxer and an unlicensed detective. He has one lung only, which makes action difficult except, it would seem, with the ladies who frequent his many books in no small measure.

American Male Private Detective operating in USA

J B O'SULLIVAN 1919- (British)

Writer: James Brendan O'SULLIVAN

Citation Record: 14 Books

The Death Card - *First*
Pillar US (1945)

Make My Coffin Big - *Last*
Ward, Lock UK (1964)

Ch Joe SILVA

is the Chief of Police in the fictional small town of Mellingham and investigates the murder of a local citizen, a crime for which the woman he is falling for has become the chief suspect.

American Policeman operating in USA

Susan OLEKSIW (American)

Citation Record: 1 Book

Family Album - *Single*
Scribner's US (1995)

Jennifer SILVER

British Female Amateur operating in France

Mary STEWART 1916- (British)

Invented 3 detectives - see Charity SELBOURNE

Citation Record: 1 Book

Thunder On The Right - *Only*
Hodder & Stoughton UK (1957); Mill US (1958)

Insp Jim SILVER
appears also in two books with the author's amateur detective, *Mike LOGAN.*

British Policeman operating in England

Henry HOLT (British)

was a crime reporter for London newspapers.

Other Detectives:

Mike LOGAN   Insp Jim SILVER and Mike LOGAN

Citation Record: 14 Books 1 Selected Short Story

The Mayfair Mystery - *First*
Harrap UK (1929)

The Mayfair Murder - *First**
Dial US (1929)

Murder, My Sweet - *Last*
Museum Press UK (1950)

The Almost Perfect Crime
is in an anthology, *Fifty Famous Detectives of Fiction.*
Odhams UK (1948)

Insp Jim SILVER and Mike LOGAN
also appear individually in other books by this author.

British Policeman and British Male Amateur operating in England

Henry HOLT (British)

Invented 3 detectives - see Insp Jim SILVER

Citation Record: 2 Books

A Wreath For A Lady - *First*
Hale UK (1959)

Don't Shoot, Darling - *Last*
Hale UK (1961); Roy US (1963)

Det Sgt Leopold SILVER
Second detective of Det Supt George MACRAE

Maud Hephzibah SILVER
is one of the genre's classic creations, appearing in a series that lasted over thirty years. Elderly, unmarried, genteel, she was once a teacher, we are led to believe. By a fortunate turn of events she was enabled to set up house on her own, employ a housekeeper, and use her undoubted cleverness and insight in investigating the nefarious doings of other people. She operates from her own drawing room, in Marsham Street, which she has kitted out as a detective's office and with a sign that simply says, 'Private Enquiries'. Although an armchair detective in the best possible sense, she is not averse to hopping around in the course of her work. She has been compared to *Miss MARPLE,* because she too is always knitting something. But, with *Maud SILVER,* this is often a cover-up operation to trap the guilty while she observes them. Amateur, yes, but a true professional!

British Female Professional Amateur operating in London

Stooge: Insp Ernest LAMB
is, in fact, not unfriendly to *Maud SILVER,* but he gets irritated at the lady's annoying ability to solve cases that continue to stump him.
British Male

Patricia WENTWORTH 1878-1961 (British)

was born in Mussoorie, India, and educated privately and at Blackheath High School, London, England. She lived in Surrey after 1920 and was the author of sixty-five criminous novels, being renowned for the creation of the immortal *Maud SILVER.*

Writer: Dora Amy ELLES

Inventor of one other detective Insp Ernest LAMB

Citation Record: 32 Books

Grey Mask - *First*
Hodder & Stoughton UK (1928); Lippincott US (1929)

The Girl In The Cellar - *Last*
Hodder & Stoughton UK (1961)

Richard SILVER and Insp Tarrant TINKLER
solve the mystery of a man's disappearance from a locked Treasure House.

British Male Amateur and British Policeman operating in England

Eden PHILLPOTTS 1862-1960 (British)

Invented 10 detectives - see Insp MIDWINTER

Citation Record: 1 Book

A Tiger's Cub - *Only*
Arrowsmith UK (1892)

SILVER TOM
American Male Detective in Pulp Magazines operating in USA

ANON

Citation Record: 1 Book

Silver Tom, The Detective; Or, Kink By Kink
US (?)

Arthur SILVERMAN
is a graduate mathematics student at Harvard who investigates the murder of a girl.

American Male Amateur operating in Massachusetts

John Alexander GRAHAM 1941- (American)

was born in New York City.

Inventor of one other detective Arnold WECHSLER

Citation Record: 1 Book

Arthur - *Only*
Harper & Row US (1969)

Lt Guy SILVESTRI
of the local police is a part-time student at the fictional Lambert University and is called on to investigate the rather frequent murders that occur there – regrettably, but perhaps understandably, of various professors.

American Policeman operating in Massachusetts

Maggie RENNERT 1922-1984 (American)

Citation Record: 3 Books

Circle Of Death - *First*
Prentice-Hall US (1974)

Operation Calpurnia - *Last*
Prentice-Hall US (1976)

Ex-Supt 'Simmy' SIMMONDS
has retired from his post at Scotland Yard and is now employed, more or less, in an amateur capacity on a case or two. A heavily built man, of a pessimistic but tolerant nature, he is shipped out from England to solve a rather difficult case of murder in the fictitious island of San Rocco, where he is given the assistance of a farcical squad.

British Male Professional Amateur operating in West Indies

Sidekick: Aubrey WILKINSON
is so keen on his own sleuthing abilities that he insists on attaching himself to *SIMMONDS* in this strange novel.
British Male - Assistant

Roger EAST 1904- (British)

saw service for the British government abroad and wrote nine rather unusual genre books.

Writer: Roger d'Este BURFORD

Inventor of one other detective Colin KNOWLES

Citation Record: 1 Book

Twenty-Five Sanitary Inspectors - *Only*
Collins UK (1935)

Bernard SIMMONS
American Male Amateur operating in New York

Frances LOCKRIDGE and Richard LOCKRIDGE (American)

were a husband-and-wife team who wrote numerous criminous novels under both combinations of their names. *Richard LOCKRIDGE* was born in St Joseph, Missouri, and educated at the University of Missouri, Columbia. He was a reporter and drama critic and married *Frances (née Davis) LOCKRIDGE*, 1922. She was born in Kansas City, Missouri, attended the University of Kansas, and was a reporter and music critic. They received the Mystery Writers of America Edgar Allan Poe award for a radio play, 1945, and their Special award, 1962.

After the death of his wife, *Richard LOCKRIDGE* continued to write criminous novels for another twenty years, mainly using the detectives they had created together.

Writers: Frances Louise Davis LOCKRIDGE 1896-1963 and Richard Orson LOCKRIDGE 1898-1992

Other Detectives:
Geoffrey BOWEN
Paul LANE
Pam NORTH and Jerry NORTH
Nathan SHAPIRO

Citation Record: 2 Books

And Left For Dead - *First*
Lippincott US (1962); Hutchinson UK (1962)

The Devious Ones - *Last*
Lippincott US (1964)

Four Hours To Fear - *Last**
Long UK (1965)

Richard LOCKRIDGE 1898-1982 (American)

Invented 3 detectives - see Capt/Insp Merton HEIMRICH

Citation Record: 5 Books

Squire Of Death - *First*
Lippincott US (1965); Long UK (1966)

Death On The Hour - *Last*
Lippincott US (1974); Long UK (1975)

Ralph SIMMONS

American Male Amateur operating in New York

Robert B GILLESPIE 1917- (American)

See main detective Rocky CAPUTO

Citation Record: 5 Books

Print-Out - *First*
Dodd, Mead US (1983)

Deathstorm - *Latest*
Carroll & Graf US (1990)

Sister SIMON

does a little gentle sleuthing when murder disturbs the nuns.

American Female Amateur operating in USA

Margaret Ann HUBBARD 1909- (American)

See main detective Mother THEODORE

Citation Record: 1 Book

Sister Simon's Murder Case - *Only*
Bruce US (1959)

Arnold SIMON

American Male Amateur operating in New York

N J MCIVER (American)

Citation Record: 1 Book

Come Back, Alice Smythereene! - *Single*
St Martin's US (1985)

Dep Commiss Benjamin SIMON

!See Appendix 2.

American Policeman operating in New York

Gregory DEAN 1883- (American)

Writer: Jacob D POSNER

Citation Record: 3 Books

The Case Of Marie Corwin - *First*
Covici US (1933); Nicholson & Watson UK (1934)

Murder On Stilts - *Last*
Hillman-Curl US (1939)

Grant SIMON and Lt PASCAL

appear together in these two books and *Lt PASCAL* appears on his own and in books with *John JERICHO*.

American Male Amateur and American Policeman operating in USA

Hugh PENTECOST 1903-1989 (American)

Invented 12 detectives - see Pierre CHAMBRUN

Citation Record: 2 Books

The Obituary Club - *First*
Dodd, Mead US (1958); Boardman UK (1959)

The Lonely Target - *Last*
Dodd, Mead US (1959); Boardman UK (1960)

Jack SIMONS

American Male Professional Investigator operating in USA

Anthony P MORRIS 1849-1921 (American)

Invented 5 detectives - see Mark MAGIC

Citation Record: 1 Book

Jack Simons, Detective - *Only*
Ivers US (1902)

The Wolves Of Washington - *Only**
was published anonymously.
Aldine US (1895)

SIMPSON, CARRUTHERS and BRIGGS

British Male Amateurs operating in England

Robert L FISH 1912-1981 (American)

Invented 4 detectives - see Schlock HOMES

Citation Record: 3 Books

The Murder League - *First*
Simon & Schuster US (1968); New English Library UK (1970)

A Gross Carriage Of Justice - *Last*
Doubleday US (1979)

Arthur Abdul SIMPSON

Male Amateur operating in Istanbul/Africa

Eric AMBLER 1909- (British)

Invented 4 detectives - see Dr Jan CZISSAR

Citation Record: 2 Books

The Light Of Day - *First*
Heinemann UK (1962); Knopf US (1963)

Topkapi - *First**
Bantam US (1964)

Dirty Story - *Last*
Bodley Head UK (1967); Atheneum US (1967)

Tim SIMPSON

is a financial and art consultant to a London merchant bank that believes in investing in antiques and paintings. It is a field, of course, that attracts crimes such as theft, forgery, confidence trickery and murder. *SIMPSON* can't help blundering into such hard cases and, often at peril to himself, he brings the perpetrators to book. He is perhaps doubly fortunate in having women around him who know more about art than he does and police friends who seem prone to passing him useful information, often, it seems, just for a friendly cup of coffee.

British Male Amateur operating in several locations

Stooge: Det 'Nobby' ROBERTS
is a member of something called 'The Art Fraud Squad'. He acts as a useful adversary, yet behaves as the friend and informant in the police that no amateur detective can very well do without these days.

British Male

John MALCOLM 1936- (British)

was born in Manchester, Lancashire. He was educated at the British School in Montevideo, Uruguay, and, in England later, at Bedford Modern School, Bedford, subsequently taking an MA in Engineering at St John's College, Cambridge, 1958.

Citation Record: 8 Books

A Back Room In Somers Town - *First*
Collins UK (1984); Scribner's US (1985)

Hung Over - *Latest*
HarperCollins UK (1994)

Yen SIN
Chinese Male Amateur

Donald E KEYHOE

Citation Record: 2 Short Stories in 1 Collection

Dr Yen Sin - *Collection 1*
Weinberg (1975)

Alec SINCLAIR
British Male Amateur operating in Scotland

D Wilson MACARTHUR 1903- (British)

Writer: David Wilson MACARTHUR

Citation Record: 2 Books

The Mystery Of The "David M" - *First*
Melrose UK (1932)

Landfall - *Last*
Melrose UK (1933)

Sir Arthur SINCLAIR
British Male Amateur operating in England

Walter S MASTERMAN 1876- (British)

Invented 3 detectives - see Dick SELDON

Citation Record: 17 Books

The Wrong Letter - *First*
Methuen UK (1926); Dutton US (1926)

The Silver Leopard - *Last*
Jarrolds UK (1941)

Cecily SINCLAIR
is, in 1908, the owner of the Pennyfoot Hotel, a discreet and comfortable establishment in the fictional seaside town of Badgers End. Unsolved murder will not do the place any good, especially when the police are as bone-headed as usual, so she does the necessary herself.

Female Amateur

Kate KINGSBURY

Citation Record: 1 Book

Check-Out Time - *Single*
Berkley US (1995)

Evangeline SINCLAIR
Second detective of Trixie DOLAN

George SINCLAIR
British Male Amateur operating in India

Elizabeth IRONSIDE (British)

Citation Record: 1 Book

A Very Private Enterprise - *Single*
Hodder & Stoughton UK (1984); Hodder & Stoughton US (1985)

S

John 'Chant' SINCLAIR
American Male Amateur operating in USA

David CROSS 1940- (American)

For writer details see Robert 'Mongo' FREDERICKSON

Citation Record: 3 Books

Chant - *First*
Jove US (1986)

Code Of Blood - *Latest*
Jove US (1987)

Matt SINCLAIR
is a non-practising lawyer, now vaguely in some aspect of the art trade, who becomes involved in gory, scandalous murders, which he brilliantly solves. Much is made of his bisexuality.

American Male Professional Amateur operating in New Orleans

Tony FENNELLY 1945- (American)

was born in Orange County, New Jersey. She has been a go-go dancer, barmaid and welfare worker.

Citation Record: 3 Books

The Glory Hole Murders - *First*
Carroll & Graf US (1985)

Murder With A Twist - *First**
Carroll & Graf US (1991)

Kiss Yourself Goodbye - *Latest*
Arlington UK (1989)

Steve (The Force) SINCLAIR
American Male Professional Investigator operating in USA

Jake DECKER (American)

Citation Record: 4 Books

Deadly Snow - *First*
Pinnacle US (1984)

Death's Little Sister - *Latest*
Pinnacle US (1984)

Judith SINGER
Second detective of Nelson SHARPE

James SINGLETON
British Male Private Detective operating in England

Frank BARRETT 1848-1926 (British)

Invented 5 detectives - see Capt Thomas VERNAN

Citation Record: 1 Book

Kitty's Father - *Only*
Heinemann UK (1893)

Horace SINNAT
solves the mystery of how a treasure was stolen from the top of an unclimbable pagoda.

American Male Amateur operating in USA

S B H HURST

Citation Record: 1 Selected Short Story

The Pagoda Of Gold
In 'Adventure' US (1931)

Harry SINTON
British Male Amateur operating in England

Roy FULLER 1912- (British)

was born in Failsworth, Lancashire. He qualified as a solicitor, 1934, and served in the Royal Navy, 1941-1946. A practising lawyer and distinguished novelist, he has achieved the highest honours for his work as a poet, receiving the Queen's Gold Medal, 1970, the Cholmondeley award, 1980, and the Heinemann prize, 1990. He was awarded an MA from Oxford and made a CBE, 1970. He has published at least eight criminous works and over thirty volumes of his poetry. He has also written several books for children and some biography.

Writer: Roy Broadbent FULLER

Inventor of one other detective George GARNER

Citation Record: 1 Book

Fantasy And Fugue - *Only*
Verschoyle UK (1954); Macmillan US (1956)

Hilda SIRENE
appeared in one dime novel. An ex-actress, now a detective, she is tough, masculine in her behaviour, adept at fighting, brilliant at knife-throwing and can see her opponents in the dark. What more can be expected of a beautiful woman?

American Female Private Detective operating in USA

Albert W AIKEN 1846-1894 (American)

Other Detectives:
CHIN CHIN
LA MARMOSET
Mignon LAWRENCE
Joe PHOENIX

Citation Record: 1 Book

The Actress Detective; Or, The Invisible Hand - *Only*
Beadle & Adams US (1889)

Sam SIX KILLER
American Male Detective in Pulp Magazines operating in USA

D W STEVENS (American)

Inventor of one other detective OLD SADDLE-BAGS

Citation Record: 1 Book

Sam Six Killer, The Cherokee Detective; Or, The James Boys Most Dangerous Foe
New York Detective Library US (1882-8)

Joe SIXSMITH

is, as he himself says, 'black, balding, and middle-aged'. He is a redundant lathe operator who – to everyone's surprise, including his own – is running a PI operation in Luton, Bedfordshire, of all places, which – as the author takes care to tell us – need not have any similarity to the real town of Luton, Bedfordshire. Indeed, no other detective in the history of detective fiction has ever operated in any town called Luton, fictional or not. Lean, mean, and streetwise *SIXSMITH* is definitely not, but he has one of the PI's greatest gifts, serendipity.

British Male Private Detective operating in England

Reginald HILL 1936- (British)

Invented 4 detectives - see Supt Andrew DALZIEL and Sgt Peter PASCOE

Citation Record: 2 Books 1 Selected Short Story

Blood Sympathy - *First*
HarperCollins UK (1993)

Born Guilty - *Latest*
HarperCollins UK (1995)

Bring Back The Cat!
appeared in the author's collection, *There Are No Ghosts In The Soviet Union.*
Collins UK (1987); Foul Play US (1988)

Insp SKANE

appears also in other books with other detectives of this author.

American Policeman operating in New York

Dwight MARFIELD 1868-1955 (American)

Invented 4 detectives - see Maj KRIM

Citation Record: 1 Book

The Mandarin's Sapphire - *Only*
Dutton US (1938)

Insp SKANE, Dudley BRENT and Maj KRIM

One American Policeman and two American Amateurs operating in New York

Dwight MARFIELD 1868-1955 (American)

Invented 4 detectives - see Maj KRIM

Citation Record: 1 Book

Mystery Of King Cobra - *Only*
Dutton US (1933)

Insp SKANE, Gail MCGURK and Dudley BRENT

One American Policeman and two American Amateurs operating in New York

Dwight MARFIELD 1868-1955 (American)

Invented 4 detectives - see Maj KRIM

Citation Record: 3 Books

Mystery Of The East Wind - *First*
Dutton US (1930)

The Man With A Paper Skull - *Last*
Dutton US (1932)

Dane SKARLE

is one of the master's minor pulp detectives.

American Male Detective in Pulp Magazines operating in New York

Erle Stanley GARDNER 1889-1970 (American)

Invented 14 detectives - see Perry MASON

No citations

Insp SKARRATT

British Policeman operating in England

J S FLETCHER 1863-1935 (British)

Invented 9 detectives - see Paul CAMPENHAYE

Citation Record: 3 Books

Manchester Royal - *First*
Everett UK (1909); Doran US (1926)

The Secret Of Secrets - *Last*
Clode US (1929)

SKILLFUL CHARLIE

American Male Detective in Pulp Magazines operating in USA

Paul WARREN (American)

See main detective Bill POOLE

Citation Record: 1 Selected Short Story

Skillful Charlie, The Giant Detective; Or, Unraveling The Most Mysterious Of Crimes
Old Cap Collier Library US (18??)

Insp SKINNER

is the head of the Edinburgh CID and, when a distinguished local lawyer is found dead in an alley, sets out on a hunt for a serial killer.

British Policeman operating in Edinburgh

Quintin JARDINE (British)

is a journalist and has been a government information officer.

Citation Record: 1 Book

Skinner's Rules - *Single*
Headline UK (1993)

Del SKINNER

is head of an agency handling a nasty case of robbery, combined with murder and mutilation.

American Male Private Detective operating in USA

Sidekick: 'Loopy' JONES
never stops complaining, especially about his pay. Even so, he can take plenty of rough stuff and still solve a nasty case for the boss.

American Male - Assistant

William DALE (American)

Citation Record: 1 Book

The Terror Of The Handless Corpse - *Only*
Gateway US (1939)

Gregory SKIPWITH

American Male Amateur operating in New Orleans

Garry WILLS 1934- (American)

Citation Record: 1 Book

At Button's - *Single*
Sheed US (1979)

Charlie SKRAGG

American Male Amateur operating in New England

Lawrence KAMARCK 1927- (American)

Citation Record: 1 Book

The Bell Ringer - *Only*
Random House US (1969)

SLADE

is a fairly typical hero-adventurer-detective up against dark forces in books that are technically thrillers of high quality.

British Male Secret Agent operating in Malta/Iceland

Desmond BAGLEY 1923-1983 (British)

See main detective Max STAFFORD

Citation Record: 2 Books

Running Blind - *First*
Collins UK (1970); Doubleday US (1970)

The Freedom Trap - *Last*
Collins UK (1971); Doubleday US (1972)

The Mackintosh Man - *Last**
Crest US (1973)

Insp SLADE

solves the mystery of how an actress disappeared on stage between curtain calls.

British Policeman operating in England

Clara Evelyn ELVY (British)

Citation Record: 1 Book

The Magic Of Chez Finnie - *Only*
Stockwell UK (1967)

Det Insp SLADE

British Policeman operating in London

Vivian GREY (British)

Writer: Harry Walter ANDERSON

Inventor of one other detective Insp WALL

Citation Record: 13 Short Stories in 1 Collection

Stories Of Scotland Yard - *Collection 1*
Everett UK (1906)

Supt Anthony SLADE

British Policeman operating in England

Leonard GRIBBLE 1908-1985 (British)

was born in London. In addition to his many criminous books, written under his real name and also under a pseudonym, he has written at least eighteen books that can loosely be called Westerns, for which he has used other (uncited) bylines. He is also the author of many non-fictional and critical works on crime and is the editor of collections of stories in related genres, especially for children.

Writer: Leonard Reginald GRIBBLE

Other Bylines:
Leo GREX Dexter MUIR

Inventor of one other detective Insp RILEY

Citation Record: 33 Books 27 Short Stories in 2 Collections

The Case Of The Marsden Rubies - *First*
Harrap UK (1929); Doubleday US (1930)

Crime On Her Hands - *Last*
Hale UK (1977)

The Case-Book Of Anthony Slade - *Collection 1*
Short stories - 12
Quality Press UK (1937)

The Velvet Mask And Other Stories - *Collection 1**
Allen UK (1952)

Superintendent Slade Investigates - *Collection 2*
Short stories - 15
Jenkins UK (1956); Roy US (1957)

Ben SLADE

American Male Amateur operating in New York

Herbert BURKHOLZ 1932- (American)

was born in New York City, but has lived largely in Spain.

Citation Record: 2 Books

The Sensitives - *First*
Atheneum US (1987); Headline UK (1988)

Strange Bedfellows - *Latest*
Atheneum US (1988); Headline UK (1989)

S

Geoffrey SLADE

British Male Amateur operating in England

Frank LESTER 1909-1976 (British)

For writer details see Insp Jim BURGESS

Citation Record: 3 Books

The Corpse Wore Rubies - *First*
Hale UK (1958)

The Golden Murder - *Last*
Hale UK (1959)

Insp John SLADE and LESSINGER

appear together, but *LESSINGER* also appears on his own in other books by this author.

British Policeman and British Male Sleuth operating in London

Richard ESSEX 1878- (British)

See main detective LESSINGER

Citation Record: 4 Books

Slade Of The Yard - *First*
Jenkins UK (1932); McBride US (1933)

Murder In The Bank - *Last*
Jenkins UK (1936)

Mac SLADE

is such an incompetent gumshoe and would-be tough guy, who falls flat on his face at every turn, that he has to be loved.

American Male Private Detective operating in New York

John BLUMENTHAL (American)

Citation Record: 2 Books

The Tinseltown Murders - *First*
Fireside US (1985)

The Case Of The Hardboiled Dicks - *Latest*
Fireside US (1985)

Nicholas SLADE

British Male Amateur operating in England

R C WOODTHORPE 1886- (British)

See main detective Matilda PERKS

Citation Record: 2 Books

Silence Of A Purple Shirt - *First*
Nicholson & Watson UK (1934)

Death Wears A Purple Shirt - *First**
Doubleday US (1934)

The Necessary Corpse - *Last*
Nicholson & Watson UK (1939); Doubleday US (1939)

Ralph SLADE

solves a *Marie Celeste*-type mystery of crews that vanished from a ship at sea.

American Male Amateur

Stewart Edward WHITE 1873-1946 and Samuel Hopkins ADAMS 1871-1958 (American)

Citation Record: 1 Book

The Mystery - *Only*
McClure US (1907); Hodder & Stoughton UK (1907)

Vince SLADER

American Male Private Detective operating in USA

Ovid DEMARIS 1919- (American)

Citation Record: 4 Books

The Hoods Take Over - *First*
Fawcett US (1957)

The Gold-Plated Sewer - *Last*
Avon US (1957)

Insp SLANE

British Policeman operating in England

Stephen MADDOCK 1897-1952 (British)

For writer details see Insp QUAILE

Inventor of one other detective Timothy TERREL

Citation Record: 3 Books

Exit Only - *First*
Collins UK (1947)

Private Line - *Last*
Collins UK (1950)

Sir Jasper SLANE

British Male Amateur operating in England

E Phillips OPPENHEIM 1866-1946 (British)

Invented 27 detectives - see Nicholas GOADE

Citation Record: 10 Short Stories in 1 Collection

Slane's Long Shots - *Collection 1*
Hodder & Stoughton UK (1930); Little, Brown US (1930)

Florian SLAPPEY

is described as 'a sepia gentleman'. Tall, slender, immaculately dressed, and called the Beau Brummell of Birmingham, Alabama, he solves some cases in his home town and then sets off to conquer Harlem in a series of humorous adventures.

American Male Amateur operating in Alabama

Octavus Roy COHEN 1891-1959 (American)

Invented 6 detectives - see Jim HANVEY

Citation Record: 21 Short Stories in 2 Collections

Florian Slappey Goes Abroad - *Collection 1*

Short stories - 9
Little, Brown US (1928)

Florian Slappey - *Collection 2*

Short stories - 12
Appleton US (1938)

Veronica SLATE

American Female Sleuth operating in Florida

Lary CREWS (American)

Citation Record: 3 Books

Kill Cue - *First*
Lynx US (1988)

Option To Die - *Latest*
Lynx US (1989)

Grant SLATTERY

foils plots without number by Russians, Japanese, and Germans, all of whom wish to invade America.

American Male Secret Agent operating in USA

E Phillips OPPENHEIM 1866-1946 (British)

Invented 27 detectives - see Nicholas GOADE

Citation Record: 1 Book

Wrath To Come - *Only*
Hodder & Stoughton UK (1925); Little, Brown US (1925)

Mike SLATTERY

Australian Male Sleuth operating in Australia

Des R DUNN (Australian)

Citation Record: 2 Books

Farewell To Peril - *First*
Cleveland AU (?)

Night Crime - *Latest*
Cleveland AU (?)

SLAUGHTER

appears in a novelization of a film.

American Male Sleuth operating in USA

Henry CLEMENT (American)

Citation Record: 1 Book

Slaughter - *Only*
Curtis US (1972)

Abel KANE (American)

Citation Record: 1 Book

Slaughter's Big Rip-Off - *Only*
Curtis US (1973)

Vitaly SLAVIN

Russian Male Sleuth operating in Russia/Africa

Julian SEMYONOV 1931- (Russian)

Writer: Julian Semenovich SEMYONOV

Citation Record: 2 Books

Tass Is Authorized To Announce - *First*
Calder UK (1987); Riverrun US (1987)

Intercontinental Knot - *Latest*
Riverrun US (1990)

Ben 'T-Man' SLAYTON

American Male Professional Investigator operating in USA

Buck SANDERS (American)

House name.

Citation Record: 1 Book

The Starshine Connection - *Single*
Warner US (1982)

Buck SANDERS 1947- (American)

For writer details see Det Neil 'Hock' HOCKADAY

Citation Record: 2 Books

A Clear And Present Danger - *First*
Warner US (1981)

Trail Of The Twisted Cross - *Latest*
Warner US (1982)

Buck SANDERS (American)

Writer: Jeffrey FRENTZEN

Citation Record: 2 Books

Star Of Egypt - *First*
Warner US (1981)

The Bayou Brigade - *Latest*
Warner US (1982)

Sam SLEEP

Second detective of William DRINK

SLENDER SAUL

American Male Detective in Pulp Magazines operating in USA

Police Captain HOWARD (American)

Invented 15 detectives - see LIGHTNING LUKE

Citation Record: 1 Book

Slender Saul, The Keenest Of Detectives
New York Detective Library US (1882-8)

Satan SLEUTH

American Male Sleuth operating in New York

Michael AVALLONE 1924- (American)

Invented 5 detectives - see Ed NOON

Citation Record: 2 Books

The Werewolf Walks Tonight - *First*
Warner US (1974)

Devil, Devil - *Last*
Warner US (1975); New English Library UK (1976)

Oscar SLICK

American Male Detective in Pulp Magazines operating in USA

Hal HAWK (American)

Inventor of one other detective The RENEGADE DETECTIVE

Citation Record: 1 Book

Oscar Slick, The Marvelous Detective; Or, Exposing A Number Of Crimes
New York Detective Library US (1882-8)

Det Insp Bill SLIDER

is a nice creation by a mistress of fine prose and characterisation. Middle-class, middle-aged, and according to his colleagues, menopausal, he is never going to make it to the Yard. His manor is West London, not the West End but the back streets and the ghastly new estates round Shepherd's Bush. Passed over for promotion, saddled with an incommodious wife and a ranch-style executive dog-kennel of a house in Ruislip, he is a most likeable modern cop, steely-eyed but with a soft centre. He is in some danger, in a late book, in being tipped by the author into what could be the morass of the romantic novel.

British Policeman operating in London

Sidekick: Sgt ATHERTON
is young, single, well-educated, literary, and sophisticated: all the things *SLIDER*, whom he loves and admires, is not. He is probably not at all suited to be a cop.

British Male - Subordinate

Cynthia HARROD-EAGLES (British)

Citation Record: 4 Books

Death Watch - *First*
Macdonald UK (1990)

Dead End - *Latest*
Little, Brown UK (1994)

Fan SLIVER

is a parody of *Patricia WENTWORTH's* detective, *Maud SILVER.*

Appears with at least two other detectives - see Mallory KING

S

Insp Christopher Dennis SLOAN

is head of the tiny CID force of Calleshire, an imaginary county of the type that British authors seem to like. Heaven knows why, as there are plenty of real ones, all different. *Insp SLOAN* appears in books that have traditional and well-researched backgrounds, but latterly their plots have shown a regrettable tendency towards the police procedural, often tiresomely so. He has a disaster of a sidekick and an exacting and overbearing boss.

British Policeman operating in England

Sidekick: Sgt William CROSBY
is the unfortunate assistant of *SLOAN.* Those around him and who know him say that he was only promoted off the beat as the result of a typist's error.
British Male - Subordinate

Stooge: Supt LEEYES
is an unusual example of a police stooge, for he is *SLOAN's* boss. Lazy and rather stupid, he rarely leaves his office and is full of stereotyped attitudes to the latter's cases. Even so, by way of conversations with this infuriating man, *SLOAN* is often able to arrive at correct solutions.
British Male

Catherine AIRD 1930- (British)
was born in Huddersfield, Yorkshire.
Writer: Kinn Hamilton MCINTOSH
Citation Record: 14 Books
The Religious Body - *First*
Macdonald UK (1966); Doubleday US (1966)
A Going Concern - *Latest*
Macmillan UK (1993)

Tim SLOAN

appeared mainly in stories in *Spicy Detective.*

American Male Detective in Pulp Magazines operating in USA

Dale BOYD (American)
No citations

Capt SLOCUM

British Male Amateur operating in several locations

H De Vere STACPOOLE 1863-1951 (British)
was born in Kingstown, Ireland, and became a physician. He later wrote a large number of popular novels and many short stories (some in the crime and mystery genres), which were usually published as collections.
Writer: Henry De Vere STACPOOLE
Other Detectives:
Mynheer AMAYAT   Jacques RADOUB
Citation Record: 6 Short Stories in 1 Collection
In Blue Waters - *Collection 1*
This collection of twenty-one of the author's stories contains six with *SLOCUM.*
Hutchinson UK (1917)

Maggie SLONE

American Female Amateur operating in New Orleans

Elizabet M STONE (American)
Citation Record: 2 Books
Poison, Poker And Pistols - *First*
Sheridan US (1946)
Murder At The Mardi Gras - *Last*
Sheridan US (1947)

Oliver SMAILE

British Male Amateur operating in England

Major General Sir John ADYE 1857-1930 (British)
Citation Record: 3 Books
At The House Of The Priest - *First*
Jenkins UK (1925)
A Flash Of Lightning - *Last*
Methuen UK (1927)

Rabbi David SMALL

has become one of the most popular of modern detectives, opening up new avenues with its background of Judaism and Jewish life in New England.

American Male Amateur operating in New England

Stooge: Ch Hugh LANIGAN
is continually and simply amazed at the sheer wisdom of *Rabbi David SMALL.*
American Male

Harry KEMELMAN 1908- (American)
was born in Boston, Massachusetts. He was educated at Boston Latin School and took an AB in English Literature at Boston University, 1930, followed by an MA in English Philology at Harvard University, Cambridge, Massachusetts, 1931. He has held senior posts in Administration and Economics with the US government, and is a private businessman and a sometime Assistant Professor of English in Boston. He received the Mystery Writers of America Edgar Allan Poe award, 1964.
Inventor of one other detective Prof Nicky WELT
Citation Record: 9 Books
Friday The Rabbi Slept Late - *First*
Crown US (1964); Hutchinson UK (1965)
One Fine Day The Rabbi Bought A Cross - *Latest*
Century Hutchinson UK (1988)

Sam SMALL

British Male Amateur operating in several locations

Eric KNIGHT 1897-1943 (British)
Writer: Eric Mowbray KNIGHT
Citation Record: 10 Short Stories in 1 Collection
Sam Small Flies Again - *Collection 1*
Harper & Row US (1942); Cassell UK (1943)

Colin SMALLPIECE

American Male Amateur operating in several locations

Frank KENMORE (American)
Citation Record: 3 Books
The Wire Window - *First*
Pinnacle US (1988)
Southeast Of Mandalay - *Latest*
Pinnacle US (1990)

Insp SMALLWAYS

British Policeman operating in England

George A BIRMINGHAM 1865-1950 (British)
Writer: James Owen HANNAY
Citation Record: 1 Book
The Hymn Tune Mystery - *Only*
Methuen UK (1930); Bobbs US (1931)

Ch Insp Joshua SMARLES

British Policeman operating in England

MacGregor URQUHART (British)
Citation Record: 8 Books
Girl On The Waterfront - *First*
Boardman UK (1962)
The Open Mouth - *Last*
Boardman UK (1967)

Alex SMART

British Policeman operating in England

Randall Howland ROBERTS (British)
Writer: Sir Randall Howland ROBERTS
Citation Record: 1 Book
Hard Held: A Sporting Novel - *Only*
Spencer Blackett UK (1889)

Maxwell SMART

American Male Sleuth operating in New York

William JOHNSTON 1924- (American)

Invented 7 detectives - see John WOODRUFF and Tony NOVELLO

Citation Record: 7 Books

Get Smart! - *First*
Tempo UK (1965)

Max Smart And The Ghastly Ghost Affair - *Last*
Tempo UK (1969)

Sam SMART

American Male Detective in Pulp Magazines operating in USA

David DRUID (American)

Other Detectives:
OLD HUMPY
OLD PITCHER
Sam STRONG

Citation Record: 1 Selected Short Story

Sam Smart, The Eastern Postal Route Detective; Or, Piping A Dark Conspiracy For The Government
Old Cap Collier Library US (18??)

George SMILEY

is, by any account, one of the truly great figures to emerge in the genre since 1945. A product of the Cold War, he is the transcendent British agent, totally patriotic, a spy certainly, a detective often, but – unlike most of the heroes of the 1930s and 1940s – supremely human. His intellect is outstanding and his detective work, tortuous at times, is perfect. The canon of his books will be read long after their immediate political origins are overtaken by events.

British Male Secret Agent operating in England

John LE CARRE 1931- (British)

was born in Poole, Dorset. He was educated at Sherborne School, Dorset, and at Berne University, 1948-1949. He took a BA in Modern Languages at Lincoln College, Oxford, 1956, after which he was, for a time, a teacher at Eton College. He was a member of the British Foreign Service, 1959-1964, and wrote his first novel of espionage in 1961. Although his novels are relatively few in number, their quality is of the highest and he is considered to be the greatest modern exponent of the novel of pure espionage, in which characterisation and extraordinarily powerful plotting play vital roles. He received the Mystery Writers of America Edgar Allan Poe award, 1965, and their Grand Master award, 1984, the Crime Writers Association Gold Dagger award twice, 1978 and 1980, and their Diamond Dagger award, 1988.

Writer: David John Moore CORNWELL

Citation Record: 6 Books

Call For The Dead - *First*
Gollancz UK (1961); Walker US (1962)

The Deadly Affair - *First**
Penguin UK (1966)

Smiley's People - *Latest*
Hodder & Stoughton UK (1980); Knopf US (1980)

Insp SMITH

Second detective of Lee VAUGHAN

Don Alverado y Miraflo SMITH

appears in a number of short stories, often of the locked-room murder variety, originally published in *Detective Weekly* during 1937. They were published in the collection cited, generally with changed titles.

Spanish Male Amateur operating in several locations

"CAPSTAN" 1904- (British)

wrote many *Sexton BLAKE* novels between 1930 and 1955 under the other byline. He reserved the unusual pseudonym, always thus written, for his other criminous works, including thirteen novels and the collection cited.

For writer details see MURPHY and MCTAVISH

Citation Record: 11 Short Stories in 1 Collection

The Polite Pirate - *Collection 1*
Wright UK (1938)

Aurelius SMITH

American Male Amateur operating in USA

R T M SCOTT 1882- (American)

Writer: Reginald Thomas Maitland SCOTT

Citation Record: 8 Books

Secret Service Smith - *First*
Dutton US (1923); Hodder & Stoughton UK (1924)

The Nameless Ones - *Last*
Dutton US (1947)

Beau SMITH and Pogy ROGERS

are partners and operate as private eyes in Nevada, providing respectively the brawn and the brains.

American Male Private Detectives operating in USA

Z H ROSS 1912- (American)

Writer: Zola Helen Girdey ROSS

Citation Record: 2 Books

Three Down Vulnerable - *First*
Bobbs US (1946)

One Corpse Missing - *Last*
Bobbs US (1948)

Policeman Black John SMITH

is in the Royal Canadian Mounted Police.

Canadian Policeman operating in Canada

James B HENDRYX 1880-1963 (Canadian)

Invented 3 detectives - see Connie MORGAN

Citation Record: 14 Books

The Way Of The North - *First*
Doubleday US (1945); Edwards UK (1946)

Sourdough Gold - *Last*
Doubleday US (1952); Hammond UK (1957)

Captain SMITH

American Policeman operating in Los Angeles

The EDINGTONS (American)

Writers: Arlo Channing EDINGTON 1890-1953 and Carmen Ballen EDINGTON 1894-

Citation Record: 3 Books

The Studio Murder Mystery - *First*
Reilly & Lee US (1929); Collins UK (1929)

The Monk's Hood Murders - *Last*
Cosmopolitan US (1931); Collins UK (1931)

Cellini SMITH

is hardboiled but can also be something of an intellectual. Neither quality seems to make him good at his job, however.

American Male Private Detective operating in New York/Los Angeles

Robert REEVES 1912?-1945 (American)

See main detective Thomas C THERON

Citation Record: 3 Books

Dead And Done For - *First*
Knopf US (1939); Cassell UK (1940)

Cellini Smith: Detective - *Last*
Houghton US (1943)

Charles SMITH

appears also in one book with the author's other detective, *Lee VAUGHAN.*

British Policeman operating in England

Simon TROY (British)

Writer: Thurman WARRINER

Inventor of one other detective pair Lee VAUGHAN and Insp SMITH

Citation Record: 9 Books

Half-Way To Murder - *First*
Gollancz UK (1955)

Blind Man's Garden - *Last*
Gollancz UK (1970)

Daye SMITH

British Female Amateur operating in London

Frank USHER 1909-1976 (British)

See main detective pair Amanda CURZON and Oscar SALLIS

Citation Record: 13 Books

Death In Error - *First*
Hale UK (1959)

The Lonely Cage - *First*
Long UK (1965)

Dudley SMITH and Det Fred UNDERHILL

American Policemen operating in Los Angeles

James ELLROY 1948- (American)

Invented 4 detectives - see Fritz BROWN

Citation Record: 4 Books

Clandestine - *First*
Avon US (1982); Allison & Busby UK (1984)

White Jazz - *Latest*
Knopf US (1992)

Mr Henry SMITH

is an investigator for the Phalanx Insurance Company. He solves a case of death by stabbing in a guarded house.

American Male Professional Investigator operating in USA

Fredric BROWN 1906-1972 (American)

Invented 8 detectives - see Ambrose HUNTER and Ed HUNTER

Citation Record: 1 Selected Short Story

Whistler's Murder
appeared first in the magazine's January number and was later included in an anthology, *The Shaggy Dog and Other Stories* (*Dutton*; US 1963; *Boardman*; UK 1964).
In 'Ellery Queen's Mystery Magazine' US (1961)

Jared SMITH

is an ex-cop as well as an ex-convict. He now works for Suicide Inc, an interplanetary investigation agency, at some time in the future. The crimes, however, seem familiar.

American Male Private Detective operating in Space

Ron GOULART 1933- (American)

Invented 15 detectives - see Jake PACE and Hildy PACE

Citation Record: 1 Book

Suicide, Inc - *Single*
Berkley US (1985)

Jill SMITH

is the lead detective in what are essentially police procedurals set in Berkeley. She is concerned not only with the crimes but the problems that lie beyond them.

American Policewoman operating in California

S

Susan DUNLAP 1943- (American)

Invented 3 detectives - see Vejay HASKELL

Citation Record: 5 Books

As A Favor - *First*
St Martin's US (1984); Hale UK (1986)

Diamond In The Buff - *Latest*
St Martin's US (1990)

John SMITH

American Male Amateur operating in USA

Wyatt BLASSINGAME 1909-

Writer: Wyatt Rainey BLASSINGAME

Citation Record: 5 Short Stories in 1 Collection

John Smith Hears Death Walking - *Collection 1*
Bartholomew US (1944)

John SMITH

American Male Amateur operating in Chicago

Mary PLUM (American)

Citation Record: 4 Books

The Killing Of Judge MacFarlane - *First*
Harper & Row US (1930); Eyre & Spottiswoode UK (1930)

Murder At The World's Fair - *Last*
Harper & Row US (1933)

The Broken Vase Mystery - *Last**
Eyre & Spottiswoode UK (1933)

John SMITH

operates in the London district of Soho and doubles as an undercover agent for British Intelligence.

American Male Private Detective operating in London/Russia

Jimmy SANGSTER 1927- (British)

Invented 3 detectives - see James REED

Citation Record: 2 Books

Private I - *First*
Triton UK (1967); Norton US (1967)

Foreign Exchange - *Last*
Triton UK (1968); Norton US (1968)

John SMITH

Second detective of Ian FIRTH

Dr John SMITH

is a psychiatrist who sleuths. He appears also in one book with one of the author's other detectives, *Luke BRADLEY*.

American Male Amateur operating in USA

Hugh PENTECOST 1903-1989 (American)

Invented 12 detectives - see Pierre CHAMBRUN

Citation Record: 2 Books 4 Short Stories in 1 Collection

Where The Snow Was Red - *First*
Dodd, Mead US (1949); Hale UK (1951)

Shadow Of Madness - *Last*
Dodd, Mead US (1950)

Death Wears A Copper Necktie And Other Stories - *Collection 1*
Edward US (1946)

Kim SMITH

British Male Amateur operating in Paris

John BOLAND 1913-1976 (British)

See main detective John Byron HYDE

Citation Record: 2 Books

Counterpol - *First*
Harrap UK (1963); Walker US (1965)

Counterpol In Paris - *Last*
Harrap UK (1964); Walker US (1965)

Det Insp Lancelot Carolus SMITH

specialises, it seems, in solving 'impossible' cases of murder.

British Policeman operating in England

Norman BERROW 1902- (British)

Invented 4 detectives - see Michael REVEL

Citation Record: 5 Books

The Three Tiers Of Fantasy - *First*
Ward, Lock UK (1947)

The Footprints Of Satan - *Last*
Ward, Lock UK (1950)

Prof MacKenzie SMITH

is a Professor of Law, close to top people in Washington, who is brought in to solve cases of murder, which have delicate political undertones.

American Male Amateur operating in Washington DC

Margaret TRUMAN 1924- (American)

Invented 9 detectives - see Mr Ron FAIRCHILD

Citation Record: 2 Books

Murder At The Kennedy Center - *First*
Random House US (1989); Severn UK (1990)

Murder At The National Cathedral - *Latest*
Random House US (1990); Severn UK (1991)

Madeline SMITH

Second detective of John INGLES

Mady SMITH

American Female Amateur operating in USA

Mignon G EBERHART 1899- (American)

Invented 9 detectives - see Sarah KEATE

Citation Record: 1 Book

Next Of Kin - *Single*
Random House US (1982)

Napoleon B SMITH

is a rather incompetent detective who has a passion for ice-cream and can easily be bribed with the right flavour.

American Male Private Detective operating in USA

Leslie ALLEN 1908- (American)

For writer details see Squire ADAMS

Citation Record: 1 Book

Murder In The Rough - *Only*
was published under the following byline in the UK.
Five Star US (1946)

Horace BROWN 1908- (American)

See main detective Squire ADAMS

Citation Record: 1 Book

Murder In The Rough - *Only*
was published under the preceding byline in the US.
Boardman UK (1948)

Oliver Trentham SMITH

British Male Amateur operating in England

Franklin DARE (British)

Citation Record: 1 Collection

The Amazing Mr Smith - *Collection 1*
contains several stories with this detective, randomly distributed among the chapters.
Amalgamated UK (1937)

Supt Owen SMITH

is a Scotland Yard man in books that are almost police procedurals. In the later ones he is more concerned with espionage, becoming involved in increasingly unbelievable situations.

British Policeman operating in London

James BARNETT 1920- (British)

was born in Scotland. After serving for thirty years with the Metropolitan Police in London he is highly knowledgeable about police and criminal procedures and his novels are full of interest.

Citation Record: 5 Books

Backfire Is Hostile! - *First*
Secker & Warburg UK (1979); St Martin's US (1979)

Diminished Responsibility - *Latest*
Secker & Warburg UK (1984); Secker & Warburg US (1986)

Peabody SMITH

was formerly in the US Secret Service and became a famous detective in stories in *Argosy* in 1922.

American Male Detective in Pulp Magazines operating in USA

W J FLYNN 1867-1952 (American)

No citations

Peregrine SMITH

British Male Amateur operating in England

Thomas KINDON

Citation Record: 1 Book

Murder In The Moor - *Only*
Methuen UK (1929); Dutton US (1929)

T B SMITH

appears also in one book with one of the author's other detectives, *Insp ELK.*

British Male Amateur operating in London

Edgar WALLACE 1875-1932 (British)

Invented 28 detectives - see J G REEDER

Citation Record: 2 Books 15 Short Stories in 1 Collection

Kate Plus Ten - *First*
Ward, Lock UK (1919); Small, Maynard US (1917)

The Secret House - *Last*
Ward, Lock UK (1917); Small, Maynard US (1919)

The Admirable Carfew - *Collection 1*
Not all the stories are criminous.
Ward, Lock UK (1914)

T B SMITH

Second detective of Sgt/Insp ELK

Tiberius SMITH

American Male Amateur operating in USA

Hugh PENDEXTER 1875-1940 (American)

Citation Record: 15 Short Stories in 1 Collection

Tiberius Smith - *Collection 1*
Harper & Row US (1907); Harper & Row UK (1907)

Tim SMITH

is the only PI in Winston, New York State.

American Male Private Detective operating in New York

Donald E WESTLAKE 1933- (American)

was born in New York City and educated at the State University of New York, Plattsburgh, 1949-1950, and Binghamton, 1956-1957. A master of the modern crime novel in all its forms, and particularly the difficult comic form, he is the author, under his real name and two main pseudonyms, of at least sixty genre novels and many short stories, as well as screenplays and books for children. He received the Mystery Writers of America Edgar Allan Poe award, 1967.

Writer: Donald Edwin WESTLAKE

Other Bylines:
Tucker COE
Samuel HOLT
Richard STARK

Inventor of one other detective John EDGARSON

Citation Record: 1 Book

Killing Time - *Only*
Random House US (1961); Boardman UK (1962)

The Operators - *Only**
Dell US (1964)

William Wilberforce SMITH

British Male Secret Agent operating in Europe

William HAGGARD 1907- (British)

Invented 4 detectives - see Col Charles RUSSELL

Citation Record: 2 Books

The Martello Tower - *First*
Hodder & Stoughton UK (1985)

The Diplomatist - *Latest*
Hodder & Stoughton UK (1987)

Xenia SMITH and Leslie WETZON

American Female Amateur and American Male Amateur operating in New York

Annette MEYERS 1934- (American)

Writer: Annette Brafman MEYERS

Citation Record: 5 Books

The Big Killing - *First*
Bantam US (1989)

Murder: The Musical - *Latest*
Bantam US (1994)

'Necessary' SMITH

Second detective of Jason JONES

Benjamin SMOKE

is a tall, heavy, man and very fit, an ex-cop from the New York Police Department who simply got fed up with the monotony of the work. He now investigates selected cases but does not wish to apply for a PI licence.

American Male Professional Amateur operating in New York

Ed MCBAIN 1926- (American)

Invented 4 detectives - see The 87th PRECINCT

Citation Record: 1 Book

Where There's Smoke - *Only*
Random House US (1975); Hamish Hamilton UK (1975)

Millard SMYTH

American Male Amateur operating in Alaska

Eunice Mays BOYD (American)

Citation Record: 3 Books

Murder Breaks Trail - *First*
Farrar, Straus US (1943)

Murder Wears Mukluks - *Last*
Farrar, Straus US (1945)

Mrs SNAGG

Female Amateur

O M POPPLEWELL (British)

Writer: Olive M POPPLEWELL

Citation Record: 1 Book

Mrs Snagg, Detective - *Play*
Deane UK (1934); Baker US (1934)

Insp Terry SNEED

is a cop whose ambition and disregard for the rules has led to his increasing corruption, although he remains an excellent detective.

British Policeman operating in England

G F NEWMAN 1945- (British)

Writer: Gordon F NEWMAN

Other Detectives:
Det Ch Insp John FORDHAM Jimmy VANESCO

Citation Record: 3 Books

Sir, You Bastard - *First*
Allen UK (1970); Simon & Schuster US (1971)

Rogue Cop - *First**
Lancer US (1973)

The Price - *Last*
New English Library UK (1974); Allen UK (1974)

Insp SNELL

solves the mystery of an old man's disappearance at his club.

British Policeman operating in London

E Phillips OPPENHEIM 1866-1946 (British)

Invented 27 detectives - see Nicholas GOADE

Citation Record: 1 Book

Sir Adam Disappeared - *Only*
Hodder & Stoughton UK (1939); Little, Brown US (1939)

S

Henrietta SNOOKS and Gus BILINSKI

American Female Amateur and American Male Amateur operating in Pittsburgh

Barbara PAUL (American)

Invented 8 detectives - see Lt TOOMEY

Citation Record: 1 Book

Your Eyes Are Growing Heavy - *Single*
Doubleday US (1981); Collins UK (1982)

Joe SNOW

is a Government agent who retraces the route of the famous lost aviatrix, Amelia Earhart, and discovers 'the truth'.

American Male Professional Investigator operating in several locations

James Stewart THAYER 1949- (American)

Citation Record: 1 Book

The Earhart Betrayal - *Single*
Putnam US (1980); Hamlyn UK (1982)

Supt John SNOW

British Policeman operating in England

Raymond H SAWKINS 1923- (British)

For writer details see TWEED

Citation Record: 3 Books

Snow On High Ground - *First*
Heinemann UK (1966); Harcourt Brace US (1967)

Snow Along The Border - *Last*
Heinemann UK (1968); Harcourt Brace US (1968)

Sylvia SNOW and Prof Charles CARSTAIRS

Sylvia SNOW, a book-keeper with artistic leanings, is hired by *Prof Charles CARSTAIRS* to sort out a bankrupt business left to him by his uncle, but she is left with a murder on her hands when he finds a body in his car.

American Female Amateur and American Male Amateur operating in Seattle

K K BECK (American)

Invented 5 detectives - see Iris COOPER

Citation Record: 1 Book

The Body In The Volvo - *Single*
Walker US (1987)

Hemlock SOAMES

British Male Professional Amateur operating in England

is a *Sherlock HOLMES* parody who has appeared in brief stories published in one of Britain's oldest and most authoritative technical journals. A brilliant chemist, he encounters laboratory mysteries, often involving unusual chemical reactions, which the reader is challenged to solve before he does.

ANON

Citation Record: 4 Selected Short Stories

The Posthumous Nobel Prize - *Pastiche 1*
In 'Chemistry and Industry' UK (1995)

The Hair In The Soup - *Pastiche 2*
In 'Chemistry and Industry' UK (1995)

A War Of Nerves - *Pastiche 3*
In 'Chemistry and Industry' UK (1995)

The Optical Illusion - *Pastiche 4*
In 'Chemistry and Industry' UK (1995)

Herlock SOAMES and Arsène LEPINE

Herlock SOAMES is a *Sherlock HOLMES* and *Arsène LEPINE* is an *Arsène LUPIN* parody. In their one encounter they parody the classic encounter between the two originals in *ARSENE LUPIN CONTRE HERLOCK SHOLMES* by *Maurice LEBLANC* (qv).

British Male Professional Amateur and French Professional Amateur operating in France

Sidekick: Dr WATTS
is his parody *WATSON*-like assistant.
British Male - Assistant

S Beach CHESTER 1880- (British)

Writer: Samuel Beach CHESTER

Citation Record: 1 Selected Short Story

The Arsène Lepine-Herlock Soames Affair - *Parody 1*
appeared first in a collection of the author's short stories and was published later in book form by Aspen (US 1976).
Paul UK (1912)

'Soc' SOCARIDES

American Male Private Detective operating in Cape Cod

Paul KEMPRECOS (American)

Citation Record: 4 Books

Death In Deep Water - *First*
Bantam US (1993)

Feeding Frenzy - *Latest*
Bantam US (1994)

A SOCIAL DETECTIVE

British Male Professional Investigator operating in London

Charles BRAMLEY (British)

Citation Record: 20 Short Stories in 1 Collection

The Adventures Of A Social Detective; Or, Life Among The Lions Of Society In Bohemia - *Collection 1*
Diprose & Bateman UK (18??)

The SOCIETY DETECTIVE

American Male Detective in Pulp Magazines operating in USA

ANON

Citation Record: 1 Book

The Society Detective
Aldine US

Kyra SOKRATESCU

is a Roumanian playgirl who regards detection as an intellectual exercise to stave off boredom.

Roumanian Female Amateur

Gilbert FRANKAU 1884-1952 (British)

Invented 3 detectives - see Giuseppe CIGARINI

Citation Record: 3 Short Stories in 2 Collections

Concerning Peter Jackson - *Collection 1*

This collection of five of the author's stories contains two with *Kyra SOKRATESCU.*

Short stories - 2
Hutchinson UK (1931)

Experiments In Crime And Other Stories - *Collection 2*

This collection of fourteen of the author's short stories contains one with *Kyra SOKRATESCU.*

Short stories - 1
Hutchinson UK (1937); Dutton US (1937)

Sgt Louis SOLDEN

British Male Sleuth operating in England

Bill TURNER 1927- (British)

See main detective Bruce KIRKWOOD

Citation Record: 3 Books

Sex Trap - *First*
Constable UK (1968)

Solden's Women - *Last*
Constable UK (1972)

Napoleon SOLO and Ilya KURYAKIN

are agents for UNCLE, the spy-catching apparatus set up to defend the Western world from the machinations of its enemies. They are derived from TV and films, have their own magazine, and appear in countless pulp stories, one of which is cited.

American Male Professional Investigators operating in several locations

Michael AVALLONE 1924- (American)

Invented 5 detectives - see Ed NOON

Citation Record: 1 Book

The Thousand Coffin Affair - *Only*
Ace US (1965)

Robert Hart DAVIS (American)

See main detective Insp Charlie CHAN

Citation Record: 1 Selected Short Story

The Ghost Rider Affair
In 'The Man From Uncle Magazine' US (1966)

Ed SOMERS

American Male Detective in Pulp Magazines operating in USA

Ernest STARK (American)

Citation Record: 1 Book

Ed Somers, The Pinkerton Detective - *Only*
Ogilvie US (1886)

Det SOMERTON

of Scotland Yard is in this one Victorian novel.

British Policeman operating in England

Mortimer COLLINS 1827-1876 (British)

Writer: Edward James Mortimer COLLINS

Citation Record: 1 Book

Who Is The Heir? - *Only*
Maxwell UK (1865)

Harry SOMMERS

is an ex-convict and ex-bouncer who accidentally gets a job with the seedy Coronet Private Detective Agency, situated above a dry-cleaning shop in Bethnal Green, East London. When the boss dies, leaving the failing business to his secretary, who was also his mistress, she takes in *Harry SOMMERS* as a partner. He is untutored, oafish, and he hasn't much going for him except a naive honesty and simplicity of outlook. He is turning out to be one of the most likeable as well as one of the most credible of modern British private eyes.

!See Appendix 2.

British Male Private Detective operating in London

Peter WHALLEY 1946- (British)

was born in Colne, Lancashire. He was educated at St Mary's College, Blackburn, Lancashire, and the University of Lancaster. Formerly a schoolteacher, he has been a full-time writer since 1977.

Citation Record: 3 Books

Robbers - *First*
Macmillan UK (1986); Walker US (1987)

Villains - *Latest*
Macmillan UK (1987)

Crooks - *Latest**
Walker US (1988)

Jaine (The Bionic Woman) SOMMERS

American Female Amateur operating in USA

Eileen LOTTMAN 1927- (American)

Writer: Eileen Shurb LOTTMAN

Citation Record: 2 Books

Extracurricular Activities - *First*
Berkley US (1976)

Welcome Home, Jaine - *Last*
Berkley US (1977)

Martin SONDES

Second detective of Raphael PHARE

Joseph SOUTH

is hired as a bodyguard, gets drunk, and wakes to find himself accused of murder; a state of affairs that, understandably, he does not like.

American Male Private Detective operating in USA

Gentry NYLAND (American)

Citation Record: 1 Book

Mr South Burned His Mouth - *Only*
Morrow US (1941)

Hot Bullets For Love - *Only**
Double Action Detective US (1943)

Run For Your Money - *Only**
Long UK (1941)

Prof John SOUTHARD

is a Professor of Modern Literature at Harvard who, at the age of thirty-three and a bachelor, ought to know better when he starts sleuthing to protect a young female colleague suspected of murder.

Male Amateur operating in Boston

Wyndham MARTYN 1875- (British)

was born in London. Trained in mining engineering, he emigrated to the USA, where he spent most of his life. He turned to writing novels, plays, thrillers and magazine stories and was the author of at least forty genre novels.

Other Detectives:
Christopher BOND   Anthony TRENT

Citation Record: 1 Book

The Bathurst Complex - *Only*
Jenkins UK (1924)

The Murder In Beacon Street - *Only**
McBride US (1930)

Sam SPACE

is the grandson of the author's other detective, *Bart CHALLIS.* He has an office on Mars at some time in the near future and goes through the same old routines, in excellent parody.

American Male Private Detective operating on Mars

William F NOLAN 1928- (American)

Invented 3 detectives - see Bart CHALLIS

Citation Record: 2 Books

Space For Hire - *First*
Lancer US (1971)

Look Out For Space - *Latest*
International Polygonics US (1984)

Danny SPADE

is an American PI, created by a British writer and rings slightly untrue.
!See Appendix 2.

American Male Private Detective operating in New York

Dail AMBLER 1919-1974 (American)

For writer details see Danny SPADE

Citation Record: 4 Books

Duet For Two Guns - *First*
Scion UK (1952)

The Virgin Collector - *Last*
New English Library UK (1971)

Danny SPADE 1919-1974 (British)

Writer: Dail AMBLER

Other Byline: Dail AMBLER

Citation Record: 32 Books

She Liked It That Way - *First*
Scion UK (1950)

That's All I Need - *Last*
Milestone UK (1954)

Richard SPADE

American Male Amateur operating in USA

B B JOHNSON (American)

Writer: UNKNOWN

Citation Record: 4 Books

Bad Day For A Black Brother - *First*
Paperback Library US (1970)

Black Is Beautiful - *Last*
Paperback Library US (1970)

Sam SPADE

is the absolutely prototypic PI of the 1930s, cool, dedicated and incorruptible. He was the model for countless others, although, in fact, he only appeared in one novel and three short stories. Still, that novel is *THE MALTESE FALCON.* He operated on Sutter Street; the agency was, of course, Spade & Archer (later just Samuel Spade); and his license number is said to have been #137596.

American Male Private Detective operating in San Francisco

Dashiell HAMMETT 1894-1961 (American)

was born in St Mary's County, Maryland, and grew up in Philadelphia. He had no formal education after his early teens and worked as a newsboy, messenger, clerk, timekeeper, yardman and stevedore, finally becoming an operative for the Pinkerton Agency, 1908-1922. After serving in the US army during the First World War, his health badly affected, he resumed his detective work and also began to write detective stories. In 1930 he went to Hollywood, beginning his long relationship with Lillian Hellman, and he stayed there until 1942. He later became a teacher of creative writing in New York, and held many posts in organisations with liberal and left views. In 1951 he was convicted of contempt of Congress for trumped-up offences relating to his left-wing activities and sentenced to six months in prison. *HAMMETT* is generally considered to be one of the three mainsprings of modern American detective fiction. His output was small, consisting of just six novels and a handful of short stories, but their impact on the genre was great. He virtually invented the modern private eye, the lonely, upright shamus, whose allegiance is to an abstract ideal of justice. *HAMMETT's* vein was, in truth, the romantic one, but he gave it a new injection. His detectives are heroes, but they are not super-heroes. His women are feminine but they can possess the vices of men. The police may be honest but they may also be corrupt. They are all identifiable by ordinary mortals.

Writer: Samuel Dashiell HAMMETT

Other Detectives:
Ned BEAUMONT
Nick CHARLES and Nora CHARLES
The CONTINENTAL OP
Alexander RUSH
SECRET AGENT X-9
Robin THIN

Citation Record: 1 Book 3 Short Stories in 1 Collection

The Maltese Falcon - *Only*
is one of the most prestigious books in the whole genre, a living legend and the subject of an equally famous film, in which Humphrey Bogart starred.
Knopf US (1930); Knopf UK (1930)

The Adventures Of Sam Spade And Other Stories - *Collection 1*
contains the only three *Sam SPADE* stories.
Spivak US (1944)

Roger SPAIN

returns home to find his father dead. He determines to catch the murderer and wreak vengeance.

British Male Amateur operating in England

Selwyn JEPSON 1899-1989 (British)

was educated at St Paul's School, London, and the Sorbing, Paris. He served in British Intelligence Corps and Special Operations during the Second World War.

Other Detectives:
Eve GILL
Ian MACARTHUR
John PERRIN

Citation Record: 1 Book

Keep Murder Quiet - *Only*
Joseph UK (1940); Doubleday US (1941)

J T 'Jake' SPANNER

is a private eye who, with the help of his ex-wives, works with the author's other detective, *Ch Insp Max KAUFFMAN,* in two ingenious caper novels and appears on his own in this one book.

American Male Private Detective operating in New York

Thomas CHASTAIN (American)

Other Byline: Nick CARTER

Other Detectives:
Lilia BEDDOES
Det Ch Insp Max KAUFFMAN and J T 'Jake' SPANNER
Perry MASON

Citation Record: 1 Book

Spanner - *Only*
Mason/Charter US (1977)

J T 'Jake' SPANNER

Second detective of Dep Ch Insp Max KAUFFMAN

Jake SPANNER

is seventy-eight years old but as tough as old boots in this, his last case.

American Male Private Detective operating in Los Angeles

L A MORSE 1945- (American)

was born in Fort Wayne, Indiana.

Writer: Larry Alan MORSE

Inventor of one other detective Sam HUNTER

Citation Record: 1 Book

The Old Dick - *Single*
Avon US (1981); Avon UK (1982)

Frank SPARGO

British Male Amateur operating in London

J S FLETCHER 1863-1935 (British)

Invented 9 detectives - see Paul CAMPENHAYE

Citation Record: 1 Book

The Middle Temple Murder - *Only*
Ward, Lock UK (1919); Knopf US (1919)

SPARROW

British Male Sleuth operating in England

Christopher MURPHY 1943- (British)

Citation Record: 2 Books

Scream At The Sea - *First*
Secker & Warburg UK (1981); St Martin's US (1983)

I, Said The Sparrow - *Latest*
Secker & Warburg UK (1984)

Charlie SPARROW

American Male Sleuth operating in Mexico

Tom ARDIES 1931- (American)

was born in Seattle, Washington. He has been a journalist and editor in the USA and Canada.

Citation Record: 3 Books

Their Man In The White House - *First*
Doubleday US (1971); Macmillan UK (1971)

Pandemic - *Last*
Doubleday US (1973); Angus UK (1974)

Luke SPEARE and Schyler COLE

Schyler COLE, not quite hardboiled, runs the Cole Detective Agency in Manhattan and is nominally assisted by *Luke SPEARE.* However, he usually has to play second fiddle to his brilliant assistant. The books appeared under the *DAVIS* byline in the USA and under the author's pseudonym, *Stephen RANSOME,* in the UK and are so cited.

American Male Private Detectives operating in New York

Frederick C DAVIS 1902-1977 (American)

was born in St Joseph, Missouri. He was a prolific writer, the author of about a thousand short stories for the pulps, for which he used many bylines. Later he wrote crime and detective novels under his own name and new pseudonyms.

Writer: Frederick Clyde DAVIS

Other Bylines:
Scott CAMPBELL
Murdo COOMBS
Stephen RANSOME
Curtis STEELE

Other Detectives:
Dr Carter COLE
Prof Syrups HATCH
Steve THATCHER

Citation Record: 6 Books

The Deadly Miss Ashley - *First*
Doubleday US (1950)

Night Drop - *Last*
Doubleday US (1955)

Stephen RANSOME 1902-1977 (American)

Invented 4 detectives - see Lt Lee BARCELLO

Citation Record: 6 Books

The Deadly Miss Ashley - *First*
Gollancz UK (1950)

Night Drop - *Last*
Gollancz UK (1956)

Prof Henry SPEARMAN

is a Professor of Economics at Harvard. He is good at using what he calls 'game matrix theory' to solve cases of murder, to the intense bafflement and pardonable irritation on the part of whichever local police force encounters this sort of thing.

American Male Amateur operating in several locations

Marshall JEVONS (American)

is the byline of two sometime Professors of Economics at the University of Virginia.

Writers: William BREIT and Kenneth Gerald ELZINGA 1947-

Citation Record: 2 Books

Murder At The Margin - *First*
Hotrod US (1978); Melbourne UK (1979)

The Fatal Equilibrium - *Latest*
MIT US (1985)

Insp SPEARPOINT

is probably the only detective who has ever worked the Fiji Islands.

British Policeman operating in Fiji

Sidekick: Insp SHARPE
is tall, young and naive.
British Male - Assistant

Frank ARTHUR 1902-1984 (British)

was born in London. He worked mainly as a civil servant but was also a playwright and poet. He lived for some years in Fiji, which he used as the background to his unusual detective novels.

Writer: Frank Arthur EBERT

Citation Record: 4 Books

Who Killed Netta Maul? - *First*
Gollancz UK (1940)

The Suva Harbour Mystery - *First**
Penguin UK (1948)

The Throbbing Dark - *Last*
Jenkins UK (1963)

Det Insp Simon SPEARS

is, in his first book, called in to solve the murder of an actor during a radio broadcast. He appeared in two more novels concerned with broadcasting.

British Policeman operating in London/Budapest

Sidekick: Julian CAIRD
is a BBC executive. Being on the spot, as it were, he is able to give much help to *SPEARS.*
British Male - Assistant

Val GIELGUD 1900-1981 (British)

was born in London, educated at Rugby School, Warwickshire, and graduated from Trinity College, Oxford. He became well known for his work as a writer and producer in radio, TV and films, writing and directing plays and scripts for all the media. He was Head of Drama for the BBC and received an OBE, 1942, and a CBE, 1958. He was the author of nearly thirty genre books, at least twenty stage plays, and around fifty radio plays.

Writer: Val Henry GIELGUD

Other Detectives:
Anthony HAVILLAND
Insp Gregory PELLEW and Viscount CLYMPING

Citation Record: 3 Books

Death At Broadcasting House - *First*
Rich & Cowan UK (1934)

London Calling - *First**
Doubleday US (1934)

Death In Budapest - *Last*
Rich & Cowan UK (1937)

SPECIAL OPERATIONS EXECUTIVE

Sleuths operating in Canada

Jack H CRISP 1923- (Canadian)

Citation Record: 2 Books

Dragon Spoor - *First*
Simon & Pierre US (1978); Futura UK (1979)

Final Act - *Latest*
Futura UK (1979)

Insp Bill SPEED
British Policeman operating in England

J B DONOVAN (British)
Writer: Jean Bernadine DONOVAN
Citation Record: 2 Books 22 Short Stories in 1 Collection
Bill Speed On Hot Ice - *First*
Kingfisher UK (1962)
Bill Speed - Special Squad - *Last*
Kingfisher UK (1963)
Meet Bill Speed - *Collection 1*
Kingfisher UK (1961)

Martin SPEED
British Male Amateur operating in England

Maurice G HUGI 1904-1947 (British)
Citation Record: 2 Books
Martin Speed Versus "The Snatcher" - *First*
Swan UK (1946)
The Tin Bath Murder - *Last*
Swan UK (1947)

John NORMAN (British)
Citation Record: 4 Books
The Concert Party Murders - *First*
Swan UK (1945)
The Case Of The Four Pages - *Last*
Swan UK (1946)

George ELLIOTT (British)
Citation Record: 2 Books
The Case Of The Missing Airman - *First*
Swan UK (1944)
The Mystery Of The Missing Corpses - *Last*
Swan UK (1945)

Maxwell SPEED
American Male Sleuth operating in Sweden/Middle East

Richard STARNES 1922- (American)
Inventor of one other detective pair Barney FORGE and Dr St George PEACHY
Citation Record: 2 Books
Requiem In Utopia - *First*
Trident Press US (1967)
The Flypaper War - *Last*
Trident Press US (1969); Hutchinson UK (1970)

Gil SPEER
American Male Private Detective operating in Washington DC

S

Don TRACEY 1905-1976 (American)
Writer: Donald Fiske TRACEY
Citation Record: 4 Books
Flats Fixed - Among Other Things - *First*
Pocket Books US (1974)
The Big Fix - *Latest*
Pocket Books US (1976)

Insp SPEIGHT
investigates the murder of a nurse at a hospital.
British Policeman operating in England

John WAKEFIELD 1921- (British)
Citation Record: 1 Book
Death The Sure Physician - *Only*
Constable UK (1965); Dodd, Mead US (1966)

Tom SPELLACY
American Male Amateur operating in USA

John Gregory DUNNE 1932- (American)
Citation Record: 1 Book
True Confessions - *Single*
Dutton US (1977); Weidenfeld & Nicolson UK (1978)

Supt Ben SPENCE
British Policeman operating in England

Michael ALLEN 1939- (British)
Writer: Michael Derek ALLEN
Citation Record: 4 Books
Spence In Petal Park - *First*
Constable UK (1977)
Spence And The Holiday Murders - *First**
Walker US (1978)
Spence At Marlby Manor - *Latest*
Walker US (1982)

Philip SPENCE
Second detective of Margo FRANKLIN

Prof Irving SPENCER
is a blind detective.
American Male Amateur operating in USA

Chester K STEELE 1862-1930 (American)
For writer details see Carolyn KEENE
Inventor of one other detective Col Robert Lee ASHLEY
Citation Record: 1 Book
The House Of Disappearances - *Only*
Chelsea US (1927)

John SPENCER
British Male Sleuth

Lou SMITH 1918- (British)
Citation Record: 3 Books
The Secret Of MI6 - *First*
Hale UK (1975); St Martin's US (1978)
Primrose: The Fourth Man - *Last*
Hale UK (1976); St Martin's US (1976)
The Fourth Man - *Last**
Signet US (1978)

Marc SPENCER
is an American detective created by a British author. In one book he investigates a case of three missing blondes.
American Male Private Detective operating in New York

Raymond MARSHALL 1906-1985 (British)
Invented 4 detectives - see Don MICKLEM
Citation Record: 1 Book
Blondes' Requiem - *Only*
Jarrolds UK (1945); Crown US (1946)

Tony SPENCER
Australian Male Amateur operating in Sydney

Otto BEEBY 1906-1981 (Australian)
Citation Record: 4 Books
A Blank Cheque For Murder - *First*
Long UK (1968)
Too Many Innocents - *Last*
Long UK (1972)

Insp SPENS
solves a case of death by shooting in a locked room.
British Policeman operating in England

Horace G HUTCHINSON 1859-1932 (British)
Writer: Horace Gordon HUTCHINSON
Inventor of one other detective Emil TABOR
Citation Record: 1 Book
The Greenwells Glory Case - *Only*
!See Appendix 2.
Hutchinson UK (1924)

Walter SPENSE
American Male Sleuth operating in Austria

Richard Martin STERN 1915- (American)
Invented 3 detectives - see Johnny ORTIZ

Citation Record: 1 Book

The Kessler Legacy *- Only*
Scribner's US (1967); Cassell UK (1968)

SPENSER

is a worthy successor, it is said, to the classic *Philip MARLOWE* and *Lew ARCHER.* A private eye in Boston, he cannot be regarded, however, as a particularly moral character, compared to his illustrious predecessors. As a sign of the times, he is depicted as being rougher and tougher, and as being fond of wenching, good food and, especially, Susan Silverman.

American Male Private Detective operating in Boston

Sidekick: Jim HAWK

is a black man who was once a mob enforcer but, in later books of the continuing canon, has become the very definite rough, tough sidekick of one of the most admired of modern fictional detectives, a move regarded by aficionados as one of the more retrograde steps in recent fiction.

American Male - Assistant

Robert B PARKER 1932- (American)

was born in Springfield, Massachusetts. He graduated with a BA at Colby College, Waterville, Maine, 1954, followed by an MA from Boston University, 1957, and a PhD, 1971. He has taught and held professorships at several US universities, is a distinguished literary critic and is acknowledged to be one of the modern masters of the private eye novel. In addition to his own series, he completed the last novel of *Raymond CHANDLER,* which was unfinished at the latter's death, and has also written a *Philip MARLOWE* pastiche novel. He received the Mystery Writers of America Edgar Allan Poe award, 1976.

Writer: Robert Brown PARKER

Adopter of one other detective Philip MARLOWE

Citation Record: 18 Books

The Godwulf Manuscript *- First*
Houghton US (1974); Deutsch UK (1974)

Walking Shadow *- Latest*
Putnam US (1994); Viking UK (1994)

Mark SPICER

American Male Detective in Pulp Magazines operating in USA

OLD SPICER (American)

Writer: UNKNOWN

Citation Record: 14 Books

The Sport Of Fate; Or, The Mystery Of Fort Hale *- First*
Street & Smith (Magnet #255) US (1902)

The Tattooed Wrist; Or, The Deed Of A Night *- Last*
Street & Smith (Magnet #327) US (1904)

Robert SPICER

is the head of a London detective agency in the 1890s.

British Male Private Detective operating in London

Sidekick: Rose COURTENAY

assists the detective in five books and appears in one book as the main detective.

British Female - Assistant

Milton DANVERS (British)

See main detective Rose COURTENAY

Citation Record: 5 Books

The Doctor's Crime; Or, Simply Horrible! *- First*
Diprose & Bateman UK (1891)

Mysterious Disappearance Of A Bride *- Last*
Diprose & Bateman UK (1895)

The SPIDER

American Male Detective in Pulp Magazines operating in USA

UNKNOWN

No citations

Capt Harry SPINK

is a sea captain who, in short stories only, does some sleuthing.

British Male Amateur operating in several locations

Morley ROBERTS 1857-1942 (British)

Writer: Morley Charles ROBERTS

Citation Record: 7 Short Stories in 1 Collection

Adventures Of Captain Spink *- Collection 1*
Nash UK (1926)

Phineas SPINNET

British Male Amateur operating in England

Andrew SOUTAR 1879-1941 (British)

Inventor of one other detective KHARDUNI

Citation Record: 9 Books

The Hanging Sword! *- First*
Hutchinson UK (1933)

Study In Suspense *- Last*
Hutchinson UK (1941)

Michael SPRAGGUE

is an ex-actor and an ex-cop, which gives him useful, if unbelievable, credentials. Wealthy in his own right, he became fed up with the world of the stage and took up the world of the private eye (which seems no better). He is a sound attempt, however, at a modern sleuth, midway in behaviour between the old-fashioned amateur and the hardboiled PI.

American Male Private Detective operating in Boston

Sidekick: Mary Spraggue HILLMAN

is the detective's elderly aunt and acts as his veritable *WATSON.*

American Female - Aunt

Linda J BARNES 1949- (American)

See main detective Carlotta CARLYLE

Citation Record: 4 Books

Blood Will Have Blood *- First*
Avon US (1982)

Cities Of The Dead *- Latest*
St Martin's US (1986); Severn UK (1986)

Calvin SPRAGUE

is a government scientist who investigates mysteries.

American Male Professional Investigator operating in USA

Francis LYNDE 1856-1930 (American)

Citation Record: 6 Short Stories in 1 Collection

Scientific Sprague *- Collection 1*
Scribner's US (1912)

Sgt SPRATT

Second detective of Insp HALLAN

Penelope SPRING

Second detective of Sir Toby GLENDOWER

Terry SPRING

American Male Amateur operating in USA

Josephine KAINS 1933- (American)

For writer details see Jake PACE and Hildy PACE

Citation Record: 6 Books

The Devil Mask Mystery *- First*
Zebra US (1978)

The Laughing Dragon Mystery *- Latest*
Zebra US (1980)

Judd SPRINGFIELD

American Male Amateur operating in Vermont

Alison SMITH 1932- (American)

was born in Boston, Massachusetts.

Citation Record: 2 Books

Someone Else's Grave - *First*
St Martin's US (1984)
Rising - *Latest*
US (1987)

Mr SPRINGFIELD

British Male Amateur operating in England

James SANDYS (British)
Invented 3 detectives - see Insp MILLWALL
Citation Record: 4 Books
Thicker Than Water - *First*
Paul UK (1941)
The Man Who Wasn't There - *Last*
Paul UK (1953)

Ms SQUAD

American Sleuth operating in USA

Mercedes ENDFIELD 1922-
Writer: Bela William VON BLOCK
Citation Record: 2 Books
Lucky Pierre - *First*
Bantam UK (1975)
On The Brink - *Last*
Bantam UK (1975)

Dominick SQUEEK

British Male Detective in Pulp Magazines operating in USA

ANON
Citation Record: 1 Selected Short Story
Dominick Squeek, The Bow Street Runner; Or, An English Detective In America
Old Cap Collier Library US (18??)

George Lombard SQUIRE

is a banker who solves the mystery of how jewels were stolen from a hotel safe.
American Male Amateur operating in USA

Walter DALLAS (American)
Citation Record: 1 Selected Short Story
The Mysterious Mirror
appeared in the April number.
In 'Mike Shayne Mystery Magazine' US (1964)

Lee SQUIRES

American Female Amateur operating in Montana

Christine ANDRAE (American)
Citation Record: 1 Book
Grizzly, A Mystery - *Single*
St Martin's US (1994)

S

ST FRANCIS SCHOOL

is a collection of schoolboy detectives.
British Male Amateurs operating in England/USA

Edwy Searles BROOKS 1889-1965 (British)
Invented 5 detectives - see Insp William (The Grouser) BEEKE
Citation Record: 3 Books
The Kidnapped School - *First*
Amalgamated UK (1924)
The New York Mystery - *Last*
Amalgamated UK (1924)

Jean Henri ST AMAND

appears also in one book with one of the author's other detectives, *Peter BLUE.*
French Male Amateur operating in Paris

Darwin L TEILHET 1904-1964 (American)
Invented 3 detectives - see Peter BLUE and Jean Henri ST AMAND
Citation Record: 1 Book
Death Flies High - *First*
Morrow US (1931); Long UK (1932)

Jean Henri ST AMAND

Second detective of Peter BLUE

Col Sir Theophilus ST CLAIR

is a serving officer in Spain during the Napoleonic Wars.
British Male Amateur operating in several locations

Arthur GRIFFITHS 1838-1908 (British)
Invented 8 detectives - see Insp FASKE
Citation Record: 14 Short Stories in 1 Collection
A Royal Rascal: Episodes In The Career Of Sir Theophilus St Clair, KCB - *Collection 1*
Unwin UK (1905)

Angus ST CLOUD

is one of this author's numerous pulp detectives, appearing mainly in stories in *Crime Busters Magazine.*
American Male Detective in Pulp Magazines operating in USA

Norwell PAGE (American)
Invented 3 detectives - see Ken CARTER
No citations

Insp ST CYR and Hermann KOHLER

are national enemies in Occupied France during the Second World War, but have to work together as policemen to solve cases of non-military murder.
French Policeman and German Policeman operating in France

J Robert JANES 1935- (Canadian)
is a mining engineer.
Writer: Joseph Robert JANES
Citation Record: 6 Books
Mayhem - *First*
Constable UK (1992)
Dollmaker - *Latest*
Constable UK (1995)

Claudine ST CYR

sleuths at some time in the future. She appears also in one book with the author's other detective, *CROYD.*
Female Sleuth

Ian WALLACE 1912- (American)
Writer: Wallace PRITCHARD
Other Detectives:
CROYD — Claudine ST CYR and CROYD
Citation Record: 3 Books
Deathstar Voyage - *First*
Putnam US (1969); Dobson UK (1972)
The Sign Of The Mute Medusa - *Latest*
Popular Library UK (1977)

Claudine ST CYR and CROYD

also appear individually in other books by this author.
Female Sleuth and Male Sleuth

Ian WALLACE 1912- (American)
Invented 3 detectives - see Claudine ST CYR
Citation Record: 1 Book
Heller's Leap - *Single*
Daw US (1979)

Philip ST IVES

is a professional intermediary between crooks and their victims and has to do a reasonable amount of sleuthing to stay in business.
American Male Professional Investigator operating in USA

Oliver BLEECK 1926- (American)
For writer details see Morgan CITRON
Citation Record: 5 Books
The Brass Go-Between - *First*
Morrow US (1969); Hodder & Stoughton UK (1970)
No Questions Asked - *Latest*
Morrow US (1976); Hamish Hamilton UK (1976)

Kiel ST JAMES and Orson BOLES
American Male Amateurs operating in Alabama

Elliott CHAZE 1915- (American)
Writer: Lewis Elliott CHAZE
Citation Record: 2 Books
Mr Yesterday - *First*
Scribner's US (1984)
The Catherine Murders - *First**
Hale UK (1986)
Little David - *Latest*
Scribner's US (1985)

Quin ST JAMES and Mike MCCLEARY
American Female Private Detective and American Male Private Detective operating in Miami

T J MACGREGOR 1947- (American)
Writer: Trish Janeschutz MACGREGOR
Citation Record: 6 Books
Dark Fields - *First*
Ballantine US (1987); Futura UK (1988)
Storm Surge - *Latest*
Hyperion US (1993)

Jeremiah ST JOHN
was once an assistant District Attorney but he quit to become a PI.
American Male Private Detective operating in San Francisco
Sidekick: Michelle FARABAUGH
was a female cop in Ohio but was fired for appearing nude in a magazine article about female police uniforms. She now shares the sidekick honours with another of *ST JOHN's* assistants.
American Female - Assistant
Sidekick: Ch MOSES
is a giant Seminole Indian.
American Male - Assistant

William BABULA 1943- (American)
Citation Record: 2 Books
St John's Baptism - *First*
Stuart US (1988); Stuart UK (1989)
According To St John - *Latest*
Stuart US (1989)

Florence ST LEONARD
sleuths in England in the early 1800s.
American Female Amateur operating in England

Anna GILBERT 1916- (British)
Writer: Marguerite LAZARDS
Citation Record: 1 Book
Miss Bede Is Staying - *Single*
Pitman UK (1982); St Martin's US (1983)

Britt (Mind Masters) ST VINCENT
American Sleuth operating in USA

Ian ROSS 1942- (American)
Writer: John Francis ROSSMAN
Citation Record: 2 Books
Amazons - *First*
Signet UK (1976)
Recycled Souls - *Latest*
Signet UK (1976)

John F ROSSMANN 1942- (American)
Citation Record: 3 Books
The Mind-Masters - *First*
Signet UK (1974)
The Door - *Last*
Signet UK (1975)

Johnny STACCATO
appeared first on TV as a PI working in New York. He was novelized in one book under the pseudonym of a well-known crime writer.
American Male Private Detective operating in New York

Frank BOYD 1912-1968 (American)
Writer: Frank KANE
Citation Record: 1 Book
Johnny Staccato - *Only*
GM US (1960); Consul UK (1964)

Colby STACK
solves a case of death by gassing on a train.
British Male Amateur operating in England

Leonard KNIGHT 1895- (British)
Writer: Leonard Alfred KNIGHT
Inventor of one other detective Jerry SCANT
Citation Record: 1 Book
Night Express Murder - *Only*
Low UK (1936)

Max STAFFORD
is a professional agent doing his best against the usual forces of evil in darkest Africa.
British Male Secret Agent operating in Kenya

Desmond BAGLEY 1923-1983 (British)
was born in Kendal, Westmoreland. He had no higher education and worked during the late 1940s in Kenya and South Africa.
Inventor of one other detective SLADE
Citation Record: 2 Books
Flyaway - *First*
Collins UK (1978); Doubleday US (1979)
Windfall - *Last*
Collins UK (1982); Summit US (1982)

Det Satan STAGG
Second detective of Pharaoh LOVE

Ch Insp Alec STAINTON
British Policeman operating in England
Sidekick: Policewoman Jayne SIMMONDS
British Female - Subordinate

Stephen MURRAY 1954- (British)
Citation Record: 5 Books
A Cool Killing - *First*
Collins UK (1987); St Martin's US (1988)
Fatal Opinions - *Latest*
HarperCollins UK (1991)

Vincent STALLARD and Cynthia GODWIN
British Male Amateur and British Female Amateur operating in Middle East

George BEARE (Australian)
is a sometime journalist, living mainly in England.
Citation Record: 2 Books
The Very Breath Of Hell - *First*
Long UK (1971); Houghton US (1971)
The Bee Sting Deal - *Last*
Long UK (1972); Houghton US (1972)

STANDIFORD
British Male Amateur operating in England

Donald SHOUBRIDGE (British)
Citation Record: 5+ Short Stories in 2 Collections
The Stories Of Donald Shoubridge - *Collection 1*
contains an uncounted number of stories.
Pendulum UK (1945)
Yard Lengths - *Collection 2*
Short stories - 5
Pendulum UK (1946)

Kaye STANDISH and Mike STANDISH
British Female Amateur and British Male Amateur operating in England

J E GURDON 1898- (British)
Writer: John Everard GURDON

Citation Record: 8 Short Stories in 1 Collection
The Sky Trackers - *Collection 1*
Warne UK (1931)

Mike STANDISH
Second detective of Kaye STANDISH

Dr Paul STANDISH
is a medical examiner who is called in to examine a murder victim and is so intrigued he goes on to discover whodunnit.
American Male Amateur operating in New York

George Harmon COXE 1901-1984 (American)
Invented 20 detectives - see Kent MURDOCK
Citation Record: 1 Book
The Ring Of Truth - *Single*
Knopf US (1966); Hammond UK (1967)

Ronald STANDISH
worked with *'Bulldog' DRUMMOND* in three novels and appeared on his own in short stories. He is simply a wealthy man who likes to do detective work and put down nasty anti-British criminals, a pastime that seemed an alternative, at the time, to foxhunting. He is, readers are assured, a first-class cricketer.
British Male Private Detective operating in England

SAPPER 1888-1937 (British)
Invented 4 detectives - see Capt Hugh 'Bulldog' DRUMMOND
Citation Record: 24 Short Stories in 2 Collections
Ronald Standish - *Collection 1*
Short stories - 12
Hodder & Stoughton UK (1933)
Ask For Ronald Standish - *Collection 2*
Short stories - 12
Hodder & Stoughton UK (1936)

Ronald STANDISH
Second detective of Capt Hugh 'Bulldog' DRUMMOND

Timothy Overbury 'Tiger' STANDISH
is the son of the Duke of Quorn and another in the line of British superheroes of the 1930s. Tall, strong, handsome, impeccably dressed, and pipe-smoking calmly in the face of personal danger, he saves his country from all manner of despicable deeds, usually contrived by nasty foreigners. In all his early books he was accompanied by one of the author's other detectives, *Sir Harker BELLAMY;* but, in his later books, he managed to deal with the villains on his own.
British Male Amateur operating in England

S

Sydney HORLER 1888-1954 (British)
Invented 20 detectives - see Sir Harker BELLAMY
Citation Record: 4 Books
Exit The Disguiser - *First*
Hodder & Stoughton UK (1948)
The House Of Jackals - *Last*
Hodder & Stoughton UK (1951)

The Hon Timothy Overbury 'Tiger' STANDISH and Sir Harker BELLAMY
also appear individually in other books by this author.
British Male Amateurs operating in England

Sydney HORLER 1888-1954 (British)
Invented 20 detectives - see Sir Harker BELLAMY
Citation Record: 8 Books
The Mystery Of The Seven Cafés: The Novel Of The Famous Wireless Play - *First*
Hodder & Stoughton UK (1935)
The Lady With The Limp - *Last*
Hodder & Stoughton UK (1944)

Policeman STANHOPE
is in the Royal Canadian Mounted Police.
Canadian Policeman operating in Canada

Lawrence L LYNCH (American)
Invented 11 detectives - see Neil J BATHURST
Citation Record: 1 Book
A Mountain Mystery; Or, The Outlaws Of The Rockies - *Only*
Ward, Lock UK (1890)

Richard STANHOPE
Second detective of Rufus CARNES

Paul STANIAL
American Male Private Detective operating in Florida

John D MACDONALD 1916-1986 (American)
Invented 3 detectives - see Travis MCGEE
Citation Record: 1 Book
The Drowner - *Only*
Fawcett US (1963); Hale UK (1964)

Hagar STANLEY
is a gypsy pawnbroker whose Romany heritage enables her to solve mysteries surrounding the appearance of several pawned objects.
Female Amateur operating in England

Fergus HUME 1859-1932 (British)
Invented 24 detectives - see Insp Samuel GORBY
Citation Record: 12 Short Stories in 1 Collection
Hagar Of The Pawnshop - *Collection 1*
Skeffington UK (1898)

Burl STANNARD
American Male Private Detective operating in California

J M FLYNN 1927-1985 (American)
Writer: Jay FLYNN
Other Byline: Jay FLYNN
Inventor of one other detective Ken MADISON
Citation Record: 1 Book
Terror Tournament - *Only*
Mystery House US (1959)

Rand STANNARD
American Male Secret Agent operating in several locations

Richard L HERSHATTER 1923- (American)
Writer: Richard Lawrence HERSHATTER
Citation Record: 3 Books
The Spy Who Hated Licorice - *First*
Signet UK (1966)
The Spy Who Hated Fudge - *Last*
Ace US (1970)

Hugh STANTON
Second detective of Insp Peter CURWEN

John STANTON
American Male Amateur operating in Chicago

Clifford S RAYMOND 1875- (American)
Writer: Clifford Samuel RAYMOND
Citation Record: 1 Book
The Men On The Dead Man's Chest - *Only*
Bobbs US (1930)

Ruth STANTON
is a novelist who investigates the disappearance and possible death of a young woman.
British Female Amateur operating in England

Gwen MOFFAT 1924- (British)
See main detective Melinda PINK
Citation Record: 1 Book
Deviant Death - *Only*
Gollancz UK (1973)

Toni STAPLETON
Second detective of Insp FROST

Det Insp Dave STARK
British Policeman operating in Nottingham

Keith WRIGHT (British)

Citation Record: 1 Book

Fair Means Or Foul? - *Single*
Constable UK (1995)

Joanna STARK
is in her forties and was once a partner in a firm providing security for art museums and galleries. She moves from San Francisco into the hinterland to provide expert help to museums in combating crime.
American Female Amateur operating in California

Marcia MULLER 1944- (American)
Invented 3 detectives - see Sharon MCCONE

Citation Record: 3 Books

The Cavalier In White - *First*
St Martin's US (1986)

Dark Star - *Latest*
St Martin's US (1989)

John STARK
British Male Sleuth operating in several locations

Joseph HEDGES 1936- (British)
For writer details see Terry HARKNETT

Citation Record: 12 Books

Arms For Oblivion - *First*
Sphere UK (1973); Pyramid US (1975)

Angel Of Destruction - *Latest*
Sphere UK (1977)

Robert STARK
American Male Sleuth operating in Hong Kong

Mark SCHORR 1953- (American)
Invented 3 detectives - see Red DIAMOND

Citation Record: 2 Books

Gunpower - *First*
Pocket Books US (1990)

Seize The Dragon - *Latest*
Pocket Books US (1990)

Dr Colin STARR
lives in the fictional small town of Laurel Falls, Ohio, where, more than once, he senses murder when people die. His medical skills enable him to prove it.
American Male Professional Amateur operating in Ohio

Rufus KING 1893-1966 (American)
Invented 5 detectives - see Cotton MOON

Citation Record: 7 Short Stories in 1 Collection

Diagnosis: Murder - *Collection 1*
Doubleday US (1941); Methuen UK (1942)

Jason STARR and Adam CYBER
American Male Sleuths operating in USA

Peter HEATH 1938- (American)

Writer: Peter Heath FINE

Citation Record: 3 Books

The Mind Brothers - *First*
Lancer UK (1967)

Men Who Die Twice - *Last*
Lancer UK (1968)

Dr Ben STARRETT
solves an 'impossible' case of stabbing, with no people around and no weapon to be seen.
American Male Sleuth operating in USA

George DYER 1903-1978 (American)

Writer: George Bell DYER

Citation Record: 1 Book

The Three-Cornered Wound - *Only*
Houghton US (1931); Skeffington UK (1932)

STARSKY and HUTCH
appear in novelizations of episodes from the TV series.
American Male Sleuths operating in Los Angeles

Max FRANKLIN 1915-1983 (American)

Writer: Richard DEMING

Citation Record: 8 Books

Death Ride - *First*
Ballantine US (1976); Futura UK (1976)

The Set-Up - *Latest*
Ballantine US (1978); Futura UK (1978)

Kate STARTE
Second detective of Roger STARTE

Roger STARTE and Kate STARTE
British Male Amateur and British Female Amateur operating in The Balkans

Eric WILLIAMS 1911- (British)

Writer: Eric Ernest WILLIAMS

Citation Record: 2 Books

Dragoman Pass - *First*
Collins UK (1959); Coward McCann US (1959)

The Borders Of Barbarism - *Last*
Heinemann UK (1961); Coward McCann US (1962)

T D STASH
lives on Key West, does a little fishing, and fits in a little unlicensed private eye work.
American Male Private Detective operating in Florida

W R PHILBRICK (American)
Invented 4 detectives - see Connie KALE

Citation Record: 3 Books

The Neon Flamingo - *First*
Onyx US (1987)

Tough Enough - *Latest*
Signet US (1988)

Gerald STAUNTON
is a lawyer's clerk who sleuths in this one Victorian novel.
British Male Amateur operating in England

Florence WARDEN 1857-1929 (British)
Invented 4 detectives - see Insp MAYNARD

Citation Record: 1 Book

A Prince Of Darkness - *Only*
Ward & Downey UK (1885)

Insp Robert STAUNTON
British Policeman operating in England

Peter HILL (British)
was formerly a police officer.
Inventor of one other detective Cdr Allan DICE

Citation Record: 3 Books

The Liars - *First*
Davies UK (1977); Houghton US (1978)

The Savages - *Latest*
Heinemann UK (1980)

STAVELEY
British Male Sleuth operating in England

Clifton ROBBINS 1890- (British)
See main detective Clay HARRISON

Citation Record: 2 Books

Six Sign-Post Murder - *First*
Rich UK (1939)

Death Forms Threes - *Last*
Rich UK (1940)

The STEAM-BOAT DETECTIVE
American Male Detective in Pulp Magazines operating in USA

Old Cap DARRELL (American)
Invented 5 detectives - see YOUNG SLEDGE

Citation Record: 1 Book

The Steam-Boat Detective; Or, Tracing A Crime On The Water
New York Detective Library US (1882-8)

Alan STEEL

British Male Sleuth operating in England

Colin ROBERTSON 1906-1980 (British)

Invented 7 detectives - see Mike REED

Citation Record: 2 Books

The Judas Spies - *First*
Hale UK (1966)

Project X - *Last*
Hale UK (1968)

Jon STEEL

American Male Sleuth operating in USA

Michael NEWTON 1951- (American)

Inventor of one other detective pair Det FLYNN and Det TANNER

Citation Record: 2 Books

The Ripper - *First*
Carousel US (1978)

The Satan Ring - *Latest*
Carousel US (1978)

Raeburn STEEL

British Male Amateur operating in England

Collin BROOKS 1893- (British)

Invented 3 detectives - see Swete MCTAVISH

Citation Record: 3 Books

The Body Snatchers - *First*
Hutchinson UK (1927)

The Ghost Hunters - *Last*
Hutchinson UK (1928); Sears US (1928)

Argus STEELE

is not just a detective, and not only a mystery writer, but also a part-time spy. This combination of careers involves him with all manner of nasty characters, at home and abroad.

American Male Private Detective operating in New York/Portugal

Babs LEE 1914- (American)

Writer: Marion Van Der Veer LEE

Citation Record: 2 Books

A Model Is Murdered - *First*
Scribner's US (1942)

Passport To Oblivion - *Last*
Scribner's US (1943)

Babs LEE and Clare Castler SAUNDERS (American)

Although *Babs LEE* wrote the first two books with this detective on her own, she wrote the third and last with a co-author.

Writer: (First author) Marion Van Der Veer LEE 1914-

Citation Record: 1 Book

Measured For Murder - *Only*
Scribner's US (1944); Muller UK (1945)

Donovan STEELE

American Male Sleuth operating in New York

J D MASTERS (American)

Citation Record: 6 Books

Cold Steele - *First*
Charter US (1989)

Renegade Steele - *Latest*
Charter US (1990)

Jim STEELE

American Male Amateur operating in New York/Connecticut

Dana CHAMBERS 1895-1946 (American)

Writer: Albert LEFFINGWELL

Other Byline: Giles JACKSON

Inventor of one other detective Nile BOYD

Citation Record: 7 Books

Some Day I'll Kill You - *First*
Dial US (1939); Hale UK (1939)

Death Against Venus - *Last*
Dial US (1946); Hale UK (1953)

John STEELE

is a reporter who becomes a PI.

American Male Private Detective operating in USA

Jerome ODLUM 1905-1954 (American)

was born in Minneapolis. He was a screenwriter in Hollywood who served time in prison on forgery charges. Of his five criminous works, three were made into acclaimed films.

Other Detectives:
Sam BOOKER and Jimmy WEBB
O'SULLIVAN

Citation Record: 2 Books

Night And No Moon - *First*
Howell Soskin US (1942)

The Mirabilis Diamond - *Last*
US (1945)

Insp Malcolm STEELE

American Policeman operating in Boston

Mansfield SCOTT (American)

Citation Record: 2 Books

The Black Circle - *First*
Clode US (1928); Lane UK (1929)

The Spider's Web - *Last*
Clode US (1929)

'Rocky' Aloysius Algernon STEELE

is a huge man, an ex-boxer, and an ex-Commando from the Second World War. He now runs Steele Special Services from an office in Manhattan and tends to solve his cases by continuing to use the violent behaviour he was accustomed to during his earlier occupations.

American Male Private Detective operating in New York

John B WEST ?-1960? (American)

was born in Washington DC, and educated at Howard University and Harvard University, Cambridge, Massachusetts. He was a doctor and a specialist in tropical diseases who practised in Liberia.

Citation Record: 6 Books

An Eye For An Eye - *First*
Signet US (1959)

Never Kill A Cop - *Last*
Signet US (1961)

'Skyrocket' STEELE

American Male Sleuth

Ron GOULART 1933- (American)

Invented 15 detectives - see Jake PACE and Hildy PACE

Citation Record: 2 Books 1 Selected Short Story

Skyrocket Steele - *First*
Pocket Books US (1980)

Galaxy Jane - *Latest*
Berkley US (1986)

Skyrocket Steele Conquers The Universe
appeared in the author's collection, *Skyrocket Steele Conquers the Universe and Other Media Tales.*
Pulphouse US (1990)

Charles STEEN

is a valet who sleuths in this one Victorian novel.

British Male Amateur operating in England

James PAYN 1830-1898 (British)

Inventor of one other detective Bow Street Runner TOWNSHEND

Citation Record: 1 Book

Found Dead - *Only*
Chapman & Hall UK (1874)

Cpl Larry STEER
Canadian Policeman operating in Canada

L C DOUTHWAITE 1878- (British)
Invented 3 detectives - see Const Jimmie WARDEN
Citation Record: 14 Short Stories in 1 Collection
Corporal Of The Mounted - *Collection 1*
Blackie UK (1939)

Stonewall STEEVENS
British Male Amateur operating in England

Maurice G KIDDY 1894- (British)
Writer: Maurice George KIDDY
Citation Record: 3 Books
Killing No Murder - *First*
Hutchinson UK (1931)
The Jade Hatpin - *Last*
Hutchinson UK (1933)

Gertrude STEIN and Alice TOKLAS
are, indeed, the famous American author and her close companion. They lived in Paris in 1937 and here they are made to go sleuthing together.
American Female Amateurs operating in Paris

Samuel M STEWARD 1909- (American)
Writer: Samuel Morris STEWARD
Citation Record: 2 Books
Murder Is Murder Is Murder - *First*
Alyson US (1985); Alyson UK (1985)
The Caravaggio Shawl - *Latest*
Alyson US (1990); Alyson UK (1990)

Bill STEMPLE
British Male Amateur operating in England

Roderic JEFFRIES 1926- (British)
Invented 4 detectives - see Insp Enrique ALVAREZ
Citation Record: 1 Book
An Embarrassing Death - *Only*
Collins UK (1964); Dodd, Mead US (1965)

Bill STENEM
British Male Amateur operating in England

Jeffrey ASHFORD 1926- (British)
Invented 9 detectives - see Det Insp Don KERRY
Citation Record: 1 Book
The Loss Of The Culion - *Single*
Walker US (1981)

Jack STENTON
British Male Amateur operating in London/New York

Ted DEXTER and Clifford MAKINS 1924-1990 (British)
Citation Record: 2 Books
Testkill - *First*
Allen UK (1976)
Deadly Putter - *Last*
Allen UK (1979)

Brad STERLING
American Male Private Detective operating in USA

Vernon WARREN 1925- (British)
Invented 5 detectives - see Johnny MAQUIS
Citation Record: 1 Book
Farewell By Death - *Only*
Gifford UK (1961)

Clarice STERLING
Second detective of Hannibal LECTER

Miba STERLING
British Amateur operating in England

Jeffrey ASHFORD 1926- (British)
Invented 9 detectives - see Det Insp Don KERRY
Citation Record: 1 Book
A Sense Of Loyalty - *Single*
Walker US (1984)

Alejandro 'Sandy' STERN
is an Argentine-Jewish attorney who brilliantly solves ingenious murders.
American Male Amateur operating in New York

Scott TUROW 1949- (American)
was born in Chicago, Illinois. He took a BA at Amherst College, Massachusetts, 1970, an MA at Stanford University, California, 1974, and a JD at Harvard University, Cambridge, Massachusetts, 1978.
Citation Record: 2 Books
Presumed Innocent - *First*
Farrar, Straus US (1987); Bloomsbury UK (1987)
The Burden Of Proof - *Latest*
Farrar, Straus US (1990); Bloomsbury UK (1990)

Joel STERN
is an attorney who investigates a case of gassing in a locked room.
American Male Amateur operating in USA

Robert ARCHER (American)
Citation Record: 1 Book
Death On The Waterfront - *Only*
Doubleday US (1941); Swan UK (1948)

Dave STEVENS
British Male Private Detective operating in England

K Allen SADDLER 1923- (British)
Writer: Ronald Charles William RICHARDS
Citation Record: 3 Books
The Great Brain Robbery - *First*
Elek UK (1966)
Talking Turkey - *Last*
Joseph UK (1968)

Edward STEVENS
is a publisher who discovers a nineteenth-century manuscript, which enables him to solve a series of crimes, old and new.
American Male Amateur operating in Philadelphia

John Dickson CARR 1906-1977 (American)
Invented 16 detectives - see Dr Gideon FELL
Citation Record: 1 Book
The Burning Court - *Only*
Harper & Row US (1937); Hamish Hamilton UK (1937)

Gavin STEVENS
is the shrewd, white-haired, rustic attorney of the author's famed Yoknapatawpha County.
American Male Amateur operating in Mississippi

William FAULKNER 1897-1962 (American)
Citation Record: 1 Book 6 Short Stories in 1 Collection
Intruder In The Dust - *Only*
Random House US (1948); Chatto UK (1949)
Knight's Gambit - *Collection 1*
Random House US (1949); Chatto UK (1951)

Jim STEVENS
American Male Amateur operating in Africa

David SMITH 1936- (American)
was born in New York, graduated in Law, and has been the sometime Dean of Harvard Law School.
Citation Record: 2 Books
The Leo Conversion - *First*
Dodd, Mead US (1980); Hale UK (1982)
Timbuktu - *Latest*
Dodd, Mead US (1983)

Supt William STEVENS and Insp Pierre ALLAIN
British Policeman and French policeman operating in Europe

Bruce GRAEME 1900-1982 (British)

Invented 6 detectives - see BLACKSHIRT

Citation Record: 10 Books

A Murder Of Some Importance - *First*
Hutchinson UK (1931); Lippincott US (1931)

News Travels By Night - *Latest*
Hutchinson UK (1943)

Alan STEWART
American Male Amateur operating in USA/Bermuda

Van SILLER (American)

Invented 3 detectives - see Richard MASSEY

Citation Record: 3 Books

A Complete Stranger - *First*
Doubleday US (1965); Ward, Lock UK (1966)

The Biltmore Call - *Last*
Ward, Lock UK (1967)

Blaine STEWART
American Female Private Detective operating in Carolina

Sharon ZUKOWSKI (American)

Citation Record: 3 Books

Dancing In The Dark - *First*
Worldwide US (1992)

Leap Of Faith - *Latest*
Dutton US (1994)

Teal STEWART
is a hot-shot corporate accountant and part-time sleuth. 'The words sexy and CPA wouldn't seem to go together but they describe...the sorceress of the spread-sheets' who investigates the financial finagling and murder that go on in so many fictional businesses.

American Female Amateur operating in USA

J Dayne LAMB (American)

was born in San Francisco and raised in Massachusetts. She is a Certified Public Accountant.

Citation Record: 2 Books

Questionable Behaviour - *First*
Zebra US (1993)

A Question Of Preference - *Latest*
Kensington US (1994)

Det Sgt STEYTLER
Policeman operating in South Africa

Shirley MILNE (South African)

Citation Record: 2 Books

The Hammer Of Justice - *First*
Hale UK (1963)

False Witness - *Last*
Hale UK (1964)

Mr STIFFSON
British Male Amateur operating in England

Herbert JENKINS 1876-1923 (British)

See main detective Malcolm SAGE

Citation Record: 1 Collection

The Stiffsons, And Other Stories - *Collection 1*
Jenkins UK (1928)

Joan STOCK
Second detective of Matthew STOCK

Matthew STOCK and Joan STOCK
are a husband and wife who live, during the sixteenth century, in Chelmsford. He is a respectable draper, but also a Constable, an important post in Elizabethan England, and is involved, often for the Crown, in cases of murder. With the considerable help of his wife, he is able to solve them.

British Policeman and British Female Amateur operating in Essex

Leonard TOURNEY (American)

is a Professor of English.

Writer: Leonard D TOURNEY

Citation Record: 4 Books

The Player's Boy Is Dead - *First*
Harper & Row US (1980); Hale UK (1982)

The Bartholomew Fair Murders - *Latest*
St Martin's US (1986); Quartet UK (1988)

Insp Pat STOCKTON
British Policeman operating in England

Cyril JOYCE ?-1992 (British)

was born in Liverpool.

Other Detectives:
Greg ALLARD CHARD

Citation Record: 1 Book

A Bullet For Betty - *Single*
Hale UK (1981)

'Spider' STOCKWELL
British Male Amateur operating in England

J Railton HOLDEN (British)

Citation Record: 2 Books

Death Flies High - *First*
Newnes UK (1935)

Spider Flies Again - *Last*
Newnes UK (1937)

Insp STODDART
British Policeman operating in England

Annie HAYNES ?-1929 (British)

See main detective Insp FURNIVAL

Citation Record: 3 Books

The Crime At Tattenham Corner - *First*
Bodley Head UK (1929)

The Crystal Beads Murder - *Last*
Bodley Head UK (1930)

Dick STODDART
American Male Amateur operating in USA

Edgar BOHLE 1909- (American)

Writer: Edgar Henry BOHLE

Citation Record: 1 Book

The Man Who Disappeared - *Only*
Random House US (1958); Boardman UK (1960)

'Doc' STOEGER
is the editor of a newspaper in a small town near Chicago. He is drawn into a complicated murder plot, which he then has to go on to solve.

American Male Amateur operating in Chicago

Fredric BROWN 1906-1972 (American)

Invented 8 detectives - see Ambrose HUNTER and Ed HUNTER

Citation Record: 1 Book

Night Of The Jabberwock - *Only*
Dutton US (1951); Boardman UK (1951)

Trevor STOKE
solves a case of death by poisoning in a locked room.

American Male Amateur operating in Washington DC

James Z ALNER (American)

Citation Record: 1 Book

The Capital Murder - *Only*
Knopf US (1932); Hurst UK (1933)

Harvey STOKES
Male Detective in Pulp Magazines operating in USA

Nicholas CARTER 1861-1909

Invented 4 detectives - see Patsy MURPHY

Citation Record: 2 Books

A Klondyke Claim; Or, Won By Sheer Nerve - *First*
Street & Smith (Magnet #1) US (1897)

The Australian Klondyke - *Last*
Street & Smith (Magnet #8) US (1897)

Peter STOKES

American Male Amateur operating in Los Angeles

Timothy CHILDS 1941- (American)

Citation Record: 1 Book

Cold Turkey - *Single*
Harper & Row US (1979); Hale UK (1981)

Leopold STOKOWSKI

Second detective of Toby PETERS

Sebastian STOLE

British Male Amateur operating in England

Charles WOGAN (British)

Citation Record: 3 Books

The Hangman's Hands - *First*
Long UK (1947)

Cyanide For The Chorister - *Last*
Long UK (1950)

Adelaide STONE

is a very large spinster lady who teaches English at a university in Michigan where some rare books are housed. The books' custodian is murdered and, although the official cop does his best, it is *Miss STONE* who solves the case. She is aided, not so much by this or that clue, but by her belief that 'evil has a special odour' – as it does indeed say in the medieval texts she is given to perusing.

American Female Amateur operating in USA

Stooge: Sgt Robert MORNINGSTAR
is no match for *Adelaide STONE.*
American Male

Carey MAGOON 1885- (American)

Writers: Elizabeth CAREY and Marian Austin Waite MAGOON 1885-

Citation Record: 1 Book

I Smell The Devil - *Only*
Farrar, Straus US (1943); Cassell UK (1949)

Curt STONE

American Male Private Detective operating in Japan

Jack SEWARD 1924- (American)

Writer: John Neil SEWARD

Citation Record: 5 Books

The Cave Of The Chinese Skeletons - *First*
Tuttle US (1964)

The Eurasian Virgins - *Last*
Tower US (1969)

Ed STONE

is an ex-prizefighter who becomes a reluctant detective in five bizarre stories in *Crime Busters.*

American Male Detective in Pulp Magazines operating in USA

Sidekick: ONE
Chinese Male - Assistant

Kenneth ROBESON (American)

See main detective 'Doc' SAVAGE

No citations

Fleming STONE

is, throughout an incredibly large series of books, able to sit in his New York office and solve his cases by cogitation. Good for him!

American Male Amateur operating in New York

Sidekick: Terrence MCGUIRE
American Male - Assistant

Carolyn WELLS 1870-1942 (American)

was born in Rahway, New Jersey and educated at public schools and privately. Deaf from the age of six, she worked as a librarian and was the author of at least a hundred and seventy novels, of which eighty-three were loosely in the criminous genre.

Other Detectives:

Bert BAYLISS	Kenneth CARLISLE
Alan FORD	Sherlock HOLMES
Lorimer LANE	Pennington WISE

Citation Record: 59 Books

The Clue - *First*
Lippincott US (1909); Hodder & Stoughton UK (1920)

Who Killed Caudwell? - *Last*
Lippincott US (1942)

George STONE, George DAVIS and FLETCHER

George STONE, of Scotland Yard, appears in this one Victorian novel, with *George DAVIS* of Scotland Yard and *FLETCHER,* a private detective.

British Policeman, British Private Detective, and British Amateur operating in London

Richard MARSH 1867-1915 (British)

Invented 10 detectives - see The Hon Augustus CHAMPNELL

Citation Record: 1 Book

Marvels And Mysteries - *Only*
Methuen UK (1900)

J Rockingham STONE

appears also with the author's other detectives, *Insp Dick MASON* and *Laura SCUDAMORE.*

British Male Amateur operating in England

Raymond ARMSTRONG 1905-1962 (British)

Invented 4 detectives - see Insp Dick MASON

Citation Record: 2 Books

Midnight Cavalier - *First*
Long UK (1954)

Cavalier Of The Night - *Last*
Long UK (1956)

J Rockingham STONE, Laura SCUDAMORE and Insp Dick MASON

British Male Amateur, British Female Amateur, and British Policeman operating in England

Raymond ARMSTRONG 1905-1962 (British)

Invented 4 detectives - see Insp Dick MASON

Citation Record: 2 Books

The Widow And The Cavalier - *First*
Long UK (1956)

The Sinister Widow Comes Back - *Last*
Long UK (1957)

Johnny STONE and Ruth DEE

Johnny STONE is hired as a football coach for the fictional State University He runs into a case of murder carried out by big gambling bosses and he investigates, with the aid of *Ruth DEE,* an attractive secretary.

American Male Amateur and American Female Amateur operating in USA

Sidekick: NIP
is the team's mascot and seems a better sleuth than the two detectives. He actually captures the villain.
Male - Pet Dog

Francis WALLACE 1894-1977 (American)

was a sportswriter for papers in New York and a feature writer for *Colliers* and *Saturday Evening Post.*

Citation Record: 1 Book

Front Man - *Only*
Rinehart US (1952)

Shep STONE

American Male Private Detective operating in New York

Jeff JACKS (American)

Citation Record: 2 Books

Murder On The Wild Side - *First*
GM US (1971)

Find The Don's Daughter - *Last*
GM US (1974)

Warren STONE

was in the CIA. He now specialises in dealing with the forces of civil corruption.

American Male Private Detective operating in Kentucky

David HARPER 1931-1981 (American)

Writer: Edwin Raymond CORLEY

Other Byline: Patrick BUCHANAN

Citation Record: 1 Book

The Hanged Men - *Single*
Dodd, Mead US (1976); Hamish Hamilton UK (1977)

Zachary STONE

is an aging, once famous shamus.

American Male Private Detective operating in USA

Lois EBY and John C FLEMING (American)

Writers: Lois Christine EBY 1908- and John Chester FLEMING 1906-1964

Inventor of one other detective Pat O'LEARY

Citation Record: 1 Book

The Case Of The Malevolent Twin - *Only*
Mystery Novel Classics US (1946)

'Rolling' STONE

British Male Amateur operating in England

Kenneth LAING (British)

Writer: Kenneth Joseph Robb LANGMAID

Citation Record: 4 Books

The Malignant Snowman - *First*
Jenkins UK (1950)

The Shadow People - *Last*
Jenkins UK (1952); Roy US (1956)

Harry STONER

is an ex-military cop who served in Vietnam. A very large man, in his thirties, he has worked for Pinkerton's and now works for himself. With a strong sense of moral purpose he can, regrettably, be as violent as the villains he meets.

American Male Private Detective operating in Cincinnati

Jonathan VALIN 1948- (American)

was born in Cincinnati, Ohio. He is a lecturer in English.

Writer: Jonathan Louis VALIN

Adopter of one other detective Philip MARLOWE

Citation Record: 11 Books

The Lime Pit - *First*
Dodd, Mead US (1980); Collins UK (1981)

Missing - *Latest*
Delacorte US (1995)

Mark STONER

Male Sleuth operating in Argentine

Ralph HAYES 1927- (American)

Writer: Ralph Eugene HAYES

Other Byline: Nick CARTER

Other Detectives:
Alexander (Check Force) CHANE and Vladimer KAR
Agent of Cominsec TAGGART John (The Hunter) YARD

Citation Record: 3 Books

The Golden God - *First*
Manor US (1976); New English Library UK (1978)

King's Ransom - *Latest*
Manor US (1978)

Det Randi STONER

Second detective of Sgt Bill CLARK

Mme Rosika STOREY

is voluptuous, cool-headed, and seemingly awesome, though actually she is quite kindly.

American Female Amateur operating in New York

Sidekick: Bella BRICKLEY

American Female - Assistant

Hulbert FOOTNER 1879-1944 (Canadian)

was born in Hamilton, Ontario. His first books were set in Northwest Canada. Later he became a playwright and actor but, between times, he wrote a considerable number of criminous novels, mainly set in New York, but sometimes in London.

Writer: William Hulbert FOOTNER

Inventor of one other detective Amos Lee MAPPIN

Citation Record: 4 Books 19 Short Stories in 4 Collections

The Under Dogs - *First*
Collins UK (1925); Doran US (1925)

Dangerous Cargo - *Last*
Collins UK (1934); Harper & Row US (1934)

Madame Storey - *Collection 1*
Short stories - 4
Collins UK (1926); Doran US (1926)

The Velvet Hand - *Collection 2*
Short stories - 4
Collins UK (1928); Doubleday US (1928)

The Casual Murderer - *Collection 3*
Short stories - 6
Collins UK (1932); Lippincott US (1937)

The Almost Perfect Murder - *Collection 4*
Short stories - 5
Collins UK (1933); Lippincott US (1937)

STORM

is hired to follow a woman, for whom he falls.

American Male Private Detective operating in USA

Roy CHANSLOR 1899- (American)

Citation Record: 1 Book

Hazard - *Only*
Simon & Schuster US (1947)

Insp STORM

British Policeman operating in England

J M WALSH 1897-1952 (British)

Invented 7 detectives - see Insp QUAILE

Citation Record: 2 Books

The Silver Greyhound - *First*
Hamilton UK (1928)

The Whisperer - *Last*
Hamilton UK (1931)

Christopher STORM

is in his thirties and in demand by the Homicide Bureau of the New York Police Department because of his abilities as an illustrator. His sketching enables them to solve several difficult cases, believe it or not.

American Male Amateur operating in New York

Willetta Ann BARBER 1911- and R F SCHABELITZ 1884-1959 (American)

Citation Record: 7 Books

Murder Draws A Line - *First*
Doubleday US (1940)

The Deed Is Drawn - *Last*
Doubleday US (1949)

Hugh STORM

American Male Amateur operating in USA

Anthony CAPUTI 1924- (American)

Writer: Anthony Francis CAPUTI

Citation Record: 1 Book

Storms And Son - *Single*
Atheneum US (1985)

John STORM

American Male Private Detective operating in New York

Francis K ALLAN 1917- (American)

Citation Record: 1 Book

First Come, First Kill - *Only*
Reynal US (1945); Boardman UK (1947)

Dr Andrew STOUGHTON

solves a case of death by bludgeoning in a locked room.

American Male Amateur operating in USA

Morrison DUPREE 1878-1945 (American)

Writer: Sherlock Bronson GASS

Citation Record: 1 Book

A Tap On The Shoulder - *Only*
Doubleday US (1929)

Roy STOVER

appeared in four books for juveniles during the 1930s.

American Male Detective in Pulp Magazines operating in USA

UNKNOWN

No citations

Donald STRACHEY

has cases that mainly seem to involve the homosexual community in New York.

American Male Private Detective operating in New York

Richard STEVENSON 1938- (American)

Writer: Richard LIPEZ

Citation Record: 3 Books

Death Trick - *First*
St Martin's US (1981); Alyson UK (1985)

Ice Blues - *Latest*
St Martin's US (1986)

Ricky STRAIGHT

British Male Amateur operating in England

Geoffrey MORGAN 1916- (British)

Citation Record: 2 Books

No Crest For The Wicked - *First*
Robertson UK (1952)

Heavenly Body - *Last*
Robertson UK (1953)

Mick STRANAHAN

is a retired investigator from the Florida State Attorney's Office. He survives an assassination attempt and backtracks his career to find out which of his cases has come back to kill him.

American Male Professional Investigator operating in Florida

Carl HIAASEN 1933- (American)

Invented 3 detectives - see R J DECKER

Citation Record: 1 Book

Skin Tight - *Single*
Putnam US (1989)

Mr STRANG

has appeared in the author's short stories over nearly twenty years and is often concerned with cases of 'impossible' murder.

American Male Amateur operating in USA

William BRITTAIN 1930- (American)

See main detective Joshua Red WING

Citation Record: 2 Selected Short Stories

Mr Strang Gives A Lecture
appeared in the March number.
In 'Ellery Queen's Mystery Magazine' US (1967)

Mr Strang Takes A Tour
appeared in the July number.
In 'Ellery Queen's Mystery Magazine' US (1983)

Jim STRANG

British Male Secret Agent operating in England

George DILNOT 1883-1951 (British)

Invented 5 detectives - see Val EMERY

Citation Record: 2 Books

The Secret Service Man - *First*
Nash UK (1916)

Counter-Spy - *Last*
Bles UK (1942)

John STRANG and Sally STRANG

British Male Amateur and British Female Amateur operating in England

Henry BRINTON 1901-1977 (British)

Citation Record: 6 Books

Death To Windward - *First*
Hutchinson UK (1954)

An Ordinary Day - *Last*
Hutchinson UK (1959)

Apprentice To Fear - *Last**
Hutchinson UK (1961)

Mike STRANG

is one of this British author's several attempts to create an American PI.
!See Appendix 2.

American Male Private Detective operating in USA

Peter CAGNEY 1918- (American)

For writer details see Al BOCCA

Citation Record: 3 Books

No Diamonds For A Doll - *First*
Jenkins UK (1960); Roy US (1961)

A Grave For Madam - *Last*
Jenkins UK (1961)

Sally STRANG

Second detective of John STRANG

James STRANGE

British Male Private Detective operating in England

E Baker QUINN (British)

Writer: Eleanor Baker QUINN

Citation Record: 2 Books

One Man's Muddle - *First*
Heinemann UK (1936); Macmillan US (1937)

Death Is A Restless Sleeper - *Last*
Heinemann UK (1940); Mystery House US (1941)

Jeff STRANGE

American Male Sleuth operating in Washington DC

Audrey GAINES (American)

See main detective Chauncey O'DAY

Citation Record: 2 Books

Omit Flowers, Please - *First*
Messner US (1946)

No Crime Like The Present - *Last*
Arcadia US (1952)

Jimmy STRANGE

British Male Amateur operating in England

Ernest DUDLEY 1908- (British)

Invented 3 detectives - see Dr MORELLE

Citation Record: 15 Short Stories in 1 Collection

The Adventures Of Jimmy Strange - *Collection 1*
Long UK (1945)

Violet STRANGE

is one of the earliest American lady detectives and appears only in short stories. She is, it seems, out of some ill-defined top drawer; but, to help an outcast sister and strapped for

cash herself, she stoops to practise this lowly form of work. Like most lady detectives of the era, she is heavily into disguises when working.
!See Appendix 2.
American Female Amateur operating in USA

Anna Katherine GREEN 1846-1935 (American)
Invented 9 detectives - see Det Ebenezer GRYCE
Citation Record: 8 Short Stories in 1 Collection
The Golden Slipper And Other Problems For Violet Strange - *Collection 1*
This collection contains eight stories with *Violet STRANGE* and one with *Ebenezer GRYCE.*
Putnam US (1915)

Peter STRANGELY
British Male Amateur operating in London/Paris

E Best BLACK 1894- (British)
Writer: Elizabeth Best BLACK
Citation Record: 2 Books
The Ravenelle Riddle - *First*
Loring UK (1933)
The Crime Of The Chromium Bowl - *Last*
Newnes UK (1937); Loring UK (1934)

Nigel STRANGEWAYS
comes from the pen of a writer who was an eminent poet and he seems to possess many of his creator's qualities. A typical amateur detective of the late 1930s, he is urbane, cultivated, literary, and a fount of academic wisdom, and the books in which he appeared are filled with detailed, often obscure, ingenious, literary plotting. An Oxford man, with apparently no profession, *Nigel STRANGEWAYS,* through his many acquaintances, just happens to be around when murder is done. The deed usually takes place in some traditional setting, to which the British detective story of the 1930s was committed. The police side of things, though inadequate as always, is fairly represented.

STRANGEWAYS, tall, thin, and with a passion for tea-drinking, ages naturally over the twenty-one years during which he appeared and during which he was twice married.
British Male Amateur operating in England/Massachusetts
Stooge: Insp BLOUNT
is the epitome of the stolid but baffled British policeman, the necessary accompaniment to the British Golden Age detective.
British Male

S

Nicholas BLAKE 1904-1972 (British)
was born in Ballintubbert, Ireland. He was educated at Sherborne School, Dorset, and took BA and MA s at Wadham College, Oxford, 1923-1927. During his distinguished career he was a schoolmaster, publishers' reader, and government information officer. However, it was as a poet that he became well known, particularly for his work during the 1930s, which leaned strongly towards the left in politics. Later he held honorary professorships at universities in England, Ireland and Canada. He was made a Companion of Literature, 1965, and received the highest honour for his poetry, being appointed Poet Laureate, 1968. He wrote, under his main pseudonym, at least twenty detective novels and a number of short stories.
Writer: Cecil Day LEWIS
Citation Record: 16 Books
A Question Of Proof - *First*
Collins UK (1935); Harper & Row US (1935)
The Morning After Death - *Last*
Collins UK (1966); Harper & Row US (1966)

Lord STRANLEIGH
British Male Amateur operating in England

Robert BARR 1850-1912 (British)
Invented 4 detectives - see Nick NICHOLSON
Citation Record: 10 Short Stories in 1 Collection
Young Lord Stranleigh - *Collection 1*
Ward, Lock UK (1908); Appleton US (1908)

George STRATFIELD
is a lawyer who sleuths in this one Victorian novel.
British Male Amateur operating in England

William LEQUEUX 1864-1927 (British)
Invented 23 detectives - see Allan KENNEDY
Citation Record: 2 Books
If Sinners Entice Thee - *First*
White UK (1898); Dillingham US (1899)
Her Majesty's Minister - *Last*
Dodd, Mead US (1901)

Insp STRATTON
of Scotland Yard is in this one Victorian novel.
British Policeman operating in London

Charles MATTHEW (British)
Citation Record: 1 Book
Bazi Bazoum; Or, A Strange Detective - *Only*
Ward, Lock UK (1889)

Bill STRATTON
Appears with at least two other detectives - see Lt MOYNAHAN

Mark STRATTON
British Male Sleuth

Richard Townshend BICKERS 1917- (British)
Writer: Richard Leslie Townshend BICKERS
Citation Record: 2 Books
The Hellions - *First*
Hale UK (1965)
Scent Of Mayhem - *Last*
Hale UK (1965)

Insp Angus STRAUN
is a modern cop, only about thirty-five, with the usual divorce behind him and a live-in mistress to provide some interest between the passages of detection. He is said to have been shot in the right arm by a bandit, and so has some sort of desk job. When not sleuthing, it seems, he writes historical novels; but his main interest is in golf, and his books to date have golfing themes.
British Policeman operating in England/Scotland

Barry CORK (British)
Citation Record: 2 Books
Dead Ball - *First*
Collins UK (1988)
Unnatural Hazard - *Latest*
Collins UK (1989)

'Twisted Face' STRAUSSMAN
appears also in books with the author's other detective, *Peter CASTLE.*
Male Amateur operating in England

G DAVISON 1892- (British)
Invented 3 detectives - see Peter CASTLE
Citation Record: 5 Books
A Traitor Unmasked - *First*
Jenkins UK (1932)
Twisted Face Defends His Title - *Last*
Jenkins UK (1940)

'Twisted Face' STRAUSSMAN
Second detective of Peter CASTLE

Victor STRAWN

was hardboiled, surrounded by available blondes and mercifully appeared only in short stories, mainly in *Spicy Detective Stories.*

American Male Private Detective operating in USA

Carl MOORE (American)

Citation Record: 1 Selected Short Story

An Eye For An Eye
can also be found in the anthology, *Spicy Detective Stories* (Editor: Tom Mason; US 1989).
In 'Spicy Detective Stories' US (1937)

Dee STREET

is a solicitor in a British, all-female, left-wing, law firm. She naturally gravitates towards cases involving feminist issues, women' s problems, revolutionaries, social justice and political correctness.

American Female Amateur operating in London

Hannah WAKEFIELD (American)

Sarah BURTON was born in New York City. She moved to London, 1972, and qualified as a solicitor. *Judith HOLLAND* was born in Boston, Massachusetts. She was educated at Tufts University, Medford, Massachusetts, and took a BA at the University of California, Berkeley, 1970. She moved to London, 1971, and is a teacher and editor of art publications. Both authors have a sometime involvement in left-wing and social reform movements in England.

Writers: Sarah BURTON and Judith HOLLAND

Citation Record: 2 Books

The Price You Pay - *First*
St Martin's US (1987); Women's Press UK (1987)

A February Mourning - *Latest*
Women's Press UK (1990)

A Woman's Own Mystery - *Latest**
St Martin's US (1991)

Joe STREETER

American Male Amateur operating in New York

J F BURKE 1915-1992 (American)

See main detective Samuel Moses KELLY

Citation Record: 2 Books

The Kama Sutra Tango - *First*
Harper & Row US (1977)

Crazy Woman Blues - *Latest*
Dutton US (1978); Constable UK (1979)

Insp STRICKLAND

British Policeman operating in England

George DILNOT 1883-1951 (British)

Invented 5 detectives - see Val EMERY

Citation Record: 2 Books

The Crooks' Game - *First*
Bles UK (1927); Houghton US (1927)

The Black Ace - *Last*
Bles UK (1929); Houghton US (1929)

Clive STRICKLAND

is, in 1865, a writer of serials for magazines. He uses his undoubted aptitude for solving puzzles to deal with a real-life murder.

British Male Amateur operating in England

John Dickson CARR 1906-1977 (American)

Writer: John Dickson CARR

Other Bylines:
Carr DICKSON — Carter DICKSON
John Carter DICKSON and John RHODE

Invented 16 detectives - see Dr Gideon FELL

Citation Record: 1 Book

Scandal At High Chimneys: A Victorian Melodrama - *Only*
Harper & Row US (1959); Hamish Hamilton UK (1959)

Insp Jack STRICKLAND

British Policeman operating in England

Hearnden BALFOUR (British)

Writers: Eva BALFOUR and Beryl HEARNDEN

Citation Record: 3 Books

The Paper Chase - *First*
Hodder & Stoughton UK (1927)

A Gentleman From Texas - *First**
Houghton US (1927)

Anything Might Happen - *Last*
Hodder & Stoughton UK (1931)

Murder And The Red-Haired Girl - *Last**
Houghton US (1933)

Jason STRIKER

American Male Sleuth operating in Brazil

Piers ANTHONY and Roberto FUENTES (American)

Writer: (First author) Piers Anthony Dillingham JACOB 1934-

Citation Record: 4 Books

Mistress Of Death - *First*
Berkley US (1974)

Amazon Slaughter - *Latest*
Berkley US (1976)

Insp STRODE

British Policeman operating in England

J B HARRIS-BURLAND 1870- (British)

Writer: John Burland HARRIS-BURLAND

Inventor of one other detective Richard LORYAT

Citation Record: 1 Book

The Curse Of Cloud - *Only*
Chapman & Hall UK (1914)

Jim STRONG

was one of this author's numerous pulp detectives, appearing mainly in stories in *Crime Busters Magazine.*

American Male Detective in Pulp Magazines operating in USA

Frank GRUBER 1904-1969 (American)

Invented 8 detectives - see Johnny FLETCHER and Sam CRAGG

No citations

Max STRONG

Male Amateur operating in several locations

Robert DUDGEON (Australian)

Citation Record: 23 Books

The Beautiful Bait - *First*
Cleveland AU (ca 1951)

My Price Is Murder - *Last*
Cleveland AU (ca 1964)

Philip STRONG and James MATTHEWS

American Male Amateurs operating in New York

Will OURSLER 1913-1985 (American)

Writer: William Charles OURSLER

Inventor of one other detective Offr Michael LA RUE

Citation Record: 2 Books

The Trial Of Vincent Doon - *First*
Simon & Schuster US (1941); Museum Press UK (1943)

Folio On Florence White - *Last*
Simon & Schuster US (1942); Art & Educational Publishers UK (1947)

Insp Robert STRONG

British Policeman operating in England

Colin ROBERTSON 1906-1980 (British)

Invented 7 detectives - see Mike REED

Citation Record: 3 Books

Painted Faces - *First*
Ward, Lock UK (1935)

Soho Spy - *Last*
Ward, Lock UK (1940)

Sam STRONG
American Male Detective in Pulp Magazines operating in USA

David DRUID (American)

Invented 4 detectives - see Sam SMART

Citation Record: 1 Selected Short Story

Sam Strong, The Cowboy Detective; Or, The Ranch Mystery
Old Cap Collier Library US (18??)

George STROUD
works for a big magazine and is set by his powerful boss the task of seeking out a witness to a murder that the latter has himself committed. He is in peril from the word go.

American Male Amateur operating in New York

Kenneth FEARING 1902-1961 (American)

was born at Oak Park, Illinois. He graduated with a BA from the University of Wisconsin, Madison, 1924. A reporter and poet, he wrote seven genre works, including the outstanding thriller cited. It was made into a classic film for which he received an Academy Award, 1945.

Writer: Kenneth Flexner FEARING

Citation Record: 1 Book

The Big Clock - *Only*
Harcourt Brace US (1946); Bodley Head UK (1947)

No Way Out - *Only**
Perennial US (1987)

Dixie T STRUTHERS
American Female Amateur operating in California

L V SIMS (American)

Citation Record: 3 Books

Death Is A Family Affair - *First*
Charter US (1987)

To Sleep, Perchance To Kill - *Latest*
Charter US (1988)

Ch Supt J V STRUTT
solves a case of death by drowning in a locked bathroom.

British Policeman operating in London

Clifford ALLEN 1902- (British)

Writer: Clifford Edward ALLEN

Citation Record: 1 Selected Short Story

A Lecture In Detection
In 'London Mystery Magazine' UK

Colin STRYKER
American Male Amateur operating in New Mexico

William CRAWFORD 1929- (American)

Writer: William Elbert CRAWFORD

Other Bylines:
Jim PETERSON
Paul ROSS

Citation Record: 4 Books

Stryker - *First*
Pinnacle US (1973)

Deadly Alliance - *Last*
Pinnacle US (1975)

Lt Jack STRYKER
is tough, obsessive, suffering, a bit of an oddball, and would be full of angst if he knew what that was. He has to solve a case of murder on a college campus, neither the location of which nor the police force involved being clear.

American Policeman operating in USA

Paula GOSLING 1939- (American)

was born in Detroit, Michigan, graduated with a BA in English from Wayne University, Detroit, 1957, and has lived in England since 1964. She received the Crime Writers Association John Creasey Memorial award, 1978, and their Golden Dagger award, 1985.

Other Detectives:
Lt Jake CHASE
Sheriff Matt GABRIEL
Mike MALCHECK
John Owen COSATELLI
Charles LLEWELLYN
Dorothy Mayotte RIGBY

Citation Record: 1 Book

Monkey Puzzle - *Single*
Macmillan UK (1985)

Det Sgt John STRYKER
is in the Los Angeles Police Department.

American Policeman operating in Los Angeles

Dallas BARNES (American)

was a sometime member of the Los Angeles Police Department.

Citation Record: 2 Books

See The Woman - *First*
Signet UK (1973); Hodder & Stoughton US (1974)

Badge Of Honor - *Last*
Signet UK (1974); Hodder & Stoughton US (1976)

Sgt Mark STRYKER
American Male Professional Investigator operating in several locations

Jonathan CAIN (American)

Writer: Nick UHERNIK

Citation Record: 9 Books

Saigon Commandos - *First*
Zebra US (1983)

Mad Minute - *Latest*
Zebra US (1985)

Bob STUART
solves a clannish murder in Scotland.

British Male Private Detective operating in Edinburgh

Winifred PECK 1832-1962 (British)

Writer: Winifred Francis Knox Lady PECK

Citation Record: 1 Book

The Warrielaw Jewel - *Only*
UK (1933); US (1933)

David STUART
is a lawyer who has quit his father's practice to become a PI. He follows the profession more seriously than most.

American Male Private Detective operating in Ohio

James K MACDOUGALL (American)

is a sometime Professor of English at US universities.

Citation Record: 2 Books

Weasel Hunt - *First*
Bobbs US (1977); Hale UK (1979)

Death And The Maiden - *Latest*
Bobbs US (1978); Hale UK (1979)

Insp Scott STUART
American Policeman operating in Washington DC

Geoffrey COFFIN (American)

Writers: Francis Van Wyck MASON 1897-1978 and Helen BRAWNER 1902-

Citation Record: 2 Books

Murder In The Senate - *First*
Dodge US (1935); Hurst UK (1936)

The Forgotten Fleet Mystery - *Last*
Dodge US (1936); Jarrolds UK (1943)

Prof John STUBBS
is a Scottish Professor of Botany. A very large man, he wears thick glasses, drives an enormous car, is impetuous, and is fond of swilling beer and smoking his obnoxious pipe. He loves sleuthing above all; for he finds the police incompetent and enjoys nothing more than teasing them with his own knowledge.

British Male Amateur operating in Scotland

Sidekick: MAX
is not up to the *Archie GOODWIN* standard.
British Male - Assistant

Stooge: Ch Insp BISHOP
British Male

R T CAMPBELL 1914- (British)
was born in Edinburgh, Scotland, but emigrated to the USA, 1948, and later became an American citizen. He was a poet, historian, and the author of books for children as well as a few detective novels.
Writer: Ruthven TODD
Citation Record: 7 Books
Unholy Dying - *First*
Westhouse UK (1945)
Take Thee A Sharp Knife - *Last*
Westhouse UK (1946)

Prof Marcus STUBBS

is assisted by other members of 'The Dilettantes' Club' and appears in a collection of short stories in which 'impossible' and locked-room crimes abound, only to be solved.
British Male Amateur operating in England

E RADFORD and M A MANGAN (British)
See main detective Dr MANSON
Citation Record: 8 Short Stories in 1 Collection
Death And The Professor - *Collection 1*
Hale UK (1961)

Dr STURGESS

investigates a death by poisoning in a locked room.
British Male Amateur operating in England

Frank BARRETT 1848-1926 (British)
Invented 5 detectives - see Capt Thomas VERNAN
Citation Record: 1 Book
Lady Judas - *Only*
Chatto UK (1903)

Bow Street Runner Jeremy STURROCK

is a member of the earliest professional police force in the world, taking its name from the station in Bow Street, in London's West End, which was set up in the middle of the eighteenth century. Telling his own tales, he elaborates on cases that are ingenious and full of the life of the period, although he does seem to use detective methods that anticipate those of a later century. In the UK the books appear under the *STURROCK* byline, but in the US they are under the pseudonym of *JEFFREYS*.
British Policeman operating in London

Sidekick: MAGSY
is a street urchin who can be used for some essential legwork and undercover sleuthing.
British Male - Aide

J G JEFFREYS 1908- (British)
For writer details see Paul HEDLEY
Citation Record: 8 Books
The Thief Taker - *First*
was published in the UK as *THE VILLAGE OF ROGUES*, under the following byline.
Walker US (1972)
The Thistlewood Plot - *Latest*
Walker US (1987)

Jeremy STURROCK 1908- (British)
For writer details see Paul HEDLEY
Citation Record: 1 Book
The Village Of Rogues - *Only*
was published in the US as *THE THIEF TAKER*, under the preceding byline.
Macmillan UK (1972)

Peter STYLES

lost a leg in an automobile accident caused by a driver on drugs, and later his wife was killed by terrorists. He now has one aim in life, to right wrongs as he sees them and to bring those responsible to justice.
American Male Amateur operating in USA

Judson PHILIPS 1903-1989 (American)
For writer details see Pierre CHAMBRUN
Other Detectives:
James W BELLAMY　COYLE and DONOVAN
Carole TREVOR and Max BLYTHE
Citation Record: 19 Books
The Laughter Trap - *First*
Dodd, Mead US (1964); Gollancz UK (1965)
Target For Tragedy - *Last*
Dodd, Mead US (1982); Hale UK (1983)

Chauncy Wayne SUGHRUE

is an alcoholic, an ex-Vietnam War criminal, an army spy, but a great private eye. Remarkably, there is a gap of sixteen years between the appearance of his two books.
American Male Private Detective operating in Montana

James CRUMLEY 1939- (American)
was born in Three Rivers, Texas. He graduated in History, served in the US Army, 1958-1961, and has been Assistant Professor of English at several Texan universities.
Inventor of one other detective Milton Chester MILODRAGOVITCH
Citation Record: 2 Books
The Last Good Kiss - *First*
Random House US (1978); Granada UK (1979)
The Mexican Tree Duck - *Latest*
Picador UK (1994)

Asst Ch Const SULLIVAN

British Policeman operating in England

John WAINWRIGHT 1921- (British)
Invented 9 detectives - see Ch Insp/Supt LENNOX
Citation Record: 1 Book
High-Class Kill - *Only*
Macmillan UK (1973)

Bob SULLIVAN

British Male Sleuth operating in Malta

Frederic MULLALLY 1920- (British)
Citation Record: 3 Books
Danse Macabre - *First*
Secker & Warburg UK (1959)
Marianne - *First**
Viking US (1960)
The Malta Conspiracy - *Last*
Hart Davis UK (1972)

Giles SULLIVAN

is a retired lawyer who solves cases of murder that always seem to involve crossword puzzles, at which he and his sidekick happen to be experts.
American Male Amateur operating in USA

Sidekick: Isobel MCKINTOSH
American Female - Friend

Herbert RESNICOW 1921- (American)
Invented 3 detectives - see Ed BAER
Citation Record: 5 Books
Murder Across And Down - *First*
Ballantine US (1985)
The Crossword Hunt - *Latest*
Ballantine US (1987)

Hank SULLIVAN

American Male Sleuth operating in Texas

Anne Reed ROOTH (American)
Citation Record: 2 Books
Fatal Stranger - *First*
Berkley US (1988)
The Eye Of The Beholder - *Latest*
Charter US (1990)

Jack (The Specialist) SULLIVAN

American Male Professional Investigator operating in USA

John CUTTER (American)
Citation Record: 11 Books
The Big One - *First*
Signet US (1984)
Vengeance Mountain - *Latest*
Signet US (1985)

William (Sultans' Harem) SULTAN

American Male Sleuth operating in New York

Hugh AUSTIN (American)
See main detective Peter QUINT
Citation Record: 2 Books
The Milkmaid's Millions - *First*
Scribner's US (1948)
Drink The Green Water - *Last*
Scribner's US (1948)

Jack SUMMER

Male American Sleuth

Ron GOULART 1933- (American)
Invented 15 detectives - see Jake PACE and Hildy PACE
Citation Record: 2 Books
Plunder - *First*
Beagle US (1972)
Galaxy Jane - *Latest*
Berkley US (1986)

Offr Jessie SUMMER

American Policewoman operating in Fort Lauderdale

Cherokee Paul MCDONALD (American)
Citation Record: 1 Book
Summer's Reason - *Single*
Fine US (1994)

Lucy SUMMERS

British Female Amateur operating in England

Josephine BELL 1897-1987 (British)
Invented 10 detectives - see Dr David WINTRINGHAM
Citation Record: 1 Book
Such A Nice Client - *Only*
Hodder & Stoughton UK (1977)
A Stroke Of Death - *Only**
Walker US (1977)

Steve SUMMERS

was formerly a cop but is now a PI who decides he likes fishing better than sleuthing.
American Male Private Detective operating in California

Jason MANOR 1920- (American)
Writer: Oakley M HALL
Citation Record: 2 Books
The Red Jaguar - *First*
Viking US (1954); Secker & Warburg UK (1955)
The Girl In The Red Jaguar - *First**
Popular Library US (1955)
The Pawns Of Fear - *Last*
Viking US (1955); Secker & Warburg UK (1955)
No Halo For Me - *Last**
Popular Library US (1956)

'Doc' SUMMERS

British Male Amateur operating in England

Francis MARLOWE (British)
Citation Record: 2 Books
The Crime Of Philip Garrison - *First*
Gray UK (1935)
In Pursuit Of A Million - *Last*
Gray UK (1936)

Ch of Plce SUTHERLAND

American Policeman operating in New York

Frederick G EBERHARD 1889- (American)
See main detective Insp O'HARE
Citation Record: 1 Book
The 13th Murder - *Only*
Macaulay US (1931)

John SUTHERLAND

appears in a few short stories adapted from a TV series in which he features.
British Male Amateur operating in England

Lindsay GALLOWAY (British)
Citation Record: 1 Collection
Sutherland's Law - *Collection 1*
contains some short stories based on a TV series.
Pan UK (1974)

Bernard SUTTON

is described as a 'private detective' in this one Victorian novel.
British Male Private Detective operating in England

Max PEMBERTON 1863-1950 (British)
Other Detectives:
Jeremy BELL
Capt BLACK
Capt Jack WARD
Citation Record: 10 Short Stories in 1 Collection
Jewel Mysteries I Have Known: From A Dealer's Notebook - *Collection 1*
Ward, Lock UK (1894)
Jewel Mysteries From A Dealer's Notebook - *Collection 1**
Fenno US (1904)

Insp Alfred SWAIN

is a cultured, rather artistic policeman at Scotland Yard during the 1880s. Assisted by the his sceptical sergeant, he becomes involved in some famous and bizarre crimes of this dark period, including the Jack the Ripper murders and the Jekyll & Hyde fantasy. A later book takes him to Greece on a mission with Byronic undertones against a background of Scotland Yard corruption, the latter episode being based on true events.
British Policeman operating in London

Sidekick: Sgt LUMLEY
is portly, stolid and incorruptible; virtues that more than once prove of value to his superior officer.
British Male - Subordinate

Donald THOMAS 1935- (British)
was born in Brighton, Sussex, is a poet and has written several biographies of Victorian writers. He is the author of some unusual novels in the criminous vein, especially those featuring Victorian detectives and policemen.
Writer: Donald THOMAS
Other Byline: Francis SELWYN
Citation Record: 4 Books
Mad Hatter Summer - *First*
Viking US (1983)
Belladonna - *First**
Macmillan UK (1984)
The Arrest Of Scotland Yard - *Latest*
Macmillan UK (1993)

Ape SWAIN

American Male Sleuth operating in Middle East

Daniel DA CRUZ 1921- (American)
See main detective Jock SERGEANT

Citation Record: 3 Books

The Pipe Dream Finesse - *First*
Ballantine US (1975)

The Captive City - *Latest*
Ballantine US (1976)

Matthew SWAIN

is a gumshoe in a city in Texas in 2083. Terrible things happen in a broken-down, fortress society, where the police hardly function but, fortunately, the private eye goes on for ever.

American Male Private Detective operating in Texas

Mike MACQUAY (American)

For writer details see William JUSTICE

Citation Record: 4 Books

Hot Time In Old Town - *First*
Bantam US (1981)

The Odds Are Murder - *Latest*
Bantam US (1982)

C J SWAN

British Male Amateur operating in England

R PHILMORE 1900- (British)

Writer: Herbert Edmund HOWARD

Inventor of one other detective GARNETT

Citation Record: 4 Books

Journey Downstairs - *First*
Gollancz UK (1934); Doubleday US (1934)

Short List - *Last*
Collins UK (1938)

Cassandra SWANN

is a fiend at Bridge, which she teaches. During this congenial pastime she encounters mysterious murders.

British Female Amateur operating in England

Susan MOODY 1940- (British)

Invented 3 detectives - see Penny WANAWAKE

Citation Record: 3 Books

Grand Slam - *First*
Headline UK (1994); Otto Penzler US (1995)

King Of Hearts - *Latest*
Headline UK (1995)

SWEENEY

is a newsman who is a periodic drunk. In this fine tale, he pulls himself together, after witnessing an attack on a beautiful woman, to hunt down and identify a serial killer.

American Male Amateur operating in Chicago

Fredric BROWN 1906-1972 (American)

Invented 8 detectives - see Ambrose HUNTER and Ed HUNTER

Citation Record: 1 Book

The Screaming Mimi - *First*
is a simple but classic tale of detection and is considered by many critics to be this prolific author's masterpiece.
Dutton US (1949); Boardman UK (1950)

Nichole SWEET

is the daughter of a policeman. Pretty but not very well balanced, she does her best but appears just the once.
!See Appendix 2.

American Female Private Detective operating in California

Fran HUSTON 1936- (American)

Writer: Ron S MILLER

Citation Record: 1 Book

The Rich Get It All - *Only*
Doubleday US (1973); Macmillan UK (1974)

Caleb SWEETWATER

appears also in books with the author's other detective, *Ebenezer GRYCE.*

American Male Sleuth operating in New York

Anna Katherine GREEN 1846-1935 (American)

Invented 9 detectives - see Det Ebenezer GRYCE

Citation Record: 3 Books

Agatha Webb - *First*
Putnam US (1899); Ward, Lock UK (1900)

The House Of The Whispering Pines - *Last*
Putnam US (1910); Nash UK (1910)

Caleb SWEETWATER

Second detective of Det Ebenezer GRYCE

Insp Tom SWETMAN and Insp CRANE

are called in to investigate the murder of two female students in a British university town. Baffled at first, they solve the case in the end.

British Policemen operating in England

Peter MALLOCH 1909-1976 (British)

See main detective Dave NORTON

Citation Record: 1 Book

Murder Of A Student - *Only*
Long UK (1968)

Leighton SWIFT

American Male Amateur operating in New York

Charles Reed JONES (American)

Inventor of one other detective Insp James CONWAY

Citation Record: 3 Books

The King Murder - *First*
Dutton US (1929)

The Van Norton Murders - *Last*
Macaulay US (1931)

Loren SWIFT

operates from Charlottesville. A Vietnam War veteran, he is always deeply concerned about the people he meets, deplores the present time, and loves the culture of the 1960s. He comes up against crimes involving big business and the government.

American Male Private Detective operating in Virginia

Doug HORNIG 1943- (American)

was born in New York City. He graduated with a BA from George Washington University, Washington DC, 1965.

Inventor of one other detective Steven KIRK

Citation Record: 4 Books

Foul Shot - *First*
Scribner's US (1984)

Deep Dive - *Latest*
Mysterious Press US (1988)

Martin SWIFT

was a detective who came rather late on a scene that had been flourishing, in juvenile magazines, since the early 1890s. He appeared in 1922 in the pages of the pink-jacketed *Boys' Magazine* and was hailed, for the post-war generation, as a new kind of 'sporting' detective – not the first, for *Aldine* had already introduced *DR GRIP, The Sport Detective,* many years earlier. However, *SWIFT* was probably the only man to have played international soccer wearing a monocle. A Cambridge triple blue, he was, in spite of his apparent monocular disability, equally proficient at boxing, sculling, fencing and football. His headquarters were filled with his trophies and here too sat his assistant, *Chick CONWAY,* who – cast in the usual mould for boy sidekicks – was a street urchin who had been taken by the great detective out of the gutter. Together they faced adversaries who, astonishingly, were prepared to spend their whole lives sabotaging British sporting events, stealing trophies, and generally making a nuisance of themselves on the playing fields. *SWIFT's* main adversary was one Claude Montana, the 'arch-crook of five continents', whose main aim in the course of his criminal career was to steal the English Foot-

S

ball Cup, which, of course, was a disgraceful thing to want to do and one for which he paid heavily.

British Male Professional Amateur operating in England

Sidekick: Chick CONWAY

was a young boy, taken off the streets. He was not only an invaluable assistant but played an important part in the stories, often by being put into terrible danger from which he would have to be rescued in the nick of time. Suspended upside down, kidnapped, threatened with being dissolved in acid, booby-trapped or worse, he could often escape on his own by using his 'mirror ring' or even releasing a miniature pigeon that, it seems, he kept concealed about his person in a perforated cricket ball. Of course he would!

Male

ANON

No citations

Sabina SWIFT

sleuths in and around high-tech crime near Washington DC, where there are some very shady goings-on.

American Female Private Detective operating in Washington DC

Sidekick: Vic NEWMAN

was a male psychiatric nurse. He got the job as *Sabina SWIFT's* assistant by answering an ad she put in the papers. His background can be useful when handling geniuses.

American Male - Assistant

Dorothy SUCHER 1933- (American)

Citation Record: 2 Books

Dead Men Don't Give Seminars - *First*
St Martin's US (1988)

Dead Men Don't Marry - *Latest*
St Martin's US (1989)

Insp SWINTON

Australian Policeman operating in Australia

Pat FLOWER 1914-1978 (British)

Writer: Patricia Mary Bryson FLOWER

Citation Record: 7 Books

Wax Flowers For Gloria - *First*
Angus UK (1958)

Fiends Of The Family - *Last*
Hale UK (1966)

Insp SWINTON

British Policeman operating in England

Ian GREIG (British)

Writer: Ian Baxter GREIG

Citation Record: 5 Books

The Tragedy Of The Chinese Mine - *First*
Benn UK (1930); Holt US (1931)

Baxter's Second Death - *Last*
Benn UK (1932); Kinsey US (1933)

S

SYALOCH

is a Martian who solves a kind of locked-room crime committed in outer space, where the Martian crown jewels are stolen from a space-craft. He is clearly a *Sherlock HOLMES* parody and refers to the latter in veneration more than once. Although he does not have a *WATSON*-like sidekick, he does come up against a stooge called *Insp Gregg.*

Martian Male Professional Amateur operating in Space

Stooge: Insp GREGG

is the conventional police stooge to the strange creation, *SYALOCH*. His name is a slight nod of the author's towards the police stooge, *GREGSON*, who appeared in several of the canonical *Sherlock HOLMES* stories.

Male

Poul ANDERSON 1926- (American)

Invented 4 detectives - see Trygve YAMAMURA

Citation Record: 1 Selected Short Story

The Martian Crown Jewels - *Parody 1*

appeared in the February number and has often been reprinted in anthologies, the latest of these being *THE MISADVENTURES OF SHERLOCK HOLMES*, (Editor: *Sebastian WOLFE).*

In 'Ellery Queen's Mystery Magazine' US (1958)

SYDENHAM

British Male Sleuth

Donald SEAMAN 1922- (British)

Writer: Donald Peter SEAMAN

Citation Record: 3 Books

The Defector - *First*
Hamish Hamilton UK (1975)

The Chameleon Course - *First**
Coward McCann US (1976)

The Terror Syndicate - *Last*
Hamish Hamilton UK (1976); Coward McCann US (1976)

Lord SYFRET

British Male Amateur operating in England

Arabella KENEALY 1864-1938 (British)

Citation Record: 6 Short Stories in 1 Collection

Belinda's Beaux And Other Stories - *Collection 1*

This collection of fourteen of the author's short stories contains six with *Lord SYFRET.*

Bliss UK (1897)

Insp SYLVESTER

is an intelligent, confident cop although, it seems, a little slow on the uptake.

British Policeman operating in England

H R F KEATING 1926- (British)

Invented 6 detectives - see Insp Ganesh GHOTE

Citation Record: 1 Book

The Rich Detective - *Single*
Macmillan UK (1993)

SYME

is a poet who is also an undercover cop. He infiltrates what appears to be (but is not) a vast anarchist organisation, believing that he can foil its plans for revolution.

British Policeman operating in England

G K CHESTERTON 1874-1936 (British)

Invented 7 detectives - see Father BROWN

Citation Record: 1 Book

The Man Who Was Thursday - *Only*

has been described as one of the best spy thrillers ever written.

Simpkin UK (1908); Dodd, Mead US (1908)

York SYMON

British Male Amateur operating in England

Edgar WALLACE 1875-1932 (British)

Invented 28 detectives - see J G REEDER

Citation Record: 9 Short Stories in 1 Collection

The Reporter - *Collection 1*
Reader's Library UK (1929)

Dr SYN

was a parson who doubled as a smuggler during the late eighteenth century.

Male Amateur operating in England

Russell THORNDYKE 1885-1972 (British)

Writer: Arthur Russell THORNDYKE

Inventor of one other detective Mr MACAULEY

Citation Record: 7 Books

Doctor Syn - *First*
Nelson UK (1915); Doubleday US (1915)

The Shadow Of Doctor Syn - *Last*
Rich UK (1944)

Chester C TABOR
American Male Sleuth operating in USA

Mark CRUZ 1928- (American)
For writer details see Michael HAWK
Citation Record: 4 Books
Dead End - *First*
Manor US (1975)
Voyage Of Death - *Last*
Manor US (1975)

Emil TABOR
solves the mystery of how a distinguished diplomat disappears.
Male Amateur

Horace G HUTCHINSON 1859-1932 (British)
See main detective Insp SPENS
Citation Record: 1 Book
The Foreign Secretary Who Vanished - *Only*
Hutchinson UK (1927)

TAFFIN
Male Sleuth

Lyndon MALLET 1946-
Citation Record: 1 Book
Taffin - *Single*
New English Library UK (1980)

Andrew TAGGART
is an investigative reporter who becomes involved with organisations that are intent on manipulating British policies for private ends.
British Male Amateur operating in England

Stooge: Insp Brian KING
is a Special Branch detective who works on the cases that the amateur *TAGGART* is investigating for his paper. They are often in conflict; but, of course, *TAGGART* provides the solutions.
British Male

Ruth BRANDON (British)
Citation Record: 2 Books
Left, Right And Centre - *First*
Collins UK (1986); St Martin's US (1986)
Out Of Body, Out Of Mind - *Latest*
Macmillan UK (1987); St Martin's US (1988)

Clayton 'Yankee' TAGGART
American Male Private Detective operating in California

Robert RAY 1935- (American)
See main detective Matt MURDOCK
Citation Record: 1 Book
Cage Of Mirrors - *Single*
Lippincott US (1980)

Agent of Cominsec TAGGART
Male Sleuth

Ralph HAYES 1927- (American)
Invented 4 detectives - see Mark STONER
Citation Record: 5 Books
The Bloody Monday Conspiracy - *First*
Belmont US (1974)
The Death Makers Conspiracy - *Last*
Belmont US (1975)

TAGGETT
investigates theft, linked with romantic passion, in this early detective novel, but does not do well at all, relying too much, it seems, on the ratiocinative process.
American Male Professional Investigator operating in New England

Thomas Bailey ALDRICH 1836-1907 (American)
See main detective Paul LYNDE
Citation Record: 1 Book
The Stillwater Tragedy - *Only*
Houghton US (1880); Douglas UK (1886)

Roger TAINE
is a man on the run; he must use his wits to out-manoeuvre those who wish to kill him, and then discover why.
British Male Amateur operating in England

Geoffrey HOUSEHOLD 1900-1988 (British)
was born in Bristol, Gloucestershire, educated at Clifton College, Bristol, and took a BA in English at Magdalene College, Oxford, 1922. He was engaged in commercial work and banking in Europe until 1935, and for a while in the USA. Later, he served in British Intelligence, 1939-1945. He is the author of at least twenty-three genre novels, most of them thrillers, including some of exceptional quality, and several books for children.
Writer: Geoffrey Edward West HOUSEHOLD
Inventor of one other detective Pedro GONZALES
Citation Record: 2 Books
A Rough Shoot - *First*
Joseph UK (1951); Little, Brown US (1951)
A Time To Kill - *Last*
Little, Brown US (1951); Joseph UK (1952)

TAINE OF SAN FRANCISCO
appeared in four stories in *Amazing Stories.*
American Male Detective in Pulp Magazines operating in San Francisco

David H KELLER 1880-1967 (American)
Writer: David Henry KELLER
No citations

Prof Michael TAIRLAINE
Second detective of John GAUNT

Spencer TAIT and DENHAM
Spencer TAIT is said to hate women.
British Male Amateur and Private Detective operating in England

Fergus HUME 1859-1932 (British)
Invented 24 detectives - see Insp Samuel GORBY
Citation Record: 1 Book
The Lone Inn: A Mystery - *Only*
!See Appendix 2.
Digby, Long UK (1894)

Cobb TAKAMURA and Charles KOENIG
American Male Sleuths operating in Hawaii

Rob SWIGART 1941- (American)
Citation Record: 2 Books
Vector - *First*
Bluejay US (1986)
Toxin - *Latest*
St Martin's US (1989)

Andrew TALBOT
is an engineer who, working in Havana, solves the murder of a man who falls to his death.
American Male Amateur operating in Havana

George Harmon COXE 1901-1984 (American)
Invented 20 detectives - see Kent MURDOCK
Citation Record: 1 Book
Murder In Havana - *Only*
Knopf US (1943); Hammond UK (1944)

Clem TALBOT
is a down-at-heel private eye who becomes involved in cases that are both morbid and comical.
American Male Private Detective operating in New York

Thomas P MULKEEN 1923- (American)
Writer: Thomas Patrick MULKEEN
Citation Record: 2 Books
Honor Thy Godfather - *First*
Stein & Day US (1973)
My Killer Doesn't Understand Me - *Last*
Stein & Day US (1973)

Jean TALBOT
Appears with at least two other detectives - see Det Jay GOLDSTEIN

Ch of Plce Munroe TALLANT
is the Chief of Police in the Grand Flamingo Islands, a fictional part of the West Indies. He and his merry men go in for high-flown adventure and some detection.
British Policeman operating in West Indies

Andrew YORK 1930- (British)
See main detective Jonas WILDE
Citation Record: 2 Books
Tallant For Trouble - *First*
Hutchinson UK (1977); Doubleday US (1977)
Tallant For Disaster - *Latest*
Hutchinson UK (1978); Doubleday US (1978)

Tom TALLEY
American Male Amateur operating in USA

Philip ROSS 1932- (American)
Writer: UNKNOWN
See main detective James MARLEY
Citation Record: 2 Books
Hovey's Deception - *First*
Tor US (1986)
Talley's Truth - *Latest*
Tor US (1987)

Roger TALLIS
British Male Secret Agent operating in several locations

John ROSSITER 1916- (British)
See main detective Supt INKBARROW
Citation Record: 4 Books
The Murder Makers - *First*
Cassell UK (1970); Walker US (1977)
The Golden Virgin - *Last*
Constable UK (1975)
The Deadly Gold - *Last**
Walker US (1975)

Ch Jack TALLON
American Policeman operating in USA

John BALL 1911-1988 (American)
Inventor of 3 detectives - see Virgil TIBBS
Citation Record: 3 Books
Police Chief - *First*
Doubleday US (1977); Hale UK (1982)
Chief Tallon And The S O R - *Latest*
Dodd, Mead US (1984)

Prof Hilary TAMAR
is a female Oxford professor who, for various reasons, comes to the aid of a cast of four barristers in Lincoln's Inn, London, and their friends, when they run into murder. She narrates the stories and solves the cases.
British Female Amateur operating in England

Sarah CAUDWELL 1939- (British)
is a barrister, the daughter of Claud Cockburn, political commentator of the left in the 1930s and 1940s.
Citation Record: 3 Books
Thus Was Adonis Murdered - *First*
Collins UK (1981); Scribner's US (1981)
The Sirens Sang Of Murder - *Latest*
Collins UK (1989); Delacorte US (1989)

TAMARA
Second detective of VALESHOFF

Tina TAMIKO
Second detective of Calico Jack WALKER

Anthony TAMWORTH
American Male Private Detective operating in USA

Anna Katherine GREEN 1846-1935 (American)
Invented 9 detectives - see Det Ebenezer GRYCE
Citation Record: 1 Book
The Forsaken Inn - *Only*
Bonner US (1890); Routledge UK (1890)

Ben TANCRED and Supt Henry WILSON
Supt WILSON is the lesser figure in these two dull books but does better in books on his own and with *The Hon Everard BLATCHINGTON.*
British Male Professional Amateur and British Policeman operating in England
Sidekick: Paul GRAHAM
assists and also narrates the two books.
British Male - Narrator
Sidekick: JELLICOE
is *Dr TANCRED's* assistant in the second of his books.
British Male - Assistant

G D H COLE and Margaret COLE (British)
Invented 7 detectives - see Supt Henry WILSON
Citation Record: 2 Books
Dr Tancred Begins; Or, The Pendexter Saga - *First*
Collins UK (1935); Doubleday US (1935)
Last Will And Testament; Or, The Pendexter Saga, Second (And Last) Canto - *Last*
Collins UK (1936); Doubleday US (1936)

Ch Insp Michael 'Napper' TANDY
British Policeman operating in London
Sidekick: Sgt HOLLAND
British Male - Subordinate

Neal SHEPHERD 1905-1986 (British)
For writer details see Mrs Palmyra Evangeline PYM
Citation Record: 4 Books
Death Flies Low - *First*
Constable UK (1938)
Exit To Music: A Problem In Detection - *Last*
Constable UK (1940)

Walter TANDY
solves an 'impossible' jewel theft.
British Male Amateur operating in England

Edmund DOWNEY (British)
Citation Record: 1 Book
The Ugly Man - *Only*
Downey UK (1896)

Peter TANGENT
American Male Sleuth operating in Africa

Lawrence SANDERS 1920- (American)
Invented 6 detectives - see Ex-Plce Edward X DELANEY
Citation Record: 2 Books
The Tangent Objective - *First*
Putnam US (1976); Hart Davis UK (1977)
The Tangent Factor - *Latest*
Putnam US (1978); Hart Davis UK (1978)

Arthur TANK
learned how to be a detective through a correspondence course, which, unfortunately, did not improve his manners or teach him how to be a regular guy.
American Male Private Detective operating in USA

William H HALLAHAN (American)

See main detective Charlie BREWER

Citation Record: 1 Book

The Ross Forgery - *Only*
Bobbs US (1973); Gollancz UK (1977)

Annie TANNENBAUM

American Female Amateur operating in USA

Sarah SHANKMAN (American)

See main detective Samantha ADAMS

Citation Record: 1 Book

Impersonal Attractions - *Single*
St Martin's US (1985)

Det TANNER

Second detective of Det FLYNN

Insp TANNER

British Policeman operating in England

Freeman Wills CROFTS 1879-1957 (British)

Invented 4 detectives - see Insp Joseph FRENCH

Citation Record: 1 Book

The Ponson Case - *Only*
Collins UK (1921); Boni US (1927)

Evan TANNER

American Male Amateur

Lawrence BLOCK 1938- (American)

Invented 6 detectives - see Leo HAIG

Citation Record: 6 Books

The Thief Who Couldn't Sleep - *First*
GM US (1966)

Two For Tanner - *Last*
GM US (1968)

John Marshall TANNER

is of indeterminate age but served in Korea with the US Army before setting up as a PI. He hates California, loves whisky, music, his old automobile, and good old-fashioned values – not necessarily in that order.

American Male Private Detective operating in San Francisco

Stephen GREENLEAF 1942- (American)

was born in Washington DC. He graduated with a BA from Carleton College, Northfield, Minnesota, 1964, and received a JD from the University of California, Berkeley, 1967. He is a senior attorney in California.

Writer: Stephen Howell GREENLEAF

Citation Record: 10 Books

Grave Error - *First*
Dial US (1979); New English Library UK (1981)

False Conception - *Latest*
US (1994)

John TANNER

American Male Amateur

Robert LUDLUM 1927- (American)

was born in New York City. He graduated at the Wesleyan University, Middletown, Connecticut, and served in the US Marine Corps, 1945-1947. He has been an actor on stage and in films, and is the author of at least seventeen genre novels, all of which are powerful tales of adventure and espionage, often with exotic locales.

Other Detectives:
Noel HOLCROFT
James MATLOCK

Citation Record: 1 Book

The Osterman Weekend - *Single*
World US (1982); Hart Davis UK (1982)

Pete TANNER and Rosemary CLEVELAND

American Male Amateur and American Female Amateur operating in New England

Sandra D WILKINSON (American)

is a senior nursing administrator.

Citation Record: 1 Book

Death On Call - *Single*
Dodd, Mead US (1984)

Insp/Ch Insp Dick TANSEY

is a senior detective in the Thames Valley Police Force.

British Policeman operating in England

Sidekick: Sgt ABBOTT
British Male - Subordinate

John PENN (British)

Invented 3 detectives - see Supt George THORNE

Citation Record: 13 Books

Outrageous Exposures - *First*
Collins UK (1988); Doubleday US (1989)

Widow's End - *Latest*
Collins UK (1993)

Kinsey TARGET

American Female Sleuth operating in USA

GRIFF 1891-1968 (British)

House name.

Real Name: F Dubrez FAWCETT
Other Byline: Ben SARTO

Invented one other detective Don DANBY

Citation Record: 3 Books

Brooklyn Moll Shoots Bedmate - *First*
Modern Fiction UK (1951)

Played The Hard Way - *First**
Modern Fiction UK (1954)

Back-Alley Blonde - *Last*
Modern Fiction UK (1952)

Dr Frank TARLETON

British Male Amateur operating in England

Allen UPWARD 1863-1926 (British)

Invented 6 detectives - see Charles PRESCOTT

Citation Record: 3 Books

The House Of Sin - *First*
Faber UK (1926); Lippincott US (1927)

The Venetian Key - *Last*
Faber UK (1927); Lippincott US (1927)

Geoffrey TARLETON

is a junior Fellow at the fictional St Michael's College, Oxford, who is recruited by a British Intelligence Unit to discover who murdered the History tutor, and why.

British Male Amateur operating in Europe

Jonathan GRAY (British)

Writer: Jack TAYLOR

Citation Record: 1 Book

Untimely Slain - *Only*
Hutchinson UK (1947)

John TARLETON

American Male Amateur operating in New York

Frederick F VAN DE WATER 1890-1968 (American)

Writer: Frederick Franklyn VAN DE WATER

Inventor of one other detective David MALLORY

Citation Record: 2 Books

Still Waters - *First*
Doubleday US (1929); Skeffington UK (1932)

Plunder - *Last*
Doubleday US (1933)

Insp TARR and Ann NELSON

American Policeman and American Female Amateur operating in USA

Ellery QUEEN 1917- (American)

See main detective Insp Omar COLLINS

Citation Record: 1 Book

A Room To Die In - *Only*
Pocket Books US (1965); Kinnell UK (1987)

Alan TARR
American Male Amateur operating in USA

Joseph HANSEN 1923- (American)

See main detective Dave BRANDSTETTER

Citation Record: 1 Book

Backtrack - *Single*
Countryman Press US (1982)

Mr Trevis TARRANT
appears only in short stories, many of which involve him in classic cases of locked-room murder.

British Male Amateur operating in England

C Daly KING 1895-1963 (American)

Invented 3 detectives - see Lt Michael LORD

Citation Record: 8 Short Stories in 1 Collection

The Curious Mr Tarrant - *Collection 1*
Collins UK (1935); Dover US (1977)

Victoria TARRANT
American Female Amateur operating in USA

Ruth FENISONG ?-1978 (American)

See main detective Capt Gridley NELSON

Citation Record: 1 Book

The Drop Of A Hat - *Only*
Doubleday US (1970); Hale UK (1971)

Gerry TATE
Second detective of Douglas PERKINS

Tyler TATLOCK
was an early attempt to follow the success of *Sherlock HOLMES* but he did not make the grade.

British Male Professional Amateur operating in England

Dick DONOVAN 1842-1924 (British)

Invented 7 detectives - see Fabian FIELD

Citation Record: 21 Short Stories in 1 Collection

The Adventures Of Tyler Tatlock, Private Detective - *Collection 1*
Chatto & Windus UK (1890)

TATTON
of Scotland Yard is in this one Victorian novel.

British Policeman operating in England

Mrs Henry WOOD 1814-1887 (British)

Invented 3 detectives - see Sgt DELVES

Citation Record: 1 Book

Within The Maze - *Only*
Bentley UK (1891)

Insp TAVERNER
British Policeman operating in England

T

Agatha CHRISTIE 1890-1976 (British)

Invented 18 detectives - see Hercule POIROT

Citation Record: 1 Book

The Crooked House - *Only*
Collins UK (1949); Dodd, Mead US (1949)

Dr TAVERNER
British Male Amateur operating in England

Dion FORTUNE 1890-1946 (British)

Writer: Violet Mary FIRTH

Citation Record: 11 Short Stories in 1 Collection

The Secrets Of Dr Taverner - *Collection 1*
Douglas UK (1926); Llewellyn US (1962)

Mark TAVERNER
is a 'private detective' in this one Victorian novel.

British Male Private Detective operating in England

Headon HILL 1857-1927 (British)

Invented 11 detectives - see Insp HERON

Citation Record: 1 Book

The Sentence Of The Court - *Only*
Pearson UK (1901)

Det Mitch TAYLOR
Second detective of Jub FREEMAN

Det Mitch TAYLOR
Appears with at least two other detectives - see Jub FREEMAN

Pete TAYLOR
is young, ignorant and ambitious; not a promising combination. He was said by one critic to have had 'all the wit and charm of Calvin Coolidge'.

American Male Private Detective operating in New York

Robert D ABRAHAMS 1905- (American)

Writer: Robert David ABRAHAMS

Citation Record: 2 Books

Death After Lunch - *First*
Phoenix Press US (1941)

Death In 1-2-3 - *Last*
Phoenix Press US (1942)

Sangamon TAYLOR
is more worried about the environment than the desperadoes.

American Male Private Detective operating in Boston

Neal STEPHENSON (American)

Citation Record: 1 Book

Zodiac: The Eco-Thriller - *Single*
Atlantic US (1988); Bloomsbury UK (1988)

Zeb TAYLOR
American Male Detective in Pulp Magazines operating in USA

Warne MILLER (American)

Invented 4 detectives - see Silas QUIRK

Citation Record: 1 Selected Short Story

Zeb Taylor, The Puritan Detective; Or, Piping The Great Treasury Case
Old Cap Collier Library US (18??)

Aurora 'Rose' TEAGARDEN
is a librarian in a small town who likes to investigate local murders that the police seem to ignore.

American Female Amateur operating in USA

Charlaine HARRIS 1951- (American)

Invented 3 detectives - see Catherine LINTON

Citation Record: 4 Books

Three Bedrooms, One Corpse - *First*
Scribner's US (1994)

The Julius House - *Latest*
Scribner's US (1995)

Insp Claude Eustace TEAL
appears as the main detective in this book but also occurs in many other *Simon TEMPLAR (The Saint)* books, usually as a stooge.

British Policeman operating in England

Leslie CHARTERIS 1907- (American)

Invented 3 detectives - see Simon (The Saint) TEMPLAR

Citation Record: 1 Book

Daredevil - *Only*
Doubleday US (1929); Ward, Lock UK (1929)

Timothy TEALEAF
American Male Professional Investigator operating in USA

W W HILL (American)

Citation Record: 10 Short Stories in 1 Collection

Timothy Tealeaf, Business Investigator - *Collection 1*
La Salle University US (1925)

Russell TEED
Canadian Male Amateur operating in Toronto

David MONTROSE 1920- (Canadian)

Writer: Charles Ross GRAHAM

Citation Record: 2 Books

The Crime On Côte Des Neiges - *First*
Collins CA (1951)

Murder Over Dorval - *Last*
Collins CA (1952)

Roger TEJEDA

American Male Amateur operating in California

Wendy HORNSBY (American)

See main detective Maggie MACGOWEN

Citation Record: 2 Books

No Harm - *First*
Dodd, Mead US (1947)

Half A Mind - *Latest*
New American Library US (1990)

Kitty TELEFAIR

American Female Amateur operating in Los Angeles

Florence STEVENSON (American)

Citation Record: 6 Books

The Witching Hour - *First*
Award US (1971)

The Sorcerer Of The Castle - *Last*
Award US (1974)

Dave TELLER

Second detective of Gene HAWKINS

Martin TELLER and Susanna PINSCHER

of the US Justice Department investigate the murder of a Supreme Court official.

American Male Amateur and American Female Amateur operating in Washington DC

Margaret TRUMAN 1924- (American)

Invented 9 detectives - see Mr Ron FAIRCHILD

Citation Record: 1 Book

Murder In The Supreme Court - *Single*
Arbor US (1982)

Jeff TELLFORD

British Male Amateur operating in England

Douglas FISHER 1902-1981 (British)

For writer details see Insp HALLAN and Sgt SPRATT

Citation Record: 3 Books

What's Wrong At Pyford? - *First*
Hodder & Stoughton UK (1950)

Death At Pyford Hall - *Last*
Hodder & Stoughton UK (1952)

Ashley TEMPEST

British Male Amateur operating in England

A C FOX-DAVIES 1871-1928 (British)

Invented 3 detectives - see Sir John KYNNERSLEY

Citation Record: 4 Books

The Mauleverer Murders - *First*
Lane UK (1907)

The Ultimate Conclusion - *Last*
Lane UK (1912)

Kate TEMPEST

is an artist who solves the mystery of a child's disappearance from a moving train.

British Female Amateur operating in England

Dorothy EDEN 1912-1982 (British)

Inventor of one other detective Grace ASHERTON

Citation Record: 1 Book

The Deadly Travellers - *Only*
Macdonald UK (1959); Ace US (1966)

William TEMPEST

is a Canadian working in London as a PI.

Canadian Male Private Detective operating in London

William SHAND (British)

Citation Record: 3 Books

A Man Called Tempest - *First*
Jenkins UK (1957)

Tempest In A Tea Cup - *Last*
Jenkins UK (1958); Roy US (1959)

Simon (The Saint) TEMPLAR

was created in 1929, in an era when British fictional detection was almost entirely in the capable hands of rich young heroes, adventurers, crooks, swashbucklers and several kinds of private admonisher. Since the detectives were usually right-wing in their political standards and could hardly be called unbiased in their attitudes to the working classes and those not fortunate enough to be British, and since they often set themselves up, as seemed only proper to themselves and their readers, outside the law, they were the natural scourge of foreigners, communists, Jews, gentlemen of non-white hue and enemies of the British Empire.

Simon TEMPLAR, however, although he is in some ways yet another example of the species, being an adventurer, a crook, a gallant gentleman to the ladies and death to villains, a man who has to indulge in many a detective role to save himself or other victims, stands out from the general run. He is himself, by British standards, a rather classless liberal. Indeed, at times he shows contempt for the ruling classes and true empathy with lower-class people. Perhaps this is why his books remain so popular and have sold in their tens of millions. Although at first he operated in Britain, in later books he operated in the USA and, during the Second World War, he naturally and properly worked as an agent. Unlike some other period pieces, he was able to develop and change over the decades, and he remains the most long-lasting and popular of the old gentleman outlaws, in a way foreshadowing the American private eyes of the 1950s. His sobriquet of *The Saint* was derived from his habit of leaving his, now famous, emblem on the scenes of his capers.

Simon TEMPLAR has appeared in so many novels and short stories (many written by the prolific author, but many others re-worked, re-published, anthologised, or derived by other authors from earlier stories or radio and TV scripts) that a definitive count probably has yet to be made. He has had various magazines entirely devoted to him and he has been the hero of many films and scripts for radio, film and TV. The citations shown here are to the first publications of the novels and the first collections. The latter, all of which are cited, sometimes contain two to four novelettes and sometimes a greater number of short stories.

British Male Professional Amateur operating in England/Europe/USA

Stooge: Insp Charles TEAL
is one of the several Scotland Yard policemen to come into conflict with *The Saint* during the many adventures of that loveable rogue.
British Male

Leslie CHARTERIS 1907- (American)

was born in Singapore. He was educated privately in Surrey, England, and spent one year at Cambridge University. He adopted the name of *CHARTERIS* legally in 1926. He worked at many kinds of jobs in England, France, and Malaya until 1935, when he went to the US, becoming a naturalised American citizen in 1946. He continued, however, to maintain close contact with Britain.

Writer: Leslie Charles Bowyer YIN

Other Detectives:

Bill KENNEDY — Insp Claude Eustace TEAL

Citation Record: 17 Books 144 Short Stories in 28 Collections

Meet The Tiger - *First*
Doubleday US (1929); Ward, Lock UK (1928)
Vendetta For The Saint - *Last*
was ghost-written by *Harry Max HARRISON.*
Doubleday US (1964); Hodder & Stoughton UK (1965)
Enter The Saint - *Collection 1*
Short stories - 3
Doubleday US (1931); Hodder & Stoughton UK (1930)
Wanted For Murder - *Collection 2*
Short stories - 6
Doubleday US (1931)
The Saint - Wanted For Murder - *Collection 2**
Sun Dial (1943)
Featuring The Saint - *Collection 3*
Short stories - 3
Hodder & Stoughton UK (1931)
Alias The Saint - *Collection 4*
Short stories - 3
Hodder & Stoughton UK (1931)
The Saint Vs Scotland Yard - *Collection 5*
Short stories - 3
Doubleday US (1932)
The Holy Terror - *Collection 5**
Hodder & Stoughton UK (1932)
The Saint And Mr Teal - *Collection 6*
Short stories - 3
Doubleday US (1933)
Once More The Saint - *Collection 6**
Hodder & Stoughton UK (1933)
The Brighter Buccaneer - *Collection 7*
Short stories - 15
Doubleday US (1933); Hodder & Stoughton UK (1933)
The Saint - The Brighter Buccaneer - *Collection 7**
Avon US (1957)
The Saint Intervenes - *Collection 8*
Short stories - 14
Doubleday US (1934)
Boodle - *Collection 8**
Hodder & Stoughton UK (1934)
The Misfortunes Of Mr Teal - *Collection 9*
Short stories - 3
Doubleday US (1934); Hodder & Stoughton UK (1934)
The Saint In England - *Collection 9**
Sun Dial (1941)
The Saint In London - *Collection 9**
Hodder & Stoughton UK (1952)
The Saint Goes On - *Collection 10*
Short stories - 3
Doubleday US (1934); Hodder & Stoughton UK (1934)
The Ace Of Knaves - *Collection 11*
Short stories - 3
Doubleday US (1937); Hodder & Stoughton UK (1937)
The Saint In Action - *Collection 11**
Sun Dial (1938)
The Saint: Ace Of Knaves - *Collection 11**
Avon US (1955)
Follow The Saint - *Collection 12*
Short stories - 3
Doubleday US (1938); Hodder & Stoughton UK (1938)
The Happy Highwayman - *Collection 13*
Short stories - 9
Doubleday US (1939); Hodder & Stoughton UK (1939)
The Saint - The Happy Highwayman - *Collection 13**
Avon US (1955)
The Saint Goes West - *Collection 14*
Short stories - 3
Doubleday US (1942); Hodder & Stoughton UK (1942)
The Saint On Guard - *Collection 15*
contains two novelettes, each of which was later published separately by *Avon* (US 1956/1958).
Short stories - 2
Doubleday US (1944); Hodder & Stoughton UK (1945)
Paging The Saint - *Collection 16*
Short stories - 2
Jacobs US (1945)
Call For The Saint - *Collection 17*
contains two novelettes. Their plots are set in New York and Chicago respectively.
Short stories - 2
Doubleday US (1948)
Saint Errant - *Collection 18*
Short stories - 9
Doubleday US (1948); Hodder & Stoughton UK (1949)
The Saint In Europe - *Collection 19*
Short stories - 7
Doubleday US (1953); Hodder & Stoughton UK (1954)
The Saint On The Spanish Main - *Collection 20*
Short stories - 6
Doubleday US (1955); Hodder & Stoughton UK (1956)
The Saint Around The World - *Collection 21*
Short stories - 6
Doubleday US (1956); Hodder & Stoughton UK (1957)
Thanks To The Saint - *Collection 22*
Short stories - 6
Doubleday US (1957); Hodder & Stoughton UK (1958)
Senor Saint - *Collection 23*
Short stories - 4
Doubleday US (1958); Hodder & Stoughton UK (1959)
Concerning The Saint - *Collection 24*
contains two novelettes.
Short stories - 2
Avon US (1958)
The Saint To The Rescue - *Collection 25*
These stories are located in California.
Short stories - 6
Doubleday US (1959); Hodder & Stoughton UK (1961)
The Saint Cleans Up - *Collection 26*
Short stories - 5
Avon US (1959)
Trust The Saint - *Collection 27*
Short stories - 6
Doubleday US (1962); Hodder & Stoughton UK (1962)
The Saint In The Sun - *Collection 28*
Short stories - 7
Doubleday US (1963); Hodder & Stoughton UK (1964)

Evelyn TEMPLE

does a lot of scientific detection but makes all the wrong deductions. She appears also in two books published under the author's other name, *Lord GORELL,* in which she is teamed with one of the latter's detectives, *Insp HEPBURN,* and does rather better at the sleuthing.

British Female Amateur operating in England

Ronald Gorell BARNES 1884-1963 (British)
Citation Record: 1 Book
In The Night - *Only*
Longman UK (1917)

Evelyn TEMPLE

Second detective of Insp Maurice HEPBURN

Paul TEMPLE

has appeared in novels, films and plays for over fifty years. He may have started as a character on radio and certainly was featured in a lengthy series during the early 1940s. He fits best into the long line of heroes who were both adventurers and detectives, and was engaged in countless tussles with the forces of evil, ranging from the simple criminal to the malevolent political agent.

British Male Professional Amateur operating in several locations

Francis DURBRIDGE 1912- (British)
was born in Hull, Yorkshire.
Writer: Francis Henry DURBRIDGE
Inventor of one other detective Tim FRAZER
Citation Record: 15 Books
Send For Paul Temple - *First*
Long UK (1938)
Paul Temple And The Conrad Case - *Latest*
BBC UK (1989)

Wayne TEMPLE
does more seduction than detection.
American Male Private Detective operating in Mississippi

M Earle PALMER (American)
Citation Record: 1 Book
Southern Exposure - *Only*
US (1967)

Paul TEMPLETON
British Male Amateur operating in England

Richard GOYNE 1902-1957 (British)
Invented 4 detectives - see Supt 'Tubby' GREENE
Citation Record: 12 Books
Murder At The Inn - *First*
Paul UK (1935)
Murderer's Moon - *Last*
Paul UK (1949)

Det Insp TENCH
Second detective of Ch Insp LUBBOCK

Irene TENNANT
American Female Amateur operating in USA

Amanda RUTTER (American)
Citation Record: 1 Book
Murder At Eastover - *Only*
Arcadia US (1958)

Maj TENNENTE
is an honest policeman serving under a foreign dictatorship.
American Policeman operating in USA

Thomas FLANAGAN 1923- (American)
See main detective Niccolo MACHIAVELLI
Citation Record: 1 Selected Short Story
The Cold Winds Of Adesta
In 'Ellery Queen's Mystery Magazine' US (1951)

Sally TEPPER
American Female Amateur operating in New York

Frank KING 1936- (American)
Writer: Franklin KING
Citation Record: 2 Books
Sleeping Dogs Die - *First*
Dutton US (1988)
Take The D Train - *Latest*
Dutton US (1990)

Theodore I TERHUNE
is a young bookseller in a small town, whose desire to live quietly is usually interrupted by murders, which he, for various complicated reasons, has to solve.
British Male Amateur operating in England

Bruce GRAEME 1900-1982 (British)
Invented 6 detectives - see BLACKSHIRT
Citation Record: 6 Books
House With Crooked Walls - *First*
Hutchinson UK (1942)
Dead Pigs At Hungry Farm - *Last*
Hutchinson UK (1951)

Bill TERN
British Male Amateur

Bryan Edgar WALLACE 1904- (British)
was the son of *Edgar WALLACE.* He was a screenwriter and served in the British Diplomatic Service.
Citation Record: 2 Books
Death Packs A Suitcase - *First*
Hodder & Stoughton UK (1961)
The Device - *Last*
Hodder & Stoughton UK (1962)

Timothy TERREL
British Male Amateur operating in England

Stephen MADDOCK 1897-1952 (British)
See main detective Insp SLANE
Citation Record: 18 Books
Danger After Dark - *First*
Collins UK (1934)
I'll Never Like Friday Again - *Last*
Collins UK (1945)

Frank TERRELL
is one of this British author's several American detectives. He appears also in another book with the author's other detectives, *Al BARNEY* and *Steve HARMAS.*
American Male Private Detective operating in California/Florida

James Hadley CHASE 1906-1985 (British)
Invented 14 detectives - see Dave FENNER
Citation Record: 6 Books
The Soft Centre - *First*
Hale UK (1964)
There's A Hippie On The Highway - *Last*
Hale UK (1970)

Frank TERRELL
Appears with at least two other detectives - see Steve HARMAS

Sam TERRELL
American Male Amateur operating in USA

William P MCGIVERN 1927-1982 (American)
Invented 5 detectives - see Dave BANNION
Citation Record: 1 Book
Night Extra - *Only*
Dodd, Mead US (1957); Collins UK (1958)

Michael TERRENCE and 'Terry' TERRENCE
British Male Amateur and British Female Amateur operating in England

Gordon BRANDON (British)
For writer details see Sgt/Det Insp Patrick Aloysius MCCARTHY
Inventor of one other detective pair Arthur Stukeley PENNINGTON and Det Insp Patrick Aloysius MCCARTHY
Citation Record: 3 Books
Murder In Maytime - *First*
Wright UK (1950)
A Mild Case Of Murder - *Last*
Wright UK (1951)

'Terry' TERRENCE
Second detective of Michael TERRENCE

Jerry THACKER
is an investigator for Cosmo Life Insurance.
American Male Professional Investigator operating in Indianapolis

G T FLEMING-ROBERTS (American)
Inventor of one other detective Jeffrey WREN
Citation Record: 1 Selected Short Story
The Death Master
In 'Ten Detective Aces' US (1935)

Const THACKERAY
Second detective of Sgt CRIBB

Det Ch Insp Colin THANE and Insp Phil MOSS
are Scottish cops in a long series of police procedurals. The cases are set in Glasgow and other parts of Scotland and introduce many subsidiary characters and transient sidekicks on the way.
British Policemen operating in Glasgow

Sidekick: Francy DUNBAR
is a motor-cycle enthusiast and part of the team.
Scottish Male - Subordinate
Sidekick: Sandra LAING
is a beautiful and bright member of the team.
Scottish Female - Subordinate

Bill KNOX 1928- (British)

For writer details see Jonathan GAUNT

Inventor of one other detective Ch Offr Webb CARRICK

Citation Record: 20 Books

Deadline For A Dream - *First*
Long UK (1957)

In At The Kill - *First**
Doubleday US (1961)

The Interface Man - *Latest*
Century Hutchinson UK (1989); Doubleday US (1990)

Det Insp Luke THANET

operates in the fictional Kent town of Sturrenden.

British Policeman operating in Kent

Sidekick: Sgt Mike LINEHAM
British Male - Subordinate

Dorothy SIMPSON 1933- (British)

was born in Blaenavon, Monmouthshire, Wales. She graduated with a BA from the University of Bristol, 1955, then worked, first as a teacher and then as a marriage guidance counsellor, 1969-1982. She received the Crime Writers Association Silver Dagger award, 1985.

Citation Record: 12 Books

The Night She Died - *First*
Scribner's US (1981)

No Laughing Matter - *Latest*
Scribner's US (1993)

Corey THATCHER

investigates murder in hospital in the year 2010.

American Male Amateur operating in USA

Geoffrey S SIMMONS 1943- (American)

Citation Record: 1 Book

Murdock - *Only*
Arbor US (1976)

J D THATCHER

Second detective of Stonewall Jackson YATES

John Putnam THATCHER

is a Wall Street banker who solves many a case of financial skulduggery, chicanery and murder, all taking place in the world of high finance.

American Male Amateur operating in New York

Sidekick: Everett GABLER
is elderly, diet-conscious and fussy; but he has a tremendous eye for detail.
American Male - Assistant

Emma LATHEN (American)

is the pseudonym of a writing team that has produced two main series of criminous works over more than three decades. *Mary J LATSIS* was raised in Illinois. She was educated at Wellesley College, Massachusetts, and graduated at Harvard University, Cambridge, Massachusetts, after which she worked as an economist for the United Nations Organisation.

Martha HENNISART was born in New York City and worked, until 1973, in corporate finance. Together the two authors received the Crime Writers Association Gold Dagger award, 1967, and the Mystery Writers of America Ellery Queen award, 1983.

Writers: Mary J LATSIS 1927- and Martha HENNISSART 1929-

Citation Record: 20 Books

Banking On Death - *First*
Macmillan US (1961); Gollancz UK (1962)

Something In The Air - *Latest*
Simon & Schuster US (1988); Gollancz UK (1989)

Steve THATCHER

was also known as The Moon Man. A kind of Robin Hood character, he was a cop who robbed the rich to give to the poor. He appeared in stories published, 1933-1937, in *Ten Detective Aces*, some of which appear in this recent collection.

American Male Detective in Pulp Magazines operating in USA

Frederick C DAVIS 1902-1977 (American)

Invented 4 detectives - see Luke SPEARE and Schyler COLE

Citation Record: 14 Short Stories in 1 Collection

The Night Nemesis - *Collection 1*
Purple Prose US (1984)

Charles THAYER

American Male Amateur operating in Detroit

A H GARNET (American)

Writer: UNKNOWN

See main detective Cyrus WILSON

Citation Record: 1 Book

The Santa Claus Killer - *Single*
Ticknor US (1981)

The THEATRE DETECTIVE

American Male Detective in Pulp Magazines operating in USA

M H WILLIAMS (American)

Invented 4 detectives - see DAVENPORT BLAKE

Citation Record: 1 Selected Short Story

The Theatre Detective; Or, A Tragedy On The Stage
Old Cap Collier Library US (18??)

Kate THEOBALD

is an intrepid reporter whose investigations involve her in murder cases, which she proceeds to solve, somewhat to the astonishment and chagrin of the police.

British Female Amateur operating in England

Sidekick: Henry THEOBALD
assists his wife
British Male - Husband

Stooge: Det Insp Roger WAKE
is the main police opposition to *KATE THEOBALD* when her cases are in the country.
British Male

Stooge: Det Insp Aloysius COMFORT
is the main police opposition to *KATE THEOBALD* when her cases are in London.
British Male

Lionel BLACK 1910-1980 (British)

was born in London. He took a BA at Oriel College, Oxford, 1933, and served as a Wing Commander in the Royal Air Force during the Second World War. A reporter and news editor for many London newspapers, he wrote fiction and non-fiction, published mainly under his real name. His works included nearly twenty criminous novels.

Writer: Dudley BARKER

Other Detectives:
Supt Francis FOY
Emma GREAVES

Citation Record: 6 Books

Swinging Murder - *First*
Cassell UK (1969); Walker US (1969)

The Eve Of The Wedding - *Last*
Avon US (1981)

Mother THEODORE

is the Superior of the fictional College of St Aurelian, deep in the bayou country. When one of three new male lay instructors is murdered, she decides to find out whodunnit.

American Female Amateur operating in Louisiana

Margaret Ann HUBBARD 1909- (American)

was born in Souris, North Dakota. She is the author of children's books and four criminous novels.

Writer: Margaret PRILEY

Inventor of one other detective Sister SIMON

T

Citation Record: 1 Book

Murder Takes The Veil - *Only*
Bruce US (1950)

Max THERINGER

Second detective of Dave ROBBINS

Thomas C THERON

is a Professor of American Civilization at a Boston college, who reluctantly turns amateur sleuth.

American Male Amateur operating in Boston

Robert REEVES (American)

was born in Birmingham, Alabama. He has been a lecturer in History at Harvard.

Writer: Robert Nicholas REEVES

Inventor of one other detective Cellini SMITH

Citation Record: 2 Books

Doubting Thomas - *First*
Crown US (1985); Collins UK (1986)

Peeping Thomas - *Latest*
Crown US (1990)

Insp H H THEW

British Male Amateur operating in England

Douglas G BROWNE 1884-1963 (British)

Invented 4 detectives - see LEGARDE

Citation Record: 2 Books

The Cotfold Conundrums - *First*
Methuen UK (1933)

Plan XVI - *Last*
Methuen UK (1934); Doubleday US (1934)

Fritz THIERINGER and Maggie MCGUANE

are partners in an agency.

American Male Private Detective and American Female Private Detective operating in Los Angeles

Brad SOLOMON 1945- (American)

See main detective Charlie QUINLAN

Citation Record: 1 Book

The Open Shadow - *Single*
Summit US (1978)

Robin THIN

was a minor and transient invention by this eminent author.

American Male Private Detective operating in USA

Dashiell HAMMETT 1894-1961 (American)

Invented 7 detectives - see Sam SPADE

Citation Record: 1 Selected Short Story

The Nails In Mr Cayterer
In 'Black Mask Magazine' US (1926)

Jock THIRLSTANE

British Male Amateur operating in Scotland

W Clark RUSSELL 1844-1911 (British)

See main detective Col KILMAIN

Citation Record: 11 Short Stories in 1 Collection

The Reminiscences Of Jock Thirlstane, Yokel And Detective, At Musselburgh Races In Days Gone By - *Collection 1*
Adams UK (ca 1914)

Insp THOMAS

was perhaps the first detective of this prolific crime writer to have appeared in print.

American Policeman operating in USA

Cleve F ADAMS 1895-1949 (American)

Invented 5 detectives - see Rex MCBRIDE

Citation Record: 1 Selected Short Story

Inspector Thomas Wins A Hat
In 'Clues' US (1933)

Bernado THOMAS

is half American and half Venezuelan. He investigates murder in a Venezuelan locale.

American Male Private Detective operating in Venezuela

Louis WILLIAMS (American)

Citation Record: 1 Book

Tropical Murder - *Single*
Tower US (1981)

Ethel THOMAS

is a wealthy old maid of good family who loves murder cases and is rather good at solving them, saying, 'Murder is like a good fire. If they must happen I want to be where I can see them'.

American Female Amateur operating in New York

Courtland FITZSIMMONS 1883-1949 (American)

Invented 4 detectives - see Det Jack KETHERIDGE

Citation Record: 4 Books

The Whispering Window - *First*
US (1936)

The Evil Men Do - *Last*
Stokes US (1941); Boardman UK (1942)

Lizzie THOMAS

is a Welsh widow in the fictional town of Flaxfield. She is zestful, curious, and, when murders take place, takes to amateur detecting like a duck to water.

Welsh Female Amateur operating in Suffolk

Sidekick: John WEBBER

is a retired policeman, plump and arthritic, but shrewd and a most useful sidekick to the lady sleuth, especially when fed.

British Male - Friend

Anthony OLIVER 1923- (Welsh)

was born in Abersychan, Wales. Once an actor, he later became the owner of a London antiques business.

Citation Record: 4 Books

The Pew Group - *First*
Heinemann UK (1980); Doubleday US (1981)

Cover-Up - *Latest*
Heinemann UK (1987); Doubleday US (1987)

George THOMASSY

American Male Amateur operating in USA

Sol STEIN 1926- (American)

Citation Record: 3 Books

The Magician - *First*
Delacorte US (1971); Joseph UK (1971)

The Touch Of Treason - *Latest*
St Martin's US (1985); Macmillan UK (1985)

Ch Insp THOMPSON

British Policeman operating in England

Peter DRAX (British)

Writer: Eric Elrington ADDIS

Citation Record: 3 Books

Murder By Chance - *First*
Hutchinson UK (1936)

Tune To A Corpse - *Last*
Hutchinson UK (1938)

Crime To Music - *Last**
Appleton US (1939)

THOMPSON

British Male Sleuth operating in England

Junius L HEMPSTEAD 1842- (British)

Writer: Junius Lackland HEMPSTEAD

Citation Record: 1 Book

Thompson The Detective - *Only*
Abbey UK (1902)

Rev Dan THOMPSON
is a popular clergyman in a small town in Kentucky. When someone starts reducing his congregation in a deadly kind of way, he gives up sermonising for sleuthing, suggesting that the Lord works in mysterious ways indeed.
American Male Amateur operating in Kentucky

Dean FELDMEYER (American)
Citation Record: 1 Book
Pitchfork Hollow - *Single*
Pocket Books US (1995)

Derek THOMPSON
sets out to find a missing child.
American Male Private Detective operating in San Francisco

Kelly BRADFORD (American)
Citation Record: 1 Book
Footprints - *Single*
Crossing Press US (1988); Crossing Press UK (1988)

Harry THOMPSON
is a failed journalist and penniless private eye who is sucked into a case of international politics and murder.
British Male Private Detective operating in England

John WAINWRIGHT 1921- (British)
Invented 9 detectives - see Ch Insp/Supt LENNOX
Citation Record: 1 Book
Blind Brag - *Single*
Macmillan UK (1988); St Martin's US (1988)

Sheriff Jack THOMPSON
American Policeman operating in Texas

Evelyn CAMERON (American)
Citation Record: 2 Books
Dead Man's Shoes - *First*
Doubleday US (1939)
Malice Domestic - *Last*
Doubleday US (1940)

Jeff THOMPSON
is in a novelization of a TV film.
American Male Private Detective operating in Miami

Evan Lee HEYMAN (American)
Citation Record: 1 Book
Miami Undercover - *Only*
Popular Library US (1961)

Mike THOMPSON
Second detective of Tracy LARRIMORE

Pat THOMPSON
works for an agency and according to his boss, is 'better drunk than most men sober'. He and his sidekick act tough but tend to talk a lot.
American Male Private Detective operating in New York
Sidekick: Sue BARKER
American Female - Assistant

Robert George DEAN (American)
See main detective Anthony HUNTER
Citation Record: 4 Books
What Gentleman Strangles A Lady? - *First*
Doubleday US (1936)
Murder On Margin - *Last*
Doubleday US (1937)

THORN
American Male Sleuth operating in Florida

Jim HALL 1947- (American)
Writer: James Wilson HALL
Citation Record: 2 Books
Under Cover Of Daylight - *First*
Norton US (1987); Heinemann UK (1988)
Tropical Freeze - *Latest*
Norton US (1989)
Squall Line - *Latest**
Heinemann UK (1989)

Bella THORN
is a female typist at the Secretarial Supply Syndicate Ltd. Her job gets her into investigations of crimes.
British Female Amateur operating in London

Tom GALLON 1866-1914 (British)
Invented 3 detectives - see Enoch VOYCE
Citation Record: 1 Book
The Girl Behind The Keys - *Only*
Hutchinson UK (1903)

Dr John Evelyn THORNDYKE
was created by *R Austin FREEMAN* and is one of the major detectives of the British Golden Age. He holds the post of Professor of Medical Jurisprudence at the fictional St Margaret's Hospital and remains one of the very few convincing scientific investigators in the whole genre, for he really knew and used scientific methodology in a way quite beyond most other fictional detectives and, indeed, was foremost in bringing the new age of forensic science to the art of detection. He operates, over a span of thirty years, from 5A King's Bench Walk in London's Inner Temple and it is there he has his wonderful but realistic laboratory, filled with technical workers. It is there, using microscopes, spectroscopes and chemistry, that he traps the most ingenious criminals, who insist on using despicable tricks like forged fingerprints, planted dust, and all manner of fake clues.
Dr THORNDYKE may not have the stature of *Sherlock HOLMES* and, certainly, he is much less interesting; but, unlike the latter, he is a real scientist and his cases are brilliantly thought out. He featured not only in novels but in many short stories, mostly appearing in the author's collections. The original five are cited here, but several later omnibuses were published. After the death of his creator, at least two other authors wrote new *THORNDYKE* novels.
British Male Professional Amateur operating in London
Sidekick: Nathaniel POLTON
is a small man of wrinkled countenance. He is one of the most important sidekicks in the genre, being, in all books, *THORNDYKE's* factotum, laboratory assistant, photographer, messenger and general aide.
British Male - Assistant
Sidekick: Dr Christopher JERVIS
is one of *THORNDYKE's* two important assistants. He is a key figure in the canon, not only because of his laboratory researches, on which the detective so often depends, but because he also narrates the cases.
British Male - Narrator

John H DIRCKX 1938-
Citation Record: 1 Book
Dr Thorndyke's Dilemma - *Pastiche 1*
Aspen US (1974)

Norman DONALDSON 1922- (British)
Citation Record: 1 Book
Goodbye, Dr Thorndyke - *Only*
Norris UK (1972)

R Austin FREEMAN 1862-1947 (British)
was born in London. He qualified as a doctor at Middlesex Hospital, London, 1887, and had several medical appointments in the Army, 1915-1919, after which he worked in general practice. He settled in Gravesend, Kent, 1903, and became a full-time writer in 1919.
Writer: Richard Austin FREEMAN

Other Detectives:
Humphrey CHALLONER
Danby CROKER
Phyllis DUDLEY
Citation Record: 21 Books 38 Short Stories in 5 Collections
The Red Thumb Mark - *First*
Collingwood UK (1907); Newton US (1911)
The Jacob Street Mystery - *Last*
Hodder & Stoughton UK (1942)
The Unconscious Witness - *Last**
Dodd, Mead US (1942)
John Thorndyke's Cases - *Collection 1*
Short stories - 8
Chatto UK (1909)
Dr Thorndyke's Cases - *Collection 1**
Dodd, Mead US (1931)
The Singing Bone - *Collection 2*
Short stories - 5
Hodder & Stoughton UK (1912); Dodd, Mead US (1923)
Dr Thorndyke's Case-Book - *Collection 3*
Short stories - 7
Hodder & Stoughton UK (1923)
The Blue Scarab - *Collection 3**
Dodd, Mead US (1924)
The Puzzle Lock - *Collection 4*
Short stories - 9
Hodder & Stoughton UK (1925); Dodd, Mead US (1926)
The Magic Casket - *Collection 5*
Short stories - 9
Hodder & Stoughton UK (1927); Dodd, Mead US (1927)

Dr John Evelyn THORNDYKE

Appears with at least two other detectives - see Sherlock HOLMES

Dr THORNE

solves the mystery of how a chef poisoned his wife; and why.

British Male Amateur operating in England

Eden PHILLPOTTS 1862-1960 (British)

Invented 10 detectives - see Insp MIDWINTER

Citation Record: 1 Book
Monkshood - *Only*
Methuen UK (1939); Macmillan US (1939)

Curtis THORNE

was a 'scientific detective' who appeared in stories in the early issues of *Amazing Stories*.

American Male Detective in Pulp Magazines operating in USA

A Hyatt VERRILL 1871-1954 (American)

No citations

Supt George THORNE

British Policeman operating in England

Sidekick: Sgt Bill ABBOT
British Male - Subordinate

John PENN (British)

is the joint pseudonym of a husband-and-wife team. *Palma HARCOURT* has written at least seventeen other books in the criminous genre, none of which features series detectives.

Writers: Palma HARCOURT and Jack H TROTMAN
Other Detectives:
John BRELAND and Mike FREEMAN
Insp/Ch Insp Dick TANSEY
Citation Record: 3 Books
A Will To Kill - *First*
Collins UK (1983); Scribner's US (1984)
A Deadly Sickness - *Latest*
Collins UK (1985); Scribner's US (1985)

Lisa THORNE

American Female Amateur operating in Cape Cod

Clare BARROLL (American)

Citation Record: 1 Book
A Strange Place For Murder - *Single*
Scribner's US (1979)

Tommy THORNE

American Male Amateur operating in USA

Charles H SNOW 1877-1967 (American)

For writer details see Frank BRIERS

Citation Record: 4 Books
The Lakeside Murder - *First*
Wright UK (1933)
The Highgrade Murder - *Last*
Wright UK (1935)

Insp Richard THORNHILL

investigates the murder of an unknown baby in the fictional town of Lydmouth.

British Policeman operating in England

Andrew TAYLOR 1951- (British)

was born in Hertfordshire. He was educated at King's School. Ely, Cambridgeshire, and took an MA in English at Emmanuel College, Cambridge, 1973, followed by an MA at the University of London, 1979. A librarian and authority on information science, he received the Crime Writers Association John Creasey Memorial award, 1982.

Writer: Andrew John Robert TAYLOR
Inventor of one other detective William DOUGAL
Citation Record: 1 Book
Just Another Angel - *First*
HarperCollins UK (1988)

Bo 'Springblade' THORNTON

American Male Sleuth operating in USA/Asia

Greg WALKER (American)

Citation Record: 6 Books
Springblade - *First*
Charter US (1989)
Machete - *Latest*
Charter US (1990)

Cassandra THORPE

is not licensed to act as a PI until sentenced by a judge to be one.

American Female Private Detective operating in San Francisco

Robert BOWMAN (American)

Citation Record: 1 Book
The House Of Blue Lights - *Single*
St Martin's US (1988)

Gilbert THRESHAM and Percy BARSTONE

are respectively a tutor and a minor poet who are joint sleuths in this one Victorian novel.

British Male Amateurs operating in England

Fergus HUME 1859-1932 (British)

Invented 24 detectives - see Insp Samuel GORBY

Citation Record: 1 Book
The White Prior: A Family Mystery - *Only*
Warne UK (1895)

Derek THRYDE

British Male Amateur operating in England

Bertie DENHAM 1927- (British)

Citation Record: 3 Books
The Man Who Lost His Shadow - *First*
Macmillan UK (1979); Scribner's US (1979)
Foxhunt - *Latest*
St Martin's US (1988)

John THUNSTONE

uses psychic powers of detection.

American Male Amateur operating in USA

Manly Wade WELLMAN 1905- (American)

Invented 5 detectives - see David RETURN

Citation Record: 15 Short Stories in 1 Collection

Lonely Vigils - *Collection 1*

This collection of twenty stories contains four with *PURSUIVANT* and fifteen with *THUNSTONE.*

Carcosa US (1981)

Roger THURSBY

British Male Amateur operating in England

Henry CECIL 1902-1976 (British)

Invented 4 detectives - see Col BRAIN

Citation Record: 3 Books

Brothers In Law - *First*

Joseph UK (1955); Harper & Row US (1955)

Sober As A Judge - *Last*

Joseph UK (1958); Harper & Row US (1958)

Max THURSDAY

works himself up from being a cheap house dick to becoming a good private eye.

American Male Private Detective operating in San Diego

Wade MILLER (American)

wrote together under this main pseudonym and used others. *Bill MILLER* was born in Garrett, Indiana. He was educated at Woodrow Wilson Junior High School, San Diego, and San Diego State College until 1942 and served with the US Air Force in the Pacific, 1942-1946. *Robert WADE* was born in San Diego, California. He was educated at Woodrow Wilson Junior High School, San Diego, and San Diego State College and served with the US Air Force in Europe during the Second World War. The two men began their collaboration while at school together and continued it until the early death of *MILLER,* after which *WADE* continued to write alone.

Writers: Robert WADE 1920- and Bill MILLER 1920-1961

Other Byline: Whit MASTERSON

Inventor of one other detective Walter JAMES

Citation Record: 6 Books

Guilty Bystander - *First*

Farrar, Straus US (1947); Low UK (1948)

Shoot To Kill - *Last*

Farrar, Straus US (1951); Allen UK (1953)

Nan THURSDAY

American Female Amateur operating in USA

Virginia DALE (American)

Citation Record: 1 Book

Nan Thursday - *Only*

Coward McCann US (1944)

T

Jimmy THURSTON

solves a case of brutal murder in a taxi.

British Male Amateur operating in England

Alan THOMAS 1896- (British)

See main detective Insp WIDGEON

Citation Record: 1 Book

The Tremayne Case - *Only*

Benn UK (1929); Lippincott US (1930)

Emmy TIBBETT

Second detective of Ch Insp/Ch Sup Henry TIBBETT

Ch Insp/Ch Sup Henry TIBBETT and Emmy TIBBETT

Henry TIBBETT is a classic Scotland Yard man; a little plodding, but one who gets there in the end. His wife, *Emmy TIBBETT,* is more than just a sidekick and truly helps him solve his cases.

British Policeman and British Female Amateur operating in England

Patricia MOYES 1923- (British)

was born in Bray, County Wicklow, Ireland. She was educated at Overstone School, Northampton, and served in the Women's Auxiliary Air Force, 1940-1945. Since 1958 she has lived at various times in Switzerland, Holland and the USA. She received the Mystery Writers of America Edgar Allan Poe award, 1971.

Citation Record: 18 Books

Dead Men Don't Ski - *First*

Collins UK (1959); Rinehart US (1960)

Black Girl, White Girl - *Latest*

Holt US (1989); Collins UK (1990)

John TIBBETT

British Male Amateur operating in England

Laurence PAYNE 1919- (British)

Invented 4 detectives - see Mark SAVAGE and Ch Insp Sam BIRKETT

Citation Record: 2 Books

Spy For Sale - *First*

Hodder & Stoughton UK (1969); Doubleday US (1970)

Even My Foot's Asleep - *Last*

Hodder & Stoughton UK (1971)

Virgil TIBBS

is a black detective, called 'a homicide specialist', operating in a police force in Pasadena. He is young, unmarried, athletic, an expert in martial arts, and he has considerable forensic knowledge. He achieved his rank and status because of his unusual skills in observation of detail and a classic deductive approach. Even so, he is subject to considerable racial prejudice during his cases and he must deal with it.

American Policeman operating in Pasadena/Los Angeles

Sidekick: Bob NAKAMURA

does a certain amount of investigative work for *TIBBS.*

American Male - Assistant

John BALL 1911-1988 (American)

was born in Schenectady, New York. He graduated as BA from Carroll College, Waukesha, Wisconsin, 1934, and served in the US Army Air Corps, 1942-1945. He has had a career in the aircraft industry, for which he has written many reports. He was a full-time writer from 1958, receiving the Mystery Writers of America Edgar Allan Poe award, 1965, and the Crime Writers Association Gold Dagger award, 1966. The author of several interesting and unusual detective novels, he was particularly concerned with the accuracy of time, place and methodology in his work. In the *TIBBS* books, he was innovatory in depicting the social implications of the protagonist's situation as a black man who is also a very good detective.

Writer: John Dudley BALL Jr

Other Detectives:

Ch Jack TALLON

Sherlock Holmes

Citation Record: 7 Books

In The Heat Of The Night - *First*

Harper & Row US (1965); Joseph UK (1966)

Singapore - *Last*

Dodd, Mead US (1986)

TICTOCQ

is a parody of the early French detective, *VIDOCQ.* He appeared in two stories (one cited) by the American master of the short story form.

French Male Professional Investigator operating in France

O HENRY 1862-1910 (American)

See main detective Shamrock JOLNES

Citation Record: 1 Selected Short Story

Tictocq - *Parody 1*

is in the author's collection, *Rolling Stones.*

Doubleday US (1912); Hodder & Stoughton UK (1916)

James TIERNEY

American Male Amateur operating in New York

John A MOROSO 1874-1957 (American)
Writer: John Antonio MOROSO
Citation Record: 1 Book 9 Short Stories in 1 Collection
The People Against Nancy Preston - *Only*
Holt US (1921); Methuen UK (1922)
The Listening Man - *Collection 1*
Appleton UK (1924)

Matthew TIERNEY
British Male Amateur operating in England

E X FERRARS 1907-1995 (British)
Invented 11 detectives - see Toby DYKE
Citation Record: 1 Book
Murderers Anonymous - *Only*
Doubleday US (1978)

Elizabeth FERRARS 1907-1995 (British)
Invented 10 detectives - see Toby DYKE
Citation Record: 1 Book
Murderers Anonymous - *Only*
Collins UK (1977)

Lord TIGRANES
sleuths in England in a book set back to 1914.
British Male Amateur operating in USA

J M BENNETT (American)
Writer: John McGrew BENNETT
Citation Record: 1 Book
A Local Matter - *Single*
Walker US (1985)

Alastair Alexandrovitch TIMUROFF
investigates murders in a creepy old house.
Male Amateur operating in USA

Reginald BRETNOR 1911- (American)
Citation Record: 1 Book
A Killing In Swords - *Single*
Pocket Books US (1978)

TINKER
British Male Amateur operating in England

Edgar JEPSON 1863-1938 (British)
Invented 3 detectives - see Lord BARRADINE
Citation Record: 14 Short Stories in 1 Collection
The Triumph Of Tinker - *Collection 1*
Not all the stories are criminous.
Hodder & Stoughton UK (1906)

Insp TINKLER
British Policeman operating in England

Fergus HUME 1859-1932 (British)
Invented 24 detectives - see Insp Samuel GORBY
Citation Record: 1 Book
The Bishop's Secret - *Only*
Long UK (1900)
Bishop Pendle; Or, The Bishop's Secret - *Only**
Random House US (1900)

Insp Tarrant TINKLER
Second detective of Richard SILVER

Lord TINTAGEL and Lady 'Ginger' TINTAGEL
British Male Amateur and British Female Amateur operating in England

F DRACO 1904- (British)
Writer: Julia DAVIS
Citation Record: 2 Books
The Devil's Church - *First*
Rinehart US (1951)
Cruise With Death - *Last*
Rinehart US (1952)

Lady 'Ginger' TINTAGEL
Second detective of Lord TINTAGEL

Maj Adrian TITTERTON
British Male Amateur operating in England

Edward BROWN (British)
Citation Record: 2 Books
A Penny To Spend - *First*
Harrap UK (1966)
Vandersley - *Last*
Harrap UK (1967)

Nicky TITUS
Second detective of Sheriff Sam TITUS

Sheriff Sam TITUS and Nicky TITUS
The sheriff and his photographer wife sleuth together.
American Policeman and American Female Amateur operating in Oklahoma

Eve K SANDSTROM (American)
Citation Record: 4 Books
Death Down Home - *First*
Scribner's US (1990)
The Down Home Heifer Heist - *Latest*
Scribner's US (1993)

TOBIN
is a short man and perhaps that makes him the short-tempered movie critic he is. He solves two cases of murder, both classically constructed. The first is that of his TV partner and the second is a death aboard ship.
American Male Amateur operating in New York/on a ship

Ed GORMAN 1941- (American)
Invented 4 detectives - see Leo GUILD
Citation Record: 2 Books
Murder On The Aisle - *First*
St Martin's US (1987)
Several Deaths Later - *Latest*
St Martin's US (1988)

Insp TOBIN
American Policeman operating in New York

Dorothy B HUGHES 1904- (American)
was born in Kansas City, Missouri. She was educated at the University of Missouri, Columbia, the University of New Mexico, Albuquerque, and Columbia University, New York, taking degrees in Journalism. She has been a reporter and is a highly esteemed critic and reviewer of books in the crime genre, for which work she received a Mystery Writers of America Edgar Allan Poe award, 1950. She received their Grand Master award, 1978.
Writer: Dorothy Belle Flanagan HUGHES
Other Detectives:
Hugh DENSMORE
Sherlock HOLMES
Det Brub NICOLAI
Citation Record: 3 Books
The So Blue Marble - *First*
Duell US (1940); Bantam UK (1979)
The Fallen Sparrow - *Last*
Duell US (1942); Nicholson & Watson UK (1948)

Art TOBIN
Second detective of E L OXMAN

Matthew TOBIN
American Male Sleuth operating in Middle East

Alan CAILLOU 1914- (American)
was born in Redhill, Surrey, England, and became a naturalised American citizen, 1978. He served in the British Army, 1939-1941, and in the Intelligence Corps, 1941-1945. He saw action all over Europe and was awarded the Military Cross and made an MBE. Later he served in the Colonial Police forces in various parts of the Middle East and Africa. After

1952 he worked as an actor and interpreter and began to write. He is the author of romantic novels, screenplays, documentaries, theatrical histories and about twenty detective novels. He received the Mystery Writers of America Edgar Allan Poe award, 1970.

Writer: Allan LYLE-SMYTHE

Other Byline: Alex WEBB

Other Detectives:
Mike BENASQUE
Cabot CAIN
Ian QUAYLE

Citation Record: 6 Books

Dead Sea Submarine - *First*
Pinnacle US (1971)

The Garonsky Missile - *Latest*
Pinnacle US (1976)

Mitch TOBIN

was dismissed from the New York Police Department for causing the death of his police partner. Unlicensed in the first books, he operates as a detective to help the weak and deviant around him. In later books he has recovered and become a licensed shamus.

American Male Private Detective operating in New York

Tucker COE 1933- (American)

For writer details see Tim SMITH

Citation Record: 5 Books

Kinds Of Love, Kinds Of Death - *First*
Random House US (1966); Souvenir UK (1967)

Don't Lie To Me - *Last*
Random House US (1972); Gollancz UK (1974)

Dr Quentin TOBY

American Male Amateur operating in Miami

Sturges Mason SCHLEY (American)

was born in New York City.

Citation Record: 2 Books

Dr Toby Finds Murder - *First*
Random House US (1941)

Dream Sinister - *Last*
Morrow US (1950)

The Starry-Eyed Chipmunk - *Last**
Gollancz UK (1951)

Insp TODD

British Policeman operating in England

John HALSTEAD (British)

Citation Record: 3 Books

The Black Templar - *First*
Paul UK (1934)

The Black Hate - *Last*
Paul UK (1937)

Charles TODD

British Male Amateur operating in England

Dick FRANCIS 1920- (British)

Invented 18 detectives - see Sid HALLEY

Citation Record: 1 Book

In The Frame - *Single*
Joseph UK (1976); Harper & Row US (1977)

Fraser TODD

British Male Amateur operating in England

H Llewellyn JONES 1890- (British)

Writer: Henry David Llewellyn JONES

Citation Record: 2 Books

Under The Shadow - *First*
Hamilton UK (1928)

The Case Is Altered - *Last*
Hamilton UK (1929)

Irving TODD

British Male Amateur operating in England

Philip CONDE (British)

Invented 3 detectives - see Dick PEMBERTY

Citation Record: 6 Books

Murder In The Cockpit - *First*
Wright UK (1936)

Murder At 10,000 Feet - *Last*
Wright UK (1938)

Jerry TODD

is a fast mover when it comes to end-of-book solutions.

American Male Private Detective operating in Chicago

Sidekick: Mary CLERKENWELL

American Female - Assistant

Martin J FREEMAN 1899- (American)

Writer: Martin Joseph FREEMAN

Inventor of one other detective Judo MARRIOTT

Citation Record: 2 Books

The Case Of The Blind Mouse - *First*
Dutton US (1935); Eldon UK (1936)

The Scarf On The Scarecrow - *Last*
Dutton US (1938)

Jerry TODD

appeared in juvenile pulp series.

American Male Detective in Pulp Magazines operating in USA

Leo EDWARDS (American)

No citations

Alice TOKLAS

Second detective of Gertrude STEIN

TOKLEY

British Policeman operating in London

Tom GALLON 1866-1914 (British)

Invented 3 detectives - see Enoch VOYCE

Citation Record: 1 Book

The Second Dandy Chater - *Only*
Hutchinson UK (1901)

Nick TOLAND

American Male Amateur operating in Boston

William L STORY (American)

Citation Record: 2 Books

Cemeteries Are For Dying - *First*
Doubleday US (1982)

Final Thesis - *Latest*
St Martin's US (1989)

Philip TOLEFREE

toils through a large number of cases, for the most part conventional period whodunnits and mainly involving financial crimes.

British Male Private Detective operating in London

R A J WALLING 1869-1949 (British)

is a journalist and newspaper editor.

Writer: Robert Alfred John WALLING

Other Detectives:
GARSTANG
Prof LAXTON

Citation Record: 21 Books

The Fatal Five Minutes - *First*
Hodder & Stoughton UK (1932); Morrow US (1932)

The Corpse With The Missing Watch - *Last*
Morrow US (1949)

Mr TOLEPAT

is a retired tallow-melter (surely the only one in the whole of detective fiction!) who is the sleuth in this one Victorian novel.

British Male Amateur operating in England

ANON

Citation Record: 1 Book

On Her Majesty's Secret Service - *Only*
is not in the British Library apparently.
Maxwell UK (1878)

Mr Samuel TOLLIVER
American Male Amateur operating in New York

William WIEGAND 1928- (American)
Writer: William George WIEGAND
Citation Record: 1 Book
At Last, Mr Tolliver - *Only*
Rinehart US (1950); Hodder & Stoughton UK (1951)

TOM and JERRY
American Male Detectives in Pulp Magazines operating in USA

Tony PASTOR 1837-1898 (American)
Invented 4 detectives - see O'Neil MCDARRAGH
Citation Record: 1 Book
Tom And Jerry; Or, The Double Detectives - *Only*
Street & Smith US (1889)

Morlock TOMES
is a *Sherlock HOLMES* parody. He is also, it would appear, an ingenious parody of an earlier parody; for, almost a century earlier, *Louis ZANGWILL* had already parodied the sage of Baker Street with his invention of *Mr WARLOCK-JONES* (qv). Even the title and the plot of *LOCKE's* story are obvious parodies of *ZANGWILL's* novel.
British Male Professional Amateur operating in London

George LOCKE
Citation Record: 2 Selected Short Stories
A Nineteenth Century Debacle - *Parody 1*
is in the anthologies, *The Art of the Impossible* (*Xanadu*; UK 1990) and *Murder Impossible* (*Carroll*; US 1990).
Ferret Fantasy UK (1979)
The Channel Tunnel Mystery - *Parody 2*
Ferret Fantasy UK (1990)

Tommy TOMPKINS
British Male Amateur operating in England

Frank BRANSTON 1939- (British)
Citation Record: 2 Books
An Up And Coming Man - *First*
Deutsch UK (1977); St Martin's US (1977)
Sergeant Ritchie's Conscience - *Latest*
Deutsch UK (1978); St Martin's US (1978)

Det Sgt Pietro TONELLI
American Policeman operating in New York

Alexander WILLIAMS 1894-1952 (American)
Writer: Alexander Hazard WILLIAMS
Citation Record: 3 Books
Death Over Newark - *First*
Payson UK (1933)
Murder In The WPA - *Last*
McBride US (1937)

Sheerback TONES
is a *Sherlock HOLMES* parody.
Male Professional Amateur
Sidekick: Dr BOPSON
is his parody *WATSON*-like assistant.
Male - Assistant

Jerry Neal WILLIAMSON (American)
Other Detectives:
Sherlock HOLMES
Sure-They-Lock HOMEZ
Citation Record: 2 Selected Short Stories
The Adventure Of The Bugged Bird - *Parody 1*
In 'Baker Street Journal' US (1960)
Bopping It In Bohemia; Or, Sheerback Tones In Basin Street - *Parody 2*
In 'Ellery Queen's Mystery Magazine' US (1961)

Harry TONG
British Male Amateur operating in England

Eric BURGESS 1912- (British)
Writer: Eric Alexander BURGESS
Citation Record: 4 Books
A Killing Frost - *First*
Collins UK (1961)
Exit Pretty Poll - *Last*
Hale UK (1968)

Det Gypsy TONNELLI
Second detective of Det Max PRIMA

Dr John TONNEMAN
is of Dutch extraction and practises in the New York of 1775. He is caught up in serial killings and plots to assassinate George Washington.
American Male Amateur operating in New York

Maan MEYERS (American)
Writers: Annette Brafman MEYERS 1934- and Martin MEYERS
Citation Record: 1 Book
The Kingsbridge Plot - *Single*
Bantam US (1994)

Lt TOOMEY
American Policeman operating in New York
Sidekick: Sgt RIZZUTO
American Male - Subordinate

Barbara PAUL (American)
Writer: Barbara OVSTEDAL
Other Detectives:
Enrico CARUSO
Enrico CARUSO and Geraldine FERRAR
Gillian CLIFFORD
Abby JAMES
Sgt Marian LARCH
Lt Janus MURTAUGH
Henrietta SNOOKS and Gus BILINSKI
Citation Record: 1 Book
But He Was Already Dead When I Got There - *Single*
Collins UK (1986)

Insp TOPE
American Policeman operating in USA

Ben Ames WILLIAMS 1889-1953 (American)
Citation Record: 2 Books
Death On Scurvy Street - *First*
Dutton US (1929)
The Bellmer Mystery - *First**
Paul UK (1930)
Money Musk - *Last*
Dutton US (1932)
Lady In Peril - *Last**
Popular Library US (1948)

Edward TOPE
British Male Amateur operating in England

Howard Charles DAVIS 1909- (British)
See main detective Hugh RUDD
Citation Record: 2 Books
Trouble In The Bank - *First*
Ward, Lock UK (1960)
The Tortured Boy - *Last*
Ward, Lock UK (1961)

Mr TOPHAM
British Male Amateur operating in England

C Ranger GULL 1876-1923 (British)
Writer: Cyril Arthur Edward GULL
Citation Record: 8 Short Stories in 1 Collection
The Adventures Of Mr Topham, Comedian - *Collection 1*
Greening UK (1903)

Kingsley TOPLITT and Sally TOPLITT

are one of those bright, witty husband-and-wife teams of the 1930s.

American Male Private Detective and American Female Private Detective operating in New York

Gail STOCKWELL (American)

Writer: Grace STOCKWELL

Citation Record: 2 Books

Death By Invitation - *First*
Macmillan US (1937)

The Embarrassed Murderer - *Last*
Macmillan US (1938); Lane UK (1938)

Sally TOPLITT

Second detective of Kingsley TOPLITT

TOPPIN

is a Scotland Yard representative at the French *Sûreté* in this one Victorian novel.

British Policeman operating in Paris

H F WOOD (British)

See main detective Insp George BYDE

Citation Record: 1 Book

The Englishman Of The Rue Cain - *Only*
Chatto & Windus UK (1889)

Capt Andrew TORRENT

American Policeman operating in New York

Lucy CORES 1914- (American)

Writer: Lucy Michaela CORES

Citation Record: 2 Books

Painted For The Kill - *First*
!See Appendix 2.
Duell US (1943); Cassell UK (1946)

Corpse De Ballet - *Last*
Duell US (1944); Cassell UK (1948)

Miranda TORRES

American Policewoman operating in USA

Dorothy UHNAK 1933- (American)

Invented 3 detectives - see Policewoman Christie OPARA

Citation Record: 1 Book

Victims - *Single*
Simon & Schuster US (1986); Century UK (1986)

Dick TORREYTON

British Male Amateur operating in England

Ernest F CHARLES (British)

Citation Record: 3 Books

Death Crosses The Line - *First*
Nelson UK (1937)

Death Comes Ashore - *Last*
Nelson UK (1938)

Mr TORRY

British Policeman operating in London

Fergus HUME 1859-1932 (British)

Invented 24 detectives - see Insp Samuel GORBY

Citation Record: 1 Book

The Red-Headed Man - *Only*
Digby, Long UK (1899)

Derek TORRY

is of Italian extraction, American-trained, and now with Scotland Yard. A tough cop with religious problems, he has continuous feelings of guilt about his non-marital sexual activities, which do not, however, seem to prevent him solving difficult cases.
!See Appendix 2.

British Policeman operating in England

John GARDNER 1926- (British)

Invented 5 detectives - see Boysie OAKES

Citation Record: 2 Books

A Complete State Of Death - *First*
Cape UK (1969); Viking US (1969)

The Corner Men - *Last*
Joseph UK (1974); Doubleday US (1976)

The Stone Killer - *Last**
Award US (1973)

Katy TOUCHFEATHER

American Female Amateur operating in Africa

Jimmy SANGSTER 1927- (British)

Invented 3 detectives - see James REED

Citation Record: 2 Books

Touchfeather - *First*
Triton UK (1968); Norton US (1968)

Touchfeather, Too - *Last*
Triton UK (1970); Norton US (1970)

Insp Broderick TOURNEUR

is a parody of *Ngaio MARSH's* detective, *Insp Roderick ALLEYN.*

Appears with at least two other detectives - see Mallory KING

Daisy TOWER

is nearing the age of seventy but is still able to run around town in her quest to solve a murder that occurred on a train.

American Female Amateur operating in New York

Freeman DANA 1909-1976 (American)

Writer: Phoebe Atwood TAYLOR

Other Byline: Alice TILTON

Citation Record: 1 Book

Murder At The New York World's Fair - *Only*
Random House US (1938)

Hugo TOWER

Second detective of Oliver GALT

Supt Robert TOWNLEY and Sgt Roger NEWMAN

British Policemen operating in England

Brian BEARSHAW (British)

Citation Record: 2 Books

The Day Of Murder - *First*
Hale UK (1978)

Practice Makes Murder - *Latest*
Hale UK (1979)

Insp TOWNSEND

solves a case of 'impossible' murder by strangulation.

British Policeman operating in England

Fred M WHITE 1859- (British)

See main detective James TRENT

Citation Record: 1 Book

The Cardinal Moth - *Only*
Ward, Lock UK (1905)

Katie MacGregor TOWNSEND

American Female Amateur operating in New York

David E FISHER 1932- (American)

See main detective Henry GRACE

Citation Record: 1 Book

Katie's Terror - *Single*
Morrow US (1982)

Schuyler TOWNSEND

American Male Sleuth Operating in USA

Fritz GORDON (American)

Writers: Frederick Gordon JARVIS Jr 1930- and Robert F VAN BEEVER

Citation Record: 2 Books

The Flight Of The Bamboo Saucer - *First*
Award US (1967)

Tonight They Die To Mendelssohn - *Last*
Award US (1968)

Sheriff TOWNSEND and Susan EYERLY

When the president of Larkin College, a fictional co-ed establishment, is stabbed to death, the local law in the shape of *Sheriff TOWNSEND* is called in; but, to solve the case, he needs the assistance of *Susan EVERLEY*, the college's publicity director.

American Policeman and American Female Amateur operating in Midwest USA

Carolyn THOMAS 1913- (American)

Writer: Actea Caroline DUNCAN

Citation Record: 1 Book

Prominent Among The Mourners - *Only*
Lippincott US (1946); Cherry Tree UK (1949)

Mr TOWNSHEND

is a private detective operating from rooms in London's fashionable Jermyn Street.

British Male Private Detective operating in London

J MacLaren COBBAN 1849-1903 (British)

Writer: James MacLaren COBBAN

Citation Record: 3 Books

Pursued By The Law - *First*
Long UK (1899); Appleton US (1899)

The Terror By Night - *Last*
Long UK (1905)

Bow Street Runner TOWNSHEND

British Policeman operating in London

James PAYN 1830-1898 (British)

See main detective Charles STEEN

Citation Record: 1 Book

Lost Sir Massingberd: A Romance Of Real Life - *Only*
Sampson, Low UK (1890)

Mike TOZZI and Bert GIBBONS

are operators for the FBI.

American Male Sleuths operating in New York

Anthony BRUNO (American)

Citation Record: 5 Books

Bad Guys - *First*
Putnam US (1988); Bantam UK (1989)

Bad Luck - *Latest*
Delacorte US (1994)

John TRACER

is a laid-off executive who, with a family to support and a large mortgage, sets up as a PI in Carmel City. A novice and inept besides, he struggles manfully and comically through his first case.

American Male Private Detective operating in California

Jeff ANDRUS (American)

Citation Record: 1 Book

Tracer Inc - *Single*
Scribner's US (1994)

Kay TRACEY

was an American schoolgirl detective appearing in magazine stories during the inter-war years.

American Female Amateur operating in USA

Frances K JUDD (American)

No citations

Martin TRACK

was a boys' detective who appeared in the pages of *Dreadnought* around 1912. Unlike others of his sort, who were content with rooms in London's City or West End, he was rather keener on personal comfort and safety, preferring to live in a barbaric palace, built on a pinnacle overlooking the North Sea. Not unreasonably, he surrounded the place with a wall a mile in circumference that had no visible entrance. Important visitors to the great man would, very properly, be met by a Chinese dwarf dressed as a monk (strange, but then again, why not?) who would blindfold them and escort them in. The less important might be netted or picked up by claws and dropped down a chute.

Martin TRACK lived in gothic luxury, surrounded by all the bizarre paraphernalia that the authors could devise. He had a formidable armoury at his disposal, for he was in incessant conflict with syndicates of arch-criminals who, for no very clear reason, seemed intent on his destruction. Mad fools, of course, for they faced 'enforced repentance' and were never seen again!

British Male Amateur operating in England

Sidekick: GRIP
was, one might think, an odd name for a Chinese dwarf.
Chinese Male - Assistant

ANON

No citations

Nat TRACKER

American Male Amateur operating in several locations

Ron STILLMAN (American)

Citation Record: 2 Books

Tracker - *First*
Charter US (1990)

Green Lightning - *Latest*
Charter US (1990)

Martin TRACKMAN

British Male Amateur operating in England

ANON

Citation Record: 1 Collection

The Cases Of Martin Trackman - *Collection 1*
Amalgamated UK (1938)

Devlin 'Trace' TRACY

appeared in 1983, mysteriously transmogrified from the author's earlier detective, *Julian BURROUGHS*. He appears also in one book with the author's pair of detectives, *Ed RAZONI* and *William JACKSON*.

American Male Private Detective operating in Las Vegas

Warren B MURPHY 1933- (American)

Invented 8 detectives - see Julian 'Digger' BURROUGHS

Citation Record: 7 Books

Trace - *First*
Signet US (1983)

Getting Up With Fleas - *Latest*
Signet US (1987)

Devlin 'Trace' TRACY

Appears with at least two other detectives - see Ed RAZONI

Dick TRACY

is a comic strip character, who has been written about by many authors.

American Male Professional Amateur operating in USA

Chester GOULD 1900-1985 (American)

Citation Record: 7 Books

The Exploits Of Dick Tracy, Detective: The Case Of The Brow - *First*
Rosdon UK (1946)

Dick Tracy: The Thirties - Tommy Guns And Hard Times - *Last*
Chelsea US (1978)

William JOHNSTON 1924- (American)

Invented 7 detectives - see John WOODRUFF and Tony NOVELLO

Citation Record: 1 Book

Dick Tracy - *Only*
Tempo UK (1970)

Jerry TRACY and Insp FITZGERALD

Jerry TRACY, a Broadway columnist, solves murders with the co-operation of *Insp FITZGERALD* of the New York Police Department. They appeared together in short stories in *Black Mask Magazine.*

American Male Amateur and American Policeman operating in New York

Theodore TINSLEY 1934- (American)

Invented 3 detectives - see Carrie CASHIN

No citations

John TRACY

British Male Amateur operating in New Guinea

Trevor WALLACE (British)

Citation Record: 4 Books

Galahad Of The Air - *First*
Wright UK (1937)

Cargo For Death - *Last*
Wright UK (1938)

Insp Noel TRACY

British Policeman operating in England/Los Angeles

Alex FRASER 1901- (British)

Writer: Henry BRINTON

Citation Record: 3 Books

Constables Don't Count - *First*
Bles UK (1957); Roy US (1960)

Bury Their Dead - *Last*
Bles UK (1959); Roy US (1960)

Philip 'Spike' TRACY

American Male Sleuth operating in New York

H ASHBROOK 1896-1946 (American)

For writer details see Christopher SAXE

Citation Record: 7 Books

The Murder Of Cecily Thane - *First*
Coward McCann US (1930); Eyre & Spottiswoode UK (1930)

The Purple Onion Mystery - *Last*
Coward McCann US (1941); Eyre & Spottiswoode UK (1950)

Murder On Friday - *Last**
Arrow UK (1944)

Sheila TRACY

is a reporter for a paper in fictional Seahaven on the South coast. When a colleague is found dead at the foot of a cliff, she investigates and discovers the truth, which is indeed tragic.

British Female Amateur operating in England

Margaret HINXMAN (British)

was a former film critic for British newspapers.

Citation Record: 1 Book

The Boy From Nowhere - *Single*
Collins UK (1985)

T

Rick TRAIN

American Male Sleuth operating in New York

Bruno FISCHER 1908- (American)

See main detective Ben HELM

Citation Record: 2 Books

The Hornet's Nest - *First*
Morrow US (1944); Quality Press UK (1947)

Kill To Fit - *Last*
Green US (1946); In 'Instructive Arts' UK (1951)

Sam TRAIN

American Male Private Detective operating in San Francisco

Ernest SAVAGE 1918- (American)

was born in Detroit, Michigan. He wrote mainly short stories.

Citation Record: 1 Selected Short Story

Count Me Out
In 'Ellery Queen's Mystery Magazine' US (1978)

Nikki TRAKOS

Female Sleuth operating in USA

Ruby HORANSKY (American)

Citation Record: 2 Books

Dead Ahead - *First*
Piatkus UK (1992)

Dead Centre - *Latest*
Piatkus UK (1993)

Hyacinth TRAMWELL and Primrose TRAMWELL

are two unusually clever English ladies who run the rather select Flowers Detective Agency in the fictional village of Chitterton Fells.

British Female Private Detectives operating in England

Dorothy CANNELL (British)

See main detective Ellie Simons HASKELL

Citation Record: 1 Book

The Widow's Club - *Single*
Bantam UK (1988); Bantam US (1988)

Primrose TRAMWELL

Second detective of Hyacinth TRAMWELL

Luther TRANT

was said to be 'a very early user of Freudian psychology for detection purposes'.

American Male Amateur operating in USA

Edwin BALMER and William MACHARG 1872-1951 (American)

Inventor of one other detective Basil SANTOINE

Citation Record: 9 Short Stories in 1 Collection

The Achievements Of Luther Trant - *Collection 1*
Small, Maynard US (1910)

Lt Timothy TRANT

was educated at Princeton. A model of sartorial elegance, he is certainly no slouch when it comes to detection. He appears in books under two of the authors' pseudonyms and also appears in a book with another of their detectives.

American Policeman operating in New York

Q PATRICK 1901- (American)

Writer: Richard Wilson WEBB

Other Detectives:
Insp BOOT
Insp Martin FIELD
Insp HORROCKS and Hilary FENTON
Insp Archibald INGE

Citation Record: 3 Books

Death For Dear Clara - *First*
Simon & Schuster US (1937); Cassell UK (1937)

Death And The Maiden - *Last*
Simon & Schuster US (1939); Cassell UK (1939)

Patrick QUENTIN (American)

Invented 6 detectives - see Peter DULUTH

Citation Record: 3 Books

The Man With Two Wives - *First*
Simon & Schuster US (1955); Gollancz UK (1955)

Family Skeletons - *Last*
Random House US (1965); Gollancz UK (1965)

Lt Timothy TRANT

Second detective of Peter DULUTH

Capt Ralph 'Rat' TRAPP

American Policeman operating in New Orleans

John William CORRINGTON 1932-1988 and Joyce H CORRINGTON (American)

Citation Record: 4 Books

So Small A Carnival - *First*
Viking US (1986); Mysterious Press UK (1987)

The White Zone - *Latest*
Viking US (1990)

Julian TRASK

solves a case of rape that has occurred in a female dormitory.

American Male Sleuth operating in USA

Ray RUSSELL 1924- (American)

Inventor of one other detective FOAMES

Citation Record: 1 Book

Incubus - *Single*
Morrow US (1976); Sphere Books UK (1977)

Mason TRASK

is a newspaperman who seeks out the murderers of his policeman brother.

American Male Amateur operating in New York

Hugh PENTECOST 1903-1989 (American)

Invented 12 detectives - see Pierre CHAMBRUN

Citation Record: 1 Book

The Kingdom Of Death - *Only*
Dodd, Mead US (1960); Boardman UK (1961)

Moroni TRAVELER

operates among the Mormon community of Salt Lake City, where he encounters cases of murder, which are often engendered by its customs and laws.

American Male Private Detective operating in Salt Lake City

Sidekick: Martin TRAVELER

American Male - Father

Robert IRVINE 1936- (American)

For writer details see Bob CHRISTOPHER

Citation Record: 4 Books

Baptism For The Dead - *First*
Dodd, Mead US (1988)

The Hosanna Shout - *Latest*
St Martin's US (1994)

Terry TRAVEN

is a strange figure. His addiction to old detective stories induces him to join the Los Angeles Police Department, with the aim of eventually getting a PI licence. He then acts like a hardboiled sleuth of the 1940s.

American Male Private Detective operating in Los Angeles

Geoffrey MILLER 1945- (American)

Writer: Geoffrey Samuel MILLER

Citation Record: 1 Book

The Black Glove - *Single*
Viking US (1981)

Felicity TRAVERS

is a lecturer at a polytechnic and notices that some of her students are missing. Accident-prone though she is, she sets out (mistakenly, it transpires) to investigate. And as she so delightfully, if non-syntactically, says, 'They don't call me Sherlock Holmes for nothing, and with good reason'. They don't, indeed!

British Female Amateur operating in England

Barbara LEIGHTON (British)

Citation Record: 1 Book

A Little Learning - *Single*
Quartet UK (1988)

Insp George TRAVERS

British Policeman operating in England

Pamela BARRINGTON 1904- (British)

Invented 3 detectives - see Insp George MARSHALL

Citation Record: 3 Books

The Mortimer Story - *First*
Barker UK (1952)

The Gentle Killer - *Last*
Hammond UK (1961)

Ludovic TRAVERS

is, apart from his detective skills, to be honoured as an extraordinary literary achievement, for he appeared first in 1926 and continued through sixty-three novels until 1968. He is a writer with private means and is the nephew of the Assistant Commissioner at the Yard, both of which assets make him well qualified to be a classical amateur detective of the British Golden Age and beyond. The ramifications of his career and of the characters in the books are, naturally, extensive. During the Second World War he is involved in cases in France, and after the war he starts the Broad Street Detective Agency in London. The cases are often elaborately involved and the detection sometimes excellent.

British Male Professional Amateur operating in England

Christopher BUSH 1885-1973 (British)

was born in East Anglia. He served in the Army in the First World War and as a Major in the Second World War. He was a schoolmaster before becoming a full-time writer.

Writer: Charlie Christmas BUSH

Other Byline: Michael HOME

Citation Record: 63 Books

The Plumley Inheritance - *First*
Jarrolds UK (1926)

The Case Of The Prodigal Daughter - *Last*
Macdonald UK (1968); Macmillan US (1968)

Mark TRAVERS

American Male Amateur operating in USA

Martha ALBRAND 1914-1981 (American)

was born in Rostock, Germany and went to the USA, 1937, becoming a naturalised citizen, 1947. She wrote several novels of espionage and detection.

Writer: Heidi Huberta FREYBE

Citation Record: 1 Book

A Day In Monte Carlo - *Only*
Random House US (1959); Hodder & Stoughton UK (1959)

Melanie TRAVIS

solves a case of murder and dog-stealing – not necessarily regarded, by this fictional doggy fraternity, as in that order of importance – in the dog-eat-dog world of championship breeding.

American Female Amateur operating in USA

Laurien BERENSON (American)

Citation Record: 1 Book

A Pedigree To Die For - *Single*
Kensington US (1995)

Norman TRAVIS

solves a case of murder on the campus.

American Male Amateur operating in USA

Hugh HOLMAN 1914-1981 (American)

See main detective Sheriff MACREADY

Citation Record: 1 Book

Death Like Thunder - *Only*
Phoenix Press US (1942)

Sheila TRAVIS

American Female Amateur operating in Georgia

Patricia Houck SPRINKLE (American)

Citation Record: 4 Books

Murder At Markham - *First*
St Martin's US (1988)

Death Of A Dunwoody Matron - *Latest*
Bantam US (1994); St Martin's US (1994)

Whit TRAXLER

Second detective of Brady RUSKIN

Pat TRAYMORE

is a TV journalist who digs into political shenanigans at the highest level.

American Female Amateur operating in Washington DC

Mary Higgins CLARK 1931- (American)

Invented 3 detectives - see Katie DEMAIO

Citation Record: 1 Book

Stillwatch - *Single*
Simon & Schuster US (1984); Collins UK (1984)

Insp TREADGOLD

British Policeman operating in England

Anthony WEYMOUTH 1887- (British)

Writer: Ivor Geikie COBB
!See Appendix 2.

Citation Record: 6 Books 14 Short Stories in 1 Collection

Frozen Death - *First*
Barker UK (1934)

Cornish Crime - *Last*
Hodder & Stoughton UK (1937)

Inspector Treadgold Investigates - *Collection 1*
Rich UK (1941)

Mr Horace B TREADGOLD

is a London tailor who does amateur detective work not only in London but, surprisingly in one book, in Canada.

British Male Amateur operating in England/Canada

Valentine WILLIAMS 1883-1946 (British)

Invented 8 detectives - see Det Sgt Trevor DENE

Citation Record: 2 Books 10 Short Stories in 1 Collection

Dead Man Manor - *First*
Hodder & Stoughton UK (1937); Houghton US (1936)

Skeleton Out Of The Cupboard - *Last*
Hodder & Stoughton UK (1946)

The Curiosity Of Mr Treadgold - *Last**
Houghton US (1937)

Mr Treadgold Cuts In - *Collection 1*
Hodder & Stoughton UK (1937)

Mark TREASURE

is a merchant banker, vice-Chairman of a renowned City firm, and comes from a wealthy family himself. He is sent by the bank into a variety of adventures to seek out the many criminals operating in the world of finance. In one of his books he finds himself in a curious detecting trio with a *Maj COPPER* and an ex-cab driver called *Benny GOLD.*

British Male Amateur operating in several locations

Sidekick: Molly TREASURE
is, in some books, the soundboard for *TREASURE's* thoughts and she reports his cases.
British Female - Wife

T

David WILLIAMS 1926- (British)

was born in Bridgend, Glamorganshire. He was educated at Cathedral School, Hereford, and took a BA at St John's College, Oxford, 1948, followed by an MA, 1953. Since then he has been a senior figure in the business world of London.

Inventor of one other detective group Mark TREASURE, Maj COPPER and Benny GOLD

Citation Record: 13 Books

Unholy Writ - *First*
Collins UK (1976); St Martin's US (1977)

Prescription For Murder - *Latest*
Macmillan UK (1990); St Martin's US (1990)

Mark TREASURE, Maj COPPER and Benny GOLD

British Male Amateurs operating in England

David WILLIAMS 1926- (British)

See main detective Mark TREASURE

Citation Record: 1 Book

Copper, Gold And Treasure - *Single*
Collins UK (1982)

Angeline TREDENNICK

American Female Amateur operating in Maine

Ruth Burr SANBORN 1894-1942 (American)

Citation Record: 2 Books

Murder By Jury - *First*
Little, Brown US (1932); Jarrolds UK (1933)

Murder On The Aphrodite - *Last*
Macmillan US (1935); Jarrolds UK (1936)

Don TREE

was one of this author's numerous pulp detectives and appeared in short stories.

American Male Detective in Pulp Magazines operating in USA

Ramon DECOLTA 1898-1945 (American)

Invented 5 detectives - see Dion DAVIES

No citations

Peter TREES

American Male Amateur operating in USA

John Q 1920- (American)

Writer: John Edward QUIRK

Citation Record: 3 Books

The Bunnies - *First*
Avon UK (1965)

The Tournament - *Last*
Signet UK (1966)

Jane TREGAR

works for a large head-hunting firm. When a senior executive is found dead in a locked computer room, she knows it is one of the staff of five who did the foul deed and decides to find out which one.

Canadian Female Amateur operating in Toronto

Ellen GODFREY 1942- (Canadian)

Citation Record: 1 Book

Murder Behind Locked Doors - *Single*
St Martin's US (1988); Virago UK (1989)

Sarah TREGARON

tracks the killer of her husband in England and then in Africa, although the police think his death was accidental.

British Female Amateur operating in England/Africa

Phyllida BARSTOW 1937- (British)

Citation Record: 1 Book

Night Is For Hunting - *Single*
Century UK (1982)

Richard TREGENNA

British Male Amateur operating in Edinburgh

Riccardo STEPHENS (British)

Citation Record: 1 Book

The Cruciform Mark: The Strange Story Of Richard Tregenna, Bachelor Of Medicine - *Only*
Chatto & Windus UK (1896)

Sydney TREHERNE

American Male Amateur operating in New York

Madelon ST DENNIS (American)

Citation Record: 2 Books

The Death Kiss - *First*
Fiction League US (1932)

The Perfumed Lure - *Last*
Clode US (1932)

TRELAWNEY

British Male Amateur operating in England

Antony MELVILLE-ROSS (British)

Citation Record: 2 Books

Blindfold - *First*
Collins UK (1978); Harper & Row US (1978)

Two Faces Of Nemesis - *Latest*
Collins UK (1979)

Edward TRELAWNEY

Second detective of Katherine 'Peter' PIPER

Edward TRELAWNY

appears also in one book with another of the author's detectives, *Katherine 'Peter' PIPER.*

American Male Amateur operating in Philadelphia

Amelia Reynolds LONG 1904-1978 (American)

Invented 4 detectives - see Katherine 'Peter' PIPER

Citation Record: 5 Books

The Shakespeare Murders - *First*
Phoenix Press US (1939); Grafton UK (1945)

Symphony In Murder - *Last*
Ziff-Davis US (1944); Quality Press UK (1953)

John Q TRELAWNY

British Male Sleuth operating in Germany

George GOODCHILD 1888-1969 (British)

Invented 5 detectives - see Insp MCLEAN

Citation Record: 3 Books

Q33 - *First*
Odhams UK (1933)

Q33 - Spy Catcher - *Last*
Newnes UK (1937)

Rev Septimus TRELOAR

British Male Amateur operating in England

Stephen CHANCE 1925- (British)

Writer: Philip William TURNER

Citation Record: 4 Books

Septimus And The Danedyke Mystery - *First*
Bodley Head UK (1971); Nelson US (1973)

Septimus And The Spy Ring - *Latest*
Bodley Head UK (1979)

Mordecai Euripides TREMAINE

British Male Amateur operating in England

Francis DUNCAN (British)

Inventor of one other detective Peter JUSTICE

Citation Record: 6 Books

They'll Never Find Out - *First*
Jenkins UK (1944)

Behold A Fair Woman - *Last*
Long UK (1954)

Det Insp Charles TREMAYNE

British Policeman operating in England

Nigel MACKENZIE (British)

Citation Record: 3 Books

Killer At Large - *First*
Wright UK (1961)

Night Of Fear - *Last*
Wright UK (1964)

Betty TRENKA

is a retired businesswoman who takes a job typing memoirs, yet has her heart set on sleuthing when she meets murder.

American Female Amateur operating in USA

Joyce CHRISTMAS (American)

See main detective Lady Margaret PRIAM

Citation Record: 2 Books

This Business Is Murder - *First*
GM US (1993)

Death At Face Value - *Latest*
GM US (1995)

Anthony TRENT

Male Amateur operating in New York/Maine

Wyndham MARTYN 1875- (British)

Invented 3 detectives - see Prof John SOUTHARD

Citation Record: 23 Books 1 Collection

Trent Of The Lone Hand - *First*
Jenkins UK (1927)

Manhunt In Murder - *Last*
Jenkins UK (1950); Roy US (1958)

Anthony Trent, Master Criminal - *Collection 1*
Moffat US (1918); Jenkins UK (1922)

Gregory TRENT

American Male Amateur operating in Missouri

Adele SEIFERT 1889-1971 (American)

Citation Record: 3 Books

Shadows Tonight - *First*
Mill US (1939); Boardman UK (1943)

3 Blind Mice - *Last*
Mill US (1942); Boardman UK (1945)

James TRENT

solves a case of death by stabbing in a guarded room.

British Male Amateur operating in England

Fred M WHITE 1859- (British)

Writer: Frederick Merrick WHITE

Inventor of one other detective Insp TOWNSEND

Citation Record: 1 Book

Who Killed James Trent? - *Only*
Pearson UK (1901)

Marla TRENT

is blonde, was very nearly a Miss America, is a brilliant graduate of Columbia, has a doctorate in abnormal psychology, was married to the Chief of Homicide in the New York Police Department, and has an office on Madison Avenue. If one needed to hire a detective, could one do better? Criminals beware! Absurd, of course, but she is in this one superbly titled book on her own and in one other with the author's main detective, *Peter CHAMBERS.*

American Female Private Detective operating in New York

Henry KANE 1918- (American)

Invented 4 detectives - see Peter CHAMBERS

Citation Record: 1 Book

The Private Eyeful - *Only*
Pyramid US (1959); Boardman UK (1960)

Marla TRENT

Second detective of PETER CHAMBERS

Philip TRENT

was created by a writer who was already well-known as a journalist and writer of humorous verse, in what was manifestly to be an attempt to expose and parody the conventional detective story of the pre-1914 era. Instead the book, *TRENT'S LAST CASE,* became famous. It has been called the best first detective story ever written and, by some critics, one of the best detective stories ever written.

Philip TRENT is a young artist who is retained by a London newspaper to investigate the murder of a wealthy financier. Instead of solving the case, however, he falls for the widow. To make matters worse, his two consecutive and ingenious solutions are both shown to be wrong. This was an extraordinary precedent; for, until then, it was virtually axiomatic that the amateur sleuth should solve the case. *TRENT* is, nevertheless, one of the earliest examples of what was to become the stereotype of the amateur detective of the Golden Age and beyond – explicitly upper-middle class and not so poor that he might be suspected of working for a living, well educated, and speaking in an extraordinary kind of infantile, but apparently clever, banter. He re-appeared, by popular request, twenty-three years later, in a second novel (written with a collaborator) and again, a little later, in a collection of short stories. The impact of the first book was, it almost goes without saying, not repeated in the sequel. It is interesting to record that the author originally called his detective 'Philip Gasket'. Fortunately for posterity, the American publishers suggested that the name might prove unattractive.

British Male Amateur operating in England

E C BENTLEY 1875-1956 (British)

was born in London, England. He was educated at St Paul's School, London, and took a BA degree at Merton College, Oxford, 1898. He studied Law and was called to the Bar in 1902. A well-known barrister, he was also a highly regarded writer in several genres, becoming famed eternally for his invention of the Clerihew, an unusual four-line verse form, usually comic in nature, which is now named after him. In the criminous genre his output was meagre, yet he is renowned as the author of one of the great, seminal detective novels, which more or less set the classic British Golden Age on its course. When, over twenty years later, he tried to repeat its success, it was with the aid of *Herbert WarnerALLEN.*

Writer: Edmund Clerihew BENTLEY

Inventor of one other detective Lord Peter WIMSEY

Citation Record: 1 Book 12 Short Stories in 1 Collection

Trent's Last Case - *Only*

is one of the best and most famous detective stories of all time. It has been reprinted many times and has been the basis of three film versions. It has the honour, according to some critics, of being the first full-length novel to have been totally conceived as a detective story. *THE MOONSTONE* is essentially a Victorian romantic novel, in which detection is an important element, and *Sir Arthur Conan DOYLE* barely managed the full-length form with *THE HOUND OF THE BASKERVILLES.*

Nelson UK (1913)

The Woman In Black - *Only**

was originally published in the US under the title cited, but it was reissued by *Knopf* (US and UK) under its original UK title and has since then has always been known by that title.

Century US (1913)

Trent Intervenes - *Collection 1*

Nelson UK (1938); Knopf US (1938)

E C BENTLEY and Warner ALLEN (British)

collaborated on the eventual but long-delayed sequel to *TRENT'S LAST CASE.* Like nearly all such attempts, it did not reach the quality of its predecessor.

Writers: Edmund Clerihew BENTLEY 1875-1956 and Herbert Warner ALLEN 1881-1969

Citation Record: 1 Book

Trent's Own Case - *Only*

Constable UK (1936); Knopf US (1936)

Rick TRENT

is an ex-convict who sets up as a PI. He appeared in four stories in *Black Mask Magazine* in the late 1940s.

American Male Detective in Pulp Magazines operating in USA

Norman DANIELS (American)

Invented 6 detectives - see Richard Curtis (Phantom) VAN LOAN

No citations

Garaway TRENTON

British Male Sleuth operating in France/Tangiers

John Paddy CARSTAIRS 1910- (British)

Citation Record: 6 Books

Gardenias Bruise Easily - *First*

Allen UK (1958); British Book Centre US (1959)

A Smell Of Peardrops - *Last*

Allen UK (1966)

Hilda TRENTON

American Female Amateur operating in California

Dana LYON 1897-1982 (American)

Writer: Mabel Dana LYON

Inventor of one other detective Jeff MILES

Citation Record: 2 Books

The Tentacles - *First*

Harper & Row US (1950)

Spin The Web Tight - *Last*

Ace US (1963)

Richard TRENTON

British Male Amateur operating in England

Anne BURTON 1922-1985 (British)

For writer details see Antony MAITLAND

Citation Record: 3 Books

The Dear Departed - *First*

Raven CA (1980); Raven US (1980)

Where There's A Will - *Latest*

Raven CA (1980); Raven US (1980)

Insp Perry TRETHOWAN

is a Scotland Yard man. He appears also in other books with the author's other detective, *Charlie PEACE.*

British Policeman operating in England

Robert BARNARD 1936- (British)

was born in Burnham-on-Crouch, Essex. He took a BA at Balliol College, Oxford, 1959, and a PhD at the University of Bergen, Norway, 1972. He has been a lecturer in English at universities in England, Australia, and Norway, and is the author of over twenty detective novels, several short stories, and works of criticism in the thriller and other genres.

Other Detectives:

Insp CROFT
Insp FAGERMO
Greg HOCKING
Helen KITTEREGE
Ch Insp MCHALE
Idwal MEREDITH
Supt Mike ODDIE
Insp PARRISH
Charlie PEACE
Insp Mike PUMFREY
Insp ROYLE
Insp Perry TRETHOWAN and Charlie PEACE

Citation Record: 3 Books

Sheer Torture - *First*

Collins UK (1981)

Death By Sheer Torture - *First**

Scribner's US (1982)

The Missing Brontë - *Latest*

Collins UK (1983)

The Case Of The Missing Brontë - *Latest**

Scribner's US (1983)

Insp Perry TRETHOWAN and Charlie PEACE

also appear individually in other books by this author.

British Policeman and British Male Amateur operating in England

Robert BARNARD 1936- (British)

Invented 13 detectives - see Insp Perry TRETHOWAN

Citation Record: 2 Books

Bodies - *First*

Collins UK (1986); Scribner's US (1986)

Death In Purple Prose - *Latest*

Collins UK (1987)

The Cherry Blossom Corpse - *Latest**

Scribner's US (1987)

Ch Insp Nick TREVELLYAN

British Policeman operating in England

Susan KELLY (British)

Writer: Susan B KELLY

See main detective Det Jack LINGEMANN and Liz CONNORS

Citation Record: 3 Books

Hope Against Hope - *First*
Piatkus UK (1990); Scribner's US (1991)

Kid's Stuff - *Latest*
Scribner's US (1994)

TREVELYAN

Australian Male Amateur operating in Australia

S J STUTLEY and A E COPP (Australian)

Citation Record: 1 Book

The Melbourne Mystery - *Only*
Bodley Head UK (1929)

Mary TREVERT

Appears with at least two other detectives - see Robin GREVE

Sgt TREVOR and Sgt GODBOLD

British Policemen operating in England

Headon HILL 1857-1927 (British)

Invented 11 detectives - see Insp HERON

Citation Record: 1 Book

Caged! The Romance Of A Lunatic Asylum - *Only*
Ward, Lock UK (1900)

Carole TREVOR and Max BLYTHE

Lovely *Carole TREVOR* is given the Old Town Detective Agency by her rich ex-husband, *Max BLYTHE,* who continues to work in it with her.

American Female Private Detective and American Male Private Detective operating in New York

Judson PHILIPS 1903-1989 (American)

Invented 4 detectives - see Peter STYLES

Citation Record: 2 Books

The Death Syndicate - *First*
Washburn US (1938); Hurst UK (1939)

Death Delivers A Postcard - *Last*
Washburn US (1939); Hurst UK (1940)

Jimmy TREYNOR

American Male Amateur operating in Long Island

Armstrong LIVINGSTON 1885- (American)

See main detective Peter CREIGHTON

Citation Record: 5 Books

The Doublecross - *First*
Henkle US (1929); Skeffington UK (1929)

Night Of Crime - *Last*
Sovereign House US (1938)

Det Vincent TRILL

of the 'Detective Service' appeared in a number of short stories by this author. He was the fashionable type of Victorian policeman, then becoming popular.

British Policeman operating in England

Dick DONOVAN 1842-1924 (British)

Invented 7 detectives - see Fabian FIELD

Citation Record: 10 Short Stories in 1 Collection

The Records Of Vincent Trill Of The Detective Service - *Collection 1*
Chatto & Windus UK (1899)

Joe TRIMO

appeared in stories in *Spicy Detective.*

American Male Detective in Pulp Magazines operating in USA

Horton JACQUES (American)

No citations

Edmund TROTHE

British Male Amateur operating in England

Richard LLEWELLYN 1906-1983 (British)

Writer: Richard David Vivian Llewellyn LLOYD

Citation Record: 4 Books

The End Of The Rug - *First*
Joseph UK (1969); Doubleday US (1968)

The Night Is A Child - *Last*
Joseph UK (1974); Doubleday US (1974)

Sgt TROTTER

Second detective of Reggie RUGGLES

Tuddleton TROTTER

American Male Amateur operating in Chicago

Harry Stephen KEELER 1890-1967 and Hazel GOODWIN (American)

Invented 3 detectives - see Angus MACWHORTER

Citation Record: 2 Books

The Matilda Hunter Murder - *First*
Dutton US (1931)

The Black Satchel - *First**
Ward, Lock UK (1931)

The Case Of The Barking Clock - *Last*
Phoenix Press US (1947)

The Barking Clock - *Last**
was a longer version of the US publication.
Ward, Lock UK (1951)

Commiss TROTTI

is a dedicated police officer in an undefined city in northern Italy, where he copes with domestic crime and political corruption, using good police methodology.

Italian Policeman operating in Italy

Sidekick: Sgt PISANELLI
is useful, if aberrant in his behaviour.
Italian Male - Subordinate

Timothy WILLIAMS (British)

was born in London and has had extensive experience as a teacher around the world. His books, to date, have been set in Italy.

Citation Record: 4 Books

Converging Parallels - *First*
Gollancz UK (1982)

The Red Citroen - *First**
St Martin's US (1983)

Black August - *Latest*
Gollancz UK (1993)

Dan TROUT

was often called 'Dumb Dan' because of his soft-heartedness. He appeared in short stories in *Detective Tales* between March 1945 and July 1947.

American Male Private Detective operating in USA

William R COX 1901-1989 (American)

Invented 4 detectives - see Tom KINCAID

Citation Record: 2 Selected Short Stories

See You At Murder Mansion
was the first of the ten stories in which *Dan TROUT* is known to have appeared.
In 'Detective Tales' US (1945)

Whose Body Are You?
was the last of the ten stories in which *Dan TROUT* is known to have appeared.
In 'Detective Tales' US (1947)

Percival TROUT

is the Dean of the Psychology Department at an unnamed American college, where two murders occur. Since he was once in US Army Intelligence and has degrees in almost every subject one could imagine, it is no wonder he is called on by the college president to help the police out of their lamentably baffled state.

American Male Amateur operating in New England

Hans C OWEN (American)

!See Appendix 2.

Citation Record: 1 Book

Ways Of Death - *Only*
Green Circle US (1937)

Fit To Kill - *Only**
Hangman's House US (1946)

Griffith TROWBRIDGE

is a lawyer who sleuths in this one Victorian novel. He precedes the author's classic *Sgt CUFF* by a decade.

British Male Amateur operating in England

Wilkie COLLINS 1824-1889 (British)

Invented 5 detectives - see Sgt CUFF

Citation Record: 1 Book

The Queen Of Hearts - *Only*
Hurst & Blackett UK (1859); Harper & Row US (1859)

Julian Morse TROWBRIDGE

American Male Sleuth operating in USA

Arthur PORGES (American)

Invented 13 detectives - see Arsène LUPIN

Citation Record: 1 Selected Short Story

The Invisible Tomb
appeared in the February number.
In 'Alfred Hitchcock's Mystery Magazine' US (1967)

George Washington TROXELL

is a bibliophile who does some amateur sleuthing.

American Male Amateur operating in USA

Vincent STARRETT 1886-1974 (American)

Invented 6 detectives - see Jimmie LAVENDER

Citation Record: 1 Collection

The Blue Door - *Collection 1*
contains a few stories with this detective.
Doubleday US (1930)

David TROY

British Male Amateur operating in England

Alan GARDNER 1925- (British)

Writer: Alan Harold GARDNER

Citation Record: 4 Books

The Escalator - *First*
Muller UK (1963)

The Man Who Was Too Much - *Last*
Muller UK (1967)

Haila TROY

Second detective of Jeff TROY

T

Jeff TROY and Haila TROY

are another of those husband-and-wife teams going in for fun and detective work, usually in New York and the theatre – in both of which locations, as is well known, cases of great interest to such couples lie thick on the ground. The books are interesting for their portrayal of an era and they are filled with love and romance as well as detection.

American Male Amateur and American Female Amateur operating in New York

Stooge: Lt George HANKINS
may act the friendly cop but he is in competition with the hero and heroine. Of course, he is always wrong.
American Male

Kelley ROOS (American)

Writers: Audrey ROOS 1912-1982 and William ROOS 1911-

Other Detectives:
Steve BARTON and Connie BARTON
Timothy O'HARA and Nancy BREWSTER

Citation Record: 9 Books

Made Up To Kill - *First*
Dodd, Mead US (1940)

Made Up For Murder - *First**
Jarrolds UK (1941)

One False Move - *Last*
Dodd, Mead US (1966)

Trixie TRUE

appears only in a stage play.

American Female Amateur operating in USA

Kelly HAMILTON (American)

was born in San Francisco and has been a writer and producer of musical plays.

Citation Record: 1 Book

Trixie True, Teen Detective - *Play*
French US (1981)

TRUE BLUE

American Male Detective in Pulp Magazines operating in USA

OLD SLEUTH (American)

Invented 40 detectives - see Brant ADAMS

Citation Record: 1 Book

True Blue, The Detective; Or, The Romance Of A Great Special - *Only*
Ogilvie US (1894)

Mr TRUEFITT

British Male Amateur operating in England

Milward KENNEDY 1894-1968 (British)

Invented 6 detectives - see Sir George BULL

Citation Record: 1 Selected Short Story

Mr Truefitt Detects
can be found in the anthologies, *Great Short Stories of Detection, Mystery, and Horror 2* (Editor; *Dorothy L SAYERS*) and *The Second Omnibus of Crime.*
Gollancz UK (1931); Coward McCann US (1932)

Roger TRULY

American Male Amateur operating in USA

Dean FULLER (American)

Citation Record: 1 Book

Passage - *Single*
Dodd, Mead US (1983); Hale UK (1984)

Insp TRUMPET

British Policeman operating in England

Fergus HUME 1859-1932 (British)

Invented 24 detectives - see Insp Samuel GORBY

Citation Record: 1 Book

The Crime Of The 'Liza Jane' - *Only*
Ward, Lock UK (1895)

Insp TRUSCOTT

is, as he says, 'of the Yard'. One of the great comic inventions of the modern British drama, *TRUSCOTT* personifies the stupid cunning for which the British stage bobby is historically renowned, playing havoc with his suspects in this one great play.

British Policeman operating in England

Joe ORTON 1933-1967 (British)

was born in Leicester and educated in local schools until the age of sixteen. He studied sporadically for the theatre, spent six months in jail for defacing library books, could rarely earn a living, never wanted to, and was outrageously immoral and anti-establishment during all his short life, which ended when he was murdered in a fit of passion by his homosexual partner. *ORTON* wrote seven plays, among which are two of the finest comedies of the twentieth century, both of them containing brilliantly observed comic detectives.

Inventor of one other detective Sgt MATCH

Citation Record: 1 Book

Loot - *Play*
Methuen UK (1967)

Bill TRUSCOTT

American Male Sleuth operating in USA

GRIFF 1896-1976 (British)

was a house name used as a byline for a number of rough, tough, action novels, mainly published between 1949 and 1953 and, although apparently written by British authors, attempting to emulate the prevailing hardboiled school of American detective fiction.

Writer: Ernest Lionel MCKEAG

Other Bylines: Mark GRIMSHAW

Citation Record: 3 Books

Dope Is For Dopes - *First*
Modern Fiction UK (1949)

Trading With Bodies - *Last*
Modern Fiction UK (1950)

Glynis TRYON

is, in the 1840s and 1850s, a young free-thinking librarian in the small town of Seneca Falls, New York. She struggles for the rights of women in 1848 and is later in the fight to abolish slavery. Meeting murder on the way, she has to turn sleuth.

American Female Amateur operating in New York

Miriam Grace MONFREDO (American)

Citation Record: 2 Books

Seneca Falls Inheritance - *First*
St Martin's US (1992)

North Star Conspiracy - *Latest*
St Martin's US (1993)

Dr Zeng TSE-LIN

was a superman hero who appeared in short stories in *Popular Detective* during the 1940s.

Chinese Male Detective in Pulp Magazines operating in USA

Walt BRUCE 1903-1980 (American)

For writer details see Bill LENNOX

No citations

Lt/Insp Richard TUCK

American Policeman operating in Los Angeles

Lange LEWIS 1915- (American)

Writer: Jane BEYNON

Citation Record: 5 Books

Murder Among Friends - *First*
Bobbs US (1942)

Death Among Friends - *First**
Bodley Head UK (1950)

The Passionate Victims - *Last*
Bobbs US (1952); Bodley Head UK (1953)

Sgt TUCKER

British Policeman operating in England

H F M PRESCOTT 1896- (British)

Writer: Hilda Frances Margaret PRESCOTT

Citation Record: 1 Book

Dead And Not Buried - *Only*
Constable UK (1938); Dodd, Mead US (1954)

Charity TUCKER

Second detective of Benjamin SHOCK

Coleridge TUCKER

seeks out an international drugs ring.

British Male Secret Agent operating in India

Ivor DRUMMOND 1929- (British)

was born in Edinburgh, Scotland. He was educated privately and took a BA in History at Magdalen College, Oxford, 1952.

Writer: Roger Erskine LONGRIGG

Other Byline: Frank PARRISH

Inventor of one other detective pair Jennifer Norrington Aless GANZARELLO and Coleridge TUCKER

Citation Record: 1 Book

The Necklace Of Skulls - *Single*
Dell US (1980)

Coleridge TUCKER

Second detective of Jennifer Norrington Aless GANZARELLO

Mike TUCKER

American Male Sleuth operating in California

Brian COFFEY 1945- (American)

Writer: Dean Ray KOONTZ

Citation Record: 3 Books

Blood Risk - *First*
Bobbs US (1973); Barker UK (1974)

Surrounded - *Last*
Bobbs US (1974); Barker UK (1975)

Roy TUCKER

American Male Sleuth operating in USA

Adam KENNEDY (American)

Citation Record: 2 Books

The Domino Principle - *First*
New English Library UK (1976)

The Domino Vendetta - *Latest*
Allen UK (1982); Viking US (1984)

Samuel Clemens TUCKER

is a Vietnam War veteran who came back without his left foot and left testicle, a combination of disabilities that only slightly hinders his operations in Carmel, California. He is helped by his ex-Army psychiatrist wife and others.

American Male Private Detective operating in California

Sidekick: Nicki HILL

is an ex-Marine and ex-football player who does most of the legwork.

American Male - Assistant

Jerry Allen POTTER (American)

Citation Record: 2 Books

A Talent For Dying - *First*
Popular Library US (1980)

If I Should Die Before I Wake - *Latest*
Popular Library US (1981)

Mark TUDOR

has the benefit of a psychically detecting dog. No kidding!

American Male Private Detective operating in California

Sidekick: SVEA

is caninely 'psychic'. He and the detective explain to each other what their case is all about.

Male - Pet Dog

Anne NASH 1890- (American)

Citation Record: 2 Books

Said With Flowers - *First*
Doubleday US (1943); Hammond UK (1953)

Death By Design - *Last*
Doubleday US (1944); Hammond UK (1954)

Matt TUDOR

investigates a death by stabbing in a locked room, which contains no weapon.

American Male Amateur operating in USA

Joseph COMMINGS (American)

Other Detectives:
Senator Brooks Urban BANNER
Mayor Thomas LANDIN

Citation Record: 1 Selected Short Story

Death Shapes The Frame
In 'Private Detective Stories' US (1949)

Harvey TUKE and Sir Bruton KAMES

Harvey TUKE is the senior legal assistant of *Bruton KAMES*, who is the Director of Public Prosecutions. Together they solve several cases, all of which have a legal background. Because of his knowledge and position, *TUKE* has considerable influence with the police. He has been described as 'a tactless bureaucrat...with a face like Mephistopheles and a sardonic sense of humour.' He has a French wife, and he studies the campaigns of Napoleon in his leisure time.

British Male Amateurs operating in London

Douglas G BROWNE 1884-1963 (British)

Invented 4 detectives - see LEGARDE

Citation Record: 7 Books

Death Wears A Mask - *First*
Hutchinson UK (1940); Macmillan US (1954)

Death In Seven Volumes - *Last*
Macdonald UK (1958)

Jasper TULLY and Mrs Annie NORRIS

Jasper TULLY is the Chief Investigator for the District Attorney in New York and appears in these two novels, which are concerned with investigations into the life and death of the reprobate General Ransom Jarvis (US Army, retired). He is aided by *Mrs Annie NORRIS*, who appears in one other book as the main detective.

American Male Professional Investigator and American Female Amateur operating in New York

Dorothy Salisbury DAVIS 1916- (American)

Invented 9 detectives - see Kate OSBORN

Citation Record: 2 Books

Death Of An Old Sinner - *First*
Scribner's US (1957); Secker & Warburg UK (1958)

A Gentleman Called - *Last*
Scribner's US (1958); Secker & Warburg UK (1958)

Hector TUMBLER

British Male Amateur operating in England

Simon CRABTREE (British)

Citation Record: 23 Short Stories in 1 Collection

Hector Tumbler Investigates - *Collection 1*
Jarrolds UK (1943)

Amy TUPPER

British Female Amateur operating in England

Josephine BELL 1897-1987 (British)

Invented 10 detectives - see Dr David WINTRINGHAM

Citation Record: 2 Books

Wolf! Wolf! - *First*
Hodder & Stoughton UK (1979); Walker US (1980)

A Question Of Inheritance - *Last*
Hodder & Stoughton UK (1980); Walker US (1981)

Henry TURNBUCKLE

American Male Amateur operating in USA

Jack RITCHIE 1922-1983 (American)

Writer: John George REITCI

Citation Record: 29 Short Stories in 1 Collection

The Adventures Of Henry Turnbuckle - *Collection 1*
Southern Illinois University US (1987)

Roger TURNBULL

British Male Sleuth operating in Middle East

John TYNDALL (British)

Citation Record: 2 Books

Death In The Jordan - *First*
Bles UK (1970)

Death In Lebanon - *Last*
Bles UK (1971)

Dan TURNER

was one of the most famous and popular of all the detectives in the heyday of American pulp magazines. A hardboiled PI who could also be comic, he appeared first in the June 1934 issue of *Spicy Detective Stories* (later *Speed Detective*) and then in several hundred short stories before 1950, about which time the author ceased writing. Known as 'Hollywood's hottest hawkshaw', he worked mainly for clients in the film industry and, after 1942, he had a magazine devoted solely to him, *Dan Turner, Hollywood Detective.*

American Male Amateur operating in USA

Robert Leslie BELLEM 1902-1968 (American)

was born in Philadelphia, Pennsylvania. He is best known, perhaps, for having written several hundred *Dan TURNER* stories for the pulps, but in all he is supposed to have written, under several names and sometimes with collaborators, upwards of three thousand short stories.

Other Byline: John A SAXON

Inventor of one other detective Duke PIZZATELLO

Citation Record: 2 Selected Short Stories 7 Short Stories in 1 Collection

Murder By Proxy
is reputedly the first story in which *Dan TURNER* appeared.
In 'Spicy Detective Stories' US (1934)

The Doomed Quartet
must be one of the very last stories written by *BELLEM*.
In 'Hollywood Detective' US (1950)

Dan Turner, Hollywood Detective - *Collection 1*
contains some of the original stories.
Popular Press US (1983)

James TURNER

is a journalist who solves a case of death by snake bite in a locked room under guard.

British Male Amateur operating in England

Rolf BENNETT (British)

Inventor of one other detective Lt/Cdr Frank H LAWLESS

Citation Record: 1 Book

The Web - *Only*
Hodder & Stoughton UK (1917)

Milo TURNER

is a reformed con-man.

American Male Private Detective operating in USA

Francis M NEVINS Jr 1943- (American)

Invented 3 detectives - see Loren MENSING

Citation Record: 2 Books

The 120-Hour Clock - *First*
Walker US (1986)

The Ninety Million Dollar Mouse - *Latest*
Walker US (1987)

Tom TURNER

American Male Detective in Pulp Magazines operating in USA

Anthony P MORRIS 1849-1921 (American)

Invented 5 detectives - see Mark MAGIC

Citation Record: 1 Selected Short Story

Tom Turner, Detective; Or, Piping The Hawks Of Baltimore
Old Cap Collier Library US (18??)

Nicodemus Dove TURTLE

of the London CID is in this one Victorian novel.

British Policeman operating in London

Hume NISBET 1849-1921? (British)

Other Detectives:
William GIBSON
Robert SCOTT

Citation Record: 1 Book

Children Of Hermes: Romance Of Love And Crime - *Only*
Hurst & Blackett UK (1901)

Ephraim TUTT

is one of the most astute lawyers in the criminous literature. Said to be born on July 4, 1869, he is Yankee to the core and practises in New York City and in his home town, Pottsville, New York. Lincolnesque in his frock coat and stove-pipe hat, he smokes endless stogies and solves mysteries, always in favour of an underdog or a helpless victim, from whom he cannot hope to collect a fee. He knows every legal loophole in the book, 'fights fire with fire' and never loses a case.

TUTT appeared in numerous collections of short and long stories, which have been recently reassembled under new titles, but only in one novel. The original collections only are cited.

American Male Amateur operating in New York/Pottsville

Stooge: Hezekia MASON

is the prosecutor who pits his wits against *Ephraim TUTT* in the Pottsville cases, but is always beaten by the shrewd old lawyer.

British Male

Arthur TRAIN 1875-1945 (American)

was born in Boston, Massachusetts. He was educated at Prince School, Boston, and St Paul's School, Concord, New Hampshire. He graduated from Harvard University, Cambridge, Massachusetts, with an AB, 1896, followed by an LLB, 1899, and was admitted to the Massachusetts Bar, 1899. He was an assistant District Attorney in New York, 1901-1908, and later became Attorney General for Massachusetts. He was the author of at least twenty-five novels, including several genre works, as well as numerous short stories, usually published in collections.

Writer: Arthur Cheney TRAIN

Other Detectives:
John DOCKRIDGE
MCALLISTER

Citation Record: 1 Book 84 Short Stories in 9 Collections

Yankee Lawyer - The Autobiography Of Ephraim Tutt - *Only*
Although *Ephraim TUTT* is the hero-detective in many of the author's short stories, he appears in only this one novel.
Scribner's US (1943)

Tutt And Mr Tutt - *Collection 1*
Short stories - 7
Scribner's US (1920)

Tut,Tut! Mr Tutt - *Collection 2*
Short stories - 8
Scribner's US (1923); Nash UK (1924)

Page Mr Tutt - *Collection 3*
Short stories - 9
Scribner's US (1926)

When Tutt Meets Tutt - *Collection 4*
Short stories - 5
Scribner's US (1927)

Tutt For Tutt - *Collection 5*
Short stories - 10
Scribner's US (1934)

Mr Tutt Takes The Stand - *Collection 6*
Short stories - 10
Scribner's US (1936)

Old Man Tutt - *Collection 7*
Short stories - 11
Scribner's US (1938)

Mr Tutt Finds A Way - *Collection 8*
Short stories - 13
Scribner's US (1945)

Mr Tutt Comes Home - *Collection 9*
Short stories - 11
Scribner's US (1945)

Erasmus TUTTLEBERRY

British Male Amateur operating in several locations

W Carter PLATTS 1864- (British)

Writer: William Carter PLATTS

Citation Record: 20 Short Stories in 1 Collection

The Whims Of Erasmus - *Collection 1*
Not all the stories are criminous.
Digby UK (1902)

TWEED

is said to be the Deputy Director of the British Secret Intelligence Service. He solves a nasty case of death by decapitation, where there is no likely suspect.

British Male Professional Investigator operating in England

Colin FORBES 1923- (British)

Writer: Raymond Harold SAWKINS

Other Bylines:
Richard RAINE
Raymond H SAWKINS

Citation Record: 1 Book

The Greek Key - *Single*
Collins UK (1989)

Det Insp TWIGG

Second detective of Dr David GARTH

Anthony Nicholas TWIN

American Male Sleuth operating in USA

Doug MASTERS (American)

Citation Record: 4 Books

The Beast - *First*
Charter US (1985)

The Devil's Claw - *Latest*
Charter US (1985)

Det Const Jason TWITTY

is young, black, of Caribbean extraction, and is one of eight children of a postman. Having won a rare scholarship to Harrow, the famous English public school usually reserved for sons of the wealthy, he simulates a well-turned-out Englishman, although rather given to far-out dress. What he is doing in the police force of an English market town is beyond comprehension, except he is yet another attempt at a clever but comic cop. In fact, he succeeds at being both.

British Policeman operating in England

Michael KENYON 1931- (British)

Invented 6 detectives - see Insp/Ch Insp Harry PECKOVER

Citation Record: 1 Book

A Healthy Way To Die - *Single*
Hodder & Stoughton UK (1986)

Jabez TWOMBLEY

American Male Amateur operating in Philadelphia

Sidney WILLIAMS 1878-1949 (American)

See main detective Ben MORRISON

Citation Record: 2 Books

The Murder Of Miss Betty Sloan - *First*
Appleton US (1935)

The Aconite Murders - *Last*
Dodd, Mead US (1936)

Tommy TWOTOES and Terry ROOKE

Terry ROOKE is employed by the eccentric, 300-lb, penguin fancier, *Tommy TWOTOES,* to investigate murders in books that touch the outer fringes of bizarrerie.

American Male Amateur and American Male Private Detective operating in New York

David ALEXANDER 1907-1973 (American)

Invented 4 detectives - see Bart HARDIN

Citation Record: 2 Books

Murder In Black And White - *First*
Random House US (1951); Hammond UK (1951)

Most Men Don't Kill - *Last*
Random House US (1951); Hammond UK (1951)

The Corpse In My Bed - *Last**
Ace US (1954)

Hal TYBERT
American Male Detective in Pulp Magazines operating in USA

F Lusk BROUGHTON (American)

Invented 10 detectives - see Harry WILLIAMS

Citation Record: 1 Selected Short Story

Hal Tybert, The Hotel Detective; Or, Shadowing Chicago Crooks
Old Cap Collier Library US (18??)

Dennis TYLER
seeks the killer of a Japanese diplomat.
American Male Professional Investigator operating in Washington DC

DIPLOMAT 1897-1967 (American)

Writer: John Franklin CARTER

Citation Record: 7 Books

Scandal In The Chancery - *First*
Cape & Smith UK (1931)

Slow Death At Geneva - *Last*
Coward McCann US (1934)

Jeff TYLER
American Male Amateur operating in New Orleans

J L POTTER (American)

Citation Record: 3 Books

Kill, Sweet Charity - Kill - *First*
Chicago Paperback House UK (1962)

Room At The Bottom - *Last*
Chicago Paperback House UK (1962)

Miss Julia TYLER
is an elderly Southern gentlewoman, a retired Latin teacher, who likes travelling and detective stories. As she moves around she runs into murders and is called on to solve them.
American Female Amateur operating in England/Maryland

Louisa REVELL ?-1985 (American)

Writer: Ellen Hart SMITH

Citation Record: 7 Books

The Bus Station Murders - *First*
Macmillan US (1947); Boardman UK (1949)

A Party For The Shooting - *Last*
Macmillan UK (1960)

Ralph TYLER
Male Sleuth

Mark VALENTINE

Citation Record: 3 Short Stories in 1 Collection

14 Bellchamber Tower - *Collection 1*
Dempsey (1987)

Nolen TYNER
American Male Private Detective operating in Miami

Elmore LEONARD 1935- (American)

Invented 6 detectives - see Frank RYAN

Citation Record: 1 Book

Cat Chaser - *Single*
Arbor US (1982); Viking UK (1986)

Steve TYNER
is hired by a New York bank to protect a young and wealthy orphan heiress and to investigate why others should want otherwise.
American Male Private Detective operating in New York

Henry SLESAR 1927- (American)

was born in Brooklyn, New York. He has been a copywriter and head of an advertising agency. He wrote few novels but many short stories, mainly for crime and detective magazines, 1956-1984.

Inventor of one other detective pair Dave ROBBINS and Max THERINGER

Citation Record: 1 Book

The Thing At The Door - *Only*
Random House US (1974); Hamilton UK (1975)

Mrs TYRELL and Mrs LEEDS
American Female Amateurs operating in USA

Ursula CURTISS 1923- (American)

Invented 5 detectives - see Lou FABIAN

Citation Record: 1 Collection

The House On Plymouth Street And Other Stories - *Collection 1*
contains some stories with these detectives.
Dodd, Mead US (1985)

James TYRONE
British Male Amateur operating in England

Dick FRANCIS 1920- (British)

Invented 18 detectives - see Sid HALLEY

Citation Record: 1 Book

Forfeit - *Only*
Joseph UK (1969); Harper & Row US (1969)

Fred TYRREL
American Male Private Detective operating in New York

Julian HAWTHORNE 1846-1934 (American)

Invented 3 detectives - see Keppel DRAKE

Citation Record: 1 Book

John Parmalee's Curse - *Only*
Cassell US (1886); Cassell UK (1886)

Judge Henry TYSON
American Male Amateur operating in Maryland

Frederic Arnold KUMMER 1873-1943 (American)

Invented 3 detectives - see Owen MORGAN

Citation Record: 2 Books

The Scarecrow Murders - *First*
Dodd, Mead US (1938); Hutchinson UK (1938)

The Twisted Face - *Last*
Dodd, Mead US (1938); Hutchinson UK (1938)

The Clue Of The Twisted Face - *Last**
Mystery Novel of the Month US (194?)

Annie TYSON-TYREE
Second detective of Whit Pynchon

T

— U —

UBIQUE
Australian Male Sleuth operating in Australia

Clarence W MARTIN (Australian)

Citation Record: 1 Book

'Ubique', The Scientific Bushranger - *Only*
Bookstall AU (1910)

Det Fred UNDERHILL
Second detective of Dudley SMITH

The UNION CLUB
American Male Amateurs operating in USA

Isaac ASIMOV 1920-1992 (American)

Invented 6 detectives - see Elijah BALEY

Citation Record: 15 Short Stories in 1 Collection

The Union Club Mysteries - *Collection 1*
Doubleday US (1983); Granada UK (1984)

Prof Heinrich UNTERMENSCH
Second detective of Insp MACE

Harriet UNWIN

is a poor orphan girl in Victorian England, brought up on the parish and receiving her name from 'the very same beadle who named Oliver Twist'. By hard work and study she obtains a lowly position as a governess, which, during the 1870s, is the only possible way for her to rise in society. Her fortunes are progressively complicated by her meeting murder wherever she goes. However, by sedate and genteel sleuthing she rises regardless.

British Female Amateur operating in England

Evelyn HERVEY 1926- (British)

For writer details see Insp Ganesh GHOTE

Citation Record: 3 Books

The Governess - *First*
Weidenfeld & Nicolson UK (1984); Doubleday US (1984)

Into The Valley Of Death - *Latest*
Weidenfeld & Nicolson UK (1986); Doubleday US (1986)

Eliot UPTON

is a middle-aged Professor of Music, at a university in the Midwest, and is in all sorts of emotional difficulties. He becomes involved in a murder most foul, which baffles the local police.

American Male Amateur operating in USA

Stooge: Capt SINCLAIR
is suitably stumped by events that are elucidated by *Eliot UPTON.*

American Male

Brian MURPHY 1939- (American)

Citation Record: 1 Book

The Enigma Variations - *Single*
Scribner's US (1981)

Robert URBAN

German Male Sleuth

C H GUENTER (German)

Writer: K H GUNTHER

Citation Record: 7 Books

Hunter Of Men - *First*
Translated from the German.
Pinnacle US (1975)

A Swindler Named Zefano - *Last*
Translated from the German.
Manor US (1979)

Mark URGENT

is said to be 'the West Country's most famous private eye', which can hardly be regarded, by the British criminal fraternity, as an accolade.

British Male Private Detective operating in England

Nicholas FORDE 1919- (British)

Writer: Arthur ELLIOTT-CANNON

Other Byline: Elliott CANNON

Citation Record: 6 Books

Urgent Enquiry - *First*
Hale UK (1973)

Urgent Conference - *Latest*
Hale UK (1981)

Miguel URIZAR

investigates murder aboard ship. He appears in one other book with the author's main detective, *Basil WILLING.*

Male Amateur operating on a ship

Helen MCCLOY 1904-1993 (American)

Invented 5 detectives - see Dr Basil WILLING

Citation Record: 1 Book

She Walks Alone - *Only*
Random House US (1948); Coker UK (1950)

Wish You Were Dead - *Only**
Bestseller US (1958)

Miguel URIZAR

Second detective of Dr Basil WILLING

Coralie URQUHART

is a lady's companion who turns sleuth.

British Female Amateur operating in England

M E BRADDON 1835-1915 (British)

Invented 9 detectives - see Robert AUDLEY

Citation Record: 1 Book

Thou Art The Man - *Only*
Simpkin UK (1894)

Sister URSULA

is a nun in the Order of Martha of Bethany and takes to sleuthing, as fictional nuns are only too prone to do.

American Female Amateur operating in USA

Anthony BOUCHER 1911-1968 (American)

Invented 7 detectives - see Fergus O'BREEN and Det Lt JACKSON

Citation Record: 2 Books 1 Collection

Nine Times Nine - *First*
was previously published under the following byline.
International Polygonics US (1989)

Rocket To The Morgue - *Last*
was previously published under the following byline.
International Polygonics US (1989)

Exeunt Murderers - *Collection 1*
contains eight *Nick NOBLE* stories and two *Sister URSULA* stories.
Southern Illinois University US (1983)

H H HOLMES 1911-1968 (American)

For writer details see Fergus O'BREEN and Det Lt JACKSON

Citation Record: 2 Books 1 Collection

Nine Times Nine - *First*
was republished under the preceding byline.
Duell US (1940)

Rocket To The Morgue - *Last*
was republished under the preceding byline.
Duell US (1942)

Frank URWIN

is a Victorian investigative journalist.

British Male Amateur operating in England

William LEQUEUX 1864-1927 (British)

Invented 23 detectives - see Allan KENNEDY

Citation Record: 1 Book

An Eye For An Eye; A Mystery - *Only*
White UK (1900)

Trooper USELESS

South African Policeman operating in South Africa

L Patrick GREENE

Invented 5 detectives - see 'Dynamite' DRURY

Citation Record: 22 Short Stories in 1 Collection

Trooper Useless - *Collection 1*
Harrap UK (1936)

Ambrose USHER

is an amorous, middle-aged bachelor, learned in the classics, philosophy and languages, who is assigned for various reasons to foreign embassies, where he invariably runs into involved and ingenious crimes. Dashing, and often with real or metaphorical cocktail in hand, he solves them with brilliant intellect, usually because of literary or arcane allusions in the plot itself. In the last book in which he appears he acts as a kind of sidekick to *Victoria MCKENZIE.*

British Male Amateur operating in Europe/USA

Jocelyn DAVEY 1908-1994 (British)

was born in Middlesborough, Yorkshire, the son of Lithuanian Jewish immigrants. Educated at Portsmouth Grammar

School, Hampshire, he was originally intended for a rabbinical career. Instead, he went to University College, Oxford, where he took BA and MA in Philosophy and Politics. He served in important liaison posts for the British government during the Second World War and later served in New York, where he stayed for fifteen years. He was awarded an OBE and later a CBE for his work. Although himself irreligious, he was an eminent Hebrew scholar and became an authority on many aspects of Hebrew and Jewish culture, writing several important books in those fields. During the 1950s and 1960s he found time to write, under the pseudonym, six detective novels. After a gap of many years, a seventh appeared.

Writer: Chaim RAPHAEL

Inventor of one other detective Victoria MCKENZIE

Citation Record: 6 Books

The Undoubted Deed - *First*
Chatto & Windus UK (1956)

A Capitol Offense - *First**
Knopf US (1956)

Murder In Paradise - *Last*
Chatto & Windus UK (1982); Walker US (1982)

Sgt Silas USHER

of the London CID is in this one Victorian novel.

British Policeman operating in London

Hawley SMART 1833-1893 (British)

Invented 8 detectives - see Insp POLLOCK

Citation Record: 1 Book

At Fault - *Only*
Chapman & Hall UK (1883); Munro US (1883)

Gabriel UTLEY

operates among the Mormon community in and around Salt Lake City.

American Male Private Detective operating in Utah

Gary STEWART (American)

was born in Salt Lake City, Utah. He is a sometime Professor of Theatre in Indiana.

Citation Record: 2 Books

The Tenth Virgin - *First*
St Martin's US (1983)

The Zarahemia Vision - *Latest*
St Martin's US (1986)

— V —

Monsieur V

French Male Amateur operating in Europe

Allen UPWARD 1863-1926 (British)

Invented 6 detectives - see Charles PRESCOTT

Citation Record: 1 Book 12 Short Stories in 1 Collection

The Phantom Torpedo-Boats - *Only*
Chatto UK (1905)

The International Spy - *Only**
Dillingham US (1905)

Secret History Of Today - *Collection 1*
Chapman & Hall UK (1904)

Supt VACHELL

British Policeman operating in Africa

Elspeth HUXLEY 1907- (British)

was born in London and lived in Kenya, 1912-1925. She was educated at the European School, Nairobi, and later attended Reading University, Berkshire, and Cornell University, Ithaca, New York, obtaining degrees in Agriculture. She farmed in Wiltshire, England, for many years and advised government bodies on farming in Africa. She was made a CBE, 1962.

Writer: Elspeth Jocelyn Grant HUXLEY

Inventor of one other detective Alexander BARTON

Citation Record: 3 Books

Murder At Government House - *First*
Methuen UK (1937); Harper & Row US (1937)

Death Of An Aryan - *Last*
Methuen UK (1939)

The African Poison Murders - *Last**
Harper & Row US (1940)

Lt VALCOUR

is in the New York Police Department and, because of his courteous manners and efficiency, is often sent to remote places to solve difficult cases.

French-Canadian Policeman operating in New York/Miami

Rufus KING 1893-1966 (American)

Invented 5 detectives - see Cotton MOON

Citation Record: 11 Books

Murder By The Clock - *First*
Doubleday US (1929); Chapman & Hall UK (1929)

Murder Masks Miami - *Last*
Doubleday US (1939); Methuen UK (1939)

Amanda VALENTINE

is an ultra-tough Homicide cop in an unidentified American town. She is, one is informed, 'unpredictable and passionate, as her adversaries and lovers soon learn, and very much her own woman'. There seems little reason to doubt it.

American Policewoman operating in USA

Rose BEECHAM (American)

Citation Record: 2 Books

The Garbage Dump Murders - *First*
Naiad US (1992); Silver Moon UK (1992)

Second Guess - *Latest*
Naiad US (1994); Silver Moon UK (1994)

Claudia VALENTINE

is an Australian female private eye, perhaps the first in the literature. In her very first outing she finds a writer dead at his computer.

Australian Female Amateur operating in Sydney

Marele DAY (Australian)

Citation Record: 3 Books

The Life And Crimes Of Harry Lavender - *First*
Allen AU (1988); Hodder & Stoughton UK (1994)

The Last Tango Of Dolores Delgardo - *Latest*
Allen AU (1992)

Daniel VALENTINE and Clarisse LOVELACE

solve murders together.

American Male Amateur and American Female Amateur operating in Boston

Nathan ALDYNE (American)

Writers: Michael MACDOWELL 1950- and Dennis SHUETZ 1947-1989

Citation Record: 2 Books

Vermilion - *First*
Avon US (1980)

Canary - *Last*
Ballantine US (1986)

Gene VALERY

Second detective of Margot ANSTRUTHER

VALESHOFF and TAMARA

Sleuths operating in Europe

Eric AMBLER 1909- (British)

Invented 4 detectives - see Dr Jan CZISSAR

Citation Record: 2 Books

Uncommon Danger - *First*
Hodder & Stoughton UK (1937)

Background To Danger - *First**
Knopf US (1937)

Cause For Alarm - *Last*
Hodder & Stoughton UK (1938); Knopf US (1939)

Eddie VALIANT

American Male Amateur operating in USA

Gary K WOLF (American)

Citation Record: 1 Book

Who Censored Roger Rabbit? - *Single*
St Martin's US (1981)

Insp Bill VALLANCE

British Policeman operating in England

Walter PROUDFOOT 1881- (British)

For writer details see Penny MERCER and Vincent MERCER

Citation Record: 3 Books

Crime In The Arcade - *First*
Hutchinson UK (1931)

Conspiracy - *Last*
Hutchinson UK (1933)

Incra VALLO

sleuths in Fascist Rome during 1927.

Italian Male Amateur operating in Rome

Carlo Emilio GADDA 1893-1973

Citation Record: 1 Book

That Awful Mess On Via Merulana - *Only*
Braziller US (1965); Secker & Warburg UK (1966)

Johnny VALLON

is head of Chennault Investigations, operating from an office in Regent Street, in London's West End.

British Male Private Detective operating in London/Bahamas

Peter CHEYNEY 1896-1951 (British)

Invented 11 detectives - see Lemmy CAUTION

Citation Record: 3 Books

You Can Call It A Day - *First*
Collins UK (1949)

The Man Nobody Saw - *First**
Dodd, Mead US (1949)

Dark Bahama - *Last*
Collins UK (1950); Dodd, Mead US (1951)

I'll Bring Her Back - *Last**
Eton US (1951)

Eugène VALMONT

is one of a large group of early detectives, whose creators attempted, with varying degrees of success, to follow in the wake of *Sherlock HOLMES*. He appears only in this one collection of untitled short stories, related by himself. He was, it seems, a senior policeman in France; but falling foul of the authorities there, he has come to England to practise as a detective. His cases are usually brought to him by a nebulous and suitably puzzled Scotland Yard officer. In truth, *VALMONT* has a low regard for the English police, although he himself is shown as slightly comic and sometimes given to failure. The stories were highly admired when they appeared and it has been said that *VALMONT's* vanity, pomposity and impeccable dress sense may have provided a prototype for *Hercule POIROT*.

French Male Professional Amateur operating in England

Stooge: Mr Spenser HALE

is a policeman at Scotland Yard who, being out of his depth, brings his cases to *VALMONT*.

British Male

Robert BARR 1850-1912 (British)

Invented 4 detectives - see Nick NICHOLSON

Citation Record: 7 Short Stories in 1 Collection

The Triumphs Of Eugène Valmont - *Collection 1*
Hurst UK (1906); Appleton US (1906)

VAN

American Male Detective in Pulp Magazines operating in USA

Harlan Page HALSEY 1837-1898 (American)

Invented 6 detectives - see Kate GOELET

Citation Record: 1 Book

Van, The Government Detective; Or, The Base Metal Coiners - *Only*
Street & Smith US (1888); Aldine US (18??)

VAN BIBBER

American Male Amateur operating in USA

Richard Harding DAVIS 1864-1901 (British)

See main detective Insp LYLE

Citation Record: 15 Short Stories in 1 Collection

Van Bibber And Others - *Collection 1*
Osgood UK (1892); Harper & Row US (1892)

Arlette VAN DER VALK

appears as the second detective in the last book of her husband and, after the author killed him off, is the detective in one more book. She has now married again, lives in France and operates vaguely as a private detective.

French Female Private Detective operating in France

Nicholas FREELING 1927- (British)

Invented 4 detectives - see Insp Piet VAN DER VALK

Citation Record: 1 Book

The Widow - *Single*
Heinemann UK (1979); Pantheon US (1979)

Arlette VAN DER VALK

Second detective of Insp Piet VAN DER VALK

Insp Piet VAN DER VALK

was a popular Dutch detective before the author killed him off and substituted his widow in one book. With the interesting backdrop of Amsterdam, the books have been much admired as examples of excellent modern police work. In the detective's final book, he shared the sleuthing honours with his wife, *Arlette VAN DER VALK*.

Dutch Policeman operating in Amsterdam

Nicholas FREELING 1927- (British)

was born in London. Educated in primary and secondary schools, he worked as a hotel and restaurant cook throughout Europe, 1945-60, and then became a full-time writer. He received the Crime Writers Association Gold Dagger award, 1964, the *Grand Prix de Roman Policier*, 1964, and the American Writers of America Award, 1966.

Other Detectives:
Insp Henri CASTANG — Arlette VAN DER VALK
Insp Piet VAN DER VALK and Arlette VAN DER VALK

Citation Record: 10 Books

Love In Amsterdam - *First*
Gollancz UK (1962); Harper & Row US (1962)

Death In Amsterdam - *First**
Ballantine US (1964)

Over The High Side - *Last*
Hamish Hamilton UK (1971)

The Lovely Ladies - *Last**
Harper & Row US (1971)

Insp Piet VAN DER VALK and Arlette VAN DER VALK

appear as joint sleuths in *Piet VAN DER VALK's* last book. They also appear individually in other books by this author.

Dutch Policeman and Dutch Female Amateur operating in Amsterdam

Nicholas FREELING 1927- (British)

Invented 4 detectives - see Insp Piet VAN DER VALK

Citation Record: 1 Book

A Long Silence - *Only*
was the last of the novels to feature *Piet VAN DER VALK*, who was killed off in it. His wife *Arlette VAN DER VALK* took over the detective work and she subsequently appeared in another book.
Hamish Hamilton UK (1972)

Auprès De Ma Blonde - *Only**
Harper US (1972)

Hannah VAN DOREN

looks like an angel, drinks like a fish, writes for crime magazines, and goes round town seeking homicides, 'the gorier the better, and with a sex angle if possible'. Not for nothing is she known as 'Homicide Hannah, the Gorgeous Ghoul'.
American Female Amateur operating in USA

Dwight V BABCOCK 1909- (American)
was born in Iowa.
Writer: Dwight Vincent BABCOCK
Citation Record: 3 Books

The Gorgeous Ghoul - *First*
Knopf US (1941); United Authors UK (1947)

The Gorgeous Ghoul Murder Case - *First**
Avon US (1943)

Hannah Says Foul Play - *Last*
Avon US (1946)

Prof Augustus S F X VAN DUSEN

is one of the most original of early detective creations and certainly the most brilliant. He appeared in forty-three short stories, which were first published in a Boston newspaper, but in only two short novels. Some stories were published in two early collections and others have appeared in more recent collections. Many of the stories include cases of 'impossible' crimes to which *VAN DUSEN*, who is credited with the most remarkable brain power, has the answer.
American Male Amateur operating in USA

Jacques FUTRELLE 1875-1912 (American)
was born in Pike County, Georgia. Mainly known as the creator of *VAN DUSEN*, The Thinking Machine, he later departed the genre and wrote romantic novels until his untimely death in the Titanic disaster.
Citation Record: 2 Books 35+ Short Stories in 5 Collections

The Chase Of The Golden Plate - *First*
Dodd, Mead US (1906)

The Diamond Master - *Last*
was republished, together with one of the author's short stories, *The Haunted Bell*, by *Burt* (US 1915).
Bobbs US (1909); Holden UK (1912)

The Thinking Machine - *Collection 1*
is the title of one story in the collection, and has been said to be the most popular story in mystery literature, except for certain adventures of *Sherlock HOLMES*. Without doubt, it is one of the most ingenious.
Short stories - 7
Chapman & Hall UK (1907)

The Problem Of Cell 13 - *Collection 1**
Dodd, Mead US (1918)

The Thinking Machine On The Case - *Collection 2*
contains an uncounted number of untitled stories.
Appleton US (1908)

The Professor On The Case - *Collection 2**
Nelson UK (1909)

The Thinking Machine - *Collection 3*
was published half a century after the first collection. It added one previously uncollected story.
Short stories - 3
Four Winds US (1957)

Best Thinking Machine Detective Stories - *Collection 4*
contains stories previously uncollected, but also some from the first collection.
Short stories - 12
Dover US (1973)

Great Cases Of The Thinking Machine - *Collection 5*
consists largely of stories hitherto uncollected.
Short stories - 13
Dover US (1977); Dover UK (1977)

Hendrik VAN KILL

is a scholarly sleuth of the 1930s, pure intellect, we are told, but hardly plausible.
American Male Private Detective operating in USA

Spencer BAYNE (American)
was born in Iowa. He graduated in Colorado and was awarded a doctorate in Chicago, Illinois, later becoming Professor of Greek at the University of Illinois and New York University.
Writers: Floyd Albert SPENCER 1899-1978 and Paula Teresa BAYNE 1907-
Citation Record: 3 Books

Murder Recalls Van Kill - *First*
Harper & Row US (1939)

Agent Extraordinary - *Last*
Dutton US (1942); Eyre & Spottiswoode UK (1944)

Richard Curtis (The Phantom) VAN LOAN

is one of those mysterious, shadowy figures, so beloved by the American school of popular fiction. They were the 'crimebusters', supermen whose self-inflicted purpose it was to right wrongs, bring criminals to justice, and rescue the good, the meek, and especially the female beautiful, from a variety of desperate and unseemly fates. The crimebusters often had meaningfully mysterious names, such as the one cited. However, unlike some of the species, *The PHANTOM* did have a real name and, in fact, was a man called *Richard Curtis VAN LOAN*, originally invented in 1933 by D L Champion. Most of the later stories appeared under the *Robert WALLACE* house name, many of them in *Phantom Detective*, until about 1954. The individual writers known are cited below
American Male Amateur operating in USA

D L CHAMPION 1903?-1968 (Australian)
Invented 4 detectives - see Insp ALLHOFF
No citations

Norman DANIELS (American)
was one of the most prolific of all American writers of detective fiction. During his work for the pulps of the 1930s, 1940s, and early 1950s he wrote hundreds of short stories, often under pseudonyms. Many have been collected and have appeared in anthologies. He invented many detectives, mainly minor and ephemeral figures in the history of the genre but often occurring in several dozen stories for one magazine under a unique byline.
Writer: Norman A DANIELS
Other Bylines:
G Wayman JONES
C K M SCANLON
Robert WALLACE
Other Detectives:
Bruce BARON
Kelly CARVEL
John KEITH
Jimmy ROSS
Rick TRENT
Citation Record: 1 Selected Short Story

Merchant Of Murder
In 'Phantom Detective' US

Robert WALLACE
House name.
Citation Record: 15 Books

The Dancing Doll Murders - *First*
Regency US (1965)

Stones Of Satan - *Last*
Regency US (1966)

Robert WALLACE

For writer details see Richard Curtis (The Phantom) VAN LOAN (Norman DANIELS)

Citation Record: 1 Book

Murder Under The Big Top - *Only*
Regency US (1965)

Robert WALLACE

Writer: Laurence DONOVAN

Citation Record: 3 Books

The Broadway Murders - *First*
Regency US (1965)

Murder Stalks A Billion - *Last*
Regency US (1966)

Robert WALLACE

Writer: Charles GREEN

Citation Record: 3 Books

Death Under Contract - *First*
Regency US (1966)

The Melody Murders - *Last*
Regency US (1966)

Mrs A J VAN RAFFLES

is a female parody of the classic British amateur sleuth, *A J RAFFLES.*

Female Amateur operating in several locations

John Kendrick BANGS 1862-1922 (American)

Invented 4 detectives - see Raffles HOLMES

Citation Record: 12 Short Stories in 1 Collection

Mrs Raffles - *Parody Collection 1*
Harper & Row US (1905)

Nicholas VAN RIJN

Male Amateur

Poul ANDERSON 1926- (American)

Invented 4 detectives - see Trygve YAMAMURA

Citation Record: 3 Short Stories in 1 Collection

Trader To The Stars - *Collection 1*
contains three novelettes.
Doubleday US (1964); Gollancz UK (1965)

Miss Nora VAN SNOOP

American Female Professional Investigator operating in London

Clarence ROOK ?-1915 (American)

seems to have been an American living for a time in London, England.

Citation Record: 1 Selected Short Story

The Stir Outside The Café Royal
In 'The Harmsworth Magazine' UK (1898)

Det Maggie VAN ZANDT

is said to be 'a shrewd, sweet, crime-stopper and a charming, pretty klutz'. That being said, in her first outing she has the straightforward job of finding a maniacal serial killer who is going around injecting his own HIV-positive blood into people.

American Policewoman operating in New York

Ken GROSS (American)

Citation Record: 1 Book

Full Blown Rage - *Single*
Forge US (1995)

Elinor VANCE

is rich and likes spending her money helping people, often by doing a little sleuthing on the side.

American Female Amateur operating in USA

Frederic Arnold KUMMER 1873-1943 (American)

Invented 3 detectives - see Owen MORGAN

Citation Record: 1 Selected Short Story

Diamond Cut Diamond
is in the anthology, *The Female of the Species* (Editor; *Ellery QUEEN).*
US (1924)

Philo VANCE

is one of the great American detectives, although now generally considered to be as outmoded as some of his British equivalents. He is a man-about-town, wealthy, a social aristocrat, drawls like the British *Peter WIMSEY,* is an expert on most things, and solves the most ingenious and erudite murder cases that, up to that time, had ever been invented. He influenced the detective genre, certainly in the US, for the next generation, which saw the domination of detective fiction by the intellectual puzzle. *Philo VANCE,* unlike several of his British counterparts, has no real sidekick but he does have a narrator as a stand-in.

American Male Amateur operating in New York

Sidekick: S S VAN DINE
is the author himself and purports to be a friend who narrates the cases of the great detective. He does not play an important part in solving them.
American Male - Narrator

Stooge: John F X MARKHAM
is an attorney and the detective's usual intellectual adversary.
American Male

S S VAN DINE 1888-1939 (American)

was born in Charlottesville, Virginia. He was educated at St Vincent College and Pomona College, California, at Harvard University, Cambridge, Massachusetts, and later in Munich and Paris, where he studied art. A distinguished man of letters, art critic and editor, he began writing his classic series of novels after a serious illness in 1923, during which, it is said, he read vast numbers of detective stories and works on criminology.

Writer: Willard Huntington WRIGHT

Inventor of one other detective pair Philo VANCE and Gracie ALLEN

Citation Record: 11 Books

The Benson Murder Case - *First*
Scribner's US (1926); Benn UK (1926)

The Winter Murder Case - *Last*
Scribner's US (1939); Cassell UK (1939)

Philo VANCE and Gracie ALLEN

It was an early custom to link a well-known detective with an equally well-known literary or movie character, the latter acting as a second detective, or, at any rate, appearing to help the main detective. Thus, in this book, the great *Philo VANCE* sleuthed with the help of *Gracie ALLEN,* the female half of the famed variety and movie duo of Burns and Allen. She was so silly she was a genius!

American Male Amateur and American Female Amateur operating in USA

S S VAN DINE 1888-1939 (American)

See main detective Philo VANCE

Citation Record: 1 Book

The Gracie Allen Murder Case - *Only*
Scribner's US (1938); Cassell UK (1938)

The Smell Of Murder - *Only**
Bantam US (1950)

Pluto VANCE

is a parody of the classic American detective, *Philo VANCE.*

American Male Amateur operating in New York

John RIDDELL 1902-1969 (American)

Writer: Corey FORD

Citation Record: 1 Book

The John Riddell Murder Case: A Philo Vance Parody - *Parody 1*
Scribner's US (1930)

George VANCOUVER
American Male Amateur operating in USA

George BOWERING (American)

Citation Record: 1 Book

Burning Water - *Single*
Beaufort US (1980)

Paul VANDERVENT
solves the mystery of some historical poisonings.
British Male Amateur operating in London

Julian SYMONS 1912-1994 (British)
Invented 11 detectives - see Insp CRAMBO

Citation Record: 1 Book

The Blackheath Poisonings: A Victorian Murder Mystery - *Only*
Collins UK (1978); Harper & Row US (1978)

Dr VANE
British Male Amateur operating in England

W E JOHNS 1893-1968 (British)
Invented 3 detectives - see BIGGLES

Citation Record: 10 Short Stories in 1 Collection

Dr Vane Answers The Call - *Collection 1*
Latimer UK (1950)

Sydney VANE
British Male Amateur operating in England

Nicholas ISLAY 1880-1929 (British)
For writer details see Ferrers LOCKE

Citation Record: 2 Books

A Brace Of Rogues - *First*
Murray UK (1920)

The Selicombe Murder - *Last*
Murray UK (1920)

Jimmy VANESCO
is a skip-tracer who, tracking down some missing men, comes up against covert CIA involvement.
American Male Private Detective operating in New York

G F NEWMAN 1945- (British)
Invented 3 detectives - see Insp Terry SNEED

Citation Record: 1 Book

The Men With The Guns - *Single*
Secker & Warburg UK (1982)

Richard VANESS
British Male Amateur operating in several locations

Mansell BLACK 1920- (British)

Writer: Elleston TREVOR

Other Byline: Simon RATTRAY

Citation Record: 4 Books

Sinister Cargo - *First*
Hodder & Stoughton UK (1951)

Steps In The Dark - *Last*
Hodder & Stoughton UK (1954)

V

Sarah VANESSA
British Female Sleuth operating in Germany

Joan STORM (British)

Citation Record: 3 Books

Dark Emerald - *First*
Hammond UK (1951)

Deadly Diamond - *Last*
Hammond UK (1953)

Rick VANNER
is an ex-Naval Intelligence man, now a private eye, and mainly interested in cases with foreign backgrounds.
!See Appendix 2.
American Male Private Detective operating in several locations

M V HEBERDEN 1906- (American)
See main detective Desmond SHANNON

Citation Record: 3 Books

Murder Cancels All Debts - *First*
Doubleday US (1946); Edwards UK (1947)

The Sleeping Witness - *Last*
Doubleday US (1951); Hale UK (1955)

Det Vic VARALLO and Jesse FALKENSTEIN
Vic VARALLO and his squad operate in Glendale, a suburban precinct of Los Angeles. His detective work is always intimately involved with the legal work of *Jesse FALKENSTEIN*, a lawyer who assists considerably with the solutions. The series deals repeatedly with the social and marital inter-relationships of the two men and their wives.
American Policeman and American Male Amateur operating in Los Angeles

Lesley EGAN 1921-1988 (American)
For writer details see Sgt Ivor MADDOX
Inventor of one other detective Delia RIORDAN

Citation Record: 24 Books

A Case For Appeal - *First*
Harper & Row US (1961); Gollancz UK (1962)

Crime For Christmas - *Latest*
Doubleday US (1979); Gollancz UK (1984)

'Chick' VARNEY
American Male Amateur operating in New York

Jerome BARRY 1894-1975 (American)

Writer: Jerome Benedict BARRY

Citation Record: 3 Books

Murder With Your Malted - *First*
Doubleday US (1941); Boardman UK (1942)

Lady Of Night - *Last*
Doubleday US (1944); Boardman UK (1945)

VASCO
American Male Detective in Pulp Magazines operating in USA

Ed STRAYER (American)
Invented 4 detectives - see Jack SHARPLEY

Citation Record: 1 Selected Short Story

Vasco, The Magician Detective; Or, The Murder In The Theatrical Car
Old Cap Collier Library US (18??)

Barry VAUGHAN and Dee VAUGHAN
British Male Amateur and British Female Amateur operating in England

Jennifer JORDAN (British)

Citation Record: 3 Books

A Good Weekend For Murder - *First*
Severn UK (1987); St Martin's US (1987)

Book Early For Murder - *Latest*
Severn UK (1990); St Martin's US (1993)

Dee VAUGHAN
Second detective of Barry VAUGHAN

Lee VAUGHAN and Insp SMITH
Lee VAUGHAN is a private investigator from London who works on a case in an English seaside town, on which *Insp. SMITH* is also working. The latter is the main detective in other books by this author.
British Male Private Detective and British Policeman operating in England

Simon TROY (British)
See main detective Charles SMITH

Citation Record: 1 Book

Road To Rhuine - *Only*
Collins UK (1952); Dodd, Mead US (1952)

Valentine VAUGHAN
British Male Amateur operating in England

R Thurston HOPKINS 1884-1958 (British)

Writer: Robert Thurston HOPKINS

Other Byline: Robert ROSTAND

Citation Record: 6 Short Stories in 1 Collection

Valentine Vaughan Omnibus - *Collection 1*
Grafton UK (1947)

Capt VAUGHN

Second detective of Dave BARNUM

Nick VELVET

is a thief who has to act as an accomplished detective in the course of his nefarious work.

American Male Sleuth operating in New York

Edward D HOCH 1930- (American)

Invented 20 detectives - see Capt LEOPOLD

Citation Record: 20 Short Stories in 2 Collections

The Spy And The Thief - *Collection 1*
has seven stories with *RAND* and seven with *Nick VELVET.*

Short stories - 7
Davis UK (1971)

The Thefts Of Nick Velvet - *Collection 2*

Short stories - 13
Mysterious Press US (1978)

Willy VELVET

Policeman

Robert L WIMBERLY

Citation Record: 1 Book

Willy Velvet, Homicide Detective - *Only*
Dramatic (1956)

Tessie VENABLE

American Female Amateur operating in USA

Helen HOLLEY (American)

Citation Record: 2 Books

Blood On The Beach - *First*
Mystery House US (1946)

Dead Run - *Last*
Mystery House US (1947)

Charles VENABLES

appears also in books with the author's other detective, *Insp Bernard BRAY.*

British Male Amateur operating in England

C St John SPRIGG 1907-1937 (British)

Invented 4 detectives - see Insp Charles MORGAN

Citation Record: 2 Books

Fatality In Fleet Street - *First*
Eldon UK (1933)

Death Of A Queen - *Last*
Nelson UK (1935)

Charles VENABLES

Second detective of Insp Bernard BRAY

Sgt VENN

British Policeman operating in England

Lynn BROCK 1877-1943 (British)

See main detective Col GORE

Citation Record: 3 Books

The Silver Sickle Case - *First*
Collins UK (1938)

Fourfingers - *Last*
Collins UK (1939)

Paul VENNEKER

appears also in one book with the author's other detective, *Ludovic FENDER.*

Male Sleuth operating in France

Paul GEDDES 1922- (British)

Other Detectives:
Ludovic FENDER
Ludovic FENDER and Paul VENNEKER

Citation Record: 1 Book

Hangman - *Single*
Faber UK (1977); St Martin's US (1977)

Code Name Hangman - *Single**
Penguin UK (1979)

Paul VENNEKER

Second detective of Ludovic FENDER

Ronnie VENTANA

American Male Private Detective operating in USA

Gloria WHITE (American)

Citation Record: 1 Book

Money To Burn - *Single*
Dell US (1993)

Gillean VERDEAN

American Female Amateur operating in USA

Tony GIBBS 1935- (American)

Writer: Wolcott GIBBS Jr

Citation Record: 2 Books

Dead Run - *First*
Random House US (1988); Headline UK (1989)

Running Fix - *Latest*
Headline UK (1990)

Bill VERECKER

is a lawyer who investigates a disappearance during a flight.

American Male Amateur operating in San Francisco

Tony KENRICK 1935- (Australian)

Invented 4 detectives - see Jimmy PELHAM

Citation Record: 1 Book

A Tough One To Lose - *Only*
Joseph UK (1972); Bobbs US (1972)

Anthony VEREKER

British Male Amateur operating in England

Robin FORSYTHE 1879- (British)

Citation Record: 5 Books

Missing Or Murdered - *First*
Lane UK (1929)

The Spirit Murder Mystery - *Last*
Lane UK (1936)

Mr VERITY and Insp RAMBLER

Mr VERITY lives in the fictional town of Amnestie, a seaside resort in Sussex. A large man, with a smooth light brown face, he always wears a chestnut Van Dyck beard. He dons a cloak in winter and, in summer, he makes frequent use of a huge purple bathing dress bought in Beirut in 1924. He is joined by *Insp RAMBLER* of the local police in solving some baffling crimes. In the last of the three books the name of *Mr VERITY* seems, unaccountably, to have been changed to *Mr FATHOM* and the book is cited thereunder.

British Male Amateur and British Policeman operating in Sussex

Peter ANTONY 1926- (British)

is the pseudonym of the most remarkable twins writing contemporary literature. They were born in Liverpool, Lancashire, were educated at St Paul's School, London, and graduated at Trinity College, Cambridge, 1950.

Anthony Joshua SHAFFER has been a barrister, 1951-1955, and a journalist, 1956-1958. He has written novels, plays and film scripts and was given the Mystery Writers of America Edgar Allan Poe award, 1973, for a screenplay.

Peter Levin SHAFFER worked as a conscripted coalminer, 1944-1947, and then had several jobs in bookstores, includ-

ing one at the New York Public Library, 1951-1954. Later he worked as a drama and music critic for several journals. He wrote his first stage play in 1958 and it was an immediate success. He has written at least a dozen more since, all of them successful, both on stage and in film. He has received many awards for his critical studies and plays and the coveted Oscar for one screenplay, 1985.
Writers: Peter Joshua SHAFFER 1926- and Anthony Levin SHAFFER 1926-
Inventor of one other detective FATHOM
Citation Record: 2 Books
The Woman In The Wardrobe - *First*
Evans UK (1951)
How Doth The Little Crocodile? - *Last*
Evans UK (1952); Macmillan US (1957)

William VERITY
is a Victorian policeman, traditionally portly and plodding, solving cases in London and (in one book) in India.
British Policeman operating in England/India

Francis SELWYN 1935- (British)
For writer details see Insp Alfred SWAIN
Citation Record: 5 Books
Sergeant Verity And The Cracksman - *First*
Deutsch UK (1974)
Cracksman On Velvet - *First**
Stein & Day US (1974)
Sergeant Verity And The Swell Mob - *Latest*
Deutsch UK (1980); Stein & Day US (1980)

Capt Thomas VERNAN
British Male Amateur operating in England

Frank BARRETT 1848-1926 (British)
Other Detectives:
KEENE
David LEIGH
James SINGLETON
Dr STURGESS
Citation Record: 1 Book
Breaking The Shackles - *Only*
MacQueen UK (1900)

Richard VERNER
calls himself 'a heuristician'. Perhaps this is why he can solve two tricky cases of death by stabbing in as many locked rooms.
American Male Amateur operating in USA

Christopher ANVIL (American)
Citation Record: 2 Selected Short Stories
The Murder Trap
appeared in the January number.
In 'The Man From Uncle Magazine' US (1967)
The Drop Of A Pin
appeared in the April number.
In 'Mike Shayne Mystery Magazine' US (1974)

Van VERNET
American Male Professional Investigator operating in USA

Lawrence L LYNCH (American)
Invented 11 detectives - see Neil J BATHURST
Citation Record: 2 Books
Dangerous Ground; Or, The Rival Detectives - *First*
Loyd US (1885)
The Rival Detectives; Or, Dangerous Ground - *First**
Ward, Lock UK (1887)
A Mountain Mystery; Or, The Outlaws Of The Rockies - *Last*
Loyd US (1886)

Larry VERNON
British Male Sleuth operating in several locations

David BATESON 1921- (British)
Citation Record: 6 Books
It's Murder, Senorita - *First*
Hale UK (1950)
I'll Do Anything - *Last*
Hale UK (1960)

Michael VERNON
is the resident CIA man in the Congo who tries to solve the murder of his ex-Air Force pal.
American Male Secret Agent operating in Africa

Warren KIEFER 1929- (American)
Writer: Warren David KIEFER
Citation Record: 1 Book
The Lingala Code - *Only*
Random House US (1972)

Val VERNON
seems more concerned with who bedded whom than whodunnit. However, he manages to solve both questions in a mystery involving a nude dead heiress, dope fiends and divers sexual matters.
American Male Private Detective operating in New York

Arthur WALLACE (American)
For writer details see Val VERNON
Citation Record: 1 Book
Passion Pulls The Trigger - *Only*
was republished, with a change of title, under the following byline, a house name.
Valhalla US (1936)

James CLAYFORD (American)
Writer: Frank ARMER
Other Byline: Arthur WALLACE
Citation Record: 1 Book
Man Crazy - *Only*
was previously published under the preceding byline.
Falcon US (1951)

VERRITER
is an agent of the British Foreign Office who sleuths in this one Victorian novel.
British Male Professional Investigator operating in England

Allen UPWARD 1863-1926 (British)
Invented 6 detectives - see Charles PRESCOTT
Citation Record: 1 Book
The Accused Princess - *Only*
Pearson UK (1900)

Horace VESEY
British Male Amateur operating in England

Wirt GERRARE 1862- (British)
Writer: William Oliver GREENER
Citation Record: 9 Short Stories in 1 Collection
Phantasms - *Collection 1*
Roxburghe UK (1895)

Baron VESSELOFFSKY
Male Amateur operating in England

Sydney HORLER 1888-1954 (British)
Invented 20 detectives - see Sir Harker BELLAMY
Citation Record: 1 Book
Miss Mystery - *Only*
Hodder & Stoughton UK (1928); Little, Brown US (1935)

Baron VESSELOFFSKY
Second detective of Sir Brian FORDINGHAME

Grant VICKARY
Male Amateur operating in England/Australia

Robertson HOBART 1905-1962 (British)
For writer details see Insp Dick MASON
Citation Record: 2 Books
The Case Of The Shaven Blonde - *First*
Hale UK (1959)
Dangerous Cargoes - *Last*
Hale UK (1960)

Michael VICKERS

returns, after being presumed dead for four years, to discover which of his associates and friends had tried to kill him. The background is the author's favourite Los Angeles landscape, replete with old movies and tough private eyes.

American Male Amateur operating in Hollywood

Leigh BRACKETT 1915-1978 (American)

Invented 3 detectives - see Edmond CLIVE

Citation Record: 1 Book

Stranger At Home - *Only*

was ghost-written for the actor, George Sanders, who was to have appeared in the movie to be made from it, and it was published originally under his name.

Simon & Schuster US (1946); Pilot Press UK (1947)

Valentine VICKERS

was called 'the specialist in the impossible', and he certainly seemed to have the knack of solving seemingly 'impossible' cases of murder, many involving deaths in various kinds of locked room. He appeared in short stories, mainly published in *Dime Mystery* in the 1940s.

American Male Sleuth operating in USA

Curtis T GARDNER (American)

Inventor of one other detective Leonard MACE

Citation Record: 1 Selected Short Story

In Bed We Die

In 'Dime Mystery' US (1944)

Emma VICTOR

is a lesbian sleuth, eager to subvert male-orientated society. Rather old-fashioned though, not very attractive to herself, and generally getting involved with gorgeous fellow lesbians, she investigates in a way that subverts the classical tenets of the genre rather than society itself, in books with suggestive titles.

American Female Private Detective operating in California

Mary WINGS 1949- (American)

was born in Chicago, Illinois, and educated at San Francisco State University, California, and Shimer College, Mount Cassoll, Illinois, 1988-1990. She is a book designer and resident in both Amsterdam and London.

Citation Record: 3 Books

She Came Too Late - *First*

Women's Press UK (1986); Crossing Press US (1987)

She Came By The Book - *Latest*

Women's Press UK (1995)

Eugène VIDOCQ

is one of the earliest 'proto-detectives' to appear in European literature and his cases are based on true or elaborated facts, taken by his creator from incidents in his own police career. Although not yet fully formed, as it were, he certainly provides one of the planks on which the modern detective story was to be based. More than half a century later, he was taken up by that voraciously prolific British writer of countless mediocre criminous stories, *Dick DONOVAN*, and made the central character of a novel. The great American short story writer, *O HENRY*, wrote at least two stories featuring a parody detective, *TICTOCQ*. More recently, a century later in fact, he has again been made the hero of a novel by an American writer, *Vincent MCCONNOR*.

French Male Professional Amateur operating in France/England

Dick DONOVAN 1842-1924 (British)

Invented 7 detectives - see Fabian FIELD

Citation Record: 1 Book

Eugène Vidocq, Soldier, Thief, Spy, Detective: A Romance Founded On Facts - *Pastiche 1*

Chatto & Windus UK (1895)

Vincent MCCONNOR 1907?- (American)

Invented 3 detectives - see Insp DAMIOT

Citation Record: 1 Book

I Am Vidocq - *Pastiche 1*

Dodd, Mead US (1985)

VIDOCQ 1775-1857 (French)

was born in Arras, the son of a baker. At first a soldier, then an acrobat, and always a thief, he was sentenced, 1796, to eight years in the galleys. After his release he offered his services to Napoleon, 1809, mainly as an informer. Rejected but unabashed, he founded the *Police de Sûreté* and became its first chief, using highly suspect informers as agents. Forced to resign, he eventually opened a private detective agency, 1832, but his methods remained dubious and it is known that he organised many of the crimes he claimed to have solved. The authorities eventually forced him out of business and he died impoverished. He appears, as a character called Vautrin, in several novels by Balzac, who befriended him. *VIDOCQ* was the earliest French writer to describe, in detail, the actual work of a detective, which was on the way to becoming a profession of sorts. He published his memoirs, 1828-9; they are regarded as the founding canon for the key French fictional detectives in the middle of the nineteenth century and were the basis for the pioneering and classic work of the following generation of mystery and detective writers in England.

Writer: Eugène François VIDOCQ

Citation Record: 1 Book

Memoirs Of Vidocq - *Only*

Although this book is generally listed as cited, the full title in the first UK publication was *Memoirs of Vidocq, Principal Agent of the French Police until 1827; and Now Proprietor of the Paper Manufactury at St Mande; Written by Himself.* It appeared in the same year in the US as *Memoirs of Vidocq, French Police Agent* and was republished by *Routledge* (UK 1866) as *Vidocq, the Police Spy.*

Hunt & Clarke UK (1828); Carey & Hart US (1828)

Viscount Anthony VILLIERS

is a detective of the future, having divers adventures around the galaxy.

British Male Private Detective operating in Space

Sidekick: Torve The TROG

is a member of a non-terrestial species.

Unknown sex - Assistant

Alexei PANSHIN 1940- (American)

Citation Record: 3 Books

Star Well - *First*

Ace US (1968)

Masque World - *Last*

Ace US (1969)

Francis VILLIERS

British Male Sleuth operating in Ireland

Bryan RODNEY (British)

Writer: Cyril EDGELEY

Citation Record: 3 Books

The Owl Hoots - *First*

Wright UK (1945)

The Owl Flies Home - *Last*

Wright UK (1952)

Johnny VINCENT

is one of this British author's American detectives.

American Male Private Detective operating in USA

Peter CHESTER 1924- (British)

For writer details see Mark PRESTON

Inventor of one other detective Johnny PRESTON

Citation Record: 1 Book

Murder Forestalled - *Only*

Jenkins UK (1960); Roy US (1961)

Johnny VINCENT
Male Sleuth operating in New Zealand and other locations

Jason CALDER 1923- (Australian)
Writer: John DUNMORE
Citation Record: 2 Books
The O'Rourke Affair - *First*
Hale UK (1979)
Target Margaret Thatcher - *Latest*
Hale UK (1981)

Gil VINE
is a hotel detective at the Plaza Royale where, it seems, murder is endemic. Narrating his own cases, he manages to stay one jump ahead of the cops, who don't like it or him.
American Male Private Detective operating in New York

Stewart STERLING 1895- (American)
See main detective Fire Marshal Ben PEDLEY
Citation Record: 8 Books
Alibi Baby - *First*
Boardman UK (1947)
Dead Certain - *Last*
Ace US (1960)

Moses VINE
changes his character greatly as the series goes on, starting as a Berkeley-based, anti-social, political activist and progressing to higher if not better things in the world of Silicon Valley.
American Male Private Detective operating in Los Angeles

Roger L SIMON 1943- (American)
Writer: Roger Lichtenberg SIMON
Adopter of one other detective Philip MARLOWE
Citation Record: 7 Books
The Big Fix - *First*
Simon & Schuster US (1973); Deutsch UK (1974)
Dead Meet - *Latest*
In 'Black Lizard' US (1988)

Jack VINTON
American Male Detective in Pulp Magazines operating in USA

ANON
Citation Record: 1 Book
Jack Vinton, The Boy Detective
Aldine US

Thomas Phillips VOKES
Irish Policeman operating in Ireland

H R ADDISON 1805?-1876 (Irish)
Writer: Henry Robert ADDISON
Citation Record: 33 Short Stories in 1 Collection
Recollections Of An Irish Police Magistrate And Other Reminiscences Of The South Of Ireland - *Collection 1*
Ward, Lock UK (1862)

V

Baron Franz Maximilian Karagos VON KAZ
was a police official in Austria before going to California, where he solves two tricky cases of murder.
Austrian Male Amateur operating in California

Darwin L TEILHET 1904-1964 and Hildegarde Tolman TEILHET 1906- (American)
Citation Record: 2 Books
The Ticking Terror Murders - *First*
Doubleday US (1935); Methuen UK (1936)
The Broken Face Murders - *Last*
Doubleday US (1940); Gollancz UK (1940)

George VORE
solves a case of death by poisoning in a locked room.
British Male Amateur operating in England

Hamilton DRUMMOND 1857-1935 (British)
Citation Record: 1 Book
Room Five - *Only*
Ward, Lock UK (1904)

Wenceslas VOROBEITCHIK
Male Sleuth operating in Paris

André STEEMAN 1908- (French)
Writer: Stanislaus André STEEMAN
Citation Record: 2 Books
Six Dead Men - *First*
Farrar, Straus US (1932); Hurst UK (1933)
The Night Of The 12th-13th - *Last*
is a translation from the French of *La Nuit du 12 au 13* (Paris, 1931).
Lippincott US (1933)

Abelard VOSS
American Male Amateur operating in New York/Massachusetts

Donald Clough CAMERON 1909?- (American)
was born in Detroit, Michigan.
Inventor of one other detective Andrew BRANT
Citation Record: 3 Books
Murder's Coming - *First*
Holt US (1939)
And So He Had To Die - *Last*
Holt US (1941)

Enoch VOYCE
solves a case of 'impossible' jewel theft from a locked hotel room.
British Male Amateur operating in England

Tom GALLON 1866-1914 (British)
Other Detectives:
Bella THORN TOKLEY
Citation Record: 1 Selected Short Story
The Mystery Of The Locked Room
appeared in the issue for June 3.
In 'Pictorial Magazine' UK (1905)

Stefan VYNALEK
operates at some time in the future in Carinthia, a planet colonised by Czechs.
Czech Male Private Detective operating in Carinthia

A Bertram CHANDLER (American)
Citation Record: 1 Book
Bring Back Yesterday - *Only*
Sphere UK (1982)

— W —

Insp Fadiman WACE
British Policeman operating in England

Roger SIMONS (American)
Writers: Margaret PUNNETT 1932- and Ivor Macaulay PUNNETT
Citation Record: 16 Books
The Houseboat Killings - *First*
Bles UK (1959)
Murder By Design - *Last*
Hale UK (1974)

Riley WADDELL
falls for his lady client and proves her innocent of the case against her.
American Male Private Detective operating in USA

Floyd MAHANNAH 1911- (American)

See main detective Cassie GIBSON

Citation Record: 1 Book

The Golden Goose - *Only*
Duell US (1951); Boardman UK (1952)

The Broken Body - *Only**
Signet US (1952)

WADE

is an ace reporter on *The Morning Creole* and investigates murder cases for his paper.

American Male Amateur operating in New Orleans

Sidekick: WIGGINS

is an ace photographer and his pictures are of inestimable help.

American Male - Aide

Gwen BRISTOW 1903-1980 and Bruce MANNING (American)

were a husband-and-wife team.

Citation Record: 2 Books

The Gutenburg Murders - *First*
Mystery League US (1931)

The Mardi Gras Murders - *Last*
Mystery League US (1932)

Nurse Hilda WADE

is a hospital nurse who sets out to be a detective, her chief assets being a photographic memory and 'the deepest feminine gift - intuition', qualities that enable her to be a most useful sleuth for the period. In an era in which the detective profession was, even more than most, considered quite unsuitable for a woman (and those who entered it nearly always did so for reasons of some great personal sentiment) she adopts the usual period device of operating under wraps. Her real name is disclosed as Maisie Yorke Bannerman, but she adopts her *nom-de-guerre* in order to prove the innocence of her husband, who has been wrongfully condemned to death for murder. She has to go all over the world in search of clues to the real culprit and the stories follow her adventures.

British Female Amateur operating in London

Grant ALLEN 1848-1899 (British)

Writer: Charles Grant Blairfindie ALLEN

Other Detectives:
Lois CAYLEY, Col CLAY, FLETCHER, SHERRARD

Citation Record: 12 Short Stories in 1 Collection

Hilda Wade: A Woman With Great Tenacity Of Purpose - *Collection 1*

appeared in Volumes XVII-XIX, 1899-1900, of the *Strand Magazine* and the collection was published in 1900, being completed by *Sir Arthur Conan DOYLE,* after the death of *Grant ALLEN.*

Richards UK (1900); Putnam US (1900)

Jerry WADE

was often called 'The Candid Camera Kid'. He was one of this prolific author's many quickly-drawn detectives, appearing, 1939-1944, in *Detective Novels Magazine.*

American Male Amateur operating in USA

John L BENTON 1900-1976 (American)

See main detective Stephen DUANE

Citation Record: 1 Selected Short Story

Murder In Pictures
In 'Detective Novels Magazine' US

John WADE

has battles mainly with the crooked and filthy rich. He appeared in several stories, mainly in *Detective Tales.*

American Policeman operating in USA

William R COX 1901-1989 (American)

Invented 4 detectives - see Tom KINCAID

No citations

Nyla WADE

American Female Amateur operating in Denver

Vicki MCCONNELL 1949?-

Citation Record: 3 Books

Mrs Porter's Letter - *First*
Naiad US (1982)

Double Daughter - *Latest*
Naiad US (1988)

Det Gabriel WAGER

is in the Denver Police Department. He is particularly skilled at using modern police technology and, being half Chicano, his mixed heritage gives him a special outlook on some of the crimes he meets.

American Policeman operating in Denver

Sidekick: Det DENBY

American Male - Partner

Rex BURNS 1935- (American)

was born in San Diego, California. He took a BA in English at Stanford University, California, and an MA, 1963, and a PhD, 1965, at the University of Minnesota, Minneapolis. After serving in the Marines Corps, 1958-1961, he began a distinguished career as Professor of English Studies in several universities in the USA and abroad. He received the Mystery Writers of America Edgar Allan Poe award, 1976.

Writer: Rex Raoul Stephen Sehler BURNS

Inventor of one other detective Devlin KIRK

Citation Record: 8 Books

The Alvarez Journal - *First*
Harper & Row US (1975); Hale UK (1976)

The Killing Zone - *Latest*
Viking US (1988); Penguin UK (1989)

Jimmy WAGHORN

British Male Amateur operating in England

John RHODE 1884-1965 (British)

Invented 3 detectives - see Dr Lancelot PRIESTLEY

Citation Record: 18 Books

Hendon's First Case - *First*
Collins UK (1935); Dodd, Mead US (1935)

Twice Dead - *Last*
Bles UK (1960); Dodd, Mead US (1960)

Roger WAGNER

has ten days in which to find a group of terrorists plotting the death of the US President.

American Male Secret Agent operating in USA

Jack D HUNTER 1921- (American)

Writer: Jack Dayton HUNTER

Citation Record: 1 Book

The Terror Alliance - *Single*
Leisure Books US (1980)

James WAINWRIGHT

British Male Secret Agent operating in Tibet

Berkley MATHER 1914- (British)

Invented 3 detectives - see Peter FELTHAM

Citation Record: 2 Books

The Springers - *First*
Collins UK (1968)

A Spy For A Spy - *First**
Scribner's US (1968)

The Break In The Line - *Last*
Collins UK (1970)

The Break - *Last**
Scribner's US (1970)

Pablo WAITZ and Maria PONCE

American Male Amateur and American Female Amateur operating in New York

Paul PINES 1941- (American)

Writer: Paul André PINES

Citation Record: 1 Book

The Tin Angel - *Single*
Morrow US (1983)

Insp WAKE

British Policeman operating in England

Charles KINGSTON (British)

Writer: Charles Kingston O'MAHONEY

Citation Record: 7 Books

Murder In Piccadilly - *First*
Ward, Lock UK (1936)

Fear Followed On - *Last*
Paul UK (1945)

Insp WAKE and Philip GAYMORE

solve a case of death by gassing in a locked room.

British Policeman and British Male Amateur operating in England

Warner ALLEN 1881-1969 (British)

Invented 3 detectives - see George B EDGEHILL and Aristide GOVIN

Citation Record: 1 Book

The Uncounted Hour - *Only*
Constable UK (1936)

Prof David WAKELY

is the Professor of History at the fictional Lowell's College in California. He solves a case of murder on the campus and wins a bride.

American Male Amateur operating in California

Charlotte ARMSTRONG 1905-1969 (American)

Invented 5 detectives - see Prof MacDougal DUFF

Citation Record: 1 Book

The Better To Eat You - *Only*
Coward McCann US (1954); Davies UK (1954)

Catherine WALDEN

American Female Amateur operating in USA

Philip LORAINE (British)

See main detective Insp KEEN

Citation Record: 1 Book

Death Wishes - *Single*
St Martin's US (1983)

Lt WALDMAN

appears in a little-known story by the master and solves a case of death by shooting in a locked house.

American Policeman operating in USA

Raymond CHANDLER 1888-1959 (American)

Invented 9 detectives - see Philip MARLOWE

Citation Record: 1 Selected Short Story

Professor Bingo's Snuff
was published posthumously.
Fantastic US (1952)

Cash WALE

was called 'the pint-size private peep' because of his small stature. He appeared in a large number of short stories and novelettes in *Dime Detective* from 1939 through the 1940s, often in the guise of letters from him to the author.

American Male Detective in Pulp Magazines operating in New York

Sidekick: 'Sailor' DUFFY
was once a boxer who is now, unfortunately, punch-drunk. However, he still makes a useful scrapping partner and assistant for *WALE*, whose adventures involve him in more than the average amount of mayhem.
American Male - Partner

Stooge: Insp Anthony J QUINN
is in the New York Police Department's Homicide division. He appears in many of the stories and hounds *WALE* incessantly, always trying to pin crimes, which he is unable to solve himself, on the little shamus.
American Male

Peter PAIGE (American)

Writer: Morton WOLSON

Citation Record: 1 Selected Short Story

When A Man Murders
In 'Dime Detective' US (1947)

Insp John WALK

British Policeman operating in England

Roland DANIEL 1880-1969 (British)

Invented 11 detectives - see Insp Neville LANGHAM

Citation Record: 5 Books

Dead Man's Vengeance - *First*
Shaylor UK (1931)

Human Vultures - *Last*
Wright UK (1939)

Insp WALKER

investigates murder at a provincial university.

British Policeman operating in England

Nina BAWDEN 1925- (British)

was born in London. She is the author of books for children, mainstream novels and some criminous works.

Writer: Nina Mary Maby KARK

Citation Record: 1 Book

Change Here For Babylon - *Only*
Collins UK (1955)

WALKER

American Male Secret Agent operating in USA

Melville Davisson POST 1871-1930 (American)

Invented 5 detectives - see Uncle ABNER

Citation Record: 13 Short Stories in 1 Collection

Walker Of The Secret Service - *Collection 1*
Appleton US (1924)

Amos WALKER

is a Vietnam War veteran, an ex-military policeman with a sociology degree, an ex-policeman, and by way of being a compassionate social introvert – all qualities that help to make him one of the best-defined and best private eyes in detective fiction. Perhaps this is why he can charge his clients $250 a day plus expenses. His cases are sordid but give a consistently excellent view of Detroit and its problems.

American Male Private Detective operating in Detroit

Loren D ESTLEMAN 1952- (American)

was born in Ann Arbor, Michigan, and took a BA in English and Journalism at Eastern Michigan University, Ypsilanti, 1974. A journalist by profession before becoming a full-time writer, he is the author of several non-genre novels and many short stories.

Other Detectives:

Sherlock HOLMES	Peter MACKLIN
Philip MARLOWE	Connie MINOR
Page MURDOCK	Ralph POTEET

Citation Record: 9 Books 10 Short Stories in 1 Collection

Motor City Blue - *First*
Houghton Mifflin US (1980); Hale UK (1982)

Sweet Woman Lie - *Latest*
Houghton Mifflin US (1990); Macmillan UK (1990)

General Murders - *Collection 1*
Houghton US (1988); Macmillan UK (1989)

Calico Jack WALKER and Tina TAMIKO

American Male Sleuth and Female Sleuth operating in Los Angeles

Paul BISHOP (American)

See main detective Det Fey CROAKER

Citation Record: 2 Books

Citadel Run - *First*
Tor US (1988)

Sand Against The Tide - *Latest*
Tor US (1990)

Harry WALKER

is an ex-foreign correspondent who senses a scoop involving international skulduggery.

British Male Amateur operating in several locations

Simon BELL 1956- (British)

Citation Record: 1 Book

Blood Money - *Single*
Heinemann UK (1991)

Josh WALKER

American Male Amateur operating in Chicago

Mary S CRAIG 1923- (American)

Citation Record: 1 Book

Gillean's Chain - *Single*
Dodd, Mead US (1983)

Richard WALKER

works for a detective agency that polices the diamond trade on behalf of private companies.

British Male Private Detective operating in London

James Broome LYNNE 1920- (British)

Writer: James Broome LYNNE
Other Byline: James QUARTERMAIN

Citation Record: 1 Book

Rogue Diamond - *Single*
Joseph UK (1980); Atheneum US (1980)

Insp WALL

solves a case of shooting in a locked room.

British Policeman operating in England

Vivian GREY (British)

See main detective Det Insp SLADE

Citation Record: 1 Selected Short Story

The Buddha Case
is in a collection, *Stories of Scotland Yard.*
!See Appendix 2.
Everett UK (1906)

Brendan WALLACE

was formerly an investigator for an insurance company but is now a security consultant.

British Male Private Detective operating in London

Mike BREWER (British)

Citation Record: 3 Books

Man In Danger - *First*
Hale UK (1961)

Man Against Fear - *Last*
Hale UK (1966)

Brett WALLACE

American Male Professional Investigator operating in USA

Wade BARKER (American)

House name.

Citation Record: 3 Books

Vengeance Is His - *First*
Warner US (1981)

The Zakka Slaughter - *Latest*
Warner US (1988)

Wade BARKER 1928- (American)

Writer: Richard S MEYERS

Citation Record: 7 Books

Mountain Of Fear - *First*
Warner US (1981)

Phoenix Sword - *Latest*
Warner US (1986)

Dirk WALLACE

American Male Private Detective operating in USA

James Hadley CHASE 1906-1985 (British)

Invented 14 detectives - see Dave FENNER

Citation Record: 1 Book

Hit Them Where It Hurts - *Single*
Hale UK (1984)

Sir Leonard WALLACE

British Male Secret Agent operating in England/Germany/India

Alexander WILSON 1893- (British)

Writer: Alexander Douglas Chesney WILSON

Citation Record: 6 Books 13 Short Stories in 2 Collections

The Mystery Of Tunnel 51 - *First*
Longman UK (1928)

Wallace Intervenes - *Last*
Jenkins UK (1939)

Wallace Of The Secret Service - *Collection 1*
Short stories - 10
Jenkins UK (1933)

Chronicles Of The Secret Service - *Collection 2*
contains three novelettes.
Short stories - 3
Jenkins UK (1940)

Michael WALLACE

British Male Amateur operating in England

Roland DANIEL 1880-1969 (British)

Invented 11 detectives - see Insp Neville LANGHAM

Citation Record: 4 Books

Lovely But Dangerous - *First*
Wright UK (1960)

The Prisoner - *Last*
Wright UK (1965)

William WALLACE

is an ex-amateur boxer, too young to have the heart attack he suffered. He is now a tough PI.

American Male Private Detective operating in USA

Ed LACY 1911-1968 (American)

Invented 8 detectives - see Toussaint 'Touie' MOORE

Citation Record: 1 Book

Bugged For Murder - *Only*
Avon US (1961)

James Rufus WALLINGFORD

appears in a great number of short stories, mainly adventures and escapades, typical of the period, and including detection.

American Male Amateur operating in USA

George Randolph CHESTER 1869-1924 (American)

Citation Record: 97 Short Stories in 4 Collections

Get-Rich-Quick Wallingford - *Collection 1*
Short stories - 27
Altemus US (1908); Richards UK (1908)

Young Wallingford - *Collection 2*
Short stories - 27
Bobbs US (1910); Hodder & Stoughton UK (1917)

Wallingford In His Prime - *Collection 3*
Short stories - 20
Bobbs US (1913); Newnes UK (1916)

Wallingford And Blackie Daw - *Collection 4*
Short stories - 23
Bobbs US (1913); Hodder & Stoughton UK (1918)

Maurice WALLION

Swedish Male Amateur operating in Sweden

Julius REGIS 1889-1925 (Swedish)

Writer: Julius PETTERSON

Citation Record: 2 Books

No 13 Toroni - *First*
is a translation from the Swedish.
Hodder & Stoughton UK (1922); Holt US (1922)

The Copper House - *Latest*
is a translation from the Swedish.
Hodder & Stoughton UK (1923); Holt US (1923)

Supt WALSH

conducts a murder enquiry within a prison.

British Policeman operating in England

Roger PARKES 1933- (British)

Invented 3 detectives - see Insp Taff ROBERTS

Citation Record: 1 Book

Riot - *Single*
Collins UK (1986)

Clint WALSH

was a cop in New York before going to Florida to search for a fugitive from Nazi Germany.

American Male Private Detective operating in New York/Florida

Jack DE WITT (American)

Citation Record: 1 Book

Murder On Shark Island - *Only*
Liveright US (1941)

Prof Jackie WALSH

is a Professor of Film, a screenwriter and a sharp sleuth. She is well known, apparently, as being just the girl to ask if one is worried about having a dead man on one's hands.

American Female Amateur operating in Hollywood

Sidekick: JAKE
is well-known too, being an essential part of the detecting team.
Male - Pet dog

Melissa CLEARY (American)

Citation Record: 1 Book

Dead And Buried - *Single*
Berkley US (1994)

Lt Marty WALSH

American Policeman operating in Los Angeles

Octavus Roy COHEN 1891-1959 (American)

Invented 6 detectives - see Jim HANVEY

Citation Record: 3 Books

My Love Wears Black - *First*
Macmillan US (1948); Barker UK (1949)

A Bullet For My Love - *Last*
Macmillan US (1950); Barker UK (1951)

Det Ch Insp Sidney WALSH

British Policeman operating in Cambridgeshire

Sidekick: Const Brenda PHIPPS
is the more attractive of *WALSH's* two assistants.
British Female - Subordinate

Sidekick: Sgt Reginald FINCH
British Male - Subordinate

Richard HUNT 1938- (British)

Citation Record: 3 Books

Death Sounds Grand - *First*
Constable UK (1991)

Death Of A Merry Widow - *Latest*
Constable UK (1992)

Howel WALTER

British Male Private Detective operating in England

Dick DONOVAN 1842-1924 (British)

Invented 7 detectives - see Fabian FIELD

Citation Record: 1 Book

The Mystery Of Jamaica Terrace - *Only*
Chatto & Windus UK (1896)

Capt Gregory WALTHAM

solves a case of 'impossible' murder by stabbing.

American Policeman operating in USA

Thomas CHASTAIN and Bill ADLER (American)

See main detective John LANGE

Citation Record: 1 Book

The Revenge Of The Robins Family - *Single*
Morrow US (1984)

John WALTZ

American Male Amateur operating in USA/Tahiti

Claire MCCORMICK 1943- (American)

Writer: Marta Haake LABUS

Citation Record: 3 Books

Resumé For Murder - *First*
Walker US (1982)

Murder In Cowboy Bronze - *Latest*
Walker US (1985)

Penny WANAWAKE

is one of the latest additions to the realm of increasingly unbelievable female detectives. She is tall, black, highly educated, liberated, sensual, beautiful, athletic, caring, and rather good at the amateur detective work. She is also very rich, being the daughter of Lady Helena Hurley and Dr Benjamin Wanawake, the Permanent Ambassador to the UN for the tiny republic of Senangaland.

In her books so far, *Penny WANAWAKE* and her rather criminal lover become involved in crimes and murders, which occur with regularity among her many acquaintances. In the course of solving them (the crimes), wealth from the undeserving rich is often redistributed to the deserving not-so-rich. The morality is dubious but the books are racy and entertaining.

British Female Amateur operating in several locations

Susan MOODY 1940- (British)

was born in Oxford. She took a BA from the Open University, 1978, and lectures on creative writing.

Writer: Susan Elizabeth MOODY

Other Detectives:
Frances BRETT
Cassandra SWANN

Citation Record: 6 Books

Penny Black - *First*
Macmillan UK (1984); Fawcett US (1984)

Penny Pinching - *Latest*
Joseph UK (1989); Ballantine US (1989)

Clayton WARD

American Male Sleuth operating in USA

Richard MERWIN (American)

Citation Record: 1 Book

Hard Sell - *Single*
TSR US (1988)

Richard MERWIN and Warren SPECTOR (American)

Citation Record: 1 Book

The Royal Pain - *Single*
TSR US (1988)

Eric WARD

British Male Amateur operating in England

Roy LEWIS 1933- (British)

Invented 3 detectives - see Arnold LANDON

Citation Record: 4 Books

A Certain Blindness - *First*
Collins UK (1980); St Martin's US (1981)

A Necessary Dealing - *Latest*
St Martin's US (1989)

Capt Jack WARD
British Male Amateur operating in several locations

Max PEMBERTON 1863-1950 (British)

Invented 4 detectives - see Bernard SUTTON

Citation Record: 8 Short Stories in 1 Collection

The Adventures Of Captain Jack - *Collection 1*
Mills UK (1909)

Peter WARD
is an example of the professional agent in what are essentially Cold War action thrillers.

American Male Secret Agent operating in several locations

David ST JOHN 1918- (American)

For writer details see Jack NOVAK

Citation Record: 10 Books

On Hazardous Duty - *First*
New American Library US (1965)

Hazardous Duty - *First**
Muller UK (1966)

The Coven - *Last*
Weybright US (1972)

Watson WARD
British Male Amateur operating in England

Burford DELANNOY (British)

Writer: Burford H DELANNOY

Other Detectives:
John GARDEN JANSON

Citation Record: 2 Books

Dead Man's Rooms - *First*
Ward, Lock UK (1905)

The Flat Beneath - *Last*
Rivers UK (1931)

Const Jimmie WARDEN
Canadian Policeman operating in Canada

L C DOUTHWAITE 1878- (British)

Writer: Louis Charles DOUTHWAITE

Other Detectives:
Sexton BLAKE Cpl Larry STEER

Citation Record: 31 Short Stories in 3 Collections

Warden Of The North - *Collection 1*
Short stories - 12
Nelson UK (1938)

The Man From Outside - *Collection 2*
This collection of seventeen of the author's short stories contains seven with *Const WARDEN.*
Short stories - 7
Nelson UK (1940)

Warden Of The Wilds - *Collection 3*
Short stories - 12
Nelson UK (1947)

Montague WARDROP
British Male Amateur operating in London

Headon HILL 1857-1927 (British)

Invented 11 detectives - see Insp HERON

Citation Record: 1 Book

The Peril Of The Prince: A Romance Of Modern Anarchism - *Only*
Pearson UK (1901)

Anthony WARE
American Male Amateur operating in California

Susan WELLS (American)

Writer: Doris SIEGEL

Citation Record: 4 Books

Murder Is Not Enough - *First*
Simon & Schuster US (1939); Cassell UK (1939)

The Witches' Pond - *Last*
Doubleday US (1947)

Drexel WARE
British Male Amateur operating in England/France

Charlton ANDREWS 1874-1939 (American)

Invented 4 detectives - see Derek WHITBY

Citation Record: 2 Books

The Affair Of The Malacca Stick - *First*
Washburn US (1936)

The Affair Of The Syrian Dagger - *Last*
Washburn US (1937)

Liz WAREHAM
is in Public Relations, but that doesn't stop her investigating murder when it occurs.

American Female Amateur operating in USA

Carol BRENNAN (American)

Citation Record: 1 Book

Full Commission - *Single*
Carroll & Graf US (1993)

Steve WARFIELD
American Male Sleuth operating in South America

David CHACKO (American)

Citation Record: 2 Books

The Black Chamber - *First*
St Martin's US (1988)

White Gamma - *Latest*
St Martin's US (1988)

Elizabeth WARING
American Female Amateur operating in Las Vegas

Thomas PERRY (American)

Citation Record: 1 Book

The Butcher's Boy - *Single*
Scribner's US (1982); Constable UK (1982)

Philip WARING
Second detective of Sgt FOGERTY

Scarsdale WARING
British Male Amateur operating in England

T Stanleyan KING (British)

See main detective Dixon BRETT

Citation Record: 3 Books

Black Magic - *First*
Mellifont UK (1934)

Vampire City - *Last*
Mellifont UK (1935)

Mike WARLOCK
American Male Amateur operating in New York

Paul HAGGARD 1907- (American)

Writer: Stephen LONGSTREET

Citation Record: 4 Books

Dead Is The Door-Nail - *First*
Lippincott US (1937)

Death Talks Shop - *Last*
Hillman-Curl US (1938)

Mr WARLOCK-JONES
is an early *Sherlock HOLMES* parody who, in this one book, solves the mystery of a drowned corpse that falls into a London studio. In a sense he was more than a parody, for the author could have been attempting to produce a successful detective, hot on the heels of *HOLMES*, who had appeared just a few years earlier.

British Male Amateur operating in London

Louis ZANGWILL 1869- (British)

Citation Record: 1 Book

A Nineteenth Century Miracle - *Parody 1*
Chatto UK (1897)

Insp Thomas WARNER

solves the mystery of a man's disappearance without trace.

British Policeman operating in England

Eden PHILLPOTTS 1862-1960 (British)

Invented 10 detectives - see Insp MIDWINTER

Citation Record: 1 Book

A Clue From The Stars - *Only*
Hutchinson UK (1932); Macmillan US (1932)

William WARNER

British Male Amateur operating in England

Martin SYLVESTER (British)

is an architect.

Citation Record: 3 Books

A Dangerous Age - *First*
Joseph UK (1986); Villard US (1988)

Rough Red - *Latest*
Joseph UK (1989); Villard US (1990)

James WARREN

was formerly in the police but has now gone private.

British Male Private Detective operating in London

James WARREN (British)

Inventor of one other detective James WESTON

Citation Record: 2 Books

The Lady Was Disturbed - *First*
Collins UK (1956)

The Runaway Corpse - *Last*
Collins UK (1957)

The Disappearing Corpse - *Last**
Washburn US (1958)

Malcolm WARREN

is a young stockbroker who progressively becomes involved in murder. The first of his cases still reads excellently, but the three later books are diminishingly effective.
!See Appendix 2.

British Male Amateur operating in London

C H B KITCHIN 1895-1967 (British)

was born in Harrogate, Yorkshire. He was educated at Clifton College, Bristol, and Exeter College, Oxford. He entered Lincoln's Inn, London and was called to the Bar, 1924.

Writer: Clifford Henry Benn KITCHIN

Citation Record: 4 Books

Death Of My Aunt - *First*
Woolf UK (1929); Harcourt Brace US (1930)

The Cornish Fox - *Last*
Secker & Warburg UK (1949)

Steve WARREN

is a returned war hero who becomes involved with a female Mossad agent, a cache of deadly germs, and a coroner with his own private crematorium.

American Male Amateur operating in USA

Lou CAMERON 1924- (American)

See main detective Sgt Morgan PRICE

Citation Record: 1 Book

Before It's Too Late - *Only*
GM US (1970); Fawcett UK (1970)

W

Mrs Elizabeth WARRENDER and James WARRENDER

There is some divergence of opinion as to which of this duo of mother and son is the main detective, some sources citing one, some the other. *James WARRENDER* is a rather ineffectual private detective and is continually being upstaged and second guessed by his mother, whom he calls 'an incurably meddling old woman'.

British Female Amateur and British Male Private Detective operating in England

G D H COLE and Margaret COLE (British)

Invented 7 detectives - see Supt Henry WILSON

Citation Record: 1 Book 5 Short Stories in 1 Collection

A Knife In The Dark - *Only*
Collins UK (1941); Macmillan US (1942)

Mrs Warrender's Profession - *Collection 1*
contains five novelettes.
Collins UK (1938); Macmillan US (1939)

James WARRENDER

Second detective of Mrs Elizabeth WARRENDER

Seth WARRINER

sleuths in a case set back into 1875.

American Male Amateur operating in Pennsylvania

Gerald TOMLINSON 1933- (American)

Citation Record: 1 Book

On A Field Of Black - *Single*
Nellin US (1980)

Claude WARRINGTON-REEVE and Insp Steven MITCHELL

Claude WARRINGTON-REEVE is a barrister who works closely with *Insp MITCHELL*, often finding important clues, which the latter usually unravels and puts into place.

British Male Amateur and British Policeman operating in England

Josephine BELL 1897-1987 (British)

Invented 10 detectives - see Dr David WINTRINGHAM

Citation Record: 3 Books

Easy Prey - *First*
Hodder & Stoughton UK (1959); Macmillan US (1959)

A Flat Tyre In Fulham - *Last*
Hodder & Stoughton UK (1963)

Fiasco In Fulham - *Last**
Macmillan US (1963)

Room For A Body - *Last**
Ballantine US (1964)

Victoria Iphigenia 'Vi' WARSHAWSKI

is one of the best and toughest detectives in Chicago and, around the place, is generally known as Vi. Only a colleague of her dead policeman father is allowed to call her Vicki and her close friends call her Vic. Of mixed Polish, Jewish and Italian extraction, she was once an attorney in Cook County but now operates on the Loop in Chicago and specialises in financial cases. She is an avowed feminist and can be a bore. However, she is progressive when it comes to ethics and morals. Naturally, she is good at most things a modern gal has to be good at; and, when it comes to the point, and it often does, she can take it as well as dish it out.

American Female Private Detective operating in Chicago

Sara PARETSKY 1947- (American)

was born in Ames, Iowa. She graduated with a BA in Political Science at the University of Kansas, Lawrence, 1967, followed by a PhD in History at the University of Chicago, Illinois, 1977. Co-founder of Sisters in Crime, 1988, she received the Crime Writers Association Silver Dagger award, 1988.

Adopter of one other detective Philip MARLOWE

Citation Record: 8 Books

Indemnity Only - *First*
Dial US (1982); Gollancz UK (1982)

Tunnel Vision - *Latest*
Atheneum US (1994); Hamish Hamilton UK (1994)

Emma WARWICK

British Female Amateur operating in New Guinea

Charlotte JAY 1919- (British)

See main detective William BROOKE

Citation Record: 1 Book

Beat Not The Bones - *Only*
Collins UK (1952); Harper & Row US (1953)

John (The Spider) WARWICK

American Male Sleuth operating in USA

Johnston MCCULLEY 1883-1958 (American)

Invented 5 detectives - see John (The Thunderbolt) FLATCHLEY

Citation Record: 2 Books

The Spider's Den - *First*
Chelsea US (1925)

The Spider's Fury - *Last*
Chelsea US (1930); Hutchinson UK (1931)

George WASHINGTON

is, indeed, the first President of America and here he solves the problem of how a spy could disappear from a locked room, the sort of thing that was not at all good for the standing of the new society.

American Male Amateur operating in USA

Steven PETERS (American)

Citation Record: 1 Selected Short Story

George Washington, Detective
appeared in the August number.
In 'Ellery Queen's Mystery Magazine' US (1967)

Trooper Sam WATCHMAN

is a State Trooper who is repeatedly passed over for promotion because of his part-Navajo ancestry. He undertakes his own quests for justice, however, on the part of fellow Indians.

American Policeman operating in Arizona

Brian GARFIELD 1939- (American)

was born in New York City. He graduated with a BA from the University of Arizona, Tucson, 1959, and received an MA, 1963. Jazz musician, teacher and producer, he has written over twenty criminous works and many short stories but rarely uses series detectives. Under his own name and several pseudonyms, he is the author of at least forty novels in other genres, especially the Western.

Writer: Brian Francis Wynne GARFIELD

Other Detectives:
Paul BENJAMIN
Simon CRANE
Charlie DARK

Citation Record: 2 Books

Relentless - *First*
World US (1972); Hodder & Stoughton UK (1973)

The Threepersons Hunt - *Last*
Evans US (1974); Coronet UK (1975)

Cdr Roger WATERLOW

British Male Amateur operating in England

Compton MACKENZIE 1883-1972 (British)

Writer: Anthony Edward Montagu Compton MACKENZIE

Citation Record: 2 Books

Extremes Meet - *First*
Cassell UK (1928); Doubleday US (1928)

The Three Couriers - *Last*
Cassell UK (1929); Doubleday US (1929)

WATERS

was the main fictional representation of the author in his detective mode.

British Policeman operating in England

WATERS (British)

was certainly connected with the police but his identity remains obscure. He was probably, however, the first author of police short stories in England, publishing his various collections purporting to be the experiences of police detectives under several pseudonyms in addition to the one cited.

Writer: William Clark RUSSELL

Other Byline: W Clark RUSSELL

Other Detectives:
Henry CLARKE
Theodore DUHAMEL
A FRENCH DETECTIVE OFFICER
INSPECTOR F
William SHARPE

Citation Record: 18 Short Stories in 2 Collections

Recollections Of A Detective Police-Officer - *Collection 1*
was published in several forms in the US and later in the UK, with stories added or subtracted.
Short stories - 10
Brown UK (1856)

The Recollections Of A Policeman - *Collection 1**
Cornish Lamport US (1952)

Diary Of A Detective Police Officer - *Collection 1**
Dick US (1864)

The Recollections Of A Detective - *Collection 1**
Loyd US (1887)

Recollections Of A Detective Police-Officer. Second Series - *Collection 2*
Short stories - 8
Kent UK (1859)

Mr WATSON

American Male Amateur operating in California

Dorothy GARDINER 1894-1979

See main detective Sheriff Moss MAGILL

Citation Record: 2 Books

The Transatlantic Ghost - *First*
Harrap UK (1933); Doubleday US (1933)

A Drink For Mr Cherry - *Last*
Doubleday US (1934)

Mr Watson Intervenes - *Last**
Hurst UK (1935)

John Conan WATSON

is a bizarre invention, half-way between a *Sherlock HOLMES* parody and a *Dr WATSON* parody. He sometimes calls himself Moriarty, which confuses everyone, probably including the readers of this very strange story.

American Male Amateur operating in USA

Joyce HARRINGTON (American)

Invented 3 detectives - see Jenny HOLLAND

Citation Record: 1 Selected Short Story

The Adventure Of The Gowanus Abduction - *Parody 1*
is in the anthology, *THE NEW ADVENTURES OF SHERLOCK HOLMES.*
Carroll & Graf US (1987)

Dr John H WATSON

is, of course, the most famous and revered sidekick in the criminous literature. However, several authors have used him as a detective in pastiches, which are all cited.

British Male Amateur operating in England

Sidekick: Mycroft HOLMES
was *Sherlock HOLMES'* brother, created by *Conan DOYLE* and appearing in one or two of the stories. He was said to be even more brilliant than the sage of Baker Street and, in fact, lends a little help to the latter when particularly sensitive matters of state are involved. In the story by *Noel DOWNING* he is made an assistant to the bumbling *Dr WATSON.*

British Male - Assistant

Noel DOWNING

Citation Record: 1 Book

Dr Watson And The Invisible Man - *Pastiche 1*
It would seem that, following the death of the famous *H G WELLS* character, The Invisible Man, his notebooks have been found and, for fairly obvious reasons, lead to murder. *Sherlock HOLMES* being away on a case, *Dr John WATSON* takes over the investigation and is fortunate in obtaining the help of a most brilliant sidekick.
Ian Henry UK (1991)

Robert Lee HALL 1941- (American)

See main detective Benjamin FRANKLIN

Citation Record: 1 Book

Exit Sherlock Holmes: The Great Detective's Final Days - *Pastiche 1*

Dr WATSON, summoned to 221B Baker Street some time in 1903, learns that Professor Moriarty had not been killed in 1891 and is still bent on evil. *Sherlock HOLMES* having retired to Sussex, the good doctor sets about investigating, only to learn the shocking truth about his old friend.

Scribner's US (1977); Murray UK (1977)

Michael HARDWICK 1924-1991 (British)

Writer: John Michael Drinkrow HARDWICK

Other Detectives:

BERGERAC　Sherlock HOLMES

Citation Record: 1 Book

The Private Life Of Dr Watson - *Pastiche 1*

Dutton US (1983)

W HEIDENFELD (American)

Adopter of one other detective Sherlock HOLMES

Citation Record: 1 Selected Short Story

The Unpleasantness At The Stooges Club - *Pastiche 1*

In this pastiche, *Dr WATSON* meets several other well-known fictional stooges to show them how a crime should be solved – except that this one is down to Professor Moriarty.

In 'Ellery Queen's Mystery Magazine' US (1953)

Mrs Sarah WATSON

is a large lady who runs the Watson Detective Agency and, for extraordinary reasons, manages to do very well out of it - which is more than anybody else in her immediate environs does. She appeared in short stories in *Detective Fiction Weekly* in the 1930s.

American Female Private Detective operating in USA

Sidekick: Ben TODD

is baffled by everything and everybody, including the redoubtable lady who is his boss.

American Male - Assistant

D B MCCANDLESS (American)

Citation Record: 1 Selected Short Story

Cash Or Credit

can also be found in the anthology, *Hard-Boiled Dames; Stories Featuring Women Detectives, Reporters, Adventurers and Criminals from the Pulp Fiction Magazines of the 1930s* (Editor; Bernard Drew; US 1986).

In 'Detective Fiction Weekly' US (1933)

Sherlock WATSON

is a *Sherlock HOLMES* parody.

British Male Professional Amateur operating in London

A F ARNOLD

Citation Record: 1 Selected Short Story

Sherlock Watson's Last Case - *Parody 1*

appeared in the March number.

In 'The Amateur Mart' (1935)

Insp WATTERSON

solves a case of death by shooting, unexplained by those present.

American Policeman operating in USA

Walter F EBERHARDT 1891?-1935 (American)

Citation Record: 1 Book

The Jig-Saw Puzzle Murder - *Only*

Grosset US (1933); Puzzle Books UK (1933)

Wally WATTS

is an eighteen-year-old correspondence school detective. He works as a grocery clerk and delivery boy to pay for his course and his cases are described in letters to the Watchful Eye Detective School of New York City.

American Male Amateur operating in New York

Paul W FAIRMAN 1916-1977 (American)

See main detective Rick MASON

Citation Record: 1 Selected Short Story

Wally, The Watchful Eye

US (1960)

Insp WAYNE

solves a case in which a man is shot in a locked room.

British Policeman operating in England

E J POND (British)

Citation Record: 1 Book

The Ince Murder Case - *Only*

Heritage UK (1934)

Morgan WAYNE

American Male Amateur operating in New York

Matthew BLOOD 1904-1977 (American)

For writer details see Michael SHAYNE

Citation Record: 2 Books

The Avenger - *First*

Fawcett US (1952); GM US (1952)

Death Is A Lovely Dame - *Last*

Fawcett US (1954); GM US (1954)

Pam WAYNE

British Female Amateur operating in England

Mairi O'NAIR 1890- (British)

Writer: Constance May EVANS

Citation Record: 12 Short Stories in 1 Collection

The Girl With The X-Ray Eyes - *Collection 1*

Mills UK (1935)

Rodney WAYNE

British Male Amateur operating in England

A G E CROMWELL (British)

Citation Record: 2 Books

Murder In Flat 14 - *First*

Wright UK (1939)

Death In The Copse - *Last*

Wright UK (1940)

Steve WAYNE

British Male Amateuroperating in England

Terry HARKNETT 1936- (British)

See main detective Ch Supt John CROWN

Citation Record: 9 Books

The Scratch On The Surface - *First*

Hale UK (1962)

The Softcover Kill - *Last*

Hale UK (1971)

Carl WAYWARD

is a criminologist. He appears also in a book with the author's other detective, *Jub FREEMAN.*

American Male Professional Investigator operating in USA

Lawrence TREAT 1903- (American)

Invented 7 detectives - see Det Jub FREEMAN, Det Bill DECKER and Det Mitch TAYLOR

Citation Record: 4 Books

B As In Banshee - *First*

Duell US (1940)

O As In Omen - *Last*

Duell US (1943)

Det Carl WAYWARD

Second detective of Det Jub FREEMAN

Lt WEARIE
American Policeman operating in USA

Sean MACGRADY (American)

Citation Record: 1 Book

Gloom Of Night - *Single*
Pocket Books US (1993)

Artie WEATHERBY
is a Vietnam War veteran and an ex-alcoholic who finally makes it as a PI.

American Male Private Detective operating in USA

J M T MILLER (American)

Writer: Janice M Tubbs MILLER

Citation Record: 2 Books

Weatherby - *First*
Ballantine US (1987)

On A Dead Man's Chest - *Latest*
Ballantine US (1989)

Kate WEATHERLY
British Female Amateur operating in several locations

Maisie BIRMINGHAM (British)

Citation Record: 2 Books

You Can Help Me - *First*
Collins UK (1974)

The Heat Of The Sun - *Latest*
Collins UK (1976)

Nicky WEAVER
American Male Sleuth operating in USA

Nicky WEAVER 1916-1975 (American)

Writer: Orrie Edwin HITT

Citation Record: 2 Books

Love, Blood And Tears - *First*
Kozy US (1963)

Love Or Kill Them All - *Last*
Kozy US (1963)

Ted S WEAVER
American Male Amateur operating in New York/France

David KEITH 1906- (American)

Writer: Francis STEEGMULLER

Citation Record: 2 Books

A Matter Of Iodine - *First*
Dodd, Mead US (1940); Cassell UK (1940)

A Matter Of Accent - *Last*
Dodd, Mead US (1943)

Anne WEBB
Second detective of John WEBB

Ch Insp David WEBB
British Policeman operating in England

Sidekick: Det Sgt Ken JACKSON

British Male - Subordinate

Anthea FRASER 1930- (British)

was born in Blundellsands, Lancashire, and educated at Cheltenham Ladies' College, Cheltenham. Her novels are English rural whodunnits of high quality.

Writer: Anthea Mary FRASER

Citation Record: 7 Books

A Shroud For Delilah - *First*
Collins UK (1984); Doubleday US (1986)

The April Rainers - *Latest*
Collins UK (1989); Doubleday US (1990)

Jimmy WEBB
Second detective of Sam BOOKER

John WEBB and Anne WEBB
American Male Amateur and American Female Amateur operating in Ohio

Frank G PRESNELL 1906- (American)

Citation Record: 2 Books

Send Another Coffin - *First*
Morrow US (1939); Heinemann UK (1939)

No Mourners Present - *Last*
Morrow US (1940); Nicholson & Watson UK (1943)

Martin WEBB
is a learned musicologist at Harvard. When he discovers two bodies in his apartment he naturally sets out to find whodunnit.

American Male Amateur operating in Boston

Vernon HINKLE 1935- (American)

See main detective Steve HERSHEY

Citation Record: 1 Book

Music To Murder By - Single
Tower US (1978)

Peter WEBB
Second detective of Dick PEMBERTY

Terry WEBB
is a female cop who, with the help of her husband, solves a murder case.

American Policewoman operating in New York

Sidekick: Glenn WEBB

American Male - Husband

Philip DEGRAVE 1952- (American)

For writer details see Matt COBB

Citation Record: 1 Book

Unholy Moses - *Single*
Doubleday US (1985)

Dallas WEBSTER
was a fighter pilot in the Second World War and is now a PI in Yavapai, Arizona. He looks like a cowboy and is, in fact, really reluctant to be a detective at all.

American Male Private Detective operating in USA

Don STANFORD 1918- (American)

Writer: Donald Kent STANFORD

Citation Record: 2 Books

The Slaughtered Lovelies - *First*
GM US (1950); Red Seal UK (1957)

Bargain In Blood - *Last*
GM US (1951); Muller UK (1958)

Det Daniel WEBSTER
solves two cases of murder that occur under strange circumstances, involving resurrectionists and death in the operating theatre.

!See Appendix 2.

American Policeman operating in Los Angeles

Richard SALE 1911- (American)

Invented 5 detectives - see Calamity QUADE

Citation Record: 2 Books

Lazarus #7 - *First*
Simon & Schuster US (1942)

Lazarus Murder Seven - *First**
Handi-Books US (1943)

Death Looks In - *First**
Cassell UK (1943)

Passing Strange - *Last*
Simon & Schuster US (1942)

Sam WEBSTER
is a black operative for a secret US agency who is sent to Israel to foil a dangerous plot.

American Male Secret Agent operating in Israel

Blaine LITTELL (American)

Citation Record: 1 Book

The Dolorosa Deal - *Only*
Collins UK (1973)

Arnold WECHSLER

is a member of the Classics department of the fictional Hewes University. He is asked by the president to investigate the kidnapping of the latter's grand-daughter. Since this is followed at once by the president's murder, he has to start detecting pretty sharply.

American Male Amateur operating in USA

John Alexander GRAHAM 1941- (American)

See main detective Arthur SILVERMAN

Citation Record: 1 Book

The Involvement Of Arnold Wechsler - *Only*
Atlantic US (1971)

Nat WEDGEWOOD

British Male Amateur operating in England

J FAIRFAX-BLAKEBOROUGH 1883-1976 (British)

Writer: John Freeman FAIRFAX-BLAKEBOROUGH

Citation Record: 7 Short Stories in 1 Collection

Nat Wedgewood, Jockey - *Collection 1*
Allan UK (1933)

WEE PUNCH

appears in one short story in the collection, *BROUGHT TO BAY,* which mainly features *M'GOVAN.*

Sleuth operating in Edinburgh

James M'GOVAN (British)

Invented 3 detectives - see James M'GOVAN

Citation Record: 1 Selected Short Story

Wee Punch, The Dog Detective
Menzies UK (1878)

Finley WEHRMANN

investigates the death of her mother, the wife of the Professor of English at the fictional Whitefield College. She gets little help and no encouragement from the police.

American Female Amateur operating in USA

Mildred DAVIS (American)

Writer: Mildred B DAVIS

Citation Record: 1 Book

Tell Them What's-Her-Name Called - *Only*
Random House US (1975); Hale UK (1976)

Raoul WEILER

Male Amateur operating in England

Hilary St George SAUNDERS 1898-1951 (British)

Writer: Hilary Aiden St George SAUNDERS

Citation Record: 1 Book

The Sleeping Bacchus - *Only*
Joseph UK (1951)

Agatha WELCH

solves local and ingenious murders involving her friends.

American Female Amateur operating in Connecticut

Veronica Parker JOHNS 1907-1988 (American)

See main detective Webster FLAGG

Citation Record: 2 Books

Hush, Gabriel! - *First*
Duell US (1941)

Shady Doings - *Last*
Duell US (1941)

Victoria WELCH

American Female Amateur operating in San Francisco

M J BOSSE 1924- (American)

Writer: Malcolm Joseph BOSSE

Citation Record: 1 Book

The Man Who Loved Zoos - *Only*
Putnam US (1974); Gollancz UK (1975)

Hugo WELCHMAN

British Male Amateur operating in England

Julian GLOAG 1930- (British)

Citation Record: 1 Book

Sleeping Dogs Lie - *Single*
Secker & Warburg UK (1980); Dutton US (1980)

Ada WELLER

American Female Amateur operating in New York

Miriam BORGENICHT 1915- (American)

See main detective Nan DUNLAP

Citation Record: 1 Book

True Or False - *Single*
St Martin's US (1982)

Prof WELLS

is doctor, chemist and amateur criminologist. He lives in Russell Square, London's intellectual heart; and, being a bachelor, middle-aged, bearded, and looking avuncular with gold-rimmed glasses, he naturally likes a pipe and a glass of sherry. Do not be fooled! Because of his brilliance, he is brought into difficult cases by his friend in the police and is actually assisted in what little legwork he thinks necessary by being given a police aide. Splendid stuff!

British Male Amateur operating in London

Sidekick: Supt SIMS
is seconded from Scotland Yard to work closely with the amateur sleuth.
!See Appendix 2.
British Male - Aide

Stooge: Sir Charles MERRIVALE
is head of the London CID and he brings in *WELLS* to solve baffling cases. He must be one of the nicest stooges in the literature.
British Male

Francis GRIERSON 1888-1972 (British)

Invented 6 detectives - see Ch Det Insp George MUIR

Citation Record: 11 Books 10 Short Stories in 1 Collection

The Limping Man - *First*
Hodder & Stoughton UK (1924); Clode US (1926)

Murder In Black - *Last*
Thornton-Butterworth UK (1935); Appleton Century US (1935)

The Double Thumb - *Collection 1*
Hodder & Stoughton UK (1925)

Prof Clifford WELLS and Lt Barney MATTINGLEY

Clifford WELLS is a lecturer in physics at John Hopkins University and uses his special skills to help *Insp Barney MATTINGLEY* solve a case of murder there.

American Male Amateur and American Policeman operating in Baltimore

Norman Stanley BORTNER (American)

Citation Record: 2 Books

Bond Grayson Murdered - *First*
McCrae, Smith US (1936)

Death Of A Merchant Of Death - *Last*
McCrae, Smith US (1937)

Gardner WELLS

specialises in investigating security frauds in high-tech companies. In his first book, however, he tries to find a missing child and runs into the dark underworld of crime and murder in Mexico.

American Male Professional Investigator operating in California/Mexico

David A VAN METER (American)

Citation Record: 1 Book

Body Of Evidence - *Single*
Piatkus UK (1990)

H G WELLS

is, indeed, the famous British writer of mainstream novels and the father figure of science fiction.

British Male Amateur operating in England

Karl ALEXANDER (American)

See main detective Sarah SCOTT

Citation Record: 1 Book

Time After Time - *Only*
Delacorte US (1979); Panther UK (1980)

John WELLS

is an investigative reporter.

American Male Amateur operating in New York

Keith PETERSON (American)

Writer: Andrew KLAVAN

Citation Record: 4 Books

The Rain - *First*
Bantam US (1988); Coronet UK (1990)

Rough Justice - *Latest*
Bantam US (1989); Coronet UK (1990)

Mike WELLS

American Male Private Detective operating in New York

Lawrence LARIAR 1908-1981 (American)

Writer: Lawrence LARIAR

Other Bylines:
Adam KNIGHT
Michael LAWRENCE
Michael STARK

Other Detectives:
Homer BULL
Steve GANT

Citation Record: 1 Book

You Can't Catch Me - *Only*
Crown US (1951)

Sam WELPTON

is a partner in Lane & Welpton Insurance Investigators and his first case fizzed with action, much gunslinging and many lovely ladies.

American Male Private Detective operating in Los Angeles

John A SAXON 1886-1947 (American)

Citation Record: 1 Book

Liability Limited - *Only*
Mill US (1947)

This Was No Accident - *Only**
Foulsham UK (1949)

John A SAXON 1902-1968 (American)

Writer: Robert Leslie BELLEM

Other Byline: Robert Leslie BELLEM

Citation Record: 1 Book

Half-Past Mortem - *Only*
was written by *John Leslie BELLEM* after the death of *John A SAXON*, although published under the latter's name.
Mill US (1947); Foulsham UK (1951)

Prof Nicky WELT

is a middle-aged Professor of English. He plays chess every Friday night with the District Attorney of Suffolk County and, by purely intellectual means, is able to solve a number of the latter's cases. A classic example of the armchair detective!

American Male Amateur operating in New England

Harry KEMELMAN 1908- (American)

See main detective Rabbi David SMALL

Citation Record: 7 Short Stories in 1 Collection

The Nine Mile Walk - *Collection 1*
Putnam US (1967); Hutchinson UK (1968)

Peter WENNICK

is a law clerk and process server who, on his firm's cases, goes outside the law to get the cases resolved. An early creation of an author who was to go far, he appeared in the pulps of the 1930s.

American Male Amateur operating in USA

Erle Stanley GARDNER 1889-1970 (American)

Invented 14 detectives - see Perry MASON

Citation Record: 1 Selected Short Story

Leg Man
In 'Black Mask Magazine' US (1938)

Bea WENTWORTH

Second detective of Lyon WENTWORTH

Lyon WENTWORTH and Bea WENTWORTH

are a liberal-minded husband-and-wife team who meet up with classic murder puzzles around the villages of Connecticut. He is a former Professor of English who is also a writer of children's stories and she is a feminist state senator who can often obtain information of use in his enquiries. They are aided in their sleuthing by a young female protester and tend to work with the local police chief.

American Male Amateur and American Female Amateur operating in Connecticut

Sidekick: Kimberly WARD
is a female activist who lends help where needed.
American Female - Assistant

Stooge: Ch Rocco HERBERT
is a large, powerful man who was once in Army Intelligence with *Lyon WENTWORTH* and is now Police Chief at Murphysville. He works with the couple, a helpful stooge, but a stooge even so as he never solves a single case.
American Male

Richard FORREST 1932- (American)

was born in Orange, New Jersey. He graduated from the University of South Carolina, Columbia, 1955, and served in the US Army in the Korean War, 1951-1954. He worked as an executive for an insurance company until 1972 and then became a full-time writer.

Writer: Richard Stockton FORREST

Citation Record: 7 Books

A Child's Garden Of Death - *First*
Bobbs Merrill US (1975); Hale UK (1979)

Death On The Mississippi - *Latest*
St Martin's US (1989)

Richard (The Spider) WENTWORTH

appears in books that have all been reprinted from pulp magazines of the 1930s.

American Male Amateur operating in New York

Grant STOCKBRIDGE 1904-1961 (American)

Writer: Norvell W PAGE

Citation Record: 12 Books

Wings Of The Black Death - *First*
Berkley US (1969)

The Prince Of Evil - *Latest*
Dimedia US (1985)

Sheridan WESLEY

is unusually rich for a PI and can afford to turn down cases that do not interest him.

American Male Private Detective operating in USA

Hillary WAUGH 1920- (American)

Invented 7 detectives - see Ch Fred FELLOWS

Citation Record: 3 Books

Madam Will Not Dine Tonight - *First*
Coward McCann US (1947); Boardman UK (1949)

If I Live To Dine - *First**
Graphic US (1949)

The Odds Run Out - *Last*
Coward McCann US (1949); Boardman UK (1950)

Ambrose WEST
British Male Amateur operating in London/Paris

Philip LEVENE 1926- (British)

Citation Record: 2 Books

Ambrose In London - *First*
Hale UK (1959)

Ambrose In Paris - *Last*
Hale UK (1960)

Delilah WEST
resigns from the Los Angeles Police Department to join her husband in his detective agency in Orange County. When he is killed she does what a girl has to do and carries on where he, regrettably, had to leave off.

American Female Private Detective operating in California

Maxine O'CALLAGHAN (American)

Citation Record: 3 Books

Death Is Forever - *First*
Raven US (1981)

Hit And Run - *Latest*
St Martin's US (1989)

Helen WEST and Det Supt Geoffrey BAILEY
Helen WEST is a crown prosecutor who joins in the sleuthing with the official police and together they are beginning to form a series team. *Geoffrey BAILEY* is also in one other book by this author.

British Female Amateur and British Policeman operating in England

Frances FYFIELD 1948- (British)

See main detective Det Supt Geoffrey BAILEY

Citation Record: 3 Books

A Question Of Guilt - *First*
Heinemann UK (1988); Pocket Books US (1989)

Shadow Play - *Latest*
Bantam UK (1993)

Henry Highland (Iceman) WEST
American Male Sleuth operating in USA

Joseph NAZEL 1944- (American)

Writer: Joseph G NAZELL Jr

Other Byline: Don GOBER

Inventor of one other detective BLACK

Citation Record: 7 Books

Billion Dollar Death - *First*
Holloway US (1974)

The Shakedown - *Last*
Holloway US (1975)

Honey WEST
operates first in California and later in New York. 'The sexiest private eye ever to pull a trigger', her tendency and willingness to remove her clothes at the slightest provocation probably makes her an embarrassment to creators of the modern female PI; for she is hardboiled, great fun and has absolutely no political correctness whatsoever. However, though she oozes sex, as far as we can tell she never gets it. Definitely the virgin tease of the 1950s, before the deluge, she nevertheless solves some strange cases without trying to be a man in girl's clothing (or absence of it). She appears also in one book with the author's other detective, *Erik MARCH*.

American Female Private Detective operating in New York/California

G G FICKLING (American)

Writers: Gloria FICKLING and Forrest E FICKLING 1925-

Other Detectives:
Erik MARCH   Honey WEST and Erik MARCH

Citation Record: 10 Books

This Girl For Hire - *First*
Pyramid US (1957)

Honey On Her Tail - *Last*
Pyramid US (1971)

Honey WEST and Erik MARCH
also appear individually in other books by this author.

American Female Private Detective and American Male Private Detective operating in Los Angeles

G G FICKLING (American)

Invented 3 detectives - see Honey WEST

Citation Record: 1 Book

Stiff As A Broad - *Only*
Pyramid US (1971)

Janine WEST
American Female Sleuth operating in Cape Cod/Florida

Elizabeth WELLES

House name.

Citation Record: 4 Books

Captain's Walk - *First*
Pocket Books US (1976)

Spaniard's Gift - *Latest*
Pocket Books US (1977)

Elizabeth WELLES 1930-

Writer: Mary Linn ROBY

Citation Record: 1 Book

Seagull Crag - *Single*
Pocket Books US (1977)

Mae WEST
Second detective of Toby PETERS

Matthew WEST
American Male Amateur operating in Chicago

Randall PARRISH 1858-1923 (American)

Citation Record: 1 Book

The Case And The Girl - *Only*
Knopf US (1922); Paul UK (1923)

Michael WEST
American Male Amateur operating in USA

Max MURRAY 1901-1956 (Australian)

was a journalist on Australian and American newspapers.

Citation Record: 1 Book

The Doctor And The Corpse - *Only*
Farrar, Straus US (1952); Joseph UK (1953)

Robert WEST and Donald SHAW
solve a case of murder in the House of Commons.

British Male Amateurs operating in London

Ellen WILKINSON 1891-1947 (British)

was a prominent Labour Party MP in the post-war British government.

Writer: Ellen Cicely WILKINSON

Citation Record: 1 Book

The Division Bell Mystery - *Only*
Harrap UK (1932); Garland US (1976)

Insp Roger 'Handsome' WEST
of Scotland Yard is one of the author's longest lasting police detectives and one of the best- known. His cases mainly deal with the London underworld, although some have international connections. The books are sometimes more thrillers than detective stories and, on the whole, do not compare in quality with the author's later books, for example those with *Insp GIDEON*.

British Policeman operating in England

John CREASEY 1908-1973 (British)

was born in Southfields, a London suburb, and educated at primary schools in London. By any account he was a publishing phenomenon; for, under his own name and at least twenty pseudonyms, he is thought to have written over 600 novels, many of which remain unpublished. During his career, he published the *John Creasey Magazine*, 1956-1965; he was a co-founder of the Crime Writers Association; he was the President of the Mystery Writers of America, 1967-1968; he was a Liberal Party candidate, 1950; he founded his own political party, 1967. He received, from the Mystery Writers of America, the Edgar Allan Poe award, 1962, and the Grand Master award, 1967, and was made an MBE in 1969.

Writer: John CREASEY

Other Bylines:

Gordon ASHE, Norman DEANE, Robert Caine FRAZER, Michael HALLIDAY, Kyle HUNT, J J MARRIC, Anthony MORTON, Jeremy YORK

Other Detectives:

Sexton BLAKE, DEPARTMENT Z, Martin FANE and Richard FANE, Dr PALFREY, Richard (The Toff) ROLLISON

Citation Record: 43 Books

Inspector West Takes Charge - *First*
Paul UK (1942); Scribner's US (1970)

A Sharp Rise In Crime - *Last*
Hodder & Stoughton UK (1978); Scribner's US (1979)

Prof Theocritus Lucius WESTBOROUGH

is a scholar specialising in Roman history. A mild but firm man, he is often called in by the local police to solve difficult cases, first in Chicago, later in California. The cases often seem to be of the 'impossible' or locked-room type.

American Male Amateur operating in Illinois/California

Stooge: Insp John MACK
is rough on suspects but, even so, is unable to solve his cases on his own.
American Male

Clyde B CLASON 1903- (American)

was born in Denver, Colorado. He was a copy writer and editor in Chicago, Illinois.

Citation Record: 10 Books

The Death Angel - *First*
Doubleday US (1936); Heinemann UK (1937)

Green Shiver - *Last*
Doubleday US (1941); Heinemann UK (1948)

Conway WESTENHANGER

British Male Amateur operating in England

J J CONNINGTON 1880-1947 (British)

Invented 5 detectives - see Mark BRAND

Citation Record: 1 Book

The Dangerfield Talisman - *Only*
Benn UK (1926); Little, Brown US (1927)

Dr Hugh WESTLAKE

is a poor country doctor in the fictional town of Kenmore, somewhere in the eastern part of the USA. A widower, he has a propensity for getting into cases of murder and, with the aid of his daughter, solving them.

American Male Amateur operating in USA

Sidekick: Dawn WESTLAKE
assists her father in his sleuthing rather than his doctoring.
American Female - Daughter

Stooge: Insp COBB
is the epitome of rural police bafflement.
American Male

Jonathan STAGGE (American)

Writers: Richard Wilson WEBB 1901- and Hugh Callingham WHEELER 1912-1987

Citation Record: 9 Books

The Dogs Do Bark - *First*
Doubleday US (1937)

Murder Gone To Earth - *First**
Joseph UK (1936)

The Three Fears - *Last*
Doubleday US (1949); Joseph UK (1949)

WESTON

is described as a 'private inquiry agent' in this one Victorian novel.

British Male Private Detective operating in England

George R SIMS 1847-1922 (British)

Invented 5 detectives - see Dorcas DENE

Citation Record: 1 Book

In London's Heart - *Only*
Chatto & Windus UK (1900)

Mrs Caywood WESTON

American Female Amateur operating in Virginia/New York

Eugene THOMAS 1894- (American)

Inventor of one other detective CHU-SHENG

Citation Record: 2 Books

Death Rides The Dragon - *First*
Sears US (1932)

The Dancing Dead - *Last*
Sears US (1933)

Policeman Dick WESTON

Canadian Policeman operating in Canada

T LUND 1886- (Canadian)

Writer: Trygve LUND

Citation Record: 2 Books 6 Short Stories in 1 Collection

The Murder Of Dave Brandon - *First*
Laurie UK (1931)

Robbery At Portage Bend - *Last*
Laurie UK (1933); Kendall US (1933)

Weston Of The Royal North-West Mounted Police - *Collection 1*
Laurie UK (1928)

Weston Of The North-West Mounted Police - *Collection 1**
Mellifont UK (1938)

Gary WESTON

is accused wrongly of a murder and has to investigate a conspiracy against him.

British Male Amateur operating in England

Jeffrey ASHFORD 1926- (British)

Invented 9 detectives - see Det Insp Don KERRY

Citation Record: 1 Book

Deadly Reunion - *Single*
HarperCollins UK (19??)

Geoffrey WESTON

British Male Amateur operating in England

Thomas Brace HAUGHEY (British)

Citation Record: 4 Books

The Case Of The Invisible Thief - *First*
Bethany UK (1978)

The Case Of The Kidnapped Shadow - *Latest*
Bethany UK (1980)

James WESTON

British Male Private Detective operating in London

James WARREN (British)

See main detective James WARREN

Citation Record: 4 Books

No Sleep At All - *First*
Collins UK (1941); Alliance US (1941)

Brush Of Death - *Last*
Collins UK (1958)

Kate WESTON

is a social worker who believes in the innocence of a young man arrested for murder and sets out to prove it.

British Female Amateur operating in Yorkshire

Patricia HALL (British)

Citation Record: 1 Book

The Poison Pool - *Single*
HarperCollins UK (199?)

Tommy WESTON

British Male Amateur operating in England

Wilfred SHERIDAN (British)

Citation Record: 2 Books

The Five Brains - *First*
Jarrolds UK (1924)

Tommy Weston, Adventuress - *Last*
Jarrolds UK (1925)

Wade WESTON

American Male Detective in Pulp Magazines operating in USA

Police Captain HOWARD (American)

Invented 15 detectives - see LIGHTNING LUKE

Citation Record: 1 Book

Wade Weston, The 'Upper Ten' Detective; Or, The Mystery Of No 20 - *Only*
New York Detective Library US (1882-8)

Leslie WETZON

Second detective of Xenia SMITH

Ch Insp Reginald WEXFORD

is burly, stolid, pragmatic, compassionate, and happily married with two daughters. He has been hailed as one of the best of the present era's crop of British police detectives and is certain to remain so. Based in the fictional town of Kingsmarkham, he and his nicely delineated assistant revel in some of the most ingenious and finely written novels that have appeared since the Golden Age came to a close. Many of the books have formed the basis for a long-running British TV series.

British Policeman operating in England

Sidekick: Insp Mike BURDEN
is straight-faced and inflexible, an indomitable assistant to the sometimes bemused detective.
British Male - Assistant

Ruth RENDELL 1930- (British)

was born in London and educated at Loughton High School, Essex. A sometime reporter for provincial papers, she began writing in the 1960s and is, under her own name and a pseudonym, the author of three different series of criminous works, including classically told detective stories. She is regarded as in the very top rank of British crime and mystery writers to have emerged since the 1930s. She received the Mystery Writers of America Edgar Allen Poe award for short stories twice, 1975 and 1984; the Crime Writers Association Silver Dagger award, 1984; and their Gold Dagger award three times, 1976, 1986 and 1989.

Inventor of one other detective Anthony JOHNSON

Citation Record: 14 Books

From Doon With Death - *First*
Long UK (1964); Doubleday US (1965)

The Veiled One - *Latest*
Pantheon US (1988)

W

Lady WEYBRIDGE

British Female Amateur operating in England

Oliver SANDYS 1894-1964 (British)

Writer: Marguerite Helen Jervis EVANS

Citation Record: 11 Short Stories in 1 Collection

Chicane - *Collection 1*
Long UK (1912)

Sam WHARTON

British Male Amateur operating in England

David BUCKINGHAM 1919- (British)

Writer: David Hugh VILLIERS

Citation Record: 2 Books

The Wind Tunnel - *First*
Macdonald UK (1959)

The Cliff Face - *Last*
Macdonald UK (1960)

Insp Tom WHARTON

British Policeman operating in England

Elizabeth LEMARCHAND 1906- (British)

See main detective Det Supt Tom POLLARD

Citation Record: 11 Books

Death Of An Old Girl - *First*
Hart Davis UK (1967); Award US (1970)

Change For The Worse - *Latest*
Piatkus UK (1980); Walker US (1981)

Whitney WHEAT

American Male Sleuth operating in New York

Jeremy LANE 1893-1963 (American)

Citation Record: 4 Books

Death To Drumbeat - *First*
Phoenix Press US (1944)

Murder Spoils Everything - *Last*
Phoenix Press US (1949)

Lt Al WHEELER

is in the Homicide division in the Sheriff's department in Pine City, a fictional location near Los Angeles.

American Policeman operating in Pine City

Sidekick: Sgt POLNICK
is just about as stupid as a police sidekick can get and the author abandoned him in later books.
American Male - Subordinate

Stooge: Sheriff LAVERS
is the superior of *WHEELER* and always at odds with him.
American Male

Carter BROWN 1923-1985 (Australian)

Invented 10 detectives - see Rick HOLMAN

Citation Record: 45 Books

The Blonde - *First*
Horwitz AU (1955); New American Library US (1958); New English Library UK (1964)

Model For Murder - *Last*
Horwitz AU (1980); Tower US (1980)

Dan WHEELER

Second detective of Arthur 'Red' BLAKE

Simon WHEELER

appears in this book by the great *Mark TWAIN*, who died before finishing it. It was published, still uncompleted, later.

American Male Amateur operating in USA

Mark TWAIN 1835-1910 (American)

Invented 5 detectives - see Tom SAWYER

Citation Record: 1 Book

Simon Wheeler, Detective - *Only*
is, by all accounts, a satiric piece.
New York Public Library US (1963)

Walt WHEELER

American Male Detective in Pulp Magazines operating in USA

Harry ROCKWOOD 1859-1932 (American)

Invented 14 detectives - see Clarice DYKE

Citation Record: 2 Books

Walt Wheeler, The Scout Detective - *First*
Ogilvie US (1884)

The Secret Of The Missing Checks And Walt Wheeler, The Scout Detective - *Last*
Street & Smith (Magnet #233) US (1902)

Dick WHELAN

American Male Amateur operating in Long Island

Laurence Dwight SMITH (American)

Citation Record: 2 Books

The Corpse With The Listening Ear - *First*
Mystery House US (1940)

Follow This Fair Corpse - *Last*
Mystery House US (1941)

The Case Of The Rented Coffin - *Last**
Mystery Novel of the Month US (1941)

Gilbert E WHELDON

of Allegheny University is an American academic on the trail of works by Dr Sam Johnson in rural England. He meets with murder and runs considerable risk to his own life.

American Male Amateur operating in England

Thomas KYD 1901-1976 (American)

Invented 3 detectives - see Det Sam PHELAN

Citation Record: 1 Book

Cover His Face - *Only*
Lippincott US (1949)

Sheriff Emil WHIPPLETREE

American Policeman operating in Minnesota

Michael T HINKEMEYER 1940- (American)

!See Appendix 2.

Writer: Michael Thomas HINKEMEYER

Citation Record: 3 Books

The Fields Of Eden - *First*
Putnam US (1977); Futura UK (1980)

Fourth Down - *Latest*
St Martin's US (1985)

The WHISPERER

was one of the large species of 'private justice, figures. He appeared in at least twenty-four novels and twenty-five short stories, 1939-1942.

American Male Detective in Pulp Magazines operating in USA

UNKNOWN

WHISTLER

is a rough and tough operative in a sleazy Hollywood that is far removed from his youthful vision of it. He hangs out at a diner at the corner of Hollywood and Vine and his cases arise from his sentimentality about rescuing women in distress, who, alas, turn out to be not what they seem.

American Male Private Detective operating in Los Angeles

Robert CAMPBELL 1927- (American)

Invented 5 detectives - see Jake HATCH

Citation Record: 4 Books

In La-La Land We Trust - *First*
Mysterious Press US (1986)

The Wizard Of La-La Land - *Latest*
Pocket Books US (1994)

Derek WHITBY

American Male Amateur operating in USA

Charlton ANDREWS 1874-1939 (American)

Other Detectives:
Mycroft HOLMES and Sherlock HOLMES
Sherlock HOLMES   Drexel WARE

Citation Record: 1 Book

The Butterfly Murder - *Only*
Sears US (1932); Allen UK (1934)

Mr WHITE

Second detective of Mr BELL

Lt Al WHITE

American Policeman operating in USA

Genevieve HOLDEN 1919- (American)

See main detective Hank FERRELL

Citation Record: 4 Books

Killer Loose! - *First*
Doubleday US (1953)

Something's Happened To Kate - *Last*
Doubleday US (1958)

Blackie WHITE

is only just over 5 feet tall, 'with the body of a tank and the eyes of a baby'. He behaves like both when excited.

American Male Private Detective operating in New York

Philip JOHNSON 1911- (American)

Writer: Philip Edward JOHNSON

Citation Record: 1 Book

Hung Until Dead - *Only*
Phoenix Press US (1940)

Blanche WHITE

is an Afro-American lady who cleans for other people, more wealthy or more elevated in society than she is. A real American working-class detective at last!

American Female Amateur operating in Maine

Barbara NEELY (American)

Citation Record: 2 Books

Blanche On The Lam - *First*
St Martin's US (1992)

Blanche Among The Talented Tenth - *Latest*
St Martin's US (1994)

Sheriff George WHITE

American Policeman operating in California

M M MANNON (American)

Writers: Martha MANNON 1909- and Mary Ellen MANNON 1913-

Citation Record: 2 Books

Here Lies Blood - *First*
Bobbs US (1942)

Murder On The Program - *Last*
Bobbs US (1944)

Jim WHITE

Second detective of Theodore ROOSEVELT

Lace WHITE

is a middle-aged spinster who writes novels and just happens to be an honorary lieutenant in the Indiana State police force. The time when that could happen, regrettably alas, seems to have passed!

American Female Amateur operating in Indiana

Jeannette Covert NOLAN 1897-1974 (American)

Citation Record: 4 Books

Final Appearance - *First*
Duell US (1943)

A Fearful Way To Die - *Last*
Washburn US (1956); Muller UK (1957)

Peregrine WHITE

is a government agent involved in Cold War espionage.

American Male Secret Agent operating in USA

Bart SPICER 1918- (American)

Invented 3 detectives - see Carney WILDE

Citation Record: 2 Books

The Day Of The Dead - *First*
Dodd, Mead US (1955); Hodder & Stoughton UK (1956)

The Burned Man - *Last*
Atheneum US (1966); Hale UK (1967)

Bob WHITFIELD

American Male Amateur operating in USA

Richard A MOORE (American)

Citation Record: 2 Books

Death In The Past - *First*
Raven US (1981)

Death Of A Source - *Last*
Raven US (1982)

Whit WHITNEY

is a tax accountant turned amateur detective who appears in books that are more high comedy than detective stories.

American Male Professional Investigator operating in Los Angeles/Nevada

Sidekick: Kitty MACLEOD
was first a girlfriend but she married the boss. She now assists him.
American Female - Wife

David DODGE 1910- (American)

Invented 4 detectives - see Al COLBY

Citation Record: 4 Books

Death And Taxes - *First*
Macmillan US (1941); Joseph UK (1947)

It Ain't Hay - *Last*
Simon & Schuster US (1946)

A Drug On The Market - *Last**
Joseph UK (1949)

Chattin WHYTE

is an associate Professor of Sociology who is present when a young girl is murdered at a ceremony in a motion picture theatre at a small town where he is staying. Since, fortunately, he was once a crime reporter in Pittsburgh, he is eminently fitted to solve the crime, which baffles the local police force.

American Male Amateur operating in Pennsylvania

W C CLARK 1907- (American)
was born in Cleveland, Ohio. He was, for many years, Professor of Journalism at Syracuse University.

Writer: Wesley Clarke CLARK

Citation Record: 1 Book

Murder Goes To Bank Night - *Only*
Hale, Cushman & Flint US (1940)

Christer WICK

Swedish Male Sleuth operating in Sweden

Maria LANG 1914- (Swedish)

Writer: Dagmar Maria LANGE

Citation Record: 3 Books

A Wreath For The Bride - *First*
is a translation from the Swedish of *Kung Liljekonvalj Av Dungen* (Stockholm, 1957).
Hodder & Stoughton UK (1966); Regnery US (1968)

Death Awaits Thee - *Last*
is a translation from the Swedish of *Se, Doden Pa Dig Vantar* (Stockholm, 1955).
Hodder & Stoughton UK (1967)

Offr Tally WICKHAM and Sgt John BOON

solve a case of strange disappearances in a police building.

American Policemen operating in USA

Jack OLSEN 1925- (American)

Citation Record: 1 Book

Missing Persons - *Single*
Atheneum US (1981); Hale UK (1982)

Mr WICKWIRE

is an elderly New York banker turned amateur sleuth

American Male Amateur operating in USA

Mignon G EBERHART 1899- (American)

Invented 9 detectives - see Sarah KEATE

Citation Record: 2 Selected Short Stories

Mr Wickwire's 'Gun Moll'
is the first of three in which *Mr WICKWIRE* appeared. It is in an anthology, *A Choice of Murders.*
Scribner's US (1958); Macdonald UK (1960)

Mr Wickwire's Widow
is the last of the three and is in an anthology, *With Malice Towards All.*
Putnam US (1968); Macmillan UK (1969)

Insp WIDGEON

British Policeman operating in England

Alan THOMAS 1896- (British)

Writer: Alan Ernest Wentworth THOMAS

Inventor of one other detective Jimmy THURSTON

Citation Record: 2 Books

The Death Of Laurence Vining - *First*
Benn UK (1928); Lippincott US (1929)

Death Of The Home Secretary - *Last*
Benn UK (1931)

Insp WIELD

British Policeman operating in England

Glint GREEN 1883-1933 (British)

Writer: Margaret Ann PETERSON

Citation Record: 4 Books

Strands Of Red - Hair! - *First*
Hutchinson UK (1931)

Poison Death - *Last*
Hutchinson UK (1933)

Lt Chester WIERLOCK

investigates the murder of the wife of a tycoon, all the time in peril as he tries to keep an innocent man from being framed.

American Policeman operating in Georgia

Richard JESSUP 1925-1982 (American)

Citation Record: 1 Book

Cry Passion - *Only*
Dell US (1956)

P C James WIGAN

British Sleuth operating in England

Bernard J FARMER 1902- (British)

Writer: Bernard James FARMER

Citation Record: 4 Books

Death At The Cascades - *First*
Heinemann UK (1953)

Murder Next Year - *Last*
Heinemann UK (1959)

'Gramps' WIGGINS

American Male Amateur operating in California

Erle Stanley GARDNER 1889-1970 (American)

Invented 14 detectives - see Perry MASON

Citation Record: 2 Books

The Case Of The Turning Tide - *First*
Morrow US (1941); Cassell UK (1942)

The Case Of The Smoking Chimney - *Last*
Morrow US (1943); Cassell UK (1945)

Augustus WIGGLESWORTH

sleuths among the smuggling fraternity on the South Coast of England during the early 1800s.

British Male Amateur operating in England

Herbert CARTER (British)

Writer: Herbert Spencer CARTER

Citation Record: 9 Short Stories in 1 Collection

Wiggles. A Story Of Smuggling Days And Ways Around Poole - *Collection 1*
Looker UK (1931)

Keightley WILBUR

British Male Amateur operating in England

Frank DANBY 1864-1916 (British)

Writer: Julia Davis FRANKAU

Citation Record: 7 Short Stories in 1 Collection

The Story Behind The Verdict - *Collection 1*
Cassell UK (1915); Dodd, Mead US (1915)

Carl WILCOX

was once a convict and a soldier. Later he became an amateur detective in a rural community, Corden, in South Dakota. A smart rustic with some of the attributes, however, of an urban PI, he operates in this bleak farming community in the years of the Great Depression and his cases are all local and intimate.

American Male Amateur operating in South Dakota

Harold ADAMS 1923- (American)

was born in Clerk, South Dakota. He took a degree in English Literature at the University of Minnesota, Minneapolis, 1950.

Inventor of one other detective Kyle CHAMPION

Citation Record: 10 Books

Murder - *First*
Charter US (1981); Chivers UK (1989)

A Perfectly Proper Murder - *Latest*
Walker US (1993)

Carney WILDE

rises from running a one-man agency in Philadelphia to being head of Wilde Protective Systems Inc, which employs a couple of hundred agents.

American Male Private Detective operating in Philadelphia

Bart SPICER 1918- (American)

Other Detectives:
Benson KELLOGG
Peregrine WHITE

Citation Record: 7 Books

The Dark Light - *First*
Dodd, Mead US (1949); Collins UK (1950)

Exit Running - *Last*
Dodd, Mead US (1959); Hodder & Stoughton UK (1960)

Jonas WILDE

is a British agent, rather akin to the prototypic *James BOND*, though he prefers to kill people with a karate chop rather than a gun.

British Male Secret Agent operating in several locations

Andrew YORK 1930- (British)

was born in Georgetown, British Guiana (now Guyana). He was educated at Harrison College, Barbados, Queen's College, Guyana, and lives in Guernsey, Channel Islands. He has written, under his real name and other pseudonyms, at least seventy mainstream novels and is the author, under the *YORK* byline, of fourteen genre novels, mainly adventure thrillers.

Writer: Christopher Robin NICOLE

Other Byline: Christopher NICOLE

Inventor of one other detective Ch of Plce Munroe TALLANT

Citation Record: 9 Books

The Eliminator - *First*
Lippincott US (1967)

The Fascinator - *Last*
Hutchinson UK (1975); Doubleday US (1975)

Oscar WILDE

is, indeed, the famous English playwright. In this one book, he is on his well-documented lecture tour of the American West in 1882. Not so documented apparently is that, fictionally, he becomes suspected of murdering prostitutes. To save himself, he sets out to identify the real murderer by the application of 'poetic imagination'.

British Male Amateur operating in USA

Walter SATTERTHWAIT (American)

Invented 3 detectives - see Rita MONDRAGON

Citation Record: 1 Book

Wilde West - *Single*
St Martin's US (1991); HarperCollins UK (1991)

Timothy WILDE

American Male Private Detective operating in San Francisco

Howard RIGSBY 1909-1975 (American)

For writer details see Johnny CHURCH

Citation Record: 1 Book

Kill And Tell - *Only*
Morrow US (1951); Muller UK (1954)

Toby WILDE

British Male Amateur operating in England

Alison CAIRNS (American)

Citation Record: 2 Books

Strained Relations - *First*
Collins UK (1983); St Martin's US (1984)

New Year's Resolution - *Latest*
Collins UK (1984); St Martin's US (1985)

Joanna WILDER and Ruth WILSON

are partners in an agency in Portland, Maine.

American Female Private Detectives operating in Maine

Agnes BUSHNELL (American)

Citation Record: 1 Book

Shadow Dance - *Single*
US (1989)

Insp WILKINS

is a deliberate and delightful parody of all those stiff, noble, English policemen of the Golden Age of whodunnits. The murders all take place, as indeed is fictionally only proper, at the country house of the Earl and Countess of Burford.

British Policeman operating in England

James ANDERSON 1936- (British)

Other Detectives:
Insp BIDWELL
Jessica FLETCHER
Insp PALMER
Mikael Josef PETROS

Citation Record: 2 Books

The Affair Of The Bloodstained Egg Cosy - *First*
Constable UK (1975); McKay US (1977)

The Affair Of The Mutilated Mink Coat - *Latest*
Avon US (1981); Avon UK (1983)

Murray THOMAS 1897- (British)

Writer: Thomas Murray RAGG

Citation Record: 3 Books

Buzzards Pick The Bones - *First*
Longman UK (1932)

Inspector Wilkins Reads The Proofs - *Last*
Jenkins UK (1935)

Insp WILKINS

appears in a book that was said by the eminent critic, *Vincent STARRETT*, to be one of the ten greatest detective stories ever written.

British Policeman operating in England

Francis BEEDING (British)

was the pseudonym of two British writers who met around 1920 when both were working for the League of Nations Permanent Secretariat, in posts that they both held until 1939. During that period they wrote many detective novels and action thrillers. *PALMER* graduated from Balliol College, Oxford, and was a drama critic before working in several posts for the British government. He wrote several novels on his own as well as nearly a dozen works of criticism and on the theatre. *SAUNDERS* graduated from Balliol College,

Oxford, and served in the Army, 1916-1919, winning the Military Cross. He also wrote novels under his own name and was the author of some officially commissioned studies of the RAF, Boy Scouts and related topics.
Writers: John Leslie PALMER 1885-1944 and Hilary Aidan St George SAUNDERS 1898-1951
Other Detectives:
Ronald BRIERCLIFFE
John COWPER
Col Alistair GRANBY
Insp George MARTIN
Thomas PRESTON
Citation Record: 2 Books
Death Walks In Eastrepps - *First*
is said, by many critics, to be the best of all the detective stories written by these authors.
Hodder & Stoughton UK (1931); Mystery League US (1931)
Murder Intended - *Last*
Hodder & Stoughton UK (1932); Little, Brown US (1932)

Supt WILKINS and Col CHIDDINGTON

solve a couple of rather horrific cases of death in a locked room.
British Policeman and British Male Amateur operating in England

Max DALMAN (British)

Inventor of one other detective David MARCHANT
Citation Record: 1 Book
Vampire Abroad - *Only*
Ward, Lock UK (1938)

Nell WILLARD

American Female Amateur operating in USA

Miriam LYNCH (American)

has written a great number of criminous and suspense novels, but rarely uses distinctive or series detectives.
Writer: Mary WALLACE
Citation Record: 2 Books
Time To Kill - *First*
Zebra US (1979)
You'll Be The Death Of Me - *Latest*
Zebra US (1979)

Sheriff WILLETS

American Policeman operating in USA

Dorothy Salisbury DAVIS 1916- (American)

Invented 9 detectives - see Kate OSBORN
Citation Record: 1 Selected Short Story
Backward, Turn Backward
is in an anthology, *Tales for a Stormy Night.*
Countryman Press US (1984)

Brother WILLIAM

is a friar, a pilgrim who arrives at a monastery in Italy and succeeds in solving one special and stupendous mystery after a number of murders have taken place.
English Male Amateur operating in Italy
Sidekick: ADSO
is the lowly assistant of *Brother WILLIAM* and relates the tale.
Male - Assistant

Umberto ECO 1932- (Italian)

is a distinguished Italian writer whose book created a sensation.
Citation Record: 1 Book
The Name Of The Rose - *Single*
is a translation from the Italian of *Il Nome Della Rosa* (Milan, 1983), one of the great genre works of the century.
Secker & Warburg UK (1983); Harcourt Brace US (1983)

Insp WILLIAMS

British Policeman operating in England

Hugh CLEVELY 1898-1964 (British)

Invented 4 detectives - see Maxwell ARCHER
Citation Record: 6 Books
Frazer Butts In - *First*
Hutchinson UK (1929); Clode US (1931)
Public Enemy - *Last*
Cassell UK (1953)

George WILLIAMS

American Male Sleuth operating in USA

Joseph DI MONA (American)

Citation Record: 3 Books
The Last Man At Arlington - *First*
Fields US (1973); Weidenfeld & Nicolson UK (1974)
To The Eagle's Nest - *Latest*
Morrow US (1980); Joseph UK (1980)

Harry WILLIAMS

American Male Detective in Pulp Magazines operating in New York

F Lusk BROUGHTON (American)

Other Detectives:
Clint CLEAVER
Dick DRANT
DURGON
HOODOOED HOWARD
Belle KINGSTON
NEMO
OLD DECEIVER
OLD MYSTAGOGNE
Hal TYBERT
Citation Record: 1 Book
Harry Williams, The New York Detective - *Only*
Ogilvie US (1887)

Ken WILLIAMS

British Male Amateur operating in England

John H BARRINGTON (British)

Writer: John Henry HARVEY
Citation Record: 2 Books
The Moving Finger - *First*
Langdon UK (1947)
Murder In White Pit - *Last*
Langdon UK (1947)

Mal WILLIAMS

is called on to solve a case involving stolen drugs.
British Male Amateur operating in England

Bill WALSH 1933- (British)

Citation Record: 1 Book
Barbs - *Single*
Hale UK (1984)

Paul WILLIAMS

Male Sleuth

Hugh C MCDONALD 1913-

Writer: Hugh Chisholm MCDONALD
Citation Record: 3 Books
Five Signs From Ruby - *First*
Pyramid US (1976)
Letter From Kiev - *Latest*
Pyramid US (1977)

Race WILLIAMS

is, after *Terry MACK*, created by the same author just a fortnight earlier, historically the second of the long series of hardboiled private detectives to appear in the canon of American crime fiction, being featured in a short story for *Black Mask Magazine*. Aged around thirty, tall, with brown hair and black eyes, he is linearly descended from the Western cowboy hero and is, in fact, not much more than a tough gunman himself. He has been a reporter, insurance investigator, cameraman, and undercover agent, but he mainly operates as a PI. He is, of course, a crack shot with a revolver and women adore him. His code is crude and simple but already includes what was to become the linchpin of PI fiction, the credo of absolute loyalty to his client, provided he is honest. His popularity was enormous.
American Male Private Detective operating in New York

Carroll John DALY 1889-1958 (American)
was born in Yonkers, New York. He was a well-known New York theatre manager who became a prolific writer of short stories for the early pulps and later of a dozen or more detective novels with his two main detectives, *Race WILLIAMS* and *Vee BROWN.*

Other Detectives:
Vee BROWN   Marty DAY
Satan HALL   Clay HOLT
Terry MACK

Citation Record: 7 Books 1 Selected Short Story 5 Short Stories in 1 Collection

Knights Of The Open Palm
was published five months before the classic first story of *Dashiell HAMMETT*, featuring *The CONTINENTAL OP.* It marks perhaps the earliest appearance of the modern American hardboiled private eye.
Nicholson & Watson UK (1923)

The Snarl Of The Beast - *First*
Clode US (1927); Hutchinson UK (1928)

Better Corpses - *Last*
does not seem to have found a US publisher.
Hale UK (1940)

The Adventures Of Race Williams - *Collection 1*
Mysterious Press US (1988)

Remo (The Destroyer) WILLIAMS

appears in books that have sold over 30 million copies in a dozen languages and so must be accounted as a pretty nice guy as well as a useful one.. Appearing first in 1971, he is a young Westerner (his odd name derives from the Indiana town in which his hospital bed pan was manufactured), a cop for a while, who has been trained in the martial arts by a fairly inscrutable oriental Master. Naturally enough, with such a background, he decides to rid the world of its main enemies and fight evil wherever he finds it, which is, fortunately for the series, everywhere. The books provide action, thrills and detection, all delivered with great imagination and no mean quality. They were written, in the main, by *Warren B MURPHY* and *Richard SAPIR* and sometimes jointly. They have, to date, always appeared under one or other of their names and are so cited. *SAPIR* did not write any of the books after about 1979 and they were then written by *MURPHY* alone or with other collaborators.

American Male Amateur operating in New York/New Jersey

Warren B MURPHY 1933- (American)
Invented 8 detectives - see Julian 'Digger' BURROUGHS

Citation Record: 43 Books

Bay City Blast - *First*
Pinnacle US (1979); Corgi UK (1981)

Death Sentence - *Last*
Signet US (1990)

Richard SAPIR 1936-1987 (American)
Inventor of one other detective Alphonse Joseph BRESSIO

Citation Record: 37 Books

Created: The Destroyer - *First*
Pinnacle US (1971); Corgi UK (1973)

Bottom Line - *Last*
Pinnacle US (1979); Corgi UK (1981)

Dr Basil WILLING

is cast in the era's classic pattern in most respects, being upright, literate, a keen observer and well versed in much of the knowledge judged essential to the amateur sleuth. However, he is perhaps the first true practising psychiatrist detective in the genre and he uses his skills to observe clues others have missed, what he calls 'psychic fingerprints' that cannot be hidden. His cases occur in several different types of location, from Connecticut to Scotland. He appears also in one book with one of the author's other detectives, *Miguel URIZAR.*

American Male Professional Investigator operating in USA/Europe

Helen MCCLOY 1904-1993 (American)
was born in New York City. She was educated at Brooklyn Friends School, 1909-1919, and later at the Sorbonne, Paris. A distinguished art critic for papers in the US and UK, she is the author of at least thirty detective novels and several short stories. She received the Mystery Writers of America Edgar Allan Poe award for her work as a critic, 1953.

Writer: Helen Worrell Clarkson MCCLOY

Other Detectives:
DEVLIN   Alec NORTON
Miguel URIZAR
Dr Basil WILLING and Miguel URIZAR

Citation Record: 11 Books

Dance Of Death - *First*
Morrow US (1938)

Design For Dying - *First**
Heinemann UK (1938)

Burn This - *Last*
Dodd, Mead US (1980); Gollancz UK (1980)

Dr Basil WILLING and Miguel URIZAR

also appear individually in other books by this author.

American Male Professional Investigator and Male Amateur operating in USA

Helen MCCLOY 1904-1993 (American)
Invented 5 detectives - see Dr Basil WILLING

Citation Record: 1 Book

The Goblin Market - *Only*
Morrow US (1943); Hale UK (1951)

Insp WILLIS

British Policeman operating in England

Freeman Wills CROFTS 1879-1957 (British)
Invented 5 detectives - see Insp Joseph FRENCH

Citation Record: 1 Book

The Pit-Prop Syndicate - *Only*
Collins UK (1922); Seltzer US (1925)

George WILLIS

British Male Amateur operating in England

William HUGHES (British)

Citation Record: 3 Books

Split On Red - *First*
Magread UK (1979); Wyndham US (1979)

Cover Zero - *Latest*
Magread UK (1980)

James WILLOP

is a black reporter who is now able to investigate the conviction of his uncle in 1944 for rape and murder. Even after a lapse of forty years, he finds himself stalked by the real killer.

American Male Amateur operating in South Carolina

David STOUT 1942- (American)

Citation Record: 1 Book

Carolina Skeletons - *Single*
Mysterious Press US (1988)

Mike WILLOUGHBY

is a journalist who investigates the death of a Defence Secretary.

British Male Amateur operating in England

Martin RUSSELL 1934- (British)
Invented 3 detectives - see Steven CASSELL

Citation Record: 1 Book

Rainblast - *Single*
Collins UK (1982)

Tuthill WILLOW

American Male Private Detective operating in Chicago

Ross H SPENCER 1921- (American)
Invented 7 detectives - see Buzz DECKARD

Citation Record: 1 Book

Death Wore Gloves - *Single*
Fine US (1988)

WILLOWDENE WILL

appears in adventures, some criminous, set in the eighteenth century.

British Male Amateur operating in England

Halliwell SUTCLIFFE 1870-1932 (British)

Citation Record: 12 Short Stories in 1 Collection

Willowdene Will - *Collection 1*
Pearson UK (1901)

Det Jack WILLOWS and Det Claire PARKER

are police detectives who are also lovers.

Canadian Policeman and Canadian Policewoman operating in Vancouver

Laurence GOUGH (Canadian)

Citation Record: 5 Books

The Goldfish Bowl - *First*
Gollancz UK (1987); St Martin's US (1988)

Killers - *Latest*
Gollancz UK (1995); Trafalgar US (11995)

Persis WILLUM

is an artist who runs a gallery for Gregor Olitsky. She has friends in high places, the sort of thing that can be of considerable help to a girl who seems to be habitually involved with murder.

American Female Amateur operating in New York/France

Clarissa WATSON (American)

Citation Record: 5 Books

The Fourth Stage Of Gainsborough Brown - *First*
McKay US (1977); Joseph UK (1978)

Last Plane From Nice - *Latest*
Atheneum US (1988); Thorndike UK (1990)

David WILSHAW

British Male Amateur operating in England

Captain A O POLLARD 1893- (British)

Writer: Captain Alfred Oliver POLLARD

Citation Record: 12 Short Stories in 1 Collection

David Wilshaw Investigates - *Collection 1*
Hutchinson UK (1948)

Cyrus WILSON

solves a case of campus murder.

American Male Amateur operating in Michigan

A H GARNET (American)

is a joint pseudonym of two unidentified writers.

Writers: UNKNOWN and UNKNOWN

Inventor of one other detective Charles THAYER

Citation Record: 1 Book

Maze - *Single*
Ticknor US (1982)

David 'Pudd'nhead' WILSON

is a lawyer who sleuths.

American Male Amateur operating in USA

Mark TWAIN 1835-1910 (American)

Invented 5 detectives - see Tom SAWYER

Citation Record: 1 Book

Pudd'nhead Wilson - *Only*
Chatto & Windus UK (1897)

Francesca WILSON

is conveniently married to a police Inspector, thus bringing her close to murder cases, which she solves before he does.

British Female Amateur operating in England

Janet NEEL 1940- (British)

Writer: Cohen Janet NEEL

Citation Record: 4 Books

Death's Bright Angel - *First*
Constable UK (1988); St Martin's US (1989)

Death Among The Dons - *Latest*
Constable UK (1993)

Supt Henry WILSON

appeared first in a novel written by *G D H COLE* and then in nineteen novels and some excellent collections of short stories written by the famous husband-and-wife team of *G D H & Margaret COLE.* A tall man, thoughtful, often agitated, he seems to have borrowed at least one of the mannerisms given to *Sherlock HOLMES,* for he also frequently closes his eyes and brings the tips of fingers together when on a case. A rather conventional and lacklustre policeman of the period, he often does the police work with the amateur sleuth, *The Hon Everard BLATCHINGTON,* and he also appears in two novels with *Dr TANCRED.*

At some time during the series, it is clear that WILSON retired from the police and set up as a private detective; for it is in that role that he seems to operate in several of the later novels and short stories. He is so colourless a character, though, that the transition is not entirely clear.

British Policeman, later a Private detective, operating in England

G D H COLE 1888-1959 (British)

wrote the first of the many books featuring *Supt Henry WILSON* on his own, before starting on the lengthy and famous collaboration with his wife.

Writer: George Douglas Howard COLE

Citation Record: 1 Book

The Brooklyn Murders - *Only*
The title does not refer to New York, but to the name of an English family.
Collins UK (1923); Seltzer US (1924)

G D H COLE and Margaret COLE (British)

were a famous husband-and-wife team who together wrote, over many years, a great number of criminous novels and short stories, featuring several police and amateur detectives. In the main the stories are conventionally, although cleverly plotted and deal with many aspects of British middle-class life. *G D H COLE* was educated at St Paul's School, London, and at Balliol College, Oxford. He was a distinguished writer, theorist and administrator in the fields of social studies, economics and politics. He was especially renowned for his pioneering work for British trade unionism and workers' education. *Margaret Isabel COLE* (née Postgate) was born in Cambridge and was a Fellow of Magdalen College, Oxford, 1912-1919. She also was a distinguished writer and historian in many of the same fields as her husband, whom she married, 1918.

Writers: George Douglas Howard COLE 1889-1959 and Margaret Isabel COLE 1893-1980

Other Detectives:
The Hon Everard BLATCHINGTON
Insp FAIRFORD
James FLINT
Ben TANCRED and Supt Henry WILSON
Mrs Elizabeth WARRENDER and James WARRENDER
Supt Henry WILSON and The Hon Everard BLATCHINGTON

Citation Record: 19 Books 27 Short Stories in 4 Collections

The Death Of A Millionaire - *First*
Collins UK (1925); Macmillan US (1925)

Toper's End - *Last*
Collins UK (1942); Macmillan US (1942)

Superintendent Wilson's Holiday - *Collection 1*
Short stories - 8
Collins UK (1928)

A Lesson In Crime - *Collection 2*
This collection contains ten stories, eight of which feature *Henry WILSON.*
Short stories - 8
Collins UK (1933)

Wilson And Some Others - *Collection 3*
This collection of thirteen of the author's stories contains seven with *Henry WILSON.*
Short stories - 7
Collins UK (1940)

Birthday Gifts And Other Stories - *Collection 4*
Short stories - 4
Polybooks UK (1946)

Supt Henry WILSON
Second detective of Ben TANCRED

Supt Henry WILSON and The Hon Everard BLATCHINGTON
The Hon Everard BLATCHINGTON is, in fact, a minor clone of the *Peter WIMSEY* period. He appeared in three books in which he set the field, as it were, for the authors' police detective, *Supt WILSON.* In his last book, however, he was on his own.
British Policeman and British Male Amateur operating in England

G D H COLE and Margaret COLE (British)
Invented 7 detectives - see Supt Henry WILSON
Citation Record: 3 Books
The Blatchington Tangle - *First*
Collins UK (1926); Macmillan US (1926)
Death In The Quarry - *Last*
Collins UK (1934); Doubleday US (1934)

John WILSON
of Scotland Yard narrates this story.
British Policeman operating in London

ANON
Citation Record: 1 Book
Who Shot The Spy? - *Only*
In 'Boys of England' UK (1887)

Murray WILSON
was a cop and then a PI in Glasgow; but, in his first book, he investigates London killings marking the centenary of the Jack the Ripper murders.
British Male Private Detective operating in Glasgow

Frederic LINDSAY (British)
Citation Record: 1 Book
Jill Rips - *Single*
Deutsch UK (1987); Deutsch US (1989)

Richard Van Ryn WILSON
is a consulting detective who gives lectures on criminology. He meets murder on four occasions, the first at the fictional Dunster College in New England.
American Male Private Detective operating in USA
Sidekick: Dr Eric DIETERLEE
American Male - Friend

Kathleen SPROUL (American)
Citation Record: 4 Books
The Birthday Murder - *First*
Dutton US (1932)
The Mystery Of The Closed Car - *Last*
Dutton US (1935)

Ruth WILSON
Second detective of Joanna WILDER

'One Week' WIMBLE
American Male Sleuth operating in New York/San Francisco

Helen BURNHAM (American)
Citation Record: 2 Books
The Murder Of Lalla Lee - *First*
McBride US (1931); Arrowsmith UK (1931)
The Telltale Telegram - *Last*
McBride US (1932)

Lord Peter WIMSEY
appears in just eleven novels and twenty-one short stories. Their excellence is such that, by universal consent, he is regarded as one of the great and classic inventions of detective literature, not just for his character and brilliance, not just for the style of the fairly small number of books in which he appeared, but because he exemplified and indeed gave his name to a whole era, a whole way of writing, to a phalanx of sleuths who came after and imitated him.

He was, it seems, born in 1890, son to the 15th Duke of Denver (the family arms were 'Sable, three mice courant, argent', the family crest was 'A domestic cat crouched as to spring' and the family motto was 'As my whimsy takes me'). He was educated at Eton and Balliol, taking First Class Honours in History. There he acquired his aristocratic style, his monocle and his foppish mannerisms to conceal his brilliant, questing mind. He served in the Army in the Second World War, being decorated with the DSO but losing his first love. His war experiences were, it is suggested, so terrible that he had a breakdown. However, he recovered and moved into his London flat, at 110A Piccadilly, pursuing his interests in history, cricket, books, music and, of course, detection. His valet, *BUNTER,* is himself one of the best known sidekicks in the literature and *Insp Charles PARKER,* his brother-in-law, is an important man at the Yard and mostly friendly, though, of course, usually baffled and sometimes actually doubting the great detective. In 1935, in the course of one of the novels, *Peter WIMSEY* meets Harriet Vane, gets her off a charge of murder and, after much pursuing, prevails on her to marry him. Although clearly the author loved him too much and indulged in some odd aberrations in some of his books, there is, indeed, nobody quite like *WIMSEY* in British detective fiction. His eminence derives from the absolute consistency of his portrayal. Like a fly in amber, he is, *sui generis,* the Golden Age incarnate and we shall not see his like again.
British Male Amateur operating in England

Sidekick: BUNTER
is the valet of one of the most famous detectives in the history of detective fiction and, as such, is one of the best-known sidekicks. *BUNTER* himself is no slouch when it comes to helping out the young master in his rather eccentric passion for sleuthing. He not only looks after important matters like the master's apartments, dress and food, but is a dab hand at photography and even dabber at obstructing the police as and when necessary.
British Male - Valet

Stooge: Insp Charles PARKER
is married to the sister of *Lord Peter WIMSEY* and rises to become one of the most senior officers at Scotland Yard. His relationship to *WIMSEY* sometimes places him in a difficult position, especially when they fail to see eye to eye over a case.
British Male

E C BENTLEY 1875-1956 (British)
See main detective Philip TRENT
Citation Record: 1 Selected Short Story
Greedy Night - *Pastiche 1*
was intended as a parody of the famous novel, *Gaudy Night,* by *Dorothy L SAYERS.* It was called, by *Ellery QUEEN,* 'The finest detective parody of our time', although it is better considered as a pastiche. It appeared in an anthology, *Stories of Detection.*
Longman UK (1939)

Geoffrey BUSH (British)

Citation Record: 1 Selected Short Story

The Last Meeting Of The Butler's Club - *Pastiche 1*
appeared in the March number. There is a murder in the billiards room of a country house, in which only the victim and the butler are present. The case is solved by *Peter WIMSEY*, who happens to be around at the time.
In 'Ellery Queen's Mystery Magazine' US (1980)

Dorothy L SAYERS 1893-1957 (British)
was born in Oxford. She was educated at Godolphin School, Salisbury, Wiltshire, and took a BA in French at Somerville, College, Oxford, 1915, followed by an MA, 1920. She was a teacher for a while, then worked as a copywriter in Benson's advertising agency, London, 1922-1929, becoming a full-time writer, 1931. Undoubtedly the *non-pareil* of the British Golden Age, she created one of the great classic amateur detectives. Indeed, many would say, the greatest of all amateur detectives. But even *WIMSEY* would not have the status he has if the books had not been so superbly plotted and integrated as to provide a true canon of work. In addition to her genre novels, *Dorothy SAYERS* wrote plays and, especially in later life, a considerable number of works on religious subjects.

Writer: Dorothy Leigh SAYERS

Inventor of one other detective Montague EGG

Citation Record: 11 Books 21 Short Stories in 3 Collections

Whose Body? - *First*
Unwin UK (1923); Boni & Liveright US (1923)

Busman's Honeymoon - *Last*
Gollancz UK (1937); Harcourt Brace US (1937)

Lord Peter Views The Body - *Collection 1*
Short stories - 12
Gollancz UK (1928); Brewer US (1929)

Hangman's Holiday - *Collection 2*
contains four *Peter WIMSEY* stories and six *Montague EGG* stories.
Short stories - 4
Gollancz UK (1933); Harcourt US (1933)

In The Teeth Of The Evidence And Other Stories - *Collection 3*
contains, in total, seventeen of the author's short stories, not all of which were included in either the UK or the US edition. However, there are two *Peter WIMSEY* stories and five *Montague EGG* stories in the original publications. A later publication (*Gollancz*; UK 1972) added the last three known *Peter WIMSEY* stories and this is the one cited under the latter detective.
Short stories - 2
Gollancz UK (1972)

Lord Peter - *Collection 4*
contains all the known *Peter WIMSEY* short stories.
Short stories - 21
Harper & Row UK (1972)

Dorothy L SAYERS and Robert EUSTACE (British)
collaborated to write this one *Peter WIMSEY* novel.

Writers: Dorothy Leigh SAYERS 1893-1957 and Robert Eustace BARTON 1868-1943

Citation Record: 1 Book

The Documents In The Case - *Only*
Benn UK (1930); Brewer US (1930)

W

Martin WINDROW

is an exceptionally violent type in a book that plumbs the depths.

American Male Private Detective operating in San Francisco

Jim NISBET (American)

Citation Record: 1 Book

The Gourmet - *Single*
Pinnacle US (1981); Black Lizard UK (1987)

The Damned Don't Die - *Single**
Black Lizard US (1986)

King of England Edward VII WINDSOR

is, indeed, the man who was King of England, 1911-1920, and he appears as a detective in books by at least two authors. Surprisingly perhaps, he was first used by *Tucker HALLERAN*, an American writer, and later by the British author, *Peter LOVESEY*, who has specialised in some delightful detective novels set in Victorian and Edwardian England. *Edward WINDSOR* was affectionately known as Bertie and, before ascending the throne, was for many years Prince of Wales. He had a well-deserved reputation for being over-fond of the ladies, at home and abroad; but, in the books cited, he is also very fond of amateur sleuthing and does rather well at it.

British Male Amateur operating in England

Tucker HALLERAN (American)

See main detective Cam MACCARDLE

Citation Record: 1 Book

The King Edward Plot - *Single*
McGraw-Hill US (1980)

Peter LOVESEY 1936- (British)

Invented 7 detectives - see Sgt CRIBB and Const THACKERAY

Citation Record: 2 Books

Bertie And The Tinman - *First*
Bodley Head UK (1987); Mysterious Press US (1988)

Bertie And The Crime Of Passion - *Latest*
Little, Brown US (1994)

King of England George V WINDSOR

is, indeed, the King of England and not at all a bad detective. A pity he only appeared once.

British Male Amateur operating in England

T E B CLARKE 1907- (British)

Writer: Thomas Ernest Bennett CLARKE

Citation Record: 1 Book

Murder At Buckingham Palace - *Only*
Hale UK (1981); St Martin's US (1982)

Carter WINFIELD

Second detective of Matt DOYLE

Jane WINFIELD

Second detective of Andrew QUENTIN

WING

American Sleuth

James REACH 1909(?)-1970 (American)

Writer: James Reach

Inventor of one other detective Michael SHAYNE

Citation Record: 2 Books

Lunatics At Large - *Play*
Samuel French US (1936)

The Case Of The Laughing Dwarf - *Play*
Samuel French US (1938)

Joshua Red WING

solves a peculiar case in which a print is left by an amputated foot.

American Male Amateur operating in USA

William BRITTAIN 1930- (American)
was born in Rochester, New York. He has published exclusively in the field of short stories, which fall into two categories. There is, first, those that begin 'The Man who Read...' and there follows a pastiche or parody of some well-known crime author, using that author's own detective. The second main series centres round a detective, *Mr STRANG*, who is a science teacher at a high school, probably much like the school at which the author himself is or has been a teacher.

Inventor of one other detective Mr STRANG

Citation Record: 1 Selected Short Story

The Impossible Footprint
appeared in the November number and is in an anthology, *Death on Arrival* (Dell; US 1979).
In 'Alfred Hitchcock's Mystery Magazine' US (1979)

Caledonia WINGATE
Second detective of Angela BENBOW

'Mac' WINGATE
American Male Sleuth operating in several locations

Brian SWIFT
House name.
Citation Record: 6 Books
Mission Code: Granite Island - *First*
Jove US (1982)
Mission Code: Volcano - *Latest*
Jove US (1982)

Brian SWIFT 1927-
Writer: William Cecil KNOTT
Citation Record: 3 Books
Mission Code: King's Pawn - *First*
Jove US (1981)
Mission Code: Symbol- *Latest*
Jove US (1982)

Brian SWIFT 1923-1982(?)
For writer details see Ned SANDERSON
Citation Record: 3 Books
Mission Code: Acropolis - *First*
Jove US (1982)
Mission Code: Scorpion - *Latest*
Jove US (1982)

Billy WINGRAVE and Nellie WINGRAVE
investigate some weird goings-on in this Victorian novelette.
British Male Amateur and British Female Amateur operating in England

Ada CAMBRIDGE 1844-1926 (British)
Writer: Ada Cambridge CROSS
Citation Record: 1 Selected Short Story
At Midnight
involves the strange disappearance of people from a locked room. It is in an anthology, *At Midnight and Other Stories.*
Ward, Lock UK (1897)

Nellie WINGRAVE
Second detective of Billy WINGRAVE

Mr WINKLEY
British Male Amateur operating in England

Harriet RUTLAND (British)
Citation Record: 2 Books
Knock, Murderer, Knock! - *First*
Skeffington UK (1938); Harrison-Hilton US (1939)
Bleeding Hooks - *Last*
Skeffington UK (1940); Harrison-Hilton US (1940)

Jake WINKMAN
American Male Sleuth operating in Hawaii

Don VON ELSNER 1909- (American)
See main detective David DANNING
Citation Record: 3 Books
How To Succeed At Murder Without Really Trying - *First*
Signet UK (1963)
The Jake Of Diamonds - *First**
Award US (1967); Tandem UK (1967)
The Jack Of Hearts - *Last*
Award US (1968)

Philip WINSLOW
seems to be just a teacher at an Oxford school but turns out to be 'somebody in the British Secret Service' when he investigates the death of a Chemistry lecturer.
British Male Secret Agent operating in Oxford

S P B MAIS 1885-1975 (British)
was born in Matlock, Derbyshire. He was a schoolmaster, journalist, mainstream novelist, man of letters and writer of at least eleven genre novels.
Writer: Stuart Petre Brodie MAIS
Citation Record: 1 Book
Who Dies? - *Only*
Hutchinson UK (1949)

Steve WINSLOW
American Male Sleuth operating in New York

J P HAILEY (American)
For writer details see Stanley HASTINGS
Citation Record: 4 Books
The Baxter Trust - *First*
Fine US (1988)
The Naked Typist - *Latest*
Fine US (1990)

Peter WINSTON
American Male Sleuth operating in Middle East

Jack LAFLIN (American)
Inventor of one other detective Gregory HILLER
Citation Record: 1 Book
The Temple At Ilumquh - *Only*
Award US (1970)

Peter WINSTON
House name.
Citation Record: 1 Book
Doomsday Vendetta - *Only*
Award US (1968)

Peter WINSTON
Writer: James BOWSER
Other Byline: Nick Carter
Citation Record: 1 Book
The Glass Cipher - *Only*
Award US (1968); Tandem US (1968)

Peter WINSTON
Writer: Paul Eiden
Other Byline: Paul EDWARDS
Citation Record: 2 Books
The ABC Affair - *First*
Award US (1967); Tandem UK (1967)
Assignment To Bahrein - *Last*
Award US (1967); Tandem UK (1967)

Stoney WINSTON
American Male Amateur operating in Los Angeles

Jim STINSON 1937- (American)
Writer: James Emerson STINSON
Citation Record: 4 Books
Double Exposure - *First*
Scribner's US (1985)
Truck Shot - *Latest*
Scribner's US (1989)

Alexandra WINTER
is a divorced lady, partly the modern woman but still with some old hangs. She works for the Abromowitz & Bailey Investigative Agency, whose motto, unsurprisingly, is 'The Agency with a Heart'.
American Female Private Detective operating in Los Angeles

Susan STEINER (American)
Citation Record: 1 Book
Murder On Her Mind - *Single*
GM US (1985)

Charles WINTER
British Male Professional Investigator operating in England

Clive EGLETON 1927- (British)

Invented 3 detectives - see Insp COGHILL

Citation Record: 2 Books

The Winter Touch - *First*
Hodder & Stoughton UK (1981)

The Eisenhower Deception - *First**
Atheneum US (1981)

The Russian Enigma - *Latest*
Atheneum US (1982); Hodder & Stoughton UK (1983)

Rabbi Daniel WINTER

is the rabbi of a Los Angeles synagogue who is forced to carry out detective work to solve the murder of a female, feminist rabbi in order to protect his congregation and principles.

American Male Amateur operating in Los Angeles

Sidekick: Brenda GOLDSTEIN

is a member of the Los Angeles Police Department. Jewish herself, she is able to provide special support to the rabbinical sleuth during his difficult and delicate detective work among his community.

American Female - Policewoman

Joseph TELUSHKIN 1948- (American)

is an ordained rabbi and a writer on Jewish history. He now lives in Jerusalem.

Citation Record: 1 Book

The Unorthodox Murder Of Rabbi Moss - *Single*
Collins UK (1986)

Holly WINTER

investigates murders with strong canine attachments, aided by her own two Alaskan beauties.

American Female Amateur operating in Boston

Susan CONANT (American)

Citation Record: 3 Books

Dead And Doggone - *First*
Diamond US (1990)

Ruffly Speaking - *Latest*
Bantam US (1994)

Stuart WINTER

works on cases concerned with environmental conservation projects.

American Male Private Detective operating in California

Alan RUSSELL (American)

Inventor of one other detective Am CAULFIELD

Citation Record: 2 Books

No Sign Of Murder - *First*
Walker US (1990)

Forest Prime Evil - *Latest*
Walker US (1992)

Insp/Supt William WINTER

Second detective of Sgt/Insp John COFFIN

Lettie WINTERBOTTOM

British Female Amateur operating in England

Leela CUTTER (American)

Citation Record: 3 Books

Murder After Tea Time - *First*
St Martin's US (1981)

Death Of The Party - *Latest*
St Martin's US (1985)

Matt WINTERS

American Male Amateur operating in New Jersey

Inez OELLRICHS 1907- (American)

Writer: Inez Hildegard OELLRICHS

Citation Record: 7 Books

The Man Who Didn't Answer - *First*
Doubleday US (1939); Davies UK (1939)

Death In A Chilly Corner - *Last*
Hammond UK (1964)

Lord WINTERSTONE

is an English Lord, also known as Lord Pig (possibly a reference to the plots of the books). The books will for ever remain obscure but must have been a moneyspinning sideline for such a well-known author to have tried her hand at them at all, even though she was only half responsible and thoughtfully used the pseudonym.

British Male Amateur operating in England

Nap LOMBARD (British)

Writers: Pamela Hansford JOHNSON 1912-1981 and Neil STEWART

Citation Record: 2 Books

Tidy Death - *First*
Cassell UK (1940)

The Grinning Pig - *Last*
Simon & Schuster US (1943)

Murder's A Swine - *Last**
Hutchinson UK (1942)

Dave WINTINO

American Male Sleuth operating in New York

Ed LACY 1911-1968 (American)

Invented 8 detectives - see Toussaint 'Touie' MOORE

Citation Record: 2 Books

Lead With Your Left - *First*
Harper & Row US (1957); Boardman UK (1957)

Double Trouble - *Last*
Boardman UK (1965); Lancer US (1967)

Dr David WINTRINGHAM

appears in many of the author's books and clearly she liked him. However, only in the very earliest books is he a detective of interest. In later books he seems merely to be around on murder cases, mainly working under the guidance of one of the author's other detectives, *Insp Steven MITCHELL*.

British Male Amateur operating in England

Josephine BELL 1897-1987 (British)

was born in Manchester, Lancashire. She began her career as a doctor, having qualified from University College Hospital, 1924. She practised at Greenwich and London until about 1935 and then in Guildford, Surrey, until 1954. She became an eminent writer of crime stories with an extraordinary wide range and was a co-founder of the Crime Writers Association. She wrote, in addition to nigh on fifty detective stories, many short stories and several novels outside the genre. She did not use a consistent series detective, preferring to create new ones as the need arose. However, some of her favourites do appear in more than one book.

Writer: Doris Bell BALL

Other Detectives:
George COLE and Amanda DREW
Dr Henry FROST
Timothy LONG
Insp Steven MITCHELL
Insp RAWLINSON
Lucy SUMMERS
Amy TUPPER
Claude WARRINGTON-REEVE and Insp Steven MITCHELL
Dr David WINTRINGHAM and Insp Steven MITCHELL

Citation Record: 7 Books

Death On The Borough Council - *First*
Longman UK (1937)

Death In Retirement - *Last*
Methuen UK (1956); Macmillan US (1956)

Dr David WINTRINGHAM and Insp Steven MITCHELL

also appear individually in other books by this author.

British Male Amateur and British Policeman operating in England

Josephine BELL 1897-1987 (British)

Invented 10 detectives - see Dr David WINTRINGHAM

Citation Record: 8 Books

W

Murder In Hospital - *First*
Longman UK (1937)
The Seeing Eye - *Last*
Hodder & Stoughton UK (1958)

Justus WISE

British Male Amateur operating in England

Alfred Wilson BARRETT 1871- (British)

Citation Record: 2 Books
Justus Wise - *First*
Ward, Lock UK (1911)
The Tower Hill Mystery - *Last*
Ward, Lock UK (1912)

Pennington WISE

American Male Amateur operating in USA

Sidekick: ZIZI
American Female - Assistant

Carolyn WELLS 1870-1942 (American)

Invented 7 detectives - see Fleming STONE
Citation Record: 7 Books
The Man Who Fell Through The Earth - *First*
Doran US (1919); Harrap UK (1924)
Wheels Within Wheels - *Last*
Doran US (1927)

Penny WISE

was a young female 'private detective' who appeared in stories in the magazine, *Girl.*

British Female Amateur operating in England

Norman PETT (British)

No citations

Leonidas WITHERALL

is a Bostonian and a retired professor who looks like William Shakespeare and is often so called. He hunts down rare books for collectors and runs into murder frequently while doing so.

American Male Amateur operating in USA

Alice TILTON 1909-1976 (American)

Writer: Phoebe Atwood TAYLOR
Other Byline: Freeman DANA
Citation Record: 8 Books
Beginning With A Bash - *First*
Collins UK (1937); Norton US (1972)
The Iron Clew - *Last*
Farrar, Straus US (1947)
The Iron Hand - *Last**
Collins UK (1947)

Insp WITHERS

British Policeman operating in England

L HIGGIN (British)

Writer: Louis HIGGIN
Citation Record: 1 Book
Lyoma Grimwood, Spinster - *Only*
Pearson UK (1900)

Adrian WITHERS

is short, red-haired, aged about thirty and a perpetual student at the fictional St Felicitas College, a Catholic institution. He investigates a disappearance.

American Male Amateur operating in Illinois

Fallon EVANS 1925- (American)

was born in Denver, Colorado. He is a sometime Associate Professor of English in Los Angeles.

Citation Record: 1 Book
Pistols And Pedagogues - *Only*
Sheed US (1963)

Hildegarde WITHERS

is, although admittedly one of the classic lady detectives, not nearly as nice a person as *Jane MARPLE* or *Maud SILVER.* In fact, she is an acid-tongued schoolteacher and a snoopy old maid, a dominant personality who will insist on treating policemen like schoolboys. Browbeaten, they accept this because, all in all, as a sleuth she really is in the first rank.

American Female Amateur operating in New York

Stooge: Insp Oscar PIPER
of the New York Police Department is a coarse, arrogant, cigar-smoking vulgarian who thinks *Hildegarde WITHERS* is a meddlesome old battle-axe but has to admit that she is probably the greatest sleuth in New York. That's why he keeps bringing her his cases to solve.
American Male

Stuart PALMER 1905-1968 (American)

was born in Baraboo, Wisconsin. He graduated from the University of Wisconsin, Madison, 1926, and took a degree at the University of California, Los Angeles, 1961.

Writer: Charles Stuart PALMER
Other Detectives:
Sherlock HOLMES   Howie ROOK
Citation Record: 13 Books 16 Short Stories in 2 Collections
The Penguin Pool Murders - *First*
Brentano's US (1931); Long UK (1932)
Cold Poison - *Last*
was the last book to be completed by *Stuart PALMER.* One other was finished by *Fletcher FLORA.*
Mill US (1954)
Exit Laughing - *Last**
Collins UK (1954)
The Riddles Of Hildegarde Withers - *Collection 1*
Short stories - 8
Jonathan US (1947)
The Monkey Murder, And Other Hildegarde Withers Stories - *Collection 2*
Short stories - 8
In 'Bestseller' UK (1950)

Stuart PALMER and Fletcher FLORA (American)

Writers: Charles Stuart PALMER 1905-1968 and Fletcher FLORA 1914-1968
Citation Record: 1 Book
Hildegarde Withers Makes The Scene - *Only*
Random House US (1969)

Hildegarde WITHERS and John J MALONE

appear together in short stories devised by these two skilled genre authors and featuring their main detectives.

American Female Amateur and American Male Amateur operating in USA

Craig RICE and Stuart PALMER (American)

Writers: Georgiana Ann Randolph CRAIG 1908-1957 and Charles Stuart PALMER 1905-1968
Citation Record: 6 Short Stories in 1 Collection
The People Vs Withers And Malone - *Collection 1*
Random House US (1963)

Insp WITTLER

investigates the death by defenestration of one of three brothers.

British Policeman operating in England

Paul MCGUIRE 1903-1978 (Australian)

Invented 4 detectives - see Insp/Supt FILLINGER
Citation Record: 1 Book
Threepence To Marble Arch - *Only*
Skeffington UK (1936)

Hazlitt WOAR

American Male Amateur operating in USA/Spain

George Worthing YATES (American)

Citation Record: 3 Books
The Body That Came By Post - *First*
Morrow US (1937); Dickson UK (1937)
If A Body - *Last*
Morrow US (1941)

Insp WOKE

British Policeman operating in England

Fergus HUME 1859-1932 (British)

Invented 24 detectives - see Insp Samuel GORBY

Citation Record: 1 Book

A Traitor In London - *Only*
Long UK (1900); Buckles US (1900)

Hannah WOLFE

is over thirty, usually broke and often alone. However, she is a rather nice girl and a rather good PI.

Female Private Detective

Sarah DUNANT 1950-

Citation Record: 3 Books

Birth Marks - *First*
Joseph UK (1991)

Under My Skin - *Latest*
Otto Penzler US (1995)

Nero WOLFE

is, although there are other contenders, perhaps the fattest detective in the whole criminous genre, weighing, as he says, one-seventh of a ton. This, however, is not his main claim to fame; for, without doubt, he is a creation in the highest ranks of the detective story in all its forms. It seems he had a somewhat obscure origin in the European principality of Montenegro; but, at any rate, he now lives in a brownstone somewhere (the exact address has been much investigated by the *cognoscenti*) on West 35th Street in Manhattan. If one is to define what is meant by a classic detective, then *Nero WOLFE* is a model. It is not just that he appears in a long and consistent saga of extraordinary brilliance. It is rather that, in the course of the canon, we come to know, understand and almost live with the great man in all his aspects. His house and its inhabitants are lovingly described, from the orchid rooms at the top, where he insists on spending exactly two hours each morning and afternoon, to the basement where his fantastic cook, Fritz Brenner, prepares the most wonderful and gigantic meals.

WOLFE, indeed, will never leave the house except on the most rare and vital occasions, leaving the legwork to others, especially, for example, to *Saul PANZER*, said to be the best in the business. *WOLFE's* relationship with his amanuensis, *Archie GOODWIN*, is of special note, for it represents one of the finest detective-sidekick liaisons in the literature, completely, reverently and beautifully illustrated in all its dimensions. In a period of over forty-one years they remain, to our delight, ageless.

WOLFE's chief assets are his ability to construct his cases by pure cerebral logic and his knowledge of every twist and turn in the law. He usually solves them by summoning his cast of suspects by pressures of various kinds and then confronting the criminal with his surprising yet obvious solution. *WOLFE* is, by any standards an intellectual giant. He reads incessantly, will only work when he is running out of money for food, the beer that he drinks whenever he can, or his beloved orchids. A *gourmet*, he would starve rather than eat a hot dog; a *flaneur*, he would rather read than work; and a *savant*, he would burn in hell rather than bend the truth.

The number of books published amounted nearly to fifty and, of these, over a dozen were, in fact, collections of three or four original novelettes (they have not been counted individually). *Nero WOLFE*, like others of his stature, has continued to exist in the hands of other authors after the death of his creator.

American Male Private Detective operating in New York

Sidekick: Archie GOODWIN
is certainly the best characterised and most famous of all American sidekicks. In his thirties, lean, athletic, intelligent and a fine detective himself, he is the indispensable aide, the essential factotum, assistant, secretary, bodyguard, and everything else of the great *Nero WOLFE*. It is *GOODWIN* who knows every detail of the great detective's cases and can report every detail of a suspect's remarks verbatim. He is the one who urges the fat man to work when funds are low, sees witnesses, obstructs the police and types the reports. Of course, he is the narrator of the stories, which include some of the most glorious in detective fiction.

American Male - Assistant

Sidekick: Saul PANZER
is a freelance detective who appears as a legman or tail in a great many of the *WOLFE* books. He is one of the best there is.

American Male - Assistant

Stooge: Insp CRAMER
of the New York Police Department is one of the best-known and best-depicted police stooges in the genre. A considerable creation in his own right, he is part of the wonderful closed world that revolves around *NERO WOLFE*. Hot, bothered, bewildered, suspicious, threatening, usually in error when it comes to suspects and always so when he matches wits with *WOLFE*, he is always won round by the end, for the fat genius is inevitably and sometimes unbelievably right in his solutions. In one book *CRAMER* has the case to himself and is listed as a detective accordingly.

American Male

Robert GOLDSBOROUGH 1937- (American)

was chosen, from many contestants apparently, to continue, after the death of *Rex STOUT*, with the series of novels featuring his detective, *Nero WOLFE*, and the rest of the cast.

Writer: Robert Gerald GOLDSBOROUGH

Citation Record: 6 Books

Murder In E Minor - *Pastiche 1*
US (1986); Collins UK (1986)

The Missing Chapter - *Pastiche 2*
Bantam US (1994)

Thomas NARCEJAC 1908- (American)

Writer: Pierre AYRAUD

Citation Record: 1 Selected Short Story

The Red Orchid - *Pastiche 1*
In 'Ellery Queen's Mystery Magazine' US (1961)

Rex STOUT 1886-1975 (American)

was born in Noblesville, Indiana, and educated at Topeka High School, Kansas, and the University of Kansas, Lawrence. He worked at many jobs until 1927, when he became a full-time writer. Always an outstanding exponent of the importance of democratic and liberal values in society, he founded a press and wrote radio programmes, several novels and a cookbook that was to become famous. He published his first criminous novel in 1934 and was rapidly established in his role as one of the giants of the American detective story. During a period that covered over forty years, he created a true canon of work, as highly regarded as is that created by *Sir Arthur Conan DOYLE* a generation earlier. No other detective series can compare with it in its delineation of place and atmosphere, the elegance of its characterisations, its extraordinary inter-action of form and content and its close-knit, almost unitary structure, all of which combine in a setting for some of the most brilliant detective stories ever written.

Rex STOUT invented several detectives, but they all stand in the shadow of his great creation, *Nero WOLFE*. He received the Mystery Writers of America Grand Master award, 1959.

Writer: Rex Todhunter STOUT

Other Detectives:
Theodora 'Dol' BONNER
Delia BRAND
Insp CRAMER
Tecumseh FOX
'Alphabet' HICKS

Citation Record: 49 Books

Fer-De-Lance - *First*
Farrar, Straus US (1934); Cassell UK (1935)

A Family Affair - *Last*
Viking US (1975); Collins UK (1976)

Nero WOLFE

Appears with at least two other detectives - see Sherlock HOLMES

Hugo WOLFRAM

American Male Sleuth operating in South America

Richard L GRAVES (American)

Writer: Richard Latshaw GRAVES

Citation Record: 3 Books

The Platinum Bullet - *First*
Stein US (1974)

Quicksilver - *Last*
Stein US (1976)

WOLVERINE WAIF

American Male Detective in Pulp Magazines operating in USA

Will WINCH (American)

Invented 5 detectives - see The LAWYER DETECTIVE

Citation Record: 1 Selected Short Story

Wolverine Waif, The Half-Breed Detective; Or, The Lost Mine Tragedy
Old Cap Collier Library US (18??)

Shamrock WOMLBS

is a *Sherlock HOLMES* parody.

British Male Professional Amateur operating in London

Sidekick: Doctored WHOPPER
is his parody *WATSON*-like assistant.
British Male - Assistant

John LENNON 1940-1980 (British)

was a member of the famous pop music group, The Beatles.

Citation Record: 1 Selected Short Story

The Singularge Experience Of Miss Anne Duffield - *Parody 1*
appeared first in the author's collection of surreal short stories, *A Spaniard in the Works*. A strange and clever tale, it can also be found in the anthology, *THE MISADVENTURES OF SHERLOCK HOLMES* (Editor; *Sebastian WOLFE*).
Cape UK (1965)

WONG

Chinese Male Amateur operating in San Francisco

Hugh WILEY (American)

Citation Record: 12 Short Stories in 1 Collection

Murder By The Dozen - *Collection 1*
Popular Library US (1951)

Will WOODFIELD

indulges in genteel sleuthing, even among a pretty murderous gang of college professors, all of them suspects.
!See Appendix 2.

American Male Private Detective operating in Illinois

Sidekick: Mercy NEWCASTLE
is a cool, attractive assistant to the gentlemanly sleuth, always hovering on the brink of seducing him.
American Female - Assistant

Elizabeth FOOTE-SMITH 1913- (American)

was born in Red Wing, Minnesota.

Citation Record: 2 Books

A Gentle Albatross - *First*
Putnam US (1976)

Never Say Die - *Latest*
Putnam US (1977)

Alister WOODHEAD

British Male Amateur operating in England/Scotland/Wales

E H CLEMENTS 1905- (British)

Writer: Eileen Helen CLEMENTS

Citation Record: 13 Books

Let Him Die - *First*
Hodder & Stoughton UK (1939); Dutton US (1940)

Let Or Hindrance - *Last*
Hale UK (1963)

Det Ch Insp Alexander 'Sandy' WOODINGS

British Policeman operating in England

Harry RYAN (Irish)

was born in Limerick, Eire. He is a doctor, a specialist in psychology, and also runs an art gallery in Yorkshire.

Citation Record: 1 Book

Sweet Summer - *Single*
Quartet UK (1987)

John WOODRUFF and Tony NOVELLO

are respectively a criminologist and a PI. They appear in a novelization of an episode from an American TV series.

American Male Professional Investigator and American Male Private Detective operating in California

William JOHNSTON 1924- (American)

Writer: William JOHNSTON

Other Byline: Ed GARTH

Other Detectives:
BANYON
BRONSON
KLUTE
Capt NICE
Maxwell SMART
Dick TRACY

Citation Record: 1 Book

My Friend Tony - *Only*
Lancer US (1968)

Insp WOODS

British Policeman operating in England

D Erskine MUIR 1889- (British)

Writer: Dorothy Erskine Sheepshanks MUIR

Citation Record: 2 Books

In Muffled Night - *First*
Methuen UK (1933)

Five To Five - *Last*
Blackie UK (1934)

Valeria WOODVILLE

appears in one book by this great Victorian writer of mysteries. She investigates murder to prove her husband's innocence – a lame excuse but almost the only one allowable for a lady sleuth at the time.

British Female Amateur operating in England

Wilkie COLLINS 1824-1889 (British)

Invented 5 detectives - see Sgt CUFF

Citation Record: 1 Book

The Law And The Lady - *Only*
Chatto & Windus UK (1875); Harper & Row US (1875)

James Rowland WOODWARD VII

Second detective of Donald BRACKEN

Dave WOOLF

is a solicitor who was once a PI. He is still prepared to take on investigations if the fee is right.

British Male Professional Amateur operating in England

Bernard BANNERMAN (British)

Citation Record: 3 Books

The Last Wednesday - *First*
Sphere Books UK (1990)

The Judge's Song - *Latest*
Sphere Books UK (1991)

Miss WOOLFE

British Female Amateur operating in England

Winifred GRAHAM 1873-1950 (British)

was the author of at least nineteen criminous novels.

Writer: Cory Matilda Winifred Muriel GRAHAM

Citation Record: 2 Books

The Last Laugh - *First*
Hutchinson UK (1930)

A Wolf Of The Evenings - *Last*
Hutchinson UK (1930)

Alexander WOOLLCOTT

Second detective of Dorothy PARKER

Tony WOOLRICH

is a New York drama critic who shows he can solve mysteries. In later books he visits Hollywood to study the drama there and is involved in other cases.

American Male Amateur operating in California

Milton M RAISON 1903-1982 (American)

was born in New York City. He worked as a reporter, screenwriter and book critic.

Writer: Milton Michael RAISON

Citation Record: 4 Books

Nobody Loves A Dead Man - *First*
Murray US (1945); Archer US (1946)

Murder In A Lighter Vein - *Last*
Murray US (1947)

Milton M RAISON and Jack HARVEY (American)

Writer: (First Author) Milton Michael RAISON 1903-1982

Citation Record: 1 Book

The Phantom Of Forty-Second Street - *Only*
Macaulay US (1936)

Pete WORDEN

American Male Private Detective operating in California

William Campbell GAULT 1910- (American)

Invented 6 detectives - see Brock (The Rock) CALLAHAN

Citation Record: 1 Book

Don't Cry For Me - *Only*
Dutton US (1952); Boardman UK (1952)

The WORKING MAN DETECTIVE

American Male Detective in Pulp Magazines operating in USA

Donald J MCKENZIE 1859-1932 (American)

Invented 3 detectives - see Det CUSH

Citation Record: 1 Book

The Working Man Detective; Or, A Crime Against The Poor - *Only*
Street & Smith (Magnet) US (1899)

Silas WORTENHEIMER

British Male Amateur operating in England

David LEARMONTH (British)

Citation Record: 2 Books

Tainted Turf - *First*
Hutchinson UK (1927)

Red Mammon - *Last*
Hutchinson UK (1928)

Checkmate And Stalemate - *Last**
Hutchinson UK (1939)

Gilbert WORTH

is a writer who is shot dead at his desk. In some sort of after-life, he senses that the police are incompetent, investigates and solves his own murder.

British Male Amateur operating in England

Guy CULLINGFORD 1907- (British)

was born in Dovercourt, Essex, and educated at Malvern Girls College.

Writer: Constance Lindsay TAYLOR

Citation Record: 1 Book

Post Mortem - *Only*
Hammond UK (1953); Lippincott US (1953)

Stuart WORTH

Second detective of Jerry 'Renegade' ROE

Christie WORTHING

American Amateur operating in USA

Rosemary GATENBY 1918- (American)

has written at least nine genre books.

Citation Record: 1 Book

The Third Identity - *Single*
Dodd, Mead US (1979); Hale UK (1981)

Matilda WORTHING

American Female Amateur operating in California

John Keith DRUMMOND (American)

Citation Record: 2 Books

Thy Sting, Oh Death - *First*
St Martin's US (1985)

'Tis The Season To Be Dying - *Latest*
St Martin's US (1988)

Elizabeth Lamb WORTHINGTON

!See Appendix 2.

American Female Amateur operating in USA

B J MORISON 1924- (American)

was born in Maine and is a sometime owner of the Criterion Theater, Bar Harbor, Maine.

Writer: Betty Jane MORISON

Citation Record: 4 Books

Champagne And A Gardener - *First*
Thorndike US (1983)

The Voyage Of The Chianti - *Latest*
North Country US (1987)

Arnold 'Tiger' WRAGGE

British Male Amateur operating in England

Paul CAPON 1912-1969 (British)

wrote about twenty genre books.

Writer: Harry Paul CAPON

Citation Record: 3 Books

The Hosts Of Midian - *First*
Nicholson & Watson UK (1946)

Image Of A Murder - *Last*
Boardman UK (1949)

Cdr WRAITHLEA

British Male Professional Investigator operating in Egypt/India

P Walker TAYLOR 1903- (British)

Writer: Philip Neville Walker TAYLOR

Citation Record: 4 Books

Murder In The Flagship - *First*
Butterworth UK (1936); Mill US (1937)

Murder In The Taj Mahal - *Last*
Butterworth UK (1938)

Daphne WRAYNE and The FOUR ADJUSTERS

have dedicated themselves to 'the adjustment of the inequalities that at present exist between the criminal and the victim'. In furtherance of this admirable proposition, the lady is said to have 'the criminal life of London at her slim fingers' ends'.

British Female Amateur and British Male Amateurs operating in England

Mark CROSS 1876-1961 (British)

Writer: Archibald Thomas PECHEY

Other Byline: VALENTINE

Citation Record: 46 Books

The Grip Of The Four - *First*
Ward, Lock UK (1934)

Perilous Hazard - *Last*
Ward, Lock UK (1961)

VALENTINE 1876-1961 (British)

For writer details see Daphne WRAYNE and The FOUR ADJUSTERS

Citation Record: 46 Books

The Adjusters - *First*
Anglo-Eastern UK (1930)

Insp WREN

British Policeman operating in England

N A TEMPLE-ELLIS 1894- (British)

Invented 3 detectives - see Montrose ARBUTHNOT

Citation Record: 3 Books

Three Went In - *First*
Hodder & Stoughton UK (1934)

Death Of A Decent Fellow - *Last*
Hodder & Stoughton UK (1941)

Chris WREN

American Male Detective in Pulp Magazines operating in USA

Gilbert JEROME (American)

Invented 5 detectives - see Jack DONAHUE

Citation Record: 1 Selected Short Story

Chris Wren, The Master Detective; Or, Piping A Parisian Tragedy
Old Cap Collier Library US (18??)

Jeffrey WREN

appeared in series of light novelettes in *Dime Detective,* solving cases that seemed to have occult backgrounds.

American Male Detective in Pulp Magazines operating in USA

G T FLEMING-ROBERTS (American)

See main detective Jerry THACKER

No citations

Russel WREN

was once a teacher. Now he is a typically down-at-heel gumshoe on the East side of Manhattan.

American Male Private Detective operating in New York

Thomas BERGER 1924- (American)

Writer: Thomas Louis BERGER

Citation Record: 2 Books

Who Is Teddy Villanova? - *First*
Delacorte US (1977); Eyre & Spottiswoode UK (1977)

Nowhere - *Latest*
Delacorte US (1985); Methuen UK (1985)

Supt WRENN

solves a case of death by shooting in a guarded, locked room.

British Policeman operating in England

James RONALD 1905- (British)

Other Detectives:
Dr Daniel BRITLING   Julian MEDOZA

Citation Record: 1 Book

They Can't Hang Me! - *Only*
Rich UK (1938); Doubleday US (1938)

David WRIGHT

British Male Amateur operating in England

J F STRAKER 1904- (British)

Invented 3 detectives - see Det Johnny INCH

Citation Record: 2 Books

A Coil Of Rope - *First*
Harrap UK (1962)

Final Witness - *Last*
Harrap UK (1963)

Jimmy WROME

solves a case of death by shooting in a locked room.

American Male Amateur operating in USA

Robert A SIMON 1897-1981 (American)

Writer: Robert Alfred SIMON

Citation Record: 1 Book

The Weekend Mystery - *Only*
Watt US (1926); Collins UK (1927)

C WRYTE

called himself a 'solutionist'. Why not? Does he not solve a most difficult case of murder by unknown means in a locked room?

British Male Professional Amateur operating in England

Wilmot E TERRIS (British)

Citation Record: 1 Book

The Mystery Of The Purple Cloak - *Only*
Modern UK (1939)

Artie WU and Quincey DURANT

run an agency called Wudu Ltd.

American Male Private Detectives operating in California

Ross THOMAS 1926- (American)

Invented 4 detectives - see Morgan CITRON

Citation Record: 1 Book

Voodoo Ltd - *Single*
Mysterious Press US (1992); Little, Brown UK (1993)

Lily WU and Janice CAMERON

American Female Amateurs operating in New York/Hawaii

Juanita SHERIDAN (American)

Citation Record: 3 Books

The Chinese Chop - *First*
Doubleday US (1949); Barker UK (1951)

The Waikiki Widow - *Latest*
Doubleday US (1953)

Burton WULFF

American Male Amateur operating in New York

Mike BARRY 1939- (American)

was born in New York City and took a BA at Syracuse University, New York, 1960. He is the author, under his real name, of several novels, some of which he wrote with *Bill PRONZINI,* and many short stories.

Writer: Barry Nathaniel MALZBERG

Citation Record: 14 Books

Night Raider - *First*
Berkley US (1973)

Philadelphia Blowup - *Last*
Berkley US (1975)

WYATT

British Male Sleuth operating in England

David GETHIN (British)

Citation Record: 4 Books

Wyatt - *First*
Gollancz UK (1983); St Martin's US (1983)

Wyatt's Orphan - *Latest*
Gollancz UK (1985)

Winston WYC

is a researcher of architectural projects who gets caught up in murder.

American Male Amateur operating in New York

Brian JOHNSTON (American)

Citation Record: 2 Books

The Gift Horse Murders - *First*
Pinnacle (1992)

With Mallets Aforethought - *Latest*
Otto Penzler US (1995)

Dr Xavier WYCHERLY

was one of the close followers on the popularity of the new 'psychological detectives' who appeared after the creation of *Luther TRANT* and *Craig KENNEDY.* His speciality was using 'a special drug' on suspects, which enabled him to pick up their thought waves to solve crimes.

British Male Amateur operating in London

Max RITTENBERG 1880- (British)

Citation Record: 1 Collection

The Strange Cases Of Dr Wycherly - *Collection 1*
In 'London Magazine' UK (1911); In 'Blue Book' US (1911)

Supt Charles WYCLIFFE

is a senior officer in the West Country CID, whose cases all have a strong rural, especially Cornish, atmosphere. He is a typical modern type of policeman and we get to know his wife, his family, his domestic problems and arrangements, whether we want to or not. He solves his cases by slow study of the characters, emulating in low key a certain French detective.

British Policeman operating in Cornwall

W J BURLEY 1914- (British)

See main detective Henry Lancaster PYM

Citation Record: 17 Books

Three-Toed Pussy - *First*
Gollancz UK (1968)

Wycliffe In The Elf Wood - *Latest*
Gollancz UK (1995)

Michael WYMAN

is, in his first book, an MI6 operator who, under pressure, has to get away and does so with £2 million. In his second book he seems to change his career. He now holds a professorship in Rome and uses his detective skills to counter a terrorist coup.

British Male Professional Investigator operating in London/Rome

Bob COOK 1922- (British)

Citation Record: 2 Books

Disorderly Elements - *First*
Gollancz UK (1985)

Question Of Identity - *Latest*
Gollancz UK (1987)

Harry WYNNE

British Male Amateur operating in England

David Christie MURRAY 1847-1907 and Henry HERMAN 1832-1894 (British)

Citation Record: 1 Book

He Fell Among Thieves - *Only*
Macmillan UK (1891)

Jeffrey WYNNE

is a professional thief-taker in the London of 1757 and solves a difficult case of murder.

British Male Professional Investigator operating in London

John Dickson CARR 1906-1977 (American)

Invented 16 detectives - see Dr Gideon FELL

Citation Record: 1 Book

The Demoniacs - *Single*
Harper & Row US (1962); Hamish Hamilton UK (1962)

Robert WYNNTON

British Male Amateur operating in England

Sydney HORLER 1888-1954 (British)

Invented 20 detectives - see Sir Harker BELLAMY

Citation Record: 2 Books

The Man In The Cloak - *First*
Eyre & Spottiswoode UK (1951)

The Man Who Used Perfume - *Last*
Wingate UK (1952)

— Y —

Alva YAEGER

is a bad lot. When a female client hires him he does her no good at all.

American Male Private Detective operating in California

Robert BLOOMFIELD 1912- (American)

Writer: Leslie EDGELEY

Citation Record: 1 Book

From This Death Forward - *Only*
Doubleday US (1952)

Sgt YALE

British Policeman operating in New York

Sylvan SHELDON (American)

Citation Record: 1 Selected Short Story

Sergeant Yale Of Scotland Yard; Or, A London Ferret In New York City
Old Cap Collier Library US (18??)

Trygve YAMAMURA

is half Norwegian, half Japanese, and was born in Hawaii. An ordinary married man with none of the vices and habits of many other American private eyes, he operates out of a little office in Berkeley, California.

American Male Private Detective operating in Berkeley

Poul ANDERSON 1926- (American)

Writer: Poul William ANDERSON

Other Detectives:
Sherlock HOLMES
SYALOCH
Nicholas VAN RIJN

Citation Record: 3 Books

Perish By The Sword - *First*
Macmillan US (1959)

Murder Bound - *Last*
Macmillan US (1962)

The YANKEE DOODLE DETECTIVE

American Male Detective in Pulp Magazines operating in USA

Arda LA CROIX (American)

Citation Record: 1 Book

The Yankee Doodle Detective - *Only*
Ogilvie US (1909)

YANKEE JED

American Male Detective in Pulp Magazines operating in USA

Allan ARNOLD (American)

Invented 6 detectives - see OLD SNAP

Citation Record: 1 Book

Yankee Jed, The Down East Detective
New York Detective Library US (1882-8)

YANKEE RUE

American Male Detective in Pulp Magazines operating in USA

OLD SLEUTH (American)

Invented 40 detectives - see Brant ADAMS

Citation Record: 1 Book

Yankie Rue, The Ex-Pugilist Detective - *Only*
Ogilvie US (1897)

The Ex-Pugilist Detective - *Only**
Ogilvie US (1900)

John (The Hunter) YARD

American Male Sleuth operating in Africa

Ralph HAYES 1927- (American)

Invented 4 detectives - see Mark STONER

Citation Record: 5 Books

A Taste Of Blood - *First*
Leisure Books US (1975)

Track Of The Beast - *Last*
Leisure Books US (1975)

Frank YARDLEY
solves a case of death by stabbing in a locked room.
British Male Amateur operating in England

Elizabeth York MILLER (British)
Citation Record: 1 Book
The Mark Of Yekel - *Only*
Bles UK (1927)

John YARDLEY
appears in one book with the author's other detective, *R I PERKINS.*
British Male Amateur operating in England

Roger GARNETT 1905-1986 (British)
Invented 4 detectives - see Ch Insp Jonathan BLACK
Citation Record: 1 Book
Death Spoke Sweetly - *Only*
Wright & Brown UK (1946)

John YARDLEY and R I PERKINS
also appear individually in other books by this author.
British Male Amateurs operating in England

Roger GARNETT 1905-1986 (British)
Invented 4 detectives - see Ch Insp Jonathan BLACK
Citation Record: 1 Book
Starr Bedford Dies - *Only*
Wright & Brown UK (1937)

Det YATES
pits his wits against two murderers on the loose in New York.
American Policeman operating in New York

Eric SAUTER 1948- (American)
Invented 3 detectives - see Robert Lee HUNTER
Citation Record: 1 Book
Predators - *Single*
Pocket Books US (1987); Sphere UK (1988)

Bill YATES
American Male Private Detective operating in Montreal

Malcolm DOUGLAS 1922- (Canadian)
For writer details see Mike GARFIN
Citation Record: 1 Book
The Deadly Dames - *Only*
GM US (1956); Consul UK (1961)

Stonewall Jackson YATES and J D THATCHER
American Male Private Detective and American Female Private Detective operating in USA

Manly Wade WELLMAN 1905- (American)
Invented 5 detectives - see David RETURN
Citation Record: 1 Book
Find My Killer - *Only*
Farrar, Straus US (1947); Low UK (1948)

Susan YATES
Second detective of Lyle CURTIS

Supt Mike YEADINGS
of the Thames Valley police is a good, careful, traditional policeman who solves cases at home and abroad. He is sometimes helped by other interesting amateur or police sleuths, male and female.
British Policeman operating in England
Sidekick: Sgt/Insp MOTT
is the detective's main assistant, a clever young man who rises to the rank of Detective Inspector as the series progresses.
British Male - Subordinate

Clare CURZON 1922- (British)
was born in Hastings, Sussex. She took a BA at the University of London, 1944. Interpreter, translator and teacher, she has written several crime novels under her main pseudonym but latterly has used her own name for this new series.
Writer: Eileen-Marie DUELL
Citation Record: 8 Books
I Give You Five Days - *First*
Collins UK (1983)
Nice People - *Latest*
Collins UK (1993)

Ira YEDDER
American Male Sleuth operating in USA

Evelyn BOND 1920- (American)
Writer: Morris HERSHMAN
Citation Record: 3 Books
Dark Sonata - *First*
Beagle US (1972)
The Girl From Nowhere - *Last*
Beagle US (1972)

YELLOWTHREAD STREET COPS
Second detective of Harry FEIFFER

Rex YELVERTON
British Male Amateur operating in England

William LEQUEUX 1864-1927 (British)
Invented 23 detectives - see Allan KENNEDY
Citation Record: 1 Book
The Crystal Claw - *Only*
Hodder & Stoughton UK (1924); Macaulay US (1924)

Pamela YEW
Second detective of John DENSON

Insp Maurice YGREC
French Policeman operating in France

Marion RIPPON 1921- (American)
Writer: Marion Edith RIPPON
Citation Record: 4 Books
The Hand Of Solange - *First*
Doubleday US (1969)
Lucien's Tomb - *Latest*
Doubleday US (1979); Hale UK (1979)

YOEMAN
British Male Sleuth operating in several locations

Robert JACKSON 1941- (British)
Citation Record: 12 Books
Hurricane Squadron - *First*
Barker UK (1978); Walker US (1984)
Hunter Squadron - *Latest*
Weidenfeld & Nicolson UK (1984)

Giles YOEMAN
Male Sleuth operating in South America

Martin WOODHOUSE 1932- (British)
Writer: Martin Charlton WOODHOUSE
Citation Record: 5 Books
Tree Frog - *First*
Heinemann UK (1966); Coward McCann US (1966)
Moon Hill - *Latest*
Macmillan UK (1976); Coward McCann US (1976)

Insp YORK
British Policeman operating in England

Mary DURHAM (British)

Inventor of one other detective Insp Rodney HILTON

Citation Record: 3 Books

Why Pick On Pickles? - *First*
Crowther UK (1945)

Murder By Multiplication - *Last*
Skeffington UK (1948)

Alan YORK

British Male Amateur operating in England

Dick FRANCIS 1920- (British)

Invented 18 detectives - see Sid HALLEY

Citation Record: 1 Book

Dead Cert - *Only*
Joseph UK (1962); Harper & Row US (1962)

Supt Richard YORK

British Policeman operating in England

Audrey WILLIAMSON 1913-1986 (British)

Writer: Audrey May WILLIAMSON

Citation Record: 2 Books

Funeral March For Siegfried - *First*
Elek UK (1979)

Death Of A Theatre Filly - *Latest*
Elek UK (1980)

Sherrett YORK

British Male Amateur operating in England

Gavin HOLT 1891- (Australian)

Invented 3 detectives - see Prof Luther BASTION

Citation Record: 2 Books

Murder Train - *First*
Hodder & Stoughton UK (1936)

Ivory Ladies - *Last*
Hodder & Stoughton UK (1937)

Alec YORKE

British Male Amateur operating in England

Lincoln SPRINGFIELD (British)

Citation Record: 2 Selected Short Stories

The Hyde Park Gardens Tragedy
In 'The Idler' UK (1884)

For Her Ladyship's Sake
In 'The Idler' UK (1885)

Hamilton YORKE

is a pretty poor PI who fails to solve a case of locked-room murder.

American Male Private Detective operating in USA

Arthur DICKSON 1888-1940? (American)

Citation Record: 1 Book

Death Bids For Corners - *Only*
Humphries US (1941)

YOUNG FEARLESS

American Male Detective in Pulp Magazines operating in USA

Police Captain HOWARD (American)

Invented 15 detectives - see LIGHTNING LUKE

Citation Record: 1 Book

Young Fearless, The Detective Of Many Disguises
New York Detective Library US (1882-8)

YOUNG SLEDGE

American Male Detective in Pulp Magazines operating in USA

Old Cap DARRELL (American)

Other Detectives:
DAUNTLESS DAN
EMERALD JIM
The OZARK DETECTIVE
The STEAM-BOAT DETECTIVE

Citation Record: 1 Book

Young Sledge, The Iron-Fisted Detective; Or, A Mystery Of The Cumberland
New York Detective Library US (1882-8)

YOUNG SLEUTH

appears generically in pulp stories by several authors.

American Male Private Detective operating in USA

Archie KUTCH (American)

Citation Record: 1 Book

Young Sleuth's Victory; Or, A Detective's Adventure - *Only*
Ogilvie US (1895)

YOUNG WEASEL

American Male Detective in Pulp Magazines operating in Baltimore

Police Captain HOWARD (American)

Invented 15 detectives - see LIGHTNING LUKE

Citation Record: 1 Book

Young Weasel, The Baltimore Detective
New York Detective Library US (1882-8)

Bernard YOUNG

Second detective of Arnold KEENE

Roger L YOUNG

is a Doctor of Divinity who solves a most remarkable mystery involving animal footprints on a ceiling.

American Male Amateur operating in USA

Fredric BROWN 1906-1972 (American)

Invented 8 detectives - see Ambrose HUNTER and Ed HUNTER

Citation Record: 1 Selected Short Story

Miracle On Vine Street
In 'The Layman's Magazine' US (1941)

Simon YOUNG

British Male Sleuth operating in China

John TRENHAILE 1949- (British)

See main detective Gen Stepan POVIN

Citation Record: 2 Books

The Gates Of Exquisite View - *First*
Collins UK (1988); Dutton US (1988)

The Scroll Of Benevolence - *Latest*
Collins UK (1988); Chivers US (1990)

Wilson YOUNG

sleuths in the Old West during the 1800s.

American Male Amateur operating in USA

Giles TIPPETTE 1936- (American)

Citation Record: 7 Books

The Bank Robber - *First*
Macmillan UK (1970)

Wilson's Woman - *Latest*
Dell US (1982)

Kyle YOUNGBLOOD

American Male Amateur operating in USA

Herb FISHER (American)

Citation Record: 2 Books

Doctor Death - *First*
Berkley US (1988)

Retribution - *Latest*
Berkley US (1988)

Eve ZABRISKIE

solves a case of murder in a wealthy planned community in California.

American Female Private Detective operating in California

Jerry OSTER 1943- (American)

Inventor of one other detective Lt NEUMAN

Citation Record: 1 Book

Rancho Maria - *Single*
US (1986)

Californian Dead - *Single**
Charter US (1988)

Mike ZACHARIAS and Steve CONSIDINE

are respectively the boss and specialist operator in an agency called Confidential Investigations.

American Male Private Detectives operating in New York

Robert Patrick WILMOT (Canadian)

was born in Montana. He was a reporter, editor and song writer.

Citation Record: 3 Books

Blood In Your Eye - *First*
Lippincott US (1952); Boardman UK (1954)

Death Rides A Painted Horse - *Last*
Lippincott US (1954); Boardman UK (1955)

Capt ZACHARY

solves the mystery of the disappearance on stage of a magician's female assistant.

American Male Amateur operating in USA

J F PEIRCE (American)

Inventor of one other detective William SHAKESPEARE

Citation Record: 1 Selected Short Story

The Magician's Wife
is in an anthology, *All But Impossible.*
Ticknor US (1981)

Prince ZALESKI

is a Russian exile of unknown origin. Appearing only in a few short stories, he is certainly one of the oddest detectives in the literature. An exotic figure, he lives, for some reason and of all places, in Wales in isolation and splendour. His brilliant mind enables him to solve the most perplexing mysteries brought to him by the narrator-author.

Russian Male Amateur operating in Wales

M P SHIEL 1865-1947 (British)

was born on Montserrat Island, West Indies. He was educated at Harrison College, Barbados, King's College, London, and St Bartholomew's Hospital Medical School, London. He wrote several novels, including some bizarre mysteries.

Writer: Matthew Phipps SHIEL

Inventor of one other detective Cummings King MONK

Citation Record: 4 Short Stories in 2 Collections

Prince Zaleski - *Collection 1*
Short stories in this collection - 3
Roberts UK (1895); Lane US (1895)

Prince Zaleski And Cummings King Monk - *Collection 2*
contains three *Cummings King MONK* stories and the three *Prince ZALESKI* stories above plus one new one.
Arkham US (1977)

Jerry ZALMAN

Second detective of Doyle Dean MCCOY

Sebastian ZAMBRA

Male Amateur operating in several locations

Headon HILL 1857-1927 (British)

Invented 11 detectives - see Insp HERON

Citation Record: 1 Book 24 Short Stories in 2 Collections

The Narrowing Circle - *Only*
Jenkins UK (1929)

Clues From A Detective's Camera - *Collection 1*
Short stories - 12
Arrowsmith UK (1893)

Zambra The Detective: Some Clues From His Notebook - *Collection 2*
Short stories - 12
Chatto UK (1894)

Martin ZANE

mainly investigates cases involving marine insurance.

American Male Private Detective operating in California/Mexico

Louis TRIMBLE 1917- (American)

Writer: Louis Preston TRIMBLE

Other Byline: Stuart BROCK

Other Detectives:
ANTHROPOL   Joseph COYLE

Citation Record: 2 Books

Cargo For The Styx - *First*
Ace US (1959)

The Dead And The Deadly - *Last*
Ace US (1963)

Thornton ZANE

American Male Amateur operating in New York/Pennsylvania

Morrell MASSEY (American)

Citation Record: 2 Books

Left Hand Left - *First*
Penn US (1932); Hutchinson UK (1932)

Through The Lens - *Last*
Penn US (1933)

Joe ZANKA

is American-Sicilian. A burned out boxer and a big fighting man, he works for a mysterious, beyond-the-law agency specialising in recovering innocent people from nasty-minded groups and citizens. He is a feature of a sub-genre, the modern crime comic, updated with technology.

American Male Professional Investigator operating in San Francisco

James N FREY (American)

is a teacher of novel-writing and suspense fiction at the University of California.

Citation Record: 1 Book

The Long Way To Die - *Single*
Bantam US (1987); Macmillan UK (1989)

Prince ZARKON

solves a case in which deaths occur, apparently at long range and with no visible weapon.

Male Sleuth operating in Novenia

Lin CARTER (American)

Citation Record: 1 Book

Invisible Death - *Only*
Doubleday US (1975)

ZED

American Male Detective in Pulp Magazines operating in USA

UNKNOWN

Commiss Aurelio ZEN

is a Police Commissioner in Rome, Italy, whose cases so far have seen him involved in various vicious crimes, including kidnapping, terrorism, corruption and murder, all of which the author uses to give an insight into the tensions in Italian society today.

Italian Policeman operating in Italy

Michael DIBDIN 1947- (British)

was born in Wolverhampton, Staffordshire. He was educated in Ireland, took a BA at the University of Sussex, Brighton,

1968, and an MA at the University of Alberta, Canada, 1969, both in English. Latterly an English teacher and language assistant at the University of Perugia, Italy, 1982-4, he has specialised to date in historical or foreign backgrounds for his several detective and crime novels.

Other Detectives:
Robert BROWNING Sherlock HOLMES

Citation Record: 4 Books

Ratking - *First*
Faber UK (1988); Bantam US (1989)

Dead Lagoon - *Latest*
Faber UK (1994); Pantheon US (1995)

F T ZEVICH

Second detective of Claude 'Snake' KIRLIN

Alexander ZHARKOV

Second detective of Justin GILEAD

Lt Al ZIMMERMAN

American Policeman operating in New York

Theodore GEORGE (American)

Writer: Theodore George BERK

Citation Record: 2 Books

The Murders On The Square - *First*
Dodd, Mead US (1971)

The Deadly Homecoming - *Last*
Dodd, Mead US (1972); Hale UK (1974)

Sidney ZOOM

was one of the author's early pulp detectives, created before he went on to greater things. Hawk-eyed, he prowls the night streets for his cases.

American Male Amateur operating in USA

Sidekick: RIP
is an honorary sidekick.
Male - Pet Dog

Erle Stanley GARDNER 1889-1970 (American)

Invented 14 detectives - see Perry MASON

Citation Record: 1 Selected Short Story

The First Stone
was republished in the US as *The Case of the Scattered Rubies.*
In 'Detective Fiction Weekly' US (1931)

Anna ZORDAN

Female Sleuth

James EASTWOOD 1918- (British)

Citation Record: 3 Books

The Chinese Visitor - *First*
Cassell UK (1965); Coward McCann US (1965)

Come Die With Me - *Last*
Macmillan UK (1970)

Diamonds Are Deadly - *Last**
McKay US (1969)

Mike ZORN

is a representative of a Hollywood film studio. He has to deal with a murder on screen that turns into real murder.

American Male Amateur operating in USA

Harry KURNITZ 1907-1968 (American)

Citation Record: 1 Book

Invasion Of Privacy - *Only*
Random House US (1955); Eyre & Spottiswoode UK (1956)

Karl ZWEIG and Charles GREY

Male Amateurs operating in England

Colin WILSON 1931- (British)

was born in Leicester and educated at local schools. The author of several important works dealing with the nature and origins of violence in society, his interests have taken him down obscure byways of mystery and the occult. He has written at least fourteen genre novels.

Writer: Colin Henry WILSON

Citation Record: 1 Book

Necessary Doubt - *Only*
Barker UK (1964); Trident Press US (1964)

The Authors

AARONS Edward Sydney	Sam DURELL
AARONS Will B	Jerry BENEDICT; ***Sam DURELL***
ABBEY Edward	George HAYDUKE
ABBOT Anthony	Commiss Thatcher COLT
ABBOTT Jeff	Jordan POTEET
ABBOTT Keith	Ernest 'Rhino' HEMINGWAY and F Scott 'Ritz' FITZGERALD
ABERCROMBIE Barbara	Sarah HOYT
ABLEMAN Paul	Eddie SHOESTRING
ABRAHAMS Peter	Rachael MONETTE
ABRAHAMS Robert D	Pete TAYLOR
ABSHIRE Richard	Jack KYLE
ABSHIRE Richard K and William R CLAIR	Det Charlie GANTS
ACKROYD Peter	Insp HAWKSMOOR
ACRE Stephen	Joe DEVLIN
ADAM Paul	Mike MACLEAN
ADAMS Bronte	Aphra COLQUHOUN
ADAMS Cleve F	***Rex MCBRIDE***; Stephen MCCLOUD; Violet MCDADE; John J SHANNON; Insp THOMAS
ADAMS Douglas	Dirk GENTLY
ADAMS George	Charlie BYRNE
ADAMS Harold	Kyle CHAMPION; ***Carl WILCOX***
ADAMS Herbert	Maj Robert BENNION; Mark BRADDON; ***Jimmie HASWELL***
ADAMS Morley	Insp PROBYN
ADAMS Samuel Hopkins	***A V R E 'Average' JONES***; Prof Willis RAVENDEN and Stanford COLTON
ADAMS Shipley	Insp HARROW
ADAMSON M J	Balthazar MARTEN
ADCOCK Thomas Larry	Det Neil 'Hock' HOCKADAY
ADDISON H R	Thomas Phillips VOKES
ADE George	Eddie PARKS
ADKINS Bill	Dave HILL
ADLER Warren	Fiona FITZGERALD
ADYE Major General Sir John	Oliver SMAILE
AFFORD Max	Insp READ and Jeffrey BLACKBURN
AFGHAN	Asaf KHAN
AGNEY Stephen H	Peter FLINT
AIKEN Albert W	CHIN CHIN; LA MARMOSET; Mignon LAWRENCE; Joe PHOENIX; ***Hilda SIRENE***
AIKEN Joan Delano	Lucy CULPEPPER
AIRD Catherine	Insp Christopher Dennis SLOAN
ALAIS E W	Sexton BLAKE
ALBERT Andrew I	Paul DECKER
ALBERT Marvin H	Tony ROME; ***Pierre-Ange SAWYER***
ALBERT Susan Wittig	China BAYLES
ALBERT T M	Const MCNINCH
ALBRAND Martha	Mark TRAVERS
ALDING Peter	Insp Robert FUSIL and Const KERR
ALDOUS Allan	Galahad Urban BROWNE
ALDRICH Thomas Bailey	***Paul LYNDE***; TAGGETT
ALDRIDGE James	Kit QUAYLE; ***Rupert ROYCE***
ALDYNE Nathan	Daniel VALENTINE and Clarisse LOVELACE
ALEXANDER Bruce	Sir John FIELDING
ALEXANDER David	Stosh COLTRAY
ALEXANDER David	***Bart HARDIN***; Marty LAND; Lt ROMANO; Tommy TWOTOES and Terry ROOKE
ALEXANDER Gary	Luis BALAM; ***Supt Bamsan KIET***
ALEXANDER Karl	***Sarah SCOTT***; H G WELLS
ALEXANDER Lawrence	Commiss Theodore ROOSEVELT
ALINGTON Adrian	Insp 'Steady as a Rock' POSSE
ALINGTON Cyril A	Mr BIRTLEY; ***John CRAGGS and James CASTLETON***
ALLAIN Marcel	FANTOMAS
ALLAN Dennis	Bruce CARVER
ALLAN Francis K	John STORM
ALLAN Joan	Valerie LAMBERT
ALLAN Luke	***BLUE PETE***; Gordon MULDREW
ALLBEURY Ted	***Tad ANDERS***; Max FARNE
ALLEGRETTO Michael	Nora HONEYCUTT; ***Jacob LOMAX***
ALLEN Austen	Insp ORD
ALLEN Clifford	Ch Supt J V STRUTT
ALLEN Grant	Lois CAYLEY; Col CLAY; FLETCHER; SHERRARD; ***Nurse Hilda WADE***
ALLEN Henry	Gordon SAULT
ALLEN Leslie	Napoleon B SMITH
ALLEN Mary Ann	Jane BRADSHAWE
ALLEN Michael	Supt Ben SPENCE
ALLEN Steve	Roger DALE
ALLEN Warner	Mr CLERIHEW; ***George B EDGEHILL and Aristide GOVIN***; Insp WAKE and Philip GAYMORE
ALLINGHAM Margery	Albert CAMPION
ALLISON E M A	Brother BARNABAS
ALLISON William	Peter KNIGHT
ALLYSON Alan	Martin ROSS
ALNER James Z	Trevor STOKE
ALVERSON Charles	***Joe GOODEY***; Alec HOERNER
AMBERLEY Richard	Insp MARTIN
AMBLER Dail	Danny SPADE
AMBLER Eric	***Dr Jan CZISSAR***; Charles LATIMER; Arthur Abdul SIMPSON; VALESHOFF and TAMARA
AMES Delano	***Dagobert BROWN and Jane BROWN***; Cpl Juan LLORCA
AMES Mel D	Det Lt Cathy CARRUTHERS
AMIS Kingsley	Christopher DANE; ***Peter FURNEAUX***
ANDERSON Frederick Irving	Oliver ARMISTON
ANDERSON Ian	Cpl John CAVANNAGH
ANDERSON J R L	Maj Peter BLAIR; ***Ch Const Piet DEVENTER***
ANDERSON James	Insp BIDWELL; Jessica FLETCHER; Insp PALMER; Mikael Josef PETROS; ***Insp WILKINS***
ANDERSON M	CREWE; ***Jason MARR***
ANDERSON Poul	Sherlock HOLMES; SYALOCH; Nicholas VAN RIJN; ***Trygve YAMAMURA***
ANDOVER Henry	Henry HOLLAND
ANDRAE Christine	Lee SQUIRES
ANDREAE Percy	JAMIESON
ANDREWS Charlton	Mycroft HOLMES and Sherlock HOLMES; Sherlock HOLMES; Drexel WARE; ***Derek WHITBY***
ANDREWS John	Nelson LEE
ANDREWS John	Ferrers LOCKE
ANDREWS V C	Chris DOLLANGANGER and Cathy DOLLANGANGER
ANDREWS Val	Sherlock HOLMES
ANDREWS Val and H PENN	Sherlock HOLMES
ANDRUS Jeff	John TRACER
ANGUS Douglas Ross	Derek CROME
ANGUS John	Caitlin O'NEAL
ANNESLEY Michael	Lawrie FENTON
ANON	The ACTRESS DETECTIVE; The ARTIST DETECTIVE; BEAUTIFUL JACK; The BOY DETECTIVE; Thad BURR; The CELEBRATED DETECTIVE; A CHICAGO DETECTIVE; The CIRCUS DETECTIVE; Capt CLEW; Shilah COOMBES; The CRACKSHOT DETECTIVE; DEATH-FACE; The DECOY DETECTIVE; Dick DOBBS; The DUMB DETECTIVE; The EAST SIDE DETECTIVE; The FAR WEST DETECTIVE; Dave FEARLESS; The FERRET DETECTIVE; Detective FLEET; Andrew FORSTER; The FRISCO DETECTIVE; The GEORGIA DETECTIVE; The GIANT DETECTIVE; The GOLD STAR DETECTIVE; Doc' GRIP; The GYPSY DETECTIVE; Tubby' HAIG; HANDSOME HARRY; Kitty HAWKE; Algernon HIGGINS; Sherlock HOLMES; Chubb-Lock HOMES;The HYPNOTIST DETECTIVE; The INDEPENDENT DETECTIVE; Jack IRWIN and Robert MARTINEAU; The JEW DETECTIVE; The KENTUCKY DETECTIVE; LIGHTNING GRIP; The LONDON DETECTIVE; LONG BRANCH DETECTIVE; LYON and GATCH; The MATCHLESS DETECTIVE; A NEW YORK DETECTIVE; OLD PURITAN; OLD TERRIBLE; The PRAIRIE DETECTIVE; The PRINCELY DETECTIVE; RAILWAY DETECTIVE; RED-LIGHT WILL; Bow Street Runner Thomas RICHMOND; The ROOKERY DETECTIVE; The SHAM DETECTIVE; SILVER TOM; Hemlock SOAMES; The SOCIETY DETECTIVE; Dominick SQUEEK; Martin SWIFT; Mr TOLEPAT; Martin TRACK; Martin TRACKMAN; Jack VINTON; John WILSON

The Authors

ANSON Lindsay	Peter ALLEN
ANTHONY David	Stanley BASS; ***Morgan BUTLER***
ANTHONY Elizabeth	Pauline LYONS
ANTHONY Evelyn	Joe DUNSTAN and Eric FISHER; ***Davina GRAHAM***
ANTHONY Michael David	Richard HARRISON
ANTHONY Piers and Roberto FUENTES	Jason STRIKER
ANTHONY Wilder	Dr NORTON
ANTILL Elizabeth	Insp Simon ASHTON
ANTONY Peter	FATHOM; ***Mr VERITY and Insp RAMBLER***
ANVIL Christopher	Richard VERNER
APPIAH Anthony	Sir Patrick SCOTT
APPLE A E	Mr CHANG
APPLIN Arthur	Andrew MORDENT
ARCHER Frank	Joe DELANEY
ARCHER Mary	Denis CHAD
ARCHER Robert	Joel STERN
ARD William	***Timothy DANE***; Danny FONTAINE; Mike FONTAINE; Barney GLINES
ARD William (William Thomas ARD)	Lou LARGO
ARD William (Lawrence BLOCK)	Lou LARGO
ARD William (John JAKES)	Lou LARGO
ARDEN William	***Kane JACKSON***; Sgt Joseph MARX
ARDIES Tom	Charlie SPARROW
ARDIN William	Charles RAMSAY
ARESBYS The	Parrish DARBY
ARLEN Michael	Gay Stanhope FALCON
ARLISS Joen	Kate GRAHAM
ARMISTEAD John	Sheriff BRAMLEY
ARMOUR R C	Sexton BLAKE
ARMSTRONG Anthony	Jimmie REZAIRE
ARMSTRONG Charlotte	Matt CUNEEN; ***Prof MacDougal DUFF***; Charley IVES; Annabel O'SHEA; Prof David WAKELY
ARMSTRONG Raymond	***Insp Dick MASON***; Insp Dick MASON and Laura SCUDAMORE; J Rockingham STONE; J Rockingham STONE, Laura SCUDAMORE and Insp Dick MASON
ARMSTRONG Vivien	***Ch Insp Ralph ARNOTT***; Insp Lawrence ERSKINE
ARNETT Jack	William JUSTICE
ARNOLD A F	Sherlock WATSON
ARNOLD Allan	The BOOT BLACK DETECTIVE; Belle BOYD; CENTERSHOT; Sherlock HOLMES; ***OLD SNAP***; YANKEE JED
ARNOLD Margot	Sir Toby GLENDOWER and Penelope SPRING
ARONSON Mark	Sherlock HOLMES
ARRIGHI Mel	***HARRINGTON***; Hank MERCER and Biff DEEGAN
ARTHUR Frank	Insp SPEARPOINT
ARTHUR Robert	Lt Oliver BAYNES and John Sherlock HOLMES; Baron DE HIRSCH; Max LONDON; Harrison MANNIX; Howard MATTHEWS and Jeff LANDRUM; ***Max MILLION***
ARVAY Harry	Max ROTH
ASBURY Herbert	Insp Thomas CONROY
ASCHER Eugene	Lucian CAROLUS
ASCOTT Adelie	Lila LISLE
ASH William	Kyle BRANDEIS
ASHBROOK H	Philip 'Spike' TRACY
ASHDOWN Clifford	Romney PRINGLE
ASHE Douglas	Insp Stephen ELIOT and Arthur CRUMP
ASHE Gordon	Patrick DAWLISH
ASHE Mary Ann	Insp CHUCKY
ASHE Rosalind	Insp BLUNT
ASHE Saxon	Saxon ASHE
ASHENHURST John M	Al BENNET
ASHFORD Jeffrey	Supt ABBOTT; Det Const ATHANA; Insp CRANE; Bob HOWE; ***Det Insp Don KERRY***; Det Sgt Peter NOYES; Bill STENEM; Miba STERLING; Gary WESTON
ASHFORTH Albert	Clinton BALL
ASHTON Charles	***Maj Jack ATHERLEY***; Insp MERTON; Richard SANGSTER
ASHTON Harold	Private PINKERTON
ASHTON Mark	John RADMELL
ASHTON Ralph A	Sherlock HOLMES
ASIMOV Isaac	***Elijah BALEY***; The BLACK WIDOWERS; Lt Jack DOHERY and Lou BRADE; Darius JUST; Wendell ORTH; The UNION CLUB
ASIMOV Isaac, Martin Harry GREENBERG and Charles G WAUGH	Sherlock HOLMES;
ASWAD Betsy	Rosalind ROTH
ATHEY Forrest	Sherlock HOLMES
ATHOLL Justin	LAKIN
ATKEY Bertram	Smiler' BUNN; Nelson CHIDDENHAM; ***Prosper FAIR***; Winnie O'WYNN
ATKINS Meg Elizabeth	Insp Henry BEAUMONT
ATLEE Philip	Joe GALL
AUBREY Edmund	Sherlock HOLMES
AUDEMARS Pierre	***Insp PINAUD***; Insp Hercule RENARD
AUSTIN Anne	Insp James F 'Bonnie' DUNDEE
AUSTIN Bliss	Sherlock HOLMES
AUSTIN F Britten	Quentin QUAYNE
AUSTIN Hugh	***Peter QUINT***; William (Sultans' Harem) SULTAN
AUSTWICK John	Insp PARKER
AVALLONE Michael	Dave DUNN; Joe MANNIX; ***Ed NOON***; Satan SLEUTH; Napoleon SOLO and Ilya KURYAKIN
AVELINE Claude	Insp Frederic BELOT
AVERY Robert	Joe KELLY
AXLER Leo	Bill HAWLEY
AYLWARD Marcus	HARPER
AYRE Thornton	Ch Insp Douglas GOSSAGE

— B —

BABCOCK Dwight V	Hannah VAN DOREN
BABSON Marion	Frances ARMITAGE; Trixie DOLAN and Evangeline SINCLAIR; Nancy HARPER; Det KNOWLES; Sarah ORPINGTON; Tom PAIGE; Douglas PERKINS and Gerry TATE; ***Douglas PERKINS***
BABULA William	Jeremiah ST JOHN
BACKHOUSE	***Insp Christopher MARSDEN***; Insp PRENTIS
BAGBY George	Insp SCHMIDT
BAGLEY Desmond	SLADE; ***Max STAFFORD***
BAILEY Elliott	Insp Geoffrey FRASER
BAILEY H C	Raoul BOMFORTUNE; Joshua CLUNK; ***Dr Reginald FORTUNE***; The Hon Victoria PUMPHREY
BAILEY Hilary	Charlotte HOLMES
BAILEY Hilea	Hilary Dunsany BAILEY III and Hilea BAILEY
BAILEY Seth	Lt HASS
BAINES Cuthbert	Dennis DOYNE
BAIRD Edwin	Herbert BARRY
BAKER Abbey Penn	Prof Myrl Adler NORTON
BAKER Asa	Jerry BURKE
BAKER Hugh	Richard LIND
BAKER Ivon	David MEYNELL
BAKER Nikki	Virginia KELLY
BAKER North and William BOLTON	Danny MICHAELS
BAKER Richard M	Franklin RUSSELL
BAKER Susan	Mavis DAVIS
BAKER W Howard	Sexton BLAKE; ***Richard QUINTAIN***
BALDWIN Michael	Patrick MATSON
BALFOUR Hearnden	Insp Jack STRICKLAND
BALHAM Joe	Det Insp Jack REGAN
BALL Brian	KEEGAN
BALL John	Sherlock HOLMES; Ch Jack TALLON; ***Virgil TIBBS***
BALLANTYNE R M	SHARP
BALLARD W T	Red DRAKE; Mark FORAN; Lt Max HUNTER; ***Bill LENNOX***
BALLENGER Dean	Mike GANNON
BALLINGER W A (House name)	Sexton BLAKE
BALLINGER W A (William Arthur Howard BAKER)	Sexton BLAKE
BALLINGER W A (William Arthur Howard BAKER and Wilfred Glassford MCNEILLY)	Sexton BLAKE
BALLINGER W A (William Arthur Howard BAKER, George Mann and Wilfred Glassford MCNEILLY)	Sexton BLAKE
BALLINGER W A (Wilfred Glassford MCNEILLY)	Sexton BLAKE
BALLINGER W A	Richard QUINTAIN
BALLINGER William S	Danny APRIL; Barr BREED; ***Joaquin HAWKS***; Van MARS; Bryce PATCH
BALMER Edwin	Joan Daisy ROYLE
BALMER Edwin and Philip WYLIE	Donald CORNWALL
BALMER Edwin and William MACHARG	Basil SANTOINE; ***Luther TRANT***
BAMBURG Lilian	Septimus MARCH
BAMFORD Francis	Sherlock HOLMES
BANDY Franklin	Kevin MACINNES
BANGS John Kendrick	Sherlock HOLMES; ***Raffles HOLMES***; Shylock HOMES; Mrs A J VAN RAFFLES
BANKIER William	Penni DANDRIDGE; ***Harry LAWSON***
BANKS Carolyn	Al AMATUCCI
BANKS Oliver	Amos HATCHER
BANKS Raymond E	Sam KING
BANNERMAN Bernard	Dave WOOLF
BANNERMAN W B	Domingo SANTOS
BANNISTER Jo	***Clio MARSH and Det Supt Harry MARSH***; Ch Insp Frank SHAPIRO and Det Insp Liz GRAHAM
BANVILLE Vincent	John BLAINE
BARBER Alex	Urban DORMER
BARBER Willetta Ann and R F SCHABELITZ	Christopher STORM
BARBETTE Jay	Harry BUTTEN
BARBOUR A Maynard	MERRICK
BARCLAY Bill	Nick ALLARD
BARCLAY Marguerite and Armiger BARCLAY	Lavie JUTT

BARDSLEY Michael	Supt Donald MARTIN
BARING Maurice	Sherlock HOLMES
BARK Conrad Voss	William HOLMES
BARKER Albert	***Reefe KING***; Hawk MACRAE
BARKER Elsa	Dexter DRAKE
BARKER Ronald	Insp HARRIS
BARKER Wade (House Name)	Brett WALLACE
BARKER Wade (Richard S MEYERS)	Brett WALLACE
BARLING Charles	***Insp HENDERSON***; Insp George MARSHALL
BARLING Tom	Charlie DANCE
BARLOW Vernon	Capt Mark FANNING
BARNAO Jack	John LOCKE
BARNARD Robert	Insp CROFT; Insp FAGERMO; Greg HOCKING; Helen KITTEREGE; Ch Insp MCHALE; Idwal MEREDITH; Supt Mike ODDIE; Insp PARRISH; Charlie PEACE; Insp Mike PUMFREY; Insp ROYLE; ***Insp Perry TRETHOWAN***; Insp Perry TRETHOWAN and Charlie PEACE
BARNES Dallas	Det Sgt John STRYKER
BARNES Linda J	***Carlotta CARLYLE***; Michael SPRAGGUE
BARNES Ronald Gorell	Evelyn TEMPLE
BARNETT Glyn	Insp GRAMPORT
BARNETT James	Supt Owen SMITH
BARNS Glenn M	Jonathan MARKS
BARR Nevada	Anna PIGEON
BARR Robert	Sherlaw KOMBS; ***Nick NICHOLSON***; Lord STRANLEIGH; Eugène VALMONT
BARR Stephen	Sherlock HOLMES; ***Dr Sylvan MOORE***
BARRE Richard	Will HARDESTY
BARRETT Alfred Wilson	Justus WISE
BARRETT Frank	KEENE; David LEIGH; James SINGLETON; Dr STURGESS; ***Capt Thomas VERNAN***
BARRETT G J	Insp BLESSINGAY
BARRETT Monte	Peter CARDIGAN
BARRETT Robert G	Les NORTON
BARRETT William E	NEEDLE MIKE
BARRIE James M	Sherlock HOLMES
BARRINGTON John H	Ken WILLIAMS
BARRINGTON Pamela	Insp HENDERSON; ***Insp George MARSHALL***; Insp George TRAVERS
BARROLL Clare	Lisa THORNE
BARRY Charles	Supt Lawrence GILMARTIN
BARRY Jerome	'Chick' VARNEY
BARRY Joe	Bill AUGUST; ***Rush HENRY***
BARRY Mike	Burton WULFF
BARSTOW Phyllida	Sarah TREGARON
BARTH Richard	Jacob BARZENY; ***Margaret BINTON***
BARTLETT E G	David LEIGH
BARTON George	Bromley BARNES
BARTON Hill	Sherlock HOLMES
BARTON William and Michael CAPOBIANCO	Sherlock HOLMES
BAR-ZOHAR Michael	Jeff SAUNDERS
BASINSKY Earle	Det Steve CONWAY
BASKERVILLE Beatrice	BRICONI
BASS Milton R	Vino ALTOBELLI; ***Benny FREEDMAN***
BATCHELOR Denzil	Insp JOHNSON
BATCHELOR Reg	Sgt FENWICK
BATESON David	Larry VERNON
BATTEN Jack	CRANG
BATTEN P W	Dixon BRETT
BATTISON Brian	Ch Insp Jim ASHWORTH
BAWDEN Nina	Insp WALKER
BAX Roger	Insp JAMES
BAXT George	Harvey GRAYMOOR and Laura GRAYMOOR; ***Det Pharaoh LOVE***; Det Pharaoh LOVE and Det Satan STAGG; Valentine NORTON; Dorothy PARKER and Alexander WOOLLCOTT; Sylvia PLOTKIN and Max Van LARSEN
BAXTER Gregory	Supt DANIELS
BAY Austin	Bill BUCHANAN
BAYER William	***Ch David BAR-LEV***; Frank JANEK
BAYFIELD William J	Sexton BLAKE
BAYLY Eric A	Percival GUNTRIP; Mr MERTON; ***Oliver POTTER and Laurence CARRINGTON***
BAYNE Isabella	Benedict BREEZE
BAYNE Spencer	Hendrik VAN KILL
BAYNES Jack	Morocco JONES
BEAL M F	Kat GUERRERA
BEAR David	Jack HUGHES
BEARE George	Vincent STALLARD and Cynthia GODWIN
BEARSHAW Brian	Supt Robert TOWNLEY and Sgt Roger NEWMAN
BEATON M C	***Insp BLAIR***; Const Hamish MACBETH; Agatha RAISIN
BEAUCHAMP Henry	Det BODKIN
BEAUFORT Tom	Sophie PARNELL
BECK Henry C	Father MICKLE
BECK K K	Michael CARUSO; Maude Teasdale CAVENDISH; ***Iris COOPER***; Jane DA SILVA; Sylvia SNOW and Prof Charles CARSTAIRS
BECKETT Arthur A	John BARMAN
BECKETT Mark	Maj Dick BURTON
BEDFORD-JONES H	Sherlock HOLMES
BEEBY Otto	Tony SPENCER
BEECHAM John Charles	KOYALA

BEECHAM Rose	Amanda VALENTINE
BEECHCROFT William	Dan FORREST
BEEDING Francis	Ronald BRIERCLIFFE; John COWPER; Col Alistair GRANBY; Insp George MARTIN; Thomas PRESTON; ***Insp WILKINS***
BEGBIE Garston	Supt Samuel QUAN
BEHM Marc	The EYE
BEINHART Larry	Tony CASSELLA
BELL Josephine	George COLE and Amanda DREW; Dr Henry FROST; Timothy LONG; Insp Steven MITCHELL; Insp RAWLINSON; Lucy SUMMERS; Amy TUPPER; Claude WARRINGTON-REEVE and Insp Steven MITCHELL; ***Dr David WINTRINGHAM***; Dr David WINTRINGHAM and Insp Steven MITCHELL
BELL Pauline	Det Ch Insp BROWNE; ***Det Sgt Jerry HUNTER***; Sgt Benedict MITCHELL
BELL Simon	Harry WALKER
BELL Vicars	Dr BAYNES
BELLAIRS George	Det Insp/Supt Thomas LITTLEJOHN
BELLAMY R L	Scout GREY
BELLEM Robert Leslie	Duke PIZZATELLO; ***Dan TURNER***
BELSKY Dick	Jenny MCKAY; ***Lucy SHANNON***
BENEDICT Gerald	Nigel MAYNE
BENGIS Nathan L	Sherlock HOLMES
BENJAMIN Paul	Max KLEIN
BENNETT Charles	Det AYLIFFE
BENNETT Dorothy	Dennis DEVORE
BENNETT J M	Lord TIGRANES
BENNETT Kem	Insp ROBINET
BENNETT Margot	John DAVIES
BENNETT Rolf	Lt/Cdr Frank H LAWLESS; ***James TURNER***
BENNETT W R	Adam KANE
BENSEN D R	Sherlock HOLMES
BENSON Benjamin	Trooper Ralph LINDSEY; ***Capt Wade PARIS***
BENSON O G	Max RAVEN
BENTLEY E C	***Philip TRENT***; Lord Peter WIMSEY
BENTLEY E C and Warner ALLEN	Philip TRENT
BENTLEY John	Glen GIBSON; ***Sir Richard HERRIVELL***; Dick MARLOW
BENTLEY Phyllis	Marian PHIPPS
BENTON John L	***Stephen DUANE***; Jerry WADE
BENTON Kenneth	Peter CRAIG
BERCKMAN Evelyn	Kirk HALSTEAD
BERCOVICI Eric	Harold SHILLING
BERENSON Laurien	Melanie TRAVIS
BERENSON Marc	Curt DENMARK
BERESFORD J D	Morgan FELLOWS
BERESFORD Leslie	Justin MARSH
BERGER Thomas	Russel WREN
BERGMAN Andrew	Jack LEVINE
BERKELEY Anthony	Ambrose CHITTERWICK; Ambrose CHITTERWICK and Roger SHERINGHAM; Lord Arthur LINTON; ***Roger SHERINGHAM***
BERNARD Robert	***Prof Richard HALSEY***; Millicent HETHEREGE; Lt MOYNAHAN, Millicent HETHEREGE and Bill STRATTON
BERNARD Trevor	Nathan BRIGHTLIGHT
BERNE Karin	Ellie GORDON
BERNEDE A	CHANTECOQ
BERNHARDT William	Ben KINCAID
BERROW Norman	Det Insp COURTENAY; MATTHEWS; ***Michael REVEL***; Det Insp Lancelot Carolus SMITH
BERRY Carole	Bonnie INDERMILL
BESTOR George Clinton	GWAYLOR
BETTERIDGE Don	***Insp DUNCAN and Capt Peter DARRELL***; Tiger' LESTER
BEYER William Gray	Cornelius DUFFY
BIBOLET R H	Sherlock HOLMES
BICKERS Richard Townshend	Mark STRATTON
BICKHAM Jack	Joe DUGGER; ***Charity ROSS***
BIDERMAN Bob	Morris KAPLAN; ***Joseph RADKIN***
BIDSTON Lester	Sexton BLAKE
BIDWELL Margaret	Mr HODSON
BIGGERS Earl Derr	Sgt/Insp Charlie CHAN
BIGGLE Lloyd	Jan DARZEK; Sherlock HOLMES; Edward Porter JONES and Sherlock HOLMES; Jay PLETCHER; ***Bill RASTIN***
BILLANY Dan	Robbie DUNCAN
BINGHAM John	***Supt 'Badger' BROCK***; Kenneth DUCANE; Det Ch Insp David MORGAN
BIRD Brandon	Hampton HUME
BIRKETT John	Michael RHINEHEART
BIRMINGHAM George A	Insp SMALLWAYS
BIRMINGHAM Maisie	Kate WEATHERLY
BISHOP Cecil	Chinese BROWN; ***Ah FOO***
BISHOP Claudia	Sarah QUILLIAM and Meg QUILLIAM
BISHOP Paul	***Det Fey CROAKER***; Calico Jack WALKER and Tina TAMIKO
BISHOP Stacey	Stephen BAYARD
BLACK E Best	Peter STRANGELY
BLACK Gavin	Paul HARRIS
BLACK Ian Stuart	Peter MUNRO
BLACK Ladbroke	Sexton BLAKE; ***Mr PREED***
BLACK Lionel	Supt Francis FOY; Emma GREAVES; ***Kate THEOBALD***
BLACK Mansell	Richard VANESS
BLACK Thomas B	Al DELANEY
BLACK Veronica	Sister JOAN and Det Sgt Alan MILL
BLACKBURN John	John CAIN; ***Gen Charles KIRK***; Marcus LEVIN; J Molden MOTT

The Authors

BLACKER Irwin R	Richard LE GRANDE
BLACKER Terence	Det Insp Simon POTTER
BLACKMON Anita	Adelaide ADAMS
BLACKWOOD Algernon	Max HENSIG; ***John SILENCE***
BLAINE Richard	Mike GARRETT
BLAIR Allan	Sexton BLAKE
BLAIR Marcia	Tory BAXTER
BLAISDELL Anne	Sgt Ivor MADDOX
BLAKE Eleanor A	John KYMMERLY
BLAKE Nicholas	Nigel STRANGEWAYS
BLAKE Stacey	Sexton BLAKE
BLAKE William Dorsey	Reggie MOON
BLAKESLEY Stephen	Sexton BLAKE; ***The CARDINAL***
BLANC Suzanne	Insp Miguel MENENDEZ
BLANKENSHIP William D	Michael SAXON
BLASSINGAME Wyatt	John SMITH
BLATTY William Peter	Bill KINDERMAN
BLAYN Hugo	Dr CARRUTHERS; ***Insp GARTH***
BLAYNE Sebastian	Sebastian BLAYNE
BLAZER J S	Donald BRACKEN and James Rowland WOODWARD VII
BLEECK Oliver	Philip ST IVES
BLISS Adam	Capt KEYES; ***Alice PENNY***
BLIZARD Marie	Eve MACWILLIAMS
BLOCHMAN Lawrence G	***Dr Daniel Webster COFFEE and Lt Max RITTER***; Bill GABRIEL; Det KILKENNY; Roderick POPLAR; Insp Leonidas PRIKE
BLOCK Barbara	Robin LIGHT
BLOCK Don	KLEIN
BLOCK Lawrence	***Leo HAIG***; Ed LONDON; MARKHAM; Bernard Grimes RHODENBARR; Matt SCUDDER; Evan TANNER
BLOOD Matthew	Morgan WAYNE
BLOOMFIELD Robert	Alva YAEGER
BLOW Lynton	Const MURDOCH
BLUMENTHAL John	Mac SLADE
BOARDMAN John	Comrade Sherslav GOLMSKY
BOBIN John William	Sexton BLAKE
BOCCA Al	Al BOCCA
BODKIN M McDonnell	***Paul BECK***; Paul BECK Jr; Dora MYRL
BOGART Stephen	R J BROOKS
BOGART William	Johnny SAXON
BOHLE Edgar	Dick STODDART
BOLAND John	***John Byron HYDE***; Kim SMITH
BOLES Paul Darcy	Luke APPLEGATE
BOLITHO Janie	Det Ch Insp Ian ROPER
BOLT Ben	Insp GODBOLD; Insp GODBOLD and Bob PONTING; Capt GRANDISON; ***Bob PONTING***; John SCARLETT
BOND Evelyn	Ira YEDDER
BOND J Harvey	Mike LANSON
BOND Michael	Monsieur Aristide PAMPLEMOUSSE
BONETT John	Insp Salvador BORGES
BONETT John and Emery BONETT	***Insp Salvador BORGES***; Prof MANDRAKE
BONFIGLIOLI Kyril	Charlie MORTDECAI
BONIFACE Marjorie	Sheriff Hiram ODOM
BONNAMY Francis	Maj Peter Utley SHANE
BONNER Geraldine	Molly MORGANTHAU
BONNER Parker	Hymie BEERMAN
BONNEY Joseph L	Simon ROLFE
BOORE W	Insp BIGGINS
BOOTH Charles G	***Anatole FLIQUE***; MCFEE; Kerry O'NEIL and Gail HOLLISTER
BOOTH Christopher B	***Jim BLISS***; Amos CLACKWORTHY; Bob FETHERSTON and Sgt QUINN
BOOTH Louis F	Maxwell FENNER
BOOTH Oliver	Wellaby JOHNSON
BOOTHBY Guy	Mr Jacob BURRELL; Simon CARNE; ***Dr NIKOLA***
BOOTHROYD Basil	Mr PITKIN
BOOTON Kage	Ida PELHAM
BORGENICHT Miriam	***Nan DUNLAP***; Ada WELLER
BORTHWICK J S	Sarah DEANE and Dr Alex MCKENZIE
BORTNER Norman Stanley	Prof Clifford WELLS and Lt Barney MATTINGLEY
BORTON D B	Cat CALIBAN
BOSAK Steven	Vernon BRADLUSKY
BOSSE M J	Victoria WELCH
BOSTON Charles K	Otis BEAGLE
BOSTROM Hank	Steve HAMM
BOSWELL Rolfe	Sherlock HOLMES
BOUCHER Anthony	Dr John ASHWIN; Sherlock HOLMES; Sherlock HOLMES and Fergus O'BREEN; Lt LIEBERMANN; Nick NOBLE; ***Fergus O'BREEN and Det Lt JACKSON***; Sister URSULA
BOURGEAU Art	Claude 'Snake' KIRLIN and F T ZEVICH
BOURJAILY Vance	'Chink' PETERS
BOURNE Mark	Sherlock HOLMES
BOWDLER Roger	Jonathan HART and Jennifer HART
BOWEN Elizabeth	Dinah DELACROIX
BOWEN Joseph	Manuel CORTINA
BOWEN Marjorie	***Brother Felipe BRUNO***; Capt HOARE
BOWEN Michael	Richard MICHAELSON
BOWEN Robert Sidney	Gerry BARNES
BOWEN Wilfred J L	Centenier PINOT
BOWERING George	George VANCOUVER
BOWERS Dorothy	***Ch Insp Dan PARDOE***; Insp RAIKES
BOWERS Elizabeth	Meg LACEY
BOWKER William Rushton	BIZZY-QUIZZY
BOWLSBY Craig	Sherlock HOLMES
BOWMAN David A	Foy LANEER
BOWMAN Gerald	Sexton BLAKE; ***Michael SHANNON***
BOWMAN Robert	Cassandra THORPE
BOX Edgar	Peter Cutler SERGEANT
BOYD Dale	Tim SLOAN
BOYD Eunice Mays	Millard SMYTH
BOYD Frank	Johnny STACCATO
BOYD Marion	Tom ALLEN
BOYD Raymond	Paul SCARF
BOYER Rick	***Dr Charlie ADAMS***; Sherlock HOLMES
BOYLAN Eleanor	Clare GAMADGE
BOYLE Denis	Cdr MORETON
BOYLE Gerry	Jack MCMORROW
BOYLE Thomas	Francis DE SALES
BOYLES William and Hank NUYER	William 'Tiny' RYDER
BRACE Timothy	Anthony ADAMS
BRACKEEN Steve	Clay MACKINNON
BRACKETT Leigh	***Edmond CLIVE***; Walter SHERRIS; Michael VICKERS
BRADDON George	Michael GAUNT
BRADDON M E	***Robert AUDLEY***; Mr Henry CARTER; Lucius DAVOREN; Mr FAUNCE; George GERRARD; Valentine HAWKEHURST; Edward HEATHCOTE; Gilbert MONKTON; Coralie URQUHART
BRADDON Russell	Ch Insp Charlie CHEADLE
BRADFORD Kelly	Derek THOMPSON
BRADLEY John	Sgt Matt MINOGUE
BRADLEY Michael	Johnny ADRANO
BRADLEY Worthen	Sherlock HOLMES
BRADY Nicholas	Rev Ebenezer BUCKLE
BRAHMS Caryl and S J SIMON	Insp Adam QUILL
BRAIN Leonard	Charlie HOWARD
BRALY David	De Ch Insp Phelim KANE
BRALY Malcolm	Andy HAMMOND
BRAMAH Ernest	Max CARRADOS
BRAMHALL Marion	Kit 'Marsden' ACTON
BRAMLEY Charles	A SOCIAL DETECTIVE
BRANCH Pamela	Clifford FLUSH
BRAND Hilary (James MOFFATT)	Hilary BRAND
BRAND Hilary (Stephen Daniel FRANCES)	Hilary BRAND
BRAND Mary Christianna	Insp BLOCK; Insp CHARLESWORTH; Insp CHUCKY; Insp COCKRILL; ***Insp COCKRILL and Insp CHARLESWORTH***; Mrs Dorinda JONES
BRAND Max	Dr KILDARE; ***Terence RADWAY***
BRANDNER Gary	Colin 'Big Brain' GARRETT
BRANDON Charles	John FORTESCUE
BRANDON Gordon	Arthur Stukeley PENNINGTON and Det Insp Patrick Aloysius MCCARTHY; ***Michael TERRENCE and 'Terry' TERRENCE***
BRANDON Jay	Raymond BOUDRO
BRANDON John G	Sexton BLAKE; BURMAN; Sgt/Det Insp Patrick Aloysius MCCARTHY; Arthur Stukeley PENNINGTON; ***Arthur Stukeley PENNINGTON and Det Insp Patrick Aloysius MCCARTHY***;
BRANDON Ruth	Andrew TAGGART
BRANDON William	Sam IRELAND
BRANSON H Clay	Dr John BENT
BRANSTON Frank	Tommy TOMPKINS
BRAUN Lillian Jackson	Jim QWILLERAN
BRAUN M G	Al GLENNE
BRAUTIGAN Richard	C CARD
BREAM Freda	Rev Jabel JARRETT
BREAN Herbert	William DEACON; ***Reynold FRAME***; Marty MALONE
BREARLEY John	Sexton BLAKE
BREBNER Percy	Christopher QUARLES
BREDE Arnold	'Bull' ROGERS
BREEN Jon L	Jerry BROGAN; Ed GORGON; ***Rachel HENNINGS***; Sherlock HOLMES; Sir Gideon MERRIMAC; Dr Sid SHOEHORN
BREITMAN Gregory	Sherlock HOLMES
BRENN George J	Charlie FENWICK
BRENNAN Carol	Liz WAREHAM
BRENNAN Joseph Payne	Lucius LEFFING
BRENNAN Robert	Insp FAVART
BRENNER John	Johnny BUCHANAN
BRENT Nigel	Barney HYDE
BRENT R L	Jake (The Liquidator) BRAND
BRETNOR Reginald	Alastair Alexandrovitch TIMUROFF
BRETT Hy and Barbara BRETT	Connie FERGUSON and Gil FERGUSON
BRETT John	John BRETT
BRETT John Michael	Hugo BARON
BRETT Martin	Mike GARFIN
BRETT Michael	Hugo BARON
BRETT Michael	Pete MCGRATH
BRETT Mike	Sam DAKKERS
BRETT Simon	Philip MARLOWE; Melita PARGETER; ***Charles PARIS***
BRETT Stephen	Rock DUGAN
BREWER Gil	Lee BARON; ***Bill MADDERN***; Al MUNDY
BREWER Mike	Brendan WALLACE
BREZ E M	Dave AXELROD
BRIDGE Ann	Julia PROBYN

BRIDGES T C	Sexton BLAKE
BRIDGMONT Leslie	Geoffrey CORDELL
BRIGHTWELL Emily	Mrs JEFFRIES and Insp WITHERSPOON
BRINTON Henry	John STRANG and Sally STRANG
BRISBANE Coutts	Sexton BLAKE
BRISTOW Gwen and Bruce MANNING	WADE
BRITTAIN William	Mr STRANG; ***Joshua Red WING***
BROCK Alan	BEACH
BROCK Lynn	***Col GORE***; Sgt VENN
BROCK Stuart	Pete CORY; Bert NORDEN; ***Steve ROURKE***
BROCKIE William	William BROCKIE
BROD D C	Quint MCCAULEY
BRODIE Gordon	John BORHAM
BRODY Marc	Marc BRODY
BROGAN Colm	Patrick HERON
BROMLEY Albert J	Rex HOMES
BROMLEY Gordon	Insp SEVERN
BRONSON Francis W	Ed BRAKELY
BRONSON-HOWARD George	Yorke NORROY
BROOKE E S	Eileen DARE
BROOKER W A H	Cleavers SETON
BROOKFIELD Charles and Edward Seymour HICKS	Sherlock HOLMES
BROOKS Clive	***Henry CHESTERFIELD***; Sherlock HOLMES
BROOKS Collin	Mr DADDY; ***Swete MCTAVISH***; Raeburn STEEL
BROOKS Edwy Searles	***Insp William (The Grouser) BEEKE***; Sexton BLAKE; Nelson LEE; Ferrers LOCKE; ST FRANCIS SCHOOL
BROOKS Leonard Harold	Sexton BLAKE
BROOME Adam	Insp BRAMLEY; ***Capt/Commiss Denzil GRIGSON***
BROUGHTON F Lusk	Clint CLEAVER; Dick DRANT; DURGON; HOODOOED HOWARD; Belle KINGSTON; NEMO; OLD DECEIVER; OLD MYSTAGOGNE; Hal TYBERT; ***Harry WILLIAMS***
BROUN Daniel	Lt CARREAU; ***Harry EGYPT***
BROWN Carter	Larry BAKER; Danny BOYD; Paul DONAVAN; Mike FARREL; ***Rick HOLMAN***; Andy KANE; Randy ROBERTS; Max ROYAL; Mavis SEIDLITZ; Lt Al WHEELER
BROWN Edward	Maj Adrian TITTERTON
BROWN Fredric	ERNIE; Jerry GRANT; ***Ambrose HUNTER and Ed HUNTER***; Det Frank RAMOS; Mr Henry SMITH; Doc' STOEGER; SWEENEY; Roger L YOUNG
BROWN George	David KENT
BROWN Gerald	Marmaduke 'Duke' MCCALE
BROWN Horace	***Squire ADAMS***; Napoleon B SMITH
BROWN Hosanna	Frank LE ROUX
BROWN Lisbie	Elizabeth BLAIR and Max SHEPHERD
BROWN R D	FRISBEE; ***Cheney HAZZARD***
BROWN Rita Mae	Mrs MURPHY
BROWN Robert Carlton	Christopher POE
BROWN Rosel George	Sybil Sue BLUE
BROWN Russell A	Sherlock HOLMES
BROWN Walter C	Det Insp Stephen HARPER
BROWN Wenzell	Peter ASWELL
BROWNE Douglas G	Maj Maurice HEMYOCK; ***LEGARDE***; Insp H H THEW; Harvey TUKE and Sir Bruton KAMES
BROWNE Howard	Ames CORYELL; ***Paul PINE***
BROWNER John	Larry HORNBLOWER
BRUCE George	Nick RONGETTI
BRUCE Jean	Hubert Bonisseur DE LA BATH
BRUCE Kennedy	Jyotish BABU
BRUCE Leo	***Sgt William BEEF***; Carolus DEENE
BRUCE Walt	Dr Zeng TSE-LIN
BRUNNER John	Max CURFEW
BRUNO Anthony	Mike TOZZI and Bert GIBBONS
BRUSSELL Jacob	Sherlock HOLMES and Arsène LUPIN
BRUTON Eric	***Insp George JUDD***; Stephen KELLY
BRYAN C D S	Sherlock HOLMES
BRYAN John	Richard SAREL

BRYANT Dorothy	Jessamyn POSEY
BRYCE Mrs Charles	Mr GIMBLET
BRYNE Leon	Dan HOLDEN
BUCHAN John	***Richard HANNAY***; Sir Edward LEITHEN; Duncan MCCUNN
BUCHANAN Madeleine	Ray BARTLEY
BUCHANAN Patrick	Benjamin SHOCK and Charity TUCKER
BUCK Peter	Marc (The Mercenary) DEAN
BUCKINGHAM Bruce	Marques Don PANCHO
BUCKINGHAM David	Sam WHARTON
BUCKLEY F R	Mr GARFIELD
BUCKLEY R J	Anthony HALLAM
BUCKLEY William F	Blackford OAKES
BUDE John	Maj BODDY; Sgt Pembury GREEN; Insp MEREDITH; ***Insp SHERWOOD***
BULLIVANT Cecil H	Henry Napoleon BAGGS; ***Garnett BELL***; May BERESFORD; Insp HAWKSHAW; Millie LYNNE
BUNCE Frank	Mr HUMBLE and Dorrit BLY
BUNN Thomas	John Thomas ROSS
BURANELLI Prosper	Nick MORRO
BURDEN Pat	Henry BASSETT
BURGESS Anthony	Sherlock HOLMES
BURGESS Eric	Harry TONG
BURKE Alan Dennis	Bill MARTELL
BURKE J F	***Samuel Moses KELLY***; Joe STREETER
BURKE James	Pat MORLEY
BURKE James Lee	Det Dave ROBICHAUX
BURKE Jan	Irene KELLY
BURKE John	Dr Alexander CASPIAN
BURKE Jonathan	Mike MERRIMAN
BURKE Richard	Quinny HITE
BURKE Thomas	Quong LEE
BURKHOLZ Herbert	Ben SLADE
BURKS Arthur J	Harlan DYCE
BURLEY W J	Henry Lancaster PYM; ***Supt Charles WYCLIFFE***
BURMAH Richard Marr	Insp David REEFE
BURNABY Nigel	Ch Insp DREWRY; ***Sir Timothy ROSSITER***
BURNETT George	Insp GULLIVER
BURNHAM David	Insp HOPKINS
BURNHAM Helen	'One Week' WIMBLE
BURNING Michael and Althea GREY	Insp HAWLING and Prof ERSKINE
BURNS Charles	El BORBAH
BURNS Rex	Devlin KIRK; ***Det Gabriel WAGER***
BURRAGE A M	Nick ROCKWELL
BURROWS Julie	Supt BOWMAN
BURT Michael	Roger POYNINGS
BURTON Anne	Richard TRENTON
BURTON Anthony	Peter KING
BURTON Miles	Desmond MERRION and Insp Henry ARNOLD
BUSBY Roger	Det Mick GARVEY; ***Det Insp LERIC***; Det Sgt Tony ROWLEY
BUSBY Roger and Gerald HOLTHAM	Maxwell DALY
BUSH Christopher	Ludovic TRAVERS
BUSH Geoffrey	Lord Peter WIMSEY
BUSHNELL Agnes	Joanna WILDER and Ruth WILSON
BUTLER Ellis Parker	Philo GUBB
BUTLER George	Dr FURNIVALL
BUTLER Gwendoline	***Sgt/Insp John COFFIN***; Sgt/Insp John COFFIN and Insp/Supt William WINTER
BUTLER John K	Tricky ENRIGHT; Rex LONERGAN; ***Steve MIDNIGHT***
BUTLER Leslie	HORTON and JORDAN
BUTLER Ragan	Capt George NASH
BUTLER Richard	Max FARNE
BUTLER William Vivian	Cdr George GIDEON
BUXTON Raymond	***Gale GALLYON***; LOU
BYERS C A	Warren BAYNE
BYFIELD Barbara Ninde	Father Simon BEDE; ***Helen BULLOCK***
BYRD Max	Mike HALLER

— C —

CADETT Herbert	Beverley GRETTON
CAFFERTY Jake	Vic MERRITT
CAGNEY Peter	Mike STRANG
CAIDIN Martin	Steve AUSTIN
CAILLOU Alan	Mike BENASQUE; Cabot CAIN; Ian QUAYLE; ***Matthew TOBIN***
CAIN Jonathan	Sgt Mark STRYKER
CAIN Nicholas	Luke ABEL
CAIN Paul	Johnny DOOLIN
CAINE Hamilton T	Ace CARPENTER
CAINE William	PILKINGTON
CAIRNS Alison	Toby WILDE
CAKE Patrick	Dion QUINCE
CALDER Jason	Johnny VINCENT
CALDWELL Alfred Betts	Freddy PHILPOTTS
CALIN Hal Jason	Edwin GREEN
CALLAHAN James	Vic MERRITT
CALLISON Brian	Brevet CABLE
CAMBRIDGE Ada	Billy WINGRAVE and Nellie WINGRAVE
CAMERON Donald Clough	Andrew BRANT; ***Abelard VOSS***
CAMERON Evelyn	Sheriff Jack THOMPSON
CAMERON Kate	***Holderly HALL***; Whispering HILLS

CAMERON Lou	***Sgt Morgan PRICE***; Steve WARREN
CAMERON Owen	Dep Sheriff Jake BROWN
CAMP Joe	Benjamin BROWNING
CAMP Wadsworth	***Bobby BLACKBURN***; GARTH; Arthur MCHUGH
CAMPBELL Alice	Insp HEADCORN; Insp HEADCORN and Tommy ROSTETTER; ***Tommy ROSTETTER***
CAMPBELL Bruce	Ken HOLT
CAMPBELL Harriette R	Simon BRADE
CAMPBELL Hazel	Olga KNARESBROOK
CAMPBELL Karen	Lisa MASSINGHAM
CAMPBELL Keith	Mike BRETT
CAMPBELL Mary E	Matthew CRAIG
CAMPBELL R T	Prof John STUBBS
CAMPBELL Robert	Jimmy FLANNERY; ***Jake HATCH***; Panama HEATH; Philip MARLOWE; WHISTLER
CAMPBELL Scott	Felix BOYD
CAMPBELL Sir Gilbert	***Insp DONOVAN***; Donald MACALPINE
CANDY Edward	Supt BURNIVAL
CANNAN Joanna	***Insp Guy NORTHEAST***; Insp Ronald PRICE
CANNELL Dorothy	***Ellie Simons HASKELL***; Hyacinth TRAMWELL and Primrose TRAMWELL

The Authors

CANNING Victor	***Rex CARVER***; Joe CHRISTOPHER; Ch Alphonse GRAND; James HELDER; Edward MERCER; Robert ROLT
CANNON Curt	Curt CANNON
CANNON Elliott	Guy FOSSE
CANNON Jack	***Det Sgt Joe KELLER and Det Sgt Joe RYKER***; Det Sgt Joe RYKER
CANNON Taffy	Nan ROBINSON
CANON Jack	Mike PARADISE
CAPES Bernard	Gilead BALM
CAPON Paul	Arnold 'Tiger' WRAGGE
"CAPSTAN"	Don Alverado y Miraflo SMITH
CAPUTI Anthony	Hugh STORM
CAREY Webster	Sheriff Buford PUSSER
CARGILL Leslie	***Maj MOSSON***; Morrison SHARPE
CARKEET David	Jeremy COOK
CARLO Philip	Frank DE NARDO
CARLON Patricia	Jefferson SHIELDS
CARLSON P M	Maggie RYAN
CARLTON Lewis	Sexton BLAKE
CARLTON Lieutenant	BLACK DOUGLASS; ***Dan DECKER***; Gideon GAULT
CARLTON Mitchell	Pat DOYLE
CARMACK Jesse	Stonewall ROUNTREE
CARMICHAEL Harry	***John PIPER***; John PIPER and QUINN; QUINN
CARMICHAEL Lt) A	A DETECTIVE
CARNAC Carol	***Ch Insp Julian RIVERS***; Insp RYVET
CARNAHAN Walter H	Abraham LINCOLN
CARPENTER Carleton	Chester LONG
CARPENTER Helen and Lorri CARPENTER	James GALVESTON
CARR A H Z	Xavier BROOKE
CARR Glyn	Sir Abercrombie LEWKER
CARR John Dickson	Juge d'Instruction Henri BENCOLIN; Jim BLAKE; Patrick BUTLER; Insp John CHEVIOT; Wilkie COLLINS; Dick DARWENT; Dr Gideon FELL and Patrick BUTLER; ***Dr Gideon FELL***; Prof Nicholas FENTON; Dr David GARTH and Det Insp TWIGG; Sherlock HOLMES; Jeff MARLE; Sir Henry MERRIVALE KC; Edward STEVENS; Clive STRICKLAND; Jeffrey WYNNE
CARR Joseph Baker	Oceola ARCHER
CARR Kirby	Mike ROSS
CARREL Mark	Andrew MCCALL
CARSON Robert	Warren HEARST and Harry HERBOLD
CARSTAIRS Henry	Lydford LONG
CARSTAIRS John Paddy	Garaway TRENTON
CARTER Herbert	Augustus WIGGLESWORTH
CARTER Lin	Prince ZARKON
CARTER Nicholas (House name)	Nick CARTER
CARTER Nicholas (ANDREWS)	Nick CARTER
CARTER Nicholas (A L ARMAGNAC)	Nick CARTER
CARTER Nicholas (BALL)	Nick CARTER
CARTER Nicholas (William Perry BROWN)	Nick CARTER
CARTER Nicholas (George Waldo BROWNE)	Nick CARTER
CARTER Nicholas (Frederick Russell BURTON)	Nick CARTER
CARTER Nicholas (O P CAYLOR)	Nick CARTER
CARTER Nicholas (Stephen CHALMERS)	Nick CARTER
CARTER Nicholas (Weldon J COBB)	Nick CARTER
CARTER Nicholas (Wiliam Wallace COOK)	Nick CARTER
CARTER Nicholas (John Russell CORYELL)	***Nick CARTER***; Wat DENTON
CARTER Nicholas (Frederick William DAVIS)	Nick CARTER
CARTER Nicholas (E C DERBY and Vincent E SCOTT)	Nick CARTER
CARTER Nicholas (Frederic Merrill Van Rensselaer DEY)	Nick CARTER
CARTER Nicholas (Frederic Merrill Van Rensselaer DEY and Charles Agnew MACLEAN)	Nick CARTER
CARTER Nicholas (Walter Bertram FOSTER)	Nick CARTER
CARTER Nicholas (Charles Witherle HOOKE)	Nick CARTER
CARTER Nicholas (Edward Cadwalader HUDSON)	Nick CARTER
CARTER Nicholas (George Charles JENKS)	Nick CARTER
CARTER Nicholas (W L LARNED)	Nick CARTER
CARTER Nicholas (MAKEE)	Nick CARTER

CARTER Nicholas (St George Henry RATHBONE)	Nick CARTER
CARTER Nicholas (RICH)	Nick CARTER
CARTER Nicholas (RUSSELL)	Nick CARTER
CARTER Nicholas (Eugene T SAWYER)	Nick CARTER
CARTER Nicholas (Samuel C SPALDING)	Nick CARTER
CARTER Nicholas (SPLINT)	Nick CARTER
CARTER Nicholas	Nick CARTER
CARTER Nicholas (Alfred B TOZER)	Nick CARTER
CARTER Nicholas (TYSON)	Nick CARTER
CARTER Nicholas	Trim CARTER; ***Patsy MURPHY***; Doctor QUARTZ; Harvey STOKES
CARTER Nicholas (House name)	Harrison KEITH
CARTER Nicholas (S A D COX)	Harrison KEITH
CARTER Nicholas (Frederick William DAVIS)	Harrison KEITH
CARTER Nicholas (Frederic Merrill Van Rensselaer DEY)	Harrison KEITH
CARTER Nicholas (Walter Bertram FOSTER)	Harrison KEITH
CARTER Nicholas (George Charles JENKS)	Harrison KEITH
CARTER Nicholas (W L LARNED)	Harrison KEITH
CARTER Nicholas (Charles Agnew MACLEAN)	Harrison KEITH
CARTER Nick (Frank ADDUCI Jr)	Nick CARTER
CARTER Nick (Bruce ALGOZIN)	Nick CARTER
CARTER Nick (Michael Angelo AVALLONE and Valerie MOOLMAN)	Nick CARTER
CARTER Nick (W T BALLARD)	Nick CARTER
CARTER Nick (James BOWSER)	Nick CARTER
CARTER Nick (Nicholas BROWNE)	Nick CARTER
CARTER Nick (Jack CANON)	Nick CARTER
CARTER Nick (Bruce Bingham CASSIDAY)	Nick CARTER
CARTER Nick (Thomas CHASTAIN)	Nick CARTER
CARTER Nick (Robert COLBY)	Nick CARTER
CARTER Nick (DeWitt S COPP)	Nick CARTER
CARTER Nick (Allen Billy CRIDER and Jack DAVIS)	Nick CARTER
CARTER Nick (Ron FELBER)	Nick CARTER
CARTER Nick (James FRITZHAND)	Nick CARTER
CARTER Nick (Jack GARSIDE)	Nick CARTER
CARTER Nick (Joseph Lee GILMORE)	Nick CARTE
CARTER Nick (Marilyn GRANBECK)	Nick CARTER
CARTER Nick (David James HAGBERG)	Nick CARTER
CARTER Nick (Ralph Eugene HAYES)	Nick CARTER
CARTER Nick (Al HINE)	Nick CARTER
CARTER Nick (Richard HUBBARD)	Nick CARTER
CARTER Nick (Frederick Vincent HUBER)	Nick CARTER
CARTER Nick (H Edward HUNSBERGER)	Nick CARTER
CARTER Nick (Joseph Michael JAHN)	Nick CARTER
CARTER Nick (Bod LATONA)	Nick CARTER
CARTER Nick (Leon LAZARUS)	Nick CARTER
CARTER Nick (Lew LOUDERBACK)	Nick CARTER
CARTER Nick (Dennis LYNDS)	Nick CARTER

CARTER Nick (Douglas MARLAND)	Nick CARTER
CARTER Nick (Arnold MARMOR)	Nick CARTER
CARTER Nick (Jon J MESSMAN)	Nick CARTER
CARTER Nick (Valerie MOOLMAN)	Nick CARTER
CARTER Nick (Homer MORRIS)	Nick CARTER
CARTER Nick (Craig NOVA)	Nick CARTER
CARTER Nick (William ODELL)	Nick CARTER
CARTER Nick (Forrest V PERRIN)	Nick CARTER
CARTER Nick (Larry POWELL)	Nick CARTER
CARTER Nick (Daniel C PRINCE)	Nick CARTER
CARTER Nick (Robert Joseph RANDISI)	Nick CARTER
CARTER Nick (Dan REARDON)	Nick CARTER
CARTER Nick (William Laurence ROHDE)	Nick CARTER
CARTER Nick (Joseph ROSENBERGER)	Nick CARTER
CARTER Nick (Steve SIMMONS)	Nick CARTER
CARTER Nick (Martin Cruz SMITH)	Nick CARTER
CARTER Nick (George SNYDER)	Nick CARTER
CARTER Nick (Robert Derek STEELEY)	Nick CARTER
CARTER Nick (John STEVENSON)	Nick CARTER
CARTER Nick (Linda STEWART)	Nick CARTER
CARTER Nick (Manning Lee STOKES)	Nick CARTER
CARTER Nick (Bob STOKESBERRY)	Nick CARTER
CARTER Nick (Dwight Vreeland SWAIN)	Nick CARTER
CARTER Nick (Lawrence VAN GELDER)	Nick CARTER
CARTER Nick (Robert E VARDEMAN)	Nick CARTER
CARTER Nick (Jeffrey Miner WALLMAN)	Nick CARTER
CARTER Nick (George WARREN)	Nick CARTER
CARTER Nick (Saul WERNICK)	Nick CARTER
CARTER Robert A	Nicholas BARLOW
CARTER Youngman	Albert CAMPION
CARVIC Heron	Emily SEETON and Supt DELPHICK
CASBERG Melvin A	Capt Prem NARAYAN
CASE Jim	John CODY
CASEY Robert J	Jim SANDS
CASLEY Dennis	Ch Insp ODHIAMBO
CASPARY Vera	Det Mark MCPHERSON
CASPER Susan	Sherlock HOLMES
CASSELLS John	***Insp FLAGG***; Ludovic (The Picaroon) SAXON
CASSIDAY Bruce	***Cash MADIGAN***; Johnny MIDAS
CASTIER Jules	Sherlock HOLMES
CASTLE Egerton	Meldrum MARSHFIELD
CASTLE Jayne	Zachariah JUSTIS and Guinevere JONES
CASTOIRE Marie and Richard POSNER	Vickie CURRAN
CATALAN Henri	Soeur ANGELE
CAUDWELL Sarah	Prof Hilary TAMAR
CAUNITZ William J	David MALONE
CAVE Hugh B	Peter KANE
CECIL Henry	***Col BRAIN***; Col BRAIN and Ambrose LOW; Rosamond CLINCH; Roger THURSBY
CHABER M E	Milo MARCH
CHACKO David	Steve WARFIELD
CHADWICK Charles	Bob ELLIS; ***Insp PRONTOUT***
CHADWICK Paul	Wade HAMMOND
CHAIS Pamela	Bud BACOLA
CHALLIS Mary	Jeremy LOCKE
CHAMBERS Dana	Nile BOYD; ***Jim STEELE***
CHAMBERS Peter	Mark PRESTON
CHAMBERS Philip	Sexton BLAKE
CHAMBERS Robert	Hank MOODY
CHAMBERS Whitman	Bill BARTLETT; Kate BLAYNE; ***Simon LAKE***; Pierre O'BRIEN
CHAMPION D L	***Insp ALLHOFF***, Mariano MERCADO; Rex SACKLER; Richard Curtis (The Phantom) VAN LOAN
CHANCE John Newton	Supt BLACK; Jonathan BLAKE; ***John Newton CHANCE***; Mr DEHAVILLAND; Mr DEHAVILLAND and Supt BLACK; JASON; KEYES; John MARSH
CHANCE Stephen	Rev Septimus TRELOAR
CHANCELLOR John	Capt FRASS; ***Supt REDARREL and David FORRESTER***
CHANDLER A Bertram	Stefan VYNALEK
CHANDLER Raymond	Pete ANGLICH; Ted CARMADY; Johnny DALMAS; Steve GRAYCE; MALLORY; Ted MALVERN; ***Philip MARLOWE***; Tony RESECK and John EVANS; Lt WALDMAN
CHANNING Mark	Colin GRAY
CHANSLOR Roy	STORM
CHANSLOR Torrey	Lutie BEAGLE and Amanda BEAGLE
CHAPMAN Robert	Rex BANNER
CHARLES Ernest F	Dick TORREYTON
CHARLES Hampton	Emily SEETON and Supt DELPHICK
CHARLES Kate	David MIDDLETON-BROWNE
CHARLES Robert	Simon LARREN; ***Supt Mark NICOLSON***
CHARLTON Dick	Sherlock HOLMES
CHARTERIS Leslie	Bill KENNEDY; Insp Claude Eustace TEAL; ***Simon (The Saint) TEMPLAR***
CHARYN Jerome	Sydney HOLDEN; ***Dep Commiss Isaac SIDEL***
CHASE Arthur M	Dan DURKIN
CHASE Elaine Raco	Roman CANTRELL
CHASE James Hadley	Al BARNEY; Lew BRANDON; ***Dave FENNER***; Mark GIRLAND; Mark GIRLAND and Herman RADNITZ; Mark GIRLAND, Lu SILK and Herman RADNITZ; Steve HARMAS; Steve HARMAS, Al BARNEY and Frank TERRELL; Floyd JACKSON; Vic MALLOY; Herman RADNITZ and Al BARNEY; Helga ROLFE; Frank TERRELL; Dirk WALLACE;
CHASE Kip	Justine CARMICHAEL
CHASTAIN Thomas	Lilia BEDDOES; Dep Ch Insp Max KAUFFMAN and J T 'Jake' SPANNER; Perry MASON; ***J T 'Jake' SPANNER***
CHASTAIN Thomas and Bill ADLER	***John LANGE***; Capt Gregory WALTHAM
CHAZE Elliott	Kiel ST JAMES and Orson BOLES
CHERNYONOK Mikhail	Anton BIRUKOV
CHESBRO George	BONE; ***Dr Robert 'Mongo' FREDERICKSON***; Dr Robert 'Mongo' FREDERICKSON and Veil KENDRY; Veil KENDRY
CHESNEY Michael	Col 'Steel' CALLAGHAN
CHESNEY Weatherby	***Edward DALE***; Richard FELTON
CHESTER George Randolph	James Rufus WALLINGFORD
CHESTER Gilbert	Sexton BLAKE
CHESTER Peter	Johnny PRESTON; ***Johnny VINCENT***
CHESTER S Beach	Herlock SOAMES and Arsène LEPINE
CHESTERTON G K	***Father BROWN***; Horne FISHER; Gabriel GALE; Rupert GRANT and Basil GRANT; Dr HYDE; Mr POND; SYME
CHETWYND Bridget	Petunia BEST and Max FREUND
CHEYNE Angela	Dorothy Mayotte RIGBY
CHEYNEY Peter	Nick BELLAMY; Rupert Patrick 'Slim' CALLAGHAN; ***Lemmy CAUTION***; Nicholas GALE; Michael KELLS; Alonzo MACTAVISH; Terence O'DAY; Cary Wylde O'HARA; Shaun O'MARA; Everard Peter QUAYLE; Johnny VALLON
CHICHESTER John Jay	***Jimmy 'Wiggly' PRICE***; Maxwell SANDERSON
CHILD Charles B	Insp Chafik J CHAFIK
CHILD Nellise	Jeremiah IRISH
CHILDERNESS George	Chet PHELPS
CHILDERS Erskine	CARRUTHERS
CHILDS Timothy	Peter STOKES
CHIN Frank	Sherlock HOLMES
CHIPPERFIELD Robert Orr	***Barry O'DELL***; Geoffrey PETERS; The SHADOWERS INC
CHISHOLM P F	Sir Robert CAREY
CHOLMONDELEY Mary	Ralph DANVERS
CHRISTIAN John	Richard DEUTSCH
CHRISTIE Agatha	Supt BATTLE; Supt BATTLE and Luke FITZWILLIAMS; Tommy BERESFORD and Tuppence BERESFORD; Lady Elaine 'Bundle' BRENT and Supt BATTLE; Dr Arthur CALGARY; Frances DERWENT and Bobby JONES; Mark EASTERBROOK and Ariadne OLIVER; Sherlock HOLMES; Victoria JONES; Jane MARPLE; Insp NARROCOTT; ***Hercule POIROT***; Hercule POIROT and Mrs Ariadne OLIVER; Hercule POIROT, Supt BATTLE, Col RACE and Mrs Ariadne OLIVER; Parker PYNE; Harley QUIN; Col RACE; Insp TAVERNER;
CHRISTIE Stephen	Sexton BLAKE
CHRISTMAS Joyce	***Lady Margaret PRIAM***; Betty TRENKA
CHRISTOPHER Laura Kinn	Insp BOSCO OF THE YARD
CHUJOY Anatole	Sherlock HOLMES
CHURCHILL Jill	Jane JEFFRY
CHUTE M G	Sheriff John Charles OLSON
CHUTE Verne	Rocky NEVINS
CILLIE François Paulus P	Sherlock HOLMES
CLANCY Tom	Jack RYAN
CLANDON Henrietta	***Penny MERCER and Vincent MERCER***; William POWER; William POWER, Penny MERCER and Vincent MERCER
CLAPPERTON Richard	Peter FLECK
CLARK Al C	KENYATTA
CLARK Benjamin S	Sherlock HOLMES
CLARK Carol Higgins	Regan REILLY
CLARK Dale	Gillian BALTIC; ***Mike O'HANNA***; Plates' O'RION; Highland PRICE
CLARK Douglas	Insp/Ch Supt George MASTERS and Ch Insp Bill GREEN
CLARK Gail	Dulcie BLIGH
CLARK Mary Higgins	***Katie DEMAIO***; Elizabeth LANGE; Pat TRAYMORE
CLARK Ronald	Samson COGG

The Authors

CLARK W C	Chattin WHYTE
CLARKE Anna	Helen BOYDEN; ***Paula GLENNING***; Richard GRIEVE, Paula GLENNING and James GOFF; Sally LIVINGSTONE
CLARKE Laurence	Terence MILNER
CLARKE Percy A	Ferrers LOCKE
CLARKE T E B	King of England George V WINDSOR
CLARKSON Stephen	Shearlock COMBS
CLASON Clyde B	Prof Theocritus Lucius WESTBOROUGH
CLAUDE M	Monsieur CLAUDE
CLAYFORD James	Val VERNON
CLAYMORE Tod	Tod CLAYMORE
CLEARY Jon	***Scobie MALONE***; Jim MCKECHNIE
CLEARY Melissa	Prof Jackie WALSH
CLEEVE Brian	***Insp O'DONOVAN***; Sean RYAN
CLEEVES Ann	George PALMER-JONES; ***Insp Stephen RAMSAY***
CLEIFE Philip	Martyn FINCH
CLEMEAU Carol	Antonia NIELSEN
CLEMENT Frank A	Supt MERSEY
CLEMENT Henry	SLAUGHTER
CLEMENTS E H	Alister WOODHEAD
CLENDENING Logan	Sherlock HOLMES
CLEVELY Hugh	***Maxwell ARCHER***; Sexton BLAKE; John MARTINSON; Insp WILLIAMS
CLIFTON Gary	MCCOY
CLINE C Terry Jr	Prof Joanne FLEMING
CLINE Edward	Chess HANRAHAN
CLINTON-BADDELEY V C	Dr R V DAVIE
CLOTHIER Peter	Jacob MOLNAR
CLOUKEY Charles	David S HARRIS
CLOUSTON J Storer	***F T CARRINGTON***; Ursula DOLLING; Sherlock HOLMES; Francis MANDELL-ESSINGTON
CLUSTER Dick	Alex GLAUBERMAN
CLYNES Michael	Roger SHALLOT
COBB Belton	Bryan ARMITAGE; ***Insp Cheviot BURMANN***; Insp Cheviot BURMANN and Bryan ARMITAGE; Supt MANNING
COBB Clayton W	Nimrod RAYMOND
COBB Irwin S	Patrick BRAY; ***Judge PRIEST***
COBB Thomas	Insp BEDISON; ***Insp PARKER***
COBBAN J MacLaren	Mr TOWNSHEND
COBDEN Guy	John CHADWICK
COBURN Andrew	Frank CHASE; ***Rita Gardella O'DEA***
COCHRAN Alan	Jason PRICE and Brooke MERIT
COCKIN Joan	Insp CAM
CODY James P	Brian PETERSEN
CODY Liza	Anna LEE
COE Tucker	Mitch TOBIN
COFFEY Brian	Mike TUCKER
COFFIN Geoffrey	Insp Scott STUART
COFFIN Peter	Peter COFFIN and Col BLACK
COFFMAN Virginia	***Lucifer COVE***; MOURA
COGGINS Mark	August HAMMOND
COGGINS Paul	Steve DART
COHEN Allen	Sherlock HOLMES
COHEN Anthea	Nurse Agnes CARMICHAEL
COHEN Barney	Asher BOCKHORN
COHEN Octavus Roy	David CARROLL; Lt Max GOLD; ***Jim HANVEY***; Eric PETERS; Florian SLAPPEY; Lt Marty WALSH
COHEN Stephen Paul	Eddie MARGOLIS
COHLER David Keith	Sam KNIGHT
COKER Carolyn	Andrea PERKINS
COLBRON Grace Isabel and Augusta GRONER	Joe MULLER
COLBURN Laura	Carol GATES
COLE G D H	Supt Henry WILSON
COLE G D H and Margaret COLE	The Hon Everard BLATCHINGTON; Insp FAIRFORD; James FLINT; Ben TANCRED and Supt Henry WILSON; Mrs Elizabeth WARRENDER and James WARRENDER; Supt Henry WILSON and The Hon Everard BLATCHINGTON; ***Supt Henry WILSON***
COLE Jackson	Jim HATFIELD
COLEMAN Reed Farrell	Dylan KLEIN and Johnny MCCLOUGH
COLES Manning	***Tommy HAMBLEDON***; Charles LATIMER and James LATIMER
COLIN Aubrey	Insp Bill MURRAY
COLLARD Teresa	Det Supt James BYRD
COLLIER Old Cap	OLD TRAMP
COLLINS Gilbert	Hugh CARDING
COLLINS Howard	Sherlock HOLMES
COLLINS Max Allan	***Nate HELLER***; MALLORY; Philip MARLOWE; NOLAN; QUARRY
COLLINS Michael	Dan FORTUNE
COLLINS Michelle	Megan MARSHALL
COLLINS Mortimer	Det SOMERTON
COLLINS Randall	Sherlock HOLMES
COLLINS Wilkie	***Sgt CUFF***; Walter HARTWRIGHT; OLD SHARON; Griffith TROWBRIDGE; Valeria WOODVILLE
COLLIS E T	Jonathan HATWOOD
COLTER Eli	Pat CAMPBELL
COLTER Frank	DEATH SQUAD
COMBER Leon	Magistrate PAO
COMFORT B	Trish MCWHINNEY
COMMINGS Joseph	Senator Brooks Urban BANNER; Mayor Thomas LANDIN; ***Matt TUDOR***
COMPTON Guy	Ben ANDERSON
CON A and O YLE	Sherlock HOLMES
CONANT Susan	Holly WINTER
CONAWAY Jim C	Jana BLAKE
CONDE Philip	***Dick PEMBERTY***; Dick PEMBERTY and Peter WEBB; Irving TODD
CONDON Richard	Capt Colin HUNTINGTON
CONDRICK George	DEADWOOD DICK
CONKLIN Bill	Fellock HOLMES
CONNELL Richard	***Matthew KELTON***; Mr POTTLE
CONNELLY Michael	Det Harry BOSCH
CONNINGTON J J	***Mark BRAND***; Ch Const Sir Clinton DRIFFIELD; Supt ROSS; Col SANDERSTEAD; Conway WESTENHANGER
CONNOR Ralph	Cpl/Sgt Allan CAMERON
CONRAD Joseph	Edgar BYRNE
CONROY Al	Johnny MORINI
CONSTANTINE K C	Ch of Plce Mario BALZIC
CONSTINER Merle	***Luther MCGAVOCK***; Dean Wardlow ROCK
CONTERIS Hiber	Philip MARLOWE
CONWAY Hugh	Philip NORRIS
CONWAY Norman	Adam HUNTER
CONWAY Peter	Lucy BECK
CONYERS Dorothea	***Mervyn HENDERSON***; Mr JONES; SANDY
COOK Bob	Michael WYMAN
COOK Bruce	Antonio 'Chico' CERVANTES
COOK Glen	GARRETT
COOK Thomas H	***Frank CLEMONS***; Tom JACKSON
COOKE Alistair	Sherlock HOLMES
COOKE David C	Peter ROURKE
COOKE G Walter	Peter MITCHELL
COOMBS Murdo	Thackeray HACKETT
COONTS Stephen	Jake GRAFTON
COOPER Barbara	Insp GIBBON
COOPER Brian	John HARRINGTON; Ch Insp LUBBOCK and Det Insp TENCH; ***Rod MCKINNON***
COOPER Craig	Matt SAVAGE
COOPER John C	Insp James DALE
COOPER Lettice	Insp CORBY
COOPER Natasha	Willow KING
COOPER Susan Rogers	***Sheriff Milton KOVAK***; Kimmy KRUSE
COOPER Will	John T MCLAREN
COPELAND Richard	Dr Gregor MACLEAN
COPPER Basil	Clyde BEATTY; Mike FARADAY; ***Solar PONS***
COPPLESTONE Bennet	Ch Insp DAWSON
CORAM Christopher	Ross MACALLISTER
CORAM Robert	Nick BROWN
CORBETT James	Insp BRIGG; ***Roy ENDICOTT***; Det Insp Alan MELFORD; John PETERSON; Victor REDMAYNE; Victor SERGE; Insp Giles SEYMOUR
CORBETT Mrs George	Mr BELL and Mr WHITE; ***Annie CORY***
CORBIN Gary	Harry REILLY
CORDER Eric	Wylie LINCOLN
CORES Lucy	Capt Andrew TORRENT
CORK Barry	Insp Angus STRAUN
CORMANY Michael	Dan KRUGER
CORNE M E	Mac MCINTYRE
CORNELL Louis	Michael JOYCE
CORNIER Vincent	Supt HAMILTON; Mervyn HENDERSON; ***Barnabas HILDRETH***
CORNWELL Patricia D	Dr Kay SCARPETTA
CORRIGAN Mark	Mark CORRIGAN
CORRINGTON John William and Joyce H CORRINGTON	Capt Ralph 'Rat' TRAPP
CORRIS Peter	***Richard BROWNING***; Ray CRAWLEY; Cliff HARDY
CORY Desmond	Mr DEE; ***Johnny FEDORA***; Lindy GREY; Mr PILGRIM
COSGRAVE Patrick	Col Allen CHEYNEY
COSTELLO Paul	Terence O'HARA
COUGHLIN William J	Rony RUSSO
COURAGE John	***William BRITTAIN***; David CANE
COURTENEY Cecil	Maj DEERING and George RYAN
COURTIER S H	***Insp 'Digger' HAIG***; Insp Ambrose MAHON
COURTNEY J W	Sherlock HOLMES
COUSINS E G	Col Richard BARNE
COVERACK Gilbert	Insp M'GUIRE
COWDROY Joan	***Ch Insp GORHAM***; Li MOH
COX A B	Sherlock HOLMES
COX S A D	BANDBOX BOB
COX Sir Edmund C	***John CARRUTHERS***; Kesho NAIK
COX William R	***Tom KINCAID***; Malachi MANATEE; Dan TROUT; John WADE
COXE George Harmon	Dave BARNUM and Capt VAUGHN; Paul BARON; Alan CARLISLE; Flashgun' CASEY; Sam CROMBIE; Jack FENNER; Max Chauncy HALE; Alan MAXWELL; Leon MORLEY; ***Kent MURDOCK***; Kent MURDOCK and Jack FENNER; Kent MURDOCK and Joyce MURDOCK; Jerry NASON; Larry PALMER; Bill RAEBURN; Knox RANDALL; Spence RANKIN; Capt Alan SCOTT; Dr Paul STANDISH; Andrew TALBOT
CRABB Arthur	Samuel LYLE
CRABTREE Simon	Hector TUMBLER
CRAGG E H	ALMACK
CRAIG Alisa	***Holly HOWE***; Dittany MONK and Osbert MONK; Policeman Madoc RHYS
CRAIG David	Stephen BELLECROIX and Sheila ROATH
CRAIG Jonathan	***Det Steve MANNING***; Det Pete SELBY
CRAIG Mary S	Josh WALKER
CRAIG Thurlow	Bunjy' HEARNE
CRAIS Robert	***Elvis COLE***; Philip MARLOWE

CRANE Caroline	Brian FRESNEY; ***Jessica HAYDEN***
CRANE Frances	Pat ABBOTT and Jean ABBOTT
CRANE Robert	Sgt Ben CORBIN
CRANSTON Claudia	Clarice CLAREMONT
CRAUFORD W H L	Insp KELLERWAY
CRAWFORD Robert	Arthur SALISBURY and Frank SHEARER
CRAWFORD William	Colin STRYKER
CRAWFURD Oswald	Purlock HONE; ***Det Insp MORGAN***
CRAWLEY Raymond	Ned SHACKLETON
CREASEY John	Sexton BLAKE; DEPARTMENT Z; Martin FANE and Richard FANE; Richard (The Toff) ROLLISON; ***Insp Roger 'Handsome' WEST***
CREIGHTON John	Ed DONOVAN; ***Matt REBER***
CREIGHTON Milt	Sherlock HOLMES
CRESPI Camilla T	Simona GRIFFO
CREWS Lary	Veronica SLATE
CRIDER Bill	***Prof Carl BURNS***; Sheriff Dan RHODES
CRISP Jack H	SPECIAL OPERATIONS EXECUTIVE
CRISP N J	Sidney KENYON
CRISPIN Edmund	***Gervase FEN***; Gervase FEN and Insp HUMBLEBY; Insp HUMBLEBY
CROFTS Freeman Wills	Insp BURNLEY, Insp LEFARGE and Insp Georges LA TOUCHE; ***Insp Joseph FRENCH***; Insp ROSS; Insp TANNER;
CROMBIE Deborah	Duncan KINCAID
CROMBIE Michael	Larry MILNER
CROMWELL A G E	Rodney WAYNE
CRONIN George P	Virgil FLETCHER
CRONIN Michael	***Sam HARRIS***; James HELLIER; Richard (The Pilgrim) MAIDMENT
CROOKER Herbert	Clay BROOKE
CROSBY John	Horatio CASSIDY
CROSBY Lee	Eric HAZARD
CROSS Amanda	Kate FANSLER and Reed AMHEARST; ***Kate FANSLER***
CROSS David	John 'Chant' SINCLAIR
CROSS Laurence	Tommy LUMB and Peter MARSHAM
CROSS Mark	Daphne WRAYNE and The FOUR ADJUSTERS
CROSS Ralph D	Ch of Plce Ira FISCHER
CROSSEN Ken	Jason JONES and 'Necessary' SMITH; ***Kim LOCKE***
CROSSLEY Barbara	Anna KNIGHT
CROSSLEY Maude	Guy BANNISTER
CROWE John	***Lee BECKETT***; Ed GRAY
CROWLEY Alistair	Simon IFF
CROWN James	Julian CASTLE
CROZIER John	FALCON
CRUIKSHANK Charles	Jack GRIFFIN
CRUMLEY James	Milton Chester MILODRAGOVITCH; ***Chauncy Wayne SUGHRUE***
CRUMP Barry	Sam CASH
CRUZ Mark	Chester C TABOR
CULLEN Carter	Robert CRAIG
CULLIMORE Alan	Harry FOSTER
CULLINGFORD Guy	Gilbert WORTH
CULLUM Ridgwell	Sgt/Insp Stanley FYLES
CULPAN Maurice	Ch Insp Bill HOUGHTON
CUMBERLAND Marten	Insp COMFORT; ***Commissaire Saturnin DAX***
CUNNINGHAM A B	Sheriff Jess RODEN
CUNNINGHAM E V	John COMADAY and Larry COHEN; Harvey KRIM; Alan MACKLIN; ***Det Sgt Masao MASUTO***
CURRINGTON O J	Jack LOVEL
CURRY Avon	Jerome AYLWIN
CURTIS Jack	Tom BULLEN
CURTIS Peter	Emma PLUME
CURTIS Richard	Dave (The Pro) BOLT
CURTIS Robert	The IRISH POLICE OFFICER
CURTIS Wade	Paul CRANE
CURTIS Wardon Allan	Mr MIDDLETON
CURTISS E M	Dr Nathaniel BUNCE
CURTISS Ursula	Caroline EMMET; ***Lou FABIAN***; Katy MEREDITH; Andrew SENTRY; Mrs TYRELL and Mrs LEEDS
CURZON Clare	Supt Mike YEADINGS
CURZON Colin	Mark ANTONY
CUSHING E Louise	Insp MACKAY
CUSHMAN Dan	CRAWFORD
CUSSLER Clive	Dirk PITT
CUTLER Stan	Rayford GOODMAN
CUTTER John	Jack (The Specialist) SULLIVAN
CUTTER Leela	Lettie WINTERBOTTOM
CUTTER Robert A	Sherlock HOLMES

— D —

DACRE Richard	Sam HOSKINS
DA CRUZ Daniel	***Jock SERGEANT***; Ape SWAIN
DAGMAR	Randy KIDD
D'AGNEAU Marcel	Sherlock HOLMES
DAHEIM Mary	Judith McMonigle FLYNN; ***Emma LORD***
DAHLINGER Susan Elizabeth	Sherlock HOLMES
DAIGER K S	Insp Everett ANDERSON
DALE Alan	Ned BACHMAN
DALE Celia	Det Insp HOGARTH
DALE Virginia	Nan THURSDAY
DALE William	Del SKINNER
DALHEATH David	Duncan KERR
DALLAS Duncan	Paul RICHARDS
DALLAS Walter	George Lombard SQUIRE
DALMAN Max	David MARCHANT; ***Supt WILKINS and Col CHIDDINGTON***
DALMAS Herbert	John FOWLER
D'ALTON Martina	Harry LANSING
DALTON Moray	***Insp Hugh COLLIER***; Norman GLADE
DALY Carroll John	Vee BROWN; Marty DAY; Satan HALL; Clay HOLT; Terry MACK; ***Race WILLIAMS***
DALY Elizabeth	Henry GAMADGE
DALY John Carroll and C H WADDELL	Red CONNORS
D'AMATO Barbara	Dr Gerritt DEGRAAF; ***Catherine 'Cat' MARSALA***
DANA Freeman	Daisy TOWER
DANBY Frank	Keightley WILBUR
DANE Clemence and Helen SIMPSON	Sir John SAUMAREZ
DANE Joel Y	Sgt Cass HARTY
DANESFORD Earle	Marise OVERTON
DANIEL David	Alex RASSMUSSEN
DANIEL Glyn	Prof Richard CHERRINGTON
DANIEL Roland	Wu FANG; Michael GRANT; John HOPKINS; ***Insp Neville LANGHAM***; Buddy MUSTARD; Brian O'MALLEY; Insp Jack PEARSON; The REMOVER; Bill SAVILLE; Insp John WALK; Michael WALLACE
DANIELS Norman	Bruce BARON; Kelly CARVEL; John KEITH; Jimmy ROSS; Rick TRENT; ***Richard Curtis (The Phantom) VAN LOAN***
DANKS Denise	Georgina POWERS
DANVERS Milton	***Rose COURTENAY***; Robert SPICER
DARBY Ruth	Peter BARRON and Janet BARRON
DARE Franklin	Oliver Trentham SMITH
DARK James	Mark HOOD
DARK Rex	Bartholomew DANE
DARRELL Old Cap	DAUNTLESS DAN; EMERALD JIM; The OZARK DETECTIVE; The STEAM-BOAT DETECTIVE; ***YOUNG SLEDGE***
DARVAS Robert, Norman V HART and Paul STERN	Sherlock HOLMES
DATESH John Nicholas	Casey CARMICHAEL
DAVEY Jocelyn	Victoria MCKENZIE; ***Ambrose USHER***
DAVIDSON Avram	Dr ESZTERHAZY
DAVIDSON Diane Mott	Goldy BEAR
DAVIDSON T L	Insp MELLISON and Dr Martin BLYTHE
DAVID-NEEL Alexandra and Lama YONGDEN	MUNPA
DAVIES David Stuart	Sherlock HOLMES
DAVIES L P	***David CONWAY***; Donald LOMAX and Peter CULLIMORE; John MORTON and Sgt DERWENT
DAVIOT Gordon	Insp Alan GRANT
DAVIS Dorothy Salisbury	Hannah BLAKE; Father DUFFY and Sgt GOLDSMITH; John EAKINS; Julia HAYES; Father MCMAHON; Mrs Annie NORRIS; ***Kate OSBORN***; Jasper TULLY and Mrs Annie NORRIS; Sheriff WILLETS
DAVIS Franklin	Quinn LELAND
DAVIS Frederick C	Dr Carter COLE; Prof Cyrus HATCH; ***Luke SPEARE and Schyler COLE***; Steve THATCHER
DAVIS George	Simon GOOD
DAVIS Gordon	Pete NOVAK
DAVIS Howard Charles	***Hugh RUDD***; Edward TOPE
DAVIS Kenn	Carver BASCOMBE
DAVIS Lavinia R	Nora Hughes BLAINE and Larry BLAINE
DAVIS Lindsey	M Didius FALCO
DAVIS Means	***James Augustus GIBBS***; Matthew HIGGINS
DAVIS Mildred	Finley WEHRMANN
DAVIS Norbert	Max CLARK; John COLLINS; DOAN; William 'Bail Bond' DODD; Mark HULL; Max LATIN; Simeon SAXON; ***Ben SHALEY***
DAVIS Richard Harding	***Insp LYLE***; VAN BIBBER
DAVIS Robert Hart	***Sgt/Insp Charlie CHAN***; Napoleon SOLO and Ilya KURYAKIN
DAVIS Tech	Aubrey NASH
DAVISON G	***Peter CASTLE***; Peter CASTLE and 'Twisted Face' STRAUSSMAN; 'Twisted Face' STRAUSSMAN
DAVISON Geoffrey	Stephen FLETCHER
DAVY Colin	David SHERIDAN
DAWE Carlton	Reginald COSWAY; ***Col Gantian LEATHERMOUTH***
DAWSON Janet	Jeri HOWARD
DAY Deforest	Chase DEFOE
DAY Lillian	Frederick HUNT
DAY Marele	Claudia VALENTINE
DAY Will B	Steven FLAGG
DEAN Amber	Albie HARRIS
DEAN Elizabeth	Emma MARSH and Hank FAIRBANKS
DEAN Gregory	Dep Commiss Benjamin SIMON
DEAN Robert George	***Anthony HUNTER***; Pat THOMPSON
DEAN S F X	Neil KELLY
DEAN Spencer	Don CADEE
DEANDREA William L	***Matt COBB***; Russ GARRETT; Ron GENTRY; Commiss Theodore ROOSEVELT
DEANE Jim	Nick MERLOTTI
DEANE Norman	The LIBERATOR; ***Bruce MURDOCH***
DEARDEN R L	Christopher PARKINS

The Authors

DEAVER Jeffrey Wilds	RUNE
DE BORCHGRAVE Arnaud and Robert MOSS	Robert HOCKNEY
DE CAIRE Edwin	Insp BOOTLE
DE CAUNES Antoine	Sam MURCHISON
DECHANCIE John	Sherlock HOLMES
DECKER Jake	Steve (The Force) SINCLAIR
DECOLTA Ramon	Don BURNEY; Ben CAREY; ***Dion DAVIES***; Jo GAR; Don TREE
DEE F J	Capt CONFETTI
DEGRAVE Philip	Terry WEBB
DE HALSALLE Henry	Olga von KOPF
DE HAMEL Herbert	Charles Hendesley MANNING and Ben HASSETT
DEIGHTON Len	Harry PALMER; ***Bernard SAMSON***
DEKKER Carl	Carl DEKKER
DEKKER Johnny	Johnny DEKKER
DEKOBRA Maurice	Bradley ADAMS
DELACORTA	Serge GORODISH and ALBA
DELANCEY Roger	Dr ARTHUR
DELANNOY Burford	John GARDEN; JANSON; ***Watson WARD***
DE LA TORRE Lillian	Sherlock HOLMES; ***Dr Sam JOHNSON***
DELLBRIDGE John	Insp Rupert HAMBLEDON
DELMAN David	Lt Jacob HOROWITZ and Helen HOROWITZ
DELMONT Joseph	Tim SHEA
DELVING Michael	Dave CANNON and Bob EDDISON; Dave CANNON; ***Bob EDDISON***
DE MARCO Gordon	Rocco CONIGLIARO; ***Riley KOVACHS***
DEMARIS Ovid	Vince SLADER
DE MILLE Nelson	***Det Sgt Joe KELLER and Det Sgt Joe RYKER***; Det Sgt Joe RYKER
DEMING Richard	Barney CALHOUN; The MOD SQUAD; ***Manville MOON***; Matt RUDD
DENBIE Roger	Quentin PACE
DENBOW Richard	Raymond CHANDLER
DENHAM Bertie	Derek THRYDE
DENNING Mark	John MARSHALL
DENNIS Ralph	Jim HARDMAN
DENNIS Robert C	Willie CARMODY; ***Paul REEDER***
DENT Lester	Foster FADE; Curt FLAGG; Lynn LASH; Mitchell LONEMAN; Chance MALLOY; John MARKS; Lee NACE; ***Click RUSH***; Oscar SAIL
DENTINGER Jane	Jocelyn O'ROARKE and Philip GERARD
DENVER Paul	CANNON
DENVERS Jake	The COWBOY 'TEC
DE O A	Dr Richard CARSTAIRS
DEPTULA Walter	Frank ARROW
DE PUY E Spence	Sam HOUSTON
DERLETH August	Tex HARRIGAN; Sherlock HOLMES; Judge Ephraim Peabody PECK; ***Solar PONS***
DERLETH August and Mack REYNOLDS	Solar PONS
DERRICK Lionel	Mark (The Penetrator) HARDIN
DE SELINCOURT Hugh	Mr BUFFUM
DESMOND Hugh	***Insp DUNNING***; Alan FRASER
DES ORMEAUX J J	Jack MCGUIRE
DE STEPHANO Anthony	MONDO
DETECTION The CLUB	Insp RUDGE
DE VILLIERS Gerard	Malko LINGE
DEVINE D M	Insp FINNEY and Graham LOUDON
DEVINE Dominic	HEMMINGS; Judy HUTCHINGS; ***Det Insp Maurice NICOLSON***; John PRESCOTT
DEWEESE Gene and Robert Stratton COULSON	Joe KARNS
DEWEY Thomas B	***Singer BATTS***; MAC; Pete SCHOFIELD
DEWHURST Eileen	Det Insp Neil CARTER; Susan HALLIDAY; ***Det Ch Supt Maurice KENDRICK and Humphrey BARNES***; Helen MARKHAM
DE WIL Ernest	Herbert HOLT
DE WITT Jack	Clint WALSH
DEXTER Colin	Insp MORSE
DEXTER Ted and Clifford MAKINS	Jack STENTON
DIAMOND Frank	Ransome DRAGOON and Vicky 'The Dish' GAINES
DIBDIN Michael	Robert BROWNING; Sherlock HOLMES; ***Commiss Aurelio ZEN***
DICHIARA Robert	Johnny HARD
DICK Philip K	Rick DECKARD
DICKENS Charles	Insp BUCKET
DICKENS Charles, Carlo FRUTTERO and Francio LUCENTINI	Sherlock HOLMES, Lew ARCHER, Nero WOLFE, Father BROWN and Hercule POIROT
DICKENSON Fred	Mack MCGANN
DICKINSON Peter	Wesley MORRIS; ***Supt James PIBBLE***; Paul ROGERS
DICKINSON Weed	Burt CALHOUN
DICKSON Arthur	Hamilton YORKE
DICKSON Carr	John GAUNT and Prof Michael TAIRLAINE
DICKSON Carter	Col MARCH; ***Sir Henry MERRIVALE KC***
DICKSON Grierson	Supt 'Cissie' MARLOW
DICKSON John Carter and John RHODE	Dr Horatio GLASS
DIDELOT Francis	Commissaire Orestes BIGNON; ***Insp LECAIN***
DIEHL V Vidal	Insp GIBSON
DIEHL William	Insp MORSE
DIETRICH Robert	Steve BENTLEY
DIETZER Karl	Rose GRAHAM
DILLARD R H W	Sir Hugh FITZ-HYFFEN
DILLON Eilis	Prof DALY
DILLON Walter	Jack HANIGAN
DILNOT George	Sexton BLAKE; Horace Augustus ELVER; ***Val EMERY***; Jim STRANG; Insp STRICKLAND
DIMENT Adam	Philip MCALPINE
DI MONA Joseph	George WILLIAMS
DINES Michael	Johnny MANNING
DI PEGO Gerald Francis	Det DELA
DIPLOMAT	Dennis TYLER
DIRCKX John H	Dr John Evelyn THORNDYKE
DISNEY Doris Miles	Rachel CAREY; ***Jefferson DIMARCO***; Griff HUGHES; Sarah LOWDEN; David MADDEN; Jim O'NEILL; Aggie SCANLON
DIX Maurice B	Sexton BLAKE; Supt Simon BULLION; ***Tommy MALINS***; Ch Insp James MILLER
DIXON George	Sgt George DIXON
DIXON W Willmott	Capt MOUNSELL
DOBSON Margaret	Jane BAILEY
DOBYNS Stephen	***Charlie BRADSHAW***; Det LAZARD
DODGE David	***Al COLBY***; John Abraham LINCOLN; John ROBIE; Whit WHITNEY
DOHERTY P C	***Hugh CORBETT***; Sir Godfrey EVESDEN; Matthew JENKYN
DOLD Gaylord	Mitch ROBERTS
DOLPH Jack	'Doc' CONNOR
DOLPHIN Rex	Sexton BLAKE
DOLSON Hildegarde	Lucy RAMSDALE and Insp James MACDOUGAL
DOMINIC R B	Benton SAFFORD
DONAHUE Jack	Harlan COLE
DONALDSON D J	Kit FRANKLYN
DONALDSON Norman	Dr John Evelyn THORNDYKE
DONAVAN John	Insp Frederick Jubilee 'Jumper' CROSS; ***Sgt Johnny LAMB***; Sir Benjamin SCARLE
DONOVAN Dick	Michael DANEVITCH and Peter BRODIE; Det Dick DONOVAN; ***Fabian FIELD***; Tyler TATLOCK; Det Vincent TRILL; Eugène VIDOCQ; Howel WALTER
DONOVAN J B	Insp Bill SPEED
DOODY Margaret	ARISTOTLE
DOOLITTLE Jerome	Tom BETHANY
DORRELL Mike	Dick BARTON
DORRINGTON Albert	Gifford RENWICK
DOSTOIEVSKI Fyodor Mikhailovich	Insp PETROVICH
DOTY William Lodevick	Mgr Thomas O MCGILLICUDDY
DOUGALL Bernard	Steve BORDEN
DOUGLAS Alexander	The ELECTRIC LIGHT DETECTIVE
DOUGLAS Arthur	Maj Jonathan CRAYTHORNE; ***Mark REGISTER***
DOUGLAS Carole Nelson	***Irene ADLER***; Kevin BLAKE; MIDNIGHT LOUIE and Temple BARR
DOUGLAS Gavin	Capt SAMSON
DOUGLAS George	***Insp HALLAN and Sgt SPRATT***; Sgt/Insp Brian 'Bonny' LEE
DOUGLAS John	***William EDMONDSON***; HARTER
DOUGLAS Lauren Wright	Caitlin REECE
DOUGLAS Malcolm	Bill YATES
DOUGLASS Donald McNutt	Sherlock HOLMES; ***Det Bolivar MANCHENIL***
DOUGLASS Ellsworth	Hermann ANDERWELT
DOUTHWAITE L C	Sexton BLAKE; Cpl Larry STEER; ***Const Jimmie WARDEN***
DOWLING Gregory	January ESPOSITO
DOWNES Quentin	Det Insp Abraham KOZMINSKI
DOWNEY Edmund	Walter TANDY
DOWNING Noel	Dr John H WATSON
DOWNING Todd	Peter BOUNTY; ***Hugh RENNERT***
DOWNING Warwick	Joe REDDMAN
DOYLE Acorn N	Neville BOYLES
DOYLE Adrian Conan and John Dickson CARR	Sherlock HOLMES
DOYLE James T	Paul BRODER; ***Dan CRONYN***
DOYLE Sir Arthur Conan	***Sherlock HOLMES***; Pharaoh JONES
DOYLIE B Conan	Sherlock HOLMES
DOZOIS Gardner and George EFFINGER	Karl JAEGER
DRACHMAN Theodore S	Dr Johnny MACK
DRACO F	Lord TINTAGEL and Lady 'Ginger' TINTAGEL
DRAKE Alison	Aline SCOTT
DRAKE Drexell	The FALCON
DRAX Peter	Ch Insp THOMPSON
DREHER Sarah	Stoner MCTAVISH
DRESSER Davis	Steve RANDOM
DREW Sidney	Sexton BLAKE
DRUID David	OLD HUMPY; OLD PITCHER; ***Sam SMART***; Sam STRONG
DRUMMOND Charles	Sgt REED
DRUMMOND Hamilton	George VORE
DRUMMOND Ivor	Jennifer Norrington, Aless GANZARELLO and Coleridge TUCKER; ***Coleridge TUCKER***
DRUMMOND J	Sexton BLAKE
DRUMMOND John Keith	Matilda WORTHING
DRUMMOND June	Insp David COPE; ***James PORBEAGLE***
DRURY W P	Pte PAGETT
DU BOIS Theodora	Dr Jeffrey MCNEILL
DU BOIS William	Jack JORDAN
DU MAURIER Daphne	Armino FABBIO
DUBOIS Brendan	Lewis COLE
DUDGEON Robert	Max STRONG
DUDLEY Ernest	Nat CRAIG; ***Dr MORELLE***; Jimmy STRANGE
DUDLEY William E	Sherlock HOLMES
DUERRENMATT Friedrich	Kommissar Hans BARLACH
DUFF James P	John P PHELAN
DUFFY Margaret	Patrick GILLARD

DUKE Madelaine	Norah NORTH
DUNANT Sarah	Hannah WOLFE
DUNCAN Allan	Maj Charles Douglas KERWOOD
DUNCAN David	Jim QUIGLEY
DUNCAN Francis	Peter JUSTICE; ***Mordecai Euripides*** TREMAINE
DUNCAN W Glenn	RAFFERTY
DUNCAN W Murdoch	Insp FLAGG; Supt GAYLORD; Mr GILLY; GREENSLEEVES; Insp Laurie HUME; Supt LESLIE; ***Supt MACNEILL***; Supt Donald (The Dreamer) REAMER
DUNDAS Lawrence	Andrew SALMOND
DUNDEE Robert	Johnny LAMB
DUNDEE Wayne D	Joe HANNIBAL
DUNLAP Susan	***Vejay HASKELL***; Kiernan O'SHAUNESSY; Jill SMITH
DUNN Des R	Mike SLATTERY
DUNNE Colin	Joe HUSSEY
DUNNE John Gregory	Tom SPELLACY
DUNNETT Alastair MacTavish	Barry RAEBURN
DUNNETT Dorothy	Johnson JOHNSON
DUNNING John	Cliff JANEWAY
DUNSANY Lord	Joseph JORKENS; ***Mr LINLEY***; RIPLEY
DUPREE Morrison	Dr Andrew STOUGHTON
DUPUY William Atherton	Bill GARD
DURBRIDGE Francis	Tim FRAZER; ***Paul TEMPLE***
DURHAM David	Fidelity DOVE; ***Insp G RASON***; Insp G RASON and Fidelity DOVE; Insp J RASON; James SEGROVE
DURHAM Mary	Insp Rodney HILTON; ***Insp YORK***
DURRANT Digby	Hamish OATH
DURST Paul	Michael CARMICHAEL
DUTTON Charles Judson	***John BARTLEY***; Prof Harley MANNERS
DVORKIN David	Sherlock HOLMES
DWIGHT Olivia	John DRYDEN and Gwyneth JONES
DYER George	Dr Ben STARRETT

—E—

E A P	Sherlock HOLMES
EADES M L	Winston BARROWS
EADIE Arlton	Wayman INSTONE
EARLY Jack	***Fortune FANELLI***; Colin MAGUIRE
EAST Roger	Colin KNOWLES; ***Ex-Supt 'Simmy' SIMMONDS***
EASTMAN Roy O	Harrison HOLT
EASTON Nat	Bill BANNING
EASTWOOD James	Anna ZORDAN
EATON Herbert	Sherlock HOLMES
EBERHARD Frederick G	***Insp O'HARE***; Ch of Plce SUTHERLAND
EBERHARDT Walter F	Insp WATTERSON
EBERHART Mignon G	Sewell BLAKE; Mallory BOOKOVER; Emmy BRACE; Det CRAFFT; Susan DARE; ***Sarah KEATE***; Sarah KEATE and Det Lance O'LEARY; Mady SMITH; Mr WICKWIRE
EBERSOHN Wessel Shalk	Dr Yudel GORDON
EBY Lois and John C FLEMING	***Pat O'LEARY***; Zachary STONE
ECCLES Marjorie	Insp Gil MAYO
ECO Umberto	Brother WILLIAM
EDEN Dorothy	Grace ASHERTON; ***Kate TEMPEST***
EDEN Matthew	Mark SAVAGE
EDENHOPE Detective	NELLIE
EDGAR Alfred	Sexton BLAKE
EDGELY Leslie	Jay ROGERS
EDGINTON May	Napoleon PRINCE
EDINGTONS The	Captain SMITH
EDMONDS Janet	Linus RINTOUL
EDMUNDS Brent	Pete MARVIN
EDWARDS Charman	Percy Aloysius HUFF
EDWARDS James G	***Insp Victor BONDURANT***; Insp Victor BONDURANT and Paul RAVEL
EDWARDS Leo	Jerry TODD
EDWARDS Martin	Harry DEVLIN
EDWARDS Paul (Paul Eiden)	John (The Expediter) EAGLE
EDWARDS Paul (Robert LORY)	John (The Expediter) EAGLE
EDWARDS Paul (Manning Lee STOKES)	John (The Expediter) EAGLE
EDWARDS Ruth Dudley	Robert AMISS
EDWARDS Walter	Sexton BLAKE
EFFINGER George Alec	***Marid AUDRAN***; Sherlock HOLMES
EGAN Lesley	Delia RIORDAN; ***Det Vic VARALLO and Jesse FALKENSTEIN***
EGGLESTON Edward	Abraham LINCOLN
EGLETON Clive	***Insp COGHILL***; David GARNETT; Charles WINTER
EHRLICH Jack	Robert W FLICK
EHRLICHMAN John	Dorothy Mayotte RIGBY
EICHLER Alfred	Martin AMES; ***Insp KNICKMAN***; Insp KNICKMAN and Martin AMES
EISENBERG Hershey H	David DAVIDOWITZ
EKSTROM Jan	Insp Bertil DURELL
ELAND Charles	Mark RANDALL
ELDREDGE Gilbert	Thibault PAREW
ELIAS David	Nell BARTLETT
ELIOT Major George F	Dan FOWLER
ELKINS Aaron J	Gideon OLIVER
ELKINS Charlotte and Aaron ELKINS	Lee OFSTED
ELLER John	Charlie ROPE
ELLERY Jan	Adrienne BISHOP
ELLIN Stanley	***Jake DEKKER***; Mel GORDON; Murray KIRK; Johnny MILANO
ELLINGTON Richard	Steve DRAKE
ELLIOTT Bruce	Lt BRISSK
ELLIOTT David	Jack CLEARY
ELLIOTT George	Martin SPEED
ELLIOTT William J	***Anthony ENGLAND***; Royston FRERE; Ed GUNNING; Bren HARDY
ELLNGER Geoffrey	Roger HARTLEY
ELLROY James	Det Dwight 'Bucky' BLEICHART; ***Fritz BROWN***; Sgt Lloyd HOPKINS; Dudley SMITH and Det Fred UNDERHILL
ELMAN Richard	Dr Robert HARMON
ELVESTAD Sven	Asbjorn (Osborne Crag) KRAG
ELVY Clara Evelyn	Insp SLADE
ELWARD James	Ginny KARR
ELY Ron	Jake SANDS
EMERSON Earl W	***Thomas BLACK***; Sheriff (temporary) Max FONTANA
EMMETT Robert	Mike (American Avenger) MCVEIGH
ENDFIELD Mercedes	Ms SQUAD
ENEFER Douglas	CANNON
ENGEL Howard	Benny COOPERMAN
ENGLEMAN Paul	Mark RENZLER
ENNEBUSKE Sarah Folsom	Georgie NAPPER
EPHESIAN	A B C HAWKES
EPSTEIN Samuel	Roger BAXTER
ERNST Paul	Sam CATES and Lt Jim RYAN; Shirley LEIGHTON and Bill HARPER; ***Lt Jim RYAN, Shirley LEIGHTON and Bill HARPER***; Dr SATAN; SEEKAY
ERSKINE Laurie York	Douglas RENFREW
ERSKINE Margaret	Insp Septimus FINCH
ESHLEMAN John M	Larry KOHARIK
ESSEX Richard	***LESSINGER***; Insp John SLADE and LESSINGER
ESTEVEN John	Miles LE BRETON; ***Insp Rae NORSE***
ESTLEMAN Loren D	Sherlock HOLMES; Peter MACKLIN; Philip MARLOWE; Connie MINOR; Page MURDOCK; Ralph POTEET; ***Amos WALKER***
ESTOW Daniel	William SCHAEFER
ETHAN John B	Victor GRANT
EUSTACE Frank J	Sherlock HOLMES
EUSTIS Helen White	Kate INNES
EVANOVICH Janet	Stephanie PLUM
EVANS E Everett	George HANLON
EVANS Fallon	Adrian WITHERS
EVANS Geraldine	Insp Joseph Aloysius RAFFERTY
EVANS Gwyn	Sexton BLAKE; Chester BRETT; Quentin DREX; ***Bill KELLAWAY***; Double O'DAY
EVANS John	Paul PINE
EVERMAY March	Insp GLOVER and Harry CURRY
EVERS Crabbe	Duffy HOUSE
EVERSON David	Robert MILES
EVERSZ Robert	Paul MARSTON
EVERTON Francis	***Det Insp ALLPORT***; Det Insp ALLPORT and Insp George ANNESLEY; Insp George ANNESLEY; Peter LINDSAY
EVOE	Sherlock HOLMES
EYLES Alfred W	Paul CHISHOLM
EYLES Leonora	Dr Joan MARVIN
EYRE Elizabeth	SIGISMONDO

—F—

FACKLER Elizabeth	Frank JAMES
FAIR A A	Bertha COOL and Donald LAM
FAIRFAX-BLAKEBOROUGH J	Nat WEDGEWOOD
FAIRLIE Gerard	Bow Street Runner Victor CARYLL; Capt Hugh 'Bulldog' DRUMMOND; ***Johnny MACALL***; Mr MALCOLM;
FAIRMAN Paul W	***Rick MASON***; Wally WATTS
FAIRWAY Sidney	Prof Richard CARFORD
FALK Lee	The PHANTOM
FALKIRK Richard	Bow Street Runner Edmund BLACKSTONE
FALLON Martin	Paul CHAVASSE
FANTINA Mary	Sherlock HOLMES
FANTONI Barry	Mike DIME

The Authors

FARJEON B L	***Robert AGNOLD***; DEVLIN; James DICKSON; Paul GODFREY; George MILLINGTON; MOLESWORTH; ROBSON and Edwin BOUSFIELD
FARJEON J Jefferson	BEN THE TRAMP; ***Paul BISHOP***; Insp KENDALL
FARMER Bernard J	P C James WIGAN
FARMER Philip Jose	Sherlock HOLMES
FARNOL Jeffrey	Sgt Jasper SHRIG
FARRAR Stewart	Insp Elwyn MORGAN
FARRELL Johnny	Johnny FARRELL
FARREN Mick	MARLOWE
FARRER Katherine	Insp Richard RINGWOOD
FAULKNER William	Gavin STEVENS
FAWCETT F Dubrez	Sexton BLAKE
FAWKES F A	Marshall HEDLEY
FEANADY S	Sherlock HOLMES
FEARING Kenneth	George STROUD
FEARN John Russell	Sawley GERSON; ***Jenkinson Talbot MERRIDREW***
FEARON Diana	Arabella FRANT
FEIFFER Jules	Roger ACKROYD
FELDMEYER Dean	Rev Dan THOMPSON
FELIX Charles	Ralph HENDERSON
FENADY Andrew J	Sam MARLOW
FENISONG Ruth	***Capt Gridley NELSON***; Victoria TARRANT
FENNELL George	Mike BRENT
FENNELLY Tony	Matt SINCLAIR
FENTON Walter	OLD NEVERSLEEP
FENWICK Elizabeth	Matthew HOLLEY
FERGUSON Frances	Det Sgt Jane PERRY
FERGUSON John	Francis MACNAB
FERGUSON Rachel	Sherlock HOLMES
FERGUSON W B M	Daniel J CLUER; ***'Biff' CORRIGAN***
FERRARS E X	Andrew BASNETT; Charlotte CAMBRY; Peter COREY; Insp CRANKSHAW; ***Toby DYKE***; Virginia FREER and Felix FREER; Peter HARKNESS; Jonas P JONAS; Martin RHYMER; Emma RITCHIE; Matthew TIERNEY
FERRARS Elizabeth	Andrew BASNETT; Charlotte CAMBRY; Peter COREY; Insp CRANKSHAW; ***Toby DYKE***; Virginia FREER and Felix FREER; Peter HARKNESS; Martin RHYMER; Emma RITCHIE; Matthew TIERNEY
FETTA Emma Lou	Lyle CURTIS and Susan YATES
FEUER Lewis	Sherlock HOLMES
FICKLING G G	Erik MARCH; Honey WEST and Erik MARCH; ***Honey WEST***
FIDLER Henry J	Dennis CHETWYND
FIELD Katherine	Det Insp Ross PATERSON
FIELD Moira	Det Insp FLOWER
FIELDHOUSE W L	Maj Clifford LANSING
FIELDING A	Hugh DUNCAN; ***Insp POINTER***
FILGATE Macartney	Charlotte ELIOT
FINDLEY Ferguson	Johnny MALONE
FINE Peter Heath	Harry LAKE
FINNEGAN Robert	Dan BANION
FINNEGAN Sam	William DRINK and Sam SLEEP
FINNEY R C	Insp BOURNE
FIRTH N Wesley	Merrick LAWRENCE; ***Al MCFEE***
FISCHER Bruno	***Ben HELM***; Rick TRAIN
FISCHER Cindy	Sherlock HOLMES
FISH Robert L	Capt Jose DA SILVA; ***Schlock HOMES***; Kek HUUYGENS; SIMPSON, CARRUTHERS and BRIGGS
FISHER Charles	Sherlock HOLMES
FISHER David E	***Henry GRACE***; Katie MacGregor TOWNSEND
FISHER Douglas	Jeff TELLFORD
FISHER Graham	Mike KING
FISHER Herb	Kyle YOUNGBLOOD
FISHER Laurence	Det Dave PITT
FISHER Norman	Nigel MORRISON
FISHER Steve	Sheridan DOOME; Kip MULDANE; Johnny RYAN; ***Joe SAXON***
FITT Mary	Insp/Supt MALLETT
FITZGERALD Kevin	Bernard FESTON
FITZGERALD Nigel	***Insp DUFFY***; Insp DUFFY and Alan RUSSELL; Alan RUSSELL
FITZGERALD Penelope	Insp MACE and Prof Heinrich UNTERMENSCH
FITZSIMMONS Courtland	***Det Jack KETHERIDGE***; Arthur MARTINSON; Prof Percy PEACOCK; Ethel THOMAS
FLAGG John	Hart MULDOON
FLANAGAN T J	Harry BLOUNT
FLANAGAN Thomas	***Niccolò MACHIAVELLI***; Maj TENNENTE
FLANNERY Sean	Wallace MAHONEY and John MAHONEY
FLEISCHMAN A S	Max BRINDLE
FLEMING Anne	Supt CHARTER
FLEMING Ian	Cdr James BOND
FLEMING Joan	Insp HOPE; ***Nuri ISKIRLAK***; Nat SAPPERTON
FLEMING Robert	Simon CROLE
FLEMING Ronald	June GAYNOR; ***Noel RAYMOND***
FLEMING-ROBERTS G T	***Jerry THACKER***; Jeffrey WREN
FLETCHER Aaron	Phillip (The Marksman) MAGELLAN
FLETCHER David	Sgt JOLLEY; A J RAFFLES; ***Det Insp RUBY***
FLETCHER Henry	Const HOBBS
FLETCHER J S	Turco BULLWORTHY; Ronald CAMBERWELL; ***Paul CAMPENHAYE***; Sgt CHARLESWORTH; Archer DAWE; Richard GOULBURN; Mr POSKITT; Insp SKARRATT; Frank SPARGO
FLETCHER Jessica and Donald BAIN	Jessica FLETCHER
FLETCHER Lucille	Robin CHODOFF
FLETCHER R J	Gilbert DAVISON

FLIEGEL Richard	Sgt Shelly LOWENKOPF
FLINN Denny Martin	Spencer HOLMES
FLORA Fletcher	Lt Joseph MARCUS
FLOWER Elliott	Policeman FLYNN
FLOWER Pat	Insp SWINTON
FLYNN Brian	Anthony BATHURST
FLYNN Carol Houlihan	Able GARRET
FLYNN Don	Ed FITZGERALD
FLYNN J M	Ken MADISON; ***Burl STANNARD***
FLYNN Jay	***Slim Jim BANNERMAN***; MCHUGH
FLYNN T T	***Mike HARRIS and Trixie MEEHAN***; Mr MADDOX
FLYNN W J	Peabody SMITH
FOLEY Rae	John HARLAND; ***Hiram POTTER***
FOLLETT Ken	Piers ROPER
FONBLANQUE Albany	Bow Street Runner BRADSHAW and Bow Street Runner FRASER
FOOTE-SMITH Elizabeth	Will WOODFIELD
FOOTMAN Robert	Harry RYDER
FOOTNER Hulbert	Amos Lee MAPPIN; ***Mme Rosika STOREY***
FORBES Bryan	Alec HILLSDEN
FORBES Colin	TWEED
FORBES J D	Michael DOUGLAS
FORBES Stanton	Constance COBBLE
FORD Corey	Sherlock HOLMES
FORD Leslie	Ben DAVIDGE; Porteus Alexander HARP; Lt Joseph KELLY; ***Grace LATHAM***; Col John PRIMROSE and Grace LATHAM; Col John PRIMROSE
FORDE Nicholas	Mark URGENT
FORKOSCH Morris D	Sherlock HOLMES
FORREST Anthony	Capt John Valcourt JUSTICE
FORREST G F	Warlock BONES
FORREST Katherine V	Det Kate DELAFIELD
FORREST Norman	John FINNEGAN
FORREST Richard	Lyon WENTWORTH and Bea WENTWORTH
FORRESTER Andrew Jr	Andrew FORRESTER Jr; ***Andrew FORRESTER***; Mrs GLADDEN
FORSTER John, Greer WOODWARD and Rick CUMMINS	Sherlock HOLMES
FORSYTE Charles	***Insp Richard LEFT***; Christopher MILNER-BROWN
FORSYTH Frederick	Commissaire LEBEL
FORSYTHE Berkley	Sherlock HOLMES
FORSYTHE Robin	Anthony VEREKER
FORTUNE Dion	Dr TAVERNER
FORWARD Robert L	Alexander L'HIBOUX
FOSTER John	Tess EVELING
FOSTER R Francis	Anthony RAVENHILL
FOSTER Richard	***Pete DRACO***; Chin Kwang KHAM
FOWLER Sydney	Prof BLINKWELL and Mr JELLIPOT; Prof BLINKWELL; Insp CAULDRON; Insp CLEVELAND; ***Mr JELLIPOT***
FOWLES Anthony	Richard POWELL
FOX David	The SHADOWERS INC
FOX James M	***Steve HARVESTER***; Sgt Jerry LONG; John MARSHALL and Suzy MARSHALL
FOX Peter	Jack LAMARRE and Alison PRENDERGAST
FOX Sebastian	George LYDNEY
FOX Tom	The ASYLUM DETECTIVE; The INSURANCE DETECTIVE; ***OLD DUDE***; The PAN HANDLE DETECIVE
FOXALL P A	Det Insp Frank DERBEN
FOXALL Raymond	***Harry ADKINS***; John CRISPIN
FOXX Jack	***Dan CONNELL***; Fergus O'HARA
FOX-DAVIES A C	***Sir John KYNNERSLEY***; Col MARWOOD; Ashley TEMPEST
FRANCE Victor	Oliver GALT and Hugo TOWER
FRANCES Stephen D	John GAIL
FRANCIS Basil	Sgt Paul DEAN; ***Insp GHENT***; Insp GHENT and Sgt Paul DEAN
FRANCIS Dick	Tony BEACH and Gregor MCGREGOR; David CLEVELAND; Freddie CROFT; Jonah DEREHAM; ***Andrew DOUGLAS***; Randall DREW; Rob FINN; Neil GRIFFON; Sid HALLEY; Gene HAWKINS and Dave TELLER; Kelly HUGHES; Thomas LYON; Philip NORE; Steven SCOTT; Matt SHORE; Charles TODD; James TYRONE; Alan YORK
FRANCIS William	Steve CASH; ***Anthony MARTIN***
FRANKAU Gilbert	***Giuseppe CIGARINI***; Marcus ORLANDO; Kyra SOKRATESCU
FRANKISH H	Richard CUNLIFFE
FRANKLIN Charles	***Insp Jim BURGESS***; Maxine DANGERFIELD; Grant GARFIELD
FRANKLIN Eugene	Berkeley Hoy BARNES
FRANKLIN Max	STARSKY and HUTCH
FRASER Alex	Insp Noel TRACY
FRASER Anthea	Ch Insp David WEBB
FRASER Antonia	Jemima SHORE
FRASER James	Insp/Supt Bill AVEYARD
FRASER John Foster	Hubert GRESHAM
FRASER T A	Dr HUDSON
FRAY Al	Barney CONROY
FRAZER Andrew	Duncan PRIDE
FRAZER Martin	Sexton BLAKE
FRAZER Robert Caine	Mark KILBY
FREDERICKS Arnold	Richard DUVALL
FREDERICKS Ernest Jason	Sam CATES
FREDMAN John	Charles DEXTER
FREDMAN Mike	Willie HALLIDAY
FREEBORN Brian	Harry GRANT
FREELING Nicholas	Insp Henri CASTANG; Arlette VAN DER VALK; ***Insp Piet VAN DER VALK***; Insp Piet VAN DER VALK and Arlette VAN DER VALK
FREEMAN Kathleen	Insp POOLE
FREEMAN Lucy	Dr William AMES and Det LONEGAN

FREEMAN Martin J	Judo MARRIOTT; ***Jerry TODD***
FREEMAN R Austin	Humphrey CHALLONER; Danby CROKER; Phyllis DUDLEY; ***Dr John Evelyn THORNDYKE***
FREEMANTLE Brian	Samuel BELL; ***Charlie MUFFIN***
FRENCH Richard P	Peter LAYTON
FREUND Philip	Sebastian ROMM
FREY James N	Joe ZANKA
FRIEDMAN Kinky	Kinky FRIEDMAN
FRIEDMAN Mickey	***Isobel ANDERS***; Georgia Lee MAXWELL
FRIEND Ed	Jonathan ARCANE and Vanessa ARCANE
FRIESNER Esther M	Brihtvic DONNE
FROEST Frank	Supt Heldon FOYLE
FROEST Frank and George DILNOT	Insp BARRACLOUGH
FROETSCHEL Susan	Jane MCBRIDE
FROME David	Maj Gregory LEWIS; Ch Insp LORD; ***Evan PINKERTON***
FROST Barbara	Marka DE LANCEY
FROST Frederick	Anthony HAMILTON
FROST Kelman	***Dr Francis FARRAR***; Insp HYND
FROST Mark	Sherlock HOLMES
FRUTTERO Carlo and Francio LUCENTINI	Sherlock HOLMES
FRY Pete	Pete FRY
FULLER Dean	Roger TRULY
FULLER Roy	George GARNER; ***Harry SINTON***
FULLER Samuel	SANDY
FULLER Timothy	Edmund 'Jupiter' JONES
FULLER William O	***Brad DOLAN***; Sherlock HOLMES
FULTON Chandos	Tom BYRNES
FULTON Eileen	Nina MCFALL and Lt Dino ROSSI
FURNIVALL Gordon	Dr Sebastian LONG
FURST Alan	Roger LEVIN
FUTRELLE Jacques	Prof Augustus S F X VAN DUSEN
FYFIELD Frances	***Det Supt Geoffrey BAILEY***; Helen WEST and Det Supt Geoffrey BAILEY

—G—

GABORIAU Emile	Monsieur LECOQ
GADDA Carlo Emilio	Incra VALLO
GAGE Edwin	Dan FALCONER
GAGNON Maurice	Deirdre O'HARA
GAINES Audrey	***Chauncey O'DAY***; Jeff STRANGE
GAINHAM Sarah	Herr MOLLNAR
GAINSLEY Sidney	Dr HAWKINS
GAIR Malcolm	Mark RAEBURN
GAITANO Nick	Det Jake PHILLIPS
GAITE Francis	Charles LATIMER and James LATIMER
GALLAGHER Gale	Gale GALLAGHER
GALLAGHER Stephen	Peter CARSON
GALLICO Paul	***Alexander HERO***; Hiram HOLLIDAY; Sally 'Sherlock Holmes' LANE
GALLISON Kate	***Mother Lavinia GREY***; Nick MAGARACZ
GALLON Tom	Bella THORN; TOKLEY; ***Enoch VOYCE***
GALLOWAY David	Lamaar RANSOM
GALLOWAY Lindsay	John SUTHERLAND
GALWAY Robert Conington	James PACKARD
GALWEY G V	Ch Insp 'Daddy' BOURNE
GANNON E J	Sexton BLAKE
GARDENHIRE Samuel M	CONNORS
GARDINER Dorothy	***Sheriff Moss MAGILL***; Mr WATSON
GARDNER Alan	David TROY
GARDNER Craig Shaw	Sherlock HOLMES
GARDNER Curtis T	Leonard MACE; ***Valentine VICKERS***
GARDNER Erle Stanley	Go Get 'Em' CARVER; Terry CLANE; Richard 'Speed' DASH; Sheriff Bill ELDON; Jax KEEN; Lester LEITH; ***Perry MASON***; Ed MIGRAINE; Paul PRY; Doug SELBY; Dane SKARLE; Peter WENNICK; Gramps' WIGGINS; Sidney ZOOM
GARDNER John	Cdr James BOND; Sherlock HOLMES; Herbie KRUGER; ***Boysie OAKES***; Derek TORRY
GARDNER Martin	Sherlock HOLMES
GARFIELD Brian	Paul BENJAMIN; Simon CRANE; Charlie DARK; ***Trooper Sam WATCHMAN***
GARFORTH John	***The AVENGERS***; Sexton BLAKE
GARLAND Lawrence	Sherlock HOLMES
GARNER Hugh	Insp Walter MCDUMONT
GARNER William	Mick JAGGER
GARNET A H	Charles THAYER; ***Cyrus WILSON***
GARNETT Roger	***Ch Insp Jonathan BLACK***; R I PERKINS; John YARDLEY; John YARDLEY and R I PERKINS
GARRETT Randall	Lord DARCY
GARRETT Robert	Alan BRETT
GARRETT William	James DREW
GARRISON Christian	Ace CHANEY
GARRITY David J	Peter BRAID
GARROWAY Pete	Pete GARROWAY
GARTH David	Zachary T ROWLAND
GARTH Ed	Matt LINCOLN
GARVE Andrew	Max EASTERBROOK; ***James RENISON and Carol RENISON***
GARVIN Richard M and Edmond G ADDEO	Barney RUSSOM
GASH Joe	Karen KOVAC and Terry FLYNN
GASH Jonathan	LOVEJOY
GASK Arthur	Gilbert LAROSE
GASTON Bill	Roy MACLEAN
GAT Dimitri	Yuri NEVSKY
GATENBY Rosemary	Christie WORTHING
GATES Clifford	Sexton BLAKE
GATES Tudor	Danny SCIPIO
GAULT William Campbell	***Brock (The Rock) CALLAHAN***; Mortimer JONES; Lee KAPRELIAN; Luke PILGRIM; Joe PUMA; Pete WORDEN
GAUNT Mary	Insp DODSON
GAVIN Catherine	Jacques BRUNEL
GAYLE Newton	James GREER
GEASON Susan	Syd FISH
GEDDES Paul	Ludovic FENDER and Paul VENNEKER; Ludovic FENDER; ***Paul VENNEKER***
GELLER Michael	***Lt Bud DUGAN***; Mickey 'Slots' RESNICK
GELLER Stephen	Oliver GAD
GELLIBRAND Edward	Kenneth O'BRIEN
GEORGE Charles	Sherlock HOLMES
GEORGE Elizabeth	The Earl of ATHERTON; ***Insp Thomas LYNLEY***
GEORGE Isaac S	Sherlock HOLMES
GEORGE Kara	Nick NICOLETTI
GEORGE Peter	Steve BRYANT
GEORGE Theodore	Lt Al ZIMMERMAN
GERARD Francis	***Sir John MEREDITH***; Commiss SANDERS
GERARD Philip	Paul POPE and Roy POPE
GERARD Ron L	Jack DEMARREST and Jane BRITLAND
GERRARE Wirt	Horace VESEY
GERRITY David J	Frank CARDOLINI
GERROLD David	Sherlock HOLMES
GERSON Jack	Insp Ernst LOHMANN
GETHIN David	WYATT
GETTEL Ronald E	Ch HAMMOND and Det BENEDETTO
GIBBON Perceval	***Miss GREGORY***; The Vrouw GROBELAAR
GIBBONS Cromwell	Rex HUXFORD
GIBBONS H H Clifford	Sexton BLAKE
GIBBS Tony	Gillean VERDEAN
GIBBS-SMITH C H	Paul HARVARD
GIBSON Theodore W	Sherlock HOLMES
GIBSON Walter B	Lamont (The Shadow) CRANSTON
GIELGUD Val	Anthony HAVILLAND; Insp Gregory PELLEW and Viscount CLYMPING; ***Det Insp Simon SPEARS***
GIESY J U and Junius B SMITH	Prince Abdull OMAR
GILBERT Anna	Florence ST LEONARD
GILBERT Anthony	***Arthur G CROOK***; Monsieur DUPUY; Scott EGERTON
GILBERT Dale L	Matt DOYLE and Carter WINFIELD
GILBERT Kenneth	Jimmy BRENNON
GILBERT Michael	Mrs ARTSIDE; Mr BEHRENS and Mr CALDER; 'Cuckoo' GOYLES; ***Insp HAZELRIGG***; Sherlock HOLMES; Ch Supt KNOTT; Peter MANCIPLE; Insp MERCER; Const/Ch Insp Patrick PETRELLA; Dorothy Mayotte RIGBY; James SCOTLAND
GILES Guy Elwyn	Brice KENT
GILES Kenneth	Insp Harry JAMES
GILES Raymond	Shamus MCCOY
GILL Anton	HUY
GILL B M	Det Ch Insp Tom MAYBRIDGE
GILL Bartholomew	Insp Peter MCGARR
GILL Elizabeth	Benvenuto BROWN
GILLESPIE Robert B	***Rocky CAPUTO***; Ralph SIMMONS
GILLETTE William	Sherlock HOLMES
GILLIAN Michael	Leith HADLEY
GILLIGAN Roy	Pat RIORDAN
GILLIS Jackson	Jonas DUNCAN
GILLMORE Rufus	Griffin SCOTT
GILMAN Dorothy	Sister JOHN and HYACINTH; Amelia JONES; ***Mrs Emily POLLIFAX***
GILPATRIC Guy	Mr GLENCANNON
GILRUTH Susan	Liane CRAWFORD and Insp Hugh GORDON
GIROUX E X	Robert FORSYTHE and Abigail 'Sandy' SANDERSON
GIVENS Charles G	Jimmy HASTINGS
GLANVILLE Alec	Insp 'Dusty' MULLER and 'Tiny' MELDRUM
GLASBY John S	Insp CHALLON
GLAZNER Joseph Mark	Billy NEVERS
GLEN Alson	Charlotte SAMS
GLIDDEN M W	Carey BRENT
GLOAG John	Lionel BUCKBY
GLOAG Julian	Hugo WELCHMAN
GLUCK Sinclair	Paul BERNARD; ***Jack CLAYTON***; Ross MCCOY
GOBER Don	James RHODES
GODDARD Norman	Sexton BLAKE
GODEY John	Jack ALBANY
GODFREY Ellen	Jane TREGAR
GODFREY Peter	Rolf LE ROUX
GOLDBERG Marshall	Dan LASSITER
GOLDMAN Lawrence	Johnny SATURDAY

The Authors

GOLDMAN Raymond Leslie	Asaph CLUME
GOLDSBOROUGH Robert	Nero WOLFE
GOLDSMITH Gene	Dan DAMON
GOLDSTEIN Arthur D	Max GUTTMAN; ***Ben LOMAX***
GOLDSTEIN William	Dr PHIBES
GOLDSWEIG Beryl	Artemus FLINT
GOLDTHWAITE Eaton K	***Lt Joseph DICKERSON***; Frank MOERSON
GOLLIN James	Alan FRENCH
GOLLOMB Joseph	GALT; ***Insp Barton HAWLEY***
GOLSWORTHY Arnold	Mr PONDERY
GONZALES John	Harry HORNE
GOODCHILD George	Insp John INCH; ***Insp MCLEAN***; Insp Laurence OGILVIE; Nigel REX; John Q TRELAWNY
GOODE George W	***KING DAN***; The POST-OFFICE DETECTIVE
GOODEN George and Frank THOMAS	Sherlock HOLMES
GOODHUE Stoddard	Dr GOODRICH
GOODRUM Charles A	Edwin GEORGE
GOODWIN John	Det/Sgt/Supt SCARFE
GORDON Alison	Kate HENRY
GORDON Fritz	Schuyler TOWNSEND
GORDON Jan	Insp PENK
GORDON Neil	***James ARNOLD***; Insp DEWAR; Peter KERRIGAN
GORDON Russell	Fred DAYMOND
GORDON Spike	Gale GALLYON
GORDONS The	GAIL and MITCH; ***D C (Darn Cat) RANDALL***; John RIPLEY
GORE William	Insp PENK
GORELL Lord	Insp Harry FARRANT; Insp Maurice HEPBURN and Evelyn TEMPLE; Insp Maurice HEPBURN; ***Insp Gordon ROSS***
GORES Joe	Neil FARGO; ***Curt HALSTEAD***; Dashiell HAMMETT; Dan KEARNEY ASSOCIATES
GORE-BROWNE Robert	Lucien CLAY
GORMAN Ed	Jack DWYER; ***Leo GUILD***; Philip MARLOWE; TOBIN
GOSLING Paula	Lt Jake CHASE; John Owen COSATELLI; Sheriff Matt GABRIEL; Charles LLEWELLYN; Mike MALCHECK; Dorothy Mayotte RIGBY; ***Lt Jack STRYKER***
GOTTLIEB Nathan	Nash KANZLER
GOUGH Laurence	Det Jack WILLOWS and Det Claire PARKER
GOULART Ron	Sam BRIMMER; Jake CONGER; John EASY; Jim HALEY; Star HAWKS; Vincent HAWTHORN; Ben JOLSON; Cleopatra JONES; Max KEARNY; Burt KURRIE; Rudy NAVARRO; ***Jake PACE and Hildy PACE***; Jared SMITH; Skyrocket' STEELE; Jack SUMMER
GOULD Chester	Dick TRACY
GOULD Heywood	Josh KRALES
GOULD Nat	Barry BROMLEY; ***Valentine MARTYN***
GOULD Stephen	Sheridan DOOME
GOYNE Richard	Sexton BLAKE; ***Supt 'Tubby' GREENE***; The PADRE; Paul TEMPLETON
GRAAF Peter	Joe DUST
GRACE Police Captain	Phil PETERSON
GRADY James	Philip MARLOWE; ***John RANKIN***
GRAEME Bruce	***BLACKSHIRT***; Lord Anthony BLACKSHIRT; Insp Auguste JANTRY; Det Sgt Robert MATHER; Supt William STEVENS and Insp Pierre ALLAIN; Theodore I TERHUNE
GRAEME David	Monsieur BLACKSHIRT
GRAEME Roderic	BLACKSHIRT
GRAFTON C W	Gilmore HENRY
GRAFTON Sue	Kinsey MILLHONE
GRAHAM Anthony	Eddie DELANEY; ***Eric MARSDEN***; Frank RICHMOND
GRAHAM Burton	Michael EVANS
GRAHAM Caroline	Det Ch Insp Tom BARNABY
GRAHAM Harold	Austin MELVILLE
GRAHAM John Alexander	***Arthur SILVERMAN***; Arnold WECHSLER
GRAHAM Neill	***James 'Solo' MALCOLM***; Mr SANDYMAN
GRAHAM Winifred	Miss WOOLFE
GRANGE John	Jim ANTHONY
GRANGER Ann	***Ursula GRETTON***; Ch Insp Alan MARKBY and Meredith MITCHELL
GRANGER Bill	***DEVEREAUX***; Karen KOVAC and Jack DONOVAN
GRANT Ben	Marty COLE
GRANT James Edward	Tip O'NEIL
GRANT James	MACE
GRANT Linda	Catherine SAYLOR
GRANT Maxwell (Walter Brown GIBSON)	Lamont (The Shadow) CRANSTON
GRANT Maxwell (William ARDEN)	Lamont (The Shadow) CRANSTON
GRANT Maxwell	NORGIL
GRANT William	Matt FARADAY
GRANT-ADAMSON Lesley	Laura FLYNN; ***Rain MORGAN***
GRAVATT Glenn	Sherlock HOLMES
GRAVES Allen	Caleb CLICKETT
GRAVES Richard L	Hugo WOLFRAM
GRAY A W	Bono PHILLIPS
GRAY Berkeley	Sexton BLAKE; ***Norman CONQUEST***
GRAY Curme	Victor MITCHEL
GRAY Dulcie	Insp CARDIFF
GRAY Jonathan	Geoffrey TARLETON
GRAY Malcolm	Alan CRAIG
GRAY Rod	Eve DRUM
GRAY Russell	Ben BRYN
GRAYDON Robert Murray	Sexton BLAKE
GRAYDON W Murray	Sexton BLAKE
GRAYLAND V Merle	Hoani MATA
GRAYLE Hubert	Mr FORDHAM
GRAYSON Richard	***John BRYANT***; Insp Jean-Paul GAUTIER
GRAYSON Rupert	Gunston COTTON
GREELEY Andrew M	***Jimmy O'NEILL***; Mgr John Blackwood 'Blackie' RYAN
GREEN Alan	John HUGO
GREEN Anna Katherine	BYRD; Sheriff Steve DILLON; Frank ETHERIDGE; ***Det Ebenezer GRYCE***; Det Ebenezer GRYCE and Caleb SWEETWATER; Det Ebenezer GRYCE and Amelia BUTTERWORTH; Violet STRANGE; Caleb SWEETWATER; Anthony TAMWORTH
GREEN Christine	Kate KINSELLA
GREEN Edith Pinero	Dearborn V PINCH
GREEN George Dawes	Romulus LEDBETTER
GREEN Glint	Insp WIELD
GREEN Richard Lancelyn	Sherlock HOLMES
GREEN Thomas J	Aaron GATES and Caro BURSA
GREENBAUM Leonard	Lt Paul GOLD and Tommy LARKIN
GREENBERG Martin H and Carol-Lynn Rossel WAUGH	Sherlock HOLMES
GREENE Graham	MASON
GREENE L Patrick	***'Dynamite' DRURY***; Sgt LANCEY; Aubrey St John MAJOR and Sgt LANCEY; Aubrey St John MAJOR; Trooper USELESS
GREENER William Oliver	Jo SALIS
GREENHALGH Katherine	Sylvia SILENCE
GREENHAM G H	A SCOTLAND YARD DETECTIVE
GREENLEAF Stephen	John Marshall TANNER
GREENWALD Ken	Sherlock HOLMES
GREENWALD Nancy	MCQUADE
GREENWOOD D M	Rev Theodora BRAITHWAITE
GREENWOOD John	Insp MOSLEY
GREENWOOD Kerry	Phryne FISHER
GREENWOOD L B	Sherlock HOLMES
GREGG Cecil Freeman	Insp Cuthbert HIGGINS; ***Henry PRINCE***
GREGORICH Barbara	Frank DRAGOVICH
GREGORY Jackson	Paul SAVOY
GREGSON J M	Supt John LAMBERT
GREIG Ian	Insp SWINTON
GRESCOE Paul	Dan RUDNICKI
GRESHAM Elizabeth	Jenny Gilette LEWIS and Hunter LEWIS
GRETH Rona	Hana SHANER
GREX Leo	Jerry DOWN; Paul IRVING; ***Phil SANDERSON***
GREY Douglas	Thorndyke FLINT
GREY Robin	Jenny Gilette LEWIS and Hunter LEWIS
GREY Vivian	***Det Insp SLADE***; Insp WALL
GRIBBLE Leonard	Insp RILEY; ***Supt Anthony SLADE***
GRIBBLE Leonard and Geraldine LAWS	Sally DEAN
GRIDBAN Volsted	Adam QUIRKE
GRIERSON Edward	Marion KERRISON
GRIERSON Francis	Supt Andrew ASH and Ch Det Insp George MUIR; Supt Andrew ASH; Richard FURLING; ***Ch Det Insp George MUIR***; Commissaire PATRAS; Prof WELLS
GRIFF	Don DANBY; ***Kinsey TARGET***
GRIFF	Gentle HOGGERTY
GRIFF	Bill TRUSCOTT
GRIFFIN John	Richard RAVEN
GRIFFIN Robert J	COOPERSMITH
GRIFFITH George	Insp LIPINSKI
GRIFFITHS Arthur	***Insp FASKE***; FLOCON; Insp LAMPETER; Mr LESLIE; Lionel MACNAUGHTEN-INNES; Insp PHILLIPSON; Plantagenet PLEWS; Col Sir Theophilus ST CLAIR
GRIFFITHS Ella	Sgt Rudolf NILSEN
GRIMES Martha	Insp Richard JURY
GRIMSHAW Mark	Colwyn DANE
GRINDAL Richard	Ian BLACKIE
GRINDLE Lucretia	Insp ROSS
GRISMAN Arnold	GOLDBERG
GRISWOLD George	Mr GROODE
GROC Leon	Henri HENRY
GROGAN Gerald	William POLLOK
GRONER Augusta	Joe MULLER
GRONER Augusta and Grace Isobel COLBRON	Joe MULLER
GROOM Mrs Sidney	Sylvia SHALE
GROOM Pelham	Peter MOHUNE
GROSS E Tudor	Kerlock SHOMES
GROSS Ken	Det Maggie VAN ZANDT
GROSSBACH Robert	Lou PECKINPAUGH
GROVE Marjorie	Maxine REYNOLDS
GRUBER Frank	Tom ALDER; Otis BEAGLE; ***Johnny FLETCHER and Sam CRAGG***; Simon LASH; Tom LOGAN; Oliver QUADE; Lt Cdr Frank SARGENT; Jim STRONG
GUENTER C H	Robert URBAN
GUILD Nicholas	***Ray GUINNESS***; William LUKES
GUISE Stanley	Frank DESPARD
GULL C Ranger	Mr TOPHAM
GUNN James	***Kirk CULLEN***; Jerry PARKER
GUNN Victor	Bill 'Ironsides' CROMWELL
GUNNING Sally	Peter BARTHOLOMEW
GUNTER Archibald Clavering	***Dr BURTON***; Thomas DUFF

GURDON J E	Kaye STANDISH and Mike STANDISH
GURR David	Jane MONTIGNY
GUTHRIE A B Jr	Sheriff Chick CHARLESTON
GUTHRIE Al	Walter MCKENZIE
GUTTERIDGE Lindsay	Matthew DILKE
GUY David	Matt GREGG
HACKFORTH-JONES Gilbert	***Paul DECKER***; Joe GARTON; Earl (of) MILLINGTON
HADDAD C A	Becky BELSKI; ***David HAHAM***
HADDAM Jane	Gregor DEMARKIAN
HADDOCK Lisa	Carmen RAMIREZ
HADDOW Denis	Det Ch Insp GREVE
HADLEY Joan	Theo BLOOMER
HAFFNER Margaret	Dr Catherine EDISON
HAGBERG David	Kirk MCGARVEY
HAGEN Miriam-Ann	Hortense CLINTON
HAGER Jean	Molly BEARPAW
HAGGARD Paul	Mike WARLOCK
HAGGARD Rider	James SHORT
HAGGARD William	Paul MARTINY; Dorothy Mayotte RIGBY; ***Col Charles RUSSELL***; William Wilberforce SMITH
HAIBLUM Isidore	James SHAW
HAIG Alec	Alec HAIG
HAILEY J P	Steve WINSLOW
HALBACH Helan	HOMONYMOUS
HALE Christopher	Lt Bill FRENCH
HALE Edgar	Montague MIGGLEWADE; ***Insp Michael REGAN***
HALL Adam	QUILLER
HALL Jim	THORN
HALL Parnell	Stanley HASTINGS
HALL Patricia	Kate WESTON
HALL Robert Lee	***Benjamin FRANKLIN***; Dr John H WATSON
HALL Vernon	Sherlock HOLMES
HALL William S	COPPER DRIFT
HALLAHAN William H	***Charlie BREWER***; Arthur TANK
HALLERAN Tucker	***Cam MACCARDLE***; King of England Edward VII WINDSOR
HALLIDAY Brett	Michael SHAYNE
HALLIDAY Dorothy	Johnson JOHNSON
HALLIDAY Fred	Stanley DELPHOND
HALLIDAY Michael	***Emmanuel CELLINI***; Martin FANE and Richard FANE
HALLINAN Timothy	Simeon GRIST
HALLIWELL Leslie	Sherlock HOLMES
HALSEY Harlan Page	Bruce ANGELO; Dudie DUNNE; Kate EDWARDS; ***Kate GOELET***; MANFRED; VAN
HALSTEAD John	Insp TODD
HAM Bob	Mark LEE and Carl BROWNE
HAMBLEDON Phyllis	Insp 'Tubby' HALL
HAMER Malcolm	Chris LUDLOW
HAMILL Edson	RYKER
HAMILL Pete	Sam BRISCOE
HAMILTON Adam	Barrington (The Peacemaker) HEWES-BRADFORD
HAMILTON Charles	Denham CROFT; ***Ferrers LOCKE***; Sedley SHARPE
HAMILTON Donald	Matt HELM
HAMILTON Elaine	Insp REYNOLDS
HAMILTON Frederic Spencer	P J DAVENANT
HAMILTON Henrietta	Sally HELDAR and Johnny HELDAR
HAMILTON Ian	Pete HEYSEN
HAMILTON Kelly	Trixie TRUE
HAMILTON Nan	Isamu OHARA
HAMMER David L	Sherlock HOLMES
HAMMETT Dashiell	Ned BEAUMONT; Nick CHARLES and Nora CHARLES; The CONTINENTAL OP; Alexander RUSH; SECRET AGENT X-9; ***Sam SPADE***; Robin THIN
HAMMOND Gerald	Deborah CALDER; ***Keith CALDER***; John CUNNINGHAM; Simon PARBITTER and Keith CALDER; 'Beau' PEPYS
HAMMOND Harry	***Allen DANE***; OLD RUFE
HAMMOND Thomas	Sherlock HOLMES
HAMMOND W F	Fiske ERRELL
HANDLER David	Stewart HOAG
HANLON Sean	Preston John RIORDAN
HANSEN Joseph	***Dave BRANDSTETTER***; Alan TARR
HANSEN Vern	BRODY
HANSHEW Hazel Phillips	Hamilton CLEEK
HANSHEW Mary E and Hazel Phillips HANSHEW	Hamilton CLEEK
HANSHEW Mary E and Thomas W HANSHEW	Hamilton CLEEK
HANSHEW Thomas W	Hamilton CLEEK
HANSON V J	Sexton BLAKE
HANSON Virginia	***Nicholas CORNISH***; Adam DREW and Kay CORNISH
HARDIE D W F	Det Insp Elwyn HUGHES
HARDING Bret	Pine-Top JONES
HARDING Eric	Toby JUDD
HARDING Paul	Brother ATHELSTAN
HARDING Richard	BONNER
HARDING Ronald S L	Insp RICHARDSON
HARDINGE Rex	Sexton BLAKE; ***MURPHY and MCTAVISH***
HARDWICK Michael	BERGERAC; Sherlock HOLMES; ***Dr John H WATSON***
HARDWICK Michael and Mollie HARDWICK	Sherlock HOLMES
HARDWICK Mollie	Doran FAIRWEATHER and Rodney CHELMARSH
HARDY A S	Sexton BLAKE
HARDY Frank	Billy BORKER
HARDY Lindsay	Gregory KEEN
HARDY William	Bob ADAMS and Anne MINER; ***Karen GORDON***
HARE Cyril	Wencelaus BOTTWINK; ***Insp MALLETT***; Insp MALLETT and Francis PETTIGREW; Francis PETTIGREW
HARING Don	Lawrence Patrick 'Larry' KENT
HARKNETT Terry	***Ch Supt John CROWN***; Steve WAYNE
HARMA Edward B	Sherlock HOLMES
HARNEY F X	Dym DARKE
HARPER David	Warren STONE
HARPER Richard	Tom RAGNON
HARRAGAN Steve	Steve HARRAGAN
HARRINGTON Joseph	Lt Francis X KERRIGAN
HARRINGTON Joyce	***Jenny HOLLAND***; Philip MARLOWE; John Conan WATSON
HARRINGTON Neil	Alexander FALLON
HARRIS Charlaine	Nickie CALLAHAN; ***Catherine LINTON***; Aurora 'Rose' TEAGARDEN
HARRIS Colver	Timothy FOWLER
HARRIS Evelyn	Largely LEE
HARRIS Larry M	John J MALONE
HARRIS Thomas	Will GRAHAM; ***Hannibal LECTER and Clarice STERLING***
HARRIS Timothy	Thomas KYD
HARRISON Chip	Leo HAIG
HARRISON Edwin	Sexton BLAKE
HARRISON Harry	***Slippery Jim DI GRIZ***; Tony HAWKIN
HARRISON Michael	***Chevalier Auguste C DUPIN***; Sherlock HOLMES
HARRISON Ray	Sgt Joseph BRAGG
HARRISON Richard	Ch Insp William BASTION
HARRISON Van	Insp BRYSON
HARRISS Will	Prof Clifford DUNBAR
HARRIS-BURLAND J B	Richard LORYAT; ***Insp STRODE***
HARROD-EAGLES Cynthia	Det Insp Bill SLIDER
HART Carolyn G	Henrietta O'Dwyer COLLINS; ***Annie LAURANCE***
HART Ellen	Sophie GREENAWAY; ***Jane LAWLESS***
HART Janet	Jinsie CARTWRIGHT
HART Jeanne	Det Carl PEDERSON
HART Roy	Supt ROPER
HARTE Bret	Hemlock JONES
HARTLAND Michael	***Sarah CABLE***; David NAIRN
HARTLEY Peter	Sherlock HOLMES
HARTMANN Michael	Ben DRYDEN
HART-DAVIS Duff	Sam SHOLTO
HARVESTER Simon	Roger FLEMING; Malcolm KENTON; Heron MURMER; ***Dorian SILK***
HARVEY John	Scott MITCHELL; ***Insp Charlie RESNICK***
HARVEY Marion	Graydon MCKELVIE
HARVEY William F	Athelstan DIGBY
HASTINGS Macdonald	Montague CORK
HASTINGS Michael	Jeff SAUNDERS
HASTINGS W S and Brian HOOKER	Prof CROSBY
HAUGHEY Thomas Brace	Geoffrey WESTON
HAUSER Thomas	Richard MARRETT
HAUSFELD Russell	Eddie GORGON
HAWES Walter	Hamo GRIFFIN
HAWK Hal	***The RENEGADE DETECTIVE***; Oscar SLICK
HAWK John	Insp LINSCOTT; ***Mortimer SARK***
HAWKES Robert	John BOLT
HAWTHORNE Julian	Insp BYRNES; ***Keppel DRAKE***; Fred TYRREL
HAWTON Hector	Asmun HILL; ***Peter MAXWELL and Susan MAXWELL***
HAY James Jr	Jefferson HASTINGS
HAY L F	Archibald BELDRUM and Nigel BLAIR
HAYES Ralph	Alexander (Check Force) CHANE and Vladimer KARLOV; ***Mark STONER***; Agent of Cominsec TAGGART; John (The Hunter) YARD
HAYES William Edward	Arthur HALSTEAD
HAYMAN Mark	Will SHAKESPEAR
HAYMON S T	Insp Ben JURNET
HAYNES Annie	***Insp FURNIVAL***; Insp STODDART
HAYNES Conrad	Prof Harry BISHOP
HAYS Lee	Lt COLUMBO
HAYTER Cecil	Derwent DUFF; ***Mortimer KANE***
HAYTER Sparkle	Robin HUDSON
HAYTHORNE John	Oliver MANDRAKE
HAYWOOD Gar Anthony	Aaron GUNNER
HAYWOOD Steve	Alan ARCHBOLD
HAZEL Fred	LOTTA
HEAD Lee	Lexey Jane PELAZONI
HEAD Matthew	Dr Mary FINNEY and Emily COLLINS
HEALD Tim	***Simon BOGNOR***; Dorothy Mayotte RIGBY
HEALEY Ben	Harcourt D'ESPINAL; ***Paul HEDLEY***; Paul HEDLEY and Harcourt D'ESPINAL
HEALEY Evelyn	Det Supt Horace PLUMMMET
HEALY Eugene P	Paul CRAINE
HEALY Jeremiah M	***John Francis CUDDY***; Philip MARLOWE
HEARD H F	Mr MYCROFT
HEARN Daniel	Giovanni Alberto NOONAN
HEATH Eric	***Dr Wade ANTHONY***; Cornelius CLIFT Jr
HEATH Lester	Sherlock JONES
HEATH Peter	Jason STARR and Adam CYBER
HEATTER Basil	Timothy DEVLIN
HEBDEN Mark	Col MOSTYN; ***Insp Clovis Desire PEL***
HEBERDEN M V	***Desmond SHANNON***; Rick VANNER
HECHT Ben	Dick MCCAREY
HECKSTALL-SMITH Anthony	Insp HYDE
HEDGES Joseph	John STARK
HEED Rufus	Dr KENT

The Authors

HEIDENFELD W	***Sherlock HOLMES***; Dr John H WATSON
HELGERSON Joel	Chet JOHNSON
HELLER Frank	Mr COLLIN
HELLER Keith	George MAN
HELM Peter	Martin RIDGWAY
HELY Elizabeth	Antoine CIRRET
HEMPSTEAD Junius L	THOMPSON
HENAGHAN Jim	Jeff PRIDE
HENDERSON C J	Jack HAGEE
HENDERSON Laurence	Det Sgt Arthur MILTON
HENDERSON M R	Jeanne DONOVAN
HENDERSON William	Ch Const William HENDERSON
HENDRICKS Michael	Rita NOONAN
HENDRICKSON Louise	Amy PRESCOTT
HENDRYX James B	Cpl DOWNEY; ***Connie MORGAN***; Policeman Black John SMITH
HENEGE Thomas	HENRICKSEN
HENRY Clay	Matt ARCHER
HENRY Michael	Det Sgt O'BRIEN and Det Sgt O'NEILL
HENRY O	***Shamrock JOLNES***; TICTOCQ
HENSLEY Joe L	Donald ROBAK
HENTOFF Nathan Irving	Det Noah GREEN and Det Sam MCKIBBON
HERBER William	James REHM
HERMAN Henry	***Insp BENDER***; George GREY
HERNDON Nancy	Det Elena JARVIS
HERNE Huxley	Mortimer HOOD
HERON-MAXWELL Beatrice	Mrs Mollie DELAMERE
HERRING Paul	Insp BOW and Capt KEETCH
HERRON Shaun	MIRO
HERSHATTER Richard L	Rand STANNARD
HERSHMAN Morris	Steve CRANE
HERVEY Evelyn	Harriet UNWIN
HERZOG Evelyn	Sherlock HOLMES
HESKY Olga	Insp Tami SHIMONI
HESS Joan	Ch Arly HANKS; ***Claire MALLOY***
HEWITT Kathleen	Glenda BLAKE
HEXT Harrington	Nicol HART; ***Insp MIDWINTER***
HEYER Georgette	Frank AMBERLEY; ***Supt HANNASYDE***; Insp HEMINGWAY
HEYES Douglas	Lee GORDON; ***Steve MALLORY***; Ray RIPLEY
HEYMAN Evan Lee	Jeff THOMPSON
HIAASEN Carl	***R J DECKER***; Brian KEYES; Mick STRANAHAN
HIGGIN L	Insp WITHERS
HIGGINS George V	***Det FOLEY***; Jerry KENNEDY
HIGGINS Jack	Paul CHAVASSE; ***Liam DEVLIN***; Nick MILLER
HIGGINS Joan	John FIELD
HIGHSMITH Patricia	Insp CORBY; ***Tom RIPLEY***
HILARY Richard	Ezell BARNES
HILD Jack (House name)	Nile BARRABAS
HILD Jack (William BAETZ)	Nile BARRABAS
HILD Jack (Jack GARSIDE)	Nile BARRABAS
HILD Jack (Roland GREEN)	Nile BARRABAS
HILD Jack E (Robin HARDY)	Nile BARRABAS
HILD Jack (Jim MADEVILLE)	Nile BARRABAS
HILD Jack (Alan PHILIPSON)	Nile BARRABAS
HILD Jack H (John PRESTON)	Nile BARRABAS
HILD Jack I (Rich RAINEY)	Nile BARRABAS
HILD Jack J (Joe ROBERTS)	Nile BARRABAS
HILL A F	Dan DENTON
HILL Frederick T	Deake GILBERT
HILL Harry Egbert	Sexton BLAKE
HILL Headon	Elisha CROWE; ***Insp HERON***; Franklin KENNARD; Pte Amos MEARS; Laura METCALF; Kala PERSAD; Radford SHONE; Mark TAVERNER; Sgt TREVOR and Sgt GODBOLD; Montague WARDROP; Sebastian ZAMBRA
HILL John Spencer	Insp Carlo ARBATI
HILL K F	Sarah BROWN
HILL Katharine	Lorna DONAHUE
HILL Lawrence	Insp MACSPORRAN
HILL Peter	Cdr Allan DICE; ***Insp Robert STAUNTON***
HILL Reginald	Insp Lev CHISLENKO; ***Supt Andrew DALZIEL and Sgt/Det Ch Insp Peter PASCOE***; Insp MCHARG; Joe SIXSMITH
HILL Richard	Randall Gatsby SIERRA
HILL W W	Timothy TEALEAF
HILLERMAN Tony	Sgt Jim CHEE; John COTTON; ***Lt Joe LEAPHORN***; Lt Joe LEAPHORN and Sgt Jim CHEE
HILLIARD A R	Judge MANFRED
HILTON James	Colin REVELL
HILTON John Buxton	***Insp Thomas BRUNT***; Supt/Ch Supt Simon KENWORTHY
HIMES Chester	Det 'Grave Digger' JONES and Det 'Coffin' Ed JOHNSON
HIMMEL Richard	John Patrick Aloysius MAGUIRE
HINCKS C Malcolm	Sexton BLAKE; ***PINCHER***
HINKEMEYER Michael T	Sheriff Emil WHIPPLETREE
HINKLE Vernon	***Steve HERSHEY***; Martin WEBB

HINXMAN Margaret	Sheila TRACY
HIRSCHBERG Cornelius	Saul HANDY
HIRSCHFIELD Burt	'Bump' HARWELL
HITCHENS Bert and Dolores HITCHENS	***COLLINS and MCKECHNIE***; John FARREL; Michael KERNEHAN, Chuck REVES and Vic MOINE
HITCHENS Dolores	Jim SADER
HITT James Alfred	Sherlock HOLMES
HJORTSBERG William	Harry ANGEL; ***Harry HOUDINI and Sir Arthur Conan DOYLE***
HOAG Tami	Ch Mitchell HOLT and Megan O'MALLEY
HOBART Donald Bayne	Ch of Plce KENNY
HOBART Robertson	Grant VICKARY
HOBSON Hank	Brad FORD
HOBSON Polly	Insp BASIL
HOCH Edward D	Simon ARK; Sebastian BLUE; Henry BOWFORT; G K CHESTERTON; Carl CRADER and Earl JAZINE; Al DARLAN; Paul DRAYER; Barney HAMET; Dr Sam HAWTHORNE; Sherlock HOLMES; Libby KNOWLES; ***Capt LEOPOLD***; Philip MARLOWE; MCLOVE; Sir Gideon PARROT; Harry PONDER; Tommy PRESTON; RAND; Sgt ROMANO; Nick VELVET
HOCKING Anne	Insp/Supt William AUSTEN
HOCKING Joseph	Jaspar POOLE
HOCKING Silas	Latimer FIELD
HODEL Michael P and Sean M WRIGHT	Mycroft HOLMES and Sherlock HOLMES
HODGES Carl G	Bob RUFF
HODGKIN M R	Nora PICKHAM
HODGSON William Hope	***CARNACKI***; Capt GAULT
HOEG Peter	Smilla JASPERSON
HOFF Ebbe Curtis and Phebe M HOFF	Sherlock HOLMES
HOFFMAN Banesh	Sherlock HOLMES
HOFFMAN E T A	Mlle DE SCUDERI
HOGAN John C	Sherlock HOLMES
HOGSTRAND Olle	Ch Insp Lars KOLLIN
HOLDEN Craig	Det Frank BRANDON and Dr Adrian LANCASTER
HOLDEN Genevieve	***Hank FERRELL***; Lt Al WHITE
HOLDEN J Railton	Spider' STOCKWELL
HOLDING Elizabeth Sanxay	Lt LEVY
HOLDING James	King DANWORTH and Martin LEROY; ***Hal JOHNSON***
HOLDSTOCK Robert P	George BULMAN
HOLLAND Isabelle	***Rev Claire ALDINGTON***; Susan GRENELLE and Ch Mark CZERNICK
HOLLANDER Nathan	HARKER
HOLLEY Helen	Tessie VENABLE
HOLLINGSWORTH Leonard	Insp/Supt ADAMS
HOLMAN Hugh	***Sheriff MACREADY***; Norman TRAVIS
HOLME Timothy	Insp Achille PERONI
HOLMES Capt Howard	The NEVER-FAIL DETECTIVE
HOLMES Gordon	Insp Charles François FURNEAUX
HOLMES Grant	Steve HARVESTER
HOLMES H H	Sister URSULA
HOLMES Samuel	Sgt FOWELL
HOLT Deben	Rickard 'Ricky' BRITTON
HOLT Gavin	***Prof Luther BASTION***; Joel SABER; Sherrett YORK
HOLT Hazel	Mrs Sheila MALLORY
HOLT Henry	Mike LOGAN; ***Insp Jim SILVER***; Insp Jim SILVER and Mike LOGAN
HOLT Samuel	Samuel HOLT
HOLTON Leonard	Father Joseph BREDDER
HOME Michael	John BENHAM
HOMES Geoffrey	Red BAILEY; ***Robin BISHOP***; Humphrey CAMPBELL; Humphrey CAMPBELL and Robin BISHOP; Jose Manuel MADERO
HOME-GALL Edward R	Sexton BLAKE
HONE Joseph	Peter MARLOW
HOOD Margaret Page	Gil DONAN
HOOD Stephen	Sexton BLAKE
HOOK S Clarke	The CARAVAN DETECTIVE
HOPE Stanton	Sexton BLAKE; ***Ferrers LOCKE***
HOPKINS Kenneth	Gerry LEE; ***Prof Gideon MANCIPLE and Dr William BLOW***
HOPKINS Nevil Monroe	Mason BRANT
HOPKINS R Thurston	Valentine VAUGHAN
HOPKINS Stanley Jr	Peter MARRELL
HORANSKY Ruby	Nikki TRAKOS
HORLER Sydney	***Sir Harker BELLAMY***; Brett CARSTAIRS; 'Bunny' CHIPSTEAD; Insp H EMP; Sir Brian FORDINGHAME and Baron VESSELOFFSKY; Sir Brian FORDINGHAME; Gerald (Nighthawk) FROST; Ian HEATH; Martin HUISH; Sir William KIRBY; Sir Charles KNIGHTLEY; Gerald LISSENDALE; Justin (The Ace) MARCH; Ch Const George MEATYARD; Sebastian QUIN; Peter SCARLETT; The Hon Timothy Overbury 'Tiger' STANDISH and Sir Harker BELLAMY; Timothy Overbury 'Tiger' STANDISH; Baron VESSELOFFSKY; Robert WYNNTON
HORNIG Doug	Steven KIRK; ***Loren SWIFT***
HORNSBY Wendy	***Maggie MACGOWEN***; Roger TEJEDA
HORNUNG E W	A J RAFFLES
HOROWITZ Floyd R	***Hairlock HOLMES***; Sherlock HOLMES
HORTON Mileson and Thomas PEMBROKE	Sgt ELLIS
HORWITZ Merle	Harvey ACE
HOSSENT Harry	Max HEALD

HOUGH S B	Det Ch Insp BRENTFORD
HOUGHAM Arthur	Amadour BEVAN
HOUSEHOLD Geoffrey	Pedro GONZALES; ***Roger TAINE***
HOWARD Hartley	***Glenn BOWMAN***; Philip SCOTT
HOWARD Jack	***John MERRY***; OLD BRIGHTON
HOWARD James A	***Steve ASHE***; Paul Kenneth KANE
HOWARD John M	Terence Everard Christopher SHARP
HOWARD Police Captain	The BORDER LINE DETECTIVE; CHIP; ***LIGHTNING LUKE***; LITTLE FERRET; MONTE; MOUNTED POLICEMAN MARK; Nick NEVERSEEN; OLD DOUBLE FACE; OLD SAFETY; OLD WOLF; SILENT; SLENDER SAUL; Wade WESTON; YOUNG WEASEL; YOUNG FEARLESS
HOWARD Robert E	***Solomon KANE***; King KULL
HOWARD Tom	Tom HOWARD
HOWARD Vechel	Johnny CHURCH
HOWE Melody Johnson	Claire CONRAD
HOWELL Wayne	Sherlock HOLMES
HOWES Royce	Ben LUCIUS
HOWIE Edith	***Peter HOLGATE***; Ross LANGDON
HOWLETT John	Joe MORGAN
HOYT Richard	James BURLANE; ***John DENSON*** and Pamela YEW; John DENSON
HUBBARD Margaret Ann	Sister SIMON; ***Mother THEODORE***
HUBBARD P M	Margaret CANNING; ***Peter GRANT***; Mark HAWKINS
HUBBELL Ned	Creighton HOLMES
HUEBNER Frederick D	Matthew RIORDAN
HUGGINS Roy	***Stuart BAILEY***; Danny FULLER
HUGHART Barry	Li KAO
HUGHES Babette Plechner	Prof Ian CRAIG
HUGHES Dorothy B	Hugh DENSMORE; Sherlock HOLMES; Det Brub NICOLAI; ***Insp TOBIN***
HUGHES G F	Bill HOLMES
HUGHES Richard	Sam MCCHESNEY
HUGHES Russell	Wilmurt ROBIN
HUGHES William	George WILLIS
HUGI Maurice G	Martin SPEED
HUGO Richard	Al BARNES
HUGO Victor Marie	Insp JAVETT
HULL Richard	Insp FENBY
HULME-BEAMAN Emeric	OZMAR
HULTMAN Helen Joan	Tim ASHER; Insp ***Dave BRATTON***
HUME David	***Mick CARDBY***; Tony CARTER; Det Insp SANDERSON
HUME Fergus	Valentine BELT; Insp BLAIR; Insp CHARD; Lucian DENZIL; DOVE; Mr DOWKER; Octavius FANKS; Gerald FOSTER; Absolom GEBB; ***Insp Samuel GORBY***; Maj Laurence JEN; Dr LUKE; Laurence MALLOW; Archie MAXWELL; Paul MEXTON; Det Sgt O'BYRNE; Insp PRINCE; Hagar STANLEY; Spencer TAIT and DENHAM; Gilbert THRESHAM and Percy BARSTONE; Insp TINKLER; Mr TORRY; Insp TRUMPET; Insp WOKE
HUNT Charlotte	Dr Paul HOLTON
HUNT E Howard	Steve BENTLEY; Pete NOVAK; ***Jack NOVAK***
HUNT Kyle	Emmanuel CELLINI
HUNT Peter	Alan MILLER
HUNT Richard	Det Ch Insp Sidney WALSH
HUNTER Alan	Insp/Ch Supt George GENTLY
HUNTER Jack D	Roger WAGNER
HUNTER John	Sexton BLAKE; ***Bill LANGLEY***
HUNTER Robin	Simon QUARRY
HUNTINGDON John	Horton FORBES
HURD Douglas	HARVEY
HURLBUT Edward H	Jack LANAGAN
HURLEY Gene	Tim FLAHERTY
HURST Norman	Herbert DARRENT
HURST S B H	Horace SINNAT
HURT Freda	Insp Herbert BROOM
HUSTON Fran	Nichole SWEET
HUSTON H C	Ch Charles BAKER
HUTCHINSON Horace G	***Insp SPENS***; Emil TABOR
HUTTON J F	Don PAULSON
HUXLEY Elspeth	Alexander BARTON; ***Supt VACHELL***
HYAMS Joe	Punch ROBERTS and Bonny CUTLER
HYDE John George Norman	John Byron HYDE
HYNE C J Cutcliffe	GRAYSON; Mr HORROCKS; ***Capt Owen KETTLE***; Cdr MCTURK

— I —

IAMS Jack	Rocky ROCKWELL
IMBERT-TERRY Sir Henry	Det Insp DU CAS
INCHBALD Peter	***Insp Franco CORTI***; Insp Frank SHORT
INCHBALD Ralph	Col PATERNOSTER
INFANTE Anne	Micky DOUGLAS
INGATE Mary	Ann HALES
INIGO Martin	Don HAWKER
INNES Hammond	John SANDS
INNES Michael	***Insp/Commiss John APPLEBY***; Insp/Commiss John APPLEBY and Prof Charles HONEYBATH; Insp CADOGAN; Prof Charles HONEYBATH
INNES Murray M	COSGROVE
ION Dr Watts	Sheerluck OHMS
IRALDI James C	Sherlock HOLMES
IRISH William	Det BURGESS
IRONSIDE Elizabeth	George SINCLAIR
IRONSIDE John	Det Insp John FREEMAN
IRVINE R R	Bob CHRISTOPHER
IRVINE Robert	Moroni TRAVELER
IRVING Alexander	Anthony POST
IRWIN Inez Haynes	Patrick O'BRIEN
IRWIN Wallace	Publius Manlius SCRIBO
ISAACS Susan	***Rosie MYERS***; Nelson SHARPE and Judith SINGER
ISLAY Nicholas	Sydney VANE
ISON Graham	***Det Ch Supt Thomas FOX***; Supt John GAFFNEY and Det Ch Supt Thomas FOX; Supt John GAFFNEY
ISRAEL Peter	**Benjamin Franklin CAGE**; Charles CAMELOT

— J —

JACK Alex	GINGKO
JACK Colin	Sherlock HOLMES
JACKS Jeff	Shep STONE
JACKSON Charles Ross	Quintus OAKES
JACKSON Donald W	Sherlock HOLMES
JACKSON Giles	Nile BOYD
JACKSON Jon A	Sgt MULHEISEN
JACKSON Ken	***Jud BLADE***; Nathan NECESSARY
JACKSON Lewis	Sexton BLAKE
JACKSON Marion J A	Abigail Patience DANFORTH
JACKSON Robert	YOEMAN
JACKSON Wallace	***Insp Clancy MARTIN***; Archibald PENNY
JACOBS T C H	***Ch Insp BARNARD***; Det Supt John BELLAMY; Temple FORTUNE; Jim MALONE; Dr Ian MCANDREW; Capt Jacques RADFORD and Tony ANDERSON; Reggie RUGGLES and Sgt TROTTER; Mike SETON
JACOBSON Edith and Ejler JACOBSON	The BLEEDER; ***Nat PERRY***
JACOBSON John	Sherlock HOLMES; ***Tide POOLES***
JACOT B L	Winslow MOULT
JACQUEMARD-SENECAL	Supt DULLAC
JACQUES Horton	Joe TRIMO
JAEDIKER Kermit	Louis LAIT
JAFFE Michael	Joe BURNS
JAFFEE Mary and Irvine JAFFEE	Sherlock HOLMES
JAHN Michael	Frank MACBRIDE and Pete RYAN; ***Jim ROCKFORD***
JAKES John	Johnny HAVOC
JAMES Bill	Ch Supt Colin HARPUR
JAMES Breni	Sgt Gunnar MATSON
JAMES Franklin	Mickey RICHARDS
JAMES P D	***Insp/Cdr Adam DALGLIESH***; Cordelia GRAY
JAMES Police Captain	***Little LIGHTNING***; The REVENUE DETECTIVE
JAMESON Storm	David PENN
JAMIESON Leland	Dan GREGORY
JANCE J A	***Det J P BEAUMONT***; Sheriff Joanna BRADY
JANES J Robert	Insp ST CYR and Hermann KOHLER
JANSON Hank (House name)	Hank JANSON
JANSON Hank (Stephen Daniel FRANCES)	Hank JANSON
JANSON Hank (Harry HOBSON)	Hank JANSON
JANSON Hank D (James MOFFATT)	Hank JANSON
JANSON Hank (Colin SIMPSON)	Hank JANSON
JANSON Hank F (Victor George Charles NORWOOD)	Hank JANSON
JAPRISOT Sebastien	Insp GRAZZONI
JARDINE Quintin	Insp SKINNER
JARDINE Warwick	Sexton BLAKE
JARRET Cora	Prof Leonidas AMES and Mr HOOPES
JASON	JASON
JASON Stuart A (House name)	The BUTCHER
JASON Stuart B (Michael Angelo AVALLONE Jr)	The BUTCHER
JASON Stuart C (Lee Floren)	The BUTCHER
JAY Charlotte	***William BROOKE***; Emma WARWICK
JAY Simon	Dr MUCH

The Authors

JEFFERIES Ian	Sgt CRAIG
JEFFERS H Paul	Sherlock HOLMES and Theodore ROOSEVELT; Harry MACNEIL; ***David MORGAN***
JEFFREYS J G	Bow Street Runner Jeremy STURROCK
JEFFRIES Roderic	***Insp Enrique ALVAREZ***; Insp CLAYTON; Supt POPE; Bill STEMPLE
JENKINS Geoffrey	Cdr Geoffrey PEACE
JENKINS Herbert	***Malcolm SAGE***; Mr STIFFSON
JENKINS Jerry	Margo FRANKLIN and Philip SPENCE; ***Jennifer GREY***; Dallas O'NEIL
JENKINS Will F	James JARNEGAN
JEPSON Edgar	***Lord BARRADINE***; Lord Rupert GARTHOYLE; TINKER
JEPSON Edgar and Maurice LEBLANC	Arsène LUPIN
JEPSON Edgar and Robert EUSTACE	Ruth KELSTERN
JEPSON Selwyn	Eve GILL; Ian MACARTHUR; John PERRIN; ***Roger SPAIN***
JERINA Carol	Jackson FURY
JEROME Gilbert	Jere CLINCH; ***Jack DONAHUE***; The GREEK DETECTIVE; Isaac LAZARUS; Chris WREN
JEROME Owen Fox	Philip MACCRAY; Philip MACCRAY and Artemus GRAHAM; ***George ROBIN***
JESSE F Tennyson	Solange FONTAINE
JESSUP Richard	Lt Chester WIERLOCK
JEVONS Marshall	Prof Henry SPEARMAN
JOBSON A E	Russell HOWARD
JOBSON Hamilton	Insp/Supt ANDERS
JOHN Hendrix	John HAMMOND
JOHN Owen	Haggai GODIN
JOHNS Gilbert	Sexton BLAKE
JOHNS Veronica Parker	***Webster FLAGG***; Agatha WELCH
JOHNS W E	***'BIGGLES'***; 'Steeley' DELAROY; Dr VANE
JOHNSON B B	Richard SPADE
JOHNSON Duff	'Gutsy' MORGAN
JOHNSON E Richard	Tony LONTO
JOHNSON Frank	CRIMSON MASK
JOHNSON James L	SEBASTIAN
JOHNSON Maurice C	Bob ROLLINS
JOHNSON Philip	Blackie WHITE
JOHNSON Ryerson	Michael SHAYNE
JOHNSON Steve	Doug ORLANDO
JOHNSON W Bolingbroke	Gilda GORHAM
JOHNSTON Brian	Winston WYC
JOHNSTON Frank	Insp DURSLEY
JOHNSTON Gunnar	SILBER
JOHNSTON J Jeremy	Sherlock HOLMES
JOHNSTON Jane	Louisa EVANS
JOHNSTON Madeleine	Noah BRADSHAW
JOHNSTON Ronald	James BRUCE
JOHNSTON Velda	***Deborah CHANNING***; Catherine MAYHEW
JOHNSTON William	BANYON; BRONSON; KLUTE; Capt NICE; Maxwell SMART; Dick TRACY; ***John WOODRUFF and Tony NOVELLO***
JON Montague	Stephen KALE
JONES Arthur E	Felix HOLLIDAY
JONES Barry	Sherlock HOLMES
JONES Bradshaw	Claude RAVEL
JONES Charles Reed	Insp James CONWAY; ***Leighton SWIFT***
JONES Cleo	Chris DANVILLE
JONES Elwyn	***Supt Charles BARLOW***; Dick BARTON
JONES Eugene	Byron HUGHES
JONES G Wayman	Tony (Black Bat) QUINN
JONES H Llewellyn	Fraser TODD
JONES Hazel Wynn	Emma SHAW
JONES J G	Sexton BLAKE
JONES James	Frank 'Lobo' DAVIES
JONES Jennifer	Daisy Jane MOTT
JONES Kelvin I	***Dr John CARTER***; Sherlock HOLMES
JONES Neil R	Miller RAND
JONES P H	Sherlock HOLMES, Insp Charlie CHAN and Hercule POIROT
JONES R W	Insp EVANS and Sgt BEDDOES
JORDAN Cathleen	Will GRAY
JORDAN David	Tom CANE and CONDON
JORDAN Jennifer	Barry VAUGHAN and Dee VAUGHAN
JOSEPH Alan	LOGAN
JOSEPH-RENAUD Jean	***Monsieur CHEVENARD***; Dr MEPHISTO and Monsieur HIGNETTE
JOYCE Cyril	Greg ALLARD; CHARD; ***Insp Pat STOCKTON***
JUDD Frances K	Kay TRACEY
JUDSON Edward Zane Carroll	The NAVAL DETECTIVE
JUNIPER Alex	Sgt Jake MURPHY
JUTA Henry	Donald FRASER

—K—

KA	Mrs Julia Herlock SHOMES
KABAL A M	David MEDINA
KAHN Michael A	Rachel GOLD
KAHN W B	Oilock COMBS
KAINS Josephine	Terry SPRING
KALISH Robert	Skipper GOULD
KALLEN Lucille	C B GREENFIELD
KAMARCK Lawrence	Charlie SKRAGG
KAMINSKY Stuart M	Maureen DIETZ and Helen KATZ; Sherlock HOLMES; Philip MARLOWE; Toby PETERS, Gary COOPER and Ernest HEMINGWAY; Toby PETERS and Bette DAVIS; Toby PETERS, William FAULKNER and Bela LUGOSI; Toby PETERS, Ian FLEMING and MARX BROTHERS; ***Toby PETERS and Errol FLYNN***; Toby PETERS and Clark GABLE; Toby PETERS and Judy GARLAND; Toby PETERS and Dashiell HAMMETT; Toby PETERS, Howard HUGHES and Basil RATHBONE; Toby PETERS and Emmett KELLY; Toby PETERS and Eleanor ROOSEVELT; Toby PETERS and Joe LOUIS; Toby PETERS and Leopold STOKOWSKI; Toby PETERS and Mae WEST; Insp Porfiry Petrovich ROSTNIKOV
KAMITSES Zoe	Courtney BROOKS
KANE Abel	SLAUGHTER
KANE Bob	BATMAN
KANE Frank	Mickey DENTON; ***Johnny LIDDELL***; Johnny LIDDELL and Mickey DENTON
KANE Henry	***Peter CHAMBERS***; Peter CHAMBERS and Marla TRENT; MCGREGOR; Marla TRENT
KANE	Martin KANE
KANTNER Rob	Ben PERKINS
KANTOR MacKinlay	***Matt EDWARDS***; Max GRAME; Lt Cliff KENNEDY; Daniel ROSS
KAPLAN Arthur	Charity BAY
KARL M S	Pete BRADY
KARLSON Katherine E	Cerlocio OLMEZ
KARMAN Mal	Jay HILLER
KARNEY Jack	Jim BREEN
KARTA Nat	Dana DALLAS
KARTUN Derek	Alfred BAUM
KASER Arthur Le Roy	MUSH and POKE
KASTLE Herbert D	Sgt Edmund ROERSCH
KATCHER Leo	Richard LANDON
KATZ Jon	Kit DELEEUW
KATZ Michael J	Murray GLICK
KATZ Robert	***Tony MCINTYRE***; Zack ROBERTS
KATZ William	Spencer CROSS-WADE
KATZENBACH John	Malcolm ANDERSON
KAUFFMAN Reginald Wright	***Frances BAIRD***; Sam BURTON and Frances BAIRD
KAUFMAN Wolfe	Dick ANDERSON
KAVANAGH Dan	Nick DUFFY
KAY Stuart	Jack HENLEY
KAYE M M	***Lash HOLDEN and Dany ASHTON***; Copper RANDAL
KAYE Marvin	***Marty GOLD***; Sherlock HOLMES; Hilary QUAYLE
KAYE William	Charles 'Chickie' FRENCH
KEANE John	Sherlock BONES
KEATE E M	Sgt/Insp/Supt MARGETSON
KEATING H R F	CRAGGS; ***Insp Ganesh GHOTE***; Sherlock HOLMES; Supt HOWARD; Dorothy Mayotte RIGBY; Insp SYLVESTER
KEECH Scott	Insp Jeff ADAMS and Kate SHAW
KEEGAN Alex	Det Const Caz FLOOD
KEELER Harry Stephen	Margaret ANNISTER; Dr BURKHALTER; Y CHEUNG; Elsa COLBY; David CROSBY; Jeff DARRELL; Simon GRUNDT; Billy HEMPLE; X JONES; Jimmie KENTLAND; Bob LANDRELL; ***Angus MACWHORTER***; Angus MACWHORTER and Sheriff Bugrus DUCKHOUSE; Terry O'ROURKE
KEELER Harry Stephen and Hazel GOODWIN	Dr Everett EDWARDS; ***Angus MACWHORTER***; Tuddleton TROTTER
KEENAN William	John MARNE
KEENE Carolyn	Nancy DREW
KEENE Day	***Johnny ALOHA***; Les FERRON
KEENE Faraday	Prof Leonidas AMES and Mr HOOPES
KEITH Carlton	Jeffrey GREEN
KEITH David	Ted S WEAVER
KELLAND Clarence Budington	Scattergood BAINES
KELLER David H	TAINE OF SAN FRANCISCO
KELLERMAN Dan	Jesse HELLER
KELLERMAN Faye	Det Peter DECKER
KELLERMAN Jonathan	Dr Alex DELAWARE
KELLEY Patrick A	Harry CALDERWOOD
KELLOCK Harold	Zinsheimer HOLMES
KELLY Bill	Pepperoni HERO
KELLY Mary	NICHOLSON; ***Insp Brett NIGHTINGALE***
KELLY Nora	Gillian ADAMS
KELLY Susan	***Det Jack LINGEMANN and Liz CONNORS***; Ch Insp Nick TREVELLYAN
KELLY Terence	Sergei ROLF
KELLY Tim J	***Insp HAWKSHAW***; Sherlock HOLMES
KELLY Tim J and Jack SHARKEY	Sherlock HOLMES
KELNER Toni L P	Laura FLEMING
KELSEY Vera	Dan CUMBERLAND; ***Lt DIEGO***
KELSO Jack	Reginald DELAMERE
KEMELMAN Harry	***Rabbi David SMALL***; Prof Nicky WELT

KEMP Harold	Insp Jimmy BRENT
KEMP Sarah	Tina MAY
KEMPRECOS Paul	'Soc' SOCARIDES
KENDRICK Baynard	Cliff CHANDLER; ***Duncan MACLAIN***; Miles Standish RICE
KENEALY Arabella	Lord SYFRET
KENMORE Frank	Colin SMALLPIECE
KENNEALY G P	Peter FLYNN
KENNEALY Jerry	Nick POLO
KENNEDY Adam	Roy TUCKER
KENNEDY Bruce	Sherlock HOLMES
KENNEDY Elliot	Griff DEXTER
KENNEDY George	George KENNEDY
KENNEDY Milward	***Gregory AMOR***; Sir George BULL; Supt COLE; Insp CORNFORD; Supt GUEST; Mr TRUEFITT
KENNEDY Robert Milward	Insp CORNFORD
KENNEY Susan	Roz HOWARD
KENNY Robert	Christian DOOM
KENRICK Tony	Hugh DECKER; Det Billy MARCUS; ***Jimmy PELHAM***; Bill VERECKER
KENT Arthur	Sexton BLAKE
KENT David	Jason BURR
KENYON Larry	Don MILES
KENYON Michael	Arthur APPLEYARD; Prof FOLEY; Supt O'MALLEY; Insp/Ch Insp Harry PECKOVER and Supt O'MALLEY; ***Insp/Ch Insp Harry PECKOVER***; Det Const Jason TWITTY
KERNAHAN Coulson	MARTEN; ***RISSLER***
KERNER Annette	Annette KERNER
KERR Philip	Yevgeni Ivanovitch GRUSHKO; Bernard GUNTHER; ***Ch Insp 'Jake' JAKOWICZ***
KETCHUM Philip	Stephen BARTH; George CLAY
KEVERNE Richard	Simon ARTIFEX; Sir Christopher HAZZARD; ***Insp MACE***; Franklin PARRY and Leonard HARRIS
KEY Sam	Prof Arnold RHYMER
KEY Sean A	CAIN
KEYES Frances Parkinson	Allan LAMBERT
KEYHOE Donald E	Yen SIN
KEYSTONE Oliver	Paul PLUSH
KIDDY Maurice G	Stonewall STEEVENS
KIEFER Warren	Michael VERNON
KIENZLE William X	Father Robert KOESLER
KIJEWSKI Karen	Kat COLORADO
KIKER Douglas	'Mac' MACFARLAND
KILGORE Axel	Hank (The Mercenary) FROST
KILLOUGH Lee	Janna BRILL and Mahlon MAXWELL
KILPATRICK Florence	ELIZABETH
KILVINGTON Edwin	Crispin QUAYNE
KINDON Thomas	Peregrine SMITH
KING C Daly	Dr Frank HAYVIER, ***Lt Michael LORD***; Dr Love Rees PONS, Dr Malcolm PLECKS and Prof Knott Coe MITTLE; Mr Trevis TARRANT
KING Frank	Insp CHAMBERS; ***Clive 'Dormouse' CONRAD***; Insp GLOOM; Dr Frank KING; Clarence KNIGHT; O'ROURKE; Sally TEPPER
KING Hilary	Sexton BLAKE
KING Laurie R	Sherlock HOLMES; Det Kate MARTINELLI and ***Det Al HAWKINS***
KING Rufus	Reginald DE PUYSTER; Prof Stuff DRISCOLL; ***Cotton MOON***; Dr Colin STARR; Lt VALCOUR
KING Sherwood	James Gaylord DURSTINE
KING Stephen	Sherlock HOLMES
KING T Stanleyan	***Dixon BRETT***; Scarsdale WARING
KING T W	Calvert COLE
KINGSBURY Kate	Cecily SINCLAIR
KINGSLEY-SMITH Terence	Pete MCCOY
KINGSMILL Hugh	Sherlock HOLMES and A J RAFFLES
KINGSTON Charles	Insp WAKE
KINGSTON Keedy	Keedy KINGSTON
KINSLEY Lawrence	Jason T O'NEIL
KIRBY Arthur (Arthur MACLEAN)	Sexton BLAKE
KIRBY Arthur (Stephen Daniel FRANCES)	Sexton BLAKE
KIRBY Dallas	Victor GARRISON
KIRK Michael	Andrew LAIRD
KIRK Philip	BUTLER
KIRST Hans Hellmut	Supt Konstantin KELLER
KITCHIN C H B	Malcolm WARREN
KITTREDGE Mary	Edwina CRUSOE; ***Charlotte KENT***
KJELL Bradley	Shrock HOLMES; ***Tide POOLES***
KLAICH Dolores	Tyler DIVINE
KLAWANS Harold L	Paul RICHARDSON
KLEIN Norman	Harvey CHURCH; ***Kennedy JONES***
KLINE Penny	Anna MCCOLL
KLINGER Henry	Lt Shomri SHOMAR
KLINGSBERG Harry M	John DOOWINKLE
KNICKMEYER Steve	Steve CRANMER
KNIGHT Adam	Steve CONACHER
KNIGHT Alanna	Insp Jeremy FARO
KNIGHT Clifford	Prof Huntoon ROGERS
KNIGHT David	Shell SCOTT
KNIGHT Edward Frederick	Arthur ALLEN
KNIGHT Eric	Sam SMALL
KNIGHT Kathleen Moore	Margot BLAIR; ***Elisha MACOMBER***
KNIGHT Kathryn Lasky	Callista JACOBS
KNIGHT Leonard	Jerry SCANT; ***Colby STACK***
KNOX Bill	Ch Offr Webb CARRICK; ***Det Ch Insp Colin THANE and Insp Phil MOSS***
KNOX Bill and Edward BOYD	Daniel PIKE
KNOX Ronald A	***Miles BREDON***; Miles BREDON and Angela BREDON; William CARMICHAEL; Sherlock HOLMES
KOBLER John	Peter QUEST
KOEHLER Robert Portner	Pecos APPLEBY; Al BRANSON; Maj Avery GREGG and Tony ELLIS; ***Les IVEY***
KOENIG Laird	Susannah BARTOK
KOMO Dolores	Clio BROWN
KOOTZ Samuel Melvin	Jason EMORY
KOTZWINKLE William	Insp MANTIS; ***Paul PICARD***
KRAFT Gabrielle	Doyle Dean MCCOY and Jerry ZALMAN
KRASNER William	Sam BIRGE
KRASNEY Samuel A	***Lt Ben KRAHMER***; Lt Abe LARSON
KRICH Rochelle Majer	Det Jessica DRAKE
KROHN William	Richard SHEILAN
KRUGER Mary	Det Matt DEVLIN
KRUGER Paul	Phil KRAMER; ***Vince LATIMER***
KUMMER Frederic Arnold	***Owen MORGAN***; Judge Henry TYSON; Elinor VANCE
KUMMER Frederic Arnold and Basil MITCHELL	Shirley HOLMES
KURLAND Michael	***Peter CARTHAGE***; Lord DARCY; Sherlock HOLMES
KURNITZ Harry	Mike ZORN
KUTAK Rosemary	Dr Marc CASTLEMAN
KUTCH Archie	YOUNG SLEUTH
KUTTNER Henry	Dr Michael GRAY
KYD Thomas	Andrew ONE; ***Det Sam PHELAN***; Gilbert E WHELDON
KYLE Duncan	Dorothy Mayotte RIGBY
KYLE Robert	Ben GATES
KYLE Sefton	Insp J RASON

—L—

LA CROIX Arda	The YANKEE DOODLE DETECTIVE
LA FRANCE Marston	Rick LARKAN
LA PLANTE Jerry	Vance (The Chameleon) GARDE
LA PLANTE Lynda	Lorraine PAGE
LA ROCHE K Alison	Ch Rufus Albert JONES and Barbara CREW
LACEY Peter	Mordecai 'Maudie' MORGAN
LACEY Sarah	Leah HUNTER
LACY Ed	Marty BOND; Hal DARLING; Barney HARRIS; Lee HAYES; ***Toussaint 'Touie' MOORE***; Matt RANZINO; William WALLACE; Dave WINTINO
LADLINE Robert	J A 'Rem' REMINGTON
LAFLIN Jack	Gregory HILLER; ***Peter WINSTON***
LAFORE Laurence Davis	Walter PAYNE and Ritchie PAYNE
LAINE Annabel	Charles DOMAY
LAING Alexander	Dr SCARLETT
LAING Kenneth	'Rolling' STONE
LAING Patrick	Patrick LAING
LAIT Jack	POLACK ANNIE
LAIT Robert	Supt BRONT
LAKE M D	Peggy O'NEILL
LAMB J Dayne	Teal STEWART
LAMB J J	Zachariah Tobias ROLF
LAMB Lynton	Supt QUILL and Insp GLOVER
LAMB Margaret	Penny MILLER
LAMBE Michael	Sherlock HOLMES
LAMBERT Rosa and Dudley LAMBERT	Glyn MORGAN
LAMBOT Isobel	Commissaire ORLOFF
LAND Jon	Blaine MCCRACKEN
LAND Myrick	Leo DURGAN
LANDON Christopher	***Harry KENT***; Bob ROSS
LANDON Herman	The GRAY PHANTOM; ***The PICAROON***
LANDON Hilary	Timothy DREWER
LANDSDOWNE Andrew	***LANDSDOWNE***; A SCOTLAND YARD DETECTIVE
LANE Gret	John BARRIN and Kate MARSH; ***Insp HOOK***; Kate MARSH
LANE Jeremy	Whitney WHEAT
LANE Willoughby	***BILLY THE PAGE***; Sherlock HOLMES
LANG Brad	Fred CROCKETT
LANG Maria	Christer WICK
LANGHAM James R	Samuel G ABBOTT
LANGLEY Bob	Martin SEGUNDO
LANGLEY Lee	Det Christopher JENSEN and Prof Natalie KEITH
LANGTON Jane	Homer KELLY
LANHAM Edwin	***Lt GRAY***; Frank LUTHER; Lt MADIGAN
LANIER Sterling E	Brig FFELLOWES
LAPIERRE Janet	Meg HALLORAN and Ch Vince GUTIEREZ
LARBALESTIER P G	Insp Michael FARRANT
LARIAR Lawrence	Homer BULL; Steve GANT; ***Mike WELLS***
LARKIN R T	The DONNA
LARSEN Gaylord D	Jason BRADLEY; Raymond CHANDLER; ***Henry GARRETT***
LARSON Charles	Nils-Frederik BLIXEN
LARSON Glen A and Roger HILL	Michael LONG
LASSITER Adam	DENNISON

The Authors

LATHAM Brad	Bill (The Hook) LOCKWOOD
LATHEN Emma	John Putnam THATCHER
LATIMER Jonathan	Richard BLAKE; ***Sam CLAY***; William CRANE; Steve CRAVEN
LATTA Gordon	ARNHOLT
LAUBEN Philip	Homer CLAY
LAUMER Keith	Joe SHAW
LAUNAY Droo	Adam FLUTE
LAURENCE Gerald	Natalie Dauntless FISHER
LAURENCE Janet	Darina LISLE
LAURENCE John	Sam BECKETT
LAURENSON R M	Marc JORDAN
LAURIA Frank	Dr Owen ORIENT
LAURISTON Victor	Harry BURNVILLE
LAW Janice	Anna PETERS
LAWRENCE David	Danny LEATHER
LAWRENCE Hilda	Mark EAST
LAWRENCE James D	Angela HARPE
LAWRENCE John	Lt Marty MARQUIS
LAWRENCE Kelly	Brian DESMOND
LAWRENCE Margery	***Miss BRANDT***; Miles PENNOYER
LAWRENCE Michael	Johnny AMSTERDAM
LE BRETON Thomas	Jo CRUPPER
LE CARRE John	George SMILEY
LE FANU Sheridan	David ARDEN
LE GRAND Leon	Michael BERESFORD
LEACOCK Stephen Butler	The GREAT DETECTIVE
LEADER Charles	David CHAN; ***Paul MASON***; Ric MCADDEN; Mike MCCALL
LEARMONTH David	Silas WORTENHEIMER
LEASOR James	***Dr Jason LOVE***; Dorothy Mayotte RIGBY
LEATHER Edwin	Rupert CONWAY
LEBLANC Maurice	***Arsène LUPIN***; Arsène LUPIN and Herlock SHOLMES; Holmlock SHEARS and Arsène LUPIN
LEDGARD Henry and Andrew SINGER	Sherlock HOLMES
LEE Austin	Flora HOGG
LEE Babs	Argus STEELE
LEE Babs and Clare Castler SAUNDERS	Argus STEELE
LEE Christopher	Insp LEONARD
LEE Edward	Arthur 'Red' BLAKE and Dan WHEELER
LEE Elsie	Sam BENEDICT
LEE Gerald	Insp CROWLEY
LEE Gypsy Rose	Gypsy Rose LEE and Biff BRANNIGAN
LEE Jennette	Millicent NEWBERRY
LEE John	Brian DOUGLAS
LEE Norma	Norma 'Nicky' LEE
LEE Old Cap	John FAY
LEE W W	Jefferson BIRCH
LEEK Margaret	Stephen MARRYAT
LEES Dan	Jeff PLUMMER
LEES R H	Peter Carstan RANDALL
LEHMANN R C	Picklock HOLES
LEIGH Robert	Sam CARROLL
LEIGHTON Barbara	Felicity TRAVERS
LEIGHTON Marie Conor	Lucille DARE; ***Michael DRED***; Joan MAR
LEITFRED Robert H	Simon CROLE
LEJEUNE Anthony	***Adam GIFFORD***; Prof James GLOWREY
LEMARCHAND Elizabeth	***Det Supt Tom POLLARD***; Insp Tom WHARTON
LENEHAN J C	***Insp KILBY***; Charlie RYAN
LENNON John	Shamrock WOMLBS
LENTON Anthony	Graham DARREN
LEON Donna	Commiss Guido BRUNETTI
LEONARD Charles L	Paul KILGERRIN
LEONARD Elmore	Raymond CRUZ; Joe LA BRAVA; Harry MITCHELL; Vincent MORA; ***Frank RYAN***; Nolen TYNER
LEQUEUX William	Raoul BECQ; Dr Villiers BEETHAM-SAUNDERS; BERYL; BLEKE; Clifton CLEEVE; DELMASSO and BRAY; DONOVAN; Theodore DROST; John DURSTON; Ronald EWART; Geoffrey FALCONER; Arthur HEATHER; Gerald INGRAM; ***Allan KENNEDY***; Kershaw KIRK; William LEQUEUX; Helen MARKLOVE; MARTIN; Harry NETTLEFIELD; SANT; George STRATFIELD; Frank URWIN; Rex YELVERTON
LEROUX Gaston	CHERI-BIBI; ***Joseph ROULETABILLE***
LESCROART John T	Auguste LUPA
LESLIE F Andrew	Sherlock HOLMES
LESLIE Francis	Jimmy LANGRY
LESLIE Jean	Peter PONSONBY
LESLIE Norman	'Jumbo' RUTHERFORD
LESLIE Peter	Father HAYES
LESTER E C	Nathaniel MOODY
LESTER Frank	Geoffrey SLADE
LEVENE Philip	Ambrose WEST
LEVERAGE Henry	Triggy DREW
LEVI Peter	Ben JONSON
LEVIN Ira	Yakov LIEBERMAN
LEVINE Paul	Jake LASSITER
LEVINREW Will	Prof Herman BRIERLY
LEVISON Eric	Dr Edward LESTER
LEWIN Elsa	Insp BERNSTEIN
LEWIN Michael Z	Adele BUFFINGTON; Lt Leroy POWDER; ***Albert SAMSON***
LEWIS Alfred Henry	A DETECTIVE
LEWIS Anthony	Sherlock HOLMES
LEWIS David	Steve SAVAGE
LEWIS Elliott	Fred BENNETT

LEWIS Irwin	Horace CLARKE
LEWIS Jack	Sexton BLAKE
LEWIS Judy	Vicky DARE
LEWIS Lange	Lt/Insp Richard TUCK
LEWIS Michael	Sgt HOBBS
LEWIS Roy Harley	Matthew COLL
LEWIS Roy	Insp CROW; ***Arnold LANDON***; Eric WARD
LEWIS Stephen	Jake LIEBERMAN
LEWIS Ted	Jack CARTER
LEY Alice Chetwynd	Anthea RUTHERFORD and Justin RUTHERFORD
LEYS John K	Insp CLARKE
LIDDON E S	Peggy FAIRFIELD
LIEBER Fritz	Sherlock HOLMES
LIEBERMAN Herbert	Paul KONIG; ***Det Sgt Francis MOONEY***
LIENTZ Gerald	Sherlock HOLMES
LILLEY Tom	Ralph CARTER
LILLY Jean	***Bruce PERKINS***; Bruce PERKINS and William Rutherford CRANE
LIMNELIUS George	***Insp MCMASTER***; Maj Weston PRYME
LINCOLN Natalie Sumner	Det FERGUSON; ***Insp MITCHELL***
LINDOP Audrey Erskine	Det GRENNON; ***KEOGH***
LINDSAY David T	Insp John Jay 'Jailbird' JACKSON
LINDSAY Frederic	Murray WILSON
LINDSAY R Howard	MCPHERSON
LINDSEY David L	Det Stuart HAYDON
LINGO Ada E	John SHIELDS
LININGTON Elizabeth	Sgt Ivor MADDOX
LINKLATER J Lane	Silas BOOTH
LINSCOTT Gillian	Nell BRAY; ***'Birdie' LINNET***
LINZEE David	Chris ROCKWELL and Sarah SABER
LITTELL Blaine	Sam WEBSTER
LITTLE C	HUMPTY DUMPTY DICK; ***Laura KEEN***
LITTLECHILD John George	Ch Insp John George LITTLECHILD
LITVINOFF Emanuel	Amos SHOMRON
LITZINGER Herman Anthony	Sherlock HOLMES
LIVINGSTON Armstrong	***Peter CREIGHTON***; Jimmy TREYNOR
LIVINGSTON Jack	Joe BINNEY
LIVINGSTON Kenneth	Cedric DODD
LIVINGSTON Nancy	G D H PRINGLE
LLEWELLYN Richard	Edmund TROTHE
LLEWELLYN Sam	Charlie AGUTTER
LLOYD Hugh	Hal KEEN
LLOYD-TAYLOR A	Sherlock HOLMES
LOCHTE Dick	***Leo G BLOODWORTH and Sarah 'Serendipity' DAHLQUIST***; Philip MARLOWE; Terry O'BANION
LOCKE Clinton W	Perry PIERCE
LOCKE G E	***Insp BURTON***; Insp BURTON and Mercedes QUERO; Mercedes QUERO
LOCKE George	Morlock TOMES
LOCKE Robert Donald	Pete BRASS
LOCKE W J	Aristide PUJOL
LOCKRIDGE Frances and Richard LOCKRIDGE	Geoffrey BOWEN; Paul LANE; Pam NORTH and Jerry NORTH; Det Nathan SHAPIRO; ***Bernard SIMMONS***
LOCKRIDGE Richard	***Capt/Insp Merton HEIMRICH***; Det Nathan SHAPIRO; Bernard SIMMONS
LOCKRIDGE Richard and Frances LOCKRIDGE	Capt/Insp Merton HEIMRICH
LODER Vernon	***Insp BREWS***; Donald CAIRN; Insp CHACE
LOFTING Hugh	Sherbert SCONES
LOFTS Norah	Emma PLUME
LOGAN Carolynne and Malcolm LOGAN	Justus DRUM
LOGUE John	John MOORE
LOMBARD Nap	Lord WINTERSTONE
LONG Amelia Reynolds	Steve CARTER; Katherine 'Peter' PIPER; ***Katherine 'Peter' PIPER*** and Edward TRELAWNEY; Edward TRELAWNY
LONG Derek	Sexton BLAKE
LONG Frank Belknap	John CARSTAIRS
LONG Harman	Franklyn KEEN
LONG Manning	Liz PARROTT
LONG Martin	Wellington COTTER
LONG Max	Komako KOA
LONG Patrick	Martyn CALE
LONGMATE Norman	Insp BRADBURY and Sgt RAYMOND
LORAC E C R	Supt KEMPSON; ***Insp/Supt MACDONALD***
LORAINE Philip	Insp KEEN; Catherine WALDEN
LORD Jeremy	Col Winston CREEVY
LORE Phillips	Leo ROI
LORENZ M K	Winston Marlowe SHERMAN
LOTT S Makepeace	Stephen RINGWAY
LOTTMAN Eileen	Jaine (The Bionic Woman) SOMMERS
LOUIS Joseph	Evan PARIS
LOVE Edmund G	George ROWE
LOVELL B E	Edge HANNEGAN
LOVELL Marc	***Jason GALT***; Appleton 'Apple' PORTER
LOVESEY Peter	Walter BARANOV; ***Sgt CRIBB and Const THACKERAY***; Insp DEW; Supt Peter DIAMOND; Warwick EASTON; Dorothy Mayotte RIGBY; King of England Edward VII WINDSOR
LOVISI J	Sherlock HOLMES
LOW Ona	Det Insp Arvo LAURILA
LOWDEN Desmond	Insp GORMAN and Const HALE
LUCAS Norman	Det Supt Bill ROWLANDS

LUCAS Warren	Lynn MELCHAN
LUDLUM Robert	Noel HOLCROFT; James MATLOCK; ***John TANNER***
LUDWIG Edward	Surly HOMES
LUGAR Hans	Phil CASEY
LUGAR Hans	Johnny FARRELL
LUGAR Hans	Det LONNIE THE FED; ***Hans LUGAR***
LUMLEY Brian	Titus CROW
LUMSBY Jim	Det Insp Carl MCCADDEN
LUND T	Policeman Dick WESTON
LUPICA Mike	Peter FINLEY
LUPOFF Richard A	Hobart LINDSEY and Det Marvia PLUM
LUSTBADER Eric Van	Philip MARLOWE
LUTHER Mark Lee	Arthur RANELEIGH
LUTZ John	***Fred CARVER***; Sherlock HOLMES; Philip MARLOWE; Milo MORGAN; Alo NUDGER
LYALL Francis	***Insp COHEN***; Supt MASON
LYALL Gavin	James CARD; Roy CASE; Bert KEMP; Maj Harry MAXIM
LYNCH Bohun and Reginald BERKELEY	Sherlock HOLMES
LYNCH Daniel	Frank MURPHY
LYNCH Jack	Peter BRAGG
LYNCH Lawrence L	***Neil J BATHURST***; Rufus CARNES and Richard STANHOPE; Sheriff COOK; Francis FERRARS; Insp HAINES; Kenneth JASPER; Carl MASTERS; Ferriss MURTAGH; Madeline PAYNE; Policeman STANHOPE; Van VERNET
LYNCH Miriam	Nell WILLARD
LYNDE Francis	Calvin SPRAGUE
LYNDS Dennis	'Slot-machine' KELLY
LYNNE James Broome	Richard WALKER
LYNWOOD Leslie J	Lester GRAYLING
LYON Dana	Jeff MILES; ***Hilda TRENTON***
LYON Winston	BATMAN
LYONS Arthur	Jacob ASCH
LYSAGHT Brian	Benjamin O'MALLEY

—M—

MACADAM Preston	Michael (The Shield) SHERIFF
MACARTHUR D Wilson	Alec SINCLAIR
MACCARGO J T	Joe MANNIX
MACCLURE Victor	Edward BLAYNE; ***Ch Insp Archie BURFORD***
MACDONALD Donald	Tommy BRIGGS
MACDONALD John D	Clifford BARTELLS; ***Travis MCGEE***; Paul STANIAL
MACDONALD John	Lew ARCHER
MACDONALD John Ross	***Lew ARCHER***; Howard CROSS; Herlock SHOLMES
MACDONALD Philip	Dr ALCAZAR; Dudley ALLWRIGHT; ***Col Anthony GETHRYN***; Supt Arnold PIKE; Supt SHANTER
MACDONALD Ross	***Lew ARCHER***; Bill GUNNERSON
MACDONALD William Colt	***Gregory QUIST***; Brady RUSKIN and Whit TRAXLER
MACDOUGALL James K	David STUART
MACDUFF David	Ch Reuben MALLOCK
MACE Merlda	Christine ANDERSEN
MACFARLANE Arthur E	Henry LANEHAM
MACGOWAN Alice and Perry NEWBERRY	Jerry BOYNE
MACGRADY Sean	Lt WEARIE
MACGRATH Harold	Cutty CLAY
MACGREGOR T J	Quin ST JAMES and Mike MCCLEARY
MACHARG William	O'MALLEY
MACHEN Arthur	DYSON and PHILIPPS
MACINTYRE John	***ASHTON-KIRK***; Duddington Pell CHALMERS
MACISAAC Fred	***Dick HADDEN***; Frank LEONARD and Foster GAINES; Addison Frank MURPHY
MACKAIL Denis	***Henry GIBSON***; Hugo PEAK
MACKAY Amanda	Hannah LAND
MACKENZIE Andrew	Supt BRANNIGAN
MACKENZIE Compton	Cdr Roger WATERLOW
MACKENZIE Donald	Henry CHALICE and Crying EDDIE; Barry JORDAN; ***John RAVEN***
MACKENZIE J Alexander	Joshua BAIN
MACKENZIE Nigel	Det Insp Charles TREMAYNE
MACKENZIE Scobie	Insp MULLINS
MACKENZIE W A	***'Slow and Sure' JACKSON***; Sir Nigel LACAITA
MACKIN Edward	August FRYE
MACKINNON Allan	Andrew CARNE; Mike DARROCH; ***Don KENDRICK***; Det Insp Duncan MACCALLUM
MACKINTOSH Ian	Tim BLACKGROVE
MACKINTOSH May	Laurie GRANT and Stewart NOBLE
MACKNIGHT Bob	Nathan HAWK
MACLEAN Alistair	Capt MALLORY
MACLEAN Arthur	Sexton BLAKE
MACLEAN Katherine	George SANDFORD
MACLEOD Angus	***Insp GILLANDREW***; Insp GILROY
MACLEOD Charlotte	Max BITTERSOHN; ***Sarah KELLING and Max BITTERSOHN***; Prof Peter SHANDY
MACLEOD Robert	Talos CORD; ***Jonathan GAUNT***; Andrew LAIRD
MACMILLAN W R Duncan	Sherlock HOLMES
MACNAMARA Brinsley	Sherlock HOLMES
MACNEIL Neil	Bert MCCALL and Tony COSTAINE
MACQUAY Mike	Matthew SWAIN
MACRAE Travis	Jim HARRIS and Kate HARRIS
MACVEIGH Sue	Capt Andy MACVEIGH
MACVICAR Angus	Rev P J MACFARLANE; ***Bruce MCLINTOCK***
MADDOCK Larry	Hannibal FORTUNE
MADDOCK Stephen	***Insp SLANE***; Timothy TERREL
MADDREN Gerry	***Jerry COOL***; Ivy MIDDAUGH and Judith PERINO
MADSEN David	Ray FALCO
MAGARSHACK David	Supt MOONEY
MAGEE Bill and Craig SCHENK	Lt COLUMBO
MAGNAY Sir William	***Maj FREEMAN***; Mr ROLF
MAGOON Carey	Adelaide STONE
MAGOWAN Ronald	Shane MACKENZIE
MAGUIRE Michael	Simon DRAKE
MAHANNAH Floyd	***Cassie GIBSON***; Riley WADDELL
MAIMAN Jaye	Robin MILLER
MAINWARING Marion	Spike BLUDGEON and Trajan BEARE; Mallory KING, Insp Jon NAPPLEBY, Jerry PASON, Atlas POIREAU, Simon QUINSEY, Fan SLIVER, Insp Broderick TOURNEUR, Spike BLUDGEON and Trajan BEARE; ***Toby SAMPSON***
MAIR George B	David GRANT
MAIS S P B	Philip WINSLOW
MAJESKI Bill	Sherlock HOLMES
MAKIN William J	***Det Insp EVANS***; Det Insp GRAVES; Jonathan JOW
MALCOLM John	Tim SIMPSON
MALET Leo	Nestor BURMA
MALIM Barbara	Simon CHARD
MALING Arthur	Calvin BIX; Walter JACKSON; ***Brockton POTTER***
MALLET Lyndon	TAFFIN
MALLETT Richard	Sherlock HOLMES
MALLOCH Peter	***Dave NORTON***; Insp Tom SWETMAN and Insp CRANE
MALLORY Arthur	Dr Kirke MONTGOMERY
MALLORY Roosevelt	RADCLIFF
MALLOY Lester	Martin MOON
MALMONT Valerie S	Tori MIRACLE
MALONE Michael	Cuddy MAGNUM and Justine SAVILE
MANCINI Anthony	Minnie SANTANGELO
MANDELKAU Jamie	Deuce RAMSEY
MANDELL Mark	Curt 'Nazi Hunter' JAEGER
MANER William	***Wilson HARLEY***; Parker ROWE
MANEY Mavis	Nancy CLUE
MANN Jack	***Rex COULSON***; Gregory George Gordon GREEN
MANN Jessica	Prof Theodora Wade CRAWFORD; ***Tamara HOYLAND***
MANN Paul	Colin LYNCH
MANNERS Margaret	Desdemona 'Squeakie' MEADOW
MANNON M M	Sheriff George WHITE
MANOR Jason	Steve SUMMERS
MANSON Will	BLACK
MANTELL Laurie	Sgt Steven ARROW
MANTHORNE Jackie	Harriet HUBBLEY
MARBLE M S	Joe GAYLORD; ***Craig MCKENZIE***
MARCH William	John LITTLETON
MARCIN Max	Dr Robert ORDWAY
MARCUS A A	Pete HUNTER
MARDER Irving	Max MORITZ
MARFIELD Dwight	***Maj KRIM***; Insp SKANE; Insp SKANE, Dudley BRENT and Maj KRIM; Insp SKANE, Gail MCGURK and Dudley BRENT
MARK Ted	Regina BLUE
MARKHAM Robert	Cdr James BOND
MARKHAM Virgil	Ed BOND; Insp FROST and Toni STAPLETON; George PETERS; ***Insp Myles RUSBY***; Supt SALT and Paula LEBETWOOD
MARKSON David	Harry FANNIN
MARLETT Melba	Sarah O'BRIEN
MARLOW Terry	Sgt Bill CLARK and Det Randi STONER
MARLOWE Dan J	Earl DRAKE; ***Johnny KILLAIN***
MARLOWE Derek	Walter BRACKETT
MARLOWE Francis	'Doc' SUMMERS
MARLOWE Greg (Leslie T Barnard)	Greg MARLOWE
MARLOWE Greg (James MCCORMICK)	Greg MARLOWE
MARLOWE Piers	***Supt Frank DRURY***; Supt Frank DRURY and Insp Bill HAZARD
MARLOWE Stephen	Chester DRUM
MARON Margaret	***Det Sigrid HAROLD***; Judge Deborah KNOTT
MAROWITZ Charles	Sherlock HOLMES
MARQUAND John P	Mr MOTO
MARRIC J J	Cdr George GIDEON
MARRIN Minette	Dorothy Mayotte RIGBY
MARRIOTT Anthony	Frank MARKER
MARSDEN Antony	Jim BEVERLEY; ***Insp BUCK***
MARSH Geoffrey	Lincoln BLACKTHORNE
MARSH Jean	Insp MANNERS
MARSH John	Ray FELTON; ***Simon LUCK***
MARSH Ngaio	Insp/Supt Roderick ALLEYN
MARSH Norman	Dan DUNN
MARSH Richard	***The Hon Augustus CHAMPNELL***; The Hon Augustus CHAMPNELL and BURCHELL; William CHARLECOT; Insp GARDNER; Matthew HOLMAN; Graham HUME; Insp IRELAND; Judith LEE; Augustus SHORT; George STONE, George DAVIS and FLETCHER

The Authors

MARSHALL Lovat	'Sugar' KANE
MARSHALL Raymond	Martin 'Brick-Top' CORRIGAN; Insp JAMES; ***Don MICKLEM***; Marc SPENCER
MARSHALL Sidney	Scott BENNET
MARSHALL William	Lt Felix ELIZALDO; ***Harry FEIFFER and YELLOWTHREAD STREET COPS***
MARSTON Edward	Nicholas BRACEWELL
MARTEL Charles	Bow Street Runner BOLTER
MARTELL Charles	Mick HALSEY
MARTIN A E	***Insp GORMLEY***; Pel PELHAM
MARTIN A Richard	Branders NOBLE
MARTIN Aylwin Lee	Matt HUGHES
MARTIN Clarence W	UBIQUE
MARTIN Ed	Jimmy BRENT
MARTIN Ian Kennedy	Det Insp Jack REGAN
MARTIN James E	Gil DISBRO
MARTIN Janet Letnes	Shirley HOLMQUIST
MARTIN Lee	Det Deb RALSTON
MARTIN Oliver	Timothy CULLINAN
MARTIN Philip	John KLINE
MARTIN Robert	Jim BENNETT
MARTIN Shane	Prof Ronald CHALLIS
MARTINI Steve	Paul MADRIANI
MARTYN Wyndham	Christopher BOND; ***Prof John SOUTHARD***; Anthony TRENT
MASKE John	***Duncan CAINSFORTH***; Jeremy FLACK and Duncan CAINSFORTH; Clarence E HEMINGWAY and Jeremy FLACK
MASON A E W	Insp HANAUD
MASON Clifford	Joe CINQUEZ
MASON Robert	Capt James Donald MACGREGOR
MASON S C	Derek GLOVER
MASON Sara Elizabeth	Sheriff Bill DAVIES
MASON Van Wyck	***Capt CATLIN***; Capt/Maj/Col Hugh NORTH
MASSEY Morrell	Thornton ZANE
MASTERMAN J C	***Ernst BRENDEL***; Sherlock HOLMES
MASTERMAN Walter S	Ch Const HENDON; ***Dick SELDON***; Sir Arthur SINCLAIR
MASTERS Anthony	Marius LARCHE
MASTERS Doug	Anthony Nicholas TWIN
MASTERS J D	Donovan STEELE
MASTERS Miles	Sherlock HOLMES
MASTERSON Whit	Mort HAGEN; ***John SHU***
MASUR Harold Q	***Scott JORDAN***; Mike RYAN
MATERA Lia	Laura DI PALMA; ***Willa JANSSON***
MATHER Berkley	***Peter FELTHAM***; Idewal REES; James WAINWRIGHT
MATHER Linda	Jo HUGHES
MATHERS Helen	Hugo HOLD
MATHESON Don	Charlie GAMBLE
MATHESON Hugh	Geoffrey BRANSCOMBE
MATHEWS Nieves	Dr Hal PHILLIPS
MATHIESON Theodore	***Leonardo DA VINCI***; Benjamin FRANKLIN; Omar KHAYYAM
MATHIS Edward	Dan ROMAN
MATHISON Volney	Samuel JONES
MATSCHAT Cecile Hulse	Andrea Reid RAMSAY and David RAMSAY
MATTESON Stefanie	Charlotte GRAHAM
MATTHEW Charles	Insp STRATTON
MATTHEWS Clayton	Lincoln PLUMMER
MATTHEWS James	Insp BARNES
MATTHEWS Lew	Horatio PARKER
MATTHIAS Lee A	Sherlock HOLMES
MAUGHAM W S	ASHENDEN
MAURO Robert	Sherlock HOLMES
MAVITY Nancy Barr	Peter PIPER
MAXIM John	Paul BANNERMAN
MAXON P B	LANDER
MAXWELL A E	FIDDLER
MAXWELL Allan	Sexton BLAKE
MAXWELL Thomas	Lew CASSIDAY
MAYHAR Ardath	Mrs HUDSON and Sherlock HOLMES
MAYLON B J	Bill KING
MAYNARD Robert	Jerry OWENS
MAYNE Talbot	Dixon BRETT
MAYO J K	Harry SEDDAL
MAYO James	Charles HOOD
MAYOR Archer	Lt Joe GUNTHER
MAYSON Walter H	JONES
MAZZARO Ed	Bruno FARRELL
MCALEER John	Austin LAYMAN
MCAULIFFE Frank	Augustus MANDRELL
MCBAIN Ed	Michael BARNES; Matthew HOPE; ***The 87th PRECINCT***; Benjamin SMOKE
MCCABE Cameron	A B C MULLER
MCCAFFERTY Taylor	Haskell BLEVINS
MCCAHERY James R	Lavinia LONDON
MCCALL John J	Al MOONEY
MCCALL K T	Johnny BUCHANAN
MCCALL Wendell	Chris KLICK
MCCANDLESS D B	Mrs Sarah WATSON
MCCARRY Charles	Paul CHRISTOPHER
MCCARTHY Shaun Lloyd	Hamilton BIGGS
MCCLINTICK Malcolm	Sgt George KELSO
MCCLOY Helen	Insp DEVLIN; Alec NORTON; Miguel URIZAR; ***Dr Basil WILLING***; Dr Basil WILLING and Miguel URIZAR
MCCLURE James	Lt Tromp KRAMER
MCCOLLUM Robert	Francesca MILLS
MCCOMAS Stanley	Sherlock HOLMES
MCCOMBS R L F	Richard DEMING
MCCONNELL Frank D	Bridget O'TOOLE
MCCONNELL Vicki	Nyla WADE
MCCONNOR Vincent	***Insp DAMIOT***; Zeke GAHAGAN; Eugène VIDOCQ
MCCORMICK Claire	John WALTZ
MCCRUMB Sharyn	Sheriff Spencer ARROWWOOD; Henry KRETZNER; ***Elizabeth MACPHERSON***; Jay OMEGA
MCCULLEY Johnston	BLACK STAR; ***John (The Thunderbolt) FLATCHLEY***; Dalton (The Crimson Clown) PROUSE; Paul SELBON and Peter SELBON; John (The Spider) WARWICK
MCCULLY Walbridge	Carey GALBREATH
MCCURTIN Peter	***Robert (The Assassin) BRIGANTI***; Phillip (The Marksman) MAGELLAN; Jim (The Death Dealer) RAINEY; Pete SHAY
MCCUTCHAN Philip	Det Ch Supt Simon SHARD; ***Cdr Esmonde SHAW***
MCCUTCHEON George Barr	Ch Anderson CROW
MCCUTCHEON Hugh	Jimmy CARROLL; Anthony HOWARD; Richard LOGAN; ***Insp MCKELLER***; Insp MCKELLER and Anthony HOWARD; Insp MCKELLER and Richard LOGAN
MCDERMID Val	Kate BRANNIGAN
MCDONALD Alan	Rosie MONAGHAN
MCDONALD Cherokee Paul	Offr Jessie SUMMER
MCDONALD Gregory	Irwin 'Fletch' FLETCHER and Insp Francis Xavier FLYNN; ***Irwin 'Fletch' FLETCHER***; Francis Xavier FLYNN
MCDONALD Hugh C	Paul WILLIAMS
MCDOUGALD Roman	Philip CABOT
MCDOWELL Emmett	***Jonathan KNOX***; Jamie MACRAE
MCDOWELL Michael	Jack BEAUMONT and Susan BRIGHT
MCDOWELL Paul	Stan GARLAND
MCDOWELL Rider	Willy DIAZ
MCELDOWNEY Eugene	Supt Ceal MCGARRY
MCELROY Hugh	Insp William BREWER
MCFARLANE Leslie	Michael BRENT
MCGERR Patricia	Sally BOWEN; ***Selena MEAD***
MCGINITY James Patrick	MANNERS
MCGIRR Edmund	PIRON
MCGIVERN William P	***Dave BANNION***; Insp HARRIGAN; Adam JAMES; Det Max PRIMA and Det Gypsy TONNELLI; Sam TERRELL
MCGOLDRICK John	Hemlock HOLMES
MCGOWN Jill	Harry CAMBERT; ***Ch Insp LLOYD***
MCGRAW Lee	Madge HATCHETT
MCGREGOR Don and Gene COLAN	Bob RAINIER and Ted DENNING
MCGREW Fenn	Lt Charles HILLARY
MCGUIRE Christine	Kathryn MACKAY
MCGUIRE Paul	***Ch Insp CUMMINGS***; Ch Insp CUMMINGS and Insp/Supt FILLINGER; Insp/Supt FILLINGER; Insp WITTLER
MCILVANNEY William	Jack LAIDLAW
MCINERNY Ralph	Andrew BROOM; ***Father Roger DOWLING***
MCINTOSH J T	Ambrose FRAYNE and Dominique FRAYNE
MCINTYRE Vonda N	Sherlock HOLMES
MCIVER N J	Arnold SIMON
MCKENNA Bridget	Det Caley BURKE
MCKENNA Marthe	Clive GRANVILLE
MCKENZIE Donald J	***Det CUSH***; The REPORTER DETECTIVE; The WORKING MAN DETECTIVE
MCLAUCHLIN Russell	Sherlock HOLMES
MCLEAN Allan Campbell	Insp Neil MACLEOD
MCLEAVE Hugh	Stephen ARMITAGE; ***Paul BRODIE***; Dr Gregor MACLEAN
MCLEISH Dougal	Insp RODERICKS
MCMAHON Thomas Patrick	Dave PECK
MCMORROW Will	Bradley AUSTIN
MCMULLEN Mary	Kells CAVENAUGH; ***Eve FITZSIMMONS***
MCNAB Claire	Insp Carol ASHTON
MCNAMARA Joseph D	Sgt Finnbar FRALEIGH
MCNEILE H C	***Capt Hugh 'Bulldog' DRUMMOND***; Capt Hugh 'Bulldog' DRUMMOND and Ronald STANDISH; Jim MAITLAND
MCNEILLY Wilfred	Sexton BLAKE
MCQUILLAN Karin	Jazz HUNTER and Wynn HUNTER
MCRAE Diana	Eliza PIREX
MCSHANE Mark	James MATRIC; ***Norman PINK***; Myra SAVAGE
MCSHEA Susannah	Forrest HAGGERTY
MCWATTERS George S	DETECTIVES
MEAD Russell	Peter CASEY
MEADE L T	CROSSLEY; Dixon DRUCE; Micah FARADAY; ***Rudolph GREY***
MEADE L T and Robert EUSTACE	John BELL; Dr Henry CHETWYND and Dr Paul CATO; George CONWAY; Florence CUSACK; Prof Christopher EKSHAW; ***Insp FROST and Dr GARLAND***; Norman HEAD
MEADE L T and Clifford HALIFAX	***Paul GILCHRIST***; Policeman William GREEN; Dr Clifford HALIFAX
MEADE Richard	John ALLISON
MEARSON Lyon	Steve MUIRHEAD
MEEK M R D	Lennox KEMP
MELVILLE Alan	MINTO

MELVILLE James	Supt Tetsuo OTANI
MELVILLE Jennie	Det Insp Charmian DANIELS
MELVILLE-ROSS Antony	TRELAWNEY
MENGERT Tom	Sharlock HOLMES
MERAK A J	Johnny MERAK and Dawn GRAHAME
MEREDITH D R	***John Lloyd BRANSON***; Sheriff Charles Timothy MATTHEWS
MERITON Peter	Sexton BLAKE; ***Capt DACK***; Bill LANGLEY
MERLAND Oliver	Sexton BLAKE
MERRICK Mark	MOONSHINER JACK; ***OLD GOLD-EYE***; OLD GRIMES
MERRICK Mollie	Red HANLON
MERRITT A	LOWELL
MERRITT Don	Frank HATCHER
MERSEREAU John	Prof James Yates BIDDLE and Kay RITCHIE
MERWIN Richard	Clayton WARD
MERWIN Richard and Warren SPECTOR	Clayton WARD
MERWIN Sam Jr	Amy BREWSTER
MESSENGER Elizabeth	Insp GREGG and Judith EVERSLEIGH
MESSMANN Jon	***Jefferson (The Handyman) BOONE***; Ben (The Revenger) MARTIN
METCALFE Herbert	Insp John HEENAN
MEYER Lawrence	Tony JORDAN
MEYER Nicholas	***Mark BRILL***; Sherlock HOLMES; Sherlock HOLMES and Sigmund FREUD
MEYERS Annette	Xenia SMITH and Leslie WETZON
MEYERS Maan	Dr John TONNEMAN
MEYERS Martin	Patrick HARDY
MEYNELL Laurence	George Stanhope BERKLEY; Sir James ERSKINE; Sir James ERSKINE and George Stanhope BERKLEY; ***Hooky HEFFERMAN***; Insp Kingsley HYLTON
M'GOVAN James	JIMSIE; ***James M'GOVAN***; WEE PUNCH
MIALL Derwent	Pusher LONG
MIALL Robert	Jason KING
MICHAELS Grant	Stan KRAYCHIK
MICHAELS Jan	Darby CASTLE
MICHAELS Melisa C	Aileen DOUGLASS and Sharon ATWOOD
MICHEL M Scott	***Dr Alexander CORNELL***; Wood JAXON
MIKSCH W F	Sherlock HOLMES
MILES John	Larry CRYSTAL
MILES Keith	Alan SAXON
MILLAR Florence N	Ch Insp Douglas GRANT
MILLAR Kenneth	Chet GORDON
MILLAR Margaret	Tomas ARAGON; Paul BLACKSHEAR; Elmer DODD; Charles DONNELLY; Howard HYATT and Michael DUNLOP; Eric MEECHAM; Steve PINATA; Dr Paul PRYE; Joe QUINN; ***Insp SANDS***; Insp SANDS and Dr Paul PRYE
MILLARD Alice	Mabelle RIVERS
MILLER Ben E	Cory BARNETT
MILLER Elizabeth York	Frank YARDLEY
MILLER Geoffrey	Terry TRAVEN
MILLER J M T	Artie WEATHERBY
MILLER John	Sgt FOGERTY and Philip WARING
MILLER Rex	Jack EICHORD
MILLER Roy S	Sherlock HOLMES
MILLER Thomas Kent	Sherlock HOLMES
MILLER Victor B	***FERNANDA***; Insp KOJAK
MILLER Wade	Walter JAMES; ***Max THURSDAY***
MILLER Warne	JOCKEY JOE; ***Silas QUIRK***; John RUGBY; Zeb TAYLOR
MILLHISER Marlys	Charlie GREENE
MILLS Hugh Travers	Franz HEPPEL
MILLS Osmington	***Insp/Supt BAKER***; Patrick C SHIRLEY and Insp Rip IRVING
MILLS Woosnam	John HOWDEN; ***John MELROSE***
MILLWARD Edward J	Insp Gil FLICKER
MILNE A A	***Anthony GILLINGHAM***; Sherlock HOLMES
MILNE Angela	Sherlock HOLMES
MILNE John	Jim JENNER
MILNE Shirley	Det Sgt STEYTLER
MILTON Joseph	Bart GOULD
MINAHAN John	'Little John' RAWLINGS
MITCHAM Gilroy	Nick MARSHALL
MITCHELL Gladys	Mrs Adela Beatrice Lestrange BRADLEY
MITCHELL James	David CALLAN; ***Joe CAVE***; Ron HOGGETT
MITCHELL Kay	Det Ch Insp John MORRISSEY
MITCHELL Scott	Brock DEVLIN
MITCHELSON Austin and Nicholas UTECHIN	Sherlock HOLMES
MITGANG Herbert	Sam LINKUM
MODIANO Patrick	Guy ROLAND
MOFFAT Gwen	***Melinda PINK***; Ruth STANTON
MOFFATT James	Virginia BOX; ***Johnny CANUCK***; Silas MANNERS
MOFFETT Cleveland	Insp BROUSSE and Alan ESTERBROOKE; ***Paul COQUENIL***
MOISEIWITSCH Maurice	***Mr PENNY***; Woolf SARASON
MOLE William	Casson DUKER
MOLLOY J Fitzgerald	Geoffrey GILLESBY
MOLLOY Michael	Lewis HORNE
MONFREDO Miriam Grace	Glynis TRYON
MONIG Christopher	Brian BRETT
MONMOUTH Jack	John EARLSTONE; ***Tom LANGLEY***
MONRO Gavin	Insp HINKLEY
MONTAGUE J J	Shauna BISHOP
MONTALBAN Manuel Vazquez	Pepe CARVALHO
MONTGOMERY Ione	Christopher GIBSON
MONTGOMERY Yvonne	Finney ALETTER
MONTROSE David	Russell TEED
MONTROSE Graham	Angel BROWN

MONTROSS David	REMSEN
MOODY Susan	Frances BRETT; Cassandra SWANN; ***Penny WANAWAKE***
MOORCOCK Michael	Jerry CORNELIUS
MOORE Amos	ROYCE
MOORE Barbara	Dr Gordon CHRISTY
MOORE Carl	Victor STRAWN
MOORE H F S	Casey PETERS
MOORE Margaret	Ch Insp BAXTER
MOORE Richard A	Bob WHITFIELD
MOORHOUSE Hopkins	Addison KENT
MORALES Pablo	Pedro MORENO
MORELLI Spike	Shaun KOVACK
MORGAN Allan (House name)	Mark BLOOD
MORGAN Allan (Marilyn GRANBECK)	Mark BLOOD
MORGAN Charles C	Ben LOGAN
MORGAN D Miller	Daisy MARLOW
MORGAN Dean	Rostron OUTFIT; ***Rogue RANSOM***
MORGAN Geoffrey	Ricky STRAIGHT
MORGAN Kate	Dewey JAMES
MORGAN Michael	Bill RYAN
MORGAN Patrick	Bill CARTWRIGHT
MORGAN Robert A	Teddy LONDON
MORGAN Roberts	Sherlock HOLMES
MORICE Anne	Tessa CRICHTON
MORISON B J	Elizabeth Lamb WORTHINGTON
MORLAND Nigel	Det Insp Rory LUCCAN; Steven MALONE; Ch Insp Andy MCMURDO; ***Mrs Palmyra Evangeline PYM***
MORLEY Christopher	Dove DULCET
MOROSO John A	James TIERNEY
MORRAH Dermot	Denys SARGENT and Humphrey CARVER
MORRIS Anthony P	BRADSHAW; ***Mark MAGIC***; Jack PARKER; Jack SIMONS; Tom TURNER
MORRIS John	Robin MCKAY
MORRIS R A V	Insp James CANDLISH
MORRIS T B	Insp HEADLEY
MORRIS W R	Sheriff Buford PUSSER
MORRISON Arthur	DORRINGTON; ***Martin HEWITT***
MORRISON Hugo	James 'Kipper' HERRING
MORROW J T	Jason PROPHET and Lynn MCCOLL
MORSE L A	Sam HUNTER; ***Jake SPANNER***
MORSON Ian	William FALCONER
MORTIMER John	Horace RUMPOLE
MORTON Anthony	John MANNERING; ***Mr QUENTIN***
MORTON Guy	Konrad ROQUE
MORTON William	Commiss Kirker CAMERON; ***'Biff' CORRIGAN***
MOSLEY Walter	Easy' RAWLINS
MOYES Patricia	Ch Insp/Ch Sup Henry TIBBETT and Emmy TIBBETT
MUDDOCK Joyce Emerson Preston	Luke BRADLEY
MUIR Augustus	Dr Louis RAPHAEL
MUIR D Erskine	Insp WOODS
MUIR Dexter	Ch Insp Max HUNTER and Prof Stephen PILGRIM
MUIR Thomas	***Prof CLEGHORN***; Roger CRAMMOND
MULKEEN Thomas P	Clem TALBOT
MULLALLY Frederic	Bob SULLIVAN
MULLEN Clarence	Tony LANTZ
MULLER Marcia	***Sharon MCCONE***; Elena OLIVEREZ; Joanna STARK
MULLER Paul	Paul MULLER
MUNDER Laura	Sara MARKS
MUNDY Max	Russell JONES
MUNDY Talbot	***Chullunder GHOSE***; James Schuyler 'Jimgrim' GRIM; James Schuyler 'Jimgrim' GRIM and Chullunder GHOSE; James Schuyler 'Jimgrim' GRIM Chullunder GHOSE and Athelstan KING; Athelstan KING; Cotswold OMMONY
MUNKITTRICK R L	Sherlock HOLMES
MUNRO Hugh	CLUTHA
MUNRO James	James CRAIG
MURPHY Brian	Eliot UPTON
MURPHY Christopher	SPARROW
MURPHY D J	Insp MALONE
MURPHY Haughton	Reuben FROST
MURPHY Warren B	***Julian 'Digger' BURROUGHS***; Justin GILEAD and Alexander ZHARKOV; Steve HOOKS; Dr David Vincent LEONARDO; Ed RAZONI and William JACKSON; Ed RAZONI, William JACKSON and Devlin 'Trace' TRACY; Devlin 'Trace' TRACY; Remo (The Destroyer) WILLIAMS
MURRAY Andrew	Sexton BLAKE
MURRAY David Christie	***Insp Joseph PRICKETT***; John PYM
MURRAY David Christie and Henry HERMAN	Harry WYNNE
MURRAY Edgar Joyce	Sexton BLAKE
MURRAY Inspector	Insp Joseph PRICKETT
MURRAY M M Lt	BRINDLE
MURRAY Max	Michael WEST
MURRAY Stephen	Ch Insp Alec STAINTON
MURRAY William	Lou 'Shifty' ANDERSON
MUSTOO Terence	Sherlock HOLMES
MUUSMANN Carl	Sherlock HOLMES
MYERS Amy	Auguste DIDIER
MYERS Isabel Briggs	Peter JERNINGHAM
MYERS Paul	Mark HOLLAND
MYLES Simon	'Apples' CARSTAIRS

The Authors

NABB Magdalen	Marshal Salva GUARNACCIA
NAHA Ed	***Lt Kevin BROSKEY***; Harry PORTER
NAPPLEBY Insp Jon	Mallory KING
NARCEJAC Thomas	Nero WOLFE
NASH Anne	Mark TUDOR
NASH Jay Robert	John Howard JOURNEY
NASH Simon	Adam LUDLOW
NASLUND Sena Jeter	Sherlock HOLMES
NASSIVERA John	Sherlock HOLMES
NATHENSON Joseph	Lt KUPFERMAN
NATSUKI Shizuko	Jane PRESCOTT
NAVA Michael	Henry RIOS
NAZEL Joseph	BLACK; ***Henry Highland (Iceman) WEST***
NEBEL Frederick	Sgt BRINKHAUS; ***Steve CARDIGAN***; Jack CARDIGAN; Donny 'Tough Dick' DONAHUE; Buck JASON; KENNEDY; Capt Steve MACBRIDE; Patricia SEAWARD
NEEBEL Richard	Erik CHATHAM
NEEL Janet	Francesca WILSON
NEELY Barbara	Blanche WHITE
NEELY Richard	Abe FRIENDLY
NELSON Hugh Lawrence	Jim DUNN and Zebulion BUCK; ***Steve JOHNSON***
NEMEC David	Frank REPPA
NETTON Budleigh	Derek CARRINGTON
NEUMAN Fredric	Policeman William MOORE; ***Abe REDDEN***
NEVILLE Margot	Insp GROGAN
NEVINS Francis M Jr	Philip MARLOWE; ***Loren MENSING***; Milo TURNER
NEWELL Audrey	Det Patrick Michael DOYLE
NEWMAN Bernard	Sgt/Insp MARSHALL; ***Papa PONTIVY***; Insp Nicholas PRINCE
NEWMAN Christopher	Lt Joe DANTE
NEWMAN G F	Det Ch Insp John FORDHAM; ***Insp Terry SNEED***; Jimmy VANESCO
NEWMAN Joel	Philip KAUFMAN
NEWTON Douglas	***Philip MANWEARING***; Raphael PHARE and Martin SONDES
NEWTON Michael	Det FLYNN and Det TANNER; ***Jon STEEL***
NICHOLAS Jerome	Bill ANSTRUTHER
NICHOLS Beverley	Horatio GREEN
NICHOLSON John	COSTELLO
NICOLAI Charles	John NOLAN
NICOLE Christopher	Jonathan ANDERS
NIELSEN Helen	Lisa BANCROFT; ***Simon DRAKE***; Ty LEANDER
NIMBLE KE	NIMBLE IKE; NORVAL
NIMERSSHEIM Jack	Sherlock HOLMES
NISBET Hume	William GIBSON; Robert SCOTT; ***Nicodemus Dove TURTLE***
NISBET Jim	Martin WINDROW
NISOT Elizabeth	Commissaire PAYRAN
NIVEN Larry	Gil HAMILTON
NIXON Alan	Lawrence MAVER
NIXON Allan	Tony GARRITY
NIZZA Paul	Doorlock HOLMES
NOEL Atanielle Annyn	Gwen GRAY and Garamond GRAY
NOEL Jeffrey	Johnny PERFECT
NOGUCHI Thomas T and Arthur LYONS Jr	Dr Eric PARKER
NOLAN Frederick	***Charles GARRETT***; Joe PETROSINO
NOLAN James Vincent	Edmond MACKELL
NOLAN Jeannette Covert	Lace WHITE
NOLAN William F	***Bart CHALLIS***; Nick CHALLIS; Sam SPACE
NORMAN Barry	Paul BAKER
NORMAN Bruce	***James MALLABY***; Jocelyn PINNER
NORMAN Earl	Burns BANNION
NORMAN Frank	Ed NELSON
NORMAN Geoffrey	Norman HUNT
NORMAN James	Gimiendo Hernande QUINTO
NORMAN John	Martin SPEED
NORRIS Margaret	Sherlock HOLMES
NORSWORTHY George	Martin CROW
NORTH Gerry	Gerry NORTH
NORTH Gil	***Sgt Caleb CLUFF***; Supt Kofi KATT
NORTH John	Sherlock HOLMES
NORTH Sam	Sam NORTH
NORTH Suzanne	Phoebe FAIRFAX
NORTON Isobel	Valerie DREW
NORWOOD Victor	JACARA
NOVAK Robert	Joe BLAZE
NOWAK Jacquelyn	Mike MINER
NOWN Graham	Sherlock HOLMES
NOY John	Rufus DEVILLE
NYLAND Gentry	Joseph SOUTH

—O—

OATES Joyce Carol	Xavier KILGARVAN
OATLEY Keith	Sherlock HOLMES and Sigmund FREUD
O'BRIEN Meg	Jessica JAMES
O'BRINE Manning	MILLS; ***Michael the O'KELLY***
OBSTFELD Raymond	***Harry GOULD***; Cliff REMINGTON
O'CALLAGHAN Maxine	Delilah WEST
O'CONNELL Carol	MALLORY and Charles BUTLER
OCORK Shannon	T T BALDWIN
ODLUM Jerome	Sam BOOKER and Jimmy WEBB; O'SULLIVAN; ***John STEELE***
O'DONNELL Lillian	Mici ANHALT; ***Policewoman Norah MULCAHANEY***; Gwen RAMADGE
O'DONNELL Peter	Modesty BLAISE
O'DONOHOE Nick	Nathan PHILLIPS
OELLRICHS Inez	Matt WINTERS
OFFORD Lenore Glen	Bill HASTINGS and Coco HASTINGS; ***Todd MCKINNON***
OGAN George F	Johnny BORDELON
O'HANLON James D	Jason CORDRY
O'HARA Kenneth	***Dr Alun BARRY***; Insp HOBDEN
O'HARA Kevin	Chico BRETT
O'HIGGINS Harvey J	Barney COOK; ***Det John DUFF***
OLBRICH Freny	Frank DESOUZA
OLCOTT Anthony	Det Ivan KUVAKIN
OLD SLEUTH	***Brant ADAMS***; AMZI; Bruce ANGELO; The BICYCLE DETECTIVE; Bertie BLAND; Henry BROCH; CLYDE; COOL TOM; The COWBOY DETECTIVE; CRESTON; Desmond DARE; DETECTIVE ARCHIE; DETECTIVE DALE; DETECTIVE GAY; DETECTIVE HANLEY; DETECTIVE KENNEDY; DETECTIVE MURDOCK; DETECTIVE PAYNE; The GIANT DETECTIVE; GIPSY ROSE; GIPSY RENO; The IRISH DETECTIVE; IRON BURGESS; JACK and GIL; KEFTON; KINGSLEY; The KING'S DETECTIVE; The LADY DETECTIVE; MAGIC DICK; MEAD; MEPHISTO; Billy MISCHIEF; MURA; OLD ELECTRICITY; OLD SLEUTH; OSCAR; RAMSEY; RED CECIL; TRUE BLUE; YANKEE RUE
OLD SPICER	Mark SPICER
OLDE Nicholas	Rowland HERN
OLDEN Marc	***Hawthorne Albert HARKER***; Robert SAND
OLECK Howard L	Sam BENEDICT
OLEKSIW Susan	Ch Joe SILVA
OLIVER Anthony	Lizzie THOMAS
OLSEN D B	***Lt Stephen MAYHEW***; Rachel MURDOCK and Jennifer MURDOCK; Rachel MURDOCK, Jennifer MURDOCK and Lt Stephen MAYHEW; Prof A PENNYFEATHER; Mr PUCKETT
OLSEN Jack	Offr Tally WICKHAM and Sgt John BOON
OLSON Donald	Devillo GREEN
O'MALLEY Frank	Mike CAVANAUGH
O'MALLEY Patrick	HARRIGAN and HOEFFLER
O'MARIE Sister Carol Anne	Sister MARY HELEN
O'NAIR Mairi	Pam WAYNE
O'NEIL Kerry	Jerry MOONEY
O'NEILL Archie	Jeff PRIDE
OPPENHEIM E Phillips	Const BENSKIN; Gen BESSERLEY; Samuel T BILLINGHAM; Miss BROWN; Gilbert CHANNAY; Joseph P CRAY; Insp DICKINS; ***Nicholas GOADE***; Malcolm GOSSETT; Commodore JASEN; JENNERTON; The Hon Algernon KNOX; Ambrose LAVENDALE; John T LAXWORTHY; Benjamin LEVY; Baroness Clara LINZ; Sir Joseph LONDE; Charles LYSON; MANNISTER; Lucie MOTT; Aaron RODD; Peter RUFF; Mr SABIN; Michael SAYERS; Sir Jasper SLANE; Grant SLATTERY; Insp SNELL
OPPENHEIM James	Kira POLLY
ORCZY Baroness	***Lady Molly DE MAZEREEN***; FERNAND; Patrick MULLIGAN; The OLD MAN IN THE CORNER; Monsieur Hector RATICHON; The SCARLET PIMPERNEL
ORDE A J	Jason LYNX
ORDE-POWLETT Nigel	Anthony RILLINGTON
ORENSTEIN Frank	***Ev FRANKLIN***; Ev FRANKLIN and Hugh MORRISON; Hugh MORRISON
ORGILL Douglas	William MALLETT
ORMEROD Roger	Harry KYLE and Angela ROLLASON; ***Philipa LOWE***; David MALLIN and George COE; Richard PATTON and Amelia PATTON
O'ROURKE Frank	Jim BRADLEY
O'ROURKE Rebecca	RATS
ORR Clifford	Joseph HARRIS; ***'Spider' MEECH***
ORTON Joe	Sgt MATCH; ***Insp TRUSCOTT***
ORUM Poul	Insp Jonas MORCK
ORVIS Kenneth	Adam BRECK
OSBORN David	Margaret BARLOW
OSBORNE Geoffrey	James DINGLE and Glyn JONES
OSBORNE Mark	Sexton BLAKE
OSBORNE Richard	Nick CURRAN
OSBORNE William Hamilton	William MURGATROYD
OSTER Jerry	Lt NEUMAN; ***Eve ZABRISKIE***
OSTRANDER Isabel	Timothy MCCARTY
O'SULLIVAN J B	Steve SILK
OTTOLENGUI Rodrigues	John BARNES; ***Robert Leroy MITCHELL and John BARNES***
OURSLER Will	Offr Michael LA RUE; ***Philip STRONG and James MATTHEWS***
OVERHOLSER Stephen	Molly OWENS
OVERTON Robert	Abel GIRDLESTONE
OWEN H Collinson	ANTOINE
OWEN Hans C	Percival TROUT
OWEN Philip	Don BURTON
OZAKI Milton K	***Prof CALDWELL***; Rusty FORBES; Carl GUARD

PACE Tom	Ben GARDEN
PACKARD Frank	Jimmie DALE
PADGETT Abigail	Bo BRADLEY
PADGETT Lewis	Seth COLMAN and Eve COLMAN
PAGE Carole Gift and Doris Elaine FELL	David BALLARD and Michelle Merrill BALLARD
PAGE Emma	Insp KELSEY
PAGE Jake	Robin DANA
PAGE Katherine Hall	Faith Sibley FAIRCHILD
PAGE Marco	Ellis BLAISE; David CALDER; ***Joel GLASS***
PAGE Martin	Louis LEPINE
PAGE Norwell	Dick BARRETT; ***Ken CARTER***; Angus ST CLOUD
PAGE Stanley Hart	Christopher HAND
PAIGE Peter	Cash WALE
PAIN Barry	Constantine DIX; ***Cdr DUMPHRY***
PAIRO Preston III	Sam HAWKINS
PALMER Frank	Det Insp 'Jacko' JACKSON
PALMER Huntley	Ed RILEY
PALMER John	Guy PLANTE and Freye MATTHEWS
PALMER M Earle	Wayne TEMPLE
PALMER P K	Jedediah KILLINGER III
PALMER Stuart	Sherlock HOLMES; Howie ROOK; ***Hildegarde WITHERS***
PALMER Stuart and Fletcher FLORA	Hildegarde WITHERS
PANSHIN Alexei	Viscount Anthony VILLIERS
PAPAZOGLU Ornia	Patience MCKENNA
PARADIS Vincent	Theodore CLAW
PARETSKY Sara	Philip MARLOWE; ***Victoria Iphigenia 'Vi' WARSHAWSKI***
PARK Owen	Tommy LEE
PARKER Maude	Jim LITTLE
PARKER Percy Spurlark	Big Bull BENSON
PARKER Robert B	Philip MARLOWE; ***SPENSER***
PARKER T Jefferson	Tom SHEPHERD
PARKES Roger	Col CALPIN; ***Insp Taff ROBERTS***; Supt WALSH
PARMER Charles	Maj Roderick AUSTEN
PARRISH Frank	Dan MALLETT
PARRISH Randall	Matthew WEST
PARSONS Anthony	Sexton BLAKE
PASSINGHAM W J	Sexton BLAKE
PASTOR Tony	FRITZ; Fritz HARMON; ***O'Neil MCDARRAGH***; TOM and JERRY
PATERNOSTER George Sidney	Randolph MANNERING
PATRICK Q	Insp BOOT; Insp Martin FIELD; Insp HORROCKS and Hilary FENTON; Insp Archibald INGE; ***Lt Timothy TRANT***
PATTERSON Harry	Nick MILLER
PATTERSON Innis	Sebald CRAFT
PATTERSON James	Det Alex CROSS
PATTERSON Richard North	Peter CAREY; Christopher PAGET; ***Adam SHAW***
PATTINSON James	Harvey LANDON
PAUL Barbara	Enrico CARUSO; Enrico CARUSO and Geraldine FERRAR; Gillian CLIFFORD; Abby JAMES; Sgt Marian LARCH; Lt Janus MURTAUGH; Henrietta SNOOKS and Gus BILINSKI; ***Lt TOOMEY***
PAUL Elliot	Homer EVANS
PAUL Ernest	George BARCLAY
PAUL Jeremy	Sherlock HOLMES
PAUL Raymond	***Lon QUINNCANNON***; Christopher RANDOLPH
PAUL William	Ch Insp David FYFE
PAULL Jessica	Tracy LARRIMORE and Mike THOMPSON
PAULSEN Gary	Lt Ronnie GOLD
PAWSON Stuart	Det Insp Charles PRIEST
PAYES Rachel C	Forsythia BROWN
PAYN James	***Charles STEEN***; Bow Street Runner TOWNSHEND
PAYNE Laurence	Ch Insp Sam BIRKETT; Mark SAVAGE; ***Mark SAVAGE and Ch Insp Sam BIRKETT***; John TIBBETT
PEARCE Michael	Capt OWEN
PEARLMAN Gilbert	Sherlock HOLMES
PEARS Iain	Gen Taddeo BOTTANDO
PEARSALL Ronald	Sherlock HOLMES
PEARSON Ann	Maggie COURTNEY
PEARSON Edmund	Sherlock HOLMES
PEARSON Ridley	Det Lou BOLDT and Daphne MATTHEWS; ***Det James DEWITT***
PECK Winifred	Bob STUART
PEDEN William Harwood	Raymond GREEN and Margaret GREEN
PEDNEAU Dave	Whit PYNCHON and Annie TYSON-TYREE
PEEBLES Niles N	Ross MCKELLAR
PEIRCE J F	William SHAKESPEARE; ***Capt ZACHARY***
PEMBERTON Max	Jeremy BELL; Capt BLACK; ***Bernard SUTTON***; Capt Jack WARD
PENDEXTER Hugh	Tiberius SMITH
PENDLETON Don	Mack (The Executioner) BOLAN; ***Joe COPP***; Ashton FORD
PENDOWER Jacques	Robert MAINE; ***Slade MCGINTY***
PENN John	John BRELAND and Mike FREEMAN; Insp/Ch Insp Dick TANSEY; ***Supt George THORNE***
PENNY Rupert	Insp Edward BEALE
PENTECOST Hugh	Luke BRADLEY; ***Pierre CHAMBRUN***; David COTTER; Uncle George CROWDER; Clyde HAVILAND; John JERICHO; John JERICHO and Lt PASCAL; Lt PASCAL; Julian QUIST; Grant SIMON and Lt PASCAL; Dr John SMITH; Mason TRASK
PENTELOW John Nix	Sexton BLAKE
PEPPE Frank	Steve BRADSHAW
PERDUE Virginia	Eleanora BURKE
PERELMAN S J	Sherlock HOLMES; ***Mike NOONAN***
PEROWNE Barry	***R J 'Rick' LEROY***; A J RAFFLES; A J RAFFLES and Sexton BLAKE; A J RAFFLES and R J 'Rick' LEROY
PERRY Anne	Insp William MONK; ***Insp Thomas PITT and Charlotte PITT***
PERRY James D	Dr NORTH
PERRY Ritchie	Frank MACALLISTER; ***Arthur PHILIS***
PERRY Thomas	Elizabeth WARING
PERRY Tyline	Sheriff Gus FLOWERS; ***Sheriff MACFARLAND***
PERTWEE Roland	Lord Louis LEWIS
PETERS Bill	Bill CANILLI
PETERS Bryan	Anthony BRANDON
PETERS Elizabeth	***Vicky BLISS***; Priest Amenhotep Sa HAPU; Jacqueline KIRBY; Amelia PEABODY
PETERS Ellis	***Brother CADFAEL***; George FELSE and Dominic FELSE; Francis KILLIAN; Det Insp MUSGRAVE
PETERS Geoffrey	Insp Trevor NICHOLLS
PETERS Ludovic	Ian FIRTH and John SMITH
PETERS Ron	Stash KOVAL
PETERS Steven	George WASHINGTON
PETERSEN Herman	'Doc' MILLER
PETERSON Audrey	Andrew QUENTIN and Jane WINFIELD
PETERSON Charles	Mr HOLBROOK
PETERSON Geoff	Boyd SHERMAN
PETERSON Jim	Mack (The Executioner) BOLAN
PETERSON Keith	John WELLS
PETIEVICH Gerald	Charles CARR and Jack KELLY
PETRIE Glen	Mycroft HOLMES
PETRIE Rhona	***Insp Marcus MACLURG***; Dr Nassim PRIDE
PETT Norman	Penny WISE
PETTEE F M	***Digby GRESHAM***; Beau QUICKSILVER
PHILBIN Tom	***Det George BENTON***; Det Joe LAWLESS, Offr Barbara BABALINO and Det Leo GRADY
PHILBRICK W R	J D HAWKINS; ***Connie KALE***; Philip MARLOWE; T D STASH
PHILIPS George Norman	Sexton BLAKE
PHILIPS Judson	James W BELLAMY; COYLE and DONOVAN; ***Peter STYLES***; Carole TREVOR and Max BLYTHE
PHILLIPS Edward O	Geoffrey CHADWICK
PHILLIPS Hubert	Insp BAILHACHE
PHILLIPS James Atlee	Joe GALL
PHILLIPS Leon	Prof Hugh MELLING
PHILLIPS Mark	Kenneth MALONE
PHILLIPS Mike	Samson DEAN
PHILLIPS R B	Elton DANCEY
PHILLIPS Stella	Insp Matthew FURNIVAL
PHILLPOTTS Eden	Avis BRYDEN; Peter GANNS; Peter HARDCASTLE; Insp Edward MAINE; ***Insp MIDWINTER***; PETERS; John RINGROSE; Richard SILVER and Insp Tarrant TINKLER; Dr THORNE; Insp Thomas WARNER
PHILMORE R	GARNETT; ***C J SWAN***
PICANO Felice	Noel CUMMINGS
PICKARD Nancy	Jennifer CAIN
PIDGIN Charles Felton	Quincy Adams SAWYER
PIDGIN Charles Felton and John M TAYLOR	Quincy Adams SAWYER
PIERCE David M	Vic DANIEL
PIERCY Rohase	Sherlock HOLMES
PIESMAN Marissa	***Nina FISCHMAN***; Nina FISCHMAN and Ida FISCHMAN
PIGGIN Julia Remine	Sarah HULL
PIKE Robert L	Lt CLANCY; ***Lt Jim REARDON***
PIKSER Jeremy	Joe POSNER
PILGRIM Chad	Ch Matt RUFFINS
PINES Paul	Pablo WAITZ and Maria PONCE
PINK Hal	Sgt/Insp DOCKER
PINKERTON A Frank	The AMERICAN DETECTIVE; Nic BROWN; Dyke DARREL; ***A Frank PINKERTON***; Det Patrick RYAN
PINKERTON Allan	Claude MELNOTTE; ***Allan PINKERTON***
PIPER H Beam	Col Jefferson Davis RAND
PIPER H Beam and John J M MCGUIRE	Sherlock HOLMES
PIPER Peter	Insp GRAY
PIRINCCI Akif	FRANCIS
PIRKIS C L	Loveday BROOKE
PLAIN Josephine	Colin ANSTRUTHER
PLATT Kin	Molly MELLINGER; ***Max ROPER***
PLATTS A Monmouth	Stephen MUNRO
PLATTS W Carter	Erasmus TUTTLEBERRY
PLEASANTS W Shepard	Paul GREEN
PLUM Mary	John SMITH
POATE Ernest M	Dr BENTIRON
POE Edgar A	Chevalier Auguste C DUPIN
POLLARD Captain A O	David WILSHAW
POLLARD Percival	Lingo DAN
POLSKY Thomas	L F 'Scoop' GRIDDLE
POND E J	Insp WAYNE
POOLE Michael	Freddie BROWNE and Jim FANSHAW
POOLE Reginald Heber	Sexton BLAKE
POPKIN Zelda	Mary CARNER
POPPLEWELL O M	Mrs SNAGG
PORCELAIN Sidney E	Stephen CLAY
PORGES Arthur	Capt (Retired) CORBETT; George Fort ELGIN; Celery GREEN; Cyriack Skinner GREY; Dr Joel HOFFMAN; Sherlock HOLMES; ***Stately HOMES***; Ben JOYCE; Alfred LEWIS; Arsène LUPIN; Ulysses Price MIDDLEBIE; Lt SELBY; Julian Morse TROWBRIDGE
PORLOCK Martin	Charles FOX-BROWNE

The Authors

PORTER Anna	Judith HAYES
PORTER Joyce	Edmund BROWN; ***Insp Wilfred DOVER***; The Hon Constance Ethel MORRISON-BURKE
POSEY Carl A	Stephen BORG
POST Melville Davisson	***Uncle ABNER***; Col BRAXTON; Sir Henry MARQUIS; Randolph MASON; WALKER
POST Mortimer	Lowell GAYLORD, Prof Angus MCDERMOTT, Lens PENGA and Prof Arthur CHURCHILL
POSTGATE Raymond	Insp HOLLY
POTTER J L	Jeff TYLER
POTTER Jeremy	Sgt/Insp HISCOCK
POTTER Jerry Allen	Samuel Clemens TUCKER
POTTS Jean	Sheriff JEFFRIES and Mr PIGEON
POURNELLE Jerry	Paul CRANE
POWELL Deborah	Hollis CARPENTER
POWELL Lester	Philip ODELL
POWELL P H	Supt GADEN
POWELL Richard	Arabella BLAKE and Andy BLAKE
POWELL Talmage	Ed RIVERS
POWERS Elizabeth	Viera KOLAROVA
POWERS James	Tom PARCHER
POYER Joe	Cole BROGAN
PRATHER Richard	Shell SCOTT
PRATHER Richard S	Shell SCOTT
PRATT Fletcher	***George Helmfleet JONES***; Ellis PARKER
PRATT Theodore	Anthony ADAMS
PREISS Byron	Philip MARLOWE
PRESCOT Julian	Julian PRESCOT
PRESCOTT H F M	Sgt TUCKER
PRESNELL Frank G	John WEBB and Anne WEBB
PRESTON James	Det Sgt Bob CHRISTIE
PRICE Anthony	***Dr David AUDLEY***; Frances FITZGIBBON; Dorothy Mayotte RIGBY
PRICE E Hoffman	Pawang ALI; ***John CARMODY***; Cliff CRAGIN; Jeff DARGAN
PRICE Frank Jr	Charles BARROW
PRICE Richard	Lt Rocco KLEIN
PRICHARD Hesketh	NOVEMBER JOE
PRICHARD K and Hesketh PRICHARD	Don Q
PRIESTLEY J B	Tim BEDFORD; Insp GOOLE ***Lionel Humphrey SALT and Maggie CULTHORPE***
PRINCE Jerome and Harold PRINCE	Insp John B MAGRUDER
PRIOR Allan	Jack EAVES
PROCTER Maurice	Det Supt Philip HUNTER; Bill KNIGHT; ***Det Insp Harry MARTINEAU***
PROCTOR Fred J	Mr KNUCKLESTONE
PRONIN Barbara	Lacey MADISON
PRONZINI Bill	Buckmaster GILLOON; Steven GIROUX; Sherlock HOLMES; ***NAMELESS DETECTIVE***; John QUINCANNON
PRONZINI Bill and John LUTZ	E L OXMAN and Art TOBIN
PRONZINI Bill and Marcia MULLER	***NAMELESS DETECTIVE and Sharon MCCONE***; Elena OLIVEREZ and John QUINCANNON
PRONZINI Bill and Collin WILCOX	NAMELESS DETECTIVE and Lt Frank HASTINGS
PROPPER Milton	Det Tommy RANKIN
PROUD Franklin M	Joe SANFORD
PROUDFOOT Walter	Insp Bill VALLANCE
PROWELL Sandra West	Phoebe SIEGEL
PRUITT Alan	Don CARSON
PRYCE Larry	Dick BARTON
PUCCETTI Roland	Harvey SHAPMAN
PUCKET Andrew	Tom JONES
PUHL Gayle Lange	Sheercrocked MOANS
PULLEIN-THOMPSON Josephine	Insp James FLECKER
PULVER Mary Monica	Sgt Peter 'Obie' BRICHTER
PUNSHON E R	Insp CARTER; ***Cdr Bobby OWEN***
PURLEY John	Sexton BLAKE
PURSER Philip	Colin PANTON
PURTILL Richard	Athena PIERCE
PYLE A M	Cesar Augustus FRANCK

—Q—

Q John	Peter TREES
QUARRY Nick	Jake BARROW
QUARTERMAIN James	CARBO
QUEEN Ellery	Ellery QUEEN
QUEEN Ellery (Gil BREWER)	Micah 'Mike' MCCALL
QUEEN Ellery (Richard DEMING)	***Tim CORRIGAN***; Micah 'Mike' MCCALL
QUEEN Ellery (Edward Dentinger HOCH)	Micah 'Mike' MCCALL
QUEEN Ellery (House name)	Ellery QUEEN; Sherlock HOLMES; ***Barney BURGESS***
QUEEN Ellery (Talmage POWELL)	Tim CORRIGAN
QUEEN Ellery (John Holbrook VANCE)	***Insp Omar COLLINS***; Insp TARR and Ann NELSON
QUENTIN Patrick	***Peter DULUTH***; Peter DULUTH and Lt Timothy TRANT; Andrew JORDAN; Mark LIDDON; Nicky ROOD; Lt Timothy TRANT
QUEST Erica	***Det Ch Insp Kate MADDOX***; Tess PENNICOTT
QUEST Rodney	Peter QUENTIN
QUICK Dorothy	Lt Peter DONNEGAN
QUILL Monica	Sister Mary Teresa DEMPSEY
QUIN B G	James CLARKSON-PARRY
QUINN E Baker	James STRANGE
QUINN Elizabeth	Lauren MAXWELL
QUINN Jake	Patrick SHANNON
QUINN John	Rod (The Terminator) GAVIN
QUINN Patrick	Pete RILEY
QUINN Seabury	Jules DE GRANDIN
QUINN Simon	Francis X (The Inquisitor) KILLY
QUINTON Ann	Det Insp James ROLAND
QUIROULE Pierre	Sexton BLAKE
QUOGAN Anthony	Matthew PRIOR

—R—

RABE Peter	Manny DEWITT
RADFORD E and M A MANGAN	***Dr MANSON***; Prof Marcus STUBBS
RADFORD John P	Joe (The Illusionist) MAGUIRE
RADLEY Sheila	Det Ch Insp Douglas QUANTRILL
RADNOR Alan	Dick BARTON
RAE Hugh C	Insp MCCAIG
RAFFERTY S S	Capt CORK
RAINE Richard	David MARTINI
RAINEY Rich	Alex (The Protector) DARTANIAN
RAISON Milton M	Tony WOOLRICH
RAISON Milton M and Jack HARVEY	Tony WOOLRICH
RALSTON Gilbert A	DAKOTA
RAMM Carl	James HAWKER
RAMSAY Diana	Lt MEREDITH
RANDALL Anthony A	Roger PATTEN
RANDALL William R	Mortimer DREXEL
RANDISI Robert J	***Sal CARLUCCI***; Nick DELVECCHIO; Miles JACOBY; Philip MARLOWE; Henry PO
RANKIN Ian	Insp REBUS
RANSOME Stephen	Jill ARCHER; Lt Lee BARCELLO; Stephen RANSOME; ***Luke SPEARE and Schyler COLE***
RASKIN Ellen	GARSON
RATH Virginia	***Rocky ALLAN***; Rocky ALLAN and Michael DUNDAS; Michael DUNDAS
RATHBONE Julian	Jan ARGAND; I; John DANBY
RATTRAY Simon	Hugo BISHOP
RAWLS Philip	Richard BRONSON
RAWSON Clayton	The Great MERLINI
RAY Robert	Matt MURDOCK; ***Clayton 'Yankee' TAGGART***
RAYMOND Clifford S	John STANTON
RAYMOND John	***George BULMAN***; DEMPSEY and MAKEPEACE
RAYNOR Claire	Dr George BARNABAS
RAYTER Joe	Johnny POWERS
RAZIO Rick	Rick RAZIO
REA M P	Lt POWLEDGE
REACH Alice Scanlon	Father Francis Xavier CRUMLISH
REACH James	Michael SHAYNE; ***WING***
REAMY Tom	Bert MALLORY
REASONER James M	CODY
REAVES J Michael	KAMUS OF KADIZAR
REAVES Sam	Cooper MACLEISH
REDMAN J M	Micky KNIGHT
REDMOND Chris	Sherlock HOLMES
REDWING Morris	Eagle GRAY
REED Barry	Dan SHERIDAN
REED Christopher	Manx MCCATTY
REED Harlan	Dan JORDAN
REED Ishmael	Papa LA BAS
REED Wallace	Sheriff Bill LLOYD
REES Arthur J	David COLWYN; Colwin GREY; ***Insp LUCKRAFT***
REES Dilwyn	Prof Richard CHERRINGTON
REES George	Sexton BLAKE
REES Olwen	Insp Felix HOBBINGDON
REESE John	Jefferson HEWITT
REEVE Arthur B	Constance DUNLAP; ***Prof Craig KENNEDY***
REEVE Joel	Patrolman MURPHY

REEVES John	Insp Andrew COGGIN
REEVES Robert	Cellini SMITH; ***Thomas C THERON***
REGAN Cass	Rusty BROWN
REGIS Julius	Maurice WALLION
REID Desmond (A CAHILL)	Sexton BLAKE
REID Desmond (W A BALLINGER)	Sexton BLAKE
REID Desmond (Sydney James BOUNDS)	Sexton BLAKE
REID Desmond (Noel BROWNE)	Sexton BLAKE
REID Desmond (John Frederick BURKE)	Sexton BLAKE
REID Desmond (John Newton CHANCE)	Sexton BLAKE
REID Desmond (Rex DOLPHIN)	Sexton BLAKE
REID Desmond (Anthony DOUSE)	Sexton BLAKE
REID Desmond (Robert Cowell ELLIOTT)	Sexton BLAKE
REID Desmond (Stephen Daniel FRANCES)	Sexton BLAKE
REID Desmond (A GARSTIN)	Sexton BLAKE
REID Desmond (Anthony Arthur GLYNN)	Sexton BLAKE
REID Desmond (Victor Joseph HANSON)	Sexton BLAKE
REID Desmond (Miss S HALL)	Sexton BLAKE
REID Desmond (Frank LAMBE)	Sexton BLAKE
REID Desmond (Christopher LOWDER)	Sexton BLAKE
REID Desmond (A L MARTIN)	Sexton BLAKE
REID Desmond (Brian MCARDLE)	Sexton BLAKE
REID Desmond (Wilfred MCNEILLY)	Sexton BLAKE
REID Desmond (Eddie PLAYER)	Sexton BLAKE
REID Desmond (Ross RICHARDS)	Sexton BLAKE
REID Desmond (Lee ROBERTS)	Sexton BLAKE
REID Desmond (Colin ROBERTSON)	Sexton BLAKE
REID Desmond (Gordon SOWMAN)	Sexton BLAKE
REID Desmond (James STAGG)	Sexton BLAKE
REID Desmond (Rosamond Mary STORY)	Sexton BLAKE
REID Desmond (George Heber TEED)	Sexton BLAKE
REILLY Helen	Insp Christopher MCKEE
REINSMITH Richard	Ray (The Bodyguard) MARTIN
REMENHAM John	***Insp BADGER***; Insp BLISS
RENARD Maurice	Jean MAREUIL
RENDALL Vernon	Christopher BELSIZE
RENDELL Ruth	Anthony JOHNSON; ***Ch Insp Reginald WEXFORD***
RENNERT Maggie	Lt Guy SILVESTRI
RENO Marie R	Karen LINDSTROM
RESNICK Laura	Sherlock HOLMES
RESNICK Mike	John Justin MALLORY
RESNICK Mike and Martin H GREENBERG	Sherlock HOLMES
RESNICOW Herbert	***Ed BAER***; Alexander Magnus GOLD; Giles SULLIVAN
RESNICOW Herbert and Fran TARHENTON	Marcus Aurelius BURR
RESNICOW Herbert and PELE	Marcus Aurelius BURR
REVELL Louisa	Miss Julia TYLER
REVELLI George	Amanda NIGHTINGALE
REVERE John D	Justin (The Assassin) PERRY
REYNOLDS Adrian	Prof Dennis BARRIE
REYNOLDS George	Victor MAURY
REYNOLDS John Lawrence	Lt Joe MCGUIRE
REYNOLDS Mack	***Rex BADER***; Sherlock HOLMES
REYNOLDS William J	NEBRASKA
REZNEK Lawrie	Dr Neal POTTER
RHEA Nicholas	Const Nick RHEA
RHOADES Knight	Lt Price PRICE
RHODE John	Insp HANSLET and Dr Lancelot PRIESTLEY; ***Dr Lancelot PRIESTLEY***; Jimmy WAGHORN
RHODES Daniel	Guilhem DE COURDEVAL
RICE Craig	Jake JUSTUS, Helene JUSTUS and John J MALONE; ***John J MALONE***; 'Bingo' RIGGS and 'Handsome' KUSAK
RICE Craig and Ed MCBAIN	'Bingo' RIGGS and 'Handsome' KUSAK
RICE Craig and Stuart PALMER	Hildegarde WITHERS and John J MALONE
RICE Jeff	Carl KOLCHAK

RICH Arthur T	Insp LIGHTFOOT
RICH Nicholas	Adam HOOD
RICH Virginia	Eugenia POTTER
RICH Willard	Insp NOONAN
RICHARDS Clay	Grant KIRBY; ***Kim LOCKE***
RICHARDS Nat	Otis DUNN
RICHARDS Paul (John J MESSMAN and George SNYDER)	Grant FOWLER
RICHARDS Paul (George SNYDER and Daniel Thomas STREIB)	Grant FOWLER
RICHARDS Paul (Daniel Thomas STREIB and Chet CUNNINGHAM)	Grant FOWLER
RICHARDSON H M	Robert HUTCH
RICHARDSON Maurice	Sherlock HOLMES
RICHARDSON Robert	Sherlock HOLMES; ***Augustus MALTRAVERS***
RICHMOND Grace	Sally HANSON
RICO Don	Burgess 'Buzz' CARDIGAN; ***Casey GRANT***
RIDDELL John	Pluto VANCE
RIDEAL Maurice Moser and Charles F RIDEAL	Insp MOSER
RIDER J W	MALONE
RIDGWAY Jason	Brian GUY
RIDLEY Arnold	Edward Gascoyne MORRISON
RIDLEY Nat Jr	Nat RIDLEY
RIEFE Alan	***Huntingdon CAGE***; Tygrus Gerald 'Tyger' DECKER
RIFKIN Shepard	Joe DUNNE; ***Damian MCQUAID***
RIGGS John R	Garth RYLAND
RIGSBY Howard	Timothy WILDE
RILEY Dick	Tom RIORDAN
RINEHART Mary Roberts	Hilda ADAMS; Jennie BRICE; ***Letitia CARBERRY***; Maj DANE; Insp HARRISON; Rachel INNES; Terrence O'BRIEN
RING Adam	Jim PIERCE
RING Raymond H	Henry DYER
RIPLEY Jack	John George DAVIS
RIPLEY Mike	Fitzroy Maclean ANGEL
RIPPERGER Walter	Carter DE RAVEN
RIPPON Marion	Insp Maurice YGREC
RISENHOOVER C C	Matt MCCALL
RITCHIE Jack	Henry TURNBUCKLE
RITCHIE Simon	John Kenneth Galbraith JANTARRO
RITTENBERG Max	Dr Xavier WYCHERLY
RIVERA William L	Arthur 'Turo' BIRONICO
ROADARMEL Paul	Tommy BERREN
ROAN Tom	Bill MANDELL and Capt Andrew LEE
ROBB Candace M	Owen ARCHER
ROBB T N	Jack CLEARY
ROBBINS Clifton	***Clay HARRISON***; STAVELEY
ROBERTS Barrie	Sherlock HOLMES
ROBERTS Carey	Det Ann FITZHUGH
ROBERTS Carl Eric Bechhofer	A B C HAWKES
ROBERTS Gillian	Amanda PEPPER
ROBERTS Lee	Andy BRICE; ***Lee FISKE***; Chad PROCTOR; Dr Clinton SHANNON
ROBERTS Les	***Milan JACOVICH***; SAXON
ROBERTS Marion	Anne LAYTON and David LAYTON
ROBERTS Morley	Capt Harry SPINK
ROBERTS Nora	Ed JACKSON
ROBERTS Ralph	Sherlock HOLMES
ROBERTS Randall Howland	Alex SMART
ROBERTS S C	Sherlock HOLMES
ROBERTS W Adolphe	Margot ANSTRUTHER and Gene VALERY
ROBERTS Willo Davis	Jane MADISON
ROBERTSON Alexander	***Detective GRIME***; OLD SPECIE
ROBERTSON Colin	Supt BRADLEY; Peter GRAYLEIGH; Victor MCBAIN; Edward NORTH; ***Mike REED***; Alan STEEL; Insp Robert STRONG
ROBERTSON Helen	Insp Lathom DYNES
ROBERTSON Manning K	Steve CARRADINE
ROBERTSON Muirhead	Percival MONTGOMERY
ROBERTSON Stephen	Ryne LANARK
ROBESON Kenneth (Paul ERNST)	Richard Henry (The Avenger) BENSON
ROBESON Kenneth (Ronald Joseph GOULART)	Richard Henry (The Avenger) BENSON
ROBESON Kenneth (William BOGART)	'Doc' SAVAGE
ROBESON Kenneth (Harold A DAVIS)	'Doc' SAVAGE
ROBESON Kenneth ((Lester DENT))	'Doc' SAVAGE
ROBESON Kenneth (Lester DENT and William BOGART)	'Doc' SAVAGE
ROBESON Kenneth (Lester DENT and Harold A DAVIS)	'Doc' SAVAGE
ROBESON Kenneth (Lester DENT and Walter Ryerson JOHNSON)	'Doc' SAVAGE
ROBESON Kenneth (Laurence DONOVAN)	'Doc' SAVAGE

The Authors

ROBESON Kenneth (Alan HATHWAY)	'Doc' SAVAGE
ROBESON Kenneth	Ed STONE
ROBINETT Stephen	Jerry JEETER
ROBINSON Abby	Nick PALLADINO
ROBINSON B Fletcher	Addington PEACE
ROBINSON B Fletcher and J Malcolm FRASER	Robert HARLAND
ROBINSON Frank M	Sherlock HOLMES
ROBINSON Gene D	Ned CAIN
ROBINSON Janice	Lorna COOPER
ROBINSON Lewis	Maj Weston PRYME
ROBINSON Lynda S	MEREN
ROBINSON Peter	Ch Insp Alan BANKS
ROBINSON Robert	Insp AUTUMN
ROBINSON Timothy	Insp MILD, Charles BLAKELOCK, Edward DONALDSON, Andrew MUIR, John QUINCE and Prof BROWNING
ROBITAILLE Julie	Kit POWELL
ROCHE Arthur Somers	Sam KERNOCHAN
ROCHESTER Geo E	Grey SHADOW
ROCKWOOD Harry	The BELL BOY DETECTIIVE; Fred DANFORD; DYKE and BURR; ***Clarice DYKE***; Mrs Donald DYKE; Donald DYKE; Abner FERRET; Nat FOSTER; Allan KEENE; Luke LEIGHTON; Neil NELSON; Harry PINKURTON; Harry SHARPE; Walt WHEELER
RODD Ralph	Anthea JUBB
RODEN H W	Sid AMES
RODERUS Frank	Carl HELLER
RODNEY Bryan	Francis VILLIERS
ROE C F	Dr Jean MONTROSE
ROEBURT John	Johnny DEVEREAUX; ***'Jigger' MORAN***
ROFFMAN Jan	***Michael HADDEN***; RATLIN
ROGAN Don	LOU
ROGERS Joel Townsley	***Kerry OTT***; Dr Henry RIDDLE and Prof Adam MACAMERON
ROGERS Samuel	Prof Paul HATFIELD
ROGERS Steve	Ferrers LOCKE
ROHDE William L	Mohawk DANIELS
ROHMER Sax	Bimbashi BAUK; Insp BRISTOL; Paul HARLEY; Ch Insp Daniel 'Red' KERRY; Morris KLAW; Gaston MAX; Capt O'HAGAN; ***Insp RYDER***; Insp SHEFFIELD
ROLFE Maro O	DIAMOND DAN
ROME Anthony	Tony ROME
RONALD E B	Rupert BRADLEY
RONALD James	Dr Daniel BRITLING; Julian MEDOZA; ***Supt WRENN***
RONNS Edward	***Jerry BENEDICT***; Reginald 'Beauty' BLACK
ROOK Clarence	Miss Nora VAN SNOOP
ROOME Annette	Chris MARTIN
ROOS Kelley	Steve BARTON and Connie BARTON; Timothy O'HARA and Nancy BREWSTER; ***Jeff TROY and Haila TROY***
ROOSEVELT Elliott	Eleanor ROOSEVELT
ROOTH Anne Reed	Hank SULLIVAN
ROPER L V	***Jerry 'Renegade' ROE and Stuart WORTH***; Michael SAXON
ROSA Dennis	Sherlock HOLMES
ROSCOE Mike	Johnny APRIL
ROSCOE Theodore	John H W KEATS
ROSEN Dorothy and Sidney ROSEN	Belle APPLEMAN
ROSEN R D	Harvey BLISSBERG
ROSEN S J	Lydia CHIN
ROSENBERG John and Elizabeth ROSENBERG	Insp HARRIS
ROSENBERG Nancy Taylor	***Dr Lily FORRESTER***; Judge Lara SANDERSTONE
ROSENBERGER Joseph	Richard (The Death Merchant) CAMELLION; ***Louis Luther (Murder Master) KING***
ROSENBLUM Robert	Pete RENO
ROSENHAYN Paul	Joe JENKINS
ROSENKJAR Pat	Sherlock HOLMES
ROSENTHAL Erik	Dan BRODSKY
ROSS Angus	***Marcus Aurelius FARROW***; Marcus Aurelius FARROW and Charlie MCGOWAN;
ROSS Barnaby	Drury LANE
ROSS Carlton	Bill MORROW and Jacqueline PINKER
ROSS Charles H	Jack JEFFCOAT
ROSS Frank	Lucas GARFIELD
ROSS Gene	Shaun O'MALLEY
ROSS Ian	Britt (Mind Masters) ST VINCENT
ROSS Ivan T	Ben GORDON
ROSS John	Maj Hutton SEARY
ROSS Jonathan	Det Supt George ROGERS
ROSS Kate	Julian KESTREL
ROSS Leonard Q	Bradford GALT
ROSS Paul (Bill AMIDON and Nathaniel FREEDLAND)	Terry (Chopper Cop) BUNKER
ROSS Paul (William Elbert CRAWFORD)	Terry (Chopper Cop) BUNKER
ROSS Paul (Daniel Thomas STREIB)	Terry (Chopper Cop) BUNKER
ROSS Philip	***James MARLEY***; Tom TALLEY
ROSS Z H	Beau SMITH and Pogy ROGERS
ROSSI Bruno (House name)	Johnny ROCK
ROSSI Bruno (Paul HOFRICHTER)	Johnny ROCK
ROSSI Bruno (Leonard LEVINSON (	Johnny ROCK
ROSSI Bruno (Russell SMITH)	Johnny ROCK
ROSSI Bruno (John STEVENSON)	Johnny ROCK
ROSSITER John	***Supt INKBARROW***; Roger TALLIS
ROSSMANN John F	Britt (Mind Masters) ST VINCENT
ROSSO Anne Oakins	Sherlock HOLMES
ROSTAND Robert	Mike LOCKEN
ROSTEN Leo	Bradford GALT; ***Sidney 'Silky' PINCUS and Mike CLANCY***
ROTH Holly	William FARLAND; Monte GORDON and Insp MEDFORD; Lt KELLY; ***Insp MEDFORD***
ROTHWELL C C	Sherwood HOAKES
ROTHWELL H T	Mike BROOKS
ROUGVIE Cameron	Robert BELCOURT
ROVIN Jeff	Roger GARRISON
ROWAN Hester	Kate PATERSON
ROWE Anne	Insp BARRY; ***Insp PETTENGILL***
ROWE Jennifer	Verity 'Birdie' BIRDWOOD
ROWLAND Henry C	Frank CLAMART
ROWLAND John	Insp SHELLEY
ROWLAND Peter	Sherlock HOLMES
ROWLANDS Betty	Melissa CRAIG
ROWLANDS D G	Father O'CONNOR
ROYCE Kenneth	Laurie GALVIN; Matt PRESTON; ***Willie 'Spider' SCOTT***
RUBEL James L	Eli DONOVAN
RUBEL Marc	Rusty CUTLER
RUD Anthony M	J C K 'Jigger' MASTERS
RUEGG Judge	Rosie BRIGHT
RUELL Patrick	Det Insp CICERO
RUNYON Charles W	Marcus GREENE
RUSCH Kristine Kathryn	Sherlock HOLMES
RUSE Gary Alan	Sherlock HOLMES
RUSHTON Charles	***Insp CADMAN***; James O'HANNAY and Floyd EAST
RUSSELL Alan	Am CAULFIELD; Stuart WINTER
RUSSELL Charles	Sergei ROLF
RUSSELL Charlotte Murray	***Jane Amanda EDWARDS***; Homer FITZGERALD; Wally KENT
RUSSELL E S	Ben LOUIS
RUSSELL Fox	Alfred DIMMOCK
RUSSELL Martin	***Steven CASSELL***; Jim LARKIN; Mike WILLOUGHBY
RUSSELL Ray	FOAMES; ***Julian TRASK***
RUSSELL Richard	Angel GRAHAM
RUSSELL W Clark	***Col KILMAIN***; Jock THIRLSTANE
RUTHERFORD Douglas	***Jay DELANEY***; Patrick MALONE
RUTLAND Harriet	Mr WINKLEY
RUTTER Amanda	Irene TENNANT
RUYLE John	Turlock LOAMS
RYAN Conall	KNIGHTSBRIDGE
RYAN Harry	Det Ch Insp Alexander 'Sandy' WOODINGS
RYAN Jessica	Gregory 'Grischa' PAVLOV
RYLAND Clive	***Ch Insp George BASSETT***; Insp BECK; Supt SHANNON
RYLAND John Knox	Insp RODWAY

— S —

SABER Robert O	***Carl GOOD***; Phil KEENE; Max KEENE
SABERHAGEN Howard M	Sherlock HOLMES
SADDLER K Allen	Dave STEVENS
SADLER Mark	Paul SHAW
SAGE Dana	Donald O'Keefe ADAMS
SAINT Eddie	Lois DULANE
SALE Medora	Insp John SANDERS
SALE Richard	Joseph 'Daffy' DILL and Insp HANLEY; Candid JONES and Insp Harry RENTANO; Penny PACKER and Det Jim SCOTT; ***Calamity QUADE***; Det Daniel WEBSTER
SALINGER Pierre	André KOHL
SALLIS James	Lew GRIFFIN
SALO Paula	Sherlock HOLMES
SALTER Elizabeth	Insp Michael HORNSLEY
SALTMARSH Max	Archie LUMSDEN
SALWAY Reginald E	Peter RUFF
SAMPSON George	PAOLA and GEORGE
SAMPSON Victor	Insp DOWNES and Sgt HOPKINS
SAN NTONIO	SAN ANTONIO
SANBORN Ruth Burr	Angeline TREDENNICK
SANDERS Bruce	Howard DIGBURN
SANDERS Buck A (House name)	Ben 'T-Man' SLAYTON
SANDERS Buck B (Thomas Larry ADCOCK)	Ben 'T-Man' SLAYTON
SANDERS Buck C (Jeffrey FRENTZEN)	Ben 'T-Man' SLAYTON

SANDERS John	Nicholas PYM
SANDERS Lawrence	Mary Lou 'Dunk' BATESON; Timothy CONE; Dora CONTI; ***Ex-Plce Edward X DELANEY***; Archie MCNALLY; Peter TANGENT
SANDERS Leonard	Clay LOOMIS
SANDFORD John	Lucas DAVENPORT
SANDFORD Kenneth	Max HALE
SANDSTROM Eve K	Sheriff Sam TITUS and Nicky TITUS
SANDYS James	James CHARLESWORTH; ***Insp MILLWALL***; Mr SPRINGFIELD
SANDYS Oliver	Lady WEYBRIDGE
SANGER Joan	Peter ALCOTT and John ELLIS
SANGSTER Jimmy	***James REED***; John SMITH; Katy TOUCHFEATHER
SANTIAGO V J	Joseph (The Vigilante) MADDEN
SAPIR Richard	Alphonse Joseph BRESSIO; ***Remo (The Destroyer) WILLIAMS***
SAPPER	***Capt Hugh 'Bulldog' DRUMMOND***; Capt Hugh 'Bulldog' DRUMMOND and Ronald STANDISH; Jim MAITLAND; Ronald STANDISH
SARIOLA Mauri	Osmo KILPI
SARRANTONIO Al	Jack PAINE
SARSFIELD Maureen	Insp Lane PARRY
SARTO Ben	Gentle HOGGERTY
SARTO Ben	Miss OTIS
SATTERTHWAIT Walter	Lizzie BORDEN; ***Rita MONDRAGON***; Oscar WILDE
SAUM Karen	Brigid DONOVAN
SAUNDERS Hilary St George	Raoul WEILER
SAUNDERS Lawrence	Wylie KING and Nels LUNDBERG
SAUTER Eric	***Robert Lee HUNTER***; Det PAIGE; Det YATES
SAVAGE Edward H	A BOSTON POLICE OFFICER
SAVAGE Ernest	Sam TRAIN
SAVAGE Jack	DEMPSEY and MAKEPEACE
SAVAGE Richard Henry	Florence RENWICK
SAVAGE Richard	Dr FERENC
SAVARIN Julian Jay	Gordon GALLAGHER; ***David PROSS***
SAVILLE Andrew	BERGERAC
SAWKINS Raymond H	Supt John SNOW
SAWYER Corrine Holt	Angela BENBOW and Caledonia WINGATE
SAWYER Eugene T	OLD QUARTZ
SAWYER Lynwood	Prof Austin LYLE
SAWYER Robert J	Sherlock HOLMES
SAXE R B	John (The Ghost) DOBBS
SAXON Peter (William Arthur Howard BAKER)	Sexton BLAKE
SAXON Peter (W A BALLINGER)	Sexton BLAKE
SAXON Peter (Sydney James BOUNDS)	Sexton BLAKE
SAXON Peter (Stephen Daniel FRANCES)	Sexton BLAKE
SAXON Peter (Wilfred MCNEILLY)	Sexton BLAKE
SAXON John (House name)	Sam WELPTON
SAXON John (Robert Leslie BELLEM)	Sam WELPTON
SAYER W W	Sexton BLAKE; ***Barnaby GRAYLE***
SAYERS Dorothy L	Montague EGG; ***Lord Peter WIMSEY***
SAYERS Dorothy L and Robert EUSTACE	Lord Peter WIMSEY
SCANLON C K M	Dan FOWLER; ***The MASKED DETECTIVE***
SCANLON Noel	QUINN
SCARLETT Roger	Insp KANE
SCARPETTA Frank	Phillip (The Marksman) MAGELLAN
SCERBANECO Giorgio	Duca LAMBERTI
SCHERF Margaret	Hal BRADY; Henry BRYCE and Emily BRYCE; ***Rev Martin BUELL***; Lt RYAN; Prof Grace SEVERANCE
SCHIER Norma	Kay BARTH
SCHIMEL Lawrence	Sherlock HOLMES
SCHISGALL Oscar	Baron IXELL
SCHLEY Sturges Mason	Dr Quentin TOBY
SCHMIDT Dan	Vic (Eagle Force) GABRIEL
SCHMITT Leo F	Jim ASBESTOS
SCHMITZ James H	Telzey AMBERDON and Trigger ARGEE
SCHOCK T A	Daniel KEEL
SCHOENFELD Howard	Jerry NELSON
SCHOLEFIELD Alan	Det Supt George MACRAE and Det Sgt Leopold SILVER
SCHOLEY Jean	Commiss Geoffrey HALLDEN
SCHOPEN Bernard	Jack ROSS
SCHORR Mark	***Red DIAMOND***; Theodore ROOSEVELT and Jim WHITE; Robert STARK
SCHUTZ Benjamin M	***Leo HAGGERTY***; Philip MARLOWE
SCHWEIK Robert C	Prof Paul ENGEL
SCOBER	Dick SAUNDERS
SCOPPETONE Sandra	Lauren LAURANO
SCOTT Bruce	Supt Steve MACLAREN
SCOTT Denis	Mike JAMES
SCOTT Don	RAKER
SCOTT Hedley	Sexton BLAKE; Ferrers LOCKE
SCOTT Jack S	Sgt ACKROYD; Ch Insp Peter PARSON; ***Det Insp Alf ROSHER***
SCOTT Justin	Ben ABBOTT
SCOTT Leroy	Bob CLIFFORD
SCOTT Mansfield	Insp Malcolm STEELE
SCOTT Mary Semple	Herbert CROSBY
SCOTT Maxwell	Martin DALE; ***Nelson LEE***; Vernon READ
SCOTT Milton	Dr Alexander CORNELL

SCOTT R T M	Aurelius SMITH
SCOTT Roney	Joe PUMA
SCOTT Sutherland	Dr Septimus DODDS
SCOTT Will	***DISHER***; GIGLAMPS
SEAFARER	Capt FIREBRACE
SEAFORTH	Lady Jane EASTINGS
SEAMAN Donald	SYDENHAM
SEAMARK	***Tommy DELAYN***; Forrest ORD
SEARLS Hank	Mike BLAIR
SEARS Edward S	Milton JARVIS
SEATON Stuart	Insp Martin LAIDMAN
SEA-LION	***Desmond DRAKE***; John PRENTICE
SECRIST Kelliher	Sham PAYNE
SEDLEY Kate	ROGER THE CHAPMAN
SEIFERT Adele	Gregory TRENT
SELA Owen	Nicholas MAASTEN
SELLERS Crighton	Sherlock HOLMES
SELLERS Michael	Cal FISHER
SELMARK George	Insp BASS
SELWYN Francis	William VERITY
SEMPHILL Ernest	Sexton BLAKE
SEMYONOV Julian	Vitaly SLAVIN
SENNOCKE T J R	Capt MALLORY
SERAFIN David	Supt Luis BERNAL
SETON Graham	Col Duncan GRANT
SEUFFERT Muir	Mike HUBBARD
SEVERN Donald	Charles GARRETT
SEVERN Richard	Jeff CASS
SEVERY Martin	George MAITLAND
SEWARD Jack	Curt STONE
SEWART Alan	Det Sgt Harry CHAMBERLANE
SEYMOUR Gerald	Harry BROWN
SHAFFER Anthony and P SHAFFER	FATHOM
SHAGAN Steve	Barney CAINE
SHAKLEY Jay	Sherlock HOLMES
SHALET Stephen A	Sherlock HOLMES
SHALLITT Joseph	Dan MORRISON
SHAND William	William TEMPEST
SHANE Susannah	Christopher SAXE
SHANKMAN Sarah	***Samantha ADAMS***; Annie TANNENBAUM
SHANNON Brad	'Lefty' O'CONNOR
SHANNON Dell	Lt Luis MENDOZA
SHANNON Jimmy	Ruff MORGAN
SHARKEY Jack	George Herbert HENRY
SHARP Alan	Harry MOSEBY
SHARP Allen	Sherlock HOLMES
SHARP David	***Prof Henry Arthur FIELDING***; Sheridan ORFORD and Prof Henry Arthur FIELDING
SHARP Luke	Sherlock HOLMES; ***Sherlaw KOMBS***
SHARP Marilyn	Richard OWEN
SHAW Howard	Insp BARNABY
SHAW Simon	Phillip FLETCHER
SHAW Stanley Gordon	Sexton BLAKE
SHAW Stanley	Sherlock HOLMES
SHAY Frank	Dan 'DeeDee' DONER
SHECKLEY Robert	Stephen DAIN
SHELDON Sidney	Catherine DOUGLAS
SHELDON Sylvan	Sgt YALE
SHELDON Walter J	Paul J BURDOCK and Joshua PRELL
SHELLEY Mike	Bernard HOLLAND; ***Barney HUGGINS***
SHEPHERD Eric	Supt Andrew PEARSON
SHEPHERD Joan	Insp JOLIVET
SHEPHERD John	Bill LENNOX
SHEPHERD Neal	Ch Insp Michael 'Napper' TANDY
SHEPHERD Stella	Insp Richard MONTGOMERY
SHERBURNE James	Paddy MORETTI
SHERIDAN Juanita	Lily WU and Janice CAMERON
SHERIDAN Wilfred	Tommy WESTON
SHERMAN Jory	Dr Russell V 'Chill' CHILDERS
SHERMAN Josepha	Sherlock HOLMES
SHERMAN Steve	Hugh QUINT
SHERROD Floyd	Sherlock HOLMES
SHERWOOD John	***Charles BLESSINGTON***; Celia GRANT
SHIEL M P	Cummings King MONK; ***Prince ZALESKI***
SHOEMAKER Bill	Coley KILLEBREW
SHORE Julian	Mark MILLNER
SHORE Viola Brothers	Shirley HOLMES; ***Gwynn LEITH and Colin KEATS***
SHOUBRIDGE Donald	STANDIFORD
SHRIBER Ione Sandberg	Lt Bill GRADY
SHROG J M	Bernard MCFOY
SHUBIN Seymour	Lt LASALA
SHUMAN M K	Micah DUNN
SHUTE Walter	Sexton BLAKE
SIBLEY Celestine	Kate MULCAY
SICILANO Sam	Sherlock HOLMES
SIKORSKI John	Sherlock HOLMES
SILBERRAD Una L	John BOLSOVER
SILER Jack	Tom FARLEY
SILLER Van	***Richard MASSEY***; Pete RECTOR; Alan STEWART
SILLIPHANT Sterling	John LOCKE
SILVERMAN Marguerite R	Insp Christopher ADRIAN
SILVERWOOD Roger	Supt CAWTHORNE
SIMENON Georges	Insp Jules MAIGRET
SIMMONS Addison	Capt PACKER and Kent BLOOMINGDALE

The Authors

SIMMONS Geoffrey S	Corey THATCHER
SIMON Robert A	Jimmy WROME
SIMON Roger L	Philip MARLOWE; ***Moses VINE***
SIMON	Insp/Supt DEERING
SIMONS Roger	Insp Fadiman WACE
SIMPSON Charles H	Charley SHIPTON
SIMPSON Dorothy	Det Insp Luke THANET
SIMPSON Howard R	Insp Roger BASTIDE
SIMS George R	Det Insp CHANCE; ***Dorcas DENE***; Jabez DUCK; Det Insp HOGARTH; WESTON
SIMS L V	Dixie T STRUTHERS
SINCLAIR Fiona	Insp Paul GRAINGER
SINCLAIR Murray	Ben CRANDEL
SINCLAIR Upton	Lanny BUDD
SINGER Bant	Denis DELANEY
SINGER Rochelle	Jake SAMSON
SINGER Shelley	Jake SAMSON
SINSTADT Gerald	Geoffrey LANDON
SIVERNS Ruth	Barlow DALE
SJOWALL Maj	Insp Martin BECK
SKENE Anthony	Sexton BLAKE
SKIRROW Desmond	John BROCK
SKLEPOWICH Edward	Urbino MACINTYRE
SKVORECKY Josef	Eve ADAM; ***Lt BORUVKA***
SLADEK John	Thackeray PHIN
SLATE John	Maria BLACK
SLATER Will	D'Arcy DEWPOND
SLEATH Frederick	Jim MARTIN
SLESAR Henry	Dave ROBBINS and Max THERINGER; ***Steve TYNER***
SLOAN Ben	Max HORN
SLOVO Gillian	Kate BAIER
SMALL Austin J	Forrest ORD
SMART Hawley	Sgt BOYCE; BULLOCK; CHISEL; COOL CARTER; John DICKINSON; Robert PEGRAM; ***Insp POLLOCK***; Sgt Silas USHER
SMITH Alison	Judd SPRINGFIELD
SMITH April	Ana GREY
SMITH Arthur D Howden	Miles MCCONAUGHY
SMITH C I D	Insp BARLOWE
SMITH Charles Merrill	Rev Cesare RANDOLLPH
SMITH Clark	Nicky MAHOUN
SMITH D O	Sherlock HOLMES
SMITH D W	Det Ch Supt Harry FATHERS
SMITH David	Jim STEVENS
SMITH Dean Wesley	Sherlock HOLMES
SMITH Derek	Algy LAWRENCE
SMITH Don	Tim PARNELL; ***Phil SHERMAN***
SMITH Evelyn E	Susan MELVILLE
SMITH Frank A	Supt PEPPER
SMITH George H	Sherlock HOLMES
SMITH George Hudson	Sherlock HOLMES
SMITH H Maynard	Insp FROST
SMITH J C S	Quentin JACOBY
SMITH Joan	Loretta LAWSON
SMITH Julie	Offr Skip LANGDON; ***Paul MACDONALD***; Philip MARLOWE; Rebecca SCHWARTZ
SMITH Kay Nolte	Edik DANTE
SMITH L Neil	Bucketeer MAV
SMITH Laurence Dwight	Dick WHELAN
SMITH Lou	John SPENCER
SMITH Mark	Arnold MAGNUSON
SMITH Martin Cruz	Dep Youngman DURAN and Hayden PAINE; ***Roman GREY***; Investigator Arkady RENKO
SMITH Michael A	Frank MONTGOMERY
SMITH Mitchell	Prof Charles BAUMAN
SMITH Neville	Eddie GINLEY
SMITH P	Sherlock HOLMES
SMITH Richard N	James Maxwell MALLORY
SMITH Shelley	Jacob CHAOS
SMITH Terrence Lore	Webster DANIELS
SMITH Willard K	Insp Dan CARR
SMITHIES Richard H R	William MCALPIN
SMOKE Stephen	Nick SANDS
SMULLYAN Raymond	Sherlock HOLMES
SNELL David	Osgood BASS
SNELL Edmund	***Reggie FAULKNER***; Peter PENNINGTON
SNOW C P	Frank BRIERS
SNOW Charles H	Tommy THORNE
SOBOL Donald J	'Encyclopedia' BROWN
SOLOMITA Stephen	Marty BLAKE; ***Stanley MOODROW***
SOLOMON Brad	***Charlie QUINLAN***; Fritz THIERINGER and Maggie MCGUANE
SOMERS Paul	Hugh CURTIS
SOUSA Innocent	Insp Raj MOHAMED
SOUTAR Andrew	KHARDUNI; ***Phineas SPINNET***
SOUTHCOTT Audley	Frank MARKER
SOUTHWORTH Louis	Insp Tom ANDERSON
SOUVESTRE Pierre and Marcel ALLAIN	FANTOMAS
SPADE Danny	Danny SPADE
SPAIN John	William RYE
SPAIN Nancy	***Miriam BIRDSEYE***; Miriam BIRDSEYE and Johnny DUVIVIEN; Johnny DUVIVIEN
SPARLING Joyce	Alex LEIGHTON
SPEIGHT T W	Lionel DERING; Supt DRUMLEY; Ursula LENORME; ***Insp MALLESON***
SPENCER John	Charley CASE
SPENCER Rick	Eric IVORSEN
SPENCER Ross H	***Buzz DECKARD***; Rip DESTON; Birch KIRBY; Luke LASSITER; Lacy LOCKINGTON; Chance PURDUE; Tuthill WILLOW
SPEWACK Samuel	Insp MARX and Dr RHINEWALD
SPICER Bart	Benson KELLOGG; Peregrine WHITE; ***Carney WILDE***
SPICER Michael	Lady Jane HILDRETH
SPIKE Paul	Father Fernando O'NEAL
SPIKOL Art	Alex BLACK
SPILLANE Mickey	***Mike HAMMER***; Dogeron KELLY; Tiger' MANN
SPILLER Andrew	Det Insp 'Duck' MALLARD
SPRIGG C St John	***Insp Bernard BRAY***; Insp Bernard BRAY and Charles VENABLES; Insp Charles MORGAN; Charles VENABLES
SPRING Michelle	Laura PRINCIPAL
SPRINGFIELD Lincoln	Alec YORKE
SPRINKLE Patricia Houck	Sheila TRAVIS
SPROUL Kathleen	Richard Van Ryn WILSON
SPRUILL Steven G	Elias KANE
SQUERENT Will	Sampson ROACH
ST CLAIR Dexter	Kirby HART
ST CLAIR Elizabeth	Marilyn AMBERS
ST DENNIS Madelon	Sydney TREHERNE
ST JAMES Bernard	Insp BLANC
ST JOHN David	Peter WARD
ST MOX E A	The HEART OF OAK DETECTIVE
STABENOW Dana	Kate SHUGAK
STACPOOLE H De Vere	Mynheer AMAYAT; Jacques RADOUB; ***Capt SLOCUM***
STAFFORD Marjorie	Donald CLIVE
STAFFORD T P	Sheerluck GNOMES
STAGG Clinton H	Thornley COLTON
STAGG James	Sexton BLAKE
STAGGE Jonathan	Dr Hugh WESTLAKE
STALLWOOD Veronica	Kate IVORY
STAMPER Joseph	Sexton BLAKE
STAND Marguerite	Bill RICE; ***Const ROBINS***
STANFORD Don	Dallas WEBSTER
STANLEY George	BIGGERS; ***BLACK PILGRIM***
STANNERS H H	Prof Charles HARDING
STANTON Coralie	Miriam LEMAIRE
STANTON Ken	William (Tiger Shark) MARTIN
STARK Ernest	Ed SOMERS
STARK Michael	Steven ERIKSON
STARK Richard	***Alan GROFIELD***; PARKER
STARNES Richard	Barney FORGE and Dr St George PEACHY; ***Maxwell SPEED***
STARR Jimmy	Joe MEDFORD
STARRETT Vincent	Riley BLACKWOOD; Sally CARDIFF; Walter GHOST; Sherlock HOLMES; ***Jimmie LAVENDER***; George Washington TROXELL
STASHOWER Daniel	Sherlock HOLMES and Harry HOUDINI
STAUFFER Frank H	Darke DARRELL
STAYNES Jill and Margaret STOREY	Supt Robert BONE
STEED Neville	Johnny BLACK; ***Peter MARKLIN***
STEEL Kurt	Hank HYER
STEELE Chester K	Col Robert Lee ASHLEY; ***Prof Irving SPENCER***
STEELE Curtis	James (Operator 5) CHRISTOPHER
STEELE Derwent	John BLACKMORE
STEELE Frederic Dorr	Sherlock HOLMES
STEEMAN André	Wenceslas VOROBEITCHIK
STEIN Aaron Marc	***Matt ERRIDGE***; Tim MULLIGAN and Elsie May HUNT
STEIN Sol	George THOMASSY
STEINER Susan	Alexandra WINTER
STEIRMAN Hy	Zachary JONES
STEPHAN Leslie	Sgt David PUTNAM
STEPHENS Hayward W	Mrs PASCHAL
STEPHENS Henry Pottinger and Warham ST LEGER	Frank COPLESTONE
STEPHENS Reed	Ginny FISTOULARI and Mick 'Brew' AXBREWDER
STEPHENS Riccardo	Richard TREGENNA
STEPHENSON Neal	Sangamon TAYLOR
STEPHENSON Ralph	Charles FINCH and 'Stalky' HERON; ***Peter JACKSON***
STERANKO	MARLOWE
STERLING Stewart	***Fire Marshal Ben PEDLEY***; Gil VINE
STERLING Thomas	Capt RIZZI
STERN Richard Martin	***Johnny OBTIZ***; Dorothy Mayotte RIGBY; Walter SPENSE
STEVENS D W	OLD SADDLE-BAGS; ***Sam SIX KILLER***
STEVENS Frank	Russell AMES
STEVENS Shane	Sherlock HOLMES
STEVENSON Burton E	***Anthony BIGELOW***; Jim GODFREY
STEVENSON Florence	Kitty TELEFAIR
STEVENSON Richard	Donald STRACHEY
STEVENSON Robert Louis and Lloyd OSBOURNE	Michael FINSBURY
STEVENSON Robert Louis and William Ernest HENLEY	Bow St Runner HUNT
STEVERMER C J	Nicholas COFFIN
STEWARD Barbara and Dwight STEWARD	Edgar Allan POE
STEWARD Donald William	Sexton BLAKE
STEWARD Dwight	Edgar Allan POE
STEWARD Paull	Don EVERHARD
STEWARD Samuel M	Gertrude STEIN and Alice TOKLAS
STEWART Douglas	Bart FRASER
STEWART Edward	Lt Vince CARDOZO

STEWART Flora	Insp NEWSOM
STEWART Gary	Gabriel UTLEY
STEWART Ian	Sherlock HOLMES
STEWART Mary	Simon LESTER and Camilla HAVEN; ***Charity SELBOURNE***; Jennifer SILVER
STEWART W T	Gaff LEE
STILLMAN Ron	Nat TRACKER
STINSON Jim	Stoney WINSTON
STOCKBRIDGE Grant	Richard (The Spider) WENTWORTH
STOCKWELL Gail	Kingsley TOPLITT and Sally TOPLITT
STODDARD Charles	Jim MALLOY
STODGHILL Dick	Henry PAIGE
STOKES Arthur M	Sherlock HOLMES
STOKES Manning Lee	Christopher FENN; ***Barnaby JONES***; Steve PAGET
STONE Elizabet M	Maggie SLONE
STONE Hampton	Jeremiah X GIBSON and MAC
STONE Nick	Ben KANE
STONE Richard	Sherlock HOLMES
STONE Simon	Sir Brian Dinsmore CONWAY
STONE Thomas H	Chester FORTUNE
STOPPARD Tom	Insp BONES
STOREY Alice	Samantha ADAMS
STOREY Michael	Michael DOVE
STORM Joan	Sarah VANESSA
STORM Michael	Nick CRANLEY
STORME Peter	Henry HALE
STORY Jack Trevor	***Albert ARGYLE***; Sexton BLAKE; Horace Spurgeon FENTON
STORY William L	Nick TOLAND
STOUT David	James WILLOP
STOUT Rex	Theodora 'Dol' BONNER; Delia BRAND; Insp CRAMER; Tecumseh FOX; 'Alphabet' HICKS; ***Nero WOLFE***
STRAHAN Kay Cleaver	Lynn MACDONALD
STRAKER J F	***Det Johnny INCH***; Insp PITT; David WRIGHT
STRAND Sidney	Frank DARRELL
STRANGE John Stephen	Barney GANTT; Lt/Capt George HONEGGER; Van Dusen ***ORMSBERRY***; Sgt POTTER
STRATFORD Michael	ADAM 12
STRATTON Chris	ADAM 12
STRATTON Roy	Scott GREGORY and Justin BASSETT
STRAYER Ed	BATTERY BOICE; PLACER DAN; ***Jack SHARPLEY***; VASCO
STREET James	Eugene MULCAHY; ***Supt ROMER***
STREIB Dan	Michael HAWK
STRIBLING T S	Prof Henry POGGIOLI
STRINGER Arthur	***James DURKIN***; Witter KERFOOT; Barbara 'Baddie' PRETLOW; Balmy RYMAL
STROBEL Marion	A Lincoln LACY
STRONG Ben	Prof Adrian CRIDDLE
STRONG L A G	Insp Ellis MCKAY

STUART Anne	***Maggie BENNETT***; Ferris BYRD
STUART Anthony	Vladimir GULL
STUART Brian	Knock-Out KAVANAGH
STUART Donald	Sexton BLAKE; ***Lionel CRANE***
STUART Ian	David GRIERSON; ***Insp Neil LAMBERT***; Graham LORIMER
STUBBS Jean	Insp John Joseph LINTOTT
STURROCK Dudley	Pixie O'HARA
STURROCK Jeremy	Bow Street Runner Jeremy STURROCK
STURT E M Leader	A DETECTIVE
STUTLEY S J and A E COPP	TREVELYAN
STYLES Showell	Sir Abercrombie LEWKER
SUCHER Dorothy	Sabina SWIFT
SUDDABY Donald	Jack JUGG
SUGAR Andrew	Alex (The Enforcer) JASON
SUTCLIFFE Halliwell	WILLOWDENE WILL
SUTER J Paul	Horatio HUMBERTON
SUTHERLAND John	Haricot BONES
SUTHERLAND William	Insp HASKELL
SUTTON Henry	Roger BRAITHWAITE
SUTTON Margaret	Judy BOLTON
SUTTON Tom	Schlomo RAVEN
SWAN Annie S	***Elizabeth GLEN***; Anne HYDE
SWAN Phyllis	Anastasia JUGEDINSKI
SWARTHOUT Glendon	Jimmie BUTTERS
SWARTWOUT R E	Angus MACNAIR
SWEET Pat	Cat O'CONNELL
SWEM Charles Lee	David LEE
SWIFT Brian (House name)	'Mac' WINGATE
SWIFT Brian (William Cecil KNOTT)	'Mac' WINGATE
SWIFT Brian (Arthur WISE)	'Mac' WINGATE
SWIGART Rob	Cobb TAKAMURA and Charles KOENIG
SWIGGETT Howard	Garrett MAYNARD
SWINSON Arthur	Sgt CORK
SYKES W Stanley	Insp Dennis DRURY
SYLVESTER John	Ferrers LOCKE
SYLVESTER Martin	William WARNER
SYLVESTER Robert	Ned SHERWOOD
SYMONDS F Addington	Sexton BLAKE; ***Insp Maxwell QUAYNE***
SYMONS Beryl	***Jane CARBERRY***; Insp Henry DOIGHT
SYMONS Julian	Charles APPLEGATE; Hugh BENNETT; Insp BLAND; Det Supt Hilary CATCHPOLE; ***Insp CRAMBO***; Sheridan HAYNES; Insp HAZELTON; Sherlock HOLMES; Dudley POTTER; Francis QUARLES; Paul VANDERVENT
SYMONS Maurice	George ROBERTS
SZANTO George	Joe LEVY

— T —

TACK Alfred	***David CROSBIE***; John HARLEY
TAFFRAIL	Joshua BILLINGS
TAIBO Paco Ignacio II	***Ch Jose Daniel FIERRO***; Philip MARLOWE; Hector SHAYNE
TALBOT Hake	Roger KINCAID
TANENBAUM Robert K	Roger 'Butch' KARP
TAPPLY William G	Brady COYNE
TARG William and Louis HERMAN	Hugh MORRIS
TAYLOR Andrew	William DOUGAL; ***Insp Richard THORNHILL***
TAYLOR Bert L	Sherlock HOLMES
TAYLOR Edith	Anne REDMOND
TAYLOR Elizabeth Atwood	Maggie ELLIOTT
TAYLOR H Baldwin	David HALLIDAY; Pete HOLLAND
TAYLOR Judson R	Gipsy BLAIR; Macon MOORE; OLD STONEWALL; ***Phil SCOTT***
TAYLOR L A	Marge BROCK; Owen DAVIS-WILLIAMS; Ethel PECK; ***Joseph 'JJ' JAMISON***
TAYLOR Mary Ann	Emil MARTIN
TAYLOR Matt	Det Dan MCGARRY
TAYLOR Merlin Moore	Robert GOODWIN
TAYLOR P Walker	Cdr WRAITHLEA
TAYLOR Phoebe Atwood	Asey MAYO
TAYLOR R M	Bob BRIDGER
TAYLOR Sam S	Neal COTTEN
TAYLOR Tom	Insp HAWKSHAW
TEED G H	Sexton BLAKE; Yvonne CARTIER; ***Roxane HARFIELD***; Lawrence MALONE; John RUMFORD; Grant RUSHTON
TEILHET Darwin L	***Peter BLUE and Jean Henri ST AMAND***; Herr KRESCH; Jean Henri ST AMAND
TEILHET Darwin L and Hildegarde Tolman TEILHET	Baron Franz Maximilian Karagos VON KAZ
TEILHET Hildegarde Tolman	Sam HOOK
TELFAIR Richard	Montgomery NASH
TELUSHKIN Joseph	Rabbi Daniel WINTER
TEMPLE Richard	Simon LEIGH
TEMPLER John	JAGGERS
TEMPLETON Jesse	Insp John INCH
TEMPLE-ELLIS N A	***Montrose ARBUTHNOT***; Montrose ARBUTHNOT and Edmund KING; Insp WREN
TERRALL Robert	Michael SHAYNE
TERRIS Wilmot E	C WRYTE
TETRICK Byron	Sherlock HOLMES

TEY Josephine	Robert BLAIR; ***Insp Alan GRANT***; Lucy PYM
THACKREY Ted Jr	PREACHER
THAYER James Stewart	Joe SNOW
THAYER Lee	Peter CLANCY
THAYER Tiffany	Abe ADAMS
THEROUX Paul	Spencer Monroe SAVAGE
THIERRY James Francis	Hemlock HOLMES
THOMAS Alan	Jimmy THURSTON; ***Insp WIDGEON***
THOMAS Carolyn	Sheriff TOWNSEND and Susan EYERLY
THOMAS Craig	Kenneth AUBREY
THOMAS Donald	Insp Alfred SWAIN
THOMAS Eugene	CHU-SHENG; ***Mrs Caywood WESTON***
THOMAS Frank	Sherlock HOLMES
THOMAS Jim	Peter CROSS
THOMAS Leslie	Dangerous DAVIES; ***George ORMEROD***
THOMAS Martin	Sexton BLAKE
THOMAS Murray	Insp WILKINS
THOMAS Ross	***Morgan CITRON***; Cyril MCCORKLE and Michael PADILLO; Jake POPE; Artie WU and Quincey DURANT
THOMPSON Gene	Dade COOLEY
THOMPSON Jim	'Bugs' MCKENNA
THOMPSON Leonard	William S GRAY
THOMPSON Lloyd S	Lt Claude GREENWAY
THOMPSON Steven L	Max MOSS
THOMPSON Vance	Mr GUELPA
THOMSEN Brian M	Sherlock HOLMES
THOMSON Basil	Lady ASENATH; Peter GRAHAM; James HATTON; Mr PEPPER; ***Insp RICHARDSON***
THOMSON June	***Det Ch Insp Jack FINCH***; Sherlock HOLMES
THOREAU David	Jimmy LUJACK
THORNDYKE Russell	Mr MACAULEY; ***Dr SYN***
THORNE Anthony	George JONES and Victoria BARTON
THORNE E P	Maj 'Brains' CUNNINGHAM; ***Quentin EADY***; Geoff FENNELL
THORNE Paul	Det CONROY and Det MCCARTHY
THORNE Paul and Mabel THORNE	***Robert FORRESTER***; Dave MORGAN
THORP Roderick	Joe LELAND
THURSTON E Temple	Const John BOODY
THYNNE Molly	Dr CONSTANTINE
TICKNER F C	Bill CHORLEY
TIDYMAN Ernest	John SHAFT

TILTON Alice	Leonidas WITHERALL
TIMINS Douglas	Philip Raines CARTWRIGHT
TIMLIN Mark	Nick SHARMAN
TINE Robert	Det Insp Samuel 'Smudge' HUDDLESTON
TINSLEY Theodore	***Carrie CASHIN***; Maj John Tattersall LACY; Jerry TRACY and Insp FITZGERALD
TIPPETTE Giles	Wilson YOUNG
TOBIN Bryan	Willie BUCHANAN
TODD Peter	Herlock SHOLMES
TOIL Cunnin	Picklock HOLES
TOKSON Elliot	Alec CAVENDER
TOLKIEN J R	Frodo BAGGINS
TOLMAN Hildegarde	Sam HOOK
TOMASHEFSKY Steven	Sherlock OHMS
TOMLINSON Gerald	Seth WARRINER
TONE Teona	Kyra KEATON
TOPOL Allan	Leora BARUCH
TOPOR Tom	Kevin FITZGERALD
TORGERSON Edwin Dial	Pierre MONTIGNY
TORRES Edwin	CARLITO
TORREY Roger	Johnny CASS; Shean CONNELL; Riley KEENAN; Pat MALONE; ***Pat MULLANCY***; Pat O'LEARY; John RYAN
TORRIE Malcolm	Timothy HERRING
TORRIO Vincente	Jim SHERIDAN
TOURNEY Leonard	Matthew STOCK and Joan STOCK
TOUSSAINT-SAMAT Jean	Monsieur JACQUOT and Monsieur LEVERT; ***Monsieur LEVERT***
TOWNE Stuart	Don DIAVOLO
TOWNEND Peter	Philip QUEST
TOWNSHEND Larry	Sherlock HOLMES
TOYE Stanley P	Anthony READ and Jacqueline NORRIS
TRACEY Don	Gil SPEER
TRACY Louis	Reginald BRETT; ***Insp Charles François FURNEAUX***
TRAIN Arthur	John DOCKRIDGE; MCALLISTER; ***Ephraim TUTT***
TRALINS Robert	Lee CROSLEY
TRAVERS Hugh	Mme AUBRY
TRAVIS Elizabeth	Ben PORTER and Carrie PORTER
TREAT Lawrence	Det Jub FREEMAN; Det Jub FREEMAN and Det Bill DECKER; Det Jub FREEMAN and Det Mitch TAYLOR; Det Jub FREEMAN and Det Carl WAYWARD; ***Det Jub FREEMAN, Det Bill DECKER and Det Mitch TAYLOR***; Hank GREENLEAF; Carl WAYWARD
TREE Gregory	Bill BRADLEY and Noel MAYBERRY; ***Insp Stephen ELIOT and Arthur CRUMP***
TREMAYNE Peter	Sister FIDELMA
TRENCH John	Martin COTTERELL
TRENHAILE John	***Gen Stepan POVIN***; Simon YOUNG
TRENT Paul	Peter QUAYLE
TREVANIAN	***Prof Jonathan HEMLOCK***; Lt Claude LAPOINTE
TREVELYAN Robert	John Hawkdale PENDRAGON
TREVOR A C	Supt ROACH
TREVOR Glen	Colin REVELL
TREVOR James	John SAVAGE
TREVOR Leslie	Sgt Pepper ANDERSON
TREVOR Ralph	***Insp Curtis BURKE***; Insp LOCKET
TREYNOR Blair	Pete BAYLISS
TRIMBLE Louis	ANTHROPOL; Joseph COYLE; ***Martin ZANE***
TRIPP Miles	Insp CROUCH; ***John SAMSON***
TRISTAM David	Insp DRAKE
TROCHECK Kathy Hogan	Callahan GARRITY
TROW M J	Insp/Supt Sholto LESTRADE
TROY Simon	***Charles SMITH***; Lee VAUGHAN and Insp SMITH
TRUMAN Margaret	Colette CAHILL; ***Mr Ron FAIRCHILD***; Mac HANRAHAN and Heather MCBEAN; Lydia JAMES; Ross LIZENBY and Chris SAKSIS; Sal MORIZIO; Joe POTOMOS; Prof MacKenzie SMITH; Martin TELLER and Susanna PINSCHER
TRUSS Seldon	Insp BASS; ***Ch Insp GIDLEIGH***; Det Insp SHANE
TUCKER Wilson	Kate BRISTOL; B G BROOKS; ***Lt DANFORTH***; Charles HORNE
TURNBULL Margaret	Juliet JACKSON
TURNBULL Peter	Insp Fabian DONOGHUE
TURNER Bill	***Bruce KIRKWOOD***; Sgt Louis SOLDEN
TURNER J V	Amos PETRIE
TURNER James	Rampion SAVAGE
TUROW Scott	Alejandro 'Sandy' STERN
TUTE Warren	George MADO
TUTTLE W C	'Hashknife' HARTLEY
TWAIN Mark	Insp BLUNT; Sherlock HOLMES; ***Tom SAWYER***; Simon WHEELER; David 'Pudd'nhead' WILSON
TYLER Alison	Jennifer HEATH
TYLER Charles W	'Blue Jean' Billy RACE
TYNAN Kathleen	Agatha CHRISTIE
TYNDALL John	Roger TURNBULL
TYRER Walter	Sexton BLAKE

—U—

UHNAK Dorothy	***Policewoman Christie OPARA***; Joe PETERS; Miranda TORRES
ULLMAN James Michael	***Julian FORBES***; Max FULLER; Michael Dane JAMES
UNDERWOOD Michael	Martin AINSWORTH; Nick ATWELL; Rosa EPTON and Martin AINSWORTH; ***Rosa EPTON***; Insp/Supt Simon MANTON; Richard MONK
UNKNOWN	Gideon BARR; Insp BLACK; BOWERY BILLY; BROADWAY BILL; BROADWAY BOB; Bob BROOKS; The CALIFORNIA DETECTIVE; Mr Sherlock COHEN; Janet DARLING; Dixon HAWKE; Insp/Supt Sholto LESTRADE and Sherlock HOLMES; MADEMOISELLE LUCIE; Nat PINKERTON; George PLUMMER; Silas SHARP; The SPIDER; Roy STOVER; The WHISPERER; ZED
UPFIELD Arthur W	Det Insp Napoleon BONAPARTE
UPTON Robert	Amos MCGUFFIN
UPWARD Allen	Mr H-LM-S; Ebenezer LOBB; Charles PRESCOTT; Dr Frank TARLETON; VERRITER; ***Monsieur V***
URQUHART MacGregor	Ch Insp Joshua SMARLES
URQUHART Paul	Sexton BLAKE
USHER Frank	***Amanda CURZON and Oscar SALLIS***; Daye SMITH
USHER Gray	***Supt Michael DREXEL***; Pete GARROWAY
USHER Jack	Stan BRADEN
UTECHIN Nicholas	Sherlock HOLMES; ***Porlock MOANS***

—V—

VACHELL Horace Annesley	IMPEY; ***Joe QUINNEY***
VACHSS Andrew	BURKE
VAILE William N	Judge DUNAWAY
VALENTINE Deborah	Kevin BRYCE
VALENTINE Douglas	Dr Adolph GRUNDT and Desmond OKEWOOD; ***Desmond OKEWOOD***
VALENTINE Mark	Ralph TYLER
VALENTINE	Daphne WRAYNE and The FOUR ADJUSTERS
VALIN Jonathan	Philip MARLOWE; ***Harry STONER***
VANARDY Varick	CREWE (BIRGE MOREAU); ***Bingham HARVARD***
VAN ARSDALE Wirt	Prof Jose APODACA
VAN ASH Cay	Sherlock HOLMES
VAN ATTA Winifred	***Jim FERGUSON***; Ken MITCHELL; Dale NELSON
VANCE Jack	***Keith GERSEN***; Miro HETZEL; Magnus RIDOLPH
VANCE John Holbrook	Sheriff Joe BAIN
VANCE Louis Joseph	***Michael LANYARD***; Terence O'ROURKE
VANCE William E	Peter KIRK
VANDAM Albert D	***Col BOTTESFORD***; DAVENPORT
VANDERCOOK John W	Bertram LYNCH
VAN DEVENTER Emma Murdoch	Kenneth JASPER
VAN DE WATER Frederick F	David MALLORY; ***John TARLETON***
VAN DE WETERING Janwillem	***Adjutent Henk GRIJPSTRA and Sgt Rufus*** DE GIER; Insp SAITO
VAN DINE S S	***Philo VANCE***; Philo VANCE and Gracie ALLEN
VANE Nigel	LI-SIN; ***Philip QUEST***
VAN GIESON Judith	Neil HAMEL
VAN GREENAWAY Peter	Insp CHERRY
VAN GULIK Robert	Judge Jen-djieh DEE
VAN LUSTBADER Eric	Nicholas LINNEAR; Philip MARLOWE; ***Jake MAROC***
VAN METER David A	Gardner WELLS
VAN URK Virginia	Tom CRAIG
VAN VORST Marie	Jimmy BULSTRODE
VAUGHAN Ralph	Sherlock HOLMES
VEDDER John K	Lt Cdr Frank SARGENT
VENNING Michael	Melville FAIRR
VERNE Jules	Det FIX
VERNER Gerald	***Supt BUDD***; Peter CHARD; Michael DENE; Simon GALE; Felix HERON; Trevor LOWE; Paul RIVINGTON
VERNES Henri	Bob MORANE
VERRILL A Hyatt	Curtis THORNE
VERRON Robert	Insp BRUMMEL
VICKERS Roy	Ch Const Colonel CRISP; Insp Peter CURWEN; Insp Peter CURWEN and Hugh STANTON; Fidelity DOVE; Insp KYLE; Insp G RASON; ***Insp J RASON***; James SEGROVE; Insp G RASON and Fidelity DOVE
VICTOR Daniel D	Sherlock HOLMES
VIDOCQ	Eugène VIDOCQ
VINCENT Lady Kitty	Gyp KIDNADZE
VIRDEN Katherine	Tom CLAYTON
VIVIAN E Charles	Insp BYRNE; ***Insp HEAD***
VIVIAN Francis	***Insp John BURNELL***; Sgt Ronnie DREW; Supt Gordon KNOLLIS
VIVIAN Margaret	Dr JAZ
VON ELSNER Don	***David DANNING***; Jake WINKMAN
VULLIAMY C E	William Arthur MALLINGHAM

WADDELL Martin	Gerald OTLEY
WADE Harrison	Johnny FURY
WADE Henry	Const John BRAGG; Supt DAWLE; Insp DOBSON; Insp DODD; Maj FAIDE; NETTERLY; ***Ch Insp POOLE***
WAGER Walter	Alison B GORDON
WAGONER David	Charlie BELL
WAHLOO Per	Ch Insp Peter JENSEN
WAINWRIGHT John	Supt GILLIANT; Harry HARKER; ***Ch Insp/Supt LENNOX***; Supt LEWIS; Insp David LYLE; Tom PILTER; RIPLEY; Asst Ch Const SULLIVAN; Harry THOMPSON
WAKEFIELD Hannah	Dee STREET
WAKEFIELD John	Insp SPEIGHT
WAKEFIELD R I	Lt MARSHALL and Judy MEADOWS
WALDMAN Frank	Insp CLOUSEAU
WALDRON Simon	Steve ESSEX
WALES Kirk	Dr Daniel BRITLING
WALK Charles Edmonds	Phineas FLINT
WALKER Greg	Bo 'Springblade' THORNTON
WALKER Ian	Sherlock HOLMES
WALKER Ira	Steve RHODEN
WALKER Irma	Steve RHODEN
WALKER Jerry	Lawrence MARLEY
WALKER Mary Willis	Molly CATES
WALKER Peter N	Det Sgt CARNABY; ***Det Supt Mark PEMBERTON***
WALKER Robert W	Dean GRANT
WALKER Rowland	***Capt MCBLAID***; Deville MCKEENE
WALKER Walter	Owen CARR; ***Hector GRONIG***
WALL William	Tony BOYLE
WALLACE Arthur	Val VERNON
WALLACE Bryan Edgar	Bill TERN
WALLACE C H	Steve RAMSAY
WALLACE Carlton	Supt Edmund BENDILOW
WALLACE David Rains	George KILGORE
WALLACE Edgar	Capt Jiggs ALLERMAN; Supt BLISS; Supt BRANBURY; Mike BRIXAN; Insp CARVER; Ch Supt Peter DAWES; DIXON; Sgt Sir Peter DUNN; Sgt/Insp ELK; Sgt/Insp ELK and T B SMITH; Educated' EVANS; FOUR JUST MEN; HEINE; Const LEE; Insp Arnold 'Betcher' LONG; Selby LOWE; Insp MASON; Leslie MAUGHAN; Commiss T X MEREDITH; Supt MINTER; Anthony NEWTON; Mrs Emily OLLERBY; Insp PARR; Oliver RATER; ***J G REEDER***; Commiss SANDERS; T B SMITH; York SYMON
WALLACE F L	Norman O HAZARD
WALLACE Francis	Johnny STONE and Ruth DEE
WALLACE Ian	CROYD; ***Claudine ST CYR***; Claudine ST CYR and CROYD
WALLACE Marilyn	***Det Jay GOLDSTEIN, Det Carlos CRUZ and Carrie RAYBORN***; Det Jay GOLDSTEIN, Det Carlos CRUZ and Jean TALBOT
WALLACE Patricia	Sydney BRYANT
WALLACE Robert	Essington HOLT;
WALLACE Robert (House name)	Richard Curtis (The Phantom) VAN LOAN
WALLACE Robert (Norman DANIELS)	Richard Curtis (The Phantom) VAN LOAN
WALLACE Robert (Laurence DONOVAN)	Richard Curtis (The Phantom) VAN LOAN
WALLACE Robert (Charles GREEN)	Richard Curtis (The Phantom) VAN LOAN
WALLACE Trevor	John TRACY
WALLING R A J	GARSTANG; Prof LAXTON; ***Philip TOLEFREE***
WALLIS J H	Insp Wilton JACKS
WALLIS Ruth Sawtell	Susan KENT; ***Eric LUND***
WALSH Bill	Mal WILLIAMS
WALSH J M	Insp GORE; Mike HARMAN; Bromley KAY; Oliver KEENE; Col ORMISTON; ***Insp QUAILE***; Insp STORM
WALSH Jill Paton	Imogen QUY
WALSH Maurice	Con MADDEN
WALSH Paul E	Paul DAMIAN
WALSH Ray	Sherlock HOLMES and Sir Arthur Conan DOYLE
WALSH William J	Sherlock HOLMES
WALTCH Lilla M	Lisa DAVIS
WALTER A E and H C WALTER	Sir Edgar EWART
WALTERS Minette	Sgt COOPER; Rosalind LEIGH and Sgt HAWKSLEY; ***Sgt Andy MCLOUGHLIN***
WALTON Marion	Insp James CARDINAL
WAMBAUGH Joseph	Det Fin FINNEGAN
WARD Alfred C	Sherlock HOLMES, Dr Reginald FORTUNE and Dr John Evelyn THORNDYKE
WARD Elizabeth C	Jake MARTIN
WARD William	Jeff CLAYTON
WARDEN Florence	Jem COLLINGHAM; Clifford KING; ***Insp MAYNARD***; Gerald STAUNTON
WARDEN Mike	Hank BRADFORD
WARGA Wayne	Jeffrey DEAN
WARMAN Erik	Insp John Isidore BLOOM
WARMBOLD Jean	Sarah CALLOWAY
WARNER Mignon	Mrs Edwina CHARLES
WARREN C Delves	Sherwood LANG
WARREN J Russell	Insp M'GUIRE
WARREN James	***James WARREN***; James WESTON
WARREN Paul	***Bill POOLE***; SKILLFUL CHARLIE
WARREN Vernon	Mark BRANDON; Clifford GRANT; ***Johnny MAQUIS***; Glen RANSOM; Brad STERLING
WARRICK Milligan	William HARKNESS
WARRINER Thurman	Mr John Cornelius SCOTTER
WARWICK Francis	Ferrers LOCKE
WASHBURN L J	Lucas HALLAM
WASHBURN Mark	Sam BOGGS
WATERS	Henry CLARKE; Theodore DUHAMEL; A FRENCH DETECTIVE OFFICER; INSPECTOR F; William SHARPE; ***WATERS***
WATSON Clarissa	Persis WILLUM
WATSON Colin	Insp PURBRIGHT
WATSON H B Marriott	Richard DERRICK; ***Dick RYDER***
WATSON John R and Arthur J REES	CREWE
WATSON Malcolm and Edward LA SERRE	Sheerluck JONES
WATSON St John	Ferrers LOCKE
WATSON Sterling	Eddie PRIEST
WAUGH Alec	Noel RAID
WAUGH Hillary	Peter CONGDON; ***Ch Fred FELLOWS***; Ch FORD; Simon KAYE; Philip MACADAM; Det Frank SESSIONS; Sheridan WESLEY
WAYDE Bernard	HARDSCRABBLE; ***Larry MURTAGH***; Rody ROGAN
WAYE Cecil	Christopher PERRIN
WAYLAND Patrick	Lloyd NICOLSON
WEATHERHEAD John	David CONNELL
WEAVER Nicky	Nicky WEAVER
WEBB Alex	Josh DEKKER
WEBB Anthony (British)	Mr PENDLEBURY
WEBB Geoffrey	David PRINCE
WEBB Geoffrey and Edward J MASON	Dick BARTON
WEBB Jack	Det Sgt Sammy GOLDEN and Father Joseph SHANLEY
WEBB Martha G	Allan CONYERS and Cheryl BURROUGHS; ***Tommy INMAN***
WEBB Victoria	Stella PIKE
WEBSTER F A M	Ebbie ENTWHISTLE
WEBSTER H M	Shamus BURKE
WEBSTER Henry Kitchell	***Prof Brinsley BUTLER***; Punch CORBIN; Arthur JEFFREY; Pete MURRAY
WEBSTER Noah	Jonathan GAUNT; ***Andrew LAIRD***
WEES Frances Shelley	Michael FORRESTER and Theresa FORRESTER
WEIL Barry	Jacob ASHER
WEINMAN Irving	Lenny SCHWARTZ
WEINSTEIN Sol	Israel 'Oy-Oy-7' BOND
WEIR Hugh C	Madelyn MACK
WEISS Mike	Ben HENRY
WELCH Timothy L	Dion QUINCE
WELCOME John	Richard GRAHAM; ***Simon HERALD***
WELLARD James	Lucius HUNT
WELLEN Edward	Sherlock HOLMES
WELLES Elizabeth (House name)	Janine WEST
WELLES Elizabeth (Mary Linn ROBY)	Janine WEST
WELLMAN Manly Wade	Sherlock HOLMES; Judge Keith Hilary PURSUIVANT; ***David RETURN***; John THUNSTONE; Stonewall Jackson YATES and J D THATCHER
WELLMAN Manly Wade and Wade WELLMAN	Sherlock HOLMES
WELLS Anna Mary	Dr Hillis OWEN; ***Grace POMEROY***
WELLS Carolyn	Bert BAYLISS; Kenneth CARLISLE; Alan FORD; Sherlock HOLMES; Lorimer LANE; ***Fleming STONE***; Pennington WISE
WELLS Charlie	Steve LEE
WELLS J W	Sherlock HOLMES
WELLS Susan	Anthony WARE
WELLS Tobias	Det Knute SEVERSON
WENDER Theodora	Glad GOLD
WENTWORTH Patricia	Insp Ernest LAMB; ***Maud Hephzibah SILVER***
WERRY Richard R	Jane D MULROY
WEST Charles	Paul CROOK
WEST Elliott	Jim BLANEY
WEST John B	'Rocky' Aloysius Algernon STEELE
WEST Morris L	George HARLEQUIN
WEST Nigel	Philip NORTH
WEST Pamela	John INGLES and Madeline SMITH
WESTALL Robert	Geoff ASHDEN
WESTBROOK Perrie D	Dr Samuel CUTTING
WESTLAKE Donald E	John EDGARSON; ***Tim SMITH***
WESTON Carolyn	Casey KELLOG and Al KRUG
WESTON Garnett	HIGHWAY
WEVERKA Robert	Wade GRIFFIN
WEYMAN Ronald C	Sherlock HOLMES
WEYMOUTH Anthony	Insp TREADGOLD
WHALLEY Peter	Harry SOMMERS
WHEAT Carolyn	Cass JAMESON
WHEATLEY Dennis	Roger BROOK; ***Julian DAY***; Duke DE RICHLEAU; Gregory SALLUST
WHEELER Benson and Claire Lee PURDY	Urgan MARCH
WHEELER Edward Lytton	DEADWOOD DICK; Denver DOLL; FRITZ; The FRONTIER DETECTIVE; The HEART OF OAK DETECTIVE; ***Nell NIBLO***
WHEELER H E	Kendal GRAYDON; ***Stephen RANT***
WHEELOCK Dorothy	Mehatibel BELLAMY
WHELTON Paul	Garry DEAN
WHIPPLE Kenneth	Clifton BRENTWOOD

WHITAKER Arthur	Sherlock HOLMES; ***Harold QUEST***
WHITAKER Beryl	John ABBOT
WHITE Alan	***Det Insp ARMSTRONG***; Capt COLSON
WHITE Ared	Capt Fox ELTON
WHITE Ethel Lina	***Iris CARR***; Alan FOAM
WHITE Frank Marshall	Sherlock HOLMES
WHITE Fred M	Insp TOWNSEND; ***James TRENT***
WHITE Gloria	Ronnie VENTANA
WHITE James Dillon	Sebastian KETTLE
WHITE Jon Manchip	Maj Morven RICKMAN
WHITE Leslie T	Capt BARNABY
WHITE Osmar	George GALBRAITH
WHITE R J	***Insp BADGERY***; Insp David BROCK
WHITE Randy Wayn	'Doc' FORD
WHITE Stewart Edward	Percy DARROW; ***Bobby ORDE***
WHITE Stewart Edward and Samuel Hopkins ADAMS	Ralph SLADE
WHITE T H	Insp BULLER
WHITE Teri	Spaceman KOWALSKI and Blue MAGUIRE
WHITECHURCH Victor L	***Det Sgt AMBROSE***; Thorpe HAZELL; Humphrey JUDD; Capt Ivan KORAVITCH; Godfrey PAGE
WHITEHOUSE F Cowley	Mark MATURIN
WHITFIELD Raoul	***Ben CASEY***; Al CONNORS; Ben JARDINN
WHITNEY Phyllis A	***Linda EARLE***; Sylvester HERING
WHITTINGTON Harry	Pat RAFFIGAN
WHITTON J Bradley	Mr JEREMY
WICKHAM Harvey	Ferris MCCLUE
WIEGAND William	Mr Samuel TOLLIVER
WIENER L E	HERRIG
WIGNALL Trevor C	Sexton BLAKE
WILCOX Collin	Alan BERNHARDT; Stephen DRAKE; ***Lt Frank HASTINGS***; MCCLOUD
WILCOX Ella Wheeler	Kitty CLOVER
WILCOX Stephen F	Timothy Seamus Wolfe SHERIDAN
WILDE Percival	Peter MORAN; ***Bill PARMELEE***
WILEY Hugh	WONG
WILHELM Kate	Charles MEIKLEJOHN and Constance LEIDL
WILKINSON Burke	Geoffrey MILDMAY
WILKINSON Ellen	Robert WEST and Donald SHAW
WILKINSON Sandra D	Pete TANNER and Rosemary CLEVELAND
WILLARD James	Clive MARSHALL
WILLEFORD Charles	Jacob C 'Jake' BLAKE; ***Sgt Hoke MOSELEY***
WILLIAMS Alan	Rupert QUINN
WILLIAMS Alexander	Det Sgt Pietro TONELLI
WILLIAMS Ben Ames	Insp TOPE
WILLIAMS Brad and W ERLICH	Sam BENEDICT
WILLIAMS Charles	John INGRAM
WILLIAMS David	***Mark TREASURE***; Mark TREASURE, Maj COPPER and Benny GOLD
WILLIAMS Eric	Roger STARTE and Kate STARTE
WILLIAMS Henry Smith	Jack HENLEY
WILLIAMS John Babington	A NEW YORK DETECTIVE
WILLIAMS Kirby	Thackeray PLACE
WILLIAMS Lew	***The DAGO DETECTIVE***; The RELIANCE DETECTIVE
WILLIAMS Louis	Bernado THOMAS
WILLIAMS M H	CROOKED COLE; ***DAVENPORT BLAKE***; DETECTIVE DAREDEATH; The THEATRE DETECTIVE
WILLIAMS P C	Mr HOYLAND
WILLIAMS Philip Lee	Hank PRINCE
WILLIAMS Richard A (William Arthur Howard BAKER)	Sexton BLAKE
WILLIAMS Richard B (Rex DOLPHIN)	Sexton BLAKE
WILLIAMS Richard C (Stephen Daniel FRANCES)	Sexton BLAKE
WILLIAMS Richard D (Bob HOPKINS and Max MARQUIS)	Sexton BLAKE
WILLIAMS Richard E (Jack Trevor STORY)	Sexton BLAKE
WILLIAMS Sidney	***Ben MORRISON***; Jabez TWOMBLEY
WILLIAMS Stephen Daniel	Shylar HOMES
WILLIAMS Timothy	Commiss TROTTI
WILLIAMS Valentine	***Det Sgt Trevor DENE***; Robin GREVE, Mary TREVERT and Insp MANDERTON; Dr Adolph (Clubfoot) GRUNDT; Dr Adolph GRUNDT and Desmond OKEWOOD; Insp MANDERTON and Det Sgt Trevor DENE; Insp MANDERTON; Desmond OKEWOOD; Mr Horace B TREADGOLD
WILLIAMSON Audrey	Supt Richard YORK
WILLIAMSON C N and A M WILLIAMSON	Christopher RACE
WILLIAMSON Jerry Neal	Sherlock HOLMES; Sure-They-Lock HOMEZ; ***Sheerback TONES***
WILLIAMSON Moncrieff	Cyrus FINNEGAN
WILLIS Ted	***Sgt George DIXON***; Cdr John KNOWLES
WILLIS Ted and Paul GRAHAM	Sgt George DIXON
WILLOCK Colin	Nathaniel GOSS
WILLS Cecil	Supt Geoffrey BOSCOBELL and Insp Roger ELLERDINE; ***Sgt/Supt Geoffrey BOSCOBELL***; Insp Roger ELLERDINE; PINKNEY

WILLS Garry	Gregory SKIPWITH
WILLS Helen and Robert W MURPHY	Insp MACMASTERS
WILLS Thomas	Barney GLINES
WILMOT Robert Patrick	Mike ZACHARIAS and Steve CONSIDINE
WILSON Alan	Sherlock HOLMES
WILSON Alexander	Sir Leonard WALLACE
WILSON Anthony C	Norman BONES
WILSON Barbara	***Pam NILSEN***; Cassandra REILLY
WILSON Charles	Lt Bret DUNNIGAN and Det Paige DUNNIGAN
WILSON Christopher	Insp OSWALD
WILSON Colin	Karl ZWEIG and Charles GREY
WILSON David	MCCLOUD
WILSON Derek	Tim LACY
WILSON Gahan	Enoch BONE; ***Eddy DECO***
WILSON Gertrude M Bryan	Insp LOVICK
WILSON Ivor	Greg FLAMM
WILSON John A	Sherlock HOLMES
WILSON Karen Ann	Samantha HOLT
WILSON P W	Sir Julian MORTHOE
WILTZ Chris	Neal RAFFERTY
WIMBERLY Robert L	Willy VELVET
WINCH Arden	Supt MEADOWS
WINCH Will	Kail HUTTON; ***The LAWYER DETECTIVE***; LITTLE BRAVO; The MARINE DETECTIVE; WOLVERINE WAIF
WINCOR Richard	Sherlock HOLMES
WINDSOR George	Nelson LORD
WINGATE Anne	Mark SHIGATA
WINGFIELD R D	Det Insp Jack FROST
WINGS Mary	Emma VICTOR
WINN Patrick	***Insp LYON***; Lee SEDDON
WINSLOW Horatio and Leslie QUIRK	Dr KLOTZ
WINSLOW Pauline Glen	Sgt/Ch Supt Merle CAPRICORN
WINSOR Diana	Tavey MARTIN
WINSOR G McLeod	Insp GILMOUR
WINSOR Roy	Prof Ira COBB
WINSTON Peter (House name)	Peter WINSTON
WINSTON Peter (James BOWSER)	Peter WINSTON
WINSTON Peter (Paul Eiden)	Peter WINSTON
WINTER Bevis	Steve CRAIG
WISE Arthur	Ned SANDERSON
WISEMAN Thomas	Bill HARDTMANN
WITHERS E L	Lt MICHAELS
WITTING Clifford	Sgt/Insp Peter BRADFIELD; ***Insp Harry CHARLTON***; Insp Harry CHARLTON and Insp Peter BRADFIELD
WODEHOUSE P G	Adrian MULLINER
WOGAN Charles	Sebastian STOLE
WOHL James P	Sam GROSS
WOLF Gary K	Eddie VALIANT
WOLF Jack	Timothy ROURKE
WOLF Sarah	Ch Philip DECKER and David BRETT
WOLFE Carson	Carlito RIVERA
WOLFE Charles	Joe FENNER
WOLFE John	Johnny MCCOY
WOLFE Michael	Michael KEEFE
WOLFE Sebastian	Sherlock HOLMES
WOLFF Benjamin	John Byron HYDE
WOLFF William Almon	Sgt/Lt Charley MITCHELL
WOLFFE Katherine	Capt Courtney BRADE
WOLK Michael	Max POPPER
WOLZIEN Valerie	Susan HENSHAW
WOMACK Steven	Harry DENTON
WOOD Andrew	***Magnus KEEBLE***; KOREGORVSKY
WOOD Christopher	Cdr James BOND
WOOD Clement	Capt/Insp COLIN; ***Skelton KYNE***; Lal REED
WOOD Eric	Arnold KEENE and Bernard YOUNG
WOOD H F	***Insp George BYDE***; TOPPIN
WOOD James	James FRASER
WOOD Mrs Henry	***Sgt DELVES***; Charlotte GUISE; TATTON
WOOD Ted	Ch of Plce Reid BENNETT
WOODBURY David O	George RIAM
WOODCROFT Robert	An ABERDEEN DETECTIVE
WOODFIN Henry	John FOLEY
WOODHOUSE Martin	Giles YOEMAN
WOODIWISS John C	Insp HOPTON
WOODRELL Daniel	Det Rene SHADE
WOODS Sara	Antony MAITLAND
WOODS Sherryl	Amanda ROBERTS and Joe DANELLI
WOODS Stuart	Det Stone BARRINGTON
WOODTHORPE R C	***Matilda PERKS***; Nicholas SLADE
WOODWARD Edward	George FENCHURCH; ***Bill MARSHALL***
WOODWARD P H	B K SHARRETTS
WOODY William	Houston MCIVER
WOOLRICH Cornell	***Hal JEFFRIES***; Angel Face' REARDON; Prudence ROBERTS
WORMSER Richard	***Lt Andy BASTIAN***; Sgt Joe DIXON
WORSLEY-GOUGH Barbara	Aloysius KELLY
WORTH Cedric	Insp SEVREL
WORTH Maurice	Derek HARING
WORTH Richard	Dixon BRETT
WRAY I	Insp DIGBY
WREN M K	Conan FLAGG

WRENN Harold A	William MITCHELL
WRIGHT Eric	Insp Charlie SALTER
WRIGHT June	Mother PAUL
WRIGHT Keith	Det Insp Dave STARK
WRIGHT L R	Sgt Karl ALBERG
WRIGHT Stephen	Dashiell HAMMETT
WRIGHT Steve	Barry DONOVAN
WRIGHT Thomas	Doll RAINBOW
WRIGHT Wade	***Paul CAMERON***; Bart CONDOR
WURR H J	Insp GRIERSON
WYLDE Jack	Dixon BRETT
WYLIE Philip	Willis PERKINS
WYLLIE John	Dr QUARSHIE
WYNNE Anthony	Dr Eustace HAILEY

—Y—

YAFFE James	***Paul DAWN***; MOM
YARBOROUGH Charlotte	Hartley RHYS
YARBRO Chelsea Quinn	Charles 'Spotted' MOON
YARDLEY Herbert O	Mr GREENLEAF
YARDLEY James A	Kiss DARLING
YATES Dornford	CHANDOS; ***Supt FALCON***; Jonah MANSEL; Bertram PLEYDELL
YATES Edmund	Dr Clement BURTON
YATES George Worthing	Hazlitt WOAR
YATES Margaret Tayler	Anne 'Davvie' Davenport MCLEAN
YATES Peter	Sandy BLUNT
YOLEN Jane	Shirlick HOLMES
YORK Andrew	***Ch of Plce Munroe TALLANT***; Jonas WILDE
YORK Jeremy	***Supt FOLLY***; Insp KENNEDY
YORKE Margaret	Nina CROWTHER; ***Stephen DAWES***; Patrick GRANT
YUILL P B	James HAZELL

—Z—

ZACKEL Fred	Michael BRENNAN
ZAKE S Joshua L	Peter KAYIRA
ZANGWILL Israel	Insp George GOODMAN
ZANGWILL Louis	Mr WARLOCK-JONES
ZAREMBA Eve	Helen KEREMOS
ZELDES Leah A	Sherlock HOLMES
ZERO	Thinlock BONES
ZIMLER Robert and Michael ZIMLER	Sherlock HOLMES
ZIMMERMAN Bruce	Quinn PARKER
ZIMMERMAN R D	Madeleine PHILLIPS
ZOCHERT Donald	***Nick CAINE***; Benjamin FRANKLIN
ZUBRO Mark Richard	Tom MASON

The Books

The	100,000 Welcomes	Supt O'MALLEY
$	106,000 Blood Money	The CONTINENTAL OP
The	10:30 From Marseilles	Insp GRAZZONI
	120 Rue De La Gare	Nestor BURMA
The	120-Hour Clock	Milo TURNER
The	12th Of Never	Lee GORDON
The	13th Murder	Ch of Plce SUTHERLAND
	14 Bellchamber Tower	Ralph TYLER
The	14th Agent	Peter ROURKE
The	180 Degrees Murder	Jason BRADLEY
	209 Thriller Road	Sam NORTH
The	22 Brothers	Donald O'Keefe ADAMS
	24th Level	Peter CRAIG
	26 Three-Minute Thrillers	Mrs Palmyra Evangeline PYM
	3 Blind Mice	Gregory TRENT
The $	3 Million Turn-Over	Dave (The Pro) BOLT
	30 For A Harry	John DENSON
	30 Manhattan East	Det Frank SESSIONS
	32 Cadillacs	Dan KEARNEY ASSOCIATES
The	3-13 Murders	Al DELANEY
	42 Days For Murder	Shean CONNELL
The	51st Sealed Room: Or, The MWA Murder	Harrison MANNIX
	7 To 12: A Detective Story	BYRD
	70,000 Witnesses	Det Jack KETHERIDGE
	77 Sunset Strip	Stuart BAILEY
	7:30 Victoria	Ch Insp CUMMINGS
The	81st Site	Jimmy PELHAM
	9 Had No Vet	Insp Christopher ADRIAN

— A —

The	Aardvark Affair	Colin 'Big Brain' GARRETT
	Aaron Rodd, Diviner	Aaron RODD
The	Abandoned Room	Bobby BLACKBURN
The	Abbey Court Murder	Insp FURNIVAL
The	ABC Affair	Peter WINSTON
	ABC Investigates	A B C HAWKES
	ABC Solves Five	A B C HAWKES
	ABC's Test Case	A B C HAWKES
The	Abductors	Sexton BLAKE
	Abel's War	Luke ABEL
The	Abergavenny Adventure	Sherlock HOLMES
The	Abernathy Affair	Sherlock HOLMES
	Abner Ferret, The Lawyer Detective	Abner FERRET
The	Abolition Of Death	Mikael Josef PETROS
	Abomination	Hank JANSON
	About Face	Johnny LIDDELL
	About The Murder Of Geraldine Foster	Commiss Thatcher COLT
	Above And Below	Guy PLANTE and Freye MATTHEWS
	Above Suspicion	Geoffrey PETERS
An	Abuse Of Justice	Insp Taff ROBERTS
An	Academic Question	William MCALPIN
	Accessory After	Insp HEAD
	Accessory To Murder	Insp HENDERSON
An	Accidental Password	Nick CARTER
The	Accomplice	Deake GILBERT
	According To Gibson	Henry GIBSON
	According To Gibson	Hugo PEAK
	According To St John	Jeremiah ST JOHN
	According To The Evidence	Col BRAIN and Ambrose LOW
The	Accused Princess	VERRITER
	Ace Of Danger	Paul IRVING
The	Ace Of Knaves	Simon (The Saint) TEMPLAR
The	Ace Of Spades Murder	Angus MACWHORTER
An	Ace Up My Sleeve	Helga ROLFE
The	Achievements Of John Carruthers	John CARRUTHERS
The	Achievements Of Luther Trant	Luther TRANT
The	Achilles Affair	Peter FELTHAM
	Acid	Det Insp DU CAS
	Acid Bath	Det Elena JARVIS
	Ackroyd	Roger ACKROYD
The	Aconite Murders	Jabez TWOMBLEY
	Acquitted!	Sexton BLAKE
	Act Of Anger	Benson KELLOGG
	Act Of Fear	Dan FORTUNE
An	Act Of War	Brevet CABLE
	Action Of The Picaroon	Ludovic (The Picaroon) SAXON
The	Activities Of Lavie Jutt	Lavie JUTT
The	Actress	Andrew MORDENT
The	Actress Detective	The ACTRESS DETECTIVE
The	Actress Detective: Or, The Invisible Hand	Hilda SIRENE
	Adam's Fall	Brian GUY
	Additional Evidence	Insp BIDWELL
	Adele & Co	Bertram PLEYDELL
The	Adjusters	Daphne WRAYNE and The FOUR ADJUSTERS
The	Admirable Carfew	T B SMITH
The	Advanced Calculus Of Murder	Dan BRODSKY
	Advantage Miss Seeton	Emily SEETON and Supt DELPHICK
	Adventure Holidays, Ltd	Donald LOMAX and Peter CULLIMORE
The	Adventure In Whitechapel	Charlotte HOLMES
The	Adventure Of Basil Rathbone	Sheercrocked MOANS
The	Adventure Of Black Peter	Sherlock HOLMES
The	Adventure Of Black, Peter	Schlock HOMES
The	Adventure Of Blue Peter	Turlock LOAMS
The	Adventure Of Buffington Old Grange	Solar PONS
The	Adventure Of Charles Augustus Milverton	Sherlock HOLMES
The	Adventure Of Foulkes Rath	Sherlock HOLMES
The	Adventure Of Isadora Persano	Sherlock OHMS
The	Adventure Of Mrs Burlingame's Diamond Stomacher	Raffles HOLMES
The	Adventure Of Ricoletti Of The Club Foot	Solar PONS
The	Adventure Of Room 407	Raffles HOLMES
The	Adventure Of Sherlock Holmes' Smarter Brother	Sherlock HOLMES
The	Adventure Of Shoscombe Old Place	Sherlock HOLMES
The	Adventure Of Sir Edward Pins	Neville BOYLES
	Adventure Of State	Col Allen CHEYNEY
An	Adventure Of Stately Homes	Stately HOMES
The	Adventure Of Stocksen Bonds	Sheercrocked MOANS
The	Adventure Of The Abbas Ruby	Sherlock HOLMES
The	Adventure Of The Abbey Grange	Sherlock HOLMES
The	Adventure Of The Adam Bomb	Schlock HOMES
The	Adventure Of The Addleton Tragedy	Sherlock HOLMES
The	Adventure Of The Alicia Cutter	Sherlock HOLMES
The	Adventure Of The Aluminium Crutch	Sherlock HOLMES
The	Adventure Of The Aluminium Crutch	Sherlock HOLMES
The	Adventure Of The Aluminium Crutch	Solar PONS
The	Adventure Of The Amateur Mendicants	Sherlock HOLMES
The	Adventure Of The Amateur Philologist	Solar PONS
The	Adventure Of The Amesbury Disappearance	Sherlock HOLMES
The	Adventure Of The Anguished Actor	Solar PONS
The	Adventure Of The Anguished Actress	Solar PONS
The	Adventure Of The Animal Fare	Schlock HOMES
The	Adventure Of The Artissium Murder	Hemlock HOLMES
The	Adventure Of The Artist's Mottle	Schlock HOMES
The	Adventure Of The Ascot Scandal	Solar PONS
The	Adventure Of The Ascot Tie	Schlock HOMES
The	Adventure Of The Ball Of Nostradamus	Solar PONS
The	Adventure Of The Belles Letters	Schlock HOMES
The	Adventure Of The Benin Bronze	Solar PONS
The	Adventure Of The Beryl Coronet	Sherlock HOLMES
The	Adventure Of The Big Plunger	Schlock HOMES
The	Adventure Of The Bishop's Companion	Solar PONS
The	Adventure Of The Black Baronet	Sherlock HOLMES
The	Adventure Of The Black Cardinal	Solar PONS
The	Adventure Of The Black Narcissus	Solar PONS
The	Adventure Of The Blanched Soldier	Sherlock HOLMES
The	Adventure Of The Blind Clairaudient	Solar PONS
The	Adventure Of The Blue Carbuncle	Sherlock HOLMES
The	Adventure Of The Bogle-Wolf	Sherlock HOLMES
The	Adventure Of The Bookseller's Clerk	Solar PONS
The	Adventure Of The Bored Professor	Tide POOLES
The	Adventure Of The Bradley Tragedy	Shylar HOMES
The	Adventure Of The Brass Check	Raffles HOLMES
The	Adventure Of The Briary School	Schlock HOMES
The	Adventure Of The Brimstone Chalice	Sherlock HOLMES
The	Adventure Of The Brixton Builder	Herlock SHOLMES
The	Adventure Of The Broken Chessman	Solar PONS
The	Adventure Of The Bruce-Partington Plans	Sherlock HOLMES

The Adventure Of The Bugged Bird	Sheerback TONES
The Adventure Of The Calabash Pipe	Sherlock HOLMES
The Adventure Of The Camberwell Beauty	Solar PONS
The Adventure Of The Cardboard Lox	Turlock LOAMS
The Adventure Of The Carved Knife	Sherlock HOLMES
The Adventure Of The Cheesemonger's Bark	Turlock LOAMS
The Adventure Of The China Cottage	Solar PONS
The Adventure Of The Christmas Visitor	Sherlock HOLMES
The Adventure Of The Chuckle-Headed Doctor: A Positively Final Story Of Sherlock Holmes	Sherlock HOLMES
The Adventure Of The Circular Room	Sherlock HOLMES
The Adventure Of The Circular Room	Solar PONS
The Adventure Of The Clawed Horrors Of Limehouse	Sherlock HOLMES
The Adventure Of The Clothes-Line	Sherlock HOLMES
The Adventure Of The Cloverdale Kennels	Solar PONS
The Adventure Of The Command Performance	Sherlock HOLMES
The Adventure Of The Common Code	Schlock HOMES
The Adventure Of The Conk-Singleton Papers	Sherlock HOLMES
The Adventure Of The Copper Beeches	Sherlock HOLMES
The Adventure Of The Copper Beeches	Sherlock HOLMES
The Adventure Of The Copper's Breeches	Sherlock HOLMES
The Adventure Of The Counterfeit Sovereign	Schlock HOMES
The Adventure Of The Crawling Horror	Solar PONS
The Adventure Of The Creeping Man	Sherlock HOLMES
The Adventure Of The Crouching Dog	Solar PONS
The Adventure Of The Dancing Hen	Turlock LOAMS
The Adventure Of The Dancing Men	Sherlock HOLMES
The Adventure Of The Dark Angels	Sherlock HOLMES
The Adventure Of The Defeated Doctor	Solar PONS
The Adventure Of The Deptford Horror	Sherlock HOLMES
The Adventure Of The Devil's Foot	Sherlock HOLMES
The Adventure Of The Devil's Footprints	Solar PONS
The Adventure Of The Diamond Necklace	Warlock BONES
The Adventure Of The Diamond Pins	Herlock SHOLMES
The Adventure Of The Disappearance Of Whistler's Mother	Schlock HOMES
The Adventure Of The Dog In The Knight	Schlock HOMES
The Adventure Of The Dog In The Manger	Solar PONS
The Adventure Of The Dorrington Inheritance	Solar PONS
The Adventure Of The Dorrington Ruby Seal	Raffles HOLMES
The Adventure Of The Double Santa Claus	Sherlock HOLMES
The Adventure Of The Double-Bogey Man	Schlock HOMES
The Adventure Of The Dover Ghost	Sherlock HOLMES
The Adventure Of The Dying Detective	Sherlock HOLMES
The Adventure Of The East Side Ball	Zinsheimer HOLMES
The Adventure Of The Eleven Cuff-Buttons	Hemlock HOLMES
The Adventure Of The Elite Type	Schlock HOMES
The Adventure Of The Empty House	Sherlock HOLMES
The Adventure Of The Engineer's Thumb	Sherlock HOLMES
The Adventure Of The Extraterrestrial	Sherlock HOLMES
The Adventure Of The Fairfax Umpire	Turlock LOAMS
The Adventure Of The Fatal Glance	Solar PONS
The Adventure Of The Field Theorems	Sherlock HOLMES
The Adventure Of The Final Problem	Schlock HOMES
The Adventure Of The First-Class Carriage	Sherlock HOLMES
The Adventure Of The Five Buffalo Chips	Turlock LOAMS
The Adventure Of The Five Green Gasogenes	Sherlock HOLMES
The Adventure Of The Five Puce Map Tacks	Doorlock HOLMES
The Adventure Of The Five Royal Coachmen	Solar PONS
The Adventure Of The Foiled Revenge	Sherlock HOLMES
The Adventure Of The Frail Codger	Turlock LOAMS
The Adventure Of The Freckled Hand	Turlock LOAMS
The Adventure Of The Frightened Baronet	Solar PONS
The Adventure Of The Frightened Governess	Solar PONS
The Adventure Of The Frying Detective	Turlock LOAMS
The Adventure Of The Giant Bat Of Sonoma	Turlock LOAMS
The Adventure Of The Giant Rat Of Sumatra	Sherlock HOLMES
The Adventure Of The Gold Hunter	Sherlock HOLMES
The Adventure Of The Golden Bracelet	Solar PONS
The Adventure Of The Golden Pince-Nez	Sherlock HOLMES
The Adventure Of The Gowanus Abduction	John Conan WATSON
The Adventure Of The Great Train Robbery	Schlock HOMES
The Adventure Of The Grice-Paterson Curse	Solar PONS
The Adventure Of The Hadderly Formula	Sherlock HOLMES
The Adventure Of The Hammer Of Hate	Solar PONS
The Adventure Of The Hansom Ransom	Schlock HOMES
The Adventure Of The Harassed Prussian	Sherlock HOLMES
The Adventure Of The Hats Of M Dulac	Solar PONS
The Adventure Of The Haunted Library	Solar PONS
The Adventure Of The Haunted Rectory	Solar PONS
The Adventure Of The Headless Monk	Sherlock HOLMES
The Adventure Of The Headless Torso	Sherlock HOLMES
The Adventure Of The Highest Beast	Sherlock HOLMES
The Adventure Of The Highgate Miracle	Sherlock HOLMES
The Adventure Of The Hired Burglar	Raffles HOLMES
The Adventure Of The Ignored Idols	Solar PONS
The Adventure Of The Illegal Alien	Sherlock HOLMES
The Adventure Of The Illustrious Client	Sherlock HOLMES
The Adventure Of The Illustrious Imposter	Sherlock HOLMES
The Adventure Of The Innkeeper's Clerk	Solar PONS
The Adventure Of The Intarsia Box	Solar PONS
The Adventure Of The Ipi Idol	Solar PONS
The Adventure Of The Iron Box	Sherlock HOLMES
The Adventure Of The Jogging Man	Turlock LOAMS
The Adventure Of The Late Mr Faversham	Solar PONS
The Adventure Of The Limping Man	Solar PONS
The Adventure Of The Lion's Mane	Sherlock HOLMES
The Adventure Of The Little Hangman	Solar PONS
The Adventure Of The Logophagous Client	Turlock LOAMS
The Adventure Of The Lost Dutchman	Solar PONS
The Adventure Of The Lost Holiday	Solar PONS
The Adventure Of The Lost Locomotive	Solar PONS
The Adventure Of The Lost Manuscripts	Sherlock HOLMES
The Adventure Of The Lost Manuscripts, And One Other	Sherlock HOLMES
The Adventure Of The Lost Prince	Schlock HOMES
The Adventure Of The Man With The Broken Face	Solar PONS
The Adventure Of The Marked Man	Sherlock HOLMES
The Adventure Of The Mazarin Stone	Sherlock HOLMES
The Adventure Of The Mazarine Blue	Solar PONS
The Adventure Of The Misleading Murder	Tide POOLES
The Adventure Of The Misplaced Hound	Sherlock HOLMES
The Adventure Of The Missing Bit	Sherlock HOLMES
The Adventure Of The Missing Bullet	Shylar HOMES
The Adventure Of The Missing Cheyne-Stroke	Schlock HOMES
The Adventure Of The Missing Coffin	Sherlock HOLMES
The Adventure Of The Missing Hatrack: A Story Of Mr Sherlock Holmes	Sherlock HOLMES
The Adventure Of The Missing Huntsman	Solar PONS
The Adventure Of The Missing Pendants	Raffles HOLMES
The Adventure Of The Missing Scuttle	Tide POOLES
The Adventure Of The Missing Tenants	Solar PONS
The Adventure Of The Missing Third Quarter	Turlock LOAMS
The Adventure Of The Missing Three-Quarter	Sherlock HOLMES
The Adventure Of The Missing Three-Quarters	Schlock HOMES
The Adventure Of The Mocking Devil	Mr HOLBROOK
The Adventure Of The Mosaic Cylinders	Solar PONS
The Adventure Of The Mowed Lawn	Tide POOLES
The Adventure Of The Murdered Art Editor: A Reminiscence Of Mr Sherlock Holmes	Sherlock HOLMES
The Adventure Of The Mysterious Lodger	Sherlock HOLMES
The Adventure Of The Noble Bachelor	Sherlock HOLMES
The Adventure Of The Norcross Riddle	Solar PONS
The Adventure Of The Norwood Builder	Sherlock HOLMES
The Adventure Of The Notorious Canary Trainer	Sherlock HOLMES
The Adventure Of The Obrisset Snuff Box	Solar PONS
The Adventure Of The Odd Lotteries	Schlock HOMES
The Adventure Of The Orient Express	Solar PONS
The Adventure Of The Out-Of-Date Murder	Sherlock HOLMES
The Adventure Of The Paradol Chamber	Sherlock HOLMES
The Adventure Of The Paradol Chamber	Sherlock HOLMES
The Adventure Of The Paradol Chamber	Sherlock HOLMES
The Adventure Of The Paralytic Mendicant	Solar PONS
The Adventure Of The Patient Resident	Schlock HOMES
The Adventure Of The Peerless Peer	Sherlock HOLMES
The Adventure Of The Pendleton Jewels	Shylar HOMES
The Adventure Of The Penny Magenta	Solar PONS
The Adventure Of The Perfect Husband	Solar PONS
The Adventure Of The Perforated Ulster	Schlock HOMES
The Adventure Of The Perilous Protoplasm	Tide POOLES
The Adventure Of The Perplexed Photographer	Solar PONS
The Adventure Of The Persecuted Millionaire	Sherlock HOLMES
The Adventure Of The Persistent Marksman	Sherlock HOLMES
The Adventure Of The Pie-Eyed Piper	Schlock HOMES
The Adventure Of The Pius Missal	Sherlock HOLMES
The Adventure Of The Politician, The Lighthouse, And The Trained Cormorant	Sherlock HOLMES
The Adventure Of The Praed Street Irregulars	Solar PONS
The Adventure Of The Printer's Inc	Schlock HOMES
The Adventure Of The Priory School	Sherlock HOLMES
The Adventure Of The Proper Comma	Solar PONS
The Adventure Of The Prophetic Poet	Sherlock HOLMES
The Adventure Of The Psychodelic Sleuth	Shrock HOLMES
The Adventure Of The Pudgy Leg	Zinsheimer HOLMES
The Adventure Of The Purloined Periapt	Solar PONS
The Adventure Of The Purple Hand	Sherlock HOLMES
The Adventure Of The Queen Bee	Shirley HOLMES
The Adventure Of The Red Circle	Sherlock HOLMES
The Adventure Of The Red Leech	Solar PONS
The Adventure Of The Red Widow	Sherlock HOLMES
The Adventure Of The Remarkable Worm	Sherlock HOLMES
The Adventure Of The Remarkable Worm	Solar PONS
The Adventure Of The Retired Colourman	Sherlock HOLMES
The Adventure Of The Retired Novelist	Solar PONS
The Adventure Of The Retired Weatherman	Turlock LOAMS
The Adventure Of The Rubber Pipe	Shilah COOMBES
The Adventure Of The Russian Grave	Sherlock HOLMES
The Adventure Of The Rydberg Numbers	Solar PONS
The Adventure Of The Sealed Room	Sherlock HOLMES
The Adventure Of The Second Generation	Sherlock HOLMES
The Adventure Of The Second Scarf	Sherlock HOLMES
The Adventure Of The Second Stain	Sherlock HOLMES
The Adventure Of The Second Stain	Sherlock HOLMES
The Adventure Of The Second Stain	Sherlock HOLMES
The Adventure Of The Second Swag	Sherlock HOLMES
The Adventure Of The Seven Clocks	Sherlock HOLMES
The Adventure Of The Seven Passengers	Solar PONS
The Adventure Of The Seven Sisters	Solar PONS
The Adventure Of The Shaft Of Death	Solar PONS
The Adventure Of The Shaplow Millions	Solar PONS
The Adventure Of The Short Fuse	Schlock HOMES
The Adventure Of The Sick Sleuth	Tide POOLES
The Adventure Of The Single Footprint	Lt Oliver BAYNES and John Sherlock HOLMES
The Adventure Of The Singular Sandwich	Solar PONS
The Adventure Of The Sinister American	Comrade Sherslav GOLMSKY
The Adventure Of The Six Gold Doubloons	Solar PONS
The Adventure Of The Six Napoleons	Sherlock HOLMES
The Adventure Of The Six Silver Spiders	Solar PONS
The Adventure Of The Smiling Judge	Sherlock HOLMES
The Adventure Of The Snared Drummer	Schlock HOMES
The Adventure Of The Snitch In Time	Solar PONS
The Adventure Of The Soledad Cyclist	Turlock LOAMS
The Adventure Of The Solitary Cyclist	Sherlock HOLMES
The Adventure Of The Soporific Cipher	Sherlock HOLMES
The Adventure Of The Sotheby Salesman	Solar PONS
The Adventure Of The Speckled Band	Sherlock HOLMES
The Adventure Of The Speckled Band	Sherlock HOLMES
The Adventure Of The Speckled Hand	Neville BOYLES
The Adventure Of The Spectacled Band	Schlock HOMES
The Adventure Of The Spot Of Tea	Tide POOLES
The Adventure Of The Spurious Tamerlane	Solar PONS
The Adventure Of The Stalwart Companions	Sherlock HOLMES and Theodore ROOSEVELT

The Adventure Of The Stockbroker's Clark	Schlock HOMES
The Adventure Of The Stolen Doormat	Mr H-LM-S
The Adventure Of The Stone Of Henge	Tide POOLES
The Adventure Of The Stone Of Scone	Solar PONS
The Adventure Of The Sussex Archers	Solar PONS
The Adventure Of The Sussex Vampire	Sherlock HOLMES
The Adventure Of The Swedenborg Signatures	Solar PONS
The Adventure Of The Swiss Banker	Picklock HOLES
The Adventure Of The Synthetic Soup	Tide POOLES
The Adventure Of The Table Foot	Thinlock BONES
The Adventure Of The Tainted Worm	Sherlock HOLMES
The Adventure Of The Tarred Captain	Neville BOYLES
The Adventure Of The Thinking(?) Machine	Sherlock HOLMES
The Adventure Of The Three Gables	Sherlock HOLMES
The Adventure Of The Three Garridebs	Sherlock HOLMES
The Adventure Of The Three Golden Chessmen	Sherlock HOLMES
The Adventure Of The Three Madmen	Sherlock HOLMES
The Adventure Of The Three Red Dwarfs	Solar PONS
The Adventure Of The Three Students	Sherlock HOLMES
The Adventure Of The Tired Captain	Sherlock HOLMES
The Adventure Of The Tired Housewife	Sherlock HOLMES
The Adventure Of The Tomato On The Wall	Mrs Julia Herlock SHOMES
The Adventure Of The Tottenham Werewolf	Solar PONS
The Adventure Of The Trained Cormorant	Solar PONS
The Adventure Of The Troubled Magistrate	Solar PONS
The Adventure Of The Two Collaborators	Sherlock HOLMES
The Adventure Of The Two Women	Sherlock HOLMES
The Adventure Of The Ukrainian Foundling Orphans	Schlock HOMES
The Adventure Of The Unique Dickensians	Solar PONS
The Adventure Of The Unique Hamlet	Sherlock HOLMES
The Adventure Of The Unique Holmes	Sherlock HOLMES
The Adventure Of The Unseen Traveler	Sherlock HOLMES
The Adventure Of The Unstrung Fiddler	Tide POOLES
The Adventure Of The Veiled Lodger	Sherlock HOLMES
The Adventure Of The Wax Gamblers	Sherlock HOLMES
The Adventure Of The Whispering Knights	Solar PONS
The Adventure Of The Widow's Weeds	Schlock HOMES
The Adventure Of The Wrong Time	Sherlock HOLMES
The Adventure Of The Zodiac Plate	Sherlock HOLMES
The Adventure Of The 'Triple Kent'	Solar PONS
The Adventure Of Vigor, The Hammersmith Wonder	Sherlock HOLMES
Adventures Of A Chemist	Marshall HEDLEY
The Adventures Of A Journalist	Beverley GRETTON
The Adventures Of A Lady Pearl-Broker	Mrs Mollie DELAMERE
The Adventures Of A Man Of Science	Dr Henry CHETWYND and Dr Paul CATO
The Adventures Of A Social Detective: Or, Life Among The Lions Of Society In Bohemia	A SOCIAL DETECTIVE
The Adventures Of A Solicitor	Edward DALE
Adventures Of Ah Foo, The Chinese Sherlock Holmes	Ah FOO
The Adventures Of Alonzo MacTavish	Alonzo MACTAVISH
The Adventures Of Antoine	ANTOINE
The Adventures Of Archer Dawe, Sleuth-Hound	Archer DAWE
The Adventures Of Augustus Short	Augustus SHORT
The Adventures Of Bill Holmes	Bill HOLMES
Adventures Of Blackshirt	BLACKSHIRT
The Adventures Of Bobby Orde	Bobby ORDE
The Adventures Of Captain Ivan Koravitch	Capt Ivan KORAVITCH
The Adventures Of Captain Jack	Capt Jack WARD
The Adventures Of Captain Kettle	Capt Owen KETTLE
The Adventures Of Captain Mounsell	Capt MOUNSELL
Adventures Of Captain Spink	Capt Harry SPINK
The Adventures Of Cardigan	Steve CARDIGAN
The Adventures Of Chubb-Lock Homes	Chubb-Lock HOMES
The Adventures Of Creighton Holmes	Creighton HOLMES
The Adventures Of Detective Barney	Barney COOK
The Adventures Of Doctor Eszterhazy	Dr ESZTERHAZY
The Adventures Of Dr Burton	Dr BURTON
The Adventures Of D'Arcy Dewpond, Detective	D'Arcy DEWPOND
The Adventures Of Ellery Queen	Ellery QUEEN
The Adventures Of Felix Boyd	Felix BOYD
The Adventures Of Harrison Keith, Detective	Harrison KEITH
The Adventures Of Heine	HEINE
The Adventures Of Henry Turnbuckle	Henry TURNBUCKLE
The Adventures Of Hiram Holliday	Hiram HOLLIDAY
The Adventures Of Inspector Lestrade	Insp/Supt Sholto LESTRADE
The Adventures Of Jerry Parker, Mobile Investigator	Jerry PARKER
The Adventures Of Jimmie Dale	Jimmie DALE
The Adventures Of Jimmy Strange	Jimmy STRANGE
The Adventures Of Judith Lee	Judith LEE
The Adventures Of Jules De Grandin	Jules DE GRANDIN
The Adventures Of Kerlock Shomes And Dr Warsaw	Kerlock SHOMES
Adventures Of Latimer Field	Latimer FIELD
The Adventures Of Lieutenant Lawless	Lt/Cdr Frank H LAWLESS
The Adventures Of Lucius Leffing	Lucius LEFFING
Adventures Of Martin Hewitt	Martin HEWITT
The Adventures Of Max Latin	Max LATIN
The Adventures Of Mike Blair	Mike BLAIR
The Adventures Of Miss Gregory	Miss GREGORY
The Adventures Of Mr Joseph P Cray	Joseph P CRAY
The Adventures Of Mr Pitkin	Mr PITKIN
The Adventures Of Mr Topham, Comedian	Mr TOPHAM
The Adventures Of Mr Wellaby Johnson	Wellaby JOHNSON
The Adventures Of Napoleon Prince	Napoleon PRINCE
The Adventures Of Picklock Holes, Together With A Perversion And A Burlesque	Picklock HOLES
The Adventures Of Picklock Holes, Together With A Perversion And A Burlesque	Picklock HOLES
The Adventures Of Porlock Moans	Porlock MOANS
The Adventures Of Race Williams	Race WILLIAMS
The Adventures Of Romney Pringle	Romney PRINGLE
The Adventures Of Russell Howard	Russell HOWARD
The Adventures Of Sam Spade And Other Stories	Sam SPADE
The Adventures Of Sandy West, Private Eye	Dashiell HAMMETT
The Adventures Of Satan Hall	Satan HALL
The Adventures Of Scout Grey	Scout GREY
The Adventures Of Shamrock Jolnes	Shamrock JOLNES
The Adventures Of Sheerluck Ohms	Sheerluck OHMS
The Adventures Of Sheerluck Ohms	Sheerluck OHMS
The Adventures Of Sherlaw Kombs	Sherlaw KOMBS
The Adventures Of Sherlock Holmes	Sherlock HOLMES
Adventures Of Sherwood Hoakes. Adventure 1 - An Interrupted Honeymoon	Sherwood HOAKES
The Adventures Of Shylar Homes	Shylar HOMES
The Adventures Of Solar Pons	Solar PONS
The Adventures Of The Black Pilgrim	BLACK PILGRIM
The Adventures Of The Ectoplasmic Man	Sherlock HOLMES and Harry HOUDINI
Adventures Of The Infallible Godahl	Oliver ARMISTON
Adventures Of The Scarlet Pimpernel	The SCARLET PIMPERNEL
The Adventures Of Turco Bullworthy	Turco BULLWORTHY
The Adventures Of Tyler Tatlock, Private Detective	Tyler TATLOCK
The Adventuress	Miriam LEMAIRE
Adversary	Guilhem DE COURDEVAL
The Adversary	David MEDINA
Adverse Report	Simon PARBITTER and Keith CALDER
Advice Limited	Baroness Clara LINZ
The Aero Clubs Mystery	Insp Gil FLICKER
The Affair At Dead End	Jonathan BLAKE
Affair At Lover's Leap	Anthony HUNTER
The Affair At The Semiramis Hotel	Insp HANAUD
The Affair In Arcady	Clive MARSHALL
The Affair Of Lady Carfax	Sherlock HOLMES
The Affair Of The Aluminium Crutch	Sherlock HOLMES
The Affair Of The Bloodstained Egg Cosy	Insp WILKINS
The Affair Of The Blue Pig	HARRIGAN and HOEFFLER
An Affair Of The Couch	Dorothy Mayotte RIGBY
The Affair Of The Fraternizing Soldier	Sexton BLAKE
The Affair Of The Malacca Stick	Drexel WARE
The Affair Of The Midnight Midget	Mrs HUDSON and Sherlock HOLMES
The Affair Of The Mutilated Mink Coat	Insp WILKINS
The Affair Of The Politician, The Lighthouse, And The Trained Cormorant	Sherlock HOLMES
The Affair Of The Razor's Edge	Sherlock HOLMES
The Affair Of The Red Mosaic	HARRIGAN and HOEFFLER
The Affair Of The Rival Cinema Kings	Sexton BLAKE
The Affair Of The Scarlet Crab	Prof Huntoon ROGERS
The Affair Of The Sixth Button	Prof Huntoon ROGERS
The Affair Of The Smuggled Millions	Sexton BLAKE
The Affair Of The Syrian Dagger	Drexel WARE
The Affair Of The Unprincipled Publisher	Sherlock HOLMES
Affairs Of Death	Insp DUFFY
The Affairs Of John Bolsover	John BOLSOVER
The Affairs Of O'Malley	O'MALLEY
African Assignment	Michael (The Shield) SHERIFF
An African Millionaire	Col CLAY
The African Poison Murders	Supt VACHELL
After All These Years	Rosie MYERS
After Darvray Died	Bill LANGLEY
After Hours	CARLITO
After Things Fell Apart	Jim HALEY
After You With The Pistol	Charlie MORTDECAI
Aftershock	Mici ANHALT
Again Sanders	Commiss SANDERS
Again The Remover	The REMOVER
Again The Three Just Men	FOUR JUST MEN
Against Odds	Carl MASTERS
Agatha	Agatha CHRISTIE
Agatha Raisin And The Quiche Of Death	Agatha RAISIN
Agatha Raisin And The Walkers Of Dembley	Agatha RAISIN
Agatha Webb	Caleb SWEETWATER
Agent B-7	Capt Fox ELTON
Agent Counter Agent	Nick CARTER
Agent Extraordinary	Hendrik VAN KILL
The Agent Of Death	Det Sgt Joe RYKER
Agents Of The League	David SHERIDAN
Agile Retrieval	Nile BARRABAS
Aground	John INGRAM
Aim For The Heart	Chris KLICK
AKA	Whit PYNCHON and Annie TYSON-TYREE
The Alarm Of The Black Cat	Rachel MURDOCK and Jennifer MURDOCK
Alaska Deception	Nile BARRABAS
Alaska Gray	Jane MCBRIDE
Alba	Serge GORODISH and ALBA
The Albert Gate Affair	Reginald BRETT
The Albert Gate Mystery	Reginald BRETT
Alias Blackshirt	BLACKSHIRT
Alias The Dead	Leon MORLEY
Alias The Masked Detective	The MASKED DETECTIVE
Alias The Night Wind	Bingham HARVARD
Alias The Saint	Simon (The Saint) TEMPLAR
Alibi	Insp BRYSON
The Alibi	Philip MARLOWE
Alibi Baby	Gil VINE
Alibi For Murder	Charley IVES
Alibi Innings	Aloysius KELLY
Alice Dies Twice	Marty COLE
Alien Archipelago	SAN ANTONIO
Alien Minds	George HANLON
Alimentary, My Dear Watson	Sherlock HOLMES
All Fall Down	Insp Ellis MCKAY
All Grass Isn't Green	Bertha COOL and Donald LAM
All I Can Get	Lou LARGO
All Is Discovered	Insp Ronald PRICE
All Leads Negative	Insp Robert FUSIL and Const KERR
All Of Our Aircraft Are Missing!	Joe (The Illusionist) MAGUIRE
All Other Perils	Andrew LAIRD
All Other Perils	Andrew LAIRD
All Points Bulletin	Ben HENRY
All Souls	Sgt Matt MINOGUE
All That Glitters	Eric IVORSEN
The All That Glitters: The Case Of The Ice-Cold Diamond	Viera KOLAROVA
All The Colors Of Darkness	Jan DARZEK

All The Lonely People	Harry DEVLIN
All The Muscle You Need	Eliza PIREX
All Things Under The Moon	Teddy LONDON
Allan Keene, The War Detective	Allan KEENE
Allen Dane, The Detective	Allen DANE
Alley Kat Blues	Kat COLORADO
The Allingham Case Book	Albert CAMPION
The Allingham Minibus	Albert CAMPION
Almack, The Detective	ALMACK
The Almost Perfect Crime	Insp Jim SILVER
The Almost Perfect Murder	Mme Rosika STOREY
Along Came A Spider	Det Alex CROSS
Alonzo MacTavish Again	Alonzo MACTAVISH
The Alpha Deception	Blaine MCCRACKEN
The Alpha List	Insp PALMER
Alphabet Hicks	'Alphabet' HICKS
The Alpine Advocate	Emma LORD
Alpine Condo Crossfire	Emmy BRACE
Alpine Encounter	Kate PATERSON
The Alpine Escape	Emma LORD
Alter Ego	Hank MERCER and Biff DEEGAN
The Alvarez Journal	Det Gabriel WAGER
The Always Anonymous Beast	Caitlin REECE
Always Lock Your Bedroom Door	Prof Ira COBB
Always Murder A Friend	Henry BRYCE and Emily BRYCE
Always The Wolf	Bill BANNING
Amanda In Berlin	Amanda NIGHTINGALE
Amateur City	Det Kate DELAFIELD
The Amateur Cracksman	A J RAFFLES
The Amateur Gentleman	Sgt Jasper SHRIG
The Amazing Adventures Of Letitia Carberry	Letitia CARBERRY
The Amazing Mr Bunn	'Smiler' BUNN
The Amazing Mr Smith	Oliver Trentham SMITH
The Amazing Test Match Crime	Insp 'Steady as a Rock' POSSE
The Amazing Web	David CROSBY
The Amazon	Nick CARTER
Amazon Slaughter	Jason STRIKER
Amazons	Britt (Mind Masters) ST VINCENT
The Amber Eyes	Pat ABBOTT and Jean ABBOTT
Ambrose In London	Ambrose WEST
Ambrose In Paris	Ambrose WEST
Ambrose Lavendale, Diplomat	Ambrose LAVENDALE
The Ambush	Sexton BLAKE
Ambush House	Hank HYER
Amends For Murder	Peggy O'NEILL
An American Monte Cristo	Keppel DRAKE
An American Penman	Insp BYRNES
American Quartet	Fiona FITZGERALD
America's Heroes	Nick BROWN
Amzi, The Detective; Or, Morning, Noon And Night In New York	AMZI
The Anatomy Lesson	Dan LASSITER
The Ancestral Precipice	Insp Bertil DURELL
An Ancient Evil	Sir Godfrey EVESDEN
Ancora Scipio	Danny SCIPIO
And Baby Will Fall	Adele BUFFINGTON
And Being Dead	Insp Septimus FINCH
And Berry Came Too	Bertram PLEYDELL
And Death Drove On	Simon CROLE
And Hope To Die	Arabella BLAKE and Andy BLAKE
... And Incidentally, Murder!	Edge HANNEGAN
And Leave Her Lay Dying	Lt Joe MCGUIRE
And Left For Dead	Bernard SIMMONS
And So He Had To Die	Abelard VOSS
And So To Bed	Lou LARGO
And Sudden Death	Rex MCBRIDE
And The Undead Sing	Mavis SEIDLITZ
And Then They Die	Francesca MILLS
And Then You Die	Gil DISBRO
And To My Beloved Husband	Insp KEEN
And Where She Stops	Pete SCHOFIELD
Anderson Crow, Detective	Ch Anderson CROW
The Andromeda Assignment	Steve SAVAGE
The Andropov File	Nick CARTER
Angel And The Red Admiral	Angel BROWN
Angel Confidential	Fitzroy Maclean ANGEL
Angel Dance	Kat GUERRERA
An Angel For Paradise	Mike PARADISE
Angel In Autumn	Nurse Agnes CARMICHAEL
Angel Maker	Det Lou BOLDT and Daphne MATTHEWS
Angel Of Death	Angel BROWN
Angel Of Death	Det Jessica DRAKE
Angel Of Destruction	John STARK
The Angel Of Light	Insp MCKELLER and Anthony HOWARD
The Angel Of The Opera	Sherlock HOLMES
The Angel Of Torremolinos	Supt Luis BERNAL
Angel Without Mercy	Nurse Agnes CARMICHAEL
Angelfish	Oscar SAIL
Anger At World's End	Sexton BLAKE
The Anger Of Fear	Det Const ATHANA
The Angry Dead	Jane BRADSHAWE
The Angry Ocean	James BRUCE
The Angst-Ridden Executive	Pepe CARVALHO
Anne Hyde, Travelling Companion	Anne HYDE
Annihilation	Timothy MCCARTY
The Anomaly Of The Empty Man	Sherlock HOLMES
Another Adventure Of Stately Homes	Stately HOMES
Another Day Toward Dying	Sarah O'BRIEN
Another Little Death	Bruce KIRKWOOD
Another Little Drink	Nick BELLAMY
Another Man's Poison	Sheriff MACREADY
Another Man's Shadow	Insp MEREDITH
Another Mug For The Bier	Barney FORGE and Dr St George PEACHY
Another Path, Another Dragon	Dan ROMAN
Another Way To Die	Lee BECKETT
Another Weeping Woman	Nick CAINE
Another's Crime	Insp BYRNES
Answer From A Dead Man	Virgil FLETCHER
Anthony Ravenhill, Crime Merchant	Anthony RAVENHILL
Anthony Trent, Master Criminal	Anthony TRENT
Anthropol	ANTHROPOL
Antique Dust	Geoff ASHDEN
The Anxious Conspirator	Insp/Supt Simon MANTON
Any Man's Death	Peter MACKLIN
Anything For A Quiet Life	Const/Ch Insp Patrick PETRELLA
Anything Might Happen	Insp Jack STRICKLAND
Anything To Declare?	Insp Joseph FRENCH
APB	Whit PYNCHON and Annie TYSON-TYREE
An Ape In Velvet	John HARLAND
The Apollo Legacy	Reefe KING
The Apothecary Rose	Owen ARCHER
Appleby And Honeybath	Insp/Commiss John APPLEBY and Prof Charles HONEYBATH
Appleby And The Ospreys	Insp/Commiss John APPLEBY
The Appleby File	Insp/Commiss John APPLEBY
Appleby Talking	Insp/Commiss John APPLEBY
Appleby Talks Again	Insp/Commiss John APPLEBY
Appointment In Andalusia	Laurie GRANT and Stewart NOBLE
Appointment In Calcutta	Alec CAVENDER
Appointment In Hell	Al MUNDY
Appointment In Hell	Glen RANSOM
Appointment To Die	David MIDDLETON-BROWNE
Appointment With Desire	Phil CASEY
Appointment With The Hangman	Reggie RUGGLES and Sgt TROTTER
Apprentice To Fear	John STRANG and Sally STRANG
The April Fool's Adventure	Sherlock HOLMES
The April Rainers	Ch Insp David WEBB
The April Robin Murders	'Bingo' RIGGS and 'Handsome' KUSAK
April Snow	Nathan PHILLIPS
April Thirteenth	Insp BLANC
The Arabian Pearl	Abigail Patience DANFORTH
Arascadero Island	Jason BRADLEY
An Arcadian Death	Insp Enrique ALVAREZ
Archdeacons Afloat	John CRAGGS and James CASTLETON
Arctic Abduction	Nick CARTER
The Argus Pheasant	KOYALA
The Ariadne Clue	Antonia NIELSEN
Arigato	Capt Colin HUNTINGTON
An Aristocratic Detective	The Hon Augustus CHAMPNELL
Aristotle, Detective	ARISTOTLE
The Armageddon Game	Sam BOGGS
Armed With A New Terror	Dr Jeffrey MCNEILL
Arms For Oblivion	John STARK
Armstrong	Det Insp ARMSTRONG
The Army Defaulter's Secret	Sexton BLAKE
The Army Of The Dead	James (Operator 5) CHRISTOPHER
Arnholt Makes His Bow	ARNHOLT
Around Dark Corners	Uncle George CROWDER
Around The World In Eighty Days	Det FIX
The Arrest Of Scotland Yard	Insp Alfred SWAIN
Arrest These Men!	R J 'Rick' LEROY
Arrested For Murder	Brian O'MALLEY
Arresting Delia	Insp CLEVELAND
The Arrow Of Death	Sgt Ronnie DREW
The Arrowmont Prison Riddle	Buckmaster GILLOON
Arsenic And Gold	'Smiler' BUNN
Arsenic For The Teacher	Paul PLUSH
Arson	Frank JAMES
The Arsène Lepine-Herlock Soames Affair	Herlock SOAMES and Arsène LEPINE
Arsène Lupin	Arsène LUPIN
Arsène Lupin Versus Holmlock Shears	Arsène LUPIN and Herlock SHOLMES
Arsène Lupin Versus Holmlock Shears	Holmlock SHEARS and Arsène LUPIN
The Art Of Survival	FIDDLER
The Art Treasure Murders	Stephen DUANE
Artemus Flint: Detective	Artemus FLINT
Arthur	Arthur SILVERMAN
Artifex Intervenes	Simon ARTIFEX
The Artist Detective	The ARTIST DETECTIVE
An Artist In Crime	Robert Leroy MITCHELL and John BARNES
As A Crook Sows; Or, An Elusive Clew	Nick CARTER
As A Favor	Jill SMITH
As Bad As I Am	Mike FONTAINE
As It Chanced	Dick RYDER
The Ascot Gamble	Sherlock HOLMES
Ashenden; Or The British Agent	ASHENDEN
Ashes By Now	Nick SHARMAN
Ashes Of Evidence	Dr Edward LESTER
Ashes To Ashes	Sgt Peter 'Obie' BRICHTER
The Ashiel Mystery	Mr GIMBLET
Ashton-Kirk: Criminologist	ASHTON-KIRK
Ashton-Kirk: Investigator	ASHTON-KIRK
Asia	Philip MARLOWE
Asimov's Mysteries	Wendell ORTH
Ask For Me Tomorrow	Tomas ARAGON
Ask For Ronald Standish	Ronald STANDISH
Ask Miss Mott	Lucie MOTT
Ask No Mercy	R J 'Rick' LEROY
Ask The Right Question	Albert SAMSON
Asking For It	Charles HOOD
Asking For Trouble	Johnny POWERS
The Assassin	Terry (Chopper Cop) BUNKER
The Assassin	Ben KANE
The Assassin	Justin (The Assassin) PERRY
Assassin	Mikael Josef PETROS
The Assassin In The Greenwood	Hugh CORBETT
Assassin - Code Name Vulture	Nick CARTER
Assassination Brigade	Nick CARTER
The Assassins	Sam HOOK
The Assassins	The PHANTOM
Assault Into Libya	John CODY
Assault On Aimata	Cabot CAIN
Assault On Loveless	Cabot CAIN

A

Assignment Afghan Dragon	Sam DURELL
Assignment For Rusty Brown	Rusty BROWN
The Assignment Haiti	Geoff FENNELL
Assignment In Algeria	Brian DOUGLAS
Assignment In Beirut	Sexton BLAKE
Assignment In Iraq	Mike DARROCH
Assignment Intercept	Nick CARTER
Assignment K	Philip SCOTT
Assignment New York	James PACKARD
Assignment Sheba	Sam DURELL
Assignment To Bahrein	Peter WINSTON
Assignment To Disaster	Sam DURELL
Assignment Tyrant's Bride	Sam DURELL
Assignment - Assassination	Bart GOULD
The Assistant Murderer	Alexander RUSH
Assisted By Lessinger	LESSINGER
The Asylum Detective: Or, The Secret Of The Chest	The ASYLUM DETECTIVE
At Button's	Gregory SKIPWITH
At Death's Door	Carolus DEENE
At Fault	Sgt Silas USHER
At Last, Mr Tolliver	Mr Samuel TOLLIVER
At Midnight	Billy WINGRAVE and Nellie WINGRAVE
At Night To Die	Sally HELDAR and Johnny HELDAR
At Odds With Scotland Yard	Patsy MURPHY
At Rest At Last	Dorothy Mayotte RIGBY
At The Edge Of The Sun	Maggie BENNETT
At The House Of The Priest	Oliver SMAILE
At The Lake Of Sudden Death	Insp Achille PERONI
At The Villa Rose	Insp HANAUD
Atlanta Burn	Mark LEE and Carl BROWNE
Atlanta Deathwatch	Jim HARDMAN
The Attack On Vienna	Lawrence MAVER
The Attempted Murder Of Malcolm Duncan: A Reminiscence Of Mr Sherlock Holmes	Sherlock HOLMES
The Attic Murder	Mr JELLIPOT
The Attic Room	Capt Courtney BRADE
The Attwater Firewitch	Sherlock HOLMES
The Auber File	John BENHAM
The Audacious Adventures Of Miles McConaughy	Miles MCCONAUGHY
Audition For Murder	Maggie RYAN
August Ice	Chase DEFOE
Auprès De Ma Blonde	Insp Piet VAN DER VALK and Arlette VAN DER VALK
Austin Melville, Turf Investigator	Austin MELVILLE
The Australian Klondyke	Harvey STOKES
Author In Distress	Sgt/Supt Geoffrey BOSCOBELL
Authorized Murder	Darius JUST
Autobiography Of A London Detective	Henry CLARKE
Autobiography Of An English Detective	Henry CLARKE
Autumn Maze	Scobie MALONE
Avenge The Belgrano	Martin SEGUNDO
The Avenger	John BLACKMORE
The Avenger	Mike BRIXAN
The Avenger	Morgan WAYNE
Avenging Angel	Sir Patrick SCOTT
The Avenging Seven	Sexton BLAKE
The Avenging Twins	Paul SELBON and Peter SELBON
The Avenging Twins Collect	Paul SELBON and Peter SELBON
Average Jones	A V R E 'Average' JONES
The Awakening Dream	Whispering HILLS
Away Went The Little Fish	John DAVIES
The Axeman's Jazz	Offr Skip LANGDON
Axes Of Hate	Det Sgt Bob CHRISTIE
Azor!	Jeff PRIDE
The Aztec Avenger	Nick CARTER

— B —

B As In Banshee	Carl WAYWARD
Babe In The Woods	Lou LARGO
The Baby Blue Rip-Off	MALLORY
The Bacchus Club Mystery	Sherlock HOLMES
The Back Bay Murders	Insp KANE
Back Country	Brad DOLAN
The Back Door Man	Ben PERKINS
Back Home	Judge PRIEST
A Back Room In Somers Town	Tim SIMPSON
Backfire Is Hostile!	Supt Owen SMITH
Background For Murder	Jacob CHAOS
Background To Danger	VALESHOFF and TAMARA
Backlash	Michael CARMICHAEL
Backlash	Steven CASSELL
Backlash	Max CURFEW
Backlash	Johnny MAQUIS
Backtrack	Alan TARR
Backward, Turn Backward	Sheriff WILLETS
Back-Alley Blonde	Kinsey TARGET
The Bacon Mystery	Herlock SHOLMES
Bad August	Giovanni Alberto NOONAN
Bad Chemistry	Gillian ADAMS
Bad Day For A Black Brother	Richard SPADE
A Bad Day In The Bahamas	Harry FOSTER
Bad Day On Baker Street	Sherlock HOLMES
Bad Debt	Jack HENLEY
Bad End Valley	Domingo SANTOS
Bad Fortune	Frank MURPHY
Bad Guys	Mike TOZZI and Bert GIBBONS
Bad Luck	Mike TOZZI and Bert GIBBONS
Bad Money	David MEDINA
Bad Neighbours	James SHAW
A Bad Night's Work	Jack LOVEL
The Bad Samaritan	G K CHESTERTON
Badge Of Honor	Det Sgt John STRYKER
Badge Of Infamy	Michael CARMICHAEL
Badmen On Halfaday Creek	Cpl DOWNEY
A Baffled Oath: Or, The Cost Of Deceit	Nick CARTER
The Bagman	Mordecai 'Maudie' MORGAN
A Bagman In Jewels	Jeremy BELL
The Bainbridge Murder	Arthur MARTINSON
The Bait	Policewoman Christie OPARA
Bait Money	NOLAN
The Baker Street Boys	KEEGAN
A Balance Of Dangers	Capt John Valcourt JUSTICE
The Balance Of Fear	Geoffrey BRANSCOMBE
Balance Of Fear	James DINGLE and Glyn JONES
Balkan Spy	'Tiger' LESTER
Ballet Of Death	Pauline LYONS
Ballet Of Fear	Pauline LYONS
The Ballot Box Mystery	Sexton BLAKE
The Ballycronin Mystery	Shamus BURKE
The Bamboo Screen	Malcolm KENTON
The Bandaged Nude	Dan BANION
Bandbox Bob, The Dandy Detective: Or, The Flying Dragon Of Devil's Gulch	BANDBOX BOB
The Bandersnatch	Doran FAIRWEATHER and Rodney CHELMARSH
Bandicoot	Capt Colin HUNTINGTON
The Bandini Affair	Benny FREEDMAN
The Bandit Trust	William HARKNESS
The Bandits Of The Air: Or, Nick Carter's Aeroplane Trail	Nick CARTER
Bang! Bang!	Eddie PARKS
The Bank Note Forger	GRAYSON
The Bank Robber	Wilson YOUNG
The Bank Vault Mystery	Maxwell FENNER
The Banker's Bones	Prof Grace SEVERANCE
Banking On Death	John Putnam THATCHER
Bannerman	Slim Jim BANNERMAN
The Bannerman Case	Col Winston CREEVY
The Bannerman Effect	Paul BANNERMAN
The Bannerman Solution	Paul BANNERMAN
Banquets Of The Black Widowers	The BLACK WIDOWERS
Banshee	Howard HYATT and Michael DUNLOP
Banyon	BANYON
Baptism For The Dead	Moroni TRAVELER
The Bar Of Soap: Or, The Jew Au Jus	Sheerluck GNOMES
The Barbarous Coast	Lew ARCHER
Barbourze	Rupert QUINN
Barbs	Mal WILLIAMS
Bare Acquaintances	Ellie GORDON
Bare Bodkin	Sir John MEREDITH
Bargain For Death	Jim BENNETT
Bargain In Blood	Dallas WEBSTER
The Barking Clock	Tuddleton TROTTER
The Barlow Casebook	Supt Charles BARLOW
Barlow Dale's Casebook	Barlow DALE
Barlow Down Under	Supt Charles BARLOW
Barlow In Charge	Supt Charles BARLOW
Baron Ixell, Crime Breaker	Baron IXELL
The Baron Of Hong Kong	Bruce BARON
The Baroness Of Bow Street	Dulcie BLIGH
Baron's Mission To Peking	Bruce BARON
The Barotique Mystery	Kent MURDOCK
The Barrabas Blitz	Nile BARRABAS
The Barrabas Creed	Nile BARRABAS
The Barrabas Edge	Nile BARRABAS
The Barrabas Fire	Nile BARRABAS
The Barrabas Fix	Nile BARRABAS
The Barrabas Heist	Nile BARRABAS
The Barrabas Hit	Nile BARRABAS
The Barrabas Kill	Nile BARRABAS
The Barrabas Rai	Nile BARRABAS
The Barrabas Strike	Nile BARRABAS
The Barrabas Sweep	Nile BARRABAS
The Barrabas War	Nile BARRABAS
Barradine Detects	Lord BARRADINE
The Barrakee Mystery	Det Insp Napoleon BONAPARTE
The Barrel Mystery: Or, A Murderer's Double	Nick CARTER
The Bartholomew Fair Murders	Matthew STOCK and Joan STOCK
Basic Instinct	Nick CURRAN
The Basilisk: A Story Of Today	Frank COPLESTONE
The Bat Woman	Rex HUXFORD
The Bath Detective	Insp LEONARD
The Bathurst Complex	Prof John SOUTHARD
Batman	BATMAN
Batman Vs The Fearsome Foursome	BATMAN
Batman Vs The Joker	BATMAN
Batman Vs The Penguin	BATMAN
Batman Vs The Three Villains Of Doom	BATMAN
Battery Boice, The Electric Detective: Or, Rounding Up The Race Track Swindlers	BATTERY BOICE
A Battle For The Rights: Or, A Clash Of Wits	Nick CARTER
Battle Pay	Jim (The Death Dealer) RAINEY
Bat-Wing	Paul HARLEY
The Baxter Trust	Steve WINSLOW
Baxter's Second Death	Insp SWINTON
Bay City Blast	Remo (The Destroyer) WILLIAMS
Bay City Burnout	BONNER
The Bay Psalm Book Murder	Prof Clifford DUNBAR
The Bayou Brigade	Ben 'T-Man' SLAYTON
Bazi Bazoum: Or, A Strange Detective	Insp STRATTON
The Beach-Front Murders	Tom HOWARD
Beacons Of Death	Tommy MALINS
The Beaded Banana	Prof Grace SEVERANCE

Beads Of Silence	Septimus MARCH
Beagle Scented Murder	Otis BEAGLE
The Bear Raid	Piers ROPER
The Bearer Plot	Nicholas MAASTEN
The Beast	Anthony Nicholas TWIN
Beast In View	Paul BLACKSHEAR
Beastmark The Spy	F T CARRINGTON
Beasts And Escapades	Tim SHEA
Beat A Distant Drum	Mike (American Avenger) MCVEIGH
Beat Not The Bones	Emma WARWICK
The Beautiful Bait	Max STRONG
A Beautiful Death	Insp Ben JURNET
The Beautiful Gunner	Norma 'Nicky' LEE
Beautiful Jack, The Double-Edged Detective	BEAUTIFUL JACK
Beauty And The Beat	Hank JANSON
Beauty Dies	Claire CONRAD
Beauty Is A Beast	Elisha MACOMBER
Beauty Sleep	Lucy RAMSDALE and Insp James MACDOUGAL
The Beauty-Mask Murder	Gwynn LEITH and Colin KEATS
The Beauty-Mask Mystery	Gwynn LEITH and Colin KEATS
Beaver To Fox	Alfred BAUM
The Becket Factor	Richard HARRISON
The Beckoning Shadow	Mike JAMES
Bed Bugs	Haskell BLEVINS
The Bee Sting Deal	Vincent STALLARD and Cynthia GODWIN
The Beekeeper	Sherlock HOLMES
The Beekeeper's Apprentice; Or, The Segregation Of The Queen	Sherlock HOLMES
The Beethoven Conspiracy	Richard MARRETT
The Beetle: A Mystery	The Hon Augustus CHAMPNELL
Before It's Too Late	Steve WARREN
Before The Crossing	David PENN
The Beggars Of Kashapore	Nelson LEE
Beggar's Choice	Dr John BENT
Beggar's Choice	Nick POLO
Beginner's Luck	Hugh CURTIS
Beginning With A Bash	Leonidas WITHERALL
The Beginnings Of Mr P J Davenant	P J DAVENANT
Begin, Murderer!	Lindy GREY
Behind Closed Doors	Sgt ROMANO
Behind Locked Doors	Dr BENTIRON
Behind Locked Doors	Sgt ELLIS
Behind That Mask	Terry O'ROURKE
Behind The Bolted Door?	Henry LANEHAM
Behind The Enemy	Greg MARLOWE
Behind The Fact	Ezell BARNES
Behind The Green Mask	Insp LOCKET
Behind The Head-Lines	Insp HASKELL
Behind The Scarlet Door	Sgt Morgan PRICE
Behind The Yellow Blind	GARSTANG
Behold A Fair Woman	Mordecai Euripides TREMAINE
The Beholder: Seven Tales For Sebastian Romm	Sebastian ROMM
The Beirut Contract	Colin LYNCH
Beirut Incident	Nick CARTER
Bejewelled Death	Sarah ORPINGTON
Belgravia	Chris ROCKWELL and Sarah SABER
Believed Violent	Mark GIRLAND, Lu SILK and Herman RADNITZ
Belinda's Beaux And Other Stories	Lord SYFRET
The Bell Boy Detective; Or, The Hotel Diamond Robbery	The BELL BOY DETECTIIVE
The Bell In The Fog	Barney GANTT
The Bell Ringer	Charlie SKRAGG
The Bell Street Murders	Prof BLINKWELL and Mr JELLIPOT
Belladonna	Insp Alfred SWAIN
The Bellamy Case	Jefferson HASTINGS
Belle Boyd, The Girl Detective; A Story Of Chicago And The West	Belle BOYD
Belle Kingston, The Detective Queen; Or, The Stolen Bonds	Belle KINGSTON
The Bellmer Mystery	Insp TOPE
The Bells At Old Bailey	Insp RAIKES
The Bells Of Old Bailey	Insp RAIKES
Below Suspicion	Dr Gideon FELL and Patrick BUTLER
Below The Clock	Amos PETRIE
Below The Dead-Line	Felix BOYD
Ben Gates Is Hot	Ben GATES
Ben Logan, The Castle Garden Detective; Or, Trading The Best Of Diamonds	Ben LOGAN
Ben On The Job	BEN THE TRAMP
Benjamin Franklin And A Case Of Artful Murder	Benjamin FRANKLIN
Benjamin Franklin Takes The Case	Benjamin FRANKLIN
The Benson Murder Case	Philo VANCE
Bent Man	Walter JACKSON
Bequest Of Evil	'Doc' SAVAGE
The Berg Case	Sir Richard HERRIVELL
Bergerac	BERGERAC
Bergerac Is Back	BERGERAC
Berlin Game	Bernard SAMSON
The Berlin Memorandum	QUILLER
Bermuda Burial	Lt Michael LORD
Bermuda Calling	Zachary T ROWLAND
Bernhardt's Edge	Alan BERNHARDT
The Berry Scene	Bertram PLEYDELL
Bertie And The Crime Of Passion	King of England Edward VII WINDSOR
Bertie And The Tinman	King of England Edward VII WINDSOR
Bertie Bland, The Detective	Bertie BLAND
Beryl Of The Biplane	BERYL
Best Dr Poggioli Detective Stories	Prof Henry POGGIOLI
The Best Go First	Mike CAVANAUGH
The Best Of Randall Garrett	Lord DARCY
The Best Story Ever	Francis MANDELL-ESSINGTON
The Best That Ever Did It	Barney HARRIS
Best Thinking Machine Detective Stories	Prof Augustus S F X VAN DUSEN
The Bet	Ben JOYCE
The Betrayal Of John Fordham	Paul GODFREY
Betrayed	Sir Edgar EWART
Better Corpses	Race WILLIAMS
Better Dead	Insp Salvador BORGES
Better Off Dead	Insp Salvador BORGES
The Better To Eat You	Prof David WAKELY
Between Murders	James Gaylord DURSTINE
Between The Lines: A Detective Story	JANSON
Beverley Hills Browning	Richard BROWNING
The Beverly Malibu	Det Kate DELAFIELD
Beware Of The Dog	Virginia FREER and Felix FREER
Beware Taurus	Jo HUGHES
Beware The Pale Horse	Capt Wade PARIS
Beyond Baker Street	Sherlock HOLMES
Beyond Hope	Helen KEREMOS
Beyond Reasonable Doubt	Insp FENBY
Beyond The Danube	John ALLISON
Beyond The Grave	Elena OLIVEREZ and John QUINCANNON
Beyond The Second Door	Marise OVERTON
Beyond The Windswept Sea	David BALLARD and Michelle Merrill BALLARD
Beyond Tolerance	Brad FORD
Bicycle Jim	The BICYCLE DETECTIVE
Bid For Beauty	Hank JANSON
A Bid For Fortune; Or Dr Nikola's Vendetta	Dr NIKOLA
The Bid Game	Pete RILEY
Bier For A Chaser	Pete DRACO
Big Ben Strikes Eleven	Supt MOONEY
The Big Black	'Apples' CARSTAIRS
The Big Boodle	Ned SHERWOOD
The Big Bow Mystery	Insp George GOODMAN
The Big C	James HELLIER
The Big Chip	Guy FOSSE
The Big Circus Mystery	Sexton BLAKE
The Big Clock	George STROUD
The Big Dark	Preston John RIORDAN
Big Deal In Veragua	Pedro MORENO
The Big Dive	Kim LOCKE
The Big Drop And Other Cliff Hardy Stories	Cliff HARDY
The Big Enchilada	Sam HUNTER
A Big Enough Wreath	Mick JAGGER
The Big Fix	Gil SPEER
The Big Fix	Moses VINE
Big Foot	Supt MINTER
Big Game	Terence RADWAY
The Big H	Anthony BRANDON
The Big Heat	Dave BANNION
The Big Killing	Xenia SMITH and Leslie WETZON
The Big Kiss-Off Of 1944	Jack LEVINE
The Big Knockover	The CONTINENTAL OP
The Big Needle	'Apples' CARSTAIRS
Big Nick	Nick MORRO
The Big One	Jack (The Specialist) SULLIVAN
The Big Payoff	Joe BLAZE
The Big Payoff	Anna PETERS
The Big Picture	Max POPPER
The Big Scratch	Manx MCCATTY
Big Shot	Det Jub FREEMAN, Det Bill DECKER and Det Mitch TAYLOR
The Big Silence	Jack ROSS
The Big Sin	Det Sgt Sammy GOLDEN and Father Joseph SHANLEY
The Big Sleep	Philip MARLOWE
The Big Stash	Stash KOVAL
The Big Steal	Det Steve CONWAY
The Big Stick	Commiss Theodore ROOSEVELT
The Big Story	George HARLEQUIN
The Big Tickle	Sam HARRIS
The Bigamist	Maxwell SANDERSON
The Bigamy Kiss	Steve HARRAGAN
The Bigger They Come	Bertha COOL and Donald LAM
Biggles And The Little Green God	'BIGGLES'
Biggles And The Pirate Treasure, And Other Biggles Adventures	'BIGGLES'
Biggles Flies Again	'BIGGLES'
Biggles Flies To Work	'BIGGLES'
Biggles Investigates	'BIGGLES'
Biggles Of The Interpol	'BIGGLES'
Biggles Of The Special Air Police	'BIGGLES'
Biggles Presses On	'BIGGLES'
Biggles Takes The Case	'BIGGLES'
Biggles - Air Detective	'BIGGLES'
Biggles - Charter Pilot	'BIGGLES'
Biggles" Of The Camel Squadron	'BIGGLES'
Biggles' Chinese Puzzle	'BIGGLES'
Bill For The Use Of A Body	Julian DAY
Bill Marshall, Turf Sleuth	Bill MARSHALL
Bill Poole, The Louisville Detective; Or, In The Lair Of The 'Red Ribbon'	Bill POOLE
Bill Speed On Hot Ice	Insp Bill SPEED
Bill Speed - Special Squad	Insp Bill SPEED
The Billiard-Room Mystery	Anthony BATHURST
Billingsgate Shoal	Dr Charlie ADAMS
Billion Dollar Death	Henry Highland (Iceman) WEST
Billy Mischief, A Regular Trained Detective	Billy MISCHIEF
The Biltmore Call	Alan STEWART
Bimbashi Baruk of Egypt	Bimbashi BAUK
Bimbo Heaven	Pierre-Ange SAWYER
Bimbos Of The Death Sun	Jay OMEGA
The Bind	Jake DEKKER
Bino	Bono PHILLIPS
Bio Blitz	Alex (The Enforcer) JASON
The Bird House	John LITTLETON
Bird In A Guilt-Edged Cage	Andy KANE
The Bird In Last Year's Nest	MIRO
A Bird In The Hand	George PALMER-JONES
Bird In The Trees	Dr Jan CZISSAR
Bird Of Prey	Edward MERCER
Birds Of One Feather	Dr Joel HOFFMAN
Birds Of Prey	Valentine HAWKEHURST

Birds Of Prey	Nelson LEE
Birth Marks	Hannah WOLFE
Birthday Gifts And Other Stories	Supt Henry WILSON
The Birthday Murder	Richard Van Ryn WILSON
Bishop Pendle: Or, The Bishop's Secret	Insp TINKLER
The Bishop's Crime	Picklock HOLES
Bishop's Gambit	Prof Harry BISHOP
The Bishop's Secret	Insp TINKLER
Bismarck Herrings	Timothy HERRING
The Bite	Wylie LINCOLN
The Bite Of The Leech	Sir Nigel LACAITA
Biting Fortune	John MELROSE
Bits And Pieces	Ernst BRENDEL
Bitter Ending	Anthony POST
Bitter Lemons	Philip MARLOWE
The Bizarre Case Expert	Sgt Joseph MARX
Bizzy-Quizzy The Great	BIZZY-QUIZZY
The Black	DIXON
Black Account	Tom CANE and CONDON
The Black Ace	Sexton BLAKE
The Black Ace	Insp STRICKLAND
Black Alibi	Insp John BURNELL
The Black And The Red	Homer EVANS
The Black Arrows	John COWPER
Black August	Gregory SALLUST
Black August	Commiss TROTTI
Black Aura	Thackeray PHIN
Black Betty	'Easy' RAWLINS
The Black Casket	Philip ODELL
The Black Chamber	Steve WARFIELD
Black Chronicle	Arthur HALSTEAD
The Black Circle	Insp Malcolm STEELE
Black Cop	James RHODES
The Black Cotton Gloves	Pete FRY
The Black Dahlia	Det Dwight 'Bucky' BLEICHART
The Black Dark Murders	Phil KEENE
The Black Death	Nick CARTER
The Black Disk	Alec NORTON
The Black Doll	Arthur HALSTEAD
The Black Door	Stephen DRAKE
The Black Door	Insp FROST and Toni STAPLETON
Black Douglass, The Jersey City Detective: Or, Tracing The Mystery Of A Great Crime	BLACK DOUGLASS
The Black Dudley Murder	Albert CAMPION
The Black Dwarf	Lewis HORNE
The Black Eagle Mystery	Molly MORGANTHAU
The Black Echo	Det Harry BOSCH
The Black Emperor	Sir John MEREDITH
Black Eye	Johnny BLACK
Black Fog	Prof Harley MANNERS
The Black Friar Murders	Mayor Thomas LANDIN
Black Girl, White Girl	Ch Insp/Ch Sup Henry TIBBETT and Emmy TIBBETT
The Black Glove	Terry TRAVEN
The Black Gold Murders	Victor GRANT
Black Gravity	KNIGHTSBRIDGE
The Black Hand	Prof Craig KENNEDY
The Black Hate	Insp TODD
Black Hawthorn	Sgt POTTER
Black Hearts And Slow Dancing	Sheriff (temporary) Max FONTANA
The Black Hearts Murder	Micah 'Mike' MCCALL
Black Hornet	Lew GRIFFIN
The Black House In Harley Street	Richard GOULBURN
Black Is Beautiful	Richard SPADE
Black Is Black	BLACK
Black Is The Fashion For Dying	Richard BLAKE
Black Justice	Insp Richard MONTGOMERY
The Black Key	Dr Alexander CORNELL
Black Knight In Red Square	Insp Porfiry Petrovich ROSTNIKOV
A Black Leather Case	Sam HARRIS
The Black Leather Murders	Jay DELANEY
Black Magic	Scarsdale WARING
Black Mail	Johnny BLACK
Black Maria, MA	Maria BLACK
The Black Mask	A J RAFFLES
Black Moon	Sal CARLUCCI
Black Moon	Aline SCOTT
The Black Moth	Marcus GREENE
Black Opal	Silas BOOTH
The Black Pawn	James MALLABY
The Black Peril	'BIGGLES'
The Black Rose Murder	Ch Insp CUMMINGS
Black Samurai	Robert SAND
The Black Satchel	Tuddleton TROTTER
The Black Seraphim	James SCOTLAND
Black Shrouds The Bride	Insp Michael FARRANT
The Black Skull Murders	Bill MORROW and Jacqueline PINKER
The Black Spider	Reginald COSWAY
The Black Spiders	DEPARTMENT Z
The Black Spot	'Doc' SAVAGE
The Black Stamp	DISHER
The Black Star	BLACK STAR
Black Star Again	BLACK STAR
The Black Star Murders	Matt DOYLE and Carter WINFIELD
Black Star's Return	BLACK STAR
Black Star's Revenge	BLACK STAR
The Black Templar	Insp TODD
Black Tide	Lewis COLE
Black Trinity	Dr Ian MCANDREW
The Black Valley Murders	Dr Kirke MONTGOMERY
Black Widow	Ch Insp William BASTION
Black Widow	Peter DULUTH
The Blackheath Poisonings: A Victorian Murder Mystery	Paul VANDERVENT
Blackmail	Rocky NEVINS
Blackmail In Red	Supt Andrew ASH
Blackmail Is Murder	Matt SAVAGE
Blackmailers Don't Shoot	MALLORY
Blackmail, Inc	Ben GATES
Blackshirt	BLACKSHIRT
Blackshirt Again	BLACKSHIRT
Blackshirt Interferes	BLACKSHIRT
Blackshirt Stirs Thing Up	BLACKSHIRT
Blackshirt Strikes Back	BLACKSHIRT
Blackshirt Takes A Hand	BLACKSHIRT
Blackshirt The Adventurer	BLACKSHIRT
Blackshirt The Audacious	BLACKSHIRT
Blackshirt, Counter-Spy	BLACKSHIRT
The Blackstock Affair	Kevin MACINNES
Blackstone	Bow Street Runner Edmund BLACKSTONE
Blackstone On Broadway	Bow Street Runner Edmund BLACKSTONE
The Black-Eyed Blonde	Philip MARLOWE
The Blade Is Bright	Gerald LISSENDALE
Blame The Dead	James CARD
Blanche Among The Talented Tenth	Blanche WHITE
Blanche On The Lam	Blanche WHITE
Bland Beginning	Insp BLAND
A Blank Cheque For Murder	Tony SPENCER
The Blank Wall	Lt LEVY
The Blatchington Tangle	Supt Henry WILSON and The Hon Everard BLATCHINGTON
The Blaydin Mystery	Det Supt Horace PLUMMMET
The Blayne Document	Adam HOOD
Bleak House	Insp BUCKET
Bleeding Hearts	Gregor DEMARKIAN
Bleeding Hooks	Mr WINKLEY
A Bleeding Of Innocents	Ch Insp Frank SHAPIRO and Det Insp Liz GRAHAM
Bleke, The Butler	BLEKE
Blessed Among Women	Insp GILROY
Blessed Are The Poor In Spirit	Mgr John Blackwood 'Blackie' RYAN
The Blessing Way	Lt Joe LEAPHORN
The Blind Beggar Murder	Insp BECK
Blind Brag	Harry THOMPSON
The Blind Cave	Richard LANDON
Blind Eye	DEMPSEY and MAKEPEACE
The Blind Fury	Ross MCCOY
The Blind Hypnotist	Jason GALT
Blind Justice	Sir John FIELDING
Blind Justice	Ben KINCAID
Blind Man With A Pistol	Det 'Grave Digger' JONES and Det 'Coffin' Ed JOHNSON
The Blind Man's Eyes	Basil SANTOINE
Blind Man's Garden	Charles SMITH
Blind Rage	Richard BRONSON
The Blind Saw Murder	Ch Charles BAKER
The Blind Side	Insp Ernest LAMB
Blind Spring Rambler	William EDMONDSON
Blind Trust	Catherine SAYLOR
The Blind Trust Contracts	Sam GROSS
Blindfold	TRELAWNEY
The Blithe Sheriff	Mr GARFIELD
The Blonde	Lt Al WHEELER
The Blonde Body	Bill RYAN
The Blonde Countess	Mr GREENLEAF
The Blonde Cried Murder	Ed DONOVAN
The Blonde Died Dancing	Steve BARTON and Connie BARTON
Blonde Dynamite	Al BOCCA
The Blonde Lady	Arsène LUPIN and Herlock SHOLMES
The Blonde Lady: Being A Record Of The Duel Of Wits Between Arsène Lupin And The English Detective	Holmlock SHEARS and Arsène LUPIN
The Blonde Target	Ray (The Bodyguard) MARTIN
Blondes Die Young	Bill CANILLI
Blondes Don't Cry	Christine ANDERSEN
Blondes' Requiem	Marc SPENCER
The Blonde, The Gangster And The Private Eye	Gillian BALTIC
Blondie Beg Your Bullet	Rick RAZIO
Blondie Kiss Your Doom	Rick RAZIO
Blood	Mark BLOOD
Blood And Judgment	Const/Ch Insp Patrick PETRELLA
Blood And Thunder	Maxwell ARCHER
The Blood Bargain	Johnny ADRANO
Blood Bath	Hank JANSON
Blood Beast	Mike GANNON
Blood Brotherhood	Insp CROFT
Blood Brother, Blood Brother	Ross MCKELLAR
Blood For Breakfast	Mike GANNON
Blood From A Stone	Susan KENT
Blood Game	Leo GUILD
Blood In The Ashes	Bart CONDOR
Blood In Your Eye	Mike ZACHARIAS and Steve CONSIDINE
Blood Is A Beggar	Det Sam PHELAN
Blood Money	Garnett BELL
Blood Money	The CONTINENTAL OP
Blood Money	Supt MEADOWS
Blood Money	Harry WALKER
Blood Mountain	William 'Tiny' RYDER
Blood Of Poets	Carver BASCOMBE
Blood Of The Falcon	Nick CARTER
Blood On His Hands!	Insp READ and Jeffrey BLACKBURN
Blood On Pale Fingers	Dave NORTON
Blood On The Bayou	Kit FRANKLYN
Blood On The Beach	Tessie VENABLE
Blood On The Block	Dr Carter COLE
Blood On The Blonde	Nile BOYD
Blood On The Bosom Divine	Det Sam PHELAN
Blood On The Moon	Asher BOCKHORN
Blood On The Moon	Sgt Lloyd HOPKINS
Blood On The Sand	Carl DEKKER
Blood On The Tracks	Henry CHESTERFIELD
Blood On The Tracks	Sherlock HOLMES
Blood Patrol	Mike BRENT

B

The Blood Pit	Andrew MCCALL
Blood Relation	William DOUGAL
Blood Relations	Insp NEWSOM
Blood Relative	Jacob LOMAX
Blood Rights	Samson DEAN
Blood Risk	Mike TUCKER
Blood Royal	CHANDOS
Blood Royal	Supt MEADOWS
Blood Run	Josh DEKKER
Blood Run	Jesse HELLER
Blood Run	Johnny MORINI
The Blood Running Cold	Det Supt George ROGERS
The Blood Runs Hot	Sam HOSKINS
Blood Sacrifice	Luis BALAM
Blood Sport	Det FLYNN and Det TANNER
Blood Sport	Gene HAWKINS and Dave TELLER
Blood Sport	Insp HUMBLEBY
Blood Sympathy	Joe SIXSMITH
Blood Tells	Ryne LANARK
Blood Ties	Ryne LANARK
The Blood Transfusion Murders	Det Tommy RANKIN
Blood Upon The Snow	Mark EAST
Blood Vessel	Dan RUDNICKI
Blood Will Have Blood	Michael SPRAGGUE
Blood Will Tell	Ulysses Price MIDDLEBIE
Blood Will Tell: Or, A Sacrifice For Nothing	Nick CARTER
The Bloodhounds Bay	Dick SELDON
Bloodmoon	Skipper GOULD
Bloodrun	Skipper GOULD
Bloodshed In Bayswater	Insp SHELLEY
Bloodstain	Marty LAND
The Bloodstained Bokhara	Lee KAPRELIAN
The Bloodstained Toy	Insp HEADCORN and Tommy ROSTETTER
Bloodstains	Tom JONES
Bloodstar	Kevin FITZGERALD
The Bloody Bokhara	Lee KAPRELIAN
The Bloody Crescendo	Sally CARDIFF
Bloody Instructions	Phillip FLETCHER
Bloody Instructions	Antony MAITLAND
Bloody Mary	Doyle Dean MCCOY and Jerry ZALMAN
The Bloody Medallion	Montgomery NASH
The Bloody Monday Conspiracy	Agent of Cominsec TAGGART
Bloody September	David HAHAM
Bloody Silks	Harvey ACE
Bloody Success	Ch Insp Bill HOUGHTON
Blown Dead	Max HORN
Blue Bayou	Terry O'BANION
Blue Chipper	Norman HUNT
Blue Diamond	Terence O'HARA
The Blue Door	George Washington TROXELL
Blue Eyes	Dep Commiss Isaac SIDEL
The Blue Hammer	Lew ARCHER
Blue Heron	James MARLEY
The Blue Ice Affair	Nick CARTER
Blue Jean Billy	'Blue Jean' Billy RACE
The Blue Lamp	Sgt George DIXON
Blue Leader	Alison B GORDON
The Blue Macaw	Percy Aloysius HUFF
The Blue Mirage	Sgt Finnbar FRALEIGH
Blue Movie	Jack CLEARY
The Blue Movies Murder	Micah 'Mike' MCCALL
Blue Murder	Alison B GORDON
Blue Murder	Montague MIGGLEWADE
Blue Murder	Duke PIZZATELLO
Blue Octavo	John CAIN
The Blue Parakeet Murders	Maj Avery GREGG and Tony ELLIS
Blue Pete And The Kid	BLUE PETE
Blue Pete: Half-Breed	BLUE PETE
The Blue Scarab	Dr John Evelyn THORNDYKE
Bluebeard's Keys	Double O'DAY
Bluefeather	Sir James ERSKINE and George Stanhope BERKLEY
Blueprint For Murder	Insp JAMES
Blues For Charlie Darwin	Det Noah GREEN and Det Sam MCKIBBON
The Blunderer	Insp CORBY
Blunt Darts	John Francis CUDDY
A Blunt Instrument	Supt HANNASYDE
The Blushing Monkey	Philip CABOT
The Boarding House Mystery	Sexton BLAKE
The Boat Race Murder	Angus MACNAIR
Bodies	Insp Perry TRETHOWAN and Charlie PEACE
Body And Soul	Amanda ROBERTS and Joe DANELLI
The Body Beautiful	Barr BREED
Body Blow	Prof Gideon MANCIPLE and Dr William BLOW
Body Count	Father Robert KOESLER
Body Farm	Dr Kay SCARPETTA
Body Guard	Insp Carol ASHTON
Body Guard	Devlin KIRK
Body In My Arms	Peter JACKSON
The Body In The Barrage Balloon: Or, Who Killed The Corpse?	Mark ANTONY
The Body In The Bed	Barr BREED
The Body In The Belfry	Faith Sibley FAIRCHILD
The Body In The Blue Room	Ben MORRISON
The Body In The Bungalow	Insp Giles SEYMOUR
The Body In The Cast	Faith Sibley FAIRCHILD
The Body In The Road	Norman GLADE
The Body In The Safe	Insp Cuthbert HIGGINS
The Body In The Shaft	Anthony RAVENHILL
The Body In The Silo	Miles BREDON
The Body In The Trawl	Insp 'Dusty' MULLER and 'Tiny' MELDRUM
The Body In The Volvo	Sylvia SNOW and Prof Charles CARSTAIRS
The Body Lies	Insp Gil FLICKER
The Body Next Door	Lt Joseph DICKERSON
The Body Of A Girl	Insp MERCER
Body Of Evidence	Gardner WELLS
Body Of Truth	Det Stuart HAYDON
The Body On The Bus	Insp/Supt ADAMS
The Body On The Floor	Peter PIPER
The Body Snatchers	Raeburn STEEL
The Body That Came By Post	Hazlitt WOAR
A Body To Dye For	Stan KRAYCHIK
The Body Vanishes	Supt DULLAC
The Body Was Of No Account	Insp James DALE
The Body Wore Brocade	Supt Tetsuo OTANI
Bogue's Fortune	Charles APPLEGATE
The Bold House Murders	Berkeley Hoy BARNES
The Bomb	Dorothy Mayotte RIGBY
Bombay Mail	Insp Leonidas PRIKE
Bomber's Moon	Insp/Ch Supt George GENTLY
Bombshell	David MARTINI
The Bomb-Makers	Theodore DROST
Bond Grayson Murdered	Prof Clifford WELLS and Lt Barney MATTINGLEY
The Bond Of Black	Clifton CLEEVE
The Bond Street Burlesque	Lon QUINNCANNON
A Bonded Villain: Or, Nick Carter In Trouble	Nick CARTER
Bone	BONE
The Bone Polisher	Simeon GRIST
Bonecrack	Neil GRIFFON
Bonepile	Mitch ROBERTS
Bones	Commiss SANDERS
Bones In London	Commiss SANDERS
Bones In The Sand	Matt PRESTON
Bones Of Contention	Supt BURNIVAL
Bones Of The River	Commiss SANDERS
Boodle	Simon (The Saint) TEMPLAR
Book Early For Murder	Barry VAUGHAN and Dee VAUGHAN
The Book Of Avis	Avis BRYDEN
The Book Of Changes	Sir Hugh FITZ-HYFFEN
The Book Of Dreams	Keith GERSEN
The Book Of Murder	Oliver ARMISTON
The Book Of Numbers	Jimmy LUJACK
The Book Of The Crime	Henry GAMADGE
The Book Of The Dead	Augustus MALTRAVERS
The Book That Squealed	Prudence ROBERTS
Booked To Die	Cliff JANEWAY
The Bookmaker's Crime	Sexton BLAKE
The Bookman's Wake	Cliff JANEWAY
The Boomerang Clue	Frances DERWENT and Bobby JONES
Boomerang Murder	Ch Det Insp George MUIR
The Boot Black Detective: Or, The Youngest Man Hunter On The Force	The BOOT BLACK DETECTIVE
Bootlegger	Jim SHERIDAN
Bootlegger's Daughter	Judge Deborah KNOTT
Bopping It In Bohemia: Or, Sheerback Tones In Basin Street	Sheerback TONES
Border Incident	Slim Jim BANNERMAN
The Border Line	Dick SELDON
The Border Line Detective: Or, Watching The Smugglers Of The Chinese	The BORDER LINE DETECTIVE
A Borderline Case	Paul BRODIE
The Borders Of Barbarism	Roger STARTE and Kate STARTE
The Borgia Cabinet	Sgt CHARLESWORTH
Born Guilty	Joe SIXSMITH
Born To Be Hanged	Milo MARCH
Borrower Of The Night	Vicky BLISS
Bosambo Of The River	Commiss SANDERS
The Boscombe Valley Mystery	Sherlock HOLMES
The Boston Crab	Amanda CURZON and Oscar SALLIS
Both Sides Of The Case	Julian PRESCOT
Bottom Line	Remo (The Destroyer) WILLIAMS
The Bottom Line Is Murder	Paul MARSTON
Bottom Of Suez	Grant RUSHTON
The Bound Of The Astorbilts: A Modern Detective Story	Sherlock HOLMES
The Bound Of The Haskervilles	Herlock SHOLMES
Bound To Kill	John CAIN
The Bournewick Murders	Const MURDOCH
A Bout With The Mildew Gang	Insp CAULDRON
Bowery Murder	Insp Dan CARR
The Bowstring Murders	John GAUNT and Prof Michael TAIRLAINE
Box Office Browning	Richard BROWNING
The Boy Detective: Or, The Crimes Of London	The BOY DETECTIVE
The Boy From Nowhere	Sheila TRACY
The Boy Scout's Craig Kennedy	Prof Craig KENNEDY
The Boys From Binjiwunyawunya	Les NORTON
The Boys From Brazil	Yakov LIEBERMAN
A Brace Of Rogues	Sydney VANE
A Brace Of Skeet	Deborah CALDER
The Bradmoor Murder	Sir Henry MARQUIS
Bradshaw, The Wide Awake Detective: Or, Piping A Very Remarkable Case	BRADSHAW
Bragg's Hunch	Peter BRAGG
The Brain Murders	Peter QUEST
The Brain Scavengers	John (The Expediter) EAGLE
Brain Twister	Kenneth MALONE
Brainwash	Insp David LYLE
Brainz, Inc	Jake PACE and Hildy PACE
Brain-Waves And Death	Insp NOONAN
The Brand Of The Beast	Sgt HOBBS
Brand Of The Black Bat	Tony (Black Bat) QUINN
The Brand Of The Broad Arrow	Insp LAMPETER
Brand T	Hilary BRAND
The Branded Spy	Sexton BLAKE
The Brandenburg Affair	Sebastian KETTLE
Brandon Is Missing	Bruce CARVER
Brandon Takes Over	Mark BRANDON
Brant Adams, The Emperor Of Detectives	Brant ADAMS
The Brass Chills	Luke BRADLEY
The Brass Cupcake	Clifford BARTELLS
The Brass Go-Between	Philip ST IVES
Brass Knuckles	Oliver QUADE

The Brass Ring	Seth COLMAN and Eve COLMAN
The Brass Shroud	Johnny MIDAS
Bravo 9	Steven FLAGG
Bravo Charlie	Charlotte ELIOT
The Bravo Of London	Max CARRADOS
Brazen Virtue	Ed JACKSON
Breach Of Promise	Supt ROPER
The Breadfruit Lotteries	Dr Robert HARMON
The Break	James WAINWRIGHT
The Break In The Line	James WAINWRIGHT
Breakaway	Supt Francis FOY
The Breaker Of Ships	Jim MARTIN
Breaking The Shackles	Capt Thomas VERNAN
Break-Out	Jack LOVEL
Breath Of Suspicion	George Fort ELGIN
Breathe No More, My Lady	Hilary Dunsany BAILEY III and Hilea BAILEY
The Breathless Hush	Dorothy Mayotte RIGBY
The Bred In The Bone	Avis BRYDEN
Bren Hardy Again	Bren HARDY
Bren Hardy, Tough Dame	Bren HARDY
Bressio	Alphonse Joseph BRESSIO
The Bridal Bed Murders	Pel PELHAM
The Bride Of A Moment	Alan FORD
The Bride Of Moat House	Emma PLUME
The Bride Of Newgate	Dick DARWENT
Bride's Castle	Sir Julian MORTHOE
Bridge Of Birds	Li KAO
The Bridled Groom	Sarah DEANE and Dr Alex MCKENZIE
Brief Candles	Charles LATIMER and James LATIMER
Brief Candles	Charles LATIMER and James LATIMER
The Brigand	Anthony NEWTON
Briggs Investigates	Tommy BRIGGS
Bright Angel	KOREGORVSKY
The Bright Blue Death	Nick CARTER
Bright Serpent	John MARSHALL and Suzy MARSHALL
The Brighter Buccaneer	Simon (The Saint) TEMPLAR
Brightlight	Nathan BRIGHTLIGHT
Bring Back The Cat!	Joe SIXSMITH
Bring Back Yesterday	Stefan VYNALEK
Bring Forth Your Dead	Supt John LAMBERT
Bring The Bride A Shroud	Prof A PENNYFEATHER
The Brink Of Murder	Simon DRAKE
Broadway Bob, The Bounder Detective	BROADWAY BOB
The Broadway Jungle	Norma 'Nicky' LEE
The Broadway Murders	Richard Curtis (The Phantom) VAN LOAN
Brock	Supt 'Badger' BROCK
Brock And The Defector	Supt 'Badger' BROCK
Broiled Alive	Marques Don PANCHO
The Broken Body	Riley WADDELL
Broken Consort	Alan FRENCH
The Broken Face Murders	Baron Franz Maximilian Karagos VON KAZ
The Broken Fang And Other Experiences Of A Specialist In Spooks	Prof Arnold RHYMER
Broken On Crime's Wheel	Nick CARTER
The Broken Spectre	Lisa MASSINGHAM
The Broken Vase	Tecumseh FOX
The Broken Vase Mystery	John SMITH
The Broken-Hearted Detective	Vino ALTOBELLI
The Broker	QUARRY
The Broker	Mike RYAN
Broker's End	Maxwell FENNER
The Bronze Mermaid	Sam CATES
The Bronze Mermaid	Lt Jim RYAN
The Bronze Perseus	Det Ch Insp BRENTFORD
A Brood Of Vipers	Roger SHALLOT
The Brookham Mystery	Herbert HOLT
Brooklyn Moll Shoots Bedmate	Kinsey TARGET
The Brooklyn Murders	Supt Henry WILSON
Brother Cadfael's Penance	Brother CADFAEL
The Brother Of Heaven	Mervyn HENDERSON
The Brother Of Heaven	Barnabas HILDRETH
The Brotherhood Of The Seven Kings	Norman HEAD
Brothers In Law	Roger THURSBY
The Brothers Sackville	Insp FAIRFORD
Brought To Bay; Or, Experiences Of A City Detective	James M'GOVAN
The Brown Murder Case	Insp Neville LANGHAM
Browne Of The Secret Service	Freddie BROWNE and Jim FANSHAW
Browne's First Case	Freddie BROWNE and Jim FANSHAW
Brown's Requiem	Fritz BROWN
Bruce Angelo, The City Detective	Bruce ANGELO
Bruce Angelo, The Old Time Detective	Bruce ANGELO
Brush Of Death	James WESTON
The Brutal Ballet	Joe HANNIBAL
The Buddha Case	Insp WALL
Bugged For Murder	William WALLACE
Build My Gallows High	Red BAILEY
The Bull Slayers	Insp Jeremy FARO
Bulldog And Rats	FANTOMAS
Bulldog Drummond On Dartmoor	Capt Hugh 'Bulldog' DRUMMOND
Bulldog Drummond: The Adventures Of A Demobilized Officer Who Found Peace Dull	Capt Hugh 'Bulldog' DRUMMOND
Bulldog Drummond Returns	Capt Hugh 'Bulldog' DRUMMOND
Bulldog Drummond: The Adventures Of A Demobilized Officer Who Found Peace Dull	Capt Hugh 'Bulldog' DRUMMOND
The Bulldog Has The Key	Ed BRAKELY
A Bullet For A Blonde	Vince LATIMER
Bullet For A Star	Toby PETERS and Errol FLYNN
A Bullet For Betty	Insp Pat STOCKTON
A Bullet For My Baby	Mavis SEIDLITZ
A Bullet For My Love	Lt Marty WALSH
A Bullet For Rhino	Insp Harry CHARLTON
A Bullet For Your Dreams	David DANNING
Bullet Hole	Alan SAXON
A Bullet In His Cap	Simon CROLE
A Bullet In The Ballet	Insp Adam QUILL
The Bullet In The Cornice	Maj Dick BURTON
Bullets And Brown Eyes	Mark CORRIGAN
Bullets Are Trumps	Sexton BLAKE
Bullets Bite Deep	Mick CARDBY
Bullets For Brandon	Mark BRANDON
Bullets Make Holes	Glen GIBSON
Bullets To Baghdad	Sexton BLAKE
The Bullet-Proof Martyr	Paul Kenneth KANE
The Bullet-Proof Toga	Martin MOON
The Bullion Mystery; Or, Nick Carter's Case From Overseas	Nick CARTER
Bullshot	Doyle Dean MCCOY and Jerry ZALMAN
Bully!	Theodore ROOSEVELT and Jim WHITE
Bull's Eye	Sir George BULL
The Bungalow Mystery	Centenier PINOT
The Bunnies	Peter TREES
Burden Of Proof	Jeremy LOCKE
The Burden Of Proof	Alejandro 'Sandy' STERN
The Burglar Who Thought He Was Bogart	Bernard Grimes RHODENBARR
Burglars Can't Be Choosers	Bernard Grimes RHODENBARR
Buried Caesars	Toby PETERS and Dashiell HAMMETT
The Buried Motive	Cash MADIGAN
Buried On Sunday	Geoffrey CHADWICK
Burma Battle	Greg MARLOWE
The Burma Ruby	Sgt CHARLESWORTH
Burn	Fred CARVER
Burn Forever	Ben DAVIDGE
Burn Sugar Burn	MCCOY
Burn This	Dr Basil WILLING
The Burned Man	Brian BRETT
The Burned Man	Peregrine WHITE
The Burning Blue Death	Richard (The Death Merchant) CAMELLION
The Burning Court	Edward STEVENS
The Burning Season	Joe HANNIBAL
Burning Water	George VANCOUVER
Burn-Out	Cdr Esmonde SHAW
Burn, Witch, Burn!	LOWELL
Bury Him Darkly	Philipa LOWE
Bury In Haste	Insp KNICKMAN
Bury It Deep	Cooper MACLEISH
Bury Me Deep	Scott JORDAN
Bury Me Not	Anthony MARTIN
Bury That Poker	Insp LOVICK
Bury The Bishop	Mother Lavinia GREY
Bury Their Dead	Insp Noel TRACY
The Bus Station Murders	Miss Julia TYLER
The Bus That Vanished	Henri HENRY
Business Unusual	Simon BOGNOR
Busman's Honeymoon	Lord Peter WIMSEY
But He Was Already Dead When I Got There	Lt TOOMEY
But Not For Love	Greg FLAMM
But Our Hero Was Not Dead	Sherlock HOLMES
But The Doctor Died	Jake JUSTUS, Helene JUSTUS and John J MALONE
But The Patient Died	Insp Victor BONDURANT
But The Patient Died	Insp Paul GRAINGER
The Butcher's Boy	Elizabeth WARING
The Butcher's Moon	Alan GROFIELD
The Butterfly	Prof Brinsley BUTLER
The Butterfly Murder	Derek WHITBY
Button, Button	Kit 'Marsden' ACTON
Button, Button	Lt KELLY
Button, Button...	Mgr Thomas O MCGILLICUDDY
The Buy Back Blues	Jim HARDMAN
Buyer Beware	Alo NUDGER
Buzzards Pick The Bones	Insp WILKINS
By A Hair's-Breadth	Laura METCALF
By Evil Means	Phoebe SIEGEL
By Force Of Circumstances	Insp Charles François FURNEAUX
By Force Of Circumstances	Insp Charles François FURNEAUX
By Frequent Anguish	Neil KELLY
By Murder's Bright Light	Brother ATHELSTAN
By Night At Dinsmore	Miles LE BRETON
By Reason Of	Jeanne DONOVAN
By Way Of Confession	Lucien CLAY
By Whose Hand?	BRICONI
The By-Pass Control	'Tiger' MANN

—C—

The Cabaret Crime	Ch Det Insp George MUIR
Cabin 3033	Paula GLENNING
A Cabinet Minister Resigns	Maj Charles Douglas KERWOOD
The Cable Car Murder	Maggie ELLIOTT
Cache On The Rocks	Cal FISHER
The Cactus	Bob ELLIS
Cad Metti, The Female Detective Strategist; Or, Dudie Dunne Again In The Field	Dudie DUNNE
Cadaver	Charlotte KENT
A Cadenza For Caruso	Enrico CARUSO
Caedmon, Caedmonk	HOMONYMOUS
The Caesar Clue	Micah DUNN
Cage Of Mirrors	Clayton 'Yankee' TAGGART
Caged! The Romance Of A Lunatic Asylum	Sgt TREVOR and Sgt GODBOLD
Cain's Chinese Puzzle	CAIN
Cain's Woman	Max RAVEN

C

	Title	Detective
	Cairo Communiqué	Capt James Donald MACGREGOR
The	Cairo Sleeper	George MADO
	Calamity In Kent	Insp SHELLEY
A	Calculated Risk	CHARD
A	Calculated Risk	Hiram POTTER
The	Calculus Of Murder	Dan BRODSKY
	Caleb Clickett, The Great Detective; Or, Tracked By A Finger-Nail	Caleb CLICKETT
	California Thriller	Mike HALLER
	Californian Dead	Eve ZABRISKIE
	Call For Simon Shard	Det Ch Supt Simon SHARD
	Call For The Dead	George SMILEY
	Call For The Saint	Simon (The Saint) TEMPLAR
	Call In The Yard	Det Insp SANDERSON
	Call Mr Fortune	Dr Reginald FORTUNE
	Callaghan Meets His Fate	Col 'Steel' CALLAGHAN
	Callaghan Of Intelligence	Col 'Steel' CALLAGHAN
	Callan	David CALLAN
	Called By A Panther	Albert SAMSON
	Called To Account; Or, Nick Carter Takes a Hand	Nick CARTER
	Calling Dr Patchwork	Jake PACE and Hildy PACE
	Calling Lord Blackshirt	Lord Anthony BLACKSHIRT
	Calling Mr Callaghan	Rupert Patrick 'Slim' CALLAGHAN
	Calling Whitehall 1212	Sexton BLAKE
The	Call-Box Murder	Insp GRAMPORT
	Calvert Cole, Of California, The Pacific Slope Detective	Calvert COLE
The	Calypso Murders	Xavier BROOKE
The	Cambri Plot	Silas MANNERS
The	Cambridge Murders	Insp BRAMLEY
The	Cambridge Murders	Prof Richard CHERRINGTON
	Camelord	Insp Taff ROBERTS
The	Camelot Conundrum	Richard RAVEN
	Camouflage	Sir James ERSKINE
The	Campanile Murders	Bill BARTLETT
The	Campden Ruby Murder	Capt KEYES
	Campus Corpse	Gerry LEE
The	Campus Murders	Micah 'Mike' MCCALL
	Can You Solve This Crime?	Insp John B MAGRUDER
The	Canal Mystery	Insp BLISS
	Canary	Daniel VALENTINE and Clarisse LOVELACE
The	Canary Trainer	Sherlock HOLMES
	Cancelled In Red	Luke BRADLEY
	Candidate For Murder	Lowell GAYLORD, Prof Angus MCDERMOTT, Lens PENGA and Prof Arthur CHURCHILL
The	Candles Are All Out	Alan RUSSELL
	Candy Floss Coast	Anna KNIGHT
The	Cannibal Who Over Ate	Pierre CHAMBRUN
The	Canterbury Cathedral Murder	Shirley HOLMES
	Canto For A Gypsy	Roman GREY
The	Canvas Coffin	Luke PILGRIM
The	Cape Cod Mystery	Asey MAYO
The	Caper Of The Politician, The Lighthouse, And Trained Cormorant	Sherlock HOLMES
A	Capital Killing	Robert MILES
The	Capital Murder	Trevor STOKE
A	Capitol Crime	Tony JORDAN
A	Capitol Offense	Ambrose USHER
The	Captain	Lt LASALA
	Captain Black	Capt BLACK
	Captain Clew, The Flying Detective	Capt CLEW
	Captain Confetti	Capt CONFETTI
	Captain Dack	Capt DACK
	Captain Firebrace	Capt FIREBRACE
	Captain Gault	Capt GAULT
	Captain Justice	Capt John Valcourt JUSTICE
	Captain Kettle On The War-Path	Capt Owen KETTLE
	Captain Kettle, KCB	Capt Owen KETTLE
	Captain Kettle's Bit	Capt Owen KETTLE
	Captain Leopold And The Vanishing Men	Capt LEOPOLD
	Captain McBlaid Of The Air Police	Capt MCBLAID
	Captain Nash And The Honour Of England	Capt George NASH
	Captain Nash And The Wroth Inheritance	Capt George NASH
	Captain Nice	Capt NICE
	Captain Samson, A B	Capt SAMSON
	Captain Shannon	RISSLER
The	Captain's Curio	Insp MIDWINTER
	Captain's Walk	Jannine WEST
	Captive Audience	Prof Theodora Wade CRAWFORD
The	Captive City	Ape SWAIN
A	Captive In The Land	Rupert ROYCE
	Captive In Time	Stoner MCTAVISH
The	Capture Of Paul Beck	Paul BECK
The	Captured Submarines	Herlock SHOLMES
The	Caravaggio Obsession	Amos HATCHER
The	Caravaggio Shawl	Gertrude STEIN and Alice TOKLAS
The	Caravan Detective	The CARAVAN DETECTIVE
	Carbon Monoxide	Supt ROMER
The	Carbuncle Clue	Octavius FANKS
	Card 13	Arthur RANELEIGH
The	Card Game	Phillip (The Marksman) MAGELLAN
The	Cardboard Box	Sherlock HOLMES
The	Cardinal And The Corpse	The CARDINAL
	Cardinal Error	Insp James CARDINAL
The	Cardinal Moth	Insp TOWNSEND
A	Cardinal Offense	Father Roger DOWLING
	Cards On The Table	Hercule POIROT, Supt BATTLE, Col RACE and Mrs Ariadne OLIVER
The	Careless Mrs Christian	Homer FITZGERALD
The	Caress Of Conquest	John GAIL
The	Cargo Club	Ray CRAWLEY
	Cargo For Death	John TRACY
	Cargo For The Styx	Martin ZANE
	Cargo Of Eagles - Special	Albert CAMPION
A	Cargo Of Spent Evil	Hugo BARON
A	Cargo Of Tin	HENRICKSEN
	Cargo To Saigon	Ric MCADDEN
The	Caribbean Account	Roger LEVIN
The	Caribbean Affair	Maj 'Brains' CUNNINGHAM
	Caribbean Caper	Hank JANSON
The	Caribbean Caper	Louis Luther (Murder Master) KING
	Caribbean Coup	Nick CARTER
The	Caribou Patrol	Jim MALLOY
	Carlito's Way	CARLITO
	Carmen Was A Virgin	Nick CRANLEY
	Carnaby And The Campaigners	Det Sgt CARNABY
	Carnaby And The Hijackers	Det Sgt CARNABY
	Carnacki, The Ghost Finder	CARNACKI
	Carnage Of The Realm	Edwin GEORGE
The	Carnation Killer	Vic MERRITT
The	Carnellian Circle	John HAMMOND
	Carney's Burlesque	Steve HARRAGAN
A	Carol In The Dark	Will GRAY
	Carolina Skeletons	James WILLOP
The	Caroline Affair	Paul HARVARD
	Caroline Minuscule	William DOUGAL
	Carpenter, Detective	Ace CARPENTER
The	Carpet-Slipper Murder	Insp Neil MACLEOD
The	Carriage Clock	Sherlock HOLMES
	Carribean Crisis	Sexton BLAKE
	Carrington's Cases	F T CARRINGTON
The	Cart Before The Crime	The Hon Constance Ethel MORRISON-BURKE
	Cartwright Is Dead, Sir!	Richard LIND
The	Carved Emerald	Oliver GALT and Hugo TOWER
	Casa Madrone	Mallory BOOKOVER
The	Case Against Butterfly	Bill BRADLEY and Noel MAYBERRY
The	Case Against Mr Ames	Sam KERNOCHAN
The	Case Against Myself	Bill BRADLEY and Noel MAYBERRY
The	Case And The Girl	Matthew WEST
The	Case Book Of Jimmie Lavender	Jimmie LAVENDER
The	Case Book Of Mr Campion	Albert CAMPION
A	Case For Appeal	Det Vic VARALLO and Jesse FALKENSTEIN
A	Case For Charley	Charley CASE
	Case For Equity	Lorna DONAHUE
	Case For Mr Fortune	Dr Reginald FORTUNE
A	Case For The Cardinal	The CARDINAL
	Case For Three Detectives	Sgt William BEEF
A	Case In Camera	Insp HUMBLEBY
The	Case Is Altered	Fraser TODD
A	Case Of Blackmail	Sexton BLAKE
The	Case Of Emily V	Sherlock HOLMES and Sigmund FREUD
A	Case Of Facsimile	Shirley HOLMES
The	Case Of His Lordship's Engagement	Herlock SHOLMES
A	Case Of Identities	Sherlock HOLMES
A	Case Of Identity	Sherlock HOLMES
A	Case Of Identity II; Or, Art In The Soup Can Take The Strangest Forms	Cerlocio OLMEZ
A	Case Of Indelicate Champagne	Stanley DELPHOND
The	Case Of Jennie Brice	Jennie BRICE
The	Case Of Larachi The Lascar	Sexton BLAKE
The	Case Of Lord Greyburn's Son	Sexton BLAKE
A	Case Of Loyalties	Det Jay GOLDSTEIN, Det Carlos CRUZ and Carrie RAYBORN
The	Case Of Marie Corwin	Dep Commiss Benjamin SIMON
The	Case Of Miss Dunstable	Jaspar POOLE
The	Case Of Miss Elliott	The OLD MAN IN THE CORNER
The	Case Of Mr Cassidy	Hugh MORRIS
The	Case Of Podgers MP	Herlock SHOLMES
The	Case Of Robert Robertson	Asbjorn (Osborne Crag) KRAG
The	Case Of The Abandoned Lighthouse	Sherlock HOLMES
The	Case Of The Absent Corpse	Lorna DONAHUE
The	Case Of The Account That Got Away	Sheerluck OHMS
The	Case Of The Ace Accomplice	Sexton BLAKE
The	Case Of The Addleton Tragedy	Sherlock HOLMES
The	Case Of The Airman's Medal	Herlock SHOLMES
The	Case Of The Alphabetical Vandal	Sheerluck OHMS
The	Case Of The Aluminium Crutch	Sherlock JONES
The	Case Of The Amateur Mendicants	Sherlock HOLMES
The	Case Of The Amateur Mendicants	Sherlock HOLMES
The	Case Of The American Clock	Herlock SHOLMES
The	Case Of The American Millionaire	Herlock SHOLMES
The	Case Of The Angry Actress	Det Sgt Masao MASUTO
The	Case Of The Anonymous Doorstep Donors	Shirley HOLMQUIST
The	Case Of The Back Seat Girl	Ch Insp George BASSETT
The	Case Of The Backward Mule	Terry CLANE
The	Case Of The Baconian Cipher	Sherlock HOLMES
The	Case Of The Baffled Policemen	Sherlock HOLMES
The	Case Of The Baker Street Irregulars	Sherlock HOLMES and Fergus O'BREEN
The	Case Of The Ball Dress	Herlock SHOLMES
The	Case Of The Barking Clock	Tuddleton TROTTER
The	Case Of The Beleaguered Detective	Sherlock HOLMES
The	Case Of The Bendigo Heirlooms	Sexton BLAKE
The	Case Of The Bewildering Barn	ERNIE
The	Case Of The Biscuit Tin	Herlock SHOLMES
The	Case Of The Blind Mouse	Jerry TODD
The	Case Of The Boat Club	Herlock SHOLMES
The	Case Of The Bolshevik!	Herlock SHOLMES
	Case Of The Brazen Beauty	Det Pete SELBY
The	Case Of The Buchanan Curse	Sherlock HOLMES
The	Case Of The Burgled Bulb	Shirley HOLMQUIST
The	Case Of The Burning Bequest	Perry MASON
The	Case Of The Calabar Bean	Sgt/Supt Geoffrey BOSCOBELL
The	Case Of The Camberwell Poisoners	Sherlock HOLMES
The	Case Of The Camberwell Poisoning	Sherlock HOLMES
The	Case Of The Canary Trainer	Sherlock HOLMES
The	Case Of The Canine Accomplice	Milo MORGAN
The	Case Of The Caterpillar's Hand	Insp MANTIS
The	Case Of The Cautious Coquette	Perry MASON
The	Case Of The Chain Reaction	Sheerluck OHMS
The	Case Of The Character Lines In Chenille	Shirley HOLMQUIST
The	Case Of The Charlady	Herlock SHOLMES
The	Case Of The Chief Rabbi's Problem	Sherlock HOLMES

The Case Of The Climbing Corpse	Chester BRETT
The Case Of The Clockport Catnapper	Sheerluck OHMS
The Case Of The Colonel's Madness	Sherlock HOLMES
The Case Of The Communist Plot To Conquer Heartsberg	Shirley HOLMQUIST
The Case Of The Concrete Corpse	Dr Carter COLE
The Case Of The Confounded Counterfeiter	Sheerluck OHMS
The Case Of The Cool-Headed Claim Jumper	Shirley HOLMQUIST
The Case Of The Copy-Book Killing	Ben LUCIUS
The Case Of The Corn-Plaster	Herlock SHOLMES
The Case Of The Counterfeit Cent	Sheerluck OHMS
The Case Of The Crawling Cockroach	Dan JORDAN
The Case Of The Crazy Americans	Sherlock HOLMES
The Case Of The Creeping Krooboy!	Herlock SHOLMES
The Case Of The Crimson Wizard	Sexton BLAKE
The Case Of The Crippled Bridegroom	Sherlock HOLMES
The Case Of The Crook Banker	Sexton BLAKE
The Case Of The Crumpled Knave	Fergus O'BREEN and Det Lt JACKSON
The Case Of The Cubist	Herlock SHOLMES
The Case Of The Cummuppance Cup	Sheerluck OHMS
The Case Of The Curious Chair	Arabella BLAKE and Andy BLAKE
The Case Of The Curious Heel	Jason JONES and 'Necessary' SMITH
The Case Of The Curious Kerchief	Sherlock HOLMES
The Case Of The Currant Bun	Herlock SHOLMES
The Case Of The Dancing Bees	Sherlock HOLMES
The Case Of The Dark Wanton	Peter QUAYLE
The Case Of The Dead Producer	Ch Insp Archie BURFORD
The Case Of The Deadly Drops	Nigel MAYNE
The Case Of The Death Computer	John MARSH
The Case Of The Demon Barber	Sherlock HOLMES
The Case Of The Dentist	Herlock SHOLMES
The Case Of The Detective's Smile	Sherlock HOLMES
The Case Of The Devil's Hoofmarks	Sherlock HOLMES
The Case Of The Diabolical Plot	Sherlock HOLMES
The Case Of The Dictator's Double	Sexton BLAKE
The Case Of The Doomed Dissertation	Sherlock HOLMES
The Case Of The Dope Dealers	Sexton BLAKE
The Case Of The Edberg Boy Who Never Married	Shirley HOLMQUIST
The Case Of The Eighteenth Ostrich	Mark ANTONY
The Case Of The Emperor's Crown	Insp MANTIS
The Case Of The Escaped Hun	Herlock SHOLMES
The Case Of The Exalted Client	Sherlock HOLMES
The Case Of The Fast Young Lady	Roger POYNINGS
The Case Of The Financier	Herlock SHOLMES
The Case Of The Fire At The Flickertail Lounge And Grill	Shirley HOLMQUIST
The Case Of The Fish That Wouldn't Keep	Sheerluck OHMS
The Case Of The Forbidden Fruit	Shirley HOLMQUIST
The Case Of The Forbidden Island	Sexton BLAKE
The Case Of The Foster Father	Eleanora BURKE
The Case Of The Four Friends	Ernst BRENDEL
The Case Of The Four Pages	Martin SPEED
The Case Of The Friesland Outrage	Sherlock HOLMES
The Case Of The Frightened Brother	Clive 'Dormouse' CONRAD
The Case Of The Frightened Fish	Jack JORDAN
The Case Of The Frightened Heiress	Sherlock HOLMES
The Case Of The Frightened Scholar	Insp MANTIS
The Case Of The Gentle Conspirators	Sherlock HOLMES
The Case Of The Gifted Amateur	Sherlock HOLMES
The Case Of The Gilded Fly	Gervase FEN
The Case Of The Girl With The Gazelle	Sherlock HOLMES
The Case Of The Good-For-Nothing Girlfriend	Nancy CLUE
The Case Of The Grieving Monkey	Eleanora BURKE
The Case Of The Gunpowder Plot	Herlock SHOLMES
The Case Of The Gushwell Ghost	Sheerluck OHMS
The Case Of The Hammersmith Wonder	Sherlock HOLMES
The Case Of The Hardboiled Dicks	Mac SLADE
The Case Of The Harley Street Specialist	Sherlock HOLMES
The Case Of The Haunted Ball Park	Sherlock HOLMES
The Case Of The Haunted Brides	Jack JORDAN
The Case Of The Haunted Coal Shed	Herlock SHOLMES
The Case Of The Headless Monster	Insp MANTIS
The Case Of The Hidden Hun	Herlock SHOLMES
The Case Of The Hook-Billed Kites	Sarah DEANE and Dr Alex MCKENZIE
The Case Of The Howling Dog	Sherlock HOLMES
The Case Of The Hula Clock	Sheriff Moss MAGILL
The Case Of The Hypnotized Virgin	'Jigger' MORAN
The Case Of The Impersonation	Sherlock HOLMES
The Case Of The Innocent Wife	Mrs Palmyra Evangeline PYM
The Case Of The Invisible Thief	Geoffrey WESTON
The Case Of The Itinerant Yeggman	Sherlock HOLMES
The Case Of The Japanese Detective	Sexton BLAKE
The Case Of The Jeweled Ragpicker	Angus MACWHORTER
The Case Of The Johannesberg Riesling	Jerry COOL
The Case Of The Journeying Boy	Insp CADOGAN
The Case Of The Judas Spoon	Christopher FENN
The Case Of The Kidnapped Shadow	Geoffrey WESTON
The Case Of The Lame Snail	Herlock SHOLMES
The Case Of The Landlady's Brother	Dr Jan CZISSAR
The Case Of The Laughing Dwarf	WING
The Case Of The Laughing Jesuit	Roger POYNINGS
The Case Of The Laundry That Came Up Short	Shirley HOLMQUIST
The Case Of The Lavender Gripsack	Elsa COLBY
The Case Of The Limping Man	Sheerluck OHMS
The Case Of The Lost Chord	Herlock SHOLMES
The Case Of The Lost Nugget	Herlock SHOLMES
The Case Of The Lost Sapphire	Herlock SHOLMES
The Case Of The Lutefisk Heist	Shirley HOLMQUIST
The Case Of The Malevolent Twin	Zachary STONE
The Case Of The Man Who Followed Himself	Sherlock HOLMES
The Case Of The Man Who Was Wanted	Sherlock HOLMES
The Case Of The Mandarin's Mask	Dixon BRETT
The Case Of The Maplestead Magpie	Sherlock HOLMES
The Case Of The Marsden Rubies	Supt Anthony SLADE
The Case Of The Maupertuis Scandal	Sherlock HOLMES
The Case Of The Mexican Knife	Jose Manuel MADERO

The Case Of The Michaelmas Goose	Insp Harry CHARLTON and Insp Peter BRADFIELD
The Case Of The Millionaire's Persecution	Sherlock HOLMES
The Case Of The Misplaced Lutheran Hymnal	Shirley HOLMQUIST
The Case Of The Misplaced Thumb	Richard 'Speed' DASH
The Case Of The Missing Airman	Martin SPEED
The Case Of The Missing Bridegroom	Sexton BLAKE
The Case Of The Missing Brontë	Insp Perry TRETHOWAN
The Case Of The Missing Butterfly	Insp MANTIS
The Case Of The Missing Corpse	Peter ALCOTT and John ELLIS
The Case Of The Missing Corpse	Lt GRAY
The Case Of The Missing Heir	Herlock SHOLMES
The Case Of The Missing Lady	Sherlock HOLMES
The Case Of The Missing Lovers	Lee FISKE
The Case Of The Missing Manuscript	Herlock SHOLMES
The Case Of The Missing Merger Pamphlets	Shirley HOLMQUIST
The Case Of The Missing Patient	Herlock SHOLMES
The Case Of The Missing Patriarchs	Sherlock HOLMES
The Case Of The Missing Pendant	Sylvia SILENCE
The Case Of The Missing Scotch	Sherlock HOLMES
The Case Of The Missing Stoker	Sexton BLAKE
The Case Of The Missing Wife	Herlock SHOLMES
The Case Of The Muckrakers	Sexton BLAKE
The Case Of The Murdered Caretaker	Sexton BLAKE
The Case Of The Murdered Financier	Sexton BLAKE
The Case Of The Murdered MacKenzie	Det Sgt Masao MASUTO
The Case Of The Murdered Madame	Peter CHAMBERS
The Case Of The Murdered Redhead	Det Nathan SHAPIRO
The Case Of The Murderer's Bride	Perry MASON
The Case Of The Murderous Mice	Max MILLION
The Case Of The Musician	Herlock SHOLMES
The Case Of The Mysterious Moll	Margaret ANNISTER
The Case Of The Mysterious Soprano	Herlock SHOLMES
The Case Of The Notorious Canary-Trainer	Sherlock HOLMES
The Case Of The Not-So-Nice Nurse	Nancy CLUE
The Case of the November Sun-Tan	Sherlock HOLMES
The Case Of The Old Russian Woman	Sherlock HOLMES
The Case Of The Orator	Herlock SHOLMES
The Case Of The Painted Girl	Insp GLOOM
The Case Of The Paradol Chamber	Sherlock HOLMES
The Case Of The Paranoid Patient	Paula GLENNING
The Case Of The Pawned Pickle Jar	Herlock SHOLMES
The Case Of The Pearls	Sherlock HOLMES
The Case Of The Perplexed Painter	Herlock SHOLMES
The Case Of The Persian Parsnip	Sheerluck OHMS
The Case Of The Phantom Fingerprints	Jason JONES and 'Necessary' SMITH
The Case Of The Philosopher's Ring	Sherlock HOLMES
The Case Of The Pink Rat	Herlock SHOLMES
The Case Of The Pipe-Clay Department	Herlock SHOLMES
The Case Of The Plastic Man	Sgt Johnny LAMB
The Case Of The Plastic Mask	Sgt Johnny LAMB
The Case Of The Pornographic Photos	MARKHAM
The Case Of The Postponed Murder	Perry MASON
The Case Of The Potato Jacket	Herlock SHOLMES
The Case Of The Presidents' Heads	Christopher FENN
The Case Of The Prodigal Daughter	Ludovic TRAVERS
The Case Of The Purloined L'isitek	Sherlock HOLMES
The Case Of The Purloined Mummy	Sherlock HOLMES
The Case Of The Purloined Pickle	Sheerluck OHMS
The Case Of The Pursuit	Sherlock HOLMES
The Case Of The R E Pipe	Supt Geoffrey BOSCOBELL and Insp Roger ELLERDINE
The Case Of The Red Leech	Sherlock HOLMES
The Case Of The Remarkable Worm	Sherlock HOLMES
The Case Of The Rented Coffin	Dick WHELAN
The Case Of The Revolutionist's Daughter: Sherlock Holmes Meets Karl Marx	Sherlock HOLMES
The Case Of The Ribbon Snatchers	Shirley HOLMQUIST
The Case Of The Russian Revolution	Herlock SHOLMES
The Case Of The Rusted Room	Sgt Johnny LAMB
The Case Of The Schweinitz Portrait	Sherlock HOLMES
The Case Of The Second Santa	Sheerluck OHMS
The Case Of The Seven Of Calvary	Dr John ASHWIN
The Case Of The Seven Sneezes	Fergus O'BREEN and Det Lt JACKSON
The Case Of The Shaven Blonde	Grant VICKARY
The Case Of The Shopkeeper's Terror	Sherlock HOLMES
The Case Of The Silent Canary	Sherlock HOLMES
The Case Of The Sinister Squeeze	Sherlock HOLMES
The Case Of The Sinn Feiners	Herlock SHOLMES
The Case Of The Six Bullets	Marc JORDAN
The Case Of The Smiling Buddha	Sherlock HOLMES
The Case Of The Smith-Mortimer Succession	Sherlock HOLMES
The Case Of The Smoking Chimney	'Gramps' WIGGINS
The Case Of The Stolen Car	Herlock SHOLMES
The Case Of The Stranded Touring Company	Sexton BLAKE
The Case Of The Strange Wireless Message	Sexton BLAKE
The Case Of The Sumatran Rat	Sherlock HOLMES
The Case Of The Sunburned Peer	Sherlock HOLMES
The Case Of The Suppressed Will	Sexton BLAKE
The Case Of The Talking Dust	Insp Frederick Jubilee 'Jumper' CROSS
The Case Of The Telltale Slop Pail	Shirley HOLMQUIST
The Case Of The Teuton's Trousers	Herlock SHOLMES
The Case Of The Thirteenth Coach	David LEIGH
The Case Of The Tootsbury Typist	Sheerluck OHMS
The Case Of The Topaz Flower	Wally KENT
The Case Of The Traveller	Sherlock HOLMES
The Case Of The Turning Tide	'Gramps' WIGGINS
The Case Of The Two Coptic Patriarchs	Sherlock HOLMES
The Case Of The Two Questions	Jonas P JONAS
The Case Of The Two Strange Ladies	Bob LANDRELL
The Case Of The Uneasy Easy Chair	Sherlock HOLMES
The Case Of The Unhappy Angels	Humphrey CAMPBELL
The Case Of The Unhappy Medium	Sherlock HOLMES
The Case Of The Vanishing Artist	Insp GLOOM
Case Of The Vanishing Beauty	Shell SCOTT
The Case Of The Vanishing Head-Waiter	Sherlock HOLMES

	Title	Detective
The	Case Of The Vanishing House	Dick BARTON
The	Case Of The Vanishing Venus	Dr Carter COLE
The	Case Of The Velvet Claws	Perry MASON
The	Case Of The Would-Be Widow	Arthur Stukeley PENNINGTON
The	Case Of Too Many Murders	Perry MASON
The	Case Of Torches	Nicky MAHOUN
The	Case Of "Eye-Strained" Door	Sheerluck OHMS
The	Case On Cloud Nine	Dr William AMES and Det LONEGAN
	Case Pending	Lt Luis MENDOZA
The	Casebook Of Jules De Grandin	Jules DE GRANDIN
The	Casebook Of Lucius Leffing	Lucius LEFFING
The	Casebook Of Solar Pons	Solar PONS
	Casebook Of The Black Widowers	The BLACK WIDOWERS
	Casefile: The Best Of The 'Nameless Detective' Stories	NAMELESS DETECTIVE
The	Cases Of Martin Trackman	Martin TRACKMAN
The	Cases Of Susan Dare	Susan DARE
The	Case-Book Of Anthony Slade	Supt Anthony SLADE
The	Case-Book Of Sherlock Holmes	Sherlock HOLMES
	Cash Or Credit	Mrs Sarah WATSON
	Casino Royale	Cdr James BOND
The	Cask	Insp BURNLEY, Insp LEFARGE and Insp Georges LA TOUCHE
The	Cask Of Amontillado	Sherlock HOLMES
	Casket For A Living Lady	Jane D MULROY
	Cassandra In Red	Dan FORTUNE
	Cassandra's Castle: Or, The Devious Disappearances	William SHAKESPEARE
The	Cassiodore Case	Branders NOBLE
	Cast A Cold Eye	Insp Gil MAYO
	Cast For Death	Patrick GRANT
	Cast Iron Alibi	Insp DUNCAN and Capt Peter DARRELL
The	Cast Of Death	Anthony RILLINGTON
The	Castilian Caper	Theodore CLAW
	Castle Sinister	Chester BRETT
	Castles In The Air	Monsieur Hector RATICHON
	Cast, In Order Of Disappearance	Charles PARIS
The	Casual Murderer	Mme Rosika STOREY
	Casual Slaughter	Nicholas BARLOW
The	Cat And Fiddle Murders	Rupert BRADLEY
	Cat And Mouse	Brock (The Rock) CALLAHAN
	Cat And Mouse	Insp CHUCKY
The	Cat And The Clock	Anatole FLIQUE
The	Cat Cay Warrant	Mark BLOOD
	Cat Chaser	Nolen TYNER
	Cat Got Your Tongue?	Maggie COURTNEY
	Cat In A Crimson Haze	MIDNIGHT LOUIE and Temple BARR
The	Cat Saw Murder	Rachel MURDOCK, Jennifer MURDOCK and Lt Stephen MAYHEW
The	Cat Who Blew The Whistle	Jim QWILLERAN
The	Cat Who Could Read Backwards	Jim QWILLERAN
The	Cat With The Moustache	Insp/Supt DEERING
	Catch A Falling Clown	Toby PETERS and Emmett KELLY
	Catch A Tiger	Dep Sheriff Jake BROWN
	Catch And Squeeze	Matt SAVAGE
	Catch As Catch Can	Geoffrey BOWEN
	Catching Fire	Edik DANTE
The	Cater Street Hangman	Insp Thomas PITT and Charlotte PITT
	Catering To Nobody	Goldy BEAR
The	Catherine Murders	Kiel ST JAMES and Orson BOLES
	Catnapped: The Further Adventures Of Undercover Cat	D C (Darn Cat) RANDALL
	Cats Don't Need Coffins	Rachel MURDOCK, Jennifer MURDOCK and Lt Stephen MAYHEW
	Catspaw	Ferris BYRD
	Catspaw II	Ferris BYRD
The	Cat's Eye	Insp Frederic BELOT
	Caught At Last! Leaves From The Notebook Of A Detective	Det Dick DONOVAN
	Caught Dead In Philadelphia	Amanda PEPPER
	Caught In The Act	Brian DOUGLAS
	Caught In The Act	Fellock HOLMES
	Caught In The Shadows	Becky BELSKI
	Caught In The Toils: Or, Nick Carter And The Train Robbers	Nick CARTER
	Cauldron Of Hell	Nick CARTER
	Cauldron, Bubble	Insp Laurence OGILVIE
	Cause And Effect	Andrew BROOM
	Cause For Alarm	VALESHOFF and TAMARA
A	Cause For Malice	Insp Herbert BROOM
The	Cause Of The Screaming	Nell BARTLETT
The	Causeway	Peter GRANT
The	Cautious Assassin	William MALLETT
The	Cavalier In White	Joanna STARK
	Cavalier Of The Night	J Rockingham STONE
The	Cavalier's Cup	Sir Henry MERRIVALE KC
	Cave Of Bats	Talos CORD
The	Cave Of The Chinese Skeletons	Curt STONE
	Caveman	Romulus LEDBETTER
	Cavern Of The Damned	James (Operator 5) CHRISTOPHER
The	Caves Of Death	JACARA
The	Caves Of Steel	Elijah BALEY
	Caves Of Terror	Athelstan KING
The	Ceiling Of Hell	Steve HOOKS
The	Celebrated Detective	The CELEBRATED DETECTIVE
The	Cell Murder Mystery	Ch of Plce KENNY
	Cellars' Market	Bart FRASER
	Cellini Smith: Detective	Cellini SMITH
	Cemeteries Are For Dying	Nick TOLAND
	Centershot, The Scout Detective: Or, The Secret Of The Indian Graves	CENTERSHOT
The	Cerebus Murders	Peter QUENTIN
A	Certain Blindness	Eric WARD
The	Chain Of Clues: Or, Nick Carter's Play To A Finish	Nick CARTER
	Chain Of Vengeance	Dan FORREST
	Chain Of Witnesses	Marian PHIPPS
	Chain Reaction	DAKOTA
	Chain Saw	Jonas DUNCAN
The	Chained Crocodile	John ABBOT
	Chains Of Gold	Penny MILLER
	Chalet Diabolique	Lucifer COVE
The	Chalice Caper	Henry CHALICE and Crying EDDIE
	Challenge	Capt Hugh 'Bulldog' DRUMMOND and Ronald STANDISH
	Challenge At Le Mans	Don MILES
	Chambered Tomb	Dr Paul HOLTON
The	Chameleon Corps	Ben JOLSON
The	Chameleon Course	SYDENHAM
	Champagne And A Gardener	Elizabeth Lamb WORTHINGTON
	Chance To Die	Emma GREAVES
A	Chance To Kill	Supt BRONT
	Chandler	Raymond CHANDLER
The	Chandler Policy	Jefferson DIMARCO
	Change For The Worse	Insp Tom WHARTON
	Change Here For Babylon	Insp WALKER
The	Channay Syndicate	Gilbert CHANNAY
The	Channel Tunnel Mystery	Morlock TOMES
	Chant	John 'Chant' SINCLAIR
	Chaos In Lagrangia	Rex BADER
The	Chapel Bell At Derby Drabbs	Sherlock HOLMES
	Charles Fort Never Mentioned Wombats	Joe KARNS
	Charley Gets The Picture	Charley CASE
	Charlie And The Ice Man	Charlie ROPE
	Charlie M	Charlie MUFFIN
	Charlie Muffin	Charlie MUFFIN
	Charlie Sent Me!	Larry BAKER
	Charlotte's Inheritance	Valentine HAWKEHURST
The	Charming Murder	Dan 'DeeDee' DONER
The	Chase Of The Golden Plate	Prof Augustus S F X VAN DUSEN
A	Chase Round The World: The Following-Up Of A Chain Of Mystery	Abel GIRDLESTONE
	Chase The Storm	Jennifer HEATH
	Chase The Wind	Jennifer HEATH
	Chasing Away The Devil	Sheriff Milton KOVAK
	Chattering Gods	Ned SHACKLETON
The	Cheap Detective	Lou PECKINPAUGH
The	Cheap Dream	Sam CARROLL
	Checked Through, Missing Trunk No 17850: A Story Of New York City Life	Florence RENWICK
The	Checkerboard Caper	Robin MCKAY
	Checkmate	David ARDEN
	Checkmate And Stalemate	Silas WORTENHEIMER
	Checkmate In Rio	Nick CARTER
The	Checkmate Kill	Rod (The Terminator) GAVIN
A	Checkmated Scoundrel: Or, After The Abductors	Nick CARTER
	Checkmate!	Sherlock HOLMES
	Checkpoint Charlie	Charlie DARK
	Check-Out Time	Cecily SINCLAIR
-	Cheer For The Dead	Pat CAMPBELL
The	Cheetah Chase	Jazz HUNTER and Wynn HUNTER
The	Cherbourg Mystery	Clarence E HEMINGWAY and Jeremy FLACK
	Cherchez La Femme	Insp Auguste JANTRY
	Cheri-Bibi and Cecily	CHERI-BIBI
The	Cherry Blossom Corpse	Insp Perry TRETHOWAN and Charlie PEACE
The	Chess Murders	James Augustus GIBBS
The	Chess Mysteries Of Sherlock Holmes	Sherlock HOLMES
The	Chessboard Spies	Stephen FLETCHER
	Cheung, Detective	Y CHEUNG
	Cheyney's Law	Col Allen CHEYNEY
	Chiaroscuro	Jacob MOLNAR
The	Chic Chic Spy	Lee CROSLEY
	Chicago Deadline	Bruno FARRELL
	Chicane	Lady WEYBRIDGE
The	Chief Inspector's Statement	Det Supt Philip HUNTER
	Chief Tallon And The S O R	Ch Jack TALLON
	Child Proof	Adele BUFFINGTON
	Child Stalker	Matt MCCALL
	Children Of Hermes: Romance Of Love And Crime	Nicodemus Dove TURTLE
	Children Of The Wind	Charles MEIKLEJOHN and Constance LEIDL
	Children's Games	Meg HALLORAN and Ch Vince GUTIEREZ
A	Child's Garden Of Death	Lyon WENTWORTH and Bea WENTWORTH
	Chill	Dr Russell V 'Chill' CHILDERS
The	Chill Of A Corpse	Insp Trevor NICHOLLS
The	Chillery Court Mystery	Anthony RAVENHILL
The	Chilling Deception	Zachariah JUSTIS and Guinevere JONES
	Chimera	Peter CARSON
	Chin Chin, The Chinese Detective: Or, The Dark Work Of The Black Hands	CHIN CHIN
	China Hand	Det Insp 'Jacko' JACKSON
	China Silk	Buck JASON
	China Spy	Harry RYDER
	China Trade	Lydia CHIN
	China White	Det Billy MARCUS
The	Chinatown Connection	Tommy LEE
The	Chinese Agent	Jerry CORNELIUS
The	Chinese Bed Mystery	Pel PELHAM
	Chinese Brown Of Scotland Yard	Chinese BROWN
The	Chinese Chop	Lily WU and Janice CAMERON
The	Chinese Doll	Charles HORNE
The	Chinese Goose	Insp Lathom DYNES
The	Chinese Hammer	Heron MURMER
The	Chinese Jar Mystery	Sgt POTTER
The	Chinese Kiss	Shauna BISHOP
The	Chinese Mask	Joaquin HAWKS
	Chinese Poison	Paul DECKER
	Chinese Restaurants Never Serve Breakfast	Pat RIORDAN
The	Chinese Visitor	Anna ZORDAN
The	Chink In The Armour	Sexton BLAKE
	Chip, The Newsboy Detective: Or, The Plot To Steal A Million	CHIP
The	Chiseller	'Gutsy' MORGAN
The	Chocolate Mousse Murders	Stanley DELPHOND
A	Choice Of Crimes	Delia RIORDAN
	Choice Of Violence	Uncle George CROWDER
The	Chopstein Venus	Herlock SHOLMES

C

	Chord In Crimson	Gale GALLAGHER
A	Chorus Of Detectives	Enrico CARUSO
	Chris Wren, The Master Detective; Or, Piping A Parisian Tragedy	Chris WREN
The	Christmas Bow Murder	Ch Insp Jim ASHWORTH
The	Christmas Egg	Insp Brett NIGHTINGALE
The	Christmas Eve Ghost	Det Lt Cathy CARRUTHERS
	Christmas Eve: An Unrecorded Adventure Of Sherlock Holmes	Sherlock HOLMES
The	Christmas Murder	Wencelaus BOTTWINK
The	Christmas Spy	Joe MORGAN
The	Christmas Tree Murders	Sgt Cass HARTY
	Christopher Parkins, RN	Christopher PARKINS
	Christopher Quarles, College Professor And Master Detective	Christopher QUARLES
The	Chromium Cat	Christopher BOND
The	Chronicles Of Addington Peace	Addington PEACE
	Chronicles Of Dennis Chetwynd	Dennis CHETWYND
The	Chronicles Of Don Q	Don Q
The	Chronicles Of Humphrey Judd	Humphrey JUDD
The	Chronicles Of Lucius Leffing	Lucius LEFFING
	Chronicles Of Martin Hewitt	Martin HEWITT
The	Chronicles Of Michael Danevitch Of The Russian Secret Service	Michael DANEVITCH and Peter BRODIE
The	Chronicles Of Quincy Adams Sawyer, Detective	Quincy Adams SAWYER
The	Chronicles Of Solar Pons	Solar PONS
	Chronicles Of The Secret Service	Sir Leonard WALLACE
A	Chronological History Of The Boston Watch And Police From 1681 To 1865	A BOSTON POLICE OFFICER
	Chutes And Adders	Robin LIGHT
	Cicely Disappears	Stephen MUNRO
	CID	Chullunder GHOSE
The	CID Of Dexter Drake	Dexter DRAKE
The	CID Room	Insp Robert FUSIL and Const KERR
	Cinderella After Midnight	Michael BRENNAN
	Cinderella Goes To The Morgue	Miriam BIRDSEYE
	"Cinders" Of Harley Street	Dr Villiers BEETHAM-SAUNDERS
The	Cinema Crime	Sexton BLAKE
The	Cinema Crook	'Tubby' HAIG
The	Cipher Detective; Or, Fighting For Fortune	Mark MAGIC
The	Cipher Detective; Or, Mark Magic On A New Trail	Mark MAGIC
	Ciphered	Insp Jeff ADAMS and Kate SHAW
	Circle Of Death	Lt Guy SILVESTRI
	Circle Of Shadows	Rickard 'Ricky' BRITTON
The	Circle Of The Snake	'Tubby' HAIG
	Circle Round A Corpse	Timothy DREWER
The	Circular Staircase	Rachel INNES
The	Circus Detective	The CIRCUS DETECTIVE
	Citadel Run	Calico Jack WALKER and Tina TAMIKO
	Citation Record: 1 Selected Short Story	Philip MARLOWE
	Cities Of The Dead	Michael SPRAGGUE
	City Of Brass, And Other Simon Ark Stories	Simon ARK
	City Of Dreams	HUY
	City Of The Dead	Paul KONIG
	City Primaeval	Raymond CRUZ
	Clandestine	Dudley SMITH and Det Fred UNDERHILL
	Clarice Dyke, The Female Detective	Clarice DYKE
	Claude Duval Of Ninety-Five: A Romance Of The Road	Valentine BELT
	Claude Melnotte As A Detective, And Other Stories	Claude MELNOTTE
The	Claw Of A Cat	Insp Trevor NICHOLLS
The	Claws Of The Scorpion	SILBER
A	Clear And Present Danger	Ben 'T-Man' SLAYTON
	Cleek Of Scotland Yard	Hamilton CLEEK
	Cleek, The Master Detective	Hamilton CLEEK
	Cleek's Government Cases	Hamilton CLEEK
	Cleek's Greatest Riddles	Hamilton CLEEK
	Cleopatra Jones	Cleopatra JONES
	Cleopatra Jones And The Casino Of Gold	Cleopatra JONES
The	Cleopatra Needle Mystery	Sexton BLAKE
The	Clever Celestial; Or, The 'Salted' Mine Case	Trim CARTER
The	Click Of The Gate	Tommy ROSTETTER
The	Cliff Face	Sam WHARTON
The	Climbing Corpse	'Bull' ROGERS
	Clint Cleaver, The Grand Street Detective; Or, The Mystery Of The Headless Woman	Clint CLEAVER
	Clio Brown: Private Investigator	Clio BROWN
The	Cloak Of Darkness	Mr ROLF
The	Clock Strikes Thirteen	Reynold FRAME
The	Clock Ticks On	Det Sgt Trevor DENE
	Clockers	Lt Rocco KLEIN
	Close Call	Kate BAIER
A	Close Call; Or, Detective Mead's Dilemma	MEAD
	Close His Eyes	John DRYDEN and Gwyneth JONES
	Close Quarters	Nina FISCHMAN
	Close Quarters	Insp HAZELRIGG
	Close Shave	William S GRAY
	Close The Door On Murder	Supt FOLLY
	Close To Death	Lee BECKETT
The	Closed Book	Allan KENNEDY
The	Closed Door	Gerald LISSENDALE
	Closet Bones	John Thomas ROSS
The	Closing Net	Frank CLAMART
	Cloud The Smiter	Gilbert LAROSE
The	Cloven Foot	George GERRARD
The	Cloze Papers	Cedric DODD
	Club Dead	Lt NEUMAN
A	Clubbable Woman	Supt Andrew DALZIEL and Sgt/Det Ch Insp Peter PASCOE
	Clubfoot The Avenger	Dr Adolph (Clubfoot) GRUNDT
The	Clue	Fleming STONE
A	Clue For Mr Fortune	Dr Reginald FORTUNE
	Clue For Murder	Insp HARRIS
The	Clue From Mars	Wayman INSTONE
A	Clue From The Stars	Insp Thomas WARNER
The	Clue In The Air	Timothy MCCARTY
The	Clue In The Clay	Lt Stephen MAYHEW
	Clue In Two Flats	Richard DEMING
The	Clue Of The Artificial Eye	Paul CAMPENHAYE
The	Clue Of The Bricklayer's Aunt	Mrs Palmyra Evangeline PYM
The	Clue Of The Burnt Candle	Derwent DUFF
The	Clue Of The Chanting Cheese	Herlock SHOLMES
The	Clue Of The Frightening Coin	Gregory 'Grischa' PAVLOV
The	Clue Of The Golden Ear-Ring	Supt Geoffrey BOSCOBELL and Insp Roger ELLERDINE
The	Clue Of The Green-Eyed Girl	Ch Insp DREWRY
The	Clue Of The Green-Eyed Girl	Sir Timothy ROSSITER
The	Clue Of The Judas Tree	Lt Joseph KELLY
The	Clue Of The New Pin	Insp CARVER
The	Clue Of The Rising Moon	Det Sgt Trevor DENE
The	Clue Of The Second Tooth	Sexton BLAKE
The	Clue Of The Twisted Candle	Commiss T X MEREDITH
The	Clue Of The Twisted Face	Judge Henry TYSON
	Clue Sinister	Ch Insp Julian RIVERS
	Clues For Dr Coffee	Dr Daniel Webster COFFEE and Lt Max RITTER
	Clues From A Detective's Camera	Sebastian ZAMBRA
	Clues Of The Caribbees, Being Certain Criminal Investigations Of Henry Poggioli, PhD	Prof Henry POGGIOLI
	Clues To Burn	Bill HASTINGS and Coco HASTINGS
	Clues; Or, Leaves From A Chief Constable's Note Book	Ch Const William HENDERSON
The	Clutching Hand	John BARTLEY
	Clutterkill	Lt Ronnie GOLD
	Clyde, The Resolute Detective; Or, His Own Mystery	CLYDE
	Coast Highway	Jake MARTIN
The	Coast Road Murder	Juliet JACKSON
	Coasts Of Fear	Jessica HAYDEN
A	Coat Of Blackmail	Ambrose FRAYNE and Dominique FRAYNE
A	Coat Of Varnish	Frank BRIERS
The	Cobra Candlestick	Dexter DRAKE
	Cobra Venom	Insp BARRY
	Cocaine And Blue Eyes	Michael BRENNAN
	Cocaine Blues	Phryne FISHER
The	Cocaine Caper	Theodore CLAW
	Cocaine Kill	MONDO
	Cockleburr	Arthur SALISBURY and Frank SHEARER
The	Cockroach Sings	Insp HEADCORN
	Cocktails And The Killer	Michael KELLS
	Coda	Kevin FITZGERALD
The	Code	Nick CARTER
	Code 1013: Assassin	Sgt Pepper ANDERSON
	Code Name Gadget	Manny DEWITT
	Code Name Hangman	Paul VENNEKER
	Code Name Sebastian	SEBASTIAN
	Code Name: Werewolf	Nick CARTER
	Code Of Blood	John 'Chant' SINCLAIR
	Code Three	Sgt Jerry LONG
The	Code-Letter-Mystery	Sheridan ORFORD and Prof Henry Arthur FIELDING
	Coffee For One	Montague MIGGLEWADE
A	Coffin For Demetrios	Charles LATIMER
	Coffin Scarcely Used	Insp PURBRIGHT
The	Coffin Tree	Sgt/Insp John COFFIN
	Coffins For Three	Prof Cyrus HATCH
	Coign Of Vantage; Or, The Boston Athenaeum Murders	Austin LAYMAN
A	Coil Of Rope	David WRIGHT
	Cold Blood	Sgt William BEEF
	Cold Blue Death	William (Tiger Shark) MARTIN
A	Cold Coming	Insp Brett NIGHTINGALE
The	Cold Finger Curse	Pierre MONTIGNY
	Cold Hearts And Gentle People	Garth RYLAND
A	Cold Killing	Chase DEFOE
The	Cold Light Of Dawn	Supt John GAFFNEY
A	Cold Mind	Det Stuart HAYDON
	Cold Night	Jack PAINE
The	Cold Ones	Phil KRAMER
	Cold Poison	Hildegarde WITHERS
	Cold Shoulder	Lorraine PAGE
The	Cold Smell Of Sacred Stone	Dr Robert 'Mongo' FREDERICKSON and Veil KENDRY
	Cold Steele	Donovan STEELE
	Cold Turkey	Peter STOKES
	Cold War In A Country Garden	Matthew DILKE
The	Cold War Swap	Cyril MCCORKLE and Michael PADILLO
The	Cold Winds Of Adesta	Maj TENNENTE
The	Collected Short Fiction Of Ngaio Marsh	Insp/Supt Roderick ALLEYN
	Collision Ahead	James BRUCE
	Colonel Dam	Ursula DOLLING
	Colonel Paternoster	Col PATERNOSTER
	Colonel Sun	Cdr James BOND
	Colonel Warburton's Madness	Sherlock HOLMES
The	Colonel's Foxhound	PINKNEY
	Columbo And The Samurai Sword	Lt COLUMBO
The	Columnist Murder	Wylie KING and Nels LUNDBERG
	Colwyn Dane - The Outlawed Detective	Colwyn DANE
	Come And Be Killed	Dennis DEVORE
	Come And Go	Charles LATIMER and James LATIMER
	Come And Go	Charles LATIMER and James LATIMER
	Come Back, Alice Smythereene!	Arnold SIMON
	Come Blonde, Come Murder	Steve BRYANT
	Come Die With Me	Anna ZORDAN
	Come Dwell With Death	Carey BRENT
	Come Home And Be Killed	Det Insp Charmian DANIELS
	Come Home To Crime	The LIBERATOR
	Come Out With Your Hands Up!	Det LONNIE THE FED
	Comets Have Long Tails	Noah BRADSHAW
	Comfort Me With Spies	Appleton 'Apple' PORTER
The	Comic Book Killer	Hobart LINDSEY and Det Marvia PLUM
The	Comic Opera Murders	Paul DAWN
	Commander Amanda Nightingale	Amanda NIGHTINGALE
	Commander Lawless, VC	Lt/Cdr Frank H LAWLESS
A	Commission To The Sultan Of Turkey	Sherlock HOLMES

The Books

C

A Common Death	Willow KING
The Common People	Pel PELHAM
Common Sense Is All You Need	Ch Const Sir Clinton DRIFFIELD
The Communicating Door	GARTH
The Communist's Corpse	Sgt Joe DIXON
Company Of Bandits	Sexton BLAKE
The Company Of Saints	Davina GRAHAM
The Compleat Crow	Titus CROW
The Complete Magnus Ridolph	Magnus RIDOLPH
A Complete State Of Death	Derek TORRY
A Complete Stranger	Alan STEWART
A Compound For Death	Jim O'NEILL
Compromising Positions	Nelson SHARPE and Judith SINGER
The Computer Kill	Sam KING
Comrade Charlie	Charlie MUFFIN
Comrades Of The Black Cross: A Romance Of Love And Crime	William GIBSON
The Con Game	Ch Fred FELLOWS
The Con Man	Paul RIVINGTON
Conan Doyle In Space	Sherlock HOLMES
Concerning Blackshirt	BLACKSHIRT
Concerning Peter Jackson	Kyra SOKRATESCU
Concerning The Saint	Simon (The Saint) TEMPLAR
The Concert Party Murders	Martin SPEED
The Concrete Blonde	Det Harry BOSCH
The Concrete Cage	Joe BLAZE
Condition Purple	Insp Fabian DONOGHUE
Confession	Jennifer CAIN
The Confession Of Hercule	Insp Hercule RENARD
Confession Of Murder	Insp George MARSHALL
Confessional	Liam DEVLIN
Confessional	Marius LARCHE
The Confessions Of A Coiner	Hermann ANDERWELT
Confessions Of A Detective	A DETECTIVE
The Confessions of Arsène Lupin	Arsène LUPIN
Confess, Fletch	Irwin 'Fletch' FLETCHER and Insp Francis Xavier FLYNN
Confetti For A Killing	Percy Aloysius HUFF
A Conflict Of Interests	Sam BENEDICT
A Conflict Of Interests	Insp COGHILL
The Conk-Singleton Affair	Sherlock HOLMES
The Connecting Link: Or, Nick Carter's Double Mystery	Nick CARTER
Connie Morgan In Alaska	Connie MORGAN
Connie Morgan In The Arctic	Connie MORGAN
Conqueror Down	Martin SEGUNDO
Conquest Before Autumn	Mark SAVAGE
Conquest Calls The Tune	Norman CONQUEST
Conquistadores	Martin SEGUNDO
Conspiracy	Insp Bill VALLANCE
Constable In The Shrubbery	Const Nick RHEA
Constable On The Hill	Const Nick RHEA
Constables Don't Count	Insp Noel TRACY
Constance Dunlap, Woman Detective	Constance DUNLAP
Consultation In The Dark	Philip MARLOWE
The Consul's File	Spencer Monroe SAVAGE
The Content Assignment	Lt KELLY
The Contents Of The Coffin	Archer DAWE
The Contessa Came Too	Richard SAREL
The Contract	Cole BROGAN
Contract For A Killer	Sexton BLAKE
Control	Nathan NECESSARY
Converging Parallels	Commiss TROTTI
Conversations With A Corpse	Paul REEDER
A Conviction Of Guilt	Horatio PARKER
The Convivial Codfish	Max BITTERSOHN
Conway, KC	Sir Brian Dinsmore CONWAY
The Cooking School Murders	Eugenia POTTER
Cool Carter, The Hocking Valley Detective: Or, Piping A Terrible Crime In The Iron Mines	COOL CARTER
A Cool Clear Death	Cam MACCARDLE
A Cool Killing	Ch Insp Alec STAINTON
Cool Tom, The Sailor Boy Detective	COOL TOM
Coopersmith	COOPERSMITH
Cop Hater	The 87th PRECINCT
Copp For Hire	Joe COPP
Copp In The Dark	Joe COPP
Copper Drift, The Lake Detective	COPPER DRIFT
The Copper House	Maurice WALLION
Copper, Gold And Treasure	Mark TREASURE, Maj COPPER and Benny GOLD
The Copsford Mystery: Or, Is He The Man?	Col KILMAIN
The Copy-Cat Killings	Sexton BLAKE
The Corbin Necklace	Punch CORBIN
The Corder Index	David MARTINI
The Cords Of Vanity	John SAMSON
Cork Of The Colonies	Capt CORK
Cork On Location	Montague CORK
Cork On The Telly	Montague CORK
Cork On The Water	Montague CORK
Corner In Crime	Det Supt Bill ROWLANDS
The Corner Men	Derek TORRY
A Corner Of Paradise	Father Joseph BREDDER
Cornish Crime	Insp TREADGOLD
The Cornish Fox	Malcolm WARREN
Corporal Cameron	Cpl/Sgt Allan CAMERON
Corporal Cameron Of The North West Mounted Police	Cpl/Sgt Allan CAMERON
Corporal Cavannagh	Cpl John CAVANNAGH
Corporal Jacques Of The Foreign Legion	Jacques RADOUB
Corporal Of The Mounted	Cpl Larry STEER
Corporal Smithers, Deceased	Sgt ACKROYD
The Corpse And The Three Ex-Husbands	Capt Andy MACVEIGH
The Corpse Awaits	George ROBIN
The Corpse Came C O D	Joe MEDFORD
The Corpse Came Too	Sexton BLAKE
Corpse De Ballet	Capt Andrew TORRENT
A Corpse For A Candidate	Lt Bud DUGAN

A Corpse For Christmas	Sexton BLAKE
A Corpse For Kofi Katt	Supt Kofi KATT
Corpse Guard Parade	Insp CORNFORD
The Corpse Hangs High	Reginald 'Beauty' BLACK
Corpse In Cold Storage	Sir George BULL
Corpse In Handcuffs	Supt PEPPER
The Corpse In My Bed	Tommy TWOTOES and Terry ROOKE
The Corpse In The Castle	Jonathan ARCANE and Vanessa ARCANE
The Corpse In The Corner Saloon	Jeremiah X GIBSON and MAC
The Corpse In The Derby Hat	Garrett MAYNARD
The Corpse In The Flannel Nightgown	Rev Martin BUELL
The Corpse In The Guest Room	Skelton KYNE
Corpse In The Wind	Les IVEY
The Corpse Maker	MCCLOUD
Corpse On London Bridge	Insp Tom ANDERSON
The Corpse On The Mat	Insp CORNFORD
Corpse On The Town	'Jigger' MORAN
The Corpse Said No	Marka DE LANCEY
The Corpse That Came Back	Insp GRAY
The Corpse That Knew Everybody	Insp SEVREL
The Corpse That Spoke	Simon CROLE
The Corpse That Traveled	Insp LUCKRAFT
The Corpse That Walked	Prof Ira COBB
Corpse To Colorado	Pine-Top JONES
Corpse To Cuba	Sexton BLAKE
The Corpse With The Knee-Action	Bill KING
The Corpse With The Listening Ear	Dick WHELAN
The Corpse With The Missing Watch	Philip TOLEFREE
Corpse Without Boots	Insp MACSPORRAN
The Corpse Wore Rubies	Geoffrey SLADE
Corpses In The Cellar	Bill (The Hook) LOCKWOOD
Corpus Christmas	Det Sigrid HAROLD
Corpus Delectable	Ed RIVERS
The Corrector Of Destinies	Randolph MASON
Corridor Of Death	Robert AMISS
Corridor Of Fear	Dr NORTH
Corrupt And Ensnare	Loren MENSING
Corsican Takeover	Tim PARNELL
Cosa Nostra Circus	Harry REILLY
Cosgrove: Detective	COSGROVE
Costello - Psychic Investigator	COSTELLO
The Cotfold Conundrums	Insp H H THEW
Cotswold Manners	Lady Jane HILDRETH
Cotswold Murders	Lady Jane HILDRETH
Cottage Sinister	Insp Archibald INGE
The Council Of Comforters	Supt LESLIE
The Counsellor	Mark BRAND
Count Me Out	Sam TRAIN
A Count Of Six	Philip ODELL
Countdown	Kirk MCGARVEY
Countdown To Crisis	Mark SAVAGE
Counterfeit Agent	Nick CARTER
Counterpol	Kim SMITH
Counterpol In Paris	Kim SMITH
Counterprobe	Kevin BLAKE
Counterspy	Sean RYAN
Counterstrike	Wallace MAHONEY and John MAHONEY
Counterstroke	Lloyd NICOLSON
Counterweight	Lt CARREAU
Counter-Spy	Jim STRANG
The Country-House Burglar	Mrs ARTSIDE
The Count's Chauffeur	Ronald EWART
Courier To Marrakesh	Dr Adolph (Clubfoot) GRUNDT
A Course Of Miss Violet De Merville	Sherlock HOLMES
A Court Intrigue	James HATTON
Court Of Shadows	Nile BOYD
A Court Tragedy	Col BOTTESFORD
Courtier To Death	Monsieur DUPUY
The Courts Of Idleness	Bertram PLEYDELL
The Courtyard Of The Fly	Supt HAMILTON
The Coven	Peter WARD
Covenant For Death	Ch Insp LUBBOCK and Det Insp TENCH
The Covent Garden Murder	Det Insp EVANS
Cover Her Face	Insp/Cdr Adam DALGLIESH
Cover Her Face	Insp MCKELLER and Anthony HOWARD
Cover His Face	Gilbert E WHELDON
Cover Zero	George WILLIS
Cover-Up	Lizzie THOMAS
Cover-Up Story	Douglas PERKINS
Coward's Kiss	Ed LONDON
Cowboy Blues	Jake LIEBERMAN
The Cowboy Detective	The COWBOY DETECTIVE
The Cowboy 'Tec	The COWBOY 'TEC
The Coyote Conection	Nick CARTER
The Coyote Cried Twice	Bill BUCHANAN
Cozumel	Jack NOVAK
Crack Down	Kate BRANNIGAN
A Cracking Of Spines	Matthew COLL
Crackshot	Det Sgt Tony ROWLEY
The Crackshot Detective	The CRACKSHOT DETECTIVE
Cracksman On Velvet	William VERITY
The Crackswoman	Insp Jack PEARSON
Craig And The Midas Touch	Peter CRAIG
Craig Kennedy Listens In	Prof Craig KENNEDY
Craig Kennedy On The Farm	Prof Craig KENNEDY
Craine's First Case	Paul CRAINE
Crang Plays The Ace	CRANG
Cranmer	Steve CRANMER
Crash And Carry	Sexton BLAKE
Crashlanding In The Congo	Steve RAMSAY
The Crawshay Jewel Mystery	Buddy MUSTARD
The Crazy Mixed-Up Nude	Erik MARCH
Crazy Woman Blues	Joe STREETER
Created: The Destroyer	Remo (The Destroyer) WILLIAMS
A Creative Kind Of Killer	Fortune FANELLI
A Creature Was Stirring	Det Knute SEVERSON

Credit For A Murder	Don CADEE
The Creeping Hours	John JERICHO and Lt PASCAL
The Creeping Siamese	The CONTINENTAL OP
The Creepy Tale	Arthur PHILIS
Creep, Shadow, Creep!	LOWELL
Creep, Shadow!	LOWELL
The Crescent Brotherhood; Or, Nick Carter's Chicago Double	Nick CARTER
Creston The Detective; Or, Following A Light Clew	CRESTON
The Crilly Court Mystery	Jimmie KENTLAND
Crime And Punishment	Insp PETROVICH
The Crime And The Criminal	Matthew HOLMAN
The Crime At Black Dudley	Albert CAMPION
Crime At Orcival	Monsieur LECOQ
The Crime At Tattenham Corner	Insp STODDART
Crime At The Villa Gloria	Martin CROW
The Crime At The "Noah's Ark"	Dr CONSTANTINE
The Crime Coast	Benvenuto BROWN
The Crime Combine	Det Insp SANDERSON
Crime De Luxe	Benvenuto BROWN
Crime For Christmas	Det Vic VARALLO and Jesse FALKENSTEIN
Crime Hound	Herbert CROSBY
Crime In Crystal	Simon BRADE
Crime In Kensington	Insp Bernard BRAY and Charles VENABLES
Crime In Quarantine	Glyn MORGAN
Crime In The Arcade	Insp Bill VALLANCE
The Crime In The Wood	Supt DRUMLEY
The Crime In Washington Mews	Clay BROOKE
Crime In Whispers	Sgt/Insp Peter BRADFIELD
The Crime Is Murder	Lisa BANCROFT
The Crime Master	Mr GILLY
The Crime Of A Christmas Toy	George GREY
The Crime Of A Countess; Or, The American Detective And the Russian Nihilist	Wat DENTON
The Crime Of Four	Sexton BLAKE
The Crime Of Philip Garrison	'Doc' SUMMERS
The Crime Of The Century	Christopher DANE
The Crime Of The Century	Robert Leroy MITCHELL and John BARNES
The Crime Of The Chromium Bowl	Peter STRANGELY
The Crime Of The Midnight Express	Dyke DARREL
The Crime Of The 'Liza Jane'	Insp TRUMPET
The Crime On Côte Des Neiges	Russell TEED
Crime On Her Hands	Theodora 'Dol' BONNER
Crime On Her Hands	Supt Anthony SLADE
The Crime On The Limited; Or, Nat Ridley In The Follies	Nat RIDLEY
The Crime On The Moor	Sexton BLAKE
Crime Partners	KENYATTA
The Crime Philosopher	The PADRE
A Crime Remembered	Det Sgt Peter NOYES
The Crime Scientist	Ebbie ENTWHISTLE
A Crime Story	John Howard JOURNEY
Crime To Music	Ch Insp THOMPSON
Crime Upon Crime	Rosa EPTON
Crime Upon Crime	Gilbert LAROSE
The Crime Without A Clue	Insp BEDISON
Crime Without Reason	Sgt/Insp Brian 'Bonny' LEE
The Crimes Of Richmond City	Capt Steve MACBRIDE
Crimes Of The Season	BERGERAC
Crimes Past	Jeremy LOCKE
Criminal Reminiscences And Detective Sketches	Allan PINKERTON
Criminals Caught; Or, Records Of A City Detective	James M'GOVAN
The Crimson Alibi	David CARROLL
The Crimson Cat Murders	Stephen CLAY
The Crimson Circle	Insp PARR
The Crimson Clown	Dalton (The Crimson Clown) PROUSE
The Crimson Clown Again	Dalton (The Crimson Clown) PROUSE
The Crimson Feather	Sheriff Bill DAVIES
The Crimson Frame	Matt HUGHES
The Crimson In The Purple	William FARLAND
The Crimson Rambler	Ch Insp Douglas GOSSAGE
The Crimson Rope	Insp Thomas CONROY
The Croaking Of The Raven	Supt MASON
Crockett On The Loose	Fred CROCKETT
Crocodile On The Sandbank	Amelia PEABODY
Crook Cargo	Sexton BLAKE
The Crook From Chicago	Sexton BLAKE
The Crook Of Fleet Street	Sexton BLAKE
Crook Stuff	Simon ARTIFEX
The Crooked Circle	Steve PAGET
Crooked Cole, The Hunchback Detective; Or, Piping The Opium Dens	CROOKED COLE
The Crooked Eye	Tom CLAYTON
The Crooked House	Insp TAVERNER
The Crooked Man	Sherlock HOLMES
The Crooked Road	George HARLEQUIN
Crooked Shadows	Ed GRAY
Crooked Wood	Nick ATWELL
Crookery Inn	Guy BANNISTER
Crooks	Harry SOMMERS
Crooks In The Sunshine	Commodore JASEN
The Crooks' Game	Insp STRICKLAND
The Crooks' Shepherd	Ch Insp GIDLEIGH
The Crook's Accomplice	Sexton BLAKE
Crook's Castle	Horace Augustus ELVER
Cross Marks The Spot	Julian MEDOZA
The Cross Of San Vincente	Ch Insp LUBBOCK and Det Insp TENCH
Cross Purposes	Peter CROSS
Cross That Palm When I Come To It	Frank MARKER
Crossed Wires; Or, A Tangle Of Crime	Nick CARTER
The Crossword Hunt	Giles SULLIVAN
The Crossword Mystery	Rocky CAPUTO
The Crouching Spy	Rev P J MACFARLANE
The Crown Swindle	Winston BARROWS
The Crown Vs Dr Watson	Sherlock HOLMES
Crowner's Quest	Capt/Commiss Denzil GRIGSON
The Crowning Murder	Prof Charles HARDING
Crown: Bamboo Shoot-Out	Ch Supt John CROWN
Crown: The Sweet And Sour Kill	Ch Supt John CROWN
The Crow's Inn Tragedy	Insp FURNIVAL
Croyd	CROYD
The Crozier Pharaohs	Mrs Adela Beatrice Lestrange BRADLEY
The Cruciform Mark: The Strange Story Of Richard Tregenna, Bachelor Of Medicine	Richard TREGENNA
Cruel As The Grave	Benedict BREEZE
The Cruise Of The Motor-Boat Conqueror	Randolph MANNERING
Cruise To Nowhere	Ben CASEY
Cruise With Death	Lord TINTAGEL and Lady 'Ginger' TINTAGEL
A Crushing Blow	Anna MCCOLL
Cry At Dusk	John MARKS
Cry For Help	Rachel CAREY
A Cry In The Night	Mr PONDERY
Cry Murder	Ross LANGDON
Cry Of The Beast	JACARA
Cry Of The Hawk	Zachary JONES
Cry Passion	Lt Chester WIERLOCK
Cry Plague!	Dr Johnny MACK
The 'Crying Pig' Murder	Edward BLAYNE
The Crystal Beads Murder	Insp STODDART
The Crystal Claw	Rex YELVERTON
The Crystal Clear Case	Lexey Jane PELAZONI
Crystal Days	MIDNIGHT LOUIE and Temple BARR
The Crystal Stopper	Arsène LUPIN
The Crystallised Carbon Pig	Supt GILLIANT
Cuckoo	Det Const Caz FLOOD
The Cuckoo Clock	Prof CALDWELL
Cult Of Darkness	Sexton BLAKE
Cul-De-Sac	Harry HARKER
Cunning As A Fox	Emmanuel CELLINI
Cunning As A Fox	Emmanuel CELLINI
The Cunning Mulatto And Other Cases Of Ellis Parker, American Detective	Ellis PARKER
The Cup And The Lip	Peter HARKNESS
The Cup And The Lip	Peter HARKNESS
The Cup Final Murder	Insp Nicholas PRINCE
The Cup Final Mystery	Sexton BLAKE
A Cup Of Death	Dade COOLEY
A Cup That Kills	Insp BLESSINGAY
The Curate Finds The Corpse	Insp LIGHTFOOT
Curiosity Didn't Kill The Cat	Conan FLAGG
Curiosity Killed The Cat	Insp CAM
The Curiosity Of Mr Treadgold	Mr Horace B TREADGOLD
The Curious Mr Tarrant	Mr Trevis TARRANT
The Curlew Coombe Mystery	John BARRIN and Kate MARSH
The Curse Of Cloud	Insp STRODE
The Curse Of Craig's End	Insp BRUMMEL
The Curse Of Doone	Ian HEATH
The Curse Of Khatra	Det Supt John BELLAMY
The Curse Of The Carringtons	Sexton BLAKE
The Curse Of The Nibelung: Being The Last Case Of Lord Holmes Of Baker Street And Sir John Watson	Sherlock HOLMES
Curse The Darkness	Rain MORGAN
The Curtain	Ted CARMADY
The Curtain Between	Richard MASSEY
Curtain Call	Richard (The Pilgrim) MAIDMENT
Curtain Fall	Det Insp Neil CARTER
A Curtain For Crime	Lt POWLEDGE
The Curtain Of Storm	GALT
Curtains For The Copper	L F 'Scoop' GRIDDLE
Curtains For The Editor	L F 'Scoop' GRIDDLE
Curtain: Hercule Poirot's Last Case	Hercule POIROT
Curves And Angles	Johnny FARRELL
The Customer's Always Wrong	Chico BRETT
Cut To The Quick	Julian KESTREL
The Cutting Edge	Jud BLADE
The CVC Murders	Thackeray PLACE
Cyanide For Christmas	Insp CHALLON
Cyanide For The Chorister	Sebastian STOLE
Cyanide!	Anthony READ and Jacqueline NORRIS
Cyborg IV	Steve AUSTIN
The Cyborg King	Star HAWKS
Cynthia	Harvey KRIM
Cynthia Wakeham's Money	Frank ETHERIDGE
C/o American Embassy	Peter ROURKE

—D—

The D Case; Or, The Truth About The Mystery Of Edwin Drood	Sherlock HOLMES, Lew ARCHER, Nero WOLFE, Father BROWN and Hercule POIROT
D E Q	Insp Maurice HEPBURN and Evelyn TEMPLE
The DA Breaks An Egg	Doug SELBY
The DA Calls It Murder	Doug SELBY
The Da Vinci Rose	Jeff PRIDE
The Dada Caper	Chance PURDUE
Daddy's Girl	Jim JENNER
Dagger Before Me	Michael the O'KELLY
Dagger Drawn	Insp MACSPORRAN
The Dago Detective; Or, The Chum Of The Police Chief	The DAGO DETECTIVE
The Dain Curse	The CONTINENTAL OP
The Daisy Dilemma	Burgess 'Buzz' CARDIGAN

Dakota Warpath	DAKOTA
The Dalehouse Murder	Det Insp ALLPORT
The Dallas Deception	Jack KYLE
Dallas Drop	Jack KYLE
Dally With A Deadly Doll	Larry CRYSTAL
A Dame Called Murder	Max KEENE
Dame On The Make	Johnny BUCHANAN
A Dame Too Many	Pete GARROWAY
Dames Take To Crime	LOU
The Dame's The Game	Barney CONROY
The Damned Don't Die	Martin WINDROW
A Damned Serious Business	Supt John GAFFNEY
Damned To Success	Supt Konstantin KELLER
Damning Trifles	Bob ROLLINS
Dan Decker, The Strongest Detective In The Northwest: Or, The Quest Of The Stolen Five Million	Dan DECKER
Dan Denton, Detective: Or, The Crime Of The Conservatory	Dan DENTON
Dan Turner, Hollywood Detective	Dan TURNER
Dance For A Dead Uncle	Insp MERTON
The Dance Of Death	Sgt/Insp HISCOCK
Dance Of Death	Dr Basil WILLING
Dance With Death	Charlie DANCE
Dance With The Devil	Charlie DANCE
Dance Without Music	Cary Wylde O'HARA
Dancer With One Leg	Det LAZARD
Dancing Bear	Milton Chester MILODRAGOVITCH
The Dancing Dead	Mrs Caywood WESTON
The Dancing Doll Murders	Richard Curtis (The Phantom) VAN LOAN
Dancing In The Dark	Blaine STEWART
The Dancing Man	Mark HAWKINS
The Danger	Andrew DOUGLAS
Danger After Dark	Timothy TERREL
Danger Below	Joe GARTON
Danger In Paradise	Lt Max GOLD
The Danger Within	'Cuckoo' GOYLES
The Dangerfield Talisman	Conway WESTENHANGER
A Dangerous Age	William WARNER
Dangerous Cargo	Mme Rosika STOREY
Dangerous Cargoes	Grant VICKARY
Dangerous Davies: The Last Detective	Dangerous DAVIES
The Dangerous Dead	Sam IRELAND
Dangerous Fortune	Temple FORTUNE
Dangerous Ground: Or, The Rival Detectives	Van VERNET
Dangerous In Love	Dangerous DAVIES
Dangerous Legacy	Spence RANKIN
A Dangerous Liaison	Victoria MCKENZIE
Dangerous Limelight	Insp Dick MASON
Dangerous Men	Don EVERHARD
The Dangerous Ones	Maxine DANGERFIELD
Dangerous Places	Roman CANTRELL
Dangerous To Know	Tom PAIGE
Dangerous To Lean Out	Bernard FESTON
Dangerous Waters	Dick MARLOW
Danse Macabre	Bob SULLIVAN
The Dante Game	Homer KELLY
The Danube Runs Red	John ALLISON
The Danvers Jewels	Ralph DANVERS
Daredevil	Insp Claude Eustace TEAL
Daredevils, Ltd	Ben JOLSON
A Daring Horse Thief	Det Patrick RYAN
The Dark And Deadly	Steve CRAIG
The Dark Arbor	Lt Bill GRADY
Dark Bahama	Johnny VALLON
The Dark Beyond Moura	MOURA
The Dark Cavalier	Michael DUNDAS
Dark Chant In A Crimson Key	Dr Robert 'Mongo' FREDERICKSON
The Dark Corner	Bradford GALT
The Dark Corner	Bradford GALT
Dark Corners	Roman CANTRELL
Dark Crusade	Steve HARVESTER
Dark Crusade	Steve HARVESTER
Dark Deeds	Det Dick DONOVAN
Dark Dream	Jim BENNETT
Dark Emerald	Sarah VANESSA
The Dark Fantastic	Johnny MILANO
Dark Fields	Quin ST JAMES and Mike MCCLEARY
Dark Frontier	Sexton BLAKE
The Dark Garden	Det CRAFFT
The Dark Gateway	Wellington COTTER
The Dark Gondola	MOURA
Dark Interlude	Shaun O'MARA
The Dark Island	Nick NICHOLSON
The Dark Light	Carney WILDE
The Dark Mirror	Mike FARADAY
Dark Moon	Sgt Ronnie DREW
The Dark Night	Justin (The Ace) MARCH
Dark Of The Moon	Dr Gideon FELL
Dark Paradise	Laurie GRANT and Stewart NOBLE
A Dark Power	Kane JACKSON
Dark Road	Jefferson DIMARCO
The Dark Side	Carver BASCOMBE
Dark Sonata	Ira YEDDER
Dark Star	Joanna STARK
Dark Swan	Callista JACOBS
The Dark Trade	Adam GIFFORD
The Dark Tunnel	Chet GORDON
Dark Wanton	Everard Peter QUAYLE
Darke Darrell, The Boy Detective	Darke DARRELL
Darkest Death	Charles FINCH and 'Stalky' HERON
The Darkest Night	Sexton BLAKE
Darkling Death	Supt Gordon KNOLLIS
Darkness At Pemberley	Insp BULLER
Darkness Of Slumber	Dr Marc CASTLEMAN
The Darkroom	Al AMATUCCI
Darkworld Detective	KAMUS OF KADIZAR
Darling Corey's Head	Allan CONYERS and Cheryl BURROUGHS
Darling, Don't Be Dumb	Insp Michael FARRANT
The Dartmouth Murders	Joseph HARRIS
A Dash Of Death	Sarah QUILLIAM and Meg QUILLIAM
The Datchet Diamonds	Insp IRELAND
A Date With Destiny	Lawrence MARLEY
The Daughter Of Anderson Crow	Ch Anderson CROW
The Daughters Of Cain	Insp MORSE
Dauntless Dan, The Boy Detective: Or, The Mysterious House In The Hollow	DAUNTLESS DAN
The Davenham Heritage	Sexton BLAKE
Davenport Blake, The Metropolitan Detective: Or, Piping The Harlem Mystery	DAVENPORT BLAKE
David Betterton	Rosie BRIGHT
David Wilshaw Investigates	David WILSHAW
The Davidson Case	Insp HANSLET and Dr Lancelot PRIESTLEY
Davis Doesn't Live Here Any More	John George DAVIS
A Day In Monte Carlo	Mark TRAVERS
A Day In The Death Of Dorothea Cassidy	Insp Stephen RAMSAY
The Day New York Trembled	Horace CLARKE
The Day Nobody Died	Insp ALLHOFF
The Day Of Murder	Supt Robert TOWNLEY and Sgt Roger NEWMAN
The Day Of The Dead	Peregrine WHITE
Day Of The Dingo	Nick CARTER
Day Of The Guns	'Tiger' MANN
The Day Of The Jackal	Commissaire LEBEL
The Day She Died	Insp Christopher MCKEE
The Day The Children Vanished	Clyde HAVILAND
The Day The Thames Caught Fire	Mark PRESTON
The Day They Invaded New York	Horace CLARKE
Daylight Murder	Ch Insp CUMMINGS and Insp/Supt FILLINGER
Days Of Thunder	Ben DRYDEN
A Daze Of Fears	Michael HADDEN
The De Bercy Affair	Insp Charles François FURNEAUX
Deacon Brodie: Or, The Double Life	Bow St Runner HUNT
Dead Ahead	Det Caley BURKE
Dead Ahead	Nikki TRAKOS
Dead Aim	Chris KLICK
Dead Air	Peter FINLEY
Dead And Buried	Benny COOPERMAN
Dead And Buried	Prof Jackie WALSH
Dead And Doggone	Holly WINTER
Dead And Done For	Cellini SMITH
Dead And Gone	Hampton HUME
Dead And Not Buried	Sgt TUCKER
Dead And Paid For	HARKER
The Dead And The Deadly	Martin ZANE
Dead Angel	'Doc' CONNOR
The Dead Are Discreet	Jacob ASCH
The Dead Are Prowling	Ed BOND
Dead As A Dummy	Jose Manuel MADERO
Dead As They Come	Molly MELLINGER
Dead At The Take-Off	Chance MALLOY
Dead Babes In The Wood	Prof A PENNYFEATHER
Dead Ball	Insp Angus STRAUN
Dead Beat	Kate BRANNIGAN
Dead Before Morning	Insp Joseph Aloysius RAFFERTY
Dead Birds	Jim JENNER
Dead Bolt	Harry GOULD
The Dead Butler Caper	Ed NELSON
Dead Calm	John INGRAM
The Dead Canary	Sgt Jerry LONG
Dead Center	Det Christopher JENSEN and Prof Natalie KEITH
Dead Centre	Det Christopher JENSEN and Prof Natalie KEITH
Dead Centre	Nikki TRAKOS
Dead Cert	Alan YORK
Dead Certain	Gil VINE
Dead Certainty	Hank JANSON
The Dead Darling	Det Pete SELBY
Dead Dinosaurs	Luis BALAM
The Dead Do Not Praise	Sgt Benedict MITCHELL
The Dead Do Talk	Dick MARLOW
Dead Dog	Catherine LINTON
Dead Dogs Bite	Dr Nathaniel BUNCE
The Dead Don't Bite	Maj Maurice HEMYOCK
The Dead Don't Scare	Supt Frank DRURY and Insp Bill HAZARD
Dead End	Det Insp Bill SLIDER
Dead End	Chester C TABOR
Dead End Game	Lt Joe DANTE
Dead End Street	Ed RAZONI and William JACKSON
Dead Even	Matt MCCALL
Dead Eye	Det Supt George ROGERS
Dead Folks' Blues	Harry DENTON
Dead For A Ducat	Mark SAVAGE and Ch Insp Sam BIRKETT
Dead For A Penny	Edwin GEORGE
Dead Game	Keith CALDER
Dead Giveaway	Mehatibel BELLAMY
Dead Giveaway	Steve JOHNSON
The Dead Hand Horrors	Ben BRYN
The Dead Have No Friends	Sir Benjamin SCARLE
Dead Heat	Harvey ACE
The Dead Heat	Carl HELLER
Dead In A Row	Sgt/Insp John COFFIN and Insp/Supt William WINTER
Dead In Bed	Johnny ALOHA
Dead In Center Field	Mark RENZLER
Dead In No Time	Montrose ARBUTHNOT
Dead In The Morning	Patrick GRANT
Dead In The Water	Ch of Plce Reid BENNETT
Dead In The Water	Rebecca SCHWARTZ
Dead In The Water	Kate SHUGAK
Dead Innocent	Insp LYON
Dead Is The Door-Nail	Mike WARLOCK
Dead Lagoon	Commiss Aurelio ZEN

	Dead Level	Fred DAYMOND
	Dead Lion	Prof MANDRAKE
The	Dead Man At The Window	Monsieur LEVERT
	Dead Man Friday	Don PAULSON
	Dead Man Killer	Nat PERRY
	Dead Man Manor	Mr Horace B TREADGOLD
A	Dead Man Out Of Mind	David MIDDLETON-BROWNE
	Dead Man Running	Sarah CALLOWAY
	Dead Man Running	J Molden MOTT
	Dead Man Talks Too Much	Burt CALHOUN
	Dead Man, Dead	Bart HARDIN
	Dead Man's Alibi	Insp/Supt ADAMS
	Dead Man's Bluff	Insp CLAYTON
	Dead Man's Fingers	Martin RIDGWAY
	Dead Man's Float	Dean GRANT
	Dead Man's Float	Albie HARRIS
	Dead Man's Island	Henrietta O'Dwyer COLLINS
	Dead Man's Mooring	Ch Offr Webb CARRICK
	Dead Man's Rooms	Watson WARD
A	Dead Man's Secret - Special	Nelson LEE
	Dead Man's Shoes	Insp/Commiss John APPLEBY
	Dead Man's Shoes	Sheriff Jack THOMPSON
A	Dead Man's Step: A Detective Story	Ferriss MURTAGH
	Dead Man's Tears	Philip KAUFMAN
	Dead Man's Thoughts	Cass JAMESON
	Dead Man's Vengeance	Insp John WALK
	Dead March In Three Keys	Emma PLUME
	Dead March In Three Keys	Emma PLUME
	Dead Meat	Yevgeni Ivanovitch GRUSHKO
	Dead Meet	Moses VINE
	Dead Men Don't Give Seminars	Sabina SWIFT
	Dead Men Don't Marry	Sabina SWIFT
	Dead Men Don't Ski	Ch Insp/Ch Sup Henry TIBBETT and Emmy TIBBETT
The	Dead Men Grin	Ben HELM
	Dead Men Leave No Fingerprints	Simon LAKE
The	Dead Men Of Eden	Hoani MATA
	Dead Men Turn Green	Kendal GRAYDON
	Dead Men's Hearts	Gideon OLIVER
	Dead Men's Plays	Sewell BLAKE
	Dead Of A Counterplot	Adam LUDLOW
	Dead Of A Physician	Insp Paul GRAINGER
The	Dead Of Summer	NICHOLSON
	Dead On Cue	Sexton BLAKE
	Dead On Departure	Don KENDRICK
	Dead On The Level	Simon DRAKE
	Dead On The Stone	Insp MARTIN
	Dead On Your Feet	Stan KRAYCHIK
	Dead Orchid	Danny LEATHER
The	Dead Past	Commiss Geoffrey HALLDEN
	Dead Pigeon	Sgt Jerry LONG
	Dead Pigeon On Beethoven Street	SANDY
	Dead Pigs At Hungry Farm	Theodore I TERHUNE
The	Dead Pull Hitter	Kate HENRY
	Dead Reckoning	Charlie AGUTTER
	Dead Reckoning	Max HALE
The	Dead Reckoning	Nick MARSHALL
	Dead Respectable	Sexton BLAKE
	Dead Right	Millicent NEWBERRY
	Dead Ringer	Laura FLEMING
	Dead Rite	Johnny LIDDELL and Mickey DENTON
The	Dead Room	Ed BAER
	Dead Run	Dan CONNELL
	Dead Run	Stephen DAIN
	Dead Run	Tessie VENABLE
	Dead Run	Gillean VERDEAN
	Dead Sand	Lewis COLE
	Dead Sea Submarine	Matthew TOBIN
	Dead Secret	Max HALE
	Dead Secret	Felix HERON
	Dead Sequence	Hugo BISHOP
	Dead Set	Chester FORTUNE
	Dead She Was Beautiful	Mort HAGEN
	Dead Skip	Dan KEARNEY ASSOCIATES
The	Dead Sleep Late	Griff DEXTER
	Dead So Soon	John BRYANT
	Dead Stop	Jefferson DIMARCO
The	Dead Take No Bows	Quinny HITE
	Dead To The World	Danny MICHAELS
	Dead Weight	Capt Gridley NELSON
	Dead Woman Of The Year	John JERICHO and Lt PASCAL
	Dead Yellow Women	The CONTINENTAL OP
	Deadeye	Charlie AGUTTER
	Deadfall	Joe SHAW
	Deadhead	Chester LONG
The	Deadlier Of The Species	Sexton BLAKE
	Deadlier Than The Male	Jana BLAKE
	Deadlier Than The Male	Hank FERRELL
The	Deadliest Game	Jim ROCKFORD
	Deadline	Jim LARKIN
	Deadline	Jack MCMORROW
	Deadline For A Diplomat	Insp BASS
	Deadline For A Dream	Det Ch Insp Colin THANE and Insp Phil MOSS
	Deadline: 2 AM	Lt Jim REARDON
The	Deadly Ackee	Theo BLOOMER
The	Deadly Affair	George SMILEY
	Deadly Aims	Jack DEMARREST and Jane BRITLAND
	Deadly Alliance	Colin STRYKER
	Deadly Beloved	Timothy DANE
The	Deadly Birdman	Marc (The Mercenary) DEAN
The	Deadly Chase	Robert CRAIG
The	Deadly Chase	Larry KOHARIK
	Deadly Climate	Margaret BINTON
The	Deadly Climate	Caroline EMMET
	Deadly Crescendo	Mark HOLLAND
	Deadly Daffodils	Supt CAWTHORNE
The	Deadly Dames	Bill YATES
	Deadly Devotion	Sydney BRYANT
	Deadly Diamond	Sarah VANESSA
The	Deadly Doctor	The BUTCHER
	Deadly Doubles	Nick CARTER
	Deadly Downbeat	Mike MERRIMAN
The	Deadly Dream	Dr Johnny MACK
	Deadly Edge	PARKER
	Deadly Ernest	Insp CAM
	Deadly Ernest	Frank MURPHY
	Deadly Errand	Kate KINSELLA
The	Deadly Gold	Roger TALLIS
The	Deadly Homecoming	Lt Al ZIMMERMAN
	Deadly Image	'Flashgun' CASEY
	Deadly In New York	James HAWKER
	Deadly Inheritance	Lorna COOPER
The	Deadly Innocent	Paul SHAW
	Deadly Intent	Insp BARRY
	Deadly Intrusion	Jack HANIGAN
	Deadly Is The Evil Tongue	Insp/Supt William AUSTEN
The	Deadly Jest	Insp Myles RUSBY
	Deadly Legacy	Kane JACKSON
A	Deadly Lie	Chris LUDLOW
The	Deadly Lovers	Frank RICHMOND
	Deadly Meeting	Lt MOYNAHAN, Millicent HETHEREGE and Bill STRATTON
The	Deadly Miss Ashley	Luke SPEARE and Schyler COLE
The	Deadly Miss Ashley	Luke SPEARE and Schyler COLE
	Deadly Nightcap	Insp NEWSOM
	Deadly Nightshade	Holderly HALL
The	Deadly Orbit Mission	Capt/Maj/Col Hugh NORTH
The	Deadly Orchid	Mike HARRIS and Trixie MEEHAN
The	Deadly Pearl	Robert SAND
	Deadly Persuasion	Sexton BLAKE
	Deadly Persuasion	Brock DEVLIN
A	Deadly Place To Stay	George COLE and Amanda DREW
	Deadly Practice	Kate KINSELLA
	Deadly Putter	Jack STENTON
	Deadly Reflections	Georgia Lee MAXWELL
	Deadly Resurrection	Dan CRONYN
	Deadly Reunion	Insp Bertil DURELL
	Deadly Reunion	Gary WESTON
	Deadly Secret	Commiss Thatcher COLT
A	Deadly Sickness	Supt George THORNE
	Deadly Sights	Jack DEMARREST and Jane BRITLAND
	Deadly Snow	Steve (The Force) SINCLAIR
A	Deadly State Of Mind	Lt COLUMBO
	Deadly Sweet	Eddie PRIEST
The	Deadly Travellers	Kate TEMPEST
	Deadly Variations	Mark HOLLAND
	Deadly Weapon	Walter JAMES
	Deadman's Bay	Jerry SCANT
	Deadpan	Daniel KEEL
	Deadwood Dick's Last Shot	DEADWOOD DICK
	Deal Me Out	Donald BRACKEN and James Rowland WOODWARD VII
	Dealer	Jim SHERIDAN
	Dealer's Choice	Philip MARLOWE
	Dear Dead Mother-In-Law	Lorna DONAHUE
	Dear Dead Professor	Ch Rufus Albert JONES and Barbara CREW
The	Dear Departed	Richard TRENTON
	Dear Irene	Irene KELLY
	Dear Laura	Insp John Joseph LINTOTT
The	Dear, Dead Girls	Mrs Palmyra Evangeline PYM
	Dear, Dead Harry	Dr Alexander CORNELL
	Death A La Provençale	Darina LISLE
	Death About Face	Johnny LIDDELL
	Death After Lunch	Pete TAYLOR
	Death Against Venus	Jim STEELE
	Death Among Friends	Lt/Insp Richard TUCK
	Death Among The Dons	Francesca WILSON
	Death Among The Writers	Insp BOOTLE
	Death And Benedict	Benedict BREEZE
	Death And Blintzes	Belle APPLEMAN
	Death And His Brother	Mr HODSON
	Death And Little Girl Blue	Sexton BLAKE
	Death And Mr Gilly	Mr GILLY
	Death And Mr Potter	Hiram POTTER
	Death And Taxes	Whit WHITNEY
	Death And The Chapman	ROGER THE CHAPMAN
	Death And The Chaste Apprentice	Charlie PEACE
	Death And The Devil	Garry DEAN
	Death And The Diplomat	Henry BRYCE and Emily BRYCE
	Death And The Dogwalker	Jason LYNX
	Death And The Good Life	Al BARNES
	Death And The Maiden	Det Ch Insp Douglas QUANTRILL
	Death And The Maiden	David STUART
	Death And The Maiden	Lt Timothy TRANT
	Death And The Pregnant Virgin	Insp Ben JURNET
	Death And The Professor	Prof Marcus STUBBS
	Death And The Single Girl	Fred BENNETT
	Death And The Trumpets Of Tuscany	Emma SHAW
	Death And Variations	David MEYNELL
The	Death Angel	Prof Theocritus Lucius WESTBOROUGH
	Death Answers The Bell	Insp MANDERTON and Det Sgt Trevor DENE
	Death At A Masquerade	Mac MCINTYRE
	Death At Appledore Towers	Sherlock HOLMES
	Death At Broadcasting House	Det Insp Simon SPEARS
	Death At Charity's Point	Brady COYNE
	Death At Court Lady	Sir Charles KNIGHTLEY
	Death At Crane's Court	Prof DALY
	Death At Dayton's Folly	Rocky ALLAN
	Death At Devil-Fish Point	Cdr MORETON
	Death At Face Value	Betty TRENKA
	Death at Flight	Nathaniel GOSS
	Death At La Fenice	Commiss Guido BRUNETTI

D

Death At Lover's Leap	Anthony HUNTER
Death At Pyford Hall	Jeff TELLFORD
A Death At St Anselm's	Rev Claire ALDINGTON
Death At Swaythling Court	Col SANDERSTEAD
A Death At The Bar	Sgt REED
Death At The Cascades	P C James WIGAN
Death At The Crossings	Mike MINER
Death At The Dog	Insp Guy NORTHEAST
Death At The Furlong Post	Sgt REED
Death At The Horse Show	Insp CHACE
Death At The Porthole	Cliff CHANDLER
Death At The President's Lodging	Insp/Commiss John APPLEBY
Death At The Salutation	Insp John BURNELL
Death At The Towers	Bill CHORLEY
Death At Three	Jake JUSTUS, Helene JUSTUS and John J MALONE
Death At Windward Hill	Tim ASHER
Death Awaits Thee	Christer WICK
Death Beat	Hank BRADFORD
Death Beckons Quietly	Insp FLAGG
Death Before Breakfast	Arabella FRANT
A Death Before Dying	Lt Frank HASTINGS
Death Before Wicket	Johnny DUVIVIEN
Death Benefits	Rachel GOLD
Death Beyond The Go-Thru	Miles Standish RICE
Death Beyond The Nile	Tamara HOYLAND
Death Bids For Corners	Hamilton YORKE
Death Blew Out The Match	Elisha MACOMBER
Death Boards The Lazy Lady	Peter BARRON and Janet BARRON
The Death Box	James CLARKSON-PARRY
The Death Bringers	William MALLETT
Death Burns The Candle	Insp Curtis BURKE
The Death Business	Frank RICHMOND
Death By Appointment	Phil CASEY
Death By Appointment	Maj Peter Utley SHANE
Death By Bequest	Insp Herbert BROOM
Death By Clue	Father MICKLE
Death By Deception	Mark SHIGATA
Death By Demonstration	Jefferson SHIELDS
Death By Design	John BLAINE
Death By Design	Mark TUDOR
Death By Dynamite	Simon ROLFE
Death By Gaslight	Sherlock HOLMES
Death By Invitation	Kingsley TOPLITT and Sally TOPLITT
Death By Marriage	Col Richard BARNE
Death By Misadventure	Phryne FISHER
Death By Sheer Torture	Insp Perry TRETHOWAN
Death By The Light Of The Moon	Claire MALLOY
Death Calls The Jester	Kendal GRAYDON
Death Came In The Studio	Bill RICE
Death Came Uninvited	Insp Christopher MARSDEN
Death Camp Columbia	Vic (Eagle Force) GABRIEL
Death Can Wait	Peter MITCHELL
Death Cancels The Evidence	Simon CROLE
The Death Card	Rita MONDRAGON
The Death Card	Steve SILK
Death Carries A Cane	James Gaylord DURSTINE
Death Casts A Lure	Noah BRADSHAW
Death Climbs A Hill	Insp PRENTIS
Death Comes Ashore	Dick TORREYTON
Death Comes On Friday	Frederick HUNT
Death Comes To Dinner	Paul BERNARD
Death Comes To Dinner	Insp Bill MURRAY
The Death Convention	Tavey MARTIN
Death Cries In The Street	Lt Abe LARSON
Death Cries Ôlé	Russell JONES
Death Croons The Blues	Julian MEDOZA
Death Crosses The Line	Dick TORREYTON
Death Cruises South	Quentin PACE
Death Dances Thrice	Charlie RYAN
Death Deal	Cory BARNETT
The Death Dealers	Lt Jack DOHERY and Lou BRADE
Death Delivers A Postcard	Carole TREVOR and Max BLYTHE
Death Down Home	Sheriff Sam TITUS and Nicky TITUS
Death Down Under	Insp Carol ASHTON
Death Elsewhere	Gillian CLIFFORD
Death Filled The Glass	Prof MacDougal DUFF
Death Flies High	Jean Henri ST AMAND
Death Flies High	'Spider' STOCKWELL
Death Flies Low	Ch Insp Michael 'Napper' TANDY
A Death For A Double	Robert FORSYTHE and Abigail 'Sandy' SANDERSON
A Death For Adonis	Robert FORSYTHE and Abigail 'Sandy' SANDERSON
Death For Auld Lang Syne	George Herbert HENRY
Death For Dear Clara	Lt Timothy TRANT
Death For Old Time's Sake	Jason LYNX
Death For Safe Custody	Sgt Paul DEAN
Death For The Surgeon	Thibault PAREW
Death Force	William JUSTICE
Death Forms Threes	STAVELEY
Death Framed In Silver	Insp HEADCORN
Death From A Top Hat	The Great MERLINI
Death From Disclosure	David GRIERSON
Death From Nowhere	Don DIAVOLO
Death From The Air	Dick PEMBERTY
Death Fugue	Insp/Supt FILLINGER
Death Gets An A	William MCALPIN
Death Goes Ashore	Insp 'Dusty' MULLER and 'Tiny' MELDRUM
Death Goes By Bus	Morrison SHARPE
Death Goes Fishing	Arthur 'Red' BLAKE and Dan WHEELER
Death Goes Native	Komako KOA
Death Goes On Skis	Miriam BIRDSEYE and Johnny DUVIVIEN
Death Goes To A Party	Joe BURNS
The Death Gong	John PERRIN
Death Greets A Guest	Maj Jack ATHERLEY
Death Had A Voice	Insp Chafik J CHAFIK
Death Has A Double	Dr Frank KING
Death Has A Thousand Doors	John T MCLAREN
Death Has A Thousand Doors	Sarah O'BRIEN
Death Has Ten Thousand Doors	Petunia BEST and Max FREUND
Death Has Two Faces	Dr MANSON
Death Has Two Hands	Danny LEATHER
Death Haunts The Lounge	Supt ROACH
Death Hunt	Phillip (The Marksman) MAGELLAN
Death In 1-2-3	Pete TAYLOR
Death In A Bowl	Ben JARDINN
Death In A Chilly Corner	Matt WINTERS
Death In A Cold Climate	Insp FAGERMO
Death In A Deckchair	Iris COOPER
Death In A High Latitude	Maj Peter BLAIR
Death In A Little Town	Matilda PERKS
Death In A Mist	Insp Michael HORNSLEY
Death In A Quiet Place	Col Richard BARNE
Death In A Serene City	Urbino MACINTYRE
Death In A Sleeping City	Supt LEWIS
Death In A Small World	Carol GATES
Death In Aberration	Insp James DALE
Death In Act IV	Insp GHENT
Death In Amsterdam	Insp Piet VAN DER VALK
Death In An Armchair	Eugene MULCAHY
Death In Ankara	Lal REED
Death In April	Jimmy O'NEILL
Death In Arms	GARNETT
Death In Budapest	Det Insp Simon SPEARS
Death In B-Minor	Bruce PERKINS
Death In Captivity	'Cuckoo' GOYLES
Death In Covert	Nathaniel GOSS
Death In Darkness	Det Insp ARMSTRONG
Death In Deakins Wood	Insp Marcus MACLURG
Death In December	Spencer CROSS-WADE
Death In Deep Water	'Soc' SOCARIDES
Death In Dockland	Sexton BLAKE
Death In Error	Daye SMITH
Death In Grease Paint	Howie ROOK
Death In Green	Micky DOUGLAS
Death In High Heels	Insp CHARLESWORTH
Death In Lebanon	Roger TURNBULL
Death In Office	Insp BRADBURY and Sgt RAYMOND
Death In Office	Sgt/Insp HISCOCK
Death In Passing	Matt RANZINO
Death In Piccadilly	Ch Insp Jonathan BLACK
Death In Ptarmigan Forest	Ross MACALLISTER
Death In Purple Prose	Insp Perry TRETHOWAN and Charlie PEACE
Death In Quiet Places	Insp Geoffrey FRASER
Death In Reserve	Roger CRAMMOND
Death In Retirement	Dr David WINTRINGHAM
Death In Seven Volumes	Harvey TUKE and Sir Bruton KAMES
Death In Silhouette	Maria BLACK
Death In Soundings	Roger CRAMMOND
Death In Store	Verity 'Birdie' BIRDWOOD
Death In Ten Point Bold	Stephen KELLY
Death In The Andamans	Copper RANDAL
Death In The Bag	Supt Michael DREXEL
Death In The Canongate	Insp GRAY
Death In The Copse	Rodney WAYNE
Death In The Dark	Stephen BAYARD
Death In The Diving-Pool	Insp RYVET
Death In The Dovecote	Insp BOOT
Death In The Dusk	Supt SALT and Paula LEBETWOOD
A Death In The Family	Dr Jean MONTROSE
Death In The Fifth Position	Peter Cutler SERGEANT
Death In The Fog	Det CRAFFT
Death In The Grand Manor	Tessa CRICHTON
Death In The Hands Of Talent	Sandy BLUNT
Death In The High Latitude	Maj Peter BLAIR
Death In The House	Lord Arthur LINTON
Death In The Jordan	Roger TURNBULL
Death In The Kettle	Supt Edmund BENDILOW
Death In The Library	Stephen BARTH
A Death In The Life	Julia HAYES
Death In The Limelight	Insp GORMLEY
Death In The Mews	Arnold KEENE and Bernard YOUNG
Death In The Morning	Det Ch Insp Douglas QUANTRILL
Death In The Night	George CLAY
Death In The Pasig	Jo GAR
Death In The Past	Bob WHITFIELD
Death In The Picture	Cyrus FINNEGAN
Death In The Picture	Michael GAUNT
Death In The Quadrangle	Prof DALY
Death In The Quarry	Supt Henry WILSON and The Hon Everard BLATCHINGTON
Death In The Stocks	Supt HANNASYDE
Death In The Wheelbarrow	Insp PENK
Death In The Wheelbarrow	Insp PENK
Death In The Wind	Lt GRAY
Death In Triplicate	Supt KEMPSON
Death In Verona	Matthew COLL
Death In View	Jim HARRIS and Kate HARRIS
Death In Willow Pattern	Henry Lancaster PYM
Death In Zanzibar	Lash HOLDEN and Dany ASHTON
The Death Inheritance	Anastasia JUGEDINSKI
Death Is A Circus	JASON
Death Is A Family Affair	Dixie T STRUTHERS
Death Is A Friend	Henry CHALICE and Crying EDDIE
Death Is A Lovely Dame	Morgan WAYNE
Death Is A Restless Sleeper	James STRANGE
Death Is A Round Black Ball	Johnny APRIL
Death Is Academic	Hannah LAND
Death Is Confidential	Steve GANT
Death Is For Losers	Bart CHALLIS
Death Is Forever	Delilah WEST

	Death Is Like That	William RYE
	Death Is Merciful	James CHARLESWORTH
	Death Is My Lover	Steve ROURKE
	Death Is No Lady	Mac MCINTYRE
	Death Is Not A Passing Grade	Insp KOJAK
	Death Is The End	Peter MITCHELL
The	Death Kiss	Sydney TREHERNE
	Death Knows No Calendar	Maj BODDY
	Death Laughs Aloft	Dick PEMBERTY
	Death Leaves A Diary	John PIPER and QUINN
	Death Like Thunder	Norman TRAVIS
	Death Likes It Hot	Peter Cutler SERGEANT
	Death Lives Next Door	Sgt/Insp John COFFIN
	Death Looks Down	Katherine 'Peter' PIPER and Edward TRELAWNEY
	Death Looks In	Det Daniel WEBSTER
The	Death Makers Conspiracy	Agent of Cominsec TAGGART
	Death Masque	Dr Gregor MACLEAN
The	Death Master	Jerry THACKER
	Death May Surprise Us	Cdr John KNOWLES
	Death Meets The Coroner	Insp RODWAY
The	Death Merchant	Richard (The Death Merchant) CAMELLION
The	Death Miser	DEPARTMENT Z
	Death Mission: Havana	Nick CARTER
	Death Must Have Laughed	Amos PETRIE
	Death Never Forgets	HIGHWAY
	Death Notice	Pete BRADY
	Death Of A Best Seller	PINKNEY
	Death Of A Big Man	RIPLEY
	Death Of A Blue Movie Star	RUNE
	Death Of A Borgia	Nicholas COFFIN
	Death Of A Bovver Boy	Carolus DEENE
	Death Of A Charming Man	Const Hamish MACBETH
	Death Of A Cheat	Larry KOHARIK
	Death Of A Citizen	Matt HELM
	Death Of A Con Man	Insp RAWLINSON
	Death Of A Corinthian	Lt GRAY
	Death Of A Dandie Dinmont	Norah NORTH
	Death Of A Dear Friend	Det Insp James ROLAND
	Death Of A Decent Fellow	Insp WREN
	Death Of A Delegate	Virgil FLETCHER
The	Death Of A Difficult Woman	Bonnie INDERMILL
	Death Of A Dissenter	Supt QUILL and Insp GLOVER
	Death Of A Dog	Dr Joan MARVIN
	Death Of A Doll	Mark EAST
	Death Of A Don	Insp BARNABY
	Death Of A Dunwoody Matron	Sheila TRAVIS
	Death Of A Favourite Girl	Ch Supt KNOTT
	Death Of A Fire-Raiser	Simon GOOD
	Death Of A Golden Girl	Nina MCFALL and Lt Dino ROSSI
	Death Of A Gossip	Insp BLAIR
	Death Of A Gossip	Const Hamish MACBETH
	Death Of A Halo	Dr Frank KING
	Death Of A Holy Murderer	Norah NORTH
	Death Of A Literary Widow	Greg HOCKING
	Death Of A Merchant Of Death	Prof Clifford WELLS and Lt Barney MATTINGLEY
	Death Of A Mermaid	Arthur Stukeley PENNINGTON and Det Insp Patrick Aloysius MCCARTHY
	Death Of A Merry Widow	Det Ch Insp Sidney WALSH
The	Death Of A Millionaire	Supt Henry WILSON
	Death Of A Minor Poet	Sam BIRGE
	Death Of A Mystery Writer	Idwal MEREDITH
	Death Of A Perfect Mother	Ch Insp MCHALE
	Death Of A Pornographer	Adam GIFFORD
	Death Of A Punk	Larry HORNBLOWER
	Death Of A Pusher	Matt RUDD
	Death Of A Queen	Charles VENABLES
	Death Of A Raven	Patrick GILLARD
	Death Of A Russian Priest	Insp Porfiry Petrovich ROSTNIKOV
	Death Of A Shadow	Dr Eustace HAILEY
	Death Of A Shipowner	HENRICKSEN
	Death Of A Shrew	Insp HENDERSON
	Death Of A Sinner	Peter QUENTIN
	Death Of A Skin Diver	Dr MUCH
	Death Of A Source	Bob WHITFIELD
	Death Of A Spinster	Insp Hugh COLLIER
	Death Of A Theatre Filly	Supt Richard YORK
	Death Of A Viewer	Maj Robert BENNION
	Death Of A Wicked Servant	Insp O'DONOVAN
	Death Of A Witch	Peter MAXWELL and Susan MAXWELL
	Death Of An Airman	Insp Bernard BRAY
	Death Of An Alderman	Supt/Ch Supt Simon KENWORTHY
	Death Of An Angel	Sgt/Ch Supt Merle CAPRICORN
	Death Of An Angel	Grant KIRBY
	Death Of An Angel	Lt POWLEDGE
	Death Of An Ardent Bibliophile	Insp Peter MCGARR
	Death Of An Artist	Insp KNICKMAN and Martin AMES
	Death Of An Aryan	Supt VACHELL
	Death Of An Editor	Insp BREWS
	Death Of An Englishman	Marshal Salva GUARNACCIA
	Death Of An Innocent	Mr DEHAVILLAND and Supt BLACK
	Death Of An Oddfellow	Arnold KEENE and Bernard YOUNG
	Death Of An Old Girl	Insp Tom WHARTON
	Death Of An Old Goat	Insp ROYLE
	Death Of An Old Sinner	Jasper TULLY and Mrs Annie NORRIS
	Death Of An Older Girl	Det Supt Tom POLLARD
	Death Of Anton	MINTO
The	Death Of Cardinal Tosca	Sherlock HOLMES
The	Death Of Daddy-O	Marty LAND
	Death Of Jezebel	Insp COCKRILL and Insp CHARLESWORTH
The	Death Of Laurence Vining	Insp WIDGEON
	Death Of Miss X	Eve FITZSIMMONS
The	Death Of Mr Dodsley	Francis MACNAB
	Death Of My Aunt	Malcolm WARREN
The	Death Of Sholmes	Herlock SHOLMES

The	Death Of The Claimant	Branders NOBLE
	Death Of The Deputy	Insp LECAIN
The	Death Of The Detective	Arnold MAGNUSON
	Death Of The Falcon	Nick CARTER
	Death Of The Home Secretary	Insp WIDGEON
	Death Of The Office Witch	Charlie GREENE
	Death Of The Party	Lettie WINTERBOTTOM
	Death Of Virginia	Insp Felix HOBBINGDON
	Death Off Stage	Insp Jean-Paul GAUTIER
	Death Off The Fairway	Maj Robert BENNION
	Death On A Broomstick	Insp LOVICK
	Death On A Ferris Wheel	Matt HUGHES
	Death On A High Note	Sexton BLAKE
	Death On A Hot Summer Night	Micky DOUGLAS
	Death On All Hallows	Insp Neil MACLEOD
	Death On Call	Pete TANNER and Rosemary CLEVELAND
	Death On Delivery	Lucien CLAY
	Death On Demand	Patrick DAWLISH
	Death On Demand	Annie LAURANCE
	Death On Jerusalem Road	Derek CROME
	Death On Location	Tom KINCAID
	Death On Milestone Buttress	Sir Abercrombie LEWKER
	Death On Paper	Sgt Pembury GREEN
	Death On Scurvy Street	Insp TOPE
	Death On The Agenda	Mr HODSON
	Death On The Barrier Reef	Insp Simon ASHTON
The	Death On The Boardwalk	Vic MERRITT
	Death On The Borough Council	Dr David WINTRINGHAM
	Death On The Campus	Capt PACKER and Kent BLOOMINGDALE
	Death On The Cliff Walk	Det Matt DEVLIN
	Death On The Doormat	Desmond SHANNON
	Death On The Doorstep	Sgt/Insp Brian 'Bonny' LEE
	Death On The Downs	Insp BUCK
	Death On The Eno	Hannah LAND
	Death On The Hour	Bernard SIMMONS
	Death On The Late Show	Darby CASTLE
	Death On The Limited	Quentin PACE
	Death On The Mississippi	Lyon WENTWORTH and Bea WENTWORTH
	Death On The Pack Road	Henry HOLLAND
	Death On The Pampas	Lal REED
	Death On The Reserve	Dr Henry FROST
	Death On The River	Hannah LAND
	Death On The Rocks	Maj Peter BLAIR
	Death On The Rocks	Jacob LOMAX
	Death On The Roof	Insp GHENT and Sgt Paul DEAN
	Death On The Slopes	Kay BARTH
	Death On The Spike	Sexton BLAKE
	Death On The Waterfront	Joel STERN
	Death On Widows Walk	Rain MORGAN
	Death Order Of A Left-Wing Student	Morris KAPLAN
	Death Out Of Thin Air	Don DIAVOLO
	Death Over Newark	Det Sgt Pietro TONELLI
	Death Packs A Suitcase	Bill TERN
	Death Paints A Picture	Desmond MERRION and Insp Henry ARNOLD
	Death Pays A Dividend	Insp HANSLET and Dr Lancelot PRIESTLEY
	Death Pays The Rose Rent	Tori MIRACLE
	Death Plays The Gramophone	Donald CLIVE
	Death Points A Finger	Prof Herman BRIERLY
The	Death Pool	Insp BREWS
	Death Pulls A Double Cross	Ed LONDON
	Death Rattle	Freddy PHILPOTTS
	Death Registers At The Eagle Arms	Insp HYND
	Death Ride	STARSKY and HUTCH
	Death Rides A Painted Horse	Mike ZACHARIAS and Steve CONSIDINE
	Death Rides Tandem	Carey GALBREATH
	Death Rides The Dragon	Mrs Caywood WESTON
	Death Rings A Bell	Prof Percy PEACOCK
	Death Sentence	Paul BENJAMIN
	Death Sentence	Det Joe LAWLESS, Offr Barbara BABALINO and Det Leo GRADY
	Death Sentence	Remo (The Destroyer) WILLIAMS
	Death Serves An Ace	Insp MACMASTERS
	Death Set In Diamonds	Trevor LOWE
	Death Set To Music	Insp Clovis Desire PEL
	Death Shapes The Frame	Matt TUDOR
The	Death Ship	Sexton BLAKE
	Death Sounds Grand	Det Ch Insp Sidney WALSH
	Death Sped The Plough	Supt Michael DREXEL
	Death Spoke Sweetly	John YARDLEY
	Death Springs The Trap	Lt Joseph DICKERSON
	Death Squad	Sgt Edmund ROERSCH
The	Death Squad	Det Sgt Joe RYKER
	Death Stalks In Soho	Arthur Stukeley PENNINGTON and Det Insp Patrick Aloysius MCCARTHY
	Death Stalks The Cobbled Square	John Newton CHANCE
	Death Stalks The Punjab	Capt Prem NARAYAN
	Death Stalks The Wakely Family	Judge Ephraim Peabody PECK
	Death Stands Round The Corner	Supt MACNEILL
	Death Stops At A Tourist Camp	Porteus Alexander HARP
	Death Stops The Bells	Franklin RUSSELL
	Death Stops The Manuscript	Franklin RUSSELL
	Death Stops The Show	Lt Claude GREENWAY
The	Death Strain	Nick CARTER
	Death Strikes At Heron House	Jerry MOONEY
	Death Strikes At Six Bells	Supt DANIELS
	Death Strikes From The Rear	Insp BUCK
	Death Strikes Home	Carey BRENT
	Death Swap	Nancy HARPER
The	Death Syndicate	Carole TREVOR and Max BLYTHE
	Death Takes A Dive	Cornelius CLIFT Jr
	Death Takes A Dive	John HARLEY
	Death Takes A Gamble	William MCALPIN
	Death Takes A Ride	Stephen RANT
	Death Takes A Sabbatical	Prof Richard HALSEY
	Death Takes An Editor	Steven MALONE
	Death Takes An Option	Bert MCCALL and Tony COSTAINE

D

The	Devil In The Belfry	Mr MACAULEY
The	Devil In The Bush	Dr Mary FINNEY and Emily COLLINS
The	Devil In Velvet	Prof Nicholas FENTON
The	Devil Knows You're Dead	Matt SCUDDER
The	Devil Loves Me	Insp SANDS and Dr Paul PRYE
The	Devil Mask Mystery	Terry SPRING
The	Devil Met A Lady	Toby PETERS and Bette DAVIS
The	Devil Of Pei-Ling	Insp Thomas CONROY
The	Devil Stirs	Dep Sheriff Jake BROWN
The	Devil That Slumbers	George B EDGEHILL and Aristide GOVIN
The	Devil Woman	Brian O'MALLEY
	Deville McKeene, The British Ace	Deville MCKEENE
	Devils Of The Deep	'Doc' SAVAGE
The	Devil-Stick	Maj Laurence JEN
	Devil, Devil	Satan SLEUTH
The	Devil's Dozen	Nick CARTER
The	Devil's Bride	Jules DE GRANDIN
The	Devil's Church	Lord TINTAGEL and Lady 'Ginger' TINTAGEL
The	Devil's Claw	Anthony Nicholas TWIN
	Devil's Daughter	Don DANBY
The	Devil's Den	Wylie KING and Nels LUNDBERG
The	Devil's Derby	Mr MADDOX
	Devil's Drum	Insp Maurice HEPBURN
The	Devil's Finger	Mike (American Avenger) MCVEIGH
The	Devil's Footsteps	Dr Alexander CASPIAN
The	Devil's Guard	James Schuyler 'JimGrim' GRIM
The	Devil's Kloof	Aubrey St John MAJOR
The	Devil's Mirror	Eric IVORSEN
The	Devil's Own	Sexton BLAKE
The	Devil's Passkey	Ruff MORGAN
The	Devil's Playground	Philip MARLOWE
	Devil's Power	Insp CADMAN
The	Devil's Suit	Jack MCGUIRE
	Devil's Tears	Insp Michael REGAN
The	Devil's Torch	Supt 'Cissie' MARLOW
The	Devine Court Mystery	Insp Henry DOIGHT
The	Devious Ones	Bernard SIMMONS
	Devlin The Barber	DEVLIN
	Devlin's Triangle	Timothy DEVLIN
The	Devouring Fire	Insp Harry FARRANT
	Dewey Decimated	Edwin GEORGE
The	DI	Det Insp Don KERRY
	Diagnosis: Homicide	Dr Daniel Webster COFFEE and Lt Max RITTER
	Diagnosis: Murder	Dr Colin STARR
	Dial 'M' For Murdock	Matt MURDOCK
A	Diamond Before You Die	Neal RAFFERTY
The	Diamond Coterie	Neil J BATHURST
The	Diamond Cross Mystery	Col Robert Lee ASHLEY
	Diamond Cut Diamond	Elinor VANCE
	Diamond Dan, The Brooklyn Divorce Detective; Or, The Strangest Tail Of Crime On Record	DIAMOND DAN
The	Diamond Exchange	Dep Ch Insp Max KAUFFMAN and J T 'Jake' SPANNER
The	Diamond Feather	Insp Christopher MCKEE
The	Diamond Fix	Hawk MACRAE
The	Diamond Hook	CARBO
The	Diamond Hostage	CARBO
	Diamond In The Buff	Jill SMITH
The	Diamond Master	Prof Augustus S F X VAN DUSEN
The	Diamond Queen	Prof Craig KENNEDY
The	Diamond Ransom Murders	Jeremiah IRISH
	Diamond Rock	Red DIAMOND
The	Diamond Thieves	Balmy RYMAL
	Diamonds Are Deadly	Anna ZORDAN
	Diamonds Bid	Col Nur BEY
	Diamonds Can Be Trouble	Sexton BLAKE
	Diamonds In The Dumplings	Christopher SAXE
The	Diamonds Of Death	Insp Clancy MARTIN
	Diamonds Wild	Mike BENASQUE
The	Diamond-Studded Typewriter	Jeffrey GREEN
	Diana Is Dead	Const ROBINS
	Diary Of A Detective Police Officer	WATERS
	Diary Of An Ex-Detective	Bow Street Runner BOLTER
The	Diary Of Death	Insp COMFORT
The	Dick And The Devil	Johnny HARD
The	Dick And The Jane	Nick PALLADINO
	Dick Barton, Special Agent	Dick BARTON
	Dick Barton, Special Agent	Dick BARTON
	Dick Drant, The Reporter Detective; Or Running Down The Bank Wreckers	Dick DRANT
	Dick Tracy	Dick TRACY
	Dick Tracy: The Thirties - Tommy Guns And Hard Times	Dick TRACY
	Dick, The Boy Detective; Or, Out Of The Streets Of New York	MAGIC DICK
	Die A Little Every Day	Det Dave PITT
	Die By Night	Joe GAYLORD
	Die Fast, Die Happy	John MARSHALL
	Die Hard	Joe LELAND
	Die My Lovely	Johnny BUCHANAN
	Die Of A Rose	Wilson HARLEY
	Die On Easy Street	Steve ASHE
	Diecast	Hugo BARON
	Died In The Red	Insp CARDIFF
The	Diehard	Sgt MULHEISEN
The	Different Night	Insp Tami SHIMONI
	Dig Me A Grave	William RYE
The	Digger 'Tec	John RUMFORD
The	Dilemma Of The Distressed Savoyard	Sherlock HOLMES
	Diminished Responsibility	Supt Owen SMITH
	Diminishing Returns	Lt MICHAELS
The	Dinard Mystery	Duncan CAINSFORTH
	Dine And Be Dead	Sgt/Insp John COFFIN
	Dinner For None	Insp Lane PARRY
The	Dinosaur	Bob MORANE
The	Diplomat And The Gold Piano	Henry BRYCE and Emily BRYCE
	Diplomatic Corpse	Asey MAYO
	Diplomatic Death	Insp Richard LEFT
The	Diplomatist	William Wilberforce SMITH
	Dirge For A Dorset Druid	Sir Toby GLENDOWER and Penelope SPRING
	Dirk Gently's Holistic Detective Agency	Dirk GENTLY
	Dirty Laundry	Sam BRISCOE
	Dirty Proof	Frank DRAGOVICH
	Dirty Story	Arthur Abdul SIMPSON
A	Dirty Way To Die	Johnny ROCK
	Dirty Weekend	Det Supt George MACRAE and Det Sgt Leopold SILVER
	Disappearance Of A Niece	Det Insp Ross PATERSON
	Disappearance Of Dr Bruderstein	Charles BLESSINGTON
The	Disappearance Of Dr Jotson	Herlock SHOLMES
The	Disappearance Of Edwin Drood	Sherlock HOLMES
The	Disappearance Of James Phillimore	Sherlock HOLMES
The	Disappearance Of Lady Francis Carfax	Sherlock HOLMES
The	Disappearance Of Lady Francis Carfax	Pharaoh JONES
The	Disappearance Of Lord Adolphus	Herlock SHOLMES
The	Disappearance Of Mr James Phillimore	Sherlock HOLMES
The	Disappearance Of Penny	Henry PO
The	Disappearing Corpse	James WARREN
The	Disappearing Diamond	James GALVESTON
The	Disappearing Monster	HERRIG
	Disaster At Dungeness	James BRUCE
	Disclosures Of A Press Agent	Pusher LONG
	Discretion	Chris ROCKWELL and Sarah SABER
	Disguise For A Dead Gentleman	Ben ANDERSON
	Disher - Detective	DISHER
	Dishonour Among Thieves	Insp/Supt MACDONALD
	Dismal Ravens Crying	Sgt JOLLEY
	Disorderly Elements	Michael WYMAN
The	Disorientated Man	Sexton BLAKE
	Displaced Persons	Supt/Ch Supt Simon KENWORTHY
The	Disposal Of The Living	Helen KITTEREGE
	Disposing Mind	William MCALPIN
The	Dispossessed	Lt Luis MENDOZA
The	Distant Clue	Capt/Insp Merton HEIMRICH
	Diva	Serge GORODISH and ALBA
The	Diva's Emeralds	Ch Insp Archie BURFORD
	Dive Deep For Danger	Mike BROOKS
The	Diversions Of Dawson	Ch Insp DAWSON
	Divide The Night	Dr Yudel GORDON
	Dividend On Death	Michael SHAYNE
The	Divinations Of Kala Persad And Other Stories	Kala PERSAD
The	Division Bell Mystery	Robert WEST and Donald SHAW
	Dixie City Jam	Det Dave ROBICHAUX
	Dixon Hawke's Case Book. No 1	Dixon HAWKE
	Dixon Hawke's Case Book. No 20	Dixon HAWKE
	Dixon Of Dock Green	Sgt George DIXON
	Dixon Of Dock Green	Sgt George DIXON
	Do Androids Dream Of Electric Sheep?	Rick DECKARD
	Do Not Murder Before Christmas	Rocky ROCKWELL
	Do Unto Others	Jordan POTEET
The	Doberman Wore Black	Dr Gordon CHRISTY
	Doc Grip, The Sporting Detective; Or, The Vendetta	'Doc' GRIP
	Docken Dead	Martin COTTERELL
The	Doctor And The Corpse	Michael WEST
	Doctor Bentiron: Detective	Dr BENTIRON
	Doctor Death	Kyle YOUNGBLOOD
The	Doctor Died At Dusk	Robin BISHOP
	Doctor Dodds' Experiment	Dr Septimus DODDS
	Doctor Jaz	Dr JAZ
The	Doctor Looks At Murder	Lt Peter DONNEGAN
	Doctor Quartz, Magician; Or, The Most Dangerous Criminal Alive	Doctor QUARTZ
	Doctor Quartz's Quick Move; Or, Cleverness Personified	Doctor QUARTZ
	Doctor Syn	Dr SYN
	Doctors Beware!	Carey GALBREATH
The	Doctor's Case	Sherlock HOLMES
The	Doctor's Crime; Or, Simply Horrible!	Robert SPICER
The	Documents In The Case	Lord Peter WIMSEY
The	Dodd Cases	Cedric DODD
The	Dog Collar Murders	Pam NILSEN
The	Dog Detective And His Young Master	BRINDLE
	Dog Eat Dog	Pierre O'BRIEN
A	Dog Fight With Death	Peter CASTLE and 'Twisted Face' STRAUSSMAN
	Dog Heavies	Lucas HALLAM
	Dog In The Dark	John CUNNINGHAM
The	Dog Track Murder	Sexton BLAKE
The	Dogs Do Bark	Dr Hugh WESTLAKE
	Dog's Body	Linus RINTOUL
	Doing Wrong	Insp Ganesh GHOTE
	Dollmaker	Insp ST CYR and Hermann KOHLER
	Dolls And Dollars	Johnny DEKKER
	Dolls Are Deadly	Michael SHAYNE
	Dolly And The Bird Of Paradise	Johnson JOHNSON
	Dolly And The Bird Of Paradise	Johnson JOHNSON
	Dolly And The Singing Bird	Johnson JOHNSON
The	Dolly Dolly Spy	Philip MCALPINE
The	Doll's Bad News	Dave FENNER
The	Dolorosa Deal	Sam WEBSTER
The	Dolphin Mystery	Don PAULSON
	Dominant Third	Antoine CIRRET
The	Dominican Affair	Nick CARTER
	Dominick Squeek, The Bow Street Runner; Or, An English Detective In America	Dominick SQUEEK
The	Domino Principle	Roy TUCKER
The	Domino Vendetta	Roy TUCKER
	Dominoes	Ch Insp/Supt LENNOX
	Don Balasco Of Key West	Thomas DUFF
	Don Q In The Sierras	Don Q
	Don Q's Love Story	Don Q
	Donald Dyke, The Down-East Detective	Donald DYKE

D

Donald Dyke, The Yankee Detective	Donald DYKE
Donavan	Paul DONAVAN
Donavan's Delight	Paul DONAVAN
The Donnington Affair	Father BROWN
The Donovan Case	Tom LANGLEY
Donovan Of Whitehall	DONOVAN
Don't Break The Seal	Nick ROCKWELL
Don't Call Tonight	Joe PUMA
Don't Catch Me	Arabella BLAKE and Andy BLAKE
Don't Count The Corpses	Brian BRETT
Don't Crowd Me!	Pete GARROWAY
Don't Cry For Me	Pete WORDEN
Don't Dig Deeper	Steve CASH
Don't Drop Dead Tomorrow	Julian QUIST
Don't Ever Love Me	Lt Max GOLD
Don't Get Caught	Milo MARCH
Don't Lie To Me	Mitch TOBIN
Don't Look Behind You!	Prof Paul HATFIELD
Don't Mess With Murder	Martin ROSS
Don't Point That Thing At Me	Charlie MORTDECAI
Don't Shoot, Darling	Insp Jim SILVER and Mike LOGAN
Don't Take It To Heart	Insp Martin LAIDMAN
Don't Turn Your Back On The Ocean	Jeri HOWARD
Don't Wake Me Up While I'm Driving	Hal BRADY
The Doomed Quartet	Dan TURNER
The Doomsday List	Adam BRECK
Doomsday Vendetta	Peter WINSTON
The Door	Insp HARRISON
The Door	Britt (Mind Masters) ST VINCENT
The Door Of Death	Insp Rae NORSE
The Door To Doom And Other Detections	Juge d'Instruction Henri BENCOLIN
The Door To Doom And Other Detections	Dr Gideon FELL
The Door To Doom And Other Detections	Sherlock HOLMES
Door To Enigma	CROYD
Doors To Death	Eric HAZARD
Doorway To Death	Johnny KILLAIN
Doowinkle DA	John DOOWINKLE
Dope	Ch Insp Daniel 'Red' KERRY
The Dope Dealers	Tommy LUMB and Peter MARSHAM
Dope Devils	Royston FRERE
Dope Is For Dopes	Bill TRUSCOTT
Dope Opera	Stan GARLAND
Doppelganger	Insp CHERRY
The Doppelganger Gambit	Janna BRILL and Mahlon MAXWELL
Dora Myrl, The Lady Detective	Dora MYRL
Dorcas Dene, Detective	Dorcas DENE
Dorcas Dene, Detective: Second Series	Dorcas DENE
The Dorking Gap Affair	Mycroft HOLMES
The Dorothy Parker Murder Case	Dorothy PARKER and Alexander WOOLLCOTT
The Dorrington Deed-Box	DORRINGTON
The Dossier	André KOHL
Dossier Closed	Mark RANDALL
Dossier Ix	Jacob ASHER
The Dossier Of Solar Pons	Solar PONS
Dossier On A Mantis	Adam KANE
Double	NAMELESS DETECTIVE and Sharon MCCONE
The Double Agent	Kenneth DUCANE
The Double Agent	Sam HOOK
The Double Alibi	Hilda ADAMS
Double Cross Purposes	Miles BREDON and Angela BREDON
Double Daughter	Nyla WADE
Double Death	Insp Richard LEFT
Double Exposure	Stoney WINSTON
Double Feature	Richard POWELL
Double For Death	Tecumseh FOX
A Double For Detection	Ch Insp Julian RIVERS
Double Identity	Alan CARLISLE
Double Jeopardy	George Helmfleet JONES
Double Jeopardy	Skelton KYNE
Double Kill	Jock SERGEANT
The Double M Man	Mike MCCALL
Double Negative	Jeremy COOK
Double Plot	Bill HAWLEY
The Double Shuffle	Steve HARMAS
The Double Take	Stuart BAILEY
Double Take	January ESPOSITO
Double Take	KLEIN
The Double Tenth	David KENT
The Double Thumb	Prof WELLS
Double Trouble	Dave WINTINO
Double Whammy	R J DECKER
The Doublecross	Jimmy TREYNOR
A Double-Barrelled Detective Story	Sherlock HOLMES
Doubtful Motives	Deirdre O'HARA
Doubting Thomas	Thomas C THERON
The Dove	Carl GOOD
Dover Beats The Band	Insp Wilfred DOVER
Dover One	Insp Wilfred DOVER
The Dover Train Mystery	Monsieur DUPUY
Down Among The Ad Men	Sexton BLAKE
Down Among The Dead Men	David NAIRN
Down For The Count	Toby PETERS and Joe LOUIS
The Down Home Heifer Heist	Sheriff Sam TITUS and Nicky TITUS
Down In The Valley	Vic DANIEL
Down In The Zero	BURKE
Down To Death	Insp Matthew FURNIVAL
Down Yonder With Judge Priest	Judge PRIEST
Downbeat For A Dirge	Hampton HUME
Downey Of The Mounted	Cpl DOWNEY
Downtown	Michael BARNES
The Downward Path	Rex BANNER
Downwind	Nathan HAWK
Dowry Of Death	Capt Prem NARAYAN
Dr Bruderstein Vanishes	Charles BLESSINGTON
Dr Burton	Dr BURTON
Dr Burton's Success	Dr BURTON
Dr Cunliffe - Investigator	Richard CUNLIFFE
Dr Death	Nick CARTER
Dr Fell, Detective, And Other Stories	Dr Gideon FELL
Dr Jekyll And Mr Holmes	Sherlock HOLMES
Dr Mephisto	Dr MEPHISTO and Monsieur HIGNETTE
Dr Morelle And The Drummer Girl	Dr MORELLE
Dr Morelle Meets Murder And Other Adventures	Dr MORELLE
Dr Orient	Dr Owen ORIENT
Dr Phibes	Dr PHIBES
Dr Phibes Rises Again	Dr PHIBES
Dr Sam: Johnson, Detector	Dr Sam JOHNSON
Dr Satan	Dr SATAN
Dr Scarlett	Dr SCARLETT
Dr Tancred Begins: Or, The Pendexter Saga	Ben TANCRED and Supt Henry WILSON
Dr Thorndyke's Cases	Dr John Evelyn THORNDYKE
Dr Thorndyke's Case-Book	Dr John Evelyn THORNDYKE
Dr Thorndyke's Dilemma	Dr John Evelyn THORNDYKE
Dr Toby Finds Murder	Dr Quentin TOBY
Dr Vane Answers The Call	Dr VANE
Dr Watson And Mr Holmes: Or, The Worm That Turned	Sherlock HOLMES
Dr Watson And The Invisible Man	Dr John H WATSON
Dr Yen Sin	Yen SIN
Drag Me Down	Johnny BUCHANAN
Dragoman Pass	Roger STARTE and Kate STARTE
Dragon	Dirk PITT
Dragon Hunt	Peter BRAID
The Dragon In Harness	Jack CLAYTON
The Dragon In Spring	Hawk MACRAE
The Dragon Of Lung Wang	Graydon MCKELVIE
Dragon Road	Dorian SILK
The Dragon Slayings	Alex (The Protector) DARTANIAN
Dragon Spoor	SPECIAL OPERATIONS EXECUTIVE
The Dragon Strikes Back	Bill MANDELL and Capt Andrew LEE
Dragon's Teeth	Janna BRILL and Mahlon MAXWELL
Draw The Blinds	Ch Insp GIDLEIGH
Draw The Curtain Close	MAC
Dread	Gentle HOGGERTY
Dread Brass Shadows	GARRETT
The Dread Cave	William BRITTAIN
The Dream	Dr William AMES and Det LONEGAN
The Dream Doctor	Prof Craig KENNEDY
The Dream Girl Caper	Angela HARPE
Dream Of A Fair Woman	Matt CUNEEN
Dream Sinister	Dr Quentin TOBY
The Dream Walker	Charley IVES
The Dreamer At Large	Supt Donald (The Dreamer) REAMER
The Dreaming Detective	Sherlock HOLMES
Dreaming Of Babylon	C CARD
The Dream-Detective	Morris KLAW
The Dress Circle Murders	Sandy BLUNT
Dressed To Kill	Lyle CURTIS and Susan YATES
Dressed To Kill	Rusty FORBES
A Dressing Of Diamond	Insp Henri CASTANG
The Drexel Dream	Sir Nigel LACAITA
Drifting Death	Roy MACLEAN
The Drill Is Death	Det Nathan SHAPIRO
Drilling For Death	Johnny MCCOY
A Drink For Mr Cherry	Mr WATSON
Drink The Green Water	William (Sultans' Harem) SULTAN
Drink To Yesterday	Tommy HAMBLEDON
Drive East On 66	Lt Andy BASTIAN
Driven Death	Anthony RILLINGTON
Driven To Death	Charlie RYAN
Driven To Kill	Sexton BLAKE
Driven To Kill	Jim O'NEILL
Driving Force	Freddie CROFT
A Drop In The Ocean	Barry DONOVAN
The Drop Of A Hat	Victoria TARRANT
The Drop Of A Pin	Richard VERNER
Drop To His Death	Dr Horatio GLASS
Drown All The Dogs	Det Neil 'Hock' HOCKADAY
Drown Him Deep	Insp GIBBON
Drown The Wind	Gil DONAN
The Drowner	Paul STANIAL
The Drowning Pool	Lew ARCHER
The Drowning Pool	Lew ARCHER
A Drug Called Power	Tim BLACKGROVE
A Drug In The Market	Dennis DOYNE
A Drug On The Market	PAOLA and GEORGE
A Drug On The Market	Whit WHITNEY
Druid's Blood	Brihtvic DONNE
Drum Beat - Marianne	Chester DRUM
The Drums Of Jeopardy	Cutty CLAY
Drums Of The Dark Gods	Richard QUINTAIN
Drury Lane's Last Case	Drury LANE
The Dry White Tear	Timothy Seamus Wolfe SHERIDAN
Duane And The Art Murders	Stephen DUANE
Duane And The G-Men	Stephen DUANE
Duane Of The FBI	Stephen DUANE
Duca And The Milan Murders	Duca LAMBERTI
Due To A Death	NICHOLSON
Duet For Two Guns	Danny SPADE
Duffy	Nick DUFFY
The Duke And The Veil	Nicholas COFFIN
The Duke Of York's Steps	Ch Insp POOLE
The Duke's Feather	Picklock HOLES
Dulcie Bligh	Dulcie BLIGH
The Dumb Detective	The DUMB DETECTIVE
The Dumb Witness And Other Stories	Nick CARTER
The Dumbo Dossier	Guy FOSSE
The Dummy Murder Case	Prof CALDWELL
The Dump	Insp BLISS
Dumphry	Cdr DUMPHRY
A Dum-Dum For The President	Mike GARFIN

D

	Title	Character
	Dupe	Anna LEE
	Dupe Negative	Richard POWELL
The	Duplicate	David HALLIDAY
	Durgon, The Detective: Or, The Clerk's Crime	DURGON
	Dusky Limelight	Edward NORTH
	Dust And The Curious Boy	Joe DUST
	Dust In Your Eyes	Insp Martin LAIDMAN
	Dusty Coinage	John HOWDEN
	Dusty Death	Peter CLANCY
	Dusty Death	Clay HARRISON
	Dusty Death	Insp HAWLING and Prof ERSKINE
	Duty Elsewhere	Insp David LYLE
The	Duveen Letter	Rupert CONWAY
	Dying Breath	Dean GRANT
	Dying Day	Ron HOGGETT
A	Dying Fall	NETTERLY
	Dying High	Jerome AYLWIN
	Dying To Help	Anna MCCOLL
The	Dying Trade	Cliff HARDY
	Dying Voices	Prof Carl BURNS
	Dyke And Burr, The Rival Detectives	DYKE and BURR
	Dyke Darrel, The Railroad Detective: Or, The Crime Of The Midnight Express	Dyke DARREL
	Dym Darke, Detective: The History Of A Celebrated Case	Dym DARKE
	Dynamite Drury	'Dynamite' DRURY
	Dynamite Drury Again	'Dynamite' DRURY
	Dynamite Drury Patrols	'Dynamite' DRURY
	Dynamite Monster Boogie Concert	Terry (Chopper Cop) BUNKER
The	Dynamiters	Sherlock HOLMES

— E —

	Title	Character
	E T A For Death	Steve RAMSAY
The	Eagle Has Landed	Liam DEVLIN
	Eagle Six	Martyn CALE
	Eagles Die Too	Jessica JAMES
The	Eames-Erskine Case	Insp POINTER
An	Ear To The Ground	Al BARNEY
An	Ear To The Ground	
The	Earhart Betrayal	Joe SNOW
	Early Morning Poison	Supt MANNING
The	Earthquake Machine	Sherlock HOLMES
	East Beach	Jake SANDS
The	East Side Detective	The EAST SIDE DETECTIVE
	Easy Prey	Claude WARRINGTON-REEVE and Insp Steven MITCHELL
	Easy To Kill	Supt BATTLE and Luke FITZWILLIAMS
An	Easy Way To Go	Kent MURDOCK
	Ebenezer Investigates	Rev Ebenezer BUCKLE
The	Ebony Bed Murder	Griffin SCOTT
The	Ebony Cross	Nick CARTER
The	Ebony Torso	Insp HOPTON
	Echo Of A Bomb	Richard MASSEY
	Echoes Of Zero	Rip DESTON
	Ed Somers, The Pinkerton Detective	Ed SOMERS
	Eddie Gorgon Calls The Tune	Eddie GORGON
	Eddie Gorgon Takes The Rap	Eddie GORGON
	Eddy Deco's Last Caper	Eddy DECO
The	Edge Of The Forest	Nick NICHOLSON
	Edited Out	Carmen RAMIREZ
	Edsel	Connie MINOR
An	Educated Death	Henry GARRETT
	Educated Evans	'Educated' EVANS
The	Educated Harpoon	Joe FENNER
The	Educated Man	'Educated' EVANS
The	Education Of Mr P J Davenant	P J DAVENANT
	Edwin Of The Iron Shoes	Sharon MCCONE
	Eenie, Meenie, Minie - Murder!	Cornelius DUFFY
	Egyptian Nights	Bimbashi BAUK
	Egypt's Choice	Harry EGYPT
The	Eiger Sanction	Prof Jonathan HEMLOCK
	Eight Card Stud	Nick CARTER
	Eight Dogs Flying	Samantha HOLT
	Eight Faces At Three	Jake JUSTUS, Helene JUSTUS and John J MALONE
	Eight Murders In The Suburbs	Insp J RASON
The	Eighth Circle	Murray KIRK
The	Eighth Commandment	Mary Lou 'Dunk' BATESON
The	Eisenhower Deception	Charles WINTER
	Eleanor's Victory	Gilbert MONKTON
	Election By Murder	Martin AMES
	Electric City	Jane DA SILVA
The	Electric Light Detective: Or, Solving The Mysteries Of An Old Graveyard	The ELECTRIC LIGHT DETECTIVE
	Elegy In A Country Graveyard	Andrew QUENTIN and Jane WINFIELD
	Elementary Pascal	Sherlock HOLMES
	Elementary, My Dear Holmes	Sherlock HOLMES
	Elementary, My Dear Watson	Sherlock HOLMES
	Elementary, My Dear Watson (The Tale Of 4 Clubs)	Sherlock HOLMES
	Elephants Can Remember	Hercule POIROT and Mrs Ariadne OLIVER
The	Elevated Railway Mystery And Other Stories	Nick CARTER
The	Elgar Variations	Insp/Ch Insp Harry PECKOVER
The	Eliminator	Jonas WILDE
	Elizabeth Finds The Body	ELIZABETH
	Elizabeth Glen, MB: The Experiences Of A Lady Doctor	Elizabeth GLEN
	Elizabeth The Sleuth	ELIZABETH
The	Elusive Mr Drago	Mike SETON
The	Elvis Murders	Claude 'Snake' KIRLIN and F T ZEVICH
	Elvis, Jesus And Coca-Cola	Kinky FRIEDMAN
The	Embarrassed Ladies Affair	Soeur ANGELE
The	Embarrassed Murderer	Kingsley TOPLITT and Sally TOPLITT
An	Embarrassing Death	Bill STEMPLE
	Embrace Of The Butcher	Peter KING
	Embrace The Wolf	Leo HAGGERTY
The	Embroidered Sunset	Lucy CULPEPPER
The	Emerald Chicks Caper	Jerry 'Renegade' ROE and Stuart WORTH
	Emerald Jim, The Irish Boy Detective	EMERALD JIM
The	Emerald Murder Trap	Paul SAVOY
	Emeralds Of Shade	Buck JASON
	Emergency Exit	John PIPER
	Emperor Of Evil	Vee BROWN
	Empire 99	Star HAWKS
The	Empty House	Peter MANCIPLE
The	Empty Sleeve	Philip MARLOWE
	Empty Tigers	Greg FLAMM
The	Enchanted Desert	Henry Napoleon BAGGS
The	Enchanted Type-Writer	Sherlock HOLMES
	Encounter Three	Steve AUSTIN
	Encyclopedia Brown And The Case Of The Secret Pitch	'Encyclopedia' BROWN
	End Of A Call Girl	Joe PUMA
The	End Of A Cigarette	Kenneth O'BRIEN
	End Of A JD	Harry HORNE
The	End Of Lieutenant Boruvka	Lt BORUVKA
The	End Of Mr Garment	Walter GHOST
The	End Of Sherlock Holmes	Sherlock HOLMES
	End Of The Game	Kommissar Hans BARLACH
	End Of The Line	John FARREL
The	End Of The Mildew Gang	Insp CAULDRON
The	End Of The Rug	Edmund TROTHE
The	Endless Game	Alec HILLSDEN
	Enemies Of The Bride	Patrick C SHIRLEY and Insp Rip IRVING
	Enemy And Brother	John EAKINS
The	Enemy Within The Gates	'Bunny' CHIPSTEAD
	Energy Zero	Colin 'Big Brain' GARRETT
An	English Murder	Wencelaus BOTTWINK
The	Englishman Of The Rue Cain	TOPPIN
	Enigma Of The Talking Wraith	Jimmy ROSS
The	Enigma Variations	Eliot UPTON
The	Enormous Hour Glass	Sam BRIMMER
	Enough!	John EDGARSON
	Enquiries Are Continuing	Det Insp Don KERRY
The	Enquiries Of Dr Eszterhazy	Dr ESZTERHAZY
	Enquiry	Kelly HUGHES
	Enrollment Cancelled	Prof A PENNYFEATHER
	Enter Craig Kennedy	Prof Craig KENNEDY
	Enter Dr Nikola	Dr NIKOLA
	Enter Second Murderer	Insp Jeremy FARO
	Enter Sir John	Sir John SAUMAREZ
	Enter The Ace	Justin (The Ace) MARCH
	Enter The Crimson Mask	CRIMSON MASK
	Enter The Dormouse	Clive 'Dormouse' CONRAD
	Enter The Lion	Mycroft HOLMES and Sherlock HOLMES
	Enter The Saint	Simon (The Saint) TEMPLAR
The	Entry From San Sebastian	Dave HILL
	Envoy On Excursion	Insp Adam QUILL
	Epitaph For A Dead Actor	Insp CARDIFF
	Epitaph For A Loser	Paul BRODER
	Epitaph For A Tramp	Harry FANNIN
	Epitaph To A Bad Cop	Charles DEXTER
	Epitaph To Treason	Sexton BLAKE
The	Eppworth Case	Sebald CRAFT
An	Equal Opportunity Death	Vejay HASKELL
The	Erection Set	Dogeron KELLY
	Eric Peters, Pullman Porter	Eric PETERS
	Errant Sleuth	Greg ALLARD
The	Escalator	David TROY
The	Escapades Of Mr Alfred Dimmock	Alfred DIMMOCK
	Escape	Dudley ALLWRIGHT
The	Escape	Maxine DANGERFIELD
	Escape And Be Secret	Paul HARVARD
	Escape From Liberty	Aubrey St John MAJOR
	Escape From Murder	Bill RICE
	Escape Into The Night	Peter CAREY
The	Escape Of Mr Trimm	Judge PRIEST
The	Escape Of The Bulldog	Picklock HOLES
	Escape Out Of Darkness	Maggie BENNETT
	Escape To Danger	Lucy BECK
	Escape To Eternity	Daniel J CLUER
	Espionage!	Greg MARLOWE
	Essence D'Orient	Philip MARLOWE
The	Essex Murders	Insp BREWS
	Estate Of Grace	Tom PARCHER
The	Ethiopian's Secret	Sexton BLAKE
The	Etruscan Bull	Tom LOGAN
	Eugène Vidocq, Soldier, Thief, Spy, Detective: A Romance Founded On Facts	Eugène VIDOCQ
The	Eurasian Virgins	Curt STONE
The	Euro-Killers	Jan ARGAND
The	Eve Of The Wedding	Kate THEOBALD
	Even Cops' Daughters	Tommy INMAN
	Even Doctors Die	Peter ALLEN
	Even My Foot's Asleep	John TIBBETT
The	Evergreen Death	Insp/Supt Bill AVEYARD
	Evermore	Edgar Allan POE
	Every Breath You Take	Laura PRINCIPAL
	Every Deadly Sin	Rev Theodora BRAITHWAITE
	Every Inch A Lady	Nat SAPPERTON
	Everybody Makes Mistakes	Craig MCKENZIE
	Everybody's Favorite Duck	Enoch BONE

E

Everything Has Its Price	Supt Konstantin KELLER
Everything You Have Is Mine	Lauren LAURANO
The Evidence I Shall Give	Ch Insp/Supt LENNOX
Evidence Of The Accused	Supt POPE
Evidence Unseen	Nora Hughes BLAINE and Larry BLAINE
Evil At Whispering Hills	Whispering HILLS
An Evil Hour	Harry CAMBERT
Evil Intent	RIPLEY
The Evil Men Do	Ethel THOMAS
The Evil Messenger	Martin HUISH
The Evil Of The Day	Capt RIZZI
The Exact Opposite	Lester LEITH
Excellent Intentions	Insp FENBY
An Excellent Knave	Geoffrey GILLESBY
An Excellent Night For Murder	Rocky ALLAN
Except For One Thing	Insp GARTH
The Exchange	Jake (The Liquidator) BRAND
The Executioners	Det Ch Supt Simon SHARD
Exercise In Terror	Maureen DIETZ and Helen KATZ
Exeunt Murderers	Nick NOBLE
Exeunt Murderers	Sister URSULA
The Exile Kiss	Marid AUDRAN
Exit Actors, Dying	Sir Toby GLENDOWER and Penelope SPRING
Exit Arnholt	ARNHOLT
Exit Laughing	Hildegarde WITHERS
Exit Mr Brent	Peter CASTLE
Exit Mr Punch	Mrs Edwina CHARLES
Exit Only	Insp SLANE
Exit Pretty Poll	Harry TONG
Exit Running	Carney WILDE
Exit Sherlock Holmes: The Great Detective's Final Days	Dr John H WATSON
Exit The Disguiser	Timothy Overbury 'Tiger' STANDISH
Exit The Harlequin	Gregory 'Grischa' PAVLOV
Exit To Music: A Problem In Detection	Ch Insp Michael 'Napper' TANDY
Exit To Violence	Insp/Supt ANDERS
The Exorcist	Bill KINDERMAN
Expect No Mercy	Quentin EADY
Expected Death	Insp/Supt MALLETT
The Expendable Man	Hugh DENSMORE
An Expensive Place To Die	Harry PALMER
Experience With Evil	Howard CROSS
Experiences Of A Bond Street Jeweller	IMPEY
The Experiences Of A French Detective Officer	Theodore DUHAMEL
The Experiences Of A French Detective Officer	A FRENCH DETECTIVE OFFICER
The Experiences Of A French Police Officer	Theodore DUHAMEL
The Experiences Of A Lady Detective	Mrs PASCHAL
Experiences Of A Real Detective	INSPECTOR F
The Experiences Of Loveday Brooke, Lady Detective	Loveday BROOKE
Experiment With Death	Emma RITCHIE
Experiment With Death	Emma RITCHIE
Experiments In Crime And Other Stories	Kyra SOKRATESCU
The Exploding Lake	'Doc' SAVAGE
The Exploits Of A Physician Detective	Dr FURNIVALL
The Exploits Of A Private Detective	Felix BOYD
The Exploits Of A Race-Course Detective	Valentine MARTYN
The Exploits Of Arsène Lupin	Arsène LUPIN
Exploits Of Asaf Khan	Asaf KHAN
Exploits Of Beau Quicksilver	Beau QUICKSILVER
The Exploits Of Billy The Page	BILLY THE PAGE
The Exploits Of Capt McKeene	Deville MCKEENE
The Exploits Of Captain O'Hagan	Capt O'HAGAN
The Exploits Of Danby Croker	Danby CROKER
The Exploits Of Dick Tracy, Detective: The Case Of The Brow	Dick TRACY
The Exploits Of Dr Sam: Johnson, Detector	Dr Sam JOHNSON
The Exploits Of Elaine	Prof Craig KENNEDY
The Exploits Of Fidelity Dove	Fidelity DOVE
The Exploits Of Fidelity Dove	Fidelity DOVE
The Exploits Of Fidelity Dove	Insp G RASON and Fidelity DOVE
The Exploits Of Fidelity Dove	Insp G RASON and Fidelity DOVE
The Exploits Of Jo Salis, A British Spy	Jo SALIS
The Exploits Of Jonathan Jow	Jonathan JOW
The Exploits Of Kesho Naik, Dacoit	Kesho NAIK
The Exploits Of Sherlock Holmes	Sherlock HOLMES
The Exploits Of The Chevalier Dupin	Chevalier Auguste C DUPIN
An Explosive Encounter	Sherlock HOLMES
Expo '98: Sherlock Holmes In Omaha	Sherlock HOLMES
Express Delivery	Mike HARMAN
The Expressman And The Detective	Allan PINKERTON
Extracurricular Activities	Jaine (The Bionic Woman) SOMMERS
The Extraordinary Case Of Mr Bell	Archibald PENNY
Extremes Meet	Cdr Roger WATERLOW
The Ex-Detective	Malcolm GOSSETT
The Ex-Pugilist Detective	YANKEE RUE
The Eye	E L OXMAN and Art TOBIN
An Eye For An Eye	'Rocky' Aloysius Algernon STEELE
An Eye For An Eye	Victor STRAWN
An Eye For An Eye: A Mystery	Frank URWIN
Eye Hath Not Seen...	Father O'CONNOR
The Eye In Attendance	Insp MANDERTON and Det Sgt Trevor DENE
The Eye In The Museum	Supt ROSS
Eye In The Ring	Miles JACOBY
The Eye Of Anna	Mark SHIGATA
The Eye Of The Beholder	The EYE
The Eye Of The Beholder	Tom PILTER
The Eye Of The Beholder	Hank SULLIVAN
The Eye Of The Hurricane	Philip SCOTT
Eye To Eye	Ashton FORD
Eye Witness	Lt/Capt George HONEGGER
The Eyes Of Death	Sir Richard HERRIVELL
The Eyes Of Max Carrados	Max CARRADOS
The Eyes Of The Tiger	Nick CARTER
The Eyes On Utopia Murders	Dr Gerritt DEGRAAF

— F —

F As In Flight	Det Jub FREEMAN and Det Bill DECKER
F Corridor	Insp Victor BONDURANT and Paul RAVEL
The Fabulous Clipjoint	Ambrose HUNTER and Ed HUNTER
The Fabulous Wink	Insp ROBINET
Face Of Danger	Mike KING
The Face Of The Abbot	Dixon DRUCE
The Face Of The Man From Saturn	Jimmie KENTLAND
The Face Of The Tiger	Lou FABIAN
The Face On The Cutting Room Floor	A B C MULLER
Face Value	Aubrey St John MAJOR
Face Value	Richard PATTON and Amelia PATTON
The Faceless Adversary	Det Nathan SHAPIRO
The Faces Of Danger	Prof Stuff DRISCOLL
The Faces Of Murder	Joe MANNIX
The Factory	Samuel BELL
Fade Into Murder	Sgt FOWELL
Fadeout	Dave BRANDSTETTER
The Fair	Sherlock HOLMES
Fair Game	Det Jessica DRAKE
Fair Game	Det Ch Insp Douglas QUANTRILL
Fair Means Or Foul?	Det Insp Dave STARK
The Fair-Haired Lady	Arsène LUPIN and Herlock SHOLMES
Faith	Bernard SAMSON
Faith, Hope And Charity	Judge PRIEST
The Fala Factor	Toby PETERS and Eleanor ROOSEVELT
The Falcon Meets A Lady	The FALCON
The Falcon Mystery	Frank DESPARD
Falconer's Crusade	William FALCONER
The Falcon's Prey	The FALCON
Falklands Gambit	Martin SEGUNDO
Fall From Grace	Nan DUNLAP
A Fall From Grace	James HELDER
The Fall Guy	Arthur PHILIS
Fall Guy For A Killer	Joe DEVLIN
Fall Guy For Murder	Johnny SATURDAY
Fall Into My Grave	Amanda CURZON and Oscar SALLIS
The Fall Of Marty Moon	Duncan PRIDE
Fallen Among Thieves: A Novel Of Interest	John BARMAN
Fallen Into The Pit	George FELSE and Dominic FELSE
The Fallen Sparrow	Insp TOBIN
Falling Angel	Harry ANGEL
The Falling Blonde	CANNON
The Falling Man	Paul SHAW
Falls The Shadow	Amos SHOMRON
False Alibi	Det Supt Mark PEMBERTON
False Cards	BULLOCK
False Conception	John Marshall TANNER
False Confessions	Doug ORLANDO
False Face	Bruce PERKINS and William Rutherford CRANE
False Impressions	Ellie GORDON
The False Inspector Dew	Walter BARANOV
The False Inspector Dew: A Murder Mystery Aboard The SS Mauretania, 1921	Insp DEW
False Pretences	Jacob ASCH
False Profit	Paul MARSTON
False Witness	Det Sgt STEYTLER
Falseface	Richard OWEN
False-Face	Sir Brian FORDINGHAME and Baron VESSELOFFSKY
The Fame Hotel	Det Insp Simon POTTER
A Family Affair	Nero WOLFE
Family Album	MEREN
Family Album	Ch Joe SILVA
Family Reunion	Jenny HOLLAND
Family Skeletons	Lt Timothy TRANT
The Family Stalker	Kit DELEEUW
The Family Vault	Sarah KELLING and Max BITTERSOHN
A Famine Of Horses	Sir Robert CAREY
The Famous McGarry Stories	Det Dan MCGARRY
The Fan Who Molded Himself	Sherlock HOLMES
The Fanatics	Cdr Allan DICE
Fangs Of The Cobra	Wade HAMMOND
The Fangs Of The Hooded Demon	Lincoln BLACKTHORNE
Fannin	Harry FANNIN
Fantasy And Fugue	Harry SINTON
Fantomas	FANTOMAS
The Far Sands	James RENISON and Carol RENISON
The Far West Detective	The FAR WEST DETECTIVE
Farewell By Death	Brad STERLING
Farewell Nikola	Dr NIKOLA
Farewell To Peril	Mike SLATTERY
Farewell, Little Sister	CANNON
Farewell, My Lovely	Philip MARLOWE
Farewell, My Lovely Appetizer	Mike NOONAN
The Fascinator	Jonas WILDE
Fashioned For Murder	Jerry NASON
Fast And Loose	Insp FASKE
Fast Company	Joel GLASS
Fat Chance	Joe SHAW
The Fat Innkeeper	Am CAULFIELD
A Fat Man With A Dollar	Joe KELLY
Fat Man's Agony	Sir Abercrombie LEWKER
Fata Morgana	Paul PICARD
Fatal Bride	Richard MASSEY

	Title	Character
	Fatal Descent	Dr Horatio GLASS
	Fatal End	Det Insp James ROLAND
The	Fatal Equilibrium	Prof Henry SPEARMAN
The	Fatal Finger Mark, Rose Courtenay's First Case	Rose COURTENAY
	Fatal Finish	Harry LANSING
The	Fatal Five Minutes	Philip TOLEFREE
	Fatal Flashback	Nina MCFALL and Lt Dino ROSSI
	Fatal Flourishes	Capt CORK
The	Fatal Foursome	Johnny LIDDELL
	Fatal Opinions	Ch Insp Alec STAINTON
	Fatal Stranger	Hank SULLIVAN
	Fatal Woman	Peter DULUTH
	Fatality In Fleet Street	Charles VENABLES
	Father Hayes	Father HAYES
	Father's Law	Det Ch Supt Harry FATHERS
The	Favor	Ray GUINNESS
	FBI Story	John RIPLEY
	Fea	Gentle HOGGERTY
	Fear And Miss Betony	Ch Insp Dan PARDOE
	Fear By Instalments	Mike MERRIMAN
	Fear Followed On	Insp WAKE
	Fear For Miss Betony	Ch Insp Dan PARDOE
	Fear Fortune, Father	Det Ch Insp BRENTFORD
	Fear In The Wind	Eve GILL
	Fear No More	Jay ROGERS
	Fear Of The Dark	Aaron GUNNER
	Fear Runs Softly	Grant GARFIELD
	Fear To Tread	Insp HAZELRIGG
	Fear Walked Behind	Sebastian QUIN
	Fearful Symmetry	Lisa DAVIS
A	Fearful Thing	Insp Gregory PELLEW and Viscount CLYMPING
A	Fearful Way To Die	Lace WHITE
	Feast Into Mourning	Det Sgt Jerry HUNTER
	Featuring The Saint	Simon (The Saint) TEMPLAR
A	February Mourning	Dee STREET
	Federal Bullets	Dan FOWLER
	Feeding Frenzy	'Soc' SOCARIDES
The	Feldisham Mystery	Insp Charles François FURNEAUX
	Felidae	FRANCIS
	Felidae On The Road	FRANCIS
	Felix Boyd's Final Problems	Felix BOYD
	Felix Boyd's Revelations	Felix BOYD
	Fell Purpose	Judge Ephraim Peabody PECK
	Fellowship Of Fear	Gideon OLIVER
The	Fellowship Of The Frog	Sgt/Insp ELK
	Fellow-Traveler	REMSEN
	Felon In Disguise	Insp Tom ANDERSON
The	Female Barber Detective: Or, Joe Phoenix In Silver City	Mignon LAWRENCE
The	Female Detective	Mrs GLADDEN
	Feminine For Spy	Howard DIGBURN
	Fen Country	Gervase FEN
	Fen Country	Gervase FEN and Insp HUMBLEBY
	Fenton Of The Foreign Service	Lawrie FENTON
The	Ferguson Affair	Bill GUNNERSON
	Fernanda	FERNANDA
	Fer-De-Lance	Nero WOLFE
	Festering Lilies	Willow KING
	Festival	Ch Const Piet DEVENTER
	Fetch Me A Rope	Paul SCARF
	Fete Fatale	Helen KITTEREGE
	Fetish	Det Carl PEDERSON
The	Feud Of Fear	Sexton BLAKE
	Fever Grass	Robin MCKAY
The	Fever Of Life	Archie MAXWELL
A	Few Dying Words	Sheriff Matt GABRIEL
A	Few Small Bones	Insp MCCAIG
	Fiasco In Fulham	Claude WARRINGTON-REEVE and Insp Steven MITCHELL
The	Fiddling Cracksman	Billy HEMPLE
The	Fidelio Score	Geoffrey LANDON
The	Fields Of Eden	Sheriff Emil WHIPPLETREE
	Fiends Of The Family	Insp SWINTON
The	Fifth Dagger	Lt Peter DONNEGAN
The	Fifth Grave	Steve CRAVEN
The	Fifth Rapunzel	Det Ch Insp Tom MAYBRIDGE
The	Fifth Script	Lacy LOCKINGTON
	Fifty-Two Pickup	Harry MITCHELL
	Fighting Against Millions; Or, The Detective In The Jewel Caves Of Kurm	Nick CARTER
	Fighting Back	Alec HOERNER
	Fighting Fool	Val EMERY
The	Figure Of Eight	Christopher PERRIN
	File For Death	Jinsie CARTWRIGHT
A	File On Death	Insp Harry JAMES
	File Under: Deceased	Leah HUNTER
	File Under: Jeopardy	Leah HUNTER
The	Film Of Fear	Richard DUVALL
	Final Act	SPECIAL OPERATIONS EXECUTIVE
The	Final Adventure	Sherlock HOLMES
	Final Appearance	Lace WHITE
	Final Copy	Harry BUTTEN
	Final Cut	Bud BACOLA
	Final Cut	Insp Charlie SALTER
	Final Edit	Nicholas BARLOW
	Final Option	Jerry JEETER
The	Final Pose	Tory BAXTER
The	Final Problem	Sherlock HOLMES
The	Final Problem	Sherlock HOLMES
	Final Proof	Karen LINDSTROM
	Final Proof Or, The Value Of Evidence	Robert Leroy MITCHELL and John BARNES
The	Final Solution	Sherlock HOLMES
	Final Thesis	Nick TOLAND
The	Final Toast	Sherlock HOLMES
	Final Witness	David WRIGHT
	Finale	Tory BAXTER
The	Finances Of Sir John Kinnersley	Sir John KYNNERSLEY
	Find A Victim	Lew ARCHER
	Find Eileen Hardin - Alive!	Duncan PRIDE
	Find Me A Villain	Nina CROWTHER
	Find My Killer	Stonewall Jackson YATES and J D THATCHER
	Find The Body	Supt FOLLY
	Find The Clock	Jeff DARRELL
	Find The Don's Daughter	Shep STONE
	Find The Innocent	Insp Peter CURWEN
	Find The Lady	Insp GRAMPORT
	Find The Woman	Tim ASHER
	Finders Weepers	Mike HALLER
	Finders, Keepers	Ben PORTER and Carrie PORTER
	Finding Maubee	Xavier BROOKE
A	Fine And Private Place	Ellery QUEEN
The	Fine Art Of Murder	Matthew PRIOR
	Fine Distinctions	Kevin BRYCE
The	Fine Italian Hand	Niccoló MACHIAVELLI
A	Fine Night For Dying	Paul CHAVASSE
The	Finger Of Saturn	Robert ROLT
	Fingers For Ransom	Michael REVEL
	Fingers Of Fear	Dr ALCAZAR
	Finish Me Off	Det Frank SESSIONS
	Finnegan's Week	Det Fin FINNEGAN
	Fire Alarm Funeral	Fire Marshal Ben PEDLEY
	Fire And Ice	'Doc' SAVAGE
The	Fire Bug	Insp George JUDD
	Fire Horse	Coley KILLEBREW
	Fire In His Hand	Prof Hugh MELLING
	Fire In The Barley	Dan MALLETT
	Fire Kill	Jock SERGEANT
The	Fire Trap	Dep Sheriff Jake BROWN
A	Firework For Oliver	Nicholas PYM
	Fire-Tongue	Paul HARLEY
	Fire, Burn!	Insp John CHEVIOT
	Firm Ambitions	Rachel GOLD
	First And Last Murder	Sam CARROLL
	First Blood	Dr George BARNABAS
The	First Body	Ch Insp Sam BIRKETT
The	First Case Of Mr Paul Savoy	Paul SAVOY
	First Come, First Kill	John STORM
The	First Deadly Sin	Ex-Plce Edward X DELANEY
	First Degree Murder	Alfred LEWIS
The	First Detective	Sgt Finnbar FRALEIGH
	First Kill All The Lawyers	Samantha ADAMS
	First Prize	Chess HANRAHAN
	First Round Murder	Amos PETRIE
The	First Stone	Sidney ZOOM
	First You Have To Find Him	Frank MOERSON
	Fish And Kill	Montague CORK
A	Fish For Murder	Arthur 'Red' BLAKE and Dan WHEELER
	Fish Story	John DENSON
	Fisherman's Luck	Ben GARDEN
	Fishing Is Dangerous	Ch Insp Douglas GRANT
	Fit For Felony	Ivy MIDDAUGH and Judith PERINO
	Fit To Kill	Michael SHAYNE
	Fit To Kill	Percival TROUT
The	Five And Dime Murders	Ray (The Bodyguard) MARTIN
The	Five Brains	Tommy WESTON
	Five Days To Oblivion	George RIAM
The	Five Faces Of Murder	MCHUGH
	Five Fatal Words	Donald CORNWALL
	Five Gates To Armageddon	Richard DEUTSCH
	Five Little Rich Girls	Leo HAIG
The	Five Orange Pips	Sherlock HOLMES
	Five O'clock Lightning	Russ GARRETT
The	Five Red Stars	Bob PONTING
	Five Signs From Ruby	Paul WILLIAMS
	Five Thousand Pounds Reward	Det AYLIFFE
	Five To Five	Insp WOODS
The	Fix	Stan BRADEN
A	Flair For Affairs	Hilary BRAND
	Flame Of The Forest	Capt/Commiss Denzil GRIGSON
The	Flaming Falcons	'Doc' SAVAGE
The	Flaming Frontier	Sexton BLAKE
	Flash Casey - Hardboiled Detective	'Flashgun' CASEY
	Flash Casey, Detective	'Flashgun' CASEY
A	Flash Of Lightning	Oliver SMAILE
	Flash - Hold For Murder	Garry DEAN
	Flashlight	Terence MILNER
	Flashpoint	Dr CARRUTHERS
	Flashpoint	Roger PATTEN
	Flashpoint For Treason	Sexton BLAKE
The	Flat Beneath	Watson WARD
A	Flat Tyre In Fulham	Claude WARRINGTON-REEVE and Insp Steven MITCHELL
	Flats Fixed - Among Other Things	Gil SPEER
A	Flaw In The System	Benton SAFFORD
	Flawless Execution	John MOORE
The	Fleetwood Mansions Mystery	Ch Insp James MILLER
	Flesh Wound	Dan RUDNICKI
	Fletch	Irwin 'Fletch' FLETCHER
	Fletch Reflected	Irwin 'Fletch' FLETCHER
	Flex	Rusty CUTLER
	Flickering Death	Jonathan GAUNT
	Flight From Montego Bay	Alec HAIG
A	Flight From Paris	Jonathan GAUNT
The	Flight Of The Bamboo Saucer	Schuyler TOWNSEND
The	Flight Of The Falcon	Armino FABBIO
	Flight Of The Intruder	Jake GRAFTON
The	Flight Of The Raven	Supt Mark NICOLSON
	Flighty Phyllis	Phyllis DUDLEY
	Flip Side	Jack CLEARY
The	Floating Admiral	Insp RUDGE
The	Floating Game	The AVENGERS

Flood	BURKE
Flood	Supt Francis FOY
Florentine Finish	Saul HANDY
Florian Slappey	Florian SLAPPEY
Florian Slappey Goes Abroad	Florian SLAPPEY
The Flower O' The Peach	'Slow and Sure' JACKSON
The Flowered Box	Aaron GATES and Caro BURSA
Flowers For Violet	Violet MCDADE
The Flung-Back Lid	Rolf LE ROUX
Flush As May	Margaret CANNING
Fly By Night	Insp READ and Jeffrey BLACKBURN
The Fly On The Wall	John COTTON
Flyaway	Max STAFFORD
Flying Blind	Tommy ROSTETTER
The Flying Dagger Murder	Li MOH
The Flying Death	Prof Willis RAVENDEN and Stanford COLTON
The Flying Goblin	'Doc' SAVAGE
Flying High	Insp COHEN
The Flying Horse	Heron MURMER
The Flying Patrol	Cpl John CAVANNAGH
The Flying Saucer Gambit	Hannibal FORTUNE
Flying Too High	Phryne FISHER
Flynn	Francis Xavier FLYNN
Flynn	Laura FLYNN
Flynn's In	Francis Xavier FLYNN
The Flypaper War	Maxwell SPEED
FOB Murder	COLLINS and MCKECHNIE
Fog Of Doubt	Insp COCKRILL and Insp CHARLESWORTH
Fog Off Weymouth	Penny MERCER and Vincent MERCER
The Folded Paper Mystery	Amos Lee MAPPIN
Folio On Florence White	Philip STRONG and James MATTHEWS
Follow That Hearse!	Harry HORNE
Follow The Leader	John MOORE
Follow The Saint	Simon (The Saint) TEMPLAR
Follow This Fair Corpse	Dick WHELAN
The Follower	Mark LIDDON
Folly's Gold	Bob CLIFFORD
Food For Felony	Bryan ARMITAGE
The Food Mystery Story	Sherbert SCONES
Fool's Mercy	Gordon SAULT
Fool's Ransom	Ch Insp Jim ASHWORTH
The Football Crooks	Ferrers LOCKE
Footnote To Murder	Marge BROCK
Footprints	Derek THOMPSON
The Footprints Of Satan	Det Insp Lancelot Carolus SMITH
The Footprints On The Ceiling	Sherlock HOLMES
Footsteps Of Death	Bill 'Ironsides' CROMWELL
For A Woman's Honour	Insp OSWALD
For Godmother And Country	The DONNA
For Her Ladyship's Sake	Alec YORKE
For Love Of Imabelle	Det 'Grave Digger' JONES and Det 'Coffin' Ed JOHNSON
For Murder I Charge More	Augustus MANDRELL
For Pete's Sake!	Pete GARROWAY
For Sale - With Corpse	Supt John LAMBERT
For The Defence	MOLESWORTH
For The Eyes Of The President Only	André KOHL
For The Love Of Murder	Rev Martin BUELL
For Your Eyes Only	Cdr James BOND
The Forbidden Hour	Guy BANNISTER
The Forbidden Territory	Duke DE RICHLEAU
Force 10 From Navarone	Capt MALLORY
A Force Of Innocence	David CONNELL
Forced Entry	Stanley MOODROW
Ford's Folly Ltd	Plantagenet PLEWS
Forecast - Murder	David CROSBIE
Foreign Bodies	Insp BASS
Foreign Bodies	Dr Nassim PRIDE
Foreign Body	Det Insp FLOWER
Foreign Exchange	John SMITH
The Foreign Secretary Who Vanished	Emil TABOR
The Foreign Spy	Herlock SHOLMES
Forest Prime Evil	Stuart WINTER
Forests Of The Night	Ch Insp BAXTER
Forfeit	James TYRONE
Forgers And Confidence Men: Or The Secrets Of The Detective Service Revealed	DETECTIVES
Forget My Fate	Eric LUND
Forgive Me, Lively Lady	Bill BANNING
The Forgotten Fleet Mystery	Insp Scott STUART
The Formula	Barney CAINE
Formula For Murder	Prof Dennis BARRIE
Formula For Murder	Van MARS
The Forsaken Inn	Anthony TAMWORTH
Forsythia Finds Murder	Forsythia BROWN
The Fortec Conspiracy	Barney RUSSOM
The Fortieth Birthday Party	Susan HENSHAW
The Fortnight Of Fear	Sexton BLAKE
Foul Shot	Loren SWIFT
Found And Fettered: A Series Of Thrilling Detective Stories	Det Dick DONOVAN
Found Dead	Charles STEEN
The Fountain At Marlieu	Insp Frederic BELOT
Four Dead Mice	Al DELANEY
The Four Defences	Mark BRAND
The Four Defenses	Mark BRAND
Four Doors To Death	David CANE
The Four False Weapons, Being The Return Of Bencolin	Juge d'Instruction Henri BENCOLIN
Four Feet In The Grave	Katherine 'Peter' PIPER
Four Hours To Fear	Bernard SIMMONS
The Four Just Men	FOUR JUST MEN
The Four Last Things	Simeon GRIST
Four More Sherlock Holmes Plays	Sherlock HOLMES
Four Of A Kind	Rostron OUTFIT
Four On The Floor	Father Roger DOWLING
Four Past Four	James SEGROVE
Four Sherlock Holmes Plays	Sherlock HOLMES
Four Times A Widower	Alice PENNY
Fourfingers	Sgt VENN
The Fourteenth Key	Lorimer LANE
The Fourteenth Trump	COYLE and DONOVAN
The Fourth Agency	Charles DEXTER
The Fourth Angel	Simon QUARRY
The Fourth Book Of Jorkens	Joseph JORKENS
The Fourth Crow	Det Ch Supt Harry FATHERS
The Fourth Deadly Sin	Ex-Plce Edward X DELANEY
Fourth Degree	Insp Everett ANDERSON
The Fourth Degree	Quentin QUAYNE
Fourth Down	Sheriff Emil WHIPPLETREE
The Fourth Man	John SPENCER
The Fourth Stage Of Gainsborough Brown	Persis WILLUM
The Fourth Wall	Abby JAMES
Fowl Murder	MCPHERSON
The Fowler Formula	John FOWLER
The Fowlhaven Werewolf	Sherlock HOLMES
Fox In The Sea	Shane MACKENZIE
The Fox Valley Murders	Sheriff Joe BAIN
The Foxbat Spiral	Jay HILLER
Foxcatcher	Charlie BREWER
Foxhunt	Derek THRYDE
Fragile Empires	Julian CASTLE
Framed Evidence	Ch Insp GORHAM
Framed In Blue	Quint MCCAULEY
A Framework Of Fate: Or, The One In Twenty	Nick CARTER
The Franchise Affair	Robert BLAIR
Francis Quarles Investigates	Francis QUARLES
The Frankenstein Factory	Carl CRADER and Earl JAZINE
Frankincense And Murder	Duncan MACLAIN
Frass	Capt FRASS
Fratricide Is A Gas	Matthew DILKE
Frazer Butts In	Insp WILLIAMS
Freak Racket	Ed GUNNING
Freaked Out Stranger	Bill CARTWRIGHT
Freak-Out	HARRINGTON
The Freckled Hand	Herlock SHOLMES
Fred Danford, The Skillful Detective: Or, The Watertown Mystery	Fred DANFORD
Fred In Situ	'Beau' PEPYS
Free Draw	Jake SAMSON
Freebooty	Fergus O'HARA
The Freedom Trap	SLADE
Freemartin	Sam KNIGHT
The French Key	Johnny FLETCHER and Sam CRAGG
French Ordinary Murder	Sgt Joseph BRAGG
Frenzy In The Flesh	Sexton BLAKE
A Frenzy Of Merchantmen	Brevet CABLE
The Friday Run	James FRASER
Friday The Rabbi Slept Late	Rabbi David SMALL
Friday To Monday	James DREW
The Friends Of Eddie Coyle	Det FOLEY
The Friesland Case	Sherlock HOLMES
Frightened Eyes	Michael GRANT
The Frightened Fiancée	Sam CROMBIE
The Frightened Fingers	Don CADEE
The Frightened Man	Hooky HEFFERMAN
The Frightened Sailor	Prof Henry Arthur FIELDING
The Frighteners	Matt HELM
Fringe Ending	Ch Insp BAXTER
The Fringe Of The Law	Henry Napoleon BAGGS
Frisbee In The Middle	FRISBEE
Frisco Blues	Riley KOVACHS
The Frisco Detective	The FRISCO DETECTIVE
Fritz To The Front	FRITZ
Fritz, The Bound Boy Detective	FRITZ
Fritz, The German Detective	FRITZ
Fritz, The German Detective	Fritz HARMON
The Frog King	Bridget O'TOOLE
From A Detective's Notebook	Adrian MULLINER
From A High Place	Dan ROMAN
From Clue To Capture: A Series Of Thrilling Detective Stories	Det Dick DONOVAN
From Doon With Death	Ch Insp Reginald WEXFORD
From Information Received	Det Dick DONOVAN
From Street To Mansion: Or, Darke Darrell's Success	Darke DARRELL
From The Diary Of Sherlock Holmes	Sherlock HOLMES
From The Notebooks Of Dr Lyndon Parker	Solar PONS
From This Death Forward	Alva YAEGER
Front Man	Johnny STONE and Ruth DEE
Front Page Murder	Insp Curtis BURKE
The Frontier Detective	The FRONTIER DETECTIVE
Frontier Of Fear	Sarah CABLE
Frontiers Of Violence	Paul MASON
Frost At Christmas	Det Insp Jack FROST
Frozen Death	Insp TREADGOLD
The Frozen Flame	Hamilton CLEEK
The Frozen Franklin	Preston John RIORDAN
Fruits Of A Poisonous Tree	Lt Joe GUNTHER
The Fugitive	Capt Jose DA SILVA
Full Blown Rage	Det Maggie VAN ZANDT
Full Circle	Alan BERNHARDT
Full Commission	Liz WAREHAM
Full Cry	Kyra KEATON
Full Fathom Five	Ch Insp 'Daddy' BOURNE
Full Stop	Loretta LAWSON
The Full Stop	Nick MARSHALL
Funeral March For Siegfried	Supt Richard YORK
The Funeral Of Figaro	Det Insp MUSGRAVE
Funeral Rites	Tamara HOYLAND
The Funeral Was In Spain	PIRON
Funnelweb	Ch Insp Charlie CHEADLE

F

Funny As A Dead Relative	Kimmy KRUSE
Furnished For Murder	Jacob BARZENY
The Further Adventures Of Batman	BATMAN
Further Adventures Of Captain Kettle	Capt Owen KETTLE
The Further Adventures Of Quincy Adams Sawyer	Quincy Adams SAWYER
The Further Adventures Of Romney Pringle	Romney PRINGLE
The Further Adventures Of Sherlock Holmes	Sherlock HOLMES
The Further Adventures Of Solar Pons	Solar PONS
Further Adventures Of The Black Pilgrim	BLACK PILGRIM
The Further Side Of Fear	Insp DEVLIN
The Fury Of Rachael Monette	Rachael MONETTE
The Future Engine	Sherlock HOLMES

—G—

Gaboreau The Terrible	Don EVERHARD
Gabriel's Flight	Steve HAMM
Gad	Oliver GAD
Gaff Lee, Detective	Gaff LEE
Galactic Effectuator	Miro HETZEL
Galactic Sybil Sue Blue	Sybil Sue BLUE
Galahad Of The Air	John TRACY
Galaxy Jane	'Skyrocket' STEELE
Galaxy Jane	Jack SUMMER
Gale Gallyon Takes A Hand	Gale GALLYON
The Gallant Affair	Brad FORD
Galloping Dick	Dick RYDER
The Gallowglass	Det Ch Insp Phelim KANE
Gallows Bait	Det Insp SHANE
The Gallows In My Garden	Manville MOON
Gallows View	Ch Insp Alan BANKS
Gallows' Foot	Insp Gregory PELLEW and Viscount CLYMPING
A Gambit For Mr Groode	Mr GROODE
The Gambler	Ch Insp Lars KOLLIN
The Gambler, The Minstrel And The Dance Hall Queen	Joe REDDMAN
The Gambler's Wax Finger And Other Startling Detective Experiences	DETECTIVES
A Game Men Play	'Chink' PETERS
A Game Of Secrets	Bill HARDTMANN
The Game Show Girls	Joe (The Illusionist) MAGUIRE
Game Without Rules	Mr BEHRENS and Mr CALDER
The Gamecock	Patrick MATSON
Gamemaker	Sam KNIGHT
Game, Set And Danger	Helen BOYDEN
The Game's Afoot	Sherlock HOLMES
Gammon	Vernon BRADLUSKY
The Gang	Sgt Edmund ROERSCH
The Gang Smasher	John MARTINSON
The Gang Smasher Again	John MARTINSON
Gang War	DEATH SQUAD
Gangster Girl	POLACK ANNIE
Gangster Movies	Max HEALD
Gangster Pay-Off	Al MCFEE
Gangsters	John KLINE
Gangsters All	BIGGERS
Gangsters #2	John KLINE
Gangsters' Glory	Insp DICKINS
The Gangster's Daughter	Buddy MUSTARD
The Gangster's Deputy	Sexton BLAKE
The Gangster's Revenge	Sexton BLAKE
The Gang's Deserter	Sexton BLAKE
The Gantry Episode	Insp David COPE
Gants	Det Charlie GANTS
The Garbage Collector	Matt ERRIDGE
The Garbage Dump Murders	Amanda VALENTINE
Garde Save The World	Vance (The Chameleon) GARDE
The Garden Game	Maj Morven RICKMAN
The Garden Of Asia	Sir Henry MARQUIS
Garden Of Malice	Roz HOWARD
Gardenias Bruise Easily	Garaway TRENTON
Garnett Bell, Detective	Garnett BELL
The Garonsky Missile	Matthew TOBIN
Garrity	Tony GARRITY
The Garston Murder Case	Joshua CLUNK
Garstons	Joshua CLUNK
Garvey's Code	Det Mick GARVEY
The Gates Of Exquisite View	Simon YOUNG
A Gathering Of Ghosts	Arnold LANDON
A Gathering Of Gunmen	Insp Roger BASTIDE
The Gathering Place	Rachel HENNINGS
Gaudi Afternoon	Cassandra REILLY
The Gaunt Stranger	Supt BLISS
The Gauntlet Of Alceste	Addison KENT
Gay Falcon	Gay Stanhope FALCON
Gay Ghastly Holiday	Sebastian BLAYNE
The Geek Interpreter	Turlock LOAMS
Gees' First Case	Gregory George Gordon GREEN
A Gem Of A Murder	Jeffrey GREEN
The Gemini Man	Det Jack LINGEMANN and Liz CONNORS
General Besserley's Puzzle Box	Gen BESSERLEY
General Besserley's Second Puzzle Box	Gen BESSERLEY
General Murders	Amos WALKER
Generous Death	Jennifer CAIN
Genesis	Edgar Allan POE
Genghis Coopersmith	COOPERSMITH
Genius In Murder	Insp CARTER
Genocide Express	William JUSTICE
A Gentle Albatross	Will WOODFIELD
The Gentle Assassin	Kim LOCKE
The Gentle Killer	Insp George TRAVERS
A Gentle Murderer	Father DUFFY and Sgt GOLDSMITH
A Gentleman Called	Jasper TULLY and Mrs Annie NORRIS
A Gentleman From Texas	Insp Jack STRICKLAND
The Gentleman With The Walrus Moustache	Mr GLENCANNON
The Gentlemen At Large	John Byron HYDE
Gently Does It	Insp/Ch Supt George GENTLY
George Washington, Detective	George WASHINGTON
The Geranium Kiss	Scott MITCHELL
Gerry North Collects	Gerry NORTH
Get Clutha	CLUTHA
Get Garrity	Tony GARRITY
Get Smart!	Maxwell SMART
Getting Away With Murder	Bill MARTELL
Getting Up With Fleas	Devlin 'Trace' TRACY
Get-Rich-Quick Wallingford	James Rufus WALLINGFORD
Ghost Fingers	Mike REED
The Ghost Girl	Arthur JEFFREY
Ghost House	MATTHEWS
The Ghost Hunters	Raeburn STEEL
Ghost In The Making	Alan RUSSELL
The Ghost Knows His Greengages	John (The Ghost) DOBBS
The Ghost Motel	Harriet HUBBLEY
Ghost Of A Cardinal	Clarence E HEMINGWAY and Jeremy FLACK
The Ghost Of Robert Forbes	Sexton BLAKE
The Ghost Of Sherlock Holmes	Sherlock HOLMES
The Ghost Of Truth	Supt BLACK
The Ghost On The Balcony	Maj KRIM
The Ghost Pulls The Jackpot	John (The Ghost) DOBBS
The Ghost Rider Affair	Napoleon SOLO and Ilya KURYAKIN
The Ghost Train	Edward Gascoyne MORRISON
The Ghost Walks	Patrick HERON
The Ghostly Xmas Knight	Herlock SHOLMES
Ghosts	Samuel LYLE
Ghosts Never Die	Dr KENT
The Ghosts' High Noon	Jim BLAKE
The Ghostway	Sgt Jim CHEE
The Ghoul	Clarence KNIGHT
The Giant Detective Among The Cowboys	The GIANT DETECTIVE
The Giant Detective In Ireland	The GIANT DETECTIVE
The Giant Detective; Or, Can't Be Downed	The GIANT DETECTIVE
The Giant Hunchback	Insp GRIERSON
The Giant Rat Of Sumatra	Sherlock HOLMES
The Giant Rat Of Sumatra	Sherlock HOLMES
The Giant Rat Of Sumatra: A Story For Which The World Is Now, At Last, Prepared	Sherlock HOLMES
Gibraltar Road	Cdr Esmonde SHAW
Gideon Gault's Red Light Case; Or, Solving The Mystery Of The Bronx River	Gideon GAULT
Gideon Of Scotland Yard	Cdr George GIDEON
Gideon's Day	Cdr George GIDEON
Gideon's Drive	Cdr George GIDEON
Gideon's Fear	Cdr George GIDEON
Gideon's Force	Cdr George GIDEON
Gideon's Raid	Cdr George GIDEON
Gift From Berlin	Reefe KING
The Gift Horse Murders	Winston WYC
Gift Of Death	Jerry BENEDICT
Gift Of Death	Jerry BENEDICT
A Gift Of The Gods; Or, The Path Of Sudden Death	Nick CARTER
The Gig Of The Man (With The Twist)	Sure-They-Lock HOMEZ
The Gigantic Shadow	Insp CRAMBO
Giglamps	GIGLAMPS
Gilbert's Last Toothache	Rev Martin BUELL
The Gilded Canary	Bill (The Hook) LOCKWOOD
The Gilded Sarcophagus	Dr Paul HOLTON
The Gilded Witch	Det Sgt Sammy GOLDEN and Father Joseph SHANLEY
Gilead Balm, Knight Errant	Gilead BALM
Gilgamesh	Clio MARSH and Det Supt Harry MARSH
Gillean's Chain	Josh WALKER
Gin And Daggers	Jessica FLETCHER
Gin And Murder	Insp James FLECKER
The Gin Monkey	Max CLARK
Giotto's Hand	Gen Taddeo BOTTANDO, Flavia DI STEFANO and Jonathan ARGYLL
Gipsy Blair, The Western Detective	Gipsy BLAIR
Gipsy In Evening Dress	Det Insp GRAVES
Gipsy Reno, The Detective	GIPSY RENO
Gipsy Rose, The Female Detective	GIPSY ROSE
The Girl At Central	Molly MORGANTHAU
The Girl Behind The Keys	Bella THORN
The Girl Cage	Robert W FLICK
A Girl Died Singing	Det Insp Rory LUCCAN
The Girl From Malta	Gerald FOSTER
The Girl From Nowhere	John HARLAND
The Girl From Nowhere	Ira YEDDER
The Girl From Scotland Yard	Leslie MAUGHAN
Girl In A Big Brass Bed	Manny DEWITT
Girl In A Net	Simon LUCK
The Girl In Ocean View	George ROBERTS
The Girl In The Cellar	Maud Hephzibah SILVER
Girl In The Dark	Insp BYRNE
The Girl In The Fog	Insp Barton HAWLEY
The Girl In The Red Jaguar	Steve SUMMERS
The Girl In The Train	John SCARLETT
The Girl In The White Mercedes	Stan BRADEN
The Girl Known As D 13	Insp J RASON
The Girl Nobody Knows	Norman PINK
The Girl On The Left Bank	Insp JOLIVET
Girl On The Waterfront	Ch Insp Joshua SMARLES
The Girl Who Cried Wolf	Philip MACADAM

G

The Girl Who Died	Gerry LEE
The Girl Who Saw Too Much	Sexton BLAKE
The Girl Who Wouldn't Talk	Insp Peter CURWEN
The Girl Who Wouldn't Talk	Insp Peter CURWEN
The Girl With The Frightened Eyes	Homer BULL
The Girl With The X-Ray Eyes	Pam WAYNE
The Girls Who Came To Murder	Mike ROSS
Giselle	Rod MCKINNON
Give A Corpse A Bad Name	Toby DYKE
Give It To Me Straight	Shaun KOVACK
Give Me Death	Peter JERNINGHAM
Give The Devil His Due	Joe DUST
The Glade Manor Murder	Det Supt Tom POLLARD
The Glass Bridge	Baron DE HIRSCH
The Glass Cipher	Peter WINSTON
The Glass Key	Ned BEAUMONT
The Glass Ladder	Rick MASON
The Glass Spear	Insp Ambrose MAHON
The Glass Too Many	Gregory George Gordon GREEN
The Glass-Sided Ants' Nest	Supt James PIBBLE
Glencannon Afloat	Mr GLENCANNON
The Glendower Conspiracy	Edward Porter JONES and Sherlock HOLMES
The Glenna Powers Case	Simon KAYE
The Glimpses Of The Moon	Gervase FEN
Glitterburn	Josh KRALES
Glitz	Vincent MORA
Gloom Of Night	Lt WEARIE
The 'Gloria Scott'	Sherlock HOLMES
The Glory Hole Murders	Matt SINCLAIR
The Gloved Saskia	Brady RUSKIN and Whit TRAXLER
The Glyphs Of Gold	John (The Expediter) EAGLE
Go For Broke	Richard GRAHAM
Go For Garrity	Tony GARRITY
The Goat	Det Johnny INCH
The Goblin Market	Dr Basil WILLING and Miguel URIZAR
The Goblins	'Doc' SAVAGE
God Is An Executioner	Charlie DANCE
The Goddess, A Demon	Graham HUME
The Godmother	The DONNA
The Godmother Caper	Angela HARPE
The Godson	Les NORTON
The Godwulf Manuscript	SPENSER
God's Defector	Kenneth DUCANE
A Going Concern	Insp Christopher Dennis SLOAN
The Going Down Of The Sun	Clio MARSH and Det Supt Harry MARSH
Going To The Dogs	Nick DUFFY
Gold And Gaiters	John CRAGGS and James CASTLETON
The Gold Bullion Swindle	Dick BARTON
Gold Coast Nocturne	Simon DRAKE
The Gold Gamble	Alexander Magnus GOLD
The Gold Gap	Lt Cdr Frank SARGENT
The Gold Hijack	Mark RANDALL
The Gold Of St Matthew	Sam SHOLTO
Gold Of The Gods	Prof Craig KENNEDY
Gold Shield	Vickie CURRAN
The Gold Solution	Alexander Magnus GOLD
The Gold Star Line	George CONWAY
Gold Was Our Grave	Ch Insp POOLE
The Golden Bull	Nick CARTER
The Golden Bullet	CANNON
The Golden Casket	Sexton BLAKE
The Golden Cat	Franklyn KEEN
The Golden Child	Insp MACE and Prof Heinrich UNTERMENSCH
The Golden Cow	Herlock SHOLMES
The Golden Crucible	Insp John Joseph LINTOTT
The Golden Dress	Christopher GIBSON
The Golden Fear	Malcolm KENTON
The Golden God	Mark STONER
The Golden Goose	Riley WADDELL
The Golden Limping Stick	Sherlock HOLMES
The Golden Lure	John MARSHALL
The Golden Lure	Ric MCADDEN
The Golden Murder	Geoffrey SLADE
The Golden Panther	Jack CLAYTON
The Golden Pheasant Mystery	Derek HARING
The Golden Scarab	Addison KENT
The Golden Slipper	Det Ebenezer GRYCE
The Golden Slipper And Other Problems For Violet Strange	Violet STRANGE
The Golden Stag	Timothy DEVLIN
The Golden Triangle	Joe SANFORD
The Golden Venus Affair	Bruce MCLINTOCK
The Golden Virgin	Roger TALLIS
Goldfish	Ted CARMADY
The Goldfish Bowl	Det Jack WILLOWS and Det Claire PARKER
Goldilocks	Matthew HOPE
Goldilocks	Rita Gardella O'DEA
The Gold-Plated Sewer	Vince SLADER
The Gold-Trackers	Sam SHOLTO
The Golf Course Mystery	Col Robert Lee ASHLEY
Gone Away	Mrs Sheila MALLORY
The Gone Man	Charlie QUINLAN
The Gone Shots	Brian DESMOND
Gone Tomorrow	Prof Cyrus HATCH
The Good Book	Jimmy LUJACK
Good By Stealth	William POWER
Good Evans!	'Educated' EVANS
The Good Fight	Laura DI PALMA
Good Girls Don't Get Murdered	Big Bull BENSON
Good Luck, Mr Cain	Harry GRANT
Good Night And Goodbye	Thomas KYD
Good Night For Murder	George CLAY
Good Night, Ladies	Pete RECTOR
A Good Place For Murder	Tony LANTZ
A Good Place To Die	Harry FOSTER
A Good Place To Work And Die	Jim FERGUSON
The Good Thief	Pete RENO
Good Time Lady	Merrick LAWRENCE
A Good Weekend For Murder	Barry VAUGHAN and Dee VAUGHAN
A Good Year For Little Roses	Nick SHARMAN
Good - But Hot	Sam MURCHISON
Goodbye Stranger	Steve MALLORY
Goodbye Tomorrow	Don DANBY
Goodbye, Dr Thorndyke	Dr John Evelyn THORNDYKE
Goodbye, L A	Ben CRANDEL
Goodbye, Nanny Gray	Supt Robert BONE
Goodey's Last Stand	Joe GOODEY
Goodnight, Mr Holmes	Irene ADLER
The Gorgeous Ghoul	Hannah VAN DOREN
The Gorgeous Ghoul Murder Case	Hannah VAN DOREN
Gorky Park	Investigator Arkady RENKO
The Gory Details	Nell BARTLETT
The Gotland Deal	Sidney KENYON
The Goulden Fleece	Harry GOULD
The Gourmet	Martin WINDROW
The Governess	Harriet UNWIN
Gown And Shroud	Insp POOLE
Gownsman's Gallows	Insp Richard RINGWOOD
Go, Lovely Rose	Sheriff JEFFRIES and Mr PIGEON
The Grace In Older Women	LOVEJOY
The Gracie Allen Murder Case	Philo VANCE and Gracie ALLEN
The Grail Murders	Roger SHALLOT
The Grand Duke's Finances	Mr COLLIN
The Grand Guignol Caper	Senator Brooks Urban BANNER
Grand Slam	Cassandra SWANN
Grandmaster	Justin GILEAD and Alexander ZHARKOV
Grant's Overture	Ch Insp Douglas GRANT
Grass Widow	Hank JANSON
The Grate Fur Koat Mistery	Rex HOMES
A Grave Case Of Murder	Insp JAMES
Grave Consequences	Trish MCWHINNEY
Grave Doubt	David MEYNELL
Grave Error	John Marshall TANNER
A Grave For Madam	Mike STRANG
A Grave For Miss Carling	Det Insp Elwyn HUGHES
A Grave Matter	John MORTON and Sgt DERWENT
Grave Matters	Bill HAWLEY
Grave Murder	Walter MCKENZIE
Grave Secrets	Amy PRESCOTT
A Grave Talent	Det Kate MARTINELLI and Det Al HAWKINS
Grave Undertaking	Lavinia LONDON
Grave Witness	Ben JONSON
Gravelhanger	Anthony HAVILLAND
Graves In Academe	Roz HOWARD
A Graveyard Of My Own	Burt KURRIE
The Graveyard Shift	Nick MILLER
The Gray Flannel Shroud	Dave ROBBINS and Max THERINGER
Gray Magic	The GRAY PHANTOM
The Gray Mask	GARTH
The Gray Phantom	The GRAY PHANTOM
The Graysons	Abraham LINCOLN
The Great Adams Express Robbery	A Frank PINKERTON
The Great Brain Robbery	Dave STEVENS
Great Cases Of The Thinking Machine	Prof Augustus S F X VAN DUSEN
The Great Cronion Mystery: Or, The Irish Patriot's Fate	A CHICAGO DETECTIVE
A Great Deliverance	Insp Thomas LYNLEY
The Great Divide	Dorothy Mayotte RIGBY
The Great Drain Robbery	Sherlock HOLMES
The Great Dumping Mystery	Sexton BLAKE
The Great Grave Robbery	'Little John' RAWLINGS
The Great Horseshoe Mystery	Bill RASTIN
The Great Hotel Murder	Riley BLACKWOOD
The Great Hotel Robbery	'Little John' RAWLINGS
The Great Merlini: The Complete Stories Of The Great Magician	The Great MERLINI
The Great Museum Mystery	Sexton BLAKE
The Great Pegram Mystery	Sherlaw KOMBS
The Great Pimlico Mystery: A Well-Kept Secret Disclosed	Keedy KINGSTON
Great Porter Square	Robert AGNOLD
The Great Pretender	Nick MERLOTTI
The Great Stores Mystery	Sexton BLAKE
The Great Tontine	Robert PEGRAM
The Great Waxworks Mystery	Herlock SHOLMES
The Greatest Batman Stories Ever Told	BATMAN
The Greatest Detective Of All Time	Sherlock HOLMES
The Greatest Tertian	Sherlock HOLMES
Greedy Night	Lord Peter WIMSEY
The Greek Detective: Or, On The Trail Of A Vitriol Thrower	The GREEK DETECTIVE
The Greek God Affair	The MOD SQUAD
The Greek Interpreter	Sherlock HOLMES
The Greek Key	TWEED
The Green Arrow	Capt GRANDISON
Green December Fills The Graveyard	Insp Lane PARRY
The Green Diamonds	Supt BRADLEY
Green Eye Of Death	Insp MILLWALL
Green For A Grave	Barnaby JONES
The Green God	Owen MORGAN
The Green Grassy Slopes	Sexton BLAKE
The Green Jacket	Millicent NEWBERRY
The Green Jade Hand	Simon GRUNDT
The Green Lantern	Insp GODBOLD
Green Lightning	Nat TRACKER
Green Mask	Supt BUDD
The Green Murder	Capt Mark FANNING
Green Murder	Alan SAXON
The Green Ray	Ronald EWART
The Green Reapers	Insp EVANS and Sgt BEDDOES
The Green Room Crime	Sexton BLAKE
The Green Shadow	Tip O'NEIL

The Green Shadow	The PICAROON
Green Shiver	Prof Theocritus Lucius WESTBOROUGH
The Green Stone	Insp Miguel MENENDEZ
The Green Toad	Ch Const HENDON
The Green Triangle	Supt LESLIE
The Green Triangle Mystery	Sgt/Insp DOCKER
Green Trigger Fingers	Celia GRANT
The Green Wound	Joe GALL
The Green Wound Contract	Joe GALL
Greenmask!	Sgt Ivor MADDOX
Greenmask!	Sgt Ivor MADDOX
The Greenwells Glory Case	Insp SPENS
The Green-Eyed Monster	Andrew JORDAN
The Grell Mystery	Supt Heldon FOYLE
Grenelle	Susan GRENELLE and Ch Mark CZERNICK
Grey Mask	Maud Hephzibah SILVER
The Grey Nun Legacy	Sherlock HOLMES
The Grey Phantom	The GRAY PHANTOM
The Grey Phantom's Triumph	The GRAY PHANTOM
The Grey Room	Peter HARDCASTLE
Grey Shadow	Grey SHADOW
Greymarsh	Colwin GREY
Griff	Wade GRIFFIN
The Grim Caretaker	Lucian CAROLUS
Grim Chancery	John MELROSE
Grim Pickings	Verity 'Birdie' BIRDWOOD
The Grinning Pig	Lord WINTERSTONE
The Grip Of The Four	Daphne WRAYNE and The FOUR ADJUSTERS
Grizzly, A Mystery	Lee SQUIRES
Groota	Sgt MULHEISEN
The Groote Park Murder	Insp ROSS
A Gross Carriage Of Justice	SIMPSON, CARRUTHERS and BRIGGS
Grounds For Murder	Tom CRAIG
The Grouser Investigates	Insp William (The Grouser) BEEKE
A Growing Concern	David GRIERSON
The Grub-And-Stakers Move A Mountain	Dittany MONK and Osbert MONK
The Grub-And-Stakers Spin A Yarn	Dittany MONK and Osbert MONK
The Grudge	John FARREL
Grushko	Yevgeni Ivanovitch GRUSHKO
The Guardians	Col CALPIN
Guardians Of The Treasure	Jim MAITLAND
The Guest With The Scythe	John BARRIN and Kate MARSH
Guild	Leo GUILD
Guilt For Innocence	Insp Jim BURGESS
Guilt With Honor	Bob HOWE
The Guilty Are Afraid	Lew BRANDON
The Guilty Bystander	Sam DAKKERS
Guilty Bystander	Max THURSDAY
Guilty Gold: A Romance Of Financial Fraud And City Crime	Insp HERON
Guilty Witness	Steve CRANE
The Guilt-Edged Cage	Andy KANE
The Gull Cove Murders	Pat CAMPBELL
Gumshoe	Eddie GINLEY
Gun Cotton In Mexico	Gunston COTTON
Gun Cotton - Adventurer	Gunston COTTON
A Gun In My Back	Pete MARVIN
Gun Music	Philip MARLOWE
Gun Play	Elton DANCEY
The Gun Runner	John ALLISON
Gunning In England	Ed GUNNING
Gunpowder Treason And Plot	Det Insp FLOWER
Gunpowder	Robert STARK
Guns At Cyrano's	Ted MALVERN
Guns In The Desert	Derek CARRINGTON
The Guns Of Heaven	Sam BRISCOE
The Guns Of Navarone	Capt MALLORY
Gunship	David PROSS
The Gutenburg Murders	WADE
The Guvnor	Det Ch Insp John FORDHAM
The Guv'nor And Other Stories	J G REEDER
The Guy Fawkes Murder	Nathaniel MOODY
A Guy Named Judas	Dana DALLAS
The Gypsy Detective	The GYPSY DETECTIVE
Gypsy In Amber	Roman GREY
G-Men On Murder Island	Dan GREGORY
The G-String Murders	Gypsy Rose LEE and Biff BRANNIGAN

—H—

H As In Hunted	Det Jub FREEMAN
The Habit Of Fear	Julia HAYES
Hacker	Det Deb RALSTON
The Hades Hello	Paul CAMERON
Hag Wood	Bernard MCFOY
Hagar Of The Pawnshop	Hagar STANLEY
Hag's Nook	Dr Gideon FELL
Hail To The Chief	Kerlock SHOMES
The Hair In The Soup	Hemlock SOAMES
Hairlock Holmes, Detective, Solves An Anachronistic Mystery	Hairlock HOLMES
The Hairpin Mystery	Insp GORE
The Hairy Arm	Mike BRIXAN
Hal Tybert, The Hotel Detective; Or, Shadowing Chicago Crooks	Hal TYBERT
Half A Mind	Roger TEJEDA
Half Devil, Half Tiger	Gilbert DAVISON
A Half Interest In Murder	Matt REBER
Half Nelson	Tom BETHANY
Half-Mast Murder	Supt GUEST
Half-Past Mortem	Sam WELPTON
Half-Seas Over	Mr GLENCANNON
Half-Way To Murder	Charles SMITH
Hallmark Of Murder	Sgt Joseph BRAGG
Hallowed Murder	Jane LAWLESS
A Halo For Nobody	Peter CHAMBERS
Halo In Blood	Paul PINE
Halo In Brass	Paul PINE
The Halo Solution	Erik CHATHAM
Halsey And The Dead Ringer	Mick HALSEY
Halsey And The Fine Art Of Murder	Mick HALSEY
The Hamlet Problem	Claude RAVEL
The Hamlet Trap	Charles MEIKLEJOHN and Constance LEIDL
The Hamlet Ultimatum	Clay LOOMIS
The Hamlet Warning	Clay LOOMIS
Hammer Island	Sir Abercrombie LEWKER
Hammer Locke	John LOCKE
The Hammer Of Justice	Det Sgt STEYTLER
Hammerhead	Charles HOOD
The Hammersmith Maggot	Casson DUKER
The Hammersmith Murders	Evan PINKERTON
Hammett	Dashiell HAMMETT
Hammett Homicides	The CONTINENTAL OP
The Hampstead Mystery	CREWE
The Hampstead Poisonings	Mycroft HOLMES
The Hand In The Cobbler's Safe	Lt HASS
The Hand In The Dark	David COLWYN
The Hand In The Glove	Theodora 'Dol' BONNER
Hand Me A Crime	Jane Amanda EDWARDS
Hand Of A Killer	Mike HUBBARD
The Hand Of Doom	Insp QUAILE
The Hand Of God	Dr BURKHALTER
The Hand Of Horror	Philip MACCRAY
The Hand Of Justice	Peter JUSTICE
The Hand Of Mary Constable	Alexander HERO
The Hand Of Solange	Insp Maurice YGREC
The Hand Of The Lion	Andrea PERKINS
The Hand Of Vengeance	Alan FRASER
The Handcuff Wizard; Or, Nick Carter's Perplexity	Nick CARTER
Handle With Care	Det LONNIE THE FED
Handle With Fear	Singer BATTS
Hands Of Death	Insp Bill MURRAY
Hands Of Doom!	Dixon BRETT
The Hands Of Healing Murder	Dr Gerritt DEGRAAF
Hands Off The Lovely	Martin KANE
The Handwriting On The Wall	The SHADOWERS INC
The Handwriting On The Wall	The SHADOWERS INC
Hang On A Minute, Mate	Sam CASH
Hang The Consequences	Lennox KEMP
Hanged By A Thread	Det Ch Insp GREVE
The Hanged Men	Warren STONE
The Hanging Captain	Supt DAWLE
The Hanging Doll Murder	Richard PATTON and Amelia PATTON
The Hanging Of Constance Hillier	Insp CLEVELAND
The Hanging Rope	Kerry OTT
The Hanging Sword!	Phineas SPINNET
The Hanging Woman	RATLIN
Hangman	Paul VENNEKER
A Hangman For Paradise	Mike PARADISE
Hangman's Hat	Lt Jim RYAN, Shirley LEIGHTON and Bill HARPER
The Hangman's Hands	Sebastian STOLE
The Hangman's Handyman	Roger KINCAID
Hangman's Harvest	Milo MARCH
Hangman's Holiday	Montague EGG
Hangman's Holiday	Lord Peter WIMSEY
Hangman's Root	China BAYLES
Hannah Says Foul Play	Hannah VAN DOREN
Hanoi	Nick CARTER
The Happiest Ghost In Town	Martin MOON
Happy Are The Meek	Mgr John Blackwood 'Blackie' RYAN
Happy Deathday	Dr Samuel CUTTING
The Happy Highwayman	Simon (The Saint) TEMPLAR
Happy Never After	Callahan GARRITY
Hard Bargains	John RANKIN
Hard Case	Catherine 'Cat' MARSALA
Hard Held: A Sporting Novel	Alex SMART
The Hard Kill	Phil SANDERSON
Hard Sell	Clayton WARD
Hardball	Catherine 'Cat' MARSALA
Hardball	James REED
Hardcover	Jeffrey DEAN
A Harder Thing Than Triumph	Father Simon BEDE
Hardscape	Ben ABBOTT
Hardscrabble, The Detective; Or, Tracked By A Hair	HARDSCRABBLE
Hardware	Carlotta CARLYLE
Hard-Boiled Defective Stories	El BORBAH
The Harker File	HARKER
The Harker File	Hawthorne Albert HARKER
Harlem Hit	RADCLIFF
Harlem Underground	Lee HAYES
Harlequin	George HARLEQUIN
Harness Bull	Capt BARNABY
The Harness Of Death	Insp Dennis DRURY
Harper's Folly	HARPER
Harper's Luck	HARPER
Harpinger's Hunch	Lydford LONG
Harrigan's File	Tex HARRIGAN

H

Harrison Keith's Abduction Tangle: Or, Lifting A Veil Of Mystery	Harrison KEITH
Harrison Keith, Sleuth: Or, The Army Puzzle	Harrison KEITH
Harrison Keith's Cyclone Clue: Or, Through The Air	Harrison KEITH
Harrison Keith's Danger: Or, Out Of The Jaws Of Death	Harrison KEITH
Harrison Keith's Death Compact	Harrison KEITH
Harrison Keith's Diamond Case: Or, The Most Exciting Case On Record	Harrison KEITH
Harrison Keith's Drag Net	Harrison KEITH
Harrison Keith's Greatest Task: Or, An Unbearable Burden	Harrison KEITH
Harrison Keith's Lucky Strike: Or, The Plot That Failed	Harrison KEITH
Harrison Keith's Perilous Contract: Or, Crime's Bitterest Foe	Harrison KEITH
Harrison Keith's Poison Problem: Or, The Quest Of The Blue Cobra	Harrison KEITH
Harrison Keith's Queer Clue: Or, Among The 'Reds'	Harrison KEITH
Harrison Keith's Triple Tragedy	Harrison KEITH
Harry Blount, The Detective: Or, The Martin Mystery Solved	Harry BLOUNT
Harry Pinkurton, The Boy Detective	Harry PINKURTON
Harry Pinkurton, The King Of Detectives	Harry PINKURTON
Harry Sharpe, The New York Detective	Harry SHARPE
Harry Williams, The New York Detective	Harry WILLIAMS
Harry's Game	Harry BROWN
Hart To Hart	Jonathan HART and Jennifer HART
The Hartland Case	Sir Richard HERRIVELL
Harvard Has A Homicide	Edmund 'Jupiter' JONES
Hashimi's Revenge	Willie 'Spider' SCOTT
Hatchet Man	Ken MITCHELL
Hatchett	Madge HATCHETT
Hatchet-Man	John Abraham LINCOLN
Hatch's Island	Frank HATCHER
Hatch's Mission	Frank HATCHER
Haunted Bells	Ray BARTLEY
The Haunted Grange	Lila LISLE
The Haunted House	CHANTECOQ
Haunted Lady	Hilda ADAMS
The Haunting Hand	Margot ANSTRUTHER and Gene VALERY
The Haunting Of Alan Mais	Sexton BLAKE
Haunts	HARTER
Have Gat - Will Travel	Shell SCOTT
Have This One On Me	Mark GIRLAND
Have You Seen This Man?	Tim FLAHERTY
Hawaii	Nick CARTER
Hawkshaw The Detective	Insp HAWKSHAW
Hawksmoor	Insp HAWKSMOOR
Hayduke Lives!	George HAYDUKE
Hazard	STORM
Hazardous Duty	Peter WARD
Hazell And The Menacing Jester	James HAZELL
Hazell Plays Solomon	James HAZELL
Hazzard	Cheney HAZZARD
He Could Not Have Slipped	Insp George MARTIN
He Didn't Mind Hanging	Peter PIPER
He Died Laughing	Homer BULL
He Died Of Murder!	Jacob CHAOS
He Dies And Makes No Sign	Dr CONSTANTINE
He Done Her Wrong	Toby PETERS and Mae WEST
He Fell Among Thieves	Harry WYNNE
He Huffed And He Puffed	Sgt Marian LARCH
He Repudiates Sherlock	Mycroft HOLMES and Sherlock HOLMES
He Should Have Died Hereafter	Insp MALLETT and Francis PETTIGREW
He Solves The Mystery Of The Man In The Iron Mask	Mycroft HOLMES and Sherlock HOLMES
He Solves The Mystery Of The Shakespearean Authorship	Mycroft HOLMES and Sherlock HOLMES
He Walked In Her Sleep	Alonzo MACTAVISH
He Was Her Man	Samantha ADAMS
Head Crusher	Johnny ROCK
Head On The Sill	Insp GROGAN
Heading For A Wreath	Mick CARDBY
Headline For Murder	Lt MADIGAN
Headlined For Murder	Lt MADIGAN
Headlong For Murder	Christine ANDERSEN
Heads You Lose	Insp COCKRILL
Heads You Lose	Morrison SHARPE
A Healthy Body	'Birdie' LINNET
The Healthy Grave	Stephen MARRYAT
A Healthy Way To Die	Det Const Jason TWITTY
Healthy, Wealthy And Dead	Phoebe FAIRFAX
Hear No Evil	Stephen RANSOME
Hear Not My Steps	Lt Claude GREENWAY
Heart In The Box	Commissaire PATRAS
The Heart Of Oak Detective	The HEART OF OAK DETECTIVE
The Heart Of Oak Detective: Or, Zig-Zag's Full Hand	The HEART OF OAK DETECTIVE
Heart To Heart	Ashton FORD
Heartbeat	Jennifer GREY
Heartless	Eddie MARGOLIS
Hearts Ease In Death	Insp/Supt Bill AVEYARD
The Heat Of The Sun	Kate WEATHERLY
Heaven Ran Last	Insp HARRIGAN
The Heaven Stone	Alex RASSMUSSEN
Heavenly Bodies	Mr John Cornelius SCOTTER
Heavenly Body	Ricky STRAIGHT
Heavy As Lead	Timothy HERRING
Heavy Gilt	Tyler DIVINE
Hector Tumbler Investigates	Hector TUMBLER
The Heel Of Achilles	Michael DENE
Heil Britannia	Martyn CALE
Heist Me Higher	Bryce PATCH
Hell Bent For Heaven	T T BALDWIN
Hell Hath No Fury	Pat O'LEARY
Hell Is A City	Det Insp Harry MARTINEAU
Hell Is Always Today	Nick MILLER
Hell Is Always Today	Nick MILLER
Hell Nest	Curt 'Nazi Hunter' JAEGER
Hell On Friday	Johnny SAXON
Hell To Pay	Tom KINCAID
Heller's Leap	Claudine ST CYR and CROYD
The Hellfire Files Of Jules De Grandin	Jules DE GRANDIN
The Hellfire Papers	Tim LACY
The Hellions	Mark STRATTON
Hello, Lemuria, Hello	Jake CONGER
Hellrider	Jesse HELLER
Hellshot	Cole BROGAN
Hell-Bent For Election	Joe BINNEY
Hell-Bent For Homicide	Joe BINNEY
Hell's Angel	Hank JANSON
Helping With Inquiries	Det Insp HOGARTH
Help! Help! Sherlock!	Sherlock HOLMES
The Helsinki Affair	Osmo KILPI
Hendon's First Case	Jimmy WAGHORN
Henry Broch, Old Sleuth's Assistant	Henry BROCH
Henry Dunbar: The Story Of An Outcast	Mr Henry CARTER
Heptameron	Insp BAILHACHE
Her Death Of Cold	Father Roger DOWLING
Her Last Bow: Or, An Adventure Of Stately Homes	Stately HOMES
Her Majesty's Minister	Gerald INGRAM
Her Majesty's Minister	George STRATFIELD
Her Mother's Husband	Jason MARR
Hercule Poirot's Casebook: Fifty Stories	Hercule POIROT
Hercules Esq	Bill KELLAWAY
Here Come The Dead	Pecos APPLEBY
Here Comes The Copper	Const John BRAGG
Here Is An SOS	Ch Const George MEATYARD
Here Lies	Griff HUGHES
Here Lies Blood	Sheriff George WHITE
Here's Murder Done	Richard SANGSTER
Herlock Sholmes At Monte Carlo	Herlock SHOLMES
Hero By Proxy	Sam HOOK
Herod's Peal	Mr MACAULEY
Heroes Also Die	Mickey 'Slots' RESNICK
Heroin Annie	Cliff HARDY
He's Late This Morning	Lt Bill FRENCH
Hidden Agenda	Judith HAYES
Hidden Eyes	Dr Edward LESTER
The Hidden Kingdom	Thomas PRESTON
The Hidden Law	Henry RIOS
The Hidden Light	David MARCHANT
A Hidden Masterpiece In Westminster	Sherlock HOLMES
Hidden Ways	David MALLORY
The Hidden Wrath	Insp Matthew FURNIVAL
Hide And Go Seek	Timothy FOWLER
Hideaway	Det Insp Harry MARTINEAU
Hideaway	Boysie OAKES
High Bid For Murder	Jeff PRIDE
The High Commissioner	Scobie MALONE
High Court	Andrew ONE
High Dive	Jim BRADLEY
High Fall	Kiernan O'SHAUNESSY
The High Game	Ludovic FENDER and Paul VENNEKER
High Heels And Homicide	Sexton BLAKE
High Midnight	Toby PETERS, Gary COOPER and Ernest HEMINGWAY
High Noon At Midnight	Ed NOON
High Priest	Justin GILEAD and Alexander ZHARKOV
High Red For Dead	Mohawk DANIELS
The High Sheriff	Maj FAIDE
High Stakes	Chance MALLOY
High Stakes	Steven SCOTT
High Strung	Adrienne BISHOP
High Summer Homicide	Sexton BLAKE
The High Toby	Dick RYDER
The High Window	Philip MARLOWE
A High Yield In Death	Nick CARTER
The Highgrade Murder	Tommy THORNE
Highland Homicide	Insp PARKER
Highly Inflammable	Archie LUMSDEN
High-Class Kill	Asst Ch Const SULLIVAN
Hilda Wade: A Woman With Great Tenacity Of Purpose	Nurse Hilda WADE
Hildegarde Withers Makes The Scene	Hildegarde WITHERS
Hill Fog	Jonathan BLAKE
The Hill Of The Terrified Monk	Jose Manuel MADERO
Hindsight	Paul ROGERS
Hire Me A Hearse	Supt Frank DRURY and Insp Bill HAZARD
His Darling Sin	Mr FAUNCE
His Eminence, Death	Francis X (The Inquisitor) KILLY
His Father's Crime	Benjamin LEVY
His First Bow	Sherlock HOLMES
His Last Bow	Sherlock HOLMES
His Last Bow: The War Service Of Sherlock Holmes	Sherlock HOLMES
His Last Scrape: Or, Holmes, Sweet Holmes	Sherlock HOLMES
His Last Vow	Turlock LOAMS
His Majesty-The Crook	Quentin DREX
His Own Appointed Day	Det Insp Maurice NICOLSON
His Own Funeral	Insp BLESSINGAY
The Hit	Simon CRANE
The Hit	The MOD SQUAD
Hit And Run	Barney CALHOUN
Hit And Run	Delilah WEST
Hit Man	Johnny ROCK
Hit Squad	Sgt Edmund ROERSCH
Hit Them Where It Hurts	Dirk WALLACE

The Hitchhike Killer	Terry (Chopper Cop) BUNKER
Hitler Needs You	Horace Spurgeon FENTON
Hitler's Legacy	Stosh COLTRAY
The Hochmann Miniatures	Kek HUUYGENS
Hocus-Pocus Homicide	Ned CAIN
Hoffman's Row	Abraham LINCOLN
The Hog Murders	Ron GENTRY
The Holcroft Covenant	Noel HOLCROFT
Holfernes	Patrick MATSON
The Holiday Adventures Of Mr P J Davenant	P J DAVENANT
Holiday Homicide	Cotton MOON
The Holladay Case	Jim GODFREY
The Hollow Man	Johnny DEVEREAUX
The Hollow Woman	John Kenneth Galbraith JANTARRO
Hollywood And Levine	Jack LEVINE
Hollywood Detective: Garrison	Roger GARRISON
Hollywood Detective: The Wolf	Roger GARRISON
Hollywood Heroes	Ace CARPENTER
The Hollywood Murder Mystery	Clay BROOKE
Hollywood Troubleshooter	Bill LENNOX
Holmes And The Dasher	Sherlock HOLMES
Holmes Ex Machina	Sherlock HOLMES
Holmes In Scotland	Sherlock HOLMES
The Holmes Team Advantage	Sherlock HOLMES
The Holmes-Dracula File	Sherlock HOLMES
Holmlock Shears Arrives Too Late	Holmlock SHEARS and Arsène LUPIN
The Holy Father's Navy	Colin PANTON
The Holy Innocents	ROGER THE CHAPMAN
The Holy Spirit	Father HAYES
The Holy Terror	Simon (The Saint) TEMPLAR
Home Office: 221b Baker Street: Or, A Study In Cement	Sherlock HOLMES and Arsène LUPIN
The Home Secretary Will See You Now	Supt John GAFFNEY and Det Ch Supt Thomas FOX
Homemade Sin	Callahan GARRITY
Hometown Heroes	Forrest HAGGERTY
Homicide	Capt BARNABY
Homicide Blues	Sexton BLAKE
Homicide Call	Lt Abe LARSON
Homicide Handicap	Nathan HAWK
Homicide House: Mr Pinkerton Returns	Evan PINKERTON
Homicide Lost	Peter KIRK
Honey On Her Tail	Honey WEST
The Honey Trap	Insp Lawrence ERSKINE
Honeybath's Haven	Insp/Commiss John APPLEBY and Prof Charles HONEYBATH
The Hong Kong Caper	Andy KANE
Hong Kong Kill	Anthony BRANDON
The Hongkong Jewel Mystery	King DANWORTH and Martin LEROY
Honky In The Woodpile	Max CURFEW
Honolulu Slay Ride	JASON
The Honor Of The Yorkshire Light Artillery	Sherlock HOLMES
Honor Thy Godfather	Clem TALBOT
The Honourable Algernon Knox, Detective	The Hon Algernon KNOX
Hood Of Death	Nick CARTER
The Hooded Man	Supt GAYLORD
The Hooded Terror	Sexton BLAKE
Hoodooed Howard, The Detective: Or, The River Pirates	HOODOOED HOWARD
The Hoods Take Over	Vince SLADER
Hoodwink	Lt Jake CHASE
Hookers Don't Go To Heaven	Michael SAXON
Hooky Hooked	Hooky HEFFERMAN
Hooligan	Joe HUSSEY
Hooligan	John Abraham LINCOLN
Hooray For Homicide	Jessica FLETCHER
Hope	Bernard SAMSON
Hope Against Hope	Ch Insp Nick TREVELLYAN
A Hopeless Case	Jane DA SILVA
The Horizontal Man	Kate INNES
The Hornet's Nest	Rick TRAIN
The Horror Chambers Of Jules De Grandin	Jules DE GRANDIN
Horror House	Sexton BLAKE
The Horror Of The Folding Bed	Richard FELTON
Horror's Head	Insp H EMP
The Horstmann Inheritance	Harcourt D'ESPINAL
The Hosanna Shout	Moroni TRAVELER
The Hospital Homicides	Sam HOUSTON
The Hospital Murders	Matthew HIGGINS
The Hostage	Matt LINCOLN
Hostage In Tokyo	Malko LINGE
The Hosts Of Midian	Arnold 'Tiger' WRAGGE
Hot Bullets For Love	Joseph SOUTH
Hot Day Hot Night	Det 'Grave Digger' JONES and Det 'Coffin' Ed JOHNSON
Hot Freeze	Mike GARFIN
Hot Ice	Steve ESSEX
Hot Money Can Cook Your Goose	Billy NEVERS
Hot Oil	Pat DOYLE
The Hot Place	Ed BAER
Hot Summer, Cold Murder	Mitch ROBERTS
Hot Tickets	MALONE
Hot Time In Old Town	Matthew SWAIN
Hot Water	Peter BARTHOLOMEW
Hot Zone	Max HORN
The Hotel Detective	Am CAULFIELD
The Hotel Richelieu Murders	Adelaide ADAMS
The Hotel X	DELMASSO and BRAY
The Hound Of Death	Insp BRIGG
The Hound Of London	Sherlock HOLMES
The Hound Of The Baskervilles	Sherlock HOLMES
The Hound Of The Baskervilles	Sherlock HOLMES
The Hound Of The Baskervilles	Sherlock HOLMES
The Hound Of The Basket-Maker	Sherlock HOLMES
Hounded Down	Insp G RASON
Hounded Down	Insp G RASON
The Hounds Of Sparta	Paul BAKER
The Hour Of Recognition	Sexton BLAKE
Hour Of The Wolf	Nick CARTER
The Hour Of The Wolf	Supt Mark NICOLSON
The House At Balnesmoor	Insp MCCAIG
The House At Pluck's Gutter	Tommy HAMBLEDON
House Dick	Pete NOVAK
The House In Hook Street	Insp Septimus FINCH
The House In Lordship Lane	Insp HANAUD
The House Is Falling	Insp DUFFY
The House Next Door	Jim GODFREY
The House Of Blue Lights	Cassandra THORPE
House Of Darkness	Det Insp Duncan MACCALLUM
The House Of Disappearances	Prof Irving SPENCER
The House Of Doom: Or, Nick Carter's Battle With The Crime Germ	Nick CARTER
The House Of Fear	Arthur MCHUGH
The House Of Green Turf	Francis KILLIAN
House Of Horror	Temple FORTUNE
The House Of Intrigue	Barbara 'Baddie' PRETLOW
The House Of Jackals	Timothy Overbury 'Tiger' STANDISH
The House Of Malory	Insp William BREWER
House Of Murder	Insp Wilton JACKS
The House Of Shade	Lash HOLDEN and Dany ASHTON
The House Of Sin	Dr Frank TARLETON
The House Of Strange Guests	Rev Ebenezer BUCKLE
The House Of Strange Secrets	Oliver POTTER and Laurence CARRINGTON
The House Of Terror	George FENCHURCH
The House Of The Four Winds	Duncan MCCUNN
The House Of The Missing	Jack CLAYTON
The House Of The Moving Room	Maxwell SANDERSON
The House Of The Opal	Paul SAVOY
The House Of The Shrill Whispers	Sir Gideon MERRIMAC
The House Of The Whispering Pines	Caleb SWEETWATER
The House On 9th Street	Barney GANTT
The House On Plymouth Street And Other Stories	Mrs TYRELL and Mrs LEEDS
The House On The Downs	Insp BURTON
The House On The Marsh	Insp MAYNARD
The House That Jack Built	Susan HALLIDAY
The House That Jack Built	Sherlock HOLMES
The House That Paid No Rent	Lord Rupert GARTHOYLE
House With Crooked Walls	Theodore I TERHUNE
The House With Green Shutters	Steve CARTER
The House With The Red Blinds	Sexton BLAKE
The House With The Red Door	Bradley AUSTIN
The House Without A Key	Sgt/Insp Charlie CHAN
The Houseboat Killings	Insp Fadiman WACE
A House-Party Mystery	Martin CROW
Houston Town	Hollis CARPENTER
A Hovering Of Vultures	Supt Mike ODDIE
Hovey's Deception	Tom TALLEY
How A Hermit Was Disturbed In His Retirement	Sherlock HOLMES
How Doth The Little Crocodile?	Mr VERITY and Insp RAMBLER
How Like An Angel	Joe QUINN
How To Succeed At Murder Without Really Trying	Jake WINKMAN
The Howard Hughes Affair	Toby PETERS, Howard HUGHES and Basil RATHBONE
Hoyland Intervenes	Mr HOYLAND
Hoyland Steps Out	Mr HOYLAND
Huckleberry Fiend	Paul MACDONALD
The Huddersfield Job	Marcus Aurelius FARROW and Charlie MCGOWAN
Hue And Cry	Singer BATTS
The Human Chase	Const BENSKIN
The Human Time Bomb	Nick CARTER
Human Vultures	Insp John WALK
Humpty Dumpty Dick: Or, The Harlequin Detective	HUMPTY DUMPTY DICK
The Hunchback Of Hatton Garden	Sexton BLAKE
The Hundred-Dollar Girl	Joe PUMA
Hung In The Balance	Philipa LOWE
Hung Over	Tim SIMPSON
Hung Until Dead	Blackie WHITE
The Hungarian Diamond	Picklock HOLES
The Hungry Goblin	Wilkie COLLINS
The Hunt Ball Mystery	Maj FREEMAN
The Hunt Club	John KEITH
The Hunt For Red October	Jack RYAN
Hunt The Lady!	Sexton BLAKE
The Hunted	Ben DRYDEN
Hunted Down: Or, Recollections Of A City Detective	James M'GOVAN
Hunter	Robert Lee HUNTER
The Hunter	Det Sgt Tony ROWLEY
Hunter And The Raven	Robert Lee HUNTER
Hunter Of Men	Robert URBAN
Hunter Squadron	YOEMAN
Hunter-Killer	Cdr Geoffrey PEACE
The Hunting Season	Harry SEDDAL
Huntingtower	Duncan MCCUNN
The Huntress Is Dead	Capt Wade PARIS
Hurricane Squadron	YOEMAN
Hurricane Warning	Sexton BLAKE
Hush Money	Benjamin Franklin CAGE
The Hush-Hush Murders	Anne 'Davvie' Davenport MCLEAN
Hush, Gabriel!	Agatha WELCH
Hyde And Seek	John Byron HYDE
Hyde In Deep Cover	John Byron HYDE
The Hyde Park Gardens Tragedy	Alec YORKE
The Hydra Conspiracy	BUTLER
Hymie And The Double-Dome	Hymie BEERMAN
Hymie On The Spot	Hymie BEERMAN
The Hymn Tune Mystery	Insp SMALLWAYS

H

I

Title	Character
I Am Not A Candidate...But	Kerlock SHOMES
I Am Saxon Ashe	Saxon ASHE
I Am The Captain	Joe GARTON
I Am The Cat	Dr Marc CASTLEMAN
I Am Vidocq	Eugène VIDOCQ
I Can Cope	Richard (The Pilgrim) MAIDMENT
I Die Slowly	Chet GORDON
I Don't Like Cats	Peter ALLEN
I Don't Scare Easy	Steve BORDEN
I Found Him Dead	Gale GALLAGHER
I Give You Five Days	Supt Mike YEADINGS
I Hate Blondes	Dick ANDERSON
I L F	Paul RICHARDS
I Left My Heart	Robin MILLER
I Like It Cool	Johnny AMSTERDAM
I Like 'Em Tough	Curt CANNON
I Never Miss Twice	Insp Cheviot BURMANN and Bryan ARMITAGE
I Saw Murder	John CHADWICK
I Smell The Devil	Adelaide STONE
I Spy	Insp MITCHELL
I Spy, You Die	Frank LE ROUX
I Was Walking Down Below	Danny SCIPIO
I Will Speak Daggers	Det Supt Philip HUNTER
Ice Before Killing	A Lincoln LACY
Ice Blues	Donald STRACHEY
Ice Bomb Zero	Nick CARTER
The Ice Goddess	John (The Expediter) EAGLE
The Ice House	Sgt Andy MCLOUGHLIN
Ice Trap Terror	Nick CARTER
Iceberg	Dirk PITT
Iced	Kit POWELL
The Iceman	Lucas DAVENPORT
The Identity Of Miss Angela Vespers	Mrs Julia Herlock SHOMES
The Idol's Eye	Sexton BLAKE
If A Body	Hazlitt WOAR
If Dying Was All	John EASY
If Ever I Return, Pretty Peggy-O	Sheriff Spencer ARROWWOOD
If I Knew What I Was Doing...	Ben LOMAX
If I Live To Dine	Sheridan WESLEY
If I Should Die	Jeanne DONOVAN
If I Should Die Before I Die	Charles CAMELOT
If I Should Die Before I Wake	Samuel Clemens TUCKER
If I Should Murder	Patrick LAING
If Looks Could Kill	Aphra COLQUHOUN
If Sherlock Holmes Were A Woman	Sherlock HOLMES
If Sinners Entice Thee	George STRATFIELD
If Wishes Were Hearses	Mike LANSON
Ifs And Ans	Richard DERRICK
Ill Gotten Gains	Sexton BLAKE
Ill Met By Moonlight	Col John PRIMROSE and Grace LATHAM
Ill Wind	Anna PIGEON
Illegal Entry	Millicent HETHEREGE
Illegal Tender	HEMMINGS
The Illegitimate Spy	Supt CAWTHORNE
The Image Killer	Parker ROWE
Image Of A Murder	Arnold 'Tiger' WRAGGE
Imagine A Murder	Prof Paul ENGEL
Imago: A Modern Comedy Of Manners	Lt Tromp KRAMER
The Immaterial Murder Case	Insp BLAND
An Imperfect Spy	Kate FANSLER
Impersonal Attractions	Annie TANNENBAUM
The Impetuous Mistress	Sam CROMBIE
The Impossible Footprint	Joshua Red WING
The Impossible Gulf	Cyriack Skinner GREY
The Impossible Murder Of Dr Satanus	Richard SHEILAN
The Impossible 'Impossible Crime'	Henry BOWFORT
In A Lonely Place	Det Brub NICOLAI
In At The Kill	Charlotte CAMBRY
In At The Kill	Charlotte CAMBRY
In At The Kill	Jonathan KNOX
In At The Kill	Det Ch Insp Colin THANE and Insp Phil MOSS
In Bed We Die	Valentine VICKERS
In Black And Whitey	Lee HAYES
In Blue Waters	Capt SLOCUM
In Comes Death	Garry DEAN
In Compartment 813	Arsène LUPIN
In Disgrace	Dorothy Mayotte RIGBY
In Full Cry	Insp GARDNER
In Full Cry	Det/Sgt/Supt SCARFE
In Garde We Trust	Vance (The Chameleon) GARDE
In Holy Terrors	Rev Theodora BRAITHWAITE
In La-La Land We Trust	WHISTLER
In London's Heart	WESTON
In Muffled Night	Insp WOODS
In Pursuit Of A Million	'Doc' SUMMERS
In Pursuit Of Evil	Franz HEPPEL
In Re Sherlock Holmes: The Adventures Of Solar Pons	Solar PONS
In Search Of A Villain	Lucien CLAY
In Secret	William LEQUEUX
In Suspicion's Shadow; Or, Nick Carter's Costly Error	Nick CARTER
In The Absence Of The Body	Insp SEVERN
In The Dark	'Bunny' CHIPSTEAD
In The Dead Of Night	Lionel DERING
In The Dead Of Winter	Prof Myrl Adler NORTON
In The Face Of Evidence; Or, The House Of The Seven Gargoyles	Nick CARTER
In The Fog	Insp LYLE
In The Frame	Charles TODD
In The Grip Of The Law	Det Dick DONOVAN
In The Heat Of The Night	Virgil TIBBS
In The Heat Of The Summer	Malcolm ANDERSON
In The House Of Secret Enemies	Dr Robert 'Mongo' FREDERICKSON
In The Jungle Of Cities	Philip MARLOWE
In The Lap Of Danger; Or, The Man Who Would Not Hide	Nick CARTER
In The Last Analysis	Kate FANSLER
In The Line Of Duty	Philip MARLOWE
In The Night	Evelyn TEMPLE
In The Shadow Of King's	Gillian ADAMS
In The Shadow Of Night	Sexton BLAKE
In The Teeth Of Adversity	Douglas PERKINS and Gerry TATE
In The Teeth Of The Evidence And Other Stories	Montague EGG
In The Teeth Of The Evidence And Other Stories	Lord Peter WIMSEY
In Tight Places: Some Experiences Of An Amateur Detective	Lionel MACNAUGHTEN-INNES
The Ince Murder Case	Insp WAYNE
Inch Of The CI	Insp John INCH
Inch Of The CI	Insp John INCH
The Incident At The Merry Hippo	Alexander BARTON
Incitement To Murder	Insp MARTIN
Inclining To Crime	Sexton BLAKE
The Inconsistent Villains	Montrose ARBUTHNOT and Edmund KING
The Incredible Adventures Of Rowland Hern	Rowland HERN
The Incredible Schlock Homes	Schlock HOMES
The Incredible Umbrella	Sherlock HOLMES
The Incredulity Of Father Brown	Father BROWN
Incubus	Julian TRASK
Indemnity Only	Victoria Iphigenia 'Vi' WARSHAWSKI
The Independent Detective	The INDEPENDENT DETECTIVE
The Indian Bangle	Laurence MALLOW
The Indian Diamond Mystery	Celery GREEN
The India-Rubber Men	Sgt/Insp ELK
The Indictment	Dan SHERIDAN
Indigo Death	Archie LUMSDEN
The Indiscretions Of Dr Carstairs	Dr Richard CARSTAIRS
The Indiscretions Of Lady Asenath	Lady ASENATH
The Infernal Device	Sherlock HOLMES
The Infernal Machine	Sherlock HOLMES
An Infinite Number Of Monkeys	SAXON
The Informant	John RIPLEY
Information Received	Cdr Bobby OWEN
Infra Blood	Dr Samuel CUTTING
Initials Only	Det Ebenezer GRYCE and Caleb SWEETWATER
Injustice For All	Det J P BEAUMONT
Inland Passage	Knox RANDALL
The Inn By The Shore	Clifford KING
The Inn Of Thirteen Swords	Monsieur BLACKSHIRT
The Inn Of Two Witches	Edgar BYRNE
The Inner Ring	Deirdre O'HARA
The Innocence Of Father Brown	Father BROWN
The Innocent	George COLE and Amanda DREW
Innocent Bystander	Marka DE LANCEY
The Innocent Bystanders	James CRAIG
The Innocent Flower	Prof MacDougal DUFF
The Innocents	Will HARDESTY
Inquest On A Lady	Capt MALLORY
Inquest On A Mistress	Capt MALLORY
The Inside Man	Tony LONTO
Insider's Price	Charlie BYRNE
Insoluble	Peter LINDSAY
Inspector Bosco And Lady Indiana	Insp BOSCO OF THE YARD
Inspector Bosco And The Cat Burglar	Insp BOSCO OF THE YARD
An Inspector Calls	Insp GOOLE
Inspector Derben's War	Det Insp Frank DERBEN
Inspector Dickens Retires	Insp DICKINS
Inspector Drake's Last Case	Insp DRAKE
Inspector French's Greatest Case	Insp Joseph FRENCH
Inspector Frost In The Background	Insp FROST
Inspector Frost's Jigsaw	Insp FROST
Inspector Ghote, His Life And Crimes	Insp Ganesh GHOTE
Inspector Gingko Tips His Hat To Sherlock Holmes	GINGKO
Inspector Jackson Goes North	Insp John Jay 'Jailbird' JACKSON
Inspector Jackson Investigates	Insp John Jay 'Jailbird' JACKSON
Inspector Kirchner's Own Case	Tide POOLES
Inspector Lestrade Lets The Cat Out Of The Bag	Sherlock HOLMES
Inspector Malone Sails In	Insp MALONE
Inspector Morgan's Dilemma	Det Ch Insp David MORGAN
Inspector Morse's Greatest Mystery	Insp MORSE
Inspector Rusby's Finale	Insp Myles RUSBY
Inspector Saito's Small Satori	Insp SAITO
Inspector Thomas Wins A Hat	Insp THOMAS
Inspector Treadgold Investigates	Insp TREADGOLD
Inspector West Takes Charge	Insp Roger 'Handsome' WEST
Inspector Wilkins Reads The Proofs	Insp WILKINS
The Instrument Of Destiny	Morgan FELLOWS
The Insurance Detective; Or, Unearthing A Great Fraud	The INSURANCE DETECTIVE
Intercontinental Knot	Vitaly SLAVIN
Interest Of Justice	Judge Lara SANDERSTONE
Interface	Neil FARGO
Interface For Murder	Jay PLETCHER
The Interface Man	Det Ch Insp Colin THANE and Insp Phil MOSS
Interloper	Johnny ORTIZ
The International Spy	Monsieur V
Interpol: The Case Of The Modern Medusa	Sebastian BLUE
The Interrogators	Jack EAVES
Intimate Kill	Stephen DAWES
Into The Valley Of Death	Harriet UNWIN
Into Thin Air	Dr KLOTZ
Into Thin Air	Lincoln PLUMMER
Introducing C B Greenfield	C B GREENFIELD
Introducing Miss Holmes And Her Friend	Charlotte HOLMES
Introducing Mr Raffles Holmes	Raffles HOLMES
Introducing The Super	Supt 'Tubby' GREENE
Introducing The Toff	Richard (The Toff) ROLLISON
Intruder In The Dust	Gavin STEVENS
Invasion Of Privacy	Mike ZORN
The Inverness Murder	Warren BAYNE
The Investigation	Joe PETERS
Investigations Are Proceeding	Det Insp Don KERRY
Investigations Of Colwin Grey	Colwin GREY
The Investigations Of Godfrey Page, Railwayac	Godfrey PAGE
The Investigations Of John Pym	John PYM

Invisible Death	Prince ZARKON
The Invisible Enemy	Prof Christopher EKSHAW
Invisible Evidence	Lee SEDDON
Invisible Green	Thackeray PHIN
The Invisible Intruder	Libby KNOWLES
The Invisible Man Murders	Chin Kwang KHAM
The Invisible Pickpocket: Or, Records Of A City Detective	James M'GOVAN
The Invisible Tomb	Julian Morse TROWBRIDGE
The Invisible Worm	Dr Paul PRYE
Invitation To Kill	Clifford GRANT
The Involvement Of Arnold Wechsler	Arnold WECHSLER
In-Laws And Outlaws	Gillian CLIFFORD
IOU Murder	Pete SCHOFIELD
IOU - Murder	Anthony MARTIN
The Ipcress File	Harry PALMER
Irene At Large	Irene ADLER
Irene, Good Night	Sherlock HOLMES
Irene's Last Waltz	Irene ADLER
The Irish Detective: Or, Fergus Connor's Greatest Case	The IRISH DETECTIVE
The Irish Police Officer	The IRISH POLICE OFFICER
Irish Stew	Mr JONES
The Iron Arm Detective	OLD TERRIBLE
Iron Burgess, The Government Detective	IRON BURGESS
The Iron Clew	Leonidas WITHERALL
The Iron Door	Timothy CULLINAN
The Iron Egg	Det Insp Elwyn HUGHES
The Iron Gates	Insp SANDS
The Iron God	Modesty BLAISE
The Iron Hand	Leonidas WITHERALL
The Iron Horse	Matt FARADAY
The Iron Horse Or Life On The Line	SHARP
The Iron Maiden	Larry BAKER
The Iron Pirate: A Plain Tale Of Strange Happenings At Sea	Capt BLACK
The Iron Ring	Margaret ANNISTER
The Iron Skull	Vernon READ
The Iron Spiders	Miles Standish RICE
The Ironing Board	Dove DULCET
A Is For Alibi	Kinsey MILLHONE
Is He The Man?	Col KILMAIN
Is Money Everything?	Al MOONEY
Is There A Traitor In The House?	Selena MEAD
Isaac Lazarus, The Egyptian Detective	Isaac LAZARUS
Island Gold	Dr Adolph (Clubfoot) GRUNDT and Desmond OKEWOOD
Island Intrigue	Michael (The Shield) SHERIFF
The Island Of Disaster	Sgt HOBBS
The Island Of Sheep	Richard HANNAY
Island Of Spies	Oliver KEENE
Island Of Steel	Eddie MARGOLIS
The Island Of Terror	Jim MAITLAND
The Israeli Connection	Nick CARTER
The Issue Of The Bishop's Blood	Dave PECK
It Ain't Hay	Whit WHITNEY
It Blows Up In Your Face	William DRINK and Sam SLEEP
It Couldn't Be Murder	Peter QUINT
It Had To Be Murder	Hal JEFFRIES
It Makes You Think	Felix HOLLIDAY
It Might Have Meant Murder	Maj MOSSON
It Takes A Thief	Robbie DUNCAN
It Walks By Night	Juge d'Instruction Henri BENCOLIN
It Was Locked	Insp LINSCOTT
It Was Murder, They Said	Glen GIBSON
It Wasn't A Nightmare	Archibald BELDRUM and Nigel BLAIR
It Wasn't Me!	Sgt CRAIG
It Won't Get You Anywhere	John BROCK
Italian Assets	Max FARNE
Italian Assets	Max FARNE
Item 7	Lawrence MAVER
It's A Free Country	Charlie HOWARD
It's Death, My Darling!	Katherine 'Peter' PIPER
It's Her Funeral	Lady Margaret PRIAM
It's Murder If You Say So	Galahad Urban BROWNE
It's Murder, Maguire	John Patrick Aloysius MAGUIRE
It's Murder, Senorita	Larry VERNON
It's My Own Funeral	Jeff MILES
It's Your Funeral	Chico BRETT
Ivory Ladies	Sherrett YORK
The Ivory Queen	Herbert DARRENT
The Ivory Snuff Box	Richard DUVALL
I, Anna	Insp BERNSTEIN
I, Said The Sparrow	SPARROW
I, Sherlock Holmes	Sherlock HOLMES
I, The Criminal	Sheridan ORFORD and Prof Henry Arthur FIELDING
I, The Jury	Mike HAMMER
I'd Rather Be In Philadelphia	Amanda PEPPER
I'll Be Judge, I'll Be Jury	Antoine CIRRET
I'll Be Waiting	Tony RESECK and John EVANS
I'll Bring Her Back	Johnny VALLON
I'll Cry When I Kill You	Charles CAMELOT
I'll Do Anything	Larry VERNON
I'll Eat You Last	Dr John BENT
I'll Find You	John Patrick Aloysius MAGUIRE
I'll Get You Yet	Steve ASHE
I'll Grind Their Bones	John H W KEATS
I'll Never Like Friday Again	Timothy TERREL
I'll Say She Does!	Lemmy CAUTION
I'm Cannon - For Hire	Curt CANNON
I'm No Murderer	R J 'Rick' LEROY
I'm Trying To Give It Up	John BROCK

— J —

The J Alfred Prufrock Murders	Angela BENBOW and Caledonia WINGATE
J For Jupiter	Edmund 'Jupiter' JONES
The Jacaranda Murders	Insp DUNNING
Jack And Susan In 1933	Jack BEAUMONT and Susan BRIGHT
Jack And Susan In 1953	Jack BEAUMONT and Susan BRIGHT
Jack Carter And The Mafia Pigeon	Jack CARTER
Jack Donahue, The Mountain Detective: Or, Unraveling A Terrible Mystery	Jack DONAHUE
The Jack Of Hearts	Jake WINKMAN
Jack Parker, The 'All-Round' Detective: Or, The Trail Of The Letter 'A'	Jack PARKER
Jack Sharpley, The Always-Ready Detective: Or, Hunting Down The Red Hand Gang	Jack SHARPLEY
Jack Simons, Detective	Jack SIMONS
Jack Vinton, The Boy Detective	Jack VINTON
Jack's Return Home	Jack CARTER
The Jacob Street Mystery	Dr John Evelyn THORNDYKE
Jacoby's First Case	Quentin JACOBY
The Jade Figurine	Dan CONNELL
The Jade Green Cats	John KYMMERLY
The Jade Hatpin	Stonewall STEEVENS
Jaggers At Bay	JAGGERS
Jaggers Swoops Again	JAGGERS
Jaggers, Air Detective	JAGGERS
The Jake Of Diamonds	Jake WINKMAN
Jamaica Run	Joe CINQUEZ
The Jamaican Exchange	Nick CARTER
James Bond And Moonraker	Cdr James BOND
James Bond, The Spy Who Loved Me	Cdr James BOND
Jane Carberry: Detective	Jane CARBERRY
Jane Carberry's Week-End	Jane CARBERRY
Janet Darling, The Love Detective	Janet DARLING
The Janus Murder	Casey CARMICHAEL
The Jason Affair	JASON
Jason Burr's First Case	Jason BURR
Jason Goes West	JASON
Jason King	Jason KING
Jealousy Pulls The Trigger	Mac MCINTYRE
Jeff Clayton's Mexican Plot	Jeff CLAYTON
Jeff Clayton's Triumph	Jeff CLAYTON
The Jefferson Nickel: An Astonishing Sherlock Holmes Adventure	Sherlock HOLMES
Jemima Shore's First Case	Jemima SHORE
Jennerton & Co	JENNERTON
Jere Clinch, The Eagle-Eyed Detective: Or, Guarding The Demdike Millions	Jere CLINCH
The Jericho Scam	DEMPSEY and MAKEPEACE
Jerry Owens, The Young Western Detective	Jerry OWENS
Jersey Tomatoes	MALONE
The Jerusalem File	Nick CARTER
Jest Of Darkness	Hoani MATA
Jethro Hammer	Melville FAIRR
Jewel Mysteries From A Dealer's Notebook	Bernard SUTTON
Jewel Mysteries I Have Known: From A Dealer's Notebook	Bernard SUTTON
Jewels In Jeopardy	George BARCLAY
Jian	Jake MAROC
Jigger Moran	'Jigger' MORAN
Jigsaw	John RINGROSE
The Jig-Saw Puzzle Murder	Insp WATTERSON
The Jig-Time Murders	Jimmy HASTINGS
Jill Rips	Murray WILSON
Jim Cummings: Or, The Great Adams Express Robbery	A Frank PINKERTON
Jim Hanvey, Detective	Jim HANVEY
Jim Maitland	Jim MAITLAND
Jim Maitland	Jim MAITLAND
Jimgrim	James Schuyler 'Jimgrim' GRIM and Chullunder GHOSE
Jimgrim Sahib	James Schuyler 'Jimgrim' GRIM and Chullunder GHOSE
Jimmie Dale And The Missing Hour	Jimmie DALE
Jimmie Rezaire	Jimmie REZAIRE
Jimsie, The Horse Detective	JIMSIE
Jinx	Kit POWELL
Jo Crupper, Bus Conductor	Jo CRUPPER
Joan Mar, Detective	Joan MAR
Jockey Joe, The Race Track Detective	JOCKEY JOE
Joe Jenkins: Detective	Joe JENKINS
Joe Jenkins' Casebook	Joe JENKINS
Joe Muller, Detective	Joe MULLER
Joe Nix Is Dead	Sgt George KELSO
Joe Phoenix, Private Detective: Or, The League Of Skeleton Keys	Joe PHOENIX
Joe Phoenix, The Police Spy	Joe PHOENIX
Joe Quinney's Jodie	Joe QUINNEY
John Boddy: Leaves From A Constable's Notebook	Const John BOODY
John Carruthers: Indian Policeman	John CARRUTHERS
John Carstairs, Space Detective	John CARSTAIRS
John Clutterbuck	Rosie BRIGHT
John Fay, Detective: Or, The Renegade's Plot	John FAY
John Merry, The Alert Detective	John MERRY
John Parmalee's Curse	Fred TYRREL
The John Riddell Murder Case: A Philo Vance Parody	Pluto VANCE
John Rugby, The Ferryboat Detective: Or, The North River Mystery	John RUGBY
John Silence, Physician Extraordinary	John SILENCE
John Smith Hears Death Walking	John SMITH

John Thorndyke's Cases	Dr John Evelyn THORNDYKE
Johnny Havoc	Johnny HAVOC
Johnny Liddell's Morgue	Johnny LIDDELL
Johnny Staccato	Johnny STACCATO
The Joker In The Deck	Helga ROLFE
Jonah And Co	Bertram PLEYDELL
The Jordan Intercept	Joshua BAIN
Jorkens Borrows Another Whisky	Joseph JORKENS
Jorkens Has A Large Whisky	Joseph JORKENS
Joseph Prickett, The Scotland Yard Detective	Insp Joseph PRICKETT
The Joshua Sequence	Matthew RIORDAN
Journey Downstairs	C J SWAN
Journey Into Danger	John MARSHALL and Suzy MARSHALL
Journey Into Stone	Det GRENNON
Journey Into Violence	William MALLETT
Journey To A Safe Place	Peter MUNRO
Journey To Genoa	Sexton BLAKE
The Journeying Boy	Insp CADOGAN
The Joyous Adventures Of Aristide Pujol	Aristide PUJOL
Judas Country	Roy CASE
The Judas Diary	Richard QUINTAIN
The Judas Figures	KEOGH
The Judas Judge	The BUTCHER
The Judas Kiss	Shauna BISHOP
The Judas Mandate	David GARNETT
The Judas Pair	LOVEJOY
The Judas Spies	Alan STEEL
Judge And Be Damned	Linus RINTOUL
The Judge And His Hangman	Kommissar Hans BARLACH
Judge Priest Turns Detective	Judge PRIEST
The Judge Sums Up	Paul BISHOP
The Judge Will Call It Murder	Stephen RINGWAY
The Judges Of Hades, And Other Simon Ark Stories	Simon ARK
The Judge's Song	Dave WOOLF
Judith Lee, Some Pages From Her Life	Judith LEE
Juice	Panama HEATH
Juke Box King	Mickey DENTON
Julia In Ireland	Julia PROBYN
The Julius Caesar Murder Case	Publius Manlius SCRIBO
The Julius House	Aurora 'Rose' TEAGARDEN
Jump Cut	Bob CHRISTOPHER
Jumpers	Insp BONES
Jumping The Cracks	RATS
The Jumpmaster	Insp Roger BASTIDE
June Mail	Sarah CALLOWAY
June, Moon, And Murder	Homer FITZGERALD
Jungle Blitz	Mark (The Penetrator) HARDIN
The Jungle Crime	Gordon MULDREW
Jungle Jest	Cotswold OMMONY
Jungle Of Steel And Stone	Veil KENDRY
Junk On The Hill	Joe POSNER
Junkyard Angel	Scott MITCHELL
The Junkyard Dog	Jimmy FLANNERY
The Juror	Nick ATWELL
Juror	Stanley HASTINGS
Just Another Angel	Fitzroy Maclean ANGEL
Just Another Angel	Insp Richard THORNHILL
Just Another Day In Paradise	FIDDLER
Just Around The Corner	Pete CORY
Just Desserts	Judith McMonigle FLYNN
Just Killing Time	Steve DRAKE
Justice Be Damned	Judge MANFRED
Justice For A Dead Spy	Silas MANNERS
Justice In Jeopardy	Insp Roger ELLERDINE
Justice Is Done	KHARDUNI
The Justice Of Sanders	Commiss SANDERS
The Justification Of Andrew Lebrun	David LEIGH
Justus Wise	Justus WISE
Juvenile Delinquent	Manville MOON
Juvenile Hoods	Dan MORRISON

— K —

K Is For Killer	Kinsey MILLHONE
The K Section	Ralph CARTER
Kail Hutton, The Cincinnati Detective; Or, The Mystery Of The Phantom Hand	Kail HUTTON
The Kaiser's Code	Herlock SHOLMES
The Kali Death Cult	Nick CARTER
The Kaligarh Fault	Tommy BERREN
The Kama Sutra Tango	Joe STREETER
Kansas City Flash	Mark HULL
Kate Plus Ten	T B SMITH
Katie's Terror	Katie MacGregor TOWNSEND
Katwalk	Kat COLORADO
Kearny's Last Case	Max KEARNY
Keegan: The No-Option Contract	KEEGAN
Keegan: The One-Way Deal	KEEGAN
Keep Cool, Mr Jones	Edmund 'Jupiter' JONES
Keep Murder Quiet	Roger SPAIN
Keeper Of The Keys	Sgt/Insp Charlie CHAN
The Keepers Of The King's Peace	Commiss SANDERS
Keeping Time	Jack HUGHES
Kefton, The Detective; Or, The Wonder Of The Age	KEFTON
Kek Huuygens, Smuggler	Kek HUUYGENS
Kellogg Junction	Benson KELLOGG
Kelly Among The Nightingales	Samuel Moses KELLY
Kennedy For The Defense	Jerry KENNEDY
Kensington Gore	Jack LAMARRE and Alison PRENDERGAST
The Kentucky Detective	The KENTUCKY DETECTIVE
Kenyatta's Last Hit	KENYATTA
The Kessler Legacy	Walter SPENSE
The Kestrel House Mystery	Ch Insp BARNARD
The Key Ring Clew; Or, On The Edge Of Doom	Nick CARTER
Key To Murder	Ch of Plce Ira FISCHER
Key Without A Door	Prof James GLOWREY
Keys For The Criminal	Insp 'Tubby' HALL
Keystone	Warwick EASTON
KGB Kill	Joe CAVE
Kharduni	KHARDUNI
The Kid From Riga	Lewis HORNE
The Kid Who Came Home With A Corpse	Jeremiah X GIBSON and MAC
Kidnapped Again	FALCON
The Kidnapped School	ST FRANCIS SCHOOL
The Kidnapper	Peter GRAHAM
The Kidnapper's Victim	Sexton BLAKE
The Kidnapping Of Mr Chasebrook	Kerlock SHOMES
Kid's Stuff	Ch Insp Nick TREVELLYAN
Kiet And The Opium War	Supt Bamsan KIET
Kiev Footprint	Stephen BORG
The Kilbourne Connection	Henry GARRETT
The Kill	Ray RIPLEY
Kill All The Lawyers	Curt DENMARK
Kill And Tell	Rolf LE ROUX
Kill And Tell	Timothy WILDE
Kill City	Alex (The Enforcer) JASON
Kill Cue	Veronica SLATE
Kill Fee	Lt Janus MURTAUGH
Kill For It	John BOLT
Kill For The Millions	Peter CHAMBERS
Kill Him Quickly, Its Raining	Pete MCGRATH
Kill Jason King	Jason KING
Kill Me In Roppongi	Burns BANNION
Kill Me In Tokyo	Burns BANNION
Kill Petrosino!	Joe PETROSINO
Kill Quick Or Die	The BUTCHER
Kill The Hundredth Monkey	Randall Gatsby SIERRA
Kill The Reporter	Hawthorne Albert HARKER
Kill To Fit	Rick TRAIN
Kill Zone	Peter MACKLIN
Kill 'Em With Kindness	Mack MCGANN
Killed In The Ratings	Matt COBB
Killed On The Rocks	Matt COBB
Killed With A Passion	Matt COBB
The Killer At Large	Mr PREED
Killer At Large	Det Insp Charles TREMAYNE
The Killer At Port Norman	Jim MALLOY
Killer Be Killed	Justine CARMICHAEL
Killer By Proxy	Eve GILL
Killer Cop	Johnny MALONE
Killer Cruise	Ben KANE
The Killer Elite	Mike LOCKEN
A Killer For A Song	Boysie OAKES
The Killer Genesis	Hank (The Mercenary) FROST
Killer In The Crowd - Special	Insp Alan GRANT
Killer In The Kitchen	Mickey RICHARDS
A Killer Is Loose	John NOLAN
The Killer Is Mine	Ed RIVERS
Killer Loose!	Lt Al WHITE
Killer Pack	Sexton BLAKE
Killer Patrol	Mike BRENT
Killers	Det Jack WILLOWS and Det Claire PARKER
Killers At Sea	LOGAN
Killers For Hire	DEATH SQUAD
Killers From The Keys	Michael SHAYNE
Killers Must Eat	Michael the O'KELLY
The Killers Of Starfish	Jonas DUNCAN
Killers Play Rough	Jim PIERCE
Killer's Choice	Bert NORDEN
Killer's Ink	Pete BRADY
Killer's Kiss	Peter CHAMBERS and Marla TRENT
Killer's Playground	Sexton BLAKE
Killer's Rights	Isamu OHARA
The Killing Circle	Neal RAFFERTY
Killing Comes Easy	Johnny PRESTON
A Killing For Charity	Charity BAY
A Killing Frost	Harry TONG
Killing Ground!	James RHODES
A Killing In Real Estate	Amos MCGUFFIN
A Killing In Real Estate	Hugh MORRISON
A Killing In Rome	Mike LOCKEN
A Killing In Swords	Alastair Alexandrovitch TIMUROFF
Killing Jazz	Jim BLISS
The Killing Kind	Jim BLANEY
The Killing Machine	Johnny ROCK
The Killing Man	Mike HAMMER
The Killing Match	Jeff CASS
Killing No Murder	Insp BARNABY
Killing No Murder	Stonewall STEEVENS
The Killing Of Judge MacFarlane	John SMITH
The Killing Of Katie Steelstock	Ch Supt KNOTT
The Killing Of Monday Brown	Phoebe SIEGEL
The Killing Of Paris Norton	R I PERKINS
Killing Time	Tim SMITH
A Killing Trade	William 'Tiny' RYDER
The Killing Wind	Brian DOUGLAS
Killing Wonder	Jessamyn POSEY
The Killing Zone	Det Gabriel WAGER
The Killings At Badger's Drift	Det Ch Insp Tom BARNABY
Killtown	PARKER

Kill-Box	Steven ERIKSON
Kill, Sweet Charity - Kill	Jeff TYLER
The Kilroy Gambit	Richard LE GRANDE
The Kimberley Diamond Mine Substitution Scandal	Shearlock COMBS
A Kind Of Homecoming	Supt Ceal MEGARRY
Kind Uncle Buckby	Lionel BUCKBY
Kinderkill	Tom RAGNON
Kindness Can Kill	Det Ch Insp Ian ROPER
Kindred Crimes	Jeri HOWARD
Kinds Of Love, Kinds Of Death	Mitch TOBIN
A King By Night	Selby LOWE
King Cobra	Colin GRAY
King Dan, The Factory Detective	KING DAN
The King Edward Plot	King of England Edward VII WINDSOR
The King In Yellow	Steve GRAYCE
The King Murder	Leighton SWIFT
King Of Diamonds	PREACHER
King Of Hearts	Cassandra SWANN
The King Of Paflagonia	Picklock HOLES
The King Of Satan's Eyes	Lincoln BLACKTHORNE
King Of The Khyber Rifles	Athelstan KING
King Of The Mountain	Conan FLAGG
King Of The Underworld: Or, With A Life At Stake	Nick CARTER
King Silky!	Sidney 'Silky' PINCUS and Mike CLANCY
The Kingdom Of Death	Clyde HAVILAND
The Kingdom Of Death	Mason TRASK
Kings In The Counting House	Sam LINKUM
The Kingsbridge Plot	Dr John TONNEMAN
Kingsley The Detective: Or, A Single Clew	KINGSLEY
King-Sized Murder	James REHM
The King's Prisoner: Or, Patsy Plays a Lone Hand	Patsy MURPHY
The King's Detective: Or, A New York Detective's Great Quest	The KING'S DETECTIVE
The King's Highway	Dick RYDER
King's Messenger	Col ORMISTON
King's Ransom	Mark STONER
The Kinsmen	Paul MARTINY
Kirby's Last Circus	Birch KIRBY
A Kiss A Day Keeps The Corpses Away	Kiss DARLING
Kiss And Kill	Barney BURGESS
Kiss And Kill	Patrick HARDY
Kiss And Kill	A Lincoln LACY
Kiss Me Once	Lew CASSIDAY
Kiss Me Twice	Lew CASSIDAY
Kiss The Boss Goodbye	Arthur SALISBURY and Frank SHEARER
Kiss The Boss Goodbye	Lt Cdr Frank SARGENT
Kiss The Boys And Make Them Die	Kiss DARLING
Kiss The Girls	Det Alex CROSS
Kiss The Killer	Dan MORRISON
Kiss The Tiger	Quinn LELAND
Kiss Yourself Goodbye	Matt SINCLAIR
The Kissed Corpse	Jerry BURKE
Kisses Leave No Fingerprints	Willie HALLIDAY
Kisses Of Death	Peter CHAMBERS and Marla TRENT
The Kiss-Off	Steve MALLORY
Kiss! Kiss! Kill! Kill!	Peter CHAMBERS
Kitty's Father	James SINGLETON
The Kiwi Club	'Jumbo' RUTHERFORD
A Klondyke Claim: Or, Won By Sheer Nerve	Harvey STOKES
Klute	KLUTE
The Knave Of Diamonds	Jim BREEN
Knaves Of Diamonds, Being Tales Of Mine And Veld	Insp LIPINSKI
The Knife	Mark BRADDON
Knife Between Brothers	David RETURN
A Knife Between The Ribs	Det Insp Alf ROSHER
A Knife In The Dark	Mrs Elizabeth WARRENDER and James WARRENDER
A Knife Is Silent	Jason BURR
A Knife To Remember	Jane JEFFRY
Knight Fall	Sgt Peter 'Obie' BRICHTER
Knight Fall	Mark SAVAGE
Knight Must Fall	Glad GOLD
Knight Rider	Michael LONG
Knight Sinister	Hugo BISHOP
Knights Of The Open Palm	Race WILLIAMS
Knight's Gambit	Supt 'Cissie' MARLOW
Knight's Gambit	Gavin STEVENS
Knit One, Drop Two	Ben JONSON
Knock And Come In	Nigel REX
Knock Down	Jonah DEREHAM
Knock-Out Kavanagh	Knock-Out KAVANAGH
Knock, Murderer, Knock!	Mr WINKLEY
Knots And Crosses	Insp REBUS
Knots Untied: Or, Ways And Byways In The Hidden Life Of American Detectives	DETECTIVES
The Komani Mystery	Insp DOWNES and Sgt HOPKINS
The Krakatoa Cult	Julian PRESCOT
The Kravonian Adventure	Charlotte HOLMES
The Kremlin Conspiracy	Wallace MAHONEY and John MAHONEY
The Kremlin File	Nick CARTER
Kyd For Hire	Thomas KYD
The Kyle Contract	Barry JORDAN
Kyril	Gen Stepan POVIN

K

—L—

La Brava	Joe LA BRAVA
La Marmoset, The Detective Queen: Or, The Lost Heir Of Morel	LA MARMOSET
The Labyrinth Makers	Dr David AUDLEY
Ladies In Ermine	Joel SABER
Ladies Won't Wait	Michael KELLS
Ladies' Night	Meg LACEY
Lady Audley's Secret	Robert AUDLEY
The Lady Can Lose	Hans LUGAR
The Lady Chapel	Owen ARCHER
The Lady Detective	Kate GOELET
The Lady Detective	The LADY DETECTIVE
The Lady From Nowhere	Absolom GEBB
The Lady Had A Tiger	John BORHAM
The Lady Hilda's Mystery	Picklock HOLES
Lady In Black	Insp Auguste JANTRY
The Lady In Blue	Joe MULLER
Lady In Danger	Christopher SAXE
Lady In Peril	Mitchell LONEMAN
Lady In Peril	Insp TOPE
The Lady In The Lake	Johnny DALMAS
The Lady In The Lake	Philip MARLOWE
The Lady In The Wood	Insp Rupert HAMBLEDON
Lady Incognito	Insp QUAILE
The Lady Is A Spy	Emma GREAVES
The Lady Is A Vamp	Bradley ADAMS
The Lady Is Afraid	Max Chauncy HALE
The Lady Is Lethal	Lois DULANE
The Lady Is The Tiger	Steve DART
Lady Judas	Dr STURGESS
Lady Kate, The Darling Detective	Kate EDWARDS
Lady Killer	Bob ADAMS and Anne MINER
The Lady Killer Affair	Kate GRAHAM
The Lady Killers	Huntingdon CAGE
The Lady Loved Too Well	Harlan COLE
Lady Molly Of Scotland Yard	Lady Molly DE MAZEREEN
Lady Of Burlesque	Gypsy Rose LEE and Biff BRANNIGAN
Lady Of Night	'Chick' VARNEY
The Lady Of The Camellias	Sherlock HOLMES
Lady Of The Impossible	Sir Gideon PARROT
The Lady Of The Night Wind	Bingham HARVARD
Lady On Fire	Julian FORBES
Lady On The Line	Kyra KEATON
The Lady Said No	Martin ROSS
A Lady Swings Her Right	Patrolman MURPHY
Lady To Kill	Chance MALLOY
Lady Turpin	Insp BENDER
The Lady Vanishes	Iris CARR
The Lady Was A Tramp	Pat RAFFIGAN
The Lady Was Disturbed	James WARREN
Lady With A Cool Eye	Melinda PINK
The Lady With The Limp	The Hon Timothy Overbury 'Tiger' STANDISH and Sir Harker BELLAMY
Ladycat	MCQUADE
Ladygrove	Dr Alexander CASPIAN
Lady, Don't Die On My Doorstep	Dan MORRISON
Lady, Drop Dead	Det Jub FREEMAN and Det Mitch TAYLOR
Lady, Drop Dead	Hank GREENLEAF
Lady, Get Your Gun	Shirley LEIGHTON and Bill HARPER
Lady, The Guy Is Dead	Jerry BENEDICT
The Lady's Not For Living	Kirby HART
Laguna Heat	Tom SHEPHERD
Laidlaw	Jack LAIDLAW
The Lake District Murder	Insp MEREDITH
The Lake Effect	Milan JACOVICH
The Lake Frome Monster	Det Insp Napoleon BONAPARTE
Lakeland Tragedy	William BRITTAIN
The Lakeside Murder	Tommy THORNE
Lam To The Slaughter	Bertha COOL and Donald LAM
Lamaar Ransom - Private Eye	Lamaar RANSOM
Lament For A Lover	Insp CORBY
Lanagan, Amateur Detective	Jack LANAGAN
Lancer Spy	Clive GRANVILLE
Land Of Always-Night	'Doc' SAVAGE
Landfall	Alec SINCLAIR
Landscape With Dead Dons	Insp AUTUMN
Lantern Hill	Aloysius KELLY
The Lantern House Affair	Kate MARSH
Large Type Killer	Sexton BLAKE
Largely Luck	Largely LEE
Largely Trouble	Largely LEE
Larry Murtagh's Missing Ear Case: Or, A Clew To The Murder Of Langley, The Broker	Larry MURTAGH
Las Vegas Vengeance	Johnny ROCK
The Lasko Tangent	Christopher PAGET
Last Act In Bermuda	Insp HOPKINS
The Last Adventures Of Christian Doom, Private I	Christian DOOM
The Last Annual Slugfest	Vejay HASKELL
The Last Appointment	Glenn BOWMAN
The Last Assignment	Nigel MORRISON
Last Bus To Woodstock	Insp MORSE
The Last Camel Died At Noon	Amelia PEABODY
The Last Castrato	Insp Carlo ARBATI
Last Chance For Glory	Marty BLAKE
Last Clear Chance	Geoffrey MILDMAY
The Last Clue	Byron HUGHES
Last Dance At Redondo Beach	Murray GLICK
The Last Days Of Louisiana Red	Papa LA BAS
Last Death Below Deck	'Mac' MACFARLAND
The Last Detective	Supt Peter DIAMOND
The Last Detective Story In The World	Sherlock HOLMES
The Last Domino Contract	Joe GALL
The Last Doorbell	Lt Francis X KERRIGAN

The Last Doorbell	Lt Cdr Frank SARGENT
The Last Escape	Insp/Supt MACDONALD
The Last Express	Duncan MACLAIN
Last Ferry From The Lido	Paul HEDLEY and Harcourt D'ESPINAL
The Last Flight To Moscow	Nick CARTER
The Last Generation	Tom HOWARD
The Last Good Kiss	Chauncy Wayne SUGHRUE
The Last Housewife	Kit DELEEUW
Last Judgement	Richard GRIEVE, Paula GLENNING and James GOFF
The Last Kill	Steve LEE
The Last Known Address	Lt Francis X KERRIGAN
The Last Laugh	Garth RYLAND
The Last Laugh	Miss WOOLFE
The Last Man At Arlington	George WILLIAMS
The Last Meeting	Insp BARNES
The Last Meeting Of The Butler's Club	Lord Peter WIMSEY
The Last Move In The Game: Or, Crime's Horror	Nick CARTER
The Last Of Mr Moto	Mr MOTO
The Last Of Sherlock Holmes	Sherlock HOLMES
The Last Of The Potatoes	Herlock SHOLMES
Last Plane From Nice	Persis WILLUM
Last Poppies Of Death	John (The Expediter) EAGLE
The Last Private Eye	Michael RHINEHEART
The Last Private Eye In Belfast	Bernard HOLLAND
The Last Reunion	Sherlock HOLMES
Last Rights	Maj Jonathan CRAYTHORNE
Last Rites	Father Fernando O'NEAL
Last Rites For The Vulture	Francis X (The Inquisitor) KILLY
The Last Samaurai	Nick CARTER
Last Seen Wearing...	Ch FORD
The Last Set	Adrienne BISHOP
The Last Shaft	John SHAFT
The Last Sherlock Holmes Story	Sherlock HOLMES
The Last Straw	Lt Bill GRADY
The Last Straw	Det Sgt O'BYRNE
The Last Straw	Jim O'NEILL
The Last Stroke	Francis FERRARS
The Last Stronghold	Harvey LANDON
The Last Supper	Paul CHRISTOPHER
The Last Suppers	Goldy BEAR
The Last Tango Of Dolores Delgardo	Claudia VALENTINE
The Last Tenant	James DICKSON
The Last Tiger	Sexton BLAKE
The Last Time I Saw Mary	Harry REILLY
The Last Trap	Paul BERNARD
The Last Voyage	Sally LIVINGSTONE
The Last Warning	Arthur MCHUGH
The Last Wednesday	Dave WOOLF
Last Will And Testament	Virginia FREER and Felix FREER
Last Will And Testament	Virginia FREER and Felix FREER
The Last Will And Testament Of Constance Cobble	Constance COBBLE
Last Will And Testament: Or, The Pendexter Saga, Second (And Last) Canto	Ben TANCRED and Supt Henry WILSON
The Last Word	Adam JAMES
The Late Candidate	Samson DEAN
The Late Edition	Dr Francis FARRAR
Late Knight	Mark SAVAGE
The Late Lady	Supt Robert BONE
Late Payments	Lt Leroy POWDER
The Late, Lamented Lady	Eve MACWILLIAMS
The Latimer Mercy	Augustus MALTRAVERS
The Laughing Buddha Murders	Chin Kwang KHAM
The Laughing Cat	Anthony READ and Jacqueline NORRIS
The Laughing Death	John (The Expediter) EAGLE
Laughing Dog	Leo G BLOODWORTH and Sarah 'Serendipity' DAHLQUIST
The Laughing Dragon Mystery	Terry SPRING
The 'Laughing Man' Murders	Insp Martin FIELD
The Laughing Policeman	Insp George JUDD
Laughter In The Alehouse	MCGREGOR
The Laughter Trap	Peter STYLES
Laura	Det Mark MCPHERSON
Laura Keen, The Queen Of Detectives	Laura KEEN
The Lavender Gripsack	Elsa COLBY
Law And Order, Unlimited	Gregory QUIST
The Law And The Lady	Valeria WOODVILLE
The Law Breakers	Sgt/Insp Stanley FYLES
The Law Of The Four Just Men	FOUR JUST MEN
The Law Of The Gun	Sgt/Insp Stanley FYLES
The Law Of The River	Commiss SANDERS
The Law Of The Three Just Men	FOUR JUST MEN
The Lawyer Detective: Or, The Mystery At Three Oaks Ranch	The LAWYER DETECTIVE
The Lawyer's Secret	Insp CLARKE
Lay Her Among The Lilies	Vic MALLOY
Lay Me Odds	Eve DRUM
Lay On, Macduff	Prof MacDougal DUFF
Layout For Murder	Jim BREEN
The Layton Court Mystery	Roger SHERINGHAM
The Lazarus Lie	Insp CHERRY
Lazarus Murder Seven	Det Daniel WEBSTER
Lazarus #7	Det Daniel WEBSTER
The Lazy Lawrence Murders	Peter BOUNTY
Lead Me To The Slaughter	Det Ch Supt Thomas FOX
Lead With Your Left	Dave WINTINO
The League Of Gentlemen	John Byron HYDE
A League Of Hawks	Ian QUAYLE
The League Of Justice	Peter JUSTICE
The League Of Missing Men	Bromley KAY
The League Of The Scarlet Pimpernel	The SCARLET PIMPERNEL
The League Of The White Hand	Det Insp MORGAN
Leap Before You Look	Steve ESSEX
Leap Of Faith	Blaine STEWART
Leathermouth	Col Gantian LEATHERMOUTH
Leave Everything To Me	Philip MACCRAY
Leave The Grave Green	Duncan KINCAID
The Leavenworth Case: A Lawyer's Story	Det Ebenezer GRYCE
Leaves From The Notebook Of A New York Detective	A NEW YORK DETECTIVE
A Lecture In Detection	Ch Supt J V STRUTT
The Ledger	Policewoman Christie OPARA
The Ledger Is Kept	Insp HOLLY
Left Hand Left	Thornton ZANE
Lefty O'Connor Moves In	'Lefty' O'CONNOR
Lefty Takes Over	'Lefty' O'CONNOR
Left, Right And Centre	Andrew TAGGART
Leg Man	Peter WENNICK
Legacy	Telzey AMBERDON and Trigger ARGEE
Legacy Of Danger	Selena MEAD
A Legacy Of Vengeance	Sheriff BRAMLEY
The Legend Of The Slain Soldiers	Elena OLIVEREZ
Legion	Bill KINDERMAN
Leipzig Manuscript	Marcus Aurelius FARROW and Charlie MCGOWAN
The Lemon Chicken Jones	SAXON
Lena Hates Men	Insp GROGAN
Lend A Hand	Donald BRACKEN and James Rowland WOODWARD VII
The Lenient Beast	Det Frank RAMOS
The Leo Conversion	Jim STEVENS
The Leo Wyoming Caper	Deuce RAMSEY
Leonardo Da Vinci, Detective	Leonardo DA VINCI
Leonardo's Law	Dr David Vincent LEONARDO
Leopold's Way	Capt LEOPOLD
Les Miserables	Insp JAVETT
The Lessing Murder Case	Sir William KIRBY
Lessinger's Lapse	LESSINGER
A Lesson In Crime	Supt Henry WILSON
A Lesson In Dying	Insp Stephen RAMSAY
Lester Grayling, KC	Lester GRAYLING
Lestrade And The Mirror Of Murder	Insp/Supt Sholto LESTRADE and Sherlock HOLMES
Lestrade And The Sign Of Nine	Insp/Supt Sholto LESTRADE
Let Him Die	Alister WOODHEAD
Let Him Stay Dead	Jim MALONE
Let Not Thy Left Hand	Insp Gordon ROSS
Let Or Hindrance	Alister WOODHEAD
Let Them Eat Bullets	Jerry NELSON
Let Them Prey	Roger FLEMING
Let Us Prey	Keith CALDER
Letter From Kiev	Paul WILLIAMS
The Letter From Spain	Allan LAMBERT
The Letter Of The Law	Bonnie INDERMILL
Level With Me	Lawrence Patrick 'Larry' KENT
Lew Archer, Private Investigator	Lew ARCHER
Li Kwang's Dagger	Insp DURSLEY
Liability Limited	Sam WELPTON
The Liars	Insp Robert STAUNTON
The Liar's League	Lt Jacob HOROWITZ and Helen HOROWITZ
The Liberators	Harvey LANDON
The Library Of Death	Insp RICHARDSON
The Libyan Contract	Colin LYNCH
Licence Renewed	Cdr James BOND
License To Kill	Kelly CARVEL
The Lies That Bind	Neil HAMEL
Lieutenant Bones	Commiss SANDERS
Lieutenant Pascal's Tastes In Homicides	Lt PASCAL
The Life And Crimes Of Harry Lavender	Claudia VALENTINE
The Life And Death Of Peter Wade	Supt Francis FOY
Life Cycle	John PIPER and QUINN
A Life For Sale	'Bunny' CHIPSTEAD
Life Goes Sleeping	Dylan KLEIN and Johnny MCCLOUGH
Life In The Far West: Or, A Detective's Adventures Among The Indians And Outlaws Of Montana	Charley SHIPTON
Life Itself	Ch Jose Daniel FIERRO
A Life's Reminiscences At Scotland Yard	LANDSDOWNE
A Life's Reminiscences Of Scotland Yard	A SCOTLAND YARD DETECTIVE
The Lift Murder	Anthony RAVENHILL
Light At Midnight	Charles RAMSAY
The Light At Three O'clock	Matt EDWARDS
The Light Of Day	Arthur Abdul SIMPSON
Light Thickens	Insp/Supt Roderick ALLEYN
The Lighthearted Quest	Julia PROBYN
Lightning Grip, The Cautious Detective: Or Piping The Nathan Murder Mystery	LIGHTNING GRIP
Lightning Luke, The Photographer Detective: Or, Caught By The Instantaneous Camera	LIGHTNING LUKE
Lightning Over Mayfair	Tom LANGLEY
The Lights That Did Not Fail	Lawrie FENTON
Lights, Camera...Murder	Osgood BASS
Lights, Camera, Murder	Bill LENNOX
Like An Evening Gone	Supt BOWMAN
Like Ice She Was	Lou LARGO
The Lime Pit	Harry STONER
Limehouse Nights	Quong LEE
The Limit	Mordecai 'Maudie' MORGAN
The Limner	Luke APPLEGATE
The Limping Man	Insp Septimus FINCH
The Limping Man	Prof WELLS
The Lincoln Diddle	Edgar Allan POE
The Lingala Code	Michael VERNON
Lingo Dan	Lingo DAN
Link By Link	Maj DEERING and George RYAN
Link By Link	Det Dick DONOVAN
The Lion Game	Telzey AMBERDON and Trigger ARGEE
Lion In Wait	Sheriff Moss MAGILL
Lion? Or Murder?	Sheriff Moss MAGILL
Liquid Desires	Urbino MACINTYRE

The Liquidator	Jake (The Liquidator) BRAND
The Liquidator	Nick CARTER
The Liquidator	Boysie OAKES
The List	Nick CARTER
The List Of Adrian Messenger	Col Anthony GETHRYN
The List Of Seven	Sherlock HOLMES
Listen For The Click	Jerry BROGAN
The Listening Man	James TIERNEY
The Listening Walls	Elmer DODD
Listening Woman	Lt Joe LEAPHORN
The Little Affair Of The Vatican Cameos	Sherlock HOLMES
A Little Cowboy In New York: Or, In Search Of His Dad	The COWBOY DETECTIVE
A Little Darling, Dead	Ch Insp Peter PARSON
Little David	Kiel ST JAMES and Orson BOLES
A Little Death Music	John FIELD
The Little Dog Barked	Insp PETTENGILL
The Little Ferret	Harry ADKINS
Little Ferret, The Boy Detective	LITTLE FERRET
A Little Gentle Sleuthing	Melissa CRAIG
A Little Giant: Or, Feats And Frolics Of An Athlete	The GIANT DETECTIVE
The Little Girls	Dinah DELACROIX
A Little Lady Killing	Stella PIKE
A Little Learning	Dorothy Mayotte RIGBY
A Little Learning	Felicity TRAVERS
Little Lightning, The Shadow Detective: Or, The Twenty-Third Street Mystery	Little LIGHTNING
A Little Local Murder	Insp PARRISH
A Little Madness	C B GREENFIELD
Little Mink, The Bravo Detective: Or, Traps And Trails Of The Southwest Border	LITTLE BRAVO
Little Murder	Andy BRICE
A Little Murder Music	Lt MEREDITH
Little Ripper	Paul CROOK
A Little Sin	Karen GORDON
The Little Sister	Philip MARLOWE
The Little Tales Of Smethers, And Other Stories	Mr LINLEY
The Little Tales Of Smethers, And Other Stories	RIPLEY
Little Victims	Insp Mike PUMFREY
Littlejohn On Leave	Det Insp/Supt Thomas LITTLEJOHN
Live Bait For Murder	James REHM
Live Now, Pay Later	Albert ARGYLE
Live Oaks Also Die	Pat RIORDAN
A Lively Game Of Death	Hilary QUAYLE
The Living Alibi	Det Insp SHANE
Living Or Dead	Philip NORRIS
Living Proof	Insp Charlie RESNICK
A Local Matter	Lord TIGRANES
Location Shots	Samuel Moses KELLY
Lock The Death House Door	Insp ALLHOFF
The Locked Door	Insp LINSCOTT
The Locked House	Dr Sylvan MOORE
Locked In	Insp HEAD
The Locked Room	Dr GOODRICH
The Locked Roomette	Penni DANDRIDGE
The Locked Tomb Mystery	Priest Amenhotep Sa HAPU
Locker 246	Philip MARLOWE
Lockestep	John LOCKE
Logan	LOGAN
Logbook Of The White Knight	Dave DUNN
The Lombard Street Mystery	Sexton BLAKE
A Lombard Street Mystery	Percival MONTGOMERY
The London Adventures Of Mr Collin	Mr COLLIN
London Calling	Det Insp Simon SPEARS
The London Connection	Simon QUARRY
The London Deal	Sidney KENYON
The London Embassy	Spencer Monroe SAVAGE
London Match	Bernard SAMSON
The London Nights Of Belsize	Christopher BELSIZE
London Particular	Insp COCKRILL and Insp CHARLESWORTH
The London Spy Murders	Peter QUAYLE
The Lone House Mystery	Supt MINTER
The Lone Inn: A Mystery	Spencer TAIT and DENHAM
The Lone Lodge Mystery	Mortimer SARK
The Lone Wolf	Michael LANYARD
The Lone Wolf's Last Prowl	Michael LANYARD
The Lonely Astronomer	Adam QUIRKE
The Lonely Cage	Daye SMITH
The Lonely Graves	Brian BRETT
Lonely Hearts	Insp Charlie RESNICK
The Lonely Hunter	Lt Frank HASTINGS
Lonely Mosaic	John MARNE
A Lonely Place To Die	Dr Yudel GORDON
A Lonely Place To Die	Peter GRAYLEIGH
The Lonely Silver Rain	Travis MCGEE
The Lonely Target	Grant SIMON and Lt PASCAL
Lonely Vigils	Judge Keith Hilary PURSUIVANT
Lonely Vigils	John THUNSTONE
A Lonely Way To Die	Claude 'Snake' KIRLIN and F T ZEVICH
The Long Arm	Rosamond CLINCH
The Long Arm	CONNORS
The Long Arm	MANNISTER
The Long Arm Of Gil Hamilton	Gil HAMILTON
The Long Arm Of Mannister	MANNISTER
The Long Branch Detective	LONG BRANCH DETECTIVE
Long Chain Of Death	Ch Philip DECKER and David BRETT
The Long Chase	Larry KOHARIK
A Long Cold Fall	Cooper MACLEISH
The Long Dark Tea-Time Of The Soul	Dirk GENTLY
The Long Escape	Al COLBY
The Long Goodbye	Philip MARLOWE
The Long Goodbyes	Virginia KELLY
The Long Hard Cure	Morgan BUTLER

The Long Island Murders	Carey BRENT
The Long Knife	Sam HOUSTON
Long Live The Spy	Sergei ROLF
Long Live The Spy	Sergei ROLF
The Long Night Through	Anthony HOWARD
The Long Night's Walk	Capt COLSON
The Long Orbit	MARLOWE
The Long Overcoat	Pete FRY
Long Run South	Rupert QUINN
The Long Silence	Capt COLSON
The Long Silence	Terence O'HARA
A Long Silence	Insp Piet VAN DER VALK and Arlette VAN DER VALK
The Long Tunnel	Prof Richard CARFORD
A Long Way Down	Matthew HOLLEY
The Long Way Down	MCLOVE
The Long Way To Die	Joe ZANKA
The Long Window	Larry KOHARIK
The Longstreet Legacy	Insp Stephen ELIOT and Arthur CRUMP
The Long-Legged Fly	Lew GRIFFIN
The Long, Dark Night Of Baron Samedi	Dr QUARSHIE
The Loo Sanction	Prof Jonathan HEMLOCK
Look Back On Murder	Alan CRAIG
Look Behind You	Harry BUTTEN
Look Out For Space	Sam SPACE
Looking For Samson	KEYES
A Loose Connection	Lennox KEMP
Loose Lips	Jerry BROGAN
The Loose Rib	Insp ORD
The Loose Screw	'Beau' PEPYS
Loot	Insp TRUSCOTT
Lord Darcy Investigates	Lord DARCY
Lord Exenham Created A Sensation	Supt BRANBURY
Lord Mullion's Secret	Prof Charles HONEYBATH
The Lord Of Terror	FANTOMAS
The Lord Of The Rings	Frodo BAGGINS
Lord Peter	Lord Peter WIMSEY
Lord Peter Views The Body	Lord Peter WIMSEY
Lorimer's Legacy	Vernon READ
Losers Take All	Zachariah Tobias ROLF
Loser's Blues	John Owen COSATELLI
Losing Bet	Anton BIRUKOV
The Loss Of The British Bark, Sophy Anderson	Sherlock HOLMES
The Loss Of The Culion	Bill STENEM
The Lost Adventures Of Sherlock Holmes	Sherlock HOLMES
The Lost And Found Man	William LUKES
Lost Daughter	Dan KRUGER
The Lost Emeralds Of Zarinthia	Det BODKIN
Lost Friday	Sam CATES
The Lost Frôulein	John ALLISON
The Lost Heir	Sherlock HOLMES
The Lost Naval Papers	Ch Insp DAWSON
The Lost Persian	Herlock SHOLMES
Lost Sir Massingberd: A Romance Of Real Life	Bow Street Runner TOWNSHEND
Lot 41 - Dead Auctioneer	George ROBERTS
Lotta, The Young Lady Detective	LOTTA
The Lottery Ticket	Herlock SHOLMES
Lotus Leaves And Larceny	Sexton BLAKE
A Lovable Man	Det Insp RUBY
Love And Dr Hawkins	Dr HAWKINS
Love Avalon	Barry DONOVAN
Love Down Under	Dr Jason LOVE
Love For The Baron	John MANNERING
Love In Amsterdam	Insp Piet VAN DER VALK
Love Is The Victim	Lt Marty MARQUIS
Love Me And Die	Joseph COYLE
Love Of Money	Ethel PECK
Love Or Kill Them All	Nicky WEAVER
Love You To Death	DEMPSEY and MAKEPEACE
Loveday Brooke	Loveday BROOKE
Lovely But Dangerous	Michael WALLACE
The Lovely Ladies	Insp Piet VAN DER VALK
A Lovely Night To Kill	Daisy MARLOW
Lover And Thief	Calvin BIX
A Lover Scorned	Rev Claire ALDINGTON
A Lover Too Many	Insp CROW
Love, Blood And Tears	Nicky WEAVER
The Low Road	James 'Kipper' HERRING
Loxfinger	Israel 'Oy-Oy-7' BOND
Lucien's Tomb	Insp Maurice YGREC
Lucifer's Weekend	Julian 'Digger' BURROUGHS
Lucille Dare, Detective	Lucille DARE
Lucius Davoren: Or, Publicans And Sinners	Lucius DAVOREN
The Luck Of Jocelyn Pinner, RN	Jocelyn PINNER
Lucky Ham	Hamilton BIGGS
Lucky Jane	Dagobert BROWN and Jane BROWN
Lucky Pierre	Ms SQUAD
Luke Leighton, The Government Detective	Luke LEIGHTON
Lullaby	The 87th PRECINCT
The Lumsden Baby	Dr Jean MONTROSE
The Lunatic At Large	Francis MANDELL-ESSINGTON
The Lunatic Fringe	Commiss Theodore ROOSEVELT
Lunatics At Large	WING
The Lure	Noel CUMMINGS
The Lure Of Sweet Death	Tina MAY
The Lure Of The Bush	Det Insp Napoleon BONAPARTE
Lust For Murder	Lt Shomri SHOMAR
Lust To Kill	Arthur 'Red' BLAKE and Dan WHEELER
Lydia	Harvey KRIM
Lying In Wait	Det J P BEAUMONT
The Lying Jade	Col John PRIMROSE and Grace LATHAM
Lyoma Grimwood, Spinster	Insp WITHERS
Lyssa	Margo FRANKLIN and Philip SPENCE
The Lyttelton Case	Insp James CANDLISH

M For Murder	Sgt/Det Insp Patrick Aloysius MCCARTHY
Mabelle Rivers, Girl Detective	Mabelle RIVERS
MacAllister	Frank MACALLISTER
Mace!	MACE
Mace's Luck	MACE
Machete	Bo 'Springblade' THORNTON
The Mackintosh Man	SLADE
MacLurg Goes West	Insp Marcus MACLURG
Macon Moore, The Southern Detective	Macon MOORE
MacTavish	Alonzo MACTAVISH
Mad Blood	Frank REPPA
Mad Hatter Summer	Insp Alfred SWAIN
The Mad Man Theory	Insp Omar COLLINS
Mad Minute	Sgt Mark STRYKER
Madam Murder - And The Corpse Brigade	SEEKAY
Madam Will Not Dine Tonight	Sheridan WESLEY
Madame Aubry And The Police	Mme AUBRY
Madame Aubry Dines With Death	Mme AUBRY
Madame Ellie's Chamber Of Horrors	Barney HUGGINS
Madame Judas	Juliet JACKSON
Madame Shadow	Supt Andrew ASH and Ch Det Insp George MUIR
Madame Storey	Mme Rosika STOREY
Madam, Will You Talk?	Charity SELBOURNE
Maddened By Mystery; Or, The Defective Detective	The GREAT DETECTIVE
The Maddox House Murder	Mortimer KANE
Made For Murder	Lt Charles HILLARY
Made In Detroit	Ben PERKINS
Made Up For Murder	Jeff TROY and Haila TROY
Made Up To Kill	Jeff TROY and Haila TROY
Madelaine	Evan PARIS
Madeline	John INGLES and Madeline SMITH
Madeline Payne, The Detective's Daughter	Madeline PAYNE
Mademoiselle De Scuderi	Mlle DE SCUDERI
Mademoiselle Lucie, The French Lady Detective	MADEMOISELLE LUCIE
The Maestro Murders	Michael FORRESTER and Theresa FORRESTER
The Mafia Diaries	John Howard JOURNEY
The Magic Bullet	Harry PONDER
The Magic Casket	Dr John Evelyn THORNDYKE
Magic Dick, A Boy Detective; Or, Out Of The Streets Of New York	MAGIC DICK
Magic Mirror	Georgia Lee MAXWELL
The Magic Of Chez Finnie	Insp SLADE
The Magician	George THOMASSY
The Magicians	Kirk CULLEN
The Magician's Wife	Capt ZACHARY
A Magnet For Murder	Mac MCINTYRE
A Magnum For Schneider	David CALLAN
The Magpie Murder	Insp M'GUIRE
The Magpie Murder	Insp M'GUIRE
Maid For Murder	Carl GUARD
Maid To Murder	Insp KYLE
Maiden Possessed	Mr DEHAVILLAND
Maigret And The Enigmatic Lett	Insp Jules MAIGRET
Maigret Bides His Time	Insp Jules MAIGRET
Maigret's Christmas	Insp Jules MAIGRET
Maigret's Pipe	Insp Jules MAIGRET
The Main	Lt Claude LAPOINTE
Main Line Kill	Maxwell DALY
Main Street Morgue	Gentle HOGGERTY
Major Adventures	Aubrey St John MAJOR
Major Crime	Paul PLUSH
Major Developments	Aubrey St John MAJOR
Major Enquiry	Det Sgt Arthur MILTON
Major Exploits	Aubrey St John MAJOR
Major Hazards	Aubrey St John MAJOR
Major League Murder	Mickey 'Slots' RESNICK
Major Occasions	Aubrey St John MAJOR
The Major Steps Out	Maj Hutton SEARY
Major Vices	Judith McMonigle FLYNN
The Major - Diamond Buyer	Aubrey St John MAJOR
The Major - Knight Errant	Aubrey St John MAJOR
The Major-General's Pepper-Pots	Raffles HOLMES
Make Mine Mavis	Lou LARGO
Make Mine Mayhem	Paul MULLER
Make Mine Murder	Gerry BARNES
Make My Coffin Big	Steve SILK
Make Out With Murder	Leo HAIG
Make Way For Murder	Pete HUNTER
Make-Up For Murder	Mother PAUL
Making It Big	Johnny HAVOC
Making The Cut	Det Insp Carl MCCADDEN
The Malabang Pearl	Joe DELANEY
Malcolm Sage, Detective	Malcolm SAGE
Malibu Tag Team	Philip MARLOWE
Malice Domestic	Bob ADAMS and Anne MINER
Malice Domestic	Doran FAIRWEATHER and Rodney CHELMARSH
Malice Domestic	Sheriff Jack THOMPSON
Malice In Maggody	Ch Arly HANKS
Malice In Wonderland	Prof Stuff DRISCOLL
Malice Poetic	Melissa CRAIG
The Malignant Snowman	'Rolling' STONE
Mallory	Martin 'Brick-Top' CORRIGAN
The Malta Conspiracy	Bob SULLIVAN
The Maltese Falcon	Sam SPADE
The Mamur Zapt And The Return Of The Carpet	Capt OWEN
The Mamur Zapt And The Spoils Of Egypt	Capt OWEN
Mam'zelle Guillotine	The SCARLET PIMPERNEL
Man Against Fear	Brendan WALLACE
Man Alive	James HELLIER
Man And Master	Carl MASTERS
A Man Called Black	BLACK
A Man Called Kyril	Gen Stepan POVIN
A Man Called Tempest	William TEMPEST
Man Crazy	Val VERNON
A Man Died Talking	Ch Insp Jonathan BLACK
The Man From Checkmate	Adam KANE
The Man From Internal Affairs	Det Noah GREEN and Det Sam MCKIBBON
The Man From M O D	Steven FLAGG
The Man From Madagascar	Commissaire PATRAS
The Man From Madrid	Sexton BLAKE
The Man From Manhattan	Jerry DOWN
The Man From Nowhere	Jake DEKKER
The Man From Outside	Const Jimmie WARDEN
The Man From Pansy	Burgess 'Buzz' CARDIGAN
The Man From Persia	Sexton BLAKE
The Man From The Norlands	Richard HANNAY
A Man From The Past	Nicholas CORNISH
The Man From White Hat	The BUTCHER
Man In A Mist	Supt QUILL and Insp GLOVER
The Man In Brown	Con MADDEN
Man In Danger	Brendan WALLACE
The Man In Grey	FERNAND
The Man In My Grave	B G BROOKS
The Man In My Shoes	John Newton CHANCE
The Man In The Blue Mask	John MANNERING
The Man In The Brown Suit	Col RACE
The Man In The Button Boots	Monsieur DUPUY
The Man In The Cloak	Robert WYNNTON
The Man In The Corner	The OLD MAN IN THE CORNER
The Man In The Dark	Francis MACNAB
The Man In The Driver's Seat	Steve RHODEN
The Man In The Green Chevy	Sheriff Milton KOVAK
The Man In The Grey Flannel Shroud	Ev FRANKLIN and Hugh MORRISON
The Man In The Jury Box	Barry O'DELL
The Man In The Middle	Charlie BELL
The Man In The Mist	Maj Peter Utley SHANE
The Man In The Queue	Insp Alan GRANT
The Man In The Sandhills	Jim BEVERLEY
The Man In The Shadow	Insp J RASON
Man In The Shadows	Cliff HARDY
The Man In The Shadows	Terry MACK
The Man In The Tricorn Hat	Cpl Juan LLORCA
A Man Lay Dead	Insp/Supt Roderick ALLEYN
Man Missing	Sarah KEATE
The Man Nobody Saw	Johnny VALLON
The Man Of Glass	Nick CAINE
A Man Of God	Dorothy Mayotte RIGBY
The Man Of Last Resort; Or, The Clients Of Randolph Mason	Randolph MASON
Man Of Many Minds	George HANLON
The Man Of Mystery	Nick CARTER
The Man Of Mystery; Or, Mephisto The Detective	MEPHISTO
The Man Of The Forty Faces	Hamilton CLEEK
Man On A String	Michael KEEFE
The Man On The Bridge	Peter MUNRO
Man On The Run	Martin FANE and Richard FANE
Man On The Run	Martin FANE and Richard FANE
Man On The Run!	Sexton BLAKE
The Man On The Spot	Derek GLOVER
Man Overboard	Don KENDRICK
Man Running	Eve GILL
The Man Who Asked Why	Gregory 'Grischa' PAVLOV
The Man Who Bombed The World	Bart GOULD
The Man Who Came Back	Richard SAREL
The Man Who Cancelled Himself	Stewart HOAG
The Man Who Convicted Himself	The SHADOWERS INC
The Man Who Convicted Himself	The SHADOWERS INC
The Man Who Couldn't Sleep	Witter KERFOOT
The Man Who Crawled Away	HORTON and JORDAN
The Man Who Didn't Answer	Matt WINTERS
The Man Who Didn't Exist	Reginald DE PUYSTER
The Man Who Didn't Mind Hanging	Peter PIPER
The Man Who Died Laughing	Stewart HOAG
The Man Who Died On Friday	Richard MONK
The Man Who Disappeared	Insp FROST and Dr GARLAND
The Man Who Disappeared	Dick STODDART
The Man Who Feared	James JARNEGAN
The Man Who Fell Through The Earth	Pennington WISE
The Man Who Followed Women	COLLINS and MCKECHNIE
The Man Who Heard Too Much	DEVEREAUX
The Man Who Invented Florida	'Doc' FORD
The Man Who Killed Fortescue	Van Dusen ORMSBERRY
The Man Who Killed His Brother	Ginny FISTOULARI and Mick 'Brew' AXBREWDER
The Man Who Killed The King	Roger BROOK
The Man Who Killed Too Soon	Richard MONK
The Man Who Knew Dick Bong	Philip MARLOWE
The Man Who Knew Hammett	Zeke GAHAGAN
The Man Who Knew Sherlock Holmes	Sherlock HOLMES
The Man Who Knew Too Much	Sexton BLAKE
The Man Who Knew Too Much And Other Stories	Horne FISHER
The Man Who Liked Dogs	Ted CARMADY
The Man Who Lost His Shadow	Derek THRYDE
The Man Who Loved Chocolates	Insp JOHNSON
The Man Who Loved Dirty Books	Matt GREGG
The Man Who Loved Spiders	Ch Const George MEATYARD
The Man Who Loved Zoos	Victoria WELCH
The Man Who Made A King	J A 'Rem' REMINGTON
The Man Who Murdered God	Lt Joe MCGUIRE
The Man Who Murdered Goliath	Robin BISHOP
The Man Who Never Blundered	Ross MCCOY
The Man Who Played Thief	Tim PARNELL
The Man Who Plundered The City	Asbjorn (Osborne Crag) KRAG
The Man Who Rang The Bell	Insp CORNFORD
The Man Who Risked His Partner	Ginny FISTOULARI and Mick 'Brew' AXBREWDER

The Man Who Shook The Earth	Sir Charles KNIGHTLEY
The Man Who Shot Birds And Other Tales	Insp/Supt MALLETT
The Man Who Slept All Day	Melville FAIRR
The Man Who Sold Death	Nick CARTER
The Man Who Sold Death	James CRAIG
The Man Who Stole The Mona Lisa	Louis LEPINE
The Man Who Used Perfume	Robert WYNNTON
The Man Who Walked With Death	Brett CARSTAIRS
The Man Who Wanted To Die	Supt BRANNIGAN
The Man Who Was Dead	Insp Dennis DRURY
The Man Who Was Not Dead	Sherlock HOLMES
The Man Who Was Not Himself	Emmanuel CELLINI
The Man Who Was Not Himself	Emmanuel CELLINI
The Man Who Was There	Montrose ARBUTHNOT and Edmund KING
The Man Who Was Thursday	SYME
The Man Who Was Too Clever	Scott EGERTON
The Man Who Was Too Much	David TROY
The Man Who Wasn't There	John ABBOT
The Man Who Wasn't There	Mr SPRINGFIELD
A Man Will Be Kidnapped	Supt ABBOTT
The Man With A Load Of Mischief	Insp Richard JURY
The Man With A Number	Sexton BLAKE
The Man With A Paper Skull	Insp SKANE, Gail MCGURK and Dudley BRENT
The Man With Bated Breath	Oceola ARCHER
The Man With Bogart's Face	Sam MARLOW
The Man With Five Enemies	Sexton BLAKE
The Man With Nine Lives	Victor REDMAYNE
The Man With No Bones	Martin RIDGWAY
The Man With The Black Cord	Joe MULLER
The Man With The Clubfoot	Dr Adolph (Clubfoot) GRUNDT and Desmond OKEWOOD
The Man With The Clubfoot	Dr Adolph (Clubfoot) GRUNDT and Desmond OKEWOOD
The Man With The Golden Gun	Cdr James BOND
The Man With The Green Eyes	Sexton BLAKE
The Man With The Iron Chest	Sexton BLAKE
The Man With The Parrots: A Story Of Events And The Shadows They Cast	Percival GUNTRIP
The Man With The Scarlet Skull And Other Tales	Quentin DREX
The Man With The Tiny Head	Jennifer Norrington Aless GANZARELLO and Coleridge TUCKER
The Man With The Twisted Face	Peter CASTLE and 'Twisted Face' STRAUSSMAN
The Man with The Twisted Lip	Sherlock HOLMES
The Man With The Wax Face	Sgt Joe DIXON
The Man With Three Passports	Cpl Juan LLORCA
The Man With Two Wives	Lt Timothy TRANT
The Man Without A Head	Manuel CORTINA
A Man Without Friends	Insp CROUCH
The Manchester Connection	Marcus Aurelius FARROW
Manchester Royal	Insp SKARRATT
The Manchester Thing	Marcus Aurelius FARROW
Manchu Jade	Ian MACARTHUR
Mandarin's Jade	Johnny DALMAS
The Mandarin's Sapphire	Insp SKANE
Mandrake In The Monastery	Oliver MANDRAKE
Maneuvers	Abe REDDEN
Manhattan Is My Beat	RUNE
Manhattan Massacre	Robert (The Assassin) BRIGANTI
Manhattan Night	Sgt/Lt Charley MITCHELL
Manhunt In Murder	Anthony TRENT
Manhunter	Will GRAHAM
The Manhunter: Stories From The Notebook Of A Detective	Det Dick DONOVAN
A Mania For Blondes	Lt Ben KRAHMER
Manila Bay	Lt Felix ELIZALDO
Mannix	Joe MANNIX
The Manor House Menace	Sexton BLAKE
The Mansfield Mystery	Insp KILBY
The Mansion On The Moor	Sexton BLAKE
The Mantle Of Ishmael	Richard GOULBURN
The Manuscript Murder	Maj Weston PRYME
The Manuscript Murder	Maj Weston PRYME
The Manville Murders	Arthur MARTINSON
Many A Monster	Dan BANION
Many A Slip	Insp Joseph FRENCH
Many A Slip	Patrick C SHIRLEY and Insp Rip IRVING
Many Thanks - Ben Hassett	Charles Hendesley MANNING and Ben HASSETT
The Many Ways Of Death	Commissaire Orestes BIGNON
The Many Worlds Of Magnus Ridolph	Magnus RIDOLPH
Man's Illegal Life	George MAN
Man's Loving Family	George MAN
The Maori Murder Case	Paul DECKER
Map Of Mistrust	Andrew CARNE
The Maple Sugar Murders	Hugh QUINT
The Marble Jungle	Grant KIRBY
The March Of Fate	George MILLINGTON
March Violets	Bernard GUNTHER
The Mardi Gras Murders	WADE
Margie	John COMADAY and Larry COHEN
Margin For Murder	Martin KANE
Margin For Terror	Johnny LIDDELL
Margo	Margo FRANKLIN and Philip SPENCE
Marianne	Bob SULLIVAN
Mariella - Spy!	David SHERIDAN
The Marine Detective: Or, Tracking The Ship Insurance	The MARINE DETECTIVE
Mark Kilby Solves A Murder	Mark KILBY
Mark Kilby Takes A Risk	Mark KILBY
Mark Magic, The Detective: Or, A Story Of A Beautiful Woman's Strange Career	Mark MAGIC
Mark Maturin, Parson	Mark MATURIN
Mark Of A Witch	Insp Jimmy BRENT
The Mark Of Cain	CAIN
A Mark Of Displeasure	Antoine CIRRET
The Mark Of The Dead	Parrish DARBY
The Mark Of Yekel	Frank YARDLEY
Marked For Murder	Insp KOJAK
A Marked Man	Ferrers LOCKE
Marked With A Cross	Insp HINKLEY
Marker Calls The Tune	Frank MARKER
A Marriage Mystery	Dr LUKE
The Marriage Of Captain Kettle	Capt Owen KETTLE
The Marriage Of Kettle	Capt Owen KETTLE
The Marriage Of Sherlock Holmes	Sherlock HOLMES
The Marshal At The Villa Torini	Marshal Salva GUARNACCIA
Marshfield The Observer	Meldrum MARSHFIELD
The Martello Tower	William Wilberforce SMITH
The Marten Mystery	Det Insp John FREEMAN
The Martian Crown Jewels	SYALOCH
The Martian Who Hated People	Surly HOMES
Martin Hewitt, Investigator	Martin HEWITT
Martin Speed Versus "The Snatcher"	Martin SPEED
Martinis And Murder	Peter CHAMBERS
Marvels And Mysteries	George STONE, George DAVIS and FLETCHER
The Mary Deare	John SANDS
The Mary Queen Of Scots Jewel	Sherlock HOLMES
Mary Regan	Bob CLIFFORD
Mary Watson Takes A Hand	Charlotte HOLMES
The Marylebone Miser	John RINGROSE
Mary's Grave	Sgt George KELSO
A Masculine Ending	Loretta LAWSON
The Mask	DISHER
A Mask For Crime	Anne LAYTON and David LAYTON
The Mask Of Demetrios	Charles LATIMER
Mask Of Innocence	Richard PATTON and Amelia PATTON
Mask Of Violence	Col MOSTYN
Mask Of Words	RATLIN
The Masked Death	Ferrers LOCKE
The Masked Forgers	Sexton BLAKE
The Masked Marauder	Sexton BLAKE
The Masked Raiders	Sexton BLAKE
Masque World	Viscount Anthony VILLIERS
Masquerade	'Biff' CORRIGAN
Masquerade Of Vengeance	Anthea RUTHERFORD and Justin RUTHERFORD
Masques	Steven GIROUX
Massacre In Milan	Nick CARTER
The Master	Andy HAMMOND
The Master Detective	Christopher QUARLES
The Master Mind	Paul COQUENIL
Master Minds At Play	Sherlock HOLMES, Insp Charlie CHAN and Hercule POIROT
The Master Must Die	Adam QUIRKE
The Master Mystery	Tommy DELAYN
A Master Of Fortune	Capt Owen KETTLE
The Master Of Greylands	Charlotte GUISE
A Master Of Mysteries	John BELL
Master Of Shadows	Miles PENNOYER
Master Plan	Graham LORIMER
The Master Spy	Anthony HALLAM
The Masterless Men	Harry SEDDAL
Mather Investigates	Det Sgt Robert MATHER
The Matilda Hunter Murder	Tuddleton TROTTER
The Matlock Paper	James MATLOCK
Matricide At St Martha's	Robert AMISS
Matter For A May Morning	Desdemona 'Squeakie' MEADOW
A Matter Of Accent	Ted S WEAVER
A Matter Of Confidence	Sam BENEDICT
A Matter Of Degree	Det George BENTON
A Matter Of Diplomacy	George MADO
A Matter Of Iodine	Ted S WEAVER
A Matter Of Love And Death	Det Knute SEVERSON
The Matter Of Mandrake	Paul BAKER
A Matter Of Observation	Det Lt Cathy CARRUTHERS
A Matter Of Policy	Amy BREWSTER
A Matter Of Speculation	The Hon Victoria PUMPHREY
The Mauleverer Murders	Ashley TEMPEST
Max Carrados	Max CARRADOS
Max Carrados Mysteries	Max CARRADOS
Max Hensig - Bacteriologist And Murderer	Max HENSIG
Max Smart And The Ghastly Ghost Affair	Maxwell SMART
May Beresford, Typist	May BERESFORD
The May Day Mystery	Jim HANVEY
May You Die In Ireland	Prof FOLEY
The Maya Stone Murders	Micah DUNN
Mayday In Magadan	Det Ivan KUVAKIN
The Mayfair Murder	Insp Jim SILVER
The Mayfair Mystery	Insp Jim SILVER
Mayhem	Insp ST CYR and Hermann KOHLER
Mayhem At Parva	G D H PRINGLE
Mayhem On The Coney Beat	Lt Bud DUGAN
The May-Week Murders	Maj Maurice HEMYOCK
May's New Fangled Mirth	Balthazar MARTEN
Mazatlan	Jack NOVAK
Maze	Cyrus WILSON
McAllister And His Double	John DOCKRIDGE
McAllister And His Double	MCALLISTER
McCloud	MCCLOUD
McGarr And The Politician's Wife	Insp Peter MCGARR
McHugh	MCHUGH
McLean Of Scotland Yard	Insp MCLEAN
McLean Takes Over	Insp MCLEAN
McNally's Risk	Archie MCNALLY
McNally's Secret	Archie MCNALLY
McQuaid	Damian MCQUAID
McQuaid In August	Damian MCQUAID

Title	Character
The Mean Season	Malcolm ANDERSON
Measured For Murder	Argus STEELE
Medal From Pamplona	Robert BELCOURT
The Medbury Fort Murder	Insp MCMASTER
Medicine Dog	Boyd SHERMAN
Medicine Maker	'Hashknife' HARTLEY
The Medicine Men	Dr Neal POTTER
The Medicine-Man	'Hashknife' HARTLEY
The Mediterranean Murder	Glyn MORGAN
Medium For Murder	Ben ANDERSON
A Medium For Murder	Mrs Edwina CHARLES
Meet Bill Speed	Insp Bill SPEED
Meet Desmond Drake	Desmond DRAKE
Meet Dr Morelle	Dr MORELLE
Meet Dr Morelle Again	Dr MORELLE
Meet Gerry North	Gerry NORTH
Meet Inspector Bourne	Insp BOURNE
Meet Me At The Morgue	Howard CROSS
Meet Me In Darkness	Sam KING
Meet Morocco Jones	Morocco JONES
Meet The Baron	John MANNERING
Meet The Dreamer	Supt Donald (The Dreamer) REAMER
Meet The Picaroon	Ludovic (The Picaroon) SAXON
Meet The Tiger	Simon (The Saint) TEMPLAR
The Megadeath Option	Marc (The Mercenary) DEAN
The Meirovitz Plan	Max ROTH
The Melancholy Virgin	Charles DOMAY
The Melbourne Mystery	TREVELYAN
The Melody Murders	Richard Curtis (The Phantom) VAN LOAN
The Melting Man	Rex CARVER
The Melwood Mystery	Jefferson HASTINGS
Memoirs Of An Aberdeen Detective	An ABERDEEN DETECTIVE
The Memoirs Of An Inspector	Insp LIPINSKI
The Memoirs Of Constantine Dix	Constantine DIX
Memoirs Of Monsieur Claude, Chief Of Police Under The Second Empire	Monsieur CLAUDE
Memoirs Of Murder	Forsythia BROWN
The Memoirs Of Professor Moriarty	Sherlock HOLMES
The Memoirs Of Schlock Homes	Schlock HOMES
The Memoirs Of Sherlock Holmes	Sherlock HOLMES
The Memoirs Of Solar Pons	Solar PONS
Memoirs Of Vidocq	Eugène VIDOCQ
Memories Of Midnight	Catherine DOUGLAS
The Memory Trap	Dr David AUDLEY
Men At Arms	Pte PAGETT
Men For Counters	Mr MALCOLM
The Men From The Boys	Marty BOND
Men In Arms	Horatio CASSIDY
The Men In Her Death	Eve MACWILLIAMS
The Men On The Dead Man's Chest	John STANTON
Men Who Die Twice	Jason STARR and Adam CYBER
The Men Who Explained Miracles	Dr Gideon FELL
The Men Who Explained Miracles	Col MARCH
The Men Who Explained Miracles	Sir Henry MERRIVALE KC
The Men With The Double Faces	Donald CAIRN
The Men With The Guns	Jimmy VANESCO
Menace	Franklin PARRY and Leonard HARRIS
The Menace Of Li-Sin	LI-SIN
Menace To Mrs Kershaw	Insp ORD
The Mendelov Conspiracy	Steve AUSTIN
Mene Tekel: A Tale Of Strange Happenings	Joe MULLER
The Menu Cypher	Dr Robert HARMON
Mercenary Kill	Rod (The Terminator) GAVIN
Merchant Of Murder	Richard Curtis (The Phantom) VAN LOAN
Merchants Of Disaster	'Doc' SAVAGE
The Mercy Man	Willy DIAZ
The Mercy Trap	Gil DISBRO
Merely Murder	Supt HANNASYDE
Mermaid	Tomas ARAGON
The Mermaid	Timothy CULLINAN
Merridrew Marches On	Jenkinson Talbot MERRIDREW
The Merrivale Mystery	Victor SERGE
The Merrlyn Mystery	Sexton BLAKE
The Merry Hippo	Alexander BARTON
Merry Jack Jugg - Highwayman	Jack JUGG
Merry-Go-Round	Li MOH
Message From A Corpse	Amy BREWSTER
The Metal Flask	Peter GRAHAM
Method In His Murder	Mr John Cornelius SCOTTER
The Methods Of Dr Scarlett	Dr SCARLETT
The Methods Of Uncle Abner	Uncle ABNER
Methylated Murder	Clay HARRISON
Mexican Standoff	Antonio 'Chico' CERVANTES
The Mexican Tree Duck	Chauncy Wayne SUGHRUE
Mexico Set	Bernard SAMSON
The Meyringen Papers	Sherlock HOLMES
Miami Blues	Sgt Hoke MOSELEY
Miami Mayhem	Tony ROME
Miami Mayhem	Tony ROME
Miami Merry-Go-Round	Rick LARKAN
Miami Undercover	Jeff THOMPSON
Micah Faraday, Adventurer	Micah FARADAY
Mice	Philip MARLOWE
The Mice Are Not Amused	Glenda BLAKE
Michael Dred, Detective	Michael DRED
Michael's Evil Deeds	Michael SAYERS
The Microbe Murders	Insp O'HARE
The Microbe Of Crime: Or, Nick Carter's Biggest Crime	Nick CARTER
The Midas Kill	BUTLER
The Midas Operation	Richard RAVEN
The Middle Temple Murder	Frank SPARGO
Midnight	David CARROLL
Midnight Baby	Maggie MACGOWEN
Midnight Cavalier	J Rockingham STONE
The Midnight Eye	Johnny APRIL
Midnight Ferry To Venice	Paul HEDLEY and Harcourt D'ESPINAL
The Midnight Lady And The Mourning Man	Morgan BUTLER
The Midnight Lorry Crime	Sexton BLAKE
The Midnight Man	MCGREGOR
Midnight Murder	Richard Henry (The Avenger) BENSON
The Midnight Murder	Insp BOW and Capt KEETCH
Midnight Murder	Lionel CRANE
The Midnight Mystery	Sexton BLAKE
The Midnight Mystery	Prosper FAIR
Midnight Sister	Johnny FARRELL
The Midnight Sonata At Colliers End	Sherlock HOLMES
Midnight Wireless	Mr BIRTLEY
Midst Balkan Perils	Sexton BLAKE
Midsummer Malice	Insp DUFFY and Alan RUSSELL
A Midsummer Night's Crime	Insp SEVERN
The Mid-Hants Affair	Sherlock HOLMES
The Miernik Dossier	Paul CHRISTOPHER
Mike Dime	Mike DIME
The Miko	Nicholas LINNEAR
The Milan Grill Room	Charles LYSON
A Mild Case Of Murder	Michael TERRENCE and 'Terry' TERRENCE
Milk And Honey	Det Peter DECKER
The Milkmaid's Millions	William (Sultans' Harem) SULTAN
The Mill House Murder	Ronald CAMBERWELL
Millie Lynne - Shop Investigator	Millie LYNNE
The Million Dollar Babe	Mike FARREL
Million Dollar Handle	Michael SHAYNE
The Million Dollar Suitcase	Jerry BOYNE
The Millionaire Mystery	Insp BLAIR
A Millionaire's Mania: Or, Nick Carter's Strange Client	Nick CARTER
A Millionaire's Love Story	Mr Jacob BURRELL
The Million-Dollar Diamond	Richard GOULBURN
Mills	MILLS
Mimic A Murderer	Insp Ambrose MAHON
The Mind Brothers	Jason STARR and Adam CYBER
The Mind Of Mr J G Reeder	J G REEDER
The Mind Readers	Albert CAMPION
The Mind Twisters	Michael HAWK
Mind Wreckers, Limited, And Other Adventures Of Barrow - Ace Insurance Detective	Charles BARROW
The Mindbenders	Patrick SHANNON
The Mind-Masters	Britt (Mind Masters) ST VINCENT
Mine Sinister Host	Barnaby GRAYLE
Ministry Of Death	Kenneth DUCANE
Mini-Mysteries	Sarah HULL
The Mini-Skirt Murders	Sexton BLAKE
The Mink-Lined Coffin	Richard BLAKE
Minnesota Strip	Pete SHAY
Minnie Santangelo And The Evil Eye	Minnie SANTANGELO
Minnie Santangelo's Mortal Sin	Minnie SANTANGELO
The Minuteman Murder	Homer KELLY
Minutes To Midnight	Miriam BIRDSEYE
The Mirabilis Diamond	John STEELE
Miracle On Vine Street	Roger L YOUNG
Miriam Lemaire, Moneylender	Miriam LEMAIRE
Miro	MIRO
The Miro Papers	MIRO
Mirror Image	Robin CHODOFF
Mirror Image	Michael LONG
Mirrors Kill	Tom BULLEN
The Misadventures Of Athelstan Digby	Athelstan DIGBY
The Misadventures Of Sherlock Holmes	Sherlock HOLMES
The Misadventures Of Sherlock Holmes	Sherlock HOLMES
The Misfortunes Of Mr Teal	Simon (The Saint) TEMPLAR
Misprision Of Felony	Lady Jane EASTINGS
Miss Bede Is Staying	Florence ST LEONARD
Miss Brandt: Adventuress	Miss BRANDT
Miss Brown Of XYO	Miss BROWN
Miss Cayley's Adventures	Lois CAYLEY
Miss Doll, Go Home	Harry FANNIN
Miss Francis Baird, Detective: A Passage From Her Memoirs	Frances BAIRD
Miss Hamblett's Ghost	BEACH
Miss Hogg's Last Case	Flora HOGG
Miss Hurd: An Enigma	Sheriff Steve DILLON
Miss Lizzie	Lizzie BORDEN
Miss Madelyn Mack, Detective	Madelyn MACK
Miss Marple: Complete Short Stories	Jane MARPLE
Miss Melville Regrets	Susan MELVILLE
Miss Melville's Revenge	Susan MELVILLE
Miss Mystery	Baron VESSELOFFSKY
Miss Otis Relents	Miss OTIS
Miss Otis Throws A Come-Back	Miss OTIS
Miss Pinkerton	Hilda ADAMS
Miss Pym Disposes	Lucy PYM
Miss Seeton, By Appointment	Emily SEETON and Supt DELPHICK
Miss Smilla's Feeling For Snow	Smilla JASPERSON
Missing	Insp KENNEDY
Missing	Harry STONER
The Missing Ace	Insp KELLERWAY
Missing At Lloyds	Lawrence MALONE
The Missing Bales	Harold QUEST
The Missing Bishop	Buzz DECKARD
The Missing Book-Keeper	Jeffrey GREEN
A Missing Boy And A Royal Connection	Charlotte HOLMES
The Missing Brontë	Insp Perry TRETHOWAN
The Missing Chapter	Nero WOLFE
The Missing Cricketer	Herlock SHOLMES
The Missing Doctor	Gilbert DAVISON
Missing In Mexico	Sexton BLAKE
Missing Joseph	The Earl of ATHERTON
The Missing Link	Insp Richard RINGWOOD
Missing Man	George SANDFORD
The Missing Margarine	Herlock SHOLMES
The Missing Mayor	Dixon BRETT

The Missing Men	CHERI-BIBI
The Missing Millionaire	Herlock SHOLMES
The Missing Minister	Herlock SHOLMES
The Missing Minx	Supt 'Tubby' GREENE
The Missing Moke	Herlock SHOLMES
The Missing Money-Lender	Insp Dennis DRURY
The Missing Mother-In-Law	Herlock SHOLMES
Missing Or Murdered	Anthony VEREKER
The Missing Partners	Insp DODD
The Missing Person	Willie BUCHANAN
Missing Person	Det Sgt Jane PERRY
Missing Person	Guy ROLAND
Missing Persons	Prof Joanne FLEMING
Missing Persons	Offr Tally WICKHAM and Sgt John BOON
The Missing Quarto	Sherlock HOLMES
The Missing Romney	Ch Supt Peter DAWES
Missing Susan	Elizabeth MACPHERSON
The Missing Tycoon	Pete HOLLAND
The Missing Walnuts	Sherlock HOLMES
Missing Woman	Insp KELSEY
Mission Accomplished	Lawrence MARLEY
Mission Code: Acropolis	'Mac' WINGATE
Mission Code: Granite Island	'Mac' WINGATE
Mission Code: King's Pawn	'Mac' WINGATE
Mission Code: Scorpion	'Mac' WINGATE
Mission Code: Symbol	'Mac' WINGATE
Mission Code: Volcano	'Mac' WINGATE
A Mission For Betty Smith	John HARRINGTON
Mission To Siena	Don MICKLEM
Mission To Venice	Don MICKLEM
Missionary Stew	Morgan CITRON
Mist Over Morro Bay	David BALLARD and Michelle Merrill BALLARD
Mistakenly In Mallorca	Insp Enrique ALVAREZ
Mister Big	Supt BUDD
Mistress Murder	Terence O'DAY
Mistress Of Death	Jason STRIKER
Mistress Of Horror House	Houston MCIVER
Mitigating Circumstances	Dr Lily FORRESTER
A Mixed Pack	Mr JONES
Mizmaze	Insp/Supt MALLETT
The Moccasin Men	Maj Hutton SEARY
Model For Murder	Lt Al WHEELER
A Model Is Murdered	Argus STEELE
Model Murder	Det Ch Insp Kate MADDOX
A Modern Wizard	John BARNES
Modesty Blaise	Modesty BLAISE
Moina	Madeline PAYNE
Moina: Or, Against The Mighty	Madeline PAYNE
Molly And The Confidence Man	Molly OWENS
Molly And The Gambler	Molly OWENS
Molly On The Spot	O'ROURKE
Mom In The Spring	MOM
Mom Meets Her Maker	MOM
Mom Sings An Aria	MOM
Moment For Murder	Insp KNICKMAN
A Moment In Time	Lucius HUNT
The Moment Of Fiction	William SCHAEFER
A Moment Of Need	Thackeray HACKETT
The Moment Of Silence	William SCHAEFER
Moment Of Untruth	Toussaint 'Touie' MOORE
Monastery Nightmares	Luke LASSITER
Monday's Child Is Dead	Ginny KARR
Mondo	MONDO
The Moneta Papers	Jefferson (The Handyman) BOONE
The Money Harvest	Jake POPE
Money Leads To Murder	Daisy MARLOW
Money Men And One-Shot Deal	Charles CARR and Jack KELLY
The Money Mountain	Jonathan GAUNT
Money Musk	Insp TOPE
Money On The Black	Det Insp Duncan MACCALLUM
Money To Burn	Rita NOONAN
Money To Burn	Ronnie VENTANA
Money With Menaces	Sam HOSKINS
Mongoose, Rip	Blackford OAKES
Monimbo	Robert HOCKNEY
The Monkey Murder, And Other Hildegarde Withers Stories	Hildegarde WITHERS
Monkey Puzzle	Lt Jack STRYKER
The Monkey Wrench Gang	George HAYDUKE
The Monkey's Raincoat	Elvis COLE
Monkshood	Dr THORNE
The Monk's Hood Murders	Captain SMITH
Monologue In Baker Street	Sherlock HOLMES
The Monomark Mystery	Sexton BLAKE
Monopoly To Murder	Shane MACKENZIE
Monsieur Blackshirt	Monsieur BLACKSHIRT
Monsieur Judas	Octavius FANKS
Monsieur Pamplemousse	Monsieur Aristide PAMPLEMOUSSE
Monsieur Pamplemousse Takes The Train	Monsieur Aristide PAMPLEMOUSSE
Monsoon Murder	John HARRINGTON
The Monster Squad	Caitlin O'NEAL
The Monstrous Regiment	Mycroft HOLMES
The Montauk Fault	Sam LINKUM
Monte Cristo Complex	Vincent HAWTHORN
Montezuma's Man	Dep Commiss Isaac SIDEL
Montezuma's Revenge	Tony HAWKIN
Monte, The French Detective: Or, The Man Of Many Disguises	MONTE
Moon Hill	Giles YOEMAN
The Moon Is Red	Insp RYDER
Moon Over Miami	Nick MERLOTTI
The Moon Was Red	Donald O'Keefe ADAMS
Moondreamer	Courtney BROOKS
Mooney Moves Around	Jerry MOONEY
Moonmilk And Murder	Tim MULLIGAN and Elsie May HUNT

Moonshiner Jack, The Mountain Detective	MOONSHINER JACK
The Moonstone	Sgt CUFF
The Moonstone Mystery	Jim BEVERLEY
Morals Squad	Lt Ben KRAHMER
The Morbid Kitchen	Det Insp Charmian DANIELS
Morbid Symptoms	Kate BAIER
More About P J, The Secret Service Boy	P J DAVENANT
More Adventures Of Captain Kettle, KCB	Capt Owen KETTLE
More Adventures Of Oilock Combs: The Succored Beauty	Oilock COMBS
More Crook Stuff	Sir Christopher HAZZARD
More Deaths Than One	Insp Gil MAYO
More Educated Evans	'Educated' EVANS
More Lives Than One	Lorimer LANE
More Murder In A Nunnery	Supt Andrew PEARSON
More News From Middle East	Capt James Donald MACGREGOR
More Tales Of The Black Widowers	The BLACK WIDOWERS
More Tish	Letitia CARBERRY
The Morgue Is Always Open	Sam BOOKER and Jimmy WEBB
Moriarty By Modem	Sherlock HOLMES
The Moriarty Gambit	Sherlock HOLMES
The Morning After Death	Nigel STRANGEWAYS
Morocco Jones In The Case Of The Golden Angel	Morocco JONES
Mortal Causes	Insp REBUS
Mortal Grace	Lt Vince CARDOZO
Mortal Remains	Insp KELSEY
Mortal Sins	Judith HAYES
Mortdecai's Endgame	Charlie MORTDECAI
The Mortimer Story	Insp George TRAVERS
Moscow At High Noon Is The Target	Grant FOWLER
The Moses Bottle	Peter CASEY
Most Men Don't Kill	Tommy TWOTOES and Terry ROOKE
Most Secret...Most Immediate	Garrett MAYNARD
Most Unnatural Murder	Insp Paul GRAINGER
The Most Wanted	Insp SCHMIDT
Moth In A Rag Shop	Hank MOODY
Mother Finds A Body	Gypsy Rose LEE and Biff BRANNIGAN
The Mother Murders	Matt DOYLE and Carter WINFIELD
The Mother Shadow	Claire CONRAD
Mother's Boys	Ch Insp MCHALE
Moths	Insp BLUNT
The Motion Menace	'Doc' SAVAGE
Motive For Murder	Sheriff Bill LLOYD
Motive For Murder	James 'Solo' MALCOLM
Motive For Murder	Insp George MARSHALL
Motive For Murder	Det Ch Insp Ian ROPER
Motive For Revenge	Lucy BECK
Motor City Blue	Amos WALKER
The Motor Coach Murder	Sexton BLAKE
The Motor Pirate	Randolph MANNERING
Mountain Cat	Delia BRAND
The Mountain Cat Murders	Delia BRAND
Mountain Madness	Ben DAVIDGE
Mountain Meadow	Sir Edward LEITHEN
A Mountain Mystery: Or, The Outlaws Of The Rockies	Policeman STANHOPE
A Mountain Mystery: Or, The Outlaws Of The Rockies	Van VERNET
Mountain Of Fear	Brett WALLACE
The Mountaineer Detective	Nimrod RAYMOND
Mounted Policeman Mark: Or, The Central Park Detective's Great Cremation Case	MOUNTED POLICEMAN MARK
Moura	MOURA
Mourner's Voyage	Prof Ronald CHALLIS
The Mournful Demeanour Of Lieutenant Boruvka	Lt BORUVKA
The Mourning After	Scott JORDAN
The Mourning Show	Jenny MCKAY
Mouse And The Master	Sherlock HOLMES
The Mouse In The Mountain	DOAN
The Moving Finger	Benny FREEDMAN
The Moving Finger	Ken WILLIAMS
The Moving House Of Foscaldo	Insp PRONTOUT
The Moving Target	Lew ARCHER
Mr Billingham, The Marquis And Madelon	Samuel T BILLINGHAM
Mr Boyer's Unexpected Will	Florence CUSACK
Mr Braddy's Bottle And Other Humorous Tales	Mr POTTLE
Mr Buffum	Mr BUFFUM
Mr Calder And Mr Behrens	Mr BEHRENS and Mr CALDER
Mr Campion And Others	Albert CAMPION
Mr Campion: Criminologist	Albert CAMPION
Mr Campion's Falcon	Albert CAMPION
Mr Campion's Farthing	Albert CAMPION
Mr Campion's Quarry	Albert CAMPION
Mr Chang Of Scotland Yard	Mr CHANG
Mr Chang's Crime Ray	Mr CHANG
Mr Clackworthy	Amos CLACKWORTHY
Mr Clackworthy, Con Man	Amos CLACKWORTHY
Mr Clerihew: Wine Merchant	Mr CLERIHEW
Mr Collin Is Ruined	Mr COLLIN
Mr Commissioner Sanders	Commiss SANDERS
Mr Daddy - Detective	Mr DADDY
Mr Death	Supt Edmund BENDILOW
Mr Death Walks Abroad	Supt Edmund BENDILOW
Mr Fairlie's Final Journey	Solar PONS
Mr Faraday's Formula	George RIAM
Mr Fortune Explains	Dr Reginald FORTUNE
Mr Fortune Here	Dr Reginald FORTUNE
Mr Fortune Objects	Dr Reginald FORTUNE
Mr Fortune Speaking	Dr Reginald FORTUNE
Mr Fortune Wonders	Dr Reginald FORTUNE
Mr Fortune, Please	Dr Reginald FORTUNE
Mr Fortune's Practice	Dr Reginald FORTUNE
Mr Fortune's Trials	Dr Reginald FORTUNE
Mr Glencannon	Mr GLENCANNON
Mr Guelpa	Mr GUELPA
Mr Hercules	Bill KELLAWAY

Mr Holmes At Sea	William HOLMES
Mr Homes Acts As Attorney For Solomon	Shylock HOMES
Mr Homes Foils A Conspiracy And Gains A Fortune	Shylock HOMES
Mr Homes Makes An Important Confession	Shylock HOMES
Mr Homes Radiates A Wireless Message	Shylock HOMES
Mr Homes Reaches An Unhistorical Conclusion	Shylock HOMES
Mr Homes Shatters A Tradition	Shylock HOMES
Mr Homes Shatters An Alibi	Shylock HOMES
Mr Homes Solves A Question Of Authorship	Shylock HOMES
Mr Homes Tackles A "Hard Case"	Shylock HOMES
Mr Horrocks, Purser	Mr HORROCKS
Mr Hoyland Looks Round	Mr HOYLAND
Mr J G Reeder Returns	J G REEDER
Mr Jeremy, Detective	Mr JEREMY
Mr Jorkens Remembers Africa	Joseph JORKENS
Mr Justice Raffles	A J RAFFLES
Mr Kettle, Third Mate	Capt Owen KETTLE
Mr Laxworthy's Adventures	John T LAXWORTHY
Mr Marlow Takes To Rye	Dick MARLOW
Mr Meeson's Will	James SHORT
Mr Moto Takes A Hand	Mr MOTO
Mr Parker Pyne, Detective	Parker PYNE
Mr Pendlebury's Hat Trick	Mr PENDLEBURY
Mr Penny	Mr PENNY
Mr Penny At War	Mr PENNY
Mr Penny Comes Down Heads	Mr PENNY
Mr Pepper, Investigator	Mr PEPPER
Mr Pidgeon's Island	Roger SHERINGHAM
Mr Poskitt	Mr POSKITT
Mr Poskitt's Nightcaps	Mr POSKITT
Mr Preed's Gangster	Mr PREED
Mr Quentin Investigates	Mr QUENTIN
Mr Sandeman Loses His Life	Paul CRAINE
Mr South Burned His Mouth	Joseph SOUTH
Mr Strang Gives A Lecture	Mr STRANG
Mr Strang Takes A Tour	Mr STRANG
Mr Treadgold Cuts In	Mr Horace B TREADGOLD
Mr Truefitt Detects	Mr TRUEFITT
Mr Tutt Comes Home	Ephraim TUTT
Mr Tutt Finds A Way	Ephraim TUTT
Mr Tutt Takes The Stand	Ephraim TUTT
Mr Watson Intervenes	Mr WATSON
Mr Wickwire's Widow	Mr WICKWIRE
Mr Wickwire's 'Gun Moll'	Mr WICKWIRE
Mr X	Det Jake PHILLIPS
Mr Yesterday	Kiel ST JAMES and Orson BOLES
MRCS	John GARDEN
Mrder Is My Business	Michael SHAYNE
Mrs Brown's Pearls	Samuel LYLE
Mrs Craggs: Crimes Cleaned Up	CRAGGS
Mrs Donald Dyke, Detective	Mrs Donald DYKE
Mrs Halliburton's Troubles	Sgt DELVES
Mrs Jeffries On The Ball	Mrs JEFFRIES and Insp WITHERSPOON
Mrs Jeffries On The Trail	Mrs JEFFRIES and Insp WITHERSPOON
Mrs Judas	Kira POLLY
Mrs Mallory Investigates	Mrs Sheila MALLORY
Mrs McGinty's Dead	Hercule POIROT and Mrs Ariadne OLIVER
Mrs Meeker's Money	David MADDEN
Mrs Murdock Takes A Case	Kent MURDOCK and Joyce MURDOCK
Mrs Murphy's Underpants	Ambrose HUNTER and Ed HUNTER
Mrs Musgrave And Her Husband	William CHARLECOT
Mrs Norris Observes	Mrs Annie NORRIS
Mrs Pollifax Pursued	Mrs Emily POLLIFAX
Mrs Pollifax, Spy	Mrs Emily POLLIFAX
Mrs Porter's Letter	Nyla WADE
Mrs Pym And Other Stories	Mrs Palmyra Evangeline PYM
Mrs Pym Of Scotland Yard	Mrs Palmyra Evangeline PYM
Mrs Raffles	Mrs A J VAN RAFFLES
Mrs Snagg, Detective	Mrs SNAGG
Mrs Vanderstein's Jewels	Mr GIMBLET
Mrs Warrender's Profession	Mrs Elizabeth WARRENDER and James WARRENDER
Mrs. Presumed Dead	Melita PARGETER
The Mule On The Minaret	Noel RAID
Multiple Murder	Jim HARRIS and Kate HARRIS
Mumbo-Jumbo	Papa LA BAS
The Mummy Case	Denys SARGENT and Humphrey CARVER
The Mummy Case Mystery	Denys SARGENT and Humphrey CARVER
The Mummy Moves	Insp DODSON
Mum's The Word	Ellie Simons HASKELL
Mum's The Word For Murder	Jerry BURKE
The Munich Posture	Dorothy Mayotte RIGBY
The Munition Mystery	Herlock SHOLMES
Mura, The Western Lady Detective	MURA
Murder	Carl WILCOX
Murder 97	Simon LASH
A Murder A Day!	Joe KELLY
Murder A La Richelieu	Adelaide ADAMS
Murder A Mile High	Emma MARSH and Hank FAIRBANKS
Murder Across And Down	Giles SULLIVAN
Murder After A Fashion	Steve HERSHEY
Murder After Tea Time	Lettie WINTERBOTTOM
Murder After The Blitz	Insp GRAY
Murder After The Fact	Clinton BALL
Murder Al Fresco	Daisy Jane MOTT
Murder Among Friends	Insp/Supt DEERING
Murder Among Friends	Bridget O'TOOLE
Murder Among Friends	Lt/Insp Richard TUCK
Murder Among The Angells	Insp KANE
Murder Among Us	Ch Insp Alan MARKBY and Meredith MITCHELL
Murder And Magic	Lord DARCY
Murder And Miss Ming	Insp 'Tubby' HALL
Murder And Music	Insp CROWLEY
Murder And The First Lady	Eleanor ROOSEVELT
Murder And The Red-Haired Girl	Insp Jack STRICKLAND
A Murder Arranged	Insp RICHARDSON
Murder As An Ornament	Sheriff Hiram ODOM
Murder As Usual	David COTTER
Murder At 10,000 Feet	Irving TODD
Murder At Arondale Farm	Mortimer SARK
Murder At Bador	Derek GLOVER
Murder At Bratton Grange	Insp HANSLET and Dr Lancelot PRIESTLEY
Murder At Buckingham Palace	King of England George V WINDSOR
Murder At Cambridge	Insp HORROCKS and Hilary FENTON
Murder At Covent Garden	Det Insp EVANS
The Murder At Crome House	James FLINT
Murder At Deer Lick	Sheriff Jess RODEN
Murder At Eastover	Irene TENNANT
Murder At Endor	Sgt/Lt Charley MITCHELL
Murder At Exbridge	Det Sgt AMBROSE
Murder At Full Moon	Det Insp GRAVES
Murder At Government House	Supt VACHELL
Murder At Grassmere Abbey	Ch Insp James MILLER
Murder At Hazelmoor	Insp NARROCOTT
Murder At High Noon	Ch Insp CUMMINGS and Insp/Supt FILLINGER
Murder At High Tide	Anatole FLIQUE
Murder At Horsethief	Jason CORDRY
Murder At HQ	Asmun HILL
Murder At La Marimba	Carlito RIVERA
Murder At Landred Hall	Rampion SAVAGE
Murder At Little Malling	Insp Jack PEARSON
Murder At Malibu	Jason CORDRY
Murder At Manor House	Insp Gordon ROSS
Murder At Markendon Court	Prof Charles HARDING
Murder At Markham	Sheila TRAVIS
Murder At Mavering	Insp Maurice HEPBURN
Murder At Midnight	GARSTANG
Murder At Midyears	Toby SAMPSON
Murder At Mocking House	Det Insp Stephen HARPER
Murder At Monticello	Mrs MURPHY
Murder At Morning Prayers	Timothy DREWER
Murder At Mt Fuji	Jane PRESCOTT
Murder At Out-Patients	Paul CHISHOLM
Murder At Plenders	Insp George ANNESLEY
Murder At Red Grange	John PETERSON
Murder At School	Colin REVELL
Murder At Scotland Yard	Horace Augustus ELVER
Murder At Sea	Matthew KELTON
Murder At The ABA	Darius JUST
Murder At The Academy Awards	Punch ROBERTS and Bonny CUTLER
Murder At The Black Crook	Andrea Reid RAMSAY and David RAMSAY
Murder At The Cat Show	Douglas PERKINS
Murder At The Club	Gordon MULDREW
Murder At The College	Det Sgt AMBROSE
Murder At The Diogenes Club	Sherlock HOLMES
Murder At The FBI	Ross LIZENBY and Chris SAKSIS
Murder At The Flea Club	Dr Mary FINNEY and Emily COLLINS
Murder At The Fringe	Rocco CONIGLIARO
Murder At The Inn	Paul TEMPLETON
Murder At The Kennedy Center	Prof MacKenzie SMITH
Murder At The Kentucky Derby	Maj Roderick AUSTEN
Murder At The Keyhole	Prof LAXTON
Murder At The Mardi Gras	Maggie SLONE
Murder At The Margin	Prof Henry SPEARMAN
Murder At The Movies	Rose GRAHAM
Murder At The National Cathedral	Prof MacKenzie SMITH
Murder At The New York World's Fair	Daisy TOWER
Murder At The Old Stone House	Jane Amanda EDWARDS
Murder At The Piano	Insp SCHMIDT
Murder At The PTA Luncheon	Susan HENSHAW
Murder At The Red October	Det Ivan KUVAKIN
Murder At The Spa	Charlotte GRAHAM
Murder At The Superbowl	Marcus Aurelius BURR
Murder At The Tower	Det Supt James BYRD
Murder At The Varsity	Insp HORROCKS and Hilary FENTON
The Murder At The Vicarage	Jane MARPLE
Murder At The War	Sgt Peter 'Obie' BRICHTER
Murder At The Women's City Club	Insp BOOT
Murder At The World's Fair	John SMITH
Murder At The Zoo	Solar PONS
Murder At Tomorrow	Nick NICOLETTI
Murder At Vassar	Maggie ELLIOTT
Murder At Willow Run	Megan MARSHALL
Murder At Wrides Park	Ronald CAMBERWELL
Murder At "The Angel"	Insp MCKELLER and Anthony HOWARD
Murder Backstairs	Insp James F 'Bonnie' DUNDEE
Murder Beat	Graham DARREN
Murder Before Breakfast	Bill HASTINGS and Coco HASTINGS
Murder Before Dinner	Insp Jim BURGESS
Murder Before Matins	Insp Andrew COGGIN
Murder Before Tuesday	Insp REYNOLDS
Murder Behind Closed Doors	Leo ROI
Murder Behind Locked Doors	Jane TREGAR
Murder Below Wall Street	Dr ARTHUR
Murder Between Dark And Dark	Komako KOA
Murder Beyond The Mountains	Sherlock HOLMES
The Murder Book Of Mr J G Reeder	J G REEDER
Murder Bound	Trygve YAMAMURA
Murder Breaks Trail	Millard SMYTH
Murder Buys A Ticket	Marty MALONE
Murder By An Aristocrat	Sarah KEATE and Det Lance O'LEARY
Murder By Arrangement	Cornelius DUFFY
Murder By Chance	Ch Insp THOMPSON
Murder By Deception	John Lloyd BRANSON
Murder By Degrees	Maggie COURTNEY
Murder By Design	Insp Fadiman WACE
Murder By Experts	Arthur G CROOK

	Murder By Formula	Insp Wilton JACKS
	Murder By Gaslight	Lon QUINNCANNON
	Murder By Impulse	John Lloyd BRANSON
	Murder By Inches	Peter MARRELL
	Murder By Invitation	Insp Neil MACLEOD
	Murder By Jury	Angeline TREDENNICK
	Murder By Mail	Peggy O'NEILL
	Murder By Mail	Patricia SEAWARD
	Murder By Moonlight	Sexton BLAKE
	Murder By Multiplication	Insp YORK
	Murder By Proxy	Sexton BLAKE
	Murder By Proxy	Johnny BORDELON
	Murder By Proxy	Simon DRAKE
	Murder By Proxy	Dan TURNER
	Murder By Request	Horatio GREEN
	Murder By The Book	Verity 'Birdie' BIRDWOOD
	Murder By The Book	Pam NORTH and Jerry NORTH
	Murder By The Clock	Lt VALCOUR
	Murder By The Day	Webster FLAGG
	Murder By The Dozen	WONG
	Murder By The Lake	Ross MACALLISTER
	Murder By The Mile	Jim LARKIN
	Murder By The Minute	Magnus KEEBLE
	Murder By The Pack	Bob RUFF
	Murder By The Yard	Anne 'Davvie' Davenport MCLEAN
	Murder By Warrant	Jonathan HATWOOD
	Murder Calls The Tune	Insp Laurie HUME
	Murder Cancels All Debts	Rick VANNER
	Murder Can't Stop	Bill LENNOX
	Murder Can't Wait	Det Nathan SHAPIRO
	Murder Case Number 33	Michael JOYCE
	Murder City	Graham DARREN
	Murder Comes Calling!	Sexton BLAKE
	Murder Comes Home	Jeremiah IRISH
	Murder Comes Smiling	Arthur Stukeley PENNINGTON and Det Insp Patrick Aloysius MCCARTHY
	Murder Comes To Dinner	Simon CROLE
	Murder Comes To Rothesay	Insp FLAGG
	Murder Cries Out	Insp/Supt William AUSTEN
	Murder Cum Laude	Sgt Cass HARTY
	Murder Day By Day	Patrick BRAY
	Murder Draws A Line	Christopher STORM
	Murder Every Monday	Clifford FLUSH
	Murder For A Hollow Shell	Paul DECKER
	Murder For A Million	Sexton BLAKE
	Murder For Art's Sake	Det Nathan SHAPIRO
	Murder For Breakfast	Alan MILLER
	Murder For Christmas	Peter HOLGATE
	Murder For Fun	Dr FERENC
	Murder For Madame	Steve CONACHER
	Murder For Miss Emily	Insp PITT
	Murder For Sale	Supt Donald MARTIN
	Murder For The Asking	Max Chauncy HALE
	Murder For The Wrong Reason	MASON
	Murder Forestalled	Johnny VINCENT
	Murder From Three Angles	Insp CHACE
The	Murder Game	Sgt FENWICK
	Murder Game	Van Dusen ORMSBERRY
	Murder Gets A Degree	Glad GOLD
	Murder Gets Around	Gerry BARNES
	Murder Gives A Lovely Light	Lt/Capt George HONEGGER
	Murder Goes Fishing	Anthony ADAMS
	Murder Goes Fishing	Anthony ADAMS
	Murder Goes Rolling Along	Casey PETERS
	Murder Goes Round And Round	Pierre CHAMBRUN
	Murder Goes To Bank Night	Chattin WHYTE
	Murder Goes To The World's Fair	Anthony ADAMS
	Murder Goes To The World's Fair	Anthony ADAMS
	Murder Gone Mad	Sir Brian Dinsmore CONWAY
	Murder Gone Mad	Supt Arnold PIKE
	Murder Gone To Earth	Dr Hugh WESTLAKE
	Murder Has No Calories	Angela BENBOW and Caledonia WINGATE
	Murder Has Your Number	Insp Walter MCDUMONT
	Murder Hath Charms	Insp Rodney HILTON
	Murder Humane	Insp Jimmy BRENT
	Murder In 25 Words Or Less	Steve RHODEN
	Murder In A Hot Flash	Charlie GREENE
	Murder In A Lighter Vein	Tony WOOLRICH
	Murder In A Nunnery	Supt Andrew PEARSON
	Murder In A Pug's Parlour	Auguste DIDIER
	Murder In Amber	Timothy FOWLER
The	Murder In Beacon Street	Prof John SOUTHARD
	Murder In Black	Prof WELLS
	Murder In Black And White	Tommy TWOTOES and Terry ROOKE
	Murder In Blue	Insp Harry CHARLTON
	Murder In Borstal	Ch Insp CUMMINGS
	Murder In Brass	Seth COLMAN and Eve COLMAN
	Murder In Church	Prof Ian CRAIG
	Murder In College	Sgt Cass HARTY
	Murder In Cowboy Bronze	John WALTZ
	Murder In E Minor	Nero WOLFE
	Murder In Earl's Court	Peter KERRIGAN
	Murder In False Face	Chet PHELPS
	Murder In Fancy Dress	Sgt Steven ARROW
	Murder In Fancy Dress	Patrick O'BRIEN
	Murder In Five Columns	Ransome DRAGOON and Vicky 'The Dish' GAINES
	Murder In Flat 14	Rodney WAYNE
	Murder In Georgetown	Joe POTOMOS
	Murder In Haste	Ch Insp CUMMINGS and Insp/Supt FILLINGER
	Murder In Haste	HIGHWAY
	Murder In Havana	Andrew TALBOT
	Murder In Hollywood	Rex HUXFORD
	Murder In Hospital	Paul CHISHOLM
	Murder In Hospital	Dr David WINTRINGHAM and Insp Steven MITCHELL
	Murder In Jackson Hole	Jim LITTLE
	Murder In Make-Up	Maj Jack ATHERLEY
	Murder In Maryland	Lt Joseph KELLY
	Murder In Mayfair	Arthur Stukeley PENNINGTON
	Murder In Maytime	Michael TERRENCE and 'Terry' TERRENCE
	Murder In Melancholy	John MARNE
	Murder In Mendocino	Charlotte KENT
	Murder In Mid-Atlantic	Insp Simon ASHTON
	Murder In Millenium Vi	Victor MITCHEL
	Murder In Mortimer Square	Richard FURLING
	Murder In New Guinea	Bertram LYNCH
	Murder In Ocean Drive	Michael GRANT
	Murder In Okefenokee	Andrea Reid RAMSAY and David RAMSAY
	Murder In Paradise	Ambrose USHER
	Murder In Pastiche	Louis Luther (Murder Master) KING
	Murder In Peking	Riley BLACKWOOD
	Murder In Piccadilly	Insp WAKE
	Murder In Pictures	Jerry WADE
	Murder In Plain Sight	Marmaduke 'Duke' MCCALE
	Murder In Public	FALCON
	Murder In Queer Street	Ch Insp George BASSETT
	Murder In Rockwater	Insp GROGAN
	Murder In Silence	Insp BASS
	Murder In Store	Quint MCCAULEY
	Murder In Style	Lyle CURTIS and Susan YATES
	Murder In Suffolk	Hugh DUNCAN
	Murder In Switzerland	Reggie FAULKNER
	Murder In Texas	John SHIELDS
	Murder In The Act	Marilyn AMBERS
	Murder In The Air	Peter BLUE and Jean Henri ST AMAND
	Murder In The Bank	Insp John SLADE and LESSINGER
	Murder In The Bath	Insp LECAIN
	Murder In The Bedroom	Joseph ROULETABILLE
	Murder In The Borough Library	Insp PARKER
	Murder In The Camp	Const ROBINS
	Murder In The Central Committee	Pepe CARVALHO
	Murder In The CIA	Colette CAHILL
	Murder In The Cockpit	Irving TODD
	Murder In The Collective	Pam NILSEN
	Murder In The Cotswolds	Sheriff Chick CHARLESTON
	Murder In The Dog Days	Maggie RYAN
	Murder In The Family	Sgt David PUTNAM
	Murder In The Family Way	Randy ROBERTS
	Murder In The Fine Arts	John NOLAN
	Murder In The Flagship	Cdr WRAITHLEA
The	Murder In The Fog	Dixon BRETT
	Murder In The Fog	Det CONROY and Det MCCARTHY
	Murder In The French Room	Insp Dave BRATTON
	Murder In The Gunroom	Col Jefferson Davis RAND
	Murder In The Haunted Sentry-Box	James GREER
	Murder In The Hellfire Club	Benjamin FRANKLIN
	Murder In The Hotel	Hamilton CLEEK
The	Murder In The Laboratory	Insp MELLISON and Dr Martin BLYTHE
	Murder In The Lords	Philip NORTH
	Murder In The Madhouse	William CRANE
	Murder In The Mails	Willie CARMODY
	Murder In The Making	'Doc' MILLER
	Murder In The Maze	Ch Const Sir Clinton DRIFFIELD
	Murder In The Mist	Pierre O'BRIEN
	Murder In The Moor	Peregrine SMITH
	Murder In The Morning	Supt BRADLEY
	Murder In The Museum	Cornelius CLIFT Jr
	Murder In The Old Jail	Det Sgt O'BRIEN and Det Sgt O'NEILL
	Murder In The Radio Department	Insp KNICKMAN and Martin AMES
	Murder In The Raw	Brock (The Rock) CALLAHAN
	Murder In The Red Room	Eleanor ROOSEVELT
	Murder In The Rough	Napoleon B SMITH
	Murder In The Rough	Napoleon B SMITH
	Murder In The Rue Royale	Chevalier Auguste C DUPIN
	Murder In The Ruins	Montrose ARBUTHNOT
	Murder In The Senate	Insp Scott STUART
	Murder In The Smithsonian	Mac HANRAHAN and Heather MCBEAN
	Murder In The Smokehouse	Auguste DIDIER
	Murder In The Stacks	Tom ALLEN
	Murder In The Stratosphere	Thibault PAREW
	Murder In The Supreme Court	Martin TELLER and Susanna PINSCHER
	Murder In The Surgery	Insp Victor BONDURANT
	Murder In The Taj Mahal	Cdr WRAITHLEA
	Murder In The Walls	Johnny ORTIZ
	Murder In The White House	Mr Ron FAIRCHILD
	Murder In The WPA	Det Sgt Pietro TONELLI
	Murder In The Zoo	Prof Ian CRAIG
	Murder In Time	Frederick HUNT
	Murder In Trinidad	Bertram LYNCH
	Murder In Two Flats	Insp Peter CURWEN and Hugh STANTON
	Murder In Venice	Capt RIZZI
	Murder In Wax	'Angel Face' REARDON
	Murder In White Pit	Ken WILLIAMS
	Murder In Yiddish	James SHAW
	Murder Included	Insp Ronald PRICE
	Murder Intended	Insp WILKINS
	Murder Is A Collector's Item	Emma MARSH and Hank FAIRBANKS
	Murder Is A Furtive Thing	Paul SCARF
	Murder Is A Gamble	Jonathan MARKS
	Murder Is A Long Time Coming	Marius LARCHE
	Murder Is A Maiden's Handicap	Marc BRODY
	Murder Is Aboard	Jimmy BRENNON
	Murder Is Contagious	Kit 'Marsden' ACTON
	Murder Is For Keeps	Mark PRESTON
	Murder Is Insane	Jonathan MARKS
	Murder Is Murder Is Murder	Gertrude STEIN and Alice TOKLAS
	Murder Is My Racket	Simon CROLE
	Murder Is Not Enough	Anthony WARE

	Murder Is Not Mute	Det Patrick Michael DOYLE
	Murder Is Relative	Brigid DONOVAN
	Murder Island	Dan GREGORY
	Murder Isn't Enough	Ed FITZGERALD
	Murder Isn't Funny	Mike LANSON
	Murder Jigsaw	Dr MANSON
	Murder Las Vegas Style	Mark FORAN
The	Murder League	SIMPSON, CARRUTHERS and BRIGGS
	Murder Loves Company	Prof James Yates BIDDLE and Kay RITCHIE
	Murder Made Easy	Sexton BLAKE
The	Murder Makers	Roger TALLIS
	Murder Makes A Merry Widow	Anthony HUNTER
	Murder Makes A Pilgrimage	Sister MARY HELEN
	Murder Makes A Villain	Mike JAMES
	Murder Makes By-Lines	Sham PAYNE
	Murder Makes Me Nervous	Lt RYAN
The	Murder Man	Insp Laurie HUME
	Murder Mansion	Insp Wilton JACKS
	Murder Maritime	Clarice CLAREMONT
The	Murder Mask	Sir Brian FORDINGHAME
	Murder Mask	Supt Samuel QUAN
	Murder Masks Miami	Lt VALCOUR
	Murder Masquerade	Patrick O'BRIEN
	Murder May Pass Unpunished	Det Insp ALLPORT and Insp George ANNESLEY
	Murder Melody	Sham PAYNE
	Murder Melody	'Doc' SAVAGE
	Murder Memo: The Carl Houston Case	Offr Michael LA RUE
	Murder Mission	Johnny MORINI
	Murder Most Artistic	Insp PENK
	Murder Most Fowl	Sheriff Dan RHODES
	Murder Most Grizzly	Lauren MAXWELL
	Murder Most Irregular	David MORGAN
	Murder Mystery	Dade COOLEY
A	Murder Mystery	Herlock SHOLMES
	Murder Needs A Name	Capt Gridley NELSON
	Murder Next Year	P C James WIGAN
	Murder Observed	Clare GAMADGE
	Murder Of A Dead Man	Hank HYER
The	Murder Of A Magnate	Maj Dick BURTON
The	Murder Of A Midget	Judo MARRIOTT
	Murder Of A Mystery Writer	Dr Wade ANTHONY
	Murder Of A Park Avenue Playgirl	Peter CHAMBERS
	Murder Of A Priest	Lt SELBY
	Murder Of A Professor	Sgt FOGERTY and Philip WARING
	Murder Of A Snob	Ch Const Colonel CRISP
	Murder Of A Student	Insp Tom SWETMAN and Insp CRANE
	Murder Of A Wife	Dr Michael GRAY
	Murder Of An MP	Lucien CLAY
The	Murder Of An Old Man	Maj Gregory LEWIS
The	Murder Of An Old-Time Movie Star	Pete MCCOY
The	Murder Of Cecily Thane	Philip 'Spike' TRACY
The	Murder Of Colonel Neville	Reginald DELAMERE
The	Murder Of Conan Doyle	FOAMES
A	Murder Of Crows	Dr Catherine EDISON
A	Murder Of Crows	Patrick GILLARD
A	Murder Of Crows	Benjamin SHOCK and Charity TUCKER
The	Murder Of Dave Brandon	Policeman Dick WESTON
The	Murder Of Eleanor Pope	Dr Michael GRAY
The	Murder Of Estelle Cantor	Henry PRINCE
The	Murder Of Geraldine Foster	Commiss Thatcher COLT
The	Murder Of Harvey Blake	Asaph CLUME
The	Murder Of Lalla Lee	'One Week' WIMBLE
The	Murder Of Margot Midnight	Insp BOW and Capt KEETCH
The	Murder Of Marion Mason	Singer BATTS
The	Murder Of Martin Fotherill	Nathaniel MOODY
The	Murder Of Miss Betty Sloan	Jabez TWOMBLEY
The	Murder Of Paul Rougier	Insp DOWNES and Sgt HOPKINS
The	Murder Of Roger Ackroyd	Hercule POIROT
The	Murder Of Sherlock Holmes	Jessica FLETCHER
A	Murder Of Some Importance	Supt William STEVENS and Insp Pierre ALLAIN
	Murder Of The Admiral	Sheridan DOOME
The	Murder Of The Maharajah	Supt HOWARD
	Murder Of The Pigboat Skipper	Sheridan DOOME
	Murder Off The Glass	Murray GLICK
	Murder Offstage	Paul DRAYER
	Murder On A Bad Trip	Insp David COPE
	Murder On A Shoestring	Det Insp 'Duck' MALLARD
	Murder On Alternate Tuesdays	Aubrey NASH
	Murder On Bag Hill	Insp BECK
	Murder On Beacon Hill	Marmaduke 'Duke' MCCALE
	Murder On Cape Cod	Dan 'DeeDee' DONER
	Murder On Capitol Hill	Lydia JAMES
	Murder On Clam Pond	'Mac' MACFARLAND
	Murder On Cue	Jocelyn O'ROARKE and Philip GERARD
	Murder On Embassy Row	Sal MORIZIO
The	Murder On Fifth Avenue	Clarice CLAREMONT
	Murder On Friday	Philip 'Spike' TRACY
	Murder On Ghost Tree Island	Insp Everett ANDERSON
	Murder On Her Mind	Johnny CHURCH
	Murder On Her Mind	Alexandra WINTER
	Murder On High	Charlotte GRAHAM
	Murder On High	George KENNEDY
	Murder On His Mind	Dan DAMON
	Murder On Holiday	Simon CHARD
	Murder On Ice	Supt Donald MARTIN
	Murder On Leave	Ch Insp 'Daddy' BOURNE
	Murder On Location	George KENNEDY
	Murder On Madison Avenue	Ev FRANKLIN
	Murder On Margin	Pat THOMPSON
	Murder On Martha's Vineyard	Timothy O'HARA and Nancy BREWSTER
	Murder On My Street	Frank LUTHER
	Murder On Page Three	Sgt Rudolf NILSEN
	Murder On Russian Hill	Bill HASTINGS and Coco HASTINGS

	Murder On Shark Island	Clint WALSH
	Murder On Show	Douglas PERKINS
	Murder On Stilts	Dep Commiss Benjamin SIMON
	Murder On The Aisle	TOBIN
	Murder On The Aphrodite	Angeline TREDENNICK
	Murder On The Brain	Insp HYDE
The	Murder On The Burrows	Insp/Supt MACDONALD
	Murder On The Chesapeake	Margaret BARLOW
	Murder On The Common	Supt SHANNON
	Murder On The Glass Floor	Gwynn LEITH and Colin KEATS
	Murder On The Line	Mohawk DANIELS
	Murder On The Long Straight	Hartley RHYS
	Murder On The Program	Sheriff George WHITE
	Murder On The Rocks	Steve BENTLEY
	Murder On The Run	Insp John SANDERS
The	Murder On The Sixth Hole	Maj Gregory LEWIS
	Murder On The Square	Evan PINKERTON
	Murder On The S-23	Sheridan DOOME
	Murder On The Ten-Yard Line	Van Dusen ORMSBERRY
	Murder On The Thirty-First Floor	Ch Insp Peter JENSEN
	Murder On The Tropic	Peter BOUNTY
	Murder On The Wild Side	Shep STONE
	Murder On The Yellow Brick Road	Toby PETERS and Judy GARLAND
	Murder On Tour	Hugh RENNERT
	Murder On Trial	Insp/Supt Simon MANTON
	Murder On Usher's Planet	Gwen GRAY and Garamond GRAY
	Murder On Wall Street	Victor GRANT
	Murder On "B" Deck	Walter GHOST
	Murder Or Manslaughter	Hugo HOLD
	Murder Out Of Court	Ch Insp GORHAM
	Murder Out Of School	Ben GORDON
	Murder Out Of Tune	Insp CADMAN
	Murder Over Dorval	Russell TEED
	Murder Over Miami	Michael SHAYNE
	Murder Paves The Way	Det Insp SHANE
	Murder Points A Finger	Lt ROMANO
The	Murder Pool	Dr Wade ANTHONY
	Murder R F D	Sgt David PUTNAM
	Murder Recalls Van Kill	Hendrik VAN KILL
	Murder Rehearsal	Colin KNOWLES
	Murder Rents A Room	Sheriff Bill DAVIES
	Murder Rides A Rocket	Ransome DRAGOON and Vicky 'The Dish' GAINES
The	Murder Room	Paul DAMIAN
	Murder Round The Clock	Pierre CHAMBRUN
	Murder Roundabout	Capt/Insp Merton HEIMRICH
	Murder Seeks An Agent	Peter ASWELL
	Murder Sits Pretty	Victor MCBAIN
	Murder Spoils Everything	Whitney WHEAT
	Murder Stalks A Billion	Richard Curtis (The Phantom) VAN LOAN
	Murder Stalks The Wakely Family	Judge Ephraim Peabody PECK
	Murder Starts From Fishguard	Hugh RUDD
	Murder Stops The Clock	Jake JUSTUS, Helene JUSTUS and John J MALONE
	Murder Strikes Pink	Insp James FLECKER
	Murder Strikes Three	Ch Reuben MALLOCK
	Murder Strikes Thrice	MCFEE
	Murder Strikes Twice	Supt Simon BULLION
	Murder Sunny Side Up	Benton SAFFORD
	Murder Sweet And Sour	Uncle George CROWDER
	Murder Takes A Ride	Steve RANDOM
	Murder Takes The Veil	Mother THEODORE
	Murder Through The Window	Insp George ANNESLEY
	Murder To Burn	Sgt Steven ARROW
	Murder To Follow	Det Insp Ross PATERSON
	Murder To Music	Sherlock HOLMES
	Murder To Music	Insp KELLERWAY
	Murder To Order	'Sugar' KANE
	Murder To Type	Steve CARTER
	Murder Train	Sherrett YORK
The	Murder Trap	Richard VERNER
	Murder Trapp	Berkeley Hoy BARNES
The	Murder Tree	Michael BRENT
	Murder Under Construction	Capt Andy MACVEIGH
	Murder Under Glass	Senator Brooks Urban BANNER
	Murder Under The Big Top	Richard Curtis (The Phantom) VAN LOAN
	Murder Under The Christmas Tree	Maj Clifford LANSING
	Murder Unleashed	Dennis DEVORE
	Murder Unlimited	Desmond SHANNON
	Murder Unsolved	Insp HARROW
	Murder Up My Sleeve	Terry CLANE
	Murder Upstairs	Alice PENNY
	Murder Walks Alone	Edmond MACKELL
	Murder Walks The Corridors	Dr NORTH
	Murder Was My Neighbour	John CHADWICK
	Murder Wears Mukluks	Millard SMYTH
	Murder Well Done	Insp HARROW
	Murder Will In	Alan FORD
	Murder Will Out	Mr HOYLAND
	Murder Will Out	Insp J RASON
	Murder With A Theme Song	Rocky ALLAN and Michael DUNDAS
	Murder With A Twist	Matt SINCLAIR
	Murder With Love	Sexton BLAKE
	Murder With Love	Johnny CHURCH
	Murder With Menaces	BRODY
	Murder With Minarets	Christopher MILNER-BROWN
	Murder With Muskets	Insp Andrew COGGIN
	Murder With Orange Blossoms	Peter BARRON and Janet BARRON
	Murder With Pictures	Kent MURDOCK and Jack FENNER
	Murder With Your Malted	'Chick' VARNEY
	Murder Without Clues	Simon ROLFE
	Murder Without Mourners	Dr Septimus DODDS
	Murder Without Regret	Insp MACKAY
	Murder Without Weapons	Matthew HIGGINS
	Murder Won't Out	Insp BASIL

Murder Won't Wait	Vee BROWN
Murder Yet To Come	Peter JERNINGHAM
Murder - And Ariadne	Insp DIGBY
Murder - But Natch	Hortense CLINTON
Murdercon	Athena PIERCE
Murdered But Not Dead	Insp James F 'Bonnie' DUNDEE
The Murdered Manservant	Insp Cuthbert HIGGINS
The Murdered Millionaire	Ellery QUEEN
The Murderer	'Biff' CORRIGAN
Murderer At Large	Insp H EMP
The Murderer Returns	Pierre MONTIGNY
The Murderer Vine	Joe DUNNE
Murderers Anonymous	Matthew TIERNEY
Murderers Anonymous	Matthew TIERNEY
Murderers Make Mistakes	Insp Joseph FRENCH
The Murderers Of Monty	Insp FENBY
Murderers Three	Bill CHORLEY
Murderer's Choice	Grace POMEROY
Murderer's Maze	Ray FELTON
Murderer's Moon	Paul TEMPLETON
Murderer's Row	Sgt FENWICK
The Murdering Kind	Sgt/Insp John COFFIN and Insp/Supt William WINTER
Murdering Mr Velfrage	Insp KYLE
A Murderous Journey	PIRON
Murderous Justice	Alan ARCHBOLD
Murders And Acquisitions	Reuben FROST
The Murders At Impasse Louvain	Insp Jean-Paul GAUTIER
The Murders At Loon Lake	Clifton BRENTWOOD
Murders At Scandal House	Alan MILLER
Murders In Sequence	Det Tommy RANKIN
The Murders In The Rue Morgue	Chevalier Auguste C DUPIN
The Murders On The Square	Lt Al ZIMMERMAN
Murder-In-Law	Mark RENZLER
Murder-On-Hudson	Daisy Jane MOTT
Murder-On-Thames	Arabella FRANT
Murder... In Full View	Michael DOUGLAS
Murder, Bless It!	Johnny DUVIVIEN
Murder, Chop Chop	Gimiendo Hernande QUINTO
Murder, Maestro, Please	George Herbert HENRY
Murder, Mr Mosley	Insp MOSLEY
Murder, Murder, Little Star	Frances ARMITAGE
Murder, My Sweet	Insp Jim SILVER
Murder: The Musical	Xenia SMITH and Leslie WETZON
Murder! Murder!	Francis QUARLES
Murder's A Swine	Lord WINTERSTONE
Murder's Coming	Abelard VOSS
Murder's Night	Jack MCGUIRE
Murder's No Accident	Max BRINDLE
Murdock	Corey THATCHER
Murdock For Hire	Matt MURDOCK
Murdock's Acid Test	Kent MURDOCK
Murky Shallows	Det Insp Arvo LAURILA
The Muscatel Ritual	Turlock LOAMS
The Museum Murder	Duddington Pell CHALMERS
The Musgrave Ritual	Sherlock HOLMES
The Musgrave Version	Sherlock HOLMES
Mush And Poke, Detectives	MUSH and POKE
The Mushroom Man	Det Insp Charles PRIEST
The Music Room	Wellington COTTER
Music To Murder By	Martin WEBB
Music When Sweet Voices Die	Charles 'Spotted' MOON
The Mussolini Murder Plot	Sgt/Insp MARSHALL
Mute Witness	Lt CLANCY
My Body	Steve BENTLEY
My Body	Steve BENTLEY
My Brother Michael	Simon LESTER and Camilla HAVEN
My Brother, The Druggist	Marty GOLD
My Dearest Holmes	Sherlock HOLMES
My First Murder	Mavis DAVIS
My Friend Tony	John WOODRUFF and Tony NOVELLO
My Heart And Stephanie: A Novel	Sam BURTON and Frances BAIRD
My Killer Doesn't Understand Me	Clem TALBOT
My Kind Of Game	Tony ROME
My Lady Dangerous	Sir Harker BELLAMY
My Lady's Money	OLD SHARON
My Love Wears Black	Lt Marty WALSH
My Masters; Or, The Strange Experiences Of Peter Ruff In Domestic Service	Peter RUFF
My Name Is Black!	BLACK
My Old Man's Badge	Johnny MALONE
My Price Is Murder	Max STRONG
My Son, The Druggist	Marty GOLD
My Son, The Murderer	Peter DULUTH and Lt Timothy TRANT
My Sweet Untraceable You	Lauren LAURANO
My Time Or Yours	Reggie MOON
My Word You Should Have Seen Us	John George DAVIS
The Mycroft Memoranda	Sherlock HOLMES and Sir Arthur Conan DOYLE
The Myopic Mermaid	Max ROYAL
Mysteries Of A Great City	Raoul BECQ
Mysteries Of Black Valley	Dr Kirke MONTGOMERY
The Mysteries Of Blair House	Harrison HOLT
Mysteries Of Winterthurn	Xavier KILGARVAN
Mysteries Suspended	Sherlock HOLMES
The Mysterious Affair At Styles	Hercule POIROT
The Mysterious Bottle	Herlock SHOLMES
The Mysterious Commission	Prof Charles HONEYBATH
Mysterious Disappearance Of A Bride	Robert SPICER
The Mysterious Disappearances	Insp GILMOUR
The Mysterious Mickey Finn; Or, Murder At The Cafè Du Dôme	Homer EVANS
The Mysterious Mirror	George Lombard SQUIRE
The Mysterious Miss Death	Chester BRETT
The Mysterious Mr Badman	Athelstan DIGBY

The Mysterious Mr Frame	Red HANLON
The Mysterious Mr Quin	Harley QUIN
The Mysterious Mr Reece	Sexton BLAKE
Mysterious Mr Sabin	Mr SABIN
The Mystery	Ralph SLADE
Mystery At A Country Inn	Don BURTON
The Mystery At Chillery	Anthony RAVENHILL
Mystery At Friar's Pardon	Charles FOX-BROWNE
The Mystery At Newton Ferry	Sir James ERSKINE
The Mystery At Pier 7	Sgt BRINKHAUS
Mystery For Mary	Adam DREW and Kay CORNISH
The Mystery Hand	Capt GRANDISON
Mystery In Glass	Crispin QUAYNE
Mystery In Kensington Gore	Dudley ALLWRIGHT
Mystery In St James Square	Hugh CARDING
The Mystery Man	Hamo GRIFFIN
The Mystery Militiaman	Sexton BLAKE
The Mystery Of A Hansom Cab	Insp Samuel GORBY
The Mystery Of Castle Royal	Cleavers SETON
The Mystery Of Headless Valley	Sherlock HOLMES
The Mystery Of High Eldersham	Desmond MERRION and Insp Henry ARNOLD
The Mystery Of Jamaica Terrace	Howel WALTER
Mystery Of King Cobra	Insp SKANE, Dudley BRENT and Maj KRIM
The Mystery Of King's Everard	John FORTESCUE
The Mystery Of Landy Court	DOVE
The Mystery Of Lone Manor	Ferrers LOCKE
The Mystery Of M Felix	Robert AGNOLD
The Mystery Of Mandeville Square	Insp DONOVAN
The Mystery Of Marie Roget	Chevalier Auguste C DUPIN
The Mystery Of Moldy Manor	Herlock SHOLMES
The Mystery Of Mr Bernard Brown	Benjamin LEVY
The Mystery Of Norman's Court	Supt REDARREL and David FORRESTER
The Mystery Of Orcival	Monsieur LECOQ
The Mystery Of Pinkham's Diamond Stud	Sherlock HOLMES
The Mystery Of St Dunstans	Doll RAINBOW
The Mystery Of The 10-20-Thirt	Kerlock SHOMES
The Mystery Of The 1c August Cover	Kerlock SHOMES
The Mystery Of The Ashes	Dr Eustace HAILEY
The Mystery Of The Carrier Of The One Cent	Kerlock SHOMES
The Mystery Of The Clasped Hands	Mr Jacob BURRELL
The Mystery Of The Closed Car	Richard Van Ryn WILSON
The Mystery Of The Corbin Necklace	Punch CORBIN
The Mystery Of The Creeping Man	Michael FORRESTER and Theresa FORRESTER
The Mystery Of The Crested Falcon	Rufus DEVILLE
The Mystery Of The Downs	CREWE
The Mystery Of The Dustbin	Herlock SHOLMES
Mystery Of The East Wind	Insp SKANE, Gail MCGURK and Dudley BRENT
The Mystery Of The Engraved Skull	Sexton BLAKE
The Mystery Of The Fabulous Laundryman	Dick MCCAREY
The Mystery Of The Fiddling Cracksman	Billy HEMPLE
The Mystery Of The Folded Paper	Amos Lee MAPPIN
The Mystery Of The Garden Suburb	Herlock SHOLMES
The Mystery Of The Glass Bullet	'Smiler' BUNN
The Mystery Of The Golconda	Judge DUNAWAY
The Mystery Of The Golden Angel	Richard FURLING
Mystery Of The Golden Palomino	Dallas O'NEIL
The Mystery Of The Goya Nude	Kerlock SHOMES
The Mystery Of The Green Ray	Ronald EWART
The Mystery Of The Hasty Arrow	Det Ebenezer GRYCE and Caleb SWEETWATER
The Mystery Of The Hidden Room	Graydon MCKELVIE
The Mystery Of The Human Bookcase	Commiss Kirker CAMERON
The Mystery Of The Hypnotic Room	Insp/Supt DEERING
The Mystery Of The Inn By The Shore	Clifford KING
The Mystery Of The Italian Ruins	Sexton BLAKE
Mystery Of The Kidnapped Kid	Dallas O'NEIL
The Mystery Of The Locked Door	Herbert BARRY
The Mystery Of The Locked Room	Enoch VOYCE
The Mystery Of The Lorry Driver	Sexton BLAKE
The Mystery Of The Louvre	CHANTECOQ
The Mystery Of The Man Who Evaporated	Howard MATTHEWS and Jeff LANDRUM
The Mystery Of The Mince-Pie	Herlock SHOLMES
The Mystery Of The Missing Corpses	Martin SPEED
The Mystery Of The Missing Envoy	Sexton BLAKE
Mystery Of The Missing Formula	Dick BARTON
The Mystery Of The Missing Refugee	Sexton BLAKE
The Mystery Of The Painted Nude	Insp PENK
The Mystery Of The Patrician Club	DAVENPORT
The Mystery Of The Purple Cloak	C WRYTE
The Mystery Of The Red Flame	Bromley BARNES
The Mystery Of The Red Tower	Sexton BLAKE
Mystery Of The Red-Haired Valet	Peter CASTLE
The Mystery Of The Scented Death	Insp J RASON
The Mystery Of The Sealed Room	Sherlock HOLMES
The Mystery Of The Seven Cafés: The Novel Of The Famous Wireless Play	The Hon Timothy Overbury 'Tiger' STANDISH and Sir Harker BELLAMY
The Mystery Of The Sleeping Car Express	Insp Joseph FRENCH
The Mystery Of The Smoking Gun	Satan HALL
The Mystery Of The Studio	Herlock SHOLMES
The Mystery Of The Studio Suite	Det Insp HOGARTH
The Mystery Of The Taxi-Cab	Herlock SHOLMES
The Mystery Of The Thirteenth Floor	Peter CLANCY
The Mystery Of The Vacant House	Herlock SHOLMES
The Mystery Of The Vanished Trainer	Sexton BLAKE
Mystery Of The Vanishing Aerodrome	Dick PEMBERTY and Peter WEBB
The Mystery Of The War	Ferrers LOCKE
The Mystery Of The Yellow Room	Joseph ROULETABILLE
The Mystery Of The "David M"	Alec SINCLAIR
The Mystery Of Tunnel 51	Sir Leonard WALLACE
Mystery On The Clyde	GREENSLEEVES

The Books

The	N3 Conspiracy	Nick CARTER
The	Nabob's Elephant	Herlock SHOLMES
The	Nails In Mr Cayterer	Robin THIN
	Naked And Alone	Johnny AMSTERDAM
	Naked Ebony	CRAWFORD
The	Naked Eye	NEBRASKA
The	Naked Five	Oliver GALT and Hugo TOWER
	Naked Mistress	Frank ARROW
	Naked Nemesis	Lois DULANE
	Naked Once More	Jacqueline KIRBY
The	Naked Typist	Steve WINSLOW
	Naked Villain	Antony MAITLAND
The	Name Is Archer	Lew ARCHER
The	Name Is Chambers	Peter CHAMBERS
The	Name Is Jordan	Scott JORDAN
The	Name Is Malone	John J MALONE
The	Name Of Annabel Lee	Dudley POTTER
The	Name Of The Game	Mr DEE
The	Name Of The Game Is Death	Earl DRAKE
The	Name Of The Rose	Brother WILLIAM
The	Nameless Ones	Aurelius SMITH
The	Name's Maguire	John Patrick Aloysius MAGUIRE
	Nan Thursday	Nan THURSDAY
The	Nantucket Diet Murders	Eugenia POTTER
	Nantucket Soap Opera	Neil KELLY
The	Napa Valley Mystery	Turlock LOAMS
	Napoleon SOLO and Ilya KURYAKIN	Ed NOON
	Narc	John BOLT
	Narcs	Nick BROWN
The	Narrowing Circle	Sebastian ZAMBRA
The	Narrowing Lust	Supt DANIELS
A	Nasty Bit Of Murder	Dr Jean MONTROSE
	Nat Foster, The Boston Detective	Nat FOSTER
	Nat Wedgewood, Jockey	Nat WEDGEWOOD
	Natural Causes	Col BRAIN
	Naughty But Dead	Erik MARCH
The	Naval Detective's Chase	The NAVAL DETECTIVE
The	Naval Treaty	Sherlock HOLMES
The	Navy Spy Murders	Dan FOWLER
The	Nazi Assassins	Johnny FEDORA
	Nazi Hunter	Curt 'Nazi Hunter' JAEGER
	Neapolitan Reel	January ESPOSITO
The	Neapolitan Streak	Insp Achille PERONI
	Nebraska Nightmare	Mark LEE and Carl BROWNE
The	Nebraska Quotient	NEBRASKA
	Necessary	Nathan NECESSARY
The	Necessary Corpse	Nicholas SLADE
A	Necessary Dealing	Eric WARD
	Necessary Doubt	Karl ZWEIG and Charles GREY
	Neck In A Noose	Toby DYKE
The	Necklace Of Skulls	Coleridge TUCKER
	Necropolis	Clyde BEATTY
	Ned Bachman, The New Orleans Detective	Ned BACHMAN
The	Needle's Eye	Arthur 'Red' BLAKE and Dan WHEELER
The	Negative Man	James PACKARD
	Neil Nelson, The Veteran Detective; Or, Tracking Mail Robbers	Neil NELSON
	Neither A Candle Nor A Pitchfork	Edmund BROWN
	Nellie, The Girl Detective; Or, The Mystery Of The Mason Mansion	NELLIE
	Nelson Lord - One Of Our Agents	Nelson LORD
	Nemo, The Shadow Detective	NEMO
The	Neon Flamingo	T D STASH
The	Neon Graveyard	Valentine NORTON
The	Neon Haystack	Max FULLER
	Neon Mirage	Nate HELLER
The	Neon Preacher	Hank MOODY
The	Neon Rain	Det Dave ROBICHAUX
The	Neon Smile	Terry O'BANION
	Neon Tough	Hugh DECKER
	Nerve	Rob FINN
	Nest Of Vultures	Talos CORD
	Never Bet Your Life	Dave BARNUM and Capt VAUGHN
The	Never Contract	Frank CARDOLINI
	Never Cross A Vampire	Toby PETERS, William FAULKNER and Bela LUGOSI
	Never Kill A Cop	'Rocky' Aloysius Algernon STEELE
	Never Put Off Till Tomorrow What You Can Kill Today	Jack ALBANY
	Never Say Die	Will WOODFIELD
	Never Send Flowers	Cdr James BOND
The	Never Summer Mystery	Sheriff Gus FLOWERS
	Never Wake A Dead Man	Hampton HUME
	Nevermore	Harry HOUDINI and Sir Arthur Conan DOYLE
	Nevsky's Demon	Yuri NEVSKY
	Nevsky's Return	Yuri NEVSKY
The	New Adventures Of Ellery Queen	Ellery QUEEN
The	New Adventures Of Sherlock Holmes	Sherlock HOLMES
The	New Chronicles Of Don Q	Don Q
The	New Idol	CHERI-BIBI
	New Jersey Showdown	RADCLIFF
The	New Mexican Connection	MCCLOUD
The	New Monster	Charlotte HOLMES
	New Orleans Holocaust	Robert (The Assassin) BRIGANTI
	New Orleans Mourning	Offr Skip LANGDON
The	New Tenant	Benjamin LEVY
	New Year's Resolution	Toby WILDE
	New York Dead	Det Stone BARRINGTON
The	New York Detective Police Officer	A NEW YORK DETECTIVE
The	New York Mystery	ST FRANCIS SCHOOL
	New York Nell, The Boy-Girl Detective	Nell NIBLO
	News Girl	Hilary BRAND
	News Of Murder	Adam GIFFORD
	News Reel Murder	Nick MORRO
	News Travels By Night	Supt William STEVENS and Insp Pierre ALLAIN
	Newspaper Murders	Karen KOVAC and Terry FLYNN
	New, Improved Murder	Jack DWYER
	Next Door To Murder	Maj MOSSON
	Next Of Kin	Mady SMITH
The	Next To Die	Sgt Shelly LOWENKOPF
	Next, After Lucifer	Guilhem DE COURDEVAL
A	Nice Class Of Corpse	Melita PARGETER
	Nice Enough To Murder	Ben LOUIS
A	Nice Girl Like You	Lt Andy BASTIAN
The	Nice Lady	Will SHAKESPEAR
A	Nice Little Business	Det Insp Neil CARTER
A	Nice Little Killing	Arthur G CROOK
A	Nice Murder For Mom	MOM
	Nice People	Supt Mike YEADINGS
A	Nice Place To Die	Ch Insp Bill HOUGHTON
A	Nice Sound Alibi	Homer CLAY
A	Nice Way To Die	Mrs Edwina CHARLES
	Nicholas Goade, Detective	Nicholas GOADE
	Nicholas Lattermole's Case	Supt Lawrence GILMARTIN
The	Nichovev Plot	Nick CARTER
	Nick Carter's Egyptian Clew; Or, The Mystery Of The Mummy's Head	Nick CARTER
	Nick Carter's Persistence; Or, At Danger's Call	Nick CARTER
	Nick Neverseen, The Invisible Detective; Or, A Startling Story Of Two Great Cities	Nick NEVERSEEN
	Nickel Jackpot	Zachariah Tobias ROLF
	Night After The Wedding	GAIL and MITCH
	Night And Morning; Or, A Detective's Shadow	AMZI
	Night And No Moon	John STEELE
	Night And The Judgement	HORTON and JORDAN
The	Night At The Lighthouse Inn On The Beach At Blackpool	Sherlock HOLMES
	Night Before The Wedding	GAIL and MITCH
	Night Cover	Lt Leroy POWDER
	Night Crime	Mike SLATTERY
	Night Drop	Luke SPEARE and Schyler COLE
	Night Drop	Luke SPEARE and Schyler COLE
	Night Express Murder	Colby STACK
	Night Extra	Sam TERRELL
	Night Freight Murders	Simon CROLE
	Night Frost	Det Insp Jack FROST
The	Night Has Eyes	Insp Christopher MARSDEN
A	Night In Havana	Ned SHERWOOD
The	Night In The Asylum At Torrence	Sherlock HOLMES
The	Night In The Burial Vault Under The Sanitarium At Soames Meadow	Sherlock HOLMES
The	Night In The Elizabethan Concert Hall In The Very Heart Of London	Sherlock HOLMES
The	Night In The Wax Museum At Llangollen	Sherlock HOLMES
The	Night Is A Child	Edmund TROTHE
	Night Is For Hunting	Sarah TREGARON
The	Night Mail; or, The Passenger From Scotland Yard	Insp George BYDE
	Night Moves	Harry MOSEBY
The	Night Nemesis	Steve THATCHER
	Night Of Crime	Jimmy TREYNOR
	Night Of Fear	Det Insp Charles TREMAYNE
	Night Of Shadows	Paul LANE
The	Night Of The 12th-13th	Wenceslas VOROBEITCHIK
The	Night Of The Garter	Amadour BEVAN
	Night Of The Garter Murder	Ben LUCIUS
	Night Of The Jabberwock	'Doc' STOEGER
	Night Of The Juggler	Det Max PRIMA and Det Gypsy TONNELLI
	Night Of The Kill	Sgt Gunnar MATSON
	Night Of The Phoenix	Det Sgt Joe KELLER and Det Sgt Joe RYKER
	Night Of The Phoenix	Det Sgt Joe KELLER and Det Sgt Joe RYKER
	Night Of The Shadow	Lamont (The Shadow) CRANSTON
	Night On The Broads	Lawrence MALONE
	Night Over Mexico	Hugh RENNERT
	Night Passage	Steve CARRADINE
	Night Raider	Burton WULFF
The	Night Remembers	Jack DWYER
	Night Run From Java	Paul HARRIS
	Night Secrets	Frank CLEMONS
The	Night She Died	Det Insp Luke THANET
	Night Sins	Ch Mitchell HOLT and Megan O'MALLEY
The	Night Stalker	Carl KOLCHAK
The	Night Strangler	Carl KOLCHAK
The	Night The Fog Came Down	Insp SHERWOOD
The	Night The Gods Smiled	Insp Charlie SALTER
	Night Train	Chet GORDON
	Night Train To Memphis	Vicky BLISS
A	Night With Sherlock Holmes	Sherlock HOLMES
	Night Without Darkness	Adam BRECK
	Nightbloom	Det Sgt Francis MOONEY
	Nightcap	Quentin JACOBY
	Nightclimber	Maj Morven RICKMAN
The	Nighthawk	Supt GAYLORD
	Nighthawk Swears Vengeance	Gerald (Nighthawk) FROST
The	Nightingale Gallery	Brother ATHELSTAN
The	Nightingale Trivet	Peter CASEY
	Nightmare Blue	Karl JAEGER
	Nightmare For Dr Morelle	Dr MORELLE
	Nightmare Island	Alexander (Check Force) CHANE and Vladimer KARLOV
	Nightmare's Nest	Insp HOBDEN
	Nightscape	Lilia BEDDOES
The	Nightshade Ring	Gregory KEEN
The	Nightwalkers	Gimiendo Hernande QUINTO
	Nightwing	Dep Youngman DURAN and Hayden PAINE
The	Night-Blooming Cereus	Theo BLOOMER
The	Night, The Woman	Lt Lee BARCELLO
	Nile Green	Tom CANE and CONDON
	Nimble Ike, The Detective; Or, Solving A Mystery	NIMBLE IKE
	Nimble Ike, The Trick Ventriloquist	NIMBLE IKE
The	Nine Bears	Sgt/Insp ELK and T B SMITH
	Nine Day's Murder	Det Insp Duncan MACCALLUM
	Nine Doctors And A Madman	Dr Nathaniel BUNCE

	Title	Detective
	Nine Lives	Colin GRAY
	Nine Lives Are Not Enough	O'SULLIVAN
The	Nine Mile Walk	Prof Nicky WELT
	Nine More Lives	Bill RYAN
	Nine Seven Juliet	Walter PAYNE and Ritchie PAYNE
	Nine Strings To Your Bow	Con MADDEN
	Nine Times Nine	Sister URSULA
	Nine Times Nine	Sister URSULA
The	Nine Unknown	James Schuyler 'Jimgrim' GRIM, Chullunder GHOSE and Athelstan KING
A	Nineteenth Century Debacle	Morlock TOMES
A	Nineteenth Century Miracle	Mr WARLOCK-JONES
The	Ninety Million Dollar Mouse	Milo TURNER
The	Ninja	Nicholas LINNEAR
	Ninth Life	Charlie GAMBLE
The	Nirvana Contracts	Sam GROSS
	No 3	Gyp KIDNADZE
	No 13 Toroni	Maurice WALLION
	No 17	BEN THE TRAMP
	No Alibi	Insp Cheviot BURMANN
	No Bail For The Judge	Col BRAIN and Ambrose LOW
	No Bones About It	Eric LUND
	No Business For A Lady	Eli DONOVAN
	No Cause To Kill	Lt MEREDITH
	No Charge For The Poison	Supt MANNING
	No Coffin For The Corpse	The Great MERLINI
	No Crest For The Wicked	Ricky STRAIGHT
	No Crime For A Lady	Mary CARNER
	No Crime Like The Present	Jeff STRANGE
	No Diamonds For A Doll	Mike STRANG
	No Earth For Foxes	MILLS
	No Epitaph For Mr Zarke	Insp BARLOWE
	No Escape	Timothy LONG
	No Exit From Brooklyn	Nick DELVECCHIO
	No Face In The Mirror	Dr Gregor MACLEAN
	No Free Lunch	Jack HAGEE
	No Gentle Lady	Gale GALLYON
	No Go On Jackson Street	Ben HENRY
	No Good From A Corpse	Edmond CLIVE
	No Grave For A Lady	Prof MANDRAKE
	No Halo For Me	Steve SUMMERS
	No Hands On The Clock	Humphrey CAMPBELL
	No Happy Ending	Hector SHAYNE
	No Harm	Roger TEJEDA
	No Hero	Mr MOTO
	No Hiding Place	Frank LUTHER
	No Honour Amongst Spies	Mike BROOKS
	No Known Grave	Kirk HALSTEAD
	No Laughing Matter	Det Insp Luke THANET
	No Lesser Plea	Roger 'Butch' KARP
	No Lilies	Mike LOGAN
	No Luck For A Lady	Cassie GIBSON
	No Man's Hand	Simon ROLFE
	No Man's Street	Horatio GREEN
	No Mardi Gras For The Dead	Kit FRANKLYN
	No Mean Tartar	Archibald BELDRUM and Nigel BLAIR
	No Mourners Present	John WEBB and Anne WEBB
	No Need For Violence	Supt BOWMAN
	No News On Monday	Peter FLECK
	No Obelisk For Emily	Insp 'Digger' HAIG
	No One Rides For Free	Tony CASSELLA
	No Orchids For Miss Blandish	Dave FENNER
	No Place For Me	Shaun KOVACK
	No Place For Murder	Jack FENNER
	No Place To Live	Jerry BENEDICT
	No Place To Live	Jerry BENEDICT
	No Pleasure In Death	Det Ch Insp BROWNE
	No Proof	Kenneth JASPER
	No Proof	Kenneth JASPER
	No Question Of Murder	Emma PLUME
	No Questions Asked	Philip ST IVES
	No Room At The Morgue	Al BOCCA
	No Safe Place	Nile BARRABAS
	No Sale For Haloes	Eddie DELANEY
	No Second Stroke	James O'HANNAY and Floyd EAST
	No Sentiment In Murder	Commissaire Saturnin DAX
	No Sign Of Life	Dave CANNON
	No Sign Of Murder	Stuart WINTER
	No Sleep At All	James WESTON
	No Smoke, No Fire	Det Insp Abraham KOZMINSKI
	No Tears For Hilda	Max EASTERBROOK
	No Thanks To The Duke	Barry RAEBURN
	No Time To Kill	Insp Salvador BORGES
	No Trial - No Error	Edward NORTH
	No Way Back	Willie 'Spider' SCOTT
	No Way Out	George STROUD
	No Wind Of Blame	Insp HEMINGWAY
	No Wings On A Cop	John J SHANNON
	No Witnesses	Det Lou BOLDT and Daphne MATTHEWS
	No Wreath From Manuela	Don KENDRICK
	No Wreaths For The Duchess	Supt Andrew ASH and Ch Det Insp George MUIR
The	Noah's Ark Murders	Mark REGISTER
	Noble Pirate	John CRISPIN
The	Noblest Experiment In The Galaxy	ANTHROPOL
	Nobody Likes Letitia	Sir Patrick SCOTT
	Nobody Loves A Dead Man	Tony WOOLRICH
	Nobody Saw Him Fall	Daniel ROSS
	Nobody Wins	Peter FLYNN
	Nobody's Perfect	Insp/Ch Supt George MASTERS and Ch Insp Bill GREEN
	Nobody's Sorry He Got Killed	Max GUTTMAN
	Nocturne For The General	Gen Stepan POVIN
The	Nocturne Murder	Andrew QUENTIN and Jane WINFIELD
The	Nominative Case	August FRYE
	None Dare Call It Treason	Jacques BRUNEL
	None Of My Business	Sheridan ORFORD and Prof Henry Arthur FIELDING
	None Of Us Cared For Kate	Oliver MANDRAKE
	None Shall Sleep Tonight	Insp MCKELLER
	Noon Street Nemesis	Pete ANGLICH
The	Noonday Devil	Andrew SENTRY
	Noose For A Lady	Simon GALE
	Norgil The Magician	NORGIL
	Norgil: More Tales Of Prestidigitection	NORGIL
	Norman Bones, Detective	Norman BONES
	Norroy, Diplomatic Agent	Yorke NORROY
	North Of Delhi, East Of Heaven	Alex LEIGHTON
	North Of Montana	Ana GREY
	North Of The Border	Neil HAMEL
The	North Shore Mystery	Const HOBBS
	North Star Conspiracy	Glynis TRYON
The	Norths Meet Murder	Pam NORTH and Jerry NORTH
	Norval The Detective: Or, A Detective's Shadow	NORVAL
The	Norwich Victims	Insp George MARTIN
The	Nose On My Face	Ch Insp Sam BIRKETT
The	Nostalgia Of Nervy Jim The Snatcher	Raffles HOLMES
The	Nostradamus Traitor	Herbie KRUGER
	Not A Blessed Thing!	Sister Mary Teresa DEMPSEY
	Not A Creature Was Stirring	Gregor DEMARKIAN
	Not One Of Us	Det Ch Insp Jack FINCH
	Not Ready To Die	John EARLSTONE
	Not Sleeping, Just Dead	Joe GOODEY
	Not Till A Hot January	Balthazar MARTEN
	Not Working	Joe LEVY
The	Notch In The Tulwar	Picklock HOLES
The	Notched Hairpin	Mr MYCROFT
	Nothing But The Truth	Insp Jonas MORCK
	Nothing Is The Number When You Die	Nuri ISKIRLAK
	Nothing Lasts Forever	Joe LELAND
	Nothing To Declare	Tommy HAMBLEDON
	Nothing To Lose	Simon LARREN
	Notorious	Les FERRON
The	Notorious Sophie Lang	Oliver ARMISTON
The	Notting Hill Murder	Supt SHANNON
The	Notting Hill Mystery	Ralph HENDERSON
	November Joe, The Detective Of The Woods	NOVEMBER JOE
The	November Man	DEVEREAUX
A	November Wind	Ludovic FENDER
A	Novena For Murder	Sister MARY HELEN
	Now Let's Talk Of Graves	Samantha ADAMS
	Now Lying Dead	Supt GADEN
	Now Seek My Bones	Insp 'Digger' HAIG
	Now You Don't	Hana SHANER
	Now You See Her, Now You Don't	Lou 'Shifty' ANDERSON
	Now You See It-Him-Them	Joe KARNS
	Nowhere	Russel WREN
The	Nowhere Weapon	Nick CARTER
	Nude In Nevada	Pete SCHOFIELD
	Nude On The Rocks	Matt ARCHER
The	Number 12 Jinx	Ed GORGON
	Number 18	Sgt/Supt Geoffrey BOSCOBELL
	Number 99	Mr LESLIE
	Number Seven Queer Street	Miles PENNOYER
	Number Seventeen	Insp Charles François FURNEAUX
The	Numbers Man	Frank CARDOLINI
A	Nun In The Closet	Sister JOHN and HYACINTH
A	Nun In The Cupboard	Sister JOHN and HYACINTH
	Nurse Hanson's Strange Case	Sally HANSON
	Nymph In The Night	Hank JANSON

—O—

	Title	Detective
	O As In Omen	Carl WAYWARD
	O Little Town Of Maggody	Ch Arly HANKS
	O Sweet McTavish	Swete MCTAVISH
	Obedience	Dave BRANDSTETTER
	Obelists At Sea	Dr Frank HAYVIER, Dr Love Rees PONS, Dr Malcolm PLECKS and Prof Knott Coe MITTLE
	Obelists En Route	Lt Michael LORD
The	Obituary Club	Grant SIMON and Lt PASCAL
	Obsequies At Oxford	Gervase FEN
	Obsession	John SAMSON
The	Obsidian And Other Stories	Dr John CARTER
	Obstacle Course	Finney ALETTER
The	Obstinate Captain Samson	Capt SAMSON
The	October Cabaret	Tess PENNICOTT
	October Heat	Riley KOVACHS
The	Octopus Of Paris	Joseph ROULETABILLE
	Octopussy	Cdr James BOND
	Octopussy And The Living Daylights	Cdr James BOND
The	Odd Job	Sarah KELLING and Max BITTERSOHN
	Odd Job #101 & Other Future Crimes And Intrigues	Jake PACE and Hildy PACE
	Odd Woman Out	George LYDNEY
	Odds Against	Sid HALLEY
The	Odds Are Murder	Matthew SWAIN
	Odds On Bluefeather	George Stanhope BERKLEY
	Odds On Miss Seeton	Emily SEETON and Supt DELPHICK
	Odds On The Hot Seat	COYLE and DONOVAN

	Title	Detective
The	Odds Run Out	Sheridan WESLEY
	Odds-On Murder	'Doc' CONNOR
	Of All The Bloody Cheek	Augustus MANDRELL
	O'Fear	Cliff HARDY
	Off Duty	Frank CHASE
	Off The Track	Donald FRASER
	Off With Her Head	Insp FAIRFORD
The	Officer From Special Branch	Ralph CARTER
An	Official Secret	Maj Charles Douglas KERWOOD
	Ogilvie, Tallant & Moon	Charles 'Spotted' MOON
	Oh Heavenly Dog	Benjamin BROWNING
"	Oh, Joshua!"	Joshua BILLINGS
	Oh, Murderer Mine	DOAN
The	Oil Rig	Carl HELLER
	Okewood Of The Secret Service	Desmond OKEWOOD
	Old Bones	'Doc' MILLER
	Old Brighton, The Coney Island Detective: Or, Solving The Great Coffin Mystery	OLD BRIGHTON
	Old Deceiver, The Private Detective: Or, Trailing His Own Cast	OLD DECEIVER
The	Old Detective's Pupil	Nick CARTER
The	Old Dick	Jake SPANNER
	Old Double Face, The Veteran Detective	OLD DOUBLE FACE
	Old Dude, The Detective: Or, Working For A Life	OLD DUDE
	Old Ebbie Returns	Ebbie ENTWHISTLE
	Old Ebbie: Detective Up-To-Date	Ebbie ENTWHISTLE
	Old Electricity, The Lightning Detective	OLD ELECTRICITY
	Old Enemies	Meg HALLORAN and Ch Vince GUTIERREZ
	Old Gold-Eye, The Miner Detective: Or, Piping The Mystery Of Sandy Gulch	OLD GOLD-EYE
	Old Grimes, The 'Get-There' Detective: Or, Tracking The Mystery Of The Vault	OLD GRIMES
	Old Humpy, The Dwarf Detective: Or, Thwarting A Career Of Crime	OLD HUMPY
	Old Judge Priest	Judge PRIEST
	Old Man Dies	Det Insp/Supt Thomas LITTLEJOHN
The	Old Man In The Corner	The OLD MAN IN THE CORNER
	Old Man Tutt	Ephraim TUTT
The	Old Mill	Sir Julian MORTHOE
	Old Mistagogne, The Protean Detective: Or, Tracking The Prince Of Rogues	OLD MYSTAGOGNE
	Old Mrs Fitzgerald	Insp/Supt William AUSTEN
The	Old Must Die	Chauncey O'DAY
	Old Neversleep, The Government Detective	OLD NEVERSLEEP
	Old Pitcher, The Baseball Detective: Or, Sharp Work On The Diamond	OLD PITCHER
	Old Quartz, The Nevada Detective	OLD QUARTZ
	Old Rufe, The Secret Service Detective	OLD RUFE
	Old Saddle-Bags, The Preacher Detective: Or, The James Boys In A Fix	OLD SADDLE-BAGS
	Old Safety, The Denver Detective: Or, Piping The Mail Robbers	OLD SAFETY
	Old Sinners Never Die	Mrs Annie NORRIS
	Old Sleuth, The Detective: Or, The Bay Ridge Mystery	OLD SLEUTH
	Old Sleuth's Greatest Case	OLD SLEUTH
	Old Snap, The Postal Service Detective	OLD SNAP
	Old Specie, The Treasury Detective: Or, The Harbor Lights Of New York	OLD SPECIE
	Old Stonewall, The Colorado Detective	OLD STONEWALL
	Old Tramp, The Hermit Detective: Or, Tracking The Opium Smugglers Of San Francisco	OLD TRAMP
	Old Ugly Face	James Schuyler 'JimGrim' GRIM
	Old Wolf, The Secret Service Detective	OLD WOLF
	Olga Knaresbrook: Detective	Olga KNARESBROOK
	Olura	Pedro GONZALES
	Omar Khayyam, Detective	Omar KHAYYAM
The	Omega Assignment	Steve SAVAGE
The	Omega Command	Blaine MCCRACKEN
The	Omega Document	Joshua BAIN
The	Omega Operation	Adam HUNTER
The	Omega Threat	Sam BOGGS
	Omega-Minus	Tad ANDERS
	Omit Flowers, Please	Jeff STRANGE
	Om: The Secret Of Ahbor Valley	Cotswold OMMONY
	On A Dead Man's Chest	Artie WEATHERBY
	On A Field Of Black	Seth WARRINER
	On Account Of Murder	Viera KOLAROVA
	On Hazardous Duty	Peter WARD
	On Her Majesty's Secret Service	Mr TOLEPAT
	On The Brink	Ms SQUAD
	On The Dead Run	Ed RAZONI and William JACKSON
	On The Edge	Lt Kevin BROSKEY
	On The Instruction Of My Government	André KOHL
"	On The Night Of The 18th..."	Insp Kingsley HYLTON
	On The Prime Minister's Account	Ch Insp Lars KOLLIN
	On The Right Wrists	Peter CREIGHTON
	On The Scent	Herlock SHOLMES
	On The Trail Of Wu Fang	Dan DUNN
	On The Trail Of 'Big Finger'	Felix BOYD
	On Ticket Of Leave	Sexton BLAKE
	Once A Spy	Harry RYDER
	Once A Widow	Dr Clinton SHANNON
	Once And Always Murder	Patience MCKENNA
	Once More The Saint	Simon (The Saint) TEMPLAR
	Once Upon A Private Eye	Pete RILEY
	Once Upon A Tombstone	Insp Michael HORNSLEY
	One Among None	Scott GREGORY and Justin BASSETT
	One Bang-Up Job	Natalie Dauntless FISHER
	One By One They Disappeared	Insp Hugh COLLIER
	One Coffee With	Det Sigrid HAROLD
	One Corpse Missing	Beau SMITH and Pogy ROGERS
	One Corpse Too Many	Brother CADFAEL
	One Cried Murder	Peter PONSONBY
	One Dead Dean	Prof Carl BURNS
	One Dead Debutante	Josh KRALES

	Title	Detective
	One Death In The Red	Bruno FARRELL
	One Deathless Hour	David MALLIN and George COE
	One False Move	Jeff TROY and Haila TROY
	One Fine Day The Rabbi Bought A Cross	Rabbi David SMALL
	One Foot In The Grave	Supt James PIBBLE
	One For The Books	Marge BROCK
	One For The Money	Cat CALIBAN
	One For The Money	Stephanie PLUM
	One For The Money	Lucy SHANNON
	One Grave Too Many	John EASY
	One Horse Race	Chester FORTUNE
	O'Neil McDarragh, The Detective	O'Neil MCDARRAGH
	One Jump Ahead	Rex BANNER
	One Last Mad Embrace	Horace Spurgeon FENTON
	One Man's Justice	Insp Robert FUSIL and Const KERR
	One Man's Muddle	James STRANGE
	One Man's Poison	George LYDNEY
	One Murder Too Many	Prof Cyrus HATCH
	One Murder Too Many	Lt MADIGAN
	One Of My Sons	Det Ebenezer GRYCE
	One Of Our Pigeons Is Missing	George BULMAN
	One Of These Seven	Justus DRUM
	One Of Those Things	Terence O'DAY
	One Of Us	Sam CASH
	One Police Plaza	David MALONE
	One Thrilling Night	Det Insp COURTENAY
	One To Jump	Insp HALLAN and Sgt SPRATT
	One Woman	Abe ADAMS
The	One-Minute Murder	BURMAN
	One-Way Ticket	Michael KERNEHAN, Chuck REVES and Vic MOINE
The	Only Game	Det Insp CICERO
	Only Half A Hoax	Joseph 'JJ' JAMISON
	Only Her Hairdresser Knew	Chester LONG
The	Only Security	Prof Theodora Wade CRAWFORD
	Only The Dead Know Brooklyn	Francis DE SALES
	Only The Rich Die Young	Lt PASCAL
The	Opal Murder Case	Insp Henry DOIGHT
The	Open Mouth	Ch Insp Joshua SMARLES
	Open Season	Lt Joe GUNTHER
	Open Season	Nathan PHILLIPS
The	Open Shadow	Fritz THIERINGER and Maggie MCGUANE
	Open Verdict	Insp MACE
The	Opera House Murders	Robbie DUNCAN
The	Opera Murder	Tide POOLES
The	Opera Murders	Thackeray PLACE
	Operation Apricot	David HAHAM
	Operation Atlantis	Al GLENNE
	Operation Calpurnia	Lt Guy SILVESTRI
	Operation Caroline	Paul HARVARD
	Operation Counterpunch	Earl DRAKE
	Operation Dancing Dog	Steve HARVESTER
	Operation Destruct	Jonathan ANDERS
	Operation Doctors	Insp MEDFORD
	Operation Mermaid	William (Tiger Shark) MARTIN
	Operation Moon Rocket	Nick CARTER
	Operation Neptune	Jonathan ANDERS
	Operation Parrot	Bob MORANE
	Operation Starvation	Nick CARTER
	Operation S-L	John KEITH
	Operation - Kill Or Be Killed	Johnny MANNING
	Operation-Deadline	Johnny MANNING
	Operation: Alpha Death	Adam HUNTER
The	Operators	Tim SMITH
The	Optical Illusion	Hemlock SOAMES
	Option To Die	Veronica SLATE
The	Orange Divan	Insp MANDERTON
The	Orator	Oliver RATER
	Orchids To Murder	Amos Lee MAPPIN
	Orchids With Murder	Insp HEADLEY
	Ordeal By Fire	Sherlock HOLMES
	Ordeal By Innocence	Dr Arthur CALGARY
The	Ordeal Of Father Crumlish	Father Francis Xavier CRUMLISH
An	Ordinary Day	John STRANG and Sally STRANG
The	Orford Mystery: Covent Garden 1734	Capt HOARE
The	Organization	Stanley BASS
	Original Sin	Insp/Cdr Adam DALGLIESH
	Ormerod's Landing	George ORMEROD
The	O'Rourke Affair	Johnny VINCENT
The	Osage Bow	Gregory QUIST
	Oscar Slick, The Marvelous Detective: Or, Exposing A Number Of Crimes	Oscar SLICK
	Oscar, The Detective	OSCAR
	Osiris Died In Autumn	Det Christopher JENSEN and Prof Natalie KEITH
The	Osterman Weekend	John TANNER
The	Other Body In Grant's Tomb	Barney FORGE and Dr St George PEACHY
	Other Byline: Scott MITCHELL	Griff DEXTER
The	Other David	Andrea PERKINS
The	Other Eye	Al DARLAN
The	Other Karen	Catherine MAYHEW
The	Other Man	Sgt/Insp ELK and T B SMITH
The	Other Side	Roger KINCAID
The	Other Side Of Midnight	Catherine DOUGLAS
The	Other Side Of The Door	Policewoman Norah MULCAHANEY
	Other Sins Only Speak	MCGREGOR
The	Other Woman	Ch Insp LLOYD
	Otis Dunn, Manhunter	Otis DUNN
	Otley	Gerald OTLEY
	Otley Victorious	Gerald OTLEY
	Our Agent In Rome Is Missing	Nick CARTER
	Our First Murder	Lutie BEAGLE and Amanda BEAGLE
	Our Mr Smith	Purlock HONE
	Our Second Murder	Lutie BEAGLE and Amanda BEAGLE
	Our Spacecraft Is Missing!	Grant FOWLER
	Out Brief Candle	Insp HARRIS

Out Of Body, Out Of Mind	Andrew TAGGART
Out Of Focus	Philip QUEST
Out Of His Head	Paul LYNDE
Out Of Nowhere	Harry FEIFFER and YELLOWTHREAD STREET COPS
Out Of Shape	Lt Paul GOLD and Tommy LARKIN
Out Of The Darkness	Det Jack LINGEMANN and Liz CONNORS
Out Of The Labyrinth	Neil J BATHURST
Outlaw Island	Judge MANFRED
Outrageous Exposures	Insp/Ch Insp Dick TANSEY
The Outrider	BONNER
Outrun The Constable	Eve GILL
An Outside Job	'Bull' ROGERS
The Outside Ledge: A Cablegram Mystery	Florence CUSACK
The Outside Man	Adam SHAW
Outsider In Amsterdam	Adjutent Henk GRIJPSTRA and Sgt Rufus DE GIER
The Outsiders	Pel PELHAM
Out, Damned Tot!	Miriam BIRDSEYE
Over The Edge	Det Jub FREEMAN and Det Bill DECKER
Over The High Side	Insp Piet VAN DER VALK
Over The Sea To Die	Ian BLACKIE
Overkill	Mick JAGGER
The Owl	Clarence KNIGHT
The Owl	Alexander L'HIBOUX
The Owl Flies Home	Francis VILLIERS
The Owl Hoots	Francis VILLIERS
The Owl In The Cellar	Lt RYAN
The Owl Of Darkness	Insp READ and Jeffrey BLACKBURN
The Owl Sang Three Times	Lt DIEGO
The Owner Lies Dead	Sheriff MACFARLAND
Oxford Exit	Kate IVORY
The Oxford Murders	Insp BRAMLEY
An Oxford Tragedy	Ernst BRENDEL
The Ozark Detective: Or, Wild Life Among The Bald Knobbers	The OZARK DETECTIVE
Ozmar The Mystic	OZMAR

— P —

P J The Secret Service Boy	P J DAVENANT
P Moran, Operative	Peter MORAN
The Package Holiday Spy Case	'Tiger' LESTER
The Packet Of Death	Insp John HEENAN
The Paddington Mystery	Dr Lancelot PRIESTLEY
The Paduan Conspiracy	Insp James CARDINAL
Pagan Pagoda	Russell JONES
Page Mr Tutt	Ephraim TUTT
Pagett Calling	Pte PAGETT
Paging The Saint	Simon (The Saint) TEMPLAR
Pagoda	Joe GALL
The Pagoda Mystery	Derek HARING
The Pagoda Of Gold	Horace SINNAT
The Painful Predicament Of Sherlock Holmes	Sherlock HOLMES
Paint Her Face Dead	Louisa EVANS
Paint It Black	J D HAWKINS
Paint Out	Essington HOLT
The Painted Doll Affair	Bruce MCLINTOCK
Painted Faces	Insp Robert STRONG
Painted For The Kill	Capt Andrew TORRENT
The Painted Monster	Insp PETTENGILL
The Palace Of Love	Keith GERSEN
The Pale Criminal	Bernard GUNTHER
The Pale Door	Chad PROCTOR
The Pale Horse	Mark EASTERBROOK and Ariadne OLIVER
The Palgrave Mummy	Digby GRESHAM
Palimpsest	Insp Henry BEAUMONT
Palomino Blonde	Tad ANDERS
The Pan Handle Detective: Or, Working Up The Great Railroad Robbery	The PAN HANDLE DETECIVE
The Panama Paradox	Michael KEEFE
The Panama Plot	Prof Craig KENNEDY
Pandemic	Charlie SPARROW
The Pandora Option	John DANBY
The Pandora Plague	Sherlock HOLMES
Pandora's Box	Dep Ch Insp Max KAUFFMAN and J T 'Jake' SPANNER
Pandora's Box	Johnny LAMB
Panic Party	Roger SHERINGHAM
Panic Walks Alone	Arthur 'Turo' BIRONICO
The Paper Chase	Charles APPLEGATE
The Paper Chase	Insp Jack STRICKLAND
The Paper Circle	Ben HELM
Paper Cuts	Joseph RADKIN
The Paper Gun	Paul PINE
Paperbag	Angel GRAHAM
The Papyrus Murder	Insp HEADLEY
A Parade Of Cockeyed Creatures: Or, Did Someone Murder Our Wandering Boy?	Sylvia PLOTKIN and Max Van LARSEN
The Paradise Gun	Hart MULDOON
Paradise Man	Sydney HOLDEN
Paradise Of Death	Ev FRANKLIN
The Paradise Plot	Harry PORTER
Paradise Spells Danger	David GRANT
Paradox Planet	Elias KANE
The Paradoxes Of Mr Pond	Mr POND
Paragon Man	Ace CHANEY
A Paramount Kill	Raymond CHANDLER
A Parcel Of Their Fortunes	Helen BULLOCK
The Parchment Key	Peter MARRELL
Pardon My Gun	Mike BRETT
The Paris Bit	Max MORITZ
The Parisian Affair	Nick CARTER
Park Avenue Executioner	MCCLOUD
Parker Pyne Investigates	Parker PYNE
Parole	Robert W FLICK
Partners In Crime	Sexton BLAKE
Partners Of The Night	Bob CLIFFORD
The Party At The Penthouse	Dan DURKIN
A Party For Lawty	Insp Lane PARRY
A Party For The Shooting	Miss Julia TYLER
The Pass Beyond Kashmir	Idewal REES
Pass The Body	Insp Bernard BRAY and Charles VENABLES
Passage	Roger TRULY
The Passenger From Scotland Yard	Insp George BYDE
The Passing Of Fan Chu Fang	Dixon BRETT
The Passing Of Gloria Munday	The AVENGERS
Passing Strange	Det Daniel WEBSTER
Passion Pulls The Trigger	Val VERNON
The Passionate Victims	Lt/Insp Richard TUCK
Passport To Oblivion	Dr Jason LOVE
Passport To Oblivion	Argus STEELE
A Past Master Of Crime: Or, Detective Cush's Clever Work	Det CUSH
Past Reason Hated	Ch Insp Alan BANKS
Past Reckoning	Det Ch Insp Jack FINCH
Past, Present, And Murder	Julian QUIST
The Patchwork Girl	Gil HAMILTON
A Path To The Bridge	Rod MCKINNON
The Patience Of Maigret	Insp Jules MAIGRET
The Patient In Room 18	Sarah KEATE and Det Lance O'LEARY
The Paton Street Case	Det Ch Insp David MORGAN
Patrick Butler For The Defense	Patrick BUTLER
The Patriot	Sir Edgar EWART
Patriots	Laurie GALVIN
The Patrol Of The Sun Dance	Cpl/Sgt Allan CAMERON
Pattern Crimes	Ch David BAR-LEV
Pattern For Murder	Insp John Isidore BLOOM
Pattern For Murder	Shell SCOTT
Pattern In Black And Red	Prof Leonidas AMES and Mr HOOPES
Pattern In Black And Red	Prof Leonidas AMES and Mr HOOPES
Pattern In Poison-Ivy	Michael SHANNON
Pattern Of Violence	Det Insp LERIC
Patterns In The Dust	Rain MORGAN
Paul Beck, Detective	Paul BECK
Paul Beck, The Rule Of Thumb Detective	Paul BECK
Paul Campenhaye, Specialist In Criminology	Paul CAMPENHAYE
Paul Richards - Detective	Paul RICHARDS
Paul Temple And The Conrad Case	Paul TEMPLE
The Pavilion By The Lake	Insp LUCKRAFT
The Pawns Of Death	Sgt/Insp Charlie CHAN
The Pawns Of Fear	Steve SUMMERS
Pay As You Die	Arthur SALISBURY and Frank SHEARER
Pay The Devil	Stosh COLTRAY
Payoff In Blood	Edwin GREEN
Payoff On Fever Street	Timothy ROURKE
Payola	Johnny ALOHA
The Pay-Off	Rush HENRY
The Pazenger Problem	Colin ANSTRUTHER
PC Richardson's First Case	Insp RICHARDSON
The Peacock Is A Bird Of Prey	Hiram POTTER
Peak Of Frenzy	Hilary BRAND
Peanut Butter & Jelly Is Not For Kids	Pepperoni HERO
The Pearl-Headed Pin	Insp J RASON
Peckover And The Bog Man	Insp/Ch Insp Harry PECKOVER
The Peculiar Exploits Of Brigadier Ffellowes	Brig FFELLOWES
A Pedigree To Die For	Melanie TRAVIS
Peeping Thomas	Thomas C THERON
Peking	Nick CARTER
The Peking Dossier	Nick CARTER
Pel And The Sepulchre Job	Insp Clovis Desire PEL
The Pelham Murder Case	Peter CARDIGAN
The Pembroke Mason Affair	Bromley BARNES
The Pemex Chart	Nick CARTER
Penance For Jerry Kennedy	Jerry KENNEDY
Pendragon, Late Of Prince Albert's Own	John Hawkdale PENDRAGON
Pendragon, The Illusionist	John Hawkdale PENDRAGON
Penelope	John COMADAY and Larry COHEN
The Penguin Pool Murders	Hildegarde WITHERS
Pennies For His Eyes	Supt MACNEILL
Penny Black	Penny WANAWAKE
A Penny For The Guy	RATLIN
Penny Pinching	Penny WANAWAKE
A Penny To Spend	Maj Adrian TITTERTON
The Pennycross Murders	Det Supt Philip HUNTER
The Penthouse Killings	Squire ADAMS
The Penthouse Mystery	Ellery QUEEN
The Penultimate Problem Of Sherlock Holmes	Sherlock HOLMES
The People Against Nancy Preston	James TIERNEY
People Of Darkness	Sgt Jim CHEE
The People Of The River	Commiss SANDERS
The People Vs Withers And Malone	Hildegarde WITHERS and John J MALONE
People Will Talk	Supt KEMPSON
Pepper Pike	Milan JACOVICH
Perchance To Dream	Philip MARLOWE
The Perdition Express	Fred CROCKETT
Peregrination 22	Colin PANTON
Peregrine Dream	Henry DYER
The Perfect Alibi	Insp Bernard BRAY and Charles VENABLES
Perfect Assignment	Virginia BOX

The Perfect Crime	Philip MARLOWE
The Perfect Frame	Timothy DANE
Perfect Justice	Ben KINCAID
A Perfect Match	Ch Insp LLOYD
The Perfect Murder	Insp Ganesh GHOTE
The Perfect Wife	Slade MCGINTY
A Perfectly Proper Murder	Carl WILCOX
The Perfumed Lure	Sydney TREHERNE
The Peril Of Helen Marklove And Other Stories	Helen MARKLOVE
The Peril Of The Prince: A Romance Of Modern Anarchism	Montague WARDROP
The Peril Pit	Ferrers LOCKE
Peril Under The Palms	Iris COOPER
Perilous Hazard	Daphne WRAYNE and The FOUR ADJUSTERS
The Perilous Transactions Of Mr Collin	Mr COLLIN
Period Stuff	Supt FALCON
Perish By The Sword	Trygve YAMAMURA
Perish The Thought	Insp Salvador BORGES
Perkins Finds $3,400,000	Willis PERKINS
Perpetual Check	Prof Harry BISHOP
The Perrin Murder Case	Konrad ROQUE
The Persecutor	Pete HEYSEN
The Persian Death-Trap	Richard DEUTSCH
The Persian Slipper	Sherlock HOLMES
The Persistent House-Hunters	A B C HAWKES
A Person Shouldn't Die Like That	Max GUTTMAN
Personal Adventures Of A Detective	A DETECTIVE
Personal Effects	Nina FISCHMAN
A Personal Possession	Det Carl PEDERSON
Pet Peeves	Haskell BLEVINS
Petals On The Wind	Chris DOLLANGANGER and Cathy DOLLANGANGER
Peter Ruff	Peter RUFF
Peter Ruff And The Double Four	Peter RUFF
Peters, Detective	PETERS
Petrella At Q	Const/Ch Insp Patrick PETRELLA
The Petticoat Lane Murders	Bill 'Ironsides' CROMWELL
The Pew Group	Lizzie THOMAS
Phantasms	Horace VESEY
The Phantom Anarchist	Sherlock HOLMES
The Phantom Chamber	Sherlock HOLMES
The Phantom Crime	Frank DARRELL
Phantom Fingers	Steve MUIRHEAD
Phantom Fleet	John PRENTICE
Phantom Hollow	Trevor LOWE
Phantom Lady	Det BURGESS
The Phantom Murderer	James CLARKSON-PARRY
The Phantom Musketeer	John FORTESCUE
The Phantom Of Forty-Second Street	Tony WOOLRICH
The Phantom Of The Barbary Coast	Sherlock HOLMES
The Phantom Of The Mill	Sexton BLAKE
The Phantom Torpedo-Boats	Monsieur V
The Phantom Train	Philip Raines CARTWRIGHT
The Phantom Violin	Monsieur CHEVENARD
Phantom Wires	James DURKIN
The Phantom-Fighter	Jules DE GRANDIN
Phil Peterson, The Detective: Or, Trailing Down A Murderer	Phil PETERSON
Phil Scott, The Indian Detective	Phil SCOTT
Philadelphia Blowup	Burton WULFF
Philip And The Flappers	Philip MANWEARING
Philip In Particular	Philip MANWEARING
Philo Gubb: Correspondence School Detective	Philo GUBB
The Philomel Foundation	Alan FRENCH
A Philosophical Investigation	Ch Insp 'Jake' JAKOWICZ
Phoenix No More	Dan FALCONER
Phoenix Sword	Brett WALLACE
The Phone Calls	Policewoman Norah MULCAHANEY
The Photogenic Soprano	Johnson JOHNSON
The Physalia Incident	Alex BLACK
Physical Evidence	Dr Eric PARKER
The Picaroon And The Burglar Tools	The PICAROON
The Piccadilly Murder	Ambrose CHITTERWICK
The Piccadilly Puzzle: A Mysterious Puzzle	Mr DOWKER
The Pickled Poodles	John J MALONE
Picklock's Disappearance	Picklock HOLES
Picky Pack, Being Passages From The Re-Incarnation Of Picklock Holes	Picklock HOLES
Picture Him Dead	Supt MERSEY
Picture Miss Seeton	Emily SEETON and Supt DELPHICK
Picture Postcard	Matthew RIORDAN
Pictures Of Perfection	Supt Andrew DALZIEL and Sgt/Det Ch Insp Peter PASCOE
The Picture-Perfect Murders	John LANGE
A Piece Of Justice	Imogen QUY
A Piece Of Resistance	David GARNETT
A Piece Of The Moon Is Missing	SEBASTIAN
A Piece Of The Silence	Joe BINNEY
Pieces Of Modesty	Modesty BLAISE
Pigeon Blood	Supt Bamsan KIET
Pigeon Blood Rubies	Paul BECK
The Pilditch Puzzle	'Biff' CORRIGAN
Pilgrim At The Gate	Mr PILGRIM
Pilgrim On The Island	Mr PILGRIM
The Pilgrims Meet Murder	Ch Insp Max HUNTER and Prof Stephen PILGRIM
Pilkington	PILKINGTON
A Pinch Of Snuff	Rosa EPTON and Martin AINSWORTH
The Pinchbeck Masterpiece	Martyn FINCH
Pincher In Peace And War	PINCHER
Pincushion	Foy LANEER
Pine-Top Jones: Renegade	Pine-Top JONES
The Pink Carnation	Dr HUDSON
The Pink Edge	Insp BARRACLOUGH
The Pink Panther Strikes Again	Insp CLOUSEAU
Pinkeye's New Year Resolution	Herlock SHOLMES
The Pinned Man	Mr GROODE
A Pint Of Murder	Policeman Madoc RHYS
The Pipe Dream	Insp CRAMBO
The Pipe Dream Finesse	Ape SWAIN
Pipeline To Death	Martin AMES
Pistols And Pedagogues	Adrian WITHERS
Pitchfork Hollow	Rev Dan THOMPSON
The Pit-Prop Syndicate	Insp WILLIS
Pixie At The Wheel	Pixie O'HARA
The Pizza House Crash	Georgina POWERS
Placer Dan, The Yukon Detective: Or, The Missing Nuggets Of Gold	PLACER DAN
The Plague Court Murders	Sir Henry MERRIVALE KC
A Plague Of Demons	Patrick DAWLISH
A Plague Of Dragons	Hugo BARON
A Plague Of Kinfolks	Kate MULCAY
A Plague Of Sailors	Brevet CABLE
A Plague Of Spies	Peter CARTHAGE
A Plague Of Violence	John JERICHO
A Plague On Both Your Causes	Max CURFEW
Plague Over London	'Bunjy' HEARNE
Plain Murder	Hana SHANER
Plain Sailing	Insp/Ch Supt George MASTERS and Ch Insp Bill GREEN
The Plains Of Fire	Nile BARRABAS
Plan XVI	Insp H H THEW
Planning For Murder	Tessa CRICHTON
Plant Me Now	Hortense CLINTON
The Platinum Bullet	Hugo WOLFRAM
Play It Again	R J BROOKS
Play It Solo	James 'Solo' MALCOLM
Play With Fire	Kate SHUGAK
Playback	Philip MARLOWE
Played The Hard Way	Kinsey TARGET
The Player	Joe REDDMAN
The Players And The Game	Insp HAZELTON
The Player's Boy Is Dead	Matthew STOCK and Joan STOCK
Playing A Lone Hand: Or, Nick Carter On Top	Nick CARTER
Playing For The Ashes	Insp Thomas LYNLEY
Playing Happy Families	Det Supt Hilary CATCHPOLE
Playing Safe	Helen MARKHAM
Playing With Fire	Frances BRETT
Playing With Fire	PAOLA and GEORGE
The Pleasant Grove Murders	Sheriff Joe BAIN
The Pleasantries Of Old Quong	Quong LEE
Please Kill My Cousin	Johnny MACALL
Pleasure Island	Nick CARTER
Plot For The Fourth Reich	Nick CARTER
The Plotters	Mike BENASQUE
Plugged Nickel	Jake HATCH
The Plumley Inheritance	Ludovic TRAVERS
Plunder	Capt DACK
Plunder	Jack SUMMER
Plunder	John TARLETON
The Plunge	Patrick HERON
The Plunger: A Turf Tragedy Of Five-And-Twenty Years Ago	Sgt BOYCE
A Pocket Full Of Clues	Samuel G ABBOTT
A Pocketful Of Clues	Samuel G ABBOTT
A Pocketful Of Khama	Nan ROBINSON
The Poellenberg Inheritance	Joe DUNSTAN and Eric FISHER
The Poet And The Lunatics: Episodes In The Life Of Gabriel Gale	Gabriel GALE
Poetic Justice	Owen DAVIS-WILLIAMS
Poetic Justice	Kate FANSLER and Reed AMHEARST
Poets And Murder	Judge Jen-djieh DEE
The Point Of A Thousand Spears	Aubrey St John MAJOR and Sgt LANCEY
Point Of Reference	Angel GRAHAM
Point Of Testimony	Bert BAYLISS
The Pointed Tower	Mr GUELPA
Pointer To A Crime	Insp POINTER
The Poison And The Root	Dr FERENC
Poison Case Number 10	Michael JOYCE
Poison Death	Insp WIELD
Poison For Teacher	Miriam BIRDSEYE and Johnny DUVIVIEN
Poison For The Prince	SIGISMONDO
The Poison Gang	John BLACKMORE
Poison In Jest	Jeff MARLE
Poison In The Parish	Supt COLE
The Poison Oracle	Wesley MORRIS
The Poison Plague	Prof Herman BRIERLY
The Poison Pool	Kate WESTON
The Poison Trail	Jimmie REZAIRE
The Poisoned Chocolates Case	Ambrose CHITTERWICK and Roger SHERINGHAM
The Poisoned Fang	Jyotish BABU
The Poisoned Pen	Prof Craig KENNEDY
The Poisoning Of Hector Alhuson	Mervyn HENDERSON
The Poisonous Angel	Gentle HOGGERTY
Poisonous Relations	Insp Ronald PRICE
Poison, Poker And Pistols	Maggie SLONE
Pokerface	Ray CRAWLEY
Polaroid Man	Dan KRUGER
Police Blotter	Lt CLANCY
Police Chief	Ch Jack TALLON
Policeman Flynn	Policeman FLYNN
Policeman's Lot	Ch Insp POOLE
The Polite Pirate	Don Alverado y Miraflo SMITH
Political Death	Jemima SHORE
The Politician, Lighthouse And Trained Cormorant	Sherlock HOLMES
Polly Put The Kettle On	Insp HOPE

	Polo Solo	Nick POLO
The	Ponson Case	Insp TANNER
	Poodle Springs	Philip MARLOWE
The	Pool	Terrence O'BRIEN
The	Pool Of Flame	Terence O'ROURKE
	Poor Butterfly	Toby PETERS and Leopold STOKOWSKI
	Poor Little Rich Girl	DOAN
The	Poor Old Lady's Dead	Det Insp Alf ROSHER
	Poor, Poor Ophelia	Casey KELLOG and Al KRUG
The	Porcelain Mask	Jimmy 'Wiggly' PRICE
The	Port Of London Murders	Insp Steven MITCHELL
A	Portion For Foxes	Det Ch Insp John MORRISSEY
The	Portland Laugher	Thomas BLACK
The	Portland Murders	Nils-Frederik BLIXEN
	Portrait In Smoke	Danny APRIL
The	Portrait Invisible	GALT
The	Portuguese Fragment	Nicholas MAASTEN
A	Position Of Trust	Supt ROPER
	Post Mortem	Gilbert WORTH
The	Post Office Case	David MADDEN
The	Postage Stamp Murder	GWAYLOR
	Postern Of Fate	Tommy BERESFORD and Tuppence BERESFORD
The	Posthumous Nobel Prize	Hemlock SOAMES
	Posthumous Papers	Greg HOCKING
	Postman's Knock	Insp PITT
The	Postmaster-General: A Further Adventure Of Sherlock Holmes	Sherlock HOLMES
	Postmortem	Dr Kay SCARPETTA
	Postscript To Murder	Insp LYON
	Post-Mark Homicide	Pete HUNTER
	Post-Mortem	Hugh CARDING
	Post-Mortem Effects	Francis DE SALES
The	Post-Office Detective: Or, A Mystery In The Mails	The POST-OFFICE DETECTIVE
The	Power Of Nothingness	MUNPA
	Power On The Scent	William POWER, Penny MERCER and Vincent MERCER
The	Power-House	Sir Edward LEITHEN
	PPC	Insp MITCHELL
	Practice Makes Murder	Supt Robert TOWNLEY and Sgt Roger NEWMAN
A	Praed Street Dossier	Solar PONS
	Pratfall	Daniel KEEL
	Pray For Ricky Foster	Louisa EVANS
	Pray For The Dawn	Toby JUDD
	Pray God To Die	Det Ann FITZHUGH
	Pray To The Hustlers' God	Harlan COLE
The	Prayer Mat	Supt Steve MACLAREN
	Preacher	PREACHER
	Precinct: Siberia	Det Joe LAWLESS, Offr Barbara BABALINO and Det Leo GRADY
The	Predators	Michael HAWK
	Predators	Det YATES
	Premeditated Murder	Nick BELLAMY
	Premiere At Willow Run	Megan MARSHALL
The	Prenatal Entreaty	Turlock LOAMS
	Prescription For Murder	Mark TREASURE
A	Present For Santa	Pat MORLEY
The	President Has Been Kidnapped!	Grant FOWLER
The	President Is Dead	Laurie GALVIN
	President Kettle	Capt Owen KETTLE
	Presidential Agent	Lanny BUDD
	Pressure Point	Steve HAMM
	Presumed Dead	Frank MACALLISTER
	Presumed Innocent	Alejandro 'Sandy' STERN
	Pretty Miss Murder	Lt Max HUNTER
The	Pretty Pink Shroud	Martin RHYMER
The	Pretty Pink Shroud	Martin RHYMER
The	Pretty Stenographer Mystery: Or, On The Trail Of A Fiend	Nick CARTER
The	Price	Insp Terry SNEED
The	Price You Pay	Dee STREET
A	Pride Of Dolphins	Col MOSTYN
	Priestess Of The Damned	Lucifer COVE
	Priestly Murders	Karen KOVAC and Terry FLYNN
The	Priest's Secret	Sexton BLAKE
	Prima Donna At Large	Enrico CARUSO and Geraldine FERRAR
	Primary Target	Det Jay GOLDSTEIN, Det Carlos CRUZ and Jean TALBOT
	Primary Target	QUARRY
The	Prime Minister's Pencil	Christopher PERRIN
	Prime Witness	Paul MADRIANI
	Primrose: The Fourth Man	John SPENCER
	Prince Has Five Aces	David PRINCE
A	Prince Of Darkness	Gerald STAUNTON
The	Prince Of Evil	Richard (The Spider) WENTWORTH
The	Prince Of Liars: Or, The Man Without A Soul	Nick CARTER
The	Prince Of Plunder	Sir Brian FORDINGHAME
A	Prince Of Swindlers	Simon CARNE
	Prince Zaleski	Prince ZALESKI
	Prince Zaleski And Cummings King Monk	Cummings King MONK
	Prince Zaleski And Cummings King Monk	Prince ZALESKI
The	Princely Detective	The PRINCELY DETECTIVE
The	Prince's Diamond	OZMAR
	Printer's Devil	Nick ALLARD
	Print-Out	Mike FARADAY
	Print-Out	Ralph SIMMONS
The	Priscilla Copperwaite Case	Simon KAYE
	Prison At Obregon	Dave HILL
The	Prisoner	Michael WALLACE
The	Prisoner In The Mask	Duke DE RICHLEAU
	Prisoner Of The Devil: Sherlock Holmes And The Dreyfus Case	Sherlock HOLMES
	Prisoners Of The Desert	Sexton BLAKE
	Private Carter's Crime	Sexton BLAKE
A	Private Enquiry	Jack JEFFCOAT
	Private Eye	Jack CLEARY
The	Private Eye	Nat CRAIG
The	Private Eye	John J SHANNON
The	Private Eyeful	Marla TRENT
	Private I	John SMITH
A	Private Investigation	Sarah SCOTT
The	Private Life Of Dr Watson	Sherlock HOLMES
The	Private Life Of Dr Watson	Dr John H WATSON
The	Private Life Of Sherlock Holmes	Sherlock HOLMES
	Private Line	Insp SLANE
The	Private Lives Of Sherlock Holmes	Sherlock HOLMES
	Private Murder	Walter MCKENZIE
The	Private Pavilion	Insp Victor BONDURANT and Paul RAVEL
	Private Pinkerton, Millionaire	Private PINKERTON
A	Private Prosecution	Det Ch Supt Maurice KENDRICK and Humphrey BARNES
The	Private Sector	Peter MARLOW
	Prized Possessions	Sgt Karl ALBERG
	Probable Cause	Det James DEWITT
	Probe	Kevin BLAKE
	Problem By Rail	Insp HEAD
The	Problem In Ciphers	MURPHY and MCTAVISH
The	Problem Of Biffley Vicarage	Sherlock HOLMES
The	Problem Of Cell 13	Prof Augustus S F X VAN DUSEN
The	Problem Of Cell 16	Dr Sam HAWTHORNE
The	Problem Of The Empty Magnums	Sherlock HOLMES
The	Problem Of The Importunate Landlady	Sherlock HOLMES
The	Problem Of The Mysterious Client	Sherlock HOLMES
The	Problem Of The Peculiar Pipes	Sherlock HOLMES
The	Problem Of The Purple Maculas: A Sherlock Holmes Adventure	Sherlock HOLMES
The	Problem Of The Sore Bridge - Among Others	Sherlock HOLMES
The	Problem Of The Vanishing Town	Dr Sid SHOEHORN
The	Problem Of Thor Bridge	Sherlock HOLMES
	Proceed At Will	Geoffrey MILDMAY
	Process Of Elimination	Harvey GRAYMOOR and Laura GRAYMOOR
	Procession Of Two	GARNETT
The	Procurator Of Justice	Sherlock HOLMES
	Professional Jealousy	Insp Cuthbert HIGGINS
	Professor Bingo's Snuff	Lt WALDMAN
	Professor In Peril	Prof James GLOWREY
The	Professor Knits A Shroud	Prof Jose APODACA
The	Professor On The Case	Prof Augustus S F X VAN DUSEN
The	Professor's Mystery	Prof CROSBY
The	Professor's Poison	James ARNOLD
The	Programmed Man	Michael SAXON
The	Progress Of A Crime	Hugh BENNETT
	Project X	Alan STEEL
The	Projects Section	Ralph CARTER
The	Prom Concert Murders	Magnus KEEBLE
	Prominent Among The Mourners	Sheriff TOWNSEND and Susan EYERLY
A	Promise Of Death	Ben (The Revenger) MARTIN
	Promise To Kill	Supt Frank DRURY
	Promises To Keep	Connie FERGUSON and Gil FERGUSON
	Proof	Tony BEACH and Gregor MCGREGOR
A	Property In Cyprus	Jonathan GAUNT
	Prophet	Jason PROPHET and Lynn MCCOLL
	Prophet Motive	Chris DANVILLE
	Prospero Drill	Stephen BORG
The	Protectors	Paul MARTINY
The	Provence Puzzle	Insp DAMIOT
The	Proverbial Murder Case	Insp HASKELL
The	Pro-Am Murders	Dion QUINCE
	Prudence Be Damned	Kells CAVENAUGH
The	Psychopath Plague	Elias KANE
The	Pub Crawler	Bill KNIGHT
	Public Enemy	Insp WILLIAMS
	Public Murders	Karen KOVAC and Jack DONOVAN
	Publicans And Sinners: Or, Lucius Davoren	Lucius DAVOREN
	Publicity For Murder	Insp GREGG and Judith EVERSLEIGH
	Publish And Perish	Loren MENSING
	Pudd'nhead Wilson	David 'Pudd'nhead' WILSON
The	Pulpcon Kill	Nick CHALLIS
A	Pulpit In The Grill Room	Charles LYSON
The	Pumpkin-Shell Wife	Forrest HAGGERTY
	Pure Murder	Cesar Augustus FRANCK
The	Purloined Letter	Chevalier Auguste C DUPIN
The	Purloined Pork	Herlock SHOLMES
The	Purple Onion Mystery	Philip 'Spike' TRACY
The	Purple Pony Murders	Stephen CLAY
The	Purple Shells	Asaph CLUME
The	Purple Twilight	Peter MOHUNE
The	Purple Zombie	Richard Henry (The Avenger) BENSON
	Pursued By The Law	Mr TOWNSHEND
	Pursuit Of A Parcel	Insp Ernest LAMB
The	Pursuit Of The House Boat	Sherlock HOLMES
The	Pushbutton Butterfly	Max ROPER
	Put On The Spot	POLACK ANNIE
A	Puzzle For Experts	Lt KUPFERMAN
A	Puzzle For Fools	Peter DULUTH
	Puzzle In Paint	Jason EMORY
	Puzzle In Paisley	Jenny Gilette LEWIS and Hunter LEWIS
	Puzzle In Parquet	Jenny Gilette LEWIS and Hunter LEWIS
	Puzzle In Petticoats	Jason EMORY
	Puzzle In Pewter	Jenny Gilette LEWIS and Hunter LEWIS
	Puzzle In Porcelain	Jenny Gilette LEWIS and Hunter LEWIS
The	Puzzle Lock	Dr John Evelyn THORNDYKE
The	Puzzle Of The Strange Visage	Sherlock HOLMES
	Puzzle Parade	Insp PROBYN
	Puzzles Of The Black Widowers	The BLACK WIDOWERS
The	Pyramid Of Lead	Prosper FAIR

Q As In Quicksand	Det Jub FREEMAN and Det Mitch TAYLOR
Q33	John Q TRELAWNY
Q33 - Spy Catcher	John Q TRELAWNY
QBI: Queen's Bureau Of Investigation	Ellery QUEEN
QED: Queen's Experiments In Detection	Ellery QUEEN
The Qualified Adventurer	Ian MACARTHUR
Quality Bill's Girl	'Blue Jean' Billy RACE
The Quality Of Mercy	Warren HEARST and Harry HERBOLD
The Quality Of The Informant	Charles CARR and Jack KELLY
The Quallsford Inheritance	Sherlock HOLMES
The Quarry	Kommissar Hans BARLACH
Quayle Of The Yard	Peter QUAYLE
Quayle's First Case	Peter QUAYLE
The Queen Against Owen	Charles PRESCOTT
The Queen City Murder Case	Johnny SAXON
The Queen Is Dead	Jocelyn O'ROARKE and Philip GERARD
The Queen Of Hearts	Griffith TROWBRIDGE
The Queen Of Night	Franklin KENNARD
Queen Victoria's Revenge	Tony HAWKIN
Queens Full	Ellery QUEEN
The Queen's Head	Nicholas BRACEWELL
The Queen's Mare	Michael RHINEHEART
The Queer Affair Of The Greek Interpreter	Sherlock HOLMES
A Queer Bag Of Bodies	Mr PENDLEBURY
A Queer Kind Of Death	Det Pharaoh LOVE
Quest For Superintendent Flagg	Insp FLAGG
Quest For The Bogeyman	Paul LANE
The Quest Of Julian Day	Julian DAY
The Quest Of Nigel Rex	Nigel REX
The Quest Of The Sacred Slipper	Insp BRISTOL
Quest Of The Spider	'Doc' SAVAGE
The Questing Hound	Earl (of) MILLINGTON
A Question Of Guilt	Helen WEST and Det Supt Geoffrey BAILEY
Question Of Identity	Michael WYMAN
A Question Of Inheritance	Amy TUPPER
A Question Of Law	Stephen KALE
A Question Of Murder	Peter Carstan RANDALL
A Question Of Negligence	Dr Gregor MACLEAN
A Question Of Preference	Teal STEWART
A Question Of Proof	Nigel STRANGEWAYS
Questionable Behaviour	Teal STEWART
The Quests Of Paul Beck	Paul BECK
The Quests Of Simon Ark	Simon ARK
The Quick And The Wed	Michael SHANNON
Quicksilver	Hugo WOLFRAM
Quiet As A Nun	Jemima SHORE
The Quiet Ones	Det Sgt Robert MATHER
Quiet Terror	Tony BOYLE
Quiet Under The Sun	Bernard FESTON
The Quiller Memorandum	QUILLER
Quiller Solitaire	QUILLER
Quincannon	John QUINCANNON
Quinn	QUINN
Quinn And The Desert Oil	QUINN
Quinney's	Joe QUINNEY
Quinney's Adventures	Joe QUINNEY
Quinney's For Quality	Joe QUINNEY
Quintus Oakes	Quintus OAKES

— R —

R Holmes & Co: Being The Remarkable Adventures Of Raffles Holmes, Esq, Detective And Amateur Cracksman By Birth	Raffles HOLMES
The Raccoon Lake Mystery	Mason BRANT
A Race For Life	Dyke DARREL
A Race For Millions	Insp Joseph PRICKETT
A Race With The Sun	Paul GILCHRIST
The Racing Adventures Of Barry Bromley	Barry BROMLEY
Radford Shone	Radford SHONE
A Radical Departure	Willa JANSSON
The Radiobuster	Samuel JONES
The Radish River Caper	Chance PURDUE
The Radium Terrors	Gifford RENWICK
Rafferty: Poor Dead Cricket	RAFFERTY
Rafferty's Rules	RAFFERTY
Raffles	A J RAFFLES
Raffles After Dark	A J RAFFLES
Raffles And The Key Man	A J RAFFLES and R J 'Rick' LEROY
Raffles In Pursuit	A J RAFFLES
Raffles Of The Albany	A J RAFFLES
Raffles Of The MCC	A J RAFFLES
Raffles Revisited	A J RAFFLES
Raffles Under Sentence	A J RAFFLES
Raffles Vs Sexton Blake	A J RAFFLES and Sexton BLAKE
Raffles, The Amateur Cracksman	A J RAFFLES
Raffles: Further Adventures Of The Amateur Cracksman	A J RAFFLES
Raffles' Crime In Gibraltar	A J RAFFLES and R J 'Rick' LEROY
The Rag Bag Clan	Margaret BINTON
The Rag Doll Murder	Harry MACNEIL
A Rage In Heaven	Det 'Grave Digger' JONES and Det 'Coffin' Ed JOHNSON
Rage Of Heaven	Charlie ROPE
A Rage Of Maidens	Caitlin REECE
A Rage To Kill	Edge HANNEGAN
The Ragged Robin Murders	Konrad ROQUE
Raid Over England	'Jumbo' RUTHERFORD
The Railroad Murder Case	Marc JORDAN
The Railway Detective	The RAILWAY DETECTIVE
The Rain	John WELLS
Rainblast	Mike WILLOUGHBY
The Rainbow Conspiracy	Jeff PLUMMER
The Rainbow Feather	Paul MEXTON
The Rainbow Mystery	John DURSTON
The Rainbow/Seagreen Case	Jedediah KILLINGER III
Rainbow's End	George FELSE and Dominic FELSE
Rainbow's End	Insp Richard JURY
The Rainy City	Thomas BLACK
Raker	RAKER
Ramsden	James Schuyler 'JimGrim' GRIM
Ramsey, The Detective	RAMSEY
Rancho Maria	Eve ZABRISKIE
Randolph Mason: The Clients	Randolph MASON
Randolph Mason: The Strange Schemes	Randolph MASON
Random Access Murder	Catherine SAYLOR
Ransom!	Jefferson (The Handyman) BOONE
Raoul: Gentleman Of Fortune	Raoul BOMFORTUNE
The Rape	Sgt Pepper ANDERSON
Rape Of A Quiet Town	Jeff PLUMMER
The Rape Of A Town	Kelly CARVEL
The Rape Of The Sherlock	Sherlock HOLMES
The Raphael Affair	Gen Taddeo BOTTANDO, Flavia DI STEFANO and Jonathan ARGYLL
Raphael, MD	Dr Louis RAPHAEL
The Rapist	Supt O'MALLEY
The Raptor Zone	Melinda PINK
The Rasp	Col Anthony GETHRYN
Rasputin's Revenge	Auguste LUPA
The Rat Began To Gnaw The Rope	Gilmore HENRY
Rat Race	Matt SHORE
Ratcatcher	Joe HUSSEY
Rather A Common Sort Of Crime	The Hon Constance Ethel MORRISON-BURKE
Rather A Vicious Gentleman	Augustus MANDRELL
Ratings Are Murder	Bob CHRISTOPHER
Ratking	Commiss Aurelio ZEN
The Rats Of Montsouris	Nestor BURMA
Rattle His Bones	Mark MILLNER
The Rattle-Rat	Adjutent Henk GRIJPSTRA and Sgt Rufus DE GIER
Raven	Schlomo RAVEN
The Ravenelle Riddle	Peter STRANGELY
Ravenmocker	Molly BEARPAW
Raven's Shadow	John RAVEN
The Ravishing Of Lady Mary Ware	Roger BROOK
Raymond Chandler's Marlowe - Anthology	Philip MARLOWE
Rays Of Darkness	Septimus MARCH
Razor Moon	Sam HAWKINS
Razzamatazz	Colin MAGUIRE
Razzle-Dazzle	Lt Kevin BROSKEY
Ready To Burn	Satan HALL
A Real Shot In The Arm	Chris MARTIN
Reardon	Lt Jim REARDON
A Reason To Kill	Helen KEREMOS
Rebecca's Pride	Det Bolivar MANCHENIL
Recipe For Homicide	Dr Daniel Webster COFFEE and Lt Max RITTER
Reckless Coulson	Rex COULSON
The Reckoning	Phillip (The Marksman) MAGELLAN
Reclining Figure	Ellis BLAISE
A Recoiling Vengeance	KEENE
The Recollections Of A Detective	WATERS
Recollections Of A Detective Police-Officer	WATERS
Recollections Of A Detective Police-Officer Second Series	WATERS
The Recollections Of A Policeman	WATERS
Recollections Of A Sheriff's Officer	William SHARPE
Recollections Of An Irish Police Magistrate And Other Reminiscences Of The South Of Ireland	Thomas Phillips VOKES
A Reconstructed Corpse	Charles PARIS
The Records Of Vincent Trill Of The Detective Service	Det Vincent TRILL
Recount	Robert MILES
Recovery	Max MOSS
The Recrudescence Of Sherlock Holmes	Sherlock HOLMES
Recycled Souls	Britt (Mind Masters) ST VINCENT
Red Aces	J G REEDER
Red Agents	Gaff LEE
Red Altars	Sgt/Det Insp Patrick Aloysius MCCARTHY
The Red Carnation	Anthony BIGELOW
The Red Carnelian	Sylvester HERING
The Red Cavalier	Insp BURTON and Mercedes QUERO
Red Cecil, The Detective; Or, A Steady Pursuit	RED CECIL
Red Cent	Jake HATCH
The Red Citroen	Commiss TROTTI
The Red Cobra	Supt Andrew ASH
The Red Colonel	Col Duncan GRANT
Red Devil Of The Air Police	Rufus DEVILLE
Red Diamond: Private Eye	Red DIAMOND
Red Dragon	Paul CRANE
Red Dragon	Paul CRANE
Red Dragon	Will GRAHAM
The Red Eyes Of Kali	Ch Insp BARNARD
Red Farm Mystery	Roy ENDICOTT
A Red File For Callan	David CALLAN
The Red Flame Of Erinpura	Chullunder GHOSE
Red Gardenias	William CRANE

Red Goose	Ben SHALEY
Red Greed	Anne LAYTON and David LAYTON
Red Harvest	The CONTINENTAL OP
Red Heroin	Paul CRANE
Red Heroin	Paul CRANE
Red Herring	Charles HORNE
The Red Horse Caper	Jerry 'Renegade' ROE and Stuart WORTH
The Red House Mystery	Anthony GILLINGHAM
Red Is For Murder	Sylvester HERING
Red Is For Shrouds	Emil MARTIN
The Red Jaguar	Steve SUMMERS
The Red Kite Clue	Philip MACCRAY and Artemus GRAHAM
Red Lilac	Insp Maurice HEPBURN and Evelyn TEMPLE
Red Mammon	Silas WORTENHEIMER
Red Mask	Det Insp EVANS
The Red Mirror Mystery	Insp HOOK
The Red Mouse	William MURGATROYD
The Red Net	Jim MALONE
Red On Wight	Tavey MARTIN
The Red Orchid	Nero WOLFE
The Red Passport	Hubert GRESHAM
The Red Redmaynes	Peter GANNS
The Red Right Hand	Dr Henry RIDDLE and Prof Adam MACAMERON
Red Rock	Philip MARLOWE
The Red Rods	Gillian BALTIC
The Red Room	Kershaw KIRK
The Red Ruth	Rudolph GREY
The Red Scream	Molly CATES
The Red Seal	Det FERGUSON
Red Snow At Darjeeling	Insp Leonidas PRIKE
Red Square	KOREGORVSKY
Red Square	Investigator Arkady RENKO
Red Sun Of Nippon	Mr GREENLEAF
The Red Symbol	Det Insp John FREEMAN
The Red Tape Mystery	Herlock SHOLMES
The Red Tassel	Al COLBY
Red Threads	Insp CRAMER
The Red Thumb Mark	Dr John Evelyn THORNDYKE
Red Tide	MARLOWE
The Red Triangle	Martin HEWITT
The Redemption Of Young Billington Rand	Raffles HOLMES
A Redhead For Free	Johnny BUCHANAN
Redheads Cool Fast	Steve CRAIG
The Redman Cave Murder	Dexter DRAKE
Redoubtable Dexter	Paul DECKER
The Red-Headed League	Sherlock HOLMES
The Red-Headed Man	Mr TORRY
The Red-Light Victim	Jason T O'NEIL
Red-Winged Angel	Mike DARROCH
Reel Murder	Trixie DOLAN and Evangeline SINCLAIR
Reflex	Philip NORE
Regan	Det Insp Jack REGAN
Regan And The Deal Of The Century	Det Insp Jack REGAN
Regan And The Snout Who Cried Wolf	Det Insp Jack REGAN
Regan And The Venetian Virgin	Det Insp Jack REGAN
The Regensburg Legacy	Joe DUGGER
Regina Blue	Regina BLUE
Regina V Rumpole	Horace RUMPOLE
Rehearsal For Murder	Mr HUMBLE and Dorrit BLY
Reich Four	Nick CARTER
The Reigate Squires	Sherlock HOLMES
The Reinhard Action	David DAVIDOWITZ
A Relative Distance	Insp CROW
Relative To Murder	Insp John Isidore BLOOM
Released For Death	Const John BRAGG
Relentless	Trooper Sam WATCHMAN
The Reliance Detective; Or, Tracking The Great Grain Steal	The RELIANCE DETECTIVE
The Religious Body	Insp Christopher Dennis SLOAN
The Reluctant Assassin	Jack ALBANY
The Reluctant Cloak And Dagger Man	George BARCLAY
The Reluctant Executioner	Simon LUCK
The Reluctant Medium	David CONWAY
The Reluctant Spy	Gregory HILLER
The Reluctant Spy	Gen Charles KIRK
The Remarkable Adventures Of Christopher Poe	Christopher POE
The Rembrandt File	Amos HATCHER
The Rembrandt Panel	Amos HATCHER
Remember That Face!	Johnny MALONE
Remembered Death	Col RACE
Remembrance Of Miranda	Ann HALES
The Remington Contract	Cliff REMINGTON
The Remington Factor	Cliff REMINGTON
The Reminiscences Of Chief-Inspector Littlechild	Ch Insp John George LITTLECHILD
The Reminiscences Of Jock Thirlstane, Yokel And Detective, At Musselburgh Races In Days Gone By	Jock THIRLSTANE
The Reminiscences Of Solar Pons	Solar PONS
The Remover	The REMOVER
Rendezvous On An Island	Tod CLAYMORE
Rendezvous With Death	Tracy LARRIMORE and Mike THOMPSON
Rendezvous With Fear	DOAN
Rendezvous With The Past	Margot BLAIR
The Renegade Detective; Or, Playing A Double Role	The RENEGADE DETECTIVE
Renegade Steele	Donovan STEELE
The Renewable Virgin	Sgt Marian LARCH
Renfrew Flies Again	Douglas RENFREW
Renfrew Of The Royal Mounted	Douglas RENFREW
Report For A Corpse	Peter CHAMBERS
Report From Argyll	Don KENDRICK
The Reporter	York SYMON
The Reporter Detective	The REPORTER DETECTIVE
Reprieve	Roderick POPLAR
Reprise	Sgt David PUTNAM
Repulse Monkey	Alex GLAUBERMAN
A Reputation Dies	Anthea RUTHERFORD and Justin RUTHERFORD
Requiem For A Cop	Insp KOJAK
Requiem For A Redhead	Gregory KEEN
Requiem For Rogues	Tony CARTER
Requiem In Utopia	Maxwell SPEED
Rescue	John Francis CUDDY
Rescue From The Rose	Insp Thomas BRUNT
The Resident Patient	Sherlock HOLMES
The Resources Of Mycroft Holmes	Mycroft HOLMES and Sherlock HOLMES
The Rest Is Silence	Insp George MARSHALL
Rest You Merry	Prof Peter SHANDY
The Restless Corpse	Don CARSON
Resumé For Murder	John WALTZ
The Resurrection Murder Case	Christopher HAND
Retribution	Kyle YOUNGBLOOD
The Return	Sherlock HOLMES
The Return Of Arsène Lupin	Arsène LUPIN
The Return Of Blackshirt	BLACKSHIRT
The Return Of Bulldog Drummond	Capt Hugh 'Bulldog' DRUMMOND
The Return Of Cardannesley	Roger HARTLEY
The Return Of Clubfoot	Dr Adolph (Clubfoot) GRUNDT and Desmond OKEWOOD
The Return Of Dr Sam: Johnson, Detector	Dr Sam JOHNSON
The Return Of Frank Clamart	Frank CLAMART
The Return Of Frass	Capt FRASS
The Return Of Grey Shadow	Grey SHADOW
The Return Of Henry Prince	Henry PRINCE
The Return Of Hercules, Esq	Bill KELLAWAY
The Return Of Herlock Sholmes	Herlock SHOLMES
The Return Of Lanny Budd	Lanny BUDD
The Return Of Lieutenant Boruvka	Lt BORUVKA
The Return Of Moriarty	Sherlock HOLMES
The Return Of Mr Campion	Albert CAMPION
The Return Of Picklock Holes	Picklock HOLES
The Return Of Raffles	A J RAFFLES
The Return Of Sanders Of The River	Commiss SANDERS
The Return Of Schlock Homes	Schlock HOMES
The Return Of Sherlock Holmes	Sherlock HOLMES
The Return Of Solar Pons	Solar PONS
The Return Of The Black Gang	Capt Hugh 'Bulldog' DRUMMOND
The Return Of The Pink Panther	Insp CLOUSEAU
The Return Of The Redheaded League	Tide POOLES
Return Of The Shadow	Lamont (The Shadow) CRANSTON
The Return Of The Speckled Band	Sherlock HOLMES
The Return Of Wu Fang	Wu FANG
The Return Of Zingrave	Nelson LEE
Return To Adventure	The LIBERATOR
Return To Murder	Emil MARTIN
Return To Sender	Alex GLAUBERMAN
The Rev Captain Kettle	Capt Owen KETTLE
The Revelations Of A Private Detective	Andrew FORRESTER Jr
The Revelations Of Inspector Morgan	Det Insp MORGAN
Revenge At Indy	Don MILES
Revenge At Nightfall	Insp Geoffrey FRASER
The Revenge Of Moriarty	Sherlock HOLMES
Revenge Of The Generals	Nick CARTER
The Revenge Of The Robins Family	Capt Gregory WALTHAM
The Revenger	Ben (The Revenger) MARTIN
The Revenue Detective	The REVENUE DETECTIVE
Reverend Randollph And The Splendid Samaritan	Rev Cesare RANDOLLPH
Reverend Randollph And The Wages Of Sin	Rev Cesare RANDOLLPH
The Revolutionist	Matt LINCOLN
Reward For A Defector	Martin AINSWORTH
Re-Enter Sir John	Sir John SAUMAREZ
Re-Enter The Blithe Sheriff	Mr GARFIELD
Rhino Ritz	Ernest 'Rhino' HEMINGWAY and F Scott 'Ritz' FITZGERALD
The Rich Detective	Insp SYLVESTER
A Rich Full Death	Robert BROWNING
The Rich Get It All	Nichole SWEET
The Richmond Enigma	Sherlock HOLMES
Richmond; Or Scenes In The Life Of A Bow Street Runner	Bow Street Runner Thomas RICHMOND
Riddle In Silk	Carrie CASHIN
The Riddle In Wax	Steve BRADSHAW
The Riddle Of The Blazing Bungalow	Sexton BLAKE
The Riddle Of The Dead Cats	Adelaide ADAMS
The Riddle Of The Eighth Guest	Urgan MARCH
The Riddle Of The Florentine Folio	Peggy FAIRFIELD
The Riddle Of The Frozen Flame	Hamilton CLEEK
The Riddle Of The Golden Fingers	Sexton BLAKE
The Riddle Of The Green Cylinder	Sexton BLAKE
The Riddle Of The Lascar's Head	Sexton BLAKE
The Riddle Of The Night	Hamilton CLEEK
The Riddle Of The Purple Emperor	Hamilton CLEEK
The Riddle Of The Rovers	Sexton BLAKE
The Riddle Of The Russian Princess	Peggy FAIRFIELD
The Riddle Of The Sands	CARRUTHERS
The Riddle Of The Spanish Circus	Mark CORRIGAN
The Riddle Of The Winged Death	Hamilton CLEEK
The Riddles Of Hildegarde Withers	Hildegarde WITHERS
Riddles Read	Det Dick DONOVAN
Ride A Paper Tiger	Kyle BRANDEIS
Ride A Tiger	William MALLETT
Ride A Tiger	Roger PATTEN
Right You Are, Mr Moto	Mr MOTO
Riley Of The Special Branch	Insp RILEY
Rim Of The Pit	Roger KINCAID
Ring Around Rosa	Brock (The Rock) CALLAHAN
Ring Of Fire	Vic (Eagle Force) GABRIEL
A Ring Of Roses	Insp CHUCKY
A Ring Of Roses	Gen Charles KIRK
The Ring Of Truth	Dr Paul STANDISH
Ring The Bell At Zero	Jim DUNN and Zebulion BUCK
The Ringer	Supt BLISS
The Ring-A-Ding UFOs	Lee CROSLEY
Riot	Supt WALSH

Title	Character
Riot '71	Ian FIRTH and John SMITH
Ripe For Development	Lionel BUCKBY
The Ripe Moment	Sherlock HOLMES
Ripley Under Water	Tom RIPLEY
Ripoff	Brockton POTTER
The Ripper	Det Supt Philip HUNTER
The Ripper	Jon STEEL
The Ripper Returns	Sexton BLAKE
A Ripple Of Murders	Supt GILLIANT
Riptide	Isobel ANDERS
RISC	Mark KILBY
Rising	Judd SPRINGFIELD
Rite Of Expiation	Tom RIORDAN
Rites For A Killer	John MARSHALL and Suzy MARSHALL
The Rites Of Murder	Paul J BURDOCK and Joshua PRELL
The Ritual Bath	Det Peter DECKER
Ritual Fire Dance	Prof Hugh MELLING
The Rival Detectives	DYKE and BURR
The Rival Detectives: Or, Dangerous Ground	Van VERNET
The River Sorrow	Det Frank BRANDON and Dr Adrian LANCASTER
The Riverside Villas Murder	Peter FURNEAUX
Riviera Blues	CRANG
The Riviera Puzzle	Insp DAMIOT
The Road House Murders	Maj Avery GREGG and Tony ELLIS
Road To Rhuine	Lee VAUGHAN and Insp SMITH
The Road To Suez	Dorothy Mayotte RIGBY
Roadhouse Girl	Sexton BLAKE
Roag's Syndicate	Simon GOOD
Robak's Firm	Donald ROBAK
Robak's Run	Donald ROBAK
Robbers	Harry SOMMERS
Robbery At Portage Bend	Policeman Dick WESTON
Robbery Blue	Det Insp LERIC
Robbery Without Violence	Sawley GERSON
Robots And Empire	Elijah BALEY
The Rock Of Justice	Robert HUTCH
Rockabye	Susannah BARTOK
The Rockefeller Gift	Sgt/Ch Supt Merle CAPRICORN
Rocket To The Morgue	Sister URSULA
Rocket To The Morgue	Sister URSULA
Rocks And Ruin	Edwin GREEN
The Rocksburg Railroad Murders	Ch of Plce Mario BALZIC
Rocky Mountain	'Gutsy' MORGAN
The Rodeo Murder Mystery	Sgt/Insp DOCKER
Rody Rogan, The Detective From Ireland: Or, In Search Of The Thug With The Yellow Club	Rody ROGAN
Rogue Cop	Insp Terry SNEED
Rogue Diamond	Richard WALKER
A Rogue In Ambush	Elisha CROWE
Rogue Ransom - Racket Buster	Rogue RANSOM
Rogue Ransom - Triggerman	Rogue RANSOM
Rogue Royal	Quentin DREX
Rogues And Vagabonds	Jabez DUCK
Rogues In Clover	Bill PARMELEE
Rogue's Gold	Jefferson BIRCH
The Rollo Boys With Sherlock In Mayfair	Sherlock HOLMES
The Roman Hat Mystery	Ellery QUEEN
The Romance Of Elaine	Prof Craig KENNEDY
The Rome Express	FLOCON
Ronald Standish	Ronald STANDISH
Rook Takes Knight	Howie ROOK
The Rookery Detective	The ROOKERY DETECTIVE
Rooksmiths	Insp BASS
Room 13	J G REEDER
Room 14: A Secret Service Adventure	Lawrie FENTON
The Room 31 Riddle	Insp GIBSON
Room At The Bottom	Jeff TYLER
Room Five	George VORE
Room For A Body	Claude WARRINGTON-REEVE and Insp Steven MITCHELL
Room For Murder	Singer BATTS
Room For Murder	Aggie SCANLON
Room Number Twenty-Three	James W BELLAMY
A Room To Die In	Insp TARR and Ann NELSON
Room To Swing	Toussaint 'Touie' MOORE
The Room With No Escape	Urban DORMER
Root Canal	Becky BELSKI
Root Of Evil	Lt Joseph DICKERSON
The Root Of His Evil	Timothy DANE
The Rope Began To Hang The Butcher	Gilmore HENRY
Rope By Arrangement	William POWER, Penny MERCER and Vincent MERCER
A Rope For A Gal Called Lou	LOU
Rope For The Judge	Asmun HILL
Rope Of Sand	Grant GARFIELD
Rope Over Jezebel	Ch Insp William BASTION
The Rosario Murder Case	Insp Neville LANGHAM
The Rosary Murders	Father Robert KOESLER
Rosa's Dilemma	Rosa EPTON
The Rose Bath Riddle	J C K 'Jigger' MASTERS
A Rose From The Dead	Shirley LEIGHTON and Bill HARPER
The Rose In Darkness	Insp CHARLESWORTH
The Rose Petal Murders	Jimmy HASTINGS
The Rose Window	Insp Miguel MENENDEZ
Roseanna	Insp Martin BECK
Roses, Roses	Ch Supt Colin HARPUR
Rosie Among Thorns	Rosie MONAGHAN
The Ross Forgery	Arthur TANK
Rostron Outfit In Mexico	Rostron OUTFIT
The Rosy Pastor	Insp DUFFY and Alan RUSSELL
Rotten Apples	Willow KING
Rotten Apples	Dearborn V PINCH
Rough Cut	Antonio 'Chico' CERVANTES
Rough Cut	Rayford GOODMAN
Rough Justice	Mr FAUNCE
Rough Justice	Lt NEUMAN
Rough Justice	John WELLS
Rough On Rats	Anthony MARTIN
Rough Red	William WARNER
A Rough Shoot	Roger TAINE
Rough Water	Peter BARTHOLOMEW
The Roumanian Envoy	Sexton BLAKE
The Round Table Murders	Prof Dennis BARRIE
Roundhead Retreat	Nicholas PYM
Rouse The Demon	Casey KELLOG and Al KRUG
Roxburghe UK (1895)	Horace VESEY
The Royal Flush	Sherlock HOLMES
The Royal Pain	Clayton WARD
A Royal Rascal: Episodes In The Career Of Sir Theophilus St Clair, KCB	Col Sir Theophilus ST CLAIR
Royce Of The Royal Mounted	ROYCE
Rubies, Emeralds And Diamonds	Petunia BEST and Max FREUND
Rubout At The Onyx	Harry MACNEIL
The Ruby Of Khitmandu	Sherlock HOLMES and A J RAFFLES
Ruby Red Death	Nick CARTER
Ruffly Speaking	Holly WINTER
Rules Of Evidence	Raymond BOUDRO
Rules Of Prey	Lucas DAVENPORT
The Rules Of The Game	Dorothy Mayotte RIGBY
The Rules Of The Knife Fight	Owen CARR
The Rum And Coca-Cola Murders	Peter ASWELL
The Rum Row Murders	Insp James CONWAY
Rumpole A La Carte	Horace RUMPOLE
Rumpole And The Age Of Miracles	Horace RUMPOLE
Rumpole And The Golden Thread	Horace RUMPOLE
Rumpole Of The Bailey	Horace RUMPOLE
Rumpole's Last Case	Horace RUMPOLE
Rumpole's Return	Horace RUMPOLE
Run Down: The World Of Alan Brett	Alan BRETT
Run For Cover	Richard GRAHAM
Run For Your Life	Sarah HOYT
Run For Your Life!	Steven ERIKSON
Run For Your Money	Joseph SOUTH
Run Rabbit Run Run Run	Dorothy Mayotte RIGBY
Run When I Say Go	Peter CONGDON
The Runaway	ADAM 12
The Runaway Corpse	James WARREN
Runner On The Streets	John RANKIN
Running Blind	SLADE
A Running Duck	Mike MALCHECK
The Running Fight	William MURGATROYD
Running Fix	Gillean VERDEAN
Running For Shelter	Laura PRINCIPAL
The Running Killer	Royston FRERE
The Ruse Of The Vanished Women	Anthony HAVILLAND
The Russian Enigma	Charles WINTER
The Russian Intelligence	Jerry CORNELIUS
Russian Leave	Vladimir GULL
Rustler's Venom	Jefferson BIRCH
The Rustling Death	'Doc' SAVAGE
Rusty Thumbs A Ride	Rusty BROWN
Ryan's Rules	Frank RYAN
Rynox	Supt SHANTER
The Rynox Murder	Supt SHANTER
The Rynox Murder Mystery	Supt SHANTER
The Rynox Mystery	Supt SHANTER

— S —

Title	Character
Saba's Treasure	Det Bolivar MANCHENIL
Sabotage	Haggai GODIN
Sabotage Unlimited	Peter MOHUNE
Sacred Clowns	Lt Joe LEAPHORN and Sgt Jim CHEE
The Sacred Shaft	David CONNELL
Sacred Sins	Ed JACKSON
The Sacrifice	Roger BRAITHWAITE
Sacrifice Play	Prof Harry BISHOP
Sacrificial Ground	Frank CLEMONS
The Sadist	RYKER
Sad-Eyed Blonde	Philip MARLOWE
Safari For Spies	Nick CARTER
Safe At Home	Kate HENRY
Safe House	Alfred BAUM
Said With Flowers	Mark TUDOR
Saigon	Nick CARTER
Saigon Commandos	Sgt Mark STRYKER
Sail	Oscar SAIL
The Saint And Mr Teal	Simon (The Saint) TEMPLAR
The Saint Around The World	Simon (The Saint) TEMPLAR
The Saint Cleans Up	Simon (The Saint) TEMPLAR
Saint Errant	Simon (The Saint) TEMPLAR
The Saint Goes On	Simon (The Saint) TEMPLAR
The Saint Goes West	Simon (The Saint) TEMPLAR
The Saint In Action	Simon (The Saint) TEMPLAR
The Saint In England	Simon (The Saint) TEMPLAR
The Saint In Europe	Simon (The Saint) TEMPLAR
The Saint In London	Simon (The Saint) TEMPLAR
The Saint In Silver	Steve MIDNIGHT
The Saint In The Sun	Simon (The Saint) TEMPLAR

The Saint Intervenes	Simon (The Saint) TEMPLAR
The Saint Maker	Father Joseph BREDDER
The Saint On Guard	Simon (The Saint) TEMPLAR
The Saint On The Spanish Main	Simon (The Saint) TEMPLAR
The Saint To The Rescue	Simon (The Saint) TEMPLAR
The Saint Vs Scotland Yard	Simon (The Saint) TEMPLAR
The Saint - The Brighter Buccaneer	Simon (The Saint) TEMPLAR
The Saint - The Happy Highwayman	Simon (The Saint) TEMPLAR
The Saint - Wanted For Murder	Simon (The Saint) TEMPLAR
The Saints Are Sinister	Anthony BATHURST
The Saint-Malo Mystery	Jeremy FLACK and Duncan CAINSFORTH
The Saint: Ace Of Knaves	Simon (The Saint) TEMPLAR
Sakhalin Breakout	Nile BARRABAS
Salesman Of Death	Mike MCCALL
Sally Of Scotland Yard	Sally DEAN
Salmon In The Soup	Jessica JAMES
Salt Is Leaving	Lionel Humphrey SALT and Maggie CULTHORPE
Salute Mr Sandyman	Mr SANDYMAN
The Salzberg Affair	Sebastian KETTLE
Sam Benedict: Cast The First Stone	Sam BENEDICT
Sam Six Killer, The Cherokee Detective; Or, The James Boys Most Dangerous Foe	Sam SIX KILLER
Sam Small Flies Again	Sam SMALL
Sam Smart, The Eastern Postal Route Detective; Or, Piping A Dark Conspiracy For The Government	Sam SMART
Sam Strong, The Cowboy Detective; Or, The Ranch Mystery	Sam STRONG
Samantha	Det Sgt Masao MASUTO
Samson's Deal	Jake SAMSON
Samuel Boyd Of Catchpole Square: A Mystery	ROBSON and Edwin BOUSFIELD
Samuel Lyle, Criminologist	Samuel LYLE
San Francisco Kills	Spencer HOLMES
The Sanctuary Club	Dr Henry CHETWYND and Dr Paul CATO
Sand Against The Tide	Calico Jack WALKER and Tina TAMIKO
The Sandal Wood Slipper; Or, Nick Carter's Isle Of Safety	Nick CARTER
Sanders	Commiss SANDERS
Sanders Of The River	Commiss SANDERS
Sanderson's Diamond Loot	Jimmy 'Wiggly' PRICE
Sandi, The King Maker	Commiss SANDERS
Sandscreen	Graham LORIMER
Sandwiches Are Not My Business	Pepperoni HERO
Sandy And Others	SANDY
The Sandycroft Mystery	Insp MALLESON
Sant Of The Secret Service	SANT
The Santa Claus Killer	Charles THAYER
Santos, Border Detective	Domingo SANTOS
The Sapphire Conference	Joe DUST
Sapphires On Wednesday	Mark RAEBURN
Sarah Brown, Detective; Or, The Mystery Of The Pavilion	Sarah BROWN
The Sarah Jane Mystery	Herlock SHOLMES
The Saranoff Murder	Arthur RANELEIGH
Saratoga Haunting	Charlie BRADSHAW
Saratoga Longshot	Charlie BRADSHAW
Satan Has Six Fingers	Lt DIEGO
Satan In St Mary's	Hugh CORBETT
Satan Is A Woman	Sylvia PLOTKIN and Max Van LARSEN
Satan Ltd	Bill KELLAWAY
The Satan Ring	Jon STEEL
Satan's Child	Sexton BLAKE
Satan's Sabbath	Mack (The Executioner) BOLAN
Satellite City	Rex BADER
Satellite City	Nick CARTER
Saturday Of Glory	Supt Luis BERNAL
Saturn Over The Water	Tim BEDFORD
Sauce For The Goose	Jimmy FLANNERY
Savage Breast	Liz PARROTT
Savage Encounter	Insp MCLEAN
The Savage Game	John SAVAGE
The Savage Height	John SAVAGE
Savage Interlude	CRAWFORD
Savage Slaughter	Johnny ROCK
The Savage Squeeze	Sexton BLAKE
The Savages	Insp Robert STAUNTON
A Savant's Vendetta	Humphrey CHALLONER
Save A Rope	Dr Reginald FORTUNE
Saved At The Scaffold; Or, Nic Brown, The Chicago Detective	Nic BROWN
Saving A Rope	Dr Reginald FORTUNE
Saving Grace	Insp EVANS and Sgt BEDDOES
Saving Grace	Philip MARLOWE
Saving The Queen	Blackford OAKES
Savings And Loam	Andrew BROOM
Saxon Ashe, Secret Agent	Saxon ASHE
Saxon's Ghost	Joe SAXON
Say It With Poison	Ch Insp Alan MARKBY and Meredith MITCHELL
Say Yes To Murder	Bill LENNOX
Say Yes, Sugar	Pete GARROWAY
The Scallywag	SHERRARD
Scandal At High Chimneys: A Victorian Melodrama	Clive STRICKLAND
Scandal At School	The Hon Everard BLATCHINGTON
Scandal At Scotland Yard	Bryan ARMITAGE
Scandal At The Home Office	Supt MERSEY
Scandal Has Two Faces	Matthew CRAIG
A Scandal In Bohemia	Sherlock HOLMES
A Scandal In Bulimia	Turlock LOAMS
Scandal In Fair Haven	Henrietta O'Dwyer COLLINS
Scandal In The Chancery	Dennis TYLER
The Scandal Of Father Brown	Father BROWN
The Scapegoat	Insp BLOCK
Scapegoat	Insp Jonas MORCK
Scar Faced Killer	Johnny ROCK
The Scarecrow Murders	Judge Henry TYSON
The Scarf On The Scarecrow	Jerry TODD
The Scarlet Flush	Mike FARREL
The Scarlet Lily	Barney HYDE
The Scarlet Macaw	Insp BURTON
The Scarlet Pimpernel	The SCARLET PIMPERNEL
The Scarlet Runner	Christopher RACE
The Scarlet Thread	Gil DONAN
The Scarlet X	Ferris MCCLUE
Scarlett Gets The Kidnapper	Peter SCARLETT
Scarlett - Special Branch	Peter SCARLETT
Scattergood Baines	Scattergood BAINES
Scattergood Baines Pulls The Strings	Scattergood BAINES
Scattergood Returns	Scattergood BAINES
Scavengers	Finney ALETTER
The Scavengers	Ch Offr Webb CARRICK
Scent Of Mayhem	Mark STRATTON
A Scent Of New-Mown Hay	Gen Charles KIRK
Schlock Homes: The Complete Bagel Street Saga	Schlock HOMES
School For Murder	Insp Mike PUMFREY
The Schulsinger Affair	Simon LEIGH
The Schwotten Ray	Herlock SHOLMES
Scientific Sprague	Calvin SPRAGUE
Scissors Cut Paper	Bow Street Runner Victor CARYLL
The Scold's Bridle	Sgt COOPER
The Score	PARKER
A Score Of Arms	John ALLISON
The Scorpio Letters	Joe CHRISTOPHER
Scotch And Water	Mr GLENCANNON
Scotland Yard	Picklock HOLES
Scotland Yard Experiences	A SCOTLAND YARD DETECTIVE
Scotland Yard Photo Crimes	Insp BLACK
Scotland Yard: Department of Queer Complaints	Col MARCH
Scoundrels & Co	MARTEN
Scout Grey - Detective	Scout GREY
Scrambled Yeggs	Jim HANVEY
The Scrambled Yeggs	Shell SCOTT
Scratch Fever	NOLAN
The Scratch On The Surface	Steve WAYNE
Scratchproof	Simon DRAKE
The Scream	Adam FLUTE
Scream And Scream Again	Sexton BLAKE
Scream At The Sea	SPARROW
Scream Street	Sam DAKKERS
Screaming Bones	Henry BASSETT
The Screaming Fog	John Newton CHANCE
The Screaming Mimi	SWEENEY
The Screwball King Murder	Max ROPER
The Scroll Of Benevolence	Simon YOUNG
The Scrutinies Of Simon Iff	Simon IFF
The Sculptress	Rosalind LEIGH and Sgt HAWKSLEY
Sea Fever	George PALMER-JONES
Sea Gold	Insp BADGER
Sea Of Green	Det Neil 'Hock' HOCKADAY
Sea Scrape	Mark HOOD
Seagull Crag	Jannine WEST
The Sealed Envelope	Glenn BOWMAN
The Sealed Room Murder	Larry MILNER
The Sealed Spire Mystery	Solar PONS
Sealed-Room Murder	Insp Edward BEALE
The Sealer	James FRASER
Seance	Myra SAVAGE
Seance For Two	Myra SAVAGE
Seance On A Wet Afternoon	Myra SAVAGE
The Search	Leo DURGAN
Search And Destroy	Richard LE GRANDE
Search And Destroy	Brian PETERSEN
The Search For My Great-Uncle's Head	Peter COFFIN and Col BLACK
The Search For Tamerlane	Hal JOHNSON
Search The Dark Woods	Leo DURGAN
Searchlight On Hambledon	Insp Rupert HAMBLEDON
A Seaside Mystery	Jim BLISS
A Season Of Knives	Sir Robert CAREY
Seattle	Peter BRAGG
The Sea-coast Of Bohemia	Insp Henri CASTANG
The Seclusion Room	Policeman William MOORE
The Second Case Of The Speckled Band	Sherlock HOLMES
The Second Chance	Det Insp Stephen HARPER
Second Curtain	George GARNER
The Second Dandy Chater	TOKLEY
Second Fiddle	Sherlock HOLMES
Second Guess	Amanda VALENTINE
The Second Longest Night	Chester DRUM
The Second Man	Marion KERRISON
Second Opinion	Dr George BARNABAS
The Second Red Dragon	William HOLMES
A Second Shot In The Dark	Chris MARTIN
Second Time Round	Stephen ARMITAGE
The Second Vanetti Affair	Jason GALT
The Second War Of Worlds	Sherlock HOLMES
A Second-Hand Tomb	Insp BADGERY
The Secret Adventure Of The Thoroughbred Ghost	Sherlock HOLMES
The Secret Adversary	Tommy BERESFORD and Tuppence BERESFORD
A Secret Agent In Port Arthur	Jo SALIS
Secret Agent Number One	Anthony HAMILTON
Secret Agent X-9	SECRET AGENT X-9
Secret Agent X-9: Book Two	SECRET AGENT X-9
The Secret Brotherhood	Sgt/Det Insp Patrick Aloysius MCCARTHY
The Secret Cargo	Paul CAMPENHAYE
The Secret Chronicles Of Sherlock Holmes	Sherlock HOLMES
The Secret Dancer	Det Insp COURTENAY
Secret Dragnet	Howard DIGBURN
Secret Errand	Bruce MURDOCH
The Secret Families	Herbie KRUGER
The Secret Files Of Sherlock Holmes	Sherlock HOLMES

The Secret Files Of Solar Pons	Solar PONS
The Secret Front	Hiram HOLLIDAY
The Secret Hand	Desmond OKEWOOD
Secret History Of Today	Monsieur V
Secret Hong Kong	Quinn LELAND
The Secret House	T B SMITH
The Secret In The Pudding Bag	Herlock SHOLMES
Secret Inquiry	Insp Cheviot BURMANN and Bryan ARMITAGE
The Secret Journals Of Sherlock Holmes	Sherlock HOLMES
Secret Kills	Dan FORREST
Secret Ministry	Johnny FEDORA
Secret Mission: Prague	Phil SHERMAN
The Secret Of Bogey House	Jimmie HASWELL
The Secret Of Chimneys	Supt BATTLE
The Secret Of Father Brown	Father BROWN
The Secret Of Gnome Head	Prof Adrian CRIDDLE
The Secret Of High Eldersham	Desmond MERRION and Insp Henry ARNOLD
The Secret Of MI6	John SPENCER
The Secret Of Sam Marlow	Sam MARLOW
The Secret Of Scotland Yard: A Mystery	Mr MERTON
The Secret Of Secrets	Insp SKARRATT
The Secret Of Sherlock Holmes	Sherlock HOLMES
The Secret Of Shoreswood Hall	Sherlock HOLMES
The Secret Of The Bucket Shop	Sexton BLAKE
The Secret Of The Elephants	Supt Steve MACLAREN
The Secret Of The Green Lagoon	Sexton BLAKE
The Secret Of The Hills	James DREW
The Secret Of The Hulk	Sexton BLAKE
The Secret Of The Jungle	Sexton BLAKE
The Secret Of The Marble Mantle	Nick CARTER
The Secret Of The Missing Checks And Walt Wheeler, The Scout Detective	Walt WHEELER
The Secret Of The Monastery	Sexton BLAKE
The Secret Of The Old Clock - Special	Nancy DREW
The Secret Of The Reef	Ferrers LOCKE
The Secret Of The Ring	Martin DALE
The Secret Of The Roman Temple	Sexton BLAKE
The Secret Of The Sandbanks	Colin ANSTRUTHER
The Secret Of The Screen	Prof BLINKWELL
The Secret Of The Sea	Peter KNIGHT
The Secret Of The Snows	Sexton BLAKE
The Secret Of The Suez Canal	Sexton BLAKE
The Secret Of The Surgery	Sexton BLAKE
The Secret Of The Ten Bales	Sexton BLAKE
The Secret Of The Tower	Ferrers LOCKE
The Secret Of Thirty-Seven Hardy Street	Jim SANDS
A Secret Rage	Nickie CALLAHAN
Secret Servant	Sgt/Insp MARSHALL
The Secret Servant	Maj Harry MAXIM
The Secret Service Man	Martin HUISH
The Secret Service Man	Jim STRANG
Secret Service Smith	Aurelius SMITH
A Secret Service Woman	Olga von KOPF
Secret Services	Marcus ORLANDO
Secret Service: Or, Recollections Of A City Detective	Andrew FORRESTER
A Secret Singing	James Maxwell MALLORY
The Secret Telephone	Arthur HEATHER
The Secret Telephone	MARTIN
The Secret Toll	Robert FORRESTER
The Secretary's Double	Herlock SHOLMES
Secrets	Frank MONTGOMERY
Secrets Of A Private Enquiry Office	Mr BELL and Mr WHITE
The Secrets Of Dr Taverner	Dr TAVERNER
The Secrets Of Monte Carlo	MARTIN
The Sedulous Ape	Insp JOHNSON
See Naples And Kill	January ESPOSITO
See The Red Blood Run	Ross MCKELLAR
See The Woman	Det Sgt John STRYKER
See You At Murder Mansion	Dan TROUT
See You At The Morgue	Det KILKENNY
Seeds Of Doom	Alexander (Check Force) CHANE and Vladimer KARLOV
Seeds Of Murder	Capt/Maj/Col Hugh NORTH
Seeds Of Yesterday	Chris DOLLANGANGER and Cathy DOLLANGANGER
The Seeing Eye	Dr David WINTRINGHAM and Insp Steven MITCHELL
Seeing Is Believing	Wilmurt ROBIN
Seeing Red	Harry KYLE and Angela ROLLASON
Seeing Red	Dr Jeffrey MCNEILL
Seek And Destroy	Steve CARRADINE
The Seen And The Unseen	The Hon Augustus CHAMPNELL and BURCHELL
The Seine Mystery	Insp BROUSSE and Alan ESTERBROOKE
Seize The Dragon	Robert STARK
Self-Defence	Dr Alex DELAWARE
The Selicombe Murder	Sydney VANE
Sellers Of Death	Barnaby GRAYLE
Selling's Murder	John HARLEY
Send Another Coffin	John WEBB and Anne WEBB
Send For Paul Temple	Paul TEMPLE
Send Him Victorious	HARVEY
Seneca Falls Inheritance	Glynis TRYON
Senor Saint	Simon (The Saint) TEMPLAR
A Sensational Case	Jem COLLINGHAM
A Sense Of Loyalty	Miba STERLING
The Sensitives	Ben SLADE
The Sentence Of The Court	Mark TAVERNER
The Sentimental Adventures Of Jimmy Bulstrode	Jimmy BULSTRODE
The Sentimental Kill	Peter FLECK
The Sentry-Box Murder	James GREER
The Sepia Siren Killer	Hobart LINDSEY and Det Marvia PLUM
September Story	Col PATERNOSTER
Septimus And The Danedyke Mystery	Rev Septimus TRELOAR
Septimus And The Spy Ring	Rev Septimus TRELOAR
Sergeant Cluff Rings True	Sgt Caleb CLUFF
Sergeant Cluff Stands Firm	Sgt Caleb CLUFF
Sergeant Cork's Casebook	Sgt CORK
Sergeant Cork's Second Casebook	Sgt CORK
Sergeant Dunn, CID	Sgt Sir Peter DUNN
Sergeant Lancey Carries On	Sgt LANCEY
Sergeant Lancey Reports	Sgt LANCEY
Sergeant Lancey Tells The Tale	Sgt LANCEY
Sergeant Ritchie's Conscience	Tommy TOMPKINS
Sergeant Sir Peter	Sgt Sir Peter DUNN
Sergeant Verity And The Cracksman	William VERITY
Sergeant Verity And The Swell Mob	William VERITY
Sergeant Yale Of Scotland Yard: Or, A London Ferret In New York City	Sgt YALE
The Sergeant's Cat And Other Stories	Adjutent Henk GRIJPSTRA and Sgt Rufus DE GIER
The Serpent Among The Lilies	Matthew JENKYN
The Serpent Under It	Anne REDMOND
The Serpent's Smile	Insp Tami SHIMONI
Servant's Problem	Webster FLAGG
Set A Thief	Louis LEPINE
Set A Thief	Patrolman MURPHY
Set A Trap	George ROWE
A Set Of Flats	Insp PHILLIPSON
The Seth Papers	Dr Owen ORIENT
Settled Out Of Court	Miles BREDON
The Set-Up	Cory BARNETT
Set-Up	George ROWE
The Set-Up	STARSKY and HUTCH
The Seven Agate Devils	'Doc' SAVAGE
The Seven Black Chessmen	Horton FORBES
Seven Black Stones	Molly BEARPAW
The Seven Clues	Michael DENE
Seven Dead	Insp KENDALL
The Seven Deadly Sisters	Sally BOWEN
The Seven Dials Mystery	Lady Elaine 'Bundle' BRENT and Supt BATTLE
Seven Died	Jose Manuel MADERO
The Seven Dreamers	Insp BLANC
Seven Gates To Nowhere	Sgt George DIXON
Seven Looked On	Simon CHARD
The Seven Of Hearts	Arsène LUPIN
The Seven Per-Cent Solution	Sherlock HOLMES and Sigmund FREUD
Seven Red Herrings	Quentin EADY
The Seven Seas Murders	Capt/Maj/Col Hugh NORTH
Seven Sins	Gaston MAX
Seven Slayers	Johnny DOOLIN
The Seven Sleepers	Thomas PRESTON
Seven Steps East	Trooper Ralph LINDSEY
Seven Steps To Treason	Sarah CABLE
Seven Suspects	Insp/Commiss John APPLEBY
Seven To Die	Franklyn KEEN
The Seventh Bullet And Others	Sherlock HOLMES
The Seventh Commandment	Dora CONTI
The Seventh Enemy	Brady COYNE
The Seventh Sinner	Jacqueline KIRBY
Several Deaths Later	TOBIN
Sex Trap	Randy ROBERTS
Sex Trap	Sgt Louis SOLDEN
Sexton Blake And The Demon God	Sexton BLAKE
Sexton Blake's Honour	Sexton BLAKE
The Sexual Adventures Of Sherlock Holmes	Sherlock HOLMES
Sgt Corbin's War	Sgt Ben CORBIN
The Shade Of Time	Jim QUIGLEY
The Shadow And The Golden Master	Lamont (The Shadow) CRANSTON
Shadow Behind The Curtain	Deborah CHANNING
The Shadow Crook	Sexton BLAKE
Shadow Crusade	John HOWDEN
Shadow Dance	Joanna WILDER and Ruth WILSON
Shadow Dancers	Det Sgt Francis MOONEY
The Shadow From The Bogue	Capt/Insp COLIN
Shadow House	Nora HONEYCUTT
Shadow In The House	Paul BERNARD
Shadow Kills	J D HAWKINS
The Shadow Laughs!	Lamont (The Shadow) CRANSTON
The Shadow Man	Det/Sgt/Supt SCARFE
Shadow Of A Broken Man	Dr Robert 'Mongo' FREDERICKSON
Shadow Of A Killer	Casson DUKER
Shadow Of A Lady	Monte GORDON and Insp MEDFORD
Shadow Of Chu-Sheng	CHU-SHENG
The Shadow Of Doctor Syn	Dr SYN
A Shadow Of Himself	Bob EDDISON
The Shadow Of His Crime	Sexton BLAKE
Shadow Of Madness	Dr John SMITH
The Shadow Of Malreward	Richard LORYAT
The Shadow Of Murder	Patrick LAING
The Shadow Of The Cobra	Duncan KERR
Shadow Of The Leopard	Ben DRYDEN
The Shadow Of Time	Harry KENT
The Shadow On The Downs	Matilda PERKS
Shadow On The Wall	Dr Reginald FORTUNE
The Shadow People	'Rolling' STONE
Shadow Play	Helen WEST and Det Supt Geoffrey BAILEY
The Shadow Strikes	Lamont (The Shadow) CRANSTON
Shadowed By Three	Francis FERRARS
Shadows	Dr Russell V 'Chill' CHILDERS
Shadows Before	Ch Insp Dan PARDOE
Shadows Don't Bleed	Paul CAMERON
Shadows In Their Blood	Trixie DOLAN and Evangeline SINCLAIR
Shadows Of The Past	Holderly HALL
Shadows On The Green	Chris LUDLOW
The Shadows On The Lawn	Sherlock HOLMES
Shadows On The Mirror	Det Supt Geoffrey BAILEY
Shadows Tonight	Gregory TRENT
The Shadowy Third	David CALDER
Shady Doings	Agatha WELCH

	Shady Lady	Rex MCBRIDE
	Shaft	John SHAFT
	Shake A Crooked Town	Johnny KILLAIN
	Shakedown	Steve DRAKE
	Shakedown	Joe PUMA
The	Shakedown	Henry Highland (Iceman) WEST
	Shakedown Hotel	Sam CATES
The	Shaken Leaf	Lindy GREY
The	Shakeout	Piers ROPER
The	Shakespeare Murders	Peter KERRIGAN
The	Shakespeare Murders	Edward TRELAWNY
	Shakespeare The Physicist	Sherlock HOLMES
The	Shake-Up	Sgt Gunnar MATSON
	Shallow Grave	Patrick SHANNON
The	Sham Detective	The SHAM DETECTIVE
The	Sham Huns	Herlock SHOLMES
The	Shaman Tree	Det Charlie GANTS
	Shamus	Shamus MCCOY
A	Shamus And A Sheba	Ed RILEY
	Shan	Jake MAROC
The	Shape Of Fear	Isamu OHARA
A	Share In Death	Duncan KINCAID
The	Shark Bait Affair	Kate GRAHAM
A	Sharp Rise In Crime	Insp Roger 'Handsome' WEST
	Sharretts The Detective	B K SHARRETTS
The	Shattered Raven	Barney HAMET
	Shattered Steel	Det Sgt Bob CHRISTIE
	Shaved Fish	Syd FISH
	Shawnee Alley Fire	HARTER
The	Shayne Case	Daniel J CLUER
	She Came By The Book	Emma VICTOR
	She Came Too Late	Emma VICTOR
	She Didn't Like Dying	Ch Insp Andy MCMURDO
	She Died Because...	Prof Gideon MANCIPLE and Dr William BLOW
	She Died Dancing	Steve BARTON and Connie BARTON
	She Died On The Stairway	Lt Price PRICE
	She Died Without Light	Dr Hal PHILLIPS
	She Faded Into Air	Alan FOAM
	She Left A Silver Slipper	Russell AMES
	She Liked It That Way	Danny SPADE
	She Married Raffles	A J RAFFLES
	She Modelled Her Coffin	Adam FLUTE
	She Screamed Blue Murder	Sham PAYNE
	She Shall Have Murder	Dagobert BROWN and Jane BROWN
	She Should Have Cried On Monday	Ben LOUIS
	She Walked In Fear	Insp J RASON
	She Walks Alone	Miguel URIZAR
	She Walks These Hills	Henry KRETZNER
	She Wore Pink Gloves	Bradley ADAMS
	Shed A Bitter Tear	Casey PETERS
	Shed Light On Death	Joseph 'JJ' JAMISON
The	Sheep And The Wolves	Insp GULLIVER
	Sheep's Clothing	Flora HOGG
	Sheer Torture	Insp Perry TRETHOWAN
	Sheerluck Jones	Sheerluck JONES
The	Shell Scott Sampler	Shell SCOTT
	Shell Scott's Seven Slaughters	Shell SCOTT
	Shellshock	Shell SCOTT
The	Sheridan Road Mystery	Dave MORGAN
The	Sheriff And The Folsom Man Murders	Sheriff Charles Timothy MATTHEWS
The	Sheriff And The Panhandle Murders	Sheriff Charles Timothy MATTHEWS
	Sheriff Olson	Sheriff John Charles OLSON
	Sherlock Bones, Tracer Of Missing Pets	Sherlock BONES
	Sherlock Holmes	Sherlock HOLMES
	Sherlock Holmes	Sherlock HOLMES
	Sherlock Holmes	Sherlock HOLMES
	Sherlock Holmes	Sherlock HOLMES
	Sherlock Holmes And A Near Case Of Murder	Sherlock HOLMES
	Sherlock Holmes And A Theatrical Mystery	Sherlock HOLMES
	Sherlock Holmes And The Arabian Princess	Sherlock HOLMES
	Sherlock Holmes And The Arthritic Clergyman	Sherlock HOLMES
	Sherlock Holmes And The Brighton Pavilion Mystery	Sherlock HOLMES
	Sherlock Holmes And The Case Of Sabina Hall	Sherlock HOLMES
	Sherlock Holmes And The Curious Adventure Of The Clockwork Prince	Sherlock HOLMES
	Sherlock Holmes And The Curse Of The Sign Of Four: Or, 'The Mark Of Timber Toe'	Sherlock HOLMES
	Sherlock Holmes And The Drood Mystery	Sherlock HOLMES
	Sherlock Holmes And The Egyptian Hall Adventure	Sherlock HOLMES
	Sherlock Holmes And The Eminent Thespian	Sherlock HOLMES
	Sherlock Holmes And The German Nanny	Sherlock HOLMES
	Sherlock Holmes And The Giant Rat Of Sumatra	Sherlock HOLMES
	Sherlock Holmes And The Golden Bird	Sherlock HOLMES
	Sherlock Holmes And The Greyfriars School Mystery	Sherlock HOLMES
	Sherlock Holmes And The Hellbirds	Sherlock HOLMES
	Sherlock Holmes And The Hentzau Affair	Sherlock HOLMES
	Sherlock Holmes And The King Of Siam	Sherlock HOLMES
	Sherlock Holmes And The London Zoo Mystery	Sherlock HOLMES
	Sherlock Holmes And The Mark Of The Beast	Sherlock HOLMES
	Sherlock Holmes And The Masquerade Murders	Sherlock HOLMES
	Sherlock Holmes And The Muffin	Sherlock HOLMES
	Sherlock Holmes And The Mysterious Friend Of Oscar Wilde	Sherlock HOLMES
	Sherlock Holmes And The Railway Maniac	Sherlock HOLMES
	Sherlock Holmes And The Raleigh Legacy	Sherlock HOLMES
	Sherlock Holmes And The Red-Headed League	Sherlock HOLMES
	Sherlock Holmes And The Sacred Sword	Sherlock HOLMES
	Sherlock Holmes And The Thistle Of Scotland	Sherlock HOLMES
	Sherlock Holmes And The Treasure Train	Sherlock HOLMES
	Sherlock Holmes And The Ultimate Disguise	Sherlock HOLMES
	Sherlock Holmes And The Wendigo	Sherlock HOLMES
	Sherlock Holmes And The Wife Of Bath	Sherlock HOLMES

	Sherlock Holmes And The Wood Green Empire Mystery	Sherlock HOLMES
	Sherlock Holmes And 'The Woman'	Sherlock HOLMES
	Sherlock Holmes At Elsinore	Sherlock HOLMES
	Sherlock Holmes At Oxford	Sherlock HOLMES
	Sherlock Holmes At The 1902 Fifth Test	Sherlock HOLMES
	Sherlock Holmes, Bridge Detective	Sherlock HOLMES
	Sherlock Holmes Comedy Trilogy	Sherlock HOLMES
	Sherlock Holmes, Consulting Detective	Sherlock HOLMES
	Sherlock Holmes' First Case	Sherlock HOLMES
	Sherlock Holmes In Dallas	Sherlock HOLMES
	Sherlock Holmes In Gibraltar	Sherlock HOLMES
	Sherlock Holmes In Hongkong	Sherlock HOLMES
	Sherlock Holmes In New York	Sherlock HOLMES
	Sherlock Holmes In Orbit	Sherlock HOLMES
	Sherlock Holmes In Tibet	Sherlock HOLMES
	Sherlock Holmes Investigates The EPR Paradox	Sherlock HOLMES
	Sherlock Holmes Investigates The Murder In Euston Square	Sherlock HOLMES
	Sherlock Holmes Meets Annie Oakley	Sherlock HOLMES
	Sherlock Holmes Meets The Phantom	Sherlock HOLMES
	Sherlock Holmes: My Life And Crimes	Sherlock HOLMES
	Sherlock Holmes On The Roof Of The World; Or, The Adventure Of The Wayfaring God	Sherlock HOLMES
	Sherlock Holmes Revisited	Sherlock HOLMES
	Sherlock Holmes Revisited: Volume 2	Sherlock HOLMES
The	Sherlock Holmes Solution	Sherlock HOLMES
	Sherlock Holmes: The Adventure Of The Ancient Gods	Sherlock HOLMES
	Sherlock Holmes Through Time And Space	Sherlock HOLMES
	Sherlock Holmes Versus Arsène Lupin: The Case Of The Golden Blonde	Sherlock HOLMES and Arsène LUPIN
	Sherlock Holmes Versus Jack The Ripper	Sherlock HOLMES
	Sherlock Holmes Versus John Thorndyke And Reginald Fortune	Sherlock HOLMES, Dr Reginald FORTUNE and Dr John Evelyn THORNDYKE
	Sherlock Holmes Vs Dracula: Or, The Adventures Of The Sanguinary Count	Sherlock HOLMES
	Sherlock Holmes's War Of The Worlds	Sherlock HOLMES
	Sherlock In Love	Sherlock HOLMES
The	Sherlock Solution	Sherlock HOLMES
	Sherlock Watson's Last Case	Sherlock WATSON
	Sherlock's Last Case	Sherlock HOLMES
A	Shilling For Candles	Insp Alan GRANT
	Ship Of Spies	Geoffrey LANDON
The	Shipyard Menace	Sexton BLAKE
	Shirley Holmquist And Aunt Wilma: Whodunnit?	Shirley HOLMQUIST
	Shirlick Holmes And The Case Of The Wandering Wardrobe	Shirlick HOLMES
The	Shivering Mountain	Hugh CURTIS
	Shoal Water	Jonah MANSEL
	Shock Treatment	Dale NELSON
	Shock Wave	Kate OSBORN
The	Shocking Secret	Lt KELLY
	Shock!	Insp FROST and Toni STAPLETON
	Shoes That Had Walked Twice	Monsieur JACQUOT and Monsieur LEVERT
	Shoestring	Eddie SHOESTRING
	Shoestring's Finest Hour	Eddie SHOESTRING
	Shoot The Moon	Robin DANA
	Shoot The Works	Steve DRAKE
	Shoot To Kill	Max THURSDAY
	Shooting At Loons	Judge Deborah KNOTT
The	Shooting Gallery	Insp MCCAIG
The	Shooting Of Sergius Leroy	John HOPKINS
The	Shooting Of The Green	Cole BROGAN
	Shoot-Out	CANNON
The	Shore House Mystery	Insp MANNERS
	Short Break In Venice	Insp Franco CORTI
The	Short Cases Of Inspector Maigret	Insp Jules MAIGRET
	Short Cut To Santa Fe	Insp John SANDERS
	Short List	C J SWAN
A	Short-Lived Ghost	Arnold LANDON
A	Shot In The Dark	Insp GODBOLD and Bob PONTING
A	Shot In The Night	Bob PONTING
	Shot Silk	Simon DRAKE
	Showdown In Sydne	Sexton BLAKE
The	Shred Of Lace	Sherlock HOLMES
The	Shredded Rose	Prof Austin LYLE
The	Shrieking Pit	David COLWYN
A	Shroud For Aquarius	MALLORY
A	Shroud For Delilah	Ch Insp David WEBB
A	Shroud For Grandmama	Insp Stephen ELIOT and Arthur CRUMP
A	Shroud For Grandmama	Insp Stephen ELIOT and Arthur CRUMP
A	Shroud For Rowena	Michael DUNDAS
A	Shroud For Shylock	Jill ARCHER
	Shroud For The Archbishop	Sister FIDELMA
The	Shroud Off Her Back	Stephen RANSOME
	Shrouded Death	Joshua CLUNK
	Shrunken Heads	Dr Alex DELAWARE
The	Shudders	Commiss Thatcher COLT
	Shylock Homes: His Posthumous Memoirs	Shylock HOMES
	Shylock Homes: His Posthumous Memoirs	Shylock HOMES
The	Shyster Lawyer	Jim ASBESTOS
	Siberian Road	Dorian SILK
The	Sicilian Affair	Laurie GRANT and Stewart NOBLE
	Sicilian Slaughter	Mack (The Executioner) BOLAN
	Sick Heart River	Sir Edward LEITHEN
	Sick Of Shadows	Elizabeth MACPHERSON
	Siege	James BURLANE
The	Sign At Six	Percy DARROW
The	Sign In The Sky	Sexton BLAKE
The	Sign Of Four	Sherlock HOLMES
The	Sign Of Fourty Four	Herlock SHOLMES
	Sign Of The Cobra	Nick CARTER
The	Sign Of The Mute Medusa	Claudine ST CYR
The	Sign Of The Prayer Shawl	Nick CARTER

The Books

The	Sign Of The '400': Being A Continuation Of The Adventures Of Sherlock Holmes	Sherlock HOLMES
	Sign On For Tokyo	Alec HAIG
	Silas Quirk, The Diamond Detective: Or, The Mystery Of The False Jewels	Silas QUIRK
	Silence After Dinner	Insp Harry CHARLTON and Insp Peter BRADFIELD
	Silence Of A Purple Shirt	Nicholas SLADE
A	Silence Of Birds	John RADMELL
The	Silence Of The Lambs	Hannibal LECTER and Clarice STERLING
	Silent Are The Dead	'Flashgun' CASEY
The	Silent Bullet: Adventures Of Craig Kennedy, Scientific Detective	Prof Craig KENNEDY
The	Silent Death	Lamont (The Shadow) CRANSTON
The	Silent House	Lucian DENZIL
The	Silent House In Pimlico: A Detective Story	Lucian DENZIL
The	Silent Jury	Sexton BLAKE
The	Silent Murders	Insp DEWAR
A	Silent Reach	George GALBRAITH
The	Silent Siren	Capt RIZZI
The	Silent Slain	Ch Matt RUFFINS
The	Silent Witness	Col BRAXTON
A	Silent Witness	Dr Clement BURTON
The	Silent Witness	Kent MURDOCK and Jack FENNER
	Silent, The Harbor Detective: Or, Tracking A Gang Of Thieves	SILENT
	Silky!	Sidney 'Silky' PINCUS and Mike CLANCY
	Silk'	Anthony ENGLAND
	Silver Blaze	Sherlock HOLMES
The	Silver Goblet	Harry ADKINS
The	Silver Greyhound	Insp STORM
	Silver Haze	Turlock LOAMS
The	Silver Jackass	Otis BEAGLE
The	Silver Jackass	Otis BEAGLE
The	Silver Key	Martin DALE
The	Silver Leopard	Sir Arthur SINCLAIR
The	Silver Phantom Murder	Knock-Out KAVANAGH
	Silver Pigs	M Didius FALCO
The	Silver Puma	Huntingdon CAGE
	Silver Sandals	Thornley COLTON
The	Silver Setup	Mike GARRETT
The	Silver Sickle Case	Sgt VENN
	Silver Star	John LOCKE
	Silver Street	Tony LONTO
The	Silver Street Killer	Tony LONTO
	Silver Tom, The Detective: Or, Kink By Kink	SILVER TOM
The	Silver Venus	Insp William BREWER
The	Silver Wishbone	Herlock SHOLMES
The	Silvered Cage	Insp GARTH
	Silverskull	John (The Expediter) EAGLE
	Simon	F T CARRINGTON
	Simon Lash, Detective	Simon LASH
	Simon Lash, Private Detective	Simon LASH
	Simon Wheeler, Detective	Simon WHEELER
A	Simple Suburban Murder	Tom MASON
	Sin And Johnny Inch	Det Johnny INCH
	Sin In Their Blood	Matt RANZINO
	Sin Me A Murder	Ty LEANDER
	Sin Of Angels	Dr Hillis OWEN
The	Sin Sniper	Insp Walter MCDUMONT
	Sing A Song Of Homicide	Samuel G ABBOTT
	Sing A Song Of Murder	Samuel G ABBOTT
	Sing A Song Of Murder	Pecos APPLEBY
	Sing A Song Of Murder	Darby CASTLE
	Singapore	Virgil TIBBS
	Singapore Transfer	Jeffrey DEAN
The	Singer Not The Song	KEOGH
The	Singing Bone	Dr John Evelyn THORNDYKE
The	Singing Corpse	Steve BORDEN
The	Singing Room	Michael REVEL
The	Singing Sands	Insp Alan GRANT
A	Single Clew	KINGSLEY
The	Singular Affair Of The Aluminium Crutch	Sherlock HOLMES
The	Singular Affair Of The Tintype Woman	Sherlock HOLMES
The	Singular Case Of The Duplicate Holmes	Sherlock HOLMES
The	Singular Case Of The Plural Twosome	Sherlock HOLMES
A	Singular Crime	Robert SCOTT
A	Singular Fury	Sam BENEDICT
The	Singularge Experience Of Miss Anne Duffield	Shamrock WOMLBS
	Sinister Cargo	Richard VANESS
	Sinister Crag	James GREER
	Sinister Errand	Michael KELLS
	Sinister House	Kerry O'NEIL and Gail HOLLISTER
	Sinister Murders	Michael KELLS
	Sinister Playhouse	Insp Dick MASON
	Sinister Street	Quinny HITE
The	Sinister Widow	Insp Dick MASON and Laura SCUDAMORE
The	Sinister Widow At Sea	Insp Dick MASON and Laura SCUDAMORE
The	Sinister Widow Comes Back	J Rockingham STONE, Laura SCUDAMORE and Insp Dick MASON
	Sinners And Shrouds	Sam CLAY
	Sinners Go Secretly	Dr Eustace HAILEY
	Sins For Father Knox	Eve ADAM
	Sins Of Commission	Paul RICHARDSON
	Sins Of The Dead	Det Fey CROAKER
The	Sins Of The Fathers	Matt SCUDDER
	Sins Of The Heart	Ch Insp Frank SHAPIRO and Det Insp Liz GRAHAM
The	Sinsiter Ray	Lynn LASH
	Sir Adam Disappeared	Insp SNELL
A	Siren Sounds Off	Max ROYAL
The	Sirens Sang Of Murder	Prof Hilary TAMAR
	Sir, You Bastard	Insp Terry SNEED
	Sister Simon's Murder Case	Sister SIMON
The	Sittaford Mystery	Insp NARROCOTT
	Sitting Up Dead	Matt ERRIDGE

	Situations Vacant	Det Supt Bill ROWLANDS
	Six Bloody Summer Days	Nick CARTER
	Six Came To Dinner	Insp Peter CURWEN and Hugh STANTON
	Six Dead Men	Wenceslas VOROBEITCHIK
	Six Deadly Dames	Donny 'Tough Dick' DONAHUE
	Six Foot Deep	Hans LUGAR
	Six Minutes Past Twelve	Prof Luther BASTION
	Six Murders In The Suburbs	Insp J RASON
The	Six Proud Walkers	Col Alistair GRANBY
The	Six Queer Things	Insp Charles MORGAN
	Six Sign-Post Murder	STAVELEY
	Six Silver Handles	Humphrey CAMPBELL
	Six Were Present	Cdr Bobby OWEN
	Six Were To Die	Dr Daniel BRITLING
	Six Were To Die	Dr Daniel BRITLING
	Sixteen Bells	Earl (of) MILLINGTON
The	Sixth Precinct	Lt Joe DANTE
The	Sixty-Fifth Tape	Lucas GARFIELD
	Sixty-Nine Diamonds	Col Winston CREEVY
The	Skeleton At The Feast	Kenneth CARLISLE
The	Skeleton Closet Of Jules De Grandin	Jules DE GRANDIN
	Skeleton Key	Todd MCKINNON
	Skeleton Out Of The Cupboard	Mr Horace B TREADGOLD
	Skeletons	Jimmie BUTTERS
	Skeletons	Det PAIGE
	Skillful Charlie, The Giant Detective: Or, Unraveling The Most Mysterious Of Crimes	SKILLFUL CHARLIE
	Skin Deep	Supt James PIBBLE
	Skin O' My Tooth	Patrick MULLIGAN
	Skin Tight	Mick STRANAHAN
	Skin Trap	Casson DUKER
	Skinner's Rules	Insp SKINNER
	Skinwalkers	Lt Joe LEAPHORN and Sgt Jim CHEE
The	Skull Beneath The Skin	Cordelia GRAY
	Skull Still Bone	Dr QUARSHIE
	Sky High	Mrs ARTSIDE
The	Sky Trackers	Kaye STANDISH and Mike STANDISH
	Skyrocket Steele	'Skyrocket' STEELE
	Skyrocket Steele Conquers The Universe	'Skyrocket' STEELE
The	Skyscraper Murder	Insp MARX and Dr RHINEWALD
	Slade Of The Yard	Insp John SLADE and LESSINGER
	Slagged	Regan REILLY
	Slane's Long Shots	Sir Jasper SLANE
	Slashback	Jake LASSITER
The	Slasher	RYKER
	Slaughter	SLAUGHTER
	Slaughter In The Sun	Sexton BLAKE
The	Slaughter Run	Hank (The Mercenary) FROST
The	Slaughtered Lovelies	Dallas WEBSTER
	Slaughter's Big Rip-Off	SLAUGHTER
The	Slave Market Of Mucar	The PHANTOM
The	Slavers	Montgomery NASH
The	Slaves Of Paris	Monsieur LECOQ
	Slaves Of The Lamp	Yorke NORROY
A	Slay At The Races	Dewey JAMES
	Slay Ride	Det FLYNN and Det TANNER
A	Slaying In September	Tim BLACKGROVE
	Slayride	David CLEVELAND
	Slease	Sam HUNTER
	Sleep Before Evening	Devillo GREEN
	Sleep Is For The Rich	Henry CHALICE and Crying EDDIE
	Sleep Long, My Love	Ch Fred FELLOWS
	Sleep No More	Neal COTTEN
	Sleep With Slander	Jim SADER
	Sleep With Strangers	Jim SADER
	Sleep With The Devil	Les FERRON
The	Sleeping Bacchus	Raoul WEILER
The	Sleeping Bomb	Silas MANNERS
The	Sleeping Car Murders	Insp GRAZZONI
The	Sleeping Death	The Hon Everard BLATCHINGTON
	Sleeping Dog	Leo G BLOODWORTH and Sarah 'Serendipity' DAHLQUIST
	Sleeping Dogs	Kenneth CARLISLE
	Sleeping Dogs	Ch Insp David FYFE
	Sleeping Dogs Die	Sally TEPPER
	Sleeping Dogs Lie	Hugo WELCHMAN
	Sleeping Dogs Lying	Dr Alun BARRY
	Sleeping Murder	Jane MARPLE
	Sleeping Pretty	Ch Insp David FYFE
The	Sleeping Tiger	John PRESCOTT
The	Sleeping Witness	Rick VANNER
The	Sleepless Man	Double O'DAY
The	Sleepwalker	Sexton BLAKE
	Sleight Of Hand	Ch Insp Ralph ARNOTT
	Sleightly Guilty	Harry CALDERWOOD
	Sleightly Murder	Harry CALDERWOOD
A	Slender Clue: Or, The Mystery Of Mardi-Gras	Rufus CARNES and Richard STANHOPE
	Slender Margin	Sgt Paul DEAN
	Slender Saul, The Keenest Of Detectives	SLENDER SAUL
The	Sleuth Hound	Joseph ROULETABILLE
The	Sleuth Of St James's Square	Sir Henry MARQUIS
	Sleuth Of The World	Anthea JUBB
The	Sleuths	Shamrock JOLNES
	Slice	Jack EICHORD
The	Slick And The Dead	Martyn FINCH
	Slickensides	Insp Thomas BRUNT
A	Slightly Bitter Taste	QUINN
The	Slip Coach	Dennis DOYNE
	Slippery As Sin	FANTOMAS
	Slit My Throat Gently	Pete MCGRATH
	Slob	Jack EICHORD
	Slow Burn	Chet JOHNSON
	Slow Burner	Col Charles RUSSELL
	Slow Dance In Autumn	Hank PRINCE
	Slow Dancer	Connie KALE
	Slow Death At Geneva	Dennis TYLER

The Slow Gallows	John SHU
Slow Grave	J D HAWKINS
Slow Poison	Insp George MARSHALL
Slug It Slay	Lt MADIGAN
The Slugger	Dave NORTON
The Slype	Mr MACAULEY
The Smack Man	Det Sgt Joe KELLER and Det Sgt Joe RYKER
The Smack Man	Det Sgt Joe KELLER and Det Sgt Joe RYKER
Small And Deadly	Ray FELTON
Small Favors	Sydney BRYANT
A Small Sacrifice	Jane LAWLESS
A Small Slain Body	Insp PINAUD
Small Venom	Casson DUKER
The Smaller Penny	Supt Lawrence GILMARTIN
The Smart Money	Laura DI PALMA
Smart Money Doesn't Sing Or Dance	Billy NEVERS
The Smartest Grave	Insp David BROCK
Smart-Aleck Kill	MALLORY
Smear Job	David CALLAN
The Smell Of Murder	Philo VANCE and Gracie ALLEN
A Smell Of Peardrops	Garaway TRENTON
Smile And Murder	Sexton BLAKE
The Smile Of Cheng Su	Maj 'Brains' CUNNINGHAM
The Smile On The Face Of The Tiger	HARVEY
The Smiler Bunn Brigade	'Smiler' BUNN
Smiler Bunn, Byewayman	'Smiler' BUNN
Smiler Bunn, Crook	'Smiler' BUNN
Smiler Bunn, Gentleman-Adventurer	'Smiler' BUNN
Smiler Bunn, Gentleman-Crook	'Smiler' BUNN
Smiler Bunn, Manhunter	'Smiler' BUNN
Smiley's People	George SMILEY
Smiling, The Boy Fell Dead	Dave CANNON
The Smith Slayer	Insp David REEFE
The Smoke	Charlie DANCE
The Smoke Filled Room	Lt LIEBERMANN
Smoke Screen	Lt Bill FRENCH
Smoke Without Fire	Andrew BASNETT
Smoke Without Fire	Andrew BASNETT
Smoked Out	Julian 'Digger' BURROUGHS
Smoker's Cough	Det Sgt Harry CHAMBERLANE
Smuggler's Pay For Firebrace	Capt FIREBRACE
Snake Doctor	Ace CHANEY
Snake Doctor	Judge PRIEST
The Snake In The Grass	Lucius HUNT
Snake In The Grasses	Ezell BARNES
The Snake Is Living Yet	Liane CRAWFORD and Insp Hugh GORDON
The Snake Of Luvercy	Jean MAREUIL
The Snake On 99	Insp Elwyn MORGAN
The Snapdragon Murders	Paul HEDLEY
The Snarl Of The Beast	Race WILLIAMS
The Snatch	NAMELESS DETECTIVE
A Snatch Of Music	Ian FIRTH and John SMITH
Sneaks	Dearborn V PINCH
Snipe Hunt	Albie HARRIS
The Sniper	ADAM 12
Sniper	John JERICHO
The Sniper	Jane MADISON
The Sniper	Det Sgt Joe RYKER
The Sniper	Det Sgt Joe RYKER
Snow Along The Border	Supt John SNOW
Snow Falcon	Kenneth AUBREY
Snow Fire	Linda EARLE
Snow Job	Mark RAEBURN
Snow On High Ground	Supt John SNOW
Snowball	Tad ANDERS
Snowball	James REED
Snowball In Hell	DENNISON
Snowfall	Kate PATERSON
Snowjob	Ch of Plce Reid BENNETT
Snowline	Idewal REES
The Snowman Cometh	Sexton BLAKE
The So Blue Marble	Insp TOBIN
So Cold, My Bed	Neal COTTEN
So Little Cause For Caroline	Harold SHILLING
So Little To Die For	Insp ROSS
So Long At The Fair	George JONES and Victoria BARTON
So Lovely To Kill	Johnny FURY
So Much For Gennaro	Guy PLANTE and Freye MATTHEWS
So Rich, So Dead	Bill MADDERN
So Small A Carnival	Capt Ralph 'Rat' TRAPP
So Sweet, So Deadly	Casey GRANT
So The Lady Died	Insp Michael REGAN
So Young A Body	Mr HUMBLE and Dorrit BLY
The Soap Opera Slaughter	Hilary QUAYLE
Sober As A Judge	Roger THURSBY
The Social Gangster	Prof Craig KENNEDY
The Society Detective	The SOCIETY DETECTIVE
Society Of The Dispossessed	John CRISPIN
The Society Of The Singing Death	Dan HOLDEN
The Society Of The Spiders	Bill SAVILLE
Soeur Angele And The Bell Ringer's Niece	Soeur ANGELE
Soeur Angele And The Embarrassed Ladies	Soeur ANGELE
The Soft Centre	Frank TERRELL
Soft In The Middle	Michael DOVE
The Softcover Kill	Steve WAYNE
Soho Spy	Insp Robert STRONG
The Solander Box Mystery	Jerry SCANT
The Solange Stories	Solange FONTAINE
The Solar Pons Omnibus	Solar PONS
Solden's Women	Sgt Louis SOLDEN
Solemn High Murder	Father Simon BEDE
Solo Blues	John Owen COSATELLI
Solo Job	Sally 'Sherlock Holmes' LANE
Solomon's Vineyard	Steve CRAVEN
Solved In Thirty-Six Hours!	Sexton BLAKE
Solved Mysteries; Or, Revelations Of A City Detective	James M'GOVAN
Some Adventures Of Samson Cogg	Samson COGG
Some Beasts No More	Insp Harry JAMES
Some Cases Of Sherwood Lang, Detective	Sherwood LANG
Some Dark Antiquities	Charles RAMSAY
Some Day I'll Kill You	Jim STEELE
Some Die Hard	Jake BARROW
Some Die Hard	Rock DUGAN
Some Die Slow	James REHM
Some Die Young	John P PHELAN
Some Further Adventures Of Mr P J Davenant	P J DAVENANT
Some Like It Hot	Scott BENNET
Some Things Come Back	Teddy LONDON
Some Unaccountable Exploits Of Sherlock Holmes	Sherlock HOLMES
Some Unknown Hand	Insp REYNOLDS
Somebody At The Door	Insp HOLLY
Somebody's Sister	Walter BRACKETT
Somebody's Walking Over My Grave	Max LONDON
Someone Else's Grave	Judd SPRINGFIELD
Someone Must Die	Commissaire Saturnin DAX
Someone's Death	Nils-Frederik BLIXEN
Someone's Stolen Nellie Gray	Steve RHODEN
Something Doing	CREWE (BIRGE MOREAU)
Something For Nothing	Jack HAGEE
Something In The Air	John Putnam THATCHER
Something Of The Night	Kells CAVENAUGH
Something Rotten	Jack HENLEY
Something To Hide	Dr ALCAZAR
Something To Kill Abou	Sexton BLAKE
Something Wicked	Andrew BASNETT
Something Wicked	Andrew BASNETT
Something Wicked	Jimmy CARROLL
Something Wrong At Chillery	Anthony RAVENHILL
Something's Happened To Kate	Lt Al WHITE
Sometimes You Could Die	Ron HOGGETT
Somewhere In The Night	Nick ALLARD
Somewhere In This City	Det Insp Harry MARTINEAU
Son Of Blackshirt	Lord Anthony BLACKSHIRT
Son Of Holmes	Auguste LUPA
A Son Of Ishmael	CROSSLEY
A Song At Twilight	Alec HILLSDEN
Soothsayer	Jane BAILEY
The Sorcerer Of The Castle	Kitty TELEFAIR
Sorcerer's House	Simon GALE
Sorry, Mr Sherlock Is Engaged Just Now	Sherlock HOLMES
A Sort Of Madness	Rupert BRADLEY
The Soul Scar	Prof Craig KENNEDY
The Sound Of Murder	'Alphabet' HICKS
The Sound Of The Weir	Ann HALES
A Sounder Of Swine	Benjamin SHOCK and Charity TUCKER
Sour Cream With Everything	Edmund BROWN
Sourdough Gold	Policeman Black John SMITH
The South Sea Soup Company	Herlock SHOLMES
Southeast Of Mandalay	Colin SMALLPIECE
Southern Exposure	Wayne TEMPLE
Southern Ghost	Annie LAURANCE
The Souvenir	Jefferson SHIELDS
Sow The Wind	Sarah LOWDEN
Space For Hire	Sam SPACE
The Spandau Warrant	Mark BLOOD
Spaniard's Gift	Jannine WEST
The Spanish Connection	Nick CARTER
Spanner	J T 'Jake' SPANNER
Sparkling Cyanide	Col RACE
Speak Ill Of The Dead	Sexton BLAKE
The Speaking Eye	Nicky MAHOUN
Speaking Of Murder	Tom CRAIG
Special Circumstances	Benjamin O'MALLEY
Special Delivery	Anthony HAVILLAND
A Special Kind Of Nightmare	Ludovic FENDER
Special Victims	Det Jake PHILLIPS
The Speckled Band	Sherlock HOLMES
Speedy Death	Mrs Adela Beatrice Lestrange BRADLEY
Spence And The Holiday Murders	Supt Ben SPENCE
Spence At Marlby Manor	Supt Ben SPENCE
Spence In Petal Park	Supt Ben SPENCE
The Spherical Ghoul	Jerry GRANT
A Spider At The Elvira	Andrew SALMOND
Spider Flies Again	'Spider' STOCKWELL
Spider House	Capt CATLIN
Spider In The Morning	Sam SHOLTO
Spider In The Web	Barney HYDE
Spider Webs	Charles DONNELLY
Spiders In The Night	Pete MARVIN
The Spider's Den	John (The Spider) WARWICK
The Spider's Fury	John (The Spider) WARWICK
The Spider's Web	Insp Malcolm STEELE
Spies Die At Dawn	Max HEALD
Spies In Spain	Col ORMISTON
The Spies Of Peace	Christopher BOND
The Spike	Robert HOCKNEY
Spin The Web Tight	Hilda TRENTON
The Spiral Path	John BRYANT
Spiral: The World Of Alan Brett	Alan BRETT
The Spirit House And Other Stories	Dick SAUNDERS
The Spirit Murder Mystery	Anthony VEREKER
Spitfire Parade	'BIGGLES'
Splash Of Red	Supt BRANNIGAN
A Splendid Sin	FLETCHER
Split On Red	George WILLIS
The Spoils Of Ararat	Tony MCINTYRE
Spoils Of War	Jim (The Death Dealer) RAINEY
The Spoilt Kill	NICHOLSON
The Sport Of Fate; Or, The Mystery Of Fort Hale	Mark SPICER
A Sporting Proposition	Kit QUAYLE

Sports Freak	T T BALDWIN
Spotlight On A Simple Case: Or, Wiggins, Who Was That Horse I Saw You With Last Night?	Sherlock HOLMES
Spotlight On Murder	Lucius HUNT
Spotlight On Murder	Insp Maxwell QUAYNE
The Spotted Men	'Doc' SAVAGE
A Sprig Of Sea Lavender	Ch Const Piet DEVENTER
Springblade	Bo 'Springblade' THORNTON
The Springers	James WAINWRIGHT
Spun Silk	Anthony ENGLAND
The Spy	Brett CARSTAIRS
Spy 222	Bartholomew DANE
Spy And Die	Patrick HARDY
The Spy And The Thief	RAND
The Spy And The Thief	Nick VELVET
The Spy At Number 10	Papa PONTIVY
A Spy At Twilight	Alec HILLSDEN
The Spy Catchers	Bert MCCALL and Tony COSTAINE
Spy Catchers	Papa PONTIVY
A Spy For A Spy	James WAINWRIGHT
Spy For Sale	John TIBBETT
Spy From The Grave	Mark HOOD
The Spy Game	Appleton 'Apple' PORTER
Spy Hook	Bernard SAMSON
The Spy Hunter	Harry NETTLEFIELD
The Spy In Khaki	Clive GRANVILLE
The Spy In The Java Sea	Joaquin HAWKS
The Spy In The Ointment	Alan GROFIELD
The Spy In The Vodka	Cyril MCCORKLE and Michael PADILLO
Spy Is A Dirty Word	Simon LEIGH
The Spy Is Dead	Sergei ROLF
The Spy Is Dead	Sergei ROLF
A Spy Is Forever	Peter LAYTON
Spy Line	Bernard SAMSON
Spy Meets Spy	Anthony HAMILTON
The Spy Net	Capt Fox ELTON
Spy Now, Pay Later	Adam HOOD
Spy Or Die	Michael EVANS
Spy Sinker	Bernard SAMSON
Spy Story	Pat MORLEY
The Spy Trap	Michael EVANS
The Spy Who Came In From The Copa	Randy KIDD
The Spy Who Died Twice	Jeff SAUNDERS
The Spy Who Hated Fudge	Rand STANNARD
The Spy Who Hated Licorice	Rand STANNARD
The Spy Who Loved America	Gregory HILLER
The Spy Who Read Latin And Other Stories	RAND
The Spy Who Swopped Shoes	Stephen FLETCHER
The Spy With The Blue Kazoo	Randy KIDD
Squall Line	THORN
The Square Emerald	Leslie MAUGHAN
Squeakie's First Case	Desdemona 'Squeakie' MEADOW
Squeeze Play	Max KLEIN
Squire Of Death	Bernard SIMMONS
The St Cloud Affair	BRICONI
St John's Baptism	Jeremiah ST JOHN
Stab In The Back	Insp Neil LAMBERT
Stacked Deck	Johnny LIDDELL
Stag Dinner Death	John BRELAND and Mike FREEMAN
Stage Fright	Nell BRAY
The Stainless Steel Rat	Slippery Jim DI GRIZ
A Stainless Steel Rat Is Born	Slippery Jim DI GRIZ
The Stairs Lead Nowhere	Garrett MAYNARD
Stalk A Long Shadow	Jeff CASS
Stalking Horse	Coley KILLEBREW
The Stalking Man	Rony RUSSO
Stalking The Angel	Elvis COLE
Stalking The Unicorn: A Fable For Tonight	John Justin MALLORY
Stamped For Death	Jonathan KNOX
Stand By - London Calling	Angus MACWHORTER
The Standish Gaunt Case	Sebald CRAFT
Stand-In For Murder	Sexton BLAKE
Stand-Up	Miles JACOBY
Stanhope Of Chester	JAMIESON
Star Bright	Philip MARLOWE
Star For A Warrior	David RETURN
The Star King	Keith GERSEN
Star Light, Star Bright	Johnny MILANO
Star Of Earth	Jim HANVEY
Star Of Egypt	Ben 'T-Man' SLAYTON
Star Well	Viscount Anthony VILLIERS
Stardust Kills	Philip MARLOWE
A Starlet For A Penny	Sexton BLAKE
Starr Bedford Dies	John YARDLEY and R I PERKINS
The Starry-Eyed Chipmunk	Dr Quentin TOBY
The Stars Are Dark	Everard Peter QUAYLE
The Stars Scream Murder	Prof Craig KENNEDY
The Starshine Connection	Ben 'T-Man' SLAYTON
Stash Spots A Murder	Stash KOVAL
State Of Fear	Sexton BLAKE
State Of Grace	Ralph POTEET
State Secrets	Sexton BLAKE
Stately Homes...And The Box: A Mystery	Stately HOMES
The Statesman's Game	Rupert ROYCE
Station Wagon In Spain	Allan LAMBERT
Stay Of Execution	Insp HAZELRIGG
The Steam Pig	Lt Tromp KRAMER
The Steam-Boat Detective: Or, Tracing A Crime On The Water	The STEAM-BOAT DETECTIVE
The Steel Casket And Other Stories	Nick CARTER
Steel Shutters	Prof Luther BASTION
The Steel Spring	Ch Insp Peter JENSEN
Steel Tiger	John LOCKE
Steeley Flies Again	'Steeley' DELAROY
A Stench Of Poppies	Jennifer Norrington Aless GANZARELLO and Coleridge TUCKER

Step Into Quicksand	Det Jub FREEMAN and Det Mitch TAYLOR
Step Up, Sucker	Shaun O'MALLEY
Steps In The Dark	Richard VANESS
Steps To Murder	Al BRANSON
The Steps To Murder	Prof Stuff DRISCOLL
The Sticking Point	Jud BLADE
Stickman	Mike DIME
Stiff As A Broad	Honey WEST and Erik MARCH
The Stiff Upper Lip	Benjamin Franklin CAGE
The Stiffsons, And Other Stories	Mr STIFFSON
Still Dead	Miles BREDON and Angela BREDON
Still Waters	John TARLETON
Still Waters Run Deadly	Commissaire ORLOFF
Stillwatch	Pat TRAYMORE
The Stillwater Tragedy	TAGGETT
The Stingaree Murders	Paul GREEN
Stinger	Nash KANZLER
Stinger	Steven KIRK
The Stir Outside The Café Royal	Miss Nora VAN SNOOP
The Stoat	Col GORE
The Stock Market Detective	Michael Dane JAMES
The Stockbroker's Clerk	Sherlock HOLMES
Stockholders In Death	Richard Henry (The Avenger) BENSON
The Stolen Boat-Train	LEGARDE
The Stolen Cigar Case	Hemlock JONES
The Stolen Fiddle	JONES
Stolen Flower	Frank DE NARDO
The Stolen Girl	Dixon BRETT
The Stolen March	Picklock HOLES
Stolen Moments	Amanda ROBERTS and Joe DANELLI
The Stolen Sapphire	Tommy PRESTON
The Stolen Squadron	Paul KILGERRIN
The Stolen White Elephant, Etc	Insp BLUNT
Stone Angel	Pierre-Ange SAWYER
Stone Blunts Scissors	Bow Street Runner Victor CARYLL
Stone City	Prof Charles BAUMAN
Stone Cold Dead	Insp Walter MCDUMONT
Stone Cold Dead In The Market	Bob ROSS
Stone Dead	Don HAWKER
Stone Dead	Insp Maxwell QUAYNE
The Stone Dormitory	Rampion SAVAGE
The Stone Killer	Derek TORRY
A Stone Of The Heart	Supt Ceal MEGARRY
Stonedust	Ben ABBOTT
Stonefish	Paul CROOK
Stoner McTavish	Stoner MCTAVISH
Stones Of Satan	Richard Curtis (The Phantom) VAN LOAN
Stop At Nothing	Simon HERALD
Stop That Man!	J A 'Rem' REMINGTON
Stopover: Tokyo	Mr MOTO
Stories From Scotland Yard	Insp MOSER
Stories From The Diary Of A Doctor (1st Series)	Dr Clifford HALIFAX
Stories From The Diary Of A Doctor (2nd Series)	Dr Clifford HALIFAX
Stories From The Note-Book Of A Detective	Det Dick DONOVAN
The Stories Of Donald Shoubridge	STANDIFORD
Stories Of Scotland Yard	Det Insp SLADE
Stories Of The Railway	Thorpe HAZELL
Storm Surge	Quin ST JAMES and Mike MCCLEARY
Stormlight	Mr DEHAVILLAND
Storms And Son	Hugh STORM
The Story Behind The Verdict	Keightley WILBUR
The Story Of The Lamplighter	Picklock HOLES
The Story Of The Lost Picklock	Picklock HOLES
The Story Of The Princess	Picklock HOLES
The Story Of The Stone	Li KAO
The Stowmarket Mystery	Reginald BRETT
Straight	Steve CRANMER
Straight Ahead For Danger	GREENSLEEVES
Strained Relations	Toby WILDE
Strands Of Red - Hair!	Insp WIELD
The Strange Adventures Of Bromley Barnes	Bromley BARNES
The Strange Adventures Of Charlotte Holmes	Charlotte HOLMES
The Strange Adventures Of Mr Collin	Mr COLLIN
The Strange Adventures Of Mr Middleton	Mr MIDDLETON
The Strange Affair Of The Widow's Diamonds	Sexton BLAKE
Strange Bedfellows	Ben SLADE
The Strange Case Of Peter The Lett	Insp Jules MAIGRET
The Strange Case Of Steinkelwintz	Max GRAME
The Strange Case Of The Antlered Man	Insp William (The Grouser) BEEKE
The Strange Case Of The Megatherium Thefts	Sherlock HOLMES
The Strange Case Of William Cook	Franklin PARRY and Leonard HARRIS
The Strange Cases Of Dr Wycherly	Dr Xavier WYCHERLY
The Strange Cases Of Magistrate Pao	Magistrate PAO
The Strange Cases Of Mason Brant	Mason BRANT
A Strange Case: With Full Particulars First Made Public	Algernon HIGGINS
Strange Clues: Or, Chronicles Of A City Detective	James M'GOVAN
Strange Corpse On Murder Mile	Cdr MORETON
The Strange Death Of Martin Green	Maj Gregory LEWIS
The Strange Death Of The Heir Apparent	Sherlock HOLMES
A Strange Desire	Det Ch Insp John MORRISSEY
The Strange Disappearance Of Mary Young	Det Tommy RANKIN
The Strange Face Of Murder	Sexton BLAKE
Strange Felony	Sgt Ivor MADDOX
Strange Felony	Sgt Ivor MADDOX
Strange Holiday	Benvenuto BROWN
Strange Inheritance	Joseph RADKIN
Strange Loyalties	Jack LAIDLAW
The Strange Murder Of Hatton, KC	Mark BRADDON
A Strange Place For Murder	Lisa THORNE
The Strange Prisoner	John BENHAM
Strange Return	Sheriff Jess RODEN
The Strange Schemes Of Randolph Mason	Randolph MASON
The Strange Smell Of Murder	Andrew SALMOND
The Strange Will	Dr Everett EDWARDS
Strangely She Died	Steven MALONE

	Stranger At Home	Michael VICKERS
A	Stranger In My Grave	Steve PINATA
A	Stranger Is Watching	Katie DEMAIO
	Strangle Hold	Sgt BRINKHAUS
	Strangled Prose	Claire MALLOY
The	Strangled Witness	Col John PRIMROSE
	Stranglehold	Mr DEE
	Stranglehold	Eve FITZSIMMONS
The	Stranglers	Page MURDOCK
	Strangler's Kill	Dean Wardlow ROCK
	Strangler's Moon	Paul MASON
The	Strausser Transfer	Phil SHERMAN
The	Straw Donkey Case	Max BRINDLE
	Strawgirl	Bo BRADLEY
	Stray Cat	Charlie GAMBLE
	Stray Shot	Simon PARBITTER and Keith CALDER
	Streaked With Crimson	Prof Harley MANNERS
The	Street Of The Crying Woman	Jose Manuel MADERO
	Streetcar To Hell	Johnny DEKKER
	Streets Of Shadow	Michael BRENT
The	Strenuous Life	Commiss Theodore ROOSEVELT
	Strike Terror	Zachary JONES
	Strike Three You're Dead	Harvey BLISSBERG
	Strikefast	Simon LARREN
The	String Glove Mystery	Simon BRADE
	Strip For Violence	Hal DARLING
	Strip Tease	Hubert Bonisseur DE LA BATH
A	Stripe For A Stripe	James CHARLESWORTH
	Stripped For Murder	Ben HELM
The	Striptease Murders	Al MCFEE
The	Strip-Tease Murders	Gypsy Rose LEE and Biff BRANNIGAN
A	Stroke Of Death	Lucy SUMMERS
The	Stroke Of One	GARSTANG
A	Stroke Of Policy; Or, The Stolen Charter	Nick CARTER
	Struck Dead	Jack IRWIN and Robert MARTINEAU
	Struck Down: A Tale Of Devon	Insp POLLOCK
The	Struldbrugg Reaction	Haricot BONES
	Stryker	Colin STRYKER
	Stud Game	Stanley BASS
	Student Body	Nora PICKHAM
The	Studio Murder Mystery	Captain SMITH
A	Study In Lavender Lace	Sherlock HOLMES
A	Study In Scarlet	Sherlock HOLMES
A	Study In Sorcery	Lord DARCY
A	Study In Stagnation	Sharlock HOLMES
	Study In Suspense	Phineas SPINNET
A	Study In Sussex	Sherlock HOLMES
A	Study In Terror	Sherlock HOLMES
	Study Of Death	Jimmy LANGRY
The	Stuffed Men	J C K 'Jigger' MASTERS
The	Subject Of Harry Egypt	Harry EGYPT
	Submarine Flotilla	Earl (of) MILLINGTON
	Subscription To Murder	Desmond SHANNON
	Such A Nice Client	Lucy SUMMERS
	Such Natural Deaths	Peter ALLEN
	Sucker Bait	Carl GOOD
	Sudden Death	Lt Jacob HOROWITZ and Helen HOROWITZ
	Sudden Death At Scotland Yard	Supt Samuel QUAN
	Sudden Death Finish	Cam MACCARDLE
The	Sudden Death Of Cardinal Tosca	Sherlock HOLMES
	Suddenly By Violence	Danny BOYD
	Suddenly In Her Sorbet	Lady Margaret PRIAM
	Suddenly, At Singapore	Paul HARRIS
	Suddenly, In The Air	Lisa MASSINGHAM
	Suddenly, In Vienna	Richard LOGAN
A	Sudden, Fearful Death	Insp William MONK
	Sugar For The Lady	'Sugar' KANE
	Sugar, You're Swell	Johnny FARRELL
	Suicide Excepted	Insp MALLETT
	Suicide Kill	Sgt Lloyd HOPKINS
	Suicide King	Jake SAMSON
The	Suicide Murders	Benny COOPERMAN
The	Suicide Notice	Benny COOPERMAN
The	Suicide Plague	Harry PORTER
	Suicide Season	Devlin KIRK
The	Suicide Seat	Nick CARTER
The	Suicide Squad	Dave (The Pro) BOLT
	Suicide, Inc	Jared SMITH
A	Suitcase In Berlin	Ed FITZGERALD
The	Sultan's Skull	Insp Dan CARR
The	Summer Soldier	Ray GUINNESS
	Summer's Reason	Offr Jessie SUMMER
The	Summons	Supt Peter DIAMOND
	Summons From Baghdad	Mike DARROCH
The	Sun Is A Witness	Tim MULLIGAN and Elsie May HUNT
	Sunburst	Johnny FEDORA
The	Sunday Fishing Club	Ch Alphonse GRAND
The	Sunday Pigeon Murders	'Bingo' RIGGS and 'Handsome' KUSAK
	Sunday's Child	Geoffrey CHADWICK
	Sunflower	Richard OWEN
The	Sunflower Plot	Celia GRANT
	Sunk Without A Trace	Judy HUTCHINGS
The	Sunken Treasure	Abigail Patience DANFORTH
	Sunshine Enemies	Ch of Plce Mario BALZIC
	Sunshine, Sunshine	Sherlock HOLMES
	Sunspot	Insp GORMAN and Const HALE
	Superfluous Death	Mrs Sheila MALLORY
	Superintendent Slade Investigates	Supt Anthony SLADE
	Superintendent Wilson's Holiday	Supt Henry WILSON
The	Superintendent's Room	Det Insp Don KERRY
	Supermind	Kenneth MALONE
The	Supreme Adventure Of Inspector Lestrade	Insp/Supt Sholto LESTRADE
A	Surfeit Of Alibis	Homer CLAY
	Surfside 6	Ken MADISON
	Surprise Party	Spencer CROSS-WADE
	Surrounded	Mike TUCKER
The	Suspect	Sgt Karl ALBERG
	Suspect	Jim DUNN and Zebulion BUCK
	Suspect	Det Ch Insp Tom MAYBRIDGE
The	Suspected Six	Sexton BLAKE
	Suspects All	David CALDER
	Suspicion	Dr Clinton SHANNON
	Suspicion Aroused	Det Dick DONOVAN
	Suspicion In Triplicate	Insp Cheviot BURMANN
	Suspicious Circumstances	Nicky ROOD
	Sutherland's Law	John SUTHERLAND
The	Suva Harbour Mystery	Insp SPEARPOINT
	Swag	Frank RYAN
	Swan Song	Insp Lathom DYNES
The	Sweat Of Fear	Paul REEDER
The	Sweeper	Lt Ronnie GOLD
	Sweet And Deadly	Frank DESOUZA
	Sweet And Deadly	Catherine LINTON
	Sweet Deals	Benjamin O'MALLEY
	Sweet Dreams, Irene	Irene KELLY
	Sweet Jeopardy	Jackson FURY
	Sweet Justice	Lt NEUMAN
	Sweet Murder	Wood JAXON
	Sweet Narcissus	Winston Marlowe SHERMAN
	Sweet Revenge	Liane CRAWFORD and Insp Hugh GORDON
The	Sweet Short Grass	Insp Frank SHORT
	Sweet Silver Blues	GARRETT
	Sweet Sister Death	Charles GARRETT
	Sweet Summer	Det Ch Insp Alexander 'Sandy' WOODINGS
	Sweet Woman Lie	Amos WALKER
	Sweetheart	Rita Gardella O'DEA
	Sweetwater Ranch	Norman HUNT
	Sweet, Savage Death	Patience MCKENNA
	Sweet, Sweet Poison	Charles MEIKLEJOHN and Constance LEIDL
The	Swimming Pool	Terrence O'BRIEN
A	Swindler Named Zefano	Robert URBAN
	Swing Low, Sweet Harriet	Det Pharaoh LOVE
	Swing Low, Swing Dead	Johnny FLETCHER and Sam CRAGG
The	Swing Music Murder	Dan JORDAN
The	Swingers	Rick HOLMAN
	Swinging Murder	Kate THEOBALD
The	Swinging Virgin	Casey GRANT
The	Swiss Deal	Max ROTH
The	Swiss Shot	Johnny ADRANO
	Switch	Frank JANEK
	Switch	Frank MACBRIDE and Pete RYAN
	Switch 2	Frank MACBRIDE and Pete RYAN
	Switchblade	Richard BRONSON
	Switcheroo	Jamie MACRAE
The	Sword Of God	Ian QUAYLE
	Sword Of The Prophet	John CODY
	Sybil Sue Blue	Sybil Sue BLUE
	Sylvia	Alan MACKLIN
The	Symbol Of The Cat	Mr SANDYMAN
	Symphony In Murder	Edward TRELAWNY
	Symphony In Two Time	Anthony POST
The	Syndicate Murders	Mortimer DREXEL

— T —

	T E C Sharp, The Football Sleuth	Terence Everard Christopher SHARP
	Tabernacle	Tom JACKSON
The	Tabloid Murders	Capt/Insp COLIN
	Taffin	TAFFIN
The	Tahitian Powder Box Mystery	King DANWORTH and Martin LEROY
	Tailor's Dummy	Lenny SCHWARTZ
The	Tainted Jade	Mike GARRETT
	Tainted Turf	Silas WORTENHEIMER
	Take A Body	Martin FANE and Richard FANE
	Take A Body	Martin FANE and Richard FANE
	Take A Pair Of Private Eyes	Ambrose FRAYNE and Dominique FRAYNE
	Take The D Train	Sally TEPPER
	Take The Money And Run	Mark SAVAGE
	Take Thee A Sharp Knife	Prof John STUBBS
	Take-Off	Kyle BRANDEIS
The	Taking Of Satcon Station	Asher BOCKHORN
The	Tale Of Copperella	Sherlock HOLMES
A	Tale Of Two Clocks	Telzey AMBERDON and Trigger ARGEE
A	Tale Of Two Murders	Insp CRANKSHAW
A	Talent For Dying	Samuel Clemens TUCKER
A	Talent For Murder	Dr Hillis OWEN
A	Talent For The Invisible	Jake CONGER
The	Talented Mr Ripley	Tom RIPLEY
	Tales Of An Ulster Detective	Const MCNINCH
The	Tales Of Mynheer Amayat	Mynheer AMAYAT
	Tales Of The Black Widowers	The BLACK WIDOWERS
	Tales Of The Mounted	William BROCKIE
The	Talk Show Murders	Roger DALE
The	Talkative Policeman	Insp Edward BEALE
The	"Talkie" Murder Mystery	Sexton BLAKE
The	Talking Sparrow Murder	Herr KRESCH
	Talking Turkey	Dave STEVENS

A	Tall Adventure Of Sherlock Holmes	Sherlock HOLMES
The	Tall Dark Alibi	Jackson FURY
The	Tall Dolores	Ed NOON
	Tallant For Disaster	Ch of Plce Munroe TALLANT
	Tallant For Trouble	Ch of Plce Munroe TALLANT
	Talley's Truth	Tom TALLEY
	Tall, Dark And Dead	Louis LAIT
The	Taming Of Tango Harris	Det Ch Supt Thomas FOX
	Taming The Furies	Det Insp Frank DERBEN
The	Tang Murders	Jack GRIFFIN
The	Tangent Factor	Peter TANGENT
The	Tangent Objective	Peter TANGENT
	Tangle	Insp Henry BEAUMONT
	Tangle	William MITCHELL
The	Tangled Miracle	Mortimer HOOD
	Tangled Roots	Nan ROBINSON
The	Tangled Skein	Sherlock HOLMES
	Tango Key	Aline SCOTT
The	Tank Of Terror	Lee NACE
A	Tap On The Shoulder	Dr Andrew STOUGHTON
The	Tarantula Strike	Nick CARTER
	Target Blue	Sgt Bill CLARK and Det Randi STONER
	Target For Malice	Insp GIBBON
	Target For Murder	Brice KENT
	Target For Terror	Mike SETON
	Target For Tragedy	Peter STYLES
The	Target Is H	Mark (The Penetrator) HARDIN
	Target Margaret Thatcher	Johnny VINCENT
	Target Practice	Mark BRILL
	Target: Charity Ross	Charity ROSS
	Target: Doomsday Island	Nick CARTER
The	Tartan Conspiracy	Ian BLACKIE
	Tass Is Authorized To Announce	Vitaly SLAVIN
A	Taste For Honey	Mr MYCROFT
A	Taste For Murder	Mr MYCROFT
A	Taste For Murder	Sarah QUILLIAM and Meg QUILLIAM
The	Taste Of Ashes	Paul PINE
A	Taste Of Blood	John (The Hunter) YARD
A	Taste Of Brass	Pete BRASS
	Taste Of Death	Lt Charles HILLARY
	Taste Of Fears	Insp SANDS
A	Taste Of Power	Henry Lancaster PYM
A	Taste Of Sangria	Jeffrey GREEN
A	Taste Of Treason	Brockton POTTER
	Taste Of Vengeance	Nora Hughes BLAINE and Larry BLAINE
The	Tattooed Potato And Other Clues	GARSON
The	Tattooed Wrist; Or, The Deed Of A Night	Mark SPICER
The	Taurus Trip	MAC
The	Taxi-Cab Murder	Sexton BLAKE
	Tea At The Abbey	William Arthur MALLINGHAM
The	Tea Leaf	Ruth KELSTERN
	Tea On Sunday	Insp CORBY
	Teacher's Blood	Ben GORDON
	Tears Of Blood	Andrew MCCALL
A	Tea-Shop In Limehouse	Quong LEE
The	Teddy-Boy Mystery	Sexton BLAKE
	Tell It To The Birds	Steve HARMAS
	Tell Them What's-Her-Name Called	Finley WEHRMANN
The	Telltale Telegram	'One Week' WIMBLE
	Telluride Smile	Henry DYER
The	Tell-Tale Clock Mystery	Stonewall ROUNTREE
The	Telzey Toy And Other Stories	Telzey AMBERDON and Trigger ARGEE
	Tempest In A Tea Cup	William TEMPEST
The	Temple At Ilumquh	Peter WINSTON
The	Temple Falls	Rev P J MACFARLANE
The	Temple Of Dawn	Peter GRAYLEIGH
A	Temporary Ghost	Georgia Lee MAXWELL
The	Temptation Of Hercule	Insp Hercule RENARD
The	Ten Black Pearls	Henry PRINCE
	Ten Days, Mr Cain	Harry GRANT
	Ten Little Wizards	Lord DARCY
	Ten Percent Of Life	Philip MARLOWE
	Ten Times Dynamite	Nick CARTER
	Ten Years Beyond Baker Street	Sherlock HOLMES
	Tenant For Death	Insp MALLETT
	Tender Is The Knife	Insp JOLIVET
The	Tender Killer	Det Ch Insp BRENTFORD
The	Tennis Murders	Dion QUINCE
The	Tentacles	Hilda TRENTON
The	Tenth Leper	Commissaire Orestes BIGNON
The	Tenth Life	Capt/Insp Merton HEIMRICH
The	Tenth Virgin	Gabriel UTLEY
	Terence O'Rourke, Gentleman Adventurer	Terence O'ROURKE
	Terminus	Tom JONES
The	Terrarium	Lexey Jane PELAZONI
The	Terrible Death Of Crosby, The Banker	Sherlock HOLMES
The	Terrible Hobby Of Sir Joseph Londe, Baronet	Sir Joseph LONDE
The	Terrible Night	Shaun O'MARA
The	Terrible People	Insp Arnold 'Betcher' LONG
The	Terrible Tide	Holly HOWE
The	Terror	Sgt/Insp ELK
The	Terror Alliance	Roger WAGNER
	Terror At Staups House	Insp CHAMBERS
	Terror By Night	Harvey CHURCH
	Terror By Night	Eric HAZARD
The	Terror By Night	Mr TOWNSHEND
	Terror In The Night	Sebastian BLAYNE
	Terror Keep	J G REEDER
The	Terror Of Her Ways	Barney HUGGINS
The	Terror Of The Handless Corpse	Del SKINNER
The	Terror Of Tibet	Ferrers LOCKE
The	Terror Of Torlands	Capt Jacques RADFORD and
		Tony ANDERSON
	Terror On Broadway	Bart HARDIN
	Terror On Compass Lake	Aubrey NASH
The	Terror Syndicate	SYDENHAM
	Terror Tournament	Burl STANNARD
The	Terrorists	Insp Martin BECK
	Terror-Go-Round	Johnny CANUCK
The	Testament Of Caspar Schultz	Paul CHAVASSE
The	Testament Of Caspar Schultz	Paul CHAVASSE
	Testimony	Det Insp 'Jacko' JACKSON
	Testkill	Jack STENTON
	Texas Wind	CODY
	Thanks To The Saint	Simon (The Saint) TEMPLAR
	That Affair At Portstead Manor	Mercedes QUERO
	That Affair Next Door	Det Ebenezer GRYCE and
		Amelia BUTTERWORTH
	That Awful Mess On Via Merulana	Incra VALLO
	That Darn Cat	D C (Darn Cat) RANDALL
	That Girl From Istanbul	Al GLENNE
	That Mainwaring Affair	MERRICK
	That Man Returns	Bow Street Runner Victor CARYLL
	That Royle Girl	Joan Daisy ROYLE
	That Was No Lady	Mike BRETT
	That Yew Tree's Shade	Francis PETTIGREW
	That's All I Need	Danny SPADE
	That's Your Man, Inspector!	Ch Insp LORD
The	Theatre Detective; Or, A Tragedy On The Stage	The THEATRE DETECTIVE
The	Theban Mysteries	Kate FANSLER and Reed AMHEARST
The	Theft Of The World's Rarest Stamp	Kerlock SHOMES
The	Thefts Of Nick Velvet	Nick VELVET
	Their Majesties' Bucketeers	Bucketeer MAV
	Their Man In The White House	Charlie SPARROW
The	Theme Is Murder	Joel SABER
	Then Came Bronson	BRONSON
	Then Hang All The Liars	Samantha ADAMS
	Then There Were Three	Humphrey CAMPBELL and Robin BISHOP
	Therapy For Murder	Sara MARKS
	There And Back	Sam CASH
	There Are No Ghosts In The Soviet Union	Insp Lev CHISLENKO
	There Are Thirteen	Col Alistair GRANBY
	There Goes Charlie	Supt CHARTER
	There Is No Return	Adelaide ADAMS
	There Was A Crooked Man	Sgt/Insp Peter BRADFIELD
	There Was A Little Girl	Matthew HOPE
	There Were No Asper Ladies	Lucian CAROLUS
	Thereby Hangs A Corpse	Tony LANTZ
	Therefore I Killed Him	Insp/Supt ANDERS
	There's A Hippie On The Highway	Frank TERRELL
	There's No Such Things As Private Eyes	August HAMMOND
	They All Came Back	David CANE
	They Called Him Nighthawk	Gerald (Nighthawk) FROST
	They Came To Baghdad	Victoria JONES
	They Came To Spy	Sexton BLAKE
	They Can't Hang Me!	Supt WRENN
	They Died Laughing	John HUGO
	They Do It With Mirrors	Jana BLAKE
	They Hadn't A Clue	Det Insp Abraham KOZMINSKI
	They Hang Them In Gibraltar	A J RAFFLES and R J 'Rick' LEROY
	They Never Came Back	Geoff FENNELL
	They Rang Up The Police	Insp Guy NORTHEAST
	They Talked Of Poison	Insp GLOVER and Harry CURRY
	They Walk In Darkness	Peter CHARD
	They Wanted Him Dead!	Dr Joan MARVIN
	They'll Never Find Out	Mordecai Euripides TREMAINE
	Thicker Than Blood	Alo NUDGER
	Thicker Than Water	Lacey MADISON
	Thicker Than Water	Quinn PARKER
	Thicker Than Water	Mr SPRINGFIELD
A	Thief In The Night	A J RAFFLES
	Thief Of Clubs	Sexton BLAKE
The	Thief Taker	Bow Street Runner Jeremy STURROCK
The	Thief Who Came To Dinner	Webster DANIELS
The	Thief Who Couldn't Sleep	Evan TANNER
	Thin Air	Ames CORYELL
	Thin Ice	George BULMAN
The	Thin Man	Nick CHARLES and Nora CHARLES
The	Thin Woman	Ellie Simons HASKELL
The	Thing At The Door	Steve TYNER
The	Thing At Their Heels	Insp MIDWINTER
The	Thing In The Brook	Henry HALE
The	Things We Do For Love	Leo HAGGERTY
	Think Inc	Philip MCALPINE
	Think Of Death	Capt/Insp Merton HEIMRICH
The	Thinking Machine	Prof Augustus S F X VAN DUSEN
The	Thinking Machine	Prof Augustus S F X VAN DUSEN
The	Thinking Machine On The Case	Prof Augustus S F X VAN DUSEN
	Thinner Than Blood	Insp Richard MONTGOMERY
The	Third Attempt	Stephen RANT
The	Third Betrayal	David NAIRN
The	Third Bullet And Other Stories	Dr Gideon FELL
The	Third Bullet And Other Stories	Sir Henry MERRIVALE KC
The	Third Case Of Mr Paul Savoy	Paul SAVOY
The	Third Degree	Rush HENRY
The	Third Degree	Quintus OAKES
The	Third Figure	Stephen DRAKE
The	Third Force	Geoffrey BRANSCOMBE
The	Third Identity	Christie WORTHING
The	Third Owl	Jim SANDS
The	Third Truth	Jeff SAUNDERS
The	Third Truth	Jeff SAUNDERS
The	Third Victim	Lisa DAVIS
The	Third Way	Sarah CALLOWAY
	Thirsty Evil	Peter CHARD
	Thirteen Days	Sgt CRAIG
	Thirteen Detectives	Father BROWN
	Thirteen Detectives	Horne FISHER
	Thirteen Detectives	Gabriel GALE
	Thirteen Detectives	Rupert GRANT and Basil GRANT
	Thirteen Detectives	Mr POND
	Thirteen Guests	Insp KENDALL

	Thirty Days Hath September	Haggai GODIN
The	Thirty-First Floor	Ch Insp Peter JENSEN
The	Thirty-Nine Steps	Richard HANNAY
	This Business Is Murder	Betty TRENKA
	This Death Was Murder	Insp GLOVER and Harry CURRY
	This Girl For Hire	Honey WEST
	This Gun For Justice	Joseph (The Vigilante) MADDEN
	This Is For Real	Mark GIRLAND and Herman RADNITZ
	This Is Mr Fortune	Dr Reginald FORTUNE
	This Is My Murder	Supt Simon BULLION
	This Is What Happened	Tod CLAYMORE
	This Little Piggy Went To Murder	Sophie GREENAWAY
	This Man Is Dangerous	Lemmy CAUTION
	This Time Forever	Johnny MERAK and Dawn GRAHAME
	This Troublesome World	Policeman William GREEN
	This Was No Accident	Sam WELPTON
	This Water Laps Gently	Ann HALES
	This Woman Is Death	Nick CRANLEY
	This Woman Is Death	John GAIL
The	Thistlewood Plot	Bow Street Runner Jeremy STURROCK
The	Thomas Street Horror	Lon QUINNCANNON
	Thompson The Detective	THOMPSON
	Thornley Colton, Blind Detective	Thornley COLTON
	Thornton Colton, Blind Reader Of Hearts	Thornley COLTON
	Those Dark Eyes	Dave AXELROD
	Those Who Prey Together Slay Together	David DANNING
	Thou Art The Man	Coralie URQUHART
The	Thousand Coffin Affair	Napoleon SOLO and Ilya KURYAKIN
The	Thousand Hands	James MALLABY
	Threats And Menaces	Det Supt George MACRAE and Det Sgt Leopold SILVER
	Three Bad Nights	Marques Don PANCHO
	Three Bedrooms, One Corpse	Aurora 'Rose' TEAGARDEN
	Three Bright Pebbles	Grace LATHAM
The	Three Couriers	Cdr Roger WATERLOW
	Three Dead	Supt MOONEY
	Three Dead That Night	Insp HOOK
	Three Dead, One Hurt	Insp MULLINS
	Three Die At Midnight	Bill LANGLEY
	Three Died Variously	Brice KENT
	Three Down Vulnerable	Beau SMITH and Pogy ROGERS
The	Three Fears	Dr Hugh WESTLAKE
The	Three Fishers	Ronald BRIERCLIFFE
	Three For The Money	Bill AUGUST
	Three For The Money	Lt Max HUNTER
	Three Frightened Men	Sexton BLAKE
The	Three Gold Feathers	John RUMFORD
The	Three Graces	Insp BASIL
	Three Hours To Hang	Nicholas CORNISH
The	Three Imposters	DYSON and PHILIPPS
	Three Is A Crowd	Cat CALIBAN
The	Three Just Men	FOUR JUST MEN
	Three Layers Of Guilt	Insp CRANE
	Three Porges Parodies And A Pastiche	Stately HOMES
	Three Sheets In The Wind	Mr GLENCANNON
	Three Short Biers	Joe MEDFORD
The	Three Short Men	Supt Gordon KNOLLIS
The	Three Taps	Miles BREDON
The	Three Tiers Of Fantasy	Det Insp Lancelot Carolus SMITH
	Three Times A Victim	Norman O HAZARD
	Three Went In	Insp WREN
	Three White Hairs	Mr FORDHAM
	Three Yards Of Cord	Swete MCTAVISH
	Threepence To Marble Arch	Insp WITTLER
The	Threepersons Hunt	Trooper Sam WATCHMAN
The	Three-Cornered Halo	Insp COCKRILL
	Three-Cornered Murder	Peter PONSONBY
The	Three-Cornered Wound	Dr Ben STARRETT
A	Three-Pipe Problem	Sheridan HAYNES
	Three-Toed Pussy	Supt Charles WYCLIFFE
The	Threshold Of Fear	Colwin GREY
The	Thrill Machine	Pete HEYSEN
The	Thrilling Adventures Of A New York Detective	A NEW YORK DETECTIVE
	Thrilling Stories Of The Railway	Thorpe HAZELL
The	Throbbing Dark	Insp SPEARPOINT
The	Throne Of Peril	Sexton BLAKE
	Through Fire And Water	Sexton BLAKE
	Through The Eyes Of The Dead	Aileen DOUGLASS and Sharon ATWOOD
	Through The Lens	Thornton ZANE
	Through The Valley Of Death	Brother BARNABAS
	Through The Wall	Paul COQUENIL
The	Thug Executive	John MARSH
	Thunder On The Right	Jennifer SILVER
The	Thunderbolt Collects	John (The Thunderbolt) FLATCHLEY
The	Thunderbolt's Jest	John (The Thunderbolt) FLATCHLEY
	Thunderstrike In Syria	Nick CARTER
The	Thursday Turkey Murders	'Bingo' RIGGS and 'Handsome' KUSAK
	Thus Was Adonis Murdered	Prof Hilary TAMAR
	Thy Guilt Is Great	Insp BARLOWE
	Thy Sting, Oh Death	Matilda WORTHING
	Tiberius Smith	Tiberius SMITH
The	Tick Of The Clock	Insp Thomas CONROY
The	Ticket-Of-Leave Man	Insp HAWKSHAW
The	Ticket-Of-Leave Man	Insp HAWKSHAW
The	Ticking Heart	Lt Stephen MAYHEW
The	Ticking Terror Murders	Baron Franz Maximilian Karagos VON KAZ
	Tictocq	TICTOCQ
	Tidy Death	Lord WINTERSTONE
	Tie And Trick: A Melodramatic Story	CHISEL
	Tied For Murder	Prof Percy PEACOCK
The	Ties That Bind	Fiona FITZGERALD
The	Tiger Among Us	Walter SHERRIS
	Tiger By The Tail	Johnny SATURDAY
	Tiger Lily	Val EMERY
	Tigers Burning	Duffy HOUSE
The	Tiger's Claws	Victor MCBAIN
A	Tiger's Cub	Richard SILVER and Insp Tarrant TINKLER
	Tight Squeeze	Brad DOLAN
	Tightrope	Spaceman KOWALSKI and Blue MAGUIRE
The	Tightrope Walker	Amelia JONES
	Tijuana Traffic	RAKER
	Till The Butchers Cut Him Down	Sharon MCCONE
	Tim Frazer Gets The Message	Tim FRAZER
	Timbuktu	Jim STEVENS
	Time After Time	H G WELLS
	Time Bomb	Lt DANFORTH
	Time For A Murder	Insp M'GUIRE
	Time For A Murder	Insp M'GUIRE
	Time For Caution	Lemmy CAUTION
A	Time For Murder	Max KEENE
A	Time For Payment	Supt Konstantin KELLER
A	Time For Scandal	Supt Konstantin KELLER
	Time For Sherlock Holmes	Sherlock HOLMES
	Time For Sleeping	Johnny CANUCK
A	Time For Vengeance	James DINGLE and Glyn JONES
	Time Limit	Stephen DAIN
The	Time Lock	Phineas FLINT
A	Time Of Predators	Curt HALSTEAD
	Time Off For Death	Michael GAUNT
	Time Right Deadly	Herr MOLLNAR
	Time Running Out	Sgt Ben CORBIN
	Time To Change Hats	John DAVIES
A	Time To Depart	M Didius FALCO
A	Time To Die	Charles GARRETT
	Time To Kill	Mike HARMAN
	Time To Kill	Sheriff Bill LLOYD
	Time To Kill	Sgt Shelly LOWENKOPF
	Time To Kill	David MALLIN and George COE
A	Time To Kill	Roger TAINE
	Time To Kill	Nell WILLARD
The	Time Trap Gambit	Hannibal FORTUNE
The	Times Square Connection	Phillip (The Marksman) MAGELLAN
The	Timetable Murder	Quentin PACE
	Time's Witnesses	Cuddy MAGNUM and Justine SAVILE
The	Timid Tycoon	Mark KILBY
	Timor Mortis	Prof Clifford DUNBAR
The	Timothy Files	Timothy CONE
	Timothy Tealeaf, Business Investigator	Timothy TEALEAF
	Timothy Twill's Secret	Mr KNUCKLESTONE
	Timothy's Game	Timothy CONE
The	Tin Angel	Pablo WAITZ and Maria PONCE
The	Tin Bath Murder	Martin SPEED
	Tinplate	Peter MARKLIN
The	Tinseltown Murders	Mac SLADE
	Tiny Carteret	Capt Hugh 'Bulldog' DRUMMOND and Ronald STANDISH
	Tiny Carteret	Capt Hugh 'Bulldog' DRUMMOND and Ronald STANDISH
	Tip On A Dead Crab	Lou 'Shifty' ANDERSON
	Tis The Season To Be Dying	Matilda WORTHING
	Tish	Letitia CARBERRY
	Tish Marches On	Letitia CARBERRY
	Tish Plays The Game	Letitia CARBERRY
A	Tisket, A Casket	Silas BOOTH
The	Title Is Murder	Steve JOHNSON
A	Titled Counterfeiter; Or, The American Detective In France	Wat DENTON
	Tje Barrabas Fallout	Nile BARRABAS
	To Catch A Forger	Essington HOLT
	To Catch A Thief	John ROBIE
	To Die In Beverly Hills	Charles CARR and Jack KELLY
	To Dusty Death	Insp MCKELLER and Richard LOGAN
	To Hell On Skates	William DRINK and Sam SLEEP
	To Hell With The Law	Jimmy BRENT
	To His Just Deserts	Det Insp Arvo LAURILA
	To Kill A Corpse	Lucian CAROLUS
	To Kill A Judge	Johnny BORDELON
	To Play The Fool	Det Kate MARTINELLI and Det Al HAWKINS
	To Sleep, Perchance To Kill	Dixie T STRUTHERS
	To Speak For The Dead	Jake LASSITER
	To Spite Her Face	Lucy RAMSDALE and Insp James MACDOUGAL
	To Study A Long Silence	Dr R V DAVIE
	To The Eagle's Nest	George WILLIAMS
	To The Tombaugh Station	Kate BRISTOL
	Todmanhowe Grange	Ronald CAMBERWELL
The	Toff And The Dead Man's Finger	Richard (The Toff) ROLLISON
The	Toledo Dagger	Insp FAVART
	Tom And Jerry; Or, The Double Detectives	TOM and JERRY
	Tom Rocket	Bow Street Runner BRADSHAW and Bow Street Runner FRASER
	Tom Sawyer Abroad, Tom Sawyer, Detective & Other Stories	Tom SAWYER
	Tom Sawyer, Detective, As Told By Huck Finn	Tom SAWYER
	Tom Turner, Detective; Or, Piping The Hawks Of Baltimore	Tom TURNER
	Tombstone Courage	Sheriff Joanna BRADY
	Tommy Weston, Adventuress	Tommy WESTON
	Tomorrow Is Another Day	Toby PETERS and Clark GABLE
	Tomorrow's Ghost	Frances FITZGIBBON
	Tondo For Short	Insp Franco CORTI
The	Toni Diamonds	ARNHOLT
	Tonight They Die To Mendelssohn	Schuyler TOWNSEND
The	Tontine Treasure	Shamus BURKE
	Too Dangerous To Be Free	Vic MALLOY
	Too Good To Be True	Don PAULSON
	Too Hot To Handle	Fire Marshal Ben PEDLEY
	Too Late For Mourning	Pete DRACO
	Too Late For Tears	Danny FULLER
	Too Late To Die	Sheriff Dan RHODES

Too Many Crooks Spoil The Caper	Ed NELSON
Too Many Doctors	Insp MEDFORD
Too Many Doors	Eric HAZARD
Too Many Ghosts	Alexander HERO
Too Many Innocents	Tony SPENCER
Too Many Magicians	Lord DARCY
Too Many Murderers	Steve PAGET
Too Many Murderers	Chet PHELPS
Too Many Women	Prof CALDWELL
Too Mini Murders	Bill CARTWRIGHT
Too Much Evidence	Alexander FALLON
Too Much Poison	Insp BARRY
Too Old A Cat	Ed RAZONI, William JACKSON and Devlin TRACY
Too Sane A Murder	Det Deb RALSTON
Top Assignment	Larry PALMER
Top End	Max MOSS
Top Ten	Hank JANSON
Toper's End	Supt Henry WILSON
Topkapi	Arthur Abdul SIMPSON
The Topless Corpse	Hank BRADFORD
The Topless Tulip Caper	Leo HAIG
The Topless Tulip Caper	Leo HAIG
Topsy And Evil	Det Pharaoh LOVE and Det Satan STAGG
Torment Was A Redhead	Sexton BLAKE
The Torrington Square Mystery	Winston BARROWS
The Tortured Boy	Edward TOPE
The Tortured Path	Kim LOCKE
A Touch Of Danger	Frank 'Lobo' DAVIES
Touch Of The Past	Rachel HENNINGS
The Touch Of Treason	George THOMASSY
Touch Play	Don HAWKER
Touchfeather	Katy TOUCHFEATHER
Touchfeather, Too	Katy TOUCHFEATHER
Touchstone	Jane BAILEY
The Tough And The Tender	Insp GILLANDREW
Tough Company	Col Gantian LEATHERMOUTH
Tough Cop	Johnny DEVEREAUX
Tough Enough	T D STASH
Tough Justice	SAN ANTONIO
Tough Luck, L A	Ben CRANDEL
A Tough One To Lose	Bill VERECKER
Tour De Force	Martyn FINCH
Tourist Season	Brian KEYES
Tourists Are For Trapping	Douglas PERKINS and Gerry TATE
The Tournament	Peter TREES
Towards Zero	Supt BATTLE
The Tower Hill Mystery	Justus WISE
The Tower Mystery	Insp/Supt FILLINGER
A Town Of Masks	Hannah BLAKE
The Town That Went Sick	Ch Insp GIDLEIGH
Toxin	Mike MACLEAN
Toxin	Cobb TAKAMURA and Charles KOENIG
Trace	Devlin 'Trace' TRACY
Trace Elements	Callista JACOBS
Traced And Tracked; Or, Memoirs Of A City Detective	James M'GOVAN
Tracer Inc	John TRACER
The Traces Of Brillhart	William DEACON
The Traces Of Merrilee	William DEACON
Track Of The Beast	John (The Hunter) YARD
Track Of The Cat	Anna PIGEON
The Track Of The Slayer	Prof Adrian CRIDDLE
Tracked And Taken: Detective Sketches	Det Dick DONOVAN
Tracked By Wireless	Geoffrey FALCONER
Tracker	Nat TRACKER
The Tracker Tracked	Dr Sebastian LONG
Trackless Death	Peter CREIGHTON
The Trackless Thing	LAKIN
The Trackwalker	Matt FARADAY
Trader To The Stars	Nicholas VAN RIJN
Trade-Off	Det Ch Insp John FORDHAM
Trading With Bodies	Bill TRUSCOTT
The Tragedy At Draythorpe	Paul IRVING
The Tragedy At Freyne	Scott EGERTON
Tragedy At Law	Insp MALLETT and Francis PETTIGREW
The Tragedy At Tiverton	Christopher RANDOLPH
The Tragedy Near Tring	Insp RODWAY
Tragedy Of A Third Class Smoker	GRAYSON
The Tragedy Of The Chinese Mine	Insp SWINTON
The Tragedy Of X	Drury LANE
The Tragic Curtain	Christopher HAND
Trail Of A Tramp	Jake BARROW
The Trail Of Blood	James O'HANNAY and Floyd EAST
The Trail Of Fear	Jimmie REZAIRE
The Trail Of The Dead	Robert HARLAND
The Trail Of The Human Tiger; Or, Nick Carter's Mysterious Shadow	Nick CARTER
The Trail Of The Reaper	Jack LAMARRE and Alison PRENDERGAST
The Trail Of The Serpent	Insp SEVREL
The Trail Of The Squid	Ferris MCCLUE
Trail Of The Twisted Cross	Ben 'T-Man' SLAYTON
Traitor And Spy	Sexton BLAKE
Traitor Betrayed	Insp/Supt BAKER
A Traitor In London	Insp WOKE
A Traitor Unmasked	'Twisted Face' STRAUSSMAN
Traitors' Doom	Dr PALFREY
Traitor's Gate	Jacques BRUNEL
The Traitor's Gate	Mrs Emily OLLERBY
Traitor's Gate	Insp Thomas PITT and Charlotte PITT
Traitor's Island	Slade MCGINTY
Traitor's Mountain	Sir Abercrombie LEWKER
Traitor's Tide	The PADRE
Traitor's Wife	REMSEN
The Transactions Of Lord Louis Lewis	Lord Louis LEWIS
The Transatlantic Ghost	Mr WATSON
The Transcendental Murder	Homer KELLY
The Transvection Machine	Carl CRADER and Earl JAZINE
A Trap For Bellamy	Nick BELLAMY
The Trap In The Tunnel	Roger HARTLEY
Trap No 6	Lt Lee BARCELLO
The Travel Tales Of Mr Joseph Jorkens	Joseph JORKENS
The Traveling Corpses	Hank HYER
Traveling With Sherlock Holmes And Dr Watson	Sherlock HOLMES
Travels In The Canadian West	Sherlock HOLMES
Treachery In Trieste	Paul KILGERRIN
Tread Gently, Death	Al BRANSON
Treason In The Egg	Insp Ellis MCKAY
Treason Remembered	Sexton BLAKE
A Treasure From Treasure Island	Sherlock HOLMES
The Treasure Hunt	Ben GARDEN
The Treasure Of The Cosa Nostra	Brian GUY
Treasure Of The Sun	Jimmy CARROLL
Treasure Royal	James DREW
The Treasure Train	Prof Craig KENNEDY
Tree Frog	Giles YOEMAN
The Tree Of Death	Elena OLIVEREZ
Trek Or Treat	Marilyn AMBERS
The Tremayne Case	Jimmy THURSTON
Trent Intervenes	Philip TRENT
Trent Of The Lone Hand	Anthony TRENT
Trent's Last Case	Philip TRENT
Trent's Own Case	Philip TRENT
Trial And Error	Ambrose CHITTERWICK
The Trial Of John And Henry Norton	Harvey SHAPMAN
The Trial Of Vincent Doon	Philip STRONG and James MATTHEWS
Trial Run	Randall DREW
The Trials Of Commander McTurk	Cdr MCTURK
The Trials Of Rumpole	Horace RUMPOLE
Triangle	Spaceman KOWALSKI and Blue MAGUIRE
Triangle Of Fire	Tom FARLEY
The Triarchs	Tim LACY
Trick Of The Light	Nick SANDS
Trick Or Treat	Brian FRESNEY
A Trifling Affair	Sherlock HOLMES
Trigger Lady	Anastasia JUGEDINSKI
Trigger Man	Johnny ROCK
Trilogy In Jeopardy	Peter CHAMBERS
Trinity In Violence	Peter CHAMBERS
The Trip To Jerusalem	Nicholas BRACEWELL
Trip Trap	Col Nur BEY
Triple Death	Insp RYVET
Triple Exposure	Philip QUEST
A Triple Knavery; Or, Link By Link	Nick CARTER
Triple Slay	Steve CONACHER
Triple Terror	Peter CHAMBERS
Tripletrap	Charlie BREWER
The Triumph Of Elaine	Prof Craig KENNEDY
The Triumph Of McLean	Insp MCLEAN
The Triumph Of Tinker	TINKER
The Triumphant Beast	Brother Felipe BRUNO
The Triumphs Of Eugène Valmont	Eugène VALMONT
The Triumphs Of Fabian Field, Criminologist	Fabian FIELD
The Triumvirate	David HALLIDAY
Trixie True, Teen Detective	Trixie TRUE
Troika	Heron MURMER
Trooper Useless	Trooper USELESS
Tropical Deathpact	Nick CARTER
Tropical Freeze	THORN
Tropical Heat	Fred CARVER
Tropical Murder	Bernado THOMAS
Trotsky's Run	James BURLANE
The Trouble At Aquitaine	G D H PRINGLE
Trouble Crossing The Pyrenees	Henry GARRETT
Trouble Follows Me	Chet GORDON
Trouble In Bugland: A Collection Of Inspector Mantis Mysteries	Insp MANTIS
Trouble In Paradise	Nick CARTER
Trouble In Paradise	Capt Jose DA SILVA
Trouble In The Bank	Edward TOPE
Trouble Looking For A Place To Happen	Laura FLEMING
Trouble Making Toys	Cesar Augustus FRANCK
A Trouble Of Fools	Carlotta CARLYLE
The Trouble With Crime	Johnny PERFECT
The Trouble With Going Home	Simona GRIFFO
The Trouble With Guns	Johnny PERFECT
The Trouble With Murder	Insp JAMES
The Trouble With Series Three	Arthur APPLEYARD
The Trouble With Stephanie	Evan PARIS
The Trouble With Tycoons	Pete HOLLAND
Troublecross	Prof Theodora Wade CRAWFORD
Troubled Waters	Harry LAKE
Troubled Waters	Cat O'CONNELL
The Troubles Of Colonel Marwood	Col MARWOOD
Troubleshooter	John Abraham LINCOLN
Trout In The Milk	Sheriff MACREADY
Truck Shot	Stoney WINSTON
Truckful Of Gold	Peter KAYIRA
The True Adventure Of The Second Stain	Sherlock HOLMES
True Blue, The Detective; Or, The Romance Of A Great Special	TRUE BLUE
True Confessions	Tom SPELLACY
True Detective	Nate HELLER
True Detective Stories	Insp MOSER
True Or False	Ada WELLER
True-Life Adventure	Paul MACDONALD
Trunch	Hamish OATH
The Trunk Mystery	Herlock SHOLMES
Trunk Show	Charlotte SAMS
Trust The Saint	Simon (The Saint) TEMPLAR
Trusted Like The Fox	Insp JAMES

The Truth At Last: An Authentic Case Of Some Baker Street Irregularities	Sherlock HOLMES
The Truthful Lady	Sherlock HOLMES
Try Anything Twice	Nicholas GALE
Try The Girl	Ted CARMADY
The Tudor Garden Mystery	Felix HERON
Tune To A Corpse	Ch Insp THOMPSON
The Tunnel Mystery	Insp KILBY
Tunnel Vision	Victoria Iphigenia 'Vi' WARSHAWSKI
Turbo	Patrick MALONE
The Turkey Buzzard Blues	Luther MCGAVOCK
Turkey Tracks	Elizabeth BLAIR and Max SHEPHERD
The Turncoat	Nick CARTER
The Turquoise Dragon	George KILGORE
Turquoise Hazard	Freddy PHILPOTTS
The Turquoise Shop	Pat ABBOTT and Jean ABBOTT
The Turquoise Spike	Joe DELANEY
The Turquoise/Yellow Case	Jedediah KILLINGER III
Turtle Baby	Bo BRADLEY
Tutt And Mr Tutt	Ephraim TUTT
Tutt For Tutt	Ephraim TUTT
Tut,Tut! Mr Tutt	Ephraim TUTT
The Twelfth Of August	Sheriff Buford PUSSER
The Twelfth Statue	Mel GORDON
Twelve Chinamen And A Woman	Dave FENNER
Twelve Chinks And A Woman	Dave FENNER
The Twelve Deaths Of Christmas	Det KNOWLES
Twelve Girls In The Garden	Prof Ronald CHALLIS
Twelve To Dine	Commissaire PAYRAN
Twenty Minutes To Kill	Dan DURKIN
Twenty Per Cent	Jim HARRIS and Kate HARRIS
Twenty Plus Two	Tom ALDER
The Twentysecond Man: Or, Re Sherlock Holmes, German Agent	Sherlock HOLMES
The Twenty-Acre Plot	Timothy Seamus Wolfe SHERIDAN
The Twenty-First Burr	Harry BURNVILLE
Twenty-Five Sanitary Inspectors	Ex-Supt 'Simmy' SIMMONDS
Twice Burned	Ch HAMMOND and Det BENEDETTO
Twice Dead	Jimmy WAGHORN
Twice Removed	Frank JANEK
Twilight At Mac's Place	Cyril MCCORKLE and Michael PADILLO
Twilight At Monticello	Raymond GREEN and Margaret GREEN
Twilight Of Death	Det Christopher JENSEN and Prof Natalie KEITH
A Twist Of Sand	Cdr Geoffrey PEACE
A Twist Of The Knife	Stanley MOODROW
A Twist Of The Rope	Insp SHERWOOD
Twisted Evidence	Tommy MALINS
The Twisted Face	Judge Henry TYSON
Twisted Face Defends His Title	'Twisted Face' STRAUSSMAN
Twixt Night And Morn	Insp Raj MOHAMED
Two Bullets For Briggs	Tommy BRIGGS
Two Clues	Sheriff Bill ELDON
Two Deaths For A Penny	Ch Insp DREWRY
Two Faces Of Death	Bart CONDOR
Two Faces Of Nemesis	TRELAWNEY
The Two Footmen	Sherlock HOLMES
Two For Tanner	Evan TANNER
Two Heads Are Better	Fred BENNETT
The Two Hundred Ghost	Sally HELDAR and Johnny HELDAR
The Two Imposters	Insp PINAUD
The Two Kings	SILBER
Two Knocks For Death	Insp Clancy MARTIN
Two Ladies In Verona	Emma GREAVES
Two Plus Two	Jason PRICE and Brooke MERIT
Two Roads, No Choices	Sherlock HOLMES
Two Shadows For Death	Timothy ROURKE
Two Smart Dames	Shaun O'MALLEY
Two Songs This Archangel Sings	Dr Robert 'Mongo' FREDERICKSON and Veil KENDRY
Two Strange Ladies	Bob LANDRELL
The Two Tickets Puzzle	Supt ROSS
The Two Undertakers	Ronald BRIERCLIFFE
Two Wonderful Detectives: Or, Jack And Gil's Marvellous Skill	JACK and GIL
Twopence For A Rat's Tail	Stephen RINGWAY
Twospot	NAMELESS DETECTIVE and Lt Frank HASTINGS
The Two-Dude Offense	Hector GRONIG
The Two-Faced Man	CREWE (BIRGE MOREAU)
Two-Gun Gerta	Red CONNORS
Tyger At Bay	Tygrus Gerald 'Tyger' DECKER
Tyger By The Tail	Tygrus Gerald 'Tyger' DECKER
Typed For A Corpse	Don CARSON

—U—

U

'Ubique', The Scientific Bushranger	UBIQUE
The Ugly Man	Walter TANDY
The Ultimate Code	Nick CARTER
The Ultimate Conclusion	Ashley TEMPEST
The Ultimate Confrontation	Sherlock HOLMES
The Umbrosa Burglary	Picklock HOLES
Unappointed Rounds	David MADDEN
Unbalanced Accounts	Nick MAGARACZ
Unbecoming Habits	Simon BOGNOR
Unbriefed Mission	Geoffrey CORDELL
Uncanny Adventures	Lucian CAROLUS
Uncivil Seasons	Cuddy MAGNUM and Justine SAVILE
Uncle Abner, Master Of Mysteries	Uncle ABNER
Uncle Happy	Modesty BLAISE
Uncle Sam, Detective	Bill GARD
Uncle Target	Maj Harry MAXIM
The Uncollected Cases Of Solar Pons	Solar PONS
Uncommon Danger	VALESHOFF and TAMARA
The Unconscious Witness	Dr John Evelyn THORNDYKE
The Uncounted Hour	Insp WAKE and Philip GAYMORE
Under A Cloud	Pete RECTOR
Under A Strange Mask	KEENE
Under Contract	Anna LEE
Under Cover Of Daylight	THORN
The Under Dogs	Mme Rosika STOREY
Under Fate's Wheel: A Story Of Mystery, Love And The Bicycle	Sheriff COOK
Under My Skin	Robin MILLER
Under My Skin	Hannah WOLFE
Under Siege	Jake GRAFTON
Under The Bright Lights	Det Rene SHADE
Under The Clock	Sherlock HOLMES
Under The Influence	Ben PORTER and Carrie PORTER
Under The Shadow	Fraser TODD
Under The Wall	Nick CARTER
Undercover Cat	D C (Darn Cat) RANDALL
The Undertaker Dies	HIGHWAY
The Underwood Mystery	John BARTLEY
The Undisclosed Client	Const LEE
The Undoubted Deed	Ambrose USHER
Undressed To Kill	Nicholas GALE
Undue Influence	Paul MADRIANI
Uneasy Lies The Head	Det Insp Samuel 'Smudge' HUDDLESTON
Uneasy Terms	Rupert Patrick 'Slim' CALLAGHAN
The Unexpected Corpse	Insp MACKAY
Unexpected Developments	Benton SAFFORD
The Unexpected Legacy	Insp CARTER
The Unexpected Mrs Pollifax	Mrs Emily POLLIFAX
Unexpected Night	Henry GAMADGE
Unfair Lady	Mr MALCOLM
Unfinished Business	Jerry JEETER
Unfit To Plead	Insp Rupert HAMBLEDON
The Unfortunate Replacement	Jim ROCKFORD
Unfriendly Persuasion	Richard QUINTAIN
The Unguarded Goal	Herlock SHOLMES
Unguarded Moment	William MITCHELL
Unhallowed Murder	Adam LUDLOW
Unhappy Hooligan	Howie ROOK
Unholy Communion	Sam MCCHESNEY
Unholy Dying	Prof John STUBBS
Unholy Ground	Sgt Matt MINOGUE
Unholy Moses	Terry WEBB
Unholy Writ	Mark TREASURE
Uninvited Guest	Capt Alan SCOTT
The Union Club Mysteries	The UNION CLUB
Unjustly Branded	Sexton BLAKE
Unknown Man #89	Frank RYAN
Unlucky Break	Insp/Supt BAKER
Unnatural Causes	Dr Eric PARKER
Unnatural Deeds	Commissaire PAYRAN
Unnatural Hazard	Insp Angus STRAUN
Unofficial Rosie	Rosie MONAGHAN
Unorthodox Methods	Kevin BRYCE
The Unorthodox Murder Of Rabbi Moss	Rabbi Daniel WINTER
Unorthodox Practices	Nina FISCHMAN and Ida FISCHMAN
The Unpleasantness At The Stooges Club	Dr John H WATSON
The Unprofessional Spy	Martin AINSWORTH
Unravelled Knots	The OLD MAN IN THE CORNER
Unruly Son	Idwal MEREDITH
The Unseen Ear	Det FERGUSON
Unseen Enemy	Harry KENT
The Unseen Hand	Insp HAINES
Unseen Hands	Barry O'DELL
The Unsolvable Crime	Capt (Retired) CORBETT
The Unsolved Case Of Sherlock Holmes	Sherlock HOLMES
An Unsuitable Job For A Woman	Cordelia GRAY
Until Proven Guilty	Kathryn MACKAY
Untimely Death	Insp MALLETT and Francis PETTIGREW
Untimely Ripped	James MATRIC
Untimely Slain	Geoffrey TARLETON
The Untold Sherlock Holmes	Sherlock HOLMES
An Untold Tale	Gyp KIDNADZE
The Untouchable Juli	Kit QUAYLE
Unusual Behaviour	Insp CORBY
Unwanted Attentions	Michael CARUSO
Unwanted Witness	Insp HALLAN and Sgt SPRATT
An Unwelcome Presence	Alan CRAIG
An Up And Coming Man	Tommy TOMPKINS
Up The Ladder: Or, Morton Merrill's Pluck	BRINDLE
Up To Her Neck	JASON
The Upfold Witch	Dr Henry FROST
Upon Reflection	Mrs Dorinda JONES
Upper Case	Red HANLON
The Upside Down Murders	Peter QUINT
The Urban District Lover	Albert ARGYLE
Urgent Conference	Mark URGENT
Urgent Enquiry	Mark URGENT
The Urgent Hangman	Rupert Patrick 'Slim' CALLAGHAN
Ursula Lenorme: Lady Companion	Ursula LENORME
Used To Kill	Gwen RAMADGE
The Uttermost Farthing	Humphrey CHALLONER

V As In Victim	Det Jub FREEMAN and Det Carl WAYWARD
Vain Escape	Insp BYRNE
Valentine Vaughan Omnibus	Valentine VAUGHAN
The Valentine Victim	Insp RODERICKS
The Valley And The Shadow	Insp BIGGINS
The Valley Of Creeping Men	Ned SHACKLETON
Valley Of Death	Terry (Chopper Cop) BUNKER
Valley Of Death	The BUTCHER
The Valley Of Fear	Sherlock HOLMES
The Valley Of Hanoi	Richard LE GRANDE
The Valley Of The Fox	Peter MARLOW
Vampire Abroad	Supt WILKINS and Col CHIDDINGTON
Vampire City	Scarsdale WARING
The Vampire's Trail: Or, Nick Carter And The Policy King	Nick CARTER
The Van Alstine Cas	Trim CARTER
Van Bibber And Others	VAN BIBBER
The Van Norton Murders	Leighton SWIFT
Vandersley	Maj Adrian TITTERTON
Vane Pursuit	Prof Peter SHANDY
Vanish In An Instant	Eric MEECHAM
The Vanished Aliens	Herlock SHOLMES
The Vanishing Celebrities	Insp 'Steady as a Rock' POSSE
The Vanishing Death	Philip QUEST
The Vanishing Diamonds: Or, The Treasure-Seekers Of Tibet	Donald MACALPINE
The Vanishing Diary	Dr Lancelot PRIESTLEY
The Vanishing Gold Truck	Angus MACWHORTER and Sheriff Bugrus DUCKHOUSE
Vanishing Men	Insp GILMOUR
The Vanishing Of Tera	Insp CHARD
The Vanishing Of Velma	Capt LEOPOLD
The Vanishing Professor	Frank LEONARD and Foster GAINES
The Vanishing Shadow	Judy BOLTON
The Vanishing Track	John PIPER
Van, The Government Detective: Or, The Base Metal Coiners	VAN
Variation On A Theme	Henry GRACE
Vasco, The Magician Detective: Or, The Murder In The Theatrical Car	VASCO
Vector	Cobb TAKAMURA and Charles KOENIG
The Veetols	Eric MARSDEN
Veil	Veil KENDRY
Veil Of Ignorance	Sister Mary Teresa DEMPSEY
The Veiled One	Ch Insp Reginald WEXFORD
Veiled Threat	Jennifer GREY
The Veils Of Death	Philip QUEST
The Velvet Hand	Mme Rosika STOREY
The Velvet Mask And Other Stories	Supt Anthony SLADE
Vendetta	Phillip (The Marksman) MAGELLAN
Vendetta For The Saint	Simon (The Saint) TEMPLAR
The Vendettists	Col Charles RUSSELL
Venetian Bird	Edward MERCER
The Venetian Key	Dr Frank TARLETON
A Venetian Reckoning	Commiss Guido BRUNETTI
Venetian Vendetta	The BUTCHER
The Vengeance Due	Insp MILLWALL
The Vengeance Game	Nick CARTER
Vengeance Is His	Brett WALLACE
Vengeance Mountain	Jack (The Specialist) SULLIVAN
The Vengeance Of Henry Jarroman	James SEGROVE
The Vengeance Of Li-Sin	LI-SIN
Venice Of The Black Sea	Insp Lathom DYNES
Venturous Lady	Bill RAEBURN
The Venus Death	Trooper Ralph LINDSEY
The Venus Figurine	Sherlock HOLMES
Venus Underground	Alex (The Protector) DARTANIAN
Venus With Pistol	Bert KEMP
The Verdict Of You All	Insp DOBSON
The Verdugo Affair	'Bump' HARWELL
Vermilion	Daniel VALENTINE and Clarisse LOVELACE
A Very Black Deed	BLACK
The Very Breath Of Hell	Vincent STALLARD and Cynthia GODWIN
The Very Great Grandson Of Sherlock Holmes	Sherlock HOLMES
A Very Private Enterprise	George SINCLAIR
A Very Proper Death	Sgt Jake MURPHY
A Very Venetian Murder	Reuben FROST
The Vespucci Papers	Harcourt D'ESPINAL
The Vessel May Carry Explosives	Roger FLEMING
The Vet It Was That Died	Insp Christopher ADRIAN
The Viaduct Murder	William CARMICHAEL
The Vicar Done It	Rev Jabel JARRETT
The Vicar Investigates	Rev Jabel JARRETT
Vicar's Roses	Jerry BROGAN
Vice Cop	Matt RUDD
Vice Squad	Capt BARNABY
The Viceroy's Protegé	Simon CARNE
Vicious Circle	Liz PARROTT
Vicious Circles	Vladimir GULL
Victim For Hire	Pedro MORENO
The Victim Of The Girl Spy	Sexton BLAKE
Victim Unknown	Sexton BLAKE
The Victim Was Important	Johnny POWERS
Victims	Det Ch Insp Tom MAYBRIDGE
Victims	Miranda TORRES
Victor	Victor GARRISON
Victor Maury, The French Detective	Victor MAURY
Victor Versus Verhasst	Victor GARRISON
The Vidocq Of New York	Tom BYRNES
The Vienna Elephant	Rupert CONWAY
The View From Daniel Pike	Daniel PIKE
A View To A Death	Dr Alun BARRY
The Villa Head	Cheney HAZZARD
Village East	Hank MOODY
The Village Of Rogues	Bow Street Runner Jeremy STURROCK
The Villain And The Virgin	Dave FENNER
The Villain Of The Earth	Phillip FLETCHER
Villain Of The Piece	Mike KING
Villains	Harry SOMMERS
The Villars-Manningham Papers	Sherlock HOLMES
The Villars-Manningham Papers And Other Stories Of Sherlock Holmes	Sherlock HOLMES
Villiger	Gordon GALLAGHER
Violent Death Of A Bitter Englishman	Sean RYAN
Violent Keepsake	Phil SANDERSON
Violent Security	Insp GULLIVER
A Viper In Her Bosom	Paul MULLER
Virgil's Ghost	Lenny SCHWARTZ
The Virgin Collector	Danny SPADE
The Virgin Kills	Al CONNORS
Virginia Box And The "Unsatisfied"	Virginia BOX
Virginia's Thing	John FOLEY
The Virtuous Vamp	Ursula DOLLING
Visa To Death	Barney HARRIS
A Voice From The Dark	John RINGROSE
Voice Of The Past	Stephen MARRYAT
Voice Out Of Darkness	Katy MEREDITH
Voiceover	Sherlock HOLMES
Voices	Charlie FENWICK
Voices From The Dark	Dan MALLETT
The Von Kessel Dossier	Michael BERESFORD
Voodoo	Insp Rae NORSE
The Voodoo Drum	Sexton BLAKE
The Voodoo Goat	Chauncey O'DAY
Voodoo Island	Grant RUSHTON
Voodoo Ltd	Artie WU and Quincey DURANT
Vortex	Jim MCKECHNIE
Vote Against Poison	Charles BLESSINGTON
Vote For Violence	Sexton BLAKE
Vote X For Treason	Sean RYAN
Voudon	Ray FALCO
A Vow Of Devotion	Sister JOAN and Det Sgt Alan MILL
A Vow Of Silence	Sister JOAN and Det Sgt Alan MILL
Voyage Of Death	Chester C TABOR
The Voyage Of The Chianti	Elizabeth Lamb WORTHINGTON
Vrouw Grobelaar And Her Leading Cases	The Vrouw GROBELAAR
The Vrouw Grobelaar's Leading Cases	The Vrouw GROBELAAR
The Vulcan Disaster	Nick CARTER
Vulture	Det Const Caz FLOOD
Vultures, Ltd	Norman CONQUEST
The Vye Murder	Insp DIGBY

—W—

The W Plan	Col Duncan GRANT
Wade Weston, The 'Upper Ten' Detective: Or, The Mystery Of No 20	Wade WESTON
The Wager	Kek HUUYGENS
The Wages Of Rascality: Or, A Terrible Reward	Nick CARTER
The Wages Of Zen	Supt Tetsuo OTANI
Waif Of The River	Sgt Jasper SHRIG
The Waikiki Widow	Lily WU and Janice CAMERON
The Wailing Rock Murders	'Spider' MEECH
Waiting For A Tiger	Paul HEDLEY
Waiting For Willa	Grace ASHERTON
The Waiting Game	Lloyd NICOLSON
Wake For A Lady	Sid AMES
A Wake For Mourning	Prof Ronald CHALLIS
Wake Up Dead	Tony BOYLE
Walk At A Steady Pace	Nigel MORRISON
A Walk At Night	Stephen BELLECROIX and Sheila ROATH
Walk In The Shadows	Sexton BLAKE
A Walk Into Murder	Martin RIDGWAY
A Walk On The Blond Side	Joe MANNIX
Walk The Dark Streets	Sam BIRGE
Walker Of The Secret Service	WALKER
Walking On Air	Robert MAINE
Walking Shadow	Todd MCKINNON
Walking Shadow	SPENSER
Walking Tall: Part 2	Sheriff Buford PUSSER
The Walking Wind	Joe SANFORD
Wall Of Eyes	Insp SANDS
Wall Of Glass	Rita MONDRAGON
A Wall Street Haul: Or, A Bold Stroke For a Fortune	Nick CARTER
Wallace Intervenes	Sir Leonard WALLACE
Wallace Of The Secret Service	Sir Leonard WALLACE
Wallingford And Blackie Daw	James Rufus WALLINGFORD
Wallingford In His Prime	James Rufus WALLINGFORD
The Wallington Case	Stephen KALE
Wally, The Watchful Eye	Wally WATTS
Walt Wheeler, The Scout Detective	Walt WHEELER
The Waltz Of Death	LANDER
The Wanderings Of Asaf	Asaf KHAN
Wanted For Killing	Simon HERALD
Wanted For Murder	Simon (The Saint) TEMPLAR
Wanted: Danny Fontaine	Danny FONTAINE
Wanted: Dude Or Alive	Dewey JAMES
Wanted! A Detective's Strange Adventures	Det Dick DONOVAN
Wanton For Murder	Lt Shomri SHOMAR
The War Against Charity Ross	Charity ROSS
War Against The Mafia	Mack (The Executioner) BOLAN
War From The Clouds	Nick CARTER

	Title	Character
The	War Model	Carl DEKKER
A	War Of Nerves	Hemlock SOAMES
The	War Terror	Prof Craig KENNEDY
	Warden Of The North	Const Jimmie WARDEN
	Warden Of The Wilds	Const Jimmie WARDEN
The	Wardour Street Mystery	Bartholomew DANE
	Warhawk	David PROSS
	Warrant For A Wanton	Leith HADLEY
The	Warrielaw Jewel	Bob STUART
	Was It Murder?	Colin REVELL
	Was It Murder?	Colin REVELL
	Washed In The Blood	Able GARRET
The	Washermen	Cdr Allan DICE
	Washington Deceased	Richard MICHAELSON
	Washington Payoff	Pete NOVAK
	Washington Whispers Murder	Col John PRIMROSE and Grace LATHAM
A	Wastrel Goes West	Eugene MULCAHY
	Watch All Night	Tess EVELING
	Watch Mr Moh	Lt MOH
	Watching The Detectives	Jan ARGAND
The	Water Widow	Sgt Rudolf NILSEN
	Waterfront	Johnny MALONE
	Waterhole	Gordon GALLAGHER
	Waterman	Steven KIRK
The	Waters Of Centaurus	Sybil Sue BLUE
The	Watertown Mystery	Fred DANFORD
	Watson's No 8 In B Minor	Sherlock HOLMES
	Wax Flowers For Gloria	Insp SWINTON
	Waxwork	Sgt CRIBB and Const THACKERAY
The	Waxworks Spies	Hugh RUDD
A	Way Of Life	Tom HOWARD
The	Way Of The North	Policeman Black John SMITH
	Way Past Dead	Harry DENTON
The	Way To Nowhere	Norman PINK
The	Way We Die Now	Sgt Hoke MOSELEY
	Ways Of Death	Percival TROUT
	Wayward Angel	Rocky NEVINS
	We Are Not Amused	Dorothy Mayotte RIGBY
	We The Condemned	Dana DALLAS
	We Walk With Death	Alan FRASER
The	Weak-Eyed Bat	Dr Paul PRYE
	Weapon Heavy	Jefferson HEWITT
	Weasel Hunt	David STUART
	Weatherby	Artie WEATHERBY
The	Web	Sexton BLAKE
The	Web	James TURNER
The	Web Of Destiny	Forrest ORD
The	Web Of Murder	Forrest ORD
The	Web Of Shadows	Insp PRENTIS
	Wedderburn's Will	Insp PARKER
The	Wedding March Murder	Peter CARDIGAN
	Wednesday Night At The Forum	Harry LAWSON
	Wee Punch, The Dog Detective	WEE PUNCH
	Weeds	Det Insp DU CAS
The	Weekend Mystery	Jimmy WROME
	Weep For Willow Green	Phil KRAMER
	Weep No More, My Lady	Elizabeth LANGE
	Welcome Death	Prof Richard CHERRINGTON
	Welcome Home, Jaine	Jaine (The Bionic Woman) SOMMERS
	Welcome Home, Lily Glow	Matt ARCHER
	Welcome, Proud Lady	James PORBEAGLE
	Werewolf	David LEE
The	Werewolf Walks Tonight	Satan SLEUTH
	Wes Hardin's Gun	Jefferson HEWITT
	West End	Arthur Stukeley PENNINGTON and Det Insp Patrick Aloysius MCCARTHY
The	West End Horror	Sherlock HOLMES
	West Of Jerusalem	Malko LINGE
The	West Shore Mystery	MANFRED
The	Western Express Robbery: Or, Nat Ridley And The Mail Thieves	Nat RIDLEY
The	Westminster Mystery	Insp REYNOLDS
	Westminster One	Cdr John KNOWLES
	Weston Of The North-West Mounted Police	Policeman Dick WESTON
	Weston Of The Royal North-West Mounted Police	Policeman Dick WESTON
A	Whale Of A Tale	HOMONYMOUS
	What A Body!	John HUGO
	What Crime Is It?	Sheriff Moss MAGILL
	What Dread Hand?	Insp COCKRILL
	What Dread Hand?	Tina MAY
	What Evil Lurks	Lavinia LONDON
	What Gentleman Strangles A Lady?	Pat THOMPSON
	What Happened To Hammond?	Dr CARRUTHERS
	What I Tell You Three Times Is False	Samuel HOLT
	What Is The Dark?	Tim CORRIGAN
	What Me, Mr Mosley?	Insp MOSLEY
	What Night Will Bring	Hilary Dunsany BAILEY III and Hilea BAILEY
	What Price Murder	Stephen MCCLOUD
	What Rhymes With Murder?	Rocky ROCKWELL
	What Rough Beast	Martin COTTERELL
	What The Butler Saw	Sgt MATCH
	What You Pay For	Jack HAGEE
	What - No Body?	Denis CHAD
	What - No Witnesses?	Denis CHAD
	Whatever Happened To Rosie Dunn?	Sophie PARNELL
	Whatever's Been Going On At Mumblesby?	Insp PURBRIGHT
	What's A Girl Gotta Do?	Robin HUDSON
	What's At The End?	Justin MARSH
	What's In A Name?	Det Insp 'Duck' MALLARD
	What's Wrong At Pyford?	Jeff TELLFORD
The	Wheel Spins	Iris CARR
	Wheels In The Forest	Mr DEHAVILLAND and Supt BLACK
	Wheels Within Wheels	Pennington WISE
	When A Man Murders	Cash WALE
	When Conscience Sleeps	Sexton BLAKE
	When Dames Get Tough	Hank JANSON
	When Danger Threatens	John PRENTICE
	When Fell The Night?	Tim CORRIGAN
	When First We Deceive	Lt Bret DUNNIGAN and Det Paige DUNNIGAN
	When Gravity Fails	Marid AUDRAN
	When Honours Pall: Or, Not For Self Gain	Nick CARTER
	When I Grow Rich	Nuri ISKIRLAK
	When Johnny Died	Robert BELCOURT
	When Love Was Not Enough	Joe CINQUEZ
	When Necessity Drives: Or, With The Speed Of Light	Nick CARTER
	When No Man Pursueth	Prof Henry Arthur FIELDING
	When Rich Men Die	Kyle CHAMPION
	When Scholars Fall	Insp MILD, Charles BLAKELOCK, Edward DONALDSON, Andrew MUIR, John QUINCE and Prof BROWNING
	When She Was Bad	Danny FONTAINE
	When The Bough Breaks	Dr Alex DELAWARE
	When The Cat's Away	Kinky FRIEDMAN
	When The Dragon Flies	MCCOY
	When The Gangs Came To London	Capt Jiggs ALLERMAN
	When The Sea Gives Up Its Dead: A Thrilling Detective Story	Annie CORY
	When The Wind Blows	Francis PETTIGREW
	When Thieves Fall Out	Insp RICHARDSON
	When Tutt Meets Tutt	Ephraim TUTT
	Where All The Girls Are Sweeter	Max FARNE
	Where All The Girls Are Sweeter	Max FARNE
	Where Dead Soldiers Walk	Jay PLETCHER
	Where is Bianca?	Tim CORRIGAN
	Where Is The Withered Man?	Bruce MURDOCH
	Where Lawyers Fear To Tread	Willa JANSSON
	Where Nobody Dies	Cass JAMESON
	Where Old Bones Lie	Ursula GRETTON
	Where The Dark Streets Go	Father MCMAHON
	Where The Snow Was Red	Dr John SMITH
	Where The Spies Are	Dr Jason LOVE
	Where There's A Will	Justine CARMICHAEL
	Where There's A Will	Richard TRENTON
	Where There's Smoke	Benjamin SMOKE
	Which Doctor?	Supt BURNIVAL
	Which Mrs Torr?	Jim LITTLE
A	Whiff Of Death	Lt Jack DOHERY and Lou BRADE
The	Whiff Of Money	Mark GIRLAND, Lu SILK and Herman RADNITZ
A	Whiff Of Sulphur	'Birdie' LINNET
	While Murder Waits	Miles LE BRETON
	While Murder Waits	Cash MADIGAN
The	Whims Of Erasmus	Erasmus TUTTLEBERRY
The	Whip Hand	Rex CARVER
	Whip Hand	Sid HALLEY
The	Whipping Boy	Insp Jonas MORCK
The	Whirligig Of Time	Jan DARZEK
	Whirlpools	MANNERS
The	Whirlwind	Dr PALFREY
	Whisper	Lt Felix ELIZALDO
	Whisper In A Lonely Place	Geoffrey LANDON
	Whisper Murder!	Dan CUMBERLAND
The	Whisper Of Death	BRODY
The	Whisperer	Insp STORM
The	Whispering Death	Dixon BRETT
The	Whispering Man	Arthur JEFFREY
The	Whispering Window	Ethel THOMAS
	Whispering Wires	Triggy DREW
	Whispers In The Dark	Oliver KEENE
	Whistle Up The Devil	Algy LAWRENCE
	Whistler's Murder	Mr Henry SMITH
The	White Cad Cross-Up	Bart CHALLIS
The	White Chalet	Tommy LUMB and Peter MARSHAM
	White Circle	Bernard MCFOY
	White Death	Luke ABEL
	White Face	Insp MASON
	White Flower	James MARLEY
	White For A Shroud	Andrew BRANT
The	White Friar	Lionel CRANE
	White Gamma	Steve WARFIELD
	White Gas	Insp MACE
	White Girls Eastward	'Bunjy' HEARNE
	White Jazz	Dudley SMITH and Det Fred UNDERHILL
	White Lie The Dead	Insp KEEN
A	White Male Running	Tommy INMAN
	White Man's Stride	Aubrey St John MAJOR
The	White Mask	Bromley KAY
	White Mercenary	Sexton BLAKE
The	White Mountain Murders	Hugh QUINT
A	White Orchid	Insp SHEFFIELD
The	White Pillar Murders	Dr HYDE
The	White Prior: A Family Mystery	Gilbert THRESHAM and Percy BARSTONE
The	White Rabbit	Herlock SHOLMES
The	White Rider	Bill KENNEDY
	White Wig	Paul RIVINGTON
The	White Witch Of The South Seas	Gregory SALLUST
The	White Zone	Capt Ralph 'Rat' TRAPP
The	Whitechapel Horrors	Sherlock HOLMES
The	Whitechapel Murders: Or, An American Detective In London	The AMERICAN DETECTIVE
The	Whittington Pact	Michael BERESFORD
	Who Called Diamonds?	John BORHAM
	Who Censored Roger Rabbit?	Eddie VALIANT
	Who Closed The Casement?	Insp BEDISON
	Who Dies Next?	Insp GRIERSON
	Who Dies There?	John P PHELAN
	Who Dies?	Philip WINSLOW
	Who Guards The Prince?	Insp MCHARG
	Who Is Teddy Villanova?	Russel WREN
	Who Is The Heir?	Det SOMERTON
	Who Is The Next?	Pete MURRAY
	Who Is This Man?	Jerry BOYNE

Who Keeps The Keys?	Jimmy LANGRY
Who Killed Brother Treasurer?	Insp Roger ELLERDINE
Who Killed Caudwell?	Fleming STONE
Who Killed Cavelotti?	Det Patrick Michael DOYLE
Who Killed Cock Robin?	Nicol HART
Who Killed Coralie?	Parrish DARBY
Who Killed Diana	Nicol HART
Who Killed Gregory?	Byron HUGHES
Who Killed James Trent?	James TRENT
Who Killed Me?	Valerie LAMBERT
Who Killed Netta Maul?	Insp SPEARPOINT
Who Killed Peter Trueman?	Andrew FORSTER
Who Killed The Little Cockney Nightingale	Charlotte HOLMES
Who Killed The Pie Man?	Leo ROI
Who Knows Julie Gordon?	Ida PELHAM
Who Murdered Reynard?	Prof BLINKWELL
Who Poisoned Hetty Duncan? And Other Detective Stories	Det Dick DONOVAN
Who Rides A Tiger	Sarah LOWDEN
Who Shot The Spy?	John WILSON
Who Spies, Who Kills?	Tim CORRIGAN
Who Told Clutha?	CLUTHA
Who Was The Killer?	Det Insp Alan MELFORD
Whoever I Am	Helen MARKHAM
The Whole Hog	Arthur APPLEYARD
Whom The Gods Love	Julian KESTREL
Whose Body Are You?	Dan TROUT
Whose Body?	Lord Peter WIMSEY
Whose Dog Are You?	John CUNNINGHAM
Whose Was The Hand?	Luke BRADLEY
Whoso Diggeth A Pit	Henry Napoleon BAGGS
Who'd Hire Brett?	John BRETT
Who'd Want To Kill Old George?	Amos MCGUFFIN
Who's Afraid Of Sherlock Holmes?	Sherlock HOLMES
Who's Next?	Valerie LAMBERT
Why Didn't They Ask Evans?	Frances DERWENT and Bobby JONES
Why Isn't Becky Twitchell Dead?	Tom MASON
Why Kill A Butler?	Supt GADEN
Why Kill Arthur Potter?	Sgt Joseph BRAGG
Why Pick On Me?	Martin 'Brick-Top' CORRIGAN
Why Pick On Pickles?	Insp YORK
Why Shoot A Butler?	Frank AMBERLEY
Why So Dead?	Tim CORRIGAN
The Whyte Hart	Matthew JENKYN
Wicked Designs	Mici ANHALT
A Wicked Slice	Lee OFSTED
The Widening Stain	Gilda GORHAM
The Widow	Arlette VAN DER VALK
The Widow And The Cavalier	J Rockingham STONE, Laura SCUDAMORE and Insp Dick MASON
The Widow Gay	Pete HUNTER
Widows Ought To Weep	Mr PUCKETT
The Widow's Club	Hyacinth TRAMWELL and Primrose TRAMWELL
Widow's End	Insp/Ch Insp Dick TANSEY
Widow's Mite	Lt LEVY
The Widow's Peak	Bill ANSTRUTHER
Widow's Peak	Nell BRAY
Widow's Pique	Pete BAYLISS
The Wife Of Ronald Sheldon	Peter DULUTH and Lt Timothy TRANT
Wiggles, A Story Of Smuggling Days And Ways Around Poole	Augustus WIGGLESWORTH
Wild	Lee BARON
Wild Horses	Thomas LYON
Wild Justice	James Maxwell MALLORY
Wild Night	Lucas HALLAM
Wild Pitch	Sheriff Chick CHARLESTON
Wild Town	'Bugs' MCKENNA
Wild Wives	Jacob C 'Jake' BLAKE
Wilde West	Oscar WILDE
Wilders Walk Away	Reynold FRAME
A Wild-Cat Scheme	Sgt/Insp/Supt MARGETSON
A Will To Kill	Supt George THORNE
William Cook - Antique Dealer	Franklin PARRY and Leonard HARRIS
William Pollok And Other Tales	William POLLOK
Willowdene Will	WILLOWDENE WILL
Willy Velvet, Homicide Detective	Willy VELVET
Wilson And Some Others	Supt Henry WILSON
Wilson's Woman	Wilson YOUNG
Win Some, Lose Some	Michael SHAYNE
The Wind Blows Death	Francis PETTIGREW
The Wind Tunnel	Sam WHARTON
The Windblow Mystery	Kenneth O'BRIEN
Windfall	Max STAFFORD
Window In The Dark	Crispin QUAYNE
Winds Of The Old Day	Rosalind ROTH
Winds Of The World	Cliff CRAGIN
Wind-Up	Peter MARKLIN
The Wine Merchant: A Hitherto Unpublished Case Of Sherlock Holmes As Recorded By Dr Watson	Sherlock HOLMES
Wine, Women And Waiters	Giuseppe CIGARINI
Wine, Women...And Death	Frank ARROW
The Winged Murderer	Dick HADDEN
Wings Of Death	Sheriff Hiram ODOM
Wings Of Romance	'Steeley' DELAROY
Wings Of The Black Death	Richard (The Spider) WENTWORTH
Wingwalker	Horatio CASSIDY
The Wink	Insp ROBINET
Wink A Hopeful Eye	Georgina POWERS
Winner Take All	Johnny MACALL
Winnie O'Wynn And The Dark Horses	Winnie O'WYNN
Winnie O'Wynn And The Wolves	Winnie O'WYNN
The Winning Streak	GOLDBERG
Winslow Moult	Winslow MOULT
Winter Kill	Johnny RYAN
The Winter Murder Case	Philo VANCE
The Winter Touch	Charles WINTER
The Winton Street Mystery	Lydford LONG
The Wire Tappers	James DURKIN
The Wire Window	Colin SMALLPIECE
The Wisdom Of Father Brown	Father BROWN
The Wisemann Originals	Rudy NAVARRO
Wish You Were Dead	Miguel URIZAR
Wish You Were Here	Mrs MURPHY
Wisteria Lodge	Sherlock HOLMES
The Witch Of The Low Tide: An Edwardian Melodrama	Dr David GARTH and Det Insp TWIGG
The Witches' Pond	Anthony WARE
The Witching Hour	Insp Edward MAINE
The Witching Hour	Kitty TELEFAIR
Witchline	Andrew LAIRD
Witchline	Andrew LAIRD
Witch-Hunt!	Sexton BLAKE
Witch's Bane	China BAYLES
The Witch's House	Annabel O'SHEA
Witch's Moon	Nile BOYD
With A Vengeance	Det DELA
With Bated Breath	Insp HEADCORN
With Cause Enough?	Mr JELLIPOT
With Extreme Prejudice	Peter FELTHAM
With Intent	Det Sgt Arthur MILTON
With Mallets Aforethought	Winston WYC
With Murder For Some	Ch Charles BAKER
With My Little Eye	Hamish OATH
The Withdrawing Room	Max BITTERSOHN
Withered Murder	FATHOM
Withered Murder	FATHOM
Within The Maze	TATTON
Without Honor	Kirk MCGARVEY
Without Love Or Licence: A Tale Of South Devon	John DICKINSON
Witness Before The Fact	Peter COREY
Witness Before The Fact	Peter COREY
Witness In Peril	Sarah O'BRIEN
The Witness Of The Sun	Jack HENLEY
Wives To Burn	Bill GABRIEL
The Wizard Of La-La Land	WHISTLER
Wobble To Death	Sgt CRIBB and Const THACKERAY
The Wolf Howls "Murder"	Barnaby JONES
Wolf In Man's Clothing	Sarah KEATE
A Wolf In The Fold	Donald CAIRN
The Wolf Of Texas	Ferrers LOCKE
A Wolf Of The Evenings	Miss WOOLFE
The Wolf Whispered Death	Dr Gordon CHRISTY
The Wolfman At Milburn	Sherlock HOLMES
Wolf! Wolf!	Lt Cliff KENNEDY
Wolf! Wolf!	Amy TUPPER
Wolverine Waif, The Half-Breed Detective; Or, The Lost Mine Tragedy	WOLVERINE WAIF
The Wolves Of Chaos	Cutty CLAY
The Wolves Of Washington	LYON and GATCH
The Wolves Of Washington	Jack SIMONS
The Woman Accused	James SEGROVE
The Woman At The Window	Margo FRANKLIN and Philip SPENCE
A Woman Called Scylla	Jane MONTIGNY
Woman Detective	Annette KERNER
The Woman In Black	Jimmie HASWELL
The Woman In Black	Philip TRENT
The Woman In Black; Or, Nick Carter's Clever Haul	Nick CARTER
The Woman In Red	Charles LLEWELLYN
Woman In The Dark	The CONTINENTAL OP
The Woman In The Wardrobe	Mr VERITY and Insp RAMBLER
The Woman In White	Walter HARTWRIGHT
Woman Of Cairo	Hart MULDOON
Woman Of Saigon	Sexton BLAKE
A Woman Of Valor	Leora BARUCH
A Woman Spy	Olga von KOPF
Woman With A Gun	Alan MAXWELL
A Woman's Burden	Insp PRINCE
A Woman's Own Mystery	Dee STREET
A Woman's Revenge	Yvonne CARTIER
Women Are Like That	Det Supt John BELLAMY
The Women Of Peasenhall	Insp David BROCK
The Women Swore Revenge	Patrick O'BRIEN
The Wonder Craft	Nelson LEE
The Wonderful Career Of Ebenezer Lobb	Ebenezer LOBB
The Wooden Overcoat	Clifford FLUSH
Woolf Sarason, Special Agent	Woolf SARASON
The Woolwich Arsenal Mystery	Sexton BLAKE
A Word For Murder	Lt Joseph MARCUS
Work For A Dead Man	John Kenneth Galbraith JANTARRO
The Working Man Detective; Or, A Crime Against The Poor	The WORKING MAN DETECTIVE
Working Murder	Clare GAMADGE
The World Championship Mystery	Sexton BLAKE
The World Cup Murders	Marcus Aurelius BURR
A World Of Hurt	Harvey BLISSBERG
The World Of Tim Frazer	Tim FRAZER
The World-Shakers	Sexton BLAKE
The World's Fair Murders	Al BENNET
A Worm Turns	Maj Jonathan CRAYTHORNE
The Worm Will Turn	Kerlock SHOMES
The Worst Case On Record; Or, A Murderer By Profession	Nick CARTER
The Worst Way TO Die	Johnny ROCK
Wrath To Come	Grant SLATTERY
A Wreath For A Lady	Insp Jim SILVER and Mike LOGAN
A Wreath For America	David MARTINI
A Wreath For The Bride	Gwen RAMADGE
A Wreath For The Bride	Christer WICK
A Wreath From Bangkok	David CHAN
A Wreath Of Cherry Blossom	David CHAN
Wreath Of Honesty	Henry BASSETT
A Wreath Of Roses	Gen Charles KIRK

The Wreck Of The Mary Deare	John SANDS
Write Me A Letter	Vic DANIEL
Written In Blood	Det Ch Insp Tom BARNABY
The Wrong Box	Michael FINSBURY
The Wrong Case	Milton Chester MILODRAGOVITCH
The Wrong Letter	Sir Arthur SINCLAIR
The Wrong Rite	Policeman Madoc RHYS
Wrong Target	Charles 'Chickie' FRENCH
The Wrong Target	Johnny MCCOY
Wrongful Death	Henry PAIGE
Wu Fang	Wu FANG
Wyatt	WYATT
Wyatt's Orphan	WYATT
Wycliffe In The Elf Wood	Supt Charles WYCLIFFE
Wyllard's Weird	Edward HEATHCOTE
The Wyndham Case	Imogen QUY
The Wyss Pursuit	Barrington (The Peacemaker) HEWES-BRADFORD

—X—

X Esquire	Bill KENNEDY
X Jones	X JONES
X Jones Of Scotland Yard	X JONES
The Xander Pursuit	Barrington (The Peacemaker) HEWES-BRADFORD
The XYY Man	Willie 'Spider' SCOTT
The X-Ray Murders	Wood JAXON

—Y—

Y Cheung, Business Detective	Y CHEUNG
The Yankee Doodle Detective	The YANKEE DOODLE DETECTIVE
Yankee Jed, The Down East Detective	YANKEE JED
Yankee Lawyer - The Autobiography Of Ephraim Tutt	Ephraim TUTT
Yankie Rue, The Ex-Pugilist Detective	YANKEE RUE
Yard Lengths	STANDIFORD
The Yarns Of Billy Borker	Billy BORKER
The Yawning Lion	William HARKNESS
Yellow Bird	Dr Charlie ADAMS
The Yellow Circle	Phineas FLINT
The Yellow Claw	Gaston MAX
The Yellow Crayon	Mr SABIN
Yellow Death	Prof Arnold RHYMER
The Yellow Dragon	Lawrence Patrick 'Larry' KENT
The Yellow Face	Sherlock HOLMES
The Yellow Hearse	Cassie GIBSON
Yellow Jacket	Peter PENNINGTON
Yellow Magic	CHU-SHENG
The Yellow Overcoat	Joe DEVLIN
The Yellow Phiz	Herlock SHOLMES
The Yellow Room	Maj DANE
The Yellow Seven	Peter PENNINGTON
Yellow Shadows	Ch Insp Daniel 'Red' KERRY
The Yellow Spider	KOYALA
The Yellow Spider	Ferrers LOCKE
The Yellow Streak	Robin GREVE, Mary TREVERT and Insp MANDERTON
The Yellow Tiger	Sexton BLAKE
The Yellow Turban	William BROOKE
The Yellow Wolf	Dixon BRETT
Yellowthread Street	Harry FEIFFER and YELLOWTHREAD STREET COPS
Yesterday's Papers	Harry DEVLIN
Yes, Sir; No, Sir	Supt INKBARROW
You Asked For It	Cdr James BOND
You Bet Your Life	Toby PETERS, Ian FLEMING and MARX BROTHERS
You Can Always Blame The Rain	Willie HALLIDAY
You Can Call It A Day	Johnny VALLON
You Can Die Trying	Aaron GUNNER
You Can Help Me	Kate WEATHERLY
You Can't Catch Me	Mike WELLS
You Could Call It Murder	MARKHAM
You Did It	Lt Joseph DICKERSON
You Get What You Pay For	Tony CASSELLA
You Have Yourself A Deal	Mark GIRLAND
You Know The Way It Is	Felix HOLLIDAY
You Leave Me Cold!	Prof Paul HATFIELD
You Never Know With Women	Floyd JACKSON
You Only Hang Once	Sid AMES
You Only Live Until You Die	Israel 'Oy-Oy-7' BOND
You Pay For Pity	Casson DUKER
You Remember The Case	Tod CLAYMORE
You See But You Do Not Observe	Sherlock HOLMES
You Will Die Today!	Lt MARSHALL and Judy MEADOWS
Young Beck, A Chip Off The Old Block	Paul BECK Jr
Young Fearless, The Detective Of Many Disguises	YOUNG FEARLESS
Young Lord Stranleigh	Lord STRANLEIGH
The Young Man From Lima	Marcus LEVIN
Young Men May Die	Stephen BELLECROIX and Sheila ROATH
Young Mrs Cavendish And The Kaiser's Men	Maude Teasdale CAVENDISH
Young Petrella	Const/Ch Insp Patrick PETRELLA
Young Sherlock Holmes	Sherlock HOLMES
Young Sledge, The Iron-Fisted Detective; Or, A Mystery Of The Cumberland	YOUNG SLEDGE
Young Sleuth's Victory; Or, A Detective's Adventure	YOUNG SLEUTH
The Young Vanish	Det Insp ALLPORT
Young Wallingford	James Rufus WALLINGFORD
Young Weasel, The Baltimore Detective	YOUNG WEASEL
Your Daughter Will Die!	Brian PETERSEN
Your Day In The Barrel	Roger LEVIN
Your Eyes Are Growing Heavy	Henrietta SNOOKS and Gus BILINSKI
Your Golden Jugular	Sampson ROACH
Your Move, Delaney	Denis DELANEY
Your Neck In A Noose	Toby DYKE
Your Turn, Mr Moto	Mr MOTO
You're Hired; You're Dead	Mike ROSS
You'd Better Believe It	Ch Supt Colin HARPUR
You'll Be The Death Of Me	Nell WILLARD
You'll Catch Your Death	Tony CARTER
You'll Die Laughing	Lt BRISSK
You'll Die Tonight	Maxine REYNOLDS
You'll Die When You Hear This	Maxine REYNOLDS
You'll Get Yours	Barney GLINES
You'll Get Yours	Barney GLINES
You'll Never Get To Heaven	Brock DEVLIN
You're A Long Time Dead	Peter FLECK
You're Dead Without Money	Herman RADNITZ and Al BARNEY
You're Lonely When You're Dead	Vic MALLOY
You're Wrong, Delaney	Denis DELANEY
The Yunnan Terminus	Erik CHATHAM

—Z—

The Z Document	Nick CARTER
The Zadda Street Affair	Archibald PENNY
The Zakka Slaughter	Brett WALLACE
Zaleski's Percentage	John RAVEN
Zambra The Detective: Some Clues From His Notebook	Sebastian ZAMBRA
The Zarahemia Vision	Gabriel UTLEY
Zeb Taylor, The Puritan Detective; Or, Piping The Great Treasury Case	Zeb TAYLOR
Zelda	Rick HOLMAN
Zero In The Gate	Insp Elwyn MORGAN
Zero The 14th	Maxwell ARCHER
Ziggurat	Zack ROBERTS
Zigzag	Insp/Ch Insp Harry PECKOVER and Supt O'MALLEY
Zodiac: The Eco-Thriller	Sangamon TAYLOR
Zombies Of The Gene Pool	Jay OMEGA
The Zone Of Fire	Pte Amos MEARS
The " Z" Ray	Reggie FAULKNER

The Sidekicks

A

Sgt Bill ABBOT	Supt George THORNE
Tony ABBOTT	Commiss Thatcher COLT
Sgt ABBOTT	Insp/Ch Insp Dick TANSEY
Father ABSINTHE	Monsieur LECOQ
Dolly ADAMS	Al DELANEY
ADSO	Brother WILLIAM
Nurse Cherry AIMLESS	Nancy CLUE
Dr Walter ALLAN	Capt/Maj/Col Hugh NORTH
Nevada ALVARADO	Violet MCDADE
Jock ANDERSON	Dick BARTON
ASTA	Nick CHARLES and Nora CHARLES
Sgt ATHERTON	Det Insp Bill SLIDER
ATSONEZ	Cerlocio OLMEZ
AUNT WILMA	Shirley HOLMQUIST
Clement AUSTIN	Mr Henry CARTER

B

Warren BAER	Ed BAER
George BAGBY	Insp SCHMIDT
Sgt Baptiste BANTOC	Lt Felix ELIZALDO
Harold BANTZ	Henry GAMADGE
Sue BARKER	Pat THOMPSON
Det Const Clive BARNARD	Det Insp Jack FROST
Steve BARNES	Prof Ira COBB
Nigel BATHGATE	Insp/Supt Roderick ALLEYN
Dave BAXTER	Ron HOGGETT
Henry BEAVER	Rev Martin BUELL
Fergus BEDE	Helen BULLOCK
Sgt BELL	Insp CARTER
BENNO	SIGISMONDO
Sgt BENWICK	Insp Lathom DYNES
Sgt BERGER	Insp/Ch Supt George MASTERS and Ch Insp Bill GREEN
Bill BEVERLEY	Anthony GILLINGHAM
Mavis BIGNELL	G D H PRINGLE
Kathy BIRCHFIELD	Thomas BLACK
Sgt William BIRD	Insp Richard MONTGOMERY
Det Ken BLACKBURN	Prof Joanne FLEMING
'Cherry' BLOSSOM	Insp Roger ELLERDINE
Det Jane BOARDMAN	Lt Francis X KERRIGAN
BODINSKY	Daniel J CLUER
Henry BONES	Norman BONES
Francis BONNAMY	Maj Peter Utley SHANE
Dr BOPSON	Sheerback TONES
Charlie BOSTON	Oliver QUADE
James BOSWELL	Dr Sam JOHNSON
Sgt Tom BOYCE	Det Ch Insp Jack FINCH
Sgt Peter BRADFIELD	Insp Harry CHARLTON
Mark BRADLEY	Rayford GOODMAN
Sgt BRAGG	Ch Insp POOLE
Det Sgt Jim BRAILEY	Det Ch Insp GREVE
Meriadoc BRANDYBUCK	Frodo BAGGINS
Joseph Payne BRENNAN	Lucius LEFFING
Mr BRETT	Martin HEWITT
Bella BRICKLEY	Mme Rosika STOREY
Bendy BRINKS	Prof CALDWELL
Sgt BROOK	Insp MCLEAN
Mrs Elizabeth Barrett BROWNING	Robert BROWNING
Sgt Phineas BUCK	Col John PRIMROSE
Mrs BUCKET	Insp BUCKET
Insp Humphrey BULL	Evan PINKERTON
Helen BULLOCK	Father Simon BEDE
BUNTER	Lord Peter WIMSEY
Insp Mike BURDEN	Ch Insp Reginald WEXFORD
Aleck BURTON	Carrie CASHIN
Polly BURTON	The OLD MAN IN THE CORNER
Jim BYRNE	Susan DARE

C

Julian CAIRD	Det Insp Simon SPEARS
Angel CANTINI	Paul MARSTON
Beth CANTRELL	John CUNNINGHAM
CARDBY	Mick CARDBY
Louis CARLYLE	Max CARRADOS
Thomas C CARLYLE	Carlotta CARLYLE
CARMEN	Kate BAIER
Insp CARON	Commissaire LEBEL
CARSTAIRS	DOAN
Policewoman Sue CARSTAIRS	Sgt Ivor MADDOX
Chick CARTER	Nick CARTER
Laura CHARME	Sebastian BLUE
Sgt CHEAL	Insp HOBDEN
CHUCK	Sherlock MONK
Jack CLANCY	Iris COOPER
Mary CLERKENWELL	Jerry TODD
Max COHN	Ben JARDINN
Sgt Chuck CONLEY	Sgt Jerry LONG
Chick CONWAY	Martin SWIFT
Det Frank COOPER	Det Mick GARVEY
Gerry CORDENT	Paul KILGERRIN
Patricia CORDRY	Jason CORDRY
Rose COURTENAY	Robert SPICER
COUSIN RENIE	Judith McMonigle FLYNN
COWBOY	RAFFERTY
CREIGHTON	Quentin QUAYNE
Joshua CROFT	Rita MONDRAGON
Supt CROMWELL	Det Insp/Supt Thomas LITTLEJOHN
Insp CROSBY	Insp George MARTIN
Sgt William CROSBY	Insp Christopher Dennis SLOAN
Ronnie CUMMINGS	Insp Rupert HAMBLEDON
'Doc' CUMMINGS	Asey MAYO
Insp CURTIS	Insp/Supt William AUSTEN

D

Ahmad DAKAR	Jane D MULROY
Det D'ARCY	Sgt Ivor MADDOX
Insp Daniel DARCY	Insp Clovis Desire PEL
Max DARLING	Annie LAURANCE
Dr DAWSON	Haricot BONES
Prof Robert DEANE	Bertram LYNCH
Danny DELEVAN	Prof Cyrus HATCH
Det DENBY	Det Gabriel WAGER
Sgt DICKENS	Insp/Supt Sholto LESTRADE
Dr Eric DIETERLEE	Richard Van Ryn WILSON
DOLLOPS	Hamilton CLEEK

The Sidekicks

Fritz DONHOFF	Pierre-Ange SAWYER
Det DONOVAN	MAC
Sgt DOVE	Sgt/Insp John COFFIN
Dr DOVER	Sherlock HOLMES
Dr DOVER	Pharaoh JONES
Paul DRAKE	Perry MASON
DREIST	Duncan MACLAIN
Avie DU POIS	Dr ALCAZAR
Sgt DUFF	Insp CHERRY
'Sailor' DUFFY	Cash WALE
Francy DUNBAR	Det Ch Insp Colin THANE and Insp Phil MOSS
Det Marge DUNN	Det Peter DECKER

E

Sgt EBERHART	Lt Janus MURTAUGH
Dennis ECKENBERG	Eliza PIREX
Sgt ELK	Insp MASON
Det Sgt Jack ELLERS	Insp Ben JURNET
Radcliff EMERSON	Amelia PEABODY
EMILY	Insp Thomas PITT and Charlotte PITT
Hump EVANS	Jim HARDMAN

F

Michelle FARABAUGH	Jeremiah ST JOHN
Dr FATSO	Turlock LOAMS
Alice FAVENDEN	Clive 'Dormouse' CONRAD
Sgt Reginald FINCH	Det Ch Insp Sidney WALSH
Huckleberry FINN	Tom SAWYER
Dr FITZBROWN	Insp/Supt MALLETT
FLASH	Valerie DREW
Jillian FLETCHER	Jackson FURY
Sgt FLYTE	Insp/Supt William AUSTEN
Insp FOX	Insp/Supt Roderick ALLEYN
Sgt FRANT	Insp MALLETT
Sgt FRANT	Insp MALLETT and Francis PETTIGREW
Garth FREDERICKSON	Dr Robert 'Mongo' FREDERICKSON
Insp Gordon FREWIN	Ch Insp James MILLER
Lt Pete FRIEDMAN	Lt Frank HASTINGS
Christine FROST	Reuben FROST

G

Everett GABLER	John Putnam THATCHER
Sam GAMGEE	Frodo BAGGINS
Wizard GANDALF	Frodo BAGGINS
Harry GARNISH	Bridget O'TOOLE
Paddy GARVAN	Nick CARTER
Sgt Frank GATENBY	Insp Charlie SALTER
GAYLORD	KNIGHTSBRIDGE
June GAYNOR	Noel RAYMOND
GENE	Hilary QUAYLE
GEORGE	Toby DYKE
Det Sgt GILMORE	Det Insp Jack FROST
Det Insp Jack GILROY	Det Ch Supt Thomas FOX
Jules GIRAUD	Auguste LUPA
Barney GLINES	Mike FONTAINE
James GOFF	Paula GLENNING
Norma GOLD	Alexander Magnus GOLD
Isadore GOLDBERG	Sidney 'Silky' PINCUS and Mike CLANCY
Brenda GOLDSTEIN	Rabbi Daniel WINTER
Carl GOOD	Max KEENE
Archie GOODWIN	Nero WOLFE
GOSWELL	Warlock BONES
Joey GRAHAM	Rex SACKLER
Paul GRAHAM	Ben TANCRED and Supt Henry WILSON
Bill GRIFFITH	Anthony HUNTER
GRIP	Martin TRACK
GUITERREZ	Max LATIN
GWEN	Stoner MCTAVISH

H

Det Arthur HACKETT	Lt Luis MENDOZA
Arthur HALLAM	John JERICHO
Mike HAMMER	Peter BRAID
Dr HARCOURT	Shrock HOLMES
Dr HARCOURT	Tide POOLES
Sgt HARKNESS	Jack LAIDLAW
Pete HARMAN	Catherine SAYLOR
Helen HARMAS	Steve HARMAS
HARRIS	Bert BAYLISS
Chip HARRISON	Leo HAIG
Capt HASTINGS	Hercule POIROT
Sgt Barbara HAVERS	Insp Thomas LYNLEY
Jim HAWK	SPENSER
Nimue HAWTHORNE	'Birdie' LINNET
Insp HEMINGWAY	Supt HANNASYDE
HICKS	DORRINGTON
Det George HIGGINS	Lt Luis MENDOZA
Judy HILL	Ch Insp LLOYD
Nicki HILL	Samuel Clemens TUCKER
Bobby HILLIARD	Julian QUIST
Mary Spraggue HILLMAN	Michael SPRAGGUE
Harry HINDS	Paul MADRIANI
HOGG	PIRON
Sgt HOLLAND	Ch Insp Michael 'Napper' TANDY
Mycroft HOLMES	Dr John H WATSON
Sgt HONEYBODY	Insp Harry JAMES
Dr Fabian HONEYCHURCH	Supt BURNIVAL
Sgt Bert HOOK	Supt John LAMBERT
Liang HOONG	Judge Jen-djieh DEE
Sgt HOPKINS	Insp Neville LANGHAM
Insp HOPKINSON	Det Insp/Supt Thomas LITTLEJOHN
Dr HOTBUN	Rex HOMES
Larry HOWE	Berkeley Hoy BARNES
Lester HOYT	Shean CONNELL
Olivia HUDSON	Charley IVES
Hubert HUMBERSTONE	Kate KINSELLA
Det Sgt Jerry HUNTER	Det Ch Insp BROWNE
Nell HUXLEIGH	Irene ADLER

I

Dr Watts ION	Sheerluck OHMS

J

Det Sgt Ken JACKSON	Ch Insp David WEBB
JAKE	Prof Jackie WALSH
Sgt Gemma JAMES	Duncan KINCAID
Walter JAMESON	Prof Craig KENNEDY
Insp JANVIER	Insp Jules MAIGRET
JELLICOE	Ben TANCRED and Supt Henry WILSON
Dr JENKINS	Raffles HOLMES
Ted JERNINGHAM	Capt Hugh 'Bulldog' DRUMMOND
Dr Christopher JERVIS	Dr John Evelyn THORNDYKE
Dr JOBSON	Purlock HONE
JOHNSTONE	A B C HAWKES
JOLLY	Richard (The Toff) ROLLISON
JONES	Joshua CLUNK
JONES	The Hon Constance Ethel MORRISON-BURKE
Fetlock JONES	Sherlock HOLMES
'Loopy' JONES	Del SKINNER
Sgt JONES	Insp/Supt Sholto LESTRADE
Dr JOTSON	Herlock SHOLMES
Sister JOYCE	Sister Mary Teresa DEMPSEY
JUGGINS	Shamrock JOLNES

K

Det Joe KAMINSKY	Lt Jake CHASE
KAPROSKI	Lt CLANCY
KARPO	Insp Porfiry Petrovich ROSTNIKOV
Sandy KEITH	Joe CAVE
Sgt Tom KELLY	Det Insp Frank DERBEN
KENNEDY	Capt Steve MACBRIDE
Jack KERMAN	Mark GIRLAND
Jack KERMAN	Vic MALLOY
Maj KETTERING-BEVIS	Prof Luther BASTION
KHAN	John MARSHALL and Suzy MARSHALL
Sister KIM	Sister Mary Teresa DEMPSEY
Insp Jiro KIMURA	Supt Tetsuo OTANI
Molly KINGSLEY	Olga KNARESBROOK
Lucy KINGSLEY	David MIDDLETON-BROWNE
Lord KIRWOOD	Paul BECK Jr
Sgt KITE	Insp Gil MAYO
Isobel KITTS	John CUNNINGHAM
Avery KNIGHT	Shamrock JOLNES
KOKO	Jim QWILLERAN
Sgt Bell KOSINSKI	Marty BLAKE
KURT	Barney HYDE

L

Sandra LAING	Det Ch Insp Colin THANE and Insp Phil MOSS
Penny LAKE	Dr Wade ANTHONY
Sgt John LAMB	Insp Frederick Jubilee 'Jumper' CROSS
Sgt LAMBERT	Insp KELSEY
Raina LAMBERT	Jay PLETCHER
'Bumpy' LANDING	Hugh DECKER
Ann LANG	William SCHAEFER
Insp LAPOINTE	Insp Jules MAIGRET
Nancy LEE	Edith DEXTER
Sgt LEEDS	Insp HARRIS
Miriam LEONARD	Homer EVANS
Emma LESTRADE	Insp/Supt Sholto LESTRADE
Tania LEVIN	J Molden MOTT
Tania LEVIN	Marcus LEVIN
Sgt LEWIS	Insp MORSE
Clare LIDDICOTE	Insp Richard RINGWOOD
LILLY	Tip O'NEIL
Sgt Mike LINEHAM	Det Insp Luke THANET
Ch Insp LINGARD	Det Supt George ROGERS
Sgt LISTER	Bill 'Ironsides' CROMWELL
Sgt Dafydd LLEWELLYN	Insp Joseph Aloysius RAFFERTY
Sgt Hilary LLOYD	Det Ch Insp Douglas QUANTRILL
Det Walt LOGAN	Det Steve MANNING
LONELY	David CALLAN
Sgt LOVE	Insp PURBRIGHT
Insp LUCAS	Insp Jules MAIGRET
Magersfontein LUGG	Albert CAMPION
Sgt LUMLEY	Insp Alfred SWAIN

M

Alexander MACBAIN	Sir Godfrey EVESDEN
Kitty MACLEOD	Whit WHITNEY
Susie MACVEIGH	Capt Andy MACVEIGH
MAGSY	Bow Street Runner Jeremy STURROCK
Pat MALONE	Dixon BRETT
Bunny MANDERS	A J RAFFLES
Butch MANERI	Steve CRANMER
Sgt Patrick MANSFIELD	Det Insp James ROLAND
Jeff MARLE	Juge d'Instruction Henri BENCOLIN
MARLOWE	Nathan PHILLIPS
Sgt MARSHALL	Insp/Supt Sholto LESTRADE
'Pulp' MARTIN	Maria BLACK
'Plugger' MARTIN	Rex HUXFORD
Sylvia MARTIN	Doug SELBY
MARY	Lady Molly DE MAZEREEN
Dabney MASON	Col BRAXTON
John MATTHEWS	Prof Herman BRIERLY
Ben MATTHEWS	Dean Wardlow ROCK
MAX	Prof John STUBBS
MAX THE SILENT	BURKE
Det MAZELLI	Lt Rocco KLEIN
Noreen MCGARR	Insp Peter MCGARR
Sgt MCGREGOR	Insp Wilfred DOVER
Terrence MCGUIRE	Fleming STONE
Isobel MCKINTOSH	Giles SULLIVAN
Anne MCNEILL	Dr Jeffrey MCNEILL
Caroline MCWILLIAMS	Miles JACOBY
MEG	Conan FLAGG
Hilary MEREDITH	Father MICKLE
MEREDITH	Dr Louis RAPHAEL
Cad METTI	Dudie DUNNE
MEYER	Travis MCGEE
MICHELLE	BURKE
MILHORNE	CRAGGS
Jeff MILTON	GINGKO
MIMI	RAFFERTY
Det Insp Kate MISKIN	Insp/Cdr Adam DALGLIESH
The MOLE	BURKE
MOLLOCK	Walter GHOST
Motilal MOOKERJI	Dr Daniel Webster COFFEE and Lt Max RITTER
Mona MOORE	Prof Clifford DUNBAR
Fausta MORENI	Manville MOON
Ralph MORETON	Victor SERGE
Const James MORTON	Sgt Joseph BRAGG
Ch MOSES	Jeremiah ST JOHN
Sgt/Insp MOTT	Supt Mike YEADINGS
Miriam The MOUTH	Hugh DECKER
S Michael MURDOCH	Wade GRIFFIN
Jane MYERS	Nick PALLADINO
Dora MYRL	Paul BECK

N

Bob NAKAMURA	Virgil TIBBS
Natasha NEVKORINA	Miriam BIRDSEYE
Mercy NEWCASTLE	Will WOODFIELD
Vic NEWMAN	Sabina SWIFT
Windermere NIKOLLS	Rupert Patrick 'Slim' CALLAGHAN
NIP	Johnny STONE and Ruth DEE
NIPPER	Nelson LEE
Insp 'Ninja' NOGUCHI	Supt Tetsuo OTANI
Nora NORAKER	Madelyn MACK
Sgt Jean-Luc NOSJEAN	Insp Clovis Desire PEL

O

Hattie O'HARA	Fergus O'HARA
R Danoel OLIVAW	Elijah BALEY
Tom O'MALLEY	William CRANE
ONE	Ed STONE

P

PANSY	BURKE
Saul PANZER	Nero WOLFE
Dr Lyndon PARKER	Solar PONS
PARKINSON	Max CARRADOS
Dep Commiss PARR	Oliver ARMISTON
Marty PEARL	Peter FINLEY
Joe PEEL	Otis BEAGLE
Bessy PETTY	Mark EAST
Const Brenda PHIPPS	Det Ch Insp Sidney WALSH
Det Sgt Tony PIDGEON	Det Insp Samuel 'Smudge' HUDDLESTON
Det Insp William PIGRAM	Darina LISLE
PIKE	Elvis COLE
Sgt PISANELLI	Commiss TROTTI
Melrose PLANT	Insp Richard JURY
Victor PLOTZ	Charlie BRADSHAW
Sgt PLUMMER	Insp Richard RINGWOOD
Sgt POLLOCK	Insp HAZELRIGG
Sgt POLNICK	Lt Al WHEELER
Nathaniel POLTON	Dr John Evelyn THORNDYKE
Grace POMEROY	Dr Hillis OWEN
Beulah POND	Mark EAST
Dr Love Rees PONS	Lt Michael LORD
Dr POTSDAM	Porlock MOANS
Dr POTSON	Sheerluck GNOMES
Dr POTSON	Picklock HOLES
Winnie PRESTON	Cornelius CLIFT Jr
Det Robin PRICE	Tessa CRICHTON
Insp PRICE	Supt ROPER
Nikky PRICE	Lt Price PRICE
Giles PRIEST	Dorian SILK
Rupert PRIGGLEY	Carolus DEENE
Sgt PRIMROSE	Insp BIDWELL
Jeremy PROCTER	Sir John FIELDING
The PROFESSOR	BURKE
Sgt Judy PULLEN	Ch Insp Ralph ARNOTT
Cletus PURCEL	Det Dave ROBICHAUX

Q

Mr Q	Det Ebenezer GRYCE
Insp Richard QUEEN	Ellery QUEEN
Orson QUICK	Hank HYER

R

Corey RALEIGH	Brock (The Rock) CALLAHAN
Squire RANDOLPH	Uncle ABNER
Det Sgt RANGER	Emily SEETON and Supt DELPHICK
RATSO	Kinky FRIEDMAN
Det Stan RAYDER	Det Pete SELBY
Mr RAYMOND	Det Ebenezer GRYCE
Sgt REDFIELD	Lt NEUMAN
Sgt REED	Insp/Ch Supt George MASTERS and Ch Insp Bill GREEN
Sgt REEVES	Insp/Supt MACDONALD
Philip REVERE	Charles CAMELOT
REX	Vicky DARE
Mr RICARDO	Insp HANAUD
Det Const RICKS	Supt BRONT
Johnny RIO	Mavis SEIDLITZ
RIP	Sidney ZOOM
Johnny RISOTTO	Hugh DECKER
Sgt RIZZUTO	Lt TOOMEY

The Sidekicks

Liatus ROANTIS	Dr Charlie ADAMS
Insp ROBERTS	Col MARCH
ROBIN	BATMAN
Sgt Derek ROBINSON	Ch Insp Charlie CHEADLE
Const George ROGERS	Insp JAMES
Maggie ROME	C B GREENFIELD
ROSSI	Jimmy PELHAM
Dr J ROTSON	Sheerluck JONES
Det Supt Alison ROWE	Marius LARCHE
Mary RUSSELL	Sherlock HOLMES

S

Rachel SABIN	Jeffrey DEAN
SAINCLAIR	Joseph ROULETABILLE
Spike SALIENO	Rex HUXFORD
Sgt SALT	Ch Insp Dan PARDOE
SAM	Ch of Plce Reid BENNETT
SASHA	Insp Porfiry Petrovich ROSTNIKOV
Sgt SAUNDERS	Ch Insp Sam BIRKETT
Sgt SAUNDERS	Mark SAVAGE and Ch Insp Sam BIRKETT
Spud SAVAGE	Duncan MACLAIN
Mr SAXON	Dorcas DENE
Bernie SCHILLER	Anna LEE
SCHNUCKE	Duncan MACLAIN
John SCOTT	Joshua CLUNK
Insp SHARPE	Insp SPEARPOINT
Dr James SHEPPARD	Hercule POIROT
SILCHESTER	Mr MYCROFT
Policewoman Jayne SIMMONDS	Ch Insp Alec STAINTON
Supt SIMS	Prof WELLS
Toby SINCLAIR	Capt Hugh 'Bulldog' DRUMMOND
Boris SLIVKA	Larry BAKER
Eddie SLOCUM	Simon LASH
Bill SLOOK	Dixon BRETT
Sir John SMYTHE	Vicky BLISS
Sgt SNELGROVE	Insp/Supt Sholto LESTRADE
SPOT	Matt COBB
Dr SPOTSON	Oilock COMBS
SQUATSON	FOAMES
Godwin STAMBERGER	Ian FIRTH and John SMITH
Bert STANLEY	Cotton MOON
STANTON	Lt CLANCY
STEPHANOS	ARISTOTLE
Cassie STORM	Chauncey O'DAY
Della STREET	Perry MASON
Sgt Fred SUMP	Insp Andrew COGGIN
Andy SUSSMAN	Murray GLICK
SVEA	Mark TUDOR
SWIFT	Insp BOOTLE
SYLVESTER	Edmund 'Jupiter' JONES

T

Gerry TATE	Douglas PERKINS
Sgt Martin TATE	Det Ch Insp Douglas QUANTRILL
Det Ed TAYLOR	Det Kate DELAFIELD
Brad TCHERNACK	Kiernan O'SHAUNESSY
Julie TENDLER	Gideon OLIVER
Dr THATSON	Shilah COOMBES
Henry THEOBALD	Kate THEOBALD
Cordelia THORN	Jane LAWLESS
TINKER	Sexton BLAKE
TINKER	LOVEJOY
TJ	Matt SCUDDER
Ben TODD	Mrs Sarah WATSON
Hooper TOLLIVER	Dr Mary FINNEY and Emily COLLINS
Peregrine TOOK	Frodo BAGGINS
Lionel TOWNSEND	Sgt William BEEF
Det Insp Gregory TOYE	Det Supt Tom POLLARD
Mike TRAPPER	Al DARLAN
Martin TRAVELER	Moroni TRAVELER
Molly TREASURE	Mark TREASURE
Arabella TRENCH	Peter MARKLIN
Lavender TREVELYAN	Lamaar RANSOM
Augustus TRIBBLE	Peter MARKLIN
Joey TRIMBLE	Uncle George CROWDER
Winton 'Ritzy' TRIPP-TYLER	Joel SABER
Torve The TROG	Viscount Anthony VILLIERS
Sgt TROY	Det Ch Insp Tom BARNABY
Russ TURNER	Wylie LINCOLN
Emma TWIGGS	James GALVESTON
Det Const Jason TWITTY	Insp/Ch Insp Harry PECKOVER

U

Insp UNDERWOOD	Dr Reginald FORTUNE
UNNAMED	BRINDLE
Ambrose USHER	Victoria MCKENZIE

V

S S VAN DINE	Philo VANCE
Dr Ivan VATSOV	Comrade Sherslav GOLMSKY
Jem VAUGHAN	Sir Christopher HAZZARD
VELDA	Mike HAMMER
Rosie VICENTE	Jake SAMSON
Svetozar VOK	Roger KINCAID

W

Insp James WAGHORN	Dr Lancelot PRIESTLEY
Policewoman Amanda WALLBRIDGE	Det Supt Mark PEMBERTON
Kimberly WARD	Lyon WENTWORTH and Bea WENTWORTH
Dr WARSAW	Kerlock SHOMES
Mr WASSERMAN	Mr Sherlock COHEN
Sun WAT	Stately HOMES
Dr WATCHPOT	Neville BOYLES
Dr WATCHSON	Surly HOMES
Dr J WATNEY	Schlock HOMES
Dr WATSDOTTER	Sheercrocked MOANS
Dr WATSIS	Padlock HOMES
Dr WATSO	Fellock HOLMES
Nigel WATSON	Sharlock HOLMES
Dr John H WATSON	Sherlock HOLMES
Dr WATSON	Sherlock HOLMES
Joan WATSON	Shirley HOLMES
Dr WATSON	Hemlock HOLMES
Jean WATSON	Shirley HOLMES
Mrs Mary WATSON	Charlotte HOLMES
Dr John H WATSON	Edward Porter JONES and Sherlock HOLMES
Bertie WATSON	Sherlock HOLMES
Dr John H WATSON	Insp/Supt Sholto LESTRADE and Sherlock HOLMES
Dr John H WATSON	Herlock SHOLMES
Henry F WATSON	Simon ROLFE
Dr WATSUP	Shamrock JOLNES
Dr WATTS	Hemlock HOLMES
Dr WATTS	Sherlock OHMS
Dr WATTS	Herlock SOAMES and Arsène LEPINE
Bobby WEATHERBY	Harrison HOLT
Glenn WEBB	Terry WEBB
John WEBBER	Lizzie THOMAS
Stu WELLMAN	Rachel HENNINGS
Nadia WELLS	Terry O'BANION
WENDOVER	Ch Const Sir Clinton DRIFFIELD
Dawn WESTLAKE	Dr Hugh WESTLAKE
John WESTON	Enoch BONE
Dr John H WESTON	Brihtvic DONNE
Dr WHATLEY	Shylar HOMES
Dr WHATSON	Doorlock HOLMES
Dr WHATSON	Sherlaw KOMBS
WHATSONAME	Thinlock BONES
Snowy WHITE	Dick BARTON
Thomas WHITNEY	Nora HONEYCUTT
Sgt WHITTAKER	Insp GARTH
'Doc' WHOOSON	Sure-They-Lock HOMEZ
Dr Ernest WHOPPER	HOMONYMOUS
Doctored WHOPPER	Shamrock WOMLBS
WIGGAR	Peter CLANCY
Sgt WIGGINS	Insp Richard JURY
Mrs Lucilla WIGGINS	Mrs Julia Herlock SHOMES
WIGGINS	WADE
Bill WILKINS	Celia GRANT
Aubrey WILKINSON	Ex-Supt 'Simmy' SIMMONDS
Lt Sid WILKS	Ch Fred FELLOWS
Sgt WILLIAMS	Insp Alan GRANT

'Doc' WILLIAMS	William CRANE
Det Grace WILLIS	Jason LYNX
Sgt WILSON	Det Supt Hilary CATCHPOLE
Mr WILSON	Capt Jose DA SILVA
Mr WILSON	Mr HOLBROOK
Sgt 'Wammo' WIMBUSH	Ch Insp Peter PARSON
Dr WITSEND	Shearlock COMBS
WOLF	Sylvia SILENCE
Mama WONG	BURKE
Eddie WRIGHT	Tony LANTZ

X

Jon X	NOLAN

Y

Lu YU	Li KAO
YUM YUM	Jim QWILLERAN

Z

ZIZI	Pennington WISE
Sgt ZONDI	Lt Tromp KRAMER

The Stooges

ABBERLINE Ch Supt	Insp/Supt Sholto LESTRADE
AKERS Supt	Insp CLAYTON
ATHELNEY Insp Tobias	Hercule POIROT
BALUSTRADE Insp	Schlock HOMES
BANCROFT Insp	Victor SERGE
BARRY Det Supt Bill	Christopher DANE
BATTLE Supt	Hercule POIROT
BAUTISTA Lt Luis	Reuben FROST
BELL Supt	Joshua CLUNK
BILES Insp	Dr Eustace HAILEY
BISHOP Ch Insp	Prof John STUBBS
BLOUNT Insp	Nigel STRANGEWAYS
BRENNAN Sheriff	MALLORY
BRISTOW Supt	John MANNERING
BURCHELL Insp	Prof Luther BASTION
BURGER Dist Att Hamilton	Perry MASON
BYRNE Lt	Hal JEFFRIES
CARACCI Lt	Antonia NIELSEN
CECCHI Lt Peter	Lauren LAURANO
CHURCH Insp	Don DIAVOLO
COBB Insp	Dr Hugh WESTLAKE
COMFORT Det Insp Aloysius	Kate THEOBALD
CRAMER Insp	Nero WOLFE
DAVIS Insp Larry	Duncan MACLAIN
DEVENISH Supt Roger	Sheridan HAYNES
DORGAN Attorney James	Prof Brinsley BUTLER
DOUGHERTY Attorney Merle K	Commiss Thatcher COLT
DRAKE Cdr	John RAVEN
DRIFT Insp Angus	Prof James Yates BIDDLE and Kay RITCHIE
DRUMMOND Det	Constance DUNLAP
DUANE Lt Tobias	Nathan HAWK
EVANS Sgt	Larry MILNER
FELLOWES Ch	Nora HONEYCUTT
FLAGG Lt	Perry MASON
FLEDGE Insp	Paul DAWN
FLUMMER Lt	David CALDER
GREGG Insp	SYALOCH
GREGORY Insp	Sherlaw KOMBS
GREGSON Insp Tobias	Sherlock HOLMES
GRIMSHAW Det Supt	Insp MOSLEY
GUILD Det John	Nick CHARLES and Nora CHARLES
HALE Mr Spenser	Eugbne VALMONT
HANKINS Lt George	Jeff TROY and Haila TROY
HANSLET Supt	Dr Lancelot PRIESTLEY
HERBERT Ch Rocco	Lyon WENTWORTH and Bea WENTWORTH
HOLCOMB Sgt	Perry MASON
HOLMES Sherlock	Insp/Supt Sholto LESTRADE
HUISH Supt	Dr Arthur CALGARY
JAPP Insp Jimmy	Hercule POIROT
JENKINS Det Lt Robert E	Hannah LAND
JONES Athelney	Sherlock HOLMES
JOWETT Insp	Sgt CRIBB and Const THACKERAY
KEEGAN Capt Phil	Father Roger DOWLING
KENNY Insp Mike	Prof DALY
KING Insp Brian	Andrew TAGGART
KOZETSKY Sgt	Matthew PRIOR
KRAUSE Lt Lemmie	Bart CHALLIS
LAMA Jimmy	Paul MADRIANI
LAMB Insp Ernest	Maud Hephzibah SILVER
LANIGAN Ch Hugh	Rabbi David SMALL
LAVERS Sheriff	Lt Al WHEELER
LE Det Insp	Mark EASTERBROOK and Ariadne OLIVER
LEEYES Supt	Insp Christopher Dennis SLOAN
LESTRADE Insp	Sherlock HOLMES
LESTRADE Insp Jules	Charlotte HOLMES
LESTRADSKY Insp	Comrade Sherslav GOLMSKY
LETSTRAYED Insp	Hemlock HOLMES
LUKE Insp Charlie	Albert CAMPION
MACK Insp John	Prof Theocritus Lucius WESTBOROUGH
MACREADY Capt	Henry HALE
MANNIE Insp	Bruce PERKINS and William Rutherford CRANE
MARKHAM John F X	Philo VANCE
MARTIN Insp	Cleavers SETON
MARTINEZ Lt Luis	Patience MCKENNA
MASON Hezekia	Ephraim TUTT
MCGREGOR Lt	Fred CARVER
MERCER Asst Commiss	Dr Jan CZISSAR
MERRIVALE Sir Charles	Prof WELLS
MIFFLIN Lt Tim	Vic MALLOY
MILNER Insp	MOM
MINARDI Lt	Father Joseph BREDDER
MONTERO Insp Herbert	Adam LUDLOW
MOONEY Lt	Albert CAMPION
MORESBY Insp	Roger SHERINGHAM
MORESBY Insp	Ambrose CHITTERWICK and Roger SHERINGHAM
MORGAN Insp 'Eyebrows'	Maria BLACK
MORNINGSTAR Sgt Robert	Adelaide STONE
MULLETT Cdr	Det Insp Jack FROST
MUNRO Ch Insp	Keith CALDER
MUNRO Ch Insp	Simon PARBITTER and Keith CALDER
MURPHY Det Kate	Sister MARY HELEN
NAPIER Sheriff 'Boss'	Prof Carl BURNS
NASEBY Insp	Auguste DIDIER
NIVEN Insp Douglas	Dr Jean MONTROSE
NOLA Det John	Scott JORDAN
OATES Ch Stanislaus	Albert CAMPION
PARKER Insp Charles	Lord Peter WIMSEY
PATTON Insp	Hilda ADAMS
PETERSON Ch	Charlie BRADSHAW
PHOENIX Joe	Mignon LAWRENCE
PICON Amer	Sgt William BEEF
PILKINS Sheriff	Bill RASTIN
PIPER Insp Oscar	Hildegarde WITHERS
PLIMSOLL Lord Simon	Sgt William BEEF
PLUMMER Insp	Martin HEWITT
POOLEY Det Sgt Ellis	Robert AMISS
QUINN Insp Anthony J	Cash WALE
RACER Ch Supt	Insp Richard JURY
RAGLAND- Insp	Hercule POIROT
REARDON Casey	Policewoman Christie OPARA
REYNOLDS Insp	Stephen KELLY
ROBERTS Det 'Nobby'	Tim SIMPSON
ROGERS Sgt	Wencelaus BOTTWINK
ROMANO Lt	Bart HARDIN
ROMANO Lt	Prof Ira COBB
ROSE Insp Egbert	Auguste DIDIER
ROSEN Lt Peter	Claire MALLOY
SALAS Ch	Insp Enrique ALVAREZ
SAMPSON Capt Phil	Shell SCOTT
SAUNDERS Insp	Lady Molly DE MAZEREEN
SEEGRAVE Supt	Sgt CUFF
SINCLAIR Capt	Eliot UPTON
SMITH	Steven KIRK
SMITH Mgr	Sgt William BEEF
SMITHERS Det Insp Colin	Patrick GRANT
TEAL Insp Charles	Simon (The Saint) TEMPLAR
TENCH Supt	Det Insp CICERO
THUMM Insp	Drury LANE
TRAYNOR Lt Grady	Molly CATES
TRIVETT Insp	Patrick DAWLISH
VANNER Insp	Toby DYKE
WAKE Det Insp Roger	Kate THEOBALD
WARSHINSKY Sgt John	Dr Catherine EDISON
WHETSTONE Insp Digby	Peter MARKLIN

Appendix 1 - Sources

1. Adey, Robert, *Locked Room Murders and Other Impossible Crimes: A Comprehensive Bibliography*. Minneapolis, Crossover, 1991.

   A fully documented bibliography of a special sub-genre, listing around 1500 detectives and their authors, with no information about either, but with information on the selected books.

2. Albert, Walter, Detective and Mystery Fiction: *An International Bibliography of Secondary Sources*. Madison, Indiana, Brownstone, 1984.

3. Barnes, Melvyn, *Murder in Print: A Guide to Two Centuries of Crime Fiction*. Lydeard St Lawrence, Somerset, Barn Owl, 1986.

   A narrative guide to selected criminous works.

4. Barzun, Jacques, and Wendell Hertig Taylor, *A Catalogue of Crime*. New York, Harper, 1971.

   This classic compilation of brief notes on over 3000 criminous works includes references to several hundred detectives.

5. Binyon, T J, *Murder Will Out: The Detective in Fiction*, Oxford, Oxford University Press, 1989.

   A selected bibliography, with narration, of a few hundred major British and American detectives, classified into types and with some author information.

6. Bunsen, Matthew E, *The Sherlock Holmes Encyclopedia: A Complete Guide to the World of the Great Detective*. London, Pavilion Book, 1995.

   A useful guide to the canon, citing virtually every character and providing information on much incidental material in the stories. There are some errors.

7. Conquest, John, *Trouble is Their Business: Private Eyes in Fiction, Film and Television, 1927-1988*. New York, Garland, 1990.

   A comprehensive bibliography with brief narrative notes on around 1500 detectives and their books.

8. Craig, Patricia, and Cadogan, Mary, *The Lady Investigates: Women Detectives and Spies in Fiction*. London, Gollancz, 1981.

   A compilation of women detectives, around 300 in number, many obscure, with short narrative details and some publication information.

9. De Waal, Ronald Burt. *The World Bibliography of Sherlock Holmes and Dr Watson: A Classified and Annotated List of Materials Relating to Their Lives and Adventures*. New York, Bramhall House, 1974.

   A definitive bibliography on the subject that includes every work on Sherlock Holmes in the world literature to 1973, including almost all the then known pastiches and parodies.

Appendix 1

10. Glover, Dorothy, and Graham Greene, *Victorian Detective Fiction: A catalogue*. London, Bodley Head, 1966.

    A selected bibliography of British and American fiction before 1901, citing about 200 detectives.

11. Goulart, Ron, *The Dime Detectives.* New York, Mysterious Press, 1988.

    A selective bibliography of detectives and their authors, with narrative, appearing in American pulp magazines and novels from the 1880s to the 1950s. Some 300 detectives are cited.

12. Hoppenstand, Gary, editor, *The Dime Novel Detective.* Bowling Green, Ohio, Popular Press, 1983.

    A list of several hundred detectives and their creators, appearing in American pulp magazines and novels from the 1880s to around 1940.

13. Hubin, Allen J, *Crime Fiction II: A Comprehensive Bibliography, 1749-1990.* New York, Garland, 1994.

    The most comprehensive bibliography of crime fiction. It is indexed by author name and cites around 4000 'series detectives' and all the books in which they are known to appear, by name only and without narrative.

14. Klein, Kathleen Gregory, *The Woman Detective: Gender and Genre.* Champaign, University Press, 1988.

    A narrative discussion of female detectives, around 100 in number, from the 1880s to the 1980s.

15. Olderr, Steven, *Mystery Index: Subjects, Settings, and Sleuths of 10,000 Titles.* Chicago, American Library Association, 1988.

    A library index to books, comprising 20th-century publications only, that were available in hardcover in US libraries. It cites around 2000 detectives and their books, but, because of the constraints, is often bibliographically incomplete. There is no information on either detectives or authors, other than names for the former and sometimes dates and pseudonyms for the latter. Although US publication information is given on the books cited , the information is often lacking for corresponding UK publications. The index, although large, contains many errors.

16. Henderson, Lesley, editor, *Twentieth Century Crime and Mystery Writers (3rd Edition).* Chicago, St James, 1991.

    A fully documented bibliography of around 700 important authors, with expansive narrative and critical discussion of their detectives, books and short stories. The large text cites around 1500 detectives and sometimes their sidekicks.

17. Nichols, Victoria, and Susan Thompson, *Silk Stalkings: When Women write of Murder: A Survey of Series created by Women Authors in Crime and Mystery Fiction.* Berkeley, California, Black Lizard, 1988.

    A critical study of the role of female authors in the criminous field, with only passing reference to their detectives.

18. Pate, Janet, *The Book of Sleuths.* London, New English Library 1977).

    An annotated reference work with narratives on around 100 detectives.

19. Penzler, Otto, Chris Steinbrunner, and Marvin Lachman, *Detectionary: A Bibliographic Dictionary of the Leading Characters in Detective and Mystery Fiction.* New York, Overlook Press, 1977.

    An selection of around 400 detectives, many of them obscure, with entertaining narrative details. There is also useful information, not found elsewhere, on sidekicks, short stories and movies.

20. Pronzini, Bill, *Gun in Cheek: A Study of 'Alternative' Crime Fiction.* New York, Coward, McCann, and Geoghegan, 1982.

    An entertaining critical narrative that deals with what the author regards as the really bad British and American crime novels. It reveals a number of obscure detectives.

21. Pronzini, Bill, *Son of Gun in Cheek.* New York, Mysterious Press, 1987.

A sequel to *Gun in Cheek,* covering similar ground.

22. Slung, Michaele, *Crime on her Mind: Fifteen Stories of Female Sleuths from the Victorian Era to the Forties.* New York, Pantheon, 1975.

In addition to the stories, a selected guide to a number of early female detectives.

23. Smith Myron J Jr, *Cloak-and-Dagger Bibliography. An Annotated Guide to Spy Fiction, 1937-1975.* Metuchen, New Jersey, Scarecrow Press, 1976.

24. Steinbrunner, Chris and Otto Penzler, *Encyclopedia of Mystery and Detection.* New York, McGraw Hill, 1976.

A large, highly entertaining encyclopedia, dealing with almost every aspect of the subject and giving information on several hundred detectives.

Appendix 2 - Source Discrepancies

Several discrepancies have been found where sources disagree with each other or with the source material. They are listed here, the sources being numbered as shown in Appendix 1. They are noted in 'The Detectives' under the Detectives shown in bold type named below.

Pat **ABBOTT** and Jean ABBOTT	Source 7 gives the detectives' names as *Abbot,* when cited under the main author citation, but correctly as *Abbott* in the subsidiary detective index.
Adelaide **ADAMS**	Source 1 erroneously gives the detective's name as *Evans.*
Frank **AMBERLEY**	Source 15 gives the title of the book erroneously as *Why Shoot The Bather?*
Prof Leonides **AMES** and Mr HOOPES	Source 13 gives the title of the book as cited. Source 15 gives *Pattern In Black And Red.*
Robert **AMISS**	Source 13 gives the title of the book as cited. Source 15 gives *Corridors of Death.*
Jan **ARGAND**	Source 15 erroneously gives the detective's name as *Aryand*
Frances **ARMITAGE**	Source 13 cites the author's real name as *Stenstreem* in the index and *Stenstrom* in the text.
Sgt Steve **ARROW**	Source 13 gives the title of the book as cited in the index but as *Murder in Fancydress* in the text.
ASHTON-KIRK	Source 13 cites this detective as *Ashton Kirk*, but Sources 1 and 26 agree with 'The Detectives'.
T T **BALDWIN**	Source 13 gives the author's name as cited. Source 15 gives *O'Cork.*
Dan **BANION**	Source 13 gives the detective's name as cited. Source 5 gives *Bannion.*
Kommissar Hans **BARLACH**	Source 15 erroneously gives the detective's name as *Borlach.*
Johnny **BORDELON**	Sources 7 gives 1983 as the publication date for *Murder By Proxy.*
William **BROOKE**	Source 13 gives the author's real name as *Geraldine Mary Jay Halls.*
Henry **BRYCE** and Emily BRYCE	Although Source 16 gives these detectives as appearing in *The Diplomat and the Gold Piano*, Source 13 cites the author's other detective, *Rev Martin Buell.*
Supt **BURNIVAL**	Source 5 gives the detective's name as cited. Source 13 gives *Burnivel.*
Sarah **CALLOWAY**	Source 13 gives this book as not identical with *June Mail.*
Paul **CAMPENHAYE**	Source 15 erroneously gives the title of the book as *The Case of the Artificial Eye*
Bill **CANILLI**	Source 13 gives the detective's name as cited. Source 15 gives *Canalli.*
Roman **CANTRELL**	Source 7 gives the detective's name as cited. Source 13 gives *Contrell.*
Det Insp **CHANCE**	Source 1 gives *David Chance.*
Monsieur **CHEVENARD**	Source 13 gives the detective's name as *Jean-Joseph Renaud.*
Morgan **CITRON**	Source 15 erroneously attributes this detective to an author, *Thomas Ross,* whose name does not appear in any other bibliography.

Appendix 2

Edmund **CLIVE**	Source 13 gives the author's middle name as Douglas, but Source 16 gives *Douglass.*
Harlan **COLE**	The author's name may be *Jackson Donahue.*
Matthew **COLL**	Source 15 erroneously gives the name as *Martin Coll* in two out of three citations.
Clive 'Dormouse' **CONRAD**	Source 13 gives the detective's name as *Clive King.*
Martin 'Brick-Top' **CORRIGAN**	Source 13 cites the detective's name erroneously as *John Craig.*
John Francis **CUDDY**	Source 15 gives the author's name as *J F Healy.*
Prof **DALY**	Source 13 gives the cited stooge, Insp *Mike Kenny*, as the detective.
Frank 'Lobo' **DAVIES**	Source 15 erroneously gives the name as *Frank Lobo Jones.*
Carolus **DEENE**	Source 13 gives the detective's name as cited. Source 5 gives *Deane.*
Alex **DELAWARE**	Source 15 erroneously gives the detective's name as *Alex Davenport.*
Johnny **DEVEREAUX**	Source 7 gives the author's other detective, *'Jigger' Moran*, in *The Hollow Man.*
Matthew **DILKE**	Source 13, in the index, gives the detective's name as cited, but as *Mathew Dilke* in the text.
DUPUY	Source 16 gives the title of the book as *The Man in Button Boots.*
Toby **DYKE**	Source 13 gives the real name of E X Ferrars as Elizabeth *Xavia* Ferrars. There is no indication in any biography that the middle name exists.
Mark **EAST**	Source 15 erroneously gives the detective's name as *Mack East.*
Ronald **EWART**	Source 20 gives the detective's name as cited. Source 13 erroneously gives George Ewart.
Horton **FORBES**	Source 15 erroneously gives the author's name as *Huntington.*
Prof James **GLOWERY**	Sources 1 and 13 both give the detective's name as cited. Source 16 gives *Glowrey.*
George **GALBRAITH**	Source 15 erroneously gives the author's name as *Whylte.*
Insp George **GOODMAN**	Source 15 erroneously gives the detective's name as *Grodman.*
Robin **GREVE**, Mary TREVERT and Insp MANDERTON	Source 1 gives these detectives for the book cited but Source 13 gives *Insp Manderton*, who appears elsewhere in 'The Detectives'.
Lindy **GREY**	Source 13 gives the detective's name as Gray in the text and as Linda Gray in the index.
Lucas **HALLAM**	Source 13 gives the title of the book as cited. Source 7 gives *Wild Nights.*
Sgt Cass **HARTY**	Source 15 gives the detective's name as *Hartly.*
Ellie Simons **HASKELL**	Source 15 erroneously gives the detective's name as *Ellie Simmons.*
Anthony **HAVILLAND**	Source 13 gives the title of the book as cited in the index but, in the text, gives it as *The Ruse of the Vanishing Women.*
Jessica **HAYDEN**	Source 13 gives the title of the book as *Coast of Fear.*
Simon **HERALD**	Source 13 erroneously gives the detective's name as *Harald.*
Gentle **HOGGERTY**	Source 13 erroneously gives the detective's name as *Hoggarty* under the Ben Sarto byline but gives it correctly in the index.
Sherlock **HOLMES**	Source 1 erroneously gives the title of the book as *The Case of the Uneasy Chair.*
Sherlock **HOLMES** and Theodore ROOSEVELT	Source 15 erroneously gives the author as *Simon Jay* and the title of the book as The Adventure of the Stalwart.
Sam **HOUSTON**	The author, *E Spence De Puy*, is sometimes listed as *De Pue.*
Anthony **HOWARD**	Source 13 gives the detective's name as cited. Source 15 gives *Howard Anthony.*
Det Insp 'Smudge' **HUDDLESTON**	Source 15 erroneously gives the name of this detective as *Smudge.*

Joe **HUSSEY**	Source 7 gives the detective's name as cited. Source 13 gives *Hussy.*
Dr **HYDE**	Source 13 gives the title of the book as *The White Pillars Murder.*
Mike **JAMES**	Source 15 gives the author for this detective correctly in its index but, in the text, erroneously attributes the detective to *Dennis Schutz.*
Wood **JAXON**	Source 7 gives the detective's name as cited. Source 13 gives *Jason.*
Barnaby **JONES**	Source 7 gives the detective's name as cited. Source 13 gives *Barnabas Jones.*
Anastasia **JUGEDINSKI**	Source 7 gives the detective's name as cited. Source 13 give *Jagedinski.*
Zachariah **JUSTIS** and Guinevere JONES	Source 13 gives only one detective, *Guinevere Jones.*
Zachariah **JUSTIS** and Guinevere JONES	Source 7 gives the title of the book as cited. Source 13 gives *The Desperate Games.*
Casey **KELLOG** and AIKUG	Source 15 erroneously gives the first detective's name as *Kellogg.*
Maj Charles Douglas **KERWOOD**	The name of this detective may be *Kerrwood.*
Stephen **KELLY**	Source 16 gives this detective in a short but detailed narrative. The distinguished Source 4 gives the cited stooge, Insp REYNOLDS,in a discussion that is hardly recognisable as being about the same book.
Det Jack **KETHERIDGE**	Source 20 gives the detective's name as *Kethridge.* Source 15 gives it as *Methridge.*
Viera **KOLAROVA**	Source 15 gives the title of the book as *All That Glitters.*
Riley **KOVACHS**	Source 13 gives the detective's name as cited. Source 7 gives *Kovacs.*
Herr **KRESCH**	Source 13 gives the title of the book as cited. Source 1 gives *The Talking Sparrow Murders.*
Jack **LAMARRE** and Alison PRENDERGAST	Source 15 erroneously gives the title of the book as *Trail of the Reaper.*
Ch Insp/Supt **LENNOX**	Sources disagree as to whether this detective or Insp David LYLE, another of the author's detectives, is the main sleuth in this book.
Roger **LEVIN**	Source 13 gives the author's name as cited. Source 7 gives *Richard Furst.*
Darina **LISLE**	Source 13 erroneously gives the title of the book as *A Deep Coffin.*
John Abraham **LINCOLN**	Source 13 gives the title of the book as *Hatchetman.*
Ben **LUCIUS**	Source 13 gives the title of the book as *The Case of the Copy-Hook Killing.*
Millie **LYNNE**	Source 13 erroneously gives the detective's name as *Lynn.*
Paul **MACDONALD**	Source 7 gives the detective's name as cited. Source 13 gives *McDonald.*
Sgt Ivor **MADDOX**	Source 16, but not Source 13, gives *Alter Ego* (1987) as the last book.
Cuddy **MAGNUM** and Justine SAVILLE	Source 15 erroneously gives the detective's name as *Saville Dollard.*
Arnold **MAGNUSON**	Source 15 erroneously gives the detective's name as *Arned Magnuson.*
Billy **MARCUS**	Source 16 states that this book was also published as *Faraday's Flowers* , which Source 13 gives as a different book (not cited).
Travis **MCGEE**	Source 13 erroneously gives the detective's name as *McGee*, although it was correctly given in the source's first edition. Source 13 also erroneously gives the title of the book as *The Deep Blue Good-by.*
Amos **MCGUFFIN**	Source 15 erroneously gives the detective's name as *McGriffin.*
Penny **MILLER**	Source 15 erroneously gives the detective's name as *Renny Miller.*
Kinsey **MILLHONE**	Source 15 erroneously gives the detective's name as *Milhone.*
Rachael **MONETTE**	Source 13 gives the detective's name as *Rachel Monette.*
Hoke **MOSELEY**	Source 15 erroneously gives the detective's name as *Mosley.*
Joe **MULLER**	Source 13 gives the detective's name correctly under the Colbrun authorship

Appendix 2

	but erroneously as *Miller* under the Groner authorship.
Insp Bill **MURRAY**	Source 15 erroneously gives the detective's name as *Burray.*
Lee **NACE**	Source 16 gives the detective's name as cited. Source 7 gives *Nayce.*
Rocky **NEVINS**	Source 7 gives the author's name as cited. Source 13 gives *Vern Chute.*
Insp **O'HARE**	Source 13 gives the author's other detective, *Ch of Plce Sutherland,* in this book.
Kate **OSBORN**	Source 15 gives the detective's name as *Osborne.*
Colin **PANTON**	Source 13 erroneously gives the detective's name as *Pauton.*
Athena **PIERCE**	Source 15 erroneously gives the title of the book as *Mudercon.*
Katherine 'Peter' **PIPER**	Source 13 gives the detective's name as cited. Source 17 gives *James Aloysius Piper* and the author as *Nancy Maritz.*
Solar **PONS**	Source 9 gives the title of the book as *The Adventure of the Fatal Glance.* Source 13 gives *The Adventure of the Fatal Silence.*
Solar **PONS**	Source 9 includes this story in the collection cited, but it is omitted from the citation in Source 13.
Thomas **PRESTON**	Sources 15 and 16 give the detective as *Professor Kreutzemark,* who is actually the villain of the piece.
Chance **PURDUE**	Source 20 erroneously gives the detective's name as *Perdue.*
Dr **QUARSHIE**	Source 15 erroneously gives the author's name as *Wylie.*
Joe **QUINNEY**	Source 13 erroneously gives the title of the book as *Quinneys'.*
Steve **RANDOM**	Source 1 erroneously attributes the story to *Michael Halliday,* a pseudonym of John Creasey, instead of Brett Halliday, the pseudonym of Davis Dresser.
John **RANKIN**	Source 7 gives the title of the book as cited. Sources 13 and 15 both give *Runner in the Street.*
John **RHINEHEART**	Source 7 gives the detective's name as cited. Source 13 gives *Rhinehart.*
Insp **RODERICKS**	Source 13 gives the author's name as cited. Source 15 gives *McLiesh.*
Balmy **RYDAL**	Source 19 gives the detective's name as cited. Source 13 gives *Rymal.*
Eddie **SHOESTRING**	Source 15 erroneously gives the author as *Abelman.*
Richard **SILVER**	is given as the detective by Source 1 but Source 10 gives *Tinkler.*
Dep Commiss Benjamin **SIMON**	Source 13 gives the detective's name as cited. Source 1 gives *Stone.*
Harry **SOMMERS**	Source 7 erroneously gives the detective's name as *Somers.*
Danny **SPADE**	Source 7 lists this detective under the author's pseudonym, *Danny Spade.*
Insp **SPENS**	Source 1 gives the title of the book as cited. Source 13 gives *The Greenwell's Glory* Case.
Mike **STRANG**	Source 7 gives the detective's name as cited. Source 13 gives *Strong.*
Violet **STRANGE**	Source 13 gives the detective's name correctly in the index but, in what might be regarded as a Freudian slip, cites her as *Violent Strange* in the text.
Spencer **TAIT** and DENHAM	Source 13 does not cite the detectives and gives different publishers for the book.
Capt Andrew **TORRENT**	Source 15 erroneously gives the title of the book as *Painted for the Ball.*
Derek **TORRY**	Source 13 gives the detective's name as cited, Source 4 gives *Torrey.*
Insp **TREADGOLD**	Source 13 gives the author's name as *Ivo Geikie Cobb.*
Percival **TROUT**	Source 13 gives the author's name as cited. Source 15 gives *Owens.*
Rick **VANNER**	Sources 7 and 13 give the detective's name as cited. Sources 4 and 15 give *Vanning.*
Will **WOODFIELD**	Source 1 erroneously gives the title of the story as *The Bhudda Case.*
Malcolm **WARREN**	Source 15 erroneously gives the detective's name as *Warren Malcolm.*
Det Daniel **WEBSTER**	Source 16 gives the detective's name as cited. Sources 13 and 15 give *Danile Webster.*

Prof **WELLS**	Source 13 gives the cited stooge, *Insp Sims*, as a joint detective with *Wells*.
Sheriff Emil **WHIPPLETREE**	Source 15 erroneously gives the author's name as *Hinkermeyer.*
Will **WOODFIELD**	Sources 7 and 13 give the detective's name as cited. Source 15 gives *Woodford.*
Elizabeth Lamb **WORTHINGTON**	Source 15 erroneously cites *Elizabeth Lamb* and *Worthington* as separate detectives.

Appendix 3 - Sherlock Holmes Parodies

Parody detective with author and author's nationality appearing in 'The Detectives'

Haricot BONES	John Sutherland	American
Sherlock BONES	John Keane	American
Thinlock BONES	Zero	British
Warlock BONES	G F Forrest	?
Neville BOYLES	Aco N Doyle	American
Oilock COMBS	W B Kahn	American
Shearlock COMBS	Stephen Clarkson	?
Shilah COMBS	Anon	?
Brihtvic DONNE	E M Friesner	?
Sherlav GOLMSKY	John Boardman	American
Sheerluck GNOMES	TP Stafford	British
A B C HAWKES	Ephesian	British
Sherwood HOAKES	C C Rothwell	British
Mr HOLBROOK	Charles Peterson	?
Picklock HOLES	R C Lehman	British
Charlotte HOLMES	Hilary Bailey	British
Creighton HOLMES	Ned Hubbell	American
Doorlock HOLMES	Paul Nizza	?
Fellock HOLMES	Bill Conklin	American
Hairlock HOLMES	Floyd R Horowitz	American
Hemlock HOLMES	John McGoldrick	American
Raffles HOLMES	John Kendrick Bangs	American
Sharlock HOLMES	Tom Mengert	American
Shirlick HOLMES	Jane Yolen	American
Shirley HOLMES	Fred A Kummer &	
Basil Mitchell	American	
Shirley HOLMES	Viola Brothers Shore	American
Shrock HOLMES	Bradley Kjell	American
Spenser HOLMES	Denny Martin Flinn	American
Zinsheimer HOLMES	Harold Kellock	?
Shirley HOLMQUIST	Janet Letnes Martin	American
Chubb-Lock HOMES	Anon	?
Padlock HOMES	Anon	American
Rex HOMES	Albert J Bromley	American
Schlock HOMES	Robert L Fish	American
Shylar HOMES	Stephen Daniel Williams	American
Shylock HOLMES	John Kendrick Bangs	American
Stately HOMES	Arthur Porges	American
Surly HOMES	Edward Ludwig	American
Sure-They-Lock HOLMEZ	Jerry Neal Williamson	American

Appendix 3

HOMONYMOUS	Helen Halbach	American
Purlock HONE	Oswald Crawfurd	British
Mr H-LM-S	Allen Upward	British
Shamrock JOLNES	O Henry	American
Hemlock JONES	Bret Harte	American
Sheerluck JONES	Malcolm Watson & Edward La Serre	American
Sherlock JONES	Lester HEATH	American
Mr Warlock JONES		
Sherlaw KOMBS	Robert Barr	British
Turlock LOAMS	John Ruyle	American
Insp MANTIS	William Kotzwinkle	American
Porlock MOANS	Nicholas Utechin	American
Sheercrocked MOANS	Gayle Lange Puhl	American
Sherlock MONK	Anon	American
Mr MYCROFT	H F Heard	British
Sheerluck OHMS	Dr Watts Ion	American
Sherlock OHMS	Steven Tomashefsky	American
Cerlocio OLMEZ	Katherine E Karlson	American
Solar PONS	August Derleth	American
Solar PONS	Basil Copper	British
Tide POOLES	John Jacobson	American
Sherbert SCONES	Hugh Lofting	American
Holmlock SHEARS	Maurice Leblanc	French
Herlock SHOLMES	John Ross Macdonald	American
Mrs Julia Herlock SHOMES	KA	British
Kerlock SHOMES	E Tudor Gross	American
Hemlock SOAMES	Anon	British
Kerlock SOAMES	S Beach Chester	British
SYLOCH	Poul Anderson	American
John Conan WATSON	Joyce Harrington	American
Sherlock WATSON	A F Arnold	?
Shamrock WOMLBS	John Lennon	British